# INFORMATION PLEASE

# READER SURVEY

Could we have some information, please?

We want **Information Please** to be as useful as possible to you. The more we know about our readers and their requirements, the better we, in "The Answer Book," can supply the answers you need.

Would you, therefore, take a moment to give *us* some answers, about yourself and the way you use this Almanac? We'll read your replies carefully, and use them to create an even more helpful book for you in future years.

Please check the sections you find most useful:

____ Special articles
____ Current Events
____ Headline History
____ Business and the Economy
____ Energy
____ Environment
____ Women
____ World and U.S. Statistics
____ Countries of the World
____ Canada
____ Calendar and Holidays
____ Science
____ Astronomy and Space
____ Religion
____ Travel
____ Aviation
____ Military
____ Disasters
____ Nutrition and Health
____ Where to Find Out More
____ Writer's Guide
____ Geography and Maps
____ U.S. History & Government
____ Postage
____ Consumers
____ U.S. Societies
____ Awards
____ People
____ Guide to Growing Older
____ Taxes
____ Education
____ Sports
____ Entertainment and Culture

Where do you use **Information Please** the most?

___At home ___At work ___In school ___In college

Do you now own

___a dictionary ___an atlas ___a multi-volume encyclopedia

___a one-volume encyclopedia

Your age?

___under 18 ___18–25 ___26–45 ___46–60 ___over 60

Your education?

___now in school ___high school graduate ___some college ___college graduate

Your occupation? ______________________________

We would be very pleased to have you make any other comments you think would be helpful.

Please return this information to the Editor, Information Please, 57 West 57 Street, New York, N.Y. 10019.

For convenience, you can remove this page simply by cutting along the dotted line. Or, if you prefer, send us a letter. In either case, we would be grateful for your help.

# INFORMATION PLEASE ALMANAC

## ATLAS & YEARBOOK

# 1979

33rd EDITION

THE VIKING PRESS
NEW YORK

---

The Information Please Almanac invites comments and suggestions from readers. Because of the many letters received, however, it is not possible to respond personally to every correspondent. Nevertheless, all suggestions are most welcome, and the editors will consider them carefully.
A limited supply of previous editions is available. Please send requests to the Back Issue Department at the address below.
(Information Please Almanac does not rule on bets or wagers.)

---

Library of Congress Catalog Number: 47-845
ISBN (Hardcover): 0-670-39820-9
ISBN (Paperback): 0-449-7-6681-0


Manufactured in the United States of America

---

INFORMATION PLEASE
PUBLISHING, INC.
57 West 57th Street, New York, N.Y. 10019

# A PROFILE OF THE UNITED STATES

This Profile was created by the editors of *Information Please* from many data sources. Most figures are, of course, approximate. For more precise details, please refer to the appropriate sections of the *Information Please Almanac* itself.

## GEOGRAPHY

Number of states: 50
Land area (1970): 3,615,122 sq mi. Share of world land area (1969): 6.9%
Northernmost point: Point Barrow, Alaska
Easternmost point: West Quoddy Head, Me.
Southernmost point: Ka Lae (South Cape), Hawaii
Westernmost point: Cape Wrangell, Alaska
Geographic center: In Butte County, S.D. (44°58′ N.lat., 103°46′ W. long.)

## POPULATION

Total (est. July 1, 1979): 220,232,000
Center of population (1970): 5 miles east-southeast of Mascoutah, Illinois
Males (est. 1979): 107,309,000
Females (est. 1979): 112,923,000
White persons (est. 1979): 190,194,000
Black and other persons (est. 1979): 30,038,000
Breakdown by age groups (est. 1979):
Under 5 years: 15,617,000
5–14 years: 34,555,000
15–24 years: 41,656,000
25–64 years: 103,972,000
65 and over: 24,432,000
Median age (est. 1979): 30.0
Rural population (est. 1978): 61,180,500
Metropolitan population (est. 1978): 157,321,500
Families (est. 1978): 56,958,000
Average family size (est. 1978): 3.33
Married couples (est. 1978): 50,000,000
Unmarried persons (14 years and over) (est. 1978): 45,000,000
Widowers (est.): 2,500,000
Widows (est.): 10,750,000
Divorced persons (est.): 7,250,000

## VITAL STATISTICS

Births (1977): 3,313,000
Deaths (1977): 1,898,000
Marriages (1977): 2,176,000
Divorces (1977): 1,097,000

## CIVILIAN LABOR FORCE

Males (July 1978): 56,629,000 (95.3% employed).
Females (1978): 33,543,000 (92% employed)
Teenagers 16–19 (July 1978): 8,881,000 (84.4% employed)

## INCOME

Gross national product (est. 1978): $2,100,000,000,000
Personal income per capita (1977): $7,057
Family income, median (1977): $16,740
Personal savings accounts (est.): $90,000,000,000
Individual shareholders (est.): 25,270,000
Home ownership (est.): 70,000,000
Number of millionaires (net worth): 200,000
Number below poverty level (1977): white, 16,416,000; black and other minorities 8,304,000

## EDUCATION

Elementary and secondary schools (1976): 85,496
Elementary and secondary pupils (est. 1979): 47,224,000
Elementary and secondary teachers (est. 1979): 2,429,000
High school graduates (1979): 3,080,000
Money spent on elementary and secondary education (est. 1979–80): $74,800,000,000
Institutions of higher learning (est. 1976): 2,765
College graduates (1979): 1,005,000

## CONVENIENCES

TV sets (1978): 138,200,000
Radios (1978): 444,000,000
TV stations (1978): 986. Radio stations (standard and FM, 1978): 8,527
Automobiles (est. 1977): 109,676,000
Telephones (1977): 155,173,000
Newspaper circulation (morning and evening, 1977): 61,495,140

## TRAVEL

Road mileage (all vehicles) (est. 1978): 1,500,000,000,000
Railroad passenger-miles (excluding commuter) (est. 1978): 10,750,000,000
Airline passenger-miles (est. 1978): 180,000,000,000

# CONTENTS

The Comprehensive Index lists in alphabetical order all the important topics, terms, and names covered and gives the page or pages on which they appear. • To find a fact, date, or idea, begin by looking under the most specific word. For example, to find the population of Des Moines, start by looking for *Des Moines.* But that city is not listed separately. Therefore, the next step is to look under *Iowa* or *Cities, U.S.* Under *Iowa* the designated page gives the latest population of Des Moines. Under *Cities, U.S.* there is a subhead, *Population figures,* with three alternatives: *Fifty largest* (of which Des Moines is not one), *Largest by state* (which refers back to *Iowa* ), and *1920–1970* (where Des Moines is listed alphabetically). • For President George Washington, look under *Washington,* before checking *President.* Where general headings (such as *Presidents, U.S.* ) are given, they refer to a section where the subject is treated at some length.

# INTRODUCTION

During the past year, the editors of *Information Please* held many long meetings to establish the ground rules for the 1979 edition, which you now hold in your hand. These and other discussions with journalists, librarians, researchers, and other users of the *Almanac* were particularly crucial this year, because we knew that we were going to use the newest and most sophisticated technology to create this 1979 version. Our use of new "electronic files"—computer memories —rather than conventional file cabinets and bookshelves to store our data gave us a special opportunity to re-examine the data and ideas that have appeared in *Information Please* over the years. Thanks to computerization, we were able to make even more revisions than we usually do each year.

As we were inundated by the reams of new data that became available for the new *Information Please,* it became apparent that the world was changing at an ever-accelerating rate. Few of us realize that 75 percent of all the information available to humankind has evolved over the past 20 years! Because *Information Please* itself was established 30 years ago, some of the premises on which it was based clearly needed re-examination. After all, many more people are being educated today, new countries and new alliances are being born, new ideas and new technologies are rapidly changing our lives. With all these developments, the world is a very different place from what it was only a few years ago. Shouldn't *Information Please* become, therefore, a different kind of almanac?

We all agreed that *Information Please* should reflect the world we live in. As the "Answer Book," it should contain today's answers to today's questions. Our readers should not be put in the position of the man who said, "I thought I had all the answers—and then they changed the questions!" Therefore, we felt we should delete any material that really didn't apply anymore, even if it were still "correct."

Let me cite one example: A table of square roots appears in virtually every almanac published anywhere in the world, just as it had been included in earlier editions of *Information Please.* It is *not* in this year's edition. As we re-examined our premises, we discovered that over 40 million calculators have been sold each year since 1975. Five years ago, about 75 percent of all students in engineering, science, and business owned their own calculators. Today, almost anyone who has the need to know square roots now owns a pocket electronic calculator. Therefore, we decided to make better use of the space occupied by these tables by including more useful, more *relevant* data.

What new data? We have always believed that *Information Please* should answer the kinds of questions most people ask:

—questions about specific personal needs or requirements

—questions about the world today, and

—questions about the past that might illuminate some aspect of the present.

The expanded sections on taxes, postage, consumerism, credit, growing older, education, and similar material have been updated and expanded to give current, specific, and practical answers to questions of the first kind. In many cases, we have chosen to go directly to experts in the field for our facts, because they are ideally equipped to know exactly what should be included in the "how-to" sections and to come up with useful answers.

As only one example, we went directly to the American Association of Retired Persons, a national, nonprofit organization specializing in the needs of older people, rather than having our own researchers dig up the data *they* thought were important. AARP experts drew on their day-to-day knowledge of their 12 million senior-citizen members to help identify those questions about growing older that are frequently asked—and then turned to their own extensive resources to come up with authoritative answers.

To help our readers cope with the present through a better understanding of the past, we completely revised our "Headline History." It now provides more detailed coverage of people, places, and events that can help the reader correlate people with events and the past with the present.

For someone trying to comprehend the quality of life in different countries around the world, we have searched for development statistics that suggest how people really live. These data give the reader another way of comparing one country with another—making the kinds of comparisons that are a necessary prerequisite to holding opinions that make sense.

That's why we added the new "Statistical History of the United States," too. Decade by decade, it illustrates how life has changed in these United States. It contains over a thousand "numbers" that help to explain how America has evolved and how our people have lived. Indeed, the changing statistics in this section alone demonstrate why the contents of *any* almanac need to be regularly reviewed.

We looked to Freedom House for its informed evaluation of social and political freedom around the world. While "human freedom" attracts a great deal of attention these days, many of us lack the fundamental information needed to think soundly about it. Since it is not sufficient simply to provide quick and easy labels, we've also included Freedom House's detailed explanations of the *criteria* by which political and social freedoms can be measured.

In this complex world, people often need more information on specific topics than any one-volume, all-purpose reference book can provide. So you will find in *Information Please* sources of additional facts, including a "Where to Find Out More" section to help you get to the bottom of things, if that is your goal.

If another goal of yours is to search for enjoyment from the amusing, if trivial, events of the day—and it's a reasonable goal these very serious days—we also want to help. Therefore, a new *Information Please* section—"The Year's Top Trivia"—provides a welcome change of pace.

It would take many more words to describe just why we added one item, deleted another, or expanded yet a third. In many cases, our reasons for doing so go back to letters from our readers. We believe that the more we know their views, the more easily we can create a book that meets their needs. Therefore, this year, we hope to organize a panel of *Information Please* readers to whom we can address specific questions about the usefulness of specific almanac features and about new information that is wanted or needed.

If you would like to become a member of this advisory panel, please let me know. We'll collect your replies and organize them according to where you live, your age, occupation, sex, and other such "demographic" criteria. Then we'll select at random a more manageable, smaller group to become our Reader Advisory Panel and represent our readers at large.

Please write me at Information Please, 57 West 57th Street, New York, N.Y. 10019, if you wish to become a member of this very special group. Be sure to include the following information about yourself: Your name, address, age, sex, marital status, occupation, and highest year of school you completed. This will help us choose a panel that is truly representative of you, our readers.

I very much look forward to hearing from you.

*Theodore B. Dolmatch*
*Editor*

# SPECIAL FEATURES

## The Year in Religion

*Dr. Billy Graham*

*Each year in Information Please,* different religious leaders review the year before, emphasizing developments of particular concern to members of their own faith and of broad interest to everyone. In the 1978 Almanac, Father Theodore M. Hesburgh wrote about American Catholicism. For this 1979 edition, Dr. Billy Graham presents *his* view of the past year's significant religious events.

A confidant of world leaders, Dr. Graham has personally addressed more than 60 million people on every continent. Ordained as a Baptist minister, he has received numerous awards from interfaith organizations and honorary degrees from universities around the world. The best-known evangelist of our time, Dr. Graham has written scores of books and articles on man and his faith.

---

Religious matters seldom receive top billing in the news, but in 1978 there were some notable exceptions. The most significant in many ways were the death of Pope Paul VI and the election of a relatively unknown cardinal as Pope John Paul I. His election was hailed not only by hundreds of millions of Roman Catholics across the world, but by countless others who hoped and prayed that he would become a symbol of peace and moral courage in the world.

Other religious issues also received their share of attention. In some of the major Christian denominations, controversy continued over such issues as homosexuality and the ordination of women to the ministry, with every indication such issues would continue to be discussed. The news media also took note of several instances of missionary martyrdom, especially in Africa, although indications were that the publicized cases were only a small part of widespread persecution in some other parts of the world as well.

Rather than attempt a complete survey of religious happenings of 1978, however, I think it is appropriate instead for me to concentrate on the particular tradition with which I am most acquainted—evangelicalism. Until a few years ago many people had never heard the term "evangelical" to describe a specific religious position. All that has changed, however. Once terms like "born again" and "conversion" were often relegated to smaller "fringe" groups within the Christian tradition. Now a steady stream of prominent politicians, entertainers, athletes, and others in the public eye can be found talking frankly about their evangelical convictions in books, magazines, and television talk shows. *Time* magazine's last issue of 1977 devoted its cover story to "The Evangelical Empire."

*What is an "evangelical"?* Those who call themselves evangelicals come from a wide variety of traditions and backgrounds, and may be widely different from one another in some respects. The thing that unites them is not organizational unity but a shared emphasis on certain key Christian beliefs. They affirm the historic creeds of the church, such as the Apostle's Creed and the Nicene Creed, and are therefore committed to the historic beliefs of Christians throughout the ages. They also share a common emphasis on the Bible as the Word of God, completely authoritative over their lives. Evangelicals also share an emphasis on the helplessness of the human race apart from the grace of God. They are convinced God did for us what we cannot do for ourselves—He provided a way through the death and resurrection of Jesus Christ whereby we may be forgiven of sin and given new life and salvation by faith in Him.

For many evangelicals the decision to turn to Jesus Christ and consciously accept Him as Master and Saviour was a deliberate act of faith that they vividly remember. It may have been in an evangelistic meeting or church service, or it may have been in the quiet of a hotel room or at home. It may have been dramatic, or it may have been very quiet and simple. Whatever the setting or the form, evangelicals stress the fact of conversion: The need—and possibility—that men and women can experience spiritual rebirth by turning to God in complete reliance and faith. At times it may seem to be only the reinforcing of beliefs held since childhood. For others it involves a radical redirection of thought and action.

*The Evangelical Visibility.* Modern evangelicals would insist they stand firmly in the mainstream of historic Biblical Christianity. Nevertheless, in the first half of the 20th Century, evangelicals in América seemed to be in steady decline. A variety of problems seemed to beset them, from assaults by an optimistic humanism to internal squabbles over peripheral doctrinal issues. Evangelicals also tended to retreat from involvement in the great social issues of the day (although they by no means lost a social concern completely), largely as a reaction to the growing "social gospel" movement. New theories from science and Biblical criticism also tended to put evangelicals on the defensive.

Now that has changed. Signs of a powerful evangelical resurgence were very much in evidence during 1978. Sales of evangelical books were at an all-time high—so much so that many large secular publishers are avidly entering the field of evangelical publishing. The growth of Christian television (such as the Christian Broadcasting Network) has been nothing short of explosive, and shows few signs of slowing down. All across the United States tens of thousands of Bible study groups have sprung up in homes, offices, factories, and colleges. New evangelistic and missionary movements and organizations have grown dramatically. The growth of the charismatic movement (which emphasizes especially the present work of the Holy Spirit) continues unabated, having a major impact especially in the more traditional and liturgical churches. While it has tended to stress spiritual experiences (such as joyous ecstatic speaking), for many it has heralded mainly a new commitment of life to God.

All of this (and more) has become newsworthy for the first time in at least half a century. Nevertheless, it is not the first time America has been gripped by an evangelical awakening. America was founded basically by people of strong Christian convictions, and from time to time those convictions have re-emerged to exert a profound effect on the whole nation.

*What of the future?* Will the present evangelical resurgence have as deep and positive influence as its predecessors? Or will it fade rapidly, with little impact on our society as a whole?

No one can answer that question right now, of course, much as I personally am optimistic about the potential good that is coming from the present evangelical renewal. I am encouraged, for example, by the strong recovery of interest in social action on the part of many evangelicals. I am also encouraged by the new emphasis on family life, particularly in an age when family relationships are under severe assault in many quarters. I am likewise encouraged by a new determination on the part of many evangelicals to be faithful disciples of their Lord in every dimension of personal and social life.

Many people today are disillusioned and even cynical about life. Materialism and humanism have shown little to our jaded world except their inability to solve the deepest problems and questions of the human heart. In the minds of many, Jean-Paul Sartre was correct when he said there was no exit from the human dilemma.

But evangelicals—with Christians throughout the centuries—have said the opposite. This life, they contend, has meaning and purpose, because God has created it and God has acted in Christ for its redemption and renewal. Perhaps the very hollowness of modern secular humanity will set the stage for an even greater spiritual renewal in 1979 —and beyond.

# Coping With Stress in 1979

*Hans Selye, C.C., M.D., Ph.D., D.Sc.*

*One of the pioneers of modern medicine, Dr. Hans Selye is world-famous for his discoveries about stress. His research has opened new avenues of treatment through the discovery that hormones participate in the development of many maladies that he calls "diseases of adaptation" or "stress diseases." Now President of the International Institute of Stress in Montreal, he was Director of the Institute of Experimental Medicine and Surgery of the University of Montreal from 1945 to 1976. Dr. Selye is the author of 38 books and 1600 articles, a Fellow of the Royal Society of Canada, and an Honorary Fellow of 43 other scientific societies around the world. The recipient of numerous awards for his contributions to science, he was invested Companion of the Order of Canada, the highest decoration awarded by his country, in 1968.*

---

In his overview on general medicine for the previous edition of this Almanac, Dr. Baruch S. Blumberg said "perhaps the most striking recent advance in medicine has been the growing realization that much of the responsibility for health must now be assumed by the people themselves. . . . In a recent national health survey, it was noted that most current illness in the United States is a consequence of the unhealthy habits of the patients."

This is particularly true of the methods designed to cope with the stress of daily life. As the president of the Rockefeller Foundation, Dr. John H. Knowles, pointed out in his remarkable book on health in the United States, *Doing Better and Feeling Worse,* we are doing better in the conquest of contagious diseases, infant mortality, and the development of technologies that extend life. Expenditures for health care in the United States have tripled in 10 years from $39 billion in 1965 to $119 billion in 1975, and yet most people are not happier and do not feel better. "The point is," he says, "most of the bad things that happen to people are at present beyond the reach of medicine." But he was careful to emphasize that they are *not* beyond the reach of individuals who try to supplement what medicine has to offer by taking the time and trouble necessary to learn how they can help themselves.

Of course, inevitably we will profit from the enormous progress made in the recognition and treatment of identifiable diseases of the body by modern medicine and surgery, but this is not enough. Now, the greatest challenge faced by the healing professions is to teach people how to live in a way that satisfies them without hurting others. I believe we can achieve this most effectively through the development of a code of behavior that assists us in coping with the stress of life in our increasingly "civilized" world.

I admit that I am prejudiced in favor of stress research, for I have worked in this area ever since I wrote the first paper on the stress syndrome in 1936. Then, I tried to demonstrate that stress is not a vague concept, somehow related to the decline in the influence of traditional codes of behavior, dissatisfaction with the world, or the rising cost of living. Rather, it is a clearly definable biological and medical phenomenon whose mechanisms can be objectively identified and with which we can cope much better once we know where the trouble lies.

Today, everyone talks about stress, but only a few people know exactly what it is. It is hard to read a newspaper or watch a television program without hearing about stress, and literally hundreds of people now lecture and write about it. They are ever ready to give advice, usually based on the teachings of an Eastern guru or Western "stressologist"—advice that works well just as long as one has absolute faith in the master's divine infallibility.

Far be it from me to suggest that such teaching has nothing to offer, but not all of us can be helped by the same teacher, and there are so many of them around that you could spend your entire life shopping for one that suits you. In any event, if you *do* succeed in finding such a "healer," you may still lose faith in what you originally thought was the creed that perfectly suited your needs, or you may "just not have the time" to follow the recommended prescription—which is another way of saying that you no longer believe it to be the best and shortest way to happiness.

There *are* alternatives. During recent years, considerable progress has been made in comprehending and controlling stress through classical scientific techniques. The results are of immense practical value for further improving the understanding of stress mechanisms by scientists, and for the treatment of certain stress-induced derangements by competent physicians.

Clearly, since 1936 a great deal of progress has been made in identifying the mechanisms of stress-induced bodily responses. At first, we knew only that they are not sudden, momentary changes provoked by nervous tension but rather non-specific, adaptive responses to the need for coping with demands of any kind, be they psychic (fear, frustration, pain, grief, job pressures, marital discord) or somatic (surgical operations, burns, loss of blood). Of course, bodily injuries also cause psychic arousal and excitement; nevertheless, the *actual, measurable* changes characteristic of stress as such are obvious, even in deeply anesthetized patients or experimental animals which are not conscious of any potentially painful or threatening situation.

However, if the troublesome "stressors" (stress-producing agents) last for weeks, months, or years, these adaptive reactions progress from the first stage of *general alarm* (so termed because it was visualized as a "call to arms" of all defense mechanisms) to the stage of *resistance,* during which we learn to deal better with the demands made upon us. The bodily expressions of exposure to stress —the visible organ changes or measurable alterations in the stress hormone content of our blood—tend to disappear. Yet our adaptability (or adaptation energy) is not infinite. Everyone breaks down sooner or later, depending upon his or her innate resistance and the intensity of the stress situation itself. If breakdown occurs, the stage of *exhaustion* is reached, the final breakdown which ends in death. This entire three-stage response to stressful situations has been called the *general adaptation syndrome* (G.A.S.).

It was clear from the outset that hormones, especially those of the pituitary (hypophysis) and the adrenals, play an important role in this response. If these glands are removed in experimental animals, or if excessive stress occurs in a person whose pituitary or adrenals have been incapacitated, the whole reaction is totally deranged and adaptation enormously diminished.

It was also clear that the nervous system plays a role, especially by starting the whole chain of events, because the pituitary receives its impulses almost exclusively from the base of the brain (hypothalamus) to which it is attached. However, both nerves and blood vessels descend to the pituitary through its stalk, and much more work was necessary in subsequent years to prove that if you cut the stalk, the adaptive mechanism is deranged almost as much as if you remove the pituitary entirely.

From the practical point of view, perhaps the most important subsequent observations were made during the 1940s. It was found that if the organs involved in resistance to stress are malfunctioning, diseases develop. These maladies are not so much due to what happens to us but to our inability to adapt, and they have therefore been called "diseases of adaptation." The most common among them are peptic ulcers in the stomach and upper intestine, high blood pressure, heart accidents, and nervous disturbances. Of course, any event makes demands upon us and, hence, causes some stress, but it is only people who cannot cope, either because of innate defects or lack of knowledge, who develop stress diseases.

We must also distinguish between the stress-producing agents (or stressors) that cause suffering or distress and the events that we appraise as pleasant because they give us satisfaction and happiness. (You also have to adapt yourself to the unexpected news of suddenly having become a multimillionaire or having found the girl you always dreamed of). They produce what we technically call *eustress* (*eu* = good, pleasant, as in euphonia, euphoria). Curiously, eustress rarely causes maladies and often actually counteracts the bad effects of distress. There are cases on record where people have died suddenly when faced with the news of a particularly pleasant, unexpected event; as a rule, however, the damage caused by eustress is negligible. After all, pleasure and satisfaction are what we want in life.

In this short essay, it is impossible to give a meaningful sketch of all that has been learned about the structure of stress hormones, the nerve pathways involved, the medicines that have been developed to combat stress, and the diagnostic aids that this approach has offered. Nevertheless, the medical, chemical or microscopic approach to the problem has been extremely fruitful.

Since the very first description of the G.A.S.—general adaptation syndrome—the most important single discovery was made only recently. It showed that the brain produces certain simple chemical substances closely related to the adrenal-stimulating or *a*dreno*c*ortico*t*rophic *h*ormone (ACTH). These substances have morphine-like, pain-killing properties, and since they come from the inside *(endo)*, they have been called *endorphins.* (I am especially proud that one of my former students, Dr. Roger Guillemin, was one of the three American scientists who shared the 1977 Nobel Prize for this remarkable discovery, although it was made quite independently of me at the Salk Institute.) The endorphins have opened up an entirely new field in medicine, particularly in stress research. Not only do they have anti-stress effects as pain-killers, but they also probably play an important role in the transmission of the alarm signal from the brain to the pituitary, and their concentration is especially high in the pituitary itself.

Significant breakthroughs have also been made with the discovery of tranquilizers and psychotherapeutic chemicals to combat mental diseases. These have reduced the number of institutionalized mental patients to an unprecedented low. Also worth mentioning are the enormously potent anti-ulcer drugs that block the pathways through which stress ulcers are produced.

However, all these purely medical discoveries are applicable only by physicians, and the general public cannot use them in daily life without constant medical supervision. Furthermore, most of these agents are not actually directed against stress but rather against some of its morbid manifestations (ulcers, high blood pressure, heart accidents). Therefore, increasing attention has been given to the development of psychological techniques and behavioral codes that anybody can use after suitable instruction to adjust to the particular demands made by his life.

Among these *not* strictly medical approaches are the *relaxation techniques.* We should spend a little time each day at complete rest, with our eyes closed, our muscles relaxed, breathing regularly and repeating words that are either meaningless or heard so often that they merely help us not think of anything in particular. This is the basis of transcendental meditation, Benson's relaxation technique, and an infinite variety of other procedures. They have been given to us by religion, from the most ancient faiths up to the Eastern sages and contemporary theologies, and include reciting the litany or standard prayers in the quiet and elevating atmosphere of a house of worship, with tranquilizing music. These practices should not be underestimated merely because science cannot explain them; they have worked for so long and in so many forms that we must respect them.

More recently, *biofeedback* has added a great deal to the psychological approach. A number of highly sophisticated instruments have been developed that inform us constantly about changes characteristic of stress, for example, blood pressure, pulse rate, body temperature, and even electrical brain waves. We do not yet have a scientific explanation for biofeedback, but if you learn to identify, instinctively or through instrumentation, when you are under stress, you can automatically avoid, or at least reduce, it.

Of course, the most important thing we must do is to live happily, and so each of us needs to develop a code of behavior that helps to achieve this. It will never be possible to discover a code or philosophy of conduct equally applicable to everybody. Any code has to be adjusted to the person involved, for we are all different.

After 40 years of research in laboratories and clinics, scientists have found enough evidence to justify trying to develop a code of behavior based only on the laws of Nature. These laws are eternal and applicable to everybody regardless of race, sex, religion, or national and political loyalties. They are equally applicable to everybody because all of us are products of Nature. They are also eternal. Water boils at 100°C at sea level; it always has and always will. These laws apply to body and mind, but we need much more scientific work to learn how to apply them in daily life and to make them easily understandable to everyone.

After four decades of clinical and laboratory research, I would to summarize the most important principles briefly as follows:

1. *Find your own stress level*—the speed at which you can run toward your own goal. Make sure that both the stress level and the goal are really your own, and

not imposed upon you by society, for only you yourself can know what you want and how fast you can accomplish it. There is no point in forcing a turtle to run like a racehorse or preventing a racehorse from running faster than a turtle because of some "moral obligation." The same is true of people.

2. *Be an altruistic egoist.* Do not try to suppress the natural instinct of all living beings to look after themselves first. Yet the wish to be of some use, to do some good to others, is also natural. We are social beings, and everybody wants somehow to earn respect and gratitude. You must be useful to others. This gives you the greatest degree of safety, because no one wishes to destroy a person who is useful.
3. *Earn they neighbor's love.* This is a contemporary modification of the maxim "Love thy neighbor as thyself." It recognizes that all neighbors are not lovable and that it is impossible to love on command.

In my first book for the layman, I tried to condense several thousand scientific articles and two dozen books into 324 pages—which may still have been too long and too technical. Perhaps two short lines can summarize what I have discovered from all my though and research:

Fight for *your* highest *attainable* aim,
but do not put up resistance in vain.

# CURRENT EVENTS

## What Happened in 1977–78

The important events of the year, from November 1977 to October 1978, organized for easy reference:



The Countries of the World section (starting on page 127) covers specific international events, country by country. Special commentaries on Business and the Economy, Energy, Medicine, Religion, Space, Travel, Weather, and Women appear in the appropriate sections (*see* Index).

## Major Events—October 1978

### 1978 Nobel Prize Winners

**Literature:** Issac Bashevis Singer, Polish-born Yiddish writer.

**Medicine:** Dr. Daniel Nathans and Dr. Hamilton Smith, both of Johns Hopkins University, and Dr. Werner Arber of the University of Basel, for discovery of restriction enzymes and their application to problems of molecular genetics.

**Economics:** Prof. Herbert A. Simon, Carnegie-Mellon University, Pittsburgh, Pa., for "his pioneering research into the decision-making process within economic organizations."

**Physics:** Dr. Arno A. Penzias and Dr. Robert W. Wilson, Bell Telephone Laboratories, N.J., for work in cosmic microwave radiation; and Dr. Piotr Leonidovich Kaplitisa, Soviet Union, for his basic inventions and discoveries in low temperature physics.

**Chemistry:** Dr. Peter Mitchell, Glynn Research Laboratories, Cornwall, England, for his contribution to the understanding of biological energy transfer.

**Lebanon Crisis Worsens (Oct. 5):** Syrians bombard Christian areas; American embassy grounds come under fire. Israeli gunboats shell Palestinian guerrillas and Syrian artillery in defense of Christians. President Carter writes Syrian President Assad expressing deep concern and calling for cease-fire. **(Oct. 7):** Syrian forces reduce shelling of Christian areas, and uneasy truce is in force after U.N. Security Council call for cease-fire **(Oct. 6).**

**ERA Deadline Extended (Oct. 8):** Senate votes 60–36 to extend deadline for Equal Rights Amendment ratification until June 30, 1982. House had previously approved.

**Panama Government Changes (Oct. 10):** Gen. Omar Torrijos Herrera turns presidency over to Aristides Rayo, a moderate. Torrijos expected to retain strong influence.

**Belgian Leader Resigns (Oct. 11):** Prime Minister Léo Tindemans quits after difficulties with his coalition government over constitutional and other issues.

**"Koreagate" Scandal Investigation Ends (Oct. 13):** Three California Democratic congressmen reprimanded. Senate Ethics Committee concludes that only two now-deceased senators violated the law.

**New Swedish Prime Minister (Oct. 13):** Liberal Party leader, Ola Ullsten, named to replace Thorbjörn Fälldin.

**Brazil Names New President (Oct. 13):** Retired General Joao Figueiredo named by Electoral College.

**Russian U.N. Employees Guilty of Espionage (Oct. 13):** Two-week trial in Newark, N.J., federal court ends in conviction of Vladik Enger and Rudolf Chernyayev.

**Humphrey-Hawkins Bill Passes at Close of 95th Congress (Oct. 15):** Diluted "full employment" measure finally approved in House with additional goals of reduced inflation, balanced budget, higher farm price supports, foreign trade surplus.

**Congress Approves Carter Energy Package (Oct. 15):** After 1½-year struggle, much-modified bill passes. Compromise measure will gradually deregulate new natural gas, increase taxes on fuel-guzzling autos, provide home and business credits for energy savings, push industrial conversion to coal power, etc.

**Tax Bill Passes Congress (Oct. 15):** Cuts of $18.7 billion made for 1979—moderate reductions meet Carter's objections to previous Congressional proposals.

**New Pope Chosen (Oct. 16):** Cardinal Karol Wojtyla, 58, Archbishop of Krakow, Poland, adopts title of Pope John Paul II. He is the first non-Italian to rule Church in 455 years.

# 1977–78

## Business and the Economy

### 1977

**I.B.M. Will Leave India (Nov. 15):** Decides to dismantle manufacturing and marketing operations, refusing to accept demands of Indian government for nationalization.

**2 Old Wall Street Investment Firms to Merge (Nov. 28):** Lehman Brothers, Inc. and Kuhn Loeb & Company merger unites two concerns with international prestige and diversified capability.

**Dock Pact Ends 60-day Walkout (Nov. 29):** Strikers vote to accept new master contract and local agreements, ending tie-up that paralyzed container shipping from Maine to Texas. Job security and guaranteed annual income provided.

**Administration Announces Plan to Aid Steel (Dec. 6):** Seeks to protect depressed industry against import competition. Would help provide financing through loan guarantees, tax breaks, and other aid.

**Nationwide Farmers' Strike Begins (Dec. 14):** Scattered picketing, rallies, and withholding of deliveries from some markets under way in move to cut off food supplies until growers get higher prices. Strike led by American Agriculture Movement, loose federation.

### 1978

**U.S. and Japan Reach Accord on Trade Tensions (Jan. 13):** Agree on bilateral economic measures expected to lead to new and more liberal era in trading relationships. Agreement follows six months of mounting tensions over Japan's trade surplus.

**Kodak Convicted in Antitrust Case (Jan. 21):** World's largest photographic manufacturer held guilty by federal court jury in New York of monopolizing much of amateur photography business. Jury finds monopoly damaged Berkey Photo Inc., a company with sales of less than $200 million yearly. **(June 16):** Jury's award reduced by judge to $27.1 million, expected to be tripled under federal laws designed to punish and discourage antitrust violators.

**1977 Trade Deficit Called U.S. Biggest (Jan. 28):** Commerce Dept. reports $26.7 billion record deficit, largely fed by mounting oil imports, more than four times 1976 deficit of $5.9 billion. Former record set with $6.4 billion in 1972. Another deficit foreseen for 1978.

**Cesar Chavez Ends Nationwide Boycotts (Jan. 31):** Halts United Farm Workers union action against lettuce, table grapes, and Gallo wine. Calls boycotts instrumental in winning labor contracts for union and helping foster labor relations law in California.

**British-U.S. Pact on Air Fares (March 17):** Reached after two-week impasse, it provides for lower fares on scheduled flights and fewer restrictions on charters. Settlement provides bargain flights between London and 14 American gateway cities. Accord is victory for Carter and Civil Aeronautics Board.

**Debtor Harassment Barred (March 20):** Fair Debt Collection Practices Act in effect, barring collectors from calling debtors at all hours, threatening them or using abusive language. Consumers also gain right to sue for damages, court costs and lawyer fees.

**U.S. Curbs Deadly Cargoes (March 23):** Dept. of Transportation orders ban on hazardous materials in freight cars with high-carbon wheels as result of recent derailments. Cars with such wheels also to be barred in any train carrying dangerous matter. End of year deadline for removing all such wheels from freight system.

**112-Day Coal Strike Ends (March 27):** Miners in major coal-producing states accept three-year contract and return to work after rejection of two earlier proposals. A total of 160,000 members of United Mine Workers involved. Contract provides hourly $4.97 increase in wages and benefits over three years; it improves pensions and health and other benefits; miners must now pay for some of health care; no curb on wildcat strikes imposed. Rise in costs over three years set at 38.8%. Highlights of strike—**(March 5):** Miners vote overwhelmingly against latest contract proposals. **(March 6):** President Carter invokes strike-halting provisions of Taft-Hartley Act, warning of widespread economic damage. **(March 9):** Administration gets Federal Court back-to-work order to begin 80-day cooling-off period under act. Union miners ignore order as settlement nears. **(March 14)** Strike settled. Industry reports tie-up cost 120 million tons in lost production, $2 billion in unretrievable sales and $200 million in vanished profits.

**AMC and Renault Join Forces (March 31):** Agree on joint manufacture and distribution of cars. Renaults will be sold by AMC in U.S. and Canada, and Renault will sell AMC Jeeps abroad. Renaults also may be manufactured by AMC in U.S.

**First VW Made in America (April 10):** White Rabbit rolls off assembly line at new Volkswagen plant at East Huntington Township, Pa. Begins era of "Made in America" cars by many foreign companies.

**J.P. Stevens Settles With Labor Board (April 28):** Company agrees not to engage in illegal anti-union tactics, without admitting guilt. Board drops request for sweeping injunction to stop tactics. Both Stevens and Textile Workers Union regard agreement as a victory.

**Jobless Rate Lowest in 3½ Years (May 5):** Nation's unemployment rate down to 6% in April, Labor Dept. reports. Total employment continued to expand sharply. But rising inflation rate causes concern.

**China Finds New Offshore Oil (May 5):** Reports oil and natural gas deposits in South China Sea and plans development as major field. China has made sizable purchases of U.S. technology on offshore oil, including fixed platforms.

**Curbs on Eyeglass Ads Lifted (May 24):** FTC ends restrictions on price advertising, move to foster competition. Eventual savings to consumers put at $400 million a year.

**Inflation at Double-Digit Annual Rate (May 31):** Consumer prices reported up by 0.9% for April, biggest monthly increase in more than year. Record 6.6% rise in beef prices led the way.

**CAB Moves on Overbooking (June 1):** Revised rules require airlines to pay up to $400 to any passenger with confirmed reservation who is denied a seat.

**Ford Orders Recall of Pintos (June 9):** Will modify fuel system in 1.5 million subcompacts to increase resistance to leakage and risk of fire. Move follows months of vigorous defense of fuel system.

**G.E. Settles Discrimination Case (June 15):** Agrees to pay $32 million to aid job advancement for women and minorities. Bias charges had been brought in 1973 by Equal Employment Opportunity Commission.

**OPEC Maintains Oil Price (June 19):** Keeps world level at present rate for rest of year. Forms committee to study ways to protect revenues, paid in dollars, against declining rate of U.S. currency.

**Import Duty Ruled Optional (June 21):** Supreme Court averts increase in prices for imported Japanese electronic products, with almost certain inflationary impact. Justices rule Treasury Secretary is not required by 1897 law to impose "countervailing duty."

**LTV-Lykes Merger Approved (June 21):** Attorney General Bell consents to proposal that would make two steel companies—Jones & Laughlin and Youngstown Sheet & Tube—third largest steel producer, in merger of two conglomerates. LTV owns J. & L., Lykes Youngstown Sheet & Tube.

**Ford Motor Co. President Quits (July 13):** Lee A. Iacocca resigns after rift with company chairman Henry Ford II. **(Sept. 14):** Philip Caldwell, 58, vice chairman, named president to succeed Iacocca.

**United Airlines Orders 767 Jets (July 14):** Places $1.2-billion order with Boeing Company for 30 new-generation middle-size airliners. It is largest commercial order, in dollars, ever placed for single airliner or package of planes.

**Agreement on Postal Contract Reached (July 21):** Postal Service and unions settle on 3-year pact providing 19.5% increase in wages and benefits, making cost-of-living increases permanent part of salaries and keeping no-layoff clause.

**Gold above $200 an Ounce in Europe (July 28):** Renewed weakness of U.S. dollar reflected in record price following heavy purchasing of metal. American failure to curb inflation blamed.

**Europe Air Travel in Chaos (July 31):** Hundreds of thousands jam airports because of slowdown by French air controllers and flood of U.S. and Canadian travelers waiting for standby seats on Atlantic flights.

**IBM Wins Verdict in Memorex Case (Aug. 12):** Judge rules in $1-billion antitrust action after jury fails to reach verdict in San Francisco trial. Court finds no evidence that IBM acts were anticompetitive or predatory. Memorex to appeal.

**Police on Strike in Memphis (Aug. 14):** About 1,200 Tennessee national guardsmen protect police stations and firehouses after hundreds of firemen join walkout by 1,000 police. Civil emergency declared, with tight curfew. Officials term firemen's action a wildcat strike.

**$25.6 Million Verdict Against Xerox (Aug. 16):** SCM. Corp. awarded damages on part of office-copier market from which federal jury in Hartford said Xerox had excluded SCM. Jury earlier had awarded SCM $11.7 million in other monopoly claims.

**A.T. & T. Cuts Overseas Rates (Aug. 17):** Reduction and special discount for overseas calls, effective Nov. 15, will total more than $230 million in first year. Plan will establish international dial rates to 46 countries.

**Slash in Air Fares Allowed (Aug. 26):** CAB gives lines authority to slash coach rates as much as 50% below existing levels on all flights and as much as 70% for off-hours flights. Also gives some leeway in raising fares.

**G.M. to Desegregate South African Plants (Aug. 29):** Plans to spend $4.5 million to improve and integrate facilities and increase training of nonwhites.

**Antitrust Suit Against Bar Dropped (Aug. 30):** Justice Dept., with federal court approval, dismisses case against American Bar Association, saying battle to allow lawyers to advertise is over. Government cites Supreme Court ruling and bar association's liberalized policy.

## The Courts

### 1977

**Ruling Bars Antitrust Immunity for A.T.&T. (Nov. 28):** Supreme Court rejects contention that far-flung communications network is immune because of existing heavy federal and state regulation. U.S. civil suit can proceed.

**Justices Relax Rule on Phone Surveillance (Dec. 7):** Supreme Court, 5–4, rules that federal district courts have authority to order telephone company to install surveillance equipment in criminal investigation.

### 1978

**Supreme Court Rejects Challenges to Press Curbs (Jan. 9):** Refuses to consider dispute over court orders limiting coverage of criminal trials in Ohio and South Carolina. Leaves standing judges' "gag orders" prohibiting statements outside courtroom by participants or officials.

**Immunity of Judges Upheld (March 28):** Supreme Court rules it is broad enough to cover "grave procedural errors." Decision reached in Indiana case involving judge's approval of sterilization of 15-year-old girl and her parents' subsequent damage suit.

**Justices Restrict Nixon Tapes (April 18):** Supreme Court refuses broadcasters and recording companies right to copy, broadcast, and sell excerpts from White House tapes that led to resignation.

**Higher Pension Costs for Women Barred (April 25):** Supreme Court rules employer guilty of illegal sex discrimination if he charges women more than men to participate in a pension plan even though women generally live longer than men.

**Corporate Spending in Elections Upheld (April 26):** Supreme Court, 5–4, rules states cannot bar corporations from spending unlimited amounts to influence outcome of public referendums. Justices hold Constitution protects their freedom of speech as it does for individuals.

**U.S. Safety Checks Restricted (May 23):** Supreme Court, 5–3, rules Occupational Safety and Health Administration cannot make spot inspections of employers' premises without obtaining a warrant. Alternative procedures suggested.

**Ban on New Press-Video Links Upheld (June 12):** Supreme Court backs FCC policy that newspapers can no longer acquire radio or television stations, as move to limit economic concentration. Existing combinations can continue.

**Double Jeopardy Ban Narrowed (June 14):** Supreme Court, 5–4, rules criminal can be tried by Government second time if charges had been dismissed "on grounds unrelated to factual guilt or innocence."

**Justices Void Anti-Dumping Law (June 23):** Supreme Court, 7–2, rules New Jersey cannot prevent other states from dumping wastes inside its borders, striking down 1974 ban on imports of material not headed for recycling or reprocessing.

**Right of News Media Curbed (June 26):** Supreme Court, 4–3, rules press has no "constitutional right of access" to jails and other government facilities beyond that granted to general public.

**Affirmative Action Programs Upheld (June 28):** Supreme Court affirms constitutionality of college admission programs giving advantage to blacks and other minorities to help remedy past discrimination. Justices also rule that Allan P. Bakke must be admitted to University of California Medical College at Davis, holding college's quota plan unjustifiably biased against white applicants. Both decisions 5–4, with Lewis F. Powell, Jr. joining four others supporting Bakke admission, then shifting to join four remaining Justices favoring flexible affirmative action plans. Ruling hailed as Court's most significant civil-rights decision since outlawing public school segregation in 1954. Attorney General Bell says he and President Carter regard decision as "great gain for affirmative action." Civil rights advocates generally pleased, with some exceptions.

**Defendants in Capital Cases Get Leeway (July 3):** Supreme Court, 6–2, rules they must be permitted to offer broad mitigating evidence in opposing death sentence. Finds narrow Ohio law deprives defendants of rights. Other death penalty laws in doubt.

**Court Backs Jobs for Minorities (July 3):** Supreme Court, without dissent, supports affirmative action to remedy past discrimination in employment, even when programs conflict with union seniority systems. Justices leave standing 1973 consent decree requiring A.T.&T. to hire more blacks and women. Three unions had charged violation of contracts.

**N.Y. Times Reporter Jailed (Aug. 4):** M.A. Farber and newspaper fail to win delay of penalties for refusal to turn over files for use by defense in murder trial of Dr. Mario E. Jascalavich. Reporter ordered jailed and *Times* fined $5,000 a day by New Jersey judge until files are given up. Supreme Court Justice Thurgood Marshall refuses to grant stay. **(Aug. 30):** After 27 days in jail, Farber is released by New Jersey Supreme Court, which suspends contempt citation against him and *The Times* pending hearing on controversy. Thirty-three large news organizations granted permission to participate.

## Crime and Violence

### 1977

**2 Guilty in Reporter's Death (Nov. 6):** Phoenix, Ariz., jury convicts Max Dunlap, 48, contractor, and James Robison, 55, plumber, in bomb assassination of Don Bolles, reporter for *The Arizona Republic*, while he was investigating organized crime in 1976. **(Jan. 10):** Judge sentences pair to gas chamber. Appeal is automatic.

**Alabaman Guilty in 1963 Church Blast (Nov. 18):** Robert E. Chambliss, 73, former Ku Klux Klansman, convicted in Birmingham of first-degree murder in bombing at Baptist church that killed four young black girls—one of the South's worst racial incidents. Chambliss gets life term. Integrated jury reflects changes in South since 1963.

**Evel Knievel Begins Jail Term (Nov. 21):** Motorcycle stunt man starts serving sentence in California for beating with a baseball bat of television executive who wrote a book about him. Must spend nights and weekends in jail for six months.

**Dutch Art Collector Convicted for World War II Killings (Dec. 14):** Pieter Menten, 78, found guilty of having participated in killing of 20 to 30 Polish Jews. Sentenced to 15 years in prison.

**Bus Kidnappers Found Guilty and Face Life (Dec. 15):** Three already convicted of kidnapping 27 captives on Chowchilla, Calif., school bus are convicted of causing bodily harm to three children. Life sentence without parole is mandatory.

### 1978

**Terms Shortened in Wilmington Bombing (Jan. 23):** North Carolina Gov. James B. Hunt, Jr., makes nine blacks of "Wilmington 10" remaining in prison eligible for parole. Affirms belief in their guilt in firebombing in which two died, and concludes that trial and appeal procedures were fair.

**Charges Against Filipino Nurses Dropped (Feb. 1):** Government abandons case against Filipina Narciso, 30, and Leonora Perez, 32, nurses who had been granted a new trial after conviction on charges of poisoning patients at a V.A. hospital in Ann Arbor, Mich.

**Bombing Shuts Down Alaska Pipeline (Feb. 14):** 800-mile project closed nearly 24 hours after bomb blows hole. **(Feb. 17):** Line back in operation after workers fit sleeve over 2-inch hole.

**Boyle Convicted Again in Slaying (Feb. 18):** Seventy-six-year-old W. A. Boyle, former United Mine Workers leader, guilty on three counts of first-degree murder in 1969 deaths of Joseph A. Yablonski, insurgent union leader; his wife, Margaret, and daughter, Charlotte. Life term mandatory under Pennsylvania law.

**Guilty Plea in "Koreagate" Case (March 17):** Former Rep. Richard T. Hanna, D.-Calif., concedes he conspired with South Korean CIA and Tongsun Park to defraud U.S. in influence peddling. First person to admit wrongdoing while in Congress.

**Korean Guilty in Bribe Plot (April 8):** Hancho C. Kim, business man, convicted by federal jury in Washington of conspiring to bribe Congressmen and lying about it under oath. Trial is first growing out of Korean influence-buying scandal.

**High Court Rebuffs Patricia Hearst (April 24):** Denies appeal for review of conviction for robbing a San Francisco bank. Miss Hearst, sentenced to seven years, free on bail of $1 million guaranteed by father, Randolph A. Hearst, California publisher. **(May 15):** Returns to Federal facility near San Francisco to serve rest of seven-year sentence for bank robbery.

**American Charged in Letelier Slaying (April 26):** Michael Vernon Townley, 35, recently extradited from Chile, accused of conspiracy to murder former Chilean Ambassador, Orlando Letelier, killed in Washington in 1976 when bomb destroyed his car. Government identifies Townley as agent of Chilean intelligence service. **(May 5):** Three anti-Castro Cuban exiles charged with conspiracy in Letelier killing: Ignacio Novo Sampol, 39, leader of a Cuban nationalist organization, José Dionisio Suarez Esquivel, 39, and Virgilio Paz Romero, 26.

**Berkowitz Pleads Guilty (May 8):** David Berkowitz publicly admits he was "Son of Sam" .44 caliber killer in New York as his guilty pleas to six charges are accepted in New York Supreme Court. He is charged with second-degree murder. **(June 12):** Berkowitz gets 25 years to life in each of six New York slayings.

**Huey Newton Arrested (May 11):** Black Panther Party chairman and two associates charged with intent to murder after a barroom brawl in Santa Cruz County, Calif. Newton faces murder and assault trials in Oakland.

**3 Killed at Paris Airport (May 20):** French police fell three terrorists who open fire on passengers at Orly. Three passengers booked on El Al flight to Tel Aviv wounded. Policeman killed. Gunmen had passports from Arab nations.

**Joan Little Returned to Prison (June 9):** Loses appeals in New York and Federal courts to avoid serving rest of 7–10 year sentence in North Carolina for breaking and entering. Miss Little, 24, acquitted in 1975 in murder of white guard, feared harm and possible death from North Carolina prison officials. **(July 12):** Miss Little pleads guilty in North Carolina court to prison-escape charges and is sentenced to six months to two years in prison additional.

**Youth Guilty in Killing (June 18):** Richard J. Herrin convicted of first-degree manslaughter in hammer-bludgeoning of former girl friend, Bonnie Joan Garland, in her Scarsdale, N.Y., home. Yale graduate, 24, jailed after bail is revoked.

**Manson Family Member Convicted Again (July 5):** Leslie Van Houten must serve life sentence on first-degree murder charge. Jury backs first verdict in 1970 on knife slayings of grocery-chain executive and wife.

**Union Head Indicted as Embezzler (July 19):** Joseph P. Tonelli, adviser to three Presidents, charged with theft of $360,000 from United Paperworkers. Other union officials also accused along with 70-year-old Tonelli, who is a vice president of AFL-CIO International Executive Council.

**Officer Killed in Philadelphia Raid (Aug. 8):** Shot to death as law forces storm barricaded house of self-styled revolutionaries with bulldozer, fire hoses and tear gas. Eighteen other persons injured. Members of group called "Move" surrender, ending long legal battle with city over health-code and weapons violations.

**Ambassador's Son Found Slain (Aug. 30):** Body of Hugo Margain, Jr., son of Mexican envoy to U.S., discovered near Mexico City 12 hours after kidnapping by abductors demanding $2 million ransom. Thirty-five-year-old director of Institute of Philosophy at University of Mexico had been shot in leg and bled to death.

**Harrises Plead Guilty (Aug. 31):** William and Emily, members of Symbionese Liberation Army, enter pleas in kidnapping of Patricia Hearst in 1974.

## Disasters

### 1977

**38 Dead in Georgia Dam Break (Nov. 6):** Earthen dam at Toccoa collapses during heavy rains. Water surges through trailer park of Bible College.

**Toll Is Heavy in India Cyclone (Nov. 19):** At least 10,000 dead as storm strikes state of Andhra Pradesh. Hundreds of villages and towns in Krishna River delta isolated by floodwaters. **(Nov. 22):** India begins major relief effort.

**Severe Quake Rocks Argentina (Nov. 23):** At least 50 dead, hundreds injured, and thousands of dwellings wrecked by tremors over wide area reaching into Chile, Peru, and Brazil.

**Hijacked Airliner Crashes in Malaysia (Dec. 4):** All 100 aboard dead after terrorists seize Boeing 737 of Malaysian Airline System.

**Basketball Team Among 29 Killed in Air Crash (Dec. 13):** Fourteen players and coach of University of Evansville (Ind.) victims when chartered DC-3 crashes in rain and fog on way to game.

**7 Students Killed in Providence Fire (Dec. 13):** Sixteen students injured in flash fire on top floor of a women's dormitory at Providence College in Rhode Island. Building had neither fire escapes nor sprinkler system.

**Two Supertankers Collide Off South Africa (Dec. 16):** 330,000-ton deadweight-on vessels catch fire in crash that costs lives of two of 84 crewmen. Crash believed first between supertankers at sea.

**Blasts Kill 56 Grain Workers (Dec. 31):** Death toll in fires and explosions of grain dust in 10-day period is greater than in all 137 elevator accidents in previous 18 years. Investigations under way by Occupational Safety and Health Administration and Agriculture Dept. Worst incident is death of 36 on Dec. 22 at Continental Grain Co., Westwego, La. Other companies with fatalities were: Farmers Export Co., Galveston, Tex., 18, and Sunshine Mills & Grain Inc., Tupelo, Miss, 2.

### 1978

**41 Dead in Canadian Plane Crash (Feb. 11):** Pacific Western Airlines passenger Boeing 737 jet overshoots runway while landing in heavy snow at Cranbrook, B.C. Seven, including flight attendant, survive. Pilot sought to avoid snowplow on runway.

**9 Dead in Tank Car Blast (Feb. 24):** Fifty-one are injured and damage is heavy in downtown Waverly, Tenn., as derailed tanker car filled with butane explodes while crew pumps contents into a truck. Accident comes two days after experts warn Congress that some liquefied gas facilities in the nation are not safe enough. **(March 3):** Government investigators find human error in operation of train. **(March 9):** National Transportation Safety Board asks emergency action to replace 150,000 sets of freight-car wheels like those involved in such recent derailments. Would restrict use of high-carbon wheels.

**8 Killed by Gas in Derailed Car (Feb. 26):** Sixty-seven hurt as chlorine spews across busy highway after freight train including tank cars derails near Youngstown, Fla. Auto engines stalled by fumes. Some of victims lived nearby or were hunting in woods. About 2,500 residents of 80-square-mile area in rural northern Florida evacuated. **(March 3):** Government investigation finds evidence that tracks were sabotaged.

**73 Perish in Bulgarian Plane Crash (March 16):** All on board killed as Bulgarian Soviet-built Tupolev-134 plunges to ground shortly after takeoff from Sofia Airport.

**51 Killed in Tower Collapse (April 27):** All workmen die as scaffolding crumbles inside a power plant cooling tower under construction at St. Mary's, W.Va. **(June 8):** U.S. charges willful or serious violations of safety regulations in collapse of scaffolding. Companies are: Research-Cottrell Inc., Pittsburgh Testing Laboratory, and United Engineers and Constructors.

**Death Toll 140 in Spanish Blast (July 11):** Hundreds engulfed in flames as tank truck carrying liquid industrial gas overturns and explodes at a Mediterranean coastal campsite near Tarragona.

**41 Drown as Bus Sinks (Aug. 5):** Mentally and physically handicapped persons killed after vehicle's brakes fail and it goes out of control on hill in Quebec and plunges into lake.

**Nearly 400 Killed in Iran Theater Fire (Aug. 20):** Arsonists pour gasoline around building in southwestern port city of Abadan and ignite it. Police blame extremists opposed to Shah's religious reforms and to attendance at cinema during Moslem holy month of Ramadan. Cinema crowd consisted mostly of youngsters.

**Antarctica Chapel Destroyed (Aug. 22):** Chapel of the Snows at McMurdo Station bulldozed to prevent fire from spreading to other structures and vital cables. One of few remaining original buildings at U.S. station opened in 1956.

**1,000 Dead in India Floods (Sept. 9):** Toll grows, with hundreds of thousands more driven from homes, as overflow from rampaging Ganges and Jamuna Rivers destroys crops and swirls into Taj Mahal gardens. Property damage estimated at over $100 million.

**Iran Earthquake Toll Climbs (Sept. 16):** Over 25,000 people reported dead or injured after quake measuring 7.7 on Richter scale in northeastern Iran. Epicenter at city of Tabas, where two thirds of 12,000 residents die.

**Worst Air Disaster in U.S. History (Sept. 25):** All 135 on Pacific Southwest jet liner approaching San

Diego dead in mid-air collision with private plane. Two in small plane and people on ground also killed, bringing toll to 144.

## Education

### 1977

**Hutchins Successor Is Selected (Nov. 21):** Center for the Study of Democratic Institutions at Santa Barbara, Calif., chooses Maurice B. Mitchell, chancellor of University of Denver, to succeed late Robert M. Hutchins as president.

**Acting Yale President to Head U. of Chicago (Dec. 10):** Hanna Holborn Gray, 47, history scholar, chosen by board of trustees of University of Chicago as 10th president.

**Scholar Named Yale's 18th President (Dec. 19):** A. Bartlett Giamatti, 39-year-old Renaissance literature scholar and one of Yale's most popular teachers, named by Yale Corporation. He succeeds Kingman Brewster, Jr.

### 1978

**Columbia Left $12 Million Bequests (April 11):** Percy Kierstede Hudson, stockbroker, gives $7 million in will, and wife, former chorus girl, $5 million. The broker had cut Columbia out of will in 1934 because he believed there were radicals on faculty.

**Supreme Court Rules for Bakke (June 28):** Holds that racial quota plan at the University of California Medical College at Davis is unjustifiably biased against white applicants. Ruling, 5–4, finds that Allan P. Bakke, who had sued, must be admitted to the Medical College.

**Teacher Strikes Widespread (Sept. 23):** School strikes in seven states affect almost 500,000 students. Nineteen-day strike in Bridgeport, Conn., which resulted in jailing of more than 260 teachers, settled.

## Energy

### 1978

**Way for Oil Drilling Cleared (Feb. 21):** Supreme Court rebuffs appeals against exploration for oil and natural gas off mid-Altantic coast. Challenges had blocked drilling for more than 18 months.

**Canada Rejects Kitimat Oil Port (Feb. 23):** Government, in surprise decision, rejects major facility in British Columbia for storing Alaskan oil to be piped to American refineries in Middle West.

**Atomic Project Doomed in California (April 17):** State legislators kill bill to remove statutory obstacles to $3-billion Sundesert power generating plant. Many in state have misgivings about nuclear perils.

**Uranium Sale to India Ordered (April 27):** President Carter overrules Nuclear Regulatory Commission and orders sale of more than eight tons of enriched uranium to India for nuclear power plant outside Bombay. Carter says denial of sale would hurt efforts to have India accept safeguards.

**Work on Seabrook Plant Halted (June 30):** Nuclear Regulatory Commission orders suspension of construction on controversial nuclear power facility in New Hampshire. Environmental Protection Agency to decide whether cooling system satisfies environmental requirements. **(Aug. 5):** EPA rejects environmentalists' arguments and approves open-ocean-cooling system for project. Action could clear way for construction.

**Breakthrough in Nuclear Fusion (Aug. 12):** Energy Dept. reports Princeton scientists use small test reactor to produce sunlike temperatures inside magnetic "bottle." Process might lead to cheap, abundant and safe power source in next century.

**Gas Discovered Off East Coast (Aug. 14):** Texaco Inc. reports finding natural gas in Baltimore Canyon about 100 miles off Atlantic City, first such discovery along Atlantic coast. Further tests scheduled.

## Entertainment and Culture

### 1977

**Metropolitan Opera Financially Sound (Dec. 18):** After eight years of operating losses, Anthony A. Bliss, executive director, reports dramatic fiscal turnaround.

### 1978

**Rubens Painting Sold for $3 Million (Jan. 27):** Self-portrait of family of 17th-century Flemish artist bought by private buyer for between $3 million and $4 million. Official of Metropolitan Museum calls work "greatest Rubens in this country."

**Sale of Brueghel Painting Sets Records (Jan. 13):** Swiss dealer pays $560,000 for still-life by Jan Brueghel the Elder at auction at Sotheby Parke Bernet in New York. Price highest in 15 years for Old Master, highest ever for Old Master still-life. Previous record $325,203.

**Avant-Garde Art in Moscow (March 7):** Soviet sanctions exhibition by 20 painters after removing score of works for ideological reasons. Showing draws crowds. Works not advanced by Western standards but are spectacular contrast to accepted Soviet art.

**"Holocaust" Draws 120 Million (April 20):** Four-night telecast dramatizing Hitler's extermination of Jews presented by NBC-TV. Audience reported second only to "Roots."

**Autograph Auction Records Set (April 26):** Publisher Malcolm Forbes pays $70,000 for Paul Revere's expense account following second ride. Highest ever paid at auction for American autograph. Forbes also buys a Lincoln letter for $30,000 and another for $31,000, exceeding previous record of $20,000 for a Lincoln letter.

**Carter Opens Newest Art Gallery (June 1):** Praises East Building of National Gallery of Art as "architectural masterpiece," Building, near foot of Capitol Hill, a striking contemporary design by I.M. Pei.

**Record $1.4 Million Auction in London (June 22):** Gothic, Romanesque, and Renaissance art works sold from collection of Robert von Hirsch, late Swiss leather merchant. Sum largest for single session in history of art auctions.

**Ban on "Offensive" Words Upheld (July 3):** Supreme Court, 5–4, affirms FCC reprimand for New York radio station WBAI-FM in "seven dirty words case." Justices rule Constitution does not bar Government prohibition of words "patently offensive."

**Fire Destroys Rio de Janeiro Art (July 8):** More than 1,000 works lost in 30 minutes—the Museum of Modern Art's entire collection of oils, sculpture, engravings and other small objects. Collection included works by Picasso, Van Gogh, and Dali.

**2 Americans Triumph in Moscow (July 10):** Gold medals in Tchaikovsky Competition go to cellist Nathaniel Rosen, 30, of Pittsburgh Symphony and violinist Elmar Oliveira, of Binghamton, N.Y. They are first Americans to win gold medals since Van Cliburn took honor in piano 20 years before.

**Paintings by Another Constable (Aug. 29):** British art historians find that a dozen major paintings attributed to John Constable, 19th-century landscape artist, were works of his fourth son, Lionel. Value of Constable paintings unaffected.

**Painter and Sculptor Share 1978 Mellon Prize (Sept. 8):** Willem de Kooning, Dutch-born American painter, and Eduardo Chillida, Spanish sculptor, each receive $25,000 from Carnegie Institute Museum of Art. The annual Andrew W. Mellon prize is intended to be art world's equivalent of the Nobel Prize.

**Fox Film Fined $25,000 (Sept. 12):** Twentieth Century-Fox Film Corp. pleads no contest in Federal Court to charge it forced theaters that wanted to show the hit *Star Wars* also to exhibit *The Other Side of Midnight,* less-popular film. U.S. had charged practice violated 1951 consent order against "block-booking."

**30th Annual Emmy Awards (Sept. 17):** *Holocaust* and *All in the Family* dominate the 1978 awards of the Academy of Television Arts and Sciences. Outstanding limited series—*Holocaust,* which also won best writer for Gerald Green, lead actor for Michael Moriarty, lead actress for Meryl Streep, supporting actress for Blanche Baker, a director's award for Marvin J. Chomsky, and two creative crafts awards. Best Comedy Series—*All in the Family,* which also won best lead actor in comedy series for Carroll O'Connor, lead actress for Jean Stapleton (both for the third time), supporting actor for Rob Reiner, a director's award for Paul Bogart, and writers' awards for Bob Weiskopf, Bob Schiller, Barry Harman, and Howe Brosten. Other awards included: Best drama or comedy special—*The Gathering;* lead actress in a special—Joanne Woodward in *See How She Runs;* lead actor in drama series—Edward Asner in *Lou Grant;* lead actress in drama series—Sada Thompson in *Family;* drama series—*The Rockford Files;* comedy-variety series—*The Muppet Show.*

## Environment

### 1977

**Concorde Flights Approved (Oct. 17):** Supreme Court lifts ban on supersonic Concorde at Kennedy Airport, imposed because of community opposition to noise. **(Oct. 19):** Plane meets Port Authority legal noise limits in flight test, and is reported slightly quieter than some subsonic jets. **(Oct. 22):** Heads back to Europe after familiarization flights from Kennedy. **(Nov. 22):** Concordes begin flight to JFK Airport from London and Paris, delayed 19 months. Noise level is modest and there is only token picketing.

**Mediterranean Pollution Treaty (Oct. 21):** Countries of region agree in principle on treaty to control discharge of industrial and other wastes into coastal waters, prompted by fears of danger to tourism, public health, and fisheries.

**Utilities' Shift to Coal Spurs Pollution (Dec. 7):** Council on Economic Priorities finds change to dirtier fuels has canceled out improvements by power companies in achieving air-quality goals.

**Eskimos Get Quota on Killing of Whales (Dec. 7):** International Whaling Commission limits Alaskans to total catch of 12 bowhead whales for 1978. Eskimo leaders warn that hungry people will be forced to violate restriction.

**Asbestos Workers to Get $1.84 Million (Dec. 28):** Attorneys for seven manufacturers and 26 who inhaled asbestos fibers at work agree to settlement approved in Federal Court. Construction workers' counsel had contended asbestos products did not have warnings of health dangers.

### 1978

**Sweden to Ban Most Aerosols (Jan. 29):** Will be first country to enact legislation against sprays in belief they may harm atmosphere. Ban effective Jan. 1, 1979, applies to sprays using Freon as propellants. Certain medical sprays exempted.

**U.S. Judge Backs Delay in Oil Lease Sales (Jan. 30):** Appeals Court in Boston refuses to stay injunction holding up sale of oil and gas exploration leases on the Georges Bank fishing grounds off Massachusetts. Judge Levin H. Campbell says: "There may be issues more serious than one involving the future of the oceans of our planet and the life within them, but surely they are few." **(Jan. 31):** Federal officials say sale of the oil and natural-gas leases is likely to be delayed several months by decision. Ruling viewed as victory for Massachusetts.

**Bald Eagle Close to Extinction (Feb. 11):** Interior Dept. says national symbol since 1782 is being declared an endangered species in 43 states, and is classified as "threatened" in several others. **(April 12):** One hatched at Centex Zoo, Waco, Tex.; the other at Columbus, Ohio. Events called extremely rare.

**Oil Pollutes Brittany Coastline (March 18):** 80,000 tons from wrecked supertanker, *Amoco Cadiz,* fouls beaches, harbors, and fishing grounds along 70 miles of coast in one of worst oil spills on record. Grave damage reported to fishing and seaweed industries and to tourist trade. Other areas affected.

**U.S. Curbs Aerosol Products (March 15):** Announces ban, effective Dec. 15, on nearly all products containing chlorofluorocarbons because of fears they are contaminating the earth's atmosphere.

**Britain Bars Imports of Kepone (April 5):** Imposes ban on 4,400 gallons of poisonous substance from Baltimore to be burned experimentally on outskirts of Welsh town by company hired by Allied Chemical. Official says action is designed to protect workers and the public.

**Supreme Court Reprieves Fish (June 15):** Justices, 6–3, rule law protecting endangered species must prevent completion of $120 million TVA Tellico Dam and reservoir, which threatens existence of snail darter, obscure three-inch variety of perch, with single remote habitat. **(June 16):** TVA Chairman S. David Freeman agrees to redesigning of water project to protect the endangered fish.

**Canada Limits Mineral Search (July 7):** Prohibits further exploration for oil, gas and other resources in Yukon wilderness area to protect roving caribou herds and other wildlife. Plans joint measures with U.S. to preserve caribou.

## Health and Medicine

### 1977

**Pneumonia Vaccine Succeeds (Oct. 26):** Medical scientists in California report successful testing of vaccine against major cause of pneumonia, meningitis, and ear infections—bacteria called pneumococci.

**Dieters Warned on Liquid Protein (Nov. 9):** FDA cites 16 deaths and says use of food supplement could be highly dangerous. **(Nov. 11):** Government asks 29 manufacturers and distributors to put warning labels on diet product immediately.

**New Pneumonia Vaccine (Nov. 21):** Food and Drug Administration approves new protection against common, potentially fatal type of pneumonia, caused by pneumococcal bacterium.

**Pipes and Cigars Banned on Planes (Nov. 22):** CAB curbs smoking on nation's commercial airliners. Moves for eventual prohibition of cigarettes as well.

**Smallpox Eradicated in Worst Form (Dec. 13):** Kind that kills, blinds, and maims, *variola major*, wiped out, World Health Organization reports. Milder form remains in Somalia.

**First use of "Total Artificial Heart" (Dec. 14):** International team of surgeons at Zurich Hospital announces device used externally and temporarily, attached by tube to natural heart and acting as blood pump until natural heart returns to normal.

**Influenza Epidemic Rages in Soviet Union (Dec. 29):** Hundreds of thousands laid low, from Kremlin to kindergartens. Bureaucracy, schools and public events all affected.

## 1978

**FDA Warns Women Smokers (Jan. 24):** Tells 4 million who use contraceptive pills and smoke to give up one or the other or suffer increased risk of heart attack or stroke.

**Drug Found to Help Remove Kepone From Body (Feb. 1):** Researchers at Medical College of Virginia at Richmond report discovery of substance that hastens elimination of pesticide. Drug cholestyramine, may help persons exposed to other pesticides and toxic chemicals.

**Russian Flu Grounds Air Force Academy (Feb. 7):** Classes and extracurricular activity halt as 65% of 4,312 students are stricken by A-variety flu. Strain that has caused epidemics in Soviet Union, Europe and Asia, definitely identified. It appeared in U.S. two weeks previously at Cheyenne, Wyo.

**Gout Drug Found to Aid Heart Victims (Feb. 8):** International reserach team finds Anturane can more than halve sudden deaths among persons with at least one previous attack. Drug's generic name is sulfinpyrazone.

**Baking Soda Fights Disease (Feb. 18):** Large doses found to increase height of very small children suffering rare kidney diseases. Therapy developed by researchers at University of California Medical Center.

**Electromagnetic Treatment in Fractures (Feb. 18):** Five-year study at New York's Columbia-Presbyterian Medical Center finds waves can help broken bones heal.

**Laetrile verdict Clears Doctor (Feb. 22):** Atlanta federal jury holds U.S. Rep. Larry McDonald, urologist, not responsible for death of cancer patients he treated with laetrile. Awards family $15,000 for medical and other expenses in death of John L. Scott, postal worker. Suit for $6 million had charged "quackery."

**Abortion Law Voted in Italy (May 18):** Italian Parliament makes operation virtually free on demand. Action after years of controversy is defeat for Vatican-backed Christian Democratic Party.

**Carter Health Plan Unveiled (July 29):** Administration program emphasizes curbing rising costs as well as care for all. If enacted, plan would be phased in over some years, starting perhaps in 1983. Health experts expect program will make heavy demands on federal budget.

**Rare Disease Kills Victim (Aug. 10):** Robert McFall, 39, asbestos worker, dies in Pittsburgh of aplastic anemia after cousin refuses to donate bone marrow. Disease caused by marrow's failure to produce enough red blood cells and platelets. Court backed decision of cousin, who doubted he could endure necessary operation.

**Woman Wins Test-Tube Baby Case (Aug. 18):** U.S. jury in New York awards Doris Del Zio and her husband, John, $50,003 in $1.5-million suit over termination of a doctor's attempt five years previously to fertilize with her husband's sperm an egg taken from her and to replant it in her womb. She had been unable to conceive normally because of blocked fallopian tubes. A principal defendant, Dr. Raymond Vande Wiele, chief gynecologist at Columbia–Presbyterian Medical Center, calls verdict absurd. Jury accepted couple's contention that the termination had illegally deprived them of property.

**Bacteria Produce Insulin (Sept. 6):** California scientists use new gene transplant technique to develop hormone identical to that made by human body, first potentially commercial biological product in years of work on recombinant DNA.

**Illinois Allows Marijuana Use (Sept. 9):** Gov. James R. Thompson signs bill permitting drug for cancer patients and victims of uncontrollable glaucoma. Still opposes general legalization.

# International Affairs

## 1977

**Panama Ratifies Canal Treaties (Oct. 23):** Voters, in heavy turnout, give two thirds approval to new treaties with U.S.

**U.N. Assembly Censures Israel (Oct. 28):** Resolution condemns establishment of settlements in occupied Arab territories. Calls actions illegal and obstruction to Middle East peace efforts.

**U.S. Quits ILO (Nov. 1):** U.N. diplomats bitterly critical after President Carter withdraws U.S. from International Labor Organization, ending American contribution of $20 million a year to oldest specialized U.N. agency. Some aid to continue.

**Giscard Supports Quebec (Nov. 3):** French President assures province of backing for right of self-determination. Takes unusual steps of making Quebec Premier René Lévesque Grand Officer of Legion of Honor, normally reserved for a chief of state.

**South Africa Embargo Ordered (Nov. 4):** U.N. Security Council imposes arms sanctions because of government's racial policies. Vote is unanimous.

**Israel Frees Archbishop (Nov. 6):** Israel, responding to Vatican request, commutes sentence of Archbishop Hilarion Capucci, serving 12-year term for smuggling arms to West Bank for Palestinian guerrillas.

**Canada Reports Illegal Mail Opening (Nov. 9):** Government says Mounted Police have tampered with and copied personal mail illegally since 1954 despite denials.

**Israeli Jets Strike Lebanon (Nov. 9):** Israelis say raids were reprisal for rocket attacks on Israeli town of Nahariya. **(Nov. 12):** Israeli bombers attack southern Lebanon for second time in three days. Artillery fire exchanged with Palestinian gunners.

**Somalia Ousts Soviet Advisers (Nov. 13):** Orders them to leave in seven days, ends Soviet use of strategic naval facilities on Indian Ocean, and breaks relations with Cuba.

**Begin Formally Invites Sadat to Jerusalem (Nov. 15):** Israeli Premier invites President Anwar el-Sadat of Egypt to address Parliament. **(Nov. 17):** Sadat formally accepts bid for trip, first by an Arab leader since Israel was founded in 1948. Uproar develops in Arab world as Syria, Iraq, and Palestine Liberation Organization condemn the trip. **(Nov. 19):** Two leaders meet on Israeli soil as Sadat arrives in Jerusalem. Sadat, addressing Israeli Parliament, says he accepts existence of Israel, reiterates stand that lasting peace depends on Israeli withdrawal from occupied Arab land and recognition of rights of Palestinians. Welcomes Israel's right to exist "with all security and safety." P.L.O. accuses Sadat of humiliating surrender and calls on Arabs to impose sanctions and isolation on him. **(Nov. 21)**: Mission ends with Sadat and Begin joining in pledges of "no more war." Disagreements still exist. **(Nov. 22)**: Sadat welcomed home and acclaimed as a "man of peace" by tens of thousands of Egyptians lining route from airport.

**Biko Inquest Absolves South African Police (Dec. 2)**: Security force cleared as inquiry ends in prison death of Steven Biko, black leader. Finding shocks blacks who attended. U.S. State Department expresses shock at verdict in face of "compelling evidence that Stephen Biko was the victim of flagrant neglect and official irresponsibility."

**Egypt Breaks With Arab Critics (Dec. 5)**: Severs diplomatic relations with Syria, Iraq, Libya, Algeria, and Southern Yemen in retaliation for efforts to prevent President Anwar el-Sadat from pursuing negotiations with Israel.

**Egypt and Israel Conference Opens (Dec. 15)**: Americans look on as negotiators meet in new effort for peace settlement in Middle East. U.N. sends representative. Three invited Arab countries—Jordan, Lebanon, and Syria—Palestine Liberation Organization, and Soviet Union refuse to send delegates.

**Carter and Begin Meet at White House (Dec. 16)**: Israeli Prime Minister tells President that Israel, in response to Sadat initiatives, is ready to restore to Egypt complete sovereignty over Sinai Peninsula and to give Palestinians control over internal affairs in the West Bank and the Gaza Strip.

**Israeli-Egyptian Peace Talks Held (Dec. 25)**: Prime Minister Begin and President Sadat meet at Ismailia, Egypt. **(Dec. 26)**: Two-day conference ends with leaders failing to reach agreement on Palestinian state and terms for Israeli withdrawal from the Sinai Peninsula, the West Bank of the Jordan, and the Gaza Strip. Pledge to continue efforts for peace and create standing committees for continued discussions. **(Dec. 27)**: In TV-radio interview, Sadat defends peace initiative. Refuses to back down from demands for Palestinian state and Israeli withdrawal from other occupied territories as well as Sinai Peninsula. **(Dec. 28)**: President Carter, in TV interview, praises Begin plan for Palestinian self-rule as "long step forward" and opposes "fairly radical new independent nation in heart of Middle East." **(Dec. 29)**: Sadat "disappointed" by Carter's views, feels remarks could delay Middle East peace settlement.

**Carter Starts Six-Nation Tour (Dec. 29)**: President reaches Warsaw on nine-day trip. At Warsaw Airport, he says old labels have lost meaning and basic goals of justice, rights, and freedom are more important than ever. President is embarrassed by gaffes of his American interpreter at airport, who was reported to translate "desire" as "lust" and to have Mr. Carter "abandoning Washington." **(Dec. 30)**: At news conference in Warsaw, equates Polish and American aspirations to human rights. He confers privately with Edward Gierek, Polish leader, and visits memorials to World War II victims. **(Dec. 31)**: Carter arrives at Teheran, Iran, for talks with Shah and King Hussein of Jordan. President and Shah agree on unspecified joint steps on Middle East and to help end fighting between Ethiopia and Somalia. **(Jan. 1)**: Thousands give President warm welcome in India. He meets for first time with Prime Minister Morarji R. Desai. **(Jan. 2)**: Carter discloses sharp disagreement with Desai over U.S. demands that India accept safeguards assuring that U.S.-supplied nuclear fuel is used for peaceful purposes. Rift revealed inadvertently over open microphone. **(Jan. 3)**: President flies to Riyadh, Saudi Arabia, for talks on Middle East peace efforts and oil. In talks described as "warm," he meets with King Khalid and Crown Prince Fahd, operating head of Saudi government. **(Jan. 4)**: At Aswan, Egypt, President meets with President Sadat. In prepared statement, Carter says Palestinians should be able to "participate in the determination of their own future." His view is shared by Egyptians. Carter comes close to calling for self-determination outright. **(Jan. 5)**: Carter visits Normandy beach and crowded cemetery to commemorate Allied invasion of Europe and to honor thousands of Allied dead. President Valéry Giscard d'Estaing is with him. **(Jan. 6)**: Carter meets in Paris with Socialist leader François Mitterrand and expresses concern about possible renewed alliance with Communists. Later he ends trip in Brussels with pledge to NATO allies that he will involve them more in negotiating strategic arms agreements with Soviet.

**Turkish Government Defeated in Parliament (Dec. 31)**: Prime Minister Suleyman Demirel's right-wing coalition loses on confidence motion and must resign. **(Jan. 1)**: Bulent Ecevit takes office as Prime Minister.

**Spain Approves Provisional Basque Home Rule (Dec. 31)**: Government defuses potentially explosive situation in turbulent provinces. Move marks further break with Franco policies.

**Egypt Gives Terms for Middle East Settlement (Dec. 31)**: Foreign Minister submits conditions to U.S. Ambassador. Says Israel must accept principle of full withdrawal from West Bank and Gaza Strip and recognize "inalienable" rights of Palestinians to self-determination.

## 1978

**Vietnamese Hold Cambodian Region (Jan. 3)**: Stalemate reached in border conflict. Skirmishing has increased to full-scale battles. Vietnam forces occupy 400 square miles in Cambodia after offensive.

**Chilean President Supported in Vote (Jan. 4)**: Augusto Pinochet wins important political victory by winning 75% vote of confidence in plebiscite. He is supported against a condemnation of Chile's military rule by U.N. General Assembly for human rights violations.

**Crown of St. Stephen Returned to Hungary (Jan. 6)**: Symbol of sovereignty and unity brought back by Secretary of State Cyrus R. Vance. Crown had been kept by U.S. for 32 years. Roman Catholic primates and clergy prominent in rites.

**15 Nations Agree on Safeguards in Nuclear Exports (Jan. 11)**: Adopt code to insure materials will not be used for military purposes. Suppliers are committed to exercise restraint in selling "sensitive facilities," weapons technology, and materials. Group includes U.S., Soviet Union, and three East Europe allies; Britain, France, West Germany, Canada, Japan, and five other West European nations.

**Italian Government Resigns Under Pressure (Jan. 16)**: Prime Minister Giulio Andreotti hands resignation to President Giovanni Leone. Minority Christian Democratic Party, in office 18 months, had faced increased Communist demands for role in Cabinet. Communists, Socialists, and Republicans withdraw support.

**U.S. Expels Vietnam Envoy to U.N. (Feb. 3)**: Dinh Ba Thi allegedly linked to espionage case involving USIA official and Vietnamese national.

**Egyptian President Meets Carter (Feb. 3)**: Anwar el-Sadat arrives in U.S. Tells President Middle East is at "historic and crucial crossroads" and urges U.S. to become "arbiter" in Arab-Israeli dispute. Carter praises Sadat's "courageous and historic" visit to Jerusalem, but stresses own neutral position. **(Feb. 4)**: Carter and Sadat open talks at Camp David, Md. Carter says U.S. seeks fair Middle East settlement. Insists Egypt as well as Israel must make compromises. **(Feb. 5)**: They return to Washington after agreeing to make "unremitting efforts" to get peace negotiations started again. **(Feb. 8)**: Carter and Sadat end discussions, pledging to continue efforts for a Middle East peace with security for Israel and a solution to Palestinian problem.

**Canada to Expel 11 Soviet Officials (Feb. 9)**: Bars two others from returning, all accused of plotting to penetrate security apparatus of Royal Canadian Mounted Police. Canada's biggest spy case since 1946.

**Nazi Who Fled Italy Dies (Feb. 9)**: Herbert Kappler, convicted war criminal, succumbs to stomach cancer at home at Soltau, West Germany. The 70-year-old colonel in Hitler's SS police made daring escape from Rome military hospital six months before.

**Accord on Rhodesian Rule Reached (Feb. 15)**: Prime Minister Ian D. Smith and three black leaders, Bishop Abel Muzorewa, Senator Jeremiah Chirau, and Dr. Elliott Gabellah, agree on major points for transfer to black majority rule. Gabellah represented Rev. Ndabaningi Sithole. After 37th round of talks they resolve differences over white representation in Parliament. Rhodesian Patriotic Front took no part in talks. **(Feb. 17)**: Four leaders reach broad agreement on future of country's armed forces. **(March 3)**: Smith and black nationalist leaders sign agreement to install black-majority government by end of year.

**12 Killed in Belfast Explosion (Feb. 17)**: Bomb goes off in crowded suburban restaurant in Protestant area. Many children among victims; 30 wounded. Provisional IRA takes responsibility. **(Feb. 18)**: Police seize 20 IRA suspects.

**Gunmen Kill Top Cairo Editor (Feb. 18)**: Two Palestinian terrorists escape on hijacked Cyprus Airways jet with 15 hostages after slaying in Nicosia Hilton Hotel. Victim was Yousef el-Sebai, board chairman, chief executive, and editor of *Al Ahram*, Egypt's most important newspaper. Permission to land refused in Kuwait and Libya. **(Feb. 19)**: Fifteen Egyptian commandos killed by Cypriot troops as Egyptians storm jetliner to rescue the hostages after plane returns to Nicosia Airport. Hostages freed and the guerrillas are captured. Cypriot government says Egyptians landed without permission and holds 57 surviving commandos. **(Feb. 20)**: Egypt says it had notified Cyprus of planned action but did not specifically say commandos were on way in military plane for rescue raid. Cyprus frees commandos, but demands recall of Egyptian military attaché. Refuses to turn over the two terrorists. Egypt withdraws diplomatic mission from Cyprus and orders Cypriot diplomats to leave Cairo. **(Feb. 22)**: Egypt breaks diplomatic relations with Cyprus after funeral for 15 slain commandos that turned into demonstrations against Cypriots and Palestinians.

**Commons Approves Scottish Home Rule (Feb. 22)**: Votes 297–257 for much-modified bill to grant limited home rule despite substantial defections by Labor M.P.'s.

**Black Leader Dead in South Africa (Feb. 27)**: Robert Mangalisco Sobukwe succumbs to lung cancer in Kimberley. Founded Pan-African Congress and envisioned democratic Africa. Sobukwe, 53, had spent his last 18 years in prison or under other severe government restrictions.

**Mrs. Gandhi Wins Power Base (Feb. 28)**: Ousted Indian Prime Minister stages comeback by winning second election in south, victory for splinter party she formed, named "Congress-I" (for Indira).

**Hua Named Chinese Premier (March 5)**: Communist Party Chairman Hua Kuo-feng re-elected by National People's Congress, nominal legislature. Decisions at Peking meeting leave Teng Hsiao-ping as only First Deputy Prime Minister and third in Red hierarchy. **(March 7)**: China adopts new Constitution approved by People's Congress. It strengthens rights of citizens and increases powers of Parliament in relation to Communist Party.

**Tito and Carter Confer (March 6)**: Yugoslav President arrives in Washington. **(March 9)**: Carter, in joint statement with Tito, affirms support for Yugoslav unity, and pledges to combat anti-Tito terrorist activities by emigré groups in U.S.

**Belgrade Conference Winds Up (March 8)**: Eight months of bitter debate on European security and cooperation end with adoption of summary document that does not mention human rights or other issues dividing East and West.

**32 Die in Raid on Israel (March 11)**: Civilians killed by Palestinian terrorists who come ashore in boats south of Haifa and seize bus. It explodes in flames near Tel Aviv in exchange of gunfire with Israeli police. Nine guerrillas killed and two are captured. Toll of wounded set at 76. Prime Minister Menachem Begin postpones trip to U.S. Raid ascribed by Palestinian spokesman to Al Fatah, largest guerrilla group in Palestine Liberation Organization. **(March 12–13)**: Begin warns twice of reprisals, vowing Israel will "cut off evil arm" of Palestinian terrorist band. **(March 14)**: President Sadat of Egypt breaks with other Arabs and denounces raid as "irresponsible" and as "sad and tragic."

**Israelis Raid Terrorists in Lebanon (March 14)**: Troops cross border to root out bases used for guerrilla operations within Israel. Drive follows Palestinian foray in which civilians were killed. Naval forces also involved. **(March 15)**: Major fighting ends. Israelis rout Palestinians from at least seven strongholds in southern Lebanon with land, air, and sea operation. Occupy "security belt" 4½–6 miles deep along 63 miles of Israel's north border. Prime Minister Begin says troops will remain until agreement to insure that area could never again be used for raids against Israel. Egypt denounces Israel's action as act of genocide and aggression periling peace efforts. **(March 19)**: U.N. Security Council, 12–0, calls on Israel to withdraw forces from Lebanon immediately. Moves to set up 4,000-man peace-keeping force for border area. **(March 21)**: Israel orders cease-fire in southern Lebanon. Israel reported 20 dead among forces and estimates Palestinian dead at 400. Lebanon reports deaths of 1,168 Lebanese and Palestinians. PLO reports 144 of its guerrillas dead, and 450 Israelis killed. **(March 22)**: Vanguard of 4,000-man U.N. peace-keeping force enters southern Lebanon. Many nations represented. Foreign troops take positions at Ghanduriye, not far from Litani River.

**Italian Leader Kidnapped and Slain (March 16)**: Former Premier Aldo Moro seized by left-wing terrorists, who also kill five bodyguards. Red Brigades claim responsibility and demand release of 15 imprisoned members in exchange for Moro. Kidnapping leads to nationwide manhunt for abductors. Government refuses to release imprisoned terrorists. Red Brigades announce they are carrying out death sentence after a "people's trial." **(May 9:)** Moro's bullet-ridden body found in parked car in Rome. **(May 10):** Moro is buried in small village north of Rome, with Christian Democratic leaders barred from funeral by embittered family. **(May 11:)** Pope Paul VI celebrates mass at state memorial service attended by government leaders and diplomats.

**Begin and Carter Confer (March 19).** Israeli Prime Minister arrives in New York with Foreign Minister Moshe Dayan. **(March 21):** U.S. President tells Begin "historic decisions" are needed to break Middle East deadlock. Each side firm in outlining disagreements on policy. **(March 22):** Two-day talks end with exchange of cold statements emphasizing differences on Middle East peace.

**Leftists Rebuffed in France (March 19):** Voters retain government coalition with 291–200 majority in Parliament in second-round election. Balloting shows France does not face imminent upheaval as Center-Right retains 20-year hold. Popular vote gives government 50.71%, Left 49.26. President Valéry Giscard d'Estaing, in post-election speech, pledges reforms in social policy.

**Rhodesian Black Leaders Take Oath (March 21):** Bishop Abel Muzorewa, Rev. Ndabaningi Sithole, and Sen. Jeremiah Chirau sworn in as co-leaders with Prime Minister Ian D. Smith of provisional government to prepare for fully black government by end of year.

**300 Storm Tokyo Airport (March 26):** Radicals crash fence and seize control tower at new base and destroy vital equipment at new $2.9-billion facility. Evicted with tear gas by police. **(March 27):** Riot police seize demonstrators' concrete fortress and arrest 51.

**Carter Begins 4-Nation Trip (March 28):** Cheered by thousands in Caracas as he ends speech in Spanish with "Viva Venezuela." He mingles with crowd. Carter confers with President Carlos Andres Pérez, and they sign pacts for maritime boundaries and cooperation in curbing drug flow to U.S. **(March 29):** President, arriving in Brazil, raises issues of human rights and nuclear non-cooperation, which have caused friction. **(March 31):** President begins three-day visit to Nigeria, first state visit by an American President to sub-Saharan African nation. **(April 1):** Carter, in policy address at Lagos, Nigeria, commits Administration to Africa "free from colonialism, racism, and military interference by outside nations." **(April 3):** In Liberia, President warns South Africa not to reject Western-backed U.N. plan for majority rule in South-West Africa. He is met by enthusiastic crowds as four-country tour ends.

**Panama Canal Treaties Voted (April 18):** Senate, 68–32, moves to turn canal over to Panama by year 2000, saving President Carter from serious political defeat. On March 16, by identical vote, Senate had approved treaty guaranteeing neutrality of canal. Action is move to establish new spirit of U.S. relations with Latin America.

**Russians Force Down Airliner (April 21):** South Korean Boeing 707 jet airliner strays over Soviet territory and is forced to land on frozen lake south of Murmansk. Two are killed and 13 are injured, two seriously. Failure of navigation equipment blamed. **(April 23):** U.S. jet carries more than 100 passengers to Helsinki to resume journey to Far East. Passengers say a Soviet plane trailed airliner and fired several cannon bursts at it.

**Afghanistan Government Overthrown (April 27):** Insurgents in military stage coup with hours of fierce fighting. Lt. Gen. Abdul Khadir heads military revolutionary council assuming power. **(April 29):** Afghan government radio says four senior members of President Mohammad Daud's government were killed with him when they resisted rebel takeover. **(April 30):** Military junta proclaims new "Revolutionary Council" headed by a civilian, Nur Mohammad Taraki, as President and Prime Minister. Soviet Union immediately extends recognition.

**Israel Celebrates 30th Anniversary (May 10):** Squares flooded with lights and music 24 hours after sirens signal onset of Memorial Day, mourning period for thousands of war dead.

**Chinese Charge Raid by Soviet (May 11):** Say Soviet forces used helicopter and military boats to cross stream on Manchurian border, first reported clash in area since 1969. **(May 12):** Soviet Union apologizes for what it calls accidental crossing.

**Zaire Reports Invasion (May 14):** President Mobotu Sese Seku of Zaire (former Belgian Congo) says 4,000 Communist-backed Katangan rebels invaded southern province of Shaba, formerly Katanga, entering from Angola. He reports rebels attacked copper town of Kolwezi with support of Soviet Union, Cuba, Algeria, and Libya. **(May 18):** Belgium and France fly paratroops in international airlift to rescue more than 2,500 Europeans and Americans trapped in copper mining area. U.S. approves sending of millions of dollars of military supplies requested by Zaire. **(May 19):** U.S. dispatches 18 Air Force C-141 transports to take part in airlift. French and Belgians drop paratroops at Kolwezi to rescue foreigners and begin evacuation. Forty-four Europeans apparently shot to death by rebels. State Dept. says Cuba is responsible for training Katangan rebels and that they are carrying Cuban-supplied Soviet weapons. **(May 21):** Last of whites evacuated from Kolwezi, reporting brutality and violence. Death toll at Kolwezi at least 120 white civilians and at least twice as many blacks. Rebels are driven back. **(May 29):** French and Belgian troops deployed in towns of Shaba mining area to protect remaining white technicians and their families.

**Fighter Plane Sale Upheld (May 15):** Senate, 54–44, approves Carter's decision to sell fighter planes in package deal to Saudi Arabia, Egypt, and Israel.

**Dissident Sentenced in Moscow (May 18):** Yuri F. Orlov, physicist who organized group to expose Soviet violations of human rights, sentenced to seven years in prison and five years in exile after trial for "anti-Soviet agitation." Punishment is defiance of appeals from West and a warning to other protesters.

**Brzezinski Opens Peking Talks (May 20):** Carter's security adviser tells Chinese U.S. seeks full diplomatic relations with China. He is feted at banquet by China's foreign minister.

**Scientists Boycott Soviet Union (May 27):** Delegation of American cancer research scientists cancels trip to protest trial of dissident Yuri F. Orlov, physicist. Group is fourth to stage protest boycott.

**Yugoslavs Seize 4 Terrorists (May 29):** Criminals wanted by West Germany as members of Red Army, including Brigitte Mohnhaupt, 28, allegedly linked to murderers of Aldo Moro, Italian political leader. Others: Rolf Clemens Wagner, 33, Peter Boock, 27, and Sieglinde Gutrun Hoffman, 33.

**U.S. Embassy in Soviet Bugged (June 1):** Officials protest to Russians after new discovery of electronic listening devices in Moscow. System included an espionage tunnel discovered leading from adjoining building to embassy chimney.

**Six Dead in Jerusalem Bus Blast (June 3):** Five killed and one fatally injured in explosion on city bus, apparently timed by Palestinian guerrillas for the 11th anniversary of Israel's capture of East Jerusalem. Twenty hurt, some critically.

**Rehabilitation Move in China (June 5):** Peking reported to have released about 110,000 detained since antirightist campaign in 1957. Lower-level officials and citizens also rehabilitated in broad new effort to restore victims of political persecution in 1975–76.

**Dispute Over Fishing Grounds (June 5):** U.S. and Canada exclude each other's vessels from respective waters after talks fail to settle fish management differences. But Coast Guard tries to avoid confiscation and arrests.

**Carter Warns Russians (June 7):** President calls on Soviet to choose between confrontation and cooperation, saying U.S. is "adequately prepared to meet either choice." In speech at Annapolis graduation, toughest yet on Soviet-American relations, President attacks Soviet interpretation of détente and warns of escalation to greater tensions. He calls on Moscow to conclude new accord on limiting strategic arms and to join in working for black rule in Rhodesia and South-West Africa. In Moscow, Soviet spokesmen call speech "strange" and accuse U.S. of vacillating between cold war and détente.

**Israelis Raid Guerrilla Base (June 9):** Commandos destroy Palestinian coastal installation in southern Lebanon, north of zone held by U.N. troops. Report Palestinians planned to use base for staging attack on civilians in Israel. Death toll fixed by Israelis at seven Palestinians and two Israeli navy lieutenants.

**Last Israeli Units Quit Lebanon (June 13):** Troops hand over six-mile-deep border strip to Lebanese Christian militia units rather than to U.N. peacekeeping force. In earlier withdrawals, positions had been handed over to U.N. forces.

**Italian President Resigns (June 15):** Giovanni Leone faces inquiry into charges of tax fraud involving business partnership in Lockheed kickback case.

**Ceremonies Conclude Panama Treaties (June 16):** President Carter and Brig. Gen. Omar Torrijos Herrera, Panamanian leader, sign and exchange five documents providing for neutrality of canal and transfer to Panama by end of century. They acclaim "new era of inter-American understanding and cooperation." **(June 17):** In speech at Canal Zone Army base, Carter warns Panama to respect civil liberties of 40,000 Americans who have operated and defended the canal for decades. Reception by crowd of 5,000 American listeners is cool.

**Terrorist Suspects Seized (June 22):** Four suspected Germans arrested by Bulgaria and returned to West Germany in first such action by Soviet-bloc nation. Three women and man sought in kidnapping of Christian Democratic leader and 1974 murder of Supreme Court justice.

**29 Sentenced in Red Brigades Trial (June 23):** Terrorists given up to 15 years in prison by Italian court. Sixteen acquitted. Those sentenced include Renato Curcio, most prominent in group held responsible for kidnapping and slaying of former Premier Aldo Moro.

**U.S. Releases 2 Soviet Citizens (June 25):** Gives ambassador custody of two U.N. employees held on \$2-million bail on espionage charges. American businessman held in Moscow on currency law charges is turned over to American ambassador. All three still face legal action.

**U.N. Votes Arms Text Compromise (June 30):** General Assembly, ending special session, approves recommendations for restraining arms race and agrees on enlarged committee to replace Geneva disarmament conference. "Papers over" differences between atomic powers and third world.

**Peking Ends Aid to Vietnamese (July 3):** Halts economic projects and recalls advisers because of treatment of Chinese in Vietnam. Diplomat see basic reason in Vietnam's admission to Soviet-bloc economic alliance, Comecon.

**Rescue of Refugees Ordered (July 5):** President Carter bids U.S. ships pick up fugitives from Southeast Asia fleeing in boats. Will allow them to settle in U.S.

**Socialist Elected President of Italy (July 8):** Sandro Pertini, 81, who spent years in Fascist prisons, named nation's seventh President by overwhelming majority of Electoral Assembly. Victory for continued cooperation between Roman Catholic Christian Democrats and the Communists.

**Andrew Young Stirs Controversy (July 12):** U.S. chief delegate to U.N., referring to Soviet dissidents, says U.S. has hundreds, perhaps thousands, of political prisoners of its own. Views given in interview with Paris newspaper. **(July 13):** After Secretary of State Cyrus R. Vance expresses displeasure, Young denies he had meant to equate struggles of Soviet dissidents with those of U.S. civil rights activists. **(July 15):** President Carter tells Young he is "very unhappy" over controversial statements.

**Namibia Guerrillas Accept West's Plan (July 12):** Agree with U.S., Britain, France, Canada, and West Germany on ending 11-year war in South-West Africa and achieving independence from South Africa for new black state. **(July 27):** U.N. Security Council, 13–0, approves Western plan for ending guerrilla war and independence for Namibia. Council also backs steps for early reintegration of port city of Walvis Bay into Namibia. South Africa has insisted on sovereignty over Walvis Bay.

**2 Soviet Dissidents Sentenced (July 13):** Aleksandr Ginzburg found guilty in Moscow of "anti-Soviet agitation and propaganda" and sentenced to eight years in strict labor camp. He had managed a fund aiding families of political prisoners. In Lithuania, Viktoras Petkus, a translator, gets 10 years in prison and 5 years exile for founding a dissident committee to publicize Soviet violations of rights pledged under 1975 Helsinki accord.

**No Arms Limitation Accord (July 13):** Secretary of State Vance and Soviet Foreign Minister Andrei Gromyko report inability to resolve major issues in two days of talks at Geneva. Vance reports "new ideas" by both sides.

**Soviet Sentences Jewish Leader (July 14):** Despite protests from West, Anatoly B. Shcharansky, 30-year-old computer specialist, gets 13 years in prison and labor camps for treason, espionage, and "anti-Soviet agitation." Prominent dissident, leader in Jewish emigration movement, had denied as "absurd" charges of giving secrets to CIA. Convicted despite President Carter's personal assurances that Shcharansky had no links to U.S. intelligence.

**Carter at Economic Summit Conference (July 14):** President, in West Germany for two-day, seven-nation meeting, is applauded by thousands in Bonn as he echoes Kennedy pledge to "defend your land as if it were our own." Carter and German Chancellor Helmut Schmidt discuss East-West relations, the economy, Africa, and the Middle East. **(July 15):** President addresses "town meeting" of 1,000 West Berliners and fields questions on everything from security of divided Berlin to his daughter's weekly allowance. East Germans slow highway traffic to West Berlin to protest presence of Schmidt. **(July 17):** As Bonn conference opens, Carter reaffirms pledge to cut U.S. dependence on imported oil and to strengthen the dollar. Schmidt and Japanese Prime Minister Takeo Fukuda promise action to stimulate economies. **(July 17):** Leaders of seven nations agree on moves to combat worldwide unemployment without rekindling inflation. Carter and other leaders pleased with results. **(July 18):** Carter and economic negotiators return, confident they had escaped being tagged as scapegoats for world's economic ills.

**2 U.S. Reporters Lose in Moscow (July 18):** Court rules Craig R. Whitney of *N.Y. Times* and Harold D. Piper of *Baltimore Sun* had libeled Soviet television employees by reporting that a televised confession by a convicted dissident had been fabricated. Orders them to print a retraction in U.S. or Soviet Union and pay court costs of $1,647 each. Reporters, who had refused to participate in trial, defend articles as unbiased; papers refuse to publish retractions. **(Aug. 3):** Moscow City Court fines reporters $72.50 each for failure to print retractions. **(Aug. 4):** Soviet lawyer pays nearly $3,500 in fines and court costs in behalf of the correspondents.

**Carter Reacts to Soviet Trials (July 18):** Decides to put U.S. exports of oil technology to Russia under Government control in response to moves against dissidents. Also will cancel sale of computer for use by Soviet press agency Tass.

**Officials Linked to Rhodesia Scandal (July 23):** White minority shaken by revelation of multi-million-dollar plan to divert secret arms-buying funds into private Swiss bank accounts. Three businessmen convicted; fined total of $314,000 after agreeing to return some funds diverted to Switzerland.

**Nonaligned Nations End Talks (July 30):** Divisive conference at Belgrade ends with compromise declarations avoiding stands on major economic and political problems. Foreign ministers seek to insulate their countries from East-West conflict.

**Albania Critical of China (July 30):** Reveals harsh letter to Peking saying falling-out had developed over many years, with principal irritant China's attempts to seek accords with Soviet and with West.

**2 Slain at Paris Embassy (July 31):** Arabic-speaking gunman holds hostages in Iraqi Embassy, then is killed by Iraqi security officers after surrendering to French police. French police inspector killed by shots from Iraqi guards. Two officers wounded. Police kill one guard.

**Israeli Jets Avenge Bombing (Aug. 3):** Strike at Palestinian terrorist training camp after terrorist bomb kills one Israeli and wounds 50 in crowded Carmel Market at Tel Aviv.

**2 PLO Men Slain in Paris (Aug. 3):** Chief representative and an aide killed by two terrorists believed to be linked to Iraq. Assailants arrested. Killings linked to feud between Palestinian factions.

**Briton Accused in Murder Plot (Aug. 4):** Jeremy Thorpe, former Liberal Party leader, and three others charged with conspiracy to kill Norman Scott, former model who said he had had homosexual relationship with Thorpe. Thorpe, 49, is well-known and respected member of House of Commons since 1959.

**98 Dead in Beirut Blast (Aug. 13):** Explosion levels 9-story apartment building containing offices of Yasser Arafat's Fatah Palestinian guerrillas and radical Palestine Liberation Front of Abdul Abbas, who is backed by Iraq.

**Canada Freezes Foreign Aid (Aug. 17):** Also orders spending cuts in many departments. Prime Minister Pierre Elliott Trudeau is committed to cutting $2 billion from planned expenditures.

**Terrorists Shoot Up Bus in London (Aug. 20):** One Arab and a stewardess are killed in Arab attack on Israeli El Al Airlines bus outside hotel. Nine wounded, including four airline employees. Popular Front for Liberation of Palestine takes responsibility. **(Aug. 21):** Israeli planes attack Palestinian guerrilla bases in Lebanon in reprisal. Five guerrillas reported killed.

**Guerrillas Attack in Nicaragua (Aug. 22):** One-hundred leftist foes of President Anastasio Somoza seize National Palace at Managua in 10-minute assault and hold many hundreds of hostages, including high officials. **(Aug. 24):** Rebels, members of Sandinista Liberal Front, free all but eight hostages after settling for release of political prisoners held by regime, $71,000 in cash, and safe passage to Panama, where they seek asylum.

**President of Kenya Dies (Aug. 22):** Possibly violent power struggle expected to follow death of Jomo Kenyatta, 87. Daniel Arap Moi, Vice President, assumes limited power until national election.

**Vietnam Returns 11 War Dead (Aug. 26):** Gives U.S. Congressional delegation remains of airmen killed in war in Southeast Asia. This brings to 76 total returned by Vietnam and Laos. Eight Congressmen feel six-day visit improved relations between Vietnam and U.S.

**Airliner Shot Down in Rhodesia (Sept. 3):** Guerrillas of Joshua Nkomo group fell Air Rhodesia plane with missile; 38 of passengers and crew presumed killed. Rhodesian army says guerrillas shot and killed 10 of 18 survivors. **(Sept. 5):** Nkomo says his men attacked craft because airline's planes also carry troops and military supplies. Denies that survivors were murdered.

**Mideast Summit Conference Held (Sept. 5):** President Sadat of Egypt and Prime Minister Begin of Israel arrive at Camp David, Md., for summit talks with President Carter on Mideast peace. **(Sept. 6):** After separate meetings with each, Carter opens three-way discussions; joint statement asks prayers for peace. **(Sept. 10):** Talks enter second week with no sign of progress. Carter, Begin, and Sadat visit Gettysburg, Pa., battlefield.

**U.S. Businessman Convicted in Moscow (Sept. 7):** Soviet judge gives Francis Crawford suspended five-year sentence sought by prosecution for currency violations. U.S. Embassy relieved.

**Turmoil Grows in Nicaragua (Sept. 11):** Guerrillas of Sandinista National Liberation Front begin fighting in capital of Managua and outlying cities as part of broadly based movement to end authoritarian rule of Gen. Anastasio Somoza. Three-week strike of businessmen intensifies. Government declares state of economic emergency and institutes currency-exchange controls.

**New Portuguese Cabinet Falls (Sept. 14):** Fifteen-man panel of specialists formed by Premier Alfredo Nobre da Costa topples after 17 days in power. Had been organized following breakup of coalition government and dismissal of Socialist Premier Mário Soares by President António Ramalho Eanes following three-week political crisis.

**Historic "Framework for Peace" in Middle East Signed (Sept. 17):** After 13-day conference at Camp David, Md., President Sadat of Egypt and Prime Minister Begin of Israel sign two documents designed to end 30-year-long enmity between countries. President Carter, who spent nearly 80 hours leading intense negotiations, hailed as architect of peace effort. Israel to withdraw from most

Arab land won in 1967 war; countries to work for peace treaty within three months and normal relations within one year. Problems of Israeli settlements in Sinai and West Bank issues remain. PLO, Arab hardliners, and Soviet Union attack agreements. Egyptian Foreign Minister Mohammed Ibrahim Kamel resigns **(Sept. 18)**. Secretary of State Vance flies to meet with King Hussein of Jordan and King Khalid of Saudi Arabia to discuss Camp David results **(Sept. 19)**.

**Israeli Parliament Approves Peace Moves (Sept. 26)**: Vote in Knesset is 2-1 for Camp David agreements. Egyptian-Israeli talks to start, aiming at peace treaty in three months.

**Chinese Negotiators Leave Vietnam (Sept. 26)**: Talks designed to settle problems of ethnic Chinese in Vietnam are broken off. Each side accuses the other of border violations.

**South African Prime Minister Quits (Sept. 20)**. After 12 years in office, Balthazar Johannes Vorster, a symbol of white resistance to black freedom, resigns. He had been in poor health **(Sept. 28)**: Pieter Willem Botha, defense minister in Vorster's National Party government, chosen as Prime Minister by parliamentary caucus. Vorster nominated as State President, basically ceremonial post. Botha expected to continue white-supremacist policies.

**Nicaraguan Anti-Government Groups Reject Talks (Sept. 26)**: Coalition will not meet with President Somoza under U.S. mediation plans unless opposition leaders are freed from jail and censorship lifted.

## National Government and Politics

### 1977

**House Rejects B-1 Bomber (Oct. 20)**: Representatives, 204–194, vote not to reinstate $1.4 billion for new plane, averting pending rebuff to President Carter.

**Helms Pleads No Contest (Oct. 31)**: Former Director of Central Intelligence faces sentence on two misdemeanor counts of failing to testify fully before Senate committee on intervention in Chile. **(Oct. 31)**: Helms fined $2,000, given two-year suspended prison term, and rebuked by federal judge for failing to testify fully. Says he considers his conviction a badge of honor.

**Carter Bars Nuclear Reactor (Nov. 5)**: In first veto, President rejects bill to authorize $80 million for reactor on Clinch River, Tenn. Says approval would imperil curb on nuclear proliferation.

**President Signs Urban Transit Bill (Nov. 16)**: Carter approves $80 million for urban mass transit despite reservations that some cities had not lived within payments.

**CIA Bars Use of Reporters (Dec. 2)**: New regulation forbids use of employees of U.S. news organizations as adjuncts of intelligence operations. Previous relationships severed.

**Compromise Reached in Abortion Dispute (Dec. 7)**: House and Senate end five-month impasse on use of Medicaid funds, which had held up appropriations for two departments. Current law liberalized to allow financing abortions for physically ill women and medical procedures to avert pregnancy for some victims of rape and incest.

**Carter Gets Social Security Bill (Dec. 15)**: Congress approves financing measure that Republicans denounce as "biggest peacetime tax increase in history." It mandates increases starting in 1979 for Social Security payroll taxes levied on more than 100 million employers, workers, and self-employed persons. Purpose is to end deficits draining cash from trust funds. **(Dec. 20)**: Carter approves measure. Says additional revenue guarantees that from 1980 through 2030 Social Security System will be sound.

**Carter Names Budget Director (Dec. 27)**: President promotes James T. McIntyre, 37, Georgia lawyer, to be director of Office of Management and Budget. McIntyre had been acting director since resignation of Bert Lance after disclosures about actions while a Georgia banker.

**New Federal Reserve Head Named (Dec. 28)**: President to replace Arthur F. Burns as chairman with G. William Miller, chairman of Textron Inc. Burns, critical of Administration economic policies had reflected conservative outlook. Miller believed to be fiscally conservative. **(March 3)**: Senate confirms Miller, with William Proxmire sole dissenter. Vote follows long investigation of Textron and $2.9-million payment by subsidiary to Iranian agent in sale of helicopters to Iran.

### 1978

**Tongsun Park Reported to Recall Gifts (Jan. 13)**: Korean businessman said to tell U.S. Justice Dept. investigators in Seoul of $750,000 covert disbursements to American officials and political campaigns. Payments said to include $200,000 to former Rep. Otto E. Passman and $20,000 to President Nixon's 1972 re-election campaign. **(Jan. 24)**: Korean reportedly tells inquiry he made financial contributions to at least five Senators, including the late former Vice President Humphrey. Park certain Humphrey did not know of campaign gift. No evidence of wrongdoing by any of the Senators.

**Humphrey's Body Lies in State in Capitol (Jan. 14)**: President Carter leads tributes to Minnesota Senator, who died Jan. 13 of cancer at 66. **(Jan. 15)**: Friends and foes honor Humphrey at memorial service in Capitol Rotunda, including President Carter and former Presidents Ford and Nixon. **(Jan. 16)**: Humphrey is buried at Lakewood Cemetery, Minneapolis. Thousands join family and President Carter, Vice President Mondale, and other public figures in tributes.

**Carter's State of the Union Address (Jan. 19)**: President lists as 1978 priorities energy, economy, and Panama Canal treaties. Proposes $25-billion tax reduction, a new federal department of education, and extensive Civil Service reform.

**New F.B.I. Director Nominated (Jan. 19)**: William H. Webster, Federal Appeals Court judge in St. Louis, chosen by President Carter and Attorney General Griffin B. Bell. Bell calls 53-year-old judge "man of strength, intellect, and integrity." Nominee promises to act "within the framework of the Constitution."

**Bell Dismisses Federal Prosecutor (Jan. 20)**: Ousts David W. Marston, U.S. Attorney in Philadelphia, a Republican, who successfully prosecuted leading Democratic politicians for corruption and was investigating at least two Democratic Congressmen. Marston, 35, calls dismissal purely political. **(Jan. 30)**: Carter says involvement in dismissal of Marston was "routine," and compatible with campaign promises.

**Carter Offers Plan for Tax Cuts and Reforms (Jan. 21)**: Hands Congress controversial package with revenue-raising revisions of tax code that he says will spur economy and make tax system "fairer and simpler." Plans to reduce taxes on incomes of less than $100,000 and raise them on higher incomes. Reforms include crackdown on deductions.

**Carter Budget Seeks Economic Gains (Jan. 23)**: President's message offers $500-billion plan for fiscal 1979. Carter thinks $25-billion tax cut and $60.6-billion budget deficit will keep economic growth at steady rate just under 5% yearly.

**New HEW Rules for Abortion Victims (Jan. 26):** U.S. will help finance operations for impoverished women who are victims of rape or incest and if crime is reported within 60 days. Secretary Joseph A. Califano, Jr., issues regulations interpreting recent legislation by Congress.

**Two Arrested as Spies for Hanoi (Jan. 31):** USIA official and a Vietnamese named in seven-count federal indictment charging espionage and related crimes. They are: Ronald L. Humphrey, 42, who once served in South Vietnam, and Truong Dinh Hung, 32, son of "peace candidate" in South Vietnam's 1967 Presidential election. **(Feb. 1):** The two plead not guilty. **(May 19):** Federal jury in Alexandria, Va., convicts pair of espionage. **(July 7):** Humphrey and Truong each sentenced to 15 years. Insist on their innocence.

**Army Selects West German Gun (Jan. 31):** Chooses weapon over British and American products for use in new U.S. battle tank in 1980s. A major step toward goal of standardizing weapons in Atlantic Alliance. Official calls German gun "significant advance" over U.S. 105-millimeter gun.

**Haldeman Book Reports Soviet War Bid (Feb. 16):** Book by Nixon White House chief of staff says Russians made overtures to U.S. in 1969 proposing joint nuclear attack on China's atomic facilities, but that Nixon rejected them. Account, in *The Ends of Power* is denied by William P. Rogers, then Secretary of State, and Henry A. Kissinger, then National Security Adviser. Book is released prematurely. In it, Haldeman says Nixon initiated Watergate break-in, participated in the cover-up from the beginning, and may have erased 18½ minutes of damaging dialogue on tape. **(Feb. 17):** Official Soviet press agency Tass calls Haldeman statement about Soviet war bid "lie from beginning to end."

**Rep. Diggs Indicted in Kickbacks (March 23):** Michigan Democrat charged by Federal jury in connection with Congressional payroll. Charles C. Diggs, Jr., 55, has served 24 years in House and became senior black member in 1970. Alleged kickbacks and improper payments said to have passed $101,000.

**Carter Offers New Urban Policy (March 27):** Proposes broad program of job aid, tax incentives, public works, and loan guarantees to help recovery of ailing cities. President will ask Congress to expand 1979 budget request by $4.4 billion.

**Passman Indicted in Korean Bribe Case (March 31):** Former Louisiana Rep. Otto E. Passman charged with conspiring with Tongsun Park to defraud U.S. and with accepting bribes from Park, an alleged covert agent for South Korea. Passman, a Democrat, once a power in foreign aid appropriations.

**Carter Signs Retirement Bill (April 6):** Approves legislation raising legal mandatory retirement age to 70 for most employees.

**Carter Delays Neutron Weapons (April 7):** Decides to defer production of controversial nuclear warhead. Says tactical weapon will not be produced in immediate future unless Soviet Union fails to exercise restraint in arms deployment.

**Former FBI Officials Indicted (April 10):** Federal jury in Washington charges L. Patrick Gray III, once acting Director, with conspiring to deprive citizens of rights by ordering break-ins and searches without warrants. Also accused are W. Mark Felt, former Acting Associate Director, and Edward S. Miller, once chief of counterintelligence section. First time a former director or high executive has been charged with a criminal act. Justice Dept. drops charges of illegal wiretapping and mail opening against John J. Kearney, low-level FBI official. Attorney General Griffin B. Bell says evidence indicated Kearney had been acting under orders. **(April 13):** J. Wallace LaPrade removed as chief of New York FBI office to answer Justice Dept. charges relating to his role in break-ins without warrants. He says FBI continues warrantless inquiries under authorization from President Carter and Bell. **(July 6):** Attorney General dismisses LaPrade from FBI. Reason given is failure to cooperate with inquiry into illegal investigative techniques against antiwar radicals. **(Aug. 4):** Neil John Welch, FBI Philadelphia chief, named to head New York office. Pledges "brick by brick" reorganization.

**Nixon's Memoirs Appear (April 30):** *The New York Times* and other newspapers begin publication of excerpts from forthcoming 400,000-word volume, *RN: The Memoirs of Richard Nixon.* He defends his role in the Watergate cover-up. He says he misled the people but terms his actions result of series of misjudgments or tactical errors as he found himself drawn into scandal. In succeeding installments he recalls the following: He preserved tape-recorded conversations in his office to protect himself against aides who might turn against him; the decision for the 1972 Christmas bombing of the Hanoi area was his most difficult of the Vietnam War, but one of the most necessary; the Watergate scandal "badly damaged" his ability to counter growing opposition to his policy of détente with Soviet Union.

**15-Cent Postage Takes Effect (May 28):** New letter rates announced by Postal Service are 15 cents for first full ounce and 13 cents for each additional ounce. Price for postcard rises from 9 to 10 cents.

**Nixon Hailed in Kentucky (July 2):** In one of first appearances since resignation, he dedicates $2.6-million Leslie County Recreation Center at Hyden, named in his honor. Addressing thousands in remote town, he attacks global Communism and defends the military, CIA, and free-enterprise system.

**Bell Held in Contempt; Wins Stay (July 6):** Order issued by Judge Thomas P. Griess in Manhattan U.S. District Court after Attorney General refuses to release files on 18 informers who spied on Socialist Workers Party. First time an Attorney General held in contempt for refusal to release information. **(July 7):** Bell wins stay of order from Judge Murray I. Gurfein in U.S. Court of Appeals.

**Judge Rules Snepp Broke Trust (July 7):** Oren R. Lewis, in U.S. District Court, finds Frank W. Snepp III, former CIA agent, violated contract in writing unauthorized book about agency. Orders author's "ill-gotten gains" to go to Government.

**American Nazis Rally in Chicago (July 9):** Twenty-five brown-uniformed members demonstrate in Marquette Park, the culmination of a year-long legal battle. Supreme Court had refused stay of Federal judge's order lifting Chicago insurance requirements and permitting rally. The Nazis, represented by ACLU, had charged that a $60,000 insurance requirement denied their free speech rights. Seventy-two arrested at park in racially tense southwest Chicago as 2,000 mill about, hundreds exchanging racial insults. Earlier, Supreme Court had denied request by Skokie, Ill., hometown of thousands of holocaust survivors, to bar Nazi march there, which the Nazis later called off. Case sharply divided civil liberties advocates.

**Mitchell Granted a Parole (July 20):** Former Attorney General to leave prison in January 1979 after serving 19 months for crimes in Watergate scandal.

**Carter's Drug Adviser Resigns (July 20):** Dr. Peter G. Bourne, 38, a psychiatrist, subject of controversy for prescribing powerful sedative for White House employee under fictitious name for recipient. Quits soon after getting indefinite leave with pay from $51,000 job. **(July 21):** Inquiries result from his statement about use of marijuana or cocaine by White House staff members. **(July 24):** President warns staff to obey drug laws even if they disagree with them or to "seek employment elsewhere."

**Carter Orders Aid for Cities (Aug. 16):** Signs four orders to focus Federal attention on urban needs.

**Ray Denies Killing Dr. King (Aug. 16):** Tells House Assassinations Committee under oath that he was set up to take blame for 1968 killing by man named "Raoul," who Ray said had been his partner in gun smuggling. Fifty-year-old convict is serving 99-year sentence for killing civil rights leader. **(Aug. 17):** Ray denies he stalked King across South before assassination. Committee finds no evidence Ray is telling the truth.

**Carter Vetoes Weapons Bill (Aug. 17):** Rejects $37-billion authorization, charging it would weaken defense by including $2.13-billion aircraft carrier he doesn't want. Prefers funds to improve air and ground forces in Europe and general military readiness.

**U.S. Adopts New Bias Guidelines (Aug. 22):** Administration policy designed to guide Federal agencies in protecting public and private employees from job discrimination.

**Susan B. Anthony Dollar (Aug. 23):** Senate unanimously votes bill for minting of coin bearing likeness of champion of women's voting rights. New dollar would be somewhat larger than a quarter. House yet to act.

**Carter Names Woman to Fed (Aug. 28):** Nancy H. Teeters, 48, liberal economist, nominated to fill term of Arthur Burns, expiring Jan. 31, 1984, with an annual salary of $52,500. She would be first woman on seven-member Federal Reserve Board. Mrs. Teeters is chief economist of House Budget Committee.

**Rep. Daniel Flood Indicted (Sept. 5):** U.S. jury charges Pennsylvania Democrat with lying to juries by denying he knew of payoff to a former aide and that he himself had received payoffs. Flood, 74, denies all charges. He is chairman of House Labor, Health, Education, and Welfare Subcommittee.

**Defense Bill Veto Upheld (Sept. 7):** House, 205–191, in major victory for Carter, easily upholds veto of defense authorization bill containing $2-billion nuclear aircraft carrier President doesn't want.

**House Panel Votes Arms Bill (Sept. 13):** Armed Services Committee, rebuffing Pentagon plea for $545-million worth of new weapons, approves $35.2-billion defense authorization bill to replace the $37-billion measure that Carter vetoed. New bill eliminates $1.93-billion aircraft carrier that President did not want but adds $209 million for Navy to settle shipbuilding claims. **(Sept. 14):** Similar measure cleared by Senate committee.

**General Services Administration Scandals Brewing (Sept. 19).** At Senate hearing, GSA Administrator Jay Solomon calls story of agency's operations an "ugly and disgusting saga." Six grand juries looking into scandals, 50 GSA employees already disciplined, 80 transferred. Investigations continuing.

## People, Places, and Things

### 1977

**Boy Is Born to Princess Anne (Nov. 15):** Queen Elizabeth's grandchild, 7 pounds, 9 ounces, is fifth in line to British throne.

**English Court Protects Mistresses (Nov. 28):** Court of Appeal rules they must get same protection as a wife against use of violence in the home.

### 1978

**Wallaces Divorced in Surprise Settlement (Jan. 4):** Alabama Gov. George C. Wallace and wife, Cornelia, agree to terms on seventh anniversary. She will receive $75,000 in lump-sum alimony and personal items.

**Husband-Beating Viewed as Problem (Jan. 29):** Two authors of book on wife beating report studies show nearly 12 million battered husbands in U.S., nearly 20% of the total. Book says there are 28 million battered wives. "Domestic violence," not just wife-beating, viewed as the real problem.

**The Smew Returns to Rhode Island (Jan. 30):** White and black Siberian duck first seen in continental U.S. two years previously. Audubon Society official reports it was seen swimming on pond at Westerly.

**Papers on Sacco-Vanzetti Case Released (Jan. 31):** Harvard University frees files of A. Lawrence Lowell 50 years after execution of two in famous case.

**Blizzard Blots Out New England Scene (Feb. 7):** Red fishing shack at Rockport, Mass., "Motif No. 1" to thousands of artists, collapses in snowstorm.

**West Point's First Black Honored (Feb. 11):** His name cleared, Lieut. Henry Ossian Flipper is reburied at Thomasville, Ga., with full military honors. Academy graduate of 1877, who died 38 years ago, had been dismissed from the Army in disgrace in an 1882 embezzling case. His discharge was changed to honorable after 94-year fight for review.

**A Number's Not a Name (Feb. 13):** Minneapolis judge denies Michael Herbert Dengler's request to assume legally the name "1069." Court rules changing a name to a number would offend "basic human dignity."

**First Wedding in Antarctica (Feb. 18):** Sgt. Carlos Alberto Sugliano and Julia Beatriz Buonamio married in headquarters building while blizzard rages outside.

**Chaplin's Body Stolen (March 2):** Taken from site in small Swiss cemetery where comedian was buried two months previously. **(May 17):** Body found in cornfield near Lake Geneva. Two suspects arrested after calling family to demand ransom for return of body. **(May 18):** Authorities say body will be reburied in solid protective vault.

**Pregnant Hippo Suffocates (March 11):** Two-ton Bubbles shot by tranquilizing dart after eluding capture for 19 days after escape from Lion Country Safari animal park in California. Rolls against tree and head is bent, shutting off breathing.

**Soviet Penalizes Rostropovich (March 15):** Revokes citizenship of expatriate cellist and conductor for "unpatriotic activity." Wife, singer Galina Vishnevskaya, also loses citizenship. Cellist had campaigned for artistic freedom in Soviet Union.

**John Wayne Has Heart Surgery (April 3):** Film actor, 70, undergoes operation at Boston hospital for replacement of defective valve.

**Betty Ford in Hospital (April 10):** Former President's wife enters Navy rehabilitation center in Long Beach, Calif., to be treated for effects of combination of alcohol and Valium, a tranquilizer. **(April**

21): Mrs. Ford says she became addicted to alcohol as well as to medicine she had been taking for arthritis.

**Ehrlichman Out of Prison (April 27):** Former Nixon aide leaves federal prison camp in Arizona on parole 18 months after beginning sentence for role in Watergate affair. Ehrlichman, 53, believes he is "different and better person."

**Hosts Liable for Intoxicated Guest (April 29):** California Supreme Court rules hosts can be sued by people who are injured by drunken guests.

**Scouts Drop Eagle Age Limit (May 5):** Scouting-USA drops restrictions for severely handicapped Cub Scouts, Scouts and Explorer Scouts. Gregory Wittine, 23, a Long Island cerebral palsy victim who had been denied the award, thus becomes an Eagle Scout after nationwide protests. Ruling means 60,000 physically or mentally handicapped Scouts will have same privilege. Age limit had been 18 years.

**Princess Margaret Plans Divorce (May 10):** She and Earl of Snowdon announce plans to end two years of formal separation and 18 years of marriage. **(May 11):** Kensington Palace says 47-year-old Princess is suffering from hepatitis and gastroenteritis.

**British Royalty Gets a Raise (May 20):** Total annual allowances increased to $4.6 million. Queen Elizabeth gets $85,000 more, for $3.5 million, tax-free. Princess Margaret, despite controversy about personal life, awarded $106,000, an increase of $7,000.

**East's First Casino Opens (May 26):** Legalized casino gambling begins officially in Atlantic City. Bettors crowd into Resorts International Hotel. New Jersey's new industry launched as Gov. Brendan Byrne cuts ribbon to open casino.

**German Embezzler Freed as Ill (May 29):** Frankfurt judge paroles Rainer Kuhn, 40, who had stolen $474,137 from employer and gambled most of it away. Court accepts defense argument that Kuhn's compulsive gambling was "illness of soul."

**Freddie Laker Knighted (June 2):** Queen Elizabeth elevates man who introduced low-price, no-frills flights between London and New York.

**Second Woman Senator (June 12):** Maryon P. Allen sworn in to succeed late husband, James Allen, Alabama Democrat. She is embraced by Senator Muriel Humphrey, who replaced husband, Hubert.

**Hussein Marries American (June 15):** Jordan's King proclaims Elizabeth Halaby, 26, new Queen of desert kingdom after brief Moslem ceremony. She will be called Queen Noor al-Hussein—Light of Hussein.

**Ali and Brezhnev Chat (June 19):** Ex-heavyweight champion exchanges hug and kisses with Soviet leader. Ali says Brezhnev "told me he'd like me to do all I can to better relations between our two countries."

**Christina Onassis Weds (Aug. 1):** Greek shipping millionaire, 27, married to Sergei Kauzov, 37, former Soviet merchant marine official, in simple Moscow ceremony. She looks forward to domestic life cooking and scrubbing in small Russian apartment, but returns to Greece "on business," cutting honeymoon short.

**3 Cross Atlantic by Balloon (Aug. 17):** Ben Abruzzo, Max Anderson, and Larry Newman, all from Albuquerque, N.M., land in French wheatfield. Two British balloonists had failed a month earlier in attempt at first Atlantic crossing.

**First Nonstop Polar Flight (Aug. 19):** Dieter Schmitt, 54, of Germany, completes first nonstop solo flight across North Pole in single-engine plane.

## Religion

### 1977

**Italy and Vatican Agree (Nov. 7):** New accord to replace 1929 Concordat between Roman Catholic Church and the state. Catholicism no longer state religion and Vatican influence on education and marriage to be cut.

**Pope Drops Remarriage Penalty (Nov. 10):** Paul VI agrees to lift penalty of excommunication for U.S. Catholics who remarry after divorce. Penalty imposed in 1884.

**Man and Wife Ordained as Episcopal Priests (Dec. 17):** Ann and Michael Coburn take vows in St. James Church, Danbury, Conn., as first married couple in nation to be ordained priests together. Both are 28. Mrs. Coburn 90th woman priest and first to be ordained in Connecticut. Rector of nearby church protests.

### 1978

**Presbyterians Name Moderator (May 16):** Rev. William P. Lytle, 54, Princeton Seminary graduate, chosen to head United Presbyterian Church in the U.S.A. Now pastor in San Antonio. **(May 22):** 190th General Assembly disapproves ordination of avowed, practicing homosexuals as clergymen.

**Mormon Church Ends Ban on Blacks (June 9):** Leaders reverse 148-year-old policy of excluding them from priesthood. President Spencer W. Kimball announces revelation, saying "every faithful, worthy man in the church" may now be ordained "without regard for race or color."

**Lutherans Choose President (July 15):** Rev. Dr. James R. Crumley named head of Lutheran Church in America at biennial convention in Chicago. Church, formed from four groups in 1962, has 3.1 million members and is third largest Protestant denomination in North America.

**Pope Paul VI Is Mourned (Aug. 6):** Giovanni Battista Montini, 262nd occupant of Throne of St. Peter, dead at 80 after heart attack at Castel Gandolfo summer home. Political and church leaders praise his work for world peace and ecumenism and for guiding church in major liturgical and organizational changes during time of religious and social unrest. **(Aug. 12):** Pope entombed in crypt of St. Peter's Basilica after requiem concelebrated in St. Peter's Square by 104 cardinals. Rosalynn Carter, Sen. Edward Kennedy, and New York Gov. Hugh Carey lead U.S. delegation at funeral.

**New Pope Is Surprise Choice (Aug. 26):** Albino Cardinal Luciani, 65, moderate Italian prelate, elected as 263rd Pope on third ballot of secret session of 111 Cardinals. He takes name of John Paul I, after Paul VI and John XXIII, his immediate predecessors. Luciani, son of a Socialist glass worker, was ordained at age 22 and became Patriarch of Venice. He opposes artificial birth control and abortion. In first speech to Cardinals, he says his goal is to "preserve the discipline of the church," but wants to carry out Vatican Council II reforms. **(Sept. 3):** John Paul I installed in simple ceremony outside St. Peter's Basilica before crowd of 250,000, including kings, queens, and presidents. **(Sept. 4):** Pope bends protocol to confer with Vice President Walter F. Mondale 30 minutes on Middle East and Carter's human rights campaign.

**Russian Prelate Dies During Audience With Pope (Sept. 5):** Orthodox Archbishop Nikodim, 49, advocate of Christian unity and a president of World Council of Churches, succumbs to heart attack after congratulating John Paul I. New Pontiff gives him absolution.

**New Pope Dies Suddenly (Sept. 28):** Pope John Paul I, after only 34 days in office, dies of a heart attack.

## Science

### 1977

**New Object in Space (Nov. 9):** Astronomers say new class of asteroid or perhaps solar system's 10th and smallest planet may be orbiting sun between Saturn and Uranus.

**Drill Pierces Antarctic Ice (Dec. 8):** Engineers report success in blasting through 1,380 feet to penetrate "lost world" extension of Pacific Ocean under Ross Ice Shelf year after earlier failure.

**New Blood Test for Cancer Reported (Dec. 21):** Research technique that won Nobel Prize used to improve detection of malignant prostate tumors in men. Method called the radioimmunoassay technique.

### 1978

**Soviet Astronauts Link Up in Space (Jan. 11):** Two in Soyuz 27 dock spaceship to main hatch of 19-ton Salyut 6 research station high over Siberia about 25½ hours after launching. They crawl through hatch to embrace two comrades who docked their craft with the station a month before. Tass calls orbital station and two spaceships a step in development of Soviet space flight. **(Jan. 16):** Astronauts blast loose from research station and parachute safely to snowy landing site in central Asia. They use Soyuz 26 craft their comrades had used to reach the station Dec. 11. Those astronauts remain in space in mission looking to creation of permanently manned orbital stations with changing crews. **(Jan. 22):** Shuttle capsule docked to orbiting Salyut 6, occupied by two astronauts. First such unmanned mission brings fuel, life support, and equipment.

**35 Selected as Astronaut Candidates (Jan. 16):** NASA picks six women, three blacks, and an Oriental-American from 8,079 applicants for space-shuttle program.

**Soviet Spy Satellite Breaks Up (Jan. 24):** Crippled Cosmos 954 with atomic reactor re-enters earth's atmosphere and disintegrates over northwestern Canada. Reactor powered ocean-scanning radar that tracked surface ships. Naval reconnaissance satellite used by Soviet for 12 years. U.S. and Soviet had cooperated to prevent possible radioactive contamination and prevent panic. **(Jan. 28):** Scientists find signs that crippled Cosmos 954 released radiation in sub-Arctic wastes of Canada. Also report aerial surveys have turned up second source of contamination from fragment of Soviet space vehicle. **(Jan. 30):** Canadian and U.S. scientists identify radioactive twisted metal object discovered in northern Canada as part of Cosmos 954. **(Jan. 30):** President Carter calls on Soviet Union to join pact to bar earth satellites from carrying radioactive material to bar possible contamination on re-entering earth's atmosphere. **(Feb. 4):** Canadian Defense Minister estimates cost of search and recovery operations at $1 million and says government is considering whether to bill Soviet Union.

**Human Teeth Clue to Ancestor of Man (Feb. 5):** Researchers dating oldest such fossil found in China believe ancestor one step from modern man lived in Asia 1.7 million years ago. This increases by more than million years age assigned to earliest fossil man in China.

**Czech Orbited With Russian (March 2):** Capt. Vladimir Remek, 29, joins Soviet Col. Aleksei A. Gubarov, 47, in Soyuz 28 capsule. **(March 3):** They rendezvous with orbiting Salyut 6 space station, where two Soviet astronauts have been orbiting the earth for 12 weeks. All feeling well. **(March 4):** A few hours later, space station astronauts, Lieut. Col. Yuri Romanenko and Georgi M. Grechko, break American record of 84 days in space. American Skylab crew sends message of congratulations. **(March 10):** Soviet and Czechoslovak astronauts return to earth after seven days in space. **(March 16):** Romanenko and Grechko ride Soyuz 27 capsule to perfect landing in central Asia after 96 days orbiting earth in longest manned mission in space flight.

**Wobbling Skylab Stabilized (June 9):** 84-ton space station responds to radio commands and leaves dangerous falling orbit. Can be controlled for future use or sent on harmless plunge back to earth.

**Major Eruption on Sun (July 11):** Flare-ups disrupt Coast Guard ship-to-shore communications, saturate X-ray detectors on two satellites and send magnetic clouds streaking through solar system.

**Child Conceived Outside Womb (July 26):** Baby girl, delivered at Oldham, England, hospital, believed to be world's first child born from egg fertilized in laboratory. Normal 5-pound, 12-ounce baby delivered by Caesarean section. Parents are John Brown, 38, truck driver, and Lesley, 32. Mrs. Brown had been unable to become pregnant because of blockage in fallopian tubes. Church leaders welcome achievement, with some reservations from Roman Catholics.

**Soviet Breaks Space Record (Aug. 2):** Soyuz 29 astronauts pass American mark of 937 astronaut days spent in space as they circle earth in Salyut 6 space laboratory. Supply capsule is separated.

**Second Venus Probe Launched (Aug. 8):** Pioneer Venus 2 begins four-month, 220-million-mile journey to study hot, dense atmosphere of earth's nearest planetary neighbor. Enters perfect flight trajectory after launching at Kennedy Space Center in Florida.

**German Astronaut in Space (Aug. 28):** Sigmund Jaehn, East Germany's first, and three Soviet colleagues begin medical and technical experiments aboard Soviet space station Salyut 6. Jaehn and Valery Bykovsky of Russia fired into space aboard Soyuz 31 capsule, joining pair already aboard.

**New Asteroid Spotted, Named Ra-Shalom (Sept. 10):** Eleanor Helin, Cal Tech astronomer, confirms existence of previously unidentified asteroid about 17 million miles from Earth. Estimated about two miles in diameter. Named in honor of Egyptian-Israeli participants at Camp David meeting.

**Cosmonauts Set Record (Sept. 20):** Vladimir Kovalenok and Alexander Ivanchenkov surpass 96-day, 10-hour space endurance record set by other Soviet spacemen in same *Salyut 6* space lab.

## Sports

### 1978

**HEW Insists on Sex Equality in Sports (Jan. 24):** Warns Oak Ridge, Tenn., school officials of loss of $850,000 in federal funds unless girls are treated same as boys in interscholastic and physical education programs.

**South Africa Names Nonwhite Player (Feb. 12):** Peter Lamb, 18, of mixed race, picked for Davis Cup team to play U.S. in Nashville, Tenn. First nonwhite named to a national squad. South Africa is facing demands for expulsion from world tennis.

**Horsemen Battle Spread of Disease (March 14):** Kentucky breeders seek to check equine venereal infection that has shut several farms, threatening operations. Malady traced to three stallions from France.

**Scottish Soccer Star Banned (June 5):** Willie Johnston ordered home after being caught using stimulant in World Cup game against Peru. Will be banned for life from Scottish national team.

**$1.5-Million Award in Skiing Case (June 6):** Vermont Supreme Court upholds verdict for James Sunday, 24, paralyzed from waist down in a spill in 1974. Rejects appeal by Stratton Mountain Corp. that sport contains inherent risks. New Vermont law now places most of responsibility on the skier, except on lifts.

**Billy Martin Quits Yankees (July 24):** Ends stormy relationship with George Steinbrenner, Yankees' owner, in second year of three-year contract. Martin, 50, had been dismissed from three previous major league managerships. Bob Lemon, 57, Hall of Fame pitcher, succeeds Martin. **(July 29):** Yankees announce Martin will return to lead team in 1980.

**Muhammad Ali Wins Again (Sept. 15):** Ex-heavyweight champion, 36, easily outpoints Leon Spinks to become first man to win title three times. Estimated 90 million people see fight over TV. New gate record set, about $4.8 million, at Louisiana Superdome in New Orleans.

**Women Sportswriters Allowed in Locker Rooms (Sept. 25):** Federal judge overrules Commissioner Bowie Kuhn's attempt to bar women reporters from baseball clubhouses.

## State and Local Governments

### 1977

**Black Elected New Orleans Mayor (Nov. 12):** Ernest N. Morial, former Louisiana Appeals Court judge, first of race to win post. Credits white support in narrow election.

### 1978

**Transit System for Miami (March 8):** Area voters approve construction of high-speed transit system using elevated tracks. $900-million Dade County, Fla., line will connect downtown Miami with Hialeah and suburbs as first stage of system that will eventually cost $2.5 billion.

**Carey Vetoes Death-Penalty Bill (April 11):** New York Governor terms capital punishment "ultimate deception" and official killing "not a proper or legitimate exercise of a government." **(May 2):** State Senate fails by one vote to override veto after two Democrats reverse themselves. Vote of 39 to 19 is legislative victory for Governor.

**Californians Vote to Limit Taxes (June 6):** Approve Proposition 13 for nearly 60% slash in property tax revenues effective July 1. Referendum resulted from voter initiative campaign. **(June 7):** Nearly every city, county and school district in state orders emergency budget cutbacks. Gov. Edmund G. Brown freezes state hiring. His administration presses plan to use remaining property tax revenue and state surplus to hold reduction in state and local budgets to 15%. Nationwide, antispending groups view vote as sign of wide tax revolt. Eight state primaries on same day show conservative, antitax, and anti-incumbent voting patterns.

**ERA Loses in Illinois (June 7):** Legislature rejects proposed Federal equal rights amendment by vote of 101 to 64, six votes short of needed majority. Amendment thus dead in state for 1978.

**Carter Signs New York Aid Bill (Aug. 8):** Enacts measure to give city $1.65 billion in Federal loan guarantees in continuing effort to avoid bankruptcy.

## Women

### 1977

**Reader's Digest Settles Suit (Nov. 4):** Agrees to pay more than $1.5 million to 2,600 former and current women employees in one of biggest settlements of sex-discrimination case. Does not acknowledge discrimination.

**Women's Parley Opens (Nov. 19):** Two thousand delegates convene at Houston for National Women's Conference on issues affecting health, homes, jobs, and institutions. **(Nov. 20):** Conference votes substitute resolution on rights of minority women stronger than proposed in leadership's agenda. Resolution decries "double discrimination" of minority women. **(Nov. 21):** Parley ends after adopting 25 points of agenda but rejecting proposal for Cabinet-level women's department.

**Justices Block Seniority Loss in Maternity Leave (Dec. 6):** Supreme Court rules, 9–0, that employer cannot deprive woman of seniority because she takes uncompensated leave to give birth to a child.

**Women Cadets Do Well at West Point (Dec. 7):** Study shows first of sex are on a par with men academically at U.S. Military Academy and show similar pattern to men in physical tasks, although ranked separately.

### 1978

**15 Women to Train for Missile Crews (Feb. 5):** Air Force officers selected for 27 weeks of training for service at a nuclear ballistics-missile site.

**Rotary Club Must Expel Women (Feb. 25):** Duarte, Calif., unit warned to oust three female members or lose charter. Club only one in international service organization to enroll women. It has voted to keep them.

**Woman Marine General Named (April 6):** Carter nominates Col. Margaret A. Brewer, 47, as first female general of corps. She will become director of information.

**Stormy Triumph for Women (May 12):** Commerce Dept. announces hurricanes will no longer be named exclusively for women. Second storm of season designated as Hurricane Bud, others as Daniel, Hector, Paul, etc.

**First Women Join White House Honor Guard (May 17):** Five in ranks at arrival ceremonies for Kenneth Kaunda, President of Zambia. One from each branch of service.

**8 Women Graduate at Kings Point (June 26):** Merchant Marine Academy midshipmen first to get diplomas from service academies. Get Navy and Coast Guard Reserve commissions.

**Sea Duty Opened to Navy Women (July 28):** U.S. District judge in Washington rules unconstitutional federal law prohibiting them from serving on other than transport and hospital ships.

**Woman Picked for White House Post (Aug. 29):** Sarah Weddington, general counsel for Agriculture Dept., chosen by President as chief assistant for women's issues, succeeding Margaret Costanza.

# The Year's Top Trivia

*Sanford Teller*

An astute federal official pointed out two seemingly contradictory Occupational Safety and Health Administration regulations. One rule requires earth-moving machines at construction sites to be equipped with bells that must be rung when the equipment is being moved backward—as a warning to workers in the area.

But another regulation "protects" the workers by making it mandatory for them to wear earplugs.

•

The year's "Tell-It-Like-It-Is" award goes to Emil Kordish, a Baltimore contractor. Kordish, whose company does millions of dollars worth of business with the state of Maryland, told a State Senate committee that bribes and kickbacks were actually in the best interests of the taxpayers. He noted that "limited corruption is less costly to taxpayers than consolidated purchasing and all this sunshine."

Senator Victor L. Crawford said that, upon hearing Kordish's testimony, he nearly fell out of his chair.

•

Bob Holt, a 20-year-old Seattle man, was quietly walking on a downtown street, disguised as a mallard duck, when he was—for no apparent reason—attacked by a husky, 6-foot-tall, bearded stranger. The perpetrator spun him around by one wing, tore off his duck bill, hit him over the head with it, and ran away.

Holt, who was dressed as a duck to promote a local radio station, had no explanation for the incident. He told police: "I didn't speak to him. I didn't flap my wings or do anything like that."

•

Philosophers may still be puzzled by that age-old question: "How many angels can dance on the head of a pin." But scientists do know how fast the average older Swedish citizen walks.

In March, a series of tests undertaken by Sweden's Road Traffic Institute revealed that a typical Swedish pensioner walks at a speed of 0.9 yard per second. Researchers also discovered that the speed could increase to 1.3 yards per second when an elderly Swede was "trying to catch a bus."

•

A man wearing a gorilla mask leaped over the counter at a McDonald's hamburger restaurant in Atlanta and attempted a holdup with an unusual weapon.

Clerks said they were startled when the culprit pulled a banana from his pocket, pointed it at them, and demanded that they open the cash register. When they refused to comply, he ran out into the street, with several employees in hot pursuit. Later, one counter clerk said, "I kept looking at the banana, trying to see if there was something inside it—perhaps a gun covered with peel."

The simian-masked bandit was captured a few moments after his abortive heist. Police reported that the banana wasn't loaded.

•

While aboard the orbiting Soviet space lab, *Salyut 6,* Poland's first spaceman, Miroslaw Hermaszewski, said he slept on the ceiling "since I am a very tall guy."

The Soviet news agency, Tass, reported that the three Russian cosmonauts slept on the walls.

Toshio Nakagawa, known to his neighbors in Western Honshu, Japan's main island, as "the garlic nut," made one of the year's most valuable contributions to romance and to human relationships in general. After 20 years of failure, the 66-year-old farmer finally fulfilled his lifelong dream—he developed an odor-free garlic.

According to Junichi Moriya, an executive with Mitsubishi Corp., the giant Japanese company now marketing the revolutionary product (known as White Nakagawa No.1 Garlic), "a team of 10 staffers tasted the odor-free garlic raw and only one of them had bad breath afterward."

•

The myth that Australian politicians don't have any fun was laid to rest with the June publication of a book by Don Chipp, a former Liberal Party colleague of Prime Minister Malcolm Fraser.

According to Chipp's account, the Prime Minister thoroughly enjoys a little practical joke now and then. Chipp wrote that Fraser rarely drinks liquor, "but his alcohol tolerance is low and he becomes affected quickly. This brings out his sense of humor, which normally takes the form of stuffing pickled onions and ice cubes into people's pockets."

•

A long-overdue comment on today's brazen criminals came from a top U.S. Capitol police official in June.

After bandits held up two Washington, D.C., police officers, stealing their service revolvers, their wallets, and their wrist watches—as well as a police portable radio—they tied them to a chair and to a doorknob with their own handcuffs.

Police Captain Harry Grevey summed it up when he said, "The gunmen apparently had no respect for the law."

•

Old wives—and most mothers—were right: Chicken soup does fight colds.

In June, Miami Beach's Mount Sinai Hospital announced that, more than any other hot liquid tested, chicken soup helps to rapidly expel germ-carrying mucus from nasal passages, thus fighting infection.

The hospital said that chicken soup was "efficacious upper respiratory tract infection therapy."

•

In April, a Portland man filed suit against the Mount Angel, Ore., Oktoberfest for injuries he sustained during the 1976 celebration.

Robert Rispler claimed that an overly boisterous crowd pushed over the portable toilet he was occupying and that he had been "violently thrown about inside said portable toilet, became intimately mixed with the contents thereof, and sustained a fracture of his right wrist."

•

Senator William Proxmire's August "Golden Fleece Award" went to the Agriculture Department.

Each month, the Senator gives his Golden Fleece to federal agencies he feels are making poor use of public funds.

The Agriculture Department received the award in recognition of its funding of a research project designed to "identify methods of reducing psychological stress and boredom" of pregnant pigs.

# Deaths in 1977–1978

**Ahn, Philip,** 72: veteran character actor; *Thank You, Mr. Moto, Thoroughly Modern Millie,* and TV's *Kung Fu* series. Feb. 28, 1978.

**Allen, James B.,** 65: Democratic Senator from Alabama since 1969. June 1, 1978.

**Baldwin, Faith,** 84: author of more than 60 novels; *Honor Bound* and *Rich Girl, Poor Girl.* March 18, 1978.

**Barrie, Wendy,** 65: actress and TV personality. Feb. 2, 1978.

**Bergen, Edgar,** 75: ventriloquist. Sept. 30, 1978.

**Best, Charles H.,** 79: co-discoverer of insulin. March 31, 1978.

**Boyer, Charles,** 78: actor; appeared in *Tovarich, Gaslight, Algiers, Hold Back the Dawn, Fanny.* Suicide, Aug. 26, 1978.

**Braden, Spruille,** 83: former Assistant Secretary of State for American Republic Affairs. Jan. 11, 1978.

**Brel, Jacques,** 49: Belgian singer and song writer. Oct. 9, 1978.

**Bruce, David K.E.,** 79: veteran diplomat was ambassador to Britain, France, and West Germany; headed first U.S. liaison office in Peking. Dec. 4, 1977.

**Burns, W. Sherman,** 86: ex-chairman of Burns International Security Services. Jan. 5, 1978.

**Byron, Goodloe E.,** 49: Democratic U.S. Representative from Maryland. Oct. 11, 1978.

**Catton, Bruce,** 78: Civil War historian; won 1954 Pulitzer Prize for *A Stillness at Appomattox;* also wrote *Mr. Lincoln's Army, Glory Road, Terrible Swift Sword.* Aug. 28, 1978.

**Chaplin, Charles,** 88: creator of screen's Little Tramp; appeared in *The Gold Rush, The Kid, City Lights, Modern Times, The Great Dictator, Limelight.* Dec. 25, 1977.

**Chase, Ilka,** 72: actress; *The Women, Barefoot in the Park:* author; *Past Imperfect.* Feb. 15, 1978.

**Chavez, Carlos,** 79: Mexican composer and conductor. Aug. 2, 1978.

**Clay, Lucius D.,** 80: commander of U.S. forces in Europe after World War II; organized Berlin Airlift in 1948–49. April 16, 1978.

**Cole, Charles W.,** 71: president of Amherst College 1946–60. Feb. 6, 1978.

**Conant, James B.,** 84: president of Harvard University 1933–53, scientist, and diplomat. Feb. 11, 1978.

**Cox, Billy,** 58: third baseman for Brooklyn Dodgers in 1950s. March 31, 1978.

**Cozzens, James Gould,** 74: novelist, won 1949 Pulitzer Prize for *Guard of Honor;* also wrote *The Last Adam* and *By Love Possessed.* Aug. 9, 1978.

**Crane, Bob,** 49: actor; star of *Hogan's Heroes* on TV. Found murdered June 29, 1978.

**Daly, James,** 59: actor; in *Major Barbara, The Glass Menagerie, J.B.* on Broadway; in *Foreign Intrigue* on TV. July 3, 1978.

**Davis, Hal,** 63: president of American Federation of Musicians. Jan. 11, 1978.

**Diederichs, Nicolaas,** 74: President of South Africa since 1975. Aug. 21, 1978.

**Eames, Charles,** 71: designer of furniture, and a documentary filmmaker. Aug. 21, 1978.

**Eccles, Marriner S.,** 87: chairman of Federal Reserve Board 1936–48, leading figure in economic policy-making in New Deal. Dec. 18, 1977.

**Eglevsky, Andre,** 60: classical ballet dancer. Dec. 4, 1977.

**Etting, Ruth,** 81: singer-actress; appeared on Broadway in *Ziegfeld Follies* and *Whoopee;* radio star in 1930s. Sept. 24, 1978.

**Evans, Bergen,** 73: authority on English language, author, and TV moderator. Feb. 4, 1978.

**Fields, Totie,** 47: comedienne. Aug. 2, 1978.

**Fine, John S.,** 85: Republican governor of Pennsylvania, 1951–55. May 20, 1978.

**Frick, Ford C.,** 83: baseball commissioner 1951–65; sportswriter and broadcaster. April 8, 1978.

**Gainza Paz, Alberto,** 78: publisher of *La Prensa* in Buenos Aires; fighter for press freedom in South America. Dec. 26, 1977.

**Gallagher, Buell G.,** 74: president of City College of New York, 1952–69. Aug. 30, 1978.

**Geer, Will,** 76: character actor appeared in *Tobacco Road,* Shakespeare plays; grandfather in *The Waltons* on TV. April 22, 1978.

**Gilliam, Jim,** 49: Brooklyn and Los Angeles Dodgers player and coach. Oct. 8, 1978.

**Goff, Norris,** 72: played Abner in the *Lum and Abner* radio comedy program from 1931 to 1955. June 7, 1978.

**Goldmark, Peter Carl,** 71: inventor of the long-playing record. Dec. 7, 1977.

**Gordon, Joe,** 63: second baseman with New York Yankees and Cleveland Indians, 1938–50. April 14, 1978.

**Haines, Jesse,** 85: knuckleball pitcher with St. Louis Cardinals' Gashouse Gang. Aug. 5, 1978.

**Harris, Henry E.,** 75: founded H. E. Harris and Company, world's largest stamp dealers. Dec. 29, 1977.

**Hasselblad, Victor,** 72: inventor of camera bearing his name. Aug. 5, 1978.

**Hawks, Howard,** 81: film director; *Sgt. York, Red River, The Crowd Roars, Scarface, The Dawn Patrol, Gentlemen Prefer Blondes.* Dec. 26, 1977.

**Highet, Gilbert,** 71: classicist, author, ex-professor of Latin at Columbia University; *The Classical Tradition.* Jan. 20, 1978.

**Homolka, Oscar,** 79: character actor; *I Remember Mama, Funeral in Berlin, The Seven Year Itch, War and Peace.* Jan. 27, 1978.

**Humphrey, Hubert H.,** 66: Democratic Senator from Minnesota and former Vice President. Jan. 13, 1978.

**Hunt, Reed O.,** 73: ex-chairman of Crown Zellerbach. Nov. 26, 1977.

**James, Gen. Daniel,** 58: first black to hold four-star rank in United States Army. Feb. 25, 1978.

**John Paul I (Albino Luciani),** 65: Roman Catholic Pontiff for 34 days. Sept. 28, 1978.

**Kachaturian, Aram,** 74: Armenian composer; "Saber Dance." May 1, 1978.

**Kenyatta, Jomo,** 87: first President of Kenya, having served since 1963. Aug. 22, 1978.

**Kipnis, Alexander,** 87: basso with Metropolitan Opera. May 14, 1978.

**Koussevitzky, Olga,** 76: widow of Serge Koussevitzky, the conductor. Jan. 5, 1978.

**Kuh, Frederick,** 82: diplomatic correspondent for *Chicago Sun-Times;* longtime foreign reporter for UPI. Jan. 2, 1978.

**Lear, William P.,** 75: inventor of automatic pilot for aircraft, eight-track stereo cartridge and car radio, and designer of *Learstar* jet. May 14, 1978.

**Leavis, Frank Raymond,** 82: influential and controversial English literary critic. April 14, 1978.

**Leibowitz, Samuel S.,** 84: noted criminal lawyer and former justice of New York State Supreme Court; defended nine youths in Scottsboro, Ala., case of 1930s. Jan. 11, 1978.

**Light, Enoch,** 71: leader of dance band. July 31, 1978.

**Lindner, Richard,** 76: American painter renowned for figures of women. April 16, 1978.

**Lombardo, Guy,** 75: led Royal Canadians dance band for 50 years. Nov. 5, 1977.

**MacArthur, John D.,** 80: self-made insurance and real estate billionaire. Jan. 6, 1978.

**Marshall, S.L.A.,** 77: military historian; author of *Pork Chop Hill, Night Drop, Bastogne.* Dec. 17, 1977.

**Martinson, Harry,** 73: Swedish poet and novelist shared 1974 Nobel Prize for Literature. Feb. 11, 1978.

**Mason, (Francis) Van Wyck,** 76: novelist; *Valley Forge, 1777, Guns for Rebellion.* Drowned, Aug. 28, 1978.

**McCarthy, Joseph V.,** 90: managed New York Yankees to eight American League pennants and seven World Series championships between 1930 and 1945. Jan. 13, 1978.

**McClellan, John L.,** 81: Arkansas Senator served 35 years; chairman of Appropriations Committee was second in seniority. Nov. 27, 1977.

**McCoy, Col. Tim,** 86: cowboy actor appeared in over 80 Westerns. Jan. 29, 1978.

**McKnight, William L.,** 90: president and chairman of Minnesota Mining and Manufacturing Company (3M) 1929–67. March 4, 1978.

**Menzies, Sir Robert Gordon,** 83: former Prime Minister of Australia. May 14, 1978.

**Messerschmitt, Willy,** 80: German aircraft designer; his Me-109 fighter was mainstay of *Luftwaffe* in World War II. Aug. 15, 1978.

**Metcalf, Lee,** 66: Democratic Senator from Montana since 1961. Jan. 12, 1978.

**Metcalfe, Ralph E.,** 68: Democratic U.S. Representative from Illinois, Olympic track champion. Oct. 10, 1978.

**Meusel, Bob,** 81: member of "Murderers' Row" while outfielder with New York Yankees. Nov. 28, 1977.

**Montoya, Joseph M.,** 62: former Democratic Senator from New Mexico; served on Watergate committee. June 5, 1978.

**Morrison, Bret,** 66: voice of The Shadow (Lamont Cranston) on radio in 1940s. Sept. 25, 1978.

**Murphy, Robert D.,** 83: veteran diplomat had major role in planning invasion of North Africa in 1942. Jan. 9, 1978.

**Noble, Ray,** 91: jazz conductor and composer; wrote "Goodnight Sweetheart," "Love Is the Sweetest Thing." April 3, 1978.

**Oakie, Jack,** 74: film comedian; *The Fleet's In, Tin Pan Alley, The Great Dictator.* Jan. 23, 1978.

**Paul VI (Giovanni Battista Montini),** 80: Roman Catholic Pontiff since 1963. Aug. 6, 1978.

**Paynter, Richard K., Jr.,** 73: chairman of New York Life Insurance Company, 1962–69. Dec. 30, 1977.

**Peckinpaugh, Roger,** 86: American League shortstop; managed Cleveland Indians. Nov. 17, 1977.

**Pei, Mario A.,** 77: linguist, author of 34 books, and Columbia U. professor. March 2, 1978.

**Prima, Louis,** 67: band leader and jazz trumpeter; wrote "Sing, Sing, Sing" and "Angelina." Aug. 25, 1978.

**Rattigan, Terence,** 66: British playwright; author of *Separate Tables* and *The Winslow Boy.* Nov. 30, 1977.

**Ritchard, Cyril,** 79: star of musicals; best known as Captain Hook in *Peter Pan* on TV. Dec. 18, 1977.

**Rockefeller, John D. III,** 72: philanthropist, patron of the arts, ex-chairman of Rockefeller Foundation. Killed in car crash July 10, 1978.

**Ross, Nellie Tayloe,** 101; nation's first woman Governor (Wyoming); ex-director of the Mint. Dec. 19, 1977.

**Rupp, Adolph F.,** 76: basketball coach at University of Kentucky for 42 years. Dec. 10, 1977.

**Schippers, Thomas,** 47: conductor laureate of Cincinnati Symphony; conducted at Metropolitan Opera and European houses. Dec. 16, 1977.

**Shaw, Robert,** 51: actor; *A Man for All Seasons, The Caretaker, The Sting, Jaws, Black Sunday, The Deep;* author and playwright. Aug. 27, 1978.

**Silone, Ignazio,** 78: author and co-founder of Italian Communist Party; wrote *Bread and Wine* and *Bitter Font.* Aug. 22, 1978.

**Spencer-Churchill, Lady Clementine,** 92: widow of Britain's wartime Prime Minister. Dec. 12, 1977.

**Steinberg, William,** 78: former music director of Pittsburgh and Boston Symphony Orchestras. May 16, 1978.

**Stone, Edward Durrell,** 76: architect designed Radio City Music Hall in New York, Kennedy Center for the Performing Arts in Washington, Stanford Medical Center. Aug. 6, 1978.

**Untermeyer, Louis,** 92: anthologist and poet; 90 published works included *Treasury of Great Poems, Modern American and British Poetry.* Dec. 18, 1977.

**Velasco Alvarado, Gen. Juan,** 67: President of Peru, 1968–75. Dec. 24, 1977.

**von Schuschnigg, Kurt,** 79: Chancellor of Austria at time of Nazi takeover in 1938. Nov. 18, 1977.

**Wallenda, Karl,** 73: founder of the Great Wallendas, circus high-wire walkers. Killed in 100-foot fall from wire March 22, 1978.

**Warner, Jack,** 86: last of four brothers who founded motion-picture studio; made *The Jazz Singer, Little Caesar, Casablanca, Treasure of Sierra Madre.* Aug. 9, 1978.

**Wengenroth, Stow,** 71: lithographer noted for New England scenes. Jan. 22, 1978.

**Wood, Peggy,** 86: actress; *Sound of Music* on screen; *I Remember Mama* on TV. March 18, 1978.

# The U.S. Economy in 1978

*Monte J. Gordon*
*Vice President–Director of Research*
*The Dreyfus Corporation*

Most of the problems which troubled the business and financial community in 1977 continued to defy solution in 1978. Progress was recorded in a few sectors, such as unemployment, which declined to as low as 5.7% in June—although it subsequently rebounded to somewhat over 6%. In general, the gains were limited, and inflation and the foreign trade deficit continued to show a stubborn resistance to improvement.

Inflation became the dominant economic problem of 1978. As a result, the most significant development during the year was the Carter Administration's shift in emphasis from overriding concern with unemployment and tax reform to a primary concern with the problem of halting inflation and its corrosive effects on the economy and society.

In the first quarter of 1978, the economy stumbled badly from the twin blows of an unusually severe winter and a three-month coal strike by the United Mineworkers. These two developments slowed the pace of economic activity sharply, and Gross National Product in real terms (constant dollars, adjusted for inflation) in the first quarter was unchanged from the fourth quarter of 1977. The concern that this could presage a further impairment of the economy proved to be fleeting, since economic activity surged during the second quarter to an annual real rate of growth of about 8.7%. These developments enabled the Administration to continue to forecast an increase in real Gross National Product of about 4% in 1978, compared with a 5.1% increase in 1977. As the year 1978 drew to a close, however, signs of a slowing pace of economic activity became more evident. For example, the Index of Leading Economic Indicators (a sensitive measure which is used to forecast the direction of the economy) fell a rather substantial 0.7% in July after five consecutive months of gain.

The foreign trade deficit (which expanded enormously in 1977 to $26 billion, up from $7 billion in 1976, primarily as a result of a huge increase in oil imports to about $42 billion) continued to plague the U.S. economy in 1978. A major shock occurred when a trade deficit of $4.52 billion was reported for the month of February—the highest in history. Although subsequent months showed some easing, the report for July indicated the fourth highest deficit ever ($2.9 billion), emphasizing the tenacity and dimensions of the problem. Forecasts of the deficit for 1978, generally, focused around the $28- to $30-billion figure, although in the closing months of 1978 there was some reduction in the level of oil imports as a result of improved conservation efforts and rising Alaskan oil production.

A major ancillary effect of the huge trade deficit was a sharp decline in the value of the U.S. dollar versus other major currencies of the world—particularly the Japanese yen, the German mark, and the Swiss franc. Against the yen and the mark, the dollar reached new postwar lows, when it purchased fewer than 200 yen and less than 2 marks. In August 1978, President Carter expressed "deep concern" about the sharp decline of the dollar and the rather disorderly condition of the foreign exchange markets. In response to these conditions and high inflation rates, the Federal Reserve raised the discount rate from 7¼% to 8% and took other actions to raise interest rates in a pattern reminiscent of 1974-75. The Treasury announced it would increase the amount of gold being auctioned each month to 750,000 ounces from 300,000 ounces with the November 1978 auction. Further, the President indicated that other actions would be considered and announced later. The net effect of these steps was to cause some rise in the value of the dollar, but foreign exchange markets remained quite nervous.

One of the major causes of the huge trade deficit and the decline in the value of the dollar abroad was the high inflation rate which continued very much in evidence. The annual inflation rate was recorded at 7.2% in the first quarter of 1978, and it increased substantially to 11% in the second quarter. The Administration raised its earlier forecast of the inflation rate for 1978 from 6.1% to 7.2%. There was some slowing in the rate of inflation toward the end of the year, primarily reflecting a decline in prices paid to farmers and in food prices generally, although prices for industrial goods continued to rise. While some easing could be anticipated from the high rate of the second quarter, as evidenced by a decline in the Producers Price Index (formerly called the Wholesale Price Index) in August—down 0.1%—the underlying rate of inflation remained uncomfortably high—with the PPI up 0.9% in September.

In 1978, capital spending for new plant and equipment continued to lag well below the levels which most economists felt were needed to sustain the forward momentum of the economy and to hold the rate of unemployment below the 6% level. The latest forecasts indicated that capital spending would grow at about 5.3% in real terms in 1978—substantially below the 8% level generally viewed as necessary to achieve these goals. This lag in capital spending has several ramifications: It affects the level of employment, the competitive position of the U.S. economy, inflation through its effect on the rate of productivity—improvement, and the growth rate of the economy. The ability of the U.S. economy to continue to grow in 1979 would be depressed by the failure of capital spending to accelerate in 1978.

A development of major significance during early 1978 was President Carter's decision not to reappoint Dr. Arthur F. Burns as Chairman of the

Federal Reserve Board. Instead, President Carter appointed G. William Miller, Chairman of Textron, Inc., to this key post. The financial community, both domestic and international, regarded the decision with some trepidation, since Dr. Burns' policies opposing inflation had been viewed favorably while Mr. Miller, a businessman and neither a banker nor an economist, was an unknown quantity. In subsequent months, Mr. Miller's action gained the confidence of the financial community as his strong anti-inflation position emerged.

As the year progressed, short-term interest rates rose to about the 8% level, while the prime rate set by banks increased in a series of one-quarter point jumps to around 10%. The major thrust of monetary policy set by the Federal Reserve Board during 1978 was to raise rates and to seek to restrain the flow of money into the economy in order to slow the rate of inflation. From the Federal Reserve's point of view, the problem was complicated by the huge deficit of the federal budget and the decline in the value of the dollar.

During 1978 the range of fluctuation in the stock market was considerable, moving from a low of 742 in February on the Dow Jones Industrial Average to a high of over 900 in September. The dominant factors which influenced the market were concern with inflation, the declining value of the dollar, the prolonged delay in the efforts of the Carter Administration to move its energy program through the Congress, the huge trade deficit, and concern that the economy could be sliding into a recession in late 1978. During the course of the year, a record volume of trading for a single day was recorded on the New York Stock Exchange at a level of 66.37 million shares, with a record trading volume of 220.58 million shares for a single week. Another interesting development during the year involved a rise in the price of gold, which broke through the $200-an-ounce level to about $220 an ounce.

As the year drew to a close, many private forecasters anticipated a marked slow-down in the economy but most continued to believe that the economy would be able to avoid a recession. The new group of difficult economic problems that had bedeviled the 1970s continued in force. Economists failed to agree on policies needed to counteract inflation. Even when there was such agreement—as in the need for an effective energy policy—political stalemates prevented effective action.

As 1979 approached, there was no question that inflation was the premier problem confronting the U.S. economy. The ingenuity and skill of the Administration, Congress, and the Federal Reserve Board will be heavily taxed to bring inflation under control in 1979.

## Money in Circulation by Denomination[1]

(in millions)

| Denomination | 1977[2] | 1976[2] | 1975[3] | 1970 | 1965 | 1960 | 1955 | 1950 | 1945 | 1939 |
|---|---|---|---|---|---|---|---|---|---|---|
| Coin | $ 9,876 | $ 9,348 | $ 8,496 | $ 6,281 | $ 4,060 | $ 2,427 | $ 1,927 | $ 1,554 | $ 1,274 | $ 590 |
| $1[4] | 2,835 | 2,703 | 2,616 | 2,310 | 1,818 | 1,533 | 1,312 | 1,113 | 1,039 | 559 |
| $2 | 636 | 621 | 135 | 136 | 127 | 88 | 75 | 64 | 73 | 36 |
| $5 | 3,816 | 3,639 | 3,571 | 3,161 | 2,489 | 2,246 | 2,151 | 2,049 | 2,313 | 1,019 |
| $10 | 10,552 | 10,213 | 10,280 | 9,170 | 7,514 | 6,691 | 6,617 | 5,998 | 6,782 | 1,772 |
| $20 | 31,060 | 28,665 | 26,798 | 18,581 | 12,974 | 10,536 | 9,940 | 8,529 | 9,201 | 1,576 |
| $50 | 9,520 | 8,577 | 7,671 | 4,896 | 3,482 | 2,815 | 2,736 | 2,422 | 2,327 | 460 |
| $100 | 29,155 | 25,405 | 21,280 | 12,084 | 8,092 | 5,954 | 5,641 | 5,043 | 4,220 | 919 |
| $500 | 170 | 173 | 177 | 215 | 243 | 249 | 307 | 368 | 454 | 191 |
| $1,000 | 197 | 200 | 206 | 252 | 286 | 316 | 438 | 588 | 801 | 425 |
| $5,000 | 2 | 2 | 2 | 3 | 3 | 3 | 3 | 4 | 7 | 20 |
| $10,000 | 4 | 4 | 4 | 4 | 4 | 10 | 12 | 12 | 24 | 32 |
| Total[5] | 97,823 | 89,549 | 81,196 | 57,093 | 42,056 | 32,869 | 31,158 | 27,741 | 28,515 | 7,598 |

1. End of year unless otherwise noted. 2. Sept. 30. 3. June 30. 4. Paper currency only. $1 coins reported under coin. 5. Includes unassorted currency. *Source:* Department of the Treasury, Bureau of Government Financial Operations.

## National Income by Type

(in billions of dollars)

| Type of share | 1978[1] | 1978 % of total | 1977 | 1975 | 1970 | 1965 | 1960 | 1955 | 1950 |
|---|---|---|---|---|---|---|---|---|---|
| National income | $1,603.1 | 100.0 | $1,515.3 | $1,215.0 | $800.5 | $564.3 | $414.5 | $331.0 | $241.1 |
| Compensation of employees | 1,241.0 | 77.4 | 1,153.4 | 931.1 | 603.9 | 393.8 | 294.2 | 224.5 | 154.6 |
| Wages and salaries | 1,050.8 | 65.4 | 983.6 | 805.9 | 542.0 | 358.9 | 270.8 | 211.3 | 146.8 |
| Supplements to wages and salaries | 190.2 | 11.9 | 169.8 | 125.2 | 61.9 | 35.0 | 23.4 | 13.2 | 7.8 |
| Proprietors' income | 105.0 | 6.6 | 99.8 | 87.0 | 66.9 | 57.3 | 46.2 | 41.7 | 37.5 |
| Business and professional | 83.1 | 5.2 | 79.5 | 63.5 | 50.0 | 42.4 | 34.2 | 30.3 | 24.0 |
| Farm | 21.9 | 1.4 | 20.2 | 23.5 | 16.9 | 14.8 | 12.0 | 11.4 | 13.5 |
| Rental income of persons | 22.8 | 1.4 | 22.5 | 22.4 | 23.9 | 19.0 | 15.8 | 13.9 | 9.4 |
| Corporate profits[2] | 132.6 | 8.3 | 144.2 | 95.9 | 69.4 | 76.1 | 49.9 | 46.9 | 37.7 |
| Net interest | 101.7 | 6.3 | 95.4 | 78.6 | 36.4 | 18.2 | 8.4 | 4.1 | 2.0 |

1. Second quarter annual rate (preliminary). 2. Includes inventory valuation adjustment. *Source:* Department of Commerce, Bureau of Economic Analysis.

## Per Capita Personal Income by States

| State | 1977[1] | 1976 |
|---|---|---|
| Alabama | $5,682 | $5,102 |
| Alaska | 9,746 | 10,404 |
| Arizona | 6,455 | 5,798 |
| Arkansas | 5,565 | 4,928 |
| California | 7,836 | 7,152 |
| Colorado | 7,022 | 6,440 |
| Connecticut | 8,154 | 7,352 |
| Delaware | 7,716 | 7,042 |
| District of Columbia | 8,900 | 8,081 |
| Florida | 6,771 | 6,021 |
| Georgia | 6,075 | 5,549 |
| Hawaii | 7,681 | 7,079 |
| Idaho | 6,000 | 5,647 |
| Illinois | 7,787 | 7,259 |
| Indiana | 6,984 | 6,230 |
| Iowa | 7,134 | 6,239 |
| Kansas | 7,050 | 6,466 |
| Kentucky | 6,025 | 5,384 |
| Louisiana | 5,916 | 5,406 |
| Maine | 5,808 | 5,375 |
| Maryland | 7,576 | 6,975 |
| Massachusetts | 7,282 | 6,596 |
| Michigan | 7,723 | 6,757 |
| Minnesota | 7,087 | 6,185 |
| Mississippi | 5,022 | 4,529 |
| Missouri | 6,684 | 5,957 |
| Montana | 6,108 | 5,691 |
| Nebraska | 6,789 | 6,092 |
| Nevada | 7,962 | 7,158 |
| New Hampshire | 6,563 | 5,984 |
| New Jersey | 8,186 | 7,405 |
| New Mexico | 5,878 | 5,325 |
| New York | 7,666 | 6,997 |
| North Carolina | 6,016 | 5,446 |
| North Dakota | 6,076 | 5,826 |
| Ohio | 7,179 | 6,409 |
| Oklahoma | 6,333 | 5,708 |
| Oregon | 6,888 | 6,265 |
| Pennsylvania | 7,146 | 6,443 |
| Rhode Island | 6,927 | 6,342 |
| South Carolina | 5,690 | 5,158 |
| South Dakota | 6,545 | 5,120 |
| Tennessee | 5,901 | 5,355 |
| Texas | 6,762 | 6,201 |
| Utah | 5,838 | 5,350 |
| Vermont | 5,908 | 5,414 |
| Virginia | 6,923 | 6,298 |
| Washington | 7,415 | 6,853 |
| West Virginia | 5,956 | 5,487 |
| Wisconsin | 6,786 | 6,131 |
| Wyoming | 7,434 | 6,634 |
| **United States** | **7,057** | **6,396** |

1. Preliminary. *Source:* Department of Commerce, Bureau of Economic Analysis.

## Gross National Product or Expenditure
(in billions)

| Item | 1978[1] | 1977 | 1976 | 1975 | 1974 | 1973 | 1972 | 1970 | 1965 | 1960 | 1955 | 1950 | 1946 | 1938 | 1933 | 1929 |
|---|---|---|---|---|---|---|---|---|---|---|---|---|---|---|---|---|
| Gross national product | $2,077 | $1,887 | $1,700 | $1,529 | $1,413 | $1,307 | $1,171 | $ 982 | $688 | $506 | $399 | $286 | $210 | $ 85 | $ 56 | $103 |
| GNP in constant (1972) dollars | 1,379 | 1,333 | 1,271 | 1,202 | 1,218 | 1,235 | 1,171 | 1,075 | 926 | 737 | 655 | 534 | 477 | 312 | 222 | 315 |
| Personal consumption expenditures | 1,324 | 1,207 | 1,090 | 980 | 890 | 810 | 733 | 619 | 430 | 325 | 254 | 192 | 144 | 64 | 46 | 77 |
| Durable goods | 197 | 178 | 157 | 133 | 122 | 124 | 111 | 85 | 63 | 43 | 39 | 31 | 16 | 6 | 3 | 9 |
| Nondurable goods | 519 | 479 | 443 | 409 | 376 | 334 | 299 | 265 | 189 | 151 | 123 | 98 | 83 | 34 | 22 | 38 |
| Services | 608 | 549 | 491 | 438 | 391 | 352 | 322 | 269 | 179 | 131 | 92 | 63 | 45 | 24 | 20 | 30 |
| Gross private domestic investment | 342 | 298 | 243 | 189 | 215 | 220 | 188 | 141 | 112 | 76 | 68 | 54 | 31 | 6 | 1 | 16 |
| Residential structures | 105 | 92 | 68 | 52 | 54 | 65 | 61 | 36 | 31 | 24 | 24 | 20 | 7 | 2 | 1 | 4 |
| Nonresidential structures | 74 | 64 | 57 | 53 | 54 | 49 | 43 | 38 | 26 | 18 | 14 | 9 | 7 | 2 | 1 | 5 |
| Producers' durable equipment | 143 | 127 | 107 | 96 | 97 | 88 | 75 | 64 | 46 | 30 | 24 | 18 | 10 | 3 | 1 | 6 |
| Change in business inventories | 21 | 16 | 10 | —11 | 9 | 18 | 9 | 4 | 10 | 4 | 6 | 7 | 6 | —1 | —2 | 2 |
| Net export of goods and services | —14 | —11 | 7 | 20 | 6 | 7 | —3 | 4 | 8 | 4 | 2 | 2 | 8 | 1 | (2) | 1 |
| Government purchases | 425 | 394 | 359 | 339 | 303 | 270 | 253 | 219 | 138 | 100 | 75 | 38 | 28 | 13 | 8 | 8 |
| Federal | 147 | 145 | 130 | 123 | 111 | 102 | 102 | 96 | 67 | 54 | 44 | 19 | 18 | 5 | 2 | 1 |
| National defense | 99 | 94 | 87 | 84 | 77 | 74 | 74 | 74 | 49 | 44 | 38 | 14 | 15 | n.a. | n.a. | n.a. |
| Other | 49 | 51 | 43 | 39 | 34 | 29 | 29 | 22 | 18 | 9 | 6 | 5 | 3 | n.a. | n.a. | n.a. |
| State and local | 277 | 249 | 230 | 216 | 192 | 167 | 151 | 123 | 71 | 47 | 31 | 20 | 10 | 8 | 6 | 7 |
| Implicit price deflator | 151 | 142 | 134 | 127 | 116 | 106 | 100 | 91 | 74 | 69 | 61 | 54 | 44 | 27 | 25 | 33 |

1. Second quarter annual rate (preliminary). 2. Less than $500 million. NOTE: n.a. = not available. *Source:* Department of Commerce, Bureau of Economic Analysis.

## Median Family Income

| Year | Median family income | Annual percent gain or loss | Year | Median family income | Annual percent gain or loss |
|---|---|---|---|---|---|
| 1970 | $14,465 | — | 1974 | $14,891 | 3.5 |
| 1971 | 14,457 | −0.1 | 1975 | 14,510 | −2.6 |
| 1972 | 15,126 | 4.7 | 1976 | 14,958 | 3.1 |
| 1973 | 15,437 | 2.1 | 1977 | 16,010 | 7.0 |

*Source:* Department of Commerce, Bureau of the Census.

## Per Capita Personal Income

| Year | Amount | Year | Amount | Year | Amount | Year | Amount | Year | Amount |
|---|---|---|---|---|---|---|---|---|---|
| 1929 | $705 | 1954 | $1,787 | 1960 | $2,219 | 1966 | $2,987 | 1972 | $4,493 |
| 1935 | 474 | 1955 | 1,881 | 1961 | 2,269 | 1967 | 3,167 | 1973 | 4,980 |
| 1940 | 593 | 1956 | 1,980 | 1962 | 2,373 | 1968 | 3,433 | 1974 | 5,428 |
| 1945 | 1,223 | 1957 | 2,050 | 1963 | 2,460 | 1969 | 3,667 | 1975 | 5,851 |
| 1950 | 1,501 | 1958 | 2,074 | 1964 | 2,592 | 1970 | 3,893 | 1976 | 6,396 |
| 1953 | 1,806 | 1959 | 2,166 | 1965 | 2,773 | 1971 | 4,132 | 1977[1] | 7,057 |

1. Preliminary. *Source:* Department of Commerce, Bureau of Economic Analysis.

## Consumer Price Indexes
(1967 = 100)

| Year | Commod-ities | Ser-vices | Hous-ing | All items | Percent change[1] | Year | Commod ities | Ser vices | Hous-ing | All items | Percent change[1] |
|---|---|---|---|---|---|---|---|---|---|---|---|
| 1940 | 40.6 | 43.6 | 52.4 | 42.0 | 1.0 | 1965 | 95.7 | 92.2 | 94.9 | 94.5 | 1.7 |
| 1945 | 56.3 | 48.2 | 59.1 | 53.9 | 2.3 | 1970 | 113.5 | 121.6 | 118.9 | 116.3 | 5.9 |
| 1950 | 78.8 | 58.7 | 72.8 | 72.1 | 1.0 | 1975 | 158.4 | 166.6 | 166.8 | 161.2 | 8.9 |
| 1955 | 85.1 | 70.9 | 82.3 | 80.2 | −0.4 | 1976 | 165.2 | 180.4 | 177.2 | 170.5 | 5.8 |
| 1960 | 91.5 | 83.5 | 90.2 | 88.7 | 1.6 | 1977 | 174.7 | 194.3 | 189.6 | 181.5 | 6.5 |

1. Over previous year. *Source:* Department of Labor, Bureau of Labor Statistics.

## Consumer Price Index for All Urban Consumers
(1967=100)

| Group | July 1978 | Percent change Jan.-July | Group | July 1978 | Percent change Jan.-July |
|---|---|---|---|---|---|
| All items | 196.7 | 9.8 | Fuel oil, coal, bottled gas | 297.5 | 4.7 |
| Food | 213.9 | 15.3 | House operation[1] | 178.3 | 7.7 |
| Alcoholic beverages | 160.1 | 7.5 | House furnishings | 154.4 | 5.5 |
| Apparel and upkeep | 159.3 | 2.7 | Transportation | 185.6 | 6.0 |
| Men's and boys' apparel | 158.0 | 1.7 | Medical care | 219.1 | 7.5 |
| Women's and girls' apparel | 148.2 | 0.1 | Personal care | 182.4 | 6.0 |
| Footwear | 163.2 | 4.3 | Tobacco products | 180.1 | 8.6 |
| Housing, total | 204.1 | 11.3 | Entertainment | 176.6 | 5.3 |
| Rent | 164.4 | 7.2 | Personal and educational expenses | 196.7 | 5.1 |
| Gas and electricity | 237.7 | 18.0 | | | |

1. Combines house furnishings and operation. *Source:* Department of Labor, Bureau of Labor Statistics.

# Consumer Price Index for Urban Wage Earners and Clerical Workers

**(1967 = 100)**

Effective January 1978, the Consumer Price Index was revised, with two indexes now being produced: A new index for All Urban Consumers covers 80% of the non-institutional population; the other index, the Consumer Price Index for Urban Wage Earners and Clerical Workers, covers about half of those included in the new index and is a major revision of the one that had been published for many years.

| | 1978[1] | 1977 | 1975 | 1970 | 1965 | 1960 | 1955 | 1950 | 1945 |
|---|---|---|---|---|---|---|---|---|---|
| All items | — | 181.5 | 161.2 | 116.3 | 94.5 | 88.7 | 80.2 | 72.1 | 53.9 |
| Food total | 213.8 | 192.2 | 175.4 | 114.9 | 94.4 | 88.0 | 81.6 | — | — |
| Apparel and upkeep | 159.5 | 154.2 | 142.3 | 116.1 | 93.7 | 89.6 | 84.1 | 79.0 | 61.5 |
| Housing total | 203.8 | 189.6 | 166.8 | 118.9 | 94.9 | 90.2 | 82.3 | 72.8 | 59.1 |
| Rent | 164.4 | 153.5 | 137.3 | 110.1 | 96.9 | 91.7 | 84.3 | 70.4 | 58.8 |
| Gas and electricity | 237.6 | 213.4 | 169.6 | 107.3 | 99.4 | 98.6 | 87.5 | 81.2 | 79.6 |
| Fuel oil and coal | 297.7 | 283.4 | 235.3 | 110.1 | 94.6 | 89.2 | 82.3 | 72.7 | 48.0 |
| House operation[2] | 177.6 | 177.0 | 158.1 | 113.4 | 95.3 | 93.8 | 89.9 | — | — |
| House furnishings | 154.1 | 156.5 | 144.4 | 111.4 | 97.1 | 99.3 | 99.2 | 95.5 | 73.3 |
| Transportation | 185.9 | 177.2 | 150.6 | 112.7 | 95.9 | 89.6 | 77.4 | 68.2 | 47.8 |
| Medical care | 219.2 | 202.4 | 168.6 | 120.6 | 89.5 | 79.1 | 64.8 | 53.7 | 42.1 |
| Personal care | 182.7 | 170.9 | 150.7 | 113.2 | 95.2 | 90.1 | 77.9 | 68.3 | 55.1 |
| Reading, recreation | 175.8[3] | 157.9 | 144.4 | 113.4 | 95.9 | 87.3 | 76.7 | 74.4 | 62.4 |

1. July. 2. Combines house furnishings and operation. 3. Includes all entertainment. *Source:* Department of Labor, Bureau of Labor Statistics.

# Total Family Income

**(figures in percent)**

| | White | | | | Black and other races | | | |
|---|---|---|---|---|---|---|---|---|
| **Family income** | **1977** | **1975** | **1970** | **1965** | **1977** | **1975** | **1970** | **1965** |
| Families (thousands)[1] | 50,530 | 49,873 | 46,535 | 43,497 | 6,685 | 6,372 | 5,413 | 4,782 |
| Under $3,000 | 2.8 | 3.1 | 3.6 | 5.1 | 9.6 | 9.5 | 10.5 | 14.6 |
| $3,000 to $4,999 | 4.8 | 5.2 | 4.9 | 6.2 | 13.2 | 12.8 | 11.8 | 15.3 |
| $5,000 to $6,999 | 6.6 | 6.7 | 6.2 | 7.1 | 12.4 | 11.4 | 11.0 | 15.3 |
| $7,000 to $9,999 | 10.5 | 11.1 | 10.4 | 12.1 | 14.2 | 14.2 | 16.1 | 18.0 |
| $10,000 to $11,999 | 7.1 | 7.6 | 7.8 | 9.9 | 7.9 | 8.8 | 9.1 | 9.1 |
| $12,000 to $14,999 | 11.5 | 12.2 | 13.2 | 15.5 | 10.0 | 11.0 | 11.3 | 10.3 |
| $15,000 to $24,999 | 33.0 | 33.4 | 34.7 | 31.3 | 22.0 | 22.9 | 21.7 | 14.3 |
| $25,000 and over | 23.9 | 20.7 | 19.3 | 12.8 | 10.8 | 9.4 | 8.4 | 3.0 |
| Median Income (1977 dollars) | $16,740 | $16,065 | $15,974 | $13,927 | $10,142 | $10,495 | $10,169 | $7,670 |

1. As of March 1978. *Source:* Department of Commerce, Bureau of the Census.

# Producer Price Indexes by Major Commodity Groups

| Commodity | 1978[1] | 1977 | 1975 | 1970 | 1965 | 1960 | 1955 |
|---|---|---|---|---|---|---|---|
| All commodities | 209.4 | 194.2 | 174.9 | 110.4 | 96.6 | 94.9 | 87.8 |
| Farm products | 219.5 | 192.5 | 186.7 | 111.0 | 98.7 | 97.2 | 98.2 |
| Processed foods | 204.6 | 186.1 | 182.6 | 112.1 | 95.5 | 89.5 | 85.0 |
| Textile products and apparel | 158.9 | 154.0 | 137.9 | 107.1 | 99.8 | 99.5 | 98.7 |
| Hides, skins, and leather products | 195.5 | 179.5 | 148.5 | 110.3 | 94.3 | 90.8 | 77.3 |
| Fuels and related products and power | 322.8 | 302.2 | 245.1 | 106.2 | 95.5 | 96.1 | 91.2 |
| Chemicals and allied products | 199.1 | 192.7 | 181.3 | 102.2 | 99.0 | 101.8 | 98.5 |
| Rubber and plastic products | 174.4 | 167.5 | 150.2 | 108.3 | 95.9 | 103.1 | 102.4 |
| Lumber and wood products | 278.5 | 236.2 | 176.9 | 113.6 | 95.9 | 95.3 | 97.1 |
| Pulp, paper, and allied products | 193.3 | 186.4 | 170.4 | 108.2 | 96.2 | 98.1 | 87.8 |
| Metals and metal products | 225.2 | 209.0 | 185.6 | 116.6 | 96.4 | 92.4 | 82.1 |
| Machinery and equipment | 195.1 | 181.7 | 161.4 | 111.4 | 93.9 | 92.0 | 75.7 |
| Furniture and household durables | 159.2 | 151.4 | 139.7 | 107.5 | 96.9 | 99.0 | 93.3 |
| Nonmetallic mineral products | 221.7 | 200.4 | 174.0 | 112.9 | 97.5 | 97.2 | 87.5 |
| Transportation equipment (Dec. 1968 = 100) | 172.5 | 161.3 | 141.5 | 104.6 | 98.5 | 98.8 | — |
| Miscellaneous products | 183.6 | 164.4 | 147.7 | 109.9 | 95.9 | 93.0 | 86.5 |

1. June. NOTE: Previous to January 1978, above table was known as Wholesale Price Indexes. *Source:* Department of Labor, Bureau of Labor Statistics.

## Federal Reserve Board Indexes of Production

(1967 = 100)

| Industry | 1978[1] | 1977 | 1975 | 1970 |
|---|---|---|---|---|
| Total industrial production | 145.3 | 137.1 | 117.8 | 106.7 |
| Total manufactures | 145.6 | 137.1 | 116.3 | 105.2 |
| Durable manufactures | 139.6 | 129.5 | 109.3 | 101.5 |
| Primary metals | 118.4 | 110.2 | 96.4 | 106.9 |
| Fabricated metal products | 142.5 | 130.9 | 109.9 | 109.4 |
| Machinery | 156.0 | 144.8 | 125.1 | 100.3 |
| Transportation equipment | 131.4 | 121.1 | 97.4 | 90.4 |
| Instruments and products | 171.5 | 159.1 | 132.3 | 110.8 |
| Clay, glass, stone products | 158.5[2] | 146.1 | 117.9 | 106.4 |
| Lumber and products | 136.7[2] | 133.4 | 107.6 | 106.3 |
| Furniture and fixtures | 154.2[2] | 140.9 | 118.2 | 99.4 |
| Nondurable manufactures | 154.3 | 148.1 | 126.4 | 110.6 |
| Textile mill products | 139.1[2] | 137.1 | 122.3 | 106.3 |
| Apparel products | 125.9[3] | 124.2 | 107.6 | 97.8 |
| Leather products | 74.4[2] | 75.3 | 76.5 | 90.8 |
| Rubber and plastics products | 253.4[2] | 232.2 | 166.7 | 115.7 |
| Paper and products | 144.4 | 137.4 | 116.3 | 113.3 |
| Printing and publishing | 128.6 | 124.7 | 113.4 | 104.1 |
| Chemicals and products | 190.2[2] | 180.7 | 147.3 | 120.3 |
| Petroleum products | 142.4 | 141.0 | 124.1 | 112.6 |
| Foods | 141.9[2] | 137.9 | 123.4 | 111.7 |
| Tobacco products | 120.2[3] | 114.3 | 111.8 | 100.0 |
| Mining | 129.3 | 117.8 | 112.8 | 109.7 |
| Coal | 137.4 | 118.0 | 113.4 | 105.7 |
| Oil and gas extraction | 128.7 | 118.0 | 113.3 | 109.7 |
| Metal mining | 121.1[2] | 105.4 | 115.8 | 131.3 |
| Stone and earth minerals | 130.0[2] | 124.9 | 107.0 | 98.8 |
| Utilities | 157.9 | 156.5 | 146.0 | 128.3 |

1. July estimate except where otherwise indicated. 2. June preliminary. 3. May. *Source: Federal Reserve Bulletin,* August 1978.

## What Americans Pay in Personal Taxes[1] and What They Save

(in billions of current dollars)

| Item | 1978[e] | 1975 | 1970 | 1965 | 1960 | 1955 | 1950 |
|---|---|---|---|---|---|---|---|
| Gross personal income | $1,682.5 | $1,249.7 | $808.3 | $538.9 | $401.0 | $310.9 | $227.6 |
| Social insurance contributions | 09.1 | 50.0 | 28.0 | 13.4 | 9.3 | 5.2 | 2.9 |
| Tax and non-tax payments to governments | 248.8 | 168.8 | 116.6 | 65.7 | 50.9 | 35.5 | 20.7 |
| Income available for spending and saving[3] | 1,433.7 | 1,080.9 | 691.7 | 473.2 | 350.0 | 275.3 | 206.9 |
| Income available per capita (dollars) | 6,572 | 5,062 | 3,376 | 2,436 | 1,937 | 1,666 | 1,364 |
| Personal saving | 75.8 | 84.0 | 56.2 | 28.4 | 17.0 | 15.8 | 13.1 |
| Rate of personal saving | 5.3 | 7.8% | 8.1% | 6.4% | 4.9% | 5.4% | 6.3% |

1. Personal income basis: direct taxes and payments only; corporate taxes and payments, paid by shareholders or customers, and hidden and consumption taxes not included. 2. Second-quarter annual rate (preliminary). 3. Disposable personal income. *Source:* Department of Commerce, Bureau of Economic Analysis.

## Business Population

(in thousands of concerns)

| Item | 1976[1] | 1975[1] | 1974[1] | 1970 | 1965[1] | 1953 | 1949 | 1941 | 1933 | 1929 |
|---|---|---|---|---|---|---|---|---|---|---|
| Total operating businesses[2] | 14,553 | 13,977 | 13,914 | 12,001 | 11,417 | 4,188 | 3,984 | 3,276 | 2,782 | 3,029 |
| Manufacturing | 467 | 469 | 458 | 410 | 408 | 331 | 322 | 230 | 167 | 257 |
| Wholesale trade | 590 | 588 | 581 | 470 | 444 | 283 | 260 | 190 | 142 | 148 |
| Retail trade | 2,439 | 2,322 | 2,357 | 2,210 | 2,044 | 1,846 | 1,783 | 1,561 | 1,291 | 1,327 |
| Service industries | 3,832 | 3,670 | 3,526 | 2,964 | 2,565 | 750 | 739 | 615 | 575 | 591 |
| Contract construction | 1,220 | 1,143 | 1,146 | 875 | 876 | 405 | 339 | 194 | 185 | 234 |
| All other[3] | 6,005 | 5,785 | 5,846 | 5,072 | 5,080 | 573 | 541 | 486 | 422 | 472 |
| New incorporations | 376 | 326 | 319 | 264 | 204 | 352 | 331 | 290 | n.a. | n.a. |
| Commercial and industrial failures[4] | 9.6 | 11.4 | 9.9 | 10.7 | 13.5 | 8.9 | 9.2 | 11.8 | 19.9 | 22.9 |

1. Data for total operating businesses are now based on tax returns; not comparable with earlier figures. 2. 1929–33, annual average; 1941–53, as of January 1. 3. Includes agriculture, forestry, and fishing; mining; transportation, communication, electric, gas, and sanitary services; financial, insurance, and real estate; wholesale and retail trade not allocable; and nature of business not allocable. 4. Closures resulting in a known loss to creditors. NOTE: New incorporations for 1977 were 436,000; failures, 7,900. n.a. = not available. *Sources:* Departments of Commerce and the Treasury; Dun & Bradstreet.

## Value of New Construction Put in Place

(in millions of dollars)

| Activity | 1977 | 1975 | 1970 | 1960 | 1950 | 1940 | 1933 | 1929 |
|---|---|---|---|---|---|---|---|---|
| Total new construction activity | $172,552 | $134,535 | $94,855 | $54,738 | $33,575 | $8,682 | $2,879 | $10,793 |
| New private construction activity | 134,724 | 93,651 | 66,759 | 38,875 | 26,709 | 5,504 | 1,231 | 8,307 |
| Residential | 80,956 | 46,472 | 31,864 | 22,975 | 18,126 | 2,985 | 470 | 3,625 |
| New dwelling units | 65,749 | 34,408 | 24,272 | 17,279 | 15,551 | 2,560 | 290 | 3,040 |
| Additions and alterations | 14,209 | 10,925 | 6,234 | 4,831 | 2,400 | 335 | 145 | 340 |
| Nonhousekeeping | 998 | 1,139 | 1,358 | 865 | 175 | 90 | 35 | 245 |
| Nonresidential building, except farm and public utility | 28,695 | 26,407 | 21,417 | 10,149 | 3,904 | 1,025 | 406 | 2,694 |
| Industrial | 7,712 | 8,018 | 6,538 | 2,851 | 1,062 | 442 | 176 | 949 |
| Commercial[1] | 14,783 | 12,806 | 9,754 | 4,180 | 1,415 | 348 | 130 | 1,135 |
| Other | 6,199 | 5,582 | 5,125 | 3,118 | 1,427 | 235 | 100 | 610 |
| Public utility | 21,072 | 17,379 | 11,020 | 4,621 | 3,045 | 771 | 261 | 1,578 |
| Railroads | 722 | 514 | 306 | n.a. | n.a. | 167 | 94 | 510 |
| Telephone and telegraph | 4,345 | 3,683 | 2,968 | 1,088 | 440 | 122 | 45 | 354 |
| Farm construction | 2,700 | 2,325 | 1,512 | 849 | 1,522 | 240 | 49 | 307 |
| New public construction activity | 37,827 | 40,884 | 28,096 | 15,863 | 6,866 | 3,628 | 1,648 | 2,486 |
| Residential | 959 | 754 | 1,107 | 716 | 345 | 200 | n.a. | n.a. |
| Nonresidential building | 11,792 | 14,719 | 9,550 | 4,395 | 2,387 | 615 | 230 | 659 |
| Industrial | 1,146 | 918 | 499 | 407 | 224 | 164 | 2 | n.a. |
| Educational | 5,433 | 7,760 | 5,619 | 2,818 | 1,133 | 156 | 52 | 389 |
| Hospital and institutional | 1,679 | 1,745 | 837 | 401 | 499 | 54 | 49 | 101 |
| Other | 3,534 | 4,296 | 2,595 | 1,169 | 531 | 241 | 127 | 169 |
| Military facilities | 1,517 | 1,389 | 718 | 1,366 | 177 | 385 | 36 | 19 |
| Highway | 9,372 | 10,854 | 9,981 | 5,437 | 2,134 | 1,302 | 847 | 1,266 |
| Sewer and water | 7,208 | 6,566 | 2,638 | 1,487 | 659 | 338 | 95 | 253 |
| Conservation and development | 3,879 | 3,257 | 1,908 | 1,175 | 942 | 528 | 359 | 115 |

1. Warehouses, office and loft buildings; stores, restaurants and garages. NOTE: n.a. = not available. *Source:* Department of Commerce, Bureau of the Census.

## Expenditures for New Plant and Equipment[1]

(in millions of dollars)

| Year | Manufacturing and mining | Transportation | All other[2] | Total[3] |
|---|---|---|---|---|
| 1945 | $4,366 | $1,122 | $3,204 | $8,692 |
| 1950 | 8,230 | 2,370 | 9,600 | 20,210 |
| 1955 | 13,200 | 2,580 | 13,770 | 29,530 |
| 1960 | 16,390 | 3,120 | 17,230 | 36,750 |
| 1965 | 24,900 | 4,890 | 24,620 | 54,420 |
| 1970 | 33,840 | 6,040 | 39,830 | 79,710 |
| 1972 | 33,770 | 5,720 | 48,960 | 88,440 |
| 1973 | 40,750 | 6,030 | 52,960 | 99,740 |
| 1974 | 49,190 | 6,660 | 56,560 | 112,400 |
| 1975 | 51,740 | 7,570 | 53,470 | 112,780 |
| 1976 | 56,480 | 7,450 | 56,570 | 120,490 |
| 1977 | 64,660 | 6,930 | 64,210 | 135,800 |
| 1978[4] | 72,330 | 7,280 | 71,070 | 150,680 |

1. Data exclude agriculture. 2. Includes electric and gas utilities, trade, service, communications, construction, and finance. 3. Details may not add up to totals because of rounding. 4. Estimates. *Source:* Department of Commerce, Bureau of Economic Analysis.

## New Housing Starts[1] and Mobile Homes Shipped

(in thousands)

| Year | No. of units started | Year | No. of units started | Year | Mobile homes shipped |
|---|---|---|---|---|---|
| 1900 | 189 | 1950 | 1,952 | 1965 | 216 |
| 1905 | 507 | 1955 | 1,646 | 1969 | 413 |
| 1910 | 387 | 1960[1] | 1,296 | 1970 | 401 |
| 1915 | 433 | 1965 | 1,510 | 1971 | 497 |
| 1920 | 247 | 1970 | 1,469 | 1972 | 576 |
| 1925 | 937 | 1973 | 2,057 | 1973 | 567 |
| 1930 | 330 | 1974 | 1,352 | 1974 | 329 |
| 1935 | 221 | 1975 | 1,171 | 1975 | 213 |
| 1940 | 603 | 1976 | 1,548 | 1976 | 246 |
| 1945 | 326 | 1977 | 1,990 | 1977 | 277 |

1. Prior to 1960, starts limited to nonfarm housing; from 1960 on, figures include farm housing. *Sources:* Department of Commerce, Housing Construction Statistics, 1900–1965, and Construction Reports, Housing Starts, 1970–77; Manufactured Housing Institute.

## Costs of Pollution Control

In 1976, industry and government spent $34.7 billion to control water and air pollution, according to a Commerce Department report in 1978. This was a 12% increase over the previous year. Expenditures to control pollution came to about 2% of the nation's output in 1976 and 1975, up from 1.6% in 1972.

## 50 Most Active Stocks in 1977

| Issue | Share volume | Issue | Share volume | Issue | Share volume |
|---|---|---|---|---|---|
| General Motors | 33,772,100 | U.S. Steel | 19,833,900 | Gulf & Western Industries | 15,248,800 |
| Sony | 32,445,800 | Atlantic Richfield | 19,067,200 | Bally Manufacturing | 15,236,200 |
| Dow Chemical | 29,580,500 | Sears, Roebuck | 18,977,200 | Standard Oil of Calif. | 15,205,100 |
| Texaco | 28,934,300 | Gulf Oil | 18,443,300 | Caterpillar Tractor | 15,104,000 |
| Occidental Petroleum | 28,219,500 | Ford Motor | 18,344,500 | Texas Utilities | 15,054,500 |
| American Tel. & Tel. | 27,502,700 | American Home Products | 18,277,800 | Federal Natl. Mortgage | 15,037,000 |
| Exxon | 27,358,400 | RCA | 17,787,800 | Gen. Tel. & Electronics | 15,033,100 |
| K Mart | 26,980,200 | Columbia Pictures | 17,194,200 | Polaroid | 14,877,200 |
| Eastman Kodak | 26,893,200 | Phillips Petroleum | 16,669,600 | Union Carbide | 14,847,200 |
| Citicorp | 25,861,500 | NCR Corporation | 16,602,700 | Sambo's Restaurants | 14,737,100 |
| Westinghouse Electric | 25,596,700 | Bethlehem Steel | 16,227,100 | Inexco Oil | 14,471,300 |
| British Petroleum | 25,169,600 | Southern Co. | 16,144,900 | Aetna Life & Casualty | 14,435,400 |
| International Tel. & Tel. | 23,053,500 | Twentieth Century-Fox Film | 16,069,400 | Schlumberger, N.V. | 14,055,500 |
| Digital Equipment | 22,991,400 | Coastal States Gas | 15,921,100 | Deere & Co. | 13,882,500 |
| Continental Oil | 21,769,100 | Chrysler | 15,913,500 | Norton Simon | 13,864,300 |
| General Electric | 21,039,200 | PepsiCo | 15,905,400 | Weyerhaeuser | 13,864,300 |
| Xerox | 20,873,800 | | | | |
| Int'l Business Machines | 19,999,100 | | | | |

*Source:* New York Stock Exchange.

## Shareholders in Public Corporations

| Characteristic | 1975 | 1970 | 1965 | 1962 | 1959 | 1956 | 1952 |
|---|---|---|---|---|---|---|---|
| Individual shareholders (thousands) | 25,270 | 30,850 | 20,120 | 17,010 | 12,490 | 8,630 | 6,490 |
| Owners of shares listed on New York Stock Exchange (thousands) | 17,950 | 18,290 | 12,430 | 11,020 | 8,510 | 6,880 | n.a. |
| Adult shareowner incidence in population | 1 in 6 | 1 in 4 | 1 in 6 | 1 in 6 | 1 in 8 | 1 in 12 | 1 in 16 |
| Median household income | $19,000 | $13,500 | $9,500 | $8,600 | $7,000 | $6,200 | $7,100 |
| Adult shareowners with household income: under $10,000 (thousands) | 3,420 | 8,170 | 10,080 | 10,340 | 9,340 | n.a. | n.a. |
| $10,000 and over (thousands) | 19,970 | 20,130 | 8,410 | 5,920 | 2,740 | n.a. | n.a. |
| Adult female shareowners (thousands) | 11,750 | 14,290 | 9,430 | 8,290 | 6,350 | 4,260 | 3,140 |
| Adult male shareowners (thousands) | 11,630 | 14,340 | 9,060 | 7,970 | 5,740 | 4,020 | 3,210 |
| Median age | 53 | 48 | 49 | 48 | 49 | 48 | 51 |

NOTE: n.a. = not available. *Source:* New York Stock Exchange.

## Interest Rates

| Instrument | 1978[1] | 1977 | 1976 | 1975 | 1974 | 1973 | 1972 | 1971 | 1970 | 1969 | 1967 |
|---|---|---|---|---|---|---|---|---|---|---|---|
| **MONEY MARKET RATES** | | | | | | | | | | | |
| Federal funds | 7.81 | 5.54 | 5.05 | 5.82 | 10.51 | 8.74 | 4.44 | 4.66 | 7.17 | 8.21 | 4.22 |
| Prime commercial paper | | | | | | | | | | | |
| 90 to 119 days | 7.85 | 5.54 | 5.24 | 6.26 | 10.05 | 8.20 | 4.66 | — | — | — | — |
| 4 to 6 months | 7.91 | 5.60 | 5.35 | 6.33 | 9.87 | 8.15 | 4.69 | 5.11 | 7.72 | 7.83 | 5.10 |
| Prime bankers acceptances, 90 days | 8.02 | 5.59 | 5.19 | 6.30 | 9.92 | 8.08 | 4.47 | 4.85 | 7.31 | 7.61 | 4.75 |
| Large negotiable certificates of deposit, 3 months, primary market | 8.00 | 5.52 | 5.15 | — | — | — | — | — | — | — | — |
| U.S. government securities: bills, 6-month yield | 7.44 | 5.53 | 5.26 | 6.11 | 7.95 | 7.20 | 4.49 | 4.52 | 6.51 | 6.86 | 4.61 |
| **CAPITAL MARKET RATES** | | | | | | | | | | | |
| U.S. Treasury | | | | | | | | | | | |
| Notes and bonds maturing in 3–5 years | 8.54 | 6.85 | 6.94 | 7.55 | 7.81 | 6.92 | 5.85 | 5.77 | 7.37 | 6.85 | 5.07 |

| Instrument | 1978[1] | 1977 | 1976 | 1975 | 1974 | 1973 | 1972 | 1971 | 1970 | 1969 | 1967 |
|---|---|---|---|---|---|---|---|---|---|---|---|
| 5 years | 8.54 | 6.99 | 7.18 | 7.77 | 7.80 | — | — | — | — | — | — |
| 10 years | 8.64 | 7.42 | 7.61 | 7.99 | 7.56 | — | — | — | — | — | — |
| State and local | | | | | | | | | | | |
| Moody's series: | | | | | | | | | | | |
| Aaa | 5.80 | 5.20 | 5.66 | 6.42 | 5.89 | — | — | — | — | — | — |
| Baa | 6.45 | 6.12 | 7.49 | 7.62 | 6.53 | — | — | — | — | — | — |
| Corporate bonds, | | | | | | | | | | | |
| seasoned issues: | | | | | | | | | | | |
| Aaa | 8.88 | 8.02 | 8.43 | 8.83 | 8.57 | — | — | — | — | — | — |
| Aa | 9.07 | 8.24 | 8.75 | 9.17 | 8.84 | — | — | — | — | — | — |
| A | 9.33 | 8.49 | 9.09 | 9.65 | 9.20 | — | — | — | — | — | — |
| Baa | 9.60 | 8.97 | 9.75 | 10.61 | 9.50 | — | — | — | — | — | — |

1. July. *Source* Federal Reserve Bulletin, August 1978.

## Largest Businesses, 1977

**(in thousands of dollars)**

*Source: Fortune* magazine.

### 50 LARGEST INDUSTRIAL CORPORATIONS

| | *Sales* | *Assets* |
|---|---|---|
| General Motors | $54,961,300 | $26,658,300 |
| Exxon | 54,126,219 | 38,453,336 |
| Ford Motor | 37,841,500 | 19,241,300 |
| Mobil | 32,125,828 | 20,575,967 |
| Texaco | 27,920,499 | 18,926,026 |
| Standard Oil of California | 20,917,331 | 14,822,347 |
| International Business Machines | 18,133,184 | 18,978,445 |
| Gulf Oil | 17,840,000 | 14,225,000 |
| General Electric | 17,518,600 | 13,696,800 |
| Chrysler | 16,708,300 | 7,668,200 |
| International Telephone & Telegraph | 13,145,664 | 12,285,522 |
| Standard Oil (Indiana) | 13,019,939 | 12,884,286 |
| Atlantic Richfield | 10,969,091 | 11,119,012 |
| Shell Oil | 10,112,062 | 8,876,754 |
| U.S. Steel | 9,609,900 | 9,914,400 |
| E. I. du Pont de Nemours | 9,434,800 | 7,430,600 |
| Continental Oil | 8,700,317 | 6,625,229 |
| Western Electric | 8,134,604 | 5,875,543 |
| Tenneco | 7,440,300 | 8,278,300 |
| Procter & Gamble | 7,284,255 | 4,487,186 |
| Union Carbide | 7,036,100 | 7,423,200 |
| Goodyear Tire & Rubber | 6,627,818 | 4,677,908 |
| Sun | 6,418,117 | 5,180,958 |
| Phillips Petroleum | 6,284,185 | 5,836,503 |
| Dow Chemical | 6,234,255 | 7,675,231 |
| Westinghouse Electric | 6,137,661 | 5,527,628 |
| Occidental Petroleum | 6,006,019 | 4,134,372 |
| International Harvester | 5,975,061 | 3,788,134 |
| Eastman Kodak | 5,966,986 | 5,904,228 |
| RCA | 5,880,900 | 4,351,700 |
| Rockwell International | 5,858,700 | 3,392,200 |
| Caterpillar Tractor | 5,848,900 | 4,345,600 |
| Union Oil of California | 5,668,520 | 4,724,516 |
| United Technologies | 5,550,670 | 2,979,303 |
| Bethlehem Steel | 5,370,000 | 4,898,900 |
| Beatrice Foods | 5,288,578 | 2,128,875 |
| Esmark | 5,280,160 | 1,799,854 |
| Kraft | 5,238,807 | 2,085,361 |
| Xerox | 5,076,900 | 4,906,296 |
| General Foods | 4,909,737 | 2,345,017 |
| R. J. Reynolds Industries | 4,816,022 | 4,333,961 |
| Ashland Oil | 4,785,578 | 2,610,391 |
| LTV | 4,703,296 | 2,065,987 |
| Monsanto | 4,594,500 | 4,350,100 |
| Amerada Hess | $4,591,253 | $2,997,954 |
| Firestone Tire & Rubber | 4,426,900 | 3,395,700 |
| Cities Service | 4,388,200 | 3,739,600 |
| Marathon Oil | 4,252,028 | 3,445,626 |
| Boeing | 4,018,800 | 2,440,400 |
| Minnesota Mining & Manufacturing | 3,980,326 | 3,529,597 |

### 50 LARGEST RETAILING COMPANIES

| | *Sales* | *Assests* |
|---|---|---|
| Sears, Roebuck | $17,224,033 | $14,746,247 |
| Safeway Stores | 11,249,398 | 2,561,784 |
| K Mart | 10,064,457 | 3,428,110 |
| J. C. Penney | 9,369,000 | 4,106,000 |
| Great Atlantic & Pacific Tea | 7,235,854 | 1,044,897 |
| Kroger | 6,747,553 | 1,413,932 |
| F. W. Woolworth | 5,534,500 | 2,214,200 |
| Federated Department Stores | 4,923,399 | 2,520,168 |
| Montgomery Ward | 4,548,029 | 2,870,054 |
| Winn-Dixie Stores | 3,996,699 | 580,884 |
| Lucky Stores | 3,914,072 | 753,223 |
| American Stores | 3,464,655 | 590,216 |
| Jewel Companies | 3,277,742 | 880,618 |
| City Products | 2,846,930 | 885,119 |
| Southland | 2,536,109 | 795,996 |
| Food Fair | 2,436,702 | 459,725 |
| May Department Stores | 2,370,281 | 1,650,533 |
| Dayton Hudson | 2,169,276 | 1,218,513 |
| Rapid-American | 2,045,864 | 1,485,296 |
| Allied Stores | 1,927,011 | 1,295,158 |
| Supermarkets General | 1,829,098 | 371,859 |
| Albertson's | 1,816,495 | 408,310 |
| R. H. Macy | 1,660,684 | 938,994 |
| Gamble-Skogmo | 1,634,122 | 810,932 |
| Grand Union | 1,622,633 | 358,368 |
| Stop and Shop Companies | 1,611,569 | 344,555 |
| ARA Services | 1,539,933 | 669,759 |
| Fisher Foods | 1,536,523 | 344,794 |
| Carter Hawley Hale Stores | 1,505,196 | 911,706 |
| Wickes | 1,487,857 | 581,949 |
| Melville | 1,473,587 | 553,696 |
| Associated Dry Goods | 1,467,755 | 814,191 |
| McDonald's | 1,384,207 | 1,645,155 |
| Zayre | 1,298,974 | 380,981 |
| Dillon Companies | 1,296,035 | 230,790 |
| Walgreen | 1,223,249 | 331,363 |
| Colonial Stores | 1,053,167 | 189,118 |

| | *Sales* | *Assets* |
|---|---|---|
| Marriott | $1,026,313 | $ 871,914 |
| Gimbel Bros. | 1,008,092 | 697,703 |
| First National Stores | 992,635 | 118,727 |
| Vornado | 988,455 | 317,696 |
| Jack Eckerd | 980,102 | 364,457 |
| Tandy | 949,267 | 474,675 |
| Allied Supermarkets | 904,305 | 139,318 |
| Skaggs Companies | 899,772 | 205,240 |
| Giant Food | 895,335 | 184,627 |
| Arlen Realty & Development | 848,989 | 1,563,297 |
| National Tea | 835,604 | 141,342 |
| Waldbaum | 826,337 | 116,164 |
| Fred Meyer | 822,478 | 270,412 |

**10 LARGEST COMMERCIAL BANKS**

| | *Assets* | *Deposits* |
|---|---|---|
| BankAmerica | $81,988,575 | $66,405,379 |
| Citicorp | 77,112,434 | 55,651,250 |
| Chase Manhattan | 53,180,295 | 43,508,258 |
| Manufacturers Hanover | 35,787,568 | 29,782,691 |
| J. P. Morgan & Co. | 31,663,815 | 23,831,026 |
| Chemical New York | 30,705,933 | 23,296,823 |
| Continental Illinois | 25,800,280 | 18,753,785 |
| Bankers Trust New York | 23,473,678 | 17,359,803 |
| First Chicago | 22,613,959 | 17,054,104 |
| Western Bancorp | 22,488,026 | 18,656,404 |

**10 LARGEST LIFE INSURANCE COMPANIES**

| | *Assets* | *Premium and annuity income* |
|---|---|---|
| Prudential | $46,423,607 | $6,742,457 |
| Metropolitan | 39,575,922 | 5,521,311 |
| Equitable Life Assurance | 24,798,678 | 3,850,290 |
| New York Life | 15,848,213 | 2,194,734 |
| John Hancock Mutual | 15,038,203 | 2,369,660 |
| Aetna Life | 13,020,007 | 3,272,035 |
| Connecticut General Life | 9,828,845 | 2,147,181 |
| Travelers | 9,384,343 | 2,842,468 |
| Northwestern Mutual | 9,062,139 | 986,260 |
| Massachusetts Mutual | 6,949,694 | 1,119,640 |

**10 LARGEST TRANSPORTATION COMPANIES**

| | *Operating revenues* | *Assets* |
|---|---|---|
| Trans World Airlines | $3,393,473 | $1,834,411 |
| UAL | 3,267,282 | 3,000,600 |
| Union Pacific | 2,528,416 | 4,116,425 |
| United Parcel Service | 2,354,265 | 849,803 |
| American Airlines | 2,277,989 | 2,069,141 |
| Burlington Northern | 2,109,442 | 3,642,992 |
| Southern Pacific | 2,098,331 | 4,028,483 |
| Eastern Air Lines | 2,035,893 | 1,243,496 |
| Pan American World Airways | 1,907,453 | 1,896,636 |
| Santa Fe Industries | 1,850,383 | 3,293,127 |

**10 LARGEST UTILITIES**

| | *Assets* | *Operating revenues* |
|---|---|---|
| American Telephone & Telegraph | $93,972,292 | $36,494,806 |
| General Telephone & Electronics | 14,686,713 | 7,680,107 |
| Southern Company | 9,043,904 | 2,660,767 |
| Pacific Gas & Electric | 7,998,013 | 3,505,541 |
| American Electric Power | 7,449,675 | 2,031,247 |
| Commonwealth Edison | 6,829,692 | 2,095,017 |
| Consolidated Edison | 6,758,553 | 3,022,900 |
| Southern California Edison | 5,646,465 | 2,064,914 |
| Public Service Electric & Gas | 5,125,497 | 2,032,795 |
| Virginia Electric & Power | 4,802,009 | 1,358,860 |

**10 LARGEST DIVERSIFIED FINANCIAL COMPANIES**

| | *Assets* | *Revenues* |
|---|---|---|
| Aetna Life & Casualty | $20,806,334 | $8,128,714 |
| Travelers Corp. | 15,090,000 | 6,617,500 |
| American Express | 12,346,178 | 3,446,229 |
| H. F. Ahmanson | 9,487,946 | 864,688 |
| INA | 9,231,669 | 3,740,693 |
| Merrill Lynch & Co. | 8,094,599 | 1,124,216 |
| First Charter Financial | 7,668,770 | 605,532 |
| Great Western Financial | 7,625,166 | 593,393 |
| Loews | 6,083,411 | 3,272,814 |
| Continental | 6,410,950 | 2,772,928 |

## 25 Companies With Largest Number of Stockholders

| Company | Stockholders |
|---|---|
| American Telephone & Telegraph | 2,897,000 |
| General Motors | 1,225,000 |
| Exxon Corporation | 684,000 |
| International Business Machines | 582,000 |
| General Electric | 545,000 |
| General Telephone & Electronics | 443,000 |
| Texaco Inc. | 414,000 |
| Gulf Oil | 357,000 |
| Ford Motor | 335,000 |
| Southern Company | 293,000 |
| Sears, Roebuck | 291,000 |
| International Telephone & Telegraph | 280,000 |
| Consolidated Edison | 275,000 |
| RCA | 273,000 |
| Standard Oil of California | 271,000 |
| Mobil Corporation | 265,000 |
| Occidental Petroleum | 264,000 |
| U.S. Steel | 249,000 |
| Eastman Kodak | 248,000 |
| American Electric Power | 245,000 |
| Philadelphia Electric | 235,000 |
| Tenneco Inc. | 232,000 |
| Commonwealth Edison | 214,000 |
| Public Service Electric & Gas | 214,000 |
| Chrysler Corporation | 211,000 |
| **Total** | **11,542,000** |

NOTE: As of early 1978. *Source:* New York Stock Exchange.

## Shirts That Suit

According to April-Marcus, Inc., merchandising consultant, the average man has 15 dress shirts: 5 striped, 3 blue, 4 white, and 3 either gold, pink, or gray. Ten years ago, the average man had 10 shirts—all of them white.

## 50 Leading Stocks in Market Value

| Stock | Listed shares (millions) | Market value (millions) |
|---|---|---|
| International Business Machines | 148.4 | $40,513 |
| American Telephone & Telegraph | 647.5 | 39,172 |
| Exxon Corporation | 453.2 | 21,754 |
| General Motors | 287.7 | 18,053 |
| General Electric | 231.4 | 11,513 |
| Sears, Roebuck | 321.8 | 9,011 |
| Eastman Kodak | 161.6 | 8,280 |
| Texaco Inc. | 274.3 | 7,577 |
| Standard Oil (Indiana) | 150.0 | 7,446 |
| Procter & Gamble | 82.6 | 7,095 |
| Mobil Corporation | 105.9 | 6,726 |
| Standard Oil of California | 170.5 | 6,608 |
| Schlumberger, N.V. | 88.6 | 6,447 |
| E. I. du Pont de Nemours | 48.5 | 5,839 |
| Gulf Oil | 211.9 | 5,642 |
| Minnesota Mining & Mfg. | 116.2 | 5,620 |
| Atlantic Richfield | 104.8 | 5,357 |
| Dow Chemical | 198.5 | 5,311 |
| Shell Oil | 146.3 | 4,901 |
| Ford Motor | 103.8 | 4,747 |
| Caterpillar Tractor | 86.3 | 4,733 |
| Phillips Petroleum | 153.7 | 4,708 |
| American Home Products | 167.8 | 4,678 |
| Coca-Cola Company | 122.6 | 4,567 |
| Johnson & Johnson | 58.6 | 4,497 |
| Merck & Company | 75.8 | 4,208 |
| General Telephone & Electronics | 133.6 | $ 4,158 |
| Getty Oil | 22.1 | 3,840 |
| Halliburton Company | 58.7 | 3,838 |
| Morris (Philip) Inc. | 59.9 | 3,708 |
| Xerox Corporation | 79.2 | 3,703 |
| Weyerhaeuser Company | 128.6 | 3,553 |
| Continental Oil | 113.0 | 3,389 |
| International Telephone & Telegraph | 104.9 | 3,331 |
| K mart Corporation | 121.6 | 3,330 |
| BankAmerica Corporation | 146.3 | 3,329 |
| Burroughs Corporation | 40.4 | 2,948 |
| Citicorp | 127.8 | 2,923 |
| Tenneco Inc. | 94.9 | 2,919 |
| Georgia-Pacific Corporation | 102.7 | 2,914 |
| Pacific Telephone & Telegraph | 168.6 | 2,866 |
| Reynolds (R.J.) Industries | 48.2 | 2,858 |
| Avon Products | 58.1 | 2,796 |
| Union Carbide | 64.7 | 2,660 |
| U.S. Steel | 84.2 | 2,651 |
| Eli Lilly | 69.5 | 2,634 |
| American Express | 71.5 | 2,582 |
| American Electric Power | 103.0 | 2,510 |
| PepsiCo Inc. | 86.9 | 2,432 |
| Southern Company | 136.1 | 2,415 |
| **Total** | **6,942.8** | **329,290** |

NOTE: As of Dec. 31, 1977. The 50 leading stocks with the largest market value at the end of 1977 totaled $329 billion, or 43% of the value of all common shares listed for the 1,549 common stocks on the New York Stock Exchange. The largest five issues were valued at $131 billion, or 17% of the total. Five corporations joined the list in 1977—K mart Corporation, American Express, American Electric Power, PepsiCo Inc., and Southern Company. *Source:* New York Stock Exchange.

## Estimated Annual Retail and Wholesale Sales by Kind of Business

**(in millions of dollars)**

| Kind of business | 1977 | 1976 |
|---|---|---|
| Retail trade, total | $708,344 | $642,507 |
| Building materials, hardware, garden supply, and mobile home dealers | 37,958 | 32,226 |
| Automotive dealers | 143,682 | 125,685 |
| Furniture, home furnishings, and equipment stores | 34,499 | 31,368 |
| General merchandise group stores | 89,231 | 79,258 |
| Food stores | 156,313 | 145,939 |
| Gasoline service stations | 56,538 | 51,265 |
| Apparel and accessory stores | 33,527 | 33,188 |
| Eating and drinking places | 63,825 | 58,008 |
| Drug stores and proprietary stores | 22,380 | 20,716 |
| Liquor stores | 13,084 | 12,734 |
| Merchant wholesale trade, total | 642,104 | 580,894 |
| Total (excluding farm-product raw materials) | 572,052 | 508,201 |
| Durable goods, total | 285,605 | 246,732 |
| Motor vehicles and automotive parts and supplies | 54,046 | 44,889 |
| Furniture and home furnishings | 11,026 | 9,594 |
| Lumber and other construction materials | $ 26,181 | $ 20,920 |
| Electrical goods | 31,745 | 27,868 |
| Hardware, plumbing, heating, and supplies | 22,404 | 19,174 |
| Machinery, equipment, supplies | 82,003 | 71,378 |
| Scrap and waste materials | 9,632 | 9,134 |
| Nondurable goods, total | 356,498 | 334,162 |
| Total (excluding farm-product raw materials) | 286,448 | 261,469 |
| Paper and paper products | 15,482 | 13,444 |
| Drugs, drug proprietaries, and druggists' sundries | 10,868 | 10,144 |
| Apparel, piece goods, and notions | 19,595 | 17,567 |
| Groceries and related products | 110,766 | 99,791 |
| Beer, wine, distilled alcoholic beverages | 23,371 | 21,587 |
| Miscellaneous nondurable goods | 48,762 | 45,492 |
| Tobacco and tobacco products | 8,868 | 8,681 |

*Source:* Department of Commerce, Bureau of the Census.

## Dow Jones Industrial Stock Averages

| Year | High | Low | Close | Year | High | Low | Close | Year | High | Low | Close |
|---|---|---|---|---|---|---|---|---|---|---|---|
| 1915 | 99.21 | 54.22 | 99.15 | 1944 | 152.53 | 134.22 | 152.32 | 1973 | 1051.70 | 788.31 | 850.86 |
| 1916 | 110.15 | 84.96 | 95.00 | 1945 | 195.82 | 151.35 | 192.91 | 1974 | 891.66 | 577.60 | 616.24 |
| 1917 | 99.18 | 65.95 | 74.38 | 1946 | 212.50 | 163.12 | 177.20 | 1975 | 881.81 | 632.04 | 852.41 |
| 1918 | 89.07 | 73.38 | 82.20 | 1947 | 186.85 | 163.21 | 181.16 | 1976 | 1014.79 | 858.71 | 1004.65 |
| 1919 | 119.62 | 79.15 | 107.97 | 1948 | 193.16 | 165.39 | 177.30 | 1977 | 999.75 | 800.85 | 835.15 |
| 1920 | 109.88 | 66.75 | 71.95 | 1949 | 200.52 | 161.60 | 200.13 | Jan. | 999.75 | 954.37 | 954.37 |
| 1921 | 81.50 | 63.90 | 81.10 | 1950 | 235.47 | 196.81 | 235.41 | Feb. | 958.36 | 931.57 | 936.42 |
| 1922 | 103.43 | 78.59 | 98.73 | 1951 | 276.37 | 238.99 | 269.23 | March | 968.00 | 919.13 | 919.13 |
| 1923 | 105.38 | 85.76 | 95.52 | 1952 | 292.00 | 256.35 | 291.90 | April | 947.76 | 914.60 | 926.90 |
| 1924 | 120.51 | 88.33 | 120.51 | 1953 | 293.79 | 255.49 | 280.90 | May | 943.44 | 898.66 | 898.66 |
| 1925 | 159.39 | 115.00 | 156.66 | 1954 | 404.39 | 279.87 | 404.39 | June | 929.70 | 896.79 | 916.30 |
| 1926 | 166.64 | 135.20 | 157.20 | 1955 | 488.40 | 388.20 | 488.40 | July | 923.42 | 888.43 | 890.07 |
| 1927 | 202.40 | 152.73 | 202.40 | 1956 | 521.05 | 462.35 | 499.47 | Aug. | 891.81 | 854.12 | 861.49 |
| 1928 | 300.00 | 191.33 | 300.00 | 1957 | 520.77 | 419.79 | 435.69 | Sept. | 876.39 | 834.72 | 847.11 |
| 1929 | 381.17 | 198.69 | 248.48 | 1958 | 583.65 | 436.89 | 583.65 | Oct. | 851.96 | 801.54 | 818.35 |
| 1930 | 294.07 | 157.51 | 164.58 | 1959 | 679.36 | 574.46 | 679.36 | Nov. | 845.89 | 800.85 | 829.70 |
| 1931 | 194.36 | 73.79 | 77.90 | 1960 | 685.47 | 566.05 | 615.89 | Dec. | 835.15 | 806.91 | 835.15 |
| 1932 | 88.78 | 41.22 | 59.93 | 1961 | 734.91 | 610.25 | 731.14 | 1978 | — | — | — |
| 1933 | 108.67 | 50.16 | 99.90 | 1962 | 726.01 | 535.76 | 652.10 | Jan. | 817.74 | 763.34 | 769.92 |
| 1934 | 110.74 | 85.51 | 104.04 | 1963 | 767.21 | 646.79 | 762.95 | Feb. | 782.66 | 742.12 | 742.12 |
| 1935 | 148.44 | 96.71 | 144.13 | 1964 | 891.71 | 766.08 | 874.13 | March | 777.81 | 742.72 | 757.36 |
| 1936 | 184.90 | 143.11 | 179.90 | 1965 | 969.26 | 840.59 | 969.26 | April | 837.32 | 766.29 | 837.32 |
| 1937 | 194.40 | 113.64 | 120.85 | 1966 | 995.15 | 744.32 | 785.69 | May | 858.37 | 822.07 | 840.61 |
| 1938 | 158.41 | 98.95 | 154.76 | 1967 | 943.08 | 786.41 | 905.11 | June | 866.51 | 812.28 | 818.95 |
| 1939 | 155.92 | 121.44 | 150.24 | 1968 | 985.21 | 825.13 | 943.75 | July | 805.79 | 862.27 | 862.27 |
| 1940 | 152.80 | 111.84 | 131.13 | 1969 | 968.85 | 769.93 | 800.36 | Aug. | 900.12 | 876.82 | 876.82 |
| 1941 | 133.59 | 106.34 | 110.96 | 1970 | 842.00 | 631.16 | 838.92 | Sept. | 907.74 | 860.19 | 865.82 |
| 1942 | 119.71 | 92.92 | 119.40 | 1971 | 950.82 | 797.97 | 890.20 | | | | |
| 1943 | 145.82 | 119.26 | 135.89 | 1972 | 1036.27 | 889.15 | 1020.02 | | | | |

NOTE: The industrial average was composed of 12 stocks before the New York Stock Exchange closed in July 1914 because of World War I. In September 1916, the list was enlarged to 20 industrial stocks and computed back to the opening of the Exchange on Dec. 12, 1914. On Oct. 1, 1928, the number of stocks making up the industrial average was increased to 30, the present number, although individual stocks have been added and deleted.

## Employed Persons 16 Years and Over, by Race and Occupational Groups

| Race and occupational group | 1977 Number | 1977 Percent distribution | 1976 Number | 1976 Percent distribution | Percent change, 1976–77 |
|---|---|---|---|---|---|
| **WHITE** | | | | | |
| White-collar workers | 41,725,000 | 51.7 | 40,420,000 | 51.8 | 3.2 |
| Professional and technical workers | 12,536,000 | 15.5 | 12,224,000 | 15.7 | 2.6 |
| Managers and administrators, except farm | 9,194,000 | 11.4 | 8,896,000 | 11.4 | 3.3 |
| Sales workers | 5,472,000 | 6.8 | 5,265,000 | 6.7 | 3.9 |
| Clerical workers | 14,523,000 | 18.0 | 14,036,000 | 18.0 | 3.5 |
| Blue-collar workers | 26,524,000 | 32.9 | 25,396,000 | 32.6 | 4.4 |
| Craft and kindred workers | 11,001,000 | 13.6 | 10,452,000 | 13.4 | 5.3 |
| Operatives, except transport | 8,871,000 | 11.0 | 8,605,000 | 11.0 | 3.1 |
| Transport equipment operatives | 2,967,000 | 3.7 | 2,804,000 | 3.6 | 5.8 |
| Nonfarm laborers | 3,685,000 | 4.6 | 3,536,000 | 4.5 | 4.2 |
| Private household workers | 744,000 | 0.9 | 708,000 | 0.9 | 5.1 |
| Service workers, except private household | 9,197,000 | 11.4 | 8,896,000 | 11.4 | 3.4 |
| Farm Workers | 2,543,000 | 3.1 | 2,601,000 | 3.3 | —2.2 |
| **Total** | **80,734,000** | **100.0** | **78,021,000** | **100.0** | **3.5** |
| **BLACK AND OTHER** | | | | | |
| White-collar workers | 3,462,000 | 35.3 | 3,279,000 | 34.7 | 5.6 |
| Professional and technical workers | 1,156,000 | 11.8 | 1,105,000 | 11.7 | 4.6 |
| Managers and administrators, except farm | 468,000 | 4.8 | 420,000 | 4.4 | 11.4 |
| Sales workers | 256,000 | 2.6 | 232,000 | 2.5 | 10.3 |
| Clerical workers | 1,583,000 | 16.1 | 1,522,000 | 16.1 | 4.0 |

| Race and occupational group | 1977 Number | 1977 Percent distribution | 1976 Number | 1976 Percent distribution | Percent change, 1976–77 |
|---|---|---|---|---|---|
| Blue-collar workers | 3,687,000 | 37.6 | 3,562,000 | 37.6 | 3.5 |
| Craft and kindred workers | 880,000 | 9.0 | 826,000 | 8.7 | 6.5 |
| Operatives, except transport | 1,483,000 | 15.1 | 1,480,000 | 15.6 | 0.2 |
| Transport equipment operatives | 508,000 | 5.2 | 467,000 | 4.9 | 8.8 |
| Nonfarm laborers | 815,000 | 8.3 | 789,000 | 8.3 | 3.3 |
| Private household workers | 414,000 | 4.2 | 417,000 | 4.4 | —0.7 |
| Service workers, except private household | 2,037,000 | 20.8 | 1,984,000 | 21.0 | 2.7 |
| Farm workers | 212,000 | 2.2 | 221,000 | 2.3 | —4.1 |
| **Total** | **9,812,000** | **100.0** | **9,464,000** | **100.0** | 3.7 |

*Source:* Department of Labor, Bureau of Labor Statistics.

## Employment and Unemployment

(in millions of persons)

| Category[1] | 1978[2] | 1977 | 1976 | 1975 | 1970 | 1959 | 1950 | 1945 | 1941 | 1932 | 1929 |
|---|---|---|---|---|---|---|---|---|---|---|---|
| **EMPLOYMENT STATUS[1]** | | | | | | | | | | | |
| Total noninstitutional population | 161.1 | 158.6 | 156.0 | 153.4 | 140.2 | 117.9 | 106.6 | 105.5 | 101.5 | — | — |
| Total labor force | 102.7 | 99.5 | 96.9 | 94.8 | 85.9 | 70.9 | 63.9 | 65.3 | 57.5 | 51.3 | 49.4 |
| Percent of population | 63.8 | 62.8 | 62.1 | 61.8 | 61.3 | 60.2 | 59.9 | 61.9 | 56.7 | — | — |
| Civilian labor force | 100.6 | 97.4 | 94.8 | 92.6 | 82.7 | 68.4 | 62.2 | 53.9 | 55.9 | 51.0 | 49.2 |
| Employed | 94.4 | 90.5 | 87.5 | 84.8 | 78.6 | 64.6 | 58.9 | 52.8 | 50.4 | 38.9 | 47.6 |
| Agriculture | 3.4 | 3.2 | 3.3 | 3.4 | 3.5 | 5.6 | 7.2 | 8.6 | 9.1 | 10.2 | 10.5 |
| Nonagricultural industries | 91.0 | 87.3 | 84.2 | 81.4 | 75.2 | 59.1 | 51.8 | 44.2 | 41.3 | 28.8 | 37.2 |
| Unemployed | 6.2 | 6.9 | 7.3 | 7.8 | 4.1 | 3.7 | 3.3 | 1.0 | 5.6 | 12.1 | 1.6 |
| Percent of labor force | 6.2 | 7.0 | 7.7 | 8.5 | 4.9 | 5.5 | 5.3 | 1.9 | 9.9 | 23.6 | 3.2 |
| Not in labor force | 58.4 | 59.0 | 59.1 | 58.7 | 54.3 | 47.0 | 42.8 | 40.2 | 44.0 | — | — |
| **INDUSTRY** | | | | | | | | | | | |
| Total nonagricultural employment | 86.0 | 82.1 | 79.4 | 77.0 | 70.9 | 53.3 | 45.2 | 40.4 | 36.6 | 23.6 | 31.3 |
| Goods-producing industries | 25.6 | 24.2 | 23.3 | 22.6 | 23.5 | 20.4 | 18.5 | 17.5 | 15.9 | 8.6 | 13.3 |
| Mining | 0.9 | 0.8 | 0.8 | 0.7 | 0.6 | 0.7 | 0.9 | 0.8 | 1.0 | 0.7 | 1.1 |
| Contract construction | 4.4 | 3.8 | 3.6 | 3.5 | 3.5 | 3.0 | 2.3 | 1.1 | 1.8 | 1.0 | 1.5 |
| Manufacturing: Durable goods | 12.1 | 11.5 | 11.0 | 10.7 | 11.2 | 9.4 | 8.1 | 9.1 | 7.0 | — | — |
| Nondurable goods | 8.2 | 8.1 | 7.9 | 7.7 | 8.2 | 7.3 | 7.1 | 6.5 | 6.2 | — | — |
| Services-producing industries | 60.4 | 57.9 | 56.1 | 54.4 | 47.7 | 32.9 | 26.7 | 22.9 | 20.6 | 15.0 | 18.1 |
| Transportation and public utilities | 4.7 | 4.6 | 4.5 | 4.5 | 4.5 | 4.0 | 4.0 | 3.9 | 3.3 | 2.8 | 3.9 |
| Trade: Wholesale | 4.6 | 4.4 | 4.3 | 4.2 | 3.8 | 2.9 | 2.5 | 1.9 | 1.9 | — | — |
| Retail | 14.5 | 13.9 | 13.4 | 12.8 | 11.2 | 8.2 | 6.9 | 5.5 | 5.4 | — | — |
| Finance, insurance, real estate | 4.8 | 4.5 | 4.3 | 4.2 | 3.7 | 2.6 | 1.9 | 1.5 | 1.5 | 1.3 | 1.5 |
| Services | 16.1 | 15.3 | 14.6 | 14.0 | 11.6 | 7.1 | 5.4 | 4.2 | 3.9 | 2.9 | 3.4 |
| Federal government | 2.8 | 2.7 | 2.7 | 2.7 | 2.7 | 2.2 | 1.9 | 2.8 | 1.3 | 0.6 | 0.5 |
| State and local government | 12.9 | 12.5 | 12.2 | 12.0 | 9.8 | 5.9 | 4.1 | 3.1 | 3.3 | 2.7 | 2.5 |

1. For 1929–45, figures on labor force status relate to persons 14 years and over; beginning 1950, 16 years and over. 2. July, seasonally adjusted (preliminary). NOTE: Figures may not add to totals due to rounding. *Source:* Department of Labor, Bureau of Labor Statistics.

## National Labor Unions With Membership Over 100,000[1]

| Members | Union |
|---|---|
| 1,358,354 | Automobile, Aerospace and Agricultural Implement Workers of America, International Union, United (Ind.) |
| 135,154 | Bakery and Confectionery Workers' International Union of America |
| 144,500 | Boilermakers, Iron Ship Builders, Blacksmiths, Forgers and Helpers, International Brotherhood of |
| 134,744 | Bricklayers and Allied Craftsmen, International Union of |
| 178,632 | Bridge and Structural Iron Workers, International Association of |
| 112,300 | California State Employees' Association (Ind.) |
| 820,000 | Carpenters and Joiners of America, United Brotherhood of |
| 207,000 | Civil Service Employees Association, Inc. (New York State Ind.) |
| 109,143 | Classified School Employees, American Association of (Ind.) |
| 502,000 | Clothing and Textile Workers Union of North America, Amalgamated |

| Members | Union |
|---|---|
| 483,238 | Communications Workers of America |
| 1,881,532 | Education Association, National (Ind.) |
| 237,693 | Electrical, Radio and Machine Workers, International Union of |
| 165,000 | Electrical, Radio and Machine Workers of America, United (Ind.) |
| 923,560 | Electrical Workers, International Brotherhood of |
| n.a. | Federal Employees, National Federation of (Ind.) |
| 174,350 | Fire Fighters, International Association of |
| 260,000 | Government Employees, American Federation of |
| 150,000 | Government Employees, National Association of (Ind.) |
| 432,171 | Hotel and Restaurant Employees and Bartenders International Union |
| 627,406 | Laborers' International Union of North America |
| 365,346 | Ladies' Garment Workers' Union, International |
| 227,221 | Letter Carriers of the United States of America, National Association of |
| 917,266 | Machinists and Aerospace Workers, International Association of |
| 119,184 | Maintenance of Way Employees, Brotherhood of |
| 509,903 | Meat Cutters and Butcher Workmen of North America, Amalgamated |
| 277,000 | Mine Workers of America, United (Ind.) |
| 330,000 | Musicians, American Federation of |
| 199,691 | Nurses' Association, American (Ind.) |
| 177,370 | Oil, Chemical and Atomic Workers International Union |
| 420,000 | Operating Engineers, International Union of |
| 195,000 | Painters and Allied Trades of the United States and Canada, International Brotherhood of |
| 300,000 | Paperworkers International Union, United |
| 228,000 | Plumbing and Pipe Fitting Industry of the United States and Canada, United Association of Journeymen and Apprentices of the |
| 135,000 | Police, Fraternal Order of (Ind.) |
| 251,551 | Postal Workers' Union, American |
| 109,000 | Printing and Graphic Communications Union, International |
| 211,293 | Railway, Airline and Steamship Clerks, Freight Handlers, Express and Station Employees, Brotherhood of |
| 699,200 | Retail Clerks International Association |
| 200,000 | Retail, Wholesale and Department Store Union |
| 211,161 | Rubber, Cork, Linoleum and Plastic Workers of America, United |
| 575,000 | Service Employees' International Union |
| 153,000 | Sheet Metal Workers' International Association |
| 750,000 | State, County and Municipal Employees of America, American Federation of |
| 1,300,000 | Steelworkers of America, United |
| 446,045 | Teachers, American Federation of |
| 1,888,895 | Teamsters, Chauffeurs, Warehousemen and Helpers of America, International Brotherhood of (Ind.) |
| 150,000 | Transit Union, Amalgamated |
| 150,000 | Transport Workers Union of America |
| 285,000 | Transportation Union, United |
| 100,449 | Typographical Union, International |
| 108,717 | Woodworkers of America, International |

1. 1976. NOTE: Unless indicated by Ind. (Independent), all unions are affiliated with the AFL-CIO. n.a.=not available. *Source:* Department of Labor, Bureau of Labor Statistics

## Persons in the Labor Force

| Year | Working population: Number (thousands) | Working population: %total population aged 10 and over[1] | Percent of working population in: Farm occupation | Percent of working population in: Nonfarm occupation | Year | Working population: Number (thousands) | Working population: %total population aged 10 and over[1] | Percent of working population in: Farm occupation | Percent of working population in: Nonfarm occupation |
|---|---|---|---|---|---|---|---|---|---|
| 1820 | 2,881 | 44.4 | 71.8 | 28.2 | 1900 | 29,073 | 50.2 | 37.5 | 62.5 |
| 1830 | 3,932 | 45.5 | 70.5 | 29.5 | 1910 | 37,371 | 52.2 | 31.0 | 69.0 |
| 1840 | 5,420 | 46.6 | 68.6 | 31.4 | 1920 | 42,434 | 51.3 | 27.0 | 73.0 |
| 1850 | 7,697 | 46.8 | 63.7 | 36.3 | 1930 | 48,830 | 49.5 | 21.4 | 78.6 |
| 1860 | 10,533 | 47.0 | 58.9 | 41.1 | 1940 | 52,966 | 52.4 | 17.0 | 83.0 |
| 1870 | 12,925 | 44.4 | 53.0 | 47.0 | 1950 | 59,671 | 53.4 | 11.5 | 88.5 |
| 1880 | 17,392 | 47.3 | 49.4 | 50.6 | 1960 | 69,877 | 55.3 | 5.9 | 94.1 |
| 1890 | 23,318 | 49.2 | 42.6 | 57.4 | 1970 | 82,897 | 55.5 | 2.9 | 97.1 |

1. For 1820 to 1930, the data relate to the population and gainful workers at ages 10 and over. For 1940 to 1970, the data relate to the population and labor force at ages 14 and over; the farm and nonfarm percentages relate only to the experienced labor force. *Source:* Department of Commerce, Bureau of the Census.

## Where the Jobs Will Be Through the Mid-'80s
**(anticipated annual job openings for selected occupations)**

| Occupation | Estimated employment 1976 | Projected requirements 1985 | Percent change, 1976–85 | Annual average openings, 1976–85[1] |
|---|---|---|---|---|
| Accountants | 865,000 | 1,050,000 | 21.3 | 51,500 |
| Airplane mechanics | 110,000 | 138,000 | 25.5 | 5,200 |
| Airplane pilots | 83,000 | 110,000 | 33.6 | 4,100 |
| Anthropologists | 3,500 | 4,300 | 22.4 | 200 |
| Architects | 49,000 | 61,600 | 25.0 | 3,100 |
| Astronomers | 2,000 | 2,100 | 5.0 | 40 |
| Automobile mechanics | 790,000 | 915,000 | 15.9 | 32,000 |
| Bank officers | 319,000 | 465,000 | 45.8 | 28,000 |
| Bookkeeping workers | 1,700,000 | 1,900,000 | 12.8 | 95,000 |
| Building custodians | 2,100,000 | 2,423,000 | 15.3 | 160,000 |
| Business-machine repairers | 58,000 | 80,000 | 37.8 | 3,400 |
| Buyers | 109,000 | 120,000 | 10.1 | 5,700 |
| Carpenters | 1,010,000 | 1,260,000 | 24.8 | 67,000 |
| Chemists | 148,000 | 175,000 | 19.0 | 6,300 |
| Commercial artists | 67,000 | 80,000 | 19.4 | 3,600 |
| Composing room occupations | 152,000 | 140,000 | −7.9 | 3,600 |
| Computer operating personnel | 565,000 | 540,000 | −4.0 | 8,500 |
| Computer programmers | 230,000 | 290,000 | 27.4 | 9,700 |
| Computer service technicians | 50,000 | 93,000 | 86.0 | 5,200 |
| Computer systems analysts | 160,000 | 210,000 | 32.9 | 7,600 |
| Construction laborers | 715,000 | 900,000 | 25.9 | 40,000 |
| Cooks and chefs | 1,065,000 | 1,350,000 | 26.6 | 79,000 |
| Cosmetologists | 534,000 | 625,000 | 16.7 | 30,000 |
| Dental hygienists | 27,000 | 60,000 | 121.9 | 5,100 |
| Dentists | 112,000 | 135,000 | 20.8 | 4,800 |
| Drafters | 320,000 | 420,000 | 30.6 | 16,500 |
| Economists | 115,000 | 148,000 | 27.4 | 6,400 |
| Electricians (construction) | 260,000 | 320,000 | 25.5 | 13,700 |
| Engineering and science technicians | 586,000 | 760,000 | 29.9 | 29,000 |
| Engineers | 1,133,000 | 1,415,000 | 25.0 | 56,500 |
| Aerospace | 50,000 | 58,500 | 14.7 | 1,500 |
| Agricultural | 12,000 | 15,000 | 25.0 | 600 |
| Biomedical | 3,000 | 3,800 | 26.7 | 150 |
| Ceramic | 12,000 | 15,000 | 25.0 | 600 |
| Chemical | 53,000 | 64,000 | 20.6 | 2,100 |
| Civil | 155,000 | 192,000 | 23.9 | 8,900 |
| Electrical | 300,000 | 370,000 | 23.3 | 12,800 |
| Industrial | 200,000 | 255,000 | 27.9 | 10,500 |
| Mechanical | 200,000 | 245,000 | 21.5 | 9,300 |
| Metallurgical | 17,000 | 22,000 | 29.4 | 900 |
| Mining | 6,000 | 8,800 | 46.7 | 600 |
| Petroleum | 20,000 | 28,000 | 40.0 | 1,300 |
| Firefighters | 210,000 | 260,000 | 21.1 | 8,300 |
| Foresters | 25,000 | 29,000 | 15.7 | 1,100 |
| Geographers | 10,000 | 12,500 | 25.3 | 600 |
| Geologists | 34,000 | 47,500 | 38.1 | 2,300 |
| Geophysicists | 12,000 | 16,700 | 38.0 | 800 |
| Health services administrators | 160,000 | 230,000 | 45.0 | 16,000 |
| Historians | 22,500 | 24,500 | 9.1 | 900 |
| Industrial machinery repairers | 320,000 | 500,000 | 57.0 | 30,000 |
| Lawyers | 396,000 | 490,000 | 25.0 | 23,400 |
| Librarians | 128,000 | 145,000 | 13.3 | 8,000 |
| Life scientists | 205,000 | 265,000 | 28.6 | 12,000 |
| Lithographic occupations | 29,000 | 39,000 | 34.5 | 1,900 |
| Locomotive engineers | 33,300 | 39,500 | 18.6 | 2,400 |
| Machine-tool operators | 508,000 | 595,000 | 16.9 | 22,000 |
| Machinists | 405,000 | 475,000 | 17.1 | 20,000 |
| Mathematicians | 38,000 | 41,000 | 8.8 | 1,000 |
| Merchant marine sailors | 33,200 | 30,600 | −7.8 | 400 |
| Meteorologists | 5,500 | 6,300 | 14.0 | 200 |
| Newspaper reporters | 40,500 | 46,000 | 13.9 | 2,100 |
| Nurses, registered | 960,000 | 1,320,000 | 37.6 | 83,000 |
| Oceanographers | 2,700 | 3,400 | 25.3 | 150 |
| Office-machine operators | 163,000 | 180,000 | 10.4 | 7,700 |
| Painters | 410,000 | 500,000 | 21.4 | 27,000 |

| Occupation | Estimated employment 1976 | Projected requirements 1985 | Percent change, 1976–85 | Annual average openings, 1976–85[1] |
|---|---|---|---|---|
| Physical therapists | 25,000 | 36,000 | 44.8 | 2,100 |
| Physicians and osteopathic physicians | 375,000 | 520,000 | 37.8 | 21,800 |
| Physicists | 48,000 | 53,000 | 8.7 | 1,100 |
| Photographers | 85,000 | 97,000 | 14.0 | 3,700 |
| Plumbers and pipefitters | 385,000 | 535,000 | 39.0 | 30,000 |
| Police officers | 500,000 | 700,000 | 40.4 | 32,500 |
| Political scientists | 14,000 | 15,300 | 7.0 | 400 |
| Psychologists | 90,000 | 120,000 | 33.8 | 5,600 |
| Radio and TV announcers | 26,000 | 34,500 | 32.2 | 1,300 |
| Receptionists | 500,000 | 640,000 | 27.5 | 38,000 |
| Secretaries and stenographers | 3,500,000 | 4,800,000 | 37.1 | 295,000 |
| Social workers | 330,000 | 440,000 | 32.7 | 25,000 |
| Sociologists | 19,000 | 21,700 | 14.5 | 800 |
| Statisticians | 24,000 | 30,000 | 26.7 | 1,500 |
| Teachers: Kindergarten and elementary | 1,364,000 | 1,498,000 | 9.8 | 70,000 |
| Secondary | 1,111,000 | 986,000 | −11.3 | 13,000 |
| College and university | 593,000 | 610,000 | 2.9 | 17,000 |
| Truck drivers: Local | 1,600,000 | 1,940,000 | 21.7 | 73,000 |
| Long-distance | 467,000 | 520,000 | 10.9 | 15,400 |
| Typists | 1,000,000 | 1,200,000 | 21.8 | 63,000 |
| Urban planners | 16,000 | 23,000 | 46.5 | 1,100 |
| Veterinarians | 30,500 | 39,500 | 27.0 | 1,800 |

1. Annual openings include jobs resulting from growth and deaths and retirements. Transfers to other fields of work are not reflected. *Source:* Department of Labor, Bureau of Labor Statistics.

## Number of Employed Persons by Major Occupations, 1977

(in thousands)

| Occupations | Total employed | Percent distribution: Female | Percent distribution: Black and other |
|---|---|---|---|
| **White-collar workers** | 45,187 | 51.3 | 7.7 |
| Professional and technical | 13,692 | 42.6 | 8.4 |
| Accountants | 868 | 27.5 | 6.8 |
| Architects | 58 | 3.4 | 5.2 |
| Computer programmers | 221 | 26.2 | 6.3 |
| Computer systems analysts | 129 | 20.2 | 5.4 |
| Engineers | 1,267 | 2.7 | 5.5 |
| Aeronautical and astronautical engineers | 54 | 1.9 | 3.7 |
| Civil engineers | 171 | 1.2 | 7.6 |
| Electrical and electronic engineers | 324 | 2.8 | 5.9 |
| Industrial engineers | 214 | 7.0 | 4.2 |
| Mechanical engineers | 215 | .9 | 5.6 |
| Lawyers and judges | 462 | 9.5 | 3.2 |
| Librarian, archivists, and curators | 208 | 79.8 | 9.1 |
| Life and physical scientists | 275 | 15.6 | 8.7 |
| Biological scientists | 55 | 36.4 | 12.7 |
| Chemists | 124 | 13.7 | 10.5 |
| Operations and systems researchers and analysts | 122 | 20.5 | 4.1 |
| Personnel and labor relations workers | 370 | 43.5 | 11.9 |
| Dentists | 105 | 2.9 | 5.7 |
| Pharmacists | 138 | 17.4 | 4.3 |
| Physicians, medical and osteopathic | 403 | 11.2 | 9.2 |
| Registered nurses | 1,063 | 96.7 | 11.3 |
| Therapists | 178 | 68.5 | 9.6 |

| Occupations | Total employed | Percent distribution: Female | Percent distribution: Black and other |
|---|---|---|---|
| Health technologists and technicians | 462 | 71.4 | 12.1 |
| Religious workers | 347 | 13.0 | 8.6 |
| Economists | 106 | 17.9 | 4.7 |
| Psychologists | 92 | 41.3 | 2.2 |
| Social workers | 325 | 61.2 | 19.1 |
| Recreation workers | 119 | 59.7 | 19.3 |
| Teachers, college and university | 562 | 31.7 | 7.5 |
| Teachers, except college and university | 3,024 | 70.9 | 9.8 |
| Engineering and science technicians | 892 | 14.9 | 7.0 |
| Airplane pilots | 64 | — | 1.6 |
| Vocational and educational counselors | 175 | 49.1 | 14.3 |
| Writers, artists, and entertainers | 1,141 | 35.5 | 5.4 |
| Athletes and kindred workers | 105 | 41.9 | 6.7 |
| Designers | 146 | 24.0 | 2.7 |
| Editors and reporters | 185 | 44.9 | 4.9 |
| Musicians and composers | 154 | 31.2 | 9.7 |
| Painters and sculptors | 177 | 44.6 | 4.5 |
| Photographers | 81 | 13.6 | 3.7 |
| Public relations specialists and publicity writers | 120 | 38.3 | 5.0 |
| Managers and administrators, except farm | 9,662 | 22.3 | 4.8 |
| Bank officials and financial managers | 543 | 27.3 | 4.4 |
| Buyers and purchasing agents | 372 | 28.0 | 3.8 |
| Buyers, wholesale and retail trade | 162 | 37.0 | 4.3 |

| Occupations | Total employed | Percent distribution: Female | Percent distribution: Black and other |
|---|---|---|---|
| Credit and collection managers | 54 | 33.3 | 1.9 |
| Health administrators | 175 | 45.1 | 5.1 |
| Officials and administrators, public administration n.e.c. | 401 | 24.9 | 8.5 |
| Officials of lodges, societies, and unions | 118 | 24.6 | 5.9 |
| Restaurant, cafeteria, and bar managers | 548 | 34.7 | 8.9 |
| Sales managers and department heads, retail trade | 345 | 36.2 | 5.2 |
| Sales managers, except retail trade | 321 | 3.7 | 7.9 |
| School administrators, college | 126 | 29.4 | 2.5 |
| School administrators, elementary and secondary | 265 | 36.2 | 7.9 |
| Sales workers | 5,728 | 43.3 | 4.5 |
| Insurance agents, brokers, and underwriters | 500 | 16.6 | 5.4 |
| Real estate agents and brokers | 502 | 43.8 | 2.0 |
| Stock and bond sales agents | 98 | 13.3 | 2.0 |
| Sales representatives, manufacturing industries | 336 | 13.1 | 3.6 |
| Sales representatives, wholesale trade | 850 | 7.6 | 2.6 |
| Sales clerks, retail trade | 2,316 | 70.4 | 5.8 |
| Sales workers, except clerks, retail trade | 486 | 14.6 | 2.9 |
| Sales workers, services and construction | 154 | 35.1 | 4.5 |
| Clerical workers | 16,106 | 78.9 | 9.8 |
| Bank tellers | 408 | 90.0 | 7.6 |
| Billing clerks | 156 | 87.8 | 5.8 |
| Bookkeepers | 1,726 | 90.0 | 4.4 |
| Cashiers | 1,326 | 87.0 | 8.8 |
| File clerks | 274 | 84.7 | 20.4 |
| Insurance adjusters, examiners, and investigators | 168 | 50.6 | 10.1 |
| Library attendants and assistants | 142 | 80.3 | 16.2 |
| Mail carriers, post office | 242 | 9.5 | 10.3 |
| Office machine operators | 759 | 73.8 | 14.9 |
| Computer and peripheral equipment operators | 302 | 54.6 | 11.6 |
| Key punch operators | 280 | 93.2 | 17.9 |
| Postal clerks | 267 | 31.8 | 26.2 |
| Receptionists | 531 | 96.8 | 8.1 |
| Secretaries | 3,421 | 99.1 | 5.4 |
| Statistical clerks | 357 | 75.6 | 11.2 |
| Stenographers | 83 | 91.6 | 12.0 |
| Stock clerks and storekeepers | 497 | 30.8 | 12.3 |
| Teachers aides, except school monitors | 320 | 93.4 | 16.9 |
| Telephone operators | 342 | 95.3 | 14.0 |
| Typists | 1,006 | 96.3 | 14.5 |

| Occupations | Total employed | Percent distribution: Female | Percent distribution: Black and other |
|---|---|---|---|
| **Blue-collar workers** | 30,211 | 17.7 | 12.2 |
| Craft and kindred workers | 11,881 | 5.0 | 7.4 |
| Carpenters | 1,171 | .9 | 4.4 |
| Brickmasons and stonemasons | 177 | — | 18.1 |
| Electricians | 588 | .2 | 4.8 |
| Excavating, grading, and road machinery operators | 406 | .2 | 9.6 |
| Painters, construction and maintenance | 461 | 3.3 | 10.2 |
| Plumbers and pipefitters | 429 | .5 | 8.2 |
| Blue-collar worker supervisors, n.e.c. | 1,554 | 9.0 | 7.4 |
| Machinists and job setters | 576 | 2.6 | 8.0 |
| Metal craft workers, excluding mechanics, machinists, and job setters | 653 | 3.1 | 6.7 |
| Mechanics, automobiles | 1,161 | .9 | 8.0 |
| Mechanics, except automobiles | 2,019 | 1.6 | 6.1 |
| Printing craft workers | 389 | 22.4 | 8.0 |
| Telephone installers and repairers | 279 | 5.0 | 6.5 |
| Operatives, except transport | 10,354 | 39.6 | 14.3 |
| Assemblers | 1,136 | 50.3 | 15.7 |
| Garage workers and gas station attendants | 427 | 5.2 | 8.9 |
| Packers and wrappers, excluding meat and produce | 610 | 63.6 | 17.4 |
| Precision machine operatives | 372 | 10.2 | 8.3 |
| Sewers and stitchers | 820 | 95.2 | 18.8 |
| Transport equipment operatives | 3,476 | 6.8 | 14.6 |
| Truck drivers | 1,898 | 1.3 | 14.3 |
| Nonfarm laborers | 4,500 | 9.4 | 18.1 |
| **Service workers** | 12,392 | 62.0 | 19.8 |
| Private households | 1,158 | 97.0 | 35.8 |
| Service workers, except private households | 11,234 | 58.3 | 18.1 |
| Cleaning workers | 2,363 | 34.9 | 28.9 |
| Bartenders | 272 | 41.9 | 6.6 |
| Cooks | 1,106 | 56.3 | 20.6 |
| Waiters | 1,310 | 90.4 | 7.6 |
| Health service workers | 1,747 | 89.2 | 22.7 |
| Dental assistants | 123 | 98.4 | 5.7 |
| Health aides and trainees, excluding nursing | 245 | 84.5 | 18.0 |
| Nursing aides, orderlies, and attendants | 1,008 | 86.3 | 26.5 |
| Practical nurses | 371 | 96.8 | 21.6 |
| Personal service workers | 1,705 | 74.0 | 13.6 |
| Fire fighters | 225 | .4 | 7.1 |
| Guards | 490 | 10.2 | 18.0 |
| Police | 498 | 3.8 | 9.2 |
| **Farm workers** | 2,756 | 17.2 | 7.7 |
| Farm laborers, wage workers | 936 | 17.0 | 17.2 |
| **Total employed** | **90,546** | **40.5** | **10.8** |

NOTE: n.e.c.="not elsewhere classified" and designates broad categories of occupations that cannot be more specifically identified. *Source:* Department of Labor, Bureau of Labor Statistics.

## Private Pilots

There were about 10% more people taking flying lessons in 1978 than in 1977, when 139,000 took up flying. From 1975 to 1978, the number of women pilots increased 27%. In 1978, it cost about $1,400 for 50–60 hours of flying time—the usual length of time required to earn a private pilot's license. The program generally takes from nine months to a year to complete.

## Strikes and Lockouts

| Year | Strikes and lockouts | Workers involved (thousands) | Man-days idle (thousands) | Year | Strikes and lockouts | Workers involved (thousands) | Man-days idle (thousands) |
|---|---|---|---|---|---|---|---|
| 1895 | 1,255 | 407 | n.a. | 1945 | 4,750 | 3,470 | 38,000 |
| 1900 | 1,839 | 568 | n.a. | 1950 | 4,843 | 2,410 | 38,800 |
| 1905 | 2,186 | 302 | n.a. | 1955 | 4,320 | 2,650 | 28,200 |
| 1915 | 1,593 | n.a. | n.a. | 1960[1] | 3,333 | 1,320 | 19,100 |
| 1920 | 3,411 | 1,463 | n.a. | 1965 | 3,963 | 1,550 | 23,300 |
| 1925 | 1,301 | 428 | n.a. | 1970 | 5,716 | 3,305 | 66,414 |
| 1930 | 637 | 183 | 3,320 | 1975 | 5,031 | 1,746 | 31,237 |
| 1935 | 2,014 | 1,120 | 15,500 | 1976 | 5,648 | 2,420 | 37,859 |
| 1940 | 2,508 | 577 | 6,700 | 1977[2] | 5,600 | 2,300 | 36,000 |

1. First year for which figures include Alaska and Hawaii. 2. Preliminary. NOTE: n.a. = not available. *Source:* Department of Labor, Bureau of Labor Statistics.

## Percent Unemployed in the Civilian Labor Force

| Year | Percent Unemployed | Year | Percent Unemployed |
|---|---|---|---|
| 1920 | 5.2 | 1973 | 4.9 |
| 1922 | 6.7 | 1974 | 5.6 |
| 1924 | 5.0 | 1975 | 8.5 |
| 1926 | 1.8 | 1976 | 7.7 |
| 1928 | 4.2 | 1977 | 7.0 |
| 1930 | 8.7 | Jan. | 7.4 |
| 1932 | 23.6 | Feb. | 7.6 |
| 1934 | 21.7 | March | 7.4 |
| 1936 | 16.9 | April | 7.1 |
| 1938 | 19.0 | May | 7.1 |
| 1940 | 14.6 | June | 7.1 |
| 1942 | 4.7 | July | 6.9 |
| 1944 | 1.2 | Aug. | 7.0 |
| 1946 | 3.9 | Sept. | 6.8 |
| 1948 | 3.8 | Oct. | 6.8 |
| 1950 | 5.3 | Nov. | 6.7 |
| 1952 | 3.0 | Dec. | 6.4 |
| 1954 | 5.5 | 1978 | |
| 1956 | 4.1 | Jan. | 6.3 |
| 1958 | 6.8 | Feb. | 6.1 |
| 1960 | 5.5 | March | 6.2 |
| 1962 | 5.5 | April | 6.0 |
| 1964 | 5.2 | May | 6.1 |
| 1966 | 3.8 | June | 5.7 |
| 1968 | 3.6 | July | 6.2 |
| 1970 | 4.9 | Aug. | 5.9 |
| 1971 | 5.9 | Sept. | 6.0 |
| 1972 | 5.6 | | |

NOTE: Estimates prior to 1940 are based on sources other than direct enumeration. *Source:* Department of Labor, Bureau of Labor Statistics.

## Women in the Working Population

| Year[1] | Number (thousands) | Percent of female population aged 10 and over[1] | Percent of total working population aged 10 and over[1] |
|---|---|---|---|
| 1880 | 2,647 | 14.7 | 15.2 |
| 1890 | 4,006 | 17.4 | 17.2 |
| 1900 | 5,319 | 18.8 | 18.3 |
| 1910 | 7,445 | 21.5 | 19.9 |
| 1920 | 8,637 | 21.4 | 20.4 |
| 1930 | 10,752 | 22.0 | 22.0 |
| 1940 | 12,845 | 25.4 | 24.3 |
| 1950 | 18,412 | 33.9 | 17.3 |
| 1960[2] | 23,272 | 37.8 | 19.4 |
| 1970 | 31,560 | 43.4 | 22.5 |
| 1977 | 40,067 | 48.5 | 25.3 |

1. For 1880–1930; data relate to population and gainful workers at ages 10 and over; for 1940, to ages 14 and over; for 1950–77, to population at ages 16 and over. 2. Beginning in 1960, figures include Alaska and Hawaii. *Sources:* Department of Commerce, Bureau of the Census, and Department of Labor, Bureau of Labor Statistics.

## Amount of Life Insurance in Force
### (in millions)

| As of Dec. 31 | Ordinary | Group | Industrial | Credit | Total |
|---|---|---|---|---|---|
| 1915 | $16,650 | $ 100 | $ 4,279 | — | $ 21,029 |
| 1925 | 52,892 | 4,247 | 12,318 | 18 | 69,475 |
| 1930 | 78,576 | 9,801 | 17,963 | 73 | 106,413 |
| 1935 | 70,684 | 10,208 | 17,471 | 101 | 98,464 |
| 1940 | 79,346 | 14,938 | 20,866 | 380 | 115,530 |
| 1945 | 101,550 | 22,172 | 27,675 | 365 | 151,762 |
| 1950 | 149,071 | 47,793 | 33,415 | 3,844 | 234,168 |
| 1955 | 216,812 | 101,345 | 39,682 | 14,493 | 373,332 |
| 1960 | 341,881 | 175,903 | 39,563 | 29,101 | 586,448 |
| 1965 | 499,638 | 308,078 | 39,818 | 53,020 | 900,554 |
| 1970 | 734,730 | 551,357 | 38,644 | 77,392 | 1,402,123 |
| 1975 | 1,083,421 | 904,695 | 39,423 | 112,032 | 2,139,571 |
| 1977 | 1,289,521 | 1,115,047 | 39,045 | 139,402 | 2,582,815 |

*Source:* Institute of Life Insurance.

## Composition of the Civilian Labor Force and Unemployment

| | July 1978 | | | | | July 1977 | | | | |
|---|---|---|---|---|---|---|---|---|---|---|
| | Civilian labor force | | Unemployed | | | Civilian labor force | | Unemployed | | |
| Race, sex, and age | Number (thousands) | Percent distribution | Number (thousands) | Percent distribution | Rate | Number (thousands) | Percent distribution | Number (thousands) | Percent distribution | Rate |
| White | | | | | | | | | | |
| Men, 20 years and older | 46,086 | 51.1 | 1,465 | 27.5 | 3.2 | 45,284 | 51.9 | 1,832 | 31.6 | 4.0 |
| Women, 20 years and older | 25,323 | 28.1 | 1,467 | 27.5 | 5.8 | 24,101 | 27.6 | 1,555 | 26.8 | 6.5 |
| Teenagers, 16 to 19 years | 7,745 | 9.0 | 984 | 18.5 | 12.7 | 7,494 | 8.6 | 987 | 17.0 | 13.2 |
| Black and other | | | | | | | | | | |
| Men, 20 years and older | 5,450 | 6.0 | 453 | 8.5 | 8.3 | 5,280 | 6.1 | 525 | 9.1 | 9.9 |
| Women, 20 years and older | 4,433 | 4.9 | 554 | 10.4 | 12.5 | 4,073 | 4.7 | 496 | 8.6 | 12.2 |
| Teenagers, 16 to 19 years | 1,136 | 1.3 | 406 | 7.6 | 35.7 | 1,036 | 1.2 | 401 | 6.9 | 38.7 |
| All races | | | | | | | | | | |
| Men, 20 years and older | 51,536 | 57.2 | 1,917 | 36.0 | 3.7 | 50,564 | 57.9 | 2,357 | 40.7 | 4.7 |
| Women, 20 years and older | 29,755 | 33.0 | 2,020 | 37.9 | 6.8 | 28,174 | 32.3 | 2,051 | 35.4 | 7.3 |
| Teenagers, 16 to 19 years | 8,881 | 9.8 | 1,389 | 26.1 | 15.6 | 8,530 | 9.8 | 1,389 | 24.0 | 16.3 |
| **Total** | **90,172** | **100.0** | **5,327** | **100.0** | **5.9** | **87,268** | **100.0** | **5,797** | **100.0** | **6.6** |

NOTE: Totals may not add due to rounding. *Source:* Department of Labor, Bureau of Labor Statistics.

## Nonmanufacturing Industries—Gross Average Weekly Earnings and Hours Worked

| | 1978[1] | | 1977 | | 1975 | | 1970 | | 1958 | |
|---|---|---|---|---|---|---|---|---|---|---|
| Industry | Earnings | Hours worked | Earnings | Hours worked | Earnings | Hours worked | Earnings | Hours worked | Earnings | Hours worked |
| Bituminous coal and lignite mining | $403.20 | 42.0 | $354.89 | 41.1[2] | $284.53 | 39.2[2] | $186.41 | 40.8 | $97.57 | 33.3 |
| Metal mining | 329.25 | 40.9 | 299.52 | 41.2 | 250.72 | 42.3 | 165.68 | 42.7 | 94.96 | 38.6 |
| Nonmetallic minerals | 293.42 | 46.5 | 259.88 | 44.5 | 213.09 | 43.4 | 155.11 | 44.7 | 88.33 | 43.3 |
| Telephone communications | 295.32 | 40.4 | 278.99 | 40.2 | 221.18 | 38.4 | 131.60 | 39.4 | 78.72 | 38.4 |
| Radio and TV broadcasting | 280.92 | 39.4 | 253.09 | 39.3 | 214.50 | 39.0 | 147.45 | 38.2 | 100.70 | 38.0 |
| Electric, gas and sanitary services | 309.50 | 41.6 | 291.87 | 41.4 | 246.79 | 41.2 | 172.64 | 41.5 | 98.57 | 40.9 |
| Local and suburban transportation | | | 233.83 | 39.7 | 196.89 | 40.1 | 142.30 | 42.1 | 87.29 | 43.0 |
| Wholesale trade | 235.38 | 39.1 | 215.90 | 38.9 | 188.75 | 38.6 | 137.60 | 40.0 | 84.02 | 40.2 |
| Retail trade | 131.56 | 31.7 | 121.41 | 31.7 | 108.22 | 32.4 | 82.47 | 33.8 | 54.10 | 38.1 |
| Hotels, tourist courts, motels | 110.72 | 31.1 | 101.70 | 31.1 | 89.64 | 31.9 | 68.16 | 34.6 | 40.89 | 39.7 |
| Laundries and dry cleaning plants | 133.38 | 35.1 | 122.50 | 35.1 | 106.05 | 35.0 | 77.47 | 35.7 | 45.28 | 38.7 |
| General building contracting | 302.78 | 36.7 | 286.83 | 36.4 | 254.88 | 36.0 | 184.40 | 36.3 | 96.92 | 35.5 |

1. June preliminary. 2. 11-month average. *Source:* Department of Labor, Bureau of Labor Statistics.

## Manufacturing Industries—Gross Average Weekly Earnings and Hours Worked

| | 1978[1] | | 1977 | | 1975 | | 1970 | | 1958 | | 1953 | |
|---|---|---|---|---|---|---|---|---|---|---|---|---|
| Industry | Earnings | Hours worked | Earnings | Hours worked | Earnings | Hours worked | Earnings | Hours worked | Earnings | Hours worked | Earnings | Hours worked |
| All manufacturing[2] | $246.64 | 40.3 | $226.89 | 40.3 | $189.51 | 39.4 | $133.73 | 39.8 | $82.71 | 39.2 | $70.47 | 40.5 |
| Durable goods | 265.61 | 40.8 | 246.22 | 40.9 | 205.09 | 39.9 | 143.07 | 40.3 | 89.27 | 39.5 | 76.63 | 41.2 |
| Primary metal industries | 340.62 | 42.0 | 306.20 | 41.1 | 246.80 | 40.0 | 159.17 | 40.5 | 101.11 | 38.3 | 84.46 | 41.0 |
| Iron and steel foundries | 306.98[3] | 42.4[3] | 277.79 | 41.4 | 220.99 | 40.4 | 151.03 | 40.6 | 86.86 | 37.6 | 77.64 | 41.3 |
| Nonferrous foundries | 252.76[3] | 40.9[3] | 232.47 | 41.0 | 190.03 | 39.1 | 138.16 | 39.7 | 90.85 | 39.5 | 79.73 | 41.1 |
| Fabricated metal products | 253.13 | 40.5 | 238.86 | 40.9 | 201.60 | 40.0 | 143.67 | 40.7 | 89.78 | 39.9 | 76.49 | 41.8 |
| Hardware, cutlery, hand tools | 238.19 | 40.1 | 230.27 | 40.9 | 187.07 | 39.3 | 132.33 | 40.1 | 82.92 | 39.3 | 71.80 | 41.5 |
| Other hardware | 254.75[3] | 40.5[3] | 244.73 | 41.2 | 195.42 | 39.4 | 133.46 | 40.2 | 84.32 | 39.4 | 72.63 | 41.5 |
| Structural metal products | 244.20[3] | 40.7[3] | 227.70 | 40.3 | 202.61 | 40.2 | 142.61 | 40.4 | 92.63 | 40.1 | 79.71 | 42.4 |

| Industry | 1978[1] Earnings | 1978[1] Hours worked | 1977 Earnings | 1977 Hours worked | 1975 Earnings | 1975 Hours worked | 1970 Earnings | 1970 Hours worked | 1958 Earnings | 1958 Hours worked | 1953 Earnings | 1953 Hours worked |
|---|---|---|---|---|---|---|---|---|---|---|---|---|
| Electrical equipment, supplies | 228.71 | 39.5 | 214.67 | 40.2 | 180.91 | 39.5 | 130.54 | 39.8 | 83.95 | 39.6 | 70.99 | 40.8 |
| Machinery, except electrical | 277.64 | 41.5 | 257.92 | 41.6 | 219.22 | 40.9 | 154.95 | 41.1 | 94.33 | 39.8 | 82.68 | 42.4 |
| Transportation equipment | 320.67 | 41.7 | 303.71 | 42.3 | 242.61 | 40.3 | 163.22 | 40.3 | 100.40 | 40.0 | 85.28 | 41.6 |
| Motor vehicles and equipment | 369.27 | 43.7 | 348.39 | 44.1 | 262.68 | 40.6 | 170.07 | 40.3 | 101.24 | 39.7 | 89.88 | 42.0 |
| Lumber and wood products | 225.83 | 39.9 | 202.91 | 40.1 | 167.35 | 39.1 | 117.51 | 39.7 | 69.09 | 38.6 | 60.76 | 39.2 |
| Furniture and fixtures | 180.96 | 39.0 | 166.84 | 38.8 | 142.13 | 37.9 | 108.58 | 39.2 | 69.95 | 39.3 | 62.99 | 40.9 |
| Nondurable goods | 218.44 | 39.5 | 199.76 | 39.4 | 168.78 | 38.8 | 120.43 | 39.1 | 74.11 | 38.8 | 62.57 | 39.6 |
| Textile mill products | 172.43 | 40.1 | 160.39 | 40.4 | 133.28 | 39.2 | 97.76 | 39.9 | 57.51 | 38.6 | 53.18 | 39.1 |
| Apparel and other textile products | 140.76 | 36.0 | 128.15 | 35.4 | 111.97 | 35.1 | 84.37 | 35.3 | 54.05 | 35.1 | 48.74 | 36.1 |
| Leather and leather products | 146.63 | 37.5 | 134.68 | 37.0 | 120.80 | 37.4 | 92.63 | 37.2 | 57.25 | 36.7 | 50.90 | 37.7 |
| Food and kindred products | 231.42 | 39.9 | 213.07 | 39.9 | 184.17 | 40.3 | 127.98 | 40.5 | 79.15 | 40.8 | 63.50 | 41.5 |
| Tobacco manufactures | 236.80 | 36.6 | 210.27 | 38.3 | 171.38 | 38.0 | 110.00 | 37.8 | 62.17 | 39.1 | 47.63 | 38.1 |
| Paper and allied products | 279.48 | 42.8 | 253.38 | 42.8 | 207.58 | 41.6 | 144.14 | 41.9 | 87.99 | 41.9 | 71.81 | 43.0 |
| Printing and publishing | 244.02 | 37.6 | 230.20 | 37.8 | 198.32 | 37.0 | 147.78 | 37.7 | 94.62 | 38.0 | 82.29 | 39.0 |
| Chemicals and allied products | 292.18 | 41.8 | 266.46 | 41.7 | 219.63 | 40.9 | 153.50 | 41.6 | 93.20 | 40.7 | 74.21 | 41.0 |
| Petroleum and coal products | 377.10 | 45.0 | 331.19 | 42.9 | 267.07 | 41.6 | 182.76 | 42.7 | 111.66 | 40.9 | 90.35 | 40.7 |

1. July preliminary. 2. Average weekly earnings in 1919 = $21.04; 1929 = $24.70; 1932 = $16.89; 1939 = $23.64. Average hours worked per week in 1914 = 49.4; 1929 = 44.2; 1932 = 38.3; 1939 = 37.7. 3. June preliminary. *Source:* Department of Labor, Bureau of Labor Statistics.

## Government Employment and Payrolls

| Year and function | Employees (in thousands) Total | Employees Federal[1] | Employees State | Employees Local | Monthly payrolls (in millions) Total | Monthly payrolls Federal[1] | Monthly payrolls State | Monthly payrolls Local |
|---|---|---|---|---|---|---|---|---|
| 1940 | 4,474 | 1,128 | 3,346 | | $566 | $177 | $389 | |
| 1945 | 6,556 | 3,375 | 3,181 | | 1,110 | 642 | 468 | |
| 1950 | 6,402 | 2,117 | 1,057 | 3,228 | 1,528 | 613 | 218 | 696 |
| 1955 | 7,432 | 2,378 | 1,199 | 1,436 | 2,265 | 846 | 326 | 1,093 |
| 1960 | 8,808 | 2,421 | 1,527 | 4,860 | 3,333 | 1,118 | 524 | 1,691 |
| 1965 | 10,589 | 2,588 | 2,028 | 5,973 | 4,884 | 1,484 | 849 | 2,551 |
| 1970 | 13,028 | 2,881 | 2,755 | 7,392 | 8,334 | 2,428 | 1,612 | 4,294 |
| 1972 | 13,759 | 2,795 | 2,957 | 8,007 | 9,950 | 2,710 | 1,937 | 5,303 |
| 1973 | 14,139 | 2,786 | 3,013 | 8,339 | 11,027 | 3,102 | 2,158 | 5,857 |
| 1974 | 14,628 | 2,874 | 3,155 | 8,599 | 12,086 | 3,294 | 2,410 | 6,382 |
| 1975 | 14,973 | 2,890 | 3,271 | 8,813 | 13,224 | 3,584 | 2,653 | 6,987 |
| 1976 | 15,012 | 2,843 | 3,343 | 8,826 | 13,924 | 3,565 | 2,894 | 7,465 |
| 1977, total | 15,406 | 2,848 | 3,467 | 9,091 | 15,198 | 3,918 | 3,200 | 8,079 |
| National defense and international relations | 989 | 989 | (2) | (2) | 1,327 | 1,327 | (2) | (2) |
| Postal service | 652 | 652 | (2) | (2) | 890 | 890 | (2) | (2) |
| Education | 6,515 | 22 | 1,483 | 5,010 | 5,782 | 29 | 1,237 | 4,516 |
| Instructional employees | 3,642 | (2) | 444 | 3,198 | 5,012 | (2) | 589 | 4,423 |
| Highways | 592 | 5 | 260 | 327 | 550 | 9 | 275 | 266 |
| Health and hospitals | 1,509 | 254 | 638 | 616 | 1,391 | 318 | 573 | 498 |
| Police protection | 684 | 56 | 70 | 558 | 785 | 89 | 88 | 607 |
| Local fire protection | 301 | (2) | (2) | 301 | 292 | (2) | (2) | 292 |
| Sewerage and sanitation | 223 | (2) | (2) | 223 | 199 | (2) | (2) | 199 |
| Local parks and recreation | 221 | (2) | (2) | 221 | 142 | (2) | (2) | 142 |
| Natural resources | 483 | 273 | 176 | 34 | 557 | 372 | 159 | 26 |
| Financial administration | 415 | 108 | 119 | 189 | 409 | 140 | 123 | 146 |
| All other | 2,822 | 489 | 721 | 1,612 | 2,874 | 744 | 745 | 1,387 |

1. Civilians only. 2. Not applicable. *Source:* Department of Commerce, Bureau of the Census.

## How Consumers Spend Their Dollar

(in billions)

| | 1977 | 1977 % of total | 1975 | 1970 | 1965 | 1960 | 1955 | 1950 | 1940 | 1930 |
|---|---|---|---|---|---|---|---|---|---|---|
| Food | $217.0 | 17.9 | $184.7 | $112.1 | $85.8 | $70.1 | $58.1 | $46.0 | $16.6 | $18.0 |
| Tobacco | 16.5 | 1.4 | 14.7 | 11.2 | 8.4 | 7.0 | 5.0 | 4.3 | 1.9 | 1.5 |
| Alcohol | 28.2 | 2.3 | 24.9 | 17.9 | 13.0 | 10.4 | 9.1 | 7.9 | 3.6 | n.a. |
| Clothing, accessories, and jewelry | 95.6 | 7.9 | 82.0 | 62.8 | 43.3 | 33.0 | 28.0 | 23.7 | 8.9 | 9.7 |
| Personal care | 16.7 | 1.4 | 14.2 | 10.4 | 7.6 | 5.3 | 3.5 | 2.4 | 1.0 | 1.0 |
| Housing | 184.6 | 15.3 | 150.2 | 90.9 | 63.5 | 46.3 | 33.7 | 21.3 | 9.4 | 11.1 |
| Household operation | 176.9 | 14.7 | 142.3 | 87.4 | 61.8 | 46.9 | 37.3 | 29.5 | 10.5 | 9.6 |
| Medical care | 118.0 | 9.8 | 89.2 | 47.4 | 28.1 | 19.1 | 12.8 | 8.8 | 3.0 | 2.8 |
| Personal business | 60.4 | 5.0 | 51.6 | 35.3 | 21.9 | 15.0 | 10.0 | 6.8 | 3.3 | 3.7 |
| Transportation | 172.1 | 14.3 | 125.5 | 77.8 | 58.2 | 43.1 | 35.6 | 24.7 | 7.1 | 6.1 |
| Recreation | 81.2 | 6.7 | 66.5 | 40.7 | 26.3 | 18.3 | 14.1 | 11.1 | 3.8 | 4.0 |
| Private education and research | 18.8 | 1.6 | 15.5 | 10.4 | 5.9 | 3.7 | 2.3 | 1.6 | 0.6 | 0.7 |
| Religious and welfare activities | 15.4 | 1.3 | 13.0 | 8.6 | 6.0 | 4.7 | 3.3 | 2.3 | 1.0 | 1.2 |
| Foreign travel and other | 5.1 | 0.4 | 5.0 | 4.8 | 3.2 | 2.2 | 1.6 | 0.6 | (1) | 0.5 |
| **Total** | **1,206.5** | **100.0** | **979.1** | **617.6** | **432.8** | **325.2** | **254.4** | **191.0** | **70.8** | **69.9** |

1. Less than $100 million. *Source:* Department of Commerce, Bureau of Economic Analysis.

## Terms on Conventional First Mortgages: All Major Types of Lenders

| Type of homes and year | Contract rate (percent) | Fees and charges (percent) | Maturity (years) | Loan-to-price ratio (percent) | Purchase price | Loan amount |
|---|---|---|---|---|---|---|
| New homes: 1978[1] | 9.23 | 1.40 | 28.3 | 75.6 | $62,600 | $45,900 |
| 1977 | 8.80 | 1.33 | 27.9 | 76.3 | 54,300 | 40,500 |
| 1976 | 8.76 | 1.44 | 27.2 | 75.8 | 48,400 | 35,900 |
| 1975 | 8.75 | 1.54 | 26.8 | 76.1 | 44,600 | 33,300 |
| 1974 | 8.72 | 1.30 | 26.3 | 75.8 | 40,100 | 29,800 |
| 1970 | 8.27 | 1.03 | 25.1 | 71.7 | 35,500 | 25,200 |
| Existing homes: 1978[1] | 9.27 | 1.21 | 26.5 | 74.8 | 53,900 | 39,200 |
| 1977 | 8.83 | 1.17 | 25.8 | 75.1 | 47,500 | 34,700 |
| 1976 | 8.92 | 1.17 | 24.5 | 73.8 | 41,300 | 29,800 |
| 1975 | 9.01 | 1.19 | 24.0 | 73.4 | 38,200 | 27,400 |
| 1974 | 8.84 | 1.09 | 23.0 | 72.4 | 34,700 | 24,500 |
| 1970 | 8.20 | 0.92 | 22.8 | 71.1 | 30,000 | 21,000 |

1. June. *Source:* Federal Home Loan Bank Board.

## Annual Budgets for 4-Person Urban Families, Autumn 1977

| Item | Lower budget | | Intermediate budget | | Higher budget | |
|---|---|---|---|---|---|---|
| | Amount | Percent increase 1976–77 | Amount | Percent increase 1976–77 | Amount | Percent increase 1976–77 |
| Total family consumption | $8,657 | 6.1 | $13,039 | 5.4 | $17,948 | 5.3 |
| Food | 3,190 | 6.2 | 4,098 | 6.2 | 5,159 | 6.2 |
| Housing | 2,083 | 6.1 | 4,016 | 4.5 | 6,085 | 4.5 |
| Transportation | 804 | 4.8 | 1,472 | 4.9 | 1,913 | 4.9 |
| Clothing | 828 | 3.6 | 1,182 | 3.6 | 1,730 | 3.6 |
| Personal care | 282 | 6.4 | 377 | 6.2 | 535 | 6.4 |
| Medical care | 980 | 9.4 | 985 | 9.4 | 1,027 | 9.4 |
| Other family consumption | 489 | 4.5 | 909 | 4.6 | 1,499 | 4.5 |
| Other items | 472 | 4.7 | 763 | 4.4 | 1,288 | 4.4 |
| Personal income taxes | 720 | −12.7 | 2,342 | 4.7 | 4,980 | 9.1 |
| Social security and disability | 632 | 4.6 | 961 | 7.0 | 985 | 8.1 |
| **Total budget** | **10,481** | **4.4** | **17,106** | **5.4** | **25,202** | **6.1** |

NOTE: Above budgets illustrate three levels of living based on estimates of costs for goods and services rather than actual expenditures. Totals may not add because of rounding. *Source:* Department of Labor, Bureau of Labor Statistics.

# Receipts and Outlays of the Federal Government

(in millions of dollars)

Effective Oct. 1, 1976, the federal fiscal year was converted from a July 1–June 30 basis to an Oct. 1–Sept. 30 basis. The transition quarter was from July 1 through Sept. 30, 1976.

| Yearly average for year ended June 30 | Receipts: Customs (including tonnage tax)[1] | Receipts: Internal revenue: Income and profits tax | Receipts: Internal revenue: Other | Receipts: Miscellaneous taxes and receipts | Receipts: Total receipts | Receipts: Net receipts[2] | Outlays: Department of Defense (Army, 1789–1950) | Outlays: Department of the Navy | Outlays: Interest on public debt | Outlays: All other | Outlays: Net outlays[3] | Surplus (+) or deficit (−) |
|---|---|---|---|---|---|---|---|---|---|---|---|---|
| 1789–1800 | $ 6 | — | — | — | $ [illegible] | $ 7 | $ 2 | — | $ 3 | $ 1 | $ 6 | — |
| 1801–1810 | 12 | — | — | — | 1[illegible] | 13 | 2 | $ 1 | 4 | 2 | 9 | +4 |
| 1811–1820 | 16 | — | $ 2 | $ 3 | 2[illegible] | 21 | 11 | 5 | 5 | 3 | 24 | −3 |
| 1821–1830 | 20 | — | — | 2 | 2[illegible] | 22 | 4 | 3 | 4 | 5 | 16 | +6 |
| 1831–1840 | 20 | — | — | 10 | 3[illegible] | 30 | 8 | 5 | — | 11 | 24 | +6 |
| 1841–1850 | 24 | — | — | 3 | 2[illegible] | 27 | 13 | 7 | 1 | 11 | 32 | −5 |
| 1851–1860 | 54 | — | — | 6 | 6[illegible] | 60 | 16 | 12 | 3 | 29 | 60 | — |
| 1861–1865 | 69 | $ 17 | 55 | 20 | 16[illegible] | 161 | 548 | 65 | 35 | 36 | 684 | −523 |
| 1866–1870 | 179 | 51 | 171 | 46 | 44[illegible] | 447 | 128 | 28 | 135 | 86 | 377 | +70 |
| 1871–1880 | 166 | 4 | 115 | 28 | 313 | 313 | 39 | 20 | 106 | 107 | 271 | +42 |
| 1881–1890 | 418 | — | 259 | 65 | 742 | 742 | 83 | 34 | 108 | 312 | 537 | +205 |
| 1891–1900 | 362 | — | 357 | 69 | 788 | 788 | 161 | 77 | 68 | 515 | 821 | −33 |
| 1901–1910 | 571 | 4 | 512 | 100 | 1,18[illegible] | 1,187 | 302 | 199 | 51 | 622 | 1,174 | +13 |
| 1915 | 210 | 80 | 335 | 72 | 693 | 683 | 202 | 142 | 23 | 379 | 746 | −63 |
| 1918 | 180 | 2,314 | 872 | 299 | 3,665 | 3,645 | 4,870 | 1,279 | 190 | 6,339 | 12,677 | −9,032 |
| 1929 | 602 | 2,331 | 607 | 493 | 4,033 | 3,862 | 426 | 365 | 678 | 1,658 | 3,127 | +734 |
| 1933 | 251 | 746 | 858 | 225 | 2,080 | 1,997 | 435 | 349 | 689 | 3,125 | 4,598 | −2,602 |
| 1939 | 319 | 2,189 | 2,972 | 188 | 5,663 | 4,979 | 695 | 673 | 941 | 6,533 | 8,841 | −3,862 |
| 1943 | 324 | 16,094 | 6,050 | 934 | 23,402 | 21,947 | 42,526 | 20,888 | 1,808 | 14,146 | 79,368 | −57,420 |
| 1944 | 431 | 34,655 | 7,030 | 3,325 | 45,44[illegible] | 43,563 | 49,438 | 26,538 | 2,609 | 16,401 | 94,986 | −51,423 |
| 1945 | 355 | 35,173 | 8,729 | 3,494 | 47,750 | 44,362 | 50,490 | 30,047 | 3,617 | 14,149 | 98,303 | −53,941 |
| 1950 | 423 | 28,263 | 11,186 | 1,439 | 41,311 | 36,422 | 5,789 | 4,130 | 5,750 | 23,875 | 39,544 | −3,122 |
| 1956[4] | 705 | 56,639 | 20,564 | 389 | 78,297 | 74,547 | 35,693 | — | 6,787 | 27,981 | 70,460 | +4,087 |
| 1960 | 1,123 | 67,151 | 28,266 | 1,190 | 97,730 | 92,492 | 43,969 | — | 9,180 | 39,075 | 92,223 | +269 |
| 1965 | 1,478 | 79,792 | 39,996 | 1,598 | 122,863 | 116,833 | 47,179 | — | 11,346 | 59,904 | 118,430 | −1,596 |
| 1970 | 2,494 | 138,689 | 65,276 | 3,424 | 209,8[illegible]3 | 193,743 | 78,360 | — | 19,304 | 98,924 | 196,588 | −2,845 |
| 1974 | 3,444 | 184,648 | 99,553 | 5,369 | 293,0[illegible]4 | 264,932 | 79,307 | — | 29,319 | 160,995 | 269,621 | −4,689 |
| 1975 | 3,782 | 202,146 | 108,371 | 6,711 | 321,0[illegible]0 | 280,997 | 87,471 | — | 32,665 | 205,969 | 326,105 | −45,108 |
| 1976 (June 30) | 4,209 | 205,752 | 115,719 | 8,028 | 333,7[illegible]8 | 300,005 | 90,160 | — | 37,063 | 239,233 | 366,456 | −66,451 |
| 1976 (Sept. 30) | 1,243 | 49,567 | 31,769 | 1,613 | 84,1[illegible]2 | 81,773 | 22,509 | — | 8,102 | 64,135 | 94,746 | −12,973 |
| 1977 | 5,287 | 246,976 | 134,378 | 6,554 | 393,1[illegible]5 | 356,861 | 98,031 | — | 41,900 | 261,965 | 401,896 | −45,035 |

1. Beginning 1933, tonnage tax incl. in "Other receipts." 2. Net receipts equal total receipts less (a) appropriations to federal old-age and survivors' insurance trust fund beginning fiscal year 1939 and (b) refunds of receipts beginning fiscal year 1933. 3. Includes Air Force 1950–65 (in millions): 1950–$3,521; 1953–$15,085; 1956–$16,750; 1960–$19,065; 1965–$18,471. 4. Beginning 1956, computed on unified budget concepts; not strictly comparable with preceding figures. NOTE: The Export-Import Bank was moved within the budget effective Oct. 1, 1976. Adjustments have been made to include it for the period it was outside the budget (Aug. 17, 1971, through Sept. 30, 1976). *Source:* Department of the Treasury, Bureau of Government Financial Operations.

## Federal Budget—Receipts and Sources

(in billions of dollars)

| Source or function | 1977 | 1978 (est.) | 1979 (est.) |
|---|---|---|---|
| **SOURCE** | | | |
| Individual income taxes | $156.7 | $178.8 | $190.1 |
| Corporation income taxes | 54.9 | 58.9 | 62.5 |
| Social insurance taxes and contributions | 108.7 | 124.1 | 141.9 |
| Employment taxes and contributions | 92.2 | 104.0 | 119.6 |
| Unemployment insurance | 11.3 | 14.4 | 16.3 |
| Contributions for other insurance and retirement | 5.2 | 5.7 | 6.0 |
| Excise taxes | 17.5 | 20.2 | 25.5 |
| Estate and gift taxes | 7.3 | 5.6 | 6.1 |
| Customs duties | 5.2 | 5.8 | 6.4 |
| Miscellaneous receipts | 6.5 | 6.9 | 7.2 |
| **FUNCTION** | | | |
| National defense | 97.5 | 107.6 | 117.8 |
| Department of Defense—military | 95.6 | 105.3 | 115.2 |
| Atomic energy defense activities | 1.9 | 2.3 | 2.5 |
| International affairs | 4.8 | 6.7 | 7.7 |
| Foreign economic and financial assistance | 4.2 | 5.3 | 5.4 |
| Military assistance | 0.5 | 0.5 | 0.5 |
| Conduct of foreign affairs | 1.0 | 1.1 | 1.2 |
| Foreign information and exchange activities | 0.4 | 0.4 | 0.5 |
| International financial programs | −0.8 | ([1]) | 0.7 |
| General science, space, and technology | 4.7 | 4.8 | 5.1 |
| General science and basic research | 1.1 | 1.2 | 1.3 |
| Space flight | 2.3 | 2.2 | 2.3 |
| Space science, applications, and technology | 1.0 | 1.0 | 1.2 |
| Energy | 4.2 | 7.8 | 9.6 |
| Supply | 3.3 | 4.2 | 4.1 |
| Conservation | 0.1 | 0.6 | 1.4 |
| Emergency energy preparedness | 0.1 | 2.3 | 3.3 |
| Information, policy, and regulation | 0.7 | 0.8 | 0.9 |
| Natural resources and environment | 10.0 | 12.1 | 12.2 |
| Water resources | 3.2 | 3.7 | 3.4 |
| Conservation and land management | 1.3 | 2.1 | 1.6 |
| Recreation resources | 1.0 | 1.3 | 1.5 |
| Pollution control and abatement | 4.3 | 4.9 | 5.6 |
| Other natural resources | 1.0 | 1.2 | 1.3 |
| Agriculture | 5.5 | 9.1 | 5.4 |
| Farm income stabilization | 4.5 | 7.9 | 4.2 |
| Research and services | 1.1 | 1.2 | 1.3 |
| Commerce and housing credit | ([1]) | 3.5 | 3.0 |
| Mortgage credit and thrift insurance | −3.3 | 0.5 | −0.3 |
| Postal Service | 2.3 | 1.8 | 1.8 |
| Other advancement and regulation of commerce | 1.1 | 1.3 | 1.4 |
| Transportation | 14.6 | 16.3 | 17.4 |
| Ground | 10.1 | 11.1 | 12.0 |
| Air | 2.8 | 3.3 | 3.4 |
| Water | 1.7 | 1.9 | 2.0 |
| Other | 0.1 | 0.1 | 0.1 |
| Community and regional development | 6.3 | 9.7 | 8.7 |
| Community development | 3.5 | 4.0 | 4.0 |
| Area and regional development | 2.1 | 4.0 | 3.7 |

| Function | 1977 | 1978 (est.) | 1979 (est.) |
|---|---|---|---|
| Disaster relief and insurance | 0.6 | 1.7 | 1.0 |
| Education, training, employment, and social services | 21.0 | 27.5 | 30.4 |
| Elementary, secondary, and vocational education | 5.1 | 5.7 | 6.5 |
| Higher education | 3.1 | 3.8 | 4.3 |
| Research and general education aids | 0.9 | 1.2 | 1.2 |
| Training and employment | 6.9 | 10.9 | 12.8 |
| Other labor services | 0.4 | 0.5 | 0.5 |
| Social services | 4.6 | 5.5 | 5.1 |
| Health | 38.8 | 44.3 | 49.7 |
| Health care services | 34.5 | 39.9 | 45.1 |
| Health research | 2.5 | 2.7 | 2.9 |
| Education and training of health-care work force | 1.0 | 0.8 | 0.8 |
| Consumer and occupational health and safety | 0.7 | 0.8 | 0.9 |
| Income security | 137.0 | 147.6 | 160.0 |
| General retirement and disability insurance | 88.6 | 98.2 | 108.4 |
| Federal employee retirement and disability | 9.5 | 10.8 | 12.0 |
| Unemployment compensation | 15.3 | 12.4 | 11.8 |
| Public assistance and other income supplements | 23.6 | 26.3 | 27.8 |
| Veterans benefits and services | 18.0 | 18.9 | 19.3 |
| Income security | 9.2 | 9.7 | 10.3 |
| Education, training, and rehabilitation | 3.7 | 3.1 | 2.6 |
| Hospital and medical care | 4.7 | 5.4 | 5.8 |
| Administration of justice | 3.6 | 4.0 | 4.2 |
| Law enforcement activities | 1.7 | 1.9 | 2.0 |
| Litigative and judicial activities | 0.8 | 1.0 | 1.1 |
| Correctional activities | 0.2 | 0.3 | 0.4 |
| Criminal justice assistance | 0.8 | 0.8 | 0.7 |
| General government | 3.4 | 4.1 | 4.3 |
| Legislative functions | 0.8 | 0.9 | 0.9 |
| Executive direction and management | 0.1 | 0.1 | 0.1 |
| Central fiscal operations | 1.9 | 2.2 | 2.4 |
| General property and records management | 0.1 | 0.4 | 0.4 |
| Central personnel management | 0.1 | 0.1 | 0.1 |
| Other general government | 0.5 | 0.6 | 0.6 |
| General purpose fiscal assistance | 9.5 | 9.9 | 9.6 |
| General revenue sharing | 6.8 | 6.8 | 6.9 |
| Other fiscal assistance | 2.7 | 3.0 | 2.8 |
| Interest | 38.1 | 43.8 | 49.0 |
| On the public debt | 41.9 | 48.6 | 55.4 |
| Other interest | −3.8 | −4.8 | −6.4 |
| Allowances | — | — | 2.8 |
| Civilian pay raises | — | — | 1.1 |
| Relatively uncontrollable programs | — | — | 1.7 |
| Undistributed offsetting receipts | −15.1 | −15.6 | −16.0 |
| Employer share, employee retirement | −4.5 | −5.0 | −5.2 |
| Interest received by trust funds | −8.1 | −8.6 | −9.1 |
| Rents and royalties on the Outer Continental Shelf | −2.4 | −2.0 | −1.8 |
| **Total receipts** | **356.9** | **400.4** | **439.6** |
| **Total outlays** | **401.9** | **462.2** | **500.2** |
| **Total deficit** | **45.0** | **61.8** | **60.6** |

1. Less than $500,000. NOTE: The fiscal year is from Oct. 1 to Sept. 30. *Source:* Executive Office of the President, Office of Management and Budget.

## Per Capita Social Welfare Expenditures Under Public Programs

(in constant prices)

| Year | Social insurance | Public aid | Health and medical programs | Veterans' programs | Education | Other social welfare | All health and medical care[1] | Total[2] | Total social welfare (in millions)[3] |
|---|---|---|---|---|---|---|---|---|---|
| 1950 | $ 75 | $ 38 | $31 | $103 | $101 | $ 7 | $ 46 | $ 355 | $ 54,467 |
| 1960 | 192 | 41 | 45 | 54 | 176 | 11 | 64 | 520 | 94,911 |
| 1965 | 242 | 54 | 54 | 51 | 242 | 18 | 82 | 664 | 130,609 |
| 1970 | 375 | 114 | 68 | 62 | 350 | 29 | 174 | 1,003 | 208,132 |
| 1971 | 432 | 139 | 73 | 68 | 371 | 33 | 188 | 1,122 | 235,192 |
| 1972 | 464 | 162 | 80 | 71 | 370 | 33 | 208 | 1,188 | 251,455 |
| 1973 | 510 | 171 | 80 | 77 | 385 | 34 | 218 | 1,270 | 270,747 |
| 1974 | 537 | 172 | 82 | 76 | 385 | 37 | 227 | 1,303 | 279,797 |
| 1975 | 599 | 199 | 85 | 83 | 381 | 37 | 249 | 1,398 | 302,762 |
| 1976 | 669 | 224 | 88 | 86 | 396 | 37 | 269 | 1,514 | 330,593 |
| **PERCENTAGE INCREASE (OR DECREASE—) FOR 1976 FROM —** | | | | | | | | | |
| 1950 | 793 | 493 | 181 | −16 | 291 | 445 | 480 | 327 | 507 |
| 1965 | 177 | 313 | 63 | 68 | 63 | 107 | 227 | 128 | 153 |
| 1970 | 78 | 97 | 29 | 40 | 13 | 29 | 55 | 51 | 59 |
| 1973 | 31 | 31 | 10 | 13 | 3 | 9 | 23 | 19 | 22 |
| 1974 | 24 | 30 | 8 | 13 | 3 | 1 | 19 | 16 | 18 |
| 1975 | 12 | 13 | 3 | 5 | 4 | 0 | 8 | 8 | 9 |

1. Combines health and medical programs with medical services provided in connection with social insurance, public aid, veterans', vocational rehabilitation, and antipoverty programs. 2. Includes housing, not shown. 3. Excludes expenditures abroad for education, veterans' benefits, civil service retirement benefits, and certain other items. NOTE: Figures are latest available. *Source:* Department of Health, Education, and Welfare, *Social Security Bulletin*, January 1977.

## Social Welfare Expenditures Under Public Programs

(in millions of dollars)

| Year and source of funds | Social insurance | Public aid | Health and medical programs | Veterans' programs | Education | Housing | Other social welfare | All health and medical care[1] | Total social welfare | Total social welfare as: Percent of gross national product | Total social welfare as: Percent of total gov't outlays |
|---|---|---|---|---|---|---|---|---|---|---|---|
| **FEDERAL** | | | | | | | | | | | |
| 1950 | $ 2,103 | $ 1,103 | $ 604 | $ 6,386 | $ 157 | $ 15 | $ 174 | $ 1,362 | $ 10,541 | 4.0 | 26.2 |
| 1955 | 6,385 | 1,504 | 1,150 | 4,772 | 485 | 75 | 252 | 2,473 | 14,623 | 3.9 | 22.3 |
| 1960 | 14,307 | 2,117 | 1,737 | 5,367 | 868 | 144 | 417 | 2,918 | 24,957 | 5.0 | 28.1 |
| 1965 | 21,807 | 3,594 | 2,781 | 6,011 | 2,470 | 238 | 812 | 4,625 | 37,712 | 5.7 | 32.6 |
| 1970 | 45,246 | 9,649 | 4,775 | 8,952 | 5,876 | 582 | 2,259 | 16,600 | 77,337 | 8.1 | 40.1 |
| 1974 | 82,830 | 20,388 | 7,145 | 13,874 | 7,007 | 2,009 | 3,902 | 27,499 | 137,155 | 10.1 | 52.3 |
| 1975 | 99,748 | 27,208 | 8,547 | 16,570 | 8,567 | 2,335 | 4,264 | 34,126 | 167,237 | 11.5 | 54.0 |
| 1976[2] | 120,809 | 33,245 | 9,353 | 18,791 | 9,168 | 2,428 | 4,534 | 39,863 | 198,328 | 12.3 | 56.0 |
| **STATE AND LOCAL** | | | | | | | | | | | |
| 1950 | 2,844 | 1,393 | 1,460 | 480 | 6,518 | (3) | 274 | 1,704 | 12,967 | 4.9 | 59.2 |
| 1955 | 3,450 | 1,499 | 1,953 | 62 | 10,672 | 15 | 367 | 2,473 | 18,017 | 4.7 | 55.3 |
| 1960 | 4,999 | 1,984 | 2,727 | 112 | 16,758 | 33 | 723 | 3,478 | 27,337 | 5.5 | 60.1 |
| 1965 | 6,316 | 2,690 | 3,466 | 20 | 25,638 | 80 | 1,254 | 4,911 | 39,464 | 6.0 | 60.4 |
| 1970 | 9,446 | 6,839 | 5,132 | 127 | 44,970 | 120 | 1,886 | 8,791 | 68,519 | 7.1 | 64.0 |
| 1974 | 16,123 | 11,133 | 7,809 | 239 | 63,492 | 545 | 2,819 | 14,013 | 102,159 | 7.5 | 64.1 |
| 1975 | 23,199 | 13,502 | 8,890 | 449 | 69,344 | 632 | 3,269 | 16,744 | 119,285 | 8.2 | 65.0 |
| 1976[2] | 25,783 | 15,701 | 9,839 | 215 | 77,257 | 700 | 3,542 | 18,957 | 133,038 | 8.3 | 66.9 |
| **TOTAL** | | | | | | | | | | | |
| 1950 | 4,947 | 2,496 | 2,064 | 6,866 | 6,674 | 15 | 448 | 3,065 | 23,508 | 8.9 | 37.4 |
| 1955 | 9,835 | 3,003 | 3,103 | 4,834 | 11,157 | 89 | 619 | 4,421 | 32,640 | 8.6 | 32.7 |
| 1960 | 19,307 | 4,101 | 4,464 | 5,479 | 17,626 | 177 | 1,139 | 6,395 | 52,293 | 10.5 | 38.4 |
| 1965 | 28,123 | 6,283 | 6,246 | 6,031 | 28,108 | 318 | 2,066 | 9,535 | 77,175 | 11.7 | 42.2 |
| 1970 | 54,691 | 16,488 | 9,907 | 9,078 | 50,846 | 701 | 4,145 | 25,391 | 145,856 | 15.2 | 48.2 |
| 1974 | 98,953 | 31,520 | 14,953 | 14,112 | 70,499 | 2,554 | 6,722 | 41,512 | 239,314 | 17.6 | 56.5 |
| 1975 | 122,947 | 40,709 | 17,437 | 17,019 | 77,911 | 2,967 | 7,533 | 50,870 | 286,522 | 19.7 | 57.9 |
| 1976[2] | 146,593 | 48,946 | 19,193 | 19,006 | 86,426 | 3,128 | 8,077 | 58,820 | 331,366 | 20.6 | 59.7 |

| Year and source of funds | Social insurance | Public aid | Health and medical programs | Veterans' programs | Education | Housing | Other social welfare | All health and medical care[1] | Total social welfare | Total social welfare as: Percent of gross national product | Percent of total gov't outlays |
|---|---|---|---|---|---|---|---|---|---|---|---|
| **PERCENT OF TOTAL, BY TYPE** | | | | | | | | | | | |
| 1950 | 21.0 | 10.6 | 8.8 | 29.2 | 28.4 | 0.1 | 1.9 | 13.0 | 100.0 | [3] | [3] |
| 1955 | 30.1 | 9.2 | 9.5 | 14.8 | 34.2 | 0.3 | 1.9 | 13.5 | 100.0 | [3] | [3] |
| 1960 | 36.9 | 7.8 | 8.5 | 10.5 | 33.7 | 0.3 | 2.2 | 12.2 | 100.0 | [3] | [3] |
| 1965 | 36.4 | 8.1 | 8.1 | 7.8 | 36.4 | 0.4 | 2.7 | 12.4 | 100.0 | [3] | [3] |
| 1970 | 37.5 | 11.3 | 6.7 | 6.2 | 34.9 | 0.5 | 3.0 | 17.2 | 100.0 | [3] | [3] |
| 1974 | 41.3 | 13.2 | 6.2 | 5.9 | 29.5 | 0.9 | 2.8 | 17.3 | 100.0 | [3] | [3] |
| 1975 | 42.9 | 14.2 | 6.1 | 5.9 | 27.2 | 1.0 | 2.6 | 17.8 | 100.0 | [3] | [3] |
| 1976[2] | 44.3 | 14.8 | 5.8 | 5.7 | 26.1 | 0.9 | 2.4 | 17.8 | 100.0 | [3] | [3] |
| **FEDERAL PERCENT OF TOTAL** | | | | | | | | | | | |
| 1950 | 42.5 | 44.2 | 29.2 | 93.0 | 2.3 | 100.0 | 38.9 | 44.4 | 44.8 | [3] | [3] |
| 1955 | 64.9 | 50.1 | 37.1 | 98.7 | 4.3 | 83.7 | 40.7 | 44.1 | 44.8 | [3] | [3] |
| 1960 | 74.1 | 51.6 | 38.9 | 98.0 | 4.9 | 81.2 | 36.6 | 45.6 | 47.7 | [3] | [3] |
| 1965 | 77.5 | 57.2 | 44.5 | 99.7 | 8.8 | 74.9 | 39.3 | 48.5 | 48.9 | [3] | [3] |
| 1970 | 82.7 | 58.5 | 48.2 | 98.6 | 11.6 | 82.9 | 54.5 | 65.4 | 53.0 | [3] | [3] |
| 1974 | 83.7 | 64.7 | 47.8 | 98.3 | 9.9 | 78.7 | 58.1 | 66.2 | 57.3 | [3] | [3] |
| 1975 | 81.1 | 66.8 | 49.0 | 97.4 | 11.0 | 78.7 | 56.6 | 67.1 | 58.4 | [3] | [3] |
| 1976[2] | 82.4 | 67.9 | 48.7 | 98.9 | 10.6 | 77.6 | 56.1 | 67.8 | 59.9 | [3] | [3] |

1. Combines health and medical programs with medical services provided in connection with social insurance, public aid, veterans, and other social welfare programs. 2. Preliminary. 3. Not applicable. NOTE: Figures are latest available. *Source:* Department of Health, Education, and Welfare, *Social Security Bulletin,* January 1977.

## Contributions to International Organizations

**(for fiscal year 1977 in millions of dollars)**

| Organization | Amount[1] |
|---|---|
| United Nations and Specialized Agencies | $219.41 |
| United Nations | 95.45 |
| Food and Agricultural Organization | 18.55 |
| International Atomic Energy Agency | 10.52 |
| International Civil Aviation Organization | 3.73 |
| Joint Financing Program | 2.36 |
| International Labor Organization | 17.36 |
| International Telecommunications Union | 1.93 |
| UNESCO | 27.04 |
| World Health Organization | 38.93 |
| World Meteorological Organization | 2.60 |
| Others | 0.94 |
| Peacekeeping Forces | 34.93 |
| United Nations Emergency Force | 25.33 |
| United Nations Force in Cyprus | 9.60 |
| Inter-American Organizations | 54.15 |
| Organization of American States | 28.87 |
| Pan American Health Organization | 18.73 |
| Inter-American Institute of Agricultural Sciences | 5.11 |
| Others | 1.44 |
| Regional Organizations | 26.93 |
| NATO Civilian Headquarters | 11.38 |
| Organization for Economic Cooperation and Development | 14.47 |
| Others | $ 1.08 |
| Other International Organizations | 9.40 |
| International Institute for Cotton | 1.50 |
| General Agreement on Tariffs and Trade | 2.08 |
| North Atlantic Ice Patrol | 4.51 |
| Others | 1.31 |
| Special Voluntary Programs | 397.14 |
| Indus Basin and Tarbela Development Funds | 15.76 |
| International Agricultural Research Institute | 18.30 |
| International Atomic Energy Agency—Operational Program | 6.05[2] |
| Organization of American States Special Development Assistance Fund | 6.30 |
| Organization of American States Special Multilateral Fund (education and science) | 7.00 |
| U.N. Children's Fund | 20.00 |
| U.N. Development Program | 100.00 |
| U.N. Environment Fund | 10.00 |
| U.N./F.A.O. World Food Program | 77.38 |
| U.N. Fund for Population Activities | 29.00 |
| U.N. Special Resettlement and Relief Programs | 27.50 |
| U.N. Relief and Works Agency (Middle East) | 48.70 |
| Others | 31.15 |
| **Total** | **741.96** |

1. Estimated. 2. Includes cash, commodities and services. *Source:* Department of State.

## Teen-Agers' Diet

A *Scholastic* magazine survey shows that 42% of U.S. teenagers prefer to make a meal of pizza, 19% choose steak, and 10% like hamburger.

# The Public Debt

| Year | Gross debt: Amount (in millions) | Gross debt: Per capita | Year | Gross debt: Amount (in millions) | Gross debt: Per capita |
|---|---|---|---|---|---|
| 1800 (Jan. 1) | $ 83 | $ 15.87 | 1950 | $257,357 | $1,696.67 |
| 1860 | 65 | 2.06 | 1955 | 274,374 | 1,660.11 |
| 1865 | 2,678 | 75.01 | 1960 | 286,331 | 1,584.70 |
| 1900 | 1,263 | 16.60 | 1965 | 317,274 | 1,630.46 |
| 1920 | 24,299 | 228.23 | 1970 | 370,919 | 1,811.12 |
| 1925 | 20,516 | 177.12 | 1975 | 533,189 | 2,496.90 |
| 1930 | 16,185 | 131.51 | 1976 | 634,702 | 2,950.15 |
| 1935 | 28,701 | 225.58 | 1977[1] | 698,840 | 3,223.18 |
| 1940 | 42,968 | 325.23 | | | |
| 1945 | 258,682 | 1,848.60 | | | |

1. Preliminary, Sept. 30, 1977. *Source:* Department of the Treasury, Bureau of Government Financial Operations.

# Foreign Assistance
(in millions of dollars)

| Calendar years | Economic assistance (net): Net new grants | Net new credits | Net other assistance | Total | Military grants (net) | Net assistance[1] |
|---|---|---|---|---|---|---|
| July 1945–50 | $18,411 | $ 8,086 | — | $ 26,496 | $ 1,981 | $ 28,477 |
| 1951–55 | 10,459 | 556 | $ 541 | 11,556 | 14,464 | 26,020 |
| 1956–60 | 8,291 | 1,503 | 2,226 | 12,021 | 11,327 | 23,348 |
| 1961–65 | 9,384 | 5,522 | 576 | 15,482 | 7,831 | 23,313 |
| 1966–70 | 8,808 | 9,430 | −564 | 17,674 | 12,028 | 29,702 |
| 1971 | 2,043 | 1,844 | 246 | 3,640 | 3,580 | 7,220 |
| 1972 | 2,173 | 1,484 | −213 | 3,444 | 4,527 | 7,971 |
| 1973 | 1,938 | 1,089 | 49 | 3,579 | 2,853 | 6,431 |
| 1974 | 4,539 | −348 | −247 | 3,944 | 2,842 | 6,785 |
| 1975 | 2,247 | 2,849 | 30 | 5,126 | 2,891 | 8,017 |
| 1976 | 2,266 | 3,275 | −53 | 5,488 | 1,339 | 6,828 |
| 1977 | 2,275 | 2,860 | −39 | 5,096 | 757 | 5,853 |
| **Total postwar period[2]** | **72,833** | **38,751** | **1,962** | **113,546** | **66,420** | **179,966** |

1. Excludes investment in international nonmonetary financial institutions of $5,982 million. 2. Includes transactions after V-J Day (Sept. 2, 1945). NOTE: Detail may not add to total due to rounding. *Source:* Department of Commerce, Bureau of Economic Analysis.

# Domestic Freight Traffic by Major Carriers
(in millions of ton-miles)[1]

| Year | Railroads: Ton-miles | Railroads: % of total | Inland waterways[2]: Ton-miles | Inland waterways[2]: % of total | Motor trucks: Ton-miles | Motor trucks: % of total | Oil pipelines: Ton-miles | Oil pipelines: % of total | Air carriers: Ton-miles | Air carriers: % of total |
|---|---|---|---|---|---|---|---|---|---|---|
| 1940 | 379,201 | 61.3 | 118,057 | 19.1 | 62,043 | 10.0 | 59,277 | 9.6 | 14 | — |
| 1945 | 690,809 | 67.3 | 142,737 | 13.9 | 66,948 | 6.5 | 126,530 | 12.3 | 91 | — |
| 1950 | 596,940 | 56.2 | 163,344 | 15.4 | 172,860 | 16.3 | 129,175 | 12.1 | 318 | — |
| 1955 | 631,385 | 49.5 | 216,508 | 17.0 | 223,254 | 17.5 | 203,244 | 16.0 | 481 | — |
| 1960 | 579,130 | 44.1 | 220,253 | 16.8 | 285,483 | 21.7 | 228,626 | 17.4 | 778 | — |
| 1965 | 708,700 | 43.3 | 262,421 | 16.0 | 359,218 | 21.9 | 306,393 | 18.7 | 1,910 | 0.1 |
| 1970 | 771,168 | 39.8 | 318,560 | 16.4 | 412,000 | 21.3 | 431,000 | 22.3 | 3,274 | 0.2 |
| 1975[3] | 759,000 | 36.7 | 342,210 | 16.5 | 454,000 | 22.0 | 507,300 | 24.6 | 3,732 | 0.2 |
| 1976[3] | 799,000 | 36.2 | 372,865 | 16.9 | 510,000 | 23.1 | 523,000 | 23.6 | 3,902 | 0.2 |
| 1977[3] | 831,000 | 36.0 | 370,000 | 16.0 | 549,000 | 23.8 | 556,000 | 24.0 | 4,181 | 0.2 |

1. Mail and express included, except railroads for 1970. 2. Rivers, canals, and domestic traffic on Great Lakes. 3. Preliminary. *Sources:* Interstate Commerce Commission; Civil Aeronautics Board; Association of American Railroads.

## Waterborne Commerce at Selected Ports, 1976

**(excluding Great Lakes; in thousands of tons)**

| | Foreign | | Domestic | | | | | |
|---|---|---|---|---|---|---|---|---|
| | | | Coastwise | | Internal | | | |
| Port or harbor | Imports | Exports | Receipts | Shipments | Receipts | Shipments | Local | Total |
| Baton Rouge, La. | 15,265 | 9,591 | 2,476 | 5,511 | 13,159 | 20,280 | 421 | 66,703 |
| Baltimore | 18,135 | 14,945 | 5,601 | 1,164 | 6,047 | 2,427 | 4,218 | 52,437 |
| Beaumont, Tex. | 17,293 | 3,898 | 1,355 | 10,496 | 6,539 | 4,187 | 171 | 43,939 |
| Boston | 7,134 | 535 | 14,295 | 2,971 | 740 | — | 1,237 | 26,172 |
| Corpus Christi, Tex. | 15,669 | 4,302 | 220 | 12,996 | 1,358 | 3,247 | 766 | 38,559 |
| Houston | 26,934 | 14,967 | 1,973 | 18,804 | 10,739 | 12,583 | 3,898 | 89,898 |
| Lake Charles, La. | 5,620 | 1,620 | 132 | 2,932 | 6,170 | 3,293 | 453 | 20,221 |
| Long Beach, Calif. | 14,950 | 5,576 | 5,936 | 2,323 | 1,233 | 974 | 464 | 31,457 |
| Los Angeles | 11,346 | 3,264 | 6,582 | 5,663 | 1,029 | 1,240 | 1,808 | 30,931 |
| Marcus Hook, Pa. | 15,330 | 150 | 3,316 | 2,764 | 3,036 | 3,580 | 505 | 28,681 |
| Mobile, Ala. | 8,216 | 5,745 | 384 | 1,817 | 7,625 | 9,519 | 2,073 | 35,379 |
| New Orleans | 16,101 | 41,555 | 2,250 | 11,698 | 57,835 | 21,923 | 4,627 | 155,990 |
| New York | 53,292 | 6,246 | 32,872 | 24,092 | 5,397 | 15,610 | 42,078 | 179,587 |
| Norfolk, Va. | 6,516 | 31,021 | 2,171 | 95 | 2,788 | 5,821 | 1,643 | 50,055 |
| Pascagoula, Miss. | 9,020 | 2,466 | 683 | 4,874 | 2,133 | 4,599 | 152 | 23,927 |
| Paulsboro, N.J. | 12,051 | 82 | 4,855 | 1,748 | 3,240 | 4,116 | 122 | 26,213 |
| Philadelphia | 26,695 | 4,714 | 2,736 | 3,919 | 8,442 | 2,548 | 1,549 | 50,604 |
| Portland, Me. | 20,054 | 37 | 4,501 | 699 | 6 | — | 77 | 25,374 |
| Portland, Ore. | 1,666 | 7,441 | 3,492 | 293 | 4,227 | 2,459 | 1,914 | 21,493 |
| Port Arthur, Tex. | 13,197 | 2,310 | 937 | 8,964 | 872 | 4,391 | 15 | 30,687 |
| Richmond, Calif. | 6,439 | 499 | 5,186 | 3,950 | 1,307 | 2,591 | 192 | 20,165 |
| St. Louis | — | — | 1 | 7 | 7,004 | 15,878 | 1,065 | 23,955 |
| Tampa, Fla. | 4,379 | 12,208 | 14,911 | 7,955 | 20 | 234 | 197 | 39,904 |
| Texas City, Tex. | 9,693 | 794 | 510 | 6,260 | 5,180 | 6,049 | 29 | 28,516 |

*Source:* Department of Commerce, Bureau of the Census.

## State Motor Vehicle Registration, 1976

**(in thousands; excluding publicly owned vehicles)**

| State | Autos[1] | Buses[2] | Trucks | Total |
|---|---|---|---|---|
| Alabama | 1,942 | 1.9 | 596 | 2,540 |
| Alaska | 154 | 1.0 | 87 | 242 |
| Arizona | 1,062 | 0.8 | 390 | 1,453 |
| Arkansas | 897 | 1.9 | 430 | 1,329 |
| California | 11,394 | 14.1 | 2,690 | 14,098 |
| Colorado | 1,504 | 1.4 | 492 | 1,997 |
| Connecticut | 1,911 | 7.4 | 142 | 2,060 |
| Delaware | 294 | 1.4 | 60 | 355 |
| D.C. | 238 | 2.2 | 13 | 253 |
| Florida | 4,788 | 3.4 | 922 | 5,713 |
| Georgia | 2,590 | 3.6 | 700 | 3,294 |
| Hawaii | 418 | 2.4 | 67 | 487 |
| Idaho | 422 | 0.6 | 240 | 663 |
| Illinois | 5,481 | 18.9 | 1,094 | 6,594 |
| Indiana | 2,642 | 7.9 | 764 | 3,414 |
| Iowa | 1,585 | 2.0 | 560 | 2,147 |
| Kansas | 1,277 | 1.3 | 568 | 1,846 |
| Kentucky | 1,719 | 1.3 | 597 | 2,317 |
| Louisiana | 1,677 | 13.5 | 621 | 2,312 |
| Maine | 553 | 0.7 | 132 | 686 |
| Maryland | 2,129 | 8.0 | 342 | 2,479 |
| Massachusetts | 2,854 | 9.5 | 300 | 3,164 |
| Michigan | 4,702 | 6.0 | 922 | 5,630 |
| Minnesota | 2,063 | 5.9 | 659 | 2,728 |
| Mississippi | 1,034 | 3.4 | 388 | 1,425 |
| Missouri | 2,226 | 3.6 | 685 | 2,915 |
| Montana | 389 | 1.1 | 238 | 628 |
| Nebraska | 905 | 1.2 | 369 | 1,275 |
| Nevada | 369 | 0.3 | 124 | 493 |
| New Hampshire | 442 | 1.1 | 75 | 518 |
| New Jersey | 3,797 | 8.4 | 354 | 4,159 |
| New Mexico | 586 | 3.1 | 276 | 865 |
| New York | 6,697 | 17.5 | 824 | 7,539 |
| North Carolina | 2,981 | 8.3 | 812 | 3,801 |
| North Dakota | 333 | 0.5 | 220 | 554 |
| Ohio | 6,159 | 8.8 | 907 | 7,075 |
| Oklahoma | 1,494 | 1.7 | 683 | 2,179 |
| Oregon | 1,421 | 2.3 | 332 | 1,755 |
| Pennsylvania | 6,921 | 20.6 | 1,115 | 8,057 |
| Rhode Island | 510 | 0.9 | 68 | 579 |
| South Carolina | 1,397 | 3.2 | 343 | 1,743 |
| South Dakota | 342 | 0.7 | 187 | 530 |
| Tennessee | 2,144 | 3.0 | 617 | 2,764 |
| Texas | 6,528 | 15.6 | 2,249 | 8,793 |
| Utah | 598 | 0.4 | 262 | 860 |
| Vermont | 242 | 0.5 | 56 | 299 |
| Virginia | 2,744 | 2.1 | 506 | 3,252 |
| Washington | 1,963 | 4.1 | 668 | 2,635 |
| West Virginia[3] | 755 | 0.8 | 225 | 981 |
| Wisconsin | 2,191 | 6.2 | 412 | 2,609 |
| Wyoming | 211 | 1.1 | 139 | 351 |
| **Total** | **109,676** | **237.3** | **26,524** | **136,437** |

1. Includes taxicabs. 2. Estimates by Federal Highway Administration of number in operation, rather than registration counts of the states. 3. Estimates by Federal Highway Administration. *Source:* Department of Transportation, Federal Highway Administration.

## Domestic and Export Factory Sales of Motor Vehicles
(in thousands)

| | From plants in United States[1] | | | | | | | | |
|---|---|---|---|---|---|---|---|---|---|
| | Passenger cars | | | Motor trucks and buses | | | Total motor vehicles | | |
| Year | Total | Domestic | Exports | Total | Domestic | Exports | Total | Domestic | Exports |
| 1965 | 9,297 | 9,092 | 205 | 1,700 | 1,564 | 136 | 10,997 | 10,656 | 341 |
| 1970 | 6,531 | 6,171 | 359 | 1,642 | 1,515 | 127 | 8,173 | 7,686 | 486 |
| 1974 | 7,322 | 6,712 | 609 | 2,678 | 2,420 | 258 | 10,000 | 9,133 | 868 |
| 1975 | 6,708 | 6,068 | 640 | 2,235 | 1,966 | 269 | 8,943 | 8,034 | 909 |
| 1976 | 8,481 | 7,821 | 660 | 2,927 | 2,682 | 245 | 11,408 | 10,503 | 905 |
| 1977 | 9,177 | 8,489 | 688 | 3,380 | 3,117 | 263 | 12,557 | 11,606 | 951 |

1. Excludes factory sales to all Federal government agencies. *Source:* Motor Vehicle Manufacturers Association of the U.S.

## Domestic Passenger-Car Sales, 1975–1977

| Company and model | 1977 | 1976 | 1975 |
|---|---|---|---|
| American Motors | 183,954 | 247,640 | 322,272 |
| Gremlin | 37,531 | 50,617 | 66,614 |
| Hornet | 79,508 | 81,780 | 97,841 |
| Pacer | 44,874 | 79,898 | 96,769 |
| Matador | 22,041 | 35,345 | 61,048 |
| Chrysler Corp. | 1,219,752 | 1,301,940 | 997,116 |
| Total Plymouth | 444,063 | 545,171 | 414,548 |
| Valiant | 2,243 | 74,924 | 228,083 |
| Volare | 304,305 | 311,259 | 6,518 |
| Voyager | 13,767 | 12,974 | 12,928 |
| Fury | 92,056 | 97,063 | 104,110 |
| Plymouth | 31,692 | 48,951 | 62,909 |
| Total Chrysler | 317,012 | 277,809 | 229,061 |
| Cordoba | 142,619 | 175,456 | 148,943 |
| Chrysler | 104,356 | 102,353 | 80,118 |
| LeBaron | 70,037 | — | — |
| Total Dodge | 458,677 | 478,960 | 353,507 |
| Dart | 1,898 | 60,946 | 166,094 |
| Aspen | 242,111 | 232,742 | 4,808 |
| Sportsman | 45,380 | 43,266 | 39,402 |
| Monaco | 59,559 | 49,299 | 67,937 |
| Charger SE | 29,099 | 53,770 | 33,701 |
| Dodge | 32,248 | 38,937 | 41,565 |
| Diplomat | 40,072 | — | — |
| Magnum | 8,310 | — | — |
| Ford Motor | 2,552,210 | 2,256,277 | 1,983,723 |
| Ford Division | 1,862,796 | 1,715,525 | 1,542,550 |
| Pinto | 220,775 | 229,536 | 202,662 |
| Fairmont/Maverick | 167,841 | 118,907 | 145,133 |
| Club Wagon | 38,761 | 32,942 | 28,324 |
| Mustang II | 170,659 | 167,201 | 201,370 |
| Granada | 355,186 | 387,423 | 306,517 |
| LTD II | 203,922 | 191,464 | 144,040 |
| T-Bird/Elite | 325,153 | 212,049 | 139,172 |
| Ford | 380,499 | 376,003 | 295,332 |
| Total Mercury | 508,132 | 418,749 | 344,671 |
| Bobcat | 35,481 | 36,365 | 37,605 |
| Zephyr/Comet | 42,234 | 27,265 | 43,570 |
| Monarch | 106,821 | 122,057 | 94,082 |
| XR-7/Cougar/Montego | 182,986 | 127,913 | 99,874 |
| Mercury | 140,610 | 105,149 | 71,540 |
| Total Lincoln | 181,282 | 122,003 | 96,502 |
| Lincoln | 92,985 | 63,781 | 52,747 |
| Mark V | 74,807 | 58,222 | 43,755 |
| Versailles | 13,490 | — | — |
| L-M Division | 689,414 | 540,752 | 441,173 |
| General Motors | 5,148,131 | 4,800,716 | 3,747,009 |
| Buick Division | 746,394 | 738,385 | 518,032 |
| Skyhawk | 24,872 | 31,128 | 30,243 |
| Skylark | 97,196 | 108,206 | 68,025 |
| Century | 279,657 | 294,989 | 195,399 |
| Buick | 323,860 | 282,492 | 209,487 |
| Riviera | 20,809 | 21,570 | 14,378 |
| Cadillac Division | 335,785 | 304,495 | 207,049 |
| Seville | 44,667 | 41,248 | 26,531 |
| Cadillac | 244,770 | 223,602 | 194,600 |
| Eldorado | 46,348 | 39,635 | 45,918 |
| Chevrolet Division | 2,280,439 | 2,104,142 | 1,822,426 |
| Chevette | 196,218 | 140,974 | 42,204 |
| Vega | 73,813 | 133,251 | 217,002 |
| Monza | 83,413 | 91,586 | 120,567 |
| Nova | 312,135 | 312,379 | 267,946 |
| Sportvan | 39,609 | 30,337 | 24,432 |
| Camaro | 208,511 | 172,846 | 145,029 |
| Malibu/Chevelle | 296,193 | 334,267 | 285,726 |
| Monte Carlo | 370,825 | 376,621 | 278,826 |
| Chevrolet | 657,151 | 470,208 | 400,087 |
| Corvette | 42,571 | 41,673 | 40,607 |
| Oldsmobile Division | 977,046 | 900,611 | 635,645 |
| Starfire | 19,120 | 27,501 | 20,354 |
| Omega | 51,724 | 56,324 | 39,157 |
| Cutlass | 527,939 | 514,593 | 342,875 |
| Oldsmobile | 349,403 | 278,004 | 204,003 |
| Toronado | 28,860 | 24,189 | 20,256 |
| Pontiac Division | 808,467 | 753,093 | 503,857 |
| Astre | 28,693 | 41,148 | 53,792 |
| Sunbird | 61,790 | 50,070 | 4,605 |
| Phoenix/Ventura | 72,520 | 61,396 | 52,380 |
| Firebird | 137,807 | 108,348 | 82,652 |
| LeMans | 73,061 | 89,178 | 93,382 |
| Grand Prix | 235,833 | 251,952 | 101,829 |
| Pontiac | 198,763 | 151,001 | 115,217 |
| **Industry Total** | **9,104,454** | **8,606,573** | **7,050,120** |

*Source: Automotive News.*

## Passenger Car Production by Makes

| Companies and models | 1977 | 1976 | 1975 | 1974 | 1970 | 1965 |
|---|---|---|---|---|---|---|
| American Motors Corporation | 156,994 | 313,918 | 323,704 | 352,088 | 276,127 | 346,367 |
| Chrysler Corporation | | | | | | |
| Plymouth | 492,063 | 658,020 | 443,550 | 602,606 | 699,031 | 679,539 |
| Dodge | 497,232 | 547,916 | 354,482 | 463,993 | 405,699 | 547,531 |
| Chrysler | 247,064 | 127,466 | 102,940 | 96,630 | 158,614 | 224,061 |
| Imperial | — | — | 1,930 | 13,433 | 10,111 | 16,422 |
| **Total** | **1,236,359** | **1,333,402** | **902,902** | **1,176,662** | **1,273,455** | **1,467,553** |
| Ford Motor Company | | | | | | |
| Ford | 1,761,373 | 1,494,054 | 1,301,414 | 1,716,975 | 1,647,918 | 2,164,902 |
| Mercury | 583,055 | 434,865 | 405,104 | 400,701 | 310,463 | 355,404 |
| Lincoln | 211,439 | 124,880 | 101,520 | 87,569 | 58,771 | 45,470 |
| **Total** | **2,555,867** | **2,053,799** | **1,808,038** | **2,205,245** | **2,017,152** | **2,565,776** |
| General Motors Corporation | | | | | | |
| Chevrolet | 2,133,403 | 2,012,412 | 1,687,091 | 1,903,861 | 1,504,614 | 2,587,509 |
| Pontiac | 875,957 | 784,631 | 523,469 | 502,083 | 422,212 | 860,652 |
| Oldsmobile | 1,079,841 | 964,425 | 654,342 | 548,658 | 439,632 | 650,801 |
| Buick | 801,202 | 817,669 | 535,820 | 400,262 | 459,931 | 653,838 |
| Cadillac | 369,254 | 312,845 | 278,404 | 230,649 | 152,859 | 196,595 |
| **Total** | **5,259,657** | **4,891,982** | **3,679,126** | **3,585,513** | **2,979,248** | **4,949,395** |
| Checker Motors Corporation | 4,777 | 4,792 | 3,181 | 4,996 | 4,146 | 6,136 |
| **Grand Total** | **9,213,654** | **8,497,893** | **6,716,951** | **7,324,504** | **6,550,128** | **9,335,227** |

*Source:* Motor Vehicle Manufacturers Association of the U.S.

## Intercity Passenger Traffic
### (in millions of passenger-miles)

| | Railroads | | Buses | | Air carriers | | Inland waterways[1] | | | |
|---|---|---|---|---|---|---|---|---|---|---|
| Year | Miles | % of total | Miles | % of total | Miles | % of total | Miles | % of total | Total commercial | Private airplanes |
| 1940 | 24,766 | 67.1 | 9,800 | 26.5 | 1,052 | 2.8 | 1,317 | 3.6 | 36,935 | — |
| 1945 | 93,535 | 74.3 | 27,027 | 21.4 | 3,362 | 2.7 | 2,056 | 1.6 | 125,980 | — |
| 1950 | 32,481 | 46.3 | 26,436 | 37.7 | 10,072 | 14.3 | 1,190 | 1.7 | 70,179 | — |
| 1955 | 28,695 | 36.5 | 25,519 | 32.4 | 22,741 | 28.9 | 1,738 | 2.2 | 78,693 | — |
| 1960 | 21,574 | 28.6 | 19,327 | 25.7 | 31,730 | 42.1 | 2,688 | 3.6 | 75,319 | 2,228 |
| 1965 | 17,557 | 17.9 | 23,775 | 24.2 | 53,719 | 54.7 | 3,101 | 3.2 | 98,152 | 4,364 |
| 1970 | 10,903 | 7.3 | 25,300 | 16.9 | 109,499 | 73.1 | 4,000 | 2.7 | 149,702 | 9,101 |
| 1975 | 10,075 | 5.8 | 25,000 | 14.2 | 136,432 | 77.7 | 4,000 | 2.3 | 175,507 | 11,500 |
| 1976 | 11,000 | 5.8 | 25,000 | 13.2 | 150,000 | 78.9 | 4,000 | 2.1 | 190,000 | 13,000 |
| 1977[2] | 10,450 | 5.1 | 25,900 | 12.7 | 163,700 | 80.2 | 4,000 | 2.0 | 204,050 | n.a. |

1. Rivers, canals, and Great Lakes. 2. Preliminary. NOTE: Beginning in 1970, data include Alaska and Hawaii. n.a. = not available. *Sources:* Interstate Commerce Commission; Civil Aeronautics Board; Association of American Railroads.

## Passenger Car Data

| | 1976 | 1960 | 1950 | 1940 |
|---|---|---|---|---|
| U.S. passenger cars and taxis registered (thousands) | 110,351 | 61,671 | 40,339 | 27,466 |
| Total mileage of U.S. passenger cars (millions) | 1,074,000 | 588,083 | 363,613 | 249,600 |
| Total fuel consumption of U.S. passenger cars (millions of gallons) | 78,291 | 41,169 | 24,305 | 16,323 |
| World registration of cars, trucks, and buses (thousands) | 341,711 | 126,908 | 70,424 | n.a. |
| U.S. registration of cars, trucks, and buses (thousands) | 138,549 | 73,858 | 49,162 | 32,453 |
| U.S. share of world registration of cars, trucks, and buses | 40.5% | 58.2% | 69.8% | n.a. |

NOTE: n.a. = not available. *Source:* Motor Vehicle Manufacturers Association of the U.S.

## Exports of Leading Commodities
(value in millions of dollars)

| Commodity | 1977 | 1976 |
|---|---|---|
| Food and live animals | $14,103 | $15,710 |
| Meat and preparations | 797 | 798 |
| Dairy products and eggs | 182 | 128 |
| Grains and preparations | 8,755 | 10,911 |
| Wheat, including wheat flour | 2,882 | 4,041 |
| Rice | 730 | 629 |
| Fruits and nuts | 1,080 | 976 |
| Vegetables | 518 | 559 |
| Feed for animals | 1,572 | 1,358 |
| Beverages and tobacco | 1,847 | 1,524 |
| Tobacco and manufactures | 1,709 | 1,432 |
| Beverages and other tobacco | 138 | 92 |
| Crude materials, inedible, except fuels | 12,815 | 10,891 |
| Hides and skins, except fur skins | 583 | 522 |
| Soybeans, other oilseeds, peanuts | 4,798 | 3,560 |
| Synthetic rubber | 327 | 329 |
| Wood in the rough | 1,000 | 945 |
| Wood pulp | 875 | 844 |
| Textile fibers and wastes | 1,902 | 1,425 |
| Ores and metal scrap | 1,197 | 1,285 |
| Mineral fuels and related materials | 4,179 | 4,226 |
| Coal | 2,655 | 2,910 |
| Petroleum and products | 1,276 | 998 |
| Animal and vegetable oils and fats | 1,341 | 978 |
| Soybean oil | 440 | 238 |
| Chemicals | 10,827 | 9,959 |
| Chemical elements and compounds | 4,376 | 3,943 |
| Medicines and pharmaceuticals | 1,081 | 997 |
| Fertilizers, manufactured | 701 | 813 |
| Plastic materials and resins | 1,733 | 1,672 |
| Machinery and transport equipment | 51,037 | 49,501 |
| Machinery | 33,426 | 32,113 |
| Machinery, nonelectrical | 23,140 | 22,835 |
| Power generating machinery | 3,540 | 3,543 |
| Aircraft engines, parts | 939 | 978 |
| Automotive engines, parts | 990 | 943 |
| Agricultural machinery | 716 | 707 |
| Tractors and parts | 868 | 928 |
| Office machines | 3,645 | 2,937 |
| Metalworking machinery | 730 | 953 |
| Textile and leather machinery | 423 | 457 |
| Electrical apparatus | 10,285 | 9,278 |
| Transport equipment | 17,611 | 17,388 |
| Road motor vehicles and parts | 10,887 | 10,132 |
| Aircraft, parts, and accessories | 5,866 | 6,104 |
| Other manufactured goods | 18,590 | 17,781 |
| Rubber manufactures | 588 | 491 |
| Paper and manufactures | 1,517 | 1,624 |
| Nonmetallic mineral manufactures | 1,275 | 1,166 |
| Metals and manufactures | 5,044 | 5,094 |
| Iron and steel-mill products | 1,608 | 1,833 |
| Nonferrous base metals | 1,058 | 1,089 |
| Other manufactures of metals | 2,339 | 2,089 |
| Textiles, other than clothing | 1,959 | 1,971 |
| Clothing | 586 | 488 |
| Scientific instruments | 979 | 878 |
| Photographic equipment, supplies | 1,453 | 1,215 |
| Printed matter | 668 | 607 |
| Other transactions | 3,224 | 2,749 |
| **Total** | **$120,163** | **$114,992** |

## Imports of Leading Commodities
(value in millions of dollars)

| Commodity | 1977 | 1976 |
|---|---|---|
| Food and live animals | $12,490 | $10,267 |
| Cattle, except for breeding | 187 | 159 |
| Meat and preparations | 1,273 | 1,447 |
| Cheese | 215 | 207 |
| Fish | 2,056 | 1,855 |
| Grains and feed for animals | 249 | 251 |
| Fruits and nuts | 959 | 760 |
| Vegetables | 592 | 426 |
| Sugar | 1,079 | 1,154 |
| Coffee, green | 3,861 | 2,632 |
| Cocoa or cacao beans | 486 | 358 |
| Tea | 176 | 96 |
| Spices | 138 | 104 |
| Beverages and tobacco | 1,663 | 1,624 |
| Alcoholic beverages | 1,282 | 1,174 |
| Tobacco, unmanufactured | 319 | 392 |
| Crude materials, inedible, except fuels | 7,944 | 7,014 |
| Hides and skins, except fur skins | 97 | 89 |
| Fur skins, undressed | 122 | 101 |
| Rubber, including latex | 645 | 513 |
| Lumber | 2,098 | 1,452 |
| Wood pulp | 1,215 | 1,237 |
| Textile fibers and wastes | 225 | 249 |
| Industrial diamonds | 61 | 46 |
| Asbestos, unmanufactured | 152 | 149 |
| Ores and metal scrap | 2,234 | 2,251 |
| Iron ore and concentrates | 957 | 982 |
| Ores and concentrates, nonferrous metals | 1,277 | 1,269 |
| Mineral fuels and related materials | 44,287 | 33,996 |
| Petroleum and products | 42,136 | 31,993 |
| Natural gas | 1,942 | 1,612 |
| Animal and vegetable oils and fats | 538 | 404 |
| Chemicals | 5,432 | 4,772 |
| Organic chemicals | 1,427 | 1,193 |
| Inorganic chemicals | 1,176 | 937 |
| Medicinal and pharmaceutical products | 318 | 269 |
| Fertilizers, manufactured | 829 | 683 |
| Machinery and transport equipment | 35,494 | 29,824 |
| Machinery | 17,937 | 15,446 |
| Machinery, nonelectrical | 9,505 | 8,021 |
| Electrical apparatus | 8,432 | 7,424 |
| Automotive engines, parts | 1,607 | 1,384 |
| Transport equipment | 17,557 | 14,378 |
| Automobiles and parts | 15,842 | 13,104 |
| Aircraft and parts | 601 | 434 |
| Other manufactured goods | 36,278 | 30,180 |
| Wood manufactures, excluding furniture | 1,028 | 825 |
| Paper and manufactures | 2,392 | 2,103 |
| Glass, glassware, and pottery | 785 | 652 |
| Diamonds, excluding industrial | 1,453 | 1,018 |
| Metals and manufactures | 12,246 | 9,899 |
| Pig iron and ferroalloys | 524 | 538 |
| Iron and steel-mill products | 5,281 | 3,809 |
| Platinum group metals | 254 | 270 |
| Nonferrous base metals | 3,369 | 2,941 |
| Textiles, other than clothing | 1,772 | 1,635 |
| Clothing | 4,154 | 3,634 |
| Footwear | 1,848 | 1,686 |
| Furniture | 671 | 550 |
| Scientific and photographic apparatus | 701 | 501 |
| Clocks and watches | 716 | 627 |
| Toys, games, and sporting goods | 1,159 | 903 |
| Artworks and antiques | 720 | 580 |
| Other transactions | 2,692 | 2,538 |
| **Total** | **$146,817** | **$120,678** |

*Source:* Department of Commerce, Office of International Economic Research.

## Exports and General Imports by Countries and Areas

**($25 million and over; value in millions)**

| Area and country | Exports, including re-exports 1977 | 1970 | 1960 | 1950 | General imports 1977 | 1970 | 1960 | 1950 |
|---|---|---|---|---|---|---|---|---|
| **NORTH AND SOUTH AMERICA** | | | | | | | | |
| Canada | $25,749 | $9,079 | $3,810 | $2,039 | $29,356 | $11,092 | $2,901 | $1,960 |
| 19 American Republics | 16,346 | 5,695 | 3,577 | 2,720 | 16,335 | 4,779 | 3,528 | 2,910 |
| Argentina | 731 | 441 | 359 | 148 | 383 | 172 | 98 | 206 |
| Bolivia | 214 | 46 | 25 | 21 | 161 | 25 | 9 | 35 |
| Brazil | 2,482 | 840 | 464 | 365 | 2,246 | 670 | 570 | 715 |
| Chile | 520 | 300 | 203 | 73 | 261 | 157 | 193 | 160 |
| Colombia | 782 | 395 | 253 | 237 | 822 | 269 | 299 | 313 |
| Costa Rica | 323 | 94 | 45 | 27 | 285 | 117 | 35 | 25 |
| Dominican Republic | 424 | 143 | 42 | 43 | 631 | 184 | 110 | 38 |
| Ecuador | 565 | 127 | 57 | 29 | 609 | 109 | 65 | 34 |
| El Salvador | 314 | 64 | 43 | 33 | 427 | 48 | 32 | 51 |
| Guatemala | 377 | 100 | 64 | 44 | 384 | 87 | 59 | 54 |
| Haiti | 203 | 34 | 25 | 25 | 169 | 32 | 18 | 23 |
| Honduras | 240 | 89 | 35 | 24 | 253 | 102 | 34 | 20 |
| Mexico | 4,806 | 1,704 | 831 | 526 | 4,685 | 1,218 | 443 | 315 |
| Nicaragua | 223 | 77 | 30 | 19 | 181 | 61 | 21 | 19 |
| Panama | 346 | 208 | 90 | 112 | 159 | 76 | 24 | 10 |
| Paraguay | 51 | 18 | 9 | 3 | 23 | 11 | 8 | 6 |
| Peru | 500 | 214 | 147 | 76 | 499 | 340 | 183 | 49 |
| Uruguay | 74 | 41 | 63 | 41 | 88 | 19 | 21 | 106 |
| Venezuela | 3,171 | 759 | 567 | 406 | 4,072 | 1,082 | 948 | 324 |
| **OTHER WESTERN HEMISPHERE** | | | | | | | | |
| Bahamas | 224 | 173 | 49 | 7 | 1,050 | 82 | 8 | 1 |
| Barbados | 59 | 22 | 6 | 1 | 32 | 9 | 1 | (1) |
| Bermuda | 87 | 92 | 32 | 10 | 6 | 1 | 2 | (1) |
| Cuba | (1) | (1) | 225 | 464 | (1) | (1) | 357 | 406 |
| French West Indies | 34 | 15 | 4 | 3 | 4 | 9 | (1) | (1) |
| Guyana | 62 | 25 | 12 | 3 | 55 | 43 | 11 | 1 |
| Jamaica | 293 | 218 | 48 | 9 | 347 | 187 | 54 | 2 |
| Leeward and Windward Islands | 65 | 32 | 6 | 1 | 9 | 6 | 2 | 2 |
| Netherlands Antilles | 304 | 126 | 65 | 70 | 1,286 | 416 | 265 | 158 |
| Surinam | 119 | 35 | 18 | 7 | 120 | 56 | 30 | 13 |
| Trinidad and Tobago | 306 | 84 | 36 | 6 | 1,658 | 232 | 55 | 9 |
| **EUROPE** | | | | | | | | |
| Western Europe | 33,752 | 14,463 | 7,204 | 3,280 | 27,417 | 11,169 | 4,187 | 1,368 |
| Austria | 245 | 74 | 80 | 106 | 281 | 120 | 49 | 16 |
| Belgium and Luxembourg | 3,117 | 1,195 | 467 | 291 | 1,441 | 696 | 364 | 140 |
| Denmark | 532 | 227 | 146 | 65 | 584 | 284 | 98 | 12 |
| Finland | 195 | 99 | 56 | 21 | 276 | 114 | 52 | 35 |
| France | 3,503 | 1,483 | 699 | 475 | 3,031 | 942 | 396 | 132 |
| Germany, West | 5,982 | 2,741 | 1,272 | (2) | 7,215 | 3,127 | 897 | — |
| Greece | 539 | 203 | 103 | 107 | 176 | 52 | 33 | 17 |
| Iceland | 36 | 13 | 12 | 6 | 159 | 47 | 10 | 4 |
| Ireland | 378 | 112 | 43 | 47 | 234 | 135 | 28 | 2 |
| Italy | 2,788 | 1,353 | 715 | 369 | 3,038 | 1,316 | 393 | 109 |
| Malta | 29 | 6 | (2) | (2) | 4 | 1 | (2) | (2) |
| Netherlands | 4,796 | 1,651 | 817 | 251 | 1,477 | 528 | 213 | 85 |
| Norway | 541 | 196 | 108 | 95 | 754 | 142 | 66 | 41 |
| Portugal | 551 | 126 | 45 | 34 | 146 | 92 | 35 | 21 |
| Spain | 1,875 | 712 | 208 | 46 | 970 | 353 | 88 | 50 |
| Sweden | 1,099 | 543 | 301 | 99 | 990 | 399 | 170 | 71 |
| Switzerland | 1,359 | 700 | 254 | 130 | 1,085 | 459 | 198 | 110 |
| Turkey | 424 | 315 | 178 | 84 | 145 | 70 | 60 | 61 |
| United Kingdom | 5,380 | 2,536 | 1,487 | 548 | 5,068 | 2,194 | 993 | 335 |
| Yugoslavia | 357 | 168 | 88 | 43 | 335 | 96 | 41 | 19 |
| Soviet Bloc | 2,544 | 354 | 194 | 27 | 914 | 226 | 81 | 81 |
| Bulgaria | 24 | 15 | 73 | 857 | 18 | 2 | 1 | 2 |
| Czechoslovakia | 75 | 22 | 5 | 11 | 37 | 24 | 12 | 27 |
| Germany, East | 36 | 32 | 4 | (2) | 17 | 9 | 3 | (2) |
| Hungary | 81 | 28 | 2 | 3 | 47 | 6 | 2 | 2 |
| Poland | 439 | 70 | 143 | 9 | 325 | 98 | 39 | 11 |
| Romania | 260 | 66 | 1 | 2 | 233 | 13 | 1 | (1) |
| U.S.S.R. | 1,628 | 119 | 39 | 1 | 234 | 72 | 23 | 38 |

| Area and country | Exports, including re-exports 1977 | 1970 | 1960 | 1950 | General imports 1977 | 1970 | 1960 | 1950 |
|---|---|---|---|---|---|---|---|---|
| **ASIA AND OCEANIA** | | | | | | | | |
| Total Asia and Oceania | 35,288 | 11,294 | 4,700 | 1,691 | 51,312 | 9,103 | 2,987 | 1,846 |
| Near East | 11,020 | 1,423 | 532 | 228 | 12,981 | 10,515 | 312 | 131 |
| Bahrain | 203 | 12 | 8 | 7 | 74 | 8 | 3 | 2 |
| Egypt | 982 | 77 | 151 | 34 | 170 | 23 | 32 | 55 |
| Iran | 2,731 | 326 | 156 | 38 | 2,789 | 67 | 51 | 24 |
| Iraq | 211 | 22 | 37 | 10 | 382 | 3 | 27 | 12 |
| Israel | 1,447 | 592 | 130 | (2) | 570 | 150 | 27 | (2) |
| Jordan | 302 | 63 | 20 | 1 | 3 | (1) | 92 | 8 |
| Kuwait | 548 | 62 | 41 | 3 | 215 | 25 | 124 | 42 |
| Lebanon | 124 | 64 | 45 | 28 | 43 | 13 | 3 | 4 |
| Oman | 57 | — | — | — | 424 | — | — | — |
| Qatar | 113 | — | — | — | 292 | — | — | — |
| Saudi Arabia | 3,575 | 141 | 46 | 34 | 6,359 | 20 | 65 | 24 |
| Syria | 134 | 11 | 38 | 11 | 16 | 2 | 7 | 12 |
| United Arab Emirates | 515 | — | — | — | 1,641 | — | — | — |
| Yemen Arab Republic | 46 | — | — | — | 1 | — | — | — |
| Far East | 21,219 | 8,682 | 1,979 | 1 | 36,405 | 8,682 | 2,406 | 1,360 |
| Bangladesh | 156 | — | — | — | 59 | — | — | — |
| Brunei | 39 | 10[3] | — | — | 119 | (1,3) | — | — |
| China | 171 | — | — | 37 | 203 | (1) | (1) | 146 |
| China (Taiwan) | 1,798 | 527 | 278 | 40 | 3,681 | 549 | 20 | 3 |
| Hong Kong | 1,292 | 406 | 125 | 104 | 2,916 | 944 | 139 | 5 |
| India | 779 | 574 | 642 | 217 | 781 | 298 | 228 | 259 |
| Indonesia | 763 | 266 | 100 | 85 | 3,491 | 182 | 216 | 156 |
| Japan | 10,522 | 4,652 | 1,447 | 418 | 18,623 | 5,875 | 1,149 | 182 |
| Korea, South | 2,371 | 643 | 231 | (2) | 2,895 | 370 | 5 | (2) |
| Malaysia[4] | 561 | 67 | 18 | (2) | 1,322 | 270 | 156 | (2) |
| Pakistan | 293 | 328 | 170 | 31 | 57 | 80 | 36 | 31 |
| Philippines | 876 | 373 | 307 | 247 | 1,103 | 472 | 307 | 236 |
| Singapore | 1,172 | 240 | 42 | (2) | 875 | 81 | 19 | (2) |
| Sri Lanka | 53 | 12 | 14 | 7 | 67 | 26 | 39 | 66 |
| Thailand | 510 | 155 | 71 | 29 | 350 | 100 | 56 | 75 |
| Australia | 2,356 | 986 | 423 | 115 | 1,185 | 611 | 142 | 141 |
| New Zealand and Samoa | 405 | 135 | 78 | 29 | 358 | 222 | 119 | 65 |
| Papua New Guinea | 19 | 18 | 1 | (1) | 79 | 12 | (1) | — |
| **AFRICA** | | | | | | | | |
| Total Africa | 4,563 | 1,425 | 793 | 376 | 16,854 | 1,067 | 534 | 494 |
| Algeria | 527 | 62 | 28 | 16 | 3,065 | 10 | 1 | 5 |
| Angola | 38 | 38 | 11 | 7 | 310 | 68 | 26 | 13 |
| Cameroon | 54 | 19 | — | 5 | 37 | 25 | 6 | — |
| Canary Islands | 85 | 22 | 14 | 6 | 47 | 4 | (1) | (1) |
| Congo | 12 | — | — | — | 32 | — | — | — |
| Ethiopia | 58 | 26 | 12 | 3 | 90 | 67 | 27 | 12 |
| Gabon | 30 | 7 | — | — | 225 | 9 | — | — |
| Ghana | 146 | 59 | 17 | 6 | 214 | 91 | 52 | 61 |
| Guinea | 16 | 7 | — | — | 45 | 77 | — | — |
| Ivory Coast | 89 | 36 | — | — | 318 | 92 | — | — |
| Kenya | 77 | 34 | — | — | 92 | 23 | — | — |
| Liberia | 91 | 46 | 36 | 25 | 107 | 51 | 39 | 21 |
| Libya | 314 | 108 | 43 | (1) | 3,796 | 39 | (1) | (1) |
| Madagascar | 7 | 7[5] | 3 | 4 | 79 | 32[5] | 13 | 8 |
| Morocco | 372 | 89 | 36 | — | 21 | 10 | 10 | — |
| Mozambique | 13 | 22 | 10 | 8 | 66 | 18 | 4 | 3 |
| Nigeria | 958 | 129 | 26 | 6 | 6,096 | 71 | 40 | 35 |
| Rhodesia | 1 | 1 | (2) | 5 | 49 | (1) | 7 | (2) |
| Senegal | 36 | 8 | — | — | 2 | 1 | — | — |
| Sierra Leone | 14 | 8 | — | — | 63 | 8 | — | — |
| South Africa[6] | 1,071 | 563 | 288 | 129 | 1,275 | 290 | 108 | 142 |
| Tanzania | 39 | 12 | — | — | 78 | 24 | — | — |
| Uganda | 14 | 4 | — | — | 248 | 48 | — | — |
| Zaire | 114 | 62 | 27 | 41 | 173 | 41 | 58 | 46 |
| Summary: | | | | | | | | |
| Developed countries | 73,837 | 29,877 | 13,250 | 6,010 | 78,206 | 29,259 | 8,605 | 3,858 |
| Developing countries | 43,282 | 12,993 | 7,131 | 4,193 | 67,480 | 10,442 | 5,965 | 4,767 |
| OPEC and other oil-exporting, less developed countries | 16,476 | 2,659 | — | — | 38,346 | 2,516 | — | — |
| **Total** | **120,163** | **43,224** | **20,575[7]** | **10,275[7]** | **146,817** | **39,952** | **14,654[7]** | **8,852[7]** |

1. Less than $500,000. 2. Not applicable. 3. Includes Bhutan, Maldives, and Portuguese Timor. 4. Excludes Sarawak and Sabah, which are included with Singpore through 1960. 5. Includes French Indian Ocean areas. 6. South-West Africa, Bechuanaland, and Swaziland included for 1950 and 1960; South-West Africa (Namibia) included for 1970 and 1977. 7. Includes Communist areas in Europe and Asia. *Source:* Department of Commerce, Office of International Economic Research.

## Balance of International Payments

**(in billions of dollars)**

| Item | 1977 | 1976 | 1975 | 1974 | 1970 | 1965 | 1960 | 1955 | 1949 |
|---|---|---|---|---|---|---|---|---|---|
| Exports of goods and services (excluding transfers under military grants) | $183.2 | $171.3 | $155.7 | $146.1 | $65.7 | $41.1 | $28.9 | $19.9 | $15.8 |
| Merchandise adjusted, excluding military | 120.6 | 114.7 | 107.1 | 98.3 | 42.5 | 26.5 | 19.7 | 14.4 | 12.2 |
| Transfers under U.S. military agency sales contracts | 7.1 | 5.2 | 3.9 | 3.0 | 1.5 | 0.8 | 0.3 | 0.2 | n.s.s. |
| Receipts of income on U.S. investments abroad | 32.1 | 29.2 | 25.4 | 27.5 | 11.8 | 7.4 | 4.6 | 2.6 | 1.5 |
| Other services | 23.5 | 22.1 | 19.3 | 17.3 | 9.9 | 6.4 | 4.3 | 2.7 | 2.1 |
| Imports of goods and services | −193.7 | −161.9 | −132.6 | −137.2 | −60.0 | −32.8 | −23.7 | −17.8 | −9.6 |
| Merchandise, adjusted, excluding military | −151.6 | −124.0 | −98.0 | −103.6 | −39.9 | −21.5 | −14.8 | −11.5 | −6.9 |
| Direct defense expenditures | −5.7 | −4.9 | −4.8 | −5.0 | −4.9 | −3.0 | −3.1 | −2.9 | −0.6 |
| Payments of income on foreign investments in U.S. | −14.6 | −13.3 | −12.6 | −12.1 | −5.5 | −2.1 | −1.2 | −0.5 | −0.3 |
| Other services | −21.7 | −19.7 | −17.2 | −16.4 | −9.8 | −6.2 | −4.6 | −2.8 | −1.8 |
| Unilateral transfers, excluding military grants, net | −4.7 | −5.0 | −4.6 | −7.2 | −3.3 | −2.9 | −2.3 | −2.5 | −5.6 |
| U.S. Government capital flows, net | −3.7 | −4.2 | −3.5 | 0.4 | −1.6 | −1.6 | −1.1 | −0.3 | −0.7 |
| U.S. private capital flows, net | −30.7 | −43.9 | −35.4 | −33.6 | −10.2 | −5.3 | −5.1 | −1.3 | −0.6 |
| Foreign capital flows, net | 50.9 | 37.0 | 15.6 | 34.7 | 6.4 | 0.7 | 2.3 | −1.4 | 0.2 |
| Transactions in U.S. official reserve assets, net | −0.2 | −2.5 | −0.6 | −1.4 | 2.5 | 1.2 | 2.1 | 0.2 | −0.3 |
| Statistical discrepancy | −1.0 | 9.3 | 5.5 | −1.7 | −0.2 | −0.5 | −1.0 | 0.4 | 0.7 |
| Balance on goods and services | −10.5 | 9.4 | 23.1 | 8.9 | 5.7 | 8.3 | 5.1 | 2.2 | 6.2 |
| Balance on goods, services, and remittances | −12.4 | 7.5 | 21.3 | 7.2 | 4.1 | 7.2 | 4.5 | 1.6 | 5.6 |
| Balance on current account | −15.2 | 4.3 | 18.4 | 1.7 | 2.4 | 5.4 | 2.8 | −0.3 | 0.6 |

NOTE: n.s.s. = not shown separately. — denotes debits; sum of credits equals sum of credits. *Source:* Department of Commerce, Bureau of Economic Analysis.

## Farm Income

**(in millions of dollars)**

| Year | Cash receipts from marketings: Crops | Cash receipts from marketings: Livestock, livestock products | Government payments | Total cash income |
|---|---|---|---|---|
| 1920 | $6,644 | $5,956 | — | $12,600 |
| 1925 | 5,545 | 5,476 | — | 11,021 |
| 1930 | 3,868 | 5,187 | — | 9,055 |
| 1935 | 2,977 | 4,143 | $ 573 | 7,693 |
| 1940 | 3,469 | 4,913 | 723 | 9,105 |
| 1945 | 9,655 | 12,008 | 742 | 22,405 |
| 1950 | 12,356 | 16,105 | 283 | 28,744 |
| 1955 | 13,523 | 15,967 | 229 | 29,719 |
| 1960 | 15,208 | 18,946 | 702 | 34,856 |
| 1965 | 17,392 | 21,958 | 2,463 | 41,813 |
| 1970 | 20,907 | 29,615 | 3,717 | 54,239 |
| 1971 | 22,276 | 30,583 | 3,145 | 56,004 |
| 1972 | 25,520 | 35,670 | 3,961 | 65,151 |
| 1973 | 41,132 | 45,936 | 2,607 | 89,675 |
| 1974 | 51,090 | 41,359 | 531 | 92,980 |
| 1975 | 45,053 | 43,024 | 807 | 88,884 |
| 1976 | 47,937 | 46,389 | 734 | 95,060 |
| 1977 | 47,572 | 47,453 | 1,864 | 96,889 |

*Source:* Department of Agriculture.

## Consumption of Principal Foods[1]

**(in pounds per capita)**

| Foods | 1977[2] | 1957–59 avg | 1935–39 avg |
|---|---|---|---|
| Red meats | 154.8 | 131.4 | 109.8 |
| Poultry | 54.1 | 33.5 | 15.6 |
| Eggs[3] | 34.5 | 45.2 | 36.4 |
| Fluid milk and cream | 237.5 | 337 | 330 |
| Cheese | 16.3 | 7.9 | 5.6 |
| Butter | 4.4 | 8.2 | 17.0 |
| Margarine | 11.6 | 8.9 | 2.9 |
| Fats and oils[4] | 42.6 | 31.5 | 29.3 |
| Fresh fruits | 82.1 | 95.5 | 135.5 |
| Processed fruits[5] | 54.3 | 47.8 | 25.5 |
| Fresh vegetables | 100.3 | 104.1 | 113.2 |
| Processed vegetables | 63.4 | 49.9 | 29.5 |
| Potatoes, sweet potatoes[6] | 83.1 | 106.6 | 139.4 |
| Sugar | 95.7 | 96.1 | 97.5 |
| Corn products[7] | n.a. | 40.1 | 51.9 |
| Wheat flour | 107.6 | 120 | 160 |
| Coffee | 6.8 | 15.7 | 14.0 |
| Cocoa | 2.7 | 3.5 | 4.4 |

1. Civilian consumption, retail equivalent basis. 2. Preliminary. 3. Pounds, not number. 4. Excludes butter and margarine. 5. Pack year. Excludes chilled fruits and juices. 6. Retail weight. 7. Corn used in food products. NOTE: n.a. = not available. *Source:* Department of Agriculture.

## Agricultural Output by States, 1977 Crops

| State | Corn (1,000 bu) | Wheat (1,000 bu) | Cotton (1,000 ba[1]) | Potatoes (1,000 cwt) | Tobacco (1,000 lb) | Cattle[2] (1,000 head) | Swine[3] (1,000 head) |
|---|---|---|---|---|---|---|---|
| Alabama | 10,875 | 2,520 | 277 | 2,010 | 1,045 | 2,130 | 650 |
| Alaska | — | — | — | — | — | 8 | 1 |
| Arizona | 3,000 | 10,080 | 1,135 | 1,755 | — | 1,135 | 102 |
| Arkansas | 2,279 | 25,740 | 1,035 | — | — | 2,120 | 400 |
| California | 28,652 | 43,700 | 2,790 | 21,890 | — | 4,430 | 150 |
| Colorado | 80,620 | 57,100 | — | 11,284 | — | 3,180 | 320 |
| Connecticut | — | — | — | 466 | 5,620 | 108 | 10 |
| Delaware | 10,360 | 1,054 | — | 1,113 | — | 31 | 60 |
| Florida | 10,465 | 377 | 5 | 6,207 | 24,798 | 2,350 | 320 |
| Georgia | 24,000 | 3,300 | 82 | — | 134,875 | 1,975 | 1,720 |
| Hawaii | — | — | — | — | — | 234 | 62 |
| Idaho | 2,408 | 50,730 | — | 88,200 | — | 1,870 | 60 |
| Illinois | 1,152,900 | 68,370 | — | 460 | — | 2,950 | 6,100 |
| Indiana | 633,420 | 55,800 | — | 1,496 | 16,560 | 2,025 | 4,100 |
| Iowa | 1,091,200 | 3,145 | — | 473 | — | 7,800 | 14,500 |
| Kansas | 161,280 | 344,850 | — | — | — | 6,000 | 2,000 |
| Kentucky | 126,900 | 10,138 | 0.7 | — | 452,024 | 3,120 | 1,140 |
| Louisiana | 3,380 | 918 | 656 | 173 | 119 | 1,425 | 160 |
| Maine | — | — | — | 28,320 | — | 132 | 7 |
| Maryland | 43,200 | 4,366 | — | 240 | 29,900 | 390 | 200 |
| Massachusetts | — | — | — | 888 | 1,906 | 99 | 60 |
| Michigan | 191,250 | 33,000 | — | 10,243 | — | 1,470 | 640 |
| Minnesota | 600,000 | 131,894 | — | 15,023 | — | 3,700 | 4,000 |
| Mississippi | 5,760 | 3,570 | 1,645 | 117 | — | 2,130 | 420 |
| Missouri | 205,200 | 60,450 | 235 | — | 5,850 | 6,000 | 3,700 |
| Montana | 748 | 130,920 | — | 2,016 | — | 2,570 | 211 |
| Nebraska | 628,650 | 103,250 | — | 1,695 | — | 6,500 | 3,200 |
| Nevada | — | 1,560 | 1.7 | 5,250 | — | 570 | 9 |
| New Hampshire | — | — | — | 71 | — | 74 | 10 |
| New Jersey | 6,650 | 1,302 | — | 2,147 | — | 114 | 76 |
| New Mexico | 10,260 | 9,137 | 173 | 551 | — | 1,550 | 60 |
| New York | 51,200 | 6,825 | — | 12,082 | — | 1,760 | 125 |
| North Carolina | 86,190 | 6,000 | 53 | 2,711 | 744,525 | 1,100 | 2,300 |
| North Dakota | 16,116 | 229,907 | — | 20,800 | — | 2,050 | 320 |
| Ohio | 380,100 | 72,380 | — | 3,086 | 22,283 | 2,025 | 1,750 |
| Oklahoma | 7,790 | 175,500 | 436 | — | — | 5,900 | 330 |
| Oregon | 1,140 | 45,320 | — | 25,774 | — | 1,490 | 100 |
| Pennsylvania | 106,720 | 8,910 | — | 6,375 | 26,190 | 1,900 | 790 |
| Rhode Island | — | — | — | 943 | — | 10 | 10 |
| South Carolina | 22,320 | 2,755 | 109 | — | 138,720 | 690 | 575 |
| South Dakota | 126,850 | 71,964 | — | 1,062 | — | 3,925 | 1,580 |
| Tennessee | 47,450 | 10,080 | 255 | 405 | 136,746 | 2,700 | 1,180 |
| Texas | 148,500 | 117,500 | 5,500 | 3,339 | — | 14,500 | 890 |
| Utah | 1,157 | 4,716 | — | 1,296 | — | 864 | 42 |
| Vermont | — | — | — | 235 | — | 336 | 7 |
| Virginia | 30,800 | 6,355 | 0.3 | 3,463 | 142,985 | 1,620 | 650 |
| Washington | 5,088 | 101,305 | — | 48,685 | — | 1,275 | 68 |
| West Virginia | 3,996 | 310 | — | 154 | 3,232 | 550 | 60 |
| Wisconsin | 286,000 | 3,075 | — | 18,038 | 24,809 | 4,100 | 1,400 |
| Wyoming | 2,550 | 5,620 | — | 1,474 | — | 1,280 | 32 |
| **Total** | **6,357,424** | **2,025,793** | **14,389** | **352,010** | **1,912,187** | **116,265** | **56,656** |

1. 480-lb net-weight bales. 2. Number on farms as of Jan. 1, 1978. 3. Number on farms as of Dec. 1, 1977. *Source:* Department of Agriculture.

## Annual Railroad Carloadings

| Year | Total | Year | Total | Year | Total | Year | Total |
|---|---|---|---|---|---|---|---|
| 1920 | 33,754,000 | 1945 | 41,918,000 | 1968 | 28,140,000 | 1973 | 27,336,000 |
| 1925 | 34,783,000 | 1950 | 38,903,000 | 1969 | 28,596,000 | 1974 | 26,184,000 |
| 1930 | 30,173,000 | 1955 | 37,636,000 | 1970 | 27,160,000 | 1975 | 23,217,000 |
| 1935 | 22,015,000 | 1960 | 30,441,000 | 1971 | 25,260,000 | 1976 | 23,460,000 |
| 1940 | 36,358,000 | 1965 | 29,248,000 | 1972 | 26,100,000 | 1977 | 22,292,000 |

*Source:* Association of American Railroads.

## Consumer Credit
(in millions of dollars)

| End of year | Installment credit | Noninstallment credit[1] | Charge accounts | Total credit outstanding |
|---|---|---|---|---|
| 1929 | $ 3,524 | $ 1,596 | $ 1,996 | $ 7,116 |
| 1930 | 3,022 | 1,496 | 1,833 | 6,351 |
| 1935 | 2,817 | 1,019 | 1,354 | 5,190 |
| 1940 | 5,514 | 1,353 | 1,471 | 8,338 |
| 1945 | 2,462 | 1,591 | 1,612 | 5,665 |
| 1950 | 14,703 | 3,401 | 3,367 | 21,471 |
| 1955 | 28,906 | 5,129 | 4,795 | 38,830 |
| 1960[2] | 42,968 | 7,844 | 5,329 | 56,141 |
| 1965 | $ 71,324 | $12,560 | $ 6,430 | $ 90,314 |
| 1970 | 101,964 | 17,131 | 7,968 | 127,063 |
| 1973 | 148,177 | 23,661 | 9,198 | 181,036 |
| 1974 | 157,457 | 24,293 | 9,506 | 191,256 |
| 1975 | 164,955 | 25,733 | 9,940 | 200,628 |
| 1976 | 185,489 | 27,784 | 10,907 | 224,180 |
| 1977 | 216,572 | 30,673 | 13,490 | 260,735 |

1. Single payment loans and service credit. 2. Beginning with 1960, data include Alaska and Hawaii. *Source:* Federal Reserve Board.

## Advertising Expenditures by Medium
(in billions)

| Medium | 1977[1] Amt. | 1977 % of total | 1975 Amt. | 1975 % of total | 1970 Amt. | 1970 % of total | 1965 Amt. | 1965 % of total | 1960 Amt. | 1960 % of total | 1950 Amt. | 1950 % of total |
|---|---|---|---|---|---|---|---|---|---|---|---|---|
| Newspapers | $11.1 | 29.1 | $8.4 | 29.9 | $5.8 | 29.3 | $4.5 | 29.2 | $3.7 | 31.0 | $2.1 | 36.4 |
| Magazines | 2.2 | 5.7 | 1.5 | 5.2 | 1.3 | 6.8 | 1.2 | 7.9 | 0.9 | 7.9 | 0.5 | 9.0 |
| Business Papers | 1.2 | 3.1 | 0.9 | 3.3 | 0.7 | 3.8 | 0.7 | 4.4 | 0.6 | 5.1 | 0.3 | 4.4 |
| Radio | 2.6 | 6.8 | 2.0 | 7.0 | 1.3 | 6.5 | 0.9 | 6.0 | 0.7 | 5.8 | 0.6 | 10.6 |
| Television | 7.6 | 20.1 | 5.3 | 18.6 | 3.7 | 18.7 | 2.5 | 16.5 | 1.6 | 13.3 | 0.2 | 3.0 |
| Direct mail | 5.3 | 14.1 | 4.2 | 14.8 | 2.7 | 13.9 | 2.3 | 15.2 | 1.8 | 15.3 | 0.8 | 14.1 |
| Outdoor | 0.4 | 1.1 | 0.3 | 1.2 | 0.2 | 1.2 | 0.2 | 1.2 | 0.2 | 1.7 | 0.1 | 2.5 |
| Miscellaneous[2] | 7.6 | 20.0 | 5.6 | 20.0 | 3.9 | 19.8 | 3.0 | 19.6 | 2.4 | 19.8 | 1.1 | 20.0 |
| **Total** | **38.0** | **100.0** | **28.2** | **100.0** | **19.6** | **100.0** | **15.3** | **100.0** | **11.9** | **100.0** | **5.7** | **100.0** |

1. Preliminary. 2. Includes regional farm papers. *Sources:* McCann-Erickson, Inc., and *Advertising Age.*

## Homes With Selected Electrical Appliances
(in millions)

| Item | 1977 Number | 1977 Percent | 1965 Number | 1965 Percent | 1960 Number | 1960 Percent | 1952 Number | 1952 Percent |
|---|---|---|---|---|---|---|---|---|
| Air conditioners, room | 42.0 | 55.3 | 13.9 | 24.2 | 7.8 | 15.1 | 0.6 | 1.3 |
| Blenders | 38.0 | 50.0 | 7.5 | 13.0 | 4.1 | 8.0 | 1.5 | 3.5 |
| Calculators, electronic | 70.4 | 92.7 | n.a. | n.a. | — | — | — | — |
| Clothes dryers (incl. gas) | 45.0 | 59.3 | 15.2 | 26.4 | 10.1 | 19.6 | 1.5 | 3.6 |
| Clothes washers | 55.6 | 73.3 | 50.3 | 87.4 | 44.1 | 85.4 | 32.2 | 76.2 |
| Coffeemakers | 75.7 | 99.7 | 41.3 | 71.7 | 30.2 | 58.3 | 21.6 | 51.0 |
| Dishwashers | 31.1 | 40.9 | 7.8 | 13.5 | 3.7 | 7.1 | 1.3 | 3.0 |
| Electric blankets | 45.4 | 59.9 | 20.0 | 34.7 | 12.2 | 23.6 | 3.6 | 8.6 |
| Food waste disposers | 32.5 | 42.8 | 7.9 | 13.6 | 5.4 | 10.5 | 1.4 | 3.3 |
| Freezers, home | 34.0 | 44.8 | 15.7 | 27.2 | 12.1 | 23.4 | 4.9 | 11.5 |
| Hair dryers, hand-held | 25.3 | 33.3 | n.a. | n.a. | — | — | — | — |
| Knives, slicing | 31.7 | 41.8 | n.a. | n.a. | — | — | — | — |
| Mixers | 70.1 | 92.4 | 41.9 | 72.8 | 29.0 | 56.0 | 12.6 | 29.7 |
| Radios[1] | 75.8 | 99.9 | 58.2 | 99.3 | 50.3 | 94.3 | 43.7 | 96.2 |
| Ranges, electrical | 54.5 | 71.9 | 24.4 | 42.3 | 19.3 | 37.3 | 10.2 | 24.1 |
| Refrigerators | 75.8 | 99.9 | 57.3 | 99.5 | 50.8 | 98.2 | 37.8 | 89.2 |
| Television: Black and white | 75.8 | 99.9 | 55.9 | 97.1 | 46.2 | 89.4 | 19.8 | 46.7 |
| Color | 61.7 | 81.3 | 5.5 | 9.5 | n.a. | n.a. | n.a. | n.a. |
| Toasters | 75.8 | 99.9 | 48.1 | 83.6 | 37.2 | 72.0 | 30.0 | 70.9 |
| Vacuum cleaners | 75.8 | 99.9 | 48.1 | 83.5 | 38.4 | 74.3 | 25.1 | 59.4 |
| **Total number of wired homes** | **76.0** | **100.0** | **57.6** | **100.0** | **51.7** | **100.0** | **42.3** | **100.0** |

1. Radio data based on 53,300,000 homes in 1960 and 58,566,000 in 1965. NOTE: Percentages based on total number of homes wired for electricity. n.a. = not available. *Sources:* Billboard Publications, Inc., and *Merchandising Week.*

# Women in 1978

*Ruth J. Abram, Executive Director, Women's Action Alliance*

To Houston and the first National Women's Conference in November 1977 came 1,959 delegates, elected by over 100,000 participants in International Women's Year meetings in every U.S. state and territory.

They hammered out the language of 26 planks of a National Plan of Action, calling for an end to sex discrimination. The wide range of issues indicated how deeply rooted sexism and sex discrimination are in our society, and the rudimentary nature of so many of the demands suggests that the nation must travel a long way before equity is realized.

Executive Order 11832, which established International Women's Year and the National Commission on its observance, provided both for the presentation of the Plan of Action to the President and his response. It was given to President Carter on March 22, 1978.

What women want, and some of the reasons why, as expressed by delegates to the first National Women's Conference included:

**1. Equity in arts and humanities.** Women hold 50% of the graduate degrees in art history, but only 25% of faculty positions in that discipline. Women make up 70% of undergraduate English majors, yet only 7% of English professors are women.

**2. A declaration that the elimination of violence in the home is a national goal.** In Boston City Hospital, 70% of emergency room assault victims were women attacked in their homes. In Kansas City, Mo., family assault calls made up 82% of all disturbance calls in 1972. The Harris Poll reports that one out of four men approved of slapping a wife (compared to less than one out of seven women). As of November 1977, there were only 30 shelters for battered women in the U.S.

**3. Equity in all aspects of business.** Women own only 4.6% of all American businesses (1972). Businesses owned by women and minorities combined received less than 1% of all contracts awarded by the federal government (1975).

**4. Prevention and treatment of abused children—** including a bill providing $50 million to implement the Child Abuse Prevention and Treatment Act. 100,000 to 200,000 children are regularly attacked by their parents with cords, sticks, fists, hot irons, cigarettes, and/or booted feet. 700,000 may be denied food, clothing, or shelter. At least 2,000 children die each year of abuse or neglect.

**5. Provision for comprehensive, voluntary, flexible-hour, bias-free, non-sexist, quality child care and developmental programs.** More than 28 million children, nearly one half of the total, have mothers in the labor force (1976). Four and a half million children live in families headed by women.

**6. Enforcement of the federal Equal Credit Opportunity Act of 1974.** Women still face discrimination when they seek credit to buy a car or home, start a business, or finance an education.

**7. Equal opportunity for handicapped women.** Over 20 million women in the United States are handicapped. Only 29% of disabled women are employed, as compared with 60% of disabled men (1972). Laws guaranteeing basic rights to handicapped persons were not accompanied by the compliance systems necessary to implement them.

**8. Equal education and training.** While women make up 63% of all elementary and secondary school teachers, less than 2% are principals in high schools and only 18% are principals in primary schools. Of the 16,000 school districts in the country, only 75 had female administrators (1975). Almost 39% of girls in vocational programs were studying homemaking; only 4.9% were training for higher-paying jobs as compared with 60% of male students (1976). Women are stereotyped, if not invisible, in many of the commonly used texts and library books.

**9. Increased numbers of women in appointive and elective office.** As long as women are absent from the political decision-making process, realization of equity will remain a dream. Except for Muriel Humphrey and Maryon Allen, appointed as temporary replacements for their husbands, there are no women in the Senate. Only 3.6% of the members of the House of Representatives are women (1978). Only 9.3% of all state legislators are women (1978). No woman has ever been appointed to the Supreme Court or elected President or Vice President. 1.1% of all federal judges are women. Only five women have ever been appointed to the Cabinet.

**10. Equal employment opportunity.** One half of all women over 16 were employed or looking for employment in the second quarter of 1978. 79% of all clerical workers and 59% of all service workers are women (1978). Women earn an average of 60% of what men earn.

**11. Adequate health care and services.** Health was the third most popular issue at state IWY meetings. Delegates called for a national health security program which covered women as individuals. Among the health-related demands were: Testing of all drugs, devices, and cosmetics by independent sources and for periods longer than 18 months. Increased research on safe, alternative forms of contraception. Appropriation of federal funds to encourage more women to enter health professions.

**12. Recognition of work in the home as work of equal value.** Homemakers have no health disability insurance, no retirement plan, no social security. Except in eight community property states, homemakers do not legally have an equal share of the couple's economic assets.

**13. Elimination of sex discrimination in insurance, including sex-based rate tables.** Pregnancy is generally not regarded as a disability for purposes of insurance. Health insurance policies often exclude maternity expenses or severely limit maternity benefits.

**14. Equity in international affairs.** Women are as absent from the process of decision-making on international policy as they are on domestic policy. Women occupy only 4.3% of the senior level positions in the State Department. The United States has failed to ratify most of the international conventions relating to women.

**15. Fair representation by and equal access to media.** Women hold only 5% of policy-making positions in media. Women hold only 6% of the technical jobs in the broadcast industry and 3% in the film industry. Women account for only 10% to 15% of presidential appointments to media commissions.

**16. Equity for minority women.** Life expectancy for minority women was 72.3 years, compared with 77.2 for white women (1975). Maternal mortality was 29 per 100,000 minority women, compared with 9.1 for white women. Minority women's unemployment is the highest. Families headed by minority women had a median income of $5,140, compared to $8,226 for those headed by white women.

**17. Elimination of sexism and sex discrimination in the criminal laws and in the treatment of female offenders.** Some states permit indeterminate sentences for women. Women are likely to be incarcerated farther from their homes than men. Women's prisons are less likely to have full-time medical staffs, counseling, library, religious, and recreational services. Men's prisons offer an average of ten vocational training programs, as compared to three for women. Those for women are likely to train for the lowest-paid jobs. Although as many as 80% of female prisoners are mothers, and half of them are the sole support of their children, very few programs exist to address their special needs.

**18. Equity for older women.** Women over 65 have the lowest median income of any age or sex group —$2,800—about half the income of their male counterparts. One third of the women robbed on our city streets are women over 65.

**19. Prevention and control of rape.** 56,000 cases of rape—or one every nine minutes—were reported in 1975. (It is estimated that the actual number of rapes range from 3.5 to 9 times those actually reported.) No arrest is made in 49% of all reported cases; only 58% of those arrested were prosecuted, and one half of those arrested were acquitted or had the charges dismissed.

**20. Support of the right of every woman to control her own reproduction.** The restriction on the use of Medicaid funds for abortion may force poor women back to the illegal abortionist or to acquiescing to compulsory pregnancy. Before the Supreme Court affirmed the right of women to choose abortion, an estimated one million women had illegal abortions per year. With the legalization of abortion, approximately the same number are performed; the only difference is that there are significantly fewer deaths and related complications.

**21. Rural women.** Almost one third of all Americans live in rural areas and account for 40% to 50% of those in poverty. A wife's labor on her farm does not legally earn her equal right to the capital she and her husband have accumulated. Migrant workers suffer a host of abuses and neglect, including low pay and serious health problems.

**22. End to discrimination based on sexual and affectional preference.**

**23. Statistics.** The Office of Management and Budget does not require all departments and agencies to collect, tabulate, and analyze data relating to persons on the basis of sex in order to assess the impact of their programs on women. The U.S. Bureau of the Census does not aggressively pursue its efforts to reduce the undercounts of minority women.

**24. Recognition and treatment of welfare and poverty as a women's issue.** 90% of the families receiving welfare are headed by women.

**25. Ratification of the Equal Rights Amendment.** Delegate support for ratification of the Equal Rights Amendment was overwhelming. Thirty-five of the necessary 38 states have ratified the ERA. The House of Representatives passed Resolution 638 which extends the deadline for ratification to 1981; it has not yet (October 1978) been voted on in the Senate.

**26. Continuing Committee.** The last plank established a Continuing Committee of 470 members throughout the nation to consider steps to achieve the recommendations of the conference. The committee held its first meeting on March 22, 1978, in Washington, D.C.

## Occupations of Employed Women

**(16 years of age and over)**

| Occupations | March 1978 (percent) | 1977[1] (percent) | 1976[1] (percent) |
|---|---|---|---|
| Professional and technical workers | 16.1 | 15.9 | 16.0 |
| Managers and administrators (except farm) | 6.2 | 5.9 | 5.5 |
| Sales workers | 6.8 | 6.8 | 6.7 |
| Clerical workers | 34.8 | 34.7 | 34.9 |

| Occupations | March 1978 (percent) | 1977[1] (percent) | 1976[1] (percent) |
|---|---|---|---|
| Craft and kindred workers | 1.7 | 1.6 | 1.6 |
| Operatives, except transport | 11.1 | 11.2 | 11.3 |
| Transport equipment operatives | .6 | .6 | .6 |
| Nonfarm laborers | 1.0 | 1.2 | 1.1 |
| Private household workers | 2.9 | 3.1 | 3.1 |
| Service workers | 17.7 | 17.9 | 17.9 |
| Farmers and farm managers | .2 | .3 | .3 |
| Farm laborers and supervisors | .9 | 1.0 | 1.0 |

1. Annual averages. NOTE: Details may not add up to totals because of rounding. *Source:* Department of Labor, Women's Bureau.

## Employment by Marital Status and Sex, March 1977
(in thousands)

| Marital status and sex (persons 16 years and over) | Population | Civilian labor force | | | | |
|---|---|---|---|---|---|---|
| | | | | | Unemployed | |
| | | Number | Labor force participation rate | Employed | Number | Percent of labor force |
| Men | 74,541 | 56,392 | 76.6 | 52,187 | 4,206 | 7.5 |
| Never married | 19,553 | 13,186 | 67.8 | 11,189 | 1,996 | 15.1 |
| Married, wife present | 48,002 | 38,704 | 82.0 | 36,987 | 1,717 | 4.4 |
| Other ever married | 6,986 | 4,503 | 65.1 | 4,011 | 492 | 10.9 |
| Married, wife absent | 1,927 | 1,436 | 76.1 | 1,252 | 184 | 12.8 |
| Widowed | 1,887 | 571 | 30.3 | 527 | 45 | 7.8 |
| Divorced | 3,172 | 2,496 | 79.3 | 2,232 | 264 | 10.6 |
| Women | 82,059 | 39,374 | 48.0 | 36,034 | 3,340 | 8.5 |
| Never married | 16,078 | 9,470 | 58.9 | 8,336 | 1,134 | 12.0 |
| Married, husband present | 47,984 | 22,377 | 46.6 | 20,854 | 1,523 | 6.8 |
| Other ever married | 17,997 | 7,526 | 41.8 | 6,844 | 683 | 9.1 |
| Married, husband absent | 3,110 | 1,716 | 55.1 | 1,477 | 237 | 13.8 |
| Widowed | 10,024 | 2,251 | 22.5 | 2,108 | 143 | 6.3 |
| Divorced | 4,863 | 3,561 | 73.2 | 3,258 | 303 | 8.5 |
| **Total: Both sexes** | **156,600** | **95,766** | **61.5** | **88,221** | **7,546** | **7.9** |

NOTE: Due to rounding, sums of individual items may not equal total. *Source:* Department of Labor, Bureau of Labor Statistics.

## Median Income Comparisons of Full-Time Workers by Educational Attainment, 1976
(persons 25 years and over)

| Years of school completed | Median income | | Income gap in dollars | Women's income as a percent of men's | Percent men's income exceeded women's |
|---|---|---|---|---|---|
| | Women | Men | | | |
| Elementary school: | | | | | |
| Less than 8 years | $ 5,644 | $ 8,991 | $ 3,347 | 62.8 | 59.3 |
| 8 years | 6,433 | 11,312 | 4,879 | 56.9 | 75.8 |
| High School: | | | | | |
| 1 to 3 years | 6,800 | 12,301 | 5,501 | 55.3 | 80.9 |
| 4 years | 8,377 | 14,295 | 5,918 | 58.6 | 70.6 |
| College: | | | | | |
| 1 to 3 years | 9,475 | 15,514 | 6,039 | 61.1 | 63.7 |
| 4 years or more | 12,109 | 19,338 | 7,229 | 62.6 | 59.7 |

*Source:* Department of Commerce, Bureau of the Census.

## Women in the Labor Force
(16 years of age and over)

| Labor force status | March 1978 (thousands) | 1977[1] (thousands) | 1976[1] (thousands) |
|---|---|---|---|
| In the labor force: | 40,974 | 39,952 | 38,414 |
| 16 to 19 years of age | 3,991 | 4,267 | 4,138 |
| 20 years and over | 36,983 | 35,685 | 34,276 |
| Employed | 38,098 | 36,685 | 35,095 |
| 16 to 19 years of age | 3,281 | 3,486 | 3,365 |
| 20 years and over | 34,817 | 33,199 | 31,730 |
| Unemployed | 2,876 | 3,267 | 3,320 |
| 16 to 19 years of age | 711 | 781 | 773 |
| 20 years and over | 2,165 | 2,486 | 2,547 |
| Not in the labor force: | 42,406 | 42,510 | 42,789 |
| Women as percent of labor force | 41.6 | 41.0 | 40.5 |
| Total civilian population | 83,380 | 82,462 | 81,203 |

1. Annual averages. *Source:* Department of Labor, Women's Bureau.

## Characteristics of Households With Female Heads

| Characteristics | 1977 |
|---|---|
| All households | 74,142,000 |
| Number with female head | 18,238,000 |
| Percent of all households | 24.6 |
| Persons per household | 2.0 |
| Under 18 years | 10,680,000 |
| Percentage under 18 years | 29.7 |
| 18 years and over | 25,287,000 |
| Percentage 18 years and over | 70.3 |
| Marital status of female head | |
| Married, husband absent | 2,351,000 |
| Widowed | 8,367,000 |
| Divorced | 3,964,000 |
| Single | 3,556,000 |

| Income bracket | Number of households, 1976 |
|---|---|
| Household income of female head | |
| Under $2,000 | 1,605,000 |
| $2,000 to $3,999 | 4,826,000 |
| $4,000 to $5,999 | 3,023,000 |
| $6,000 to $7,999 | 2,148,000 |
| $8,000 to $9,999 | 1,779,000 |
| $10,000 to $14,999 | 2,746,000 |
| $15,000 to $24,999 | 1,642,000 |
| $25,000 to $49,999 | 438,000 |
| $50,000 and over | 31,000 |
| Median income | $5,762 |

*Source:* Department of Commerce, Bureau of the Census.

## Comparison of Median Earnings of Full-Time Workers by Sex
(persons 14 years and over)

| Year | Median earnings: Women | Median earnings: Men | Earnings gap in dollars | Women's earnings as a percent of men's | Percent men's earnings exceeded women's | Earnings gap in constant 1967 dollars |
|---|---|---|---|---|---|---|
| 1960 | $3,293 | $5,417 | $2,124 | 60.8 | 64.5 | $2,394 |
| 1965 | 3,823 | 6,375 | 2,552 | 60.0 | 66.8 | 2,700 |
| 1970 | 5,323 | 8,966 | 3,643 | 59.4 | 68.4 | 3,133 |
| 1971 | 5,593 | 9,399 | 3,806 | 59.5 | 68.0 | 3,136 |
| 1972 | 5,903 | 10,202 | 4,299 | 57.9 | 72.8 | 3,435 |
| 1973 | 6,335 | 11,186 | 4,851 | 56.6 | 76.6 | 3,649 |
| 1974 | 6,772 | 11,835 | 5,063 | 57.2 | 74.8 | 3,433 |
| 1975 | 7,504 | 12,758 | 5,254 | 58.8 | 70.0 | 3,264 |
| 1976 | 8,099 | 13,455 | 5,356 | 60.2 | 66.1 | 3,114 |

NOTE: For 1970–74, data include wage and salary income and earnings from self-employment; for 1960 and 1965, data include wage and salary income only. *Source:* Department of Commerce, Bureau of the Census.

## Earnings Distribution of Full-Time Workers, by Sex, 1976
(persons 14 years old and over)

| Earnings group | Number (in thousands) | | Distribution (percent) | | Likelihood of a woman rather than a man to be in each earnings group (percent)[1] |
|---|---|---|---|---|---|
| | Women | Men | Women | Men | |
| Less than $3,000 | 704 | 1,137 | 3.9 | 3.0 | 1.3 |
| $3,000 to $4,999 | 1,887 | 1,136 | 10.4 | 3.0 | 3.5 |
| $5,000 to $6,999 | 4,201 | 2,515 | 23.2 | 6.7 | 3.5 |
| $7,000 to $9,999 | 5,716 | 5,702 | 31.6 | 14.9 | 3.1 |
| $10,000 to $14,999 | 4,259 | 11,671 | 23.6 | 30.6 | .8 |
| $15,000 and over | 1,305 | 16,022 | 7.2 | 42.0 | .2 |
| Total with earnings | 18,073 | 38,184 | 100.0 | 100.0 | 1.0 |

1. Figures obtained by dividing percentages for women by percentages for men. *Source:* Department of Commerce, Bureau of the Census.

## Unemployment Rate, 1977

| Race and age | Unemployment rate in 1977 | |
|---|---|---|
| | Women | Men |
| All races: | 8.2 | 6.2 |
| 16 to 19 years | 18.3 | 17.3 |
| 20 years and over | 7.0 | 5.2 |
| White | 7.3 | 5.5 |
| 16 to 19 years | 15.9 | 15.0 |
| 20 years and over | 6.2 | 4.6 |
| Minority races | 14.0 | 12.4 |
| 16 to 19 years | 39.9 | 37.0 |
| 20 years and over | 11.7 | 10.0 |

*Source:* Department of Labor, Women's Bureau.

## Median Incomes of Full-Time Women Workers
(persons 14 years and over)

| Major occupation group | 1976 income | As percent of men's income |
|---|---|---|
| Professional and technical workers | $11.081 | 68 |
| Nonfarm managers and administrators | 10.177 | 59 |
| Clerical workers | 8,138 | 64 |
| Sales workers | 6,350 | 44 |
| Operatives (including transport) | 6,696 | 57 |
| Service workers (except private household | 5,969 | 59 |

*Source:* Department of Labor, Women's Bureau.

## Mothers Participating in Labor Force
(figures in percentage)

| Year | Mothers with children | | |
|---|---|---|---|
| | Under 18 years | 6 to 17 years | Under 6 years[1] |
| 1977 | 50.7 | 58.3 | 40.9 |
| 1976 | 48.8 | 56.2 | 39.7 |
| 1975 | 47.4 | 54.8 | 38.9 |
| 1965 | 35.0 | 45.7 | 25.3 |
| 1955 | 27.0 | 38.4 | 18.2 |
| 1950 | 21.6 | 32.8 | 13.6 |

1. May also have older children. NOTE: For 1950 and 1955, data are for April; for 1965 and 1975–77, data are for March. *Source:* Department of Labor, Women's Bureau.

## Desirable Weights[1]

### Men Age 25 and Over

| Height (with shoes on—1-inch heels) feet | inches | Small frame | Medium frame | Large frame |
|---|---|---|---|---|
| 5 | 2 | 112–120 | 118–129 | 126–141 |
| 5 | 3 | 115–123 | 121–133 | 129–144 |
| 5 | 4 | 118–126 | 124–136 | 132–148 |
| 5 | 5 | 121–129 | 127–139 | 135–152 |
| 5 | 6 | 124–133 | 130–143 | 138–156 |
| 5 | 7 | 128–137 | 134–147 | 142–161 |
| 5 | 8 | 132–141 | 138–152 | 147–166 |
| 5 | 9 | 136–145 | 142–156 | 151–170 |
| 5 | 10 | 140–150 | 146–160 | 155–174 |
| 5 | 11 | 144–154 | 150–165 | 159–179 |
| 6 | 0 | 148–158 | 154–170 | 164–184 |
| 6 | 1 | 152–162 | 158–175 | 168–189 |
| 6 | 2 | 156–167 | 162–180 | 173–194 |
| 6 | 3 | 160–171 | 167–185 | 178–199 |
| 6 | 4 | 164–175 | 172–190 | 182–204 |

### Women Age 25 and Over[2]

| Height (with shoes on—2-inch heels) feet | inches | Small frame | Medium frame | Large frame |
|---|---|---|---|---|
| 4 | 10 | 92–98 | 96–107 | 104–119 |
| 4 | 11 | 94–101 | 98–110 | 106–122 |
| 5 | 0 | 96–104 | 101–113 | 109–125 |
| 5 | 1 | 99–107 | 104–116 | 112–128 |
| 5 | 2 | 102–110 | 107–119 | 115–131 |
| 5 | 3 | 105–113 | 110–122 | 118–134 |
| 5 | 4 | 108–116 | 113–126 | 121–138 |
| 5 | 5 | 111–119 | 116–130 | 125–142 |
| 5 | 6 | 114–123 | 120–135 | 129–146 |
| 5 | 7 | 118–127 | 124–139 | 133–150 |
| 5 | 8 | 122–131 | 128–143 | 137–154 |
| 5 | 9 | 126–135 | 132–147 | 141–158 |
| 5 | 10 | 130–140 | 136–151 | 145–163 |
| 5 | 11 | 134–144 | 140–155 | 149–168 |
| 6 | 0 | 138–148 | 144–159 | 153–173 |

1. Weight in pounds according to frame (in indoor clothing). 2. For girls between 18 and 25, subtract 1 pound for each year under 25. *Source:* Metropolitan Life Insurance Company.

## Hospital Facilities, 1976

| State | Hospitals[1] | Beds | Admissions during year |
|---|---|---|---|
| Alabama | 146 | 25,005 | 704,339 |
| Alaska | 25 | 1,571 | 54,672 |
| Arizona | 80 | 11,057 | 360,870 |
| Arkansas | 96 | 13,295 | 422,504 |
| California | 631 | 119,409 | 3,315,128 |
| Colorado | 100 | 14,726 | 468,238 |
| Connecticut | 67 | 19,535 | 456,123 |
| Delaware | 15 | 4,567 | 81,263 |
| D.C. | 20 | 10,612 | 214,397 |
| Florida | 243 | 53,365 | 1,515,993 |
| Georgia | 186 | 30,883 | 916,492 |
| Hawaii | 27 | 3,883 | 115,934 |
| Idaho | 52 | 3,668 | 133,020 |
| Illinois | 287 | 77,312 | 2,022,420 |
| Indiana | 139 | 34,862 | 868,354 |
| Iowa | 143 | 21,721 | 572,307 |
| Kansas | 164 | 18,183 | 459,820 |
| Kentucky | 125 | 19,432 | 637,073 |
| Louisiana | 154 | 24,726 | 731,915 |
| Maine | 54 | 7,294 | 181,191 |
| Maryland | 81 | 25,103 | 536,568 |
| Massachusetts | 190 | 48,329 | 956,789 |
| Michigan | 253 | 53,223 | 1,457,691 |
| Minnesota | 189 | 31,385 | 740,388 |
| Mississippi | 111 | 17,262 | 451,897 |
| Missouri | 171 | 35,139 | 958,841 |
| Montana | 65 | 4,397 | 144,183 |
| Nebraska | 108 | 11,403 | 310,450 |
| Nevada | 23 | 3,248 | 101,586 |
| New Hampshire | 33 | 5,113 | 134,971 |
| New Jersey | 144 | 47,645 | 1,078,263 |
| New Mexico | 54 | 6,629 | 189,763 |
| New York | 394 | 151,997 | 2,825,305 |
| North Carolina | 159 | 34,064 | 909,927 |
| North Dakota | 60 | 5,740 | 146,838 |
| Ohio | 248 | 70,378 | 1,857,212 |
| Oklahoma | 140 | 17,123 | 505,483 |
| Oregon | 87 | 12,085 | 370,712 |
| Pennsylvania | 318 | 92,565 | 1,982,043 |
| Rhode Island | 21 | 7,315 | 145,945 |
| South Carolina | 88 | 17,627 | 466,935 |
| South Dakota | 70 | 5,828 | 146,771 |
| Tennessee | 154 | 30,543 | 861,418 |
| Texas | 563 | 77,605 | 2,355,994 |
| Utah | 38 | 4,954 | 192,944 |
| Vermont | 21 | 3,568 | 79,149 |
| Virginia | 129 | 32,217 | 788,342 |
| Washington | 129 | 16,295 | 581,817 |
| West Virginia | 85 | 15,827 | 406,943 |
| Wisconsin | 172 | 31,146 | 790,694 |
| Wyoming | 30 | 2,656 | 67,855 |
| **Total** | **7,582** | **1,433,505** | **36,775,770** |

1. All registered hospitals. Data estimated for nonreporting hospitals. NOTE: Data are latest available. *Source:* American Hospital Association.

## Major Nutrients and Where to Find Them

For Recommended Daily Dietary Allowances and Nutritional Values, see page 85.

| Nutrient[1] [2] | What they do | Where found |
|---|---|---|
| Protein | Keeps body processes working. Carries oxygen into system. Produces antibodies in blood stream that fight off disease and infection. Builds muscle tissue. | Meat, poultry, fish, milk, cheese, eggs, bread, cereal, and vegetables (soybeans, dry beans, and peanuts). |
| Fats | Provide energy. Some contain vitamins A,D,E, and K. Protect vital organs by providing a cushion around them. | Butter, margarine, shortening, salad oils and dressings, cream, most cheeses, mayonnaise, nuts, and bacon. |
| Carbohydrates | Major source of energy. Help body make best use of other nutrients. | Wheat, oats, corn and rice and foods made from them, such as bread and pasta. Potatoes, sweet potatoes, peas, dry beans, peanuts, and soybeans. Dried fruits. |
| Minerals | | |
| Calcium | Builds bones and teeth. Aids blood clotting and heart function. Aids nervous system. | Milk and cheese. Dark green leafy vegetables (collards, mustard or turnip greens). Salmon and sardine bones. |
| Iron | Combines with protein to make hemoglobin. Needed to prevent iron deficiency anemia. | Liver, heart, kidney, shellfish (especially oysters). Enriched bread and cereals. Dark leafy green vegetables. |
| Iodine | Assists thyroid gland function. Prevents goiter | Iodized salt and seafood. |
| Vitamins | | |
| Vitamin A (retinol) | Needed for normal vision. Protects against night blindness. Keeps skin and mucous membranes resistant to infection. | Spinach, beet and turnip greens, carrots, squash, sweet potatoes. Yellow peaches, apricots, cantaloupe, and papayas also help. Liver and whole milk. |
| Vitamin $B_1$ (thiamin) | Promotes normal appetite and digestion. Necessary for a healthy nervous system. | Lean pork, dry beans, some of the organ meats, some nuts. Enriched or whole-grain breads and cereals. |
| Vitamin $B_2$ (riboflavin) | Helps cells use oxygen. Helps maintain good vision. Needed for good skin. | Meats, milk, whole grain or enriched breads and cereals. Green leafy vegetables. |
| Vitamin $B_6$ and $B_{12}$, Folacin | Maintain normal hemoglobin (carry oxygen to tissues). | Occur in foods of animal origin, brown rice, bananas, pears. |
| Vitamin C (ascorbic acid) | Maintains cementing material that holds body cells together. Needed for healthy gums. Aids body to resist infection. | Citrus fruits and juices, potatoes, sweet potatoes, tomatoes, peppers, green vegetables (broccoli, turnip greens, raw cabbage, and collards.) |
| Vitamin D | Builds strong bones and teeth. Aids calcium absorption. | Milk fortified with vitamin D, egg yolk, fish liver, liver, oils. Sunlight. |
| Vitamin E | Not fully understood. | Abundant in vegetable oils and margarines. Wheat germ and lettuce. |
| Vitamin K | Aids blood clotting. | Green and leafy vegetables, tomatoes, cauliflower, egg yolks, soybean oil, and liver. |

1. The body also requires zinc, copper, sodium, potassium, magnesium and phosphorus. These show up in most foods of the above. Magnesium abounds in nuts, whole grain products, dry beans and dark green vegetables. Phosphorus is in the same foods that supply you with protein and calcium. 2. The B-Vitamins should be taken together because an inadequate intake of one may impair the utilization of the other. *Source:* Department of Agriculture, Science and Education Administration.

## Calories, Minerals, and Vitamins of Selected Foods

| Food and amount | Energy (calories) | Nutrients: Protein (gm) | Nutrients: Fat (gm) | Minerals: Calcium (mg) | Minerals: Iron (mg) | Vitamins: Vitamin A (IU) | Vitamins: Vitamin B₁ (thiamin) (mg) | Vitamins: Vitamin B₂ (riboflavin) (mg) | Vitamins: Niacin (mg) | Vitamins: Vitamin C (ascorbic acid) (mg) |
|---|---|---|---|---|---|---|---|---|---|---|
| Apple, 1 medium, raw | 80 | — | 1 | 10 | .4 | 120 | .04 | .03 | .1 | 6 |
| Applesauce, 1 cup, canned, unsweetened | 100 | — | — | 10 | 1.2 | 100 | .05 | .02 | .1 | 2 |
| Bacon, 2 slices, crisp | 85 | 4 | 8 | 2 | .5 | — | .08 | .05 | .8 | — |
| Banana, 1 medium | 100 | 1 | — | 10 | .8 | 230 | .06 | .07 | .8 | 12 |
| Beans, snap green, 1 cup cooked | 30 | 2 | — | 63 | .8 | 680 | .09 | .11 | .6 | 15 |
| Beans, red kidney, 1 cup canned | 230 | 15 | 1 | 74 | 4.6 | 10 | .13 | .10 | 1.5 | — |
| Beans, baked, pork and molasses, 1 cup | 385 | 16 | 12 | 161 | 5.9 | — | .15 | .10 | 1.3 | — |
| Beef cuts, cooked: Chuck, boned, 3 ounces | 245 | 23 | 16 | 10 | 2.9 | 30 | .04 | .18 | 3.6 | — |
| Hamburger, 3 ounces | 235 | 20 | 17 | 9 | 2.6 | 30 | .07 | .17 | 4.4 | — |
| Rib roast, 3 ounces boned | 375 | 17 | 33 | 8 | 2.2 | 70 | .05 | .13 | 3.1 | — |
| Round, 3 ounces boned | 220 | 24 | 13 | 10 | 3.0 | 20 | .07 | .19 | 4.8 | — |
| Sirloin, 3 ounces boned | 330 | 20 | 27 | 9 | 2.5 | 50 | .05 | .15 | 4.0 | — |
| Beef stew with vegetables, 1 cup | 220 | 16 | 11 | 29 | 2.9 | 2,400 | .15 | .17 | 4.7 | 17 |
| Beets, 1 cup cooked | 55 | 2 | — | 24 | .9 | 30 | .05 | .07 | .5 | 10 |
| Breads: Cracked wheat, ½-inch slice | 65 | 2 | 1 | 22 | .5 | — | .08 | .06 | .8 | — |
| Italian, average slice, enriched | 85 | 3 | — | 5 | .7 | — | .12 | .07 | 1.0 | — |
| Raisin, ½-inch slice enriched | 65 | 2 | 1 | 18 | .6 | — | .09 | .06 | .6 | — |
| Rye (American), ½-inch slice | 60 | 2 | — | 19 | .5 | — | .07 | .05 | .7 | — |
| White, ½-inch slice enriched | 70 | 2 | 1 | 21 | .6 | — | .10 | .06 | .8 | — |
| Whole wheat, ½-inch slice | 65 | 3 | 1 | 24 | .8 | — | .09 | .03 | .8 | — |
| Butter, 1 tbsp. | 100 | — | 12 | 3 | — | 430 | — | — | — | — |
| Cabbage, 1 cup, raw, coarsely shredded | 15 | 1 | — | 34 | .3 | 90 | .04 | .04 | .2 | 33 |
| Cake: Sponge, average slice | 195 | 5 | 4 | 20 | 1.1 | 300 | .09 | .14 | .6 | — |
| Pound, average slice | 160 | 2 | 10 | 6 | .5 | 80 | .05 | .06 | .4 | — |
| Candies: Caramels, 1 ounce | 115 | 1 | 3 | 42 | .4 | — | .01 | .05 | .1 | — |
| Chocolate, milk, 1 ounce | 145 | 2 | 9 | 65 | .3 | 80 | .02 | .10 | .1 | — |
| Cantaloup, ½ melon | 80 | 2 | — | 38 | 1.1 | 9,240 | .11 | .08 | 1.6 | 90 |
| Carrot, raw, 1 average size | 30 | 1 | — | 27 | .5 | 7,930 | .04 | .04 | .4 | 6 |
| Catsup, 1 tbsp. | 15 | — | — | 3 | .1 | 210 | .01 | .01 | .2 | 2 |
| Cheese: Cheddar, 1 ounce | 115 | 7 | 9 | 204 | .2 | 300 | .01 | .11 | — | — |
| Cottage, creamed, 1 cup | 235 | 28 | 10 | 135 | .3 | 370 | .05 | .37 | .3 | — |
| Cottage, uncreamed, 1 cup | 125 | 25 | 1 | 46 | .3 | 40 | .04 | .21 | .2 | — |
| Cream cheese, 1 ounce | 100 | 2 | 10 | 23 | .3 | 400 | — | .06 | — | — |
| Swiss, natural, 1 ounce | 105 | 8 | 8 | 272 | — | 240 | .01 | .10 | — | — |
| Swiss, process, 1 ounce | 95 | 7 | 7 | 219 | .2 | 230 | — | .08 | — | — |
| Chicken, broiled, 3 ounces | 115 | 20 | 3 | 8 | 1.4 | 80 | .05 | .16 | 7.4 | — |

| | | | | | | | | | | |
|---|---|---|---|---|---|---|---|---|---|---|
| Chicken, fried, ½ breast, 3.3 ounces | 160 | 26 | 5 | 9 | 1.3 | 70 | .04 | .17 | 11.6 | — |
| Chicken, canned, boned, 3 ounces | 170 | 18 | 10 | 13 | 1.3 | 200 | .03 | .11 | 3.7 | 3 |
| Clams, raw, 3 ounces | 65 | 11 | 1 | 59 | 5.2 | 90 | .08 | .15 | 1.1 | 8 |
| Cocoa, 1 cup, homemade | 220 | 9 | 9 | 298 | .8 | 320 | .10 | .44 | .4 | 2 |
| Coffee; black, 1 cup | — | — | — | — | — | — | — | — | — | — |
| Cola, carbonated, 12 ounces | 145 | — | — | — | — | — | — | — | — | — |
| Corn, average ear | 70 | 2 | 1 | 2 | .5 | 310 | .09 | .08 | 1.1 | 7 |
| Corn flakes, 1 cup | 95 | 2 | — | 3 | .6 | 1,180 | .29 | .35 | 2.9 | 9 |
| Crabmeat, canned, 3 ounces | 85 | 15 | 2 | 38 | .7 | — | .07 | .07 | 1.6 | — |
| Crackers, Graham, 4 | 110 | 2 | 3 | 11 | 1.0 | — | .04 | .16 | 1.0 | — |
| Saltines, 4 | 50 | 1 | 1 | 2 | .5 | — | .05 | .05 | .4 | — |
| Cream: Light, table, 1 cup | 470 | 6 | 46 | 231 | .1 | 1,730 | .08 | .36 | .1 | 2 |
| Heavy, whipping, 1 cup | 820 | 5 | 88 | 154 | .1 | 3,500 | .05 | .26 | .1 | 1 |
| Sour, 1 cup | 495 | 7 | 48 | 268 | .1 | 1,820 | .08 | .34 | .2 | 2 |
| Whipped topping (pressurized), 1 cup | 155 | 2 | 13 | 61 | — | 550 | .02 | .04 | — | — |
| Doughnut, 1 plain | 100 | 1 | 5 | 10 | .4 | 20 | .05 | .05 | .4 | — |
| Egg: Raw or cooked in shell, 1 | 80 | 6 | 6 | 28 | 1.0 | 260 | .04 | .14 | — | — |
| Omelet, scrambled, 1 | 95 | 6 | 7 | 47 | .9 | 310 | .04 | .16 | — | — |
| Frankfurter, 1 | 170 | 7 | 15 | 3 | .8 | — | .08 | .11 | 1.4 | — |
| Fruit cocktail, 1 cup canned | 195 | 1 | — | 23 | 1.0 | 360 | .05 | .03 | 1.0 | 5 |
| Grapefruit: Raw, ½ | 45 | 1 | — | 19 | .5 | 10 | .05 | .02 | .2 | 44 |
| Canned, syrup, 1 cup | 180 | 2 | — | 33 | .8 | 30 | .08 | .05 | .5 | 76 |
| Juice, fresh, 1 cup | 95 | 1 | — | 22 | .5 | 20 | .10 | .05 | .5 | 93 |
| Haddock, breaded, fried, 3 ounces | 140 | 17 | 5 | 34 | 1.0 | — | .03 | .06 | 2.7 | 2 |
| Honey, strained, 1 tbsp. | 65 | — | — | 1 | .1 | — | — | .01 | .1 | — |
| Ice cream, 1 cup | 270 | 5 | 14 | 176 | .1 | 540 | .05 | .33 | .1 | 1 |
| Jellies, 1 tbsp. | 50 | — | — | 4 | .3 | — | — | .01 | — | 1 |
| Lamb: Rib chop, boned, 4 ounces | 400 | 25 | 33 | 10 | 1.5 | — | .14 | .25 | 5.6 | — |
| Leg roast, 3 ounces, boned | 235 | 22 | 16 | 9 | 1.4 | — | .13 | .23 | 4.7 | — |
| Lemon, 1 medium | 20 | 1 | — | 19 | .4 | 10 | .03 | .01 | .1 | 39 |
| Liver: Beef, fried, 2 ounces | 130 | 15 | 6 | 6 | 5.0 | 30,280 | .15 | 2.37 | 9.4 | 15 |
| Luncheon meat: Boiled ham, 2 ounces | 135 | 11 | 10 | 6 | 1.6 | — | .25 | .09 | 1.5 | — |
| Canned, spiced or unspiced, 2 ounces | 165 | 8 | 14 | 5 | 1.2 | — | .18 | .12 | 1.6 | — |
| Macaroni, enriched, 1 cup | 155 | 5 | 1 | 11 | 1.3 | — | .20 | .11 | 1.5 | — |
| Macaroni and cheese, 1 cup | 430 | 17 | 22 | 362 | 1.8 | 860 | .20 | .40 | 1.8 | — |
| Margarine, 1 tbsp. | 100 | — | 12 | 3 | — | 470 | — | — | — | — |
| Mayonnaise, 1 tbsp. | 100 | — | 11 | 3 | .1 | 40 | — | .01 | — | — |
| Milk: Whole, 1 cup | 150 | 8 | 8 | 291 | .1 | 310 | .09 | .40 | .2 | 2 |
| Skim (non-fat), 1 cup | 85 | 8 | — | 302 | .1 | 500 | .09 | .34 | .2 | 2 |
| Buttermilk, 1 cup | 100 | 8 | 2 | 285 | .1 | 80 | .08 | .38 | .1 | 2 |
| Mushrooms, canned, 1 cup | 40 | 5 | — | 15 | 1.2 | — | .04 | .60 | 4.8 | 4 |
| Nuts: Almonds, 1 cup shelled | 850 | 26 | 77 | 332 | 6.7 | — | .34 | 1.31 | 5.0 | — |
| Peanuts, roasted, 1 cup | 840 | 37 | 72 | 107 | 3.0 | — | .46 | .19 | 24.8 | — |
| Oatmeal, 1 cup cooked | 130 | 5 | 2 | 22 | 1.4 | — | .19 | .05 | .2 | — |
| Oils, salad, cooking, 1 tbsp. | 120 | — | 14 | — | — | — | — | — | — | — |
| Orange, 1 medium | 65 | 1 | — | 54 | .5 | 260 | .13 | .05 | .5 | 66 |

| Food and amount | Energy (calories) | Nutrients: Protein (gm) | Nutrients: Fat (gm) | Minerals: Calcium (mg) | Minerals: Iron (mg) | Vitamins: Vitamin A (IU) | Vitamins: Vitamin B₁ (thiamin) (mg) | Vitamins: Vitamin B₂ (riboflabin) (mg) | Vitamins: Niacin (mg) | Vitamins: Vitamin C (ascorbic acid) (mg) |
|---|---|---|---|---|---|---|---|---|---|---|
| Orange juice, fresh, 1 cup | 110 | 2 | — | 27 | .5 | 500 | .22 | .07 | 1.0 | 124 |
| Frozen, diluted with 3 parts water, 1 cup | 120 | 2 | — | 25 | .2 | 540 | .23 | .03 | .9 | 120 |
| Oysters, raw, 1 cup | 160 | 20 | 4 | 226 | 13.2 | 740 | .34 | .43 | 6.0 | — |
| Pancake, wheat, 1 average | 60 | 2 | 2 | 27 | .4 | 30 | .06 | .07 | .5 | — |
| Peach, raw, 1 medium | 40 | 1 | — | 9 | .5 | 1,330 | .02 | .05 | 1.0 | 7 |
| Peanut butter, 1 tbsp. | 95 | 4 | 8 | 9 | .3 | — | .02 | .02 | 2.4 | — |
| Peas, green, 1 cup | 115 | 9 | 1 | 37 | 2.9 | 860 | .45 | .18 | 3.7 | 32 |
| Pie: Apple, 4-inch wedge | 345 | 3 | 15 | 11 | .9 | 40 | .15 | .11 | 1.3 | 2 |
| Cherry, 4-inch wedge | 350 | 4 | 15 | 19 | .9 | 590 | .16 | .12 | 1.4 | — |
| Lemon meringue, 4-inch wedge | 305 | 4 | 12 | 17 | 1.0 | 200 | .09 | .12 | .7 | 4 |
| Pineapple, raw, 1 cup diced | 80 | 1 | — | 26 | .8 | 110 | .14 | .05 | .3 | 26 |
| Pineapple juice, canned, 1 cup | 140 | 1 | — | 38 | .8 | 130 | .13 | .05 | .5 | 23 |
| Pizza (cheese), 4¾-inch wedge | 145 | 6 | 4 | 86 | 1.1 | 230 | .16 | .18 | 1.6 | 4 |
| Pork: Roast, 3 ounces | 310 | 21 | 24 | 9 | 2.7 | — | .78 | .22 | 4.8 | — |
| Chop, with bone, 2.7 ounces | 305 | 19 | 25 | 9 | 2.7 | — | .75 | .22 | 4.5 | — |
| Potatoes: Baked, 1 medium | 145 | 4 | — | 14 | 1.1 | — | .15 | .07 | 2.7 | 31 |
| French fried, deep fat, 10 pieces | 135 | 2 | 7 | 8 | .7 | — | .07 | .04 | 1.6 | 11 |
| Mashed with milk, 1 cup | 135 | 4 | 2 | 50 | .8 | 40 | .17 | .11 | 2.1 | 21 |
| Potato chips, 10 | 115 | 1 | 8 | 8 | .4 | — | .04 | .01 | 1.0 | 3 |
| Prune juice, 1 cup canned | 195 | 1 | — | 36 | 1.8 | — | .03 | .03 | 1.0 | 5 |
| Rice: White, enriched, 1 cup cooked | 225 | 4 | — | 21 | 1.8 | — | .23 | .02 | 2.1 | — |
| Puffed, 1 cup | 60 | 1 | — | 3 | .3 | — | .07 | .01 | .7 | — |
| Salad dressings: Mayonnaise type, 1 tbsp. | 65 | — | 6 | 2 | — | 30 | — | — | — | — |
| French, 1 tbsp. | 65 | — | 6 | 2 | .1 | — | — | — | — | — |
| French, low calorie, 1 tbsp. | 15 | — | 1 | 2 | .1 | — | — | — | — | — |
| Salmon: Canned, 3 ounces | 120 | 17 | 5 | 167 | .7 | 60 | .03 | .16 | 6.8 | — |
| Sardines, canned, 3 ounces | 175 | 20 | 9 | 372 | 2.5 | 190 | .02 | .17 | 4.6 | — |
| Spaghetti, 1 cup cooked | 155 | 5 | 1 | 11 | 1.3 | — | .20 | .11 | 1.5 | — |
| Spinach, 1 cup cooked | 40 | 5 | 1 | 167 | 4.0 | 14,580 | .13 | .25 | .9 | 50 |
| Sugar, 1 teaspoon | 15 | — | — | — | — | — | — | — | — | — |
| Tomato juice, canned, 1 cup | 45 | 2 | — | 17 | 2.2 | 1,940 | .12 | .07 | 1.9 | 39 |
| Tuna fish, 3 ounces | 170 | 24 | 7 | 7 | 1.6 | 70 | .04 | .10 | 10.1 | — |
| Veal, 3-ounce cutlet | 185 | 23 | 9 | 9 | 2.7 | — | .06 | .21 | 4.6 | — |
| Yogurt, from lowfat milk, 8-oz. container, plain | 145 | 12 | 4 | 415 | .2 | 150 | .10 | .49 | .3 | 2 |

NOTE: Gm—gram; Mg—milligram; IU—International Unit. A dash in a column indicates little or no basis for assigning value. *Source:* Department of Agriculture, Science and Education Administration.

## Recommended Daily Dietary Allowances[1]

**Designed for the maintenance of good nutrition of practically all healthy persons in the U.S. (revised 1974)**

| Persons | Age (years) | Wgt. (lbs) | Wgt. (kg) | Hgt. (in.) | Hgt. (cm) | Fat-Soluble Vitamins: Vitamin A Activity (IU) | Vitamin D (IU) | Vitamin E Activity[2] (IU) | Water-Soluble Vitamins: Ascorbic Acid (mg) | Folacin[3] (μg) | Niacin[4] (mg) | Riboflavin (mg) | Thiamin (mg) | Vitamin $B_6$ (mg) | Vitamin $B_{12}$ (μg) | Minerals: Calcium (mg) | Phosphorus (mg) | Iodine (μg) | Iron (mg) | Magnesium (mg) | Zinc (mg) |
|---|---|---|---|---|---|---|---|---|---|---|---|---|---|---|---|---|---|---|---|---|---|
| Infants | 0.0–0.5 | 14 | 6 | 24 | 60 | 1,400 | 400 | 4 | 35 | 50 | 5 | 0.4 | 0.3 | 0.3 | 0.3 | 360 | 240 | 35 | 10 | 60 | 3 |
| | 0.5–1.0 | 20 | 9 | 28 | 71 | 2,000 | 400 | 5 | 35 | 50 | 8 | 0.6 | 0.5 | 0.4 | 0.3 | 540 | 400 | 45 | 15 | 70 | 5 |
| Children | 1–3 | 28 | 13 | 34 | 86 | 2,000 | 400 | 7 | 40 | 100 | 9 | 0.8 | 0.7 | 0.6 | 1.0 | 800 | 800 | 60 | 15 | 150 | 10 |
| | 4–6 | 44 | 20 | 44 | 110 | 2,500 | 400 | 9 | 40 | 200 | 12 | 1.1 | 0.9 | 0.9 | 1.5 | 800 | 800 | 80 | 10 | 200 | 10 |
| | 7–10 | 66 | 30 | 54 | 135 | 3,500 | 400 | 10 | 40 | 300 | 16 | 1.2 | 1.2 | 1.2 | 2.0 | 800 | 800 | 110 | 10 | 250 | 10 |
| Males | 11–14 | 97 | 44 | 63 | 158 | 5,000 | 400 | 12 | 45 | 400 | 18 | 1.5 | 1.4 | 1.6 | 3.0 | 1,200 | 1,200 | 130 | 18 | 350 | 15 |
| | 15–18 | 134 | 61 | 69 | 172 | 5,000 | 400 | 15 | 45 | 400 | 20 | 1.8 | 1.5 | 2.0 | 3.0 | 1,200 | 1,200 | 150 | 18 | 400 | 15 |
| | 19–22 | 147 | 67 | 69 | 172 | 5,000 | 400 | 15 | 45 | 400 | 20 | 1.8 | 1.5 | 2.0 | 3.0 | 800 | 800 | 140 | 10 | 350 | 15 |
| | 23–50 | 154 | 70 | 69 | 172 | 5,000 | — | 15 | 45 | 400 | 18 | 1.6 | 1.4 | 2.0 | 3.0 | 800 | 800 | 130 | 10 | 350 | 15 |
| | 51+ | 154 | 70 | 69 | 172 | 5,000 | — | 15 | 45 | 400 | 16 | 1.5 | 1.2 | 2.0 | 3.0 | 800 | 800 | 110 | 10 | 350 | 15 |
| Females | 11–14 | 97 | 44 | 62 | 155 | 4,000 | 400 | 12 | 45 | 400 | 16 | 1.3 | 1.2 | 1.6 | 3.0 | 1,200 | 1,200 | 115 | 18 | 300 | 15 |
| | 15–18 | 119 | 54 | 65 | 162 | 4,000 | 400 | 12 | 45 | 400 | 14 | 1.4 | 1.1 | 2.0 | 3.0 | 1,200 | 1,200 | 115 | 18 | 300 | 15 |
| | 19–22 | 128 | 58 | 65 | 162 | 4,000 | 400 | 12 | 45 | 400 | 14 | 1.4 | 1.1 | 2.0 | 3.0 | 800 | 800 | 100 | 18 | 300 | 15 |
| | 23–50 | 128 | 58 | 65 | 162 | 4,000 | — | 12 | 45 | 400 | 13 | 1.2 | 1.0 | 2.0 | 3.0 | 800 | 800 | 100 | 18 | 300 | 15 |
| | 51+ | 128 | 58 | 65 | 162 | 4,000 | — | 12 | 45 | 400 | 12 | 1.1 | 1.0 | 2.0 | 3.0 | 800 | 800 | 80 | 10 | 300 | 15 |
| Pregnant | — | — | — | — | — | 5,000 | 400 | 15 | 60 | 800 | +2 | +0.3 | +0.3 | 2.5 | 4.0 | 1,200 | 1,200 | 125 | 18+[5] | 450 | 20 |
| Lactating | — | — | — | — | — | 6,000 | 400 | 15 | 80 | 600 | +4 | +0.5 | +0.3 | 2.5 | 4.0 | 1,200 | 1,200 | 150 | 18 | 450 | 25 |

1. Allowances provide for individual variances among most normal persons living in the United States under usual environmental stresses. 2. Total vitamin E activity, estimated to be 80 percent as *a*-tocopherol and 20 percent other tocopherols. 3. Pure forms of folacin may be effective in doses of less than one-fourth. 4. Although expressed as niacin, the average 1 mg. of niacin is derived from each 60 mg. of dietary tryptophan. 5. Cannot be met by ordinary diets; use of supplemental iron is recommended. NOTE: mg—milligram; μg—microgram; IU—International Units; Lbs—Pounds; Wgt.—Weight; Hgt.—Height. *Source:* Food and Nutrition Board, National Academy of Sciences—National Research Council.

## Health Care Expenditures Per Person, 1977[1]

| Type of expenditure | Direct payments | Third-party payments: Private health insurance | Government | Philanthropy and industry | Total | Total |
|---|---|---|---|---|---|---|
| Hospital care | $17.52 | $108.85 | $164.03 | $6.98 | $279.86 | $297.38 |
| Physicians' services | 56.64 | 53.55 | 35.45 | .19 | 89.19 | 145.84 |
| Dentists' services | 36.01 | 7.04 | 2.27 | — | 9.31 | 45.41 |
| Other professional services | 6.34 | 3.52 | 4.19 | .51 | 8.22 | 14.56 |
| Drugs and drug sundries | 47.13 | 4.41 | 5.18 | — | 9.59 | 56.72 |
| Eyeglasses and appliances | 8.69 | .18 | .59 | — | .77 | 9.45 |
| Nursing-home care | 23.68 | .53 | 32.55 | .41 | 33.49 | 57.18 |
| Other health services | — | — | 14.58 | 5.10 | 19.58 | 19.59 |
| **Total per person** | **196.09** | **178.08** | **258.84** | **13.10** | **450.02** | **646.11** |

1. Year ending Sept. 30, preliminary. NOTE: Figures may not add up to totals due to rounding. *Source:* Department of Health, Education, and Welfare, Social Security Administration.

## Annual Increase in Cost of Medical Care
(in percent)

| Year | All consumer prices | Total medical care | Hospital semi-private room charges | Physicians' fees | Dentists' fees |
|---|---|---|---|---|---|
| 1965 | 1.7 | 2.1 | 5.3 | 3.1 | 2.9 |
| 1966 | 2.9 | 2.9 | 6.1 | 3.9 | 2.9 |
| 1967 | 2.9 | 6.5 | 17.3 | 7.4 | 4.5 |
| 1968 | 4.2 | 6.4 | 15.9 | 6.1 | 5.2 |
| 1969 | 5.4 | 6.5 | 13.5 | 6.1 | 5.8 |
| 1970 | 5.9 | 6.4 | 12.8 | 7.2 | 6.8 |
| 1971 | 4.3 | 6.9 | 13.3 | 7.5 | 6.0 |
| 1972 | 3.3 | 4.7 | 9.4 | 5.2 | 5.7 |
| 1973 | 6.2 | 3.1 | 5.0 | 2.6 | 3.1 |
| 1974 | 11.0 | 5.7 | 6.0 | 5.0 | 4.4 |
| 1975 | 9.1 | 12.5 | 16.4 | 12.8 | 10.8 |
| 1976 | 5.8 | 10.2 | 15.2 | 11.4 | 7.7 |
| 1977 | 6.5 | 9.6 | 11.5 | 9.3 | 7.5 |

*Source:* Department of Health, Education, and Welfare; Social Security Administration.

## Physicians, Dentists, and Nurses
(numbers in thousands)

| Profession | 1975 | 1974 | 1973 | 1970 | 1965 | 1960 | 1955 | 1950 |
|---|---|---|---|---|---|---|---|---|
| Physicians, number | 409 | 394 | 381 | 348 | 305 | 275 | 255 | 233 |
| Rate per 100,000 resident population[1] | 188 | 183 | 178 | 166 | 153 | 148 | 150 | 149 |
| Active (exc. physicians in Federal serv.) | 338 | 324 | 312 | 282 | 255 | n.a. | n.a. | n.a. |
| Rate per 100,000 resident population[1] | 155 | 150 | 146 | 135 | 129 | n.a. | n.a. | n.a. |
| Doctors of medicine[2] | 394 | 380 | 366 | 334 | 292 | 260 | 242 | 220 |
| Doctors of osteopathy | 15[3] | 15[3] | 15[3] | 14 | 13 | 14 | 14 | 13 |
| Physicians admitted to U.S. as immigrants[4] | 7.1 | 6.3 | 7.1 | 3.2 | 2.0 | 1.6 | 1.0 | 1.9 |
| Dentists, number[5] | n.a. | n.a. | 122 | 116 | 109 | 103 | 95 | 87 |
| Active (excl. dentists in Federal service) | 108 | n.a. | 101 | 96 | 86 | 85 | 76 | 75 |
| Rate per 100,000 resident population[1] | 50 | n.a. | 48 | 47 | 45 | 47 | 47 | 50 |
| Nurses, number (active registered) | 906 | 857 | 815 | 700 | 613 | 504 | 430 | 375 |
| Rate per 100,000 resident population[1] | 427 | 404 | 390 | 345 | 319 | 282 | 259 | 249 |

1. Based on Bureau of the Census population estimates. 2. Excludes non-Federal physicians with temporary foreign addresses. 3. Estimated. 4. Immigration and Naturalization Service figures. 5. Beginning 1960, excludes graduates of year stated. NOTE: n.a. = not available. *Source:* Department of Health, Education, and Welfare, National Center for Health Statistics.

## Communicable Diseases

| Disease | Incubation period[1] | Period of communicability |
|---|---|---|
| Chickenpox (varicella) | 2 to 3 weeks | From 5 days before appearance of vesicles to 6 days after |
| Common Cold | 12 to 72 hours; usually 24 hrs | From 1 day before onset to 5 days after |
| Conjunctivitis | 1 to 3 days | During course of active infection |
| Diphtheria | 2 to 5 days | Usually 2 weeks or less; seldom more than 4 weeks |
| Dysentery, amebic | 2 to 4 weeks (varies widely) | During intestinal infection; possibly for years if untreated |
| Enterobiasis (pinworm) | 3 to 6 weeks | Not directly transmitted |
| Food poisoning: Botulism | 12 to 36 hours | Not applicable |
| Salmonella infection | 6 to 72 hours; usually 36 | 3 days to 3 weeks (extremely variable) |
| Staphylococcus intoxication | 2 to 4 hours | Not applicable |
| German measles (rubella) | 8 to 10 days; usually 14 | 1 week before and at least 4 days after onset of rash |
| Gonorrhea | 2 to 5 days; sometimes longer | Indefinite unless treated |
| Hepatitis (serum) | 45 to 160 days; usually 80 to 100 | Many weeks before onset of symptoms |
| Herpes Simplex | Up to 2 weeks | As long as 7 weeks after recovery |
| Impetigo contagiosa | 4 to 10 days; sometimes longer | Until lesions are healed |
| Infectious mononucleosis | Varies 2 to 6 weeks | Unknown |
| Influenza | Usually 1 to 3 days | Probably limited to 3 days from clinical onset |
| Measles (rubeola) | 10 days (to onset): 14 days (to rash) | From beginning of prodromal period to 4 days after onset of rash |
| Meningitis, meningococcal | 2 to 10 days | Usually 1 day after appropriate medication |
| Mumps | 12 to 26 days; commonly 18 | From 6 days before distinctive symptoms up to 9 days after |
| Pediculosis | Apprx. 2 weeks | While lice remain alive |
| Pneumonia: Bacterial | Usually 1 to 3 days | Unknown |
| Viral | Believed to be 1 to 3 days | Unknown |
| Poliomyelitis | 3 to 21 days; commonly 7 to 12 | 7 to 10 days before and after onset of symptoms |
| Rabies | 2 to 8 weeks or longer | From animals, 3 to 5 days before onset and during course of the disease |
| Respiratory (acute viral) | Few days to 1 week or more | Duration of active disease |
| Ringworm (of body) | 4 to 10 days | As long as lesions are present |
| (Athlete's foot) | Unknown | As long as lesions are present |
| Scarlet fever and streptococcal sore throat | 1 to 3 days | Uncomplicated cases apprx 10 to 21 days; in untreated cases, weeks or months |
| Smallpox | 7 to 17 days; commonly 10 to 12 | During first week |
| Syphilis | 10 days to 10 weeks; usually 3 weeks | Variable and indefinite |
| Tetanus | 4 days to 3 weeks | Not applicable |
| Trichinosis | 2 to 28 days after ingestion of infected meat; usually 9 days | Not directly transmitted |
| Tuberculosis | 4 to 12 weeks (to primary phase) | As long as tubercle bacilli are discharged by patient |
| Typhoid fever | 1 to 3 weeks, average 2 weeks | As long as typhoid bacilli appear in excreta; 2 to 5% of patients become permanent carriers |
| Whooping cough (pertussis) | Commonly 7 days, almost uniformly within 10 days, and not exceeding 21 days | From 7 days after exposure to 3 weeks after onset of typical paroxysms |

1. Usual limits. NOTE: This list is incomplete, but includes those diseases that are most common and widespread.

## Income: Doctors and Dentists

| Year | Self-employed physicians | Self-employed dentists | Male professional and technical workers | All U.S. full-time employees |
|---|---|---|---|---|
| 1955 | $16,107 | $11,533 | $ 5,055 | $ 3,923 |
| 1967 | 34,740 | 22,850 | 8,882 | 6,307 |
| 1970 | 43,100 | 28,100 | 10,722 | 7,713 |
| 1974 | 54,140 | 30,500 | 13,391 | 9,991 |
| 1976 | 62,799 | 35,000 | 14,400 | 11,623 |

*Source:* Council on Wage and Price Stability.

# HEADLINE HISTORY

Headline History has been completely revised for this edition. Beyond the broader coverage of world events now provided, the changes in this section reflect the editor's concern that the reader be able to perceive crucial correlations between events, people, and ideas.

In any broad overview of history, arbitrary compartmentalization of facts is self-defeating (and makes locating interrelated people, places, and things that much harder). Therefore, Headline History is designed as a "time-line"—a chronology that highlights both the march of time and interesting, sometimes surprising, juxtapositions.

*Also see* related sections of *Information Please*, particularly the Statistical History of the United States, Inventions and Discoveries, Countries of the World, etc.

## B.C.

**Before Christ or Before Common Era (B.C.E.)**

**4500–3000 B.C.** Sumerians in the Tigris and Euphrates valleys develop a city-state civilization; first phonetic writing (**c.3500 B.C.**). Egyptian agriculture develops. Western Europe is Neolithic, without metals or written records. Earliest recorded date in Egyptian calendar (**4241 B.C.**). First year of Jewish calendar (**3760 B.C.**). Copper used by Egyptians and Sumerians.

**3000–2000 B.C.** Pharaonic rule begins in Egypt. Cheops, 4th dynasty (**2700–2675 B.C.**). The Great Sphinx of Giza. Earliest Egyptian mummies. Papyrus. Phoenician settlements on coast of what is now Syria and Lebanon. Semitic tribes settle in Assyria. Sargon, first Akkadian king, builds Mesopotamian empire. The Gilgamesh epic (**c.3000 B.C.**). Abraham leaves Ur (**c.2000 B.C.**). Systematic astronomy in Egypt, Babylon, India, China.

**2000–1500 B.C.** Hyksos invaders drive Egyptians from Lower Egypt (**17th century B.C.**). Amosis I frees Egypt from Hyksos (**c.1600 B.C.**). Assyrians rise to power—cities of Ashur and Nineveh. Twenty-four-character alphabet in Egypt. Israelites enslaved in Egypt. Cuneiform inscriptions used by Hittites. Peak of Minoan culture on Isle of Crete—earliest form of written Greek. Hammurabi, king of Babylon, develops oldest existing code of laws (**18th century B.C.**). In Britain, Stonehenge erected on some unknown astronomical rationale.

**1500–1000 B.C.** Ikhnaton develops monotheistic religion in Egypt (**c.1375 B.C.**). His successor, Tutankhamen, returns to earlier gods. Moses leads Israelites out of Egypt into Canaan—Ten Commandments. Greeks destroy Troy (**c.1193 B.C.**). End of Greek civilization in Mycenae with invasion of Dorians. Chinese civilization develops under Shang dynasty. Olmec civilization in Mexico—stone monuments; picture writing.

**1000–900 B.C.** Solomon succeeds King David, builds Jerusalem temple. After Solomon's death, kingdom divided into Israel and Judah. Hebrew elders begin to write Old Testament books of Bible. Phoenicians colonize Spain with settlement at Cadiz.

**900–800 B.C.** Phoenicians establish Carthage (**c.810 B.C.**). The *Iliad* and the *Odyssey*, perhaps composed by Greek poet Homer.

**800–700 B.C.** Prophets Amos, Hosea, Isaiah. First recorded Olympic games (**776 B.C.**). Legendary founding of Rome by Romulus (**753 B.C.**). Assyrian king Sargon II conquers Hittites, Chaldeans, Samaria (end of Kingdom of Israel). Earliest written music. Chariots introduced into Italy by Etruscans.

**700–600 B.C.** End of Assyrian Empire (**616 B.C.**)—Nineveh destroyed by Chaldeans (Neo-Babylonians) and Medes (**612 B.C.**). Founding of Byzantium by Greeks (**c.660 B.C.**). Building of the Acropolis in Athens. Solon, Greek lawgiver (**640–560 B.C.**). Sappho of Lesbos, Greek poetess. Lao-Tse, Chinese philosopher and founder of Taoism (born **c.604 B.C.**).

**600–500 B.C.** Babylonian king Nebuchadnezzar builds empire, destroys Jerusalem (**586 B.C.**). Babylonian Captivity of the Jews (starting **587 B.C.**). Hanging Gardens of Babylon. Cyrus the Great of Persia creates great empire, conquers Babylon (**539 B.C.**), frees the Jews. Athenian democracy develops. Aeschylus, Greek dramatist (**525–465 B.C.**). Confucius (**551–479 B.C.**) develops philosophy-religion in China. Buddha (**563–483 B.C.**) founds Buddhism in India.

**500–400 B.C.** Greeks defeat Persians: battles of Marathon (**490 B.C.**), Thermopylae (**480 B.C.**), Salamis (**480 B.C.**). Peloponnesian Wars between Athens and Sparta (**431–404 B.C.**)—Sparta victorious. Pericles comes to power in Athens (**462**

## Some Ancient Civilizations

| Name | Approximate dates | Location | Major cities |
|---|---|---|---|
| Akkadian | 2350–2230 B.C. | Mesopotamia, parts of Syria, Asia Minor, Iran | Akkad, Ur, Erich |
| Assyrian | 1800–889 B.C. | Mesopotamia, Syria | Assur, Nineveh, Calah |
| Babylonian | 1728–1686 B.C. (old) 625–539 B.C. (new) | Mesopotamia, Syria, Palestine | Babylon |
| Cimmerian | 750–500 B.C. | Caucasus, northern Asia Minor | — |
| Egyptian | 2850–715 B.C. | Nile valley | Thebes, Memphis, Tanis |
| Etruscan | 900–396 B.C. | Northern Italy | — |
| Greek | 900–200 B.C. | Greece | Athens, Sparta, Thebes, Mycenae, Corinth |
| Hittite | 1640–1200 B.C. | Asia Minor, Syria | Hattusas, Nesa |
| Lydian | 700–547 B.C. | Western Asia Minor | Sardis, Miletus |
| Mede | 835–550 B.C. | Iran | Media |
| Minoan | 3000–1100 B.C. | Crete | Knossos |
| Persian | 559–330 B.C. | Iran, Asia Minor, Syria | Persepolis, Pasargadae |
| Phoenician | 1100–332 B.C. | Palestine (colonies: Gibralter, Carthage Sardinia) | Tyre, Sidon, Byblos |
| Phrygian | 1000–547 B.C. | Central Asia Minor | Gordion |
| Roman | 500 B.C.- 300 A.D. | Italy, Mediterranean region, Asia Minor, western Europe | Rome, Byzantium |
| Scythian | 800–300 B.C. | Caucasus | — |
| Sumerian | 3200–2360 B.C. | Mesopotamia | Ur, Nippur |

B.C.). Flowering of Greek culture during the Age of Pericles (**450–400** B.C.). Sophocles, Greek dramatist (**496–c.406** B.C.). Hippocrates, Greek "Father of Medicine" (born **400** B.C.). Xerxes I, king of Persia (rules **485–465** B.C.).

**400–300** B.C. Pentateuch—first five books of the Old Testament evolve in final form. Philip of Macedon assassinated (**336** B.C.) after conquering Greece; succeeded by son, Alexander the Great (**356–323** B.C.), who destroys Thebes (**335** B.C.), conquers Tyre and Jerusalem (**332** B.C.), occupies Babylon (**330** B.C.), invades India, and dies in Babylon. His empire is divided among his generals; one of them, Seleucis I, establishes Middle East empire with capitals at Antioch (Syria) and Seleucia (in Iraq). Trial and execution of Greek philosopher Socrates (**399** B.C.). Dialogues recorded by his student, Plato. Euclid's work on geometry (**323** B.C.). Aristotle, Greek philosopher (**354–322** B.C.). Demosthenes, Greek orator (**384–322** B.C.). Praxiteles, Greek sculptor (**400–330** B.C.).

**300–251** B.C. First Punic War (**264–241** B.C.): Rome defeats the Carthaginians and begins its domination of the Mediterranean. Temple of the Sun at Teotihuacan, Mexico (**c.300** B.C.). Invention of Mayan calendar in Yucatán—more exact than older calendars. First Roman gladiatorial games (**264** B.C.). Archimedes, Greek mathematician (**287 212** B.C.).

**250–201** B.C. Second Punic War (**219–201** B.C.): Hannibal, Carthaginian general (**246–142** B.C.), crosses the Alps (**218** B.C.), reaches gates of Rome (**211** B.C.), retreats, and is defeated by Scipio Africanus at Zama (**202** B.C.). Great Wall of China built (**c.215** B.C.).

**200–151** B.C. Romans defeat Seleucid King Antiochus III at Thermopylae (**191** B.C.)—beginning of Roman world domination. Maccabean revolt against Romans (**167** B.C.).

**150–101** B.C. Third Punic War (**149–146** B.C.): Rome destroys Carthage, killing 450,000 and enslaving the remaining 50,000 inhabitants. Roman armies conquer Macedonia, Greece, Turkey, Balearic Islands, and southern France. Venus de Milo (**c.140** B.C.). Cicero, Roman orator (**106–43** B.C.).

**100–51** B.C. Julius Caesar (**100–44** B.C.) invades Britain (**55** B.C.) and conquers Gaul (France) (**c.50** B.C.). Spartacus leads slave revolt against Rome (**71** B.C.). Romans conquer Seleucid empire. Roman general Pompey conquers Jerusalem (**63** B.C.). Cleopatra on Egyptian throne (**51–31** B.C.). Chinese develop use of paper (**c.100** B.C.). Virgil, Roman poet (**70–19** B.C.). Horace, Roman poet (**65–8** B.C.).

**50–1 B.C.** Caesar crosses Rubicon to fight Pompey (**50 B.C.**). Herod made Roman governor of Judea (**47 B.C.**). Caesar murdered (**44 B.C.**). Caesar's nephew, Octavian, defeats Mark Antony and Cleopatra at Battle of Actium (**31 B.C.**), and establishes Roman empire as Emperor Augustus—rules **27 B.C.-A.D. 14**. Birth of Jesus Christ (variously given from **4 B.C. to A.D. 7**). Ovid, Roman poet (**43 B.C.-A.D. 18**).

# A.D.

## The Christian or Common Era (C.E.)

**1–49** After Augustus, Tiberius becomes emperor (dies, **37**), succeeded by Caligula (assassinated, **42**), who is followed by Claudius. Crucifixion of Jesus (probably **30**). Han dynasty in China founded by Emperor Kuang Wu Ti. Buddhism introduced to China.

**50–99** Claudius poisoned (**54**), succeeded by Nero (commits suicide, **68**). Missionary journeys of Paul the Apostle (**34–60**). Jews revolt against Rome; Jerusalem destroyed (**70**). Roman persecutions of Christians begin (**64**). Colosseum built in Rome (**71–80**). Trajan (rules **98–116**); Roman empire extends to Mesopotamia, Arabia, Balkans. First Gospels of St. Mark, St. John, St. Matthew.

**100–149** Hadrian rules Rome (**117–138**); codifies Roman law, establishes postal system, builds wall between England and Scotland. Jews revolt under Bar Kokhba (**122–135**); final *Diaspora* (dispersion) of Jews begins.

**150–199** Marcus Aurelius (rules Rome **161–180**). Oldest Mayan temples in Central America (**c.200**). Mayan civilization develops writing, astronomy, mathematics.

**200–249** Goths invade Asia Minor (**c.220**). Roman persecutions of Christians increase. Persian (Sassanid) empire re-established. End of Chinese Han dynasty.

**250–299** Increasing invasions of the Roman empire by Franks and Goths. Buddhism spreads in China.

**300–349** Constantine the Great (rules **312–337**) reunites eastern and western Roman empires, with new capital (Constantinople) on site of Byzantium (**330**); issues Edict of Milan legalizing Christianity (**313**); becomes a Christian on his deathbed (**337**). Council of Nicaea (**325**) defines orthodox Christian doctrine. First Gupta dynasty in India (**c.320**).

**350–399** Huns (Mongols) invade Europe (**c.360**). Theodosius the Great (rules **392–395**)—last emperor of a united Roman empire. Roman empire permanently divided in **395**: western empire ruled from Rome; eastern empire ruled from Constantinople.

**400–449** Western Roman empire disintegrates under weak emperors. Alaric, king of the Visigoths, sacks Rome (**410**). Attila, Hun chieftain, attacks Roman provinces (**433**). St. Patrick returns to Ireland (**432**). St. Augustine's *City of God* (**411**).

**450–499** Vandals destroy Rome (**455**). Western Roman empire ends as Odoacer, German chieftain, overthrows last Roman emperor, Romulus Augustulus, and becomes king of Italy (**476**). Ostrogothic kingdom of Italy established by Theodoric the Great (**493**). Clovis, ruler of the Franks, is converted to Christianity (**496**). First schism between western and eastern churches (**484**). Peak of Mayan culture in Mexico (**c.460**).

**500–549** Eastern and western churches reconciled (**519**). Justinian I, the Great (**483–565**), becomes Byzantine emperor (**527**), issues his first code of civil laws (**529**), conquers North Africa, Italy, and part of Spain. Plague spreads through Europe (from **542**). Arthur, semi-legendary king of the Britons (killed, **c.537**). Boëthius, Roman scholar (executed, **524**).

**550–599** Beginnings of European silk industry after Justinian's missionaries smuggle silkworms out of China (**553**). Mohammed, founder of Islam (**570–632**). Buddhism in Japan (**c.560**). St. Augustine of Canterbury brings Christianity to Britain (**597**). After killing about half the population, plague in Europe subsides (**594**).

**600–649** Mohammed flees from Mecca to Medina (the *Hegira*); first year of the Muslim calendar (**622**). Muslim empire grows (**634**). Arabs conquer Jerusalem (**637**), destroy Alexandrian library (**641**), conquer Persians (**641**). Fatima, Mohammed's daughter (**606–632**).

**650–699** Arabs attack North Africa (**670**), destroy Carthage (**697**). Venerable Bede, English monk (**672–735**).

**700–749** Arab empire extends from Lisbon to China (by **716**). Charles Martel, Frankish leader, defeats Arabs at Tours/Poitiers, halting Arab advance in Europe (**732**). Charlemagne (**742–814**).

**750–799** Caliph Harun al-Rashid rules Arab empire (**786–809**): the "golden age" of Arab culture. Vikings begin attacks on Britain (**790**), land in

Ireland (795). Charlemagne becomes king of the Franks (771). City of Machu Picchu flourishes in Peru.

**800–849** Charlemagne (Charles the Great) crowned first Holy Roman Emperor in Rome (**800**). Arabs conquer Crete, Sicily, and Sardinia (**826–827**). Charlemagne dies (**814**), succeeded by his son, Louis the Pious, who divides France among his sons (**817**).

**850–899** Norsemen attack as far south as the Mediterranean but are repulsed (**859**), discover Iceland (**861**). Alfred the Great becomes king of Britain (**871**), defeats Danish invaders (**878**). Russian nation founded by Vikings under Prince Rurik, establishing capital at Novgorod (**855–879**).

**900–949** Vikings discover Greenland (**c.900**). Arab Spain under Abd ar-Rahman III becomes center of learning (**912–961**).

**950–999** Eric the Red establishes first Viking colony in Greenland (**982**). Mieczyslaw I becomes first ruler of Poland (**960**). Hugh Capet elected King of France in **987**; Capetian dynasty to rule until **1328**. Musical notation systematized (**c.990**). Vikings and Danes attack Britain (**988–999**). Holy Roman Empire founded by Otto I, King of Germany since **936**, crowned by Pope John XII in **962**.

---

**c.1000** Hungary and Scandinavia converted to Christianity. Viking raider Leif Ericson discovers North America, calls it *Vinland*. Chinese invent gunpowder. *Beowulf*, Old English epic.

**1009** Moslems destroy Holy Sepulchre in Jerusalem.

**1013** Danes control England. Canute takes throne (**1016**), conquers Norway (**1028**), dies (**1035**); kingdom divided among his sons: Harold Harefoot (England), Sweyn (Norway), Hardecanute (Denmark).

**1040** Macbeth murders Duncan, king of Scotland.

**1053** Robert Guiscard, Norman invader, establishes kingdom in Italy, conquers Sicily (**1072**).

**1054** Final separation between Eastern (Orthodox) and Western (Roman) churches.

**1055** Seljuk Turks, Asian nomads, move west, capture Baghdad, Armenia (**1064**), Syria, and Palestine (**1075**).

**1066** William of Normandy invades England, defeats last Saxon king, Harold II, at Battle of Hastings, crowned William I of England ("the Conqueror").

**1073** Emergence of strong papacy when Gregory VII is elected. Conflict with English and French kings and German emperors will continue throughout medieval period.

**1095** *(See* special material on "The Crusades.")

Omar Khayyám, *Persian poet* (1027?–1123)
El Cid, *Spanish national hero* (1040–1099)
Peter Abelard, *French theologian* (1079–1142)
Judah Halevi, *Jewish poet* (1085–1140)

---

**1150–67** Universities of Paris and Oxford founded in France and England.

**1162** Thomas à Becket named Archbishop of Canterbury, murdered by Henry II's men (**1170**). Troubadours (wandering minstrels) glorify romantic concepts of feudalism.

**1189** Richard I ("the Lionhearted") succeeds Henry II in England, killed in France (**1199**), succeeded by King John.

---

**1211** Genghis Khan invades China, captures Peking (**1214**), conquers Persia (**1218**), invades Russia (**1223**), dies (**1227**).

**1215** King John forced by barons to sign Magna Carta at Runneymede, limiting royal power.

**1233** The Inquisition begins as Pope Gregory IX assigns Dominicans responsibility for combatting heresy. Torture used (**1252**). Ferdinand and Isabella establish Spanish Inquisition (**1478**). Tourquemada, Grand Inquisitor, forces conversion or expulsion of Spanish Jews (**1492**). Forced conversion of Moors (**1499**). Inquisition in Portugal (**1531**). First Protestants burned at the stake in Spain (**1543**). Spanish Inquisition abolished (**1834**).

**1241** Mongols defeat Germans in Silesia, invade Poland and Hungary, with-

Thomas à Becket, *English prelate and martyr* (1118–1170)
Moses Maimonides, *Jewish philosopher* (1135–1204)
Genghis Khan, *Mongol emperor* (1162–1227)
St. Francis of Assisi, *founder of Franciscans* (1182–1226)
Roger Bacon, *English scientist* (1214–1294)
Kublai Khan, *Mongol ruler* (1216–1294)
St. Thomas Aquinas, *Catholic theologian* (1225–1274)
Marco Polo, *Venetian explorer* (1254–1323)
Dante Alighieri, *Italian poet* (1265–1321)

---

### THE CRUSADES (1096–1291)

In **1095** Pope Urban II calls for war to rescue Holy Land from Moslem infidels at Council of Clermont. *First Crusade* (**1096**) —about 500,000 peasants led by Peter the Hermit prove so troublesome that Byzantine Emperor Alexius ships them to Asia Minor; only 25,000 survive return after massacre by Seljuk Turks. Followed by organized army, led by nobility, which reaches Constantinople (**1097**), conquers Jerusalem (**1099**), Acre (**1104**), establishes Latin Kingdom protected by Knights of St. John the Hospitaller (**1100**), and Knights Templar (**1123**). Seljuk Turks start series of counterattacks (**1144**). *Second Crusade* (**1146**) led by King Louis VII of France and Emperor Conrad III. Crusaders perish in Asia Minor (**1147**). Saladin controls Egypt (**1171**), unites Islam in Holy War *(Jihad)* against Christians, recaptures Jerusalem (**1187**). *Third Crusade* (**1189**) under kings of France, England, and Germany fails to reduce Saladin's power. *Fourth Crusade* (**1200–1204**) —French knights sack Greek Christian Constantinople, establish Latin empire in Byzantium. Greeks re-establish Orthodox faith (**1262**).

*Children's Crusade* (**1212**)—Only 1 of 30,000 French children and about 200 of 20,000 German children survive to return home. Other Crusades—against Egypt (**1217**), *Sixth* (**1228**), *Seventh* (**1248**), *Eighth* (**1270**). Mamelukes conquer Acre; end of the Crusades (**1291**).

draw from Europe after Ughetai, Mongol leader, dies.
**1251** Kublai Khan governs China, becomes ruler of Mongols **(1259)**, establishes Yuan dynasty in China **(1280)**, invades Burma **(1287)**, dies **(1294)**.
**1271** Marco Polo of Venice travels to China, in court of Kublai Khan **(1275–1292)**, returns to Genoa **(1295)** and writes *Travels*.
**1272** English King Edward I conquers Wales and Scotland; Great Britain unified. Summons the Model Parliament in **1295**.

---

**1312–37** Mali Empire reaches its height in Africa under King Mansa Musa.
**1337–1453** Hundred Years' War—English and French kings fight for control of France.
**c.1325** The beginning of the Renaissance in Italy: writers Dante, Petrarch, Boccaccio; painter Giotto. Development of *No* drama in Japan. Aztecs establish capital on site of modern Mexico City. Peak of Moslem culture in Spain. Small cannon in use.
**1347–1351** At least 25 million people die in Europe's "Black Death" (bubonic plague).
**1368** Ming dynasty begins in China.
**1376–82** John Wycliffe, pre-Reformation religious reformer and followers translate Latin bible into English.
**1378** The Great Schism **(to 1417)**—rival popes in Rome and Avignon, France, fight for control of Roman Catholic Church.
**c.1387** Chaucer's *Canterbury Tales*.

---

**1415** Henry V defeats French at Agincourt. Jan Hus, Bohemian preacher and follower of Wycliffe, burned at stake in Constance as heretic.
**1418–60** Portugal's Prince Henry the Navigator sponsors exploration of Africa's coast.
**1428** Joan of Arc leads French against English, captured by Burgundians **(1430)** and turned over to the English, burned at the stake as a witch after ecclesiastical trial **(1431)**.
**1438** Inca rule in Peru.
**1450** Florence becomes center of Renaissance arts and learning under the Medicis.
**1453** Turks conquer Constantinople, end of the Byzantine empire. Hundred Years' War between France and England ends.
**1455** The Wars of the Roses, civil wars between rival noble factions, begin in England **(to 1485)**. Having invented printing with movable type at Mainz, Germany, Johann Gutenberg completes first bible.
**1462** Ivan the Great rules Russia until **1505** as first czar; ends payment of tribute to Mongols.
**1492** Moors conquered in Spain by troops of Ferdinand and Isabella. Columbus discovers Caribbean islands, returns to Spain **(1493)**. Second voyage to Dominica, Jamaica, Puerto Rico **(1493–1496)**. Third voyage to Orinoco **(1498)**. Fourth voyage to Honduras and Panama **(1502–1504)**.
**1497** Vasco da Gama sails around Africa and discovers sea route to India **(1498)**. Establishes Portuguese colony in India **(1502)**. John Cabot, employed by England, reaches and explores Canadian coast. Michelangelo's *Bacchus* sculpture.

Duns Scotus, *Scottish theologian* (1265–1308)
Giotto, *Italian painter* (1276–1337)

Guillaume de Machaut, *French composer* (1300–1377)
Petrarch (Francesco Petrarca), *Italian poet* (1304–1374)
Giovanni Boccaccio, *Florentine novelist* (1313–1375)
John Wycliffe, *English church reformer* (1320–1384)
Geoffrey Chaucer, *English writer* (c.1340–1400)
Jan Hus, *Bohemian religious reformer* (c.1369–1415)
Thomas à Kempis, *German mystic* (1380–1471)
Donatello, *Italian sculptor* (1386–1466)
Fra Angelico, *Italian painter* (1387–1455)
Johann Gutenberg, *inventor of movable type* (1398–1468)
Luca della Robbia, *Italian sculptor* (1400–1482)
Guillaume Dufay, *French composer* (c.1400–1474)
Fra Filippo Lippi, *Italian painter* (1406–1469)
Joan of Arc, *French saint and national heroine* (1412–1431)
Tomas de Torquemada, *Spanish Inquisitor* (1420–1498)
Giovanni Bellini, *Italian painter* (1430–1516)
François Villon, *French poet* (1431–1465?)
Sandro Botticelli, *Italian painter* (1444–1510)
Lorenzo de'Medici, *Renaissance ruler* (1449–1492)
Hieronymus Bosch, *Dutch painter* (1450–1516)
Josquin des Prés, *Dutch composer* (1450–1521)
Isabella I, *Queen of Spain* (1451–1504)
Christopher Columbus, *Italian explorer* (1451–1506)
Amerigo Vespucci, *Italian navigator* (1451–1512)
Savonarola, *Italian churchman* (1452–1498)

Leonardo da Vinci, *Renaissance artistic and scientific genius* (1452–1519)
Vasco da Gama, *Portuguese explorer* (1460–1524)
Juan Ponce de León, *Spanish explorer* (1460–1521)
Hans Holbein (the Elder), *German painter* (1465?–1524)
Niccolo Machiavelli, *Italian author* (1468–1527)
Albrecht Dürer, *German painter* (1471–1528)
Nicolaus Copernicus, *Polish scientist* (1473–1543)
Michelangelo Buonarroti, *Italian painter, sculptor, architect* (1475–1564)
Cesare Borgia, *Renaissance prince* (1476–1507)
Titian, *Italian painter* (1477–1576)
Sir Thomas More, *English statesman* (1478–1535)
Lucrezia Borgia, *Italian patron of the arts* (1480–1519)
Ferdinand Magellan, *Portuguese explorer* (1480–1521)
Martin Luther, *German Reformation leader* (1483–1546)
Raphael, *Italian painter* (1483–1520)
Ulrich Zwingli, *Swiss humanist* (1484–1531)
Hernando Cortes, *Spanish Conquistador* (1485–1547)
Andrea del Sarto, *Florentine painter* (1486–1531)
Thomas Cranmer, *English churchman* (1489–1556)
François Rabelais, *French writer* (1490–1553)
Jacques Cartier, *French explorer* (1491–1557)
St. Ignatius de Loyola, *founder of Jesuits* (1491–1556)
Paracelsus, *Swiss physician* (1493–1541)
Correggio, *Italian painter* (1494–1534)
Hans Holbein (the Younger) *German painter* (1497–1543)
Hernando De Soto, *Spanish explorer* (1499–1542)

1501 First black slaves in America brought to Spanish colony of Santo Domingo.
c.1503 Leonardo da Vinci paints the *Mona Lisa.*
1506 St. Peter's Church started in Rome; designed and decorated by such artists and architects as Bramante, Michelangelo, da Vinci, Raphael, and Bernini before its completion in **1626**.
1509 Henry VIII ascends English throne. Michelangelo paints the ceiling of the Sistine Chapel.
1517 Turks conquer Egypt, control Arabia. Martin Luther posts his 95 theses denouncing church abuses on church door in Wittenberg—start of the Reformation in Germany.
1519 Ulrich Zwingli begins Reformation in Switzerland. Hernando Cortes conquers Mexico for Spain. Charles I of Spain is chosen Holy Roman Emperor Charles V. Spanish explorer Fernando Magellan sets out to circumnavigate the globe.
1520 Luther excommunicated by Pope Leo X. Suleiman I ("the Magnificent") becomes Sultan of Turkey, invades Hungary **(1521)**, Rhodes **(1522)**, attacks Austria **(1529)**, annexes Hungary **(1541)**, Tripoli **(1551)**, makes peace with Persia **(1553)**, destroys Spanish fleet **(1560)**, dies **(1566)**. Magellan reaches the Pacific, is killed by Philippine natives **(1521)**. One of his ships under Juan Sebastián del Cano continues around the world, reaches Spain **(1522)**.
1524 Verrazano, sailing under the French flag, explores the New England coast and New York Bay.
1527 Troops of the Holy Roman Empire attack Rome, imprison Pope Clement VII—the end of the Italian Renaissance. Castiglione writes *The Courtier.* The Medici expelled from Florence.
1532 Pizarro marches from Panama to Peru, kills the Inca chieftain, Atahualpa, of Peru **(1533)**. Machiavelli's *Prince* published posthumously.
1535 Reformation begins as Henry VIII makes himself head of English Church after being excommunicated by Pope. Sir Thomas More executed as traitor for refusal to acknowledge king's religious authority. Jacques Cartier sails up the St. Lawrence River, basis of French claims to Canada.
1536 Henry VIII executes second wife, Anne Boleyn. John Calvin establishes Presbyterian form of Protestantism in Switzerland, writes *Institutes of the Christian Religion.* Danish and Norwegian Reformations. Michelangelo's *Last Judgment.*
1541 John Knox leads Reformation in Scotland, establishes Presbyterian church **(1560)**.
1543 Publication of *On the Revolution of Heavenly Bodies* by Polish scholar Nicolaus Copernicus—giving his theory that the earth revolves around the sun.
1545 Council of Trent to meet intermittently until **1563** to define Catholic dogma and doctrine, reiterate papal authority.
1547 Ivan IV ("the Terrible") crowned as Czar of Russia, begins conquest of Astrakhan and Kazan **(1552)**, battles nobles (boyars) for power **(1564)**, kills his son **(1580)**, dies, and is succeeded by a son who gives power to Boris Godunov **(1584)**.
1553 Roman Catholicism restored in England by Queen Mary I, who rules until **1558**. Religious radical Michael Servetus burned as heretic in Geneva by order of John Calvin.
1554 Benvenuto Cellini completes the bronze *Perseus.*
1556 Akbar the Great becomes Mogul emperor of India, conquers Afghanistan **(1581)**, continues wars of conquest (until **1605**).
1558 Queen Elizabeth I ascends the throne (rules to **1603**). Restores Protestantism, establishes state Church of England (Anglicanism). Renaissance will reach height in England—Shakespeare, Marlowe, Spenser.
1561 Persecution of Huguenots in France stopped by Edict of Orleans. French religious wars begin again with massacre of Huguenots at Vassy. St. Bartholomew's Day Massacre—thousands of Huguenots murdered **(1572)**. Amnesty granted **(1573)**. Persecution continues periodically until Edict of Nantes **(1598)** gives Huguenots religious freedom (until **1685**).
1568 Protestant Netherlands revolts against Catholic Spain; independence will be acknowledged by Spain in **1648**. High point of Dutch Renaissance —painters Rubens, Van Dyck, Hals, and Rembrandt.
1570 Japan permits visits of foreign ships. Queen Elizabeth I excommunicated by Pope. Turks attack Cyprus and war on Venice. Turkish fleet defeated at Battle of Lepanto by Spanish and Italian fleets **(1571)**. Peace of Constantinople **(1572)** ends Turkish attacks on Europe.
1580 Francis Drake returns to England after circumnavigating the globe. Knighted by Queen Elizabeth I **(1581)**. Montaigne's *Essays* published.
1583 William of Orange rules The Netherlands; assassinated on orders of Philip II of Spain **(1584)**.

Benvenuto Cellini, *Florentine sculptor* (1500–1571)
Nostradamus, *French astrologer* (1503–1566)
John Knox, *Scottish church reformer* (1505–1572)
St. Francis Xavier, *Jesuit missionary* (1506–1552)
John Calvin, *Swiss theologian* (1509–1564)
Giorgio Vasari, *Italian art historian* (1511–1574)
Andreas Vesalius, *Dutch anatomist* (1515–1564)
Andrea Palladio, *Italian architect* (1518–1580)
Tintoretto (Jacopo Robusti), *Italian painter* (1518–1594)
Pieter Brueghel (the Elder), *Dutch painter* (1520–1569)
Pierre de Ronsard, *French poet* (1524–1585)
Giovanni Palestrina, *Italian composer* (1526–1594)
Paolo Veronese, *Italian painter* (1528–1588)
Queen Elizabeth, *English ruler* (1533?–1603)
Michel de Montaigne, *French author* (1533–1592)
El Greco, *Spanish-Greek painter* (1542–1614)
Tycho Brahe, *Danish astronomer* (1546–1601)
Miguel de Cervantes, *Spanish writer* (1547–1616)
Giordano Bruno, *Italian philosopher* (1548–1600)
Sir Walter Raleigh, *English courtier* (1552–1618)
Edmund Spenser, *English poet* (1552–1599)
Giovanni Gabrieli, *Italian composer* (c.1557–1612)
Francis Bacon, *English philosopher* (1561–1626)
Christopher Marlowe, *English dramatist* (1564–1593)
Galileo Galilei, *Italian scientist* (1564–1642)
William Shakespeare, *English dramatist and poet* (1564–1616)
Michelangelo da Caravaggio, *Italian painter* (c.1565–1609)
Claudio Monteverdi, *Italian composer* (1567–1643)
Johannes Kepler, *German astronomer* (1571–1630)
John Donne, *English poet* (1573–1631)
Inigo Jones, *English architect* (1573–1652)
Ben Jonson, *English dramatist* (1573–1637)
Peter Paul Rubens, *Flemish painter* (1577–1652)
William Harvey, *English physician and anatomist* (1578–1657)

**1587** Mary, Queen of Scots, executed for treason by order of Queen Elizabeth I. Monteverdi's *First Book of Madrigals.*
**1588** Defeat of the Spanish Armada by English. Henry, King of Navarre and Protestant leader, recognized as Henry IV, first Bourbon king of France. Converts to Roman Catholicism in **1593** in attempt to end religious wars.
**1590** Henry IV enters Paris, wars on Spain **(1595)**, marries Maria de Medici **(1600)**, assassinated **(1610)**. Spenser's *The Faerie Queen,* El Greco's *St. Jerome.* Galileo's experiments with falling objects.
**1598** Boris Godunov becomes Russian Czar. Tycho Brahe describes his astronomical experiments.

---

**1600** Giordano Bruno burned as a heretic. Ieyasu rules Japan, moves capital to Edo (Tokyo). Shakespeare's *Hamlet* begins his most productive decade. English East India Company established to develop overseas trade.
**1607** Jamestown, Virginia, established—first permanent English colony on American mainland.
**1609** Samuel de Champlain establishes French colony of Quebec.
**1611** Gustavus Adolphus elected King of Sweden. King James Version of the Bible published in England. Rubens paints his *Descent from the Cross.*
**1614** John Napier discovers logarithms.
**1618** Start of the Thirty Years' War (to **1648**)—Protestant revolt against Catholic oppression; Denmark, Sweden, and France will invade Germany in later phases of war. Kepler proposes his Third Law of planetary motion.
**1620** Pilgrims, after three-month voyage in *Mayflower,* land at Plymouth Rock. Francis Bacon's *Novum Organum.*
**1633** Inquisition forces Galileo to recant his belief in Copernican theory.
**1642** English Civil War. Cavaliers, supporters of Charles I, against Roundheads, parliamentary forces. Oliver Cromwell defeats Royalists **(1646)**. Parliament demands reforms. Charles I offers concessions, brought to trial **(1648)**, beheaded **(1649)**. Cromwell becomes Lord Protector **(1653)**. Rembrandt paints his *Night Watch.*
**1644** End of Ming Dynasty in China—Manchus come to power. Descartes' *Principles of Philosophy.* John Milton's *Areopagitica* on the freedom of the press.
**1648** End of the Thirty Years' War. German population about half of what it was in **1618** because of war and pestilence.
**1658** Cromwell dies; his son, Richard, resigns and Puritan government collapses.
**1660** English Parliament calls for the restoration of the monarchy; invites Charles II to return from France.
**1661** Charles II is crowned King of England. Louis XIV begins personal rule as absolute monarch; starts to build Versailles.
**1664** British take New Amsterdam from the Dutch. English limit "Nonconformity" with re-established Anglican Church. Isaac Newton's experiments with gravity.
**1665** Great Plague in London kills 75,000.
**1666** Great Fire of London. Molière's *Misanthrope.*
**1683** War of European powers against the Turks (to **1699**). Vienna withstands three-month Turkish siege; high point of Turkish advance in Europe.

Frans Hals, *Dutch painter* (1581–1666)
Phineas Fletcher, *English dramatist* (1582–1650)
Francis Beaumont, *English dramatist* (1584–1616)
Cardinal Richelieu, *French prelate* (1585–1642)
Thomas Hobbes, *English philosopher* (1588–1679)
John Winthrop, *first governor of Massachusetts* (1588–1649)
Robert Herrick, *English poet* (1591–1674)
Johann Amos Comenius, *Moravian educational reformer* (1592–1670)
Peter Stuyvesant, *Dutch administrator in America* (1592–1672)
George Herbert, *English poet* (1593–1633)
Izaak Walton, *English biographer* (1593–1683)
Nicola Amati, *Italian violin maker* (1594–1684)
Nicolas Poussin, *French painter* (1594–1665)
Pocahontas, *Indian princess* (1595–1617)
René Descartes, *French philosopher* (1596–1650)
Oliver Cromwell, *English general and statesman* (1599–1658)
Anthony Van Dyck, *Flemish painter* (1599–1641)
Diego Velázquez, *Spanish painter* (1599–1660)
Pedro Calderón de la Barca, *Spanish dramatist* (1600–1681)
Roger Williams, *American religious leader* (1604–1683)
Pierre Corneille, *French dramatist* (1606–1684)
Rembrandt van Rijn, *Dutch painter* (1606–1669)

---

## THE FOUNDING OF THE AMERICAN NATION

Colonization of America begins: Jamestown, Va. **(1607)**; Pilgrims in Plymouth **(1620)**; Massachusetts Bay Colony **(1630)**; New Netherland founded by Dutch West India Company **(1623)**, captured by English **(1664)**. Delaware established by Swedish trading company **(1638)**, absorbed later by Penn family. Proprietorships by royal grants to Lord Baltimore (Maryland, **1632**); Captain John Mason (New Hampshire, **1635**); Sir William Berkeley and Sir George Carteret (New Jersey, **1663**); friends of Charles II (the Carolinas, **1663**); William Penn (Pennsylvania, **1682**); James Oglethorpe and others (Georgia, **1732**).

Increasing conflict between colonists and Britain on western frontier because of royal edict limiting western expansion **(1763)**, and regulation of colonial trade and increased taxation of colonies (Writs of Assistance allow search for illegal shipments, **1761**; Sugar Act, **1764**; Currency Act, **1764**; Stamp Act, **1765**; Quartering Act, **1765**; Duty Act, **1767**.) Boston Massacre **(1770)**. Lord North attempts conciliation **(1770)**. Boston Tea Party **(1773)**, followed by punitive measures passed by Parliament—the "Intolerable Acts."

First Continental Congress **(1774)** sends "Declaration of Rights and Grievances" to King, urges colonies to form Continental Association. Paul Revere's Ride and Lexington and Concord battle between Massachusetts minutemen and British **(1775)**.

Second Continental Congress **(1775)**, while sending "olive branch" to the king, begins to raise army, appoints Washington commander-in-chief, and seeks alliance with France. Some colonial legislatures urge their delegates to vote for independence. Declaration of Independence **(July 4, 1776)**.

Major Battles of the Revolutionary War: *Long Island:* Howe defeats Putnam's division of Washington's Army in Brooklyn Heights, but Americans escape across East River **(1776)**. *Trenton and Princeton:* Washington defeats Hessians at Trenton, British at Princeton, winters at Morristown **(1776–77)**. Howe winters in Philadelphia; Washington at Valley Forge **(1777–78)**. Burgoyne surrenders British army to General Gates at *Saratoga* **(1777)**.

France recognizes American independence **(1778)**. The War moves south: Savannah captured by British **(1778)**; Charleston occupied **(1780)**; Americans fight successful guerrilla actions under Marion, Pickens, and Sumter. In the West, George Rogers Clark attacks Forts Kaskaskia and Vincennes **(1778–1779)**, defeating British in the region. Cornwallis surrenders at *Yorktown,* Virginia **(Oct. 19, 1781)**. By **1782**, Britain is eager for peace because of conflicts with European nations. *Peace of Paris* **(1783)**: Britain recognizes American independence.

**1685** James II succeeds Charles II in England, calls for freedom of conscience **(1687)**. Protestants fear restoration of Catholicism and demand "Glorious Revolution." William of Orange invited to England and James II escapes to France **(1688)**. William III and his wife, Mary, crowned. In France, Edict of Nantes of 1598, granting freedom of worship to Huguenots (French Protestants), is revoked by Louis XIV; thousands of Protestants flee.

**1689** Peter the Great becomes Czar of Russia—attempts to westernize nation and build Russia as military power. Defeats Charles XII of Sweden at Poltava **(1709)**. Beginning of the French and Indian Wars (to **1763**), campaigns in America linked to a series of wars between France and England for domination of Europe.

**1690** William III of England defeats former King James II and Irish rebels at Battle of the Boyne in Ireland. John Locke's *Human Understanding.*

John Milton, *English poet* (1608–1674)
François de La Rouchefoucauld, *French author* (1613–1680)
Henry More, *English philosopher* (1614–1687)
Cyrano de Bergerac, *French poet* (1619–1655)
Andrew Marvell, *English poet* (1621–1678)
Molière (Jean-Baptiste Poquelin), *French dramatist* (1622–1673)
Blaise Pascal, *French philosopher* (1623–1662)
Robert Boyle, *English scientist* (1627–1691)
John Bunyan, *English author* (1628–1688)
John Dryden, *English dramatist* (1631–1700)
John Locke, *English philosopher* (1631–1704)
Luca Giordano, *Italian painter* (1632–1705)
Anton van Leeuwenhoek, *Dutch zoologist* (1632–1723)

Jan Vermeer, *Dutch painter* (1632–1675)
Baruch Spinoza, *Dutch philosopher* (1632–1677)
Christopher Wren, *English architect* (1632–1723)
Samuel Pepys, *English diarist* (1633–1703)
Jean Baptiste Lully, *French composer* (1639–1687)
Jean Racine, *French dramatist* (1639–1699)
Sir Isaac Newton, *English philosopher and mathematician* (1642–1727)
William Penn, *founder of Pennsylvania* (1644–1718)
Antonio Stradivari, *Italian violin maker* (1644–1737)
Gottfried W. von Leibniz, *German scientist* (1646–1716)
Arcangelo Corelli, *Italian composer* (1653–1713)
Jacques Bernoulli, *Swiss scientist* (1654–1705)

Edmund Halley, *English astronomer* (1656–1742)
Henry Purcell, *English composer* (1658–1695)
Daniel Defoe, *English author* (1659–1731)
Alessandro Scarlatti, *Italian composer* (1659–1725)
Cotton Mather, *Massachusetts churchman* (1663–1728)
François Couperin, *French composer* (1668–1733)
Giovanni Battista Vico, *Italian philosopher* (1668–1744)
William Congreve, *English dramatist* (1670–1730)
Peter the Great, *Russian czar* (1672–1725)
Antonio Vivaldi, *Italian composer* (1678–1741)

George Phillip Telemann, *German composer* (1681–1767)
Jean Philippe Rameau, *French composer* (1683–1764)
Jean Antoine Watteau, *French painter* (1684–1721)
J.S. Bach, *German composer* (1685–1750)
George Frederick Handel, *German-English composer* (1685–1759)
Domenico Scarlatti, *Italian composer* (1685–1757)
Gabriel Fahrenheit, *German physicist* (1686–1736)
Alexander Pope, *English poet* (1688–1744)
Emanuel Swedenborg, *Swedish mystic* (1688–1772)
Baron de Montesquieu, *French philosopher* (1689–1755)
François de Voltaire, *French philosopher* (1694–1778)
Canaletto (Antonio Canale), *Italian painter* (1697–1768)
William Hogarth, *English painter* (1697–1764)

---

**1701** War of the Spanish Succession begins—the last of Louis XIV's wars for domination of the continent. The Peace of Utrecht **(1714)** will end the conflict and mark the rise of the British Empire. Called Queen Anne's War in America, it ends with the British taking New Foundland, Acadia, and Hudson's Bay Territory from France, and Gibraltar and Minorca from Spain.

**1704** Deerfield (Conn.) Massacre of English colonists by French and Indians. Bach's first cantata. Jonathan Swift's *Tale of a Tub. Boston News Letter* —first newspaper in America.

**1707** United Kingdom of Great Britain formed—England, Wales, and Scotland joined by parliamentary Act of Union.

**1729** J. S. Bach's *St. Matthew's Passion.* Isaac Newton's *Principia* translated from Latin into English.

**1735** John Peter Zenger, New York editor, acquitted of libel in New York, establishing press freedom.

**1740** Capt. Vitus Bering, Dane employed by Russia, discovers Alaska.

**1746** British defeat Scots under Stuart Pretender Prince Charles at Culloden Moor. Last battle fought on British soil.

**1751** Publication of the *Encyclopédie* begins in France, the "bible" of the Enlightenment.

**1755** Samuel Johnson's *Dictionary* first published. Great earthquake in Lisbon, Portugal—over 60,000 die.

**1756** Seven Years' War (called French and Indian War in America) (to **1763**), in which Britain and Prussia defeat France, Spain, Austria, and Russia.

François Boucher, *French painter* (1703–1770)
Jonathan Edwards, *American theologian* (1703–1758)
John Wesley, *founder of Methodism* (1703–1791)
Benjamin Franklin, *American statesman* (1706–1790)
Henry Fielding, *English novelist* (1707–1754)
Leonhard Euler, *Swiss mathematician* (1707–1783)
Linnaeus (Carl von Linné), *Swedish botanist* (1707–1778)
Samuel Johnson, *English author* (1709–1784)
William Boyce, *English composer* (1710–1779)
Giovanni Pergolesi, *Italian composer* (1710–1736)
David Hume, *Scottish philosopher* (1711–1776)

France loses North American colonies; Spain cedes Florida to Britain in exchange for Cuba. In India, over 100 British prisoners die in "Black Hole of Calcutta."

**1757** Beginning of British Empire in India as Robert Clive, British commander, defeats Nawab of Bengal at Plassey.

**1759** British capture Quebec from French. Voltaire's *Candide.* Haydn's *Symphony No. 1.*

**1762** Catherine II ("the Great") becomes Czarina of Russia. J. J. Rousseau's *Social Contract.* Mozart tours Europe as six-year-old prodigy.

**1769** Sir William Arkwright patents a spinning machine—an early step in the Industrial Revolution.

**1772** Joseph Priestley and Daniel Rutherford independently discover nitrogen. Partition of Poland—in **1772, 1793,** and **1795,** Austria, Prussia, and Russia divide land and people of Poland, end its independence.

**1775** The American Revolution *(see* "The Founding of the American Nation"). James Watt invents the steam engine. Priestley discovers hydrochloric and sulfuric acids.

**1776** Adam Smith's *Wealth of Nations.* Edward Gibbon's *Decline and Fall of the Roman Empire.* Thomas Paine's *Common Sense.* Fragonard's *Washerwoman.* Mozart's *Haffner Serenade.*

**1778** Capt. James Cook discovers Hawaii. Franz Mesmer uses hypnotism.

**1781** Immanuel Kant's *Critique of Pure Reason.* Herschel discovers Uranus.

**1783** End of Revolutionary War *(see* special material on "The Founding of the American Nation"). William Blake's poems. Beethoven's first printed works.

**1784** Crimea annexed by Russia. John Wesley's *Deed of Declaration,* the basic work of Methodism.

**1785** Russians settle Aleutian Islands.

**1787** The Constitution of the United States signed. Lavoisier's work on chemical nomenclature. Mozart's *Don Giovanni.*

**1788** French *Parlement* presents grievances to Louis XVI who agrees to convening of Estates-General in **1789**—not called since **1613**. Goethe's *Egmont.* Laplace's *Laws of the Planetary System.*

**1789** French Revolution *(see* special material on the "French Revolution"). In U.S., George Washington elected President with all 69 votes of the Electoral College, takes oath of office in New York City. Vice President: John Adams. Secretary of State: Thomas Jefferson. Secretary of Treasury: Alexander Hamilton.

Jean-Jacques Rousseau, *French philosopher* (1712–1778)
Denis Diderot, *French encyclopedist* (1713–1784)
Laurance Sterne, *English novelist* (1713–1768)
K.P.E. Bach, *German composer* (1714–1788)
David Garrick, *English actor* (1717–1779)
Horace Walpole, *English statesman and novelist* (1717–1797)
Thomas Chippendale, *English artisan* (1718?–1779)
Bernardo Canaletto, *Italian painter* (1720–1780)
Giambattista Piranesi, *Italian artist* (1720–1778)
Baron von Münchhausen, *German anecdotist* (1720–1797)
Mme. de Pompadour, *French courtesan* (1721–1764)
Tobias Smollet, *English novelist* (1721–1771)
Samuel Adams, *American patriot* (1722–1803)
Joshua Reynolds, *English painter* (1723–1792)
Adam Smith, *English economist* (1723–1790)
Immanuel Kant, *German philosopher* (1724–1804)
Giovanni Casanova, *Italian adventurer* (1725–1798)
Thomas Gainsborough, *English painter* (1727–1788)
Oliver Goldsmith, *English writer* (1728–1774)
Catherine II (Catherine the Great), *Russian empress* (1729–1796)
Edmund Burke, *English statesman* (1729–1797)
William Cowper, *English poet* (1731–1800)

George Washington, *first American President* (1732–1799)
J.H. Fragonard, *French painter* (1732–1800)
Josef Haydn, *Austrian composer* (1732–1809)
Franz Anton Mesmer, *Austrian hypnotist* (1733–1815)
Joseph Priestley, *English scientist* (1733–1804)
John Adams, *American President* (1735–1836)
Daniel Boone, *American frontiersman* (1735–1820)
Patrick Henry, *American patriot* (1736–1799)
James Watt, *Scottish inventor* (1736–1819)
John S. Copley, *American painter* (1737–1815)
Edward Gibbon, *English historian* (1737–1794)

Thomas Paine, *American author and patriot* (1737–1809)
William Herschel, *English astronomer* (1738–1822)
Prince Potemkin, *Russian statesman* (1739–1791)
James Boswell, *Scottish writer* (1740–1795)
Marquis de Sade, *French libertine and writer* (1741–1814)
Benedict Arnold, *American general and traitor* (1741–1801)
Luigi Boccherini, *Italian composer* (1743–1805)
Antoine Lavoisier, *French chemist* (1743–1794)

Jean-Paul Marat, *French revolutionist* (1743–1793)
Thomas Jefferson, *American President* (1743–1826)
Jean-Baptiste de Lamark, *French scientist* (1744–1829)
Alessandro Volta, *Italian scientist* (1745–1827)
Francisco de Goya, *Spanish painter* (1746–1828)
Johann Pestalozzi, *Swiss educator* (1746–1827)
John Paul Jones, *American naval officer* (1747–1792)
Jeremy Bentham *English economist* (1748–1832)
Jacques David, *French painter* (1748–1825)
Count Casimir Pulaski, *Polish-American patriot* (1748–1779)
Johann Wolfgang von Goethe, *German writer* (1749–1832)

### FRENCH REVOLUTION (1789–1799)

Revolution begins when Third Estate (Commons) delegates swear not to disband until France has a constitution. Paris mob storms Bastille, symbol of royal power **(July 14, 1789)**. National Assembly votes for Constitution, Declaration of the Rights of Man, a limited monarchy, and other reforms **(1789–90)**. Legislative Assembly elected, Revolutionary Commune formed, and French Republic proclaimed **(1792)**. War of the First Coalition—Austria, Prussia, Britain, Netherlands, and Spain fight to restore French nobility **(1792–97)**. Start of series of wars between France and European powers that will last, almost without interruption, for 23 years. Louis XVI and Marie Antoinette executed. Committee of Public Safety begins Reign of Terror as political control measure. Interfactional rivalry leads to mass killings. Danton and Robespierre executed. Third French Constitution sets up Directory government **(1795)**.

**1790** H.M.S. *Bounty* mutineers settle on Pitcairn Island. Aloisio Galvani experiments on electrical stimulation of the muscles. Philadelphia temporary capital of U.S. as Congress votes to establish new capital on Potomac. U.S. population about 3,929,000, including 698,000 slaves. Lavoisier formulates *Table of 31 chemical elements.*
**1791** U.S. Bill of Rights ratified. Boswell's *Life of Johnson.*
**1794** Kosciusko's uprising in Poland quelled by the Russians. In U.S., Whiskey Rebellion in Pennsylvania as farmers object to liquor taxes. U.S. Navy and Post Office Department established.
**1796** Napoleon Bonaparte, French general, defeats Austrians. In the U.S., Washington's Farewell Address **(Sept. 17)**; John Adams elected President; Thomas Jefferson, Vice President. Edward Jenner introduces smallpox vaccination.
**1798** Napoleon extends French conquests to Rome and Egypt.
**1799** Napoleon leads coup that overthrows Directory, becomes First Consul —one of three who rule France.

James Madison, *American President* (1751–1836)
Richard Brinsley Sheridan, *Irish dramatist* (1751–1816)
Fanny Burney, *English writer* (1752–1840)
Betsy Ross, *American flagmaker* (1752–1836)
C. de Talleyrand-Périgord, *French statesman* (1754–1838)
Marie Antoinette, *French queen* (1755–1793)
Alexander Hamilton, *American statesman* (1755–1804)
Gilbert Stuart, *American painter* (1755–1828)
Aaron Burr, *American statesman* (1756–1836)
Wolfgang Amadeus Mozart, *Austrian composer* (1756–1791)
William Blake, *English poet* (1757–1827)
Marquis de Lafayette, *French general in America* (1757–1834)

James Monroe, *American President* (1758–1831)
Horatio Nelson, *English admiral* (1758–1805)
Maximilien de Robespierre, *French revolutionist* (1758–1794)
Noah Webster, *American lexicographer* (1758–1843)
Robert Burns, *Scottish poet* (1759–1796)
Katsuhika Hokusai, *Japanese artist* (1760–1849)
Luigi Cherubini, *Italian composer* (1760–1842)
Robert Fulton, *American inventor* (1765–1815)
Eli Whitney, *American inventor* (1765–1825)
John Dalton, *English chemist* (1766–1844)
T. R. Malthus, *English economist* (1766–1834)
John Quincy Adams, *American President* (1767–1848)
Andrew Jackson, *American President* (1767–1845)

Jacques Lafitte, *French pirate* (1767–1844)
Tecumseh, *American Indian chief* (1768?–1813)
Napoleon Bonaparte, *French emperor* (1769–1821)
Duke of Wellington, *English general* (1769–1852)
Ludwig van Beethoven, *German composer* (1770–1827)
G. W. F. Hegel, *German philosopher* (1770–1831)
William Wordsworth, *English writer* (1770–1850)
Robert Owen, *English social reformer* (1771–1858)
Walter Scott, *Scottish novelist* (1771–1832)
Friedrich von Schlegel, *German philosopher* (1772–1829)

Prince K. von Metternich, *Austrian statesman* (1773–1859)
Jane Austen, *English novelist* (1775–1817)
J. W. Turner, *English painter* (1775–1851)
John Constable, *English painter* (1776–1837)
Henry Clay, *American statesman* (1777–1852)
Heinrich von Kleist, *German poet* (1777–1811)
Karl von Clausewitz, *German military strategist* (1780–1831)
J.A. Ingres, *French painter* (1780–1867)
Nicolo Paganini, *Italian composer* (1782–1840)
Daniel Webster, *American statesman* (1782–1852)
Simón Bolívar, *Latin American patriot* (1783–1830)
Washington Irving, *American writer* (1783–1859)
Stendahl (Marie Henri Beyle), *French novelist* (1783–1842)
J. J. Audubon, *American naturalist* (1785–1851)

**1800** Napoleon conquers Italy, firmly establishes himself as First Consul in France. In the U.S., Federal Government moves to Washington. Robert Owen's social reforms in England. William Herschel discovers infrared rays. Alessandro Volta produces electricity.
**1801** Austria makes temporary peace with France. United Kingdom of Great Britain and Ireland established with one monarch and one parliament, Catholics excluded from voting.
**1803** U.S. negotiates Louisiana Purchase from France: For $15 million, U.S. doubles its domain, increasing its territory by 827,000 sq mi. (2,144,500 sq km), from Mississippi River to Rockies and from Gulf of Mexico to British North America.
**1804** Haiti declares independence from France; first black nation to gain freedom from European colonial rule. Napoleon proclaims himself emperor of France, systematizes French law under *Code Napoleon.* In the U.S., Alexander Hamilton is mortally wounded in duel with Aaron Burr. Lewis and Clark expedition begins exploration of what is now northwestern U.S.
**1805** Lord Nelson defeats the French-Spanish fleets in the Battle of Trafalgar. Napoleon victorious over Austrian and Russian forces at the Battle of Austerlitz.
**1807** Robert Fulton makes first successful steamboat trip on *Clermont* between New York City and Albany.

Davy Crockett, *American frontiersman* (1786–1836)
Carl Maria von Weber, *German composer* (1786–1826)
Louis Daguerre, *French photographic pioneer* (1787–1851)
Lord Byron, *English poet* (1788–1824)
Arthur Schopenhauer, *German philosopher* (1788–1860)
James Fenimore Cooper, *American writer* (1789–1851)
Michael Faraday, *English physicist* (1791–1867)
Samuel F. B. Morse, *American inventor* (1791–1872)

1808 French armies occupy Rome and Spain, extending Napoleon's empire. Britain begins aiding Spanish guerrillas against Napoleon in Peninsular War. In the U.S., Congress bars importation of slaves. Beethoven's *Fifth* and *Sixth Symphonies* performed.

1812 Napoleon's Grand Army invades Russia in June. Forced to retreat in winter, most of Napoleon's 600,000 men are lost. In the U.S., war with Britain declared over freedom of the seas for U.S. vessels. U.S.S. *Constitution* sinks British frigate. *(See* special material on the "War of 1812.")

1814 French defeated by allies (Britain, Austria, Russia, Prussia, Sweden, and Portugal) in War of Liberation. Napoleon exiled to Elba, off Italian coast. Bourbon King Louis XVIII takes French throne. George Stephenson builds first practical steam locomotive.

1815 Napoleon returns: "Hundred Days" begin. Napoleon defeated by Wellington at Waterloo, banished again to St. Helena in South Atlantic. Congress of Vienna: victorious allies change the map of Europe.

1817 Simón Bolívar establishes independent Venezuela, as Spain loses hold on South American countries. Bolívar named President of Colombia **(1819)**. Peru, Guatemala, Panama, and Santo Domingo proclaim independence from Spain **(1821)**.

1820 Missouri Compromise—Missouri admitted as slave state but slavery barred in rest of Louisiana Purchase north of 36°30′ N.

1822 Greeks proclaim a republic and independence from Turkey. Turks invade Greece. Russia declares war on Turkey **(1828)**. Greece also aided by France and Britain. War ends and Turks recognize Greek independence **(1829)**. Brazil becomes independent of Portugal. Schubert's *Eighth Symphony* ("The Unfinished").

1823 U.S. Monroe Doctrine warns European nations not to interfere in Western Hemisphere.

1824 Mexico becomes a republic, three years after declaring independence from Spain. Beethoven's *Ninth Symphony.*

1825 First passenger-carrying railroad in England.

1830 French invade Algeria. Louis Philippe becomes "Citizen King" as revolution forces Charles X to abdicate. Mormon church formed in U.S. by Joseph Smith.

1831 Polish revolt against Russia fails. Belgium separates from the Netherlands. In U.S., Nat Turner leads unsuccessful slave rebellion.

1833 Slavery abolished in British Empire.

1834 Charles Babbage invents "analytical engine," precursor of computer. McCormick patents reaper.

1836 Boer farmers start "Great Trek"—Natal, Transvaal, and Orange Free State founded in South Africa. Mexican army besieges Texans in Alamo. Entire garrison, including Davy Crockett and Jim Bowie, wiped out. Texans gain independence from Mexico after winning Battle of San Jacinto. Dickens's *Pickwick Papers.*

1837 Victoria becomes Queen of Great Britain. Mob kills Elijah P. Lovejoy, Illinois abolitionist publisher.

1839 First Opium War (to **1842**) between Britain and China, over importation of drug into China.

1840 Lower and Upper Canada united.

1841 U.S. President Harrison dies **(April 4)** one month after inauguration; John Tyler becomes first Vice President to succeed to Presidency.

1844 Democratic convention calls for annexation of Texas and acquisition of Oregon ("Fifty-four-forty-or-fight"). Five Chinese ports opened to U.S. ships. Samuel F. B. Morse patents telegraph.

1845 Congress adopts joint resolution for annexation of Texas.

1846 Failure of potato crop causes famine in Ireland. U.S. declares war on Mexico. California and New Mexico annexed by U.S. Brigham Young leads Mormons to Great Salt Lake. W. T. Morton uses ether as anesthetic. Sewing machine patented by Elias Howe.

1848 Revolt in Paris: Louis Philippe abdicates; Louis Napoleon elected President of French Republic. Revolutions in Vienna, Venice, Berlin, Milan, Rome, and Warsaw. Put down by royal troops in **1848–49**. U.S.-Mexico War ends; Mexico cedes claims to Texas, California, Arizona, New Mexico, Utah, Nevada. U.S. treaty with Britain sets Oregon Territory boundary at 49th parallel. Karl Marx and Friedrich Engels' *Communist Manifesto.*

1849 California gold rush begins.

Percy Bysshe Shelley, *English poet* (1792–1822)
Gioacchino Rossini, *Italian composer* (1792–1868)
Sam Houston, *Texas political leader* (1793–1863)
John Keats, *English poet* (1795–1821)
Thomas Carlyle, *British historian* (1795–1881)
Heinrich Heine, *German poet* (1797–1856)
Ando Hiroshige, *Japanese painter* (1797–1858)
Franz Schubert, *Austrian composer* (1797–1828)
Adam Mickiewicz, *Polish poet* (1798–1855)
Auguste Comte, *French philosopher* (1798–1857)
Ferdinand Delacroix, *French painter* (1798–1863)
Honoré de Balzac, *French novelist* (1799–1850)
Aleksander Pushkin, *Russian poet* (1799–1837)
John Henry Newman, *English prelate* (1801–1890)
Brigham Young, *Mormon leader* (1801–1877)
Lajos Kossuth, *Hungarian patriot* (1802–1894)
Alexander Dumas, père, *French novelist* (1802–1870)
Victor Hugo, *French novelist* (1802–1885)
Ralph Waldo Emerson, *American philosopher* (1803–1882)
Hector Berlioz, *French composer* (1803–1869)
Benjamin Disraeli, *British statesman* (1804–1881)
Nathaniel Hawthorne, *American novelist* (1804–1864)
George Sand, *French writer* (1804–1876)
Giuseppe Mazzini, *Italian patriot* (1805–1872)
Hans Christian Andersen, *Danish writer* (1805–1875)
Alexis de Tocqueville, *French writer* (1805–1859)
Elizabeth Barrett Browning, *English poet* (1806–1861)
John Stuart Mill, *English philosopher* (1806–1873)
Giuseppe Garibaldi, *Italian patriot* (1807–1882)
Henry Wadsworth Longfellow, *American poet* (1807–1882)
Honoré Daumier, *French artist* (1808–1879)

**WAR OF 1812**

British interference with American trade, impressment of American seamen, and "War Hawks" drive for western expansion lead to war. American attacks on Canada foiled; U.S. Commodore Perry wins battle of Lake Erie **(1813)**. British capture and burn Washington **(1814)** but fail to take Fort McHenry at Baltimore. Andrew Jackson repulses assault on New Orleans after treaty of Ghent ends war **(1815)**. War settles little but strengthens U.S. as independent nation.

1850 Henry Clay opens great debate on slavery, warns South against secession.
1851 Herman Melville's *Moby Dick*. Harriet Beecher Stowe's *Uncle Tom's Cabin*.
1852 South African Republic established. Louis Napoleon proclaims himself Napoleon III ("Second Empire").
1853 Crimean War begins as Turkey declares war on Russia. Commodore Perry reaches Tokyo.
1854 Britain and France join Turkey in war on Russia. In U.S., Kansas-Nebraska Act permits local option on slavery; rioting and bloodshed. Japanese allow American trade. Antislavery men in Michigan form Republican Party. Tennyson's *Charge of the Light Brigade*. Thoreau's *Walden*.
1855 Armed clashes in Kansas between pro- and anti- slavery forces. Florence Nightingale nurses wounded in Crimea. Walt Whitman's *Leaves of Grass*.
1856 Flaubert's *Madame Bovary*.
1857 Supreme Court, in Dred Scott decision, rules that a slave is not a citizen. Financial crisis in Europe and U.S. Great Mutiny (Sepoy Rebellion) begins in India. India placed under crown rule as a result.
1858 Pro-slavery constitution rejected in Kansas. Abraham Lincoln makes strong antislavery speech in Springfield, Ill.: " . . . this Government cannot endure permanently half slave and half free." Lincoln-Douglas debates. First trans-Atlantic telegraph cable completed by Cyrus W. Field.
1859 John Brown raids Harpers Ferry; is captured and hanged. Work begins on Suez Canal. Unification of Italy starts under leadership of Count Cavour, Sardinian premier. Joined by France in war against Austria. Edward Fitzgerald's *Rubaiyat of Omar Khayyam*. Charles Darwin's *Origin of Species*. J. S. Mill's *On Liberty*
1861 U.S. Civil War begins as attempts at compromise fail *(see* special material on "The Civil War"). Congress creates Colorado, Dakota, and Nevada territories; adopts income tax; Lincoln inaugurated. Serfs emancipated in Russia. Pasteur's theory of germs. Independent Kingdom of Italy proclaimed under Sardinian King Victor Emmanuel II.
1863 French capture Mexico City; proclaim Archduke Maximilian of Austria emperor.
1865 Lincoln fatally shot at Ford's Theater by John Wilkes Booth. Vice President Johnson sworn as successor. Booth caught and dies of gunshot wounds; four conspirators are hanged. Joseph Lister begins antiseptic surgery. Gregor Mendel's Law of Heredity. Lewis Carroll's *Alice's Adventures in Wonderland*.
1866 Alfred Nobel invents dynamite. Seven Weeks' War: Austria defeated by Prussia and Italy.
1867 Austria-Hungary Dual Monarchy established. French leave Mexico; Maximilian executed. Dominion of Canada established. U.S. buys Alaska from Russia for $7,200,000. South African diamond field discovered. Volume I of Marx's *Das Kapital*. Strauss's *Blue Danube*.
1868 Revolution in Spain; Queen Isabella deposed, flees to France. In U.S., Fourteenth Amendment giving civil rights to blacks is ratified. Georgia under military government after legislature expels blacks.

Abraham Lincoln, *American president* (1809–1865)
Nicolai Gogol, *Russian writer* (1809–1852)
Edgar Allan Poe, *American writer* (1809–1849)
Alfred, Lord Tennyson, *English poet* (1809–1892)
William Ewart Gladstone, *British statesman* (1809–1898)
Charles Darwin, *English scientist* (1809–1882)
Felix Mendelssohn, *German composer* (1809–1847)
Louis Braille, *French inventor of touch alphabet for blind* (1809–1852)
Frédéric Chopin, *Polish composer* (1810–1849)
Robert Schumann, *German composer* (1810–1856)
Phineas T. Barnum, *American showman* (1810–1891)
Harriet Beecher Stowe, *American writer* (1811–1896)
William M. Thackeray, *English novelist* (1811–1863)
Franz Liszt, *Hungarian composer* (1811–1896)
Robert Browning, *English poet* (1812–1889)
Charles Dickens, *English novelist* (1812–1870)
Alfred Krupp, *German munitions magnate* (1812–1887)
Sören Kierkegaard, *Danish philosopher* (1813–1855)
Giuseppe Verdi, *Italian composer* (1813–1901)
Richard Wagner, *German composer* (1813–1883)
Otto von Bismarck, *Prussian statesman* (1815–1898)
Charlotte Brontë, *English writer* (1816–1855)

## THE CIVIL WAR (1861–1865)
**(The War Between the States or the War of the Rebellion)**

Apart from the matter of slavery, the Civil War arose out of both the economic and political rivalry between an agrarian South and an industrial North and the issue of the right of states to secede from the Union.

**1861** After South Carolina secedes (**Dec. 20, 1860**), Mississippi, Florida, Alabama, Georgia, Louisiana, and Texas follow, forming the Confederate States of America, with Jefferson Davis as president (**Jan.-March**). War begins as Confederates fire on Fort Sumter (**April 12**). Lincoln calls for 75,000 volunteers. Southern ports blockaded by superior Union naval forces. Virginia, Arkansas, Tennessee, and North Carolina secede to complete 11-state Confederacy. Union army advancing on Richmond repulsed at first Battle of Bull Run (**July**).

**1862** Edwin M. Stanton named Secretary of War (**Jan.**). Grant wins first important Union victory in West, at Fort Donelson; Nashville falls (**Feb.**). Ironclads, Union's *Monitor* and Confederate's *Virginia (Merrimac)* duel at Hampton Roads (**March**). New Orleans falls to Union fleet under Farragut; city occupied (**April**). Grant's army escapes defeat at Shiloh. Memphis falls as Union gunboats control upper Mississippi (**June**). Confederate general Robert E. Lee victorious at second Battle of Bull Run (**Aug.**). Union army under McClellan halts Lee's attack on Washington in the Battle of Antietam (**Sept.**). Lincoln removes McClellan for lack of aggressiveness. Burnside's drive on Richmond fails at Fredericksburg (**Dec.**). Union forces under Rosecrans chase Bragg through Tennessee; battle of Murfreesboro (**Oct.-Jan. 1863**).

**1863** Lee defeats Hooker at Chancellorsville; "Stonewall" Jackson, Confederate general, dies of wounds (**May**). Confederate invasion of Pennsylvania stopped at Gettysburg by George Meade—Lee loses 20,000 men—the greatest battle of the War (**July**). It and the Union victory at Vicksburg mark the war's turning point. Union general George H. Thomas, the "Rock of Chickamauga," holds Bragg's forces on Georgia-Tennessee border (**Sept.**). Sherman, Hooker, and Thomas drive Bragg back to Georgia. Tennessee restored to the Union (**Nov.**).

**1864** Ulysses S. Grant named commander-in-chief of Union forces (**March**). In the Wilderness campaign, Grant forces Lee's Army of Northern Virginia back toward Richmond (**May-June**). Sherman's Atlanta campaign and "march to the sea" (**May-Sept.**). Farragut's victory at Mobile Bay (**Aug.**). Hood's Confederate army defeated at Nashville. Sherman takes Savannah (**Dec.**).

**1865** Sheridan defeats Confederates at Five Forks; Confederates evacuate Richmond (**April**). On **April 9**, Lee surrenders to Grant at Appomattox.

**1869** First U.S. transcontinental rail route completed. James Fisk and Jay Gould attempt to control gold market causes Black Friday panic. Suez Canal opened. Mendeleev's periodic table of elements.
**1870** Franco-Prussian War (to **1871**): Napoleon III capitulates at Sedan. Revolt in Paris; Third Republic proclaimed.
**1871** France surrenders Alsace-Lorraine to Germany; war ends. German Empire proclaimed with Prussian King as Kaiser Wilhelm I. Fighting with Apaches begins in American West. Boss Tweed corruption exposed in New York. The Chicago Fire, with 300 deaths and $200-million damage. Stanley meets Livingston in Africa.
**1872** Congress gives amnesty to most Confederates. Jules Verne's *Around the World in 80 Days.*
**1873** Economic crisis in Europe. U.S. establishes gold standard.
**1875** First Kentucky Derby.
**1876** Sioux kill Gen. George A. Custer and 264 troopers at Little Big Horn River. Alexander Graham Bell patents the telephone.
**1877** After Presidential election of **1876**, Electoral Commission gives disputed Electoral College votes to Rutherford B. Hayes despite Tilden's popular majority. Russo-Turkish war (ends in **1878** with power of Turkey in Europe broken). Reconstruction ends in the American South. Thomas Edison patents phonograph.
**1878** Congress of Berlin revises Treaty of San Stefano ending Russo-Turkish War; makes extensive redivision of southeastern Europe. First commercial telephone exchange opened in New Haven, Conn.
**1880** U.S.-China treaty allows U.S. to restrict immigration of Chinese labor.
**1881** President Garfield fatally shot by assassin; Vice President Arthur succeeds him. Charles J. Guiteau convicted and executed (in **1882**).
**1882** Terrorism in Ireland after land evictions. Britain invades and conquers Egypt. Germany, Austria, and Italy form Triple Alliance. In U.S., Congress adopts Chinese Exclusion Act. Rockefeller's Standard Oil Trust is first industrial monopoly. In Berlin, Robert Koch announces discovery of tuberculosis germ.
**1883** Congress creates Civil Service Commission. Brooklyn Bridge and Metropolitan Opera House completed.
**1885** British Gen. Charles G. "Chinese" Gordon killed at Khartoum in Egyptian Sudan.
**1886** Bombing at Haymarket Square, Chicago, kills seven policemen and injures many others. Eight alleged anarchists accused—three imprisoned, one commits suicide, four hanged. (In **1893**, Illinois Governor Altgeld pardons three survivors and is critical of trial.) Statue of Liberty dedicated. Geronimo, Apache Indian chief, surrenders.
**1887** Queen Victoria's Golden Jubilee. Sir Arthur Conan Doyle's first Sherlock Holmes story, "A Study in Scarlet."
**1888** Historic March blizzard in Northeast U.S.—many perish, property damage exceeds $25 million. George Eastman's box camera (the Kodak). J.B. Dunlop devises pneumatic tire. Jack the Ripper murders in London.
**1889** Second (Socialist) International founded in Paris. Indian Territory in Oklahoma opened to settlement. Thousands die in Johnstown, Pa., flood. Mark Twain's *A Connecticut Yankee in King Arthur's Court.*
**1890** Congress votes Sherman Antitrust Act. Sitting Bull killed in Sioux uprising.
**1892** Battle between steel strikers and Pinkerton guards at Homestead, Pa.; union defeated after militia intervenes. Silver mine strikers in Idaho fight non-union workers; U.S. troops dispatched. Diesel engine patented.
**1894** Sino-Japanese War begins (ends in **1895** with China's defeat). In France, Capt. Alfred Dreyfus convicted on false treason charge (pardoned in **1906**). In U.S., Jacob S. Coxey of Ohio leads "Coxey's Army" of unemployed on Washington. Eugene V. Debs calls general strike of rail workers to support Pullman Company strikers; strike broken, Debs jailed for six months. Thomas A. Edison's kinetoscope given first public showing in New York City.
**1895** X-rays discovered by German physicist, Wilhelm Roentgen.
**1896** Supreme Court's *Plessy* v. *Ferguson* decision—"separate but equal"

Henry David Thoreau, *American writer* (1817–1862)
Ivan Turgenev, *Russian writer* (1818–1883)
Karl Marx, *German political philosopher* (1818–1883)
Queen Victoria, *British monarch* (1819–1901)
George Eliot, *English novelist* (1819–1880)
Walt Whitman, *American poet* (1819–1892)
Friedrich Engels, *German political philosopher* (1820–1895)
Florence Nightingale, *English nurse* (1820–1910)
Charles Baudelaire, *French poet* (1821–1867)
Feodor Dostoevsky, *Russian writer* (1821–1881)
Gustave Flaubert, *French novelist* (1821–1880)
Mary Baker Eddy, *founder of Christian Science* (1821–1910)
Ulysses S. Grant, *American President* (1822–1885)
Gregor Mendel, *Austrian scientist* (1822–1884)
Louis Pasteur, *French scientist* (1822–1895)
Alexandre Dumas, fils, *French writer* (1824–1895)
Johann Strauss, *Austrian "waltz king"* (1825–1899)
Stephen Foster, *American composer* (1826–1864)
Joseph Lister, *English surgeon* (1827–1912)
Henrik Ibsen, *Norwegian dramatist* (1828–1906)
Leo Tolstoi, *Russian novelist* (1828–1910)
Jules Verne, *French author* (1828–1905)
William Booth, *Salvation Army founder* (1829–1912)
Emily Dickinson, *American poet* (1830–1886)
James Clerk Maxwell, *Scottish astronomer and physicist* (1831–1879)
Louisa May Alcott, *American author* (1832–1888)
Horatio Alger, *American author* (1834–1899)
Lewis Carroll (Charles Lutwidge Dodgson), *English author* (1832–1898)

## SPANISH-AMERICAN WAR (1898–1899)

War fires stoked by "jingo journalism" as American people support Cuban rebels against Spain. American business sees economic gain in Cuban trade and resources and American power zones in Latin America. Outstanding events: Submarine mine explodes U.S. battleship *Maine* in Havana Harbor (**Feb. 15**); 260 killed; responsibility never fixed. Congress declares independence of Cuba (**April 19**). Spain declares war on U.S. (**Apr. 24**); Congress (**Apr. 25**) formally declares nation has been at war with Spain since Apr. 21. Commodore George Dewey wins seven-hour battle of Manila Bay (**May 1**). Spanish fleet destroyed off Santiago, Cuba (**July 3**); city surrenders (**July 17**). Treaty of Paris (ratified by Senate in **1899**) ends war. U.S. given Guam and Puerto Rico and agrees to pay Spain $20 million for Philippines. Cuba independent of Spain; under U.S. military control for three years until **May 20, 1902**. Yellow fever is eradicated and political reforms achieved.

doctrine. Alfred Nobel's will establishes prizes for peace, science, and literature. Marconi receives first wireless patent in Britain. William Jennings Bryan delivers "Cross of Gold" speech at Democratic Convention in Chicago. First modern Olympic games held in Athens, Greece.

**1898** Chinese "Boxers," anti-foreign organization, established. They stage uprisings against Europeans in **1900**; U.S. and other Western troops relieve Peking legations. Spanish-American War (*see* special material on the "Spanish-American War"). Pierre and Marie Curie discover radium and polonium.

**1899** Boer War (or South African War). Conflict between British and Boers (descendants of Dutch settlers of South Africa). Causes rooted in long-standing territorial disputes and in friction over political rights for English and other "uitlanders" following 1886 discovery of vast gold deposits in Transvaal. (British victorious as war ends in **1902**.) Casualties: 5,774 British dead, about 4,000 Boers. Union of South Africa established in **1908** as confederation of colonies; becomes British dominion in **1910**.

---

**1900** Hurricane ravages Galveston, Tex.; 6,000 drown. Sigmund Freud's *The Interpretation of Dreams.*

**1901** Queen Victoria dies; succeeded by son, Edward VII. As President McKinley begins second term, he is shot fatally by anarchist Leon Czolgosz. Theodore Roosevelt sworn in as successor.

**1902** Enrico Caruso's first gramophone recording.

**1903** Wright brothers, Orville and Wilbur, fly first powered, controlled, heavier-than-air plane at Kitty Hawk, N.C. Henry Ford organizes Ford Motor Company.

**1904** Russo-Japanese War—competition for Korea and Manchuria: In **1905**, Port Arthur surrenders to Japanese and Russia suffers other defeats; President Roosevelt mediates Treaty of Portsmouth, N.H., ending war with concessions for Japan. *Entente Cordiale:* Britain and France settle their international differences. General theory of radioactivity by Rutherford and Soddy. New York City subway opened.

**1905** General strike in Russia; first workers' soviet set up in St. Petersburg. Sailors on battleship *Potemkin* mutiny; reforms including first Duma (parliament) established by Czar's "October Manifesto." Albert Einstein's special theory of relativity and other key theories in physics. Franz Lehar's *Merry Widow.*

**1906** San Francisco earthquake and three-day fire; 500 dead. Roald Amundsen, Norwegian explorer, fixes magnetic North Pole.

**1907** Second Hague Peace Conference, of 46 nations, adopts 10 conventions on rules of war. Financial panic of **1907** in U.S.

**1908** Earthquake kills 150,000 in southern Italy and Sicily. U.S. Supreme Court, in Danbury Hatters' case, outlaws secondary union boycotts.

**1909** North Pole reached by American explorers Robert E. Peary and Matthew Henson.

**1910** Boy Scouts of America incorporated.

**1911** First use of aircraft as offensive weapon in Turkish-Italian War. Italy defeats Turks and annexes Tripoli and Libya. Chinese Republic proclaimed after revolution overthrows Manchu dynasty. Sun Yat-sen named president. Mexican Revolution: Porfirio Diaz, president since 1877, replaced by Francisco Madero. Triangle Shirtwaist Company fire in New York; 145 killed. Richard Strauss's *Der Rosenkavalier.* Irving Berlin's *Alexander's Ragtime Band.* Amundsen reaches South Pole.

**1912** Balkan Wars **(1912–13)** resulting from territorial disputes: Turkey defeated by alliance of Bulgaria, Serbia, Greece, and Montenegro; London peace treaty **(1913)** partitions most of European Turkey among the victors. In second war **(1913)**, Bulgaria attacks Serbia and Greece and is defeated after Romania intervenes and Turks recapture Adrianople. *Titanic* sinks on maiden voyage; over 1,500 drown.

**1913** Suffragettes demonstrate in London. Garment workers strike in New York and Boston; win pay raise and shorter hours. Sixteenth Amendment (income tax) and 17th (popular election of U.S. senators) adopted. Act creating U.S. Federal Reserve System becomes law. Stravinsky's *The Rite of Spring.*

**1914** World War I begins (*see* special material on "World War I"). Panama Canal officially opened. Congress sets up Federal Trade Commission, adopts Clayton Antitrust Act. U.S. Marines occupy Veracruz, Mexico, intervening in civil war to protect American interests.

**1915** U.S. protests German submarine actions and British blockade of Germany. U.S. banks lend $500 million to France and Britain. D. W. Griffith's film *Birth of a Nation.* Albert Einstein's General Theory of Relativity.

**1916** Congress expands armed forces. Tom Mooney arrested for San Francisco bombing (pardoned in **1939**). Pershing fails in raid into Mexico in

Edouard Manet, *French painter* (1832–1883)
Johannes Brahms, *German composer* (1833–1897)
Alfred Nobel, *Swedish industrialist* (1833–1896)
Edgar Dégas, *French painter* (1834–1917)
James McNeill Whistler, *American painter* (1834–1903)
Dmitri Mendeleev, *Russian chemist* (1834–1907)
Mark Twain (Samuel L. Clemens), *American author* (1835–1910)
Camille Saint-Saëns, *French composer* (1835–1910)
Andrew Carnegie, *American industrialist* (1835–1919)
W. S. Gilbert, *English librettist* (1836–1911)
Bret Harte, *American novelist* (1836–1902)
Winslow Homer, *American painter* (1836–1910)
Sitting Bull, *American Indian chief* (1837–1890)
J. P. Morgan, *American financier* (1837–1913)
Georges Bizet, *French composer* (1838–1875)
Paul Cézanne, *French painter* (1839–1906)
John D. Rockefeller, *American industrialist* (1839–1937)
Thomas Hardy, *English novelist* (1840–1928)
Emile Zola, *French novelist* (1840–1902)
Claude Monet, *French painter* (1840–1926)
Pierre Renoir, *French painter* (1840–1919)
Auguste Rodin, *French sculptor* (1840–1917)
Peter Ilich Tchaikovsky, *Russian composer* (1840–1893)
Ambrose Bierce, *American author* (1842–1914)
William James, *American philosopher* (1842–1910)
Arthur Sullivan, *English composer* (1842–1900)
Henry James, *American novelist* (1843–1916)
Edvard Grieg, *Norwegian composer* (1843–1907)
Sarah Bernhardt, *French actress* (1844–1923)
Anatole France (Jacques Anatole Thibault), *French author* (1844–1924)
Gerard Manley Hopkins, *English poet* (1844–1899)
Friedrich Nietzsche, *German philosopher* (1844–1900)
Nikolai Rimski-Korsakov, *Russian composer* (1844–1908)

quest of rebel Pancho Villa. U.S. buys Virgin Islands from Denmark for $25 million. President Wilson re-elected with "he kept us out of war" slogan. "Black Tom" explosion at munitions dock in Jersey City, N.Y., $40,000,000 damages; traced to German saboteurs. Margaret Sanger opens first birth control clinic. Easter Rebellion in Ireland put down by British troops.

**1917** First U.S. combat troops in France as U.S. declares war (**April 6**). Russian Revolution—climax of long unrest under czars. February Revolution—Czar forced to abdicate, liberal government created. Kerensky becomes prime minister and forms provisional government (**July**). In October Revolution, Bolsheviks seize power in armed coup d'état led by Lenin and Trotsky. Kerensky flees. Revolutionaries execute the czar and his family (**1918**). Reds set up Third International in Moscow (**1919**). Balfour Declaration promises Jewish homeland in Palestine. Sigmund Freud's *Introduction to Psychoanalysis.*

**1918** Russian Civil War between Reds (Bolsheviks) and Whites (anti-Bolsheviks); Reds win in **1920**. Allied troops (U.S., British, French) intervene (**March**); leave in **1919**. Japanese hold Vladivostok until 1922. World-wide influenza epidemic strikes; by **1920**, nearly 20 million are dead. In U.S. alone, 500,000 perish.

**1919** Third International (Comintern) establishes Soviet control over international Communist movements. Paris peace conference. Versailles Treaty, incorporating Wilson's draft Covenant of League of Nations, signed by Allies and Germany; rejected by U.S. Senate. Congress formally ends war in **1921**. Eighteenth (Prohibition) Amendment adopted. Alcock and Brown make first trans-Atlantic non-stop flight.

**1920** League of Nations holds first meeting at Geneva, Switzerland. U.S. Dept. of Justice "red hunt" nets thousands of radicals; aliens deported. Woman suffrage (19th) amendment ratified. First Agatha Christie mystery. Sinclair Lewis's *Main Street.*

**1921** Reparations Commission fixes German liability at 132 billion gold marks. German inflation begins. Major treaties signed at Washington Disarmament Conference limit naval tonnage and pledge to respect territorial integrity of China. Irish Free State formed in southern Ireland as self-governing dominion of British Empire. In U.S., Nicola Sacco and Bartolomeo Vanzetti, Italian-born anarchists, convicted of armed robbery murder; case stirs world-wide protests; they are executed in **1927**.

**1922** Mussolini marches on Rome; forms Fascist government. Irish Free State officially proclaimed.

**1923** Adolf Hitler's "Beer Hall Putsch" in Munich fails; in **1924** he is sentenced to five years in prison where he writes *Mein Kampf;* released after eight months. Occupation of Ruhr by French and Belgian troops to enforce reparations payments. Widespread Ku Klux Klan violence in U.S. George Gershwin's *Rhapsody in Blue.*

**1924** Death of Lenin; Stalin wins power struggle, rules as Soviet dictator until death in **1953**. Italian Fascists murder Socialist leader Giacomo Matteotti. Interior Secretary Albert B. Fall and oilmen Harry Sinclair and Edward L. Doheny are charged with conspiracy and bribery in the Teapot Dome scandal, involving fraudulent leases of naval oil reserves. In **1931**,

Wilhelm Conrad Roentgen, *German discoverer of X-rays* (1845–1923)
Gabriel Fauré, *French composer* (1845–1924)
Thomas Alva Edison, *American inventor* (1847–1931)
Alexander Graham Bell, *American inventor* (1847–1922)
Paul Gauguin, *French painter* (1848–1903)
August Strindberg, *Swedish dramatist* (1849–1912)
Luther Burbank, *American horticulturist* (1849–1926)
Guy de Maupassant, *French author* (1850–1893)
Robert Louis Stevenson, *English author* (1850–1894)
Vincent Van Gogh, *Dutch painter* (1853–1890)
George Eastman, *American photographic pioneer* (1854–1932)
George Bernard Shaw, *Irish dramatist* (1856–1950)
Oscar Wilde, *Anglo-Irish author* (1856–1900)
Sigmund Freud, *Austrian founder of psychoanalysis* (1856–1939)
Robert E. Peary, *American explorer* (1856–1920)
Booker T. Washington, *American educator* (1856–1915)
Joseph Conrad, *Anglo-Polish novelist* (1857–1924)
Giacomo Puccini, *Italian composer* (1858–1924)
Theodore Roosevelt, *American President* (1858–1919)
Max Planck, *German physicist* (1858–1947)

## WORLD WAR I (1914–1918)

Imperial, territorial, and economic rivalries lead to the "Great War" between the Central Powers (Austria-Hungary, Germany, Bulgaria, and Turkey) and the Allies (U.S., Britain, France, Russia, Belgium, Serbia, Greece, Romania, Montenegro, Portugal, Italy, Japan). About 10 million combatants killed, 20 million wounded.

**1914** Austrian Archduke Francis Ferdinand and wife assassinated in Sarajevo by Serbian nationalist, Gavrilo Princip (**June 28**). Austria declares war on Serbia (**July 28**). Germany declares war on Russia (**Aug. 1**), on France (**Aug. 3**), invades Belgium (**Aug. 4**). Britain declares war on Germany (**Aug. 4**). Germans defeat Russians in Battle of Tannenberg on Eastern Front (**Aug.**). First Battle of the Marne (**Sept.**). German drive stopped 25 miles from Paris. By end of year, war on the Western Front is "positional" in the trenches.

**1915** German submarine blockade of Great Britain begins (**Feb.**). Dardanelles Campaign—British land in Turkey (**April**), withdraw from Gallipoli (**Dec. to Jan. 1916**). Germans use gas at second Battle of Ypres (**April-May**). *Lusitania* sunk by German submarine—1,198 lost, including 128 Americans (**May 7**). On Eastern Front, German and Austrian "great offensive" conquers all of Poland and Lithuania; Russians lose 1 million men (**by Sept. 6**). "Great Fall Offensive" by Allies results in little change from 1914 (**Sept.-Oct.**). Britain and France declare war on Bulgaria (**Oct. 14**).

**1916** Battle of Verdun—Germans and French each lose about 350,000 men (**Feb.**). Extended submarine warfare begins (**March**). British-German sea battle of Jutland (**May**); British lose more ships, but German fleet never ventures forth again. On Eastern front, the Brusilov offensive demoralizes Russians, costs them 1 million men (**June-Sept.**). Battle of the Somme—British lose over 400,000; French, 200,000; Germans, about 450,000; all with no strategic results (**July-Nov.**). Romania declares war on Austria-Hungary (**Aug. 27**). Bucharest captured (**Dec.**).

**1917** U.S. declares war on Germany (**April 6**). Submarine warfare at peak (**April**). On Italian Front, Battle of Caporetto—Italians retreat, losing 600,000 prisoners and deserters (**Oct.-Dec.**). On Western Front, Battles of Arras, Champagne, Ypres (third battle), etc. First large British tank attack (**Nov.**). U.S. declares war on Austria-Hungary (**Dec. 7**). Armistice between new Russian Bolshevik government and Germans (**Dec. 15**).

**1918** Great offensive by Germans (**March-June**). Americans' first important battle role at Château-Thierry—as they and French stop German advance (**June**). Second Battle of the Marne (**July-Aug.**)—start of Allied offensive at Amiens, St. Mihiel, etc. Battles of the Argonne and Ypres panic German leadership (**Sept.-Oct.**). British offensive in Palestine (**Sept.**). Germans ask for armistice (**Oct. 4**). British armistice with Turkey (**Oct.**). German Kaiser abdicates (**Nov.**). Hostilities cease on Western Front (**Nov. 11**).

Fall is sentenced to year in prison; Doheny and Sinclair acquitted of bribery. Nellie Tayloe Ross elected governor of Wyoming; first woman governor elected in U.S. Nathan Leopold and Richard Loeb convicted in "thrill killing" of Bobby Franks in Chicago; defended by Clarence Darrow; sentenced to life imprisonment. (Loeb killed by fellow convict in **1936**; Leopold paroled in **1958**, dies in **1971**.)

**1925** Locarno conferences seek to secure European peace by mutual guarantees. John T. Scopes convicted and fined for teaching evolution in a public school in Tennessee "Monkey Trial"; sentence set aside. John Logie Baird, Scottish inventor, transmits human features by television. Adolf Hitler publishes Volume I of *Mein Kampf*.

**1926** General strike in Britain brings nation's activities to standstill. U.S. marines dispatched to Nicaragua during revolt; they remain until **1933**. Gertrude Ederle of U.S. is first woman to swim English Channel.

**1927** German economy collapses. Socialists riot in Vienna; general strike follows acquittal of Nazis for political murder. Trotsky expelled from Russian Communist Party. Charles A. Lindbergh flies first successful solo non-stop flight from New York to Paris. Ruth Snyder and Judd Gray convicted of murder of Albert Snyder; they are executed at Sing Sing prison in **1928**. *The Jazz Singer,* with Al Jolson, first part-talking motion picture.

**1928** Kellogg-Briand Pact, outlawing war, signed in Paris by 65 nations. Alexander Fleming discovers penicillin. Richard E. Byrd starts expedition to Antarctic; returns in **1930**.

**1929** Trotsky expelled from U.S.S.R. Lateran Treaty establishes independent Vatican City. In U.S., stock market prices collapse, with U.S. securities losing $26 billion—first phase of Depression and world economic crisis. St. Valentine's Day gangland massacre in Chicago.

**1930** Britain, U.S., Japan, France, and Italy sign naval disarmament treaty. Nazis gain in German elections. Cyclotron developed by Ernest O. Lawrence, U.S. physicist.

**1931** Spain becomes a republic with overthrow of King Alfonso XIII. German industrialists finance 800,000-strong Nazi party. British parliament enacts statute of Westminster, legalizing dominion equality with Britain. Mukden Incident begins Japanese occupation of Manchuria. In U.S., Hoover proposes one-year moratorium of war debts. Harold C. Urey discovers heavy hydrogen. Gangster Al Capone sentenced to 11 years in prison for tax evasion (freed in **1939**; dies in **1947**).

**1932** Nazis lead in German election with 230 Reichstag seats. Famine in U.S.S.R. In U.S., Congress sets up Reconstruction Finance Corporation to stimulate economy. Veterans march on Washington—most leave after Senate rejects payment of cash bonuses; others removed by troops under Douglas MacArthur. U.S. protests Japanese aggression in Manchuria. Amelia Earhart is first woman to fly Atlantic solo. Charles A. Lindbergh's baby son kidnapped, killed. (Bruno Richard Hauptmann arrested in **1934**, convicted in **1935**, executed in **1936**.)

**1933** Hitler appointed German chancellor, gets dictatorial powers. Reichstag fire in Berlin; Nazi terror begins. (*See* special material on "The Holocaust.") Germany and Japan withdraw from League of Nations. Giuseppe Zangara executed for attempted assassination of President-elect Roosevelt in which Chicago Mayor Cermak is fatally shot. Roosevelt inaugurated ("the only thing we have to fear is fear itself"); launches New Deal. Prohibition repealed. U.S.S.R. recognized by U.S.

Arthur Conan Doyle, *English writer* (1859–1930)
Knut Hamsun, *Swedish novelist* (1859–1952)
Henri Bergson, *French philosopher* (1859–1941)
John Dewey, *American philosopher* (1859–1952)
Georges Seurat, *French painter* (1859–1891)
Pierre Curie, *French physicist* (1859–1906)
Anton Chekhov, *Russian dramatist* (1860–1904)
Gustav Mahler, *German composer* (1860–1911)
Rabindranath Tagore, *Indian poet* (1861–1941)
Alfred North Whitehead, *British philosopher-mathematician* (1861–1947)
Edith Wharton, *American author* (1862–1937)
Claude Debussy, *French composer* (1862–1918)
David Lloyd George, *British statesman* (1863–1945)
Henry Ford, *American automobile pioneer* (1863–1947)
William Randolph Hearst, *American newspaper magnate* (1863–1951)
Henri Toulouse-Lautrec, *French painter* (1864–1901)
George Washington Carver, *American botanist* (1864–1943)
Richard Strauss, *German composer* (1864–1949)
Rudyard Kipling, *English writer* (1865–1936)
William Butler Yeats, *Irish poet* (1865–1939)
Jean Sibelius, *Finnish composer* (1865–1957)
Sun Yat-sen, *Chinese statesman* (1866–1927)
Benedetto Croce, *Italian philosopher* (1866–1952)

## THE HOLOCAUST (1933–1945)

"Holocaust" is the term describing the Nazi annihilation of about 6 million Jews (two thirds of the pre-World War II European Jewish population), including 4,500,000 from Russia, Poland, and the Baltic; 750,000 from Hungary and Romania; 290,000 from Germany and Austria; 105,000 from The Netherlands; 90,000 from France; 54,000 from Greece, etc.

The Holocaust was unique in its being *genocide*—the systematic destruction of a people solely because of religion, race, ethnicity, or nationality—on an unmatched scale. Of the millions killed during this period, only the Gypsies and the Jews were victims of this crime.

The only comparable act of genocide in modern times was launched in April 1915, when 1.5 million Armenians were massacred by the Turks.

**1933** Hitler named German Chancellor (**Jan.**). Dachau, first concentration camp, established (**March**). Boycotts against Jews begin (**April**).

**1935** Anti-Semitic Nuremberg Laws passed by Reichstag (**Sept.**).

**1937** Buchenwald concentration camp opens (**July**).

**1938** Extension of anti-Semitic laws to Austria after annexation (**March**). *Kristallnacht* (Night of Broken Glass)—anti-Semitic riots in Germany and Austria (**Nov. 9**). 26,000 Jews sent to concentration camps; Jewish children expelled from schools (**Nov.**). Expropriation of Jewish property and businesses (**Dec.**).

**1940** As war continues, Nazi acts against Jews extended to German-conquered areas.

**1941** Deportation of German Jews begins; massacres of Jews in Odessa and Kiev—68,000 killed (**Nov.**); in Riga and Vilna—almost 60,000 killed (**Dec.**).

**1942** Unified Jewish resistance in ghettos begins (**Jan.**). 300,000 Jews from Warsaw Ghetto deported to Treblinka death camp (**July**).

**1943** Warsaw Ghetto uprisings (**Jan. and April**); Ghetto exterminated (**May**).

**1944** 476,000 Hungarian Jews sent to Auschwitz (**May-June**). D-day (**June 6**). Soviet Army liberates Maidanek death camp (**July**). Nazis try to hide evidence of death camps (**Nov.**).

**1945** Americans liberate Buchenwald, Bergen-Belsen camps (**April**). Nuremberg War Crimes Trial (**Nov. 1945 to Oct. 1946**).

**1934** Chancellor Dollfuss of Austria assassinated by Nazis. Hitler becomes Führer. U.S.S.R. admitted to League of Nations. Dionne sisters, first quintuplets to survive beyond infancy, born in Canada.

**1935** Saar incorporated into Germany after plebiscite. Nazis repudiate Versailles Treaty, introduce compulsory military service. Mussolini invades Ethiopia; League invokes sanctions. Roosevelt opens second phase of New Deal in U.S., calling for social security, better housing, equitable taxation, and farm assistance. Huey Long assassinated in Louisiana.

**1936** Germans occupy Rhineland. Italy annexes Ethiopia. Rome-Berlin Axis proclaimed (Japan to join in **1940**). Trotsky exiled to Mexico. King George V dies; succeeded by son, Edward VIII, who soon abdicates to marry American-born divorcée, and is succeeded by brother, George VI. Spanish civil war begins. (Franco's fascist forces defeat Loyalist forces by **1939**, when Madrid falls.) War between China and Japan begins, to continue through World War II. Japan and Germany sign anti-Commintern pact; joined by Italy in **1937**.

**1937** Hitler repudiates war guilt clause of Versailles Treaty; continues to build German power. Italy withdraws from League of Nations. U.S. gunboat *Panay* sunk by Japanese in Yangtze River. Japan invades China, conquers most of coastal area. Amelia Earhart lost somewhere in Pacific on round-the-world flight.

**1938** Hitler marches into Austria; political and geographical union of Germany and Austria proclaimed. Munich Pact—Britain, France, and Italy agree to let Germany partition Czechoslovakia. Germany occupies Sudetenland, about one third of Czechoslovakia. Douglas "Wrong-Way" Corrigan flies from New York to Dublin.

**1939** Germany occupies Bohemia and Moravia; renounces pacts with Poland and England and concludes 10-year non-aggression pact with U.S.S.R. Russo-Finnish War begins; Finns to lose one tenth of territory in **1940** peace treaty. World War II begins (*see* special material on "World War II"). In U.S., Roosevelt submits $1,319-million defense budget, proclaims U.S. neutrality, and declares limited emergency. Albert Einstein writes FDR about feasibility of atomic bomb. New York World's Fair opens.

**1940** Trotsky assassinated in Mexico. Estonia, Latvia, and Lithuania annexed by U.S.S.R. U.S. trades 50 destroyers for leases on British bases in Western Hemisphere. Selective Service Act signed.

**1941** Japanese surprise attack on U.S. fleet at Pearl Harbor brings U.S. into World War II. Manhattan Project (atomic bomb research) begins. Roosevelt enunciates "four freedoms," signs lend-lease act, declares national emergency, promises aid to U.S.S.R.

Wilbur Wright, *American aviation pioneer* (1867–1912)
Arturo Toscanini, *Italian conductor* (1867–1957)
Marie (Sklodowska) Curie, *Polish-French scientist* (1867–1937)
Maxim Gorki, *Russian writer* (1868–1936)
Robert A. Millikan, *American physicist* (1869–1953)
Mohandas Gandhi, *Indian leader* (1869–1948)
André Gide, *French author* (1869–1951)
Henri Matisse, *French painter* (1869–1954)
Frank Lloyd Wright, *American architect* (1869–1959)
Nikolai Lenin, *Russian revolutionist* (1870–1924)
Orville Wright, *American aviation pioneer* (1871–1948)
Rasputin, *Russian monk* (1871–1916)
Stephen Crane, *American author* (1871–1900)
Theodore Dreiser, *American novelist* (1871–1945)
Marcel Proust, *French author* (1871–1922)
Bertrand Russell, *English philosopher* (1872–1970)
Enrico Caruso, *Italian tenor* (1873–1921)
Chaim Weizmann, *first president of Israel* (1874–1952)

## WORLD WAR II (1939–1945)

Axis powers (Germany, Italy, Japan, Hungary, Romania, Bulgaria) *vs.* Allies (U.S., Britain, France, U.S.S.R., Australia, Belgium, Brazil, Canada, China, Denmark, Greece, Netherlands, New Zealand, Norway, Poland, South Africa, Yugoslavia).

**1939** Germany invades Poland and annexes Danzig; Britain and France give Hitler ultimatum (**Sept. 1**), declare war (**Sept. 3**). Disabled German pocket battleship Admiral Graf Spee blown up off Montevideo, Uruguay, on Hitler's orders (**Dec. 17**). Limited activity ("Sitzkrieg") on Western Front.

**1940** Nazis invade Netherlands, Belgium, and Luxembourg (**May 10**). Chamberlain resigns as Prime Minister; Churchill takes over (**May 10**). Germans cross French frontier (**May 12**) using air/tank/infantry "Blitzkrieg" tactics. Dunkerque evacuation—about 335,000 out of 400,000 Allied soldiers rescued from Belgium by British civilian and naval craft (**May 26-June 3**). Italy declares war on France and Britain; invades France (**June 10**). Germans enter Paris; city undefended (**June 14**). France and Germany sign armistice at Compiegne (**June 22**). Nazis bomb Coventry, England (**Nov. 14**).

**1941** Germans launch attacks in Balkans. Yugoslavia surrenders—General Mihajlovic continues guerrilla warfare; Tito leads left-wing guerrillas (**April 17**). Nazi tanks enter Athens; remnants of British Army quit Greece (**April 27**). Hitler attacks Russia (**June 22**). Atlantic Charter—FDR and Churchill agree on war aims (**Aug. 14**). Japanese attacks on Pearl Harbor, Philippines, Guam force U.S. into war; U.S. Pacific fleet crippled (**Dec. 7**). U.S. and Britain declare war on Japan. Germany and Italy declare war on U.S.; Congress declares war on those countries (**Dec. 11**).

**1942** British surrender Singapore to Japanese (**Feb. 15**). U.S. forces on Bataan peninsula in Philippines surrender (**April 9**). U.S. and Filipino troops on Corregidor island in Manila Bay surrender to Japanese (**May 6**). Village of Lidice in Czechoslovakia razed by Nazis (**June 10**). U.S. and Britain land in French North Africa (**Nov. 8**).

**1943** Casablanca Conference—Churchill and FDR agree on unconditional surrender goal (**Jan. 14–24**). German 6th Army surrenders at Stalingrad—turning point of war in Russia (**Feb. 1–2**). Remnants of Nazis trapped on Cape Bon, ending war in Africa (**May 12**). Mussolini deposed; Badoglio named premier (**July 25**). Allied troops land on Italian mainland after conquest of Sicily (**Sept. 3**). Italy surrenders (**Sept. 8**). Nazis seize Rome (**Sept. 10**). Cairo Conference: FDR, Churchill, Chiang Kai-shek pledge defeat of Japan, free Korea (**Nov. 22–26**). Teheran Conference: FDR, Churchill, Stalin agree on invasion plans (**Nov. 28-Dec. 1**).

**1944** U.S. and British troops land at Anzio on west Italian coast and hold beachhead (**Jan. 22**). U.S. and British troops enter Rome (**June 4**). D-Day—Allies launch Normandy invasion (**June 6**). Hitler wounded in bomb plot (**July 20**). Paris liberated (**Aug. 25**). Athens freed by Allies (**Oct. 13**). Americans invade Philippines (**Oct. 20**). Germans launch counteroffensive in Belgium—Battle of Bulge (**Dec. 16**).

**1945** Yalta Agreement signed by FDR, Churchill, Stalin—establishes basis for occupation of Germany, returns to Soviet Union lands taken by Germany and Japan; U.S.S.R. agrees to friendship pact with China (**Feb. 11**). Mussolini killed at Lake Como (**April 28**). Admiral Doenitz takes command in Germany; suicide of Hitler announced (**May 1**). Berlin falls (**May 2**). V-E Day—Germany signs unconditional surrender terms at Rheims (**May 7**). Potsdam Conference—Truman, Churchill, Atlee (after **July 28**), Stalin establish council of foreign ministers to prepare peace treaties; plan German postwar government and reparations (**July 17-Aug. 2**). A-bomb blasts Hiroshima (**Aug. 6**). U.S.S.R. declares war on Japan (**Aug. 8**). Nagasaki hit by A-bomb (**Aug. 9**). Japan surrenders (**Aug. 14**). V-J Day—Japanese sign surrender terms aboard battleship *Missouri* (**Sept. 2**).

1942 Declaration of United Nations signed in Washington. Women's military services established. Enrico Fermi achieves nuclear chain reaction. Japanese and persons of Japanese ancestry moved inland from Pacific Coast. Cocoanut Grove nightclub fire in Boston kills 498.

1943 President freezes prices, salaries, and wages to prevent inflation. Income tax withholding introduced.

1944 G.I. Bill of Rights enacted. Bretton Woods Conference creates International Monetary Fund and World Bank. Dumbarton Oaks Conference—U.S., British Commonwealth, and U.S.S.R. propose establishment of United Nations.

1945 Yalta Conference (Roosevelt, Churchill, Stalin) plans final defeat of Germany **(Feb.)**. San Francisco Conference establishes U.N. **(April-June)**. FDR dies **(April 12)**. Potsdam Conference (Truman, Churchill, Stalin) establishes basis of German reconstruction **(July-Aug)**.

1946 First meeting of U.N. General Assembly opens in London **(Jan. 10)**. League of Nations dissolved **(April)**. Italy abolishes monarchy **(June)**. Verdict in Nuremberg war trial: 12 Nazi leaders (including 1 tried in absentia) sentenced to hang; 7 imprisoned; 3 acquitted **(Oct. 1)**. Goering commits suicide a few hours before 10 other Nazis are executed **(Oct. 15)**. Winston Churchill's "Iron Curtain" speech warns against Soviet expansion. Xerography invented by Chester Carlson.

1947 Britain nationalizes coal mines **(Jan. 1)**. Peace treaties for Italy, Romania, Bulgaria, Hungary, Finland signed in Paris **(Feb. 10)**. Soviet Union rejects U.S. plan for U.N. atomic-energy control **(March 4)**. Truman Doctrine proposed—the first significant U.S. attempt to "contain" communist expansion **(March 12)**. Marshall Plan for European recovery proposed—a coordinated program to help European nations recover from ravages of war **(June)**. (By **1951**, this "European Recovery Program" had cost $11 billion.) India and Pakistan gain independence from Britain **(Aug. 15)**. Cominform (Communist Information Bureau) founded under Soviet auspices to rebuild contacts among European Communist parties, missing since dissolution of Comintern in **1943 (Sept.)**. (Yugoslav party expelled in **1948** and Cominform disbanded in **1956**.)

1948 Gandhi assassinated in New Delhi by Hindu fanatic **(Jan. 30)**. Communists seize power in Czechoslovakia **(Feb. 23–25)**. Burma and Ceylon granted independence by Britain. Organization of American States (OAS) Charter signed at Bogotá, Colombia **(April 30)**. Nation of Israel proclaimed; British end Mandate at midnight; Arab armies attack **(May 14)**. Berlin airlift begins **(June 21)**; ends **May 12, 1949.** Stalin and Tito break **(June 28)**. Independent Republic of Korea is proclaimed, following election supervised by U.N. **(Aug. 15)**. Verdict in Japanese war trial: Tojo and six others sentenced to hang (hanged **Dec. 23**); 18 imprisoned **(Nov. 12)**. United States of Indonesia established as Dutch and Indonesians settle conflict **(Dec. 27)**. Alger Hiss, former U.S. State Department official, indicted on perjury charges after denying passing secret documents to communist spy ring. Convicted in second trial **(1950)** and sentenced to five-year prison term.

1949 Cease-fire in Palestine **(Jan. 7)**. Truman proposes Point Four Program to help world's backward areas **(Jan. 20)**. Israel signs armistice with Egypt **(Feb. 24)**. Start of North Atlantic Treaty Organization (NATO)—treaty signed by 12 nations **(April 4)**. German Federal Republic (West Germany) established **(Sept. 21)**. Truman discloses Soviet Union has set off atomic explosion **(Sept. 23)**. Communist People's Republic of China formally proclaimed **(Oct. 1)**.

1950 Truman orders development of hydrogen bomb **(Jan. 31)**. Korean War *(see special material on the "Korean War")*. Assassination attempt on President Truman by Puerto Rican nationalists **(Nov. 1)**. Brink's robbery in Boston; almost $3 million stolen **(Jan. 17)**.

1951 Six nations agree to Schuman Plan to pool European coal and steel **(March 19)**—in effect **Feb. 10, 1953.** Julius and Ethel Rosenberg sentenced to death for passing atomic secrets to Russians **(March)**. Japanese peace treaty signed in San Francisco by 49 nations **(Sept. 8)**. Color television introduced in U.S.

1952 George VI dies; his daughter becomes Elizabeth II **(Feb. 6)**. NATO

Winston Churchill, *British statesman* (1874–1965)
Gertrude Stein, *American writer* (1874–1946)
Arnold Schönberg, *Austrian composer* (1874–1951)
Guglielmo Marconi, *Italian physicist* (1874–1935)
Thomas Mann, *German novelist* (1875–1955)
C. G. Jung, *Swiss psychiatrist* (1875–1961)
Carl Sandburg, *American poet* (1878–1967)
Martin Buber, *Jewish philosopher* (1878–1965)
Joseph Stalin, *Russian dictator* (1879–1953)
Leon Trotsky, *Russian revolutionist* (1879–1940)
Paul Klee, *Swiss painter* (1879–1940)
Albert Einstein, *German-American physicist* (1879–1955)
Douglas MacArthur, *American general* (1880–1964)
Pablo Picasso, *Spanish-born French painter* (1881–1973)
Béla Bartók, *Hungarian composer* (1881–1945)
Alexander Fleming, *English scientist* (1881–1955)
Franklin D. Roosevelt, *American President* (1882–1945)
Eamon de Valera, *Irish statesman* (1882–1975)
James Joyce, *Irish author* (1882–1941)
Georges Braque, *French painter* (1882–1963)
Igor Stravinsky, *Russian composer* (1882–1971)
Benito Mussolini, *Italian dictator* (1883–1945)
Franz Kafka, *Czechoslovakian-born Austrian author* (1883–1924)
John Maynard Keynes, *English economist* (1883–1946)
Walter Gropius, *German architect* (1883–1969)
Harry S. Truman, *American President* (1884–1972)
Eduard Benes, *Czechoslovakian statesman* (1884–1948)
D. H. Lawrence, *English writer* (1885–1930)

**KOREAN WAR (1950–1953)**

**1950** North Korean Communist forces invade South Korea **(June 25)**. U.N. calls for cease-fire and asks U.N. members to assist South Korea **(June 27)**. Truman orders U.S. forces into Korea **(June 27)**. North Koreans capture Seoul **(June 28)**. Gen. Douglas MacArthur designated commander of unified U.N. forces **(July 8)**. Pusan Beachhead—U.N. forces counterattack and capture Seoul **(Aug.-Sept.)**, capture Pyongyang, North Korean capital **(Oct.)**. Chinese Communists enter war **(Oct. 26)**, force U.N. retreat toward 39th parallel **(Dec.)**.

**1951** Gen. Matthew B. Ridgeway replaces MacArthur after he threatens Chinese with massive retaliation **(April 11)**. Armistice negotiations **(July)** continue with interruptions until **June 1953.**

**1953** Armistice signed **(June 26)**. Chinese troops withdraw from North Korea **(Oct. 26, 1958)**, but over 200 violations of armistice noted to **1959.**

conference approves European army (**Feb.**). AEC announces "satisfactory" experiments in hydrogen-weapons research; eyewitnesses tell of blasts near Eniwetok (**Nov.**).

**1953** Gen. Dwight D. Eisenhower inaugurated President of United States (**Jan. 20**). Stalin dies (**March 5**). Malenkov becomes Soviet Premier; Beria, Minister of Interior; Molotov, Foreign Minister (**March 6**). Dag Hammarskjold begins term as U.N. Secretary-General (**April 10**). Edmund Hillary, of New Zealand, and Tenzing Norkay, of Nepal, reach top of Mt. Everest (**May 29**). East Berliners rise against Communist rule; quelled by tanks (**June 17**). Egypt becomes republic ruled by military junta (**June 18**). Julius and Ethel Rosenberg executed in Sing Sing prison (**June 19**). Korean armistice signed (**July 27**). Moscow announces explosion of hydrogen bomb (**Aug. 20**).

**1954** First atomic submarine *Nautilus*, launched (**Jan. 21**). Five U.S. Congressmen shot on floor of House as Puerto Rican nationalists fire from spectators' gallery; all five recover (**March 1**). Army *vs.* McCarthy inquiry—Senate subcommittee report blames both sides (**Apr. 22-June 17**). Dien Bien Phu, French military outpost in Vietnam, falls to Vietminh army (**May 7**). *(See* special material on the "Vietnam War.") U.S. Supreme Court (in *Brown* v. *Board of Education of Topeka*) unanimously bans racial segregation in public schools (**May 17**). Eisenhower launches world atomic pool without Soviet Union (**Sept. 6**). Eight-nation Southeast Asia defense treaty (SEATO) signed at Manila (**Sept. 8**). West Germany is granted sovereignty, admitted to NATO and Western European Union (**Oct. 23**). Dr. Jonas Salk starts innoculating children against polio. Algerian War of Independence against France begins (**Nov.**); France struggles to maintain colonial rule until 1962 when it agrees to Algeria's independence.

**1955** Nikolai A. Bulganin becomes Soviet Premier, replacing Malenkov (**Feb. 8**). Churchill resigns; Anthony Eden succeeds him (**April 6**). Federal Republic of West Germany becomes a sovereign state (**May 5**). Warsaw Pact, east European mutual defense agreement, signed (**May 14**). Argentina ousts Perón (**Sept. 19**). President Eisenhower suffers coronary thrombosis in Denver (**Sept. 24**). Martin Luther King, Jr., leads black boycott of Montgomery, Ala., bus system (**Dec. 1**); desegregated service begun (**Dec. 21**). AFL and CIO become one organization—AFL-CIO (**Dec. 5**).

**1956** Nikita Khrushchev, First Secretary of U.S.S.R. Communist Party, denounces Stalin's excesses (**Feb. 24**). First aerial H-bomb tested over Namu islet, Bikini Atoll—10 million tons TNT equivalent (**May 21**). Worker's uprising against Communist rule in Poznan, Poland, is crushed (**June 28–30**). Egypt takes control of Suez Canal (**July 26**). Israel launches attack

Ezra Pound, *American poet* (1885–1972)
Sinclair Lewis, *American novelist* (1885–1951)
Alban Berg, *Austrian composer* (1885–1935)
Niels Bohr, *Danish physicist* (1885–1962)
David Ben-Gurion, *Israeli statesman* (1886–1973)
Chiang Kai-shek, *Chinese statesman* (1887–1975)
Le Corbusier (C.E. Jeanneret), *Swiss-born French architect* (1887–1965)
T. S. Eliot, *Anglo-American poet* (1888–1965)
Eugene O'Neill, *American dramatist* (1888–1953)
Ludwig Wittgenstein, *Austrian philosopher* (1889–1951)
Adolf Hitler, *German dictator* (1889–1945)
Charles Chaplin, *English screen actor-director* (1889–1977)
Dwight D. Eisenhower, *American President* (1890–1969)
Charles de Gaulle, *French soldier and statesman* (1890–1970)
Sergei Prokofiev, *Russian composer* (1891–1953)
Frederick Banting, *Canadian discoverer of insulin* (1891–1941)

## VIETNAM WAR (1950–1975)

U.S., South Vietnam, and Allies versus North Vietnam and National Liberation Front (Viet Cong). Outstanding events:

**1950** President Truman sends 35-man military advisory group to aid French fighting to maintain colonial power in Vietnam.

**1954** After defeat of French at Dienbienphu, Geneva Agreements (**July**) provide for withdrawal of French and Vietminh to either side of demarcation zone (DMZ) pending reunification elections, which are never held. Presidents Eisenhower and Kennedy (from **1954** onward) send civilian advisors and, later, military personnel to train South Vietnamese.

**1960** Communists form National Liberation Front in South.

**1963** Ngo Dinh Diem, South Vietnam's premier, slain in coup (**Nov. 1**).

**1961–1963** U.S. military advisors rise from 2,000 to 15,000.

**1964** North Vietnamese torpedo boats reportedly attack U.S. destroyers in Gulf of Tonkin (**Aug. 2**). President Johnson orders retaliatory air strikes. Congress approves Gulf of Tonkin resolution (**Aug. 7**) authorizing President to take necessary steps to "maintain peace."

**1965** U.S. planes begin combat missions over South Vietnam. In **June**, 23,000 American advisors committed to combat. By end of year over 184,000 U.S. troops in area.

**1966** B-52s bomb DMZ, reportedly used by North Vietnam for entry into South (**July 31**).

**1967** South Vietnam National Assembly approves election of Nguyen Van Thieu as President (**Oct. 21**).

**1968** U.S. has almost 525,000 men in Vietnam. In Tet offensive (**Jan.-Feb.**), Viet Cong guerrillas attack Saigon, Hue, and some provincial capitals. President Johnson orders halt to U.S. bombardment of North Vietnam (**Oct. 31**). Saigon and N.L.F. join U.S. and North Vietnam in Paris peace talks.

**1969** President Nixon announces Vietnam peace offer (**May 14**)—begins troop withdrawals (**June**). Viet Cong forms Provisional Revolutionary Government. U.S. Senate calls for curb on commitments (**June 25**). Ho Chi Minh, 79, North Vietnam president, dies (**Sept. 3**); collective leadership chosen. Some 6,000 U.S. troops pulled back from Thailand and 1,000 marines from Vietnam (announced **Sept. 30**). Massive demonstrations in U.S. protest or support war policies (**Oct. 15**).

**1970** Nixon announces sending of troops to Cambodia (**April 30**). Last U.S. troops removed from Cambodia (**June 29**).

**1971** Congress bars use of combat troops, but not air power, in Laos and Cambodia (**Jan. 1**). South Vietnamese troops, with U.S. air cover, fail in Laos thrust. Many American ground forces withdrawn from Vietnam combat. *New York Times* publishes Pentagon papers, classified material on expansion of war (**June**).

**1972** Nixon responds to North Vietnamese drive across DMZ by ordering mining of North Vietnam ports and heavy bombing of Hanoi-Haiphong area (**April 1**). Nixon orders "Christmas bombing" of north to get North Vietnamese back to conference table (**Dec.**).

**1973** President orders halt to offensive operations in North Vietnam (**Jan. 15**). Representatives of North and South Vietnam, U.S., and N.L.F. sign peace pacts in Paris, ending longest war in U.S. history (**Jan. 27**).

**1974** Both sides accuse each other of frequent violations of cease-fire agreement.

**1975** Full-scale warfare resumes. Communists victorious (**April 30**). South Vietnam Premier Nguyen Van Thieu resigns (**April 21**). American troops evacuated (**April 30**). More than 140,000 Vietnamese refugees leave by air and sea, many to settle in U.S. Provisional Revolutionary Government takes control (**June 6**).

**1976** Election of National Assembly paves way for reunification of North and South.

on Egypt's Sinai peninsula and drives toward Suez Canal (**Oct. 29**). British and French invade Egypt at Port Said (**Nov. 5**). Cease-fire forced by U.S. pressure stops British, French, and Israeli advance (**Nov. 6**). Revolt starts in Hungary—Soviet troops and tanks crush anti-Communist rebellion (**Nov.**).

**1957** Eisenhower Doctrine calls for aid to Mideast countries which resist armed aggression from Communist-controlled nations (**Jan. 5**). Eisenhower sends troops to Little Rock, Ark., to quell mob and protect school integration (**Sept. 24**). Russians launch *Sputnik I,* first earth-orbiting satellite—the Space Age begins (**Oct. 4**).

**1958** Army's Jupiter-C rocket fires first U.S. earth satellite, *Explorer I,* into orbit (**Jan. 31**). Egypt and Syria merge into United Arab Republic (**Feb. 1**). European Economic Community (Common Market) established by Rome Treaty becomes effective **Jan. 1, 1958**. Khrushchev becomes Premier of Soviet Union as Bulganin resigns (**Mar. 27**). Gen. Charles de Gaulle becomes French premier (**June 1**), remaining in power until **1969**. New French constitution adopted (**Sept. 28**), de Gaulle elected president of 5th Republic (**Dec. 21**). Eisenhower orders U.S. Marines into Lebanon at request of President Chamoun, who fears overthrow (**July 15**).

**1959** Cuban President Batista resigns and flees—Castro takes over (**Jan. 1**). Tibet's Dalai Lama escapes to India (**Mar. 31**). St. Lawrence Seaway opens, allowing ocean ships to reach Midwest (**April 25**).

**1960** American U-2 spy plane, piloted by Francis Gary Powers, shot down over Russia (**May 5**). Khrushchev kills Paris summit conference because of U-2 (**May 16**). Powers sentenced to prison for 10 years (**Aug. 19**)—freed in **February 1962** in exchange for Soviet spy. Top Nazi murderer of Jews, Adolf Eichmann, captured by Israelis in Argentina (**May 23**)—executed in Israel in **1962**. Communist China and Soviet Union split in conflict over Communist ideology. Belgium starts to break up its African colonial empire, gives independence to Belgian Congo (Zaire) on **June 30**. Cuba begins confiscation of $770 million of U.S. property (**Aug. 7**).

**1961** U.S. breaks diplomatic relations with Cuba (**Jan. 3**). John F. Kennedy inaugurated President of U.S. (**Jan. 20**). Kennedy proposes Alliance for Progress—10-year plan to raise Latin American living standards (**Mar. 13**). Moscow announces putting first man in orbit around earth, Maj. Yuri A. Gagarin (**April 12**). Cuba invaded at Bay of Pigs by an estimated 1,200 anti-Castro exiles aided by U.S.; invasion crushed (**April 17**). First U.S. spaceman, Navy Cmdr. Alan B. Shepard, Jr., rockets 116.5 miles up in 302-mile trip (**May 5**). Virgil Grissom becomes second American astronaut, making 118-mile-high, 303-mile-long rocket flight over Atlantic (**July 21**). Gherman Stepanovich Titov is launched in Soviet spaceship *Vostok II;* makes 17½ orbits in 25 hours, covering 434,960 miles before landing safely (**Aug. 6**). East Germans erect Berlin Wall between East and West Berlin to halt flood of refugees (**Aug. 13**). U.S.S.R. fires 50-megaton hydrogen bomb, biggest explosion in history (**Oct. 29**).

**1962** Lt. Col. John H. Glenn, Jr., is first American to orbit earth—three times in 4 hr 55 min (**Feb. 20**). Adolf Eichmann hanged in Israel for his part in Nazi extermination of six million Jews (**May 31**). France transfers sovereignty to new republic of Algeria (**July 3**). Cuban missile crisis—U.S.S.R. to build missile bases in Cuba; Kennedy orders Cuban blockade, lifts blockade after Russians back down (**Aug.-Nov.**). James H. Meredith, escorted by Federal marshals, registers in University of Mississippi (**Oct. 1**). Pope John XXIII opens Second Vatican Council (**Oct. 11**)—Council holds four sessions, finally closing Dec. 8, 1965. Cuba releases 1,113 prisoners of 1961 invasion attempt (**Dec. 24**).

**1963** France and West Germany sign treaty of cooperation ending four centuries of conflict (**Jan. 22**). Pope John XXIII dies (**June 3**)—succeeded June 21 by Cardinal Montini, who becomes Paul VI. U.S. Supreme Court rules no locality may require recitation of Lord's Prayer or Bible verses in public schools (**June 17**). Civil rights rally held by 200,000 blacks and whites in Washington, D.C. (**Aug. 28**). Washington-to-Moscow "hot line" communications link opens, designed to reduce risk of accidental war (**Aug. 30**). President Kennedy shot and killed by sniper in Dallas, Tex. Lyndon B. Johnson becomes President same day (**Nov. 22**). Lee Harvey Oswald, accused assassin of President Kennedy, is shot and killed by Jack Ruby, Dallas nightclub owner (**Nov. 24**).

**1964** U.S. Supreme Court rules that Congressional districts should be roughly equal in population (**Feb. 17**). Jack Ruby convicted of murder in slaying of Lee Harvey Oswald; sentenced to death by Dallas jury (**March 14**) —conviction reversed **Oct. 5, 1966**; Ruby dies **Jan. 3, 1967**, before second trial can be held. Three civil rights workers—Schwerner, Goodman, and Cheney—murdered in Mississippi (**June**). Twenty-one arrests result in trial and conviction of seven by Federal jury. President's Commission on the Assassination of President Kennedy issues Warren Report con-

Tito (Josip Broz), *Yugoslavian President* (1892– )
Haile Selassie, *Ethiopian emperor* (1892–1975)
Hermann Goering, *Nazi leader* (1893–1946)
Mao Tse-tung, *Chinese Communist leader* (1893–1976)
Nikita Khrushchev, *Russian leader* (1894–1971)
Martha Graham, *American dancer* (1894– )
Paul Hindemith, *German-American composer* (1895–1963)
Bertolt Brecht, *German dramatist* (1898–1956)
Ernest Hemingway, *American author* (1898–1961)
Federico García Lorca, *Spanish author* (1899–1936)
Francis Poulenc, *French composer* (1899–1963)
Kurt Weill, *German-American composer* (1900–1950)
Aaron Copland, *American composer* (1900– )
Werner Heisenberg, *German physicist* (1901– )
Walt Disney, *American cartoonist* (1901–1966)
Enrico Fermi, *Italian-American physicist* (1901–1954)
John Steinbeck, *American novelist* (1902–1968)
Dmitri Shostakovich, *Russian composer* (1906–1975)
W. H. Auden, *English poet* (1907–1973)
Albert Camus, *French author* (1913–1960)
John F. Kennedy *American President* (1917–1963)

cluding that Lee Harvey Oswald acted alone in assassination of President (**Sept. 27**).

**1965** Rev. Dr. Martin Luther King, Jr., and more than 2,600 other blacks arrested in Selma, Ala., during three-day demonstrations against voter-registration rules (**Feb. 1**). Malcolm X, black-nationalist leader, shot to death at Harlem rally in New York City (**Feb. 21**). U.S. Marines land in Dominican Republic as fighting persists between rebels and Dominican army (**April 28**). Medicare, senior citizens' government medical assistance program, begins (**July 1**). Blacks riot for six days in Watts section of Los Angeles: 34 dead, over 1,000 injured, nearly 4,000 arrested, fire damage put at $175 million (**Aug. 11–16**). Power failure in Ontario plant blacks out parts of eight northeastern states of U.S. and two provinces of southeastern Canada (**Nov. 9**).

**1966** Black teen-agers riot in Watts, Los Angeles; two men killed and at least 25 injured (**March 15**). Michael E. De Bakey implants artificial heart in human for first time at Houston hospital; plastic device functions and patient lives (**April 21**). U.S. Supreme Court gives police strict new guidelines to protect suspects from self-incrimination (**June 13**).

**1967** Three Apollo astronauts—Col. Virgil I. Grissom, Col. Edward White II, and Lt. Cmdr. Roger B. Chaffee—killed in spacecraft fire during simulated launch (**Jan. 27**). Israeli and Arab forces battle; six-day war ends with Israel occupying Sinai Peninsula, Golan Heights, Gaza Strip, and east bank of Suez Canal (**June 5**). Red China announces explosion of its first hydrogen bomb (**June 17**). Racial violence in Detroit; 7,000 National Guardsmen aid police after night of rioting. Similar outbreaks occur in New York City's Spanish Harlem, Rochester, N.Y., Birmingham, Ala., and New Britain, Conn. (**July 23**). Thurgood Marshall sworn in as first black U.S. Supreme Court justice (**Oct. 2**). Dr. Christiaan N. Barnard and team of South African surgeons perform world's first successful human heart transplant (**Dec. 3**)—patient dies 18 days later.

**1968** North Korea seizes U.S. Navy ship *Pueblo;* holds 83 on board as spies (**Jan. 23**). President Johnson announces he will not seek or accept presidential renomination (**March 31**). Martin Luther King, Jr., civil rights leader, is slain in Memphis (**April 4**)—James Earl Ray, indicted in murder, captured in London on **June 8**. In **1969** Ray pleads guilty and is sentenced to 99 years. Sen. Robert F. Kennedy is shot and critically wounded in Los Angeles hotel after winning California primary (**June 5**)—dies **June 6**. Sirhan Bishara Sirhan convicted in **1969**. Czechoslovakia is invaded by Russians and four other Warsaw Pact forces to crush liberal regime (**Aug. 20**).

**1969** Richard M. Nixon is inaugurated 37th President of the U.S. (**Jan. 20**). Apollo 11 astronauts—Neil A. Armstrong, Edwin E. Aldrin, Jr., and Michael Collins—take man's first walk on moon (**July 20**). Sen. Edward M. Kennedy pleads guilty to leaving scene of fatal accident at Chappaquiddick, Mass. (**July 18**) in which Mary Jo Kopechne was drowned—gets two-month suspended sentence (**July 25**).

**1970** Biafra surrenders after 32-month fight for independence from Nigeria (**Jan. 12**). Rhodesia severs last tie with British Crown and declares itself a racially segregated republic (**March 1**). Four students at Kent State University in Ohio slain by National Guardsmen at demonstration protesting April 30 incursion into Cambodia (**May 4**). President Nixon signs bill lowering voting age in national elections from 21 to 18. (**June 22**). Senate repeals Gulf of Tonkin resolution (**June 24**). Nation's gross national product reaches $1 trillion (**Dec. 15**).

**1971** Supreme Court rules unanimously that busing of students may be ordered to achieve racial desegregation (**April 20**). Anti-war militants attempt to disrupt government business in Washington (**May 3**)—police and military units arrest as many as 12,000; most are later released. Twenty-sixth Amendment to U.S. Constitution lowers voting age to 18. U.N. seats Communist China and expels Nationalist China (**Oct. 25**). India invades East Pakistan (**Nov. 22**).

**1972** President Nixon makes unprecedented eight-day visit to Communist China (**Feb.**). Britain takes over direct rule of Northern Ireland in bid for peace (**March 24**). Okinawa reverts to Japan after 27 years of U.S. rule (**May 14**). Gov. George C. Wallace of Alabama is shot by Arthur H. Bremer at Laurel, Md., political rally (**May 15**)—Wallace paralyzed for life from the waist down. Bremer is sentenced to 63 years in prison on **Aug. 4**. Five men are apprehended by police in attempt to bug Democratic National Committee headquarters in Washington D.C.'s Watergate complex—start of the Watergate scandal (**June 17**). Supreme Court rules that death penalty is unconstitutional (**June 29**). Bobby Fischer becomes first American world chess champion, defeating Boris Spassky of U.S.S.R. (**Sept. 1**). Eleven Israeli athletes at Olympic Games in Munich are killed after eight members of the Arab terrorist group invade Olympic Village; five guerrillas and one policeman are also killed (**Sept. 5**).

**1973** Great Britain, Ireland, and Denmark enter European Common Market (**Jan. 1**). Indians hold 10 hostages after seizing settlement of Wounded Knee, S.D., demand Government discuss their grievances (**Feb. 28**)—surrender on **May 9**. Nixon, on national TV, accepts responsibility, but not blame, for Watergate; accepts resignations of advisers H. R. Haldeman and John D. Ehrlichman, fires John W. Dean III as counsel. He pledges "no whitewash" at White House (**April 30**). Greek military junta abolishes monarchy and proclaims republic (**June 1**). U.S. bombing of Cambodia ends, marking official halt to 12 years of combat activity in Southeast Asia (**Aug. 15**). Violent military coup in Chile deposes President Salvador Allende Gossens, who reportedly commits suicide (**Sept. 11**). Fourth and biggest Arab-Israeli War begins as Egyptian and Syrian forces attack Israel as Jews mark Yom Kippur, holiest day in their calendar. Fierce tank battles rage on Sinai Peninsula and Golan Heights (**Oct. 6**). Spiro T. Agnew resigns as Vice President and then, in Federal Court in Baltimore, pleads no contest to charges of evasion of income taxes on $29,500 he received in 1967 while Governor of Maryland. He is fined $10,000 and put on three years' probation (**Oct. 10**). In the "Saturday Night Massacre," Nixon fires special Watergate prosecutor Archibald Cox and Deputy Attorney General William D. Ruckelshaus; Attorney General Elliot L. Richardson resigns (**Oct. 20**). Egypt and Israel sign U.S.-sponsored cease-fire agreement (**Nov. 11**).

**1974** Patricia Hearst, 19-year-old daughter of publisher Randolph Hearst, kidnapped by Symbionese Liberation Army, which demands $2-million ransom (**Feb. 5**)—later, $230 million in free food for California's poor is also sought. Bloodless coup restores Portuguese democracy (**April 25**). House Judiciary Committee adopts three articles of impeachment charging President Nixon with obstruction of justice, failure to uphold laws, and refusal to produce material subpoenaed by the committee (**July 30**). Richard M. Nixon announces he will resign the next day, the first President to do so (**Aug. 8**). Vice President Gerald R. Ford of Michigan is sworn in as 38th President of the U.S. (**Aug. 9**). Ford grants "full, free, and absolute pardon" to ex-President Nixon (**Sept. 8**). Franklin National Bank, country's 20th largest, is declared insolvent in biggest bank failure in U.S. history (**Sept. 8**).

**1975** John N. Mitchell, H. R. Haldeman, John D. Ehrlichman, and Robert C. Mardian found guilty of Watergate cover-up. Mitchell, Haldeman, and Ehrlichman are sentenced on Feb. 21 to 30 months-8 years in jail and Mardian to 10 months-3 years (**Jan. 1**). King Faisal of Saudi Arabia is assassinated by a nephew (**March 25**); assassin beheaded June 18. Chiang Kai-shek, President of Nationalist China, dies at 87 (**April 5**). South Vietnam surrenders to Communists (**April 30**); Saigon captured by North Vietnamese troops, ending 16-year Vietnam War. American merchant ship *Mayaguez*, seized by Cambodian forces, is rescued in operation by U.S. Navy and Marines, 38 of whom are killed (**May 15**). Suez Canal reopens after eight years (**June 5**). Mozambique becomes independent after 470 years of Portuguese rule (**June 24**). *Apollo* and *Soyuz* spacecraft take off for U.S.-Soviet link-up in space (**July 15**)—on **July 17**, Brig. Gen. Thomas P. Stafford, Donald K. Slayton, and Vance D. Brand exchange visits with Col. Aleksei A. Leonov and Valery N. Kubasov 140 miles above earth. *Soyuz* spacecraft lands safely in Soviet; Apollo astronauts splash down in Pacific three days later (**July 21**). Federal jury clears Gov. James A. Rhodes of Ohio; Robert J. White, former Kent State University President, and 27 Ohio National Guardsmen in $46-million damage suit brought by 9 wounded students and parents of 4 slain on campus in **1970** (**Aug. 27**). President Ford escapes assassination attempt in Sacramento, Calif., when Lynette Alice Fromme, member of the Charles Manson "family," points pistol at him and is subdued (**Sept. 5**). She is convicted of attempted assassination (**Nov. 26**), later sentenced to life imprisonment. Patricia Hearst, kidnapped **Feb. 5, 1974**, apprehended by FBI in San Francisco and faces bank-robbery charges (**Sept. 18**). President Ford escapes second assassination attempt in 17 days when a woman fires at him in San Francisco (**Sept. 22**)—police seize Sara Jane Moore, 45, said to be former FBI informant. She pleads guilty (**Dec. 12**) and is sentenced to life imprisonment (**Jan. 15**). Israel signs Sinai accord with Egypt, calling for withdrawal from about 1,900 square miles of territory within five months (**Oct. 10**). World Health Organization reports that Asia is free of smallpox (**Nov. 13**).

**1976** Environmental Protection Agency orders U.S. Steel to close Gary, Ind., coke plants for violation of clean air standards (**Jan. 1**). Palestine Liberation Organization seated at U.N. (**Jan. 13**). U.S. and Spain sign five-year treaty of friendship and cooperation; U.S. gets air and naval bases for

$1.2 billion in credits and grants (**Jan. 25**). U.S. vetoes Security Council resolution for independent Palestinian state and total withdrawal by Israel from post-1967 Arab lands (**Jan. 27**). Indian Parliament grants government permanent press censorship (**Jan. 30**). Supreme Court rules that blacks and other minorities are entitled to retroactive job seniority (**March 24**). Argentine military junta proclaims martial law after bloodless coup; President Isabel Martinez de Perón under arrest (**March 25**). Hua Kuo-feng named Premier and Deputy First Chairman of Chinese Communist Party, seen as successor to Mao Tse-tung (**April 8**). Senate Select Intelligence Committee reports that FBI, CIA, Army Intelligence, and other agencies created files on 500,000 citizens, opened 500,000 pieces of mail, and monitored telegrams and overseas phone calls; illegally investigated citizen groups; charges that all Presidents since FDR used information from FBI about their opponents; makes sweeping recommendations to control intelligence community (**April 28**). United Airlines agrees to pay $1,050,000 to minority group members and women to settle discrimination complaints brought by Equal Employment Opportunity Commission (**May 1**). Ford signs Federal Election Campaign Act—measure limits individual contributions to $1,000 and spending in primaries to $10.9 million for each candidate. Each major-party candidate to get $21.8 million for general election campaign, money coming from income tax check-offs (**May 11**). Don Bolles, newspaper reporter investigating corruption involving Mafia in Arizona, dies after bomb explosion in his car (**June 12**). Many killed and wounded when South African police fire on students in Soweto, near Johannesburg, largest black urban center in country. Students were demonstrating against use of Afrikaans as language of school instruction. Violence continues for several months, with death toll rising into the hundreds (**June 16**). Francis E. Meloy, Jr., U.S. Ambassador to Lebanon, assassinated in Beirut; all Americans advised to leave country as civil war continues; deaths exceed 30,000 (**June 17**). Supreme Court rules that Civil Rights Act protects whites against racial discrimination to same extent as blacks (**June 26**). Supreme Court rules that death penalty is not inherently cruel or unusual and is a constitutionally acceptable form of punishment (**July 3**). Nation celebrates Bicentennial (**July 4**). Israeli airborne commandos attack Uganda's Entebbe Airport and free 103 hostages held by pro-Palestinian hijackers of Air France plane—one Israeli and several Ugandan soldiers killed in raid (**July 4**). New York disbars ex-President Nixon on charges relating to Watergate (**July 8**). Democratic National Convention opens in New York. Jimmy Carter nominated on first roll-call vote. He later picks Sen. Walter F. Mondale of Minnesota to be running mate (**July 12**). Taiwan withdraws from Olympic Games in Montreal when denied right to compete as Republic of China. Later, 17 nations drop out in protest against New Zealand rugby team's tour of South Africa (**July 16**). Twenty-six school children and bus driver from Chowchilla, Calif., disappear in rural central California. Next day all escape from underground cell fashioned from truck body; three men later held as abductors (**July 17**). Britain's Ambassador to Ireland and aide are killed when land mine explodes under their car in Dublin (**July 22**). Ex-Premier Kakuei Tanaka of Japan arrested on charges of accepting bribe from Lockheed Aircraft; later indicted for taking $1.6 million (**July 28**). Worst earthquake in 400 years devastates Tientsin-Tangshan area of China; 655,000 reported dead (**July 28**). Mysterious disease that eventually claims 29 lives strikes American Legion convention in Philadelphia (**Aug. 4**). Republican National Convention opens in Kansas City, Mo. President Ford defeats Ronald Reagan for nomination; later picks Senator Robert J. Dole of Kansas as Vice-Presidential running mate. Ford challenges Democratic rival Jimmy Carter to debate issues on TV and challenge is accepted (**Aug. 16**). Premier Jacques Chirac of France quits, charging he was not given enough authority to deal with nation's problems—replaced by Raymond Barre (**Aug. 25**). Prince Bernhard of the Netherlands, caught up in Lockheed Aircraft bribery scandal, resigns all military and business posts (**Aug. 26**). Prime Minister Ian D. Smith of Rhodesia accepts plan for black rule based on temporary biracial government and majority rule in two years (**Sept. 24**). Supreme Court lifts stay on death penalties as it decides not to reconsider recent decision upholding capital punishment for murder (**Oct. 4**). Military seizes power in Thailand after battles with students in which many are killed; democratic rights abolished (**Oct. 6**). Clarence Norris, last survivor of "Scottsboro Boys" of 1930s, pardoned by Gov. George C. Wallace of Alabama (**Oct. 27**). Geneva conference opens on Rhodesia concerning transfer of power from minority white to majority black rule (**Oct. 28**). Jimmy Carter elected U.S. President (**Nov. 2**). Lebanese civil war calms as Syrian army forces truce (**Nov. 15**). Chinese explode atmospheric nuclear device; fallout over U.S. (**Nov. 17**). 4,000 dead in Turkish earthquake (**Nov. 24**). Italy and Vatican revise 1929 Concordat (**Nov. 26**). Oil tanker *Argo Merchant* breaks up off Nantucket, spilling 13.5 million gallons of heavy crude oil (**Dec. 21–22**).

**1977** First woman Episcopal priest ordained (**Jan. 1**). International Monetary Fund approves its largest single credit ever, $3.9 billion, to Britain (**Jan. 3**). French arrest, then free, Abu Daoud, PLO terrorist, despite German extradition request (**Jan. 9–17**). Scientists identify previously unknown bacterium as cause of mysterious "legionnaire's disease" (**Jan. 18**). Astronomers discover water outside of Earth's galaxy, indicating possibility of life in outer space (**Jan. 19**). New Chinese government allows films, plays, and artists previously banned by Cultural Revolution (**Jan. 21**). Carter pardons Vietnam draft evaders (**Jan. 21**). Supreme Court modifies Miranda rule for suspects not under arrest (**Jan. 25**). TV adaptation of *Roots* has total of 130 million viewers, breaking all records (**Jan. 30**). Senate approves reorganization of its committee structure (**Feb. 4**). Uganda archbishop killed after arrest by Amin government (**Feb. 16**). First flight test of space shuttle, designed to be orbital shuttle vehicle (**Feb. 18**). Supreme Court upholds use of racial quotas in state reapportionment plans (**March 1**). U.S. extends its control of the sea to 200-mile limit (**March 1**.) Hanafi Moslems invade Washington, D.C., buildings, kill 1, wound 11, hold hundreds hostage, then surrender (**March 9–11**). Indira Gandhi ousted in Indian election which repudiates her repressive "emergency" rule (**March 20**). Two jumbo jets collide in Canary Islands; 582 killed in worst aviation disaster (**March 27**). NASA reports planet Uranus has five rings (**March 30**). Senate adopts strict ethics code (**April 1**). Spain legalizes Communist party after 38-year ban (**April 9**). Carter proposes national energy program to increase fuel costs, cut waste, and promote major conservation efforts (**April 21**). Oil well blowout in North Sea creates 20-mile slick (**April 23–30**). In TV interview (**May 4**), Nixon concedes he lied, "let the American people down." Israeli Labor government defeated in general election by "hawkish" Likud party (**May 17**). Scientists report using bacteria in lab to make insulin (**May 23**). South Moluccan extremists seize 161 hostages in the Netherlands (**May 23**). Lockheed under-the-table payments to foreign nationals to win aircraft contracts revealed to reach $38 million (**May 26**). Tongsun Park identified as Korean agent who allegedly spent millions to influence U.S. officials (**June 4**). Soviets charge Anatoly Shcharansky, Jewish human-rights activist, with treason (**June 4**). Hostages released, six terrorists killed, in rescue by Dutch marines (**June 11**). Laetrile found useless as cancer cure (**June 15**). Supreme Court rules that states are not required to spend Medicaid funds on elective abortions (**June 20**). Nixon aides' sentences confirmed; Haldeman and Mitchell go to jail (**June 21–22**). Supreme Court upholds 1974 law giving Government control over Nixon tapes (**June 28**). Carter rejects B-1 bomber (**June 30**). New York City blackout, with business losses of $135–150 million from theft and property damage (**July 13**). CIA reveals 14-year behavior-control project using chemical and other means (**July 20**). Teng Hsiao-ping, purged Chinese leader, restored to power as "Gang of Four" is expelled from Communist Party (**July 22**). Bandaranaike party loses power in Sri Lanka (**July 22**). First oil from Alaska's Prudhoe Bay fields pours from 799-mile pipeline at ice-free port of Valdez (**July 28**). Military coup in Pakistan; Prime Minister Bhutto jailed (**Aug. 5**). U.S. and Panama agree "in principle" on transfer of Panama Canal and Canal Zone to Panamanian control by year 2000 (**Aug. 10**). New Chinese leadership elected by first Communist Party Congress since Mao's death (**Aug. 20**). *Voyager* spacecrafts launched to explore interplanetary space (**Aug. 20, Sept. 5**). Japan opens atom plant (**Sept. 1**). U.S. and Cuban Missions open as significant step to restore official relations broken off about 17 years ago (**Sept. 1**). Twelve Hanafis sentenced to long prison terms for March raid (**Sept. 6**). Carter and General Torrijos, Panamanian chief of state, approve pacts that would transfer Canal to Panama, if ratified (**Sept. 7**). Tongsun Park charged by U.S. Justice Department with influence-buying (**Sept. 8**). Cholera epidemic in Arab countries (**Sept. 12**). Steven Biko, influential Black activist, dies while detained by South African police (**Sept. 15**). Bert Lance, U.S. Budget Director, criticized for banking practices prior to joining government (**Aug. 18**), supported by President Carter. Defends himself at Senate committee hearings (**Sept. 15**); resigns (**Sept. 21**). Nuclear proliferation pact, curbing spread of nuclear weapons, signed by 15 countries, including U.S. and U.S.S.R. (**Sept. 21**). First National Women's Conference held in Houston (**Nov. 19**).

(For later events, *see* Current Events, 1977–78, in Table of Contents.)

# WORLD STATISTICS

## Area and Population by Country

| Country | Area[1] | Population | Year[2] |
|---|---|---|---|
| Afghanistan | 249,999 | 20,900,000 | 1978E |
| Albania | 11,100 | 2,690,000 | 1978E |
| Algeria | 919,595 | 18,500,000 | 1978E |
| Andorra | 175 | 25,000 | 1978E |
| Angola | 481,350 | 6,761,000 | 1976E |
| Argentina | 1,068,296 | 26,400,000 | 1978E |
| Australia | 2,967,892 | 14,220,000[3] | 1978E |
| Austria | 32,375 | 7,500,000 | 1978E |
| Bahamas | 5,382 | 230,000 | 1978E |
| Bahrain | 240 | 280,000 | 1978E |
| Bangladesh | 55,598 | 82,500,000 | 1978E |
| Barbados | 166 | 260,000 | 1978E |
| Belgium | 11,781 | 9,845,000 | 1978E |
| Benin (Dahomey) | 43,483 | 3,380,000 | 1978E |
| Bhutan | 18,147 | 1,235,000 | 1977E |
| Bolivia | 424,162 | 6,110,000 | 1978E |
| Bophuthatswana | 15,610 | 1,039,000 | 1976E |
| Botswana | 231,804 | 725,000 | 1978E |
| Brazil | 3,286,487 | 115,450,000 | 1978E |
| Bulgaria | 42,823 | 8,840,000 | 1978E |
| Burma | 261,217 | 32,200,000 | 1978E |
| Burundi | 10,747 | 4,100,000 | 1978E |
| Cambodia (Democratic Kampuchea) | 69,898 | 8,890,000 | 1978E |
| Cameroon | 183,569 | 6,820,000 | 1978E |
| Canada | 3,851,809 | 23,445,200 | 1978E |
| Cape Verde | 1,557 | 310,000 | 1978E |
| Central African Empire | 240,535 | 2,000,000 | 1978E |
| Chad | 495,752 | 4,290,000 | 1978E |
| Chile | 292,257 | 10,880,000 | 1978E |
| China, People's Rep. of[4] | 3,705,387 | 880,000,000 | 1978E |
| China, Republic of[5] | 13,893 | 16,678,000 | 1977E |
| Colombia | 439,735 | 25,800,000 | 1978E |
| Comoro Islands | 838 | 370,000 | 1978E |
| Congo | 132,046 | 1,500,000 | 1978E |
| Costa Rica | 19,575 | 2,120,000 | 1978E |
| Cuba | 44,218 | 9,590,000 | 1977E |
| Cyprus | 3,572 | 700,000 | 1978E |
| Czechoslovakia | 49,373 | 15,150,000 | 1978E |
| Denmark[6] | 16,629 | 5,110,000 | 1978E |
| Djibouti | 8,494 | 225,000 | 1978E |
| Dominican Republic | 18,816 | 5,170,000 | 1978E |
| Ecuador | 109,483 | 7,825,000 | 1978E |
| Egypt | 386,661 | 39,500,000 | 1978E |
| El Salvador | 8,124 | 4,340,000 | 1978E |
| Equatorial Guinea | 10,830 | 325,000 | 1978E |
| Ethiopia | 471,778 | 29,700,000 | 1978E |
| Fiji | 7,055 | 620,000 | 1978E |
| Finland | 130,119 | 4,750,000 | 1978E |
| France | 211,208 | 53,250,000 | 1978E |
| Gabon | 103,346 | 540,000 | 1978E |
| Gambia | 4,361 | 560,000 | 1978E |
| Germany (East)[7] | 41,923 | 16,570,000 | 1978E |
| Germany (West)[8] | 95,791 | 61,250,000 | 1978E |
| Ghana | 92,100 | 10,650,000 | 1978E |
| Greece | 50,944 | 9,300,000 | 1977E |
| Grenada | 133 | 110,000 | 1978E |
| Guatemala | 42,042 | 6,630,000 | 1978E |
| Guinea | 94,925 | 4,775,000 | 1978E |
| Guinea-Bissau | 13,948 | 545,000 | 1978E |
| Guyana | 83,000 | 825,000 | 1978E |
| Haiti | 10,714 | 4,830,000 | 1978E |
| Honduras | 43,277 | 2,900,000 | 1977E |
| Hungary | 35,919 | 10,700,000 | 1978E |
| Iceland | 39,768 | 227,000 | 1978E |
| India[9] | 1,269,338 | 643,000,000 | 1978E |
| Indonesia[10] | 741,031 | 147,000,000 | 1978E |
| Iran | 636,296 | 34,200,000 | 1977E |
| Iraq | 167,924 | 12,350,000 | 1978E |
| Ireland | 27,136 | 3,240,000 | 1978E |
| Israel | 8,019[11] | 3,700,000 | 1978E |
| Italy | 116,304 | 56,675,000 | 1978E |
| Ivory Coast | 124,502 | 6,714,000 | 1978E |
| Jamaica | 4,244 | 2,110,000 | 1978E |
| Japan | 143,750 | 114,850,000 | 1978E |
| Jordan | 37,738 | 2,080,000 | 1977 [12] |
| Kenya | 224,960 | 14,800,000 | 1978E |
| Korea (North) | 46,540 | 17,000,000 | 1978E |
| Korea (South) | 38,022 | 37,000,000 | 1978E |
| Kuwait | 6,880 | 1,190,000 | 1978E |
| Laos | 91,429 | 3,540,000 | 1978E |
| Lebanon | 4,015 | 3,165,000 | 1978E |
| Lesotho | 11,720 | 1,090,000 | 1977E |
| Liberia | 43,000 | 1,850,000 | 1978E |
| Libya | 679,362 | 2,600,000 | 1977E |
| Liechtenstein | 61 | 22,850 | 1978E |
| Luxembourg | 999 | 370,000 | 1978E |
| Madagascar | 226,658 | 8,775,000 | 1978E |
| Malawi | 45,747 | 5,530,000 | 1977 [12] |
| Malaysia | 127,316 | 12,950,000 | 1978E |
| Maldives | 115 | 145,000 | 1978E |
| Mali | 478,766 | 6,150,000 | 1978E |
| Malta | 122 | 330,000 | 1978E |
| Mauritania | 397,955 | 1,400,000 | 1977E |
| Mauritius | 790 | 890,000 | 1978E |
| Mexico | 761,600 | 66,950,000 | 1978E |
| Monaco | ([13]) | 30,000 | 1978E |
| Mongolia | 604,250 | 1,575,000 | 1978E |
| Morocco | 172,414 | 18,675,000 | 1978E |
| Mozambique | 302,328 | 9,950,000 | 1978E |
| Nauru | 8.2 | 8,000 | 1978E |
| Nepal | 54,362 | 13,420,000 | 1978E |
| Netherlands | 15,700 | 13,930,000 | 1978E |
| New Zealand[14] | 103,736 | 3,130,000 | 1978E |
| Nicaragua | 50,193 | 2,390,000 | 1978E |
| Niger | 489,191 | 5,000,000 | 1978E |
| Nigeria | 356,669 | 66,650,000 | 1978E |
| Norway | 125,182 | 4,050,000 | 1978E |
| Oman[15] | 82,030 | 850,000 | 1978E |
| Pakistan[16] | 310,403 | 77,500,000 | 1978E |
| Panama | 29,208 | 1,820,000 | 1978E |
| Papua New Guinea | 178,259 | 2,980,000 | 1978E |
| Paraguay | 157,047 | 2,870,000 | 1978E |
| Peru | 496,222 | 17,000,000 | 1978E |
| Philippines | 115,831 | 46,400,000 | 1978E |
| Poland | 120,725 | 35,050,000 | 1978E |
| Portugal | 35,553 | 10,000,000 | 1977E |
| Qatar | 4,274 | 200,000 | 1978E |
| Rhodesia | 150,803 | 6,950,000 | 1978E |
| Romania | 91,700 | 21,630,000 | 1978E |
| Rwanda | 10,169 | 4,600,000 | 1978E |
| San Marino | 23.6 | 20,500 | 1978E |
| São Tomé and Príncipe | 372 | 85,500 | 1978E |
| Saudi Arabia | 829,995 | 9,800,000 | 1978E |
| Senegal | 75,750 | 5,090,000 | 1976 [12] |
| Seychelles | 108 | 65,000 | 1978E |

| Country | Area[1] | Population | Year[2] |
|---|---|---|---|
| Sierra Leone | 27,699 | 3,470,000 | 1977[12] |
| Singapore | 226 | 2,340,000 | 1978E |
| Solomon Islands | 10,983 | 200,000 | 1978E |
| Somalia | 246,201 | 3,440,000 | 1978E |
| South Africa[17] | 440,521 | 26,765,000 | 1977E |
| Spain[18] | 194,897 | 36,730,000 | 1978E |
| Sri Lanka | 25,332 | 14,200,000 | 1978E |
| Sudan | 967,494 | 16,550,000 | 1977E |
| Surinam | 63,037 | 460,000 | 1978E |
| Swaziland | 6,704 | 520,000 | 1978E |
| Sweden | 173,732 | 8,300,000 | 1978E |
| Switzerland | 15,941 | 6,310,000 | 1978E |
| Syria | 71,498 | 8,000,000 | 1978E |
| Tanzania[19] | 364,900 | 16,450,000 | 1978E |
| Thailand | 198,455 | 45,380,000 | 1978E |
| Togo | 21,622 | 2,410,000 | 1978E |
| Tonga | 270 | 100,000 | 1978E |
| Transkei | 15,831 | 2,050,000 | 1976E |
| Trinidad and Tobago | 1,980 | 1,120,000 | 1977E |
| Tunisia | 63,170 | 6,400,000 | 1978E |
| Turkey | 301,380 | 43,120,000 | 1978E |
| Uganda | 91,134 | 12,775,000 | 1978E |
| U.S.S.R. | 8,649,489 | 260,750,000 | 1978E |
| United Arab Emirates | 32,278 | 656,000 | 1978E |
| United Kingdom | 94,250 | 55,800,000 | 1978E |
| England and Wales | 58,383 | 49,120,000 | 1977E |
| Scotland | 30,415 | 5,196,000 | 1977E |
| Northern Ireland | 5,452 | 1,537,000 | 1977E |
| United States | 3,540,939 | 218,525,000 | 1978E |
| Upper Volta | 105,870 | 6,480,000 | 1978E |
| Uruguay | 68,037 | 2,825,000 | 1978E |
| Vatican City State | ([20]) | 1,000 | 1978E |
| Venezuela | 352,143 | 13,150,000 | 1978E |
| Vietnam | 127,242 | 49,275,000 | 1978E |
| Western Samoa | 1,097 | 155,000 | 1978E |
| Yemen Arab Republic | 75,290 | 7,300,000 | 1978E |
| Yemen, People's Dem. Rep. of[21] | 111,074 | 1,850,000 | 1978E |
| Yugoslavia | 98,766 | 21,900,000 | 1978E |
| Zaire | 905,562 | 27,150,000 | 1978E |
| Zambia | 290,586 | 5,500,000 | 1978E |

1. Square miles. 2. E = *Information Please* estimate. 3. Including aborigines. 4. Including Manchuria and Tibet. 5. Excluding Quemoy and Matsu. 6. Excluding Faeroe Islands and Greenland. 7. Including East Berlin. 8. Excluding West Berlin. 9. Including Jammu and Kashmir and Sikkim. 10. Including Portuguese East Timor, annexed in 1976, and Irian Jaya (former Netherlands New Guinea and later West Irian). 11. Excluding territory occupied in 1967 war. 12. United Nations estimate. 13. 0.65 square mile. 14. Excluding dependencies. 15. Excluding Kuria Muria Islands. 16. Excluding Jammu and Kashmir. 17. Excluding South-West Africa (Namibia). 18. Including Balearic and Canary Islands. 19. Including Zanzibar. 20. 0.17 square mile. 21. Excluding Perim and Kamaran Islands.

## Largest Cities of the World

Census figures and population estimates in the following table are based on data reflecting different years. Some cities include metropolitan areas or contiguous suburbs, while others report only those residing within precise geographical or physical boundaries. Therefore, the ratings in this listing must be considered approximate.

| City | Population | Year[1] |
|---|---|---|
| Shanghai, China | 10,888,000 | 1975E |
| Mexico City | 8,941,900 | 1977E |
| Tokyo | 8,643,000 | 1975E |
| Peking | 8,487,000 | 1975E |
| Manila | 7,800,000 | 1976E |
| Moscow | 7,734,000 | 1976E |
| New York | 7,481,600 | 1975E |
| São Paulo, Brazil | 7,198,000 | 1977E |
| London | 7,028,200 | 1976E |
| Seoul, South Korea | 6,899,470 | 1975C |
| Jakarta, Indonesia | 6,178,500 | 1977E |
| Cairo | 6,133,000 | 1976E |
| Bombay | 5,970,575 | 1975E |
| Rio de Janeiro | 4,857,500 | 1977E |
| Bangkok, Thailand | 4,545,600 | 1977E |
| Karachi, Pakistan | 4,465,000 | 1975E |
| Leningrad | 4,372,000 | 1976E |
| Tientsin, China | 4,280,000 | 1970E |
| Teheran, Iran | 4,000,000 | 1975E |
| Lima, Peru | 3,901,000 | 1975E |

*Source:* United Nations *Demographic Yearbook, 1976,* and official estimates.

## Some Other Large Foreign Cities

| City | Population | Year[1] |
|---|---|---|
| Addis Ababa, Ethiopia | 1,242,500 | 1976E |
| Ahmedabad, India | 1,585,544 | 1971C |
| Alexandria, Egypt | 2,259,000 | 1974E |
| Algiers | 2,000,000 | 1978E |
| Alma Ata, U.S.S.R. | 851,000 | 1976E |
| Amsterdam | 975,500 | 1977E |
| Ankara, Turkey | 1,700,000 | 1975C |
| Antwerp, Belgium | 673,000 | 1974E |
| Athens | 1,378,586[2] | 1971C |
| Auckland, New Zealand | 150,700 | 1976C |
| Baghdad, Iraq | 2,987,000 | 1975E |
| Baku, U.S.S.R. | 1,406,000 | 1976E |
| Badung, Indonesia | 1,201,730 | 1971C |
| Bangalore, India | 1,540,741 | 1971C |
| Barcelona | 1,846,250 | 1976E |
| Barranquilla, Colombia | 664,533 | 1973C |
| Belfast, Northern Ireland | 363,000 | 1976E |
| Belgrade, Yugoslavia | 870,000 | 1975E |
| Belo Horizonte, Brazil | 1,557,500 | 1977E |
| Berlin[3] | 3,073,000 | 1977E |
| Bern, Switzerland | 149,800 | 1976E |
| Birmingham, England | 1,058,800 | 1976E |
| Bogotá, Colombia | 3,618,800 | 1977E |
| Bonn, West Germany | 285,000 | 1977E |

| City | Population | Year[1] |
|---|---|---|
| Brasilia, Brazil | 763,250 | 1977E |
| Brisbane, Australia | 957,710 | 1976C |
| Brussels | 1,042,000 | 1977E |
| Bucharest | 1,807,000 | 1977E |
| Budapest | 2,081,700 | 1977E |
| Buenos Aires | 2,980,000[2] | 1977E |
| Calgary, Canada | 469,917 | 1976C |
| Cali, Colombia | 898,253 | 1973C |
| Canton, China | 2,300,000 | 1970E |
| Cape Town, South Africa | 842,600 | 1976E |
| Caracas, Venezuela | 2,664,000[2] | 1977E |
| Casablanca, Morocco | 1,856,000 | 1975E |
| Chungking, China | 3,500,000 | 1970E |
| Cologne, West Germany | 1,010,400 | 1977E |
| Copenhagen | 1,380,000[2] | 1974E |
| Córdoba, Argentina | 798,663[2] | 1970C |
| Dacca, Bangladesh | 1,679,600 | 1974E |
| Damascus, Syria | 1,054,000 | 1976E |
| Delhi, India | 3,287,883 | 1971C |
| Dnepropetrovsk, U.S.S.R. | 976,000 | 1976E |
| Donetsk, U.S.S.R. | 967,000 | 1976E |
| Dublin | 566,034 | 1971C |
| Edinburgh, Scotland | 467,100 | 1976E |
| Florence, Italy | 457,803 | 1971C |
| Frankfurt, West Germany | 631,300 | 1977E |
| Fukuoka, Japan | 1,000,000[2] | 1975E |
| Geneva | 155,800 | 1976E |
| Genoa, Italy | 806,400 | 1975E |
| Glasgow, Scotland | 856,000 | 1976E |
| Gorki, U.S.S.R. | 1,305,000 | 1976E |
| Guadalajara, Mexico | 1,640,900 | 1976E |
| Guyaquil, Ecuador | 823,200 | 1974C |
| The Hague | 677,500 | 1977E |
| Haifa, Israel | 227,200 | 1976E |
| Hamburg | 1,707,400 | 1977E |
| Harbin, China | 2,750,000 | 1970E |
| Havana | 1,861,400 | 1975E |
| Helsinki, Finland | 493,300 | 1977E |
| Ho Chi Minh City (Saigon), Vietnam | 3,460,500 | 1976E |
| Hyderabad, India | 1,607,396 | 1971C |
| Hyderabad, Pakistan | 628,310 | 1972C |
| Ibadan, Nigeria | 847,000 | 1975E |
| Istanbul | 2,500,000 | 1975C |
| Jerusalem | 366,300 | 1977E |
| Johannesburg, South Africa | 1,371,000 | 1976E |
| Kanpur, India | 1,154,388 | 1971C |
| Kharkov, U.S.S.R. | 1,385,000 | 1976E |
| Kiev, U.S.S.R. | 2,013,000 | 1976E |
| Kinshasa, Zaire | 2,008,250 | 1974E |
| Kitakyushu, Japan | 1,060,000[2] | 1975E |
| Kobe, Japan | 1,360,000[2] | 1975E |
| Kuibyshev, U.S.S.R. | 1,186,000 | 1976E |
| Kunming, China | 1,700,000 | 1970E |
| Lahore, Pakistan | 2,165,372 | 1972C |
| La Paz, Bolivia | 654,700 | 1976E |
| Lausanne, Switzerland | 134,300 | 1976E |
| Liège, Belgium | 444,000 | 1974E |
| Lisbon | 847,300 | 1976E |
| Liverpool, England | 539,700 | 1976E |
| Lódz, Poland | 804,300 | 1976E |
| Lucknow, India | 749,239 | 1971C |
| Lyallpur, Pakistan | 822,263 | 1972C |
| Lyons, France | 462,841 | 1975C |
| Madras, India | 2,469,449 | 1971C |
| Madrid | 3,870,900 | 1977E |
| Marseilles, France | 914,356 | 1975C |
| Medellín, Colombia | 1,064,741 | 1973C |
| Melbourne | 2,603,578 | 1976C |
| Milan, Italy | 1,700,000 | 1976E |
| Minsk, U.S.S.R. | 1,189,000 | 1976E |
| Monterrey, Mexico | 1,090,200 | 1976E |
| Montevideo, Uruguay | 1,229,700 | 1975E |
| Montreal | 1,080,546 | 1976C |
| Munich, West Germany | 1,311,300 | 1977E |
| Nagoya, Japan | 2,080,000 | 1975E |
| Nagpur, India | 866,076 | 1971C |
| Nanking, China | 2,000,000 | 1970E |
| Nantes, France | 263,689 | 1975C |
| Naples, Italy | 1,300,000 | 1975E |
| Nice, France | 346,620 | 1975C |
| Novosibirsk, U.S.S.R. | 1,286,000 | 1976E |
| Odessa, U.S.S.R. | 1,023,000 | 1976E |
| Osaka, Japan | 2,780,000[2] | 1975E |
| Oslo | 462,500 | 1977E |
| Ottawa | 394,462 | 1976C |
| Paris | 2,317,227 | 1975C |
| Poona, India | 856,105 | 1971C |
| Porto Alegre, Brazil | 869,795[2] | 1973E |
| Prague | 1,179,600 | 1977E |
| Pusan, South Korea | 1,842,259 | 1970C |
| Quebec | 177,082 | 1976C |
| Quezon City, Philippines | 994,700 | 1975E |
| Quito, Ecuador | 977,400 | 1977E |
| Rangoon, Burma | 2,056,100[2] | 1973E |
| Recife, Brazil | 1,249,800 | 1977E |
| Rome | 2,884,000 | 1977E |
| Rosario, Argentina | 810,840[2] | 1970C |
| Rostov-on-Don, U.S.S.R. | 907,000 | 1976E |
| Rotterdam | 1,022,700 | 1977E |
| Salvador, Brazil | 1,000,647[2] | |
| Santiago, Chile | 3,263,000[2] | 1975E |
| Sapporo, Japan | 1,240,000[2] | 1975E |
| Seville, Spain | 612,900 | 1976E |
| Shenyang, China | 3,750,000[2] | 1970E |
| Singapore, Singapore | 2,249,900 | 1975E |
| Sofia, Bulgaria | 965,700 | 1975E |
| Stockholm | 661,300 | 1977E |
| Surabaja, Indonesia | 1,556,255 | 1971C |
| Sverdlovsk, U.S.S.R. | 1,171,000 | 1976E |
| Sydney, Australia | 3,021,299 | 1976C |
| Taipai, Taiwan | 2,130,800 | 1978E |
| Tashkent, U.S.S.R. | 1,643,000 | 1976E |
| Tblisi, U.S.S.R. | 1,030,000 | 1976E |
| Tel Aviv-Jaffa, Israel | 348,500 | 1977E |
| Toronto | 633,318 | 1976C |
| Tunis, Tunisia | 960,000 | 1976E |
| Turin, Italy | 1,200,000 | 1975E |
| Valencia, Spain | 748,730 | 1976E |
| Vancouver, Canada | 410,188 | 1976C |
| Venice | 364,900 | 1975E |
| Vienna | 1,592,800 | 1976E |
| Volgograd, U.S.S.R. | 918,000 | 1976E |
| Warsaw | 1,448,900 | 1976E |
| Wellington, New Zealand | 139,600 | 1976C |
| Winnipeg, Canada | 560,874 | 1976C |
| Wuhan, China | 3,000,000 | 1970E |
| Yokohama, Japan | 2,620,000[2] | 1975E |
| Zurich | 389,600 | 1976E |

1. E = estimated; C = census. 2. Figure is for urban agglomeration and may include suburbs, metropolitan areas, or some rural population. 3. West Berlin, 1,966,700; East Berlin, 1,106,300. NOTE: The population of many other cities will be found throughout the World History section under individual countries. *See* Table of Contents.

# Expectation of Life by Age and Sex for Selected Countries

| Country | Period | Males 0 | Males 1 | Males 10 | Males 20 | Males 40 | Males 60 | Females 0 | Females 1 | Females 10 | Females 20 | Females 40 | Females 60 |
|---|---|---|---|---|---|---|---|---|---|---|---|---|---|
| | | Average future lifetime in years at stated age | | | | | | | | | | | |
| **NORTH AMERICA** | | | | | | | | | | | | | |
| United States | 1975 | 68.7 | 68.9 | 60.3 | 50.8 | 32.6 | 16.8 | 76.5 | 76.6 | 67.9 | 58.1 | 39.0 | 21.8 |
| Canada | 1970–72 | 69.3 | 69.8 | 61.2 | 51.7 | 33.2 | 17.0 | 76.4 | 76.6 | 67.9 | 58.2 | 39.0 | 21.4 |
| Mexico | 1975 | 62.8 | 68.0 | 59.2 | 49.9 | 32.7 | 17.9 | 66.6 | 69.3 | 62.6 | 53.1 | 35.3 | 19.1 |
| Puerto Rico | 1971–73 | 68.9 | 70.1 | 61.4 | 51.9 | 34.2 | 18.6 | 76.1 | 76.9 | 68.2 | 58.0 | 39.0 | 21.5 |
| Trinidad and Tobago | 1970 | 64.1 | 65.6 | 57.3 | 47.8 | 29.5 | 13.6 | 68.1 | 69.3 | 60.9 | 51.3 | 32.7 | 16.3 |
| **CENTRAL AND SOUTH AMERICA** | | | | | | | | | | | | | |
| Brazil | 1960–70 | 57.6 | — | 56.2 | 47.0 | 30.0 | 15.0 | 61.1 | — | 58.9 | 49.7 | 32.5 | 16.6 |
| Chile | 1969–70 | 60.5 | 64.9 | 56.7 | 47.3 | 29.9 | 15.5 | 66.0 | 70.0 | 62.2 | 52.7 | 34.5 | 18.0 |
| Colombia | 1950–52 | 44.2 | 50.4 | 48.2 | 39.6 | 24.8 | 11.8 | 45.9 | 51.1 | 49.4 | 40.9 | 26.6 | 12.8 |
| Costa Rica | 1962–64 | 61.9 | 66.8 | 60.4 | 51.1 | 33.2 | 17.0 | 64.8 | 68.9 | 62.5 | 53.0 | 34.8 | 18.2 |
| Ecuador | 1961–63 | 51.0 | 57.1 | 54.7 | 46.3 | 30.2 | 14.9 | 53.7 | 59.0 | 56.8 | 48.1 | 31.9 | 16.6 |
| Guatemala | 1963–65 | 48.3 | 52.5 | 51.3 | 43.2 | 28.1 | 14.8 | 49.7 | 53.4 | 52.8 | 44.6 | 29.2 | 14.7 |
| Panama | 1970 | 64.3 | 66.4 | 59.9 | 50.8 | 33.4 | 17.0 | 67.5 | 69.4 | 62.7 | 53.6 | 36.1 | 19.9 |
| Uruguay | 1963–64 | 65.5 | 68.0 | 59.5 | 50.0 | 31.7 | 15.9 | 71.6 | 73.7 | 65.2 | 55.5 | 36.7 | 19.5 |
| Venezuela[1] | 1961 | 66.4 | 68.8 | 61.8 | 52.4 | 34.6 | 18.9 | — | — | — | — | — | — |
| **EUROPE** | | | | | | | | | | | | | |
| Austria | 1975 | 67.7 | — | 59.7 | 50.2 | 31.8 | 15.6 | 74.9 | — | 66.5 | 56.7 | 37.4 | 19.6 |
| Belgium | 1968–72 | 67.8 | 68.4 | 59.9 | 50.3 | 31.6 | 15.2 | 74.2 | 74.5 | 65.9 | 56.1 | 36.9 | 19.2 |
| Czechoslovakia | 1970 | 66.2 | 67.0 | 58.4 | 49.9 | 30.6 | 14.6 | 72.9 | 72.6 | 64.9 | 55.2 | 35.9 | 18.3 |
| Denmark[2] | 1972–73 | 70.8 | 70.8 | 62.2 | 52.6 | 33.7 | 17.0 | 76.3 | 76.1 | 67.4 | 57.6 | 38.3 | 20.8 |
| England and Wales | 1970–72 | 68.9 | 69.3 | 60.6 | 52.0 | 31.9 | 15.3 | 75.1 | 75.3 | 66.6 | 56.8 | 37.4 | 19.9 |
| Finland | 1974 | 66.0 | 66.8 | 58.1 | 48.5 | 30.1 | 14.9 | 75.4 | 75.2 | 66.5 | 56.7 | 37.3 | 19.4 |
| France | 1972 | 68.6 | 68.6 | 60.0 | 51.0 | 32.2 | 16.3 | 76.4 | 76.3 | 67.6 | 57.9 | 38.7 | 21.1 |
| Germany, East[2] | 1969–70 | 68.9 | 69.3 | 60.8 | 51.2 | 32.7 | 16.1 | 74.2 | 74.4 | 65.8 | 56.1 | 36.9 | 16.3 |
| Germany, West[3] | 1973–75 | 68.0 | 68.7 | 60.1 | 50.6 | 32.0 | 15.5 | 74.5 | 74.9 | 66.3 | 56.5 | 37.2 | 19.5 |
| Greece | 1960–62 | 67.5 | 70.5 | 62.5 | 52.9 | 34.0 | 17.0 | 70.7 | 73.5 | 65.5 | 55.8 | 36.7 | 18.9 |
| Hungary | 1974 | 66.5 | 68.2 | 59.5 | 49.9 | 31.5 | 15.5 | 72.4 | 73.7 | 65.1 | 55.3 | 36.1 | 18.7 |
| Iceland | 1971–75 | 71.6 | 71.5 | 62.9 | 53.4 | 35.0 | 18.6 | 77.5 | 77.2 | 68.5 | 58.7 | 39.4 | 21.7 |
| Ireland | 1965–67 | 68.6 | 69.5 | 60.8 | 51.2 | 32.2 | 15.6 | 72.9 | 73.4 | 64.8 | 54.9 | 35.7 | 18.4 |
| Italy | 1970–72 | 69.0 | 70.1 | 61.6 | 52.0 | 33.2 | 16.7 | 74.9 | 75.8 | 67.1 | 57.3 | 38.1 | 20.2 |
| Netherlands | 1971–75 | 71.2 | 71.1 | 62.6 | 52.9 | 33.9 | 17.0 | 77.2 | 77.0 | 68.3 | 58.5 | 39.0 | 21.0 |
| Norway | 1973–74 | 71.5 | 71.5 | 62.9 | 53.3 | 34.4 | 17.5 | 77.8 | 77.5 | 68.8 | 59.0 | 39.5 | 21.3 |
| Poland | 1970–72 | 66.8 | 68.0 | 59.4 | 49.8 | 31.6 | 15.5 | 73.8 | 74.6 | 66.0 | 56.2 | 37.0 | 19.3 |
| Portugal | 1974 | 65.3 | 67.2 | 59.0 | 49.6 | 31.5 | 15.4 | 72.0 | 73.5 | 65.3 | 55.6 | 36.5 | 18.7 |
| Scotland | 1971–73 | 67.2 | 67.8 | 59.2 | 49.8 | 31.3 | 15.0 | 73.6 | 74.1 | 65.4 | 55.6 | 36.3 | 18.9 |
| Spain | 1970 | 69.7 | — | 62.0 | 52.4 | 33.7 | 17.0 | 75.0 | — | 66.9 | 57.1 | 38.0 | 20.1 |
| Sweden | 1971–75 | 72.1 | 71.9 | 63.2 | 53.5 | 34.7 | 17.7 | 77.7 | 77.3 | 68.5 | 58.7 | 39.4 | 21.3 |
| Switzerland | 1968–73 | 70.3 | 70.5 | 62.0 | 52.4 | 33.6 | 16.7 | 76.2 | 76.2 | 67.6 | 57.8 | 38.4 | 20.4 |
| U.S.S.R. | 1971–72 | 64.0 | — | — | — | — | — | 74.0 | — | — | — | — | — |
| Yugoslavia | 1970–72 | 65.4 | 68.0 | 59.7 | 50.1 | 31.8 | 15.7 | 70.2 | 72.8 | 64.6 | 54.9 | 35.8 | 18.2 |
| **ASIA** | | | | | | | | | | | | | |
| Burma | 1954 | 40.8 | 49.8 | 45.5 | 36.8 | 21.1 | 10.6 | 43.8 | 51.6 | 47.0 | 38.3 | 23.7 | 12.4 |
| India | 1951–60 | 41.9 | 48.4 | 45.2 | 36.9 | 22.1 | 11.8 | 40.6 | 46.0 | 43.8 | 35.6 | 22.4 | 12.9 |
| Israel | 1975 | 70.3 | 71.1 | 62.5 | 53.1 | 34.5 | 17.4 | 73.9 | 74.5 | 65.9 | 56.1 | 36.9 | 19.2 |
| Japan[4] | 1974 | 71.2 | 71.0 | 62.5 | 52.8 | 33.0 | 17.0 | 76.3 | 76.0 | 67.4 | 57.5 | 38.3 | 20.3 |
| Jordan | 1959–63 | 52.6 | 58.2 | 52.7 | 44.1 | 28.6 | 14.4 | 52.0 | 58.2 | 54.4 | 46.0 | 30.7 | 15.7 |
| Korea, South | 1970 | 63.0 | 66.0 | 58.0 | 49.0 | 31.0 | 16.0 | 67.0 | 69.0 | 61.0 | 52.0 | 34.0 | 17.0 |
| Sri Lanka | 1967 | 64.8 | 67.4 | 60.5 | 51.2 | 33.2 | 17.0 | 66.9 | 68.9 | 62.4 | 53.0 | 35.0 | 17.8 |
| Syria | 1970 | 54.5 | 60.7 | 56.4 | 47.4 | 30.5 | 15.2 | 58.7 | 64.1 | 59.5 | 50.5 | 33.3 | 17.3 |
| **AFRICA** | | | | | | | | | | | | | |
| Egypt | 1960 | 51.6 | 56.2 | 56.6 | 47.7 | 30.5 | 15.1 | 53.8 | 59.9 | 62.0 | 52.9 | 35.0 | 18.0 |
| Kenya | 1969 | 46.9 | 52.6 | 51.0 | 43.0 | 28.3 | 14.5 | 51.2 | 56.6 | 54.1 | 45.7 | 30.3 | 15.7 |
| South Africa (white population) | 1959–61 | 64.7 | 65.9 | 57.5 | 48.0 | 30.2 | 15.0 | 71.7 | 72.5 | 64.1 | 54.4 | 35.5 | 18.6 |
| **OCEANIA** | | | | | | | | | | | | | |
| Australia[5] | 1965–67 | 67.6 | 68.1 | 59.5 | 50.0 | 31.4 | 15.8 | 74.2 | 74.4 | 65.8 | 56.0 | 36.9 | 19.5 |
| New Zealand | 1970–72 | 68.5 | — | — | — | — | — | 74.6 | — | — | — | — | — |

1. Figures for male and female together. 2. Excluding data for Faeroe Islands and Greenland. 3. Includes relevant data relating to Berlin. No separate data have been supplied. 4. Japanese nationals in Japan only. 5. Excludes full-blooded aborigines. *Source:* United Nations *Demographic Yearbook, 1976.*

## Estimates of World Population by Regions

| Year | North America[1] | Latin America[2] | Europe[3] | U.S.S.R. | Asia[4] | Africa | Oceania | World total |
|---|---|---|---|---|---|---|---|---|
| | Estimated population in millions | | | | | | | |
| 1650 | 1 | 7 | 103 | [5] | 257 | 100 | 2 | 470 |
| 1750 | 1 | 10 | 144 | [5] | 437 | 100 | 2 | 694 |
| 1850 | 26 | 33 | 274 | [5] | 656 | 100 | 2 | 1,091 |
| 1900 | 81 | 63 | 423 | [5] | 857 | 141 | 6 | 1,571 |
| 1930 | 134 | 108 | 355[6] | 179 | 1,120[7] | 164 | 10 | 2,070 |
| 1950 | 166 | 164 | 392[6] | 180 | 1,368[7] | 219 | 13 | 2,501 |
| 1960 | 199 | 216 | 425[6] | 214 | 1,644[7] | 273 | 16 | 2,986 |
| 1970 | 226 | 283 | 459[6] | 243 | 2,027[7] | 352 | 19 | 3,610 |
| 1976 | 239 | 333 | 476[6] | 258 | 2,304[7] | 412 | 22 | 4,044 |

1. U.S. (including Alaska and Hawaii), Bermuda, Canada, Greenland, and St. Pierre and Miquelon. 2. Mexico, Central and South America, and Caribbean Islands. 3. Includes Russia 1650–1900. 4. Excludes Russia (U.S.S.R.). 5. Included in Europe. 6. Excludes European Turkey, which is included in Asia. 7. Includes both Asian and European Turkey. *Sources:* W.F. Willcox, 1650–1900; United Nations, 1930–76.

## Crude Birth and Death Rates for Selected Countries

(per 1,000 population)

| Country | Birth rates 1977 | 1976 | 1975 | 1970 | 1965 | Death rates 1977 | 1976 | 1975 | 1970 | 1965 |
|---|---|---|---|---|---|---|---|---|---|---|
| Australia | 16.1 | 16.7 | 17.3 | 20.6 | 19.6 | 7.7 | 8.3 | 8.1 | 9.0 | 8.8 |
| Austria | 11.3 | 11.6 | 12.5 | 15.2 | 17.9 | 12.2 | 12.7 | 12.8 | 13.4 | 13.0 |
| Belgium | 12.5 | 12.3 | 12.2 | 14.7 | 16.4 | 11.6 | 12.1 | 12.2 | 12.3 | 12.5 |
| Canada | 15.5 | 15.8 | 15.7 | 17.4 | 21.4 | 7.3 | 7.2 | 7.3 | 7.3 | 7.5 |
| Czechoslovakia | 18.7 | 19.2 | 19.6 | 15.9 | 16.4 | 11.5 | 11.4 | 11.5 | 11.6 | 10.0 |
| Denmark | 12.2 | 12.9 | 14.2 | 14.4 | 18.2 | 9.9 | 10.6 | 10.1 | 9.8 | 10.1 |
| El Salvador | 41.7 | 40.2 | 38.9 | 40.0 | 46.5 | 7.8 | 7.5 | 7.9 | 9.9 | 10.6 |
| Finland | 13.9 | 14.1 | 13.9 | 14.0 | 17.0 | 9.4 | 9.5 | 9.3 | 9.6 | 7.9 |
| France | 14.0 | 13.6 | 14.1 | 16.8 | 17.7 | 10.1 | 10.5 | 10.6 | 10.7 | 11.1 |
| Germany, East | 13.3 | 11.6 | 10.8 | 13.9 | 16.5 | 13.4 | 14.0 | 14.3 | 14.1 | 13.3 |
| Germany, West | 9.5 | 9.8 | 9.7 | 11.4 | 17.9 | 11.5 | 11.9 | 12.1 | 12.1 | 11.2 |
| Greece | 15.4 | 15.7 | 15.7 | 16.5 | 17.7 | 8.9 | 8.2 | 8.9 | 8.4 | 7.9 |
| Hungary | 16.7 | 17.5 | 18.4 | 14.7 | 13.1 | 12.4 | 12.5 | 12.4 | 11.6 | 10.7 |
| Ireland | n.a. | 21.6 | 21.5 | 21.8 | 22.2 | n.a. | 10.5 | 10.6 | 11.4 | 11.5 |
| Israel | 26.1 | 27.6 | 28.2 | 26.9 | 25.4 | 6.8 | 6.8 | 7.1 | 7.1 | 6.2 |
| Italy | 13.2 | 14.0 | 14.8 | 16.8 | 19.2 | 9.6 | 9.7 | 9.9 | 9.7 | 10.0 |
| Japan | 15.4 | 16.3 | 17.2 | 18.9 | 18.6 | 6.1 | 6.3 | 6.4 | 6.9 | 7.1 |
| Luxembourg | 11.4 | 11.0 | 11.2 | 13.2 | 15.6 | 11.5 | 12.6 | 12.2 | 12.3 | 11.8 |
| Malta | 18.0 | 18.0 | 18.3 | 16.3 | 17.6 | 8.9 | 9.0 | 8.8 | 9.4 | 9.4 |
| Mauritius | 25.8 | 25.6 | 25.1 | 26.0 | 35.4 | 7.9 | 7.8 | 8.1 | 7.8 | 8.6 |
| Mexico | n.a. | 34.6 | 37.5 | 42.1 | 45.3 | n.a. | 6.5 | 6.7 | 9.6 | 9.5 |
| Netherlands | 12.5 | 12.9 | 13.0 | 18.3 | 19.9 | 7.9 | 8.3 | 8.3 | 8.4 | 8.0 |
| New Zealand | n.a. | 17.8 | 18.4 | 22.1 | 22.8 | n.a. | 8.2 | 8.1 | 8.8 | 8.7 |
| Norway | 12.6 | 13.3 | 14.0 | 16.6 | 17.5 | 9.7 | 9.9 | 9.9 | 10.0 | 9.1 |
| Panama | 28.8 | 32.2 | 32.3 | 37.2 | 39.1 | n.a. | 5.2 | n.a. | 8.8[1] | 7.3 |
| Poland | 19.1 | 19.5 | 18.9 | 16.8 | 17.3 | 9.0 | 8.8 | 8.7 | 8.2 | 7.4 |
| Portugal | n.a. | 19.2 | 19.0 | 20.0 | 22.9 | n.a. | 10.5 | 10.4 | 10.8 | 10.1 |
| Singapore | 16.8 | 18.5 | 17.7 | 23.0 | 31.1 | 5.2 | 5.1 | 5.1 | 5.2 | 5.6 |
| Spain | 18.0 | 18.2 | 19.1 | 19.5 | 21.3 | n.a. | 8.0 | 8.3 | 8.3 | 8.7 |
| Sweden | 11.6 | 11.9 | 12.6 | 13.7 | 15.9 | 10.7 | 11.0 | 10.8 | 9.9 | 10.1 |
| Switzerland | 11.6 | 12.0 | 12.4 | 15.8 | 18.7 | 8.6 | 8.8 | 8.6 | 9.1 | 9.3 |
| Tunisia | n.a. | 36.4 | 36.6 | 36.4 | 44.3 | n.a. | n.a. | n.a. | 17.6[1] | 11.8 |
| United Kingdom | 11.8 | 12.1 | 12.4 | 16.3 | 18.4 | 11.7 | 14.2 | 11.8 | 11.8 | 11.5 |
| United States | 15.3 | 14.7 | 14.8 | 18.3 | 19.4 | 8.8 | 8.9 | 8.9 | 9.4 | 9.4 |
| Yugoslavia | 17.6 | 18.0 | 18.1 | 17.8 | 20.9 | 8.4 | 8.2 | 8.6 | 8.9 | 8.7 |

1. 1969–70 figure. NOTE: n.a. = not available. *Source:* United Nations, Department of Economic and Social Affairs, Statistical Office.

## Suicide Rates for Selected Countries

(per 100,000 population)

| Country | Year | Rate | Country | Year | Rate | Country | Year | Rate |
|---|---|---|---|---|---|---|---|---|
| Angola | 1972 | 1.0 | Hong Kong | 1975 | 10.9 | Singapore | 1975 | 11.2 |
| Australia | 1974 | 11.7 | Hungary | 1975 | 38.4 | South Africa | | |
| Austria | 1975 | 24.1 | Iceland | 1975 | 10.1 | Black | 1971 | 5.6 |
| Barbados | 1972 | 1.7 | Ireland | 1973 | 3.5 | White | 1971 | 14.5 |
| Belgium | 1973 | 14.9 | Israel | 1974 | 4.9 | Spain | 1974 | 4.0 |
| Bulgaria | 1974 | 12.7 | Italy | 1972 | 5.8 | Sweden | 1974 | 20.0 |
| Canada | 1974 | 12.9 | Jamaica | 1971 | 1.0 | Switzerland | 1975 | 1.5 |
| Chile | 1972 | 5.4 | Japan | 1975 | 18.1 | Trinidad and Tobago | 1974 | 7.0 |
| Costa Rica | 1975 | 4.1 | Mauritius | 1975 | 7.8 | Turkey | 1971 | 1.9 |
| Cuba | 1971 | 15.0 | Mexico | 1974 | 2.1 | United Kingdom | | |
| Czechoslovakia | 1973 | 22.4 | Netherlands | 1974 | 9.2 | England and Wales | 1974 | 7.9 |
| Denmark | 1973 | 23.8 | New Zealand | 1974 | 8.8 | Northern Ireland | 1975 | 3.6 |
| Ecuador | 1974 | 2.6 | Norway | 1975 | 9.9 | Scotland | 1975 | 8.2 |
| El Salvador | 1971 | 8.7 | Panama | 1974 | 3.0 | United States | 1975 | 12.7 |
| Finland | 1974 | 25.1 | Paraguay | 1974 | 1.6 | Uruguay | 1974 | 10.4 |
| France | 1970 | 15.4 | Peru | 1972 | 1.8 | Venezuela | 1974 | 4.7 |
| Germany, East | 1970 | 30.5 | Philippines | 1974 | 1.1 | | | |
| Germany, West | 1974 | 21.0 | Poland | 1975 | 11.4 | | | |
| Greece | 1975 | 2.8 | Portugal | 1974 | 8.6 | | | |
| Guatemala | 1972 | 3.4 | Puerto Rico | 1973 | 9.1 | | | |

*Source:* United Nations *Demographic Yearbook, 1976.*

## Cost of Living of United Nations Personnel in Selected Cities as Reflected by Index of Retail Prices, 1977

(New York City = 100)

| City | Index | City | Index |
|---|---|---|---|
| Addis Ababa, Ethiopia | 92 | Kinshasha, Zaire | 137 |
| Amman, Jordan | 111 | La Paz, Bolivia | 99 |
| Ankara, Turkey | 91 | Lima, Peru | 87 |
| Athens | 99 | London | 97 |
| Baghdad, Iraq | 87 | Manila | 86 |
| Bangkok, Thailand | 78 | Mexico City | 73 |
| Belgrade, Yugoslavia | 94 | Montevideo, Uruguay | 85 |
| Bogotá, Colombia | 78 | Montreal | 84 |
| Bonn, West Germany | 132 | Nairobi, Kenya | 91 |
| Budapest | 95 | New Delhi, India | 75 |
| Buenos Aires | 90 | Paris | 121 |
| Cairo | 77 | Quito, Ecuador | 80 |
| Caracas, Venezuela | 106 | Rabat, Morocco | 103 |
| Colombo, Sri Lanka | 77 | Rio de Janeiro | 105 |
| Copenhagen | 122 | Rome | 86 |
| Dacca, Bangladesh | 90 | San José, Costa Rica | 83 |
| Damascus, Syria | 104 | San Salvador, El Salvador | 91 |
| Dar es Salaam, Tanzania | 88 | Santiago, Chile | 92 |
| Geneva | 136 | Seoul, South Korea | 99 |
| Guatemala City, Guatemala | 90 | Sofia, Bulgaria | 102 |
| The Hague, The Netherlands | 127 | Teheran, Iran | 111 |
| Havana | 82 | Tokyo | 156 |
| Jakarta, Indonesia | 115 | Tunis, Tunisia | 113 |
| Kabul, Afghanistan | 83 | Vienna | 121 |
| Islamabad, Pakistan | 79 | Vientiane, Laos | 96 |
| Katmandu, Nepal | 76 | Warsaw | 75 |
| Kingston, Jamaica | 83 | Washington, D.C. | 95 |

*Source:* United Nations, *Monthly Bulletin of Statistics, May 1978.*

## Value of Exports and Imports

**(in millions of U.S. dollars)**

| Country | Exports[1] | Imports[1] |
|---|---|---|
| Afghanistan | $ 327 | $ 308 |
| Algeria | 5,812 | 7,085 |
| Angola | 1,227[2] | 625[2] |
| Argentina | 3,916[3] | 3,033[3] |
| Australia | 13,002 | 12,175 |
| Austria | 9,808 | 14,248 |
| Bahamas | 2,879[3] | 3,560[3] |
| Bahrain | 1,821 | 2,030 |
| Bangladesh | 414 | 764[3] |
| Barbados | 96 | 275 |
| Belgium-Luxembourg | 37,457 | 40,142 |
| Benin | 46[4] | 150[4] |
| Bolivia | 637[3] | 554[3] |
| Brazil | 10,128[3] | 13,622[3] |
| Bulgaria | 6,329 | 6,329 |
| Burma | 223 | 185 |
| Burundi | 95 | 74 |
| Cameroon | 658 | 994 |
| Canada | 41,452 | 39,561 |
| Central African Empire | 58[3] | 54[3] |
| Chad | 70[4] | 133[4] |
| Chile | 2,083[3] | 1,684[3] |
| Colombia | 1,745[3] | 1,708[3] |
| Congo | 182[3] | 177[3] |
| Costa Rica | 584[3] | 774[3] |
| Cyprus | 318 | 620 |
| Czechoslovakia | 10,818 | 11,149 |
| Denmark | 10,117 | 13,239 |
| Dominican Republic | 794 | 793 |
| Ecuador | 1,127[3] | 993[3] |
| Egypt | 1,726 | 4,823 |
| El Salvador | 959 | 950 |
| Ethiopia | 330 | 349 |
| Fiji | 173 | 306 |
| Finland | 7,670 | 7,603 |
| France | 63,560 | 70,498 |
| Gabon | 1,014 | 498[3] |
| Gambia | 48 | 72 |
| Germany, East | 11,361[3] | 13,196[3] |
| Germany, West | 117,895 | 100,672 |
| Ghana | 760[4] | 805[4] |
| Greece | 2,724 | 6,778 |
| Guatemala | 760[3] | 839[3] |
| Guyana | 269[3] | 363[3] |
| Haiti | 125[3] | 121[4] |
| Honduras | 373[3] | 453[3] |
| Hungary | 5,832 | 6,522 |
| Iceland | 513 | 607 |
| India | 5,412 | 5,798 |
| Indonesia | 10,853 | 6,230 |
| Iran | 24,250 | 13,750 |
| Iraq | 9,664 | 3,470[3] |
| Ireland | 4,396 | 5,378 |
| Israel | 2,959 | 4,663 |
| Italy | 45,063 | 47,580 |
| Ivory Coast | 2,170 | 1,761 |
| Jamaica | 633[3] | 913[3] |
| Japan | 80,470 | 70,660 |
| Jordan | 249 | 1,276 |
| Kenya | 656 | 941 |
| Korea, South | 10,062 | 10,798 |
| Kuwait | 9,835 | 3,321[3] |
| Laos | 5[5] | 65[2] |
| Lebanon | 497[5] | 1,224[5] |
| Liberia | 447 | 464 |
| Libya | 10,113 | 3,212[3] |
| Madagascar | 292[4] | 363[4] |
| Malawi | 195 | 235 |
| Malaysia | 6,507 | 4,966 |
| Mali | 97[3] | 150[3] |
| Malta | 289 | 513 |
| Mauritania | 178[3] | 180[3] |
| Mauritius | 312 | 442 |
| Mexico | 4,123 | 5,487 |
| Morocco | 1,300 | 3,197 |
| Mozambique | 202[4] | 417[4] |
| Netherlands | 43,703 | 45,616 |
| New Zealand | 3,142 | 3,363 |
| Nicaragua | 542[3] | 721 |
| Niger | 89[3] | 100[4] |
| Nigeria | 11,737 | 6,041[3] |
| Norway | 8,717 | 12,877 |
| Pakistan | 1,149 | 2,447 |
| Panama | 227 | 838 |
| Papua New Guinea | 635 | 430[3] |
| Paraguay | 274 | 301 |
| Peru | 1,365[3] | 2,183[3] |
| Philippines | 3,151 | 4,219 |
| Poland | 12,336 | 14,674 |
| Portugal | 2,023 | 4,963 |
| Rhodesia | 650[5] | 541[5] |
| Romania | 6,138[3] | 6,095[3] |
| Saudi Arabia | 41,490 | 8,694[3] |
| Senegal | 461[4] | 576[4] |
| Sierra Leone | 127 | 153 |
| Singapore | 8,241 | 10,472 |
| Somalia | 85[3] | 162[4] |
| Spain | 10,230 | 17,846 |
| Sri Lanka | 714 | 695 |
| Sudan | 661 | 1,767 |
| Surinam | 227[4] | 262[4] |
| Sweden | 18,823 | 19,566 |
| Switzerland | 17,682 | 17,979 |
| Syria | 1,063 | 2,672 |
| Tanzania | 459[3] | 566[3] |
| Thailand | 2,980[3] | 3,572[3] |
| Togo | 126[4] | 174[4] |
| Trinidad and Tobago | 2,174 | 1,862 |
| Tunisia | 910 | 1,767 |
| Turkey | 1,753 | 5,694 |
| Uganda | 360[3] | 80[3] |
| U.S.S.R. | 45,161 | 40,817 |
| United Kingdom | 57,547 | 63,677 |
| United States | 119,042 | 156,758 |
| Upper Volta | 53[3] | 144[3] |
| Uruguay | 546[3] | 587[3] |
| Venezuela | 9,149[3] | 6,023[3] |
| Vietnam | 59[5] | 618[5] |
| Western Samoa | 13 | 41 |
| Yemen Arab Republic | 8[3] | 410[3] |
| Yemen, Dem. Rep. of | 249[3] | 414[3] |
| Yugoslavia | 5,254 | 9,634 |
| Zaire | 982 | 606 |
| Zambia | 1,046[3] | 800[3] |

1. 1977 unless otherwise indicated. 2. 1974. 3. 1976. 4. 1975. 5. 1973. *Source:* United Nations, *Monthly Bulletin of Statistics*, July 1978.

## Annual Increases in Worldwide Consumer Prices
(in percent)

| Country | 1977 | 1976 |
|---|---|---|
| North America | | |
| Bahamas | 3.3 | 4.3 |
| Canada | 8.0 | 7.5 |
| Dominican Republic | 12.9 | 7.7 |
| El Salvador | 11.9 | 7.0 |
| Guatemala | 12.6 | 10.7 |
| Jamaica | 11.4 | 9.6 |
| Mexico | 26.4 | 16.1 |
| Trinidad & Tobago | 11.9 | 10.5 |
| United States | 6.5 | 5.8 |
| South America | | |
| Argentina | 176.1 | 443.2 |
| Brazil | 43.7 | 41.9 |
| Chile | 92.0 | 211.9 |
| Colombia | 30.0 | 17.4 |
| Ecuador | 13.0 | 10.7 |
| Peru | 38.1 | 33.5 |
| Uruguay | 58.3 | 50.5 |
| Venezuela | 7.7 | 7.6 |
| Asia | | |
| China, Republic of | 7.0 | 2.5 |
| Egypt | 12.7 | 10.3 |
| India | 8.5 | −7.8 |
| Indonesia | 11.0 | 19.8 |
| Iran | 27.3 | 11.3 |
| Iraq | — | 10.3 |
| Israel | 34.6 | 31.4 |
| Japan | 8.1 | 9.3 |
| Jordan | 35.2 | 11.5 |
| Kuwait | 8.2 | 5.5 |
| Korea, South | 10.3 | 15.4 |
| Malaysia | 4.8 | 2.6 |
| Pakistan | 10.1 | 7.2 |
| Philippines | 7.9 | 6.1 |
| Saudi Arabia | 11.3 | 31.6 |
| Sri Lanka | 1.3 | 1.2 |
| Syrian Arab Republic | 12.6 | 11.0 |
| Thailand | 8.4 | 5.0 |
| Europe | | |
| Austria | 5.5 | 7.3 |
| Belgium | 7.1 | 9.2 |
| Denmark | 11.1 | 9.0 |
| Finland | 12.7 | 14.4 |
| France | 9.5 | 9.2 |
| Germany, West | 3.9 | 4.5 |
| Greece | 12.2 | 13.3 |
| Ireland | 13.6 | 18.0 |
| Italy | 17.0 | 16.8 |
| Netherlands | 6.4 | 8.8 |
| Norway | 9.2 | 9.1 |
| Portugal | 24.3 | 21.1 |
| Spain | 24.5 | 15.1 |
| Sweden | 11.4 | 10.3 |
| Switzerland | 1.3 | 1.7 |
| Turkey | 27.2 | 17.3 |
| United Kingdom | 15.8 | 16.6 |
| Yugoslavia | 14.6 | 11.2 |
| Africa | | |
| Cameroon | 14.6 | 9.9 |
| Ethiopia | 16.6 | 28.6 |
| Ghana | — | 52.7 |
| Ivory Coast | 27.5 | 12.0 |
| Kenya | 10.4 | 13.5 |
| Madagascar | 3.0 | 5.0 |
| Morocco | 12.5 | 8.6 |
| Nigeria | 21.6 | 22.0 |
| South Africa | 11.3 | 11.1 |
| Sudan | — | 1.7 |
| Tanzania | — | 6.9 |
| Tunisia | 6.6 | 5.4 |
| Zaire | 63.3 | 85.1 |
| Zambia | 19.8 | 18.7 |
| Oceania | | |
| Australia | 12.3 | 13.5 |
| New Zealand | 14.4 | 16.9 |

*Source:* International Monetary Fund.

## Mortality From Motor Vehicle Accidents, 1976

| Country | Motor vehicles[1] | Death rate[2] | Death rate[3] |
|---|---|---|---|
| United States | 670 | 21 | 32 |
| France | 450 | 28 | 63 |
| Denmark | 320 | 17 | 53 |
| Netherlands | 410 | 18 | 43 |
| Norway | 320 | 12 | 36 |
| West Germany | 360 | 24 | 67 |
| Austria | 340 | 28 | 82 |
| Finland | 300 | 17 | 57 |
| United Kingdom | 310 | 12 | 38 |
| Italy | 390 | 17 | 44 |
| Ireland | 210 | 17 | 81 |
| Spain | 210 | 17 | 82 |
| Sweden | 380 | 14 | 38 |
| Switzerland | 440 | 19 | 43 |
| Czechoslovakia | 160 | 18 | 113 |
| East Germany | 350 | 16 | 44 |
| Hungary | 140 | 15 | 108 |
| Poland | 110 | 17 | 159 |
| Australia | 490 | 26 | 54 |
| Japan | 340 | 11 | 33 |

1. Per 1,000 population. 2. Deaths per 100,000 population. 3. Deaths per 100,000 registered motor vehicles. *Source:* Department of Transportation, National Highway Traffic Safety Administration.

## Corn, Meat, and Sugar—Production by Country
(in thousands of metric tons)

| | Corn | | | Meat[1] | | | Sugar[2] | | |
|---|---|---|---|---|---|---|---|---|---|
| Country | 1975 | 1974 | 1967–1971 average | 1975 | 1974 | 1967–1971 average | 1975 | 1974 | 1967–1971 average |
| Argentina | 7,700 | 9,900 | 8,244 | 2,778 | 2,525 | 2,935 | 1,367 | 1,514 | 932 |
| Australia | 133 | 106 | 182 | 2,256[5] | 1,978[5] | 1,959[4] | 2,930 | 2,938 | 2,539 |
| Austria | 981 | 857 | 549 | 482 | 475 | 411 | 523 | 403 | 314 |
| Belgium | 38 | 25 | 8 | 892 | 921 | 659 | 800 | 531 | 649 |
| Brazil[6] | 16,354 | 16,285 | 13,335 | 2,953 | 2,903 | 2,519 | 6,299 | 6,931 | 4,630[7] |

| Country | Corn 1975 | Corn 1974 | Corn 1967–1971 average | Meat[1] 1975 | Meat[1] 1974 | Meat[1] 1967–1971 average | Sugar[2] 1975 | Sugar[2] 1974 | Sugar[2] 1967–1971 average |
|---|---|---|---|---|---|---|---|---|---|
| Bulgaria | 2,822 | 1,626 | 2,209 | 427 | 352 | 326 | 215 | 230 | 205 |
| Canada | 3,645 | 2,577 | 2,284 | 1,552 | 1,561 | 1,456 | 120 | 98 | 136 |
| Chile | 329 | 366 | 267 | 269 | 247 | 238 | 219 | 116 | 184 |
| China, People's Rep. of[6] | 33,138[8] | 31,107[8] | 27,695[8] | 12,423[8] | 12,285[8] | 10,814 | 4,000 | 3,900 | 2,785 |
| China (Taiwan) | 138[9] | 107[9] | 36 | 395[9] | 462[9] | n.a. | n.a. | n.a. | n.a. |
| Colombia[6] | 800 | 775 | 887 | 509 | 460 | 586 | 970 | 895 | 678 |
| Cuba[6] | 125 | 125 | 118 | 227 | 223 | 222 | 6,427 | 5,926 | 6,119 |
| Czechoslovakia | 843 | 574 | 481 | 1,176[10 11] | 1,141[10 11] | 958[10 11] | 780 | 750 | 775 |
| Denmark | n.a. | n.a. | n.a. | 971 | 983 | 927 | 410 | 409 | 341 |
| Dominican Republic[6] | 55 | 49 | 43 | 56 | 57 | 41[12] | 1,170 | 1,230 | 905 |
| Egypt | 2,640 | 2,508 | 2,315 | 285 | 276 | 256[11] | 537 | 534 | 467 |
| El Salvador | 439 | 353 | 297 | n.a. | n.a. | n.a. | 244[13] | 261[13] | 129[13] |
| Ethiopia[6] | 1,470 | 877 | 882 | 321 | 339 | n.a. | 135 | 130 | 88 |
| France[6] | 8,163 | 8,885 | 6,362 | 3,524 | 3,499 | 3,088 | 2,712 | 2,709 | 2,343 |
| Germany, East | 2 | 3 | 6 | 1,563 | 1,443 | 1,169 | 683 | 570 | 465 |
| Germany, West | 531 | 521 | 397 | 3,664 | 3,754 | 3,438 | 2,571 | 2,506 | 2,135 |
| Ghana[6] | 400 | 486 | 355 | 39 | 37 | n.a. | 8 | 5 | 5 |
| Greece | 468 | 459 | 430 | 317 | 335 | 214 | 308 | 202 | 141 |
| Guatemala | 683 | 669 | 710 | 82 | 80 | n.a. | 384 | 366 | 181 |
| Hungary | 7,215 | 6,333 | 4,217 | 973 | 933 | 451 | 335 | 290 | 380 |
| India | 7,036 | 5,559 | 6,061 | 631 | 627 | 586 | 5,048 | 4,489 | 3,503 |
| Indonesia | 2,638 | 3,011 | 2,652 | 298[14] | 295[14] | 287[14] | 1,000[7] | 935[7] | 698[7] |
| Iran[6] | 40[8] | 30[8] | 26[8] | 337 | 330 | 297 | 606 | 524 | 545 |
| Ireland | n.a. | n.a. | n.a. | 546 | 514 | 392 | n.a. | 197[15] | 149 |
| Italy | 5,326 | 5,043 | 4,330 | 1,799 | 1,860 | 1,609 | 1,429 | 982 | 1,336 |
| Japan[6] | 11 | 14 | 42 | 1,392[14] | 1,397[14] | 901[14] | 459 | 626 | 631 |
| Kenya | 1,600 | 1,400[8] | 1,363 | 141 | 134 | n.a. | 174 | 179 | 112 |
| Malaysia | 24 | 23[8] | 13 | 70 | 70 | n.a. | 59 | 20 | (Z) |
| Mexico | 8,459 | 7,784 | 8,812 | 971 | 961 | 831[12] | 2,724 | 2,838 | 2,440 |
| Morocco | 371 | 389 | 362 | 164 | 167 | n.a. | 268 | 260 | 129 |
| Netherlands | 6 | 10 | 3[8] | 1,303 | 1,293 | 993 | 924 | 767 | 758 |
| Nigeria | 1,000[8] | 980[8] | 843 | 314 | 296 | n.a. | 40 | 40 | 26 |
| Pakistan[6] | 802 | 747 | 702 | 277 | 269 | 260 | 540 | 520 | 577[16] |
| Peru | 625 | 472 | 585 | 208 | 211 | 183 | 964 | 992 | 754 |
| Philippines[6] | 2,697 | 2,414 | 1,878 | 528 | 518 | 413[17] | 2,672 | 2,656 | 1,788 |
| Poland | 79 | 19 | 13 | 2,569 | 2,533 | 1,838[10] | 1,847 | 1,595 | 1,748 |
| Portugal | 506 | 486 | 603 | 228 | 229 | 195 | 13[7] | 9[7] | 12[7] |
| Rhodesia[6] | 1,400 | 1,700 | 970[8] | 160[14] | 159[14] | 103[14 18] | 257 | 255 | 151 |
| Romania[6] | 9,241 | 7,440 | 7,205 | 1,088[14] | 1,069[14] | 726[14] | 583 | 600 | 460 |
| South Africa | 9,140 | 11,105 | 7,011 | 676 | 723 | 668 | 1,968 | 1,970 | 1,677 |
| Spain[6] | 1,792 | 1,993 | 1,611 | 1,204 | 1,281 | 851 | 800 | 667 | 802 |
| Sweden | n.a. | n.a. | n.a. | 431 | 425 | 399 | 278 | 301 | 250 |
| Switzerland | 139 | 128 | 46 | 381 | 387 | 324 | 65 | 72 | 65 |
| Thailand[6] | 3,023 | 2,550 | 1,752 | 409[14] | 400[14] | 299[14] | 1,216[7] | 985[7] | 376[7 13] |
| Turkey | 1,200 | 1,200 | 1,045 | 534[14] | 569[14] | 388[14] | 758 | 834 | 719 |
| Uganda | 523 | 430 | 325[8] | 79 | 77 | 75 | 27 | 44 | 149[7] |
| U.S.S.R. | 7,328 | 12,104 | 9,594 | 13,440[10 11] | 12,910[10 11] | 10,899 | 8,200 | 8,526 | 9,266 |
| United Kingdom | n.a. | n.a. | n.a. | 2,301 | 2,310 | 2,041 | 725 | 837 | 980 |
| United States | 147,251 | 118,461 | 120,858 | 16,690 | 17,189 | 16,211 | 5,680 | 5,136 | 5,096 |
| Uruguay[6] | 157 | 225 | 134 | 420 | 391 | 380 | 95 | 90 | 56 |
| Venezuela[6] | 653 | 554 | 677 | 366 | 312 | 245[12] | 535 | 551 | 425 |
| Vietnam | 320[8] | 315[8] | 266 | 522 | 518 | n.a. | (Z) | (Z) | 2 |
| Yugoslavia | 9,389 | 8,031 | 7,243 | 766 | 748 | 627 | 500 | 560 | 440 |
| Zaire | 420 | 418 | 327 | n.a. | n.a. | n.a. | 62 | 67 | 45 |
| **World, total** | **324,721** | **293,224** | **270,600** | **94,757** | **93,484** | **82,676** | **81,691** | **78,853** | **69,900** |

1. Beef and veal (incl. buffalo meat), pork (incl. bacon and ham), and mutton and lamb (incl. goat meat). Except as noted, relates to commercial and farm slaughter and excludes lard, tallow, and edible offals. 2. Beet and cane. Data generally in terms of raw sugar. 3. Excludes Alaska and Hawaii. 4. Year beginning July. 5. Year ending June 30. 6. For meat, production from indigenous animals only, including, where applicable, meat equivalent of exported live animals. 7. Polarization or grade unknown. For Brazil, 1967 and 1970; for Uganda, 1967 and 1968. 8. FAO estimate. 9. Source: Republic of China, *Monthly Bulletin of Statistics*. 10. Includes slaughter fat. 11. Includes edible offals. 12. Commercial production. 13. Crop year. For Thailand, prior to 1968 only. 14. Inspected production. 15. For 1973. 16. Prior to 1972, data for Bangladesh included with Pakistan. 17. Year beginning March 1. 18. Year ending Sept. For 1967–1971, production on farms and estates. NOTES: Data for each country pertain to the calendar year in which all or most of the crop was harvested. n.a. =not available. (Z) = less than 500 metric tons. *Source:* Except as noted, Statistical Office of the United Nations, New York, N.Y., *Statistical Yearbook.* (Copyright.)

# Labor Force, Manufacturing, Steel, Iron Ore, Cement, Cotton Yarn, and Fish, 1975

| Country | Economically active population[1] (thousands) | Persons engaged in Manufacturing[2] (thousands) | Steel: Production[3] (mil. metric tons) | Steel: Consumption[4] Total (mil. metric tons) | Steel: Consumption[4] Per capita (kilograms) | Production: Iron ore[5] (iron content) (mil. metric tons) | Production: Cement[6] (mil. metric tons) | Production: Cotton yarn[7] (thousands metric tons) | Fish catches[8] (thousands metric tons) |
|---|---|---|---|---|---|---|---|---|---|
| Algeria | 2,565 | n.a. | n.a. | 1.2 | 73 | 2 | n.a. | 8[12] | 38 |
| Argentina | 9,011 | n.a. | 1.5 | 4.4 | 172 | (Z) | 5 | 89 | 224[17] |
| Australia | 5,330 | 1,263[18] | 8.1[18] | 6.3 | 467 | 61[18] | 5 | 24[15,18] | 103[18] |
| Austria | 3,098 | 738[19,20] | 4.1 | 2.2 | 286 | 1 | 6 | 16 | n.a. |
| Belgium | 3,638 | 1,215[21] | 11.6 | 3.2[22] | 314[22] | (Z) | 7 | 44 | 49[23] |
| Brazil | 29,557 | 3,199[12,24] | 8.3[25] | 11.2 | 105 | 47 | 18 | 60[26] | 675[17] |
| Bulgaria | 4,268 | 1,156[27] | 2.3 | 2.2 | 252 | 1 | 4 | 79 | 158 |
| Canada | 8,162[28] | 1,792[19] | 13.0 | 13.2 | 577 | 28[29] | 10 | 78[15,19] | 1,024[23] |
| Chile | 2,607 | 254[19,30] | .5[31] | .6 | 55 | 7 | 1 | 23[12] | 1,128[32] |
| China, People's Rep. of | n.a. | n.a. | 29.0[31] | 35.2 | 42 | 33 | 30 | 1,450[33] | 6,880 |
| China (Taiwan) | 5,978[21,34] | n.a. | .5[35] | n.a. | n.a. | n.a. | 7[35] | n.a. | 780[35] |
| Colombia | 5,134 | 448[19,36] | .3 | .6 | 27 | 1 | 3 | 22[12] | 67[17] |
| Cuba | 2,633 | n.a. | .3 | .8 | 85 | n.a. | 2 | 12[37] | 165 |
| Czechoslovakia | 6,996 | 2,457[27] | 14.3 | 10.8 | 733 | (Z) | 9 | 129 | 17 |
| Denmark | 2,313 | 415[19,38] | .6 | 1.8 | 358 | (Z) | 2 | 2 | 1,767[23] |
| Dominican Rep | 856 | 139[11,19,39] | n.a. | .1 | 29 | n.a. | 1 | 1[19] | n.a. |
| Ecuador | 1,443 | 66[19,24] | n.a. | .2 | 27 | n.a. | 1 | 2[21] | 223[16,17] |
| Egypt | 7,782 | 651[18,21,40] | .3 | 1.6 | 42 | 1 | 4 | 181 | 107[17] |
| El Salvador | 1,315 | 42[21,39] | n.a. | (Z) | 11 | n.a. | (Z) | 6[19] | n.a. |
| Finland | 2,129 | 521[41] | 1.6 | 2.0 | 430 | 1 | 2[19] | 15[19] | 114 |
| France | 20,439 | 5,865[42] | 21.5 | 18.5 | 350 | 15 | 30 | 232[15] | 806[23] |
| Germany (East) | 8,214 | 3,063[43] | 6.5 | 9.5 | 566 | (Z) | 11 | 59[15,44] | 375[17] |
| Germany (West) | 26,494 | 7,332[36] | 40.4 | 30.3 | 490 | 1 | 34 | 192[15] | 442 |
| Ghana | 3,332 | 61[21,45] | n.a. | (Z) | 9 | n.a. | 1 | n.a. | 255[46] |
| Greece | 3,388[47] | 306[12,36] | .6 | 1.3 | 143 | 1 | 8 | 70[19] | 71[17,48,49] |
| Guatemala | 1,364 | 61[12,24] | n.a. | .1 | 14 | n.a. | (Z) | n.a. | n.a. |
| Hong Kong | 1,655 | 679 | n.a. | .6 | 138 | (Z) | 1 | 194 | 152 |
| Hungary | 4,989 | 1,553[27] | 3.7 | 3.8 | 361 | (Z) | 4 | 61[44] | 31 |
| India | 180,373 | 5,252[19,50,51] | 7.9 | 8.4 | 14 | 26 | 16 | 989[52] | 2,328 |
| Indonesia | 40,100 | 932[12,36] | n.a. | 1.3 | 10 | n.a. | 1 | 54[12] | 1,390 |
| Iran | 7,584 | 362[19,36,53] | n.a. | 5.4 | 163 | 6[54] | 4 | 42[21] | n.a. |
| Iraq | n.a. | 125[19,55] | n.a. | 2.0 | 181 | n.a. | 2 | 2[19] | n.a. |
| Ireland | 1,120 | 203[12,56] | .1 | .3 | 106 | n.a. | 2 | 4 | 85[57] |
| Israel | 956 | 265[10,50] | .1 | .7 | 221 | n.a. | 2 | 24 | 24[58] |
| Italy | 18,750 | 3,633[19,59] | 21.6 | 17.8 | 319 | (Z) | 34 | 200 | 406[48] |
| Japan | 53,321 | 12,024[19] | 102.3 | 64.7 | 583 | (Z) | 66 | 460 | 10,509 |
| Korea, North | na. | n.a. | 2.8 | 4.0 | 251 | 4 | 6 | n.a. | 800 |
| Korea, South | 10,378 | 1,298[19,24] | 2.0[31] | 3.0 | 85 | (Z) | 10 | 134 | 2,133 |
| Lebanon | n.a. | n.a. | n.a. | .3 | 101 | n.a. | 2[19] | 5[12] | n.a. |
| Liberia | 412 | n.a. | n.a. | (Z) | 10 | 17 | (Z) | n.a. | 17[17] |
| Luxembourg | 131 | 46[19,59] | 4.6 | ([22]) | ([22]) | 1 | (Z) | n.a. | n.a. |
| Malaysia | 3,430 | 318[12] | n.a. | .5 | 46 | (Z) | 1[60] | n.a. | 474 |
| Mexico | 12,910 | n.a. | 5.2 | 6.2 | 103 | 3 | 12 | 158 | 499 |
| Morocco | 3,981 | n.a. | (Z) | .5 | 28 | (Z) | 2 | 15[37] | 211[17] |
| Netherlands | 4,169 | 1,089[61] | 4.8 | 4.5 | 330 | n.a. | 4 | 30 | 351[57] |
| New Zealand | 1,026[9] | 248[19,50,62] | n.a. | .9 | 300 | (Z) | 1 | n.a. | 66 |
| Nigeria | 18,036 | 174[11,19,55] | n.a. | 1.4 | 22 | n.a. | 1 | 5 | 507[17] |
| Norway | 1,469 | 369[19,24] | .9 | 2.1 | 514 | 3 | 3 | 2 | 2,550[23,63] |
| Pakistan | 39,591 | 427[11,18,55,64] | n.a. | .5 | 7 | (Z) | 3[18] | 351[18,52] | 195 |
| Peru | 3,872 | 258[12,24] | .4 | 1.0 | 61 | 5 | 2 | 20[65] | 3,448 |
| Philippines | 11,355 | 532[19,24] | n.a. | 1.0 | 22 | 1 | 4 | 36[44] | 1,342[66] |
| Poland | 16,944 | 4,171[27] | 14.6 | 17.8 | 524 | (Z) | 19 | 212[15] | 801 |
| Portugal | 3,424 | 607[19] | .4 | 1.0 | 118 | (Z) | 3 | 96[15] | 369[48] |
| Romania | 10,362 | 2,802[67] | 9.5 | 9.8 | 464 | 1 | 12 | 145[15,44] | 137[17] |
| South Africa | 7,986[69] | 1,125[11,18,21] | 6.6[70] | 7.5[71] | 263[71] | 8 | 7 | 73[19] | 1,315[17,48,72] |
| Rhodesia | 110 | 144[11,12] | .4 | .3 | 45 | (Z) | 1 | n.a. | n.a. |
| Spain | 11,865 | 2,247[19] | 11.1 | 10.1 | 284 | 4 | 24 | 138 | 1,524[16,17,73] |
| Sri Lanka | 3,459 | 115[11,19,74] | n.a. | .1 | 4 | n.a. | (Z) | 6[19] | 129[48] |
| Sweden | 3,413 | 917[19,24] | 5.6 | 6.3 | 772 | 20 | 3 | 7 | 215[23] |
| Switzerland | 3,005 | 707[75] | .4 | 1.5 | 232 | (Z) | 4 | 39[12] | n.a. |

| Country | Economically active population[1] (thousands) | Persons engaged in manufacturing[2] (thousands) | Steel: Production[3] (mil. metric tons) | Steel: Consumption[4] Total (mil. metric tons) | Steel: Consumption[4] Per capita (kilograms) | Production: Iron ore[5] (iron content) (mil. metric tons) | Production: Cement[6] (mil. metric tons) | Production: Cotton yarn[7] (thousands metric tons) | Fish catches[8] (thousands metric tons) |
|---|---|---|---|---|---|---|---|---|---|
| Syria | 1,525 | 156 | n.a. | .5 | 64 | n.a. | 1 | 32 | n.a. |
| Thailand | 16,850 | 309[36 64] | n.a. | .8 | 20 | (Z) | 4 | 11[44 64] | 1,370 |
| Tunisia | 1,094 | 70[19] | .1 | .3 | 56 | (Z) | 1 | 9[12] | 43 |
| Turkey | 15,829 | 666[19 36] | 1.5 | 2.7 | 69 | 1 | 11 | 189[19 52] | 259 |
| U.S.S.R. | 115,204 | 29,596 | 141.3 | 141.0 | 554 | 127 | 122 | 1,573[15] | 9,876 |
| United Kingdom | 22,754[76] | 7,680[19] | 20.2 | 21.5 | 385 | 1[77] | 17 | 125 | 980[48] |
| United States | 82,897[9] | 18,772[10 11 12] | 105.8[13] | 116.8 | 549 | 49[14] | 62 | 1,142[15] | 2,799[16 17] |
| Uruguay | 1,012 | n.a. | (Z) | .1 | 21 | (Z) | 1 | n.a. | 26 |
| Venezuela | 3.015 | 298[19] | 1.1 | 2.3 | 194 | 15 | 3 | 16[21] | 153 |
| Vietnam | 5,742[68] | n.a. | n.a. | .2 | 5 | n.a. | 1 | 10[12 68] | 1,014[17 68] |
| Yugoslavia | 8,890 | 1,577[19] | 2.9 | 4.4 | 205 | 2 | 7 | 107 | 57[48] |
| **World, total** | **n.a.** | **n.a.** | **643.0** | **n.a.** | **n.a.** | **500** | **690** | **n.a.** | **69,700** |

1. Comprises all persons engaged in or actively seeking productive work in some branch of the economy during a specified period of time. Generally, data are for a specific date in the 1960's and 1970's. 2. Comprises average number of employees, working proprietors, and unpaid family workers engaged in production of manufactured goods, including assembly of component parts and, except in the case of consumer goods, repair services. Excludes gas manufacture and electricity. 3. Total production of crude steel, both ingots and steel for castings. Excludes wrought (puddled) iron. 4. Data represent apparent consumption (i.e., production plus imports minus exports) and do not take into account changes in stocks. 5. Refers generally to iron content of marketable ores mined, including manganiferous iron ores but excluding pyrites. Some data are rough estimates obtained by applying a fixed percentage to figures for crude ore production. 6. Covers, as far as possible, all hydraulic cements used for construction (portland, metallurgic, aluminous, natural, etc.). 7. Covers pure and mixed yarn and excludes tire cord yarn, except as noted. 8. Covers both sea and inland fisheries, in terms of live weight. Includes shellfish; excludes whales, dolphins, etc. 9. Excludes Armed Forces abroad. 10. Establishments with 1 or more employees. 11. Paid employees, excluding working proprietors. 12. For 1973. 13. Excludes steel for castings made in foundries operated by companies not producing ingots. 14. Excludes manganiferous iron ore containing 5 percent or more of manganese. 15. Includes tire cord yarn. 16. Excludes landings by foreign craft in domestic ports. 17. FAO estimate. 18. Year ending June 30. 19. For 1974. 20. Establishments with 20 or more employees. 21. For 1972. 22. Luxembourg included with Belgium. 23. Includes landings by domestic craft in foreign ports and excludes landings by foreign craft in domestic ports. 24. Establishments with 5 or more engaged. 25. Excludes alloy steel. 26. Production in São Paulo only. 27. All enterprises in socialist sector except publishing. 28. Excludes armed services. 29. Shipment from mines. 30. Establishments with 50 or more engaged. 31. Ingots only. 32. Includes landings by foreign craft in domestic ports. 33. For 1969. 34. Source: U.S. Bureau of the Census, International Statistical Programs Center. 35. Source: Republic of China, *Monthly Bulletin of Statistics*. 36. Establishments with 10 or more engaged. 37. For 1970. 38. Establishments with 6 or more employees. 39. Establishments with 5 or more employees. 40. Private establishments with 10 or more engaged and all public establishments. 41. Establishments with 5 or more engaged, or equivalent in terms of installed power equipment. 42. Total mining and manufacturing. 43. Includes mining, electricity, gas, and water. 44. Excludes yarn made from waste. 45. Establishments with 30 or more engaged. 46. Excludes catches by chartered foreign vessels. 47. Includes Armed Forces abroad. 48. Excludes both landing by domestic craft in foreign ports and by foreign craft in domestic ports. 49. Data refer only to marine catches of motor vessels. 50. Year ending March 31. 51. Establishments with 10 or more persons engaged using power or with 20 or more persons engaged not using power. 52. Factory production only. 53. Year ending March 20. 54. Year beginning March 21. 55. Establishments with 10 or more employees. 56. Establishments with 3 or more engaged. 57. Excludes landings by domestic craft in foreign ports and includes landings by foreign craft in domestic ports. 58. Includes both landings by domestic craft in foreign ports and by foreign craft in domestic ports. 59. Enterprises with 20 or more engaged. 60. Data refer to West Malaysia only. 61. Man-years. 62. Establishments with 2 or more engaged. 63. Includes Svalbard. 64. For 1971. 65. For 1967. 66. Excludes mollusks used for duck feeding. 67. State enterprises under direction of central government. 68. Data for former Republic of South Vietnam only. 69. Walvis Bay included in Namibia. 70. Includes concast steel billets. 71. Includes data for Botswana, Lesotho, Namibia, and Swaziland. 72. Includes Walvis Bay. 73. Includes Ceuta, Melilla, Balearic Islands, and Canary Islands. 74. Registered establishments. 75. Establishments subject to labor laws. 76. For England and Wales only. 77. 53 weeks. NOTES: n.a.=not available. (Z) =less than 50,000 or 500,000 metric tons. *Source:* Except as noted, Statistical Office of the United Nations, New York, N.Y., *Statistical Yearbook* and *Demographic Yearbook*. (Copyright).

## Wheat and Rice—Production by Country

**(in thousands of metric tons)[1]**

| Country | Wheat 1975 | Wheat 1974 | Wheat 1973 | Wheat 1966–70 average | Wheat 1961–65 average | Rice 1975 | Rice 1974 | Rice 1973 | Rice 1966–70 average | Rice 1961–65 average |
|---|---|---|---|---|---|---|---|---|---|---|
| Afghanistan | 2,800 | 2,750 | 2,750 | 2,240 | 2,207 | 450 | 420 | 420 | 382 | 343 |
| Argentina | 8,570 | 5,370 | 6,560 | 6,249 | 7,541 | 351 | 316 | 260 | 283 | 193 |
| Australia | 11,980 | 11,357 | 11,987 | 10,697 | 8,222 | 388 | 409 | 309 | 224 | 136 |
| Austria | 945 | 1,102 | 939 | 949 | 704 | ([2]) | ([2]) | ([2]) | ([2]) | ([2]) |
| Bangladesh | 117 | 111 | 91 | 70 | 37 | 19,143 | 16,930 | 17,863 | 16,560 | 15,048 |
| Belgium | 724 | 1,078 | 1,049 | 763 | 826 | ([2]) | ([2]) | ([2]) | ([2]) | ([2]) |
| Brazil | 1,788 | 2,859 | 2,031 | 1,064 | 574 | 7,538 | 6,483 | 7,167 | 6,639 | 6,123 |
| Bulgaria | 2,771 | 2,911 | 3,258 | 2,920 | 2,213 | 68 | 58 | 62 | 54 | 37 |

| Country | Wheat | | | | | Rice | | | | |
|---|---|---|---|---|---|---|---|---|---|---|
| | 1975 | 1974 | 1973 | 1966–70 average | 1961–65 average | 1975 | 1974 | 1973 | 1966–70 average | 1961–65 average |
| Burma | 64 | 25 | 36 | 55 | 38 | 9,221 | 8,583 | 8,602 | 7,715 | 7,786 |
| Cambodia | (2) | (2) | (2) | (2) | (2) | 1,500[3] | 635 | 1,050 | 2,880 | 2,461 |
| Canada | 17,078 | 13,295 | 16,159 | 16,727 | 15,364 | (2) | (2) | (2) | (2) | (2) |
| Chile | 1,002 | 939 | 747 | 1,258 | 1,082 | 76 | 34 | 55 | 73 | 85 |
| China, People's Rep.[3] | 41,003 | 37,001 | 36,001 | 28,057 | 22,230 | 116,267 | 115,213 | 111,954 | 96,769 | 86,038 |
| China (Taiwan) | 3[4] | 1[4] | 1[4] | n.a. | 36 | 2,494[4,5] | 2,452[4,5] | 2,244[4,5] | n.a. | 3,448 |
| Colombia | 57 | 63 | 91 | 87 | 118 | 1,614 | 1,540 | 1,151 | 711 | 576 |
| Cuba | (2) | (2) | (2) | (2) | (2) | 420[3] | 400 | 375 | 165 | 151 |
| Czechoslovakia | 4,202 | 5,059 | 4,646 | 2,869 | 1,779 | (2) | (2) | (2) | (2) | (2) |
| Denmark | 520 | 592 | 542 | 445 | 535 | (2) | (2) | (2) | (2) | (2) |
| Ecuador | 65 | 55 | 45 | 78 | 61 | 348 | 265 | 235 | 191 | 173 |
| Egypt | 2,033 | 1,884 | 1,838 | 1,417 | 1,459 | 2,423 | 2,242 | 2,274 | 2,343 | 1,845 |
| Ethiopia | 734 | 576 | 653 | 762 | 663 | (2) | (2) | (2) | (2) | (2) |
| Finland | 622 | 593 | 462 | 456 | 448 | (2) | (2) | (2) | (2) | (2) |
| France | 15,041 | 19,100 | 17,850 | 13,590 | 12,495 | 48 | 49 | 69 | 98 | 120 |
| Germany, East | 2,736 | 3,154 | 2,861 | 2,006 | 1,357 | (2) | (2) | (2) | (2) | (2) |
| Germany, West | 7,014 | 7,761 | 7,134 | 5,642 | 4,607 | (2) | (2) | (2) | (2) | (2) |
| Greece | 2,140 | 2,153 | 1,659 | 1,836 | 1,765 | 104 | 105 | 84 | 91 | 88 |
| Hungary | 4,007 | 4,971 | 4,502 | 3,008 | 2,020 | 69 | 56 | 69 | 42 | 36 |
| India | 24,104 | 21,778 | 24,735 | 15,414 | 11,191 | 74,186 | 59,368 | 66,077 | 57,140 | 52,733 |
| Indonesia | (2) | (2) | (2) | (2) | (2) | 22,570 | 22,473 | 21,490 | 16,277 | 12,396 |
| Iran | 5,483 | 4,700 | 4,600 | 4,244 | 2,873 | 1,615 | 1,380 | 1,334 | 1,143 | 851 |
| Iraq | 845 | 1,339 | 957 | 1,128 | 849 | 61 | 69 | 157 | 268 | 138 |
| Ireland | 207 | 245 | 229 | 325 | 343 | (2) | (2) | (2) | (2) | (2) |
| Israel | 243 | 274 | 242 | 156 | 90 | (2) | (2) | (2) | (2) | (2) |
| Italy | 9,610 | 9,695 | 8,920 | 9,585 | 8,857 | 1,009 | 1,047 | 1,045 | 737 | 612 |
| Japan | 241 | 232 | 202 | 853 | 1,332 | 17,097 | 15,964 | 15,778 | 17,764 | 16,444 |
| Korea, North | 150[3] | 140[3] | 130[3] | 96[3] | 85 | 3,700[3] | 3,500[3] | 3,300[3] | 2,740[3] | 2,480 |
| Korea, South | 97 | 136 | 162 | 339 | 227 | 6,485 | 6,178 | 5,854 | 5,212 | 4,809 |
| Laos | (2) | (2) | (2) | (2) | (2) | 910[3] | 905 | 884 | 827 | 609 |
| Madagascar | (2) | (2) | (2) | (2) | (2) | 1,844 | 1,852 | 1,730 | 1,836 | 1,563 |
| Malaysia | (2) | (2) | (2) | (2) | (2) | 2,013 | 2,093 | 1,867 | 1,424 | 1,140 |
| Mexico | 2,798 | 2,789 | 2,091 | 1,903 | 1,549 | 510 | 469 | 450 | 385 | 314 |
| Nepal | 331 | 332 | 308 | 202 | 135 | 2,582 | 2,453 | 2,416 | 2,170 | 2,147 |
| Netherlands | 528 | 746 | 725 | 667 | 606 | (2) | (2) | (2) | (2) | (2) |
| New Zealand | 203 | 248 | 398 | 365 | 248 | (2) | (2) | (2) | (2) | (2) |
| Pakistan | 7,673 | 7,629 | 7,443 | 5,716 | 4,152 | 3,926 | 3,470 | 3,682 | 2,848 | 1,824 |
| Panama | (2) | (2) | (2) | (2) | (2) | 185 | 178 | 162 | 149 | 122 |
| Peru | 143 | 117 | 115 | 128 | 150 | 537 | 361 | 451 | 429 | 324 |
| Philippines | (2) | (2) | (2) | (2) | (2) | 6,217 | 5,660 | 5,594 | 4,735 | 3,957 |
| Poland | 5,207 | 6,408 | 5,807 | 4,260 | 2,988 | (2) | (2) | (2) | (2) | (2) |
| Portugal | 611 | 546 | 533 | 552 | 562 | 133 | 130 | 168 | 164 | 167 |
| Romania | 4,862 | 5,007 | 5,489 | 4,688 | 4,321 | 69 | 53 | 50 | 63 | 40 |
| South Africa | 1,792 | 1,596 | 1,871 | 1,101 | 840 | (2) | (2) | (2) | (2) | (2) |
| Spain | 4,302 | 4,535 | 3,967 | 4,907 | 4,365 | 379 | 367 | 387 | 380 | 386 |
| Sri Lanka | (2) | (2) | (2) | (2) | (2) | 1,154 | 1,603 | 1,312 | 1,298 | 967 |
| Sweden | 1,481 | 1,826 | 1,335 | 932 | 909 | (2) | (2) | (2) | (2) | (2) |
| Switzerland | 345 | 411 | 345 | 383 | 355 | (2) | (2) | (2) | (2) | (2) |
| Syria | 1,550 | 1,630 | 593 | 767 | 1,093 | (2) | (2) | (2) | (2) | (2) |
| Thailand | (2) | (2) | (2) | (2) | (2) | 15,300 | 13,386 | 14,898 | 12,774 | 11,267 |
| Turkey | 14,830 | 11,080 | 10,080 | 10,020 | 8,585 | 240 | 250 | 255 | 233 | 222 |
| U.S.S.R. | 66,224 | 83,913 | 109,784 | 90,192 | 64,207 | 2,009 | 1,913 | 1,765 | 1,011 | 390 |
| United Kingdom | 4,488 | 6,132 | 5,005 | 3,689 | 3,520 | (2) | (2) | (2) | (2) | (2) |
| United States | 58,102 | 48,885 | 46,408 | 38,992 | 33,040 | 5,805 | 5,098 | 4,208 | 4,121 | 3,084 |
| Uruguay | 456 | 526 | 297 | 356 | 465 | 193 | 158 | 137 | 115 | 67 |
| Venezuela | (2) | (2) | (2) | (2) | (2) | 363 | 297 | 302 | 227 | 136 |
| Vietnam | (2) | (2) | (2) | (2) | (2) | 12,000 | 11,023 | 11,125 | 9,130 | 9,629 |
| Yugoslavia | 4,405 | 6,283 | 4,751 | 4,493 | 3,599 | 37 | 31 | 32 | 24 | 23 |
| **World, total** | **355,895** | **359,803** | **376,592** | **314,700** | **254,400** | **348,374** | **320,097** | **323,270** | **284,700** | **253,200** |

1. Rice data cover rough and paddy, except as noted. Data for each country pertain to the calendar year in which all or most of the crop was harvested. 2. None or negligible. 3. FAO estimate. 4. Source: Republic of China, *Monthly Bulletin of Statistics.* 5. Paddy only. NOTE: n.a. = not available. *Source:* Except as noted, Statistical Office of the United Nations, New York, N.Y. *Statistical Yearbook.* (Copyright.)

# Communications

(telephones, mail, newspapers, radio, and television)

| Country | Telephones, in use,[1] 1975 (thousands) | Telephones per 100 population, 1975 | Pieces of mail sent, domestic,[2] 1975 (millions) | Daily newspapers,[3] 1975: Number | Daily newspapers,[3] 1975: Circulation: Total (thousands) | Daily newspapers,[3] 1975: Circulation: Copies per 1,000 population | Receiving sets, 1974: Radio[4] (thousands) | Receiving sets, 1974: Television[5] (thousands) |
|---|---|---|---|---|---|---|---|---|
| Algeria | 250 | 1.4 | 194 | 4 | 275 | 17 | 3,220[8] | 410[8] |
| Argentina | 1,996 | 7.8 | 738 | 167 | 3,683[9] | n.a. | 21,000[7] | 4,500 |
| Australia | 5,267[10] | 39.0[10] | 2,344[11 12] | 58[7] | 5,126[7] | 386[7] | 2,815[7 8] | 3,013[7 8] |
| Austria | 2,133 | 28.1 | 1,394[7] | 30 | 2,316 | 308 | 2,170[8] | 1,856[8] |
| Bangladesh | 80 | .1 | 233 | 25 | 398[13] | n.a. | n.a. | n.a. |
| Belgium | 2,798 | 28.5 | 2,026 | 31 | 2,416 | 247 | 3,769[8] | 2,464[8] |
| Bolivia | 49[7] | .9[7] | 3 | 14 | 135 | 25 | 425 | 11[14] |
| Brazil | 3,371 | 3.1 | 1,239[15] | 280[7] | 4,050[7] | 39[7] | 6,275 | 8,650 |
| Bulgaria | 777 | 8.9 | n.a. | 13 | 1,971 | 227 | 2,273[8] | 1,457[8] |
| Burma | 31 | .1 | 75 | 7 | 319 | 11 | 659[8] | — |
| Cambodia | 71 | 11.2 | 1,402[7] | 17 | n.a. | n.a. | 112 | 26 |
| Canada | 13,142 | 57.2 | 4,768[16] | 121[7] | 5,207[7] | 235[7] | 20,252 | 8,232 |
| Chile | 437 | 4.5 | 129 | 45 | n.a. | n.a. | 3,100 | 750 |
| China, People's Rep. of | n.a. | n.a. | n.a. | n.a. | n.a. | n.a. | 12,000[17] | 500[7] |
| China (Taiwan) | 599[11 18] | 3.8[11 18] | 793[11 18] | 31[18] | n.a. | n.a. | 1,464[14 19] | 835[14 19] |
| Colombia | 1,280 | 5.5 | 119[11] | 36 | 1,449 | 69 | 2,805 | 971[14] |
| Costa Rica | 112 | 5.6 | 29 | 6 | 186 | 97 | 142 | 150 |
| Cuba | 289[11] | 3.2[11] | 34[11] | 14 | n.a. | n.a. | 1,805 | 595 |
| Cyprus | 68[11] | 10.7[11] | 21 | 12 | 78[20] | n.a. | 206[8] | 85[8] |
| Czechoslovakia | 2,616 | 17.6 | 2,216[7 21] | 29 | 4,231 | 288 | 3,910[8] | 3,602[8] |
| Denmark | 2,295[22] | 45.4[22] | 1,209[16] | 51 | 1,792 | 355 | 1,693[8] | 1,556[8] |
| Dominican Republic | 108 | 2.4 | 6 | 10 | 197 | 43 | 185 | 156 |
| Ecuador | 182 | 2.7 | 7 | 22 | 285 | 41 | 1,700[17] | 250 |
| Egypt | 503[11] | 1.4[11] | 133 | 14[14] | 773[14] | 21[14] | 5,115[8] | 610[8] |
| El Salvador | 56 | 1.4 | 20 | 6 | 201 | 51 | 300[17] | 111 |
| Ethiopia | 69 | .3 | 21[7] | 7 | 51 | 2 | 200 | 20 |
| Finland | 1,834 | 38.9 | 626 | 62 | 2,058 | 440 | 1,997[8] | 1,261[8] |
| France | 13,833 | 26.2 | 11,033 | 103[7] | 11,458[7] | 220[7] | 17,000[8] | 12,335[8] |
| Germany (East) | 2,570 | 15.2 | 905 | 40 | 7,753 | 452 | 6,114[8] | 5,096[8] |
| Germany (West) | 19,603 | 31.7 | 11,343 | 320 | 17,872 | 289 | 20,909[8] | 18,920[8] |
| Ghana | 60 | .6 | 187[16] | 6[7] | 381[7] | 41[7] | 1,060 | 33 |
| Greece | 2,009 | 22.1 | 240 | 105 | 962 | 107 | 2,500 | 950 |
| Guatemala | 53[7] | 1.0[7] | 25 | 11 | 91[23] | n.a. | 261 | 106 |
| Honduras | 20 | .7 | 15 | 7 | 99[24] | n.a. | 158 | 46 |
| Hong Kong | 1,034 | 33.6 | 135[16] | 73 | n.a. | n.a. | 1,000 | 785[8] |
| Hungary | 1,048 | 9.9 | 1,839 | 27 | 2,431 | 232 | 2,541[8] | 2,296[8] |
| Iceland | 91 | 41.7 | 11[11] | 5 | 95 | 436 | 64[8] | 50 |
| India | 1,817 | 3 | 6,898[16] | 822 | 9,222 | 16 | 14,848[8] | 275[8] |
| Indonesia | 305 | .2 | 159 | 170 | 2,035[25] | n.a. | 5,000[8] | 95[26] |
| Iran | 688 | 2.0 | 858[26] | 20 | 484 | 15 | 8,000 | 1,500 |
| Iraq | 185 | 1.7 | 168[14] | 5 | n.a. | n.a. | 1,250 | 520[7] |
| Ireland | 444 | 14.1 | 308[11 16] | 7 | 729 | 236 | 886[8] | 550[8] |
| Israel | 813 | 23.1 | 292[11 16] | 23 | 1,330[13] | n.a. | 680[8 14] | 441[8] |
| Italy | 14,496 | 25.9 | 5,781 | 79 | 6,963 | 126 | 12,641[8] | 11,817[8] |
| Jamaica | 100 | 5.0 | 75[11] | 3 | 180 | 90 | 633[7] | 97 |
| Japan | 45,515[27] | 40.5[27] | 13,202[16] | 180 | 57,820[25] | 526[25] | 70,794[14] | 25,564 |
| Kenya | 122 | .9 | 143[11] | 4 | 97 | 8 | 510[8] | 37[8] |
| Korea, South | 1,400 | 4.0 | 484 | 44 | 5,867 | 175 | 4,812 | 1,619[8] |
| Kuwait | 128 | 12.3 | 3[16] | 6 | 80 | 86 | 215 | 182 |
| Lebanon | 227[14] | 7.7[14] | 26[28] | 37 | 293[29] | n.a. | 1,321 | 375 |
| Luxembourg | 147 | 41.1 | 46 | 7 | 161[23] | n.a. | 176[8] | 88[8] |
| Madagascar | 31 | .4 | 22 | 9 | 59 | 9 | 855 | 8 |
| Malaysia | 292 | 7.1 | 298[30] | 31 | 1,038 | 89 | 365[8] | 390[8] |
| Mexico | 2,915 | 2.8 | 1,032 | 249 | n.a. | n.a. | 17,514 | 4,885 |
| Morocco | 168 | 1.0 | 79 | 6 | 235 | 14 | 1,300 | 382[8] |
| Netherlands | 5,047 | 36.8 | 3,456 | 93[7] | 4,175 | 311[7] | 3,846[8] | 3,510[8] |
| New Zealand | 1,571[27] | 50.2[27] | 644[16] | 40 | n.a. | n.a. | 2,700 | 791[8] |
| Nigeria | 111[11] | 2[11] | 781[15] | 12 | 660 | 9 | 5,000[8] | 110[8] |
| Norway | 1,407 | 35.0 | 886[12] | 75 | 1,567 | 391 | 1,277[8] | 1,021[8] |
| Pakistan | 240 | .3 | 340[14] | 93 | 358[31] | n.a. | 1,015[8] | 125 |
| Panama | 142 | 8.5 | 7[7] | 9[7] | 145[7] | 92[7] | 260 | 183 |
| Paraguay | 37 | 1.4 | n.a. | 11[7] | 89[7 24] | n.a. | 176 | 53 |

| Country | Telephones, in use,[1] 1975 (thousands) | Telephones per 100 population, 1975 | Pieces of mail sent, domestic,[2] 1975 (millions) | Daily newspapers,[3] 1975: Number | Daily newspapers,[3] 1975: Circulation: Total (thousands) | Daily newspapers,[3] 1975: Circulation: Copies per 1,000 population | Receiving sets, 1974: Radio[4] (thousands) | Receiving sets, 1974: Television[5] (thousands) |
|---|---|---|---|---|---|---|---|---|
| Peru | 333[11] | 2.1[11] | n.a. | 67 | 1,436[32] | n.a. | 2,010 | 425 |
| Philippines | 490 | 1.2 | 630[28] | 13 | 772 | 18 | 1,825 | 711 |
| Poland | 2,578 | 7.5 | 1,300[33] | 44 | 7,994 | 237 | 7,988[8] | 6,100[8] |
| Puerto Rico | 474 | 15.2 | | 5 | 405 | 132 | 1,755 | 625 |
| Romania | 1,076[11] | 5.1[11] | 639[11] | 20 | 2,716 | 129 | 3,066[8] | 2,405[8] |
| Saudi Arabia | 85[7] | 1.0[7] | 31[28] | 11 | 96 | 11 | 85[17] | 122 |
| South Africa | 1,936 | 7.8 | 1,327 | 24 | 1,738[35] | n.a. | 2,335[8] | — |
| Rhodesia | 183 | 2.8 | 97 | 2 | 100 | 16 | 225 | 57[14] |
| Spain | 7,836 | 22.0 | 3,888 | 115 | 3,396 | 96 | 8,050 | 6,125 |
| Sri Lanka | 72 | .5 | 894[11 16] | 26 | n.a. | n.a. | 505[8] | — |
| Sudan | 56[11] | .3[11] | 35 | 3[7] | 140[7] | 8[7] | 1,310[8 14] | 100 |
| Sweden | 5,423 | 66.1 | 2,384 | 111 | 4,362 | 536 | 3,086[8] | 2,841[8] |
| Switzerland | 3,913 | 61.1 | 2,704 | 92 | 2,535 | 391 | 2,036[8] | 1,714[8] |
| Syria | 152[11] | 2.1[11] | 23[7] | 6 | 64[36] | n.a. | 2,500[14] | 224 |
| Thailand | 312 | .7 | 133 | 27 | n.a. | n.a. | 5,111 | 715 |
| Tunisia | 129 | 2.3 | 69 | 4 | 156 | 28 | 277[8] | 147[7 8] |
| Turkey | 1,012 | 2.5 | 471 | 450[7] | n.a. | n.a. | 4,096[8] | 458 |
| U.S.S.R. | 16,949 | 6.6 | 8,969 | 675 | 97,664 | 388 | 116,100 | 52,500 |
| United Kingdom | 21,244 | 37.9 | 9,278[16] | 109 | 24,800 | 443 | 42,000[8] | 17,641[8] |
| United States | 149,012 | 69.5 | 87,661[6 7] | 1,798 | 62,156 | 293 | 401,600 | 121,100 |
| Uruguay | 250 | 9.0 | n.a. | 30 | n.a. | n.a. | 1,500 | 350 |
| Venezuela | 650 | 5.3 | 202[11] | 47 | 1,082[37] | n.a. | 1,709 | 1,200 |
| Vietnam[34] | 47[7] | .3[7] | 59[7] | 28[7] | 412[7] | 21[7] | 1,550 | 500 |
| Yugoslavia | 1,301 | 6.1 | 1,096[7] | 25 | 1,850 | 87 | 4,081[8] | 2,784[8] |
| **World, total** | **379,524** | **9.6** | n.a. | n.a. | n.a. | n.a. | n.a. | n.a. |

1. Comprises public and private telephones installed which can be connected to a central exchange. 2. Items mailed for distribution within national territories. Comprises letters, postcards, printed matter, merchandise samples, small packets, and phonopost packets. Includes mail carried without charge, but excludes ordinary packages, and insured letters and boxes. 3. Publications containing general news and appearing at least 4 times a week; may range in size from a single sheet to 50 or more pages. Circulation data include copies sold outside the country. 4. Data cover estimated number of receivers in use, except as noted, and apply to all types of receivers for radio broadcasts to the public, including receivers connected to a radio "redistribution system" but excluding television sets. 5. Estimated number of sets in use, except as noted. 6. Includes ordinary packages as well as insured letters and boxes. 7. For 1973. 8. Number of licenses issued. 9. For 149 dailies only. 10. Year ending June 30. 11. For 1974. 12. Year beginning July 1. 13. For 19 dailies only. 14. For 1972. 15. Excludes postcards. 16. Year beginning April 1. 17. For 1970. 18. Source: Republic of China, *Taiwan Statistical Data Book, 1975.* 19. Source: U.S. Bureau of the Census, International Statistical Programs Center. 20. For 10 dailies only. 21. Domestic and foreign. 22. Includes Faeroe Islands and Greenland. 23. For 6 dailies only. 24. For 4 dailies only. 25. For 52 dailies only. 26. For 1971. 27. Year ending March 31. 28. For 1969. 29. For 16 dailies only. 30. Data refer to West Malaysia only. 31. For 18 dailies only. 32. For 41 dailies only. 33. For 1968. 34. Data are for the former Rep. of South Vietnam only. 35. For 22 dailies only. 36. For 5 dailies only. 37. For 31 dailies only. NOTE: n.a. = not available. *Source:* Except as noted, Statistical Office of the United Nations, New York, N.Y., *Statistical Yearbook.* (Copyright.)

## Energy, Petroleum, and Coal, by Country

| Country | Energy consumed[1] (coal equiv.): Total (mil. metric tons) 1975 | Total 1970 | Per capita (kilograms) 1975 | Per capita 1970 | Electric energy production[2] (bil. kwh) 1975 | 1970 | Crude petroleum production[3] (mil. metric tons) 1975 | 1970 | Coal production[4] (mil. metric tons) 1975 | 1970 |
|---|---|---|---|---|---|---|---|---|---|---|
| Algeria | 12.66 | 6.59 | 754 | 460 | 3.7 | 2.0 | 45.1 | 47.2 | (Z) | (Z) |
| Argentina | 44.52 | 39.24 | 1,754 | 1,691 | 29.5 | 21.7 | 20.8 | 20.0 | .5 | .6 |
| Australia | 87.56 | 67.24 | 6,485 | 5,375 | 73.9 | 53.9 | 20.2 | 8.5 | 61.7 | 45.2 |
| Austria | 27.84 | 25.30 | 3,700 | 3,424 | 35.2 | 30.0 | 2.0 | 2.8 | — | — |
| Bahrain | 3.09 | 1.01 | 12,079 | 4,720 | .4 | .2 | 3.1 | 3.8 | n.a. | n.a. |
| Belgium | 54.70 | 59.32 | 5,584 | 5,923 | 41.5 | 30.5 | n.a. | n.a. | 7.5 | 11.4 |
| Brazil | 71.79 | 44.64 | 670 | 478 | 78.1[5] | 45.5[5] | 8.5 | 8.1 | 2.7 | 2.4 |
| Bulgaria | 41.70 | 33.42 | 4,781 | 3,937 | 25.2 | 19.5 | .1 | .3 | .3 | .4 |
| Canada | 225.57 | 201.07 | 9,880 | 9,393 | 272.6 | 204.7 | 67.8 | 60.2 | 21.7 | 11.6 |
| Chile | 7.84 | 12.51 | 765 | 1,287 | 8.7[5] | 7.6[5] | 1.2 | 1.6 | 1.3 | 1.3 |
| China, People's Rep. | 570.47 | 391.20 | 693 | 515 | n.a. | n.a. | n.a. | 20.1 | 470.0[6] | 360.0[6] |
| China (Taiwan)[7] | n.a. | n.a. | n.a. | n.a. | 22.9 | 13.2 | .2 | .1 | 3.1 | 4.5 |
| Colombia | 15.81 | 12.70 | 671 | 601 | 14.1 | 18.8 | 8.1 | 11.3 | 3.2 | 2.8 |

| Country | Energy consumed[1] (coal equiv.) Total (mil. metric tons) 1975 | 1970 | Per capita (kilograms) 1975 | 1970 | Electric energy production[2] (bil. kwh) 1975 | 1970 | Crude petroleum production[3] (mil. metric tons) 1975 | 1970 | Coal production[4] (mil. metric tons) 1975 | 1970 |
|---|---|---|---|---|---|---|---|---|---|---|
| Cuba | 10.82 | 9.39 | 1,157 | 1,109 | 6.2 | 4.9 | .2 | .2 | n.a. | n.a. |
| Czechoslovakia | 105.86 | 93.30 | 7,151 | 6,510 | 59.3 | 45.2 | .1 | .2 | 28.4[8] | 28.2 |
| Denmark | 26.65 | 28.76 | 5,268 | 5,838 | 17.6[5] | 18.9[5] | .2 | — | n.a. | n.a. |
| Ecuador | 2.98 | 1.79 | 442 | 293 | 1.3 | .9 | 8.2 | .2 | n.a. | n.a. |
| Egypt | 15.09 | 8.83 | 405 | 265 | 10.4 | 7.6 | 8.4 | 16.4 | — | — |
| Finland | 22.43[9] | 19.17 | 4,766[9] | 4,159 | 25.3[5] | 21.2[5] | n.a. | n.a. | n.a. | n.a. |
| France | 208.88 | 192.80 | 3,944 | 3,794 | 178.5[5] | 140.7[5] | 1.0 | 2.3 | 23.7[8] | 37.8[8] |
| Germany, East | 115.17 | 102.05 | 6,835 | 5,984 | 84.5 | 67.7 | .1 | .1 | .5 | 1.0 |
| Germany, West | 330.49 | 317.75 | 5,345 | 5,239 | 301.8 | 242.6 | 5.7 | 7.5 | 96.8[10] | 116.3[10] |
| Greece | 18.91 | 11.19 | 2,090 | 1,274 | 15.2 | 9.4 | — | — | n.a. | n.a. |
| Hong Kong | 4.89 | 4.00 | 1,119 | 1,010 | 7.4 | 5.1 | n.a. | n.a. | n.a. | n.a. |
| Hungary | 38.20 | 32.92 | 3,624 | 3,185 | 20.5 | 14.5 | 2.0 | 1.9 | 3.0[8] | 4.2[8] |
| India | 132.05 | 96.80 | 221 | 179 | 85.6 | 61.2 | 8.3 | 6.8 | 95.9 | 73.7 |
| Indonesia | 24.21 | 13.25 | 178 | 112 | 3.3 | 2.1 | 64.1 | 42.3 | .2 | .2 |
| Iran | 44.66 | 27.09 | 1,353 | 945 | 15.0 | 7.0 | 267.6 | 191.3 | 1.2 | .5 |
| Iraq | 7.93 | 5.82 | 713 | 617 | 3.4 | 1.9 | 111.2 | 76.5 | n.a. | n.a. |
| Ireland | 9.68[9] | 9.02[9] | 3,097[9] | 3,064[9] | 7.7 | 6.1 | n.a. | n.a. | (Z) | .2 |
| Israel | 9.46 | 7.35 | 2,806 | 2,524 | 9.7 | 6.8 | 4.9[11] | 4.6[11] | n.a. | n.a. |
| Italy | 168.09 | 144.06 | 3,012 | 2,689 | 145.6 | 117.4 | 1.0 | 1.4 | — | .3 |
| Jamaica | 2.90 | 2.57 | 1,427 | 1,377 | 2.3 | 1.5 | | | | |
| Japan | 401.88 | 332.37 | 3,622 | 3,215 | 475.8 | 359.5 | .6 | .8 | 19.0[12] | 39.7[12] |
| Korea, North | 44.52 | 28.16 | 2,808 | 2,027 | n.a. | n.a. | n.a. | n.a. | 35.0 | 21.8 |
| Korea, South | 35.98 | 25.42 | 1,038 | 819 | 20.8 | 9.6 | n.a. | n.a. | 17.6 | 12.4 |
| Kuwait | 8.68[13] | 10.01 | 8,718[13] | 13,352 | 4.7 | 2.2 | 105.2[13] | 150.6[13] | n.a. | n.a. |
| Libya | 3.18 | 1.12 | 1,299 | 577 | .9 | .4 | 71.5 | 159.7 | n.a. | n.a. |
| Malaysia | 5.52[14] | 4.28[14] | 552[14] | 468[14] | 5.4[14] | 3.3[14] | 4.2[15] | .9[15] | n.a. | n.a. |
| Mexico | 73.43 | 60.72 | 1,221 | 1,241 | 43.3[5] | 28.6[5] | 36.5 | 21.5 | 5.1 | 3.0 |
| Netherlands | 78.96 | 66.01 | 5,784 | 5,066 | 54.3 | 40.9 | 1.4 | 1.9 | — | 4.3 |
| New Zealand | 9.60 | 7.97 | 3,111 | 2,835 | 20.1 | 13.7 | .1[16] | .1[16] | .5 | .5 |
| Nigeria | 5.64 | 2.51 | 90 | 45 | 3.2 | 1.6 | 88.4 | 54.2 | .2 | .1 |
| Norway | 18.46 | 18.70 | 4,607 | 4,822 | 77.6 | 57.6 | 9.3 | — | .4[17] | .5[17] |
| Pakistan | 12.83 | 12.16[18] | 183 | 93[18] | 8.8 | 6.5 | .4 | .5 | 1.1[6] | 1.3[6] |
| Peru | 10.65 | 8.60 | 682 | 633 | 8.3 | 5.5 | 3.6 | 3.6 | .1 | .2 |
| Philippines | 13.85 | 10.75 | 326 | 292 | 12.4 | 8.7 | n.a. | n.a. | .1 | (Z) |
| Poland | 170.34 | 138.92 | 5,007 | 4,270 | 97.2 | 64.5 | .6 | .4 | 171.6 | 140.1 |
| Romania | 80.80 | 58.39 | 3,803 | 2,883 | 53.7 | 35.1 | 14.6 | 13.4 | 7.3[8] | 6.4[8] |
| Saudi Arabia | 12.53[13] | 6.25 | 1,398[13] | 808 | 2.0 | .7 | 352.4[13] | 188.4[13] | n.a. | n.a. |
| South Africa | 84.23[20] | 63.19[20] | 2,953[20] | 2,618[20] | 74.9 | 50.8 | n.a. | n.a. | n.a. | 54.6 |
| Spain | 76.17 | 50.15[21] | 2,147 | 1,485[21] | 82.4 | 56.5 | 2.2 | .2 | 10.8[8] | 10.8[8] |
| Sweden | 50.63 | 49.73 | 6,178 | 6,183 | 80.6 | 60.6 | n.a. | n.a. | (Z) | (Z) |
| Switzerland | 23.41 | 21.58 | 3,642 | 3,475 | 42.3[5] | 33.2[5] | n.a. | n.a. | n.a. | n.a. |
| Syria | 3.51 | 2.85 | 477 | 457 | 1.7 | .9 | 9.6 | 4.2 | n.a. | n.a. |
| Thailand | 11.90 | 8.79 | 284 | 256 | 7.9 | 4.5 | (Z) | (Z) | n.a. | n.a. |
| Tunisia | 2.58 | 1.32 | 447 | 257 | 1.3 | .8 | 4.6 | 4.2 | n.a. | n.a. |
| Turkey | 24.70 | 16.90 | 630 | 480 | 15.6 | 8.6 | 3.1 | 3.5 | 5.1[8] | 4.6[8] |
| U.S.S.R. | 1,410.78[9] | 1,054.69[9] | 5,546[9] | 4,345[9] | 1,038.6 | 740.9 | 491.0[16] | 353.0[16] | 484.7 | 432.7 |
| United Arab Emirates | 3.04[22] | 1.38 | 13,699[22] | 7,446 | .5[22] | .1[22] | 80.5 | 37.7 | n.a. | n.a. |
| United Kingdom | 295.33 | 300.20 | 5,265 | 5,377 | 272.2 | 249.2 | 1.2 | .1 | 128.6[8] | 147.1[8] |
| United States | 2,349.55 | 2,269.49 | 10,999 | 11,077 | 2,355.7[5] | 1,897.9[5] | 413.1 | 475.3 | 568.2 | 550.4 |
| Venezuela | 31.65 | 25.55 | 2,639 | 2,457 | 21.2 | 12.7 | 122.2 | 194.3 | .1 | (Z) |
| Vietnam | 8.41 | 5.54[19] | 186 | 302[19] | 1.3 | 1.2 | n.a. | n.a. | 4.3 | 3.0 |
| Yugoslavia | 41.21 | 29.30 | 1,930 | 1,438 | 40.0 | 26.0 | 3.7 | 2.9 | .6 | .6 |
| Zaire | 1.95 | 1.75 | 78 | 81 | 3.4 | 3.2 | .1 | — | .1 | .1 |
| Zambia | 2.47 | 2.05 | 504 | 494 | 6.2[5] | .9[5] | n.a. | n.a. | .8 | .6 |
| **World, total** | **8,002.20** | **6,820.07** | **2,028** | **1,892** | **6,438.9** | **4,915.3** | **2,646.3** | **2,274.4** | **2,367.9** | **2,141.9** |

1. Based on apparent consumption of coal, lignite, petroleum products, natural gas, and hydro and nuclear electricity. 2. Comprises utilities generating primarily for public use. Relates to production at generating centers, including station use and transmission losses. 3. Includes shale oil, but excludes natural gasoline. 4. Excludes lignite and brown coal, except as noted. 5. Net production, i.e., excluding station use. 6. Includes lignite and brown coal. 7. Source: Republic of China, *Monthly Bulletin of Statistics*. 8. Includes slurries. 9. Includes peat. 10. Includes low grade coal at its hard-coal equivalent. 11. Includes estimated production in the occupied Sinai Peninsula (1970, 4.5 million metric tons; and 1975, 4.0 million metric tons). 12. Includes brown coal. 13. Includes share of production and consumption in the Neutral Zone. 14. West Malaysia only. 15. Production in East Malaysia: Sarawak only. 16. Includes gas condensates. 17. Svalbard: Norwegian operated mines only. 18. Includes Bangladesh. 19. Former South Vietnam only. 20. Includes data for Botswana, Lesotho, Namibia, and Swaziland. 21. Includes Canary Islands and Ceuta. 22. Abu Dhabi only. NOTES: Metric ton = 1.1023 short tons. n.a. = not available. (Z) = less than 50,000 metric tons. A dash represents zero. *Source:* Except as noted, Statistical Office of the United States, New York, N.Y., *Statistical Yearbook.* (Copyright.)

# COUNTRIES OF THE WORLD

## Freedom in the World

Any almanac, almost by definition, deals with "facts." Yet a fact in a vacuum can be more misleading than a non-fact, and an idea which cannot be quantified at all may be more important than a hundred neat, numeric formulations.

Facts about the nations of the world are reported in this section. Yet an abstract concept — *freedom* — impinges on each of these countries, and is more crucial to an understanding of the world than any list of names and numbers.

Therefore, the editors of *Information Please* have turned to Freedom House for its annual *Comparative Survey of Freedom.* "For 35 years," said President Jimmy Carter, "the vigilance of Freedom House in the pursuit of democratic ideals has nourished those ideals throughout the world."

Freedom House, a national organization dedicated to strengthening democratic institutions, issues this survey annually. The complete study is available from Freedom House, 20 West 40th Street, New York, N.Y. 10018.

## The Criteria of Freedom

The Freedom House Survey defines freedom in terms of both civil and political freedoms, as traditionally understood in constitutional democratic countries.

### Political Rights

In the area of *political rights* the Survey asks whether leaders are chosen, or decisions made, on the basis of an open voting process. If they are, then the question arises whether recent votes suggest that a significant opposition is allowed to compete. This would be demonstrated by the size of the opposition and, particularly, whether a recent change of government had resulted from an election or vote. Are there multiple political parties, or at least candidates not selected by the government? Does the polling and counting of votes appear to be generally without coercion and fraud? What share of the political power is exercised by elected representatives?

Also, how is political power allocated among central, regional, and local authorities? A wide dispersion of power is particularly critical in large states, or in states in which most people are isolated from participation in national life by lack of educational and economic development. Even if elections are not important in a country, one needs to ask if power is divided among a wide variety of persons and groups. In some cases a *de facto* balance of power may offer as much political freedom as an ineffective electoral system. Finally, the Survey asks how free the political system is from foreign or military control or influence.

### Civil Liberties

*Civil liberties* generally imply independent news media, free from censorship. The Survey is interested primarily in censorship that is applied in defense of a ruling party or its policies; it has only marginal interest in censorship applied for social or religious reasons. Perhaps the most important civil liberties for the average person are the right to openly express oneself, the right to discuss public affairs with one's fellows without fear, and the right to belong to an independent private organization free of government supervision. Civil liberties include the right to a fair trial, and thus imply that the judiciary is to a degree independent. There is little detailed information readily available on the behavior of many judicial systems, but there often are indications as to whether an individual in a particular country can win a case against the government in court.

Closely allied to this question is the degree to which the security forces of a state respect individual rights. The number of political prisoners (arrested for opinions rather than violent action) and the existence of torture or brutality are important indicators. Finally, civil liberties are usually more operative when a nation is at peace, for increasing numbers of persons feel cowed into silence as levels of political violence rise. The Freedom House Survey also takes some account of the partial denial of rights implied by illiteracy, except on the local level.

The reader should be aware that judgments of civil and political rights are always on a comparative basis, and that Freedom House bases its conclusions on behavior rather than laws or formal systems. One might realize the imperfections of all systems and that the *pattern* of rights, not a simple list of pluses and minuses, is critical.

### Political and Economic Systems

Freedom House further classifies countries according to their political and economic systems. *These classifications appear under each country in the **Countries, Territories, and Dependencies** section.*

Theoretically, the most democratic countries should be those with *decentralized multi-party systems.* More common are *centralized multi-party systems* (such as in France or Japan) in which the central government organizes lower levels of government primarily for reasons of efficiency.

*Dominant party systems* allow the forms of democracy, but structure the political process so that opposition groups do not have a realistic chance of achieving power.

The now classical form of one-party rule is that of the *communist one-party states* (such as the U.S.S.R. or Vietnam). The slightly larger number of *socialist one-party states* are ruled by groups that

# Freedom in the World—1978

Movement in 26 countries toward greater freedom reversed a four-year downward trend. The most significant improvement in 1977 came in India where an unprecedented election restored political rights to 622 million persons, 58% of all who gained a freer status last year. Other notable improvements came in Spain, where 36.5 millions tasted freedom for the first time, and in the new nation of Djibouti (formerly Afars and Issas, under French control). All three countries went from partly free to free.

Going from not free to partly free were 40.4 millions in Ghana, Kuwait, Madagascar, Nepal and Syria. There were improvements within their previous categories, ranging from free to not free, for 379.5 million inhabitants of 17 nations: Bangladesh, China (Taiwan), Hungary, Poland, Yugoslavia, Iran, Mauritius, Morocco, Nigeria, Panama, Senegal, Sierra Leone, Sri Lanka, Sudan, Comoros, Thailand, and Upper Volta. Greatest advances were in Ghana, China (Taiwan), Morocco, Nigeria, Senegal, and Sri Lanka.

In nine countries with 123.8 million people, the state of personal freedom declined. These included free countries, Malta and Jamaica, and partly free, South Africa, all of which continued in their previous categories. Freedom declined further in already not-free Angola, Argentina, Burma, Congo, Equatorial Guinea, and Ethiopia.

There are 4,082.7 million persons living in 155 sovereign nations and 58 related territories. Personal political and civil freedoms may be shown statistically:

**Not free** are 1,753.9 millions (42.95% of the world's population), of whom 1,752.9 millions (42.93%) live in 64 (41.3%) of the nations; and 1 million (.02%) in 5 (7.2%) of the territories.

**Partly free:** 874.3 millions (21.4% of the people), of whom 867.9 millions (21.3%) reside in 47 (30.3%) of the countries; and 6.4 millions (.02%) in 28 (50%) of the dependent territories.

**Free:** 1,454.5 millions (35.7% of the population), of whom 1,449.2 millions (35.6%) live in 44 (28.4%) of the nations; and 5.3 millions (.02%) in 25 (42.8%) of the territories.

## Six-Year Record of the Survey

(population in millions)

| Survey date | Free | | Partly free | | Not free | | World population |
|---|---|---|---|---|---|---|---|
| Jan. 1973 | 1.029 | (32%) | 720 | (21%) | 1,583 | (47%) | 3,334 |
| Jan. 1974 | 1,351 | (36%) | 812 | (22%) | 1,618 | (42%) | 3,784 |
| Jan. 1975 | 1,366 | (35%) | 899 | (23%) | 1,602 | (42%) | 3,867 |
| Jan. 1976 | 803.6 | (19.8%) | 1,435.8 | (35.3%) | 1,823.4 | (44.9%) | 4,062.9 |
| Jan. 1977 | 789.9 | (19.6%) | 1,464 | (36.4%) | 1,765.9 | (43.9%) | 4,019.8 |
| Jan. 1978 | 1,454.5 | (35.7%) | 874.3 | (21.4%) | 1,753.9 | (42.9%) | 4,082.7 |

use Marxist-Leninist rhetoric and organize ruling parties much along communist lines, but either do not have the disciplined organization of communist states or have explicitly rejected one or another aspect of communism. A final group of *nationalist one-party states* adopt the political form popularized by the communists (and the fascists in the last generation), but the leaders either reject entirely the revolutionary ideologies of socialist or communist states or show little inclination to develop the totalitarian controls that characterize these states. There are several borderline states that might be switched between socialist and nationalist categories (*e.g.*, Libya or Syria). It should also be noted that "socialist" is used here to designate a political rather than economic system. A socialist "vanguard party" will almost surely develop a socialist economy, but a state with a socialist economy need not be ruled by a quasi-communist vanguard party.

Non-party systems can be relatively democratic, as in the small island of Nauru, but generally they are not. Such systems may be *traditional non-party systems,* ranging from Tonga to Saudi Arabia. Much more important are the many *military non-party systems,* such as those in Argentina or Uganda.

States with *industrial capitalist* forms are generally developed states in which the ruling assumption remains reliance on the operation of the market and on private provision for individual welfare. A larger number of states are classified as *pre-industrial capitalist.* These are generally poor states, with a small part of the population involved in a capitalist modern economy and the bulk of the population still living in traditional terms. In such states the traditional economy may be individual, communal, or feudal, but the direction of change as development proceeds is capitalistic.

*Capitalist-statist nations* (such as Brazil, Turkey, or Saudi Arabia) have very large government productive enterprises, either because of an elitist development philosophy or major dependence on a key source such as oil. Government interferes in the economy in a major way in such states, but not primarily because of egalitarian motives.

*Capitalist-socialist systems* (such as those in Israel, the Netherlands, or Sweden) provide social services on a large scale through governmental or other nonprofit institutions. These nations still see capitalism as legitimate, but its legitimacy is accepted grudgingly by many in government. Governments of other states grouped here (such as Iraq or Poland) proclaim themselves to be socialist, but in fact allow rather large portions of the economy to remain in the private domain. Both variants also have *pre-industrial versions* (such as Iraq or Peru).

*Socialist economies,* on the other hand, strive to place an entire national economy under direct or indirect government control. States such as the U.S.S.R. or Cuba may allow some modest private productive property, but this is only by exception, and right to such property can be revoked at any time. The leaders of *pre-industrial socialist states* have the same goals as the leaders of industrial socialist states, but their relatively primitive economies and untrained peoples cannot yet be completely socialized. Such states generally have a small socialized modern economy and a large pre-industrial economy in which the organization of production and trade is still largely traditional. It should be understood that the classifications given are impressionistic; along the continuum between capitalist and socialist systems the division into categories must, of course, be judgmental.

## The Comparative Survey of Freedom

### Table of Nations

| | Political Rights[1] | Civil Liberties[1] | Status of Freedom[2] | Outlook[3] |
|---|---|---|---|---|
| Afghanistan | 7 | 6 | NF | 0 |
| Albania | 7 | 7 | NF | 0 |
| Algeria | 6 | 6 | NF | 0 |
| Angola | 7– | 7– | NF | 0 |
| Argentina | 6 | 6– | NF | + |
| Australia | 1 | 1 | F | 0 |
| Austria | 1 | 1 | F | 0 |
| Bahamas | 1 | 2 | F | 0 |
| Bahrain | 6 | 4 | PF | + |
| Bangladesh[6] | 4+ | 4 | PF | 0 |
| Barbados | 1 | 1 | F | 0 |
| Belgium | 1 | 1 | F | 0 |
| Benin (Dahomey) | 7 | 7 | NF | 0 |
| Bhutan | 4 | 4 | PF | 0 |
| Bolivia | 6 | 4 | PF | + |
| Botswana | 2 | 3 | F | 0 |
| Brazil | 4 | 5 | PF | 0 |
| Bulgaria | 7 | 7 | NF | 0 |
| Burma | 7– | 6 | NF | 0 |
| Burundi | 7 | 6 | NF | 0 |
| Cameroon | 6 | 5 | NF | 0 |
| Canada | 1 | 1 | F | 0 |
| Cape Verde Islands | 6 | 6 | NF | 0 |
| Central African Emp. | 7 | 7 | NF | 0 |
| Chad | 7 | 6 | NF | 0 |
| Chile[6] | 6+ | 5 | NF | + |
| China, Peoples Rep. of | 6 | 6 | NF | 0 |
| China, Republic of | 5 | 4+ | PF | 0 |
| Colombia | 2 | 3 | F | 0 |
| Comoro Islands | 4+ | 3 | PF | 0 |
| Congo | 7– | 6 | NF– | 0 |
| Costa Rica | 1 | 1 | F | 0 |
| Cuba | 6 | 6 | NF | 0 |
| Cyprus | 3 | 4 | PF | 0 |
| Czechoslovakia | 7 | 6 | NF | 0 |
| Denmark | 1 | 1 | F | 0 |
| Djibouti[4,6] | 3 | 4 | PF | 0 |
| Dominican Republic[6] | 3+ | 2 | PF | + |
| Ecuador | 6 | 4 | PF | + |
| Egypt | 5 | 4 | PF | 0 |
| El Salvador | 3 | 4– | PF | 0 |
| Equatorial Guinea | 7– | 7 | NF | 0 |
| Ethiopia | 7 | 7– | NF | 0 |
| Fiji | 2 | 2 | F | 0 |
| Finland | 2 | 2 | F | 0 |
| France | 1 | 2 | F | 0 |
| Gabon | 6 | 6 | NF | 0 |
| Gambia | 2 | 2 | F | 0 |
| Germany, East | 7 | 6 | NF | 0 |
| Germany, West | 1 | 2 | F | 0 |
| Ghana | 6+ | 5 | PF+ | + |
| Greece | 2 | 2 | F | 0 |

| | Political Rights[1] | Civil Liberties[1] | Status of Freedom[2] | Outlook[3] |
|---|---|---|---|---|
| Grenada | 2 | 3+ | F+ | 0 |
| Guatemala | 3+ | 4 | PF | 0 |
| Guinea | 7 | 7 | NF | 0 |
| Guinea-Bissau | 6 | 6 | NF | 0 |
| Guyana | 3 | 3 | PF | 0 |
| Haiti | 7 | 6 | NF | 0 |
| Honduras | 6 | 3 | PF | 0 |
| Hungary | 6 | 5+ | NF | 0 |
| Iceland | 1 | 1 | F | 0 |
| India | 2+ | 2+ | F+ | 0 |
| Indonesia | 5 | 5 | PF | + |
| Iran | 6 | 5+ | NF | 0 |
| Iraq | 7 | 7 | NF | 0 |
| Ireland | 1 | 1 | F | 0 |
| Israel | 2 | 2 | F | 0 |
| Italy | 2 | 2 | F | 0 |
| Ivory Coast | 6 | 5 | NF | 0 |
| Jamaica | 2– | 3 | F | – |
| Japan | 2 | 1 | F | 0 |
| Jordan | 6 | 6 | NF | 0 |
| Kampuchea[5] | 7 | 7 | NF | 0 |
| Kenya | 5 | 5 | PF | 0 |
| Korea, North | 7 | 7 | NF | 0 |
| Korea, South | 5 | 5 | PF | 0 |
| Kuwait | 6 | 4+ | PF+ | 0 |
| Laos | 7 | 7 | NF | 0 |
| Lebanon | 4 | 4 | PF | 0 |
| Lesotho | 5 | 4 | PF | 0 |
| Liberia | 6 | 4 | PF | 0 |
| Libya | 7 | 6 | NF | 0 |
| Luxembourg | 1 | 1 | F | 0 |
| Madagascar | 5+ | 5 | PF+ | 0 |
| Malawi | 6+ | 6 | NF | 0 |
| Malaysia | 3 | 4 | PF | 0 |
| Maldives | 4 | 4 | PF | 0 |
| Mali | 7 | 7 | NF | 0 |
| Malta | 2– | 2 | F | 0 |
| Mauritania | 6 | 6 | NF | 0 |
| Mauritius | 2+ | 2 | F | 0 |
| Mexico | 4 | 4 | PF | + |
| Mongolia | 7 | 7 | NF | 0 |
| Morocco | 4+ | 3+ | PF | + |
| Mozambique | 7 | 7 | NF | 0 |
| Nauru | 2 | 2 | F | 0 |
| Nepal | 6 | 5 | PF+ | 0 |
| Netherlands | 1 | 1 | F | 0 |
| New Zealand | 1 | 1 | F | 0 |
| Nicaragua | 5 | 5 | PF | 0 |
| Niger | 7 | 6 | NF | 0 |
| Nigeria | 5+ | 4 | PF | + |
| Norway | 1 | 1 | F | 0 |
| Oman | 6 | 6 | NF | 0 |
| Pakistan | 6– | 4+ | PF | 0 |

| | Political Rights[1] | Civil Liberties[1] | Status of Freedom[2] | Outlook[3] |
|---|---|---|---|---|
| Panama[6] | 5+ | 4+ | PF | + |
| Papua and New Guinea | 2 | 2 | F | 0 |
| Paraguay | 5 | 6 | NF | 0 |
| Peru[6] | 5+ | 4 | PF+ | + |
| Philippines | 5 | 5 | PF | 0 |
| Poland | 6 | 5+ | NF | 0 |
| Portugal | 2 | 2 | F | 0 |
| Qatar | 5 | 5 | PF | 0 |
| Rhodesia[6] | 5+ | 4+ | PF+ | 0 |
| Romania | 7 | 6 | NF | 0 |
| Rwanda | 7 | 5 | NF | 0 |
| São Tomé and Príncipe | 6 | 5 | NF | 0 |
| Saudi Arabia | 6 | 6 | NF | 0 |
| Senegal[6] | 4+ | 3 | PF | + |
| Seychelles | 6– | 3– | PF– | 0 |
| Sierra Leone | 5+ | 5 | PF | 0 |
| Singapore | 5 | 5 | PF | 0 |
| Solomon Islands | 2 | 2 | F | |
| Somalia | 7 | 7 | NF | 0 |
| South Africa | 5– | 6– | PF | 0 |
| Spain | 2 | 3 | F | 0 |
| Sri Lanka | 2 | 3 | F | 0 |
| Sudan | 5+ | 5 | PF+ | 0 |
| Surinam | 2 | 2 | F | 0 |
| Swaziland | 6 | 4 | PF | 0 |
| Sweden | 1 | 1 | F | 0 |
| Switzerland | 1 | 1 | F | 0 |
| Syria | 5+ | 6 | PF+ | 0 |
| Tanzania | 6 | 6 | NF | 0 |
| Thailand | 6 | 5+ | NF | + |
| Togo | 7 | 6 | NF | 0 |
| Tonga | 5 | 3 | PF | 0 |
| Transkei | 5+ | 5 | PF+ | 0 |
| Trinidad and Tobago | 2 | 2 | F | 0 |
| Tunisia | 6 | 5 | NF | 0 |
| Turkey | 2 | 3 | F | 0 |
| Uganda | 7 | 7 | NF | 0 |
| U.S.S.R. | 7 | 6 | NF | 0 |
| United Arab Emirates | 5 | 5 | PF | 0 |
| United Kingdom | 1 | 1 | F | 0 |
| United States | 1 | 1 | F | 0 |
| Upper Volta[6] | 2+ | 3+ | F+ | + |
| Uruguay | 6 | 6 | NF | 0 |
| Venezuela | 1 | 2 | F | 0 |
| Vietnam | 7 | 7 | NF | 0 |
| Western Samoa | 4 | 2 | PF | 0 |
| Yemen Arab Republic | 6 | 5 | NF | 0 |
| Yemen | 7 | 7 | NF | 0 |
| Yugoslavia | 6 | 5 | NF | 0 |
| Zaire | 7 | 6 | NF | 0 |
| Zambia | 5 | 5 | PF | 0 |

1. The scales use the numbers 1–7, with 1 comparatively offering the highest level of political or civil rights, and 7 the lowest. A plus or minus following a rating indicates an improvement or decline in the rating since January 1977. For further information on the scale and survey *see Freedom in the World: Political Rights and Civil Liberties, 1978,* available from Freedom House. 2. A free state is designated by F, a partly free state by PF, and a not free state by NF. 3. A positive outlook for freedom is indicated by a plus sign, a negative outlook, by a minus sign, and relative stability of ratings by a zero. The outlook for freedom is based on the problems the country is facing, the way the government and people are reacting to these problems, and the longer run political traditions of the society. A judgment of outlook may also reflect an imminent change, such as the expected adoption of a meaningful new constitution. 4. Formerly the French Territory of the Afars and Issas. 5. Formerly Cambodia. 6. Preliminary judgment, Fall 1978.

# International Treaties, Agreements, and Organizations

## Alliance for Progress Agreement

Embodied in the Declaration of Punta del Este, adopted Aug. 17, 1961, by the U.S. and 19 other American republics, Cuba abstaining. The U.S. agreed to provide most of $20 billion needed over the next 10 years for Latin-American economic development. The other nations pledged themselves to increase their own contributions to economic and social development and to make the reforms necessary for all to share fully in the benefits gained under the Alliance for Progress.

## Arab League

Formed at Cairo on March 22, 1945, as a loose confederation of Arab states seeking Arab unity. Founding members were Egypt, Iraq, Jordan, Lebanon, Saudi Arabia, Syria, and the Yemen Arab Republic, joined later by Algeria, Bahrain, Djibouti, Kuwait, Libya, Mauritania, Morocco, Oman, Qatar, Somalia, the Sudan, Tunisia, the United Arab Emirates, the Yemen People's Democratic Republic, and the Palestine Liberation Organization. Military cooperation has been hampered by differences among the members, except in the Suez Canal crisis of 1956. The league has proved more effective in economic and cultural affairs. A permanent secretariat was set up at Cairo.

## Central Treaty Organization (CENTO)

Created in 1955 to provide a defense shield on the northern tier of the Middle East against Soviet penetration. Its original members were Turkey, Iran, U.K., Pakistan, and Iraq (which withdrew in 1959). In 1958, the U.S. signed a declaration of collective security to cooperate with the member states. CENTO was known as the Baghdad Pact until 1958, when its headquarters were moved to Ankara, Turkey.

## Commonwealth of Nations

An association of equal and independent nations and subordinate areas formerly part of the old British Empire and united by their symbolic allegiance to the Crown. Member nations gained equal status with the U.K. under the Statute of Westminster of 1931, which formally initiated the Commonwealth. Its members consult and cooperate and share trade and other economic benefits. For a list of members, *see* Countries of the World by Groupings.

## Countries of the World by Groupings

**KEY**

1—Member of the Organization of American States (OAS)
2—Member of the Organization of African Unity (OAU)
3—Member of the Organization of Petroleum Exporting Countries (OPEC)
4—Member of the North Atlantic Treaty Organization (NATO)
5—Member of the Association of Southeast Asian Nations
6—Member of the Central Treaty Organization (CENTO)
7—Member of the Arab League
8—Member of the Warsaw Pact
9—Member of the European Economic Community (EEC)
10—Member of the European Free Trade Association (EFTA)
11—Member of the British Commonwealth
12—Member of the Economic Community of West African States
13—Member of the Organization for Economic Cooperation and Development (OECD)

**NORTH AMERICA**

Canada: 4, 11, 13
Mexico: 1
United States: 1, 4, 13

**SOUTH AMERICA**

Argentina: 1
Bolivia: 1
Brazil: 1
Chile: 1
Colombia: 1
Ecuador:1, 3
Guyana: 11
Paraguay: 1
Peru: 1
Surinam: 1
Uruguay: 1
Venezuela: 1,3

**CENTRAL AMERICA**

Costa Rica: 1
El Salvador: 1
Guatemala: 1
Honduras: 1
Nicaragua: 1
Panama: 1

**CARIBBEAN REGION**

Bahamas: 11
Barbados: 1, 11
Cuba
Dominican Republic: 1
Grenada: 1, 11
Haiti: 1
Jamaica: 1, 11
Trinidad and Tobago: 1, 11

**EUROPE**

Albania
Andorra
Austria: 10, 13
Belgium: 4, 9, 13
Bulgaria: 8
Cyprus: 11
Czechoslovakia: 8
Denmark: 4, 9, 13
Finland: 10 (assoc. mem.), 13
France: 4, 9, 13
Germany, East: 8
Germany, West: 4, 9, 13
Greece: 4, 13
Hungary: 8
Iceland: 4, 10, 13
Ireland: 9, 13
Italy: 4, 9, 13
Liechtenstein
Luxembourg: 4, 9, 13
Malta: 11
Monaco
Netherlands: 4, 9, 13
Norway: 4, 10, 13
Poland: 8
Portugal: 4, 10, 13
Romania: 8
San Marino
Spain: 13
Sweden: 10, 13
Switzerland, 10, 13
U.S.S.R.: 8
United Kingdom: 4, 6, 9, 11, 13
Vatican City State
Yugoslavia

**MIDDLE EAST**

Bahrain: 7
Iran: 3, 6
Iraq: 3, 7
Israel
Jordan: 7
Kuwait: 3, 7
Lebanon: 7
Oman: 7
Qatar: 3, 7
Saudi Arabia: 3, 7
Syria: 7
Turkey: 4, 6, 13
United Arab Emirates: 3, 7
Yemen, People's Dem. Rep. of: 7
Yemen Arab Republic: 7

**FAR EAST**

China
China, Rep. of (Taiwan)
Japan: 13
Korea, North
Korea, South
Mongolian People's Rep.
Philippines: 5

**SOUTHEAST ASIA**

Cambodia
Indonesia: 3, 5
Laos
Malaysia: 5, 11
Singapore: 5, 11
Thailand: 5
Vietnam

**SOUTH ASIA**

Afghanistan
Bangladesh: 11
Bhutan
Burma
India: 11
Maldives
Nepal
Pakistan: 6
Sri Lanka: 11

**OCEANIA**

Australia: 11
Fiji: 11
Nauru: 11
New Zealand: 11,13
Papua New Guinea: 11
Solomon Islands: 11
Tonga: 11
Western Samoa: 11

**AFRICA**

Algeria: 2, 3, 7
Angola: 2
Benin: 2, 12
Bophuthatswana
Botswana: 2, 11
Burundi: 2
Cameroon: 2, 12
Cape Verde: 2
Central African Empire: 2
Chad: 2, 12
Comoro Islands: 2
Congo: 2
Djibouti: 7
Egypt: 2, 7
Equatorial Guinea: 2
Ethiopia: 2
Gabon: 2, 3
Gambia: 2, 11, 12
Ghana: 2, 11, 12
Guinea: 12
Guinea-Bissau: 2, 12
Ivory Coast: 2, 12
Kenya: 2, 11
Lesotho: 2, 11
Liberia: 2, 12
Libya: 2, 3, 7
Madagascar: 2
Malawi: 2, 11
Mali: 2, 12
Mauritania: 2, 7, 12
Mauritius: 2, 11
Morocco: 2, 7
Mozambique: 2
Namibia (South-West Africa)
Niger: 2, 12
Nigeria: 2, 3, 11, 12
Rhodesia
Rwanda: 2
São Tomé and Príncipe: 2
Senegal: 2, 12
Seychelles: 11
Sierra Leone: 2, 11, 12
Somalia: 2, 7
South Africa, Rep. of
Sudan: 2, 7
Swaziland, 2, 11
Tanzania: 2, 11
Togo: 2, 12
Transkei
Tunisia: 2, 7
Uganda: 2, 11
Upper Volta: 2, 12
Zaire: 2
Zambia: 2, 11

## The European Community

In 1950, the then French Foreign Minister, Robert Schumann, proposed a "Community" of the French and German coal and steel industries, with membership open to other European countries. The *European Coal and Steel Community (ECSC)* was established in 1952; it eliminated customs duties and reduced currency and trade restrictions on coal, iron ore, and scrap. Original members were France, Germany, Italy, Belgium, the Netherlands, and Luxembourg.

By 1955, discussions began on other ways of increasing European economic integration. The *European Economic Community* (the *Common Market* or *EEC*) was established by a treaty, signed in Rome in 1957, by the original members of the ECSC. In 1970, the U.K., Ireland, Denmark, and Norway were invited to join. All except Norway did so in 1972; the enlarged "Community of the Nine" formally came into existence on January 1, 1973.

The purposes of the EEC include the removal of trade barriers, coordination of economic policies, and increased mobility of labor and capital among its members—much of which had been achieved by 1978. Its aim is eventual economic union of the member nations and ultimate political confederation.

A second treaty was signed in Rome in 1957 establishing the *European Atomic Energy Community (Euratom)* to integrate activities of member nations concerned with nuclear power and technology.

The three Communities (ECSC, EEC, and Euratom) make up the *European Community,* with a Council of Ministers and a European Parliament. A European Court of Justice and the European Investment Bank also function within the European Community. (*See* R.C. Mowat, *Creating the European Community,* 1973.)

## European Free Trade Association (EFTA)

Formed in 1959 (formally begun 1960) to promote economic growth and fair competition, equalize the supply of raw materials among the member states, and to expand world trade. Members now include Austria, Iceland, Norway, Portugal, Sweden, Switzerland, and Finland (associate). Denmark and the U.K., originally members, withdrew before becoming members of the EEC in 1973; at that time a new trade agreement was made between the EFTA and the Common Market. By 1966, custom duties between members had virtually been eliminated. The EFTA is based in Geneva.

## The Helsinki Agreement

Popular name for declaration adopted Aug. 1, 1975, by 35 nations—including the United States and the Soviet Union—participating in the Conference on Security and Cooperation in Europe held at Helsinki, Finland. The declaration particularly stressed "fundamental rights, economic and social progress and well-being for all peoples," as well as the need for joint action to promote world peace and security. The participating states reaffirmed their full support for the United Nations and pledged to respect each other's "sovereign equality and individuality. . . . " They pledged to broaden and deepen détente, and renounced the "threat or use of force" and subversion in settling international disputes.

Outstanding in the declaration was the section on cooperation in humanitarian and cultural fields. The signers pledged themselves to respect "fundamental freedoms, including the freedom of thought, conscience, religion or belief."

Among the stated objectives were: Freer movement among persons, institutions, and organizations; wider exchange of information; increased cultural exchanges and broader dissemination of books, films, other media, and artistic works. The agreement was reviewed in an eight-month conference at Belgrade, Yugoslavia, ending in March 1978, which was attended by representatives of the U.S. and Canada, 32 European countries, and the Vatican. After bitter debate, the conference adopted a summary document that did not mention human rights or other issues dividing East and West. The review will be continued at Madrid in 1980.

## Marshall Plan (European Recovery Program)

Proposed in June 1947 by Gen. George C. Marshall, U.S. Secretary of State, to meet the need for integrated recovery efforts against "hunger, poverty, desperation, and chaos" in Europe. A July conference of 16 nations (the U.S.S.R. and its satellites refusing to participate) estimated four-year-aid requirements at $22.4 billion. In April 1948, Congress appropriated $5.4 billion. The U.S. established the Economic Cooperation Administration; European nations set up the Organization for European Economic Cooperation (OEEC). Each participating country set aside, in its own currency, sums matching the aid it received. The ERP ended in December 1951, a year ahead of schedule, with a total cost of $11 billion. Emphasis by then had been shifted to rearmament. (*See* S.E. Harris, ed., *Foreign Economic Policy for the U.S.,* 1948, 1968.)

## North Atlantic Treaty Organization (NATO)

Set up April 4, 1949, under a regional defense treaty for the North Atlantic area stating that "an armed attack against one . . . shall be considered an attack against . . . all" and that participating nations will take necessary joint counteraction under the United Nations Charter, including the use of armed force. The founding members were the U.S., Canada, Iceland, Norway, Great Britain, the Netherlands, Denmark, Belgium, Luxembourg, Portugal, France, and Italy. Greece, Turkey, and West Germany were added later. NATO marked the first time that the United States pledged to go to war to support allies before the outbreak of hostilities. The member nations are represented on the governing NATO Council. Its organization comprises their top foreign, economic, defense, and financial ministers. Its major military commands are SACEUR for Europe and SACLANT for the Atlantic Ocean area. (*See* James Huntley, *The NATO Story,* 1969.)

## Organization for Economic Cooperation and Development (OECD)

Founded in 1961 to encourage world trade and economic progress and aid underdeveloped nations. The OECD superseded the Organization for European Economic Cooperation, which had been established under the Marshall Plan in 1948. Members are Austria, Belgium, Canada, Denmark, Finland, France, West Germany, Greece, Iceland, Ireland, Italy, Japan, Luxembourg, the Netherlands, New Zealand, Norway, Portugal, Spain, Sweden, Switzerland, Turkey, the U.K. and the U.S. (Australia and Yugoslavia have a special association). Its structure is consultative; its decisions, not binding.

## Organization of African Unity (OAU)

Founded in May 1963 by 32 African countries, the OAU has grown to include most independent African countries; Rhodesia and South Africa are specifically excluded. Its charter reflects historical Pan-African concern for the political sovereignty, economic advancement, and cultural cooperation of all African peoples. The charter affirms allegiance to United Nations principles; its key section emphasizes the eradication of colonialism and promotion of international cooperation. The OAU has assisted in the relaxation or settlement of border disputes and helped resolve internal crises. In economic cooperation, it has stressed transportation and telecommunications. It maintains a close relationship with the U.N. OAU headquarters are at Addis Ababa, Ethiopia.

## Organization of American States (OAS)

Created in April 1948 as a regional agency working with the UN to promote peace, justice, hemispheric solidarity, and economic development; and to defend the sovereignty of member nations. Original members were Argentina, Bolivia, Brazil, Chile, Colombia, Costa Rica, Cuba, the Dominican Republic, Ecuador, El Salvador, Guatemala, Haiti, Honduras, Mexico, Nicaragua, Panama, Paraguay, Peru, the U.S., Uruguay, and Venezuela. Barbados, Grenada, Jamaica, Surinam, and Trinidad and Tobago were admitted later. In 1962 Cuba was suspended. The permanent body of the OAS is the General Secretariat, formerly the Pan-American Union Headquarters, Washington, D.C.

## Organization of Petroleum Exporting Countries (OPEC)

Founded in 1960 at Baghdad, Iraq, to advance its members' interests in trade and development and in relations with other oil-producing nations. Venezuela took the initiative; other founders were Iran, Iraq, Kuwait, and Saudi Arabia. They were joined by Algeria, Ecuador, Gabon, Indonesia, Libya, Nigeria, Qatar, and the United Arab Emirates. Through such practices as the 1973–74 embargo, OPEC has maintained high oil prices and has generally fixed the price of oil in international trade.

## Panama Canal Treaties

Approved by the U.S. Senate in March and April of 1978. The basic treaty provides for turning the canal over to Panama by the year 2000. Until noon Dec. 31, 1999, the canal will be operated by a new U.S. agency, the Panama Canal Commission, with five Americans and four Panamanians on the board. Until 2000 the U.S. will have primary responsibility for defending the canal; Panama will assume jurisdiction over the 533-square-mile Canal Zone.

The Neutrality Treaty, also effective Dec. 31, 1999, provides that the U.S. and Panama will each have the right to defend the canal against threats to its neutrality or the peaceful passage of ships. A Senate reservation gave the U.S. the unilateral right to use force if necessary to reopen the canal or restore its operations. The Senate specified that any intervention would be only to keep the canal open, not to interfere in Panama's internal affairs. (See *Panama*, also *Canal Zone*, under States and Territories in the United States section.)

## Treaty for a Partial Nuclear Test Ban

Agreement, effective Oct. 10, 1963, signed in Moscow Aug. 8, 1963, by the U.S., U.K., and the U.S.S.R. Although over 100 nations have since signed, France and China have not. The treaty banned nuclear testing in the atmosphere, in outer space, or under water. The signatories can withdraw under certain conditions.

## The Potsdam Declaration

Issued at Potsdam, Germany, July 26, 1945, after a conference of President Truman, Prime Minister Churchill (later, Clement Attlee), and Prime Minister Stalin. Pending entry of the U.S.S.R. into the war against Japan, it was issued in the names of Truman, Churchill, and Chiang Kai-shek (reached by radio). The declaration, designed to clarify and implement the Yalta Agreement, demanded unconditional surrender of Japan and outlined surrender terms. It called for elimination of "irresponsible militarism" and for Allied occupation until Japan's war-making power was destroyed. Other major points included "stern justice" for war criminals, democratic reforms, and respect for fundamental human rights. Successful U.S. testing of the atom bomb was revealed to Stalin at Potsdam.

## Strategic Arms Limitation Talks (SALT)

Two agreements limiting American and Soviet nuclear weapons were signed in Moscow in 1972 after three years of negotiations. One was a five-year interim pact limiting some offensive strategic weapons and the number of launchers for intercontinental ballistic missiles carrying nuclear warheads. The other, a treaty of indefinite duration, restricted antiballistic or defensive missiles to 200 on each side. The agreements were signed by President Richard M. Nixon and Leonid I. Brezhnev, the Soviet Communist Party leader. The talks originated with discussions at Glassboro, N.J., in 1967 between President Lyndon B. Johnson and the Soviet Prime Minister, Aleksei N. Kosygin. On Nov. 24, 1974, President Gerald R. Ford reached agreement in principle with Mr. Brezhnev at Vladivostok on limiting the numbers of all offensive strategic weapons and delivery systems until Dec. 31, 1985.

## Warsaw Pact

Signed May 14, 1955, by Albania, Czechoslovakia, East Germany, Hungary, Poland, Romania, and the U.S.S.R. Albania, barred from meetings in 1962, withdrew in 1968 after ideological differences. The pact is the Communist equivalent of NATO, providing that an attack on one shall be regarded as an attack on all.

## The Yalta Agreement

Signed Feb. 11, 1945, at conference of President Roosevelt and Prime Ministers Churchill and Stalin. The U.S., U.K., and the U.S.S.R. agreed to require Germany's unconditional surrender and on dividing Germany into separate zones for occupation, with France invited to join as the fourth occupying power. The agreement pledged disarmament of Germany, breakup of the arms industry, punishment of war criminals, reparations for destruction by the Germans, and the wiping out of nazism and militarism. The conference also agreed on terms for Russia to enter the war against Japan. (See R.F. Fenno, ed., *The Yalta Conference*, 2nd ed., 1972.)

# Quality of Life

## Selected National Development Statistics

The World Bank, in producing its *World Development Report, 1978,* has collected statistics that provide concise information about economic and social development in a large number of countries. A number of these statistics have been extracted from the Report and organized by *Information Please* editors around the concept of "Quality of Life." It should be obvious that the items listed are not the only criteria involved in this elusive concept. "Quality of Life" includes other factors, not quantified here and, indeed, probably not objectively measurable at all. Yet these items allow the reader to draw certain interesting inferences about living conditions, national priorities, and other important matters.

| Country | Population, mid-1976 (in millions) | Area (in thousands of sq km) | GNP Per capita, 1976 (in U.S. dollars) | Energy consumption per capita, 1975 (in kg of coal equivalent) | Average annual inflation rate 1970–1976 (percent) | Labor force in agriculture 1970 (percent) | Crude birth rate, 1975 (per thousand population) | Crude death rate, 1975 (per thousand population) | Projected population in year 2000 (in millions) | Life expectancy at birth, 1975 | Infant mortality, 1975[1] (per thousand) | Population per physician 1974[1] | Persons enrolled in primary school, 1975 (percent of age group)[1,2] | Persons enrolled in higher education, 1975 (percent of population aged 20–24)[1] | Adult literacy rate, 1974 (percent) |
|---|---|---|---|---|---|---|---|---|---|---|---|---|---|---|---|
| Afganistan | 14.0 | 648 | 160 | 52 | 3.1 | 82 | 51 | 31 | 24 | 35 | 269 | 26,100 | 23 | 1 | 14 |
| Albania | 2.5 | 29 | 540 | 741 | n.a. | 66 | 32 | 7 | 4 | 69 | n.a. | 1,200 | 106 | 17 | n.a. |
| Algeria | 16.2 | 2,382 | 990 | 754 | 14.8 | 61 | 48 | 14 | 35 | 53 | n.a. | n.a. | 89 | 3 | 35 |
| Angola | 5.5 | 1,247 | 330 | 174 | 13.5 | 64 | 47 | 24 | 12 | 39 | 24 | 15,170 | 79 | 1 | n.a. |
| Argentina | 25.7 | 2,767 | 1,550 | 1,754 | 88.7 | 16 | 21 | 8 | 33 | 68 | 59 | 450 | 108 | 28 | 93 |
| Australia | 13.7 | 7,687 | 6,100 | 6,485 | 13.5 | 8 | 19 | 8 | 17 | 72 | 17 | 720 | 98 | 22 | 100 |
| Austria | 7.5 | 84 | 5,330 | 3,700 | 7.9 | 15 | 14 | 12 | 8 | 71 | 21 | 500 | 102 | 17 | 99 |
| Bangladesh | 80.4 | 144 | 110 | 28 | 20.7 | 86 | 46 | 18 | 146 | 42 | 140 | 9,350 | 73 | 3 | 23 |
| Belgium | 9.8 | 31 | 6,780 | 5,584 | 8.8 | 5 | 14 | 12 | 10 | 73 | 15 | 570 | 105 | 22 | 99 |
| Benin | 3.2 | 113 | 130 | 52 | 8.3 | 50 | 49 | 22 | 5 | 41 | n.a. | 36,060 | 44 | 1 | 10 |
| Bolivia | 5.8 | 1,099 | 390 | 303 | 25.9 | 56 | 44 | 17 | 9 | 47 | n.a. | 2,120 | 72 | 10 | 40 |
| Brazil | 110.0 | 8,512 | 1,140 | 670 | 26.1 | 46 | 38 | 8 | 205 | 61 | n.a. | 1,660 | 90 | 10 | 64 |
| Bulgaria | 8.8 | 111 | 2,310 | 4,781 | n.a. | 47 | 16 | 10 | 10 | 72 | n.a. | 480 | 96 | 19 | n.a. |
| Burma | 30.8 | 677 | 120 | 51 | 16.1 | 67 | 34 | 11 | 50 | 50 | 56 | 6,910 | 85 | 2 | 67 |
| Burundi | 3.8 | 28 | 120 | 13 | 8.7 | 87 | 48 | 24 | 7 | 39 | 138 | 45,990 | 23 | ([4]) | 10 |
| Cambodia | 8.1 | 181 | n.a. | 16 | 98.6[1] | 78 | 47 | 18 | 15 | 45 | n.a. | 15,910 | 38 | 2 | n.a. |
| Canada | 23.2 | 9,976 | 7,510 | 9,880 | 9.2 | 8 | 17 | 8 | 28 | 72 | 15 | 600 | 104 | 35 | 98 |
| Central African Empire | 1.8 | 623 | 200 | 34 | 8.3 | 91 | 43 | 22 | 3 | 41 | n.a. | 27,970 | 79 | ([4]) | n.a. |
| Chad | 4.1 | 1,284 | 120 | 39 | 6.6 | 90 | 44 | 24 | 6 | 39 | n.a. | 44,370 | 37 | ([4]) | 15 |
| Chile | 10.5 | 757 | 1,050 | 765 | 273.6 | 24 | 23 | 8 | 15 | 63 | 79 | 2,420 | 119 | 17 | 90 |
| China, People's Rep. of | 835.8 | 9,597 | 410 | 693 | n.a. | 68 | 26 | 9 | 1,093 | 62 | n.a. | n.a. | n.a. | n.a. | n.a. |
| China, Republic of | 16.3 | 36 | 1,070 | 1,427 | 11.9 | 37 | 23 | 5 | 25 | 71 | 14 | 1,592 | n.a. | n.a. | 82 |
| Colombia | 24.2 | 1,139 | 630 | 671 | 20.7 | 38 | 33 | 8 | 37 | 61 | 56 | 2,180 | 105 | 7 | 74 |
| Congo | 1.4 | 342 | 520 | 209 | 9.3 | 42 | 45 | 20 | 3 | 44 | n.a. | 6,160 | 153 | 3 | 50 |
| Costa Rica | 2.0 | 51 | 1,040 | 544 | 13.7 | 42 | 29 | 6 | 3 | 68 | 38 | 1,580 | 109 | 17 | 89 |
| Cuba | 9.5 | 115 | 860 | 1,157 | n.a. | 31 | 21 | 6 | 14 | 70 | n.a. | n.a. | 126 | 9 | n.a. |
| Czechoslovakia | 14.9 | 128 | 3,840 | 7,151 | n.a. | 17 | 17 | 11 | 17 | 70 | n.a. | 430 | 96 | 11 | n.a. |
| Denmark | 5.1 | 43 | 7,450 | 5,268 | 9.8 | 11 | 15 | 10 | 6 | 74 | 10 | 620 | 102 | 29 | 99 |
| Dominican Republic | 4.8 | 49 | 780 | 458 | 8.9 | 61 | 38 | 10 | 9 | 58 | 43 | 1,870 | 104 | 19 | 9 |
| Egypt | 38.1 | 1,001 | 280 | 405 | 5.2 | 54 | 35 | 13 | 59 | 52 | 101 | 2,340 | 72 | 40 | 13 |
| El Salvador | 4.1 | 21 | 490 | 248 | 7.1 | 56 | 40 | 10 | 7 | 58 | 58 | 4,070 | 71 | 8 | 63 |

| | | | | | | | | | | | | | | | |
|---|---|---|---|---|---|---|---|---|---|---|---|---|---|---|---|
| Ethiopia | 28.7 | 1,222 | 100 | 29 | 2.3 | 84 | 49 | 25 | 54 | 38 | n.a. | 69,340 | 23 | (4) | 7 |
| Finland | 4.7 | 337 | 5,620 | 4,766 | 1[illegible].6 | 21 | 14 | 9 | 5 | 70 | 10 | 750 | 87 | 17 | 100 |
| France | 52.9 | 547 | 6,550 | 3,944 | 9.3 | 14 | 16 | 10 | 60 | 73 | 14 | 680 | 109 | 18 | 99 |
| Germany, East | 16.8 | 108 | 4,220 | 6,835 | n.a. | 13 | 12 | 13 | 17 | 73 | n.a. | 560 | 95 | 25 | n.a. |
| Germany, West | 62.0 | 249 | 7,380 | 5,345 | 6.4 | 8 | 12 | 12 | 63 | 71 | 20 | 520 | 129 | 20 | 99 |
| Ghana | 10.1 | 239 | 580 | 182 | 2[illegible].5 | 58 | 49 | 21 | 20 | 44 | 63 | 11,220 | 60 | 1 | 25 |
| Greece | 9.1 | 132 | 2,590 | 2,090 | 1[illegible].3 | 41 | 16 | 10 | 10 | 72 | 24 | 500 | 105 | 14 | 82 |
| Guatemala | 6.5 | 109 | 630 | 237 | 9.4 | 61 | 43 | 13 | 12 | 53 | 75 | n.a. | 62 | 4 | 47 |
| Guinea | 5.7 | 246 | 150 | 92 | [illegible].2 | 85 | 46 | 22 | 10 | 41 | n.a. | 22,380 | 28 | 1 | n.a. |
| Haiti | 4.7 | 28 | 200 | 30 | 1[illegible].5 | 74 | 45 | 16 | 9 | 50 | 150 | 8,510 | 50 | n.a. | 20 |
| Hong Kong | 4.5 | 1 | 2,110 | 1,119 | 8.6 | 4 | 18 | 5 | 6 | 70 | 15 | 1,490 | 120 | 9 | 90 |
| Hungary | 10.6 | 93 | 2,280 | 3,624 | n.a. | 25 | 16 | 12 | 11 | 70 | n.a. | 460 | 99 | 11 | 98 |
| India | 620.4 | 3,288 | 150 | 221 | 9.2 | 69 | 36 | 15 | 958 | 50 | 122 | 4,160 | 65 | 5 | 36 |
| Indonesia | 135.2 | 1,904 | 240 | 178 | 2[illegible].7 | 66 | 40 | 17 | 198 | 48 | n.a. | 18,160 | 81 | 2 | 62 |
| Iran | 34.3 | 1,648 | 1,930 | 1,353 | 2[illegible].2 | 46 | 45 | 15 | 60 | 51 | 120 | 2,570 | 90 | 5 | 50 |
| Iraq | 11.5 | 435 | 1,390 | 713 | 1[illegible].5 | 47 | 48 | 14 | 25 | 53 | 104 | 2,370 | 93 | 9 | 26 |
| Ireland | 3.2 | 70 | 2,590 | 3,097 | 1[illegible].9 | 27 | 22 | 10 | 4 | 72 | 18 | 850 | 108 | 16 | 98 |
| Israel | 3.6 | 21 | 3,920 | 2,806 | 2[illegible].7 | 10 | 26 | 7 | 5 | 71 | 22 | 350 | 128 | 24 | 84 |
| Italy | 56.2 | 301 | 3,050 | 3,012 | 1[illegible].9 | 19 | 16 | 10 | 63 | 72 | 21 | 500 | 107 | 24 | 98 |
| Ivory Coast | 7.0 | 323 | 610 | 366 | 1[illegible].0 | 85 | 45 | 20 | 14 | 44 | n.a. | 15,270 | 86 | 2 | 20 |
| Jamaica | 2.1 | 11 | 1,070 | 1,427 | 1[illegible].5 | 30 | 30 | 7 | 4 | 70 | 20 | 3,510 | 111 | 7 | 86 |
| Japan | 112.8 | 372 | 4,910 | 3,622 | 1[illegible].1 | 20 | 18 | 7 | 133 | 73 | 10 | 810 | 100 | 25 | 99 |
| Jordan | 2.8 | 98 | 610 | 408 | [illegible].6 | 34 | 47 | 14 | 5 | 53 | 22 | 2,440 | 83 | 4 | 62 |
| Kenya | 13.8 | 583 | 240 | 174 | 11.1 | 82 | 50 | 15 | 31 | 50 | 51 | 5,800 | 109 | 1 | 40 |
| Korea, North | 16.3 | 121 | 470 | 2,808 | n.a. | 55 | 37 | 9 | 26 | 61 | n.a. | n.a. | n.a. | n.a. | n.a. |
| Korea, South | 36.0 | 99 | 670 | 1,038 | 1[illegible].5 | 51 | 24 | 8 | 53 | 61 | 38 | 2,010 | 109 | 10 | 92 |
| Kuwait | 1.1 | 18 | 15,480 | 8,718 | 3[illegible].6[3] | 2 | 46 | 5 | 2 | 67 | 44 | 1,140 | 90 | 7 | 55 |
| Laos | 3.3 | 237 | 90 | 63 | 2[illegible].3 | 79 | 42 | 22 | 5 | 40 | n.a. | 21,570 | 57 | (4) | n.a. |
| Lebanon | 3.2 | 10 | n.a. | 928 | [illegible].4 | 20 | 40 | 9 | 5 | 63 | n.a. | 1,330 | 132 | 23 | 68 |
| Lesotho | 1.2 | 30 | 170 | n.a. | 3.8 | 90 | 40 | 19 | 2 | 46 | 114 | 20,320 | 102 | 1 | 40 |
| Liberia | 1.6 | 111 | 450 | 404 | 10.3 | 76 | 50 | 20 | 3 | 44 | 159 | 11,500 | 62 | 2 | 15 |
| Madagascar | 9.1 | 587 | 200 | 71 | 10.2 | 89 | 50 | 20 | 19 | 44 | 53 | 11,610 | 80 | 1 | 40 |
| Malaysia | 12.7 | 330 | 860 | 560 | [illegible].0 | 50 | 31 | 6 | 19 | 59 | 35 | 4,400 | 93 | 3 | 60 |
| Mali | 5.8 | 1,240 | 100 | 25 | [illegible].1 | 91 | 50 | 25 | 11 | 38 | 120 | 33,000 | 22 | 1 | 10 |
| Mauritania | 1.4 | 1,031 | 340 | 108 | 10.3 | 88 | 45 | 24 | 2 | 39 | n.a. | 17,770 | 17 | n.a. | 10 |
| Mexico | 62.0 | 1,973 | 1,090 | 1,221 | 1[illegible].2 | 45 | 40 | 8 | 126 | 63 | 50 | n.a. | 112 | 9 | 76 |
| Mongolia | 1.5 | 1,565 | 860 | 1,091 | n.a. | 62 | 38 | 9 | 2 | 61 | n.a. | n.a. | 85 | 6 | n.a. |
| Morocco | 17.2 | 447 | 540 | 274 | 9.3 | 57 | 48 | 14 | 35 | 53 | 117 | 13,800 | 61 | 3 | 26 |
| Mozambique | 9.5 | 783 | 170 | 186 | 6.9 | 74 | 43 | 20 | 17 | 44 | 93 | 16,680 | 52 | (4) | n.a. |
| Nepal | 12.9 | 141 | 120 | 10 | 8.4 | 94 | 46 | 20 | 22 | 44 | n.a. | 36,450 | 27 | 2 | 19 |
| Netherlands | 13.8 | 41 | 6,200 | 5,784 | 8.9 | 8 | 15 | 8 | 16 | 74 | 11 | 670 | 100 | 24 | 99 |
| New Zealand | 3.1 | 269 | 4,250 | 3,111 | 11.6 | 12 | 21 | 8 | 4 | 72 | 16 | 850 | 111 | 27 | 99 |
| Nicaragua | 2.3 | 130 | 750 | 479 | 10.8 | 51 | 46 | 13 | 5 | 53 | 46 | 1,720 | 85 | 6 | 57 |
| Niger | 4.7 | 1,267 | 160 | 35 | 1.7 | 93 | 52 | 25 | 9 | 39 | 162 | 41,060 | 17 | (4) | n.a. |
| Nigeria | 77.1 | 924 | 380 | 90 | 15.1 | 62 | 49 | 22 | 154 | 41 | 163 | 25,440 | 49 | 1 | n.a. |
| Norway | 4.0 | 324 | 7,420 | 4,607 | 8.6 | 12 | 16 | 10 | 4 | 75 | 11 | 610 | 102 | 21 | 99 |
| Pakistan | 71.3 | 804 | 170 | 183 | 15.2 | 59 | 47 | 16 | 135 | 51 | 113 | 3,970 | 51 | 3 | 21 |
| Panama | 1.7 | 76 | 1,310 | 865 | 11.2 | 42 | 31 | 7 | 3 | 67 | 36 | 1,240 | 124 | 18 | 82 |

| Country | Population, mid-1976 (in millions) | Area (in thousands of sq km) | GNP Per capita, 1976 (in U.S. dollars) | Energy consumption per capita, 1975 (in kg of coal equivalent) | Average annual inflation rate 1970–1976 (percent) | Labor force in agriculture 1970 (percent) | Crude birth rate, 1975 (per thousand population) | Crude death rate, 1975 (per thousand population) | Projected population in year 2000 (in millions) | Life expectancy at birth, 1975 | Infant mortality, 1975[1] (per thousand) | Population per physician 1974[1] | Persons enrolled in primary school, 1975 (percent of age group)[1,2] | Persons enrolled in higher education, 1975 (percent of population aged 20–24)[1] | Adult literacy rate, 1974 (percent) |
|---|---|---|---|---|---|---|---|---|---|---|---|---|---|---|---|
| Paraguay | 2.6 | 407 | 640 | 153 | 13.6 | 53 | 39 | 9 | 5 | 62 | 84 | 2,220 | 106 | 6 | 81 |
| Peru | 15.8 | 1,285 | 800 | 682 | 15.6 | 45 | 42 | 13 | 29 | 56 | 65 | 1,800 | 111 | 14 | 72 |
| Philippines | 43.3 | 300 | 410 | 326 | 15.1 | 53 | 36 | 10 | 75 | 58 | 72 | n.a. | 105 | 20 | 87 |
| Poland | 34.3 | 313 | 2,860 | 5,007 | n.a. | 39 | 18 | 9 | 41 | 70 | n.a. | 590 | 100 | 16 | 98 |
| Rhodesia | 6.5 | 391 | 550 | 764 | 7.5 | 64 | 47 | 14 | 15 | 52 | n.a. | 5,700 | 99 | n.a. | n.a. |
| Romania | 21.4 | 238 | 1,450 | 3,803 | n.a. | 49 | 19 | 9 | 26 | 69 | 35 | 630 | 109 | 9 | 98 |
| Rwanda | 4.2 | 26 | 110 | 14 | 13.1 | 93 | 51 | 22 | 8 | 41 | 133 | 53,550 | 58 | (4) | 23 |
| Saudi Arabia | 8.6 | 2,150 | 4,480 | 1,398 | 33.3 | 66 | 48 | 19 | 19 | 45 | n.a. | 6,660 | 44 | 3 | 15 |
| Senegal | 5.1 | 196 | 390 | 195 | 12.1 | 80 | 47 | 22 | 9 | 40 | 158 | 15,360 | 53 | 2 | 10 |
| Sierra Leone | 3.1 | 72 | 200 | 116 | 10.2 | 72 | 45 | 20 | 5 | 44 | n.a. | n.a. | 35 | 1 | 15 |
| South Africa | 26.0 | 1,221 | 1,340 | n.a. | 11.3 | 31 | 42 | 15 | 46 | 52 | n.a. | 1,970 | 107 | 5 | n.a. |
| Spain | 35.7 | 505 | 2,920 | 2,147 | 12.8 | 26 | 19 | 9 | 45 | 72 | 12 | 670 | 115 | 18 | 94 |
| Sri Lanka | 13.8 | 66 | 200 | 127 | 11.5 | 55 | 27 | 9 | 21 | 68 | 45 | 6,295 | 77 | 1 | 78 |
| Sudan | 15.9 | 2,506 | 290 | 140 | 3.5 | 82 | 49 | 17 | 30 | 49 | 132 | 12,370 | 40 | 2 | 15 |
| Sweden | 8.2 | 450 | 8,670 | 6,178 | 8.8 | 8 | 13 | 11 | 8 | 73 | 8 | 650 | 97 | 22 | 99 |
| Switzerland | 6.4 | 41 | 8,880 | 3,642 | 7.4 | 8 | 14 | 10 | 7 | 72 | 11 | 590 | 92 | 8 | 99 |
| Syria | 7.7 | 185 | 780 | 477 | 18.8 | 51 | 46 | 14 | 15 | 54 | 22 | 2,910 | 102 | 11 | 53 |
| Thailand | 43.0 | 514 | 380 | 284 | 10.3 | 80 | 34 | 10 | 76 | 58 | 27 | 8,530 | 78 | 2 | 82 |
| Togo | 2.3 | 56 | 260 | 65 | 8.6 | 73 | 50 | 23 | 4 | 41 | 121 | 22,280 | 98 | (4) | 12 |
| Tunisia | 5.7 | 164 | 840 | 447 | 7.7 | 50 | 34 | 13 | 9 | 54 | 63 | 6,350 | 95 | 4 | 55 |
| Turkey | 41.2 | 781 | 990 | 630 | 19.8 | 71 | 34 | 12 | 63 | 57 | n.a. | 2,130 | 104 | 7 | 55 |
| Uganda | 11.9 | 236 | 240 | 55 | 17.1 | 86 | 47 | 15 | 23 | 50 | n.a. | 20,690 | 53 | 1 | 25 |
| U.S.S.R. | 256.7 | 22,402 | 2,760 | 5,546 | n.a. | 26 | 18 | 8 | 320 | 70 | n.a. | 340 | 99 | 22 | 99 |
| United Kingdom | 56.1 | 244 | 4,020 | 5,265 | 13.3 | 3 | 15 | 11 | 61 | 72 | 16 | 750 | 116 | 16 | 98 |
| United States | 215.1 | 9,363 | 7,890 | 0,999 | 6.8 | 4 | 16 | 9 | 254 | 71 | 16 | 610 | 104 | 54 | 99 |
| Upper Volta | 6.2 | 274 | 110 | 20 | 6.3 | 87 | 49 | 25 | 9 | 38 | n.a. | 59,570 | 14 | (4) | n.a. |
| Uruguay | 2.8 | 178 | 1,390 | 942 | 70.5 | 15 | 20 | 9 | 4 | 70 | 48 | 910 | 103 | 14 | 91 |
| Venezuela | 12.4 | 912 | 2,570 | 2,639 | 13.4 | 26 | 37 | 7 | 24 | 65 | 46 | 870 | 96 | 19 | 82 |
| Vietnam | 47.6 | 333 | n.a. | n.a. | n.a. | 76 | 41 | 16 | 86 | 45 | n.a. | n.a. | n.a. | n.a. | n.a. |
| Yemen, People's Dem. Rep. of | 1.7 | 333 | 280 | 328 | n.a. | 65 | 49 | 20 | 3 | 45 | 44 | n.a. | 78 | 1 | 10 |
| Yemen, Arab Rep. | 6.0 | 195 | 250 | 49 | n.a. | 79 | 50 | 20 | 9 | 45 | 160 | 26,440 | 25 | (4) | 10 |
| Yugoslavia | 21.5 | 256 | 1,680 | 1,930 | 16.3 | 50 | 18 | 9 | 26 | 68 | 41 | 850 | 97 | 19 | 85 |
| Zaire | 25.4 | 2,345 | 140 | 78 | 15.7 | 79 | 44 | 20 | 47 | 44 | n.a. | 27,950 | 90 | 1 | 15 |
| Zambia | 5.1 | 753 | 440 | 504 | 3.8 | 73 | 51 | 19 | 11 | 45 | n.a. | 8,110 | 96 | 1 | 43 |

1. Data reported for some countries are for years other than those specified, although generally not more than three years distant. 2. Primary school age is generally considered to be six to eleven years; however, the educational systems of countries may differ. For countries with universal primary education, gross enrollment ratios may exceed 100% since some pupils may be above or below the official primary school age. 3. 1975. 4. Less than half of one percent. NOTE: n.a. = not available. *Source:* World Bank, *World Development Report 1978* (New York: Oxford University Press, 1978). Reprinted by permission.

# Countries, Territories, and Dependencies

For later developments, *see* Current Events

## AFGHANISTAN

**Democratic Republic of Afghanistan**
**Chairman of Revolutionary Council:** Noor Mohammad Taraki (1978)
**Area:** 249,999 sq mi. (647,497 sq km)
**Population (est. 1978):** 20,900,000 (Pushtu, 60.5%; Tajik, 30.7%; Uzbek, 5%)
**Density per square mile:** 83.6
**Capital:** Kabul
**Largest cities (est. 1976):** Kabul, 749,000; (est. 1973): Kandahar, 140,000; Baghlan, 110,900; Herat, 108,750
**Monetary unit:** Afghani
**Languages:** Pushtu and Dari Persian (both official)
**Religion:** Islam (Sunni, 90%; Shiah, 10%)
**Gross national product (1976):** $2.3 billion
**National name:** Jamhouriat Afghánistán
**Freedom House classification:** Capitalist-statist pre-industrial, non-party military

**Geography.** Afghanistan, approximately the size of Texas, lies wedged between the U.S.S.R., China, Pakistan, and Iran. The country is split east to west by the Hindu Kush mountain range, rising in the east to heights of 24,000 feet (7,315 m). With the exception of the southwest, most of the country is covered by high snow-capped mountains and is traversed by deep valleys.

**Government.** A limited monarchy ended July 17, 1973, in a coup ousting King Mohammad Zahir Shah. Mohammed Daud, a former Prime Minister and brother-in-law of the King, proclaimed a republic, suspended the 1964 Constitution, and abolished the Shura (parliament). On April 27, 1978, Daud himself was overthrown and Noor Mohammad Taraki installed as President.

**History.** Afghanistan occupies the land route to India trod by many conquerors, among them Darius I and Alexander the Great. The Moslems conquered the country from the west, beginning in the 7th century A.D. Genghis Khan in the 13th century and Tamerlane in the 14th century were later conquerors. Tamerlane's descendant, Baber, used the Afghanistan town of Kabul from 1504 to achieve the Mogul conquest of India. The country was torn by tribal and family warfare until Nadir Shah of Persia conquered the area in the 18th century. His commander, Ahmad Shah, established an emirate in 1747 and unified the country.

A later ruler, Dost Mohammed, reigned as the British and Czarist Russia began their struggle for central Asia. The Afghan Wars (1838–42 and 1878–81), that he, his son, and his grandson waged against the British are remembered for the massacre of the British at Kabul in 1842 and for the subsequent assaults on the Khyber Pass.

Afghanistan regained independence, though still under British influence, by the Anglo-Russian agreement of 1907, and full sovereignty by the Treaty of Rawalpindi in 1919. Emir Amanullah founded the kingdom in 1926.

The 1973 coup that ended the monarchy also cut off a 10-year experiment in democracy when Mohammed Daud seized all powers. The April 27, 1978, coup that brought Noor Mohammed Taraki to power resulted not only in the death of Daud but also, according to press reports, deaths of thousands of officials and supporters of his government.

Taraki, described as pro-Soviet, denied the reported killings as "imperialist propaganda," contending in a May 6 statement that only 72 or 73 persons died and 20 to 25 were arrested and later released. Taraki declared the Central Committee of his People's Democratic Party to be the supreme power in the nation, with a 35-member Revolutionary Council setting "routine policy."

**Economy.** Only a fifth of the soil is under cultivation, the greater part of the country being mountainous and rocky. Farming is confined to the fertile valleys and plains, sometimes with the aid of irrigation. Two crops a year are usually grown. Important ones include fruits and nuts, castor beans, cereals, madder, tobacco, cotton, and vegetables. Wheat is the staple food in Afghanistan. The fat-tailed indigenous sheep is a principal source of meat and wearing apparel.

Industry is still in a primary stage of development in Afghanistan. Manufactures include cotton and woolen textiles and clothing, soap, leather, matches, beet sugar, and furniture.

The country's mineral and forest resources are largely unexploited.

Afghanistan has no railways or navigable streams. Camels and pack horses are still used.

Chief exports in 1972–73 were fruits and nuts (29%), natural gas (20%), cotton (13%), carpets (7%), and karakul (Persian lamb) skins (5%). Leading customers in 1972–73 were U.S.S.R. (29%), India (24%), U.K. (16%), West Germany (6%). Leading suppliers in 1973–74 were U.S.S.R. (21%), Japan (17%), U.S. (12%), India (10%), West Germany (6%).

## ALBANIA

**People's Socialist Republic of Albania**
**President of Presidium:** Haxhi Leshi (1953)
**Premier:** Mehmet Shehu (1953)
**Area:** 11,100 sq mi. (28,748 sq km)
**Population (est. 1978):** 2,690,000
**Density per square mile:** 242.3
**Capital and largest city (est. 1975):** Tirana, 192,000
**Monetary unit:** Lek
**Language:** Albanian
**Religions:** Historically Islam 70%; Greek Orthodox, 20%; Roman Catholic, 10%
**Gross national product:** $1.3 billion
**National name:** Republika Popullore Socialiste e Shqipërisë
**Freedom House classifications:** Socialist industrial, one-party communist

**Geography.** Albania is situated on the eastern shore of the Adriatic Sea, with Yugoslavia to the north and east and Greece to the south. Slightly larger than Maryland, it is a mountainous country, mostly over 3,000 feet above sea level with a narrow, marshy coastal plain crossed by several rivers. The centers of population are contained in the interior mountain plateaus and basins.

**Government.** Under the Constitution that Albania adopted in 1946, supreme power is vested in the popularly elected National Assembly, to which the Cabinet, headed by the Premier, is responsible. The 240 members of the National Assembly all belong to the Labor Party and Democratic Front. The only political party is Labor (Communist), led by First Secretary Enver Hoxha.

**History.** Albania proclaimed its independence on Nov. 28, 1912, after a history of Roman, Byzantine, and Turkish dominion.

A battlefield in World War I, Albania reasserted its independence in 1920. A chief, Ahmet Zogu, proclaimed himself president in 1925 and monarch (King Zog) in 1928. Italy, under Benito Mussolini, drove him into exile in 1939 and annexed the country. The Communists under Enver Hoxha established a government in 1944, issuing a Constitution in 1946, amended in 1950, declaring the country a people's republic. Close relations with the U.S.S.R. ended in 1961 with the Soviet-Chinese rupture. Thereafter, Albania functioned as a Peking satellite, receiving massive Chinese aid to offset the Soviet boycott.

In 1967, the regime closed all of the nation's 2,169 churches and mosques in a move to make the country "the first atheist state in the world."

Albania's long alliance with China ended with the announcement on July 13, 1978, that China was cutting off all aid to its one-time partner. Albanian criticism of Peking following the death of Mao Tse-tung was cited as the reason, but Tirana called the action "arbitrary." Since 1954, Chinese aid had amounted to $5 billion. There was no indication from Tirana that Albania was ready to return to the Soviet sphere.

**Economy.** Albania is still a primitive country where each family tries to provide most of its own needs. Nearly the whole population is engaged in combined farming and stock-raising. Only a small portion of the central part is fit for tilling. Corn is the chief crop. Others are grains, tobacco, olives, and citrus fruit.

Factories produce food products, cement, and textiles; a large dam and power station were completed near Tirana in 1950.

Mineral wealth, thought to be considerable, is relatively unexploited.

## ALGERIA

**Democratic and Popular Republic of Algeria**
**President:** Col. Houari Boumediène (1965)
**Area:** 919,595 sq mi. (2,381,741 sq km)
**Population (est. 1978):** 18,500,000
**Density per square mile:** 20.1
**Capital:** Algiers
**Largest cities (est. 1978):** Algiers, 2,000,000; Oran, 700,000; Constantine, 600,000; Annaba (Bône), 500,000
**Monetary unit:** Dinar
**Languages:** Arabic, French, Berber
**Religion:** Islam
**Gross national product (1976):** $16.1 billion
**National name:** République Algérienne Democratiqe et Populaire—El Djemouria El Djazaïria Demokratia Echaabia
**Freedom House classifications:** Socialist industrial, one-party socialist

**Geography.** Nearly four times the size of Texas, Algeria is bordered on the west by Morocco and on the east by Tunisia and Libya. To the south are Mauritania, Mali, and Niger. Low plains cover small areas near the Mediterranean coast, with 68% of the country a plateau between 2,625 and 5,250 feet (800 and 1,600 m) above sea level. The highest point is Mt. Tahat in the Sahara, which rises 9,850 feet (3,000 m).

**Government.** Algeria is governed by a National Revolutionary Council of 24 members, presided over by President Houari Boumediène, who also heads the Cabinet and is Minister of Defense. Under a new Constitution approved by voters Nov. 19, 1976, Boumediène was elected President on December 10 for a six-year term after having ruled by decree since June 19, 1965.

A National Popular Assembly of 261 members was elected Feb. 25, 1977, the first since the dismissal of a predecessor body early in 1965. The National Liberation Front, which led the struggle for independence from France, is the only legal party.

**History.** As ancient Numidia, Algeria became a Roman colony at the close of the Punic Wars (145 B.C.). Conquered by the Vandals about A.D. 440, it fell from a high state of civilization to virtual barbarism, from which it partially recovered after invasion by the Moslems about A.D. 650.

In 1492 the Moors and Jews, who had been expelled from Spain, settled in Algeria. Falling under Turkish control in 1518, Algiers became for three centuries the headquarters of the Barbary pirates. The French took Algiers in 1830 and made it a part of France in 1848.

The fight by Algerian nationalists for independence had widespread political, diplomatic, military, and financial repercussions in France. Politically, it brought Gen. Charles de Gaulle to power when the Army and extremist French colonist virtually seceded, set up a "Committee of Public Safety," and demanded that de Gaulle be given power. Ironically, it was de Gaulle who determined to end the fighting by granting Algeria self-determination and independence, while his former Army and French colonial supporters in Algeria joined to create a Secret Army Organization (OAS), a terrorist group that tried to block independence. But metropolitan France, weary of continued warfare, voted by some 15 million to 5 million in January 1961 to approve de Gaulle's proposals.

On July 5, 1962, Algeria was proclaimed independent. In October 1963, Ahmed Ben Bella was elected President. He began to nationalize foreign holdings and aroused opposition. He was overthrown in a military coup on June 19, 1965, by Col. Houari Boumediène, who suspended the Constitution and sought to restore financial stability. While retaining close economic and financial relations with France and the U.S., Algeria entered the Arab bloc and joined the war against Israel in 1967. Thereafter, the U.S.S.R. stepped up development aid.

Friction with Morocco continued in 1976 as Algeria opposed the annexation of the Spanish Sahara by Morocco and Mauritania following a mass invasion of the former Spanish colony by Moroccan civilians. Algeria formally recognized a Saharan Arab Democratic Republic—composed of Polisario front leaders who fought unsuccessfully for an independent Sahara—on Feb. 27, 1976. The move was accompanied by a break in diplomatic relations with Morocco.

From an agricultural economy closely linked to

France even after independence, Algeria became an exporter of energy in the form of petroleum products and then liquefied natural gas. The U.S. replaced France as Algeria's chief trading partner in 1976, buying 40% of Algerian crude oil production. In common with other oil-exporting countries in 1977 and 1978, however, Algeria slowed its general industrial expansion and shifted investment toward increasing oil and gas output and strengthening agriculture. Non-energy industry had proved too costly in relation to income produced and agricultural imports had become a drain on a weakened economy.

U.S. exports to Algeria, estimated at $480 million for 1976, included grain, machinery, vehicles, and aircraft.

**Economy.** The principal crops are wheat, barley, and oats. Algeria is a leading wine producer.

The government's Third Development plan (1978–81) envisions expanded steel and nonferrous metals production as well as increased output of electrical goods and construction materials.

In addition to oil and gas, Algeria remains an important producer of phosphates, iron ore, zinc, lead, and salt.

Chief exports in 1975 were crude oil (86%) and petroleum products (5%). Leading customers in 1975 were U.S. (27%), West Germany (19%), France (15%), Italy (11%). Leading suppliers were France (34%), West Germany (12%), U.S. (11%), Italy (8%).

## ANDORRA

**Valleys of Andorra**
**Episcopal Co-Prince:** Msgr. Joan Martí Alanis, Bishop of Urgel
**French Co-Prince:** Valéry Giscard d'Estaing, President of France
**First Syndic:** Julià Reig-Ribó (1974)
**Area:** 175 sq mi. (453 sq km)
**Population (est. 1978):** 25,000
**Density per square mile:** 142.9
**Capital (est. 1975):** Andorra la Vella, 10,900
**Monetary units:** French franc and Spanish peseta
**Languages:** Catalán (official); French, Spanish
**Religion:** Roman Catholic
**National names:** Les Vallées d'Andorre-Valls d'Andorra

**Geography.** Andorra lies high in the Pyrenees Mountains on the French-Spanish border. The country is drained by the Valira River.

**Government.** A Council General of 24 members, elected for four years, chooses the First Syndic and Second Syndic. In November 1976 the Andorran Democratic Association, the principality's first political party, was formed.

**History.** An autonomous and semi-independent coprincipality, Andorra has been under the joint suzerainty of the French state and the Spanish bishops of Urgel since 1278.

**Economy.** With animal husbandry the principal occupation, the country survives as an example of medieval agrarian communal organization. The inhabitants enjoy the cheapest electricity, gasoline, tobacco, and alcoholic beverages in Europe. They also have no social services. Tourism is increasingly important, with 4 million visitors in 1976.

## ANGOLA

**People's Republic of Angola**
**President:** Agostinho Neto (1976)
**Prime Minister:** Lópo do Nascimento (1976)
**Area:** 481,350 sq mi. (1,246,700 sq km)
**Population (est. 1976)** 6,761,000
**Density per square mile:** 14.0
**Capital and largest city (est. 1970):** Luanda, 480,600
**Monetary unit:** Kwanza
**Languages:** Bantu, Portuguese (official)
**Religions:** Animist, 50%; Roman Catholic, 38%; Protestant, 12%
**Gross national product (1976):** $1.8 billion
**Freedom House classifications:** Socialist pre-industrial, one-party socialist

**Geography.** Angola, more than three times the size of California, extends for more than 1,000 miles along the South Atlantic in southwestern Africa. Zaire is to the north and east; Zambia to the east, and South-West Africa (Namibia) to the south. A plateau averaging 6,000 feet (1,829 m) above sea level rises abruptly from the coastal lowlands. Nearly all the land is desert or savanna, with hardwood forests in the northeast.

**Government.** Last of Portugal's African colonies to gain independence, Angola was born amid civil war Nov. 11, 1975. Four months later, the Popular Movement for the Liberation of Angola (MPLA) claimed victory over two rival factions with the aid of Soviet weapons and advisers and Cuban troops. Cuban Premier Fidel Castro's pledge to withdraw all his troops by the end of 1976 was still unredeemed two years later, and the situation in Angola remained one of the root causes of U.S.-U.S.S.R. conflict in Africa.

Because of the troop presence, the U.S. vetoed Angolan U.N. membership June 23, 1976. It abstained in a second vote by the Security Council Nov. 22, 1976, and Angola on December 1 became the 147th member of the world organization.

**History.** Discovered by Portuguese navigator Diego Cao in 1482, Angola became a link in trade with India and the Far East. Later it was a major source of slaves for Portugal's New World colony of Brazil. Development of the interior began after the Treaty of Berlin in 1885 fixed the colony's borders, and British and Portuguese investment pushed mining, railways, and agriculture.

Following World War II, independence movements began but were sternly suppressed by military force. The April revolution of 1974 brought about a reversal of Portugal's policy, and President Francisco da Costa Gomes, on Jan. 15, 1975, signed an agreement to liberate Angola. The plan called for election of a constituent assembly and a settlement of differences by the MPLA and the National Front for the Liberation of Angola (FNLA) and the National Union for the Total Independence of Angola (UNITA).

Despite covert aid to FNLA by the U.S. and open support by neighboring Zaire for the Front's leader, Holden Roberto, the MPLA had the initial advantage of strength in the capital region. Cuban troops were introduced in October and soon routed the poorly trained and equipped FNLA and UNITA forces.

The Organization of African Unity, split over the issue earlier, recognized the MPLA government led by Agostinho Neto on Feb. 11, 1976, and the People's Republic of Angola became the 47th member of the organization.

The new government nationalized 19 major industries on May 19, mostly Portuguese-owned. This, together with Lisbon's objection to the refueling of Cuban troop transports in the Azores, led to a break between the former mother country and Angola on May 19.

Although militarily victorious, Neto's regime had yet to consolidate its power in opposition strongholds in the east and south. Less militantly Marxist than their colleagues in the former East African colony of Mozambique, the new leaders sought help from both the Western and Eastern worlds.

In March 1977, Zairean refugees in Angola invaded Shaba province, Zaire, bringing charges by Zairean President Mobutu Sese Seko that the unsuccessful invasion was Soviet-backed with the collaboration of Angola. The Neto regime, the U.S.S.R., and Cuba all denied complicity. In May 1978, a repetition occurred, and this time the U.S. and France joined Mobutu in accusing Angola, the U.S.S.R., and Cuba, who again denied guilt.

**Economy.** Angola is agriculturally rich among African nations, exporting coffee, cotton, corn, rice, sisal, sugar, and timber before independence. Light industrial products included cigarettes, textiles, processed foods, and fish meal. Diamonds, gold, iron, and other minerals are traditional exports, and in recent years oil produced by the Gulf Oil Corporation in the exclave of Cabinda has become an important source of revenue. Dislocation by the war was reported to have reduced the Angolan economy to 20% of its pre-independence volume.

## ARGENTINA

**Argentine Republic**
**President:** Lt. Gen. Jorge Rafaél Videla (1976)
**Area:** 1,068,296 sq mi. (2,766,889 sq km)
**Population (est. 1978):** 26,400,000
**Density per square mile:** 24.7
**Capital:** Buenos Aires
**Largest cities (est. 1977):** Buenos Aires, 2,980,000; **(1970 census for urban agglomeration):** Rosario, 810,840; Córdoba, 798,663; La Plata, 506,287; Mendoza, 470,896
**Monetary unit:** Peso
**Language:** Spanish
**Religion:** Predominantly Roman Catholic
**Gross national product (1976):** $39.9 billion
**National name:** República Argentina
**Freedom House classifications:** Capitalist-statist industrial, non-party military

**Geography.** With an area slightly less than one third of the United States and second in South America only to its eastern neighbor, Brazil, in size and population, Argentina is a plain, rising from the Atlantic to the Chilean border and the towering Andes peaks. Aconcagua (23,034 ft.; 7,021 m) is the highest peak in the world outside Asia. The northern area is the swampy and partly wooded Gran Chaco, bordering on Bolivia and Paraguay. South of that are the rolling, fertile pampas, rich for agriculture and grazing and supporting most of the population. Next southward is Patagonia, a region of cool, arid steppes with some wooded and fertile sections. The eastern part of Tierra del Fuego, the island southern tip of South America, belongs to Argentina.

**Government.** Argentina is a federal union of 22 provinces, one national territory, and the Federal District. Under the Constitution of 1853 (restored by a Constituent National Convention in 1957 and amended in 1972), the President and Vice President were elected every four years by direct vote. The President appointed his Cabinet. The Vice President presided over the Senate but had no other powers. The Congress consisted of two houses: a 69-member Senate and a 243-member Chamber of Deputies. All legislators were elected by direct vote for four-year terms.

All political parties have been suspended, along with Congress, since the military coup of March 24, 1976. Meetings or statements by political parties are forbidden.

**History.** Discovered in 1516 by Juan Díaz de Solis, Argentina developed slowly under Spanish colonial rule. Buenos Aires was settled in 1580; the cattle industry was thriving as early as 1600.

Invading British forces were expelled in 1806–07, and when Napoleon conquered Spain, the Argentinians set up their own government in the name of the Spanish King in 1810. On July 9, 1816, independence was formally declared.

As in World War I, Argentina proclaimed neutrality at the outbreak of World War II, but in the closing phase declared war on the Axis on March 27, 1945, and became a founding member of the United Nations. Juan D. Perón, an army colonel, emerged as the strongman of the postwar era, winning the Presidential elections of 1946 and 1951.

Opposition to Perón's increasing authoritarianism, fanned by worsening relations with the Roman Catholic Church, brought a coup by the armed forces that sent Perón into exile Sept. 19, 1955. The Peronist party and Congress dissolved, Argentina entered a long period of military dictatorships with brief intervals of constitutional government.

In the first free election since 1951, a Perón-endorsed candidate, Hector Campóra, narrowly won the Presidency in 1973. He resigned July 13, 1973, seven weeks after his inauguration, in an effort to hand power back to Perón. The former dictator returned from exile and, with his third wife, Maria Estela (Isabel) Martinez de Perón, as Vice-Presidential candidate, swept the election on Sept. 23, 1973, winning 61% of the vote.

Perón launched a three-year plan to double the economic growth rate and boost family incomes by a third; it involved price freezes, wage boosts, and increased government spending. He persuaded subsidiaries of two U.S. auto firms to sell vehicles to Cuba under a $1.2-billion export grant. It was an early break in the hemispheric boycott of Cuba.

Perón died of a heart attack at the age of 78 on July 1, 1974. His widow became the hemisphere's first woman chief of state, but she took over a nation racked by acute economic and political polarization reflected in mounting civil disorders.

Mrs. Perón was re-elected head of the Peronist movement Aug. 24, 1975, at a tumultuous party Congress at which 118 of 238 delegates walked out before the vote. In mid-September she announced she would take a month-long leave of absence to recover from nervous strain and turned the presidential duties over to Italo A. Luder, president of the Senate.

Returning to take up her duties again October 16, Mrs. Perón was greeted with demands for her resignation as both the economic recession and terrorism increased. The inflation rate for 1975 was 334.8%, compared with 40% for 1974, and labor protest mounted despite massive wage boosts.

The long-anticipated military revolt came March 24, 1976, with a junta composed of Army Lt. Gen.

Jorge Rafaél Videla, Adm. Eduardo Massera, and Air Force Brig. Gen. Orlando Agosti taking power. Mrs. Perón and her closest advisers were arrested and subsequently charged with misuse of government funds, while thousands of Peronist government officials and labor leaders were placed under detention.

Videla took office as President on March 29 and formed a government of six military officers and two civilians, one of them the industrialist José Martinéz de Hoz, as Minister of the Economy. The new regime suspended the Justicialista (Peronist) party as well as all others and decreed new security laws and censorship.

Political murders and terrorism under the Videla regime mounted, together with allegations of police torture. Testimony at the United Nations Human Rights Commission in February 1977 said 2,300 had died, 10,000 had been jailed for political reasons, and more than 20,000 had disappeared since the new government took power.

The U.S. State Department earlier listed Argentina as a violator of human rights, and in reaction the Videla regime announced that it would refuse further U.S. military aid. A $700,000 military training program was scheduled to continue but the U.S. House of Representatives voted in June to eliminate the appropriation.

The twin plagues of inflation and terrorism continued in 1978. The cost-of-living rose 31.9% in the first quarter for a projected annual increase of 120%. More favorable economic news was the $1.5 billion favorable balance of trade for 1977 and a 15-year low in unemployment with a rate of 3.3%.

On April 11, 1978, Miguel Tobias Padilla, undersecretary for economic coordination under Martinez de Hoz, was assassinated by terrorists after the government was reported to have reached a truce with the Montonero to apply during the World Cup soccer tournament in Buenos Aires in June. Argentina won the quadrennial event June 25 in a final match before 77,000 spectators, beating the Netherlands 3–1.

An Argentine human rights organization charged on Aug. 9, 1978, that at least 150 persons had disappeared in Argentina during the first half of 1978, raising the total number of missing persons to 3,000.

**Economy.** A farming and stock-raising nation, Argentina devotes some 40% of its area to pasture and 10% to cultivation. Cotton, sugarcane, and fruits are important, and Argentina is the world's largest producer of yerba maté (Paraguay tea).

Cattle-raising predominates on the pampas, especially in Buenos Aires Province. Sheep-raising is more important in Patagonia.

The principal industry is meat packing, followed by flour milling, textiles, sugar refining, and dairy products.

Argentina must import most of nearly every mineral it uses. Oil is produced in Patagonia. The government announced discovery of uranium deposits in Argentina in February 1947.

## AUSTRALIA

**Commonwealth of Australia**
**Sovereign:** Queen Elizabeth II
**Governor-General:** Sir Zelman Cowen (1977)
**Prime Minister:** Malcolm Fraser (1975)
**Area:** 2,967,892 sq mi. (7,686,848 sq km)
**Population (est. 1978):** 14,220,000 (including aborigines)
**Density per square mile:** 4.8
**Capital (1976 census):** Canberra, 215,414
**Largest cities (1976 census):** Sydney, 3,021,299; Melbourne, 2,603,578; Brisbane, 957,710; Adelaide, 900,379; Perth, 805,489; Hobart (on Tasmania), 162,059
**Monetary unit:** Australian dollar
**Language:** English
**Religions (1971 census):** Anglican, 31%; Roman Catholic, 27%; Uniting Church, 17%
**Gross national product (1976):** $93.2 billion
**Member of Commonwealth of Nations**
**Freedom House classifications:** Capitalist industrial, multi-party decentralized

**Geography.** The continent of Australia, with the island state of Tasmania, is approximately equal in area to the United States (excluding Alaska and Hawaii), and is more than three fourths the size of Europe.

Mountain ranges run from north to south along the east coast, reaching their highest point in Mt. Kosciusko (7,328 ft; 2,234 m). The western half of the continent is occupied by a desert plateau that rises into barren, rolling hills near the west coast. It includes the Great Victoria Desert to the south and the Great Sandy Desert to the north. The Great Barrier Reef lies along the northeast coast.

The island of Tasmania (26,215 sq mi.; 67,897 sq km) is off the southeastern coast.

**Government.** The Federal Parliament consists of a bicameral legislature. The House of Representatives has 124 members elected for three years by adult (male and female) suffrage. The Senate has 64 members elected by popular vote for six years. One half of the Senate is elected every three years. Voting is compulsory at 18. Federal judicial power is vested in a Federal Supreme Court of seven justices, appointed by the Governor-General in Council. Each of the states has its own judicial system.

The major political parties are the Liberal Party (67 seats in the House of Representatives), led by Prime Minister Malcolm Fraser; Labor Party (38 seats), led by William G. Hayden; National Country Party (19 seats), led by J. Douglas Anthony.

**History.** Dutch, Portuguese, and Spanish ships sighted Australia in the 17th century; the Dutch landed at the Gulf of Carpentaria in March 1606. In 1642, Abel Tasman (for whom Tasmania was named) proved that Australia was not part of the Antarctic Continent. Australia was called New Holland, Botany Bay, and New South Wales until about 1820.

Captain James Cook, in 1770, claimed possession for Great Britain. A British penal colony was set up at what is now Sydney, then Port Jackson, in 1788, and about 161,000 transported English convicts were settled there until the system was suspended in 1839.

Free settlers established six colonies: New South Wales (1786), Tasmania (then Van Diemen's Land) (1825), Western Australia (1829), South Australia (1834), Victoria (1851), and Queensland (1859).

Sheep raising and wheat growing built the economy, and the white population, which had dwindled to 34,000 in 1820, grew to 400,000 by 1850. Discovery of gold in Victoria in 1851 led immigrants to pour in. The six colonies became states and in 1901 federated into the Commonwealth of Australia with a constitution merging British parliamentary tradition and U.S. federal experience. Australia became known for liberal legislation: free compulsory education, protected trade unionism with industrial conciliation and arbitration, the "Australian" ballot facilitating selection, the secret ballot, women's suffrage, maternity allowances, and sickness and old age pensions.

The Labor Government of Prime Minister Gough Whitlam, elected in 1972, was itself a victim of the twin economic troubles that hit Australia along with most of the rest of the world—inflation and recession. Opposition parties blocked passage of government budget requests to force Whitlam to resign and, in what was called an unconstitutional action, Gov. Gen. Sir John Kerr dissolved both houses of Parliament on Nov. 11, 1975. Kerr asked Malcolm Fraser, the Liberal Party chief, to form a caretaker government until a new general election on December 13. Kerr resigned in 1977.

On May 17, 1978, the government announced that it would accept 9,000 Indochinese refugees in the year beginning July 1. Australia had already admitted 10,000, including 1,500 "boat people" who had made the perilous journey from Vietnam in small craft.

**Economy.** About 55% of Australia's total area is suitable (mining excepted) only for grazing.

Sugar and cotton are grown in Queensland and New South Wales, tobacco in Northeast Victoria, and vines chiefly in South Australia and Victoria.

New South Wales is the leading industrial state. Power for industry comes mainly from coal.

Spurred by the rise in world prices, Australian gold production in 1977 set a five-year record with an output of 43,120 pounds compared to 34,400 pounds in 1976. After gold, the most important mineral production is iron ore, coal, bauxite, copper, silver, lead, zinc, tin, and uranium. On May 31, 1978, after a suspension of uranium mining under union pressure, legislation was passed to provide environmental protection of mine sites, impose safeguards in mining, and insure that uranium exports be used only for peaceful purposes.

Oil, discovered in Western Australia in 1953, provided 70% of domestic requirements in 1977 with production of 209.1 million barrels, up 3% from the previous year.

Forest products of Australia include timber (rough sawn), eucalyptus oil, sandalwood oil, tanbark, and yacca gum. Sea products include bêche-de-mer, oysters, pearls, pearl shell, tortoise shell, and agar-agar.

Chief exports in 1976 were wool (12%), coal (10%), wheat (9%), and iron ore (8%). Leading customers were Japan (33%), U.S. (9%), New Zealand (5%), U.K. (5%). Leading suppliers were Japan (21%), U.S. (20%), U.K. (12%), West Germany (7%).

## Australian External Territories

**Norfolk Island** (14 sq mi.; 36.3 sq km) was placed under Australian administration in 1914. Population in 1977 was about 1,600.

**The Ashmore and Cartier Islands** (.8 sq mi.) were placed under Australian administration in 1931. In 1938 the islands, which are uninhabited, were annexed to the Northern Territory.

**The Australian Antarctic Territory** (2,360,000 sq mi.; 6,112,400 sq km), comprising all the islands and territories, other than Adélie Land, situated south of lat. 60° S and lying between long. 160° to 45° E, was placed under Australian administration in 1936.

**Heard Island and the McDonald Islands** (158 sq mi.; 409.2 sq km), lying in the sub-Antarctic, were placed under Australian administration in 1947.

**The Cocos (Keeling) Islands** (5.5 sq mi.; 14.2 sq. km) placed under Australian administration in 1955. Population in 1977 was 447.

**Christmas Island** (52 sq mi.; 134.7 sq km) was placed under Australian administration in 1958. Population in 1977 was about 3,300.

**Coral Sea Islands** (400,000 sq mi.; 1,036,000 sq km, but only a few sq mi. of land) became a territory of Australia in 1969. There is no permanent population on the islands.

# AUSTRIA

**Republic of Austria**
**President:** Rudolf Kirchschläger (1974)
**Chancellor:** Bruno Kreisky (1970)
**Area:** 32,375 sq mi. (83,849 sq km)
**Population (est. 1978):** 7,500,000
**Density per square mile:** 231.7
**Capital:** Vienna
**Largest cities (est. 1976):** Vienna, 1,592,800; **(1971 census):** Graz, 248,500; Linz, 202,874; Salzburg, 128,845; Innsbruck, 115,197; Klagenfurt, 74,326
**Monetary unit:** Schilling
**Language:** German
**Religion (1977):** Roman Catholic, 90%
**Gross national product (1976):** $40.6 billion
**National name:** Republik Österreich
**Freedom House classifications:** Capitalist-socialist industrial, multi-party centralized

**Geography.** Slightly smaller than Maine, Austria includes much of the mountainous territory of the eastern Alps (about 75% of the area). The country contains many snowfields, glaciers, and snow-capped peaks, the highest being the Grossglockner (12,530 ft; 3,819 m). The Danube is the principal river. Forests and woodlands cover about 40% of the land area.

Almost at the heart of Europe, Austria has as its neighbors Italy, Switzerland, West Germany, Czechoslovakia, Hungary, Yugoslavia, and Liechtenstein.

**Government.** The federal republic of Austria is composed of nine provinces (Bundesländer), including Vienna. The President is elected by the people directly for a term of six years. The bicameral legislature consists of the Bundesrat, with 58 members chosen by the provincial assemblies, and the Nationalrat, with 183 members popularly elected for four years. Presidency of the Bundesrat revolves each six months, going to the provinces in alphabetical order.

The major political parties are the Socialist Party (93 of 183 seats in Nationalrat), led by Chancellor Bruno Kreisky; People's Party (80 seats); Freiheitliche Partei (10 seats).

**History.** Settled in prehistoric times, the Central European land that is now Austria was overrun in pre-Roman times by various tribes, including the Celts. Charlemagne conquered the area in 788 and encouraged colonization and Christianity. In 1252, Ottokar, King of Bohemia, gained possession, only to lose the territories to Rudolf of Hapsburg in 1278. Thereafter, until World War I, Austria's history was largely that of its ruling house, the Hapsburgs.

Austria emerged from the Congress of Vienna in 1815 as the Continent's dominant power. The *Ausgleich* of 1867 provided for a dual sovereignty, the empire of Austria and the kingdom of Hungary, under Francis Joseph I, who ruled until his death on Nov. 21, 1916. He was succeeded by his grandnephew, Charles I.

During World War I, Austria-Hungary was one of the Central Powers with Germany, Bulgaria, and Turkey; and the war left the country in political chaos and economic ruin. Austria, shorn of Hungary, was proclaimed a republic in 1918, and the monarchy was dissolved in 1919.

A parliamentary democracy was set up by the Constitution of Nov. 10, 1920. To check the power of Nazis advocating union with Germany, Chancellor Engelbert Dollfuss in 1933 established a dictatorship, but was assassinated by the Nazis on July 25, 1934. Kurt von Schuschnigg, his successor, struggled to keep Austria independent, but on March 12, 1938, German troops occupied the country, and Hitler proclaimed its *Anschluss* (union) with Germany, annexing it to the Third Reich.

After World War II the U.S. and U.K. declared the Austrians a "liberated" people. But the Russians prolonged the occupation. Finally Austria concluded a state treaty with the U.S.S.R. and the other occupying powers and regained her independence on May 15, 1955. The second Austrian republic, established Dec. 19, 1945, on the basis of the 1920 Constitution amended in 1929, was declared by the federal parliament to be permanently neutral. Austria became a member of the Council of Europe in 1956.

Vienna has become a headquarters for international organizations, such as the International Atomic Energy Agency and the Organization of Petroleum Exporting Countries (OPEC).

**Economy.** Agriculture employs approximately one third of the population, but the country is heavily dependent on imported foodstuffs. Mixed farming predominates. Rye and wheat are the leading cereals. Stock-raising and dairy farming are of importance.

Forty-one percent of the population is engaged in industry. Most important are the metallurgical, engineering, textile, and food-processing industries. Nationalized plants employ one fifth of the industrial labor force. Major steel and aluminum plants are in Upper Austria.

Austria possesses valuable mineral resources. In Styria lies one of the largest European deposits of iron ore. Copper is mined in Salzburg, Tyrol, and Lower Austria, and lead and zinc in Carinthia. Large supplies of coal and coke must be imported, but extensive water power resources are available for exploitation. Petroleum fields are in the Zistersdorf and Mühlberg areas. Austria's tourist trade annually covers almost completely the country's balance-of-trade deficit.

## BAHAMAS

**Commonwealth of the Bahamas**

**Governor-General:** Sir Milo Butler, Sr. (1973)
**Prime Minister:** Lynden O. Pindling (1967)
**Area:** 5,382 sq mi. (13,935 sq km)
**Population (est. 1978):** 230,000
**Density per square mile:** 42.7
**Capital and largest city (est. 1976 for urban agglomeration):** Nassau, 125,000
**Monetary unit:** Bahamian dollar
**Language:** English
**Religions:** Baptist, 29%; Anglican, 23%; Roman Catholic, 23%; Methodist, 7%
**Gross national product (1976):** $700 million
**Member of Commonwealth of Nations**
**Freedom House classifications:** Capitalist industrial, multi-party centralized

**Geography.** The Bahamas are an archipelago of about 700 islands, east of Florida and north of Cuba, extending from northwest to southeast for about 800 miles. Only 29 of the islands are inhabited; the most important is New Providence (83 sq mi.), on which Nassau is located. Other islands include Grand Bahama, Abaco, Eleuthera, Andros, Cat Island, San Salvador (or Watling's Island), Exuma, Long Island, Crooked Island, Acklins Island, Mayaguana, and Inagua.

The islands are mainly flat, few rising above 200 feet. There are a few streams, one river (on Andros), and one large lake (on Inagua).

**Government.** The Bahamas moved toward greater autonomy in 1968 after the overwhelming victory in general elections of the Progressive Liberal Party, led by Prime Minister Pindling. The black leader's party won 29 seats in the House of Assembly to only 7 for the predominantly white United Bahamians, who had controlled the islands for decades before Pindling became Prime Minister in 1967.

With its new mandate from the 85%-black population, Pindling's government negotiated a new Constitution with the U.K. under which the colony became the Commonwealth of the Bahama Islands in 1969. On July 10, 1973, the Bahamas became an independent nation as Commonwealth of the Bahamas. The islands established diplomatic relations with Cuba in 1974.

In the 1977 election, Pindling's Progressive Liberal Party won 30 of 38 seats in Parliament; the Bahamian Democratic Party, 6; the Free National Movement, 2.

**History.** The islands were reached by Columbus in October 1492, and were a favorite pirate area in the early 18th century. The Bahamas were a crown colony from 1717 until they were granted internal self-government on Jan. 7, 1964.

**Economy.** Pindling's government pushed for greater government participation in economic enterprises. The principal agriculture products are tomatoes, citrus fruit, and sisal. From the sea come sponges, lobsters, and crayfish.

Tourism is the main source of foreign exchange. In 1977, almost 1.4 million visitors spent over $412 million in the islands.

Chief exports in 1975 were crude oil (56%) and petroleum products (40%). Leading customers were U.S. (76%), Liberia (5%). Leading suppliers were Saudi Arabia (38%), Nigeria (18%), Libya (14%), Indonesia (7%), U.S. (7%), Iran (5%).

## BAHRAIN

**State of Bahrain**

**Amir:** Sheik Isa bin-Sulman al-Khalifa (1961)
**Prime Minister:** Khalifa bin Sulman al-Khalifa

**Area:** 240 sq mi. (622 sq km)
**Population (est. 1978):** 280,000
**Density per square mile:** 105.4
**Capital (est. 1976):** Manama, 105,400
**Monetary unit:** Bahrain dinar
**Languages:** Arabic (official); Persian, English
**Religion:** Islam
**Gross national product (1976):** $660 million
**Freedom House classifications:** Capitalist-statist industrial, non-party traditional

**Geography.** Bahrain is an archipelago in the Persian Gulf off the coast of Saudi Arabia. The islands for the most part are level expanses of sand and rock.

**Government.** A new Constitution was approved in 1973. It created the first elected parliament in the country's history. Called the National Council, it consisted of 30 members elected by male citizens for four-year terms, plus up to 14 cabinet ministers as ex-officio members. In August 1975, the Amir dissolved the National Council.

**History.** A sheikdom which passed from the Persians to the al-Khalifa family from Arabia in 1782, Bahrain became, by treaty, a British protectorate in 1820. It has become a major Middle Eastern oil center and, through use of oil revenues, is one of the most developed of the Persian Gulf sheikdoms. The Amir, Sheik Isa bin-Sulman al-Khalifa, who succeeded to the post in 1961, is a member of the al-Khalifa family that has governed Bahrain since 1782. Bahrain announced its independence as a sovereign state on Aug. 14, 1971.

**Economy.** Bahrain is becoming an offshore financial center for the oil-rich Middle East. The refinery on Bahrain Island is the second largest in the Middle East. Citrus fruits, dates, and vegetables are grown on Bahrain Island. Manufactures include sailcloth and reed mats. The principal port is Manama on the Persian Gulf.

Chief exports in 1975 were petroleum products (74%) and aluminum (8%).

## BANGLADESH

**People's Republic of Bangladesh**
**President:** Gen. Ziaur Rahman (1977)
**Area:** 55,598 sq mi. (143,998 sq km)
**Population (est. 1978):** 82,500,000
**Density per square mile:** 1,483.9
**Capital and largest city (est. 1974):** Dacca, 1,679,600
**Monetary unit:** Taka
**Principal languages:** Bengali (official), English
**Religions:** Islam, 85%; Hindu, 13%
**Gross national product (1976):** $8.5 billion
**Member of the Commonwealth of Nations**
**Freedom House classifications:** Capitalist-statist pre-industrial, non-party military

**Geography.** Bangladesh, on the northern coast of the Bay of Bengal, is surrounded by India, with a small common border with Burma in the southeast. It is approximately the size of Wisconsin. The country is low-lying riverine land traversed by the many branches and tributaries of the Ganges and Brahmaputra rivers. Elevation averages less than 600 feet above sea level. Tropical monsoons and frequent floods and cyclones inflict heavy damage in the delta region.

**Government.** Bangladesh, formerly East Pakistan, achieved independence in December 1971 when Indian and Bengali troops defeated West Pakistan after a two-week war. The new nation was established as a parliamentary democracy, with the leader of the independence movement, Sheik Mujibur Rahman, as its first Prime Minister. A Constitution approved in December 1972 provided for a 315-seat National Assembly.

The Assembly voted unanimously on Jan. 25, 1975, to amend the Constitution to make Mujibur President and to give him full executive powers.

Mujibur's assassination on Aug. 15, 1975, ended constitutional government and brought the first of a series of martial-law administrations that have governed Bangladesh since.

In January 1975, the National Assembly outlawed all parties except the Awami League, dominant party in the independence movement. The regime that succeeded Mujibur dissolved the League on Aug. 30, 1975, and banned formation of any new parties. However, more than a score of parties, including the Awami League and Muslim League, campaigned in the 1977 municipal-council elections.

**History.** The former East Pakistan, like West Pakistan and India, was part of imperial British India until Britain withdrew in 1947. The two Pakistans were united by religion (Moslem), but their peoples were separated by culture, physical features, and 1,000 miles of Indian territory. Bangladesh consists primarily of East Bengal (West Bengal is part of India and its people are primarily Hindu) plus the Sylhet district of the Indian state of Assam. For almost 25 years after independence from the U.K., its history was as part of Pakistan (*see* Pakistan).

The East Pakistanis unsuccessfully sought greater autonomy from West Pakistan. The first general elections in Pakistani history, in December 1970, saw virtually all 171 seats of the region (out of 300 for both East and West Pakistan) go to Sheik Mujibur Rahman's Awami League, with the rest to other similarly independence-minded minor parties.

Attempts to write an all-Pakistan Constitution to replace the military regime of Gen. Yahya Khan failed. General strikes in East Pakistan followed at Mujibur's direction; he also told his followers to stop paying taxes. Yahya bloodily put down his revolt in March 1971. An estimated one million Bengalis were killed in the fighting or later slaughtered. Ten million more took refuge in India.

In December 1971, India invaded East Pakistan, routed the West Pakistani occupation forces, and created Bangladesh. The U.S. opposed its violent creation, but recognized Bangladesh in April 1972 and provided several hundred million dollars in relief aid.

In February 1974, Pakistan agreed to recognize the independence of Bangladesh. India, Pakistan, and Bangladesh signed an agreement April 19, 1974, that provided for release of all Pakistani prisoners, improved conditions for the Bihari minority seeking to emigrate from Bangladesh to Pakistan, and negotiations to restore normal communication between the three states.

The charismatic Mujibur had a following of millions and near-dictatorial powers, but he failed to cope with poverty, starvation, sporadic political violence, and widespread government corruption. In June, after press criticism, his government nationalized the press, closing down all but four daily newspapers.

Before dawn on Aug. 15, 1975, Mujibur, his wife, and several relatives were assassinated in a coup led by young Army officers. As the new President, they installed Khondakar Mushtaque Ahmed, a founder of the Awami League who was then serving as Minister of Foreign Trade and Commerce. After sporadic fighting in which a reported 200 persons died, borders were sealed, martial law was imposed, and Ahmed was established at the head of a government run mostly by ministers inherited from Mujibur.

A military coup forced Ahmed from power Nov. 6, 1975, and installed former Supreme Court Chief Justice Abu Sadat Mohammed Sayem as President and "chief martial law administrator." On Nov. 30, 1976, Gen Ziaur Rahman, Army Chief of Staff, took over Sayem's powers and blocked the national elections scheduled for early 1977. On April 21, 1977, Ziaur became President following Sayem's resignation.

**Economy.** Predominantly a rural economy, Bangladesh's principal crops are rice, tea, and jute.

Chief exports in 1976 were jute products (46%), jute (28%), and leather (9%). Leading customers were U.S. (16%), U.K. (9%), Italy (6%), Mozambique (5%). Leading suppliers were U.S. (16%), Australia (9%), Canada (7%), India (7%), Japan (7%), U.K. (6%), Iran (5%).

## BARBADOS

**Sovereign:** Queen Elizabeth II
**Governor-General:** Sir Deighton L. Ward
**Prime Minister:** J. M. G. Adams (1976)
**Area:** 166 sq mi. (431 sq km)
**Population (est. 1978):** 260,000
**Density per square mile:** 1,566.3
**Capital and largest city (1970 census):** Bridgetown, 8,900
**Monetary unit:** Barbados dollar
**Language:** English
**Religions:** Anglican, 53%; Methodist, 9%; Roman Catholic, 4%
**Gross national product (1976):** $380 million
**Member of Commonwealth of Nations**
**Freedom House classifications:** Capitalist industrialist, multi-party centralized

**Geography.** An island in the Atlantic about 300 miles north of Venezuela, Barbados is only 21 miles long and 14 miles across at its widest point. It is circled by fine beaches and narrow coastal plains. The highest point is Mount Hillaby (1,105 ft; 337 m) in the north central area.

**Government.** The Barbados legislature dates from 1627. It is bicameral, with a Senate of 21 appointed members and an Assembly of 24 elected members.

The major political parties are the Barbados Labour Party (17 seats in Assembly), led by Prime Minister J. M. G. Adams; Democratic Labour Party (7 seats), led by Errol Barrow.

**History.** Barbados, with a population 90% black, was settled by the British in 1627. It became a crown colony in 1885. It was a member of the Federation of the West Indies from 1958 to 1962. Britain granted the colony independence on Nov. 30, 1966, and it became a parliamentary democracy.

While retaining membership in the Commonwealth of Nations and economic ties with the U.K., Barbados seeks broader economic and political relations with Western Hemisphere countries. Diplomatic ties with Cuba were established in 1972.

**Economy.** Although unemployment is high, tourism and light industry give Barbados a higher standard of living than most other Caribbean islands. Agricultural products are sugar, cotton, maize, and cassava. Manufactures are rum and molasses.

Chief exports in 1975 were sugar (47%), petroleum and products (13%), clothing (12%), and molasses (5%). Leading customers were U.S. (30%), U.K. (27%), Canada (6%), Trinidad and Tobago (6%), Windward Islands (5%). Leading suppliers were U.K. (22%), U.S. (19%), Trinidad and Tobago (10%), Venezuela (10%), Canada (9%).

## BELGIUM

**Kingdom of Belgium**
**Sovereign:** King Baudouin I (1951)
**Premier:** Léo Tindemans (1974)
**Area:** 11,781 sq mi. (30,513 sq km)
**Population (est. 1978):** 9,845,000
**Density per square mile:** 835.7
**Capital:** Brussels
**Largest cities (est. urban area 1977):** Brussels, 1,042,000; **(est. 1974):** Antwerp, 673,000; Liège, 444,000; Ghent, 235,000
**Monetary unit:** Belgian franc
**Languages:** Dutch, 56%; French, 32%; bilingual (Brussels), 11%
**Religion:** Roman Catholic, 97%
**Gross national product (1976):** $68.5 billion
**National name:** Royaume de Belgique—Koninkrijk België
**Freedom House classifications:** Capitalist industrial, multi-party decentralized

**Geography.** A neighbor of France, West Germany, the Netherlands, and Luxembourg, Belgium has about 40 miles of seacoast on the North Sea at the Strait of Dover. In area, it is approximately the size of Maryland. The northern third of the country is a plain extending eastward from the seacoast. North of the Sambre and Meuse Rivers is a low plateau; to the south lies the heavily wooded Ardennes plateau, attaining an elevation of about 2,300 feet (700 m).

The Schelde River, which rises in France and flows through Belgium, emptying into the Schelde estuaries, enables Antwerp to be an ocean port.

**Government.** Belgium is a parliamentary democracy under a constitutional monarch, consisting of nine provinces. Its bicameral legislature has a Senate, with its 181 members elected for four years, 106 by general election, 50 by provincial councillors and 25 by the Senate itself. The 212-member Chamber of Representatives is directly elected for four years by proportional representation. There is universal suffrage, and those who do not vote are fined.

Belgium joined the North Atlantic Alliance in April 1949 and is a member of the European Community. NATO and the European Community have their headquarters in Brussels. The present Cabinet is a coalition of the Social Christians (CVP/PSC), Socialists (BSP/PSB), Flemish nationalists (VU), and Brussels Francophones (FDF).

The sovereign, Baudouin I, was born Sept. 7, 1930, the son of King Leopold III and Queen Astrid. He became King on July 17, 1951, after the abdication of his father. He married Doña Fabiola de Mora y Aragón on Dec. 15, 1960. Since he has no children, his brother, Prince Albert, is heir to the throne.

The major political parties are the Social Christian parties (70 Senators, 80 Representatives), Socialist parties (52 Senators, 62 Representatives), Liberal parties (26 Senators, 33 Representatives), Volksunie (Flemish Nationalist Party) (17 Senators, 20 Representatives), Rassemblement Wallon-Democratic Front of Francophones (15 Senators, and 5 and 10 Representatives respectively), and the Communists (1 Senator, 2 Representatives).

**History.** Belgium occupies part of the Roman province of Belgica, named after the Belgae, a people of ancient Gaul. The area was conquered by Julius Caesar in 57–50 B.C., then was overrun by the Franks in the 5th century. It was part of Charlemagne's empire in the 8th century, then in the next century was absorbed into Lotharingia and later into the Duchy of Lower Lorraine. In the 12th century it was partitioned into the Duchies of Brabant and Luxembourg, the Bishopric of Liège, and the domain of the Count of Hainaut, which included Flanders.

The rise of the wool industry brought prosperity and power to the country, particularly to the semi-independent cities—Ghent, Bruges, and Ypres. In the 16th century, Belgium, with most of the area of the Low Countries, passed to the Duchy of Burgundy and was the marriage portion of Archduke Maximilian of Hapsburg and the inheritance of his grandson, Charles V, who incorporated it into his empire. Then, in 1555, they were united with Spain.

By the treaty of Utrecht in 1713, the country's sovereignty passed to Austria. During the wars that followed the French Revolution, Belgium was occupied and later annexed to France. But with the downfall of Napoleon, the Congress of Vienna in 1815 gave the country to the Netherlands. The Belgians revolted in 1830 and declared their independence.

Germany's invasion of Belgium in 1914 set off World War I. The Treaty of Versailles (1919) gave the areas of Eupen, Malmédy, and Moresnet to Belgium. Leopold III succeeded Albert, King during World War I, in 1934. In World War II, Belgium was overwhelmed by Nazi Germany, and Leopold III was made prisoner. When he attempted to return in 1950, Socialists and Liberals revolted. He abdicated July 16, 1951, and his son, Baudouin, became King the next day.

The country has long been torn by language disputes between the Dutch-speaking Flemish people and the French-speaking Walloons. The three largest political parties have two leaders, one from each community. Constant compromises must be struck within the government to allow the country to remain unified. In 1972, a major clash occurred over transferring six small hamlets from Flemish to Walloon administrative jurisdiction. When a balancing change was not implemented, the government fell. A new one under Edmond Leburton was formed; this, in turn, was replaced in April 1974 by one under Léo Tindemans of the Flemish Social Christian party (CVP).

Tindemans' coalition reached agreement Jan. 17, 1978, on a plan to begin in January 1979 the transformation of the nation into a federated state by the mid-80's. The plan would divide Belgium into Dutch- and French-speaking areas.

Belgium sent 1,700 troops to the combat area when Katangese rebels invaded Zaire's Shaba province in May although they were used only for evacuation of Europeans and for relief work. French troops moved in more quickly and drove the rebels back, performing so aggressively that Belgians complained that the French were seeking to displace Belgian influence in the former Belgian colony. In Paris, Belgium attended the post-Shaba meeting of participants in the rescue operation and backed the creation of a permanent African peacekeeping force.

**Economy.** About 60% of the total area of Belgium is under cultivation, and one half the farmed area is devoted to forage crops. Other crops are fodder beets, flax, and fruit. The pastoral industry, especially dairy farming, flourishes.

Industry chiefly processes imported raw materials for re-export in semifinished or finished form. Of primary importance are iron and steel, nonferrous metals, fabricated metal products, and textiles. Associated with iron and steel are a considerable engineering industry, ship-building in Antwerp, and machinery and railway stock in Brussels. The centuries-old textile industry produces linen (Courtrai), cotton (the southeast), and synthetic fibers. Antwerp rivals Amsterdam in diamond cutting. The principal mineral is coal.

Chief exports in 1976 were chemicals (12%), machinery (12%), iron and steel (12%), motor vehicles (11%), food (8%), textile yarns and fabrics (7%), and petroleum products (5%). Leading customer was EEC (76%; incl. West Germany 23%, France 21%, Netherlands 17%, U.K. 6%, Italy 5%). Leading suppliers were EEC (68%; incl. West Germany 23%, Netherlands 17%, France 16%, U.K. 7%), U.S. (6%).

# BENIN

**People's Republic of Benin**
**President:** Lt. Col. Mathieu Kerekou (1972)
**Area:** 43,483 sq mi. (112,622 sq km)
**Population (est. 1978):** 3,380,000
**Density per square mile:** 77.7
**Capital:** Porto-Novo
**Largest cities (est. 1972):** Cotonou, 175,000; Porto-Novo, 100,000; Abomey, 50,000; Ouidah, 30,000
**Monetary unit:** Franc CFA
**Ethnic groups:** Fons and Adjas, Boribas, Yorubas, Mahis
**Languages:** French, African languages
**Religions:** Animist, Christian, Islam
**Gross national product (1976):** $430 million
**National name:** République Populaire du Benin
**Freedom House classifications:** Socialist pre-industrial, one-party socialist

**Geography.** This West African nation on the Gulf of Guinea, between Togo on the west and Nigeria on the east, is about the size of Tennessee. The land consists of a narrow coastal strip that rises to a swampy, forested plateau and then to highlands in the north. A hot and humid climate blankets the entire country.

**Government.** The change in name from Dahomey to Benin was announced by President Mathieu Kerekou Nov. 30, 1975. Benin commemorates an African kingdom that flourished in the 17th century. At the same time, Kerekou announced the formation of a political organization, the Party of the People's Revolution of Benin, to mark the first anniversary of his declaration of a "new society" guided by Marxist-Leninist principles.

One of the smallest and most densely populated states in Africa, Benin was annexed by the French in 1893. The area was incorporated into French West Africa in 1904. After World War II it became in 1958 an autonomous republic within the French

Community, and on Aug. 1, 1960, was granted its independence within the Community.

General Christophe Soglo deposed the first President, Hubert Maga, in an army coup in 1963, dismissed the civilian government in 1965, proclaimed himself chief of state. A group of young army officers seized power in December 1967, deposing Soglo. They promulgated a new Constitution in 1968.

On Dec. 10, 1969, Benin had its fifth coup of the decade, with the Army again taking power. In May 1970, a three-man presidential commission was created to take over the government. The commission had a six-year term; each member serves as President for two years. Maga turned over power as scheduled to Justin Ahomadegbe in May 1972, but six months later yet another Army coup ousted the triumvirate and installed Lt. Col. Mathieu Kerekou as President.

**Economy.** The most important economic activity is the production of palm oil. Other agricultural products include cassava, peanuts, cottonseed, sweet potatoes, corn, and coffee.

Chief exports in 1972 were cotton (28%), cocoa (19%), palm products (17%), cottonseed (5%), and coffee (5%). Leading customers in 1973 were France (36%), West Germany (12%), Netherlands (10%), Italy (6%), Japan (5%). Leading suppliers were France (36%), West Germany (7%), China (7%), U.K. (5%), Netherlands (5%), U.S. (5%).

## BHUTAN

**Kingdom of Bhutan**
**Ruler:** King Jigme Singye Wangchuk (1972)
**Area:** 18,147 sq mi. (47,000 sq km)
**Population (est. 1977):** 1,235,000
**Density per square mile:** 68.1
**Capital (est. 1974):** Thimphu, 15,000
**Monetary unit:** Ngultrum and Indian rupee
**Language:** Dzongkha
**Religions:** Buddhist, 75%; Hindu, 25%
**Gross national product (1976):** $90 million
**National name:** Druk-yul
**Freedom House classifications:** Capitalist pre-industrial, non-party traditional

**Geography.** Mountainous Bhutan, half the size of Indiana, is situated on the southeast slope of the Himalayas, bordered on the north and east by Tibet and on the south and west by India. The landscape consists of a succession of lofty and rugged mountains running generally from north to south and separated by deep valleys. In the north, towering peaks reach a height of 24,000 feet (7,315 m).

**Government.** Bhutan is a constitutional monarchy. The King rules with a Council of Ministers and a nine-member Advisory Council, of whom five are elected by the people; two represent the monastic order and two are named by the King. There is a National Assembly (Parliament), which meets semiannually, but no political parties.

**History.** After almost a century of conflict, British troops invaded the country in 1865 and negotiated an agreement under which Britain undertook to pay an annual allowance to Bhutan on condition of good behavior. A treaty with India in 1949 increased this subsidy and placed Bhutan's foreign affairs under Indian control.

In the 1960s, Bhutan undertook modernization, abolishing slavery and the caste system, emancipating women, breaking up estates, and limiting farms to 30 acres.

**Economy.** The chief crops are rice, corn, and millet; the fields, laid out on hillside terraces, are watered by an ingenious system of irrigation. Bhutan is famous for its small though sturdy mountain ponies.

The chief industries are metal work, cloth weaving, and fine basket and mat work. Trade is insignificant, much of it by barter. About 95% of external trade is with India.

Chief exports are timber, coal, fruit and fruit products, and alcoholic spirits.

## BOLIVIA

**Republic of Bolivia**
**President:** Gen. Juan Pereda Asbún (1978)
**Area:** 424,162 sq mi. (1,098,581 sq km)
**Population (est. 1978):** 6,110,000 (Indian, 53%; mestizo, 32%; white, 15%)
**Density per square mile:** 14.4
**Judicial capital (est. 1976):** Sucre, 90,000
**Administrative capital:** La Paz
**Largest cities (est. 1976 by U.N.):** La Paz, 654,700; Santa Cruz, 237,100; Cochabamba, 194,150; Oruro, 124,100
**Monetary unit:** Peso boliviano
**Languages:** Spanish, Quechua, Aymara
**Religion:** Roman Catholic, 94%
**Gross national product (1976):** $2.3 billion
**National name:** República de Bolivia
**Freedom House classifications:** Capitalist-socialist pre-industrial, non-party military

**Geography.** Landlocked Bolivia, equal in size to California and Texas combined, lies to the west of Brazil. It is a low alluvial plain throughout 60% of its area toward the east, drained by the Amazon and Plata river systems. The western part, enclosed by two chains of the Andes, is a great plateau—the Altiplano, with an average altitude of 12,000 feet (3,658 m). More than 80% of the population lives on the plateau, which also contains La Paz, the highest capital city in the world.

Lake Titicaca, half the size of Lake Ontario, is one of the highest large lakes in the world, at an altitude of 12,507 feet (3,812 m). Islands in the lake hold ruins of the ancient Incas.

**Government.** Bolivia is a republic, electing by popular vote a President every four years, a 27-member Senate every six years, and a 102-member Chamber of Deputies every four years. The President appoints the members of his Cabinet. Congress was dissolved in September 1969 and has not been reconvened.

In 1967, a new Constitution replaced the Constitution of 1947.

A succession of coups d'etat in recent years has produced an average of one new President a year, ending with the seizure of power by Col. Hugo Banzer Suárez in August 1971. Banzer's seven-year tenure set a record for continuous leadership in Bolivia.

The major political parties are Falange Socialista Boliviana (FSB) and Movimiento Nacionalista Revolucionario (MNR).

**History.** Famous since Spanish colonial days for its mineral wealth, modern Bolivia was once a part of the ancient Incan Empire. After the Spaniards had defeated the Incas in the 16th century, Bolivia's predominantly Indian population was reduced to slavery. The country won its independence in 1825; the new republic was named after Simón Bolívar, the famed liberator.

Since 1825 Bolivia has had more than sixty revolutions, seventy Presidents, and eleven Constitutions.

Harassed by internal strife, Bolivia lost great slices of territory to three neighbor nations. Several thousand square miles and its outlet to the Pacific were taken by Chile after the War of the Pacific (1879–84). In 1903 a piece of Bolivia's Acre province, rich in rubber, was ceded to Brazil. And in 1938, after a war with Paraguay, Bolivia gave up claim to nearly 100,000 square miles of the Gran Chaco.

Great prosperity came with World War II and its demand for two important Bolivian products, tin and wolframite. But rising prices provoked strikes that were ruthlessly broken and promoted growth of the leftist National Revolutionary Movement. The movement seized power in 1943 but was ousted by a moderate government in 1947.

In 1965 a guerrilla movement mounted from Cuba and headed by Maj. Ernesto (Ché) Guevara began a revolutionary war. With the aid of U.S. military advisers, the Bolivian Army, helped by the peasants, smashed the guerrilla movement, wounding and capturing Guevara on Oct. 8, 1967, and shooting him to death the next day.

Banzer, on accession in 1971, promised that general elections would be held, but this was rescinded in November 1974, when the armed forces took control following suppression of a revolt by disaffected troops.

In January 1976, Banzer appointed a commission to study a proposal by Chile to grant Bolivia a corridor to the Pacific. Peruvian agreement would be required, because the coastal area under consideration was ceded to Chile by Peru after the War of the Pacific.

A counterproposal by Bolivia was rejected by Chile in December, and in early 1977 any solution seemed imperiled by rising tensions between Chile and Peru.

In common with many of its Latin neighbors, Bolivia was charged with violations of human rights by the U.S. State Department report of March 1977.

When Assistant Secretary of State for Inter-American Affairs Terence Todman visited Bolivia in May, he was told that the Government had made political arrests, shut down labor unions, and deported journalists. Although the government denied the charges, Catholic, Lutheran, and Methodist representatives formed a Permanent Assembly on Human Rights on May 14, with former President Luis Adolfo Siles Salinas as the group's head.

Banzer authorized the first elections since 1966 to take place July 9, but after charges of fraud, Gen. Juan Pereda Asbún, the disputed winner, declared himself President with the backing of the armed forces. Opposition candidates called for new elections soon but Pereda said they could not be held before 1980. In 1979, he said, he wishes to concentrate national energies on regaining the access to the sea that Bolivia had lost to Chile in 1884.

The elections of July 9 were voided by the National Electoral Court on the basis of irregularities. Supporters of General Juan Pereda Asbún seized power. On July 24, General Pereda, as President, installed his new cabinet and promised a continuation of the democratization process.

In August 1978, the United States announced that it would continue economic aid to Bolivia, while reserving decision on its military assistance program. The U.S. foreign aid program for Bolivia, the largest for any Latin American nation, ($56.1 million proposed for fiscal 1979) had been held up as a sign of U.S. displeasure over the military coup which followed the cancellation of Bolivia's presidential elections.

**Economy.** U.S. Economic aid to Bolivia approached $100,000,000 a year in 1978. Private foreign banks lent Bolivia $240,000,000 in 1977.

Production of such basic foodstuffs as wheat and rice is insufficient for domestic needs, and considerable quantities must be imported. Cattle are raised in the more temperate regions of the east and south, sheep in the departments of La Paz and Cochabamba, and llamas, alpacas, vicuñas, and chinchillas are raised on the plateaus.

Mining is the backbone of the economy. Tin is by far the most important mineral.

Because Bolivia has no access to the sea, foreign trade must pass through free ports in Chile and river ports on the Amazon.

Chief exports in 1975 were tin (44%), crude oil (22%), natural gas (11%), zinc (8%), tungsten (7%), antimony (6%), and silver (5%). Leading customers were U.S. (31%), Argentina (25%), U.K. (11%). Leading suppliers were U.S. (25%), Japan (16%), Argentina (14%), Brazil (14%), West Germany (8%).

## BOPHUTHATSWANA

**See South Africa**

# BOTSWANA

**Republic of Botswana**
**President:** Sir Seretse Khama (1966)
**Area:** 231,804 sq mi. (600,372 sq km)
**Population (est. 1978):** 725,000
**Density per square mile:** 3.1
**Capital and largest city** (est. 1976): Gaborone, 36,900
**Monetary unit:** Pula
**Languages:** English, Setswana
**Religions:** Christian, 60%; Animist
**Gross national product (1976):** $280 million
**Member of Commonwealth of Nations**
**Freedom House classifications:** Capitalist pre-industrial, multi-party decentralized

**Geography.** Twice the size of Arizona, Botswana is in south central Africa, bounded by South-West Africa, Zambia, Rhodesia, and South Africa. Most of the country is near-desert, with the Kalahari occupying the western part of the country. The eastern part is hilly, with salt lakes in the north.

**Government.** The Botswana Constitution provides, in addition to the unicameral National Assembly, for a House of Chiefs, which has a voice on bills affecting tribal affairs. There is universal adult suffrage.

The major political parties are the Democratic Party (27 of 32 elective seats in 36-man Legislative Assembly), led by President Seretse Khama; People's Party (2 seats), led by Philip Matante; National Front (2 seats), led by Kenneth Koma; Independence Party (1 seat), led by Motsamai Mpho.

**History.** Botswana is the land of the Batawana tribes, who, when threatened by the Boers in Transvaal, got the U.K., in 1885, to establish a protectorate over the country, then known as Bechuanaland. In 1961, the U.K. granted a Constitution to the country. Self-government began in 1965. On Sept. 30, 1966, the country became an independent member of the Commonwealth of Nations. In 1971, it was offered associate membership in the European Common Market. The association was ratified in 1975.

**Economy.** The country was essentially pastoral, chiefly cattle-raising and dairy farming, but during the past five years mining investment for diamonds, nickel, copper, and coal deposits has increased.

Chief exports in 1975 were mineral products (mainly diamonds, 49%) and meat and meat products (36%).

## BRAZIL

**Federative Republic of Brazil**
President: Gen. Ernesto Geisel (1974)
Area: 3,286,487 sq mi. (8,511,965 sq km)
Population (est. 1978): 115,450,000 (approx.: white, 60%; mestizo, 26%; black, 11%)
Density per square mile: 35.1
Capital (est. 1977): Brasília, 763,250
Largest cities (est. 1977): São Paulo, 7,198,600; Rio de Janeiro, 4,857,500; Belo Horizonte, 1,557,500; Recife, 1,249,800
Monetary unit: Cruzeiro
Language: Portuguese
Religion: Roman Catholic, 89%
Gross national product (1976): $125.0 billion
National name: Brasil
Freedom House classifications: Capitalist-statist industrial, multi-party decentralized

**Geography.** Brazil covers about three sevenths of South America, extends 2,965 miles north-south, 2,691 miles east-west, and borders every South American state except Chile and Ecuador. It is the fifth largest country in the world, ranking after the U.S.S.R., China, Canada, and the U.S.

More than a third of Brazil is drained by the Amazon and its more than 200 tributaries. The Amazon is navigable for ocean steamers to Iquitos, Peru, 2,300 miles (3,700 km) upstream. Southern Brazil is drained by the Plata system—the Paraguay, Uruguay, and Paraná rivers. The most important stream entirely within Brazil is the São Francisco, navigable for a thousand miles, but broken near its mouth by the 275-foot (84 m) Paulo Afonso Falls.

**Government.** Under the Constitution, Brazil is a union of 21 states, 5 territories, and 1 federal district. The President is elected by the vote of an electoral college for a term of five years. The National Congress is composed of two houses—the Senate, whose members serve for eight-year terms, and the Chamber of Deputies, elected for four-year terms. Members of Congress are elected by equal, direct, compulsory, and secret suffrage under proportional representation.

The military took control in 1964, ousting the last elected civilian President and installing a military man (with the Congress ratifying the junta's choice). Gen. Arthur Costa e Silva became President in 1966, but when he died suddenly three years later, the junta (composed of three service ministers) brushed aside the legitimate successor, Vice President Pedro Aleixo, a civilian, and named Gen. Emilio Garrastazu Médici as President. Congress then elected him to the post. In 1970, Médici announced that the military would rule indefinitely (until "economic, social, racial and political democracy" is attained).

Médici and the military chose Gen. Ernesto Geisel to become his successor in 1974.

The major political parties are Alianca Renovadora Nacional (ARENA), led by Sen. Petronio Portela; Movimento Democratico Brasileiro (MDB), led by Congressman Ulysses Guimarães.

**History.** Brazil is the only Latin American nation deriving its language and culture from Portugal. Adm. Pedro Alvares Cabral claimed the territory for the Portuguese in 1500. He brought to Portugal a cargo of wood, pau-brasil, from which the land received its name. Portugal began colonization in 1532 and made the area a royal colony in 1549.

During the Napoleonic wars, King João VI, then Prince Regent, fled the country in 1807 in advance of the French armies and in 1808 set up his court in Rio de Janeiro. João was drawn home in 1820 by a revolution, leaving his son as Regent. When Portugal sought to reduce Brazil again to colonial status, the prince declared Brazil's independence on Sept. 7, 1822, and became Pedro I, Emperor of Brazil.

Harassed by his parliament, Pedro I abdicated in 1831 in favor of his five-year-old son, who became Emperor in 1840 as Pedro II. The son was a popular monarch, but discontent built up and, in 1889, following a military revolt, he had to abdicate. A republic was set up, but until 1893 Brazil was under two military dictatorships. A revolt permitted a gradual return to stability under civilian presidents. Slavery was abolished in 1888.

The President during World War I, Wenceslau Braz, cooperated with the Allies and declared war on Germany. The President from 1926 to 1930, Washington Luiz Pereira da Souza, was overthrown by a revolutionary group under Getulio Vargas, who took over as provisional President.

Vargas' 1934 Constitution curtailed states' rights and established a nationalistic policy. In 1937, Vargas seized absolute power and adopted another Constitution, extending his term indefinitely. In World War II, Brazil cooperated with the Western Allies, welcoming Allied air bases, patrolling the South Atlantic, and joining the invasion of Italy after declaring war on the Axis.

Vargas was overthrown on Oct. 29, 1945. Succeeding presidents were Gen. Eurico Gaspar Dutra (1945–50); Getulio Vargas (1950–54); João Cafe Filho (1954–55); Juscelino Kubitschek de Oliveira (1955–60); Janio Quadros (1960); João Goulart (1960–63); Gen. Humberto de Alencar Castelo Branco (1963–66); Gen. Arthur Costa e Silva (1966–69); Gen. Emilio Garrastazu Médici (1970–74); Gen. Ernesto Geisel (1974– ).

Elections in November 1974 brought sharp gains for the MDB party. These were interpreted as a rebuke to Geisel and the ruling ARENA party for violations of human rights and an inflation rate estimated at 33%. The election was the freest in a decade and the least violent in many years. Press censorship was relaxed under a policy of "decompression."

Geisel tightened political controls in 1977, suspending Congress on April 1 when opposition legislators balked at approving election procedures guaranteeing ARENA control over state governments. On Jan. 5, 1978, Geisel announced his choice for ARENA's candidate in the 1979 presidential election, Gen. João Baptista de Oliveira Figueiredo, a choice criticized by the Army because Figueiredo was not a commander but a staff officer and by civilians because they had hoped for a return to direct elections.

Relations with the U.S. remained cool following Geisel's 1977 repudiation of a mutual defense pact after a U.S. State Department report cited the military regime's repression of human rights, and Brazil emphasized that President Carter was coming on his own request when he visited Brazil in March. The U.S. also opposed Brazil's purchase of German nuclear equipment capable of reprocessing spent nuclear fuel into plutonium of weapons grade.

**Economy.** Agriculture is a mainstay of Brazil's economy, but only 4% of its area is under cultivation, the rest being grazing, forest, or nonproductive land. Brazil leads the world in production of coffee and castor beans and ranks third in cacao. Export of both coffee and cacao is government controlled.

Livestock is raised nearly everywhere, with the great centers in the central and northern states.

Industry is now an important segment of the economy. The principal fields are automobile manufacturing, electric-power production, cement production, shipbuilding, and oil refining.

Brazil's vast mineral resources are among her least developed assets. Important minerals are coal, iron ore, gold, manganese ore, crude petroleum, bauxite, diamonds, silver, quartz crystals, and uranium.

The nation's first nuclear power plant, near Rio de Janeiro, was the first producing unit in South America.

The largest single forest commodities are timber, chiefly pine from the southern states, and the wax of the carnauba palm, used for insulation and phonograph records and produced commercially only in Brazil.

Chief exports in 1975 were sugar (13%), coffee (11%), iron ore (11%), soybeans (8%), machinery (7%), and animal fodder (6%). Leading customers in 1976 were U.S. (18%), West Germany (9%), Netherlands (7%), Japan (6%). Leading suppliers were U.S. (23%), Saudi Arabia (9%), Iraq (9%), West Germany (8%), Japan (7%).

## BULGARIA

**People's Republic of Bulgaria**
**Chairman of the State Council:** Todor Zhivkov (1971)
**Prime Minister (Chairman of Council of Ministers):** Stanko Todorov (1971)
**Area:** 42,823 sq mi. (110,912 sq km)
**Population (est. 1978):** 8,840,000
**Density per square mile:** 206.4
**Capital:** Sofia
**Largest cities (est. 1975):** Sofia, 965,700; (est. 1974 by U.N.): Plovdiv, 305,100; Varna, 270,000; Ruse, 171,300; Burgas, 148,200; Stara Zagora, 121,500
**Monetary unit:** Lev
**Language:** Bulgarian
**Religions:** Orthodox, 84%; Islam, 14%
**Gross national product (1976):** $20.3 billion
**National name:** Narodna Republika Bŭlgariya
**Freedom House classifications:** Socialist industrial, one-party communist

**Geography.** Two mountain ranges and two great valleys mark the topography of Bulgaria, a country the size of Tennessee. Situated on the Black Sea in the eastern part of the Balkan peninsula, it shares borders with Yugoslavia, Romania, Greece, and Turkey. The Balkan belt crosses the center of the country, almost due east-west, rising to a height of 7,800 feet (2,377 m). The Rhodope range breaks off from the Balkans in the west, curves, and then straightens out to run nearly parallel along the southern border. Between the two ranges, is the valley of the Maritsa, Bulgaria's principal river. Between the Balkan range and the Danube, which forms most of the northern boundary with Romania, is the Danubian tableland.

Southern Dobruja, a fertile region of 2,900 square miles (7,511 sq km), below the Danube delta, is an area of low hills, fens, and sandy steppes.

**Government.** The present Constitution has been in effect since May 18, 1971. The National Assembly, consisting of 400 members elected for five-year terms, is the governing body. It elects the State Council and the Council of Ministers.

The Communist Party is led by the chairman of the State Council, Todor Zhivkov.

**History.** The first Bulgarians, a tribe of wild horsemen akin to the Huns, crossed the Danube from the north in A.D. 679 and subjugated the Slavic population of Moesia. They adopted a Slav dialect and Slavic customs and twice conquered most of the Balkan peninsula between 893 and 1280. After the Serbs subjected their kingdom in 1330, the Bulgars gradually fell prey to the Turks, and from 1396 to 1878 Bulgaria was a Turkish province. In 1878, Russia forced Turkey to give the country its independence; but the European powers, fearing that Bulgaria might become a Russian dependency, intervened. By the Treaty of Berlin (July 1878), Bulgaria became autonomous under Turkish sovereignty.

In 1887, Prince Ferdinand of Saxe-Coburg-Gotha was elected ruler of Bulgaria; on Oct. 5, 1908, he declared the country independent and took the title of Tsar.

Bulgaria joined Germany in World War I and lost. On Oct. 3, 1918, Tsar Ferdinand abdicated in favor of his son, Tsar Boris III. Boris assumed dictatorial powers in 1934–35. When Hitler awarded Bulgaria Southern Dobruja, taken from Romania in 1940, the weak but land-hungry Boris joined the Nazis in war the next year and occupied parts of Yugoslavia and Greece. Later the Germans tried to force Boris to send his troops against the Russians. Boris resisted and died under mysterious circumstances on Aug. 28, 1943.

Simeon II, infant son of Boris, became nominal ruler under a regency. Russia declared war on Bulgaria on Sept. 5, 1944. An armistice was agreed to three days later, after Bulgaria had declared war on Germany. Russian troops streamed in the next day, and under an informal armistice a coalition "Fatherland Front" Cabinet was set up under Kimon Georgiev.

A peace treaty negotiated in 1947 permitted Bulgaria to keep southern Dobruja. A Constitution was adopted in 1947 establishing a Soviet-type people's republic.

**Economy.** Bulgaria is still predominantly agrarian, with most of the population engaged in agriculture. Because of the mountainous character of the country, however, less than half of the land is tilled or used for pasture. Collectivization is well advanced. More than half the cultivated area is devoted to cereals, including wheat, corn, barley, oats, and rye. Other crops are tobacco, alfalfa, cotton, flax, potatoes, and sugar. There are extensive vineyards in the southern valleys.

Industries are of minor importance and with few exceptions—tobacco, wines and liquors, fertilizers, and flour—confined to domestic markets.

Soft coal is Bulgaria's principal mineral; others include chromite, gypsum, iron ore, manganese ore, rock salt, and silver.

Chief exports in 1974 were machinery (30%), tobacco and cigarettes (11%), transport equipment (9%), fruit and vegetables (8%), nonferrous metals (6%), chemicals (6%), iron and steel (6%), and wines and spirits (5%). Leading customers in 1975 were U.S.S.R. (55%), East Germany (7%), Czechoslovakia (5%). Leading suppliers were U.S.S.R. (51%), West Germany (8%), East Germany (7%), Poland (5%).

## BURMA

**Socialist Republic of the Union of Burma**
**President:** U Ne Win (1974)
**Prime Minister:** U Maung Maung Kha (1977)
**Area:** 261,217 sq mi. (676,552 sq km)
**Population (est. 1978):** 32,200,000
**Density per square mile:** 123.3
**Capital:** Rangoon
**Largest cities (est. 1973 for urban agglomeration):** Rangoon, 2,056,100; Mandalay, 417,300; Moulmein, 171,800; Bassein, 126,150
**Monetary unit:** Kyat
**Language:** Burmese
**Religions:** Buddhist, 80%; Christian, Islam, Hindu
**Gross national product (1976):** $3.7 billion
**National name:** Pyidaungsu Socialist Thammada Myanma Naingngandau
**Freedom House classifications:** Capitalist-socialist pre-industrial, one-party socialist.

**Geography.** Burma occupies the northwest portion of the former Indochinese peninsula. India lies to the northwest and China to the northeast. The Bay of Bengal touches the southwestern coast.

Slightly smaller than Texas, the country is divided into three natural regions: the Arakan Yoma, a long, narrow mountain range forming the barrier between Burma and India; the Shan Plateau in the east, extending southward into Tenasserim; and the Central Basin, running down to the flat fertile delta of the Irrawaddy in the south. This delta contains a network of intercommunicating canals and nine principal river mouths.

**Government.** On March 2, 1962, the government of U Nu was overthrown and replaced by a Revolutionary Council, which assumed all power in the state. Gen. U Ne Win, as chairman of the Revolutionary Council, became the chief executive.

A new Constitution was approved in 1973 and took effect Jan. 4, 1974. Under it, Burma is a Socialist Democratic Republic with a 451-seat unicameral legislature called the People's Congress. In 1972, Ne Win and his colleagues resigned their military titles and thereafter ruled as "civilians." In March 1974, Ne Win dissolved the Revolutionary Council and became President under the new Constitution; he is also chairman of the Council of State. The Burmese Socialist Program Party (the only legal party) is led by Ne Win.

**History.** In 1612, the British East India Company sent agents to Burma, but the Burmese long resisted efforts of British traders, and Dutch and Portuguese as well, to establish posts on the Bay of Bengal. By the Anglo-Burmese War in 1824–26 and two following wars, the British East India Company expanded to the whole of Burma by 1886. Burma was annexed to India. It became a separate colony in 1937.

During World War II, Burma was a key battleground; the 800-mile Burma Road was the Allies' vital supply line to China. The Japanese invaded the country in December 1941, and by May 1942 had occupied most of it, cutting the Burma Road. After one of the most difficult campaigns of the war, Allied forces liberated most of Burma prior to the Japanese surrender in August 1945. Burma became independent on Jan. 4, 1948. The new government was soon faced by armed uprisings of Communists and of Karen tribesmen. In 1949 the Karen rebels won a large degree of autonomy.

In 1951 and 1952 the Socialists achieved power, and Burma became the first Asian country to introduce social legislation.

In 1968, after the government had made headway against the Communist rebels, the military regime adopted a policy of strict nonalignment and followed "the Burmese Way" to socialism. But the insurgents, reportedly numbering several thousand and armed by China, continued active.

**Economy.** Burma is essentially agricultural, with crop growing concentrated in the delta and river valleys. It is a leading producer of rice, the staple food, which occupies two thirds of the cultivated area. Crops grown in the dry zone in upper Burma include millet, cotton, peanuts, and sesame. Other crops include tobacco, fruit, vegetables, and cereals. The number of rubber plantations has increased.

The principal domestic animals are water buffalo, which are used as beasts of burden in the delta, and small-humped oxen, which predominate in other areas.

Under the Socialist regime, all industry and rice production were nationalized and made monopolies of the state. All banks were also nationalized.

Leading industries are silk weaving and dyeing, rice husking, oil refining, and wood carving. The Baluchaung hydroelectric plant, one of the largest in Southeast Asia, was completed in 1960.

Mineral resources are lead, silver, zinc, nickel, cobalt, copper, gold, iron ore, molybdenum, coal, rubies, sapphires, and jade.

More than half of Burma is forested. Teak, valuable for naval construction, is the main timber product. Its cutting is strictly controlled.

Chief exports in 1975 were rice (58%) and teak (23%). Leading customers were Indonesia (14%), Singapore (13%), Sri Lanka (11%), Japan (10%), Netherlands (6%), Mauritius (6%). Leading suppliers were Japan (33%), China (9%), U.K. (8%), U.S. (7%), West Germany (7%), South Korea (5%).

## BURUNDI

**Republic of Burundi**
**President:** Lt. Col. Jean-Baptiste Bagaza (1976)
**Prime Minister:** Lt. Col. Edouard Nzambimana (1976)
**Area:** 10,747 sq mi. (27,834 sq km)
**Population (est. 1978):** 4,100,000

**Density per square mile:** 381.5
**Capital and largest city (est. 1970 for urban agglomeration):** Bujumbura, 110,000
**Monetary unit:** Burundi franc
**Languages:** Kirundi (official), French
**Religions:** Roman Catholic, 61%; Animist, 35%; Protestant, 4%
**Gross national product (1976):** $460 million
**National name:** Republika Y'Uburundi
**Freedom House classifications:** Capitalist-socialist pre-industrial, one-party socialist

**Geography.** Wedged between Tanzania and Zaire in east central Africa, Burundi occupies a high plateau divided by several deep valleys. It is equal in size to Maryland.

**Government.** Legislative and executive power is vested in the President.

Burundi's first Constitution, approved July 11, 1974, placed UPRONA (Unity and National Progress), the only political party, in control of national policy and automatically made Lt. Gen. Michel Micombero President.

**History.** Burundi was once part of German East Africa. An integrated society developed among the Watusi, a tall, warlike people and nomad cattle raisers, and the Bahutu, a Bantu people, who were subject farmers. Belgium won a League of Nations mandate in 1923, and subsequently Burundi, with Rwanda, was transferred to the status of a United Nations trust territory.

In 1962, Burundi gained independence and became a kingdom under Mwami Mwambutsa IV, with his son, Louis Rwangasore, as Premier. Shortly after, the son was assassinated. The second man to succeed him, Pierre Ngendandumwe, who took office in 1963, was assassinated in 1965 when an unsuccessful coup against the Watusi led to the massacre of many Bahutus.

Crown Prince Charles, returning from Europe, rallied Watusi extremists, ousted the Premier, suspended the Constitution, and renewed relations with Communist China. He deposed his father in 1966, reigned as Ntare V, with Micombero as Premier. Three months later, Micombero, in a military coup, overthrew the Mwami and established a republic, installing himself as President.

One of Africa's worst tribal wars, which became genocide, occurred in Burundi in April 1972, following the return of Ntare. He was given a safe-conduct promise in writing by Micombero but was "judged and immediately executed" by the Burundi leader. His return was apparently attended by an invasion of exiles of Burundi's Hutu tribe. Although Hutus make up 85% of the population, they have been dominated for centuries by the minority Tutsi tribe of Micombero. Whether Hutus living in Burundi joined the invasion is unclear, but after it failed, the victorious Tutsis proceeded to massacre some 100,000 persons in six weeks, with possibly 100,000 more slain by summer.

On Nov. 1, 1976, a military coup led by Lt. Col. Jean-Baptiste Bagaza ousted Micombero, who was serving his second term. Bagaza assumed the presidency Nov. 3, suspended the Constitution, and announced that a 30-member Supreme Revolutionary Council would be the governing body.

On Jan. 7, 1977, the Council gave Bagaza a mandate for a renewable 5-year term and proposed its own dissolution, once UPRONA is reorganized.

**Economy.** Because of overpopulation, poor soil, and irregular rainfall, Burundi, principally an agricultural and cattle-raising country, is just able to feed itself.

Agricultural products are sweet potatoes, dry beans, coffee, and cotton. Livestock include cattle and sheep.

Chief export in 1976 was coffee (89%). Leading customers were U.S. (43%), West Germany (17%), Belgium-Luxembourg (5%), U.K. (5%). Leading suppliers were Belgium-Luxembourg (18%), France (13%), West Germany (11%), Iran (8%), Netherlands (6%), Italy (6%), Kenya (5%), U.S. (5%).

## CAMBODIA

**Democratic Kampuchea**
**Head of State:** Khieu Samphan (1976)
**Premier:** Pol Pot (1977)
**Area:** 69,898 sq mi. (181,035 sq km)
**Population (est. 1978):** 8,890,000
**Density per square mile:** 127.2
**Capital and largest city (est. 1976):** Phnom Penh, 40,000–100,000
**Monetary unit:** Riel
**Ethnic groups:** Cambodian, 85%; Annamese, 5%; Chinese, 6%
**Languages:** Khmer (official), French, Vietnamese, Chinese, Cham, English
**Religion:** Theravada Buddhist
**Freedom House classifications:** Socialist industrial, one-party communist

**Geography.** Situated on the Indochinese peninsula, Cambodia is bordered by Thailand and Laos on the north and Vietnam on the east and south. The Gulf of Siam is off the western coast. The country, the size of Missouri, consists chiefly of a large alluvial plain ringed in by mountains and on the east by the Mekong River. The plain is centered on Lake Tonle Sap, which is a natural storage basin of the Mekong.

**Government.** A bloodless coup toppled Prince Sihanouk in March 1970. It was led by Lon Nol and Prince Sisowath Sirik Matak (Sihanouk's cousin). The National Assembly approved the coup and gave "full power" to Lon Nol. Sihanouk moved to Peking to head a government-in-exile. On Oct. 9, 1970, Cambodia became the Khmer Republic, and Lon Nol proclaimed himself President.

The Lon Nol regime was overthrown in April 1975 and replaced by xenophobic leaders of the Communist Khmer Rouge forces, who rule through revolutionary cadres.

**History.** Cambodia came under Khmer rule about A.D. 600. Under the Khmers, magnificent temples were built at Angkor. The Khmer kingdom once ruled over most of Southeast Asia, but attacks by the Thai and the Vietnamese almost annihilated the empire until the French joined Cambodia, Laos, and Vietnam into French Indochina.

Under Norodom Sihanouk, enthroned in 1941, and particularly under Japanese occupation during World War II, nationalism revived. After the ouster of the Japanese, the Cambodians sought independence, but the French returned in 1946, granting the country a Constitution in 1947 and independence within the French Union in 1949. Sihanouk won full military control during the French-Indochinese War in 1953. He abdicated in 1955 in favor of his parents, remaining head of the government, and when his father died in 1960, became chief of state without returning to the throne. In 1963, he sought a guarantee of Cambodia's neutrality from all parties to the Vietnam War.

Sihanouk first favored the Communist-backed Vietcong in Vietnam, but in 1967 he accused the Communists of planning a revolt and veered away from them. In 1968 he announced that under certain conditions he would not oppose "hot pursuit" by American troops of Communist forces across the Cambodian border.

On March 18, 1970, while Sihanouk was abroad trying to get North Vietnamese and the Vietcong out of border sanctuaries near Vietnam, anti-Vietnamese riots occurred, and Sihanouk was overthrown, a move legalized by the legislature. The historically anti-Vietnamese (north and south) Cambodians largely stayed with the government.

North Vietnamese and Vietcong units in border sanctuaries began moving deeper into Cambodia, threatening rapid overthrow of Lon Nol. President Nixon sent South Vietnamese and U.S. troops across the border April 30. U.S. ground forces, limited to 30-kilometer penetration, withdrew by June 30.

The Vietnam peace agreement of 1973 stipulated withdrawal of foreign forces from Cambodia, but fighting continued between Hanoi-backed insurgents and U.S.-supplied government troops. U.S. air support for the government forces was ended by Congress on Aug. 15, 1973. Lon Nol made overtures for a negotiated settlement, but neither Sihanouk nor leaders of the Khmer Rouge rebels would deal with him.

Fighting continued through 1974, then reached a quick climax early in 1975. In January, the rebels cut off the Mekong River as a supply route to Phnom Penh and fought their way to the outskirts of the capital and began shelling it. In February, the U.S. Congress ignored a request from President Ford for $222 million to supplement Phnom Penh's dwindling arms stores, but a U.S. food airlift to the besieged capital went forward.

As government troops fell back in bitter fighting, there were student protests in Phnom Penh, and foreigners began leaving the country. Lon Nol fled by air April 1, leaving the government under the interim control of Premier Long Boret. On April 16, the government's capitulation ended the five-year war, but not the travails of war-ravaged Cambodia.

The new regime embarked immediately on a sweeping, inward-looking agrarian revolution. Cambodian borders were closed, but 6,000 refugees escaped to Thailand. They reported that all cities had been evacuated, with inhabitants marched off to found new farm settlements in the jungle. They said policy was enforced by Communist troops and teen-aged revolutionaries who summarily shot dissidents and former government soldiers.

The leadership of the new regime was obscure, although Khieu Samphan, wartime leader of the Khmer Rouge and Deputy Premier when the new government was established, appeared to be the strong man of the egalitarian regime. Sihanouk, the nominal chief of state, who had been in exile in Peking, returned to Phnom Penh in September 1975 for the first time since the 1970 coup that had overthrown him.

A new Constitution was proclaimed in December, establishing a 250-member People's Assembly, a State Presidium with a President and two Vice Presidents, and a Supreme Judicial Tribunal. The Assembly was elected as of March 20, 1976, and Sihanouk, until then described as Chief of State, resigned on April 7. Samphan replaced him as Head of State.

President Carter, on April 21, 1978, called the Cambodian government "the worst violator of human rights in the world," and former Cambodian Information Minister Chhang Song charged that 1 million of his countrymen have died since the Communist takeover. In May, fighting between Cambodia and Vietnam stepped up, with the Vietnamese reported to be using U.S. tanks and other heavy equipment. Saigon offered a truce June 6, with a demilitarized zone to be established along the disputed border, followed by a peace conference.

By August 1978, Cambodian casualties in the war with Vietnam seemed to be increasing. Vietnamese diplomats in Southeast Asia generated rumors that there was serious internal friction within the Cambodian leadership. The Phnom Penh radio confirmed some changes in the government.

American Senator George McGovern charged in August that as many as 2.5 million Cambodians had died of starvation or disease or had been executed since the Communist takeover.

**Economy.** Agriculture is the basis of the economy. The chief crop is rice, grown principally in the Battambang area. Second in importance is rubber. Other crops are tobacco, kapok, cotton, pepper, and maize. Cattle breeding is of major importance. Native industries include silk and cotton weaving, rice milling, and the salting of fish obtained from Lake Tonle Sap during the low-water season.

Forests cover 75% of the land, but most are unexploited. Deposits of iron ore, limestone, and phosphate are undeveloped.

The Cambodian government seems to be creating a subsistence economy, with little external trade. Its major trading partner seems to be China.

## CAMEROON

**United Republic of Cameroon**
**President:** Ahmadou Ahidjo (1960)
**Prime Minister:** Paul Biya (1975)
**Area:** 183,569 sq mi. (475,442 sq km)
**Population (est. 1978):** 6,820,000
**Density per square mile:** 37.2
**Capital:** Yaoundé
**Largest cities (est. 1975):** Douala, 485,800; Yaoundé, 274,400
**Monetary unit:** Franc CFA
**Languages:** French and English (both official); Foulbé, Bamiléke, Ewondo, Donala, Mungaka, Bassa
**Religions:** Animist, Christian, Islam
**Gross national product (1976):** $2.2 billion
**National name:** République Unie du Cameroun
**Freedom House classifications:** Capitalist pre-industrial, one-party nationalist

**Geography.** Cameroon is a West African nation on the Gulf of Guinea, bordered by Nigeria, Chad, the Central African Empire, the Congo, Equatorial Guinea, and Gabon. It is nearly twice the size of Oregon.

The interior consists of a high plateau, rising to 4,500 feet (1,372 m), with the land descending to a lower, densely wooded plateau and then to swamps and plains along the coast. Mount Cameroon (13,350 ft.; 4,069 m), near the coast, is the highest elevation in the country. The main rivers are the Benue, Nyong, and Sanaga.

**Government.** After a 1972 plebiscite, a unitary nation was formed out of East and West Cameroon to replace the former Federal Republic. A Constitution was adopted, providing for election of a President every five years and of a 120-seat National Assembly, whose nominal five-year term can be extended or shortened by the President. The Cameroon National Union is the only political party.

**History.** The United Republic of Cameroon is inhabited by Hamitic and Semitic peoples in the north, where Islam is the principal religion, and by Bantu peoples in the central and southern regions, where native animism prevails. The tribes were conquered by many invaders.

The land escaped colonial rule until 1884, when treaties with tribal chiefs brought the area under German domination. After World War I, the League of Nations gave the French a mandate over 80% of the area, and the British 20% adjacent to Nigeria. After World War II, when the country came under a U.N. trusteeship in 1946, self-government was granted, and the Cameroun People's Union emerged as the dominant party by campaigning for reunification of French and British Cameroon and for independence. Accused of being under Communist control, it waged a campaign of revolutionary terror from 1955 to 1958, when it was crushed. In British Cameroon, unification was pressed also by the leading party, the Kamerun National Democratic Party led by John Foncha.

France set up Cameroun as an autonomous state in 1957, and in 1958 its legislative assembly voted for independence by 1960. In 1959 a fully autonomous government of Cameroun was formed under Ahmadou Ahidjo, who immediately began consultations on unification with Foncha. Cameroun became an independent republic on Jan. 1, 1960, adopted a Constitution in a referendum in February, and chose a National Assembly in April. The Assembly elected Ahidjo President. A federal Constitution was approved in 1961, and the Federal Republic of Cameroon came into being in October, 1961, headed by Ahidjo and Foncha.

Ahidjo was re-elected in 1975 for a fourth five-year term. Paul Biya was named Prime Minister.

**Economy.** Agricultural products are sweet potatoes, cassava, coffee, cocoa, bananas, peanuts, rubber, cotton, corn, dry beans, millet and sorghum, palm kernels and oil, and timber. Mineral resources include titanium, tin, and gold.

Chief exports in 1975 were cocoa (25%), coffee (24%), and timber (7%). Leading customers were France (27%), Netherlands (22%), U.S.S.R. (10%), West Germany (7%), Gabon (5%). Leading suppliers were France (46%), West Germany (8%), U.S. (7%), Italy (6%), Gabon (5%).

## CANADA

**See separate Canada section**

## CAPE VERDE

**Republic of Cape Verde**
**President:** Aristide Pereira (1975)
**Premier:** Maj. Pedro Pires (1975)
**Area:** 1,557 sq mi. (4,033 sq km)
**Population: (est. 1978):** 310,000
**Density per square mile:** 199.1
**Capital (1970 census):** Praia, 21,494
**Largest city:** Mindelo (est. 1970): 28,800
**Monetary unit:** Cape Verde escudo
**Language:** Portuguese
**Religions:** Mainly Roman Catholic, Protestant, and Christian Racionalist
**National name:** República de Cabo-Verde.
**Freedom House classifications:** Socialist pre-industrial, one-party socialist

**Geography:** Cape Verde, only slightly larger than Rhode Island, is an archipelago in the Atlantic 385 miles west of Dakar, Senegal.

The islands are divided into two groups: Barlavento in the north, comprising Santo Antão (291 sq mi.; 754 sq km), Boa Vista (240 sq mi.; 622 sq km), São Nicolau (132 sq mi.; 342 sq km), São Vicente (88 sq mi.; 246 sq km), Sal Rei (83 sq mi.; 298 sq km), and Santa Luzia (13 sq mi.; 34 sq km); and Sotavento in the south, consisting of São Tiago (383 sq mi.; 992 sq km), Fogo (184 sq mi.; 477 sq km), Maio (103 sq mi.; 267 sq km), and Brava (25 sq mi.; 65 sq km). The islands are mostly mountainous, with the land deeply scarred by erosion. There is an active volcano on Fogo.

**Government.** The islands became Africa's 44th independent nation July 5, 1975, under an agreement negotiated with Portugal in 1974. A 56-member National Assembly elected June 30 chose Aristide Pereira as President and Maj. Pedro Pires as Premier. All members of the Assembly belong to the African Party for the Independence of Portuguese Guinea and Cape Verde (P.A.I.C.G.), then the only party that entered candidates in the election. P.A.I.C.G. is committed to union with Guinea-Bissau, another former Portuguese colony.

**History.** Uninhabited upon its discovery in 1456, the Cape Verde islands became part of the Portuguese empire in 1495. There are 10 principal islands. A majority of their modern inhabitants are of mixed Portuguese and African ancestry. A coaling station developed during the 19th century on the island of São Vicente has grown in recent years to an oil and gasoline storage depot for ships and aircraft. Portugal's desire to retain the depot complicated the joint P.A.I.C.G. negotiations on independence. Lisbon agreed to independence for the Cape Verdes on Dec. 18, 1974, and accepted the P.A.I.C.G. as the only ruling party during the transitional period.

**Economy.** The main occupations are livestock breeding and fishing. Because of a drought that has lasted since 1968 and antiquated agricultural methods, there is little farming. The main crops are bananas, sugar cane, maize, sweet potatoes, and beans.

Chief exports in 1975 were fish (18%; shellfish 7%) and fish products (6%). Leading customer was Portugal (89%). Leading suppliers were Portugal (63%), Angola (11%).

## CENTRAL AFRICAN EMPIRE

**Head of State:** Emperor Bokassa I (1976)
**Prime Minister:** Ange Patassé (1976)
**Area:** 240,535 sq mi. (622,984 sq km)
**Population (est. 1978):** 2,000,000
**Density per square mile:** 8.0
**Capital and largest city (est. 1976):** Bangui, 320,000
**Monetary unit:** Franc CFA
**Ethnic groups:** Mandja-Baya, Banda, Mbaka, Azande

**Languages:** French (official) and Sango
**Religions:** Animist, 60%; Christian, 35%; Islam, 5%
**Gross national product (1976):** $420 million
**National name:** L'Empire Centrafricain
**Member of French Community**
**Freedom House classifications:** Capitalist pre-industrial, one-party nationalist

**Geography.** Situated about 500 miles north of the equator, the Central African Empire is a landlocked nation bordered by Cameroon, Chad, the Sudan, Zaire, and the Congo. Twice the size of New Mexico, it is covered by tropical forests in the south and semidesert land in the east. The Ubangi and Shari are the largest of many rivers.

**Government.** On Dec. 4, 1976, the Central African Republic became the Central African Empire. Marshal Jean-Bédel Bokassa, who had ruled the republic since he took power in a military coup Dec. 31, 1965, was declared Emperor Bokassa I.

MESAN (Mouvement d'Evolution Sociale de l'Afrique Noire), led by Emperor Bakassa, is the only political party.

**History.** As the colony of Ubangi-Shari, what is now the Central African Empire was united with Chad in 1905 and joined with Gabon and Middle Congo in French Equatorial Africa in 1910. After World War II a rebellion in 1946 forced the French to grant self-government. In 1958 the territory voted to become an autonomous republic within the French Community, but on Aug. 13, 1960, President David Dacko proclaimed the republic's independence from France.

Dacko undertook to move the country into Peking's orbit, but was overthrown in a coup on Dec. 31, 1965, by the then Col. Jean-Bédel Bokassa, Army Chief of Staff. In August 1977, the U.S. State Department protested the Emperor's jailing of American and British newsmen.

Bokassa staged an elaborate coronation ceremony on the first anniversary of the Empire, inviting 3,500 guests to see him place a diamond-studded crown on his head and sit on a 2.5-ton gilded bronze throne in the shape of an eagle. The cost of the ceremony was one fourth of the annual foreign exchange earnings of the country, one of the 25 poorest in the world.

**Economy.** Coffee, cotton, sesame, diamonds, and lumber are the leading products.

Chief exports in 1975 were coffee (23%), diamonds (20%), and cotton (18%). Leading customers were France (42%), Belgium-Luxembourg (9%), U.S. (8%), Italy (8%), Chad (5%), South Africa (5%), Israel (5%). Leading suppliers were France (58%), Yugoslavia (9%), West Germany (7%).

## CHAD

**Republic of Chad**
**Chief of State:** Brig. Gen. Félix Malloum (1975)
**Area:** 495,752 sq mi. (1,284,000 sq km)
**Population (est. 1978):** 4,290,000
**Density per square mile:** 8.7
**Capital and largest city (est. 1975):** N'djamena, 224,000
**Monetary unit:** Franc CFA
**Ethnic groups:** Baguirmiens, Kanembous, Saras, Massas, Arabs, Toubous, Goranes
**Languages:** French (official), Sara, Kanembou, Ouddai, Massa, Arabic, Gorane
**Religions:** Islam, 52%; Animist, 43%; Roman Catholic, 5%
**Gross national product (1976):** $510 million
**National name:** République de Tchad
**Freedom House classifications:** Capitalist pre-industrial, non-party military

**Geography.** A landlocked country in north central Africa, Chad is about 85% the size of Alaska. Its neighbors are Niger, Libya, the Sudan, the Central African Empire, Cameroon, and Nigeria.

Lake Chad, from which the country gets its name, lies on the western border with Niger and Nigeria. In the north is a desert that runs into the Sahara.

**Government.** After a coup on April 13, 1975, a nine-member military council took over all governmental functions, including those of the 75-member Legislative Assembly. Political parties were banned.

**History.** Chad was absorbed into the colony of French Equatorial Africa, as part of Ubangi-Shari, in 1910. France began the country's development after 1920, when it became a separate colony. In 1946, French Equatorial Africa was admitted to the French Union. The Chad territory by referendum in 1958 became an autonomous republic within the French Union.

An independence movement led by the first Premier and President, François (later Ngarta) Tombalbaye, achieved complete independence on Aug. 11, 1960. After a coup failed in 1963, Tombalbaye as President and chief of state promulgated a new Constitution and organized a new government dominated by the south.

A six-year sub-Sahara drought caused mass migrations, thousands of deaths, and famine conditions for some 2 million Chadians in 1974. International relief efforts were disrupted October 25, when President Tombalbaye ordered rejection of U.S. grain shipments (45% of the total). He charged that U.S. officials had barred Chadians from policy roles.

Tombalbaye was killed in the 1975 coup and was succeeded by Gen. Malloum, who has faced a Libyan-financed rebel movement, the Chadian National Liberation Front (Frolinat), throughout his tenure in office. A ceasefire backed by Libya, Niger, and Sudan on Feb. 24, 1978, failed to end the fighting, and French military aid, both troops and supplies, was increased.

**Economy.** The principal agricultural product of Chad is cotton. Rice and peanuts are also cultivated. Livestock include camels, cattle, and sheep.

Chief export in 1974 was cotton (67%). Leading customers not separately distinguished (74%), Zaire (5%). Leading suppliers were France (37%), Nigeria (12%), U.S. (10%).

## CHILE

**Republic of Chile**
**President:** Gen. Augusto Pinochet Ugarte (1973)
**Area:** 292,257 sq mi. (756,945 sq km)
**Population (est. 1978):** 10,880,000
**Density per square mile:** 37.2
**Capital:** Santiago
**Largest cities (est. 1975 for urban agglomeration):** Santiago, 3,263,000; (est. 1971 by U.N.): Valparaiso, 250,400; Viña del Mar, 179,600; Concepción, 161,000; Talcahuano, 148,000; Antofagasta, 125,100

**Monetary unit:** Peso
**Language:** Spanish
**Religion:** Roman Catholic
**Gross national product (1976):** $11.1 billion
**National name:** República de Chile
**Freedom House classifications:** Capitalist industrial, non-party military

**Geography.** Situated south of Peru and west of Bolivia and Argentina, Chile fills a narrow 1,800-mile strip between the Andes and the Pacific. Its area is nearly twice that of Montana.

One third of Chile is covered by the towering ranges of the Andes. In the north is the mineral-rich Atacama Desert, between the coast mountains and the Andes. In the center is a 700-mile-long valley, thickly populated, between the Andes and the coastal plateau. In the south, the Andes border on the ocean.

At the southern tip of Chile's mainland is Punta Arenas, the southernmost city in the world, and beyond that lies the Strait of Magellan and Tierra del Fuego, an island divided between Chile and Argentina. The southernmost point of South America is Cape Horn, a 1,390-foot (424-m) rock on Horn Island in the Wollaston group, which belongs to Chile.

The Juan Fernández Islands, in the South Pacific about 400 miles (644 km) west of the mainland, and Easter Island, about 2,000 miles (3,219 km) west, are Chilean possessions.

**Government.** Under the pre-coup constitution, the nation elected a President every six years, a Senate of 50 members, every eight years (one-half renewable every four years), and a Chamber of Deputies of 150 members every four years.

Leftist parties were abolished immediately after the 1973 military coup that ousted President Salvador Allende Gossens. Other parties were placed "in recess," and on March 12, 1977, the government officially dissolved them.

**History.** Chile was originally under the control of the Incas in the north and the fierce Araucanian people in the south. In 1541, a Spaniard, Pedro de Valdiva, founded Santiago. Chile won its independence from Spain in 1818 under Bernardo O'Higgins and an Argentinian, José de San Martin. O'Higgins, dictator until 1823, laid the foundations of the modern state with a two-party system and a centralized government.

The dictator from 1830 to 1837, Diego Portales, fought a war with Peru in 1836–39 that expanded Chilean territory. The Conservatives were in power from 1831 to 1861. Then the Liberals, winning a share of power for the next 30 years, disestablished the church and limited presidential power. Chile fought the war of the Pacific with Peru and Bolivia from 1879 to 1883, winning Antofagasta, Bolivia's only outlet to the sea, and extensive areas from Peru. A revolt in 1890 led by Jorge Montt overthrew, in 1891, José Balmaceda and established a parliamentary dictatorship that persisted until a new Constitution was adopted in 1925. Industrialization began before World War I and led to the formation of Marxist groups.

Juan Antonio Ríos, President during World War II, was originally pro-Nazi but in 1944 led his country into the war on the side of the U.S. After the war Gabriel González Videla, elected by a coalition including the Communists, turned on them. The Communist Party was outlawed until 1958.

A small abortive army uprising in 1969 raised fear of military intervention to prevent a Marxist, Salvador Allende Gossens, from taking office after his election to the presidency on Sept. 4, 1970, with 36.3% of the vote in a three-way battle. Dr. Allende was the first President in a non-Communist country freely elected on a Marxist-Leninist program.

Allende quickly established relations with Cuba and the People's Republic of China and nationalized several American companies. He promised compensation but imposed retroactive taxes to cancel out most claims, leading to cool but proper relations with the U.S. By 1972, inflation was running over 100% annually.

A middle-class general strike led to a military coup Sept. 11, 1973, then to Allende's overthrow and mysterious death in an army assault on the presidential palace. More than 2,700 deaths were reported in the coup, and many thousands were arrested. The coup ended a 46-year era of constitutional government in Chile, which had boasted the longest such record in Latin America.

The takeover was run by a four-man junta headed by Army chief of staff Augusto Pinochet Ugarte, who assumed the office of President and governed under a state of siege that was kept in force by extensions every six months. In March 1978, Pinochet lifted the state of siege because of "support for government" by the public, reported by a Gallup poll to be 75%.

Committed to "exterminate Marxism," the junta embarked on a right-wing dictatorship. It suspended parliament, banned political activity, and broke relations with Cuba. Mexico, which recognized the Havana regime, severed relations with Chile in 1974.

The Human Rights Commission of the Organization of American States charged the junta with "most grave violations" of basic liberties, but the O.A.S. voted in May 1975 not to hear the report until further evidence was supplied. In July, Chile denied entry to a U.N. investigatory panel. On June 9, 1978, the government reversed that policy to permit the U.N. Human Rights Commission to send an investigative mission to Cuba.

In September 1974, it was disclosed that the U.S. Central Intelligence Agency had secretly aided Allende's opponents before his election and had later worked covertly to "destabilize" his government. President Ford admitted that there had been a clandestine U.S. effort under the Nixon Administration to "assist the preservation" of opposition news media and political parties, but said the U.S. had "no involvement in any way with the coup itself."

With an economy depressed by a slump in world copper prices, the military regime in October 1975 designated a new currency, the peso, equivalent to 1,000 escudos, the much-devalued former monetary unit. Under the impact of an austerity program launched earlier, the rate of inflation—375% for 1975—slowed to 10% a month for the first half of 1976.

Pinochet, in a speech marking his fourth year in power, on September 11, 1977, promised elections by 1985 if conditions warranted. Earlier, he had abolished DINA, the secret police, and decreed an amnesty for political prisoners, an action Amnesty International said might affect only 200–400 of some 1,500 political prisoners. He permitted the deportation of Michael V. Townley to the U.S. on April 8, 1978, where he and three Cuban exiles were charged with the murder of Orlando Letelier, a former Chilean foreign minister who had taken refuge in Washington. Pinochet's softening was attributed partly to increasing stability at home and partly to U.S. pressure.

**Economy.** Chilean agriculture is mostly confined to the temperate central valley, similar to that of California. Productive land is extremely limited, and most of it must be irrigated. Wheat is the leading crop. Grapes are next to wheat in acreage. Feudal-type estates averaging 2,500 acres predominate.

The basis of the country's economy is its mineral resources in the northern desert provinces of Atacama, Antofagasta, and Tarapacá, where the only natural nitrate in the world is found. Some 60% of the world's iodine is obtained as a by-product of nitrate processing. Chile's world monopoly in nitrate, however, declined with the development of the synthetic product.

The world's largest copper reserve, estimated at 134 billion pounds, is in Chile, as are more than 900 million tons of high-grade iron ore. The reserve of Chilean coal, noted for quantity rather than quality, exceeds two billion tons.

Chief export in 1975 was copper (60%). Leading customers were West Germany (14%), Japan (11%), Argentina (10%), U.S. (9%), U.K. (8%), Brazil (6%), Netherlands (5%), Italy (5%). Leading suppliers were U.S. (31%), Argentina (17%), West Germany (7%), Japan (6%), U.K. (5%), Brazil (5%).

## CHINA

**People's Republic of China**
**Premier:** Hua Kuo-feng (1976)
**Area:** 3,705,387 sq mi. (9,596,961 sq km)[1]
**Population (est. 1978):** 880,000,000
**Density per square mile:** 237.4
**Capital:** Peking
**Largest cities (est. 1975):** Shanghai, 10,888,000; Peking, 8,487,000; (est. 1970): Tientsin, 4,280,000; Wuhan, 4,250,000; Lüta (Port Arthur and Dairen), 4,000,000, Mukden, 3,750,000; Chungking, 3,500,000; Harbin, 2,750,000; Taiyüan, 2,725,000; Canton, 2,300,000; Nanking, 2,000,000
**Monetary unit:** Yuan
**Language:** Chinese, (Mandarin, Cantonese, and local dialects)
**Religions:** Principally Confucianist, Buddhist, and Taoist
**Gross national product (1976):** $343.1 billion
**National name:** Chung Hua Jen Min Kung-Ho Kuo
**Freedom House classifications:** Socialist industrial, one-party communist

**Geography.** China, which occupies the eastern part of Asia, is slightly larger in area than the U.S. Its coastline is roughly a semicircle, about 2,150 miles long. The greater part of the country is mountainous, and only in the lower reaches of the Yellow and Yangtze rivers are there extensive low plains.

The principal mountain ranges are the Tien Shan, to the northwest; the Kunlun chain, running south of the Takla Makan and Gobi deserts; and the Trans-Himalaya, connecting the Kunlun with the borders of China and Tibet. Manchuria is largely an undulating plain connected with the north China plain by a narrow lowland corridor. Inner Mongolia contains the relatively fertile southern and eastern portions of the Gobi. The large island of Hainan (13,500 sq mi.; 34,965 sq km) lies off the southern coast.

Hydrographically, China proper consists of three great river systems. The northern part of the country is drained by the Yellow River (Hwang Ho), 2,900 miles long (4,667 km) and mostly unnavigable. The central part is drained by the Yangtze Kiang, the fourth longest river in the world: 3,602 miles (5,797 km). The Si Kiang in the south is 1,236 miles long (1,989 km) and navigable for a considerable distance. In addition, the Amur (2,704 mi.; 4,352 km) forms part of the northeastern boundary.

**Government.** With 3,040 deputies, elected for four-year terms by universal suffrage, the National People's Congress is the chief legislative organ. A State Council has the executive authority. The Congress elects the Premier and Vice Premier. The State Council, headed by Premier Hua Kuo-feng, has under it all ministries.

The Communist Party controls the government.

**History.** By 2000 B.C., the Chinese were living in the Hwang Ho basin, and they had achieved an advanced stage of civilization by 1200 B.C. The great philosophers Lao-tse, Confucius, Mo Ti, and Mencius lived during the Chou dynasty (1122–249 B.C.). The warring feudal states were first united under Emperor Ch'in Shih Huang Ti, during whose reign (246–210 B.C.) work was begun on the Great Wall. Under the Han dynasty (206 B.C.-A.D. 220) China prospered and traded with the West.

In the T'ang dynasty (618–907), often called the golden age of Chinese history, painting, sculpture, and poetry flourished, and printing made its earliest known appearance.

The Mings, last of the native rulers (1368–1644), overthrew the Mongol, or Yuan, dynasty (1280–1368) established by Kublai Khan. The Mings in turn were overthrown in 1644 by invaders from the north, the Manchus.

China closely restricted foreign activities, and by the end of the 18th century only Canton and the Portuguese port of Macao were open to European merchants. Following the Anglo-Chinese War of 1839–42, however, several treaty ports were opened, and Hong Kong was ceded to the U.K. Treaties signed after further hostilities (1856–60) weakened Chinese sovereignty and removed foreigners from Chinese jurisdiction. The disastrous Chinese-Japanese War of 1894–95 was followed by a scramble for Chinese concessions by European powers, leading to the Boxer Rebellion (1900), suppressed by an international force.

The death of the Empress Dowager Tzu Hsi in 1908 and the accession of the infant Emperor Hsüan T'ung (Pu-Yi) were followed by a nationwide rebellion led by Dr. Sun Yat-sen, who became first President of the Provisional Chinese Republic in 1911. The Manchus abdicated on Feb. 12, 1912. Dr. Sun resigned in favor of Yuan Shih-k'ai, who suppressed the republicans but was forced by a serious rising in 1915–16 to abandon his intention of declaring himself Emperor. Yuan's death in June 1916 was followed by years of civil war between rival militarists and Dr. Sun's republicans.

Nationalist forces, led by Gen. Chiang Kai-shek and with the advice of Communist experts, soon occupied most of China, setting up a Kuomintang regime in 1928. Internal strife continued, however, and Chiang broke with the Communists.

An alleged explosion on the South Manchurian Railway on Sept. 18, 1931, brought invasion of Manchuria by Japanese forces, who installed the last Manchu Emperor, Henry Pu-Yi, as nominal ruler of the puppet state of "Manchukuo." Japanese efforts to take China's northern provinces in July 1937 were resisted by Chiang Kai-shek, who meanwhile had succeeded in uniting most of China be-

1. Including Manchuria and Tibet.

hind him. Within two years, however, Japan seized most of the ports and railways. The Kuomintang government retreated first to Hankow and then to Chungking, while the Japanese set up a puppet government at Nanking headed by Wang Ching-wei.

Japan's surrender in 1945 touched off civil war between Nationalist forces under Chiang Kai-shek and Communist forces led by Mao Tse-tung, the party chairman. Despite U. S. aid, the Chiang forces were overcome by the Maoists, backed by the Soviet bloc, and were expelled from the mainland. The Mao regime, established in Peking as the new capital, proclaimed the People's Republic of China on Oct. 1, 1949, with Chou En-lai as Premier.

The soviet-type government, after prolonged negotiations, signed a 30-year treaty of friendship and mutual aid with the U.S.S.R. on Feb. 14, 1950. Its published terms provided for return of the Changchun railroad to China and the eventual return of Port Arthur and Dairen, occupied by Soviet troops. Later in the year, Chinese troops invaded Tibet and began its subjugation, a campaign that brought China into conflict with India. After the Korean War began in June 1950, China led the Communist bloc in supporting North Korea, and on Nov. 26, 1950, the Mao regime intervened openly.

A deterioration of relations between Peking and Moscow was indicated in 1958 when Peking emerged as an independent center of Communist power, challenging the leadership role of the U.S.S.R. in the Soviet bloc.

In 1958, Mao undertook the "Great Leap Forward" campaign, which combined the establishment of rural communes with a crash program of village industrialization. These efforts also failed, causing Mao to lose influence to Liu Shao-chi, who became President in 1959, to Premier Chou, and to Party Secretary Teng Hsiao-ping. Meanwhile China's backing of subversive movements in Asia soured relations with India and Burma, although it very nearly achieved the conquest of Indonesia, and culminated in war on the borders of India late in 1962. By 1963 the break with the U.S.S.R. was complete.

Mao, with the backing of supporters—his wife, Chiang Ching; the Defense Minister, Marshal Lin Piao; his former secretary, Chen Po-ta; and Premier Chou—began a struggle to regain power. Chou proposed the movement that became known as the Cultural Revolution at the party congress in 1964, the same year China exploded its first atomic (fission) bomb (it achieved the fusion bomb in 1967).

Mao moved to Shanghai, and from that base he and his supporters waged their own Cultural Revolution. President Liu and the party secretary, Teng, took over, and their followers denounced hundreds of party and government officials at rallies and in wall posters. Then, in 1966, Chen became director of the Cultural Revolution; the army chief of staff, Lo Juiching, was purged; and Lin replaced Liu as second in the hierarchy. In the spring of 1966 the Mao group formed Red Guard units dominated by youths and students, closing the schools to free the students for agitation. On Aug. 18, 1966, a few days after a Central Committee session at which Liu and Teng retained membership, a rally was held in Peking at which hundreds of thousands of Red Guards took part. During the fall more than 11 million Red Guards went to Peking to take part in rallies, demonstrations, and purges.

The Red Guards campaigned against "old ideas, old culture, old habits, and old customs." Often they were no more than uncontrolled mobs, and brutality was frequent. Early in 1967 efforts were made to restore control. The Red Guards were urged to return home. Schools started opening. But the height of violence was only reached in September 1967 when in Canton the opposing factions used tanks and artillery against each other.

Persistent overtures by the Nixon Administration (relaxed trade and travel restrictions) abruptly climaxed in an invitation to a U.S. table tennis team to visit Peking in April 1971. This was followed by the dramatic announcement in July that Henry Kissinger, Mr. Nixon's national security adviser, had secretly visited Peking and reached agreement on a visit by the President to Red China.

The movement toward reconciliation, which signaled the end of the U.S. containment policy toward China, provided irresistible momentum for Chinese admission to the U.N. Despite U.S. opposition to expelling Taiwan (Nationalist China), the world body overwhelmingly ousted Chiang Kai-shek in seating Peking.

Mr. Nixon went to Peking for a week early in 1972, meeting Mao as well as Chou. The summit ended with a historic communiqué on February 28, in which both nations promised to work toward improved relations. They differed over Vietnam as well as Taiwan, although the U.S. noted it was withdrawing from Vietnam and said its ultimate goal was withdrawal from Taiwan as well, with interim reductions of those forces as tension in the area diminished.

In 1973, the U.S. and China agreed to set up "liaison offices" in each other's capitals, which constituted de facto diplomatic relations. Full diplo-

## Provinces and Regions of China

| Name | Area (sq mi.) | Capital |
|---|---|---|
| Provinces | | |
| Anhwei | 54,015 | Ho-fei |
| Chekiang | 39,305 | Hangchow |
| Fukien | 47,529 | Foochow |
| Heilungkiang[1] | 178,996 | Harbin |
| Honan | 64,479 | Cheng-chou |
| Hopeh | 81,479 | Shih-chia-chuang |
| Hunan | 81,274 | Ch'ang-sha |
| Hupeh | 72,394 | Wu-ch'ang |
| Kansu | 137,104 | Lan-chou |
| Kiangsi | 63,629 | Nan-ch'ang |
| Kiangsu | 40,927 | Nanking |
| Kirin[1] | 72,201 | Ch'ang-ch'un |
| Kwangtung | 89,344 | Canton |
| Kweichow | 67,181 | Kuei-yang |
| Liaoning[1] | 58,301 | Mukden |
| Shansi | 60,656 | T'ai-yüan |
| Shantung | 59,189 | Tsinan |
| Shensi | 75,598 | Sian |
| Szechwan | 219,691 | Ch'eng-tu |
| Tsinghai | 278,378 | Hsi-ning |
| Yunnan | 168,417 | K'un-ming |
| Autonomous Regions | | |
| Inner Mongolia[1] | 454,633 | Huhehot |
| Kwangsi Chuang | 85,096 | Nan-ning |
| Ningsia Hui | 30,039 | Yin-ch'uan |
| Sinkiang Uighur[1] | 635,829 | Urumchi |
| Tibet[1] | 471,660 | Lhasa |

1. Together constitute (with Taiwan) what has been traditionally known as Outer China, the remaining territory forming the historical China Proper.

matic relations were barred by China as long as the U.S. continued to recognize Nationalist China.

The National People's Congress held its first meeting in a decade in Peking, Jan. 13–17, 1975. With Mao absent, it re-elected Chou as Premier. It approved a government realignment that placed Marshal Yeh Chien-ying, 77, in the post of Defense Minister, vacant since Lin's death. It revised the 1954 Constitution to reassert the primacy of the Communist Party and to specify limited rights of citizens to strike and demonstrate, to hold private farm plots, and to work for themselves.

Chou predicted in a keynote address that "fierce contention" between the U.S. and the U.S.S.R. "is bound to lead to world war some day." He said there is "no détente, let alone lasting peace in the world today."

The same warnings against détente were made during President Ford's visit to China, Dec. 8–12, 1975, by Vice Premier Teng Hsiao-Ping. Teng served as chief host because Chou was now seriously ill with cancer and Mao, visibly failing, saw the visitor only briefly.

On Jan. 8, 1976, amid a national outpouring of grief, Chou died. Demonstrations in the capital turned into near riots when mourners suspected the government of trying to suppress the display of emotion. Teng, who had been rehabilitated by Chou and designated as his successor, was supplanted within a month by Hua Kuo-feng, 54, former Minister of Public Security. Hua, believed to be a compromise between radicals and the moderates represented by the ousted Teng, became permanent Premier in April. In October he was named successor to Mao as Chairman of the Communist Party.

Mao died September 10, apparently of Parkinson's disease, and China for the second time in a year went into a period of national mourning. Almost immediately afterward, a campaign against his widow, Chiang Ch'ing, and three of her "radical" colleagues began. The "Gang of Four" was denounced for having undermined the party, the government, and the economy.

While the despised four were reviled throughout China, there was evidence by late 1976 that Teng was to be rehabilitated. At the Central Committee meeting of 1977, Teng was reinstated on July 22 as Deputy Premier, Chief of Staff of the Army, and member of the Central Committee of the Politburo. He was ranked behind Yeh Chien-ying, the Defense Minister, in the third-ranking place in the government.

At the same time, Chiang Ch'ing, Wang Hung-wen, Chang Chun-Chiao, and Yao Wen-yuan—the notorious "Gang of Four"—were removed from all official posts and banished from the party. The final resolution of the committee meeting declared national unity restored and "a new leap forward taking shape in the national economy."

In addition to political reconstruction, China still faced the task of repairing the damage done by the enormous earthquake of July 28, 1976, which devastated the northern part of the country. Casualty estimates ranged from 100,000 to 600,000 dead in Tangshan, Tientsin, and Peking.

In August 1977, the 11th national Communist Party Congress and the election of a new Politburo took place as U.S. Secretary of State Cyrus Vance visited China to call for efforts by both China and the U.S. to normalize relations.

The Fifth National People's Congress adopted a new Constitution on March 5, 1978, strengthening civil rights such as free speech and the right to file complaints against the government. The Congress also approved a 10-year plan to increase farm production and add 120 industrial complexes to the nation's industrial base. Hua Kuo-feng was affirmed as Premier despite rumors that Deputy Premier Teng Hsiao-ping might take the post.

In May 1978, expulsion of ethnic Chinese by Vietnam produced an open rupture. China withdrew aid technicians and on July 3 announced a complete cutoff, disclosing for the first time that it had given $10 billion to Vietnam in the past 20 years. Peking sided with Cambodia in the border fighting that flared between Vietnam and Cambodia, charging Hanoi with aggression.

China loudly denounced Soviet-Cuban intervention in Africa, offering aid to both Somalia and, after the May invasion of Shaba province, Zaire. National Security Adviser Zbigniew Brzezinski visited Peking during May 20–22 and joined in the chorus of anti-Soviet declarations. He also briefed Chinese leaders on the SALT negotiations with Moscow and returned with hints that the Chinese had softened their insistence that Washington break with Taiwan before a closer relationship would be possible.

On Aug. 12, 1978, China and Japan signed a treaty of peace and friendship. The key portion of the treaty declared that each country is opposed to efforts by any other country or group of countries to establish a hegemony in the Asia-Pacific region. The U.S.S.R. contended that this clause was directed specifically at the Soviet Union because of China's bitter enmity.

In August, Premier Hua while visiting Romania and Yugoslavia, continued to attack the U.S.S.R. for seeking "hegemony"—authority over other Communist states.

**Economy.** In China, nearly 80% of the population depends on the land for livelihood. Subsistence crops are necessarily emphasized, but China is still not self-sufficient in food.

In northern China, wheat, barley, corn, sorghum, millet and other cereals, and beans and peas predominate, whereas in the south, rice, sugar, and indigo are most important.

The Yangtze basin, one of the most favored agricultural regions in the world, is China's premier granary. Tea is grown mainly in the central uplands, coastal ranges, and Szechwan.

Silkworm culture is practiced widely, especially in the lower Yangtze valley. Soybeans and cotton are of ever-increasing importance. Other crops include fibers, tobacco, vegetable oils, cane sugar, and many medicinal plants and spices.

Industrially, China is still in its infancy although, in 1978, an ambitious development program was planned. Development has been mainly in the erection of textile mills, silk and flour mills, match factories, tanneries, and a few steel and cement mills. The production of consumer's goods far exceeds that of producer's goods, which must still be imported.

Mineral resources are considerable. Iron ore, far less plentiful than coal, is mined principally in the lower Yangtze valley and in north China. Tin, mined in Yunnan and southwest Szechwan, has been a major mineral export. Of some rarer minerals, notably antimony and tungsten, China is sometimes the world's leading producer. Lead, zinc, silver, mercury, and gold are also mined. The discovery of uranium has been reported.

China urgently needs reforestation. Most remaining forests are on inaccessible mountain slopes. Bamboo is cultivated in groves throughout the country south of the Tsinling mountains.

Chief exports in 1975 were foodstuffs (meat and products, cereals, fruits and vegetables) (30%), textiles and clothing (20%), and crude oil (12%). Leading customers were Japan (20%), Hong Kong (18%). Leading suppliers were Japan (34%), West Germany (8%), France (6%), Canada (6%), Australia (5%), U.S. (5%).

## CHINA (TAIWAN)

**Republic of China**
**President:** Chiang Ching-kuo (1978)
**Premier:** Sun Yun-suan (1978)
**Area:** 13,893 sq mi. (35,566 sq km)[1]
**Population (est. 1977):** 16,678,000
**Density per square mile:** 1,200.5
**Capital:** Taipei
**Largest cities (est. 1978):** Taipei, 2,130,800; Kao-hsiung, 1,042,000; T'ai-chung, 570,750; T'ai-nan, 547,000; Chi-lung, 341,700
**Monetary unit:** New Taiwan dollar
**Language:** Chinese (Mandarin)
**Religions:** Confucianist, Buddhist, Christian, Taoist
**Gross national product (1976):** $17.1 billion
**Freedom House classifications:** Capitalist-statist industrial, dominant party

**Geography.** The Republic of China today consists of the former Taiwan Province, including Taiwan, an island 100 miles off the Asian mainland in the Pacific; two offshore islands, Quemoy and Matsu; and the nearby islets of the Pescadores chain. It is slightly larger than the combined areas of Massachusetts and Connecticut.

The country is divided by a central mountain range that runs from north to south, rising sharply on the east coast and descending gradually to a broad western plain, where cultivation is concentrated.

**Government.** The President and the Vice President are elected by the National Assembly for a term of six years. There are five major governing bodies called Yuans: Executive, Legislative, Judicial, Control, and Examination. Taiwan's internal affairs are administered by the Taiwan Provincial Government under the supervision of the Provincial Assembly, which is popularly elected.

The majority and ruling party is the Kuomintang (Nationalist Party) led by Chiang Ching-kuo. There are also two minority parties: the China Democratic Socialist Party and the Young China Party.

**History.** Taiwan was inhabited by aborigines of Malayan descent when Chinese from the areas now designated as Fukien and Kwangtung began settling it beginning in the 7th century, becoming the majority.

The Portuguese explored the area in 1590, naming it The Beautiful (Formosa). In 1624 the Dutch set up forts in the South, the Spanish in the North. The Dutch threw out the Spanish in 1641 and controlled the island until 1661, when the Chinese General Koxinga took it over, established an independent kingdom, and expelled the Dutch. The Manchus seized the island in 1683 and held it until 1895 when it passed to Japan after the first Sino-Japanese War. Japan developed and exploited it, and it was heavily bombed by American planes during World War II, after which it was restored to China.

1. Excluding Quemoy and Matsu.

After the defeat of its armies on the mainland, the Nationalist Government of Generalissimo Chiang retreated to Taiwan on Dec. 8, 1949. With only 15% of the population consisting of the 1949 immigrants, Chiang dominated the island, maintaining a 600,000-man army in the hope of eventually recovering the mainland. Japan renounced its claim to the island by the San Francisco Peace Treaty of 1951.

By a fleet in the Strait of Formosa the U.S. prevented a mainland invasion in 1953, and in 1955 the U.S. signed a mutual defense treaty by which it is committed to defend Taiwan and the neighboring islands.

The "China seat" in the U.N., which the Nationalists held with U.S. help for over two decades, was lost in October 1971, when the People's Republic of China was admitted and Taiwan ousted by the world body. Mr. Nixon's summit meeting with Chinese leaders and the February 1972 Sino-American communiqué further eroded Taiwan's position. In it, the U.S. said its eventual goal was complete withdrawal of its forces from Taiwan and progressive cutbacks as tensions in the area eased. With the end of U.S. participation in the war in Vietnam, withdrawal of U.S. air-support forces on the island began in 1973.

The U.S. on March 11, 1976, announced that it would reduce by an indefinite number its forces on Taiwan, estimated in 1972 to be about 2,500.

Chiang Kai-shek died at 87 of a heart attack on April 5, 1975. His son, Chiang Ching-kuo, continued as Premier and dominant power in the Taipei regime.

Continuing U.S. relations with Taiwan were cited by Peking from the beginning of its rapprochement with the U.S. in 1971 as a barrier to closer ties. In 1978, however, there were indications that Peking was willing to overlook the issue in order to form a bond with Washington in opposition to Soviet "expansionist" policies in Southeast Asia and Africa.

**Economy.** Taiwan is increasingly being industralized, although much of the population is dependent on farming. It is self-sufficient in most basic foodstuffs and produces surpluses of a number of others, notably rice and sugar. Farms are generally small. Cattle and water buffalo are the chief livestock.

Chief exports in 1975 were clothing (17%), electrical machinery and equipment (13%), textile yarns and fabrics (12%), footwear (6%), fruit and vegetables (5%), and sugar (5%). Leading customers in 1976 were U.S. (38%), Japan (14%), Hong Kong (7%), West Germany (5%). Leading suppliers were Japan (32%), U.S. (24%), Kuwait (9%), Saudi Arabia (5%), West Germany (5%).

## COLOMBIA

**Republic of Colombia**
**President:** Julio César Turbay Ayala (1978)
**Area:** 439,735 sq mi. (1,138,914 sq km)
**Population (est. 1978):** 25,800,000; (mestizo, 68%; white, 20%; Indian, 7%; black, 5%)
**Density per square mile:** 58.7
**Capital:** Bogotá
**Largest cities (est. 1977):** Bogotá, 3,618,800; **(1973 census):** Medellín, 1,064,741; Cali, 898,253; Barranquilla, 664,533; Cartagena, 356,424; Bucaramanga, 328,328
**Monetary unit:** Peso
**Language:** Spanish

**Religion:** Roman Catholic
**Gross national product (1976):** $15.4 billion
**National name:** República de Colombia
**Freedom House classifications:** Capitalist industrial, multi-party centralized

**Geography.** Colombia, in the northwestern part of South America, is the only country on that continent that borders on both the Atlantic and Pacific Oceans. It is nearly equal to the combined areas of California and Texas.

Through the western half of the country, three Andean ranges run north and south, merging into one at the Ecuadorean border. The eastern half is a low, jungle-covered plain, drained by spurs of the Amazon and Orinoco, inhabited mostly by isolated, tropical-forest Indian tribes. The fertile plateau and valley of the eastern range are the most densely populated parts of the country.

**Government.** Colombia's President, who appoints his own Cabinet, serves for a four-year term. The Senate, the upper house of Congress, has 113 members elected for four years by direct vote. The Chamber of Deputies of 199 members is directly elected for four years.

The major political parties are the Liberal Party (62 of 112 seats in Senate, 109 of 199 seats in House), Conservative Party (49 seats in Senate, 86 seats in House), and National Opposition Union, a leftist coalition (1 seat in Senate, 4 seats in House).

**History.** Spaniards in 1510 founded Darien, the first permanent European settlement on the American mainland. In 1538 the Spaniards established the colony of New Granada, the area's name until 1861. After a 14-year struggle, in which Simón Bolívar's Venezuelan troops won the battle of Boyacá in Colombia on Aug. 7, 1819, independence was attained in 1824. Bolívar united Colombia, Venezuela, Panama, and Ecuador in the Republic of Greater Colombia (1819–30), but lost Venezuela and Ecuador to separatists. Bolívar's Vice President, Francisco de Paula Santander, founded the Liberal Party as the Federalists while Bolívar established the Conservatives as the Centralists.

Santander's presidency (1832–36) re-established order, but later periods of Liberal dominance (1849–57 and 1861–80), when the Liberals sought to disestablish the Roman Catholic Church, were marked by insurrection and even civil war. Rafael Nuñez, in a 15-year-presidency, restored the power of the central government and the church, which led in 1899 to a bloody civil war and the loss in 1903 of Panama over ratification of a lease to the U.S. of the Canal Zone. For 21 years, until 1930, the Conservatives held power as revolutionary pressures built up.

The Liberal administrations of Enrique Olaya Herrera and Alfonso López (1930–38) were marked by social reforms that failed to solve the country's problems and in 1946, after World War II, insurrection and banditry broke out, which claimed hundreds of thousands of lives by 1958. Laureano Gómez (1950–53), the army chief of staff, Gen. Gustavo Rojas Pinilla (1953–56), and a military junta (1956–57) sought to curb disorder by repression.

Subsequent Presidents were Alberto Lleras Camargo (1957–62); Guillermo León Valencia (1962–66); Carlos Lleras Restrepo (1966–70); Misael Pastrana Borrero (1970–74); and Alfonso López Michelson (1974–78).

Julio César Turbay Ayala, Liberal Party candidate in 1978, won a narrow victory—approximately 140,000 of a total of nearly 2,500,000 votes—over the Conservative Party candidate, who accused President López of illegally aiding his party's candidate. The Liberals also retained control of both the Senate and House.

**Economy.** Most of the people live by farming and cattle herding, but only a small part of the land is cultivated, and that by primitive means. Colombia's coffee, the nation's principal crop, is a mild variety that does not compete with Brazilian types.

The leading manufacturing industries are foodstuff processing, textiles, and beverages.

Rich in minerals, Colombia has the third largest oil industry in Latin America (70% controlled by U.S. interests). The country is also rich in platinum and has world-famous emerald mines at Muzc in the eastern Andes.

Forest products are vanilla, quinine, ipecac, sarsaparilla, gums and balsams, tanning agents, and dyewoods.

Chief exports in 1975 were coffee (53%) and textile yarns and fabric (7%). Leading customers were U.S. (32%), West Germany (15%), Netherlands (6%), Venezuela (6%). Leading suppliers were U.S. (43%), West Germany (9%), Japan (9%).

## COMORO ISLANDS

**Co-leaders of Government:** Ahmed Abdallah and Mohammed Ahmed (1978)
**Area:** 838 sq mi. (2,171 sq km)
**Population (oct. 1978):** 370,000
**Density per square mile:** 441.5
**Capital and largest city (est. 1976):** Moroni (on Grande Comoro), 18,300
**Monetary unit:** Franc CFA
**Language:** French
**Religions:** Islam and Christian
**Gross national product (1976):** $60 million
**National name:** État Comorien
**Freedom House classifications:** Capitalist-socialist pre-industrial, multi-party centralized

**Geography.** The Comoro Islands—Grande Comoro, Anjouan, Mohéli, and Mayotte (which retains ties to France)—are an archipelago of volcanic origin in the Indian Ocean between Mozambique and Madagascar.

**Government.** The National Council of the Revolution and the National Executive Council of the republican government on Jan. 2, 1976, elected Ali Soilih, Minister of Justice and Defense, as head of state, succeeding Prince Said Mohamed Jaffar.

**History.** Under French rule since 1886, the Comoros declared themselves independent July 6, 1975. However, Mayotte, with a Christian majority, voted against joining the other, mainly Islamic islands, in the move to independence and continues to remain French.

On May 13, 1978, French mercenaries landed in Moroni and captured Ali Soilih, who had gained power with the help of some of the same mercenaries three years earlier. An eccentric, Soilih had lowered the voting age to 14, burned all records, and massacred a number of Comorans. Shortly after, Soilih was shot while trying to escape. Ahmed Abdallah, the first leader of the islands after independence, returned from exile with Mohammed Ahmed, and they declared themselves co-leaders of a new pro-French government.

**Economy.** Agriculture is the principal industry of the Comoro Islands. The chief crop is aromatic plants, whose essences are important to the perfume industry. The islands also produce cassava, yams, rice, and maize. The chief exports are vanilla, copra, and cloves.

Chief exports in 1972 were vanilla (41%), essential oils (33%), cloves (11%), and copra (6%). Leading customers in 1974 were France (75%), Madagascar (9%), Italy (7%). Leading suppliers were France (50%), Madagascar (15%), Kenya (5%).

## CONGO

**People's Republic of the Congo**
**President:** Col. Joachim Yhombi-Opango (1977)
**Prime Minister:** Maj. Louis Sylvain Ngoma (1977)
**Area:** 132,046 sq mi. (342,000 sq km)
**Population (est. 1978):** 1,500,000
**Density per sq mi.:** 11.4
**Capital and largest city (est. 1974):** Brazzaville, 310,500
**Monetary unit:** Franc CFA
**Ethnic groups:** Bavilis, Balalis, Batékés, M'Bochis
**Languages:** French, Lingala, Kokongo
**Religions:** Animist, 60%; Roman Catholic, 38%
**Gross national product (1976):** $700 million
**National name:** République Populaire du Congo
**Member of French Community**
**Freedom House classifications:** Capitalist-socialist pre-industrial, one-party socialist.

**Geography.** The Congo is situated in west central Africa astride the Equator. It borders on Gabon, Cameroon, the Central African Empire, Zaire, and the Angola exclave of Cabinda, with a short stretch of coast on the South Atlantic. Its area is nearly three times that of Pennsylvania.

Most of the inland is tropical rain forest, drained by tributaries of the Zaire (Congo) River, which flows south along the eastern border with Zaire to Stanley Pool. The narrow coastal plain rises to highlands separated from the inland plateaus by the 200-mile-wide Niari River Valley, which gives passage to the coast.

**Government.** Since the coup d'état of September 1968 the country has been governed by a National Council of the Revolution. The Congolese Labor Party (PCT) is the only party.

**History.** The inhabitants of the former French Congo, mainly Bantu peoples with Pygmies in the north, were subjects of several kingdoms in earlier times.

The Frenchman Pierre Savorgnan de Brazza signed a treaty with Makoko, ruler of the Bateke people, in 1880, which established French control. The area, with Gabon and Ubangi-Shari, was constituted the colony of French Equatorial Africa in 1910. It joined Chad in supporting the Free French cause in World War II. It proclaimed its independence without leaving the French Community in 1960. The republic was a target of Chinese Communist subversion, and in 1965 the United States broke off relations with it.

Maj. Marien Ngouabi, head of the National Council of the Revolution, took power as President on Jan. 1, 1969. He was sworn in for a second five-year term in January 1975. A visit to Moscow by Ngouabi in March ended with the signing of a Soviet-Congolese economic and technical aid pact.

A four-man commando squad assassinated Ngouabi in Brazzaville on March 18, 1977. Five days later the assassination of Émile Cardinal Biayenda, Archbishop of Brazzaville, was announced. Former President Alphonse Massamba-Débat, accused by the government of plotting both deaths, was executed March 25.

Col. Joachim Yhombi-Opango, Army Chief of Staff, assumed the Presidency April 4. In June, the new government agreed to resume diplomatic relations with the U.S.

**Economy.** The chief agricultural products of the Congo are cocoa, coffee, and tobacco. Okoumé and limba woods are important forest products. Lead and cassiterite (tin) are the principal minerals.

Chief export in 1973 was crude oil (54%). Leading customers were France (29%), Italy (14%), West Germany (10%), South Africa (9%), Netherlands (7%). Leading suppliers were France (56%), West Germany (7%), U.S. (6%), Netherlands (6%).

## COSTA RICA

**Republic of Costa Rica**
**President:** Rodrigo Carazo Odio (1978)
**Area:** 19,575 sq mi. (50,700 sq km)
**Population (est. 1978):** 2,120,000 (approx.: white and Mestizo, 97.6%; black, 1.9%; Indian, .4%; Asiatic, .1%)
**Density per square mile:** 108.3
**Capital and largest city (est. 1977):** San José, 547,200
**Monetary unit:** Colón
**Language:** Spanish
**Religion:** Roman Catholic
**Gross national product (1976):** $2.3 billion
**National name:** República de Costa Rica
**Freedom House classifications:** Capitalist industrial, multi-party centralized

**Geography.** This Central American country lies between Nicaragua to the north and Panama to the south. Its area slightly exceeds that of Vermont and New Hampshire combined.

Most of Costa Rica is tableland, from 3,000 to 6,000 feet (914 to 1,829 m) above sea level. Cocos Island (10 sq mi.), about 300 miles off the Pacific Coast, is under Costa Rican sovereignty; although it is mostly tropical jungle, it is of potential strategic importance in defense of the Panama Canal.

**Government.** Under the 1949 Constitution, the President and the one-house Legislative Assembly of 57 members are elected for terms of four years.

The army was abolished in 1949. There is a civil guard of 3,000 and a rural guard of 2,500.

The major political parties are Unity Party (27 of 57 seats in Legislative Assembly), led by Rafael A. Grillo; National Liberation Party (25 seats), led by Armando Arauz; Pueblo Unido Party (3 seats), led by Humberto Vargas Carbonel; Agricola Cartagines Party (1 seat), led by Martin Brenes; Frente Popular Party (1 seat), led by Dr. Rodolfo Cerdas Cruz.

**History.** Costa Rica was inhabited by 25,000 Indians when Columbus discovered it and probably named it in 1502. Few of the Indians survived the Spanish conquest, which began in 1563. The region was administered as a Spanish province. It achieved independence in 1821 but was absorbed for two years by Agustín de Iturbide in his Mexican Empire. It was established as a republic in 1848.

Except for the military dictatorship of Tomás Guardia from 1870 to 1882, Costa Rica has enjoyed one of the most democratic governments in Latin America.

On Feb. 5, 1978, Rodrigo Carazo Odio, leader of a four-party opposition coalition called the Unity Party, defeated the candidate of the ruling National Liberation Party (PLN). His victory was attributed partly to the fact that the government had granted protection to Robert L. Vesco, a fugitive U.S. financier. On his inauguration in May, Carazo ordered that Vesco be barred from Costa Rica.

**Economy.** Coffee, bananas, abaca, fiber, cacao, and sugar are the basic agricultural products. The mountain slopes yield such forest products as balsa, cedar, dyewood, mahogany, and rosewood. Per capita income is the highest in Central America.

Chief exports in 1975 were coffee (26%), bananas (25%), sugar (10%), and meat (8%). Leading customers were U.S. (40%), West Germany (11%), Nicaragua (8%), Guatemala (7%), El Salvador (6%). Leading suppliers were U.S. (37%), Japan (10%), Guatemala (6%), West Germany (6%), Nicaragua (6%), El Salvador (5%).

## CUBA

**Republic of Cuba**
**Premier:** Fidel Castro (1956)
**Area:** 44,218 sq mi. (114,524, sq km)
**Population (est. 1977):** 9,590,000
**Density per square mile:** 216.9
**Capital:** Havana
**Largest cities (est. 1975 by U.N.):** Havana, 1,861,400; Santiago de Cuba, 315,800; Camagüey, 221,800; Holguín, 151,900; Guantánamo, 148,800; Santa Clara, 146,650
**Monetary unit:** Peso
**Language:** Spanish
**Religion:** Roman Catholic
**Gross national product (1976):** $8.1 billion
**National name:** República de Cuba
**Freedom House classifications:** Socialist industrial, one-party communist

**Geography.** The largest island of the West Indies group (equal in area to Pennsylvania), Cuba is also the westernmost—just west of Hispaniola (Haiti and the Dominican Republic), and 90 miles south of Key West, Fla., at the entrance to the Gulf of Mexico.

The island has mountainous areas in the southeast, central area, and the west (Sierra Maestra). The rest of the country is flat or rolling.

**Government.** There have been no national elections since 1958. Fidel Castro heads the Council of Ministers, the chief governing body.

The only political party is the Cuban Communist Party, with a 100-member Central Committee; the power rests with a Politbureau of 8 and a Secretariat of 6.

**History.** Cuba was occupied by the Arawak Indians when Columbus discovered the island in 1492; they died off from diseases brought by sailors and settlers. By 1511, Spaniards under Diego Velásquez were founding settlements that served as bases for Spanish exploration. Cuba soon after served as an assembly point for treasure looted by the conquistadores, attracting French and English pirates.

Black slaves and free laborers were imported to work sugar and tobacco plantations, and waves of chiefly Spanish immigrants maintained a European character in the island's culture. Early slave rebellions and conflicts between colonials and Spanish rulers laid the foundation for an independence movement that turned into open warfare from 1867 to 1878. The poet, José Marti, in 1895 led the struggle that finally ended Spanish rule, thanks largely to U.S. intervention in 1898 after the sinking of the battleship *Maine* in Havana harbor. An 1899 treaty made Cuba an independent republic under U.S. protection. A U.S. occupation, ending in 1902, suppressed yellow fever and brought large American investment. Washington in 1906–09 invoked the Platt amendment to the treaty, which gave it the right to intervene in order to suppress any revolt. U.S. troops came back in 1912 and again in 1917 to restore order.

Gerardo Machado, President during the depression, planned vast social reforms but abandoned them. The U.S., under President Franklin D. Roosevelt, scrapped the Platt Amendment in 1934. Fulgencio Batista, an army sergeant, led a revolt in 1934 that overthrew the Machado regime and developed into a Batista dictatorship. A succession of constitutionally elected Presidents—Ramón Grau San Martín, Carlos Mendieta, Miguel Mariano Gómez, Carlos Prío Socarrás—pushed through social reforms, hampered by overwhelming corruption manipulated by Batista. Batista seized power in 1952.

Fidel Castro staged a hopeless revolt in 1953. Captured and paroled he went to Oriente Province and, aided by an Argentinian adventurer, Ernesto (Ché) Guevara, rebuilt his forces and waged a guerrilla war. The U.S. withdrew support from Batista in 1958. With funds from Soviet sources, Castro bought off the leaders of Batista's army. This and popular support from the intellectual and laboring classes demoralized the army, and Castro's forces grew as he marched on Havana. Batista fled to the Dominican Republic on Jan. 1, 1959.

Executions and torture by the new Castro regime caused a world outcry. Castro antagonized the U.S. in 1959 by confiscating U.S. investments in banks and industries and by seizing large U.S. landholdings, turning them at first into collective farms, then into Soviet-type state farms.

The U.S. broke off relations on Jan. 3, 1961, and Castro disclosed his alliance with the U.S.S.R. and the Soviet bloc. Thousands of Cubans fled to the U.S. From their ranks an invasion force was recruited by an all-party coalition financed and guided by the U.S. Central Intelligence Agency and trained in Florida and Guatemala. It landed in the Bay of Pigs, Cuba, on April 17, 1961, but when John F. Kennedy, then President, refused it air support under Soviet and Latin American pressure, the effort collapsed.

In 1962 the U.S.S.R. built missile sites in Cuba and provided Castro's army with troops, planes, and submarines. Alarmed, President Kennedy on Oct. 22, 1962, served notice that the U.S. was willing to risk war to enforce a demand that the Soviets remove weapons and troops considered to threaten U.S. security. The U.S. confronted Soviet vessels with U.S. warships. Nikita Khrushchev, then Soviet Premier, agreed to remove the missiles, and the blockade was lifted on November 20. Shortly before Christmas, Castro released 1,113 Bay of Pigs prisoners.

Russia, spending over $1 million a day (about $400 million a year) to keep Cuba afloat, had to increase its contribution by over $100 million in 1971, but gained greater control over Cuba's economy by setting up a joint Soviet-Cuban economic commission on management and efficiency.

Neither nation formally admitted it, but U.S.-Cuban relations began to thaw with negotiation of a 1973 agreement to end air hijacking. Except for political refugees, criminal hijackers will be extradited to their home country or tried for the crime where they land; also, both nations pledged to forbid attacks on the other to be mounted from their territory.

In 1975, both sides signaled readiness to improve relations. U.S. curbs on travel by Cuba'a United Nations delegation were eased in February. On July 29, the U.S. joined 15 Latin American republics in voting to scrap economic and diplomatic sanctions the O.A.S. had imposed against Cuba in 1964.

The improving U.S.-Cuban climate cooled in late 1975 with the disclosure that Cuban troops were being used to bolster the Popular Movement for the Liberation of Angola in the former Portuguese African colony. President Ford warned on December 20 that the Angolan intervention as well as continued Cuban support for a Puerto Rican independence faction "erodes any chance for improvement of relations."

Despite a May 1976 commitment by Cuba to begin withdrawal from Angola, there were reports of Cuban troops in the Congo, Somalia, and the Mideast continuing to "export revolution."

The Carter Administration signaled its intention to end the long estrangement when it signd two fishing agreements with Cuba on April 27 after removing restrictions on March 9 on travel to the island by Americans. In May, the Senate Foreign Relations Committee approved a modification of the boycott, which would permit Cuba to buy medicine, food, and agricultural supplies.

Sept. 1, 1977, Cuban diplomats opened a Cuban interests section in their old embassy in Washington and 10 Americans reopened a similar office in the former U.S. embassy in Havana. The new harmony was shattered early in 1978, however, when Washington charged that Cuban troops were fighting in Ethiopia against Somali and Eritrean rebels. National Security Adviser Zbigniew Brzezinski asserted February 24 that 10,000 to 11,000 Cubans were serving in Ethiopia under the command of a Soviet general.

A repetition in May 1978 of the 1977 invasion of Shaba province in Zaire touched off a world-wide furor as Cuba was accused by the U.S., France, and Zaire of training, arming, and even taking part in the new invasion. Castro called in Lyle Lane, head of the U.S. interest section in Havana, on May 17 to deny the charges. He later told U.S. congressmen and newsmen he tried to halt the invasion. Although President Carter insisted that he had evidence, Congressional foreign relations committee members expressed doubts about the White House claims.

As 1978 ended, Castro was believed to have been withdrawing troops from Ethiopia, but Cubans remained a strong presence there and in Mozambique, Angola, and elsewhere in Africa. U.S. intelligence sources put Cuban losses in Africa at 1,500 men out of a total of 40,000 sent there.

**Economy.** Half of the employed are engaged in agriculture, which normally accounts for more than 90% of the exports. About two thirds of the cultivated area is devoted to sugar-cane. Other important crops are tobacco, coffee, cacao, fruits, vegetables, henequen, corn, pineapples, and rice.

Manufactured products are sugar, molasses, syrup, brandy, rum, alcohol, cigars, cigarettes, cigar boxes, sponges, cement, cordage, salt, dressed hides, dairy products, and canned goods.

Rich mineral beds, mostly in the eastern province of Oriente, include iron, copper, manganese, chromium, and nickel.

Chief exports in 1974 were sugar (86%) and nickel and copper ores (6%). Leading customers were U.S.S.R. (36%), Japan (17%), Spain (7%), East Germany (5%). Leading suppliers were U.S.S.R. (47%), Japan (8%), U.K. (5%).

## CYPRUS

**Republic of Cyprus**
**President:** Spyros Kyprianou (1977)
**Area:** 3,572 sq mi (9,251 sq km)
**Population (est. 1978):** 700,000 (Greek, 82%, Turkish, 18%)
**Density per square mile:** 196.0
**Capital and largest city (est. 1977):** Nicosia, 120,000
**Monetary unit:** Cyprus pound
**Languages:** Greek, Turkish, English
**Religions:** Greek Orthodox, 77%; Islam, 18%
**Gross national product (1976):** $789 million
**National name:** Kypriaki Dimokratia—Kibris Cumhuriyeti
**Member of Commonwealth of Nations**
**Freedom House classifications:** Capitalist industrial, multi-party decentralized

**Geography.** The third largest island in the Mediterranean (half again larger than Delaware), Cyprus lies off the southern coast of Turkey and the western shore of Syria. Most of the country consists of a wide plain lying between two mountain ranges that cross the island. The highest peak is Mt. Olympus at 6,406 feet (1,953 m).

**Government.** Under the republic's Constitution, for the protection of the Turkish minority the Vice President as well as three of the ten Cabinet ministers must be from the Turkish community, while the House of Representatives shall be elected by each community separately, 70% Greek Cypriote and 30% Turkish Cypriote representatives.

The Greek and Turkish communities are self-governing in questions of religion, education, and culture. Other governmental matters are under the jurisdiction of the central government. Each community is entitled to a Communal Chamber.

The Greek Communal Chamber, which had 23 members, was abolished in March 1965 and its function was absorbed by the Ministry of Education. The Turkish Communal Chamber, however, has continued to function.

The members of the Parliament were elected Sept. 5, 1976. Thirty-five seats are held by Greeks and 15 by Turks. The following is a breakdown of the 35 seats held by Greeks: Democratic Front of Spyros Kyprianou (19); AKEL (Progressive Party of the Working People) (9); EDEK Socialist Party of Dr. Vassos Lyssarides (4); Independents (3). The 15 Turkish members have not attended sessions of the House since January 1964.

**History.** Cyprus was the site of early Phoenician and Greek colonies. For centuries its rule passed through many hands. It fell to the Turks in 1571, and a large Turkish colony settled on the island.

In World War I, on the outbreak of hostilities with Turkey, the U.K. annexed the island. It was declared a crown colony in 1925.

For centuries the Greek population of the island, regarding Greece as its mother country, has sought self-determination and reunion with it *(enosis)*. The resulting quarrel with Turkey threatened the North Atlantic Alliance. Cyprus became an independent nation on Aug. 16, 1960, with the U.K., Greece, and Turkey as guarantor powers.

After troubled years, a crisis was averted in 1968 when an American mediator, Cyrus Vance, induced Turkey, Greece, and Cyprus to accept a solution proposed by U.N. Secretary General Thant for withdrawal of the Greek troops and the dismantling of Turkish invasion forces. The ethnic blocs began long direct negotiations for a new Constitution.

Archbishop Makarios, who had been president since 1959, was overthrown July 15, 1974, by a military coup led by the Cypriot National Guard. The new regime named Nikos Giorgiades Sampson as president and Bishop Gennadios as head of the Cypriot Church to replace Makarios. The rebels were led by rightist Greek officers who supported *enosis*.

Diplomacy failed to resolve the crisis. Turkey invaded Cyprus by sea and air July 20, 1974, asserting its right to protect the Turkish Cypriote minority. Greece rejected a Turkish demand for withdrawal of the 650 Greek officers who had engineered the coup. The crisis forced resignation of the military junta that had ruled Greece for seven years.

Geneva talks involving Greece, Turkey, the U.K., and the two Cypriote factions failed in mid-August, and the Turks kept control of 40% of the island. Greece made no armed response to the superior Turkish force, but bitterly suspended military participation in the NATO alliance.

On Cyprus, U.S. Ambassador Rodger P. Davies was shot to death in August during Greek Cypriote riots. The tension continued after Makarios returned to replace Sampson in the presidency on Dec. 7, 1974. He offered self-government to the Turkish minority, but rejected any solution "involving transfer of populations and amounting to partition of Cyprus."

Turkish Cypriots proclaimed a separate state in the northern 40% of the island and proposed a "bi-regional federation." Some 200,000 Greek Cypriots demanded return to homes in the Turkish zone and an estimated three fourths of the 45,000 ethnic Turks in the Greek zone crossed into the Turkish area.

Makarios died on Aug. 3, 1977, and Spyros Kiprianou was elected to serve the remaining five months of his term. On Jan. 26, 1978, Kiprianou, running unopposed, won a full five-year term.

Despite intense pressure from the U.S. and other NATO allies anxious to end the dispute that kept both Greece and Turkey from functioning as defenders of the strategic eastern Mediterranean, intercommunal negotiations were still deadlocked in the latter half of 1978.

**Economy.** Agriculture is the principal industry of the island. Products include barley, wheat, potatoes, wine, and fruit. Mining is also important.

Chief exports in 1976 were potatoes (17%), cement (9%), clothing (8%), cigarettes (6%), wine (5%), and citrus fruit (5%). Leading customers were U.K. (28%), Lebanon (17%), Syria (6%), Saudi Arabia (6%), Libya (6%), U.S.S.R. (5%). Leading suppliers were U.K. (20%), Greece (10%), Italy (9%), West Germany (7%), Turkey (6%), U.S. (6%), France (5%).

## CZECHOSLOVAKIA

**Czechoslovak Socialist Republic**
**President:** Gustav Husak (1975)
**Premier:** Lubomir Strougal (1970)
**Area:** 49,373 sq mi. (127,869 sq km)
**Population (est. 1978):** 15,150,000 (Czech 68%; Slovak, 32%)
**Density per square mile:** 306.8
**Capital:** Prague
**Largest cities (est. 1977):** 1,179,600; Prague, 1,179,600; (est. 1974 by U.N.): Brno, 343,860; Bratislava, 328,765; Ostrava, 292,404; Košice, 166,240; Plzeň, 154,126
**Monetary unit:** Koruna
**Languages:** Czech, Slovak, Hungarian
**Religions:** Roman Catholic, 70%; Czechoslovak Church, 8%; Protestant, 7%; Greek Orthodox, 5%.
**Gross national product (1976):** $57.3 billion
**National name:** Ceskoslovenská Socialistická Republika
**Freedom House classifications:** Socialist industrial, one-party communist

**Geography.** Czechoslovakia lies in central Europe, a neighbor of East and West Germany, Poland, the U.S.S.R., Hungary, and Austria. It is equal in size to New York State. The principal rivers—the Elbe, Danube, Oder, and Moldau—are vital commercially to this landlocked country, both for waterborne commerce and agriculture, which flourishes in fertile valleys irrigated by these rivers and their tributaries.

**Government.** Since 1969 the supreme organ of the state has been the Federal Assembly with two equal chambers: the Chamber of People with 200 deputies and the Chamber of Nations with 150 deputies (75 from the Czech Socialist Republic and 75 from the Slovak Socialist Republic). The chief executive is the President, who is elected by the Federal Assembly for a five-year term. The Premier and his Cabinet are appointed by the President but are responsible to the Federal Assembly.

The major political parties are the Communist Party, led by First Secretary Gustav Husak in both republics; Socialist Party; People's Party in the Czech Socialist Republic; Slovak Freedom Party and Slovak Reconstruction Party in the Slovak Socialist Republic. Together with trade unions, youth organizations, and other organizations, they form the National Front.

**History.** Probably about the 5th century A.D., Slavic tribes from the Vistula basin settled in the region of modern Czechoslovakia. Slovakia came under Magyar domination. The Czechs founded the kingdom of Bohemia, the Premyslide dynasty, which ruled Bohemia and Moravia from the 10th to the 16th century. One of the Bohemian kings, Charles IV, Holy Roman Emperor, made Prague an imperial capital and a center of Latin scholarship. The Hussite movement founded by Jan Hus (1369?–1415) linked the Slavs to the Reformation and revived Czech nationalism, previously under German domination. A Hapsburg, Ferdinand I, ascended the throne in 1526. The Czechs rebelled in 1618. Defeated in 1620, they were ruled for the next 300 years as part of the Austrian Empire.

In World War I, Czech and Slovak patriots, notably Thomas G. Masaryk and Milan Stefanik, promoted Czech-Slovak independence from abroad while their followers fought against the Central Powers. On Oct. 28, 1918, Czechoslovakia proclaimed itself a republic. Shortly thereafter Masaryk was unanimously elected first President.

Hitler, dictator of Nazi Germany, provoked the country's German minority in the Sudetenland, led by Konrad Henlein, to agitate for autonomy. At the Munich Conference on Sept. 30, 1938, France and the U.K., seeking to avoid World War II, agreed that the Nazis could take the Czech Sudetenland. Dr. Eduard Beneš, who had succeeded Masaryk, resigned on Oct. 5, 1938, and fled to London. Czechoslovakia became a state within the German orbit and was known as Czecho-Slovakia. In March 1939, the Nazis occupied the country. Beneš organized a government-in-exile in London in 1940.

Soon after Czechoslovakia was liberated in World War II and the government returned in April 1945, it was obliged to cede Ruthenia to the U.S.S.R. On July 3, 1946, a Communist, Klement Gottwald, formed a six-party coalition Cabinet. Pressure from Moscow increased until Feb. 23–25, 1948, when the Communists seized complete control in a coup d'état. Following constituent assembly elections in which the Communists and their allies were unopposed, a new Constitution was adopted.

Beneš refused to sign it and resigned on June 7, 1948; he died mysteriously on Sept. 3, 1948. The Constitution was promulgated June 9, 1948. Thereafter agriculture was collectivized, industry almost completely socialized, and foreign trade conducted chiefly with the Soviet bloc. Industrialization was intensified and concentrated upon heavy industry. The "people's democracy" was converted into a "socialist" state by a new Constitution adopted June 11, 1960.

After the death of the Soviet dictator Joseph Stalin and the relaxing of Soviet controls, Czechoslovakia witnessed a nationalist awakening. In 1968 conservative Stalinists were driven from power and replaced by more liberal, reform-minded Communists.

In more orthodox circles of the U.S.S.R. and her East European satellites, fears arose that the trend was undermining Communist rule. Soviet military maneuvers on Czechoslovak soil in May 1968 were followed in July by a meeting of the U.S.S.R. with Poland, Bulgaria, East Germany, and Hungary in Warsaw that demanded an accounting, which Prague refused. Czechoslovak-Soviet talks on Czechoslovak territory, at Cierna, in late July 1968 led to an accord. But the Russians charged that the Czechoslovaks reneged on pledges to modify their policies, and on Aug. 20–21, 1968, troops of the five powers, estimated at 600,000, executed lightning invasion and occupation.

Soviet secret police seized the Czechoslovak top leadership and detained it for several days in Moscow. But Soviet efforts to establish a puppet regime failed. President Ludvik Svoboda negotiated an accord providing for a gradual troop withdrawal in return for "normalization" of political policy.

The purge of liberals was virtually completed in 1970. Only Svoboda remained from 1968. Husak, who became Secretary General of the Communist Party in 1969, promised no show trials, but most liberals were punished. Czechoslovakia signed a new friendship treaty with the U.S.S.R. that codified the "Brezhnev doctrine," under which Russia can invade any Eastern European socialist nation that threatens to leave the satellite camp.

Continuing ferment surfaced early in 1975 with publication in the West of a long letter of protest against repression written by Alexander Dubček, First Secretary of the Czechoslovak Communist Party during the 1968 "Prague Spring." The letter, addressed to the Presidium of Czechoslovakia's Federal Assembly, charged that the regime had purged thousands of creative workers. Dubček was later reported transferred to a menial forester's job.

One of the most vigorous of the Eastern European groups formed to support human rights in the wake of the 1975 Helsinki Conference on Security and Cooperation in Europe was the Czech "Charter 77," an association of 240 intellectuals who signed a New Year manifesto protesting the suppression of freedom. Detentions of the signers began immediately, and a second manifesto appeared on January 8 with 300 signatures condemning the official reaction to the first. On January 28, the government offered to let five of the dissidents leave the country, but they refused.

Despite warnings from the U.S., British, and other western governments, arrests of members of the group continued, and five were sentenced to jail terms in October 1977. Playwright Vaclav Havel, given a suspended sentence, predicted more persecution for the group. Charter 77 adherents marked the first anniversary of their founding by issuing a manifesto Jan. 1, 1978, calling on the government to permit open debate on the observance of human rights in Czechoslovakia. But, by mid-1978, the government had not responded to their appeals.

**Economy.** Nationalization of all enterprises with more than 50 employees as well as concerns of any size operating in key industries was completed between 1945 and 1948. Distribution of large estates had already been accomplished by the 1919 Land Reform Law. Total collectivization of agriculture was the professed aim of the Communist regime.

Sugar beets, wheat, corn, and high-grade barley and hops for beer brewing are cultivated in the low-lying areas. In more elevated regions, the cultivation of potatoes, rye, and oats predominates. Higher lands are also used for growing fodder crops or for grazing.

Abundance of coal and presence of iron ore give the country a big metallurgical industry. The Skoda steel works at Plzeň are among the largest in Europe.

Other industries are glass, porcelain, and pottery making, while large forest areas provide raw material for the timber, paper, and cellulose industries. Also highly developed are the textile industries, including cotton, wool flax, and jute production, and the shoe industry. The famous Bat'a shoe factories, now nationalized, are at Gottwaldov, formerly Zlin.

Most important of Czechoslovakia's varied minerals are pit coal and lignite, with the principal coal fields in the Ostrava-Karvinná area, connected with the Polish fields of Upper Silesia.

Iron ore is produced in Czechoslovakia, but much ore is imported to meet the demands of the flourishing iron and steel industry. Excellent porcelain raw materials, particularly kaolin, are obtained in western Bohemia and southern Moravia. Other minerals are antimony, gold, magnesite, oil, uranium, silver, and zinc.

Chief exports in 1975 were machinery (36%), iron and steel (11%), motor vehicles (8%) and chemicals (5%). Leading customers were U.S.S.R. (33%), East Germany (12%), Poland (9%), Hungary (6%), West Germany (6%). Leading suppliers were U.S.S.R. (32%), East Germany (12%), Poland (10%), West Germany (6%), Hungary (5%).

## DENMARK

**Kingdom of Denmark**
**Sovereign:** Queen Margrethe II (1972)
**Premier:** Anker Jørgensen (1975)
**Area:** 16,629 sq mi. (43,069 sq km)[1]

**Population (est. 1978):** 5,110,000[1]
**Density per square mile:** 367.3
**Capital:** Copenhagen
**Largest cities (est. 1974):** Copenhagen (including Frederiksberg) 1,380,000; (est. 1974 by U.N.): Århus, 245,900; Odense, 168,200; Ålborg, 154,600
**Monetary unit:** Krone
**Language:** Danish
**Religion:** Lutheran (established)
**Gross national product (1976):** $38.2 billion
**National name:** Kongeriget Danmark
**Freedom House classifications:** Capitalist-socialist industrial, multi-party centralized

**Geography.** Smallest of the Scandinavian countries (half the size of Maine), Denmark occupies the Jutland peninsula, which extends north from Germany between the tips of Norway and Sweden. To the west is the North Sea and to the east the Baltic.

The country also consists of several Baltic islands; the two largest are Sjaelland, the site of Copenhagen, and Fyn. The narrow waters off the north coast are called the Skagerrak and those off the east, the Kattegat.

**Government.** Denmark has been a constitutional monarch since 1849. Legislative power is held jointly by the Sovereign and parliament. The Constitution of 1953 provides for a unicameral parliament called the Folketing consisting of 179 popularly elected members serving for four years. The Cabinet is presided over by the Sovereign, who appoints the Prime Minister.

The Sovereign, Queen Margrethe II, was born April 16, 1940, and became Queen—the first in Denmark's history—Jan. 15, 1972, the day after her father, King Frederik IX, died at 72 in the 25th year of his reign. Margrethe was the eldest of his three daughters (by Princess Ingrid of Sweden). The nation's Constitution was amended in 1953 to permit her to succeed her father in the absence of a male heir to the throne. (Denmark was ruled six centuries ago by Margrethe I, but she was never crowned queen since there was no female right of succession.) Margrethe's sisters are Benedikte (born 1944) and Anne Marie (born 1946), now the former Queen of Greece.

The major political parties are the Social Democratic Party (65 seats in Folketing), led by Premier Anker Jørgensen; Progress Party (26 seats), led by Mogens Glistrup; Liberal Democratic Party (21 seats), led by Poul Hartling; Conservative Party (15 seats), led by Poul Schlüter; Center Democratic Party (11 seats); Socialist People's Party (7 seats), led by Gert Petersen; Communist Party (7 seats), led by Knud Jespersen; Radical Liberal Party (6 seats); Single Tax Party (6 seats); Christian People's Party (6 seats).

**History.** Denmark emerged with establishment of the Norwegian dynasty of the Ynglinger in Jutland at the end of the 8th century. Danish mariners played a major role in the raids of the Vikings or Norsemen on Western Europe and particularly England. It was Christianized by St. Ansgar and Harald Blaatand (Bluetooth)—the first Christian king—in the 10th century. Harald's son, Sweyn, conquered England in 1013. His son, Canute the Great, who reigned from 1014 to 1035, united Denmark, England, and Norway under his rule; the southern part of Sweden was part of Denmark until the 17th century. On Canute's death, civil war tore the country until Waldemar I (1157–82) re-established Danish hegemony over the north.

In 1282 the nobles won the Great Charter, and Eric V was forced to share power with parliament and a Council of Nobles. Waldemar IV (1340–75) restored Danish power, checked only by the Hanseatic League of North German cities allied with ports from Holland to Poland. His daughter, Margaret, in 1397 united under her rule Denmark, Norway, and Sweden. But Sweden achieved autonomy and in 1523, under Gustavus I, independence.

Denmark supported Napoleon, for which she was punished at the Congress of Vienna in 1815 by the loss of Norway to Sweden. In 1864 Bismarck, together with the Austrians, made war on the little country as an initial step in the unification of Germany. Denmark was neutral in World War I. In 1939 Denmark signed a 10-year pact with Hitler, but less than a year later she was invaded by the Nazis. King Christian X cautioned his fellow countrymen to accept the occupation, but there was widespread resistance against the Nazi occupation. In 1944, Iceland declared its independence from Denmark, thus putting an end to a union that had existed since 1380.

Liberated by British troops in May 1945, Denmark joined the United Nations in 1945 and the North Atlantic Treaty Organization in 1949. The country staged a fast recovery after World War II in both agriculture and manufacturing and was a leader in liberalizing trade.

The Social Democrats largely ran Denmark after the war but were ousted in 1973 when, in a December election dominated by protests against high taxes, all established parties lost heavily. The big winner was the new Progress Party. A minority government was formed by the Liberal Democrats, with their leader, Poul Hartling, as Premier. After losing a vote of confidence in January 1975, Hartling resigned and was succeeded by Anker Jørgensen, a Social Democrat who was Premier in 1972–73.

In 1969, Denmark became the first Western nation to legalize the sale of written and pictorial pornography; police reported sex crimes down 30% to 50% in the following year.

Denmark's application to join the European Economic Community (Common Market) was approved in 1972 along with those of the U.K., Norway, and Ireland.

In May 1978, legislation was introduced in the Folketing to give Greenland home rule in May 1979. The island would remain part of the monarchy, and Copenhagen would retain responsibility for its defense and foreign affairs.

**Economy.** Denmark's principal agricultural products are wheat, barley, oats, rye, potatoes, and sugar beets.

The largest industries are food processing and iron and metal. Others are chemicals and pharmaceuticals, wood and paper, clothing, textiles, machinery, beverages, and leather.

The fishing industry, centered at Copenhagen but carried on also in the shallow fiords and in the deeper waters of the Baltic, North Sea, and Skagerrak, is a basic part of the Danish economy.

Chief exports in 1976 were machinery (21%), meat (14%), chemicals (7%), dairy products (6%), and ships and boats (5%). Leading customers were EEC (45%; incl. U.K. 17%, West Germany 14%, Italy 5%), Sweden (16%), Norway (7%), U.S. (6%). Leading suppliers were EEC (47%; incl. West Germany 21%, U.K. 10%, Netherlands 5%), Sweden

1. Excluding Faeroe Islands and Greenland.

(14%), U.S. (5%), Norway (5%).

## Outlying Territories of Denmark

### FAEROE ISLANDS

**Status:** Autonomous part of Denmark
**Commissioner:** L. Groth (1972)
**Area:** 540 sq mi. (1,399 sq km)
**Population (est. 1978):** 43,000
**Density per square mile:** 79.9
**Capital (est. 1975):** Thorshavn, 11,300
**Monetary unit:** Faeroese krone

This group of 21 islands, lying in the North Atlantic about 200 miles northwest of the Shetland Islands, joined Denmark in 1386 and has since been part of the Danish kingdom. The islands were occupied by British troops during World War II, after the German occupation of Denmark. The principal pursuits are fishing and sheep grazing. The Faeroes have home rule under a bill enacted in 1948; they also have two representatives in the Danish Folketing.

Chief exports in 1975 were fish and products (80%; incl fish meal 16%). Leading customers were Denmark (19%), U.S. (15%), U.K. (13%), Portugal (11%), Spain (10%), Italy (9%), West Germany (5%), France (5%). Leading suppliers were Denmark (66%), Norway (19%).

### GREENLAND

**Status:** Integral part of Kingdom of Denmark.
**Governor:** H. J. Lassen (1973).
**Area:** 839,999 sq mi. (incl. 708,069 sq mi. covered by icecap) (2,175,600 sq km).
**Population (est. 1978):** 57,500.
**Capital (est. 1975):** Godthaab, 8,300.
**Chief exports:** fish, fur skins, cryolite.

Greenland, the world's largest island, was colonized in 985–86 by Eric the Red. Danish sovereignty, which covered only the west coast, was extended over the whole island in 1917. In 1941 the U.S. signed an agreement with the Danish minister in Washington, placing it under U.S. protection during World War II but maintaining Danish sovereignty. A definitive agreement for the joint defense of Greenland within the framework of NATO was signed on April 27, 1951. A large U.S. air base at Thule in the far north was completed in 1953.

Under 1953 amendments to the Danish Constitution, Greenland is part of Denmark and has two representatives in the Danish Folketing. There is a popularly elected council.

Greenland is the world's only source of natural cryolite, important in making aluminum.

Chief exports in 1975 were zinc ores (47%), fish and products (40%), and lead ores (7%). Leading customers were Denmark (38%), Finland (18%), Spain (14%), France (11%), West Germany (6%). Leading suppliers were Denmark (89%), U.K. (7%).

## DJIBOUTI

**Republic of Djibouti**
**President:** Hassan Gouled Aptidon (1977)
**Prime Minister:** Abdallah Mohamed Kamil (1978)
**Area:** 8,494 sq mi. (22,000 sq km)
**Population (est. 1978):** 225,000
**Density per sq mi.:** 26.5
**Capital (est. 1977):** Djibouti, 160,000
**Monetary unit:** Djibouti franc
**Languages:** Arabic, French, Saho-Afar, Somali
**Religions:** Islam and Christian
**Freedom House classifications:** Capitalist industrial, multi-party centralized

**Geography.** Djibouti lies in northeastern Africa on the Gulf of Aden at the southern entrance to the Red Sea. It borders on Ethiopia and Somalia. The country, the size of Massachusetts, is mainly a stony desert, with scattered plateaus and highlands.

**Government.** On May 8, 1977, the population of the French Territory of the Afars and Issas voted by more than 98% for independence. Voters at the same time approved a 65-member interim Constituent Assembly. France transferred sovereignty to the new nation of Djibouti on June 27 and on the same day it became the 49th member of the Organization of African Unity. There are four major political parties.

**History.** The territory that makes up Djibouti was acquired by France between 1843 and 1886 by treaties with the Somali sultans. Small, arid, and sparsely populated, Djibouti is important chiefly because of the capital city's port, the terminal of the Djibouti-Addis Ababa railway that carries 60% of Ethiopia's foreign trade.

Originally known as French Somaliland, the colony voted in 1958 and 1967 to remain under French rule. It was renamed the Territory of the Afars and Issas in 1967 and took the name of its capital city on attaining independence.

Somali rebels in Ethiopia's Ogaden province cut the railway to Djibouti in June 1977 and there was fear that the new nation might be absorbed by Somalia. Earlier, Somalia rejected a Soviet proposal for a federation with Djibouti and Ethiopia.

**Economy.** Among the poorest nations in the world, Djibouti has a per capita income of less than $50 a year. It exports boats, leather, and shoes, but its principal income has come from rail and port transit fees and salaries of French civil servants, some of whom were to remain and continue to be paid by France.

Chief exports in 1973 were ships and boats (16%) and leather and shoes (7%). Leading customer was France (84%). Leading suppliers were France (49%), Ethiopia (12%), Japan (6%).

## DOMINICAN REPUBLIC

**President:** Antonio Guzmán (1978)
**Area:** 18,816 sq mi. (48,734 sq km)
**Population (est. 1978):** 5,170,000 (approx.: mestizo and mulatto, 73%; white, 16%; black, 11%
**Density per square mile:** 274.8
**Capital:** Santo Domingo[1]
**Largest cities (est. 1977):** Santo Domingo, 1,000,000; **(1970 census):** Santiago de los Caballeros, 155,151
**Monetary unit:** Peso
**Language:** Spanish
**Religion:** Roman Catholic
**Gross national product (1976):** $3.8 billion
**National name:** República Dominicana
**Freedom House classifications:** Capitalist industrial, multi-party centralized

1. Called Ciudad Trujillo from 1936 to 1961.

**Geography.** The Dominican Republic in the West Indies, occupies the eastern two thirds of the island of Hispaniola, which it shares with Haiti. Its area equals that of Vermont and New Hampshire combined.

Crossed from northwest to southeast by a moutain range with elevations exceeding 10,000 feet (3,048 m), the country has fertile, well-watered land in the northeast, where nearly two thirds of the population lives. The southwest part is arid and has poor soil, except around Santo Domingo.

**Government.** The President is elected by direct vote every four years. Legislative powers rest with a Senate and a Chamber of Deputies, both elected by direct vote, also for four years. All citizens must vote when 18 years old or even before that age if they are married.

The major political parties are the Reformist Party, led by former President Joaquín Balaguer; Dominican Liberation Party, led by Juan Bosch; PQD (Partido Quisquellano Demócrata), led by Elías Wessin y Wessin); MIDA (Movimiento de Integración Democrática Anti-Releccionista), led by Augusto Lora.

**History.** The Dominican Republic was discovered by Columbus in 1492. He named it La Española, and his son, Diego, was its first viceroy. The capital, Santo Domingo, founded in 1496, is the oldest European settlement in the Western Hemisphere. Spain ceded the colony to France in 1795, and Haitian blacks under Toussaint L'Ouverture conquered it in 1801.

In 1808 the people revolted and in 1809 captured Santo Domingo, setting up the first republic. Spain regained title to the colony in 1814. In 1821 the people overthrew Spanish rule, but in 1822 they were reconquered by the Haitians. They revolted again in 1844, threw out the Haitians, and established the Dominican Republic headed by Pedro Santana. Uprisings and Haitian attacks led Santana to make the country a province of Spain from 1861 to 1865. The U.S. Senate refused to ratify a treaty of annexation. Disorder continued until Ulíses Heureaux established a ruthless dictatorship from 1882 to 1899. With further disorder, U.S. Marines occupied the country from 1916 to 1934.

A sergeant in the Dominican Army trained by the marines, Rafaél Leonides Trujillo Molina, overthrew Horacio Vásquez in 1930 and established a dictatorship that lasted until his assassination. To end border clashes, Trujillo mounted an invasion of Haiti in 1937, killing more than 10,000 Haitians. Trujillo established a ruthless dictatorship, developing the country but running it for his own benefit and that of his followers; he wound up owning much of the economy.

After Trujillo's assassination on May 30, 1961, disorders forced out the President, Joaquín Balaguer, but a governing council, in spite of an abortive military coup, steered the country to a return to constitutional government.

A new Constitution was adopted in 1962, and the first free elections since 1924 put Juan Bosch, a leftist leader, in office in December. A planned program of reforms with U.S. support was cut off in September by a rightwing military coup that replaced Bosch with a civilian triumvirate.

Leftists rebelled April 24, 1965, and President Lyndon Johnson sent in 400 Marines to help evacuate U.S. citizens. After an OAS ceasefire request May 6, a compromise installed Hector Garcia-Godoy as provisional President. Balaguer won in free elections in June 1966 against Bosch, and an OAS force of 9,000 U.S. troops and 2,000 from other countries withdrew. Balaguer restored political and economic stability and launched a 15-year development program.

Balaguer's longtime support for free elections faltered in 1978, when the army suspended the counting of ballots in the May 16 vote as he trailed in a fourth-term bid. After a warning from President Jimmy Carter, however, Balaguer accepted the victory of Antonio Guzmán of the opposition Dominican Revolutionary Party, who denied predictions that he would recognize Cuba and the U.S.S.R. and install a socialist regime.

**Economy.** Primarily agricultural, the country produces sugar, coffee, cacao, tobacco, bananas, rice, corn, cassava, beans, and sweet potatoes. Cattle raising is of growing importance. Sugar refining is the only important industry, although several new industries have been established in recent years.

Chief exports in 1976 were sugar (38%), coffee (14%), cocoa (7%), and tobacco (5%). Leading customers were U.S. (70%), Netherlands (7%), Switzerland (7%). Leading suppliers were U.S. (68%), Japan (9%).

# ECUADOR

**Republic of Ecuador**
**President of Supreme Council:** Vice Adm. Alfredo Poveda (1976)
**Area:** 109,483 sq mi. (283,561 sq km)
**Population (est. 1978):** 7,825,000
**Density per square mile:** 71.5
**Capital:** Quito
**Largest cities (est. 1977):** Quito, 977,400; **(1974 census):** Guayaquil, 823,200
**Monetary unit:** Sucre
**Languages:** Spanish, Quéchua, Jibaro
**Religion:** Roman Catholic
**Gross national product (1976):** $4.8 billion
**National name:** República del Ecuador
**Freedom House classifications:** Capitalist pre-industrial, non-party military

**Geography.** Ecuador, equal in area to Nevada, is in the northwest part of South America fronting on the Pacific. To the north is Colombia and to the east and south is Peru. Two high and parallel ranges of the Andes, traversing the country from north to south, are topped by tall volcanic peaks. The highest is Chimborazo at 20,577 feet (6,272 m).

The Galápagos Islands (or Colón Archipelago) (3,029 sq mi.; 7,845 sq km) in the Pacific Ocean about 600 miles (966 km) west of the South American mainland, became part of Ecuador in 1832.

**Government.** A bloodless military coup on Jan. 11, 1976 brought to power a three-man military junta headed by Vice Adm. Alfredo Poveda, deposing Brig. Gen. Guillermo Rodríguez Lara. Lara led a three-man junta in a similar coup Feb. 15, 1972, and subsequently assumed the Presidency.

Poveda did not immediately take the title, but as of August 1976 styled himself only President of the Supreme Council. The other members of the junta also constituting the Supreme Council were Army Brig. Gen. Guillermo Durán Arcentales and Air Force Brig. Gen. Luís Leoro Franco.

In discussions with political, labor and business leaders, the junta promised that it would return Ecuador to constitutional rule by 1979.

**History.** Ecuador was inhabited in early times by many peoples. The tribes in the northern highlands formed the Kingdom of Quito around A.D. 1000. It was absorbed, by conquest and marriage, into the Inca Empire. Pizarro conquered the land in 1532, and through the 17th century a thriving colony was built by exploitation of the Indians. The first revolt against Spain occurred in 1809. Ecuador then joined Venezuela, Colombia, and Panama in a confederacy founded by Simón Bolívar and known as Greater Colombia.

On the collapse of this union in 1830, Ecuador became independent. Subsequent history was one of revolts and dictatorships; it had 48 Presidents during the first 131 years of the republic. Conservatives ruled until the Revolution of 1895 ushered in nearly a half century of Radical Liberal rule, when the church was disestablished and freedom of worship, speech, and press was introduced.

On June 23, 1970, following six months of strife between University students and police, President José María Velasco Ibarra, who was elected in 1968 for the fifth time, took supreme powers to "avoid social and economic chaos." He closed universities, jailed some professors and businessmen, and demanded "reform" of the Supreme Court. Opposition political leaders were arrested and a military shake-up ensued.

Velasco was ousted nine months later by the junta, which sharply increased fees charged to foreign oil companies. Ecuador had already launched a "tuna war" in 1971, seizing more than a score of U.S. boats fishing within the 200-mile coastal zone claimed by Ecuador and seven other Latin American nations. The U.S. government repaid to the fishermen more than $1 million in fines levied by Ecuador and cut off military sales, a ban lifted in 1976 after general recognition of 200-mile coastal zones.

The Poveda government presented a new Constitution, which received majority approval on Jan. 15, 1978, as the first step toward a return to civilian rule. In the first round in presidential elections on July 9, Sixto Duran Ballen, candidate of the National Constitutional Front, and Raul Clemente Huerta of the Liberal Party placed highest among a field of six. A run-off was scheduled for fall.

**Economy.** Although agriculture is the basis of Ecuador's economy, less than 12 million acres are devoted to it. Cacao, the chief crop, is grown in coastal regions and lower river valleys. The plateaus and mountain valleys are used for grazing and dairying, and raising cereals and potatoes. After textiles, one of Ecuador's main industries is the manufacture of Panama hats, which are made of toquilla straw.

Ecuador produces gold, silver, copper, lead, and petroleum. It is the world's chief source of light, strong balsa wood.

Chief exports in 1975 were crude oil (49%), coffee (18%), and bananas (15%). Leading customers were U.S. (47%), Panama (15%), Chile (8%), Peru (7%). Leading suppliers were U.S. (40%), Japan (13%), West Germany (10%).

## EGYPT

**Arab Republic of Egypt**
**President:** Anwar el-Sadat (1970)
**Premier:** Mamdouh Salem (1975)
**Area:** 386,661 sq mi. (1,001,449 sq km)
**Population (est. 1978):** 39,500,000
**Density per square mile:** 102.2
**Capital:** Cairo
**Largest cities (est. 1976):** Cairo, 6,133,000; **(est. 1974 by U.N.):** Alexandria, 2,259,000; Giza, 853,700; Suez, 368,000; Subra el Khema, 346,000; Port Said, 342,000; El Mahalla el Kûbra, 287,800
**Monetary unit:** Egyptian pound
**Language:** Arabic
**Religions:** Islam, 93%; Christian (mostly Copt), 7%
**Gross national product (1976):** $10.5 billion
**Freedom House classifications:** Capitalist-socialist industrial, dominant party

**Geography.** Egypt, at the northeast corner of Africa on the Mediterranean Sea, is bordered on the west by Libya, on the south by the Sudan, and on the east by the Red Sea and Israel. It is nearly half again the size of Texas.

The historic Nile flows through the eastern third of the country. On either side of the Nile valley are desert plateaus, spotted with oases. In the north, toward the Mediterranean, plateaus are low, while south of Cairo they rise to a maximum of 1,015 feet (309 m) above sea level. At the head of the Red Sea is the Sinai Peninsula, between the Suez Canal and Israel.

Navigable throughout its course in Egypt, the Nile is used largely as a means of cheap transport for heavy goods. The principal port is Alexandria.

The Nile delta starts 100 miles south of the Mediterranean and fans out to a sea front of 155 miles between the cities of Alexandria and Port Said. From Cairo north, the Nile branches into many streams, the principal ones being the Damietta and the Rosetta.

Except for a narrow belt along the Mediterranean, Egypt lies in an almost rainless area, in which high daytime temperatures fall quickly at night.

**Government.** Executive power is held by the President, who appoints the Premier and one or more Vice Presidents.

The major political parties are the Egypt-Arab Socialist Party, Free Socialist Party, Nationalist Progressive Party, and Independent Front.

**History.** Egyptian history dates back to about 4000 B.C., when the kingdoms of upper and lower Egypt, already highly civilized, were united. Egypt's "Golden Age" coincided with the 18th and 19th dynasties (16th to 13th centuries B.C.), during which the empire was established. Persia conquered Egypt in 525 B.C.; Alexander the Great subdued it in 332 B.C.; and then the dynasty of the Ptolemies ruled the land until 30 B.C., when Cleopatra, last of the line, committed suicide, and, Egypt became a Roman province. From 641 to 1517 the Arab caliphs ruled Egypt, and then the Turks took it for their Ottoman Empire.

Napoleon's armies occupied the country from 1798 to 1801. In 1805, Mohammed Ali, leader of a band of Albanian soldiers, became Pasha of Egypt. After completion of the Suez Canal in 1869, both the French and British took increasing interest in Egypt.

British troops occupied Egypt in 1882, and British resident agents became its actual administrators, though it remained under nominal Turkish sovereignty. On Dec. 18, 1914, this fiction was ended, and Egypt became a protectorate of Britain.

Pressure by Egyptian nationalists forced Britain to declare Egypt an independent, sovereign state on Feb. 28, 1922, although the British reserved rights for the protection of the Suez Canal and the defense of Egypt. On Aug. 26, 1936, by an Anglo-Egyptian treaty of alliance, all British troops and officials were to be withdrawn, except from the Suez Canal zone. When World War II started, Egypt remained neutral. British imperial troops finally ended the Nazi threat to Suez in 1942 in the battle of El Alamein, which took place west of Alexandria.

In October 1951, Egypt abrogated the 1936 treaty and the 1899 Anglo-Egyptian condominium of the Sudan (*See* Sudan.) Rioting and attacks on British troops in the Suez Canal zone followed, reaching a climax in January 1952. The army, led by Gen. Mohammed Naguib, seized power on July 23, 1952. On July 26, King Farouk abdicated in favor of his infant son. Naguib took over the premiership on Sept. 7, 1952, and promised far-reaching reforms. The monarchy was abolished, and a republic proclaimed on June 18, 1953, with Naguib holding the posts of both Provisional President and Premier. He relinquished the latter post on April 18, 1954, to Gamal Abdel Nasser, leader of the ruling military junta. Naguib was deposed on Nov. 14, 1954. Nasser was confirmed as President in a popular referendum on June 23, 1956.

Nasser's policies embroiled his country in continual conflict. In July 1956, the U.S. and U.K. withdrew their pledges of financial aid for the building of the Aswan High Dam. In reply, Nasser nationalized the Suez Canal and expelled British oil and embassy officials. Israel, barred from the canal and exasperated by terrorist raids, invaded the Gaza Strip and the Sinai Peninsula. The U.K. and France, after demanding Egyptian evacuation of the canal zone, attacked Egypt on Oct. 31, 1956. Worldwide pressure forced the U.K., France, and Israel to halt the hostilities. A U.N. emergency force occupied the canal zone, and all troops were evacuated in the spring of 1957.

On Feb. 1, 1958, Egypt and Syria formed the United Arab Republic, which was joined by Yemen on March 8 in an association known as the United Arab States. However, Syria withdrew from the United Arab Republic on Sept. 29, 1961, and on December 26, Egypt dissolved its ties with Yemen in the United Arab States. On Sept. 2, 1971, Egypt finally shed the name United Arab Republic.

On June 5, 1967, Israel invaded the Sinai Peninsula, the east bank of the Jordan River, and the zone around the Gulf of Aqaba. Only a U.N. cease-fire on June 10 saved the Arabs from complete rout. The war left the U.A.R. army, its prestige, and its economy in ruins. The Suez Canal was blocked by wrecks and closed to all traffic. Nasser at first resigned as President, then withdrew the resignation, getting increased power to rebuild the stricken nation. He obtained economic and financial help from the U.S.S.R., the People's Republic of China, Kuwait, and former King Suad.

Nasser declared the 1967 cease-fire void along the canal on April 23, 1969, and began a war of attrition. Egyptian artillery fire across the canal sparked Israeli "deep penetration" raids that attempted to topple Nasser. He went to Moscow in January 1970, and by March, Russians were flying planes with Egyptian markings to defend the Nile delta and were manning some antiaircraft missiles. An estimated 10,000 to 12,000 Russians were in Egypt in 1970. Missiles were moved into the canal zone, challenging Israeli air superiority. The U.S. peace plan of June 19, 1970, resulted in Egypt's agreement to reinstate the cease-fire for at least three months, (from August) and to accept Israel's existence within "recognized and secure" frontiers that might emerge from U.N.-mediated talks. In return, Israel accepted the principle of withdrawing from occupied territories.

Then, on Sept. 28, 1970, Nasser died, at 52, of a heart attack in the midst of Jordanian-Palestinian guerrilla hostilities and the hijacking by these guerrillas of four Western jet planes. The new President was Anwar el-Sadat.

With Nasser's death, the pan-Arabism he advocated disintegrated. Sadat seemed more willing to reach a peace settlement with Israel. While receiving more arms from the U.S.S.R. (matched by U.S. sales to Israel), he responded to U.S. peace initiatives by promising to sign a peace agreement if Israel withdrew to its pre-war 1967 borders. The Israelis refused, however.

In 1971, Sadat signed a 15-year treaty of friendship and cooperation with Moscow that legitimized Soviet penetration of Egypt.

The Aswan High Dam, whose financing by the U.S.S.R. was its first step into Egypt, was completed and dedicated in January 1971.

In July 1972, Sadat ordered the expulsion of Soviet "advisors and experts" from Egypt because the Russians had not provided the sophisticated weapons he felt were needed to retake territory lost to Israel in 1967. Moscow pulled out virtually all of its 18,000 men.

The fourth major Arab-Israeli war broke out Oct. 6, 1973, while Israelis were commemorating Yom Kippur, the Jewish high holy day. Egypt swept deep into the Sinai, while Syria strove to throw Israel off the Golan Heights. Arab oil-producing countries cut off shipments to the U.S. and other Western nations, helping to precipitate a worldwide energy crisis.

A U.N.-sponsored truce was called October 22, with Egyptian forces in the Sinai split by an Israeli invasion into Egypt itself. In January 1974, the two nations agreed to a six-point settlement, negotiated by U.S. Secretary of State Henry A. Kissinger, which left Egypt in possession of a narrow strip along the entire Sinai bank of the Suez Canal.

President Nixon, in June 1974, made the first visit by a U.S. President to Egypt following a Kissinger-mediated settlement between Israel and Syria. A joint Egyptian-American economic commission was set up that promised U.S. aid to Egypt, and relatively large U.S. atomic reactors were to be provided Egypt for making electricity. Full diplomatic relations between the countries were resumed.

On June 5, 1975, Egypt reopened the Suez Canal to traffic after basic repairs of damage caused by the 1967 war. Quiet, three-cornered disengagement negotiations resumed, with the U.S. acting as middleman between Cairo and Jerusalem. The principal sticking-point was Egypt's insistence on return of the strategic Mitla and Giddi passes and captured oil fields at Abu Rudeis.

Kissinger resumed his "shuttle diplomacy" August 21 and midwifed an agreement that was formally initialed in Alexandria the night of September 1. It was not a peace accord, but it was a concrete step toward a possible Mideastern settlement. It called for Israeli withdrawal from the Mitla and Giddi passes and the Abu Rudeis oil fields. It committed both governments to resolve disputes by peaceful means and required annual renewal of the mandate of the U.N. peace-keeping force.

The agreement drew the U.S. directly into the Middle Eastern diplomatic picture. It also undercut Egypt's relations with the U.S.S.R., which criticized the U.S. presence in the Sinai. Sadat was denounced by Syria and the Palestine Liberation Organization for selling out the Arab cause. The accord gave the Sadat government leeway for fulfillment of programs to strengthen the economy of Egypt, which was beset by 30% inflation and serious unemployment.

In a referendum on Sept. 16, 1976, Sadat, running unopposed, was nominated for a second six-year term, winning a 99.9% vote of approval.

Sadat won promises of major economic help on March 25, 1977, when Saudi Arabia and other Gulf states agreed to lend Egypt $1.5 billion. In May, a consortium of the International Monetary Fund, the European Economic Community, and others recommended loans and credits of $13.1 billion for 1977–80. May 10, the Ford Motor Co. said it would resume manufacture of trucks and diesel engines in an Alexandria plant shut down by the Arab boycott in the 1960s. Goodyear, Union Carbide, and Coca-Cola were also reported ready to begin operations in Egypt.

In the most audacious act of his career, Sadat flew to Jerusalem at the invitation of Prime Minister Menachem Begin and pleaded before Israel's Knesset on Nov. 20, 1977, for a permanent peace settlement. The Arab world reacted with fury—only Morocco, Tunisia, Sudan, and Oman voiced approval—and Egyptian Foreign Minister Ismail Fahmy resigned. Hope for progress cooled when political talks in Jerusalem snagged, and Sadat ordered his negotiators home Jan. 17, 1978. The Egyptian was angered by Begin's defense of new settlements on the West Bank and his refusal to discuss the ultimate status of the West Bank and Gaza Strip, which Sadat proposed be placed under Jordanian and Egyptian administration respectively.

Sadat maintained an image of cooperation while Begin reflected intransigence, a perception that U.S. Senators apparently shared as they voted May 15 for Carter's requested package sale of fighter jets to Egypt, Saudi Arabia, and Israel. At U.S. insistence, the two sides met with Secretary of State Cyrus Vance at Leeds Castle, England, July 17–19, for inconclusive political talks. Sadat warned that a "big test" could come with the October 21 expiration of the mandate for the U.N. Emergency Force, the peace-keeping force in the Sinai Peninsula.

**Economy.** Agriculture is the chief industry, engaging more than half the population. Only about 3.5% of the total area is arable, and only about 6 million acres are actually under cultivation, almost entirely in the Nile valley and delta. More than half the cultivated area comprises farms of less than 20 acres. Irrigation is indispensable to agriculture; the Aswan reservoir above the first cataract of the Nile holds up to 5.5 billion cubic meters of water and the reservoir of Gebel Aulia, in the Sudan, 2 billion cubic meters. In the delta and in middle Egypt, where perennial or canal irrigation is possible, two or three crops a year can be grown. The chief cash crop is cotton.

Industry includes sugar refining, cotton ginning, cement manufacture, milling and pottery, and soap and perfume making.

The most important mineral deposits in Egypt are manganese ore, phosphate, and petroleum. Gold, iron ochres, nickel, sodium carbonate, sulfate talc, and tungsten also are mined.

Chief exports in 1975 were cotton (37%) and cotton yarn (11%). Leading customers were U.S.S.R. (43%), Czechoslovakia (7%), East Germany (6%), Romania (5%). Leading suppliers were U.S. (19%), France (11%), West Germany (8%), U.S.S.R. (6%), Italy (6%), U.K. (5%).

**Suez Canal.** The Suez Canal, in Egyptian territory between the Arabian Desert and the Sinai Peninsula, is an artificial waterway about 100 miles long between Port Said on the Mediterranean and Suez on the Red Sea. Construction work, directed by the French engineer Ferdinand de Lesseps, was begun April 25, 1859, and the canal was opened Nov. 17, 1869. The cost was 432,807,882 francs. The concession was held by an Egyptian joint stock company, *Compagnie Universelle du Canal Maritime de Suez,* in which the British government held 353,504 out of a total of 800,000 shares. The concession was to expire Nov. 17, 1968, but the company was nationalized July 26, 1956, by unilateral action of the Egyptian government.

The canal was closed in June 1967 after the Arab-Israeli conflict. With the help of the U.S. Navy, work was begun on clearing the canal in 1974, after the cease-fire ending the Arab-Israeli war. It was reopened to traffic June 5, 1975.

## EL SALVADOR

**Republic of El Salvador**
**President:** Gen. Carlos Humberto Romero (1977)
**Area:** 8,124 sq mi. (21,041 sq km)
**Population (est. 1978):** 4,340,000
**Density per square mile:** 534.2
**Capital:** San Salvador
**Largest cities (est. 1976):** San Salvador, 500,000; (est. 1969): Santa Ana, 168,000
**Monetary unit:** Colón
**Language:** Spanish
**Religion:** Roman Catholic
**Gross national product (1976):** $2.2 billion
**National name:** República de El Salvador
**Freedom House classifications:** Capitalist industrial, multi-party centralized

**Geography.** Situated on the Pacific coast of Central America, El Salvador has Guatemala to the west and Honduras to the north and east. It is the smallest of the Central American countries, its area equal to that of Massachusetts, and the only one without an Atlantic coastline.

Most of the country is a fertile volcanic plateau about 2,000 feet (607 m) high. There are some active volcanoes and many scenic crater lakes.

**Government.** The Constitution provides for a President, popularly elected for five years and ineligible to succeed himself, and a unicameral legislature, the National Assembly, consisting of 52 members elected by universal popular vote for two years.

The National Conciliation Party (48 Assembly seats), led by President Carlos Humberto Romero, is the leading political party.

**History.** Pedro de Alvarado, a lieutenant of Cortés, conquered El Salvador in 1525. El Salvador, with the other countries of Central America, declared its independence from Spain on Sept. 15, 1821, and was part of a federation of Central American states until that union was dissolved in 1838. Its independent career for several decades thereafter was marked by numerous revolutions and wars against other Central American republics.

In January 1931, the first free election in 20 years was held, but Gen. Maximiliano Hernández Martínez took power in December of that year and maintained a dictatorship until ousted in May 1944. For nearly two decades, politics remained turbulent and unstable, until the 1962 elections.

The new President, Julio Adalberto Rivera, restored free elections. In the next few years, El Salvador assumed a leading role in the Central American Common Market. But in 1968, a drop in exports of coffee and cotton produced a slump. Widespread unemployment in El Salvador and land hunger in Honduras resulted in a conflict between El Salvador and Honduras in July 1969. Deportation from Honduras of several thousand Salvadorans led to an invasion by El Salvador. Under threats of economic sanctions and military intervention El Salvador withdrew its troops. The clash left 1,000 dead, tens of thousands homeless.

By June 1970, with land trade to the south hurt by Honduran roadblocks to its goods on the Pan American Highway, El Salvador agreed with Honduras on a demilitarized zone of 1.8 miles on each side of their poorly defined border. They also agreed to restore diplomatic relations and work toward a peace agreement as well as toward reviving the common market, but the peace talks broke down in 1973.

Presidential elections on Feb. 20, 1972, gave none of four candidates a clear majority, so the National Assembly, where the National Conciliation Party had an overwhelming majority, proclaimed its candidate, Col. Arturo Armando Molina, as President.

The 1977 Presidential elections were marked by at least eight deaths and massive protest demonstrations by the National Opposition Union (UNO), which charged extensive voter fraud on February 20. Gen. Carlos Humberto Romero, candidate of the governing National Conciliation Party, claimed 812,080 votes to 394,661 for Lt. Col. Ernesto Claramount, the UNO candidate, who chose exile rather than prison after the election.

Reports of fraud were heard by a U.S. Congressional subcommittee the following month after publication of a State Department report listing human rights violations. On March 16, the Salvadoran government became the fifth Latin nation to reject U.S. military aid because of human rights charges. El Salvador had been scheduled to receive $2.5 million in military assistance in fiscal 1978.

**Economy.** El Salvador is one of the most intensively cultivated countries in Latin America. Important agricultural products are coffee, cotton, lint, sugar, rice, and corn. There has been considerable recent development in industry. Products include cement, steel, and electricty.

Gold, silver, coal, copper, iron, zinc, mercury, and sulfur are the nation's chief minerals. Forest resources are dyewood, mahogany, cedar, and walnut. El Salvador is a leading source of balsam.

Chief exports in 1975 were coffee (33%), sugar (16%), cotton (15%), chemicals (6%), and textile (6%). Leading customers were U.S. (27%), Guatemala (15%), West Germany (13%), Japan (12%), Costa Rica (6%), Netherlands (6%), Nicaragua (6%). Leading suppliers were U.S. (31%), Guatemala (14%), Venezuela (8%), Japan (7%). West Germany (6%), Costa Rica (5%).

## EQUATORIAL GUINEA

**Republic of Equatorial Guinea**
**President:** Francisco Macías Nguema Ñegue Ndong
**Area:** 10,830 sq mi. (28,051 sq km)
**Population (est. 1978):** 325,000
**Density per square mile:** 30.0
**Capital and largest city (est. 1970):** Malabo (formerly Santa Isabel), 19,300
**Monetary unit:** Ekpwele
**Languages:** Spanish, Fang, Bubi
**Religions:** Roman Catholic, Protestant, Animist
**Gross national product (1976):** $110 million
**National name:** Républica de Guinea Ecuatorial
**Freedom House classifications:** Capitalist-statist pre-industrial, one-party nationalist

**Geography.** Equatorial Guinea, formerly Spanish Guinea, consists of Rio Muni (10,045 sq mi.; 26,117 sq km), on the western coast of Africa, and several islands in the Gulf of Guinea, the largest of which is Macias Nguema Biyogo (formerly Fernando Po) (785 sq mi.; 2,033 sq km). The other islands are Pagalu (formerly Annobón), Corisco, Elobey Grande, and Elobey Chico. The total area is twice that of Connecticut.

**Government.** Executive power is vested in a Council of Ministers appointed by and responsible to the President. Legislative power is vested in a 60-member People's National Assembly.

A new Constitution was approved in 1973 and the capital's name was changed from Santa Isabel to Malabo.

The Partido Unico Nacional de Trabajadores (PUNT), headed by the President, is the only political party.

**History.** Fernando Po and Annobón came under Spanish control in 1778. From 1827 to 1844, with Spanish consent, the U.K. administered Fernando Po, but in the latter year Spain reclaimed the island. Río Muni was given to Spain in 1885 by the Treaty of Berlin.

Negotiations with Spain led to independence on Oct. 12, 1968.

In February 1969, anti-Spanish incidents in Río Muni, including the tearing down of a Spanish flag by national troops, caused 5,000 Spanish residents to flee for their safety, and diplomatic relations between the two nations became strained. The United Nations sent a Bolivian official as mediator. A month later the President claimed a coup had been attempted against him. He seized dictatorial powers and arrested 80 opposition politicians and even several of his Cabinet ministers and the secretary of the National Assembly. Refugees from his regime reached record numbers in 1977, and dissident intellectuals, now in Barcelona, have set up the Organización Nacional de la Oposición de Guinea Ecuatorial en el Exilio.

**Economy.** Agricultural products include cocoa, coffee, palm kernels and oil, and timber.

Chief exports in 1970 were cocoa (66%), coffee (24%), and timber (9%). Leading customer was Spain (91%). Leading supplier was Spain (80%).

## ETHIOPIA

**Head of State:** Lt. Col. Mengistu Haile Mariam (1977)
**Area:** 471,778 sq mi. (1,221,900 sq km)
**Population (est. 1978):** 29,700,000 (Amhara, 20%; Gala, 40%, others 40%)
**Density per square mile:** 63.0
**Capital:** Addis Ababa
**Largest cities (est. 1977):** Addis Ababa, 1,327,200; Asmara, 340,200
**Monetary unit:** Birr
**Languages:** Amharic (official), Galligna, Tigrigna
**Religions:** Copt (Christian), Islam

**Gross national product (1976):** $2.9 billion
**Freedom House classifications:** Socialist pre-industrial, non-party military

**Geography.** Ethiopia is in east central Africa, bordered on the west by the Sudan, the east by Somalia and Djibouti, the south by Kenya, and the north by the Red Sea. It is nearly three times the size of California.

Over its main plateau land, Ethiopia has several high mountains, the highest of which is Ras Dashan at 15,158 feet (4,620 m). The Blue Nile, or Abbai, rises in the northwest and flows in a great semicircle east, south, and northwest before entering Sudan. Its chief reservoir, Lake Tana, lies in the northwestern part of the plateau.

**Government.** A provisional military government headed by a 120-member officers' committee (the Dirgue) deposed Ethiopia's traditional monarchy in 1974, suspended parliament, and ruled by decree. It proclaimed Ethiopia a socialist state.

**History.** Black Africa's oldest state, Ethiopia can trace 2,000 years of recorded history. Its now-deposed royal line claimed descent from King Menelik I, by tradition the son of the Queen of Sheba and King Solomon. The present nation is a consolidation of smaller kingdoms that owed feudal allegiance to the Ethiopian Emperor.

Hamitic peoples migrated to Ethiopia from Asia Minor in prehistoric times. Semitic traders from Arabia penetrated the region in the 7th Century B.C. Its Red Sea ports were important to the Roman and Byzantine Empires. Coptic Christianity came to the country in A.D. 341, and a variant of that communion became Ethiopia's state religion.

Ancient Ethiopia reached its peak in the 5th Century, then was isolated by the rise of Islam and weakened by feudal wars. Modern Ethiopia emerged under Emperor Menelik II, who established its independence by routing an Italian invasion in 1896. He expanded Ethiopia by conquest.

Disorders that followed Menelik's death brought his daughter to the throne in 1917, with his cousin, Tafari Makonnen, as regent, heir presumptive, and strong man. When the Empress died in 1930, Tafari was crowned Emperor Haile Selassie I.

As regent, Haile Selassie outlawed slavery. As Emperor, he worked for centralization of his diffuse realm, in which 70 languages are spoken, and for moderate reform. In 1931, he granted a Constitution, revised in 1955, that created a parliament with an appointed Senate and an elected Chamber of Deputies, and a system of courts. But basic power remained with the Emperor.

Bent on colonial empire, fascist Italy invaded Ethiopia on Oct. 3, 1935, forcing Haile Selassie into exile in May 1936. Ethiopia was annexed to Eritrea, then an Italian colony, and Italian Somaliland to form Italian East Africa, losing its independence for the first time in recorded history. In 1941, British troops routed the Italians, and Haile Selassie returned to Addis Ababa.

The Emperor's gradual reforms failed to make headway against key problems. Although 85% of Ethiopians were subsistence farmers, feudal laws vested ownership of 55% of its land in the crown, the church, and the nobility; there was strong pressure for land reform. There was also mounting insurgency in Eritrea, a culturally distinct province where Christians and Moslems have long vied for control, which the United Nations placed under Ethiopian rule in 1952. Violent agitation for Eritrean independence was begun in 1969 by the Moslem-led Eritrean Liberation Front (ELF), which used Arab-supplied arms to field a 4,000-man guerrilla force.

Deep discontent erupted in the fall of 1973. A long drought had caused famine that killed 100,000 peasants and drove thousands of others to cities, where food was scarce and inflation was rampant. Charges of mismanagement of drought relief sparked riots in Addis Ababa in February 1974, and unpaid troops in Asmara, capital of Eritrea, mutinied to protest conditions. The Cabinet headed by Premier Aklilou Habte-wold resigned.

The Emperor named Endalkachew Makonnen, a moderate, to succeed as Prime Minister and agreed to call a constitutional convention. But there was a general strike, students rioted, and mutiny spread to the Air Force. In mid-April, with disorders growing, Army and police units arrested over 200 prominent persons. Late in June the Army took virtual control of Addis Ababa and made more arrests.

Endalkachew was ousted as Prime Minister on July 24, arrested, and later executed. Under his successor, Michael Imru, a draft constitution proposing a constitutional monarchy was put forward, but power shifted relentlessly to a new Armed Forces Committee (AFC).

In August, the AFC nationalized Haile Selassie's palace and estates and directed him not to leave Addis Ababa. On Sept. 12, 1974, Haile Selassie was peacefully deposed after nearly 58 years as regent and emperor. The 82-year-old "Lion of Judah" was placed under guard. Parliament was dissolved and the Constitution suspended; and a provisional military government took over pending elections for which no date was set.

On December 20, the AFC announced that Ethiopia would become a socialist state directed by one political organization called the Supreme Progressive Council. All financial concerns were nationalized in January 1975. In March, the regime proclaimed nationalization of all rural land, ending 2,000 years of feudal tenure.

On Aug. 27, 1975, Haile Selassie died in a small apartment in his former Addis Ababa palace where he had been treated as a state prisoner. He was 83.

After the coup, revolt in Eritrea escalated from guerrilla conflict to open war. The ELF, armed by Libya and other Arab states, demanded full independence. The regime tried and failed to negotiate with the ELF and then began vigorous military action. Some 22,000 government troops were in combat in Eritrea by February 1975, and 6,000 deaths, mostly of civilians, were said to have resulted in March. There were reports of atrocities by government troops against Eritrean villages, but rigid censorship blocked verification.

U.S. military aid, which had been going to Ethiopia since World War II, was suspended after the 1974 coup and only briefly resumed in 1976 as the military government turned increasingly toward the U.S.S.R. In retaliation for the Carter administration's ruling out further aid to Ethiopia because of human rights violations, the regime in April and May of 1977 shut down the Kagnew communications center in Asmara and other U.S. military and diplomatic offices, ordering some 300 Americans to leave.

Lt. Col. Mengistu Haile Mariam was named head of state Feb. 2, 1977, to replace Brig. Gen. Teferi Benti, killed in a factional fight of the Dirgue after having ruled since 1974. The government was losing its fight to hold Eritrea and in the southeastern region of Ogaden, Somali guerrillas backed by Somali regular forces threatened the ancient city of

Harar. In October, the U.S.S.R. announced it would end military aid to Somalia and henceforth back its new ally, Ethiopia. This, together with the intervention of Cuban troops in Ogaden, turned the tide for Mengistu. By March 1978, the badly beaten Somalis had retreated to Somalia. Mengistu sought more Cuban and Soviet help for his battle in Eritrea, but his allies—reluctant to interfere in an obviously more internal situation—counseled mediation.

In late July 1978, the Ethiopian government reported that it had gained its first victory over Eritrean rebels in three years in a campaign aimed at cutting off Eritrean rebels from their supply lines to the Sudan.

**Economy.** Ethiopia is generally fertile, predominantly agricultural and pastoral, with many regions yielding two crops a year. The chief crops are maize, wheat, barley, rye, cotton, sugarcane, millet, hemp, vegetables, coffee, and teff (the common bread grain). The country's inadequate transport system, however, makes crop-growing largely a local industry.

A number of industries have been established under consecutive five-year plans, such as sugar, beverages, cement, and iron. Hydroelectric power has been developed.

Gold, produced from placer mines worked by natives in the south and west, is Ethiopia's main mineral. Platinum also is mined in fair commercial quantities. Other minerals are rock salt, cinnabar, copper, iron, mercury, mica, potash, and sulfur. Oil deposits are believed to exist, and all drilling rights have been sold to the Sinclair Refining Company of the U.S.

Chief exports in 1975 were coffee (56%), beans (10%), hides and skins (10%), and oilseeds (5%). Leading customers were U.S. (20), Saudi Arabia (14%), Djibouti (10%), Egypt (9%), Japan (9%), West Germany (8%), Italy (5%). Leading suppliers were Saudi Arabia (15%), Japan (12%), Italy (11%), West Germany (10%), U.K. (8%), U.S. (8%), France (5%).

## FIJI

**Dominion of Fiji**
**Governor General:** Sir George Cakobau
**Prime Minister:** Sir Kamisese Mara (1970)
**Area:** 7,055 sq mi. (18,272 sq km)
**Population (est. 1978):** 620,000
**Density per square mile:** 87.9
**Capital (est. 1976):** Suva (on Viti Levu), 63,600
**Monotary unit:** Fijian dollar
**Languages:** Fijian, Hindustani, English, Chinese
**Religions:** Christian, Hindu, Islam
**Gross national product (1976):** $670 million
**Member of Commonwealth of Nations**
**Freedom House classifications:** Capitalist pre-industrial, multi-party centralized

**Geography.** Fiji consists of more than 500 islands in the southwestern Pacific Ocean about 1,960 miles from Sydney, Australia. The two largest islands are Viti Levu (4,109 sq mi.; 10,642 sq km) and Vanua Levu (2,242 sq mi.; 5,807 sq km). The island of Rotuma (18 sq mi.; 47 sq km), about 400 miles (644 km) to the north, is a dependency of Fiji. Overall, Fiji is nearly as large as New Jersey.

The largest islands in the group are mountainous and volcanic, with the tallest peak being Mount Victoria (4,341 ft; 1,323 m) on Viti Levu. The islands in the south have dense forests on the windward side and grasslands on the leeward.

**Government.** Executive authority is vested in the Cabinet and legislative authority in a bicameral 74-member Parliament. The major political parties are the Alliance Party, led by Sir Kamisese Mara; National Federation Party, led by Jai Ram Reddy, and Fijian Nationalist Party, led by Sakeasi Butadroka.

**History.** In 1874, an offer of cession by the Fijian chiefs was accepted, and Fiji was proclaimed a possession and dependency of the British Crown.

During World War II, the archipelago was an important air and naval station on the route from the U.S. and Hawaii to Australia and New Zealand.

Fiji became an independent nation on Oct. 10, 1970. The next year it joined the five-island South Pacific Forum, which intends to become a permanent regional group to promote collective diplomacy of the newly independent members. Besides Fiji, the Forum includes Western Samoa, Tonga, Nauru, and the self-governing segments of the Cook Islands.

**Economy.** Tourism is important. Agricultural products include sugar, coconut oil, copra, bananas, and pineapples.

Chief exports in 1974 were sugar (54%), petroleum products (12%), coconut products (9%), and gold (7%). Leading customers in 1976 were U.K. (40%), Australia (18%), New Zealand (10%), Singapore (5%). Leading suppliers were Australia (29%), Japan (18%), New Zealand (14%), U.K. (11%), Singapore (9%).

## FINLAND

**Republic of Finland**
**President:** Urho K. Kekkonen (1956)
**Premier:** Kalevi Sorsa (1977)
**Area:** 130,119 sq mi. (337,009 sq km)
**Population (est. 1978):** 4,750,000 (Finnish, 90%; Swedish, 10%)
**Density per square mile:** 36.5
**Capital:** Helsinki
**Largest cities (est. 1977):** Helsinki, 493,300; **(est. 1974 by U.N.):** Tampere, 165,500; Turku, 162,500
**Monetary unit:** Markka
**Languages:** Finnish, Swedish
**Religions:** Lutheran, 98.6%; Orthodox, 1.3%
**Gross national product (1976):** $27.7 billion
**National name:** Suomen Tasavalta—Republiken Finland
**Freedom House classifications:** Capitalist-socialist industrial, multi-party centralized

**Geography.** Finland stretches 700 miles (1,127 km) from the Gulf of Finland on the south to Soviet Petsamo, north of the Arctic Circle. The U.S.S.R. extends along the entire eastern frontier. In area, Finland is three times the size of Ohio.

Off the southwest coast are the Aland Islands, controlling the entrance to the Gulf of Bothnia. Finland has more than 60,000 lakes. Of the few rivers, only the Oulu (Ulea) is navigable to any important extent.

The Swedish-populated Aland Islands (581 sq mi.; 1,505 sq km) have an autonomous status under a law passed in 1951.

**Government.** The President of the Republic of Finland, chosen for six years by the Electoral College of 300 members who are elected by the people, appoints the Cabinet. The one-chamber Diet, the Eduskunta, consists of 200 members elected for four-year terms by proportional representation.

The major political parties are the Social Democratic Party (54 seats in Eduskanta), led by Premier Kalevi Sorsa; People's Democratic League (Communist) (40 seats); Center Party (39 seats), led by Dr. Johannes Virolainen; Conservative Party (35 seats); Swedish People's Party (10 seats); Liberal Party (9 seats); Christian League (9 seats). Premier Sorsa leads a coalition of the Social Democratic, Communist, Center, and Liberal party members totaling 142 seats.

**History.** At the end of the 7th century, the Finns came to Finland from their Volga settlements, taking the country from the Lapps, who retreated northward. The Finns' repeated raids on the Scandinavian coast impelled Eric IX, the Swedish King, to conquer the country in 1157 and bring it into contact with Western Christendom. By 1809 the whole of Finland was conquered by Alexander I of Russia, who set up Finland as a Grand Duchy.

The first period of Russification (1899–1905) resulted in a lessening of the powers of the Finnish Diet. The Russian language was made official, and the Finnish military system was superseded by the Russian. The pace of Russification was intensified from 1908 to 1914. When Russian control was weakened as a consequence of the March Revolution of 1917, the Finnish Diet on July 20, 1917, proclaimed Finland's independence, which became complete on Dec. 6, 1917.

When its territorial demands on Finland were rejected, the U.S.S.R. attacked Finland on Nov. 30, 1939. The Finns made an amazing stand of three months. Finland finally capitulated, ceding 16,000 square miles to the U.S.S.R. Under German pressure the Finns joined the Nazis against Russia in 1941, but were defeated again and ceded the Petsamo area to the U.S.S.R. In 1948, a 20-year treaty of friendship and mutual assistance was signed by the two nations and renewed for another 20 years in 1970.

In 1970 Finland entered into a trade agreement with the enlarged European Economic Community (Common Market), which includes Norway and Denmark, and also with Comecom, the Communist East European Economic Group.

The world oil crisis added a practical new reason for maintenance of an unimpaired relationship with Moscow, for Finland imports two thirds of its oil from the U.S.S.R. In October 1974, the two nations signed a 10-year energy cooperation pact providing for delivery to Finland of two 440-megawatt nuclear power stations to go into operation in 1981–82.

Helsinki was the site in late July 1975 of a summit conference of 35 heads of government convened for the signing of a European security agreement. It was the most inclusive gathering of European leaders since the Congress of Vienna in 1815.

With inflation running at 14% and unemployment at 6% for 1976, economic problems remained in 1977, and Miettunen resigned May 11 when Kalevi Sorsa, Chairman of the Social Democratic Party, was able to assemble a majority coalition. Earlier, President Kekkonen, whose scheduled 1974 expiration of his third term was postponed until 1978 to allow time for negotiating Finland's entry into the European Economic Community, said he would oppose a further extension without an election.

**Economy.** The chief crops are oats, barley, rye, and potatoes. Other food must be imported, such as wheat, rye, sugar, fruits, and vegetables, to supplement local production. Grazing lands are extensive.

A government program to stimulate the stagnant economy was begun in 1977.

Leading industrial products include wood and paper, cement, cellulose, food, luxury items, machinery, and textiles. With the cession of the Karelian Isthmus and the city of Viipuri to the U.S.S.R., Finland lost valuable manufacturing areas. Helsinki is the principal industrial center.

Finland has no coal or oil, and many of its ore deposits are remote from transportation. Hydroelectricity supplies 70% or more of the total power supply. Finland's sulfide ore is 4% copper, 26% sulfur, and 27% iron, with some zinc, cobalt, gold, and silver. Limestone, soapstone, and red granite deposits are extensive, and uranium deposits are believed to exist. Wood and peat are the only natural fuels.

Chief exports in 1976 were paper (25%), machinery (14%), ships (8%), timber (8%), wood pulp (6%), and clothing (6%). Leading customers were U.S.S.R. (20%), Sweden (17%), U.K. (14%), West Germany (9%). Leading suppliers were U.S.S.R. (18%), Sweden (16%), West Germany (15%), U.K. (8%). U.S. (5%).

# FRANCE

**French Republic**
**President:** Valéry Giscard d'Estang (1974)
**Premier:** Raymond Barre (1976)
**Area:** 211,208 sq mi. (547,026 sq km)
**Population (est. 1978):** 53,250,000
**Density per square mile:** 252.1
**Capital:** Paris
**Largest cities (1975 census):** Paris, 2,317,227; Marseilles, 914,356; Lyons, 462,841; Toulouse, 383,176; Nice, 346,620; Nantes, 263,689; Strasbourg, 257,300; Bordeaux, 226,281
**Monetary unit:** Franc
**Religion (est.):** Roman Catholic, 90%; Protestant, Jewish, Islam, and others, 10%
**Gross national product (1976):** $346.7 billion
**National name:** République Française
**Freedom House classifications:** Capitalist industrial, multi-party centralized

**Geography.** France (80% the size of Texas) is second in size to Russia among Europe's nations. In the Alps near the Italian and Swiss borders is France's highest point—Mont Blanc (15,781 ft; 4,810 m). The forest-covered Vosges Mountains are in the northeast, and the Pyrenees are along the Spanish border.

Except for extreme Northern France, which is part of the Flanders plain, the country may be described as four river basins and a plateau. Three of the streams flow west—the Seine into the English Channel, the Loire into the Atlantic, and the Garonne into the Bay of Biscay. The Rhône flows south into the Mediterranean. For about a hundred miles, the Rhine is France's eastern border.

West of the Rhône and northeast of the Garonne lies the Central Plateau, covering about 15% of France's area and rising to a maximum elevation of 6,188 feet (1,886 m). In the Mediterranean, about 115 miles (185 km) east-southeast of Nice, is Corsica (3,367 sq mi.; 8,721 sq km).

**Government.** The President is elected for seven years by universal suffrage. He appoints the Premier, and the Cabinet is responsible to Parliament. The President has the right to dissolve the National Assembly or to ask Parliament for reconsideration of a law. The Parliament consists of two Houses: the National Assembly and the Senate.

The major political parties are the Rally for the Republic (154 of 491 seats in National Assembly), led by Claude Labbé; Union for French Democracy (119 seats), led by Roger Chinaud; Socialists (115 seats), led by Gaston Defferre; Communists (86 seats), led by Robert Ballanger.[1]

**History.** The history of France, as distinct from ancient Gaul, begins with the Treaty of Verdun (843), dividing the territories corresponding roughly to France, Germany, and Italy among the three grandsons of Charlemagne. Julius Caesar had conquered part of Gaul in 57–52 B.C., and it remained Roman until Franks invaded it in the 5th century.

Charles the Bald, inheritor of *Francia Occidentalis,* founded the Carolingian dynasty, which ruled over a kingdom increasingly feudalized. By 987, the crown passed to Hugh Capet, a princeling who controlled only the Île-de-France, the region surrounding Paris. For 350 years, an unbroken Capetian line added to its domain and consolidated royal authority until the accession in 1328 of Philip VI, first of the Valois line. France was then the most powerful nation in Europe, with a population of 15 million.

The missing pieces in Philip's domain were the French provinces still held by the Plantagenet kings of England, who also claimed the French crown. Beginning in 1338, the Hundred Years' War eventually settled the contest. English longbows defeated French armored knights at Crécy (1346) and the English also won the second landmark battle at Agincourt (1415), but the final victory went to the French peasant girl, Joan of Arc, at Orléans (1429).

Absolute monarchy reached its apogee in the reign of Louis XIV (1643–1715), the Sun King, whose brilliant court was the center of the Western world. Neither Louis XV, nor his grandson, Louis XVI, could sustain the role, however, and the Ancien Régime tottered under the weight of an outmoded society, crushing taxes, and the infiltration of egalitarian philosophy. The monarchy lost French Canada in the Battle of Quebec Sept. 13, 1759, and in its last gasp under Louis XVI aided the American British colonists to gain their freedom.

Revolution plunged France into a blood bath beginning in 1789 and ending with a new authoritarianism under Napoleon Bonaparte, who had successfully defended the infant republic from foreign attack and then made himself First Consul in 1799, Emperor in 1804. Napoleon set patterns in government, education, and law visible today, and his conquests spread them throughout Europe.

The Congress of Vienna (1815) sought to restore the pre-Napoleonic order in the person of Louis XVIII, but industrialization and the middle class, both fostered under Napoleon, built pressure for change, and a revolution in 1848 drove Louis Philippe, last of the Bourbons, into exile.

A second republic elected as its president Prince Louis Napoleon, a nephew of Napoleon I, who declared a Second Empire in 1852 and took the throne as Napoleon III. His opposition to the rising power of Prussia ignited the Franco-Prussian war (1870–71), ending in his defeat and abdication.

Reconstruction after the War of 1870 was rapid, and a new France emerged from World War I as the continent's dominant power. But four years of hostile occupation had reduced northeast France to ruins. The postwar Third Republic was plagued by political instability and economic chaos.

From 1919, French foreign policy aimed at keeping Germany weak through a system of alliances, but it failed to halt the rise of Adolf Hitler and the Nazi war machine. On May 10, 1940, mechanized Nazi troops attacked and, as they approached Paris, Italy joined with Germany. The Germans marched into an undefended Paris and Marshal Henri Philippe Pétain signed an armistice June 22. France was split into an occupied North and an unoccupied South, the latter becoming a totalitarian state with Pétain as its chief.

Allied armies liberated France in August 1944. The French Committee of National Liberation, formed in Algiers in 1943, established a provisional government in Paris headed by Gen. Charles de Gaulle. The Fourth Republic was born Dec. 24, 1946.

The Empire became the French Union, the National Assembly was strengthened and the Presidency weakened, and France joined the North Atlantic Treaty Organization. A war against Communist insurgents in Indochina was abandoned after the defeat at Dien Bien Phu. A new rebellion in Algeria (*see* Algeria) threatened a military coup, and on June 1, 1958, the Assembly invited de Gaulle to return as Premier with extraordinary powers. He drafted a new Constitution for a Fifth Republic, adopted September 28, which strengthened the Presidency and reduced legislative power. He was elected President December 21.

The new President negotiated the independence of Algeria July 5, 1962, nearly all of the other French possessions in Africa having already received their freedom. De Gaulle cultivated the ex-colonies along with other new nations of what he called the Third World—nations aligned with neither the West nor the Soviet bloc—as a base for French leadership. In 1960, de Gaulle exploded an atomic bomb; in 1963 he negotiated a Franco-German friendship treaty; and the following year he recognized Peking, at the same time improving relations with the U.S.S.R.

De Gaulle took France out of NATO in 1967, expelling all foreign-controlled troops from the country, and in a visit to Canada aroused a storm by speaking out for a "free Quebec." Although he had been re-elected to a seven-year term in 1965, the end of his reign was foreshadowed in 1968 by a rebellion of students. The disorders spread to the workers, who seized plants across the country, resulting in a general strike supported by half the labor force. Obtaining assurances of support from his army commanders, de Gaulle offered, then canceled a referendum and held elections on the promise of reforms, which gave his supporters an overwhelming victory.

In September and October 1968, de Gaulle reformed the universities to give students and faculty a voice in choosing presidents and in controlling most major policy areas. De Gaulle went on to attempt to achieve a long cherished plan of regional reform. This, however, aroused wide opposition. He decided to stake his fate on a referendum. At the voting on April 27, 1969, the electorate defeated the plan, 53% to 47%. His successor, Georges Pompidou, de Gaulle's Premier for six years, reversed the de Gaulle policy of opposing the unification of Europe, which had led de Gaulle to oppose the entrance of the U.K. into the Common Market in 1963.

Pompidou continued the de Gaulle policies of seeking to expand France's influence in the

1. Figures include both members enrolled and members affiliated with party. In addition, there are 13 unaffiliated members in the National Assembly.

## Rulers of France

| Name | Born | Ruled[1] |
|---|---|---|
| **CAROLINGIAN DYNASTY** | | |
| Pepin the Short | c. 714 | 751–768 |
| Charlemagne[2] | 742 | 768–814 |
| Louis I the Debonair[3] | 778 | 814–840 |
| Charles I the Bald[4] | 823 | 840–877 |
| Louis II the Stammerer | 846 | 877–879 |
| Louis III[5] | c. 863 | 879–882 |
| Carloman[5] | ? | 879–884 |
| Charles II the Fat[6] | 839 | 884–887[7] |
| Eudes (Odo), Count of Paris | ? | 888–898 |
| Charles III the Simple[8] | 879 | 893–923[9] |
| Robert I[10] | c. 865 | 922–923 |
| Rudolf (Raoul), Duke of Burgundy | ? | 923–936 |
| Louis IV d'Outremer | c. 921 | 936–954 |
| Lothair | 941 | 954–986 |
| Louis V the Sluggard | c. 967 | 986–987 |
| **CAPETIAN DYNASTY** | | |
| Hugh Capet | c. 940 | 987–996 |
| Robert II the Pious[11] | c. 970 | 996–1031 |
| Henry I | 1008 | 1031–1060 |
| Philip I | 1052 | 1060–1108 |
| Louis VI the Fat | 1081 | 1108–1137 |
| Louis VII the Young | c.1121 | 1137–1180 |
| Philip II (Philip Augustus) | 1165 | 1180–1223 |
| Louis VIII the Lion | 1187 | 1223–1226 |
| Louis IX (St. Louis) | 1214 | 1226–1270 |
| Philip III the Bold | 1245 | 1270–1285 |
| Philip IV the Fair | 1268 | 1285–1314 |
| Louis X the Quarreler | 1289 | 1314–1316 |
| John I | 1316 | 1316–1316 |
| Philip V the Tall | 1294 | 1316–1322 |
| Charles IV the Fair | 1294 | 1322–1328 |
| **HOUSE OF VALOIS** | | |
| Philip VI | 1293 | 1328–1350 |
| John II the Good | 1319 | 1350–1364 |
| Charles V the Wise | 1337 | 1364–1380 |
| Charles VI the Well-Beloved | 1368 | 1380–1422 |
| Charles VII | 1403 | 1422–1461 |
| Louis XI | 1423 | 1461–1483 |
| Charles VIII | 1470 | 1483–1498 |
| Louis XII the Father of the People | 1462 | 1498–1515 |
| Francis I | 1494 | 1515–1547 |
| Henry II | 1519 | 1547–1559 |
| Francis II | 1544 | 1559–1560 |
| Charles IX | 1550 | 1560–1574 |
| Henry III | 1551 | 1574–1589 |
| **HOUSE OF BOURBON** | | |
| Henry IV of Navarre | 1553 | 1589–1610 |
| Louis XIII | 1601 | 1610–1643 |
| Louis XIV the Great | 1638 | 1643–1715 |
| Louis XV the Well-Beloved | 1710 | 1715–1774 |
| Louis XVI | 1754 | 1774–1792[12] |
| Louis XVII (Louis Charles de France)[13] | 1785 | 1793–1795 |

| Name | Born | Ruled[1] |
|---|---|---|
| **FIRST REPUBLIC** | | |
| National Convention | — | 1792–1795 |
| Directory (Directoire) | — | 1795–1799 |
| **CONSULATE** | | |
| Napoleon Bonaparte[14] | 1769 | 1799–1804 |
| **FIRST EMPIRE** | | |
| Napoleon I | 1769 | 1804–1815[15] |
| **RESTORATION OF HOUSE OF BOURBON** | | |
| Louis XVIII le Désiré | 1755 | 1814–1824 |
| Charles X | 1757 | 1824–1830[16] |
| **BOURBON-ORLEANS LINE** | | |
| Louis Philippe ("Citizen King") | 1773 | 1830–1848[17] |
| **SECOND REPUBLIC** | | |
| Louis Napoleon[18] | 1808 | 1848–1852 |
| **SECOND EMPIRE** | | |
| Napoleon III (Louis Napoleon) | 1808 | 1852–1871[19] |
| **THIRD REPUBLIC (PRESIDENTS)** | | |
| Louis Adolphe Thiers | 1797 | 1871–1873 |
| Marie E. P. M. de MacMahon | 1808 | 1873–1879 |
| François P. J. Grévy | 1807 | 1879–1887 |
| Sadi Carnot | 1837 | 1887–1894 |
| Jean Casimir-Périer | 1847 | 1894–1895 |
| François Félix Faure | 1841 | 1895–1899 |
| Émile Loubet | 1838 | 1899–1906 |
| Clement Armand Fallières | 1841 | 1906–1913 |
| Raymond Poincaré | 1860 | 1913–1920 |
| Paul E. L. Deschanel | 1856 | 1920–1920 |
| Alexandre Millerand | 1859 | 1920–1924 |
| Gaston Doumergue | 1863 | 1924–1931 |
| Paul Doumer | 1857 | 1931–1932 |
| Albert Lebrun | 1871 | 1932–1940 |
| **VICHY GOVERNMENT (CHIEF OF STATE)** | | |
| Henri Philippe Pétain | 1856 | 1940–1944 |
| **PROVISIONAL GOVERNMENT (PRESIDENTS)** | | |
| Charles de Gaulle | 1890 | 1944–1946 |
| Félix Gouin | 1884 | 1946–1946 |
| Georges Bidault | 1899 | 1946–1947 |
| **FOURTH REPUBLIC (PRESIDENTS)** | | |
| Vincent Auriol | 1884 | 1947–1954 |
| René Coty | 1882 | 1954–1959 |
| **FIFTH REPUBLIC (PRESIDENTS)** | | |
| Charles de Gaulle | 1890 | 1959–1969 |
| Georges Pompidou | 1911 | 1969–1974 |
| Valéry Giscard d'Estaing | 1926 | 1974– |

1. For Kings and Emperors through the Second Empire, year of end of rule is also that of death, unless otherwise indicated. 2. Crowned Emperor of the West in 1800. 3. Holy Roman Emperor 814–840. 4. Holy Roman Emperor 875–877 as Charles II. 5. Ruled jointly 879–882. 6. Holy Roman Emperor 881–887 as Charles III. 7. Died 888. 8. King 893–898 in opposition to Eudes. 9. Died 929. 10. Not counted in regular line of Kings of France by some authorities. Elected by nobles but killed in Battle of Soissons. 11. Sometimes called Robert I. 12. Executed 1793. 13. Titular King only. He died in prison according to official reports, but many pretenders appeared during the Bourbon restoration. 14. As First Consul, Napoleon held the power of government. In 1804, he became Emperor. 15. Abdicated first time June 1814. Re-entered Paris March 1815, after escape from Elba; Louis XVIII fled to Ghent. Abdicated second time June 1815. He named as his successor his son, Napoleon II, who was not acceptable to the Allies. He died 1821. 16. Died 1836. 17. Died 1850. 18. President; became Emperor in 1852. 19. Died 1873.

Mideast and Africa, selling arms to South Africa (despite the U.N. embargo), to Libya, and to Greece. He also continued de Gaulle's efforts to improve relations between France and individual members of the Communist bloc, notably the U.S.S.R. and China, and in 1971 he endorsed British entry into the Common Market.

Pompidou died of cancer in April 1974 and was succeeded by Valéry Giscard d'Estaing, the first non-Gaullist President in 15 years. He narrowly defeated the Socialist leader, François Mitterrand, who had Communist backing, by less than 1% of 26 million votes cast.

Giscard was no Gaullist, but depended on Gaullist votes for parliamentary support. He adhered to basic foreign policies set by de Gaulle and Pompidou, but was more cordial and flexible in relations with the U.S. He maintained French aloofness from military participation in NATO, asserting that he did not wish to encourage Soviet fears of military pressure from the West. He cultivated good relations with China. Domestically, he successfully suppported liberalized abortion and divorce laws and lowering of the voting age to 18.

Under Giscard's leadership, the French National Planning Council in January 1975, adopted a 10-year program to reduce dependence on foreign fuel to below 60% from the 76% prevailing in 1973.

Giscard's uneasy alliance with the Gaullists ended Aug. 25, 1976, with the resignation of his Premier, Jacques Chirac, who protested that he needed greater powers to tackle rising political and economic problems. The President, saying he could brook no challenge to his own authority, appointed as Chirac's successor a technician without party affiliation, Raymond Barre.

France continued her independent nuclear arms program and emerged as a supplier of nuclear technology to other nations with the sale of five 1,000-megawatt reactors to Iran in 1974 and a $1-billion power plant to South Africa in 1976. In January 1977, over U.S. and Canadian objections, Pakistan announced its intention to buy a French reprocessing plant to make plutonium from spent fuel. In August, however, France was reported to have acceded to a request by President Carter to join a study to find safeguards against the use of nuclear power reactors to develop weapons.

Giscard showed less willingness to compromise in his opposition to Carter's other foreign policy plank, the public pursuit of human rights. Aided by West German Chancellor Helmut Schmidt, the French President warned that too zealous a campaign could threaten the benefits of détente with the U.S.S.R.

With the establishment of the Republic of Djibouti on June 27, France released its last possession in mainland Africa. Giscard had made it clear earlier, however, that France would continue to play an active role in Africa when he supplied the airlift for Moroccan troops to help President Mobutu Sese Seko of Zaire fight a rebellion in Shaba province. The action was hailed by most of the former French African colonies and conservative nations throughout the continent.

France responded even more boldly to a second Shaba invasion in May 1978, moving 1,000 troops to the scene with U.S. aid and repelling the Katangese, again to the applause of most of Africa but to the displeasure of leftists. France was attaining the reputation of a world policeman, with a contingent in the U.N. peacekeeping force in Southern Lebanon and a total of 12,000 troops stationed in Djibouti, Chad, and Mauritania—in the last two nations aiding the governments in suppression of guerrilla opposition.

At home, Giscard won a surprise victory in general elections March 19 when pro-government forces won 291 seats and a narrow margin of the popular vote to retain control of the 491-seat National Assembly. The strongest leftist challenge in 20 years was predicted to win, but a Socialist-Communist alliance cracked before the election as the Communists changed their terms for cooperation with the Socialists on reported orders from Moscow.

**Religion.** The predominant faith is Roman Catholicism, but church and state were separated in 1905. Diplomatic relations with the Vatican were resumed in 1921, and lesser church property was returned to diocesan associations in 1924.

**Economy.** Silk culture once thrived in the lower Rhône valley, but production fell sharply between wars.

Principal industrial areas are Paris, Artois, lower Seine, and Lyons; the textile industry is concentrated in the north. Leading manufactures are iron, steel, chemicals, textiles, automobiles, machinery, and beet sugar.

French coalfields, most extensive in the northeast, ordinarily supply about 70% of domestic needs. Lorraine, Anjou, and Normandy have valuable iron ore deposits. Provence has bauxite. Alsace has potash and oil. Limousin has kaolin, zinc, lead, and tar.

France produces forest products, including resin, turpentine, timber, and nuts. The annual fish catch is among the largest in Europe.

Chief exports in 1976 were machinery (19%), motor vehicles (12%), chemicals (11%), and iron and steel (9%). Leading customers were EEC (51%; incl. West Germany 17%, Italy 11%, Belgium-Luxembourg 10%, U.K. 6%, Netherlands 5%), U.S. (5%). Leading suppliers were EEC (50%; incl. West Germany 19%, Belgium-Luxembourg 10%, Italy 9%, Netherlands 6%, U.K. 5%), U.S. (7%), Saudi Arabia (6%).

## Overseas Departments and Territories of France

### FRENCH GUIANA (including ININI)

**Status:** Overseas Department
**Prefect:** Jean Le Direach (1977)
**Area:** 35,135 sq mi. (91,000 sq km)
**Population (est. 1978):** 62,000
**Capital (1974 census):** Cayenne, 29,404
**Agricultural products:** bananas, cacao, corn, manioc, rice, sugar cane
**Mineral:** gold

French Guiana, lying north of Brazil and east of Surinam on the northeast coast of South America, was first settled in 1626. Penal settlements, embracing the area around the mouth of the Maroni River and the Iles du Salut (including Devil's Island), were founded in 1852; they have since been abolished.

During World War II, French Guiana at first adhered to the Vichy government, but the Free French took over in March 1943. French Guiana accepted in September 1958 the new Constitution of the French Fifth Republic and remained an Overseas Department of the French Republic.

Chief exports in 1975 were shrimp (44%), timber (14%), transport equipment (9%), and hides and skins (5%). Leading customers were U.S. (46%), France (25%), Guadeloupe (8%), Martinique (8%), Brazil (8%). Leading suppliers were France (71%), Trinidad and Tobago (6%).

## FRENCH POLYNESIA

**Status:** Overseas Territory
**High Commissioner:** Paul Cousseran (1977)
**Area:** 1,544 sq mi. (4,000 sq km)
**Population (est. 1978):** 140,000
**Capital (1971):** Papeete (on Tahiti), 25,300
**Agricultural products:** copra, vanilla, coffee
**Mineral:** phosphates

The term French Polynesia is applied to the scattered French possessions in the eastern Pacific—Mangareva (Gambier), Makatea, Marquesas Islands, Rapa, Rurutu, Rimatara, Society Islands, Tuamotu Archipelago, Tubuai, Raivavae, and the island of Clipperton—which were organized into a single colony in 1903. The High Commissioner is assisted by a Privy Council and a popularly elected Representative Assembly. The principal and most populous island—Tahiti, in the Society group—was claimed as French in 1768. In September 1958, French Polynesia voted in favor of the new Constitution of the French Fifth Republic and remained an Overseas Territory of the French Republic. The natives are mostly Polynesians.

Chief exports in 1975 were copra, vanilla, mother of pearl, and coffee. Leading customer was France (84%). Leading suppliers were France (54%), U.S. (17%).

## GUADELOUPE

**Status:** Overseas Department
**Prefect:** Jean-Claude Aurousseau
**Area:** 687 sq mi. (1,779 sq km)
**Population (est. 1978):** 375,000
**Capital (1974 census):** Basse-Terre, 15,778
**Largest city (1974 census):** Pointe-à-Pitre-Les Abymes, 77,937
**Agricultural products:** sugar, bananas, coffee, cacao, vanilla, tobacco
**Manufactures:** rum, sugar

Guadeloupe, lying in the West Indies about 300 miles southeast of Puerto Rico, was discovered by Columbus in 1493. French colonization began in 1635. In September 1958, Guadeloupe voted in favor of the new Constitution of the French Fifth Republic and remained an Overseas Department of the French Republic.

Chief exports in 1975 were sugar (41%), bananas (37%), rum (7%), and wheat meal and flour (6%). Leading customers were France (73%), U.K. (12%), Martinique (10%). Leading suppliers in 1976 were France (74%), Martinique (5%), Puerto Rico (5%), United States (5%).

## MARTINIQUE

**Status:** Overseas Department
**Prefect:** Raymond Heim (1978)
**Area:** 425 sq mi. (1,102 sq km)
**Population (est. 1978):** 375,000
**Capital (1974 census):** Fort-de-France 100,576
**Agricultural products:** sugar, bananas, pineapples, cacao, coffee
**Manufactures:** rum, sugar

Martinique, lying in the Lesser Antilles about 300 miles northeast of Venezuela, was probably discovered by Columbus in 1502 and was taken for France in 1635. Following the Franco-German armistice of 1940 it had a semiautonomous status under the High Commissioner, Adm. Georges Robert, until 1943, when he relinquished his authority to the Free French. The area, administered by a Prefect assisted by an elected council, is represented in the French Parliament. In September 1958, Martinique voted in favor of the new Constitution of the French Fifth Republic and remained an Overseas Department of the French Republic.

Chief exports in 1975 were bananas (48%), petroleum products (20%), rum (13%), and fruit preserves (7%). Leading customer in 1976 was France (69%). Leading suppliers were France (65%), Venezuela (6%).

## MAYOTTE

**Status:** Territorial collectivity
**Representative of French Government:** Jean-Marie Coussirou (1976)
**Area:** 146 sq mi. (378 sq km)
**Population (est. 1976):** 40,000
**Capital:** Dzaoudzi, (about 3,200)
**Principal products:** vanilla, essential oils, copra

The most populous of the Comoro Islands in the Indian Ocean, with a Christian majority, Mayotte voted in 1974 and 1976 against joining the other, predominantly Moslem islands, in declaring themselves independent. It continues to retain its ties to France.

## NEW CALEDONIA AND DEPENDENCIES

**Status:** Overseas Territory
**High Commissioner:** Gabriel Eriau
**Area:** 7,358 sq mi. (19,058 sq km)[1]
**Population (est. 1978):** 140,000
**Capital (1976 census):** Nouméa, 56,100
**Agricultural products:** coffee, copra, corn, cotton, manioc, rice, tobacco
**Minerals:** nickel, chromite, iron ore
**Sea product:** mother-of-pearl

New Caledonia (6,466 sq mi.), lying about 1,070 miles northeast of Sydney, Austrialia, was discovered by Capt. James Cook in 1774 and annexed by France in 1853. The government also administers the Isle of Pines, the Loyalty Islands (Uvéa, Lifu, and Maré), and the Belep Islands.

New Caledonia chose in 1958 to remain an Overseas Territory of the French Republic. The natives are Melanesians; about one-third of the population is white and one fifth Indochinese and Javanese.

Chief exports in 1975 were ferronickel (53%), nickel (22%), and nickel castings (20%). Leading customers were France (59%), Japan (23%), U.S. (12%). Leading suppliers were France (41%), Australia (9%), Singapore (5%).

1. Including dependencies.

## NEW HEBRIDES

**Status:** Anglo-French condominium

**British Resident Commissioner:** Colin Hamilton Allan
**French Resident Commissioner:** Gabriel Eriau
**Area:** 5,700 sq mi. (14,763 sq km)
**Population (est. 1978):** 100,000
**Capital (est. 1976):** Vila (metropolitan area), 17,400
**Agricultural products:** copra, cocoa, coffee
**Sea products:** trochus and burghaus shell

The New Hebrides, under joint Anglo-French administration since October 1906, lie northeast of New Caledonia. The islands, about 40 in number, joined the Free French movement after a plebiscite in July 1940. Most of the natives are Melanesians of mixed blood. The largest island is Espiritu Santo (875 sq mi.). The French and British high commissioners in the Pacific are represented by resident commissioners.

Chief exports in 1975 were copra (43%), fish (33%), manganese (9%), beef and veal (8%), and cocoa (5%). Leading customers were France (43%), U.S. (28%), Japan (15%), New Caledonia (8%). Leading suppliers were Australia (30%), France (25%), Japan (8%), New Caledonia (7%), U.S. (5%).

## REUNION (BOURBON)

**Status:** Overseas Department
**Prefect:** Bernard Landouzy
**Area:** 970 sq mi. (2,510 sq km)
**Population (est. 1978):** 500,000
**Capital (1974 census):** Saint-Denis, 104,603
**Agricultural products:** sugar, vanilla, tea, tobacco.

Discovered by Portuguese navigators in the 16th century, the island of Réunion, then uninhabited, was taken as a French possession in 1643. It is located about 450 miles (724 km) east of Madagascar, in the Indian Ocean. In September 1958, Réunion approved the Constitution of the Fifth French Republic and remained an Overseas Department of the French Republic.

Chief exports in 1975 were sugar (82%), rum (7%), and essential oils (5%). Leading customer was France (94%). Leading suppliers were France (63%), Madagascar (8%), Italy (6%), South Africa (5%).

## ST. PIERRE AND MIQUELON

**Status:** Overseas Department
**Prefect:** Pierre Eydoux (1977)
**Area:** 93 sq mi. (242 sq km)
**Population (est. 1976):** 6,000
**Capital (1974 census):** St. Pierre, 5,232
**Industries:** Fishing and canneries.

The sole remnant of the French colonial empire in North America, these islands were first occupied by the French in 1604. Their only importance arises from proximity to the Grand Banks, located 10 miles south of Newfoundland, making them the center of the French Atlantic cod fisheries. In September 1958, St. Pierre and Miquelon voted in favor of the new Constitution of the French Fifth Republic. On July 19, 1976, the islands became an Overseas Department of the French Republic.

Chief exports in 1974 were petroleum products (as ship's stores) (53%), cattle (30%), and fish (12%). Leading customers (excl. ship's stores) were Canada (70%), U.S. (25%), France (5%). Leading suppliers were Canada (54%), France (38%).

## SOUTHERN AND ANTARCTIC LANDS

**Status:** Overseas Territory
**Administrator:** Roger Barberot
**Area:** 169,614 sq mi. (439,300 sq km)
**Population (1972):** 189
**Capital (1972):** Port-au-Français: 93

This territory is uninhabited except for the personnel of scientific bases. It consists of Adélie Land (166,752 sq mi.; 431,888 sq km) on the Antarctic mainland and the following islands in the southern Indian Ocean: the Kerguelen and Crozet archipelagos and the islands of Saint-Paul and New Amsterdam.

## WALLIS AND FUTUNA ISLANDS

**Status:** Overseas Territory
**Administrator Superior:** Henri Beaux (1976)
**Area:** 77 sq mi. (200 sq km)
**Population (est. 1978):** 9,200
**Capital:** Mata-Utu (on Uvea), (1969): 600
**Agricultural products:** copra, taro, hams, cassava, bananas

The two islands groups in the South Pacific between Fiji and Samoa were settled by French missionaries at the beginning of the 19th century. A protectorate was established in the 1880s. Following a referendum by the Polynesian inhabitants, the status was changed to that of an Overseas Territory in July 1961.

# GABON

**Gabon Republic**
**President:** Omar Dongo (1967)
**Premier:** Léon Mébiame (1975)
**Area:** 103,346 sq mi. (267,667 sq km)
**Population (est. 1978):** 540,000
**Density per square mile:** 5.2
**Capital and largest city (est. 1975 for urban agglomeration):** Libreville, 169,200
**Monetary unit:** Franc CFA
**Ethnic groups:** Bateke, Obamba, Bakota, Shake, Pongwés, Adumas, Chiras, Punu, and Lumbu
**Languages:** French (official) and Bantu dialects
**Religions:** Animist, Christian, Islam
**Gross national product (1976):** $1.4 billion
**National name:** République Gabonaise
**Member of French Community**
**Freedom House classifications:** Capitalist pre-industrial, one-party nationalist

**Geography.** This west African land with the Atlantic as its western border is also bounded by Equatorial Guinea, Cameroon, and the Congo. Its area is slightly less than Kentucky's.

From mangrove swamps on the coast, the land becomes divided plateaus in the north and east and mountains in the north. Most of the country is covered by a dense tropical forest.

**Government.** The President is elected for a seven-year term. Legislative powers are exercised by a National Assembly, which is elected for a seven-year term. After his conversion to Islam in 1973, President Bongo changed his given name, Albert Bernard, to Omar. The Parti Démocratique Gabonais (all National Assembly seats) is led by President Bongo. Bongo was re-elected without opposition in 1973.

**History.** Little is known of Gabon's history, even in oral tradition, but Pygmies are believed to be the original inhabitants. Now there are many tribal groups in the country, the largest being the Fang people who constitute a third of the population.

Gabon was first visited by the Portuguese navigator Diego Cam in the 15th century. In 1839, the French founded their first settlement on the left bank of the Gabon Estuary and gradually occupied the hinterland during the second half of the 19th century. It was organized as a French territory in 1888 and became an autonomous republic within the French Union after World War II and an independent republic on Aug. 17, 1960.

Immense resources in oil, uranium, manganese, and iron help give Gabon's inhabitants a per capita annual income of $225 to $250, the highest in Black Africa. To speed exploitation of a billion-ton iron ore reserve in the Belinga-Mekambo region, the government began work in 1969 on a 350-mile railroad leading from the coast into the area. The project was initiated by President León Mba, who died in 1967, and has been continued by his hand-picked successor, President Omar Bongo.

In 1974, Bongo negotiated 60% control of an iron-ore venture half-owned by the Bethlehem Steel Corp. In October of that year, he visited Peking and concluded an economic and technical agreement with China.

**Economy.** Agricultural products include corn, coffee, cocoa, bananas, and timber.

Chief export in 1975 was crude oil (82%). Leading customers were France (21%), U.S. (19%), Spain (13%), Bahamas (11%), West Germany (9%). Leading suppliers were France (63%), U.S. (11%), Belgium-Luxembourg (5%).

## GAMBIA

**Republic of the Gambia**
**President:** Sir Dawda K. Jawara (1970)
**Area:** 4,361 sq mi. (11,295 sq km)
**Population (est. 1978):** 560,000
**Density per square mile:** 128.4
**Capital and largest city (est. 1975):** Banjul, 42,400
**Monetary unit:** Dalasi
**Languages:** Native tongues, English (official)
**Religions:** Islam, Christian, Animist
**Gross national product (1976):** $100 million
**Member of Commonwealth of Nations**
**Freedom House classifications:** Capitalist pre-industrial, multi-party centralized

**Geography.** Situated on the Atlantic coast in westernmost Africa and surrounded on three sides by Senegal, Gambia is twice the size of Delaware. The Gambia River flows for 200 miles (322 km) through Gambia on its way to the Atlantic. The country, the smallest on the continent, averages only 20 miles (32 km) in width.

**Government.** The President's five-year terms are linked to the 35-member unicameral House of Representatives, from which he appoints his Cabinet members and a vice president.

The major political party is the People's Progressive Party (29 seats in House of Representatives), led by President Jawara.

**History.** During the 17th century, Gambia was settled by various companies of English merchants. Slavery was the chief source of revenue until it was abolished in 1807. Gambia became a crown colony in 1843 and an independent nation within the Commonwealth of Nations on Feb. 18, 1965.

A proposal to convert from a monarchy to a republic was approved in a 1970 referendum, and on April 24 of that year Gambia proclaimed itself a republic.

**Economy.** The principal economic activity of Gambia is the cultivation of peanuts.

Tourism increased after 1977 because, in *Roots,* Alex Haley had traced his family's origins back to the Mandinka tribe in Juffure, a Gambian village.

Chief exports in 1976 were peanut products (91%). Leading customers were U.K. (30%), Netherlands (22%), France (10%), Italy (7%), Switzerland (6%), Portugal (5%). Leading suppliers were U.K. (25%), China (13%), Netherlands (6%), Japan (6%), France (5%), Burma (5%), West Germany (5%).

## GERMANY, EAST

**German Democratic Republic**
**Chairman of Council of State:** Erich Honecker (1976)
**Chairman of Council of Ministers:** Willi Stoph (1976)
**Area:** 41,923 sq mi. (108,178 sq km)[1]
**Population (est. 1978):** 16,570,000
**Density per square mile:** 395.2
**Capital:** Berlin (eastern sector)
**Largest cities (est. 1977):** East Berlin, 1,106,300; **(est. 1976 by U.N.):** Leipzig, 565,400; Dresden, 509,250; Karl-Marx Stadt, 305,900; Magdeburg, 278,000; Halle, 235,550; Rostock, 215,000; Erfurt, 204,500
**Monetary unit:** Mark of the Deutsche Demokratische Republik
**Language:** German
**Religions (est. 1969):** Protestant, 80%; Roman Catholic, 10%
**Gross national product (1976):** $70.9 billion
**National name:** Deutsche Demokratische Republik
**Freedom House classifications:** Socialist industrial, one-party communist

**Geography.** East Germany lies on the Baltic Sea with Poland to the east and Czechoslovakia to the south. The border with West Germany is roughly a line running south from Lübeck for about 250 miles. The main river is the Elbe, which flows from Dresden in the southeast to the North Sea in the northwest. The Oder and Neisse rivers form the border with Poland. Most of the country, which is the size of Tennessee, is situated in the north German plain.

**Government.** The People's Chamber, composed of 500 deputies elected for five-year terms, chooses the chairman and Council of State and the chairman and Council of Ministers, which carries on executive functions.

The major political party is the Socialist Unity (Communist) Party, led by Secretary General Erich Honecker. Other political groupings include the Christian Democratic Union, Liberal Democratic Party, Democratic Farmers' Party, National Democratic Party.

**History.** (For history before 1945, *see* Germany, West. The area now occupied by East Germany, as well as adjacent areas in Eastern Europe, consists

1. Including East Berlin (156 square miles), which has been incorporated into the German Democratic Republic.

of Mecklenburg, Brandenburg, Lusatia, Saxony, and Thuringia. Soviet armies conquered the five territories by 1945. In the division of 1945 they were allotted to the U.S.S.R. Soviet forces created a State controlled by the secret police with a single party, the Socialist Unity (Communist) party. The Russians appropriated East German plants to restore their war-ravaged industry.

When the Federal Republic of Germany was established in West Germany, the East German states adopted a more centralized constitution for the Democratic Republic of Germany, and it was put into effect on Oct. 7, 1949. The U.S.S.R. thereupon dissolved its occupation zone, but Soviet troops remained. The Western Allies declared that the East German Republic was a Soviet creation undertaken without self-determination and refused to recognize it. It was recognized only within the Soviet bloc.

In June 1953, the U.S.S.R. transferred control of East Germany from the military commander to a civilian commissioner and announced a more liberal policy. Continued austerity and political repression led to workers' riots in East Berlin and other cities, allegedly instigated by the Soviet secret police as part of a power struggle within the Kremlin. Soviet troops ruthlessly reestablished order. But the Soviet authorities made efforts to revive the East German economy.

In 1955, Walter Ulbricht, hard-line dictator, won Soviet recognition of the East German republic and joined the Warsaw Treaty Organization, organizing troops under the guise of police forces. In the middle and late 1960s East Germany also came to enjoy economic prosperity. Trade, formerly limited largely to the Soviet bloc, expanded to West Germany and developing nations. But trade agreements obliging the East Germans to sell to Russia at low fixed prices and to buy from the Soviets at prices higher than the world market held per capita income well below that of West Germany.

East German troops took part in the Soviet-bloc occupation of Czechoslovakia in August 1968, but reportedly were withdrawn after the U.S.S.R. questioned whether the 1945 Potsdam agreements permitted German troops on foreign soil. A new Constitution adopted in April 1968 reaffirmed one-party rule and narrowed civil rights. Ulbricht continued pressure on West Berlin, opposed liberalization in Czechoslovakia and other parts of the Soviet bloc, impeded Bonn's establishment of ties with East Europe, and pressured Bonn to acknowledge the existence of the two German states.

Talks between the two German states on normalization began in 1970, with the East seeking recognition of its existence and the West wanting easing of pressure on Berlin. West Germany's nonaggression treaty with the U.S.S.R. was cooly received by Ulbricht. In 1971 he resigned and rapprochement between the two Germanys accelerated with agreement on a variety of issues (for details, *see* West Germany). By 1973, normal relations were established, and the two states entered the United Nations.

A new Constitution unanimously approved by the East German parliament on Sept. 27, 1974, pointedly deleted any reference to eventual reunification of the two Germanys, a principle maintained in the West German constitution.

The 25-year diplomatic hiatus between East Germany and the U.S. ended Sept. 4, 1974, with the establishment of formal relations.

The East German government has repeatedly challenged the Western powers' right of access to Berlin, most recently at the time of President Carter's July 15, 1978, visit to West Berlin. Autobahn traffic between the city and West Germany was deliberately slowed and, as in a similar 1977 case, the U.S., U.K., and France protested to the U.S.S.R. and the East Germans that such action was illegal under the 1971 Four Power Agreement.

Increased Soviet action in Africa in 1978 revealed that East Germany as well as Cuba was actively engaged as a Soviet agent. The East German "Afrika Korps" was reported to number about 4,500 soldiers, with an equal number of civilian technicians. Defense Minister Heinz Hoffmann visited Angola just before the Zaire invasion was launched in May. In Angola, 1,000 East German troops were reported serving with the army, and a small number of pilots were flying combat strikes against anti-government guerrillas.

**Economy.** In 1978, East Germany sought to increase its exports to the West, to decrease its indebtedness to non-Communist countries. About 22% of the population is engaged in agricultural pursuits, and the area is almost self-sufficient in foodstuffs. Postwar yields have, however, suffered from droughts and shortages of fertilizers.

Most of the industrial establishments, particularly in heavy industry, have been nationalized. The area accounted for 26% of prewar Germany's industrial production, ranking first in textiles, paper and pulp, and ceramics and glass (especially optical glass produced by the famous Jena works). In the first quarter of 1974, trade with the West increased 8%.

The area is not rich in minerals. It has only minor deposits of coal, but it does have important deposits of lignite and crude potash.

Chief exports in 1975 were machinery (31%), transport equipment (9%), chemicals, and textiles. Leading customers in 1974 were U.S.S.R. (33%), Czechoslovakia (10%), West Germany (10%), Poland (9%), Hungary (6%). Leading suppliers were U.S.S.R. (30%), West Germany (9%), Czechoslovakia (7%), Poland (7%), Hungary (5%).

## GERMANY, WEST

**Federal Republic of Germany**
**President:** Walter Scheel (1974)
**Chancellor:** Helmut Schmidt (1974)
**Area:** 95,791 sq mi. (248,577 sq km)[1]
**Population (est. 1978):** 61,250,000[1]
**Density per square mile:** 639.4
**Capital (est. 1977):** Bonn, 285,000
**Largest cities (est. 1977):** Hamburg, 1,707,400; Munich, 1,311,300; Cologne, 1,010,400; Essen, 674,000; Düsseldorf, 658,400; Frankfurt, 631,000; Dortmund, 627,600; Stuttgart, 594,100; Bremen, 570,700; Hannover, 549,100
**Monetary unit:** Deutsche Mark
**Language:** German
**Religions:** Protestant, 51%; Roman Catholic, 45%
**Gross national product (1976):** $446.7 billion
**National name:** Bundesrepublik Deutschland
**Freedom House classifications:** Capitalist industrial, multi-party decentralized

**Geography.** The Federal Republic of Germany occupies the western half of the central European area historically regarded as German. This was the part of Germany occupied by the U.S., U.K., and

1. Excluding West Berlin (184 square miles with 1977 population of 1,966,700).

France after the German defeat in World War II, when the eastern half of prewar Germany was split roughly between a Soviet-occupied zone, which became the present German Democratic Republic, and an area annexed by Poland.

The northern plain, the central hill country, and the southern mountain district constitute the main physical divisions of West Germany, which is slightly smaller than Oregon. The Bavarian plateau in the southwest averages 1,600 feet (488 m) above sea level, but it reaches 9,721 feet (2,963 m) in the Zugspitze, which is the highest point in Germany.

There are several important navigable rivers. In the south the Danube, rising in the Black Forest, flows east across Bavaria into Austria. The other important rivers flow north. The Rhine, which rises in Switzerland and flows across the Netherlands in two channels to the North Sea, is navigable by smaller vessels as far as Cologne. The Rhine and the Elbe, which also empties into the North Sea, are navigable within Germany for ships of 400 tons. The Weser, flowing into the North Sea, and the Main and Mosel (Moselle), both tributaries of the Rhine, are also important.

**Government.** Under the Constitution of May 23, 1949, the Federal Republic was established as a parliamentary democracy. The Parliament consists of the Bundesrat, an upper chamber representing and appointed by the 10 Länder, or states (plus West Berlin), and the Bundestag, a lower house elected for four years by universal suffrage. Each house has non-voting representatives from West Berlin. The entire legislature elects the President of the Republic for a five-year term; the Bundestag alone chooses the Chancellor, or Prime Minister. Each of the Länder and West Berlin have an assembly popularly elected for a four-year term.

The major political parties are the Social Democratic Party (214 of 496 seats in the Bundestag), led by former Chancellor Willy Brandt; Christian Democratic Union-Christian Social Union (243 seats), led by Helmut Kohl; and the Free Democratic Party (39 seats), led by Hans-Dietrich Genscher. Schmidt's government is a coalition with the Free Democrats.

**History.** Immediately before the Christian era, when the Roman Empire had pushed its frontier to the Rhine, what is now Germany was inhabited by several tribes believed to have migrated from Central Asia in the 6th to 4th centuries B.C. One of these Germanic tribes, the Franks, attained supremacy in western Europe under Charlemagne, who was crowned Holy Roman Emperor A.D. 800. By the Treaty of Verdun (843), Charlemagne's lands east of the Rhine were ceded to the German Prince Louis. Additional territory acquired by the Treaty of Mersen (870) gave Germany approximately the area it maintained throughout the Middle Ages. For several centuries after Otto the Great was crowned King in 936, the German rulers were also usually heads of the Holy Roman Empire.

Relations between state and church were changed by the Reformation, which began with Martin Luther's 95 theses, and came to a head in 1547, when Charles V scattered the forces of the Protestant League at Mühlberg. Freedom of worship was obtained by the Peace of Augsburg (1555), but a Counter Reformation took place later, and a dispute over the succession to the Bohemian throne brought on the Thirty Years' War (1618–48), which devastated Germany and left the empire divided into hundreds of small principalities virtually independent of the Emperor.

Meanwhile, Prussia was developing into a state of considerable strength. Frederick the Great (1740–86) reorganized the Prussian army and defeated Maria Theresa of Austria in a struggle over Silesia. The conflict with revolutionary France hastened the disintegration of the empire. After the defeat of Napoleon at Waterloo (1815), the struggle between Austria and Prussia for supremacy in Germany continued, reaching its climax in the defeat of Austria in the Seven Weeks' War (1866) and the formation of the Prussian-dominated North German Confederation (1867).

The architect of German unity was Otto von Bismarck, a conservative, monarchist, and militaristic Prussian Junker who had no use for "empty phrase-making and constitutions." From 1862 until his retirement in 1890 he dominated not only the German but also the entire European scene. He

## Rulers of Germany and Prussia

| Name | Born | Ruled[1] |
|---|---|---|
| **KINGS OF PRUSSIA** | | |
| Frederick I[2] | 1657 | 1701–1713 |
| Frederick William I | 1688 | 1713–1740 |
| Frederick II the Great | 1712 | 1740–1786 |
| Frederick William II | 1744 | 1786–1797 |
| Frederick William III | 1770 | 1797–1840 |
| Frederick William IV | 1795 | 1840–1861 |
| William I | 1797 | 1861–1871[3] |
| **EMPERORS OF GERMANY** | | |
| William I | 1797 | 1871–1888 |
| Frederick III | 1831 | 1888–1888 |
| William II | 1859 | 1888–1918[4] |
| **HEADS OF THE REICH** | | |
| Fredrich Ebert[5] | 1871 | 1919–1925 |
| Paul von Hindenburg[5] | 1847 | 1925–1934 |
| Adolf Hitler[6 7] | 1889 | 1934–1945 |
| Karl Doenitz[6] | 1891 | 1945–1945 |
| **GERMAN FEDERAL REPUBLIC (WESTERN)** | | |
| Theodor Heuss[5] | 1884 | 1949–1959[9] |
| Heinrich Luebke[5] | 1895 | 1959–1969[8] |
| Gustav Heinemann[5 12] | 1899 | 1969–1974 |
| Walter Scheel[5] | 1919 | 1974– |
| **GERMAN DEMOCRATIC REPUBLIC (EASTERN)** | | |
| Wilheim Pieck[5] | 1876 | 1949–1960 |
| Walter Ulbricht[10] | 1893 | 1960–1973 |
| Willi Stoph[11] | 1914 | 1973– |

1. Year of end of rule is also that of death, unless otherwise indicated. 2. Was Elector of Brandenburg (1688–1701) as Frederick III. 3. Became Emperor of Germany in 1871. 4. Died 1941. 5. President. 6. Führer. 7. Named Chancellor by President Hindenburg in 1933. 8. Died 1972. 9. Died 1963. 10. Chairman of Council of State. Died 1973. 11. Chairman Council of State. 12. Died 1976.

unified all Germany in a series of three wars against Denmark (1864), Austria (1866), and France (1870–71). Historians differ on the responsibility for these wars, but many believe they were instigated and promoted by Bismarck in his zeal to obtain national unity through "blood and iron."

On Jan. 18, 1871, King Wilhelm I of Prussia was proclaimed William I, German Emperor, in the Hall of Mirrors, Versailles. The North German Confederation, created in 1867, was abolished, and the new Second German Reich, consisting of both North and South German states, was born. As King of Prussia, the German Emperor exercised what amounted to dictatorial control over all Germany. With a powerful army, an efficient bureaucracy, and a loyal bourgeoisie, Chancellor Bismarck consolidated a powerful centralized state.

Wilhelm II dismissed Bismarck in 1890 and embarked upon a "New Course," stressing an intensified colonialism and a powerful navy. His chaotic foreign policy gradually culminated in the diplomatic isolation of Germany and the disastrous defeat in World War I (1914–18).

The Second German Empire collapsed following the defeat of the German armies in 1918, the naval mutiny at Kiel, and the flight of Wilhelm II to The Netherlands on November 10. The Social Democrats, led by Friedrich Ebert and Philipp Scheidemann, crushed the Communists and established a moderate republic with Ebert as President.

The Weimar Constitution of 1919 provided for a President to be elected for seven years by direct universal suffrage and a bicameral legislature, consisting of the Reichsrat, representing the states, and the Reichstag, representing the people. It contained a model Bill of Rights. It was weakened by including a provision (Article 48) enabling the President to rule by decree.

President Ebert died Feb. 28, 1925, and on April 26, Field Marshal Paul von Hindenburg was elected President of Germany.

The mass of Germans regarded the Weimar Republic as a child of defeat, imposed upon a Germany whose legitimate aspirations to world leadership had been thwarted by a world conspiracy. Added to this were a crippling currency debacle, a tremendous burden of reparations, and acute economic distress.

Adolf Hitler, an Austrian war veteran and a fanatical nationalist, capitalized on the situation. He fanned discontent by promising a Greater Germany, the abrogation of the Treaty of Versailles, the restoration of Germany's lost colonies, and the destruction of the Jews. When the Social Democrats and the Communists refused to combine against the Nazi threat, President Hindenburg made Hitler Chancellor on Jan. 30, 1933.

With the death of President Hindenburg on Aug. 2, 1934, Hitler became complete master of Germany. He repudiated the Treaty of Versailles and began full-scale rearmament. In 1935 he withdrew from the League of Nations, and in 1936 he reoccupied the Rhineland and signed the anti-Comintern pact with Japan, at the same time strengthening relations with Italy. Austria was annexed in March 1938. By the Munich agreement (September 1938) he gained the Czech Sudetenland, and in violation of this agreement he completed the dismemberment of Czechoslovakia in March 1939. But his invasion of Poland on Sept. 1, 1939, precipitated World War II.

On May 8, 1945, Germany surrendered unconditionally to Allied and Soviet military commanders, and on June 5 the four-nation Allied Control Council became the *de facto* government of Germany.

For details of World War II (1939–45), *see* Headline History.

At the Berlin (or Potsdam) Conference (July 17–Aug. 2, 1945) Truman, Stalin, and Attlee set forth the principles by which the Allied Control Council was to be guided. They were Germany's complete disarmament and demilitarization, destruction of its war potential, rigid control of industry, and decentralization of the political and economic structure. Pending final determination of territorial questions at a peace conference, the three victors agreed in principle to the ultimate transfer of the city of Königsberg (now Kaliningrad) and its adjacent area to the U.S.S.R. and to the administration by Poland of former German territories lying generally east of the Oder-Neisse Line.

For purposes of control Germany was divided in 1945 into four national occupation zones, each headed by a Military Governor, assisted by appropriate supervisory and operating staffs.

Efforts to unify Germany were totally unsuccessful, and the Western powers were unable to agree with the U.S.S.R. on any fundamental issue. Work of the Allied Control Council was hamstrung by repeated Soviet vetoes; and finally, on March 20, 1948, Russia walked out of the Council. Meanwhile, the U.S. and U.K. had taken steps to merge their zones economically (Bizone); and on May 31, 1948, the U.S., U.K., France, and the Benelux countries agreed to set up a German state comprising the three western zones. At the same time the Western powers introduced a new German currency.

The U.S.S.R. reacted by clamping a blockade on all ground communications between the Western Zones and Berlin, an enclave in the Soviet Zone. The Western Allies countered by organizing a gigantic airlift to fly supplies into the beleaguered city, assigning 60,000 men to it. The U.S.S.R. was finally forced to lift the blockade on May 12, 1949.

The Federal Republic of Germany was proclaimed on May 23, 1949, with its capital at Bonn. In free elections West German voters gave a majority in the Constituent Assembly to the Christian Democrats, with the Social Democrats largely making up the opposition. Konrad Adenauer became Chancellor, and Theodor Heuss of the Free Democrats was elected first President.

With admission into the European Coal and Steel Community and later into the Common Market, West German prosperity was strengthened. In 1950 a Constitution was given West Berlin which provided for autonomous municipal government and representation in the Bundestag. A peace contract was given West Germany on May 26, 1952, which created within the North Atlantic Treaty Organization a European Defense Community but it was later vetoed by France.

A conference at Paris reached agreements signed on Oct. 23, 1954, giving the Federal Republic full independence and complete sovereignty; it came into force on May 5, 1955. Under it, West Germany and Italy became members of the Brussels treaty organization created in 1948 and renamed the Western European Union. West Germany also became a member of NATO. In 1955 the U.S.S.R. recognized the Federal Republic. The Saar territory, under an agreement between France and West Germany, held a plebiscite and despite economic links to France voted to rejoin West Germany. It became a state of West Germany on Jan. 1, 1957.

On Jan. 22, 1963, Chancellor Adenauer concluded a treaty of mutual cooperation and friendship with France and then retired. He was succeeded by his chief inner-party critic, Ludwig Erhard, who was followed in 1966 by Kurt Georg Kiesinger. He, in turn, was succeeded in 1969 by Willy Brandt, former Mayor of West Berlin.

The division between West Germany and East Germany was signalized when the Communists erected the Berlin Wall in 1961. In June, 1968, the East German Communist leader, Walter Ulbricht, imposed restrictions on West German movements into West Berlin. The Soviet-bloc invasion of Czechoslovakia in August 1968 added to the tension.

Willy Brandt's Socialist government pushed through an "Ostpolitik" policy that led to the first official meetings of leaders of East and West Germany on March 19, 1970. A treaty with the U.S.S.R. was signed in Moscow in August 1970 in which force was renounced and respect for the "territorial integrity" of present European states declared.

Three months later, Germany signed a similar treaty with Poland, renouncing force and setting Poland's western border as the Oder-Neisse Line (which acknowledged Poland's post-war annexation of 40,000 square miles of former German territory) and subsequently resumed formal relations with Czechoslovakia in a pact that "voided" the Munich treaty that gave Nazi Germany the Sudetenland.

Both German states were admitted to the United Nations in 1973.

Brandt, winner of a Nobel Peace Prize for his foreign policies, was forced to quit in May 1974 when an East German Communist spy was discovered as one of his top staff members. Succeeding him was a moderate Social Democrat, Helmut Schmidt.

Schmidt's government was plagued with mounting terrorism by urban guerrillas known as the Baader-Meinhof gang. Andreas Baader and two of the gang's survivors were sentenced to life imprisonment on May 29, 1977. Ulrike Meinhof had committed suicide a year earlier. On September 5, members of the gang kidnapped Hanns-Martin Schleyer, president of the Federation of West German Industries, in Cologne, and demanded the freedom of 11 imprisoned terrorists as ransom.

On October 18, a spectacular assault by a crack West German commando unit freed 86 passengers and crew members of a hijacked Lufthansa jet in Mogadishu, Somalia, killing three of the four hijackers who had also sought the terrorist prisoners' release. Hours after the capture, Baader and two other prisoners committed suicide, and the next day Schleyer's bullet-riddled body was found in France.

West Germany hosted the fourth annual summit meeting of the seven leading industrial nations July 16–17, 1978. Schmidt, whose economy was Europe's strongest with a trade surplus of $5 billion in 1977, was critical of U.S. failure to curb both its oil consumption and inflation. He showed a reluctance, however, to meet U.S. demands for stimulating a sluggish German economy. Schmidt had differed with Carter previously, questioning his emphasis on human rights as a threat to détente and refusing to accept U.S. restrictions on the export of nuclear reactors unless all nations accepted such controls.

**Economy.** Agriculture is characterized by mixed farming, the climate and the soil permitting cultivation of a variety of crops and most types of livestock. Rye and potatoes are staple crops in the north; grains and sugar beets in the central regions.

The northwestern and southern areas are noted for dairying, while the west is the chief fruit- and wine-producing region. The soil is generally poor, and high crop yields are dependent upon large-scale use of fertilizers.

West Germany's industry is well developed and diversified. It accounted for about two thirds of Germany's prewar industrial production and for a large part of iron and steel production. Shipbuilding has regained its former prominence.

West Germany is a member of the European Coal and Steel Community, which commenced activities on Aug. 10, 1952. It has jurisdiction over the production and allocation of coal and steel by its member nations.

Aside from rich deposits of coal and potash, West Germany's mineral wealth is not considerable. The Ruhr, Krefeld, and Aachen districts constitute one of the world's greatest coal-mining regions.

About 23% of the total area of West Germany is covered by commercial forests, which yield timber as well as material for paper, wood fiber, cellulose, and other products.

Shipping on the Rhine is controlled by the Central Commission of the Rhine—an international body composed provisionally of U.S., British, French, Swiss, Dutch, and Belgian representatives —which was reconvened in October 1945.

Chief exports in 1976 were machinery (29%), motor vehicles (15%), chemicals (13%), iron and steel (9%), and textiles and clothing (6%). Leading customers were EEC (46%; incl. France 13%, Netherlands 10%, Belgium-Luxembourg 8%, Italy 7%, U.K. 5%), U.S. (6%), Austria (5%). Leading suppliers were EEC (49%; incl. Netherlands 14%, France 12%, Belgium-Luxembourg 9%, Italy 9%), U.S. (8%).

## BERLIN

**Status:** West Berlin: State of West Germany; East Berlin: capital of East Germany
**Governing Mayor,** West Berlin: Dietrich Stobbe (1977).
**Mayor, East Berlin:** Erhard Krack.
**Area:** 340 square miles (West Berlin, 184; East Berlin, 156
**Population (est. 1977):** 3,057,000 (West Berlin, 1,950,700; East Berlin, 1,106,300)

Berlin, the capital of prewar Germany, is surrounded by East Germany. After the war, Berlin was occupied by the forces of the U.S., the U.K., France, and the U.S.S.R. The three western sectors, now known as West Berlin, contain 55% of the area and two thirds of the population.

West Berlin is a state of the Federal Republic of Germany, but supreme authority remains in the hands of the three Western powers in accordance with postwar agreements. The government is composed of the Governing Mayor, the 11-member Senate (his Cabinet), and the House of Representatives, a popularly elected legislative body that elects the Governing Mayor and the Senate.

East Berlin is governed by a City Assembly elected by Communist Party members, and a Magistrat (city council) chosen by the Assembly and headed by the Mayor. In violation of the Four Power Agreements, the Soviet Sector has been incorporated into the German Democratic Republic and is now the capital of that country.

Major anti-Communist riots broke out in East Berlin in June 1953 and, since Aug. 13, 1961, the Soviet Sector has been virtually sealed off by a

Communist-built wall, 26½ miles long, running through the city. It was built to stem the flood of refugees seeking freedom in the West, 200,000 having fled in 1961 before the wall was erected.

## GHANA

**Republic of Ghana**
**Head of State and Government:** Lt. Gen. Frederick W. K. Akuffo (1978)
**Area:** 92,100 sq mi. (238,537 sq km)
**Population (est. 1978):** 10,650,000
**Density per square mile:** 115.6
**Capital:** Accra
**Largest cities (est. 1975):** Accra, 716,600; **(est. 1972):** Kumasi, 342,982; Sekondi-Takoradi, 161,071
**Monetary unit:** New cedi
**Languages:** Native tongues (Twi, Fanti, Ga, Ewe, Dagbani); English
**Religions:** Christian 43%, Islam, 12%, Animist 38%
**Gross national product (1976):** $5.9 billion
**Member of Commonwealth of Nations**
**Freedom House classifications:** Capitalist-statist industrial, non-party military

**Geography.** A West African country bordering on the Gulf of Guinea, Ghana has the Ivory Coast to the west, Upper Volta to the north, and Togo to the east. It compares in size to Oregon.

The coastal belt, extending about 270 miles (435 km), is sandy, marshy, and generally exposed. Behind it is a gradually widening grass strip. The forested plateau region to the north is broken by ridges and hills. The largest river is the Volta.

**Government.** On Jan. 13, 1972, a military coup led by Col. Ignatius Kutu Acheampong seized power bloodlessly and deposed Kofi A. Busia, who had been Premier since 1969. The Constitution was suspended, Parliament dissolved, and a National Redemption Council was set up. It consists of nine members, seven of whom are military men, an Inspector-General of Police, and a civilian Attorney General. The activities of political parties were banned.

**History.** Created an independent country on March 6, 1957, Ghana is the former British colony of the Gold Coast. The area was first seen by Portuguese traders in 1470. They were followed by the English (1553), the Dutch (1595), and the Swedes (1640). British rule over the Gold Coast began in 1820, but it was not until after quelling the severe resistance of the Ashanti in 1901 that it was firmly established. British Togoland, formerly a colony of Germany, was incorporated into Ghana by referendum in 1956. As the result of a plebiscite, Ghana became a republic on July 1, 1960.

Premier Kwame Nkrumah attempted to take leadership of the Pan-African Movement, holding the All-African People's Congress in his capital, Accra, in 1958 and organizing the Union of African States with Guinea and Mali in 1961. But he oriented his country toward the Soviet Union and China and built an autocratic rule over all aspects of Ghanaian life.

In February 1966, while Nkrumah was visiting Peking and Hanoi, he was deposed by a military coup led by Emmanuel K. Kotoka. The U.S. recognized it and gave it financial aid. In April 1967, a military junta was crushed, but General Kotoka was killed. The military leaders took steps to restore civilian rule and a new Constitution was approved in May 1969.

Another military group took over in January 1972. Its leader, Col. Acheampong, proclaimed himself Head of State and chairman of the National Redemption Council, which replaced Parliament. The new regime proposed a union government of military, police, and civilian elements in a referendum approved by the voters on March 30, 1978. Before the plan could be implemented, however, Lt. Gen. Frederick W. K. Akuffo of the military governing council ousted Acheampong on July 5. The shift was apparently related to food shortages and Ghana's raging inflation, running at an annual rate of more than 100%.

**Economy.** The mainstay of the economy is the cultivation of cacao, in the production of which Ghana leads the rest of the world. Secondary export crops include palm kernels, copra, kola nuts, coffee, rubber, and timber.

Mineral resources are abundant. Most important is gold, mined at Tarkwa, Bibiani, and Obuasi. Others include diamonds, manganese ore, and bauxite. Forest resources are extensive and large amounts of hardwoods, notably mahogany, are exported from the forests in the interior.

Chief exports in 1975 were cocoa (59%) and timber (8%). Leading customers were U.K. (15%), U.S. (11%), Netherlands (10%), Switzerland (8%), West Germany (8%), Japan (7%), U.S.S.R. (7%), Yugoslavia (5%). Leading suppliers were U.S. (16%), U.K. (15%), West Germany (11%), Nigeria (7%), Japan (6%), Libya (5%).

## GREECE

**Hellenic Republic**
**President:** Constantine Tsatsos (1975)
**Prime Minister:** Constantine Caramanlis (1974)
**Area:** 50,944 sq mi. (131,944 sq km)
**Population (est. 1977):** 9,300,000
**Density per square mile:** 182.6
**Capital:** Athens
**Largest cities (1971 census):** Athens (metropolitan area), 1,378,586; Salonika, 302,634; Patras, 94,192; Volos, 73,877
**Monetary unit:** Drachma
**Language:** Greek
**Religion:** Greek Orthodox
**Gross national product (1976):** $22.9 billion
**National name:** Elliniki Dimokratia
**Freedom House classifications:** Capitalist industrial, multi-party centralized

**Geography.** Greece, on the Mediterranean Sea, is the southernmost country on the Balkan Peninsula in Eastern Europe. It is bordered on the north by Albania, Yugoslavia, and Bulgaria; on the west by the Ionian Sea; and on the east by the Aegean Sea and Turkey. It is slightly smaller than Alabama.

North central Greece, Epirus, and western Macedonia all are mountainous. The main chain of the Pindus Mountains rises to 9,000 feet (2,743 m) in places, separating Epirus from the plains of Thessaly. Greek Thrace is mostly a lowland region separated from European Turkey by the lower Maritsa River.

Among the many islands are the Ionian group off the west coast; the Cyclades group to the southeast; other islands in the eastern Aegean, including Lesbos, Samos, and Chios; and Crete, the fourth largest

Mediterranean island.

The Dodecanese, a group of islands in the Aegean Sea near the coast of Asia Minor, were ceded to Greece by the 1947 Italian peace treaty and were formally transferred on March 7, 1948.

**Government.** Greece returned to democratic government when the military dictatorship imposed in April 1967, collapsed July 23, 1974. A referendum in December 1974, resulted in 69.18% support for a republic to replace the monarchy. Constantine Tsatsos was elected President and Constantine Caramanlis Prime Minister.

The major political parties are the New Democracy Party (172 of 300 seats in the unicameral parliament), led by Premier Caramanlis; Panhellenic Socialist Movement (93 seats), led by Andreas Papandreou; Union of Democratic Center (15 seats), led by George Mavros; Communist Party (11 seats); National Alignment Party (5 seats); Alliance of the Left (2 seats); and Neo-Liberal Party (2 seats).

**History.** Greece, with a recorded history going back to 766 B.C., reached the peak of its glory in the 5th century B.C., and by the middle of the 2nd century B.C., it had declined to the status of a Roman province. It remained within the Eastern Roman Empire until Constantinople fell to the Crusaders in 1204.

In 1453, the Turks took Constantinople, and by 1460 Greece was a Turkish province. The insurrection made famous by the poet Lord Byron broke out in 1821, and in 1827 Greece was set up as an independent nation, with sovereignty guaranteed by the U.K., France, and Russia.

The protecting powers chose Prince Otto of Bavaria as the first King of modern Greece in 1832 to reign over an area only slightly larger than the Peloponnese peninsula. Chiefly under the next King, George I, chosen by the protecting powers in 1863, Greece acquired much of its present territory. During his 57-year tenure, a period in which he encouraged parliamentary democracy, Thessaly, Epirus, Macedonia, Crete, and most of the Aegean islands were added from the disintegrating Turkish empire. An unsuccessful war against Turkey after World War I brought down the monarchy, to be replaced by a republic in 1923.

Two military dictatorships and a financial crisis brought George II back from exile, but only until 1941, when Italian and German invaders defeated tough Greek resistance. After British and Greek troops liberated the country in October 1944, Communist guerrillas staged a long campaign in which the government received U.S. aid under the Truman doctrine, the predecessor of the Marshall Plan.

A military junta seized power in April 1967, sending young King Constantine II into exile December 14. Col. George Papadopoulos as Premier converted the government to republican form in 1973 and as President ended martial law and was moving to restore democracy when he was ousted in November 1974 by his military colleagues. The regime of the "colonels," which had tortured its opponents and scoffed at human rights, resigned meekly July 23, 1974, after bungling an attempt to seize Cyprus.

Former Premier Caramanlis returned from exile to become Premier of Greece's first civilian government since 1967. Elections Nov. 17, 1974, gave him 54.37% backing and a new republican constitution was adopted June 7, 1975.

Greece cut its military ties with the North Atlantic Treaty Organization in mid-August 1974 because of the failure of the U.S. and other members to restrain Turkey, also a member, from invading Cyprus. Efforts to settle the Cyprus problem failed and in January 1978 Opposition leader Andreas Papandreou demanded the closing of U.S. bases remaining in Greece.

A meeting between Caramanlis and Turkish Premier Bülent Ecevit in Switzerland March 10–11 was reported to have eased differences over air and sea rights in the Aegean, but Ecevit broke off in anger at U.S. Secretary of State Cyrus Vance's statement that the provision of U.S. arms to Turkey would be linked with progress in Cyprus. The Carter administration in August 1978 obtained a reluctant Congressional reversal of an arms embargo imposed when Turkey intervened in Cyprus. Greece supported a continuing embargo as long as Turkish troops remained on the island.

**Economy.** About three quarters of the population engages in agricultural pursuits, although only one fifth of the land is arable. Most of the cultivated area is devoted to cereals: wheat, barley, and maize. There are also olive trees, vines, tobacco, and currants. The principal fruits are oranges, lemons, figs, mandarins, apples, and pears.

Development of large-scale Greek manufacturing is blocked by lack of coal resources and of capital. The most valuable products are textiles, chemicals, and food items. Among other processed or manufactured products are olive oil, wine, spirits, flour, carpets, leather, cigarettes, and building materials.

Greek minerals are varied but are exploited only moderately. Principal ones are lignite, iron ore, iron pyrites, magnesite, chromite, lead, bauxite, molybdenum, emery, marine salt, and marble.

A fifth of the country is forested, largely with pine, fir, and oak. Resin and turpentine are main forest products. The major sea product is sponges.

Chief exports in 1975 were fruits and vegetables (19%), petroleum products (11%), textile yarns and fabrics (8%), tobacco (7%) and iron and steel (7%). Leading customers were EEC (50%; incl. West Germany 21%, Italy 8%, France 7%, Netherlands 6%, U.K. 5%), Libya (6%), U.S. (5%). Leading suppliers were EEC (43%; incl. West Germany 16%, Italy 8%, France 6%, U.K. 5%), Saudi Arabia (8%), Japan (8%), U.S. (7%).

# GRENADA

**State of Grenada**
**Prime Minister:** Sir Eric M. Gairy (1974)
**Governor General:** Leo de Gale
**Area:** 133 sq mi. (344 sq km)
**Population (est. 1978):** 110,000 (black, 53%; mixed, 42%)
**Density per square mile:** 827.1
**Capital and largest city (est. 1974):** St. George's, 6,600
**Monetary unit:** East Caribbean dollar
**Ethnic groups:** Caribs and Indians
**Language:** English
**Religions:** Roman Catholic, Anglican, Methodist
**Gross national product (1976):** $50 million
**Member of Commonwealth of Nations**
**Freedom House classifications:** Capitalist industrial, multi-party centralized

**Geography.** Grenada (the first "a" is pronounced as in "gray") is the most southerly of the Windward

Islands, about 100 miles from the South American coast. It is a volcanic island traversed by a mountain range, the highest peak of which is Mount St. Catherine (2,756 ft.; 840 m).

**History.** Grenada was discovered by Columbus in 1498. After more than 200 years of British rule, most recently as part of the West Indies Associated States, it became independent Feb. 7, 1974.

The country began its independence in chaos, as opponents of Prime Minister Gairy's curbs on civil liberties—notably the professionals and educated class, as well as some union leaders and businessmen—paralyzed Grenada with a general strike that ended after two weeks when Gairy promised to disband his secret police force.

In September 1974, Grenada became a member of the United Nations and in 1975 of the Organization of American States. In June 1977, it was host to the OAS General Assembly.

The United Labor Party, led by Prime Minister Gairy, won only 9 of 15 seats in the House of Assembly, the island's parliament in 1976.

**Economy.** The principal sources of revenue are derived from tourism, bananas, nutmeg, and cocoa.

Chief exports in 1974 were cocoa (29%), nutmeg (28%), bananas (16%), and mace (9%). Leading customers in 1973 were U.K. (33%), West Germany (19%), Netherlands and possessions (14%), U.S. (8%), Belgium-Luxembourg (5%). Leading suppliers were U.K. (27%), Trinidad and Tobago (20%), U.S. (9%), Canada (8%).

## GUATEMALA

**Republic of Guatemala**
**President:** Gen. Romeo Lucas Garcia (1978)
**Area:** 42,042 sq mi. (108,889 sq km)
**Population (est. 1978):** 6,630,000
**Density per square mile:** 157.7
**Capital and largest city (est. 1978):** Guatemala City, 1,227,800
**Monetary unit:** Quetzal
**Languages:** Spanish, some Indian dialects
**Religion:** Roman Catholic
**Gross national product (1976):** $4.1 billion
**National name:** República de Guatemala
**Freedom House classifications:** Capitalist pre-industrial, multi-party centralized

**Geography.** The northernmost of the Central American nations, Guatemala is the size of Tennessee. The country consists of two main regions—the cool highlands with the heaviest population and the tropical area along the Pacific and Caribbean coasts. The principal mountain range rises to the highest elevation in Central America and contains many volcanic peaks. Volcanic eruptions are frequent.

**Government.** Executive power is vested in the President, who is elected for a term of four years, and his Cabinet of 10 members. Legislative power is vested in the 61-member National Congress.

The major political parties are National Liberation Movement (20 seats in National Congress); Democratic Institutional Party (17 seats); Revolutionary Party (14 seats); Christian Democratic Party (7 seats); and the Aranista Union Party (3 seats).

**History.** Once the site of the ancient Mayan civilization, Guatemala, conquered by Spain in 1524, set itself up as a republic in 1839. From 1898 to 1920, the dictator Manuel Estrada Cabrera ran the country, and from 1931 to 1944, Gen. Jorge Ubico Castaneda was the "strong man." In July 1944 the National Assembly elected Gen. Federico Ponce President, but he was overthrown in October. In December Dr. Juan José Arévalo was elected as the head of a leftist regime that continued to press its reform program. Jacobo Arbenz Guzmán, administration candidate with pro-Communist leanings, won the 1950 elections.

Arbenz expropriated the large estates, including plantations of the United Fruit Company, and exterminated his political enemies. With covert U.S. backing, a revolt was led by Col. Carlos Castillo Armas, and Arbenz took refuge in Havana. Castillo Armas became President but was assassinated in 1957. Constitutional government was restored in 1958, and Gen. Miguel Ydigoras Fuentes was elected President. He was host to the Cuban force that trained for the disastrous landing at the Bay of Pigs in April 1961.

In 1963 the Ydigoras government was overthrown by Enrique Peralta Azurdia, who ruled until 1966, when elections, under a new Constitution, led to Congress's choice of Dr. Julio César Méndez Montenegro.

In 1967, terrorists of the Left and Right began plaguing the country. The U.S. military and naval attachés were assassinated in Guatemala City in January 1968, and the U.S. Ambassador, John Gordon Mein, was slain in August 1968, when he resisted kidnapping. In a little over two years at least 1,000 people—some estimates make it 4,000—were murdered by extremists.

The left-wing terrorists, abetted by counterterrorists of the right, created widespread fear of anarchy, which led to the election of the Coalition's conservative, business-backed Carlos Arana Osorio on March 1, 1970. Arana had won fame as an army chief who bloodily put down one rural guerrilla movement (1,500–3,000 peasants killed). On taking office, Arana surprisingly pledged social reform.

Gen. Kjell Laugerud won the March 1974 elections for President. Political violence attended his inauguration in July and continued after he took office.

A devastating earthquake struck Guatemala on Feb. 4, 1976, killing an estimated 22,000 and injuring 74,000. Despite the heavy casualties, little damage was done to the nation's small, but growing, industrial base.

A long-standing feud with the U.K. over Guatemalan claims to Belize, a British possession formerly known as British Honduras, sharpened in 1977. On June 18, Guatemala warned that it would fight for the territory if it were declared independent by Britain, and troops were dispatched from London to bolster Belize's defenses. The Organization of American States announced on March 1 that it supported Guatemala's claim, but on June 16 five Caribbean member states declared their backing for the territory's independence.

Guatemala became the fourth Latin nation to reject U.S. military aid after publication of a State Department report in March about human rights abuses under the Laugerud regime. Guatemala had been scheduled to receive $1.2 million in military assistance in fiscal 1978.

**Economy.** Agricultural products include corn, cotton, cane sugar, coffee, and bananas. The country's vast forests, mostly in the Petén region, yield chicle for chewing gum, cinchona bark, some rubber, and dyewoods and cabinet woods.

Chief exports in 1975 were coffee (26%), sugar (18%), cotton (12%), and bananas (5%). Leading customers were U.S. (23%), El Salvador (12%), West Germany (10%), U.K. (8%), Italy (6%), Costa Rica (6%), Nicaragua (5%), Japan (5%). Leading suppliers were U.S. (34%), Venezuela (11%), Japan (9%), El Salvador (8%), West Germany (8%).

## GUINEA

**Republic of Guinea**
**President:** Ahmed Sékou Touré (1958)
**Premier:** Lansana Beavogui
**Area:** 94,925 sq mi. (245,857 sq km)
**Population (est. 1978):** 4,775,000 (chiefly Fulani, Malinké, and Susu)
**Density per square mile:** 50.3
**Capital and largest city (est. 1977):** Conakry, 600,000
**Monetary unit:** Syli
**Languages:** French (official), native tongues (Malinké, Soussou, Fulani)
**Religions:** Islam and animist
**Gross national product (1976):** $880 million
**National name:** République de Guinée
**Freedom House classifications:** Socialist pre-industrial, one-party socialist

**Geography.** Guinea, in western Africa on the Atlantic, is also bordered by Guinea-Bissau, Senegal, Mali, the Ivory Coast, Liberia, and Sierra Leone. Slightly smaller than Oregon, the country consists of a coastal plain, a mountainous region, a savanna interior, and a forest area in the Guinea Highlands. The highest peak is Mt. Nimba at about 6,000 feet (1,829 m).

**Government.** The National Assembly has 150 members elected by universal suffrage from a list prepared and presented by the Parti Démocratique de Guinée, the only political party, led by President Touré (Secretary General of the party).

**History.** Previously part of French West Africa, Guinea achieved independence by rejecting the new French Constitution, and on Oct. 2, 1958, became an independent State with Sékou Touré as President. Touré led the country into being the first avowedly Marxist state in Africa. Diplomatic relations with France were suspended in 1965, with the Soviet Union replacing France as the country's chief source of economic and technical assistance.

In 1966, when a Ghanian military coup deposed Kwame Nkrumah as President, Touré welcomed him to Guinea and declared him joint President and party leader. The titles proved to be only honorary. Touré accused Ghana of being an American imperialist puppet, and the U.S. embassy in his capital, Conakry, was sacked. In retaliation the United States ended financial aid. An exchange of letters between the Guinea and U.S. presidents restored relations.

In 1968, President Touré sought to establish more normal relations with his neighbors. Prosperity came in 1969 after the start of exploitation of bauxite deposits. Touré was re-elected to a seven-year term in December 1974.

**Economy.** Guinea is well equipped economically to be independent. It is the second richest country in French Africa. It is rich in bauxite and has great reserves of hydraulic power.

Chief exports in 1971 were alumina and bauxite (72%), pineapples (10%), coffee (6%), and palm kernels (6%). Leading customers in 1975 were U.S. (16%), Spain (14%), U.S.S.R. (12%), Canada (9%), West Germany (8%), Cameroon (8%), France (7%), Yugoslavia (6%), Switzerland (6%). Leading suppliers were France (24%), U.S.S.R. (15%), U.S. (15%), Morocco (8%), Belgium-Luxembourg (7%), U.K. (5%).

## GUINEA-BISSAU

**Republic of Guinea-Bissau**
**President:** Luis Cabral (1974)
**Principal Commissioner:** João Bernardo Vieira
**Area:** 13,948 sq mi. (36,125 sq km)
**Population (est. 1978):** 545,000
**Density per square mile:** 39.1
**Capital and largest city (est. 1970 for urban agglomeration):** Bissau, 71,200
**Monetary unit:** Guinea-Bissau peso
**Language:** French (official)
**Religions:** Animist, Islam, Roman Catholic
**Gross national product (1976):** $70 million
**National name:** Guiné Bissau
**Freedom House classifications:** Socialist pre-industrial, one-party socialist

**Geography.** A neighbor of Senegal and Guinea in western Africa, on the Atlantic coast, Guinea-Bissau is about half the size of South Carolina.

The country is a low-lying coastal region of swamps, rain forests, and mangrove-covered wetlands, with about 60 islands off the coast. The Bissagos archipelago extends 30 miles out to sea. Internal communications depend mainly on deep estuaries and meandering rivers, since there are no railroads. Bissau, the capital, is the main port.

**Government.** The President and a 15-member Council of State were elected in 1977 by a National Assembly of 150 members chosen from regional councils elected in 1976 and 1977 from lists provided by the sole political party, the African Party for the Independence of Guinea-Bissau and Cape Verde.

**History.** Guinea-Bissau was discovered in 1446 by the Portuguese Nuno Tristão, and colonists in the Cape Verde Islands obtained trading rights in the territory. In 1879 the connection with the Cape Verde Islands was broken. Early in the 1900s the Portuguese managed to pacify some tribesmen, although resistance to colonial rule remained.

The African Party for the Independence of Guinea-Bissau and Cape Verde was founded in 1956 and several years later began guerrilla warfare that grew increasingly effective. By 1974 the rebels controlled most of the countryside, where they formed a government that was soon recognized by scores of countries. The military coup in Portugal in April 1974 brightened the prospects for freedom, and in August the Lisbon government signed an agreement granting independence to the province as of Sept. 10. The new republic took the name of Guinea-Bissau. Its government was immediately recognized by the United States.

On July 7, 1978, Francisco Mendès, who had been Premier since 1975, was assassinated.

**Economy.** Agriculture is the principal industry, the leading exports being peanuts. Cattle breeding provides hides for export.

Deposits of bauxite, oil, and minerals have been found, but the years of guerrilla war prevented any development.

Chief exports in 1973 were peanuts (46%), transport equipment (transit) (21%), petroleum and products (transit) (8%), palm kernels (7%), metals (6%), and timber (5%). Leading customer was Portugal (90%). Leading suppliers were Portugal (56%), Spain (7%), U.K. (5%), Japan (5%).

## GUYANA

**Republic of Guyana**
**President:** Arthur Chung (1970)
**Prime Minister:** Forbes Burnham (1964)
**Area:** 83,000 sq mi. (214,969 sq km)
**Population (est. 1978):** 825,000 (East Indian, 52%; African, 31%; mixed 10%; Amerindian, 5%)
**Density per square mile:** 9.9
**Capital and largest city (est. 1972):** Georgetown, 101,000
**Monetary unit:** Guyanan dollar
**Languages:** English (official), Hindi, Urdu
**Religions:** Protestant, Islam, Roman Catholic, Hindu
**Gross national product (1976):** $430 million
**Member of Commonwealth of Nations**
**Freedom House classifications:** Capitalist-socialist industrial, multi-party centralized

**Geography.** Guyana is situated on the northern coast of South America to the east of Venezuela and north of Brazil. The country consists of a low coastal area and the Guiana Highlands in the south. There is an extensive north-south network of rivers. Guyana is the size of Idaho.

**Government.** Guyana proclaimed itself a republic on Feb. 23, 1970, ending its tie with Britain while remaining in the Commonwealth.

Guyana has a unicameral legislature, the National Assembly, with 53 members elected for four-year terms. A 24-member Cabinet is headed by the Prime Minister.

The major political parties are the People's National Congress (37 of 53 seats in National Assembly), led by Prime Minister Burnham; People's Progressive Party (14 seats), led by Dr. Cheddi B. Jagan.

**History.** Formerly British Guiana, this independent nation, a member of the Commonwealth of Nations, won internal self-government in 1952. The next year the People's Progressive Party, headed by Cheddi Jagan, an East Indian dentist, won the elections and Jagan became Prime Minister. British authorities deposed him for alleged Communist connections. In 1962, conservatives rioted over his first effort at fiscal reform. A coalition ousted Jagan in 1964, installing a moderate Socialist, Forbes Burnham, a black, as Prime Minister. On May 26, 1966, the country became an independent member of the Commonwealth and resumed its traditional name, Guyana.

The government nationalized mining operations of the U.S.-owned Reynolds Metals Co. on Jan. 1, 1975.

In August 1978, the International Monetary Fund approved an $18.7-million loan for Guyana, which is trying to overcome a $60-million deficit in balance of payments.

**Economy.** Agricultural products include cane sugar and rice. Minerals include bauxite, manganese, and diamonds.

Chief exports in 1975 were sugar (50%), bauxite (24%), rice (10%), and alumina (8%). Leading customers were U.K. (28%), U.S. (23%), U.S.S.R. (9%), Jamaica (6%), Trinidad and Tobago (5%). Leading suppliers were U.S. (30%), U.K. (22%), Trinidad and Tobago (18%).

## HAITI

**Republic of Haiti**
**Life President:** Jean-Claude Duvalier (1971)
**Area:** 10,714 sq mi. (27,750 sq km)
**Population (est. 1978):** 4,830,000
**Density per square mile:** 450.8
**Capital and largest city (est. 1976):** Port-au-Prince, 652,900
**Monetary unit:** Gourde
**Languages:** French, Creole
**Religion:** Roman Catholic
**Gross national product (1976):** $930 million
**National name:** République d'Haïti
**Freedom house classifications:** Capitalist pre-industrial, one-party nationalist

**Geography.** Haiti, in the West Indies, occupies the western third of the island of Hispaniola, which it shares with the Dominican Republic. About the size of Maryland, Haiti is two thirds mountainous, with the rest of the country marked by great valleys, extensive plateaus, and small plains. The most densely populated region is the Cul-de-Sac plain near Port-au-Prince.

**Government.** In 1964, the late President, François Duvalier, known as "Papa Doc," made himself President for life, a tenure that his son, Jean-Claude, 19, known as "Baby Doc," inherited on his father's death, April 21, 1971. Under a Constitution revised in 1964, the President in periods of crisis may dismiss the National Assembly and Cabinet and govern by decree. The Parti d'Unité Nationale (all 58 seats in National Assembly), led by President Duvalier, is the only legal party in the country.

**History.** Discovered by Columbus, who landed at Môle Saint Nicolas on Dec. 6, 1492, Haiti in 1697 became a French possession known as Saint Domingue, occupying the western third of the island of Hispaniola. An insurrection among a slave population of 500,000 in 1791 ended with a declaration of independence by Pierre-Dominique Toussaint l'Ouverture in 1801. Napoleon Bonaparte suppressed the independence movement, but it eventually triumphed in 1804 under Jean-Jacques Dessalines, who gave the new nation the aboriginal name Haiti.

Its prosperity dissipated in internal strife as well as disputes with neighboring Santo Domingo during a succession of 19th-century dictatorships, a bankrupt Haiti accepted a U.S. customs receivership from 1905 to 1941. Direct U.S. rule from 1915 to 1930 brought a measure of stability and a population growth that made Haiti the most densely populated nation in the hemisphere.

In December 1949, after four years of democratic rule by President Dumarsais Estimé, dictatorship returned under Gen. Paul Magloire, who was succeeded by François Duvalier in September 1957.

Duvalier established a dictatorship based on a

secret police known as the "Ton-ton Macoutes," which gunned down opponents of the regime. In 1964 he amended the Constitution, making himself President for life.

Frequent assassinations and the famine in the interior led to the loss of the tourist trade, and the country's modern hotels were largely empty as terror and stagnation ravaged the country, the poorest nation in the Western Hemisphere.

Three months before he died in 1971 of natural causes at age 64, Duvalier named his son, then 19 years old, his successor.

An economic comeback of sorts attended Jean-Claude Duvalier's regime. With urban unemployment at 60% and the minimum wage at $1.30 a day, some 150 foreign firms established Haitian branches to take advantage of cheap labor and the order enforced by a still-authoritarian government. The rate of new investment was estimated at $100 million yearly, but per capita income for the masses was about $70 in 1975.

**Economy.** Haiti is predominantly agricultural. Coffee is the principal crop, followed by sisal, sugarcane, cotton, bananas, and cacao. Manufacturing is almost entirely for local consumption.

Mineral resources in Haiti include gold, silver, tin, and copper.

Chief exports in 1975 were coffee (27%) and bauxite (18%). Leading customers were U.S. (74%), France (8%), Belgium-Luxembourg (5%). Leading suppliers were U.S. (54%), Netherlands Antilles (8%), Japan (7%), Canada (5%), France (5%).

## HONDURAS

**Republic of Honduras**
**Chief of State:** Gen. Policarpio Paz Garcia (1978)
**Area:** 43,277 sq mi. (112,088 sq km)
**Population (est. 1977):** 2,900,000 (90% mestizo)
**Density per square mile:** 67.0
**Capital and largest city (est. 1975):** Tegucigalpa, 350,000
**Monetary unit:** Lempira
**Languages:** Spanish, some Indian dialects
**Religion:** Roman Catholic
**Gross national product (1976):** $1.2 billion
**National name:** República de Honduras
**Freedom House classifications:** Capitalist pre-industrial, non-party military

**Geography.** Honduras, in the north central part of Central America, has a 400-mile (644-km) Caribbean coastline and a 40-mile (64-km) Pacific frontage. Its neighbors are Guatemala to the west, El Salvador to the south, and Nicaragua to the east. Honduras is slightly larger than Tennessee.

Generally mountainous, the country is marked by fertile plateaus, river valleys, and narrow coastal plains.

**Government.** The 1965 Constitution, providing for a President to be elected to a single six-year term and for a unicameral legislature of 64 members, was suspended in 1973 by Gen. Oswaldo López Arellano. López was ousted by the armed forces April 22, 1975, after he was charged with having received a bribe of $1,250,000 from the United Brands Company, a multinational banana exporter. He was replaced by Col. Juan Alberto Melgar Castro, who on Jan. 1, 1978 authorized political party activity and set April 1980 as the date for election of an assembly to write a new Constitution.

The National Party and the Liberal Party are the principal political parties.

**History.** Columbus discovered Honduras on his last voyage in 1502. Honduras, with four other countries of Central America, declared its independence from Spain in 1821 and was part of a federation of Central American states until 1838. In that year it seceded from the federation and became a completely independent country.

It has been troubled by revolution and war ever since. American Marines intervened in 1903 and 1923. In 1931, 1932, and 1937, major revolutions were crushed by force.

In July 1969, El Salvador invaded Honduras after Honduran landowners had deported several thousand Salvadorans. The fighting left 1,000 dead and tens of thousands homeless. By threatening economic sanctions and military intervention, the OAS induced El Salvador to withdraw.

In June 1970, Honduras and El Salvador agreed to a demilitarized zone of 1.8 miles on each side of their ill-defined border and accepted an OAS police force. A year later they agreed, despite two more border flare-ups, to negotiate a peace settlement. Honduras remained largely out of the five-nation Central America Common Market, however, until the Pan-American Highway link with El Salvador was reopened in 1972.

In 1971, Ramon Ernesto Cruz, a lawyer, diplomat, and teacher, became Honduras's first freely elected President since 1949. But strongman Oswaldo López Arellano, citing "chaos and weakness" under the coalition, again seized control (for the third time in two decades). He served until his ouster in 1975.

On Aug. 7, 1978, the Honduran military ousted President Juan Alberto Melgar Castro as President, naming Gen. Policarpio Paz Garcia as chief of state. This was the second military-originated change of government in three years resulting from charges of corruption.

**Economy.** Agricultural products include corn, rice, coffee, sugar, and bananas. Gold and silver are the most important mineral products.

Chief exports in 1975 were coffee (20%), bananas (16%), timber (14%), lead and zinc (8%), meat (6%), and silver (5%). Leading customers were U.S. (52%), West Germany (11%), Dominican Republic (5%). Leading suppliers were U.S. (42%), Venezuela (16%), Japan (7%), Guatemala (6%).

## HUNGARY

**Hungarian People's Republic**
**President:** Pál Losonczi (1967)
**Premier:** Gyorgy Lazar (1975)
**Area:** 35,919 sq mi. (93,030 sq km)
**Population (est. 1978):** 10,700,000 (Magyar, German, Slovak)
**Density per square mile:** 297.9
**Capital:** Budapest
**Largest cities (est. 1977):** Budapest, 2,081,700 **(est. 1975 by U.N.):** Miskolc, 198,000; Debrecen, 184,700; Szeged, 168,800; Pécs, 162,350; Györ, 117,500
**Monetary unit:** Forint
**Language:** Magyar
**Religions:** Roman Catholic, 60%; Protestant, atheist
**Gross national product:** (1976): $24.1 billion
**National name:** Magyar Népköztársaság
**Freedom House classifications:** Socialist industrial, one-party communist

**Geography.** This central European country the size of Indiana is bordered by Austria to the west, Czechoslovakia to the north, the U.S.S.R. and Romania to the east, and Yugoslavia to the south.

Most of Hungary is a fertile, rolling plain lying east of the Danube River and drained by the Danube and Tisza rivers. In the extreme northwest is the Little Hungarian Plain. South of that area is Lake Balaton (250 sq mi.; 648 sq km).

**Government.** According to the 1949 Constitution, Hungary is a People's Republic. Legislative power is vested in the unicameral National Assembly, whose 352 members are elected by the people for four-year terms. The supreme body of state power is the 21-member Presidential Council elected by the National Assembly. The supreme body of state administration is the Council of Ministers, headed by the Premier.

The Hungarian Socialist Workers (Communist) Party, led by János Kádár, is the only political party.

**History.** About 2,000 years ago, Hungary was part of the Roman provinces of Pannonia and Dacia. In A.D. 896 it was invaded by the Magyars, who founded a kingdom. Christianity was accepted during the reign of Stephen I (St. Stephen) (997–1038).

The peak of Hungary's great period of medieval power came during the reign of Louis I the Great (1342–82), whose dominions touched the Baltic, Black, and Mediterranean seas.

War with the Turks broke out in 1389, as for more than 100 years the Turks advanced through the Balkans. When the Turks smashed a Hungarian army in 1526, western and northern Hungary accepted Hapsburg rule to escape Turkish occupation. Transylvania became independent under Hungarian princes. Intermittent war with the Turks was waged until a peace treaty was signed in 1699.

After the suppression of the 1848 revolt against Hapsburg rule, led by Louis Kossuth, the dual monarchy of Austria-Hungary was set up in 1867.

The dual monarchy was defeated with the other Central Powers in World War I, and the new Hungary underwent hard times. First there was a short-lived republic in 1918. The chaotic Communist rule of 1919 under Béla Kun ended with the Romanians occupying Budapest on Aug. 4, 1919. When the Romanians left, Adm. Nicholas Horthy entered the capital with a national army. The Treaty of Trianon of June 4, 1920, cost Hungary 67.8% of its land and 58% of its population. Meanwhile, the National Assembly had restored the legal continuity of the old monarchy, and, on March 1, 1920, Horthy was elected Regent.

Following the German invasion of Russia on June 22, 1941, Hungary joined the attack against the Soviet Union, but the war was not popular and Hungarian troops were almost entirely withdrawn from the eastern front by May 1943. German occupation troops set up a puppet government after Admiral Horthy's appeal for an armistice with advancing Soviet troops on Oct. 15, 1944, had resulted in his overthrow. The German regime soon fled the capital, however, and on December 23 a provisional government was formed in Soviet-occupied eastern Hungary. On Jan. 20, 1945, it signed an armistice in Moscow. On Feb. 1, 1946, the National Assembly approved a constitutional law abolishing the thousand-year-old monarchy and establishing a republic.

By the Treaty of Paris (1947) Hungary had to give up all territory it had acquired since 1937 and to pay $300 million reparations to the U.S.S.R., Czechoslovakia, and Yugoslavia. A coalition government instituted land reform. In 1948 the Communist Party, with the support of Soviet bayonets, seized control. Hungary was proclaimed a People's Republic and one-party state in 1949. Industry was nationalized, the land collectivized into State farms, and the opposition terrorized by the secret police.

The terror, modeled after that of the U.S.S.R., reached its height with the trial of Jozsef Cardinal Mindszenty, Roman Catholic primate. He confessed to fantastic charges under duress of drugs or brainwashing and was sentenced to life imprisonment on Feb. 8, 1949. Protests were voiced in all parts of the world.

On Oct. 23, 1956, anti-Communist revolution broke out in Budapest. To cope with it the Communists set up a coalition government and called former Premier Imre Nagy back to head it. But he and most of his ministers were swept by the logic of events into the anti-Communist opposition, and he declared Hungary a neutral power, withdrawing from the Warsaw Treaty and appealing to the United Nations for help. One of his ministers, János Kádár, established a counter-regime and asked the U.S.S.R. to send in military power. Soviet troops and tanks suppressed the revolution in bloody fighting after 190,000 people had fled the country and Mindszenty, freed from jail on October 30, had taken refuge in the U.S. Embassy. By treachery, Nagy and some of his ministers were abducted by the Soviet occupation troops and executed.

Kádár was succeeded as Premier, but not party secretary, by Gyula Kallai in 1965. In 1966 the party announced drastic economic reforms to raise living standards and improve productive efficiency. Continuing his program of national reconciliation, Kádár emptied prisons, reformed the secret police, and eased travel restrictions. But 60,000 Soviet troops remained in Hungary. Further sweeping reforms liberalized the economy in 1968.

Hungary developed the reputation of being the freest East European state, with Kádár's new motto —"If you're not against us, you're with us"—replacing previous police state suspicions. Significant Western capitalist investment was welcomed and some capitalistic methods embraced.

After 15 years' asylum in the U.S. Embassy, Mindszenty, under an agreement between the Vatican and the Hungarian regime, was allowed to travel into exile to Rome in September 1971. In a move applauded by Kádár, Pope Paul VI removed Mindszenty from his honorary post as Primate of Hungary in February 1974. The Cardinal died in Vienna in 1975.

Relations with the U.S. improved in 1972 when World War II debt claims between the two nations were settled. On Jan. 6, 1978, the U.S. returned to Hungary, over anti-Communist protests, the 977-year-old crown of St. Stephen, held at Fort Knox since World War II.

**Economy.** Agriculture is the basis of Hungarian economic life, engaging about a third of the population. The Land Reform Act issued in March 1945 provided for the confiscation of all estates over 284 acres; about 8,000,000 acres were divided among some 500,000 families. Cereals grown in the fertile Danubian plains are the chief crops. Leading crops are corn, sugar beets, wheat, potatoes, barley, rye, and oats.

In addition, cultivation of vines, fruit, and garden produce is important. The famous Tokay wine is produced on the southern slopes of the Hegyalja in the northeast part of the country.

The dominant industries are all based on agriculture, with flour milling in first place, followed by sugar refining, brewing, and canning. The second group of industries makes hardware and machinery. Most of the machine industry is concentrated in Budapest and Györ. Cotton leads the textile industry, especially in Budapest, which is also a center of woolen manufactures.

While Hungary generally is mineral-poor, it has about 20% of the world's known reserves of bauxite.

Chief exports in 1976 were machinery (26%), motor vehicles (10%), chemicals (8%), iron and steel (6%), meat and meat preparations (5%), and fruit and vegetables (5%). Leading customers were U.S.S.R. (30%), East Germany (9%), West Germany (8%), Czechoslovakia (7%). Leading suppliers were U.S.S.R. (27%), West Germany (10%), East Germany (9%), Czechoslovakia (6%), Austria (5%).

## ICELAND

**Republic of Iceland**
**President:** Kristjan Eldjarn (1968)
**Prime Minister:** Olfur Johannesson (1978)
**Area:** 39,768 sq mi. (103,000 sq km)
**Population (est. 1978):** 227,000
**Density per square mile:** 5.7[1]
**Capital and largest city (est. 1976):** Reykjavik, 84,500
**Monetary unit:** Króna
**Language:** Icelandic
**Religion:** Evangelical Lutheran
**Gross national product (1976):** $1.4 billion
**National name:** Lýoveldio Island
**Freedom House classifications:** Capitalist industrial, multi-party centralized

**Geography.** Iceland, a bleak island about the size of Kentucky, lies in the north Atlantic Ocean east of Greenland and just touches the Arctic Circle. It is one of the most volcanic regions in the world.

Small fresh-water lakes are to be found throughout the island, and there are many natural oddities, including hot springs, geysers, sulfur beds, canyons, waterfalls, and swift rivers. More than 13% of the area is covered by snowfields and glaciers, and most of the people live in the 7% of the island comprising fertile coastlands.

**Government.** Constitutionally, the President of Iceland is elected for four years by popular vote. Executive power of the state resides in the Prime Minister and his Cabinet. The Althing (Parliament) is composed of 60 members in two houses. At an election the 60 members elect 20 of themselves to constitute the Upper House, the remaining 40 members representing henceforth the Lower House.

The major political parties are the Independence Party (20 of 60 seats in the Althing), led by Geir Hallgrimsson; Social Democratic Party (14 seats), led by Benedikt Grndal; Progressive Party (12 seats), led by Einar Agustsson; People's Alliance (14 seats), a Marxist group dominated by Communists.

**History.** Iceland was first settled shortly before 900, mainly by Norse. A Constitution drawn up about 930 created a form of democracy and provided for an Althing, or General Assembly.

In 1262–64, Iceland came under Norwegian rule and passed to ultimate Danish control through the formation of the Union of Kalmar in 1483. In 1874, Icelanders obtained their own Constitution. In 1918, Denmark recognized Iceland as a separate state with unlimited sovereignty but still nominally under the Danish king.

On June 17, 1944, after a popular referendum, the Althing proclaimed Iceland a completely independent republic.

The British occupied Iceland in 1940, immediately after the German invasion of Denmark. In 1942, the U.S. took over the burden of protection. Iceland refused to abandon its neutrality in World War II and thus forfeited charter membership in the United Nations, but it was cooperative with the Allies throughout. Iceland joined the North Atlantic Treaty Organization in 1949.

Iceland unilaterally extended her territorial waters from 12 to 50 nautical miles in 1972, precipitating a running dispute with the U.K. known as the "cod war." Icelandic warships harassed British trawlers, which then received aid from British gunboats; some trawlers were shelled, and Icelandic and British warships collided in 1973. The World Court ruled in July 1974 that the 50-mile limit could not be applied unilaterally, but Iceland rejected the ruling.

Another "cod war" broke out in late 1975 at the expiration of a two-year agreement reached in 1973 and Britain sent warships to guard its fishing boats. Iceland closed its airspace and ports to British military aircraft and ships and on February 19 broke diplomatic relations with the U.K.

A June 2 agreement calling for registration of all British trawlers fishing within 200 miles of Iceland and a 24-hour time limit on incursions brought a resumption of relations on June 3.

**Economy.** Approximately six sevenths of Iceland is unproductive, and only about 1% is under cultivation. With about 20% of the population engaged in farming, sheep raising is the most important branch of this industry. Hay, potatoes, and turnips are the principal crops. Vegetation is of the Arctic type, mostly stunted.

About one tenth of the people are engaged in fishing. Many European fishing craft visit Iceland's fisheries, which lead the world in cod and are important for herring, plaice, and halibut.

Chief exports in 1976 were fish and products (73%) and aluminum (17%). Leading customers were U.S. (29%), U.K. (12%), West Germany (11%), Portugal (10%), U.S.S.R. (5%). Leading suppliers were U.S.S.R. (12%), West Germany (11%), U.S. (11%), U.K. (10%), Denmark (10%), Norway (8%), Sweden (6%), Netherlands (6%).

1. Including some offshore islands.

## INDIA

**Republic of India**
**President:** Neelam Sanjiva Reddy (1977)
**Prime Minister:** Morarji R. Desai (1977)
**Area:** 1,269,338 sq mi. (3,287,590 sq km)
**Population (est. 1978):** 643,000,000

**Density per square mile:** 506.6
**Capital (1971 census):** New Delhi, 301,801
**Largest cities (1971 census):** Calcutta, 7,031,382; Greater Bombay, 5,970,575; Delhi, 3,287,883; Madras, 2,469,449; Bangalore, 1,540,741; Ahmedabad, 1,585,544; Kanpur, 1,154,388
**Monetary unit:** Rupee
**Principal languages;** Hindi (official), Bengali, Sindhi, Gujarati, Kannarese, Kashmiri, Malayalam, Marathi, Oriya, Punjabi, Tamil, Telugu, Urdu, English
**Religions:** Hindu, 83%; Islam, 11%; Christian, 3%; Sikh, 2%
**Gross national product (1976):** $95.9 billion
**National name:** Bharat
**Member of Commonwealth of Nations**
**Freedom House classifications:** Capitalist-statist, pre-industrial, multi-party decentralized

**Geography.** One third the area of the United States, the Republic of India occupies most of the subcontinent of India in south Asia. It borders on China in the northeast.

The country contains a large part of the great Indo-Gangetic plain, which extends from the Bay of Bengal on the east to the Afghan frontier on the Arabian Sea on the west. This plain is the richest and most densely settled part of the subcontinent. Another distinct natural region is the Deccan, a plateau of 2,000 to 3,000 feet (610 to 914 m) in elevation, occupying the southern portion of the subcontinent.

Forming a part of the republic are several groups of islands—the Laccadives (14 islands) in the Arabian Sea and the Andamans (204 islands) and the Nicobars (19 islands) in the Bay of Bengal.

India's three great river systems, all rising in the Himalayas, have extensive deltas. The Ganges flows south and then east for 1,540 miles (2,478 km) across the northern plain to the Bay of Bengal; part of its delta, which begins 220 miles (354 km) from the sea, is within the republic. The Indus, starting in Tibet, flows northwest for several hundred miles in Kashmir before turning southwest toward the Arabian Sea; it is important for irrigation in Pakistan. The Brahmaputra, also rising in Tibet, flows eastward first through India and then south into Bangladesh and the Bay of Bengal.

**Government.** India is a federal republic. It is also a member of the Commonwealth of Nations, a status defined at the London Conference of Prime Ministers on April 27, 1949, by which India recognizes the Queen as head of the Commonwealth. Under the Constitution passed by the Constituent Assembly on Nov. 26, 1949, and effective Jan. 26, 1950, India has a parliamentary type of government.

The constitutional head of the state is the President, who is elected every five years. He is advised by the Prime Minister and a Cabinet based on a majority of the bicameral Parliament, which consists of a Council of States (Rajya Sabha) representing the constituent units of the republic and a House of the People (Lok Sabha) elected every five years by universal adult (21 years) suffrage.

The major political parties are Janata (295 of 542 seats in the Lok Sabha), led by Prime Minister Morarji R. Desai; Congress Party (153 seats), led by K. Bramananda Reddy; Communist Party of India (Marxist) (22 seats); Communist Party of India (pro-Congress Party) (6 seats).

**History.** The Aryans or Hindus who invaded India between 2400 and 1500 B.C. from the northwest found a land already well civilized. Buddhism was founded in the sixth century B.C. and spread through northern India. The first exact date in Indian history is 327 B.C., when Alexander the Great invaded India.

In 1526, Mohammedan invaders founded the great Mogul empire, centered on Delhi, which lasted at least in name until 1857. Akbar the Great (1542–1605) strengthened this empire and became the ruler of a greater portion of India than had ever before acknowledged the suzerainty of one man. The long reign of his great-grandson, Aurangzeb (1658–1707) represents both the culmination of Mogul power and the beginning of its decay.

Vasco da Gama, the Portuguese explorer, visited India first in 1498, and for the next hundred years the Portuguese had a virtual monopoly on trade with the subcontinent. Meanwhile, the English founded the East India Company, which set up its first factory at Surat in 1612 and began expanding its influence, fighting against the Indian rulers and the French, Dutch, and Portuguese traders simultaneously.

Bombay, taken from the Portuguese, became the seat of English rule in 1687. The defeat of French and Islamic armies by Lord Clive in the decade ending in 1760 laid the foundation of the British Empire in India. From then until 1858, when the administration of India was formally transferred to the British crown following the great mutiny of native troops in 1857, the East India Company suppressed native uprisings and extended British rule.

After World War I, in which the Indian states sent more than 6 million troops to fight beside the Allies, Indian nationalist unrest rose to new heights under the leadership of a little Hindu lawyer, Mohandas K. Gandhi, called Mahatma Gandhi. His tactics called for nonviolent revolts against British authority. He soon became the leading spirit of the All-India Congress Party, which was the spearhead of Indian revolt. In 1919 the British gave added responsibility to Indian officials, and in 1935 India was given a federal form of government and a measure of self-rule.

In 1942, with the Japanese pressing hard on the eastern borders of India, the British war cabinet tried and failed to reach a political settlement with nationalist leaders. The Congress Party took the position that the British must quit India. In August 1942, fearing mass civil disobedience, the government of India carried out widespread arrests of Congress leaders, including Gandhi.

Gandhi was released in May 1944 and other leaders later. Negotiations for a settlement were resumed, but they proved fruitless. Finally, in February 1947, the Labour government announced its determination to transfer power to "responsible Indian hands" by June 1948 even if a Constitution had not been worked out.

With the appointment at the same time of Lord Mountbatten as Governor-General, events moved swiftly. By early June 1947, agreement was reached on the partitioning of India along religious lines (a plan previously opposed by the predominant Hindus and by the U.K.) and on the splitting of the provinces of Bengal and the Punjab, which the Moslems had claimed.

The Indian Independence Act, passed quickly by both houses of the British Parliament, received royal assent on July 18, 1947, and on August 15 the Indian Empire passed into history.

Jawdharlal Nehru, leader of the Congress Party,

## Political Subdivisions of Republic of India

| Subdivisions | Area sq mi. | Population 1971 census |
|---|---|---|
| **STATES** | | |
| Andhra Pradesh | 106,052 | 43,502,708 |
| Assam | 30,400[1] | 14,625,152[1] |
| Bihar | 67,198 | 56,353,369 |
| Gujarat | 72,154 | 26,697,475 |
| Haryana | 16,670 | 10,036,808 |
| Himachal Pradesh | 10,880 | 3,460,434 |
| Jammu and Kashmir[2] | 85,861 | 4,616,632 |
| Karnataka[3] | 74,122 | 29,299,014 |
| Kerala | 15,003 | 21,347,375 |
| Madhya Pradesh | 171,210 | 41,654,119 |
| Maharashtra | 118,530 | 50,412,235 |
| Manipur | 8,628 | 1,072,753 |
| Meghalaya | 8,700[1] | 1,011,699[1] |
| Nagaland | 6,236 | 516,449 |
| Orissa | 60,182 | 21,944,615 |
| Punjab | 21,630 | 13,551,060 |
| Rajasthan | 132,151 | 25,765,806 |
| Sikkim[4] | 2,744 | 215,000 |
| Tamil Nadu[5] | 50,132 | 41,199,168 |
| Tripura | 4,022 | 1,556,342 |
| Uttar Pradesh | 113,452 | 88,341,144 |
| West Bengal | 33,928 | 44,312,011 |
| **UNION TERRITORIES** | | |
| Andaman and Nicobar Islands | 3,215 | 115,133 |
| Arunachal Pradesh | 31,400 | 467,511 |
| Chandigarh | 44 | 257,251 |
| Dadra and Nagar-Haveli | 189 | 74,170 |
| Delhi | 573 | 4,065,698 |
| Goa, Daman, and Diu | 1,619 | 857,771 |
| Lakshadweep[6] | 11 | 31,810 |
| Mizoram | 8,100 | 332,390 |
| Pondicherry | 196 | 471,707 |

1. After reorganization of North East Frontier Agency in December 1971. 2. Status in dispute with Pakistan. 3. Formerly Mysore. 4. Sikkim became an Indian state in May 1975. Population figure is 1974 estimate. 5. Formerly Madras. 6. Formerly Laccadive, Minicoy, and Amindivi Islands.

was made Prime Minister of India. Before an exchange of populations could be arranged, terrible riots occurred among the communal groups, and armed conflict broke out over rival claims to the princely state of Jammu and Kashmir. Peace was restored only with the greatest difficulty. In 1949 a Constitution, along the lines of the U.S. Constitution, was adopted making India a sovereign republic, an independent member of the Commonwealth of Nations. Under a federal structure the states were organized on linguistic lines.

For a considerable period the dominance of the Congress Party contributed stability. In 1956 the republic absorbed the former French settlements. Five years later it forcibly annexed the Portuguese enclaves of Goa, Damão, and Diu. After a decade of independence India was once again the target of invasion. Communist China provoked a border dispute in 1957 which proceeded by local skirmishes until Oct. 20, 1962, when the Chinese mounted a massive offensive against Ladakh in Kashmir and against the North East Frontier Agency. After gaining much territory claimed by India, the Chinese announced a cease-fire on Nov. 20, 1962. An uneasy truce has since prevailed.

Nehru died in 1964. His successor, Lal Bahadur Shastri, died on Jan. 10, 1966, a few hours after concluding talks with President Ayub Khan of Pakistan arranging for an interim settlement of their differences. Nehru's daughter, Mrs. Indira Gandhi, became Prime Minister on Jan. 19, 1966. She continued the policy of nonalignment and made it clear that India's only concern with Communist China was its threat to India's borders.

In 1971 the Pakistani Army moved in to quash the independence movement in East Pakistan that was supported by clandestine aid from India, and some 10 million Bengali refugees poured across the border into India, creating social, economic, and health problems. In August, India signed a friendship treaty with the U.S.S.R. and quantities of Soviet arms began to enter India. After numerous border incidents, India invaded East Pakistan and in two weeks forced the surrender of the Pakistani Army and took 93,000 prisoners. East Pakistan was established as an independent state and renamed Bangladesh.

India moved further toward the U.S.S.R. in 1973 with a 15-year economic, technological, and trade cooperation agreement.

India startled the world on May 18, 1974, by exploding an atomic device made of plutonium it had surreptitiously removed from a peaceful reactor given by Canada. It became the sixth nation of the world to set off a nuclear blast, and while India disclaimed any intention to make nuclear weapons, there were widespread misgivings about its aims.

In the summer of 1975, the world's largest democracy veered suddenly toward authoritarianism when a judge in Allahabad, Mrs. Gandhi's home constituency, found her landslide victory in the 1971 elections invalid because civil servants had illegally aided her campaign. An appeal to the Supreme Court produced an interim order permitting her to continue as Prime Minister but without a vote in Parliament.

Amid demands for her resignation, Mrs. Gandhi decreed a state of emergency on June 26 and ordered mass arrests of her critics, including all opposition party leaders except the Communists. The government later admitted to 4,400 arrests; opponents put the figure at 54,000. Rigid censorship was clamped on both the national press and foreign correspondents.

Legislation extending the emergency indefinitely passed Parliament July 23. Opposition members walked out after the vote. Their boycott was still in force during the next fortnight, when unhampered Congress Party majorities successively enacted: a bill forbidding courts to invalidate the government's emergency decrees; a constitutional amendment retroactively barring lawsuits challenging the elections of high government officers, including the Prime Minister, and a bill retroactively wiping out Mrs. Gandhi's conviction in the 1971 election case.

As she effectively suspended India's equivalent of the U.S. Bill of Rights and took apparent steps toward one-party government, Mrs. Gandhi also initiated actions that she said would improve the lot of India's largely apolitical masses. On July 1, she announced a 21-point program of social and economic reforms that could make up the Congress Party platform in the next general elections, which should have been held by March 1976 under India's Constitution but were delayed indefinitely.

Even before the reform program was announced, there were signs of improvement in India's long-troubled economy. A year of conservative fiscal policy had reduced the inflation rate from 30% in 1974 to 10% in 1975, and good rains appeared to have ensured a better-than-average 1975 harvest of basic food crops.

On July 24, 1976, India and Pakistan formally renewed diplomatic relations, which had been broken off in 1971. Air and land transportation between the two nations was also restored.

Despite strong opposition to her repressive measures and particularly the resentment against compulsory birth control programs, Mrs. Gandhi in January 1977 announced parliamentary elections for March 16–20. At the same time, she freed most political prisoners, including her former Deputy Prime Minister, Morarji R. Desai, and L. K. Advani, a right-wing Hindu nationalist. Press censorship was relaxed and serious defections from the ruling Congress Party began.

The landslide victory of Desai and his allies unseated Mrs. Gandhi and also defeated a bid for office by her son, Sanjay, himself a focus of much criticism as the recipient of official favors. Taking office on March 24, the 81-year-old Desai promised to "drive fear from the society" and restore morality to government.

In state elections in April, Desai's Janata Party toppled the Congress Party in eight of 10 states where the Congress Party had held power, as in the national government, since independence.

In July, Neelam Sanjiva Reddy was elected President, replacing Fakhruddin Ali Ahmed, who died February 11.

Desai moved away from Mrs. Gandhi's pro-Soviet policy, receiving a visit from President Carter Jan. 1–3, 1978, and himself visiting Carter in June. A dispute over the supply of enriched uranium to India, in which the U.S. Nuclear Regulatory Agency sought greater safeguards over its use, was resolved by Carter in India's favor in the hope that India would eventually sign the Non-Proliferation Treaty. Desai's success abroad was not matched at home, however, as economic problems and party squabbles lowered enthusiasm for the new regime.

In August 1978, former Prime Minister Indira Gandhi launched a so-called "Save India" campaign against the government.

**Native States.** Most of the 560-odd native states and subdivisions of pre-1947 India acceded to the new nation, and the central government pursued a vigorous policy of integration. This took three forms: merger into adjacent provinces, conversion into centrally administered areas, and grouping into unions of states. Finally, under a controversial reorganization plan effective Nov. 1, 1956, the unions of states were abolished and merged into adjacent states, and India became a union of 15 states and 8 centrally administered areas. A 16th state was added in 1962, and in 1966, the Punjab was partitioned into two states.

The status of the large princely state of Jammu and Kashmir on the northwest frontier is in dispute with Pakistan. It is 85% Islamic, but its Hindu ruling prince acceded to India, which took over administration following invasion by Moslem troops in late 1947. The U.N. Security Council voted on April 21, 1948, to hold a plebiscite in the area, but it was never held. The part occupied by India was incorporated into India in 1957.

The controversy over Jammu and Kashmir was waged in the halls of the U.N. until 1965, when India announced that its civil servants would assume administration of the state. Pakistan sent guerrillas into the territory, and India, in response, invaded in August 1965. In September the U.N. sponsored a cease-fire and stationed observers to make sure it was honored, but there were violations.

The U.S.S.R. intervened and arranged a meeting in Tashkent between Prime Minister Shastri of India and President Ayub Khan of Pakistan. With the U.S.S.R. as mediator, they reached an interim settlement, the Declaration of Tashkent, in January 1966. It provided for the withdrawal of troops, observance of the U.N. cease-fire, and continued attempts to resolve their disputes by diplomatic means.

Resolution of the territorial dispute over Kashmir grew out of peace negotiations following the two-week India-Pakistan war of 1971. After sporadic skirmishing, an accord reached July 3, 1972, committed both powers to withdraw troops from a temporary cease-fire line after the border was fixed. Agreement on the border was reached Dec. 7, 1972.

In April 1975, the Indian Parliament voted to make the 300-year-old kingdom of Sikkim a full-fledged Indian state, and the annexation took effect May 16.

Situated in the Himalayas, Sikkim was a virtual dependency of Tibet until the early 19th century. Under an 1890 treaty between China and Great Britain, it became a British protectorate, and was made an Indian protectorate after Britain quit the subcontinent.

**Economy.** Agricultural products include wheat, rice, barley, corn, potatoes, cassava, tea, sugar, millet, sorghum, and peanuts. Industrial products include pig iron, crude steel, aluminum, cement, yarn and fabrics, and jute manufactures.

The republic has rich mineral resources, including coal, iron ore, monazite, diamonds, magnesite, uranium, zircon, silver, graphite, gypsum, tungsten, and sapphires. Assam and the Punjab produce oil.

Chief exports in 1975–76 were sugar (12%), jute fabrics (6%), tea (6%), iron ore (5%), cotton fabrics (5%), clothing (5%), and leather (5%). Leading customers were U.S. (13%), Japan (11%), U.S.S.R. (10%), U.K. (10%), Iran (7%). Leading suppliers were U.S. (25%), Iran (9%), West Germany (7%), Japan (7%), U.S.S.R. (6%), Saudi Arabia (6%), U.K. (5%), Iraq (5%).

## INDONESIA

**Republic of Indonesia**
**President and Prime Minister:** General Suharto (1969)[1]
**Area:** 741,031 sq mi. (1,919,270 sq km)[2]
**Population (est. 1978):** 147,000,000
**Density per square mile:** 198.4

**Capital:** Jakarta
**Largest cities (est. 1977):** Jakarta, 6,178,500; **(1971 census):** Surabaja, 1,556,255; Bandung, 1,201,730; Semarang, 646,590; Medan, 635,562; Palembang, 582,961
**Monetary unit:** Rupiah
**Languages:** Bahasa Indonesia (Malay) (official), Dutch, Javanese, Sundanese, Madurese
**Religions:** Islam, 89%; Christian, 7%; Hindu, Buddhist
**Gross national product (1976):** $36.2 billion
**National name:** Republik Indonesia
**Freedom House classifications:** Capitalist-statist pre-industrial, dominant party

**Geography.** Indonesia is part of the Malay archipelago in Southeast Asia with an area nearly three times that of Texas. It consists of the islands of Sumatra, Java, Madura, central and southern Borneo, the Celebes, and the Moluccas. Its neighbor to the north is Malaysia and to the east Papua and New Guinea.

A backbone of mountain ranges extends throughout the main islands of the archipelago. Earthquakes are frequent, and there are many active volcanoes.

**Government.** The President is elected by the People's Consultative Assembly, whose 920 members include the functioning legislative arm, the 460-member House of Representatives. Meeting at least once every five years, the Assembly has broad policy functions. The House, 100 of whose members are appointed by the President, meets at least once annually. Gen. Suharto was elected unopposed to a third five-year term March 22, 1978.

The major political parties are Sekber Golkar, 232 of 360 contested seats in the House; Islamic United Development Party, 99 seats; Democratic Party, 29 seats.

**History.** Indonesia is inhabited by Malayan and Papuan peoples ranging from the more advanced Javanese and Balinese to the more primitive Dyaks of Borneo. Invasions from China and India contributed Chinese and Indian admixtures.

During the first few centuries of the Christian era, most of the islands came under the influence of Hindu priests and traders, who spread their culture and religion. Moslem invasions began in the 13th century, and most of the area was Moslem by the 15th century. Portuguese traders arrived early in the 16th century but were ousted by the Dutch about 1595. After Napoleon subjugated the Netherlands homeland in 1811, the British seized the islands but returned them to the Dutch in 1816. In 1922 the islands were made an integral part of the Netherlands kingdom.

In World War II, the Japanese military occupation with nominal native self-government continued until August 1945. About the time of the Japanese surrender, a self-styled Indonesian Republic headed by Achmed Sukarno took over effective control of parts of Sumatra and Java. Allied forces, mostly British Indian troops, moved in, and fought the nationalists until Nov. 15, 1946, when Dutch-Indonesian parleys resulted in a draft agreement that contemplated the formation by Jan. 1, 1949, of a Netherlands-Indonesian Union. This would consist on the one hand of the Netherlands, the Netherlands Antilles, and Surinam and on the other of the United States of Indonesia, which was to be a sovereign nation composed of three equal states—the Republic of Indonesia, East Indonesia, and Borneo. Differences of interpretation ensued, and the Dutch resorted to force on July 20, 1947. Both sides issued cease-fire orders on Aug. 4, 1947, in response to a call from the U.N. Security Council.

On Nov. 2, 1949, Dutch and Indonesian leaders agreed upon the terms of union. Dr. Sukarno was elected President of the federation on December 16 and the first all-Indonesian Cabinet was formed with Mohammed Hatta as Premier. The transfer of sovereignty took place at Amsterdam on December 27, 1949.

In 1963, Netherlands New Guinea was transferred to Indonesia, and it was renamed West Irian. In 1973 it became Irian Jaya.

Sukarno, who had himself declared "President for Life," launched a series of guerrilla raids in September 1963 to scuttle formation of the new Federation of Malaysia. A treaty between Indonesia and Malaysia in August 1966 ended the open conflict. Meanwhile, with Sukarno's encouragement, Communist influence increased.

Early in 1966, led by Moslem students, the masses undertook an anti-Communist campaign that is believed to have assassinated more than 300,000 Indonesians suspected of Communist ties. Sukarno was forced in March 1966 to yield power to General Suharto, whom Sukarno had made army chief of staff. He began a series of trials of Sukarno's associates. The Communist Party was outlawed. Sukarno was forced to give up all power on Feb. 22, 1967, and Suharto became acting President in March 1967.

He ended hostilities against Malaysia and established close ties with the Western democracies, including the U.S. Suharto introduced a "New Order" emphasizing austerity and fiscal responsibility and with Western aid of $200 million—a third provided by the U.S.—began rebuilding the country. In March 1968, the Consultative Assembly elected Suharto President for a five-year term.

Suharto also permitted national elections, which moved the nation back toward representative government. The Consultative Assembly elected him unanimously for a second five-year term in 1973. He was unopposed.

The economic and political stability achieved by the Suharto regime was tested by external events in 1975. Tightening of world money markets put serious pressures on ambitious industrial development plans underwritten by Pertamina, the state-owned oil company. Communist triumphs in Vietnam and Cambodia encouraged Jakarta toward a policy of non-alignment with any great power and toward closer relationships with other members of the Association of Southeast Asian Nations, a regional grouping of five non-Communist states.

Indonesia annexed the former Portuguese half of the island of Timor after the provisional government of the area requested annexation May 31, 1976.

Bankruptcy of Pertamina in 1976, and the arrest of Gen. Ibnu Sutowo as an investigation of $10 billion in debts began, dramatically reduced for-

1. General Suharto served as Acting President of Indonesia from 1967 to 1969. 2. Includes West Irian (former Netherlands New Guinea), renamed Irian Jaya in March 1973 (159,355 sq mi.; 412,731 sq km), and former Portuguese Timor (5,763 sq mi.; 14,925 sq km), annexed in 1976.

eign investment. A total of $2 billion in 1975 was cut to $423 million in 1976. The government estimated that debt service for 1977–78 would offset an expected 18% gain in oil revenues.

**Economy.** Agriculture engages about 70% of the adult males. Rich in a variety of crops, the islands prior to World War II produced about 31% of the world's copra, 37% of its rubber, 83% of its pepper, and nearly all of its quinine. The big-estate agriculture on Java and Sumatra is devoted mainly to export. The rest is subsistence agriculture. Rice is the staple food and chief crop. Major plantation crops are rubber, tea, coffee, cinchona bark, palm kernels, and sugar. Others are copra, cacao, spices, agava fiber, and Kapok. In addition to rice, the chief food crops are maize, cassava, sweet potatoes, peanuts, and soybeans.

Industry, especially in Java, developed rapidly after 1930. In addition to industries connected with the processing of the rich natural products, there were established chemical works, textile and paper mills, soap factories, breweries, shipyards, a Goodyear tire and rubber plant, and a General Motors assembly plant.

Petroleum is the principal product of modern Indonesia. The tin industry attained pre-war levels more rapidly than others after World War II. Other important minerals include bauxite, coal, salt, nickel, and manganese.

Most valuable timber is teak. Ebony, sandalwood, and ironwood also are cut.

Chief exports in 1976 were crude oil (66%), timber (9%), and rubber (6%). Leading customers were Japan (42%), U.S. (29%), Singapore (8%), Trinidad and Tobago (7%). Leading suppliers were Japan (26%), U.S. (17%), Singapore (10%), West Germany (9%).

## IRAN

**Empire of Iran**

**Monarch:** Shah Mohammad Reza Pahlavi (1941)
**Premier:** Jafar Sharif-Emami (1978)
**Area:** 636,296 sq mi. (1,648,000 sq km)
**Population (est. 1977):** 34,200,000 (Iranian, Kurdish, Azerbaijani)
**Density per square mile:** 53.7
**Capital:** Teheran
**Largest cities (est. 1976):** Teheran, 4,002,000; Isfahan, 700,000; Mashed, 600,000; Tabriz, 510,000
**Monetary unit:** Rial
**Languages:** Farsi (Persian), Kurdish, Azerbaijani
**Religions:** Shi'ite Moslem, 93%; Sunni Moslem, 5%
**Gross national product (1976):** $66.7 billion
**National name:** Keshvaré Shahanshahiyé Iran
**Freedom House classifications:** Capitalist-statist pre-industrial, one-party nationalist

**Geography.** Iran, a Middle Eastern country south of the Caspian Sea and north of the Persian Gulf, is three times the size of Arizona. It shares borders with Iraq, Turkey, the U.S.S.R., Afghanistan, and Pakistan.

In general, the country is a plateau averaging 4,000 feet (1,219 m) elevation. There are also maritime lowlands along the Persian Gulf and the Caspian Sea. The Elburz Mountains in the north rise to 18,603 feet (5,670 m) at Mt. Damavend. From northwest to southeast, the country is crossed by a desert 800 miles (1,287 km) long.

**Government.** Iran is a monarchy, and the Shah has the usual powers of the head of a parliamentary state. Executive power is exercised by a Cabinet headed by the Premier, who is appointed by the Shah and who is responsible to Parliament, the lower house of which (Majles) has 268 popularly elected members and the upper house of which (Senate) has 60 members, half of whom are appointed by the Shah.

One-party rule was imposed March 2, 1975, when the Shah decreed that the National Resurgence Party, headed by former Premier Jamshid Amouzegar, would be the state's only political organization for "at least the next two years." The decree dissolved two existing parties. Iran Novin (New Iran) Party, led by Manouchehr Kalali, and the Mardom Party, led by Yahya Adl.

**History.** Oil-rich Iran was called Persia before 1935. Its key location blocks the lower land gate to Asia and also stands in the way of traditional Russian ambitions for access to the Indian Ocean. After periods of Assyrian, Median, and Achaemenidian rule, Persia became a powerful empire under Cyrus the Great, reaching from the Indus to the Nile at its zenith in 525 B.C. It fell to Alexander in 331–30 B.C. and to the Seleucids in 312–02 B.C., and a native Persian regime arose about 130 B.C. Another Persian regime arose about A.D. 224, but it fell to the Arabs in 637. In the 12th century, the Mongols took their turn ruling Persia, and in the early part of the 18th century, the Turks occupied it.

An Anglo-Russian convention of 1907 divided Iran into two spheres of influence. British attempts to impose a protectorate over all of Iran were defeated in 1919. On Feb. 26, 1921, General Reza Pahlavi seized the government and was elected hereditary Shah in 1925. Subsequently he did much to modernize the country and abolished all foreign extraterritorial rights.

Increased pro-Axis activity led to Anglo-Russian occupation of Iran in August 1941, and deposition of the Shah in favor of his son, Mohammad Reza Pahlavi.

Ali Razmara became Premier on June 26, 1950, and pledged to restore efficient and honest government, but he was assassinated March 7, 1951. Mohammed Mossadegh took over April 29. Parliament completed action on a bill nationalizing the oil industry over strong British protests.

Mossadegh was ousted Aug. 19, 1953, by Fazollah Zahedi, whom the Shah had named Premier. The oil dispute was settled in August 1954.

Iran established closer relations with the U.S. and the West, and the U.S. began a vast program of economic and military aid. In 1955 the country joined the Central Treaty Organization (then called the Baghdad Pact). At the Shah's insistence the government undertook a broad program of reform, especially agrarian land reform, distributing crown lands and estates to the landless peasants.

The Shah maintained continuing cordial relations with the West, despite Iran's role as a founding member of the Organization of Petroleum Exporting Countries. Iran did not participate in OPEC's 1973 embargo on oil shipments to the West, and it continued to supply Israel with oil during the 1973 Arab-Israeli war. But it benefited hugely from the fivefold boost in world oil prices forced by OPEC, realizing $18 billion in oil revenues in 1974. The oil profits have financed an extraordinary modernization program of education, industrialization, and construction, which is expected to cost over $400 billion in the next 13 years.

Iran also embarked on an enormous military buildup, contracting for over $2 billion in U.S. military equipment, including modern aircraft, naval vessels, and sophisticated electronic devices. As he has built Iran's forces, the Shah has worked to exclude the superpowers from the Persian Gulf area and to ease disputes in the region. A March 1975, agreement ended long-standing border frictions with Iraq, and Iranian relations with Saudi Arabia and Egypt warmed noticeably in 1975.

A non-Arab Moslem nation, Iran has never shared Arab antipathy toward Israel and its military buildup was not welcomed by Arab Socialist states, which accused the Shah of subservience to the U.S. Iranian radicals have taken to guerrilla operations; they killed one U.S. adviser in 1973 and two in 1975.

Iran led nine other members of OPEC in raising oil prices at the end of 1976, and the refusal of Saudi Arabia and the United Arab Emirates to go along resulted in a 38% drop in Iranian oil exports. The loss of revenues forced the government to curtail its aid program. In June 1977, a $2.2-billion final contract for the purchase of 160 F-16 fighter planes was signed with the U.S.

Iran was among the nations cited by the U.S. State Department for abuse of human rights in a report made public in January 1977. The report said, however, that Iran's strategic importance justified continuing arms sales. In 1978, the State Department reported that the human-rights situation had "improved."

On Aug. 11, 1978, martial law was declared in Isfahan, after rioting left four dead and many injured. The Shah had warned Moslem religious extremists not to try to block his moves toward political liberalization.

In late August, the sixth theater fire blamed on Moslem extremists killed almost 400 people.

**Economy.** Iran is predominantly agricultural, and irrigation is common, especially on the central plateau. The principal crops are wheat and barley. Other important crops are rice, grapes, dates, apricots, tobacco, tea, cotton, sugar beets and corn. There are extensive grazing lands.

Although Iran was famous for centuries for her handicrafts and carpets, her Western-style industrialization began only in the 1920s and took momentum in the postwar era. The main industrial products are textiles, sugar, cement, copper, refractory material, chemicals and pharmaceuticals, plastics, rubber and tires, automobile assemblies, etc.

Oil is Iran's major resource, developed by the Anglo-Iranian Oil Co. in 1901. Anglo-Iranian's property was nationalized in 1951, and in 1954 a consortium of eight Western oil companies took over production, refining, and marketing, with 50% of the profits going to Iran. On March 20, 1973, the Shah announced the abrogation of a 25-year contract with the consortium, and the National Iranian Oil Co. took control of production and refining although the international companies continued to market the oil.

Chief exports in 1976 were crude oil (93%), and petroleum products (5%). Leading customers were Japan (22%), West Germany (10%), U.K. (9%), Netherlands (8%), U.S. (8%), France (7%), Italy (6%), U.S. Virgin Islands (6%), Spain (5%). Leading suppliers were West Germany (18%), U.S. (17%), Japan (16%), U.K. (8%), Italy (5%), France (5%).

## IRAQ

**Republic of Iraq**
**President:** Gen. Ahmed Hassan al-Bakr (1968)
**Area:** 167,924 sq mi. (434,924 sq km)
**Population (est. 1978):** 12,350,000 (Arab, 75%; Kurdish, 15%; Iranian, 3.8%)
**Density per square mile:** 73.5
**Capital:** Baghdad
**Largest cities (est. 1975):** Baghdad, 2,987,000; (1965 census): Basra, 310,950, Mosul, 264,146; Kirkuk, 175,303; An Najaf, 134,027
**Monetary unit:** Iraqi dinar
**Languages:** Arabic and Kurdish
**Religions:** Islam, 96%; Christian, 3%
**Gross national product (1975):** $13.6 billion
**National name:** Al Jumhouriya Al Iraqia
**Freedom House classifications:** One-party socialist, socialist pre-industrial

**Geography.** Iraq, a triangle of mountains, desert, and fertile river valley, is bounded on the east by Iran, on the north by Turkey, the west by Syria and Jordan, and the south by Saudi Arabia. It is twice the size of Idaho.

The country has arid desertland west of the Euphrates, a broad central valley between the Euphrates and Tigris, and mountains in the northeast. The fertile lower valley is formed by the delta of the two rivers, which join about 120 miles from the head of the Persian Gulf. The gulf coastline is 26 miles (42 km).

**Government.** Since the coup d'etat of July 1968, Iraq has been governed by the Arab Ba'ath Socialist Party through a Council of Command of the Revolution headed by the President. There is also a Council of Ministers headed by the President.

**History.** From earliest times Iraq was known as Mesopotamia—the land between the rivers—for it embraces a large part of the alluvial plains of the Tigris and Euphrates.

An advanced civilization existed by 4000 B.C. Sometime after 2000 B.C. it became the center of the ancient Babylonian and Assyrian empires. It was conquered by Cyrus the Great of Persia in 538 B.C., and by Alexander in 331 B.C. After an Arab conquest in A.D. 637–40, Baghdad became capital of the ruling caliphate. The country was cruelly pillaged by the Mongols in 1258, and during the 16th, 17th, and 18th centuries was the object of repeated Turkish-Persian competition.

Nominal Turkish suzerainty imposed in 1638 was replaced by direct Turkish rule in 1831. In World War I an Anglo-Indian force occupied most of the country, and Britain was given a mandate over the area in 1920. The British recognized Iraq as a kingdom in 1922 and terminated the mandate in 1932 when Iraq was admitted to the League of Nations. In World War II, Iraq generally adhered to its 1930 treaty of alliance with the U.K., but in 1941, British troops were compelled to put down a pro-Axis revolt led by Premier Rashid Ali.

Iraq became a charter member of the Arab League in March 1945, and Iraqi troops took part in the Arab invasion of Palestine in 1948. The 1930 treaty of alliance with the U.K. was terminated in April 1955, and replaced by a defense cooperation agreement.

King Faisal II, born on May 2, 1935, succeeded his father, Ghazi I, who was killed in an automobile accident on April 4, 1939. King Faisal and his uncle, Crown Prince Abdul-Ilah, were assassinated in August 1958 in a swift revolutionary coup that brought to power a military junta headed by Abdul Karem Kassim. The short-lived "Arab Union," formed by the federation of Iraq and Jordan in February 1958, came abruptly to an end with recognition by the United Arab Republic (Egypt) of the rebel government of Iraq. Kassim, in turn, was overthrown and killed in a coup staged March 8, 1963, by the Ba'ath Socialist Party.

President Abdel Salam Arif, a leader in the March coup, staged another coup in November 1963, driving the Ba'ath members of the revolutionary council from power. He adopted a new Constitution in 1964. In 1966, he, two Cabinet members, and other supporters died in a helicopter crash. His brother, General Abdel Rahman Arif, assumed the presidency, crushed the opposition, and won an indefinite extension of his term in April 1967. In May he took over the premiership, but his regime was ousted in July 1968 by a junta led by Maj. Gen. Ahmed Hassan al-Bakr.

In March 1970, the Baghdad government announced a settlement of the 8½-year sporadic war with the Kurds of northeastern Iraq (who spread over the border into Turkey and Iran), accepting two nationalities in Iraq (Arabs and Kurds) and promising a Kurdish Vice President of Iraq and proportional Kurdish representation in a new parliament. The Kurds ultimately refused the government's terms.

The Kurdish rebellion flared anew in April 1974, following collapse of an Iraqi plan for Kurdish self-rule. The rebels, armed and reinforced from Iran, withstood Soviet-supplied Iraqi forces until Iran ended its aid under an agreement with Iraq reached March 5, 1975. Some 200,000 Kurds fled to Iran and the revolt was liquidated within a month.

In April 1972, Iraq signed a 15-year treaty of friendship and cooperation with the U.S.S.R. Although relations with Moscow subsequently cooled, Iraq was the only Arab nation still maintaining such a treaty in 1978.

**Economy.** The chief economic activity is agriculture, dependent upon irrigation and confined to the valleys of the Tigris and Euphrates. Iraq supplies about 80% of the world's dates. Chief among the cereal products of Iraq are barley, wheat, rice, sorghum, maize, and millet. Many fruits and some tobacco and cotton are grown. Herding is the principal occupation of the many nomadic and seminomadic tribes.

Industry is still embryonic. Of some 100 firms, the most important are those making brick, tile, woolen textiles, vegetable oils, soap, glass, and cigarettes.

Oil production is concentrated at the Baba Gurgur fields near Kirkuk, which are operated on behalf of an international group by the British-managed Iraq Petroleum Company. Associated companies operate fields at Zubair and Rumaila near Basra and at Ain Zalah and Butmah.

Oil is piped to Tripoli in Lebanon, Baniyas in Syria, and Fao on the Persian Gulf.

The only port for seagoing vessels is Basra, which is on the Shatt-al-Arab River near the head of the Persian Gulf.

Chief export in 1975 was crude oil (98%). Leading customers were Italy (17%), France (11%), Brazil (6%), Turkey (5%), U.S.S.R. (5%), Spain (5%). Leading suppliers were Japan (18%), West Germany (18%), U.S. (9%), France (6%), U.K. (6%), Brazil (5%).

## IRELAND

**Republic of Ireland**
**President:** Patrick J. Hillery (1977)
**Taoiseach (Prime Minister):** John Lynch (1977)
**Area:** 27,136 sq mi. (70,283 sq km)
**Population (est. 1978):** 3,240,000
**Density per square mile:** 119.4
**Capital:** Dublin
**Largest cities (1971 census):** Dublin, 566,034; Cork, 128,235
**Monetary unit:** Irish pound
**Languages:** Irish, English
**Religions:** Roman Catholic, 95%; Protestant, 5%
**Gross national product (1976):** \$8.1 billion
**National name:** Saorstát Éireann
**Freedom House classifications:** Capitalist industrial, multi-party centralized

**Geography.** Ireland is situated on the island in the Atlantic Ocean that is the second largest of the British Isles. Half the size of Arkansas, it occupies the entire island except for the six northern counties of Ulster.

Ireland resembles a basin—a central plain rimmed with mountains, except in the Dublin region. The mountains are low, with the highest peak, Carrantuohill in County Kerry, rising to 3,415 feet (1,041 m).

The principal river is the Shannon, which begins in the north central area, flows south and southwest for about 240 miles (386 km), and empties into the Atlantic.

**Government.** Ireland is a sovereign, independent, democratic state. The President is elected by direct vote for a term of seven years. The Oireachtas (National Parliament) consists of the President and two Houses, Dáil Éireann (House of Representatives) and Seanad Éireann (Senate), which have a maximum term of five years. The House of Representatives has 148 members elected by proportional representation, while the Senate has 60 members, of whom 11 are nominated directly by the Prime Minister, 6 are elected by the universities, and the remaining 43 are elected from five vocational panels. The Taoiseach (Prime Minister) is appointed by the President on the nomination of the Dáil.

The major political parties are Fianna Fáil (84 of 148 seats in the Dáil), led by Lynch; Fianna Gael (43 seats), led by Garret FitzGerald; Labour Party (17 seats), led by Frank Cluskey.

**History.** In the Stone and Bronze Ages, Ireland was inhabited by Picts in the north and a people called the Erainn in the south, the same stock, apparently, as in all the isles before the Anglo-Saxon invasion of Britain. About the fourth century B.C. tall, red-haired Celts arrived from Gaul or Galicia. They subdued and assimilated the inhabitants and established a Gaelic civilization.

By the beginning of the Christian Era, Ireland was divided into five kingdoms—Ulster, Connacht, Leinster, Meath, and Munster. St. Patrick introduced Christianity in 432 and the country developed into a center of Gaelic and Latin learning. Irish monasteries, the equivalent of universities, attracted intellectuals as well as the pious and sent out missionaries to many parts of Europe and, some believe, to North America.

Norse depredations along the coasts, starting in

795, ended in 1014 with Norse defeat at the Battle of Clontarf by forces under Brian Boru. In the 12th century, the Pope gave all Ireland to the English Crown as a papal fief. In 1171, Henry II of England was acknowledged "Lord of Ireland," but local sectional rule continued for centuries, and English control over the whole island was not reasonably absolute until the 17th century. By the Act of Union (1800), England and Ireland became the "United Kingdom of Great Britain and Ireland."

A steady decline in the Irish economy followed in the next decades. The population had reached 8¼ million when the great potato famine of 1846–48 took many lives and drove millions to emigrate to America. By 1921 it was down to 4.3 million.

In the meantime, anti-British agitation continued along with demands for Irish home rule. The advent of World War I delayed the institution of home rule and resulted in the Easter Rebellion in Dublin (April 24–29, 1916), in which Irish nationalists unsuccessfully attempted to throw off British rule. Guerrilla warfare against British forces followed proclamation of a republic by the rebels in 1919.

The Irish Free State was established as a dominion on Dec. 6, 1921, with the six northern counties as part of the United Kingdom. Ireland was neutral in World War II.

In 1948, Eamon de Valera, leader of the Sinn Fein, who had won establishment of the Free State in 1921 in negotiations with Britain's David Lloyd George, was defeated by John A. Costello, who demanded final independence from the U.K. The Republic of Ireland was proclaimed on April 18, 1949. It withdrew from the Commonwealth but in 1955 entered the United Nations. Since 1949 the prime concern of successive governments has been economic development.

De Valera, who retired in 1973 after two terms in the largely ceremonial presidency, died Aug. 29, 1975, at the age of 92.

Through the 1960s two antagonistic currents dominated Irish politics. One sought to bind the wounds of the rebellion and civil war, symbolized in 1967 by the merger of Protestant Trinity College and Catholic University College into the University of Dublin. The other was the effort of the outlawed extremist Irish Republican Army to bring Northern Ireland into the republic. Despite public sympathy for unification of Ireland, the Dublin government dealt rigorously with IRA guerrillas caught inside the republic's borders.

The 1973 elections brought to power Liam Cosgrave, at the head of a coalition of the Fianna Gael and the Labour Party, unseating the Fianna Fáil which had governed for 35 of 41 years of the Republic. Cosgrave cooperated with the British government in attempts to control IRA terrorism and, after the assassination of the British Ambassador to Ireland on July 21, 1976, pushed through an Emergency Powers Act to strengthen police and court powers in combatting terrorists. The unpopularity of the Act became evident after President Cearbhail Ó Dalaigh resigned when he was criticized by one of Cosgrave's ministers for questioning the law's constitutionality. The Fianna Fáil nominated Patrick J. Hillery to succeed Ó Dalaigh and the government named no candidate to oppose him.

The June 16, 1977, election gave the Fianna Fáil a record 84 seats and aroused British fears that the new government of Prime Minister Lynch would repeal the emergency powers and reduce Irish controls on the northern border.

Lynch aroused protests in Ulster and Britain and among his political opponents at home when he declared his support on Jan. 8, 1978, for eventual unification of Ireland and an amnesty for the IRA. He somewhat repaired his position the next month with a public appeal to the Irish abroad, particularly in the U.S., to stop sending money to the IRA and other extremists in Ulster.

**Economy.** Agriculture is still the principal occupation in Ireland, although participation in the European Economic Community and a campaign for investment by foreign companies is increasing Ireland's industrial growth. The main crops are wheat, oats, potatoes, and sugar beets. Other staple crops are rye, flax, turnips, cabbage, hay.

Ireland supplies most of its own consumer goods and is now producing a wide variety of goods for world markets. Leading manufactures are ordinarily beverages, tobacco, wood, paper, clothing, textiles, and metals.

Chief exports in 1976 were machinery (12%), dairy products (11%), beef and veal (9%), chemicals (9%), textile yarns and fabrics (6%), and livestock (6%).

# ISRAEL

**State of Israel**
**President:** Yitzhak Navon (1978)
**Prime Minister:** Menahem Begin (1977)
**Area:** 8,019 sq mi. (20,770 sq km)[1]
**Population (est. 1978):** 3,700,000
**Density per square mile:** 461.4
**Capital:** Jerusalem
**Largest cities (est. 1977):** Jerusalem, 366,300[2] (est. 1976): Tel Aviv, 348,500; Haifa, 227,200; Ramat-Gan, 121,000
**Monetary unit:** Israeli pound
**Languages:** Hebrew, Arabic, English
**Religions:** Jewish, 85%; Islam, Christian
**Gross national product (1976):** $12 billion
**National name:** Medinat Israel
**Freedom House classifications:** Capitalist-socialist industrial, multi-party centralized

**Geography.** Israel, slightly smaller than Massachusetts, lies at the eastern end of the Mediterranean Sea. It is bordered by Egypt on the west, Syria and Jordan on the east, and Lebanon on the north.

Northern Israel is largely a plateau traversed from north to south by mountains and broken by great depressions also running from north to south.

The maritime plain of Israel is remarkably fertile. The southern Negev region, which comprises almost half the total area, is largely a wide desert steppe area. The National Water Project irrigation scheme is now transforming it into fertile land. The Jordan, the only important river, flows from the north through Lake Hule (Waters of Merom) and Lake Kinneret (Sea of Galilee or Sea of Tiberias), finally entering the Dead Sea, 1,290 feet (393 m) below sea level. This "sea," which is actually a salt lake (394 sq mi.; 1,020 sq km), has no outlet, its water balance being maintained by evaporation.

**Government.** Israel, which does not have a written Constitution, has a republican form of government headed by a President elected for a five-year term by the Knesset, a one-chamber legislature. He may be elected twice. The Knesset has 120 members who are elected by universal suffrage under pro-

1. Excluding 26,473 sq mi. (68,565 sq km) occupied in 1967 war. 2. Includes East Jerusalem.

portional representation for four years. The government is administered by the Cabinet, which is headed by the Prime Minister.

The Knesset decided in June 1950 that Israel would acquire a Constitution gradually through the years by the enactment of fundamental laws. Israel grants automatic citizenship to every Jew who desires to settle within its borders, subject to control of the Knesset.

The major political parties are Likud (45 of 120 seats in Knesset), led by Prime Minister Menahem Begin; Labour Party (32 seats), led by Shimon Peres; Democratic Movement for Change Party (15 seats), led by Yigael Yadin; National Religious Party (12 seats).

**History.** Palestine, cradle of two great religions and homeland of the modern state of Israel, was known to the ancient Hebrews as the "Land of Canaan." Palestine's name derives from the Philistines, a people who occupied the southern coastal part of the country in the 12th Century B.C.

A Hebrew kingdom established in 1000 B.C. was later split into the kingdoms of Judah and Israel and subsequently invaded by Assyrians, Babylonians, Egyptians, Persians, Macedonians, Romans, and Byzantines. The Arabs took Palestine from the Byzantine Empire A.D. 634–40. With the exception of a Frankish Crusader kingdom from 1099 to 1187, Palestine remained under Moslem rule until the 20th century (Turkish rule from 1516) when British forces under Gen. Sir Edmund Allenby defeated the Turks and captured Jerusalem Dec. 9, 1917. The League of Nations granted the U.K. a mandate to govern Palestine, effective in 1923.

Jewish colonies—Jews from Russia established one as early as 1882—multiplied after Theodor Herzl's 1897 call for a Jewish state. The Zionist movement received official approval with the publication of a letter Nov. 2, 1917, from Arthur Balfour, British Foreign Secretary, to Lord Rothschild, a British Jewish leader. Balfour promised support for the establishment of a Jewish homeland in Palestine on the understanding that the civil and religious rights of non-Jewish Palestinians would be safeguarded.

A 1937 British proposal called for an Arab and a Jewish state separated by a mandated area incorporating Jerusalem and Nazareth. Arabs opposed this, demanding a single state with minority rights for Jews, and a 1939 British White Paper retreated, offering instead a single state with further Jewish immigration to be limited to 75,000. Although the White Paper satisfied neither side, further discussion ended on the outbreak of World War II, when the Jewish population stood at nearly 500,000, or 30% of the whole. Illegal and legal immigration through the war brought the Jewish population to 678,000 in 1946, compared with 1,269,000 Arabs. Unable to reach a compromise, the U.K. turned the problem over to the United Nations in 1947, which on November 29 voted for partition—despite strong Arab opposition.

The U.K. did not help implement the U.N. decision and withdrew on expiration of its mandate May 14, 1948. Zionists had already seized control of areas designated as Jewish and, on the day of British departure, the Jewish National Council proclaimed the state of Israel.

U.S. recognition came within hours and, on May 15, Jordanian and Egyptian forces invaded the new nation. At the cease-fire Jan. 7, 1949, Israel increased its original territory by 50%, taking western Galilee, a broad corridor through central Palestine to Jerusalem and part of modern Jerusalem. (In April 1950, Jordan annexed areas of eastern and central Palestine that had been designated for an Arab state, together with the old city of Jerusalem.)

The provisional leaders of the Jewish state, Chaim Weizmann and David Ben-Gurion, became Israel's first President and Prime Minister. The new government was admitted to the U.N. May 11, 1949.

The next clash with Arab neighbors came when Egypt nationalized the Suez Canal in 1956 and barred Israeli shipping. Coordinating with an Anglo-French force, Israeli troops seized the Gaza strip and drove through the Sinai to the East Bank of the Suez Canal, but withdrew under U.S. and U.N. pressure. In 1967, Israel threatened retaliation against Syrian border raids, and Syria asked Egyptian aid. Egypt demanded the removal of U.N. peace-keeping forces from Suez, staged a national mobilization, closed the Gulf of Aqaba, and moved troops into Sinai. Israel replied with a simultaneous air attack June 5 against Syrian, Jordanian, and Egyptian bases and in a six-day war totally defeated its Arab enemies. Expanding its territory by 200%, Israel at the cease-fire held the Golan Heights, the West Bank of the Jordan River, the Old City, and all of the Sinai and the East Bank of the Suez.

Israel asserted as its new terms for peace with her Arab neighbors a guarantee that any occupied territory returned could never be used as a base for aggression. She also insisted that Jerusalem remain a unified city and that peace negotiations be conducted directly—something the Arab states had refused to do because it would constitute a recognition of their Jewish neighbor.

Egypt's President Gamal Abdel Nasser renounced the 1967 cease-fire April 23, 1969, to begin a "war of attrition" against Israel, firing Soviet artillery at Israeli forces on the East Bank of the Suez. Israel used its U.S. Phantom aircraft to stage heavy raids against Egyptian industrial and population centers, prompting Nasser to travel to Moscow twice in 1970 to ask for additional planes, antiaircraft missiles, and Soviet advisers. The U.S. in June 1970 launched a peace initiative seeking to reopen negotiations after President Anwar Sadat succeeded Nasser.

In the face of Israeli reluctance even to discuss the return of occupied territories, the fourth Mideast war erupted Oct. 6, 1973, with a surprise Egyptian and Syrian assault on the Jewish high holy day, Yom Kippur. Initial Arab gains were reversed when a cease-fire took effect two weeks later, but Israeli losses in manpower were serious. The U.S. supplied over $2 billion worth of weapons and, at a point when the U.S.S.R. threatened to intervene, put its nuclear forces on world-wide alert.

U.S. Secretary of State Henry Kissinger arranged a disengagement of forces on both the Egyptian and Syrian fronts, which permitted the two Arab nations to recover small amounts of territory they lost in 1967. The disengagement was supervised by U.N. peace-keeping forces, with the U.S.S.R. for the first time sharing the cost. Geneva talks, aimed at a lasting peace, foundered, however, when Israel balked at inclusion of the Palestine Liberation Organization, a guerrilla front increasingly active in terrorism directed against Israel.

At home, criticism of the ruling Labour Party's lack of preparedness cost it five seats in 1973 elections, and Prime Minister Golda Meir was forced to head a minority government until her retirement April 10, 1974. Former General Yitzhak Rabin formed a successor government to win narrow approval in the Knesset and, in October 1974, assembled a majority coalition. In the same month, the PLO won recognition as the "representative of the Palestine people" in a resolution passed by the U.N. General Assembly and at an Arab summit meeting in Rabat, Morocco, where the Arab states pledged $2.3 billion in military aid to Israel's neighbors. Amid continuing terrorist attacks and counterattacks by Israeli forces, Rabin refused to negotiate with the PLO on grounds that a Palestinian homeland should be discussed between Israel and Jordan, which opposed PLO claims to the West Bank.

When Kissinger in January 1975 sought a second-stage agreement between Israel and Egypt for disengagement in the Sinai, Israel insisted on a formal Egyptian pledge of non-belligerency but eventually signed a three-year agreement in Geneva September 4.

The agreement required Israel to give up the strategic Mitla and Gidi passes and to return the captured Abu Rudeis oil fields. Egypt guaranteed passage of Israeli cargoes through the reopened Suez Canal, and both sides renounced force in the settlement of disputes. Two hundred U.S. civilian technicians were stationed in a widened U.N. buffer zone to monitor and warn either side of truce violations. After approval by the Knesset September 3, U.S. commitments to give Israel $400 million in economic aid and $1 billion in U.S. weapons were disclosed, along with the assurance of a coordinated U.S.-Israeli position in any renewed Geneva negotiations. Nevertheless, an estrangement between Washington and Jerusalem, which began with the 1974 Arab oil boycott, persisted and the solidity of the alliance became increasingly an issue in domestic politics.

For the Israelis, the July 4, 1976, rescue of 103 hostages in a hijacked Air France airliner at Entebbe, Uganda, was a stunning victory against Arab terrorism. The hijacking was the first in a year and a half to be carried out by Palestinians, in this case the Popular Front for the Liberation of Palestine. Rabin contravened government policy in opening negotiations with the terrorists but secretly prepared a commando raid on the airport. When he learned that the hostages faced death in any event, Rabin launched the airborne raid, which killed the terrorists and a score of Ugandan soldiers, losing only two hostages and one rescuer. Uganda unsuccessfully appealed to the U.N. Security Council to condemn Israel for aggression, but Israeli Ambassador Chaim Herzog claimed that international law sanctioned his government's action.

With no progress toward permanent peace and rampant inflation causing severe economic strain, the malaise in the ruling Labour Party deepened in early 1977 when Rabin confessed to maintaining an illegal bank account in the United States. He resigned April 8 and Defense Minister Shimon Peres was named as the party's leader for general elections May 17, in which the Labour Party was defeated for the first time since Israel's founding.

Menahem Begin, 63, took office June 21 as the leader of the Likud, a coalition of conservative parties. Begin founded the Irgun Zvai Leumi (National Military Organization) to fight British rule during the Palestine Mandate. His election victory provoked a wave of negative reaction throughout the Arab world and misgivings on the part of western proponents of a Mideast peace. Attempting to modify his image, the Likud platform on the inauguration of the new government omitted an election claim of permanent sovereignty over the West Bank and agreed to suspend the application of Israeli law to the occupied territories in general while peace negotiations are under way.

A dramatic breakthrough in the tortuous history of Mideast peace efforts occurred Nov. 9, 1977, when Egypt's President Anwar el-Sadat declared his willingness to go anywhere to talk peace. Begin on November 15 extended an invitation to the Egyptian leader to address the Knesset. Sadat's arrival in Israel four days later raised worldwide hopes. But optimism ebbed even before Begin was invited to Ismailia by Sadat, December 25–26.

An Israeli peace plan unveiled by Begin on his return, and approved by the Knesset, offered to end military administration in the West Bank and the Gaza Strip, with a degree of Arab self-rule but no relinquishment of sovereignty by Israel. Sadat severed talks January 18 and, despite U.S. condemnation, Begin approved new West Bank settlements by Israelis. Dissidents within the cabinet, notably Defense Minister Ezer Weizman, kept the door open for negotiations, however, and a foreign ministerial meeting of the two antagonists with U.S. Secretary of State Cyrus Vance took place in an English castle July 18.

Amid the continuing tension over peace negotiations, a PLO raid on Israel's coast on March 11 killed 30 civilians and provoked a full-scale invasion of southern Lebanon by Israel March 14 to attack PLO bases. Israel withdrew three months later, turning over strongpoints to Lebanese Christian militia wherever possible rather than to a U.N. peacekeeping force installed in the area.

**Economy.** Agriculture is the chief economic activity, but industrialization has been the most important feature of Israel's economic development recently. The maritime plain, the plain of Esdraelon, and the northern Jordan valley are the principal agricultural areas. Citrus growing, confined largely to the maritime plain, normally furnishes the major export crop. Others include olives, rice, fruits and vegetables, figs, tobacco, wheat, barley, corn, sesame, and potatoes.

Industry is developing rapidly, especially the food-processing, textile, metalworking, and chemical groups. Diamond cutting, although dependent on rough diamond imports, is of major importance; and there are oil refineries and storage tanks at Haifa, serving Israel's needs for petroleum products.

Mineral resources are limited. They include gypsum, sulfur, limestone, and rock salt, together with potash, phosphates, and bromine from the Dead Sea.

Chief exports in 1976 were diamonds (33%), chemicals (10%), citrus fruits (7%), machinery (7%), metal manufactures (6%), and clothing (5%). Leading customers were U.S. (18%), West Germany (8%), U.K. (8%), Netherlands (7%), Hong Kong (6%), France (6%), Iran (5%). Leading suppliers were U.S. (22%), U.K. (16%), West Germany (10%), Netherlands (6%).

# ITALY

**Italian Republic**
**President:** Sandro Pertini (1978)
**Premier:** Giulio Andreotti (1976)
**Area:** 116,304 sq mi. (301,225 sq km)
**Population (est. 1978):** 56,675,000
**Density per square mile:** 487.3
**Capital:** Rome
**Largest cities (est. 1977):** Rome, 2,884,000; **(est. 1976):** Milan, 1,700,000; Palermo, 700,000; (est. 1975): Naples, 1,300,000; Turin, 1,200,000; Genoa, 806,400; Bologna, 493,000; Venice, 364,900; (1971 census): Florence, 457,803; Catania, 400,886
**Monetary unit:** Lira
**Language:** Italian
**Religion:** Roman Catholic
**Gross national product (1976):** $170.0 billion
**National name:** Repubblica Italiana
**Freedom House classifications:** Capitalist industrial, multi-party centralized

**Geography.** Italy is a long peninsula shaped like a boot bounded on the west by the Tyrrhenian Sea and on the east by the Adriatic. Slightly larger than Arizona, it has for neighbors France, Switzerland, Austria, and Yugoslavia.

Approximately 600 of Italy's 708 miles (1,139 km) of length are in the long peninsula that projects into the Mediterranean from the fertile basin of the Po River. The Apennines, branching off from the Alps between Nice and Genoa, form the peninsula's backbone, and rise to a maximum height of 9,560 feet at the Gran Sasso d'Italia (Corno). The Alps form Italy's northern boundary.

Several islands form part of Italy. Sicily (9,926 sq mi.; 2,769 sq km) lies off the toe of the boot, across the Strait of Messina, with a steep and rock bound northern coast and gentler slopes to the sea in the west and south. Mt. Etna, an active volcano, rises to 10,741 feet (3,274 m), and most of Sicily is more than 500 feet (152 m) in elevation. Sixty-two miles (100 km) southwest of Sicily lies Pantelleria (45 sq mi.; 117 sq km), and south of that are Lampedusa and Linosa. Sardinia (9,301 sq mi.; 2,409 sq km), which is located just south of Corsica and about 125 miles (200 km) west of the mainland, is mountainous, stony, and unproductive.

Italy has many northern lakes, lying below the snow-covered peaks of the Alps. The largest are Garda (143 sq mi.; 370 sq km), Maggiore (83 sq mi.; 215 sq km), and Como (55 sq mi.; 142 sq km).

The Po, the principal river, flows from the Alps on Italy's western border and crosses the Lombard plain to the Adriatic.

**Government.** The President is elected for a term of seven years by Parliament in joint session with regional representatives. The President nominates the Premier and, upon the Premier's recommendations, the members of the Cabinet. Parliament is composed of two houses: a Senate with 315 elective members and a Chamber of Deputies of 630 members elected by the people for a five-year term.

The major political parties are Christian Democratic Party (263 seats in Chamber of Deputies), led by Benigno Zaccagnini; Italian Community Party (220 seats), led by Enrico Berlinguer; Socialist Party (57 seats), led by Bettino Craxi; Social Movement Party (17 seats), led by Giorgio Almirante; National Democracy Party (17 seats), led by Ernesto De Marzio; Socialist Democratic Party (15 seats), led by Pierluigi Romita; Republican Party (14 seats), led by Oddo Biasini; Proletarian Democracy Party (6 seats), led by Massimo Gorla; Liberal Party (5 seats), led by Valerio Zanone; Radical Party (4 seats), led by Adelaide Aglietta.

**History.** Until A.D. 476, when the German Odoacer became head of the Roman Empire in the west, the history of Italy was largely the history of Rome. From A.D. 800 on, the Holy Roman Emperors, Popes, Normans, and Saracens all vied for control over various segments of the Italian peninsula. Numerous city states, such as Venice and Genoa, and many small principalities flourished in the late Middle Ages.

In 1713, after the War of the Spanish Succession, Milan, Naples, and Sardinia were handed over to Austria, which lost some of its Italian territories in 1735. After 1800, Italy was unified by Napoleon, who crowned himself King of Italy on May 26, 1805; but after the Congress of Vienna in 1815, Austria once again became the dominant power in Italy.

The tyranny of the Restoration met with opposition by the Carbonari (charcoal burners), a secret society that demanded constitutional government and national unification. But Austrian armies crushed Italian uprisings in 1820, 1821, and 1831. In the 1830s Giuseppe Mazzini, brilliant liberal nationalist, organized the Risorgimento (Resurrection), which laid the foundation for Italian unity.

Disappointed Italian patriots looked to the House of Savoy for leadership. Count Camille di Cavour (1810–61), Prime Minister of Sardinia in 1852 and the architect of United Italy, joined England and France in the Crimean War (1853–56), and in 1859 helped France in a war against Austria, thereby obtaining Lombardy. By plebiscite in 1860, Modena, Parma, Tuscany, and the Romagna voted to join Sardinia. In 1860, Giuseppe Garibaldi conquered Sicily and Naples and turned them over to Sardinia. Victor Emmanuel II, King of Sardinia, was proclaimed King of Italy on March 17, 1861.

Allied with Germany and Austria-Hungary in the Triple Alliance of 1882, Italy declared her neutrality upon the outbreak of World War I on the ground that Germany had embarked upon an offensive war. In 1915, Italy entered the war on the side of the Allies.

Benito Mussolini, a former Socialist, organized discontented Italians in 1919 into the Fascist Party to "rescue Italy from Bolshevism." He led his Black Shirts in a march on Rome and, on Oct. 28, 1922, became Premier. He transformed Italy into a dictatorship, embarking on an expansionist foreign policy with the invasion and annexation of Ethiopia in 1935 and allying himself with Adolf Hitler in the Rome-Berlin Axis in 1936. Il Duce was executed by Partisans at Dongo on Lake Como, April 28, 1945.

Following the overthrow of Mussolini's dictatorship and the armistice with the Allies (Sept. 3, 1943), Italy joined the war against Germany as a co-belligerent. King Victor Emmanuel III abdicated May 9, 1946, and left the country after installing his son as King Humbert II. However, a provisional government held a popular plebiscite on June 2, and the Italians voted to establish a republic. On June 13, King Humbert followed his father into exile.

The peace treaty that took effect Sept. 15, 1947, required Italian renunciation of all claims in Ethiopia and Greece and the cession of the Dodecanese to Greece and of five small Alpine areas to France. In addition, the major part of the Istrian

Peninsula, including Fiume and Pola, went to Yugoslavia.

The Trieste area west of the new Yugoslav territory was made a free territory (until 1954, when the city and a 90-square-mile zone were transferred to Italy and the rest to Yugoslavia). Italy was required to pay nearly $400 million in reparations, chiefly to the Soviet Union, Yugoslavia, Greece, Ethiopia, and Albania.

Economic problems vied with political discord as Italy's greatest impediment to stability in the 1970s.

The Rumor government fell Oct. 3, 1974, following setbacks that included failure by the Christian Democrats to persuade voters in a May referendum to repeal the 1970 divorce law. After a 51-day crisis, a government was formed under Aldo Moro, a left-centrist Christian Democrat who had been Premier three times before.

The economy appeared to stabilize in the summer of 1975. Provincial and regional elections in June resulted in Communist gains and in left-wing administrators being seated in all major cities north of Rome.

Withdrawal of the Socialists from Moro's coalition—the 32nd government since World War II—brought his resignation Jan. 7, 1976. In the June 20 elections, the Communists gained but the Christian Democrats still led and, warned by the U.S. and West Germany against a Communist coalition, they chose to govern as a minority under Giulio Andreotti. Petro Ingrao, a Communist, became President of the Chamber of Deputies, however, and Communists won 7 of 26 parliamentary chairmanships.

Andreotti had Communist cooperation in imposing wage limits and taxes to meet International Monetary Fund conditions for a $530-million loan. He also got Communist backing to combat a wave of kidnappings and political terrorism, culminating in the seizure of former Premier Moro in Rome on March 16, 1978, by the ultra-left Red Brigades. The discovery on May 9 of Moro's bullet-ridden body near the site of his kidnapping caused worldwide shock and in Italy was held responsible for a drop in Communist strength and a gain for the Christian Democrats in the May 16th local elections.

A second political shock was the resignation of President Giovanni Leone on June 15, six months before the end of his term, because of his involvement in Lockheed bribery scandals. Moro had been the leading candidate to replace him, but in the wide-open contest that ensued, 81-year-old Sandro Pertini became Italy's first Socialist President.

**Religion.** Although the country is predominantly Roman Catholic, religious freedom is permitted. Catholic religious teaching is given in all elementary and intermediate schools. Relations with the Church were regulated until 1977 by the treaty with the Holy See of Feb. 11, 1929, which established the temporal power of the Pope over Vatican City. In November 1977 a new accord replaced the 1929 Corcordat; Catholicism is no longer to be considered as the state religion and Vatican influence on education and marriage has been reduced.

**Economy.** Agriculture engages more than a third of the population. It is extremely diversified; differences of altitude, soil, and climate allow the production of all European crops from rye to rice, from apples to oranges, and from hemp to cotton. Italy ranks next to France in wine production and next to Spain in olive-oil production.

Livestock and dairy farming are important in Italy. Of the 50-odd varieties of Italian cheese, the best known are the hard parmesan and pecorino (the latter made from ewe's milk) and the soft bel paese and gorgonzola.

Industrial production is centered in the north. The nature of the Fascist corporate state had a tendency to foster industrial concentration prior to World War II. The textile industry is the largest and most important and supplies the home market as well as furnishing a large proportion of Italy's exports. The metal industries are handicapped by lack of coal, which must be imported in large quantities, and by insufficient iron-ore reserves. The chemical, clothing, and food industries are also important.

Italy is a member of the European Coal and Steel Community.

Production includes cotton yarn, woven cotton fabrics, rayon yarn, pig iron and ferroalloys, raw steel, cement, automobiles, and trucks.

Italy is ordinarily the world's largest producer of mercury; it is also an important producer of sulfur.

In Alto Adige and in the central Apennines, there are abundant hydroelectric power resources and deposits of natural gas.

Chief exports in 1975 were machinery (24%), motor vehicles (9%), chemicals (8%), iron and steel (7%), textile yarns and fabrics (6%), petroleum products (5%), and clothing (5%). Leading customers in 1976 were EEC (48%; incl. West Germany 19%, France 15%, U.K. 5%), U.S. (6%). Leading suppliers were EEC (44%; incl. West Germany 17%, France 14%, Netherlands 5%), U.S. (8%), Saudi Arabia (6%).

## IVORY COAST

**Republic of Ivory Coast**
**President:** Félix Houphouët-Boigny (1960)
**Area:** 124,502 sq mi. (322,462 sq km)
**Population (est. 1978):** 6,714,000
**Density per square mile:** 53.9
**Capital and largest city (est. 1975):** Abidjan, 685,800
**Monetary unit:** Franc CFA
**Ethnic groups:** Agnis, Baoulés, Senoufos, Kroumen, Mandes, Dan-Gouros
**Languages:** French and African languages
**Religions:** Animist, 65%; Islam, 23%; Christian, 12%
**National name:** République de la Côte d'Ivoire
**Gross national product (1976):** $4.3 billion
**Freedom House classifications:** Capitalist pre-industrial, one-party nationalist

**Geography.** The Ivory Coast, in western Africa on the Gulf of Guinea, is a little larger than New Mexico. Its neighbors are Liberia, Guinea, Mali, Upper Volta, and Ghana.

The country consists of a coastal strip in the south, dense forests in the interior, and savannas in the north. Rainfall is heavy, especially along the coast.

**Government.** The government is headed by a President who is elected every five years by universal direct suffrage, together with a National Assembly of 120 members.

The Parti Démocratique de la Côte d'Ivoire, member of Rassemblement Démocratique Africain (P.D.C.I./R.D.A.), is the only political party.

**History.** The Ivory Coast attracted both French and Portuguese merchants in the 15th century. French traders set up establishments early in the 19th century, and in 1842, the French obtained territorial concessions from local tribes, gradually extending their influence along the coast and inland. The area was organized as a territory in 1893, became an autonomous republic in the French Union after World War II, and achieved independence on Aug. 7, 1960.

Ivory Coast formed a customs union in 1959 with Dahomey, Niger, and Upper Volta. The country is one of the most prosperous and stable in West Africa. Ivory Coast succeeded in getting a $10-million loan from European and U.S. private capital in April 1960 for low-cost housing and other development work. It also obtained a $30-million U.S. loan to assist in construction of a $96.5-million hydroelectric project.

Ivory Coast joined a seven-nation Economic Community for West Africa Jan. 1, 1973, to promote regional economic development.

**Economy.** Agricultural products include corn, sweet potatoes, cassava, coffee, cocoa, bananas, and peanuts. With coffee and cocoa prices at world highs, the economy in 1977 showed siginificant growth.

Chief exports in 1976 were coffee (34%), cocoa (24%), and timber (20%). Leading customers were France (25%), Netherlands (13%), U.S. (10%), Italy (9%), West Germany (7%). Leading suppliers were France (38%), U.S. (7%), West Germany (7%), Japan (5%).

## JAMAICA

**Governor-General:** Florizel Glasspole (1973)
**Prime Minister:** Michael Manley (1972)
**Area:** 4,244 sq mi. (10,991 sq km)
**Population (1978):** 2,110,000
**Density per square mile:** 497.2
**Capital and largest city (est. 1974):** Kingston, 169,800
**Monetary unit:** Jamaican dollar
**Language:** English
**Religions:** Anglican, Baptist, Roman Catholic
**Gross national product (1976):** $2.9 billion
**Member of Commonwealth of Nations**
**Freedom House classifications:** Multi-party centralized, capitalist-socialist industrial

**Geography.** Jamaica is an island in the West Indies, 90 miles south of Cuba and west of Haiti. It is a little smaller than Connecticut.

The island is made up of a plateau and the Blue Mountains, a group of volcanic hills, in the east. Blue Mountain (7,402 ft.; 2,256 m) is the tallest peak.

**Government.** The island legislature is a 60-member House of Representatives elected by universal suffrage, and an appointed Senate of 21 members. The Prime Minister is appointed by the Governor-General and must in the Governor-General's opinion be the person best able to command the confidence of a majority of the members of the House of Representatives.

The major political parties are the People's National Party (47 seats in the House of Representatives), led by Prime Minister Michael Manley; and Jamaica Labour Party (13 seats), led by Edward P. G. Seaga.

**History.** Jamaica was inhabited by Arawak Indians when Columbus discovered it in 1494 and named it St. Iago. It remained under Spanish rule until 1655, then became a British possession. Jamaica prospered from wealth brought by buccaneers to their base, Port Royal, the capital, until the city disappeared in the sea in 1692 after an earthquake. The Arawaks died off from disease and exploitation, and slaves, mostly black, were imported to work sugar plantations. Abolition of the slave trade (1807), emancipation of the slaves (1833), and a gradual drop in sugar prices led to depressed economic conditions that resulted in an uprising in 1865.

The following year the government was changed to that of a colony, and conditions improved considerably. Introduction of banana cultivation made the island less dependent on the sugar crop for its well-being. Overpopulation and problems inherited from the colonial era, such as illiteracy, produced chronic substantial unemployment, leading to much emigration to the Caribbean countries and to the U.S.

On May 5, 1953, the island of Jamaica attained internal autonomy, and in 1958 it led in organizing the West Indies Federation. This effort at Caribbean unification failed. A nationalist labor leader, Sir Alexander Bustamente, led a campaign for withdrawal from the federation. As the result of a popular referendum in 1961, Jamaica became an independent nation on Aug. 6, 1962.

Manley became Prime Minister in 1972 and initiated a socialist program with higher taxes on land and luxuries and on the production of bauxite. In February and March 1977, the government agreed to buy 51% of the Kaiser and Reynolds bauxite operations in Jamaica, ending a dispute with the U.S. companies over heavy taxes imposed earlier. After a visit by Rosalynn Carter in May, U.S. aid was resumed in September, bringing to an end a two-year cutoff stemming from the takeover of a U.S. company without compensation. Although Jamaica's chronic economic problems continued, the restoration of public order brought a revival in 1978 of the tourist industry, hit by civil unrest in the previous two years.

**Economy.** Jamaica is the world's largest producer of bauxite. Its most important agricultural products are sugar, bananas, tobacco, and citrus fruits.

Chief exports in 1976 were alumina (43%), bauxite (23%), and sugar (9%). Leading customers were U.S. (43%), U.K. (17%), Norway (12%), Sweden (5%). Leading suppliers were U.S. (37%), Venezuela (14%), U.K. (11%), Canada (6%), Netherlands Antilles (6%).

## JAPAN

**Emperor:** Hirohito (1926)
**Prime Minister:** Takeo Fukuda (1976)
**Area:** 143,750 sq mi. (372,313 sq km)
**Population (est. 1978):** 114,850,000
**Density per square mile:** 799.0
**Capital:** Tokyo
**Largest cities (est. 1977)**[1]: Tokyo, 8,568,700; **(est. 1975):** Osaka, 2,779,000; Yokohama, 2,622,000; Nagoya, 2,080,000; Kyoto, 1,461,000; Kobe, 1,361,000; Sapporo, 1,241,000; Kitakyushu, 1,058,000
**Monetary unit:** Yen
**Language:** Japanese

1. Except for Tokyo, figures refer to *shi*, a minor division that may include some scattered or rural population as well as an urban center.

**Religions:** Shintoist, Buddhist, Christian
**Gross national product (1976):** $554.4 billion
**National name:** Nippon
**Freedom House classifications:** Multi-party centralized, capitalist industrial.

**Geography.** An archipelago extending more than 1,000 miles from north to south in the Pacific, Japan is separated from the east coast of Asia by the Sea of Japan. It is approximately the size of Montana.

Japan's four main islands are Honshu, Hokkaido, Kyushu, and Shikoku. The Ryukyu chain to the southwest was U.S.-occupied and the Kuriles to the northeast are Russian-occupied. The surface of the main islands consists largely of mountains separated by narrow valleys. There are about 50 more or less active volcanoes, of which the best-known is Mount Fuji.

**Government.** Japan's Constitution, promulgated on Nov. 3, 1946, replaced the Meiji Constitution of 1889. The 1946 Constitution, sponsored by the U.S. during its occupation of Japan, brought fundamental changes to the Japanese political system, including the abandonment of the Emperor's divine rights. The Diet (Parliament) consists of a House of Representatives of 511 members, elected for four years, and a House of Councilors of 252 members, half of whom are elected every three years for six-year terms. Executive power is vested in the Cabinet, which is headed by a Prime Minister, nominated by the Diet from its members.

Emperor Hirohito, who was born April 29, 1901, succeeded his father, Yoshihito, on Dec. 25, 1926. He was married on Jan. 26, 1924, to Princess Nagako, born in 1903. They have two sons—Crown Prince Akihito (born Dec. 23, 1933) and Prince Hitachi (born Nov. 28, 1935)—and four daughters. Succession to the Japanese throne is in the male line only.

The major political parties are the Liberal Democratic Party (258 of 511 seats in House of Representatives), led by Prime Minister Takeo Fukuda; Socialist Party (122 seats), led by Tomomi Narita; Clean Government Party (56 seats), led by Yoshikatsu Takeiri; Democratic Socialist Party (28 seats), led by Ikko Kasuga; Communist Party (19 seats), led by Sanzo Nosaka; New Liberal Club (18 seats).

**History.** A series of legends attributes creation of Japan to the sun goddess, from whom the later emperors were allegedly descended. The first of them was Jimmu Tenno, supposed to have ascended the throne in 660 B.C.

Recorded Japanese history begins with the first contact with China in the fifth century A.D. Japan was then divided into strong feudal states, all nominally under the Emperor, but with real power often held by a court minister or clan. In 1185, Yoritomo, chief of the Minamoto clan, was designated Shogun (Generalissimo) with the administration of the islands under his control. A dual government system —Shogun and Emperor—persisted till 1867.

First contact with the West came about 1542, when a Portuguese ship off course arrived in Japanese waters. Portuguese traders, Jesuit missionaries, and Spanish, Dutch, and English traders followed. Suspicious of Christianity and of Portuguese support of a local Japanese revolt, the shoguns prohibited all trade with foreign countries; only a Dutch trading post at Nagasaki was permitted. Western attempts to renew trading relations failed until 1853, when Commodore Matthew Perry sailed an American fleet into Tokyo Bay.

Japan now quickly made the transition from a medieval to a modern power. Feudalism was abolished and industrialization was speeded. An imperial army was established with conscription. The shogun system was abolished in 1868 by Emperor Meiji, and parliamentary government was established in 1889. After a brief war with China in 1894–95, Japan acquired Formosa (Taiwan), the Pescadores islands, and part of southern Manchuria. China also recognized the independence of Korea (Chosen), which Japan later annexed (1910).

In 1904–05, Japan defeated Russia in the Russo-Japanese War, gaining the territory of southern Sakhalin (Karafuto) and Russia's port and rail rights in Manchuria. In World War I, Japan, which took a negligible part in military operations, seized Germany's Pacific islands and leased areas in China. The Treaty of Versailles then awarded her a mandate over the islands.

At the Washington Conference of 1921–22, Japan agreed to respect Chinese national integrity. The series of Japanese aggressions that was to lead to the nation's downfall began in 1931 with the invasion of Manchuria. The following year, Japan set up this area as a puppet state, "Manchukuo," under Emperor Henry Pu-Yi, last of China's Manchu dynasty. On Nov. 25, 1936, Japan joined the Axis by signing the anti-Comintern pact. The invasion of China came the next year and the Pearl Harbor attack on Dec. 7, 1941.

For many months after Pearl Harbor, the Japanese army and navy enjoyed spectacular success, but by the end of 1942 the tide had begun to turn. Three years later the dropping of atomic bombs on Hiroshima and Nagasaki knocked Japan swiftly into surrender.

Japan surrendered formally on Sept. 2, 1945, aboard the battleship *Missouri* in Tokyo Bay. Southern Sakhalin and the Kurile Islands reverted to Russia, and Formosa (Taiwan) and Manchuria to China. The Pacific islands remained under U.S. occupation. General of the Army Douglas MacArthur was appointed Supreme Commander for the Allied Powers (SCAP) on Aug. 14, 1945.

A new Japanese Constitution was approved in 1946 and went into effect in 1947. In 1949, many of the responsibilities of government were returned to the Japanese. Full sovereignty was granted to Japan by the Japanese Peace Treaty in 1951.

The treaty took effect on April 28, 1952, when Japan returned to full status as a nation. It was admitted into the United Nations in 1958. Japan regained its former economic position in Asia, becoming a leading producer of cotton textiles and ships. Much agitation led the U.S. to withdraw its troops in 1958.

Following the visit of Prime Minister Eisaku Sato to Washington in November 1969, the U.S. agreed to return Okinawa and other Ryukyu Islands to Japan in 1972, and both nations renewed the security treaty in June 1970.

Events of the 1970s tested Japan's special relationship with the U.S. Trade ties were strained in 1972 by Washington's inconclusive effort to curb textile imports from Japan. The focus of Japanese diplomacy was altered when President Nixon opened a dialogue with Peking in 1972. Prime Minister Kakuei Tanaka, who succeeded Sako in July 1972, quickly established diplomatic relations with the mainland Chinese and severed ties with Formosa.

The jump in world oil prices that followed the 1973 Arab boycott squeezed Japan, which imports 85% of its oil from the Middle East. Japan greatly expanded its exports to the oil states and accepted some Arab investments.

Following Communist triumphs in Southeast Asia in the spring of 1975, Japan began moving into the diplomatic and commercial vacuum that followed U.S. withdrawal from the area.

Spending on defense in 1975 was less than 1% of the gross national product, and Japan's all-volunteer Self-Defense Forces numbered only 232,000 —12% below authorized strength.

President Ford visited Japan Nov. 18–24, 1974, the first U.S. President to do so. Substantive results were minimized by Tanaka's domestic political troubles. Tanaka resigned Nov. 26, 1974, and was succeeded December 2 by Takeo Miki, a compromise choice from the progressive wing of the Liberal Democrats.

While economic recovery continued in 1976, the Lockheed scandal pursued the ruling Liberal Democrats. With the disclosure by the U.S. Senate in February that $6.3 million in "promotion" money had been paid by the aircraft company to Yoshio Kodama, a rightwing political "fixer," Miki was placed under strong pressure to investigate the ultimate recipients.

Former Prime Minister Tanaka himself was jailed in August, charged with having received $1.7 million of the Lockheed money in violation of exchange controls. The scandal cost the party its control of the lower House in elections December 5, but nine independents affiliated with the Liberal Democrats to provide a narrow majority. Miki resigned, accepting responsibility for the first defeat since the party took control of the government in 1955, turning over leadership to Takeo Fukuda.

Fukuda, concentrating on economic recovery, achieved a record year in 1977, with exports exceeding imports by $9 billion, nearly twice the previous record of $5.1 billion in 1972. With the U.S. alone, Japan's favorable balance was $7.3 billion, despite a steadily falling dollar in yen terms.

Visiting Washington on May 3, 1978, Fukuda promised "massive efforts" to reduce Japan's surplus, currently running at an annual rate of $14 billion, but cutting automobile, color television, and steel exports and by buying U.S. aircraft. In return, like other U.S. trade partners, he urged Washington to curb inflation at home and support the dollar in foreign markets.

On Aug. 12, 1978, Japan and China signed a treaty of peace and friendship that was viewed by both countries' leaders as a foreign policy landmark. The U.S.S.R. contended that this treaty was anti-Soviet. Japanese diplomats maintained that Japan's policy toward the U.S.S.R. would not change because of the pact. This pact follows an 8-year, $20-billion economic pact signed in February in which Japanese business leaders agreed to provide China with modern technology in return for Chinese natural resources.

**Economy.** Prewar Japan was one of the world's leading industrial nations and the only country in the Far East with highly developed textile, steel, machinery, chemical, and electrical industries. The textile industry was dominant but, after 1931, considerable expansion took place in the heavy industries—metal, machinery-building, and chemical —that were adaptable to war purposes.

Postwar industrial rehabilitation proceeded slowly at first but, by the end of 1956, average industrial output was more than twice the 1934–36 level. Since the end of World War II, Japan's shipbuilding industry had consistently ranked among the world leaders.

The huge interlocking monopolies *(Zaibatsu)*, controlling prewar business and finance were dissolved in 1945, and reconcentration was prohibited by postwar legislation. However, there has been a growing tendency toward "bigness" in the last few years.

Japan is relatively poor in minerals, and large imports of coal, petroleum, and iron ore are necessary. Other minerals include lead, silver, gold, and copper.

Before World War II the merchant marine carried almost 80% of the foreign trade and was surpassed only by those of the U.S. and U.K. Wartime losses were enormous, but by 1974 it ranked second in the world to Liberia-flag ("flag of convenience) shipping.

Chief exports in 1976 were machinery (25%) (telecommunications apparatus 7%), iron and steel (18%), motor vehicles (18%), ships (10%), chemicals (8%), instruments (6%), and textile yarns and fabrics (6%). Leading customers were U.S. (24%), South Korea (4%). Leading suppliers were U.S. (18%), Saudi Arabia (12%), Australia (8%), Iran (7%), Indonesia (6%).

## JORDAN

**The Hashemite Kingdom of Jordan**
**Ruler:** King Hussein I (1952)
**Prime Minister:** Mudar Badran (1976)
**Area:** 37,738 sq mi. (97,740 sq km)[1]
**Population (est. 1977 by U.N.):** 2,080,000
**Capital:** Amman
**Largest cities (est. 1976):** Amman, 691,100. (est. 1973 by U.N.): Zarka, 220,000; Irbid, 116,000
**Monetary unit:** Jordanian dinar
**Language:** Arabic
**Religions:** Islam, 94%, Christian, 6%
**Gross national product (1976):** $1.6 billion
**National name:** Al Mamlaka al Urduniya al Hashemiyah
**Freedom House classifications:** Capitalist industrial, non-party traditional

**Geography.** The Middle Eastern country of Jordan is bordered on the west by Israel and the Dead Sea, on the north by Syria, on the east by Iraq, and on the south Saudi Arabia. It is comparable in size to Indiana.

Arid hills and mountains make up most of the country. The southern section of the Jordan River flows through the country.

**Government.** Jordan is a constitutional monarchy with a bicameral parliament. Its Chamber of Deputies of 60 members is elected for four years by the people, and the 30 members of the senate are appointed by the King.

All political parties were banned in 1957.

**History.** In biblical times, the country that is now Jordan contained the lands of Edom, Moab, Ammon, and Bashan. In A.D. 106 it became part of the Roman province of Arabia and in 633–36 was conquered by the Arabs.

Taken from the Turks by the British in World War I, Jordan (formerly known as Transjordan) was separated from the Palestine mandate in 1920, and in 1921, placed under the rule of Abdullah ibn Hussein.

In 1923, the U.K. recognized Jordan's independence, subject to the mandate. In 1946, grateful for

1. Includes territory occupied by Israel in 1967 war.

Jordan's loyalty in World War II, U.K. abolished the mandate. That part of Palestine occupied by Jordanian troops was formally incorporated by action of the Jordanian Parliament on April 24, 1950. Jordan's rejection of the Baghdad Pact in December 1955 set off a period of instability.

Abdullah was assassinated June 20, 1951. His son Talal was deposed as mentally ill on Aug. 11, 1952. Talal's son Hussein, born May 2, 1935, succeeded him.

King Hussein, formally enthroned May 2, 1953, sought close association with the U.S. and the U.K. to get aid against nationalists seeking union with the United Arab Republic. The government's decision to join the Central Treaty Organization (then the Baghdad Pact) in 1955 caused riots. Israel's invasion of the U.A.R. and the intervention by U.K. and France at the Suez strengthened the nationalists. An agreement on Oct. 25, 1956, put the Jordanian Army under the nominal command of an Egyptian, supreme commander of the armies of Syria and the U.A.R.

The break-up of the U.A.R. in September 1961 reduced the threat to Hussein, who was the first to recognize Syria when it withdrew from the U.A.R. Hussein established diplomatic relations with the U.S.S.R. in 1966. In that year Israel charged Jordan was sheltering terrorists who raided Israel. In the six-day Israeli-Arab war of June 1967, Jordan lost the old city of Jerusalem and territory west of the Jordan River.

The power of the Palestinian guerrillas grew until they mocked the throne and the army. Clashes occurred and after the guerrillas hijacked four Western airliners in September 1970 a full-scale civil war ensued. Thousands of casualties were reported.

Syria intervened with tanks on the side of the guerrillas. Apparently the Jordanians defeated the Syrians alone, but the U.S. implicitly threatened to intervene on Hussein's side unless the Syrians withdrew. About 20,000 U.S. troops in Europe were alerted, and the U.S. Seventh Fleet in the Eastern Mediterranean was reinforced before the U.S.S.R. urged the Syrians to pull back. Another factor was Israeli armor massing on the Golan Heights to strike into Syria if she did not leave Jordan. The 12,000 Iraqi troops in Jordan since the 1967 war were asked to leave by Hussein, now clearly in control of his country. He ignored calls, demands, and warnings from other Arab countries to go easy on the guerrillas and by mid-1971 had crushed the Palestinians to the point where some fled to Israeli jails in preference to those of fellow Arabs.

The U.S. supplied an average of $30 million annually in military arms to keep Jordan secure. In the Arab-Israeli war of 1973, Jordan remained virtually aloof from the fighting.

At an Arab summit conference in Rabat, Morocco, in October 1974, Hussein concurred in resolutions calling for creation of an independent Palestinian state on any land liberated from Israel and recognizing the Palestinian Liberation Organization as "the sole legitimate representative of the Palestinian people."

Despite Rabat, growing Arab dissatisfaction with the PLO and the continued refusal of Israel to negotiate with the guerrillas brought a reversal of the situation by 1977. Arab states proposed that a Palestinian state on the West Bank of the Jordan be linked with Jordan to make it more acceptable to Israel. Hussein and Yasser Arafat, leader of the PLO, met to reconcile their differences in March and Hussein once again referred publicly to the unity of the people on both banks of the river. The King celebrated on August 11 the 25th anniversary of his accession to the throne, a survivor of one of the more fiery furnaces of Middle East politics.

On June 15, 1978, Hussein married Elizabeth Halaby, 26, daughter of Najeeb Halaby, former president of Pan American World Airways. In an unexpected gesture, the monarch's fourth wife—his previous wife was killed and the first two divorced—was proclaimed Queen and given the name Noor al-Hussein.

**Economy.** Agriculture and tourism constitute Jordan's main sources of national income. The area of cultivable land is estimated at 4,000 square miles. Agricultural products are grains, cereals, vegetables, and fruits such as bananas, citrus fruits, grapes, quinces, pears, apples, peaches, almonds, figs, and olives. The Ghor area, which is situated on both banks of the Jordan River, has the most fertile land. Limited but growing mineral exploitation also contributes to Jordan's national income. Minerals include phosphates, marble, and potash.

Industry is expanding in Jordan. There are now industries producing canned vegetables, cement, cigarettes, aluminum products, and other light consumer goods.

Chief exports in 1975 were phosphates (40%), oranges (11%), and vegetables (6%). Leading customers in 1976 were Saudi Arabia (11%), Syria (9%), Iran (9%), Kuwait (5%). Leading suppliers were West Germany (17%), U.S. (9%), U.K. (8%), Japan (7%), Italy (6%).

## KAMPUCHEA

**See Cambodia**

## KENYA

**Republic of Kenya**
**Acting President:** Daniel Arap Moi (1978)
**Area:** 224,960 sq mi. (582,646 sq km)
**Population (est. 1978):** 14,800,000
**Density per square mile:** 65.8
**Capital:** Nairobi
**Largest cities (est. 1976 by U.N.):** Nairobi, 736,000; Mombasa, 351,000
**Monetary unit:** Kenyan shilling
**Languages:** Swahili (official), Bantu, Kikuyu, English
**Religions:** Protestant, 36%; Roman Catholic, 22%; Islam, 6%; Animist
**Gross national product 1976):** $3.3 billion
**Member of Commonwealth of Nations**
**Freedom House classifications:** Capitalist pre-industrial, one-party nationalist

**Geography.** Kenya lies on the equator in east central Africa on the coast of the Indian Ocean. It is twice the size of Nevada. Kenya's neighbors are Tanzania, Uganda, the Sudan, Ethiopia, and Somalia.

In the north, the land is arid; the southwestern corner is in the fertile Lake Victoria Basin; and a length of the eastern depression of Great Rift Valley separates western highlands from those that rise from the lowland coastal strip. Large game reserves have been developed.

**Government.** Under its Constitution of 1963, amended in 1964, Kenya has a one-house National Assembly of 171 members, elected for five years by universal adult suffrage. Since 1969, the President has been chosen by the public through a general election.

The Kenya African National Union, led by the President, is the only political party.

President Jomo Kenyatta died in his sleep on August 22, 1978. Vice President Daniel Arap Moi was sworn in as Acting President for 90 days pending election of a new President.

**History.** Kenya, formerly a British colony and protectorate, was made a crown colony in 1920. The whites' domination of the rich plateau area, the White Highlands, long regarded by the Kikiyu people as their territory, was a factor leading to native terrorism, called the Mau Mau movement, in 1952. In 1954 the British began preparing the territory for African rule and independence. In 1961 Jomo Kenyatta was freed from banishment to become leader of the Kenya African National Union.

Internal self-government was granted in 1963; Kenya became an independent republic on Dec. 12, 1963, with Kenyatta the first President. Kenya obtained economic and technical assistance from Communist China beginning in 1964 and later a World Bank loan.

In 1967 Kenya, Uganda, and Tanzania agreed to establish an East African trading community and a development bank. Kenya also sought to end dominance of retail trade by the Indian community of 188,000. In 1968 it began a drive against the Asians, and 20,000 left the country. In 1972, Kenyatta ordered all Asians with Kenyan passports to leave, allegedly for foreign-currency manipulations.

Kenya's relations with Uganda and Tanzania, her partners in a once closely cooperating East African Community, continued to deteriorate in 1977. Uganda's Idi Amin, embittered since Kenya's ill-concealed aid to Israel in mounting the July 4, 1976, raid on Entebbe airport, made new charges of Kenyan aggression and participation in plots against him. Tanzania closed its border April 18 in a dispute over division of the assets of East African Airways, which began with Kenya's unilateral withdrawal from the trilateral venture in February.

**Economy.** The country is predominantly agricultural, and a large area is cultivated by Europeans. The altitude ranges from sea level to more than 9,000 feet, allowing for tropical, subtropical, and temperate climate crops.

The principal agricultural products are coffee, tea, and sisal. Minerals include gold, silver, salt, and sodium carbonate.

Chief exports in 1976 were coffee (37%), petroleum products (12%), tea (12%), and fruit and vegetables (6%). Leading customers were West Germany (13%), U.K. (11%), Tanzania (10%), Uganda (10%), U.S. (6%), Netherlands (5%). Leading suppliers were U.K. (19%), Iran (17%), Japan (11%), West Germany (10%), Saudi Arabia (6%), U.S. (6%).

## KOREA, NORTH

**Democratic People's Republic of Korea**
**President:** Marshal Kim Il Sung (1948)
**Premier:** Li Jong-ok (1977)
**Area:** 46,540 sq mi. (120,538 sq km)
**Population (est. 1978):** 17,000,000
**Density per square mile:** 365.3
**Capital and largest city (est. 1976):** Pyongyang, 1,500,000
**Monetary unit:** Won
**Language:** Korean
**Religions:** None
**National name:** Chosun Minchu-chui Inmin Konghwa-guk
**Gross national product (1976):** $7.6 billion
**Freedom House classifications:** Socialist industrial, one-party communist

**Geography.** Korea is a 600-mile peninsula jutting from Manchuria and China (and a small portion of the U.S.S.R.) into the Sea of Japan and the Yellow Sea off eastern Asia. North Korea occupies an area slightly smaller than Pennsylvania north of the 38th parallel.

The country is almost completely covered by a series of north-south mountain ranges separated by narrow valleys. The Yalu River forms part of the northern border with Manchuria.

**Government.** The elected Supreme People's Assembly, as the chief organ of government, chooses a Presidium and a Cabinet. The Cabinet, which exercises executive authority, is subject to approval by the Assembly and the Presidium.

The Korean Workers (Communist) Party, led by President Kim Il Sung, is the only political party.

**History.** According to myth, Korea was founded in 2333 B.C. by Tangun. In the 17th century, it became a vassal of China and was isolated from all but Chinese influence and contact until 1876, when Japan forced Korea to negotiate a commercial treaty, opening the land to the U. S. and Europe. Japan achieved control as the result of its war with China (1894–95) and with Russia (1904–05) and annexed Korea in 1910. Japan developed the country but never won over the Korean nationalists.

After the Japanese surrender in 1945, the country was divided into two occupation zones, the U.S.S.R. north of and the U.S. south of the 38th parallel. When the cold war developed between the U.S. and U.S.S.R., trade between the zones was cut off. In 1948, the division between the zones was made permanent with the establishment of separate regimes in the north and south. By mid-1949, the U.S. and U.S.S.R. withdrew all troops. The Democratic People's Republic of Korea (North Korea) was established on May 1, 1948. The Communist Party, headed by Kim Il Sung, was established in power.

On June 25, 1950, the North Korean Army launched a surprise attack on South Korea. On June 26, the U.N. Security Council condemned the invasion as aggression and ordered withdrawal of the invading forces. On June 27, U.S. President Truman ordered air and naval units into action to enforce the U.N. order. The British government did the same and soon a multinational U.N. command was set up to aid the South Koreans. The North Korean invaders took Seoul and pushed the South Koreans into the southeast corner of their country.

Gen. Douglas MacArthur, U.N. commander, made an amphibious landing at Inchon on September 15 behind the North Korean lines, which resulted in the complete rout of the North Korean Army. The U.N. forces drove north across the 38th parallel, approaching the Yalu River. Then Communist China entered the war, forcing the U.N. forces into headlong retreat. Seoul was lost again, then regained; ultimately the war stabilized near the 38th parallel but dragged on for two years while the belligerents negotiated. An armistice was achieved July 27, 1953.

In 1966, North Korea proclaimed its ideological independence from both Moscow and Peking, a move that in effect aligned North Korea with the U.S.S.R. North Korea became embroiled with the

U.S. again on Jan. 23, 1968, when it seized the American intelligence ship *Pueblo* and its crew of 83. After more than a year, the crew was released.

On July 4, 1972, North and South Korea announced an agreement to work for peaceful reunification. A series of talks failed to produce concrete results and, on April 19, 1975, President Kim Il Sung declared during a Peking visit that Korean peace would depend on withdrawal of U.S. troops from the South.

When a U.S. helicopter strayed across the 38th parallel July 13, 1977, and was shot down by North Koreans, with the loss of three crewmen, the reaction was much more restrained. President Carter acknowledged U.S. error and, after seven hours of talks at Panmunjom, the North Koreans sent back the three bodies and the lone survivor. The absence of invective was attributed to Northern appreciation of the withdrawal plan for U.S. forces in the South and there were reports that Kim wished to open direct contact with the Carter administration.

Although Kim appears to be revered, economic troubles have beset his rigidly collectivist country. World bankers say a record of unpaid accounts due the U.S.S.R., as well as non-Communist states, has demolished North Korea's international credit standing. Its armed forces, numbering 467,000, are about three fourths of the South's military establishment, but the North's 600-plane air force holds a 3-to-1 edge over its potential foes, who have relied on U.S. air support in the event of war.

**Economy.** The chief agricultural products of North Korea are rice, corn, and other grains. The chief industrial products are pig iron, steel, rolled metals, cement, fertilizers, and electricity. The chief mineral products are coal and iron ore.

Chief exports in 1965 were metals (zinc, lead, magnesite, steel) (50%), minerals (12%), and farm produce (11%). Leading customers in 1975 were China (60%), U.S.S.R. (17%), Japan (5%). Leading suppliers were China (30%), U.S.S.R. (20%), Japan (13%).

## KOREA, SOUTH

**Republic of Korea**
**President:** Park Chung Hee (1963)
**Premier:** Choi Kyu Ha (1975)
**Area:** 38,022 sq mi. (98,484 sq km)
**Population (est. 1978):** 37,000,000
**Density per square mile:** 973.1
**Capital:** Seoul
**Largest cities (1975 census):** Seoul, 6,899,470; Pusan, 2,454,051; Taegu, 1,311,078; Inchon, 799,982; Kwangju, 607,058; Taujon, 506,703; Chonju, 311,432.
**Monetary unit:** Won
**Language:** Korean
**Religions:** Buddhist, Confucianist, Taoist, Christian
**Gross national product (1976):** $25.1 billion
**National name:** Han Kook
**Freedom House classifications:** Capitalist industrial, multi-party centralized

**Geography.** Slightly larger than Indiana, South Korea lies below the 38th parallel on the Korean peninsula. It is mountainous in the east; in the west and south are many harbors on the mainland and offshore islands.

**Government.** The Constitution, modified by President Park in 1972, provides for a one-house legislature. The National Assembly has 219 members, two thirds of whom are elected by direct popular vote for six-year terms and the rest appointed by the President for three-year terms.

The Constitution was also amended to allow Park to run for re-election indefinitely (initially there was a two-term limit) and to extend the presidential terms from four to six years each. Park was re-elected to his fourth term in 1972. Instead of popular vote, the President is now chosen by between 2,000 and 5,000 electors, who are elected by popular vote. Park now may also reduce parliament's powers and curb civil liberties by decree.

The major political parties are the Democratic Republican Party (68 of 219 seats in the National Assembly), led by President Park; New Democratic Party (57 seats); Democratic Unification Party (3 seats); and 14 independents. Beyond this election result (1973), Park appointed 73 supporters to the Assembly, of whom at least 25 were aligned with his Democratic Republican Party.

**History.** South Korea came into being in the aftermath of World War II as the result of a 1945 agreement making the 38th parallel the boundary between a northern zone occupied by the U.S.S.R. and a southern zone occupied by U.S. forces. (For details, *see* North Korea.)

Elections were held in the U.S. zone on May 10, 1948 for a national assembly, which on July 12 adopted a republican Constitution and on July 20 elected Syngman Rhee President. The new republic was proclaimed on August 15 and was recognized as the legal government of Korea by the U.N. General Assembly on Dec. 12, 1948.

On June 25, 1950, South Korea was attacked by North Korean Communist forces. U.S. armed intervention was ordered on June 27 by President Truman, and on the same day the U.N. invoked military sanctions against North Korea. Gen. Douglas MacArthur was named commander of the U.N. forces on July 7. U.S. and South Korean troops fought a heroic holding action but, by the first week of August, they had been forced back to a 4,000-square-mile beachhead in southeast Korea.

There they stood off superior North Korean forces until September 15, when a major U.N. amphibious attack was launched far behind the Communist lines at Inchon, port of Seoul. By September 30, U.N. forces were in complete control of South Korea. They then invaded North Korea and were nearing the Manchurian and Siberian borders when several hundred thousand Chinese Communist troops entered the conflict in late October. U.N. forces were then forced to retreat below the 38th parallel.

On May 24, 1951, U.N. forces recrossed the parallel and had made important new inroads into North Korea when truce negotiations began on July 10. An armistice was finally signed at Panmunjom on July 27, 1953, leaving a devastated Korea in need of large-scale rehabilitation. The armistice contemplated an international political conference on the status of Korea, but negotiations for arranging it broke down.

The U.S. and South Korea signed a mutual-defense treaty on Oct. 1, 1953.

Syngman Rhee, President since his election in 1948, resigned on April 27, 1960, in the face of rising disorders.

Posun Yun was elected to succeed Rhee as President, but political instability continued. In 1961, Gen. Park Chung Hee took power in a coup. He built up the country, maintaining an average growth rate in the economy of 8.5%. The U.S.

stepped up military aid, building up South Korea's armed forces to 600,000 men. The South Koreans sent 50,000 troops to Vietnam, most of their cost paid by the U.S.

In mid-1972, following President Nixon's summit meetings in Moscow and Peking, the two Koreas issued a mutual declaration setting a goal of peaceful reunification. (For details, *see* North Korea).

The prospective détente with North Korea failed to materialize, and agitation against Park's repressive regime was on the rise when President Ford visited the country Nov. 22–23, 1974. In talks with Park, Mr. Ford affirmed that U.S. forces would remain in South Korea and supported negotiations for unification of the country.

An announcement by President Carter on March 9, 1977, that he would withdraw U.S. ground troops from South Korea within four to five years brought protests from both the Park government and opposition leaders. A U.S. pledge of $2 billion in arms aid—close to the estimated amount of savings in the troop reduction—together with a commitment that U.S. air and naval forces would stay indefinitely appeared to have reassured Koreans.

Tension between Seoul and Washington also arose over human rights as South Korean dissidents appealed for U.S. support in their demands that Park rescind both the 1972 Constitution and his 1975 emergency powers. U.S. Secretary of State Cyrus Vance told a Congressional committee Feb. 24, 1977, of his "great concern" about the human rights situation, but said the strategic importance of South Korea precluded aid cuts like those made in other countries guilty of rights abuses. Park responded to pressure by releasing 14 political detainees, including several Christian leaders, but not Kim Dae Jung, a former opposition presidential candidate kidnapped from Tokyo in 1973 by the Korean Central Intelligence Agency.

A growing scandal over Korean bribery of U.S. Congressmen accelerated in 1977 with testimony by a defecting ex-Director of the KCIA who named a Washington influence man, Tongsun Park, as a KCIA agent. Two former Democratic Representatives, Richard T. Hanna of California and Otto E. Passman of Louisiana, were indicted in 1978 for accepting bribes, with Hanna sentenced to six months in prison.

A Congressional investigation on July 13 charged four sitting Democratic Representatives, Charles H. Wilson, Edward R. Roybal, and John J. McFall of California, and Edward J. Patten of New Jersey, with having accepted money improperly from Park. The House June 22 voted 273–125 to cut $56 million in food aid for Korea because President Park had refused to permit his former Ambassador to the U.S., Kim Dong Jo, to testify before Congressional committees. But other, larger aid programs were not reduced.

**Economy.** South Korea, with 43% of the peninsula's area and over two thirds of its population, is predominantly agricultural. The major agricultural products are rice, barley, sweet potatoes, and yams. Although industrial development was speeded in the peninsula during the last years of Japanese rule, by far the smaller part of the industry is located in South Korea.

Mineral products include iron ore, copper ore, tungsten, graphite, kaolin, talc, fluorite, limestone, coal, gold, and silver.

Chief exports in 1975 were clothing (23%), textile yarns and fabrics (13%), electrical machinery and equipment (9%), fish (7%), and iron and steel (5%). Leading customers were U.S. (32%), Japan (23%), West Germany (5%). Leading suppliers were Japan (35%), U.S. (22%), Saudi Arabia (8%), Kuwait (8%).

## KUWAIT

**State of Kuwait**
**Emir:** Sheik Jaber al-Ahmad al-Sabah (1978)
**Prime Minister:** Sheik Sa'ad Abdullah al-Sabah (1978)
**Area:** 6,880 sq mi. (17,818 sq km)
**Population (est. 1978):** 1,190,000
**Density per square mile:** 173.0
**Capital (est. 1975):** Al-Kuwait, 78,000
**Largest city (est. 1975):** Hawalli, 130,300
**Monetary unit:** Kuwaiti dinar
**Languages:** Arabic and English
**Religions:** Islam, 95%; Christian, 5%
**Gross national product (1976):** $16.5 billion
**National name:** Dowlat al Kuwait
**Freedom House classifications:** Capitalist-statist industrial, non-party traditional

**Geography.** Kuwait is situated northeast of Saudi Arabia at the northern end of the Persian Gulf, south of Iraq. It is slightly larger than Hawaii. The low-lying land is mainly sandy and barren.

**Government.** Sheik Jaber al-Ahmad al-Sabah rules as Emir of Kuwait and appoints the Prime Minister, who appoints his Cabinet (Council of Ministers). The National Assembly, consisting of 50 members elected by adult males, has been suspended. Servicemen and policemen are not eligible to vote. There are no political parties in Kuwait.

**History.** Kuwait obtained British protection in 1897 when the Sheik feared that the Turks would take over the area. In 1961, Britain ended the protectorate, giving Kuwait independence, but agreed to give military aid on request. Iraq immediately threatened to occupy the area and Sheik Sabah al-Salem al-Sabah called in British troops in July 1961. Soon afterward the Arab League sent in troops replacing the British. The prize was oil.

Oil was discovered in the 1930s. Kuwait proved to have 20% of the world's known oil resources. It has been a major producer since 1946, the world's second largest oil exporter, with the main concession held by a British-American concern. The Sheik, who gets half the profits, devotes most of them for the education, welfare, and modernization of his kingdom. In 1966, Sheik Sabah designated a relative, Jaber al-Ahmad al-Sabah, as his successor. By 1968 the sheikdom had established a model welfare state, and it sought to establish dominance among the sheikdoms and emirates of the Persian Gulf.

Kuwait contributed handsomely to Egypt and Jordan after the 1967 war with Israel and supported the 1973 war against Israel with funds and by joining the Arab oil boycott of Western nations.

Quadrupling of prices following the embargo sent Kuwait's oil profits rocketing from $2 billion in 1973 to almost $9 billion in 1974, with $7 billion estimated for 1975, when the oil output was reduced somewhat. With per capita income at about $11,000—nearly twice that of the U.S.—little Kuwait became an overnight financial power. It financed domestic improvements on a lavish scale, sponsored a foreign-aid program for favored Arab and African states, and ploughed over $10 billion into profitable corporate investments overseas.

In March 1975, the government nationalized

Kuwaiti operations of Gulf Oil and British Petroleum. The acquisition, which cost about $180 million, gave Kuwait full control of an estimated 60 billion barrels of petroleum reserves.

**Economy.** Chief exports in 1975 were crude oil (75%) and petroleum products (17%). Leading customers were Japan (25%), Netherlands (9%), U.K. (8%), France (6%), Brazil (5%). Leading suppliers were U.S. (18%), Japan (16%), West Germany (11%), U.K. (10%), Italy (5%).

## LAOS

**Lao People's Democratic Republic**
**President:** Souphanouvong (1975)
**Prime Minister:** Kaysone Phomvihane (1975)
**Area:** 91,429 sq mi. (236,800 sq km)
**Population (est. 1978):** 3,540,000
**Density per square mile:** 38.7
**Capital and largest city (est. 1973):** Vientiane, 176,600
**Monetary unit:** New kip
**Languages:** Lao (official); French, English
**Religion:** Buddhist
**Gross national product (1976):** $310 million
**Freedom House classifications:** Socialist pre-industrial, one-party communist

**Geography.** A landlocked nation in Southeast Asia occupying the northwestern portion of the Indochinese peninsula, Laos is surrounded by China, Vietnam, Cambodia, Thailand, and Burma. It is twice the size of Pennsylvania.

Laos is a mountainous country, especially in the north, where peaks rise above 8,000 feet (2,438 m). Dense forests cover the northern and eastern areas. The Mekong River flows through the country for 300 miles (483 km) of its course.

**Government.** Laos is a People's Democratic Republic with executive power in the hands of the Premier. The monarchy was abolished Dec. 2, 1975, when the Pathet Lao ousted a coalition government and King Sisavang Vatthana abdicated. The King was appointed "Supreme Adviser" to the President, the former Prince Souphanouvong. Former Prince Souvanna Phouma, Premier since 1962, was made an "adviser" to the government. The Lao People's Revolutionary Party (the Pathet Lao), led by President Souphanouvong and Premier Kaysone Phomvihane, is the only political party.

**History.** Laos became a French protectorate in 1893, and the territory was incorporated into the union of Indo-China. A strong nationalist movement developed during World War II, but France re-established control in 1946 and made the King of Luang Prabang constitutional monarch of all Laos. France granted semiautonomy in 1949 and then, spurred by the Viet Minh rebellion in Vietnam, full independence within the French Union in 1950. In 1951, Prince Souphanouvong organized the Pathet Lao, a Communist independence movement, in North Vietnam. The Viet Minh in 1953 established the Pathet Lao in power at Samneua. Viet Minh and Pathet Lao forces invaded central Laos, and civil war resulted.

By the Geneva Agreements of 1954 and an armistice of 1955, two northern provinces were given the Pathet Lao, the royal regime the rest. Full sovereignty was given the kingdom by the Paris agreements of Dec. 29, 1954. In 1957, Prince Souvanna Phouma, the royal Premier, and the Pathet Lao leader, Prince Souphanouvong, the Premier's half-brother, agreed to re-establishment of a unified government with Pathet Lao participation and integration of Pathet Lao forces into the royal army. The agreement broke down in 1959, and armed conflict broke out again.

In 1960, the struggle became three-way as Gen. Phoumi Nosavan, controlling the bulk of the royal army, set up in the south a pro-Western revolutionary government headed by Prince Boun Gum. General Phoumi took Vientiane in December 1960, driving Souvanna Phouma into exile in Cambodia. The Soviet bloc supported Souvanna Phouma. In May 1961, a cease-fire was arranged and, in October, the three princes agreed to a coalition government headed by Souvanna Phouma.

But North Vietnam, the U.S. (in the form of Central Intelligence Agency personnel), and China remained active in Laos after the settlement. North Vietnam used a supply line (Ho Chi Minh trail) running down the mountain valleys of eastern Laos into Cambodia and South Vietnam, particularly after the U.S.-South Vietnamese incursion into Cambodia in 1970 stopped supplies via Cambodian seaports.

An agreement, reached in September 1973 and implemented the following April, revived coalition government. Royal Laotian rule continued in populous areas, the Pathet Lao controlled the mountainous east, and the two groups exercised joint rule over Vientiane Province. With Souvanna Phouma as Premier and Souphanouvong as President of a 42-member National Political Council representing both factions, joint operation of the government began.

On March 12, 1977, former King Sisavang Vatthana and his family were arrested at the old royal capital of Luang Prabang as royalist Meo tribesmen attacked government forces near the town. March 19 and 20, an official U.S. mission led by Leonard Woodcock reported "substantial improvement in atmosphere" after a discussion of the return of missing servicemen's bodies, but Laotian officials insisted, like their Vietnamese counterparts, that the question be linked to U.S. aid.

**Economy.** About 95% of the Laotians are farmers. The chief food crop is rice; other crops are maize, vegetables, cotton, cardamom, and tobacco.

Chief exports in 1974 were timber (81%) and tin (11%). Leading customers were Thailand (73%), Malaysia (11%), Hong Kong (10%). Leading suppliers were Thailand (49%), Japan (19%), France (7%), West Germany (7%), U.S. (5%).

## LEBANON

**Republic of Lebanon**
**President:** Elias Sarkis (1976)
**Premier:** Selim al-Hoss (1976)
**Area:** 4,015 sq mi. (10,400 sq km)
**Population (est. 1978):** 3,165,000 (Arabian and Armenian).
**Density per square mile:** 788.3
**Capital:** Beirut
**Largest cities (est. 1975):** Beirut, 1,172,000; (est. 1964): Tripoli, 127,611
**Monetary unit:** Lebanese pound
**Languages:** Arabic (official); French, English
**Religions:** Christian and Islam
**National name:** Al-Joumhouriya al-Lubnaniya
**Freedom House classifications:** Capitalist industrial, multi-party decentralized

**Geography.** Lebanon lies at the eastern end of the Mediterranean Sea north of Israel and west of

Syria. It is four fifths the size of Connecticut.

The Lebanon Mountains, which parallel the coast on the west, cover most of the country, while on the eastern border is the Anti-Lebanon range. Between the two lies the El Bika Valley, the principal agricultural area.

**Government.** Lebanon is governed by a President, elected by Parliament for a six-year term, and a Cabinet of Ministers appointed by the President but responsible to Parliament.

Parliament has 99 members elected for a four-year term by universal suffrage and chosen by proportional division of religious groups.

Party breakdown of the Chamber of Deputies is difficult because of the religious groupings required by law and because of the fact that many deputies join in major parliamentary blocs—Democratic Front, Tri-Partite Coalition, and National Struggle Front. The parties represented in Parliament are: Al-Kataib, led by Pierre Al-Jumayeh; Al-Wataniyin Al-Ahrar, led by Camille Chamoun; Al-Takadumi Al-Ishteraki; Al-Kutla Al-Wataniya, led by Raymond Edde; Al-Dimocrati Al-Eshteraki, led by Kamel El-Assad.

**History.** In ancient times Lebanon was the mountainous hinterland of the Phoenician coast towns. From the 7th to the 11th century there infiltrated into southern Lebanon the heretics of Islam, who finally coalesced into the Druse community.

In the 19th century the Turkish Sultanate encouraged the Druses to wage civil war against the Christian Maronites. After a massacre of 2,500 Christians in 1860, Lebanon was occupied by the French for a year. From 1864 to 1914, a Christian military government ruled the area under nominal Turkish sovereignty. After World War I, France received a League of Nations mandate over Syria and Lebanon. The French drew a Lebanese border in 1920 to offset predominantly Moslem Syria and proclaimed the area a republic under French control on May 23, 1926. Complete independence came on Nov. 26, 1941. Lebanon joined the Arab League and took part in the invasion of Palestine on May 15, 1948.

In May 1958, a civil war broke out, with the Moslems Kamal Jumblatt and Saeb Salam leading the opposition to the Maronite Christian government. Threatened with defeat, President Camille Chamoun obtained the intervention of the U.S. military forces. In September 1958, a Maronite Christian military man, Gen. Fouad Chehab, took over the presidency. After a U.N. resolution demanded it, the U.S. forces withdrew.

Palestinian guerrillas using Lebanese territory drew Lebanon into conflict with Israel. Terrorist attacks on Israeli airliners led to an Israeli raid on Arab airlines at Beirut, and terrorist assaults on Israel's northern settlements drew punitive raids against guerrillas in Lebanon by Israeli army and air units. Lebanon appeared powerless.

In May and June 1975, repeated clashes between guerrilla sympathizers and conservative Christian Phalangist militiamen left more than 400 dead in street fighting in Beirut.

Intensifying civil war through 1976 led to the ousting of President Suleiman Franjieh by Parliament in May after the virtual destruction of Beirut. Franjieh refused to step down until the end of his six-year term in October when his successor, Elias Sarkis, took office.

At the time of Sarkis' inauguration, Lebanon was divided into a northern sector, controlled by Syrian troops who had entered the country to restore order, and a coastal region under Christian control, with enclaves where leftist Moslems and the Palestine Liberation Organization dominated. With the economy shattered and an estimated 40,000 dead in 18 months of war, many felt that the country might be dismembered. Notwithstanding flare-ups of civil strife, an Arab League committee of Syria, Egypt, Saudi Arabia, and Kuwait appeared by mid-1977 to have stabilized a reunited Lebanon. Banks had reopened in January and reconstruction of Beirut began. Although Palestinian guerrilla strength had been reduced, those who remained in Lebanon still constituted a threat to peace and the Christian Lebanese Front called on the Arab League to resolve the problem of the Palestinians' "illegal presence."

A new crisis began for Lebanon on March 14, 1978, with the invasion of Israeli forces across the entire 60-mile northern border to a depth of from 4 to 10 miles. The invasion was in retaliation for a PLO terrorist raid on Israel and the chief targets were PLO bases in Southern Lebanon. On March 19, the U.N. Security Council called for immediate withdrawal and authorized a 4,000-man peacekeeping force to occupy the area, a force later enlarged to 6,000.

Israeli troops withdrew by June 13 but turned over more strongpoints to Lebanese Christian militia than to Unifil, the U.N. force. Israel protested that Unifil was allowing PLO guerrillas to return to their areas, where they threatened Israel as well as local Lebanese Christians.

By the summer, Syrian forces were attacking Christian strongholds and President Sarkis threatened to resign unless the killing stopped. Disorders continued with more than 200 civilians, mainly in the Christian districts of Beirut, estimated killed in July alone.

**Economy.** The civil war significantly damaged the Lebanese economy. Traditionally, Lebanon produces tobacco, olives, grapes and other fruits, wheat, and silk. Manufacturing is confined mainly to local consumers' goods. The silk industry is important in Beirut and Tripoli. Tobacco manufacturing is a government monopoly.

Chief exports in 1973 were machinery (14%), fruit and vegetables (12%), chemicals (8%), aircraft (6%), clothing (6%), textile yarns and fabrics (5%), and motor vehicles (5%). Leading customers were Saudi Arabia (15%), France (9%), U.K. (8%), Libya (7%), Kuwait (6%), Syria (5%). Leading suppliers were U.S. (12%), West Germany (11%), France (10%), Italy (10%), U.K. (8%).

## LESOTHO

**Kingdom of Lesotho**
**Sovereign:** King Moshoeshoe II (1966)
**Prime Minister:** Chief Leabua Jonathan (1966)
**Area:** 11,720 sq mi. (30,355 sq km)
**Population (est. 1977):** 1,090,000
**Density per square mile:** 93.0
**Capital and largest city (est. 1976):** Maseru, 14,700
**Monetary unit:** South African rand
**Languages:** English and Sesotho (official)
**Religions:** Roman Catholic (38.7%), Lesotho Evangelical Church (24.3%), Anglican (10.4%), non-Christian (18.2%).
**Gross national product (1976):** $210 million
**Member of Commonwealth of Nations**
**Freedom House classifications:** Capitalist pre-industrial, multi-party centralized

**Geography.** Mountainous Lesotho, the size of Maryland, is surrounded by the Republic of South Africa in the east central part of that country except for short borders on the east and south with two discontinuous units of the Republic of Transkei. The Drakensberg Mountains in the east are Lesotho's principal chain. Elsewhere the region consists of rocky tableland.

**Government.** There is a 93-member interim National Assembly made up of 60 representatives of various political parties, 22 leading chiefs, and 11 appointees.

The major political parties are the Basotho National Party, led by Prime Minister Jonathan and the Basutoland Congress Party led by G. P. Ramoreboli.

**History.** Lesotho (formerly Basutoland) was constituted a native state under British protection by a treaty signed with the native chief Moshesh in 1843. It was annexed to Cape Colony in 1871, but in 1884 it was restored to direct control by the crown.

The colony of Basutoland became the independent nation of Lesotho on Oct. 4, 1966.

In the January 1970 elections, Ntsu Mokhehle, then head of the Basutoland Congress Party, claimed a victory, but Jonathan declared a state of emergency, suspended the Constitution, and arrested Mokhehle. The major issue in the election was relations with South Africa, with Jonathan for close ties to the surrounding white nation, while Mokhehle was for more independent policy. Jonathan jailed 45 opposition politicians, declared the King had "technically abdicated" by siding with the opposition party, exiled him to the Netherlands in April, and named his Queen and her seven-year-old son as regent.

The King returned after a compromise with Jonathan in which the new Constitution would name him head of state but forbid his participation in politics.

**Economy.** Agricultural products include corn, wheat, and sorghum. Sheep raising is highly developed.

Chief exports in 1974 were wool (35%), mohair (16%), livestock (16%), and diamonds (9%). Leading customer and supplier is South Africa, which employs over 90,000 Lesotho miners. Various development programs supported by the European Economic Community and other countries have been announced.

## LIBERIA

**Republic of Liberia**
**President:** William R. Tolbert, Jr. (1971)
**Area:** 43,000 sq mi. (11,369 sq km)
**Population (est. 1978):** 1,850,000
**Density per square mile:** 43.0
**Capital and largest city (est. 1977):** Monrovia, 172,100
**Monetary unit:** Liberian dollar
**Languages:** English (official) and tribal dialects
**Religions:** Protestant Christian, Islam, Catholic, Animist
**Gross national product (1976):** $720 million
**Freedom House classifications:** Capitalist pre-industrial, one-party nationalist

**Geography.** Lying on the Atlantic in the southern part of west Africa, Liberia is bordered by Sierra Leone, Guinea, and the Ivory Coast. It is comparable in size to Tennessee.

Most of the country is a plateau covered by dense tropical forests, which thrive under an annual rainfall of about 160 inches a year.

**Government.** The President and the Vice President are popularly elected for a single eight-year term. The members of the House of Representatives are elected for four years and the members of the Senate for six years.

The True Whig Party is the only political party.

**History.** Liberia was founded in 1822 as a result of the efforts of the American Colonization Society to settle freed American slaves in west Africa. In 1847, it became the Free and Independent Republic of Liberia.

The government of Africa's first republic was modeled after that of the United States, and Joseph J. Roberts of Virginia was elected the first President. He laid the foundations of a modern state and initiated efforts, never too successful but pursued for more than a century, to bring the aboriginal inhabitants of the territory to the level of the emigrants. The English-speaking descendants of U.S. blacks, known as Americo-Liberians, are the intellectual and ruling class. The indigenous inhabitants, divided, constitute 99% of the population. The Americo-Liberians amount to only 0.8% of the population.

The country's only big enterprises are the million-acre concession granted in 1925 to the Firestone Plantations Co. for rubber cultivation, and a large iron ore concession developed by Republic Steel Corp., beginning in 1951. After 1920, considerable progress was made toward opening up the interior, a process that was spurred in 1951 by the establishment of a 43-mile railroad to the Bomi Hills from Monrovia.

In July 1971, while serving his sixth term as President of Africa's oldest independent republic, William V. S. Tubman died following surgery and was succeeded by his long-time associate, Vice President William R. Tolbert, Jr.

**Economy.** Agricultural products include rice, cassava, rubber, cocoa, and coffee. In 1977, new profit-sharing agreements with foreign concessionaires and increased foreign investment spurred the growth of the Liberian economy.

Chief exports in 1976 were iron ore (72%) and rubber (12%). Leading customers were West Germany (28%), U.S. (19%), Italy (14%), France (8%), Belgium-Luxembourg (8%), Netherlands (6%), Spain (5%). Leading suppliers were U.S. (30%), Saudi Arabia (13%), West Germany (12%), U.K. (8%), Japan (7%), Netherlands (6%).

## LIBYA

**People's Socialist Libyan Arab Public**
**Secretary-General of the General People's Congress:** Col. Muammar el-Qaddafi (1969)
**Premier:** Maj. Abdul Salam Jallud (1972)
**Area:** 679,362 sq mi. (1,759,540 sq km)
**Population (est. 1977):** 2,600,000
**Density per square mile:** 3.8
**Capital:** Tripoli
**Largest cities (1973 census):** Tripoli, 551,477; Bengasi, 282,192
**Monetary unit:** Libyan dinar
**Language:** Arabic

**Religion:** Islam
**Gross national product (1976):** $16.0 billion
**National name:** Al-Jumhuria al-Arabia al-Libya
**Freedom House classifications:** Capitalist-statist industrial, one-party socialist

**Geography.** Libya stretches along the northeastern coast of Africa between Tunisia and Algeria on the west and Egypt on the east; to the south are Chad and Niger. It is one sixth larger than Alaska.

A greater part of the country lies within the Sahara. There are many oases along the Mediterranean coast; farther inland is arable plateau land.

**Government.** In a bloodless coup d'etat on Sept. 1, 1969, the military seized power in Libya. King Idris I, who had ruled since 1951, was deposed and the Libyan Arab Republic proclaimed. The official name was changed in 1977 to People's Socialist Libyan Arab Public. The Revolutionary Council that had governed since the coup was renamed the General Secretariat of the General People's Congress. The Arab Socialist Union Organization is the only political party.

**History.** Libya was a part of the Turkish dominions from the 16th century until 1911. Following the outbreak of hostilities between Italy and Turkey in that year, Italian troops occupied Tripoli; Italian sovereignty was recognized in 1912.

Libya was the scene of much desert fighting during World War II. After the fall of Tripoli on Jan. 23, 1943, it came under Allied administration. The United Nations General Assembly voted on Nov. 21, 1949, that Libya should become independent by 1952.

Discovery of oil in the Libyan Desert promised financial stability and funds for economic development. Although maintaining cordial relations with the U.S., the government asked for evacuation of the U.S. Wheelus air base by 1971. The first crude oil moved in January 1967 through the 320-mile pipeline from the Sarir oil field to Tobruk, where it was loaded on British tankers. The flow was halted in June 1967, when Libya joined the Arab oil boycott of the U.K. and U.S. as a result of the Middle Eastern war but was soon resumed thereafter.

President Muammar el-Qaddafi attacked Egypt's conduct of the 1973 war with Israel, and Egypt accused Qaddafi, a very volatile person, of financing an attempted coup against President Anwar el-Sadat in 1974. Qaddafi, in April 1974, gave up his domestic political powers to Premier Abdul Salam Jallud, but remained Libya's leader in foreign affairs.

In May 1975, following a visit by Soviet Premier Alexei N. Kosygin, a major deal for Soviet arms sales to Libya, reported to involve $1 billion to $4 billion in modern military equipment, was concluded. It was followed by a Soviet agreement to supply Libya with a nuclear research reactor in the 2–10 megawatt range.

On July 21, 1977, a four-day war broke out between Libya and Egypt, with Egypt charging that Libyans had attacked a frontier post. Superior Egyptian air power and armor inflicted losses on their opponents and the clash ended after Algerian President Houari Boumédienne intervened as peacemaker.

On Feb. 20, 1978, Libya announced a cease-fire in the 13-year guerrilla war by Frolinat, the Chad National Liberation Front, against the Chadian government in which Libya had aided the rebels. Four days later, Qaddafi and leaders of Chad, the Sudan, and Niger signed an agreement to end the war, but by April there were reports of renewed fighting.

**Economy.** Animal husbandry, which was the basic economic activity of Libya, has been superseded by petroleum and natural gas.

Agriculture is possible only in the Mediterranean coastal region, where dates, olives, citrus fruit, wheat, and barley are grown, and in oases in the Fezzan and elsewhere; here the principal product is dates.

Sponge and tuna fisheries are carried on off the Libyan coast.

The chief export in 1975 was crude oil (100%). Leading customers were U.S. (22%), Italy (22%), West Germany (19%), Spain (5%). Leading suppliers were Italy (26%), West Germany (12%), France (9%), Japan (8%), U.K. (5%).

## LIECHTENSTEIN

**Principality of Liechtenstein**
**Ruler:** Prince Franz Josef II (1938)
**Prime Minister:** Hans Brunhart (1978).
**Area:** 61 sq mi. (157 sq km).
**Population (est. 1978):** 22,850.
**Density per square mile:** 374.6.
**Capital and largest city** (est. 1975: Vaduz, 4,500.
**Monetary unit:** Swiss franc.
**Language:** German (Alemannish dialect).
**Religion:** Roman Catholic.

**Geography.** Tiny Liechtenstein, not quite as large as Washington, D.C., lies on the east bank of the Rhine River south of Lake Constance between Austria and Switzerland. It consists of low valley land and Alpine peaks. Falknis (8,401 ft.; 2,561 m) and Naatkopf (8,432 ft.; 2,570 m) are the tallest.

**Government.** The Constitution of 1921, amended in 1972, provides for a legislature, the Landtag, of 15 members elected by direct suffrage.

The ruler, Prince Franz Josef II, was born in 1906 and succeeded his great uncle, Franz I, in 1938. In 1943 he married Countess Gina Wilczek of Austria.

The major political parties are the Homeland Union (8 of 15 seats in the Landtag) and the Progressive Citizens Party (7 seats).

**History.** Founded in 1719, Liechtenstein was a member of the German Confederation from 1815 to 1866, when it became an independent principality. It abolished its army in 1868 and has managed to stay neutral and undamaged in all European wars since then. It also remained free of ties until after World War I. Since then, it has been oriented toward Switzerland.

**Economy.** Liechtenstein adopted Swiss currency in 1921 and has been part of the Swiss Customs Union since 1924. Switzerland administers Liechtenstein's telegraph and postal services and its foreign affairs.

Wheat, wine, and fruit are the chief agricultural products. There are small manufactures of cotton products, leather, and pottery.

Registration of foreign firms in the country is a source of tax income.

Chief exports in 1975 were metal manufactures, furniture, and pottery. Leading customers were Switzerland (41%), EEC (27%), EFTA (other than Switzerland) (9%).

## LUXEMBOURG

**Grand Duchy of Luxembourg**
**Ruler:** Grand Duke Jean (1964)
**Premier:** Gaston Thorn (1974)
**Area:** 999 sq mi. (2,586 sq km)
**Population (est. 1978):** 370,000. (Luxembourgian, French, German)
**Density per square mile:** 370.4
**Capital and largest city (est. 1975):** Luxembourg, 78,300
**Monetary unit:** Luxembourg franc
**Languages:** Letzeburgesch, French, German
**Religion:** Mainly Roman Catholic
**Gross national product (1976):** $2.3 billion
**National name:** Grand-Duché de Luxembourg
**Freedom House classifications:** Capitalist industrial, multi-party centralized

**Geography.** Luxembourg is a neighbor of Belgium on the west, Germany on the east, and France on the south. The Ardennes Mountains extend from Belgium into the northern section of Luxembourg.

**Government.** Luxembourg's unicameral legislature, the Chamber of Deputies, consists of 59 members elected for five years.

The major political parties are the Christian Social Party (18 of 59 seats in Chamber of Deputies), led by Jacques Senter; Socialist-Labor (17 seats), led by Lydie Schmit; Democratic Party (14 seats), led by Gaston Thorn; Social Democratic Party (5 seats), led by Henry Cravatte; Communist Party (5 seats), led by René Urbany.

**History.** Sigefroi, Count of Ardennes, an offspring of Charlemagne, was Luxembourg's first sovereign ruler. In 1060, the country came under the rule of the House of Luxembourg. From the 15th to the 18th century, Spain, France, and Austria held it in turn. The Congress of Vienna in 1815 made it a Grand Duchy and gave it to William I, King of the Netherlands. In 1839 the Treaty of London ceded the western part of Luxembourg to Belgium.

The eastern part, continuing in personal union with the Netherlands and a member of the German Confederation, became autonomous in 1848 and a neutral territory by decision of the London Conference of 1867, governed by its Grand Duke. Germany occupied the duchy in World Wars I and II. Allied troops liberated the enclave in 1944.

In 1961, Prince Jean, son and heir of Grand Duchess Charlotte, was made head of the state, acting for his mother. She abdicated in 1964, and Prince Jean became Grand Duke.

**Economy.** Because the soil is not very fertile, agriculture is not widely engaged in. Principal crops are potatoes, oats, wheat, rye, and grapes.

The mining and metallurgical industries, based on iron ore found in the south, are the most important.

By a customs union between Belgium and Luxembourg, which came into force on May 1, 1922, to last for 50 years, customs frontiers between the two countries were abolished. On Jan. 1, 1948, an economic union with Belgium and the Netherlands (Benelux) came into existence. Luxembourg's foreign-trade figures are included in those of Belgium, and no separate statistics are available. Exports consist chiefly of iron and steel products.

Luxembourg's prosperity depends largely on its steel mills.

## MADAGASCAR

**Democratic Republic of Madagascar**
**President and Head of State:** Comdr. Didier Ratsiraka (1975)
**Prime Minister:** Lt. Col. Desiré Rakotoarijaona (1977)
**Area:** 226,658 sq mi. (587,041 sq km)
**Population (est. 1978):** 8,775,000
**Density per square mile:** 38.7
**Capital and largest city (est. 1975):** Antananarivo (Tananarive), 438,800
**Monetary unit:** Malagasy franc
**Languages:** Malagasy, French
**Ethnic groups:** Merina (or Hova), Betsimisaraka, Betsileo, Tsimihety, Antaisaka, Sakalava, Antandroy
**Religions:** Christian, 50%; Animist
**Gross national product (1976):** $1.9 billion
**National name:** Repoblika Demokratika Malagasy
**Freedom House classifications:** Capitalist-socialist pre-industrial, one-party nationalist

**Geography.** Madagascar lies in the Indian Ocean off the southeast coast of Africa opposite Mozambique. The world's fourth-largest island, it is twice the size of Arizona. The country's low-lying coastal area gives way to a central plateau. The once densely wooded interior has largely been cut down.

**Government.** The legislature had two houses—a Senate with 18 appointed members and 36 elected, and a lower chamber with 107 members, all elected. Both houses were closed in 1972 by the then President, Gen. Gabriel Ramanantsoa.

The assassination of President Richard Ratsimandrava in 1975 led to the take-over of the government by an 18-member Supreme Council of the Revolution, which ruled by modified martial law and suspended political party activities. Comdr. Didier Ratsiraka, a former Foreign Minister, was named President.

**History.** The present population is of black and Malay stock, with perhaps some Polynesian, called Malagasy. The French took over a protectorate in 1885, and then in 1894–95 ended the monarchy, exiling Queen Rànavàlona III to Algiers. A colonial administration was set up to which the Comoro Islands were attached in 1908, and other territories later. In World War II, the British occupied Madagascar, which adhered to Vichy France.

An autonomous republic within the French Community since October 1958, Madagascar became an independent member of the Community on June 25, 1960. In May 1973, an army coup led by Maj. Gen. Gabriel Ramanantsoa ousted Philbert Tsiranana, who had been President since 1959.

With unemployment and inflation both high, Ramanantsoa resigned Feb. 5, 1975, five weeks after an abortive military coup. His leftist-leaning successor, Interior Minister Richard Ratsimandrava, an Army lieutenant colonel, was killed February 11 by a machine-gun ambush in Antananarivo, the capital.

On June 15, 1975, Comdr. Didier Ratsiraka was named President. He announced that he would follow a socialist course and, after nationalizing banks and insurance companies, declared all mineral resources nationalized.

**Economy.** Leading agricultural products are rice, cassava, corn, peanuts, sugarcane, coffee, sisal, vanilla, rubber, and tobacco. Livestock include sheep, cattle, goats, pigs, and poultry.

Chief exports in 1974 were coffee (27%), petroleum products (9%), vanilla (8%), meat (7%), cloves (7%), and fish (6%). Leading customer was France (34%). Leading supplier was France (36%).

## MALAWI

**Republic of Malawi**
**Life President:** Hastings Kamuzu Banda (1966)
**Area:** 45,747 sq mi. (118,484 sq km)
**Population (est. 1977 by U.N.):** 5,530,000
**Density per square mile:** 120.9
**Capital (est. 1976):** Lilongwe, 75,000
**Largest city (est. 1976):** Blantyre, 219,000
**Monetary unit:** Kwacha
**Languages:** English (official), Chichewa
**Religion:** Animist
**Gross national product (1976):** $703 million
**Member of Commonwealth of Nations**
**Freedom House classifications:** Capitalist pre-industrial, one-party nationalist

**Geography.** Malawi is a landlocked country the size of Pennsylvania in southeastern Africa, surrounded by Mozambique, Zambia, and Tanzania. Lake Malawi, formerly Lake Nyasa, occupies most of the country's eastern border. The north-south Rift Valley is flanked by mountain ranges and high plateau areas.

**Government.** Under a new Constitution that came in effect on July 6, 1966, the President is the sole head of state; there is neither a Prime Minister nor a Vice President. The National Assembly has 87 members.

Under the 1966 Constitution, there is only one national party—the Malawi Congress Party (all 87 seats in the National Assembly), led by President Banda.

**History.** The first European to make extensive explorations in the area was David Livingstone in the 1850s and 1860s. In 1884, Cecil Rhodes's British South African Company received a charter to develop the country. The company came into conflict with the Arab slavers in 1887–89 and after Britain annexed the Nyasaland territory in 1891, making it a protectorate in 1892, Sir Harry Johnstone, the first high commissioner, using Royal Navy gunboats, wiped out the slavers.

Nyasaland became the independent nation of Malawi on July 6, 1964. Two years later, on July 6, 1966, it became a republic within the Commonwealth of Nations.

Dr. Hastings K. Banda, Malawi's first Prime Minister, became its first President. He pledged to follow a policy of "discretionary nonalignment." Banda alienated much of Black Africa by maintaining good relations with such white-ruled nations as South Africa and Rhodesia. He argued that his landlocked country had to rely on white-ruled countries for access to the sea and trade.

**Economy.** Malawi's principal export is labor—men who work in the copper mines in Zambia. The country is usually self-supporting in agricultural products, except for sugar and wheat flour.

Chief exports in 1976 were tobacco (45%), tea (18%), and peanuts (8%). Leading customers were U.K. (42%), U.S. (11%), Netherlands (6%), South Africa (5%). Leading suppliers were South Africa (29%), U.K. (22%), Japan (8%), Rhodesia (5%), Canada (5%), Netherlands (5%).

## MALAYSIA

**Federation of Malaysia**
**Paramount Ruler:** Yahya Petra, Sultan of Kelantan (1975)
**Prime Minister:** Hussein bin Onn (1976)
**Area:** 127,316 sq mi. (329,749 sq km)
**Population (est. 1978):** 12,950,000
**Density per square mile:** 101.7
**Capital:** Kuala Lumpur
**Largest cities (est. 1975 by U.N.):** Kuala Lumpur, 557,000; **(1970 census):** Pulau Pinang, 270,019; Ipoh, 247,689
**Monetary unit:** Ringgit
**Languages:** Malay (official), Chinese, Tamil, English
**Religions:** Islam, Buddhist, Hindu.
**Gross national product (1976):** $10.6 billion
**Member of Commonwealth of Nations**
**Freedom House classifications:** Capitalist-industrial, multi-party decentralized

**Geography.** Malaysia is at the southern end of the Malay Peninsula in southeast Asia. The nation also includes Sabah and Sarawak on the island of Borneo to the southeast. Its area slightly exceeds that of New Mexico.

Most of Malaysia is covered by dense jungle and swamps, with a mountain range running the length of the peninsula. Extensive forests provide ebony, sandalwood, teak, and other woods.

**Government.** Malaysia is a sovereign constitutional monarchy within the Commonwealth of Nations. The Paramount Ruler is elected by the hereditary rulers of the states from among themselves, for a five-year term. He is advised by the Prime Minister and his Cabinet. There is a bicameral legislature. The Senate, whose role is comparable more to that of the British House of Lords than to the U.S. Senate, has 58 members, partly appointed by the Paramount Ruler to represent minority and special interests, and partly elected by the legislative assemblies of the various states.

The House of Representatives, or lower house, is made up of 154 members who are elected for five-year terms.

The major political parties are the National Front, a coalition of 10 parties (128 of 154 seats in House of Representatives); Islamic Party (13 seats); Democratic Action Party (9 seats).

**History.** Malaysia came into existence on Sept. 16, 1963, as a federation of Malaya, Singapore, Sabah (North Borneo), and Sarawak. On Aug. 9, 1965, Singapore withdrew from the federation. Since 1966, the 11 states of former Malaya have been known as West Malaysia, and Sabah and Sarawak have been known as East Malaysia.

The Union of Malaya was established April 1, 1946, being formed from the Federated Malay States of Negri Sembilan, Pahang, Perak, and Selangor; the Unfederated Malay States of Johore, Kedah, Kelantan, Perlis, and Trengganu; and two of the Straits Settlements—Malacca and Penang. The Malay states had been brought under British administration during the late 19th and early 20th centuries.

It became the Federation of Malaya on Feb. 1, 1948, and the Federation attained full independence within the Commonwealth of Nations on Aug. 31, 1957.

Sabah (formerly North Borneo), constituting the extreme northern portion of the island of Borneo, was a British protectorate administered under charter by the British North Borneo Company from

1881 to July 15, 1946, when it assumed the status of a colony. It was occupied by Japanese troops from 1942 to 1945.

Sarawak extends along the northwestern coast of Borneo for about 500 miles. In 1841, part of the present territory was granted by the Sultan of Brunei to Sir James Brooke. Sarawak continued to be ruled by members of the Brooke family until the Japanese occupation.

From 1963, when Malaysia became independent, it was the target of guerrilla infiltration from Indonesia, but beat off invasion attempts. In 1966, when Sukarno fell and the Communist Party was liquidated in Indonesia, hostilities ended.

In the late 1960s, the country was torn by communal rioting directed against Chinese and Indians, who controlled a disproportionate share of the country's wealth. Beginning in 1968, the government moved to achieve greater economic balance through a rural development program.

**Economy.** Agricultural products are timber, rubber, palm oil, copra, rice, tea, and bananas.

Malaysia is the largest tin producer in the world, and it also produces iron ore, bauxite, crude oil, and gold.

Chief exports in 1976 were rubber (23%), timber (18%), crude oil (13%), tin (11%) and palm oil (9%). Leading customers were Japan (21%), Singapore (18%), U.S. (16%), Netherlands (7%), U.K. (5%). Leading suppliers were Japan (21%), U.S. (13%), Singapore (9%), U.K. (7%), Australia (7%), West Germany (6%).

## MALDIVES

**Republic of Maldives**
**President:** Ibrahim Nasir (1968)
**Vice-President:** Amir Ahmed Hilmy Didi
**Area:** 115 sq mi. (298 sq km)
**Population (est. 1978):** 145,000
**Density per square mile:** 1,260.9
**Capital and largest city (est. 1977):** Male, 29,500
**Monetary unit:** Maldivian rupee
**Languages:** Divehi
**Religion:** Islam
**Freedom House classifications:** Capitalist pre-industrial, non-party traditional

**Geography.** The Republic of Maldives is a group of atolls in the Indian Ocean about 500 miles southwest of Sri Lanka. Its 1,087 coral islets stretch over an area of 45,000 square miles (116,550 sq km).

**Government.** The 11-member Cabinet is headed by the President. The Majlis (People's Council) is a unicameral legislature consisting of 48 members. Eight of these are appointed by the President. The other 40 are elected for three-year terms, 2 from the capital island of Male and 2 from each of the 19 administrative atolls.

There are no political parties in the Maldives.

**History.** Maldives (formerly called the Maldive Islands) is inhabited by an Islamic seafaring people. Originally the islands were under the suzerainty of Ceylon. They came under British protection in 1887 and were a dependency of the then colony of Ceylon until 1948. The independence agreement with Britain was signed July 26, 1965.

For centuries a sultanate, the islands adopted a republican form of government in 1952, but the sultanate was restored in 1954. On Nov. 11, 1968, however, as the result of a March referendum, a republic was again established in the islands.

**Economy.** The people are great traders and fishermen. Besides fishing, coir making is the chief local industry. Exports include fish, fish meal, coir yarn, and copra.

Chief exports in 1975 (in metric tons) were fresh fish (5,870), dried fish (1,960), fish meal (75), and shells (62). Leading customers were Sri Lanka, Japan, and India.

## MALI

**Republic of Mali**
**Chief of State and Head of Government:** Col. Moussa Traoré (1968)
**Area:** 478,766 sq mi. (1,240,000 sq km)
**Population (est. 1978):** 6,150,000
**Density per square mile:** 12.8
**Capital and largest city (est. 1976):** Bamako, 404,000
**Monetary unit:** Mali franc
**Ethnic groups:** Bambara, Peul, Soninke, Malinke, Songhai, Dogon, Senoufo, Minianka, Berbers, and Moors
**Languages:** French (official), African languages
**Religions:** Islam, 65%; Animist, 30%; Christian
**Gross national product (1976):** $590 million
**National name:** République de Mali
**Freedom House classifications:** Capitalist-socialist pre-industrial, one-party nationalist

**Geography.** Most of Mali, in western Africa, lies in the Sahara. A landlocked country four fifths the size of Alaska, it is bordered by Guinea, Senegal, Mauritania, Algeria, Niger, Upper Volta, and the Ivory Coast.

The only fertile area is in the south, where the Niger and Senegal Rivers provide irrigation.

**Government.** The army overthrew the government on Nov. 19, 1968, and formed a provisional government. The Military Committee of National Liberation (CMLN) consists of 14 members and forms the decision-making body.

In late 1969 an attempted coup was foiled, and Lt. Moussa Traoré, president of the CMLN, assumed the powers of chief of state and head of government, ousting Capt. Yoro Diakité as Premier.

The Malian People's Democratic Union, established in 1976, is the only political party.

**History.** Subjugated by France by the end of the 19th century, this area became a colony in 1904 (named French Sudan in 1920) and in 1946 became part of the French Union. On June 20, 1960, it became independent and, under the name of Sudanese Republic, was federated with the Republic of Senegal in the Mali Federation. However, Senegal seceded from the Federation on Aug. 20, 1960, and the Sudanese Republic then changed its name to the Republic of Mali on September 22.

In the 1960s, Mali concentrated on economic development, continuing to accept aid from both Soviet bloc and Western nations, as well as international agencies. In the late 1960s, it began retreating from close ties with Communist China. But a purge of conservative opponents brought greater power to Pres. Modibo Keita, and in 1968 the influence of the Communist Chinese and their Malian sympathizers increased. By a treaty signed in Peking in May 1968, China agreed to help build a railroad from Mali to Guinea, providing Mali with vital access to the sea.

Mali, with Mauritania, Ivory Coast, Senegal, Dahomey, Niger, and Upper Volta signed a treaty establishing the Economic Community for West Africa to promote economic development among the seven nations. It came into force on Jan. 1, 1973.

A six-year sub-Sahara drought devastated Mali before disastrously heavy rains began in August 1974. Emergency shipments from a dozen nations and international organizations helped alleviate a famine that affected 1.8 million Malians and killed thousands.

**Economy.** Mali's agricultural products include rice, cotton, and peanuts. Only about one fifth of the land is suitable for cultivation. The raising of livestock is an important industry.

Chief exports in 1972 were cotton (34%), livestock (25%), peanuts (6%), fish (6%), and textile yarns and fabrics (5%). Leading customers in 1974 were France (27%), China (17%), Ivory Coast (15%), Senegal (11%), West Germany (5%). Leading suppliers were France (24%), U.S. (13%), Ivory Coast (9%), China (9%), U.S.S.R. (7%), West Germany (7%), Senegal (5%), Pakistan (5%).

## MALTA

**Republic of Malta**
**President:** Anton Buttigieg (1976)
**Prime Minister:** Dom Mintoff (1971)
**Area:** 122 sq mi. (316 sq km)
**Population** (est. 1978): 330,000
**Density per square mile:** 2,704.9
**Capital (est. 1977):** Valetta, 14,100
**Largest city (est. 1977):** Sliema, 20,100
**Monetary unit:** Maltese pound
**Languages:** Maltese and English
**Religion:** Roman Catholic
**Gross national product (1976):** $522 million
**National name:** Repubblika Ta Malta
**Member of Commonwealth of Nations**
**Freedom House classifications:** Capitalist-statist industrial, multi-party centralized

**Geography.** The five Maltese islands—with a combined land area smaller than Philadelphia—are in the Mediterranean about 60 miles south of the southeastern tip of Sicily.

**Government.** The government is headed by a Prime Minister, responsible to a 65-member House of Representatives elected by universal suffrage.

The major political parties are Malta Labor Party (34 of 65 seats in House of Representatives), led by Prime Minister Dom Mintoff; Nationalist Party (31 seats), led by Edward Fenech Adami.

**History.** The strategic importance of Malta was recognized by the Phoenicians, who occupied it, as did in their turn the Greeks, Carthaginians, and Romans. The apostle Paul was shipwrecked there in A.D. 58.

The Knights of St. John (Malta), who obtained the three habitable Maltese islands of Malta, Gozo, and Comino from Charles V in 1530, reached their highest fame when they withstood an attack by superior Turkish forces in 1565.

Napoleon seized Malta in 1798, but the French forces were ousted by British troops in 1799, and British rule was confirmed by the Treaty of Paris in 1814.

Malta was heavily attacked by German and Italian aircraft during World War II, but was never invaded by the Axis.

Malta became an independent nation on Sept. 21, 1964. By vote of its parliament, Malta became a republic Dec. 13, 1974, but retained its formal ties with the British Commonwealth. Governor-General Mamo was sworn in as first President and Mintoff remained Prime Minister.

The new government proposed to Parliament a seven-year plan to end economic dependence on foreign military bases by 1980. It called for a $568-million investment program to create 20,000 new jobs. Britain announced its intention to withdraw from Malta in 1979, thus ending its annual subsidy of $33 million for use of the island's port facilities.

**Economy.** Much of Malta's economy has depended on expenditures at the large British naval installations, but with the gradual withdrawal of some of the military forces, Britain agreed to provide economic assistance valued at $140 million during the first 10 years of independence. Some local industrialization has been started. The principal agricultural products are potatoes, cereals, onions, and fruit. There are also some livestock raising and a fishing industry.

Chief exports in 1976 were clothing (42%), petroleum products (7%), food (6%), textile yarns and fabrics (5%), and ships (5%). Leading customers were West Germany (24%), U.K. (18%), Libya (13%), Italy (5%). Leading suppliers were U.K. (24%), Italy (17%), West Germany (10%), U.S. (10%), France (5%).

## MAURITANIA

**Islamic Republic of Mauritania**
**President:** Lt. Col. Moustapha Ould Saleck (1978)
**Area:** 397,955 sq mi. (1,030,700 sq km)[1]
**Population (est. 1977):** 1,400,000
**Density per square mile:** 3.5
**Capital and largest city (1976 census):** Nouakchott, 135,000
**Monetary unit:** Ouguyia
**Ethnic groups:** Moors; a black minority (Poulars, Soninkes, and Wolofs)
**Languages:** Arabic and French
**Religion:** Islam
**Gross national product (1976):** $460 million
**National name:** République Islamique de Mauritanie
**Freedom House classifications:** Capitalist-socialist pre-industrial, one-party nationalist

**Geography.** Mauritania, three times the size of Arizona, is situated in northwest Africa with about 350 miles (592 km) of coastline on the Atlantic Ocean. It is bordered by Morocco on the north, Algeria and Mali on the east, and Senegal on the south.

The country is mostly desert, with the exception of the fertile Senegal River valley in the south and grazing land in the north.

**Government.** An Army coup on July 10, 1978, deposed Moktar Ould Daddah, who had been President since Mauritania achieved independence in 1960. A 13-man Committee for National Recovery, headed by Lt. Col. Moustapha Ould Saleck, took over executive and legislative power,

1. Does not include any of Spanish Sahara, reportedly divided between Mauritania and Morocco.

suspending the National Assembly and the nation's single political party.

**History.** Mauritania was first explored by the Portuguese. The French organized the area as a territory in 1904.

Mauritania became an independent nation on Nov. 28, 1960, and was admitted to the United Nations in 1961 over the strenuous opposition of Morocco, which claimed the territory. With Moors, Arabs, Berbers, and Blacks frequently in conflict, the government in the late 1960s sought to make Arab culture dominant to unify the land. Iron ore was discovered at Feyreck in the north, and commercial exploitation was begun in 1968.

Sizable deposits of copper also have been found, and an Atlantic fishing industry is being developed. But the dispersed, largely nomadic population is a handicap to modernization.

Mauritania and Morocco planned to divide the territory of the former Spanish Sahara after the departure of the colonial administration. Mauritanian troops moved into the territory but encountered resistance from the Polisario Front, a Saharan independence movement backed by Algeria. Mauritania broke diplomatic relations with Algeria in March 1976, after Algerian recognition of the area as an independent state.

The task of pacifying the approximately one third of the former Spanish Sahara (the exact amount of territory acquired by Mauritania is unknown) proved a heavy burden. Increased military spending and rising casualties, with no evidence of progress, were cited as possible causes for Ould Daddah's overthrow.

**Economy.** Livestock raising is the principal economic activity in Mauritania. Some crops are produced. Minerals include iron and copper.

Chief export in 1975 was iron ore (82%). Leading customers were France (20%), U.K. (16%), Italy (13%), Japan (11%), Spain (11%), Belgium-Luxembourg (8%), West Germany (5%). Leading suppliers were France (56%), U.S. (8%), West Germany (8%), Senegal (5%), U.K. (5%).

## MAURITIUS

**Governor-General:** Dayendranath Burrenchobay (1978)
**Prime Minister:** Sir Seewoosagur Ramgoolam (1961)
**Area:** 790 sq mi. (2,045 sq km)
**Population (est. 1978):** 890,000 (Indian, 51%; Creole, 33%, Pakistani, 16%)
**Density per square mile:** 1,113.9
**Capital and largest city (est. 1977):** Port Louis, 141,300
**Monetary unit:** Mauritius rupee
**Languages:** English (official), French, Creole.
**Religions:** Hindu, 51%, Christian (mainly Roman Catholic), 30%; Islam, 16%; Buddhist, 3%
**Gross national product (1976):** $600 million
**Member of Commonwealth of Nations**
**Freedom House classifications:** Capitalist industrial, multi-party centralized

**Geography.** Mauritius is a mountainous island in the Indian Ocean east of Madagascar.

**Government.** Mauritius is a member of the British Commonwealth, with Queen Elizabeth II as Head of State. She is represented by a Governor-General, who chooses the Prime Minister from the unicameral Legislative Assembly. The Legislative Assembly has 70 members, 62 of whom are elected by direct suffrage. The remaining 8 are chosen from among the unsuccessful candidates.

The major political parties are the Mouvement Militant Mauricien (30 seats in Legislative Assembly); Labour Party (25 seats); Social Democratic Party (7 seats).

**History.** Mauritius was seized from France by British troops in 1810 and ceded to Britain by the Treaty of Paris in 1814. Until 1903, Mauritius and the Seychelles were administered as a single colony. The colony of Mauritius became an independent nation on March 12, 1968.

The nation has an Indian majority, descendants of laborers imported from India to work the sugar plantations after the abolition of slavery in 1834. The native blacks speak French and are Roman Catholics.

Overpopulation and unemployment continue to be major problems.

**Economy.** Agricultural products include cane sugar, tea, and tobacco; and industrial products include alcohol and molasses.

Chief export in 1975 was sugar (77%). Leading customers were U.K. (77%), U.S. (6%), France (6%). Leading suppliers were U.K. (17%), South Africa (10%), Iran (9%), France (9%), Japan (8%), West Germany (7%), Australia (6%), U.S. (5%).

## MEXICO

**United Mexican States**
**President:** José López Portillo (1976)
**Area:** 761,600 sq mi. (1,972,547 sq km)
**Population (est. 1978):** 66,950,000 (55% mestizo; 29% Indian)
**Density per square mile:** 87.9
**Capital:** Mexico City
**Largest cities (est 1977):** Mexico City, 8,941,900; (est. 1976 by U.N.): Guadalajara, 1,640,900; Monterrey, 1,090,200; Juarez, 544,900
**Monetary unit:** Peso
**Languages:** Spanish, Indian languages
**Religion:** Mainly Roman Catholic
**Gross national product (1976):** $67.6 billion
**National name:** Estados Unidos Mexicanos
**Freedom House classifications:** Capitalist-statist industrial, dominant party

**Geography.** The United States' neighbor to the south, Mexico is about one fifth its size. Baja California in the west, an 800-mile (1,287-km) peninsula, forms the Gulf of California. In the east are the Gulf of Mexico and the Bay of Campeche, which is formed by Mexico's other peninsula, the Yucatán.

Mexico is a great, high plateau, open to the north, with mountain chains on east and west and with ocean-front lowlands lying outside of them.

**Government.** The President, who is popularly elected for six years and is ineligible to succeed himself, governs with a Cabinet of ministers. Congress has two houses—a 250-member Chamber of Deputies (one member for each 250,000 of population), elected for three years, and a 64-member Senate, elected for six years.

Each of the 31 states has considerable autonomy, with a popularly elected governor, a legislature, and a local judiciary. The President of Mexico appoints the governor of the Federal District.

The major political parties are the Partido Revolucionario Institucional (PRI), led by Carlos Sansores Pérez; Authentic Party of the Mexican

Revolution (PARM); National Action Party (PAN); and Popular Socialist Party (PPS).

**History.** Mexico's early history is shrouded in mystery. At least two civilized races—the Mayas and later the Toltecs—preceded the wealthy Aztec empire, conquered in 1519–21 by the Spanish under Hernando Cortés. Spain ruled for the next 300 years until 1810 (the date was Sept. 16 and is now celebrated as Independence Day), when the Mexicans first revolted. They continued the struggle and finally won independence in 1821.

Turbulent years followed. From 1821 to 1877, there were two emperors, several dictators, and enough presidents and provisional executives to make a new government on the average of every nine months. Mexico lost Texas (1836), and after defeat in the war with the U.S. (1846–48) it lost the area comprising the present states of California, Nevada, and Utah, most of Arizona and New Mexico, and parts of Wyoming and Colorado:

In 1855, the Indian patriot Benito Juárez began a series of liberal reforms, including the disestablishment of the Catholic Church, which had acquired vast property. A subsequent civil war was interrupted by the French invasion of Mexico (1861), the crowning of Maximilian of Austria as Emperor (1864), and then his overthrow and execution by forces under Juárez, who again became President in 1867.

The years after the fall of the dictator Porfirio Diaz (1877–80 and 1884–1911) were marked by bloody political military strife and trouble with the U.S. culminating in the punitive expedition into northern Mexico (1916–17) in unsuccessful pursuit of the revolutionary Pancho Villa. There was a continuous succession of various presidents and of internal strife until 1917, when a new Congress was elected and a liberal Constitution adopted. Since a brief period of civil war in 1920, Mexico has enjoyed a period of gradual agricultural, political, and social reforms. Relations with the U.S. were again disturbed in 1938 when all foreign oil wells were expropriated. Agreement on compensation was finally reached in 1941.

Lázaro Cardenas (1934–40), President during the oil seizures, also began a program of distributing land to the peasants and of broad labor reforms. Manual Avila Camacho, President during World War II, followed Cardenas' policy at home but cooperated closely with the United Nations, and established cordial relations with the U.S. His policy was followed by his immediate successors, Miguel Alemán, Adolfo Ruíz Cortines, and Adolfo López Mateos. López Mateos redefined Mexican foreign policy as "independent" rather than neutral or partial, a course followed by Gustavo Díaz Ordaz, who became President in 1964.

Mexico maintained ties with Cuba after the Organization of American States approved a U.S.-sponsored boycott of Fidel Castro's regime in 1962. Mexico opposed the boycott until the OAS repealed it July 29, 1975.

Luis Echeverría Alvarez, who was elected President in 1970, worked vigorously in Latin America and elsewhere in the underdeveloped world to promote more benefits for developing nations from the raw materials they export.

Mexico and Venezuela proposed formation of a Latin American economic system (SELA) to promote regional economic development, and the organization held its first meeting in Caracas in January 1976.

Despite a drastic devaluation of the peso in 1976 that quadrupled the price of goods imported from the U.S., the government cut the rate of inflation by mid-1977 to 20%, compared with a rate of 45% for 1976. Recession kept unemployment at 11%, but Mexico's trade deficit with the United States was only $91.5 million for the first quarter, compared with $426.3 million a year earlier. A key factor in the improved payments was a 60% increase in tourism from the United States, hard hit earlier by terrorism and Echevarría's support for Palestine Liberation Organization presence in the United Nations.

Another factor in the improvement of the economy was a 64% increase in export oil sales in 1977, worth nearly $1 billion to the foreign trade balance. The confirmation in June 1978 of new oil reserves in Yucatán, adding 16 billion barrels to the nation's proven reserves, also improved the economic outlook.

In July 1978, the army and police were used as strikebreakers to control independent trade unions that challenged government control of the labor movement.

**Economy.** Primitive agricultural methods are steadily giving way to modern practices. The Yucatán peninsula, at the southern end of the Gulf of Mexico, raises more than half of the world supply of sisal hemp. Stockraising is important on nonarable land.

The leading industrial products are cotton cloth and thread, beer, sugar, iron, and steel. Important minerals are silver, gold, lead, copper, zinc, antimony, tin, coal, and iron ore.

Most of the Mexican mining properties are foreign-owned, and the industry is declining in relative importance.

Mexico's forests are of considerable importance; they include pine, oak, fir, mahogany, red and white cedar, and primavera. Resins, turpentine, and vegetable wax are also produced. Yucatán produces nearly all of the world's chicle, used as the base of chewing gum.

Chief exports in 1976 were crude oil (16%), coffee (10%), chemicals (9%), cotton (8%), metal and ores (8%), machinery (6%), shrimps (5%), and textile yarns and fabrics (5%). Leading customers were U.S. (56%), Brazil (5%). Leading suppliers were U.S. (63%), West Germany (7%), Japan (5%).

# MONACO

**Principality of Monaco**
**Ruler:** Prince Rainier III (1949)
**Minister of State:** André Saint-Mleux
**Area:** 0.73 square mile (465 acres)
**Population (est. 1978):** 30,000, of whom 5,500 are Monégasque citizens
**Density per square mile:** 41,095.9
**Largest city (1968 census):** Monte Carlo, 9,948
**Monetary unit:** French franc
**Languages:** French and Monégasque
**Religion:** Roman Catholic
**National name:** Principauté de Monaco

**Geography.** Monaco is a tiny, hilly wedge driven into the French Mediterranean coast nine miles east of Nice.

**Government.** Prince Albert of Monaco gave the principality a Constitution in 1911, creating a National Council of 18 members popularly elected for five years. The head of government is the Minister of State.

Prince Rainier III, born May 31, 1923, succeeded his grandfather, Louis II, on the latter's death, May 9, 1949. Rainier was married April 18, 1956, to Grace Kelly, U.S. actress. A daughter, Princess Caroline Louise Marguerite, was born on Jan. 23, 1957 (married to Philippe Junot June 28, 1978); a son, Prince Albert Louis Pierre, on March 14, 1958; and another daughter, Princess Stéphanie Marie Elisabeth, on Feb. 1, 1965.

The special significance attached to the birth of descendants to Prince Rainier stems from a clause in the Treaty of July 17, 1919, between France and Monaco stipulating that in the event of vacancy of the Crown, the Monégasque territory would become an autonomous state under a French protectorate.

The National and Democratic Union (all 18 seats in National Council), led by Auguste Medecin, is the only political party.

**History.** Monaco is a little land of pleasure with a tourist business that runs as high as 1.5 million visitors a year. It had popular gaming tables as early as 1856. Five years later, a 50-year concession to operate the games was granted to François Blanc, of Bad Homburg. This concession passed into the hand of a private company in 1898.

The Phoenicians, and after them the Greeks, had a temple on the Monacan headland honoring Hercules. From *Monoikos,* the Greek surname for this mythological strong man, the principality took its name. After being independent for 800 years, Monaco was annexed to France in 1793 and was placed under Sardinia's protection in 1815. In 1861, it went under French guardianship but continued to be independent.

By a treaty in 1918, France stipulated that the French government be given a veto over the succession to the throne.

Monaco's practice of providing a tax shelter for French businessmen resulted in a dispute between the countries. When Rainier refused to end the practice, France retaliated with a customs tax. In 1967, Rainier took control of the Société des Bains de Mer, operator of the famous Monte Carlo gambling casino, in a program to increase hotel and convention space, paying $8 million to Greek shipping magnate Aristotle Onassis for his shares.

## MONGOLIA

**Mongolian People's Republic**
**Chairman of Presidium of Great People's Khural (President):** Yumjaagiin Tsedenbal (1973)
**Chairman of Council of Ministers (Premier):** Jambyn Batmunkh (1973)
**Area:** 604,250 sq mi. (1,565,000 sq km)
**Population (est. 1978):** 1,575,000
**Density per square mile:** 2.2
**Capital and largest city (est. 1976):** Ulan Bator, 331,800
**Monetary unit:** Tugrik
**Language:** Khalkha Mongolian
**Religion:** Lamaistic Buddhism
**Gross national product (1976):** $1.3 billion
**National name:** Bugd Nayramdakh Mongol Ard Uls
**Freedom House classifications:** Socialist industrial, one-party communist

**Geography.** Mongolia lies in eastern Asia between Soviet Siberia on the north and China on the south. It is slightly larger than Alaska.

The productive regions of Outer Mongolia—a tableland ranging from 3,000 to 5,000 feet (914 to 1,524 m) in elevation—are in the north, which is well drained by numerous rivers, including the Hovd, Onon, Selenga, and Tula.

Much of the Gobi Desert falls within Mongolia. There several mountain ranges, one of which, the Altai Mountains, contains the highest peak in the country—Tabun Bogdo at 15,266 feet (4,653 m).

**Government.** The Mongolian People's Republic is a socialist state in the form of a people's democracy. The highest organ of state power is the Great People's Khural (Parliament), which is elected for a term of four years and is convened once a year. The Great People's Khural elects the Presidium, which consists of a chairman, vice-chairman, secretary, and six members. The Council of Ministers is set up by the Great People's Khural and consists of a chairman, vice-chairman, and ministers.

The Mongolian People's Revolutionary Party, led by President Tsedenbal, is the only political party.

**History.** The Mongolian People's Republic, known as Outer Mongolia, is a Russian satellite. It contains the original homeland of the historic Mongols, whose power reached its zenith during the 13th century under Kublai Khan. The area accepted Manchu rule in 1689, but after the Chinese Revolution of 1911 and the fall of the Manchus in 1912, the northern Mongol princes expelled the Chinese officials and declared independence under the Khutukhtu or "Living Buddha."

In 1921, Soviet troops entered the country and facilitated the establishment of a republic by Mongolian revolutionaries in 1924 after the death of the last Living Buddha. China, meanwhile, continued to claim Outer Mongolia but was unable to back the claim with any strength. Under the 1945 Chinese-Russian Treaty, China agreed to give up Outer Mongolia, which, after a plebiscite, became a nominally independent country.

The country allied itself with the U.S.S.R. in its dispute with China. It has mobilized troops along its borders since 1968 when the two powers became involved in border clashes on the Kazakh-Sinkiang frontier to the west and on the Amur and Ussuri rivers. Under a 20-year treaty of friendship and cooperation signed in 1966, it was entitled to call upon the U.S.S.R. for military aid in the event of invasion.

**Economy.** The country is largely pastoral. There are few areas suitable for crop growing, but some millet, rye, and wheat are produced. Most of the people are essentially nomadic or seminomadic; flocks and herds remain the chief source of wealth.

Reserves of 500 million tons of coal are said to exist in the Nalaikha field near Ulan Bator. Some gold is mined. Deposits of antimony, copper, iron ore, lead, graphite, mercury, sulfur, and silver exist.

Chief exports in 1975 were livestock (27%), meat (19%), and wool (16%). Leading customers were U.S.S.R. (79%), Czechoslovakia (6%). Leading supplier was U.S.S.R. (90%).

## MOROCCO

**Kingdom of Morocco**
**Ruler:** King Hassan II (1961)
**Premier:** Ahmed Osman (1972)
**Area:** 172,414 sq mi. (446,550 sq km)[1]
**Population: (est. 1978):** 18,675,000

1. Does not include any of Spanish Sahara, reportedly divided between Morocco and Mauritania.

**Density per square mile:** 108.3
**Capital:** Rabat
**Largest cities (est. 1975 by U.N.):** Casablanca, 1,856,000; (1971 census): Rabat, 435,510; Marrakech, 330,400; Fez, 321,460
**Monetary unit:** Dirham
**Languages:** Arabic, French, Spanish
**Religions:** Chiefly Islam
**Gross national product (1976):** $8.5 billion
**National name:** al-Mamlaka al-Maghrebia
**Freedom House classifications:** Capitalist pre-industrial, multi-party centralized

**Geography.** Morocco, about one tenth larger than California, is just south of Spain across the Strait of Gibraltar and looks out on the Atlantic from the northwest shoulder of Africa. Algeria is to the east and Mauritania to the south.

On the Atlantic coast there is a fertile plain. The Mediterranean coast is mountainous. The Atlas Mountains, running northeastward from the south to the Algerian frontier, average 11,000 feet (3,353 m) in elevation.

**Government.** The King, after suspending the 1962 Constitution and dissolving Parliament in 1965, promulgated a new Constitution in 1972. He continued to rule by decree until June 3, 1977, when the first free elections since 1962 took place. The new 264-member Chamber of Deputies has 176 elected seats, with the balance chosen by local councils and groups.

A coalition of independents loyal to the King and small right-wing parties has 114 of the 176 elected seats; Istiqlal, principal opposition group, 45 seats; Socialist Union of Popular Forces, 16 seats; and the Communist Party of Progress and Socialism, one seat.

**History.** Morocco was once the home of the Berbers, who helped the Arabs invade Spain in A.D. 711 and then revolted against them and gradually won control of large areas of Spain for a time after 739.

The country was ruled successively by various native dynasties and maintained regular commercial relations with Europe, even during the 17th and 18th centuries when it was the headquarters of the famous Salé pirates. In the 19th century clashes with the French and Spanish became frequent. Finally, in 1904, France and Spain divided Morocco into zones of French and Spanish influence, and these were established as protectorates in 1912.

Meanwhile, Morocco had become the object of big-power rivalry, which almost led to a European war in 1905 when Germany attempted to gain a foothold in the rich mineral country. By terms of the Algeciras Conference (1906), Morocco was internationalized economically, and France's privileges were limited.

The Tangier Statute, concluded by U.K., France, and Spain in 1923, created an international zone at the port of Tangier, permanently neutralized and demilitarized. In World War II, Spain occupied the zone, ostensibly to ensure order, but was forced to withdraw in 1945.

Sultan Mohammed V was deposed by the French in August 1953 and replaced by his uncle, but nationalist agitation forced his return in November 1955. On his death on Feb. 26, 1961, his son, Hassan, became King.

France recognized the independence and sovereignty of Morocco on March 2, 1956. Spain followed on April 7, 1956. The Tangier international zone was abolished by a declaration signed Oct. 29, 1956. Morocco was admitted to the United Nations on Nov. 12, 1956.

In the Middle East War of 1967, Morocco joined the Arab States in their attack on Israel. In 1968 the country embarked on a $1-billion 5-year plan designed to make it self-sufficient in agricultural products and the granary of Europe through multiplying irrigated lands six times.

On Nov. 6, 1975, tens of thousands of Moroccans crossed the border into Spanish Sahara to back their government's contention that the northern part of the territory was historically part of Morocco. At the same time, Mauritania occupied the southern half of the territory in defiance of Spanish threats to resist such a takeover. Abandoning its commitment to self-determination for the territory, Spain withdrew and only Algeria protested. Algerian recognition of a Saharan republic in March 1976 led to a break in relations among the three North African states, and Algerian-backed Polisario Front guerrillas continued to fight Moroccan and Mauritanian forces, preventing exploitation of the region's rich phosphate deposits.

Although Polisario guerrillas were still active in 1977, Hassan dispatched 1,500 troops to Zaire April 9 to help President Mobutu defeat an invasion from Angola. Radical African states criticized Morocco, but most hailed the successful operation, in which France supplied the airlift.

In the May 1978 invasion of Zaire's Shaba province, Morocco once again supplied troops, this time only a small number, who were transported to Zaire by the U.S. Air Force. Hassan was one of the few chiefs of government who volunteered to contribute to a permanent pan-African peacekeeping force, discussed but not activated after the second Shaba invasion.

**Economy.** Morocco is essentially agricultural. Corn, beans, peas, hemp, wheat, barley, sorghum, citrus fruits, olives, and dates are raised.

Since independence, large-scale efforts to industrialize the country have been undertaken. Manufacturing industries produce chemicals, flour, leather, beverages, and textiles. Native industries include carpet weaving and making Turkish slippers.

Major minerals are phosphates, antimony, coal, cobalt, iron ore, manganese ore, molybdenum, tin, zinc, and lead.

Casablanca has perhaps the world's largest artificial port.

Chief exports in 1976 were phosphates (39%) and citrus fruit (11%). Leading customers were France (24%), West Germany (10%), Italy (7%), U.K. (6%), Belgium-Luxembourg (6%), Spain (5%), Poland (5%). Leading suppliers were France (29%), U.S. (9%), West Germany (8%), Spain (6%), Italy (6%), Iraq (5%).

## MOZAMBIQUE

**People's Republic of Mozambique**
**President:** Samora Moises Machel (1975)
**Area:** 302,328 sq mi. (783,030 sq km)
**Population (est. 1978):** 9,950,000
**Density per square mile:** 32.9
**Capital and largest city (est. 1978):** Maputo, 500,000
**Monetary unit:** Mozambique escudo
**Languages:** Portuguese (official); Bantu languages
**Religions:** Animist, 70%; Christian, 15%; Islam, 13%
**Gross national product (1976):** $1.6 billion

**National name:** República Popular de Moçambique
**Freedom House classifications:** Socialist pre-industrial, one-party socialist.

**Geography.** Mozambique stretches for 1,535 miles (2,470 km) along Africa's southeast coast. It is nearly twice the size of California. Tanzania is to the north; Malawi, Zambia, and Rhodesia to the west; and South Africa and Swaziland to the south.

The country is generally a low-lying plateau broken up by 25 sizable rivers that flow into the Indian Ocean. The largest is the Zambezi, which provides access to central Africa.

**Government.** After being under Portuguese colonial rule for 470 years, Mozambique became independent on June 25, 1975. It is a Marxist state. The first President, Samora Moises Machel, is a militant Maoist and a former nurse who headed the National Front for the Liberation of Mozambique (FRELIMO) in its 10-year guerrilla war for independence.

**History.** Mozambique was discovered by Vasco da Gama in 1498, although the Arabs had penetrated into the area as early as the 10th century. It was first colonized in 1505, and by 1510, the Portuguese were masters of all the former Arab sultanates on the east African coast.

FRELIMO was organized in 1963. Guerrilla activity had become so extensive by 1973 that Portugal had dispatched 40,000 troops to fight the rebels. A cease-fire was signed in September 1974, when Portugal agreed to grant Mozambique independence.

After a brief period of cooperation with neighboring white-ruled Rhodesia, Mozambique closed its border on March 3, 1976, cutting off Rhodesia's most direct link to the sea. A series of border clashes between Rhodesian forces and guerrillas based in Mozambique continued.

**Economy.** Ninety percent of the population is engaged in agriculture, with the principal crops being cotton, cashew nuts, tea, copra, and sugar. Livestock production is limited because of the widespread presence of the tsetse fly.

The country's mineral resources include gold, coal, graphite, and mica. The forests produce large quantities of timber.

The chief ports are Maputo and Beira, which is also the port for Rhodesia.

Chief exports in 1974 were sugar (22%), fruit and nut preserves (14%), cotton (11%), copra (8%), cashew nuts (6%), and petroleum products (5%). Leading customers were Portugal (33%), U.S. (11%), South Africa (9%), India (6%), Netherlands (5%). Leading suppliers were South Africa (20%), Portugal (17%), West Germany (14%), Japan (7%), U.K. (6%), U.S. (6%), France (5%), Saudi Arabia (5%).

## NAMIBIA

**See South-West Africa**

## NAURU

**Republic of Nauru**
**President and Premier:** Hammer DeRoburt (1978)
**Area:** 8.2 sq mi. (21 sq km)
**Population (est. 1978):** 8,000
**Density per square mile:** 1,000.0
**Capital:** Yaren
**Monetary unit:** Australian dollar
**Languages:** Nauruan, English
**Religions:** Nauruan Protestant and Roman Catholic
**Special relationship within the Commonwealth of Nations**
**Freedom House classifications:** Capitalist-statist industrial, non-party traditional

**Geography.** Nauru is an island in the Pacific just south of the equator, about 2,500 miles southwest of Honolulu.

**Government.** Legislative power is invested in a popularly elected 18-member Parliament, which elects the President from among its members. Executive power is invested in the President, who is assisted by a five-member Cabinet.

**History.** Nauru was annexed by Germany in 1888. It was placed under joint Australian, New Zealand, and British mandate after World War I, and in 1947 it became a U.N. trusteeship administered by the same three powers. On Jan. 31, 1968, Nauru became an independent republic.

The tiny republic is one of the world's chief phosphate producers. The islanders earn an annual $4,000 per capita in royalties from production of 1.6 million tons out of a reserve of 61.4 million tons.

**Economy.** Chief export in 1974 was phosphate. Leading customers were Australia (c. 57%), Japan (c. 23%), New Zealand (c. 18%). Leading suppliers were Australia (c. 58%), Netherlands (c. 30%).

## NEPAL

**Kingdom of Nepal**
**Ruler:** King Birendra Bír Bikram Shah Deva (1972)
**Prime Minister:** Kirtinidhi Bista (1977)
**Area:** 54,362 sq mi. (140,797 sq km)
**Population (est. 1978):** 13,420,000 (Magar, Gurung, Bhotia, Newar)
**Density per square mile:** 246.9
**Capital and largest city (est. 1976):** Katmandu, 171,400
**Monetary unit:** Nepalese rupee
**Languages:** Nepali (official), Newari, Bhutia
**Religions:** Hindu, 89.4%; Buddhist, 7.5%
**Gross national product (1976):** $1.5 billion
**Freedom House classifications:** Capitalist pre-industrial, non-party traditional

**Geography.** A landlocked country the size of Arkansas, lying between India and the Tibetan Autonomous Region of China, Nepal contains Mt. Everest (29,028 ft.; 8,848 m), the tallest mountain in the world. Along its southern border, Nepal has a strip of level land that is partly forested, partly cultivated. North of that is the slope of the main section of the Himalayan range, including Everest and many other peaks higher than 20,000 feet (6,096 m).

**Government.** A new Constitution promulgated by King Mahendra in December 1962 provided for a unicameral legislature called the National Panchayat. All political parties were banned in 1960.

**History.** The Kingdom of Nepal was unified in 1768 by King Prithwi Narayan Shah. A commercial treaty was signed with Britain in 1792, and in 1816, after more than a year's hostilities, the Nepalese agreed to allow British residents to live in Katmandu, the capital. In 1923, Britain recognized the absolute independence of Nepal. Between 1846 and 1951, the country was ruled by the Rana family, which always held the office of Premier. In 1951, however, the King took over all power and proclaimed a constitutional monarchy. Nepal was admitted to the United Nations in 1955.

Mahendra Bir Bikram Shah became King in 1955. Tension developed between India and Nepal in the 1950s. Nepal and Communist China settled their differences in 1956, and thereafter Nepal accepted economic aid from the Chinese. The U.S. and the U.S.S.R. also provide aid.

After Mahendra, who had ruled since 1955, died of a heart attack in 1972, Prince Birendra, at 26, succeeded to the throne.

**Economy.** Cultivated and irrigated where possible, the main valley of Nepal grows rice, wheat, pulse, fruits, vegetables, spices, sugarcane, and potatoes. A few sheep and cattle are grazed. Manufacturing is limited to native handicraft, but jute and textile mills are being established.

Mineral resources, nearly all unexploited, include lignite, copper, zinc, lead, sulfur, marble, and iron. Southern Nepal has valuable forests that yield gum, timber, resin, and dye. Hemp plants grow wild.

Chief exports in 1974–75 were jute goods (33%), raw jute (13%), curio goods (11%), and jute cuttings (7%). Leading customers in 1975 were India (56%), Pakistan (6%). Leading suppliers were India (58%), Japan (15%), U.K. (5%), West Germany (5%).

## THE NETHERLANDS

**Kingdom of the Netherlands**
**Sovereign:** Queen Juliana (1948)
**Premier:** Andries van Agt (1977)
**Area:** 15,700 sq mi. (40,844 sq km)
**Population (est. 1978):** 13,930,000
**Density per square mile:** 887.3
**Capital:** Amsterdam; seat of government: The Hague
**Largest cities (est. 1977):** Rotterdam, 1,022,700; Amsterdam, 975,500; The Hague, 677,500; Utrecht, 467,900
**Monetary unit:** Guilder
**Language:** Dutch
**Religions:** Roman Catholic, 40%; Dutch Reformed, 24%; unaffiliated, 24%
**Gross national product (1976):** $89.5 billion
**National name:** Koninkrijk der Nederlanden
**Freedom House classifications:** Capitalist-socialist industrial, multi-party centralized

**Geography.** The Netherlands, on the coast of the North Sea, has West Germany to the east and Belgium to the south. It is twice the size of New Jersey.

Part of the great plain of north and west Europe, the Netherlands has maximum dimensions of 190 by 160 miles (360 by 257 km) and is low and flat except in Limburg in the southeast, where some hills rise to 300 feet (92 m). About half the country's area is below sea level, making the famous Dutch dikes a requisite to the use of much land. Reclamation of land from the sea through dikes has continued through recent times.

All drainage reaches the North Sea, and the principal rivers—Rhine, Maas (Meuse), and Schelde—have their sources outside the country. The Rhine is the most heavily used waterway in Europe.

**Government.** The Netherlands and its former colony of the Netherlands Antilles form the Kingdom of the Netherlands.

The Netherlands is a constitutional monarchy with a bicameral Parliament. The Upper Chamber has 75 members elected for six years by representative bodies of the provinces, half of the members retiring every three years. The Lower Chamber has 150 members elected by universal suffrage for four years. The two Chambers have the right of investigation and interpellation; the Lower Chamber can initiate legislation and amend bills.

The sovereign, Queen Juliana, born April 30, 1909, was married on Jan. 7, 1937, to Prince Bernhard of Lippe-Biesterfeld (born 1911). They have four daughters: Beatrix (born 1938); Irene (born 1939); Margriet Francisca (born 1943); and Maria Christina (born 1947). Crown Princess Beatrix in 1966 married a former West German diplomat, Claus von Amsberg, who served in the German army in World War II. In 1967, she gave birth to a son, Willem Alexander, a male heir to the throne, the first since 1884.

Premier Andries van Agt leads a coalition of center-right parties with 77 seats in the 150 seats in the lower house. The coalition consists of his Christian Democratic Appeal (49 seats) and the conservative liberal Party for Freedom and Democracy (28 seats). A dissident bloc of the Christian Democrats objected to the Liberal alliance, but said they would support van Agt in confidence votes, and a half-dozen members of splinter right-wing parties were expected to vote with the government.

**History.** Julius Caesar found the low-lying Netherlands inhabited by Germanic tribes—the Nervii, Frisii, and Batavi. The Batavi on the Roman frontier did not submit to Rome's rule until 13 B.C., and then only as allies.

A part of Charlemagne's empire in the 8th and 9th centuries A.D., the area later passed into the hands of Burgundy and the Austrian Hapsburgs, and finally in the 16th century came under Spanish rule.

When Philip II of Spain suppressed political liberties and the growing Protestant movement in the Netherlands, a revolt led by William of Orange broke out in 1568. Under the Union of Utrecht (1579), the seven northern provinces became the Republic of the United Netherlands.

The Dutch East India Company was established in 1602, and by the end of the 17th century Holland was one of the great sea and colonial powers of Europe.

The nation's independence was not completely established until after the Thirty Years' War (1618–48), after which the country's rise as a commercial and maritime power began. In 1814, all the provinces of Holland and Belgium were merged into one kingdom, but in 1830 the southern provinces broke away to form the Kingdom of Belgium. A liberal Constitution was adopted by the Netherlands in 1848.

In spite of its neutrality in World War II, the Netherlands was invaded by the Nazis in May 1940, and the East Indies were later taken by the Japanese. The nation was liberated in May 1945. In 1948, after a reign of 50 years, Queen Wilhelmina resigned and was succeeded by her daughter Juliana.

In 1949, after a four-year war, the Netherlands granted independence to the East Indies, which became the Republic of Indonesia. In 1963, it turned over the western half of New Guinea to the new nation, ending 300 years of Dutch presence in Asia. Attainment of independence by Surinam on

Nov. 25, 1975, left the Dutch Antilles as the Netherlands' only overseas territory.

The Lockheed bribery scandals, which caused a major scandal in Japan, also brushed the House of Orange in 1976. Prince Bernhard, reported to have been the high official whom a Lockheed Aircraft Corporation executive said was paid more than $1 million to influence the choice of a fighter plane by the Dutch air force, was cleared of the bribe charge by a government panel. Because he was criticized for his business connections by the group, however, Bernhard resigned all his business and military posts.

On May 23, 1977, South Moluccan militants seized 50 persons on a hijacked train and 105 schoolchildren with 6 teachers. The Moluccans, who sided with the Dutch in the war for the independence of Indonesia and were given refuge in the Netherlands, have repeatedly committed acts of terrorism to dramatize their demand for freedom of their home island from Indonesian rule. Dutch Marines freed the hostages.

A seven-month constitutional crisis during which Prime Minister Joop den Uyl had unsuccessfully sought to form a majority coalition ended Dec. 19 when van Agt was able to organize the center-right coalition. Van Agt said in a Jan. 16, 1978, statement that his government would aim chiefly at bringing down both inflation and the 5% unemployment rate.

**Economy.** Dutch farms are characteristically small, with only a few larger than 250 acres. Dairying is more important than crop growing; production of cheese, milk, butter, and eggs is under state control.

An important industry is the raising of tulip, hyacinth, and other flower bulbs in the area around Haarlem.

The Netherlands is a highly industrialized nation, utilizing both overseas raw materials and domestic agricultural products. Leading industries are textiles, clothing, shipbuilding, shoes, food, and building materials.

A major discovery of natural gas in the 1960s made the Netherlands an exporter of energy. As of 1976, reserves were reported at 2.4 billion cubic meters and in 1978 there was discussion of limiting exports after 1980 to conserve gas for domestic use. Sales of gas abroad accounted for the Netherlands' favorable trade balances through the 1970s. Other important minerals are coal, petroleum, and salt.

Chief exports in 1976 were food (19%), chemicals (15%), machinery (13%), petroleum products (12%), transport equipment (6%), and natural gas (5%). Leading customers were EEC (71%; incl. West Germany 31%, Belgium-Luxembourg 15%, France 11%, U.K. 8%, Italy 5%). Leading suppliers were EEC (55%; incl. West Germany 24%, Belgium-Luxembourg 13%, France 7%, U.K. 6%), U.S. 9%.

## Netherlands Autonomous Country

### NETHERLANDS ANTILLES

**Status:** Part of the Kingdom of the Netherlands
**Governor:** B. M. Leito (1970)
**Premier:** S.M.G. Rozendal
**Area:** 371 sq mi. (961 sq km)
**Population (est. 1978):** 250,000.
**Capital (est. 1978):** Willemstad, 152,000

**Geography.** The Netherlands Antilles comprise two groups of Caribbean islands 500 miles apart: one, about 40 miles off the Venezuelan coast, consists of Curaçao (173 sq mi.; 448 sq km), Bonaire (95 sq mi.; 246 sq km), and Aruba (69 sq mi.; 179 sq km); the other, lying to the northeast, consists of three small islands with a total area of 34 square miles (88 sq km). The Dutch acquired the island of Curaçao from Spain in 1643.

**Government.** There is a constitutional government formed by the Governor and Cabinet and an elected Legislative Council. The area has complete autonomy in domestic affairs.

**Economy.** The islands manufacture petroleum products from imported crude oil. The agricultural output consists of aloes, beans, and corn. Lime phosphate and salt are the principal mineral resources.

Chief exports in 1974 were petroleum products (80%) and crude oil (16%). Leading customers in 1975 were U.S. (62%), Netherlands (5%). Leading suppliers were Venezuela (57%), Saudi Arabia (17%), Nigeria (6%), U.S. (6%).

## NEW ZEALAND

**Dominion of New Zealand**
**Sovereign:** Queen Elizabeth II
**Governor-General:** Sir Keith Holyoake (1977)
**Prime Minister:** Robert D. Muldoon (1975)
**Area:** 103,736 sq mi. (268,676 sq km) (excluding dependencies)
**Population (est. 1978):** 3,130,000 (European, 90%; Maori and other Polynesian, 10%)
**Density per square mile:** 30.2
**Capital:** Wellington
**Largest cities (1976 census):** Christchurch, 172,000; Auckland, 150,700; Wellington, 139,600
**Monetary unit:** New Zealand dollar
**Languages:** English, Maori
**Religions (1971):** Church of England (31%); Presbyterian (20%); Roman Catholic (16%)
**Gross national product (1976):** $12.8 billion
**Member of Commonwealth of Nations**
**Freedom House classifications:** Capitalist industrial, multi-party centralized

**Geography.** New Zealand, about 1,250 miles east of Australia, consists of two main islands and a number of smaller, outlying islands so scattered that they range from the tropical to the antarctic. The country is the size of Colorado.

New Zealand's two main components are North Island and South Island, separated by Cook Strait, which varies from 16 to 190 miles (25.7 to 305.8 km) in width. North Island (44,281 sq mi.; 114,688 sq km) is 515 miles (828.8 km) long and volcanic in its south-central part. It contains many hot springs and beautiful geysers. South Island (58,093 sq mi.; 150,461 sq km) has the Southern Alps along its west coast, with Mt. Cook (12,349 ft; 3,764 m) the highest point.

The largest of the outlying islands are the Auckland Islands (234 sq mi.; 606 sq km), Campbell Island (44 sq mi.; 114 sq km), the Antipodes Islands (24 sq mi.; 62.2 sq km), and the Kermadec Islands (13 sq mi.; 33.7 sq km).

**Government.** New Zealand was granted self-government in 1852, a full parliamentary system and ministries in 1856, and dominion status on Sept. 26, 1907. Meanwhile, from 1861 to 1871 there was fierce intermittent fighting with the native Maoris. The Queen is represented by a Governor-General, and the Cabinet is responsible to a unicameral Parliament of 87 members who are elected by popular vote for three years.

The major political parties are the National Party (53 of 87 seats in House of Representatives), led by Prime Minister Robert D. Muldoon; Labor Party (33 seats) led by Wallace E. Rowling; and Social Credit Party (1 seat).

**History.** New Zealand was discovered and named in 1642 by Abel Tasman, a Dutch navigator. Captain James Cook explored the islands in 1769. On Jan. 22, 1840, Britain formally annexed them.

From the first, the country has been in the forefront in adopting social welfare legislation. It adopted old age pensions (1898); a national child welfare program (1907); social security for the aged, widows, and orphans along with family benefit payments; minimum wages; a 40-hour week and unemployment and health insurance (1938); and socialized medicine (1941). The currency was converted to the decimal system based on the dollar in 1967.

New Zealand supported U.S. policy in Vietnam and supplied military aid to South Vietnam in the orientation of its policy toward the U.S. and Asian neighbors after the U.K.'s entry into the European Common Market. To replace the lost British market —the once prosperous islands had fallen into a local recession since 1972—New Zealand sought to sell more agricultural products to Japan. On May 23, 1978, Prime Minister Muldoon announced a pact with Japan enlarging quotas for New Zealand beef, reducing the tariffs on New Zealand fish, and providing for Japanese purchase of butter, skim milk, and other food products.

**Economy.** New Zealand is primarily a grazing country. The chief crops are grass, wheat, oats, barley, potatoes, onions, tobacco, fruits, and vegetables.

Principal minerals are coal and gold. Other minerals of importance include tungsten, pumice, silica sand, asbestos, scheelite, iron ore, and phosphate. About 30% of the total area is forested.

Numerous rushing streams provide New Zealand with a great source of hydroelectric power.

Chief exports in 1975–76 were meat and meat preparations (25%), wool (19%), butter (9%), and wood pulp and paper (5%). Leading customers were U.K. (19%), Japan (14%), Australia (13%), U.S. (12%). Leading suppliers were Australia (20%), U.K. (17%), Japan (15%), U.S. (14%), Iran (5%).

## Cook Islands and Overseas Territories

**The Cook Islands** (93 sq mi.; 241 sq km) were placed under New Zealand administration in 1901. They achieved self-governing status in association with New Zealand in 1965. Population in 1975 was 18,068. The seat of government is on Rarotonga Island.

Chief exports in 1973 were citrus juice (41%), bananas (6%), canned fruit (6%), and pineapple juice (5%). Leading customer in 1970 was New Zealand (98%). Leading suppliers were New Zealand (83%), Japan (5%).

**Niue** (100 sq mi.; 259 sq km) was formerly administered as part of the Cook Islands. It was placed under separate New Zealand administration in 1901 and achieved self-governing status in association with New Zealand in 1974. The capital is Alofi.

Chief exports in 1973 were passion fruit (23%), copra (15%), plaited ware (10%), and honey (8%). Leading customer in 1975 was New Zealand (73%). Leading supplier was New Zealand (79%).

**The Ross Dependency** (160,000 sq mi.; 414,400 sq km), an Antarctic region, was placed under New Zealand administration in 1923.

**Tokelau** (4 sq mi.; 10 sq km) was formerly administered as part of the Gilbert and Ellice Islands colony. It was placed under New Zealand administration in 1925. Its population in 1975 was 1,603.

# NICARAGUA

**Republic of Nicaragua**
**President:** Anastasio Somoza Debayle (1974)
**Area:** 50,193 sq mi. (130,000 sq km)
**Population (est. 1978):** 2,390,000 (mestizo, 70%; white, 17%; black, 9%; Indian, 4%)
**Density per square mile:** 47.6
**Capital and largest city (est. 1976):** Managua, 400,000
**Monetary unit:** Cordoba
**Language:** Spanish
**Religion:** Roman Catholic
**Gross national product (1976):** $1.8 billion
**National name:** República de Nicaragua
**Freedom House classifications:** Capitalist pre-industrial, dominant party

**Geography.** Largest but most sparsely populated of the Central American nations, Nicaragua borders on Honduras to the north and Costa Rica to the south. It is slightly larger than New York State.

Nicaragua is mountainous in the west, with fertile valleys. A plateau slopes eastward toward the Caribbean.

Two big lakes—Nicaragua, about 100 miles long (161 km), and Managua, about 38 miles long (61 km)—are connected by the Tipitapa River. The Pacific coast is bald and rocky. The Caribbean coast, swampy and indented, is aptly called the "Mosquito Coast."

**Government.** Anastasio Somoza Debayle, whose family has ruled Nicaragua since 1934, was elected President in 1974 after a two-year constitutional crisis in which Congress and the Constitution were suspended. A new Constituent Assembly, elected in 1972, rewrote the Constitution to permit Somoza to run for a second term. During the interim, Nicaragua was ruled by a triumvirate friendly to him.

The major political parties are the National Liberal party (60 seats in Assembly), led by Anastasio Somoza Debayle; Conservative Party, led by Edmundo Paguaga-Irias.

**History.** Nicaragua, which established independence in 1838, was first visited by the Spaniards in 1522. The chief of the country's leading Indian tribe at that time was called Nicaragua, from whom the nation derived its name. A U.S. naval force intervened in 1909 after two American citizens had been executed, and a few U.S. Marines were kept in the country from 1912 to 1925. The Bryan-Chamorro Treaty of 1916 (terminated in 1970) gave the U.S. an option on a canal route through Nicaragua, and naval bases. Disorder after the 1924 elections brought in U.S. Marines again.

A guerrilla leader, Gen. César Augusto Sandino, began fighting the Marine occupation force in 1927. He fought the U.S. troops successfully until their withdrawal in 1933. They trained Gen. Anastasio (Tacho) Somoza García to head a National Guard. In 1934, Somoza assassinated Sandino and overthrew the Liberal President Juan Batista Sacassa, establishing a military dictatorship that he headed as President. He spurred the economic development of the country, meanwhile enriching his family through estates in the countryside and investments in air and shipping lines, pursuing a pro-U.S. policy. On his assassination in 1956, he was succeeded by his son Luis, who alternated with trusted family friends in the Presidency until his death in 1967. Another son, Maj. Gen. Anastasio Somoza Debayle, became President for a five-year term on May 1, 1967.

Somoza resigned the presidency in May 1972, but remained commander-in-chief and national strongman while the Constitution was rewritten to permit him to run for a second term. The civilian triumvirate exercised nominal rule until Sept. 3, 1974, when Somoza was declared the winner of a runaway election. Critics called his 20–1 victory margin farcical because special laws disqualified most opponents.

One of the worst earthquakes in Nicaragua's history struck Managua on Dec. 23, 1972, destroying an estimated 90% of its commercial establishments and 70% of its housing. Over 6,000 were killed, 20,000 injured, and 300,000 made homeless, and 60,000 were jobless as a result. Rebuilding costs were put at $772 million.

Following his inauguration on Dec. 1, 1974, Somoza obtained loans from the U.S. and international banks totaling $127 million for the reconstruction of Managua. Shortly afterward, he declared martial law after leftist guerrillas kidnapped 14 prominent officials, and Nicaragua remained under martial law in 1976.

Although the Somoza regime was cited in 1977 by a U.S. State Department report for human-rights violations and Nicaragua's Catholic hierarchy testified to the government's repression and terror, it was not until 1978 that the Carter Administration moved to cut military aid to Somoza.

The situation was aggravated by the murder on January 10 of Pedro Joaquin Chamorro, the opposition leader, causing student strikes and wide public protest. In an uncharacteristic response, Somoza made concessions to protesters and announced an inquiry into Chamorro's death. On May 16, the U.S. Congress acted to restore $12 million in military aid to Nicaragua.

Since the murder of a prominent newspaper editor in February 1978, anti-government activity has increased. A new Broad Opposition Front has demanded President Somoza's resignation. On July 24, four Opposition workers were shot, allegedly by right-wing para-military groups supporting the Somoza regime.

After holding hundreds of hostages in the National Palace in Managua for several days, Sandinista guerrillas flew to Panama on Aug. 24, 1978, with 59 released political prisoners and $500,000. President Somoza's concessions to the rebels were made, he said, "to save lives." Despite this, in the fall of 1978 there was increasing unrest and military action.

**Economy.** More than half of Nicaragua is junglecovered. Agriculture, the leading industry, utilizes only 10% of the total land.

Since 1961, the economic situation has constantly improved. Production of cotton, coffee, and meat products has increased substantially.

Gold and silver are the most important minerals. One-third wooded, Nicaragua produces mahogany, rosewood, cedar, rubber, and ipecac root.

Chief exports in 1975 were cotton (24%), coffee (22%), sugar (10%), and meat (7%). Leading customers were U.S. (28%), Japan (13%), Costa Rica (10%), West Germany (9%), Guatemala (6%), El Salvador (6%). Leading suppliers were U.S. (32%), Venezuela (12%), Japan (7%), Costa Rica (7%), Guatemala (7%), West Germany (6%), El Salvador (6%).

# NIGER

**Republic of Niger**
**Chief of State:** Lt. Col. Seyni Kountché (1974)
**Area:** 489,191 sq mi. (1,267,000 sq km)
**Population (est. 1978):** 5,000,000
**Density per square mile:** 10.2
**Capital and largest city (est. 1975):** Niamey, 130,000
**Monetary unit:** Franc CFA
**Ethnic groups:** Hausa, 53.7%; Djerma and Songhai, 23.6%; Peul, 10.6%
**Languages:** French (official); Hausa, Songhai; Arabic
**Religions:** Islam, Animist, Christian
**Gross national product (1976):** $740 million
**National name:** République du Niger
**Freedom House classifications:** Capitalist pre-industrial, non-party military

**Geography.** Niger, in western Africa's Sahara region, is four fifths the size of Alaska. It is surrounded by Mali, Algeria, Libya, Chad, Nigeria, Benin, and Upper Volta.

The Niger River in the southwest flows through the country's only fertile area. Elsewhere the land is semiarid.

**Government.** After a military coup on April 15, 1974, Lt. Col. Seyni Kountché suspended the Constitution and instituted rule by decree. Previously, the President was elected by direct universal suffrage for a five-year term and a National House of Assembly of 50 members was elected for the same term.

Parti Progressiste Nigérien-Rassemblement Démocratique Africain, the only political party, was dissolved by the military government in 1974.

**History.** Niger was incorporated into French West Africa in 1896. Rebellions were constant, but when order was restored in 1922, the French made the area a colony. In 1958 the voters approved the French Constitution and voted to make the territory an autonomous republic within the French Community. The republic adopted a Constitution in 1959 and in 1960 withdrew from the Community, proclaiming its independence.

The 1974 army coup ousted President Hamani Diori, who had held office since 1960, claiming Diori had mishandled relief for the terrible drought that has devastated Niger and five neighboring sub-Saharan nations for several years. An estimated 2 million people were starving in Niger, but 200,000 tons of imported food, half U.S.-supplied, substantially ended famine conditions by the year's end. The new President, Lt. Col. Seyni Kountché, chief of staff of the army, installed a 12-man military government. A predominantly civilian government was formed by President Kountché on Feb. 21, 1976.

**Economy.** Agricultural products include peanuts, rice, and dates. Livestock raising is an important activity.

Chief exports in 1974 were uranium (50%), livestock (17%), peanut oil (9%), and textile yarns and fabrics (5%). Leading customers were France (54%), Nigeria (27%), West Germany (7%). Leading suppliers were France (37%), U.S. (13%), Nigeria (9%), West Germany (8%).

## NIGERIA

**Federal Republic of Nigeria**
**Head of State:** Lt. Gen. Olusegun Obasanjo (1976)
**Area:** 356,669 sq mi. (923,768 sq km)
**Population (est. 1978):** 66,650,000[1]
**Density per square mile:** 186.9
**Capital:** Lagos
**Largest cities (est. 1975 by U.N.):** Lagos, 1,060,850; Ibadan, 847,000; Ogbomosho, 432,000; Kano, 399,000
**Monetary unit:** Naira
**Languages:** English (official) and native tongues
**Religions:** Islam, 47%; Christian, 34%; Animist
**Gross national product (1976):** $29.3 billion
**Member of Commonwealth of Nations**
**Freedom House classifications:** Capitalist-statist pre-industrial, non-party military

**Geography.** Nigeria, one third larger than Texas, is situated on the Gulf of Guinea in West Africa. Its neighbors are Benin, Niger, and Cameroon.

The lower course of the Niger River flows south through the western part of the country into the Gulf of Guinea. Swamps and mangrove forests border the southern coast; inland are hardwood forests.

**Government.** Since January 1966 a Supreme Military Council has been running the government of the country. But in August 1977 new local-government councils elected a 203-member national Constituent Assembly, which held its opening session in October and was to begin work on the draft constitution completed in 1976. It was hoped that party politics would be resumed in 1978 and that the country could return to civilian rule early in 1979.

**History.** Between 1879 and 1914, private colonial developments by the British, with reorganizations of the crown's interest in the region, resulted in the formation of Nigeria as it exists today. During World War I, native troops of the West African frontier force joined with French forces to defeat the German garrison in the Cameroons.

Nigeria became independent on Oct. 1, 1960. It is black Africa's most populous nation.

Organized as a loose federation of self-governing states, the independent nation faced an overwhelming task of unifying a country with 250 ethnic and linguistic groups. The largest were the Hausa and Fulani in the north and the Ibo and Yoruba in the south, each of which had kingdoms in the late Middle Ages.

The people of the northern section of the British Cameroons voted to join the federation in 1961. In 1963, the people of Benin and Delta provinces, mainly of the Edo tribe, voted to form a new region, the Midwest. Full independence within the Commonwealth was achieved in 1963.

Rioting broke out again in 1966, the military commander was seized, and Col. Yakubu Gowon took power. Also in that year, the Moslem Hausas in the north massacred the predominantly Christian Ibos in the east, many of whom had been driven from the north. Thousands of Ibos took refuge in the Eastern Region. The military government there asked Ibos to return to the region and, in May 1967, the assembly voted to secede from the federation and set up the Republic of Biafra. Civil war broke out.

In January 1970, after 31 months of civil war, Biafra surrendered to the federal government. An estimated one million persons, mostly Ibos of the defeated state, were homeless and hungry, but a massive international relief operation kept the death toll down. The overall cost of the civil war was estimated at $840 million.

Gowon's nine-year rule was ended July 29, 1975, by a bloodless coup that made Army Brigadier Muritala Rufai Mohammed the new chief of state. Gowon was attending a summit meeting of the Organization of African Unity in Uganda at the time of the coup and accepted its results.

Mohammed was assassinated Feb. 13, 1976, by a group of seven young officers, who failed to seize control of the government. The 20-member Supreme Military Council chose Lt. Gen. Olusegun Obasanjo, chief of staff of the armed forces, as the new head of the Council and President. The assassins were publicly executed by firing squads on March 11.

In December 1976, the military government for the first time conducted local elections as a step toward the restoration of full democratic rule by 1979.

Although Nigeria ranked seventh in world oil production in 1977 with revenues of $10 billion, a deficit in its balance of payments of $960 million for the year forced the government to impose severe restrictions on imported consumer goods. Nevertheless, Nigeria's prestige as the richest black African nation was emphasized by the visit of President Carter to Lagos on March 31, 1978, the first visit by an American President to black Africa since a brief stopover in Liberia by President Franklin D. Roosevelt during World War II. In a speech, Obasanjo called for Cuban withdrawal from Africa and urged majority rule in Southern Africa. He pointedly criticized the U.S. and its allies for having failed to apply enough economic pressure on South Africa to bring about change.

**Economy.** Aside from small industry, there is little manufacturing in Nigeria.

Nigeria is a leading tin producer from mines on the Bauchi plateau. Other minerals are coal, gold, lead, silver, tungsten, and petroleum. Over half the area is forested.

Chief export in 1975 was crude oil (94%). Leading customers were U.S. (29%), U.K. (14%), Netherlands (11%), France (11%), Netherlands Antilles (7%), West Germany (7%). Leading suppliers were U.K. (23%), West Germany (15%), U.S. (11%), Japan (10%), France (8%), Italy (6%).

1. While U.N. and similar sources continue to report this figure, interpretations of election data by demographers suggest that, in reality, the population of Nigeria in 1978 approached 100,000,000.

## NORWAY

**Kingdom of Norway**
**Sovereign:** King Olav V (1957)
**Prime Minister:** Odvar Nordli (1976)

**Area:** 125,182 sq mi. (324,219 sq km)
**Population (est. 1978):** 4,050,000
**Density per square mile:** 32.4
**Capital:** Oslo
**Largest cities (est. 1977):** Oslo, 462,500; Bergen, 212,750; Trondheim, 135,550
**Monetary unit:** Krone
**Language:** Norwegian
**Religions:** Evangelical Lutheran (state), 94%
**Gross national product (1976):** $29.9 billion
**National name:** Kongeriket Norge
**Freedom House classifications:** Capitalist-socialist industrial, multi-party centralized

**Geography.** Norway is situated in the western part of the Scandinavian peninsula. It extends about 1,100 miles (1,770 km) from the North Sea along the Norwegian Sea to more than 300 miles (483 km) above the Arctic Circle, the farthest north of any European country. It is slightly larger than New Mexico. Sweden borders on most of the eastern frontier, with Finland and the U.S.S.R. in the northeast.

Nearly 70% of Norway is uninhabitable and covered by mountains, glaciers, moors, and rivers. The hundreds of deep fiords that cut into the coastline give Norway an overall oceanfront of more than 12,000 miles (19,312 km). Nearly 150,000 islands off the coast form a breakwater and make a safe coastal shipping channel.

**Government.** Norway is a constitutional hereditary monarchy. Executive power is vested in the King together with a Cabinet, or Council of State, consisting of a Prime Minister and at least seven other members. The Storting, or Parliament, is composed of 155 members elected by the people under proportional representation. The Storting discusses and votes on political and financial questions, but divides itself into two sections (Lagting and Odelsting) to discuss and pass on legislative matters. The King cannot dissolve the Storting before the expiration of its term.

The sovereign is Olav V, born July 2, 1903, only son of Haakon VII and Princess Maud (1869–1938), third daughter of Edward VII of England. He succeeded to the throne on the death of his father Sept. 20, 1957. He married Princess Märtha of Sweden (1901–1954) on March 21, 1929. Their children are Princess Ragnhild Alexandra (born 1930), Princess Astrid (born 1932), and Crown Prince Harald (born 1937). In 1968, the Crown Prince married Sonja Haraldsen, a commoner.

The major political parties are the Labour Party (76 of 155 seats in the Storting), led by Prime Minister Odvar Nordli; Conservative Party (41 seats), led by Kåre Willoch; Christian Democrats (22 seats), led by Lars Korvald; Center Party (12 seats), led by Johan J. Jakobsen; Socialist Left Party (2 seats).

**History.** Norwegians, like the Danes and Swedes, are of Teutonic origin. The Norsemen, also known as Vikings, ravaged the coasts of northwestern Europe from the 8th to the 11th century.

In 1815, Norway, contrary to her wishes, fell under the control of Sweden. The union of Norway, inhabited by fishermen, sailors, merchants, and peasants, and Sweden, an aristocratic country of large estates and tenant farmers, was not a happy one, but it lasted for nearly a century. In 1905, the Norwegian Parliament arranged a peaceful separation and invited a Danish prince to the Norwegian throne—King Haakon VII. A treaty with Sweden provided that all disputes be settled by arbitration and that no fortifications be erected on the common frontier. Since the separation the two countries have lived amicably as neighbors.

When World War I broke out, Norway joined with Sweden and Denmark in a decision to remain neutral and to cooperate in the joint interest of the three countries. In World War II, Norway was invaded by the Germans on April 9, 1940. She resisted for two months before the Nazis took over complete control. King Haakon and his government fled to London, where they established a government-in-exile. Maj. Vidkun Quisling, who collaborated with the Nazis, was executed by the Norwegians on Oct. 24, 1945.

Despite severe war losses, Norway recovered quickly. The country led the world in social experimentation. A neighbor of the U.S.S.R., Norway sought to retain good relations with it without losing its identity with the West. It entered the North Atlantic Treaty Organization in 1949.

Verification of U.S. and Soviet oil strikes in separated areas of Norway's sector of the North Sea bottom led the Storting in May 1975 to impose stiff tax and royalty rates on concession holders. Following discovery of a new North Sea field expected to produce 900,000 barrels a day by 1984, Parliament on Jan. 7, 1976 approved establishment of a national refining and distributing company to market petroleum products at home and abroad.

**Economy.** Land suitable for cultivation, estimated at less than 5% of the total area, consists of strips in the deep narrow valleys and around fiords and lakes. Foodstuff production is insufficient to meet domestic needs. Leading crops are potatoes, barley, oats, wheat, and rye. The country is more adapted to stock raising than to crop growing.

Raw materials produced in Norway form the basis of most of the manufactures. The most important industries are food, machinery, metals, wood, paper, and electro-chemicals.

Mineral resources are extensive, but coal deposits are entirely lacking except in Spitsbergen. Important minerals are iron ore, aluminum, pyrite ore, zinc, copper ore, molybdenum ore, tungsten, antimony ore, tin, and silver.

Cheap electric power, produced mainly by hydroelectric plants, makes possible the extraction of nitrogen from the air and manufacture of potassium nitrate, an important fertilizer. The forests, largely in the south and southeast, are one of the chief natural resources. Fishing is one of the principal industries.

Chief exports in 1976 were crude oil (15%), ships (11%), machinery (10%), aluminum (7%), iron and steel (7%), chemicals (6%), fish (6%), and paper (5%). Leading customers were U.K. (29%), Sweden (14%), West Germany (10%), Denmark (7%), U.S. (5%). Leading suppliers were Sweden (18%), West Germany (15%), U.K. (10%), Japan (7%), U.S. (6%), Denmark (6%), Netherlands (5%).

## Dependencies of Norway

**Svalbard** (23,957 sq mi.; 62,049 sq km), in the Arctic Ocean about 360 miles north of Norway, consists of the Spitsbergen group and several smaller islands, including Bear Island, Hope Island, King Charles Land, and White Island (or Gillis Land). It came under Norwegian administration in 1925. The population in 1975 was 3,500.

**Bouvet Island** (23 sq mi.; 60 sq km), in the South

Atlantic about 1,600 miles south-southwest of the Cape of Good Hope, came under Norwegian administration in 1928.

**Jan Mayen Island** (144 sq mi.; 273 sq km), in the Arctic Ocean between Norway and Greenland, came under Norwegian administration in 1929. Its population in 1973 was 37.

**Peter I Island** (96 sq mi.; 249 sq km), lying off Antarctica in the Bellinghausen Sea, came under Norwegian administration in 1931.

**Queen Maud Land,** a section of Antarctica, came under Norwegian administration in 1939.

## OMAN

**Sultanate of Oman**
**Sultan:** Qabus Bin Said (1970)
**Area:** 82,030 sq mi. (212,457 sq km)
**Population (est. 1978):** 850,000[1]
**Density per square mile:** 10.4
**Capital (est. 1973):** Muscat, 15,000
**Largest city (est. 1973):** Matrah, 18,000
**Monetary unit:** Omani rial
**Language:** Arabic
**Religion:** Islam
**Gross national product (1976):** $2.1 billion
**National name:** Saltanat Oman
**Freedom House classifications:** Capitalist-statist pre-industrial, non-party traditional

**Geography.** Oman is a 1,000-mile (1,609-km) long coastal plain at the southeastern tip of the Arabian peninsula lying on the Arabian Sea and the Gulf of Oman. The interior is a plateau. The country is the size of Kansas.

**Government.** The Sultan of Oman (formerly called Muscat and Oman), an absolute monarch, is assisted by several Personal Advisers, 17 Ministers, and other government officials.

There are no political parties.

**History.** Although Oman is an independent state under the rule of the Sultan, it has been under British protection since the early 19th century.

Muscat, the capital of the geographical area known as Oman, was occupied by the Portuguese from 1508 to 1648. Then it fell to Persian princes and later was regained by the Sultan.

The Kuria Muria Islands, formerly part of Aden, were given to Oman by the British in 1967.

In a palace coup on July 23, 1970, the Sultan, Sa'id bin Taimur, who had ruled since 1932, was overthrown by his son, who promised to establish a modern government and use new-found wealth to aid the people of this very isolated state.

With the shrinkage of British power, oil-rich Oman has moved into the Iranian military orbit. Iranian troops were detailed in 1973–74 to help the Omani army put down Marxist rebels in Dhofar Province.

**Economy.** Chief export in 1975 was crude oil (100%). Leading customers were Japan (35%), Spain (17%), U.K. (16%), West Germany (6%), Brazil (5%). Leading suppliers in 1976 were U.K. (19%), United Arab Emirates (17%), Japan (12%), West Germany (6%), U.S. (6%), India (5%).

1. Excluding the Kuria Muria Islands.

## PAKISTAN

**Islamic Republic of Pakistan**
**President:** Fazal Elahi Chaudhry (1973)
**Chief Martial Law Administrator:** Gen. Mohammad Zia ul-Haq (1977)
**Area:** 310,403 sq mi. (803,943 sq km)[1]
**Population (est. 1978):** 77,500,000
**Density per square mile:** 249.7
**Capital (1972 census):** Islamabad, 77,000
**Largest cities (est. 1975):** Karachi, 4,465,000; **(1972 census):** Lahore, 2,165,372; Lyallpur, 822,263; Hyderabad, 628,310; Rawalpindi, 615,392
**Monetary unit:** Pakistan rupee
**Principal languages:** Urdu (national), English (official), Punjabi, Sindhi, Pashtu, and Baluchi
**Religions:** Islam, 90%; Hindu, Christian, Buddhist
**Gross national product (1976):** $13.4 billion
**Freedom House classifications:** Capitalist-statist pre-industrial, non-party military

**Geography.** Pakistan is situated in the western part of the Indian subcontinent, with Afghanistan and Iran on the west, India on the east, and the Arabian Sea on the south.

Nearly twice the size of California, Pakistan consists of towering mountains, including the Hindu Kush in the west; a desert area in the east, the Punjab plains in the north, and an expanse of alluvial plains. The 1,000-mile-long Indus River flows through the country from the Kashmir to the Arabian Sea.

**Government.** On July 5, 1977, martial law returned to Pakistan when Gen. Mohammad Zia ul-Haq, Army chief of staff, ousted the civilian government of Prime Minister Zulfikar Ali Bhutto. President Fazal Elahi Chaudhry remained in office and Zia declared himself Chief Administrator of Martial Law as head of a four-man council. The National and state assemblies were dissolved and all political parties banned, while the Chief Justices of the four states replaced the governors.

Zia said his action was not a coup, but only a "de-fusing" of political tension until new elections could be held and civilian government restored. On Sept. 3, 1977, Bhutto was arrested and charged with having conspired to murder a political opponent in 1974.

**History.** Pakistan was one of the two original successor states to British India. For almost 25 years following independence in 1947, it consisted of two separate regions. East and West Pakistan, but now comprises only the western sector. It consists of Sind, Baluchistan, the former North-West Frontier Province, western Punjab, the princely state of Bahawalpur, and several other smaller native states.

The British became the dominant power in the region in 1797 following Lord Clive's military victory, but rebellious tribes have kept the northwest in turmoil. In the northeast, the formation of the Moslem League in 1906 estranged the Moslems from the Hindus. In 1930, the league, led by Mohammed Ali Jinnah, demanded creation of a Moslem state wherever Moslems were in the majority. He supported the U.K. during the war. Afterward, the league received almost a unanimous Moslem vote in 1946 and the U.K. agreed to the formation of Pakistan as a separate dominion.

1. Excluding Kashmir and Jammu.

Pakistan was proclaimed a republic March 23, 1956, and Iskander Mirza, then Governor General, was elected Provisional President. H. S. Suhrawardy, the first non-Moslem League Prime Minister, took office Sept. 12, 1956.

On Oct. 27, 1958, President Iskander Mirza surrendered his power to Gen. Ayub Khan, who purged corrupt and inefficient officeholders, broke up the feudal land system, eliminated much of the black market, tax evasion, and hoarding, and revolutionized education. A vote of confidence in February 1960 extended Ayub's dictatorial rule for five years and gave him power to write a new Constitution. It went into effect in June 1962. In March 1969, Gen. Yahya Khan ousted Ayub and took over as President.

The election of Dec. 7, 1970—the first direct general elections in Pakistani history—set the stage for bloody civil war. The Awami League, led by Sheik Mujibur Rahman, swept all Assembly seats allotted the more populous East Pakistan, while the major West Pakistani party, the People's Party, led by Zulfikar Ali Bhutto, won only 82 seats. General Yahya directed the newly elected Assembly to meet March 1, 1971, and in 120 days write a Constitution. The Assembly never convened. Sheik Mujibur called general strikes, which turned bloody, and told East Pakistanis to stop paying taxes to the central government. West Pakistan troops moved in and fighting began. The independent state of Bangladesh, or Bengali nation, was proclaimed March 26, 1971.

The intervention of Indian troops permitted the new state to emerge and brought Yahya down. Bhutto took over and accepted Bangladesh as an independent entity and met with Indian Premier Indira Gandhi in July 1972 and reached a first-step peace agreement that calls for disputes to be negotiated. India appeared to have also gained a permanent partition of Kashmir along cease-fire lines of 1971. The overall effect was to leave Pakistan a much smaller and weaker nation, no longer able to seriously challenge India.

Diplomatically, 1976 saw the resumption of formal relations between India and Pakistan on July 21. At the same time, civilian air traffic between the two nations was restored after an 11-year interruption.

Pakistan's first elections under civilian rule took place on March 7, 1977, and provoked bitter opposition protest when Bhutto's party was declared to have won 155 of the 200 elected seats in the 216-member National Assembly. A rising tide of violent protest and political deadlock led to a military takeover on July 5. Gen. Mohammed Zia ul-Haq promised new elections, but on October 1 postponed them indefinitely because of disorderly campaigning.

Bhutto was tried for the murder of a former political opponent and was found guilty and sentenced to death on March 18, 1978, by the Lahore High Court. Anti-government riots by his supporters and numerous foreign pleas for clemency produced no response from Zia other than a tightening of martial law.

**Economy.** Pakistan, poor in industry and natural resources, is mainly an agricultural nation. The Punjab contains important wheat-growing areas.

Mineral resources are limited to petroleum, coal, lignite, chromite, and gypsum. Vast quantities of natural gas were discovered at Sui, Baluchistan, in 1952.

Chief exports in 1975–76 were rice (22%), cotton yarn (13%), cotton fabrics (12%), leather (9%), cotton (9%), and carpets (6%). Leading customers were Hong Kong (11%), Saudi Arabia (7%), Japan (7%), U.K. (6%), U.S. (6%), West Germany (5%), Iraq (5%). Leading suppliers were U.S. (19%), Japan (12%), Saudi Arabia (8%), U.K. (8%), West Germany (6%), United Arab Emirates (5%).

## PANAMA

**Republic of Panama**
**President:** Demetrio Lakas Bahas (1972)
**Head of Government:** Gen. Omar Torrijos Herrera (1972)
**Area:** 29,208 sq mi. (75,650 sq km)
**Population (est. 1978):** 1,820,000 (mestizo, 65.34%; black, 13.31%; white, 11.07%; Indian, 9.53%; others, .75%)
**Density per square mile:** 62.3
**Capital and largest city (est. 1977):** Panama City, 427,700
**Monetary unit:** Balboa
**Language:** Spanish (official)
**Religion:** Roman Catholic, 90%, Protestant
**Gross national product (1976):** $2.0 billion
**National name:** República de Panamá
**Freedom House classifications:** Capitalist-statist industrial, non-party military

**Geography.** The southernmost of the Central American nations, Panama is south of Costa Rica and north of Colombia. The Panama Canal bisects the isthmus at its narrowest and lowest point, allowing passage from the Caribbean Sea to the Pacific Ocean.

Panama is slightly smaller than South Carolina. It is marked by a chain of volcanic mountains in the west, moderate hills in the interior, and a low range on the east coast. There are extensive forests in the fertile Caribbean area.

**Government.** Following a military coup in 1968, a two-man junta ruled briefly but was in turn overthrown by Gen. Omar Torrijos, head of the National Guard (which is Panama's army). The Constitution was suspended.

In 1972, a new Constitution was approved by a new 505-seat National Assembly of Community Representatives (corregidores), which was created in the first election in five years. The Charter provides for indirect election of the President by the Assembly. The Assembly elected Demetrio Lakas Bahas President but named General Torrijos as Head of Government with all civil and military powers for six years. Otherwise the Assembly is more a consultative than legislative body. Torrijos named a legislative committee to assist him in drafting laws.

All political parties were suspended in 1968, but a pro-Torrijos New Panama movement operated before the 1972 elections.

**History.** Visited by Columbus in 1502 on his fourth voyage and explored by Balboa in 1513, Panama was the principal transshipment point for Spanish treasure and supplies to and from South and Central America in colonial days. In 1821, when Central America revolted against Spain, Panama joined Colombia, which already had declared its independence. For the next 82 years, Panama attempted unsuccessfully to break away from Colombia. After U. S. proposals for canal rights over the narrow isthmus had been rejected by Colombia, Panama proclaimed its independence with U.S. backing in 1903.

For canal rights in perpetuity, the U.S. paid Panama $10 million and agreed to pay $250,000 each year, increased to $430,000 after devaluation of the U.S. dollar in 1933 and was further increased under a revised treaty signed Jan. 25, 1955. The figure is now $2,328,200 a year. In exchange, the U.S. got the Canal Zone—a 10-mile-wide strip across the isthmus—and a considerable degree of influence in Panama's affairs.

In 1968, Dr. Arnulfo Arias was elected President for the third time in three decades. And for the third time, he was thrown out of office by the military. A two-man junta, Col. José M. Pinilla and Col. Bolivar Urrutia, took control. They were ousted by Gen. Omar Torrijos, who named a new junta, with Lakas as President and Albert Surce as deputy.

Panama and the U.S. agreed in February 1974 to negotiate the eventual reversion of the canal to Panama, despite strongly expressed opposition in the U.S. Congress. The texts of two treaties—one governing the transfer of the canal and the other guaranteeing its neutrality after transfer—were negotiated by August 1977 and were signed by Torrijos and President Carter in Washington on September 7. A Panamanian referendum approved the treaties by more than two thirds on October 23, but further changes were insisted upon by the U.S. Senate.

The principal change was a reservation sponsored by Senator Dennis De Concini, an Arizona Democrat, specifying that despite the neutrality treaty's specification that only Panama shall maintain forces in its territory after transfer of the canal Dec. 31, 1999, the U.S. should have the right to use military force to keep the canal operating if it should become obstructed. After lengthy debate, the Senate approved the neutrality treaty on March 16, 1978, by 68–32 and by the same vote approved the basic treaty governing the transfer on April 18. On June 16, Carter and Torrijos exchanged instruments of ratification in Panama City.

The basic treaty provides an increase from the present $2.3 million a year in royalties to $10 million a year during the transition period, with an additional annual payment of $10 million if it can be obtained from tolls. It also requires the use of more Panamanians as canal employees in the interim and pledges the U.S. not to pursue the development of another canal without the agreement of Panama.

**Economy.** About five eighths of the nation is unoccupied. A fourth of the population is in Colón and in Panama City, the oldest white settlement on the Pacific coast of the Americas. In the cities, the lower classes are descendants of British West Indian laborers on the canal.

The Panama Canal is the country's biggest economic asset. The main railway is the U.S. government-owned Panama Railroad (47.64 mi.; 77 km), bridging the isthmus from Panama City to Colón. In recent years many foreign ships have been registered in Panama to escape high labor costs and governmental regulations in other nations.

Revenues from canal tolls are of decreasing importance, and the country is beginning to exploit natural resources that have not been touched since independence was achieved. A steel mill has been built, a manganese mine has been opened, and farm land is being extended.

Chief exports in 1975 were petroleum products (29%), bananas (27%), shrimps (15%), and sugar (12%). Leading customers were U.S. (59%), Canal Zone (12%), West Germany (6%), Italy (5%). Leading suppliers were U.S. (27%), Saudi Arabia (17%), Ecuador (15%), Venezuela (8%), Japan (5%).

## PAPUA NEW GUINEA

**Sovereign:** Queen Elizabeth II
**Prime Minister:** Michael Somare (1975)
**Governor General:** Sir Tore Lokoloko
**Area:** 178,259 sq mi. (461,691 sq km)
**Population (est. 1978):** 2,980,000
**Density per square mile:** 16.7
**Capital and largest city (1976 census):** Port Moresby, 113,449
**Monetary unit:** Kina
**Languages:** English, Police Motu, Pidgin English (all official)
**Religions:** Roman Catholic, Lutheran, Anglican
**Gross national product (1976):** $1.4 billion
**Member of Commonwealth of Nations**
**Freedom House classifications:** Capitalist pre-industrial, multi-party centralized

**Geography.** Papua New Guinea occupies the eastern half of the island of New Guinea, just north of Australia, and many outlying islands. The Indonesian province of Irian Jaya is to the west. To the north and east are the islands of Manus, New Britain, New Ireland, and Bougainville.

Papua New Guinea is about one tenth larger than California. Its mountainous interior has only recently been explored. The high-plateau climate is temperate, in contrast to the tropical climate of the coastal plains. Two major rivers, the Sepik and the Fly, are navigable for shallow-draft vessels.

**Government.** Papua New Guinea attained independence Sept. 16, 1975, ending a United Nations trusteeship under the administration of Australia. Chief Minister Michael Somare became the first Prime Minister, heading a coalition Cabinet. Parliamentary democracy was established by a Constitution that invests power in a single-chamber national legislature.

Just before independence, dissidents on the island of Bougainville, whose copper resources provide the chief foreign earnings for the central government, declared their intention to secede. The central government responded by taking direct control on Oct. 16, 1975, amid warnings from Australia that it would oppose secession. Somare met with pro-secessionists early in 1976 and, after conceding extra powers for a restored provincial government, appeared to have resolved the dispute.

Pangu Party (senior in the coalition government) and United Party (the main opposition) are largest of half a dozen political parties.

**History.** The eastern half of New Guinea was first visited by Spanish and Portuguese explorers in the 16th century, but a permanent European presence was not established until 1884, when Germany declared a protectorate over the northern coast and Britain took similar action in the south. Both nations formally annexed their protectorates and, in 1901, Britain transferred its rights to a newly independent Australia. Australian troops invaded German New Guinea in World War I and retained control under a League of Nations mandate that eventually became a United Nations trusteeship, incorporating a territorial government in the southern region, known as Papua.

Australia granted limited home rule in 1951 and, in 1964, organized elections for the first House of Assembly. Autonomy in internal affairs came nine years later.

**Economy.** Papua New Guinea is heavily dependent on foreign aid, 90% of which comes from Australia.

Copper leads the mineral production, with gold an important export and extensive exploration for oil in progress.

Chief exports in 1974–75 were copper ores (56%), cocoa (9%), coffee (8%), and copra (7%). Leading customers in 1975 were Japan (30%), West Germany (29%), Australia (14%), U.K. (6%), U.S. (6%), Spain (5%). Leading suppliers were Australia (46%), Japan (14%), U.S. (9%), U.K. (5%).

## PARAGUAY

**Republic of Paraguay**
**President:** Gen. Alfredo Stroessner (1954)
**Area:** 157,047 sq mi. (406,752 sq km)
**Population (est. 1978):** 2,870,000 (mestizo, 94.9%; white, 3.0%; Indian, 2.1%)
**Density per square mile:** 18.3
**Capital and largest city (est. 1975 by U.N.):** Asunción, 574,000
**Monetary unit:** Guaraní
**Languages:** Spanish (official), Guaraní
**Religion:** Roman Catholic (official)
**Gross national product** (1976): $1.7 billion
**National name:** República del Paraguay
**Freedom House classifications:** Capitalist-statist pre-industrial, dominant party

**Geography.** California-size Paraguay is surrounded by Brazil, Bolivia, and Argentina in south central South America. Eastern Paraguay, between the Paraná and Paraguay Rivers, is upland country with the thickest population settled on the grassy slope that inclines toward the Paraguay River. The greater part of the Chaco region to the west is covered with marshes, lagoons, dense forests, and jungles.

**Government.** The President is elected by popular vote for five years. The legislature is bicameral, consisting of a Senate of 30 members and a Chamber of Representatives of 60 members. There is also a Council of State, whose members are nominated by the government.

The governing Partido Colorado was even further strengthened in 1977 when the Partido Liberal Unido, a merger of the Partido Liberal Radical and Partido Liberal, was declared illegal.

**History.** In 1526 and again in 1529, Sebastian Cabot explored Paraguay when he sailed up the Paraná and Paraguay Rivers. From 1608 until their expulsion from the Spanish dominions in 1767, the Jesuits maintained an extensive establishment in the south and east of Paraguay. In 1811, Paraguay revolted against Spanish rule and became a nominal republic under two Consuls.

Actually, Paraguay was governed by three dictators during the first 60 years of independence. The third, Francisco López, declared war on both Brazil and Argentina in 1864–65, a conflict in which the male population was almost wiped out. A new Constitution in 1870, designed to prevent dictatorships and internal strife, failed to do so, and not until 1912 did a period of comparative economic and political stability begin. The dispute between Paraguay and Bolivia over the Chaco region led to war in 1932 and was finally settled by the 1935 Buenos Aires peace conference, which gave most of the Chaco to Paraguay.

After World War II, politics became particularly unstable. Juan Natalicio González was elected President in the 1948 elections, and took office in August. Successive revolts on Jan. 30 and Feb. 26, 1949, ousted him and his successor. The leader of the second revolt, Felipe Molas López, was elected President in April but gave way to Federico Chaves. Re-elected in 1953, he was ousted by the army, and Gen. Alfredo Stroessner was elected to complete his term.

Stroessner ruled under a state of siege until 1965, when the dictatorship was relaxed and exiles returned. The Constitution was revised in 1967 to permit Stroessner to be re-elected, and press freedom was briefly restored before the regime again moved to repress opposition.

U.S. companies began exploration for oil in 1974 in the desolate Chaco Boreal section of northwest Paraguay under 40-year contracts that the regime's critics denounced as overgenerous. No oil has been found.

Paraguay was criticized by the U.S. State Department for violation of human rights, but was not one of the countries for which the Carter administration recommended aid cuts. Stroessner in January and February of 1977 released three Communist leaders jailed in 1958 together with 11 other political prisoners. He was reported to have acted after a visit by OAS Sec. Gen. Alejandro Orfila, who carried an urgent message from Carter. Amnesty International estimated that about 350 political prisoners remained.

On Aug. 8, 1978, opposition leader Domingo Laino was freed after the court ruled that President Stroessner's regime had not proved its charges that Laino had connections with leftist subversives. Laino's arrest in July had provoked sharp protest from the U.S.

**Economy.** A well-favored land, Paraguay is predominantly a cattle country, keeping about four million head. The chief cash crop is cotton.

Forest resources are considerable, especially in the Chaco. Quebracho—the "axe-breaker," a wood so heavy that it will not float—is the principal commercial tree. The wood has many uses, from paving blocks to oxcart wheels. Quebracho tannic extract is the chief product.

Chief exports in 1976 were cotton (19%), meat (12%), vegetable oils (9%), tobacco (8%), and timber (7%). Leading customers were Netherlands (15%), U.S. (12%), West Germany (11%), Argentina (10%), Switzerland (10%), U.K. (6%), France (6%), Brazil (6%), Uruguay (5%). Leading suppliers were Argentina (21%), Brazil (17%), Algeria (13%), U.S. (10%), West Germany (8%), U.K. (8%), Japan (5%).

## PERU

**Republic of Peru**
**President:** Gen. Francisco Morales Bermúdez (1975)
**Premier:** Gen. Oscar Molina Pallochia (1978)
**Area:** 496,222 sq mi. (1,285,216 sq km)
**Population (est. 1978):** 17,000,000 (white and mestizo, 52%; Indian, 46%; Asiatic, black, and other, 2%
**Density per square mile:** 34.3
**Capital:** Lima
**Largest cities (est. 1975 by U.N. for metropolitan area):** Lima, 3,901,000. Arequipa, 304,600; Callao, 296,200; Trujillo, 241,900
**Monetary unit:** Sol
**Languages:** Spanish, Quéchua
**Religion:** Roman Catholic
**Gross national product (1976):** $13.2 billion
**National name:** República del Perú

**Freedom House classifications:** Capitalist-socialist pre-industrial, non-party military

**Geography.** Peru, in western South America, extends for nearly 1,500 miles (2,414 km) along the Pacific Ocean. Colombia and Ecuador are to the north, Brazil and Bolivia to the east, and Chile to the south.

Five sixths the size of Alaska, Peru is divided by the Andes Mountains into three sharply differentiated zones. To the west is the coastline, much of it arid, extending 50 to 100 miles inland. The mountain area, with peaks over 20,000 feet (6,096 m), lofty plateaus, and deep valleys, lies centrally. Beyond the mountains to the east is the heavily forested slope leading to the Amazonian plains.

**Government.** Since the bloodless coup d'état of Oct. 3, 1968, the Constitution has remained suspended, and the country has been governed by a military junta. Its leader, Gen. Francisco Morales Bermúdez, is President.

The major political parties are Acción Popular, led by Fernando Belaunde Terry; Partido Aprista Peruano, led by Victor R. Haya de la Torre; Partido Democrático Cristiano, led by Héctor Cornejo Chávez; Partido Popular Cristiano, led by Luis Bedoya Reyes; Movimiento Democrático Peruano.

**History.** Peru was once part of the great Incan empire and later the major vice-royalty of Spanish South America. It was conquered in 1531–33 by Francisco Pizarro. On July 28, 1821, Peru proclaimed its independence, but the Spanish were not finally defeated until 1824.

For a hundred years thereafter, revolutions were frequent, and a new war was fought with Spain in 1864–66. A dispute with Chile over Tacna and Arica was not finally settled until 1929.

Peru emerged from 20 years of dictatorship in 1945 with the inauguration of President José Luis Bustamente y Rivero after the first free election in many decades. But he served for only three years and was succeeded in turn by Gen. Manuel A. Odria, Manuel Prado y Ugarteche, and Fernando Belaunde Terry. On Oct. 3, 1968, Belaunde was overthrown in a bloodless coup by Gen. Juan Velasco Alvarado.

Velasco nationalized the nation's second biggest bank and turned two large newspapers over to Marxists in 1970, but he also allowed a new agreement with a copper-mining consortium of four American firms.

On May 31, 1970, the country suffered the hemisphere's worst natural disaster, an earthquake which, together with a mud slide it caused, took an estimated 50,000 lives.

The World Bank granted Peru $470 million in credits in 1973, which appeared to end a boycott by international financial institutions in which the U.S. has a strong influence. American copper and fishing firms were seized in 1974, but compensation was paid. Peru also became in 1974 the first nation in the Western Hemisphere to receive Soviet military advisers.

On Aug. 29, 1975, President Velasco was replaced in a bloodless coup by his Premier, Gen. Francisco Morales Bermúdez. Morales eased censorship, which had caused public unrest, and in the summer of 1976 was enlisting aid from foreign banks to overcome severe economic problems.

To meet International Monetary Fund requirements for the extension of credit, Morales decreed a severe economic austerity program in 1977, touching off student and leftist demonstrations. Even stiffer measures, ranging from 50% to 100% increases in the prices of essentials, were ordered in 1978. The Communist General Confederation of Peruvian Workers called a general strike for May 22–23, paralyzing major cities and leading to clashes with police that caused at least five deaths.

The disorders delayed Peru's first free vote in more than a decade until June 18, when 3.7 million electors chose 100 members of a special assembly to write a new constitution. Although Morales retired from the Army at the beginning of 1978, he indicated he would remain in the Presidency at least until 1980, when he promised that civilian rule would return.

**Economy.** Land under cultivation is estimated at only slightly more than 10% of the total area, with more than 50% of the population being dependent on agriculture. Cotton is an important crop. Stock raising supplies domestic needs and valuable exports. Llamas, used as beasts of burden, and vicuñas and alpacas, noted for their wool, are native to Peru.

Peru has vast mineral resources. Important products are petroleum, coal, iron ore, lead, zinc, copper, tungsten, silver, and gold.

An important industry on the outlying islands is the gathering of guano (bird excrement), a valuable fertilizer.

Chief exports in 1974 were copper (17%), fish meal (13%), zinc (11%) silver (11%), coffee (9%), sugar (7%), cotton (6%), and iron ore (5%). Leading customers were U.S. (36%), Japan (13%), West Germany (8%), China (5%). Leading suppliers were U.S. (31%), Japan (12%), West Germany (10%), Ecuador (5%).

## THE PHILIPPINES

**Republic of the Philippines**
**President and Prime Minister:** Ferdinand E. Marcos (1965)
**Area:** 115,831 sq mi. (300,000 sq km)
**Population (est. 1978):** 46,400,000
**Density per square mile:** 400.6
**Capital:** Manila
**Largest cities (est. 1976 for urban agglomeration):** Manila, 7,800,000; **(est. 1975 by U.N.):** Quezon City, 994,700; Davao, 515,500, Cebu, 418,500
**Monetary unit:** Peso
**Languages:** Filipino, English, Tagalog, Visayan, Spanish, Ilocano, Bicol
**Religions:** Roman Catholic, 85%; Islam, 4%; Aglipayan (Independent Philippine Christian), 4%; Protestant, 3%
**Gross national product (1976):** $17.7 billion
**National name:** República de Filipinas—Republike ñg Pilipinas
**Freedom House classifications:** Capitalist pre-industrial, one-party nationalist

**Geography.** The Philippine Islands are an archipelago of over 7,000 islands lying about 500 miles (805 km) off the southeast coast of Asia. The overall land area is comparable to that of Arizona. The northernmost island, Y'Ami, is 65 miles (105 km) from Taiwan, while the southernmost, Saluag, is 40 miles (48 km) east of Borneo.

Only about 7% of the islands are larger than one square mile, and only one third have names. The largest are Luzon in the north (40,420 sq mi.; 104,687 sq km), Mindanao in the south (36,537 sq mi.; 94,631 sq km), Samar (5,124 sq mi.; 13,271 sq km), Negros (4,903 sq mi.; 12,699 sq km), and Palawan (4,550 sq km).

The islands are of volcanic origin, with the larger ones crossed by mountain ranges. The highest peak is Mt. Apo (9,690 ft.; 2,954 m) on Mindanao.

**Government.** President Ferdinand E. Marcos proclaimed a new Constitution in 1973, replacing the previous Presidential style of government with a parliamentary system. The President became the symbolic head of state and the Prime Minister the head of government, with Marcos holding both posts. Marcos has ruled by decree since Sept. 21, 1972, and the new Constitution dissolved the previous legislature. A new National Assembly of 165 elected and 28 appointed members was chosen April 7, 1978. Its powers are limited, within the framework of what Marcos has called "constitutional authoritarianism."

**History.** Fernando Magellan, the Portuguese navigator in the service of Spain, discovered the Philippines on March 16, 1521. Twenty-one years later, a Spanish exploration party named the group of islands in honor of Prince Philip, later Philip II of Spain. Spain retained possession of the islands for the next 350 years.

The Philippines were ceded to the U.S. in 1899 by the Treaty of Paris after the Spanish-American War. Meanwhile, the Filipinos, led by Emilio Aguinaldo, had declared their independence. They continued guerrilla warfare against U.S. troops until the capture of Aguinaldo in March 1901. By July 1902, peace was established except among the Moros.

The first U.S. civilian Governor-General was William Howard Taft (1901–04). The Jones Law (1916) provided for the establishment of a Philippine Legislature composed of an elective Senate and House of Representatives. The Tydings-McDuffie Act (1934) provided for a transitional period until 1946, at which time the Philippines would become completely independent.

Under a Constitution approved by the people of the Philippines on May 14, 1935, the Commonwealth of the Philippines was inaugurated on Nov. 15, 1935. Manuel Quezon y Molina was elected President on Sept. 17, 1935.

On Dec. 8, 1941, the Philippines were invaded by Japanese troops. Following the fall of Bataan and Corregidor, President Quezon established a government-in-exile, which he headed until his death in 1944. He was succeeded by Vice President Sergio Osmeña.

U.S. forces led by Gen. Douglas MacArthur reinvaded the Philippines in October 1944 and, after the liberation of Manila in February 1945, Osmeña re-established the government.

The Philippines achieved full independence on July 4, 1946. Manuel A. Roxas y Acuña was elected President on April 23, 1946. Subsequent Presidents have been Elpidio Quirino (1948–53), Ramón Magsaysay (1953–57). Carlos P. García (1957–61), Diosdado Macapagal (1961–65), and Ferdinand E. Marcos (from Dec. 30, 1965).

Marcos became the first President in Philippine history to win re-election, Nov. 11, 1969, when he overwhelmingly defeated Sergio Osmeña, Jr., with campaign promises to become less dependent on the U.S. and to establish ties with Communist countries. The campaign violence led to 59 deaths. After inauguration, the worst peacetime riots in Philippine history occurred when a student-led demonstration tried to storm the presidential palace, with 5 dead and 157 injured, to protest government corruption.

Political, civil, and religious unrest was responsible for the deaths of almost 500 persons in 1971, and disastrous month-long rains that caused enormous flooding added to the toll in 1972. In September 1972, Marcos declared martial law and arrested hundreds of political opponents, journalists, and leftists.

The legality of martial rule was affirmed Feb. 1, 1975, by a 10–1 vote of the Philippine Supreme Court. After a referendum four weeks later, the government said its continuance was approved by 90% of the voters.

Nearly 5,000 persons died Aug. 16, 1976, when an earthquake measuring 8 on the Richter scale hit Mindanao and other southern islands. The disaster temporarily quelled a rebellion by the Moslem majority in Mindanao, but fighting resumed until a truce was reached in December. Rebel representatives and Manila officials signed an agreement in Tripoli, March 20, 1977, providing a degree of autonomy for the Moslem region. After voters opposed autonomy in a plebiscite boycotted by the rebels, new talks beginning in Manila April 30 failed to bridge the differences and on June 11 the government warned all rebels to surrender.

The Philippines was one of six nations criticized by the U.S. State Department for human rights violations in a report made public Jan. 1, 1977, although the department recommended continuing aid because of the importance of U.S. bases in the Philippines. Marcos at first asserted he would reject any aid and threatened to close the bases but later softened, saying they could remain if the U.S. pledged that the bases would be used to defend the Philippines in the event of an attack. June 3, Marcos announced that he would phase out the military tribunals he established in 1972 and in the next two months freed about 1,000 of 4,774 prisoners being held for military trial.

Political restraints were eased for the legislative elections of April 7, 1978. The suppressed Liberal Party and other opposition groups formed the People's Force Party and contested the 21 seats assigned to Manila. Amid charges of fraud, Marcos' New Society Movement won all 21. A purely local opposition party, the Pusyon Bisaya, won 13 seats allotted to the island of Cebu, and one seat on the island of Mindanao was won by the Mindanao Alliance Party. Marcos freed many political prisoners before his inauguration as Prime Minister on June 12 and pledged to move toward "making democracy real" although he retained his powers under martial law.

By August 1978, Moslem rebels had expanded their operations in the southern islands to strengthen their bargaining position before pending peace talks with the government.

**Economy.** Agriculture is the chief industry. Average size of the farms is 10 acres, but there are many large plantations. Rice (palay) is the staple native food cereal, but production is insufficient to meet home consumption. The Philippines normally produce about half the world's copra supply and a large proportion of the abacá (Manila hemp) supply. They are also a leading source of sugar and sugar products. Other crops are sisal, kapok, cotton, corn, tobacco, coffee, rubber, cacao, citrus fruits, and bananas.

There are no large industrial establishments, and activity is limited primarily to the processing of agricultural and forest products, such as sugarcane, coconuts, tobacco, abacá, and timber. The preparation of fine embroideries is important.

The Philippines possess large but relatively undeveloped mineral resources. Most important are gold, silver, iron ore, copper ore, chromite, manganese ore, lead, and zinc.

Chief exports in 1976 were sugar (18%), coconut oil (12%), copper ores (10%), timber (8%), fruit and vegetables (7%), and copra (6%). Leading customers were U.S. (36%), Japan (24%), Netherlands (8%). Leading suppliers were Japan (27%), U.S. (22%), Saudi Arabia (8%), Kuwait (6%).

## POLAND

**Polish People's Republic**
**President of the Council of State:** Henryk Jablonski (1972)
**Prime Minister:** Piotr Jaroszewicz (1972)
**Area:** 120,725 sq mi. (312,677 sq km)
**Population (est. 1978):** 35,050,000
**Density per square mile:** 290.3
**Capital:** Warsaw
**Largest cities (est. 1976 by U.N.):** Warsaw, 1,448,900; Lódz, 804,300; Kraków, 693,800; Wroclaw, 579,600; Poznan, 521,600; Gdansk, 426,800; Szczecin, 372,900
**Monetary unit:** Zloty
**Language:** Polish (more than 90%)
**Religions:** Roman Catholic, Greek Orthodox, Protestant, Jewish
**Gross national product (1976):** $98.1 billion
**National name:** Polska Rzeczpospolita Ludowa
**Freedom House classifications:** Capitalist-socialist industrial, one-party communist

**Geography.** Poland, a country the size of New Mexico in north Central Europe, borders on East Germany to the west, Czechoslovakia to the south, and the U.S.S.R. to the east. In the north is the Baltic Sea.

Most of the country is a plain with no natural boundaries except the Carpathian Mountains in the south and the Oder and Neisse Rivers in the east. Other major rivers, which are important to commerce, are the Warta, Bug, and Vistula.

**Government.** The 1952 Constitution describes Poland as a People's Republic. The supreme organ of state authority is the Sejm (Parliament), which is composed of 460 members elected for four years.

The major political parties are the Polish United Workers' (Communist) Party (255 of 460 seats in Sejm), led by First Secretary Edward Gierek; United Peasant Party (117 seats), led by Stanislaw Gucwa; Democratic Party (39 seats), led by Tadeusz W. Mlynczak; non-party members and Catholic organizations (49 seats).

**History.** Little of certainty is known about Polish history before the 11th century, when King Boleslaus I (the Brave) ruled over Bohemia, Saxony, and Moravia. Mongol invasions in 1241 and 1259 were repelled. Meanwhile, the Teutonic knights were erecting in Prussia a state that included part of Poland and barred the latter's access to the Baltic. The knights were defeated by Wladislaus II at Tannenberg in 1410 and became Polish vassals, and Poland regained a Baltic shoreline. Poland reached the peak of power between the 14th and 16th centuries. Poles scored military successes against the Russians and Turks. In 1683, John III (John Sobieski) turned back the Turkish tide at Vienna.

These successes did not halt the process of decline that resulted from the lack of strong central authority, and Prussia, Russia, and Austria were able to carry out a first partition of the country in 1772, a second in 1792, and a third in 1795–96. For more than a century thereafter, there was no Polish state, but the Poles never ceased their efforts to regain their independence.

The independence of Poland was formally proclaimed in November 1918, and Marshal Josef Pilsudski was made Chief of State. In 1919, Ignace Paderewski, the famous pianist and patriot, became the first Premier.

On April 25, 1920, in an attempt to wrest the Ukraine from the Bolsheviks, Poland attacked Russia. The Poles reached Kiev in May, but in June the Russians launched a counterattack, driving the Poles back to Warsaw by August. The Poles, under Józef Pilsudski and aided by the French, then drove back the Russians, forcing them to abandon their conquests in Poland.

On May 12, 1926, Marshal Pilsudski seized complete power in a coup d'état and ruled the country dictatorially until his death on May 12, 1935, when he was succeeded as commander of the army by Marshal Edward Smigly-Rydz.

Despite a 10-year nonaggression pact signed with Germany in 1934, Hitler attacked Poland on Sept. 1, 1939. Russian troops invaded from the east on September 17, and on September 28 a German-Russian agreement was signed dividing Poland between Russia and Germany. Wladyslaw Raczkiewicz formed a government-in-exile in France with Gen. Wladyslaw Sikorski as Premier. This government moved to London after France's defeat in 1940.

All of Poland was occupied by Germany after the Nazi attack on the U.S.S.R. in June 1941. On July 30, 1941, the government-in-exile signed an agreement with the U.S.S.R. in which the latter voided all German-Soviet agreements effected after Sept. 1, 1939.

The legal Polish government soon fell out with the Russians, however, and, in July 1944, a Communist-dominated Polish Committee of National Liberation received Soviet recognition. Moving to Lublin after that city's liberation, it proclaimed itself the Provisional Government of Poland on Dec. 31, 1944. Some former members of the Polish government in London joined with the Lublin government to form the Polish Government of National Unity on June 28, 1945. The U.K. and U.S. recognized this government in 1945.

On Aug. 2, 1945, in Berlin, President Truman, Marshal Stalin and Prime Minister Attlee established a new *de facto* western frontier for Poland along the Oder and Neisse rivers. (The border was finally agreed to by West Germany in a nonaggression pact signed Dec. 7, 1970.) On Aug. 16, 1945, the U.S.S.R. and Poland signed a treaty delimiting the Soviet-Polish frontier. Under these agreements, Poland was shifted westward. In the east it lost 69,860 square miles (180,934 sq km) with 10,772,000 inhabitants; in the west it gained (subject to final peace-conference approval) 38,986 square miles (100,973 sq km) with a prewar population of 8,621,000.

In 1946, a unicameral Parliament was established by referendum. A limited legal opposition was countenanced at first. Then, in 1947, the government bloc won a huge majority in government-controlled elections and after much fighting the underground opposition was suppressed and the Sovietization of Poland begun, with Soviet Marshal Konstantin Rokossovsky as Defense Minister and army commander.

In 1952, a Constitution was promulgated making Poland a "people's democracy" of the Soviet type. In 1955, Poland, which had joined the Council for Economic Mutual Assistance in 1949, became a member of the Warsaw Treaty Organization, and its foreign policy became identical with that of the U.S.S.R. The government undertook persecution of the Roman Catholic Church as one of the remaining foci of opposition and in 1953 arrested the primate, Stefan Cardinal Wyszynski. But in 1956, worker and student riots in Poznan (June 28–30) forced reconsideration of the repression.

Wladyslaw Gomulka was elected leader of the United Workers (Communist) Party in October 1956. He denounced the Stalinist terror, ousted many Stalinists, relieved Rokossovsky, freed Wyszynski, and improved relations with the church. Most collective farms were dissolved, and the press became freer.

Much as the Poznan bread riots of 1956 brought Gomulka to power, so pre-Christmas rioting in 1970 in Gdansk and other Baltic coastal towns caused Gomulka to fall and elevated Gierek to the key post of party boss. Cause of the worker riots, in which at least 45 and probably over 200 died when police and army troops crushed the protest, was steep price rises on meat and other foods. Significantly, no students or intellectuals were involved.

Serious resistance to increased food prices again brought rioting in Polish cities in the summer of 1976 after the government announced on June 24 a new schedule of prices.

As a result of the riots, the government in 1977 revised its economic goals to put more emphasis on production of consumer goods and reduced foreign borrowing for capital investment, slowing industrial development. In response to the activities of a Workers Defense Committee, the government on February 4 freed 30 prisoners still imprisoned from the food riots. On March 27, a group of professionals formed a Movement for the Defense of Human and Civil Rights to cooperate with the Workers Defense Committee and to seek freedom of expression for all political groups.

In January 1978, 14 Communist Party members petitioned Gierek to grant more political freedoms, including participation of non-Communist parties in the government. In April, the Polish Writers' Union elected four dissidents to its 25-member board.

**Economy.** Industrial facilities, although severely damaged during World War II, were not greatly affected by territorial concessions to the U.S.S.R., with the exception of the Lwów area. On the other hand, important German industrial areas, especially Silesia and the city of Stettin, are located in the territories under *de facto* Polish administration.

The acquisition of large coal deposits in German Silesia, combined with much larger reserves in the southwestern region, makes Poland one of the world's leading coal producers. Iron ore deposits are located in the Kielce and Radom districts and in German Silesia (metal content 34%). Zinc and lead ores are located chiefly in Upper Silesia and the voivodships of Kielce and Kraków. Pre-war Poland's principal oil-producing areas, Boryslaw-Drohobycz, are in the territory ceded to the U.S.S.R. Among other deposits, Poland possesses copper, sulfur, chalk, clay, kaolin, marble, and granite.

Chief exports in 1976 were machinery (44%), fuel and energy (18%), textiles and clothing (9%), chemicals (9%), and food (7%). Leading customers were U.S.S.R. (30%), East Germany (10%), Czechoslovakia (8%), West Germany (6%). Leading suppliers were U.S.S.R. (26%), West Germany (9%), East Germany (8%), U.S. (6%), Czechoslovakia (6%), France (6%), U.K. (5%).

# PORTUGAL

**Republic of Portugal**
**President:** Gen. António Ramalho Eanes (1976)
**Premier:** Alfredo Nobre da Costa (1978)
**Area:** 35,553 sq mi. (92,082 sq km)
**Population (est. 1977):** 10,000,000
**Density per square mile:** 281.3
**Capital:** Lisbon
**Largest cities (est. 1976):** Lisbon, 847,300; (**est. 1974 by U.N.**): Oporto, 311,800
**Monetary unit:** Escudo
**Language:** Portuguese
**Religion:** Roman Catholic
**Gross national product (1976):** $16.5 billion
**National name:** República Portuguesa
**Freedom House classifications:** Capitalist-socialist industrial, multi-party centralized

**Geography.** Portugal occupies the western part of the Iberian Peninsula, bordering on the Atlantic Ocean to the west and Spain to the north and east. It is slightly smaller than Indiana.

The country is crossed by many small rivers, and also by three large ones that rise in Spain, flow into the Atlantic, and divide the country into three geographic areas. The Minho (Miño in Spain) River, part of the northern boundary, cuts through a mountainous area that extends south to the vicinity of the Douro (Duero) River. South of the Douro, the mountains slope to the plains about the Tagus (Tejo) River. The remaining division is the southern one of Alentejo.

The Azores, stretching over 340 miles (547 km) in the Atlantic, consist of nine islands divided into three groups, with a total area of 924 square miles (2,393 sq km). The nearest continental land is Cape da Roca, Portugal, about 900 miles (1,448 km) to the east. The Azores are an important station on Atlantic air routes, and both the U.K. and U.S. established air bases there during World War II.

Madeira, consisting of two inhabited islands, Madeira and Porto Santo, and two groups of uninhabited islands, lies in the Atlantic about 535 (861 km) southwest of Lisbon.

**Government.** The new Portuguese Constitution, adopted in April 1976, provides for a President elected by universal suffrage for a term of five years and for a legislature, the Assembly of the Republic, of 265 members elected for four-year terms.

A military coup on April 25, 1974, dissolved the former bicameral legislature and also dissolved what had been for 40 years the only authorized political party, the National Popular Action Party.

The major political parties are the Socialist Party (102 seats in the Assembly), led by former Premier Mário Soares; Social Democratic Party (73 seats), led by Dr. Francisco Sá Carneiro; Democratic Social Center Party (41 seats), led by Prof. Diogo Freitas do Amaral; and Communist Party (40 seats), led by Dr. Alvaro Cunhal.

**History.** Portugal was a part of Spain until it won its independence in the middle of the 12th century. King John I (1385–1433) unified his country at the expense of the Castilians and the Moors of Morocco. The expansion of Portugal was brilliantly coordinated by John's son, Prince Henry the Navigator. In 1488, Bartholomew Diaz reached the Cape of Good Hope, proving that the Far East was accessible by sea. In 1498, Vasco da Gama reached the west coast of India. By the middle of the 16th century, the Portuguese Empire included West and East Africa, Brazil, Persia, Indo-China, and Malaya.

In 1581, Philip II of Spain invaded Portugal and held it captive for 60 years. There followed a catastrophic decline of Portuguese commerce. Courageous and shrewd explorers, the Portuguese proved to be inefficient and corrupt colonizers. By the time the Portuguese dynasty was restored in 1640, Dutch, English, and French competitors began to seize the lion's share of the world's colonies and commerce. Portugal retained Angola and Mozambique in Africa, and Brazil (until 1822).

In the first half of the 19th century, Portugal's political history was distinguished by dynasty quarrels and factional strife. The corrupt King Carlos, who ascended the throne in 1889, made João Franco the Premier with dictatorial power in 1906. In 1908, Carlos and his heir were shot dead on the streets of Lisbon. The new King, Manoel II, was driven from the throne in the Revolution of 1910. Portugal was proclaimed a republic with a system modeled upon that of France.

Traditionally friendly to the U.K., Portugal entered World War I on the Allies' side, and Portuguese troops fought on the Western Front and in Africa. In 1926, a revolution drove out the President, and six years later the dictatorship of Antonio Oliveira Salazar began. He kept Portugal neutral in World War II but gave the Allied powers naval and air bases in 1943.

In 1961, Indian forces took Goa, Daman, and Diu, but Portugal crushed an insurrection in Angola and thereafter fought a disastrous war against guerrillas. Through the 1960s, the country opposed nationalists also in its other African possessions. U.N. resolutions calling for self-determination in these territories were ignored.

In September 1968, Premier Salazar suffered a cerebral hemorrhage and lapsed into a coma. (He died in 1970.) Marcello Caetano was named to succeed him. He continued to support military suppression of independence movements in various overseas territories. In 1971, however, Portugal granted greater autonomy for her overseas territories, particularly Angola and Mozambique.

The military coup of April 25, 1974, installed Gen. António de Spinola as Provisional President and promised sweeping domestic reforms and peace to the African colonies. The coup leaders were younger officers, notably Col. Vasco dos Santos Gonçalves, who later became Premier. The Communist Party leader was included in the Cabinet, and Socialist leader Mário Soares became Foreign Minister. Caetano and former President Américo Tomás were sent into exile. Relatively little blood was shed in the coup. Amnesty was declared for all political prisoners, and press curbs were removed.

Called the "happy revolution" because it easily unseated a detested rightist dictatorship, the coup headed by the Armed Forces Movement (M.F.A.) had a strong leftward thrust. Spinola appointed a moderate-left Cabinet that failed to deal with the political ferment that followed the coup. On July 14, 1974, the M.F.A. named Gonçalves Premier. Spinola resigned as President on September 30 after having failed to organize moderate sentiment, and was replaced by Gen. Francisco da Costa Gomes, Chief of Staff of the armed forces. Communist influences accelerated under Gonçalves.

While the far left was strong in Lisbon, resistance elsewhere in conservative Portugal surfaced when elections were held April 25, 1975, for delegates to a Constituent Assembly empowered to draft a democratic Constitution. The Socialists won 38% of the vote, the Popular Democrats 26%, and the Communists trailed badly with 12.5%. But the message was blunted by a pre-election deal between the parties and the Supreme Revolutionary Council of the M.F.A., which specified that changes in government could be made solely by the President on the advice of the Premier and the Revolutionary Council.

Anti-Communist violence in rural areas and intense pressure from non-Communists in the government and the M.F.A. led to Gonçalves' ouster on Aug. 29, 1975. His replacement was Vice Adm. José Pinheiro de Azevedo, Vice President of the provisional government. On September 19, a new government—Portugal's fifth since the "happy revolution"—was sworn in amid hopes that it could survive until the Constituent Assembly finished drafting the Constitution.

Despite pre-election violence, the first elections under the new Constitution were carried out on June 27, 1976, with Gen. António Ramalho Eanes, army Chief of Staff, winning a landslide victory. Eanes promised austerity measures to restore an economy that showed signs of recovery, measures expected to meet resistance from the left.

Inflation averaged nearly 30% in 1977 and the balance of payments deficit was $1.5 billion. When Soares sought the aid of other parties in carrying out an economic austerity program, he lost a vote of confidence on Dec. 8, 1977. Soares formed a new government seven weeks later, with a pledge of support for his economic program by the conservative Democratic Social Center Party.

The alliance held as the Assembly adopted a 30% sales tax, income tax surcharges, and other stiff measures in April 1978. Soares was committed to cut the 1978 payments deficit to $900 million and to devalue the escudo by a further 12% in order to receive $800 million in loans from the International Monetary Fund, the U.S., and 12 other industrial nations. In July, the Center Democrats left the governing coalition, depriving Soares of his majority in the legislature. However, Soares continued in office until his dismissal on July 27, 1978, by President Eanes. The president chose a nonparty industrialist, Alfredo Nobre da Costa, to replace Soares on Aug. 9, but Soares insisted that his party stay out of any coalition government.

**Economy.** Portugal's corporate state has a planned economy in which each producing unit regulates itself in the interest of the nation. Corporate units have been established in agriculture, industry, and finance.

One of the world's leading wine-makers, Portugal produces two famous kinds—Port in the vicinity of Oporto, and Madeira in the islands of the same name.

Leading crops include wheat, barley, oats, rye, maize, rice, and potatoes. Portugal is a leading producer of olive oil.

Mineral resources have not been fully developed, but wolfram, coal, iron ore, copper, manganese, iron pyrites, lead, tin, and other ores are found.

Portugal is one of the world's leading producers of cork.

The fishing industry is a basic part of the national economy. Of special importance is the sardine industry centered at Setúbal.

Chief exports in 1975 were textile yarns and fabrics (16%), clothing (11%), machinery (11%), food (8%), wine (7%), chemicals (6%), cork and manufactures (6%), and motor vehicles (5%). Leading customers in 1976 were U.K. (18%), West Germany

(11%), France (8%), Sweden (8%), U.S. (7%). Leading suppliers were West Germany (12%), U.K. (9%), U.S. (9%), France (9%), Spain (5%), Italy (5%).

## Portuguese Overseas Territory

After the April 1974 revolution, the military junta moved to grant independence to the territories, beginning with Portuguese Guinea in September 1974, which became the republic of Guinea-Bissau.

Mozambique and Angola followed, leaving only Portuguese Timor and Macao of the former Empire. Despite Lisbon's objections, Indonesia annexed Timor.

## MACAO

**Status:** Territory
**Governor:** Major José Garcia Leandro
**Area:** 6 sq mi. (15.5 sq km)
**Population (est. 1978):** 280,000
**Capital (1970 census):** Macao, 241,413

Macao comprises the peninsula of Macao and the two small islands of Taipa and Colôane on the South China coast, about 35 miles from Hong Kong. Established by the Portuguese in 1557, it is the oldest European outpost in the China trade, but Portugal's sovereign rights to the port were not recognized by China until 1887, and its boundaries are still not delimited. The port has been eclipsed in importance by Hong Kong, but it is still a busy distribution center and also has an important fishing industry. It is notorious for its opium trade and gambling houses. Most of the population is Chinese.

Macao's future is under negotiation between Portugal and China, which asserted a claim to the enclave in 1972.

**Economy.** Macao manufactures textiles, firecrackers, footwear, and porcelain.

Chief exports in 1975 were clothing (48%) and textile yarns and fabrics (36%). Leading customers were France (21%), West Germany (14%), U.S. (11%), Hong Kong (10%), Portugal (6%), Netherlands (6%), U.K. (6%). Leading suppliers were Hong Kong (71%), China (19%).

## QATAR

**State of Qatar**
**Ruler:** Sheik Khalifa bin Hamad al-Thani (1972)
**Area:** 4,274 sq mi. (11,000 sq km)
**Population (est. 1978):** 200,000
**Density per square mile:** 33.9
**Capital (est. 1977):** Doha, 150,000
**Monetary unit:** Qatari riyal
**Language:** Arabic
**Religion:** Islam
**Gross national product (1976):** $2.4 billion
**Freedom House classifications:** Capitalist-statist industrial, non-party traditional.

**Geography.** Qatar occupies a small peninsula that extends into the Persian Gulf from the east side of the Arabian Peninsula. Saudi Arabia is to the west and the United Arab Emirates to the south. The country is mainly barren.

**Government.** Qatar is one of the Persian Gulf sheikdoms, between Bahrain and Oman. For a long time, it was under Turkish protection, but in 1916, the sultan took British protection. After the discovery of oil in the 1940s and its exploitation in the 1950s and 1960s, political unrest spread to the sheikdoms. Qatar declared its independence in 1971. The next year the current Sheik, Khalifa bin Hamad al-Thani, ousted his cousin, then ruler, in a bloodless coup.

**Economy.** Chief export in 1976 was crude oil (96%). Leading customers in 1975 were U.K. (18%), U.S. Virgin Islands (17%), France (11%), Italy (7%), West Germany (6%), Thailand (6%). Leading suppliers were U.K. (21%), Japan (15%), U.S. (13%), West Germany (9%).

## RHODESIA

**President:** John J. Wrathall (1976)
**Prime Minister:** Ian Smith (1964)
**Area:** 150,803 sq mi. (390,580 sq km)
**Population (est. 1978):** 6,950,000 (black, 96%; white, 4%)
**Density per square mile:** 46.1
**Capital:** Salisbury
**Largest cities (est. 1977 for urban agglomeration):** Salisbury, 561,000; Bulawayo, 339,000
**Monetary unit:** Rhodesian dollar
**Languages:** English (official), Sindebele, Shona
**Religions:** Christian, 20%; Animist
**Gross national product (1976):** $3.6 billion
**Freedom House classifications:** Capitalist-statist pre-industrial, multi-party centralized

**Geography.** Rhodesia, a landlocked country in south central Africa, is slightly smaller than California. It is bordered by Botswana on the west, Zambia on the north, Mozambique on the east, and South Africa on the south.

A high veld up to 6,000 feet (1,829 m) crosses the country from northeast to southwest. This is flanked by a somewhat lower veld that contains ranching country. Tropical forests that yield hardwoods lie in the southeast.

In the north, on the border with Zambia, is the 175-mile-long (128-m) Kariba Lake, formed by the Kariba Dam across the Zambezi River. It is the site of one of the world's largest hydroelectric projects.

**Government.** Executive authority is vested in a 18-minister Cabinet, which is headed by the Prime Minister, and legislative authority is vested in a Legislative Assembly of 66 members.

The major political parties are the Rhodesian Front (all 50 white seats of the Legislative Assembly), led by Prime Minister Ian Smith; Rhodesia Party (7 of the 8 black elective seats). Eight more black members are selected by tribal leaders.

**History.** Rhodesia, formerly called Southern Rhodesia, was part of the Federation of Rhodesia and Nyasaland, which came to an end on Dec. 31, 1963. In 1964, both Northern Rhodesia and Nyasaland became independent states, but Rhodesia remained a British colony.

Rhodesia was opened by Cecil Rhodes's British South Africa Company, which administered the area until 1923. At that time, in a referendum, the Europeans voted to become a self-governing colony rather than merge with what was then the Union of South Africa.

On Nov. 11, 1965, the white-minority government of Rhodesia unilaterally declared its independence from the U.K.

In 1967, Rhodesia became the first country against which the United Nations ever imposed mandatory sanctions. The U.S. stopped virtually all trade with Rhodesia. The country refused to cave in, but began a slow movement toward meeting the demands of the Black Africans. The white minority regime of Prime Minister Ian Smith withstood British pressure, economic sanctions, guerrilla attacks, and a Right-wing assault.

On March 1, 1970, Rhodesia formally proclaimed itself a republic, and within the month nine nations, including the U.S., closed their consulates there.

In 1972 the international economic boycott of Rhodesia began to break down. The U.S. was one country that resumed trade by buying Rhodesian chrome ore, but restored the ban one year later.

Black terrorism, which began late in 1972, resulted in the death of several hundred black rebels and several dozen white citizens and soldiers. The army draft size was doubled and other steps were taken to counter the security threat, including uprooting 8,000 black Africans from the area bordering Mozambique in an attempt to create a 200-mile-long buffer zone.

Heightened guerrilla war and a withdrawal of South African military aid—particularly helicopters—marked the beginning of the collapse of Smith's 11 years of resistance in the spring of 1976. Under pressure from South African Prime Minister Johannes Vorster, Smith agreed with U.S. Secretary of State Henry A. Kissinger on September 19 that majority rule should come within two years.

Smith met with black nationalist leaders in Geneva, Oct. 28, 1976, under the chairmanship of Ivor Richard, British representative to the U.N. The meeting broke up December 12 as the Rhodesian Premier insisted that whites must retain control of the police and armed forces during the transition to majority rule. A British proposal called for Britons to take over these powers.

In January 1977, Richard began a "mini-shuttle" among the capitals of the neighboring black countries, the "front line" nations, and Salisbury and Pretoria. Divisions sharpened between Rhodesian blacks—Bishop Abel Muzorewa of the African National Congress and Ndabaningi Sithole as moderates versus Robert Mugabe and Joshua Nkomo of the Patriotic Front as advocates of guerrilla force—and no agreement was reached. In July, with white residents leaving in increasing numbers and the economy showing the strain of war, Smith rejected outside mediation and called for general elections in order to work out an "internal solution" of the transfer of power.

On March 3, 1978, Smith, Muzorewa, Sithole, and Chief Jeremiah Chirau signed an agreement to transfer power to the black majority by Dec. 31, 1978. They constituted themselves an Executive Council, with chairmanship rotating but Smith retaining the title of Prime Minister. Blacks were named to each cabinet ministry, serving as co-ministers with the whites already holding these posts. African nations and the Patriotic Front leaders immediately denounced the action, but Western governments were more reserved, although none granted recognition to the new regime.

An appeal for a cease-fire was ignored and guerrilla action increased, with white missionaries the targets of brutal killings. The death toll for the first half of 1978 reached nearly 2,000.

Black guerrilla raids continued, reaching within 17 miles of Salisbury. At least 28 deaths were reported over the August 19 weekend as Prime Minister Smith promised to step up efforts to obtain a cease-fire.

The government announced on July 26 its plan for holding universal suffrage elections and for the promised accession to black majority rule, presumably on December 31, 1978. Also in July, the U.S. Senate rejected a move to repeal economic sanctions against Rhodesia.

**Economy.** Agricultural products include tobacco, corn, tea, sugar, and peanuts. Minerals include coal, chrome ore, asbestos, iron ore, and gold.

Chief exports in 1965 were tobacco (33%), food (10%) and asbestos (8%). Leading customers were Zambia (25%), U.K. (22%), South Africa (10%), West Germany (9%), Malawi (5%), Japan (5%). Leading suppliers were U.K. (30%), South Africa (23%), U.S. (7%), Japan (6%).

## ROMANIA

**Socialist Republic of Romania**
**President:** Nicolae Ceausescu (1967)
**Premier:** Manea Manescu (1974)
**Area:** 91,700 sq mi. (237,500 sq km)
**Population (est. 1978):** 21,630,000 (Romanian, 88%; Hungarian, 8%)
**Density per square mile:** 235.9
**Capital:** Bucharest
**Largest cities (est. 1977):** Bucharest, 1,807,000; Timisoara, 268,800; Iasi, 265,000; Cluj-Napoca, 262,400; Brasov, 257,100; Constanta, 256,900; Galati, 239,300; Craiova, 222,400
**Monetary unit:** Leu
**Languages:** Romanian, Hungarian, Serbian, German, Turkish
**Religions:** Romanian Orthodox, 85%; Catholic and Protestant, 15%
**Gross national product (1976):** $31.1 billion
**National name:** Republica Socialistă România
**Freedom House classifications:** Socialist industrial, one-party communist

**Geography.** A country in southeastern Europe slightly smaller than Oregon, Romania is bordered on the west by Hungary and Yugoslavia, on the north and east by the U.S.S.R., on the east by the Black Sea, and on the south by Bulgaria.

The Carpathian Mountains divide Romania's upper half from north to south and connect near the center of the country with the Transylvanian Alps, running east and west.

North and west of these ranges lies the Transylvanian plateau, and to the south and east are the plains of Moldavia and Walachia. In its last 190 miles (306 km), the Danube River flows through Romania only. It enters the Black Sea in northern Dobruja, just south of the border with the Soviet Union.

**Government.** The supreme body of state power and the sole legislative body is the Grand National Assembly, with 465 members elected for five-year terms. It elects a State Council to provide continuity of state power and to settle problems between sessions of the Assembly. The supreme executive and administrative body is the Council of Ministers elected by the Assembly.

The Communist Party, led by Secretary General Nicolae Ceausescu, is the only political party.

**History.** Most of Romania was the Roman province of Dacia from about A.D. 100 to 275. From the 6th to the 12th centuries, wave after wave of barbarian conquerors—Vlachs, Bulgars, and others—passed over the area. By the 15th century, the main

Romanian principalities of Moldavia and Walachia had become satellites within the Ottoman Empire, although they retained much independence. After the Russo-Turkish War of 1828–29, they became Russian protectorates. In 1848 the Romanians rose in rebellion but were suppressed by the Russians. The nation became a kingdom in 1881 after the Congress of Berlin.

King Ferdinand acceded to the throne in 1914. At the start of World War I Romania proclaimed its neutrality, but later joined the Allied side and in 1916 declared war on the Central Powers. The armistice of Nov. 11, 1918, gave Romania vast territories from Russia and the Austro-Hungarian Empire.

The gains of World War I, making Romania the largest Balkan state, included Bessarabia, Transylvania, and Bukovina. The Banat, a Hungarian area, was divided with Yugoslavia.

In 1925, Crown Prince Carol renounced his rights to the throne, and when King Ferdinand died on July 20, 1927, Carol's son, Michael (Mihai) became King under a regency. However, Carol returned from exile in 1930, was crowned King Carol II, and gradually became a powerful political force in the country. On Feb. 10, 1938, he abolished the democratic Constitution of 1923.

On June 21, 1940, the country was reorganized along Fascist lines, and the Fascist Iron Guard became the nucleus of the new totalitarian party. On June 27, the Soviet Union occupied Bessarabia and northern Bukovina. By the Axis-dictated Vienna Award of 1940, two fifths of Transylvania went to Hungary, after which the King dissolved Parliament and granted the new Premier, Ion Antonescu, full power. Carol abdicated and again went into exile.

Romania subsequently signed the Axis Pact on Nov. 23, 1940, and the following June joined in Germany's attack on the Soviet Union, reoccupying Bessarabia. Following the invasion of Romania by the Red Army in August 1944, King Michael led a coup d'état that ousted the Antonescu government. An armistice with the Soviet Union was signed Sept. 12, 1944, in Moscow.

Elections held Nov. 19, 1946, resulted in a victory for the Communist-dominated government bloc. Michael abdicated on Dec. 30, 1947, and thereafter the nation was declared a "people's republic."

A new Constitution in 1952 made Romania a "people's democracy" of the Soviet type. In 1955, Romania joined the Warsaw Treaty Organization and the United Nations. A new Constitution was adopted in 1965, which, while proclaiming Romania a socialist republic, emphasized national autonomy.

Through the decade, Romania under Nicolae Ceausescu grew more independent of Moscow, exchanging trade and military delegations with China and Albania and, on Aug. 2–3, 1969, hosting the visit of President Richard M. Nixon. Ceausescu continued his rapport with Peking and visited China in 1971. In contrast to his flexibility in foreign affairs, he clamped down on liberal tendencies at home and took increasing personal power, becoming chief of the armed forces.

In its first postwar accord with Washington, Romania exchanged cultural and scientific agreements with the U.S. in December 1974.

For the first time in 29 years, Romanians were offered some choice of candidates when they voted, on March 9, 1975, in parliamentary and local elections. There were contests for 39% of the parliamentary seats, but all candidates were Communist Party members. Officials said 99.9% of the voters turned out.

On March 4, 1977, an earthquake measuring 7.1 on the Richter scale struck Bucharest and other cities. The official death toll was 1,541, but the total was believed higher. The government said 11,275 were injured and 80,000 left homeless, with damage exceeding $2 billion.

**Economy.** Romania is predominantly agricultural, with about 65% of the population engaged on the soil. In wheat, rye, and other grains, it is one of the richest countries of southeastern Europe. The largest acreage is usually devoted to corn and wheat. Other crops are flax, hemp, fruit, vegetables, potatoes, sugar beets, sunflower seeds, tobacco, and grapes. Stock raising is important.

Probably the most important industries are food processing, textiles, metals, chemicals, wood, and paper. All but small business enterprises are nationalized.

By far the most valuable of Romanian resources is oil, produced chiefly in the Ploesti region about 35 miles north of Bucharest.

Natural gas from Transylvania is the second most important resource. Important minerals are iron ore, lignite, copper, gold, and silver. Uranium deposits have been reported.

Chief exports in 1975 were machinery and transport equipment (25%), petroleum products and metals (22%), chemicals (11%), and food (11%). Leading customers were U.S.S.R. (20%), West Germany (8%), East Germany (5%). Leading suppliers were U.S.S.R. (17%), West Germany (11%), East Germany (6%), Switzerland (5%), Czechoslovakia (5%).

## RWANDA

**Republic of Rwanda**
**President:** Maj. Gen. Juvénal Habyarimana (1973)
**Area:** 10,169 sq mi. (26,338 sq km)
**Population (est. 1978):** 4,600,000
**Density per square mile:** 452.4
**Capital and largest city (est. 1977):** Kigali, 90,000
**Monetary unit:** Rwanda franc
**Languages:** Kinyarwanda and French
**Religions:** Roman Catholic, 50%; Protestant, 40%; Islam, 5%; Animist
**Gross national products (1976):** $480 million
**Freedom House classifications:** Capitalist-socialist pre-industrial, one-party nationalist

**Geography.** Rwanda, in east central Africa, is surrounded by Zaire, Uganda, Tanzania, and Burundi. It is slightly smaller than Maryland.

Steep mountains and deep valleys cover most of the country. Lake Kivu in the northwest, at an altitude of 4,829 feet (1,472 m) is the highest lake in Africa. From it, extending south, are the Virunga Mountains, which include Volcan Karisimbi (14,187 ft.; 4,324 m), Rwanda's highest point.

**Government.** Grégoire Kayibanda was President from 1962 until he was overthrown in a bloodless coup July 5, 1973, by the military led by Gen. Juvénal Habyarimana. The legislative Assembly was dissolved and all activities of Kayibanda's Parmenhutu Party, the only one permitted at the time, were suspended.

**History.** Rwanda, which was part of German East Africa, was first visited by European explorers in 1854. During World War I it was occupied in 1916 by Belgian troops. After the war it became a Belgian League of Nations mandate, along with Burundi, under the name of Ruanda-Urundi. The mandate was made a U.N. trust territory in 1946. Until the Belgian Congo achieved independence on June 30, 1960, Ruanda-Urundi was administered as part of that colony.

Ruanda became the independent nation of Rwanda on July 1, 1962.

**Economy.** Rwanda is primarily an agricultural and cattle-raising country. Among its natural resources are tin, tungsten, beryllium, methane, and hydroelectric potential. It also produces pyrethrum, coffee, tea, cotton, tobacco, and food crops. There is little industry because of the lack of cheap power.

Chief exports in 1975 were coffee (77%), tea (7%), and tin (6%). Leading customers were Kenya (68%), Belgium-Luxembourg (17%). Leading suppliers were Belgium-Luxembourg (16%), West Germany (10%), Kenya (10%), France (7%), Japan (7%), Iran (6%), U.S. (6%), Italy (6%).

## SAN MARINO

**Republic of San Marino**

**Co-Regents:** Two selected every six months by Grand and General Council
**Area:** 23.6 sq mi. (62 sq km)
**Population (est. 1978):** 20,500 (mostly Italian)
**Density per square mile:** 868.6
**Capital and largest city (est. 1976 for metropolitan area):** San Marino, 4,600
**Monetary unit:** Italian lira
**Language:** Italian
**Religion:** Roman Catholic
**National name:** Repubblica di San Marino

**Geography:** One tenth the size of New York City, San Marino is surrounded by Italy. It is situated in the Apennines, a little inland from the Adriatic Sea near Rimini.

**Government.** The country is governed by two co-regents. Executive power is exercised by two secretaries of state—one for foreign and political affairs and one for internal affairs. In April 1959, the Grand Council granted women the vote.

The major political parties are the Christian Democratic Party (26 of 60 seats in Grand and General Council); Communist Party (16 seats), Democratic Socialist Party (11 seats), Socialist Party (7 seats).

**History.** According to tradition, San Marino was founded about A.D. 350 and had good luck for centuries in staying out of the interminable wars and feuds on the Italian peninsula. It is the oldest republic in the world.

A person born in San Marino remains a citizen and can vote no matter where he lives.

**Economy.** San Marino derives much revenue from the exporting of its postage stamps, which are changed often to keep philatelists buying. Other exports are barley, wine and cattle, as well as building stone from Mount Titano.

## SÃO TOMÉ AND PRÍNCIPE

**Democratic Republic of São Tomé and Príncipe**

**President:** Manuel Pinto da Costa (1975)
**Premier:** Miguel Trovoada (1975)
**Area:** 372 sq mi. (964 sq km)
**Population (est. 1978):** 85,500
**Density per square mile:** 229.8
**Capital and largest city (est. 1977):** São Tomé, 20,000
**Monetary unit:** São Tomé and Príncipe escudo
**Language:** Portuguese
**Religion:** Roman Catholic
**Gross national product (1976):** $40 million
**Freedom House classifications:** Socialist pre-industrial, one-party socialist

**Geography.** The tiny volcanic islands of São Tomé and Príncipe lie in the Gulf of Guinea about 150 miles off West Africa. São Tomé (about 330 sq mi.; 855 sq km) is covered by a dense mountainous jungle, out of which have been carved large plantations. Príncipe (about 40 sq mi.; 104 sq km) consists of jagged mountains. Other islands in the republic are Pedras Tinhosas and Rolas.

**History.** São Tomé and Príncipe became independent of Portugal on July 12, 1975. They were discovered by the Portuguese in 1471. The majority of the early inhabitants were convicts, Jews from Portugal, and slaves from Brazil and the mainland.

**Economy.** The principal industry is commercial agriculture. There are about 110 coffee and cocoa plantations on São Tomé, nearly all owned by Portuguese companies. Fishing is being developed slowly.

Chief exports in 1973 were cocoa (87%) and copra (8%). Leading customers in 1975 were Netherlands (52%), Portugal (33%), West Germany (8%). Leading suppliers were Portugal (61%), Angola (13%).

## SAUDI ARABIA

**Kingdom of Saudi Arabia**

**Ruler and Prime Minister:** King Khalid Bin Abdul-Aziz (1975)
**Area:** 829,995 sq mi. (2,149,690 sq km)
**Population (est. 1978):** 9,800,000
**Density per square mile:** 11.8
**Capital:** Riyadh
**Largest cities (1974 census):** Riyadh, 666,840; Jiddah, 561,104; Mecca, 366,801
**Monetary unit:** Riyal
**Language:** Arabic
**Religion:** Islam
**Gross national product (1976):** $41.2 billion
**National name:** Al-Mamlaka al-'Arabiya as-Sa'udiya
**Freedom House classifications:** Capitalist-statist industrial, non-party traditional

**Geography.** The Middle East oil country of Saudi Arabia occupies most of the Arabian Peninsula, with the Red Sea and the Gulf of Aqaba on the west and the Persian Gulf on the east. Neighbors are Jordan, Iraq, and Kuwait in the north, and, along the perimeter from southwest to east, the two Yemens, Oman, and the United Arab Emirates. The country is more than three times the size of Texas.

Saudi Arabia's oil region lies along the Persian Gulf. The country is mostly desert. The Asir Mountains inland rise to a height of 9,000 feet (2,743 m).

**Government.** Saudi Arabia is a monarchy whose legitimacy rests on *Shariah* (the Law of Islam) and custom. A Council of Ministers was formed in

November 1953. It acts as a Cabinet under the leadership of the King and is composed of 21 ministries.

Royal and ministerial decrees account for most of the promulgated legislation, treaties, and conventions.

There are no political parties in Saudi Arabia.

**History.** Mohammed united the Arabs in the seventh century, and his followers, led by the caliphs, founded a great empire with its capital at Medina. Later, the caliphate capital was transferred to Damascus and then Baghdad, but Arabia retained its importance because of the holy cities of Mecca and Medina. In the 16th and 17th centuries, the Turks established at least nominal rule over much of Arabia, and in the middle of the 18th century, it was divided into separate principalities.

The kingdom of Saudi Arabia is almost entirely the creation of King Ibn Saud (1882–1953). A descendant of earlier Wahabi rulers, he seized Riyadh, the capital of Nejd, in 1901 and set himself up as leader of the Arab nationalist movement. By 1906 he had established Wahabi dominance in Nejd. He conquered Hejaz in 1924–25, consolidating it and Nejd into a dual kingdom in 1926. In 1932, Hejaz and Nejd became a single kingdom, which was officially named Saudi Arabia. A year later the region of Asir was incorporated into the kingdom.

Oil was discovered in 1936, and commercial production began during World War II. Saudi Arabia was neutral until nearly the end of the war, but it was permitted to be a charter member of the United Nations. The country joined the Arab League in 1945 and took part in the 1948–49 war against Israel, but followed a less extremist policy as opposed to the line of the 1958–61 United Arab Republic. In 1951, the U.S. was allowed to build an air base at Dhahran.

On Ibn Saud's death in 1953, the eldest son, Saud, began an 11-year reign marked by an increasing hostility toward the radical Arabism of Egypt's Gamal Abdel Nasser. In 1964, the ailing Saud was deposed and replaced by the Premier, Crown Prince Faisal, who gave vocal support but no military help to Egypt in the 1967 Mideast war. He sent a token force of 1,000 to Syria in the 1973 Arab-Israeli war and joined the five-month oil boycott of the West afterward.

Faisal's assassination by a deranged kinsman March 25, 1975, shook the Middle East, but failed to alter his kingdom's course. His successor was his brother, Prince Khalid, chosen within hours by five senior princes of the House of Saud. King Khalid gave influential support to Egypt during negotiations on Israeli withdrawal from the Sinai desert. His government made it clear to the industrial West that Saudi Arabia's relatively moderate oil pricing policies could change if consumer nations flouted Saudi views.

The Saudi Council of Ministers approved in May 1975 a $140-billion five-year plan to develop industry, transportation, and education to service the welfare state created under Faisal and to modernize the armed forces.

Saudi Arabia has exercised a moderating influence in the Organization of Petroleum Exporting Countries (OPEC) to restrain price increases, and has become an economic power. As of July 1, 1978, the Saudi Arabian riyal and Iranian rial replaced the Danish krone and the South African rand in the 16 currencies used as the basis for the International Monetary Fund's special drawing rights. As a measure of Saudi influence, the U.S. Senate on May 15, 1978, backed an Administration request for the sale of F-15 jet warplanes to Saudi Arabia despite strong objections from pro-Israel members.

**Economy.** The majority of the inhabitants are Bedouin—nomads following their flocks over the desert. The population is predominantly Sunni Moslem, and the religious law of Islam is the common law of the land. Mecca and Medina are the leading religious centers of Islam, and the annual influx of pilgrims to those cities is the most important commercial activity outside the oil industry.

Oil, discovered in 1936 in the province of al-Hasa along the Persian Gulf, is produced by the Arabian American Oil Co. (Aramco), owned 60% by the Saudi government and 40% by four U.S. companies that operate it. The main production centers are in Ghawar, Abqaiq, Safaniya, Dammam, Qatif, and Khursaniya. Production has skyrocketed since World War II. The company's expenditures and payroll are important invisible exports, and oil revenues have greatly strengthened the financial position of the kingdom, which receives one half the company's profits. The oil fields are connected by pipeline with the port of Sidon, Lebanon.

Chief exports in 1974 were crude oil (94%) and petroleum products (6%). Leading customers were Japan (16%), France (12%), Italy (10%), U.K. (9%), Spain (6%). Leading suppliers were U.S. (17%), Japan (16%), Lebanon (15%), West Germany (6%), U.K. (5%).

# SENEGAL

**Republic of Senegal**
**President:** Léopold Sédar Senghor (1960)
**Premier:** Abdou Diouf (1970)
**Area:** 75,750 sq mi. (196,192 sq km)
**Population (est. 1976 by U.N.):** 5,090,000
**Density per square mile:** 67.2
**Capital and largest city (est. 1976):** Dakar, 798,800
**Monetary unit:** Franc CFA
**Ethnic groups:** Wolofs, Sereres, Peuls, Tukulers, and others
**Language:** French (official); Wolof, Serer, other tribal dialects
**Religion:** Islam, 80%; Christian, 10%
**Gross national product (1976):** $2 billion
**National name:** République du Sénégal
**Freedom House classifications:** Capitalist-socialist industrial, dominant party

**Geography.** The capital of Senegal, Dakar, is the westernmost point in Africa. The country, slightly smaller than South Dakota, surrounds Gambia on three sides and is bordered on the north by Mauritania, on the east by Mali, and on the south by Guinea and Guinea-Bissau.

Senegal is mainly a low-lying country, with a semidesert area in the north and northeast and forests in the southwest. The largest rivers include the Senegal in the north and the Gambia in the central region.

**Government.** There is a National Assembly of 100 members, elected every five years. There is universal suffrage and a constitutional guarantee of equality before the law.

The major political party is the Socialist Party, led by President Senghor. Legal opposition was reconstituted in 1974 with formation of the Senegalese Democratic Party, headed by Abdoulaye Wade, which urged reduction in French and Western influences. The African Independence Party was reorganized in 1976 and a right-wing Senegalese Republican Movement party was projected in 1977.

**History.** The Portuguese had some stations on the banks of the Senegal River in the 15th century, and the first French settlement was made at Saint-Louis about 1650. The British took parts of Senegal at various times, but the French gained possession in 1840 and organized Sudan as a territory in 1904. In 1946, together with other parts of French West Africa, Senegal became part of the French Union. On June 20, 1960, it became an independent republic federated with the Sudanese Republic in the Mali Federation, from which it withdrew on August 20.

On Jan. 1, 1973, Senegal joined with six other states to create the West African Economic Community to promote economic development within the region.

**Economy.** Agricultural products include peanuts, millet, cassava, cotton, tobacco, and sisal.

Chief exports in 1974 were phosphates (28%), peanut oil (22%), fish and products (7%), and peanut oil cake (7%). Leading customers were France (50%), Netherlands (7%), U.K. (6%), Ivory Coast (6%), Mauritania (5%). Leading suppliers were France (41%), West Germany (6%), U.S. (6%), Nigeria (6%).

## SEYCHELLES

**Republic of Seychelles**
**President:** Albert René (1977)
**Area:** 108 sq mi. (280 sq km)
**Population (est. 1978):** 65,000
**Density per square mile:** 602
**Capital (est. 1976):** Victoria, 14,500
**Monetary unit:** Seychelles rupee
**Languages:** English, French (both official), Creole patois
**Religions:** Roman Catholic, 91%; Anglican, 8%
**Member of Commonwealth of Nations**
**Freedom House classifications:** Capitalist-socialist industrial, one-party nationalist

**Geography.** Seychelles consists of an archipelago of 89 islands in the Indian Ocean northeast of Madagascar. The principal islands are Mahé (55 sq mi.; 142 sq km), Praslin (15 sq mi.; 38 sq km), and La Digue (4 sq mi.; 10 sq km). The Aldabra, Farquhar, and Desroches groups are included in the territory of the republic.

**Government.** Seized from France by Britain in 1810, the Seychelles Islands remained a colony until June 28, 1974. The new state is an independent republic within the Commonwealth.

On June 5, 1977, Prime Minister Albert René ousted the islands' first President, James Mancham, suspending the Constitution and the 25-member National Assembly. Mancham, whose "lavish spending" and flamboyance were cited by René in seizing power, charged Soviet influence was at work. The new President denied this and, while more left than his predecessor, pledged to keep the Seychelles in the Commonwealth.

A new cabinet was formed with members only from Seychelles People's United Party, none from Mancham's Seychelles Democratic Party.

**Economy.** Chief exports in 1975 were fuels (47%), copra (21%), and cinnamon bark (10%). Leading customer was Pakistan (21%). Leading suppliers were U.K. (27%), Kenya (19%), Australia (8%), South Africa (8%), Japan (5%).

## SIERRA LEONE

**Republic of Sierra Leone**
**President:** Dr. Siaka P. Stevens (1971)
**Prime minister:** Christian A. Kamara-Taylor (1975)
**Area:** 27,699 sq mi. (71,740 sq km)
**Population (U.N. est. 1977):** 3,470,000
**Density per square mile:** 125.3
**Capital and largest city (est. 1974):** Freetown, 314,340
**Monetary unit:** Leone
**Languages:** English (official), Mende, Temne, Creole
**Religions:** Animist, 66%; Islam, 28%; Christian, 6%
**Gross national product (1976):** $542 million
**Member of Commonwealth of Nations**
**Freedom House classifications:** Capitalist pre-industrial, dominant party

**Geography.** Sierra Leone, on the Atlantic Ocean in West Africa, is half the size of Illinois. Guinea, in the north and east, and Liberia, in the south, are its neighbors.

Mangrove swamps lie along the coast, with wooded hills and a plateau in the interior. The eastern region is mountainous.

**Government.** Sierra Leone became an independent nation on April 27, 1961, and declared itself a republic, with former Prime Minister Siaka P. Stevens as executive president for a five-year term, on April 19, 1971.

The major political parties are the All People's Congress Party (APC), with 70 seats in Parliament, and the Sierra Leone People's Party (SLPP), with 15, in 1977 (with elections for other seats postponed because of civil disturbances).

**History.** The coastal area of Sierra Leone was ceded to English settlers in 1788 as a home for blacks discharged from the British armed forces and also for runaway slaves who had found asylum in London. The British protectorate over the hinterland was proclaimed in 1896.

After elections in 1967, the British Governor-General replaced Sir Albert Margai, head of SLPP, which had held power since independence, with Dr. Stevens, head of APC, as Prime Minister. The Army took over the government; then another coup in April 1968 restored civilian rule and put the military leaders in jail.

A coup attempt early in 1971 by the army commander was apparently foiled by loyal army officers, but the then Prime Minister Stevens called in troops of neighboring Guinea's army, under a 1970 mutual defense pact, to guard his residence. After perfunctorily blaming the U.S. for the coup attempt, Stevens switched Governors-General, changed the Constitution, and ended up with a Republic, of which he was first President. He was accused of taking "sweeping dictatorial powers," but was re-elected President in 1976.

**Economy.** Agricultural products include palm kernels and coffee. Sierra Leone is one of seven nations that produce 63% of the world's bauxite.

Chief exports in 1974 were diamonds (54%) and iron ore (11%). Leading customers were U.K. (61%), Netherlands (15%), U.S. (6%), Japan (5%). Leading suppliers were U.K. (21%), Japan (10%), Nigeria (8%), West Germany (7%), Pakistan (5%), France (5%), China (5%).

## SINGAPORE

**Republic of Singapore**
**President:** Benjamin Sheares (1970)
**Prime Minister:** Lee Kuan Yew (1959)
**Area:** 226 sq mi. (581 sq km)
**Population** (est. 1978): 2,340,000 (Chinese, 76%; Malay, 15%; Indian, 7%)
**Density per square mile:** 10,354.0
**Capital (est. 1975 by U.N.):** Singapore, 2,249,900
**Monetary unit:** Singapore dollar
**Languages:** Malay, Chinese (Mandarin), Tamil, English
**Religions:** Islam, Christian, Buddhist, Hindu, Confucianist, Taoist
**Gross national product (1976):** $5.8 billion
**Member of Commonwealth of Nations**
**Freedom House classifications:** Capitalist-statist industrial, dominant party

**Geography.** The Republic of Singapore consists of the main island of Singapore, off the southern tip of the Malay Peninsula between the South China Sea and the Indian Ocean, and 60 nearby islands.

There are extensive mangrove swamps extending inland from the coast, which is broken by many inlets.

**Government.** The head of state is the President. There is a Cabinet, headed by the Prime Minister, and a Parliament of 69 members elected by universal suffrage.

The People's Action Party (all 69 seats in Parliament), led by Prime Minister Lee, is the only political party.

**History.** Singapore, founded in 1819 by Sir Stamford Raffles, became a separate crown colony of the U.K. on April 1, 1946, when the former colony of the Straits Settlements was dissolved. The other two settlements—Penang and Malacca—were transferred to the Union of Malaya, and the small island of Labuan was transferred to North Borneo. The Cocos (or Keeling) Islands were transferred to Australia in 1951 and Christmas Island in 1958.

Singapore attained full internal self-government in 1959. On Sept. 16, 1963, it joined Malaya, Sabah (North Borneo), and Sarawak in the federation of Malaysia. It withdrew from the federation on Aug. 9, 1965 and proclaimed itself a republic in September of that year.

**Economy.** The basis of Singapore's prosperity is its entrepôt trade. It handled a large part of the export trade of the Federation of Malaysia, and it conducts a large volume of trade with Indonesia.

Fruits and vegetables are the chief agricultural products of Singapore. Industries include shipbuilding and oil refining. Offshore fishing is also an important economic activity.

Chief exports in 1976 were petroleum products (23%), machinery (19%), rubber (12%), ship and aircraft stores (7%), and food (6%). Leading customers were Malaysia (15%), U.S. (15%), Japan (10%), Hong Kong (8%), Australia (5%). Leading suppliers were Japan (16%), Saudi Arabia (16%), Malaysia (14%), U.S. (13%).

## SOLOMON ISLANDS

**Governor-General:** Baddeley Devesi (1978)
**Prime Minister:** Peter Kenilorea (1978)
**Area:** 10,983 sq mi. (28,446 sq km)
**Population (est. 1978):** 200,000
**Density per square mile:** 18.2
**Capital and largest city (est. 1977):** Honiara (on Guadalcanal), 15,600
**Languages:** Pidgin English, English, Melanesian dialects
**Member of British Commonwealth.**

**Geography:** Lying east of New Guinea, this island nation consists of the southern islands of the Solomon group: Guadalcanal, Malaita, Santa Isabel, San Cristóbal, Choiseul, New Georgia, and numerous smaller islands.

**Government.** After 85 years of British rule, the Solomons achieved independence July 7, 1978. The crown is represented by a Governor-General and legislative power is vested in a unicameral legislature of 38 members, led by a Prime Minister.

**History.** First discovered in 1567 by Alvaro de Mendana, the Solomons were not visited again for about 200 years. In 1886, Great Britain and Germany divided the islands between them. In 1914, Australian forces took over the German islands and the Solomons became an Australian mandate in 1920. In World War II, most of the islands were occupied by the Japanese. American forces landed on Guadalcanal on Aug. 7, 1942. The islands were the scene of several important U.S. naval and military victories. They are still largely undeveloped, with only 60 miles of paved road and fewer than 1,000 motor vehicles.

**Economy.** Chief exports in 1975 were copra (39%), timber (27%), fish (11%), and canned fish (10%). Leading customers were Japan (29%), U.K. (11%), France (8%), Denmark (8%), West Germany (7%), Netherlands (6%), Norway (6%), Sweden (5%). Leading suppliers were Australia (35%), U.K. (14%), Japan (13%), Singapore (10%).

## SOMALIA

**Somali Democratic Republic**
**President:** Maj. Gen. Mohamed Siad Barre
**Area:** 246,201 sq mi. (637,657 sq km)
**Population (est. 1978):** 3,440,000
**Density per square mile:** 14.0
**Capital and largest city (est. 1976 by U.N.):** Mogadishu, 286,000
**Monetary unit:** Somali shilling
**Language:** Somali
**Religion:** Islam
**Gross national product: (1976):** $370 million
**National name:** Al Jumhouriya As-Somalya Dimocradia
**Freedom House classifications:** Capitalist-socialist pre-industrial, one-party socialist

**Geography.** Somalia, situated in what is known as the Horn of Africa, lies along the Gulf of Aden and the Indian Ocean. It is bounded by Djibouti in the northwest, Ethiopia in the east, and Kenya in the southwest. In area it is slightly smaller than Texas.

Generally arid and barren, Somalia has two chief rivers, the Shebeli and the Juba.

**Government.** Maj. Gen. Mohamed Siad Barre took power on Oct. 21, 1969, in a bloodless coup that established a Supreme Revolutionary Council as the governing body, replacing a previous parliamentary government. On July 1, 1976, Barre dissolved the Council and transferred its powers to the Somali Socialist Party, organized that day as the nation's only legal political party. Council members all became members of the party's Central Committee, of which Barre is Secretary General.

**History.** From the 7th to the 10th centuries, Arab and Persian trading posts were established along the coast of present-day Somalia. Nomadic tribes occupied the interior, occasionally pushing into Ethiopian territory. In the 16th century, Turkish rule extended to the northern coast and the Sultans of Zanzibar gained control in the south.

After British occupation of Aden in 1839, the Somali coast became its food source. The French established a coaling station in 1862 at the site of Djibouti and the Italians planted a settlement in Eritrea. Egypt, which for a time claimed Turkish rights in the area, was succeeded by the U.K., and by 1920 a British protectorate and an Italian protectorate occupied what is now Somalia. The British ruled the entire area after 1941, Italy returning in 1950 to serve as United Nations trustee for its former territory.

The U.K. granted independence to its sector June 26, 1960, and on July 1 the Italian sector gained its freedom, enabling the two to join as the Republic of Somalia on that day. Somalia broke diplomatic relations with the U.K. in 1963 when the British granted the Somali-populated Northern Frontier District of Kenya to the Republic of Kenya.

On Oct. 15, 1969, President Abdi Rashid Ali Shermarke was assassinated and the army seized power, dissolving the legislature and arresting all government leaders. Maj. Gen. Mohamed Siad Barre, as President of a renamed Somali Democratic Republic, leaned heavily toward the U.S.S.R., which had largely trained and equipped the nation's 9,000-man army. A Soviet naval base was established at Berbera.

In 1977, Somalia openly backed rebels in the westernmost area of Ethiopia, the Ogaden desert, which had been seized by Ethiopia at the turn of the century. The action was an embarrassment to the U.S.S.R., which was heavily involved in Ethiopia's new Marxist government after the ouster of Emperor Haile Selassie in 1974. After denying Barre's pleas for aid, the U.S.S.R. announced in October 1977 the cutoff of military aid to Somalia and provision of "defensive weapons" to Ethiopia. Somalia then expelled an estimated 1,500 Soviet military and civilian aid personnel and broke diplomatic relations with Cuba, which had furnished military advisers to the Ethiopian troops fighting in the Ogaden.

Somalia acknowledged defeat in an eight-month war against the Ethiopians, having lost many of what had become a 32,000-man army and most of its tanks and planes. In March 1978, the U.S. agreed to supply $7 million in food over six months, in addition to $6 million in emergency food relief provided in December. The U.S. refused to consider weapons sales, however, unless Somalia gave up all claims to northern Kenya, the Ogaden, and the Republic of Djibouti, all once claimed as "Greater Somalia." Barre refused to do this.

In April, Barre visited China and signed a treaty of economic and technical cooperation, but there was no indication that he was able to obtain arms.

**Economy.** Somalia is primarily a pastoral and agricultural country; about 80% of the population are engaged in livestock raising. Agricultural products include sugarcane, bananas, and maize.

In 1968, Somalia reported discovery of major reserves of uranium and other rare minerals.

Chief exports in 1974 were livestock (61%), bananas (16%), and hides and skins (8%). Leading customers were Saudi Arabia (65%), Italy (12%), Iran (7%), U.S.S.R. (6%), Kuwait (5%). Leading suppliers were Italy (38%), U.S.S.R. (17%), China (9%), Kenya (7%), France (5%), Thailand (5%), Japan (5%), U.K. (5%), West Germany (5%).

# SOUTH AFRICA

**Republic of South Africa**
**State President:** *See* Current Events
**Prime Minister:** *See* Current Events
**Area:** 440,521 sq mi. (1,140,943 sq km)[1]
**Population (est. 1977):** 26,765,000 (Bantu, 71%, white, 17%; colored (mixed), 9%; Asian, 3%
**Density per square mile:** 56.8[1]
**Administrative capital:** Pretoria
**Legislative capital:** Cape Town
**Judicial capital:** Bloemfontein
**Largest cities (est. 1976):** Johannesburg, 1,371,000; Cape Town, 842,600; Pretoria, 634,400; Bloemfontein, 234,900; (est. 1975): Durban, 837,000; Port Elizabeth, 468,800
**Monetary unit:** Rand
**Languages:** English, Afrikaans, Bantu languages
**Religions (1970):** Dutch Reformed, 16%; Methodist, 10%; Roman Catholic, 9%; Anglican, 8%; other Christian, 55%
**Gross national product (1976):** $31.9 billion
**National name:** Republiek van Suid-Afrika
**Freedom House classifications:** Capitalist-statist industrial, multi-party centralized

**Geography.** South Africa, on the continent's southern tip, is washed by the Atlantic Ocean on the west and by the Indian Ocean on the south and east. Its neighbors are South-West Africa (Namibia) in the northwest, Rhodesia and Botswana in the north, and Mozambique and Swaziland in the northeast. Lesotho, Bophuthatswana, and Transkei are independent enclaves within South Africa, which occupies an area three times that of California.

The country has a high interior plateau, or veld, nearly half of which averages 4,000 feet (1,219 m) in elevation.

There are no important mountain ranges, although the Great Escarpment, separating the veld from the coastal plain, rises to over 11,000 feet (3,350 m) in the Drakensberg Mountains in the east. The principal river is the Orange, rising in Lesotho and flowing westward for 1,300 miles (2,092 km) to the Atlantic.

The southernmost point of Africa is Cape Agulhas, located in Cape Province about 100 miles (161 km) southeast of the Cape of Good Hope.

**Government.** The Republic is divided into four provinces (Cape, Transvaal, Orange Free State, and Natal), each with a Provincial Council. A 50-member Senate and 165-member House of Assembly make up the Parliament. Members have five-year terms unless Parliament is dissolved earlier. The President of the Republic is chosen by Parliament for a seven-year term.

Seven "Bantustans," or black homelands, exist within the country. They have unicameral legislatures elected by black voters. (Only whites vote in parliamentary elections.) There are also a Colored (mixed race) Representative Council of 60 members (40 elected) and an Indian Council of 30 mem-

1. Excluding South-West Africa (Namibia), Transkei, and Bophuthatswana.

bers (all elected), which give some representation for these minorities.

The major political parties are the National Party (135 of 165 seats in the House of Assembly), led by Prime Minister Vorster; Progressive Federal Party (17 seats), led by Colin Eglin; New Republic Party (10 seats), led by Vause Raw, and the South Africa Party (3 seats).

**History.** Dutch settlers arrived in South Africa in 1652 and by the beginning of the 18th century numbered nearly 2,000.

Britain seized the Cape Colony in 1814 and within seven years settled 5,000 Britons there, freeing the slaves on whom the Boer (Dutch) farmers relied for labor. The Boers pushed north of the Orange and Vaal rivers to escape the British, but in 1877 the British annexed the Transvaal territory. Despite the relinquishment of the territory in 1881, Dutch resentment smoldered and the Jameson Raid of 1899 touched off the Boer War, ending in Dutch defeat in 1902.

The four provinces were united in the Union of South Africa in 1910. Louis Botha, the first Prime Minister and a Boer, allied the dominion with the U.K. in the first World War. The Unionist party, led by Jan Christiaan Smuts, advocated a pro-British line and a more liberal racial policy in the period between wars, while the Nationalist party urged withdrawal from the Commonwealth and racial separation.

Smuts brought the nation into World War II on the Allied Side against Nationalist opposition, and South Africa became a charter member of the United Nations in 1945, but refused to sign the Universal Declaration of Human Rights. Apartheid—racial separation—dominated domestic politics as the Nationalists gained power and imposed greater restrictions on Bantus, Coloreds, and Asians.

Boer hostility to the U.K. triumphed in 1961 with the declaration on May 31 of the Republic of South Africa and the severing of ties with the Commonwealth. Nationalist Prime Minister H. F. Verwoerd's government in 1963 asserted the power to restrict freedom of those who opposed rigid racial laws. Three years later, amid increasing racial tension and criticism from the outside world, Verwoerd was assassinated. His Nationalist successor, B. J. Vorster, launched a campaign of conciliation toward conservative black African states, offering development loans and trade concessions. He accelerated the program for developing Bantustans, giving independence to the Transkei in 1976 and to Bophuthatswana in 1977.

The late 1960s and early 1970s were economic boom years for South Africa, giving blacks there the highest incomes in Africa, even though two thirds of the national income was going to the white fifth of the population. The 1974 elections swelled the Nationalist majority, and Vorster continued to wield a harsh hand against domestic opposition and aided white Rhodesians in their fight against black guerrillas, but also sought to improve relations with black Africa.

A critical issue was South-West Africa, the former German territory ruled by South Africa since World War I, a rule challenged by the United Nations when it asserted responsibility for the territory in 1974 under the name of Namibia. African demands for immediate freedom for Namibia led to an attempt to expel South Africa from the U.N. in October 1974, blocked by a U.S., British, and French veto. The General Assembly barred South Africa from its seat anyway, and the seat has remained empty since.

In the 1975–76 Angolan civil war, Vorster engaged 4,000 troops on the side of UNITA, which lost to the Soviet-backed Popular Movement for the Liberation of Angola (MPLA). Defeat in Angola was followed by a wave of riots in black townships in South Africa, originating in protests against the use of the Afrikaans language in schools. More than 300 died as the movement widened to ask more freedoms, the strongest challenge to the white regime in a generation.

At the same time, outside pressure forced Vorster to withdraw military aid to Rhodesia in mid-1976. He met with U.S. Secretary of State Henry A. Kissinger in Zurich in September. As a result, Premier Ian Smith of Rhodesia's white government agreed to negotiate with nationalists in Rhodesia for a majority rule.

Unrest in Soweto, the principal black township near Johannesburg, continued through 1978 despite the elimination of compulsory schooling in Afrikaans and relaxation of "petty apartheid." Under white as well as black pressure, the government in March 1978 desegregated theaters and opera houses although movie theaters in white areas remained segregated. The death of Steven Biko on Sept. 12, 1977, caused widespread protest when the anti-apartheid activist was discovered to have died from a brain injury while jailed. The U.S. expressed shock that an official inquest had held nobody responsible.

Economic restrictions tightened on South Africa following a vote by the Security Council on Nov. 4, 1977, imposing a mandatory embargo on arms in retaliation for South Africa's crackdown on opponents of apartheid. Although the U.S., U.K., and France vetoed mandatory economic sanctions against South Africa, U.S. and European businesses, unions, and church groups acted to cut trade with it.

Reflecting this as well as global economic recession, the 1978–79 South African budget of $11.3 billion projected a deficit of nearly $500 million to stimulate an economy, which grew at only 1.3% in 1977. Unemployment was up and immigration figures for 1977 showed a net loss of 1,178—the first decline since 1960.

Beginning with the meeting between Vorster and U.S. Vice President Walter F. Mondale in Vienna in May 1977, South Africa moved more quickly toward giving independence to South-West Africa. Although the five Western members of the Security Council acting as intermediaries wanted Vorster to deal with the South-West Africa People's Organization (SWAPO) in the process, Vorster chose an "internal" solution and ordered the election of a constituent assembly by residents of the territory in September 1978. Pretoria ended South-West African representation in the national legislature, where it had been allotted four Senate seats and six in the Assembly.

**Economy.** South Africa is predominantly a pastoral country, with less than 15% of its area considered arable. Sheep and cattle raising are the principal occupations.

Climate and differences in terrain combine to give South Africa a great variety of agricultural products. The staple crop is maize, which is grown widely. In southwest Cape Province, products of the Mediterranean type predominate, while in the coastal belt of Natal and in northern Transvaal, subtropical crops, especially sugar, are grown.

Food, beverages, and tobacco, and metal goods are leading products.

As a result of the need for armaments, a wartime

iron and steel industry was established, and cement, chemical, textile, and auto assembly plants were expanded.

Extensive mineral resources account for the economic prosperity. South Africa is the world's leading gold producer. Diamond production is now surpassed in importance by coal. Uranium, gypsum, tin, and tungsten also are mined.

The whaling industry, centered at Durban on the east coast, produces considerable amounts of whale oil. South Africa has extensive fishery resources.

Chief exports in 1976 were gold specie (34%), food (8%), diamonds (8%), iron and steel (7%), and gold coin (5%). Leading customers (excl. gold) were U.K. (25%), Japan (13%), West Germany (12%), U.S. (12%), Belgium-Luxembourg (5%). Leading customers were U.S. (22%), West Germany (18%), U.K. (18%), Japan (10%.

## BOPHUTHATSWANA

**Republic of Bophuthatswana**
**President:** Chief Lucas Mangope (1977)
**Area:** 15,610 sq mi. (40,430 sq km)
**Population (est. 1976):** 1,039,000 (Bantu 99.6%)
**Density per square mile:** 66.5
**Capital:** Mmabatho
**Largest city (est. 1973):** Ga-Rankuwa, 64,200
**Monetary unit:** South African rand
**Languages:** Central Tswana, English, Afrikaans
**Religions:** Methodist, Lutheran, Anglican, and Bantu Christian

**Geography.** Bophuthatswana consists of half a dozen discontinuous areas within the boundaries of South Africa, most of them in the northern sector near Botswana.

**Government.** The republic has a 99-member Legislative Assembly, approximately half of whom are elected and the others appointed. President Mangope's Democratic party is the majority party.

**History.** Bophuthatswana was given independence by South Africa Dec. 6, 1977, following Transkei as the second "homeland" to be established by Pretoria. The new state and Transkei are recognized only by South Africa and each other.

Mangope, as chief minister in the pre-independence period, sought linkage of the six units into a consolidated area, but was unable to achieve his objective. A second issue, the citizenship of Tswanas in South Africa who wished to remain South African nationals, was settled by enabling them to have citizenship in South African homelands not yet independent.

About two thirds of the population of Bophuthatswana live permanently or as migrants in white areas of South Africa.

**Economy.** Bophuthatswana is richer than many other South African homelands, as it has more than half of the republic's platinum deposits. All foreign trade is included with South Africa's, and it is economically dependent at present on that country.

## SOUTH-WEST AFRICA (NAMIBIA)

**Status:** Mandate
**Area:** 318,251 sq mi. (824,292 sq km)
**Population (est. 1977):** 920,000
**Density per square mile:** 2.9
**Administrator:** Justice Marthinus Steyn
**Capital (est. 1975):** Windhoek, 77,400
**Summer capital:** Swakopmund (est. 1975): 13,700
**Monetary unit:** South African rand
**National name:** Suidwes-Afrika

**Geography.** The mandate, bounded on the north by Angola and Zambia and on the east by Botswana and South Africa, was discovered by the Portuguese explorer Diaz in the late 15th century. It is for the most part a portion of the high plateau of southern Africa with a general elevation of from 3,000 to 4,000 feet.

**History.** It became a German colony in 1884 but was conquered by South African forces in 1915, becoming a South African mandate by the terms of the Treaty of Versailles.

South Africa's application for incorporation of the territory was rejected by the U.N. General Assembly on Dec. 14, 1946, and South Africa was invited to prepare a trusteeship agreement instead. By a law passed in April 1949, however, the territory was brought into much closer association with South Africa—including representation in the South African Parliament.

In 1969, South Africa extended its laws to the mandate over the objection of the U.N., particularly its black African members. When South Africa refused to withdraw them, the U.N. Security Council condemned it in December.

Under a 1974 Security Council resolution, South Africa was required to begin the transfer of power to the Namibians by May 30, 1975, or face U.N. action, but 10 days before the deadline Vorster rejected U.N. supervision. He said, however, that his government was prepared to negotiate Namibian independence, but not with the Southwest African People's Organization, the principal black separatist group. Meanwhile, the all-white legislature of South-West Africa eased several laws on apartheid in public places.

Despite international opposition, the Turnhalle conference in Windhoek drafted a constitution to organize an interim government based on racial divisions, a proposal overwhelmingly endorsed by white voters in the territory on May 17, 1977. At the urging of ambassadors of the five Western members of the Security Council—the U.S., the U.K., France, West Germany, and Canada—South Africa on June 11 announced rejection of the Turnhalle constitution and acceptance of the Western proposal to include the South-West Africa People's Organization (SWAPO) in negotiations.

With the approval of SWAPO, a militant nationalist group, Justice Marthinus T. Steyn was appointed by South Africa to serve as administrator of the territory during the transition to independence. At the same time, Pretoria announced that it would retain control of Walvis Bay, the territory's only deepwater port.

Apartheid laws were repealed by Steyn, and South-West representation in the South African parliament ended, but in February 1978, South African Foreign Minister Roelof Botha walked out of a New York meeting with SWAPO and Western representatives who demanded that South African troops in the territory be reduced from 3,000 to 1,500 before a U.N.-supervised election would be held. Botha charged that the Western plan would deliver Namibia to a "Marxist terrorist organization."

South Africa blamed SWAPO for the killing on March 27 of Chief Clemens Kapuuo, a moderate leader, and a South African raid on SWAPO guerrilla bases in Angola on May 4 brought Security Council condemnation and cast doubt on progress toward Namibian independence.

**Economy.** Chief exports (incl. in South African customs union) in 1972 were diamonds (40%), fish and fish products (20%), livestock (15%), and karakul pelts (14%). Leading customer was South Africa (50%). Leading supplier was South Africa (80%).

## TRANSKEI

**Republic of Transkei**
**President:** Paramount Chief Botha Sigcau (1976)
**Prime Minister:** Paramount Chief Kaiser Matanzima (1976)
**Area:** 15,831 sq mi. (41,002 sq km)
**Population (est. 1976):** 2,050,000
**Density per square mile:** 129.5
**Capital (est. 1977):** Umtala, 30,000
**Monetary unit:** South African rand
**Languages:** English, Xhosa, Southern Sotho
**Religions:** Christian, tribal
**Freedom House classifications:** Capitalist pre-industrial, dominant party

**Geography.** Transkei occupies three discontinuous enclaves within southeast South Africa that add up to twice the size of Massachusetts. It has a 270-mile (435 km) coastline on the Indian Ocean but no port. The capital, Umtata, is connected by rail to the South African port of East London, 100 miles (160 km) to the southwest.

**Government.** Transkei was granted independence by South Africa as of Oct. 26, 1976. A new Constitution called for organization of a parliament composed of 75 representative chiefs and 75 elected members, with a ceremonial President and executive power in the hands of a Prime Minister.

The Organization of African States and the chairman of the United Nations Special Committee against Apartheid denounced the new state as a sham and urged governments not to recognize it, because South Africa has declared 1.3 million Xhosas living there to be Transkei citizens, depriving them of South African citizenship.

**History.** British rule was established over the Transkei region between 1866 and 1894, and the Transkeian Territories were formed in 1903. Under the Native Land Act of 1913, the Territories were reserved for black occupation. In 1963, Transkei was given internal self-government and a legislature that elected Paramount Chief Kaiser Matanzima as Chief Minister, a post he retained in subsequent elections in 1968 and 1973.

**Economy.** Some 60% of Transkei is cultivated, producing corn, wheat, beans, and sorghum. Grazing is important. Some light industry has been established.

Most of Transkei's trade is with South Africa.

## SOVIET UNION

**Union of Soviet Socialist Republics**
**Chairman of Presidium (President):** Leonid I. Brezhnev (1977)
**Chairman of Council of Ministers (Premier):** Aleksei N. Kosygin (1964)
**Area:** 8,649,489 sq mi. (22,402,200 sq km)
**Population (est. 1978):** 260,750,000 (Russian, 53%; Ukrainian, 17%; Byelorussian, 4%; Uzbek, 4%; Tatar, 2%; others, 20%)
**Density per square mile:** 30.1
**Capital:** Moscow
**Largest cities (est. 1976 by U.N.):** Moscow, 7,734,000; Leningrad, 4,372,000; Kiev, 2,013,000; Tashkent, 1,643,000; Baku, 1,406,000; Kharkov, 1,385,000; Gorky, 1,305,000; Novosibirsk, 1,286,000; Minsk, 1,189,000; Kuibyshev, 1,186,000; Tblisi, 1,030,000; Odessa, 1,023,000; Chelyabinsk, 989,999; Dnepropetrovsk, 976,000; Donetsk, 967,000
**Monetary unit;** Ruble
**Languages:** *See* Population, above
**Religions:** Russian Orthodox (predominant), Islam, Roman Catholic, Jewish, Lutheran
**Gross national product (1976):** $708.2 billion
**National name:** Soyuz Sovyetskikh Sotsialisticheskikh Respublik
**Freedom House classifications:** Socialist industrial, one-party communist

**Geography.** The U.S.S.R. is the largest unbroken political unit in the world, occupying more than one seventh of the land surface of the globe. The greater part of its territory is a vast plain stretching from eastern Europe to the Pacific Ocean. This plain, relieved only occasionally by low mountain ranges (notably the Urals), consists of three zones running east and west: the frozen marshy tundra of the Arctic; the more temperate forest belt; and the steppes or prairies to the south, which in southern Soviet Asia become sandy deserts.

The topography is more varied in the south, particularly in the Caucasus between the Caspian and Black Seas, and in the Tien-Pamir mountain system bordering Afghanistan, Sinkiang, and Mongolia. Mountains (Stanovoi and Kolyma) and great rivers (Amur, Yenisei, Lena) also break up the sweep of the plain in Siberia.

In the west, the major rivers are the Volga, Dnieper, Don, Kama, and Southern Bug.

**Government.** Legislative authority is vested in the Supreme Soviet of the U.S.S.R., which consists of two chambers—the Soviet of the Union, with 767 members, and the Soviet of Nationalities, with 750 members. All members of the Supreme Soviet are elected for five years by the people of the Soviet Union.

A Presidium is elected by the Supreme Soviet to deal with state matters when the latter is not in session. It consists of a chairman, first vice chairman, 15 vice chairmen (one for each Union Republic), 21 members, and a secretary. The chairman of the Presidium is sometimes referred to as the President of the Soviet Union.

Executive authority is vested in the Council of Ministers. It is appointed by the Supreme Soviet and includes a chairman, a first vice chairman, and various vice chairmen, chairmen of state committees, ministers, etc. The chairman of the Council of Ministers is often referred to as the Premier of the Soviet Union.

Judicial authority is vested in the Supreme Court of the U.S.S.R. It consists of a chairman, vice chairmen, members, and people's assessors, who are elected by the Supreme Soviet for five years.

Each of the 15 Union Republics and the 20 Autonomous Republics has a Supreme Soviet (with a Presidium), a Council of Ministers, and a Supreme Court. Each of the eight Autonomous Regions has a Soviet of People's Deputies.

The Communist Party of the Soviet Union (CPSU) is the only party. It is the basic power in the country and today has a membership of over 16,-800,000.

## Republics of the U.S.S.R.

| Republic and capital | Area sq mi. | Population est. 1977 (thousands) |
|---|---|---|
| Russian S.F.S.R. (Moscow) | 6,593,391 | 135,600 |
| Ukraine (Kiev) | 233,089 | 49,300 |
| Kazakhstan (Alma-Ata) | 1,064,092 | 14,498 |
| Byelorussia (Minsk) | 80,154 | 9,414 |
| Uzbekistan (Tashkent) | 158,069 | 14,474 |
| Georgia (Tbilisi) | 26,872 | 4,999 |
| Azerbaijan (Baku) | 33,475 | 5,776 |
| Lithuania[1] (Vilnius) | 25,174 | 3,342 |
| Moldavia (Kishinev) | 13,012 | 3,885 |
| Latvia[1] (Riga) | 24,595 | 2,512 |
| Kirghizia (Frunze) | 76,641 | 3,443 |
| Tadzhikistan (Duschambe) | 55,019 | 3,591 |
| Armenia (Erevan) | 11,506 | 2,893 |
| Turkmenistan (Ashkhabad) | 188,417 | 2,650 |
| Estonia[1] (Tallinn) | 17,413 | 1,447 |

1. Soviet jurisdiction not recognized by the United States.

The supreme organ of the party is the Party Congress, which meets at least once in five years. It elects a Central Committee, consisting of 287 members and 139 candidate members, to carry on party work between sessions of the Congress.

Within the Central Committee is a Political Bureau (Politburo), which was called the Presidium from 1952 to 1966. It functions between sessions of the Central Committee. Also within the Central Committee is the Secretariat. The present General Secretary of the Central Committee of CPSU, Leonid I. Brezhnev, has served since Oct. 15, 1964. Named President in June 1977 to succeed Nikolai V. Podgorny, he is the first man in Soviet history to hold both posts simultaneously. Earlier First Secretaries were Nikita S. Khrushchev (1953–64), Georgi M. Malenkov (briefly in 1953), and Joseph Stalin (1922–53).

**History.** Tradition says the Viking Rurik came to Russia in A.D. 862 and founded the first Russian dynasty in Novgorod. The various tribes were united by the spread of Christianity in the 10th and 11th centuries; Vladimir "the Saint" was converted in 988. During the 11th century, the grand dukes of Kiev held such centralizing power as existed. In 1240, Kiev was destroyed by the Mongols, and the Russian territory was split into numerous smaller dukedoms, out of which three large centers emerged—Galicia, Moscow, and Novgorod. The early dukes of Moscow extended their dominions through their office of tribute collector for the Mongols.

In the late 15th century, Duke Ivan III acquired Novgorod and Tver and threw off the Mongol yoke. Ivan IV, the Terrible (1533–84), first Muscovite Tsar, is considered to have founded the Russian State. He crushed the power of rival princes and boyars (great landowners), but Russia remained largely medieval until the reign of Peter the Great (1682–1725), grandson of the first Romanov Tsar, Michael (1613–45). Peter made extensive reforms aimed at westernization and, through his defeat of Charles XII of Sweden at the Battle of Poltava (1709), he extended Russia's boundaries to the west.

Catherine the Great (1762–96) continued Peter's westernization program and also expanded Russian territory, acquiring the Crimea and part of Poland. During the reign of Alexander I (1801–25), Napoleon's attempt to subdue Russia was defeated (1812–13), and new territory was gained, including Finland (1809) and Bessarabia (1812). Alexander originated the Holy Alliance, which for a time crushed Europe's rising liberal movement.

Alexander II (1855–81) pushed Russia's borders to the Pacific and into central Asia. Serfdom was abolished in 1861, but heavy restrictions were imposed on the emancipated class. Revolutionary strikes following Russia's defeat in the war with Japan forced Nicholas II (1894–1917) to grant a representative national body (Duma), elected by narrowly limited suffrage. It met for the first time in 1906. Nicholas continued in his reactionary course, however, and the overwhelmingly liberal Duma had little or no influence.

World War I demonstrated tsarist corruption and the inefficiency of the tsarist regime, although the call of patriotism held the poorly-equipped army together for a time. Disorders broke out in Petrograd (now Leningrad) in March 1917, and defection of the Petrograd garrison launched the revolution. Nicholas II was forced to abdicate on March 15, 1917, and he and his family were killed by revolutionists on July 16, 1918.

A provisional government composed of conservative and radical elements under the successive premierships of Prince Lvov and moderate Alexander Kerensky lost ground to the radical, or Bolshevik, wing of the Socialist Democratic Labor Party. On Nov. 7, 1917, came the Bolshevik revolution, engineered by N. Lenin[1] and Leon Trotsky. The Kerensky government was overthrown, and authority was vested in a Council of People's Commissars, with Lenin as Premier.

The humiliating Treaty of Brest-Litovsk (March 3, 1918) concluded the war with Germany, but civil war and foreign intervention delayed Communist control of all Russia until 1920. A brief war with Poland in 1920 resulted in Russian defeat.

The Union of Soviet Socialist Republics was established as a federation on Dec. 30, 1922.

The death of Lenin on Jan. 21, 1924, precipitated an intraparty struggle between Stalin, General Secretary of the party, and Trotsky, who favored swifter socialization at home and fomentation of revolution abroad. Stalin won. Trotsky was dismissed as Commissar of War in 1925 and banished from the Soviet Union in 1929. He was murdered in Mexico City on Aug. 21, 1940, by a political agent.

Stalin further consolidated his power by a series of purges in the late 1930s. Among the many victims were prominent party leaders and military officers. Stalin assumed the premiership May 6, 1941.

Soviet foreign policy—first featured by friendship with Germany and antagonism toward England and France and then, after Hitler's rise to power in 1933, by participation in the League of Nations and an anti-Fascist program—took another abrupt turn on Aug. 24, 1939, with the signing of a Soviet-German nonaggression pact.

Territory seized from Poland (September 1939) became part of the Ukrainian and Byelorussian S.S.R.'s; that secured from Finland at the conclusion of the Finnish war of 1939–40, part of the Karelian S.S.R. set up March 31, 1940; that secured from Romania (Bessarabia and northern Bukovina), part of the Moldavian S.S.R. set up Aug. 2, 1940; and finally the formerly independent states of Es-

1. N. Lenin was the pseudonym taken by Vladimir Ilich Ulyanov. It is sometimes given as Nikolai Lenin or V. I. Lenin.

## Rulers of Russia Since 1533

| Name | Born | Ruled[1] |
|---|---|---|
| Ivan IV the Terrible | 1530 | 1533–1584 |
| Theodore I | 1557 | 1584–1598 |
| Boris Godunov | c.1551 | 1598–1605 |
| Theodore II | 1589 | 1605–1605 |
| Demetrius I[2] | ? | 1605–1606 |
| Basil IV Shuiski | ? | 1606–1610[3] |
| "Time of Troubles" | — | 1610–1613 |
| Michael Romanov | 1596 | 1613–1645 |
| Alexis I | 1629 | 1645–1676 |
| Theodore III | 1656 | 1676–1682 |
| Ivan V[4] | 1666 | 1682–1689[5] |
| Peter I the Great[4] | 1672 | 1682–1725 |
| Catherine I | c.1684 | 1725–1727 |
| Peter II | 1715 | 1727–1730 |
| Anna | 1693 | 1730–1740 |
| Ivan VI | 1740 | 1740–1741[6] |
| Elizabeth | 1709 | 1741–1762 |
| Peter III | 1728 | 1762–1762 |
| Catherine II the Great | 1729 | 1762–1796 |
| Paul I | 1754 | 1796–1801 |
| Alexander I | 1777 | 1801–1825 |
| Nicholas I | 1796 | 1825–1855 |
| Alexander II | 1818 | 1855–1881 |
| Alexander III | 1845 | 1881–1894 |
| Nicholas II | 1868 | 1894–1917[7] |
| **PROVISIONAL GOVERNMENT (PREMIERS)** | | |
| Prince Georgi Lvov | 1861 | 1917–1917 |
| Alexander Kerensky | 1881 | 1917–1917 |
| **U.S.S.R. (PREMIERS)** | | |
| N. Lenin | 1870 | 1917–1924 |
| Joseph Stalin[8] | 1879 | 1924–1953 |
| Georgi M. Malenkov | 1902 | 1953–1955 |
| Nikolai A. Bulganin | 1895 | 1955–1958 |
| Nikita S. Khrushchev | 1894 | 1958–1964 |
| Aleksei N. Kosygin | 1904 | 1964– |

1. For Czars through Nicholas II, year of end of rule is also that of death, unless otherwise indicated. 2. Also known as Pseudo-Demetrius. 3. Died 1612. 4. Ruled jointly until 1689, when Ivan was deposed. 5. Died 1696. 6. Died 1764. 7. Killed 1918. 8. General Secretary of Communist Party; Premier 1941–53.

tonia, Latvia, and Lithuania, occupied in June 1940, were absorbed into the U.S.S.R. as the 14th, 15th, and 16th Soviet Republics. The latter annexations have not been recognized by the U.S., U.K., and the majority of other nations.

Immediately following their attack (June 22, 1941), the Germans seized approximately 500,000 square miles of Soviet territory, but Soviet forces resisted stubbornly, aided by increasing amounts of matériel from the U.S. and U.K. The great Soviet counteroffensive in the Stalingrad area (November 1942–February 1943) marked the turning point. Soviet troops gradually pushed the Nazis back and unleashed their final great offensive on Jan. 12, 1945. The nonaggression pact with Japan (1941) was denounced in April 1945 and, following the declaration of war on Japan (Aug. 8, 1945), Soviet Far Eastern forces quickly occupied Manchuria, Karafuto, and the Kuriles.

Postwar territorial acquisitions include the Carpatho-Ukraine (12,617 sq mi.; 32,678 sq km) obtained from Czechoslovakia June 29, 1945, incorporated into the Ukrainian S.S.R.; the Republic of Tannu Tuva in central Asia (64,000 sq mi.; 165,760 sq km), incorporated early in 1945 into the Russian Soviet Federal Socialist Republic (R.S.F.S.R.); Karafuto or southern Sakhalin (13,935 sq mi.; 36,092 sq km) and the Kurile Islands (3,944 sq mi.; 10,215 sq km), occupied by Soviet troops in August 1945 and incorporated into the R.S.F.S.R.; the northern part of eastern Prussia (about 7,000 sq mi.; 18,130 sq km), placed under *de facto* Soviet administration at the Potsdam Conference and incorporated into the R.S.F.S.R.; the Petsamo district of Finland, obtained *de jure* under the 1947 treaty and incorporated into the R.S.F.S.R.; and Poland east of the Curzon Line (69,860 sq mi.; 180,937 sq km), under terms of the Soviet-Polish treaty of Aug. 16, 1945, incorporated into the Ukrainian and Byelorussian S.S.R.'s.

In all the Eastern European countries where Soviet troops were in occupation at the war's end, the U.S.S.R. achieved a cordon of satellite Communist states running from Poland in the north to Albania and Bulgaria and including East Germany, Czechoslovakia, Hungary, and Romania.

With its Eastern European satellites drawn together into a solid bloc, the U.S.S.R. launched a full-scale political offensive against the non-Communist world. At Berlin, Soviet troops blockaded communication through East Germany. The Western powers countered with an airlift, completed unification of West Germany, and united Western Europe into opposition to Communist aggression through the North Atlantic Treaty Organization Pact.

Stalin died March 6, 1953. The next day Malenkov succeeded him as Premier. Malenkov's chief rivals for power—Lavrenti P. Beria, chief of the Secret Police; Nikolai A. Bulganin and Lazar M. Kaganovich—were named First Deputy Premiers. The expected intraparty struggle for power was revealed by the announcement of July 10, 1953, of the purging of Beria. He was executed Dec. 23, 1953.

There followed a rise in importance of Nikita S. Khrushchev, First Secretary of the Communist Party. On Feb. 8, 1955, Malenkov was replaced as Premier by Bulganin. In July 1957, Khrushchev removed Vyacheslav M. Molotov, Malenkov, Kaganovich, and several others from the governing group. At the 20th Party Congress in 1956, Khrushchev denounced the rule and "personality cult" of Stalin. He replaced Bulganin as Premier on March 27, 1958, heading the state as well as the party.

A seven-year plan begun in 1959 was integrated in 1961 with a longer range plan for economic development. The U.S.S.R. formalized its East European system with a Council for Mutual Economic Assistance and a Warsaw Pact Treaty Organization. Poland, Romania, and Czechoslovakia later gained a measure of independence, and Albania joined China, which became Communist in 1950, in a struggle against Soviet hegemony in the Communist world.

The 1956 uprising in Hungary was ruthlessly quelled, as was the 1968 political struggle for liberalization in Czechoslovakia, when, in August, Soviet troops led forces of four other satellites in an invasion that penetrated to Prague. But elsewhere the Soviet iron fist was gloved.

In its technological race with the U.S., the U.S.S.R. exploded a hydrogen bomb in 1953, developed the intercontinental ballistic missile by 1957, sent the first artificial satellite into space (Sputnik I) in 1957, put Yuri Gagarin in the first orbital flight around the earth in 1961, and later put astronauts into space who "walked" between space vehicles. On July 24, 1975, the 44-hour link-up of a Soviet Soyuz bearing two cosmonauts and a U.S. Apollo with a three-man crew ended successfully. After this well-publicized first step toward space cooperation, Moscow tightened up again on news about its space program.

Although the U.S.S.R. emphasized collective leadership after the death of Stalin, Khrushchev achieved great personal power. But he was blamed for two fiascos of Soviet strategy. One was the arming of Cuba with missiles and the provoking of a confrontation with the U.S. in 1962, when the willingness of the U.S. to face the threat of nuclear war forced the U.S.S.R. to back down and remove the missiles. Khrushchev was blamed for the ideological dispute and break with Communist China beginning in 1963. He also was accused of establishing a personality cult of his own. On Oct. 15, 1964, he was retired. Brezhnev became First Secretary, and Aleksei Kosygin became Premier.

President Nixon visited the U.S.S.R. for a week of summit talks in May 1972 and concluded agreements on a wide variety of issues, notably strategic arms limitations and a declaration of principles that were to guide mutual relations in the future. The fact that the U.S.S.R. received Nixon while the U.S. was bombing and blockading North Vietnam indicated a search for détente after 25 years of the Cold War. There were parallel Soviet moves in Europe. The U.S.S.R. and Poland signed nonaggression treaties with West Germany that were tantamount to a World War II settlement.

The 1972 Strategic Arms Limitation Treaty (SALT I) set a ceiling of 200 anti-ballistic missiles (ABMs) for each side and the U.S.S.R. was frozen at 1,618 land-based intercontinental missiles (ICBMs), with the U.S. held to 1,054. Submarine-based missiles were restricted by a complicated formula giving the U.S.S.R. a numerical advantage, balanced by permitting the U.S. more warheads for its more reliable and accurate missiles.

Brezhnev visited the U.S. June 16–25, 1973, to discuss further arms limitations, but a return visit to Moscow by Nixon June 27–July 3, 1974, failed to produce an expected permanent treaty. The two sides agreed to reduce ABMs to 100 each and to partly limit underground nuclear testing (air, sea, and space tests were already prohibited), but there was no agreement to stop the proliferation of multi-warhead missiles (MIRVs).

Presidents Gerald R. Ford and Brezhnev met in Vladivostok Nov. 23–24 and reached tentative agreements to be incorporated into a treaty at the Geneva SALT talks in 1975. They proposed a ceiling of 2,400 ICBMs for each side, of which no more than 1,320 could be MIRVs. There was hard bargaining but no decision on verification methods and whether the new U.S. subsonic Cruise missile and the Soviet Backfire bomber should be covered.

Ford and Brezhnev renewed the discussions without progress at the 35-nation Conference on Security and Cooperation in Europe. This 1975 Helsinki conference recognized Europe's post-World War II boundaries, a long-sought goal of Soviet policy. It also, however, pledged participants to recognize basic human rights of their citizens.

President Jimmy Carter, actively pursuing both human rights and disarmament, joined with the Soviet Union in September 1977 to declare that the SALT I accord, which would have expired October 1 without further action, be maintained in effect while the two sides sought a new agreement (SALT II). At the United Nations on October 4, Carter said the U.S. and the U.S.S.R. were "within sight" of significant limitations of strategic weapons. Although negotiations continued, SALT II was still awaited in mid-1978 when the U.N. Special Assembly on Disarmament adjourned.

Despite recurrent friction, desire for détente appeared to moderate the Kremlin's policies toward the U.S. after the 1972 summit. There was a near-confrontation during the Arab-Israeli war of October 1973, when a Soviet threat to intervene to aid trapped Egyptian forces led Washington to call a world-wide nuclear alert, but the crisis was eased when the United Nations approved a truce plan developed by the U.S. and the U.S.S.R. After the war, Moscow provided arms and encouragement to militant Arab states, but did not actively resist the Israeli-Egyptian interim accord of 1975. The Kremlin made no overt move to capitalize on the fall of U.S.-backed governments in Indochina in the spring of 1975, but hailed the war's end as an incentive to improvement in relations with the U.S.

Brezhnev's 1977 election to the presidency followed publication of a new Constitution on June 6, supplanting the one adopted in 1936. It specified the dominance of the Communist Party, previously unstated, and in what was taken to be a weapon against dissidents, declared that "rights and freedoms shall be inseparable from the performance by citizens of their duties." This was thought to restrict dissidents when they cited constitutional guarantees of individual freedom.

Although Brezhnev, in a speech to the Party Central Committee made public June 5, promised an end to the "illegal repressions" of the Stalin era, the issue of human rights remained a major one in both domestic and foreign policy. Dissidents continued to cite the Helsinki Agreement, and President Carter's public support for Anatoly Shcharansky drew the angry charge from Brezhnev that Carter was conducting "ideological warfare" against the U.S.S.R. Amid the verbal fireworks, there was serious concern about the extent to which human rights might become an obstacle to SALT negotiations and to Soviet-U.S. relations in general.

Charges by Carter and particularly by National Security Adviser Zbigniew Brzezinski of Soviet interference in Africa brought heated comments from Moscow in 1978. The State Department warned, after Brezhnev had complained of SALT delays, that Soviet military aid to Ethiopia threatened all U.S.-Soviet relations. Similar friction occurred following the May invasion by rebels from Soviet-allied Angola, culminating in a speech by Carter on June 7 to graduates of the U.S. Naval Academy telling the Russians they must "choose either confrontation or cooperation." The speech did not reduce tensions, and increased Soviet uneasiness about American intentions.

Other incidents marred Soviet-U.S. relations. A U.S. businessman, Francis Jay Crawford, was arrested June 12 for currency speculation in apparent retaliation for the arrest of two accused Soviet spies in New York, Rudolf Chernayev and Vladik Enger. He was found guilty on Sept. 7 and given a 5-year suspended sentence. On June 27, correspondents Craig R. Whitney of *The New York Times* and Harold D. Piper of *The Baltimore Sun* were arrested on charges of slander, in contravention of the Helsinki Agreements' guarantee of journalistic freedom. They were found guilty and fined, but no further action against them was taken.

A crisis arose July 10 when, despite warnings from the Carter administration, the government brought two prominent Jewish dissidents to trial, only two days before the opening of a new round of SALT negotiations in Geneva. Amid worldwide protest, a Moscow judge on July 14 sentenced Anatoly Shcharansky to three years in prison and 10 years in a forced labor camp on charges of treason. Shcharansky, a leading spokesman for Jews seeking to emigrate to Israel, was accused of passing classified information to U.S. agents.

Aleksandr Ginzburg, manager of a fund established by exiled writer Aleksandr Solzhenytsin to aid political prisoners, was sentenced July 13 to eight years in a labor camp. Ginzburg was found guilty of "anti-Soviet agitation."

President Carter condemned the action as an attack on freedom and ordered cancellation of the sale of a $2 million computer to Tass, the Soviet news agency. He also delayed until Aug. 10 sales of oil-drilling equipment and technology by Dresser Industries, Inc., of Dallas.

**Economy.** Formerly an agricultural country, the U.S.S.R. has grown since about 1920 into an industrial-agricultural power.

Almost all industry in the U.S.S.R. is carried on by organizations owned or controlled by the state. Industrialization of the country has been a major objective of its leaders. Completion of the first two five-year plans (1928–32, 1933–37) and of most of the third (1938–42) saw a great increase in the volume and versatility of Soviet industry.

The large-scale evacuation of plants to the East and the construction of new plants there during World War II, coupled with the eastward orientation of industry prior to the war, has shifted the balance to newly developed regions in Central Asia and Siberia from the Moscow-Leningrad area and the Ukraine. The new regions are now the center of Soviet industrial power, accounting for almost all magnesium and aluminum production and more than 60% of the pig iron and steel production. The production of consumers' goods continues to be subordinate to the production of heavy capital equipment.

The U.S.S.R. is probably the richest country in the world in natural resources, containing deposits of almost every known mineral. It ranks among the top producing nations in coal, chromite, iron ore, petroleum, gold, copper, manganese, and other products. The richest mineral region is that of the Ural Mountains, which lacks only good coking coal.

With a forested area of about 2.5 billion acres, the U.S.S.R. possesses a large proportion of the world's timber reserves. Most of the forested area is in Siberia, but there are also valuable stands in the Caucasus. Plans were made late in 1948 for the planting of huge forest belts 60 to 90 miles wide in the southern steppes to protect fertile food-producing areas from the dry winds.

The rivers, lakes, and surrounding seas (except the Black Sea) are rich in fish. The acquisition of former Japanese fisheries in Karafuto and the Kuriles greatly increased output of the Far Eastern fish industry. Trapping is an important secondary industry, especially in eastern Siberia.

Soviet foreign trade is a state monopoly, and foreign goods are purchased in accordance with an overall plan conducted under the supervision of the Foreign Trade Ministry.

Chief exports in 1976 were machinery and transport equipment (19%), crude oil (18%), petroleum products (9%), iron and steel (7%), and timber (5%). Leading customers were Eastern Europe (47%; incl. East Germany 11%, Poland 10%, Czechoslovakia 8%, Bulgaria 8%, Hungary 6%), Cuba (5%). Leading suppliers were Eastern Europe (43%; incl. East Germany 10%, Poland 9%, Czechoslovakia 8%, Bulgaria 8%, Hungary 6%), U.S. (7%), West Germany (7%), Cuba (5%), Japan (5%).

## SPAIN

**Spanish State**
**Ruler:** King Juan Carlos I (1975)
**Premier:** Adolfo Suárez González (1976)
**Area:** 194,897 sq mi. (504,782 sq km)[1]
**Population (est. 1978):** 36,730,000 (Spanish, Basque, Catalan)
**Density per square mile:** 188.5
**Capital:** Madrid
**Largest cities (est. 1977):** Madrid, 3,870,900; (est. 1976): Barcelona, 1,846,250; Valencia, 748,730; Seville, 612,900; Zaragoza, 589,600; Bilbao, 486,600
**Monetary unit:** Peseta
**Languages:** Spanish, Basque, Catalan, Galician
**Religion:** Roman Catholic
**Gross national product (1976):** $104.1 billion
**National name:** Estado Español
**Freedom House classifications:** Capitalist industrial, multi-party centralized.

**Geography.** Spain occupies 85% of the Iberian Peninsula in southwestern Europe, which it shares with Portugal; France is to the northeast. It is touched by the Bay of Biscay in the north, the Atlantic Ocean in the west, and the Mediterranean Sea in the south and east.

Spain, less than 10 miles (16 km) from Africa at the Strait of Gibraltar, is separated from France by the Pyrenees. The country is generally a broad plateau sloping to south and east and crossed by a series of mountain ranges and river valleys.

Principal rivers are the Ebro in the northeast, the Tagus in the central region, and the Guadalquivir in the south.

Off Spain's east coast in the Mediterranean are the Balearic Islands (1,936 sq mi.; 5,014 sq km), the largest of which is Majorca. Sixty miles (97 km) west of Africa are the Canary Islands (2,808 sq mi.; 7,273 sq km).

**Government.** King Juan Carlos I (born Jan. 5, 1938) succeeded Generalissimo Francisco Franco Bahamonde as Chief of State Nov. 22, 1975. The King appoints the Premier from a list of three candidates submitted by the Council of the Realm.

The Cortes, or Parliament, consists of a Chamber of Deputies of 350 members and a Senate of 248, of whom 207 are elected and the remainder appointed by the King. The new Cortes, replacing one that was largely appointed or elected by special constituencies, is expected to write a new constitution.

The major political parties are the 12-party coalition of the Union of the Democratic Center (165 of 350 seats in the Chamber of Deputies, 106 of 207 elected Senate seats), led by Premier Adolfo Suárez González; Spanish Socialist Workers Party (118 seats in the Chamber, 35 in the Senate), led by Felipe González; Communist Party (18 seats in the Chamber, 8 in the Senate), led by Santiago Carrillo;

1. Including the Balearie and Canary Islands.

Popular Alliance (17 seats in the Chamber, 3 in the Senate), led by Manuel Fraga Iribarne.

**History.** Spain, originally inhabited by Celts, Iberians, and Basques, became a part of the Roman Empire in 201 B.C., when it was conquered by Scipio Africanus. In A.D. 412, the barbarian Visigothic leader Ataulf crossed the Pyrenees and ruled Spain, first in the name of the Roman emperor and then independently. In 711, the Moslems under Tariq entered Spain from Africa and within a few years completed the subjugation of the country. In 732, the Franks, led by Charles Martel, defeated the Moslems near Poitiers, thus preventing the further expansion of Islam in southern Europe. Internal dissension of Spanish Islam invited a steady Christian conquest from the north.

Aragon and Castile became the most important Spanish states from the 13th to the 15th centuries, in time absorbing all the other peoples of Spain. Aragon and Castile were consolidated by the marriage of Ferdinand II and Isabella I. The last Moslem stronghold, Granada, was captured in January 1492, the same year in which Columbus, under the sponsorship of Isabella, discovered America. With Moslem control ended, Roman Catholicism was established as the official state religion. The Jews (1492) and the Moslems (1502) were expelled from Spain at the cost of incalculable suffering and loss of life.

In the era of exploration, discovery, and colonization, Spain won tremendous wealth and a vast colonial empire. The conquest of Peru by Pizarro (1532–33) and of Mexico by Cortés (1519–21) brought great prosperity to the motherland. The Spanish Hapsburg monarchy, through wars, diplomatic negotiations, and marriages, became for a time one of the most powerful in the world.

In 1588, Philip II sent his Invincible Armada to invade England, but its destruction cost Spain her supremacy on the seas and paved the way for England's colonization of America. Spain then sank rapidly to the status of a second-rate power and never again played a major role in European politics. Its colonial empire in the Americas and the Philippines vanished in wars and revolutions during the 18th and 19th centuries.

In World War I, Spain maintained a position of neutrality. In 1923, General Miguel Primo de Rivera became dictator. In 1930, Alfonso XIII revoked the dictatorship, but a strong antimonarchist and republican movement led to his leaving Spain in 1931.[2] The new Constitution declared Spain a workers' republic, broke up the large estates, separated church and state, and secularized the schools. The elections held in 1936 returned a strong Popular Front majority, with Manuel Azaña as President.

But political chaos persisted. On July 18, 1936, a conservative army officer in Morocco, Francisco Franco Bahamonde, led a mutiny against the government. The terrible civil war that followed lasted for three years and cost the lives of nearly a million people. It was, in effect, a dress rehearsal for World War II. Franco was aided by Fascist Italy and Nazi Germany, while Soviet Russia helped the Loyalist side. Several hundred leftist Americans served in the Abraham Lincoln brigade on the side of the republic. The war ended when Franco took Madrid on March 28, 1939.

Franco became head of the state, national chief of the Falange Party (the governing party), and Premier and Caudillo (leader). The country was ruled by Franco's Cabinet, the National Council of the Falange Party, and the Cortes, which formulated laws subject to Franco's veto. At first the jails were filled with Franco opponents. But after the dictator consolidated his power, he undertook a policy of reconciliation under which the wounds of civil war slowly healed.

In a referendum held July 6, 1947, the Spanish people approved a Franco-drafted succession law declaring Spain a monarchy again. Franco, however, continued as Chief of State.

In 1969, Franco and the Cortes designated Prince Juan Carlos Alfonso Victor María de Borbón (who married Princess Sophia of Greece on May 14, 1962) to become King of Spain when the provisional government headed by Franco came to an end. He is the grandson of Alfonso XIII and the son of Don Juan, pretender to the throne.

Spain concluded in 1967 its first economic-social development plan, which had raised levels of living dramatically within a decade and, combined with Spanish migration to higher-wage countries in Western Europe, had virtually extinguished unemployment. A new Constitution, adopted in 1966, allowed for the direct election of a fourth of the Cortes.

Franco died of a heart attack on Nov. 20, 1975, after more than a year of ill health, and Juan Carlos was proclaimed King two days later.

Over strong rightist opposition, the government legalized the Communist party in advance of the June 1977 elections and permitted the return of Dolores Ibarruri, "La Pasionaria" of the Thirties, from long exile in Moscow. Suárez's Union of the Democratic Center, a coalition of a dozen centrist and rightist parties, claimed 34.3% of the popular vote in the June 15 election.

The Spanish Socialist Workers Party (PSOE) ran the strongest oppostion campaign to win 28.5% of the vote, with the Communists following at 9% and the right-wing Popular Alliance trailing with 8.2%. The UDC's thin margin in the Chamber of Deputies presaged difficulties for Suárez's legislative program.

Carrillo's strong stand for the "Eurocommunist" philosophy of separation from Moscow's leadership was a feature of the election and drew a sharp attack from the Soviet Union.

In September 1977, the central government granted limited autonomy to Catalonia, permitting the return from exile of Josep Tarradellas as President of the Generalitat, the ancient Catalonian governing body suppressed by Franco in 1938. Basque Day was celebrated for the first time since 1939 on March 26, 1978, marking the recognition of another major ethnic group that had long sought a degree of independence.

**Economy.** Leading agricultural products include wheat, barley, corn, and potatoes.

The textile industry, concentrated in Catalonia, leads all others. The paper and chemical industries are also important, as well as pig iron and steel.

Spain's mineral wealth, second to agriculture in the national economy, yields millions of tons of ore, including coal, lignite, iron ore (metal content 50%), potash ore, lead ore, zinc ore, and mercury. Spain also produces copper, gold, magnesite, sulfur, tungsten, phosphates, silver, and, reportedly, uranium. Spanish forests yield lumber, pine resins, cork, and esparto.

Chief exports in 1976 were machinery (12%), iron and steel (10%), fruit and vegetables (10%), chemicals (9%), motor vehicles (7%), footwear

2. However, he did not abdicate. In 1941, shortly before his death, he renounced his claim to the throne in favor of his third son, Don Juan.

(6%), textiles and clothing (5%), and ships and boats (5%). Leading customers were EEC (46%; incl. France 14%, West Germany 11%, U.K. 7%, Netherlands 5%), U.S. (10%). Leading suppliers were EEC (33%; incl. West Germany 10%, France 8%, U.K. 5%, Italy 5%), U.S. (14%), Saudi Arabia (9%), Iran (5%).

## SRI LANKA

**Republic of Sri Lanka**
**President:** J. R. Jayawardene (1978)
**Prime Minister:** Ranasingle Premadasa (1978)
**Area:** 25,332 sq mi. (65,610 sq km)
**Population (est. 1978):** 14,200,000 (Sinhalese, 72%; Tamil, 21%; Moors, 7%)
**Density per square mile:** 560.6
**Capital:** Colombo
**Largest cities (est. 1976):** Colombo, 607,000; Dehiwela, 166,000; Jaffna, 117,000
**Monetary unit:** Sri Lanka rupee
**Languages:** Sinhalese, Tamil, English
**Religions:** Buddhist, 67%; Hindu, 18%; Christian, 8%; Islam, 7%
**Gross national product** (1976): $3.1 billion
**Member of Commonwealth of Nations**
**Freedom House classifications:** Capitalist-statist industrial, multi-party centralized.

**Geography.** An island in the Indian Ocean off the southeast tip of India, Sri Lanka is about half the size of Alabama. Most of the land is flat and rolling; mountains in the south central region rise to over 8,000 feet (2,438 m).

**Government.** After 24 years as a British Dominion, Ceylon became an independent republic and reverted to the traditional name Sri Lanka (resplendent island) on May 22, 1972. A new Constitution was adopted, replacing the 1948 one. The island remains a part of the Commonwealth. William Gopallawa, the former Governor-General, was named President and Mrs. Sirimavo R. D. Bandaranaike remained Prime Minister.

The new Constitution set up the National State Assembly, which consists of such number of elected representatives of the people as a Delimitation Commission may determine. The Assembly is a unicameral legislature and serves for six years unless dissolved earlier. There are presently 168 members.

The major political parties are the United National Party (141 of 168 seats in National Assembly), led by President Jayawardene; Tamil United Liberation Front (17 seats); Sri Lanka Freedom Party (9 seats), led by former Prime Minister Bandaranaike.

**History.** Following Portuguese and Dutch rule, Ceylon became an English crown colony in 1798. The British developed coffee, tea, and rubber plantations and granted four Constitutions between 1798 and 1910. A fifth in 1920 granted partial self-government, a sixth in 1924 enlarging the powers of a legislative council. The Constitution of 1931 gave a large measure of self-government.

Ceylon became a self-governing dominion of the Commonwealth of Nations in 1948. Rioting by the Tamils seeking a separate state within a federal system occurred in 1958 and 1961, resulting in the outlawing of their party. In 1962, the Prime Minister, Mrs. Bandaranaike, a radical, nationalized Western oil and other business facilities and became embroiled with the U.S. and U.K. over compensation. She was ousted in the 1965 elections by a multiparty coalition.

Following considerable pre-election violence, Mrs. Bandaranaike was returned to power in a landslide victory on May 27, 1970, with her three-party leftist coalition capturing over two thirds of parliament. An important factor was the 800,000 youths 18-to-21 years old given the vote for the first time; they proved largely left-leaning.

Worsening economic conditions and charges of corruption combined to produce a crushing defeat for Mrs. Bandaranaike in general elections July 21, 1977. Junius Richard Jayawardene, 73-year-old leader of the small United National Party, became Prime Minister.

Amid opposition criticism, Jayawardene was sworn in as President on Feb. 3, 1978, in a constitutional change to the presidential system of government. He named his deputy party leader, Ranasingle Premadasa, as Prime Minister.

**Economy.** Sri Lanka is heavily dependent on food imports, particularly rice, the staple food. A large part of the cultivated land (25% of the total area) is devoted to the chief export crops—tea, rubber, and coconut products, all of which are grown for the most part on plantations. Other crops are rice, fruits, cinnamon, and citronella.

Mineral resources include graphite (plumbago), gem stones, mica, magnesite, and vanadium.

Chief exports in 1975 were tea (44%), rubber (18%), and coconut products (8%). Leading customers were China (13%), Pakistan (10%), U.K. (9%), U.S. (6%), Iraq (5%), Japan (5%). Leading suppliers were China (13%), Saudi Arabia (12%), Japan (9%), Australia (8%), France (8%), Thailand (7%), Pakistan (6%), U.S. (6%), West Germany (5%).

## SUDAN

**Democratic Republic of the Sudan**
**President:** Maj. Gen. Gaafar Mohamed Nimeiri (1969)
**Prime Minister:** Rashid Bakr (1976)
**Area:** 967,494 sq mi. (2,505,813 sq km)
**Population (est. 1977):** 16,550,000
**Density per square mile:** 17.1
**Capital:** Khartoum
**Largest cities** (est. 1973): Khartoum, 321,700; Omdurman, 250,000; Port Sudan, 130,000
**Monetary unit:** Sudanese pound
**Languages:** Arabic, English, tribal dialects
**Religions:** Sunni Moslem, Christian, Animist
**Gross national product (1976):** $4.6 billion
**National name:** Jamhuryat es-Sudan Al-Democratia
**Freedom House classifications:** Capitalist-socialist pre-industrial, one-party national.

**Geography.** The Sudan, in northeast Africa, is the largest country on the continent, measuring about one fourth the size of the United States. Its neighbors are Chad and the Central African Empire on the west, Egypt on the north, Ethiopia on the east, and Kenya, Uganda, and Zaire on the south. The Red Sea washes about 500 miles of the eastern coast.

The country extends from north to south about 1,200 miles (1,931 km) and west to east about 1,000 miles (1,609 km). The northern region is a continuation of the Libyan Desert. The southern region is fertile, abundantly watered, and, in places, heavily forested. It is traversed from north to south by the Nile, all of whose great tributaries are partly or entirely within its borders.

**Government.** Since the revolution of May 25, 1969, the Sudan has been governed by a 10-member Council for the Revolution. The provisional Constitution was abrogated. All political parties were dissolved by the Council for the Revolution.

**History.** The early history of the Sudan (known as the Anglo-Egyptian Sudan between 1898 and 1955) is connected with that of Nubia, where a powerful local kingdom was formed in Roman times with its capital at Dongola. After conversion to Christianity in the 6th century, it joined with Ethiopia and resisted Mohammedanization until the 14th century. Thereafter the area was broken up into many small states until 1820–22, when it was conquered by Mohammed Ali, Pasha of Egypt. Egyptian forces were evacuated during the Mahdist revolt (1881–98), but the Sudan was reconquered by the Anglo-Egyptian expeditions of 1896–98, and in 1899 became an Anglo-Egyptian condominium, which was reaffirmed by the Anglo-Egyptian treaty of 1936.

Egypt and Britain agreed in February 1953 to grant self-government to the Sudan under an appointed Governor-General. Under the self-government statute of March 21, 1953, an all-Sudanese Parliament was elected in November-December 1953, and an all-Sudanese government was formed. In December 1955, the Parliament declared the independence of the Sudan, which, with the approval of U.K. and Egypt, was proclaimed on Jan. 1, 1956.

In October 1969, Maj. Gen. Gaafar Mohamed Nimeiri, the President of the Council for the Revolution, took over the office of Prime Minister. He was elected the nation's first President in October 1971 by a reported 98.6% of the vote in a national referendum. His term was for six years. In July 1972, Sudan and the U.S. resumed diplomatic relations that were broken as a result of the Arab-Israeli War of 1967.

On March 2, 1973, eight Palestinian terrorists invaded the Saudi Arabian embassy in Khartoum and killed one Belgian and two American diplomats after their demands for the release of Arab terrorist prisoners in different countries were refused. The terrorists surrendered after three days and were captured, but Nimeiri postponed bringing them to trial in the face of Arab calls for their release.

The terrorists were convicted of murder June 24, 1974, but Nimeiri freed them the next day and turned them over to the Palestine Liberation Army, which flew them to Cairo. The U.S. withdrew its Ambassador in protest, but he returned in October 1974 after the men were imprisoned in Egypt. All new U.S. aid programs and military sales to the Sudan were suspended for two years.

On July 2 and 3, 1976, a third attempted coup against Nimeiri left 1,000 rebels and loyal troops dead after a fierce battle in Khartoum. Nimeiri accused President Muammar el-Quaddifi of Libya of having instigated the attempt and broke relations with Libya. On August 4, firing squads executed 81 convicted rebels.

Nimeiri also charged Soviet involvement in the attempt and in May 1977 expelled 90 Soviet advisers. He moved closer to Egypt—he was one of the few Arab leaders who supported Sadat's dramatic visit to Israel in November 1977—and the U.S. Nimeiri publicly backed the Eritrean rebel movement in 1977 in its fight against the pro-Soviet Ethiopian central government, which accused him of giving material aid as well as moral support to the rebels.

**Economy.** Long-staple cotton, the chief export crop, is grown under irrigation in the Kassala and Tokar areas of the north and in narrow strips along the main Nile; durra, peanuts, corn, and oilseeds are grown elsewhere.

Livestock raising is the occupation of most of the population of the Sudan.

Salt is produced at Port Sudan, and gold deposits are worked at Gebeit, near the Red Sea. Most of the world's gum arabic comes from the semiarid Kordofan area of the west.

Chief exports in 1976 were cotton (51%), peanuts (20%), and gum arabic (6%). Leading customers were Italy (20%), Japan (7%), France (7%), West Germany (7%), Yugoslavia (5%), Netherlands (5%). Leading suppliers were U.K. (20%), U.S. (9%), West Germany (8%), Italy (8%), Iraq (8%), Japan (7%), India (6%).

## SURINAM

**Republic of Surinam**
**President:** Johan H. E. Ferrier (1975)
**Prime Minister:** Henck A. E. Arron (1975)
**Area:** 63,037 sq mi. (163,265 sq km)
**Population (est. 1978):** 460,000 (approx.: Hindustani, 37%; Creole, 30.8%; Indonesian, 15.3%; Bush Negro, 10.3%)
**Density per square mile:** 7.3
**Capital and largest city (est. 1973):** Paramaribo, 150,000
**Monetary unit:** Surinam guilder
**Language:** Dutch, Taki-taki (lingua franca)
**Religions:** Protestant, Roman Catholic, Hindu, Islam
**Freedom House classifications:** Capitalist industrial, multi-party centralized

**Geography.** Surinam lies on the northeast coast of South America, with Guyana to the west, French Guiana to the east, and Brazil to the south. It is about one tenth larger than Michigan. The principal rivers are the Courantyne on the Guyana border, the Maroni in the east, and the Suriname, on which the capital city of Paramaribo is situated. The Tumuc-Humac Mountains are on the border with Brazil.

**Government.** Surinam became an independent republic on Nov. 25, 1975, after 308 years of British, French, and Dutch rule, the last continuous from 1815 and it was known as Dutch Guiana before independence.

The major political coalitions are the National Party Alliance (24 of 39 seats in the National Assembly), led by Prime Minister Arron; United Democratic Parties (15 seats), led by Jaggernath Lachmon.

**History.** After gradual progress toward internal autonomy, Surinam was offered complete independence by the Netherlands in 1973, following race riots over unemployment and inflation. Arron, leader of a coalition of Creole (Surinamese of African descent) parties, backed independence as Jaggernath Lachmon, leader of the Vatan Hitkaric (Progressive Reform Party, largely Surinamese of East Indian descent), strove for a delay.

In the first post-independence legislative elections on Oct. 31, 1977, Arron's coalition retained power despite severe economic problems.

**Economy.** Surinam is third among the world's bauxite producers, exporting 7 million metric tons annually. Bauxite earnings accounted for 92% of the nation's 1975 income of $156 million. Other exports include rice, gold, and timber.

Chief exports in 1974 were alumina (43%), bauxite (18%), and aluminum (8%). Leading customers were U.S. (19%), West Germany (8%), Netherlands, (7%), Norway (6%). Leading suppliers were U.S. (24%), Netherlands (10%), Trinidad and Tobago (6%), Japan (5%).

## SWAZILAND

**Kingdom of Swaziland**
**Ruler:** King Sobhuza II (1967)
**Prime Minister:** Col. Maphevu Dlamini (1976)
**Area:** 6,704 sq mi. (17,363 sq km)
**Population (est. 1978):** 520,000
**Density per square mile:** 77.6
**Capital and largest city (est. 1975):** Mbabane, 24,000
**Monetary unit:** Lilangeni
**Languages:** English and Siswati (official)
**Religions:** Christian, 60%, and Animist.
**Gross national product** (1976): $240 million
**Member of Commonwealth of Nations**
**Freedom House classifications:** Capitalist pre-industrial, non-party traditional

**Geography.** Swaziland, 85% the size of New Jersey, is surrounded by South Africa and Mozambique. The country consists of a high veld in the west and a series of plateaus descending from a maximum of 6,000 feet (1,829 m) to a low veld of 1,500 feet (457 m).

**Government.** In 1967, a new Constitution established King Sobhuza II as head of state and provided for an Assembly of 24 members elected by universal suffrage, together with a Senate of 12 members—half appointed by the Assembly and half by the King. But on April 12, 1973, the King renounced the Constitution, suspended political parties, and took total power for himself. On March 12, 1977, he replaced the Parliament with an assembly of tribal leaders.

**History.** Bantu peoples migrated southwest to the area of Mozambique in the 16th century. A number of clans broke away from the main body in the 18th century and settled in Swaziland. In the 19th century they organized as a tribe, partly because they were in constant conflict with the Zulu. Their ruler, Mswazi, applied to the British in the 1840s for help against the Zulu. The British and the Transvaal governments guaranteed the independence of Swaziland in 1881. In 1890 a provisional government, representing the Swazi, the British, and the Transvaal, was established.

South Africa held Swaziland as a protectorate from 1894 to 1899, but after the close of the Boer War, in 1902, Swaziland was transferred to British administration. An elected European advisory council was established in 1921. The Paramount Chief was recognized as the native authority in 1941.

In 1963 the territory was constituted a protectorate, and on Sept. 6, 1968, it became the independent nation of Swaziland.

**Economy.** Herding is the principal native occupation. Tropical and subtropical crops are raised in the lower areas.

Important agricultural products are sugar, sorghums, corn, rice, cotton lint, peanuts, and tobacco. Mineral products include iron ore, coal, asbestos, and gold. There are timber and paper pulp industries.

Chief exports in 1970 were sugar (54%), wood pulp (9%), iron ore (9%), and asbestos (7%). Leading customers were U.K. (25%), Japan (24%), South Africa (21%).

## SWEDEN

**Kingdom of Sweden**
**Sovereign:** King Carl XVI Gustaf (1973)
**Prime Minster:** Thorbjörn Fälldin (1976)
**Area:** 173,732 sq mi. (449,964 sq km)
**Population (est. 1978):** 8,300,000
**Density per square mile:** 47.8
**Capital:** Stockholm
**Largest cities (est. 1977):** Stockholm, 661,300; (est. 1976): Göteborg, 442,500; Malmö, 240,300
**Monetary unit:** Krona
**Language:** Swedish
**Religion:** Swedish Lutheran, 95%
**Gross national product (1976):** $71.3 billion
**National name:** Konungariket Sverige
**Freedom House classifications:** Capitalist-socialist industrial, multi-party centralized

**Geography.** Sweden occupies the eastern part of the Scandinavian peninsula, with Norway to the west, Finland and the Gulf of Bothnia to the east, and Denmark and the Baltic Sea in the south. It is one tenth larger than California.

The country slopes eastward and southward from the Kjølen Mountains along the Norwegian border, where the peak elevation is Kebnekaise at 6,965 feet (2,123 m) in Lapland. In the north are mountains and many lakes. To the south and east are central lowlands and south of them are fertile areas of forest, valley, and plain.

Along Sweden's rocky coast, chopped up by bays and inlets, are many islands, the largest of which are Gotland and Öland.

**Government.** Sweden is a constitutional monarchy. Under the new Constitution, which became effective Jan. 1, 1975, the Riksdag is the sole governing body. The Prime Minister is the political chief executive.

In 1967, agreement was reached on part of a new Constitution after 13 years of work. It provided for a single-house Riksdag of 350 members (later amended to 349 seats) to replace the 104-year old bicameral Riksdag. The members are popularly elected for a term of three years. The first Riksdag under the new Constitution was installed in January 1971. Eighty present members of the Riksdag are women.

The King, Carl XVI Gustaf, was born April 30, 1946, and became the world's youngest reigning monarch when he succeeded to the throne Sept. 19, 1973, on the death at 90 of his grandfather, Gustaf VI Adolf. Carl Gustaf was married on June 19, 1976, to Silvia Sommerlath, a West German commoner. Their first child, Princess Victoria, born July 14, 1977, could inherit the throne under a proposed change in the law abolishing the priority of male successors.

The major political parties are the Center Party (86 of 349 seats), led by Prime Minister Fälldin; Moderate Party (55 seats), led by Gösta Bohman; Liberal Party (39 seats), led by Ola Ullsten; Social Democratic Party (152 seats), led by former Prime Minister, Olof Palme; Leftist (Communist) Party, (17 seats). The first three parties constitute the governing coalition with a total of 180 seats.

**History.** The earliest historical mention of Sweden

is found in Tacitus' *Germania*, where reference is made to the powerful king and strong fleet of the Suiones. Toward the end of the 10th century, Olaf Sköttkonung established a Christian stronghold in Sweden. Around 1400, an attempt was made to unite the northern nations into one kingdom, but this led to bitter strife between the Danes and the Swedes.

In 1520, the Danish King, Christian II, conquered Sweden and in the "Stockholm Blood-Bath" put leading Swedish personalities to death. Gustavus Vasa (1523–60) broke away from Denmark and fashioned the modern Swedish state.

Sweden played a leading role in the second phase (1630–35) of the Thirty Years' War (1618–48). By the Treaty of Westphalia (1648), Sweden obtained western Pomerania and some neighboring territory on the Baltic. In 1700, a coalition of Russia, Poland, and Denmark united against Sweden and by the Peace of Nystad (1721) forced her to relinquish Livonia, Ingria, Estonia, and parts of Finland.

From the Napoleonic wars, Sweden emerged with the gain of Norway from Denmark and with a new royal dynasty stemming from Marshal Jean Bernadotte of France, who became King Charles XIV (1818–44). The artificial union between Sweden and Norway led to an unhappy feud. It was finally dissolved in 1905.

Sweden maintained a position of neutrality in both World Wars.

An elaborate structure of welfare legislation, imitated by many larger nations, began with the establishment of old-age pensions in 1911. Economic prosperity based on its neutralist policy enabled Sweden, together with Norway, to pioneer in public health, housing, and job security programs.

Forty-four years of Socialist government was ended Sept. 19, 1976, by a conservative coalition headed by Thorbjörn Fälldin, a 50-year-old sheep farmer. The surprise conservative victory was credited to public opposition to a nuclear power program backed by the Socialists and to a program that would have given control of all businesses to labor unions within 20 years.

**Economy.** Milk, butter, meat, grain, potatoes, and sugar beets are products of the broad fertile plains of the south; the north is limited to cattle raising and dairy farming.

The highly specialized machine industry produces separators, motors, electrical machines and apparatus, agricultural machinery, ball bearings, telephone equipment, and harbor works.

There are also large woolen, glass, and porcelain industries. Shipyards build for Swedish and foreign fleets. Timber and woodworking industries are extensive.

Sweden's iron ore deposits (metal content 60%) are among the world's richest. Those in central Sweden produce principally for domestic use, while the ones in Lapland to the north are worked largely for export, with much of the output being shipped through the Norwegian port of Narvik. Other minerals are copper, gold, lead, arsenic ore, manganese ore, and silver. Coal production is insignificant; imports of several million tons a year are therefore necessary.

About 60% of Sweden is forested, mostly conifers, and there are vast forest products industries in the north. Sweden supplies a large percentage of the world's mechanical and chemical pulp.

Chief exports in 1976 were machinery (26%), motor vehicles (10%), paper (9%), ships and boats (7%), wood pulp (7%), iron and steel (7%), timber (5%), and chemicals (5%). Leading customers were U.K. (11%), Norway (11%), West Germany (10%), Denmark (10%), Finland (6%), France (5%), U.S. (5%). Leading suppliers were West Germany (19%), U.K. (11%), Denmark (7%), U.S. (7%), Norway (6%), Finland (6%).

## SWITZERLAND

**Swiss Confederation**
**President:** Willi Ritchard (1978)
**Vice President:** Hans Hürlimann (1978)
**Area:** 15,941 sq mi. (41,288 sq km)
**Population (est. 1978):** 6,310,000 (Swiss, 85%; Italian, 8%; German, 2%; Spanish, 2%; French, 1%—figures by place of birth)
**Density per square mile:** 395.8
**Capital:** Bern
**Largest cities (est. 1976 by U.N.):** Zurich, 389,600; Basel, 192,800; Geneva, 155,800; Bern, 149,800; Lausanne, 134,300
**Monetary unit:** Swiss franc
**Languages:** German, 65%; French, 18%; Italian, 12%; Romansch, 1%
**Religions:** Roman Catholic, 49.4%; Protestant, 47.8%
**Gross national product (1976):** $58.4 billion
**National name:** Schweiz/Suisse/Svizzera
**Freedom House classifications:** Capitalist industrial, multi-party decentralized

**Geography.** Switzerland, in central Europe, is the land of the Alps. The tallest peak in Switzerland is the Dufourspitze at 15,203 feet (4,634 m) on the Swiss side of the Italian border, one of 10 summits of the Monte Rose massif in the Pennine Alps. The tallest peak in all of the Alps, Mont Blanc (15,771 ft, 4,807 m), is actually in France.

Most of Switzerland comprises a mountainous plateau bordered by the great bulk of the Alps on the south and by the Jura Mountains on the northwest. About a fourth of the total area is covered by mountains and glaciers.

The country's largest lakes—Geneva, Constance (Bodensee), and Maggiore—straddle the French, German-Austrian, and Italian borders, respectively.

The Rhine, navigable from Basel to the North Sea, is the principal inland waterway. Other rivers are the Aare and the Rhône.

Switzerland, twice the size of New Jersey, is surrounded by France, West Germany, Austria, Liechtenstein, and Italy.

**Government.** The Swiss Confederation consists of 22 sovereign cantons. Federal authority is vested in a bicameral legislature. The Ständerat, or State Council, consists of 44 members, two from each canton. The lower house, the Nationalrat, or National Council, has 200 deputies, elected for four-year terms.

Executive authority is lodged in a board called the Bundesrat, or Federal Council, of seven members chosen by parliament. The parliament elects the President, who serves for a term of one year and is ordinarily succeeded by the Vice President. The federal government regulates matters of foreign policy, railroads, postal service, and the national mint. Each canton reserves for itself important local powers.

A constitutional amendment adopted in February 1971 by referendum gave women the vote in federal elections and right to hold federal office for the first time. Women previously had the rights in some cantons and now have them in all but one.

The major political parties are the Social Democratic Party (55 of 200 seats in National Council), led by Helmut Hubacher; Radical Democratic Party (47 seats), led by Yann Richter; Conservative Christian-Social Party (46 seats), led by Hans Wyer; People's Party (21 seats), led by Fritz Hofmann; Independent Party (11 seats), led by Walter Biel.

**History.** Called Helvetia in ancient times, Switzerland in the Middle Ages was a league of cantons of the Holy Roman Empire. Fashioned around the nucleus of three German forest districts of Schwyz, Uri, and Unterwalden, the Swiss Confederation slowly added new cantons. In 1648 the Treaty of Westphalia gave Switzerland her independence from the Holy Roman Empire.

French revolutionary troops occupied Switzerland in 1798 and named it the Helvetic Republic, but Napoleon in 1803 restored its federal government. At this time, and again in 1815, the French- and Italian-speaking peoples of Switzerland were raised to political equality.

In 1815, the Congress of Vienna guaranteed the neutrality and recognized the independence of Switzerland. In the revolutionary period of 1847 the Catholic cantons seceded and organized a separate union called the *Sonderbund*. In 1848 the new Swiss Constitution established a union modeled upon that of the U.S. The Federal Constitution of 1874 established a strong central government while maintaining large powers of control in each canton.

National unity and political conservatism grew as the country prospered from its neutrality. Its banking system became the world's leading repository for international accounts. Armed neutrality was its policy through World Wars I and II. Geneva was the seat of the League of Nations, and Geneva, along with The Hague in The Netherlands, became the headquarters of a number of international organizations.

In 1971, the Swiss Supreme Court ruled that Swiss banks must show U.S. tax officials records of U.S. citizens suspected of tax fraud, thus significantly modifying a 1934 law that had seemed to forbid any bank disclosures.

**Economy.** Leading agricultural products include wheat, barley, oats, rye, potatoes, and fruit.

Chief exports in 1976 were machinery (31%), chemicals (22%), watches and clocks (8%), and textile yarns and fabrics (6%). Leading customers were EEC (45%; incl. West Germany 16%, France 9%, Italy 7%, U.K. 6%), U.S. (7%), Austria (5%). Leading suppliers were EEC (67%; incl. West Germany 28%, France 13%, Italy 10%, U.K. 7%), U.S. (7%).

## SYRIA

**Syrian Arab Republic**
**President:** Hafez al-Assad (1971)
**Premier:** Mohamad Ali al-Halabi (1978)
**Area:** 71,498 sq mi. (185,180 sq km)
**Population (est. 1978):** 8,000,000
**Density per square mile:** 111.9
**Capital:** Damascus
**Largest cities (est. 1976):** Damascus, 1,054,000; (est. 1975): Aleppo, 778,500; Homs, 267,100; Hama, 162,000
**Monetary unit:** Syrian pound
**Languages:** Arabic (official), Kurdish, Armenian, Turkish, Circassian
**Religions:** Islam, 83%; Christian, 17%
**Gross national product (1976):** $6.0 billion
**National name:** Al-Jamhouriya al Arabiya As-Souriya
**Freedom House classifications:** Capitalist-socialist industrial, dominant party

**Geography.** Slightly larger than North Dakota, Syria lies at the eastern end of the Mediterranean Sea. It is bordered by Lebanon and Israel on the west, Turkey on the north, Iraq on the east, and Jordan on the south.

Coastal Syria is a narrow plain, in back of which is a range of coastal mountains, and still farther inland a steppe area. In the east is the Syrian Desert, and in the south is the Jebel Druze Range. The highest point in Syria is Mt. Hermon (9,232 ft.; 2,814 m) on the Lebanese border.

**Government.** Following a coup by the military wing of the Ba'ath Arab Socialist Party against its political wing in November 1970, the new leadership appointed a People's Assembly (parliament) but retained all effective powers.

Syria's first permanent Constitution was approved in 1973, replacing a provisional charter that had been in force for 10 years. It provides for a 186-member People's Assembly as the legislature. No national religion is specified, although Islamic law is the basis of the state law.

In the first election in 10 years, in 1973, the Ba'ath Arab Socialist Party of President Hafez al-Assad, running on a unified National Progressive ticket with the Communists and Socialist parties, won 70% of the vote and a commensurate proportion of the seats for a four-year term in the People's Assembly. In the August 1977 Assembly elections, the ruling Ba'athists won 125 of the now 195 seats; the National Progressive Front coalition, 34 seats; various rightist candidates, 36 seats.

**History.** Ancient Syria was conquered by Egypt about 1500 B.C., and after that by Hebrews, Phoenicians, Assyrians, Chaldeans, Persians, and Greeks. From 64 B.C. until the Arab conquest in A.D. 636, it was part of the Roman Empire except during brief periods. The Arabs made it a trade center for their whole empire, but it suffered severely from the Mongol invasion in 1260 and fell to the Ottoman Turks in 1516. Syria remained a Turkish province until World War I.

A secret Anglo-French pact of 1916 put Syria in the French zone of influence. The League of Nations gave France a mandate over Syria after World War I, but the French were forced to put down several nationalist uprisings. In 1930, France recognized Syria as an independent republic, but still subject to the mandate. After nationalist demonstrations in 1939, the French High Commissioner suspended the Syrian Constitution. In 1941, British and Free French forces invaded Syria to eliminate Vichy control. During the rest of World War II, Syria was an Allied base.

Again in 1945, nationalist demonstrations broke into actual fighting, and British troops had to restore order. Syrian forces met a series of reverses while participating in the Arab invasion of Palestine in 1948. On Feb. 1, 1958, with the formation of the United Arab Republic through the union of Egypt and Syria, Gamal Abdel Nasser became President of the new republic. However, Syria became independent again on Sept. 29, 1961, following a revolution.

In the Middle Eastern War of 1967, Israel quickly vanquished the Syrian army. Before acceding to the U.N. cease-fire, the Israeli forces took over control of the fortified Golan Heights commanding the Sea of Galilee.

Syria joined Egypt in attacking Israel in October 1973 in the fourth Arab-Israeli war, but was pushed back from initial successes on the Golan Heights to end up losing more land. However, in the settlement worked out by U.S. Secretary of State Henry A. Kissinger in May 1974, the Syrians recovered all the territory lost in 1973 and a token amount of territory, including the deserted town of Quneitra, lost in 1967. Syria agreed to negotiate a permanent settlement with Israel, its first de facto recognition of Israel.

Relations between the U.S. and Syria, severed since the 1967 war, were renewed June 16, 1974, and Syria somewhat moderated the tone, but not the goals, of its policies toward Israel. Syria joined with Egypt in September 1974 in a statement declaring the Palestine Liberation Army to be "the sole representative of the Palestinian people" and initiated a resolution asserting this principle, which passed the U.N. General Assembly the following month.

Syria became involved in the Christian-Moslem civil war in neighboring Lebanon after warning in January 1976 against any attempt at partition. After an early truce failed, Syria increased its troop strength to 20,000 men and became the major element in an Arab League peace-keeping force. By late November, Syrian forces controlled all of Lebanon except a narrow strip along the Israeli border. In January 1977, the Syrians moved into this area also but, under U.S. and Israeli pressure, withdrew in February.

Assad met May 9, 1977, with President Carter in Geneva and for the first time stated his willingness to accept demilitarized zones as the price of a settlement with Israel. Assad was reported also to have supported the linking of a Palestinian homeland on the West Bank with Jordan, a proposal also backed by Egypt and Saudi Arabia.

The 30,000-man Syrian peacekeeping force in Lebanon did not interfere when Israeli troops invaded southern Lebanon on March 14, 1978, although the Syrian government joined Lebanon in calling for Israel's withdrawal. In July, however, Syrian forces clashed with Christian Lebanese militiamen in Beirut in the sharpest fighting since the Lebanese civil war ended in mid-1977.

**Economy.** Agriculture and animal breeding are the main industries. Only half the land is arable, and only a third is actually cultivated. Most crops require irrigation. Leading crops are sorghum, olives, cotton, wheat, barley, grapes, lentils, and tobacco. Stock raising is important among the nomads.

Chief exports in 1975 were crude oil (62%) and cotton (15%). Leading customers were Italy (18%), Belgium-Luxembourg (11%), West Germany (10%), U.K. (8%), U.S.S.R. (7%), Yugoslavia (6%), Greece (6%). Leading suppliers were West Germany (13%), Italy (9%), France (7%), U.S. (6%), Japan (5%), Brazil (5%).

## TANZANIA

**United Republic of Tanzania**
**President:** Julius K. Nyerere (1964)
**Prime Minister:** Edward Sokoine (1977)
**Area:** 364,900 sq mi. (945,087 sq km)[1]
**Population (est. 1978):** 16,450,000
**Density per square mile:** 45.1
**Capital and largest city (est. 1977):** Dar es Salaam, 460,000
**Monetary unit:** Tanzanian shilling
**Languages:** Swahili, Bantu, Arabic, English
**Religions:** Animist, 34.6%; Christian, 30.6%; Islam, 30.5%
**Gross national product (1976):** $2.7 billion
**Member of Commonwealth of Nations**
**Freedom House classifications:** Socialist pre-industrial, one-party socialist

1. Including Zanzibar.

**Geography.** Tanzania is in East Africa on the Indian Ocean. To the north are Uganda and Kenya; to the west, Burundi, Rwanda, and Zaire; and to the south, Mozambique, Zambia, and Malawi. Its area is three times that of New Mexico.

Tanzania contains three of Africa's best-known lakes—Victoria in the north, Tanganyika in the west, and Nyasa in the south. Mount Kilimanjaro in the north, 19,340 feet (5,895 m), is the highest point on the continent.

**Government.** Under the republican form of government, Tanzania has a President elected by universal suffrage who appoints the Cabinet ministers. The 218-member National Assembly is composed of 96 elected members from the mainland, 10 members appointed by the President (from both Tanganyika and Zanzibar), 35 National members (elected by the National Assembly after nomination by various national institutions), 32 members of the Zanzibar Revolutionary Council, 20 other Zanzibar members appointed by the President in agreement with the President of Zanzibar, and up to 20 other Zanzibar members appointed by the President in agreement with the first Vice President, who represents Zanzibar.

The Tanganyika African National Union (TANU), the only authorized party on the mainland, and the Afro-Shirazi Party, the only party in Zanzibar and Pemba, merged Feb. 5, 1977, as the Revolutionary Party (Chama Cha Mapinduzi) and elected Julius K. Nyerere as its head.

**History.** Arab traders first began to colonize the area in A.D. 700. Portuguese explorers reached the coastal regions in 1500 and held some control until the 17th century, when the Sultan of Oman took power. With what are now Burundi and Rwanda, Tanganyika became the colony of German East Africa in 1885. After World War I, it was administered by the U.K. under a League of Nations mandate and later as a U.N. trust territory.

Although not mentioned in old histories until the 12th century, Zanzibar was believed always to have had connections with southern Arabia. The Portuguese made it one of their tributaries in 1503 and later established a trading post, but they were driven out by Arabs from Oman in 1698. Zanzibar was declared independent of Oman in 1861 and, in 1890, it became a British protectorate.

Tanganyika became an independent nation on Dec. 9, 1961; Zanzibar, on Dec. 10, 1963. On April 26, 1964, the two nations merged into a single nation—the United Republic of Tanganyika and Zanzibar. The name was changed to Tanzania on Oct. 29, 1964.

On Oct. 23, 1975, the 1,163-mile (1,872 km) Tanzam railway linking the Tanzanian port of Dar es Salaam with Zambia was officially opened. Built and financed by China, the railway provided a direct route for Zambian copper exports to the sea, replacing a longer route through white-ruled Rhodesia to Mozambique.

In May 1977, Tanzania closed its border with Kenya permanently because of a dispute over the operation of East African Airways, an entity of the East African Community. The breakup of the airline left the East African Posts and Telecommunications Corporation as the only community agency still functioning.

**Economy.** The mainland portion of Tanzania is sparsely populated, and two thirds of it is uninhabited. It is the world's largest producer of sisal hemp. Production of cloves is the chief industry of the island of Zanzibar.

Chief exports in 1976 were cotton (16%), coffee (13%), cloves (8%), sisal (6%), tobacco (5%), cashew nuts (5%), and petroleum products (5%). Leading customers were West Germany (14%), U.K. (13%), U.S. (9%), Singapore (7%), Italy (6%), Kenya (6%), Hong Kong (5%), India (5%). Leading suppliers were U.K. (12%), Kenya (11%), Iran (9%), West Germany (8%), Japan (7%), China (6%), U.S. (6%).

## THAILAND

**Kingdom of Thailand**
**Ruler:** King Bhumibol Adulyadej (1946)
**Prime Minister:** Gen. Kriangsak Chamanan (1977)
**Area:** 198,455 sq mi. (514,000 sq km)
**Population (est. 1978):** 45,380,000 (incl. 2.5 million of Chinese descent born in Thailand; Chinese 1.6%; others, 0.2%)
**Density per square mile:** 228.7
**Capital and largest city (est. 1977):** Bangkok, 4,545,600
**Monetary unit:** Baht
**Languages:** Thai (Siamese), Chinese, English
**Religions:** Buddhist, 95%; Islam, 4%
**Gross national product (1976):** $16.2 billion
**National name:** Muang Thai
**Freedom House classifications:** Capitalist pre-industrial, non-party military.

**Geography.** Thailand occupies the western half of the former Indochinese peninsula and the northern two thirds of the Malay peninsula in southeast Asia. Its neighbors are Burma on the north and west, Laos on the east, and Cambodia and Malaysia on the south. Thailand is about three fourths the size of Texas.

Most of the population is supported in the fertile central alluvial plain, which is drained by the Chao Phnaya River and its tributaries.

**Government.** King Bhumibol Adulyadej, who was born Dec. 5, 1927, second son of Prince Mahidol of Songkhla, succeeded to the throne on June 9, 1946, when his brother, King Ananda Mahidol, died of a gunshot wound. He was married on April 28, 1950, to Queen Sirikit; their son, Vajiralongkorn, born July 28, 1952, is the Crown Prince.

Thailand is once again under military rule after a brief interval of civilian government from 1973 to 1976—the first in 20 years. All political parties were abolished in the coup of Oct. 6, 1976.

**History.** The Thais first began moving down into their present homeland from the Asiatic continent in the 6th century A.D., and by the end of the 13th century ruled most of the western portion. During the next 400 years, the Thais fought sporadically with the Cambodians to the east and the Burmese to the west. The British obtained recognition of paramount interest in Thailand in 1824, and in 1896 an Anglo-French accord guaranteed the independence of Thailand.

A coup on June 24, 1932, changed the absolute monarchy into a representative government with universal suffrage. After five hours of token resistance on Dec. 8, 1941, Thailand yielded to Japanese occupation and became one of the springboards in World War II for the Japanese campaign against Malaya.

After the fall of its pro-Japanese puppet government in July 1944, Thailand pursued a policy of passive resistance against the Japanese, and on Aug. 16, 1945, after the Japanese surrender, Thailand repudiated the declaration of war it had been forced to make against the U.K. and U.S. in 1942. By a treaty signed with the U.K. and India on Jan. 1, 1946, Thailand renounced all wartime acquisitions of Malayan territory.

Thailand's major problem in the late 1960s was suppressing Communist guerrilla action by invaders in the north. The prospect of a U.S. withdrawal from Southeast Asia alarmed the Thais, who sought and obtained reassurance from the U.S. that they would not be abandoned.

Although Thailand had received $2 billion in U.S. economic and military aid since 1950 and had sent troops (paid by the U.S.) to Vietnam while permitting U.S. bomber bases on its territory, the collapse of South Vietnam and Cambodia in the spring of 1975 brought rapid changes in the country's diplomatic posture.

At the Thai government's insistence, the U.S. agreed in June 1975 to withdraw all 23,000 U.S. military personnel remaining in Thailand by March 1976. Diplomatic relations with China were established July 1, 1975. Meanwhile, overtures toward an accommodation with the new regime in South Vietnam were initiated.

Thailand protested vigorously when 1,100 U.S. Marines were airlifted to Thai bases May 14 for use in the rescue of the crew of the cargo ship Mayaguez after its seizure by a Cambodian gunboat. The marines were withdrawn May 15 and Thailand later accepted a U.S. apology for unauthorized use of its territory.

From Oct. 14, 1973, when Field Marshal Thanom Kittikachorn resigned under the pressure of massive student demonstrations, Thailand had a civilian government and in January 1975 had its first general elections. Prime Minister Seni Pramoj, this time after rioting by leftist students, was ousted Oct. 6, 1976, by Admiral Sa-Ngad Chaloryu and the "National Administrative Reform Council." The Junta appointed Thanin Kraivichien, a Supreme Court Justice, as Premier and appointed a 340-member National Assembly, 110 of them military officers.

As insurgent activity increased and skirmishes along the Cambodian border continued despite Thai efforts to make peace with the Communist regime in Phnom Penh, the military, on Oct. 20, 1977, ousted Thanin as "weak," replacing him on November 11 with Gen. Kriangsak Chamanan.

In 1978, Thailand experienced a growing influx of refugees from Laos, Cambodia, and Vietnam and sought Western help in handling the problem. Vice President Walter F. Mondale, visiting Bangkok May 5–6, brought assurances that the U.S. would take refugees and would also supply arms for the beleaguered regime.

**Economy.** Almost 80% of the population work at agriculture. Rice is the principal crop, the staple food, and the leading export. It is the basis of Thailand's whole economy and the key to its prosperity. Next most important is rubber. Other products include teak, tin, cassava, coconuts, corn, tobacco, sesame, sugarcane, and soybeans. Livestock is fair in quality.

Industry is of growing importance. Industrial products include cement and tin, tungsten, and lead concentrates.

There are small deposits of many important minerals and some precious stones. Only tin, gold, tungsten, and salt are in commercial production.

Almost 70% of Thailand's total land area is forested. Teak, the principal forest product, covers over one third of this area, chiefly in the northern hill country.

Chief exports in 1976 were rice (14%), tapioca (12%), sugar (11%), corn (9%), rubber (9%), and tin (5%). Leading customers were Japan (26%), Netherlands (13%), U.S. (10%), Singapore (7%), Indonesia (5%), Hong Kong (5%). Leading suppliers were Japan (32%), U.S. (13%), Saudi Arabia (8%), Qatar (6%), West Germany (5%).

## TOGO

**Republic of Togo**
**President:** Gnassingbé Eyadema (1967)
**Area:** 21,622 sq mi. (56,000 sq km)
**Population (est. 1978):** 2,410,000
**Density per square mile:** 111.5
**Capital and largest city (est. 1976):** Lomé, 229,400
**Monetary unit:** Franc CFA
**Languages:** Ewé, Mina (south), Kabyé, Cotocoli (north), French (official), and many dialects
**Religions:** Animist, Christian, Islam
**Gross national product (1976):** $600 million
**National name:** République Togolaise
**Freedom House classifications:** Capitalist-socialist pre-industrial, one-party nationalist

**Geography.** Togo, twice the size of Maryland, is on the south coast of West Africa bordering on Ghana to the west, Upper Volta to the north and Benin to the east.

The Gulf of Guinea coastline, only 32 miles long (51 km), is low, sandy, and without harbors. The Togo hills traverse the central section.

**Government.** The government of Nicolas Grunitzky was overthrown in a bloodless coup on Jan. 13, 1967, led by Lt. Col. Etienne Eyadema (now Gen. Gnassingbé Eyadema). A National Reconciliation Committee was set up to rule the country. In April, however, Eyadema dissolved the Committee and took over as President. The Assembly of the Togolese People is the only political party.

**History.** Brazilians were the first traders to settle in Togo. Established as a German colony (Togoland) in 1884, the area was split between the British and the French as League of Nations mandates after World War I and subsequently administered as U. N. trusteeships. The British portion voted for incorporation with Ghana.

Togo became an independent nation on April 27, 1960.

Sylvanus Olympio, who became first President of the African republic in 1961, was assassinated in 1963 and succeeded by Grunitzky.

**Economy.** Agriculture and herding are the chief industries, with coffee, cacao, palm kernels and oil, cotton, and copra the principal exports. Togo also produces dyewoods and oil palms and some iron ore.

Chief exports in 1975 were phosphates (65%), cocoa (17%), and coffee (7%). Leading customers were France (39%), Netherlands (32%), West Germany (10%), Belgium-Luxembourg (6%). Leading suppliers were France (35%), U.K. (11%), West Germany (11%), Netherlands (7%), U.S. (5%).

## TONGA

**Kingdom of Tonga**
**Sovereign:** King Taufa'ahau Tupou IV (1965)
**Prime Minister:** Prince Tu'ipelehake (1965)
**Area:** 270 sq mi. (699 sq km)
**Population (est. 1978):** 100,000
**Density per square mile:** 370.4
**Capital (est. 1976):** Nuku'alofa, 18,400
**Monetary unit:** Pa'anga
**Languages:** Tongan, English
**Religion:** Christian
**Member of Commonwealth of Nations**
**Freedom House classifications:** Capitalist pre-industrial, non-party traditional

**Geography.** Situated east of the Fiji Islands in the South Pacific, Tonga (also called the Friendly Islands) consists of some 150 islands, of which 36 are inhabited.

Most of the islands contain active volcanic craters; others are coral atolls.

**Government.** Tonga is a constitutional monarchy. Executive authority is vested in the Sovereign, a Privy Council, and a Cabinet headed by the Prime Minister. Legislative authority is vested in the Legislative Assembly.

**History.** The present dynasty of Tonga was founded in 1831 by Taufa'ahau Tupou, who took the name of George I. He consolidated the kingdom by conquest, and in 1875 he granted a Constitution.

In 1900, his great-grandson, George II, signed a treaty of friendship with the U.K., and the country became a British protected state. The treaty was revised in 1959.

Queen Salote Tupou reigned from 1918 to 1964 and was succeeded by her son, who became King Taufa'ahau Tupou IV.

Tonga became an independent nation on June 4, 1970.

**Economy.** Tonga is primarily an agricultural country.

Chief exports in 1976 were copra (54%), desiccated coconut (11%), bananas (8%), kava (6%), and watermelons (5%). Leading customers were Netherlands (30%), Australia (29%), New Zealand (19%), West Germany (11%), U.K. (6%), Fiji (5%). Leading suppliers were New Zealand (40%), Australia (22%), U.K. (11%), Japan (6%), Fiji (5%).

### TRANSKEI

**See South Africa**

## TRINIDAD AND TOBAGO

**Republic of Trinidad and Tobago**
**President:** Sir Ellis Clarke (1976)
**Prime Minister:** Dr. Eric E. Williams (1962)
**Area:** 1,980 sq mi. (5,128 sq km)
**Population (est. 1977):** 1,120,000 (black, 43%; East Indian, 40%; mixed, 14%)
**Density per square mile:** 565.7
**Capital and largest city (est. 1973):** Port-of-Spain, 60,400

**Monetary unit:** Trinidad and Tobago dollar
**Languages:** English (official); Hindi, French, Spanish
**Religions:** Christian, 64%; Hindu, 25%; Islam, 6%
**Gross national product (1976):** $2.4 billion
**Member of Commonwealth of Nations**
**Freedom House classifications:** Capitalist industrial, multi-party centralized

**Geography.** Trinidad and Tobago lies in the Caribbean Sea off the northeast coast of Venezuela. The area of the two islands is slightly less than that of Delaware.

Trinidad, the larger, is mainly flat and rolling, with mountains in the north that reach a height of 3,085 feet (940 m) at Mount Aripo. Tobago is heavily forested with hardwood trees.

**Government.** The legislature consists of a 24-member Senate and a 36-member House of Representatives.

The major political parties are the People's National Movement, led by Prime Minister Williams (24 seats in the House of Representatives); United Labor Front (10 seats), led by George Weekes and Panday Shah; Democratic Action Congress (2 seats).

**History.** Trinidad was discovered by Columbus in 1498 and remained in Spanish possession, despite raids by other European nations, until it capitulated to the British in 1797 during a war between Great Britain and Spain.

Trinidad was ceded to the U.K. in 1802, and in 1899 it was united with Tobago as a colony. From 1958 to 1962, Trinidad and Tobago was a part of the West Indies Federation, and on Aug. 31, 1962, it became an independent nation.

On Aug. 1, 1976, Trinidad and Tobago cut its ties with the U.K. and became a republic, remaining within the Commonwealth and recognizing Queen Elizabeth II only as head of that organization.

**Economy.** Petroleum and petroleum products are the most important part of the nation's economy. Although wells were drilled as early as 1867, no oil was exported until 1910. Now much of it is refined on the island, whose refineries also handle Venezuelan, Colombian, and Saudi Arabian crude oil. Asphalt, which is taken from the apparently inexhaustible supplies of Pitch Lake, is another important natural resource. Sugar, cacao, and coconuts are grown in the rich soil, which yields many tropical crops. The principal products of Tobago are copra and cocoa.

Chief exports in 1976 were petroleum products (58%) and crude oil (34%). Leading customers were U.S. (69%), U.K. (5%). Leading suppliers were Saudi Arabia (26%), U.S. (20%), Indonesia (16%), Iran (11%), U.K. (8%).

## TUNISIA

**Republic of Tunisia**
**President:** Habib Bourguiba (1957)
**Premier:** Hédi Nouira (1970)
**Area:** 63,170 sq mi. (163,610 sq km)
**Population (est. 1978):** 6,400,000
**Density per square mile:** 101.3
**Capital and largest city (est. 1976):** Tunis, 960,000
**Monetary unit:** Tunisian dinar
**Languages:** Arabic, French
**Religions:** Predominantly Islam; Roman Catholic, Jewish, Greek Orthodox
**Gross national product (1976):** $4.4 billion
**National name:** Al-Djoumhouria Attunusia
**Freedom House classifications:** Capitalist-socialist industrial, one-party socialist

**Geography.** Tunisia, at the northernmost bulge of Africa, thrusts out toward Sicily to mark the division between the eastern and western Mediterranean Sea. Twice the size of South Carolina, it is bordered on the west by Algeria and Libya on the east.

The country is covered by plains in the east and projects southward to the Sahara. In the north, the Atlas Mountains continue from Algeria but do not attain great altitude.

**Government.** The executive power is vested by the Constitution in the President, who was to be elected for five years and could have been re-elected for two additional terms. Legislative power is vested in a National Assembly elected by universal suffrage.

In March 1975, the National Assembly amended Tunisia's Constitution to make Habib Bourguiba President for life. At 71, Bourguiba was re-elected to a fourth five-year term when he ran unopposed in November 1974. The only party, the Socialist Destourian, is led by President Bourguiba.

**History.** Tunisia was settled by the Phoenicians and Carthaginians in ancient times. Except for an interval of Vandal conquest in A.D. 439–533, it was part of the Roman Empire until the Arab conquest of 648–69. It was ruled by various Arab and Berber dynasties until the Turks took it in 1570–74.

Throughout much of its history, Tunisia was essentially a pirate state, preying on Mediterranean shipping. In modern times, Italy became the foremost economic power in the area, but after French troops occupied the country in 1881, the Bey signed a treaty acknowledging a French protectorate.

Nationalist agitation forced France to grant internal autonomy to Tunisia in June 1955 and to recognize Tunisian independence and sovereignty in March 1956. Tunisia was admitted to the United Nations on Nov. 12, 1956. The Constituent Assembly deposed the Bey on July 25, 1957, declared Tunisia a republic, and elected Habib Bourguiba as the first President.

Bourguiba maintained a pro-Western foreign policy that earned him enemies. Tunisia refused to break relations wht the U.S. during the Israeli-Arab war in June 1967, and it cracked down on anti-U.S. demonstrators.

**Economy.** Agriculture is the chief industry. Over a quarter of the arable land is in wheat. Other important crops are barley, oats, corn, sorghum, beans, and peas. The Cape Bon region is largely devoted to citrus fruits, the southern oases to dates.

Leading industries include flour milling, oil refining, lead smelting, and distilling. Native industries include the spinning and weaving of wool and the making of pottery and leather goods.

Tunisia's extremely rich deposits of phosphates are mined principally in the Gafsa and Kef regions. The iron ore is of good quality (55% metal content). Other minerals are lead, zinc, mercury, manganese, copper, and salt.

Chief exports in 1975 were crude oil (41%), phosphates (11%), and olive oil (11%). Leading customers were France (19%), Italy (17%), Greece (14%), U.S. (10%), West Germany (8%), Libya (6%). Leading suppliers were France (35%), Italy (9%), West Germany (8%), U.S. (7%), U.K. (5%).

## TURKEY

**Republic of Turkey**
**President:** Fahri Korutürk (1973)
**Premier:** Bülent Ecevit (1978)
**Area:** 301,380 sq mi. (incl. 9,121 in Europe) (780,576 sq km)
**Population (est. 1978):** 43,120,000
**Density per square mile:** 143.1
**Capital:** Ankara
**Largest cities (1975 census):** Istanbul, 2,500,000; Ankara, 1,700,000; Izmir (Smyrna), 640,000; Adana, 470,000; Bursa, 350,000; Gaziantep, 300,000
**Monetary unit:** Turkish lira
**Language:** Turkish
**Religion:** Islam
**Gross national product (1976):** $41.4 billion
**National name:** Türkiye Cumhuriyeti
**Freedom House classifications:** Capitalist-statist industrial, multi-party centralized

**Geography.** Turkey is at the northeastern end of the Mediterranean Sea in southeast Europe and southwest Asia. To the north is the Black Sea and to the west the Aegean Sea. Its neighbors are Greece and Bulgaria to the west, the U.S.S.R. to the north, Iran to the east, and Syria and Iraq to the south. Overall, it is more than twice the size of Montana.

The country is divided into two natural areas by the historic waterway formed by the Dardanelles, the Sea of Marmara, and the Bosporus.

Turkey in Europe comprises an area about equal to the state of Massachusetts. It is hilly country drained by the Maritsa River and its tributaries. Almost all the population is concentrated in and near the three important towns, Istanbul (Constantinople), Ankara, and Edirne (Adrianople).

Turkey in Asia, or Anatolia, about the size of Texas, is roughly a rectangle in shape with its short sides on the east and west. Its center is a treeless plateau rimmed by mountains.

**Government.** Turkey's President is elected by the Grand National Assembly for a seven-year term and is not eligible for re-election. The government operates under an amended Constitution approved in 1961. The bicameral Grand National Assembly has a Senate of 150 members and a National Assembly of 450 members.

The major political parties are the Republican People's Party (215 seats in National Assembly), led by Premier Bülent Ecevit; Justice Party (177 seats), led by former Premier Suleyman Demirel; National Salvation Party (24 seats); National Action Party (16 seats).

**History.** The Ottoman Turks first appeared in the early 13th century. Under the leadership of their Sultans, they gradually spread their hegemony over most of the Near East and the Balkans, capturing Constantinople in 1453 and storming the gates of Vienna in the 17th century. At the height of its power, the empire stretched from the Persian Gulf to the frontiers of Poland and from the shores of the Caspian Sea to Oran in Algeria.

The defeat of the Turkish navy at Lepanto in 1571 by the Holy League and of Turkish forces besieging Vienna in 1683 portended the decline of Ottoman power. Russia moved into the Balkans in the 18th century and made herself official protector of the Balkan Christians. Fear of a Russian drive on Constantinople prompted England and France to declare war on Russia, and the Crimean War (1853–56) followed. As a result of the Russo-Turkish war (1877–78), Bulgaria became practically independent, and Romania and Serbia threw off their nominal allegiance to the sultan. Further defeats were suffered by Turkey in a war with Italy (1911–12) and in the Balkan Wars (1912–13). Meanwhile, a revolt led by the Young Turks, an organization of youthful liberals, had forced the abdication of Sultan Abdul-Hamid in 1909 and established a constitutional regime.

On Aug. 2, 1914, at the outbreak of World War I, a secret alliance was signed between Germany and Turkey, whose army was advised by a German military mission, and in September the Allies declared war on Turkey. Turkish forces successfully defended the strategic Dardanelles, but British forces seized Palestine, Mesopotamia, and Syria; and the Hejaz revolted. By 1918, Allied forces held the territory along the Dardanelles and the Bosporus, and later Greek forces occupied Smyrna.

In 1919, the new Nationalist movement, headed by Mustafa Kemal, was organized to resist the Allied occupation and, in 1920, a National Assembly elected him President of both the Assembly and the government. Under his leadership, the Nationalist government was recognized by foreign powers, the Greeks were driven out of Smyrna, and other Allied forces were withdrawn.

The present Turkish boundaries (with the exception of Alexandretta, ceded to Turkey by France in 1939) were fixed by the Treaty of Lausanne (1923) and later negotiations. The caliphate and sultanate were separated, and the sultanate was abolished Oct. 1, 1922. On Oct. 29, 1923, Turkey formally became a republic with Mustafa Kemal, who took the name of Kemal Atatürk, as its first President. The caliphate was abolished Mar. 3, 1924, and Atatürk proceeded to carry out an extensive program of reform, modernization, and industrialization.

Gen. Ismet Inönü was elected to succeed Kemal Atatürk on the latter's death in 1938 and was re-elected in 1939, 1943, and 1946. However, he was defeated in 1950 and was succeeded by Celâl Bayar. On Oct. 19, 1939, a mutual assistance pact was concluded with the U.K. and France. Turkey followed a neutral course during most of World War II. However, on Feb. 23, 1945, it declared war on Germany and Japan, but took no active part in the conflict.

Turkey became a full member of NATO in 1952.

In March 1971, the Turkish military demanded the ouster of Ismet Inönu, Premier since 1961, who was replaced by Nihat Erim. He pushed through a law that forbade growing of opium poppies after 1972. The move was taken under strong U.S. requests because about two thirds of the illicit heroin reaching U.S. markets is grown in Turkey.

The poppy-growing ban was shelved after Bülent Ecevit, a liberal, became Premier in January 1974. Instead, the government required bulk-harvesting of all poppies and consignment of dried "poppy hay" to legal refineries abroad, maintaining that the method would prevent farmers from diverting raw opium to illicit channels. The system was continued after conservative Premier Suleyman Demirel took over the government March 31, 1975.

Turkey invaded Cyprus by sea and air July 20, 1974, following the failure of diplomatic efforts to resolve the crisis caused by Archbishop Makarios' ouster. Turkey, asserting its right to protect the minority Turkish Cypriot community, demanded the withdrawal of the 650 Greek officers who had led the coup. Greece refused the demand.

Talks in Geneva between Greece, Turkey, U.K., Greek Cypriot, and Turkish Cypriot leaders broke down in mid-August. Turkey was apparently determined to achieve through military means what it had failed to achieve in negotiations: the establishment of an autonomous Turkish Cypriot region encompassing the northern third of Cyprus. Turkey unilaterally announced a cease-fire August 16, after gaining control of 40% of Cyprus.

More than a year of diplomatic negotiations failed to produce a settlement on Cyprus, where tensions were compounded after Turkish Cypriots established their own state on the northern 40% of the island Feb. 13, 1975.

U.S.-Turkish relations, excellent for a generation, were seriously damaged when Congress voted to end arms sales to Turkey on Feb. 5, 1975, because arms the U.S. had supplied for mutual defense had been used in the invasion of Cyprus. Congress maintained the ban despite warnings from President Ford that it would imperil the future of 20 U.S. air and intelligence bases in Turkey and could affect Turkey's role as NATO's anchor in the Eastern Mediterranean.

On July 25, 1975, after a 30-day warning, Turkey took over control of all the installations except the big joint defense base at Incirlik, which it reserved for "NATO tasks alone." Some 7,000 U.S. military men remained on duty under Turkish orders, but relations between Ankara and Washington hit a 30-year low.

Tension between Turkey and Greece over Cyprus also continued, although in late 1976 the two nations reached agreement on submitting to arbitration their conflicting claims in the Aegean sea, where oil exploration was under way. Neither Turkey nor Greece responded favorably to a Carter emissary's request in February 1977 that the two countries return their forces to NATO.

Former Premier Bülent Ecevit fell only 12 seats short of a majority in elections on June 5, 1977, governed briefly, and was defeated in a vote of confidence that brought Conservative Premier Suleyman Demirel back on July 19 as head of a coalition. Demirel himself lost a vote of confidence on December 31, and Ecevit formed a new government the next day. In March 1978, the new leader met in Montreux, Switzerland, with Greek Premier Constantine Caramanlis to repair relations, but a comment by U.S. Secretary of State Cyrus R. Vance linking future arms aid to Turkey with peace in Cyprus broke up the talks as Ecevit accused the U.S. of attempting to pressure Turkey.

As the debate over lifting of the embargo on arms for Turkey went on in the U.S., Ecevit pointedly paid a visit to Moscow, and on June 23 signed a non-aggression pact and trade agreements, but said he neither sought nor was offered Soviet arms. In August 1978 the Carter administration obtained a reluctant Congressional reversal of the arms embargo.

**Economy.** Agriculture is the principal economic activity, engaging about 41% of the population. Only about 30% of the land is under cultivation, but the government has made great efforts to modernize and improve farming. The most important cash crops are tobacco, cotton, fruits, and nuts. Cotton is grown in the south of Asia Minor, while figs come exclusively from the Smyrna region. Grain crops are wheat and barley. Turkey is a leading producer of olive oil; the Bursa region and the Ionian coast are the principal areas of cultivation. Opium poppies are grown in the Smyrna, Malatia, and Tokat regions.

Staple industries have been established in iron, steel, textiles, paper, glass, sugar, and cement. A large proportion of the factories are government-operated. Istanbul is the major industrial area.

Turkey's rich mineral resources are still comparatively unexploited. Deposits of copper are found in the large field at Arghana, near the Iraqi-Syrian frontier. Turkey is also relatively rich in coal, with large deposits in the Eregli region on the Pontic coast some 150 miles (241 km) from Istanbul. A virtual world monopoly is enjoyed in meerschaum, found in the Eskisehir district. Other important minerals are chromite, petroleum, manganese ore, iron ore (metal content 65%), emery, and antimony.

Chief exports in 1976 were cotton (22%), tobacco (21%), and hazelnuts (11%). Leading customers were West Germany (19%), U.S. (10%), Switzerland (9%), Italy (9%), U.K. (7%), France (6%). Leading suppliers were West Germany (17%), Iraq (13%), U.S. (9%), U.K. (8%), Italy (8%), France (6%), Switzerland (6%), Libya (5%), Japan (5%).

# UGANDA

**Republic of Uganda**
**President for Life:** Gen. Idi Amin (1971)
**Area:** 91,134 sq mi. (236,036 sq km)
**Population (est. 1978):** 12,775,000
**Density per square mile:** 140.2
**Capital and largest city (est. 1975 by U.N.):** Kampala, 542,000
**Monetary unit:** Ugandan shilling
**Languages:** English (official), Swahili, Luganda, Ateso, Luo
**Religions:** Christian, Islam
**Gross national product (1976):** $2.8 billion
**Member of Commonwealth of Nations**
**Freedom House classifications:** Capitalist pre-industrial, non-party military

**Geography.** Uganda, twice the size of Pennsylvania, is in east central Africa. It is bordered on the west by Zaire, on the north by the Sudan, on the east by Kenya, and on the south by Tanzania and Rwanda.

The country, which lies across the Equator, is divided into three main areas—swampy lowlands, a fertile plateau with wooded hills, and a desert region. Lake Victoria forms part of the southern border.

**Government.** Following the military coup against President Milton Obote, who had been in office since 1962, Gen. Idi Amin assumed all legislative and executive powers and appointed a council of ministers to help him run the country. He banned all political activity. (Obote's People's Congress had been the only legal party.)

**History.** Uganda was first visited by European explorers as well as Arab traders in 1844. An Anglo-German agreement of 1890 declared it to be in the British sphere of influence in Africa, and the Imperial British East Africa Company was chartered to develop the area. The company did not prosper financially, and in 1894 a British protectorate was proclaimed.

Uganda became an independent nation on Oct. 9, 1962.

As first President, the country chose Mutesa II, King of the ancient kingdom of Buganda. Dr. Milton Obote had been Prime Minister. In 1965, he suspended the Constitution and assumed the powers of the government, later abolishing the offices of President and Vice President.

Obote in 1970 passed laws declaring that 40,000 British Asians—Asian-born persons, mostly Indian, who live in Uganda but chose British citizenship in 1962 rather than Ugandian—needed a variety of passes and permits to remain in the country and keep business there; and, further, that all non-citizens would lose their jobs. President Amin, an unpredictable former Army sergeant, began expelling the Asians in 1972. He also expelled Israeli advisors rather than pay Israel's military aid bill and applauded Hitler's treatment of Jews.

With his country's potentially rich agricultural economy in turmoil, partly because of large purchases of weapons for its 20,000-man army, Amin nationalized all its land in June 1975, without compensation to former owners.

On June 25, 1976, Amin had himself proclaimed President for Life by the Defense Council, which replaced the Council of Ministers as Uganda's ruling body.

An Israeli commando raid against Entebbe airport on July 4, 1977, freed 103 hostages in a hijacked French airliner that had been held at the airport for a week by Palestinian guerrillas. Hostages, and the government of Israel, charged that Amin had collaborated with the hijackers. Amin demanded U.N. Security Council condemnation of Israel but was unable to muster sufficient support.

The announcement on Feb. 17, 1977, that Janani Luwum, Anglican archbishop of Uganda, Rwanda, and Burundi, had died in an automobile accident the day before brought worldwide condemnation of Amin. Government spokesmen said the archbishop and two cabinet ministers, also killed, tried to overpower the driver as they were being taken to a military post for questioning about a plot to kill Amin.

President Carter and other leaders denounced the action as "assassination." Shortly before, Amnesty International reported that 300,000 persons may have died in purges since Amin took power.

Amin was barred by the U.K. from the June meeting of Commonwealth heads in London and his regime censured but, at the conference of the Organization of African Unity in Gabon a month later, the Marshal was lionized by radical Africans.

**Economy.** Agriculture, including livestock, is the basis of the economy.

Chief exports in 1976 were coffee (83%) and cotton (6%). Leading customers were U.S. (33%), U.K. (20%), France (6%), Italy (6%), Japan (6%). Leading suppliers were Kenya (50%), U.K. (15%), West Germany (9%).

## UNION OF SOVIET SOCIALIST REPUBLICS

**See Soviet Union**

## UNITED ARAB EMIRATES

**Head of State:** Sheik Zayed Bin Sultan Al-Nahayan (1971)
**Prime Minister:** Sheik Maktoum Bin Rashid (1972)
**Area:** 32,278 sq mi. (83,600 sq km)
**Population (est. 1978):** 656,000
**Density per square mile:** 20.3
**Capital and largest city (est. 1975):** Abu Dhabi, 95,000
**Monetary unit:** Dirham
**Language:** Arabic
**Religion:** Islam
**Gross national product (1976):** $9.7 billion
**Freedom House classifications:** Capitalist-statist industrial, non-party traditional

**Geography.** The United Arab Emirates, in the eastern part of the Arabian Peninsula, extend along part of the Gulf of Oman and the southern coast of the Persian Gulf. They are the size of Maine. Their neighbors are Saudi Arabia in the west and south, Qatar in the north, and Oman in the east. Most of the land is barren and sandy.

**Government.** The United Arab Emirates was formed in 1971 by seven emirates known as the Trucial States—Abu Dhabi (the largest), Dubai, Sharjah, Ajman, Fujairah, Ras al Khaimah and Umm al-Qaiwain.

The loose federation allows joint policies in foreign relations, defense, and development, with each member state keeping its internal local system of government headed by its own ruler. A 40-member legislature consists of eight seats each for Abu Dhabi and Dubai, six seats each for Ras al Khaimah and Sharjah, and four each for the others. It is a member of the Arab League. The United Arab Emirates was admitted to the U.N. and signed a treaty of friendship with the U.K.

**History.** Originally the area was inhabited by a seafaring people who were converted to Islam in the seventh century. Later, a dissident sect, the Carmathians established a powerful sheikdom, and its army conquered Mecca. After the sheikdom disintegrated, its people became pirates.

Threatening the sultanate of Muscat and Oman in the early 19th century, the pirates provoked the intervention of the British, who in 1820 enforced a partial truce and in 1853 a permanent truce. Thus what had been called the Pirate Coast was renamed the Trucial Coast.

**Economy.** Chief export in 1975 was crude oil (96%). Leading customers were Japan (24%), France (15%), U.S. (10%), West Germany (10%), Netherlands (7%), U.K. (5%). Leading suppliers were U.K. (19%), Japan (18%), U.S. (16%), West Germany (6%), France (6%).

## UNITED KINGDOM

**United Kingdom of Great Britain and Northern Ireland**

**Sovereign:** Queen Elizabeth II (1952)
**Prime Minister:** James Callaghan (1976)
**Area:** 94,250 sq mi. (244,108 sq km)
**Population (est. 1978):** 55,800,000 (English, Scottish, Welsh, Northern Irish)
**Density per square mile:** 592.0
**Capital:** London, England
**Largest cities (est. 1976):** London (Greater), 7,028,200; Birmingham, England, 1,058,800; Glasgow, Scotland, 856,000; Leeds, England, 744,500; Sheffield, England, 558,000; Liverpool, England, 539,700; Manchester, England, 490,000; Edinburgh, Scotland, 467,100; Bradford, England, 458,900
**Monetary unit:** Pound sterling (£)
**Languages:** English, Welsh, Gaelic
**Religions:** Church of England (established church); Church of Wales (disestablished); Church of Scotland (established church—Presbyterian); Church of Ireland (disestablished); Roman Catholic; Methodist; Congregational; Baptist; Jewish
**Gross national product (1976):** $222.2 billion
**Freedom House classifications:** Capitalist-socialist industrial, multi-party centralized

**Geography.** The United Kingdom, consisting of England, Wales, Scotland, and Northern Ireland, is twice the size of New York State. England, in the southeast part of the British Isles, is separated from Scotland on the north by the granite Cheviot Hills; from them the Pennine chain of uplands extends south through the center of England, reaching its highest point in the Lake District in the northwest. To the west along the border of Wales—a land of steep hills and valleys—are the Cambrian Mountains, while the Cotswolds, a range of hills in Gloucestershire, extend into the surrounding shires.

The remainder of England is plain land, though not necessarily flat, with the rocky sand-topped moors in the southwest, the rolling Downs in the south and southeast, and the reclaimed marshes of the low-lying Fens in the east central districts.

Scotland is divided into three physical regions—the Highlands, the Central Lowlands, containing two-thirds of the population, and the Southern Uplands. The western Highland coast is intersected throughout by long, narrow sea-lochs, or fiords. Scotland also includes the Outer and Inner Hebrides and other islands off the west coast and the Orkney and Shetland Islands off the north coast.

Wales is generally hilly; the Snowdon range in the northern part culminates in Mt. Snowdon (3,560 ft, 1,085 m), highest in both England and Wales.

Important rivers flowing into the North Sea are the Thames, Humber, Tees, and Tyne. In the west are the Severn and Wye, which empty into the Bristol Channel and are navigable, as are the Mersey and Ribble.

**Government.** The United Kingdom is a constitutional monarchy, with a Queen and a Parliament that has two houses: the House of Lords with about 830 hereditary peers, 26 spiritual peers, about 270 life peers and peeresses, and 9 law-lords, who are hereditary or life peers, and the House of Commons, which has numbered, since 1974, 635 members elected by practically universal suffrage. Supreme legislative power is vested in Parliament, which remains in being for five years unless sooner dissolved.

The executive power of the Crown is exercised by the Cabinet, headed by the Prime Minister. The latter, normally the head of the party commanding a majority in the House of Commons, is appointed by the sovereign, with whose consent he in turn appoints the rest of the Cabinet. All ministers must be members of one or the other house of Parliament; they are individually and collectively responsible to the Crown and Parliament. The Cabinet proposes bills and arranges the business of Parliament, but it depends entirely on the votes in the House of Commons. The Lords cannot hold up "money" bills, but they can delay other bills for a period of at most one year.

By the Act of Union (1707), the Scottish Parliament was assimilated with that of England, and Scotland is now represented in Commons by 71 members. The Secretary of State for Scotland, a member of the Cabinet, is responsible for the administration of Scottish affairs.

**Ruler:** Queen Elizabeth II, born April 21, 1926, elder daughter of King George VI and Queen Elizabeth, succeeded to the throne on the death of her father, Feb. 6, 1952; married Nov. 20, 1947, to Prince Philip, Duke of Edinburgh, born June 10, 1921; their children are Prince Charles[1] (heir presumptive), born Nov. 14, 1948; Princess Anne, born Aug. 15, 1950; Prince Andrew, born Feb. 19, 1960; and Prince Edward, born March 10, 1964. The Queen's sister is Princess Margaret, born Aug. 21, 1930.

The major political parties are the Labor Party (306 seats in House of Commons), led by Prime Minister James Callaghan; Conservative Party (282 seats), led by Margaret Thatcher; Liberal Party (13 seats), led by David Steel; Scottish National Party (11 seats); Ulster Unionists and other Northern Irish parties (11 seats); Plaid Cymru (Welsh nationalist) (3 seats); Scottish Labor (2 seats); Social Democratic and Labor Party (1 seat).

**History.** Roman invasions of the 1st century B.C. brought Britain into contact with the continent. When the Roman legions withdrew in the 5th century A.D., Britain fell easy prey to the invading hordes of Angles, Saxons, and Jutes from Scandinavia and the Low Countries. Seven large kingdoms were established, and the original Britons were forced into Wales and Scotland. It was not until the 11th century that the country finally became united under the Danish King Canute. Following the death of Edward the Confessor (1066), a dispute about the succession arose, and William, Duke of Normandy, invaded England, defeating the Saxon king, Harold II, at the Battle of Hastings (1066). The Norman conquest was accompanied by the introduction of Norman law and feudalism, changing the customs of England.

The reign of Henry II (1154–89), first of the Plantagenets, saw an increasing centralization of royal power at the expense of the nobles, but in 1215 John (1199–1216) was forced to sign the Magna Carta, which awarded the people, especially the nobles, certain basic rights. Edward I (1272–1307) continued the conquest of Ireland, reduced Wales to subjection and made some gains in Scotland. In 1314, however, English forces led by Edward II were ousted from Scotland after the battle of Bannockburn. The late 13th and early 14th centuries saw the development of a separate House of Commons with tax-raising powers.

Edward III's claim to the throne of France led to the Hundred Years' War (1338–1453), which ended with the loss of almost all the large English territory in France. In England the great poverty and discontent caused by the war were intensified by the Black Death, a plague that reduced the population by about one third. The Wars of the Roses (1455–85), a struggle for the throne between the House of York and the House of Lancaster, were ended by the victory of Henry Tudor (Henry VII) at Bosworth Field (1485).

During the reign of Henry VIII (1509–47), the

## Area and Population of United Kingdom

| Subdivision | Area sq mi. | Population (est. 1977) |
|---|---|---|
| England and Wales | 58,383 | 49,120,000 |
| Scotland | 30,415 | 5,196,000 |
| Northern Ireland | 5,452 | 1,537,000 |
| **Total** | **94,250** | **55,853,000** |

1. The title Prince of Wales, which is not inherited, was conferred on Prince Charles by his mother on July 26, 1958. The investiture ceremony took place on July 1, 1969. The previous Prince of Wales was Prince Edward Albert, who held the title from 1911 to 1936 before he became Edward VIII.

## Rulers of England and Great Britain

| Name | Born | Ruled[1] |
|---|---|---|
| **SAXONS[2]** | | |
| Egbert[3] | c. 775 | 828–839 |
| Ethelwulf | ? | 839–858 |
| Ethelbald | ? | 858–860 |
| Ethelbert | ? | 860–866 |
| Ethelred I | ? | 866–871 |
| Alfred the Great | 849 | 871–899 |
| Edward the Elder | c. 870 | 899–924 |
| Athelstan | 895 | 924–939 |
| Edmund I the Deed-doer | 921 | 939–946 |
| Edred | c. 925 | 946–955 |
| Edwy the Fair | c. 943 | 955–959 |
| Edgar the Peaceful | 943 | 959–975 |
| Edward the Martyr | c. 962 | 975–979 |
| Ethelred II the Unready | 968 | 979–1016 |
| Edmund II Ironside | c. 993 | 1016–1016 |
| **DANES** | | |
| Canute | 995 | 1016–1035 |
| Harold I Harefoot | c.1016 | 1035–1040 |
| Hardecanute | c.1018 | 1040–1042 |
| **SAXONS** | | |
| Edward the Confessor | c.1004 | 1042–1066 |
| Harold II | c.1020 | 1066–1066 |
| **HOUSE OF NORMANDY** | | |
| William I the Conqueror | 1027 | 1066–1087 |
| William II Rufus | c.1056 | 1087–1100 |
| Henry I Beauclerc | 1068 | 1100–1135 |
| Stephen of Blois | c.1100 | 1135–1154 |
| **HOUSE OF PLANTAGENET** | | |
| Henry II | 1133 | 1154–1189 |
| Richard I Coeur de Lion | 1157 | 1189–1199 |
| John Lackland | 1167 | 1199–1216 |
| Henry III | 1207 | 1216–1272 |
| Edward I Longshanks | 1239 | 1272–1307 |
| Edward II | 1284 | 1307–1327 |
| Edward III | 1312 | 1327–1377 |
| Richard II | 1367 | 1377–1399[4] |
| **HOUSE OF LANCASTER** | | |
| Henry IV Bolingbroke | 1367 | 1399–1413 |
| Henry V | 1387 | 1413–1422 |
| Henry VI | 1421 | 1422–1461[5] |

| Name | Born | Ruled[1] |
|---|---|---|
| **HOUSE OF YORK** | | |
| Edward IV | 1442 | 1461–1483[5] |
| Edward V | 1470 | 1483–1483 |
| Richard III | 1452 | 1483–1485 |
| **HOUSE OF TUDOR** | | |
| Henry VII | 1457 | 1485–1509 |
| Henry VIII | 1491 | 1509–1547 |
| Edward VI | 1537 | 1547–1553 |
| Jane (Lady Jane Grey)[6] | 1537 | 1553–1553 |
| Mary I ("Bloody Mary") | 1516 | 1553–1558 |
| Elizabeth I | 1533 | 1558–1603 |
| **HOUSE OF STUART** | | |
| James I[7] | 1566 | 1603–1625 |
| Charles I | 1600 | 1625–1649 |
| **COMMONWEALTH** | | |
| Council of State | — | 1649–1653 |
| Oliver Cromwell[8] | 1599 | 1653–1658 |
| Richard Cromwell[8] | 1626 | 1658–1659[9] |
| **RESTORATION OF HOUSE OF STUART** | | |
| Charles II | 1630 | 1660–1685 |
| James II | 1633 | 1685–1688[10] |
| William III[11] | 1650 | 1689–1702 |
| Mary II[11] | 1662 | 1689–1694 |
| Anne | 1665 | 1702–1714 |
| **HOUSE OF HANOVER** | | |
| George I | 1660 | 1714–1727 |
| George II | 1683 | 1727–1760 |
| George III | 1738 | 1760–1820 |
| George IV | 1762 | 1820–1830 |
| William IV | 1765 | 1830–1837 |
| Victoria | 1819 | 1837–1901 |
| **HOUSE OF SAXE-COBURG[12]** | | |
| Edward VII | 1841 | 1901–1910 |
| **HOUSE OF WINDSOR[12]** | | |
| George V | 1865 | 1910–1936 |
| Edward VIII | 1894 | 1936–1936[13] |
| George VI | 1895 | 1936–1952 |
| Elizabeth II | 1926 | 1952– |

1. Year of end of rule is also that of death, unless otherwise indicated. 2. Dates for Saxon kings are still subject of controversy. 3. Became King of West Saxons in 802; considered (from 828) first King of all England. 4. Died 1400. 5. Henry VI reigned again briefly 1470–71. 6. Nominal Queen for 9 days; not counted as Queen by some authorities. She was beheaded in 1554. 7. Ruled in Scotland as James VI (1567–1625). 8. Lord Protector. 9. Died 1712. 10. Died 1701. 11. Joint rulers (1689–1694). 12. Name changed from Saxe-Coburg to Windsor in 1917. 13. Was known after his abdication as the Duke of Windsor; died 1972.

Church in England asserted its independence from the Roman Catholic Church. Under Edward VI and Mary, the two extremes of religious fanaticism were reached, and it remained for Henry's daughter, Elizabeth I (1558–1603) to set up the Church of England on a moderate basis. In 1588, the Spanish Armada, a fleet sent out by Catholic King Philip II of Spain, was defeated by the English and destroyed during a storm. During Elizabeth's reign, England became a world power.

Elizabeth's heir was of the house of Stuart—James VI of Scotland—who joined the two crowns as James I (1603–25). The Stuart kings incurred large debts and were forced either to depend on Parliament for taxes or to raise money by illegal means. In 1642, war broke out between Charles I and a large portion of the Parliament; Charles was defeated and executed in 1649, and the monarchy was then abolished. The Puritan Commonwealth endured for ten years but, after the death (1658) of Oliver Cromwell, the Lord Protector, the government fell to pieces and Charles II was restored to the throne in 1660. The struggle between the King and Parliament continued, but Charles II knew when to compromise. His brother James II (1685–88) possessed none of his ability and was ousted by the Revolution of 1688, which confirmed the predominant position of Parliament. James's daughter, Mary, and her husband, William of Orange, were now the rulers.

Queen Anne's reign (1702–14) was marked by the Duke of Marlborough's victories over France at Blenheim, Oudenarde, and Malplaquet in the War of the Spanish Succession. England and Scotland meanwhile were joined together by the Act of Union (1707). Upon the death of Anne, the distant claims of the elector of Hanover were recognized, and he became King of Great Britain and Ireland as George I.

The 18th century was a period of gradual growth and change. At home, the unwillingness of the Hanoverian kings to rule resulted in the formation by the King's ministers of a Cabinet, headed by a Prime Minister, which directed all public business. Abroad, the constant wars with France resulted in expansion of the British Empire all over the globe, particularly in North America and India. This imperial growth was checked by the revolt of the American colonies (1775–81).

Struggles with France broke out again in 1793 and, during the lengthy Napoleonic Wars, which ended at Waterloo (1815), Britain was pitted at one time against almost all of Europe.

The Victorian era, named after Queen Victoria (1837–1901), saw the growth of a democratic system of government that had begun with the Reform Bill of 1832. The two important wars in Victoria's reign were the Crimean War against Russia (1853–56) and the Boer War (1899–1902). The latter was accompanied by enormous extension of Britain's sway in Africa.

Increasing uneasiness at home and abroad marked the reign of Edward VII (1901–10). Within four years after the accession of George V (1910), Britain entered World War I when Germany invaded Belgium. The nation was led by coalition Cabinets, headed first by Herbert Asquith and then (December 1916) by the Welsh statesman, David Lloyd George. The years after the war were marked by labor unrest, which culminated in the general strike of 1926.

King Edward VIII succeeded to the throne on Jan. 20, 1936, at his father's death, but abdicated on Dec. 11, 1936 (in order to marry an American, Wallis Warfield Simpson, whose second divorce was then pending) in favor of his brother, who became King George VI.

The efforts of Prime Minister Neville Chamberlain to meet by peaceful means the rising threat of Nazism in Germany failed with the German invasion of Poland (Sept. 1, 1939), which was followed by the U.K.'s entry into World War II (September 3). Serious Allied reverses in the spring of 1940 led to Chamberlain's resignation and the formation of another coalition war Cabinet by Conservative leader Winston Churchill, who led the U.K. through most of World War II. Churchill resigned as the coalition leader shortly after V-E Day, but then formed a "caretaker" government that remained in office until after the parliamentary elections of July 5, 1945, in which the Labor party won an overwhelming victory. The government formed by Clement R. Attlee on July 26 began a moderate, socialistic program.

For details of World War II (1939–45), *see* Headline History.

In 1951, Winston Churchill again became Prime Minister at the head of a Conservative government. George VI died Feb. 6, 1952, and was succeeded by his daughter, Elizabeth II.

Churchill voluntarily stepped down on April 5, 1955, in favor of Sir Anthony Eden, who led the Conservatives to another victory in elections held May 26, 1955. He resigned on grounds of ill health (Jan. 9, 1957) and was succeeded in turn by Harold Macmillan and Sir Alec Douglas-Home (Oct. 18, 1963). In 1964, Harold Wilson led the Labor Party to victory and became Prime Minister on October 16.

Wilson, the first Labor Prime Minister in 13 years, was a skilled strategist from the party's center who instituted no great changes domestically. His ambition for success abroad was thwarted by the French veto of the U.K.'s bid for entry into the European Economic Community and by his own inept handling of the unilateral declaration of independence by Southern Rhodesia, the last sizable British colony.

A lagging economy brought the Conservatives back to power in 1970. Prime Minister Edward Heath won the U.K.'s admission to the European Community, a move affirmed by 67.2% in the nation's first referendum. Heath narrowly lost a February 1974 election overshadowed by a coal strike, returning Wilson to the leadership and the first minority government since 1929. A bare three-seat majority resulted from an election nine months later, but an alliance with the Liberal party assured control.

Party elections after Wilson's announcement of his intention to retire elevated James Callaghan from the Foreign Ministry to the Prime Minister's office April 5, 1976.

Despite economic troubles, unemployment, and continuing conflict in Northern Ireland and Rhodesia, Britons in June 1977 celebrated the Silver Jubilee of Queen Elizabeth II with genuine affection. The Queen's first grandchild, Peter Mark Andrew Phillips, son of Princess Anne, was born November 14. On May 24, 1978, the first divorce in the immediate royal family in more than 150 years took place when Princess Margaret's 18-year marriage to the Earl of Snowdon was legally ended.

**Economy.** Agriculture remains one of the U.K.'s chief industries, employing about 800,000 persons. Cattle occupy a predominant position in British agriculture, accounting for about 40% of the total farm output.

The most important British manufacture is heavy goods such as machinery, tools, bridges, and locomotives; industry is concentrated in the north and Midlands of England. South Wales produces 26% of the total crude steel output, and Sheffield produces 11% of it. The china industry is concentrated in the Midlands. The cotton industry is centered in Lancashire; Liverpool, Manchester, Oldham, Preston, and Bolton are the main manufacturing towns.

The wool industry, England's oldest large industry, is located just east of the cotton towns, at Leeds, Bradford, and Hull, in Yorkshire. An important industrial region is the central Lowlands of Scotland, where woolens and other fabrics, lace, glass, paper, steel, and pig iron are produced. Important shipyards are located along the coast.

Historically, coal has been Britain's most important mineral resource, the base for her industrial supremacy in the 18th and 19th centuries. Nationalized in 1946, the mines recorded a decline in production and profit during the last decade until oil price increases raised coal demand and prices for 1974–75, reversing the deficits of recent years.

Discovery of oil beneath the North Sea in 1969 raised hopes for a valuable new energy resource in addition to natural gas already discovered offshore. The first oil was pumped June 11, 1975.

Even with the arrival of long-awaited oil from the North Sea, the economy remained a problem, particularly in an annual rate of inflation that was still

## British Prime Ministers Since 1770

| Name | Term |
|---|---|
| Lord North (Tory) | 1770–1782 |
| Marquis of Rockingham (Whig) | 1782–1782 |
| Earl of Shelburne (Whig) | 1782–1783 |
| Duke of Portland (Coalition) | 1783–1783 |
| William Pitt, the Younger (Tory) | 1783–1801 |
| Henry Addington (Tory) | 1801–1804 |
| William Pitt, the Younger (Tory) | 1804–1806 |
| Baron Grenville (Whig) | 1806–1807 |
| Duke of Portland (Tory) | 1807–1809 |
| Spencer Perceval (Tory) | 1809–1812 |
| Earl of Liverpool (Tory) | 1812–1827 |
| George Canning (Tory) | 1827–1827 |
| Viscount Goderich (Tory) | 1827–1828 |
| Duke of Wellington (Tory) | 1828–1830 |
| Earl Grey (Whig) | 1830–1834 |
| Viscount Melbourne (Whig) | 1834–1834 |
| Sir Robert Peel (Tory) | 1834–1835 |
| Viscount Melbourne (Whig) | 1835–1841 |
| Sir Robert Peel (Tory) | 1841–1846 |
| Earl Russell (Whig) | 1846–1852 |
| Earl of Derby (Tory) | 1852–1852 |
| Earl of Aberdeen (Coalition) | 1852–1855 |
| Viscount Palmerston (Liberal) | 1855–1858 |
| Earl of Derby (Conservative) | 1858–1859 |
| Viscount Palmerston (Liberal) | 1859–1865 |
| Earl Russell (Liberal) | 1865–1866 |
| Earl of Derby (Conservative) | 1866–1868 |
| Benjamin Disraeli (Conservative) | 1868–1868 |
| William E. Gladstone (Liberal) | 1868–1874 |
| Benjamin Disraeli (Conservative) | 1874–1880 |
| William E. Gladstone (Liberal) | 1880–1885 |
| Marquis of Salisbury (Conservative) | 1885–1886 |
| William E. Gladstone (Liberal) | 1886–1886 |
| Marquis of Salisbury (Conservative) | 1886–1892 |
| William E. Gladstone (Liberal) | 1892–1894 |
| Earl of Rosebery (Liberal) | 1894–1895 |
| Marquis of Salisbury (Conservative) | 1895–1902 |
| Earl Balfour (Conservative) | 1902–1905 |
| Sir H. Campbell-Bannerman (Liberal) | 1905–1908 |
| Herbert H. Asquith (Liberal) | 1908–1915 |
| Herbert H. Asquith (Coalition) | 1915–1916 |
| David Lloyd George (Coalition) | 1916–1922 |
| Andrew Bonar Law (Conservative) | 1922–1923 |
| Stanley Baldwin (Conservative) | 1923–1924 |
| James Ramsay MacDonald (Labour) | 1924–1924 |
| Stanley Baldwin (Conservative) | 1924–1929 |
| James Ramsay MacDonald (Labour) | 1929–1931 |
| James Ramsay MacDonald (Coalition) | 1931–1935 |
| Stanley Baldwin (Coalition) | 1935–1937 |
| Neville Chamberlain (Coalition) | 1937–1940 |
| Winston Churchill (Coalition) | 1940–1945 |
| Clement R. Attlee (Labour) | 1945–1951 |
| Sir Winston Churchill (Conservative) | 1951–1955 |
| Sir Anthony Eden (Conservative) | 1955–1957 |
| Harold Macmillan (Conservative) | 1957–1963 |
| Sir Alec Frederick Douglas-Home (Conservative) | 1963–1964 |
| Harold Wilson (Labour) | 1964–1970 |
| Edward Heath (Conservative) | 1970–1974 |
| Harold Wilson (Labour) | 1974–1976 |
| James Callaghan (Labour) | 1976– |

15.6% at the end of 1977. Improving trade balances pushed the British pound sterling up by fall of 1978 to over $1.90, the highest point since 1976.

Petroleum production is expected to meet consumption by 1980. Continental shelf reserves were estimated in 1976 at 2.3 billion tons.

The country produces small quantities of iron, tin, copper, lead, and zinc. The entire supply of china clay (kaolin)—important to the ceramic, paper-making, bleaching, and chemical industries—comes from Cornwall.

The U.K. is among the world's leaders in sea fishing. Salted herring normally represents about 70% of the exports.

Chief exports in 1976 were nonelectrical machinery (20%), chemicals (12%), motor vehicles (9%), electrical machinery and equipment (8%), and diamonds (5%). Leading customers were EEC (36%; incl. West Germany 7%, France 7%, Netherlands 6%, Belgium-Luxembourg 5%, Ireland 5%), U.S. (10%). Leading suppliers were EEC (37%; incl. West Germany 9%, Netherlands 8%, France 7%), U.S. (10%).

## NORTHERN IRELAND

**Status:** Part of United Kingdom
**Secretary of State:** Roy Mason (1976)
**Area:** 5,452 sq mi. (14,121 sq km)
**Population (est. 1977):** 1,537,000
**Density per square mile:** 281.9
**Capital and largest city (est. 1976):** Belfast, 363,000
**Monetary Unit:** British pound sterling
**Languages:** English, Gaelic
**Religions:** Roman Catholic, 34.9%; Presbyterian, 29%; Church of Ireland, 24.2%; Methodist, 5%

**Geography.** Northern Ireland comprises the counties of Antrim, Armagh, Down, Fermanagh, Londonderry, and Tyrone, which make up predominantly Protestant Ulster and form the northern part of the island of Ireland, westernmost of the British Isles. It is slightly larger than Connecticut.

**Government.** Northern Ireland is an integral part of the United Kingdom (it has 12 representatives in the British House of Commons), but under the terms of the Government of Ireland Act (1920), it had a semiautonomous government. But on March 28, 1972, after three years of internal strife resulted in over 400 dead and thousands injured, the U.K. suspended the Ulster parliament, and the Ulster counties became governed directly from London after an attempt to return certain powers to an elected Assembly in Belfast.

The Northern Ireland Assembly was dissolved March 28, 1975, and a Constitutional Convention was elected on May 1 to write a Constitution acceptable to Protestants and Catholics. The convention failed to reach agreement and was dissolved March 5, 1976.

The major political parties are the United Ulster Unionist Coalition (Protestant) (46 of 78 delegates to Constitutional Convention); Social Democratic Labor Party (Catholic) (17 delegates); Alliance Party (8 delegates); New Unionist Party of Northern Ireland (Protestant) (5 delegates).

**History.** Ulster was part of Catholic Ireland until the reign of Elizabeth I (1558–1603) when, after crushing three Irish rebellions, the crown confiscated lands in Ireland and settled in Ulster the Scot Presbyterians who became rooted there. Another rebellion in 1641–51, crushed as brutally by Oliver Cromwell, resulted in the settlement of Anglican Englishmen in Ulster. Subsequent political policy favoring Protestants and disadvantaging Catholics encouraged further settlement in Northern Ireland.

But the North did not separate from the South until William Gladstone presented in 1886 his proposal for home rule in Ireland as a means of settling the Irish Question. The Protestants in the north, although they had grievances like the Catholics in the south, feared domination by the Catholic majority. Industry, moreover, was concentrated in the north and depended on the British market.

When World War I began, civil war threatened between the regions. Northern Ireland, however, did not become a political entity until the six counties accepted the Home Rule Bill of 1920. This set up a semiautonomous Parliament in Belfast and a crown-appointed Governor advised by a Cabinet of the Prime Minister and eight ministers, as well as a 12-member representation in the House of Commons at London.

As the Republic of Ireland gained its sovereignty, relations improved between North and South, although the Irish Republican Army, outlawed in recent years, continued the struggle to end the partition of Ireland. In 1966–69, communal rioting and street fighting between Protestants and Catholics occurred in Londonderry, fomented by extremist nationalist Protestants, who feared the Catholics might attain a local majority, and by Catholics demonstrating for civil rights.

Rioting, terrorism, and sniping killed more than 1,800 persons from 1969 through 1978, and the religious communities, Catholic and Protestant, became hostile armed camps. British troops were brought in to separate them but themselves became a target of Catholics.

The bloodshed intensified in 1972, forcing the U.K. to impose direct rule from London after dissolving the Ulster parliament, which was unable to end the strife.

Catholics boycotted a March 8, 1973, referendum that produced a 591,820-to-6,463 vote for Ulster's continuance in the United Kingdom.

Two weeks later, a new British charter created a 78-member Assembly elected by proportional representation that gave more weight to Catholic strength. It created a Province Executive with committee chairmen of the Assembly heading all government departments except law enforcement, which remained under London's control. Assembly elections June 28, 1973, produced a majority for the new Constitution that included Catholic assemblymen. Dublin urged Ulster Catholics to work with the new system.

Ulster's leaders agreed in November 1973 to create an 11-member Executive Body with six seats assigned to Unionists (Protestants) and four to members of Catholic parties. Unionist leader Brian Faulkner headed the Executive. Also agreed to was a Council of Ireland, with 14 seats evenly divided between Dublin and Belfast, which could act only by unanimous vote.

Although the Council lacked real authority, its creation sparked a general strike by Protestant extremists in May 1974. The two-week strike caused Faulkner's resignation from the Executive and resumption of direct rule from London.

Return of a Labor government in the U.K. in February 1974 led promptly to the assignment of Merlyn Rees to replace the less conciliatory William Whitelaw as Secretary of State for Northern Ireland. In April 1974, London instituted a new program that responded to some Catholic grievances, but assigned more British troops to cut off movement of arms and munitions to Ulster's violence-racked cities.

In addition to pledging recruitment of more Catholics in the overwhelmingly Protestant Royal Ulster Constabulary, the London government proposed phased release of suspected terrorists whose imprisonment without trial had caused Catholic protests. The releases were made contingent on an end to the violence.

Violence continued unabated, with new heights reached early in 1976 when the British government announced the end of special privileges for political prisoners in Northern Ireland. British Prime Minister James Callaghan visited Belfast in July and pledged that Ulster would remain part of the United Kingdom unless a clear majority wished to separate.

In October 1977, the 1976 Nobel Prize for Peace was belatedly awarded to Mairead Corrigan and Betty Williams for their campaign against violence and for peace in Northern Ireland. Despite their work and the efforts of many others through 1978, there was little reconciliation in Northern Ireland.

**Economy.** Agriculture is the largest single industry; about two thirds of the country is devoted to crops and pasture under a system of mixed farming. The leading crops include potatoes, oats, and flax.

The two principal manufacturing industries are linen and shipbuilding, both centered in Belfast. The linen industry was established by Huguenot weavers who fled France after the revocation of the Edict of Nantes in 1685.

# Dependencies of the United Kingdom

## ANGUILLA, ANTIGUA

**See West Indies Associated States**

## BELIZE

**Status:** Self-governing dependency
**Governor:** Peter McEntee (1976)
**Prime Minister:** George C. Price (1961)
**Area:** 8,867 sq mi. (22,965 sq km)
**Population (est. 1978):** 150,000
**Capital: (est. 1975):** Belpoman, 5,300
**Monetary unit:** Belize dollar

Formerly known as British Honduras, Belize became a British Crown Colony in 1884. It is situated in Central America south of Mexico and east and north of Guatemala on the Caribbean sea. Belize was probably overrun by Hernando Cortés in 1524. British buccaneers settled the former capital, Belize, in the 17th century.

In the first popular election in 1954, the People's United Party, nationalistic and anti-British, came to power. Eventually the nationalists won a Constitution, which, effective in 1964, established self-government under a British-appointed Governor.

The agricultural output consists of bananas, sugarcane, and citrus fruits. Cedar lumber and logs, mahogany lumber and logs, and pine lumber are the principal forest products.

Chief exports in 1970 were sugar (48%), timber (8%), orange juice (7%), clothing (6%), grapefruit segments (5%), and lobster (5%). Leading customers were U.S. (30%), U.K. (24%), Mexico (22%), Canada (13%). Leading suppliers were U.S. (34%), U.K. (25%), Jamaica (7%), Netherlands (7%).

## BERMUDA

**Status:** Self-governing dependency
**Governor:** Sir Peter Ramsbotham (1977)
**Prime Minister:** J. David Gibbons (1977)
**Area:** 20 sq mi. (52 sq km)
**Population (est. 1978):** 65,000
**Capital (1970 census):** Hamilton, 2,100
**Monetary unit:** Bermuda dollar

Bermuda is an archipelago of about 360 small islands, 580 miles (934 km) east of North Carolina. The largest is (Great) Bermuda, or Long Island. Discovered by Juan de Bermúdez, a shipwrecked Spaniard, early in the 16th century, the islands were settled in 1612 by an offshoot of the Virginia Company and became a crown colony in 1684.

In 1940, sites on the islands were leased for 99 years to the U.S. for air and navy bases. Bermuda is also the headquarters of the West Indies and Atlantic squadron of the Royal Navy.

In 1968, Bermuda was granted a new Constitution, its first Prime Minister, and autonomy, except for foreign relations, defense, and internal security. The predominantly white United Bermuda Party has retained power in three elections against the opposition—the black-led Progressive Laborites—although Bermuda's population is 60% black. Serious rioting occurred in December 1977 after two blacks were hanged for a series of murders including the 1973 assassination of the Governor, Sir Richard Sharples, and British troops were summoned to restore order.

Bermuda's major industry is tourism, with more than 500,000 visitors in 1977.

The agricultural output consists of lily bulbs, potatoes, vegetables, and arrowroot.

Chief exports in 1977 were drugs (50%) and liquor (20%). Leading customers were U.S. (25%), Argentina (19%), Spain (16%), U.K. (9%). Leading suppliers were U.S. (51%), U.K. (11%), Netherlands Antilles (10%), Canada (9%), others (19%).

## BRITISH ANTARCTIC TERRITORY

**Status:** Dependency
**High Commissioner:** James R. Parker
**Area:** 500,000 sq mi. (1,395,000 sq km)
**Population (1972):** 79

The British Antarctic Territory consists of the South Shetland Islands, South Orkney Islands, and Nearby Graham Land on the Antarctic continent, largely uninhabited. They were dependencies of the British crown colony of the Falkland Islands but received a separate administration in 1962, being governed by a British-appointed high commissioner who is governor of the Falklands.

## BRITISH INDIAN OCEAN TERRITORY

**Status:** Dependency
**Commissioner:** Philip Mansfield
**Administrator:** Martin Ewens
**Administrative headquarters:** Victoria, Seychelles
**Area:** 85 sq mi, (220 sq km)

This dependency, consisting of the Chagos Archipelago and other small island groups, was formed in November 1965 by agreement with Mauritius and the Seychelles, There is no permanent civilian population in the territory.

## BRITISH VIRGIN ISLANDS

**Status:** Dependency
**Governor:** Walter W. Wallace
**Area:** 59 sq mi. (153 sq km)
**Population (est. 1977):** 12,000
**Capital (est. 1975):** Road Town (on Tortola): 3,500
**Monetary unit:** U.S. dollar

Some 36 islands in the Caribbean Sea northeast of Puerto Rico and west of the Leeward Islands, the British Virgin Islands are economically interdependent with the U.S. Virgin Islands to the south. They were formerly part of the administration of the Leeward Islands. They received a separate administration in 1956 as a crown colony. In 1967 a new Constitution was promulgated that provided for a ministerial system of government headed by the Governor. The principal islands are Tortola, Virgin Corda, Anegada and Jost Van Dyke.

Chief exports in 1973 were motor vehicles (re-exports) (15%), nonelectric machines (re-exports) (14%), sand (10%), fish (9%), timber (re-exports) (6%), and beverages (re-exports) (5%). Leading customers were U.S. Virgin Islands (59%), Netherlands Antilles (12%), St. Martin (8%), U.K. (7%). Leading suppliers were U.S. (21%), Puerto Rico (19%), U.K. (16%), U.S. Virgin Islands (15%), Trinidad and Tobago (8%).

## BRUNEI

**Status:** Independent state
**Sultan:** Hassanel Bolkiah (1968)
**High Commissioner:** J. A. Davidson
**Area:** 2,226 sq mi. (5,765 sq km)
**Population (est. 1977):** 185,000
**Capital (est. 1976):** Bandar Seri Begawan, 48,000
**Monetary unit:** Brunei dollar

A sultanate on the northwest coast of the island of Borneo on the South China Sea, Brunei consists of two prongs into the territory of Sarawak, East Malaysia. It was a powerful state from the 16th to the 19th century, ruling over the northern part of Borneo and adjacent island chains. But it fell into decay and lost Sarawak in 1841, becoming a British protectorate in 1888 and a British dependency in 1905.

The Sultan regained control over internal affairs by a Constitution he instituted in 1959, along with an agreement with the Crown delegating responsibility for defense and foreign affairs. The U.K. which is responsible for foreign affairs, is represented by a High Commissioner; government is by a Privy Council and Council of Ministers, both presided over by the Sultan, and a Legislative Council.

Sultan Bolkiah was crowned in August 1968 at the age of 22. He succeeded his father, Sir Omar Ali Saifuddin, who abdicated.

Most of the inhabitants are Malays and Borneans; in the 1971 census, 23.4% were Chinese and only 1.5% European. The bulk of the population lives in and around the capital, situated on the Brunei River nine miles from its mouth. The interior is largely forested and contains rich timber. All petroleum is exported to Sarawak for refining.

Chief exports in 1975 were crude oil (78%) and natural gas (17%). Leading customers were Japan (78%), South Africa (7%), U.S. (7%), Malaysia (5%). Leading suppliers were U.S. (23%), Japan (22%), Singapore (17%), U.K. (12%), Netherlands (5%), Malaysia (5%).

## CAYMAN ISLANDS

**Status:** Dependency
**Governor:** T. Russell (1974)
**Area:** 118 sq mi. (306 sq km)
**Population (est. 1977):** 14,000
**Capital (1970 census):** Georgetown (on Grand Cayman), 3,800
**Monetary unit:** Cayman Islands dollar

This dependency consists of three islands—Grand Cayman (76 sq mi.), Cayman Brac (22 sq mi.), and Little Cayman (20 sq mi.)—situated about 180 miles northwest of Jamaica. They were dependencies of Jamaica until 1959, when they became a unit territory within the Federation of the West Indies. In 1962, upon the dissolution of the Federation, the Cayman Islands became a British dependency.

Chief exports in 1974 were turtle products (93%). Leading customers and suppliers were U.S., Jamaica.

## CHANNEL ISLANDS

**Status:** Crown dependencies
**Lieutenant Governor of Jersey:** Gen. Sir Desmond Fitzpatrick
**Lieutenant Governor of Guernsey:** Vice Adm. Sir John Martin (1974)
**Area:** 75 sq mi. (194 sq km)
**Population (est. 1977):** 125,000
**Capital of Jersey:** St. Helier
**Capital of Guernsey:** St. Peter Port
**Monetary units:** Guernsey pound; Jersey pound

This group of islands, lying in the English Channel off the northwest coast of France, is the only portion of the Duchy of Normandy belonging to the English Crown, to which it has been attached since the conquest of 1066. It was the only British possession occupied by Germany during World War II.

For purposes of government, the islands are divided into the Bailiwick of Jersey (45 sq mi.; 117 sq km) and the Bailiwick of Guernsey (30 sq mi.; 78 sq km), including Alderney (3 sq mi.; 7.8 sq km); Sark (2 sq mi.; 5.2 sq km), Herm, Jethou, etc. The islands are administered according to their own laws and customs by local governments. Acts of Parliament in London are not binding on the islands unless they are specifically mentioned. The Queen is represented in each Bailiwick by a Lieutenant Governor.

English is now the language in daily use, although the French patois is still spoken by some people. New legislation is drafted in English, but French has been retained for ceremonial purposes in the legislative bodies.

## DOMINICA

**See West Indies Associated States**

## FALKLAND ISLANDS AND DEPENDENCIES

**Status:** Dependency
**Governor:** James R. Parker
**Area:** 6,270 sq mi. (16,239 sq km)
**Population: est. (1977):** 2,000
**Capital (est. 1976):** Stanley (on East Falkland), 1,100
**Monetary unit:** Falkland Island pound

This sparsely inhabited dependency consists of a group of islands in the south Atlantic, about 250 miles (402 km) east of the South American mainland. The largest islands are East Falkland and West Falkland. Dependencies are South Georgia Island (1,450 sq mi.; 3,756 sq km), the South Sandwich Islands, and other islets. Three former dependencies—Graham Land, the South Shetland Islands, and the South Orkney Islands—were established as a new British dependency, the British Antarctic Territory, in 1962.

The chief industry is sheep raising and, apart from the production of wool, hides and skins, and tallow, there are no known resources. The whaling industry is carried on from South Georgia Island.

Chief export was wool. Leading customer in 1971 was U.K. (93%). Leading supplier was U.K. (83%).

## GIBRALTAR

**Status:** Self-governing dependency
**Governor:** Sir William Jackson (1978)
**Chief Minister:** Sir Joshua Hassan
**Area:** 2.25 sq mi. (5.8 sq km)
**Population (est. 1978):** 30,000
**Monetary unit:** Gibraltar pound

Gibraltar, at the south end of the Iberian Peninsula, is a rocky promonotory commanding the western entrance to the Mediterranean. Aside from its strategic importance, it is also a free port, naval base, and coaling station. It was captured by the Arabs crossing from Africa into Spain in A.D. 711. In the 15th century, it passed to the Moorish ruler of Granada and later became Spanish. It was captured by an Anglo-Dutch force in 1704 during the War of the Spanish Succession and passed to Great Britain by the Treaty of Utrecht in 1713. Most of the inhabitants of Gibraltar are of Spanish, Italian, and Maltese descent.

Spanish efforts to recover Gibraltar culminated in a referendum in September 1967 in which the residents voted overwhelmingly to retain their link with the U.K. This vote followed months of discussions, marked by Spanish restrictions on travel from the mainland or by air to Gibraltar.

Chief re-exports in 1971 were petroleum products (89%) and tobacco (9%). Leading customers were EEC (31%; U.K. 16%). Leading supplier was U.K. (71%).

## GILBERT ISLANDS

**Status:** Territory
**Governor:** Reginald Wallace (1978)
**Area:** 102 sq mi. (264 sq km)
**Population (est. 1978):** 60,000
**Seat of government (est. 1974):** Bairiki (on Tarawa Atoll), 17,100
**Monetary unit:** Australian dollar

Formerly the Gilbert and Ellice Islands, the islands in these groups (the Gilbert Islands; Ellice Islands; Ocean Island; Fanning, Washington, and Christmas Islands of the Line Islands; and the Phoenix Islands) were proclaimed a British protectorate in 1892 and annexed as a colony in 1915. The most important product is high-grade phosphate.

Ownership of Canton and Enderbury Islands in the Phoenix group was long in dispute between the U.K. and the U.S. until 1939, when an agreement for "use in common" was reached by the two governments. Several of the Gilbert islands were occupied by Japanese forces in World War II, and Tarawa was the scene of one of the fiercest battles in U.S. Marine Corps history in November 1943.

In 1975, the Gilbert and Ellice Islands were divided into two colonies, the Gilberts retaining the name and the Ellice group becoming Tuvalu.

Chief exports in 1974 were phosphates (86%) and copra (14%). Leading customers were New Zealand (62%), Australia (30%). Leading suppliers were Australia (54%), U.K. (14%).

## HONG KONG

**Status:** Dependency
**Governor:** Sir Murray MacLehose (1971)
**Area:** 404 sq mi. (1,045 sq km)
**Population (est. 1978):** 4,580,000
**Capital (est. 1971):** Victoria (Hong Kong Island), 520,900
**Monetary unit:** Hong Kong dollar

The crown colony of Hong Kong comprises the island of Hong Kong (32 sq mi.; 83 sq km), Stonecutters' Island, Kowloon peninsula, and the New Territories on the adjoining mainland. The island of Hong Kong, located at the mouth of the Pearl River about 90 miles (145 km) southeast of Canton, was ceded to Britain in 1841.

Stonecutters' Island and Kowloon were annexed in 1860, and the New Territories, which are mainly agricultural lands, were leased from China in 1898 for 99 years. Hong Kong was attacked by Japanese troops Dec. 7, 1941, and surrendered the following Christmas. It remained under Japanese occupation until August 1945.

Possessing an excellent natural harbor, the only safe deep-sea anchorage between Shanghai and Southeast Asia, Hong Kong is the entrepôt for trade throughout southern China and the western Pacific.

Major industries are shipbuilding, rope making, cement, textiles, and electrical products. Chief agricultural products are vegetables, poultry, and pigs.

The cities of Victoria and Kowloon contain the greater part of the population, which is overwhelmingly Chinese. Besides those Chinese engaged in agriculture or industry, many live in sampans or junks either in Victoria harbor or neighboring bays, supporting themselves by fishing or by performing labor on the wharves.

In November 1974, Hong Kong rescinded a policy of accepting illegal immigrants from China that had, since 1968, made the crowded city a sanctuary for thousands of Chinese refugees.

Chief exports in 1976 were clothing (35%), instruments (13%), electrical machinery (12%), textile yarns and fabrics (10%), and toys (5%). Leading customers were U.S. (29%), West Germany (10%), U.K. (8%), Japan (7%). Leading suppliers were Japan (22%), China (18%), U.S. (12%), Republic of China, (7%), Singapore (6%).

## ISLE OF MAN

**Status:** Dependency
**Lieutenant Governor:** Sir John Paul (1973)
**Area:** 227 sq mi. (588 sq km)
**Population (est. 1977):** 60,500
**Capital (1971 census):** Douglas, 20,389
**Monetary unit:** Isle of Man pound

Located in the Irish Sea, equidistant from Scotland, Ireland, and England, the Isle of Man is administered according to its own laws by a government composed of the Lieutenant Governor, a Legislative Council, and a House of Keys, one of the most ancient legislative assemblies in the world.

The chief exports are beef and lamb, fish, and livestock.

## LEEWARD ISLANDS

**See British Virgin Islands; Montserrat; West Indies Associated States**

## MONTSERRAT

**Status:** Dependency
**Governor:** Wyn Jones
**Area:** 40 sq mi. (104 sq km)
**Population (est. 1977):** 13,500
**Capital (est. 1974):** Plymouth, 3,000
**Monetary unit:** East Caribbean dollar

The island of Montserrat is in the Lesser Antilles of the West Indies. Until 1956, it was a division of the Leeward Islands. It did not join the West Indies Associated States established in 1967.

Chief exports in 1975 were cattle (25%), potatoes (24%), cotton, lint (18%), recapped tires (10%), mangoes (7%), and tomatoes (5%). Leading customers were Guadeloupe (22%), U.K. (18%), St. Kitts-Nevis (17%), Antigua (14%), Trinidad and Tobago (7%), Dominica (6%). Leading suppliers were U.K. (29%), Trinidad and Tobago (18%), U.S. (18%), Canada (10%).

## PITCAIRN ISLAND

**Status:** Dependency
**Governor:** Sir Harold Smedley
**Island Magistrate:** Pervis Young
**Area:** 18 sq mi. (47 sq km)
**Population (1976 census):** 74
**Capital:** Adamstown

Pitcairn Island, located in the South Pacific about midway between Australia and South America, consists of the island of Pitcairn and the three uninhabited islands of Henderson, Ducie, and Oeno. The island of Pitcairn was settled in 1790 by British mutineers from the ship *Bounty*, commanded by Capt. William Bligh. It was annexed as a British colony in 1838. Overpopulation forced removal of the settlement to Norfolk Island in 1856, but about 40 persons soon returned.

The colony is governed by a 10-member Council presided over by the Island Magistrate, who is elected for a three-year term.

## ST. HELENA

**Status:** Dependency
**Governor:** G. C. Guy (1976)
**Area:** 47 sq mi. (122 sq km)
**Population (est 1978):** 5,200
**Capital (est. 1974):** Jamestown, 1,600
**Monetary unit:** Pound sterling

St. Helena is a volcanic island in the South Atlantic about 1,100 miles (1,770 km) from the west coast of Africa. It is famous as the place of exile of Napoleon (1815–21).

It was taken for England in 1659 by the East India Company and was brought under the direct government of the Crown in 1834.

St. Helena has two dependencies: Ascension (34

sq mi.; 88 sq km), an island about 700 miles (1,127 km) northwest of St. Helena; and Tristan da Cunha (40 sq mi.; 104 sq km), a group of six islands about 1,500 miles (2,414 km) south-southwest of St. Helena.

Leading suppliers in 1968 were U.K. (61%), South Africa (28%).

## ST. KITTS-NEVIS, ST. LUCIA, ST. VINCENT

**See West Indies Associated States**

## TURKS AND CAICOS ISLANDS

**Status:** Dependency
**Governor:** A. C. Watson
**Area:** 166 sq mi. (430 sq km)
**Population (est. 1978):** 6,200
**Capital (est. 1970):** Grand Turk, 2,300
**Monetary unit:** U.S. dollar

These two groups of islands are situated at the southeast end of the Bahamas. The principal islands in the Turks group are Grand Turk and Salt Cay; the principal ones in the Caicos group are South Caicos, East Caicos, Middle (or Grand) Caicos, North Caicos, Providenciales, and West Caicos.

The Turks and Caicos Islands were dependencies of Jamaica until 1959, when they became a unit territory within the Federation of the West Indies. In 1962, when Jamaica became independent, the Turks and Caicos became a British crown colony. The present Constitution has been in force since June 18, 1969.

Chief exports in 1974 were crayfish (73%) and conch (25%).

## TUVALU

**Status:** Dependency
**Commissioner:** T. H. Layng
**Area:** 10 sq mi. (26 sq km)
**Population (est. 1978):** 6,600
**Seat of government: (est. 1976):** Funafuti, 1,300
**Monetary unit:** Australian dollar

Formerly the Ellice Islands, Tuvalu was separated from the Gilbert and Ellice Islands in 1975 and became a separate dependency. The group consists of nine main islands just south of the equator in the western Pacific.

Britain is granting independence to Tuvalu effective Oct. 1, 1978.

The chief exports are copra and phosphates.

## VIRGIN ISLANDS

**See British Virgin Islands**

## WEST INDIES ASSOCIATED STATES

**Status:** Self-governing territories in free association with the United Kingdom, which is responsible for defense and external affairs. The British Government conducts its affairs with the West Indies Associated States through an official representative, whose office is in Bridgetown, Barbados.
**British Representative:** J. S. Arthur (1978)
**Area:** Antigua, 171 sq mi. (443 sq km); Dominica, 290 sq mi. (751 sq km); St. Christopher (Kitts)-Nevis-Anguilla, 153 sq mi. (397 sq km); St. Lucia, 238 sq mi. (616 sq km); St. Vincent, 150 sq mi. (389 sq km)
**Population (est. 1978):** Antigua, 75,000; Dominica, 80,000; St. Christopher (Kitts)-Nevis-Anguilla, 70,000; St. Lucia, 113,000; St. Vincent, 111,000
**Capitals:** Antigua: St. Johns, 23,500; Dominica: Roseau, 10,200; St. Christopher (Kitts)-Nevis-Anguilla: Basseterre (on St. Kitts), 15,900; St. Lucia: Castries, 3,600; St. Vincent: Kingstown, 22,000
**Monetary unit:** East Caribbean dollar

The West Indies Associated States were established in February-March 1967 and consisted of Antigua and St. Kitts-Nevis-Anguilla of the Leeward Islands, and Dominica, Grenada (which became independent in 1974), St. Lucia, and St. Vincent of the Windward Islands. Statehood for St. Vincent was held up until October 1969 because of local political uncertainties.

Two members of the Leeward group—the British Virgin Islands and Montserrat—did not become Associated States.

Each of the Associated States is fully self-governing in its internal affairs.

The association between the U.K. and each state is to be free and voluntary. As a guarantee of its voluntary nature, association will be terminable by either party. On termination of association, the state would become independent of the U.K.

In July 1967, Anguilla declared its independence from the St. Kitts-Nevis-Anguilla federation. The U.K., however, did not recognize this action. In February 1969, Anguilla voted to cut all ties with the U.K. and become an independent republic. In March, the U.K. landed troops on the island and, on March 30, a truce was signed. In July 1971, Anguilla became a dependency of the U.K. and two months later the U.K. ordered the withdrawal of all her troops.

A new Constitution for Anguilla, effective in February 1976, provides for separate administration and a government of elected representatives. The Associated State of St. Kitts-Nevis-Anguilla remains in being, but Anguilla has a separate relationship with the U.K.

Chief exports of Antigua in 1973 were petroleum products (84%) and aircraft and engines (re-exports, 6%). Leading customers were U.S. (21%), Switzerland (11%), Canada (9%), Bermuda (5%). Leading suppliers were Venezuela (31%), U.K. (22%), U.S. (16%), Canada (6%).

Chief exports of Dominica in 1975 were bananas (58%) and grapefruit (11%). Leading customer was U.K. (78%). Leading suppliers were U.K. (30%), U.S. (10%), Canada (10%).

Chief exports of St. Kitts-Nevis-Anguilla in 1971 were sugar (65%) and electrical equipment (24%). Leading customers were U.K. (61%), Puerto Rico (22%). Leading suppliers were U.K. (35%). Puerto Rico (14%), U.S. (10%), Trinidad and Tobago (9%), Canada (8%).

Chief exports of St. Lucia in 1974 were bananas (64%), cardboard boxes (10%), and coconut oil (10%). Leading customers in 1973 were U.K. (60%), Jamaica (10%), Barbados (8%), U.S. (6%). Leading suppliers were U.K. (30%), U.S. (16%), Trinidad and Tobago (13%), Canada (5%).

Chief exports of St. Vincent in 1972 were bananas (49%), animal and vegetable oils (14%), and arrowroot (11%). Leading customers were U.K. (61%), Barbados (15%), Trinidad and Tobago (11%), U.S. (6%). Leading suppliers were U.K. (28%), Trinidad and Tobago (17%), Canada (9%), U.S. (9%).

## WINDWARD ISLANDS

**See West Indies Associated States**

## UPPER VOLTA

**Republic of Upper Volta**
**President and Premier:** Gen. Sangoulé Lamizana (1966)
**Area:** 105,870 sq mi. (274,200 sq km)
**Population (est 1978):** 6,480,000
**Density per square mile:** 61.2
**Capital and largest city (est. 1975):** Ouagadougou, 168,600
**Monetary unit:** Franc CFA
**Ethnic groups:** Mossis, Bobos
**Languages:** French, African languages
**Religion:** Animist, 75%; Islam, 20%; Christian, 5%
**Gross national product (1976):** $710 million
**National name:** République de Haute-Volta
**Freedom House classifications:** Capitalist pre-industrial, non-party military

**Geography.** Slightly larger than Colorado, Upper Volta is a landlocked country in West Africa. Its neighbors are the Ivory Coast, Mali, Niger, Benin, Togo, and Ghana. The country consists of extensive plains, low hills, high savannas, and a desert area in the north.

**Government.** On Jan. 3, 1966, the President was deposed and the then Col. Sangoulé Lamizana dissolved the National Assembly, suspended the Constitution, and became President. In that same year, a new Constitution was adopted, providing for a National Assembly of 57 members, to be elected every four years.

Dissension within the Volta Democratic Union, the major political party, led to a take-over by the military on Feb. 8, 1974. The Constitution was suspended, the National Assembly was dissolved, and all political activity banned. Lamizana remained President and formed a mostly military Cabinet.

**History.** Upper Volta consists chiefly of the lands of the Mossi Empire, where France established a protectorate over the Kingdom of Ouagadougou in 1897. Upper Volta became a separate colony in 1919, was partitioned among Niger, Sudan, and the Ivory Coast in 1933 and was reconstituted in 1947. An autonomous republic within the French Community, it became independent on Aug. 5, 1960. On Jan. 4, 1966, Colonel Lamizana became chief of state.

On Jan. 1, 1973, Upper Volta formed, with six other nations, the Economic Community for West Africa to promote economic development in the region.

After a referendum favoring a return to civilian rule, the first legislative elections in four years took place on April 30, 1978. The Volta Democratic Union won 28 of the National Assembly's 57 seats. Lamizana was elected President on May 28, defeating Macaire Ouedraogo.

**Economy.** Agricultural products include millet, sorghum, peanuts, beans, and maize.

Chief exports in 1974 were livestock (36%), hides and skins (18%), cotton (16%), peanuts (15%), karité nuts (7%), and sesame seeds (6%). Leading customers were France (36%), Ivory Coast (34%), Ghana (7%). Leading suppliers were France (40%), Ivory Coast (14%), West Germany (12%), U.S. (9%), Belgium-Luxembourg (5%).

## URUGUAY

**Oriental Republic of Uruguay**
**President:** Aparicio Méndez (1976)
**Area:** 68,037 sq mi. (176,215 sq km)
**Population (est. 1978):** 2,825,000
**Density per square mile:** 41.5
**Capital and largest city (est. 1975):** Montevideo, 1,229,700
**Monetary unit:** New peso
**Language:** Spanish
**Religion:** Roman Catholic
**Gross national product** (1976): $3.9 billion
**National name:** República Oriental del Uruguay
**Freedom House classifications:** Capitalist-socialist industrial, non-party military

**Geography.** Uruguay, on the east coast of South America south of Brazil and east of Argentina, is comparable in size to the State of Washington.

The country consists of a low, rolling plain in the south and a low plateau in the north. It has a 120-mile (193 km) Atlantic shore line, a 235-mile (378 km) frontage on the Rio de la Plata, and 270 miles (435 km) on the Uruguay River, its western boundary.

**Government.** The President serves for a term of five years. He appoints a Council of 11 ministers to assist him. Congress consisted of two houses—a Senate and a House of Deputies. Members remained in office for five years.

In June 1973, President Juan María Bordaberry yielded to military pressure and dissolved Congress, thus ending 40 years of constitutional rule. The June decree announced creation of a Council of State to perform Congressional functions, oversee presidential activities, and formulate constitutional reforms for a national plebiscite.

The major political parties are the Colorado Party (41 of 99 seats in House of Deputies), led by Bordaberry; National Party (40 seats), and Broad Front (18 seats). Political activity has been banned since Congress was dissolved in 1973.

**History.** Juan Díaz de Solís, a Spaniard, discovered Uruguay in 1516, but the Portuguese were first to settle it when they founded Colonia in 1680. After a long struggle, Spain wrested the country from Portugal in 1778. Uruguay revolted against Spain in 1811, only to be conquered in 1816–20 by the Portuguese from Brazil. Independence was reasserted with Argentine help in 1825, and the republic was set up in 1830.

Independence, however, did not restore order, and a revolt in 1836 touched off nearly fifty years of factional strife with occasional armed intervention from Argentina and Brazil. Since 1900, there has been social and economic progress.

In 1951, the Constitution of 1934 was amended to place executive power in a National Council of nine members rather than in an individual President. The chairmanship of the council was rotated each year.

In 1966, Uruguayans voted to replace the National Council with a one-man chief executive.

Alberto Heber, who became President in 1966, vigorously championed reform, and a referendum authorized revision of the Constitution to vest executive powers in a President and a Cabinet of Ministers. Oscar Diego Gestido, elected President in 1966, devoted much effort to improving the ailing economy. But he died in November 1967 and was succeeded by Jorge Pacheco Areco.

Siege-state regulations continued as the "Tupamaros," first urban guerrilla organization, kept up spectacular kidnappings, bank and casino robberies (one gold haul netted over $250,000), and arms raids on military arsenals to embarrass what was then the most democratic government in South America. In 1970, the Tupamaros kidnapped a U.S. aid adviser, Dan Mitrione, and killed him when their ransom demands were not met.

The continuing economic, political, and guerrilla problems precipitated impeachment proceedings against Pacheco in 1971. A bitterly fought election followed, with Juan María Bordaberry, Pacheco's hand-picked choice, the winner.

Disputes between the government and the military, coupled with worsening economic problems (the peso was devalued 32 times during Bordaberry's first three years in office), led to a military revolt in February 1973 that ended in an agreement with Bordaberry in which the military promised to maintain the constitutional system but virtually took over control of the government.

Despite the military takeover, inflation soared at a 100% yearly rate and the Tupamaros continued to be active. Their assassinations and bombings were matched by government repression; an estimated 3,500 persons were arrested on political charges in the year after Congress was dissolved, and the press was kept tightly in line.

Military leaders, citing Bordaberry's opposition to the return of constitutional government, removed him from office June 12, 1976. The National Council of 25 military officers and 21 civilians designated Aparicio Méndez to take over the Presidency on September 1 for a five-year term.

Although the government in January 1977 reported that sentences for political prisoners would be reduced, Amnesty International estimated that 5,000 such prisoners were being held in Uruguay, more than in any other Latin nation. On February 24, the Carter administration cut economic aid from $220,000 to $25,000 and eliminated military sales credits of $3 million for Uruguay because of the human rights situation. The Uruguayan government declared March 1 that it would refuse any U.S. aid. On Aug. 9, 1977, the government announced that the country would return to civil rule through general elections in 1981.

**Economy.** Cattle, sheep, meat, and wool dominate the Uruguyan economy. The chief crop is wheat.

Chief exports in 1975 were wool (23%) and meat (19%). Leading customers were Brazil (17%), West Germany (11%), Argentina (7%), Netherlands (7%), U.S. (6%), Italy (5%). Leading suppliers were Kuwait (16%), Brazil (13%), U.S. (10%), Argentina (9%), West Germany (8%), U.K. (5%).

## VATICAN CITY STATE

**Ruler:** Pope John Paul I (1978) (died Sept. 28, 1978)
**Area:** 0.17 sq mi. (0.44 sq km)
**Population (est. 1978):** 1,000 (Italian, 85%; Swiss and others, 15%)
**Density per square mile:** 5,882.4
**Monetary unit:** Lira
**Languages:** Latin, Italian
**Religion:** Roman Catholic
**National name:** Stato della Città del Vaticano

**Geography.** The Vatican City State is situated on the Vatican hill, on the right bank of the Tiber River, within the commune of Rome.

**Government.** The Pope has full legal, executive, and judicial powers. Executive power over the area is in the hands of a Governor appointed by the Pope. The College of Cardinals is the Pope's chief advisory body, and upon his death the cardinals elect his successor for life. The cardinals themselves are created for life by the Pope.

In the Vatican the central administration of the Roman Catholic Church throughout the world is carried on by twelve congregations, three tribunals, three main secretariats, and numerous councils, committees, and commissions. In its diplomatic relations, the Holy See is represented by the Papal Secretary of State.

On Aug. 26, 1978, Cardinal Albino Luciani was chosen by the College of Cardinals to succeed Pope Paul VI, who had died of a heart attack on Aug. 6. The new Pope, who took the name John Paul I, was born on Oct. 17, 1912, at Forno di Canale in Italy.

**History.** The Vatican City State, sovereign and independent, together with the Lateran palaces, have been intimately associated with the history of the Roman Catholic Church since the time of the martyrdom of St. Peter. From these areas the Pope exercised temporal sway for many centuries over a large part of central Italy; in 1859, the Papal States comprised an area of some 17,000 square miles. During the struggle for Italian unification, from 1860 to 1870, most of this area became part of Italy.

By an Italian law of May 13, 1871, the temporal power of the Pope was abrogated, and the territory of the Papacy was confined to the Vatican and Lateran palaces and the villa of Castel Gandolfo. The Popes consistently refused to recognize this arrangement and, by the Lateran Treaty of Feb. 11, 1929 between the Vatican and the Kingdom of Italy, the exclusive dominion and sovereign jurisdiction of the Holy See over the city of the Vatican was again recognized, thus restoring the Pope's temporal authority over the area.

The first session of Ecumenical Council Vatican II was opened by John XXIII on Oct. 11, 1962, to plan and set policies for the modernization of the Roman Catholic Church. Paul VI continued the Council, opening the second session on Sept. 29, 1963.

Pope John Paul I succeeded a pontiff who stood implacably against relaxing the church's traditional stand against birth control, on the Latin rite's insistence upon clerical celibacy, and on conservatism in theological speculation. During his reign, however, he paid much attention to improving ecumenical relations with other denominations.

(For a listing of all the Popes, *see* the Index.)

## VENEZUELA

**Republic of Venezuela**
**President:** Carlos Andrés Pérez (1974)
**Area:** 352,143 sq mi. (912,050 sq km)
**Population (est. 1978):** 13,150,000 (mestizo, 69%; white, 20%; black, 9%; Indian, 2%)
**Density per square mile:** 37.3
**Capital:** Caracas
**Largest cities (est. 1977):** Caracas (metropolitan area): 2,664,000; (1971 census): Maracaibo, 651,574; Valencia, 366,154; Barquisimeto, 334,333
**Monetary unit:** Bolívar
**Language:** Spanish
**Religion:** Roman Catholic
**Gross national product (1976):** $31.1 billion
**National name:** República de Venezuela
**Freedom House classifications:** Capitalist-statist industrial, multi-party centralized

**Geography.** Venezuela, a third larger than Texas, occupies most of the northern coast of South America on the Caribbean Sea. It is bordered by Colombia to the west, Guyana to the east, and Brazil to the south.

Mountain systems break Venezuela into four distinct areas: (1) the Maracaibo lowlands; (2) the mountainous region in the north and northwest; (3) the Orinoco basin, with the llanos (vast grass-covered plains) on its northern border and great forest areas in the south and southeast; (4) the Guiana Highlands, south of the Orinoco, accounting for nearly half the national territory. About 80% of Venezuela is drained by the Orinoco and its tributaries.

**Government.** Venezuela has a bicameral Congress, the 52 members of the Senate and the 213 members of the Chamber of Deputies being elected by direct popular vote to five-year terms. The President is also elected for five years. He must be a Venezuelan by birth and over 30 years old. He is not eligible for re-election until 10 years after the end of his term.

The major political parties are the Democratic Action Party, with 28 of 52 Senate seats and 102 of 213 seats in the Chamber of Deputies; Social Christian Party, People's Electoral Movement, Democratic Republican Union.

**History.** Venezuela is the Western Hemisphere's second greatest producer of oil, following the U.S. Simón Bolívar, who led the liberation of much of the continent from Spain, was born in Caracas in 1783.

Columbus discovered Venezuela on his third voyage in 1498. A subsequent Spanish explorer gave the country its name, meaning "Little Venice." There were no important settlements until Caracas was founded in 1567. With Bolívar taking part, Venezuela was one of the first South American colonies to revolt against Spain in 1810, but it was not until 1821 that independence was won. Federated at first with Colombia and Ecuador, the country set up a republic in 1830 and then sank for many decades into a condition of revolt, dictatorship, and corruption.

From 1908 to 1935, Gen. Juan Vicente Gómez ruled tyrannically over the nation, picking satellites to alternate with him in the presidential palace. Thereafter, there was a struggle between democratic forces and those backing a return to strong-man rule. Dr. Rómulo Betancourt and the liberal Acción Democrática Party won a majority of seats in a constituent assembly to draft a new Constitution in 1946. A well-known writer, Rómulo Gallegos, candidate of Betancourt's party, easily won the presidential election of 1947. But in 1948, the army ousted Gallegos and instituted a military junta.

Following elections in 1952, the junta presented its resignations to the army, which named Col. Marcos Pérez Jiménez as Provisional President. He re-established strong-man rule. But the country overthrew the dictatorship in 1958 and thereafter enjoyed democratic government. Rafael Caldera Rodríguez. President from 1969 to 1974, legalized the Communist Party and established diplomatic relations with Moscow.

Venezuela and neighboring Guyana in 1970 called a 12-year moratorium on their border dispute (Venezuela claims 50,000 square miles of Guyana's 83,000).

As a charter member of the Organization of Petroleum Exporting Countries (OPEC), Venezuela shared the benefits of the tripled oil prices engineered by OPEC, but did not join the 1973 Arab oil boycott. President Carlos Andrés Pérez took office in March 1974, committed to give all Venezuelans a stake in the oil bonanza that made his country the richest in South America.

On Jan. 1, 1976, Venezuela nationalized 21 oil companies, mostly subsidiaries of U.S. firms, offering compensation of $1.28 billion. Oil income in that year was $9.9 billion, and although production decreased 2.2%, revenue remained at the same level in 1977 because of higher prices, largely financing an ambitious social welfare program.

A continuing decline in oil production as world markets slackened forced the government to impose austerity measures on Feb. 28, 1978. Economic problems raised the hopes of Pérez's opponents that they might defeat his party's choice to succeed him in the presidential election scheduled for December 1, Luís Piñerúa Ordaz.

Despite his difficulties at home, Pérez continued to play an active foreign role in extending economic aid to Latin neighbors, in backing the human rights policy of President Carter, and in supporting Mr. Carter's return of the Panama Canal to Panama.

**Economy.** Agricultural production has failed to keep pace with the food needs of the rapidly increasing population. The principal crop is coffee, grown on 60,000 plantations on the slopes of the coastal mountains. Stock raising, which is centered east of Lake Maracaibo and on the llanos, is important.

There are few industries, the most important being woodworking, cotton textiles, and tobacco products. Electric power is plentiful.

Oil, most of which is found on the shore of Lake Maracaibo, gives the country a big foreign trade balance and a treasury surplus.

Chief exports in 1975 were crude oil (65%) and petroleum products (29%). Leading customers were U.S. (33%), Netherlands Antilles (20%), Canada (13%). Leading suppliers were U.S. (48%), West Germany (8%), Japan (8%), Italy (6%).

## VIETNAM

**Socialist Republic of Vietnam**
**President:** Ton Duc Thang (1976)
**Premier:** Pham Van Dong (1976)
**Area:** 127,242 sq mi. (329,556 sq km)
**Population (est. 1978):** 49,275,000
**Density per square mile:** 387.3
**Capital:** Hanoi
**Largest cities (est. 1976):** Ho Chi Minh City (Saigon),[1] 3,460,500; Hanoi, 1,443,500; (est. 1973): Da Nang, 492,200; Na Trang, 216,200; Qui Non, 213,750; Hue, 209,000; (1960 census): Haiphong, 182,490
**Monetary unit:** Dong
**Languages:** Vietnamese, French, Chinese
**Religions:** Buddhist, Roman Catholic, Cao-Dai, Hoa-Hao, Confucian
**National name:** Công Hòa Xã Hôi Chú Nghĩa Viêt Nam
**Freedom House classifications:** Socialist industrial, one-party communist

**Geography.** Vietnam occupies the eastern and southern part of the former Indochinese peninsula in Southeast Asia, with the South China Sea along

1. Includes suburb of Cholon.

its entire coast. China is to the north and Laos and Cambodia to the west. Long and narrow on a north-south axis, Vietnam is about twice the size of Arizona.

The Mekong River delta lies in the south and the Red River delta in the north. Heavily forested mountain and plateau regions make up most of the country.

**Government.** Less than a year after the capitulation of the former Republic of Vietnam (South Vietnam) on April 30, 1975, a joint National Assembly convened with 249 deputies representing the North and 243 representing the South. At a session beginning June 24, the Assembly set July 2, 1976, as the official reunification date. Hanoi became the capital and Ton Duc Thang, President of the Northern regime since 1969, became President of the new republic.

Pham Van Dong, Premier in Hanoi since 1955, took over the new administration, and the Northern flag, anthem, and crest became the symbols of the new Vietnam. The only concession to the former Provisional Revolutionary Government of South Vietnam, which nominally administered the South in the interim period of less than a year after South Vietnam surrendered, was the installation of its President, Nguyen Huu Tho, as one of its two Vice Presidents.

Lao Dong (Communist) Party, led by First Secretary Le Duan, is the only political party.

**History.** The Vietnamese are descendants of Mongoloid nomads from China and migrants from Indonesia. The Vietnamese recognized Chinese suzerainty until the 15th century, an era of nationalistic expansion when Cambodians were pushed out of the southern area of what is now Vietnam.

A century later, the Portuguese were the first Europeans to enter the area. France established its influence early in the 19th century and within 80 years conquered the three regions into which the country was then divided—Cochin-China in the south, Annam in the center, and Tongking in the north.

France first unified Vietnam in 1887 when a single governor-generalship was created, followed by the first physical links between north and south—a rail and road system. Even at the beginning of World War II, however, there were internal differences among the three regions.

Japan took over military bases in Vietnam in 1940 and a pro-Vichy French administration remained until 1945. A veteran Communist leader, Ho Chi Minh, organized an independence movement known as the Vietminh to exploit a confused situation. At the end of the war, Ho's followers seized Hanoi and declared a short-lived republic, which ended with the arrival of French forces in 1946.

Paris proposed a unified government within the French Union under the former Annamite emperor, Bao Dai. Cochin-China and Annam accepted the proposal, and Bao Dai was proclaimed emperor of all Vietnam in 1949. Ho and the Vietminh withheld support, and the revolution in China gave them the outside help needed for a war of resistance against French and Vietnamese troops armed largely by the U.S.

A bitter defeat at Dien Bien Phu in northwest Vietnam on May 5, 1954, broke the French military campaign and brought the division of Vietnam at the conference of Geneva that year. More than 1 million North Vietnamese, mainly Christians, fled south across the 17th parallel dividing line.

In the new South, Ngo Dinh Diem, Premier under Bao Dai, deposed the monarch in 1955 and established a republic with himself as President. Diem used strong U.S. backing to create an authoritarian regime that suppressed all opposition but could not eradicate the Northern-supplied Communist Viet Cong.

Skirmishing grew into a full-scale war, with escalating U.S. involvement. A military coup, U.S.-inspired in the view of many, ousted Diem Nov. 1, 1963, and a kaleidoscope of military governments followed. The most savage fighting of the war occurred in early 1968, during the Tet holidays.

Although the Viet Cong failed to overthrow the Saigon government, U.S. public reaction to the apparently endless war forced a limitation of U.S. troops to 550,000 and a new emphasis on shifting the burden of further combat to the South Vietnamese. Ho Chi Minh's death on Sept. 3, 1969, brought a quadrumvirate to replace him but no flagging in Northern will to fight.

U.S. bombing and invasion of Cambodia in the summer of 1970—an effort to destroy Viet Cong bases in the neighboring state—marked the end of major U.S. participation in the fighting. Most American ground troops were withdrawn from combat by mid-1971 as heavy bombing of the Ho Chi Minh trail from North Vietnam appeared to cut the supply of men and matériel to the South.

Secret negotiations for peace by Secretary of State Henry A. Kissinger with North Vietnamese officials during 1972 after heavy bombing of Hanoi and Haiphong brought the two sides near agreement in October. When the Northerners demanded the removal of the South's President Nguyen Van Thieu as their price, President Nixon ordered the "Christmas bombing" of the North. The conference resumed and a peace settlement was signed in Paris on Jan. 27, 1973. It called for release of all U.S. prisoners, withdrawal of U.S. forces, limitation of both sides' forces inside South Vietnam, and a commitment to peaceful reunification.

Despite Chinese and Soviet endorsement, the agreement foundered in a welter of charges and countercharges—the North asserting that the U.S. was violating the limitation on arms supplies, Washington and Saigon accusing Hanoi of infiltrating troops to the south. U.S. bombing of Communist-held areas in Cambodia was halted by Congress in August 1973, and in the following year Communist action in South Vietnam increased.

An armored attack across the 17th parallel in January 1975 panicked the South Vietnamese army and brought the invasion within 40 miles of Saigon by April 9. Thieu resigned on April 21 and fled, to be replaced by Vice President Tran Van Huong, who quit a week later, turning over the office to Gen. Duong Van Minh. "Big Minh" surrendered Saigon on April 30, ending a war that took 1.3 million Vietnamese and 56,000 American lives, at the cost of $141 billion in U.S. aid.

U.S. helicopters evacuated 1,373 Americans and 5,595 Vietnamese from Saigon in the final days, and 135,000 other South Vietnamese escaped in small boats to seek refuge in the U.S. Congress appropriated $405 million to resettle 130,000 Indochinese refugees—mostly Vietnamese—in the U.S.

Although the new regime in the South at first appeared to be taking a moderate line, "reeducation" of former South Vietnamese government and army personnel began immediately. By mid-1976, virtually all foreigners were expelled, even those married to Vietnamese. There were reports of pressure on city residents to return to the countryside, although there was no forced exodus as in Cambodia. There were also reports that Northern carpetbaggers were moving into government posts in the South.

On May 3, 1977, the U.S. and Vietnam opened negotiations in Paris to normalize relations. One of the first results was the withdrawal of U.S. opposition to Vietnamese membership in the United Nations, formalized in the Security Council on July 20 when the Council accepted the application without a vote. Two major issues remained to be settled, however: the return of the bodies of some 2,500 U.S. servicemen missing in the war and the claim by Hanoi that former President Nixon had promised reconstruction aid under the 1973 agreement.

Negotiations in Paris during 1977 failed to resolve these issues, and the question of recognition appeared to have been shelved indefinitely when the U.S. expelled the Vietnamese Ambassador to the United Nations, Dinh Ba Thi, on Feb. 10, 1978. Thi was accused of complicity in an espionage case in which a U.S. citizen and a Vietnamese refugee were later convicted of delivering U.S. intelligence to Hanoi.

The new year also brought an intensification of border clashes between Vietnam and Cambodia and accusations by China that Chinese residents of Vietnam were being subjected to persecution. On May 12, 1978, Peking cut off all aid and withdrew 800 technicians. By June, 133,000 Chinese were reported to have fled Vietnam and as many as 300,000 of the estimated 1.8 million Chinese in Vietnam were expected to leave eventually. This would exceed the number of Vietnamese who have fled, mainly by boat to the south, since the Communist victory.

On August 21, 1978, a large U. S. Congressional delegation visited Hanoi to gather facts about Americans missing in action in the Vietnamese War and to discuss improving Vietnam-U.S. relations.

In August 1978, a World Bank affiliate approved $60 million in interest-free loans to Vietnam to expand rice production.

**Economy.** Vietnam is basically an agricultural economy, the Mekong delta being one of the leading rice-exporting regions of the world. High-quality coal is found in the North, but there is no heavy industry in either North or South. Aside from rice, Vietnam also produces tea, coffee, tobacco, rubber, and spices.

Chief exports in 1974 were clothing (10%), fish (10%), rubber (10%), coal (5%), and beverages (5%). Leading customers in 1975 were U.S.S.R. (15%), China (11%), East Germany (10%), Japan (9%). Leading suppliers were China (23%), U.S.S.R. (20%), U.S. (19%), Singapore (7%), Japan (7%).

**(For a Vietnam War chronology, see Headline History.)**

## WESTERN SAMOA

**Head of State:** Malietoa Tanumafili II (1962)
**Prime Minister:** Taisi Tupuola Efi (1976)
**Area:** 1,097 sq mi. (2,842 sq km)
**Population (est. 1978):** 155,000
**Density per square mile:** 141.3
**Capital and largest city (1976 census):** Apia, 32,100
**Monetary unit:** Tala
**Languages:** Samoan and English
**Religions:** Congregational, 51%; Roman Catholic, 22%; Methodist, 16%
**Gross national product (1976):** $50 million
**National name:** Samoa i Sisifo
**Member of Commonwealth of Nations**
**Freedom House classifications:** Capitalist pre-industrial, non-party traditional

**Geography.** Western Samoa, the size of Rhode Island, is in the South Pacific Ocean about 2,200 miles south of Hawaii midway to Sydney, Australia, and about 800 miles northeast of Fiji. The larger islands in the Samoan chain are mountainous and of volcanic origin. There is little level land except in the coastal areas, where most cultivation takes place.

**Government.** Western Samoa has a 46-member Legislature, consisting mainly of the titleholders (chiefs) of family or tribal groups, with two members elected by universal suffrage to represent those not belonging to such groups. When the present Chiefs of State die, successors will be elected by the Legislature.

**History.** The Samoan islands were discovered in the 18th century and visited by Dutch and French traders. Toward the end of the 19th century, conflicting interests of the U.S., U.K., and Germany resulted in a treaty signed in 1899. It recognized the paramount interests of the U.S. in those islands east of 171° west longitude (American Samoa) and Germany's interests in the other islands (Western Samoa); the British withdrew in return for recognition of their rights in Tonga and the Solomons.

New Zealand occupied Western Samoa in August 1914, and was granted a League of Nations mandate. In 1947, the islands became a U.N. trust territory administered by New Zealand.

Western Samoa became an independent nation on Jan. 1, 1962.

**Economy.** Agriculture in the coastal areas is the basis of Western Samoa's economy.

Chief exports in 1976 were cocoa (41%) and copra (35%). Leading customers were New Zealand (36%), West Germany (35%), Japan (8%), Netherlands (6%), American Samoa (5%). Leading suppliers were New Zealand (28%), Australia (20%), Japan (15%), U.S. (8%), Fiji (7%), Singapore (5%).

## YEMEN

**People's Democratic Republic of Yemen**
**Chairman of Presidential Council (1978) and Premier (1972):** Ali Nasser Mohammed
**Area:** 111,074 sq mi. (287,683 sq km)[1]
**Population (est. 1978):** 1,850,000
**Density per square mile:** 16.7[1]
**National capital and largest city (est. 1973 by U.N.):** Aden, 264,300
**Administrative capital:** Madinat ash Sha'b
**Monetary unit:** Yemen dinar
**Language:** Arabic
**Religion:** Islam
**Gross national product (1976):** $480 million
**National name:** Jumhurijah al-Yemen al Dimuqratiyah al Sha'abijah
**Freedom House classifications:** Socialist pre-industrial,

1. Excluding Perim and Kamaran islands.

one-party socialist

**Geography.** Formerly known as Southern Yemen, the People's Democratic Republic of Yemen extends along the southern part of the Arabian Peninsula on the Gulf of Aden and the Indian Ocean. It is comparable in size to Nevada. The Yemen Arab Republic is to the northwest, Saudia Arabia to the north, and Oman to the east.

A 700-mile (1,130-km) narrow coastal plain gives way to a mountainous region and then a plateau area.

**Government.** On June 23, 1969, President Qahtan Mohammed al Shaabi resigned and was replaced by a five-man Presidential Council.

A Constitution published in 1970 changed the state's name from Southern Yemen and established a 101-seat legislature, the People's Supreme Council. The only legal political party is the National Liberation Front.

**History.** The People's Republic of Southern Yemen was established Nov. 30, 1967, when the U.K. granted independence to the Federation of South Arabia. This Federation consisted of the state (once the colony) of Aden and 16 of the 20 states of the Protectorate of South Arabia (once the Aden Protectorate). The four states of the Protectorate that did not join the Federation then later became part of Southern Yemen.

Salim Robea Ali, Chairman of the Presidential Council since its establishment in 1969, was ousted and executed June 26, 1978, two days after the assassination of President Ahmed Hussein al-Ghashmi of the Yemen Arab Republic. Premier Ali Nasser Mohammed assumed the added duty of Council head.

Robea was reported have been blamed by a faction of the National Liberation Front for the assassination, which occurred when a bomb exploded in the briefcase of a Robea representative during a meeting with al-Ghashmi. Other reports said Robea had been deposed by the dominant pro-Soviet faction of the party because he had shown leanings toward the West as the U.S.S.R. increased its reliance on Aden as a naval and air base since the loss of its bases in Somalia.

**Economy.** The city of Aden is essentially a transshipment point and bunkering station and is also the commercial center for Yemen and the African coast opposite. The chief industry is petroleum refining.

Chief exports in 1975 were petroleum products (93%). Leading customers were Canada (65%), Australia (8%), Angola (5%), Yemen Arab Republic (5%). Leading suppliers were U.K. (21%), Japan (8%), China (8%), Netherlands (5%), Thailand (5%).

## YEMEN ARAB REPUBLIC

**Chief of State:** Abdel Karim al-Arshi (1978)
**Premier:** Abdul Ghani (1975)
**Area:** 75,290 sq mi. (195,000 sq km)
**Population (est. 1978):** 7,300,000
**Density per square mile:** 97.0
**Capital and largest city (est. 1975):** San'a', 134,600
**Monetary unit:** Rial
**Language:** Arabic
**Religion:** Islam
**Gross national product (1976):** $1.5 billion
**National name:** Al Jamhuriya al Arabiya Yamaniya
**Freedom House classifications:** Capitalist pre-industrial, non-party military

**Geography.** The Yemen Arab Republic occupies the southwestern tip of the Arabian Peninsula, with its western coast on the Red Sea opposite Ethiopia. Its neighbors are Saudi Arabia to the north and east and the People's Democratic Republic of Yemen to the south. Its area is slightly less than that of South Dakota.

A north-south coastal plain 20–50 miles wide lies in the west; eastward, there are the interior highlands, which attain a height of 12,000 feet (3,660 m), and the expanse of the Rub 'al-Khali Desert.

**Government.** The country's first permanent Constitution was submitted to the National Assembly in 1971. It provides for a 179-member legislature, the Consultative Council, 20 of whose members would be chosen by the President and the rest elected every four years. A five-man executive Presidential Council is to be chosen by the Consultative Council.

A merger agreement between Yemen and the People's Democratic Republic of Yemen (Southern Yemen) was signed by the two states Oct. 28, 1972, after bitter border clashes between them over a five-year period. A new Constitution was to be drafted, but meanwhile the joint government was to be "republican, nationalist and democratic," ruled by a single, merged Presidential Council and unified legislative, executive, and judicial branches. However, renewed fighting was reported in 1973, with one Yemeni leader assassinated, allegedly by Southern Yemeni forces.

In June 1974, the army ousted the government in a bloodless coup and suspended the Constitution and its various legislative bodies. No political organizations are permitted.

**History.** The history of Yemen dates back to the Minaean kingdom (1200–650 B.C.). It accepted Islam in A.D. 628, and in the 10th century came under the control of the Rassite dynasty of the Zaidi sect. The Turks occupied the area from 1538 to 1630 and from 1849 to 1918. The sovereign status of Yemen was confirmed by treaties signed with Saudi Arabia and the U.K. in 1934.

Yemen joined the Arab League in 1945, established diplomatic relations with the U.S. in 1946, and joined the United Nations in 1947.

In 1962, a military revolt of elements favoring President Gamal Abdel Nasser of Egypt broke out. A ruling junta proclaimed a republic, and Yemen became an international battleground, with Egypt and the U.S.S.R. supporting the revolutionaries, and King Saud of Saudi Arabia and King Hussein of Jordan the royalists. The civil war continued until the Middle Eastern War between the Arab States and Israel broke out in June 1967. Nasser had to pull out many of his troops and agree at a conference in Khartoum to a cease-fire and withdrawal of foreign forces.

The war finally ended with the defeat of the royalists in mid-1969. On Oct. 10, 1977, Col. Ibrahim al-Hamidi was assassinated after three years as head of government and was succeeded by Lt. Col. Ahmed Hussein al-Ghashmi as head of the Presidential Council. On June 24, 1978, al-Ghashmi was killed by a bomb as he received the credentials of a new ambassador from the People's Democratic Republic of Yemen. Abdel Karim al-Arshi was named chief of state.

**Economy.** Unlike most of Arabia, the Yemen highlands are well adapted to agriculture; they produce grain, fruit, vegetables, and mocha coffee. Stock raising flourishes.

Chief exports in 1976 were cotton (33%), hides and skin (20%), and coffee (20%). Leading customers were Japan (42%), China (33%), Yemen (Aden; 27%), Italy (18%), Saudi Arabia (16%). Leading suppliers were Saudi Arabia (12%), Japan (10%), India (7%), Australia (7%), U.K. (6%), China (6%), Netherlands (6%).

## YUGOSLAVIA

**Socialist Federal Republic of Yugoslavia**
**President:** Marshal Tito (Josip Broz) (1953)
**President of Federal Executive Council (Premier):** Veselin Djuranovic (1977)
**Area:** 98,766 sq mi. (255,804 sq km)
**Population (est. 1978):** 21,900,000 (Serbian, 42%; Croatian, 24%; Slovene, 9%; Macedonian, 5%; Albanian, 4%)
**Density per square mile:** 221.7
**Capital:** Belgrade
**Largest cities (est. 1975 by U.N.):** Belgrade, 870,000; (1971 census): Zagreb, 566,224; Skopje, 312,980; Sarajevo, 243,980; Ljubljana, 173,853; Split, 152,905
**Monetary unit:** Dinar
**Languages:** Serbo-Croatian, Slovene, Macedonian (all official)
**Religions:** Greek Orthodox, 41%; Roman Catholic, 32%; Islam, 12%
**Gross national product (1976):** $36.2 billion
**National name:** Socijalistička Federativna Republika Jugoslavija
**Freedom House classifications:** Capitalist-socialist industrial, one-party communist

**Geography.** Yugoslavia fronts on the eastern coast of the Adriatic Sea opposite Italy. Its neighbors are Austria, Italy, and Hungary to the north, Romania and Bulgaria to the east, and Greece and Albania to the south. It is slightly larger than Wyoming.

About half of Yugoslavia is mountainous. In the north, the Dinaric Alps rise abruptly from the sea and progress eastward as a barren limestone plateau called the Karst. Montenegro is a jumbled mass of mountains, containing also some grassy slopes and fertile river valleys. Southern Serbia, too, is mountainous. A rich plain in the north and northeast, drained by the Danube, is the most fertile area of the country.

**Government.** Yugoslavia is a federal republic composed of six socialist republics—Serbia (which includes provinces of Vojvodina and Kosovo), Croatia, Slovenia, Bosnia-Herzegovina, Macedonia, and Montenegro. Actual administration is carried on by the Federal Executive Council and its secretaries.

The League of Communists, led by President Tito, and the Socialist Alliance of the Working People are the major political parties.

**History.** Yugoslavia was formed Dec. 1, 1918, from the patchwork of Balkan states and territories where World War I began with the assassination of Archduke Ferdinand of Austria at Sarajevo on June 28, 1914. The new Kingdom of Serbs, Croats, and Slovenes included the former kingdoms of Serbia and Montenegro; Bosnia-Herzegovina, previously administered jointly by Austria and Hungary; Croatia-Slavonia, a semi-autonomous region of Hungary, and Dalmatia, formerly administered by Austria. King Peter I of Serbia became the first monarch, his son acting as regent until his accession as Alexander I on Aug. 16, 1921.

Croat demands for a federal state forced Alexander to assume dictatorial powers in 1929 and to change the country's name to Yugoslavia. Serbian dominance continued despite his efforts, amid the resentment of other regions. A Macedonian associated with Croat dissidents assassinated Alexander on Oct. 9, 1934, and his cousin, Prince Paul, became regent for the King's son, Prince Peter.

Paul's pro-Axis policy brought Yugoslavia to sign the Axis Pact on March 25, 1941, and opponents overthrew the government two days later. On April 6 the Nazis occupied the country, and the young King and his government fled. Two guerrilla armies —the Chetniks under Draza Mihajlovic supporting the monarchy and the Partisans under Tito (Josip Broz) leaning toward the U.S.S.R.—fought the Nazis for the duration of the war. In November 1943, Tito established an Executive National Committee of Liberation to function as a provisional government.

Tito won the elections of Nov. 11, 1945, as monarchists boycotted the vote. A new Assembly on November 29 abolished the monarchy and proclaimed the Federal People's Republic of Yugoslavia with Tito as Prime Minister.

Ruthlessly eliminating opposition, the Tito government executed Mihajlovic in 1946. With Soviet aid, Tito annexed the greater part of Italian Istria under the 1947 peace treaty with Italy but failed in his claim to the key port of Trieste. Zone B of the former free territory of Trieste went to Yugoslavia in 1954.

Tito broke with the Soviet bloc in 1948 and Yugoslavia has since followed a middle road, combining orthodox Communist control of politics and general overall economic policy with a varying degree of freedom in the arts, travel, and individual enterprise. Tito, who became President in 1953 and President for life under a revised Constitution adopted April 7, 1963, has played a major part in the creation of a "non-aligned" group of states, the so-called "third world."

The Marshal supported his one-time Soviet mentors in their quarrel with Communist China but, even though he imprisoned the writer Mihajlo Mihajlov and other dissenters at home, criticized Soviet repression of Czecholovakia in 1968.

Tito welcomed President Nixon to Yugoslavia in 1970 for the first U.S. Presidential visit, and Tito went to the U.S. the following year, but the relationship has been touchy. On May 21, 1977, Vice President Walter F. Mondale met with the 85-year-old dictator in Yugoslavia and was reported surprised by his subsequent attack on President Carter's position on human rights, since there had been no discussion of the issue. The U.S. had sought to smooth Mondale's visit by approving the export of components for a nuclear generator to Yugoslavia.

The regime had sought to provide continuity after Tito's death by a constitutional change in 1974 which would transmit the Presidency to a group of nine persons, each to be President for a year on a rotating basis. Divisions still exist among the nationalities, however. Most militant are the Croats, who have hijacked planes and attacked Yugoslav diplomatic missions around the world to publicize their demands for independence.

**Economy.** The principal crops are corn, wheat, sugar beets, hemp, hops, opium (in Macedonia), and tobacco (chiefly in Macedonia and Herzegovina).

Yugoslavia is the principal mineral producer of the Balkans. Important minerals are iron, bauxite, antimony, chrome, manganese, copper, lead, zinc, and aluminum.

Chief exports in 1976 were machinery (16%), transport equipment (12%), food (10%), nonferrous metals (8%), chemicals (7%), timber (5%), clothing (5%), and textile yarns and fabrics (5%). Leading customers were U.S.S.R. (23%), Italy (12%), West Germany (9%), U.S. (7%), Czechoslovakia (5%). Leading suppliers were West Germany (17%), U.S.S.R. (14%), Italy (10%), Iraq (6%), U.S. (5%).

## ZAIRE

**Republic of Zaire**
**President:** Mobutu Sese Seko (1965)
**Prime Minister:** Mpinga Kasenga (1977)
**Area:** 905,562 sq mi. (2,345,409 sq km)
**Population (est. 1978):** 27,150,000
**Density per square mile:** 30.0
**Capital:** Kinshasa
**Largest cities (1974 by U.N.):** Kinshasa, 2,008,250; Kananga, 601,250; Lubumbashi, 403,600
**Monetary unit:** Zaire.
**Languages:** French; Bantu dialects, mainly Swahili, Lingala, Ishiluba, and Kikongo
**Religions:** Animist, 50%; Roman Catholic, Protestant, Islam
**Ethnic groups:** Bantu, Sudanese, Nilotics, Pygmies, Hamites
**Gross national product (1976):** $3.5 billion
**National name:** République du Zaïre
**Freedom House classifications:** Capitalist-statist pre-industrial, one-party nationalist

**Geography.** Zaire is situated in west central Africa and is bordered by the Congo, the Central African Empire, the Sudan, Uganda, Rwanda, Burundi, Tanzania, Zambia, Angola, and the Atlantic Ocean. It is one quarter the size of the U.S.

The principal rivers are the Ubangi and Bomu in the north and the Zaire (Congo) in the west, which flows into the Atlantic. The entire length of Lake Tanganyika lies along the eastern border with Tanzania and Burundi.

**Government.** Under the Constitution approved by referendum in June 1967 and amended in 1974, the third Constitution since 1960, the President and a unicameral Legislature were to have been elected by universal suffrage for five-year terms.

In 1971, the government proclaimed that the Democratic Republic of the Congo would be known as the Republic of Zaire, since the Congo River's name had been changed to the Zaire. In addition, President Joseph D. Mobutu took the name Mobutu Sese Seko and Katanga province became Shaba.

There is only one political party: the Popular Movement of the Revolution, led by President Mobutu.

**History.** Formerly the Belgian Congo, this territory was inhabited by ancient Negrito peoples (Pygmies), who were pushed into the mountains by Bantu and Nilotic invaders. The American correspondent Henry M. Stanley navigated the Congo River in 1877 and opened the interior to exploration. Commissioned by King Leopold II of Belgium, Stanley made treaties with native chiefs that enabled the King to obtain personal title to the territory at the Berlin Conference of 1885.

Criticism of forced labor under royal exploitation prompted the Belgian government to take over administration of the Congo, which remained a colony until agitation for independence prompted Brussels to grant freedom on June 30, 1960. Moise Tshombe, Premier of the then Katanga Province—now known as Shaba—seceded from the new republic on July 11, 1960, and another mining province, South Kasai, followed. Belgium sent paratroopers to quell the civil war, and with President Joseph Kasavubu and Premier Patrice Lumumba of the national government in conflict, the United Nations flew in a peacekeeping force.

Kasavubu staged an army coup in September 1960 and handed Lumumba over to the Katangan forces. A U.N. investigating commission found that Lumumba had been killed by a Belgian mercenary in the presence of Tshombe. Dag Hammarskjold, U.N. Secretary-General, died in a plane crash en route to a peace conference with Tshombe on Sept. 17, 1961.

U.S. Secretary-General U Thant submitted a national reconciliation plan in August 1962 that Tshombe rejected. His troops fired on the U.N. force in December, and in the ensuing conflict Tshombe capitulated on Jan. 14, 1963. The peacekeeping force withdrew on June 30, 1964, and, in a complete about-face, Kasavubu named Tshombe Premier to fight a spreading rebellion. Tshombe used foreign mercenaries and, with the help of Belgian paratroops airlifted by U.S. planes, defeated the most serious opposition, a Communist-backed regime in the northeast.

Kasavubu abruptly dismissed Tshombe in October 1965 and was himself ousted by Gen. Joseph-Desiré Mobutu, Army Chief of Staff. The new President nationalized the Union Minière, the Belgian copper mining enterprise that had been a dominant force in the Congo since colonial days. The plane carrying the exiled Tshombe was hijacked in June 1967 and he was held prisoner in Algeria until his death from a heart attack was announced by the Algerian government June 29, 1969.

Mobutu eliminated opposition to win election in 1970 to a term of seven years, which was renewed in a 1977 presidential election. He invited U.S., South African, and Japanese investment to replace Belgian interests. In January 1975, he nationalized much of the economy, barred religious instruction in schools, and decreed the adoption of African names, changing his own to Sese Seko and that of the country and its chief river to Zaire.

In the Angolan civil war of 1975–76, Mobutu backed the National Front for the Liberation of Angola (FNLA), whose leader, Holden Roberto, is related to him by marriage. The Zairean government opposed the recognition of the Soviet-backed Popular Movement for the Liberation of Angola (MPLA) and reluctantly accepted its victory.

On March 8, 1977, invaders from Angola calling themselves the Congolese National Liberation Front (FLNC) pushed into Shaba and threatened the important mining center of Kolwezi. France and Belgium responded to Mobutu's pleas for help with weapons, but the U.S. gave only nonmilitary supplies.

In April, France flew 1,500 Moroccan troops to Shaba to defeat the invaders, who were, Mobutu charged. Soviet-inspired and Cuban-led. U.S. intelligence sources, however, confirmed Soviet and Cuban denials of any participation and identified the rebels as former Katanga gendarmes who had fled to Angola after their 1963 defeat.

On May 15, 1978, a new assault from Angola

resulted in the capture of Kolwezi and the death of 100 whites and 300 blacks. In this second invasion, France and Belgium intervened directly as 1,000 Foreign Legion paratroopers repelled the Katangese and 1,750 Belgian soldiers helped evacuate 2,000 Europeans. The U.S. supplied 18 air transports for both the troop movement and the evacuation. This time President Carter himself backed Mobutu's renewed assertions of Soviet-Cuban participation.

France led in organizing Western aid for the restoration of the shattered mining operations at Kolwezi, an important part of the Shaba industry that is the mainstay of Zaire's economy.

**Economy.** Mineral-rich Zaire is one of the world's most important sources of uranium. It also is a source of copper, tin, diamonds (mainly industrial), gold, cobalt, and zinc.

Agricultural products include palm oil and kernels, cottonseed, rubber, cotton lint, coffee, peanuts, sweet potatoes and yams, and cassava.

Chief exports in 1975 were copper (42%), coffee (14%), and diamonds (6%). Leading customers were Belgium-Luxembourg (38%), Italy (14%), France (6%), West Germany (6%), U.S. (6%), U.K. (6%), Japan (5%). Leading suppliers were U.S. (18%), Belgium-Luxembourg (15%), West Germany (13%), Italy (6%), U.K. (5%).

## ZAMBIA

**Republic of Zambia**
**President:** Kenneth D. Kaunda (1964)
**Prime Minister:** Mainza Chona (1977)
**Area:** 290,586 sq mi. (752,614 sq km)
**Population (est. 1978):** 5,500,000
**Density per square mile:** 18.9
**Capital:** Lusaka
**Largest cities (est. 1976 for urban agglomeration):** Lusaka, 483,000; (est. 1972 by U.N.): Ndola, 350,000; Kitwe, 290,100; Chingola, 181,500
**Monetary unit:** Kwacha
**Languages:** English and Bantu
**Religion:** Animist
**Gross national product (1976):** $2.4 billion
**Member of Commonwealth of Nations**
**Freedom House classifications:** Capitalist-socialist pre-industrial, one-party socialist

**Geography.** Zambia, a landlocked country in south central Africa, is about one tenth larger than Texas. It is surrounded by Angola, Zaire, Tanzania, Malawi, Mozambique, Rhodesia, and South-West Africa (Namibia). The country is mostly a plateau that rises to 8,000 feet (2,434 m) in the east.

**Government.** Zambia (formerly Northern Rhodesia) is governed by a President, elected by universal suffrage, and a Legislative Assembly, consisting of 105 members elected by universal suffrage and up to 5 additional members nominated by the President.

The Assembly, in December 1972, passed a law making the ruling United National Independence Party, led by President Kaunda, the only legal political party.

**History.** Empire builder Cecil Rhodes obtained mining concessions in 1889 from King Lewanika of the Barotse and sent settlers to the area soon thereafter. It was ruled by the British South Africa Company, which he established, until 1924, when the British government took over the administration.

From 1953 to 1964, Northern Rhodesia was federated with Southern Rhodesia and Nyasaland in the Federation of Rhodesia and Nyasaland. On Oct. 24, 1964, Northern Rhodesia became the independent nation of Zambia.

Kenneth Kaunda, the first President, kept Zambia within the Commonwealth of Nations. The country's economy, dependent on copper exports, was threatened when Rhodesia declared its independence from British rule in 1965 and defied U.N. sanctions, which Zambia supported, an action that deprived Zambia of its trade route through Rhodesia. The U.S., U.K., and Canada organized an airlift in 1966 to ship gasoline into Zambia. In 1967, the U.K. agreed to finance new trade routes for Zambia.

Kaunda visited Communist China in 1967, and China later agreed to finance a 1,000-mile railroad from the copper fields to Dar es Salaam in Tanzania. A pipeline was opened in 1968 from Ndola in Zambia's copper belt to the Indian Ocean at Dar es Salaam, ending the three-year oil drought.

In August 1969, Kaunda announced the nationalization of the foreign copper-mining industry, with Zambia to take 51% (over $1 billion, estimated), and by October an agreement was reached with the companies on payment. He then announced a similar take-over of foreign oil producers.

Falling world copper prices halved Zambia's 1974–75 receipts from its principal source of foreign exchange. In a move to aid the ailing economy, Kaunda announced sweeping new nationalization moves. One result was to put all mass communications under state control.

Despite the opening of the Tanzam railroad in 1975, congestion at the port of Dar es-Salaam, eastern terminal of the line, reduced the value of Zambia's new link to the Indian Ocean. Fighting in Angola during the latter part of 1975 and early 1976 brought the Benguela railway to a halt, forcing Zambia to stockpile a third of its copper production.

Improved port facilities, together with higher copper prices, resulted in copper revenues of nearly $1 billion in 1976, a gain of 20% over the previous year. The economy remained in critical condition in 1977, however, with imports running double the value of exports even after severe government curbs.

Falling copper prices in 1978 meant a renewed deficit operation for Zambia's chief industry, forcing Kaunda to seek additional economic aid from the U.S. and U.K. He nevertheless remained critical of Anglo-American failure to take a hard line against the rebel regime in Rhodesia. Kaunda continued his support for Joshua Nkomo, whose faction of the militant nationalist Patriotic Front was headquartered in Zambia, and who threatened to invite Soviet-Cuban participation in guerrilla warfare in Rhodesia.

**Economy.** In addition to copper, Zambia supplies zinc, lead, cobalt, and manganese. Its principal agricultural crops are tobacco, corn, and peanuts.

Chief export in 1975 was copper (91%). Leading customers were U.K. (22%), Japan (17%), West Germany (14%), Italy (13%), France (8%). Leading suppliers were U.K. (20%), U.S. (12%), Japan (9%), West Germany (7%), South Africa (7%).

**(For late reports, see Current Events of 1977–78.)**

# CANADA

**Sovereign:** Queen Elizabeth II
**Governor General:** Jules Léger (1974)
**Prime Minister:** Pierre Elliott Trudeau (1968)
**Area:** 3,851,809 sq mi. (9,976,139 sq km)
**Population (est. 1978):** 23,445,200 (British, 44.6%; French, 28.7%; other European, 23%; Indian and Eskimo, 1.4%)
**Density per square mile:** 6.1
**Capital:** Ottawa, Ont.
**Largest cities (1976 census):** Montreal, Que., 1,080,546; Toronto, Ont., 633,318; Winnipeg, Man., 560,874; Calgary, Alta., 469,917; Edmonton, Alta., 461,361; Vancouver, B.C., 410,188; Hamilton, Ont., 312,003; Ottawa, Ont., 304,462; London, Ont., 240,392; Windsor, Ont., 196,526; Quebec, Que., 177,082; Regina, Sask., 149,593
**Monetary Unit:** Canadian dollar
**Languages:** English, French
**Religions:** Roman Catholic, 46.2%; United Church, 17.5%; Anglican, 11.8%; Presbyterian, 4%; Lutheran, 3.3%; Baptist, 3.1%; others, 14.1%
**Gross national product (1976):** $1,707 billion
**Freedom House classifications:** Capitalist industrial, multi-party decentralized

**Geography.** Covering most of the northern part of the North American continent and with an area larger than that of the United States, Canada has an extremely varied topography. The northeastern region, including most of Quebec, northern Ontario and Manitoba, and the Northwest Territories, with Hudson Bay in the center, is an important source of minerals, wood pulp, and water power. In the east the mountainous maritime provinces have an irregular coast line on the Gulf of St. Lawrence and the Atlantic. The St. Lawrence plain, covering most of southern Quebec and Ontario, and the interior continental plain, covering southern Manitoba and Saskatchewan and most of Alberta, are the principal cultivable areas. They are separated by a forested plateau rising from lakes Superior and Huron. Westward toward the Pacific, most of British Columbia, Yukon, and part of western Alberta are covered by parallel mountain ranges including the Rockies. The Pacific border of the coast range is ragged with fiords and channels. The highest point in Canada is Mt. Logan (19,850 ft; 6,050 m), which is in the Yukon.

Canada has an abundance of large and small lakes. In addition to the Great Lakes on the U.S. border, there are 9 others that are more than 100 miles long and 35 that are more than 50 miles long.

The two principal river systems are the Mackenzie and the St. Lawrence. The St. Lawrence, with its tributaries, is navigable for over 1,900 miles (3,058 km).

**Government.** Canada, a self-governing member of the Commonwealth of Nations, is a federal union of ten provinces whose powers are laid down in the British North America Act of 1867. The executive powers nominally rest in the hands of the Governor General, who represents the Queen and is appointed by her upon the recommendation of the Canadian government.

Actually the Governor General acts only with the advice of the Canadian Prime Minister and the members of the Cabinet who at the same time sit in the federal Parliament. The Parliament has two houses: a Senate numbering 104 members appointed for life, and a House of Commons numbering 264 members apportioned according to provincial population. Elections are held at least every five years or whenever the party in power is voted down in the House of Commons or considers it expedient to appeal to the people. The Prime Minister is the leader of the majority party in the House of Commons—or, if no single party holds a majority, the leader of the party able to command the support of a majority of members of the House. Laws must be passed by both houses of Parliament and signed by the Governor General in the Queen's name.

The ten provincial governments are nominally headed by Lieutenant Governors appointed by the federal government, but the executive power in each actually is vested in a Cabinet headed by a Premier, who is leader of the majority party. The provincial legislatures are composed of one-house assemblies whose members are elected for four-year terms. They are known as Legislative Assemblies, except in Newfoundland, where it is the House of Assembly, and Quebec, where it is the National Assembly.

The judicial system consists of a Supreme Court in Ottawa (established in 1875), with appellate jurisdiction, and a Supreme Court in each province, as well as county courts with limited jurisdiction in most of the provinces. The Governor General in Council appoints these judges.

The major political parties are the Liberal Party (134 of 264 seats in House of Commons), led by Prime Minister Pierre Elliott Trudeau; Progressive Conservatives (87 seats), led by Charles Joseph Clark; New Democratic Party (15 seats), led by John Edward Broadbent; Social Credit (8 seats), led by Lorne Reznowski; Independent (4 seats); vacant (15 seats).

**History.** The Norse explorer Leif Ericson probably reached the shores of Canada (Labrador or Nova Scotia) in A.D. 1000, but the history of the white man in the country actually began in 1497, when John Cabot, an Italian in the service of Henry VII of England, reached the shore of Newfoundland or Nova Scotia. Canada was taken for France in 1534 by Jacques Cartier. The actual settlement of New France, as it was then called, began in 1604 at Port Royal in what is now Nova Scotia; in 1608 Quebec was founded. France's colonization efforts were not very successful, but French explorers by the end of the 17th century had penetrated beyond the Great Lakes to the western prairies and south along the Mississippi to the Gulf of Mexico. Meanwhile, the English Hudson's Bay Company had been established in 1670. Because of the valuable fisheries and fur trade, a conflict developed between the French and English; in 1713, Newfoundland, Hudson Bay, and Nova Scotia (Acadia) were lost to England.

During the Seven Years' War (1756–63), England extended its conquest, and the British general Wolfe won his famous victory over Montcalm outside Quebec (Sept. 13, 1759). The Treaty of Paris (1763) gave England control.

At that time the population of Canada was almost entirely French, but in the next few decades, thou-

## Canadian Governors General and Prime Ministers Since 1867

| Term of office | Governor General | Term | Prime Minister | Party |
|---|---|---|---|---|
| 1867–1868 | Viscount Monck[1] | 1867–1873 | Sir John A. Macdonald | Conservative |
| 1869–1872 | Baron Lisgar | 1873–1878 | Alexander Mackenzie | Liberal |
| 1872–1878 | Earl of Dufferin | 1878–1891 | Sir John A. Macdonald | Conservative |
| 1878–1883 | Marquess of Lorne | 1891–1892 | Sir John J. C. Abbott | Conservative |
| 1883–1888 | Marquess of Lansdowne | 1892–1894 | Sir John S. D. Thompson | Conservative |
| 1888–1893 | Baron Stanley of Preston | 1894–1896 | Sir Mackenzie Bowell | Conservative |
| 1893–1898 | Earl of Aberdeen | 1896 | Sir Charles Tupper | Conservative |
| 1898–1904 | Earl of Minto | 1896–1911 | Sir Wilfrid Laurier | Liberal |
| 1904–1911 | Earl Grey | 1911–1917 | Sir Robert L. Borden | Conservative |
| 1911–1916 | Duke of Connaught | 1917–1920 | Sir Robert L. Borden | Unionist |
| 1916–1921 | Duke of Devonshire | 1920–1921 | Arthur Meighen | Unionist |
| 1921–1926 | Baron Byng of Vimy | 1921–1926 | W. L. Mackenzie King | Liberal |
| 1926–1931 | Viscount Willingdon | 1926 | Arthur Meighen | Conservative |
| 1931–1935 | Earl of Bessborough | 1926–1930 | W. L. Mackenzie King | Liberal |
| 1935–1940 | Baron Tweedsmuir | 1930–1935 | Richard B. Bennett | Conservative |
| 1940–1946 | Earl of Athlone | 1935–1948 | W. L. Mackenzie King | Liberal |
| 1946–1952 | Viscount Alexander | 1948–1957 | Louis S. St. Laurent | Liberal |
| 1952–1959 | Vincent Massey | 1957–1963 | John G. Diefenbaker | Progressive-Conservative |
| 1959–1967 | George P. Vanier | | | |
| 1967–1973 | Roland Michener | 1963–1968 | Lester B. Pearson | Liberal |
| 1974– | Jules Léger | 1968– | Pierre Elliott Trudeau | Liberal |

1. Became Governor General of British North America in 1861.

sands of British colonists emigrated to Canada from the British Isles and from the American colonies. In 1849 the right of Canada to self-government was recognized. By the British North America Act of 1867, the Dominion of Canada was created through the confederation of Upper and Lower Canada, Nova Scotia, and New Brunswick. Prince Edward Island joined the Dominion in 1873. In 1869 Canada had purchased from the Hudson's Bay Company the vast middle west (Rupert's Land) from which the provinces of Manitoba (1870), Alberta, and Saskatchewan (1905) were later formed. In 1871, British Columbia joined the Dominion. The country was linked from coast to coast in 1885 by the Canadian Pacific Railway.

During the formative years between 1866 and 1896, the Conservative Party, led by Sir John A. Macdonald, governed the country, except during the years 1873–78. In 1896, the Liberal Party took over and, under Sir Wilfrid Laurier, an eminent French Canadian, ruled until 1911.

In World War I, more than 500,000 Canadian soldiers fought for the Allied cause. After the Treaty of Versailles, Canada, a full-fledged nation, was admitted to the League of Nations and appointed its own representatives in foreign countries. By the Statute of Westminster (1931) the British Dominions, including Canada, were formally declared to be partner nations with Britian, "equal in status, in no way subordinate to each other," and bound together only by allegiance to a common crown.

Newfoundland became Canada's 10th province on March 31, 1949, following a plebiscite. Besides the provinces, Canada includes two territories—the Yukon Territory, the area north of British Columbia and east of Alaska, and the Northwest Territories, including all of Canada north of 60° North latitude except Yukon and the northernmost sections of Quebec and Newfoundland. This area includes all of the Arctic north of the mainland, Norway having recognized Canadian sovereignty over the Svendrup Islands in the Arctic in 1931.

The Liberal Party of Sir Wilfrid Laurier and William Lyon Mackenzie King, Prime Minister in 1935–48, remained in power until 1957, when it was succeeded by the Progressive Conservatives. The Liberals, under the leadership of Lester B. Pearson, returned to power in 1963. Pearson remained Prime Minister until 1968, when he retired at 71, and was replaced as party leader and Prime Minister by a former law professor, Pierre Elliott Trudeau. Trudeau maintained Canada's defensive alliance with the United States, but began moving toward a more independent policy in world affairs.

Trudeau set about creating what he termed a "just society," stressing domestic reforms. Trudeau's election was considered in part a response to the most serious problem confronting the country, the division between French- and English-speaking Canadians, which had led to a separatist movement in the predominantly French province of Quebec. Trudeau, himself a French Canadian, supported programs for bilingualism and an increased measure of provincial autonomy, although he would not tolerate the idea of separatism. In July 1974 the provincial government voted to make French the official language of Quebec.

Capturing the Quebec provincial government from the long-entrenched local Liberal Party, René Lévesque and his separatist Parti Québécois pledged that they would seek independence for the province. He shocked English-speaking Canadians with a New York speech two months after his election in which he said the question was not when but *how* Quebec would attain independence. Early in November 1977, he paid an official visit to France, telling French legislators that "a new country will soon appear democratically on the map."

Conflicts over the law establishing French as the dominant language in Quebec, particularly in schooling, kept separatism as a national issue, but by-elections in May 1977 produced easy victories for Trudeau's ruling Liberals in four Quebec seats in the national legislature and polls showed a decline in separatist support both in the province and elsewhere in Canada. In an interview on Jan. 1,

1978, Trudeau declared that he would use force to prevent any illegal declaration of independence by Lévesque.

Economic problems appeared to take precedence over politics in 1978, as the Sun Life Assurance Company of Canada, the nation's largest insurance firm, announced in January that it would move its headquarters from Montreal to Toronto. Many businesses had left the province earlier, but Sun Life was the first to cite the language law as the reason for its departure.

Trudeau met with the 10 provincial Premiers in Ottawa in February to discuss an 8% unemployment rate and an inflation rate of over 9%. He removed unpopular wage and price controls instituted in 1975 and claimed improvement, but his concern over the economy was believed to have dictated an announcement on May 11 that elections would be postponed, probably until 1979. No Canadian government since 1935 has exercised its constitutional right to a full five-year term, the custom being to go to the polls within four years of the most recent vote.

On June 12, Trudeau presented proposals for a new constitution to replace the 111-year-old British North America Act by 1981. He offered to share with provincial governments the appointment of members of the federal Supreme Court and Senate. Without specifics, he also suggested a re-division of other powers, reopening an old and unresolved conflict between Ottawa and the provinces. Lévesque denounced Trudeau's initiative in advance of its disclosure.

Trudeau's first three national elections ranged from his "Trudeaumania" triumph in 1968 to near defeat in 1972 and strong recovery in 1974. Despite his long tenure, he remains an enigmatic figure. The request of his young wife, Margaret, for a separation in May 1977, leaving him with custody of their three sons, brought a wave of public sympathy for him, countering to some extent the loss of support he suffered because of the nation's economic problems.

U.S.-Canadian relations, strained during the 1974 energy crisis when Canada increased its oil export prices and restricted gas supplies to the U.S., improved with the visit of U.S. Vice President Walter F. Mondale in January 1978. The gas freeze was ended in exchange for a Canadian option to buy U.S. Alaskan gas on completion of the Alcan pipeline. The U.S. also increased duty-free allowances for U.S. tourists returning from Canada and eased the restriction on tax benefits for Americans attending conventions in Canada.

**Economy.** Agriculture, including horticulture, fruit growing, and the raising of stock and poultry, is the largest single industry. Canada is one of the world's greatest wheat-exporting countries; production is concentrated in Manitoba, Saskatchewan, and Alberta.

Stock raising and dairy farming have grown greatly since 1920. Ontario and Quebec are the most important dairying provinces.

Canadian manufactures rely mainly on domestic raw materials; growing industries that depend largely on material imported in a raw or semifinished state include the manufacture of automobiles, sugar, and rubber goods, as well as the iron and steel industry in Nova Scotia, Quebec, and Ontario. The latter two provinces account for more than 80% of all manufactures. The abundance of cheap water power is one of the chief factors in the growth of Canadian industry.

The most important industries in terms of output are pulp and paper, nonferrous-metals smelting and refining, petroleum products, meatpacking, motor vehicles, and sawmill products.

Canada's mineral resources are both rich and varied. Metals come mainly from two widely separated regions, the mountain ranges of the Pacific coast and the province of Ontario. Copper ore also exists in Quebec, Manitoba, and Newfoundland. Production of petroleum centers in Alberta. There are deposits of uranium in the Northwest Territories.

The total area of land covered by forests is estimated at 1,300,000 square miles (3,367,000 sq km), of which only 435,000 square miles (1,126,650 sq km) are commercially productive and accessible. The manufacture of pulp and paper is one of the leading industries.

Fishing, Canada's oldest industry, is carried on along the Atlantic and Pacific coasts and on the inland lakes.

Chief exports in 1976 were motor vehicles (22%), metal ores (7%), crude oil (6%), wood pulp (6%), aluminum (6%), newsprint (5%), and wheat

## Provinces and Territories

| | Land area sq mi. | Population (1976 census) | Capital | Premier 1978 |
|---|---|---|---|---|
| **PROVINCES** | | | | |
| Alberta | 255,285 | 1,799,771 | Edmonton | E. Peter Lougheed[1] |
| British Columbia | 366,255 | 2,406,212 | Victoria | William R. Bennett[2] |
| Manitoba | 251,000 | 1,005,953 | Winnipeg | Edward Schreyer[3] |
| New Brunswick | 28,354 | 664,525 | Fredericton | Richard B. Hatfield[1] |
| Newfoundland | 156,185 | 548,789 | St. John's | Frank D. Moores[1] |
| Nova Scotia | 21,425 | 812,127 | Halifax | Gerald A. Regan[4] |
| Ontario | 412,582 | 8,131,618 | Toronto | William G. Davis[1] |
| Prince Edward Island | 2,184 | 116,251 | Charlottetown | Alexander B. Campbell[4] |
| Quebec | 594,860 | 6,141,491 | Quebec | René Lévesque[5] |
| Saskatchewan | 251,700 | 907,650 | Regina | A. E. Blakeney[3] |
| **TERRITORIES** | | | | |
| Northwest Territories | 1,304,903 | 42,237 | Yellowknife | Stuart M. Hodgson[6] |
| Yukon Territory | 207,076 | 21,392 | Whitehorse | A. M. Pearson[6] |

1. Progressive Conservative. 2. Social Credit. 3. New Democratic Party. 4. Liberal. 5. Parti Québécois. 6. Commissioner.

(5%). Leading customers were U.S. (68%), EEC (12%; incl. U.K. 5%), Japan (6%). Leading suppliers were U.S. (69%), EEC (9%).

In 1978, Canada's inflation rate was 9.2% and unemployment reached 8.6%, a post-Depression record. These figures, heavy budget deficits, and a drop in the value of the Canadian dollar prompted Prime Minister Trudeau on August 1 to promise a $2-billion cut in government spending, tax cuts, and other measures to stimulate the Canadian economy.

## Government of Canada

**Governor General and Commander-in-Chief:** His Excellency The Right Honourable Jules Léger, C.C., C.M.M., C.D.

### GOVERNOR GENERAL'S HOUSEHOLD

**Secretary to the Governor General and Secretary General of the Order of Canada, and Secretary General of the Order of Military Merit:** Esmond U. Butler, Esq., C.V.O.
**Comptroller of the Household:** D. C. McKinnon, C.V.O., C.D.
**Director of Honors:** Roger de C. Nantel, Esq., C.D.
**Administrative Secretary:** Edmond A. C. Joly de Lotbinière
**Cultural Advisor to the Governor General:** Robert H. Hubbard
**Press Secretary to the Governor General:** Gerald B. McDuff

### THE CANADIAN MINISTRY

**Prime Minister:** The Rt. Hon. Pierre Elliott Trudeau
**President of the Queen's Privy Council for Canada:** The Hon. Allan J. MacEachen
**Minister of Finance:** The Hon. Jean Chrétien
**Minister of Labor:** The Hon. John Munro
**Minister of Justice and Attorney General:** The Hon. Stanley Ronald Basford
**Secretary of State for External Affairs:** The Hon. Donald D. Jamieson
**President of the Treasury Bd.:** The Hon. Robert K. Andras
**Minister of Transport:** The Hon. Otto Lang
**Minister of Supply and Services:** The Hon. Jean-Pierre Goyer
**Minister of Energy, Mines, and Resources:** The Hon. Alastair W. Gillespie
**Minister of Agriculture:** The Hon. Eugene F. Whelan
**Minister of Consumer and Corporate Affairs:** The Hon. Warren Allmand
**Minister of Indian Affairs and Northern Development:** The Hon. J. Hugh Faulkner
**Minister of State for Urban Affairs:** The Hon. André Ouellet
**Minister of Veterans Affairs:** The Hon. Daniel J. MacDonald
**Minister of National Revenue:** The Hon. Joseph Guay
**Minister of Communications:** The Hon. Jeanne Sauvé
**Leader of the Government in the Senate:** The Hon. Raymond J. Perrault
**Minister of National Defense:** The Hon. Barnett J. Danson
**Minister of Public Works, and Minister of State for Science and Technology:** The Hon. J. Judd Buchanan
**Minister of Fisheries and the Environment:** The Hon. Roméo LeBlanc
**Minister of Regional Economic Expansion:** The Hon. Marcel Lessard
**Minister of Employment & Immigration:** The Hon. Jack S. G. Cullen
**Minister of State (Environment):** The Hon. Leonard S. Marchand
**Secretary of State:** The Hon. John Roberts
**Minister of National Health and Welfare:** The Hon. Monique Begin
**Postmaster General:** The Hon. Jean Jacques Blais
**Solicitor General:** The Hon. Francis Fox
**Minister of State (Small Businesses):** The Hon. Anthony Abbott
**Minister of State (Fitness & Amateur Sport):** The Hon. Iona Campagnolo
**Minister of National Revenue:** The Hon. Joseph Guay
**Ministry of Industry, Trade, and Commerce:** The Hon. Jack Horner
**Minister of State for Multiculturalism:** The Hon. Norman Cafik

### PARLIAMENTARY SECRETARIES

**To President of the Privy Council:** Yvon Pinard
**To Minister of Industry, Trade, and Commerce:** Bernard Loiselle
**To Minister of Finance:** Edward Lumley
**To Minister of Labor:** Jacques Olivier
**To Minister of Justice and Attorney General:** Roger Young
**To Secretary of State for External Affairs:** Maurice Dupras
**To President of the Treasury Bd.:** Thomas Lefebvre
**To Minister of National Defense:** Jacques Guilbault
**To Minister of Transport:** Charles Lapointe
**To Minister of Supply and Services:** Aideen Nicholson
**To Minister of Agriculture:** Yves Caron
**To Minister of Indian Affairs and Northern Development:** Ross Milne
**To Minister of Veterans Affairs:** Gilbert Parent
**To Minister of National Health and Welfare:** Kenneth Robinson
**To Minister of Communications:** Crawford Douglas
**To Minister of State for Urban Affairs:** Maurice Harquail
**To Minister of Public Works and Minister of State for Science and Technology:** Frank Maine
**To Minister of Fisheries and the Environment:** Hugh Anderson
**To Minister of Regional Economic Expansion:** Donald Wood
**To Minister of Employment and Immigration:** Raymond Dupont
**To Secretary of State for Canada:** Robert Daudlin
**To Minister of National Revenue:** Yves Demers
**To Solicitor General:** Rod Blaker
**To Minister of Consumer and Corporate Affairs:** Alan Martin
**To Minister of State (Environment):** Michael Landers
**To Minister of State (Multiculturalism):** William Andres
**To Minister of Energy, Mines, and Resources:** Gilles Lamontagne

## Fathers of Confederation

Three conferences helped to pave the way for Confederation—those held at Charlottetown (September 1864), Quebec City (October 1864), and London (December 1866). As all the delegates who were at the Charlottetown conferences were also in attendance at Quebec, the following list includes the names of all those who attended one or more of the three conferences.

### Delegates to the Confederation Conferences, 1864–1866

**Legend:**
Charlottetown, September 1, 1864 — C
Quebec, October 10, 1864 — Q
London, December 4, 1866 — L

| | | | |
|---|---|---|---|
| **Canada** | | | |
| John A. Macdonald | C | Q | L |
| George E. Cartier | C | Q | L |
| Alexander T. Galt | C | Q | L |
| William McDougall | C | Q | L |
| Hector L. Langevin | C | Q | L |
| George Brown | C | Q | |
| Thomas D'Arcy McGee | C | Q | |
| Alexander Campbell | C | Q | |
| Sir Etienne P. Taché | | Q | |
| Oliver Mowat | | Q | |
| J. C. Chapais | | Q | |
| James Cockburn | | Q | |
| W. P. Howland | | | L |
| Hewitt Bernard[1] | | | |
| **Nova Scotia** | | | |
| Charles Tupper | C | Q | L |
| William A. Henry | C | Q | L |
| Jonathan McCully | C | Q | L |
| Adams G. Archibald | C | Q | L |
| Robert B. Dickey | | Q | |
| J. W. Ritchie | | | L |
| **New Brunswick** | | | |
| Samuel L. Tilley | C | Q | L |
| J. M. Johnson | C | Q | L |
| William H. Steeves | C | Q | |
| E. B. Chandler | C | Q | |
| John Hamilton Gray | C | Q | |
| Peter Mitchell | | Q | L |
| Charles Fisher | | Q | L |
| R. D. Wilmot | | | L |
| **Prince Edward Island** | | | |
| John Hamilton Gray | C | Q | |
| Edward Palmer | C | Q | |
| William H. Pope | C | Q | |
| A. A. Macdonald | C | Q | |
| George Coles | C | Q | |
| T. H. Haviland | | Q | |
| Edward Whelan | | Q | |
| **Newfoundland** | | | |
| F. B. T. Carter | | Q | |
| Ambrose Shea | | Q | |

1. Hewitt Bernard was John A. Macdonald's private secretary. He served as secretary of both the Quebec and London conferences.

## Floral Emblems

**Alberta:** Wild Rose *(Rosa acicularis).* Chosen in the Floral Emblem Act of 1930.
**British Columbia:** Dogwood (*Cornus nuttallii,* Audubon). Adopted under the Floral Emblem Act, 1956.
**Manitoba:** Pasque Flower, known locally as Prairie Crocus *(Anemone patens).* Adopted 1906.
**New Brunswick:** Purple Violet *(Viola cuculata).* Adopted by Order-in-Council, Dec. 1, 1936, at the request of the New Brunswick Women's Institute.
**Newfoundland:** Pitcher Plant *(Sarracenia purpurea).* Adopted in June 1954.
**Nova Scotia:** Trailing Arbutus, also known as Mayflower *(Epigaea repens).* Adopted in April 1901.
**Ontario:** White Trillium *(Trillium grandiflorum).* Adopted March 25, 1937.
**Prince Edward Island:** Lady's Slipper *(Cypripedium acaule).* Designated as the province's floral emblem by the Legislative Assembly in 1947. A more precise botanical name was included in an amendment to the Floral Emblem Act in 1965.
**Quebec:** White Garden (Madonna) Lily *(Lilium candidum).* Adopted in January 1963.
**Saskatchewan:** Wild Wood Lily *(Lilium philadelphicum andinum),* also known as Prairie Lily. Adopted April 8, 1941.
**Northwest Territories:** Mountain Avens *(Dryan integrifolia).* Adopted by the Council on June 7, 1959.
**Yukon Territory:** Fireweed *(Epilobium angustifolium).* Adopted Nov. 16, 1957.

## National Flag

The National Flag of Canada, otherwise known as the Canadian Flag, was approved by Parliament and proclaimed by Her Majesty the Queen on February 15, 1965, and is described as a red flag of the proportions two by length and one by width, containing in its center a white square the width of the flag, bearing a single red maple leaf.

The Flag is flown on land daily from sunrise to sunset at all federal government buildings, airports, and military bases and establishments within and outside Canada, and may appropriately be flown or displayed by individuals and organizations.

The Canada Shipping Act provides that the National Flag is the proper national colors for all Canadian ships and boats; and it is the flag flown on Canadian Naval vessels.

## Armorial Bearings of Canada, Authorized 1957

The arms are those of England, Scotland, Ireland, and France, with a "difference" to mark them as Canadian, namely, on the lower third of the shield, a sprig of maple on a silver shield. The crest is a lion holding in its paw a red maple leaf, a symbol of sacrifice. The supporters are, with some slight distinctions, the lion and unicorn of the Royal Arms; the lion upholds the Union Jack and the unicorn the ancient banner of France.

The motto—*A mari usque ad mare* ("From sea to sea")—is from the Latin version of Psalm LXXII: 8: "He shall have dominion also from sea to sea, and from the river unto the ends of the earth."

## Provinces and Territories of Canada, Dates of Admission to Confederation, and Legislative Processes by Which Admission Was Effected

| Province, territory, or district | Date of admission or creation | Legislative process |
|---|---|---|
| Ontario | July 1, 1867 | Act of Imperial Parliament—The British North America Act, 1867 (Br. Stat 1867, c. 3) and Imperial Order in Council, May 22, 1867 |
| Quebec | July 1, 1867 | |
| Nova Scotia | July 1, 1867 | |
| New Brunswick | July 1, 1867 | |
| Manitoba | July 15, 1870 | Manitoba Act, 1870 (SC 1870, C. 3) and Imperial Order in Council, June 23, 1870 |
| British Columbia | July 20, 1871 | Imperial Order in Council, May 16, 1871 |
| Prince Edward Island | July 1, 1873 | Imperial Order in Council, June 26, 1873 |
| Saskatchewan | Sept. 1, 1905 | Saskatchewan Act, 1905 (SC 1905, C. 42) |
| Alberta | Sept. 1, 1905 | Alberta Act, 1905 (SC 1905, C. 3) |
| Newfoundland | March 31, 1949 | The British North America Act, 1949 (Br. Stat. 1949, c. 22) |
| Northwest Territories | July 15, 1870 | Act of Imperial Parliament—Rupert's Land Act, 1868 (Br. Stat. 1868, c. 105) and Imperial Order in Council, June 23, 1870 |
| Mackenzie | Jan. 1, 1920 | |
| Keewatin | Jan. 1, 1920 | Order in Council, March 16, 1918 |
| Franklin | Jan. 1, 1920 | |
| Yukon Territory | June 13, 1898 | Yukon Territory Act, 1898 (SC 1898, c. 6) |

## Population of Canada by Provinces and Territories

| Province | 1978 (Estimate) | 1971 (Census) | 1961 (Census) | 1951 (Census) | 1941 (Census) |
|---|---|---|---|---|---|
| Alberta | 1,948,000 | 1,627,874 | 1,331,944 | 939,501 | 796,169 |
| British Columbia | 2,530,100 | 2,184,621 | 1,629,082 | 1,165,210 | 817,861 |
| Manitoba | 1,036,000 | 988,247 | 921,686 | 776,541 | 729,744 |
| New Brunswick | 693,200 | 634,557 | 597,936 | 515,697 | 457,401 |
| Newfoundland | 565,200 | 522,104 | 457,853 | 361,416 | |
| Nova Scotia | 840,700 | 788,960 | 737,007 | 642,584 | 577,962 |
| Ontario | 8,460,900 | 7,703,106 | 6,236,092 | 4,597,542 | 3,787,655 |
| Prince Edward Island | 122,200 | 111,641 | 104,629 | 98,429 | 95,047 |
| Quebec | 6,290,000 | 6,027,764 | 5,259,211 | 4,055,681 | 3,331,882 |
| Saskatchewan | 945,600 | 926,242 | 925,181 | 831,728 | 895,992 |
| Northwest Territories | 43,700 | 34,807 | 22,998 | 16,004 | 12,028 |
| Yukon Territory | 22,100 | 18,388 | 14,628 | 9,096 | 4,914 |
| **Total** | **23,497,700** | **21,568,311** | **18,238,247** | **14,009,429** | **11,506,655** |
| Rural | — | 5,157,525 | 5,537,857 | 5,381,176 | 5,254,239 |
| Urban | — | 16,410,785 | 12,700,390 | 8,628,253 | 6,252,416 |

## Percentage Distribution of Canadian Population by Provinces and Territories

| Province or territory | 1971 | 1961 | 1951 | 1941 | 1931 | 1911 | 1901 |
|---|---|---|---|---|---|---|---|
| Alberta | 7.55 | 7.30 | 6.71 | 6.92 | 7.05 | 5.19 | 1.36 |
| British Columbia | 10.13 | 8.93 | 8.32 | 7.11 | 6.69 | 5.45 | 3.33 |
| Manitoba | 4.58 | 5.05 | 5.54 | 6.34 | 6.75 | 6.40 | 4.75 |
| New Brunswick | 2.94 | 3.28 | 3.68 | 3.97 | 3.94 | 4.88 | 6.16 |
| Newfoundland | 2.42 | 2.51 | 2.58 | — | — | — | — |
| Nova Scotia | 3.66 | 4.04 | 4.59 | 5.02 | 4.94 | 6.83 | 8.56 |
| Ontario | 35.71 | 34.19 | 32.82 | 32.92 | 33.07 | 35.07 | 40.64 |
| Prince Edward Island | 0.52 | 0.58 | 0.70 | 0.83 | 0.85 | 1.30 | 1.92 |
| Quebec | 27.95 | 28.84 | 28.95 | 28.96 | 27.70 | 27.83 | 30.70 |
| Saskatchewan | 4.29 | 5.07 | 5.94 | 7.79 | 8.88 | 6.84 | 1.70 |
| Northwest Territories | 0.16 | 0.13 | 0.11 | 0.10 | 0.09 | 0.09 | 0.37 |
| Yukon Territory | 0.09 | 0.08 | 0.06 | 0.04 | 0.04 | 0.12 | 0.51 |
| **Totals** | **100.00** | **100.00** | **100.00** | **100.00** | **100.00** | **100.00** | **100.00** |

## Growth Components of Canada's Population

| Period | Total population growth (thousands) | Births (thousands) | Deaths (thousands) | Natural increase (thousands) | Ratio of natural increase to total growth (percent) | Immigration (thousands) | Emigration (thousands) | Net migration (thousands) | Ratio of net migration to total growth (percent) |
|---|---|---|---|---|---|---|---|---|---|
| 1851–1861 | 793 | 1,281 | 670 | 611 | 77.0 | 352 | 170 | 182 | 23.0 |
| 1861–1871 | 460 | 1,370 | 760 | 610 | 132.6 | 260 | 410 | −150 | −32.6 |
| 1871–1881 | 636 | 1,480 | 790 | 690 | 108.5 | 350 | 404 | −54 | −8.5 |
| 1881–1891 | 508 | 1,524 | 870 | 654 | 128.7 | 680 | 826 | −146 | −28.7 |
| 1891–1901 | 538 | 1,548 | 880 | 668 | 124.2 | 250 | 380 | −130 | −24.2 |
| 1901–1911 | 1,835 | 1,925 | 900 | 1,025 | 55.9 | 1,550 | 740 | 810 | 44.1 |
| 1911–1921 | 1,581 | 2,340 | 1,070 | 1,270 | 80.3 | 1,400 | 1,089 | 311 | 19.7 |
| 1921–1931 | 1,589 | 2,420 | 1,060 | 1,360 | 85.5 | 1,200 | 970 | 230 | 14.5 |
| 1931–1941 | 1,130 | 2,294 | 1,072 | 1,222 | 108.1 | 149 | 241 | −92 | −8.1 |
| 1941–1951[1] | 2,503 | 3,212 | 1,220 | 1,992 | 92.3 | 548 | 382 | 166 | 7.7 |
| 1951–1961 | 4,228 | 4,468 | 1,320 | 3,148 | 74.5 | 1,543 | 463 | 1,080 | 25.5 |
| 1961–1971 | 3,330 | 4,105 | 1,497 | 2,608 | 78.3 | 1,429 | 707 | 722 | 21.7 |

1. Includes Newfoundland in 1951 but not in 1941.

## Party Standings—House of Commons

**Thirtieth Parliament—Speaker, Hon. James Jerome; The Clerk of the House of Commons, Alistair Fraser**

| Province | Lib.[1] | P.C.[2] | N.D.P.[3] | S.Cr.[4] | Ind. | Vacancies | Seats by provinces |
|---|---|---|---|---|---|---|---|
| Alberta | 1 | 17 | — | — | 1 | — | 19 |
| British Columbia | 8 | 12 | 2 | — | — | 1 | 23 |
| Manitoba | — | 9 | 2 | — | 1 | 1 | 13 |
| New Brunswick | 6 | 2 | — | — | 1 | 1 | 10 |
| Newfoundland | 4 | 2 | — | — | — | 1 | 7 |
| Nova Scotia | 2 | 7 | 1 | — | — | 1 | 11 |
| Ontario | 49 | 25 | 7 | — | — | 7 | 88 |
| Prince Edward Island | 2 | 2 | — | — | — | — | 4 |
| Quebec | 59 | 2 | — | 8 | 2 | 3 | 74 |
| Saskatchewan | 3 | 8 | 2 | — | — | — | 13 |
| Northwest Territories | — | — | 1 | — | — | — | 1 |
| Yukon Territory | — | 1 | — | — | — | — | 1 |
| **National totals** | **134** | **87** | **15** | **8** | **5** | **15** | **264** |

1. Liberal Party—Leader, Rt. Hon. Pierre Elliott Trudeau. 2. Progressive Conservative Party—Leader, Joseph Clark. 3. New Democratic Party—Leader, John Edward Broadbent. 4. Social Credit Party—C. A. Gauthier, Parliamentary Leader. NOTE: Last three General Elections were held on June 25, 1968, October 30, 1972, and July 8, 1974. The legal duration is five years.

## Growth Statistics
(in Canadian dollars)

| Year | Exports (including re-exports (millions of dollars) | Imports (millions of dollars) | Wholesale prices index no. 1935–39 = 100 | Railway gross revenues[1] (millions of dollars) | Railway operating expenses[1] (millions of dollars) | Tons of revenue freight carried one mile[1] (millions) | Freight carried on welland canal (thousands of tons) | Vessels other than coastal entered & cleared (thousands of reg net tons) |
|---|---|---|---|---|---|---|---|---|
| 1881 | n.a. | n.a. | 72.4 | $ 28 | $ 20 | n.a. | 687 | 13,802 |
| 1891 | n.a. | n.a. | 67.1 | 48 | 35 | n.a. | 975 | 18,803 |
| 1901 | n.a. | n.a. | 63.7 | 73 | 50 | n.a. | 620 | 26,030 |
| 1911 | n.a. | n.a. | 81.1 | 189 | 131 | 16,048 | 2,538 | 47,430 |
| 1921 | $ 814 | $ 799 | 143.4 | 458 | 423 | 26,622 | 3,076 | 54,649 |
| 1941 | 1,640 | 1,449 | 116.4 | 538 | 404 | 49,982 | 13,230 | 64,766 |
| 1951 | 3,963 | 4,085 | 240.2 | 1,089 | 978 | 64,300 | 16,198 | 100,259 |
| 1961 | 5,896 | 5,771 | 223.3 | 1,156 | 1,053 | 65,828 | 31,404 | 156,987 |
| 1965 | 8,767 | 8,633 | 250.4 | 1,369 | 1,288 | 87,052 | 53,437 | 199,454 |
| 1966 | 10,326 | 9,866 | 259.5 | 1,476 | 1,367 | 94,944 | 59,137 | 202,170 |
| 1967 | 11,411 | 11,075 | 264.1 | 1,514 | 1,438 | 92,239 | 52,850 | 197,422 |
| 1968 | 13,624 | 12,358 | 269.9 | 1,528 | 1,433 | 93,147 | 58,105 | 204,777 |
| 1969 | 14,890 | 14,130 | 282.4 | 1,579 | 1,496 | 94,688 | 53,532 | 197,391 |
| 1970 | 16,819 | 13,952 | 286.4 | 1,672 | 1,570 | 108,210 | 62,963 | 217,621 |
| 1971 | 17,820 | 15,618 | 289.9 | 1,797 | 1,693 | 119,412 | 63,058 | 228,561 |
| 1972 | 20,140 | 18,669 | 310.3 | 1,843 | 1,750 | 119,135 | 64,194 | 243,376 |
| 1973 | 25,301 | 23,303 | 376.9 | 2,029 | 1,935 | 125,471 | 67,195 | 244,466 |
| 1974 | 32,177 | 31,639 | 461.3 | 2,476 | 2,394 | 133,554 | 52,360 | 227,175 |
| 1975 | 32,755 | 34,668 | 491.3 | 2,618 | 2,668 | 130,997 | 59,849 | 231,345 |
| 1976 | 38,028 | 37,391 | 512.6 | 3,058 | 2,927 | 132,589 | 64,340 | — |

1. Six major railways, representing 97% of the industry in terms of ton miles, account for 95% of revenues and operate 94% of first main track mileage. NOTE: n.a. = not available.

## Growth Statistics
(in Canadian dollars)

| Year | Motor vehicle regis-trations (thousands) | Tele-phones in use (thousands) | Post office and money order revenue (thousands) | Index numbers of weekly earnings 1961 = 100 | Strikes and lockouts: Em-ployees affected (thousands) | Strikes and lockouts: Time lost working days (thousands) | Federal finance: Total revenue (millions of dollars) | Federal finance: Total expendi-ture (millions of dollars) | Federal finance: Net debt (millions of dollars) |
|---|---|---|---|---|---|---|---|---|---|
| 1881 | n.a. | n.a. | 1,345 | n.a. | n.a. | n.a. | $ 30 | $ 34 | $ 155 |
| 1891 | n.a. | n.a. | 2,516 | n.a. | n.a. | n.a. | 39 | 41 | 238 |
| 1901 | n.a. | n.a. | 3,421 | n.a. | 24 | 738 | 53 | 58 | 268 |
| 1911 | 22 | 303 | 9,147 | n.a. | 29 | 1,821 | 118 | 123 | 340 |
| 1921 | 465 | 902 | 26,331 | n.a. | 28 | 1,049 | 436 | 528 | 2,341 |
| 1931 | 1,201 | 1,364 | 30,416 | n.a. | 11 | 204 | 356 | 442 | 2,262 |
| 1941 | 1,573 | 1,562 | 40,383 | 34.1 | 87 | 434 | 872 | 1,250 | 3,649 |
| 1951 | 2,872 | 3,114 | 90,455 | 64.0 | 103 | 902 | 3,113 | 2,901 | 11,645 |
| 1961 | 5,517 | 6,014 | 202,004 | 100.0 | 98 | 1,335 | 5,618 | 5,958 | 12,437 |
| 1965 | 6,669 | 7,445 | 263,704 | 116.2 | 172 | 2,350 | 7,180 | 7,218 | 15,504 |
| 1966 | 7,035 | 7,883 | 275,994 | 127.8 | 411 | 5,178 | 7,696 | 7,735 | 15,543 |
| 1967 | 7,482 | 8,358 | 295,529 | 130.6 | 252 | 3,975 | 8,358 | 8,780 | 15,965 |
| 1968 | 7,877 | 8,818 | 337,023 | 140.3 | 224 | 5,083 | 9,029 | 9,824 | 16,760 |
| 1969 | 8,254 | 9,296 | 374,902 | 150.8 | 307 | 7,752 | 10,163 | 11,938 | 17,336 |
| 1970 | 8,497 | 9,750 | 444,069 | 162.8 | 262 | 6,540 | 12,321 | 11,928 | 16,943 |
| 1971 | 9,022 | 10,269 | 432,911 | 176.7 | 240 | 2,867 | 12,803 | 13,182 | 17,322 |
| 1972 | 9,481 | 10,987 | 504,211 | 191.4 | 706 | 7,754 | 14,227 | 14,841 | 17,937 |
| 1973 | 10,158 | 11,677 | 563,159 | 205.4 | 348 | 5,776 | 16,602 | 16,121 | 17,456 |
| 1974 | 11,002 | 12,454 | 591,133 | 227.6 | 592 | 9,255 | 19,383 | 20,056 | 18,128 |
| 1975 | 11,443 | 13,165 | 617,743 | 261.7 | 479 | 10,859 | 24,909 | 26,055 | 19,275 |
| 1976 | n.a. | n.a. | 568,190 | 295.8 | 741 | 10,821 | 29,956 | 33,978 | 23,296 |

NOTE: n.a. = not available.

## Canadian Consumer Price Index
(1971 = 100)

| Year | Food | Housing | Clothing | Trans-portation | Health and personal care | Recreation and reading | Tobacco and alcohol | All-item index |
|---|---|---|---|---|---|---|---|---|
| 1961 | 76.1 | 73.1 | 77.7 | 77.0 | 70.2 | 73.7 | 77.8 | 75.0 |
| 1962 | 77.5 | 74.0 | 78.4 | 76.9 | 71.6 | 74.3 | 78.8 | 75.9 |
| 1963 | 80.0 | 74.8 | 80.3 | 76.9 | 73.5 | 75.4 | 78.9 | 77.2 |
| 1964 | 81.3 | 76.0 | 82.4 | 77.8 | 75.8 | 76.6 | 80.4 | 78.6 |
| 1965 | 83.4 | 77.3 | 83.8 | 80.7 | 79.4 | 77.9 | 81.7 | 80.5 |
| 1966 | 88.7 | 79.5 | 87.0 | 82.6 | 81.8 | 80.1 | 83.7 | 83.5 |
| 1967 | 89.9 | 82.9 | 91.4 | 86.1 | 86.0 | 84.1 | 85.8 | 86.5 |
| 1968 | 92.8 | 86.7 | 94.1 | 88.3 | 89.5 | 88.3 | 93.6 | 90.0 |
| 1969 | 96.7 | 91.2 | 96.7 | 92.4 | 93.8 | 93.5 | 97.2 | 94.1 |
| 1970 | 98.9 | 95.7 | 98.5 | 96.1 | 98.0 | 96.8 | 98.4 | 97.2 |
| 1971 | 100.0 | 100.0 | 100.0 | 100.0 | 100.0 | 100.0 | 100.0 | 100.0 |
| 1972 | 107.6 | 104.7 | 102.6 | 102.6 | 104.8 | 102.8 | 102.7 | 104.8 |
| 1973 | 123.3 | 111.4 | 107.7 | 105.3 | 109.8 | 107.1 | 106.0 | 112.7 |
| 1974 | 143.4 | 121.1 | 118.0 | 115.8 | 119.4 | 116.4 | 111.8 | 125.0 |
| 1975 | 161.9 | 133.2 | 125.1 | 129.4 | 133.0 | 128.5 | 125.3 | 138.5 |
| 1976 | 166.2 | 145.7 | 132.0 | 143.3 | 144.3 | 136.2 | 134.3 | 148.9 |
| 1977 | 180.1 | 161.9 | 141.0 | 153.3 | 155.1 | 142.7 | 143.8 | 160.8 |
| April 1978 | 200.4 | 171.3 | 143.2 | 159.8 | 163.3 | 145.8 | 154.0 | 171.2 |

## Estimates of the Civilian Labor Force and Its Main Components, Annual Averages
(in thousands)

| Year | Civilian population[1] | Civilian labor force[1] | | | Persons not in the labor force[1] | Unemployment rate percent | Participation rate percent |
|---|---|---|---|---|---|---|---|
| | | Employed | Unemployed | Total labor force | | | |
| 1965 | 13,128 | 6,862 | 280 | 7,141 | 5,986 | 3.9 | 54.4 |
| 1966 | 13,475 | 7,152 | 267 | 7,420 | 6,055 | 3.6 | 55.1 |
| 1967 | 13,874 | 7,379 | 315 | 7,694 | 6,179 | 4.1 | 55.5 |
| 1968 | 14,264 | 7,537 | 382 | 7,919 | 6,344 | 4.8 | 55.5 |
| 1969 | 14,638 | 7,780 | 382 | 8,162 | 6,475 | 4.7 | 55.8 |
| 1970 | 15,016 | 7,879 | 495 | 8,374 | 6,642 | 5.9 | 55.8 |
| 1971 | 15,388 | 8,079 | 552 | 8,631 | 6,757 | 6.4 | 56.1 |
| 1972 | 15,747 | 8,329 | 562 | 8,891 | 6,856 | 6.3 | 56.5 |
| 1973 | 16,125 | 8,759 | 520 | 9,279 | 6,846 | 5.6 | 57.5 |
| 1974 | 16,562 | 9,137 | 525 | 9,662 | 6,900 | 5.4 | 58.3 |
| 1975 | 16,470 | 9,363 | 697 | 10,060 | 6,410 | 6.9 | 61.1 |
| 1976 | 16,873 | 9,572 | 736 | 10,308 | 6,565 | 7.1 | 61.1 |
| 1977 | 17,250 | 9,754 | 862 | 10,616 | 6,634 | 8.1 | 61.5 |

1. 14 years of age, or over.

## Canadian Motor Vehicle Registrations, 1977
(estimate)

| Province or territory | Passenger cars | Motor trucks | Motor buses | Motor-cycles | Other motor vehicles[1] | Total motor vehicles |
|---|---|---|---|---|---|---|
| Alberta | 801,000 | 380,000 | 6,300 | 35,000 | (2) | 1,222,300 |
| British Columbia | 1,242,000 | 415,000 | (2) | 35,000[3] | (2) | 1,692,000 |
| Manitoba | 435,000 | 150,000 | 400 | 12,000 | 600 | 598,000 |
| New Brunswick | 244,000 | 64,000 | 1,500 | 12,000 | 5,000 | 326,600 |
| Newfoundland | 141,000 | 41,000 | 1,300 | 4,000 | 5,000 | 192,300 |
| Nova Scotia | 293,000 | 83,000 | 1,000 | 10,000 | 500 | 387,500 |
| Ontario | 3,780,000 | 685,000 | 16,000 | 100,000 | (2) | 4,581,000 |

| Province or territory | Passenger cars | Motor trucks | Motor buses | Motor-cycles | Other motor vehicles[1] | Total motor vehicles |
|---|---|---|---|---|---|---|
| Prince Edward Island | 45,000 | 14,000 | 500 | 2,500 | ([2]) | 52,000 |
| Quebec | 2,464,000 | 330,000 | 19,000 | 175,000 | 36,000 | 3,024,000 |
| Saskatchewan | 383,000 | 267,000 | 4,500 | 12,000[3] | 12,000 | 678,500 |
| N.W.T. | 5,500 | 6,500 | 200 | 900 | 100 | 13,200 |
| Yukon T. | 7,500 | 5,500 | 200 | 600[3] | 1,600 | 15,400 |
| **Total** | **9,841,000** | **1,331,000** | **51,000** | **399,000** | **60,800** | **12,792,800** |

1. Includes farm tractors, snowmobiles, and logging tractors. 2. Included with passenger cars or trucks. 3. Includes mopeds. *Source:* Motor Vehicle Manufacturers' Association.

## Principal Trading Partners in 1977

**(in thousands of Canadian dollars)**

| Selected countries | Imports | Exports |
|---|---|---|
| United States | $29,542,843 | $30,187,091 |
| Japan | 1,799,451 | 2,500,780 |
| United Kingdom | 1,152,384 | 1,927,303 |
| Venezuela | 1,377,279 | 510,945 |
| West Germany | 958,760 | 766,609 |
| Iran | 695,425 | 142,207 |
| Italy | 399,021 | 497,892 |
| France | 521,313 | 359,973 |
| Saudi Arabia | 690,995 | 108,732 |
| Netherlands | 188,537 | 512,254 |
| Belgium/Luxembourg | 160,312 | 508,449 |
| U.S.S.R. | 56,368 | 357,708 |
| People's Republic of China | 81,903 | 369,151 |
| Sweden | 260,166 | 105,493 |
| Brazil | 214,499 | 275,240 |
| Mexico | 194,913 | 216,825 |
| South Africa | 144,100 | 82,740 |
| Cuba | 45,375 | 182,640 |
| Norway | 69,179 | 223,381 |
| India | 55,686 | 135,327 |
| Spain | 113,987 | 129,733 |
| Poland | 46,237 | 147,527 |
| Pakistan | 8,833 | 72,399 |
| Algeria | 47,822 | 180,948 |
| Bangladesh | 7,101 | 52,018 |
| Peru | 37,526 | 46,988 |
| **Totals selected countries** | **$38,872,805** | **$40,600,438** |
| **Total all countries** | **$42,053,103** | **$43,268,843** |

## Average Temperature and Precipitation Data

| STATION (A = Airport) | Eleva-tion (ft) | Temperature °C: Mean daily Ann. | Temperature °C: Extreme Max. | Temperature °C: Extreme Min. | Average frost dates: Last in spring | Average frost dates: First in fall | Average total annual precip. (mm) | Aver. ann. snow-fall (cm) |
|---|---|---|---|---|---|---|---|---|
| St. John's A, Nfld. | 463 | 4.9 | 31 | −23 | June 8 | Oct. 12 | 1,511.5 | 363.9 |
| Charlottetown A, P.E.I. | 186 | 5.5 | 34 | −28 | May 17 | Oct. 15 | 1,127.8 | 305.6 |
| Halifax Int. A, N.S. | 461 | 6.0 | 34 | −26 | May 15 | Oct. 15 | 1,405.0 | 300.0 |
| Sydney A, N.S. | 197 | 6.0 | 35 | −25 | May 23 | Oct. 16 | 1,340.9 | 288.1 |
| Yarmouth A, N.S. | 136 | 7.0 | 30 | −21 | May 2 | Oct. 24 | 1,282.7 | 204.5 |
| Chatham A, N.B. | 112 | 4.9 | 38 | −35 | May 22 | Sept. 21 | 1,051.0 | 309.4 |
| Fredericton A, N.B. | 74 | 5.5 | 37 | −37 | May 21 | Sept. 26 | 1,060.3 | 28.4 |
| Saint John A, N.B. | 352 | 5.0 | 33 | −37 | May 18 | Oct. 2 | 1,400.3 | 296.7 |

| STATION (A = Airport) | Elevation (ft) | Temperature °C: Mean daily Ann. | Temperature °C: Extreme Max. | Temperature °C: Extreme Min. | Average frost dates: Last in spring | Average frost dates: First in fall | Average total annual precip. (mm) | Aver. ann. snowfall (cm) |
|---|---|---|---|---|---|---|---|---|
| Arvida, Que. | 335 | 3.1 | 36 | −42 | May 22 | Sept. 19 | 924.8 | 278.1 |
| Knob Lake, Que. | 1,681 | −4.0 | 32 | −51 | June 18 | Aug. 31 | 721.5 | 335.5 |
| Montreal Int. A, Que. | 98 | 6.5 | 36 | −38 | May 5 | Oct. 7 | 941.2 | 239.6 |
| Quebec A, Que. | 245 | 4.4 | 36 | −36 | May 18 | Sept. 28 | 1,088.6 | 326.7 |
| Sherbrooke A, Que. | 782 | 4.0 | 37 | −39 | June 1 | Sept. 11 | 1,065.5 | 279.3 |
| London A, Ont. | 912 | 7.5 | 37 | −32 | May 9 | Oct. 6 | 924.5 | 201.1 |
| Ottawa Int. A, Ont. | 413 | 5.8 | 38 | −36 | May 11 | Oct. 1 | 850.9 | 215.9 |
| Thunder Bay A, Ont. | 644 | 2.4 | 36 | −41 | May 31 | Sept. 10 | 738.5 | 222.1 |
| Toronto, Ont. | 379 | 8.9 | 41 | −33 | April 20 | Oct. 30 | 789.9 | 141.1 |
| Churchill A, Man. | 115 | −7.3 | 33 | −45 | June 22 | Sept. 12 | 396.2 | 183.9 |
| The Pas A, Man. | 894 | −0.6 | 37 | −49 | May 28 | Sept. 20 | 449.6 | 157.2 |
| Winnipeg Int. A, Man. | 786 | 2.3 | 41 | −45 | May 25 | Sept. 21 | 535.2 | 131.3 |
| Prince Albert A, Sask. | 1,414 | 0.1 | 38 | −50 | June 5 | Sept. 7 | 388.7 | 124.5 |
| Regina A, Sask. | 1,884 | 2.1 | 43 | −50 | May 27 | Sept. 12 | 397.9 | 114.8 |
| Beaverlodge CDA, Alta. | 2,500 | 1.8 | 37 | −48 | May 22 | Sept. 7 | 454.7 | 183.6 |
| Calgary Int. A, Alta. | 3,540 | 3.4 | 36 | −45 | May 28 | Sept. 12 | 437.1 | 153.9 |
| Edmonton Int. A, Alta. | 2,219 | 2.8 | 34 | −48 | May 14 | Sept. 19 | 446.5 | 132.1 |
| Kamloops A, B.C. | 1,133 | 8.4 | 39 | −37 | May 5 | Sept. 28 | 320.2 | 78.6 |
| Prince George A, B.C. | 2,218 | 3.2 | 34 | −50 | June 10 | Aug. 28 | 620.7 | 233.4 |
| Prince Rupert A, B.C. | 110 | 6.8 | 32 | −21 | May 8 | Oct. 20 | 2,428.0 | 113.0 |
| Vancouver Int. A, B.C. | 16 | 9.8 | 33 | −18 | March 31 | Oct. 30 | 1,068.1 | 52.4 |
| Dawson, Y.T. | 1,062 | −4.7 | 35 | −58 | May 26 | Aug. 27 | 325.1 | 136.3 |
| Whitehouse A, Y.T. | 2,289 | −0.9 | 34 | −52 | June 5 | Sept. 1 | 260.3 | 127.8 |
| Aklavik, N.W.T. | 30 | −8.9 | 34 | −52 | June 12 | Aug. 30 | 236.0 | 136.9 |
| Frobisher Bay A, N.W.T. | 68 | −9.0 | 24 | −46 | June 30 | Aug. 29 | 414.0 | 246.9 |
| Resolute A, N.W.T. | 209 | −16.4 | 18 | −52 | July 10 | July 20 | 136.4 | 78.7 |
| Yellowknife A, N.W.T. | 682 | −5.6 | 32 | −51 | May 30 | Sept. 16 | 249.9 | 119.4 |

## Mileage Between Principal Points in Canada
(via rail or water)

| Approximate distances by rail or water | Nfld. St. John's | N.S. Halifax | P.E.I. Charlottetown | N.B. Saint John | N.B. Fredericton | Que. Quebec | Que. Montreal | Ont. Ottawa | Ont. Toronto | Ont. Thunder Bay | Man. Winnipeg | Sask. Regina | Sask. Saskatoon | Alta. Calgary | Alta. Edmonton | B.C. Vancouver | B.C. Victoria | B.C. Pr. Rupert |
|---|---|---|---|---|---|---|---|---|---|---|---|---|---|---|---|---|---|---|
| St. John's | 0 | 930 | 1,041 | 1,081 | 1,094 | 1,466 | 1,563 | 1,675 | 1,897 | 2,521 | 2,797 | 3,153 | 3,268 | 3,531 | 3,646 | 4,262 | 4,362 | 4,543 |
| Halifax | 930 | 0 | 239 | 279 | 292 | 664 | 761 | 873 | 1,095 | 1,719 | 1,995 | 2,351 | 2,466 | 2,729 | 2,844 | 3,460 | 3,560 | 3,741 |
| Charlottetown | 1,041 | 239 | 0 | 215 | 230 | 600 | 684 | 795 | 1,018 | 1,653 | 1,950 | 2,305 | 2,421 | 2,772 | 2,751 | 3,413 | 3,498 | 3,707 |
| Saint John | 1,081 | 279 | 215 | 0 | 67 | 425 | 482 | 594 | 816 | 1,470 | 1,894 | 2,250 | 2,374 | 2,726 | 2,699 | 3,368 | 3,324 | 3,655 |
| Fredericton | 1,094 | 292 | 230 | 67 | 0 | 403 | 454 | 565 | 788 | 1,423 | 1,753 | 2,108 | 2,224 | 2,575 | 2,554 | 3,216 | 3,301 | 3,510 |
| Quebec City | 1,466 | 664 | 600 | 425 | 403 | 0 | 164 | 276 | 498 | 1,152 | 1,521 | 1,877 | 1,992 | 2,353 | 2,323 | 2,995 | 2,898 | 3,279 |
| Montreal | 1,563 | 761 | 684 | 482 | 454 | 164 | 0 | 112 | 334 | 988 | 1,357 | 1,713 | 1,828 | 2,244 | 2,151 | 2,886 | 2,900 | 3,115 |
| Ottawa | 1,675 | 873 | 795 | 594 | 565 | 276 | 112 | 0 | 247 | 887 | 1,301 | 1,658 | 1,772 | 2,133 | 2,098 | 2,775 | 2,789 | 3,054 |
| Toronto | 1,897 | 1,095 | 1,018 | 816 | 788 | 498 | 334 | 247 | 0 | 809 | 1,233 | 1,590 | 1,704 | 2,065 | 2,030 | 2,707 | 2,755 | 2,986 |
| Thunder Bay | 2,521 | 1,719 | 1,653 | 1,470 | 1,423 | 1,152 | 988 | 877 | 809 | 0 | 424 | 781 | 895 | 1,256 | 1,221 | 1,898 | 1,967 | 2,177 |
| Winnipeg | 2,797 | 1,995 | 1,950 | 1,894 | 1,753 | 1,521 | 1,357 | 1,301 | 1,233 | 424 | 0 | 356 | 471 | 832 | 797 | 1,474 | 1,548 | 1,753 |
| Regina | 3,153 | 2,351 | 2,305 | 2,250 | 2,108 | 1,877 | 1,713 | 1,658 | 1,590 | 781 | 356 | 0 | 161 | 476 | 487 | 1,118 | 1,193 | 1,443 |
| Saskatoon | 3,268 | 2,466 | 2,421 | 2,374 | 2,224 | 1,992 | 1,828 | 1,772 | 1,704 | 895 | 471 | 161 | 0 | 399 | 326 | 1,097 | 1,131 | 1,282 |
| Calgary | 3,531 | 2,729 | 2,772 | 2,726 | 2,575 | 2,353 | 2,244 | 2,133 | 2,065 | 1,256 | 832 | 476 | 399 | 0 | 195 | 642 | 727 | 1,151 |
| Edmonton | 3,646 | 2,844 | 2,751 | 2,699 | 2,554 | 2,323 | 2,151 | 2,098 | 2,030 | 1,221 | 797 | 487 | 326 | 195 | 0 | 771 | 846 | 956 |
| Vancouver | 4,262 | 3,460 | 3,413 | 3,368 | 3,216 | 2,995 | 2,886 | 2,775 | 2,707 | 1,898 | 1,474 | 1,118 | 1,097 | 642 | 771 | 0 | 85 | 546 |
| Victoria | 4,362 | 3,560 | 3,498 | 3,324 | 3,301 | 2,898 | 2,900 | 2,789 | 2,755 | 1,967 | 1,548 | 1,193 | 1,131 | 727 | 846 | 85 | 0 | 631 |
| Prince Rupert | 4,543 | 3,741 | 3,707 | 3,655 | 3,510 | 3,279 | 3,115 | 3,054 | 2,986 | 2,177 | 1,753 | 1,443 | 1,282 | 1,151 | 956 | 546 | 641 | 0 |

## Air Distances Between Cities
(via Air Canada)

| From | To | Miles[1] | From | To | Miles[1] |
|---|---|---|---|---|---|
| Gander | Montreal | 1,109 | Montreal | Toronto | 326 |
| Gander | Toronto | 1,494 | Montreal | Vancouver | 2,444 |
| Halifax | Moncton | 120 | Montreal | Windsor | 521 |
| Halifax | Montreal | 571 | Ottawa | Winnipeg | 1,174 |
| Halifax | North Bay | 1,034 | St. John's, Nfld. | Montreal | 1,147 |
| Halifax | Ottawa | 665 | Sydney | Halifax | 200 |
| Halifax | Toronto | 897 | Toronto | Chicago | 435 |
| Halifax | Vancouver | 3,015 | Toronto | Cleveland | 195 |
| Halifax | Winnipeg | 1,893 | Toronto | Edmonton | 1,693 |
| Lethbridge | Calgary | 124 | Toronto | New York | 375 |
| Lethbridge | Edmonton | 301 | Toronto | Tampa | 1,119 |
| Montreal | Boston | 778 | Toronto | Vancouver | 2,118 |
| Montreal | Edmonton | 2,019 | Toronto | Winnipeg | 942 |
| Montreal | Goose Bay | 824 | Vancouver | Victoria | 47 |
| Montreal | Moncton | 451 | Winnipeg | Calgary | 750 |
| Montreal | New York | 350 | Winnipeg | Edmonton | 753 |
| Montreal | Ottawa | 94 | | | |

1. Statute miles. *Source:* Air Canada.

## Land and Fresh Water Areas of Canada

| Province, territory, or district | Land sq miles | Fresh water sq miles | Total sq miles | Percent of total area |
|---|---|---|---|---|
| Alberta | 248,800 | 6,485 | 255,285 | 6.6 |
| British Columbia | 359,279 | 6,976 | 366,255 | 9.5 |
| Manitoba | 211,775 | 39,225 | 251,000 | 6.5 |
| New Brunswick | 27,835 | 519 | 28,354 | 0.7 |
| Newfoundland | 143,045 | 13,140 | 156,185 | 4.1 |
| Nova Scotia | 20,402 | 1,023 | 21,425 | 0.6 |
| Ontario | 344,092 | 68,490 | 412,582 | 10.7 |
| Prince Edward Island | 2,184 | — | 2,184 | 0.1 |
| Quebec | 523,860 | 71,000 | 594,860 | 15.4 |
| Saskatchewan | 220,182 | 31,518 | 251,700 | 6.5 |
| Northwest Territories | 1,253,438 | 51,465 | 1,304,903 | 33.9 |
| Franklin | 541,753 | 7,500 | 549,253 | 14.3 |
| Keewatin | 218,460 | 9,700 | 228,160 | 5.9 |
| Mackenzie | 493,225 | 34,265 | 527,490 | 13.7 |
| Yukon Territory | 205,346 | 1,730 | 207,076 | 5.4 |
| **Totals** | **3,560,238** | **291,571** | **3,851,809** | **100.0** |

## Highest Elevations

| Province or territory | Height in feet | Height in meters |
|---|---|---|
| Alberta—Mount Columbia | 12,294 | 3,747 |
| British Columbia—Mt. Fairweather | 15,300 | 4,663 |
| Manitoba—Baldy Mountain | 2,729 | 832 |
| New Brunswick—Mount Carleton | 2,690 | 820 |
| Newfoundland—Cirque Mt., Labrador Penin. | 5,160 | 1,573 |
| Nova Scotia—North Barren Mt., Cape Breton Island | 1,747 | 532 |
| Ontario—Ogidaki Mt. | 2,183 | 665 |
| Prince Edward Island—highest point Queens County | 465 | 142 |
| Quebec—Mt. Jacques Cartier, Gaspé Penin. | 4,160 | 1,268 |
| Saskatchewan—Cypress Hills | 4,546 | 1,386 |
| Northwest Territories—Mt. Sir James MacBrien | 9,062 | 2,762 |
| Yukon Territory—Mount Logan | 19,850 | 6,050 |

## Institutions, Full-time Teachers, Full-time Enrollment and Expenditures, Canada and Provinces[1]

| Level and subgroup | Institutions | Full-time teachers | Full-time enrollment | Total expenditures on education (millions of dollars) |
|---|---|---|---|---|
| **Newfoundland** | | | | |
| Elementary-Secondary | 722 | 7,477 | 158,175 | 181.6 |
| Post-secondary | 6 | 845 | 8,145 | 70.7 |
| Trade Level | — | — | — | 36.2 |
| Total all levels | — | — | 166,320 | 288.5 |
| **Prince Edward Island** | | | | |
| Elementary-Secondary | 98 | 1,452 | 27,922 | 40.6 |
| Post-secondary | 3 | 189 | 2,171 | 12.5 |
| Trade Level | — | — | — | 6.9 |
| Total all levels | — | — | 30,093 | 60.0 |
| **Nova Scotia** | | | | |
| Elementary-Secondary | 640 | 11,040 | 205,141 | 257.2 |
| Post-secondary | 24 | 1,816 | 20,788 | 126.0 |
| Trade Level | — | — | — | 49.5 |
| Total all levels | — | — | 225,929 | 432.7 |
| **New Brunswick** | | | | |
| Elementary-Secondary | 533 | 7,954 | 166,258 | 225.7 |
| Post-secondary | 13 | 1,180 | 12,476 | 80.9 |
| Trade Level | — | — | — | 30.9 |
| Total all levels | — | — | 178,734 | 337.5 |
| **Quebec** | | | | |
| Elementary-Secondary | 3,007 | 76,590 | 1,468,571 | 2,358.1 |
| Post-secondary | 83 | 15,570 | 194,437 | 1,140.4 |
| Trade Level | — | — | — | 204.0 |
| Total all levels | — | — | 1,663,008 | 3,702.5 |
| **Ontario** | | | | |
| Elementary-Secondary | 5,015 | 97,432 | 2,057,775 | 2,944.4 |
| Post-secondary | 52 | 16,870 | 219,341 | 1,402.7 |
| Trade Level | — | — | — | 217.4 |
| Total all levels | — | — | 2,277,116 | 4,564.5 |
| **Manitoba** | | | | |
| Elementary-Secondary | 821 | 11,935 | 242,671 | 359.0 |
| Post-secondary | 13 | 1,872 | 21,776 | 157.7 |
| Trade Level | — | — | — | 31.9 |
| Total all levels | — | — | 264,447 | 548.6 |
| **Saskatchewan** | | | | |
| Elementary-Secondary | 1,056 | 11,154 | 228,106 | 317.1 |
| Post-secondary | 9 | 1,570 | 16,747 | 111.4 |
| Trade Level | — | — | — | 44.1 |
| Total all levels | — | — | 244,853 | 472.6 |
| **Alberta** | | | | |
| Elementary-Secondary | 1,347 | 22,063 | 448,900 | 754.1 |
| Post-secondary | 25 | 3,941 | 47,452 | 302.6 |
| Trade Level | — | — | — | 101.0 |
| Total all levels | — | — | 496,352 | 1,157.7 |
| **British Columbia** | | | | |
| Elementary-Secondary | 1,784 | 26,618 | 568,287 | 840.9 |
| Post-secondary | 30 | 4,256 | 48,775 | 321.3 |
| Trade Level | — | — | — | 74.3 |
| Total all levels | — | — | 617,062 | 1,236.5 |
| **Yukon and Northwest Territories** | | | | |
| Total Elementary and Secondary Schools | 85 | 950 | 17,471 | 42.8 |

1. For 1975–76.

# Major Canadian Awards, 1977

## Governor General's Literary Awards

**Fiction:** English: Timothy Findley for *The Wars;* French: Gabrielle Roy, *Ces enfants de ma vie*
**Poetry and Drama:** English: Douglas Gordon Jons for *Under the Thunder the Flowers Light Up the Earth;* French: Michel Garneau, for *Les Célébrations* and *Adidou Adidouce,* two plays in one volume
**Nonfiction:** English: Frank Scott for *Essays on the Constitution;* French: Denis Monière, *Le développement des idéologies au Québec*

## Juno Award Winners

**Female Vocalist:** Patsy Gallant
**Male Vocalist:** Dan Hill
**Group:** Rush
**Country Female Vocalist:** Carroll Baker
**Country Male Vocalist:** Ronnie Prophet
**Country Group:** The Good Brothers
**Best New Female Vocalist:** Lisa Dal Bello
**Best New Male Vocalist:** Dave Bradstreet
**Best Selling Album:** Dan Hill ("Longer Fuse")
**Best Selling Single:** Patsy Gallant ("Sugar Daddy")
**Folksinger:** Gordon Lightfoot
**Instrumental Artist:** André Gagnon
**Composer:** Dan Hill ("Sometimes When We Touch")
**Best Jazz Recording:** Rob McConnell and the Boss Brass for Big Band Jazz
**Classical Recording:** Toronto Symphony for Three Borodin Symphonies
**Best New Group:** Hometown Band

## National Newspaper Awards

**Spot News Reporting:** Gerald Utting, Toronto Star
**Editorial Writing:** David Ablett, Vancouver Sun
**Feature Writing:** Brenda Zosky, Toronto Star
**Cartooning:** Terry Mosher, Montreal Gazette
**Spot News Photography:** Douglas Ball, Canadian Press
**Feature News Photography:** Boris Spremo, Toronto Star
**Sports Writing:** Brodie Snyder and Dick Bacon, Montreal Gazette
**Enterprise Reporting:** Gerald Utting, Toronto Star
**Critical Writing:** William French, Literary Editor, Globe & Mail

## Actra Awards

**The Earle Grey Award for the Best Acting Performance in Television in a Leading Role:** Donald Sutherland
**The Andrew Allan Award for the Best Acting Performance in Radio:** Joan Gregson
**Best Variety Performance in Television:** Entire cast of *Second City*
**Best Variety Performance in Radio:** Nancy White
**The Foster Hewitt Award for excellence in Sportscasting:** Don Wittman
**Best Dramatic Writer—Television:** Tony Sheer
**Best Dramatic Writer—Radio:** Rod Coneybeare
**Best Television Program of the Year:** Opera, *Aberfan*
**Best Radio Program of the Year:** *A Bite of the Big Apple*
**Gordon Sinclair Award for outspoken opinions and integrity in broadcasting:** Linden McIntyre
**The John Drainie Award for Distinguished Contribution to Broadcasting:** (The recipient of this Award is decided by the previous winner.) Johnny Wayne and Frank Shuster
**Best Public Affairs Broadcaster in Television:** Jack McGaw and Ruth Fremes
**Best Documentary Writer in Television:** Bill McAdam and Martyn Burke
**Best Documentary Writer in Radio:** Jim Winter
**Best Acting Performance in a Supporting Role in Television:** Les Carlson

## Canadian Association of Broadcasters

The CAB Annual Awards competition gives private broadcasters in Canada a national showcase to display achievements in programming, public service and charitable work, news, engineering, and other areas where a high degree of ingenuity, dedication, imagination, and innovation often are key elements.

**John J. Gillin, Jr. (AM Station of the Year Award):** Established in 1951, this prestigious award goes to the AM station making the greatest charitable or public service contribution within its community. Winner: CKBI, Prince Albert.

**J.E. Campeau (TV Station of the Year Award):** This award, established in 1962, honors the television station making the greatest single or continuing contribution to any form of community service. Winner: CFQC-TV, Saskatoon.

**Lloyd E. Moffat (FM Station of the Year Award):** First presented in 1968, this award honors excellence and originality by the FM station making the greatest single or continuing contribution of outstanding value to any form of community service. Winner: CKFM-FM, Toronto.

**Ted Rogers, Sr./Velma Rogers Graham Award:** Presented for the first time in 1975, this award honors the person making the most significant contribution, in a single or continuing fashion, to the Canadian broadcasting system, or for exceptional community service in a role as broadcaster. Winner: CHIN, AM-FM, Toronto.

**The CGE Colonel Keith S. Rogers Engineering Award:** This award, given only for highly significant engineering achievements, was initiated in 1950 by Canadian General Electric. It goes to the station or individual most successfully developing engineering or technical ideas, approaches, or methods to improve the extent or quality of service in technical terms, or to extend existing services. Last winner, 1975: Ernie Rose, CHAN-TV, Vancouver. No winner 1976 or 1977.

**H. Gordon Love News Trophy (station or individual):** Presented annually since 1968 to the station or individual for best quality of news work in broadcasting. Winner: CKY-TV, Winnipeg.

## Canadian Football—Grey Cup Records

| Year | Date | Site | Score | | Winning Coach |
|---|---|---|---|---|---|
| 1909 | Dec. 4 | Toronto | Toronto U 26 | Parkdale 6 | Harry Griffith |
| 1910 | Nov. 26 | Hamilton | Toronto U 16 | Hamilton 7 | Harry Griffith |
| 1911 | Nov. 25 | Toronto | Toronto U 14 | Toronto 7 | Dr. A.B. Wright |
| 1912 | Nov. 30 | Hamilton | Hamilton 11 | Toronto 4 | Liz Marriott |
| 1913 | Nov. 29 | Hamilton | Hamilton 44 | Parkdale 2 | Liz Marriott |
| 1914 | Dec. 5 | Toronto | Toronto 14 | Toronto U 2 | Billy Foulds |
| 1915 | Nov. 20 | Toronto | Hamilton 13 | Toronto 7 | Liz Marriott |
| 1916–19 | No Games, War | | | | |
| 1920 | Dec. 4 | Toronto | Toronto U 16 | Toronto 3 | Laddie Cassels |
| 1921 | Dec. 3 | Toronto | Toronto 23 | Edmonton 0 | Sinc McEvenue |
| 1922 | Dec. 2 | Kingston | Queen's U 13 | Edmonton 1 | Billy Hughes |
| 1923 | Dec. 1 | Toronto | Queen's U 54 | Regina 0 | Billy Hughes |
| 1924 | Nov. 29 | Toronto | Queen's U 11 | Balmy Beach 3 | Billy Hughes |
| 1925 | Dec. 5 | Ottawa | Ottawa 24 | Winnipeg 1 | Dave McCann |
| 1926 | Dec. 4 | Toronto | Ottawa 10 | Toronto U 7 | Dave McCann |
| 1927 | Nov. 26 | Toronto | Balmy Beach 9 | Hamilton 6 | Dr. H. Hobbs |
| 1928 | Dec. 1 | Hamilton | Hamilton 30 | Regina 0 | Mike Rodden |
| 1929 | Nov. 30 | Hamilton | Hamilton 14 | Regina 3 | Mike Rodden |
| 1930 | Dec. 6 | Toronto | Balmy Beach 11 | Regina 6 | Alex Ponton |
| 1931 | Dec. 5 | Montreal | Montreal 22 | Regina 0 | Clary Foran |
| 1932 | Dec. 3 | Hamilton | Hamilton 25 | Regina 6 | Billy Hughes |
| 1933 | Dec. 9 | Sarnia | Toronto 4 | Sarnia 3 | Lew Hayman |
| 1934 | Nov. 24 | Toronto | Sarnia 20 | Regina 12 | Art Massucci |
| 1935 | Dec. 7 | Hamilton | Winnipeg 18 | Hamilton 12 | Bob Fritz |
| 1936 | Dec. 5 | Toronto | Sarnia 26 | Ottawa 20 | Art Massucci |
| 1937 | Dec. 11 | Toronto | Toronto 4 | Winnipeg 3 | Lew Hayman |
| 1938 | Dec. 10 | Toronto | Toronto 30 | Winnipeg 7 | Lew Hayman |
| 1939 | Dec. 9 | Ottawa | Winnipeg 8 | Ottawa 7 | Reg Threlfall |
| 1940 | Nov. 30 | Toronto | Ottawa 8 | Balmy Beach 2 | Ross Trimble |
| | Dec. 7 | Ottawa | Ottawa 12 | Balmy Beach 5 | Ross Trimble |
| 1941 | Nov. 29 | Toronto | Winnipeg 18 | Ottawa 16 | Reg Threlfall |
| 1942 | Dec. 5 | Toronto | Toronto 8 | Winnipeg 5 | Lew Hayman |
| 1943 | Nov. 27 | Toronto | Hamilton 23 | Winnipeg 14 | Brian Timmis |
| 1944 | Nov. 25 | Hamilton | Montreal 7 | Hamilton 6 | Glen Brown |
| 1945 | Dec. 1 | Toronto | Toronto 35 | Winnipeg 0 | Ted Morris |
| 1946 | Nov. 30 | Toronto | Toronto 28 | Winnipeg 6 | Ted Morris |
| 1947 | Nov. 29 | Toronto | Toronto 10 | Winnipeg 9 | Ted Morris |
| 1948 | Nov. 27 | Toronto | Calgary 12 | Ottawa 7 | Les Lear |
| 1949 | Nov. 26 | Toronto | Montreal 28 | Calgary 15 | Lew Hayman |
| 1950 | Nov. 25 | Toronto | Toronto 13 | Winnipeg 0 | Frank Clair |
| 1951 | Nov. 24 | Toronto | Ottawa 21 | Saskatchewan 14 | Clem Crowe |
| 1952 | Nov. 29 | Toronto | Toronto 21 | Edmonton 11 | Frank Clair |
| 1953 | Nov. 28 | Toronto | Hamilton 12 | Winnipeg 6 | Carl Voyles |
| 1954 | Nov. 27 | Toronto | Edmonton 26 | Montreal 25 | Frank Ivy |
| 1955 | Nov. 26 | Vancouver | Edmonton 34 | Montreal 19 | Frank Ivy |
| 1956 | Nov. 24 | Toronto | Edmonton 50 | Montreal 27 | Frank Ivy |
| 1957 | Nov. 30 | Toronto | Hamilton 32 | Winnipeg 7 | Jim Trimble |
| 1958 | Nov. 29 | Vancouver | Winnipeg 35 | Hamilton 28 | Bud Grant |
| 1959 | Nov. 28 | Toronto | Winnipeg 21 | Hamilton 7 | Bud Grant |
| 1960 | Nov. 26 | Vancouver | Ottawa 16 | Edmonton 6 | Frank Clair |
| 1961 | Dec. 2 | Toronto | Winnipeg 21 | Hamilton 14 | Bud Grant |
| 1962 | Dec. 1 | Toronto | Winnipeg 28 | Hamilton 27 | Bud Grant |
| 1963 | Nov. 30 | Vancouver | Hamilton 21 | B.C. 10 | Ralph Sazio |
| 1964 | Nov. 28 | Toronto | B.C. 34 | Hamilton 24 | Dave Skrien |
| 1965 | Nov. 27 | Toronto | Hamilton 22 | Winnipeg 16 | Ralph Sazio |
| 1966 | Nov. 26 | Vancouver | Saskatchewan 29 | Ottawa 14 | Eagle Keys |
| 1967 | Dec. 2 | Ottawa | Hamilton 24 | Saskatchewan 1 | Ralph Sazio |
| 1968 | Nov. 30 | Toronto | Ottawa 24 | Calgary 21 | Frank Clair |
| 1969 | Nov. 30 | Montreal | Ottawa 29 | Saskatchewan 11 | Frank Clair |
| 1970 | Nov. 28 | Toronto | Montreal 23 | Calgary 10 | Sam Etcheverry |
| 1971 | Nov. 28 | Vancouver | Calgary 14 | Toronto 11 | Jim Duncan |
| 1972 | Dec. 3 | Hamilton | Hamilton 13 | Saskatchewan 10 | Jerry Williams |
| 1973 | Nov. 25 | Toronto | Ottawa 22 | Edmonton 18 | Jack Gotta |
| 1974 | Nov. 24 | Vancouver | Montreal 20 | Edmonton 7 | Marv Levey |
| 1975 | Nov. 23 | Calgary | Edmonton 9 | Montreal 8 | Ray Jauch |
| 1976 | Nov. 28 | Toronto | Ottawa 23 | Saskatchewan 20 | George Brancato |
| 1977 | Nov. 27 | Montreal | Montreal 41 | Edmonton 6 | Marv Levey |

### Schenley Award — Most Outstanding Player[1]

| | |
|---|---|
| 1953 | Billy Vessels, Edmonton |
| 1954 | Sam Etcheverry, Montreal |
| 1955 | Pat Abbruzzi, Montreal |
| 1956 | Hal Patterson, Montreal |
| 1957 | Jackie Parker, Edmonton |
| 1958 | Jackie Parker, Edmonton |
| 1959 | Johnny Bright, Edmonton |
| 1960 | Jackie Parker, Edmonton |
| 1961 | Bernie Faloney, Hamilton |
| 1962 | George Dixon, Montreal |
| 1963 | Russ Jackson, Ottawa |
| 1964 | Lovell Coleman, Calgary |
| 1965 | George Reed, Saskatchewan |
| 1966 | Russ Jackson, Ottawa |
| 1967 | Peter Liske, Calgary |
| 1968 | Bill Symons, Toronto |
| 1969 | Russ Jackson, Ottawa |
| 1970 | Ron Lancaster, Saskatchewan |
| 1971 | Don Jonas, Winnipeg |
| 1972 | Garney Henley, Hamilton |
| 1973 | George McGowan, Edmonton |
| 1974 | Tom Wilkinson, Edmonton |
| 1975 | Willie Burden, Calgary |
| 1976 | Ron Lancaster, Saskatchewan |
| 1977 | Jimmy Edwards, Hamilton |

1. Chosen by a vote of qualified football reporters across Canada.

### Schenley Award — Most Outstanding Canadian Player

| | |
|---|---|
| 1954 | Jerry James, Winnipeg |
| 1955 | Normie Kwong, Edmonton |
| 1956 | Normie Kwong, Edmonton |
| 1957 | Jerry James, Winnipeg |
| 1958 | Ron Howell, Hamilton |
| 1959 | Russ Jackson, Ottawa |
| 1960 | Ron Stewart, Ottawa |
| 1961 | Tony Pajaczkowski, Calgary |
| 1962 | Harvey Wylie, Calgary |
| 1963 | Russ Jackson, Ottawa |
| 1964 | Tommy Grant, Hamilton |
| 1965 | Zeno Karcz, Hamilton |
| 1966 | Russ Jackson, Ottawa |
| 1967 | Terry Evanshen, Calgary |
| 1968 | Ken Nielsen, Winnipeg |
| 1969 | Russ Jackson, Ottawa |
| 1970 | Jim Young, British Columbia |
| 1971 | Terry Evanshen, Montreal |
| 1972 | Jim Young, British Columbia |
| 1973 | Gerry Organ, Ottawa |
| 1974 | Tony Gabriel, Hamilton |
| 1975 | Jim Foley, Ottawa |
| 1976 | Tony Gabriel, Ottawa |
| 1977 | Tony Gabriel, Ottawa |

## Canadian Curling Championships

### MACDONALD'S BRIER TANKARD

**1933** **Alberta** (Royal Curling Club, Edmonton) C. R. Manahan
**1934** **Manitoba** (Strathcona Curling Club, Winnipeg) Leo Johnson
**1935** **Ontario** (Thistle Curling Club, Hamilton) Gordon Campbell
**1936** **Manitoba** (Strathcona Curling Club, Winnipeg) J. K. Watson
**1937** **Alberta** (Royal Curling Club, Edmonton) C. R. Manahan
**1938** **Manitoba** (Glenboro Curling Club, Glenboro) A. Gowanlock
**1939** **Ontario** (Granite Curling Club, Kitchener) Bert C. Hall
**1940** **Manitoba** (Granite Curling Club, Winnipeg) Howard Wood
**1941** **Alberta** (Calgary Curling Club, Calgary) T. F. H. Palmer
**1942** **Manitoba** (Strathcona Curling Club, Winnipeg) J. K. Watson
**1946** **Alberta** (Sedgewick Curling Club, Sedgewick) W. Rose
**1947** **Manitoba** (Deer Lodge Curling Club, Winnipeg) J. Welsh
**1948** **British Columbia** (Trail Curling Club, Trail) T. D'Amour
**1949** **Manitoba** (Strathcona Curling Club, Winnipeg) J. K. Watson
**1950** **Northern Ont.** (Kirkland Lake C.C., Kirkland Lake) T. Ramsy
**1951** **Nova Scotia** (Glooscap Curling Club, Kentville) H. D. Oyler
**1952** **Manitoba** (Fort Rouge Curling Club, Winnipeg) W. Walsh
**1953** **Manitoba** (Dauphin Curling Club, Dauphin) A. Gowanlock
**1954** **Alberta** (Granite Curling Club, Edmonton) Matt Baldwin
**1955** **Saskatchewan** (Avonlea Curling Club, Avonlea) Garnet Campbell
**1956** **Manitoba** (Fort Rouge Curling Club, Winnipeg) W. Walsh
**1957** **Alberta** (Granite Curling Club, Edmonton) Matt Baldwin
**1958** **Alberta** (Granite Curling Club, Edmonton) Matt Baldwin
**1959** **Saskatchewan** (Regina Civil Service Club) E. M. Richardson
**1960** **Saskatchewan** (Regina Civil Service Club) E. M. Richardson
**1961** **Alberta** (Alberta Ave. Curling Club, Edmonton) H. J. Gervais
**1962** **Saskatchewan** (Regina Curling Club) E. M. Richardson
**1963** **Saskatchewan** (Regina Curling Club) E. M. Richardson
**1964** **British Columbia** (Vancouver Curling Club) Lyall A. Dagg
**1965** **Manitoba** (Granite Curling Club, Winnipeg) T. Braunstein
**1966** **Alberta** (Calgary Curling Club) R. Northcott
**1967** **Ontario** (Parkway Curling Club, Toronto) A. Phillips, Jr
**1968** **Alberta** (Calgary Curling Club) R. Northcott
**1969** **Alberta** (Calgary Curling Club) R. Northcott
**1970** **Manitoba** (Granite Curling Club, Winnipeg) D. G. Duguid
**1971** **Manitoba** (Granite Curling Club, Winnipeg) D. G. Duguid
**1972** **Manitoba** (Fort Rouge Curling Club, Winnipeg) O. Meleschuk
**1973** **Saskatchewan** (Regina Curling Club) Harvey G. Maezinke
**1974** **Alberta** (St. Albert Curling Club) H. J. Gervais
**1975** **Northern Ontario** (Fort William Curling Club) W. R. Tetley
**1976** **Newfoundland** (St. John's Curling Club) J. A. MacDuff
**1977** **Quebec** (St. Laurent Curling Club) J. W. Ursel
**1978** **Alberta** (Medicine Hat Curling Club) Ed Lukowich

# The Year in Travel

*Doran Jacobs*
*President, Air Charter Tour Operators of America*

The only way to characterize air travel in 1978 is to say it was changing. There will be still more changes in 1979, because the Civil Aeronautics Board, under its new Chairman, Dr. Alfred Kahn, has revised many of its views.

## In the U.S.

Continuing the trend which began with the first discount fares initiated by American Airlines in April 1977, deeply discounted fares swept across the entire country in 1978. Initially, these discounted fares were made because regularly scheduled airlines believed that new CAB regulations for charter flights would be a significant threat to them. The scheduled airlines used discounts to compete more effectively with charters. However, the airlines discovered that lower fares did a very good job in filling empty seats on many flights, so fare discounting spread to virtually every city and every market in the U.S.

By the middle of 1978, the many discounted fares with their conditions and restrictions made it almost impossible for the public to figure out what the cheapest fare to a given destination would be. Indeed, because the airline phones were so jammed by the increased number of travelers' questions, people were often unable to get correct information from the carriers themselves.

It is likely that the high discounts will continue in 1979, but there will be a trend toward simplification of the fares because of increased computer efficiency and increased public familiarity with discount schedules. In addition, a trend which has already begun in Europe will probably develop in the U.S. We should begin to see *three* different types of service on aircraft: First Class, Regular Coach or "Club Car," and a special no-frills section of the aircraft, with less comfortable seating and little or no service, for people traveling on a discount.

Not all routes will have discount fares, and not all discounts will be substantial. To the Miami area, for example, where deep discounting proved to be not particularly profitable for the airlines, such discounts will be reduced. In general, however, the consumer will enjoy a range of discounted airline fares that is unprecedented in the history of U.S. commercial aviation.

## Public Charter

In 1978, charter services were cut back sharply because of fare discounting by scheduled airlines. In July 1978, to help charter tour operators and the supplemental air carriers, the Civil Aeronautics Board liberalized its rules to an extraordinary extent. The CAB formulated a so-called "Public Charter," a form of charter flight with virtually no restrictions. In short, the tour operator who chartered aircraft would perform very much like a scheduled airline.

Most charter traffic in the U.S. and, indeed, by the summer of 1979—throughout the world, will use public charters. The CAB has retained other forms of charters which have existed for a long time—military, affinity, and single-entity charters—but all other kinds of charter flights are eliminated effective December 31, 1978, to be replaced by public charter.

The first test of public charter will be on travel to the Caribbean and other warm places during the early months of 1979. Experience on these routes at that time will be useful in determining what will happen in the summer of 1979.

## Overseas

High discounts, particularly for stand-by and budget fares, were common in 1978 for flights to Europe. There should be fewer discounted fares to Europe in 1979, especially in peak periods. During the peak summer periods, it is anticipated that scheduled airline discounts will not be as high, nor will as many seats be available, as there were in 1978.

Despite the fact that fares on regularly scheduled overseas airlines will be more expensive in 1979, the trend toward "sky train" (dense, no-frills, one-class seating to major gateway cities such as London, Brussels, and Frankfurt) will continue and, indeed, increase. The first "sky train" begun by Freddie Laker in the fall of 1977 was extraordinarily successful in 1978. The supplemental air carriers—the traditional charter airlines—have asked for scheduled routes to major European gateway cities, following Laker's lead. The CAB is expected to grant their requests. Therefore, in 1979, it is likely that there will be fewer charter flights except during the peak summer season, higher prices charged by scheduled airlines, and an expansion of one-class service across the Atlantic by charter-type carriers operating "sky train" service.

This trend will gradually spread. There will be increasing acceptance of deeply-discounted fares to South America, the Far East, Africa, and other areas. Many governments in these regions are now suspicious of discounting on scheduled flights, and have been slow to react to agreements that would permit discounted fares and liberalized charter rules. But it seems inevitable that charter rules will be increasingly liberalized and a wide variety of discount fares instituted in 1979. For example, the Japanese government—which had strictly controlled discounted fares and charters—announced in the fall of 1978 that it was willing to liberalize its rules. This trend will continue for other countries, too.

While the public charter rule will be immediately useful within the U.S., foreign countries may very well not accept liberalized charter regulations, despite the fact that the U.S. government is pressing for agreements with foreign countries that would simplify the charter situation. With the exception of the Benelux countries and Spain, most countries have been reluctant to accept U.S. proposals.

There should be a large selection of charters available to Mexico and the Caribbean, as well as international charters to Brazil, Peru, and Colombia. During the 1979 summer season, there should be a large number of public charters across the Atlantic, and special-interest charters to Yugoslavia, Romania, Hungary, Africa, Egypt, and Israel.

## U.S. Travel Industry Statistics

| Volume, receipts, employment | 1977 | 1976 | 1975 |
|---|---|---|---|
| Domestic travel volume[1] (in billions of passenger miles) | | | |
| Automobile | 1,104.4 | 1,078.1 | n.a. |
| Air | 154.8 | 144.5 | 131.8 |
| Bus | 16.6 | 15.9 | n.a. |
| Rail | 4.2 | 4.2 | 3.8 |
| **Total** | **1,280.1** | **1,242.9** | n.a. |
| Industry receipts[2] (in billions of dollars) | | | |
| Transportation | $ 67.7 | $ 63.2 | $ 57.7 |
| Lodging | 17.1 | 15.7 | 13.7 |
| Food service | 63.8 | 57.8 | 51.4 |
| Amusements | 22.8 | 20.6 | 18.0 |
| **Total** | **$171.4** | **$157.4** | **$140.8** |
| Employment[3] (in millions of jobs) | | | |
| Transportation | 1.04 | 1.04 | 1.02 |
| Lodging | .86 | .86 | .82 |
| Food service | 3.85 | 3.62 | 3.33 |
| **Total** | **5.76** | **5.52** | **5.17** |

1. Includes: Auto: Main rural road passenger-miles; Air: Domestic certified air carrier revenue passenger-miles; Bus: All intercity bus passenger miles; Rail: Amtrak passenger-miles. 2. Includes: Transportation: Air and rail transportation companies, gasoline service stations; Lodging: Commercial lodging places; Food Service: Eating and drinking places; Amusements: Amusement and recreation services. 3. Includes: Transportation: Air transportation, intercity highway transportation and gasoline service stations; Lodging: Commercial lodging places; Food Service: Eating and drinking places. NOTE: n.a. = not available. *Source:* U.S. Travel Data Center.

## Expenditures of Temporary Visitors in U.S.
(in millions of dollars)

| Country or region of permanent residence | 1977 | 1976 | 1975 | 1974 | 1973 |
|---|---|---|---|---|---|
| Transportation—U.S. Flag Carriers | $1,025 | $ 937 | $ 767 | $ 813 | $ 718 |
| Expenditures in U.S. | 6,164 | 5,806 | 4,839 | 4,032 | 3,412 |
| Canada | 2,150 | 1,983 | 1,561 | 1,225 | 1,072 |
| Mexico | 1,414 | 1,428 | 1,453 | 1,142 | 830 |
| Overseas Visitors | 2,600 | 2,395 | 1,825 | 1,665 | 1,510 |
| Western Europe | 988 | 852 | 611 | 570 | 559 |
| United Kingdom | 199 | 183 | 144 | 142 | 126 |
| Germany | 261 | 206 | 145 | 126 | 137 |
| France | 120 | 96 | 68 | 63 | 76 |
| Italy | 60 | 59 | 41 | 43 | 46 |
| Netherlands | 57 | 49 | 36 | 28 | 27 |
| Belgium | 27 | 23 | 14 | 14 | n.a. |
| Sweden | 40 | 37 | 23 | 22 | 19 |
| Switzerland | 51 | 43 | 32 | 27 | 23 |
| Other | 173 | 156 | 122 | 119 | 105 |
| Caribbean and Central America | 270 | 289 | 206 | 216 | 205 |
| South America | 444 | 360 | 303 | 237 | 198 |
| Other Areas | 898 | 894 | 705 | 642 | 548 |
| Japan | 436 | 439 | 410 | 402 | 334 |
| **Total expenditures** | **7,189** | **6,743** | **5,606** | **4,845** | **4,130** |

NOTE: n.a. = not available. *Source:* Department of Commerce, Bureau of Economic Analysis.

## Expenditures of U.S. Travelers to Foreign Countries
(in millions of dollars)

| Type of expense | 1977 | 1976 | 1975 | 1974 | 1973 |
|---|---|---|---|---|---|
| Transportation fare payments | $4,473 | $4,012 | $3,726 | $3,426 | $2,946 |
| Foreign-flag carriers | 2,843 | 2,568 | 2,380 | 2,095 | 1,790 |
| U.S.-flag carriers | 1,630 | 1,444 | 1,346 | 1,331 | 1,156 |
| Travel payments in foreign countries | 7,451 | 6,856 | 6,417 | 5,980 | 5,526 |
| Canada | 1,433 | 1,371 | 1,306 | 1,359 | 1,158 |
| Mexico | 1,918 | 1,723 | 1,637 | 1,475 | 1,264 |
| Mexican border zone | 1,165 | 1,007 | 1,047 | 904 | 715 |
| Total overseas areas | 4,100 | 3,762 | 3,474 | 3,146 | 3,104 |
| Europe and Mediterranean | 2,398 | 2,150 | 1,918 | 1,802 | 1,993 |
| Western Europe | 2,104 | 1,885 | 1,709 | 1,600 | 1,800 |
| United Kingdom | 585 | 494 | 404 | 368 | 354 |
| France | 233 | 254 | 226 | 198 | 237 |
| Italy | 240 | 207 | 194 | 188 | 218 |
| Switzerland | 147 | 129 | 121 | 117 | 135 |
| West Germany | 203 | 195 | 174 | 153 | 170 |
| Austria | 73 | 70 | 65 | 61 | 77 |
| Denmark | 51 | 38 | 43 | 43 | 42 |
| Sweden | 40 | 37 | 29 | 32 | 27 |
| Norway | 38 | 40 | 44 | 31 | 33 |
| Netherlands | 49 | 58 | 60 | 47 | 63 |
| Belgium–Luxembourg | 34 | 35 | 39 | 31 | 25 |
| Spain | 153 | 117 | 135 | 138 | 201 |
| Portugal | 37 | 14 | 19 | 36 | 58 |
| Iceland | n.a. | n.a. | 55 | 47 | 45 |
| Greece | 98 | 90 | 73 | 84 | 88 |
| Other Western Europe | 26 | 24 | 28 | 26 | 27 |
| Other Europe and Mediterranean | 288 | 265 | 209 | 202 | 193 |
| Israel | 146 | 118 | 57 | 95 | 100 |
| Other[1] | 142 | 147 | 152 | 107 | 93 |
| Caribbean Area and Central America | 790 | 784 | 787 | 685 | 570 |
| Bermuda | 123 | 133 | 118 | 110 | 80 |
| Bahamas | 158 | 168 | 161 | 151 | 136 |
| Jamaica | 100 | 109 | 118 | 122 | 109 |
| Other British West Indies | 144 | 125 | 103 | 87 | 95 |
| Netherlands West Indies | 106 | 102 | 97 | 60 | 55 |
| Other West Indies and Central America | 159 | 147 | 190 | 155 | 95 |
| South America | 254 | 232 | 242 | 209 | 132 |
| Other overseas areas | 658 | 596 | 527 | 450 | 409 |
| Japan | 149 | 145 | 131 | 102 | 123 |
| Hong Kong | 87 | 74 | 75 | 75 | 65 |
| Australia—New Zealand | 92 | 82 | 54 | 55 | 48 |
| Other | 330 | 295 | 267 | 218 | 173 |
| **Total expenses[2]** | **11,924** | **10,868** | **10,143** | **9,406** | **8,472** |

1. Includes U.S.S.R. 2. Cruise passenger fare payments included in transportation payments (predominantly foreign flag carriers). Shore expenditures included in regional and country totals. NOTE: n.a. = not available. *Source:* Department of Commerce, Bureau of Economic Analysis.

## International Tourist Arrivals and Receipts, 1976

| Area | Arrivals (thousands) | Receipts (millions of $) |
|---|---|---|
| Africa | 3,625 | $3,325 |
| Americas | 48,200 | 8,550 |
| Europe | 155,300 | 21,400 |
| Middle East | 3,350 | 600 |
| Pacific and East Asia | 6,925 | 5,800 |
| South Asia | 1,600 | 325 |
| **Total** | **219,000** | **$40,000** |

*Source:* World Tourism Organization.

## Worldwide Travel Volume and Expenditures

| Global totals | 1976 | 1975 |
|---|---|---|
| **Total travel volume (millions)** | **1,095** | **1,065** |
| International arrivals | 219 | 213 |
| Domestic arrivals | 876 | 852 |
| **Total travel expenditures (in $ billions)** | **$250.0** | **$216.0** |
| International travel expenditures | $ 50.5 | $ 43.0 |
| Spent at destinations | $ 40.0 | $ 34.0 |
| Spent on transportation | $ 10.5 | $ 9.0 |
| Domestic travel expenditures | $199.5 | $173.0 |

*Source:* World Tourism Organization

## Domestic Travel Expenditures
(in billions of dollars)

| Trips 100 miles or more away from home | 1976 | 1975 | 1974 |
|---|---|---|---|
| Total[1] | $115.0 | $89.7 | $72.0 |
| U.S. residents | 98.5 | 75.2 | 60.3 |
| By type of expenditure | | | |
| Transportation | 33.8 | 28.6 | 21.9 |
| Food | 34.2 | 22.5 | 17.9 |
| Lodging | 10.9 | 9.4 | 9.0 |
| Gifts and incidentals | 12.8 | 9.1 | 7.3 |
| Entertainment and recreation | 6.8 | 5.6 | 4.1 |
| By mode of transportation | | | |
| Auto and truck travelers | 68.5 | 54.6 | 39.0 |
| Air travelers | 24.9 | 16.8 | 15.2 |
| Bus travelers | 2.3 | 1.8 | 1.5 |
| Train travelers | 0.6 | 0.5 | 0.5 |
| Boat/ship travelers | 0.2 | 0.2 | 0.05 |
| Other travelers | 2.0 | 1.3 | 1.1 |
| By purpose of trip | | | |
| Visiting friends and relatives | 37.1 | 26.4 | 20.9 |
| Business | 17.0 | 11.3 | 8.2 |
| Convention | 3.8 | 3.7 | 2.7 |
| Outdoor recreation | 11.0 | 7.5 | 6.3 |
| Sightseeing and entertainment | 15.3 | 14.3 | 12.0 |
| Personal and family | 8.4 | 7.5 | 5.8 |
| Other | 6.0 | 4.5 | 4.4 |
| By type of trip | | | |
| Weekend travel | 28.8 | 19.8 | 14.5 |
| Vacation trips | 58.6 | 46.4 | 38.7 |

1. Includes U.S. expenditures by foreign visitors and expenditures on trips of 50–100 miles that included an overnight stay. Estimated total for 1977 is $126 billion; for U.S. residents, $120 billion. *Source:* U.S. Travel Data Center.

## Temporary Visitors to U.S. by Country or Region of Permanent Residence
(in thousands)

| Country or region of permanent residence | 1977 | 1976 | 1975 | 1974 | 1973 |
|---|---|---|---|---|---|
| Canada | 12,083 | 11,164 | 9,915 | 8,665 | 8,809 |
| Mexico | 2,030 | 1,921 | 2,156 | 1,841 | 1,619 |
| Total Overseas | 4,497 | 4,439 | 3,624 | 3,618 | 3,527 |
| Europe | 1,881 | 1,886 | 1,478 | 1,508 | 1,605 |
| Austria | 26 | 25 | 19 | 21 | 20 |
| Belgium | 45 | 45 | 31 | 33 | 34 |
| Denmark | 34 | 34 | 24 | 23 | 26 |
| Finland | 19 | 20 | 17 | 13 | 15 |
| France | 216 | 217 | 157 | 166 | 189 |
| Germany | 369 | 366 | 298 | 296 | 332 |
| Greece | 32 | 33 | 28 | 31 | 31 |
| Iceland | 6 | 6 | 4 | 4 | 4 |
| Ireland | 32 | 32 | 25 | 29 | 31 |
| Italy | 122 | 131 | 102 | 109 | 120 |
| Luxembourg | 2 | 2 | 2 | 1 | 2 |
| Netherlands | 104 | 95 | 74 | 71 | 73 |
| Norway | 41 | 39 | 32 | 31 | 32 |
| Portugal | 18 | 18 | 14 | 12 | 14 |
| Spain | 59 | 57 | 44 | 44 | 46 |
| Sweden | 76 | 75 | 54 | 50 | 51 |
| Switzerland | 89 | 91 | 66 | 68 | 60 |
| U.K. | 533 | 538 | 438 | 450 | 479 |
| U.S.S.R. | 7 | 6 | 6 | 6 | 5 |
| Yugoslavia | 15 | 16 | 13 | 16 | 14 |
| Other Europe | 36 | 39 | 29 | 36 | 26 |
| South America | 574 | 510 | 431 | 395 | 355 |
| Argentina | 77 | 55 | 69 | 62 | 40 |

| Country or region of permanent residence | 1977 | 1976 | 1975 | 1974 | 1973 |
|---|---|---|---|---|---|
| Brazil | 66 | 105 | 102 | 85 | 79 |
| Colombia | 89 | 76 | 59 | 60 | 64 |
| Venezuela | 208 | 152 | 104 | 89 | 81 |
| Central America | 194 | 177 | 138 | 142 | 133 |
| West Indies | 384 | 396 | 338 | 359 | 360 |
| Bahamas | 101 | 96 | 78 | 92 | 104 |
| Dominican Republic | 68 | 67 | 65 | 75 | 62 |
| Jamaica | 60 | 83 | 72 | 62 | 59 |
| Asia | 1,146 | 1,146 | 1,002 | 992 | 845 |
| Japan | 749 | 772 | 746 | 763 | 638 |
| Oceania | 236 | 250 | 185 | 172 | 187 |
| Australia | 155 | 168 | 121 | 113 | 109 |
| New Zealand | 66 | 65 | 51 | 48 | 48 |
| Africa | 81 | 74 | 53 | 48 | 41 |
| Other Overseas | 79 | 47 | 64 | 634 | 30 |
| **Total** | **18,610** | **17,523** | **15,696** | **14,123** | **13,955** |

*Source:* Department of Commerce, U.S. Travel Service.

## Travelers from the U.S. to Foreign Countries[1] by Country and Region Visited

(in thousands)

| Country or region visited | 1977 | 1976 | 1975 | 1974 | 1973 |
|---|---|---|---|---|---|
| Canada[2] | 11,460[3] | 11,658 | 12,499 | 12,735 | 13,523 |
| Mexico[4] | 2,751 | 2,640 | 2,735 | 2,857 | 2,742 |
| Total Overseas | 7,390 | 6,897 | 6,354 | 6,467 | 6,933 |
| Europe and Mediterranean | 3,920 | 3,523 | 3,185 | 3,325 | 3,915 |
| Western Europe | 3,663 | 3,295 | 2,990 | 3,118 | 3,720 |
| Austria | 359 | 395 | 377 | 335 | 516 |
| Belgium-Luxembourg | 240 | 290 | 289 | 246 | 342 |
| Denmark | 238 | 214 | 230 | 239 | 274 |
| France | 786 | 902 | 809 | 824 | 1,106 |
| Greece | 257 | 229 | 178 | 226 | 315 |
| Ireland | 303 | 251 | 191 | 175 | 210 |
| Italy | 715 | 665 | 650 | 657 | 897 |
| Netherlands | 317 | 432 | 416 | 352 | 572 |
| Norway | 147 | 133 | 135 | 134 | 170 |
| Portugal | 134 | 57 | 95 | 179 | 332 |
| Spain | 334 | 309 | 370 | 468 | 784 |
| Sweden | 180 | 154 | 150 | 164 | 184 |
| Switzerland | 620 | 585 | 567 | 544 | 772 |
| United Kingdom | 1,559 | 1,386 | 1,199 | 1,227 | 1,334 |
| West Germany | 768 | 802 | 733 | 712 | 915 |
| Other, Western Europe | 122 | 140 | 142 | 131 | 260 |
| Israel | 316 | 264 | 138 | 231 | 261 |
| Other[5] | 489 | 494 | 515 | 430 | 496 |
| Caribbean Areas & Central America | 2,203 | 2,201 | 2,065 | 2,147 | 2,032 |
| South America | 483 | 436 | 447 | 423 | 383 |
| Other Overseas Areas | 784 | 737 | 657 | 572 | 603 |
| **Total** | **21,601** | **21,195** | **22,253** | **22,760** | **23,948** |

1. Excludes travel by military personnel and other government employees stationed abroad. 2. Visitors staying one or more nights. 3. Preliminary figure. 4. Data from the Bank of Mexico, adjusted to exclude all except U.S. travel by multiplying by .85. 5. Includes the U.S.S.R. *Source:* Department of Commerce, Bureau of Economic Analysis, and Statistics Canada.

## Foreign Study

Young people who want to study in Western Europe will find useful information in a guidebook published by the European Common Market. It lists school fees, entrance requirements, etc., mainly for Common Market countries. *The Handbook for Students* costs about $4.40, and it can be obtained from the European Community Information Service, 2100 M Street, N.W., Washington, D.C. 20037.

## Object of Travel by Passport Recipients[1]

| Object | 1977 | 1973 | 1969 |
|---|---|---|---|
| Personal Reasons | 32.4% | 45.6% | 81.1% |
| Pleasure | 35.5 | 39.5 | 7.2 |
| Business | 6.1 | 5.7 | 1.4 |
| Education | 2.5 | 3.5 | .9 |
| Religious | .3 | .3 | .1 |
| Scientific | .03 | .02 | .2 |
| Health | .04 | .04 | .01 |
| Government | 5.0 | 4.6 | 9.1 |
| Not Stated | 18.2 | .8 | .07 |

1. Percentages rounded off. *Source:* Department of State, Passport Office.

## Passport Recipients by Sex and Age Groups, 1977

| Age group | Male | Female | Total |
|---|---|---|---|
| Under 5 | 49,310 | 44,840 | 94,150 |
| 5–14 | 90,440 | 90,830 | 181,270 |
| 15–24 | 205,990 | 305,330 | 511,320 |
| 25–44 | 515,460 | 484,530 | 999,990 |
| 45–59 | 381,890 | 385,720 | 767,610 |
| 60–69 | 174,070 | 200,190 | 374,260 |
| 70–over | 79,090 | 99,432 | 178,522 |
| **Total** | **1,496,250** | **1,610,872** | **3,107,122** |

*Source:* Department of State, Passport Office.

## Volume of Domestic Travel by U.S. Residents
**(in millions of person trips)**

| Domestic Travel | 1976 | 1975 | 1974 |
|---|---|---|---|
| Mode of transportation: | | | |
| Auto, truck | 595.0 | 570.0 | 504.3 |
| Air | 79.4 | 59.5 | 62.3 |
| Other | 31.3 | 31.2 | 25.2 |
| Purpose of trip: | | | |
| Visiting friends and relatives | 252.7 | 265.3 | 237.4 |
| Other pleasure | 226.5 | 194.8 | 158.7 |
| Business and convention | 150.5 | 117.2 | 91.3 |
| Other | 76.0 | 83.0 | 104.5 |
| Type of trip: | | | |
| Weekend | 325.5 | 298.8 | 263.9 |
| Vacation | 328.8 | 285.9 | 268.0 |
| Total | 705.7 | 660.3 | 591.8 |

*Source:* U.S. Travel Data Center.

# U.S. Passport and Customs Information

*Source:* Department of State, Passport Office and Customs Service

## Passports

With a few exceptions, a passport is required for all United States citizens to depart from and enter the United States and to enter most foreign countries. A United States citizen is not required by United States laws or regulations to have a valid passport for travel to or in North, South, or Central America, except Cuba. It is, however, recommended that a passport be obtained for travel to Central and South America since many of the countries require that United States citizens be in possession of a valid passport. United States travelers should carry documentary evidence of their United States citizenship and identity to facilitate re-entry into the United States. Travelers should check passport and visa requirements with consular officials of the countries to be visited well in advance of their departure date.

Applications for passport may be made to any Passport Agent or to a clerk of any Federal court, a clerk of any State court of record or a judge or clerk of any probate court accepting applications, or at a Post Office selected to accept passport applications. Passport agencies are located in Boston; Chicago; Detroit; Honolulu; Houston; Los Angeles; Miami; New Orleans; New York; Philadelphia; San Francisco; Seattle; Stamford, Conn.; and Washington, D.C.

A first passport must be applied for in person. Applicants must present evidence of citizenship (e.g., a birth certificate), personal identification (e.g., driver's license), two identical photographs taken within six months (2 x 2 inches, with the image size measured from the bottom of the chin to the top of the head [including hair] not less than 1 inch nor more than 1⅜ inches, signed on the front left-hand side and in the center on the reverse; vending machine photographs not acceptable), plus two identical photographs of any inclusions, and the application. A fee of $10 plus a $3 execution fee is charged.

You may apply by mail if you have been the bearer of a passport issued within eight years prior to the date of a new application; are able to submit your most recent United States passport with your new application; your previous passport was not issued before your 18th birthday; you are not applying for an official, diplomatic, or no-fee passport; you do not wish to include a member of your family. This procedure may be used only in the United States. If you are eligible to apply by mail, include your previous passport, completed and signed Application for Passport by Mail, new signed photographs, and the $10 passport fee. The $3 execution fee is not required when applying by mail.

If you claim Citizenship by Naturalization, a Certificate of Naturalization is required.

Passports may be amended to show a married name or legal change of name, to correct descriptive data to include your wife/husband or any children or brothers and sisters under 13 years of age, or to exclude a person previously included. You must personally present the amendment form and have it executed by an authorized person if the amendment is an inclusion.

Any alterations by the bearer other than change of address and notification data appearing on the inside cover of the passport are forbidden.

Your passport is valid for five years from date of issue unless specifically limited by the Secretary of State to a shorter period of validity.

The passport is a traveler's principal means of identification abroad, and its loss is very serious. It should be reported immediately to the nearest United States embassy or consular office. Loss of a passport in the United States should be reported in writing to the Passport Office, Department of State, Washington, D.C. 20524, or the nearest Passport Agency.

## Customs

United States residents must declare all articles acquired abroad and in their possession at the time of their return. The wearing or use of an article acquired abroad does *not* exempt it from duty. Customs declaration forms are distributed on vessels and planes, and should be prepared in advance of arrival for presentation to the immigration and customs inspectors.

If you have not exceeded the duty-free exemption allowed, you may make an oral declaration to the customs inspector. A written declaration is necessary when (1) total fair retail value of articles exceeds $100 (keep your sales slips); (2) over 1 quart of liquor or 100 cigars are included; (3) items are not intended for your personal or household use, or articles brought home for another person; and (4) when a customs duty or internal revenue tax is collectible on any article in your possession.

An exception to the above are regulations applicable to articles purchased in the Virgin Islands, American Samoa, or Guam where you may receive a customs exemption of $200.

Other exemptions include in part: automobiles, boats, planes, or other vehicles taken abroad for noncommercial use. Foreign-made personal articles (e.g., watches, cameras, etc.) taken abroad should be registered with Customs before departure. Gifts of not more than $10 can be shipped back to the United States tax and duty free ($20 if mailed from the Virgin Islands, American Samoa, or Guam). Household effects and tools of trade which you take out of the United States are duty free at time of return.

Prohibited and restricted articles include in part: absinthe, narcotics and dangerous drugs, obscene articles and publications, seditious and treasonable materials, hazardous articles (e.g., fireworks, dangerous toys, toxic and poisonous substances) and switchblade knives, biological materials of public health or veterinary importance, fruit, vegetables and plants, meats, poultry and products thereof, birds, monkeys, and turtles.

If you understate the value of an article you declare, or if you otherwise misrepresent an article in your declaration, the article may be liable to seizure and forfeiture. Duty must be paid even if the article is seized, and you may be liable for a personal penalty and in some cases criminal prosecution.

If you carry more than $5,000 into or out of the United States in currency (either United States or foreign money), negotiable instruments in bearer form, or travelers checks, a report must be filed with United States Customs at the time you arrive or depart with such amounts.

As U.S. restrictions on travel to Cuba, North Korea, Vietnam, and Cambodia have been eased, the Office of Foreign Assets Control (FAC) issued a general license, effective March 21, 1977, which allows visitors to those countries to purchase a maximum of $100 worth of goods. This amount is based on foreign market or retail value in the country where acquired.

These articles must be for personal use—not for resale—and must accompany the traveler on his entry into the U.S. This allowance may be used only once every 6 months. A license from FAC will be required for any merchandise exceeding $100.

Articles from Rhodesia are subject to FAC sanctions and may not be imported without a license from FAC.

# Health Facts for the International Traveler

*Source:* American Express Company.

## Immunizations

Protecting one's health while traveling, especially internationally, should be a primary consideration for the tourist or business traveler. An early visit to the physician (who will also advise what should be taken along as part of your traveling medical kit) will enable you to determine, with him, what immunizations, if any, will be required for your intended destination(s).[1]

No immunization is required for travel between the United States, Canada or Europe, but it is

1. Women in any stage of pregnancy must inquire as to the safety of certain immunizations before undergoing inoculation.

recommended that some general immunizations—those for poliomyelitis, tetanus, and diptheria, for example—be brought up-to-date.

Travelers to other areas of the world should review their projected itineraries with a physician or local health authorities; the changing world health picture necessitates continual adjustment of immunization requirements from country to country, and determination must be made at the time of your trip as to what inoculations are currently indicated.

Be sure that whoever you consult understands the purpose and duration of your planned visits to places where an endemic disease may be present. A business visitor staying at a first-class hotel in a large city for a brief period needs far less protection than someone interested in exploring primitive areas.

A distinction must be made between immunizations that are required and those that are recommended. If a traveler arrives at a destination requiring a documented certificate of required immunization against a disease, failure to produce it could result in his being turned away.

**Required for Certain Destinations.** Far fewer immunizations are required now than formerly: **Smallpox** has been confined to Somalia and should soon disappear entirely. Certain countries in South America and Africa require vaccination against **yellow fever. Cholera** immunization is required for travel to and from some areas.

**Recommended for Certain Destinations.** Typhoid immunization is not required, but is recommended for travelers planning long exposure to areas where the disease is endemic—Africa, Asia, Central and South America.

Immune serum globulin offers partial protection against hepatitis A, when indicated.

Travelers to malarial areas should take an oral dose of chloroquine phosphate once a week, beginning one week before arrival in the area, continuing throughout the visit, and for six weeks following departure from the area.

Just as important as these precautions is an awareness on the part of the returning traveler that symptoms experienced subsequent to travels abroad may have a connection with exposure to some of these diseases. Preventive measures may not always provide absolute immunity. If the physician is informed as to where his patient has been, he will be better able to make a correct diagnosis.

## Food and Water

The traveler in primitive or developing parts of the world can help himself avoid intestinal disorders which, even if not serious, may still last up to a week and disrupt vacation or business plans. Drinking water, and ice made from it, should be avoided unless it is boiled or comes from a sealed bottle. Fresh milk, rare meat, undercooked fish, and rich sauces can also cause serious trouble in many instances. Raw produce, if peeled just before eating, is fairly safe, but not lettuce or melons. Hot foods are usually safe in any area.

## Jet Lag

En route—jetting across several time zones at ever-increasing speeds—the traveler may experience "jet lag"—a physiological disorder caused by upset to the body's "biological clock." It can be minimized by getting enough rest; by eating and drinking very moderately before, during, and immediately after flight; and by moderating one's activities in the first few days after arrival. Some large companies instruct their executives who travel far and fast not to undertake crucial business negotiations until a few days after arriving at their destinations if they are more than three time zones away.

## Average Daily Temperatures (°F) in Tourist Cities

| | January | | April | | July | | October | |
|---|---|---|---|---|---|---|---|---|
| Location | High | Low | High | Low | High | Low | High | Low |
| **U.S. CITIES** | | | | | | | | |
| (See Weather and Climate Section) | | | | | | | | |
| **CANADA** | | | | | | | | |
| (See Canadian Section) | | | | | | | | |
| **MEXICO** | | | | | | | | |
| Acapulco | 85 | 70 | 87 | 71 | 89 | 75 | 88 | 74 |
| Mexico City | 66 | 42 | 78 | 52 | 74 | 54 | 70 | 50 |
| **OVERSEAS** | | | | | | | | |
| Australia (Sydney) | 78 | 65 | 71 | 58 | 60 | 46 | 71 | 56 |
| Austria (Vienna) | 34 | 26 | 57 | 41 | 75 | 59 | 55 | 44 |
| Bahamas (Nassau) | 77 | 65 | 81 | 69 | 88 | 75 | 85 | 73 |
| Bermuda (Hamilton) | 68 | 58 | 71 | 59 | 85 | 73 | 79 | 69 |
| Brazil (Rio de Janeiro) | 84 | 73 | 80 | 69 | 75 | 63 | 77 | 66 |
| Denmark (Copenhagen) | 36 | 29 | 50 | 37 | 72 | 55 | 53 | 42 |
| Egypt (Cairo) | 65 | 47 | 83 | 57 | 96 | 70 | 86 | 65 |
| France (Paris) | 42 | 32 | 60 | 41 | 76 | 55 | 59 | 44 |
| Germany (Berlin) | 35 | 26 | 55 | 38 | 74 | 55 | 55 | 41 |
| Greece (Athens) | 54 | 42 | 67 | 52 | 90 | 72 | 74 | 60 |

| Location | January High | January Low | April High | April Low | July High | July Low | October High | October Low |
|---|---|---|---|---|---|---|---|---|
| Hong Kong | 64 | 56 | 75 | 67 | 87 | 78 | 81 | 73 |
| India (Calcutta) | 80 | 55 | 97 | 76 | 90 | 79 | 89 | 74 |
| Italy (Rome) | 54 | 39 | 68 | 46 | 88 | 64 | 73 | 53 |
| Israel (Jerusalem) | 55 | 41 | 73 | 50 | 87 | 63 | 81 | 59 |
| Japan (Tokyo) | 47 | 29 | 63 | 46 | 83 | 70 | 69 | 55 |
| Nigeria (Lagos) | 88 | 74 | 89 | 77 | 83 | 74 | 85 | 74 |
| Netherlands (Amsterdam) | 40 | 34 | 52 | 43 | 69 | 59 | 56 | 48 |
| Puerto Rico (San Juan) | 81 | 67 | 84 | 69 | 87 | 74 | 87 | 73 |
| South Africa (Cape Town) | 78 | 60 | 72 | 53 | 63 | 45 | 70 | 52 |
| Spain (Madrid) | 47 | 33 | 64 | 44 | 87 | 62 | 66 | 48 |
| United Kingdom (London) | 44 | 35 | 56 | 40 | 73 | 55 | 58 | 44 |
| United Kingdom (Edinburgh) | 43 | 35 | 50 | 39 | 65 | 52 | 53 | 44 |
| U.S.S.R. (Moscow) | 21 | 9 | 47 | 31 | 76 | 55 | 46 | 34 |
| Venezuela (Caracas) | 75 | 56 | 81 | 60 | 78 | 61 | 79 | 61 |
| Yugoslavia (Belgrade) | 37 | 27 | 64 | 45 | 84 | 61 | 65 | 47 |

## Foreign Currency Exchange

Visitors to foreign countries can usually change their U.S. dollars into the appropriate currency at their point of departure. Most airports have currency exchange facilities, generally open from 9:00 A.M. to 10:00 P.M. The Deak-Perera Group, the largest private organization specializing in foreign money exchange, has offices in some airports. It is generally advisable for an American traveling to a foreign destination to have a small amount of the foreign currency on hand on arrival. Currency can usually be exchanged at foreign entry points.

Visitors to the United States can usually exchange their currency into U.S. dollars at their port of entry. A large number of banks also exchange foreign currency during normal banking hours.

## Foreign Exchange Rates

**(Monday, Aug. 7, 1978)**

| | Dollar value per unit of foreign currency | Units of foreign currency per dollar |
|---|---|---|
| Argentina (New Peso) | .0012 | 802.00 |
| Australia (Dollar) | 1.1565 | .8647 |
| Austria (Schilling) | .0684 | 14.63 |
| Belgium (Franc) | .0316 | 31.65 |
| Bolivia (Peso Boliviano) | .0495 | 20.20 |
| Brazil (New Cruzeiro) | .0544 | 18.36 |
| Britain (Pound) | 1.9325 | .5175 |
| Canada (Dollar) | .8781 | 1.1388 |
| Chile (Peso) | .0308 | 32.41 |
| Colombia (Peso) | .0262 | 38.08 |
| Denmark (Krone) | .1820 | 5.4945 |
| Egypt (Pound)[1] | 2.53 | .3905 |
| Ecuador (Sucre)[1] | .0402 | 24.87 |
| France (Franc) | .2292 | 4.3637 |
| Greece (Drachma) | .0275 | 36.36 |
| Holland (Guilder) | .4592 | 2.1807 |
| Hong Kong (Dollar) | .2141 | 4.6700 |
| India (Rupee)[1] | .1247 | 8.0192 |
| Indonesia (Rupiah) | .0024 | 415.00 |
| Iran (Rial) | .01441 | 70.45 |
| Israel (Pound)[2] | .0551 | 18.12 |
| Italy (Lire) | .001191 | 839.40 |
| Japan (Yen) | .005313 | 188.20 |
| Jordan (Dinar) | 3.3057 | .3025 |
| Kuwait (Dinar) | 3.6812 | .2717 |
| Lebanon (Pound) | .3355 | 2.9800 |
| Mexico (Peso) | .0438 | 22.85 |
| Norway (Krone) | .1892 | 5.2850 |
| Peru (Sol)[1] | .0064 | 154.20 |
| Philippines (Peso) | .1365 | 7.3529 |
| Portugal (Escudo) | .0203 | 45.40 |
| Saudi Arabia (Riyal) | .2950 | 3.3900 |
| Singapore (Dollar) | .4433 | 2.2560 |
| South Africa (Rand) | 1.1517 | .8683 |
| Spain (Peseta) | .0131 | 76.09 |
| Sweden (Krona) | .2246 | 4.4515 |
| Switzerland (Franc) | .5875 | 1.7020 |
| Uruguay (New Peso) | .1811 | 6.2050 |
| Venezuela (Bolivar) | .2328 | 4.2937 |
| West Germany (Mark) | .4984 | 2.0065 |

1. Official rate. 2. Floating. NOTE: Prices for foreign currencies represent rates quoted in New York by the Bank of America in the late afternoon of the date indicated. These rates are indicative of market conditions for large business transactions, not the rates available to individuals or tourists, which may differ.

## Travel Phone U.S.A.

Foreign visitors to the United States who are unfamiliar with English can dial 1-800-255-3050, a toll-free number, in order to obtain travel information in French, German, Japanese, Spanish, and Italian. Operators are on duty from 7 a.m. to 1 a.m. In an emergency, the multilingual operator at that number will also act as an interpreter over the phone.

# Information for Air Travelers

## Baggage

**Baggage allowances.** Baggage allowances may differ for different airlines, but most U.S. airlines allow you to check two pieces of baggage on domestic flights at no additional cost. In addition, you may bring on board one piece of baggage if it will fit under the seat. If you try to bring on anything too large, the airlines may ask you to check it through and pay excess baggage charges.

If you have a question, check with the airline on which you plan to travel to be sure you understand their baggage allowance regulations.

**Lost, delayed, or damaged baggage.** Loss or delay of baggage is one of the most irritating problems that can beset the air traveler. Statistics show that the overwhelming majority of bags are promptly delivered to their owners at their destinations, but statistics are of little comfort to the traveler whose baggage does not arrive with him. In an effort to minimize the number of bags that are separated from their owners, airlines have adopted an industry agreement requiring passengers to put a label showing the passenger's name on every piece of checked baggage. Carriers supply these labels at no additional charge to ticketed passengers. For the passenger who does not want his name and address to be visible, concealed labels are available from some carriers.

As a passenger, you also can take other precautions to lessen the chances that your baggage will be lost or damaged.

1. Arrive at the airport well ahead of your departure time. If you arrive at the last minute, you may make it to the flight but your baggage may not.
2. Put your name, address, and telephone number on the **inside** as well as the outside of each piece of baggage. If the outside label is torn off accidentally, airline employees will be able to identify your baggage by checking the inside label.
3. Mark your luggage in such a way that it is easily identifiable as yours—by attaching a strip of tape or a distinctive name tag on the handle, for example.
4. Remove old baggage checks at the end of a trip. Don't try to collect bag tags on your luggage showing all the places you've traveled. It only confuses the baggage handlers and increases the probability that your baggage will be sent to the wrong destination. The only label on your baggage should be the one for the current trip.
5. Lock your luggage.
6. Don't overpack. If you have to sit on a piece of luggage to close it, it's too full. Air carriers usually will not pay for damage to overstuffed luggage that breaks.

If your baggage should be lost or damaged, you should take prompt action to alert the carrier.

Failure to do so may result in the carrier's denial of your claim if the bag is not found.

Several air carriers have filed tariff rules disclaiming liability for missing baggage if it is not reported in writing within four hours of flight arrival.

See that airline personnel fill out a report form on your lost or damaged baggage.

Each airline has a special form made up for reporting lost or damaged baggage. It is usually entitled "Property Irregularity Report." Airline personnel usually will fill out the form for you. You will be asked to describe the bag and its contents.

However, this form is not considered a claim by air carriers. Usually, the airline will send claim forms to you after your baggage has been traced for three days. On the claim form you will be asked to supply additional details, including a complete description of each item in your baggage, date and place of purchase, and original cost.

Claim forms should be completed and returned to the airline as quickly as possible to expedite processing of your claim. At present, the time limit for filing claims is 45 days.

If you have not received claim forms within two weeks after the mishandling, write to the airline to request the forms, enclosing a copy of the report you filed at the airport. This will serve to protect the validity of your claim.

Remember, the amount you claim should include all costs associated with your loss. Be certain to include any consequential expenses which you have had because of the loss, damage, or delay in delivery of your baggage. Such consequential costs include, but are not limited to, phone calls, costs of obtaining estimates or other documents required by the carrier, interim purchases, services of a notary, and other expenses which you would not have incurred if your baggage had been delivered without incident.

When airline personnel receive your claim, they will evaluate it and determine the amount to offer you in settlement. You may be asked to substantiate your claim with sales receipts for missing items. Also, airlines frequently make an allowance for depreciation, based on the age of the missing items.

In general, claims involving travel on one airline only are settled within four to six weeks. Claims for baggage lost during periods of heavy travel, such as the Christmas season, and claims involving travel on more than one airline take longer, however.

Hold onto your baggage claim check—don't surrender it until you have received your baggage.

If your baggage is found, the airlines will notify you so that you can pick it up. Many airlines deliver delayed baggage to your home.

If the airline damages your baggage by dropping it, tearing off handles, or damaging it in any other way which could have been prevented, they will pay for the damage. They will not pay for damage for which you are responsible, such as breakage of fragile items packed in your baggage, or damage caused by packing luggage too full. Report damaged baggage as soon as you discover it. Airlines will not honor damage claims if you wait too long to report them. Report the damage to airline personnel at the airport or ticket office. The agent will complete a property irregularity report form, and ask you to describe the bag and the damage.

Misunderstanding on the part of consumers as to the limits of an air carrier's liability for lost or damaged baggage accounts for a large number of complaints received by the CAB. Briefly, on domestic flights, the certificated carrier's liability is usually $750 per fare-paying passenger.

Commuter air carriers usually assume a lower liability limit. If a segment of your travel is on a commuter air carrier, it is a wise idea to check with the certificated carrier to find out whether the commuter air carrier's maximum liability or the $750 limit applies to your travel.

To say that the carrier's liability is $750 does not mean that your baggage is insured for that amount.

It means simply that the maximum the airline will pay is $750, but the company may pay you any amount up to $750 or they may deny your claim, based on their assessment of your loss. CAB does not tell airline companies how much to pay to settle a claim.

According to CAB regulations, the carrier's liability limit must be printed on every ticket and on signs posted in ticket offices and where baggage is checked in. You may also see liability limit notices in the carrier's published schedules.

If your baggage is worth more than $750, you may want to obtain additional coverage above that amount by declaring excess value and paying a fee for the extra coverage. The current charge is usually 10¢ for each additional $100 in coverage. To declare excess value, you must check your bags in at the airline's ticket counter in the terminal and inform the agent of the value you wish to declare.

## Denied Boarding—"Bumping"

Starting in September 1978, new CAB regulations concerning "bumping" went into effect.

Under the new regulations, before anyone may be bumped against his will, airlines must seek volunteers who will agree to be bumped in return for a payment of the airlines' choosing. This requirement makes it possible for travelers who have more flexible schedules to accept the airline's payment and take a later flight so that passengers with tighter travel schedules are not denied seats.

If there are too few volunteers, the airlines may involuntarily bump passengers according to a priority seating plan approved by the CAB and available at all ticket counters.

Passengers who are bumped against their will now receive more compensation: The full value of their ticket coupons up to their destination or first stopover (with a minimum of $37.50, maximum of $200). In addition, should an airline fail to provide alternate transportation that brings the bumped passenger to his destination within two hours of his originally scheduled arrival time, it would have to double the monetary compensation to the passenger (minimum $75, maximum $400).

Also, airlines will have to provide a written statement that explains denied boarding compensation and passengers' rights in an oversale situation. That statement must be given to anyone who requests it at ticket counters.

These new regulations apply to scheduled flights of U.S. airlines and also to foreign airlines on flights to or from U.S. points.

## Refunds

**Unused tickets.** Refunds usually are processed by the airline that issued the ticket, regardless of the carrier listed on the unused flight coupon. The same form of payment used in purchasing the ticket is used in issuing the refund. If you paid cash, you will receive a cash refund. If you used a credit card, a credit will be processed to your account. Be prepared to wait a couple of months before the credit appears on your statement.

Keep a record of your ticket number—in case your original application is lost, the airline will need the number to trace your refund request. Request refunds for unused tickets promptly to insure that the airline will honor your claim. Some carriers have time limits for unused ticket refunds (from 18 months to 4 years from the date the ticket was issued) and, if you wait too long to turn in the ticket, you may lose the money you paid for it.

**Lost tickets.** Lost tickets also should be reported to the issuing carrier. Most carriers charge $5.00 for processing a lost ticket application.

As a precaution, you should make a note of your ticket number at the time of purchase. Write the number on your check stub or credit form. If you pay cash, make a note of the number in a place where you are not likely to lose it.

Contact the airline promptly if you lose your ticket. Most carriers require you to submit a lost ticket refund application within a limited time period.

A waiting period of 120 days usually is required before an air carrier will issue a refund for a lost ticket. However, airline tickets are good for passage for one year from the date of issue. If the ticket is used, the purchaser must bear the loss.

## In-Flight Services—Smoking

As a minimum, the price you pay for an airline ticket includes transportation from airport to airport for one passenger and a limited amount of baggage. Meals on flights are provided at the discretion of the airline management. Meals generally are not considered part of the fare which the passenger pays, and therefore no refund is due to the passenger if he finds the meal unsatisfactory or if he doesn't get one.

Usually, soft drinks, coffee, and tea are provided at no charge. Normally there is a charge for alcoholic beverages in coach.

Charges also may be assessed for headphones for stereo music and for in-flight movies.

The airline sometimes provides additional services at no extra cost, such as reserving rental cars or hotel rooms at your destination. However, the carrier does not assume any liability if the car or hotel room is not available or is unsatisfactory.

CAB regulations require U.S. certificated air carriers to provide no-smoking sections for each class of scheduled service and for charter service and to take whatever action is necessary to prevent smoking in those areas. Airlines are required to make sure each person who requests a seat in the no-smoking section is accommodated.

# Information Sources for Travel

Many government and private organizations provide tourist information as a public service. Almost all of the 50 states and the various territories of the U.S. have government-financed tourism offices to provide information about their areas. Many states have welcome centers located on major highways near their borders. Nearly every city has a visitor's bureau, convention center, or chamber of commerce—people very willing to inform visitors about their city or region. Travel agencies—which are business organizations financed by commissions from airlines, cruise lines, hotels, and other elements of the travel industry—make available a variety of travel brochures and general information, almost always without charge. International travel organizations, like American Express, also offer travel information.

Libraries and bookstores have many tour guides to the United States on their shelves. Among the best known are:

**Fodor's USA** (1 volume and 11 regional guides) (David McKay)
**Mobil Travel Guides** (7 volumes) (Mobil Oil Corp. and Rand McNally)
**National Park Guide** (Rand McNally)
**Vacationland, USA** (National Geographic Society)

Some publications covering accommodations are:

**AYH Hostel Guide and Handbook** (American Youth Hostels)
**Country Inns and Back Roads** (Berkshire Traveller Press)
**Directory** (Budget Motels & Hotels of America)
**National Directory of Budget Motels** (Pilot Industries)
**Hotel and Motel Red Book** (American Hotel Association)
**Where to Stay USA** (Council on International Educational Exchange)

For camping—including recreational vehicles and trailers:

**Campground and Trailer Park Guide** (Rand McNally)
**KOA Kampground Directory and RV Buyers Guide** (Kampgrounds of America)
**Trailering Parks & Campgrounds** (Woodall)

Many foreign governments maintain tourist offices in major American cities. International airlines generally have available detailed information about cities and countries along their routes. Travel agencies and international travel organizations like American Express and Thomas Cook also offer travel information, almost always without charge.

Libraries and bookstores have many guides to specific countries. Among the best known are:

**Fodor's Europe** (David McKay) (plus 19 guides to individual countries)
**Fielding's Travel Guide to Europe** (Fielding)
**Let's Go: Europe** (Harvard Student Agencies)
**Let's Go: Britain & Ireland** (Harvard Student Agencies)
**Let's Go: France** (Harvard Student Agencies)
**Arthur Frommer's Guides** (Frommer/Pasmantier) (18 guides to European countries and cities)
**Michelin Guides** (Michelin Tyre Co.)
**Eurail Guide** (Saltzman)
**Nagel's Guides** (Nagel) (76 guides in English)

## State and City Tourism Offices

The following is a selected list of state, territorial, and city tourism offices. Where a toll-free telephone number is available, it is given.

**ALABAMA**
Bureau of Publicity and Information
State Highway Building
Montgomery, Ala. 36130
800–633–5761

**ALASKA**
Alaska Division of Tourism
Pouch E
Juneau, Alaska 99811

**AMERICAN SAMOA**
Director of the Office of Tourism
Pago Pago, American Samoa 96799

**ARIZONA**
Arizona Office of Tourism
1656 West Jefferson, Room 417
Phoenix, Ariz. 85007

**Phoenix**
Tourist Development Department
805 N. Second St.
Phoenix, Ariz. 85004

**Tucson**
Visitor's Bureau
P.O. Box 991
Tucson, Ariz. 85702

**ARKANSAS**
Arkansas Department of Parks and Tourism
149 State Capitol Building
Little Rock, Ark. 72201

**Hot Springs**
Hot Springs Convention Bureau
P.O. Box 1500
Hot Springs, Ark. 71901

**CALIFORNIA**
Southern California Visitor's Council
705 West 7th Street
Los Angeles, Calif. 90017

**San Francisco**
San Francisco Convention and Visitor's Bureau
1390 Market Street, Suite 260
San Francisco, Calif. 94102

**COLORADO**
Travel Marketing Section
Colorado Division of Commerce and Development
602 State Capitol Annex
Denver, Colo. 80203
800—525–3083

**CONNECTICUT**
Tourism Promotion Service
Connecticut Department of Commerce
210 Washington St.
Hartford, Conn. 06106

**DELAWARE**
Delaware State Visitors Service
45 the Green
Dover, Del. 19901

**DISTRICT OF COLUMBIA**
Washington Area Convention and Visitor's Bureau
1129 20th St., NW
Washington, D.C. 20036

Public Citizen Visitors Center
1200 15th St., NW
Washington, D.C. 20005

**FLORIDA**
Division of Tourism
107 West Gaines Street
Tallahassee, Fla. 32304

**Miami**
Miami Metro Department of Publicity & Tourism
499 Biscayne Blvd.
Miami, Fla. 33132

**GEORGIA**
Tourist Division
P.O. Box 38097
Atlanta, Ga. 30334

**GUAM**
Guam Visitors Bureau
P.O. Box 3520
Agana, Guam 96910

**HAWAII**
Hawaii Visitors Bureau
P.O. Box 2274
Honolulu, Hawaii 96804

**IDAHO**
Division of Tourism and Industrial Development
State Capitol Building, Room 108
Boise, Idaho 83720

**ILLINOIS**
Office of Tourism
205 W. Wacker Drive, Room 1100
Chicago, Ill. 60606

**Chicago**
Convention and Tourism Bureau
332 S. Michigan Avenue, Room 2050
Chicago, Ill. 60604

**INDIANA**
Tourism Development Division
State House, Room 336
Indianapolis, Ind. 46204

**IOWA**
Travel Development Division
250 Jewett Building
Des Moines, Iowa 50309

**KANSAS**
Tourist Division
122 South State Office Building
Topeka, Kan. 66612

**KENTUCKY**
Division of Advertising and Travel Promotion
Capitol Annex
Frankfort, Ky. 40601

**LOUISIANA**
Louisiana Tourist Development Commission
P.O. Box 44291, Capitol Station
Baton Rouge, La. 70804

**New Orleans**
Greater New Orleans Tourist & Convention Commission
334 Royal Street
New Orleans, La. 70130

**MAINE**
Contact: Maine Publicity Bureau
3 St. John Street
Portland, Maine 04102

**MARYLAND**
Division of Tourist Development
1748 Forest Drive
Annapolis, Md. 21401

**MASSACHUSETTS**
Division of Tourism
100 Cambridge Street
Boston, Mass. 02202

**Boston**
Convention and Tourist Bureau, Inc.
900 Boylston Street
Boston, Mass. 02215

**MICHIGAN**
Michigan Travel Commission
300 S. Capitol Avenue, Suite 102
Lansing, Mich. 48926
800-248-5456

**MINNESOTA**
Tourism Division
480 Cedar St., Hanover Bldg.
St. Paul, Minn. 55101

**MISSISSIPPI**
Travel and Tourism Department
1504 Walter Sillers Building
Jackson, Miss. 39205

**MISSOURI**
Missouri Division of Tourism
P.O. Box 1055
Jefferson City, Mo. 65101

**MONTANA**
Travel Promotion Unit
Helena, Mont. 59601

**NEBRASKA**
Division of Travel and Tourism
P.O. Box 94666, State Capitol
Lincoln, Neb. 68509

**NEVADA**
Tourism Division
Capitol Complex
Carson City, Nev. 89701

**Las Vegas**
Las Vegas Chamber of Commerce
2301 E. Sahara Avenue
Las Vegas, Nev. 89105

**NEW HAMPSHIRE**
Office of Vacation Travel
P.O. Box 856
Concord, N.H. 03301

**NEW JERSEY**
Office of Tourism and Promotion
P.O. Box 400
Trenton, N.J. 08625

**Atlantic City**
Greater Atlantic City Chamber of Commerce
10 Central Pier
Atlantic City, N.J. 08401

**NEW MEXICO**
Tourist Division
113 Washington Avenue
Santa Fe, N.M. 87503
800-545-9876

**NEW YORK**
Travel Bureau
New York State
99 Washington Avenue
Albany, N.Y. 12245

**New York City**
New York Convention and Visitor's Bureau
90 East 42nd Street
New York, N.Y. 10017

**NORTH CAROLINA**
Travel Development Section
P.O. Box 27687
Raleigh, N.C. 27611

**NORTH DAKOTA**
North Dakota Travel Division
Capitol Grounds
Bismarck, N.D. 58501

**OHIO**
Travel Bureau
30 East Broad Street
Columbus, Ohio 43215

**OKLAHOMA**
Tourism Promotion Division
500 Will Rogers Building
Oklahoma City, Okla. 73105

**OREGON**
Travel Information Section
101 Highway Building
Salem, Oreg. 97310
800-547-4901

**PENNSYLVANIA**
Bureau of Travel Development
431 South Office Building
Harrisburg, Pa. 17120

**Philadelphia**
Convention and Visitor's Bureau
1525 John F. Kennedy Blvd.
Philadelphia, Pa. 19102

**PUERTO RICO**
Puerto Rico Tourism Development Company
GPO Box BN
San Juan, Puerto Rico 00936

**RHODE ISLAND**
Tourist Promotion Division
1 Weybosset Hill
Providence, R.I. 02903

**SOUTH CAROLINA**
Division of Tourism
1205 Pendleton St.
Columbia, S.C. 29202

**SOUTH DAKOTA**
Division of Tourism
Joe Foss Building
Pierre, S.D. 57501
800-843-1930

**TENNESSEE**
Tourist Development Division
1028 Andrew Jackson Bldg.
Nashville, Tenn. 37219

**TEXAS**
Texas Tourist Development Agency
Box 12008, Capitol Station
Austin, Tex. 78711

**UTAH**
Utah Travel Council
Council Hall, Capitol Hill
Salt Lake City, Utah 84114

**VERMONT**
Office of Information
61 Elm Street
Montpelier, Vt. 05602

**VIRGIN ISLANDS**
Division of Tourism
P.O. Box 1692
St. Thomas, Virgin Islands
00801

**VIRGINIA**
Virginia State Travel Service
6 North Sixth Street
Richmond, Va. 23219

**WASHINGTON**
Travel Development Division
General Administration Bldg.
Olympia, Wash. 98504

**WASHINGTON, D.C.**
*See* District of Columbia

**WEST VIRGINIA**
Travel Development Division
1900 Washington Street, East
Charleston, W.Va. 25311

**WISCONSIN**
Division of Tourism
123 W. Washington Avenue
Madison, Wis. 53702

**WYOMING**
Wyoming Travel Commission
2320 Capitol Avenue
Cheyenne, Wyo. 82002

## Homes of the Presidents and Presidential Libraries–Museums

*Source:* American Automobile Association *Tour Books* and *Information Please* questionnaires.

**GEORGE WASHINGTON**
**George Washington Birthplace National Monument:** Washingtons Birthplace, Va. 22575. Open: daily 9–5 (closed Jan. 1, Dec. 25). Free admission.
**Mount Vernon:** on George Washington Memorial Parkway, Mount Vernon, Va. 22121 (16 mi. south of Washington, D.C.). Open: March 1–Oct. 31 daily 9–5; Nov. 1–Feb. 28–daily 9–4. Adm. $2 (children 6–11, $1; under 6, free).
*Washington's home*

**JOHN ADAMS and JOHN QUINCY ADAMS**
**John Adams and John Quincy Adams Birthplaces:** 133–141 Franklin St., South Quincy, Mass. 02169. Open: April 19–Sept. 30, daily 9–5. Adm. $1 (children under 16, 50¢).
*Family home of the Adamses.*

**Adams National Historic Site:** 135 Adams St., Quincy, Mass. 02169. Open: April 19–Nov. 10—daily 9–5. Adm. 50¢ (children under 16 free).
*Home of Adams family from 1788 to 1927; built in 1731. Contains furnishings used by four Adams generations.*

**THOMAS JEFFERSON**
**Monticello:** on Route 53, 3 mi. southeast of Charlottesville, Va. 22902. Open: March 1–Oct. 31—daily 8–5; Nov. 1–Feb. 28—daily. 9–4:30 (closed Dec. 25). Adm. $2 (children 6–11, 50¢).
*Home of Jefferson; begun in 1769; finished in 1809. National shrine contains Jefferson mementos.*

**JAMES MADISON**
**Montpelier:** Montpelier Station, Va., 22957; on Route 20, 5 mi. west of Orange, Va. Estate not open to public, but graveyard may be visited.
*Madison's home.*

**JAMES MONROE**
**Ash Lawn:** off Route 53, 2½ mi. beyond Monticello, near Charlottesville, Va. 22901. Open: daily, March–Oct. 9–6, Nov.-Feb. 10–5. Adm. $1.50 (children 6–11, 75¢; under 6, free).
*Monroe's home from 1799 to 1823; a working farm with crafts planned in 1798 by Jefferson; owned by College of William and Mary.*

**ANDREW JACKSON**
**The Hermitage:** near I–40 east on U.S. 70N, 13 mi. east of Nashville, Tenn. 37076. Open: June 1–Labor Day, daily 8–6; rest of year, daily 9–5 (closed Dec. 25). Adm. $2.50 (children 6–13, 75¢; under 6, free). Student rates available.
*Jackson's home.*

**MARTIN VAN BUREN**
**Lindenwald:** on Route 9H, 2½ mi. south of Kinderhook, N.Y. 12106. Open: daily, May-Sept.
*Van Buren's home from 1839 to 1862. Designated a National Historic Site in 1974, the house is now undergoing restoration by the National Park Service; not open to visitors. Daily tours of site, May-Sept.*

**WILLIAM HENRY HARRISON**
**Berkeley Plantation (Harrison's Landing):** halfway between Richmond and Williamsburg, Va., on Virginia Route 5. Open daily 8–5. Adm. $2.50 (children 6–12, $1.25). Group rate $2.
*Ancestral home of William Henry and Benjamin Harrison. Site of first official Thanksgiving in America, in 1619.*

**JOHN TYLER**
**Sherwood Forest:** on Virginia Route 5, 20 mi. west of Colonial Williamsburg, Charles City, Va. 23030. Open: daily 9–5.
*Tyler's home; built circa 1730, it is the longest frame residence in America—300 feet in length. Original furnishings. Still occupied by Tyler family.*

**FRANKLIN PIERCE**
**Franklin Pierce Homestead:** near junction of Routes 9 and 31, northwest of Hillsboro, N.H. 03244. Open: mid-June-Labor Day, Tues.-Sun. 9–5. Adm. 50¢ (visitors under 18 free).
*Pierce's home.*

**JAMES BUCHANAN**
**Wheatland:** 1120 Marietta Ave., Route 23, Lancaster, Pa. 17603. Open: April 1–Nov. 30—Mon.-Sat. 10–5, Sun. 10–5. Last tour: 4:30. Adm. $2 (students, $1.50; children under 12, 50¢). Group rate $1.
*Home of the nation's only bachelor President; built in 1828. It contains 19th-century American furniture and decorative arts.*

**ABRAHAM LINCOLN**
**Lincoln Home National Historic Site:** 430 South 8th St., Springfield, Ill. 62701. Open: daily, 8–5 (closed Jan. 1, Dec. 25). Free admission.
*House is only home owned by Lincoln.*

**ANDREW JOHNSON**
**Andrew Johnson National Historic Site:** Greeneville, Tenn. 37743. Open: daily 9–5 (closed Dec. 25). Adm. to Homestead (June 1–Sept. 15): 50¢ (children under 16 free).
*Contains two houses where Johnson lived, tailor shop where he worked, and Andrew Johnson National Cemetery.*

**ULYSSES S. GRANT**
**U. S. Grant Home State Historic Site:** 511 Bouthillier, Galena, Ill. 61036. Open: daily 9–5 (closed Jan. 1, Thanksgiving, Dec. 25). Free admission.

**RUTHERFORD B. HAYES**
**Rutherford B. Hayes Library and Museum Site Memorial:** 1337 Hayes Ave., Fremont, Ohio 43420. Museum open: Mon.-Sat 9–5, Sun and hldys. 1:30–5. Adm.: $1.25 (children 6–12, 50¢). Library open: Mon.-Fri. 9–5, Sat. 9–12 (closed Sun.); free. Home open (tours only): Wed.-Sat. 9–5, Sun.-Tues. and hldys. 2–5. Adm.: $1.25 (children 6–12, 50¢; under 6, free). All three sites closed Jan. 1, Thanksgiving, and Dec. 25.
*Estate is known as Spiegel Grove. It contains Hayes' home, his tomb, and White House gates.*

**JAMES A. GARFIELD**
**Lawnfield:** 8095 Mentor Ave., Mentor, Ohio 44060. Open: May 1–Oct. 31—Tues.-Sat. 9–5, Sun and hldys. 1–5. Adm. $1.50 (children 12–18, $1; under 12 with adult, free). Group rates available.
*Garfield's home and Lake County Historical Society Museum.*

**BENJAMIN HARRISON**
**Benjamin Harrison Memorial Home:** 1230 North Delaware St., Indianapolis, Ind. 46202. Open: Mon.-Sat. 10–4, Sun. 12:30–4 (closed Thanksgiving, Dec. 25–Jan. 1). Adm. $1 (students, 50¢).
*Harrison's home; completed in 1875.*

**THEODORE ROOSEVELT**
**Theodore Roosevelt Birthplace National Historic Site:** 28 E. 20th St., New York, N.Y. 10003. Open: Daily in summer 9–4:30; other months, Wed.-Sun. 9–4 (closed major hldys.). Adm. 50¢. (children under 16 and persons 62 and over, free).
**Sagamore Hill National Historic Site:** 3 mi. east of Oyster Bay, L.I., N.Y. 11771, via E. Main St. Open: daily 9:30–5; July-Aug. 9:30–6 (closed Jan. 1, Thanksgiving, Dec. 25). Adm. 50¢ (children under 16 and persons 62 and over, free).

**WOODROW WILSON**
**Birthplace of Woodrow Wilson:** Coalter and Frederick Sts., Staunton, Va. 24401. Open: daily 9–5 (closed Sun., Dec.-Feb.; Jan. 1, Thanksgiving, Dec. 25). Adm. $1.50 (children 6–16 and students, 75¢).
**Woodrow Wilson House:** 2340 S St. N.W., Washington, D.C. 20008. Open: Mon.-Fri. 10–2; Sat.-Sun. 12–4 (closed Jan. 1, Thanksgiving, Dec. 25). Adm.: $1.50 (students and senior citizens, 50¢).
*Wilson retired to this house after his second term and died here three years later in 1924.*

**WARREN G. HARDING**
**Warren G. Harding Home and Museum:** 380 Mt. Vernon Ave., Marion, Ohio 43302. Open: March 15–Nov. 15, Tues.-Sun. 1–5 (closed Mon.). Adm. $1 (children 6–18, 50¢).

**CALVIN COOLIDGE**
**Calvin Coolidge Home:** Route 100A, Plymouth, Vt. 05056. Open: Memorial Day to mid-Oct.—daily 9:30–5:30. Adm. $1 (children under 14 free).

**HERBERT HOOVER**
**Herbert Hoover National Historic Site:** ½ mi. north of I-80, exit 63, West Branch, Iowa 52358. Grounds open daily 8–5. (closed Jan. 1, Thanksgiving, Dec. 25). Free admission.
*Restored two-room cottage where Hoover was born; replica of his father's blacksmith shop. Quaker meetinghouse, grave site.*
**Herbert Hoover Presidential Library–Museum:** Interstate 80, West Branch, Iowa 52358. Open: Labor Day-April 30—Mon.-Sat. 9–5, Sun. 2–5; May 1–Labor Day—Mon.-Sat. 9–6, Sun. 10–6. (closed Jan. 1, Thanksgiving, Dec. 25). Adm. 50¢.
*Exhibits portray Hoover as engineer, public servant, and humanitarian. Located in surrounding park are birthplace cottage. Quaker Meeting House, replica of Jesse Hoover's blacksmith shop, and graves of President and Mrs. Hoover.*

**FRANKLIN D. ROOSEVELT**
**Home of Franklin D. Roosevelt National Historic Site:** on U.S. 9, south end of Hyde Park, N.Y. 12538. Open: daily 9–5 (closed Jan. 1, Dec. 25). Adm. $1.50 (children under 16 and adults over 62, free). Fee includes admission to Vanderbilt Mansion and the Library–Museum.
**Franklin D. Roosevelt Library and Museum:** Albany Post Road, Hyde Park, N.Y. 12538. Open: daily 9–5 (closed Jan. 1, Dec. 25). Adm. $1.50, includes admission to Roosevelt Home and Vanderbilt Mansion (children under 16 and adults over 62, free). Archives open Mon-Fri. 9–5 (closed natl. hldys).
*Exhibits feature lives and special interests of Franklin D. and Eleanor Roosevelt. Archives contain historic papers of President and Mrs. Roosevelt and of prominent figures in his Administration. Near the Library are Roosevelt family home, which is open to public, and graves of President and Mrs. Roosevelt.*

**HARRY S. TRUMAN**
**Harry S. Truman Birthplace State Historic Site:** Truman Ave. & 11th St., Lamar, Mo. 64759. Open: Mon.-Sat. 10–4; Sun.: May 1–Nov. 1, noon–6; rest of year, noon–5 (closed Jan. 1, Easter, Thanksgiving, Dec. 25). Free.
**Harry S. Truman Library and Museum:** U.S. Highway 24 and Delaware St., Independence, Mo. 64050. Open: daily, 9–5 (closed Jan. 1, Thanksgiving, Dec. 25). Adm 50¢.
*Copy of Truman's White House office, United Nations Charter Table, state gifts and Japanese surrender documents. Film programs. Mural by Thomas Hart Benton decorates entrance hall. Truman gravesite in courtyard is open 9–5 daily.*

**DWIGHT D. EISENHOWER**
**Eisenhower Birthplace State Historical Site:** 208 E. Day St., Denison, Tex. 75020. Open: June 1–Aug. 31, daily, 8–5; Sept. 1–May 31, daily, 10–12, 1–5 (closed Dec. 25). Adm.: 25¢ (children under 16 with adult, free).
**Dwight D. Eisenhower Library:** Kansas Highway 15, Abilene, Kan. 67410. Open: daily 9–4:45 (closed Jan. 1, Thanksgiving, Dec. 25). Adm. 50¢.
*Exhibits of paintings and memorabilia relating to Eisenhower Administration are on display in Library and Museum. Place of Meditation, where*

*Eisenhower is buried, and his boyhood home are nearby and are open to visitors.*

**JOHN F. KENNEDY**

**John F. Kennedy National Historic Site:** 83 Beals St., Brookline, Mass. 02146. Open: daily 9–4:30 (closed Jan. 1, Thanksgiving, Dec. 25). Adm. 50¢ (children under 16 with adult, free).

*Kennedy's birthplace.*

**John Fitzgerald Kennedy Library:** Open for research and some other library activities in Federal Records Center, 380 Trapelo Road, Waltham, Mass. 02154, pending construction of permanent building.

*When completed, Library will house papers and memorabilia of Kennedy and other political figures and exhibits relating to John Kennedy's life and times.*

**LYNDON B. JOHNSON**

**Lyndon B. Johnson National Historic Site:** P.O. Box 329, Johnson City, Tex. 78636. Open: daily 9–5 (closed Dec. 25). Free.

*Site includes LBJ Ranch, birthplace and family cemetery at Stonewall (15 miles west of Johnson City) and his boyhood home and grandfather's ranch headquarters in Johnson City.*

**Lyndon Baines Johnson Library:** 2313 Red River, Austin, Tex. 78705. Open daily 9–5 (closed Dec. 25). Free.

*Documents, photographs, art objects and memorabilia concerning the Presidency are exhibited. Audio tapes and film recreate four decades of U.S. history. Archives house 31 million documents. Replica of Oval Office during Johnson's Presidency is on view.*

## American Consuls for the Traveler Abroad

American consuls will advise or help you if you are in serious difficulty or distress. However, they cannot do the work of travel agencies, information bureaus, banks and the police; nor can they help you find work or get residence or driving permits; and it is not a part of their duties to act as travel couriers or interpreters, to search for missing luggage or to settle disputes with hotel managers.

**Legal Aid.** If you find yourself in a dispute which could lead to legal or police action, it is wise to consult the consul.

**If Detained.** If you are detained by the police or other authorities in a foreign country, you should ask at once to be allowed to communicate with the consul.

**If Destitute.** The consul may be able to assist you to make inquiries of your family, friends, bankers and employers, or anyone else you may designate, to see if there is any way of getting you out of your difficulties.

**Finances.** The American consul is not provided with funds to disburse to American citizens who find themselves in financial difficulties while abroad; nor can he cash or guarantee checks for you.

## Boating Statistics

In 1977, there were over 10.5 million recreational boats: 980,000 inboard boats, including auxiliary sailboats; 6,200,000 outboard boats: 840,000 sailboats; 2,495,000 miscellaneous crafts. About 400,000 boats are added to the nation's waterways each year. The number of outboard motors owned in 1977 reached 7.76 million. There are almost 6,000 marinas, boatyards, and yacht clubs with waterfront property. Boatmen spent $5.9 billion on boats, accessories, and boating services.

## U.S. Motor Vehicle Travel

U.S. highway travel in 1976 amounted to 1,390 billion vehicles miles. This was a 4.5% increase over 1975, below the average annual rate of increase of 5.6% for the five years preceding the energy crisis.

Seven states reported 1975 travel in excess of 60 billion vehicle miles and accounted for 40% of all U.S. travel. California accounted for approximately 10% of the total at 132.6 billion; followed by Texas, 84.6 billion; New York, 65.1 billion; Ohio, 64.1 billion; Pennsylvania, 63.7 billion; Florida, 61.7 billion; and Illinois, 60.9 billion.

With less than 17% of the nation's total of 3.8 million route miles, main rural roads served 35% of the 1975 travel. Urban streets accounted for 54.8% of the total travel, although they represented only 17% of the total mileage. Local rural roads accounted for 10.2% of the travel on approximately 66% of the mileage.

The Interstate System accounted for about 1% of the total mileage of roads and streets and carried 19.5% of the travel.

Passenger cars represented nearly 77% of the vehicles and accounted for 77% of the travel; motorcycles, 3.6% of all vehicles and 1.7% of all travel; trucks and truck combinations, 19% of all vehicles and 21% of all travel.

Annual miles per vehicle rose from 9,530 in 1974 to 9,644 in 1975. Gallons of fuel consumed per vehicle rose from 788 in 1974 to 790 in 1975.

Between 1966 and 1973 fuel efficiency had dropped from 12.47 miles per gallon to 11.85 miles per gallon. (These are averages for all vehicles, including trucks and buses.) In 1974, fuel efficiency increased to 12.09 miles per gallon, and in 1975 it rose to 12.20 miles per gallon. A number of factors produced this improvement: reduced speed limits, changes in driving habits, and the increasing number of smaller cars.

# Road Mileages Between U.S. Cities[1]

| Cities | Birmingham | Boston | Buffalo | Chicago | Cleveland | Dallas | Denver |
|---|---|---|---|---|---|---|---|
| Birmingham, Ala. | — | 1,194 | 947 | 657 | 734 | 653 | 1,318 |
| Boston, Mass. | 1,194 | — | 457 | 983 | 639 | 1,815 | 1,991 |
| Buffalo, N.Y. | 947 | 457 | — | 536 | 192 | 1,387 | 1,561 |
| Chicago, Ill. | 657 | 983 | 536 | — | 344 | 931 | 1,050 |
| Cleveland, Ohio | 734 | 639 | 192 | 344 | — | 1,205 | 1,369 |
| Dallas, Tex. | 653 | 1,815 | 1,387 | 931 | 1,205 | — | 801 |
| Denver, Colo | 1,318 | 1,991 | 1,561 | 1,050 | 1,369 | 801 | — |
| Detroit, Mich. | 754 | 702 | 252 | 279 | 175 | 1,167 | 1,301 |
| El Paso, Tex. | 1,278 | 2,358 | 1,928 | 1,439 | 1,746 | 625 | 652 |
| Houston, Tex. | 692 | 1,886 | 1,532 | 1,092 | 1,358 | 242 | 1,032 |
| Indianapolis, Ind. | 492 | 940 | 510 | 189 | 318 | 877 | 1,051 |
| Kansas City, Mo. | 703 | 1,427 | 997 | 503 | 815 | 508 | 616 |
| Los Angeles, Calif. | 2,078 | 3,036 | 2,606 | 2,112 | 2,424 | 1,425 | 1,174 |
| Louisville, Ky. | 378 | 996 | 571 | 305 | 379 | 865 | 1,135 |
| Memphis, Tenn. | 249 | 1,345 | 965 | 546 | 773 | 470 | 1,069 |
| Miami, Fla. | 777 | 1,539 | 1,445 | 1,390 | 1,325 | 1,332 | 2,094 |
| Minneapolis, Minn. | 1,067 | 1,402 | 955 | 411 | 763 | 969 | 867 |
| New Orleans, La. | 347 | 1,541 | 1,294 | 947 | 1,102 | 504 | 1,305 |
| New York, N.Y. | 983 | 213 | 436 | 840 | 514 | 1,604 | 1,780 |
| Omaha, Neb. | 907 | 1,458 | 1,011 | 493 | 819 | 661 | 559 |
| Philadelphia, Pa. | 894 | 304 | 383 | 758 | 432 | 1,515 | 1,698 |
| Phoenix, Ariz. | 1,680 | 2,664 | 2,234 | 1,729 | 2,052 | 1,027 | 836 |
| Pittsburgh, Pa. | 792 | 597 | 219 | 457 | 131 | 1,237 | 1,411 |
| St. Louis, Mo. | 508 | 1,179 | 749 | 293 | 567 | 638 | 871 |
| Salt Lake City, Utah | 1,805 | 2,425 | 1,978 | 1,458 | 1,786 | 1,239 | 512 |
| San Francisco, Calif. | 2,385 | 3,179 | 2,732 | 2,212 | 2,540 | 1,765 | 1,266 |
| Seattle, Wash. | 2,612 | 3,043 | 2,596 | 2,052 | 2,404 | 2,122 | 1,373 |
| Washington, D.C. | 751 | 440 | 386 | 695 | 369 | 1,372 | 1,635 |

| Cities | Detroit | El Paso | Houston | Indianapolis | Kansas City | Los Angeles | Louisville |
|---|---|---|---|---|---|---|---|
| Birmingham, Ala. | 754 | 1,278 | 692 | 492 | 703 | 2,078 | 378 |
| Boston, Mass. | 702 | 2,358 | 1,886 | 940 | 1,427 | 3,036 | 996 |
| Buffalo, N.Y. | 252 | 1,928 | 1,532 | 510 | 997 | 2,606 | 571 |
| Chicago, Ill. | 279 | 1,439 | 1,092 | 189 | 503 | 2,112 | 305 |
| Cleveland, Ohio | 175 | 1,746 | 1,358 | 318 | 815 | 2,424 | 379 |
| Dallas, Tex. | 1,167 | 625 | 242 | 877 | 508 | 1,425 | 865 |
| Denver, Colo. | 1,310 | 652 | 1,032 | 1,051 | 616 | 1,174 | 1,135 |
| Detroit, Mich. | — | 1,696 | 1,312 | 290 | 760 | 2,369 | 378 |
| El Paso, Tex. | 1,696 | — | 756 | 1,418 | 936 | 800 | 1,443 |
| Houston, Tex. | 1,312 | 756 | — | 1,022 | 750 | 1,556 | 981 |
| Indianapolis, Ind. | 290 | 1,418 | 1,022 | — | 487 | 2,096 | 114 |
| Kansas City, Mo. | 760 | 936 | 750 | 487 | — | 1,609 | 519 |
| Los Angeles, Calif. | 2,369 | 800 | 1,556 | 2,096 | 1,609 | — | 2,128 |
| Louisville, Ky. | 378 | 1,443 | 981 | 114 | 519 | 2,128 | — |
| Memphis, Tenn. | 756 | 1,095 | 586 | 466 | 454 | 1,847 | 396 |
| Miami, Fla. | 1,409 | 1,957 | 1,237 | 1,225 | 1,479 | 2,757 | 1,111 |
| Minneapolis, Minn. | 698 | 1,353 | 1,211 | 600 | 466 | 2,041 | 716 |
| New Orleans, La. | 1,101 | 1,121 | 365 | 839 | 839 | 1,921 | 725 |
| New York, N.Y. | 671 | 2,147 | 1,675 | 729 | 1,216 | 2,825 | 785 |
| Omaha, Neb. | 754 | 1,015 | 903 | 590 | 204 | 1,733 | 704 |
| Philadelphia, Pa. | 589 | 2,065 | 1,586 | 647 | 1,134 | 2,743 | 703 |
| Phoenix, Ariz. | 1,986 | 402 | 1,158 | 1,713 | 1,226 | 398 | 1,749 |
| Pittsburgh, Pa. | 288 | 1,778 | 1,395 | 360 | 847 | 2,456 | 416 |
| St. Louis, Mo. | 529 | 1,179 | 799 | 239 | 255 | 1,864 | 264 |
| Salt Lake City, Utah | 1,721 | 877 | 1,465 | 1,545 | 1,128 | 728 | 1,647 |
| San Francisco, Calif. | 2,475 | 1,202 | 1,958 | 2,299 | 1,882 | 403 | 2,401 |
| Seattle, Wash. | 2,339 | 1,760 | 2,348 | 2,241 | 1,909 | 1,150 | 2,355 |
| Washington, D.C. | 526 | 1,997 | 1,443 | 565 | 1,071 | 2,680 | 601 |

1. These figures represent estimates and are subject to change.

## Road Mileages Between U.S. Cities

| Cities | Memphis | Miami | Minne-apolis | New Orleans | New York | Omaha | Phila-delphia |
|---|---|---|---|---|---|---|---|
| Birmingham, Ala. | 249 | 777 | 1,067 | 347 | 983 | 907 | 894 |
| Boston, Mass. | 1,345 | 1,539 | 1,402 | 1,541 | 213 | 1,458 | 304 |
| Buffalo, N.Y. | 965 | 1,445 | 955 | 1,294 | 436 | 1,011 | 383 |
| Chicago, Ill. | 546 | 1,390 | 411 | 947 | 840 | 493 | 758 |
| Cleveland, Ohio | 773 | 1,325 | 763 | 1,102 | 514 | 819 | 432 |
| Dallas, Tex. | 470 | 1,332 | 969 | 504 | 1,604 | 661 | 1,515 |
| Denver, Colo. | 1,069 | 2,094 | 867 | 1,305 | 1,780 | 559 | 1,698 |
| Detroit, Mich. | 756 | 1,409 | 698 | 1,101 | 671 | 754 | 589 |
| El Paso, Tex. | 1,095 | 1,957 | 1,353 | 1,121 | 2,147 | 1,015 | 2,065 |
| Houston, Tex. | 586 | 1,237 | 1,211 | 365 | 1,675 | 903 | 1,586 |
| Indianapolis, Ind. | 466 | 1,225 | 600 | 839 | 729 | 590 | 647 |
| Kansas City, Mo. | 454 | 1,479 | 466 | 839 | 1,216 | 204 | 1,134 |
| Los Angeles, Calif. | 1,847 | 2,757 | 2,041 | 1,921 | 2,825 | 1,733 | 2,743 |
| Louisville, Ky. | 396 | 1,111 | 716 | 725 | 785 | 704 | 703 |
| Memphis, Tenn. | — | 1,025 | 854 | 401 | 1,134 | 658 | 1,045 |
| Miami, Fla. | 1,025 | — | 1,801 | 892 | 1,328 | 1,683 | 1,239 |
| Minneapolis, Minn. | 854 | 1,801 | — | 1,255 | 1,259 | 373 | 1,177 |
| New Orleans, La. | 401 | 892 | 1,255 | — | 1,330 | 1,043 | 1,241 |
| New York, N.Y. | 1,134 | 1,328 | 1,259 | 1,330 | — | 1,315 | 93 |
| Omaha, Neb. | 658 | 1,683 | 373 | 1,043 | 1,315 | — | 1,233 |
| Philadelphia, Pa. | 1,045 | 1,239 | 1,177 | 1,241 | 93 | 1,233 | — |
| Phoenix, Ariz. | 1,464 | 2,359 | 1,644 | 1,523 | 2,442 | 1,305 | 2,300 |
| Pittsburgh, Pa. | 810 | 1,250 | 876 | 1,118 | 386 | 932 | 304 |
| St. Louis, Mo. | 295 | 1,241 | 559 | 696 | 968 | 459 | 886 |
| Salt Lake City, Utah | 1,556 | 2,571 | 1,243 | 1,743 | 2,282 | 967 | 2,200 |
| San Francisco, Calif. | 2,151 | 3,097 | 1,997 | 2,269 | 3,036 | 1,721 | 2,954 |
| Seattle, Wash. | 2,363 | 3,389 | 1,641 | 2,606 | 2,900 | 1,705 | 2,818 |
| Washington, D.C. | 902 | 1,101 | 1,114 | 1,098 | 229 | 1,170 | 140 |

| Cities | Phoenix | Pitts-burgh | St. Louis | Salt Lake City | San Francisco | Seattle | Wash-ington |
|---|---|---|---|---|---|---|---|
| Birmingham, Ala. | 1,680 | 792 | 508 | 1,805 | 2,385 | 2,612 | 751 |
| Boston, Mass. | 2,664 | 597 | 1,179 | 2,425 | 3,179 | 3,043 | 440 |
| Buffalo, N.Y. | 2,234 | 219 | 749 | 1,978 | 2,732 | 2,596 | 386 |
| Chicago, Ill. | 1,729 | 457 | 293 | 1,458 | 2,212 | 2,052 | 695 |
| Cleveland, Ohio | 2,052 | 131 | 567 | 1,786 | 2,540 | 2,404 | 369 |
| Dallas, Tex. | 1,027 | 1,237 | 638 | 1,239 | 1,765 | 2,122 | 1,372 |
| Denver, Colo. | 836 | 1,411 | 871 | 512 | 1,266 | 1,373 | 1,635 |
| Detroit, Mich. | 1,986 | 288 | 529 | 1,721 | 2,475 | 2,339 | 526 |
| El Paso, Tex. | 402 | 1,778 | 1,179 | 877 | 1,202 | 1,760 | 1,997 |
| Houston, Tex. | 1,158 | 1,395 | 799 | 1,465 | 1,958 | 2,348 | 1,443 |
| Indianapolis, Ind. | 1,713 | 360 | 239 | 1,545 | 2,299 | 2,241 | 565 |
| Kansas City, Mo. | 1,226 | 847 | 255 | 1,128 | 1,882 | 1,909 | 1,071 |
| Los Angeles, Calif. | 398 | 2,456 | 1,864 | 728 | 403 | 1,150 | 2,680 |
| Louisville, Ky. | 1,749 | 416 | 264 | 1,647 | 2,401 | 2,355 | 601 |
| Memphis, Tenn. | 1,464 | 810 | 295 | 1,556 | 2,151 | 2,363 | 902 |
| Miami, Fla. | 2,359 | 1,250 | 1,241 | 2,571 | 3,097 | 3,389 | 1,101 |
| Minneapolis, Minn. | 1,644 | 876 | 559 | 1,243 | 1,997 | 1,641 | 1,114 |
| New Orleans, La. | 1,523 | 1,118 | 696 | 1,743 | 2,269 | 2,626 | 1,098 |
| New York, N.Y. | 2,442 | 386 | 968 | 2,282 | 3,036 | 2,900 | 229 |
| Omaha, Neb. | 1,305 | 932 | 459 | 967 | 1,721 | 1,705 | 1,178 |
| Philadelphia, Pa. | 2,360 | 304 | 886 | 2,200 | 2,954 | 2,818 | 140 |
| Phoenix, Ariz. | — | 2,073 | 1,485 | 651 | 800 | 1,482 | 2,278 |
| Pittsburgh, Pa. | 2,073 | — | 599 | 1,899 | 2,653 | 2,517 | 241 |
| St. Louis, Mo. | 1,485 | 599 | — | 1,383 | 2,137 | 2,164 | 836 |
| Salt Lake City, Utah | 651 | 1,899 | 1,383 | — | 754 | 883 | 2,110 |
| San Francisco, Calif. | 800 | 2,653 | 2,137 | 754 | — | 817 | 2,864 |
| Seattle, Wash. | 1,482 | 2,517 | 2,164 | 883 | 817 | — | 2,755 |
| Washington, D.C. | 2,278 | 241 | 836 | 2,110 | 2,864 | 2,755 | — |

## Air Distances Between U.S. Cities in Statute Miles

| Cities | Birmingham | Boston | Buffalo | Chicago | Cleveland | Dallas | Denver |
|---|---|---|---|---|---|---|---|
| Birmingham, Ala. | — | 1,052 | 776 | 578 | 618 | 581 | 1,095 |
| Boston, Mass. | 1,052 | — | 400 | 851 | 551 | 1,551 | 1,769 |
| Buffalo, N. Y. | 776 | 400 | — | 454 | 173 | 1,198 | 1,370 |
| Chicago, Ill. | 578 | 851 | 454 | — | 308 | 803 | 920 |
| Cleveland, Ohio | 618 | 551 | 173 | 308 | — | 1,025 | 1,227 |
| Dallas, Tex. | 581 | 1,551 | 1,198 | 803 | 1,025 | — | 663 |
| Denver, Colo. | 1,095 | 1,769 | 1,370 | 920 | 1,227 | 663 | — |
| Detroit, Mich. | 641 | 613 | 216 | 238 | 90 | 999 | 1,156 |
| El Paso, Tex. | 1,152 | 2,072 | 1,692 | 1,252 | 1,525 | 572 | 557 |
| Houston, Tex. | 567 | 1,605 | 1,286 | 940 | 1,114 | 225 | 879 |
| Indianapolis, Ind. | 433 | 807 | 435 | 165 | 263 | 763 | 1,000 |
| Kansas City, Mo. | 579 | 1,251 | 861 | 414 | 700 | 451 | 558 |
| Los Angeles, Calif. | 1,802 | 2,596 | 2,198 | 1,745 | 2,049 | 1,240 | 831 |
| Louisville, Ky. | 331 | 826 | 483 | 269 | 311 | 726 | 1,038 |
| Memphis, Tenn. | 217 | 1,137 | 803 | 482 | 630 | 420 | 879 |
| Miami, Fla. | 665 | 1,255 | 1,181 | 1,188 | 1,087 | 1,111 | 1,726 |
| Minneapolis, Minn. | 862 | 1,123 | 731 | 355 | 630 | 862 | 700 |
| New Orleans, La. | 312 | 1,359 | 1,086 | 833 | 924 | 443 | 1,082 |
| New York, N. Y. | 864 | 188 | 292 | 713 | 405 | 1,374 | 1,631 |
| Omaha, Neb. | 732 | 1,282 | 883 | 432 | 739 | 586 | 488 |
| Philadelphia, Pa. | 783 | 271 | 279 | 666 | 360 | 1,299 | 1,579 |
| Phoenix, Ariz. | 1,456 | 2,300 | 1,906 | 1,453 | 1,749 | 887 | 586 |
| Pittsburgh, Pa. | 608 | 483 | 178 | 410 | 115 | 1,070 | 1,320 |
| St. Louis, Mo. | 400 | 1,038 | 662 | 262 | 492 | 547 | 796 |
| Salt Lake City, Utah | 1,466 | 2,099 | 1,699 | 1,260 | 1,568 | 999 | 371 |
| San Francisco, Calif. | 2,013 | 2,699 | 2,300 | 1,858 | 2,166 | 1,483 | 949 |
| Seattle, Wash. | 2,082 | 2,493 | 2,117 | 1,737 | 2,026 | 1,681 | 1,021 |
| Washington, D.C. | 661 | 393 | 292 | 597 | 306 | 1,185 | 1,494 |

| Cities | Detroit | El Paso | Houston | Indianapolis | Kansas City | Los Angeles | Louisville |
|---|---|---|---|---|---|---|---|
| Birmingham, Ala. | 641 | 1,152 | 567 | 433 | 579 | 1,802 | 331 |
| Boston, Mass. | 613 | 2,072 | 1,605 | 807 | 1,251 | 2,596 | 826 |
| Buffalo, N. Y. | 216 | 1,692 | 1,286 | 435 | 861 | 2,198 | 483 |
| Chicago, Ill. | 238 | 1,252 | 940 | 165 | 414 | 1,745 | 269 |
| Cleveland, Ohio | 90 | 1,525 | 1,114 | 263 | 700 | 2,049 | 311 |
| Dallas, Tex. | 999 | 572 | 225 | 763 | 451 | 1,240 | 726 |
| Denver, Colo. | 1,156 | 557 | 879 | 1,000 | 558 | 831 | 1,038 |
| Detroit, Mich. | — | 1,479 | 1,105 | 240 | 645 | 1,983 | 316 |
| El Paso, Tex. | 1,479 | — | 676 | 1,264 | 839 | 701 | 1,254 |
| Houston, Tex. | 1,105 | 676 | — | 865 | 644 | 1,374 | 803 |
| Indianapolis, Ind. | 240 | 1,264 | 865 | — | 453 | 1,809 | 107 |
| Kansas City, Mo. | 645 | 839 | 644 | 453 | — | 1,356 | 480 |
| Los Angeles, Calif. | 1,983 | 701 | 1,374 | 1,809 | 1,356 | — | 1,829 |
| Louisville, Ky. | 316 | 1,254 | 803 | 107 | 480 | 1,829 | — |
| Memphis, Tenn. | 623 | 976 | 484 | 384 | 369 | 1,603 | 320 |
| Miami, Fla. | 1,152 | 1,643 | 968 | 1,024 | 1,241 | 2,339 | 919 |
| Minneapolis, Minn. | 543 | 1,157 | 1,056 | 511 | 413 | 1,524 | 605 |
| New Orleans, La. | 939 | 983 | 318 | 712 | 680 | 1,673 | 623 |
| New York, N. Y. | 482 | 1,905 | 1,420 | 646 | 1,097 | 2,451 | 652 |
| Omaha, Neb. | 669 | 878 | 794 | 525 | 166 | 1,315 | 580 |
| Philadelphia, Pa. | 443 | 1,836 | 1,341 | 585 | 1,038 | 2,394 | 582 |
| Phoenix, Ariz. | 1,690 | 346 | 1,017 | 1,499 | 1,049 | 357 | 1,508 |
| Pittsburgh, Pa. | 205 | 1,590 | 1,137 | 330 | 781 | 2,136 | 344 |
| St. Louis, Mo. | 455 | 1,034 | 679 | 231 | 238 | 1,589 | 242 |
| Salt Lake City, Utah | 1,492 | 689 | 1,200 | 1,356 | 925 | 579 | 1,402 |
| San Francisco, Calif. | 2,091 | 995 | 1,645 | 1,949 | 1,506 | 347 | 1,986 |
| Seattle, Wash. | 1,938 | 1,376 | 1,891 | 1,872 | 1,506 | 959 | 1,943 |
| Washington, D.C. | 396 | 1,728 | 1,220 | 494 | 945 | 2,300 | 476 |

*Source:* National Geodetic Survey.

## Air Distances Between U.S. Cities in Statute Miles

| Cities | Memphis | Miami | Minneapolis | New Orleans | New York | Omaha | Philadelphia |
|---|---|---|---|---|---|---|---|
| Birmingham, Ala. | 217 | 665 | 862 | 312 | 864 | 732 | 783 |
| Boston, Mass. | 1,137 | 1,255 | 1,123 | 1,359 | 188 | 1,282 | 271 |
| Buffalo, N. Y. | 803 | 1,181 | 731 | 1,086 | 292 | 883 | 279 |
| Chicago, Ill. | 482 | 1,188 | 355 | 833 | 713 | 432 | 666 |
| Cleveland, Ohio | 630 | 1,087 | 630 | 924 | 405 | 739 | 360 |
| Dallas, Tex. | 420 | 1,111 | 862 | 443 | 1,374 | 586 | 1,299 |
| Denver, Colo. | 879 | 1,726 | 700 | 1,082 | 1,631 | 488 | 1,579 |
| Detroit, Mich. | 623 | 1,152 | 543 | 939 | 482 | 669 | 443 |
| El Paso, Tex. | 976 | 1,643 | 1,157 | 983 | 1,905 | 878 | 1,836 |
| Houston, Tex. | 484 | 968 | 1,056 | 318 | 1,420 | 794 | 1,341 |
| Indianapolis, Ind. | 384 | 1,024 | 511 | 712 | 646 | 525 | 585 |
| Kansas City, Mo. | 369 | 1,241 | 413 | 680 | 1,097 | 166 | 1,038 |
| Los Angeles, Calif. | 1,603 | 2,339 | 1,524 | 1,673 | 2,451 | 1,315 | 2,394 |
| Louisville, Ky. | 320 | 919 | 605 | 623 | 652 | 580 | 582 |
| Memphis, Tenn. | — | 872 | 699 | 358 | 957 | 529 | 881 |
| Miami, Fla. | 872 | — | 1,511 | 669 | 1,092 | 1,397 | 1,019 |
| Minneapolis, Minn. | 699 | 1,511 | — | 1,051 | 1,018 | 290 | 985 |
| New Orleans, La. | 358 | 669 | 1,051 | — | 1,171 | 847 | 1,089 |
| New York, N. Y. | 957 | 1,092 | 1,018 | 1,171 | — | 1,144 | 83 |
| Omaha, Neb. | 529 | 1,397 | 290 | 847 | 1,144 | — | 1,094 |
| Philadelphia, Pa. | 881 | 1,019 | 985 | 1,089 | 83 | 1,094 | — |
| Phoenix, Ariz. | 1,263 | 1,982 | 1,280 | 1,316 | 2,145 | 1,036 | 2,083 |
| Pittsburgh, Pa. | 660 | 1,010 | 743 | 919 | 317 | 836 | 259 |
| St. Louis, Mo. | 240 | 1,061 | 466 | 598 | 875 | 354 | 811 |
| Salt Lake City, Utah | 1,250 | 2,089 | 987 | 1,434 | 1,972 | 833 | 1,925 |
| San Francisco, Calif. | 1,802 | 2,594 | 1,584 | 1,926 | 2,571 | 1,429 | 2,523 |
| Seattle, Wash. | 1,867 | 2,734 | 1,395 | 2,101 | 2,408 | 1,369 | 2,380 |
| Washington, D.C. | 765 | 923 | 934 | 966 | 205 | 1,014 | 123 |

| Cities | Phoenix | Pittsburgh | St. Louis | Salt Lake City | San Francisco | Seattle | Washington |
|---|---|---|---|---|---|---|---|
| Birmingham, Ala. | 1,456 | 608 | 400 | 1,466 | 2,013 | 2,082 | 661 |
| Boston, Mass. | 2,300 | 483 | 1,038 | 2,099 | 2,699 | 2,493 | 393 |
| Buffalo, N. Y. | 1,906 | 178 | 662 | 1,699 | 2,300 | 2,117 | 292 |
| Chicago, Ill. | 1,453 | 410 | 262 | 1,260 | 1,858 | 1,737 | 597 |
| Cleveland, Ohio | 1,749 | 115 | 492 | 1,568 | 2,166 | 2,026 | 306 |
| Dallas, Tex. | 887 | 1,070 | 547 | 999 | 1,483 | 1,681 | 1,185 |
| Denver, Colo. | 586 | 1,320 | 796 | 371 | 949 | 1,021 | 1,494 |
| Detroit, Mich. | 1,690 | 205 | 455 | 1,492 | 2,091 | 1,938 | 396 |
| El Paso, Tex. | 346 | 1,590 | 1,034 | 689 | 995 | 1,376 | 1,728 |
| Houston, Tex. | 1,017 | 1,137 | 679 | 1,200 | 1,645 | 1,891 | 1,220 |
| Indianapolis, Ind. | 1,499 | 330 | 231 | 1,356 | 1,949 | 1,872 | 494 |
| Kansas City, Mo. | 1,049 | 781 | 238 | 925 | 1,506 | 1,506 | 945 |
| Los Angeles, Calif. | 357 | 2,136 | 1,589 | 579 | 347 | 959 | 2,300 |
| Louisville, Ky. | 1,508 | 344 | 242 | 1,402 | 1,986 | 1,943 | 476 |
| Memphis, Tenn. | 1,263 | 660 | 240 | 1,250 | 1,802 | 1,867 | 765 |
| Miami, Fla. | 1,982 | 1,010 | 1,061 | 2,089 | 2,594 | 2,734 | 923 |
| Minneapolis, Minn. | 1,280 | 743 | 466 | 987 | 1,584 | 1,395 | 934 |
| New Orleans, La. | 1,316 | 919 | 598 | 1,434 | 1,926 | 2,101 | 966 |
| New York, N. Y. | 2,145 | 317 | 875 | 1,972 | 2,571 | 2,408 | 205 |
| Omaha, Neb. | 1,036 | 836 | 354 | 833 | 1,429 | 1,369 | 1,014 |
| Philadelphia, Pa. | 2,083 | 259 | 811 | 1,925 | 2,523 | 2,380 | 123 |
| Phoenix, Ariz. | — | 1,828 | 1,272 | 504 | 653 | 1,114 | 1,983 |
| Pittsburgh, Pa. | 1,828 | — | 559 | 1,668 | 2,264 | 2,138 | 192 |
| St. Louis, Mo. | 1,272 | 559 | — | 1,162 | 1,744 | 1,724 | 712 |
| Salt Lake City, Utah | 504 | 1,668 | 1,162 | — | 600 | 701 | 1,848 |
| San Francisco, Calif. | 653 | 2,264 | 1,744 | 600 | — | 678 | 2,442 |
| Seattle, Wash. | 1,114 | 2,138 | 1,724 | 701 | 678 | — | 2,329 |
| Washington, D.C. | 1,983 | 192 | 712 | 1,848 | 2,442 | 2,329 | — |

*Source:* National Geodetic Survey.

## Air Distances Between World Cities in Statute Miles

| Cities | Berlin | Buenos Aires | Cairo | Calcutta | Cape Town | Caracas | Chicago |
|---|---|---|---|---|---|---|---|
| Berlin | — | 7,402 | 1,795 | 4,368 | 5,981 | 5,247 | 4,405 |
| Buenos Aires | 7,402 | — | 7,345 | 10,265 | 4,269 | 3,168 | 5,598 |
| Cairo | 1,795 | 7,345 | — | 3,539 | 4,500 | 6,338 | 6,129 |
| Calcutta | 4,368 | 10,265 | 3,539 | — | 6,024 | 9,605 | 7,980 |
| Cape Town, South Africa | 5,981 | 4,269 | 4,500 | 6,024 | — | 6,365 | 8,494 |
| Caracas, Venezuela | 5,247 | 3,168 | 6,338 | 9,605 | 6,365 | — | 2,501 |
| Chicago | 4,405 | 5,598 | 6,129 | 7,980 | 8,494 | 2,501 | — |
| Hong Kong | 5,440 | 11,472 | 5,061 | 1,648 | 7,375 | 10,167 | 7,793 |
| Honolulu, Hawaii | 7,309 | 7,561 | 8,838 | 7,047 | 11,534 | 6,013 | 4,250 |
| Istanbul | 1,078 | 7,611 | 768 | 3,638 | 5,154 | 6,048 | 5,477 |
| Lisbon | 1,436 | 5,956 | 2,363 | 5,638 | 5,325 | 4,041 | 3,990 |
| London | 579 | 6,916 | 2,181 | 4,947 | 6,012 | 4,660 | 3,950 |
| Los Angeles | 5,724 | 6,170 | 7,520 | 8,090 | 9,992 | 3,632 | 1,745 |
| Manila | 6,132 | 11,051 | 5,704 | 2,203 | 7,486 | 10,620 | 8,143 |
| Mexico City | 6,047 | 4,592 | 7,688 | 9,492 | 8,517 | 2,232 | 1,691 |
| Montreal | 3,729 | 5,615 | 5,414 | 7,607 | 7,931 | 2,449 | 744 |
| Moscow | 1,004 | 8,376 | 1,803 | 3,321 | 6,300 | 6,173 | 4,974 |
| New York | 3,965 | 5,297 | 5,602 | 7,918 | 7,764 | 2,132 | 713 |
| Paris | 545 | 6,870 | 1,995 | 4,883 | 5,807 | 4,736 | 4,134 |
| Rio de Janeiro | 6,220 | 1,200 | 6,146 | 9,377 | 3,773 | 2,810 | 5,296 |
| Rome | 734 | 6,929 | 1,320 | 4,482 | 5,249 | 5,196 | 4,808 |
| San Francisco | 5,661 | 6,467 | 7,364 | 7,814 | 10,247 | 3,904 | 1,858 |
| Shanghai, China | 5,218 | 12,201 | 5,183 | 2,117 | 8,061 | 9,501 | 7,061 |
| Stockholm | 504 | 7,808 | 2,111 | 4,195 | 6,444 | 5,420 | 4,278 |
| Sydney, Australia | 10,006 | 7,330 | 8,952 | 5,685 | 6,843 | 9,513 | 9,272 |
| Tokyo | 5,540 | 11,408 | 5,935 | 3,194 | 9,156 | 8,799 | 6,299 |
| Warsaw | 320 | 7,662 | 1,630 | 4,048 | 5,958 | 5,517 | 4,667 |
| Washington, D.C. | 4,169 | 5,218 | 5,800 | 8,084 | 7,901 | 2,059 | 597 |

| Cities | Hong Kong | Honolulu | Istanbul | Lisbon | London | Los Angeles | Manila |
|---|---|---|---|---|---|---|---|
| Berlin | 5,440 | 7,309 | 1,078 | 1,436 | 579 | 5,724 | 6,132 |
| Buenos Aires | 11,472 | 7,561 | 7,611 | 5,956 | 6,916 | 6,170 | 11,051 |
| Cairo | 5,061 | 8,838 | 768 | 2,363 | 2,181 | 7,520 | 5,704 |
| Calcutta | 1,648 | 7,047 | 3,638 | 5,638 | 4,947 | 8,090 | 2,203 |
| Cape Town, South Africa | 7,375 | 11,534 | 5,154 | 5,325 | 6,012 | 9,992 | 7,486 |
| Caracas, Venezuela | 10,167 | 6,013 | 6,048 | 4,041 | 4,660 | 3,632 | 10,620 |
| Chicago | 7,793 | 4,250 | 5,477 | 3,990 | 3,950 | 1,745 | 8,143 |
| Hong Kong | — | 5,549 | 4,984 | 6,853 | 5,982 | 7,195 | 693 |
| Honolulu, Hawaii | 5,549 | — | 8,109 | 7,820 | 7,228 | 2,574 | 5,299 |
| Istanbul | 4,984 | 8,109 | — | 2,012 | 1,552 | 6,783 | 5,664 |
| Lisbon | 6,853 | 7,820 | 2,012 | — | 985 | 5,621 | 7,546 |
| London | 5,982 | 7,228 | 1,552 | 985 | — | 5,382 | 6,672 |
| Los Angeles, Calif. | 7,195 | 2,574 | 6,783 | 5,621 | 5,382 | — | 7,261 |
| Manila | 693 | 5,299 | 5,664 | 7,546 | 6,672 | 7,261 | — |
| Mexico City | 8,782 | 3,779 | 7,110 | 5,390 | 5,550 | 1,589 | 8,835 |
| Montreal | 7,729 | 4,910 | 4,789 | 3,246 | 3,282 | 2,427 | 8,186 |
| Moscow | 4,439 | 7,037 | 1,091 | 2,427 | 1,555 | 6,003 | 5,131 |
| New York | 8,054 | 4,964 | 4,975 | 3,364 | 3,458 | 2,451 | 8,498 |
| Paris | 5,985 | 7,438 | 1,400 | 904 | 213 | 5,588 | 6,677 |
| Rio de Janeiro | 11,021 | 8,285 | 6,389 | 4,796 | 5,766 | 6,331 | 11,259 |
| Rome | 5,768 | 8,022 | 843 | 1,161 | 887 | 6,732 | 6,457 |
| San Francisco | 6,897 | 2,393 | 6,703 | 5,666 | 5,357 | 347 | 6,967 |
| Shanghai, China | 764 | 4,941 | 4,962 | 6,654 | 5,715 | 6,438 | 1,150 |
| Stockholm | 5,113 | 6,862 | 1,348 | 1,856 | 890 | 5,454 | 5,797 |
| Sydney, Australia | 4,584 | 4,943 | 9,294 | 11,302 | 10,564 | 7,530 | 3,944 |
| Tokyo | 1,794 | 3,853 | 5,560 | 6,915 | 5,940 | 5,433 | 1,866 |
| Warsaw | 5,144 | 7,355 | 863 | 1,715 | 899 | 5,922 | 5,837 |
| Washington, D.C. | 8,147 | 4,519 | 5,215 | 3,562 | 3,663 | 2,300 | 8,562 |

*Source: Encyclopaedia Britannica.*

## Air Distances Between World Cities in Statute Miles

| Cities | Mexico City | Montreal | Moscow | New York | Paris | Rio de Janeiro | Rome |
|---|---|---|---|---|---|---|---|
| Berlin | 6,047 | 3,729 | 1,004 | 3,965 | 545 | 6,220 | 734 |
| Buenos Aires | 4,592 | 5,615 | 8,376 | 5,297 | 6,870 | 1,200 | 6,929 |
| Cairo | 7,688 | 5,414 | 1,803 | 5,602 | 1,995 | 6,146 | 1,320 |
| Calcutta | 9,492 | 7,607 | 3,321 | 7,918 | 4,883 | 9,377 | 4,482 |
| Cape Town, South Africa | 8,517 | 7,931 | 6,300 | 7,764 | 5,807 | 3,773 | 5,249 |
| Caracas, Venezuela | 2,232 | 2,449 | 6,173 | 2,132 | 4,736 | 2,810 | 5,196 |
| Chicago | 1,691 | 744 | 4,974 | 713 | 4,134 | 5,296 | 4,808 |
| Hong Kong | 8,782 | 7,729 | 4,439 | 8,054 | 5,985 | 11,021 | 5,768 |
| Honolulu | 3,779 | 4,910 | 7,037 | 4,964 | 7,438 | 8,285 | 8,022 |
| Istanbul | 7,110 | 4,789 | 1,091 | 4,975 | 1,400 | 6,389 | 843 |
| Lisbon | 5,390 | 3,246 | 2,427 | 3,364 | 904 | 4,796 | 1,161 |
| London | 5,550 | 3,282 | 1,555 | 3,458 | 213 | 5,766 | 887 |
| Los Angeles | 1,589 | 2,427 | 6,003 | 2,451 | 5,588 | 6,331 | 6,732 |
| Manila | 8,835 | 8,186 | 5,131 | 8,498 | 6,677 | 11,259 | 6,457 |
| Mexico City | — | 2,318 | 6,663 | 2,094 | 5,716 | 4,771 | 6,366 |
| Montreal | 2,318 | — | 4,386 | 320 | 3,422 | 5,097 | 4,080 |
| Moscow | 6,663 | 4,386 | — | 4,665 | 1,544 | 7,175 | 1,474 |
| New York | 2,094 | 320 | 4,665 | — | 3,624 | 4,817 | 4,281 |
| Paris | 5,716 | 3,422 | 1,544 | 3,624 | — | 5,699 | 697 |
| Rio de Janeiro | 4,771 | 5,097 | 7,175 | 4,817 | 5,699 | — | 5,684 |
| Rome | 6,366 | 4,080 | 1,474 | 4,281 | 697 | 5,684 | — |
| San Francisco | 1,887 | 2,539 | 5,871 | 2,571 | 5,558 | 6,621 | 6,240 |
| Shanghai, China | 8,022 | 7,053 | 4,235 | 7,371 | 5,754 | 11,336 | 5,677 |
| Stockholm | 5,959 | 3,667 | 762 | 3,924 | 958 | 6,651 | 1,234 |
| Sydney, Australia | 8,052 | 9,954 | 9,012 | 9,933 | 10,544 | 8,306 | 10,136 |
| Tokyo | 7,021 | 6,383 | 4,647 | 6,740 | 6,034 | 11,533 | 6,135 |
| Warsaw | 6,365 | 4,009 | 715 | 4,344 | 849 | 6,467 | 817 |
| Washington, D.C. | 1,887 | 488 | 4,858 | 205 | 3,829 | 4,796 | 4,434 |

| Cities | San Francisco | Shanghai | Stockholm | Sydney | Tokyo | Warsaw | Washington |
|---|---|---|---|---|---|---|---|
| Berlin | 5,661 | 5,218 | 504 | 10,006 | 5,540 | 320 | 4,169 |
| Buenos Aires | 6,467 | 12,201 | 7,808 | 7,330 | 11,408 | 7,662 | 5,218 |
| Cairo | 7,364 | 5,183 | 2,111 | 8,952 | 5,935 | 1,630 | 5,800 |
| Calcutta | 7,814 | 2,117 | 4,195 | 5,685 | 3,194 | 4,048 | 8,084 |
| Cape Town, South Africa | 10,247 | 8,061 | 6,444 | 6,843 | 9,156 | 5,958 | 7,901 |
| Caracas, Venezuela | 3,904 | 9,501 | 5,420 | 9,513 | 8,799 | 5,517 | 2,059 |
| Chicago | 1,858 | 7,061 | 4,278 | 9,272 | 6,299 | 4,667 | 597 |
| Hong Kong | 6,897 | 764 | 5,113 | 4,584 | 1,794 | 5,144 | 8,147 |
| Honolulu | 2,393 | 4,941 | 6,862 | 4,943 | 3,853 | 7,355 | 4,519 |
| Istanbul | 6,703 | 4,962 | 1,348 | 9,294 | 5,560 | 863 | 5,215 |
| Lisbon | 5,666 | 6,654 | 1,856 | 11,302 | 6,915 | 1,715 | 3,562 |
| London | 5,357 | 5,715 | 890 | 10,564 | 5,940 | 899 | 3,663 |
| Los Angeles | 347 | 6,438 | 5,454 | 7,530 | 5,433 | 5,922 | 2,300 |
| Manila | 6,967 | 1,150 | 5,797 | 3,944 | 1,866 | 5,837 | 8,562 |
| Mexico City | 1,887 | 8,022 | 5,959 | 8,052 | 7,021 | 6,365 | 1,887 |
| Montreal | 2,539 | 7,053 | 3,667 | 9,954 | 6,383 | 4,009 | 488 |
| Moscow | 5,871 | 4,235 | 762 | 9,012 | 4,647 | 715 | 4,858 |
| New York | 2,571 | 7,371 | 3,924 | 9,933 | 6,740 | 4,344 | 205 |
| Paris | 5,558 | 5,754 | 958 | 10,544 | 6,034 | 849 | 3,829 |
| Rio de Janeiro | 6,621 | 11,336 | 6,651 | 8,306 | 11,533 | 6,467 | 4,796 |
| Rome | 6,240 | 5,677 | 1,234 | 10,136 | 6,135 | 817 | 4,434 |
| San Francisco | — | 6,140 | 5,361 | 7,416 | 5,135 | 5,841 | 2,442 |
| Shanghai, China | 6,140 | — | 4,825 | 4,899 | 1,097 | 4,951 | 7,448 |
| Stockholm | 5,361 | 4,825 | — | 9,696 | 5,051 | 501 | 4,123 |
| Sydney, Australia | 7,416 | 4,899 | 9,696 | — | 4,866 | 9,696 | 9,758 |
| Tokyo | 5,135 | 1,097 | 5,051 | 4,866 | — | 5,249 | 6,772 |
| Warsaw | 5,841 | 4,951 | 501 | 9,696 | 5,249 | — | 4,457 |
| Washington, D.C. | 2,442 | 7,448 | 4,123 | 9,758 | 6,772 | 4,457 | — |

*Source: Encyclopedia Britannica.*

# STRUCTURES

## The Seven Wonders of the World

(Not all classical writers list the same items as the Seven Wonders, but most of them agree on the following.)

**The Pyramids of Egypt.** A group of three pyramids, *Khufu, Khafra,* and *Menkaura* at Giza, outside modern Cairo, is often called the first wonder of the world. The largest pyramid, built by Khufu (Cheops), a king of the fourth Dynasty, had an original estimated height of 482 ft (now approximately 450 ft). The base has sides 755 ft long. It contains 2,300,000 blocks; the average weight of each is 2.5 tons. Estimated date of construction is 2800 B.C. Of all the Seven Wonders, the pyramids alone survive.

**Hanging Gardens of Babylon.** Often listed as the second wonder, these gardens were supposedly built by Nebuchadnezzar about 600 B.C. to please his queen, Amuhia. They are also associated with the mythical Assyrian Queen, Semiramis. Archeologists surmise that the gardens were laid out atop a vaulted building, with provisions for raising water. The terraces were said to rise from 75 to 300 ft.

The Walls of Babylon, also built by Nebuchadnezzar, are sometimes referred to as the second (or the seventh) wonder instead of the Hanging Gardens.

**Statue of Zeus (Jupiter) at Olympia.** The work of Phidias (5th century B.C.), this colossal figure in gold and ivory was reputedly 40 ft high. All trace of it is lost, except for reproductions on coins.

**Temple of Artemis (Diana) at Ephesus.** A beautiful structure, begun about 350 B.C. in honor of a non-Hellenic goddess who later became identified with the Greek goddess of the same name. The temple, with Ionic columns 60 ft high, was destroyed by invading Goths in A.D. 262.

**Mausoleum at Halicarnassus.** This famous monument was erected by Queen Artemisia in memory of her husband, King Mausolus of Caria in Asia Minor, who died in 353 B.C. Some remains of the structure are in the British Museum. This shrine is the source of the modern word "mausoleum."

**Colossus at Rhodes.** This bronze statue of Helios (Apollo), about 105 ft high, was the work of the sculptor Chares, who reputedly labored for 12 years before completing it in 280 B.C. It was destroyed during an earthquake in 224 B.C.

**Pharos of Alexandria.** The seventh wonder was the Pharos (lighthouse) of Alexandria, built by Sostratus of Cnidus during the 3rd century B.C. on the island of Pharos off the coast of Egypt. It was destroyed by an earthquake in the 13th century.

## Famous Structures

### Ancient

The *Great Sphinx of Egypt,* one of the wonders of ancient Egyptian architecture, adjoins the pyramids of Giza and has a length of 240 ft. It was built in the 4th dynasty.

Other Egyptian buildings of note include the *Temples of Karnak* and *Edfu* and the *Tombs at Beni Hassan.*

The *Parthenon of Greece,* built on the Acropolis in Athens, was the chief temple to the goddess Athena. It was believed to have been completed by 438 B.C. The present temple remained intact until the 5th century A.D. Today, though the Parthenon is in ruins, its majestic proportions are still discernible.

Other great structures of ancient Greece were the *Temples at Paestum* (about 540 and 420 B.C.); the *Temple of Poseidon* (about 460 B.C.); the *Temple of Apollo* at Corinth (about 540 B.C.); the *Temple of Apollo* at Bassae (about 450–420 B.C.); the famous *Erechtheum* atop the Acropolis (about 421–405 B.C.); the *Temple of Athena Niké* at Athens (about 426 B.C.); the *Olympieum* at Athens (174 B.C.–A.D. 131); the *Athenian Treasury* at Delphi (about 515 B.C.); the *Propylaea* of the Acropolis at Athens (437–432 B.C.); the *Theater of Dionysus* at Athens (about 350–325 B.C.); the *House of Cleopatra* at Delos (138 B.C.) and the *Theater* at Epidaurus (about 325 B.C.).

The *Colosseum (Flavian Amphitheater) of Rome,* the largest and most famous of the Roman amphitheaters, was opened for use A.D. 80. Elliptical in shape, it consisted of three stories and an upper gallery, rebuilt in stone in its present form in the third century A.D. Its seats rise in tiers, which in turn are buttressed by concrete vaults and stone piers. It could seat between 40,000 and 50,000 spectators. It was principally used for gladiatorial combat.

The *Pantheon* at Rome, begun by Agrippa in 27 B.C. as a temple, was rebuilt in its present circular form by Hadrian (A.D. 110–25). Literally the Pantheon was intended as a temple of "all the gods." It is remarkable for its perfect preservation today, and it has served continuously for 20 centuries as a place of worship.

Famous Roman arches include the *Arch of Constantine* (about A.D. 315) and the *Arch of Titus* (about A.D. 80).

### Later European

*St. Mark's Cathedral* in Venice (1063–67), one of the great examples of Byzantine architecture, was begun in the 9th century. Partly destroyed by fire in 976, it was later rebuilt as a Byzantine edifice.

Other famous Byzantine examples of architecture are *St. Sophia* in Istanbul (A.D. 532–37); *San Vitale* in Ravenna (542); *St. Paul's Outside the Walls,* Rome (5th century); the *Kremlin* baptism and marriage church, Moscow (begun in 1397); and *St. Lorenzo Outside the Walls*, Rome, begun in 588.

The *Cathedral Group* at Pisa (1067–1173), one of the most celebrated groups of structures built in Romanesque style, consists of the cathedral, the cathedral's baptistery, and the *Leaning Tower*. This trio forms a group by itself in the northwest corner of the city. The cathedral and baptistery are built in varicolored marble. The campanile *(Leaning Tower)* is 179 ft. high and leans more than 16 ft out of the perpendicular. There is little reason to believe that the architects intended to have the tower lean.

Other examples of Romanesque architecture include the *Vézelay Abbey* in France (1130); the *Church of Notre-Dame-du-Port* at Clermont-Ferrand in France (1100); the *Church of San Zeno* (begun in 1138) at Verona, and *Durham Cathedral* in England.

The *Alhambra* (1248–1354), located in Granada, Spain, is universally esteemed as one of the greatest masterpieces of Moslem architecture. Designed as a palace and fortress for the Moorish monarchs of Granada, it is surrounded by a heavily fortified wall more than a mile in perimeter. The location of the Alhambra in the Sierra Nevada provides a magnificent setting for this jewel of Moorish Spain.

The *Tower of London* is a group of buildings and towers covering 13 acres along the north bank of the Thames. The central *White Tower*, begun in 1078 during the reign of William the Conqueror, was originally a fortress and royal residence, but was later used as a prison. The *Bloody Tower* is associated with Anne Boleyn and other notables.

*Westminster Abbey*, in London, was begun in 1045 and completed in 1065. It was rebuilt and enlarged in 1245–50.

*Notre-Dame de Paris* (begun in 1163), one of the great examples of Gothic architecture, is a twin-towered church with a steeple over the crossing and immense flying buttresses supporting the masonry at the rear of the church.

Other famous Gothic structures are *Chartres Cathedral* (12th century); *Sainte Chapelle*, Paris (1246–48); *Laon Cathedral*, France (1160–1205); *Reims Cathedral* (about 1210–50; rebuilt after its almost complete destruction in World War I); *Rouen Cathedral* (13th–16th centuries); *Amiens Cathedral* (1218–69), *Beauvais Cathedral* (begun 1247); *Salisbury Cathedral* (1220–60); *York Minster* or the *Cathedral of St. Peter* (begun in the 7th century); *Milan Cathedral* (begun 1386); and *Cologne Cathedral* (13th–19th centuries; badly damaged in World War II.

*The Duomo* (cathedral) in Florence was founded in 1298, completed by Brunelleschi and consecrated in 1436. The oval-shaped dome dominates the entire structure.

The *Vatican* is a group of buildings in Rome comprising the official residence of the Pope. The *Basilica of St. Peter*, the largest church in the Christian world, was begun in 1450. The *Sistine Chapel*, begun in 1473, is noted for the art masterpieces of Michelangelo, Botticelli, and others. The *Basilica of the Savior* (known as *St. John Lateran*) is the first-ranking Catholic Church in the world, for it is the cathedral of the Pope.

Other examples of Renaissance architecture are the *Palazzo Riccardi*, the *Palazzo Pitti* and the *Palazzo Strozzi* in Florence; the *Farnese Palace* in Rome; *Palazzo Grimani* (completed about 1550) in Venice; the *Escorial* (1563–93) near Madrid; the *Town Hall* of Seville (1527–32); the *Louvre*, Paris; the *Château* at Blois, France; *St. Paul's Cathedral*, London (1675–1710; badly damaged in World War II); the *École Militaire*, Paris (1752); the *Pazzi Chapel*, Florence, designed by Brunelleschi (1429); the Palace of *Fontainebleau* and the *Château de Chambord* in France.

The *Palace of Versailles*, containing the famous Hall of Mirros, was built during the reign of Louis XIV and served as the royal palace until 1793.

Outstanding European buildings of the 18th and 19th centuries are the *Superga* at Turin, the *Hôtel-Dieu* in Lyons, the *Belvedere Palace* at Vienna, the *Royal Palace* of Stockholm, the *Opera House* of Paris (1863–75); the *Bank of England*, the *British Museum*, the *University of London*, and the *Houses of Parliament*, all in London; the *Panthéon*, the *Church of the Madeleine*, the *Bourse*, and the *Palais de Justice* in Paris.

The *Eiffel Tower*, in Paris, was built for the Exposition of 1889 by Alexandre Eiffel. It is 984 ft high.[1]

### Asiatic and African

The *Taj Mahal* (1632–50), at Agra, India, built by Shah Jahan as a tomb for his wife, is considered by some as the most perfect example of the Mogul style and by others as the most beautiful building in the world. Four slim white minarets flank the building, which is topped by a white dome; the entire structure is of marble.

Other examples of Indian architecture are the temples at Benares and Tanjore.

Among famed Moslem edifices are the *Dome of the Rock* or *Mosque of Omar*, Jerusalem (A.D. 691); the *Citadel* (1166), and the *Tombs of the Mamelukes* (15th century), in Cairo; the *Tomb of Humayun* in Delhi; the *Blue Mosque* (1468) at Tabriz, and the *Tamerlane Mausoleum* at Samarkand.

*Angkor Wat*, outside the city of Angkor Thom, Cambodia, is one of the most beautiful examples of Cambodian or Khmer architecture. The sanctuary was built during the 12th century.

*Great Wall of China* (228 B.C.?), designed specifically as a defense against nomadic tribes, has numerous large watch towers which could be called buildings. It was erected by Emperor Ch'in Shih Huang Ti and is 1,400 miles long. Built mainly of earth and stone, it varies in height between 18 and 30 ft.

Typical of Chinese architecture are the pagodas or temple towers. Among some of the better-known pagodas are the *Great Pagoda of the Wild Geese* at Sian (founded in 652); *Nan t'a* (11th century) at Fang Shan; the *Pagoda of Sung Yueh Ssu* (A.D. 523) at Sung Shan, Honan.

Other well-known Chinese buildings are the *Drum Tower* (1273), the *Three Great Halls* in the Purple Forbidden City (1627), *Buddha's Perfume Tower* (19th century), the *Porcelain Pagoda*, and the *Summer Palace*, all at Peking.

### United States

*Rockefeller Center*, in New York City, extends from 5th Ave. to the Avenue of the Americas between 48th and 52nd Sts. (and halfway to 7th Ave. between 47th and 51st Sts.). It occupies more than 22 acres and has 19 buildings.

*The Cathedral Church of St. John the Divine*, at 112th St. and Amsterdam Ave. in New York City, was begun in 1892 and is now in the final stages of completion. When completed, it will be the largest cathedral in the world: 601 ft long, 146 ft wide at the nave, 320 ft wide at the transept. The east end

1. 1,056 ft, including the television tower.

is designed in Romanesque-Byzantine style, and the nave and west end are Gothic.

*St. Patrick's Cathedral,* at Fifth Ave. and 50th St. in New York City, has a seating capacity of 2,500. The nave was opened in 1877, and the cathedral was dedicated in 1879.

*Louisiana Superdome,* in New Orleans, is the largest arena in the history of mankind. The main area can accommodate up to 95,000 people. It is the world's largest steel-constructed room. Unobstructed by posts, it covers 13 ac. and reaches 27 stories at its peak.

*World Trade Center,* in New York City, was dedicated in 1973. Its twin towers are 110 stories high (1,353 ft), and the complex contains over 9 million sq ft of office space. The world's highest observation deck is at the top of the South Tower. A restaurant is located on the top floor of the North Tower.

## World's Highest Dams

| Name | River | Maximum height | | Reservoir capacity in acre-feet | Reservoir capacity in millions of cubic meters | Year completed |
|---|---|---|---|---|---|---|
| | | feet | meters | | | |
| Rogunsky | Vakhsh, U.S.S.R. | 1,066 | 325 | 9,485,000 | 11,700 | UC |
| Nurek | Vakhsh, U.S.S.R. | 1,040 | 317 | 8,424,000 | 10,400 | UC |
| Grand Dixence | Dixence, Switzerland | 935 | 285 | 325,000 | 401 | 1962 |
| Inguri | Inguri, U.S.S.R. | 892 | 272 | 801,000 | 1,100 | UC |
| Vaiont | Vaiont, Italy | 858 | 262 | 137,000 | 169 | 1961 |
| Chicoasen | Grijalva, Mexico | 820 | 250 | 1,346,000 | 1,660 | UC |
| Mica | Columbia, Canada | 794 | 242 | 20,000,000 | 24,670 | 1974 |
| Sayanskaya | Yenesei, U.S.S.R. | 794 | 242 | 25,353,000 | 31,300 | UC |
| Chivor | Bata, Colombia | 778 | 237 | 661,000 | 815 | 1975 |
| Mauvoisin | Drance de Bagnes, Switzerland | 777 | 237 | 148,000 | 182 | 1957 |
| Oroville | Feather, California | 770 | 235 | 3,538,000 | 4,299 | 1968 |
| Chirkey | Sulak, U.S.S.R. | 764 | 233 | 2,252,000 | 2,780 | 1975 |
| Bhakra | Sutlej, India | 742 | 226 | 8,000,000 | 9,868 | 1963 |
| Hoover | Colorado, Arizona-Nevada | 726 | 221 | 29,755,000 | 36,703 | 1936 |
| Contra | Verzasca, Switzerland | 722 | 220 | 86,000 | 106 | 1965 |
| Piva (Mratinje) | Piva, Yugoslavia | 722 | 220 | 713,000 | 880 | 1975 |
| Dworshak | North Fork, Clearwater, Idaho | 717 | 219 | 3,453,000 | 4,259 | 1974 |
| Glen Canyon | Colorado, Arizona | 710 | 216 | 27,000,000 | 33,305 | 1964 |
| Daniel Johnson | Manicougan, Canada | 703 | 214 | 115,000,000 | 141,852 | 1968 |
| Luzzone | Brenno di Luzzone, Switzerland | 682 | 208 | 71,000 | 88 | 1963 |
| Keban | Firat, Turkey | 679 | 207 | 25,110,000 | 31,000 | 1974 |
| Mohamed Reza Shah Pahlavi | Dez, Iran | 666 | 203 | 2,707,000 | 3,340 | 1963 |
| Almendra | Turmes-Douro, Spain | 662 | 202 | 2,148,000 | 2,649 | 1970 |
| Reza Shah Kabir | Karoun, Iran | 656 | 200 | 2,351,000 | 2,900 | 1975 |
| New Bullard's Bar | North Yuba, California | 637 | 194 | 960,000 | 1,184 | 1970 |
| New Melones | Stanislaus, California | 625 | 191 | 2,400,000 | 2,960 | 1975 |
| Kurobe No. 4 | Kurobe, Japan | 610 | 186 | 162,000 | 199 | 1964 |
| Swift | Lewis, Washington | 610 | 186 | 756,000 | 932 | 1958 |
| Mossyrock | Cowlitz, Washington | 605 | 184 | 1,300,000 | 1,603 | 1968 |
| Shasta | Sacramento, California | 602 | 183 | 4,552,000 | 5,615 | 1945 |
| W.A.C. Bennett | Peace, Canada | 600 | 183 | 57,006,000 | 70,309 | 1967 |
| Tignes | Isere, France | 591 | 180 | 186,000 | 230 | 1952 |
| Amir Kabir (Karad) | Karadj, Iran | 591 | 180 | 166,000 | 205 | 1962 |
| Tachien (Techi) | Tachia, Taiwan | 591 | 180 | 207,000 | 255 | 1974 |
| Itaipu | Parana, Brazil-Paraguay | 591 | 180 | 23,510,000 | 29,000 | UC |
| Dartmouth | Mitta-Mitta, Australia | 591 | 180 | 5,232,000 | 4,000 | 1978 |
| Emosson | Barberine, Switzerland | 590 | 180 | 184,000 | 227 | 1974 |
| Don Pedro | Tuolume, California | 585 | 178 | 2,030,000 | 2,504 | 1971 |
| Alpa-Gera | Cormor, Italy | 584 | 178 | 53,000 | 65 | 1965 |
| Kopperston Tailings No. 3 | Jones Branch, West Virginia | 580 | 177 | — | — | 1963 |
| Hungry Horse | South Fork, Flathead, Montana | 564 | 172 | 3,468,000 | 4,278 | 1953 |
| Idikki | Periyar, India | 561 | 171 | 1,182,000 | 1,460 | 1974 |
| Cabora Bassa | Zambezi, Mozambique | 561 | 171 | 51,900,000 | 64,000 | 1974 |
| Charvak | Chirchik, U.S.S.R. | 551 | 168 | 1,620,000 | 2,000 | 1970 |
| Grand Coulee | Columbia, Washington | 550 | 168 | 9,724,000 | 11,795 | 1942 |
| Vidraru | Arges-Danube, Romania | 547 | 167 | 380,000 | 465 | 1966 |
| Kremasta (King Paul) | Acheloos, Greece | 541 | 165 | 3,850,000 | 4,750 | 1965 |
| Ross | Skagit, Washington | 540 | 165 | 1,435,000 | 1,770 | 1949 |
| Trinity | Trinity, California | 537 | 164 | 2,448,000 | 3,020 | 1962 |
| Talbingo | Tumut, Australia | 530 | 162 | 747,000 | 921 | 1971 |
| Yellowtail | Bighorn, Montana | 525 | 160 | 1,375,000 | 1,696 | 1966 |

| Name | River | Maximum height feet | Maximum height meters | Reservoir capacity in acre-feet | Reservoir capacity in millions of cubic meters | Year completed |
|---|---|---|---|---|---|---|
| Gokcekaya | Sakarya, Turkey | 525 | 160 | 737,000 | 910 | 1973 |
| Cougar | South Fork, McKenzie, Oregon | 519 | 158 | 219,000 | 270 | 1964 |
| Curnera | Rein de Curnera, Switzerland | 518 | 158 | 33,000 | 41 | 1966 |
| Okutadami | Tadami, Japan | 515 | 157 | 487,000 | 601 | 1961 |
| Speccheri | Leno di Vallarsa, Italy | 514 | 157 | 8,000 | 10 | 1957 |
| Zeuzier | Lienne, Switzerland | 512 | 156 | 41,000 | 51 | 1957 |
| Sakuma | Tenryu, Japan | 510 | 156 | 265,000 | 327 | 1956 |
| Monteynard | Drac, France | 509 | 155 | 195,000 | 240 | 1962 |
| Nagawado | Azusa, Japan | 509 | 155 | 99,000 | 123 | 1969 |
| Göscheneralp | Göschenerreuss, Switzerland | 508 | 155 | 62,000 | 76 | 1960 |
| Bhumiphol (Yanhee) | Ping-Chao Phaya, Thailand | 505 | 154 | 10,914,000 | 13,462 | 1964 |
| Flaming Gorge | Green, Utah | 502 | 153 | 3,789,000 | 4,674 | 1964 |
| Place Moulin | Buthier, Italy | 502 | 153 | 81,000 | 100 | 1965 |
| Gepatsch | Faggenbach, Austria | 500 | 153 | 113,000 | 139 | 1965 |
| Santa Giustina | Noce-Adige, Italy | 500 | 153 | 148,000 | 183 | 1950 |
| Zervreila | Valserrhein, Switzerland | 495 | 151 | 81,000 | 100 | 1957 |
| Roselend | Doron-de-Beaufort, France | 492 | 150 | 152,000 | 187 | 1961 |
| Canelles | Noguera, Spain | 492 | 150 | 549,000 | 678 | 1960 |

NOTE: UC = under construction in 1977. *Source:* Department of the Interior, Bureau of Reclamation.

## World's Largest Hydroelectric Plants

| Name of dam | Location | Rated capacity (Mw) Present | Rated capacity (Mw) Ultimate | Year of initial operation |
|---|---|---|---|---|
| Itaipu | Brazil–Paraguay | — | 12,870 | UC |
| Grand Coulee | Washington | 4,163 | 10,080 | 1941 |
| Guri | Venezuela | 524 | 6,500 | 1967 |
| Sayanskaya | U.S.S.R. | — | 6,400 | UC |
| Krasnoyarsk | U.S.S.R. | 6,096 | 6,096 | 1968 |
| La Grande 2 | Canada | — | 5,328 | UC |
| Churchill Falls | Canada | 5,225 | 5,225 | 1971 |
| Bratsk | U.S.S.R. | 4,100 | 4,600 | 1964 |
| Sukhovo | U.S.S.R. | — | 4,500 | UC |
| Ust-Ipimsk | U.S.S.R. | 720 | 4,320 | 1974 |
| Cabora Bassa | Mozambique | 2,000 | 4,000 | 1975 |
| Paulo Afonso | Brazil | 1,524 | 3,409 | 1955 |
| Solteira | Brazil | 3,200 | 3,200 | 1973 |
| Inga 1 | Zaire | 360 | 2,820 | 1974 |
| John Day | Oregon–Washington | 2,160 | 2,700 | 1968 |
| Volgograd—22nd Congress | U.S.S.R. | 2,560 | 2,560 | 1958 |
| Volga—V.I. Lenin (Kuibisher) | U.S.S.R. | 2,300 | 2,300 | 1955 |
| Iron Gates 1 | Romania–Yugoslavia | 2,300 | 2,300 | 1970 |
| W.A.C. Bennett | Canada | 1,816 | 2,270 | 1969 |
| High Aswan (Sadd-el-Aali) | Egypt | 2,100 | 2,100 | 1967 |
| Tarbela | Pakistan | 700 | 2,100 | 1977 |
| Chief Joseph | Washington | 1,024 | 2,069 | 1956 |
| Robert Moses-Niagara | New York | 1,950 | 1,950 | 1961 |
| Ludington | Michigan | 1,872 | 1,872 | 1973 |
| St. Lawrence Power Dam | U.S.A.–Canada | 1,824 | 1,824 | 1958 |
| The Dalles | Washington | 1,807 | 1,807 | 1957 |
| Kemano | Canada | 813 | 1,670 | 1954 |
| Beauharnois | Canada | 1,021 | 1,574 | 1950 |
| Kariba | Rhodesia–Zambia | 1,266 | 1,566 | 1959 |
| Raccoon Mountain | Tennessee | 1,530 | 1,530 | 1975 |
| Tumut 3 | Australia | 1,500 | 1,500 | 1972 |
| Jupia | Brazil | 1,411 | 1,411 | 1966 |
| McNary | Oregon | 980 | 1,406 | 1953 |
| Cheboksary | U.S.S.R. | 1,404 | 1,404 | 1972 |
| Marimbondo | Brazil | 1,400 | 1,400 | 1975 |

NOTE: UC = under construction in 1977. *Source:* Department of the Interior, Bureau of Reclamation.

# Notable Tunnels

**Railroad, excluding subways**

| Name | Location | Length mi. | Length km | Year completed |
|---|---|---|---|---|
| Seikan | Tsugara Straits, Japan | 33.1 | 53.3 | UC |
| Simplon (I and II) | Alps, Switzerland-Italy | 12.3 | 19.8 | 1906 & 1922 |
| Kammon Straits | Honshu to Kyoshu Islands, Japan | 11.6 | 18.7 | UC |
| Apennine | Genoa, Italy | 11.5 | 18.5 | 1934 |
| St. Gotthard | Swiss Alps | 9.3 | 14.9 | 1881 |
| Lötschberg | Swiss Alps | 9.1 | 14.6 | 1911 |
| Nakayama | Komochi Mt., Japan | 8.8 | 14.2 | UC |
| Mont Cénis | French Alps | 8.5[1] | 13.7 | 1871 |
| New Cascade | Cascade Mts., Washington | 7.8 | 12.6 | 1929 |
| Vosges | Vosges, France | 7.0 | 11.3 | 1940 |
| Arlberg | Austrian Alps | 6.3 | 10.1 | 1884 |
| Moffat | Rocky Mts., Colorado | 6.2 | 9.9 | 1928 |
| Shimuzu | Shimuzu, Japan | 6.1 | 9.8 | 1931 |
| Rimutaka | Wairarapa, New Zealand | 5.5 | 8.9 | 1955 |

**Vehicular**

| Name | Location | Length mi. | Length km | Year completed |
|---|---|---|---|---|
| St. Gotthard | Alps, Switzerland | 10.2 | 16.4 | UC |
| Mt. Blanc | Alps, France-Italy | 7.5 | 12.1 | 1965 |
| Mt. Ena | Japan Alps, Japan | 5.3 | 8.5 | 1976[2] |
| Great St. Bernard | Alps, Switzerland-Italy | 3.4 | 5.5 | 1964 |
| Mount Royal | Montreal, Canada | 3.2 | 5.1 | 1918 |
| Lincoln | Hudson River, New York-New Jersey | 2.5 | 4.0 | 1937 |
| Queensway Road | Mersey River, Liverpool, England | 2.2 | 3.5 | 1934 |
| Brooklyn-Battery | East River, New York City | 2.1 | 3.4 | 1950 |
| Holland | Hudson River, New York-New Jersey | 1.7 | 2.7 | 1927 |
| Hampton Roads | Norfolk, Virginia | 1.4 | 2.3 | 1957 |
| Queens-Midtown | East River, New York City | 1.3 | 2.1 | 1940 |
| Liberty Tubes | Pittsburgh, Pennsylvania | 1.2 | 1.9 | 1923 |
| Baltimore Harbor | Baltimore, Maryland | 1.2 | 1.9 | 1957 |
| Allegheny Tunnels | Pennsylvania Turnpike | 1.2 | 1.9 | 1940[3] |

1. Lengthened to its present 8.5 miles in 1881. 2. Parallel tunnel begun in 1976. 3. Parallel tunnel built in 1965, twin tunnel in 1966. NOTE: UC = under construction. *Source:* American Society of Civil Engineers.

# America's Tallest Buildings

| City | Building | Stories | Height ft | Height m |
|---|---|---|---|---|
| Chicago | Sears Tower | 110 | 1,454 | 443 |
| New York | World Trade Center | 110 | 1,369 | 417 |
| New York | Empire State | 102 | 1,250 | 381 |
| Chicago | Standard Oil (Indiana) | 80 | 1,136 | 346 |
| Chicago | John Hancock Center | 100 | 1,127 | 343 |
| New York | Chrysler | 77 | 1,046 | 319 |
| New York | American International | 66 | 952 | 290 |
| New York | Citicorp Center | 59 | 915 | 279 |
| New York | 40 Wall Tower | 71 | 900 | 274 |
| Chicago | Water Tower Place | 74 | 859 | 262 |
| Los Angeles | United California Bank | 62 | 858 | 261 |
| San Francisco | Transamerica Pyramid | 61 | 853 | 260 |
| Chicago | First National Bank | 60 | 851 | 259 |
| New York | RCA | 70 | 850 | 259 |
| Pittsburgh | U.S. Steel Headquarters | 64 | 841 | 256 |
| New York | Chase Manhattan | 60 | 813 | 248 |
| New York | Pan Am | 59 | 808 | 246 |
| Boston | John Hancock Tower | 60 | 790 | 241 |
| San Francisco | Bank of America | 52 | 779 | 237 |
| Minneapolis | IDS Tower | 57 | 775 | 236 |
| New York | One Liberty Plaza | 54 | 775 | 236 |
| New York | One Penn Plaza | 57 | 774 | 236 |
| Atlanta | Peachtree Plaza | 73 | 754 | 230 |
| New York | Woolworth | 55 | 750 | 229 |
| New York | Exxon | 54 | 750 | 229 |
| Boston | Prudential Tower | 52 | 750 | 229 |
| Detroit | Detroit Plaza Hotel | 73 | 747 | 228 |
| Los Angeles | Security Pacific Plaza | 55 | 743 | 226 |
| New York | One Astor Plaza | 54 | 730 | 222 |
| New York | Marine Midland | 52 | 724 | 221 |
| Houston | One Shell Plaza | 50 | 714 | 218 |
| Dallas | First International | 56 | 710 | 216 |
| Cleveland | Terminal Tower | 52 | 708 | 216 |
| New York | Union Carbide | 52 | 707 | 215 |
| New York | General Motors | 50 | 705 | 215 |
| New York | Metropolitan Life | 50 | 700 | 213 |

NOTE: Does not include buildings under construction and not completed in 1978. Height does not include TV towers and antennas. *Source: Information Please* questionnaires to buildings.

# Notable Modern Bridges

## Suspension

| Name | Location | Length of main span, ft | m | Year completed |
|---|---|---|---|---|
| Humber | Hull, Britain | 4,626 | 1,410 | UC |
| Verrazano-Narrows | Lower New York Bay | 4,260 | 1,298 | 1964 |
| Golden Gate | San Francisco Bay | 4,200 | 1,280 | 1937 |
| Mackinac Straits | Michigan | 3,800 | 1,158 | 1957 |
| Bosporus | Istanbul | 3,524 | 1,074 | 1973 |
| George Washington | Hudson River at New York City | 3,500 | 1,067 | 1931 |
| Ponte 25 de Abril | Tagus River at Lisbon | 3,323 | 1,013 | 1966 |
| Forth Road | Queensferry, Scotland | 3,300 | 1,006 | 1964 |
| Severn | Severn River at Beachley, England | 3,240 | 988 | 1966 |
| Tacoma Narrows | Puget Sound at Tacoma, Wash. | 2,800 | 853 | 1950 |
| Kanmon Straits | Kyushu-Honshu, Japan | 2,336 | 712 | 1973 |
| Angostura | Orinoco River at Ciudad Bolívar, Venezuela | 2,336 | 712 | 1967 |
| Transbay (twin spans) | San Francisco Bay | 2,310 | 704 | 1936 |
| Bronx-Whitestone | East River, New York City | 2,300 | 701 | 1939 |
| Pierre Laporte | St. Lawrence River at Quebec, Canada | 2,190 | 668 | 1970 |
| Delaware Memorial (twin bridges) | Delaware River near Wilmington, Del. | 2,150 | 655 | 1951, 1968 |
| Seaway Skyway | St. Lawrence River at Ogdensburg, N.Y. | 2,150 | 655 | 1960 |
| Gas Pipe Line | Atchafalaya River, La. | 2,000 | 610 | 1951 |
| Walt Whitman | Delaware River at Philadelphia | 2,000 | 610 | 1957 |
| Tancarville | Seine River at Tancarville, France | 1,995 | 608 | 1959 |
| Lillebaelt | Lillebaelt Strait, Denmark | 1,969 | 600 | 1970 |
| Ambassador International | Detroit River at Detroit | 1,850 | 564 | 1929 |
| Throgs Neck | East River, New York City | 1,800 | 549 | 1961 |
| Benjamin Franklin | Delaware River at Philadelphia | 1,750 | 533 | 1926 |
| Skjomen | Narvik, Norway | 1,722 | 525 | 1972 |
| Kvalsund | Hammerfest, Norway | 1,722 | 525 | 1977 |
| Emmerich | Rhine River at Emmerich, West Germany | 1,640 | 500 | 1965 |
| Bear Mountain | Hudson River at Peekskill, N.Y. | 1,632 | 497 | 1924 |
| Wm. Preston Lane, Jr., Memorial (twin bridges) | Near Annapolis, Md. | 1,600 | 488 | 1952, 1973 |
| Williamsburg | East River, New York City | 1,600 | 488 | 1903 |
| Newport | Narragansett Bay at Newport, R.I. | 1,600 | 488 | 1969 |
| Brooklyn | East River, New York City | 1,595 | 486 | 1883 |

## Cantilever

| Name | Location | ft | m | Year completed |
|---|---|---|---|---|
| Quebec Railway | St. Lawrence River at Quebec, Canada | 1,800 | 549 | 1917 |
| Forth Railway (twin spans) | Queensferry, Scotland | 1,710 | 521 | 1890 |
| Minato Ohashi | Osaka, Japan | 1,673 | 510 | 1974 |
| Commodore John Barry | Chester, Pa. | 1,644 | 501 | 1974 |
| Greater New Orleans | Mississippi River, La. | 1,576 | 480 | 1958 |
| Howrah | Hooghly River at Calcutta | 1,500 | 457 | 1943 |
| Transbay Bridge | San Francisco Bay | 1,400 | 427 | 1936 |
| Baton Rouge | Mississippi River, La. | 1,235 | 376 | 1968 |
| Tappan Zee | Hudson River at Tarrytown, N.Y. | 1,212 | 369 | 1955 |
| Longview | Columbia River at Longview, Wash. | 1,200 | 366 | 1930 |
| Patapsco River | Baltimore Outer Harbor Crossing | 1,200 | 366 | 1976 |
| Queensboro | East River, New York City | 1,182 | 360 | 1909 |

## Steel Arch

| Name | Location | ft | m | Year completed |
|---|---|---|---|---|
| New River Gorge | Fayetteville, W. Va. | 1,700 | 518 | 1977 |
| Bayonne | Kill Van Kull at Bayonne, N.J. | 1,652 | 504 | 1931 |
| Sydney Harbour | Sydney, Australia | 1,650 | 503 | 1932 |
| Fremont | Portland, Ore. | 1,255 | 383 | 1973 |
| Port Mann | Fraser River at Vancouver, British Columbia | 1,200 | 366 | 1964 |
| Thatcher Ferry | Panama Canal, Panama | 1,128 | 344 | 1962 |
| Laviolette | St. Lawrence River, Trois Rivieres, Quebec | 1,100 | 335 | 1967 |
| Zdákov | Vltava River, Czechoslovakia | 1,083 | 330 | 1967 |
| Runcorn-Widnes | Mersey River, England | 1,082 | 330 | 1961 |
| Birchenough | Sabi River at Fort Victoria, Rhodesia | 1,080 | 329 | 1935 |

**Cable-Stayed**

| Name | Location | Length of main span, ft | m | Year completed |
|---|---|---|---|---|
| Second Hooghly | Calcutta | 1,500 | 457 | UC |
| St.-Nazaire | Loire River, St.-Nazaire, France | 1,325 | 404 | 1975 |
| Mississippi River | Luling, La. | 1,235 | 376 | UC |
| Düsseldorf-Flehe | Rhine River, West Germany | 1,205 | 367 | UC |
| Duisburg-Neuenkamp | Duisburg, West Germany | 1,148 | 350 | 1970 |
| Mesopotamia | Corrientes, Argentina | 1,116 | 340 | 1972 |
| West Gate | Lower Yarra River at Melbourne, Australia | 1,102 | 336 | 1970 |
| Zárate | Paraná River, Argentina | 1,083 | 330 | 1976 |
| Brazo Largo | Paraná River, Argentina | 1,083 | 330 | 1977 |
| Köhlbrand | Hamburg, West Germany | 1,066 | 325 | 1974 |
| Kniebrücke | Rhine River at Düsseldorf, Germany | 1,050 | 320 | 1969 |
| Brotonne[1] | Seine River, France | 1,050 | 320 | 1976 |
| Erskine | Clyde River at Glasgow, Scotland | 1,000 | 305 | 1971 |

**Continuous Truss**

| Name | Location | ft | m | Year completed |
|---|---|---|---|---|
| Astoria | Columbia River at Astoria, Oregon | 1,232 | 376 | 1966 |
| Oshima | Oshima Island, Japan | 1,066 | 325 | 1976 |
| Croton Reservoir | Croton, N.Y. | 1,052 | 321 | 1970 |
| Tenmon | Kumamoto, Japan | 984 | 300 | 1966 |
| Kuronoseto | Nagashima-Kyushu, Japan | 984 | 300 | 1974 |
| Ravenswood | Ohio River, Ravenswood, W. Va. | 902 | 275 | UC |
| Dubuque | Mississippi River at Dubuque, Iowa | 845 | 258 | 1943 |
| Braga Memorial | Taunton River at Somerset, Mass. | 840 | 256 | 1966 |
| Graf Spee | Germany | 839 | 256 | 1936 |

**Concrete Arch**

| Name | Location | ft | m | Year completed |
|---|---|---|---|---|
| Gladesville | Parramatta River at Sydney, Australia | 1,000 | 305 | 1964 |
| Amizade | Paraná River at Foz do Iguassu, Brazil | 951 | 290 | 1964 |
| Arrábida | Porto, Portugal | 886 | 270 | 1963 |
| Sandö | Angerman River at Kramfors, Sweden | 866 | 264 | 1943 |
| Shibenik | Krka River, Yugoslavia | 808 | 246 | 1966 |
| Fiumarella | Catanzaro, Italy | 758 | 231 | 1961 |
| Zaporozhe | Old Dnepr River, U.S.S.R. | 748 | 228 | 1952 |
| Novi Sad | Danube River, Yugoslavia | 692 | 211 | 1961 |

1. Concrete bridge. NOTE: UC = under construction. *Source: Encyclopaedia Britannica* and American Society of Civil Engineers.

# Famous Ship Canals

| Name | Location | Length (miles)[1] | Width (feet) | Depth (feet) | Locks | Year opened |
|---|---|---|---|---|---|---|
| Albert | Belgium | 80.0 | 53.0 | 16.5 | 6 | 1939 |
| Amsterdam–Rhine | Netherlands | 45.0 | 164.0 | 41.0 | 3 | 1952 |
| Beaumont–Port Arthur | United States | 40.0 | 200.0 | 34.0 | — | 1916 |
| Chesapeake and Delaware | United States | 19.0 | 250.0 | 27.0 | — | 1927 |
| Houston | United States | 43.0 | 300.0 | 34.0 | — | 1914 |
| Kiel (Nord-Ostsee Kanal) | Germany | 61.3 | 144.0 | 36.0 | 4 | 1895 |
| Panama | Canal Zone | 50.7 | 110.0 | 41.0 | 12 | 1914 |
| St. Lawrence Seaway | U.S. and Canada | 2,400.0[2] | [3] | — | — | 1959 |
| Montreal to Prescott | U.S. and Canada | 11.5 | 80.0 | 30.0 | 7 | 1959 |
| Welland | Canada | 27.5 | 80.0 | 27.0 | 8 | 1931 |
| Sault Ste. Marie | Canada | 1.2 | 60.0 | 16.8 | 1 | 1895 |
| Sault Ste. Marie | United States | 1.6 | 80.0 | 25.0 | 4 | 1915 |
| Suez | Egypt | 100.6[4] | 197.0 | 36.0 | — | 1869 |

1. Statute miles. 2. From Montreal to Duluth. 3. 442–550 feet; there are 11.5 miles of locks, 80 feet wide and 30 feet deep. 4. From Port Said lighthouse to entrance channel in Suez roads. *Source:* American Society of Civil Engineers.

## World's Largest Dams

| Dam | Location | Volume (thousands) Cubic meters | Cubic yards | Year completed |
|---|---|---|---|---|
| New Cornelia Tailings | Arizona | 209,500 | 274,026 | 1973 |
| Tarbela | Pakistan | 121,000 | 158,268 | 1975 |
| Fort Peck | Montana | 96,034 | 125,612 | 1940 |
| Guri | Venezuela | 70,762 | 92,557 | UC |
| Oahe | South Dakota | 70,343 | 92,008 | 1963 |
| Oosterschelde | Netherlands | 70,000 | 91,560 | UC |
| Yacyreta-Apipe | Argentina–Paraguay | 70,000 | 91,560 | UC |
| Mangla | Pakistan | 65,651 | 85,872 | 1967 |
| Gardiner | Canada | 65,553 | 85,743 | 1968 |
| Afsluitdijk | Netherlands | 63,400 | 82,927 | 1932 |
| Oroville | California | 59,639 | 78,008 | 1968 |
| San Luis | California | 59,378 | 77,666 | 1967 |
| Nurek | U.S.S.R. | 58,000 | 75,864 | UC |
| Garrison | North Dakota | 50,846 | 66,506 | 1956 |
| Cochiti | New Mexico | 49,417 | 64,631 | 1975 |
| Tabka | Syria | 46,000 | 60,168 | 1975 |
| Kiev | U.S.S.R. | 44,000 | 57,552 | 1964 |
| W.A.C. Bennett | Canada | 43,733 | 57,203 | 1967 |
| High Aswan (Sadd-el-Aall) | Egypt | 43,733 | 57,203 | 1970 |
| Dantiwada Left Earthen Bank | India | 41,040 | 53,680 | 1965 |
| Saratov | U.S.S.R. | 40,400 | 52,843 | 1967 |
| Mission Tailings #2 | Arizona | 40,088 | 52,435 | 1973 |
| Fort Randall | South Dakota | 38,383 | 50,205 | 1956 |
| Kanev | U.S.S.R. | 37,860 | 49,520 | 1974 |
| Kakhova | U.S.S.R. | 35,640 | 46,617 | 1955 |
| Tsimlyanska | U.S.S.R. | 33,891 | 44,323 | 1952 |

NOTE: Based on total volume of dam structure. All dams listed are predominantly earth or rockfill and may contain masonry sections. UC = under construction in 1977. *Source:* Department of the Interior, Bureau of Reclamation.

## Flowing Diamonds

The highest steady pressure ever produced in the laboratory is 25.2 million pounds per square inch—700 times the pressure produced by Mount Everest on the earth's crust. This pressure, generated at Carnegie's Geographical Laboratory in 1978, was enough to cause a diamond to flow like plastic.

## Chinese Calendar

The Chinese lunar year is divided into 12 months of 29 or 30 days. The calendar is adjusted to the length of the solar year by the addition of extra months at regular intervals.

The years are arranged in major cycles of 60 years. Each successive year is named after one of 12 animals. These 12-year cycles are continuously repeated. The Chinese New Year is celebrated at the first new moon after the sun enters Aquarius—sometime between Jan. 21 and Feb. 19.

| Rat | Ox | Tiger | Cat (Rabbit) | Dragon | Snake | Horse | Sheep (Goat) | Monkey | Rooster | Dog | Pig |
|---|---|---|---|---|---|---|---|---|---|---|---|
| 1864 | 1865 | 1866 | 1867 | 1868 | 1869 | 1870 | 1871 | 1872 | 1873 | 1874 | 1875 |
| 1876 | 1877 | 1878 | 1879 | 1880 | 1881 | 1882 | 1883 | 1884 | 1885 | 1886 | 1887 |
| 1888 | 1889 | 1890 | 1891 | 1892 | 1893 | 1894 | 1895 | 1896 | 1897 | 1898 | 1899 |
| 1900 | 1901 | 1902 | 1903 | 1904 | 1905 | 1906 | 1907 | 1908 | 1909 | 1910 | 1911 |
| 1912 | 1913 | 1914 | 1915 | 1916 | 1917 | 1918 | 1919 | 1920 | 1921 | 1922 | 1923 |
| 1924 | 1925 | 1926 | 1927 | 1928 | 1929 | 1930 | 1931 | 1932 | 1933 | 1934 | 1935 |
| 1936 | 1937 | 1938 | 1939 | 1940 | 1941 | 1942 | 1943 | 1944 | 1945 | 1946 | 1947 |
| 1948 | 1949 | 1950 | 1951 | 1952 | 1953 | 1954 | 1955 | 1956 | 1957 | 1958 | 1959 |
| 1960 | 1961 | 1962 | 1963 | 1964 | 1965 | 1966 | 1967 | 1968 | 1969 | 1970 | 1971 |
| 1972 | 1973 | 1974 | 1975 | 1976 | 1977 | 1978 | 1979 | 1980 | 1981 | 1982 | 1983 |

# UNITED NATIONS

## The 150 Members of the United Nations

| Country | Joined U.N.[1] | Country | Joined U.N.[1] | Country | Joined U.N.[1] |
|---|---|---|---|---|---|
| Afghanistan | 1946 | Germany, West | 1973 | Oman | 1971 |
| Albania | 1955 | Ghana | 1957 | Pakistan | 1947 |
| Algeria | 1962 | Greece | 1945 | Panama | 1945 |
| Angola | 1976 | Grenada | 1974 | Papua New Guinea | 1975 |
| Argentina | 1945 | Guatemala | 1945 | Paraguay | 1945 |
| Australia | 1945 | Guinea | 1958 | Peru | 1945 |
| Austria | 1955 | Guinea-Bissau | 1974 | Philippines | 1945 |
| Bahamas | 1973 | Guyana | 1966 | Poland | 1945 |
| Bahrain | 1971 | Haiti | 1945 | Portugal | 1955 |
| Bangladesh | 1974 | Honduras | 1945 | Qatar | 1971 |
| Barbados | 1966 | Hungary | 1955 | Romania | 1955 |
| Belgium | 1945 | Iceland | 1946 | Rwanda | 1962 |
| Benin (Dahomey) | 1960 | India | 1945 | São Tomé and Príncipe | 1975 |
| Bhutan | 1971 | Indonesia | 1950 | Saudi Arabia | 1945 |
| Bolivia | 1945 | Iran | 1945 | Senegal | 1960 |
| Botswana | 1966 | Iraq | 1945 | Seychelles | 1976 |
| Brazil | 1945 | Ireland | 1955 | Sierra Leone | 1961 |
| Bulgaria | 1955 | Israel | 1949 | Singapore | 1965 |
| Burma | 1948 | Italy | 1955 | Solomon Islands | 1978 |
| Burundi | 1962 | Ivory Coast | 1960 | Somalia | 1960 |
| Byelorussian S.S.R. | 1945 | Jamaica | 1962 | South Africa | 1945 |
| Cameroon | 1960 | Japan | 1956 | Spain | 1955 |
| Canada | 1945 | Jordan | 1955 | Sri Lanka | 1955 |
| Cape Verde | 1975 | Kenya | 1963 | Sudan | 1956 |
| Central African Empire | 1960 | Kuwait | 1963 | Surinam | 1975 |
| Chad | 1960 | Laos[2] | 1955 | Swaziland | 1968 |
| Chile | 1945 | Lebanon | 1945 | Sweden | 1946 |
| China[2] | 1945 | Lesotho | 1966 | Syria | 1945 |
| Colombia | 1945 | Liberia | 1945 | Tanzania | 1961 |
| Comoro Islands | 1975 | Libya | 1955 | Thailand | 1946 |
| Congo | 1960 | Luxembourg | 1945 | Togo | 1960 |
| Costa Rica | 1945 | Madagascar | 1960 | Trinidad and Tobago | 1962 |
| Cuba | 1945 | Malawi | 1964 | Tunisia | 1956 |
| Cyprus | 1960 | Malaysia | 1957 | Turkey | 1945 |
| Czechoslovakia | 1945 | Maldives | 1965 | Uganda | 1962 |
| Democratic Kampuchea |  | Mali | 1960 | Ukrainian S.S.R. | 1945 |
| (Cambodia) | 1955 | Malta | 1964 | U.S.S.R. | 1945 |
| Denmark | 1945 | Mauritania | 1961 | United Arab Emirates | 1971 |
| Djibouti | 1977 | Mauritius | 1968 | United Kingdom | 1945 |
| Dominican Republic | 1945 | Mexico | 1945 | United States | 1945 |
| Ecuador | 1945 | Mongolia | 1961 | Upper Volta | 1960 |
| Egypt | 1945 | Morocco | 1956 | Uruguay | 1945 |
| El Salvador | 1945 | Mozambique | 1975 | Venezuela | 1945 |
| Equatorial Guinea | 1968 | Nepal | 1955 | Vietnam | 1977 |
| Ethiopia | 1945 | Netherlands | 1945 | Western Samoa | 1976 |
| Fiji | 1970 | New Zealand | 1945 | Yemen, Arab Republic | 1947 |
| Finland | 1955 | Nicaragua | 1945 | Yemen, People's Dem. |  |
| France | 1945 | Niger | 1960 | Rep. of | 1967 |
| Gabon | 1960 | Nigeria | 1960 | Yugoslavia | 1945 |
| Gambia | 1965 | Norway | 1945 | Zaire | 1960 |
| Germany, East | 1973 |  |  | Zambia | 1964 |

1. The U.N. officially came into existence on Oct. 24, 1945. 2. On Oct. 25, 1971, the U.N. voted membership to the People's Republic of China, which replaced Nationalist China (Taiwan) in the world body.

## United Nations Costs

In December 1977, the General Assembly adopted a budget of $986 million for the two-year period 1978–79.

## Member Countries' Assessments to U.N. Budget, 1977

| Country | Total | Country | Total | Country | Total |
|---|---|---|---|---|---|
| Afghanistan | $ 67,607 | Germany, West | $26,163,917 | Norway | $ 1,453,550 |
| Albania | 67,607 | Ghana | 67,607 | Oman | 67,607 |
| Algeria | 338,035 | Greece | 1,318,337 | Pakistan | 202,821 |
| Argentina | 2,805,691 | Grenada | 67,607 | Panama | 67,607 |
| Australia | 5,138,134 | Guatemala | 67,607 | Papua New Guinea | 67,607 |
| Austria | 2,129,621 | Guinea | 67,607 | Paraguay | 67,607 |
| Bahamas | 67,607 | Guinea-Bissau | 67,607 | Peru | 202,821 |
| Bahrain | 67,607 | Guyana | 67,607 | Philippines | 338,035 |
| Bangladesh | 135,214 | Haiti | 67,607 | Poland | 4,732,492 |
| Barbados | 67,607 | Honduras | 67,607 | Portugal | 676,071 |
| Belgium | 3,616,976 | Hungary | 1,149,320 | Qatar | 67,607 |
| Benin (Dahomey) | 67,607 | Iceland | 67,607 | Romania | 878,892 |
| Bhutan | 67,607 | India | 2,366,245 | Rwanda | 67,607 |
| Bolivia | 67,607 | Indonesia | 473,249 | São Tomé and Principe | 67,607 |
| Botswana | 67,607 | Iran | 1,453,550 | Saudi Arabia | 811,284 |
| Brazil | 3,515,565 | Iraq | 338,035 | Senegal | 67,607 |
| Bulgaria | 439,446 | Ireland | 507,053 | Sierra Leone | 67,607 |
| Burma | 67,607 | Israel | 811,284 | Singapore | 270,428 |
| Burundi | 67,607 | Italy | 11,155,158 | Somalia | 67,607 |
| Byelorussian S.S.R. | 1,352,140 | Ivory Coast | 67,607 | South Africa | 1,352,140 |
| Cameroon | 67,607 | Jamaica | 67,607 | Spain | 5,172,699 |
| Canada | 10,013,904 | Japan | 29,273,840 | Sri Lanka | 67,607 |
| Cape Verde | 67,607 | Jordan | 67,607 | Sudan | 67,607 |
| Central African Empire | 67,607 | Kenya | 67,607 | Surinam | 67,607 |
| Chad | 67,607 | Kuwait | 540,856 | Swaziland | 67,607 |
| Chile | 304,232 | Laos | 67,607 | Sweden | 4,056,422 |
| China | 18,591,931 | Lebanon | 101,410 | Syria | 67,607 |
| Colombia | 372,194 | Lesotho | 67,607 | Tanzania | 71,727 |
| Comoros | 67,607 | Liberia | 67,607 | Thailand | 338,035 |
| Congo | 67,607 | Libya | 574,660 | Togo | 67,607 |
| Costa Rica | 67,607 | Luxembourg | 135,214 | Trinidad and Tobago | 67,607 |
| Cuba | 439,446 | Madagascar | 67,977 | Tunisia | 67,607 |
| Cyprus | 67,607 | Malawi | 67,607 | Turkey | 1,019,951 |
| Czechoslovakia | 2,940,905 | Malaysia | 304,232 | Uganda | 69,383 |
| Democratic Kampuchea | | Maldives | 67,607 | Ukrainian S.S.R. | 5,070,526 |
| (Cambodia) | 67,607 | Mali | 67,607 | U.S.S.R. | 38,299,377 |
| Denmark | 2,129,621 | Malta | 67,607 | United Arab Emirates | 270,428 |
| Dominican Republic | 67,607 | Mauritania | 67,607 | United Kingdom | 15,008,759 |
| Ecuador | 67,607 | Mauritius | 67,607 | United States | 99,397,207 |
| Egypt | 270,428 | Mexico | 2,636,674 | Upper Volta | 67,607 |
| El Salvador | 67,607 | Mongolia | 67,607 | Uruguay | 135,214 |
| Equatorial Guinea | 67,607 | Morocco | 169,018 | Venezuela | 1,352,140 |
| Ethiopia | 67,607 | Mozambique | 67,607 | Yemen, People's Dem. | |
| Fiji | 67,607 | Nepal | 67,607 | Rep. of | 67,607 |
| Finland | 1,385,944 | Netherlands | 4,664,885 | Yemen Arab Republic | 67,607 |
| France | 19,132,788 | New Zealand | 946,498 | Yugoslavia | 1,284,534 |
| Gabon | 67,607 | Nicaragua | 67,607 | Zaire | 72,543 |
| Gambia | 67,607 | Niger | 67,607 | Zambia | 67,607 |
| Germany, East | 4,563,474 | Nigeria | 439,446 | | |

## United Nations Headquarters

The first regular session of the General Assembly held at Central Hall, Westminster, London, voted that interim headquarters of the Organization should be located in New York. From London the U.N. moved to Hunter College in the Bronx. In August 1946, an interim headquarters was set up at Lake Success on Long Island, in a part of the Sperry Gyroscope Co.'s plant. The New York City building at Flushing Meadows, site of the 1939 World's Fair, was converted for the use of the General Assembly. The search for a permanent home ended in December 1946, when the General Assembly accepted an offer from John D. Rockefeller, Jr., of $8,500,000[1] for the purchase of the present Headquarters site—an 18-acre tract in Manhattan, alongside the East River. The U.S. Government lent the U.N. $65,000,000 interest free, which is being repaid in annual installments.

Architectural plans drawn up by an international Board of Design were approved by the Assembly, and construction began in September 1948. By mid-1950, the 39-story Secretariat Building was ready for occupancy, and in the spring of 1951 "United Nations, New York" became the Organization's permanent address.

1. This amount paid for two-thirds of the land; New York City gave one-third.

# Preamble of the United Nations Charter

The Charter of the United Nations was adopted at the San Francisco Conference of 1945. The complete text may be obtained by writing to the United Nations Sales Section, United Nations, New York, N.Y. 10017, and enclosing $1.

We the peoples of the United Nations determined to save succeeding generations from the scourge of war, which twice in our lifetime has brought untold sorrow to mankind, and

To reaffirm faith in fundamental human rights, in the dignity and worth of the human person, in the equal rights of men and women and of nations large and small, and

To establish conditions under which justice and respect for the obligations arising from treaties and other sources of international law can be maintained, and

To promote social progress and better standards of life in larger freedom, and for these ends

To practice tolerance and live together in peace with one another as good neighbors, and

To unite our strength to maintain international peace and security, and

To insure, by the acceptance of principles and the institution of methods, that armed force shall not be used, save in the common interest, and

To employ international machinery for the promotion of the economic and social advancement of all peoples, have resolved to combine our efforts to accomplish these aims.

Accordingly, our respective Governments, through representatives assembled in the city of San Francisco, who have exhibited their full powers found to be in good and due form, have agreed to the present Charter of the United Nations and do hereby establish an international organization to be known as the United Nations.

# Principal Organs of the United Nations

## Secretariat

This is the directorate on U.N. operations, apart from political decisions. All members contribute to its upkeep. Its staff of over 4,000 specialists is recruited from member nations in proportion to their budget contributions. The staff works under the Secretary-General, whom it assists and advises.

### Secretaries-General

Kurt Waldheim, Austria, Jan. 1, 1972.
U Thant, Burma, Nov. 3, 1961, to Dec. 31, 1971.
Dag Hammarskjöld, Sweden, April 11, 1953, to Sept. 17, 1961.
Trygve Lie, Norway, Feb. 1, 1946, to April 10, 1953.

## General Assembly

The General Assembly is the world's forum for discussing matters affecting world peace and security, and for making recommendations concerning them. It has no power of its own to enforce decisions.

The Assembly is composed of the 51 original member nations and those admitted since, a total of 149. Each nation has one vote. On major questions involving international peace and security, a two-thirds majority of those present and voting is required. Decisions on other questions are made by a simple majority.

The Assembly's agenda can be as broad as the Charter. It can make recommendations to member nations, the Security Council, or both. Emphasis is given questions relating to international peace and security brought before it by any member, the Security Council, or nonmembers.

The Assembly also maintains a broad program of international cooperation in economic, social, cultural, educational, and health fields, and for assisting in human rights and freedoms.

Among other duties, the Assembly has functions relating to the trusteeship system, and considers and approves the U.N. Budget. Every member contributes to operating expenses according to its means.

The President of the Assembly in 1978 was Lazar Mojsov of Yugoslavia.

## Security Council

The Security Council is the primary instrument for implementing the United Nations' purposes and principles. Its main purpose is to prevent war by settling disputes between nations and by limiting armaments.

Under the Charter, the Council is permitted to dispatch a U.N. force to stop aggression and restore law and order. All member nations undertake to make available armed forces, assistance, and facilities to maintain international peace and security.

Any member may bring a dispute before the Security Council or the General Assembly. Any nonmember may do so if it accepts the charter obligations of pacific settlement.

The Security Council has five permanent members: the United States, the Soviet Union, Britain, France, and China. There are also 10 temporary members elected by the General Assembly for two-year terms, with different regions of the world rotating.

Voting on procedural matters requires a nine-vote majority to carry. However, on questions of substance, the vote of each of the five permanent members is required. Thus, any one of the five possess a veto. A vetoed motion can be passed on to the General Assembly by a vote of any seven members.

Current temporary members are (term expires Dec. 31, 1978): Canada, Federal Republic of Germany, India, Mauritius, Venezuela; (term expires Dec. 31, 1979): Bolivia, Czechoslovakia, Gabon, Kuwait, Nigeria.

## Economic and Social Council

This council is composed of 54 members elected by the General Assembly to 3-year terms. It works closely with the General Assembly as a link with groups formed within the U.N. to help peoples in such fields as education, health, and human rights. It insures that there is no overlapping and sets up commissions to deal with economic conditions and collect facts and figures on conditions over the world. It issues studies and reports and may make recommendations to the Assembly and specialized agencies.

### Functional Commissions

Statistical Commission; Population Commission; Commission for Social Development; Commission on Human Rights; Commission on the Status of Women; Commission on Narcotic Drugs; Commission on Transnational Corporations.

### Regional Economic Commissions

Economic Commission for Europe; Economic and Social Commission for Asia and the Pacific; Economic Commission for Latin America; Economic Commission for Africa; Economic Commission for Western Asia.

## Trusteeship Council

This council supervises territories that had been ruled as colonies by another nation. It appoints a member nation to administer each territory. This nation is charged with developing the self-government of the territory and preserving and advancing the cultural, political, economic, and other forms of welfare of the people.

The Trusteeship Council is currently composed of 5 members: 1 member—the United States—that administers trust territories, and 4 members—China, France, the Soviet Union, and the United Kingdom—that are permanent members of the Security Council but do not administer trust territories.

The following countries ceased to be administering members because of the independence of territories they had administered: Italy and France in 1960, Belgium in 1962, New Zealand and the United Kingdom in 1968 and Australia in 1975. France and the U. K. became nonadministering members.

As of October 1978 there was only one trust territory: the Trust Territory of the Pacific Islands (administered by the United States).

## International Court of Justice

The International Court of Justice sits at The Hague, the Netherlands. Its 15-judge bench was established to hear disputes among U.N. members, who must agree to accept its verdicts. Its judges, charged with administering justice under international law, deal mainly with territorial and transportation disputes.

Following are the members of the Court and the years in which their terms expire:

President: Eduardo Jiménez de Aréchaga, Uruguay (1979)
Vice President: Nagendra Singh, India (1982)
Isaac Forster, Senegal (1982)
André Gros, France (1982)
Hardy C. Dillard, U.S. (1979)
Louis-Ignacio-Pinto, Benin (1979)
Federico de Castro, Spain (1979)
Platon D. Morozov, U.S.S.R. (1979)
Sir Humphrey Waldock, U.K. (1982)
José María Ruda, Argentina (1982)
Taslim Olawale Elias, Nigeria (1985)
Manfred Lachs, Poland (1985)
Hermann Mösler, West Germany (1985)
Shigeru Oda, Japan (1985)
Salah El Dine Tarazi, Syria (1985)

## Agencies of the United Nations

### INTERNATIONAL ATOMIC ENERGY AGENCY (IAEA)

**Established:** Statute for IAEA, approved on Oct. 26, 1956, at a conference held at U.N. Headquarters, New York, came into force on July 29, 1957. The Agency is under the aegis of the U.N., but unlike the following, it is not a specialized agency.

**Purpose:** To promote the peaceful uses of atomic energy; to ensure that assistance provided by it or at its request or under its supervision or control is not used in such a way as to further any military purpose.

**Headquarters:** Kaerntnerring 11, A-1010, Vienna, Austria.

### FOOD AND AGRICULTURE ORGANIZATION OF THE UNITED NATIONS (FAO)

**Established:** October 16, 1945, when constitution became effective.

**Purpose:** To raise nutrition levels and living standards; to secure improvements in production and distribution of food and agricultural products.

**Headquarters:** Viale delle Terme di Caracalla, Rome, Italy.

### GENERAL AGREEMENT ON TARIFFS AND TRADE (GATT)

**Established:** Jan. 1, 1948.

**Purpose:** An International Trade Organization (ITO) was planned when the U.N. Agencies were first set up. Although this agency has not materialized, some of its objectives have been embodied in an international commercial treaty, the General Agreement on Tariffs and Trade. Its purpose is to sponsor trade negotiations.

**Headquarters:** Villa le Bocage, Palais des Nations, 1211 Geneva 10, Switzerland.

### INTER-GOVERNMENTAL MARITIME CONSULTATIVE ORGANIZATION (IMCO)

**Established:** March 17, 1958.

**Purpose:** To give advisory and consultative help to promote international cooperation in maritime navigation and to encourage the highest standards of safety and navigation. Its aim is to bring about a uniform system of measuring ship tonnage; systems now vary widely in different parts of the world. Other activities include cooperation with other U.N. agencies on matters affecting the maritime field.

**Headquarters:** 101–104 Piccadilly, London, W. 1, England.

### INTERNATIONAL BANK FOR RECONSTRUCTION AND DEVELOPMENT (IBRD) (WORLD BANK)

**Established:** December 27, 1945, when Articles of Agreement drawn up at Bretton Woods Conference in July 1944 came into force. Began operations on June 25, 1946.

**Purpose:** To assist in reconstruction and development of economies of members by making loans to governments and by furnishing technical advice.

**Headquarters:** 1818 H St., N.W., Washington, D.C. 20433.

### INTERNATIONAL CIVIL AVIATION ORGANIZATION (ICAO)

**Established:** April 4, 1947, after working as a provisional organization since June 1945.

**Purpose:** To study problems of international civil aviation; to establish international standards and regulations; to promote safety measures, uniform regulations for operation, simpler procedures at international borders, and the use of new technical methods and equipment. It has evolved standards for meteorological services, traffic control, communications, radio beacons and ranges, search and rescue organization, and other facilities. It has brought about much simplification of customs, immigration, and public health regulations as they apply to international air transport. It drafts international air law conventions, and is concerned with economic aspects of air travel.

**Headquarters:** International Aviation Square, 1000 Sherbrooke St. West, Montreal, Quebec, Canada H3A 2R2.

### INTERNATIONAL DEVELOPMENT ASSOCIATION (IDA)

**Established:** Sept. 24, 1960. An affiliate of the World Bank, IDA has the same officers and staff as the Bank.

**Purpose:** To further economic development of its members by providing finance on terms which bear less heavily on balance of payments of members than those of conventional loans.

**Headquarters:** 1818 H St., N.W., Washington, D.C. 20433.

### INTERNATIONAL FINANCE CORPORATION (IFC)

**Established:** Charter of IFC came into force on July 20, 1956. Although IFC is affiliated with the World Bank, it is a separate legal entity, and its funds are entirely separate from those of the Bank. However, membership in the Corporation is open only to Bank members.

**Purpose:** To further economic development by encouraging the growth of productive private enterprise in its member countries, particularly in the less developed areas; to invest in productive private enterprises in association with private investors, without government guarantee of repayment where sufficient private capital is not available on reasonable terms; to serve as a clearing house to bring together investment opportunities, private capital (both foreign and domestic), and experienced management.

**Headquarters:** 1818 H St., N.W., Washington, D.C. 20433.

### INTERNATIONAL LABOR ORGANIZATION (ILO)

**Established:** April 11, 1919, when constitution was adopted as Part XIII of Treaty of Versailles. Became specialized agency of U.N. in 1946.

**Purpose:** To contribute to establishment of lasting peace by promoting social justice; to improve labor conditions and living standards through international action; to promote economic and social stability. The U.S. withdrew from the ILO in 1977.

**Headquarters:** 4 route des Morillons, 1211 Geneva 22, Switzerland.

### INTERNATIONAL MONETARY FUND (IMF)

**Established:** Dec. 27, 1945, when Articles of Agreement drawn up at Bretton Woods Conference in July 1944 came into force. Fund began operations on March 1, 1947.

**Purpose:** To promote international monetary cooperation and expansion of international trade; to promote exchange stability; to assist in establishment of multilateral system of payments in respect of current transactions between members.

**Headquarters:** 700 19th St., N.W., Washington, D.C. 20431.

### INTERNATIONAL TELECOMMUNICATION UNION (ITU)

**Established:** 1865. Became specialized agency of U.N. in 1947.

**Purpose:** To extend technical assistance to help members keep up with present day telecommunication needs; to standardize communications equipment and procedures; to lower costs. It also works for orderly sharing of radio frequencies and makes studies and recommendations to benefit its members.

**Headquarters:** Place des Nations, 1211 Geneva 20, Switzerland.

### UNITED NATIONS EDUCATIONAL, SCIENTIFIC, AND CULTURAL ORGANIZATION (UNESCO)

**Established:** Nov. 4, 1946, when twentieth signatory to constitution deposited instrument of acceptance with government of U.K.

**Purpose:** To promote collaboration among nations through education, science, and culture in order to further justice, rule of law, and human rights and freedoms without distinction of race, sex, language, or religion.

**Headquarters:** UNESCO House, Place de Fontenoy, Paris 7e, France.

### UNIVERSAL POSTAL UNION (UPU)

**Established:** Oct. 9, 1874. Became specialized agency of U.N. in 1947.

**Purpose:** To facilitate reciprocal exchange of correspondence by uniform procedures by all UPU members; to help governments modernize and speed up mailing procedures.

**Headquarters:** Weltpostrasse 4, 3000 Berne 15, Switzerland.

### WORLD HEALTH ORGANIZATION (WHO)

**Established:** April 7, 1948, when 26 members of the U.N. had accepted its constitution, adopted July 22, 1946, by the International Health Conference in New York City.

**Purpose:** To aid attainment by all people of highest possible level of health.

**Headquarters:** 20 Avenue Appia, 1211 Geneva, Switzerland.

### WORLD INTELLECTUAL PROPERTY ORGANIZATION (WIPO)

**Established:** April 26, 1970, when its Convention came into force. Originated as International Bureau of Paris Union (1883) and Berne Union (1886), later succeeded by United International Bureau for the Protection of Intellectual Property (BIRPI). Became a specialized agency of the U.N. in December 1974.

**Purpose:** To promote legal protection of intellectual property, including artistic and scientific works, artistic performances, sound recordings, broadcasts, inventions, trademarks, industrial designs, and commercial names.

**Headquarters:** 32 Chemin des Colombettes, 1211 Geneva 20, Switzerland.

### WORLD METEOROLOGICAL ORGANIZATION (WMO)

**Established:** March 23, 1950, succeeding the International Meteorological Organization, a nongovernmental organization founded in 1878.

**Purpose:** To promote international exchange of weather reports and maximum standardization of observations; to help developing countries establish weather services for their own economic needs; to fill gaps in observation stations; to promote meteorological investigations affecting jet aircraft, satellites, energy resources, etc.

**Headquarters:** 41 Avenue Giuseppe Motta, Geneva, Switzerland.

# Diplomatic Personnel To and From the U.S.

| Country | U.S. Representative to[1] | Rank | Representative from[2] | Rank |
|---|---|---|---|---|
| Afghanistan | Theodore L. Eliot, Jr. | Amb. | Ghulam Farouk Turabaz | Cd'A. |
| Algeria | Ulric St. Clair Haynes, Jr. | Amb. | Abdelaziz Maoui | Amb. |
| Argentina | Raul H. Castro | Amb. | Jorge A. Aja Espil | Amb. |
| Australia | Philip H. Alston, Jr. | Amb. | Alan Philip Renouf | Amb. |
| Austria | Milton A. Wolf | Amb. | Karl Herbert Schober | Amb. |
| Bahamas | William B. Schwartz, Jr. | Amb. | Livingston B. Johnson | Amb. |
| Bahrain | Wat Tyler Cluverius IV | Amb. | Abdulaziz A. Buali | Amb. |
| Bangladesh | David T. Schneider | Amb. | Mustafizur R. Siddiqi | Amb. |
| Barbados | Frank V. Ortiz, Jr. | Amb. | Oliver H. Jackman | Amb. |
| Belgium | Anne Cox Chambers | Amb. | Willy Van Cauwenberg | Amb. |
| Benin | W. Kenneth Thompson | Cd'A. | Thomas S. Boya | Amb. |
| Bolivia | Paul H. Boeker | Amb. | Carlos Iturralde B. | Amb. |
| Botswana | Donald R. Norland | Amb. | Bias Mookodi | Amb. |
| Brazil | John H. Crimmins | Amb. | Joao Baptista Pinheiro | Amb. |
| Bulgaria | Raymond L. Garthoff | Amb. | Konstantin N. Grigorov | Amb. |
| Burma | Maurice D. Bean | Amb. | U Tin Lat | Amb. |
| Burundi | (Vacancy) | | Laurent Nzeyimana | Amb. |
| Cameroon | Mabel M. Smythe | Amb. | Benoit Bindzi | Amb. |
| Canada | Thomas O. Enders | Amb. | Peter M. Towe | Amb. |
| Cape Verde | Edward Marks | Amb. | Dr. Raul Querido Varela | Amb. |
| Central African Empire | Anthony C. E. Quainton | Amb. | Christophe Maidou | Amb. |
| Chad | William G. Bradford | Amb. | Pierre Toura Gaba | Amb. |
| Chile | George W. Landau | Amb. | Jose Miguel Barros | Amb. |
| China (Taiwan) | Leonard Unger | Amb. | James C. H. Shen | Amb. |
| Colombia | Diego C. Asencio | Amb. | Virgilio Barco | Amb. |
| Congo, People's Republic of the | Jay Katzen | Cd'A. | (No Embassy) | |
| Costa Rica | Marvin Weissman | Amb. | Jose Rafael Echeverria | Amb. |
| Cyprus | William R. Crawford, Jr. | Amb. | Nicos G. Dimitriou | Amb. |
| Czechoslovakia | Thomas R. Byrne | Amb. | Dr. Jaromir Johanes | Amb. |
| Denmark | John Gunther Dean | Amb. | Otto R. Borch | Amb. |
| Djibouti | Walter S. Clarke | Cd'A. | (No Embassy) | |
| Dominican Republic | Robert A. Hurwitch | Amb. | Dr. Horacio Vicioso-Soto | Amb. |
| Ecuador | (Vacancy) | | Gustavo Ycaza Borja | Amb. |
| Egypt, Arab Republic of | Hermann F. Eilts | Amb. | Dr. Ashraf A. Ghorbal | Amb. |
| El Salvador | Frank J. Devine | Amb. | Roberto Quinonez Meza | Amb. |
| Ethiopia | Richard C. Matheron | Cd'A. | Tibabu Bekele | Cd'A. |
| Fiji | John P. Condon | Amb. | Berenado Vunibobo | Amb. |
| Finland | Rozanne L. Ridgway | Amb. | Jaakko Iloniemi | Amb. |
| France | Arthur A. Hartman | Amb. | Francois de Laboulaye | Amb. |
| Gabon | (Vacancy) | | Jean-Daniel Mambouka | Amb. |
| Gambia | Herman J. Cohen[3] | Amb. | (No Embassy) | |
| Germany, East | David B. Bolen | Amb. | Dr. Rolf Sieber | Amb. |
| Germany, West | Walter J. Stoessel, Jr. | Amb. | Berndt von Staden | Amb. |
| Ghana | Robert P. Smith | Amb. | Dr. Alex Quaison-Sackey | Amb. |
| Great Britain | Kingman Brewster, Jr. | Amb. | Peter Jay | Amb. |
| Greece | (Vacancy) | | Menelas D. Alexandrakis | Amb. |
| Grenada | Frank V. Ortiz, Jr. | Amb. | George Ashley Griffith | Amb. |
| Guatemala | Davis E. Boster | Amb. | Jorge Lamport-Rodil | Amb. |
| Guinea | Oliver S. Crosby | Amb. | Ibrahima Camara | Amb. |
| Guinea-Bissau | Edward Marks | Amb. | Gil Vicente Vaz Fernandes | Amb. |
| Guyana | John R. Burke | Amb. | Laurence E. Mann | Amb. |
| Haiti | William B. Jones | Amb. | Georges Salomon | Amb. |
| Honduras | Mari-Luci Jaramillo | Amb. | Dr. Roberto Lazarus | Amb. |
| Hungary | Philip M. Kaiser | Amb. | Ferenc Esztergalyos | Amb. |
| Iceland | James J. Blake | Amb. | Hans G. Andersen | Amb. |
| India | Robert F. Goheen | Amb. | N. A. Palkhivala | Amb. |
| Indonesia | Edward E. Masters | Amb. | D. Ashari | Amb. |
| Iran | William H. Sullivan | Amb. | Ardeshir Zahedi | Amb. |
| Ireland | William V. Shannon | Amb. | John G. Molloy | Amb. |
| Israel | Samuel W. Lewis | Amb. | Simcha Dinitz | Amb. |
| Italy | Richard N. Gardner | Amb. | Paolo Pansa Cedronio | Amb. |
| Ivory Coast | Monteagle Stearns | Amb. | Timothée N' Guetta Ahoua | Amb. |
| Jamaica | Frederick Irving | Amb. | Alfred A. Rattray | Amb. |
| Japan | Michael J. Mansfield | Amb. | Fumihiko Togo | Amb. |
| Jordan | Thomas R. Pickering | Amb. | Abdullah Salah | Amb. |
| Kenya | Wilbert J. Le Melle | Amb. | John P. Mbogua | Amb. |
| Korea, South | Richard L. Sneider | Amb. | Yong Shik Kim | Amb. |

| Country | U.S. Representative to[1] | Rank | Representative from[2] | Rank |
|---|---|---|---|---|
| Kuwait | Frank E. Maestrone | Amb. | Khalid M. Jaffar | Amb. |
| Laos | (Vacancy) | | Somphong Vanitsaveth | Cd'A. |
| Lebanon | Richard B. Parker | Amb. | Najati Kabbani | Amb. |
| Lesotho | Donald R. Norland[4] | Amb. | Thabo R. Makeka | Amb. |
| Liberia | W. Beverly Carter | Amb. | Francis A. Dennis | Amb. |
| Libya | (Vacancy) | | Ahmed Dia Addin Madfai | Cd'A. |
| Luxembourg | James G. Lowenstein | Amb. | Adrien Meisch | Amb. |
| Madagascar | Robert S. Barett | Cd'A. | Norbert Rakotomalala | Cd'A. |
| Malawi | Robert A. Stevenson | Amb. | Jacob T. X. Muwamba | Amb. |
| Malaysia | Robert H. Miller | Amb. | Zain Azraai | Amb. |
| Mali | Patricia M. Byrne | Amb. | Alpha Amadou Diaw | Cd'A. |
| Malta | L. Bruce Laingen | Amb. | Victor Gauci | Cd'A. |
| Mauritania | E. Gregory Kryza | Amb. | Mohamed Nassim Kochman | Amb. |
| Mauritius | Robert V. Keeley | Amb. | Pierre Guy Girald Balancy | Amb. |
| Mexico | Patrick J. Lucey | Amb. | Hugo B. Margain | Amb. |
| Morocco | Robert Anderson | Amb. | Ali Bengelloun | Amb. |
| Mozambique | Willard A. De Pree | Amb. | (No Embassy) | |
| Nepal | L. Douglas Heck | Amb. | Padma Bahadur Khatri | Amb. |
| Netherlands | Robert J. McCloskey | Amb. | Age R. Tammenoms Bakker | Amb. |
| New Zealand | Armistead I. Selden, Jr. | Amb. | Merwyn Norrish | Amb. |
| Nicaragua | Mauricio Solaun | Amb. | Dr. Guillermo Sevilla-Sacasa | Amb. |
| Niger | Charles A. James | Amb. | Andre Wright | Amb. |
| Nigeria | Donald B. Easum | Amb. | Olujimi Jolaoso | Amb. |
| Norway | Louis A. Lerner | Amb. | Soren Christian Sommerfelt | Amb. |
| Oman | William D. Wolle | Amb. | Farid Mbarak Ali Al-Hinai | Amb. |
| Pakistan | Arthur W. Hummel, Jr. | Amb. | Sahabzada Yaqub-Khan | Amb. |
| Panama | William J. Jorden | Amb. | Gabriel Lewis | Amb. |
| Papua New Guinea | Mary S. Olmsted | Amb. | Paulias Nguna Matane | Amb. |
| Paraguay | Robert E. White | Amb. | Mario Lopez Escobar | Amb. |
| Peru | Harry W. Shlaudeman | Amb. | Carlos Garcia-Bedoya | Amb. |
| Philippines | David D. Newson | Amb. | Eduardo Z. Romualdez | Amb. |
| Poland | Richard T. Davies | Amb. | Romuald Spasowski | Amb. |
| Portugal | Richard J. Bloomfield | Amb. | Joao Hall Themido | Amb. |
| Qatar | Andrew I. Killgore | Amb. | Abdullah Saleh Al-Mana | Amb. |
| Romania | O. Rudolph Aggrey | Amb. | Nicolae M. Nicolae | Amb. |
| Rwanda | T. Frank Crigler | Amb. | Bonaventure Ubalijoro | Amb. |
| Saudi Arabia | John C. West | Amb. | Ali Abdallah Alireza | Amb. |
| Senegal | Herman J. Cohen | Amb. | Andre Coulbary | Amb. |
| Seychelles | Wilbert J. Le Melle[5] | Amb. | (No Embassy) | |
| Sierra Leone | John Andrew Linehan | Amb. | Philip J. Palmer | Amb. |
| Singapore | John H. Holdridge | Amb. | Punch Coomaraswamy | Amb. |
| Somalia | John L. Loughran | Amb. | Dr. Abdullahi Ahmed Addou | Amb. |
| South Africa | William G. Bowdler | Amb. | Donald B. Sole | Amb. |
| Spain | Wells Stabler | Amb. | Juan Jose Rovira | Amb. |
| Sri Lanka[6] | (Vacancy) | | Dr. W. S. Karunaratne | Amb. |
| Sudan | Donald C. Bergus | Amb. | Omer Salih Eissa | Amb. |
| Surinam | J. Owen Zurhellen, Jr. | Amb. | Roel F. Karamat | Amb. |
| Swaziland | Donald R. Norland[4] | Amb. | Simon M. Kunene | Amb. |
| Sweden | Rodney Kennedy-Minott | Amb. | Count Wilhelm Wachtmeister | Amb. |
| Switzerland | Marvin Warner | Amb. | Raymond Probst | Amb. |
| Syrian Arab Republic | Richard W. Murphy | Amb. | Dr. Sabah Kabbani | Amb. |
| Tanzania | James W. Spain | Amb. | Paul Bomani | Amb. |
| Thailand | Charles S. Whitehouse | Amb. | Sukho Suwansiri | Cd'A. |
| Togo | Ronald D. Palmer | Amb. | Messanvi Kokou Kekeh | Amb. |
| Trinidad and Tobago | Richard K. Fox, Jr. | Amb. | Victor C. McIntyre | Amb. |
| Tunisia | Edward W. Mulcahy | Amb. | Ali Hedda | Amb. |
| Turkey | Ronald I. Spiers | Amb. | Melih Esenbel | Amb. |
| U.S.S.R. | Malcolm Toon | Amb. | Anatoliy F. Dobrynin | Amb. |
| United Arab Emirates | Francois M. Dickman | Amb. | Hamad Abdul Rahman Al Madfa | Amb. |
| Upper Volta | Pierre R. Graham | Amb. | Telesphore Yaguibou | Amb. |
| Uruguay | Lawrence H. Pezzullo | Amb. | Jose Perez Caldas | Amb. |
| Venezuela | Viron P. Vaky | Amb. | Ignacio Iribarren | Amb. |
| Yemen Arab Republic | Thomas J. Scotes | Amb. | Yahya M. Al-Mutawakel | Amb. |
| Yugoslavia | Lawrence S. Eagleburger | Amb. | Dimce Belovski | Amb. |
| Zaire | Walter L. Cutler | Amb. | Kasongo Mutuale | Amb. |
| Zambia | Stephen Low | Amb. | Putteho M. Ngonda | Amb. |

1. As of March 1978. 2. As of May 1978. 3. Resident in Dakar, Senegal. 4. Resident in Gaborone, Botswana. 5. Resident in Nairobi, Kenya. 6. Formerly Ceylon. NOTE: Amb. = Ambassador; Cd'A. = Chargé d'Affaires. *Source:* U.S. Department of State.

# Energy in 1978

Energy was demoted from "crisis" to "serious problem" in 1978, but the basic conditions which last year led many experts to think in terms of crisis still exist. The U.S. still depends too much on imported oil. All known sources of natural fuel are being depleted, and it costs more both to discover and to exploit new oil, coal, and gas deposits. Nuclear energy development has been stalled by acrimonious debate over its environmental impact and the related issue of proliferation of nuclear weapons. Alternate sources of power—solar, windmills, biomass—still face tremendous economic and technological problems before they can contribute much to the energy package.

But, early in 1978, it became apparent that the American economy was adjusting itself to the most immediate and most apparent component of the "crisis," the phenomenal increase in the price of imported crude oil, about $14.50 a barrel in 1978.

During the first six months of 1978 we imported 7.9 million barrels a day of foreign crude oil. In the same period a year earlier, the figure was more than 9 million barrels a day. Much of this decrease in imports was accounted for by the start of the full flow of crude oil down the Alaska pipeline in the beginning of 1978.

Of the almost 8 million barrels imported each day, 140,000 barrels were being diverted to a stored strategic petroleum reserve. By the end of the year we expect to have 50 million barrels in reserve. The Energy Department expects the reserve to reach 500 million by 1980, giving the nation a two-month's supply at current use rates.

But indications are that imports will decrease still further. The high price of crude oil has stimulated greater exploration efforts all over the world. New fields have been found in Mexico, Southeast Asia, and in what is called the Overthrust Belt in the American Rockies. In addition, vast new reserves of natural gas have been discovered in Western Canada.

The demand for fuel has lessened as the rate of growth of the industrialized nations has slowed. In addition, industry has learned to use energy more efficiently.

The use of coal has increased at a greater rate than the use of oil. Those industrial facilities that could easily switch from oil to coal have done so. But the burning of coal poses environmental problems. The Environmental Protection Service's air-quality standards could slow down considerably the growth rate in use of coal.

The higher cost of energy has also contributed to the adoption of conservation measures, both by industry and by the public at large. The sales of home insulation have spurted, and there has been some increase in the use of solar water- and space-heating units. Solar tax credits, a non-controversial part of the President's energy program that was held up in Congress for so long, are retroactive to April 1977.

Congressional delay on final passage of the President's program was another indication that there was no crisis mood in the nation. Congressmen felt free to wrangle over the issues of price fixing for natural gas and the crude oil equalization tax.

Despite the fact that, over the short term, the American economy is learning to cope with the higher cost of energy, experts recognize that, over the long term, new energy policies and new ways of using energy and conserving it will have to be evolved.

One step already taken toward long-term planning was the establishment in August 1977 of a new Department of Energy with James R. Schlesinger as its Secretary.

The Department took over the functions of the Energy Research and Development Administration which, in turn, had replaced the old Atomic Energy Commission. It also swallowed the Federal Energy Administration, and took over, on a quasi-independent basis, the Federal Power Commission, which became the Federal Energy Regulatory Commission. Detached from the Department of Interior and placed in the new department were most of its functions in the power area, including the use of public lands for energy purposes. The Navy Department's oil reserves, including Teapot Dome and Elk Hills, were transferred to the new Energy Department.

A major function of the new office is research and development in all energy technologies, old and new. Its Energy Research and Energy Technology divisions hope to bring solar energy and other alternate energy systems to the point where they are economically competitive with the older energy systems. And they are concentrating on methods of cleaning up the burning of fossil fuels, especially coal, to bring them in line with clean air standards.

The new Department of Energy with its more than 19,000 employees has had its growing pains. One has been the reluctance of Congress to approve a comprehensive energy policy. Another is the conflict within the Carter Administration over how strict should be the environmental standards with which energy sources must comply.

But these problems are being resolved, both for the new Department and for the nation at large. There is no feeling of panic in the nation about energy. There is realization that energy presents serious, long-term problems, but there is confidence that we can find solutions without too much upheaval.

*Wadsworth Likely*

## U.S. Energy Consumption

| Type | 1978 | 1977 |
|---|---|---|
| Household and commercial | 37.0% | 37.3% |
| Industry | 36.8 | 37.0 |
| Transportation | 26.2 | 25.7 |
| **Total** | **100.0** | **100.0** |

*Source:* Department of Energy, Energy Information Administration.

## Comparing Energy Sources[1]

**(converting energy sources into BTU equivalents)**

One British Thermal Unit (BTU) = the amount of heat needed to increase the temperature of one pound of water by 1° F. (252 calories).

| | BTU (in thousands) |
|---|---|
| Bituminous Coal and Lignite | |
| Production, average/short ton | 23,500.0 |
| Consumption, average/short ton | 22,800.0 |
| Electricity generation/short ton | 21,630.0 |
| Anthracite, short ton | 25,400.0 |
| Crude petroleum, barrel (42 gallons) | 5,800.0 |
| Natural gas, dry, cubic foot | 1.021 |
| Nuclear power, kilowatt-hour | 10.66 |
| Hydropower[2] kilowatt-hour | 10.38 |

1. For helpful conversion factors, *see* the "Science" section of this *Almanac*. 2. Calculated from national average heat rates for fossil-fueled steam-electric plants.

## U.S. and World Energy Projections

**(in quadrillion BTUs)**

| Activity and fuel source | United States 1980 | United States 1985 | United States 1990 | World 1980 | World 1985 | World 1990 |
|---|---|---|---|---|---|---|
| Consumption | | | | | | |
| Coal | 17.2 | 21.3 | 25.1 | 76.8 | 84.1 | 89.9 |
| Petroleum | 41.0 | 46.2 | 49.5 | 136.2 | 151.0 | 167.9 |
| Natural gas | 20.6 | 20.1 | 19.9 | 54.2 | 62.7 | 70.4 |
| Hydropower and geothermal | 3.4 | 3.9 | 4.5 | 14.8 | 16.2 | 17.7 |
| Nuclear | 4.3 | 11.4 | 18.1 | 12.1 | 32.5 | 60.2 |
| Total | 86.5 | 102.9 | 117.1 | 294.1 | 346.5 | 406.1 |
| Production | | | | | | |
| Coal | 19.1 | 23.4 | 27.3 | 76.8 | 84.1 | 89.9 |
| Petroleum | 24.0 | 25.7 | 28.0 | 136.2 | 151.0 | 167.9 |
| Natural gas | 19.5 | 18.8 | 19.6 | 54.2 | 62.7 | 70.4 |
| Hydropower and geothermal | 3.4 | 3.9 | 4.5 | 14.8 | 16.2 | 17.7 |
| Nuclear | 4.3 | 11.4 | 18.1 | 12.1 | 32.5 | 60.2 |
| Total | 70.3 | 83.2 | 97.5 | 294.1 | 346.5 | 406.1 |
| Estimated shortage | 16.2 | 19.7 | 19.6 | — | — | — |

*Source:* Department of the Interior, Bureau of Mines.

## World's Ten Largest Electric Energy Producers, 1976

**(in million kilowatt hours)**

| Country | Production Hydro | Production Nuclear | Production Thermal | Production Total |
|---|---|---|---|---|
| United States | 290,499 | 191,108 | 1,641,799 | 2,123,406 |
| USSR | 135,735 | 14,000[2] | 961,685[2] | 1,111,420 |
| Japan | 88,741[1] | 34,079 | 388,956 | 511,776 |
| West Germany | 14,052 | 24,262 | 295,337 | 333,651 |
| Canada | 213,049 | 16,430 | 63,888 | 293,367 |
| United Kingdom | 5,121 | 36,155 | 235,700 | 276,976 |
| France | 49,287 | 15,763 | 138,044 | 203,094 |
| Italy | 43,466[1] | 3,807 | 116,277 | 163,550 |
| China | 37,500[2] | — | 100,500[2] | 138,000[2] |
| Poland | 2,098 | — | 102,003 | 104,101 |
| Sub-total | 879,548 | 335,604 | 4,044,189 | 5,259,341 |
| All others | 576,608 | 62,165 | 1,018,540 | 1,657,313 |
| **World total** | **1,456,156** | **397,769** | **5,062,729** | **6,916,654** |

1. Production from geothermal sources included. 2. Estimate. *Source:* United Nations, *World Energy Supplies, 1972–1976.*

## Per Capita Electric Energy Consumption, 1976
(20 highest per capita consumers)

| Country | kwh per capita[1] | Population (thousands) | Production plus net import[2] | Country | kwh per capita[1] | Population (thousands) | Production plus net imports[2] |
|---|---|---|---|---|---|---|---|
| Norway | 18,769 | 4,026 | 75,565 | Qatar | 8,589 | 95 | 816 |
| Panama Canal Zone | 16,250 | 40 | 650 | U.S. Virgin Islands | 7,579 | 95 | 720 |
| Canada | 12,278 | 23,143 | 284,153 | Finland | 6,721 | 4,727 | 31,770 |
| New Caledonia | 11,844 | 135 | 1,599 | New Zealand | 6,663 | 3,138 | 20,910 |
| Luxembourg | 11,682 | 358 | 4,182 | Netherland Antilles | 6,639 | 241 | 1,600 |
| Guam | 11,183 | 93 | 1,040 | Australia | 5,614 | 13,643 | 76,598 |
| Iceland | 11,027 | 220 | 2,426 | Kuwait | 5,502 | 1,030 | 5,667 |
| Sweden | 10,766 | 8,222 | 88,518 | West Germany | 5,440 | 61,513 | 334,608 |
| United States | 9,911 | 215,118 | 2,132,018 | Bermuda | 5,439 | 57 | 310 |
| Christmas Island | 9,333 | 3 | 28 | Puerto Rico | 5,336 | 3,214 | 17,150 |
| | | | | **World** | **1,720** | — | — |

1. Production plus net imports divided by total population. 2. In million kilowatt hours. NOTE: Data on consumption are derived from the formula "production plus imports minus exports." Accordingly, apparent consumption may occasionally be only an indication of the magnitude of actual gross inland availability. Where relatively small populations are involved, large fluctuations in per capita consumption series may derive from small quantitative variations. *Source:* United Nations, *World Energy Supplies, 1972–76.*

## World Production, Trade, and Consumption of Commercial Energy, 1976
(in million metric tons of coal equivalent)

| Activity | World | Developed countries[1] | Developing countries[2] | Centrally planned economic[3] | U.S. | U.S.S.R. | Saudi Arabia |
|---|---|---|---|---|---|---|---|
| Total primary energy production | 8,951 | 3,229 | 2,890 | 2,832 | 2,060 | 1,674 | 644 |
| Imports of commercial energy | — | 2,455 | 557 | 212 | 577 | 35 | 1 |
| Exports of commercial energy | — | 469 | 2,422 | 364 | 62 | 276 | 602 |
| Total energy consumption | | | | | | | |
| Solid fuels | 2,696 | 1,157 | 156 | 1,383 | 544 | 485 | — |
| Liquid fuels | 3,733 | 2,491 | 534 | 708 | 1,128 | 486 | 9 |
| Natural gas | 1,662 | 1,089 | 123 | 450 | 753 | 362 | 8 |
| Hydro/nuclear electricity | 228 | 100 | 00 | 00 | 60 | 17 | — |
| **Total commercial energy in kg per capita** | **2,069** | **6,388** | **426** | **2,030** | **11,554** | **5,259** | **1,901** |

1. Australia, Canada, Israel, Japan, New Zealand, South Africa, U.S., Western Europe (incl. Yugoslovia). 2. Developing market economies of Africa, Caribbean, Middle East (incl. Turkey), Far East, etc. 3. Albania, Bulgaria, Czechoslovakia, East Germany, Hungary, Poland, Romania, U.S.S.R. *Source:* United Nations, *World Energy Supplies, 1972–1976.*

## Leading Exporters of Crude Oil to U.S.
(in millions of 42-gallon barrels)

| Country | 1976 | 1974 | 1970 | 1960 | Country | 1976 | 1974 | 1970 | 1960 |
|---|---|---|---|---|---|---|---|---|---|
| Nigeria | 371 | 254 | 17 | 0 | Angola | 2 | 18 | 0 | 0 |
| Saudi Arabia | 447 | 160 | 15 | 28 | Mexico | 32 | 0.6 | 0 | 0.8 |
| Canada | 136 | 289 | 245 | 41 | Ecuador | 19 | 15 | 0 | 0 |
| Venezuela | 88 | 116 | 98 | 173 | Gabon | — | 9 | 0 | 0 |
| Indonesia | 196 | 103 | 26 | 27 | Qatar | — | 6 | 0 | 2 |
| Iran | 109 | 169 | 12 | 13 | Egypt | 6 | 3 | 8 | 1 |
| Algeria | 149 | 66 | 2 | (1) | Bolivia | — | 2 | 1 | 0 |
| Libya | 162 | 1 | 17 | 0 | Tunisia | — | 5 | 0 | 0 |
| United Arab Emirates | 93 | 25 | 23 | 0 | Kuwait | (1) | 2 | 12 | 48 |
| Trinidad | 38 | 23 | (1) | 0 | **Total all countries** | **1,935** | **1,269** | **483** | **372** |

1. Less than 500,000 barrels. *Source:* Department of the Interior, Bureau of Mines.

## Production of Crude Petroleum by Countries
(in thousands of 42-gallon barrels)

| Area and country | 1977 | 1976 | Percent change |
|---|---|---|---|
| Western Hemisphere | 5,156,355 | 5,020,210 | 2.7 |
| Argentina | 156,950 | 145,270 | 8.0 |
| Bolivia | 12,775 | 14,600 | −12.5 |
| Brazil | 60,955 | 60,955 | — |
| Canada | 509,905 | 475,595 | 7.2 |
| Chile | 8,395 | 8,395 | — |
| Colombia | 50,370 | 53,290 | −5.5 |
| Ecuador | 65,700 | 68,255 | −3.7 |
| Mexico | 358,065 | 292,365 | 22.5 |
| Peru | 31,390 | 27,375 | 14.7 |
| Trinidad and Tobago | 83,950 | 77,015 | 9.0 |
| United States | 3,002,125 | 2,961,245 | 1.4 |
| Venezuela | 815,410 | 835,850 | −2.4 |
| Western Europe | 498,225 | 313,170 | 59.1 |
| Austria | 13,140 | 13,140 | — |
| Denmark | 3,285 | 1,460 | 125.0 |
| France | 7,300 | 7,300 | — |
| West Germany | 39,055 | 40,150 | −2.7 |
| Italy | 6,570 | 7,665 | −14.3 |
| Netherlands | 10,950 | 11,315 | −3.2 |
| Norway | 102,200 | 101,835 | 0.4 |
| Spain | 5,840 | 11,680 | −50.0 |
| United Kingdom | 280,320 | 90,155 | 210.9 |
| Yugoslavia | 29,200 | 28,835 | 1.3 |
| Middle East | 8,085,480 | 7,984,010 | 1.3 |
| Abu Dhabi | 607,725 | 580,350 | 4.7 |
| Bahrain | 20,440 | 21,170 | −3.4 |
| Dubai | 116,435 | 114,245 | 1.9 |
| Iran | 2,066,995 | 2,147,295 | −3.7 |
| Iraq | 808,475 | 784,750 | 3.0 |
| Israel | 365 | 365 | — |
| Kuwait | 650,795 | 698,975 | −6.9 |
| Neutral Zone [1] | 133,225 | 171,915 | −22.5 |
| Oman | 124,465 | 133,590 | −6.8 |
| Qatar | 160,600 | 177,755 | −9.7 |
| Saudi Arabia [2] | 3,293,395 | 3,045,560 | 8.1 |
| Sharjah | 10,220 | 13,505 | −24.3 |
| Syria | 74,095 | 69,715 | 6.3 |
| Turkey | 18,250 | 25,185 | −27.5 |
| Asia-Pacific | 1,009,955 | 919,070 | 9.9 |
| Australia | 157,315 | 155,490 | 1.2 |
| Burma | 8,760 | 8,395 | 4.3 |
| Brunei-Malaysia | 146,365 | 133,225 | 9.9 |
| India | 72,635 | 64,240 | 13.1 |
| Indonesia | 615,390 | 549,325 | 12.0 |
| Japan | 3,650 | 4,380 | −16.7 |
| Pakistan | 3,650 | 2,555 | 42.9 |
| Taiwan | 1,825 | 1,825 | — |
| Africa | 2,279,790 | 2,120,285 | 7.5 |
| Algeria | 398,215 | 382,520 | 4.1 |
| Angola | 19,710 | 4,380 | 350.0 |
| Cabinda | 51,100 | 32,120 | 59.1 |
| Congo | 12,045 | 14,965 | −19.5 |
| Egypt | 152,570 | 119,720 | 27.4 |
| Gabon | 82,125 | 79,205 | 3.7 |
| Libya | 753,725 | 701,165 | 7.5 |
| Morocco | 365 | 365 | — |
| Nigeria | 766,500 | 748,250 | 2.4 |
| Tunisia | 34,675 | 28,470 | 21.8 |
| Zaire | 8,760 | 9,125 | −4.0 |
| Communist bloc | 4,786,245 | 4,544,615 | 5.3 |
| China | 652,620 | 616,120 | 5.9 |
| Romania | 107,675 | 105,850 | 1.7 |
| U.S.S.R. [3] | 3,985,800 | 3,782,860 | 5.4 |
| Other | 40,150 | 40,150 | — |
| **World Total** | **21,815,685** | **20,901,725** | **4.4** |

1. Shared by Kuwait and Saudi Arabia. 2. Estimated. 3. Includes gas liquids. *Source: Oil & Gas Journal.*

## Oil Production by States
(in thousands of 42-gallon barrels)

| State | 1975[1] Barrels | 1975[1] Percent total U.S. | 1970 Barrels | 1970 Percent total U.S. | 1966 Barrels | 1966 Percent total U.S. |
|---|---|---|---|---|---|---|
| Texas | 1,221,929 | 40.0 | 1,249,697 | 35.5 | 1,057,706 | 34.9 |
| Louisiana | 650,840 | 21.3 | 906,907 | 25.8 | 674,318 | 22.3 |
| California | 322,199 | 10.5 | 372,191 | 10.6 | 345,295 | 11.4 |
| Oklahoma | 163,123 | 5.3 | 223,574 | 6.4 | 224,839 | 7.4 |
| Wyoming | 135,943 | 4.4 | 160,345 | 4.6 | 134,470 | 4.4 |
| New Mexico | 95,063 | 3.1 | 128,184 | 3.6 | 124,154 | 4.1 |
| Alaska | 69,834 | 2.3 | 83,616 | 2.4 | 14,358 | 0.5 |
| Kansas | 59,106 | 1.9 | 84,853 | 2.4 | 103,738 | 3.4 |
| Mississippi | 46,614 | 1.5 | 65,119 | 1.9 | 55,227 | 1.8 |
| Utah | 42,301 | 1.4 | 23,370 | 0.7 | 24,112 | 0.8 |
| Colorado | 38,089 | 1.2 | 24,723 | 0.7 | 33,492 | 1.1 |
| Montana | 32,844 | 1.1 | 37,879 | 1.1 | 35,380 | 1.2 |
| Illinois | 26,067 | 0.9 | 43,747 | 1.2 | 61,661 | 2.0 |
| Michigan | 24,420 | 0.8 | 11,693 | 0.3 | 14,273 | 0.5 |
| North Dakota | 20,452 | 0.7 | 21,998 | 0.6 | 27,126 | 0.9 |
| Arkansas | 16,133 | 0.5 | 18,035 | 0.5 | 23,824 | 0.8 |
| Kentucky | 7,837 | 0.3 | 11,575 | 0.3 | 18,066 | 0.6 |
| Nebraska | 6,120 | 0.2 | 11,451 | 0.3 | 13,850 | 0.5 |
| Others | 78,146 | 2.6 | 38,493 | 1.1 | 41,874 | 1.4 |
| **Total U.S.** | **3,056,779** | **100.0** | **3,517,450** | **100.0** | **3,027,763** | **100.0** |

1. Preliminary. *Source:* Department of the Interior, Bureau of Mines.

## U.S. Consumption of Primary Energy Resources and Selected Related Products

| Resource or product | 1976 estimate | Percentage change from 1975 |
|---|---|---|
| Coal-bituminous & lignite (million short tons) | 597.2 | + 7.4 |
| Coal-anthracite (million short tons) | 5.2 | + 2.0 |
| Crude petroleum (million barrels) | 4,892.9 | + 7.7 |
| Dry natural gas[1] (billion cubic feet) | 19,800.0 | + 1.3 |
| Liquid natural gas (million barrels) | 588.7 | − 1.2 |
| Hydropower, utility[2] (million kilowatt-hours) | 291,900.0 | − 5.1 |
| Hydropower, industrial (million kilowatt-hours) | 3,210.0 | − 3.9 |
| All oils, domestic product demand[3] (million barrels) | 6,349.7 | + 6.6 |
| Coke (million short-tons) | 57.4 | + 6.9 |
| Electricity from nuclear plants, utility (million kilowatt-hours) | 190,600.0 | +10.9 |
| Electricity from conventional plants, utility (million kilowatt-hours) | 1,559,900.0 | + 8.0 |
| Electricity from industrial plants (million kilowatt-hours) | 83,790.0 | + 2.7 |

1. Excludes shrinkage. 2. Net generation, adjusted to include net imports. 3. Includes natural gas liquids. *Source:* Department of the Interior, Bureau of Mines.

## U.S. Electric Energy Production

| Producer | 1977 Million megawatt hours | 1977 Percent | 1976 Million megawatt hours | 1976 Percent |
|---|---|---|---|---|
| Utilities | | | | |
| From Coal | 985.4 | 46.4 | 943.9 | 46.4 |
| Oil | 357.9 | 16.8 | 319.5 | 15.7 |
| Gas | 305.4 | 14.4 | 294.4 | 14.4 |
| Nuclear | 250.9 | 11.8 | 191.1 | 9.4 |
| Hydroelectric | 220.4 | 10.4 | 283.7 | 13.9 |
| Other | 4.1 | 0.2 | 3.9 | 0.2 |
| Total Utilities | 2124.1[1] | 100.0 | 2,036.5[2] | 100.0 |
| Industrial power plants | 87.0[3] | | 87.1 | |

1. Privately owned utilities generated 1,683.8 million megawatt hours; publicly owned utilities, 440.3 million megawatt hours (municipal, 83.3; federal, 213.6; cooperatives, 45.1; power districts and state projects 98.2). 2. An increase of 6.2% over 1975. Privately owned utilities generated 1,583.0 million megawatt hours; publicly owned utilities, 454.5 (municipal, 77.8; federal 235.9; cooperative, 40.6; power districts and state projects, 100.2). 3. A decrease of 0.2% compared to 1976. NOTE: If a direct comparison is made between 1977 and 1976 with the additional "leap year" day in February of 1976 excluded, total production for 365 days in 1977 increased by 4.5% above the production for the same number of days in 1976. *Source:* Department of Energy, Energy Information Administration.

## U.S. Motor Vehicle Fuel Consumption
(1976 estimate)

| Type of vehicle | Total travel (million vehicle miles) | Number of registered vehicles (thousands) | Average miles traveled per vehicle | Fuel consumed (million gallons) | Average fuel consumption per vehicle (gallons) | Average miles per gallon |
|---|---|---|---|---|---|---|
| All passenger vehicles | 1,102,213 | 115,818.9 | 9,517 | 79,703.8 | 688 | 13.83 |
| Total personal passenger vehicles | 1,096,452 | 115,340.6 | 9,506 | 78,739.8 | 683 | 13.93 |
| Cars | 1,074,000 | 110,351.4 | 9,733 | 78,290.8 | 709 | 13.72 |
| Motorcycles | 22,452 | 4,989.2 | 4,500 | 449.0 | 90 | 50.00 |
| All buses | 5,761 | 478.3 | 12,045 | 964.0 | 2,015 | 5.98 |
| Commercial | 2,899 | 96.8 | 29,948 | 574.1 | 5,931 | 5.05 |
| School and other nonrevenue | 2,862 | 381.5 | 7,502 | 389.9 | 1,022 | 7.34 |
| All cargo vehicles | 306,950 | 27,719.6 | 11,073 | 35,996.3 | 1,299 | 8.53 |
| Single unit trucks | 247,895 | 26,498.6 | 9,355 | 25,039.9 | 945 | 9.90 |
| Combinations | 59,055 | 1,221.0 | 48,366 | 10,956.4 | 8,973 | 5.39 |
| **All motor vehicles** | **1,409,163** | **143,538.5** | **9,817** | **115,700.1** | **800** | **12.18** |

*Source:* Department of Transportation, Federal Highway Administration.

## U.S. Petroleum Consumption[1] by Major Product and Major Consuming Sector, 1975

| Type of energy | Household & commercial (percent) | Industrial (percent) | Transportation[2] (percent) | Electricity generation, utilities (percent) | Misc. (percent) | Total domestic product demand (percent) |
|---|---|---|---|---|---|---|
| Fuel and power: | | | | | | |
| Liquified gases | 2.0 | 0.8 | 0.3 | — | — | 3.2 |
| Jet Fuels | — | — | 6.2 | 0.1 | — | 6.3 |
| Gasoline | — | — | 39.3 | — | — | 39.3 |
| Kerosene | 0.8 | 0.2 | — | — | — | 1.0 |
| Distillate Fuel | 8.7 | 2.3 | 6.3 | 1.1 | 0.2 | 18.5 |
| Residual Fuel | 3.0 | 3.2 | 2.2 | 8.7 | 0.1 | 17.2 |
| Still Gas | — | 3.2 | — | — | — | 3.2 |
| Petroleum Coke | — | 1.2 | — | — | — | 1.2 |
| Total | 14.5 | 10.9 | 54.3 | 9.9 | 0.3 | 89.9 |
| Raw Material | 3.1 | 6.0 | 0.4 | — | 0.6 | 10.1 |
| **Grand Total, domestic product demand** | **17.6** | **16.9** | **54.7** | **9.9** | **0.9** | **100.0** |

1. Percent distribution, derived from consumption in BTU. Includes liquified natural gas and natural gas liquids. 2. Includes bunkers, military transportation and military use of fuel oils. *Source:* Department of the Interior, Bureau of Mines.

## Largest Nuclear Power Plants in the United States

| Location | Operating utility | Capacity (kilowatts) | Year operative |
|---|---|---|---|
| Columbia County, Ore. | Portland General Electric Co. | 1,130,000 | 1975 |
| Salem County, N.J. (Unit 1) | Public Service Electric & Gas Co. | 1,090,000 | 1976 |
| Decatur, Ala. (Unit 1) | Tennessee Valley Authority | 1,065,000 | 1973 |
| Decatur, Ala. (Unit 2) | Tennessee Valley Authority | 1,065,000 | 1974 |
| Decatur, Ala. (Unit 3) | Tennessee Valley Authority | 1,065,000 | 1976 |
| Peach Bottom, Pa. (Unit 2) | Philadelphia Electric Co. | 1,065,000 | 1974 |
| Peach Bottom, Pa. (Unit 3) | Philadelphia Electric Co. | 1,065,000 | 1974 |
| Zion, Ill. (Unit 1) | Commonwealth Edison Co. | 1,050,000 | 1973 |
| Zion, Ill. (Unit 2) | Commonwealth Edison Co. | 1,050,000 | 1974 |
| Bridgman, Mich. (Unit 1) | Indiana & Michigan Power Electric Co. | 1,050,000 | 1975 |
| Clay Station, Calif. | Sacramento Municipal Utility District | 913,000 | 1975 |
| Louisa, Va. (Unit 1) | Virginia Electric & Power Co. | 907,000 | 1978 |
| Goldsboro, Pa. (Unit 2) | Metropolitan Edison Co. | 906,000 | 1978 |
| Ottawa County, Ohio (Unit 1) | Toledo Edison Co. | 906,000 | 1977 |
| Seneca, S.C. (Unit 1) | Duke Power Co. | 886,000 | 1973 |
| Seneca, S.C. (Unit 2) | Duke Power Co. | 886,000 | 1974 |
| Seneca, S.C. (Unit 3) | Duke Power Co. | 886,000 | 1974 |
| Indian Point, N.Y. (Unit 2) | Consolidated Edison Co. | 873,000 | 1973 |
| Buchanan, N.Y. (Unit 3) | New York State Power Authority | 873,000 | 1976 |
| Beaver County, Pa. (Unit 1) | Duquesne Light Co. | 852,000 | 1976 |
| Russellville, Ark. | Arkansas Power & Light Co. | 850,000 | 1974 |
| Richland, Wash. | Energy Research and Development Administration | 850,000 | 1966 |
| Lusby, Md. (Unit 1) | Baltimore Gas & Electric Co. | 845,000 | 1975 |
| Lusby, Md. (Unit 2) | Baltimore Gas & Electric Co. | 845,000 | 1976 |
| Waterford, Conn. (Unit 2) | Northeast Nuclear Energy Co. | 828,000 | 1975 |
| Surry, Va. (Unit 1) | Virginia Electric & Power Co. | 822,000 | 1972 |
| Surry, Va. (Unit 2) | Virginia Electric & Power Co. | 822,000 | 1973 |
| Scriba, N.Y. | New York State Power Authority | 821,000 | 1975 |
| Southport, N.C. | Carolina Power & Light Co. | 821,000 | 1975 |
| Southport, N.C. (Unit 1) | Carolina Power & Light Co. | 821,000 | 1976 |
| Goldsboro, Pa. (Unit 1) | Metropolitan Edison Co. | 819,000 | 1974 |
| Ft. Pierce, Fla. (Unit 1) | Florida Power & Light Co. | 810,000 | 1976 |
| Morris, Ill. (Unit 2) | Commonwealth Edison Co. | 809,000 | 1970 |
| Morris, Ill. (Unit 3) | Commonwealth Edison Co. | 809,000 | 1971 |
| **Total all plants** | — | **47,813,000** | — |

NOTE: Construction permits have been issued for 90 plants with a total capacity of 98 million kilowatts; construction permits have been sought for 41 plants, totaling 46 million kilowatts; 20 plants with a total capacity of 24 million kilowatts have been ordered or announced. Sixty-eight units, including those listed above (with the exception of the Richland, Wash., plant, which is government-owned), are licensed to operate. *Source:* Nuclear Regulatory Commission.

## Energy Consumption—Total and Per Capita

| Year | All energy[1] Total (tril. BTU) | All energy[1] Per capita (mil. BTU) | Natural gas[2] Total (tril. BTU) | Natural gas[2] Per capita (mil. BTU) | Coal[3] Total (tril. BTU) | Coal[3] Per capita (mil. BTU) | Crude petroleum[4] Total (tril. BTU) | Crude petroleum[4] Per capita (mil. BTU) |
|---|---|---|---|---|---|---|---|---|
| 1920 | 19,782 | 186 | 827 | 8 | 15,504 | 146 | 2,634 | 25 |
| 1925 | 20,899 | 180 | 1,212 | 10 | 14,706 | 127 | 4,156 | 36 |
| 1930 | 22,288 | 181 | 1,969 | 16 | 13,639 | 111 | 5,652 | 46 |
| 1935 | 19,107 | 150 | 1,974 | 16 | 10,634 | 84 | 5,499 | 43 |
| 1940 | 23,908 | 181 | 2,726 | 21 | 12,535 | 95 | 7,487 | 57 |
| 1945 | 31,541 | 238 | 3,973 | 30 | 15,972 | 121 | 9,619 | 73 |
| 1950 | 33,992 | 223 | 6,150 | 40 | 12,913 | 85 | 13,489 | 88 |
| 1955 | 39,703 | 239 | 9,232 | 56 | 11,540 | 70 | 17,524 | 106 |
| 1960 | 44,569 | 247 | 12,699 | 70 | 10,140 | 56 | 20,067 | 111 |
| 1965 | 53,343 | 274 | 16,098 | 83 | 11,908 | 61 | 23,241 | 120 |
| 1970 | 66,909 | 327 | 21,795 | 106 | 12,698 | 62 | 29,537 | 144 |
| 1971 | 68,348 | 330 | 22,469 | 109 | 12,043 | 58 | 30,570 | 148 |
| 1972 | 71,609 | 344 | 22,698 | 109 | 12,423 | 60 | 32,966 | 158 |
| 1973 | 74,555 | 356 | 22,512 | 108 | 13,294 | 64 | 34,852 | 167 |
| 1974 | 72,668 | 344 | 21,733 | 103 | 12,889 | 61 | 33,467 | 158 |
| 1975 | 70,580 | 331 | 19,948 | 93 | 12,828 | 60 | 32,742 | 153 |
| 1976[5] | 73,999 | 344 | 20,216 | 94 | 13,749 | 64 | 34,938 | 162 |

1. Includes electricity, not shown separately. 2. Dry gas only. Marketed production minus shrinkage caused by liquids extraction (34 cubic feet per gallon produced). 3. Includes bituminous coal, lignite, and anthracite coal. 4. Includes petroleum products and, beginning 1950, natural gas liquids. 5. Estimate. *Source:* 1920–1972, U.S. Library of Congress, *Energy Facts,* November 1973; thereafter, Department of the Interior, Bureau of Mines, *Minerals Yearbook* and *Mineral Industry Surveys.*

## U.S. Sources of Energy

| Fuel | 1978 | 1977 |
|---|---|---|
| Imported oil | 25.8% | 20.3% |
| Domestic oil | 22.8 | 26.7 |
| Natural gas | 25.9 | 27.0 |
| Coal | 18.8 | 19.2 |
| Hydroelectric and geothermal | 3.2 | 4.1 |
| Nuclear fuels | 3.5 | 2.7 |
| **Total** | **100.0** | **100.0** |

*Source:* Department of Energy, Energy Information Administration.

## Uranium Production, 1976
**(metric tons of ore with uranium content)**

| | |
|---|---|
| United States | 9,800 |
| Canada | 4,850 |
| South Africa | 3,412 |
| France | 2,063 |
| Niger | 1,460 |
| **World** | **22,268** |

*Source:* United Nations, *World Energy Supplies, 1972–76.*

## Cloning Could Be Good for Us!

Cloning techniques may be able to lead toward a cure for cancer and hereditary diseases and the production of better cattle and better food plants—but they cannot produce identical human beings.

Cloning is reproduction without sex. It occurs naturally with the simplest forms of living things: Amoebas and other protozoa divide to reproduce themselves. Man helps nature along by another form of cloning: the reproduction of plants by growing their cuttings. Research biologists, investigating how cells reproduce both normally and abnormally, are utilizing cloning techniques in their search for cures for cancer and hereditary diseases. Other scientists are trying to perfect a two-step cloning process to reproduce exact duplicates of particularly good breeds of cattle.

In 1978, serious scientific researchers were outraged by a book called *In His Image,* which claimed to be the true story of how a genetically exact duplicate of a 65-year-old millionaire was secretly cloned. Before a congressional committee, four scientists testified that the book was a hoax, that cloning an adult human being is at present impossible and never may be possible. They were outraged because they believed the book might arouse fears that would result in legal restrictions on legitimate scientific research. They went on to describe the work currently going on in the nation's laboratories utilizing cloning and similar techniques that, if successful, could bring immeasurable benefits to humankind.

For example, Dr. Clement Markert of Yale University told of his work with scientists at Colorado State University on a project aimed at cloning valuable beef and dairy cattle "in a few years." But if and when perfected, he said, these techniques would be unacceptable for human beings, since they produce too many abnormal fetuses. Cattle with abnormalities can be easily discarded, but human beings cannot.

Dr. Markert would take an egg from a female immediately after it had been penetrated by a male sperm. At that point, the egg would contain both an egg nucleus and a sperm nucleus. Dr. Markert would then remove the sperm nucleus and place the egg in a nutrient chemical until it divided and grew. The growing embryo would be reinserted into the mother, and if normal growth continued, a normal female would be born. This female would not be a clone, but the eggs she produced would exactly match her genes, and by repeating the process with these eggs, exact clones of her would be born. The ability to produce exact genetic duplicates of especially productive beef and dairy cattle would be of great benefit, Dr. Markert told the House Committee.

Dr. Beatrice Mintz of the Institute for Cancer Research in Philadelphia has produced mice from fertilized egg cells whose cell nuclei have been replaced with the nuclei of cancer cells. Surprisingly, normal mice were born. She believes that this suggests that a natural process was at work at the cellular level to make the cancerous cell not malignant. Dr. Mintz believes that within a short time she may be able to produce at will large numbers of mice that will have almost any human genetic disease scientists wish to study. Although a cloning-like technique would be used, these mice would not be clones, she said.

Meanwhile, a thriving business is already based on a form of cloning applied to houseplants, such as ferns. Nurserymen cut half-inch pieces of fern stems and place them in a solution containing hormones that trigger the reproductive process. The stem pieces are transferred to a second solution that quickens the growth of branches. Each branch is a potential fern. This process is considerably faster and takes up much less space than the old-fashioned method of transplanting cuttings in soil. Scientists hope eventually to produce food crops which are free of viruses and other disease-causing factors. Already, scientists in Taiwan have been able to increase the potato crop by 30% by using a virus-free stock produced by cloning.

The first successful cloning of an animal was carried out in 1952 by Dr. Robert Briggs of Indiana University and Dr. Thomas King of the National Cancer Institute. They destroyed the nuclei of frogs' eggs and replaced them with cells from very young tadpoles, thus producing genetically identical tadpoles. But of more than 700 transplants, only six tadpoles were born. Since that time, these scientists have been trying to repeat the experiment using nuclei from the cells of adult frogs, without success. Scientists believe that as organisms grow older, their cells lose their ability to differentiate and can no longer form the many kinds of cells that comprise a living creature.

Primarily for this reason, scientists are convinced that the author of *In His Image* was writing science fiction when he claimed that the nucleus of a cell from a 65-year-old man was implanted in a female egg to produce a normal infant son. Adult cells just cannot do this, they say.

Biologists don't like to be distracted by fantasies about reproducing human beings by cloning when they see so many future benefits for humankind from the more humdrum laboratory techniques they are working on right now. They don't believe the story told in *In His Image.* Nor do they believe that it would be possible to reproduce 50 Hitlers, as one recent science fiction novel postulates. Even if such a thing *were* possible, they point out, it takes more than genes to determine a person's character. A person born with Hitler's genes might, in a different environment, turn out to be quite a nice person, one scientist said.

A test tube baby is not a clone. The little girl born in England last summer was the result of the normal procreation method in mammals except in one "technically minor" respect: The egg was removed from the mother and was fertilized by the father's sperm in a glass vessel outside the body. Thus, little Louise Brown inherited the genetic characteristics of both her father and mother, even as you and I.

Can women who are infertile because of a blockage in their oviducts, or fallopian tubes, now begin to have babies by test tube? The answer for now is "no," for both medical and ethical reasons. Louise was the first successful result in more than 30 attempts by Drs. Patrick Steptoe and Robert Edwards of Great Britain. A medical procedure must have been proven to be successful far more than once in 30 times before it is routinely prescribed. Further, in this procedure eggs fertilized outside the body are destroyed if they show any evidence of abnormality or birth defects. Theologians and physicians concerned with basic issues of medical ethics have yet to come to terms with the fundamental questions that have been raised by this successful experiment.

*Wadsworth Likely*

# Measures and Weights

*Source:* Department of Commerce, National Bureau of Standards.

## The International System (Metric)

The International System of Units is a modernized version of the metric system, established by international agreement, i.e. provides a logical and interconnected framework for all measurements in science, industry, and commerce. The system is built on a foundation of seven basic units, and all other units are derived from them. (Use of metric weights and measures was legalized in the United States in 1866, and our customary units of weights and measures are defined in terms of the meter and kilogram.)

**Length.** Meter. The meter is defined as 1,650,763.73 wavelengths in vacuum of the orange-red line of the spectrum of krypton-86.

**Time.** Second. The second is defined as the duration of 9,192,631,770 cycles of the radiation associated with a specified transition of the cesium 133 atom.

**Mass.** Kilogram. The standard for the kilogram is a cylinder of platinum iridium alloy kept by the International Bureau of Weights and Measures at Paris. A duplicate at the National Bureau of Standards serves as the mass standard for the United States. The kilogram is the only base unit still defined by a physical object.

**Temperature.** Kelvin. The kelvin is defined as the fraction 1/273.16 of the thermodynamic temperature of the triple point of water; that is, the point at which water forms an interface of solid, liquid and vapor. This is defined as 0.01°C on the Centigrade or Celsius scale and 32.02°F on the Fahrenheit scale. The temperature 0°K is called "absolute zero."

**Electric Current.** Ampere. The ampere is defined as that current that, if maintained in each of two long parallel wires separated by one meter in free space, would produce a force between the two wires (due to their magnetic fields) of $2 \times 10^{-7}$ newton for each meter of length. (A newton is the unit of force which when applied to one kilogram mass would experience an acceleration of one meter per second per second.)

**Luminous Intensity.** Candela. The candela is defined as the luminous intensity of 1/600,000 of a square meter of a cavity at the temperature of freezing platinum (2,042K).

**Amount of Substance.** Mole. The mole is the amount of substance of a system that contains as many elementary entities as there are atoms in 0.012 kilograms of carbon-12.

# Tables of Metric Weights and Measures

### LINEAR MEASURE

10 millimeters (mm) = 1 centimeter (cm)
10 centimeters = 1 decimeter (dm) = 100 millimeters
10 decimeters = 1 meter (m) = 1,000 millimeters
10 meters = 1 dekameter (dam)
10 dekameters = 1 hectometer (hm) = 100 meters
10 hectometers = 1 kilometer (km) = 1,000 meters

### AREA MEASURE

100 square millimeters ($mm^2$) = 1 sq centimeter ($cm^2$)
10,000 square centimeters = 1 sq meter ($m^2$) = 1,000,000 sq millimeters
100 square meters = 1 are (a)
100 ares = 1 hectare (ha) = 10,000 sq meters
100 hectares = 1 sq kilometer ($km^2$) = 1,000,000 sq meters

### VOLUME MEASURE

10 milliliters (ml) = 1 centiliter (cl)
10 centiliters = 1 deciliter (dl) = 100 milliliters
10 deciliters = 1 liter (1) = 1,000 milliliters
10 liters = 1 dekaliter (dal)
10 dekaliters = 1 hectoliter (hl) = 100 liters
10 hectoliters = 1 kiloliter (kl) = 1,000 liters

### CUBIC MEASURE

1,000 cubic millimeters ($mm^3$) = 1 cu centimeter ($cm^3$)
1,000 cubic centimeters = 1 cu decimeter ($dm^3$) = 1,000,000 cu millimeters
1,000 cubic decimeters = 1 cu meter ($m^3$) = 1 stere = 1,000,000 cu centimeters = 1,000,000,000 cu millimeters

### WEIGHT

10 milligrams (mg) = 1 centigram (cg)
10 centigrams = 1 decigram (dg) = 100 milligrams
10 decigrams = 1 gram (g) = 1,000 milligrams
10 grams = 1 dekagram (dag)
10 dekagrams = 1 hectogram (hg) = 100 grams
10 hectograms = 1 kilogram (kg) = 1,000 grams
1,000 kilograms = 1 metric ton (t)

# Tables of Customary U.S. Weights and Measures

## LINEAR MEASURE

12 inches (in.) = 1 foot (ft)
3 feet = 1 yard (yd)
5 1/2 yards = 1 rod (rd), pole, or perch (16 1/2 ft)
40 rods = 1 furlong (fur) = 220 yds = 660 ft
8 furlongs = 1 statute mile (mi.) = 1,760 yds = 5,280 ft
3 land miles = 1 league
5,280 feet = 1 statute or land mile
6,076.11549 feet = 1 international nautical mile

## AREA MEASURE

144 square inches = 1 sq ft
9 square feet = 1 sq yd = 1,296 sq in.
30 1/4 square yards = 1 sq rd = 272 1/4 sq ft
160 square rods = 1 acre = 4,840 sq yds = 43,560 sq ft
640 acres = 1 sq mi.
1 mile square = 1 section (of land)
6 miles square = 1 township = 36 sections = 36 sq mi.

## CUBIC MEASURE

1,728 cubic inches = 1 cu ft
27 cubic feet = 1 cu yd

## LIQUID MEASURE

When necessary to distinguish the liquid pint or quart from the dry pint or quart, the word "liquid" or the abbreviation "liq" should be used in combination with the name or abbreviation of the liquid unit.

4 gills (gi) = 1 pint (pt) (= 28.875 cu in.)
2 pints = 1 quart (qt) (= 57.75 cu in.)
4 quarts = 1 gallon (gal) (= 231 cu in.) = 8 pts = 32 gills

## APOTHECARIES FLUID MEASURE

60 minims (min.) = 1 fluid dram (fl dr) (= 0.2256 cu in.)
8 fluid drams = 1 fluid ounce (fl oz) (= 1.8047 cu in.)
16 fluid ounces = 1 pt (= 28.875 cu in.) = 128 fl drs
2 pints = 1 qt (= 57.75 cu in.) = 32 fl oz = 256 fl drs
4 quarts = 1 gal (= 231 cu in.) = 128 fl oz = 1,024 fl drs

## DRY MEASURE

When necessary to distinguish the dry pint or quart from the liquid pint or quart; the word "dry" should be used in combination with the name or abbreviation of the dry unit.

2 pints = 1 qt (=67.2006 cu in.)
8 quarts = 1 peck (pk) (=537.605 cu in.) = 16 pts
4 pecks = 1 bushel (bu) (= 2,150.42 cu in.) = 32 qts

## AVOIRDUPOIS WEIGHT

When necessary to distinguish the avoirdupois dram from the apothecaries dram, or to distinguish the avoirdupois dram or ounce from the fluid dram or ounce, or to distinguish the avoirdupois ounce or pound from the troy or apothecaries ounce or pound, the word "avoirdupois" or the abbreviation "avdp" should be used in combination with the name or abbreviation of the avoirdupois unit.

(The "grain" is the same in avoirdupois, troy, and apothecaries weights.)

27 11/32 grains = 1 dram (dr)
16 drams = 1 oz = 437 1/2 grains
16 ounces = 1 lb = 256 drams = 7,000 grains
100 pounds = 1 hundredweight (cwt)[1]
20 hundredweights = 1 ton (tn) = 2,000 lbs[1]

In "gross" or "long" measure, the following values are recognized:

112 pounds = 1 gross or long cwt[1]
20 gross or long hundredweights = 1 gross or long ton = 2,240 lbs[1]

1. When the terms "hundredweight" and "ton" are used unmodified, they are commonly understood to mean the 100-pound hundredweight and the 2,000-pound ton, respectively; these units may be designated "net" or "short" when necessary to distinguish them from the corresponding units in gross or long measure.

## UNITS OF CIRCULAR MEASURE

Second (") = —
Minute (') = 60 seconds
Degree (°) = 60 minutes
Right angle = 90 degrees
Straight angle = 180 degrees
Circle = 360 degrees

## TROY WEIGHT

24 grains = 1 pennyweight (dwt)
20 pennyweights = 1 ounce troy (oz t) = 480 grains
12 ounces troy = 1 pound troy (lb t) = 240 pennyweights = 5,760 grains

## APOTHECARIES WEIGHT

20 grains = 1 scruple (s ap)
3 scruples = 1 dram apothecaries (dr ap) = 60 grains
8 drams apothecaries = 1 ounce apothecaries (oz ap) = 24 scruples = 480 grains
12 ounces apothecaries = 1 pound apothecaries (lb ap) = 96 drams apothecaries = 288 scruples = 5,760 grains

## GUNTER'S OR SURVEYOR'S CHAIN MEASURE

7.92 inches = 1 link (li)
100 links = 1 chain (ch) = 4 rods = 66 ft
80 chains = 1 statute mile = 320 rods = 5,280 ft

# Metric and U.S. Equivalents

| | |
|---|---|
| 1 angstrom[1] (light wave measurement) | 0.1 millimicron<br>0.000 1 micron<br>0.000 000 1 millimeter<br>0.000 000 004 inch |
| 1 cable's length | 120 fathoms<br>720 feet<br>219.456 meters |
| 1 centimeter | 0.3937 inch |
| 1 chain (Gunter's or surveyor's) | 66 feet<br>20.1168 meters |
| 1 decimeter | 3.937 inches |
| 1 dekameter | 32.808 feet |
| 1 fathom | 6 feet<br>1.8288 meters |
| 1 foot | 0.3048 meter |
| 1 furlong | 10 chains (surveyor's)<br>660 feet<br>220 yards<br>1/8 statute mile<br>201.168 meters |

| | |
|---|---|
| 1 inch | 2.54 centimeters |
| 1 kilometer | 0.621 mile |
| 1 league (land) | 3 statute miles<br>4.828 kilometers |
| 1 link (Gunter's or surveyor's) | 7.92 inches<br>0.201 168 meter |
| 1 meter | 39.37 inches<br>1.094 yards |
| 1 micron | 0.001 millimeter<br>0.000 039 37 inch |
| 1 mil | 0.001 inch<br>0.025 4 millimeter |
| 1 mile (statute or land) | 5,280 feet<br>1.609 kilometers |
| 1 mile (nautical international) | 1.852 kilometers<br>1.151 statute miles<br>0.999 U.S. nautical miles |
| 1 millimeter | 0.03937 inch |
| 1 millimicron (mμ) | 0.001 micron<br>0.000 000 039 37 inch |
| 1 nanometer | 0.001 micrometer or<br>0.000 000 039 37 inch |
| 1 point (typography) | 0.013 837 inch<br>1/72 inch (approximately)<br>0.351 millimeter |
| 1 rod, pole, or perch | 16 1/2 feet<br>5.0292 meters |
| 1 yard | 0.9144 meter |

## AREAS OR SURFACES

| | |
|---|---|
| 1 acre | 43,560 square feet<br>4,840 square yards<br>0.405 hectare |
| 1 are | 119.599 square yards<br>0.025 acre |
| 1 hectare | 2.471 acres |
| 1 square centimeter | 0.155 square inch |
| 1 square decimeter | 15.5 square inches |
| 1 square foot | 929.030 square centimeters |
| 1 square inch | 6.4516 square centimeters |
| 1 square kilometer | 0.386 square mile<br>247.105 acres |
| 1 square meter | 1.196 square yards<br>10.764 square feet |
| 1 square mile | 258.999 hectares |
| 1 square millimeter | 0.002 square inch |
| 1 square rod, square pole or square perch | 25.293 square meters |
| 1 square yard | 0.836 square meters |

## CAPACITIES OR VOLUMES

| | |
|---|---|
| 1 barrel, liquid | 31 to 42 gallons[2] |
| 1 barrel, standard for fruits, vegetables, and other dry commodities except cranberries | 7,056 cubic inches<br>105 dry quarts<br>3.281 bushels, struck measure |
| 1 barrel, standard, cranberry | 5.286 cubic inches<br>86 45/64 dry quarts<br>2.709 bushels, struck measure |
| 1 bushel (U.S.) struck measure | 2,150.42 cubic inches<br>35.238 liters |
| 1 bushel, heaped (U.S.) | 2,747.715 cubic inches<br>1.278 bushels, struck measure[3] |
| 1 cord (firewood) | 128 cubic feet |
| 1 cubic centimeter | 0.061 cubic inches |
| 1 cubic decimeter | 61.024 cubic inches |
| 1 cubic foot | 7.481 gallons<br>28.316 cubic decimeters |
| 1 cubic inch | 0.554 fluid ounce<br>4.433 fluid drams<br>16.387 cubic centimeters |
| 1 cubic meter | 1.308 cubic yards |
| 1 cubic yard | 0.765 cubic meter |
| 1 cup, measuring | 8 fluid ounces<br>1/2 liquid pint |
| 1 dram, fluid or liquid (U.S.) | 1/8 fluid ounces<br>0.226 cubic inch<br>3.697 milliliters<br>1.041 British fluid drachms |
| 1 dekaliter | 2.642 gallons<br>1.135 pecks |
| 1 gallon (U.S.) | 231 cubic inches<br>3.785 liters<br>0.833 British gallon<br>128 U.S. fluid ounces |
| 1 gallon (British Imperial) | 277.42 cubic inches<br>1.201 U.S. gallons<br>4.546 liters<br>160 British fluid ounces |
| 1 gill | 7.219 cubic inches<br>4 fluid ounces<br>0.118 liter |
| 1 hectoliter | 26.418 gallons<br>2.838 bushels |
| 1 liter | 1.057 liquid quarts<br>0.908 dry quart<br>61.024 cubic inches |
| 1 milliliter | 0.271 fluid drams<br>16.231 minims<br>0.061 cubic inch |
| 1 ounce, fluid or liquid (U.S.) | 1.805 cubic inch<br>29.574 milliliters<br>1.041 British fluid ounces |

| | |
|---|---|
| 1 peck | 8.810 liters |
| 1 pint, dry | 33.600 cubic inches<br>0.551 liter |
| 1 pint, liquid | 28.875 cubic inches<br>0.473 liter |
| 1 quart, dry (U.S.) | 67.201 cubic inches<br>1.101 liters<br>0.969 British quart |
| 1 quart, liquid (U.S.) | 57.75 cubic inches<br>0.946 liter<br>0.833 British quart |
| 1 quart (British) | 69.354 cubic inches<br>1.032 U.S. dry quarts<br>1.201 U.S. liquid quarts |
| 1 tablespoon, measuring | 3 teaspoons<br>4 fluid drams<br>1/2 fluid ounce |
| 1 teaspoon, measuring | 1/3 tablespoon<br>1 1/3 fluid drams |
| 1 assay ton[4] | 29.167 grams |
| 1 carat | 200 milligrams<br>3.086 grains |
| 1 dram, apothecaries | 60 grains<br>3.888 grams |
| 1 dram, avoirdupois | 27 11/32 (=27.344) grains<br>1.772 grams |
| 1 grain | 64.798 91 milligrams |
| 1 gram | 15.432 grains<br>0.035 ounce, avoirdupois |
| 1 hundredweight, gross or long[5] | 112 pounds<br>50.802 kilograms |
| 1 hundredweight, net or short | 100 pounds<br>45.359 kilograms |
| 1 kilogram | 2.205 pounds |
| 1 microgram [$\mu$g (the Greek letter mu in combination with the letter g)] | 0.000 001 gram |
| 1 milligram | 0.015 grain |
| 1 ounce, avoirdupois | 437.5 grains<br>0.911 troy or apothecaries ounce<br>28.350 grams |
| 1 ounce, troy or apothecaries | 480 grains<br>1.097 avoirdupois ounces<br>31.103 grams |
| 1 pennyweight | 1.555 grams |
| 1 point | 0.01 carat<br>2 milligrams |
| 1 pound, avoirdupois | 7,000 grains<br>1.215 troy or apothecaries pounds<br>453.592 37 grams |
| 1 pound, troy or apothecaries | 5,760 grains<br>0.823 avoirdupois pound<br>373.242 grams |
| 1 ton, gross or long[5] | 2,204 pounds<br>1.12 net tons<br>1.016 metric tons |
| 1 ton, metric | 2,204.623 pounds<br>0.984 gross ton<br>1.102 net tons |
| 1 ton, net or short | 2,000 pounds<br>0.893 gross ton<br>0.907 metric ton |

1. The angstrom is basically defined as $10^{-10}$ meter. 2. There is a variety of "barrels" established by law or usage. For example, federal taxes on fermented liquors are based on a barrel of 31 gallons; many state laws fix the "barrel for liquids" at 31 1/2 gallons; one state fixes a 36-gallon barrel for cistern measurement; federal law recognizes a 40-gallon barrel for "proof spirits"; by custom, 42 gallons comprise a barrel of crude oil or petroleum products for statistical purposes, and this equivalent is recognized "for liquids" by four states. 3. Frequently recognized as 1¼ bushels, struck measure. 4. Used in assaying. The assay ton bears the same relation to the milligram that a ton of 2,000 pounds avoirdupois bears to the ounce troy; hence the weight in milligrams of precious metal obtained from one assay ton of ore gives directly the number of troy ounces to the net ton. 5. The gross or long ton and hundredweight are used commercially in the United States to only a limited extent, usually in restricted industrial fields. These units are the same as the British "ton" and "hundredweight."

## Miscellaneous Units of Measure

**Acre:** An area of 43,560 square feet. Originally, the area a yoke of oxen could plow in one day.

**Agate:** Originally a measurement of type size (5 1/2 points). Now equal to 1/14 inch. Used in printing for measuring column length.

**Ampere:** Unit of electric current. A potential difference of one volt across a resistance of one ohm produces a current of one ampere.

**Astronomical Unit (A.U.):** 93,000,000 miles, the average distance of the earth from the sun. Used in astronomy.

**Bale:** A large bundle of goods. In the U.S., the approximate weight of a bale of cotton is 500 pounds. The weight varies in other countries.

**Board Foot** (fbm): 144 cubic inches (12 in. x 12 in. x 1 in.). Used for lumber.

**Bolt:** 40 yards. Used for measuring cloth.

**BTU:** British thermal unit. Amount of heat needed to increase the temperature of one pound of water by one degree Fahrenheit (252 calories).

**Carat (c):** 200 milligrams or 3.086 grains troy.

Originally the weight of a seed of the carob tree in the Mediterranean region. Used for weighing precious stones. *See also* Karat.

**Chain (ch):** a chain 66 feet or one-tenth of a furlong in length, divided into 100 parts called links. One mile is equal to 80 chains. Used in surveying and sometimes called Gunter's or surveyor's chain.

**Cubit:** 18 inches or 45.72 cm. Derived from distance between elbow and tip of middle finger.

**Decibel:** Unit of relative loudness. One decibel is the smallest amount of change detectable by the human ear.

**Ell, English:** 1 1/4 yards or 1/32 bolt. Used for measuring cloth.

**Freight Ton (also called Measurement Ton):** 40 cubic feet of merchandise. Used for cargo freight.

**Great Gross:** 12 gross or 1728.

**Gross:** 12 dozen or 144.

**Hand:** 4 inches or 10.16 cm. Derived from the width of the hand. Used for measuring the height of horses at withers.

**Hertz:** Modern unit for measurement of electromagnetic wave frequencies (equivalent to "cycles per second").

**Hogshead:** (hhd): 2 liquid barrels or 14,653 cubic inches.

**Horsepower:** The power needed to lift 33,000 pounds a distance of one foot in one minute (about 1 1/2 times the power an average horse can exert). Used for measuring power of steam engines, etc.

**Karat (kt):** A measure of the purity of gold, indicating how many parts out of 24 are pure. For example, 18 karat gold is 3/4 pure. Sometimes spelled *carat.*

**Knot:** Not a distance, but the rate of speed of one nautical mile per hour. Used for measuring speed of ships.

**League:** Rather indefinite and varying measure, but usually estimated at 3 miles in English-speaking countries.

**Light-Year:** 5,880,000,000,000 miles, the distance light travels in a year at the rate of 186,281.7 miles per second. (If an astronomical unit were represented by one inch, a light-year would be represented by about one mile.) Used for measurements in interstellar space.

**Magnum:** Two-quart bottle. Used for measuring wine, etc.

**Ohm:** Unit of electrical resistance. A circuit in which a potential difference of one volt produces a current of one ampere has a resistance of one ohm.

**Parsec:** Approximately 3.26 light-years of 19.2 trillion miles. Term is combination of first syllables of *par*allax and *sec*ond, and distance is that of imaginary star when lines drawn from it to both earth and sun form a maximum angle or parallax of one second (1/3600 degree). Used for measuring interstellar distances.

**Pi ($\pi$):** 3.14159265+. The ratio of the circumference of a circle to its diameter. For practical purposes, the value is used to four decimal places: 3.1416.

**Pica:** 1/6 inch or 12 points. Used in printing for measuring column width, etc.

**Pipe:** 2 hogsheads. Used for measuring wine and other liquids.

**Point:** .013837 (approximately 1/72) inch or 1/12 pica. Used in printing for measuring type size.

**Quintal:** 100,000 grams or 220.46 pounds avoirdupois.

**Quire:** Used for measuring paper. Sometimes 24 sheets but more often 25. There are 20 quires in a ream.

**Ream:** Used for measuring paper. Sometimes 480 sheets, but more often 500 sheets.

**Roentgen:** Dosage unit of radiation exposure produced by X-rays.

**Score:** 20 units.

**Sound, Speed of:** Usually placed at 1,088 ft per second at 32°F at sea level. It varies at other temperatures and in different media.

**Span:** 9 inches or 22.86 cm. Derived from the distance between the end of the thumb and the end of the little finger when both are outstretched.

**Square:** 100 square feet. Used in building.

**Stone:** Legally 14 pounds avoirdupois in Great Britain.

**Therm:** 100,000 BTU's.

**Township:** U. S. land measurement of almost 36 square miles. The south border is 6 miles long. The east and west borders, also 6 miles long, follow the meridians, making the north border slightly less than 6 miles long. Used in surveying.

**Tun:** 252 gallons, but often larger. Used for measuring wine and other liquids.

**Watt:** Unit of power. The power used by a current of one ampere across a potential difference of one volt equals one watt.

## Kelvin Scale

Absolute zero, −273.16° on the Celcius (Centigrade) scale, is 0° Kelvin. Thus, degrees Kelvin are equivalent to degrees Celsius plus 273.16. The freezing point of water, 0°C. and 32°F., is 273.16°K. The conversion formula is K° = C° + 273.16.

## Conversion of Miles to Kilometers and Kilometers to Miles

| Miles | Kilometers | Miles | Kilometers | Miles | Kilometers | Kilometers | Miles | Kilometers | Miles | Kilometers | Miles |
|---|---|---|---|---|---|---|---|---|---|---|---|
| 1 | 1.6 | 8 | 12.8 | 60 | 96.5 | 1 | 0.6 | 8 | 4.9 | 60 | 37.2 |
| 2 | 3.2 | 9 | 14.4 | 70 | 112.6 | 2 | 1.2 | 9 | 5.5 | 70 | 43.4 |
| 3 | 4.8 | 10 | 16.0 | 80 | 128.7 | 3 | 1.8 | 10 | 6.2 | 80 | 49.7 |
| 4 | 6.4 | 20 | 32.1 | 90 | 144.8 | 4 | 2.4 | 20 | 12.4 | 90 | 55.9 |
| 5 | 8.0 | 30 | 48.2 | 100 | 160.9 | 5 | 3.1 | 30 | 18.6 | 100 | 62.1 |
| 6 | 9.6 | 40 | 64.3 | 1,000 | 1609 | 6 | 3.7 | 40 | 24.8 | 1,000 | 621 |
| 7 | 11.2 | 50 | 80.4 | | | 7 | 4.3 | 50 | 31.0 | | |

## Bolts and Screws: Conversion from Fractions of an Inch to Millimeters

| Inch | mm | Inch | mm | Inch | mm | Inch | mm |
|---|---|---|---|---|---|---|---|
| 1/64 | 0.40 | 17/64 | 6.75 | 33/64 | 13.10 | 49/64 | 19.45 |
| 1/32 | 0/79 | 9/32 | 7.14 | 17/32 | 13.50 | 25/32 | 19.84 |
| 3/64 | 1.19 | 19/64 | 7.54 | 35/64 | 13.90 | 51/64 | 20.24 |
| 1/16 | 1.59 | 5/16 | 7.94 | 9/16 | 14.29 | 13/16 | 20.64 |
| 5/64 | 1.98 | 21/64 | 8.33 | 37/64 | 14.69 | 53/64 | 21.03 |
| 3/32 | 2.38 | 11/32 | 8.73 | 19/32 | 15.08 | 27/32 | 21.43 |
| 7/64 | 2.78 | 23/64 | 9.13 | 39/64 | 15.48 | 55/64 | 21.83 |
| 1/8 | 3.18 | 3/8 | 9.53 | 5/8 | 15.88 | 7/8 | 22.23 |
| 9/64 | 3.57 | 25/64 | 9.92 | 41/64 | 16.27 | 57/64 | 22.62 |
| 5/32 | 3.97 | 13/32 | 10.32 | 21/32 | 16.67 | 29/32 | 23.02 |
| 11/64 | 4.37 | 27/64 | 10.72 | 43/64 | 17.06 | 59/64 | 23.42 |
| 3/16 | 4.76 | 7/16 | 11.11 | 11/64 | 17.46 | 15/16 | 23.81 |
| 13/64 | 5.16 | 29/64 | 11.51 | 45/64 | 17.86 | 61/64 | 24.21 |
| 7/32 | 5.56 | 15/32 | 11.91 | 23/32 | 18.26 | 31/32 | 24.61 |
| 15/64 | 5.95 | 31/64 | 12.30 | 47/64 | 18.65 | 63/64 | 25.00 |
| 1/4 | 6.35 | 1/2 | 12.70 | 3/4 | 19.05 | 1 | 25.40 |

## U.S.—Metric Cooking Conversions

| U.S. customary system | | | | Metric | | | |
|---|---|---|---|---|---|---|---|
| Capacity | | Weight | | Capacity | | Weight | |
| 1/5 teaspoon | 1 milliliter | 1 fluid oz | 30 milliliters | 1 milliliter | 1/5 teaspoon | 1 gram | .035 ounce |
| 1 teaspoon | 5 ml | | 28 grams | 5 ml | 1 teaspoon | 100 grams | 3.5 ounces |
| 1 tablespoon | 15 ml | 1 pound | 454 grams | 15 ml | 1 tablespoon | 500 grams | 1.10 pounds |
| 1/5 cup | 50 ml | | | 34 ml | 1 fluid oz | 1 kilogram | 2.205 pounds |
| 1 cup | 240 ml | | | 100 ml | 3.4 fluid oz | | 35 oz |
| 2 cups (1 pint) | 470 ml | | | 240 ml | 1 cup | | |
| 4 cups (1 quart) | .95 liter | | | 1 liter | 34 fluid oz | | |
| 4 quarts (1 gal.) | 3.8 liters | | | | 4.2 cups | | |
| | | | | | 2.1 pints | | |
| | | | | | 1.06 quarts | | |
| | | | | | 0.26 gallon | | |

## Cooking Measurement Equivalents

16 tablespoons = 1 cup
12 tablespoons = 3/4 cup
10 tablespoons + 2 teaspoons = 2/3 cup
8 tablespoons = 1/2 cup
6 tablespoons = 3/8 cup
5 tablespoons + 1 teaspoon = 1/3 cup
4 tablespoons = 1/4 cup

2 tablespoons = 1/8 cup
2 tablespoons + 2 teaspoons = 1/6 cup
1 tablespoon = 1/16 cup
2 cups = 1 pint
2 pints = 1 quart
3 teaspoons = 1 tablespoon
48 teaspoons = 1 cup

## Conversion Factors

| To change | To | Multiply by | To change | To | Multiply by |
|---|---|---|---|---|---|
| acres | hectares | .4047 | liters | pints (dry) | 1.8162 |
| acres | square feet | 43,560 | liters | pints (liquid) | 2.1134 |
| acres | square miles | .001562 | liters | quarts (dry) | .9081 |
| atmospheres | cms. of mercury | 76 | liters | quarts (liquid) | 1.0567 |
| BTU | horsepower-hour | .0003931 | meters | feet | 3.2808 |
| BTU | kilowatt-hour | .0002928 | meters | miles | .0006214 |
| BTU/hour | watts | .2931 | meters | yards | 1.0936 |
| bushels | cubic inches | 2150.4 | metric tons | tons (long) | .9842 |
| bushels (U.S.) | hectoliters | .3524 | metric tons | tons (short) | 1.1023 |
| centimeters | inches | .3937 | miles | kilometers | 1.6093 |
| centimeters | feet | .03281 | miles | feet | 5280 |
| circumference | radians | 6.283 | miles (nautical) | miles (statute) | 1.1516 |
| cubic feet | cubic meters | .0283 | miles (statute) | miles (nautical) | .8684 |
| cubic meters | cubic feet | 35.3145 | miles/hour | feet/minute | 88 |
| cubic meters | cubic yards | 1.3079 | millimeters | inches | .0394 |
| cubic yards | cubic meters | .7646 | ounces avdp. | grams | 28.3495 |
| degrees | radians | .01745 | ounces | pounds | .0625 |
| dynes | grams | .00102 | ounces (troy) | ounces (avdp) | 1.09714 |
| fathoms | feet | 6.0 | pecks | liters | 8.8096 |
| feet | meters | .3048 | pints (dry) | liters | .5506 |
| feet | miles (nautical) | .0001645 | pints (liquid) | liters | .4732 |
| feet | miles (statute) | .0001894 | pounds ap or t | kilograms | .3782 |
| feet/second | miles/hour | .6818 | pounds avdp | kilograms | .4536 |
| furlongs | feet | 660.0 | pounds | ounces | 16 |
| furlongs | miles | .125 | quarts (dry) | liters | 1.1012 |
| gallons (U.S.) | liters | 3.7853 | quarts (liquid) | liters | .9463 |
| grains | grams | .0648 | radians | degrees | 57.30 |
| grams | grains | 15.4324 | rods | meters | 5.029 |
| grams | ounces avdp | .0353 | rods | foot | 16.5 |
| grams | pounds | .002205 | square feet | square meters | .0929 |
| hectares | acres | 2.4710 | square kilometers | square miles | .3861 |
| hectoliters | bushels (U.S.) | 2.8378 | square meters | square feet | 10.7639 |
| horsepower | watts | 745.7 | square meters | square yards | 1.1960 |
| hours | days | .04167 | square miles | square kilometers | 2.5900 |
| inches | millimeters | 25.4000 | square yards | square meters | .8361 |
| inches | centimeters | 2.5400 | tons (long) | metric tons | 1.1060 |
| kilograms | pounds avdp or t | 2.2046 | tons (short) | metric tons | .9072 |
| kilometers | miles | .6214 | tons (long) | pounds | 2240 |
| kilowatts | horsepower | 1.341 | tons (short) | pounds | 2000 |
| knots | nautical miles/hour | 1.0 | watts | BTU/hour | 3.4129 |
| knots | statute miles/hour | 1.151 | watts | horsepower | .001341 |
| liters | gallons (U.S.) | .2642 | yards | meters | .9144 |
| liters | pecks | .1135 | yards | miles | .0005682 |

## Fahrenheit and Celsius (Centigrade) Scales

Zero on the Fahrenheit scale represents the temperature produced by the mixing of equal weights of snow and common salt.

| | F | C |
|---|---|---|
| Boiling point of water | 212° | 100° |
| Freezing point of water | 32° | 0° |
| Absolute zero | −459.6° | −273.1° |

Absolute zero is theoretically the lowest possible temperature, the point at which all molecular motion would cease.

To convert Fahrenheit to Celsius (Centigrade), subtract 32 and multiply by 5/9.

To convert Celsius (Centigrade) to Fahrenheit, multiply by 9/5 and add 32.

| ° Centigrade | ° Fahrenheit | ° Centigrade | ° Fahrenheit |
|---|---|---|---|
| **−273.1** | **−459.6** | 30 | 86 |
| −250 | −418 | 35 | 95 |
| −200 | −328 | 40 | 104 |
| −150 | −238 | 45 | 113 |
| −100 | −148 | 50 | 122 |
| − 50 | − 58 | 55 | 131 |
| − 40 | − 40 | 60 | 140 |
| − 30 | − 22 | 65 | 149 |
| − 20 | − 4 | 70 | 158 |
| − 10 | 14 | 75 | 167 |
| **0** | **32** | 80 | 176 |
| 5 | 41 | 85 | 185 |
| 10 | 50 | 90 | 194 |
| 15 | 59 | 95 | 203 |
| 20 | 68 | **100** | **212** |
| 25 | 77 | | |

## Prefixes and Multiples

| Prefix | Symbol | Equivalent | Multiple/ submultiple | Prefix | Symbol | Equivalent | Multiple/ submultiple |
|---|---|---|---|---|---|---|---|
| atto | a | quintillionth part | $10^{-18}$ | deci | d | tenth part | $10^{-1}$ |
| femto | f | quadrillionth part | $10^{-15}$ | deka | da | tenfold | 10 |
| pico | p | trillionth part | $10^{-12}$ | hecto | h | hundredfold | $10^{2}$ |
| nano | n | billionth part | $10^{-9}$ | kilo | k | thousandfold | $10^{3}$ |
| micro | $\mu$ | millionth part | $10^{-6}$ | mega | M | millionfold | $10^{6}$ |
| milli | m | thousandth part | $10^{-3}$ | giga | G | billionfold | $10^{9}$ |
| centi | c | hundredth part | $10^{-2}$ | tera | T | trillionfold | $10^{12}$ |

## Common Formulas

### Circumference

**Circle:** $C=\pi d$, in which $\pi$ is 3.1416 and $d$ the diameter.

### Area

**Triangle:** $A=\frac{ab}{2}$, in which $a$ is the base and $b$ the height.

**Square:** $A=a^2$, in which $a$ is one of the sides.

**Rectangle:** $A=ab$, in which $a$ is the base and $b$ the height.

**Trapezoid:** $A=\frac{h(a+b)}{2}$, in which $h$ is the height, $a$ the longer parallel side, and $b$ the shorter.

**Regular pentagon:** $A=1.720a^2$, in which $a$ is one of the sides.

**Regular hexagon:** $A=2.598a^2$, in which $a$ is one of the sides.

**Regular octagon:** $A=4.828a^2$, in which $a$ is one of the sides.

**Circle:** $A=\pi r^2$, in which $\pi$ is 3.1416 and $r$ the radius.

### Volume

**Cube:** $V=a^3$, in which $a$ is one of the edges.

**Rectangular prism:** $V=abc$, in which $a$ is the length, $b$ the width, and $c$ the depth.

**Pyramid:** $V=\frac{Ah}{3}$, in which $A$ is the area of the base and $h$ the height.

**Cylinder:** $V=\pi r^2 h$, in which $\pi$ is 3.1416, $r$ the radius of the base, and $h$ the height.

**Cone:** $V=\frac{\pi r^2 h}{3}$, in which $\pi$ is 3.1416, $r$ the radius of the base, and $h$ the height.

**Sphere:** $V=\frac{4\pi r^3}{3}$, in which $\pi$ is 3.1416 and $r$ the radius.

### Miscellaneous

**Speed per second acquired by falling body:** $v=32t$, in which $t$ is the time in seconds.

**Distance in feet traveled by falling body:** $d=16t^2$, in which $t$ is the time in seconds.

**Speed of sound in feet per second through any given temperature of air:** $V=\frac{1087\sqrt{273+t}}{16.52}$, in which $t$ is the temperature Centigrade.

**Cost in cents of operation of electrical device:** $C=\frac{Wtc}{1000}$, in which $W$ is the number of watts, $t$ the time in hours, and $c$ the cost in cents per kilowatt-hour.

**Conversion of matter into energy (Einstein's Theorem):** $E=mc^2$, in which $E$ is the energy in ergs, $m$ the mass of the matter in grams, and $c$ the speed of light in centimeters per second. ($c^2=9\cdot10^{20}$).

## Decimal Equivalents of Common Fractions

| | | | | | | | | | | | |
|---|---|---|---|---|---|---|---|---|---|---|---|
| 1/2 | .5000 | 1/10 | .1000 | 2/7 | .2857 | 3/11 | .2727 | 5/9 | .5556 | 7/11 | .6364 |
| 1/3 | .3333 | 1/11 | .0909 | 2/9 | .2222 | 4/5 | .8000 | 5/11 | .4545 | 7/12 | .5833 |
| 1/4 | .2500 | 1/12 | .0833 | 2/11 | .1818 | 4/7 | .5714 | 5/12 | .4167 | 8/9 | .8889 |
| 1/5 | .2000 | 1/16 | .0625 | 3/4 | .7500 | 4/9 | .4444 | 6/7 | .8571 | 8/11 | .7273 |
| 1/6 | .1667 | 1/32 | .0313 | 3/5 | .6000 | 4/11 | .3636 | 6/11 | .5455 | 9/10 | .9000 |
| 1/7 | .1429 | 1/64 | .0156 | 3/7 | .4286 | 5/6 | .8333 | 7/8 | .8750 | 9/11 | .8182 |
| 1/8 | .1250 | 2/3 | .6667 | 3/8 | .3750 | 5/7 | .7143 | 7/9 | .7778 | 10/11 | .9091 |
| 1/9 | .1111 | 2/5 | .4000 | 3/10 | .3000 | 5/8 | .6250 | 7/10 | .7000 | 11/12 | .9167 |

## Roman Numerals

Roman numerals are expressed by letters of the alphabet and are rarely used today except for formality or variety.

There are three basic principles for reading Roman numerals:

1. A letter repeated once or twice repeats its value that many times. (XXX=30, CC=200, etc.).

2. One or more letters placed after another letter of greater value increases the greater value by the amount of the smaller. (VI=6, LXX=70, MCC=1200, etc.).

3. A letter placed before another letter of greater value decreases the greater value by the amount of the smaller. (IV=4, XC=90, CM=900, etc.).

| Letter | Value | Letter | Value | Letter | Value | Letter | Value | Letter | Value |
|---|---|---|---|---|---|---|---|---|---|
| I | 1 | VII | 7 | XXX | 30 | LXXX | 80 | $\overline{V}$ | 5,000 |
| II | 2 | VIII | 8 | XL | 40 | XC | 90 | $\overline{X}$ | 10,000 |
| III | 3 | IX | 9 | L | 50 | C | 100 | $\overline{L}$ | 50,000 |
| IV | 4 | X | 10 | LX | 60 | D | 500 | $\overline{C}$ | 100,000 |
| V | 5 | XX | 20 | LXX | 70 | M | 1,000 | $\overline{D}$ | 500,000 |
| VI | 6 | | | | | | | $\overline{M}$ | 1,000,000 |

## Mean and Median

The mean, also called the average, of a series of quantities is obtained by finding the sum of the quantities and dividing it by the number of quantities. In the series 1,3,5,18,19,20,25, the mean or average is 13—i.e., 91 divided by 7.

The median of a series is that point which so divides it that half the quantities are on one side, half on the other. In the above series, the median is 18.

The median often better expresses the common-run, since it is not, as is the mean, affected by an excessively high or low figure. In the series 1,3,4,7,-55, the median of 4 is a truer expression of the common-run than is the mean of 14.

## Prime Numbers Between 1 and 1,000

| | | | | | | | | | |
|---|---|---|---|---|---|---|---|---|---|
| 1 | 2 | 3 | 5 | 7 | 11 | 13 | 17 | 19 | 23 |
| 29 | 31 | 37 | 41 | 43 | 47 | 53 | 59 | 61 | 67 |
| 71 | 73 | 79 | 83 | 89 | 97 | 101 | 103 | 107 | 109 |
| 113 | 127 | 131 | 137 | 139 | 149 | 151 | 157 | 163 | 167 |
| 173 | 179 | 181 | 191 | 193 | 197 | 199 | 211 | 223 | 227 |
| 229 | 233 | 239 | 241 | 251 | 257 | 263 | 269 | 271 | 277 |
| 281 | 283 | 293 | 307 | 311 | 313 | 317 | 331 | 337 | 347 |
| 349 | 353 | 359 | 367 | 373 | 379 | 383 | 389 | 397 | 401 |
| 409 | 419 | 421 | 431 | 433 | 439 | 443 | 449 | 457 | 461 |
| 463 | 467 | 479 | 487 | 491 | 499 | 503 | 509 | 521 | 523 |
| 541 | 547 | 557 | 563 | 569 | 571 | 577 | 587 | 593 | 599 |
| 601 | 607 | 613 | 617 | 619 | 631 | 641 | 643 | 647 | 653 |
| 659 | 661 | 673 | 677 | 683 | 691 | 701 | 709 | 719 | 727 |
| 733 | 739 | 743 | 751 | 757 | 761 | 769 | 773 | 787 | 797 |
| 809 | 811 | 821 | 823 | 827 | 829 | 839 | 853 | 857 | 859 |
| 863 | 877 | 881 | 883 | 887 | 907 | 911 | 919 | 929 | 937 |
| 941 | 947 | 953 | 967 | 971 | 977 | 983 | 991 | 997 | (1009) |

## U.S. Budget Outlays for General Science, Space, and Technology

(in millions of dollars)

| | 1979[2] | 1978[2] | 1977 | TQ[1] | 1976 | 1975 | 1974 | 1973 | 1972 | 1971 | 1970 |
|---|---|---|---|---|---|---|---|---|---|---|---|
| General science and basic research | $1,274 | $1,190 | $1,078 | 292 | $1,035 | $1,038 | $1,018 | $961 | $978 | $1,009 | $947 |
| Space flight | 2,264 | 2,192 | 2,252 | 525 | 2,000 | 1,661 | 1,694 | 1,726 | 1,906 | 1,988 | 2,340 |
| Space science, applications, and technology | 1,150 | 1,018 | 1,006 | 251 | 980 | 958 | 947 | 1,041 | 952 | 830 | 853 |
| Supporting space activities | 390 | 358 | 343 | 94 | 358 | 334 | 322 | 304 | 338 | 355 | 370 |
| Deductions for offsetting receipts | −2 | −2 | −2 | −1 | −3 | −2 | −3 | −1 | −2 | −2 | −3 |
| Total | $5,077 | $4,757 | $4,677 | $1,161 | $4,370 | $3,989 | $3,977 | $4,030 | $4,174 | $4,180 | $4,508 |

1. Transition quarter, July 1–Oct. 1, 1976. 2. Estimated NOTE: These figures are not precisely comparable with earlier data because the Budget now reports expenses under "function" rather than for each government agency. *Source:* Office of Management and Budget, *The Budget of the United States Government,* annual.

# Atomic Energy

Just as the Space Age is said to have started with the orbiting of Sputnik I, the Atomic Age is said to have started with the explosion of a test bomb on July 16, 1945, near Alamogordo, N.M., at 5:30 A.M. local time. The bomb was placed on top of a steel tower, and observers were stationed in bunkers 10,000 yards away. The explosion vaporized the steel tower, produced a mushroom cloud rising to 40,000 feet, and melted the desert sand into glass for distances up to 800 yards from the tower.

The first operational use of an atom bomb took place only three weeks later, when a uranium bomb was exploded over Hiroshima, Japan, on Aug. 6, 1945. The bomb, cylindrical in shape, 10 feet long with a diameter of 2 feet 4 inches, weighed about 9,000 pounds. Its explosive force was equal to 20,000 tons of TNT, hence the term "20-kiloton bomb." Three days later another atomic bomb, this time of plutonium, was exploded over Nagasaki.

Of course, the Atomic Age did not begin with the explosion of the test bomb at Alamogordo, just as the Space Age did not begin with the orbiting of the first artificial satellite. In both cases these visible feats were just experiments which proved the theory that had been built up patiently over decades.

At the turn of the century, scientists began to wonder whether the atoms of the chemical elements might not be composed of smaller particles. This was actually a contradiction in terms, because the Greek word *atomos,* from which the word *atom* was derived, meant "indivisible." But there were some indications of particles smaller than an atom —the electrons. In 1905, Albert Einstein suggested that matter might just be "condensed energy" and gave the conversion formula $E = mc^2$, in which $E$ represents the energy, $m$ the mass, and $c$ the velocity of light. If this formula was correct, a small piece of matter should represent enormous amounts of energy.

## Fission and Fusion

As is now generally known, atomic energy can be released in two ways. One is the *fission* of elements with very heavy atoms, such as uranium and plutonium, which will split when struck by a neutron, a sub-atomic particle. The splitting of the heavy atom releases more neutrons, which are then available to split other atoms—the so-called chain reaction. The other way of obtaining atomic energy is *fusion;* four light atoms (hydrogen) are fused together into the next heavier element (helium). The fusion reaction requires enormous heat and very high pressures. These pressures, coupled with very high temperatures, can most easily be produced by exploding a fission bomb, which is the reason why it is often said that a fission bomb is the trigger for a fusion (hydrogen) bomb.

Interestingly enough, the fusion reaction was discovered first, though only on paper. For the period from, say, 1910 to 1930, most physicists believed that the release of atomic energy, if it could be done, would be of no practical value. They asserted that causing the release would require more energy than could be obtained. Most astronomers, on the other hand, were convinced that atomic energy was released in the sun and the other stars because there was no other way to account for the energy the stars radiated into space. Trying to account for the energy radiated by the stars led to theoretical papers predicting what we now call the fusion reaction. At the time (1930), atomic fission was still unknown; it was discovered first by Enrico Fermi in 1934. But nobody yet knew that the sudden bursts of energy observed in the experiments were due to the fission of the uranium-235 atom. This was established (by way of calculation) by Dr. Lise Meitner. Once it was known what happened, the way to a premeditated release of atomic energy was clear.

But nobody could be quite certain whether the release would take the form of an explosion or whether it would be slow enough to be used to generate power. American scientists proceeded under the assumption that the release would be sudden and violent (and the Alamogordo test proved them right), while Professor Heisenberg in Germany thought the slow release to be more likely, which is the reason why the Germans did not start a large-scale atomic energy project.

## International Scoreboard

On May 18, 1974, India exploded an underground nuclear device of 10 to 15 kilotons, becoming the world's sixth nuclear power. The international scoreboard is now as follows:

**Fission bomb explosions:** U.S., Britain, France, U.S.S.R., China, India.

**Fusion bomb explosions:** U.S., Britain, France, U.S.S.R., China.

**Power reactors:** U.S., Britain, France, U.S.S.R., Norway, Sweden, Israel, Belgium, West Germany and probably Egypt.

**Atomic rocket propulsion:** Under development in U.S. and probably in U.S.S.R.

The beneficial aspects of atomic energy lie in the field of research (physical, chemical, and medical); it provides both new materials and new techniques. Practical applications of the slow release of fission energy are the power reactors, including the power plants for seagoing vessels.

## Atoms for Peace

The *peaceful* Atomic Age can be said to have been born in 1954, when the original U.S. Atomic Energy Act was amended to release many so-called "secrets" of nuclear energy so that nuclear power plants could be built and radioactive isotopes be used in medicine. The next year, the first International Conference on the Peaceful Uses of the Atom was convened at Geneva, bringing together scientists from all over the world to discuss what hitherto had been considered to be secret.

Actually there was little that was really secret about nuclear energy. When the results of the 1938 experiments were brought to the United States, scientists from different parts of the world openly stated that the possibility of atomic bombs was inherent in the scientific findings.

Once the veil of "secrecy" had been dispelled by revision of the Atomic Energy Act and the Geneva meeting, construction of plants to produce electricity by controlled fission of uranium atoms got under way in the United States and several other industrialized nations. Electric power was first produced as a result of nuclear fission in December 1951 at the National Reactor Testing Station in Idaho. When a reactor was connected to a generator, the nuclear power plant produced enough electricity for about 50 homes.

From that early beginning, the nuclear power industry has grown until, in 1978, 71 nuclear plants were in operation in the United States, supplying about 12% of the nation's electric power. Another 89 power reactors have construction permits from the U.S. Nuclear Regulatory Commission, four have limited work authorizations, and 42 more are on order. If all are built, they will have a total capacity of 200,968 electrical megawatts.

Twenty-one other nations have nuclear power plants in operation and 41 nations have firm commitments to build nuclear plants. Foreign countries have in operation and plan to build nuclear power plants producing 363,000 electrical megawatts.

Both in the United States and other countries, construction of nuclear power plants has been slowed by a combination of public concern over their environmental effects, the possibility of using them as clandestine sources of weapons-grade plutonium, and the general decline in the demand for electric power.

## Scientific Inventions, Discoveries, and Theories

Most inventions are the results of the discoveries, theories, experiments, and improvements of many people. This list tries to suggest the development of certain particularly important ideas. In some instances, it tries to connect the fundamental theory with the ultimate practical invention.

**Abacus:** *See* Calculating machine
**Adding machine:** *See* Calculating machine; Computer
**Adrenaline:** (isolation of) Jokichi Takamine, U.S., 1901
**Air brake:** George Westinghouse, U.S., 1868
**Air conditioning:** Willis Carrier, U.S., 1911
**Airplane:** (first powered, sustained, controlled flight) Orville and Wilbur Wright, U.S., 1903. *See also* Jet propulsion, aircraft
**Airship:** (non-rigid) Henri Giffard, France, 1852; (rigid) Ferdinand von Zeppelin, Germany, 1900
**Aluminum manufacture:** (by electrolytic action) Charles M. Hall, U.S., 1866
**Anesthetic:** (first use of anesthetic—ether—on man) Crawford W. Long, U.S., 1842
**Antibiotics:** (first demonstration of antibiotic effect) Louis Pasteur, Jules-François Joubert, France, 1887; (penicillin, first modern antibiotic) Alexander Fleming, England, 1928
**Antiseptic:** (surgery) Joseph Lister, England, 1867
**Antitoxin, diphtheria:** Emil von Behring, Germany, 1890
**Atomic theory:** (ancient) Leucippus, Democritus, Greece, c.500 B.C.; Lucretius, Rome, c.100 B.C.; (modern) John Dalton, England, 1808
**Automobile:** (first with internal combustion engine, 250 rpm) Karl Benz, Germany, 1885; (first with practical high-speed internal combustion engine, 900 rpm) Gottlieb Daimler, Germany, 1885; (first true automobile, not carriage with motor) René Panhard, Emile Lavassor, France, 1891; (carburetor, spray) Charles E. Duryea, U.S., 1892
**Bacteria:** Anton van Leeuwenhoek, The Netherlands, 1683
**Bakelite:** *See* Plastics
**Balloon, hot-air:** Joseph and Jacques Montgolfier, France, 1783
**Ball-point pen:** *See* Pen
**Barometer:** Evangelista Torricelli, Italy, 1643
**Bicycle:** Karl D. von Sauerbronn, Germany, 1816; (first modern model) James Starley, England, 1884
**Bifocal lens:** *See* Lens, bifocal
**Blood, circulation of:** William Harvey, England, 1628
**Braille:** Louis Braille, France, 1829
**Bullet:** (conical) Claude Minié, France, 1849
**Calculating machine:** (Abacus) China, c.190; (logarithms: made multiplying easier and thus calculators practical) John Napier, Scotland, 1614; (slide rule) William Oughtred, England, 1632; (digital calculator) Blaise Pascal, 1642; (multiplication machine) Gottfried Leibnitz, Germany, 1671; (important 19th-century contributors to modern machine) Frank S. Baldwin, Jay R. Monroe, Dorr E. Felt, W. T. Ohdner, William Burroughs, all U.S.; ("analytical engine" design, included concepts of programming, taping) Charles Babbage, England, 1835. *See also* Computer
**Camera:** (hand-held) George Eastman, U.S., 1888; (Polaroid Land) Edwin Land, U.S., 1948. *See also* Photography
**Carburator:** *See* Automobile
**Celanese:** *See* Fibers, man-made
**Celluloid:** *See* Plastics
**Classification of plants and animals:** (by genera and species) Carolus Linnaeus, Sweden, 1737–53
**Clock, pendulum:** Christian Huygens, The Netherlands, 1656
**Combustion:** (nature of) Antoine Lavoisier, France, 1777
**Computer:** (differential analyzer, mechanically operated) Vannevar Bush, U.S., 1928; (Mark I, first information-processing digital computer) Howard Aiken, U.S., 1944; (ENIAC, Electronic Numerical Integrator and Calculator, first all-electronic) J. Presper Eckert, John W. Mauchly, U.S., 1946; (stored-program concept) John von Neumann, U.S., 1947
**Conditioned reflex:** Ivan Pavlov, Russia, c.1910
**Converter, Bessemer:** William Kelly, U.S., 1851
**Cosmetics:** Egypt, c.4000 B.C.
**Cotton gin:** Eli Whitney, U.S., 1793
**Crossbow:** China, c.300 B.C.
**Cyclotron:** Ernest O. Lawrence, U.S., 1931
**Deuterium:** (heavy hydrogen) Harold Urey, U.S., 1931
**DNA:** (deoxyribonucleic acid) Friedrich Meischer, Germany, 1869; (determination of double-helical structure) F. H. Crick, England, James D. Watson, U.S., 1953
**Dynamite:** Alfred Nobel, Sweden, 1867
**Electric generator (dynamo):** (laboratory model) Michael Faraday, England, 1832; Joseph Henry, U.S., c.1832; (hand-driven model) Hippolyte Pixii, France, 1833; (alternating-current generator) Nikola Tesla, U.S., 1892
**Electric lamp:** (arc lamp) Sir Humphrey Davy, England, 1801; (fluorescent lamp) A. E. Becquerel, France, 1867; (incandescent lamp) Sir Joseph Swann, England, Thomas A. Edison, U.S., contemporaneously, 1870s; (carbon arc street lamp) Charles F. Brush, U.S., 1879; (first widely marketed incandescent lamp) Thomas A. Edison, U.S., 1879; (mercury vapor lamp) Peter Cooper Hewitt,

U.S., 1903; (neon lamp) Georges Claude, France, 1911; (tungsten filament) Irving Langmuir, U.S., 1915
**Electric motor:** *See* Motor
**Electromagnet:** William Sturgeon, England, 1823
**Electron:** Sir Joseph J. Thompson, England, 1897
**Elevator, passenger:** (safety device permitting use by passengers) Elisha G. Otis, U.S., 1852; (elevator utilizing safety device) 1857
**E = mc²:** (equivalence of mass and energy) Albert Einstein, Switzerland, 1905
**Engine, internal combustion:** No single inventor. Fundamental theory established by Sadi Carnot, France, 1824; (two-stroke) Étienne Lenoir, France, 1860; (ideal operating cycle for four-stroke) Alphonse Beau de Rochet, France, 1862; (operating four-stroke) Nikolaus Otto, Germany, 1876; (diesel) Rudolf Diesel, Germany, 1892; (rotary) Felix Wankel, Germany, 1956. *See also* Automobile
**Engine, steam:** *See* Steam engine
**Evolution:** (by natural selection) Charles Darwin, England, 1859
**Falling bodies, law of:** Galileo Galilei, Italy, 1590
**Fermentation:** (micro-organisms as cause of) Louis Pasteur, France, c.1860
**Fibers, man-made:** (nitrocellulose fibers treated to change flammable nitrocellulose to harmless cellulose, precursor of rayon) Sir Joseph Swann, England, 1883; (rayon) Count Hilaire de Chardonnet, France, 1889; (Celanese) Henry and Camille Dreyfuss, U.S., England, 1921; (research on polyesters and polyamides, basis for modern man-made fibers) U.S., England, Germany, 1930s; (nylon) Wallace H. Carothers, U.S., 1935
**Fountain pen:** *See* Pen
**Geometry, elements of:** Euclid, Alexandria, Egypt, c.300 B.C.
**Gravitation, law of:** Sir Isaac Newton, England, c.1665 (published 1687)
**Gunpowder:** China, c.700
**Gyrocompass:** Elmer A. Sperry, U.S., 1905
**Gyroscope:** Léon Foucault, France, 1852
**Helicopter:** Igor Sikorsky, U.S., 1939
**Helium first observed on sun:** Sir Joseph Lockyer, England, 1868
**Heredity, laws of:** Gregor Mendel, Austria, 1865
**Induction, electric:** Joseph Henry, U.S., 1828
**Insulin:** Sir Frederick G. Banting, J. J. R. MacLeod, Canada, 1922
**Intelligence testing:** Alfred Binet, Theodore Simon, France, 1905
**Isotopes:** (concept of) Frederick Soddy, England, 1912; (stable isotopes) J. J. Thompson, England, 1913; (existence demonstrated by mass spectrography) Francis W. Ashton, 1919
**Jet propulsion, aircraft:** Sir Frank Whittle, England, 1930
**Laser:** (theoretical work on) Charles H. Townes, Arthur L. Schawlow, U.S., N. Basov, A. Prokhorov, U.S.S.R., 1958; (first working model) T. H. Maiman, U.S., 1960
**Lens, bifocal:** Benjamin Franklin, U.S., c.1760
**Light, nature of:** (wave theory) Christian Huygens, Denmark, 1678; (electromagnetic theory) James Clerk Maxwell, England, 1873
**Light, speed of:** (theory that light has finite velocity) Olaus Roemer, Denmark, 1675
**Lightning rod:** Benjamin Franklin, U.S., 1752
**Linotype:** *See* Printing
**Lithography:** *See* Printing
**Locomotive:** (steam-powered) Richard Trevithick, England, 1804; (first practical, due to multiple-fire-tube boiler) George Stephenson, England, 1829; (largest steam-powered) Union Pacific's "Big Boy," U.S., 1941
**Logarithms:** *See* Calculating machine
**Loom:** (horizontal, two-beamed) Egypt, c.4400 B.C.; (Jacquard drawloom, pattern controlled by punch cards) Jacques de Vaucanson, France, 1745, Joseph-Marie Jacquard, 1801; (flying shuttle) John Kay, England, 1733; (power-driven loom) Edmund Cartwright, England, 1785
**Machine gun:** James Puckle, England, 1718; Richard J. Gatling, U.S., 1861
**Match:** (phosphorus) François Derosne, France, 1816; (friction) Charles Sauria, France, 1831; (safety) J. E. Lundstrom, Sweden, 1855
**Mendelian law:** *See* Heredity
**Microscope:** (compound) Zacharias Janssen, The Netherlands, 1590; (electron) Vladimir Zworykin et al., U.S., Canada, Germany, 1932–1939
**Motion pictures:** Thomas A. Edison, U.S., 1893
**Motion pictures, sound:** Product of various inventions. First picture with synchronized musical score: *Don Juan,* 1926; with spoken dialogue: *The Jazz Singer,* 1927; both Warner Bros.
**Motor, electric:** Michael Faraday, England, 1822; (alternating-current) Nikola Tesla, U.S., 1892
**Motor, gasoline:** *See* Engine, internal combustion
**Motorcycle:** (motor tricycle) Edward Butler, England, 1884; (gasoline-engine motorcycle) Gottlieb Daimler, Germany, 1885
**Neptunium:** (first transuranic element, synthesis of) Edward M. McMillan, Philip H. Abelson, U.S., 1940
**Neutron:** James Chadwick, England, 1832
**Neutron-induced radiation:** Enrico Fermi et al., Italy, 1934
**Nitroglycerin:** Ascanio Sobrero, Italy, 1846
**Nuclear fission:** Otto Hahn, Fritz Strassmann, Germany, 1938
**Nuclear reactor:** Enrico Fermi et al., U.S., 1942
**Nylon:** *See* Fibers, man-made
**Ohm's law:** (relationship between strength of electric current, electromotive force, and circuit resistance) Georg S. Ohm, Germany, 1827
**Ozone:** Christian Schönbein, Germany, 1839
**Paper:** China, c.100 B.C.
**Parachute:** Louis S. Lenormand, France, 1783
**Pen:** (fountain) Lewis E. Waterman, U.S., 1884; (ball-point, for marking on rough surfaces) John H. Loud, U.S., 1888; (ball-point, for handwriting) Lazlo Biro, Argentina, 1944
**Penicillin:** *See* Antibiotics
**Periodic law:** (that properties of elements are functions of their atomic weights) Dmitri Mendeleev, Russia, 1869
**Periodic table:** (arrangement of chemical elements based on periodic law) Dmitri Mendeleev, Russia, 1869
**Phonograph:** Thomas A. Edison, U.S., 1877
**Photography:** (first paper negative, first photograph, on metal) Joseph Nicéphore Niepce, France, 1816–1827; (discovery of fixative powers of hyposulfite of soda) Sir John Herschel, England, 1819; (first direct positive image on silver plate, the daguerreotype) Louis Daguerre, based on work with Niepce, France, 1839; (first paper negative from which a number of positive prints could be made) William Talbot, England, 1841. Work of these four men, taken together, forms basis for all modern photography. (First color images) Alexandre Becquerel, Claude Niepce de Saint-Victor, France, 1848–60; (commercial color film with three emulsion layers, Kodachrome) U.S., 1935. *See also* Camera
**Plastics:** (first material, nitrocellulose softened by vegetable oil, camphor, precursor to Celluloid)

Alexander Parkes, England, 1855; (Celluloid, involving recognition of vital effect of camphor) John W. Hyatt, U.S., 1869; (Bakelite, first completely synthetic plastic) Leo H. Baekeland, U.S., 1910; (theoretical background of macromolecules and process of polymerization on which modern plastics industry rests) Hermann Staudinger, Germany, 1922. *See also* Fibers, man-made

**Plow, forked:** Mesopotamia, before 3000 B.C.

**Plutonium, synthesis of:** Glenn T. Seaborg, Edwin M. McMillan, Arthur C. Wahl, Joseph W. Kennedy, U.S., 1941

**Polaroid Land camera:** *See* Camera

**Polio, vaccine against:** (vaccine made from dead virus strains) Jonas E. Salk, U.S., 1955; (vaccine made from live virus strains) Albert Sabin, U.S., 1960

**Positron:** Carl D. Anderson, U.S., 1932

**Pressure cooker:** (early version) Denis Papin, France, 1679

**Printing:** (block) Japan, c.700; (movable type) Korea, c.1400; Johann Gutenberg, Germany, c.1450 (lithography, offset) Aloys Senefelder, Germany, 1796; (rotary press) Richard Hoe, U.S., 1844; (linotype) Ottman Mergenthaler, U.S. 1884

**Programming, information:** *See* Calculating machine

**Propeller, screw:** Sir Francis P. Smith, England, 1836; John Ericsson, England, worked independently of and simultaneously with Smith, 1837

**Proton:** Ernest Rutherford, England, 1919

**Psychoanalysis:** Sigmund Freud, Austria, c.1904

**Quantum theory:** Max Planck, Germany, 1901

**Rabies immunization:** Louis Pasteur, France, 1885

**Radar:** (limited to one-mile range) Christian Hulsmeyer, Germany, 1904; (pulse modulation, used for measuring height of ionosphere) Gregory Breit, Merle Tuve, U.S., 1925; (first practical radar—radio detection and ranging) Sir Robert Watson-Watt, England, 1934–35

**Radio:** (electromagnetism, theory of) James Clerk Maxwell, England, 1873; (spark coil, generator of electromagnetic waves) Heinrich Hertz, Germany, 1886; (first practical system of wireless telegraphy) Guglielmo Marconi, Italy, 1895; (vacuum electron tube, basis for radio telephony) Sir John Fleming, England, 1904; (triode amplifying tube) Lee de Forest, U.S., 1906; (regenerative circuit, allowing long-distance sound reception) Edwin H. Armstrong, U.S., 1912; (frequency modulation—FM) Edwin H. Armstrong, U.S., 1933

**Radioactivity:** (X-rays) William K. Roentgen, Germany, 1895; (radioactivity of uranium) Henri Becquerel, France, 1896; (radioactive elements, radium and polonium in uranium ore) Marie Sklodowska-Curie, Pierre Curie, France, 1898; (classification of alpha and beta particle radiation) Pierre Curie, France, 1900; (gamma radiation) Paul-Ulrich Villard, France, 1900; (carbon dating) Willard F. Libby et al., U.S., 1955

**Rayon:** *See* Fibers, man-made

**Reaper:** Cyrus McCormick, U.S., 1834

**Relativity:** (special and general theories of) Albert Einstein, Switzerland, Germany, U.S., 1905–53

**Revolver:** Samuel Colt, U.S., 1835

**Rifle:** (muzzle-loaded) Italy, Germany, c.1475; (breech-loaded) England, France, Germany, U.S., c.1866; (bolt-action) Paul von Mauser, Germany, 1889; (automatic) John Browning, U.S., 1918

**Roller bearing:** (wooden for cartwheel) Germany or France, c.100 B.C.

**Rubber:** (vulcanization process) Charles Goodyear, U.S., 1839

**Safety match:** *See* Match

**Solar system, universe:** (sun-centered universe) Nicolaus Copernicus, Warsaw, 1543; (establishment of planetary orbits as elliptical) Johannes Kepler, Germany, 1609; (infinity of universe) Giordano Bruno, Italian monk, 1584

**Spectrum:** (heterogeneity of light) Sir Isaac Newton, England, 1665–66

**Spermatozoa:** Anton van Leeuwenhoek, The Netherlands, 1683

**Spinning:** (spinning wheel) India, introduced to Europe in Middle Ages; (Saxony wheel, continuous spinning of wool or cotton yarn) England, c.1500–1600; (spinning jenny) James Hargreaves, England, 1764; (spinning frame) Sir Richard Arkwright, England, 1769; (spinning mule, completed mechanization of spinning, permitting production of yarn to keep up with demands of modern looms) Samuel Crompton, England, 1779

**Steam engine:** (first commercial version based on principles of French physicist Denis Papin) Thomas Savery, England, 1639; (atmospheric steam engine) Thomas Newcomen, England, 1705; (steam engine for pumping water from collieries) Savery, Newcomen, 1725; (modern condensing, double-acting) James Watt, England, 1782

**Steam engine, railroad:** *See* Locomotive

**Steamship:** Claude de Jouffroy d'Abbans, France, 1783; James Rumsey, U.S., 1787; John Fitch, U.S., 1790. All preceded Robert Fulton, U.S., 1807, credited with launching first commercially successful steamship

**Sulfa drugs:** (parent compound, para-aminobenzenesulfanomide) Paul Gelmo, Austria, 1908; (antibacterial activity) Gerhard Domagk, Germany, 1935

**Syphilis, test for:** *See* Wasserman test

**Tank, military:** Sir Ernest Swinton, England, 1914

**Telegraph:** Samuel F. B. Morse, U.S., 1837

**Telephone:** Alexander Graham Bell, U.S., 1876

**Telescope:** Hans Lippershey, The Netherlands, 1608

**Television:** (mechanical disk-scanning method) successfully demonstrated by J. L. Baird, England, C. F. Jenkins, U.S., 1926; (electronic scanning method) Vladimir K. Zworykin, U.S., 1928; (color, all-electronic) Zworykin, 1925; (color, mechanical disk) Baird, 1928; (color, compatible with black and white) George Valensi, France, 1938; (color, sequential rotating filter) Peter Goldmark, U.S., first introduced, 1951; (color, compatible with black and white) commercially introduced in U.S., National Television Systems Committee, 1953

**Thermometer:** (open-column) Galileo Galilei, c.1593; (clinical) Santorio Santorio, Padua, c.1615; (mercury, also Fahrenheit scale) Gabriel D. Fahrenheit, Germany, 1714; (centigrade scale) Anders Celsius, Sweden, 1742; (absolute-temperature, or Kelvin, scale) William Thompson, Lord Kelvin, England, 1848

**Tire, pneumatic:** Robert W. Thompson, England, 1845; (bicycle tire) John B. Dunlop, Northern Ireland, 1888

**Toilet, flush:** Product of Minoan civilization, Crete, c.2000 B.C. Alleged invention by "Thomas Crapper" is untrue.

**Tractor:** Benjamin Holt, U.S., 1900

**Transformer, electric:** William Stanley, U.S., 1885

**Transistor:** John Bardeen, William Shockley, Walter Brattain, U.S., 1948

**Uncertainty principle:** (that position and velocity of an object cannot both be measured exactly, at the same time) Werner Heisenberg, Germany, 1927

**Vaccination:** Edward Jenner, England, 1796

**Vacuum tube:** *See* Radio

**Van Allen (radiation) Belt:** (around the earth) James Van Allen, U.S., 1958

**Vitamins:** (hypothesis of disease deficiency) Sir F. G. Hopkins, Casimir Funk, England, 1912; (vitamin A) Elmer V. McCollum, M. Davis, U.S., 1912–14; (vitamin B) Elmer V. McCollum, U.S., 1915–16; (thiamin, $B_1$) Casimir Funk, England, 1912; (riboflavin, $B_2$) D. T. Smith, E. G. Hendrick, U.S., 1926; (niacin) Conrad Elvehjem, U.S., 1937; ($B_6$) Paul Gyorgy, U.S., 1934; (vitamin C) C. A. Holst, T. Froelich, Norway, 1912; (vitamin D) Elmer V. McCollum, U.S., 1922; (folic acid) Lucy Wills, England, 1933

**Wassermann test:** (for syphilis) August von Wassermann, Germany, 1906

**Weaving, cloth:** *See* Loom

**Wheel:** (cart, solid wood) Mesopotamia, c.3800–3600 B.C.

**Windmill:** Persia, c.600

**X-ray:** *See* Radioactivity

**Xerography:** Chester Carlson, U.S., 1938

**Zero:** Mayas, Central America, c.325; India, c.600; (absolute zero, cessation of all molecular energy) William Thompson, Lord Kelvin, England, 1848

## The Stages of Invention

Alexander von Humbolt (1769–1859), the German naturalist, said that an invention goes through three stages: doubt of its existence, denial of its importance, and, finally, credit for its discovery going to someone else.

One example of the truth in this perception is the invention of the "Pullman," the railroad sleeping car. The first sleeper was built by Richard Imlay of Philadelphia. It ran between Chambersburg and Harrisburg, Pa., in 1838. At least eight railroads advertised some kind of sleeping car before 1850. Pullman's first car was not built until 1859. George M. Pullman and his friend Ben Field patented the folding upper berth in 1864. Pullman seems to have been a better businessman and a better promoter.

## Chemical Elements

| Element | Symbol | Atomic no. | Atomic weight | Specific gravity | Melting point °C | Boiling point °C | Number of isotopes[1] | Discoverer | Year |
|---|---|---|---|---|---|---|---|---|---|
| Actinium | Ac | 89 | 227[2] | 10.07[2] | 1050 | 3200±300 | 11 | Debierne | 1899 |
| Aluminum | Al | 13 | 26.9815 | 2.6989 | 660.37 | 2467 | 8 | Wöhler | 1827 |
| Americium | Am | 95 | 243[6] | 13.67 | 994±4 | 2607 | 13[3] | Seaborg et al. | 1944 |
| Antimony | Sb | 51 | 121.75 | 6.691 | 630.74 | 1750 | 29 | Early historic times | — |
| Argon | Ar | 18 | 39.948 | 1.7837[4] | −189.2 | −185.7 | 8 | Rayleigh and Ramsay | 1894 |
| Arsenic (gray) | As | 33 | 74.9216 | 5.73 | 817 (28 atm.) | 613[5] | 14 | Albertus Magnus | 1250? |
| Astatine | At | 85 | ~210 | — | 302 | 337 | 21 | Corson et al. | 1940 |
| Barium | Ba | 56 | 137.34 | 3.5 | 725 | 1640 | 25 | Davy | 1808 |
| Berkelium | Bk | 97 | 247[6] | 14.00[7] | — | — | 8[3] | Seaborg et al. | 1949 |
| Beryllium | Be | 4 | 9.01218 | 1.848 | 1278±5 | 2970 (5 mm.) | 6 | Vauquelin | 1798 |
| Bismuth | Bi | 83 | 208.9806 | 9.747 | 271.3 | ·1560±5 | 19 | Geoffroy | 1753 |
| Boron | B | 5 | 10.81 | 2.37[8] | 2300 | 2550[5] | 6 | Gay-Lussac and Thénard; Davy | 1808 |
| Bromine | Br | 35 | 79.904 | 3.12[4] | −7.2 | 58.78 | 19 | Balard | 1826 |
| Cadmium | Cd | 48 | 112.40 | 8.65 | 320.9 | 765 | 22 | Stromeyer | 1817 |
| Calcium | Ca | 20 | 40.08 | 1.55 | 839±2 | 1484 | 14 | Davy | 1808 |
| Californium | Cf | 98 | 251[6] | — | — | — | 12[3] | Seaborg et al. | 1950 |
| Carbon | C | 6 | 12.011 | 1.8–3.5[9] | ~3550 | 4827 | 7 | Prehistoric | — |
| Cerium | Ce | 58 | 140.12 | 6.771 | 798±3 | 3257 | 19 | Berzelius and Hisinger; Klaproth | 1803 |
| Cesium | Cs | 55 | 132.9055 | 1.873 | 28.40 | 678.4 | 22 | Bunsen and Kirchhoff | 1860 |
| Chlorine | Cl | 17 | 35.453 | 1.56[4] | −100.98 | −34.6 | 11 | Scheele | 1774 |
| Chromium | Cr | 24 | 51.996 | 7.18–7.20 | 1857±20 | 2672 | 9 | Vauquelin | 1797 |
| Cobalt | Co | 27 | 58.9332 | 8.9 | 1495 | 2870 | 14 | Brandt | c.1735 |
| Copper | Cu | 29 | 63.546 | 8.96 | 1083.4±0.2 | 2567 | 11 | Prehistoric | — |
| Curium | Cm | 96 | 247[6] | 13.51[2] | 1340±40 | — | 13[3] | Seaborg et al. | 1944 |
| Dysprosium | Dy | 66 | 162.50 | 8.540 | 1409 | 2335 | 21 | Boisbaudran | 1886 |
| Einsteinium | Es | 99 | 254[6] | — | — | — | 12[3] | Ghiorso et al | 1952 |
| Erbium | Er | 68 | 167.26 | 9.045 | 1522 | 2510 | 16 | Mosander | 1843 |
| Europium | Eu | 63 | 151.96 | 5.283 | 822±5 | 1597 | 21 | Demarcay | 1896 |
| Fermium | Fm | 100 | 257[6] | — | — | — | 10[3] | Ghiorso et al | 1953 |
| Fluorine | F | 9 | 18.9984 | 1.108[4] | −219.62 | −188.14 | 6 | Moissan | 1886 |
| Francium | Fr | 87 | 223[6] | — | 27[2] | 677[2] | 21 | Perey | 1939 |
| Gadolinium | Gd | 64 | 157.25 | 7.898 | 1311±1 | 3233 | 17 | Marignac | 1880 |
| Gallium | Ga | 31 | 69.72 | 5.904 | 29.78 | 2403 | 14 | Boisbaudran | 1875 |
| Germanium | Ge | 32 | 72.59 | 5.323 | 937.4 | 2830 | 17 | Winkler | 1886 |
| Gold | Au | 79 | 196.9665 | 19.32 | 1064.43 | 2807 | 21 | Prehistoric | — |
| Hafnium | Hf | 72 | 178.49 | 13.31 | 2227±20 | 4602 | 17 | Coster and von Hevesy | 1923 |
| Helium | He | 2 | 4.00260 | 0.1785[4] | −272.2 (26 atm.) | −268.934 | 5 | Janssen | 1868 |
| Holmium | Ho | 67 | 164.9303 | 8.781 | 1470 | 2720 | 29 | Delafontaine and Soret | 1878 |
| Hydrogen | H | 1 | 1.0080 | 0.070[4] | −259.14 | −252.87 | 3 | Cavendish | 1766 |
| Indium | In | 49 | 114.82 | 7.31 | 156.61 | 2080 | 34 | Reich and Richter | 1863 |

| Element | Symbol | Atomic no. | Atomic weight | Specific gravity | Melting point °C | Boiling point °C | Number of isotopes[1] | Discoverer | Year |
|---|---|---|---|---|---|---|---|---|---|
| Iodine | I | 53 | 126.9045 | 4.93 | 113.5 | 184.35 | 24 | Courtois | 1811 |
| Iridium | Ir | 77 | 192.22 | 22.42 | 2410 | 4130 | 25 | Tennant | 1803 |
| Iron | Fe | 26 | 55.847 | 7.894 | 1535 | 2750 | 10 | Prehistoric | — |
| Krypton | Kr | 36 | 83.80 | 3.733[4] | −156.6 | −152.30 ± 0.10 | 23 | Ramsay and Travers | 1898 |
| Lanthanum | La | 57 | 138.9055 | 6.166 | 920 ± 5 | 3454 | 19 | Mosander | 1839 |
| Lawrencium | Lr | 103 | 257[6] | — | — | — | 20[3] | Ghiorso et al. | 1961 |
| Lead | Pb | 82 | 207.2 | 11.35 | 327.502 | 1740 | 29 | Prehistoric | — |
| Lithium | Li | 3 | 6.941 | 0.534 | 180.54 | 1347 | 5 | Arfvedson | 1817 |
| Lutetium | Lu | 71 | 174.97 | 9.835 | 1656 ± 5 | 3315 | 22 | Urbain | 1907 |
| Magnesium | Mg | 12 | 24.305 | 1.738 | 648.8 ± 0.5 | 1090 | 8 | Black | 1755 |
| Manganese | Mn | 25 | 54.9380 | 7.21–7.44[10] | 1244 ± 3 | 1962 | 11 | Gahn, Scheele, and Bergman | 1774 |
| Mendelevium | Md | 101 | 256[6] | — | — | — | 3[3] | Ghiorso et al. | 1955 |
| Mercury | Hg | 80 | 200.59 | 13.546 | −38.87 | 356.58 | 26 | Prehistoric | — |
| Molybdenum | Mo | 42 | 95.94 | 10.22 | 2617 | 4612 | 20 | Scheele | 1778 |
| Neodymium | Nd | 60 | 144.24 | 6.80 & 7.004[10] | 1010 | 3127 | 16 | von Welsbach | 1885 |
| Neon | Ne | 10 | 20.179 | 0.89990 (g/1 0°C/1 atm) | −248.67 | −246.048 | 8 | Ramsay and Travers | 1898 |
| Neptunium | Np | 93 | 237.0482 | 20.25 | 640 ± 1 | 3902 | 15[3] | McMillan and Abelson | 1940 |
| Nickel | Ni | 28 | 58.71 | 8.902 | 1453 | 2732 | 11 | Cronstedt | 1751 |
| Niobium (Columbium) | Nb | 41 | 92.9064 | 8.57 | 2468 ± 10 | 4742 | 24 | Hatchett | 1801 |
| Nitrogen | N | 7 | 14.0067 | 0.808[4] | −209.86 | −195.8 | 8 | Rutherford | 1772 |
| Nobelium | No | 102 | 254[6] | — | — | — | 7[3] | Ghiorso et al. | 1957 |
| Osmium | Os | 76 | 190.2 | 22.57 | 3045 ± 30 | 5027 ± 100 | 19 | Tennant | 1803 |
| Oxygen | O | 8 | 15.9994 | 1.14[4] | −218.4 | −182.962 | 8 | Priestley | 1774 |
| Palladium | Pd | 46 | 106.4 | 12.02 | 1552 | 3140 | 21 | Wollaston | 1803 |
| Phosphorus | P | 15 | 30.9738 | 1.82 (white) | 44.1 | 280 | 7 | Brand | 1669 |
| Platinum | Pt | 78 | 195.09 | 21.45 | 1772 | 3827 ± 100 | 32 | Ulloa | 1735 |
| Plutonium | Pu | 94 | 244[6] | 19.84 | 641 | 3232 | 16[3] | Seaborg et al. | 1940 |
| Polonium | Po | 84 | ~210[6] | 9.32 | 254 | 962 | 34 | Curie | 1898 |
| Potassium | K | 19 | 39.102 | 0.862 | 63.65 | 774 | 10 | Davy | 1807 |
| Praseodymium | Pr | 59 | 140.9077 | 6.772 | 931 ± 4 | 3212 | 15 | von Welsbach | 1885 |
| Promethium | Pm | 61 | 145[6] | — | ~1080 | 2460? | 14 | Marinsky et al. | 1945 |
| Protactinium | Pa | 91 | 231.0359 | 15.37[2] | <1600 | — | 14 | Hahn and Meitner | 1917 |
| Radium | Ra | 88 | 226.0254 | 5.0? | 700 | 1140 | 15 | P. and M. Curie | 1898 |
| Radon | Rn | 86 | 222[6] | 4.4[4] | 71 | 61.8 | 20 | Dorn | 1900 |
| Rhenium | Re | 75 | 186.2 | 21.02 | 3180 | 5627[7] | 21 | Noddack, Berg, and Tacke | 1925 |
| Rhodium | Rh | 45 | 102.9055 | 12.41 | 1966 ± 3 | 3727 ± 100 | 20 | Wollaston | 1803 |
| Rubidium | Rb | 37 | 85.4678 | 1.532 | 38.89 | 688 | 20 | Bunsen and Kirchhoff | 1861 |
| Ruthenium | Ru | 44 | 101.07 | 12.44 | 2310 | 3900 | 16 | Klaus | 1844 |
| Samarium | Sm | 62 | 150.4 | 7.536 | 1072 ± 5 | 1778 | 17 | Boisbaudran | 1879 |
| Scandium | Sc | 21 | 44.9559 | 2.989 | 1539 | 2832 | 15 | Nilson | 1879 |
| Selenium | Se | 34 | 78.96 | 4.79 (gray) | 217 | 684.9 ± 1 | 20 | Berzelius | 1817 |
| Silicon | Si | 14 | 28.086 | 2.33 | 1410 | 2355 | 8 | Berzelius | 1824 |
| Silver | Ag | 47 | 107.868 | 10.50 | 961.93 | 2212 | 27 | Prehistoric | — |
| Sodium | Na | 11 | 22.9898 | 0.971 | 97.81 ± 0.03 | 882.9 | 7 | Davy | 1807 |
| Strontium | Sr | 38 | 87.62 | 2.54 | 769 | 1384 | 18 | Davy | 1808 |
| Sulfur | S | 16 | 32.06 | 2.07[11] | 112.8 | 444.674 | 10 | Prehistoric | — |
| Tantalum | Ta | 73 | 180.9479 | 16.654 | 2996 | 5425 ± 100 | 19 | Ekeberg | 1801 |
| Technetium | Tc | 43 | 98.9062 | 11.50[2] | 2172 | 4877 | 23 | Perrier and Segrè | 1937 |
| Tellurium | Te | 52 | 127.60 | 6.24 | 449.5 ± 0.3 | 989.8 ± 3.8 | 29 | von Reichenstein | 1782 |
| Terbium | Tb | 65 | 158.9254 | 8.234 | 1360 ± 4 | 3041 | 24 | Mosander | 1843 |
| Thallium | Tl | 81 | 204.37 | 11.85 | 303.5 | 1457 ± 10 | 28 | Crookes | 1861 |
| Thorium | Th | 90 | 232.0381 | 11.72 | 1750 | ~4790 | 12 | Berzelius | 1828 |
| Thulium | Tm | 69 | 168.9342 | 9.314 | 1545 + 15 | 1727 | 18 | Cleve | 1879 |
| Tin | Sn | 50 | 118.69 | 7.31 (white) | 231.9681 | 2270 | 28 | Prehistoric | — |
| Titanium | Ti | 22 | 47.90 | 4.55 | 1660 ± 10 | 3287 | 9 | Gregor | 1791 |
| Tungsten (Wolfram) | W | 74 | 183.85 | 19.3 | 3410 ± 20 | 5660 | 22 | J. and F. d'Elhuyar | 1783 |
| Uranium | U | 92 | 238.029 | ~18.95 | 1132.3 ± 0.8 | 3818 | 15 | Peligot | 1841 |
| Vanadium | V | 23 | 50.9414 | 6.11 | 1890 ± 10 | 3380 | 9 | del Rio | 1801 |
| Xenon | Xe | 54 | 131.30 | 3.52[4] | −111.9 | −107.1 ± 3 | 31 | Ramsay and Travers | 1898 |
| Ytterbium | Yb | 70 | 173.04 | 6.972 | 824 ± 5 | 1193 | 16 | Marignac | 1878 |
| Yttrium | Y | 39 | 88.9059 | 4.457 | 1523 ± 8 | 3337 | 21 | Gadolin | 1794 |
| Zinc | Zn | 30 | 65.38 | 7.133 | 419.58 | 907 | 15 | Prehistoric | — |
| Zirconium | Zr | 40 | 91.22 | 6.506[2] | 1852 ± 2 | 4377 | 20 | Klaproth | 1789 |

1. Isotopes are different forms of the same element having the same atomic number but different atomic weights. 2. Calculated figure. 3. Artificially produced. 4. Liquid. 5. Sublimation point. 6. Mass number of the isotope of longest known life. 7. Estimated. 8. Amorphous. 9. Depending on whether amorphous, graphite or diamond. 10. Depending on allotropic form. 11. Rhombic. ~ Is approximately. < Is less than. NOTE: There is a dispute between groups at the Lawrence Berkeley Laboratory of the University of California and at the Dubna Laboratory in the Soviet Union concerning the discovery of elements 104, 105, and 106. The Lawrence Berkeley Laboratory claims that 104 and 105 were discovered in 1969 and 1970, respectively, by Ghiorso et al. and has suggested the names Rutherfordium and Hafnium. The U.S. laboratory claims also that Ghiorso et al. discovered element 106 in 1974. No name has yet been suggested for this element. Names will not be official until the controversy is resolved and they have been approved by the International Union for Pure and Applied Chemistry.

## The Year in Space

The first Space Shuttle, marking a new phase of the nation's space program, is scheduled to take off from Cape Canaveral in the late summer or fall of 1979, remain in orbit for 53 hours, and then land at Edwards Air Force Base in California, ready to take off again.

"Ready to take off *again*" is the new element in the space program. Unlike all the space vehicles that have left earth before, the Space Shuttle is to be reusable. National Aeronautical and Space Administration officials contend that operation of the Shuttle will drop the cost of space vehicle launches to $200 per pound, from the $10,000-per-pound cost in the 1960s. In the 1990s, costs could drop even further, to $25 per pound.

NASA and other supporters of the nation's space program contend that we get a lot more out of space even in dollars-and-cents terms than we put into it. The Midwest Research Institute in Kansas City, Mo., reports that while the space effort cost the taxpayer $25 billion through 1969, it returned $52 billion to the economy in that time. They point to all the new technologies, instrumentation, and products that had to be developed for successful space flight and then could be—and were—adapted to industry on earth. These include new products in medicine, agriculture, and education; longer-lasting metals, and consumer products.

The Shuttle program is based on the premise that less costly entry into space will be of economic benefit to the nation, though many industrialists question whether this offers enough of an economic advantage in terms of manufacturing and materials processing to be worthwhile.

The first phase of the Shuttle's approach and landing tests at Edwards AFB was successfully completed in 1978. The Shuttle orbiter was taken high into the atmosphere by a Boeing 747. The 150,000-pound vehicle landed smoothly and safely five out of five times. Meanwhile, the main engines were test fired at the National Science Testing Laboratories in Michoud, La.

The Shuttle that landed safely five times at Edwards was officially called Orbiting Vehicle (or OV) 101, and named the Enterprise. OV-102 will make the first flight into orbit. Work on it is being completed at Rockwell International's aerospace division, in Palmdale, Calif. It will be delivered to Cape Canaveral early in 1979.

Another space vehicle was having problems. Skylab, which was put into orbit in 1973, had problems in late 1977 and 1978. It was losing altitude at a rate much faster than had been anticipated, so fast that there was fear it might soon crash onto earth. In 1978, attempts were made to reactivate Skylab's controls by radio command from Houston. These attempts were at least temporarily successful. Skylab's orbit was corrected. If Skylab is still in orbit two years from now, NASA hopes to send its second Shuttle mission to its rescue. If this is done, the Shuttle will carry a remotely-operated retrieval system to be attached to Skylab. It will have the capability of either kicking Skylab into a higher, more permanent orbit for future use by scientists, or of bringing it back to earth in a controlled reentry.

The Shuttle can carry new communications or scientific satellites into orbit. It can operate in orbit for up to 30 days. Its crews can make repairs on other satellites while they remain in orbit, and it can bring back to earth damaged satellites or satellites that have outlived their usefulness. Not too far into the future, the Shuttle may have to make a "garbage run"—cleaning up the thousands of pieces of metal and plastic that have been thrown into orbit and will begin to interfere with newer space operations.

Meanwhile, NASA is training 35 new astronauts to man the Shuttles. The first class of astronauts to be selected in 11 years began its training in the summer of 1978 in Houston. Fifteen of the newcomers will be designated as "pilot astronauts," while the other 20 will be "mission specialists." NASA describes them as a new category of generalists "who will have over-all responsibility for the coordination, with the commander and pilot, of Space Shuttle operations in the areas of crew activity planning, consumables usage, and other Space Shuttle activities affecting experiment operations."

The six women selected are to be trained as mission specialists. This new group is more diversified than were the previous crews.

None of the freshmen astronauts will get to make the first flights of the Shuttle. They face a two-year training program, to be finished in 1980, about the time initial flight testing of the Shuttle is completed.

They will fly in a space age when missions will be more routine, when Shuttles will take off on a timetable, and when taxpayers will be looking for a more tangible payoff for their tax dollars.

*Wadsworth Likely*

## Chronology of Unmanned Lunar and Interplanetary Probes

| Spacecraft | Launch date | Destination | Remarks |
|---|---|---|---|
| Pioneer 1 (U.S.) | Oct. 11, 1958 | Moon | Max. alt.: 71,300 mi. Flight duration: 43 h 17.5 min |
| Pioneer 2 (U.S.) | Nov. 8, 1958 | Moon | Third stage failure |
| Pioneer 3 (U.S.) | Dec. 6, 1958 | Moon | Max. alt.: 66,654 mi. Discovered outer Van Allen layer. |
| Metchta (U.S.S.R.) | Jan. 2, 1959 | Moon | Missed moon by 4,600 mi. |
| Pioneer 4 (U.S.) | March 3, 1959 | Moon | 13.4 lb. Passed 37,300 mi. from Moon. |

| Spacecraft | Launch date | Destination | Remarks |
|---|---|---|---|
| Lunik 1 (U.S.S.R.) | Sept. 12, 1959 | Moon | Landed in area of Mare Serenitatis. |
| Pioneer 5 (U.S.) | March 11, 1960 | Inter-planetary | Orbited sun between Earth & Venus. Radio transmission over record distance of 20 million miles. |
| Venus probe (USSR) | Feb. 12, 1961 | Venus | Fired from orbiting Sputnik 8. No signals received. |
| Ranger 3 (U.S.) | Jan. 26, 1962 | Moon | 727-lb instrument capsule to impact on Moon. Missed target. |
| Ranger 4 (U.S.) | April 23, 1962 | Moon | 730-lb probe. Impacted on Moon's far side April 26. No transmission. |
| Mariner 1 (U.S.) | July 22, 1962 | Venus | Atlas Agena rocket off course. Destroyed. |
| Mariner 2 (U.S.) | Aug. 27, 1962 | Venus | Venus probe. Successful mid-course correction. Passed 21,648 mi. from Venus Dec. 14, 1962. Reported 800°F. surface temp. Contact lost Jan. 3, 1963 at 54 million mi. |
| Ranger 5 (U.S.) | Oct. 18, 1962 | Moon | 755 lb. To take TV pictures of Moon before landing. Power lost. Passed 450 mi. from Moon Oct. 20. |
| Mars 1 (U.S.S.R.) | Nov. 1, 1962 | Mars | Fired from parking orbit. Radio contact lost March 31, 1963. |
| Luna 4 (U.S.S.R.) | April 2, 1963 | Moon | Fired from parking orbit, possibly for soft landing. Passed 5,300 mi. from Moon. |
| Ranger 6 (U.S.) | Jan. 30, 1964 | Moon | Impacted on target near Crater Arago, but TV cameras failed. |
| Zond 1 (U.S.S.R.) | April 2, 1964 | Venus | No data |
| Ranger 7 (U.S.) | July 28, 1964 | Moon | Impacted near Crater Guericke 68.5 h after launch. Sent 4,316 pictures during last 15 min of flight as close as 1,000 ft above lunar surface. |
| Mariner 3 (U.S.) | Nov. 5, 1964 | Mars | Malfunctioned. Solar panels did not unfold. |
| Mariner 4 (U.S.) | Nov. 28, 1964 | Mars | After mid-course correction, passed behind Mars July 14, 1965, taking 22 pictures from about 6,000 mi. |
| Zond 2 (U.S.S.R.) | Nov. 30, 1964 | Mars | Power supply failed. |
| Ranger 8 (U.S.) | Feb. 17, 1965 | Moon | 809 lb. After 64.9 h, crashed into Mare Tranquilitatis, 2.59° N of lunar equator. Sent 7,137 pictures. |
| Ranger 9 (U.S.) | March 21, 1965 | Moon | After 64.5 h, hit Crater Alphonsus. Sent 5,814 pictures. |
| Luna 5 (U.S.S.R.) | May 9, 1965 | Moon | Crashed on Moon instead of soft landing (May 12) |
| Luna 6 (U.S.S.R.) | June 8, 1965 | Moon | Missed Moon and is in solar orbit |
| Zond 3 (U.S.S.R.) | July 18, 1965 | Moon | Sent close-ups of 3 million sq mi. of Moon. Now in solar orbit. |
| Luna 7 (U.S.S.R.) | Oct. 4, 1965 | Moon | Designed for soft landing. Crashed on Moon Oct. 7. |
| Venera 2 (U.S.S.R.) | Nov. 12, 1965 | Venus | 2,112 lb. Passed 14,912 mi. from Venus (Feb. 27, 1966). No data sent. |
| Venera 3 (U.S.S.R.) | Nov. 16, 1965 | Venus | 2,112 lb. Entered Venus atmosphere (March 1, 1966). No data sent. |
| Luna 8 (U.S.S.R.) | Dec. 3, 1965 | Moon | Intended to soft-land, but crashed on Moon Dec. 6, 1965. |
| Pioneer 6 (U.S.) | Dec. 16, 1965 | Inter-planetary | Successfully orbiting Sun (every 311 days) to check space conditions between Earth & Venus. Perihelion: 75.6 million mi. Aphelion: 90.7 million mi. |
| Luna 9 (U.S.S.R.) | Jan. 31, 1966 | Moon | 3,428 lb. Instrument capsule of 220 lb soft-landed Feb. 3, 1966. Sent back about 30 pictures. |
| Luna 10 (U.S.S.R.) | March 31, 1966 | Moon | 540 lb. Orbit achieved April 2, 1966. |
| Surveyor 1 (U.S.) | May 30, 1966 | Moon | Landed June 2, 1966. Sent almost 10,400 pictures, a number after surviving the 14-day lunar night. |
| Lunar Orbiter 1 (U.S.) | Aug. 10, 1966 | Moon | Orbited Moon Aug. 14. 21 pictures sent |
| Pioneer 7 (U.S.) | Aug. 17, 1966 | Sun Orbit | Orbiting sun (400 days). Perihelion: 92 million mi. Aphelion: 102 million mi. |
| Luna 11 (U.S.S.R.) | Aug. 24, 1966 | Moon | Moon orbit achieved Aug. 27. |
| Surveyor 2 (U.S.) | Sept. 20, 1966 | Moon | Tumbled in flight. Crashed on Moon Sept. 23. |
| Luna 12 (U.S.S.R.) | Oct. 22, 1966 | Moon | Moon orbit achieved Oct. 25 for 3.5 h. Transmission difficulties. |
| Lunar Orbiter 2 (U.S.) | Nov. 7, 1966 | Moon | Orbit achieved Nov. 10. Sent hundreds of excellent pictures. |
| Luna 13 (U.S.S.R.) | Dec. 21, 1966 | Moon | Soft-landed 80 h after launch. Good pictures. Drove spike into Moon's surface. |
| Lunar Orbiter 3 (U.S.) | Feb. 4, 1967 | Moon | Orbited Moon Feb. 8. Terminated Oct. 9, 1967. Excellent pictures. |
| Surveyor 3 (U.S.) | April 17, 1967 | Moon | Soft-landed 65 h after launch on Oceanus Procellarum. Scooped and tested lunar soil. |
| Lunar Orbiter 4 (U.S.) | May 4, 1967 | Moon | Achieved orbit May 7. Changed orbit on command. |
| Venera 4 (U.S.S.R.) | June 12, 1967 | Venus | Arrived Oct. 17. Instrument capsule sent temperature and chemical data. |
| Mariner 5 (U.S.) | June 14, 1967 | Venus | Fly-by Oct. 19, confirming Mariner 2 and Venera 4 findings |
| Surveyor 4 (U.S.) | July 14, 1967 | Moon | Contact lost 2.5 min before landing |
| Explorer 35 (U.S.) | July 19, 1967 | Moon | Orbit July 22. Perilune: 500 mi.; apolune: 4000 mi. |
| Lunar Orbiter 5 (U.S.) | Aug. 2, 1967 | Moon | Orbited Aug. 5, Perilune: 125 mi.; apolune: 3,760 mi. Time 3 h 50 min. After filming, was crashed on Moon. |
| Surveyor 5 (U.S.) | Sept. 8, 1967 | Moon | Landed near lunar equator Sept. 10. Radiological analysis of lunar soil. Mechanical claw for digging soil. |
| Surveyor 6 (U.S.) | Nov. 7, 1967 | Moon | Landed in Sinus Medii Nov. 10. Jumped 8 ft to photograph original position. Sent back 11,524 pictures. |
| Pioneer 8 (U.S.) | Dec. 12, 1967 | Sun Orbit | Achieved Solar orbit. Stopped functioning April 28, 1968. |
| Surveyor 7 (U.S.) | Jan. 6, 1968 | Moon | Landed near Crater Tycho Jan. 10. Soil analysis. Sent 3,343 pictures. |

| Spacecraft | Launch date | Destination | Remarks |
|---|---|---|---|
| Zond 4 (U.S.S.R.) | March 2, 1968 | Unknown | Achieved parking orbit but was unable to leave. Re-entered March 3. |
| Luna 14 (U.S.S.R.) | April 7, 1968 | Moon | Orbited moon April 10 |
| Zond 5 (U.S.S.R.) | Sept. 14, 1968 | Moon | Circumlunar flight |
| Pioneer 9 (U.S.) | Nov. 8, 1968 | Sun Orbit | Achieved orbit. Six experiments returned solar radiation data. |
| Zond 6 (U.S.S.R.) | Nov. 10, 1968 | Moon | Circumlunar flight |
| Venera 5 (U.S.S.R.) | Jan. 5, 1969 | Venus | Landed May 16, 1969. Returned atmospheric data. |
| Venera 6 (U.S.S.R.) | Jan. 10, 1969 | Venus | Landed May 17, 1969. Sent data as Venera 5. |
| Mariner 6 (U.S.) | Feb. 24, 1969 | Mars | Came within 2000 mi. of Mars July 31, 1969. Sent back data & TV pictures. |
| Mariner 7 (U.S.) | March 27, 1969 | Mars | Came within 2000 mi. of Mars Aug. 5, 1969. Sent back data & TV pictures. |
| Luna 15 (U.S.S.R.) | July 13, 1969 | Moon | Lunar orbiter landed on Moon July 21, 1969 after completing varying orbits. |
| Zond 7 (U.S.S.R.) | Aug. 8, 1969 | Moon | Circumlunar. Recovered Aug. 14, 1969. |
| Pioneer E (U.S.) | Aug. 27, 1969 | Inter-planetary | To obtain data on particles and magnetic fields, but failed to achieve orbit. |
| Venera 7 (U.S.S.R.) | Aug. 17, 1970 | Venus | Reached Venus Dec. 15, 1970. Sent data, apparently from surface, for 58 min. |
| Luna 16 (U.S.S.R.) | Sept. 12, 1970 | Moon | Soft-landed Sept. 20, scooped up rock, returned to earth Sept. 24. |
| Zond 8 (U.S.S.R.) | Oct. 20, 1970 | Moon | Circumlunar. Photographed Moon and Earth. Returned Oct. 27, 1970. |
| Luna 17 (U.S.S.R.) | Nov. 10, 1970 | Moon | Soft-landed on Sea of Rains Nov. 17. Lunokhod 1, self-propelled vehicle, used for first time. Sent TV photos, made soil analysis, etc. |
| Mariner 8 (U.S.) | May 8, 1971 | Mars | Designed to orbit Mars. Lost, vehicle failed. |
| Mars 2 (U.S.S.R.) | May 19, 1971 | Mars | Reached Mars Nov. 27. Dropped landing capsule on surface. |
| Mars 3 (U.S.S.R.) | May 28, 1971 | Mars | Like Mars 2. Capsule landed Dec. 2. TV transmission cut short. |
| Mariner 9 (U.S.) | May 30, 1971 | Mars | First craft to orbit Mars, Nov. 13. 7,300 pictures, 1st close-ups of Mars' moon. Transmission ended Oct. 27, 1972. |
| Luna 18 (U.S.S.R.) | Sept. 2, 1971 | Moon | Crashed into Moon after 54 orbits |
| Luna 19 (U.S.S.R.) | Sept. 28, 1971 | Moon | Orbited Moon, making measurements & taking photos. Soft-landed Feb. 21 in Sea of Fertility. Returned Feb. 25 with rock samples. |
| Pioneer 10 (U.S.) | March 3, 1972 | Jupiter | 620-million-mile flight path through asteroid belt passed Jupiter Dec. 3, 1973, to give man first close-up of giant planet. In 1986, will become first man-made object to escape solar system. |
| Venera 8 (U.S.S.R.) | March 27, 1972 | Venus | Landed July 22. Sent signals for 50 min. Capsule burned or crushed because of surface heat and pressure. Sent data on atmosphere and surface. |
| Luna 21 (U.S.S.R.) | Jan. 8, 1973 | Moon | Soft-landed Jan. 16. Lunokhod 2 (moon-car) scooped up soil samples, returned them to Earth Jan. 27. |
| Pioneer 11 (U.S.) | April 6, 1973 | Jupiter | Flew by 25,000 mi. from Jupiter Dec. 1974—3 times closer than Pioneer 10. |
| Mars 4 (U.S.S.R.) | July 21, 1973 | Mars | Arrived Feb. 1974, briefly sending back photos |
| Mars 5 (U.S.S.R.) | July 25, 1973 | Mars | Sister craft of Mars 4 |
| Mars 6 (U.S.S.R.) | Aug. 5, 1973 | Mars | Scheduled to arrive March 1974. Missed. |
| Mars 7 (U.S.S.R.) | Aug. 9, 1973 | Mars | To arrive March 1974. Missed its target. |
| Mariner 10 (U.S.) | Nov. 3, 1973 | Venus, Mercury | Passed Venus Feb. 5, 1974. Arrived Mercury March 29, 1974, for man's first close-up look at planet. First time gravity of one planet (Venus) used to whip spacecraft toward another (Mercury). |
| Luna 22 (U.S.S.R.) | May 29, 1974 | Moon | Orbited Moon June 2, 1974 |
| Luna 23 (U.S.S.R.) | Oct. 28, 1974 | Moon | Crashed into Moon Nov. 6, 1974 |
| Venera 9 (U.S.S.R.) | June 14, 1975 | Venus | Venera 9 & 10 comprised a double-barreled probe. Soft-landed Oct. 25, 1976. |
| Venera 10 (U.S.S.R.) | June 14, 1975 | Venus | (See Venera 9) |
| Viking 1 (U.S.) | Aug. 20, 1975 | Mars | Carrying life-detection labs. Landed July 20, 1976 for detailed scientific research, incl. pictures. |
| Viking 2 (U.S.) | Sept. 9, 1975 | Mars | Like Viking 1. Landed Sept. 3, 1976. |
| Luna 24 (U.S.S.R.) | Aug. 9, 1976 | Moon | Soft-landed Aug. 18, 1976. Returned soil samples Aug. 22, 1976. |
| Voyager 1 (U.S.) | Sept. 5, 1977 | Jupiter, Saturn, Uranus | Designed to fly by outer planets. Encounter dates Jupiter 1979; Saturn 1981; Uranus 1986. |
| Voyager 2 (U.S.) | Sept. 20, 1977 | Jupiter, Saturn, Uranus | (Like Voyager 1) |
| Pioneer Venus 1 (U.S.) | May 20, 1978 | Venus | Designed to measure Venus atmosphere. Encounter date Dec. 4, 1978. |
| Pioneer Venus 2 (U.S.) | Aug. 8, 1978 | Venus | (Like Pioneer Venus 1) Encounter date Dec. 9, 1978. |

# Major U.S. Space Projects

## Scientific Satellites

**Applications Technology Satellite (ATS).** Series of spacecraft designed to test techniques and equipment in space for future communications, weather, and navigational systems. Weight: Approximately 700 lb Scientific equipment: 100 to 300 lb. Orbit: 6,500 miles or 22,200 miles. *ATS-1* was launched Dec. 6, 1966. *ATS-6,* the most powerful and versatile communications satellite ever developed, was launched on May 30, 1974. It is transmitting educational TV programs and health services to scores of isolated communities in Appalachia, the Rocky Mountains, and Alaska, as well as to school children and adults in 5,000 isolated villages and cities in India.

**Biosatellite.** Earth-orbiting biological laboratory, carrying a variety of plants and animals into space to determine effects of weightlessness (zero gravity). *Biosatellite 1,* launched Dec. 14, 1966, was unrecovered. *Biosatellite 2,* launched Sept. 7, 1967, was highly successful. The last in the series, *Biosatellite 3,* launched June 29, 1969, was returned to Earth because of deteriorating condition of its primate passenger.

**Explorer.** Largest group of satellites in U.S. space program, used for a variety of scientific purposes in atmosphere, ionosphere and interplanetary space. *Explorer 1,* launched July 1, 1958, was America's first successful satellite. It confirmed the existence of the Van Allen radiation belts which girdle the Earth. *Explorer 55 (Atmosphere Explorer E)* was launched Nov. 20, 1975. First Explorer weighed about 18 lb; current spacecraft average about 100 lb, but some weigh as much as 500 lb. Orbits and design vary.

**Geostationary Scientific Satellite (GEOS).** A series of satellites designed to study the magnetosphere, that region of near-Earth space where the magnetic field of the Earth still plays a dominating role. *GEOS-2,* launched July 14, 1978, for the European Space Agency (ESA), carried out the mission originally conceived for *GEOS-1,* which did not achieve proper orbit April 20, 1977, due to a premature separation of the Delta second and third stages. The *GEOS-1* mission was modified to achieve some scientific return.

**Helios.** A joint U.S.-German program to obtain new information on interplanetary space in the region close to the Sun. *Helios 1,* launched Dec. 10, 1974, flew within 28 million miles of the Sun—closer than any previous spacecraft—at times encountering temperatures hot enough to melt lead (700 degrees F). *Helios 2* was launched on Jan. 15, 1976.

**High Energy Astronomy Observatory (HEAO).** Series of space platforms designed for research in high-energy astrophysics—the domain of peculiar astronomical objects such as quasars, pulsars, and black holes in space. Weighing 2,200 lb, *HEAO-1* was launched into a 225-mile Earth orbit Aug. 12, 1977, to perform a detailed X-ray survey of the celestial sphere. *HEAO-2,* 1978; *HEAO-3,* 1979. After that, HEAO scientific instruments will be carried into space by NASA's Space Shuttle.

**Intelsat.** Series of communications satellites launched by NASA on a reimbursable basis for the Communications Satellite Corporation (Comsat) to form a commercial, worldwide communications satellite system. Comsat is the U.S. member of the 50-nation consortium that owns the Intelsat network. *Early Bird,* launched April 6, 1965, was the world's first operational commercial communications satellite. The network now is composed of more than nine satellites, furnishing communications service including telecasts for North America, Europe and Asia. The satellites are positioned about 22,000 miles above the Equator and, moving at the same speed as Earth, appear to hover permanently over one spot. *Intelsat* IVA-C was launched on May 26, 1977. *Intelsat* IVA-D was launched on Sept. 29, 1977.

**Landsat.** Series of NASA satellites conducting a variety of earth resources observations (mineralogy, geography, mapping, land use) from space. *ERTS-1* (now called *Landsat 1)* was launched July 23, 1972, into a 570-mile circular polar-orbit around Earth. Weight: 1,800 lb. *Landsat 2* (formerly called *ERTS-2)* was launched April 9, 1975. Orbiting Earth 14 times a day, Landsats scan a swath 115 miles wide in four bands of the spectrum that reveal much about Earth's natural resources that can be used to help manage them more wisely. The satellites pass over almost the entire globe every 18 days. More than 100,000 pictures have been radioed back since the first launch, showing all the U.S. repeatedly and three fourths of the world's land masses and coastal areas. Research investigators in 43 states and 48 countries use the Landsat data.

**Laser Geodynamic Satellite (LAGEOS).** Laser-carrying satellite designed to make detailed measurements of plate tectonic (continental drift) motions, regional fault motions, and the rotation and wobble of Earth. Weighing about 900 lb each, LAGEOS is a solid sphere fitted with 600 laser retroreflectors. Laser beams from ground stations are bounced off it and returned to Earth, permitting very accurate positioning of both ground station and satellite. The first *LAGEOS,* launched on May 4, 1976, is in a circular Earth orbit at 3,440 miles.

**Large Space Telescope (LST).** The LST program calls for the construction of a 10-ton telescope orbiting the Earth at a distance of 380 miles. This national facility, with a 2.4-meter (8-foot) aperture, would make possible astronomical observations 10 times deeper and with more detail than has ever been possible. It would be placed in orbit via the United States' Space Shuttle in 1981 or 1982.

**Marisat.** Series of three satellites that will make up the first Maritime Communications Satellite systems, owned by the Communications Satellite Corp. (Comsat). *Marisat I* was launched on Feb. 19, 1976, into a geosynchronous (appearing to hover over one spot on Earth) orbit. *Marisats 2* and *3* were launched June 9 and Oct. 14, 1976, respectively.

**Nimbus.** Advanced meteorological satellites for detailed global weather and atmosphere soundings. Equipped with advanced television cameras and a high resolution infrared camera system, Nimbus can provide both day and night pictures of Earth's cloud cover. *Nimbus 1* was launched Aug. 28, 1964. *Nimbus 6* was launched June 11, 1975.

**Orbiting Astronomical Observatory (OAO).** Earth-orbiting observatory, operating above the obscuring effects of Earth's atmosphere, is able to study entire celestial sphere in electromagnetic wavelengths not easily accessible from the ground. *OAO-3* carrying 11 telescopes, is heaviest U.S. unmanned satellite (4,900 lb). It was launched Aug. 21, 1972, into a nearly circular 740-mile Earth orbit.

**Orbiting Geophysical Observatory (OGO).** Large (1,000 lb) multipurpose space platforms designed to study Earth, Sun, and the interplanetary space in between. Carrying many scientific instruments, OGO has the advantage over smaller satellites of being able to observe numerous phenomena simultaneously over prolonged periods of time. *OGO 1* was launched Sept. 5, 1964, into a 13,910–92,845-mile orbit around Earth. The last *OGO* in the series was launched June 5, 1969

**Orbiting Solar Observatory (OSO).** Series of one-ton space platforms designed to study the Sun and phenomena such as solar flares above the obscuring effects of Earth's atmosphere. Most sophisticated version, *OSO-I,* was launched June 20, 1975. Carrying such instruments as X-ray and gamma-ray monitors, the OSO's have provided scientists with invaluable basic details about the functioning of the Sun. They orbit Earth at a distance of about 300 miles.

**Pegasus.** Among the heaviest (3,000 lb) of U.S. scientific satellites, with a wing-like structure spanning 96 feet. Designed to determine the frequency and depth of punctures by micrometeoroids (tiny particles of matter speeding through space faster than a bullet). Data from Pegasus helped prepare man for the Apollo lunar landing mission. *Pegasus I,* was launched Feb. 16, 1965; *Pegasus 2,* May 25, 1965; *Pegasus 3,* July 30, 1965.

**Relay.** Communications satellite system designed to demonstrate feasibility of intercontinental and transoceanic transmission of television and radio signals with a medium-altitude (up to 12,000 miles) radio-equipped satellite. *Relay I* was launched Dec. 13, 1962. *SAS-3* was launched in May 1976.

**Small Astronomy Satellite (SAS).** X-ray satellites designed to monitor the intensity of X-ray sources in our Galaxy and beyond. *SAS-1,* weighing about 400 lb, was launched Dec. 12, 1970.

**Seasat.** Series of satellites which are the first to study ocean data exclusively. It circles the globe 14 times a day. *Seasat 1* was launched June 26, 1978. Its mission is to determine if microwave instruments scanning the oceans from space can provide useful scientific data for oceanographers, meteorologists and commercial users of the seas. The spacecraft sends back information on surface winds and temperatures, currents, wave heights, ice conditions, ocean topography, and coastal storm activity.

**Synchronous Meteorological Satellite (SMS).** Series of geostationary (hovering over same spot above Earth) satellites designed to keep continuous watch on fast-changing storms, such as hurricanes and tornadoes, sending back high resolution pictures every 30 minutes. *SMS-1* was launched May 17, 1974. With the launch of a second *SMS,* on Feb. 6, 1975, day-and-night surveillance is provided over the U.S. and adjacent ocean areas.

**Syncom.** First communications satellite to be placed in a synchronous Earth orbit for global communication. Three Syncom satellites were launched between Feb. 14, 1963, and Aug. 19, 1964.

**Telstar.** Early experimental communications satellite system operated by American Telephone and Telegraph Co. *Telstar 1* was launched July 1, 1962 by NASA for AT&T on a reimbursable basis.

**Tiros.** Spectacularly successful early weather satellite system developed by NASA. *Tiros 1,* launched April 1, 1960, took more than 22,000 cloud-cover pictures in 78 days and transmitted them to ground stations. Operational system, called ITOS (Improved Tiros), is now handled by the National Oceanic and Atmospheric Administration (NOAA) of the Department of Commerce. Tiros stands for Television and Infrared Observation Satellite. Contributes significantly to early detection of hurricanes and other destructive storms. Provides weathermen with daily pictures of weather over the entire globe. Weight: Approximately 750 lb. Orbits Earth at distance of about 450 miles. *ITOS-I (TIROS-M)* was launched Jan. 23, 1970, and was deactivated by NOAA on June 17, 1971. *ITOS-H (NOAA-5)* was launched on July 29, 1976. More satellites are planned in the Tiros series.

**Transit.** Department of Defense navigational satellite system for military vessels. Consisting of four satellites, system is designed to allow ships to determine their precise position regardless of weather or time of day.

**Vanguard.** Earth-orbiting geodetic survey satellites. *Vanguard 1,* launched March 17, 1958, determined that Earth is slightly pear-shaped.

**Westar.** Domestic communications system developed by Western Union. Spacecraft are launched into a 200-by-19,500-mile Earth orbit. Program was begun in 1974, with the launch of *Westar 1* on April 13. *Westar 2* was launched Oct. 10, 1974.

## Unmanned Planetary and Lunar Programs

**Lunar Orbiter.** Series of spacecraft designed to orbit the Moon, taking pictures and obtaining data in support of the subsequent manned Apollo landings. The U.S. launched five *Lunar Orbiters* between Aug. 10, 1966 and Aug. 2, 1967.

**Mariner.** Designation for a series of unmanned spacecraft designed to fly past or orbit the planets, particularly Mercury, Venus and Mars. Mariners provided the early information on Venus and Mars. *Mariner 9,* orbiting Mars in 1971, returned the most startling photographs of that planet to date, and helped pave the way for a Viking landing in 1976.

**Pioneer.** Designation for the United States' first series of sophisticated planetary spacecraft. Two Pioneers have flown past Jupiter, and are headed for Saturn and the outer reaches of the solar system. They are providing us with the first information on the giant outer planets—Jupiter, Saturn, Uranus, Neptune and Pluto. *Pioneer Venus,* launched in 1978, is expected to provide the most detailed look yet at that cloud-shrouded planet.

**Ranger.** NASA's earliest moon exploration program. Spacecraft were designed for a crash landing on the Moon, taking pictures and returning scientific data up to the moment of impact. Provided mankind with the first closeup views of the lunar surface. The Rangers provided more than 17,000 closeup pictures, giving us more information about the Moon in a few years than in all the time that had gone before.

**Surveyor.** Series of unmanned spacecraft designed to land gently on the Moon and provide information on the surface in preparation for the manned lunar landings. Their legs were instrumented to return data on the surface hardness of the Moon. Surveyor dispelled once and for all the fear that Apollo spacecraft might sink several feet or more into the lunar dust.

**Viking.** Designation for two spacecraft designed to conduct detailed scientific examination of the planet Mars, including a search for life. Viking 1 landed on July 20, 1976; Viking 2, Sept. 3, 1976. More was learned about the Red Planet in a few short months than in all the time that had gone before. But the question of life on Mars remains unresolved.

## Manned Space Flight Projects

**Mercury.** Project Mercury, America's first manned space program, was designed to accumulate knowledge about man's capabilities in space. Mercury 7, with astronaut Gordon L. Cooper, was the longest flight. It proved conclusively that man can live and work in space for at least 34 hours, despite the high-gravity forces of launch and re-entry, and weightlessness.

**Gemini.** Gemini was an extension of Project Mercury, to determine the effects of prolonged space flight on man—two weeks or longer. "Walks in space" provided invaluable information for astronauts' later walks on the Moon. The Gemini spacecraft, twice as large as the Mercury capsule, accommodated two men.

**Apollo.** Apollo was the designation for the United States' effort to land a man on the Moon and return him safely to Earth. The goal was successfully accomplished with Apollo 11 on July 20, 1969, culminating eight years of rehearsal and centuries of dreaming. Astronauts Neil A. Armstrong and Col. Edwin E. Aldrin, Jr., scooped up and brought back the first lunar rocks ever seen on Earth—about 47 pounds. Six Apollo flights followed, ending with Apollo 17 in December, 1972. The last three Apollos carried mechanized vehicles called lunar rovers for wide-ranging surface exploration of the Moon by astronauts. The rendezvous and docking of an Apollo spacecraft with a Russian Soyuz craft in Earth orbit on July 18, 1975, closed out the Apollo program.

**Skylab.** America's first Earth-orbiting space station. Project Skylab was designed to demonstrate that men can work and live in space for prolonged periods without ill effects. Actually the spent third stage of a Saturn 5 moon rocket, Skylab measured 118 feet from stem to stern, and carried the most varied assortment of experimental equipment ever assembled in a single spacecraft. Three three-man crews visited the space stations spending more than 740 hours observing the Sun and bringing home more than 175,000 solar pictures. These were the first recordings of solar activity above Earth's obscuring atmosphere. Skylab also evaluated systems designed to gather information on Earth's resources and environmental conditions. Skylab biomedical findings indicated that man adapts well to space for at least a period of three months, provided he has a proper diet and adequately programmed exercise, sleep, work and recreation periods. Skylab orbited Earth at a distance of about 300 miles. In mid-1978, technical problems developed in the orbiting Skylab that made its future uncertain.

**Space Shuttle.** The Space Shuttle is a new manned space transportation system being developed by NASA to reduce the cost of using space for commercial, scientific, and defense needs. In effect, the Shuttle is a manned rocket which, after depositing its payload in space, can be flown back to Earth like a conventional airplane and be available for re-use. Because of its versatility and large cargo-carrying capacity, the Space Shuttle can combine missions. For example, on one trip to space the Shuttle might place a weather satellite and a scientific satellite into different orbits, and then retrieve a communications satellite and return it to Earth for servicing. Or, if the repairs required by the communications satellite were relatively simple, the Shuttle might carry technicians who would repair it in orbit. Although most of its cargoes will be unmanned, the Shuttle can serve as an inhabited Earth-orbiting laboratory for up to 30 days. Shuttle test flights began in the summer of 1977. The system is scheduled to become operational in late 1979.

# Major Soviet Space Projects

## Scientific Satellites

**Cosmos.** Cosmos appeared as a designator in 1962 to be used for explaining many different Soviet activities in space without giving specific details each time. *Cosmos 936* was launched Aug. 3, 1977.

**Elektron.** Satellites launched in pairs to map radiation belts. Apogee: 40,000 miles; perigee: 4,000 miles. Four Elektron satellites were launched in 1964.

**Intercosmos.** Russian scientific satellites carrying experiments from other countries. The announced countries participating are from the Soviet bloc. *Intercosmos I* was launched October 14, 1969. *Intercosmos 14* was launched Dec. 11, 1975.

**Oreol.** Scientific satellites designed to study the upper atmosphere. Launched jointly with France. *Oreol I* was launched in 1971; *Oreol 2,* 1973.

**Meteor.** Earth-orbiting weather satellites. Twenty-one have been launched over the past eight years, beginning with *Meteor I* in 1967. The program continues with at least 3 Meteor satellites being launched in 1977.

**Molniya.** A communications satellite appearing in a highly elliptical orbit over the same portion of Earth each day on each of its climbs to apogee (the highest point), giving good coverage to the Soviet Union. *Molniya 1* and *2* were launched October 14, 1965.

**Prognoz.** A solar irradiation and magnetosphere satellite for the study of the solar wind. The last *Prognoz* was launched Dec. 22, 1975.

**Polyot.** Earth satellites incorporating on-board propulsion systems which enable them to change their orbits. Only two have been launched to date, in 1963 and 1964.

**Sputnik.** An early designation for Soviet unmanned spacecraft. *Sputnik 1,* launched October 4, 1957, was the world's first Earth-orbiting satellite, and is considered to have ushered in the Space Age.

## Unmanned Planetary and Lunar Programs

**Luna.** Unmanned spacecraft launched to the Moon. These include lunar orbiters, lunar landers, and lunar lander return missions.

**Mars.** Unmanned spacecraft launched to explore the planet Mars. Three spacecraft, each weighing about 1,940 lb, were launched in 1962, but failed to reach their target. *Mars 4* was launched July 21, 1973, arriving at Mars in February, 1974, and briefly transmitting photographs of the planet back to Earth. *Mars 5, 6,* and *7* were launched between July 25 and August 9, 1974, but missed the planet.

**Venus (Venera).** Unmanned spacecraft launched to explore the planet Venus. The program was begun in 1961 but, out of 10 known tries, only four can be termed successful. *Venera 9* and *10* were launched June 8 and June 14, 1975, respectively. They reached Venus on Oct. 25, 1976.

**Zond.** Soviet lunar and planetary probes not otherwise designated. Zond spacecraft have been launched to Venus, Mars and the Moon.

## Manned Space Flight Programs

**Vostok.** The Soviets' first manned capsule, roughly spherical, used to place the first six cosmonauts in Earth orbit (1961–65).

**Voskhod.** Adaptation of the Vostok capsule to accommodate two and three cosmonauts. *Voskhod 1* orbited three persons, and *Voskhod 2* orbited two persons performing the world's first manned extravehicular activity.

**Soyuz.** Late-model manned spacecraft with provisions for three cosmonauts and a "working compartment" accessible through a hatch. Soyuz is the Russian word for "union". *Soyuz 24,* carrying two cosmonauts, was launched Feb. 7, 1977, and linked up with *Salyut 5* for a 17-day study. *(See* Salyut entries.)

**Salyut.** Earth-orbiting space station intended for prolonged occupancy and re-visitation by cosmonauts. They are usually launched by Soviet Proton rockets. *Salyut 1* was launched April 19, 1971, and decayed on Oct. 11, 1971. *Salyut 2,* launched April 3, 1973, malfunctioned in orbit and was never occupied. It decayed May 28, 1973. *Salyut 3,* visited by the *Soyuz 14* and *16* cosmonauts, was launched June 25, 1974, and decayed Jan. 24, 1975. *Salyut 4* was launched Dec. 26, 1974, and is still in orbit. *Soyuz 18* docked with the space station on May 24, 1975. *Salyut 5* was launched June 22, 1976. *Soyuz 19,* launched July 15, 1975, docked with the American Apollo spacecraft. An unmanned spacecraft, *Soyuz 20,* was launched Nov. 17, 1975 and docked with the *Salyut 4* on Nov. 19, 1975. *Soyuz 21,* launched July 6, 1976, docked with *Salyut 5* on July 7; mission duration was seven days, 21 hours and 54 minutes. The *Soyuz 23,* launched on Oct. 14, 1976, failed to dock with *Salyut 5,* and the mission ended after 48 hours and six minutes. *Soyuz 24,* launched on Feb. 7, 1977, docked with *Salyut 5* and returned to Earth on February 25, 1977. *Salyut 6* was launched Sept. 29, 1977. *Soyuz 25,* launched on Oct. 9, 1977, failed in an attempt to dock with *Salyut 6* and returned to Earth after 48 hrs. and 46 minutes. *Soyuz 26,* was launched on Dec. 10, 1977, and docked with *Salyut 6* on Dec. 11 and was joined by *Soyuz 27,* launched on Jan. 10, 1978. After *Soyuz 26* returned to Earth, after a record-breaking 2,-314-hour mission duration, *Soyuz 28,* launched March 2, 1978, joined *Salyut 6* and *Soyuz 27* in another multiple mission. *Soyuz 29,* launched June 15, 1978, remaining in orbit, docked with *Salyut 6* and was joined by *Soyuz 30,* launched June 27, 1978, which returned to earth on July 5, 1978.

## The American's Creed

*William Tyler Page*

"I believe in the United States of America as a government of the people, by the people, for the people; whose just powers are derived from the consent of the governed; a democracy in a republic; a sovereign Nation of many sovereign States; a perfect union, one and inseparable; established upon those principles of freedom, equality, justice, and humanity for which American patriots sacrificed their lives and fortunes.

"I therefore believe it is my duty to my country to love it, to support its Constitution, to obey its laws, to respect its flag, and to defend it against all enemies."

NOTE: William Tyler Page, Clerk of the U.S. House of Representatives, wrote "The American's Creed" in 1917. It was accepted by the House on behalf of the American people on April 3, 1918.

# Chronology of Manned Flights

| Designation and country | Date | Astronauts | Orbit: perigee/apogee (km) | Orbital period (min) | Number of orbits | Flight time (h/min) | Remarks |
|---|---|---|---|---|---|---|---|
| Vostok 1(USSR) | April 12, 1961 | Yuri A. Gagarin | 181/327 | 89.1 | 1 | 1/48 | First manned orbital flight |
| MR III(US) | May 5, 1961 | Alan B. Shepard, Jr. | — | — | (2) | 0/15 | Range 486 km (302 mi.), peak 187 km (116.5 mi.); capsule recovered |
| MR IV (US) | July 21, 1961 | Virgil I. Grissom | — | — | (2) | 0/16 | Range 487 km, peak 190 km; capsule lost |
| Vostok 2 (USSR) | Aug. 6–7, 1961 | Gherman S. Titov | 178/257 | 88.6 | 17.5 | 25/18 | First long-duration flight |
| MA VI (US) | Feb. 20, 1962 | John H. Glenn, Jr. | 161/261 | 88.5 | 3 | 4/55 | First American in orbit |
| MA VII (US) | May 24, 1962 | M. Scott Carpenter | 161/268 | 88.3 | 3 | 4/56 | Overshot landing area; otherwise fine |
| Vostok 3 (USSR) | Aug. 11–15, 1962 | Ardrian G. Nikolavev | 173/221 | 88.1 | 64 | 94/22 | Vostoks 3 and 4 approached within 5 km |
| Vostok 4 (USSR) | Aug. 12–15, 1962 | Pavel R. Popovich | 179/254 | 88.5 | 48 | 70/57 | |
| MA VIII (US) | Oct. 3, 1962 | Walter M. Schirra, Jr. | 161/283 | 88.5 | 6 | 9/13 | First splashdown close to aiming point |
| MA IX (US) | May 15–16, 1963 | L. Gordon Cooper, Jr. | 161/267 | 88.4 | 22 | 34/20 | Longest Mercury flight |
| Vostok 5 (USSR) | June 14–19, 1963 | Valery F. Bykovsky | 180/235 | 88.4 | 81 | 119/6 | Longest Russian orbital flight to date |
| Vostok 6 (USSR) | June 16–19, 1963 | Valentina V. Tereshkova | 183/233 | 88.3 | 48 | 70/50 | First orbital flight by female cosmonaut |
| Voskhod 1 (USSR) | Oct. 12, 1964 | Vladimir M. Komarov; Konstantin P. Feoktistov; Boris G. Yegorov | 177/409 | 90.1 | 16 | 24/17 | First 3-man orbital flight; also first flight without space suits |
| Voskhod 2 (USSR) | March 18, 1965 | Alexei A. Leonov; Pavel I. Belyayev | 174/495 | 90.9 | 17 | 26/2 | First "space walk" (by Leonov), 10 min |
| GT III (US) | March 23, 1965 | Virgil I. Grissom; John W. Young | 161/224 | 88.3 | 3 | 4/53 | First manned test of Gemini spacecraft |
| GT IV (US) | June 3–7, 1965 | James A. McDivitt; Edward H. White 2d | 161/282 | 89.0 | 62 | 97/48 | First American "space walk" (by White), lasting slightly over 20 min |
| GT V (US) | Aug. 21–29, 1965 | L. Gordon Cooper, Jr.; Charles Conrad, Jr. | 161/352 | 89.0 | 120 | 190/56 | Longest flight to date |
| GT VII (US) | Dec. 4–18, 1965 | Frank Borman; James A. Lovell, Jr. | 161/330 | 89.0 | 206 | 330/35 | Longest space flight to date |
| GT VI (US) | Dec. 15–16, 1965 | Walter M. Schirra, Jr.; Thomas P. Stafford | 151/258 | 88.7 | 16 | 25/52 | Orbit was extended to 298 km to make rendezvous with orbiting GT VII |
| GT VIII (US) | March 16–17, 1966 | Neil A. Armstrong; David R. Scott | 160/270 | 88.8 | 6.5 | 10/42 | Only Gemini flight cut short by malfunction: one thruster kept firing after rendezvous and docking with an orbiting Agena rocket had been accomplished |
| GT IX (US) | June 3–6, 1966 | Thomas P. Stafford; Eugene A. Cernan | 167/169 | 90.0 | 44 | 72/21 | Rendezvous (but no docking) |
| GT X (US) | July 18–21, 1966 | John W. Young; Michael Collins | 165/274 | 88.8 | 43 | 70/47 | Docking with orbiting Agena rocket |
| GT XI (US) | Sept. 12–15, 1966 | Charles Conrad, Jr.; Richard F. Gordon, Jr. | 161/281 | 89.0 | 44 | 71/17 | Docking with orbiting Agena on first orbit; apogee of orbit then extended to 1,368 km (850 mi.) |
| GT XII (US) | Nov. 11–15, 1966 | James A. Lovell, Jr.; Edwin E. Aldrin, Jr. | 161/282 | 89.0 | 59 | 94/33 | Docking with Agena visually, without computer; co-pilot outside spacecraft for total of 5½ hours |

| Designation and country | Date | Astronauts | Orbit: perigee/apogee (km) | Orbital period (min) | Number of orbits | Flight time (h/min) | Remarks |
|---|---|---|---|---|---|---|---|
| Soyuz 1 (USSR) | April 23, 1967 | Vladimir M. Komarov | 201/224 | 88.6 | 17 | 26/40 | First test of Soyuz spacecraft; crashed after re-entry, killing Komarov |
| Apollo 7 (US) | Oct. 11–22, 1968 | Walter M. Schirra, Jr.; Donn F. Eisele; R. Walter Cunningham | 233/285 | 89.9 | 163 | 260/9 | First manned test of Apollo command module; first live TV transmissions from orbit |
| Soyuz 3 (USSR) | Oct. 26–30, 1968 | Georgi T. Beregovoi | 204/224 | 88.6 | 64 | 94/51 | First manned rendezvous and possible docking by Soviet cosmonaut |
| Apollo 8 (US) | Dec. 21–27, 1968 | Frank Borman; James A. Lovell, Jr.; William A. Anders | — | — | 10[4] | 147/00 | First spacecraft in circumlunar orbit; TV transmissions from this orbit |
| Soyuz 4 (USSR) | Jan. 14–17, 1969 | Vladamir A. Shatalov | 204/224 | 88.7 | 48 | 71/14 | Rendezvoused and docked with Soyuz 5 |
| Soyuz 5 (USSR) | Jan. 15–18, 1969 | Boris V. Volynov; Alexei S. Yeliseyev; Yevgeny V. Khrunov | 208/232 | 88.8 | 49 | 72/46 | Rendezvoused and docked with Soyuz 4; Khrunov and Yeliseyev perform EVA and transfer to Soyuz 4 |
| Apollo 9 (US) | Mar. 3–13, 1969 | James A. McDivitt; David R. Scott; Russell L. Schweikart | 197/508 | 91.5 | 151 | 241/1 | First manned flight of Lunar Module |
| Apollo 10 (US) | May 18–26, 1969 | Thomas P. Stafford; Eugene A. Cernan; John W. Young | — | — | — | 192/3 | First descent to within 9 miles of Moon's surface by manned craft |
| Apollo 11 (US) | July 16–24, 1969 | Neil A. Armstrong; Edwin E. Aldrin, Jr.; Michael Collins | — | — | — | 195/18 | First manned landing and EVA on Moon; soil and rock samples collected; experiments left on lunar surface |
| Apollo 12 (US) | Nov. 14–24, 1969 | Charles Conrad, Jr.; Richard F. Gordon, Jr.; Alan Bean | — | — | — | 244/36 | Manned lunar landing mission; investigated Surveyor 3 spacecraft; collected lunar samples. EVA time: 15 h 30 min |
| Apollo 13 (US) | April 11–17, 1970 | James A. Lovell, Jr.; Fred W. Haise, Jr.; John L. Swigert, Jr. | — | — | — | 142/54 | Third manned lunar landing attempt aborted due to loss of pressure in liquid oxygen in Service Module and failure of fuel cells |
| Soyuz 6 (USSR) | Oct. 11–16, 1969 | Gorgiy Shonin; Valriy Kabasov | 186/221 | 88.4 | 80 | 118/42 | Three spacecraft and seven men put into earth orbit simultaneously for first time |
| Soyuz 7 (USSR) | Oct. 12–17, 1969 | Anatoley Filipchenko; Viktor Gorbakov; Vladislav Volkov | 206/226 | 88.6 | 80 | 118/42 | |
| Soyuz 8 (USSR) | Oct. 13–18, 1969 | Vladimir Shatalov; Aleksey Yeliseyev | 208/224 | 88.6 | 80 | 118/42 | |
| Soyuz 9 (USSR) | June 1–17, 1970 | Andreiyan Nikolayez; Vitaly Sevastianov | 236/249 | 89.3 | 287 | 424/59 | Longest manned flight in history; designed to test man's ability to withstand long periods of weightlessness |
| Apollo 14 (US) | Jan. 31–Feb. 9, 1971 | Alan B. Shepard; Stuart A. Roosa; Edgar D. Mitchell | — | — | — | 216/42 | Third manned lunar landing: returned largest amount of lunar material |

| | | | | | | | |
|---|---|---|---|---|---|---|---|
| Soyuz 10 (USSR) | April 22–24, 1971 | Vladimir A. Shatalov; Alexei S. Yeliseyev; Nikolai Rukavishnikov | 208/246 | 88.9 | — | 47/46 | Linked up for 5½ hours with orbiting space station, Salyut 1 |
| Soyuz 11 (USSR) | June 6–30, 1971 | Georgiy Tomofeyevich Dobrovolskiy; Vladislav Nikolayevich Volkov; Viktor Ivanovich Patsyev | 185/217 | 88.3 | — | 569/40 | Linked up with first space station, Salyut 1. Astronauts died just before re-entry due to loss of pressurization in spacecraft |
| Apollo 15 (US) | July 26–Aug. 7, 1971 | David R. Scott; James B. Irwin; Alfred M. Worden | — | — | — | 295/12 | Fourth manned lunar landing; first use of Lunar Rover propelled by Scott and Worden; first live pictures of LM lift-off from Moon; longest exploration time on Moon surface (18 hours) |
| Apollo 16 (US) | April 16–27, 1972 | John W. Young; Thomas K. Mattingly; Charles M. Duke, Jr. | — | — | — | 265/51 | Fifth manned lunar landing; second use of Lunar Rover Vehicle, propelled by Young and Duke. Total exploration time on the Moon was 20 h 14 min, setting new record. Mattingly's in-flight "walk in space" was 1 h 23 min. Approximately 213 lb of lunar rock returned |
| Apollo 17 (US) | Dec. 7, 1972-Dec. 19, 1972 | Eugene A. Cernan; Ronald E. Evans; Harrison H. Schmitt | — | — | — | 301/51 | Sixth and last manned lunar landing; third to carry lunar rover. Cernan and Schmitt, during three EVA's, completed total of 22 h 05 min 3 sec. USS Ticonderoga recovered crew and about 250 lbs of lunar samples. |
| SKYLAB SL-1 (US) | May 14, 1973 | — | 423/440 | 93.4 | — | — | Unmanned portion of Skylab comprised of Orbital Workshop (OWS), Airlock Module (AM), Multiple Docking Adapter (MDA), Apollo Telescope Mount (ATM), Instrument Unit (IU), and Payload Shroud (PS) |
| SKYLAB SL-2 (US) | May 25, 1973 | Charles Conrad, Jr.; Joseph P. Kerwin; Paul J. Weitz | 401/424 | 93.2 | — | 672/50 | First manned Skylab launch. Objectives: Establish the Skylab Orbital Assembly in Earth orbit, occupy it and conduct a series of scientific experiments and medical experiments associated with long-duration manned space flight. |
| SKYLAB SL-3 (US) | July 28, 1973 | Alan L. Bean, Jr.; Jack R. Lousma; Owen K. Garriott | 401/424 | 93.2 | — | 1427/9 | Second manned Skylab launch. New crew remained in space for 59 days, continuing scientific and medical experiments and earth observations from orbit. |
| SKYLAB SL-4 (US) | Nov. 16, 1973 | Gerald Carr; Edward Gibson William Pogue | 401/424 | 93.2 | — | 2017/16 | Third manned Skylab launch; obtained medical data on crew for use in extending the duration of manned space flight; crews "walked in space" 4 times, totaling 44 h 40 min. Splashdown in Pacific, Feb. 9, 1974. |

| Designation and country | Date | Astronauts | Orbit: perigee/apogee (km) | Orbital period (min) | Number of orbits | Flight time (h/min) | Remarks |
|---|---|---|---|---|---|---|---|
| Soyuz 12 (USSR) | Sept. 27, 1973 | Vasily G. Lazarev; Oleg K. Makarov | 202/231 | 88.7 | — | 50/12 | Two-day test flight. First Soviet manned flight since ill-fated Soyuz 11. |
| Soyuz 13 (USSR) | Dec. 18, 1973 | Pyotr Klimuk; Valentin Lebedev | 188/246 | 88.9 | — | 188/55 | Modified spacecraft to be used for rendezvous with U.S. spacemen in 1975 |
| Soyuz 14 (USSR) | July 3, 1974 | Pavel Popovich; Yuri Artyukhin | 201/338 | 89.9 | — | 377/29 | Crewmen spent two weeks on board Soviet space station Salyut 3 |
| Soyuz 15 (USSR) | Aug. 26, 1974 | Lt. Col. Sarafanov; Lev Demin | 188/210 | 88.5 | — | 48/12 | Overshot Salyut 4 space station and failed to dock. Cosmonauts returned to earth. |
| Soyuz 16 (USSR) | Dec. 2, 1974 | Col. Filipchenck, Nikolay Rukavishnikov | 194/280 | 89.3 | — | 142/24 | Docked with Salyut 4 |
| Soyuz 17 (USSR) | Jan. 11, 1975 | Col. Aleksey Gubarev; Georgi Grechko | | | | 709/20 | Crew spent 30 days in Salyut 4 space station, which was launched Dec. 26, 1974 and placed in Earth orbit |
| Soyuz 18 (USSR) | May 24, 1975 | Lt. Col. Pyotr Klimuk; Vitaly Sevastyanov | 198/229 | 88.6 | — | — | Second Soviet crew to visit orbiting space station Salyut 4 |
| Apollo/Soyuz Test Project (US and USSR) | July 15, 1975 (US) | U.S.: Brig. Gen. Thomas P. Stafford, Vance D. Brand, Donald K. Slayton | 152/166 | 87.7<br>89.0<br>(docked) | 138<br>(docked) | 216/05 | World's first international manned rendezvous and docking in space; aimed at developing a space rescue capability. |
| | July 16, 1975 (USSR) | USSR: Col. A. A. Leonov, V. N. Kubasov | 191/218 | 91.0<br>89.0<br>(docked) | 138<br>(docked) | 223/35 | Apollo and Soyuz docked and crewmen exchanged visits on July 17, 1975. Mission duration for Soyuz: 142 h 31 min. For Apollo: 217 h, 28 min. |
| Soyuz 21 (USSR) | July 6, 1976 | Col. Boris Volynov; Lt. Col. Vitali Zholobov | 114/409 | 89.7 | — | 1218/24 | Crew spent 50 days aboard Salyut 5 space station, which was launched June 22, 1976 |
| Soyuz 22 (USSR) | Sept. 15, 1976 | Col. V. Bykovskiy; V. V. Aksenov | 251/257 | 85.1 | — | 189/54 | Flight believed to have been for purpose of intensive photography of Earth |
| Soyuz 23 (USSR) | Oct. 14, 1976 | Col. V. D. Zudov; Lt. Col. Rozhdostvenskity | 118/224 | 88.6 | — | 48/6 | Failed attempted docking with Salyut 5 and returned to Earth |
| Soyuz 24 (USSR) | Feb. 7, 1977 | Col. V. Gorbatko; Lt. Col. Yuri Glaszkov | 173/323 | 89.5 | — | 425/23 | Docked and transferred to Salyut 5 on Feb. 8. Returned Feb. 25 |
| Soyuz 25 (USSR) | Oct. 9, 1977 | Lt. Col. Kavalenak; V. Ryomin | — | — | — | 48/46 | Failed docking with Salyut 6 |
| Soyuz 26 (USSR) | Dec. 10, 1977 | Lt. Col. Romanenko; G. Grechko | — | — | — | 2314/0 | Record-breaking duration |
| Soyuz 27 (USSR) | Jan. 10, 1978 | Vladim Dzhanibekov; Oleg Makarov | — | — | — | 142/0 | Multiple mission with Soyuz 26 and Salyut 6 |
| Soyuz 28 (USSR) | March 2, 1978 | Aleksey Gubarev; Vladimir Remek | — | — | — | 190/17 | Multiple mission with Soyuz 27 and Salyut 6 |
| Soyuz 29 (USSR) | June 15, 1978 | Col. V. Kovalenok; A. Ivanchenkov | — | — | — | — | Still in orbit |
| Soyuz 30 (USSR) | June 27, 1978 | Pyotr Klimvk; Miroslaw Giermaszewski | — | — | — | — | Docked with Salyut 6 and Soyuz 29. Returned July 5, 1978. |

1. Ground level. 2. Suborbital flight. 3. Approximate time. 4. Number of orbits around moon. NOTE: The letters MR stand for Mercury (capsule) and Redstone (rocket); MA, for Mercury and Atlas (rocket); GT, for Gemini (capsule) and Titan-II (rocket). The first astronaut listed in the Gemini and Apollo flights is the command pilot. The Mercury capsules had names: MR-III was *Freedom 7*, MR-IV was *Liberty Bell 7*, MA-VI was *Friendship 7*, MA-VII was *Aurora 7*, MA-VIII was *Sigma 7*, and MA-IX was *Faith 7*. The figure 7 referred to the fact that the first group of U.S. astronauts numbered seven men. Only one Gemini capsule had a name: GT-III was called *Molly Brown* (after the Broadway musical *The Unsinkable Molly Brown*); thereafter the practice of naming the capsules was discontinued.

## NASA Launch Vehicles

| | Scout | Thor-Agena D | Delta | Atlas-Agena D | Atlas-Centaur | Titan 3E/Centaur | Saturn I | Uprated Saturn I | Saturn V |
|---|---|---|---|---|---|---|---|---|---|
| Overall height (ft) | 68 | 76.3 | 90 | 91 | 100 | 109[2] | 190[2] | 225[2] | 365[2] |
| Overall weight (lb) | 38,500 | — | 114,200 | — | 300,000 | 300,000 | 1,165,000 | 1,300,000 | 6,200,000 |
| Payload capacity (lb) | 240 | 1,600 | 380/150[1] | 5,950 | 8,500/2,300[1] | 7,000 | 22,500 | 40,000 | 285,000/100,000[1] |
| First stage | Algol IIB | DM-21 | DM-21 | Atlas D | Atlas D | — | S-I | S-IB | S-IC |
| Length (ft) | 30.8 | 55.9 | 55.9 | 67.4 | 75 | 71 | 82 | 80 | 138 |
| Diameter (ft) | 4 | 8 | 8 | 10 | 10 | 10 | 21.6 | 21.6 | 33 |
| Thrust (lb) | 88,000 | 170,000 | 170,000 | 388,000 | 388,000 | 430,000 | 1,504,000 | 1,600,000 | 7,500,000 |
| Second stage | Castor | Agena D | — | Agena D | Centaur | — | S-IV | S-IVB | S-II |
| Length (ft) | 20.7 | 20.9 | 20.6 | 20.9 | 32 | 19 | 40 | 59 | 80 |
| Diameter (ft) | 31 in. | 5 | 4.3 | 5 | 10 | 10 | 18 | 21.7 | 33 |
| Thrust (lb) | 61,000 | 16,000 | 7,500 | 16,000 | 30,000 | 100,000 | 90,000 | 200,000 | 1,000,000 |
| Third stage | Antares X-259 | — | Altair | — | — | — | — | — | S-IVB |
| Length (ft) | 11.5 | — | 59 in. | — | — | — | — | — | 59 |
| Diameter (in.) | 30 | — | 18 | — | — | — | — | — | 21.7 |
| Thrust (lb) | 23,000 | — | 5,800 | — | — | — | — | — | 200,000 |
| Fourth stage | Altair | — | — | — | — | — | — | — | — |
| Length (in.) | 59 | — | — | — | — | — | — | — | — |
| Diameter (in.) | 18 | — | — | — | — | — | — | — | — |
| Thrust (lb) | 5,800 | — | — | — | — | — | — | — | — |
| Programs | Explorer, San Marco, re-entry, probes, ISIS, ESRO | Alouette, OGO, Nimbus, Sert II, PAGEOS | Biosatellite, OSO, Explorer, Tiros, Syncom, Relay, ESSA, Telstar, TOS, Ariel, Pioneer, Early Bird, Nimbus | Lunar Orbiter, OAO, Mariner Ranger, OGO, ATS | Mariner, Surveyor Pioneer | Gemini, Viking, Voyager | Apollo (unmanned tests), Pegasus | Apollo (Earth orbit tests, including manned Apollo 7) | Apollo (moon flights) |

1. Payload capacity for escape of earth's gravity; first entry is earth orbit capacity. 2. Height includes payload.

# MILITARY

## U.S. Armed Forces Personnel

| Year | Army | Air Force[1] | Navy | Marines | Men[2] | Women[2] | Coast Guard[3] |
|---|---|---|---|---|---|---|---|
| 1940 | 269,023 | — | 160,997 | 28,345 | 456,984 | 1,381 | 13,621 |
| 1941 | 1,462,315 | — | 284,427 | 54,359 | 1,794,997 | 6,104 | 19,036 |
| 1942 | 3,075,608 | — | 640,570 | 142,613 | 3,844,538 | 14,253 | 58,998 |
| 1943 | 6,994,472 | — | 1,741,750 | 308,523 | 8,918,574 | 126,171 | 154,976 |
| 1944 | 7,994,750 | — | 2,981,365 | 475,604 | 11,241,173 | 210,542 | 169,264 |
| 1945 | 8,267,958 | — | 3,380,817 | 474,680 | 11,858,499 | 265,006 | 171,518 |
| 1946 | 1,891,011 | — | 983,398 | 155,679 | 2,972,081 | 58,007 | 29,736 |
| 1947 | 991,285 | — | 498,661 | 93,053 | 1,563,241 | 19,758 | 18,972 |
| 1950 | 593,167 | 411,277 | 381,538 | 74,279 | 1,438,192 | 22,069 | 23,190 |
| 1951 | 1,531,774 | 788,381 | 736,680 | 192,620 | 3,209,830 | 39,625 | 29,000 |
| 1955 | 1,109,296 | 959,946 | 660,695 | 205,170 | 2,899,916 | 35,191 | 28,500 |
| 1957 | 997,994 | 919,835 | 677,108 | 200,861 | 2,763,625 | 32,173 | 28,322 |
| 1959 | 861,964 | 840,435 | 626,340 | 175,571 | 2,472,456 | 31,718 | 29,984 |
| 1962 | 1,066,404 | 884,025 | 666,428 | 190,962 | 2,775,606 | 32,213 | 31,500 |
| 1966 | 1,199,784 | 887,353 | 745,205 | 261,716 | 3,061,469 | 32,589 | 34,767 |
| 1968 | 1,570,343 | 904,850 | 765,457 | 307,252 | 3,509,505 | 38,397 | 36,534 |
| 1969 | 1,512,169 | 862,353 | 775,869 | 309,771 | 3,420,656 | 39,506 | 38,331 |
| 1970 | 1,322,548 | 791,349 | 692,660 | 259,737 | 3,024,815 | 41,479 | 38,172 |
| 1971 | 1,123,810 | 755,300 | 623,248 | 212,369 | 2,671,952 | 42,775 | 38,029 |
| 1972 | 810,960 | 725,838 | 588,043 | 198,238 | 2,278,046 | 45,033 | 37,866 |
| 1973 | 800,812 | 688,414 | 566,953 | 193,602 | 2,249,781 | n.a. | 36,588 |
| 1974 | 779,642 | 646,624 | 542,737 | 187,200 | 2,151,203 | 69,229 | 36,407 |
| 1975 | 778,792 | 623,209 | 548,369 | 194,730 | 2,145,100 | 89,714 | 35,952 |
| 1976 | 771,301 | 595,650 | 527,296 | 193,409 | 1,982,460 | 107,196 | 37,898 |
| 1977 | 778,839 | 580,185 | 528,700 | 188,938 | 2,076,662 | 114,254 | 38,918 |
| 1978[4] | 769,627 | 573,862 | 524,573 | 190,397 | 1,940,676 | 119,724 | 38,059[5] |

1. Before July 26, 1947, when the National Military Establishment was established, the Air Force was a part of the Army. 2. Not including Coast Guard personnel. 3. In peacetime, Coast Guard operates under Dept. of Transportation; in time of war or at direction of President, it is attached to Navy Dept. 4. Preliminary figures as of March 31. 5. As of Jan. 31. Includes 761 women. NOTE: n.a. = not available. *Sources:* Department of Defense and the Coast Guard.

## History of the Armed Services

*Source:* Department of Defense.

### U.S. Army

On June 14, 1775, the Continental Congress "adopted" the New England Army—a mixed force of militia and volunteers besieging the British in Boston—by appointing a committee to draft "Rules and regulations for the government of the Army" and voting to raise 10 rifle companies as a reinforcement. The next day, it appointed Washington commander-in-chief of the "Continental forces to be raised for the defense of liberty," and he took command at Boston on July 3, 1775. The Continental Army that fought the Revolution was our first national military organization, and hence the Army is the senior service. After the war, the Continental Army was radically reduced but enough survived to form a small Regular Army of about 700 men under the Constitution in 1789, a nucleus for expansion in the 1970s to successfully meet threats from the Indians and from France. From these humble beginnings, the U.S. Army has developed, normally expanding rapidly by absorbing citizen soldiers in wartime and contracting just as rapidly after each war.

### U.S. Navy

The antecedents of the U.S. Navy go back to September 1775, when Gen. Washington commissioned 7 schooners and brigantines to prey on British supply vessels bound for the Colonies or Canada. In Oct. 1775, a motion in the Continental Congress called for the construction of 2 vessels for the purpose of intercepting enemy transports. With its passage a Naval Committee of 7 men was formed, and they rapidly obtained passage of legislation calling for construction of additional vessels. The Continental Navy was supplemented by privateers and ships operated as state navies, but soon after the British surrender it was disestablished.

In 1794, because of dissatisfaction with the payment of tribute to the Barbary pirates, Congress authorized construction of 6 frigates. The first, *United States,* was launched May 10, 1797, but the Navy still remained under the control of the Secretary of War until April 1798, when the Secretary of the Navy was given full Cabinet rank and the U.S. Navy came into its own.

## U.S. Air Force

Until creation of the National Military Establishment in September 1947, which united the services under one department, military aviation was a part of the U.S. Army. In the Army, aeronautical operations came under the Signal Corps from 1907 to 1918, when the U.S. Air Service was established. In 1926, the U.S. Air Corps came into being and remained until 1942, when the Army Air Forces succeeded it as the Army's air arm. In 1947, the U.S. Air Force was established as an independent military service under the National Military Establishment. At that time, the name "Army Air Forces" was abolished.

## U.S. Coast Guard

Our country's oldest continuous seagoing service, the U.S. Coast Guard, traces its history back to 1790, when the first Congress authorized the construction of ten vessels for the collection of revenue. Known first as the Revenue Marine, and later as the Revenue Cutter Service, the Coast Guard received its present name in 1915 under an act of Congress combining the Revenue Cutter Service with the Life-Saving Service. In 1939, the Lighthouse Service was also consolidated with this unit. The Bureau of Marine Inspection and Navigation was transferred temporarily to the Coast Guard in 1942, permanently in 1946. Through its antecedents, the Coast Guard is one of the oldest organizations under the federal government and, until the Navy Department was established in 1798, served as the only U.S. armed force afloat. In times of peace, it operates under the Department of Transportation, serving as the nation's primary agency for promoting marine safety and enforcing federal maritime laws. In times of war, or on direction of the President, it is attached to the Navy Department.

## U.S. Marine Corps

Founded in 1775 and observing its official birthday on Nov. 10, the U.S. Marine Corps was developed to serve on land, on sea, and in the air.

Marines have fought in every U.S. war. From an initial two battalions in the Revolution, the Corps reached a peak strength of six divisions and five aircraft wings in World War II. Its present strength is three active divisions and aircraft wings and a Reserve division/aircraft wing team. In 1947, the National Security Act set Marine Corps strength at not less than three divisions and three aircraft wings.

# Service Academies

## U.S. Military Academy

*Source:* U.S. Military Academy.

Established in 1802 by an act of Congress, the U.S. Military Academy is located on the west bank of the Hudson River some 50 miles north of New York City. To gain admission a candidate must first secure a nomination from an authorized source. These sources, and the number of cadetships allocated to each, are:

### Congressional

| | |
|---|---|
| Representatives | 5 each |
| Senators | 5 each |
| Other: Vice Presidential | 5 |
| District of Columbia | 5 |
| Puerto Rico | 6 |
| Am. Samoa, Canal Zone, Guam, Virgin Is. | 1 each |

### Military-Service-Connected Nominations (Each Class)

| | |
|---|---|
| Presidential | 100 |
| Enlisted members of Army | 85 |
| Enlisted members of Army Reserve/ National Guard | 85 |
| Sons and daughters of deceased and disabled veterans (approximately) | 10 |
| Honor military, naval schools and ROTC | 20 |
| Sons and daughters of persons awarded the Medal of Honor | (unlimited) |

Any number of applicants can meet the requirements for a *nomination* in these categories. *Appointments* (offers of admission), however, can only be made to the number of applicants shown above.

Candidates may be nominated for vacancies during the year preceding the day of admission, which occurs in early July. The best time to apply is during the junior year in high school.

Candidates must be citizens of the U.S., be unmarried, be at least 17 but not yet 22 years old on July 1 of the year admitted, have a secondary-school education or its equivalent, and be able to meet the academic, medical, and physical aptitude requirements. Academic qualification is determined by an analysis of entire scholastic record, and performance on either the American College Testing (ACT) Assessment Program Test or the College Entrance Examination Board Scholastic Aptitude Test (SAT). Entrance requirements and procedures for appointment are described in the Admissions Bulletin, available without charge from Admissions, U.S. Military Academy, West Point, N.Y. 10996.

Cadets are members of the Regular Army. As such they receive full scholarships and annual salaries from which they pay for their uniforms, textbooks, and incidental expenses. Upon successful completion of the four-year course, the graduate receives the degree of Bachelor of Science and is commissioned a second lieutenant in the Regular Army with a requirement to serve as an officer for a minimum of five years.

## U.S. Naval Academy

*Source:* U.S. Naval Academy.

The Naval School, established in 1845 at Fort Severn, Annapolis, Md., was renamed the U.S. Naval Academy in 1850. A four-year course was adopted a year later.

The Superintendent is an admiral. A civilian academic dean heads the academic program. A rear admiral captain heads the 4,200-man Brigade of Midshipmen and military, professional, and physical training. The faculty is half military and half civilian.

Graduates are awarded the Bachelor of Science or Bachelor of Science in Engineering and are commissioned as officers in the U.S. Navy or Marine Corps.

The primary avenues to selection for appointment as midshipmen follow. Congressmen, the Vice President, the Mayor of Washington, D. C., and the Resident Commissioner of Puerto Rico may each have 5 midshipmen at the Academy at any one time. Ten candidates may be nominated for each vacancy. Well over half of the more than 1,300 appointments as midshipmen made annually originate from these sources.

The President appoints the 65 best-qualified sons and daughters of deceased or disabled veterans, or sons and daughters of prisoners of war or servicemen missing in action, and the 100 best-qualified sons and daughters of officers and enlisted men in the regular Armed Services. He also appoints sons and daughters of Medal of Honor holders.

The Secretary of the Navy awards 170 (85 + 85) appointments to regular and reserve personnel of the Navy or Marine Corps; 150 to congressional alternate nominees, all on a competitive, best-qualified basis; and 20 outstanding graduates of NROTC or Honor Naval and Military Schools. He may also make additional appointments each year, to bring the Brigade up to authorized strength, from among qualified congressional and competitive nominees, again on a best-qualified basis. Three fourths of these additional appointments must, by law, be congressional nominees.

There are also limited numbers of appointments available from the Philippines, Canal Zone, Virgin Islands, Guam, American Samoa, and the American republics.

To have basic eligibility for admission, candidates must be citizens of the U.S., of good moral character, at least 17 and not more than 22 years of age on July 1 of their entering year, in the top 40% of their high school class, and unmarried.

In order to be considered for admission, a candidate must obtain a nomination from one of the sources of appointments listed above. The Admissions Board at the Naval Academy examines the candidate's school record, College Board or ACT scores, recommendations from school officials, extracurricular activities, and evidence from other sources concerning his or her character, leadership potential, academic preparation, and physical fitness. Qualification for admission is based on all of the above factors.

Tuition, board, lodging, and medical and dental care are provided. Midshipmen receive $317.10 a month for books, uniforms, and personal needs.

For a catalogue or answers to specific questions, write: Superintendent, U.S. Naval Academy, (Attention: Candidate Guidance), Annapolis, Md. 21402.

## U.S. Air Force Academy

*Source:* U.S. Air Force Academy.

The bill establishing the Air Force Academy was signed by President Eisenhower on April 1, 1954. The first class of 306 cadets was sworn in on July 11, 1955, at Lowry Air Force Base, Denver, the Academy's temporary location. The Cadet Wing moved into the Academy's permanent home north of Colorado Springs in 1958.

Cadets receive four years of academic, military, and physical education to prepare them for leadership as officers in the Air Force. The Academy is authorized a total of 4,417 cadets. Each new class averages 1,500. This includes approximately 1,350 men and 150 women. The candidates for the Academy must be at least 17 but less than 22 on July 1 of the year for which they seek admission, must be a United States citizen, be single, and be able to meet the mental and physical requirements. A candidate is required to take the following examinations and tests: (1) the Service Academies' Qualifying Medical Examination; (2) either the American College Testing (ACT) Assessment Program test or the College Entrance Examination Board Scholastic Aptitude Test (SAT), and (3) a Physical Aptitude Examination.

Cadets receive their entire education at Government expense and, in addition, are paid one half the pay of a second lieutenant. From this sum, they pay for their uniforms, textbooks, tailoring, laundry, entertainment tickets, etc. Upon completion of the four-year course, leading to a Bachelor of Science degree, a cadet who meets the physical qualifications is commissioned a second lieutenant in the regular U.S. Air Force. Many go on to pilot or aerospace training. For details on admissions, write: Director of Cadet Admissions, USAF Academy, Colo. 80840.

## U.S. Coast Guard Academy

*Source:* U.S. Coast Guard Academy.

The U.S. Coast Guard Academy, New London, Conn., was founded on July 31, 1876, to serve as the "School of Instruction" for the Revenue Cutter Service, predecessor to the Coast Guard.

The J.C. Dobbin, a converted schooner, housed the first Coast Guard Academy, and was succeeded in 1878 by the barque Chase, a ship built for cadet training. First winter quarters were in a sail loft at New Bedford, Mass. The school was moved in 1900 to Curtis Bay, Md., to provide a more technical education, and in 1910 was moved back to New England to Fort Trumbull, New London, Conn. In 1932 the Academy moved to its present location in New London.

The Academy today offers a four-year curriculum for the professional and academic training of cadets, which leads to a Bachelor of Science degree and a commission as ensign in the Coast Guard.

Cadets receive appointment through nationwide competition, which includes either the December administration of the College Entrance Examination Board tests, or the American College Testing (ACT) Program tests. Applications must be submitted to the Coast Guard not later than December 15 and to the College Entrance Examination Board, 30 days prior to the tests.

Women were admitted to the Coast Guard Academy for the first time during 1976 as members of the Class of 1980. Candidates must be between 17 and 22 years of age, physically sound, and unmarried. They must agree to remain unmarried until graduation and to serve at least five years on active duty. Cadets receive $4,140 per year to cover their uniform and incidental expenses and are furnished their rations and quarters. Applications may be made to Director of Admissions, U.S. Coast Guard Academy, New London, Conn. 06320.

## U.S. Merchant Marine Academy

*Source:* U.S. Merchant Marine Academy.

The U.S. Merchant Marine Academy, situated at Kings Point, N.Y., on the south shore of Long Island Sound, was dedicated Sept. 30, 1943. It is maintained by the Department of Commerce under direction of the Maritime Administration.

The Academy has a complement of 1,000 men and women representing every state, D.C., the Canal Zone, Puerto Rico, Guam, American Samoa, and the Virgin Islands. It is also authorized to admit up to 12 candidates from Central and South America.

Competitive examinations are held annually among candidates nominated by Senators and members of the House of Representatives. Appointments to the Academy are governed by a state and territory quota system based on population and the results of the College Entrance Examination Board tests.

A candidate must be a citizen not less than 17 and not yet 22 years of age by July 1 of the year in which admission is sought. Fifteen high school credits, including 3 units in mathematics (from algebra, geometry and/or trigonometry), 1 unit in science (physics or chemistry) and 3 in English are required.

The course is four years and includes one year of practical training aboard a merchant ship. Study includes marine engineering including nuclear studies, navigation, satellite navigation and communications, electricity, ship construction, naval science and tactics, economics, business, languages, history, etc.

Upon completion of the course of study, a graduate receives a Bachelor of Science degree, a license as a merchant marine deck or engineering officer, and a commission as an ensign in the Naval Reserve.

# The National Guard

*Source:* Departments of the Army and the Air Force, National Guard Bureau.

The National Guard of the U.S. originated with the Old North and East Regiments of the Colonial Militia in Massachusetts in 1636. It is the oldest military force in the country. Guardsmen have served overseas in every major conflict in which the U.S. has participated.

As of Feb. 28, 1977, the Army and Air National Guard totaled about 448,282 men and women serving in 5,907 Army and Air units in all 50 states, Puerto Rico, the Virgin Islands, and the District of Columbia.

In peacetime, the National Guard is commanded by the governors of the respective states/territories and may be called to state active duty by the governor to assist in state emergencies, disasters, and civil disturbances. During a war or national emergency, the National Guard may be called to active duty by the President or Congress. The National Guard serves as the primary source of augmentation for the Army and the Air Force.

Budget requests for fiscal 1979 are $1.6 billion for the Army National Guard and $1.2 billion for the Air National Guard. Additional money is appropriated directly for the National Guard by the states. Substantial support is also provided by state, county, and municipal governments in land, police and fire protection, maintenance of roads, and the provision of direct county and municipal fiscal support to local units.

The Army National Guard provides 30% of the Army's entire organized structure and about 46% of its combat elements. That support consists of 8 combat divisions, 17 separate combat brigades and 4 brigades that round out active component divisions, 4 armored cavalry units, 2 special forces groups, 1 infantry group arctic recon, 15 major command headquarters, and 1,122 other separate battalions, companies, headquarters, and detachments.

Army National Guard forces are an integral part of the nation's first-line defenses. For example, the 29th Infantry Brigade in the Hawaii National Guard is a round-out brigade for the active Army's 25th Infantry Division. Under the round-out concept, National Guard units work and train with the active Army unit to which they would be assigned upon mobilization. Under the total force policy, the program for increasing readiness is continually being improved. In 1978, 44 Army National Guard units will deploy overseas to participate in realistic contingency mission-oriented training. Three of these units will participate in an exchange with units from England and Norway, and selected individuals from other units with a NATO contingency mission will participate in orientation training in Germany. In order to improve readiness of the individual soldier, a modified Skill Qualification Training (Test) Program is being phased-in during 1978. National Guard units take part in Joint Chiefs of Staff and Army exercises with the active forces to further develop the readiness of both units and individuals.

The Air National Guard has 91 flying units and 231 specialized ground support units which, upon mobilization, would be gained by one of six major commands of the USAF. The gaining major commands are Tactical Air Command (TAC), Strategic Air Command (SAC), Military Airlift Command (MAC), Air Force Communications Service (AFCS), Pacific Air Forces (PACAF), and Air Defense Command (ADC).

Within the Air National Guard force are tactical fighter, tactical airlift, tactical reconnaissance, tactical electronic warfare, tactical air support, interceptor, defense system evaluation, strategic air refueling, and rescue-and-recovery flying units. These are supported by communications, flight facilities, tactical air control, electronics installation, civil engineering, medical, and weather units.

The National Guard is administered by the National Guard Bureau, a joint Army and Air Force office in the Pentagon. Chief of the Bureau is Maj. Gen. LaVern E. Weber of Oklahoma.

The Army National Guard offers its young men and women a broad spectrum of educational opportunities. These not only include skill training associated with their military assignment, but in many instances embrace civilian occupations as well. The list of skills is not limited to those that are equipment oriented but includes management, medical, and other career fields. Some of these educational opportunities may even be pursued in civilian institutions, specifically that of the Clinical Specialist, which is compatible with a Licensed

Practical Nurse or Licensed Vocational Nurse.

Participation in the military education system by Army National Guard personnel is not limited to initial entry-skill-level training. There are opportunities available to become a qualified aviator, improve managerial and leadership abilities through attendance at courses designed for the functioning middle managers, and, finally, there are the courses offered at the prestigious Senior Service Colleges that address the needs of personnel at the executive level and positions of greater responsibilities.

If openings exist, young men and women between the ages of 17 and 35 may enlist for a period of six years. In certain circumstances the period of active participation may be less than six years. Upon enlistment, they serve a minimum of 12 weeks on active duty, training with the U.S. Army or the U.S. Air Force, depending upon which branch of the National Guard they choose. The remainder of their six weeks is spent in part-time training with their Guard unit.

A woman between the ages of 17 and 35 who has no previous military experience may also enlist in the National Guard for a period of six years. Women in the Army National Guard will receive basic training at either Fort McClellan, Ala., or Fort Jackson, S.C.; women in the Air National Guard train at Lackland Air Force Base, Tex. Advanced individual training will be received at an appropriate training center. Pay, promotion, and retirement benefits are the same as for men.

A Guardsman receives a full day's pay of his military rank for each unit assembly he attends. Additionally, he receives a day's pay of his military rank for each day of his 15 days of annual training, plus any other days on active duty for training at military schools or special assignments. All such training counts toward retirement eligibility at age 60 with 20 or more years of service.

## Pay Grades of Commissioned Officers and Warrant Officers

| Rank | | | |
|---|---|---|---|
| Army, Air Force, and Marine Corps | Navy, Coast Guard, and National Oceanic and Atmospheric Adm. (NOAA) | Public Health Service | Pay grade |
| General | Admiral[1] | — | 0–10 |
| Lieutenant General | Vice Admiral | — | 0–9 |
| Major General | Rear Admiral (upper half) | Surgeon General; Deputy Surgeon General; Assistant Surgeon General | 0–8 |
| Brigadier General | Rear Admiral (lower half) and Commodore | Assistant Surgeon General | 0–7 |
| Colonel | Captain | Director Grade | 0–6 |
| Lieutenant Colonel | Commander | Senior Grade | 0–5 |
| Major | Lieutenant Commander | Full Grade | 0–4 |
| Captain | Lieutenant | Senior Assistant Grade | 0–3 |
| First Lieutenant | Lieutenant (junior grade) | Assistant Grade | 0–2 |
| Second Lieutenant | Ensign | Junior Assistant Grade | 0–1 |
| Chief Warrant Officer | Chief Warrant Officer[1] | — | W–4 |
| Chief Warrant Officer | Warrant Officer[1] | — | W–3 |
| Chief Warrant Officer | Warrant Officer[1] | — | W–2 |
| Warrant Officer | Warrant Officer[1] | — | W–1 |

1. Not applicable to National Oceanic and Atmospheric Administration (NOAA). *Source:* Department of Defense.

## Pay Grades of Enlisted Personnel

| Army ranks[1] | Air Force ranks | Marine ranks | Navy and Coast Guard ranks | Pay grades |
|---|---|---|---|---|
| Command Sergeant Major and Staff Sergeant Major | Chief Master Sergeant | Sergeant Major and Master Gunnery Sergeant | Master Chief Petty Officer | E-9 |
| 1st Sergeant and Master Sergeant | Senior Master Sergeant | 1st Sergeant and Master Sergeant | Senior Chief Petty Officer | E-8 |
| Sergeant 1st Class | Master Sergeant | Gunnery Sergeant | Chief Petty Officer | E-7 |
| Staff Sergeant | Technical Sergeant | Staff Sergeant | Petty Officer 1st Class | E-6 |
| Sergeant | Staff Sergeant | Sergeant | Petty Officer 2nd Class | E-5 |
| Corporal | Sergeant | Corporal | Petty Officer 3rd Class | E-4 |
| Private 1st Class | Airman 1st Class | Lance Corporal | Seaman | E-3 |
| Private | Airman | Private 1st Class | Seaman Apprentice | E-2 |
| Private | Airman/Basic | Private | Seaman Recruit | E-1 |

1. Army specialist pay grades correspond to numbers: Specialist 4 (E-4), etc. *Source:* Department of Defense

# Monthly Basic Pay and Allowance for Quarters Rates by Pay Grades

| Pay Grade | Pay rates: Years of service: Under 2 | 2 | 3 | 4 | 6 | 8 | 10 | 12 | 14 | 16 | 18 | 20 | 22 | 26 | Allowance for quarters: Without dependents: Full rate[1] | Partial rate[2] | With dependents |
|---|---|---|---|---|---|---|---|---|---|---|---|---|---|---|---|---|---|
| **COMMISSIONED OFFICERS** | | | | | | | | | | | | | | | | | |
| 0–10[3] | $ 3,126.30 | $3,236.40 | $3,236.40 | $3,236.40 | $3,236.40 | $3,360.30 | $3,360.30 | $3,618.00 | $3,618.00 | $3,876.60 | $3,876.60 | $4,136.10[4] | $4,136.10[4] | $4,393.80[4] | $339.30 | $50.70 | $424.20 |
| 0–9 | 2,770.80 | 2,843.70 | 2,904.00 | 2,904.00 | 2,904.00 | 2,978.10 | 2,978.10 | 3,101.40 | 3,101.40 | 3,360.30 | 3,360.30 | 3,618.00 | 3,618.00 | 3,876.60 | 339.30 | 50.70 | 424.20 |
| 0–8 | 2,509.50 | 2,584.80 | 2,646.30 | 2,646.30 | 2,646.30 | 2,843.70 | 2,843.70 | 2,978.10 | 2,978.10 | 3,101.40 | 3,236.40 | 3,360.30 | 3,495.00 | 3,495.00 | 339.30 | 50.70 | 424.20 |
| 0–7 | 2,085.30 | 2,227.20 | 2,227.20 | 2,227.20 | 2,326.80 | 2,326.80 | 2,462.10 | 2,462.10 | 2,584.80 | 2,843.70 | 3,039.00 | 3,039.00 | 3,039.00 | 3,039.00 | 339.30 | 50.70 | 424.20 |
| 0–6 | 1,545.60 | 1,698.60 | 1,809.00 | 1,809.00 | 1,809.00 | 1,809.00 | 1,809.00 | 1,809.00 | 1,870.50 | 2,166.90 | 2,277.60 | 2,326.80 | 2,462.10 | 2,670.00 | 304.50 | 39.60 | 371.40 |
| 0–5 | 1,236.30 | 1,452.00 | 1,551.90 | 1,551.90 | 1,551.90 | 1,551.90 | 1,599.30 | 1,684.80 | 1,797.30 | 1,932.30 | 2,043.30 | 2,104.80 | 2,178.60 | 2,178.60 | 280.80 | 33.00 | 338.10 |
| 0–4 | 1,042.20 | 1,268.40 | 1,353.60 | 1,353.60 | 1,378.20 | 1,439.70 | 1,537.50 | 1,624.20 | 1,698.60 | 1,772.40 | 1,821.90 | 1,821.90 | 1,821.90 | 1,821.90 | 249.90 | 26.70 | 301.80 |
| 0–3 | 968.40 | 1,082.70 | 1,157.10 | 1,280.40 | 1,341.60 | 1,390.20 | 1,464.60 | 1,537.50 | 1,575.30 | 1,575.30 | 1,575.30 | 1,575.30 | 1,575.30 | 1,575.30 | 219.90 | 22.20 | 271.20 |
| 0–2 | 844.20 | 922.20 | 1,107.90 | 1,145.10 | 1,168.80 | 1,168.80 | 1,168.80 | 1,168.80 | 1,168.80 | 1,168.80 | 1,168.80 | 1,168.80 | 1,168.80 | 1,168.80 | 190.80 | 17.70 | 241.50 |
| 0–1 | 732.90 | 762.90 | 922.20 | 922.20 | 922.20 | 922.20 | 922.20 | 922.20 | 922.20 | 922.20 | 922.20 | 922.20 | 922.20 | 922.20 | 148.80 | 13.20 | 193.80 |
| **COMMISSIONED OFFICERS WITH OVER 4 YEARS ACTIVE SERVICE AS ENLISTED MEMBERS** | | | | | | | | | | | | | | | | | |
| 0–3 | 0. | 0. | 0. | 1,280.40 | 1,341.60 | 1,390.20 | 1,464.60 | 1,537.50 | 1,599.30 | 1,599.30 | 1,599.30 | 1,599.30 | 1,599.30 | 1,599.30 | — | — | — |
| 0–2 | 0. | 0. | 0. | 1,145.10 | 1,168.80 | 1,206.00 | 1,268.40 | 1,317.30 | 1,353.60 | 1,353.60 | 1,353.60 | 1,353.60 | 1,353.60 | 1,353.60 | — | — | — |
| 0–1 | 0. | 0. | 0. | 922.20 | 984.90 | 1,021.50 | 1,058.40 | 1,095.30 | 1,145.10 | 1,145.10 | 1,145.10 | 1,145.10 | 1,145.10 | 1,145.10 | — | — | — |
| **WARRANT OFFICERS** | | | | | | | | | | | | | | | | | |
| W-4 | 986.40 | 1,058.40 | 1,058.40 | 1,082.70 | 1,131.90 | 1,181.70 | 1,231.20 | 1,317.30 | 1,378.20 | 1,427.10 | 1,464.60 | 1,512.90 | 1,563.30 | 1,684.80 | 240.90 | 25.20 | 290.70 |
| W-3 | 897.00 | 972.90 | 972.90 | 984.90 | 996.60 | 1,069.50 | 1,131.90 | 1,168.80 | 1,206.00 | 1,242.00 | 1,280.40 | 1,329.90 | 1,378.20 | 1,427.10 | 214.80 | 20.70 | 264.60 |
| W-2 | 785.40 | 849.30 | 849.30 | 874.20 | 922.20 | 972.90 | 1,009.50 | 1,046.40 | 1,082.70 | 1,120.50 | 1,157.10 | 1,193.70 | 1,242.00 | 1,242.00 | 186.90 | 15.90 | 237.30 |
| W-1 | 654.30 | 750.30 | 750.30 | 812.70 | 849.30 | 886.20 | 922.20 | 960.30 | 996.60 | 1,033.50 | 1,069.58 | 1,107.90 | 1,107.90 | 1,107.90 | 168.60 | 13.80 | 218.40 |
| **ENLISTED MEMBERS** | | | | | | | | | | | | | | | | | |
| E-9[5] | 0. | 0. | 0. | 0. | 0. | 0. | 1,120.80 | 1,146.30 | 1,172.40 | 1,199.40 | 1,225.80 | 1,249.80 | 1,315.80 | 1,443.30 | 181.80 | 18.60 | 255.60 |
| E-8 | 0. | 0. | 0. | 0. | 0. | 940.50 | 966.60 | 992.40 | 1,018.50 | 1,044.30 | 1,069.20 | 1,095.60 | 1,159.80 | 1,289.40 | 167.40 | 15.30 | 236.40 |
| E-7 | 656.70 | 708.60 | 735.00 | 760.50 | 786.90 | 811.50 | 837.30 | 863.70 | 902.70 | 928.20 | 954.30 | 966.60 | 1,031.70 | 1,159.80 | 142.50 | 12.00 | 219.90 |
| E-6 | 567.00 | 618.30 | 644.10 | 671.10 | 696.00 | 721.80 | 748.20 | 786.90 | 811.50 | 837.30 | 850.20 | 850.20 | 850.20 | 850.20 | 129.30 | 9.90 | 202.20 |
| E-5 | 498.00 | 541.80 | 568.20 | 592.80 | 631.50 | 657.30 | 683.70 | 708.60 | 721.80 | 721.80 | 721.80 | 721.80 | 721.80 | 721.80 | 124.20 | 8.70 | 185.70 |
| E-4 | 478.50 | 505.20 | 534.90 | 576.60 | 599.40 | 599.40 | 599.40 | 599.40 | 599.40 | 599.40 | 599.40 | 599.40 | 599.40 | 599.40 | 109.80 | 8.10 | 163.50 |
| E-3 | 460.20 | 485.40 | 504.90 | 525.00 | 525.00 | 525.00 | 525.00 | 525.00 | 525.00 | 525.00 | 525.00 | 525.00 | 525.00 | 525.00 | 98.10 | 7.80 | 142.50 |
| E-2 | 443.10 | 443.10 | 443.10 | 443.10 | 443.10 | 443.10 | 443.10 | 443.10 | 443.10 | 443.10 | 443.10 | 443.10 | 443.10 | 443.10 | 86.70 | 7.20 | 142.50 |
| E-1 | 397.50 | 397.50 | 397.50 | 397.50 | 397.50 | 397.50 | 397.50 | 397.50 | 397.50 | 397.50 | 397.50 | 397.50 | 397.50 | 397.50 | 81.90 | 6.90 | 142.50 |

1. Payment of the full rate of basic allowance for quarters at these rates for members of the uniformed services to personnel without dependents is authorized by 37 U.S. Code 403 and Part IV of Executive Order 11157, as amended. 2. Payment of the partial rate of basic allowance for quarters at these rates to members of the uniformed services without dependents who, under 37 U.S. Code 403(b) or 403(c), are not entitled to the full rate of basic allowance for quarters, is authorized by 37 U.S. Code 1009(d) and Part IV of Executive Order 11157, as amended. 3. For duration of service as Chairman of the Joint Chiefs of Staff, Chief of Staff of the Army, Chief of Naval Operations, Chief of Staff of the Air Force, or Commandant of the Marine Corps, basic pay for this grade is $4,848.00 regardless of cumulative years of service. 4. Basic pay is limited to $3,958.20 by Level V of the Executive Schedule. 5. Highest Enlisted Rank. For duration of service as Sergeant Major of the Army, Master Chief Petty Officer of the Navy, Chief Master Sergeant of the Air Force, or Sergeant Major of the Marine Corps, basic pay for this grade is $1,754.40 regardless of cumulative years of service. *Source:* Department of Defense.

## Extra Pay for Service During Hostilities

Act of March 3, 1847, during the Mexican War, provided for $2 a month extra pay for "distinguished service." This continued beyond the war and applied in the Civil War.

In the Spanish-American War, there was a 20% increase in enlisted men's pay for war service.

In World War I, additional incentive pay was offered for all types of services. Among these items was pay for certificate of merit of $2 a month. By the law passed in 1920, the reasons for additional pay had expanded. Recipients of the Medal of Honor, Distinguished Service Cross, and Distinguished Service Medal received $2 a month extra, while each bar in lieu of these medals also added another $2 a month. Added to this was a foreign service bonus of 20%.

Act of June 30, 1944, authorized $5 a month to enlisted men qualified as expert infantrymen and $10 to those qualified as combat infantrymen. Amounts were payable for the duration of war and 6 months thereafter.

By the Act of July 6, 1945, for the duration of war and for 6 months thereafter, enlisted men entitled to wear Medical Badges received additional pay of $10 a month.

Act of July 10, 1952, authorized $45 a month for each month beginning after May 31, 1950, for which the member was entitled to receive basic pay and during which he was a member of a combat unit in Korea.

The Combat Duty Pay Act of 1952 was repealed by the Uniformed Services Pay Act of 1963, which authorized special pay for duty subject to hostile fire under certain conditions at the rate of $55 (now $65) a month.

## Family Separation Allowance

Military members with dependents in grades E-4 (over 4 years of service) and above are entitled to an allowance of $30 a month in addition to allowances or per diem when on a permanent change of station, with movement of dependents not authorized and dependents not residing near his station; or be on board ship or temporary duty for more than 30 days, with dependents not residing near the temporary duty station.

A second type of family separation allowance at the rate equal to the quarters allowance for a member in the same grade without dependents is payable to a member with dependents when assigned to permanent duty outside the United States or in Alaska when government quarters, or quarters under the jurisdiction of a uniformed service, are not available to the member. Further, the member's dependents must not be residing at or near his permanent duty station and are not authorized to movement to or near the permanent duty station at Government expense.

## Allowances for Subsistence

Officers receive $59.53 per month. Enlisted personnel receive allowances for subsistence under the following provisions: (1) when rations in kind are not available, $3.20 per day; (2) when on leave or authorized to mess separately, $2.84 per day; (3) when assigned to duty under emergency conditions where no messing facilities of the U.S. are available, $4.25 per day.

## Special Pay

### Medical, Dental, Optometry, and Veterinary Officers

Monthly special pay for medical officers is based on cumulative service: 0–2 years, $100; 2 or more years, $350. For dental officers: 0–2 years, $100; 2–6 years, $150; 6–10 years, $250; 10 or more years, $350.

Monthly special pay for optometry and veterinary officers who entered on active duty before July 1, 1975, is $100 regardless of years of service. Those who entered after July 1, 1975, are not eligible for the special pay.

### Variable Incentive Pay for Physicians

Selected physicians who are serving in critical specialties and have completed at least 4 years of an initial active-duty obligation may, if otherwise qualified and approved, agree in writing to remain on active duty for a specified number of years for which they may be paid not more than $13,500 for each year of the agreement. This is in addition to other pays and allowances.

### Diving Duty

The monthly pay is not more than $110 for periods during which diving duty is actually performed. It may not be paid in addition to incentive pay.

### Sea Duty and Duty at Certain Places

An enlisted member of a uniformed service is entitled to special pay while on sea duty to or while on duty at a designated place outside the contiguous 48 states and the District of Columbia.

The monthly rates are: E-9, E-8, and E-7, $22.50; E-6, $20; E-5, $16; E-4, $13; E-3, $9; E-2 and E-1, $8.

### Proficiency Pay for Enlisted Members

1. A qualified career member serving in a designated specialty may receive shortage specialty pay. This type of proficiency pay is paid to personnel in high training cost specialties in which there is a critical shortage of career members. Monthly rates authorized for FY 79 are $50, $100, or $150.

2. A qualified member serving in a designated duty assignment may receive special duty assignment pay. This is paid to individuals on special duty assignments for which the number of volunteers is inadequate. Monthly rates authorized for FY 79 are $30, $50, $75, $100, or $150.

3. When employed, eligible members serving in a specialty not designated for receipt of another type of proficiency pay may compete for superior performance pay. Monthly rates authorized were $30 and $50. (Not currently being used.)

### Duty Subject to Hostile Fire

Except in time of war declared by Congress and under regulations prescribed by the Secretary of Defense, special pay at the rate of $65 a month will be paid to a member of the uniformed services for any month during which he was subject to hostile fire.

## Incentive Pay for Hazardous Duty

Members of the uniformed services are entitled to incentive pay for special kinds of hazardous duty. For the following kinds, an officer is entitled to $110 a month, and an enlisted man to $55 a month:

1. Frequent and regular participation in aerial flights *not* as a crew member.
2. Frequent and regular participation in glider flights.
3. Parachute jumping as an essential part of military duty.
4. Duty involving contact with lepers.
5. Demolition of explosives as primary duty (including training).
6. Duty inside a high- or low-pressure chamber.
7. Duty as a human acceleration or deceleration experimental subject.
8. Duty as a human test subject in thermal stress experiments.
9. Frequent and regular participation in flight operations on the flight deck of an aircraft carrier.

For duty as an enlisted crew member of an aircraft or a crew member of a submarine, the rates for incentive pay are as follows:

O–10—$165 regardless of yrs of service.
O–9—$165 regardless of yrs of service.
O–8—Under 3 yrs service, $155; over 3 yrs, $165.
O–7—Under 3 yrs service, $150; over 3 yrs, $160.
O–6—Under 3 yrs service, $200; 3–16 yrs, $215; 16–18 yrs, $220; over 18 yrs, $245.
O–5—Under 3 yrs service, $190; 3–12 yrs, $205; 12–14 yrs, $210; 14–16 yrs, $225; 16–18 yrs, $230; over 18 yrs, $245.
O–4—Under 3 yrs service, $170; 3–8 yrs, $185; 8–10 yrs, $195; 10–12 yrs, $210; 12–14 yrs. $215; 14–16 yrs, $220; 16–18 yrs, $230; over 18 yrs, $240.
O–3—Under 3 yrs service, $145; 3–4 yrs, $155; 4–6 yrs, $165; 6–8 yrs, $180; 8–10 yrs, $185; 10–12 yrs, $190; 12–14 yrs, $200; over 14 yrs, $205.
O–2—Under 2 yrs service, $115; 2–3 yrs, $125; 3–6 yrs, $150; 6–8 yrs, $160; 8–10 yrs, $165; 10–12 yrs, $170; 12–14 yrs, $180; over 14 yrs, $185.
O–1—Under 2 yrs service, $100; 2–3 yrs, $105; 3–6 yrs, $135; 6–8 yrs, $140; 8–10 yrs, $145; 10–12 yrs, $155; 12–14 yrs, $160; over 14 yrs, $170.
W–4—Under 6 yrs service, $115; 6–8 yrs, $120; 8–10 yrs, $125; 10–12 yrs, $135; 12–14 yrs, $145; 14–16 yrs, $155; 16–18 yrs, $160; over 18 yrs, $165.
W–3—Under 2 yrs service, $110; 2–6 yrs, $115; 6–10 yrs, $120; 10–12 yrs, $125; 12–14 yrs, $135; over 14 yrs, $140.
W–2—Under 2 yrs service, $105; 2–6 yrs, $110; 6–8 yrs, $115; 8–10 yrs, $120; 10–12 yrs, $125; 12–14 yrs, $130; over 14 yrs, $135.
W–1—Under 2 yrs service, $100; 2–6 yrs, $105; 6–8 yrs, $110; 8–10 yrs, $120; 10–12 yrs, $125; over 12 yrs, $130.
E–9—$105 regardless of yrs of service.
E–8—$105 regardless of yrs of service.
E–7—Under 2 yrs service, $80; 2–6 yrs, $85; 6–8 yrs, $90; 8–10 yrs, $95; 10–12 yrs, $100; over 12 yrs, $105.
E–6—Under 2 yrs service, $70; 2–4 yrs, $75; 4–6 yrs, $80; 6–8 yrs, $85; 8–10 yrs, $90; 10–14 yrs, $95; over 14 yrs, $100.
E–5—Under 2 yrs service, $60; 2–4 yrs, $70; 4–8 yrs, $80; 8–10 yrs, $85; 10–12 yrs, $90; over 12 years, $95.
E–4—Under 2 yrs service, $55; 2–4 yrs, $65; 4–6 yrs, $70; 6–8 yrs, $75; over 8 yrs, $80.
E–3—Under 2 yrs service, $55; over 2 yrs, $60.
E–2—Under 2 yrs service, $50; over 2 yrs, $60.
E–1—Under 2 yrs service, $50; over 2 yrs, $55.

# Veterans' Benefits

Although benefits of various kinds date back to Colonial days, veterans of World War I were the first to receive disability compensation, allotments for dependents, life insurance, medical care, and vocational rehabilitation. In 1940, these benefits were slowly broadened.

The following benefits available to veterans require certain minimum periods of active duty during qualifying periods of service and, except for service personnel, are applicable only to those whose discharges are not dishonorable.

**Unemployment allowances.** Every effort is being made to secure employment for Vietnam veterans. Unemployment benefits are administered by the U.S. Department of Labor.

**Loans.** GI loans are made for a variety of purposes, such as: to buy or build a home; to purchase a mobile home with or without a lot; and to refinance a home presently owned and occupied by the veteran. The VA will guarantee the lender against loss up to 60% of a home loan with a maximum of $17,500. On mobile home loans, the amount of the guaranty is 50% of the loan. The interest rate may not exceed the maximum rate set by the VA and in effect when the loan is made.

**Compensation and rehabilitation benefits.** These are available to those having some service-connected illness or disability.

**Disability compensation.** The VA pays from $41 to $754 per month, and for specific conditions up to $1,875 per month, plus allowances for dependents, where the disability is rated 50% or more.

**Vocational rehabilitation.** Necessary training expenses, special equipment, etc., toward a definite job objective are paid for, plus a monthly allowance of up to $226, with increased amounts for dependents, in addition to compensation.

**Medical and dental care.** This includes care in VA and, in certain instances, in non-VA, or other federal hospitals. It also covers outpatient treatment at a VA field facility or, in some cases, by an approved private physician or dentist. Full domiciliary care is also provided where necessary. Nursing home care may be provided at certain VA medical facilities or in approved community nursing homes. Hospital and other medical care may also be provided for the spouse and child dependents of a veteran who is permanently and totally disabled due to a service-connected disability; or for survivors of a veteran who dies from a service-connected disability; or for survivors of a veteran who at the time of death had a total disability, permanent in nature, resulting from a service-connected disability. These latter benefits are usually provided in nonfederal facilities. Eligibility criteria for these benefits vary, and veterans and/or their dependents or survivors should always apply in advance. Contact the nearest VA medical facility.

**Dependents' Educational Assistance.** The VA pays $292 a month for up to 45 months of schooling to sons and daughters of veterans who died of service-connected causes or who were permanently and totally disabled from service-connected causes or while permanently and totally disabled or who are missing in action, captured in the line of duty, or forcibly detained or interned in line of duty by a foreign power for more than 90 days. Students must usually be between 18 and 26.

Spouses of veterans whose deaths are adjudged to be service-connected, and spouses of veterans who are permanently and totally disabled due to service-connected causes or who are prisoners of war or are missing in action are also eligible for this educational benefit.

**Veterans readjustment education.** Veterans who served on active duty for at least 181 days after Jan. 31, 1955, but before Jan. 1, 1977, may receive monthly educational assistance under the new GI Bill for post-Korean conflict veterans, varying from $311 for single full-time students to $422 for veterans with two dependents, plus $26 for each additional dependent. Veterans and servicepersons who initially entered the military on or after Jan. 1, 1977, may receive educational assistance under a contributory plan. Individuals contribute $50 to $75 from military pay, up to a maximum of $2,700. Participants receive monthly payments for the number of months they contributed, or for 36 months, whichever is less.

**Pensions.** The Veterans Pension Act of 1959, effective July 1, 1960, provides a sliding-scale formula for pension benefits for wartime veterans totally disabled from non-service-connected causes. These benefits are based on need. Surviving spouses and orphans of Mexican Border service, World War II, Korea, and Vietnam veterans have the same eligibility status.

**Insurance.** The VA life insurance programs have approximately 8.3 million policyholders with total coverage of about $102.4 billion. Detailed information on NSLI (National Service Life Insurance), USGLI (United States Government Life Insurance), and VMLI (Veterans Mortgage Life Insurance) may be obtained at any VA Office. Information regarding SGLI (Servicemen's Group Life Insurance) and VGLI (Veterans Group Life Insurance) may be obtained from the VA Center, P.O. Box 8079, Philadelphia, Pa. 19101, or the Office of Servicemen's Group Life Insurance, 212 Washington St., Newark, N.J. 07102

## Highest Ranking Officers in the Armed Forces

### ARMY[1]

**General of the Army:** Omar N. Bradley
**Generals:** Bernard W. Rogers, Chief of Staff; George S. Blanchard; William E. DePuy; John R. Guthrie; Alexander M. Haig, Jr.; John J. Hennessey; Walter T. Kerwin, Jr.; William A. Knowlton; Frederick J. Kroesen; John W. Vessey, Jr.

### AIR FORCE

**Generals:** David C. Jones, Chairman, Joint Chiefs of Staff; Robert J. Dixon; Richard H. Ellis; William J. Evans; William G. Moore, Jr.; John W. Roberts; F. Michael Rogers.

### NAVY

**Admirals:** Thomas B. Hayward, Chief of Naval Operations; David H. Bagley; Isaac C. Kidd, Jr.; Frederick H. Michaelis; Daniel J. Murphy; Harold E. Shear; Stansfield Turner; John P. Weinel; Maurice F. Weisner.

### MARINE CORPS

**Generals:** Louis H. Wilson, Commandant of the Marine Corps; Samuel Jaskilka, Assistant Commandant.
**Lieutenant Generals:** Robert H. Barrow; Leslie E. Brown; Joseph C. Fegan, Jr.; Thomas H. Miller, Jr.; Robert L. Nichols; Lawrence F. Snowden; Andrew W. O'Donnell.

### COAST GUARD

**Admiral:** John B. Hayes, Commandant.
**Vice Admirals:** Robert H. Scarborough, Jr., Assistant Commandant; William F. Rea III; Austin C. Wagner.

1. On March 15, 1978, George Washington, the commander of the Continental Army in the American Revolution and our first President, was promoted to the newly-created rank of General of the Armies of the United States. Congress authorized this title two years ago to make it clear that Washington is the Army's senior general. *Source:* Department of Defense.

## Department of Defense Outlays by Branch of Service

| Year | Outlays (in millions of dollars) | | | | | Percent distribution | | | |
|---|---|---|---|---|---|---|---|---|---|
| | Total | Army | Navy | Air Force | Other | Army | Navy | Air Force | Other |
| 1965 | 47,098 | 11,552 | 13,339 | 18,146 | 4,061 | 24.5 | 28.3 | 38.5 | 8.6 |
| 1968 | 78,027 | 25,223 | 22,071 | 25,734 | 4,999 | 32.3 | 28.3 | 33.0 | 6.4 |
| 1969 | 78,660 | 25,610 | 22,691 | 26,114 | 4,245 | 32.6 | 28.8 | 33.2 | 5.4 |
| 1970 | 78,349 | 25,147 | 22,656 | 25,233 | 5,313 | 32.1 | 28.9 | 32.2 | 6.8 |
| 1971 | 76,005 | 23,909 | 22,374 | 24,749 | 4,973 | 31.5 | 29.4 | 32.6 | 6.5 |
| 1972 | 76,674 | 23,473 | 22,736 | 24,845 | 5,620 | 30.6 | 29.7 | 32.4 | 7.3 |
| 1973 | 74,473 | 21,140 | 22,985 | 24,538 | 5,811 | 28.4 | 30.9 | 32.9 | 7.8 |
| 1974 | 77,651 | 22,371 | 24,616 | 25,736 | 4,927 | 28.8 | 31.7 | 33.1 | 6.4 |
| 1975 | 84,988 | 23,678 | 28,299 | 26,709 | 6,303 | 27.9 | 33.3 | 31.4 | 7.4 |
| 1976 | 87,950 | 25,025 | 30,404 | 28,248 | 4,272 | 28.5 | 34.6 | 32.1 | 4.9 |
| 1976, TQ[1] | 21,444 | 6,268 | 7,590 | 7,158 | 428 | 29.2 | 35.4 | 33.4 | 2.0 |

1. Transition quarter, July-Sept. 1976. NOTE: Excludes civil functions. Includes military assistance to foreign countries. *Source:* Department of the Treasury.

## Federal Budget Outlays for National Defense and Veterans Benefits and Services

(in billions of dollars, except percent)

| | | | National defense | | | | | | Veterans benefits and services | |
|---|---|---|---|---|---|---|---|---|---|---|
| | | | Total | | Current dollars as percent of— | | Southeast Asia | | | |
| Year | Total federal outlays, all functions | Total national defense and veterans outlays | Current dollars | 1977 dollars | Total federal outlays | GNP[1] | Full costs[2] | Incremental costs[3] | Total | Percent of total federal outlays |
| 1950 | 42.6 | 21.2 | 12.4 | 44.0 | 29.1 | 4.7 | — | — | 8.8 | 20.7 |
| 1955 | 68.5 | 44.6 | 39.9 | 113.7 | 58.2 | 10.5 | — | — | 4.7 | 6.9 |
| 1960 | 92.2 | 50.7 | 45.2 | 110.7 | 49.0 | 9.1 | — | — | 5.5 | 6.0 |
| 1962 | 106.8 | 56.0 | 50.4 | 118.0 | 47.2 | 9.2 | — | — | 5.6 | 5.3 |
| 1963 | 111.3 | 57.0 | 51.5 | 118.3 | 46.3 | 8.9 | — | — | 5.5 | 5.0 |
| 1964 | 118.6 | 58.4 | 52.7 | 118.1 | 44.4 | 8.5 | — | — | 5.7 | 4.8 |
| 1965 | 118.4 | 54.3 | 48.6 | 106.3 | 41.0 | 7.4 | .1 | .1 | 5.7 | 4.8 |
| 1966 | 134.7 | 61.8 | 55.9 | 116.4 | 41.5 | 7.7 | 5.8 | 5.8 | 5.9 | 4.4 |
| 1967 | 158.3 | 76.0 | 69.1 | 139.5 | 43.7 | 8.9 | 20.1 | 18.4 | 6.9 | 4.4 |
| 1968 | 178.8 | 86.3 | 79.4 | 153.0 | 44.4 | 9.6 | 26.5 | 20.0 | 6.9 | 3.8 |
| 1969 | 184.5 | 87.8 | 80.2 | 148.0 | 43.5 | 8.9 | 28.8 | 21.5 | 7.6 | 4.1 |
| 1970 | 196.6 | 88.0 | 79.3 | 136.4 | 40.3 | 8.3 | 23.1 | 17.4 | 8.7 | 4.4 |
| 1971 | 211.4 | 86.6 | 76.8 | 123.1 | 36.3 | 7.5 | 14.7 | 11.5 | 9.8 | 4.6 |
| 1972 | 231.9 | 88.1 | 77.4 | 115.8 | 33.4 | 7.0 | 9.4 | 7.2 | 10.7 | 4.6 |
| 1973 | 246.5 | 87.1 | 75.1 | 105.0 | 30.5 | 6.1 | 6.3 | 5.3 | 12.0 | 4.9 |
| 1974 | 268.4 | 92.0 | 78.6 | 102.2 | 29.3 | 5.8 | 3.1 | 2.7 | 13.4 | 5.0 |
| 1975 | 324.6 | 103.2 | 86.6 | 100.2 | 26.7 | 6.0 | 1.4 | 1.1 | 16.6 | 5.1 |
| 1976 | 366.5 | 108.4 | 90.0 | 96.6 | 24.6 | 5.6 | .3 | .3 | 18.4 | 6.0 |
| 1976, TQ[4] | 94.7 | 26.6 | 22.5 | 23.4 | 23.8 | n.a. | .3 | .1 | 4.0 | 4.2 |
| 1977 | 411.2 | 118.5 | 100.1 | 100.1 | 24.3 | 5.5 | — | — | 18.4 | 4.5 |

1. Gross national product. 2. Included in national defense total. 3. Incremental war cost figures reflect the estimated costs being incurred over and above the normal peacetime operating costs of the base line force. 4. Transition quarter, July-Sept. 1976. NOTE: Through 1976, for years ending June 30, except as noted; 1977, year ending Sept. 30. Includes outlays of Department of Defense, Veterans Administration, and other agencies for activities primarily related to national defense and veterans programs. n.a. = not available. *Source:* Office of Management and Budget and the Department of Defense.

## Budget Outlays for National Defense Functions

(in billions of dollars, except as indicated)

| Item | 1977 | 1976, TQ[1] | 1976 | 1975 | 1974 | 1972 | 1970 | 1968 |
|---|---|---|---|---|---|---|---|---|
| Defense Dept., military | 98.0 | 21.9 | 88.0 | 85.0 | 77.6 | 75.2 | 77.2 | 77.4 |
| Military personnel | 26.2 | 6.4 | 25.1 | 25.0 | 23.7 | 23.0 | 23.0 | 19.9 |
| Percent of military | 26.7 | 29.0 | 28.5 | 29.4 | 30.6 | 30.7 | 29.9 | 25.7 |
| Active forces | 24.3 | 5.8 | 23.3 | 23.2 | 22.1 | 21.6 | 22.0 | 19.0 |
| Reserve forces | 1.9 | .5 | 1.8 | 1.7 | 1.6 | 1.4 | 1.1 | .9 |
| Military retirees | 8.2 | 1.9 | 7.3 | 6.2 | 5.1 | 3.9 | 2.8 | 2.1 |
| Operation, maintenance | 31.1 | 7.3 | 27.9 | 26.3 | 22.5 | 21.7 | 21.6 | 20.6 |
| Procurement[2] | 18.7 | 3.8 | 16.0 | 16.0 | 15.2 | 17.1 | 21.6 | 23.3 |
| Army | 2.6 | .2 | 1.4 | 2.5 | 2.6 | 3.9 | 5.2 | 5.8 |
| Navy[3] | 8.9 | 1.9 | 8.0 | 8.1 | 7.3 | 7.1 | 7.9 | 8.0 |
| Air Force | 7.0 | 1.6 | 6.5 | 5.3 | 5.4 | 6.0 | 8.4 | 9.4 |
| Research and develop | 10.9 | 2.2 | 8.9 | 8.9 | 8.6 | 7.9 | 7.2 | 7.7 |
| Military construction | 2.1 | .4 | 2.0 | 1.5 | 1.4 | 1.1 | 1.2 | 1.3 |
| Family housing | 1.4 | .3 | 1.2 | 1.1 | .9 | .7 | .6 | .5 |
| Civil defense | .1 | (6) | .1 | .1 | .1 | .1 | .1 | .1 |
| Other[4] | .1 | −.3 | −.4 | −.1 | −.2 | −.3 | −1.0 | 1.9 |
| Military assistance | .2 | .2 | .5 | 1.0 | .8 | .8 | .7 | .7 |
| Atomic energy activities[5] | 1.8 | .4 | 1.6 | 1.5 | 1.5 | 1.4 | 1.4 | 1.3 |
| Defense-related activities | −.1 | (6) | −.1 | −.9 | −1.3 | — | — | .1 |
| **Total** | **100.1** | **22.5** | **90.0** | **86.6** | **78.6** | **77.4** | **79.3** | **79.4** |

1. Transition quarter, July-Sept. 1976. 2. Includes other defense agencies not shown separately. 3. Includes Marine Corps. 4. Revolving and management funds, trust funds, special foreign currency program, allowances, and offsetting receipts. 5. Defense activities only. 6. Less than $50 million. NOTE: Through 1976, for year ending June 30, except as noted; 1977 year ending Sept. 30, 1977, data are estimates. *Source:* Office of Management and Budget.

## Department of Defense Personnel and Payroll

| | Personnel (in thousands) | | | | Payroll (in billions of dollars) | | | |
|---|---|---|---|---|---|---|---|---|
| Year | Total | Active duty military | Direct hire civilian | Military retirees | Total | Active duty military[2] | Direct hire civilian[3] | Military pensions payments[4] |
| 1950 | 2,213 | 1,460 | 753 | 132 | 8.2 | 5.3 | 2.9 | n.a. |
| 1955 | 4,122 | 2,935 | 1,187 | 180 | 13.8 | 9.1 | 4.7 | n.a. |
| 1960 | 3,523 | 2,476 | 1,047 | 256 | 15.1 | 9.3 | 5.8 | n.a. |
| 1965 | 3,689 | 2,655 | 1,034 | 481 | 18.5 | 11.4 | 7.1 | n.a. |
| 1967 | 4,680 | 3,377 | 1,303 | 590 | 23.5 | 14.8 | 8.7 | n.a. |
| 1968 | 4,865 | 3,548 | 1,317 | 651 | 25.8 | 16.4 | 9.4 | 2.0 |
| 1969 | 4,802 | 3,460 | 1,342 | 714 | 28.2 | 17.9 | 10.3 | 2.2 |
| 1970 | 4,260 | 3,066 | 1,194[1] | 773 | 30.7 | 19.4 | 11.3 | 2.5 |
| 1971 | 3,842 | 2,715 | 1,127[1] | 831 | 30.8 | 19.2 | 11.6 | 3.1 |
| 1972 | 3,406 | 2,323 | 1,083[1] | 890 | 32.0 | 19.8 | 12.2 | 3.6 |
| 1973 | 3,284 | 2,253 | 1,031[1] | 948 | 32.6 | 20.3 | 12.3 | 4.1 |
| 1974 | 3,233 | 2,162 | 1,071 | 1,012 | 32.7 | 19.9 | 12.8 | 4.9 |
| 1975 | 3,170 | 2,128 | 1,042 | 1,073 | 34.0 | 20.2 | 13.8 | 6.1 |
| 1976 | 3,092 | 2,082 | 1,010 | 1,132 | 35.0 | 20.4 | 14.6 | 7.2 |

1. Excludes special students and disadvantaged youth in special employment categories. 2. Excludes troop subsistence, transportation, movement of personnel, etc. 3. Excludes benefits, etc. 4. Retired military payroll for U.S. only. NOTE: Figures exclude "indirect hire" civilians. n.a. = not available. *Source:* Department of Defense.

## U.S. Navy Combatant Vessels

| Type | Number | Type | Number |
|---|---|---|---|
| Carriers | 13 | Mine warfare | 3 |
| Destroyers | 64 | Patrol ships | 3 |
| Cruisers | 27 | Amphibious warfare | 63 |
| Frigates | 65 | Auxiliaries | 101 |
| Submarines | 120 | Total | 459 |

NOTE: As of Feb. 28, 1978, exact figures are classified information. *Source:* Department of Defense.

## Insignia and Ranks of the Armed Forces

| Army, Air Force, and Marines | | Navy and Coast Guard | | |
|---|---|---|---|---|
| Insignia | Rank | Insignia | Rank | Stripes[1] |
| Five silver stars | General of the Army, AF | Five silver stars | Fleet Admiral | 1—4—0 |
| Four silver stars | General | Four silver stars | Admiral | 1—3—0 |
| Three silver stars | Lieutenant General | Three silver stars | Vice Admiral | 1—2—0 |
| Two silver stars | Major General | Two silver stars | Rear Admiral | 1—1—0 |
| One silver star | Brigadier General | One silver star | Commodore | 1—0—0[2] |
| Silver eagle | Colonel | Silver eagle | Captain | 0—4—0 |
| Silver oak leaf | Lieutenant Colonel | Silver oak leaf | Commander | 0—3—0 |
| Gold oak leaf | Major | Gold oak leaf | Lt. Commander | 0—2—1 |
| Two silver bars | Captain | Two silver bars | Lieutenant | 0—2—0 |
| One silver bar | First Lieutenant | One silver bar | Lieutenant (jg) | 0—1—1 |
| One gold bar | Second Lieutenant | One gold bar | Ensign | 0—1—0 |
| Silver bar with 3 enamel bands[3] | Chief Warrant Officer (W-4) | Silver bar with 3 enamel bands[3] | Chief Warrant Officer (W-4) | 0—1—0[4] |
| Silver bar with 2 enamel bands[3] | Chief Warrant Officer (W-3) | Silver bar with 2 enamel bands[3] | Chief Warrant Officer (W-3) | 0—1—0[5] |
| Gold bar with 3 enamel bands[3] | Chief Warrant Officer (W-2) | Gold bar with 3 enamel bands[3] | Chief Warrant Officer (W-2) | 0—1—0[6] |
| Gold bar with 2 enamel bands[3] | Warrant Officer (W-1) | Gold bar with 2 enamel bands[3] | Warrant Officer (W-1) | 0—0—1[6] |

1. Of gold embroidery; first figure is number of 2-in. stripes, second is number of ½-inch strips, third is number of ¼-in. stripes. 2. Wartime only. 3. Navy and Marine Corps use same size insignia as Army when worn on shoulder straps, but miniature size on shirt collars. Enamel bands are black for Army, scarlet for Marines, medium blue for Air Force, and blue for Navy and Coast Guard. 4. One break. 5. Two breaks. 6. Three breaks.

## U.S. Military Actions Other Than Declared Wars

**Hawaii (1893):** U.S. Marines, ordered to land by U.S. Minister John L. Stevens, aided the revolutionary Committee of Safety in overthrowing the native government. Stevens then proclaimed Hawaii a U.S. protectorate. Annexation, resisted by the Democratic administration in Washington, was not formally accomplished until 1898.

**China (1900):** Boxers (a group of Chinese revolutionists) occupied Peking and laid siege to foreign legations. U.S. troops joined an international expedition which relieved the city.

**Panama (1903):** After Colombia had rejected a proposed agreement for relinquishing sovereignty over the Panama Canal Zone, revolution broke out, aided by promoters of the Panama Canal Co. Two U.S. warships were standing by to protect American privileges. The U.S. recognized the Republic of Panama on November 6.

**Dominican Republic (1904):** When the Dominican Republic failed to meet debts owed to the U.S. and foreign creditors, President Theodore Roosevelt declared the U.S. intention of exercising "international police power" in the Western Hemisphere whenever necessary. The U.S. accordingly administered customs and managed debt payments of the Dominican Republic from 1905 to 1907.

**Nicaragua (1911):** The possibility of foreign control over Nicaragua's canal route led to U.S. intervention and agreement. The U.S. landed Marines in Nicaragua (Aug. 14, 1912) to protect American interests there. A small detachment remained until 1933.

**Mexico (1914):** Mexican dictator Victoriano Huerta, opposed by President Woodrow Wilson, had the support of European governments. An incident involving unarmed U.S. sailors in Tampico led to the landing of U.S. forces on Mexican soil. Veracruz was bombarded by the Navy to prevent the landing of munitions from a German vessel. At the point of war, both powers agreed to mediation by Argentina, Brazil, and Chile. Huerta abdicated, and Venustiano Carranza succeeded to the presidency.

**Haiti (1915):** U.S. Marines imposed a military occupation. Haiti signed a treaty making it a virtual protectorate of the U.S. until troops were withdrawn in 1934.

**Mexico (1916):** Raids by Pancho Villa cost American lives on both sides of the border. President Carranza consented to a punitive expedition led by Gen. John J. Pershing, but antagonism grew in Mexico. Wilson withdrew the U.S. force when war with Germany became imminent.

**Dominican Republic (1916):** Renewed intervention in the Dominican Republic with internal administration by U.S. naval officers lasted until 1924.

**Korea (1950):** In this undeclared war, which terminated with the July 27, 1953, truce at Panmunjom and the establishment of a neutral nations' supervisory commission, the U.S. and 15 member-nations of the U.N. came to the aid of the Republic of South Korea, whose 38th-parallel border was crossed by the invading Russian Communist-controlled North Koreans, who were later joined by the Chinese Communists.

**Lebanon (1958):** Fearful of the newly formed U.A.R. abetting the rebels of his politically and economically torn country, President Camille Chamoun appealed to the U.S. for military assistance. U.S. troops landed in Beirut in mid-July and left before the end of the year, after internal and external quiet were restored.

**Dominican Republic (1965):** On April 28, when a political coup-turned-civil war endangered the lives of American nationals, President Lyndon B. Johnson rushed 400 marines into Santo Domingo, the beginning of an eventual U.S. peak-commitment of 30,000 troops, constituting the preponderant military strength of the OAS-created Inter-American Peace Force, and 6,500 troops, including 5,000 Americans, remained until after the peaceful inauguration of President Joaquín Balaguer on July 1, 1966, and the entire force left the country on September 20.

**Vietnam:** This longest war in U.S. history began with economic and technical assistance after 1954 Geneva accords ending the Indochinese War. By 1964 it had escalated into a major conflict.

This involvement spanning the administrations of five Presidents led to domestic discontent in the late 1960s. By April 1969, U.S. troop strength reached a peak of 543,400. Peace negotiations began in Paris in 1968 but proved fruitless. Finally, on Jan. 27, 1973, a peace accord was signed in Paris by the U.S., North and South Vietnam, and the Vietcong. Within 60 days, U.S. POWs were returned, and the U.S. withdrew all military forces from South Vietnam.

## Casualties in World War I

| Country | Total mobilized forces | Killed or died[1] | Wounded | Prisoners or missing | Total casualties |
|---|---|---|---|---|---|
| Austria-Hungary | 7,800,000 | 1,200,000 | 3,620,000 | 2,200,000 | 7,020,000 |
| Belgium | 267,000 | 13,716 | 44,686 | 34,659 | 93,061 |
| British Empire[2] | 8,904,467 | 908,371 | 2,090,212 | 191,652 | 3,190,235 |
| Bulgaria | 1,200,000 | 87,500 | 152,390 | 27,029 | 266,919 |
| France[2] | 8,410,000 | 1,357,800 | 4,266,000 | 537,000 | 6,160,800 |
| Germany | 11,000,000 | 1,773,700 | 4,216,058 | 1,152,800 | 7,142,558 |
| Greece | 230,000 | 5,000 | 21,000 | 1,000 | 27,000 |

| Country | Total mobilized forces | Killed or died[1] | Wounded | Prisoners or missing | Total casualties |
|---|---|---|---|---|---|
| Italy | 5,615,000 | 650,000 | 947,000 | 600,000 | 2,197,000 |
| Japan | 800,000 | 300 | 907 | 3 | 1,210 |
| Montenegro | 50,000 | 3,000 | 10,000 | 7,000 | 20,000 |
| Portugal | 100,000 | 7,222 | 13,751 | 12,318 | 33,291 |
| Romania | 750,000 | 335,706 | 120,000 | 80,000 | 535,706 |
| Russia | 12,000,000 | 1,700,000 | 4,950,000 | 2,500,000 | 9,150,000 |
| Serbia | 707,343 | 45,000 | 133,148 | 152,958 | 331,106 |
| Turkey | 2,850,000 | 325,000 | 400,000 | 250,000 | 975,000 |
| United States | 4,734,991 | 116,516 | 204,002 | — | 320,518 |

1. Includes deaths from all causes. 2. Official figures. NOTE: For additional U.S. figures, *see* the table on U.S. Casualties in Major Wars in this section.

## Casualties in World War II

| Country | Men in war | Battle deaths | Wounded |
|---|---|---|---|
| Australia | 1,000,000 | 26,976 | 180,864 |
| Austria | 800,000 | 280,000 | 350,117 |
| Belgium | 625,000 | 8,460 | 55,513[1] |
| Brazil[2] | 40,334 | 943 | 4,222 |
| Bulgaria | 339,760 | 6,671 | 21,878 |
| Canada | 1,041,080 | 32,412 | 53,145 |
| China[3] | 17,250,521 | 1,324,516 | 1,762,006 |
| Czechoslovakia | — | 6,683[4] | 8,017 |
| Denmark | — | 4,339 | — |
| Finland | 500,000 | 79,047 | 50,000 |
| France | — | 201,568 | 400,000 |
| Germany | 20,000,000 | 3,250,000[4] | 7,250,000 |
| Greece | — | 17,024 | 47,290 |
| Hungary | — | 147,435 | 89,313 |
| India | 2,393,891 | 32,121 | 64,354 |
| Italy | 3,100,000 | 149,496[4] | 66,716 |
| Japan | 9,700,000 | 1,270,000 | 140,000 |
| Netherlands | 280,000 | 6,500 | 2,860 |
| New Zealand | 194,000 | 11,625[4] | 17,000 |
| Norway | 75,000 | 2,000 | — |
| Poland | — | 664,000 | 530,000 |
| Romania | 650,000[5] | 350,000[6] | — |
| South Africa | 410,056 | 2,473 | — |
| U.S.S.R. | — | 6,115,000[4] | 14,012,000 |
| United Kingdom | 5,896,000 | 357,116[4] | 369,267 |
| United States | 16,112,566 | 291,557 | 670,846 |
| Yugoslavia | 3,741,000 | 305,000 | 425,000 |

1. Civilians only. 2. Army and navy figures. 3. Figures cover period July 7, 1937–Sept. 2, 1945, and concern only Chinese regular troops. They do not include casualties suffered by guerrillas and local military corps. 4. Deaths from all causes. 5. Against Soviet Russia; 385,847 against Nazi Germany. 6. Against Soviet Russia; 169,822 against Nazi Germany. NOTE: The figures in this table are unofficial estimates obtained from various sources. For additional U.S. Figures, *see* the tables on U.S. Casualties in Major Wars in this section.

## U.S. Casualties in Major Wars

| War | Branch of service | Numbers engaged | Battle deaths | Other deaths | Total deaths | Wounds not mortal | Total casualties[1] |
|---|---|---|---|---|---|---|---|
| Revolutionary War 1775 to 1783 | Army | n.a. | 4,044 | n.a. | n.a. | 6,004 | n.a. |
| | Navy | n.a. | 342 | n.a. | n.a. | 114 | n.a. |
| | Marines | n.a. | 49 | n.a. | n.a. | 70 | n.a. |
| | **Total** | **n.a.** | **4,435** | **n.a.** | **n.a.** | **6,188** | **n.a.** |
| War of 1812 1812 to 1815 | Army | n.a. | 1,950 | n.a. | n.a. | 4,000 | n.a. |
| | Navy | n.a. | 265 | n.a. | n.a. | 439 | n.a. |
| | Marines | n.a. | 45 | n.a. | n.a. | 66 | n.a. |
| | **Total** | **286,730** | **2,260** | **n.a.** | **n.a.** | **4,505** | **n.a.** |

| War | Branch of service | Numbers engaged | Battle deaths | Other deaths | Total deaths | Wounds not mortal | Total casualties[1] |
|---|---|---|---|---|---|---|---|
| Mexican War 1846 to 1848 | Army | n.a. | 1,721 | 11,550 | 13,271 | 4,102 | 17,373 |
| | Navy | n.a. | 1 | n.a. | n.a. | 3 | n.a. |
| | Marines | n.a. | 11 | n.a. | n.a. | 47 | n.a. |
| | **Total** | **78,718** | **1,733** | n.a. | n.a. | **4,152** | n.a. |
| Civil War[2] 1861 to 1865 | Army | 2,128,948 | 138,154 | 221,374 | 359,528 | 280,040 | 639,568 |
| | Navy | 84,415 | 2,112 | 2,411 | 4,523 | 1,710 | 6,233 |
| | Marines | | 148 | 312 | 460 | 131 | 591 |
| | **Total** | **2,213,363** | **140,414** | **224,097** | **364,511** | **281,881** | **646,392** |
| Spanish-American War 1898 | Army | 280,564 | 369 | 2,061 | 2,430 | 1,594 | 4,024 |
| | Navy | 22,875 | 10 | 0 | 10 | 47 | 57 |
| | Marines | 3,321 | 6 | 0 | 6 | 21 | 27 |
| | **Total** | **306,760** | **385** | **2,061** | **2,446** | **1,662** | **4,108** |
| World War I 1917 to 1918 | Army | 4,057,101 | 50,510 | 55,868 | 106,378 | 193,663 | 300,041 |
| | Navy | 599,051 | 431 | 6,856 | 7,287 | 819 | 8,106 |
| | Marines | 78,839 | 2,461 | 390 | 2,851 | 9,520 | 12,371 |
| | **Total** | **4,734,991** | **53,402** | **63,114** | **116,516** | **204,002** | **320,518** |
| World War II 1941 to 1946 | Army[3] | 11,260,000 | 234,874 | 83,400 | 318,274 | 565,861 | 884,135 |
| | Navy | 4,183,466 | 36,950 | 25,664 | 62,614 | 37,778 | 100,392 |
| | Marines | 669,100 | 19,733 | 4,778 | 24,511 | 67,207 | 91,718 |
| | **Total** | **16,112,566** | **291,557** | **113,842** | **405,399** | **670,846** | **1,076,245** |
| Korean War 1950 to 1953 | Army | 2,834,000 | 27,704 | 9,429 | 37,133 | 77,596 | 114,729 |
| | Navy | 1,177,000 | 458 | 4,043 | 4,501 | 1,576 | 6,077 |
| | Marines | 424,000 | 4,267 | 1,261 | 5,528 | 23,744 | 29,272 |
| | Air Force | 1,285,000 | 1,200 | 5,884 | 7,084 | 368 | 7,452 |
| | **Total** | **5,720,000** | **33,629** | **20,617** | **54,246** | **103,284** | **157,530** |
| War in Southeast Asia[4] | Army | 4,386,000 | 30,717 | 7,194 | 37,911 | 201,536 | 239,447 |
| | Navy[5] | 1,842,000 | 1,535 | 909 | 2,444 | 10,078 | 12,522 |
| | Marines | 794,000 | 13,025 | 1,680 | 14,705 | 88,633 | 103,338 |
| | Air Force | 1,740,000 | 1,339 | 603 | 1,942 | 3,457 | 5,399 |
| | **Total** | **8,744,000** | **46,616** | **10,386** | **57,002** | **303,704** | **360,706** |

1. Excludes captured or interned and missing in action who were subsequently returned to military control. 2. Union forces only. Totals should probably be somewhat larger as data or disposition of prisoners are far from complete. Final Confederate deaths, based on incomplete returns, were 133,821, to which should be added 26,000–31,000 personnel who died in Union prisons. 3. Army data include Air Force. 4. As of Sept. 30, 1977. 5. Includes a small number of Coast Guard. NOTE: All data are subject to revision. For wars before World War I, information represents best data from available records. However, due to incomplete records and possible difference in usage of terminology, reporting systems, etc., figures should be considered estimates. n.a. = not available. *Source:* Department of Defense.

# U.S. and Soviet Strategic Force Levels

| Offensive and Defense forces | Mid-1977 U.S. | Mid-1977 U.S.S.R. | Mid-1976 U.S. | Mid-1976 U.S.S.R. |
|---|---|---|---|---|
| Intercontinental ballistic missile launchers[1,2] | 1,054 | 1,450 | 1,054 | 1,550 |
| Submarine-launched ballistic missile launchers[1,3] | 656 | 880 | 656 | 800 |
| Long range bombers[4,5] | 418 | 210 | 419 | 190 |
| Force loadings weapons[6] | 8,500 | 4,000 | 8,400 | 3,300 |
| Air defense surveillance radars[7] | 59 | 6,500 | 59 | 6,000 |
| Air defense interceptors[7,8] | 341 | 2,540 | 416 | 2,590 |
| Surface-to-air launchers[7,9] | — | 10,000 | — | 10,000 |
| Antiballistic missile launchers | — | 64 | — | 64 |

1. Includes on-line missile launchers as well as those in the final stages of construction, in overhaul, repair, conversion and modernization. 2. Does not include test and training launchers, but, for the U.S.S.R., does not include at test ranges which are probably part of the operational force. 3. Includes launchers on all nuclear-powered submarines, and, for the U.S.S.R., operational launchers for modern SLBMs on G-class diesel submarines. 4. The following long-range bombers are placed in this category: for the U.S.: B-52s, FB-111, B-1; for the U.S.S.R.: Bear, Bison, Backfire. 5. Includes deployed, strike-configured aircraft only. 6. Total force loadings reflect only those independently-targetable weapons associated with on-line ICBMs/SLBMs and UE aircraft. Weapons reserved for restrike and weapons on inactive status are not included. 7. Excludes radars and launchers at test sites or outside CONUS. 8. These numbers represent Total Active Inventory (TAI). 9. These 10,000 launchers accommodate about 12,000 SAM interceptors. Some of the launchers have multiple rails. *Source:* U.S. Department of Defense.

# Military Strengths of World Nations, 1977

| Country | Expenditures: Total (millions) | Expenditures: Per person | Expenditures: % of govt. spending | Expenditures: % of GNP[1] (1976) | Manpower (in thousands): Total in armed forces | Army | Navy | Air Forces | Estimated reservists[2] | Para-military forces |
|---|---|---|---|---|---|---|---|---|---|---|
| United States | $113,000 | $523 | 24.4 | 6.0 | 2,088.0 | 789.0 | 728.0 | 571.0 | 870.5 | — |
| Canada | 3,348 | 144 | n.a. | 1.9 | 80.0 | 28.5 | 13.4 | 36.6 | 19.1 | — |
| U.S.S.R. | 130,000[3] | n.a. | n.a. | n.a. | 3,675.0 | 1,825.0[4] | 450.0[4] | 475.0[4] | 4,200.0 | 450.0 |
| China | n.a. | n.a. | n.a. | n.a. | 3,950.0 | 3,250.0 | 300.0 | 400.0 | n.a. | n.a. |
| **NATO** (not including U.S. and Canada) | | | | | | | | | | |
| Belgium | 2,476 | 253 | 10.4 | 3.0 | 85.7 | 62.1 | 4.2 | 19.4 | 55.5 | 16.0 |
| Britain | 11,214 | 201 | 11.4 | 5.1 | 339.2[5] | 175.3[5] | 76.7[5] | 87.2[5] | 248.6[5] | — |
| Denmark | 1,103 | 217 | 6.8 | 2.8 | 34.7 | 21.8 | 5.8 | 7.1 | 153.2 | — |
| France | 13,740 | 256 | 20.4 | 3.7 | 502.1 | 330.0 | 68.5 | 103.6 | 450.0 | 76.2 |
| Germany, West[6] | 21,092 | 333 | 29.2 | 4.2 | 489.0 | 341.0 | 38.0 | 110.0 | 1,179.5 | 20.0 |
| Greece | 1,100 | 120 | n.a. | 5.5 | 200.0 | 160.0 | 17.5 | 22.5 | 310.0 | 118.0 |
| Italy | 4,416 | 78 | 8.3 | 2.6 | 330.0 | 218.0 | 42.0 | 70.0 | 694.8 | 90.0 |
| Luxembourg | 28 | 80 | 2.9 | 1.2[7] | 0.6 | 0.6 | — | — | — | 0.4 |
| Netherlands | 3,357 | 241 | 9.7 | 3.4 | 109.7 | 75.0 | 17.0 | 17.7 | 176.5 | 7.7 |
| Norway | 1,194 | 295 | 9.9 | 3.1 | 39.0 | 20.0 | 9.0 | 10.0 | 240.0 | — |
| Portugal | 508 | 52 | 19.2 | 3.9 | 58.8 | 36.0 | 12.8 | 10.0 | n.a. | 23.4 |
| Turkey | 2,653 | 64 | 21.1 | 5.6 | 465.0 | 375.0 | 43.0 | 47.0 | 725.0 | 75.0 |
| **WARSAW PACT[8]** (not including U.S.S.R.) | | | | | | | | | | |
| Bulgaria | 538 | 61 | 7.3 | 2.6 | 148.5 | 115.0 | 8.5 | 25.0 | 235.0 | 40.0 |
| Czechoslovakia | 1,614 | 108 | 6.2 | 3.5 | 181.0 | 135.0 | — | 46.0 | 350.0 | 10.0 |
| Germany, East | 2,889 | 167 | 7.8 | 6.0 | 157.0 | 105.0 | 16.0 | 36.0 | 255.0 | 73.0 |
| Hungary | 590 | 56 | 3.6 | 2.6 | 103.0 | 83.0 | — | 20.0 | 143.0 | 20.0 |
| Poland | 2,438 | 70 | n.a. | 3.6 | 307.0 | 220.0 | 25.0 | 62.0 | 605.0 | 97.0 |
| Romania | 824 | 38 | n.a. | 1.8 | 180.0 | 140.0 | 10.0 | 30.0 | 345.5 | 37.0 |
| **OTHER EUROPEAN COUNTRIES** | | | | | | | | | | |
| Austria | 534 | 68 | 3.7 | 1.1 | 37.3 | 33.0 | — | 4.3 | 112.7 | 11.3 |
| Finland | 426 | 90 | n.a. | 1.1 | 39.9 | 34.4 | 2.5 | 3.0 | 690.0 | 4.0 |
| Ireland | 146 | 45 | 4.2 | 1.6 | 14.7 | 13.4 | 0.6 | 0.7 | 18.7 | — |
| Spain | 2,154 | 59 | 15.3 | 1.7 | 309.0 | 220.0 | 48.0 | 41.0 | n.a. | 65.0 |
| Sweden | 2,833 | 343 | n.a. | 3.7 | 68.6 | 46.0 | 12.0 | 10.6 | 500.0 | — |
| Switzerland | 1,280 | 204 | 20.3 | 2.3 | 18.5 | 18.5 | — | — | 621.5 | — |
| Yugoslavia[7] | 1,640 | 76 | 41.0 | n.a. | 260.0 | 193.0 | 27.0 | 40.0 | 500.0 | 616.0 |

| | | | | | | | | | | |
|---|---|---|---|---|---|---|---|---|---|---|
| **MIDDLE EAST** | | | | | | | | | | |
| Algeria[7] | 387 | 23 | 5.8 | n.a. | 75.8 | 67.0 | 3.8 | 5.0 | 100.0 | 10.0 |
| Egypt | 4,365 | 112 | 25.0 | 37.0 | 345.0 | 300.0 | 20.0 | 25.0 | 515.0 | 50.0 |
| Iran[7] | 7,898 | 227 | 16.1 | 12.0 | 342.0 | 220.0 | 22.0 | 100.0 | 300.0 | 70.0 |
| Iraq | 1,660 | 141 | 17.6 | n.a. | 188.0 | 160.0 | 3.0 | 25.0 | 250.0 | 54.8 |
| Israel | 4,268 | 1,178 | 32.4 | 35.3 | 164.0 | 138.0 | 5.0 | 21.0 | 460.0 | 9.5 |
| Jordan | 201 | 69 | 20.2 | 11.7 | 67.8 | 61.0 | 0.2 | 6.7 | 30.0 | 10.0 |
| Libya | n.a. | n.a. | n.a. | n.a. | 29.2 | 22.0 | 2.7 | 4.5 | n.a. | n.a. |
| Morocco | 346 | 19 | 7.8 | 3.2[7] | 84.7 | 75.0 | 4.0 | 5.7 | n.a. | 30.0 |
| Saudi Arabia | 7,538 | 1,005 | 24.0 | n.a. | 61.5 | 45.0 | 1.5 | 15.0 | n.a. | 41.5 |
| Sudan | n.a. | n.a. | n.a. | n.a. | 52.1 | 50.0 | 0.6 | 1.5 | n.a. | 3.5 |
| Syria[7] | 1,067 | 137 | 23.0 | n.a. | 227.5 | 200.0 | 2.5 | 25.0 | 102.5 | 9.5 |
| **AFRICA** | | | | | | | | | | |
| Ethiopia | n.a. | n.a. | n.a. | n.a. | 53.5 | 50.0 | 1.5 | 2.0 | 20.0 | 84.0 |
| Nigeria | n.a. | n.a. | n.a. | n.a. | 230.5 | 221.0 | 3.5 | 6.0 | 2.0 | — |
| Rhodesia | 159 | 23 | 20.0 | 3.8 | 9.6 | 8.3 | — | 1.3 | 55.0 | 44.0 |
| South Africa | 1,897 | 70 | n.a. | 4.7 | 55.0 | 41.0 | 5.5 | 8.5 | 165.5 | 125.5 |
| **ASIA** (not including China) | | | | | | | | | | |
| Australia | n.a. | n.a. | n.a. | 2.8 | 69.7 | 31.8 | 16.2 | 21.7 | 32.2 | — |
| China (Taiwan) | n.a. | n.a. | n.a. | n.a. | 460.0 | 320.0 | 70.0 | 70.0 | 1,170.0 | 100.0 |
| India | 3,445 | 6 | 19.5 | n.a. | 1,096.0 | 950.0 | 46.0 | 100.0 | 240.0 | 300.0 |
| Indonesia | 1,349 | 10 | 14.0 | n.a. | 247.0 | 180.0 | 39.0 | 28.0 | n.a. | 112.0 |
| Japan | 6,090 | 49 | 5.9 | 0.9 | 238.0 | 155.0 | 40.0 | 43.0 | 39.6 | — |
| Korea, South | 1,800 | 51 | n.a. | n.a. | 635.0 | 560.0 | 45.0 | 30.0 | 1,240.0 | 1,000.0 |
| Malaysia | 544 | 41 | n.a. | n.a. | 64.0 | 52.5 | 5.5 | 6.0 | 27.0 | 213.0 |
| New Zealand | n.a. | n.a. | n.a. | 1.7 | 12.5 | 5.5 | 2.7 | 4.3 | 12.2 | — |
| Pakistan | 819 | 11 | 22.0 | 6.2 | 428.0 | 400.0 | 11.0 | 17.0 | 513.0 | 157.0 |
| Philippines | 420 | 9 | n.a. | 2.4 | 99.0 | 63.0 | 20.0 | 16.0 | 45.0 | 65.0 |
| Singapore | n.a. | n.a. | n.a. | n.a. | 36.0 | 30.0 | 3.0 | 3.0 | 45.0 | 37.5 |
| Thailand | n.a. | n.a. | n.a. | n.a. | 211.0 | 141.0 | 28.0 | 42.0 | 500.0 | 66.0 |
| **LATIN AMERICA** | | | | | | | | | | |
| Argentina | 1,415 | 54 | 14.7 | 2.8 | 129.9 | 80.0 | 32.9 | 17.0 | 250.0 | 51.0 |
| Brazil | 2,073 | 18 | 9.4 | 1.3 | 271.8 | 180.0 | 49.0 | 42.8 | n.a. | 200.0 |
| Colombia | 140 | 5 | 8.2 | 0.9 | 56.5 | 42.0 | 8.0 | 6.5 | 250.0 | 5.0 |
| Mexico[7] | 542 | 8 | 3.9 | 0.8 | 95.5 | 72.0 | 17.5 | 6.0 | n.a. | n.a. |
| Peru | 406 | 24 | 13.5 | n.a. | 70.0 | 46.0 | 14.0 | 10.0 | n.a. | 20.0 |
| Uruguay | 75 | 24 | 17.2 | 1.8 | 27.0 | 20.0 | 4.0 | 3.0 | n.a. | 2.2 |
| Venezuela | 513 | 52 | 6.1 | 1.3 | 44.0 | 28.0 | 8.0 | 8.0 | n.a. | 10.0 |

1. Based on local currency. GNP estimated where official figures are unavailable. 2. Reservists with recent training. 3. *Information Please* estimate. 4. Excludes Strategic Rocket Forces. 5. Includes men enlisted outside Britain. 6. Includes aid to West Berlin. 7. Gross domestic product at market prices. 8. This section not directly comparable to others. Difficulty of calculating suitable exchange rates makes conversion to dollars imprecise. GNP estimates are at factor-cost (market price for U.S.S.R.). NOTE: n.a. - not available. *Source:* International Institute for Strategic Studies, London.

## U.S. Military Sales Deliveries to Foreign Governments

(in millions of dollars)

| Country | 1970–1976[1] | 1976 | 1975 | 1974 | 1960–1969 |
|---|---|---|---|---|---|
| Argentina | 70.6 | 8.5 | 8.3 | 11.1 | 57.7 |
| Australia | 486.2 | 25.8 | 29.0 | 173.8 | 487.5 |
| Austria | 21.6 | 2.3 | 2.1 | 1.8 | 42.1 |
| Belgium | 50.6 | 6 | 6 | 5 | 76.4 |
| Bolivia | .9 | ([4]) | ([4]) | ([4]) | .5 |
| Brazil | 143.4 | 32.8 | 38.8 | 20.9 | 61.9 |
| Burma | 1.2 | ([4]) | .1 | .2 | 1.3 |
| Canada | 401.0 | 81.1 | 78.2 | 52.0 | 243.3 |
| Chile | 73.0 | 24.5 | 12.5 | 4.8 | 18.6 |
| China[3] | 529.5 | 124.7 | 114.7 | 93.3 | 29.1 |
| Colombia | 10.3 | 1.1 | .8 | 3.9 | 2.6 |
| Denmark | 92.0 | 11.5 | 25.2 | 10.1 | 52.0 |
| Dominican Rep. | .5 | ([4]) | ([4]) | ([4]) | .9 |
| Ecuador | 5.9 | 3.9 | 1.4 | ([4]) | 2.7 |
| El Salvador | .9 | .3 | .3 | .1 | .8 |
| Ethiopia | 29.6 | 15.8 | 9.7 | — | .2 |
| France | 66.3 | 12.9 | 5.3 | 3.4 | 258.9 |
| Germany | 2,455.6 | 375.8 | 395.7 | 413.6 | 2,471.1 |
| Greece | 538.4 | 135.3 | 134.9 | 101.2 | 22.7 |
| Guatemala | 17.8 | 1.4 | 3.4 | 1.5 | 2.0 |
| Honduras | 6.3 | 4.7 | .6 | .8 | .2 |
| India | 9.2 | 2.7 | 2.4 | .1 | 19.3 |
| Indonesia | 16.2 | 4.1 | 8.0 | .1 | .6 |
| Iran | 3,812.3 | 1,231.6 | 956.4 | 510.3 | 237.8 |
| Israel | 3,447.0 | 683.8 | 667.7 | 978.1 | 156.2 |
| Italy | 302.7 | 40.0 | 51.5 | 20.9 | 322.8 |
| Japan | 195.8 | 21.4 | 34.1 | 23.1 | 179.6 |
| Jordan | 211.9 | 70.5 | 16.7 | 14.8 | 74.7 |
| Korea | 236.8 | 138.0 | 57.5 | 13.4 | 2.2 |
| Kuwait | 30.0 | 16.6 | 7.6 | ([4]) | — |
| Lebanon | 11.2 | 2.3 | 1.0 | .8 | 1.7 |
| Libya | 12.3 | — | ([4]) | .3 | 17.3 |
| Malaysia | 47.1 | 12.4 | 29.0 | 2.1 | 3.9 |
| Mexico | 4.1 | .7 | .2 | .9 | 7.9 |
| Morocco | 45.0 | 12.6 | 2.7 | 4.1 | 9.8 |
| Netherlands | 114.1 | 18.2 | 25.6 | 25.0 | 74.3 |
| New Zealand | 59.2 | 3.7 | 4.6 | 4.5 | 53.0 |
| Norway | 153.6 | 18.9 | 22.5 | 12.9 | 101.9 |
| Pakistan | 78.4 | 12.9 | 13.7 | 18.0 | 40.3 |
| Peru | 49.7 | 29.2 | 8.3 | 4.4 | 16.4 |
| Philippines | 26.7 | 10.4 | 5.4 | 1.7 | 3.5 |
| Portugal | 5.5 | .7 | .8 | .5 | 5.9 |
| Saudi Arabia | 1,488.9 | 429.4 | 300.4 | 226.5 | 126.6 |
| Singapore | 24.3 | 5.5 | 7.6 | 3.7 | .8 |
| Spain | 347.7 | 118.9 | 42.0 | 24.6 | 60.0 |
| Sweden | 13.6 | .3 | 1.5 | 1.6 | 29.7 |
| Switzerland | 94.1 | 6.0 | 8.3 | 6.9 | 50.5 |
| Thailand | 70.8 | 17.8 | 17.2 | 3.6 | .5 |
| Turkey | 229.7 | 105.3 | 91.0 | 17.1 | 1.5 |
| U.K. | 811.1 | 148.9 | 67.4 | 64.7 | 948.4 |
| Uruguay | 7.6 | 1.1 | 2.0 | 1.6 | 1.5 |
| Venezuela | 76.4 | 11.4 | 17.2 | 25.5 | 71.9 |
| Vietnam | 1.2 | — | ([4]) | 1.2 | ([4]) |
| Yugoslavia | .8 | .2 | ([4]) | ([4]) | 8.9 |
| Zaire | 22.0 | 2.9 | .8 | 1.3 | 1.4 |
| International organizations | 187.7 | 27.0 | 31.7 | 22.5 | 166.5 |
| **Worldwide[2]** | **17,274.8** | **4,081.2** | **3,379.7** | **2,937.9** | **6,650.6** |

1. Includes transactions for fiscal year 1976 and the transition quarter, July-Sept. 1976. 2. Includes countries not shown separately. 3. Taiwan. 4. Less than $50,000. *Source:* Defense Security Assistance Agency.

## Strengths of Military Formations, 1977–1978

| Type of unit | U.S. | U.S.S.R. | China |
|---|---|---|---|
| Division: Armored | | | |
| Men | 16,500 | 11,000 | 10,000 |
| Tanks | 324 | 325[1] | 270 |
| Mechanized | | | |
| Men | 16,000 | 12,700 | 12,000[2] |
| Tanks | 216 | 266[1] | 30[2] |
| Airborne | | | |
| Men | 15,000 | 7,000 | 9,000 |
| Brigade: Armored | | | |
| Men | 4,200 | 1,300 | 1,200[3] |
| Tanks | 108 | 95[3] | 90[3] |
| Mechanized | | | |
| Men | 4,500 | 2,300[3] | 2,000[3] |
| Tanks | 54 | 40[3] | — |
| Squadron: Fighter | | | |
| Aircraft | 12–14 | 10–14 | 9–10 |

1. Tank strengths are for Soviet divisions in Eastern Europe; other divisions have fewer. 2. Infantry division. 3. Strength of a regiment, which is equivalent formation in Soviet and Chinese command structures. Particularly in West European countries, "regiment" often describes a battalion-size unit. It is so used here. *Source:* International Institute for Strategic Studies, London.

## NATO and Warsaw Pact Military Balance, 1977–1978

| Category | Northern and Central Europe[1] NATO | Warsaw Pact | (of which) U.S.S.R. | Southern Europe[2] NATO | Warsaw Pact | (of which) U.S.S.R |
|---|---|---|---|---|---|---|
| Ground forces available in peacetime (division equivalents): | | | | | | |
| Armored | 10 | 32 | 22 | 4 | 6 | 2 |
| Infantry, mechanized and airborne | 17 | 38 | 23 | 33 | 27 | 9 |
| Combat and direct support troops available (thousands) | 630 | 945 | 640 | 560 | 390 | 145 |
| Main battle tanks available in peacetime | 7,000 | 20,500 | 13,500 | 4,000 | 6,700 | 2,500 |
| Tactical aircraft in operational service: | | | | | | |
| Light bombers | 150 | 125 | 125 | — | 50 | 50 |
| Fighter/ground attack | 1,500 | 1,350 | 925 | 625 | 325 | 125 |
| Interceptors | 400 | 2,050 | 900 | 200 | 1,000 | 425 |
| Reconnaissance | 300 | 550 | 350 | 125 | 200 | 150 |

| Missile strength (all theaters) | Intercontinental ballistic missiles | Submarine launched ballistic missiles | Long-range bombers |
|---|---|---|---|
| United States[3] | 1,054 | 656 | 373 |
| Soviet Union[3] | 1,477 | 909 | 135 |

1. On NATO side, the commands for which Allied Forces, Central Europe, and Allied Forces, Northern Europe, commanders have responsibility. France (not part of NATO's integrated commands) is not included. On Warsaw Pact side, armed forces of Bulgaria, Hungary, and Romania are not included. 2. On NATO side, includes Italian, Greek, and Turkish land forces and such U.S. and British units as would be committed to Mediterranean theater of operations. On Warsaw Pact side, includes land forces of Bulgaria, Hungary, and Romania and such Soviet units normally stationed in Hungary and southwestern U.S.S.R. as might be committed to Mediterranean theater of operations. 3. 1977. *Source:* International Institute for Strategic Studies, London.

## Value of Arms Exports and Imports, Supplier and Recipient Countries

(in millions of constant 1974 dollars)

| Country | 1975 | 1974 | 1973 | 1971–1972 | 1966–1970 |
|---|---|---|---|---|---|
| **SUPPLIERS** | | | | | |
| United States | 4,440 | 4,160 | 5,520 | 8,870 | 18,630 |
| U.S.S.R. | 2,390 | 2,870 | 3,150 | 4,770 | 10,980 |
| France | 461 | 561 | 621 | 809 | 1,250 |
| United Kingdom | 346 | 463 | 366 | 579 | 960 |
| China, People's Rep | 175 | 321 | 255 | 765 | 1,166 |
| Germany, West | 235 | 223 | 29 | 421 | 703 |
| Czechoslovakia | 108 | 76 | 117 | 289 | 950 |
| Canada | 67 | 109 | 81 | 405 | 825 |
| Poland | 38 | 20 | 67 | 316 | 1,039 |
| Other | 630 | 487 | 324 | 606 | 797 |
| **RECIPIENTS—DEVELOPED COUNTRIES** | 2,380 | 2,620 | 1,660 | 4,450 | 11,930 |
| Germany, West | 442 | 470 | 305 | 736 | 1,258 |
| Germany, East | 338 | 410 | 116 | 526 | 974 |
| U.S.S.R. | 27 | 40 | 110 | 352 | 1,490 |
| Poland | 252 | 290 | 110 | 400 | 925 |
| United States | 132 | 116 | 188 | 368 | 1,060 |
| U.K. | 101 | 73 | 42 | 128 | 1,406 |
| Czechoslovakia | 178 | 275 | 83 | 250 | 623 |
| Australia | 28 | 55 | 219 | 111 | 624 |
| Italy | 72 | 182 | 92 | 298 | 387 |
| Japan | 47 | 91 | 80 | 151 | 361 |
| Hungary | 101 | 130 | 22 | 128 | 256 |
| Romania | 111 | 60 | 44 | 140 | 269 |
| Other | 551 | 428 | 249 | 862 | 2,297 |

| Country | 1975 | 1974 | 1973 | 1971–1972 | 1966–1970 |
|---|---|---|---|---|---|
| **RECIPIENTS—DEVELOPING COUNTRIES** | 6,510 | 6,670 | 8,870 | 13,380 | 25,370 |
| Vietnam, South | 829 | 665 | 1,250 | 2,504 | 5,291 |
| Vietnam, North | 142 | 400 | 358 | 1,243 | 3,570 |
| Israel | 650 | 636 | 1,880 | 553 | 683 |
| Iran | 1,020 | 870 | 530 | 871 | 930 |
| Egypt | 211 | 118 | 655 | 765 | 1,612 |
| Korea, South | 166 | 114 | 167 | 864 | 1,773 |
| Turkey | 152 | 205 | 292 | 700 | 1,498 |
| India | 139 | 129 | 198 | 524 | 1,126 |
| Syria | 202 | 465 | 797 | 323 | 306 |
| China, Rep. of | 151 | 126 | 160 | 546 | 1,090 |
| Iraq | 413 | 416 | 394 | 141 | 529 |
| Greece | 177 | 169 | 54 | 567 | 641 |
| Libya | 330 | 159 | 231 | 326 | 149 |
| Pakistan | 62 | 93 | 145 | 169 | 580 |
| Korea, North | 16 | 60 | 154 | 357 | 416 |
| Laos | 20 | 68 | 106 | 262 | 457 |
| Spain | 112 | 83 | 116 | 257 | 231 |
| Cambodia | 117 | 302 | 87 | 162 | 108 |
| Brazil | 66 | 71 | 128 | 131 | 226 |
| Peru | 99 | 74 | 85 | 157 | 140 |
| Cuba | 35 | 18 | 28 | 59 | 261 |
| Indonesia | 16 | 35 | 22 | 70 | 51 |
| Other | 1,385 | 1,394 | 1,033 | 1,829 | 3,702 |
| **World, total** | **8,890** | **9,290** | **10,530** | **17,830** | **37,300** |

*Source:* U.S. Arms Control and Disarmament Agency.

## U.S. Ballistic Missiles of Operational or Near-Operational Status

| Name | Branch of service | Maximum length (ft) | Maximum launch weight (lb) | Maximum thrust (lb) | Maximum range (nautical mi.) |
|---|---|---|---|---|---|
| **SURFACE-TO-SURFACE** | | | | | |
| Minuteman 3 | USAF | 60 | 78,000 | 205,000 | 7,000+ |
| Polaris A3 | USN | 31 | 35,000 | — | 2,500 |
| Poseidon C3 | USN | 34 | 65,000 | — | 2,500 |
| Tomahawk | USN | 18 | — | 600 | 2,000+ |
| Titan 2 | USAF | 104 | 330,000 | 530,000 | 6,300 |
| Trident C4 | USN | 34 | 65,000 | — | 4,000 |
| **SURFACE-TO-AIR** | | | | | |
| Hawk (Improved) | Army | 17 | 1,398 | — | 22 |
| Nike Hercules | Army | 41 | 10,000 | — | 75+ |
| Redeye | Army | 4 | 29 | — | — |
| Standard Missile (ER) | USN | 27 | 3,000 | — | 30+ |
| Talos | USN | 33 | 7,800 | 20,000 | 65+ |
| Tartar | USN | 15 | 1,425 | — | 10+ |
| Terrier | USN | 26.5 | 3,070 | — | 20+ |
| **AIR-TO-SURFACE** | | | | | |
| ALCM | USAF | 19.5 | 2,800 | 600 | — |
| ASALM | USAF | 14 | 2,700 | — | — |
| HARM | USN | 13.5 | 770 | — | — |
| Harpoon | USN | 12.5 | 1,200 | 660 | 50+ |
| Hound Dog | USAF | 43 | 10,000 | 7,500 | 600+ |
| Quail | USAF | 13 | 1,200 | 2,450 | 345 |
| SRAM | USAF | 14 | 2,200 | — | 120 |
| Standard ARM | USAF/USN | 15 | 1,300 | — | — |
| Walleye 2 | USN | 13 | 2,400 | — | — |
| **AIR-TO-AIR** | | | | | |
| Falcon | USAF | 7 | 140 | 4,440 | 5 |
| Superfalcon | USAF | 7 | 250 | 5,600 | — |

| Name | Branch of service | Maximum length (ft) | Maximum launch weight (lb) | Maximum thrust (lb) | Maximum range (nautical mi.) |
|---|---|---|---|---|---|
| Genie | USAF | 10 | 800 | 36,000 | 6 |
| Phoenix | USN | 13 | 1,000 | — | — |
| Sidewinder | USN/AF | 10 | 170–185 | — | — |
| Sparrow | USN/AF | 12 | 500 | — | 24+ |
| **ANTI-SUBMARINE** | | | | | |
| Subroc | USN | 22 | 4,000 | — | — |

## Russian Missiles

| Name (nickname) | Length (ft) | Launch weight, lb[1] | Range (miles) | Launch thrust, lb[1] | Remarks |
|---|---|---|---|---|---|
| **GROUND-TO-GROUND:** | | | | | |
| Scud-A | 32 | 9,000 | 100 | 15,000 | Liquid fuel; operational |
| Scud-B | 37 | 10,000 | 135 | 17,000 | Liquid fuel; status unknown |
| Shaddock | 36 | 14,000 | 245 | 20,000 | Probably solid fuel |
| Sandal | 66.5 | 50,000 | 350 | 80,000 | Liquid fuel; obsolescent |
| SS-2 | 52 | 32,000 | 300 | 50,000 | Liquid fuel; production stopped |
| Shyster | 75 | 45,000 | 900+ | 75,000 | Liquid fuel; larger version known to exist |
| SS-5 | 85 | 90,000 | 1,900 | 125,000 | Liquid fuel; obsolescent |
| Iron Maiden | c. 40 | 70,000 | 1,200+ | 100,000 | Solid fuel |
| SS-6 | 110 | 200,000 | 6,000 | 350,000 | Liquid fuel; ICBM |
| SS-7 | 80 | 150,000 | 7,500 | 250,000 | Storable liquid; ICBM |
| Snark[2] | 47.5 | — | 1,500 | — | Solid fuel |
| **SURFACE-TO-AIR:** | | | | | |
| Guideline | 35 | 5,000 | 25–30 | 9,500 | First stage solid, second stage liquid |
| Guild | 38 | 6,000 | 18–20 | 11,000 | Liquid fuel; deployed |
| Gammon | 49 | 5,000 | up to 100 | 9,000 | First stage solid, second stage liquid |
| Goa | 22 | 1,000 | 17 | 2,000 | Truck-launched, solid fuel |
| Little Sister | 55 | 30,000 | — | — | Solid fuel |
| **TACTICAL, UNGUIDED:** | | | | | |
| Frog II | 30 | 4,800 | 17 | 9,000 | Solid fuel; operational |
| Frog III | 35 | 4,400 | up to 28 | 9,000 | Solid fuel; operational |
| Frog IV | 35 | 4,200 | 31 | 8,000 | Solid fuel; probably operational |
| Gannef[3] | 26 | 4,200 | 30–35 | 8,000 | See notes |
| **AIR-TO-AIR:** | | | | | |
| Anab | 12 | — | 12 | — | Solid power plant |
| Ash | 18 | — | 12 | — | Four carried by Fiddler |
| Acrid | 19 | — | 20 | — | Four carried by Foxbat |
| Apex | — | — | 15 | — | Carried on MiG–23 |
| Aphid | — | — | 3–4 | — | Carried on MiG–23 |

1. Estimated. 2. *Snark* (NATO designation) is a submarine-launched Polaris-type missile. It is uncertain whether underwater launch is possible or whether submarine has to surface for launch. Said to have a land-based version. 3. *Gannef* may be a solid fuel missile, but the solid-fuel units are believed to be take-off help only, with ramjet propulsion acting as a sustainer engine. Could be a dual-purpose weapon, both for antiaircraft use and for tactical support. The rocket nicknamed *Big Brother* is a three-stage solid-fuel missile of a length of about 120 feet. Its take-off thrust is believed to exceed one million pounds. Claims that *Big Brother* was the rocket that launched the *Vostok* and *Voskhod* manned spacecraft turned out to be wrong. The *Vostok* rocket, shown in Paris in 1967, was a special design.

## U.S. Lacks Diplomatic Relations With 13 Countries

The State Department notes that the United States does not have diplomatic relations with 13 countries. They are: Albania, Angola, Cambodia (Democratic Kampuchea), People's Republic of China, Comoro Islands, Cuba, Equatorial Guinea, Iraq, North Korea, Mongolia, Rhodesia, Uganda, and Vietnam.

## Predictions of the Third Kind

When scientists try to figure out what the world's climate will be in the year 2000, 2050, or even 3000, they make what they call "predictions of the first kind" and "predictions of the second kind." Predictions of the *first* kind are weather and climate forecasts based on natural processes: the input of the sun's energy and its movement through the atmosphere and the oceans, from the tropics to the arctic and antarctic regions and back again. Predictions of the *second* kind are based on the effects of man-made processes on weather or climate. The most important of these is the carbon dioxide produced from burning fuels in factories and power plants all over the world since the beginning of the Industrial Revolution more than 200 years ago.

Scientists don't believe they are far enough advanced to make predictions of the first kind far into the future. They think that they can make pretty good predictions of the second kind. When they get it all together, they hope they can combine the two and come up with reasonably accurate "predictions of the third kind" based on the combined effects of natural and man-made processes. If the climatologists have enough data, they believe that they can create a computer model which will allow reasonable predictions on which governments can base their agricultural policies.

Right now we know less about the effect of natural processes on the weather than we do about man-made influences. We just don't have enough weather stations collecting temperature and wind data, measurements of strength of the sun's radiation, and other information to be able to make reasonably accurate, useful weather predictions for more than a few days ahead, let alone 20 or 50 years into the future. However, we *can* accurately measure the amount of carbon dioxide that factories and power plants spew into the air every year. Based on our estimates of $CO_2$ emissions in the past, we can use our current data to predict future conditions. For example, according to United Nations statistics, the use of fossil fuel has been increasing each year since 1860 at a constant rate of 4.3%. In 1860, it is estimated, there were about 285 parts per million of carbon dioxide in the air. Today that figure is about 327. At this rate, the figures will reach 375 by the year 2000 and more than 500 parts per million by 2040.

Scientists warn that this increase in carbon dioxide in the atmosphere will almost certainly mean that the climate will grow steadily warmer because $CO_2$ absorbs the heat that normally would be radiated from the earth into space in the form of infrared rays. Unless much of the heat that is constantly reaching us from the sun can escape into space, we will inevitably warm up.

We have known about the carbon dioxide buildup for a long time, but only in the past few years has concern about possible changes in our climate become general. This has been because we have had several years in a row of "unusual" weather. As everybody remembers, the winter of 1977 was especially cold. The winter of 1978, in its own way, was also abnormal. West of the Continental Divide the winter was wetter than usual, with floods in Southern California. Meteorologists attribute the heavy rain and snow in the West to a shift in the jet stream, which in 1977–1978 pushed west to east directly across the Rockies. In the East, heavy winter storms were caused by a greater-than-normal temperature difference between the cold air over the land on the East Coast and the warm moist air over the Atlantic Ocean. When these air masses met: blizzards.

Concern about abnormal weather patterns and about what man is doing to his climate have at last produced some action on the part of the government. In the summer of 1978, Congress passed the National Climate Program Act. Tens of millions of dollars, in addition to what the government is already spending on research and forecasting, will be appropriated to do three things: (1) gather all weather information and services in several central locations to make them more easily available to scientific researchers, farmers, and energy officials; (2) concentrate research on the two most important problems—better predictions of the first and second kind; (3) study in detail the impact on society of changes in climate.

The Department of Energy has already begun a concentrated investigation of the effects of increasing amounts of carbon dioxide in the atmosphere and what the government can do about it.

Scientists now agree that man is changing the climate by his own activities. They are not sure *how* the climate is being changed, although most of them believe it is getting warmer. These scientists are reluctant to make predictions until they are reasonably sure that they have all the data and that they can put information together in such a fashion that it makes sense. It is for politicians—or statesmen—to act in time to avoid whatever possible deleterious effects these climate changes might bring.

Passage of the National Climate Program Act seems to be one step forward.

*Wadsworth Likely*

### Tropical Storms and Hurricanes, 1886–1977

| | Jan.–Apr. | May | June | July | Aug. | Sept. | Oct. | Nov. | Dec. | Total |
|---|---|---|---|---|---|---|---|---|---|---|
| Number of tropical storms (incl. hurricanes) | 2 | 11 | 48 | 57 | 174 | 251 | 162 | 31 | 4 | 740 |
| Number of tropical storms that reached hurricane intensity | 1 | 3 | 21 | 32 | 128 | 162 | 78 | 14 | 2 | 441 |

# Devastating North Atlantic Hurricanes of the 20th Century

The following is a selected list of North Atlantic hurricanes based on casualties, damage, and general public interest. Facts about each storm are taken from Weather records, although in some cases only estimates of wind speed are available. Data given in this list pertain only to U.S. land areas except where indicated otherwise.

| Date | Areas hardest hit | Land stations with highest wind speed | Deaths (U.S. only) | Est. damage (millions) | Remarks |
|---|---|---|---|---|---|
| 1900, Aug. 27-Sept. 15 | Galveston, Tex. | Galveston, Tex. (120[1] mph) | 6,000 | $30 | Damage due to both winds and storm wave. Galveston Is. inundated. |
| 1909, Sept. 10–21 | Louisiana and Mississippi | New Orleans, La. (53 mph) | 350 | 5 | Winds 50–75 mi. W of New Orleans, where deaths occurred, were stronger than 68 mph. |
| 1915, Aug. 5–23 | East Texas and Louisiana | Galveston, Tex. (120 mph) | 275 | 50 | Water 5–6 ft deep in Galveston business district. 90% of homes demolished. Warnings issued well ahead of time. |
| 1915, Sept. 22-Oct. 1 | Mid-Gulf Coast | Burrwood, La. (140 mph) | 275 | 13 | Many casualties due to persons insisting on staying in low-lying areas despite warnings. |
| 1919, Sept. 2–15 | Florida, Louisiana, and Texas | Sand Key, Fla. (84[1] mph) | 287 | 22 | 488 persons drowned at sea. |
| 1926, Sept. 11–22 | Florida and Alabama | Miami, Fla. (138 mph) | 243 | 112 | Most deaths were in Miami area. Said to have been one of most destructive storms of century. |
| 1928, Sept. 6–20 | Southern Florida | Lake Okeechobee, Fla. (75[1] mph) | 1,836 | 25 | 1,870 injured. Nearly all deaths were in Lake Okeechobee area. Winds estimated as high as 160 mph caused Lake to overflow into populated areas. |
| 1935, Aug. 29-Sept. 10 | Southern Florida | Tampa, Fla. (86 mph) | 408 | 6 | Sustained winds over Florida Keys est. 150–200 mph. Remembered as "Labor Day Storm." |
| 1938, Sept. 10–22 | Long Island and Southern New England | Blue Hills Obs., Mass. (183 mph) | 600 | 306 | Unusually destructive. Storm center moved as fast as 56 mph at times. 1,754 injured. |
| 1944, Sept. 9–16 | North Carolina to New England | Cape Henry, Va. (150[1] mph) | 46 | 100 | 344 deaths at sea. Shipping lanes were crowded with war-time activity. |
| 1944, Oct. 12–23 | Florida | Dry Tortugas Is. (120 mph) | 18 | 100 | About 300 were killed in Cuba area before storm reached U.S. Evacuation of thousands from threatened areas in Fla. prevented higher toll. |
| 1947, Sept. 4–21 | Florida and Mid-Gulf Coast | Hillsboro Light, Fla. (155 mph) | 51 | 110 | Wind damage especially heavy Along Gulf Coast and Florida east coast. |
| 1954, Aug. 25–31 | North Carolina to New England | Block Island, R.I. (135 mph) | 60 | 461 | "CAROL"—more damage than any other single storm to this date. Water and high waves flooded low-lying areas; 1,000 injuries in Long Island–New England area. |
| 1954, Sept. 2–14 | New Jersey to New England | Block Island, R.I. (87 mph) | 21 | 40 | "EDNA"—New England again heavily hit. Gusts of 120 mph at Martha's Vineyard, Mass. |
| 1954, Oct. 5–18 | South Carolina to New York | New York, N.Y. (113 mph) (See Remarks) | 95 | 252 | "HAZEL"—several N.C. localities had winds of 130–150 mph with unusually heavy wave damage resulting. Est. 400–1,000 casualties in Haiti. In Canada there were 78 deaths, mostly due to flooding. |
| 1955, Aug. 7–21 | North Carolina to New England | Wilmington, N.C. (83 mph) | 184 | 832 | "DIANE"—worst floods in history in Southern New England. 16 in. of rain in Hartford area. |
| 1957, June 25–28 | Texas to Alabama | Sabine Pass, Tex. (100 mph) | 390 | 150 | "AUDREY"—gave an early start to the hurricane season and wiped out Cameron, La. Two |

| Date | Areas hardest hit | Land stations with highest wind speed | Deaths (U.S. only) | Est. damage (millions) | Remarks |
|---|---|---|---|---|---|
| | | | | | weeks later "BERTHA" struck same area. |
| 1960, Aug. 29-Sept. 13 | Florida to New England | Ft. Myers, Fla. (92 mph) Block Island, R.I. (130 mph) (See Remarks) | 50 | 500 | "DONNA"—hurricane winds from a single storm swept the entire Atlantic seaboard from Florida to New England for the first time in a 75-year record. Winds estimated near 140 mph with gusts 175–180 mph on Central Keys and lower southwest Florida coast. 115 deaths in Antilles, most from flash floods in Puerto Rico. |
| 1961, Sept. 3–15 | Texas coast | Port Lavaca, Tex. (145 mph) | 46 | 408 | "CARLA"—devastated Texas Gulf Coast Cities with 15-foot tides and 15-inch rains. Gusts to 175 mph at Port Lavaca. |
| 1964, Aug. 20-Sept. 5 | Southern Florida, Eastern Virginia | Miami, Fla. (110 mph) | 3 | 129 | "CLEO"—first hurricane in Miami area since 1950. Killed 214 in Caribbean Islands. |
| 1964, Aug. 28-Sept. 16 | Northeastern Florida, Southern Georgia | St. Augustine, Fla. (125 mph) | 5 | 250 | "DORA"—first storm of full hurricane force on record to move inland from east over northeastern Florida. |
| 1965, Aug. 27-Sept. 12 | Southern Florida and Louisiana | Port Sulphur, La. (136 mph) | 75 | 1,420 | "BETSY"—Damage in Louisiana, $1.2 billion. 27,000 homes destroyed, 17,500 injured or ill, 300,000 evacuated. Gusts of 165 mph at Pine Key, Fla. |
| 1967, Sept. 5–22 | Southern Texas | Brownsville, Texas (109 mph gust) | 15 | 200 | "BEULAH"—main damage was caused by torrential rains. |
| 1969, Aug. 14–22 | Mississippi, Louisiana, Alabama, Virginia, W. Virginia | Oil drilling rig east of Boothville, La. (172 mph) | 256 | 1,420 | "CAMILLE"—68 additional persons missing. One of most destructive killer storms ever to hit U.S. |
| 1970, July 23-Aug. 5 | Texas coast | Corpus Christi, Tex. (130 mph) | 11 | 453.8 | "CELIA"—Costliest storm in history to hit Texas coast. Gusts of 161 mph recorded. |
| 1972, June 14–23 | Florida to New York | Key West, Fla. (43 mph) | 117 | 3,097 | "AGNES"—Devastating floods with many record-breaking river crests. Pa. hardest hit, with 50 deaths. |
| 1975, Sept. 13–24 | Florida and Southern Alabama | Ozark, Ala. (104 mph) | 21 | 490 | "ELOISE"—Structures destroyed from Panama City Beach, Fla., to Ft. Walton Beach, Fla. Major flooding from rainfall. |
| 1976, Aug. 6–10 | New York, New Jersey, and Southern New England | Bridgeport, Conn. (77 mph gust) | 5 | 100 | "BELLE"—Crop damage in the Northeast. Considerable Inland stream and road flooding. |

1. Wind-measuring equipment disabled at speed indicated. NOTE: Additional hurricanes may be listed in *News Chronology*. *Source:* Department of Commerce, National Oceanic and Atmospheric Administration.

## Forest Resources of the United States

*Source:* Department of Agriculture, Forest Service.

One third of the U.S. is forest land. Commercial areas include land capable of producing timber of commercial quantity and quality. Noncommercial areas include alpine, semidesert, and other forest types of low timber productivity. Also included in noncommercial areas are 19.5 million acres of land in public ownership suitable for growing timber, but withdrawn for such uses as state and national parks and wilderness areas (17.2 million acres) or National Forest areas deferred while under study for possible inclusion in the wilderness system (4.6 million acres).

### U.S. Forest Land in Acres, 1978

| | |
|---|---|
| Sawtimber stands | 211,782,500 |
| Pole timber stands | 136,748,700 |
| Seedling and sapling stands | 121,187,700 |
| Nonstocked and other areas | 18,007,000 |
| Total, commercial forest lands | 487,725,800 |
| Noncommercial forest | 252,421,600 |
| Total, all forest land | 740,147,400 |

# World and U.S. Extremes of Climate

**Highest recorded temperature**

| | Place | Date | Degree Fahrenheit | Degree Centigrade |
|---|---|---|---|---|
| World (Africa) | El Azizia, Libya | Sept. 13, 1922 | 136 | 58 |
| North America (U.S.) | Death Valley, Calif. | July 10, 1913 | 134 | 57 |
| Asia | Tirat Tsvi, Israel | June 21, 1942 | 129 | 54 |
| Australia | Cloncurry, Queensland | Jan. 16, 1889 | 128 | 53 |
| Europe | Seville, Spain | Aug. 4, 1881 | 122 | 50 |
| South America | Rivadavia, Argentina | Dec. 11, 1905 | 120 | 49 |
| Antarctica | Esperanza, Palmer Peninsula | Oct. 20, 1956 | 58 | 14 |

**Lowest recorded temperature**

| | Place | Date | Degree Fahrenheit | Degree Centigrade |
|---|---|---|---|---|
| World (Antarctica) | Vostok | Aug. 24, 1960 | −127 | −88 |
| Asia | Verkhoyansk/Oimekon | Feb. 6, 1933 | −90 | −68 |
| Greenland | Northice | Jan. 9, 1954 | −87 | −66 |
| North America (excl. Greenland) | Snag, Yukon, Canada | Feb. 3, 1947 | −81 | −63 |
| Europe | Ust 'Shchugor, U.S.S.R. | n.a. | −67 | −55 |
| South America | Sarmiento, Argentina | Jan. 1, 1907 | −27 | −33 |
| Africa | Ifrane, Morocco | Feb. 11, 1935 | −11 | −24 |
| Australia | Charlotte Pass, N.S.W. | July 22, 1947 | −8 | −22 |
| United States | Prospect Creek, Alaska | Jan. 23, 1971 | −80 | −62 |

**Greatest rainfalls**

| | Place | Date | Inches | Centimeters |
|---|---|---|---|---|
| 1 minute (U.S.) | Unionville, Md. | — | 1.23 | 3.1 |
| 20 minutes (Romania) | Curtea-de-Arges | — | 8.1 | 20.6 |
| 42 minutes (U.S.) | Holt, Mo. | — | 12 | 30 |
| 12 hours (Indian Ocean) | Belouve, La Réunion | — | 53 | 135 |
| 24 hours (Indian Ocean) | Cilaos, La Réunion | — | 74 | 188 |
| 5 days (Indian Ocean) | Cilaos, La Réunion | — | 152 | 386 |
| 1 month (India) | Cherrapunji | — | 366 | 930 |
| 1 month (U.S.) | Kukui, Maui, Hawaii | — | 460 | 1,168 |
| 12 months (India) | Cherrapunji | — | 1,042 | 2,647 |

**Greatest snowfalls**

| | Place | Date | Inches | Centimeters |
|---|---|---|---|---|
| 1 month (U.S.) | Tamarack, Calif. | Jan. 1911 | 390 | 991 |
| 24 hours (U.S.) | Silver Lake, Colo. | April 14–15, 1921 | 76 | 193 |
| 19 hours (France) | Bessans | — | 68 | 173 |
| 1 storm (U.S.) | Mt. Shasta Ski Bowl, Calif. | — | 189 | 480 |
| 1 season (U.S.) | Paradise Ranger Sta., Wash. | — | 1,122 | 2,850 |

NOTE: n.a. = not available. *Source:* National Oceanic and Atmospheric Administration, Environmental Data Service.

# Other Recorded Extremes

**Highest average annual temperature (World):** Dallol, Ethiopia (1960–66), 94°F (34.4°C). **(U.S.):** Key West, Fla. (30-year normal), 78.2°F (25.7°C).

**Lowest average annual temperature (Antarctica):** Plateau Station −70°F (−56.7°C). **(U.S.):** Barrow, Alaska (30-year normal), 9.3°F (−12.6°C).

**Greatest average yearly rainfall (U.S.):** Mt. Waialeale, Kauai, Hawaii (1912–58), 460 in. (1,168 cm). **(India):** Cherrapunji (74-year avg), 450 in. (1,143 cm).

**Minimum average yearly rainfall (Chile):** Arica (59-year avg), 0.03 in. (0.08 cm) (no rainfall for 14 consecutive years). **(U.S.):** Death Valley, Calif. (49-year avg), 1.63 in. (4.14 cm). (Bagdad, Calif., holds the U.S. record for the longest period with no measurable rain, 767 days, from Oct. 3, 1912 to Nov. 8, 1914).

**Hottest summer avg in Western Hemisphere (U.S.):** Death Valley, Calif., 98°F (36.7°C).

**Longest hot spell (W. Australia):** Marble Bar, 100°F (37.8°C) (or above) for 162 consecutive days.

**Largest hailstone (U.S.):** Potter, Neb., 1½ lb (.68 kg).

## Climate of Selected U.S. Cities, 1977

(T = trace)

| Month | Temperature, °F: Average maximum | Average minimum | Record high | Record low | Precipitation: Rainfall, inches | Snowfall, inches | Days with precipitation | Percentage possible sunshine | Percentage relative humidity at noon |
|---|---|---|---|---|---|---|---|---|---|
| **Bakersfield, California (Kern County Air Terminal): lat. 35° 25′ N, long. 119° 03′ W; elevation: 475 ft** | | | | | | | | | |
| January | 52.6 | 40.8 | 67 | 32 | 0.58 | 0.0 | 4 | — | 86 |
| April | 81.8 | 53.3 | 95 | 46 | T | 0.0 | 0 | — | 35 |
| July | 99.7 | 71.7 | 107 | 63 | 0.02 | 0.0 | 1 | — | 30 |
| October | 83.4 | 58.9 | 93 | 48 | T | 0.0 | 0 | — | 45 |
| Annual | 79.4 | 56.2 | 111 | 32 | 5.52 | 0.0 | 30 | — | 50 |
| **Caribou, Maine (Municipal Airport): lat. 46° 52′ N, long. 68° 01′ W; elevation: 624 ft** | | | | | | | | | |
| January | 16.4 | −4.5 | 33 | −25 | 3.42 | 39.1 | 12 | — | 60 |
| April | 45.9 | 26.9 | 68 | 4 | 1.83 | 10.6 | 10 | — | 43 |
| July | 76.9 | 53.5 | 91 | 44 | 1.75 | 0.0 | 11 | — | 54 |
| October | 51.2 | 35.7 | 66 | 23 | 5.30 | 0.0 | 14 | — | 63 |
| Annual | 48.7 | 30.3 | 96 | −25 | 41.45 | 143.3 | 159 | — | 60 |
| **Charleston, South Carolina (Municipal Airport): lat. 32° 54′ N, long. 80° 02′ W; elevation: 40 ft** | | | | | | | | | |
| January | 48.6 | 28.7 | 65 | 17 | 2.72 | 1.0 | 9 | 55 | 50 |
| April | 79.2 | 53.6 | 87 | 38 | 0.45 | 0.0 | 3 | 90 | 45 |
| July | 93.6 | 73.9 | 101 | 67 | 3.86 | 0.0 | 8 | 86 | 51 |
| October | 74.8 | 52.2 | 91 | 37 | 2.49 | 0.0 | 6 | 71 | 53 |
| Annual | 76.0 | 54.7 | 101 | 17 | 41.24 | 1.3 | 105 | 77 | 52 |
| **Chicago, Illinois (Midway Airport): lat. 41° 47′ N, long. 87° 45′ W; elevation: 607 ft** | | | | | | | | | |
| January | 18.3 | 1.9 | 30 | −19 | 0.72 | 19.9 | 13 | 46 | 65 |
| April | 65.9 | 43.2 | 88 | 25 | 2.46 | 0.5 | 12 | 63 | 53 |
| July | 87.9 | 69.0 | 99 | 55 | 1.40 | 0.0 | 9 | 78 | 55 |
| October | 60.5 | 43.1 | 74 | 33 | 1.66 | 0.0 | 12 | 47 | 59 |
| Annual | 59.5 | 41.9 | 99 | −19 | 41.29 | 64.3 | 134 | 56 | 59 |
| **Dallas-Fort Worth, Texas (Regional Airport): lat. 32° 54′ N, long. 97° 02′ W; elevation: 551 ft** | | | | | | | | | |
| January | 43.8 | 25.6 | 67 | 10 | 2.39 | 5.4 | 11 | — | 64 |
| April | 77.5 | 56.0 | 89 | 43 | 4.31 | 0.0 | 10 | — | 55 |
| July | 100.1 | 74.1 | 108 | 71 | 2.20 | 0.0 | 6 | — | 44 |
| October | 79.6 | 53.7 | 98 | 35 | 2.96 | 0.0 | 6 | — | 52 |
| Annual | 77.5 | 54.8 | 108 | 10 | 27.19 | 5.4 | 68 | — | 54 |
| **Denver, Colorado (Stapleton International Airport): lat. 39° 45′ N, long. 104° 52′ W; elevation: 5,283 ft** | | | | | | | | | |
| January | 43.9 | 14.4 | 60 | −4 | 0.16 | 2.4 | 5 | 86 | 44 |
| April | 63.3 | 38.8 | 81 | 25 | 2.13 | 4.7 | 12 | 65 | 42 |
| July | 87.8 | 60.7 | 98 | 51 | 2.98 | 0.0 | 10 | 75 | 39 |
| October | 69.4 | 37.1 | 83 | 25 | 0.48 | 3.3 | 4 | 78 | 29 |
| Annual | 66.6 | 38.4 | 98 | −4 | 10.34 | 27.9 | 81 | 75 | 36 |
| **Duluth, Minnesota (International Airport): lat. 46° 50′ N, long. 92° 11′ W; elevation: 1,428 ft** | | | | | | | | | |
| January | 8.4 | −8.7 | 29 | −35 | 0.36 | 8.8 | 13 | 51 | 65 |
| April | 55.5 | 33.2 | 84 | 15 | 1.27 | 0.1 | 8 | 59 | 48 |
| July | 76.3 | 55.4 | 89 | 47 | 3.91 | 0.0 | 9 | 58 | 62 |
| October | 52.6 | 35.9 | 65 | 27 | 3.20 | 1.7 | 8 | 53 | 55 |
| Annual | 48.1 | 30.4 | 89 | −35 | 34.02 | 59.0 | 139 | 50 | 62 |

| Month | Temperature, °F | | | | Precipitation | | | Percentage possible sunshine | Percentage relative humidity at noon |
|---|---|---|---|---|---|---|---|---|---|
| | Average maximum | Average minimum | Record high | Record low | Rainfall, inches | Snowfall, inches | Days with precipitation | | |
| **Great Falls, Montana (International Airport): lat. 47° 29′ N, long. 111° 22′ W; elevation: 3,662 ft** | | | | | | | | | |
| January | 31.8 | 11.4 | 53 | −19 | 1.04 | 13.9 | 12 | 30 | 64 |
| April | 61.5 | 32.7 | 79 | 7 | 0.26 | 1.0 | 5 | 70 | 36 |
| July | 82.7 | 53.3 | 95 | 45 | 1.87 | 0.0 | 10 | 68 | 33 |
| October | 59.8 | 35.8 | 78 | 20 | 0.51 | 3.2 | 4 | 57 | 50 |
| Annual | 57.1 | 33.0 | 95 | −27 | 14.93 | 66.5 | 113 | 55 | 48 |
| **Kansas City, Missouri (International Airport): lat. 39° 17′ N, long. 94° 43′ W; elevation: 1,014 ft** | | | | | | | | | |
| January | 24.4 | 6.7 | 42 | −13 | 1.15 | 14.2 | 12 | 59 | 69 |
| April | 69.6 | 49.7 | 83 | 31 | 2.35 | 0.6 | 10 | 84 | 56 |
| July | 89.2 | 70.2 | 96 | 57 | 2.74 | 0.0 | 6 | 70 | 61 |
| October | 65.0 | 46.3 | 84 | 34 | 7.67 | 0.0 | 13 | 64 | 64 |
| Annual | 63.6 | 45.1 | 97 | −13 | 49.74 | 16.3 | 120 | 68 | 64 |
| **Los Angeles, California (International Airport): lat. 33° 56′ N, long. 118° 24′ W; elevation: 97 ft** | | | | | | | | | |
| January | 65.7 | 49.4 | 82 | 41 | 3.21 | 0.0 | 7 | — | 69 |
| April | 68.3 | 53.8 | 77 | 48 | T | 0.0 | 0 | — | 70 |
| July | 75.4 | 61.8 | 87 | 59 | 0.00 | 0.0 | 0 | — | 72 |
| October | 72.9 | 59.5 | 83 | 52 | T | 0.0 | 0 | — | 78 |
| Annual | 70.8 | 56.1 | 91 | 40 | 13.68 | 0.0 | 32 | — | 69 |
| **Miami, Florida (International Airport): lat. 25° 48′ N, long. 80° 16′ W; elevation: 7 ft** | | | | | | | | | |
| January | 70.5 | 51.7 | 83 | 31 | 1.44 | 0.0 | 5 | 60 | 58 |
| April | 80.9 | 68.7 | 91 | 59 | 1.97 | 0.0 | 6 | 85 | 53 |
| July | 88.5 | 78.8 | 92 | 73 | 5.23 | 0.0 | 13 | 79 | 65 |
| October | 83.0 | 70.0 | 92 | 58 | 1.25 | 0.0 | 7 | 76 | 59 |
| Annual | 81.6 | 69.2 | 92 | 31 | 64.95 | 0.0 | 118 | 69 | 62 |
| **New Orleans, Louisiana (International Airport): lat. 29° 59′ N, long. 90° 15′ W; elevation: 4 ft** | | | | | | | | | |
| January | 52.5 | 34.2 | 73 | 19 | 5.62 | T | 9 | 51 | 59 |
| April | 80.4 | 57.5 | 84 | 41 | 6.38 | 0.0 | 6 | 72 | 59 |
| July | 93.3 | 74.4 | 97 | 71 | 2.91 | 0.0 | 14 | 61 | 66 |
| October | 77.7 | 58.7 | 92 | 42 | 4.33 | 0.0 | 5 | 63 | 63 |
| Annual | 77.8 | 59.0 | 97 | 19 | 72.80 | T | 132 | 58 | 65 |
| **New York, New York (Central Park): lat. 40° 47′ N, long. 73° 58′ W; elevation: 132 ft** | | | | | | | | | |
| January | 27.7 | 16.4 | 44 | −2 | 2.25 | 13.0 | 8 | 66 | 58 |
| April | 63.6 | 43.8 | 90 | 25 | 3.75 | T | 7 | 69 | 44 |
| July | 88.2 | 69.7 | 104 | 58 | 1.60 | 0.0 | 7 | — | 48 |
| October | 61.0 | 48.8 | 70 | 40 | 5.03 | 0.0 | 11 | — | 66 |
| Annual | 61.6 | 47.0 | 104 | −2 | 54.73 | 20.0 | 114 | — | 57 |
| **Phoenix, Arizona (Sky Harbor International Airport): lat. 33° 26′ N, long. 112° 01′ W; elevation: 1,112 ft** | | | | | | | | | |
| January | 64.8 | 42.8 | 76 | 31 | 0.35 | 0.0 | 5 | 82 | 53 |
| April | 88.2 | 58.8 | 99 | 40 | 0.06 | 0.0 | 1 | 49 | 19 |
| July | 106.1 | 83.8 | 112 | 78 | 0.30 | 0.0 | 4 | 79 | 29 |
| October | 91.0 | 66.4 | 102 | 56 | 0.61 | 0.0 | 3 | 87 | 35 |
| Annual | 87.6 | 62.1 | 114 | 31 | 3.16 | 0.0 | 28 | 86 | 29 |
| **Salt Lake City, Utah (International Airport): lat. 40° 46′ N, long. 111° 58′ W; elevation: 4,220 ft** | | | | | | | | | |
| January | 35.6 | 18.0 | 49 | −2 | 0.76 | 8.6 | 4 | 68 | 74 |
| April | 67.4 | 40.8 | 85 | 27 | 0.59 | 4.8 | 3 | 83 | 34 |

| Month | Temperature, °F: Average maximum | Average minimum | Record high | Record low | Precipitation: Rainfall, inches | Snowfall, inches | Days with precipitation | Percentage possible sunshine | Percentage relative humidity at noon |
|---|---|---|---|---|---|---|---|---|---|
| July | 91.7 | 62.9 | 100 | 53 | 0.61 | 0.0 | 6 | 83 | 28 |
| October | 69.4 | 41.8 | 80 | 33 | 0.83 | 0.2 | 5 | 78 | 40 |
| Annual | 65.1 | 41.2 | 101 | −2 | 17.67 | 76.0 | 96 | 71 | 45 |
| **San Francisco, California (International Airport): lat. 37° 37′ N, long. 122° 23′ W; elevation: 8 ft** | | | | | | | | | |
| January | 53.9 | 40.1 | 63 | 35 | 2.22 | 0.0 | 5 | — | 78 |
| April | 64.4 | 46.6 | 77 | 41 | T | 0.0 | 0 | — | 61 |
| July | 71.6 | 53.2 | 97 | 50 | 0.35 | 0.0 | 1 | — | 59 |
| October | 68.6 | 52.3 | 82 | 47 | 0.15 | 0.0 | 3 | — | 63 |
| Annual | 64.5 | 48.9 | 97 | 35 | 12.54 | 0.0 | 50 | — | 67 |
| **Seattle, Washington (Seattle-Tacoma Airport): lat. 47° 27′ N, long. 122° 18′ W; elevation: 400 ft** | | | | | | | | | |
| January | 44.7 | 34.1 | 57 | 24 | 1.77 | 1.0 | 13 | 13 | 84 |
| April | 63.2 | 43.9 | 78 | 37 | 0.55 | 0.0 | 9 | — | 68 |
| July | 75.2 | 55.0 | 87 | 52 | 0.42 | 0.0 | 5 | 63 | 64 |
| October | 59.0 | 45.4 | 69 | 41 | 2.60 | 0.0 | 13 | 30 | 71 |
| Annual | 60.5 | 45.4 | 96 | 21 | 32.84 | 5.4 | 147 | — | 70 |
| **Washington, D.C. (National Airport): lat. 38° 51′ N, long. 77° 02′ W; elevation: 10 ft** | | | | | | | | | |
| January | 33.3 | 17.5 | 49 | 2 | 1.50 | 9.7 | 8 | 67 | 50 |
| April | 71.5 | 48.7 | 90 | 30 | 2.66 | T | 7 | 79 | 45 |
| July | 90.2 | 71.5 | 100 | 60 | 4.06 | 0.0 | 11 | 77 | 51 |
| October | 67.2 | 50.8 | 82 | 37 | 5.35 | 0.0 | 11 | 51 | 49 |
| Annual | 67.5 | 49.7 | 100 | 2 | 36.14 | 10.0 | 113 | 64 | 51 |

*Source:* Department of Commerce, National Oceanic and Atmospheric Administration, Environmental Data Service.

# Wind Chill Factors

| Wind speed (mph) | Thermometer reading (degrees Fahrenheit): 35 | 30 | 25 | 20 | 15 | 10 | 5 | 0 | −5 | −10 | −15 | −20 | −25 | −30 | −35 | −40 | −45 |
|---|---|---|---|---|---|---|---|---|---|---|---|---|---|---|---|---|---|
| 5 | 33 | 27 | 21 | 19 | 12 | 7 | 0 | −5 | −10 | −15 | −21 | −26 | −31 | −36 | −42 | −47 | −52 |
| 10 | 22 | 16 | 10 | 3 | −3 | −9 | −15 | −22 | −27 | −34 | −40 | −46 | −52 | −58 | −64 | −71 | −77 |
| 15 | 16 | 9 | 2 | −5 | −11 | −18 | −25 | −31 | −38 | −45 | −51 | −58 | −65 | −72 | −78 | −85 | −92 |
| 20 | 12 | 4 | −3 | −10 | −17 | −24 | −31 | −39 | −46 | −53 | −60 | −67 | −74 | −81 | −88 | −95 | −103 |
| 25 | 8 | 1 | −7 | −15 | −22 | −29 | −36 | −44 | −51 | −59 | −66 | −74 | −81 | −88 | −96 | −103 | −110 |
| 30 | 6 | −2 | −10 | −18 | −25 | −33 | −41 | −49 | −56 | −64 | −71 | −79 | −86 | −93 | −101 | −109 | −116 |
| 35 | 4 | −4 | −12 | −20 | −27 | −35 | −43 | −52 | −58 | −67 | −74 | −82 | −89 | −97 | −105 | −113 | −120 |
| 40 | 3 | −5 | −13 | −21 | −29 | −37 | −45 | −53 | −60 | −69 | −76 | −84 | −92 | −100 | −107 | −115 | −123 |
| 45 | 2 | −6 | −14 | −22 | −30 | −38 | −46 | −54 | −62 | −70 | −78 | −85 | −93 | −102 | −109 | −117 | −125 |

NOTES: This chart gives equivalent temperatures for combinations of wind speed and temperatures. For example, the combination of a temperature of 10° Fahrenheit and a wind blowing at 10 mph has a cooling power equal to −9° F. Wind speeds of higher than 45 mph have little additional cooling effect.

# Weather Glossary

**blizzard:** storm characterized by strong winds, low temperatures, and large amounts of snow.

**blowing snow:** snow lifted from ground surface by wind; restricts visibility.

**cold wave warning:** indicates that a change to abnormally cold weather is expected; greater than normal protective measures will be required.

**cyclone:** circulation of winds rotating counterclockwise in the northern hemisphere and clockwise in the southern hemisphere. Hurricanes and tornadoes are both examples of cyclones.

**drifting snow:** strong winds will blow loose or falling snow into significant drifts.

**drizzle:** uniform close precipitation of tiny drops with diameter of less than .02 inch.

**flash flood:** dangerous rapid rise of water levels in streams, rivers, or over land area.

**freezing rain or drizzle:** rain or drizzle that freezes

on contact with the ground or other objects forming a coating of ice on exposed surfaces.
**gale warning:** winds in the 33–48 knot (38–55 mph) range forecast.
**hail:** small balls of ice falling separately or in lumps; usually associated with thunderstorms and temperatures that may be well above freezing.
**hazardous driving warnings:** indicates that drizzle, freezing rain, snow, sleet, or strong winds make driving conditions difficult.
**heavy snow warnings:** issued when 4 inches or more of snow are expected to fall in a 12-hour period or when 6 inches or more are anticipated in a 24-hour period.
**hurricane:** devastating cyclonic storm; winds over 74 mph near storm center; usually tropical in origin; called cyclone in Indian Ocean, typhoon in the Pacific.
**hurricane warning:** winds in excess of 64 knots (74 mph) in connection with hurricane.
**livestock warning:** alerts farmers and ranchers that livestock will require protection from bad weather conditions.
**rain:** precipitation of liquid particles with diameters larger than .02 inch.
**sleet:** translucent or transparent ice pellets; frozen rain; generally a winter phenomenon.
**small craft warning:** indicates winds as high as 33 knots (38 mph) and sea conditions dangerous to small boats.
**snow:** precipitation of ice crystals.
**snow flurries:** snow falling for a short time at intermittent periods; accumulations are usually small.
**snow squall:** brief, intense falls of snow, usually accompanied by gusty winds.
**storm warnings:** winds greater than 48 knots (55 mph) are forecast.
**temperature-humidity index** (THI): measure of personal discomfort based on the combined effects of temperature and humidity. Most people are uncomfortable when the THI is 75. A THI of 80 produces acute discomfort for almost everyone.
**tidal waves:** series of ocean waves caused by earthquakes; can reach speeds of 600 mph; they grow in height as they reach shore and can crest as high as 100 feet.
**thunder:** the sound produced by the rapid expansion of air heated by lightning.
**tornado:** dangerous whirlwind associated with the cumulonimbus clouds of severe thunderstorms; winds up to 300 mph.
**tornado warning:** tornado has actually been detected by radar or sighted in designated area.
**tornado watch:** potential exists in the watch area for storms that could contain tornadoes.
**travelers' warning:** *see* hazardous driving warning.
**tsunami:** *see* tidal waves.
**warning:** the designated condition is imminent.
**wind-chill factor:** combined effect of temperature and wind speed as compared to equivalent temperature in calm air.

## Tornadoes That Caused Outstanding Damage

| Date | Number of tornadoes | Deaths | Property losses | States in which storms occurred |
|---|---|---|---|---|
| 1884, Feb. 19 | 60 | 800 | (1) | Mississippi, Alabama, North and South Carolina, Tennessee, Kentucky, Indiana |
| 1917, May 26–27 | (1) | 249 | $ 5,555,000 | Illinois, Indiana, Arkansas, Kentucky, Tennessee, Alabama, Mississippi |
| 1920, April 20 | 6 | 220 | 3,525,000 | Mississippi, Alabama, Tennessee |
| 1924, April 29–30 | 22 | 115 | 4,372,300 | Oklahoma, Arkansas, Alabama, Georgia, Louisiana, North and South Carolina, Virginia |
| 1924, June 28 | 4 | 96 | 13,050,000 | Ohio and Pennsylvania |
| 1925, March 18 | 8 | 792 | 17,872,000 | Missouri, Illinois, Indiana, Kentucky, Tennessee, Alabama |
| 1927, May 8–9 | 36 | 227 | 7,877,000 | Texas, Louisiana, Missouri, Nebraska, Indiana, Michigan |
| 1932, March 21 | 27 | 321 | 5,514,000 | Alabama, Mississippi, Georgia, Tennessee |
| 1936, April 5–6 | 22 | 498 | 21,800,000 | Arkansas, Alabama, Tennessee, Georgia, South Carolina |
| 1944, June 23 | 4 | 153 | 5,160,000 | Pennsylvania, West Virginia, Maryland |
| 1947, April 9–10 | 8 | 167 | 10,030,750 | Texas, Oklahoma, Kansas |
| 1952, March 21–22 | 31 | 343 | 15,327,100 | Arkansas, Tennessee, Missouri, Mississippi, Alabama, Kentucky |
| 1953, June 7–9 | 12 | 234 | 93,230,840 | Michigan, Ohio, and New England states |
| 1953, May 11 | 1 | 114 | 39,500,000 | Texas |
| 1955, May 25 | 13 | 102 | 11,747,500 | Oklahoma and Kansas |
| 1965, April 11–12 | 47 | 257 | 200,000,000 | Iowa, Illinois, Wisconsin, Michigan, Indiana, Ohio |
| 1968, May 15 | 7 | 63 | 65,000,000 | Arkansas, Iowa, Illinois |
| 1970, May 11 | 1 | 26 | 135,000,000 | Texas |
| 1971, Feb. 21 | (1) | 117 | 17,000,000 | Louisiana, Mississippi |
| 1973, March 31 | 2 | 9 | 115,000,000 | Georgia, South Carolina |
| 1973, May 26–28 | 96 | 22 | (1) | Hawaii and 18 states in South, Southwest, Midwest, and East |
| 1974, April 3–4 | 144 | 307 | 500,000,000+ | 13 states in East, South, and Midwest |
| 1975, May 6 | 3 | 3 | 400,000,000+ | Nebraska |
| 1977, April 4 | 7 | 22 | 15,000,000 | Alabama |

1. Not definitely known; believed to be large. NOTE: Additional storms may be listed in the *Current Events* section. *Source:* Data for 1884–1953, reprinted from *Tornadoes of the United States,* by S. D. Flora, copyright 1954, by University of Oklahoma Press. Used by permission. Also, Department of Commerce, National Oceanic and Atmospheric Administration.

# ASTRONOMY

## Astronomical Terms

*Planet* is the term used for a body in orbit around the sun. Its origin is Greek; even in antiquity it was known that a number of "stars" did not stay in the same relative positions to the others. There were five such restless "stars" known—Mercury, Venus, Mars, Jupiter, and Saturn—and the Greeks referred to them as *planetes,* a word which means "wanderers." That the earth is one of the planets was realized later. The additional planets were discovered after the invention of the telescope.

*Satellite* (or *moon*) is the term for a body in orbit around a planet. As long as our own Moon was the only moon known, there was no need for a general term for the moons of planets. But when Galileo Galilei discovered the four main moons of the planet Jupiter, Johannes Kepler (in a letter to Galileo) suggested "satellite" (from the Latin *satelles,* which means attendant) as a general term for such bodies. The word is used interchangeably with "moons": astronomers speak and write about the moons of Neptune, Saturn, etc. A satellite may be any size.

*Orbit* is the term for the path traveled by a body in space. It comes from the Latin *orbis,* which means circle, circuit, etc., and *orbita,* which means a rut or a wheel track. Theoretically, four mathematical figures are possible orbits: two are open (hyperbola and parabola) and two are closed (ellipse and circle), but in reality all closed orbits are ellipses. These ellipses can be nearly circular, as are the orbits of most planets, or very elongated, as are the orbits of most comets. In these orbits, the sun is in one focal point of the ellipse, and the other focal point is empty. In the orbits of satellites, the planet stands in one focal point of the orbit. The *primary* of an orbit is the body in the focal point. For planets, the point of the orbit closest to the Sun is the *perihelion,* and the point farthest from the Sun is the *aphelion.* For orbits around the Earth, the corresponding terms are *perigee* and *apogee;* for orbits around other planets, corresponding terms are coined when necessary.

Two heavenly bodies are in *inferior* or *superior conjunction* when they have the same Right Ascension, or are in the same meridian; that is, when one is due north or south of the other. If the bodies appear near each other as seen from the Earth, they will rise and set at the same time. They are in *opposition* when they are opposite each other in the heavens: when one rises as the other is setting. *Greatest elongation* is the greatest apparent angular distance from the Sun, when a planet is most favorably suited for observation. Mercury can be seen with the naked eye only at about this time. An *occultation* of a planet or star is an eclipse of it by some other body, usually the Moon.

*Stars* are the basic units of population in the universe. Our Sun is the nearest star. Stars are very large (our Sun has a diameter of 865,400 miles—a comparatively small star). Stars are composed of intensely hot gasses, deriving their energy from nuclear reactions going on in their interiors.

*Galaxies* are immense systems containing billions of stars. All that you can see in the sky (with a very few exceptions) belongs to our galaxy—a system of roughly 100 billion stars. The few exceptions are other galaxies. Our own galaxy, the rim of which we see as the "Milky Way," is about 100,000 light-years in diameter and about 10,000 light-years in thickness. Its shape is roughly that of a thick lens; more precisely it is a "spiral nebula," a term first used for other galaxies when they were discovered and before it was realized that these were separate and distant galaxies. The spiral galaxy nearest to ours is in the constellation

## Astronomical Constants

| | |
|---|---|
| Light-year (distance traveled by light in one year) | 5,880,000,000,000 mi. |
| Parsec (parallax of one second, for stellar distances) | 3.259 light-yrs. |
| Velocity of light | 186,281.7 mi./sec. |
| Astronomical unit (A.U.), or mean distance earth-to-sun | ca. 93,000,000 mi.[1] |
| Mean distance, earth to moon | 238,860 mi. |
| General precession | 50".26 |
| Obliquity of the ecliptic | 23° 27′ 8".26–0".4684(t – 1900)[2] |
| Equatorial radius of the earth | 3963.34 statute mi. |
| Polar radius of the earth | 3949.99 statute mi. |
| Earth's mean radius | 3958.89 statute mi. |
| Oblateness of the earth | 1/297 |
| Equatorial horizontal parallax of the moon | 57′ 2".70 |
| Earth's mean velocity in orbit | 18.5 mi./sec. |
| Sidereal year | 365d.2564 |
| Tropical year | 365d.2422 |
| Sidereal month | 27d.3217 |
| Synodic month | 29d.5306 |
| Mean sidereal day | 23h56m4s.091 of mean solar time |
| Mean solar day | 24h3m56s.555 of sidereal time |

1. Actual mean distance derived from radar bounces: 92,935,700 mi. The value of 92,897,400 mi. (based on parallax of 8".80) is used in calculations. 2. *t* refers to the year in question, for example, 1980.

Andromeda. It is somewhat larger than our own galaxy and is visible to the naked eye.

Recent developments in radio astronomy have revealed additional celestial objects that are still incompletely understood.

*Quasars* ("quasi-stellar" objects), originally thought to be peculiar stars in our own galaxy, are now believed to be the most remote objects in the Universe. Spectral studies of quasars indicate that some are 9 billion light years away and moving away from us at the incredible rate of 150,000 miles per second. Quasars emit tremendous amounts of light and microwave radiation. Although they appear to be far smaller than ordinary galaxies, some quasars emit as much as 100 times more energy. Some astronomers believe that quasars are the cores of violently exploding galaxies.

*Pulsars* are believed to be rapidly spinning neutron stars, so crushed by their own gravity that a million tons of their matter would hardly fill a thimble. Pulsars are so named because they emit bursts of radio energy at regular intervals. Some have pulse rates as rapid as 10 per second.

A *black hole* is the theoretical end-product of the total gravitational collapse of a massive star or group of stars. Crushed even smaller than an incredibly dense neutron star, such a body may become so dense that not even light can escape its gravitational field. It has been suggested that black holes may be detectable in proximity to normal stars when they draw matter away from their visible neighbors. Strong sources of X-rays in our galaxy and beyond may also indicate the presence of black holes. One possible black hole now being studied is the invisible companion to a supergiant star in the constellation Cygnus.

## Origin of the Universe

Evidence uncovered in recent years tends to confirm that the universe began its existence about 15 billion years ago as a dense, hot globule of gas expanding rapidly outward. At that time, the universe contained nothing but hydrogen and a small amount of helium. There were no stars and no planets. The first stars probably began to condense out of the primordial hydrogen when the universe was about 100 million years old and continued to form as the universe aged. The Sun arose in this way 4.5 billion years ago. Many stars came into being before the Sun was formed; many others formed after the Sun appeared. This process continues, and through telescopes we can now see stars forming out of compressed pockets of hydrogen in outer space.

## Birth and Death of a Star

When a star begins to form as a dense cloud of gas, the individual hydrogen atoms fall toward the center of the cloud under the force of the star's gravity. As they fall, they pick up speed, and their energy increases. The increase in energy heats the gas. When this process has continued for some millions of years, the temperature reaches about 20 million degrees Fahrenheit. At this temperature,

## The Brightest Stars

| Star | Constellation | Position, Jan. 1979 R.A. h m | Position, Jan. 1979 Dec. ° ′ | Mag. | Dist. (l.-y.) | On meridian 9 p.m. |
|---|---|---|---|---|---|---|
| Sirius | Canis Major | 6 44.1 | −16 39 | −1.6 | 8 | Feb. 16 |
| Canopus | Carina | 6 23.3 | 52 41 | −0.9 | 650 | Feb. 11 |
| Alpha Centauri | Centaurus | 14 38.1 | −60 44 | +0.1 | 4 | June 16 |
| Vega | Lyra | 18 36.1 | +38 45 | 0.1 | 23 | Aug. 15 |
| Capella | Auriga | 5 15.1 | +45 58 | 0.2 | 42 | Jan. 24 |
| Arcturus | Boötes | 14 14.4 | −41 04 | 0.2 | 32 | June 10 |
| Rigel | Orion | 5 13.3 | −08 13 | 0.3 | 545 | Jan. 24 |
| Procyon | Canis Minor | 7 38.1 | +05 16 | 0.5 | 10 | March 2 |
| Achernar | Eridanus | 1 36.6 | −57 20 | 0.6 | 70 | Nov. 30 |
| Beta Centauri | Centaurus | 14 02.2 | −60 16 | 0.9 | 130 | June 7 |
| Altair | Aquila | 19 49.5 | +08 48 | 0.9 | 18 | Sept. 3 |
| Betelgeuse | Orion | 5 54.0 | +07 24 | 0.9 | 300 | Feb. 3 |
| Aldebaran | Taurus | 4 34.4 | +16 28 | 1.1 | 54 | Jan. 14 |
| Spica | Virgo | 13 24.0 | −11 03 | 1.2 | 190 | May 28 |
| Pollux | Gemini | 7 44.0 | +28 04 | 1.2 | 31 | March 3 |
| Antares | Scorpius | 16 28.1 | −26 23 | 1.2 | 170 | July 14 |
| Fomalhaut | Piscis Austrinus | 22 56.3 | −29 44 | 1.3 | 27 | Oct. 20 |
| Deneb | Cygnus | 20 40.4 | +45 12 | 1.3 | 465 | Sept. 16 |
| Regulus | Leo | 10 07.2 | +12 04 | 1.3 | 70 | April 9 |
| Beta Crucis | Crux | 12 44.2 | −60 52 | 1.5 | 465 | May 18 |
| Eta Carinae | Carina | 10 43.1 | −59 25 | 1–7 | — | April 17 |
| Alpha-one Crucis | Crux | 12 25.3 | −62 59 | 1.6 | 150 | May 13 |
| Castor | Gemini | 7 33.2 | +31 56 | 1.6 | 44 | Feb. 28 |
| Gamma Crucis | Crux | 12 29.6 | −56 50 | 1.6 | — | May 15 |
| Epsilon Canis Majoris | Canis Major | 6 57.5 | −28 56 | 1.6 | 325 | Feb. 19 |
| Epsilon Ursae Majoris | Ursa Major | 12 53 | +56 04 | 1.7 | 50 | May 20 |
| Bellatrix | Orion | 5 24.0 | +06 20 | 1.7 | 215 | Jan. 27 |
| Lambda Scorpii | Scorpius | 17 32.1 | −37 05 | 1.7 | 205 | July 30 |
| Epsilon Carinae | Carina | 8 22.1 | −59 26 | 1.7 | 325 | March 13 |
| Mira | Cetus | 2 18.2 | −03 04 | 2–10 | 250 | Dec. 11 |

## Data for Sun, Moon, and Planets

| | Mean distance from Sun in millions of miles | Period of revo-lution around the Sun | Eccen-tricity of orbit | Incli-nation to ecliptic ° ′ | Diam-eter (miles) | Period of rotation on axis | Incli-nation of equa-tor to orbit plane ° | Surface gravity (earth = 1) | Density $H_2O$ = 1 | Number of satellites | Mean velocity in orbit (mi./sec.) | Max. stellar mag. |
|---|---|---|---|---|---|---|---|---|---|---|---|---|
| Sun | — | — | — | — | 865,400 | 24d.64[2] | 7.2 | 28 | 1.4 | 0 | — | −26.7 |
| Moon | — | (27d.322)[1] | 0.05 | 5 8 | 2,160 | 27d.322 | 6.7 | 0.16 | 3.3 | 0 | 0.63 | −12.6 |
| Mercury | 36.00 | 87d.969 | 0.21 | 7 0 | 3,100 | 58.66d | 7 | 0.28 | 3.8 | 0 | 30 | −1.2 |
| Venus | 67.27 | 224d.701 | 0.01 | 3 24 | 7,700 | 243.2d | — | 0.85 | 5.1 | 0 | 22 | −4.4 |
| Earth | 93.00 | 365d.256 | 0.02 | 0 0 | 7,927[3] | 23h56m | 23.4 | 1.00 | 5.5 | 1 | 18.5 | — |
| Mars | 141.71 | 1y.881 | 0.09 | 1 51 | 4,200 | 24h37m | 25.2 | 0.38 | 4.0 | 2 | 15 | −2.8 |
| Jupiter | 483.88 | 11y.862 | 0.05 | 1 18 | 88,700[3] | 9h50m[2] | 3.1 | 2.6 | 1.3 | 13[4] | 8 | −2.5 |
| Saturn | 887.14 | 29y.458 | 0.06 | 2 29 | 75,100[3] | 10h14m[2] | 26.8 | 1.2 | 0.7 | 10 | 6 | −0.4 |
| Uranus | 1783.98 | 84y.013 | 0.05 | 0 46 | 32,000 | 10¾y | 98 | 1.1 | 1.3 | 5 | 4 | +5.7 |
| Neptune | 2795.46 | 164y.794 | 0.01 | 1 46 | 27,700 | 15h.8 | 29 | 1.4 | 2.2 | 2 | 3 | +7.8 |
| Pluto | 3675.27 | 248h.430 | 0.25 | 17 9 | 1,500(?) | 6d8h(?) | — | — | >1.0 | 1 | <3 | +14 |

1. Period of revolution around the earth. 2. At the equator. 3. The equatorial diameters of the earth, Jupiter, and Saturn are given; polar diameters are: earth, 7,900.0 mi., Jupiter 82,789 mi., Saturn 67,170 mi. 4. Recent analysis indicates the presence of a fourteenth satellite. OTHER DATA ON THE EARTH: Equatorial circumference, 24,902.4 mi.; total area, 196,949,970 sq mi.; mass, 6.6 sextillion tons; mean diameter, 7,917.8 mi.

the hydrogen within the star ignites and burns in a continuing series of nuclear reactions in which all the elements in the universe are manufactured from hydrogen and helium. The onset of these reactions marks the birth of a star. When a star begins to exhaust its hydrogen supply, its life nears an end. The first sign of old age is a swelling and reddening of its outer regions. Such an aging, swollen star is called a red giant. The Sun, a middle-aged star, will probably swell to a red giant in 5 billion years, vaporizing the earth and any creatures that may be left on its surface. When all its fuel has been exhausted, a star cannot generate sufficient pressure at its center to balance the crushing force of gravity. The star collapses under the force of its own weight; if it is a small star, it collapses gently and remains collapsed. Such a collapsed star, at its life's end, is called a white dwarf. The Sun will probably end its life in this way. A different fate awaits a large star. Its final collapse generates a violent explosion, blowing the innards of the star out into space. There, the materials of the exploded star mix with the primeval hydrogen of the universe. Later in the history of the galaxy, other stars are formed out of this mixture. The Sun is one of these stars. It contains the debris of countless other stars that exploded before the Sun was born.

### Formation of the Solar System

The Sun, like other stars, seems to have been formed 4.6 billion years ago from a cloud of hydrogen mixed with small amounts of other substances that had been manufactured in the bodies of other stars before the Sun was born. This was the parent cloud of the solar system. The dense hot gas at the center of the cloud gave rise to the Sun; the outer regions of the cloud—cooler and less dense—gave birth to the planets.

Our solar system consists of one star (the Sun), nine planets and all their moons, several thousand minor planets called asteroids or planetoids, and an equally large number of comets.

### The Sun

All the stars, including our Sun, are gigantic balls of superheated gas, kept hot by atomic reactions in their centers. In our Sun, this atomic reaction is hydrogen fusion: four hydrogen atoms are combined to form one helium atom. The temperature at the core of our Sun must be 20 million degrees centigrade, the surface temperature is around 6,000 degrees centigrade, or about 11,000 degrees Fahrenheit. The diameter of the sun is 865,400 miles, and its surface area is approximately 12,000 times that of the Earth. Compared with other stars, our Sun is just a bit below average in size and temperature. Its fuel supply (hydrogen) is estimated to last for another 5 billion years.

Our Sun is not motionless in space; in fact it has two proper motions. One is a seemingly straight-line motion in the direction of the constellation Hercules at the rate of about 12 miles per second. But since the Sun is a part of the Milky Way system and since the whole system rotates slowly around its own center, the Sun also moves at the rate of 175 miles per second as part of the rotating Milky Way system.

In addition to this motion, the Sun rotates on its axis. Observing the motion of sun spots (darkish areas which look like enormous whirling storms) and solar flares, which are usually associated with sun spots, has shown that the rotational period of our Sun is just short of 25 days. But this figure is valid for the Sun's equator only; the sections near the Sun's poles seem to have a rotational period of 34 days. Naturally, since the Sun generates its own heat and light, there is no temperature difference between poles and equator.

What we call the Sun's "surface" is technically known as the photosphere. Since the whole Sun is a ball of very hot gas, there is really no such thing as a surface; it is a question of visual impression. The next layer outside the photosphere is known as the chromosphere, which extends several thousand miles beyond the photosphere. It is in steady motion, and often enormous prominences can be seen to burst from it, extending as much as 100,000 miles into space. Outside the chromosphere is the corona. The corona consists of very tenuous gases (essentially hydrogen) and makes a magnificent sight when the Sun is eclipsed.

## The Moon

Mercury and Venus do not have any moons. Therefore, the Earth is the planet nearest the Sun to be orbited by a moon.

The next planet farther out, Mars, has two very small moons. Jupiter has four major moons and nine or ten minor ones. Saturn, the ringed planet, has ten known moons, of which one (Titan) is larger than the planet Mercury. Uranus has five known moons (four of them large) as well as rings, while Neptune has one large and one small moon. Pluto has one moon, discovered in 1978. Some astronomers still consider Pluto to be a "runaway moon" of Neptune.

Our own Moon, with a diameter of 2,160 miles, is one of the larger moons in our solar system and is especially large when compared with the planet that it orbits. In fact, the common center of gravity of the Earth-Moon system is only about 1,000 miles below the Earth's surface. The closest our Moon can come to us (its perigee) is 221,463 miles; the farthest it can go away (its apogee) is 252,710 miles. The period of rotation of our Moon is equal to its period of revolution around the Earth. Hence from Earth we can see only one hemisphere of the Moon. Both periods are 27 days, 7 hours, 43 minutes and 11.47 seconds. But while the rotation of the Moon is constant, its velocity in its orbit is not, since it moves more slowly in apogee than in perigee. Consequently, some portions near the rim which are not normally visible will appear briefly. This phenomenon is called "libration," and by taking advantage of the librations, astronomers have succeeded in mapping approximately 59% of the lunar surface. The other 41% can never be seen from the earth but has been mapped by American and Russian Moon-orbiting spacecraft.

Though the Moon goes around the Earth in the time mentioned, the interval from new Moon to new Moon is 29 days, 12 hours, 44 minutes and 2.78 seconds. This delay of nearly two days is due to the fact that the Earth is moving around the Sun, so that the Moon needs two extra days to reach a spot in its orbit where no part is illuminated by the Sun, as seen from Earth.

If the plane of the Earth's orbit around the Sun (the ecliptic) and the plane of the Moon's orbit around the Earth were the same, the Moon would be eclipsed by the Earth every time it is full, and the Sun would be eclipsed by the Moon every time the Moon is "new" (it would be better to call it the "black Moon" when it is in this position). But because the two orbits do not coincide, the Moon's shadow normally misses the Earth and the Earth's shadow misses the Moon. The inclination of the two orbital planes to each other is 5 degrees. The tides are, of course, caused by the Moon with the help of the Sun, but in the open ocean they are surprisingly low, amounting to about one yard. The very high tides which can be observed near the shore in some places are due to funnelling effects of the shorelines. At new Moon and at full Moon the tides raised by the Moon are reinforced by the Sun; these are the "spring tides." If the Sun's tidal power acts at right angles to that of the Moon (quarter moons) we get the low "neap tides."

## Our Planet Earth

The Earth, circling the Sun at an average distance of 93 million miles, is the fifth largest planet and the third from the Sun. It orbits the Sun at a speed of 67,000 miles per hour, making one revolution in 365 days, 5 hours, 48 minutes, and 45.51 seconds. The Earth completes one rotation on its axis every 23 hours, 56 minutes, and 4.09 seconds. Actually a bit pear-shaped rather than a true sphere, the Earth has a diameter of 7,927 miles at the Equator and a few miles less at the poles. It has an estimated mass of about 6.6 sextillion tons, with an average density of 5.52 grams per cubic centimeter. The Earth's surface area encompasses 196,-949,970 square miles, of which about three-fourths is water.

**Origin of the Earth.** The Earth, along with the other planets, is believed to have been born 4.6 billion years ago as a solidified cloud of dust and gases left over from the creation of the Sun. For perhaps 500 million years, the interior of the Earth stayed solid and relatively cool, perhaps 2000° F. The main ingredients, according to the best available evidence, were iron and silicates, with small amounts of other elements, some of them radioactive. As millions of years passed, energy released by radioactive decay —mostly of uranium, thorium, and potassium— gradually heated the Earth, melting some of its constituents. The iron melted before the silicates, and, being heavier, sank toward the center. This forced upward the silicates that it found there. After many years, the iron reached the center, almost 4,000 miles deep, and began to accumulate. No eyes were around at that time to view the turmoil which must have taken place on the face of the Earth—gigantic heaves and bubbling of the surface, exploding volcanoes, and flowing lava covering everything in sight. Finally, the iron in the center accumulated as the core. Around it, a thin but fairly stable crust of solid rock formed as the Earth cooled. Depressions in the crust were natural basins in which water, rising from the interior of the planet through volcanoes and fissures, collected to form the oceans. Slowly the Earth acquired its present appearance.

**The Earth Today.** As a result of radioactive heating over millions of years, the Earth's molten *core* is probably fairly hot today, around 11,000° F. By comparison, lead melts at around 800° F. Most of the Earth's 2,100-mile-thick core is liquid, but there is evidence that the center of the core is solid. The liquid outer portion, about 95% of the core, is constantly in motion, causing the Earth to have a magnetic field that makes compass needles point north and south. The details are not known, but the latest evidence suggests that planets which have a magnetic field probably have a solid core or a partially liquid one.

Outside the core is the Earth's *mantle,* 1,800 miles thick, and extending nearly to the surface. The mantle is composed of heavy silicate rock, similar to that brought up by volcanic eruptions. It is somewhere between liquid and solid, slightly yielding, and therefore contributing to an active, moving Earth. Most of the Earth's radioactive material is in the thin *crust* which covers the mantle, but some is in the mantle and continues to give off heat. The crust's thickness ranges from 5 to 25 miles.

**Continental Drift.** A great deal of recent evidence confirms the long-disputed theory that the continents of the Earth, made mostly of relatively light granite, float in the slightly yielding mantle, like logs in a pond. For many years it had been noticed that if North and South America could be pushed toward western and southern Europe and western Africa, they would fit like pieces in a jigsaw puzzle. Today, there is little question—the continents have drifted widely and continue to do so.

In 10 million years, the world as we know it may be unrecognizable, with California drifting out to sea, Florida joining South America, and Africa moving farther away from Europe and Asia.

**The Earth's Atmosphere.** The thin blanket of atmosphere that envelops the Earth extends several hundred miles into space. From sea level—the very bottom of the ocean of air—to a height of about 60 miles, the air in the atmosphere is made up of the same gases in the same ratio: about 78% nitrogen, 21% oxygen, and the remaining 1% being a mixture of argon, carbon dioxide, and tiny amounts of neon, helium, krypton, xenon, and other gases. The atmosphere becomes less dense with increasing altitude: more than three-fourths of the Earth's huge envelope is concentrated in the first 5 to 10 miles above the surface. At sea level, a cubic foot of the atmosphere weighs about an ounce and a quarter. The entire atmosphere weighs 5,700,000,000,000,000 tons, and the force with which gravity holds it in place causes it to exert a pressure of nearly 15 pounds per square inch. Going out from the Earth's surface, the atmosphere is divided into five regions. The regions, and the heights to which they extend, are: *Troposphere,* 0 to 7 miles (at middle latitudes); *stratosphere,* 7 to 30 miles; *mesosphere,* 30 to 50 miles; *thermosphere,* 50 to 400 miles; and *exosphere,* above 400 miles. The boundaries between each of the regions are known respectively as the *tropopause, stratopause, mesopause,* and *thermopause.* Alternate terms often used for the layers above the troposphere are *ozonosphere* (for stratosphere) and *ionosphere* for the remaining upper layers.

**The Seasons.** Seasons are caused by the 23.4 degree tilt of the Earth's axis, which alternately turns the North and South Poles toward the Sun. Times when the Sun's apparent path crosses the Equator are known as *equinoxes.* Times when the Sun's apparent path is at the greatest distance from the Equator are known as *solstices.* The lengths of the days are most extreme at each solstice. If the Earth's axis were perpendicular to the plane of the Earth's orbit around the Sun, there would be no seasons, and the days always would be equal in length. Since the Earth's axis is at an angle, the Sun strikes the Earth directly at the Equator only twice a year: in March (vernal equinox) and September (autumnal equinox). In the Northern Hemisphere, spring begins at the vernal equinox, summer at the summer solstice, fall at the autumnal equinox, and winter at the winter solstice. The situation is reversed in the Southern Hemisphere.

## Mercury

Mercury is the planet nearest the Sun. Appropriately named for the wing-footed Roman messenger of the gods, Mercury whizzes around the Sun at a speed of 30 miles per second, completing one circuit in 88 days. The planet rotates on its axis over a period of nearly 59 days. Daytime on cratered Mercury is hot, about 800 degrees F., although at night the temperature may fall to room temperature. Mercury has no moons, but it does have a trace of atmosphere and a weak magnetic field, according to findings of Mariner 10. Until this spacecraft flew by Mercury in 1974 and 1975, very little was known about the planet, primarily because of its short angular distance from the Sun as seen from Earth, which puts it too close to the Sun to be easily observed.

• Mercury is a naked eye object at morning or evening twilight, when it is at greatest elongation.

## Venus

Although Venus is Earth's nearest neighbor, little is known about this planet because it is permanently covered by thick clouds. In 1962, Soviet and American space probes, coupled with Earth-based radar and infrared spectroscopy, began slowly unraveling some of the mystery surrounding Venus. According to these results, Venus' atmosphere is nearly 100% carbon dioxide, exerting a pressure at the surface 100 times greater than Earth's. Walking on Venus would be as difficult as walking a half-mile beneath the ocean. Because of the thick blanket of carbon dioxide, a "greenhouse effect" exists on Venus: Venus intercepts twice as much of the Sun's light as does the Earth. The light enters freely through carbon dioxide gas and is changed to heat radiation in molecular collisions. But carbon dioxide prevents the heat from escaping. Consequently, the temperature of the surface of Venus is nearly 800 degrees F., hot enough to melt lead. Radar bounced off the planet recently revealed what appear to be large craters. In 1978, NASA launched a multi-probe spacecraft toward Venus to conduct a detailed scientific examination of this enigmatic planet. Unlike other planets, Venus rotates in retrograde (clockwise) motion. Reason is not known.

• Venus is the brightest of all the planets and is often visible in the morning or evening, when it is frequently referred to as the Morning Star or Evening Star. At its brightest, it can sometimes be seen with the naked eye in full daylight, if one knows where to look.

## Mars

Mars, on the other side of the Earth from Venus, is Venus' direct opposite in terms of physical properties. Its atmosphere is cold, thin, and transparent, and readily permits observation of the planet's features. We know more about Mars than any other planet except Earth. Mars is a forbidding, rugged planet with huge volcanoes and deep chasms. The largest volcano, Nix Olympia, rises 78,000 feet above the surface, higher than Mount Everest. The plains of Mars are pockmarked by the hits of thousands of meteors over the years. Most of our information about Mars comes from the Mariner 9 spacecraft, which orbited the planet in 1971. Mariner 9, photographing 100% of the planet, uncovered spectacular geological formations, including a Martian Grand Canyon that dwarfs the one on Earth. The spacecraft's cameras also recorded what appeared to be dried riverbeds, suggesting the onetime presence of water on the planet. The latter idea gives encouragement to scientists looking for life on Mars, for where there is water, there may be life. However, by 1978, no evidence of life has been found. Temperatures near the equator range from −17 degrees F. in the daytime to −130 degrees F. at night. Mars rotates upon its axis in nearly the same period as Earth—24 hours, 37 minutes—so that a Mars day is almost identical to an Earth day. Mars takes 687 days to make one trip around the Sun. Because of its eccentric orbit Mars' distance from the Sun can vary by about 36 million miles. Its distance from Earth can vary by as much as 200 million miles. The atmosphere of Mars is much thinner than Earth's; atmospheric pressure is about 1% that of our planet. Its gravity is one-third of Earth's. Major constituents are carbon dioxide and nitrogen. Water vapor and oxygen are minor constituents. Mars' polar caps, composed mostly of carbon dioxide, recede and advance according to the Martian seasons. Mars was named for the Roman god of war, because when seen from Earth its distinct red color reminded the ancient people of blood. We know now that the reddish hue reflects the oxidized (rusted) iron in the surface material. The landing of two robot Viking spacecraft on the surface of Mars in 1976 provided more information about Mars in a few months than in all the time that has gone before.

• Mars becomes especially bright when nearest to us because we then see its daylight side fully illuminated by the Sun. This happens roughly every two years and two months. The last time was in December 1975.

## Jupiter

Jupiter, with an equatorial diameter of 88,000 miles, is the largest of a group of planets which differ markedly from the terrestrial planets. The others in the group are Saturn, Uranus and Neptune. All are large, with very dense atmospheres, and indeed may be giant balls of gas without any perceptible surfaces. They all whirl rapidly around their axes, but more slowly around the Sun, resulting in short days and long years. They have many moons. Majestic Jupiter, named for the king of the Roman gods, rotates so fast that it is greatly flattened at the poles. According to Pioneers 10 and 11, which flew past Jupiter in 1974 and 1975, this planet is a whirling ball of liquid hydrogen with perhaps an Earth-sized iron core. Other atmospheric constituents are helium, methane, and ammonia. Its clouds are probably ammonia ice crystals, becoming ammonia droplets deeper towards the "surface." Temperatures range from perhaps minus 300 degrees F. at the tops of the cloud decks to 100,000 degrees F. or more deep down at the center. The pressure at the center of the planet is estimated to be a crushing 10 million pounds per square inch. The most prominent feature on Jupiter is the Great Red Spot, the size of four Earths. According to Pioneer scientists, the Red Spot is the vortex of a huge 25,000-mile-wide hurricane which has been raging for at least 379 years, since Galileo first saw it through his telescope. Jupiter has possibly 14 satellites, more than any other planet. The four largest moons, called Galilean moons, are Europa, Ganymede, Io, and Callisto.

• Even when nearest the Earth, Jupiter is still almost 400 million miles away. But because of its size, it may rival Venus in brilliance when near. Jupiter's four large moons may be seen through field glasses, moving rapidly around Jupiter and changing their position from night to night.

## Saturn

Saturn, one of the giant planets in the solar system, is also the least dense. It would float in an ocean if there were one big enough to hold it. Aside from its rings, Saturn is very similar to Jupiter except that it is probably colder, being twice as far from the Sun. Recent radar observations of Saturn's rings indicate that they are no more than 10 miles thick, and probably composed of chunks of rock and ice averaging a meter in size. There are four rings. The system begins about 7000 miles from the planet's disk, and extends out to about 35,000 miles. Saturn has 10 satellites. The U.S. launched two Voyager spacecraft to Jupiter in August and September 1977. After flying past Jupiter in 1981, taking pictures and making measurements, the spacecraft will go on to Saturn and possibly Uranus.

• Saturn is the last of the planets visible to the naked eye. Saturn is never an object of overwhelming brilliance, but it looks like a bright star. The rings can be seen with a small telescope.

## Uranus and Neptune

Little is known about the distant giant planets Uranus and Neptune, but they are believed to be similar to Saturn and Jupiter. Being twice as far from the Sun as Saturn, Uranus must be a grim frozen world, and Neptune, 11 A.U. beyond Uranus, must be even colder and darker. The axis of Uranus is tilted at 98 degrees, so it goes around the Sun nearly lying on its side. In 1977, American astronomers made the startling discovery that Uranus has rings, like Saturn. The first Voyager to Uranus may take pictures of the rings in 1986. Uranus has five known moons; Neptune, two. Neptune's Triton, Jupiter's Ganymede and Callisto, and Saturn's Titan are the four largest moons in the solar system.

• Uranus and Neptune can—on rare occasion—become bright enough to be seen with the naked eye, if one knows exactly where to look; normally, they are objects for good field glasses or small portable telescopes.

## Pluto

Pluto, the outermost and smallest planet in the solar system, looks more like a terrestrial planet than a gaseous planet. But so little is known about it, that it is difficult to classify. Appropriately named for the Roman god of the underworld, it must be frozen, dark and dead.

In 1978, light curve studies gave evidence of a moon revolving around Pluto with the same period as Pluto's rotation. Therefore, it stays over the same point on Pluto's surface. In addition, it keeps the same face toward the planet. The discovery of this moon of 500–600 miles in diameter reduces the previously estimated diameter of Pluto to little more than 1,500 miles, making the pair more like a double planet than any other in the solar system. Previously, the Earth-Moon system held this distinction. The density of Pluto is slightly greater than that of water.

Pluto was predicted by calculation when Percival Lowell noticed irregularities in the orbits of Uranus and Neptune. Clyde Tombaugh discovered the planet in 1930, precisely where Lowell predicted it would be. The name Pluto was chosen because the first two letters represent the initials of Percival Lowell.

• Pluto has the most eccentric orbit in the solar system, bringing it at times closer to the Sun than Neptune. Pluto is now approaching the perihelion of its orbit, and for the rest of this century will be closer to the Sun than Neptune. Even then, it can be seen only with a large telescope.

## The First Ten Minor Planets (Asteroids)

| Name | Year of discovery | Mean distance from sun (millions of miles) | Orbital period (years) | Diameter (miles) | Magnitude |
|---|---|---|---|---|---|
| 1. Ceres | 1801 | 257.0 | 4.60 | 485 | 7.4 |
| 2. Pallas | 1802 | 257.4 | 4.61 | 304 | 8.0 |
| 3. Juno | 1804 | 247.8 | 4.36 | 118 | 8.7 |
| 4. Vesta | 1807 | 219.3 | 3.63 | 243 | 6.5 |
| 5. Astraea | 1845 | 239.3 | 4.14 | 50 | 9.9 |
| 6. Hebe | 1847 | 225.2 | 3.78 | 121 | 8.5 |
| 7. Iris | 1847 | 221.4 | 3.68 | 121 | 8.4 |
| 8. Flora | 1847 | 204.4 | 3.27 | 56 | 8.9 |
| 9. Metis | 1848 | 221.7 | 3.69 | 78 | 8.9 |
| 10. Hygeia | 1849 | 292.6 | 5.59 | 40(?) | 9.5 |

## The Asteroids

Between the orbits of Mars and Jupiter are an estimated 30,000 pieces of rocky debris, known collectively as the asteroids, or planetoids. The first and, incidentally, the largest was discovered during the New Year's night of 1801 by the Italian astronomer Father Piazzi, and its orbit was calculated by the German mathematician Karl Friedrich Gauss. (Gauss invented a new method of calculating orbits on that occasion.) A German amateur astronomer, the physician Olbers, discovered the second asteroid. The number now known, catalogued, and named is around 1,600; the estimated total is about 20 times that figure. A few asteroids do not move in orbits beyond the orbit of Mars, but in orbits which cross the orbit of Mars. The first of them was named Eros because of this peculiar orbit. It had become the rule to bestow female names on the asteroids, but when it was found that Eros crossed the orbit of a major planet, it received a male name. Since then around two dozen orbit-crossers have been discovered, and they are often referred to as the "male asteroids." A few of them—Albert, Adonis, Apollo, Amor, and Icarus—cross the orbit of the Earth, and two of them may come closer than our Moon; but the crossing is like a bridge crossing a highway, not like two highways intersecting. Hence there is very little danger of collision from these bodies. They are all small, three to five miles in diameter, and therefore very difficult objects to identify, even when quite close. Some scientists believe the asteroids represent the remains of an exploded planet.

## Comets

Comets, according to the noted astronomer, Fred L. Whipple, are enormous "snowballs" of frozen gases (mostly carbon dioxide, methane, and water vapor) and contain very little solid material. The whole behavior of comets can then be explained as the behavior of frozen gas being heated by the Sun. When the comet Kohoutek made its first appearance to man in 1973, its behavior seemed to confirm this Whipple theory of the make-up of comets.

Kohoutek will probably not appear in view for another 75,000 years. The next comet large and brilliant enough to be very easily seen is predicted for 1986, when Halley's comet will approach perihelion (the point of its orbit closest to the Sun) again.

But a large and brilliant comet is possible at any time. More than 1,000 comets are on the lists now, with several new ones being discovered every year. But while there is a comet visible to the unaided eye almost every year, none of them since the last appearance of Halley's comet in 1910–11 has been conspicuous to a casual watcher.

Since comets appear in the sky without any warning, people in classical times and especially during the Middle Ages believed that they had a special meaning, which, of course, was bad. Since a natural catastrophe of some sort or a military conflict occurs every year, it was quite simple to blame the comet that happened to be visible. But even in the past, there were some people who used logical reasoning. When, in Roman times, a comet was blamed for the loss of a battle and hence was called a "bad omen," a Roman writer observed that the victors in the battle probably did not think so.

Up until the middle of the sixteenth century, comets were believed to be phenomena of the upper atmosphere; they were usually "explained" as "burning vapors" which had risen from "distant swamps." That nobody had ever actually seen burning vapors rise from a swamp did not matter.

## 21 Famous Comets

| Year and no. | Name of comet | Period (years) |
|---|---|---|
| 1744 | De Chéseaux's Comet | — |
| 1806 | Biela's Comet | 6.7 |
| 1811 I | Great Comet of 1811 | 3000 |
| 1812 | Di Vico's Comet | 70.7 |
| 1815 | Olbers' Comet | 74.0 |
| 1819 I | Encke's Comet | 3.3 |
| 1819 | Pons-Winnecke Comet | 6.0 |
| 1835 III | Halley's Comet | 76.3 |
| 1843 I | Great Comet of 1843 | 512.4 |
| 1844 II | Great Comet of 1844 | 102,050 |
| 1858 VI | Donati's Comet | 2,040(?) |
| 1864 II | Great Comet of 1864 | 2,800,000 |
| 1871 III | Tuttle's Comet | 13.8 |
| 1874 III | Coggia's Comet | 6,000(?) |
| 1879 | Brorsen's Comet | 5.6 |
| 1881 II | Tebbutt's Comet | — |
| 1889 VI | Swift's 2nd Comet | 7.0 |
| 1892 III | Holmes' Comet | 6.9 |
| 1923 | d'Arrest's Comet | 6.6 |
| 1925 II | Comet Schwassmann-Wachmann | 16.2 |
| 1973 I | Comet Kohoutek | 75,000(?) |

But a large comet which appeared in 1577 was carefully observed by Tycho Brahe, a Danish astronomer who is often, and with the best of reasons, called "eccentric" but who insisted on precise measurements for everything. It was Tycho Brahe's accumulation of literally thousands of precise measurements which later enabled his younger collaborator, Johannes Kepler, to discover the laws of planetary motion. Measuring the motion of the comet of 1577, Tycho Brahe could show that it had been far beyond the atmosphere, even though he could not give figures for the distance. Tycho Brahe's work proved that comets were astronomical and not meteorological phenomena.

In 1682, the second Astronomer Royal of Great Britain, Dr. Edmond Halley, checked the orbit of a bright comet that was in the sky then and compared it with earlier comet orbits which were known in part. Halley found that the comet of 1682 was the third to move through what appeared to be the same orbit. And the three appearances were roughly 76 years apart. Halley concluded that this was the same comet, moving around the Sun in a closed orbit, like the planets. He predicted that it would reappear in 1758 or 1759. Halley himself died in 1742, but a large comet appeared sixteen years after his death as predicted and was immediately referred to as "Halley's comet."

In the Spring of 1974, the discovery of comet Kohoutek, apparently headed for a close-Christmastime rendezvous with the Sun, created worldwide excitement. The comet was a visual disappointment, but turned out to be a treasure trove of information on these little-understood celestial objects. Given an unprecedented advance notice of nine months on the advent of the fiery object, scientists were able to study the comet in visible, ultraviolet and infrared light; with optical telescopes, radio telescopes and radar. They observed it from the ground, from high-flying aircraft, with instruments aboard unmanned satellites, with sounding rockets, and telescopes and cameras on the Earth-orbiting Skylab space station. Kohoutek may well have been the most-scrutinized object in the history of astronomy. Scientists learned more about the nature of comets from this single event than from all the cometary observations that had gone before.

Astronomers refer to comets as "periodic" or as "non-periodic" comets, but the latter term does not mean that these comets have no period; it merely means that their period is not known. The actual periods of comets run from 3.3 years (the shortest known) to many thousands of years. Their orbits are elliptical, like those of the planets, but they are very eccentric, long and narrow ellipses. Only comet Schwassmann-Wachmann has an orbit which has such a low eccentricity (for a cometary orbit) that it could be the orbit of a minor planet.

When a comet, coming from deep space, approaches the Sun, it is at first indistinguishable from a minor planet. Somewhere between the orbits of Mars and Jupiter its outline becomes fuzzy; it is said to develop a "coma" (the word used here is the Latin word *coma,* which means "hair," not the phonetically identical Greek word which means "deep sleep"). Then, near the orbit of Mars, the comet develops its tail, which at first trails behind. This grows steadily as the comet comes closer and closer to the Sun. As it rounds the Sun (as first noticed by Girolamo Fracastoro) the tail always points away from the Sun so that the comet, when moving away from the Sun, points its tail ahead like the landing lights of an airplane.

The reason for this behavior is that the tail is pushed in these directions by the radiation pressure of the Sun. It sometimes happens that a comet loses its tail at perihelion; it then grows another one. Although the tail is clearly visible against the black of the sky, it is very tenuous. It has been said that if the tail of Halley's comet could be compressed to the density of iron, it would fit into a small suitcase.

## Meteors and Meteorites

The term "meteor" for what is usually called a "shooting star" bears an unfortunate resemblance to the term "meteorology," the science of weather and weather forecasting. This resemblance is due to an ancient misunderstanding which wrongly considered meteors an atmospheric phenomenon. Actually, the streak of light in the sky that scientists call a meteor is essentially an astronomical phenomenon: the entry of a small piece of cosmic matter into our atmosphere.

The distinction between "meteors" and "fireballs" (formerly also called "bolides") is merely one of convenience; a fireball is an unusually bright meteor. Incidentally, it also means that a fireball is larger than a faint meteor.

Bodies which enter our atmosphere become visible when they are about 60 miles above the ground. The fact that they grow hot enough to emit light is not due to the "friction" of the atmosphere, as one can often read. The phenomenon responsible for the heating is one of compression. Since unconfined air cannot move faster than the speed of sound while the entering meteorite moves with 30 to 60 times the speed of sound, the air simply cannot get out of the way. Therefore, it is compressed like the air in the cylinder of a Diesel engine and is heated by compression. This heat—or part of it—is transferred to the moving body. The details of this process are now fairly well understood as a result of re-entry tests with ballistic-missile nose cones.

The average weight of a body producing a faint

### Important Meteor Showers

| Approx. date | Name of meteor stream | Radiant in constellation |
|---|---|---|
| Jan. 1–4 | Quadrantids | Boötes |
| Feb. 5–10 | Alpha Aurigids | Auriga |
| March 10–12 | Zeta Boötids | Boötes |
| April 19–23 | Lyrids | Hercules |
| May 1–6 | May Aquarids | Aquarius |
| May 30 | Eta Pegasids | Pegasus |
| June 27–30 | Pons-Winnecke meteors | Draco |
| July 14 | Alpha Cygnids | Cygnus |
| July 26–31 | Delta Aquarids | Aquarius |
| Aug. 10–14 | Perseids | Cassiopeia |
| Aug. 10–20 | Kappa Cygnids | Cygnus |
| Aug. 21–31 | Zeta Draconids | Draco |
| Sept. 22 | Alpha Aurigids | Auriga |
| Oct. 2 | Quadrantids | Boötes |
| Oct. 9 | Giacobinids | Draco |
| Oct. 18–23 | Orionids | Orion |
| Nov. 14–18 | Leonids | Leo |
| Dec. 10–13 | Geminids | Gemini |

## The 88 Recognized Constellations

In astronomical works, the Latin names of the constellations are used. The letter N or S following the Latin name indicates whether the constellation is located to the north or south of the Zodiac. The letter Z indicates that the constellation is within the Zodiac.

| Latin name | Letter | English version | Latin name | Letter | English version | Latin name | Letter | English version |
|---|---|---|---|---|---|---|---|---|
| Andromeda | N | Andromeda | Delphinus | N | Dolphin | Pavo | S | Peacock |
| Antlia | S | Airpump | Dorado | S | Swordfish (Goldfish) | Pegasus | N | Pegasus |
| Apus | S | Bird of Paradise | Draco | N | Dragon | Perseus | N | Perseus |
| Aquarius | Z | Water Bearer | Equuleus | N | Filly | Phoenix | S | Phoenix |
| Aquila | N | Eagle | Eridanus | S | Eridanus (river) | Pictor | S | Painter (or his Easel) |
| Ara | S | Altar | Fornax | S | Furnace | Pisces | Z | Fishes |
| Aries | Z | Ram | Gemini | Z | Twins | Piscis Austrinus | S | Southern Fish |
| Auriga | N | Charioteer | Grus | S | Crane | Puppis | S | Poop (of Argo)[1] |
| Boötes | N | Herdsmen | Hercules | N | Hercules | Pyxis | S | Mariner's Compass |
| Caelum | S | Sculptor's Tool | Horologium | S | Clock | Reticulum | S | Net |
| Camelopardalis | N | Giraffe | Hydra | N | Sea Serpent | Sagitta | N | Arrow |
| Cancer | Z | Crab | Hydrus | S | Water Snake | Sagittarius | Z | Archer |
| Canes Venatici | N | Hunting Dogs | Indus | S | Indian | Scorpius | Z | Scorpion |
| Canis Major | S | Great Dog | Lacerta | N | Lizard | Sculptor | S | Sculptor |
| Canis Minor | S | Little Dog | Leo | Z | Lion | Scutum | N | Shield |
| Capricornus | Z | Goat (or Sea-Goat) | Leo Minor | N | Little Lion | Serpens | N | Serpent |
| Carina | S | Keel (of Argo)[1] | Lepus | S | Hare | Sextans | S | Sextant |
| Cassiopeia | N | Cassiopeia | Libra | Z | Scales | Taurus | Z | Bull |
| Centaurus | S | Centaur | Lupus | S | Wolf | Telescopium | S | Telescope |
| Cepheus | N | Cepheus | Lynx | N | Lynx | Triangulum | N | Triangle |
| Cetus | S | Whale | Lyra | N | Lyre (Harp) | Triangulum Australe | S | Southern Triangle |
| Chamaeleon | S | Chameleon | Mensa | S | Table (mountain) | Tucana | S | Toucan |
| Circinus | S | Compasses | Microscopium | S | Microscope | Ursa Major | N | Big Dipper |
| Columba | S | Dove | Monoceros | S | Unicorn | Ursa Minor | N | Little Dipper |
| Coma Berenices | N | Berenice's Hair | Musca | S | Southern Fly | Vela | S | Sail (of Argo)[1] |
| Corona Australis | S | Southern Crown | Norma | S | Rule (straightedge) | Virgo | Z | Virgin |
| Corona Borealis | N | Northern Crown | Octans | S | Octant | Volans | S | Flying Fish |
| Corvus | S | Crow (Raven) | Ophiuchus | N | Serpent-Bearer | Vulpecula | N | Fox |
| Crater | S | Cup | Orion | S | Orion | | | |
| Crux | S | Southern Cross | | | | | | |
| Cygnus | N | Swan | | | | | | |

1. The original constellation Argo Navis (the Ship Argo) has been divided into Carina, Puppis, and Vela. Normally the brightest star in each constellation is designated by alpha, the first letter of the Greek alphabet, the second brightest by beta, the second letter of the Greek alphabet, and so forth. But the Greek letters run through Carina, Puppis, and Vela as if it were still one constellation.

"shooting star" is only a small fraction of an ounce. Even a bright fireball may not weigh more than 2 or 3 pounds. Naturally, the smaller bodies are worn to dust by the passage through the atmosphere; only rather large ones reach the ground. Those that are found are called meteorites. (The "meteor," to repeat, is the term for the light streak in the sky.)

The largest meteorite known is still imbedded in the ground near Grootfontein in SW Africa and is estimated to weight 70 tons. The second largest known is the 34-ton Anighito (on exhibit in the Hayden Planetarium, New York), which was found by Admiral Peary at Cape York in Greenland. The largest meteorite found in the United States is the Willamette meteorite (found in Oregon, weight ca. 15 tons), but large portions of this meteorite weathered away before it was found. Its weight as it struck the ground may have been 20 tons.

All these are iron meteorites (an iron meteorite normally contains about 7% nickel), which form one class of meteorites. The other class consists of the stony meteorites, and between them there are the so-called "stony irons." The so-called "tektites" consist of glass similar to our volcanic glass obsidian, and because of the similarity, there is doubt in a number of cases whether the glass is of terrestrial or of extra-terrestrial origin.

Though no meteorite larger than the Grootfontein is actually known, we do know that the Earth has, on occasion, been struck by much larger bodies. Evidence for such hits are the meteorite craters, of which an especially good example is located near the Cañon Diablo in Arizona. Another meteor crater in the United States is a rather old crater near Odessa, Texas. A large number of others are known, especially in eastern Canada; and for many "probables," meteoric origin has now been proved.

The meteor showers are caused by multitudes of very small bodies travelling in swarms. The Earth travels in its orbit through these swarms like a car driving through falling snow. The point from which the meteors seem to emanate is called the *radiant* and is named for the constellation in that area. The Perseid meteor shower in August is the most spectacular of the year, boasting at peak roughly 60 meteors per hour under good atmospheric conditions. The presence of a bright moon diminishes the number of visible meteors.

## The Constellations

Constellations are groupings of stars which form patterns that can be easily recognized and remembered, for example, Orion and the Big Dipper. Actually, the stars of the majority of all constellations do not "belong together." Usually they are at greatly varying distances from the Earth and just happen to lie more or less in the same line of sight as seen from our solar system. But in a few cases the stars of a constellation are actually associated; most of the bright stars of the Big Dipper travel together and form what astronomers call an open cluster.

If you observe a planet, say Mars, for one complete revolution, you will see that it passes successively through twelve constellations. All planets (except Pluto at certain times) can be observed only in these twelve constellations, which form the so-called Zodiac, and the Sun also moves through the signs of the Zodiac, though the Sun's apparent movement is actually caused by the movement of the Earth. The twelve signs of the Zodiac are listed elsewhere in this section.

Although the constellations are due mainly to the optical accident of line of sight and have no real significance, astronomers have retained them as reference areas. It is much easier to speak of a star in Orion than to give its geometrical position in the sky. During the Astronomical Congress of 1928, it was decided to recognize 88 constellations. A description of their agreed-upon boundaries was published at Cambridge, England, in 1930, under the title *Atlas Céleste.*

## The Auroras

The "northern lights" *(Aurora borealis)* as well as the "southern lights" *(Aurora australis)* are upper-atmosphere phenoma of astronomical origin. The auroras center around the magnetic (not the geographical) poles of the Earth, which explains why, in the Western Hemisphere, they have been seen as far to the south as New Orleans and Florida while the equivalent latitude in the Eastern Hemisphere never sees an aurora. The northern magnetic pole happens to be in the Western Hemisphere.

The lower limit of an aurora is at about 50 miles. Upper limits have been estimated to be as high as 400 miles. Since about 1880, a connection between the auroras on Earth and the sun spots has been suspected and has gradually come to be accepted. It was said that the sun spots probably eject "particles" (later the word *electrons* was substituted) which on striking the Earth's atmosphere, cause the auroras. But this explanation suffered from certain difficulties. Sometimes a very large sun spot group on the Sun, with individual spots bigger than the Earth itself, would not cause an aurora. Moreover, even if a sun spot caused an aurora, the time that passed between the appearance of the one and the occurrence of the other was highly unpredictable.

This problem of the time lag is, in all probability, answered by the discovery of the Van Allen layer by artificial satellite *Explorer I.* The Van Allen layer is a double layer of charged sub-atomic particles around the Earth. The inner layer, with its center some 1,500 miles from the ground, reaches from about 40°N. to about 40°S. and does not touch the atmosphere. The outer layer, much larger and with its center several thousand miles from the ground, does touch the atmosphere in the vicinity of the magnetic poles.

It seems probable that the "leakage" of electrons from the outer Van Allen layer causes the auroras. A new burst of electrons from the Sun seems to be caught in the outer layer first. Under the assumption that all electrons are first caught in the outer layer, the time lag can be understood. There has to be an "overflow" from the outer layer to produce an aurora.

## The Atmosphere

Astronomically speaking, the presence of our atmosphere is deplorable. Though reasonably transparent to visible light, the atmosphere may absorb as much as 60% of the visible and near-visible light. It is opaque to most other wave-lengths, except certain fairly short radio waves. In addition to absorbing much light, our atmosphere bends light rays entering at a slant (for a given observer) so that the true position of a star close to the horizon is not what it seems to be. One effect is that we see the Sun above the horizon before it actually is. And the unsteady movement of the atmosphere causes the "twinkling" of the stars, which may be romantic but is a nuisance when it comes to observing.

The composition of our atmosphere near the ground is 78% nitrogen and 21% oxygen, the remaining 1% consisting of other gases, most of it argon. The composition stays the same to an altitude of at least 70 miles (except that higher up two impurities, carbon dioxide and water vapor, are missing), but the pressure drops very fast. At 18,000 feet, half of the total mass of the atmosphere is below, and at 100,000 feet, 99% of the mass of the atmosphere is below. The upper limit of the atmosphere is usually given as 120 miles; no definitive figure is possible, since there is no boundary line between the incredibly attenuated gases 120 miles up and space.

## Astronomical Telescopes

Optical telescopes used in astronomy are of two basic kinds: refracting and reflecting. In the *refractor telescope,* a lens is used to collect light from a distant object and bring it to a focus. A second lens, the eyepiece, then magnifies the image which may be examined visually or photographed directly. The *reflector telescope* uses a concave mirror instead of a lens, which reflects the light rays back toward the upper end of the telescope where they are magnified and observed or photographed. Most large optical telescopes now being built are reflectors.

*Radio telescopes* are used to study radio waves coming from outside the Earth's atmosphere. The waves are gathered by an antenna or "dish," which is a parabolic reflecting surface made of metal or finely meshed wire. Radio signals have been received from the Sun, Moon, and planets, and from the center of our galaxy and other galaxies. Radio signals are the means by which the distant and mysterious quasars and pulsars were recently discovered.

## Symbols

| | | | | | |
|---|---|---|---|---|---|
| ☉ the sun | ♀ Venus | ♃ Jupiter | ♆ Neptune | occultation | ☽ first quarter |
| ☾ the moon | ⊕ the earth | ♄ Saturn | ♇ Pluto | ☍ opposition | ○ full moon |
| ☿ Mercury | ♂ Mars | ♅ Uranus | ☌ conjunction | ● new moon | ☾ last quarter |

## Notable Reflector Telescopes

| Diameter in inches | Observatory | Location |
|---|---|---|
| 236 | Academy of Sciences | Zelenchukskaya, U.S.S.R. |
| 200 | Hale | Mount Palomar, Calif. |
| 158 | Kitt Peak National | Tucson, Ariz. |
| 158 | Inter-American | Cerro Tololo, Chile |
| 150 | Anglo Australian | Siding Spring Mt., Australia |
| 142 | European Southern | Cerro La Silla, Chile |
| 140[1] | French, Canadian, Hawaiian | Mauna Loa, Hawaii |
| 120 | Lick | Mount Hamilton, Calif. |
| 107 | McDonald | Mount Locke, Tex. |
| 102 | Crimean Astrophysical | Nauchny, U.S.S.R. |
| 101 | Carnegie Southern | Cerro Las Campanas, Chile |
| 100 | Hale | Mount Wilson, Calif. |
| 98 | Royal Greenwich | Herstmonceux, England |
| 90 | Steward | Tucson, Ariz. |

1. Under construction. *Source:* American Astronomical Society.

## Notable Radio Telescopes

| Diameter in feet | Observatory | Location |
|---|---|---|
| ([1]) | National Radio Astronomy Observatory | Socorro, New Mexico |
| 9842[2] | Solar Physics | Culgoora, Australia |
| 5249[3] | Westerbork Radio | Hooghalen, Netherlands |
| 1900[4] | U.S.S.R. Academy of Sciences | Caucasus, U.S.S.R. |
| 1001 | Arecibo | Arecibo, Puerto Rico |
| 3000/397 | Mullard Radio Astronomy | Cambridge, England |
| 328 | Effelsberg Radiotelescope | Bonn, West Germany |
| 300 | National Radio Astronomy | Green Bank, W. Va. |
| 656/131 | Paris-Meudon | Nancy, France |
| 249 | Nuffield Radio Astronomy | Jodrell Bank, Macclesfield, England |
| 210 | Australian National Radio Astronomy | New South Wales, Australia |
| 210 | NASA/JPL Goldstone Deep Space Communications Complex | Goldstone, Calif. |
| 341/70 | Ohio State–Ohio Wesleyan Radio | Delaware, Ohio |
| 150 | Stanford Center for Radar Astronomy | Stanford, Calif. |
| 150 | Sagamore Hill Radio | Hamilton, Mass. |
| 150 | Algonquin Radio | Lake Traverse, Canada |
| 140 | National Radio Astronomy | Green Bank, W. Va. |
| 130 | Owens Valley Radio | Big Pine, Calif. |
| 118 | Haystack | Tyngsboro, Mass. |

1. Symmetrical Y, each arm 7 miles long and consisting of nine 25-meter telescopes. 2. Diameter of 96-telescope circular array. 3. Length of 12-telescope array. 4. Under construction. *Source:* American Astronomical Society.

## Phenomena, 1979

### Configurations of Sun, Moon and Planets

**JANUARY**

| d | h | |
|---|---|---|
| 1 | 19 | Juno 0°.2 S of Moon |
| 4 | 22 | Earth at perihelion |
| 5 | 11 | FIRST QUARTER |
| 9 | 18 | Aldebaran 0°.5 S of Moon |
| 13 | 07 | FULL MOON |
| 14 | 09 | Pallas in conjunction with Sun |
| 14 | 11 | Jupiter 4° N of Moon |
| 15 | 03 | Moon at apogee |
| 15 | 18 | Venus 8° N of Antares |
| 17 | 16 | Saturn 2° N of Moon |
| 18 | 06 | Venus greatest elong. W (47°) |
| 20 | 12 | Mars in conjunction with Sun |
| 21 | 11 | LAST QUARTER |
| 22 | 21 | Uranus 4° S of Moon |
| 24 | 15 | Jupiter at opposition |
| 24 | 22 | Venus 2° S of Moon |
| 25 | 01 | Neptune 4° S of Moon |
| 26 | 18 | Venus 1°.9 N of Neptune |
| 28 | 06 | NEW MOON |
| 28 | 10 | Moon at perigee |
| 28 | 18 | Pluto stationary |
| 30 | 02 | Juno 0°.4 S of Moon |

**FEBRUARY**

| d | h | |
|---|---|---|
| 4 | 01 | FIRST QUARTER |
| 6 | 00 | Aldebaran 0°.3 S of Moon |
| 9 | 06 | Mercury in superior conjunction |
| 10 | 10 | Jupiter 4° N of Moon |
| 11 | 03 | Moon at apogee |
| 12 | 03 | FULL MOON |
| 13 | 19 | Saturn 3° N of Moon |
| 18 | 05 | Ceres in conjunction with Sun |
| 19 | 05 | Uranus 4° S of Moon |
| 20 | 01 | LAST QUARTER |
| 21 | 11 | Neptune 4° S of Moon |
| 23 | 15 | Venus 3° S of Moon |
| 24 | 13 | Uranus stationary |
| 24 | 22 | Vesta in conjunction with Sun |
| 25 | 22 | Moon at perigee |
| 26 | 17 | NEW MOON Eclipse |
| 27 | 12 | Juno 0°.5 S of Moon |
| 27 | 18 | Mercury 0°.6 N of Moon |

**MARCH**

| d | h | |
|---|---|---|
| 1 | 18 | Saturn at opposition |
| 5 | 07 | Aldebaran 0°.2 S of Moon |
| 5 | 16 | FIRST QUARTER |
| 8 | 01 | Mercury greatest elong. E (18°) |
| 9 | 12 | Jupiter 5° N of Moon |
| 10 | 10 | Moon at apogee |
| 12 | 21 | Saturn 3° N of Moon |
| 13 | 21 | FULL MOON Eclipse |
| 14 | 15 | Mercury stationary |
| 18 | 11 | Uranus 4° S of Moon |
| 20 | 18 | Neptune 4° S of Moon |
| 21 | 05 | Equinox |
| 21 | 11 | LAST QUARTER |
| 22 | 23 | Juno in conjunction with Sun |
| 24 | 14 | Mercury in inferior conjunction |

| d | h | |
|---|---|---|
| 25 | 09 | Venus 2° S of Moon |
| 26 | 01 | Jupiter stationary |
| 26 | 06 | Moon at perigee |
| 27 | 02 | Mars 0°.7 S of Moon |
| 28 | 03 | NEW MOON |

**APRIL**

| d | h | |
|---|---|---|
| 1 | 16 | Aldebaran 0°.3 S of Moon |
| 1 | 22 | Mercury 3° N of Mars |
| 4 | 10 | FIRST QUARTER |
| 5 | 18 | Jupiter 5° N of Moon |
| 6 | 01 | Mercury stationary |
| 7 | 03 | Moon at apogee |
| 8 | 07 | Pluto at opposition |
| 9 | 01 | Saturn 3° N of Moon |
| 12 | 13 | FULL MOON |
| 14 | 15 | Uranus 4° S of Moon |
| 16 | 23 | Neptune 4° S of Moon |
| 19 | 19 | LAST QUARTER |
| 21 | 13 | Mercury greatest elong. W (27°) |
| 22 | 22 | Moon at perigee |
| 24 | 03 | Venus 0°.3 S of Moon |
| 24 | 13 | Mercury 1° S of Moon |
| 24 | 23 | Mars 2° N of Moon |
| 25 | 11 | Juno 0°.7 S of Moon |
| 26 | 13 | NEW MOON |
| 29 | 01 | Aldebaran 0°.4 S of Moon |

**MAY**

| d | h | |
|---|---|---|
| 3 | 06 | Jupiter 4° N of Moon |
| 4 | 04 | FIRST QUARTER |
| 4 | 22 | Moon at apogee |
| 5 | 08 | Mercury 2° S of Mars |
| 6 | 07 | Saturn 3° N of Moon |
| 10 | 04 | Saturn stationary |
| 10 | 06 | Uranus at opposition |
| 11 | 21 | Uranus 4° S of Moon |
| 12 | 02 | FULL MOON |
| 14 | 05 | Neptune 4° S of Moon |
| 18 | 09 | Moon at perigee |
| 19 | 00 | LAST QUARTER |
| 20 | 06 | Venus 1°.1 S of Mars |
| 23 | 19 | Mars 3° N of Moon |
| 23 | 22 | Juno 1° S of Moon |
| 23 | 22 | Venus 3° N of Moon |
| 26 | 00 | NEW MOON |
| 29 | 23 | Mercury in superior conjunction |
| 30 | 22 | Jupiter 4° N of Moon |

**JUNE**

| d | h | |
|---|---|---|
| 1 | 17 | Moon at apogee |
| 2 | 16 | Saturn 2° N of Moon |
| 2 | 23 | FIRST QUARTER |
| 8 | 04 | Uranus 4° S of Moon |
| 10 | 12 | FULL MOON |
| 10 | 12 | Neptune 4° S of Moon |
| 10 | 15 | Neptune at opposition |
| 13 | 16 | Moon at perigee |
| 14 | 04 | Pallas stationary |
| 17 | 05 | LAST QUARTER |
| 20 | 03 | Venus 5° N of Aldebaran |
| 21 | 16 | Mars 5° N of Moon |
| 22 | 00 | Solstice |
| 22 | 17 | Aldebaran 0°.4 S of Moon |
| 22 | 22 | Mercury 5° S of Pollux |
| 23 | 00 | Venus 4° N of Moon |
| 24 | 12 | NEW MOON |
| 26 | 18 | Mercury 5° N of Moon |
| 27 | 16 | Jupiter 3° N of Moon |
| 29 | 11 | Moon at apogee |
| 30 | 03 | Saturn 2° N of Moon |

**JULY**

| d | h | |
|---|---|---|
| 2 | 15 | FIRST QUARTER |
| 3 | 22 | Earth at aphelion |
| 3 | 22 | Mercury greatest elong. E (26°) |
| 4 | 09 | Pluto stationary |
| 5 | 11 | Uranus 5° S of Moon |
| 7 | 20 | Neptune 4° S of Moon |
| 9 | 20 | FULL MOON |
| 10 | 16 | Mars 5° N of Aldebaran |
| 11 | 12 | Moon at perigee |
| 16 | 11 | LAST QUARTER |
| 17 | 02 | Mercury stationary |
| 19 | 23 | Aldebaran 0°.3 S of Moon |
| 20 | 12 | Mars 5° N of Moon |
| 24 | 02 | NEW MOON |
| 26 | 15 | Uranus stationary |
| 27 | 00 | Moon at apogee |
| 27 | 14 | Saturn 2° N of Moon |
| 31 | 17 | Mercury in inferior conjunction |

**AUGUST**

| d | h | |
|---|---|---|
| 1 | 06 | FIRST QUARTER |
| 1 | 20 | Uranus 5° S of Moon |
| 4 | 05 | Neptune 4° S of Moon |
| 8 | 03 | FULL MOON |
| 8 | 19 | Moon at perigee |
| 10 | 12 | Mercury stationary |
| 13 | 09 | Jupiter in conjunction with Sun |
| 14 | 19 | LAST QUARTER |
| 16 | 04 | Aldebaran 0°.2 S of Moon |
| 17 | 01 | Pallas at opposition |
| 18 | 08 | Mars 5° N of Moon |
| 19 | 04 | Mercury greatest elong. W (19°) |
| 19 | 14 | Ceres stationary |
| 21 | 02 | Mercury 2° N of Moon |
| 22 | 17 | NEW MOON Eclipse |
| 23 | 07 | Moon at apogee |
| 25 | 12 | Venus in superior conjunction |
| 29 | 03 | Uranus 5° S of Moon |
| 30 | 11 | Mercury 0°.7 N of Jupiter |
| 30 | 15 | Neptune stationary |
| 30 | 18 | FIRST QUARTER |
| 31 | 13 | Neptune 4° S of Moon |

**SEPTEMBER**

| d | h | |
|---|---|---|
| 2 | 11 | Mercury 1°.2 N of Regulus |
| 6 | 05 | Moon at perigee |
| 6 | 11 | FULL MOON Eclipse |
| 10 | 14 | Saturn in conjunction with Sun |
| 12 | 11 | Aldebaran 0°.2 S of Moon |
| 13 | 05 | Mercury in superior conjunction |
| 13 | 06 | LAST QUARTER |
| 14 | 23 | Mars 6° S of Pollux |
| 16 | 03 | Mars 5° N of Moon |
| 17 | 01 | Vesta stationary |
| 18 | 22 | Jupiter 2° N of Moon |
| 19 | 10 | Moon at apogee |
| 21 | 10 | NEW MOON |
| 23 | 15 | Equinox |
| 25 | 11 | Uranus 5° S of Moon |
| 26 | 13 | Jupiter 0°.3 N of Regulus |
| 27 | 20 | Neptune 4° S of Moon |
| 29 | 04 | FIRST QUARTER |

**OCTOBER**

| d | h | |
|---|---|---|
| 2 | 12 | Mercury 1°.9 N of Spica |
| 4 | 15 | Pallas stationary |
| 4 | 15 | Moon at perigee |
| 5 | 07 | Venus 3° N of Spica |
| 5 | 20 | FULL MOON |
| 6 | 06 | Ceres at opposition |
| 9 | 20 | Aldebaran 0°.3 S of Moon |
| 12 | 21 | LAST QUARTER |
| 13 | 02 | Pluto in conjunction with Sun |
| 14 | 20 | Mars 4° N of Moon |
| 16 | 15 | Jupiter 1° N of Moon |
| 16 | 20 | Moon at apogee |
| 18 | 05 | Saturn 0°.7 N of Moon |
| 21 | 02 | NEW MOON |
| 22 | 00 | Mercury 3° S of Uranus |
| 22 | 08 | Venus 5° S of Moon |
| 22 | 20 | Uranus 5° S of Moon |
| 22 | 22 | Mercury 8° S of Moon |
| 25 | 03 | Neptune 4° S of Moon |
| 27 | 16 | Venus 0°.2 S of Uranus |
| 28 | 13 | FIRST QUARTER |
| 29 | 16 | Mercury greatest elong. E (24°) |

**NOVEMBER**

| d | h | |
|---|---|---|
| 1 | 20 | Moon at perigee |
| 3 | 12 | Vesta at opposition |
| 4 | 06 | FULL MOON |
| 6 | 06 | Aldebaran 0°.4 S of Moon |
| 8 | 20 | Mercury 2° S of Venus |
| 9 | 18 | Mercury stationary |
| 11 | 14 | Venus 4° N of Antares |
| 11 | 16 | LAST QUARTER |
| 12 | 10 | Mars 3° N of Moon |
| 12 | 15 | Regulus 1° N of Moon |
| 13 | 07 | Jupiter 0°.8 N of Moon |
| 13 | 14 | Moon at apogee |
| 14 | 07 | Uranus in conjunction with Sun |
| 14 | 18 | Saturn 0°.3 N of Moon |
| 17 | 17 | Mars 1°.6 N of Regulus |
| 19 | 18 | NEW MOON |
| 20 | 04 | Mercury in inferior conjunction |
| 20 | 05 | Venus 2° S of Neptune |
| 21 | 11 | Neptune 4° S of Moon |
| 21 | 14 | Venus 6° S of Moon |
| 25 | 02 | Mercury 1°.7 N of Uranus |
| 26 | 21 | FIRST QUARTER |
| 29 | 00 | Moon at perigee |
| 29 | 10 | Mercury stationary |
| 30 | 05 | Juno stationary |

**DECEMBER**

| d | h | |
|---|---|---|
| 1 | 12 | Ceres stationary |
| 3 | 16 | Aldebaran 0°.5 S of Moon |
| 3 | 18 | FULL MOON |
| 5 | 00 | Mercury 2° N of Uranus |
| 7 | 16 | Mercury greatest elong. W (21°) |
| 9 | 23 | Regulus 0°.8 N of Moon |
| 10 | 18 | Mars 2° N of Moon |
| 10 | 20 | Jupiter 0°.4 N of Moon |
| 11 | 11 | Moon at apogee |
| 11 | 14 | LAST QUARTER |
| 12 | 05 | Saturn 0°.01 S of Moon |
| 12 | 20 | Neptune in conjunction with Sun |
| 13 | 17 | Mars 1°.7 N of Jupiter |
| 16 | 18 | Uranus 5° S of Moon |
| 17 | 20 | Mercury 4° S of Moon |
| 18 | 22 | Mercury 6° N of Antares |
| 19 | 08 | NEW MOON |
| 21 | 17 | Venus 5° S of Moon |
| 22 | 11 | Solstice |
| 23 | 16 | Moon at perigee |
| 24 | 05 | Vesta stationary |
| 26 | 05 | FIRST QUARTER |
| 27 | 05 | Jupiter stationary |
| 27 | 07 | Mercury 1°.4 S of Neptune |
| 31 | 00 | Aldebaran 0°.4 S of Moon |

NOTE: The hour listings are in Universal Time. For conversion to U.S. time zones, see conversion table in this section. For lunar phases and positions, for perihelion and aphelion passages of the planets, and for conjunctions of Mercury, see separate tables.

## Phases of the Moon for 1979

| Phase | Date | U.T. | E.S.T. | C.S.T. | M.S.T. | P.S.T. |
|---|---|---|---|---|---|---|
| First Quarter **JANUARY** | 5 | 11 | 6A | 5A | 4A | 3A |
| Full Moon | 13 | 07 | 2A | 1A | M | *11P |
| Last Quarter | 21 | 11 | 6A | 5A | 4A | 3A |
| New Moon | 28 | 06 | 1A | M | *11P | *10P |
| First Quarter **FEBRUARY** | 4 | 00 | * 7P | * 6P | * 5P | * 4P |
| Full Moon | 12 | 02 | * 9P | * 8P | * 7P | * 6P |
| Last Quarter | 20 | 01 | * 8P | * 7P | * 6P | * 5P |
| New Moon | 26 | 16 | 11A | 10A | 9A | 8A |
| First Quarter **MARCH** | 5 | 16 | 11A | 10A | 9A | 8A |
| Full Moon | 13 | 21 | 4P | 3P | 2P | 1P |
| Last Quarter | 21 | 11 | 6A | 5A | 4A | 3A |
| New Moon | 28 | 03 | *10P | * 9P | * 8P | * 7P |
| First Quarter **APRIL** | 4 | 09 | 4A | 3A | 2A | 1A |
| Full Moon | 12 | 13 | 8A | 7A | 6A | 5A |
| Last Quarter | 19 | 18 | 1P | N | 11A | 10A |
| New Moon | 26 | 13 | 8A | 7A | 6A | 5A |
| First Quarter **MAY** | 4 | 04 | *11P | *10P | * 9P | * 8P |
| Full Moon | 12 | 02 | * 9P | * 8P | * 7P | * 6P |
| Last Quarter | 18 | 23 | 6P | 5P | 4P | 3P |
| New Moon | 26 | 00 | * 7P | * 6P | * 5P | * 4P |
| First Quarter **JUNE** | 2 | 22 | 5P | 4P | 3P | 2P |
| Full Moon | 10 | 11 | 6A | 5A | 4A | 3A |
| Last Quarter | 17 | 05 | M | *11P | *10P | * 9P |
| New Moon | 24 | 11 | 6A | 5A | 4A | 3A |
| First Quarter **JULY** | 2 | 15 | 10A | 9A | 8A | 7A |
| Full Moon | 9 | 19 | 2P | 1P | N | 11A |
| Last Quarter | 16 | 10 | 5A | 4A | 3A | 2A |
| New Moon | 24 | 01 | * 8P | * 7P | * 6P | * 5P |
| First Quarter **AUGUST** | 1 | 05 | M | *11P | *10P | * 9P |
| Full Moon | 8 | 03 | *10P | * 9P | * 8P | * 7P |
| Last Quarter | 14 | 19 | 2P | 1P | N | 11A |
| New Moon | 22 | 17 | N | 11A | 10A | 9A |
| First Quarter | 30 | 18 | 1P | N | 11A | 10A |
| Full Moon **SEPTEMBER** | 6 | 10 | 5A | 4A | 3A | 2A |
| Last Quarter | 13 | 06 | 1A | M | *11P | *10P |
| New Moon | 21 | 09 | 4A | 3A | 2A | 1A |
| First Quarter | 29 | 04 | *11P | *10P | * 9P | * 8P |
| Full Moon **OCTOBER** | 5 | 19 | 2P | 1P | N | 11A |
| Last Quarter | 12 | 21 | 4P | 3P | 2P | 1P |
| New Moon | 21 | 02 | * 9P | * 8P | * 7P | * 6P |
| First Quarter | 28 | 13 | 8A | 7A | 6A | 5A |
| Full Moon **NOVEMBER** | 4 | 05 | M | *11P | *10P | * 9P |
| Last Quarter | 11 | 16 | 11A | 10A | 9A | 8A |
| New Moon | 19 | 18 | 1P | N | 11A | 10A |
| First Quarter | 26 | 21 | 4P | 3P | 2P | 1P |
| Full Moon **DECEMBER** | 3 | 18 | 1P | N | 11A | 10A |
| Last Quarter | 11 | 13 | 8A | 7A | 6A | 5A |
| New Moon | 19 | 08 | 3A | 2A | 1A | M |
| First Quarter | 26 | 05 | M | *11P | *10P | * 9P |

NOTE: * Denotes the previous day; dates are given in Universal Time, in which 05 corresponds to midnight E.S.T.

## Conversion of Universal Time (U. T.) to Civil Time

| U.T. | E.D.T.[1] | E.S.T.[2] | C.S.T.[3] | M.S.T.[4] | P.S.T.[5] | U.T. | E.D.T.[1] | E.S.T.[2] | C.S.T.[3] | M.S.T.[4] | P.S.T.[5] |
|---|---|---|---|---|---|---|---|---|---|---|---|
| 00 | *8P | *7P | *6P | *5P | *4P | 12 | 8A | 7A | 6A | 5A | 4A |
| 01 | *9P | *8P | *7P | *6P | *5P | 13 | 9A | 8A | 7A | 6A | 5A |
| 02 | *10P | *9P | *8P | *7P | *6P | 14 | 10A | 9A | 8A | 7A | 6A |
| 03 | *11P | *10P | *9P | *8P | *7P | 15 | 11A | 10A | 9A | 8A | 7A |
| 04 | M | *11P | *10P | *9P | *8P | 16 | N | 11A | 10A | 9A | 8A |
| 05 | 1A | M | *11P | *10P | *9P | 17 | 1P | N | 11A | 10A | 9A |
| 06 | 2A | 1A | M | *11P | *10P | 18 | 2P | 1P | N | 11A | 10A |
| 07 | 3A | 2A | 1A | M | *11P | 19 | 3P | 2P | 1P | N | 11A |
| 08 | 4A | 3A | 2A | 1A | M | 20 | 4P | 3P | 2P | 1P | N |
| 09 | 5A | 4A | 3A | 2A | 1A | 21 | 5P | 4P | 3P | 2P | 1P |
| 10 | 6A | 5A | 4A | 3A | 2A | 22 | 6P | 5P | 4P | 3P | 2P |
| 11 | 7A | 6A | 5A | 4A | 3A | 23 | 7P | 6P | 5P | 4P | 3P |

1. Eastern Daylight Time. 2. Eastern Standard Time, same as Central Daylight Time. 3. Central Standard Time, same as Mountain Daylight Time. 4. Mountain Standard Time, same as Pacific Daylight Time. 5. Pacific Standard Time. NOTES: *denotes previous day. N = noon. M = midnight.

## Morning and Evening Stars, 1979

| Planet | Morning | Evening |
|---|---|---|
| Mercury | Jan. 1—Feb. 8 | Feb. 9—March 24 |
| | March 25—May 29 | May 30—July 31 |
| | Aug. 1—Sept. 12 | Sept. 13—Nov. 19 |
| | Nov. 20—Dec. 31 | |
| Venus | Jan. 1—Aug. 25 | Aug. 25—Dec. 31 |
| Mars | | Jan. 1—Jan. 20 |
| | Jan. 20—Dec. 31 | |
| Jupiter | Jan. 1—Jan. 24 | Jan. 25—Aug. 12 |
| | Aug. 13—Dec. 31 | |
| Saturn | Jan.—March 1 | March 2—Sept. 10 |
| | Sept. 11—Dec. 31 | |
| Uranus | Jan. 1—May 9 | May 10—Nov. 13 |
| | Nov. 14—Dec. 31 | |
| Neptune | Jan. 1—June 10 | June 11—Dec. 12 |
| | Dec. 13—Dec. 31 | |
| Pluto | Jan. 1—April 7 | April 8—Oct. 12 |
| | Oct. 13—Dec. 31 | |

Dates approximate. An *evening star* is any planet that is above the horizon at sunset, and a *morning star* is any planet that is above the horizon at sunrise. Periods of best visibility for the five "naked eye" planets are given above. *Evening stars* appear in the western sky; *morning stars* appear in the eastern sky.

## Perigee and Apogee Positions of the Moon, 1979

| Perigee | U.T. | E.S.T. | Apogee | U.T. | E.S.T. |
|---|---|---|---|---|---|
| Dec. 30, 1978 | 22 | 5P | Jan. 15 | 03 | *10P |
| Jan. 28 | 10 | 5A | Feb. 11 | 03 | *10P |
| Feb. 25 | 22 | 5P | March 10 | 10 | 5A |
| March 26 | 06 | 1A | April 7 | 03 | *10P |
| April 22 | 22 | 5P | May 4 | 22 | 5P |
| May 18 | 08 | 4A | June 1 | 17 | N |
| June 13 | 16 | 11A | June 29 | 11 | 6A |
| July 11 | 12 | 7A | July 27 | 00 | *7P |
| Aug. 8 | 19 | 2P | Aug. 23 | 07 | 2A |
| Sep. 6 | 05 | M | Sep. 19 | 10 | 5A |
| Oct. 4 | 15 | 10A | Oct. 16 | 20 | 3P |
| Nov. 1 | 20 | 3P | Nov. 13 | 14 | 9A |
| Nov. 29 | 00 | *7P | Dec. 11 | 11 | 6A |
| Dec. 23 | 16 | 11A | Jan. 8, 1980 | 08 | 3A |

NOTES: *Denotes previous day. N = noon. M = midnight.

## Conjunctions of Mercury, 1979

| Inferior conjunction | U.T. | E.S.T. | Superior conjunction | U.T. | E.S.T. |
|---|---|---|---|---|---|
| March 24 | 14 | 9A | Feb. 9 | 06 | 1A |
| July 31 | 17 | N | May 29 | 23 | 6P |
| Nov. 20 | 04 | *11P | Sept. 13 | 05 | M |

NOTES: *Denotes previous day N = noon. M = midnight.

## Perihelion and Aphelion Passages, 1979

| Planet | Passes through its: Perihelion | Aphelion |
|---|---|---|
| Mercury | — | Jan. 19 |
| | March 4 | April 17 |
| | May 31 | July 14 |
| | Aug. 27 | Oct. 10 |
| | Nov. 23 | — |
| Venus | — | April 22 |
| | Aug. 12 | Dec. 3 |
| Mars | March 18 | — |

NOTE: There are no perihelion or aphelion passages by Jupiter, Saturn, Uranus, Neptune, or Pluto in 1979.

## Eclipses of the Sun and the Moon, 1979

**February 26: Total eclipse of the Sun.** Visible in North America except West Alaska, Central America, Arctic regions, Greenland except its northeast, Iceland, Western Europe.

**March 13: Partial eclipse of the Moon.** Visible in Australia, Asia, Africa, Europe, part of Antarctica, eastern South America, Arctic regions, Greenland, northeastern North America.

**August 22: Annular eclipse of the Sun.** Visible in southern part of South America, part of Antarctica.

**September 6: Total eclipse of the Moon.** Visible in South America except extreme eastern part, North America except the northeast, New Zealand, Australia, part of Antarctica; eastern Asia.

# CALENDAR & HOLIDAYS

## 1979

**JANUARY**

| S | M | T | W | T | F | S |
|---|---|---|---|---|---|---|
| – | 1 | 2 | 3 | 4 | 5 | 6 |
| 7 | 8 | 9 | 10 | 11 | 12 | 13 |
| 14 | 15 | 16 | 17 | 18 | 19 | 20 |
| 21 | 22 | 23 | 24 | 25 | 26 | 27 |
| 28 | 29 | 30 | 31 | | | |

1– New Year's Day
6– Epiphany

**FEBRUARY**

| S | M | T | W | T | F | S |
|---|---|---|---|---|---|---|
| – | – | – | – | 1 | 2 | 3 |
| 4 | 5 | 6 | 7 | 8 | 9 | 10 |
| 11 | 12 | 13 | 14 | 15 | 16 | 17 |
| 18 | 19 | 20 | 21 | 22 | 23 | 24 |
| 25 | 26 | 27 | 28 | | | |

2–Groundhog Day
12–Lincoln s Birthday
14–St. Valentine's Day
19–Washington's Birthday
28–Ash Wednesday

**MARCH**

| S | M | T | W | T | F | S |
|---|---|---|---|---|---|---|
| – | – | – | – | 1 | 2 | 3 |
| 4 | 5 | 6 | 7 | 8 | 9 | 10 |
| 11 | 12 | 13 | 14 | 15 | 16 | 17 |
| 18 | 19 | 20 | 21 | 22 | 23 | 24 |
| 25 | 26 | 27 | 28 | 29 | 30 | 31 |

13– Purim
17– St. Patrick s Day

**APRIL**

| S | M | T | W | T | F | S |
|---|---|---|---|---|---|---|
| 1 | 2 | 3 | 4 | 5 | 6 | 7 |
| 8 | 9 | 10 | 11 | 12 | 13 | 14 |
| 15 | 16 | 17 | 18 | 19 | 20 | 21 |
| 22 | 23 | 24 | 25 | 26 | 27 | 28 |
| 29 | 30 | | | | | |

8– Palm Sunday
12– 1st Day of Passover
13– Good Friday
15– Easter
29– Daylight Savings Time begins

**MAY**

| S | M | T | W | T | F | S |
|---|---|---|---|---|---|---|
| – | – | 1 | 2 | 3 | 4 | 5 |
| 6 | 7 | 8 | 9 | 10 | 11 | 12 |
| 13 | 14 | 15 | 16 | 17 | 18 | 19 |
| 20 | 21 | 22 | 23 | 24 | 25 | 26 |
| 27 | 28 | 29 | 30 | 31 | | |

13– Mother's Day
24– Ascension Day
28– Memorial Day

**JUNE**

| S | M | T | W | T | F | S |
|---|---|---|---|---|---|---|
| – | – | – | – | – | 1 | 2 |
| 3 | 4 | 5 | 6 | 7 | 8 | 9 |
| 10 | 11 | 12 | 13 | 14 | 15 | 16 |
| 17 | 18 | 19 | 20 | 21 | 22 | 23 |
| 24 | 25 | 26 | 27 | 28 | 29 | 30 |

1–1st Day of Shabuoth
3–Pentecost
10–Trinity Sunday
14–Flag Day
17–Father's Day

**JULY**

| S | M | T | W | T | F | S |
|---|---|---|---|---|---|---|
| 1 | 2 | 3 | 4 | 5 | 6 | 7 |
| 8 | 9 | 10 | 11 | 12 | 13 | 14 |
| 15 | 16 | 17 | 18 | 19 | 20 | 21 |
| 22 | 23 | 24 | 25 | 26 | 27 | 28 |
| 29 | 30 | 31 | | | | |

4– Independence Day

**AUGUST**

| S | M | T | W | T | F | S |
|---|---|---|---|---|---|---|
| – | – | – | 1 | 2 | 3 | 4 |
| 5 | 6 | 7 | 8 | 9 | 10 | 11 |
| 12 | 13 | 14 | 15 | 16 | 17 | 18 |
| 19 | 20 | 21 | 22 | 23 | 24 | 25 |
| 26 | 27 | 28 | 29 | 30 | 31 | |

**SEPTEMBER**

| S | M | T | W | T | F | S |
|---|---|---|---|---|---|---|
| – | – | – | – | – | – | 1 |
| 2 | 3 | 4 | 5 | 6 | 7 | 8 |
| 9 | 10 | 11 | 12 | 13 | 14 | 15 |
| 16 | 17 | 18 | 19 | 20 | 21 | 22 |
| 23 | 24 | 25 | 26 | 27 | 28 | 29 |
| 30 | | | | | | |

3– Labor Day
22– 1st Day of Rosh Hashana

**OCTOBER**

| S | M | T | W | T | F | S |
|---|---|---|---|---|---|---|
| – | 1 | 2 | 3 | 4 | 5 | 6 |
| 7 | 8 | 9 | 10 | 11 | 12 | 13 |
| 14 | 15 | 16 | 17 | 18 | 19 | 20 |
| 21 | 22 | 23 | 24 | 25 | 26 | 27 |
| 28 | 29 | 30 | 31 | | | |

1– Yom Kippur
6– 1st Day of Sukkoth
8– Columbus Day
28– Daylight Savings Time ends
31– Halloween

**NOVEMBER**

| S | M | T | W | T | F | S |
|---|---|---|---|---|---|---|
| – | – | – | – | 1 | 2 | 3 |
| 4 | 5 | 6 | 7 | 8 | 9 | 10 |
| 11 | 12 | 13 | 14 | 15 | 16 | 17 |
| 18 | 19 | 20 | 21 | 22 | 23 | 24 |
| 25 | 26 | 27 | 28 | 29 | 30 | |

1– All Saints' Day
6– Election Day
11– Veterans Day
22– Thanksgiving Day

**DECEMBER**

| S | M | T | W | T | F | S |
|---|---|---|---|---|---|---|
| – | – | – | – | – | – | 1 |
| 2 | 3 | 4 | 5 | 6 | 7 | 8 |
| 9 | 10 | 11 | 12 | 13 | 14 | 15 |
| 16 | 17 | 18 | 19 | 20 | 21 | 22 |
| 23 | 24 | 25 | 26 | 27 | 28 | 29 |
| 30 | 31 | | | | | |

2– 1st Sunday of Advent
15– 1st Day of Hanukkah
25– Christmas

### Seasons for the Northern Hemisphere, 1979

**Eastern Standard Time**

March 21, 12:22 a.m., sun enters sign of Aries; spring begins

June 21, 6:56 p.m., sun enters sign of Cancer; summer begins

Sept. 23, 10:17 a.m., sun enters sign of Libra; fall begins

Dec. 22, 6:10 a.m., sun enters sign of Capricorn; winter begins

# 1978

### JANUARY

| S | M | T | W | T | F | S |
|---|---|---|---|---|---|---|
| 1 | 2 | 3 | 4 | 5 | 6 | 7 |
| 8 | 9 | 10 | 11 | 12 | 13 | 14 |
| 15 | 16 | 17 | 18 | 19 | 20 | 21 |
| 22 | 23 | 24 | 25 | 26 | 27 | 28 |
| 29 | 30 | 31 | | | | |

### FEBRUARY

| S | M | T | W | T | F | S |
|---|---|---|---|---|---|---|
| – | – | – | 1 | 2 | 3 | 4 |
| 5 | 6 | 7 | 8 | 9 | 10 | 11 |
| 12 | 13 | 14 | 15 | 16 | 17 | 18 |
| 19 | 20 | 21 | 22 | 23 | 24 | 25 |
| 26 | 27 | 28 | | | | |

### MARCH

| S | M | T | W | T | F | S |
|---|---|---|---|---|---|---|
| – | – | – | 1 | 2 | 3 | 4 |
| 5 | 6 | 7 | 8 | 9 | 10 | 11 |
| 12 | 13 | 14 | 15 | 16 | 17 | 18 |
| 19 | 20 | 21 | 22 | 23 | 24 | 25 |
| 26 | 27 | 28 | 29 | 30 | 31 | |

### APRIL

| S | M | T | W | T | F | S |
|---|---|---|---|---|---|---|
| – | – | – | – | – | – | 1 |
| 2 | 3 | 4 | 5 | 6 | 7 | 8 |
| 9 | 10 | 11 | 12 | 13 | 14 | 15 |
| 16 | 17 | 18 | 19 | 20 | 21 | 22 |
| 23 | 24 | 25 | 26 | 27 | 28 | 29 |
| 30 | | | | | | |

### MAY

| S | M | T | W | T | F | S |
|---|---|---|---|---|---|---|
| – | 1 | 2 | 3 | 4 | 5 | 6 |
| 7 | 8 | 9 | 10 | 11 | 12 | 13 |
| 14 | 15 | 16 | 17 | 18 | 19 | 20 |
| 21 | 22 | 23 | 24 | 25 | 26 | 27 |
| 28 | 29 | 30 | 31 | | | |

### JUNE

| S | M | T | W | T | F | S |
|---|---|---|---|---|---|---|
| – | – | – | – | 1 | 2 | 3 |
| 4 | 5 | 6 | 7 | 8 | 9 | 10 |
| 11 | 12 | 13 | 14 | 15 | 16 | 17 |
| 18 | 19 | 20 | 21 | 22 | 23 | 24 |
| 25 | 26 | 27 | 28 | 29 | 30 | |

### JULY

| S | M | T | W | T | F | S |
|---|---|---|---|---|---|---|
| – | – | – | – | – | – | 1 |
| 2 | 3 | 4 | 5 | 6 | 7 | 8 |
| 9 | 10 | 11 | 12 | 13 | 14 | 15 |
| 16 | 17 | 18 | 19 | 20 | 21 | 22 |
| 23 | 24 | 25 | 26 | 27 | 28 | 29 |
| 30 | 31 | | | | | |

### AUGUST

| S | M | T | W | T | F | S |
|---|---|---|---|---|---|---|
| – | – | 1 | 2 | 3 | 4 | 5 |
| 6 | 7 | 8 | 9 | 10 | 11 | 12 |
| 13 | 14 | 15 | 16 | 17 | 18 | 19 |
| 20 | 21 | 22 | 23 | 24 | 25 | 26 |
| 27 | 28 | 29 | 30 | 31 | | |

### SEPTEMBER

| S | M | T | W | T | F | S |
|---|---|---|---|---|---|---|
| – | – | – | – | – | 1 | 2 |
| 3 | 4 | 5 | 6 | 7 | 8 | 9 |
| 10 | 11 | 12 | 13 | 14 | 15 | 16 |
| 17 | 18 | 19 | 20 | 21 | 22 | 23 |
| 24 | 25 | 26 | 27 | 28 | 29 | 30 |

### OCTOBER

| S | M | T | W | T | F | S |
|---|---|---|---|---|---|---|
| 1 | 2 | 3 | 4 | 5 | 6 | 7 |
| 8 | 9 | 10 | 11 | 12 | 13 | 14 |
| 15 | 16 | 17 | 18 | 19 | 20 | 21 |
| 22 | 23 | 24 | 25 | 26 | 27 | 28 |
| 29 | 30 | 31 | | | | |

### NOVEMBER

| S | M | T | W | T | F | S |
|---|---|---|---|---|---|---|
| – | – | – | 1 | 2 | 3 | 4 |
| 5 | 6 | 7 | 8 | 9 | 10 | 11 |
| 12 | 13 | 14 | 15 | 16 | 17 | 18 |
| 19 | 20 | 21 | 22 | 23 | 24 | 25 |
| 26 | 27 | 28 | 29 | 30 | | |

### DECEMBER

| S | M | T | W | T | F | S |
|---|---|---|---|---|---|---|
| – | – | – | – | – | 1 | 2 |
| 3 | 4 | 5 | 6 | 7 | 8 | 9 |
| 10 | 11 | 12 | 13 | 14 | 15 | 16 |
| 17 | 18 | 19 | 20 | 21 | 22 | 23 |
| 24 | 25 | 26 | 27 | 28 | 29 | 30 |
| 31 | | | | | | |

# 1980

### JANUARY

| S | M | T | W | T | F | S |
|---|---|---|---|---|---|---|
| – | – | 1 | 2 | 3 | 4 | 5 |
| 6 | 7 | 8 | 9 | 10 | 11 | 12 |
| 13 | 14 | 15 | 16 | 17 | 18 | 19 |
| 20 | 21 | 22 | 23 | 24 | 25 | 26 |
| 27 | 28 | 29 | 30 | 31 | | |

### FEBRUARY

| S | M | T | W | T | F | S |
|---|---|---|---|---|---|---|
| – | – | – | – | – | 1 | 2 |
| 3 | 4 | 5 | 6 | 7 | 8 | 9 |
| 10 | 11 | 12 | 13 | 14 | 15 | 16 |
| 17 | 18 | 19 | 20 | 21 | 22 | 23 |
| 24 | 25 | 26 | 27 | 28 | 29 | |

### MARCH

| S | M | T | W | T | F | S |
|---|---|---|---|---|---|---|
| – | – | – | – | – | – | 1 |
| 2 | 3 | 4 | 5 | 6 | 7 | 8 |
| 9 | 10 | 11 | 12 | 13 | 14 | 15 |
| 16 | 17 | 18 | 19 | 20 | 21 | 22 |
| 23 | 24 | 25 | 26 | 27 | 28 | 29 |
| 30 | 31 | | | | | |

### APRIL

| S | M | T | W | T | F | S |
|---|---|---|---|---|---|---|
| – | – | 1 | 2 | 3 | 4 | 5 |
| 6 | 7 | 8 | 9 | 10 | 11 | 12 |
| 13 | 14 | 15 | 16 | 17 | 18 | 19 |
| 20 | 21 | 22 | 23 | 24 | 25 | 26 |
| 27 | 28 | 29 | 30 | | | |

### MAY

| S | M | T | W | T | F | S |
|---|---|---|---|---|---|---|
| – | – | – | – | 1 | 2 | 3 |
| 4 | 5 | 6 | 7 | 8 | 9 | 10 |
| 11 | 12 | 13 | 14 | 15 | 16 | 17 |
| 18 | 19 | 20 | 21 | 22 | 23 | 24 |
| 25 | 26 | 27 | 28 | 29 | 30 | 31 |

### JUNE

| S | M | T | W | T | F | S |
|---|---|---|---|---|---|---|
| 1 | 2 | 3 | 4 | 5 | 6 | 7 |
| 8 | 9 | 10 | 11 | 12 | 13 | 14 |
| 15 | 16 | 17 | 18 | 19 | 20 | 21 |
| 22 | 23 | 24 | 25 | 26 | 27 | 28 |
| 29 | 30 | | | | | |

### JULY

| S | M | T | W | T | F | S |
|---|---|---|---|---|---|---|
| – | – | 1 | 2 | 3 | 4 | 5 |
| 6 | 7 | 8 | 9 | 10 | 11 | 12 |
| 13 | 14 | 15 | 16 | 17 | 18 | 19 |
| 20 | 21 | 22 | 23 | 24 | 25 | 26 |
| 27 | 28 | 29 | 30 | 31 | | |

### AUGUST

| S | M | T | W | T | F | S |
|---|---|---|---|---|---|---|
| – | – | – | – | – | 1 | 2 |
| 3 | 4 | 5 | 6 | 7 | 8 | 9 |
| 10 | 11 | 12 | 13 | 14 | 15 | 16 |
| 17 | 18 | 19 | 20 | 21 | 22 | 23 |
| 24 | 25 | 26 | 27 | 28 | 29 | 30 |
| 31 | | | | | | |

### SEPTEMBER

| S | M | T | W | T | F | S |
|---|---|---|---|---|---|---|
| – | 1 | 2 | 3 | 4 | 5 | 6 |
| 7 | 8 | 9 | 10 | 11 | 12 | 13 |
| 14 | 15 | 16 | 17 | 18 | 19 | 20 |
| 21 | 22 | 23 | 24 | 25 | 26 | 27 |
| 28 | 29 | 30 | | | | |

### OCTOBER

| S | M | T | W | T | F | S |
|---|---|---|---|---|---|---|
| – | – | – | 1 | 2 | 3 | 4 |
| 5 | 6 | 7 | 8 | 9 | 10 | 11 |
| 12 | 13 | 14 | 15 | 16 | 17 | 18 |
| 19 | 20 | 21 | 22 | 23 | 24 | 25 |
| 26 | 27 | 28 | 29 | 30 | 31 | |

### NOVEMBER

| S | M | T | W | T | F | S |
|---|---|---|---|---|---|---|
| – | – | – | – | – | – | 1 |
| 2 | 3 | 4 | 5 | 6 | 7 | 8 |
| 9 | 10 | 11 | 12 | 13 | 14 | 15 |
| 16 | 17 | 18 | 19 | 20 | 21 | 22 |
| 23 | 24 | 25 | 26 | 27 | 28 | 29 |
| 30 | | | | | | |

### DECEMBER

| S | M | T | W | T | F | S |
|---|---|---|---|---|---|---|
| – | 1 | 2 | 3 | 4 | 5 | 6 |
| 7 | 8 | 9 | 10 | 11 | 12 | 13 |
| 14 | 15 | 16 | 17 | 18 | 19 | 20 |
| 21 | 22 | 23 | 24 | 25 | 26 | 27 |
| 28 | 29 | 30 | 31 | | | |

## PERPETUAL CALENDAR

| | | | | | | | | | | | | | |
|---|---|---|---|---|---|---|---|---|---|---|---|---|---|
| 1800 | 4 | 1844 | 9 | 1888 | 8 | 1932 | 13 | 1976 | 12 | 2020 | 11 |
| 1801 | 5 | 1845 | 4 | 1889 | 3 | 1933 | 1 | 1977 | 7 | 2021 | 6 |
| 1802 | 6 | 1846 | 5 | 1890 | 4 | 1934 | 2 | 1978 | 1 | 2022 | 7 |
| 1803 | 7 | 1847 | 6 | 1891 | 5 | 1935 | 3 | 1979 | 2 | 2023 | 1 |
| 1804 | 8 | 1848 | 14 | 1892 | 13 | 1936 | 11 | 1980 | 10 | 2024 | 9 |
| 1805 | 3 | 1849 | 2 | 1893 | 1 | 1937 | 6 | 1981 | 5 | 2025 | 4 |
| 1806 | 4 | 1850 | 3 | 1894 | 2 | 1938 | 7 | 1982 | 6 | 2026 | 5 |
| 1807 | 5 | 1851 | 4 | 1895 | 3 | 1939 | 1 | 1983 | 7 | 2027 | 6 |
| 1808 | 13 | 1852 | 12 | 1896 | 11 | 1940 | 9 | 1984 | 8 | 2028 | 14 |
| 1809 | 1 | 1853 | 7 | 1897 | 6 | 1941 | 4 | 1985 | 3 | 2029 | 2 |
| 1810 | 2 | 1854 | 1 | 1898 | 7 | 1942 | 5 | 1986 | 4 | 2030 | 3 |
| 1811 | 3 | 1855 | 2 | 1899 | 1 | 1943 | 6 | 1987 | 5 | 2031 | 4 |
| 1812 | 11 | 1856 | 10 | 1900 | 2 | 1944 | 14 | 1988 | 13 | 2032 | 12 |
| 1813 | 6 | 1857 | 5 | 1901 | 3 | 1945 | 2 | 1989 | 1 | 2033 | 7 |
| 1814 | 7 | 1858 | 6 | 1902 | 4 | 1946 | 3 | 1990 | 2 | 2034 | 1 |
| 1815 | 1 | 1859 | 7 | 1903 | 5 | 1947 | 4 | 1991 | 3 | 2035 | 2 |
| 1816 | 9 | 1860 | 8 | 1904 | 13 | 1948 | 12 | 1992 | 11 | 2036 | 10 |
| 1817 | 4 | 1861 | 3 | 1905 | 1 | 1949 | 7 | 1993 | 6 | 2037 | 5 |
| 1818 | 5 | 1862 | 4 | 1906 | 2 | 1950 | 1 | 1994 | 7 | 2038 | 6 |
| 1819 | 6 | 1863 | 5 | 1907 | 3 | 1951 | 2 | 1995 | 1 | 2039 | 7 |
| 1820 | 14 | 1864 | 13 | 1908 | 11 | 1952 | 10 | 1996 | 9 | 2040 | 8 |
| 1821 | 2 | 1865 | 1 | 1909 | 6 | 1953 | 5 | 1997 | 4 | 2041 | 3 |
| 1822 | 3 | 1866 | 2 | 1910 | 7 | 1954 | 6 | 1998 | 5 | 2042 | 4 |
| 1823 | 4 | 1867 | 3 | 1911 | 1 | 1955 | 7 | 1999 | 6 | 2043 | 5 |
| 1824 | 12 | 1868 | 11 | 1912 | 9 | 1956 | 8 | 2000 | 14 | 2044 | 13 |
| 1825 | 7 | 1869 | 6 | 1913 | 4 | 1957 | 3 | 2001 | 2 | 2045 | 1 |
| 1826 | 1 | 1870 | 7 | 1914 | 5 | 1958 | 4 | 2002 | 3 | 2046 | 2 |
| 1827 | 2 | 1871 | 1 | 1915 | 6 | 1959 | 5 | 2003 | 4 | 2047 | 3 |
| 1828 | 10 | 1872 | 9 | 1916 | 14 | 1960 | 13 | 2004 | 12 | 2048 | 11 |
| 1829 | 5 | 1873 | 4 | 1917 | 2 | 1961 | 1 | 2005 | 7 | 2049 | 6 |
| 1830 | 6 | 1874 | 5 | 1918 | 3 | 1962 | 2 | 2006 | 1 | 2050 | 7 |
| 1831 | 7 | 1875 | 6 | 1919 | 4 | 1963 | 3 | 2007 | 2 | 2051 | 1 |
| 1832 | 8 | 1876 | 14 | 1920 | 12 | 1964 | 11 | 2008 | 10 | 2052 | 9 |
| 1833 | 3 | 1877 | 2 | 1921 | 7 | 1965 | 6 | 2009 | 5 | 2053 | 4 |
| 1834 | 4 | 1878 | 3 | 1922 | 1 | 1966 | 7 | 2010 | 6 | 2054 | 5 |
| 1835 | 5 | 1879 | 4 | 1923 | 2 | 1967 | 1 | 2011 | 7 | 2055 | 6 |
| 1836 | 13 | 1880 | 12 | 1924 | 10 | 1968 | 9 | 2012 | 8 | 2056 | 14 |
| 1837 | 1 | 1881 | 7 | 1925 | 5 | 1969 | 4 | 2013 | 3 | 2057 | 2 |
| 1838 | 2 | 1882 | 1 | 1926 | 6 | 1970 | 5 | 2014 | 4 | 2058 | 3 |
| 1839 | 3 | 1883 | 2 | 1927 | 7 | 1971 | 6 | 2015 | 5 | 2059 | 4 |
| 1840 | 11 | 1884 | 10 | 1928 | 8 | 1972 | 14 | 2016 | 13 | 2060 | 12 |
| 1841 | 6 | 1885 | 5 | 1929 | 3 | 1973 | 2 | 2017 | 1 | 2061 | 7 |
| 1842 | 7 | 1886 | 6 | 1930 | 4 | 1974 | 3 | 2018 | 2 | 2062 | 1 |
| 1843 | 1 | 1887 | 7 | 1931 | 5 | 1975 | 4 | 2019 | 3 | 2063 | 2 |

DIRECTIONS: The number given with each year in the key above is number of calendar to use for that year

### 1

**JANUARY**

| S | M | T | W | T | F | S |
|---|---|---|---|---|---|---|
| 1 | 2 | 3 | 4 | 5 | 6 | 7 |
| 8 | 9 | 10 | 11 | 12 | 13 | 14 |
| 15 | 16 | 17 | 18 | 19 | 20 | 21 |
| 22 | 23 | 24 | 25 | 26 | 27 | 28 |
| 29 | 30 | 31 | | | | |

**FEBRUARY**

| S | M | T | W | T | F | S |
|---|---|---|---|---|---|---|
| | | | 1 | 2 | 3 | 4 |
| 5 | 6 | 7 | 8 | 9 | 10 | 11 |
| 12 | 13 | 14 | 15 | 16 | 17 | 18 |
| 19 | 20 | 21 | 22 | 23 | 24 | 25 |
| 26 | 27 | 28 | | | | |

**MARCH**

| S | M | T | W | T | F | S |
|---|---|---|---|---|---|---|
| | | | 1 | 2 | 3 | 4 |
| 5 | 6 | 7 | 8 | 9 | 10 | 11 |
| 12 | 13 | 14 | 15 | 16 | 17 | 18 |
| 19 | 20 | 21 | 22 | 23 | 24 | 25 |
| 26 | 27 | 28 | 29 | 30 | 31 | |

**APRIL**

| S | M | T | W | T | F | S |
|---|---|---|---|---|---|---|
| | | | | | | 1 |
| 2 | 3 | 4 | 5 | 6 | 7 | 8 |
| 9 | 10 | 11 | 12 | 13 | 14 | 15 |
| 16 | 17 | 18 | 19 | 20 | 21 | 22 |
| 23 | 24 | 25 | 26 | 27 | 28 | 29 |
| 30 | | | | | | |

**MAY**

| S | M | T | W | T | F | S |
|---|---|---|---|---|---|---|
| | 1 | 2 | 3 | 4 | 5 | 6 |
| 7 | 8 | 9 | 10 | 11 | 12 | 13 |
| 14 | 15 | 16 | 17 | 18 | 19 | 20 |
| 21 | 22 | 23 | 24 | 25 | 26 | 27 |
| 28 | 29 | 30 | 31 | | | |

**JUNE**

| S | M | T | W | T | F | S |
|---|---|---|---|---|---|---|
| | | | | 1 | 2 | 3 |
| 4 | 5 | 6 | 7 | 8 | 9 | 10 |
| 11 | 12 | 13 | 14 | 15 | 16 | 17 |
| 18 | 19 | 20 | 21 | 22 | 23 | 24 |
| 25 | 26 | 27 | 28 | 29 | 30 | |

**JULY**

| S | M | T | W | T | F | S |
|---|---|---|---|---|---|---|
| | | | | | | 1 |
| 2 | 3 | 4 | 5 | 6 | 7 | 8 |
| 9 | 10 | 11 | 12 | 13 | 14 | 15 |
| 16 | 17 | 18 | 19 | 20 | 21 | 22 |
| 23 | 24 | 25 | 26 | 27 | 28 | 29 |
| 30 | 31 | | | | | |

**AUGUST**

| S | M | T | W | T | F | S |
|---|---|---|---|---|---|---|
| | | 1 | 2 | 3 | 4 | 5 |
| 6 | 7 | 8 | 9 | 10 | 11 | 12 |
| 13 | 14 | 15 | 16 | 17 | 18 | 19 |
| 20 | 21 | 22 | 23 | 24 | 25 | 26 |
| 27 | 28 | 29 | 30 | 31 | | |

**SEPTEMBER**

| S | M | T | W | T | F | S |
|---|---|---|---|---|---|---|
| | | | | | 1 | 2 |
| 3 | 4 | 5 | 6 | 7 | 8 | 9 |
| 10 | 11 | 12 | 13 | 14 | 15 | 16 |
| 17 | 18 | 19 | 20 | 21 | 22 | 23 |
| 24 | 25 | 26 | 27 | 28 | 29 | 30 |

**OCTOBER**

| S | M | T | W | T | F | S |
|---|---|---|---|---|---|---|
| 1 | 2 | 3 | 4 | 5 | 6 | 7 |
| 8 | 9 | 10 | 11 | 12 | 13 | 14 |
| 15 | 16 | 17 | 18 | 19 | 20 | 21 |
| 22 | 23 | 24 | 25 | 26 | 27 | 28 |
| 29 | 30 | 31 | | | | |

**NOVEMBER**

| S | M | T | W | T | F | S |
|---|---|---|---|---|---|---|
| | | | 1 | 2 | 3 | 4 |
| 5 | 6 | 7 | 8 | 9 | 10 | 11 |
| 12 | 13 | 14 | 15 | 16 | 17 | 18 |
| 19 | 20 | 21 | 22 | 23 | 24 | 25 |
| 26 | 27 | 28 | 29 | 30 | | |

**DECEMBER**

| S | M | T | W | T | F | S |
|---|---|---|---|---|---|---|
| | | | | | 1 | 2 |
| 3 | 4 | 5 | 6 | 7 | 8 | 9 |
| 10 | 11 | 12 | 13 | 14 | 15 | 16 |
| 17 | 18 | 19 | 20 | 21 | 22 | 23 |
| 24 | 25 | 26 | 27 | 28 | 29 | 30 |
| 31 | | | | | | |

### 2

**JANUARY**

| S | M | T | W | T | F | S |
|---|---|---|---|---|---|---|
| | 1 | 2 | 3 | 4 | 5 | 6 |
| 7 | 8 | 9 | 10 | 11 | 12 | 13 |
| 14 | 15 | 16 | 17 | 18 | 19 | 20 |
| 21 | 22 | 23 | 24 | 25 | 26 | 27 |
| 28 | 29 | 30 | 31 | | | |

**FEBRUARY**

| S | M | T | W | T | F | S |
|---|---|---|---|---|---|---|
| | | | | 1 | 2 | 3 |
| 4 | 5 | 6 | 7 | 8 | 9 | 10 |
| 11 | 12 | 13 | 14 | 15 | 16 | 17 |
| 18 | 19 | 20 | 21 | 22 | 23 | 24 |
| 25 | 26 | 27 | 28 | | | |

**MARCH**

| S | M | T | W | T | F | S |
|---|---|---|---|---|---|---|
| | | | | 1 | 2 | 3 |
| 4 | 5 | 6 | 7 | 8 | 9 | 10 |
| 11 | 12 | 13 | 14 | 15 | 16 | 17 |
| 18 | 19 | 20 | 21 | 22 | 23 | 24 |
| 25 | 26 | 27 | 28 | 29 | 30 | 31 |

**APRIL**

| S | M | T | W | T | F | S |
|---|---|---|---|---|---|---|
| 1 | 2 | 3 | 4 | 5 | 6 | 7 |
| 8 | 9 | 10 | 11 | 12 | 13 | 14 |
| 15 | 16 | 17 | 18 | 19 | 20 | 21 |
| 22 | 23 | 24 | 25 | 26 | 27 | 28 |
| 29 | 30 | | | | | |

**MAY**

| S | M | T | W | T | F | S |
|---|---|---|---|---|---|---|
| | | 1 | 2 | 3 | 4 | 5 |
| 6 | 7 | 8 | 9 | 10 | 11 | 12 |
| 13 | 14 | 15 | 16 | 17 | 18 | 19 |
| 20 | 21 | 22 | 23 | 24 | 25 | 26 |
| 27 | 28 | 29 | 30 | 31 | | |

**JUNE**

| S | M | T | W | T | F | S |
|---|---|---|---|---|---|---|
| | | | | | 1 | 2 |
| 3 | 4 | 5 | 6 | 7 | 8 | 9 |
| 10 | 11 | 12 | 13 | 14 | 15 | 16 |
| 17 | 18 | 19 | 20 | 21 | 22 | 23 |
| 24 | 25 | 26 | 27 | 28 | 29 | 30 |

**JULY**

| S | M | T | W | T | F | S |
|---|---|---|---|---|---|---|
| 1 | 2 | 3 | 4 | 5 | 6 | 7 |
| 8 | 9 | 10 | 11 | 12 | 13 | 14 |
| 15 | 16 | 17 | 18 | 19 | 20 | 21 |
| 22 | 23 | 24 | 25 | 26 | 27 | 28 |
| 29 | 30 | 31 | | | | |

**AUGUST**

| S | M | T | W | T | F | S |
|---|---|---|---|---|---|---|
| | | | 1 | 2 | 3 | 4 |
| 5 | 6 | 7 | 8 | 9 | 10 | 11 |
| 12 | 13 | 14 | 15 | 16 | 17 | 18 |
| 19 | 20 | 21 | 22 | 23 | 24 | 25 |
| 26 | 27 | 28 | 29 | 30 | 31 | |

**SEPTEMBER**

| S | M | T | W | T | F | S |
|---|---|---|---|---|---|---|
| | | | | | | 1 |
| 2 | 3 | 4 | 5 | 6 | 7 | 8 |
| 9 | 10 | 11 | 12 | 13 | 14 | 15 |
| 16 | 17 | 18 | 19 | 20 | 21 | 22 |
| 23 | 24 | 25 | 26 | 27 | 28 | 29 |
| 30 | | | | | | |

**OCTOBER**

| S | M | T | W | T | F | S |
|---|---|---|---|---|---|---|
| | 1 | 2 | 3 | 4 | 5 | 6 |
| 7 | 8 | 9 | 10 | 11 | 12 | 13 |
| 14 | 15 | 16 | 17 | 18 | 19 | 20 |
| 21 | 22 | 23 | 24 | 25 | 26 | 27 |
| 28 | 29 | 30 | 31 | | | |

**NOVEMBER**

| S | M | T | W | T | F | S |
|---|---|---|---|---|---|---|
| | | | | 1 | 2 | 3 |
| 4 | 5 | 6 | 7 | 8 | 9 | 10 |
| 11 | 12 | 13 | 14 | 15 | 16 | 17 |
| 18 | 19 | 20 | 21 | 22 | 23 | 24 |
| 25 | 26 | 27 | 28 | 29 | 30 | |

**DECEMBER**

| S | M | T | W | T | F | S |
|---|---|---|---|---|---|---|
| | | | | | | 1 |
| 2 | 3 | 4 | 5 | 6 | 7 | 8 |
| 9 | 10 | 11 | 12 | 13 | 14 | 15 |
| 16 | 17 | 18 | 19 | 20 | 21 | 22 |
| 23 | 24 | 25 | 26 | 27 | 28 | 29 |
| 30 | 31 | | | | | |

### 3

**JANUARY**

| S | M | T | W | T | F | S |
|---|---|---|---|---|---|---|
| | | 1 | 2 | 3 | 4 | 5 |
| 6 | 7 | 8 | 9 | 10 | 11 | 12 |
| 13 | 14 | 15 | 16 | 17 | 18 | 19 |
| 20 | 21 | 22 | 23 | 24 | 25 | 26 |
| 27 | 28 | 29 | 30 | 31 | | |

**FEBRUARY**

| S | M | T | W | T | F | S |
|---|---|---|---|---|---|---|
| | | | | | 1 | 2 |
| 3 | 4 | 5 | 6 | 7 | 8 | 9 |
| 10 | 11 | 12 | 13 | 14 | 15 | 16 |
| 17 | 18 | 19 | 20 | 21 | 22 | 23 |
| 24 | 25 | 26 | 27 | 28 | | |

**MARCH**

| S | M | T | W | T | F | S |
|---|---|---|---|---|---|---|
| | | | | | 1 | 2 |
| 3 | 4 | 5 | 6 | 7 | 8 | 9 |
| 10 | 11 | 12 | 13 | 14 | 15 | 16 |
| 17 | 18 | 19 | 20 | 21 | 22 | 23 |
| 24 | 25 | 26 | 27 | 28 | 29 | 30 |
| 31 | | | | | | |

**APRIL**

| S | M | T | W | T | F | S |
|---|---|---|---|---|---|---|
| | 1 | 2 | 3 | 4 | 5 | 6 |
| 7 | 8 | 9 | 10 | 11 | 12 | 13 |
| 14 | 15 | 16 | 17 | 18 | 19 | 20 |
| 21 | 22 | 23 | 24 | 25 | 26 | 27 |
| 28 | 29 | 30 | | | | |

**MAY**

| S | M | T | W | T | F | S |
|---|---|---|---|---|---|---|
| | | | 1 | 2 | 3 | 4 |
| 5 | 6 | 7 | 8 | 9 | 10 | 11 |
| 12 | 13 | 14 | 15 | 16 | 17 | 18 |
| 19 | 20 | 21 | 22 | 23 | 24 | 25 |
| 26 | 27 | 28 | 29 | 30 | 31 | |

**JUNE**

| S | M | T | W | T | F | S |
|---|---|---|---|---|---|---|
| | | | | | | 1 |
| 2 | 3 | 4 | 5 | 6 | 7 | 8 |
| 9 | 10 | 11 | 12 | 13 | 14 | 15 |
| 16 | 17 | 18 | 19 | 20 | 21 | 22 |
| 23 | 24 | 25 | 26 | 27 | 28 | 29 |
| 30 | | | | | | |

**JULY**

| S | M | T | W | T | F | S |
|---|---|---|---|---|---|---|
| | 1 | 2 | 3 | 4 | 5 | 6 |
| 7 | 8 | 9 | 10 | 11 | 12 | 13 |
| 14 | 15 | 16 | 17 | 18 | 19 | 20 |
| 21 | 22 | 23 | 24 | 25 | 26 | 27 |
| 28 | 29 | 30 | 31 | | | |

**AUGUST**

| S | M | T | W | T | F | S |
|---|---|---|---|---|---|---|
| | | | | 1 | 2 | 3 |
| 4 | 5 | 6 | 7 | 8 | 9 | 10 |
| 11 | 12 | 13 | 14 | 15 | 16 | 17 |
| 18 | 19 | 20 | 21 | 22 | 23 | 24 |
| 25 | 26 | 27 | 28 | 29 | 30 | 31 |

**SEPTEMBER**

| S | M | T | W | T | F | S |
|---|---|---|---|---|---|---|
| 1 | 2 | 3 | 4 | 5 | 6 | 7 |
| 8 | 9 | 10 | 11 | 12 | 13 | 14 |
| 15 | 16 | 17 | 18 | 19 | 20 | 21 |
| 22 | 23 | 24 | 25 | 26 | 27 | 28 |
| 29 | 30 | | | | | |

**OCTOBER**

| S | M | T | W | T | F | S |
|---|---|---|---|---|---|---|
| | | 1 | 2 | 3 | 4 | 5 |
| 6 | 7 | 8 | 9 | 10 | 11 | 12 |
| 13 | 14 | 15 | 16 | 17 | 18 | 19 |
| 20 | 21 | 22 | 23 | 24 | 25 | 26 |
| 27 | 28 | 29 | 30 | 31 | | |

**NOVEMBER**

| S | M | T | W | T | F | S |
|---|---|---|---|---|---|---|
| | | | | | 1 | 2 |
| 3 | 4 | 5 | 6 | 7 | 8 | 9 |
| 10 | 11 | 12 | 13 | 14 | 15 | 16 |
| 17 | 18 | 19 | 20 | 21 | 22 | 23 |
| 24 | 25 | 26 | 27 | 28 | 29 | 30 |

**DECEMBER**

| S | M | T | W | T | F | S |
|---|---|---|---|---|---|---|
| 1 | 2 | 3 | 4 | 5 | 6 | 7 |
| 8 | 9 | 10 | 11 | 12 | 13 | 14 |
| 15 | 16 | 17 | 18 | 19 | 20 | 21 |
| 22 | 23 | 24 | 25 | 26 | 27 | 28 |
| 29 | 30 | 31 | | | | |

### 4

**JANUARY**

| S | M | T | W | T | F | S |
|---|---|---|---|---|---|---|
| | | | 1 | 2 | 3 | 4 |
| 5 | 6 | 7 | 8 | 9 | 10 | 11 |
| 12 | 13 | 14 | 15 | 16 | 17 | 18 |
| 19 | 20 | 21 | 22 | 23 | 24 | 25 |
| 26 | 27 | 28 | 29 | 30 | 31 | |

**FEBRUARY**

| S | M | T | W | T | F | S |
|---|---|---|---|---|---|---|
| | | | | | | 1 |
| 2 | 3 | 4 | 5 | 6 | 7 | 8 |
| 9 | 10 | 11 | 12 | 13 | 14 | 15 |
| 16 | 17 | 18 | 19 | 20 | 21 | 22 |
| 23 | 24 | 25 | 26 | 27 | 28 | |

**MARCH**

| S | M | T | W | T | F | S |
|---|---|---|---|---|---|---|
| | | | | | | 1 |
| 2 | 3 | 4 | 5 | 6 | 7 | 8 |
| 9 | 10 | 11 | 12 | 13 | 14 | 15 |
| 16 | 17 | 18 | 19 | 20 | 21 | 22 |
| 23 | 24 | 25 | 26 | 27 | 28 | 29 |
| 30 | 31 | | | | | |

**APRIL**

| S | M | T | W | T | F | S |
|---|---|---|---|---|---|---|
| | | 1 | 2 | 3 | 4 | 5 |
| 6 | 7 | 8 | 9 | 10 | 11 | 12 |
| 13 | 14 | 15 | 16 | 17 | 18 | 19 |
| 20 | 21 | 22 | 23 | 24 | 25 | 26 |
| 27 | 28 | 29 | 30 | | | |

**MAY**

| S | M | T | W | T | F | S |
|---|---|---|---|---|---|---|
| | | | | 1 | 2 | 3 |
| 4 | 5 | 6 | 7 | 8 | 9 | 10 |
| 11 | 12 | 13 | 14 | 15 | 16 | 17 |
| 18 | 19 | 20 | 21 | 22 | 23 | 24 |
| 25 | 26 | 27 | 28 | 29 | 30 | 31 |

**JUNE**

| S | M | T | W | T | F | S |
|---|---|---|---|---|---|---|
| 1 | 2 | 3 | 4 | 5 | 6 | 7 |
| 8 | 9 | 10 | 11 | 12 | 13 | 14 |
| 15 | 16 | 17 | 18 | 19 | 20 | 21 |
| 22 | 23 | 24 | 25 | 26 | 27 | 28 |
| 29 | 30 | | | | | |

**JULY**

| S | M | T | W | T | F | S |
|---|---|---|---|---|---|---|
| | | 1 | 2 | 3 | 4 | 5 |
| 6 | 7 | 8 | 9 | 10 | 11 | 12 |
| 13 | 14 | 15 | 16 | 17 | 18 | 19 |
| 20 | 21 | 22 | 23 | 24 | 25 | 26 |
| 27 | 28 | 29 | 30 | 31 | | |

**AUGUST**

| S | M | T | W | T | F | S |
|---|---|---|---|---|---|---|
| | | | | | 1 | 2 |
| 3 | 4 | 5 | 6 | 7 | 8 | 9 |
| 10 | 11 | 12 | 13 | 14 | 15 | 16 |
| 17 | 18 | 19 | 20 | 21 | 22 | 23 |
| 24 | 25 | 26 | 27 | 28 | 29 | 30 |
| 31 | | | | | | |

**SEPTEMBER**

| S | M | T | W | T | F | S |
|---|---|---|---|---|---|---|
| | 1 | 2 | 3 | 4 | 5 | 6 |
| 7 | 8 | 9 | 10 | 11 | 12 | 13 |
| 14 | 15 | 16 | 17 | 18 | 19 | 20 |
| 21 | 22 | 23 | 24 | 25 | 26 | 27 |
| 28 | 29 | 30 | | | | |

**OCTOBER**

| S | M | T | W | T | F | S |
|---|---|---|---|---|---|---|
| | | | 1 | 2 | 3 | 4 |
| 5 | 6 | 7 | 8 | 9 | 10 | 11 |
| 12 | 13 | 14 | 15 | 16 | 17 | 18 |
| 19 | 20 | 21 | 22 | 23 | 24 | 25 |
| 26 | 27 | 28 | 29 | 30 | 31 | |

**NOVEMBER**

| S | M | T | W | T | F | S |
|---|---|---|---|---|---|---|
| | | | | | | 1 |
| 2 | 3 | 4 | 5 | 6 | 7 | 8 |
| 9 | 10 | 11 | 12 | 13 | 14 | 15 |
| 16 | 17 | 18 | 19 | 20 | 21 | 22 |
| 23 | 24 | 25 | 26 | 27 | 28 | 29 |
| 30 | | | | | | |

**DECEMBER**

| S | M | T | W | T | F | S |
|---|---|---|---|---|---|---|
| | 1 | 2 | 3 | 4 | 5 | 6 |
| 7 | 8 | 9 | 10 | 11 | 12 | 13 |
| 14 | 15 | 16 | 17 | 18 | 19 | 20 |
| 21 | 22 | 23 | 24 | 25 | 26 | 27 |
| 28 | 29 | 30 | 31 | | | |

### 5

**JANUARY**

| S | M | T | W | T | F | S |
|---|---|---|---|---|---|---|
| | | | | 1 | 2 | 3 |
| 4 | 5 | 6 | 7 | 8 | 9 | 10 |
| 11 | 12 | 13 | 14 | 15 | 16 | 17 |
| 18 | 19 | 20 | 21 | 22 | 23 | 24 |
| 25 | 26 | 27 | 28 | 29 | 30 | 31 |

**FEBRUARY**

| S | M | T | W | T | F | S |
|---|---|---|---|---|---|---|
| 1 | 2 | 3 | 4 | 5 | 6 | 7 |
| 8 | 9 | 10 | 11 | 12 | 13 | 14 |
| 15 | 16 | 17 | 18 | 19 | 20 | 21 |
| 22 | 23 | 24 | 25 | 26 | 27 | 28 |

**MARCH**

| S | M | T | W | T | F | S |
|---|---|---|---|---|---|---|
| 1 | 2 | 3 | 4 | 5 | 6 | 7 |
| 8 | 9 | 10 | 11 | 12 | 13 | 14 |
| 15 | 16 | 17 | 18 | 19 | 20 | 21 |
| 22 | 23 | 24 | 25 | 26 | 27 | 28 |
| 29 | 30 | 31 | | | | |

**APRIL**

| S | M | T | W | T | F | S |
|---|---|---|---|---|---|---|
| | | | 1 | 2 | 3 | 4 |
| 5 | 6 | 7 | 8 | 9 | 10 | 11 |
| 12 | 13 | 14 | 15 | 16 | 17 | 18 |
| 19 | 20 | 21 | 22 | 23 | 24 | 25 |
| 26 | 27 | 28 | 29 | 30 | | |

**MAY**

| S | M | T | W | T | F | S |
|---|---|---|---|---|---|---|
| | | | | | 1 | 2 |
| 3 | 4 | 5 | 6 | 7 | 8 | 9 |
| 10 | 11 | 12 | 13 | 14 | 15 | 16 |
| 17 | 18 | 19 | 20 | 21 | 22 | 23 |
| 24 | 25 | 26 | 27 | 28 | 29 | 30 |
| 31 | | | | | | |

**JUNE**

| S | M | T | W | T | F | S |
|---|---|---|---|---|---|---|
| | 1 | 2 | 3 | 4 | 5 | 6 |
| 7 | 8 | 9 | 10 | 11 | 12 | 13 |
| 14 | 15 | 16 | 17 | 18 | 19 | 20 |
| 21 | 22 | 23 | 24 | 25 | 26 | 27 |
| 28 | 29 | 30 | | | | |

**JULY**

| S | M | T | W | T | F | S |
|---|---|---|---|---|---|---|
| | | | 1 | 2 | 3 | 4 |
| 5 | 6 | 7 | 8 | 9 | 10 | 11 |
| 12 | 13 | 14 | 15 | 16 | 17 | 18 |
| 19 | 20 | 21 | 22 | 23 | 24 | 25 |
| 26 | 27 | 28 | 29 | 30 | 31 | |

**AUGUST**

| S | M | T | W | T | F | S |
|---|---|---|---|---|---|---|
| | | | | | | 1 |
| 2 | 3 | 4 | 5 | 6 | 7 | 8 |
| 9 | 10 | 11 | 12 | 13 | 14 | 15 |
| 16 | 17 | 18 | 19 | 20 | 21 | 22 |
| 23 | 24 | 25 | 26 | 27 | 28 | 29 |
| 30 | 31 | | | | | |

**SEPTEMBER**

| S | M | T | W | T | F | S |
|---|---|---|---|---|---|---|
| | | 1 | 2 | 3 | 4 | 5 |
| 6 | 7 | 8 | 9 | 10 | 11 | 12 |
| 13 | 14 | 15 | 16 | 17 | 18 | 19 |
| 20 | 21 | 22 | 23 | 24 | 25 | 26 |
| 27 | 28 | 29 | 30 | | | |

**OCTOBER**

| S | M | T | W | T | F | S |
|---|---|---|---|---|---|---|
| | | | | 1 | 2 | 3 |
| 4 | 5 | 6 | 7 | 8 | 9 | 10 |
| 11 | 12 | 13 | 14 | 15 | 16 | 17 |
| 18 | 19 | 20 | 21 | 22 | 23 | 24 |
| 25 | 26 | 27 | 28 | 29 | 30 | 31 |

**NOVEMBER**

| S | M | T | W | T | F | S |
|---|---|---|---|---|---|---|
| 1 | 2 | 3 | 4 | 5 | 6 | 7 |
| 8 | 9 | 10 | 11 | 12 | 13 | 14 |
| 15 | 16 | 17 | 18 | 19 | 20 | 21 |
| 22 | 23 | 24 | 25 | 26 | 27 | 28 |
| 29 | 30 | | | | | |

**DECEMBER**

| S | M | T | W | T | F | S |
|---|---|---|---|---|---|---|
| | | 1 | 2 | 3 | 4 | 5 |
| 6 | 7 | 8 | 9 | 10 | 11 | 12 |
| 13 | 14 | 15 | 16 | 17 | 18 | 19 |
| 20 | 21 | 22 | 23 | 24 | 25 | 26 |
| 27 | 28 | 29 | 30 | 31 | | |

### 6

**JANUARY**

| S | M | T | W | T | F | S |
|---|---|---|---|---|---|---|
| | | | | | 1 | 2 |
| 3 | 4 | 5 | 6 | 7 | 8 | 9 |
| 10 | 11 | 12 | 13 | 14 | 15 | 16 |
| 17 | 18 | 19 | 20 | 21 | 22 | 23 |
| 24 | 25 | 26 | 27 | 28 | 29 | 30 |
| 31 | | | | | | |

**FEBRUARY**

| S | M | T | W | T | F | S |
|---|---|---|---|---|---|---|
| | 1 | 2 | 3 | 4 | 5 | 6 |
| 7 | 8 | 9 | 10 | 11 | 12 | 13 |
| 14 | 15 | 16 | 17 | 18 | 19 | 20 |
| 21 | 22 | 23 | 24 | 25 | 26 | 27 |
| 28 | | | | | | |

**MARCH**

| S | M | T | W | T | F | S |
|---|---|---|---|---|---|---|
| | 1 | 2 | 3 | 4 | 5 | 6 |
| 7 | 8 | 9 | 10 | 11 | 12 | 13 |
| 14 | 15 | 16 | 17 | 18 | 19 | 20 |
| 21 | 22 | 23 | 24 | 25 | 26 | 27 |
| 28 | 29 | 30 | 31 | | | |

**APRIL**

| S | M | T | W | T | F | S |
|---|---|---|---|---|---|---|
| | | | | 1 | 2 | 3 |
| 4 | 5 | 6 | 7 | 8 | 9 | 10 |
| 11 | 12 | 13 | 14 | 15 | 16 | 17 |
| 18 | 19 | 20 | 21 | 22 | 23 | 24 |
| 25 | 26 | 27 | 28 | 29 | 30 | |

**MAY**

| S | M | T | W | T | F | S |
|---|---|---|---|---|---|---|
| | | | | | | 1 |
| 2 | 3 | 4 | 5 | 6 | 7 | 8 |
| 9 | 10 | 11 | 12 | 13 | 14 | 15 |
| 16 | 17 | 18 | 19 | 20 | 21 | 22 |
| 23 | 24 | 25 | 26 | 27 | 28 | 29 |
| 30 | 31 | | | | | |

**JUNE**

| S | M | T | W | T | F | S |
|---|---|---|---|---|---|---|
| | | 1 | 2 | 3 | 4 | 5 |
| 6 | 7 | 8 | 9 | 10 | 11 | 12 |
| 13 | 14 | 15 | 16 | 17 | 18 | 19 |
| 20 | 21 | 22 | 23 | 24 | 25 | 26 |
| 27 | 28 | 29 | 30 | | | |

**JULY**

| S | M | T | W | T | F | S |
|---|---|---|---|---|---|---|
| | | | | 1 | 2 | 3 |
| 4 | 5 | 6 | 7 | 8 | 9 | 10 |
| 11 | 12 | 13 | 14 | 15 | 16 | 17 |
| 18 | 19 | 20 | 21 | 22 | 23 | 24 |
| 25 | 26 | 27 | 28 | 29 | 30 | 31 |

**AUGUST**

| S | M | T | W | T | F | S |
|---|---|---|---|---|---|---|
| 1 | 2 | 3 | 4 | 5 | 6 | 7 |
| 8 | 9 | 10 | 11 | 12 | 13 | 14 |
| 15 | 16 | 17 | 18 | 19 | 20 | 21 |
| 22 | 23 | 24 | 25 | 26 | 27 | 28 |
| 29 | 30 | 31 | | | | |

**SEPTEMBER**

| S | M | T | W | T | F | S |
|---|---|---|---|---|---|---|
| | | | 1 | 2 | 3 | 4 |
| 5 | 6 | 7 | 8 | 9 | 10 | 11 |
| 12 | 13 | 14 | 15 | 16 | 17 | 18 |
| 19 | 20 | 21 | 22 | 23 | 24 | 25 |
| 26 | 27 | 28 | 29 | 30 | | |

**OCTOBER**

| S | M | T | W | T | F | S |
|---|---|---|---|---|---|---|
| | | | | | 1 | 2 |
| 3 | 4 | 5 | 6 | 7 | 8 | 9 |
| 10 | 11 | 12 | 13 | 14 | 15 | 16 |
| 17 | 18 | 19 | 20 | 21 | 22 | 23 |
| 24 | 25 | 26 | 27 | 28 | 29 | 30 |
| 31 | | | | | | |

**NOVEMBER**

| S | M | T | W | T | F | S |
|---|---|---|---|---|---|---|
| | 1 | 2 | 3 | 4 | 5 | 6 |
| 7 | 8 | 9 | 10 | 11 | 12 | 13 |
| 14 | 15 | 16 | 17 | 18 | 19 | 20 |
| 21 | 22 | 23 | 24 | 25 | 26 | 27 |
| 28 | 29 | 30 | | | | |

**DECEMBER**

| S | M | T | W | T | F | S |
|---|---|---|---|---|---|---|
| | | | 1 | 2 | 3 | 4 |
| 5 | 6 | 7 | 8 | 9 | 10 | 11 |
| 12 | 13 | 14 | 15 | 16 | 17 | 18 |
| 19 | 20 | 21 | 22 | 23 | 24 | 25 |
| 26 | 27 | 28 | 29 | 30 | 31 | |

## 7

**JANUARY**

| S | M | T | W | T | F | S |
|---|---|---|---|---|---|---|
| | | | | | | 1 |
| 2 | 3 | 4 | 5 | 6 | 7 | 8 |
| 9 | 10 | 11 | 12 | 13 | 14 | 15 |
| 16 | 17 | 18 | 19 | 20 | 21 | 22 |
| 23 | 24 | 25 | 26 | 27 | 28 | 29 |
| 30 | 31 | | | | | |

**FEBRUARY**

| S | M | T | W | T | F | S |
|---|---|---|---|---|---|---|
| | | 1 | 2 | 3 | 4 | 5 |
| 6 | 7 | 8 | 9 | 10 | 11 | 12 |
| 13 | 14 | 15 | 16 | 17 | 18 | 19 |
| 20 | 21 | 22 | 23 | 24 | 25 | 26 |
| 27 | 28 | | | | | |

**MARCH**

| S | M | T | W | T | F | S |
|---|---|---|---|---|---|---|
| | | 1 | 2 | 3 | 4 | 5 |
| 6 | 7 | 8 | 9 | 10 | 11 | 12 |
| 13 | 14 | 15 | 16 | 17 | 18 | 19 |
| 20 | 21 | 22 | 23 | 24 | 25 | 26 |
| 27 | 28 | 29 | 30 | 31 | | |

**APRIL**

| S | M | T | W | T | F | S |
|---|---|---|---|---|---|---|
| | | | | | 1 | 2 |
| 3 | 4 | 5 | 6 | 7 | 8 | 9 |
| 10 | 11 | 12 | 13 | 14 | 15 | 16 |
| 17 | 18 | 19 | 20 | 21 | 22 | 23 |
| 24 | 25 | 26 | 27 | 28 | 29 | 30 |

**MAY**

| S | M | T | W | T | F | S |
|---|---|---|---|---|---|---|
| 1 | 2 | 3 | 4 | 5 | 6 | 7 |
| 8 | 9 | 10 | 11 | 12 | 13 | 14 |
| 15 | 16 | 17 | 18 | 19 | 20 | 21 |
| 22 | 23 | 24 | 25 | 26 | 27 | 28 |
| 29 | 30 | 31 | | | | |

**JUNE**

| S | M | T | W | T | F | S |
|---|---|---|---|---|---|---|
| | | | 1 | 2 | 3 | 4 |
| 5 | 6 | 7 | 8 | 9 | 10 | 11 |
| 12 | 13 | 14 | 15 | 16 | 17 | 18 |
| 19 | 20 | 21 | 22 | 23 | 24 | 25 |
| 26 | 27 | 28 | 29 | 30 | | |

**JULY**

| S | M | T | W | T | F | S |
|---|---|---|---|---|---|---|
| | | | | | 1 | 2 |
| 3 | 4 | 5 | 6 | 7 | 8 | 9 |
| 10 | 11 | 12 | 13 | 14 | 15 | 16 |
| 17 | 18 | 19 | 20 | 21 | 22 | 23 |
| 24 | 25 | 26 | 27 | 28 | 29 | 30 |
| 31 | | | | | | |

**AUGUST**

| S | M | T | W | T | F | S |
|---|---|---|---|---|---|---|
| | 1 | 2 | 3 | 4 | 5 | 6 |
| 7 | 8 | 9 | 10 | 11 | 12 | 13 |
| 14 | 15 | 16 | 17 | 18 | 19 | 20 |
| 21 | 22 | 23 | 24 | 25 | 26 | 27 |
| 28 | 29 | 30 | 31 | | | |

**SEPTEMBER**

| S | M | T | W | T | F | S |
|---|---|---|---|---|---|---|
| | | | | 1 | 2 | 3 |
| 4 | 5 | 6 | 7 | 8 | 9 | 10 |
| 11 | 12 | 13 | 14 | 15 | 16 | 17 |
| 18 | 19 | 20 | 21 | 22 | 23 | 24 |
| 25 | 26 | 27 | 28 | 29 | 30 | |

**OCTOBER**

| S | M | T | W | T | F | S |
|---|---|---|---|---|---|---|
| | | | | | | 1 |
| 2 | 3 | 4 | 5 | 6 | 7 | 8 |
| 9 | 10 | 11 | 12 | 13 | 14 | 15 |
| 16 | 17 | 18 | 19 | 20 | 21 | 22 |
| 23 | 24 | 25 | 26 | 27 | 28 | 29 |
| 30 | 31 | | | | | |

**NOVEMBER**

| S | M | T | W | T | F | S |
|---|---|---|---|---|---|---|
| | | 1 | 2 | 3 | 4 | 5 |
| 6 | 7 | 8 | 9 | 10 | 11 | 12 |
| 13 | 14 | 15 | 16 | 17 | 18 | 19 |
| 20 | 21 | 22 | 23 | 24 | 25 | 26 |
| 27 | 28 | 29 | 30 | | | |

**DECEMBER**

| S | M | T | W | T | F | S |
|---|---|---|---|---|---|---|
| | | | | 1 | 2 | 3 |
| 4 | 5 | 6 | 7 | 8 | 9 | 10 |
| 11 | 12 | 13 | 14 | 15 | 16 | 17 |
| 18 | 19 | 20 | 21 | 22 | 23 | 24 |
| 25 | 26 | 27 | 28 | 29 | 30 | 31 |

## 8

**JANUARY**

| S | M | T | W | T | F | S |
|---|---|---|---|---|---|---|
| 1 | 2 | 3 | 4 | 5 | 6 | 7 |
| 8 | 9 | 10 | 11 | 12 | 13 | 14 |
| 15 | 16 | 17 | 18 | 19 | 20 | 21 |
| 22 | 23 | 24 | 25 | 26 | 27 | 28 |
| 29 | 30 | 31 | | | | |

**FEBRUARY**

| S | M | T | W | T | F | S |
|---|---|---|---|---|---|---|
| | | | 1 | 2 | 3 | 4 |
| 5 | 6 | 7 | 8 | 9 | 10 | 11 |
| 12 | 13 | 14 | 15 | 16 | 17 | 18 |
| 19 | 20 | 21 | 22 | 23 | 24 | 25 |
| 26 | 27 | 28 | 29 | | | |

**MARCH**

| S | M | T | W | T | F | S |
|---|---|---|---|---|---|---|
| | | | | 1 | 2 | 3 |
| 4 | 5 | 6 | 7 | 8 | 9 | 10 |
| 11 | 12 | 13 | 14 | 15 | 16 | 17 |
| 18 | 19 | 20 | 21 | 22 | 23 | 24 |
| 25 | 26 | 27 | 28 | 29 | 30 | 31 |

**APRIL**

| S | M | T | W | T | F | S |
|---|---|---|---|---|---|---|
| 1 | 2 | 3 | 4 | 5 | 6 | 7 |
| 8 | 9 | 10 | 11 | 12 | 13 | 14 |
| 15 | 16 | 17 | 18 | 19 | 20 | 21 |
| 22 | 23 | 24 | 25 | 26 | 27 | 28 |
| 29 | 30 | | | | | |

**MAY**

| S | M | T | W | T | F | S |
|---|---|---|---|---|---|---|
| | | 1 | 2 | 3 | 4 | 5 |
| 6 | 7 | 8 | 9 | 10 | 11 | 12 |
| 13 | 14 | 15 | 16 | 17 | 18 | 19 |
| 20 | 21 | 22 | 23 | 24 | 25 | 26 |
| 27 | 28 | 29 | 30 | 31 | | |

**JUNE**

| S | M | T | W | T | F | S |
|---|---|---|---|---|---|---|
| | | | | | 1 | 2 |
| 3 | 4 | 5 | 6 | 7 | 8 | 9 |
| 10 | 11 | 12 | 13 | 14 | 15 | 16 |
| 17 | 18 | 19 | 20 | 21 | 22 | 23 |
| 24 | 25 | 26 | 27 | 28 | 29 | 30 |

**JULY**

| S | M | T | W | T | F | S |
|---|---|---|---|---|---|---|
| 1 | 2 | 3 | 4 | 5 | 6 | 7 |
| 8 | 9 | 10 | 11 | 12 | 13 | 14 |
| 15 | 16 | 17 | 18 | 19 | 20 | 21 |
| 22 | 23 | 24 | 25 | 26 | 27 | 28 |
| 29 | 30 | 31 | | | | |

**AUGUST**

| S | M | T | W | T | F | S |
|---|---|---|---|---|---|---|
| | | | 1 | 2 | 3 | 4 |
| 5 | 6 | 7 | 8 | 9 | 10 | 11 |
| 12 | 13 | 14 | 15 | 16 | 17 | 18 |
| 19 | 20 | 21 | 22 | 23 | 24 | 25 |
| 26 | 27 | 28 | 29 | 30 | 31 | |

**SEPTEMBER**

| S | M | T | W | T | F | S |
|---|---|---|---|---|---|---|
| | | | | | | 1 |
| 2 | 3 | 4 | 5 | 6 | 7 | 8 |
| 9 | 10 | 11 | 12 | 13 | 14 | 15 |
| 16 | 17 | 18 | 19 | 20 | 21 | 22 |
| 23 | 24 | 25 | 26 | 27 | 28 | 29 |
| 30 | | | | | | |

**OCTOBER**

| S | M | T | W | T | F | S |
|---|---|---|---|---|---|---|
| | 1 | 2 | 3 | 4 | 5 | 6 |
| 7 | 8 | 9 | 10 | 11 | 12 | 13 |
| 14 | 15 | 16 | 17 | 18 | 19 | 20 |
| 21 | 22 | 23 | 24 | 25 | 26 | 27 |
| 28 | 29 | 30 | 31 | | | |

**NOVEMBER**

| S | M | T | W | T | F | S |
|---|---|---|---|---|---|---|
| | | | | 1 | 2 | 3 |
| 4 | 5 | 6 | 7 | 8 | 9 | 10 |
| 11 | 12 | 13 | 14 | 15 | 16 | 17 |
| 18 | 19 | 20 | 21 | 22 | 23 | 24 |
| 25 | 26 | 27 | 28 | 29 | 30 | |

**DECEMBER**

| S | M | T | W | T | F | S |
|---|---|---|---|---|---|---|
| | | | | | | 1 |
| 2 | 3 | 4 | 5 | 6 | 7 | 8 |
| 9 | 10 | 11 | 12 | 13 | 14 | 15 |
| 16 | 17 | 18 | 19 | 20 | 21 | 22 |
| 23 | 24 | 25 | 26 | 27 | 28 | 29 |
| 30 | 31 | | | | | |

## 9

**JANUARY**

| S | M | T | W | T | F | S |
|---|---|---|---|---|---|---|
| | 1 | 2 | 3 | 4 | 5 | 6 |
| 7 | 8 | 9 | 10 | 11 | 12 | 13 |
| 14 | 15 | 16 | 17 | 18 | 19 | 20 |
| 21 | 22 | 23 | 24 | 25 | 26 | 27 |
| 28 | 29 | 30 | 31 | | | |

**FEBRUARY**

| S | M | T | W | T | F | S |
|---|---|---|---|---|---|---|
| | | | | 1 | 2 | 3 |
| 4 | 5 | 6 | 7 | 8 | 9 | 10 |
| 11 | 12 | 13 | 14 | 15 | 16 | 17 |
| 18 | 19 | 20 | 21 | 22 | 23 | 24 |
| 25 | 26 | 27 | 28 | 29 | | |

**MARCH**

| S | M | T | W | T | F | S |
|---|---|---|---|---|---|---|
| | | | | | 1 | 2 |
| 3 | 4 | 5 | 6 | 7 | 8 | 9 |
| 10 | 11 | 12 | 13 | 14 | 15 | 16 |
| 17 | 18 | 19 | 20 | 21 | 22 | 23 |
| 24 | 25 | 26 | 27 | 28 | 29 | 30 |
| 31 | | | | | | |

**APRIL**

| S | M | T | W | T | F | S |
|---|---|---|---|---|---|---|
| | 1 | 2 | 3 | 4 | 5 | 6 |
| 7 | 8 | 9 | 10 | 11 | 12 | 13 |
| 14 | 15 | 16 | 17 | 18 | 19 | 20 |
| 21 | 22 | 23 | 24 | 25 | 26 | 27 |
| 28 | 29 | 30 | | | | |

**MAY**

| S | M | T | W | T | F | S |
|---|---|---|---|---|---|---|
| | | | 1 | 2 | 3 | 4 |
| 5 | 6 | 7 | 8 | 9 | 10 | 11 |
| 12 | 13 | 14 | 15 | 16 | 17 | 18 |
| 19 | 20 | 21 | 22 | 23 | 24 | 25 |
| 26 | 27 | 28 | 29 | 30 | 31 | |

**JUNE**

| S | M | T | W | T | F | S |
|---|---|---|---|---|---|---|
| | | | | | | 1 |
| 2 | 3 | 4 | 5 | 6 | 7 | 8 |
| 9 | 10 | 11 | 12 | 13 | 14 | 15 |
| 16 | 17 | 18 | 19 | 20 | 21 | 22 |
| 23 | 24 | 25 | 26 | 27 | 28 | 29 |
| 30 | | | | | | |

**JULY**

| S | M | T | W | T | F | S |
|---|---|---|---|---|---|---|
| | 1 | 2 | 3 | 4 | 5 | 6 |
| 7 | 8 | 9 | 10 | 11 | 12 | 13 |
| 14 | 15 | 16 | 17 | 18 | 19 | 20 |
| 21 | 22 | 23 | 24 | 25 | 26 | 27 |
| 28 | 29 | 30 | 31 | | | |

**AUGUST**

| S | M | T | W | T | F | S |
|---|---|---|---|---|---|---|
| | | | | 1 | 2 | 3 |
| 4 | 5 | 6 | 7 | 8 | 9 | 10 |
| 11 | 12 | 13 | 14 | 15 | 16 | 17 |
| 18 | 19 | 20 | 21 | 22 | 23 | 24 |
| 25 | 26 | 27 | 28 | 29 | 30 | 31 |

**SEPTEMBER**

| S | M | T | W | T | F | S |
|---|---|---|---|---|---|---|
| 1 | 2 | 3 | 4 | 5 | 6 | 7 |
| 8 | 9 | 10 | 11 | 12 | 13 | 14 |
| 15 | 16 | 17 | 18 | 19 | 20 | 21 |
| 22 | 23 | 24 | 25 | 26 | 27 | 28 |
| 29 | 30 | | | | | |

**OCTOBER**

| S | M | T | W | T | F | S |
|---|---|---|---|---|---|---|
| | | 1 | 2 | 3 | 4 | 5 |
| 6 | 7 | 8 | 9 | 10 | 11 | 12 |
| 13 | 14 | 15 | 16 | 17 | 18 | 19 |
| 20 | 21 | 22 | 23 | 24 | 25 | 26 |
| 27 | 28 | 29 | 30 | 31 | | |

**NOVEMBER**

| S | M | T | W | T | F | S |
|---|---|---|---|---|---|---|
| | | | | | 1 | 2 |
| 3 | 4 | 5 | 6 | 7 | 8 | 9 |
| 10 | 11 | 12 | 13 | 14 | 15 | 16 |
| 17 | 18 | 19 | 20 | 21 | 22 | 23 |
| 24 | 25 | 26 | 27 | 28 | 29 | 30 |

**DECEMBER**

| S | M | T | W | T | F | S |
|---|---|---|---|---|---|---|
| 1 | 2 | 3 | 4 | 5 | 6 | 7 |
| 8 | 9 | 10 | 11 | 12 | 13 | 14 |
| 15 | 16 | 17 | 18 | 19 | 20 | 21 |
| 22 | 23 | 24 | 25 | 26 | 27 | 28 |
| 29 | 30 | 31 | | | | |

## 10

**JANUARY**

| S | M | T | W | T | F | S |
|---|---|---|---|---|---|---|
| | | 1 | 2 | 3 | 4 | 5 |
| 6 | 7 | 8 | 9 | 10 | 11 | 12 |
| 13 | 14 | 15 | 16 | 17 | 18 | 19 |
| 20 | 21 | 22 | 23 | 24 | 25 | 26 |
| 27 | 28 | 29 | 30 | 31 | | |

**FEBRUARY**

| S | M | T | W | T | F | S |
|---|---|---|---|---|---|---|
| | | | | | 1 | 2 |
| 3 | 4 | 5 | 6 | 7 | 8 | 9 |
| 10 | 11 | 12 | 13 | 14 | 15 | 16 |
| 17 | 18 | 19 | 20 | 21 | 22 | 23 |
| 24 | 25 | 26 | 27 | 28 | 29 | |

**MARCH**

| S | M | T | W | T | F | S |
|---|---|---|---|---|---|---|
| | | | | | | 1 |
| 2 | 3 | 4 | 5 | 6 | 7 | 8 |
| 9 | 10 | 11 | 12 | 13 | 14 | 15 |
| 16 | 17 | 18 | 19 | 20 | 21 | 22 |
| 23 | 24 | 25 | 26 | 27 | 28 | 29 |
| 30 | 31 | | | | | |

**APRIL**

| S | M | T | W | T | F | S |
|---|---|---|---|---|---|---|
| | | 1 | 2 | 3 | 4 | 5 |
| 6 | 7 | 8 | 9 | 10 | 11 | 12 |
| 13 | 14 | 15 | 16 | 17 | 18 | 19 |
| 20 | 21 | 22 | 23 | 24 | 25 | 26 |
| 27 | 28 | 29 | 30 | | | |

**MAY**

| S | M | T | W | T | F | S |
|---|---|---|---|---|---|---|
| | | | | 1 | 2 | 3 |
| 4 | 5 | 6 | 7 | 8 | 9 | 10 |
| 11 | 12 | 13 | 14 | 15 | 16 | 17 |
| 18 | 19 | 20 | 21 | 22 | 23 | 24 |
| 25 | 26 | 27 | 28 | 29 | 30 | 31 |

**JUNE**

| S | M | T | W | T | F | S |
|---|---|---|---|---|---|---|
| 1 | 2 | 3 | 4 | 5 | 6 | 7 |
| 8 | 9 | 10 | 11 | 12 | 13 | 14 |
| 15 | 16 | 17 | 18 | 19 | 20 | 21 |
| 22 | 23 | 24 | 25 | 26 | 27 | 28 |
| 29 | 30 | | | | | |

**JULY**

| S | M | T | W | T | F | S |
|---|---|---|---|---|---|---|
| | | 1 | 2 | 3 | 4 | 5 |
| 6 | 7 | 8 | 9 | 10 | 11 | 12 |
| 13 | 14 | 15 | 16 | 17 | 18 | 19 |
| 20 | 21 | 22 | 23 | 24 | 25 | 26 |
| 27 | 28 | 29 | 30 | 31 | | |

**AUGUST**

| S | M | T | W | T | F | S |
|---|---|---|---|---|---|---|
| | | | | | 1 | 2 |
| 3 | 4 | 5 | 6 | 7 | 8 | 9 |
| 10 | 11 | 12 | 13 | 14 | 15 | 16 |
| 17 | 18 | 19 | 20 | 21 | 22 | 23 |
| 24 | 25 | 26 | 27 | 28 | 29 | 30 |
| 31 | | | | | | |

**SEPTEMBER**

| S | M | T | W | T | F | S |
|---|---|---|---|---|---|---|
| | 1 | 2 | 3 | 4 | 5 | 6 |
| 7 | 8 | 9 | 10 | 11 | 12 | 13 |
| 14 | 15 | 16 | 17 | 18 | 19 | 20 |
| 21 | 22 | 23 | 24 | 25 | 26 | 27 |
| 28 | 29 | 30 | | | | |

**OCTOBER**

| S | M | T | W | T | F | S |
|---|---|---|---|---|---|---|
| | | | 1 | 2 | 3 | 4 |
| 5 | 6 | 7 | 8 | 9 | 10 | 11 |
| 12 | 13 | 14 | 15 | 16 | 17 | 18 |
| 19 | 20 | 21 | 22 | 23 | 24 | 25 |
| 26 | 27 | 28 | 29 | 30 | 31 | |

**NOVEMBER**

| S | M | T | W | T | F | S |
|---|---|---|---|---|---|---|
| | | | | | | 1 |
| 2 | 3 | 4 | 5 | 6 | 7 | 8 |
| 9 | 10 | 11 | 12 | 13 | 14 | 15 |
| 16 | 17 | 18 | 19 | 20 | 21 | 22 |
| 23 | 24 | 25 | 26 | 27 | 28 | 29 |
| 30 | | | | | | |

**DECEMBER**

| S | M | T | W | T | F | S |
|---|---|---|---|---|---|---|
| | 1 | 2 | 3 | 4 | 5 | 6 |
| 7 | 8 | 9 | 10 | 11 | 12 | 13 |
| 14 | 15 | 16 | 17 | 18 | 19 | 20 |
| 21 | 22 | 23 | 24 | 25 | 26 | 27 |
| 28 | 29 | 30 | 31 | | | |

## 11

**JANUARY**

| S | M | T | W | T | F | S |
|---|---|---|---|---|---|---|
| | | | 1 | 2 | 3 | 4 |
| 5 | 6 | 7 | 8 | 9 | 10 | 11 |
| 12 | 13 | 14 | 15 | 16 | 17 | 18 |
| 19 | 20 | 21 | 22 | 23 | 24 | 25 |
| 26 | 27 | 28 | 29 | 30 | 31 | |

**FEBRUARY**

| S | M | T | W | T | F | S |
|---|---|---|---|---|---|---|
| | | | | | | 1 |
| 2 | 3 | 4 | 5 | 6 | 7 | 8 |
| 9 | 10 | 11 | 12 | 13 | 14 | 15 |
| 16 | 17 | 18 | 19 | 20 | 21 | 22 |
| 23 | 24 | 25 | 26 | 27 | 28 | 29 |

**MARCH**

| S | M | T | W | T | F | S |
|---|---|---|---|---|---|---|
| 1 | 2 | 3 | 4 | 5 | 6 | 7 |
| 8 | 9 | 10 | 11 | 12 | 13 | 14 |
| 15 | 16 | 17 | 18 | 19 | 20 | 21 |
| 22 | 23 | 24 | 25 | 26 | 27 | 28 |
| 29 | 30 | 31 | | | | |

**APRIL**

| S | M | T | W | T | F | S |
|---|---|---|---|---|---|---|
| | | | 1 | 2 | 3 | 4 |
| 5 | 6 | 7 | 8 | 9 | 10 | 11 |
| 12 | 13 | 14 | 15 | 16 | 17 | 18 |
| 19 | 20 | 21 | 22 | 23 | 24 | 25 |
| 26 | 27 | 28 | 29 | 30 | | |

**MAY**

| S | M | T | W | T | F | S |
|---|---|---|---|---|---|---|
| | | | | | 1 | 2 |
| 3 | 4 | 5 | 6 | 7 | 8 | 9 |
| 10 | 11 | 12 | 13 | 14 | 15 | 16 |
| 17 | 18 | 19 | 20 | 21 | 22 | 23 |
| 24 | 25 | 26 | 27 | 28 | 29 | 30 |
| 31 | | | | | | |

**JUNE**

| S | M | T | W | T | F | S |
|---|---|---|---|---|---|---|
| | 1 | 2 | 3 | 4 | 5 | 6 |
| 7 | 8 | 9 | 10 | 11 | 12 | 13 |
| 14 | 15 | 16 | 17 | 18 | 19 | 20 |
| 21 | 22 | 23 | 24 | 25 | 26 | 27 |
| 28 | 29 | 30 | | | | |

**JULY**

| S | M | T | W | T | F | S |
|---|---|---|---|---|---|---|
| | | | 1 | 2 | 3 | 4 |
| 5 | 6 | 7 | 8 | 9 | 10 | 11 |
| 12 | 13 | 14 | 15 | 16 | 17 | 18 |
| 19 | 20 | 21 | 22 | 23 | 24 | 25 |
| 26 | 27 | 28 | 29 | 30 | 31 | |

**AUGUST**

| S | M | T | W | T | F | S |
|---|---|---|---|---|---|---|
| | | | | | | 1 |
| 2 | 3 | 4 | 5 | 6 | 7 | 8 |
| 9 | 10 | 11 | 12 | 13 | 14 | 15 |
| 16 | 17 | 18 | 19 | 20 | 21 | 22 |
| 23 | 24 | 25 | 26 | 27 | 28 | 29 |
| 30 | 31 | | | | | |

**SEPTEMBER**

| S | M | T | W | T | F | S |
|---|---|---|---|---|---|---|
| | | 1 | 2 | 3 | 4 | 5 |
| 6 | 7 | 8 | 9 | 10 | 11 | 12 |
| 13 | 14 | 15 | 16 | 17 | 18 | 19 |
| 20 | 21 | 22 | 23 | 24 | 25 | 26 |
| 27 | 28 | 29 | 30 | | | |

**OCTOBER**

| S | M | T | W | T | F | S |
|---|---|---|---|---|---|---|
| | | | | 1 | 2 | 3 |
| 4 | 5 | 6 | 7 | 8 | 9 | 10 |
| 11 | 12 | 13 | 14 | 15 | 16 | 17 |
| 18 | 19 | 20 | 21 | 22 | 23 | 24 |
| 25 | 26 | 27 | 28 | 29 | 30 | 31 |

**NOVEMBER**

| S | M | T | W | T | F | S |
|---|---|---|---|---|---|---|
| 1 | 2 | 3 | 4 | 5 | 6 | 7 |
| 8 | 9 | 10 | 11 | 12 | 13 | 14 |
| 15 | 16 | 17 | 18 | 19 | 20 | 21 |
| 22 | 23 | 24 | 25 | 26 | 27 | 28 |
| 29 | 30 | | | | | |

**DECEMBER**

| S | M | T | W | T | F | S |
|---|---|---|---|---|---|---|
| | | 1 | 2 | 3 | 4 | 5 |
| 6 | 7 | 8 | 9 | 10 | 11 | 12 |
| 13 | 14 | 15 | 16 | 17 | 18 | 19 |
| 20 | 21 | 22 | 23 | 24 | 25 | 26 |
| 27 | 28 | 29 | 30 | 31 | | |

## 12

**JANUARY**

| S | M | T | W | T | F | S |
|---|---|---|---|---|---|---|
| | | | | 1 | 2 | 3 |
| 4 | 5 | 6 | 7 | 8 | 9 | 10 |
| 11 | 12 | 13 | 14 | 15 | 16 | 17 |
| 18 | 19 | 20 | 21 | 22 | 23 | 24 |
| 25 | 26 | 27 | 28 | 29 | 30 | 31 |

**FEBRUARY**

| S | M | T | W | T | F | S |
|---|---|---|---|---|---|---|
| 1 | 2 | 3 | 4 | 5 | 6 | 7 |
| 8 | 9 | 10 | 11 | 12 | 13 | 14 |
| 15 | 16 | 17 | 18 | 19 | 20 | 21 |
| 22 | 23 | 24 | 25 | 26 | 27 | 28 |
| 29 | | | | | | |

**MARCH**

| S | M | T | W | T | F | S |
|---|---|---|---|---|---|---|
| | 1 | 2 | 3 | 4 | 5 | 6 |
| 7 | 8 | 9 | 10 | 11 | 12 | 13 |
| 14 | 15 | 16 | 17 | 18 | 19 | 20 |
| 21 | 22 | 23 | 24 | 25 | 26 | 27 |
| 28 | 29 | 30 | 31 | | | |

**APRIL**

| S | M | T | W | T | F | S |
|---|---|---|---|---|---|---|
| | | | | 1 | 2 | 3 |
| 4 | 5 | 6 | 7 | 8 | 9 | 10 |
| 11 | 12 | 13 | 14 | 15 | 16 | 17 |
| 18 | 19 | 20 | 21 | 22 | 23 | 24 |
| 25 | 26 | 27 | 28 | 29 | 30 | |

**MAY**

| S | M | T | W | T | F | S |
|---|---|---|---|---|---|---|
| | | | | | | 1 |
| 2 | 3 | 4 | 5 | 6 | 7 | 8 |
| 9 | 10 | 11 | 12 | 13 | 14 | 15 |
| 16 | 17 | 18 | 19 | 20 | 21 | 22 |
| 23 | 24 | 25 | 26 | 27 | 28 | 29 |
| 30 | 31 | | | | | |

**JUNE**

| S | M | T | W | T | F | S |
|---|---|---|---|---|---|---|
| | | 1 | 2 | 3 | 4 | 5 |
| 6 | 7 | 8 | 9 | 10 | 11 | 12 |
| 13 | 14 | 15 | 16 | 17 | 18 | 19 |
| 20 | 21 | 22 | 23 | 24 | 25 | 26 |
| 27 | 28 | 29 | 30 | | | |

**JULY**

| S | M | T | W | T | F | S |
|---|---|---|---|---|---|---|
| | | | | 1 | 2 | 3 |
| 4 | 5 | 6 | 7 | 8 | 9 | 10 |
| 11 | 12 | 13 | 14 | 15 | 16 | 17 |
| 18 | 19 | 20 | 21 | 22 | 23 | 24 |
| 25 | 26 | 27 | 28 | 29 | 30 | 31 |

**AUGUST**

| S | M | T | W | T | F | S |
|---|---|---|---|---|---|---|
| 1 | 2 | 3 | 4 | 5 | 6 | 7 |
| 8 | 9 | 10 | 11 | 12 | 13 | 14 |
| 15 | 16 | 17 | 18 | 19 | 20 | 21 |
| 22 | 23 | 24 | 25 | 26 | 27 | 28 |
| 29 | 30 | 31 | | | | |

**SEPTEMBER**

| S | M | T | W | T | F | S |
|---|---|---|---|---|---|---|
| | | | 1 | 2 | 3 | 4 |
| 5 | 6 | 7 | 8 | 9 | 10 | 11 |
| 12 | 13 | 14 | 15 | 16 | 17 | 18 |
| 19 | 20 | 21 | 22 | 23 | 24 | 25 |
| 26 | 27 | 28 | 29 | 30 | | |

**OCTOBER**

| S | M | T | W | T | F | S |
|---|---|---|---|---|---|---|
| | | | | | 1 | 2 |
| 3 | 4 | 5 | 6 | 7 | 8 | 9 |
| 10 | 11 | 12 | 13 | 14 | 15 | 16 |
| 17 | 18 | 19 | 20 | 21 | 22 | 23 |
| 24 | 25 | 26 | 27 | 28 | 29 | 30 |
| 31 | | | | | | |

**NOVEMBER**

| S | M | T | W | T | F | S |
|---|---|---|---|---|---|---|
| | 1 | 2 | 3 | 4 | 5 | 6 |
| 7 | 8 | 9 | 10 | 11 | 12 | 13 |
| 14 | 15 | 16 | 17 | 18 | 19 | 20 |
| 21 | 22 | 23 | 24 | 25 | 26 | 27 |
| 28 | 29 | 30 | | | | |

**DECEMBER**

| S | M | T | W | T | F | S |
|---|---|---|---|---|---|---|
| | | | 1 | 2 | 3 | 4 |
| 5 | 6 | 7 | 8 | 9 | 10 | 11 |
| 12 | 13 | 14 | 15 | 16 | 17 | 18 |
| 19 | 20 | 21 | 22 | 23 | 24 | 25 |
| 26 | 27 | 28 | 29 | 30 | 31 | |

## 13

**JANUARY**

| S | M | T | W | T | F | S |
|---|---|---|---|---|---|---|
| | | | | | 1 | 2 |
| 3 | 4 | 5 | 6 | 7 | 8 | 9 |
| 10 | 11 | 12 | 13 | 14 | 15 | 16 |
| 17 | 18 | 19 | 20 | 21 | 22 | 23 |
| 24 | 25 | 26 | 27 | 28 | 29 | 30 |
| 31 | | | | | | |

**FEBRUARY**

| S | M | T | W | T | F | S |
|---|---|---|---|---|---|---|
| | 1 | 2 | 3 | 4 | 5 | 6 |
| 7 | 8 | 9 | 10 | 11 | 12 | 13 |
| 14 | 15 | 16 | 17 | 18 | 19 | 20 |
| 21 | 22 | 23 | 24 | 25 | 26 | 27 |
| 28 | 29 | | | | | |

**MARCH**

| S | M | T | W | T | F | S |
|---|---|---|---|---|---|---|
| | | 1 | 2 | 3 | 4 | 5 |
| 6 | 7 | 8 | 9 | 10 | 11 | 12 |
| 13 | 14 | 15 | 16 | 17 | 18 | 19 |
| 20 | 21 | 22 | 23 | 24 | 25 | 26 |
| 27 | 28 | 29 | 30 | 31 | | |

**APRIL**

| S | M | T | W | T | F | S |
|---|---|---|---|---|---|---|
| | | | | | 1 | 2 |
| 3 | 4 | 5 | 6 | 7 | 8 | 9 |
| 10 | 11 | 12 | 13 | 14 | 15 | 16 |
| 17 | 18 | 19 | 20 | 21 | 22 | 23 |
| 24 | 25 | 26 | 27 | 28 | 29 | 30 |

**MAY**

| S | M | T | W | T | F | S |
|---|---|---|---|---|---|---|
| 1 | 2 | 3 | 4 | 5 | 6 | 7 |
| 8 | 9 | 10 | 11 | 12 | 13 | 14 |
| 15 | 16 | 17 | 18 | 19 | 20 | 21 |
| 22 | 23 | 24 | 25 | 26 | 27 | 28 |
| 29 | 30 | 31 | | | | |

**JUNE**

| S | M | T | W | T | F | S |
|---|---|---|---|---|---|---|
| | | | 1 | 2 | 3 | 4 |
| 5 | 6 | 7 | 8 | 9 | 10 | 11 |
| 12 | 13 | 14 | 15 | 16 | 17 | 18 |
| 19 | 20 | 21 | 22 | 23 | 24 | 25 |
| 26 | 27 | 28 | 29 | 30 | | |

**JULY**

| S | M | T | W | T | F | S |
|---|---|---|---|---|---|---|
| | | | | | 1 | 2 |
| 3 | 4 | 5 | 6 | 7 | 8 | 9 |
| 10 | 11 | 12 | 13 | 14 | 15 | 16 |
| 17 | 18 | 19 | 20 | 21 | 22 | 23 |
| 24 | 25 | 26 | 27 | 28 | 29 | 30 |
| 31 | | | | | | |

**AUGUST**

| S | M | T | W | T | F | S |
|---|---|---|---|---|---|---|
| | 1 | 2 | 3 | 4 | 5 | 6 |
| 7 | 8 | 9 | 10 | 11 | 12 | 13 |
| 14 | 15 | 16 | 17 | 18 | 19 | 20 |
| 21 | 22 | 23 | 24 | 25 | 26 | 27 |
| 28 | 29 | 30 | 31 | | | |

**SEPTEMBER**

| S | M | T | W | T | F | S |
|---|---|---|---|---|---|---|
| | | | | 1 | 2 | 3 |
| 4 | 5 | 6 | 7 | 8 | 9 | 10 |
| 11 | 12 | 13 | 14 | 15 | 16 | 17 |
| 18 | 19 | 20 | 21 | 22 | 23 | 24 |
| 25 | 26 | 27 | 28 | 29 | 30 | |

**OCTOBER**

| S | M | T | W | T | F | S |
|---|---|---|---|---|---|---|
| | | | | | | 1 |
| 2 | 3 | 4 | 5 | 6 | 7 | 8 |
| 9 | 10 | 11 | 12 | 13 | 14 | 15 |
| 16 | 17 | 18 | 19 | 20 | 21 | 22 |
| 23 | 24 | 25 | 26 | 27 | 28 | 29 |
| 30 | 31 | | | | | |

**NOVEMBER**

| S | M | T | W | T | F | S |
|---|---|---|---|---|---|---|
| | | 1 | 2 | 3 | 4 | 5 |
| 6 | 7 | 8 | 9 | 10 | 11 | 12 |
| 13 | 14 | 15 | 16 | 17 | 18 | 19 |
| 20 | 21 | 22 | 23 | 24 | 25 | 26 |
| 27 | 28 | 29 | 30 | | | |

**DECEMBER**

| S | M | T | W | T | F | S |
|---|---|---|---|---|---|---|
| | | | | 1 | 2 | 3 |
| 4 | 5 | 6 | 7 | 8 | 9 | 10 |
| 11 | 12 | 13 | 14 | 15 | 16 | 17 |
| 18 | 19 | 20 | 21 | 22 | 23 | 24 |
| 25 | 26 | 27 | 28 | 29 | 30 | 31 |

## 14

**JANUARY**

| S | M | T | W | T | F | S |
|---|---|---|---|---|---|---|
| | | | | | | 1 |
| 2 | 3 | 4 | 5 | 6 | 7 | 8 |
| 9 | 10 | 11 | 12 | 13 | 14 | 15 |
| 16 | 17 | 18 | 19 | 20 | 21 | 22 |
| 23 | 24 | 25 | 26 | 27 | 28 | 29 |
| 30 | 31 | | | | | |

**FEBRUARY**

| S | M | T | W | T | F | S |
|---|---|---|---|---|---|---|
| | | 1 | 2 | 3 | 4 | 5 |
| 6 | 7 | 8 | 9 | 10 | 11 | 12 |
| 13 | 14 | 15 | 16 | 17 | 18 | 19 |
| 20 | 21 | 22 | 23 | 24 | 25 | 26 |
| 27 | 28 | 29 | | | | |

**MARCH**

| S | M | T | W | T | F | S |
|---|---|---|---|---|---|---|
| | | | 1 | 2 | 3 | 4 |
| 5 | 6 | 7 | 8 | 9 | 10 | 11 |
| 12 | 13 | 14 | 15 | 16 | 17 | 18 |
| 19 | 20 | 21 | 22 | 23 | 24 | 25 |
| 26 | 27 | 28 | 29 | 30 | 31 | |

**APRIL**

| S | M | T | W | T | F | S |
|---|---|---|---|---|---|---|
| | | | | | | 1 |
| 2 | 3 | 4 | 5 | 6 | 7 | 8 |
| 9 | 10 | 11 | 12 | 13 | 14 | 15 |
| 16 | 17 | 18 | 19 | 20 | 21 | 22 |
| 23 | 24 | 25 | 26 | 27 | 28 | 29 |
| 30 | | | | | | |

**MAY**

| S | M | T | W | T | F | S |
|---|---|---|---|---|---|---|
| | 1 | 2 | 3 | 4 | 5 | 6 |
| 7 | 8 | 9 | 10 | 11 | 12 | 13 |
| 14 | 15 | 16 | 17 | 18 | 19 | 20 |
| 21 | 22 | 23 | 24 | 25 | 26 | 27 |
| 28 | 29 | 30 | 31 | | | |

**JUNE**

| S | M | T | W | T | F | S |
|---|---|---|---|---|---|---|
| | | | | 1 | 2 | 3 |
| 4 | 5 | 6 | 7 | 8 | 9 | 10 |
| 11 | 12 | 13 | 14 | 15 | 16 | 17 |
| 18 | 19 | 20 | 21 | 22 | 23 | 24 |
| 25 | 26 | 27 | 28 | 29 | 30 | |

**JULY**

| S | M | T | W | T | F | S |
|---|---|---|---|---|---|---|
| | | | | | | 1 |
| 2 | 3 | 4 | 5 | 6 | 7 | 8 |
| 9 | 10 | 11 | 12 | 13 | 14 | 15 |
| 16 | 17 | 18 | 19 | 20 | 21 | 22 |
| 23 | 24 | 25 | 26 | 27 | 28 | 29 |
| 30 | 31 | | | | | |

**AUGUST**

| S | M | T | W | T | F | S |
|---|---|---|---|---|---|---|
| | | 1 | 2 | 3 | 4 | 5 |
| 6 | 7 | 8 | 9 | 10 | 11 | 12 |
| 13 | 14 | 15 | 16 | 17 | 18 | 19 |
| 20 | 21 | 22 | 23 | 24 | 25 | 26 |
| 27 | 28 | 29 | 30 | 31 | | |

**SEPTEMBER**

| S | M | T | W | T | F | S |
|---|---|---|---|---|---|---|
| | | | | | 1 | 2 |
| 3 | 4 | 5 | 6 | 7 | 8 | 9 |
| 10 | 11 | 12 | 13 | 14 | 15 | 16 |
| 17 | 18 | 19 | 20 | 21 | 22 | 23 |
| 24 | 25 | 26 | 27 | 28 | 29 | 30 |

**OCTOBER**

| S | M | T | W | T | F | S |
|---|---|---|---|---|---|---|
| 1 | 2 | 3 | 4 | 5 | 6 | 7 |
| 8 | 9 | 10 | 11 | 12 | 13 | 14 |
| 15 | 16 | 17 | 18 | 19 | 20 | 21 |
| 22 | 23 | 24 | 25 | 26 | 27 | 28 |
| 29 | 30 | 31 | | | | |

**NOVEMBER**

| S | M | T | W | T | F | S |
|---|---|---|---|---|---|---|
| | | | 1 | 2 | 3 | 4 |
| 5 | 6 | 7 | 8 | 9 | 10 | 11 |
| 12 | 13 | 14 | 15 | 16 | 17 | 18 |
| 19 | 20 | 21 | 22 | 23 | 24 | 25 |
| 26 | 27 | 28 | 29 | 30 | | |

**DECEMBER**

| S | M | T | W | T | F | S |
|---|---|---|---|---|---|---|
| | | | | | 1 | 2 |
| 3 | 4 | 5 | 6 | 7 | 8 | 9 |
| 10 | 11 | 12 | 13 | 14 | 15 | 16 |
| 17 | 18 | 19 | 20 | 21 | 22 | 23 |
| 24 | 25 | 26 | 27 | 28 | 29 | 30 |
| 31 | | | | | | |

# The Calendar

## History of the Calendar

The purpose of a calendar is to reckon time in advance, to show how many days have to elapse until a certain event takes place—the harvest, a religious festival, or whatever. The earliest calendars, naturally, were crude, and they must have been strongly influenced by the geographical location of the people who made them. In the Scandinavian countries, for example, where the seasons are pronounced, the concept of the year was determined by the seasons, specifically by the end of winter. The Norsemen, before becoming Christians, are said to have had a calendar consisting of ten months of 30 days each.

But in warmer countries, where the seasons are less pronounced, the Moon became the basic unit for time reckoning; an old Jewish book actually makes the statement that "the Moon was created for the counting of the days." All the oldest calendars of which we have reliable information were lunar calendars, based on the time interval from one new moon to the next—a so-called "lunation." But even in a warm climate there are annual events that pay no attention to the phases of the Moon. In some areas it was a rainy season; in Egypt it was the annual flooding of the Nile. It was, therefore, necessary to regulate daily life and religious festivals by lunations, but to take care of the annual event in some other manner.

The calendar of the Assyrians was based on the phases of the Moon. The month began with the first appearance of the lunar crescent, and since this can best be observed in the evening, the day began with sunset. They knew that a lunation was 29½ days long, so their lunar year had a duration of 354 days, falling eleven days short of the solar year.[1] After three years such a lunar calendar would be off by 33 days, or more than one lunation. We know that the Assyrians added an extra month from time to time, but we do not know whether they had developed a special rule for doing so or whether the priests proclaimed the necessity for an extra month from observation. If they made every third year a year of 13 lunations, their three-year period would cover 1,091½ days (using their value of 29½ days for one lunation), or just about four days too short. In one century this mistake would add up to 133 days by their reckoning (in reality closer to 134 days), requiring four extra lunations per century.

We now know that an eight-year period, consisting of five years with 12 months and three years with 13 months would lead to a difference of only 20 days per century, but we do not know whether such a calendar was actually used.

The best approximation that was possible in antiquity was a 19-year period, with seven of these 19 years having 13 months. This means that the period contained 235 months. This, still using the old value for a lunation, made a total of 6,932½ days, while 19 solar years added up to 6,939.7 days, a difference of just one week per period and about five weeks per century. Even the 19-year period required constant adjustment, but it was the period that became the basis of the religious calendar of the Jews. The Arabs used the same calendar at first, but Mohammed forbade shifting from 12 months to 13 months, so that the Islamic religious calendar, even today, has a lunar year of 354 days. As a result the Islamic religious festivals run through all the seasons of the year three times per century.

The Egyptians had a traditional calendar with 12 months of 30 days each. At one time they added five extra days at the end of every year. These turned into a five-day festival because it was thought to be unlucky to work during that time.

When Rome emerged as a world power, the difficulties of making a calendar were well known, but the Romans complicated their lives because of their superstition that even numbers were unlucky. Hence their months were 29 or 31 days long, with the exception of February, which had 28 days. However, four months of 31 days, seven months of 29 days, and one month of 28 days added up to only 355 days. Therefore, the Romans invented an extra month called Mercedonius of 22 or 23 days. It was added every second year.

Even with Mercedonius, the Roman calendar was so far off that Caesar, advised by the astronomer Sosigenes, ordered a sweeping reform in 45 B.C. One year, made 445 days long by imperial decree, brought the calendar back in step with the seasons. Then the solar year (with the value of 365 days and 6 hours) was made the basis of the calendar. The months were 30 or 31 days in length, and to take care of the six hours, every fourth year was made a 366-day year. Moreover, Caesar decreed, the year began with the first of January, not with the vernal equinox in late March.

This was the Julian calendar, named after Julius Caesar. It is still the calendar of the Eastern Orthodox churches.

However, the year is 11½ minutes shorter than the figure written into Caesar's calendar by Sosigenes, and after a number of centuries, even 11½ minutes add up, as the table below shows.

While Caesar could decree that the vernal equinox should not be used as the first day of the new year, the vernal equinox is still a fact of Nature that could not be disregarded. One of the first (as far as we know) to become alarmed about this was Roger Bacon. He sent a memorandum to Pope Clement IV, who apparently was not impressed. But Pope Sixtus IV (reigned 1471 to 1484) decided that another reform was needed and called the German astronomer Regiomontanus to Rome to advise him. Regiomontanus arrived in 1475, but one year later he died in an epidemic, one of the recurrent outbreaks of the plague. The Pope himself survived, but his reform plans died with Regiomontanus.

Less than a hundred years later, in 1545, the Council of Trent authorized the then Pope, Gregory XIII, to reform the calendar once more. Most of the mathematical and astronomical work was done by Father Christopher Clavius, S.J. The immediate correction, advised by Father Clavius and ordered by Pope Gregory XIII, was that Thursday, Oct. 4, 1582, was to be the last day of the Julian calendar. The next day was Friday, with the date of October 15. For long-range accuracy, a formula suggested by the Vatican librarian Aloysius Giglio (latinized into Lilius) was adopted: every fourth year is a leap year *unless* it is a century year like 1700 or 1800. Century years can be leap years *only* when they are divisible by 400 (e.g., 1600).

1. The correct figures are: lunation: 29 d, 12 h, 44 min, 2.8 sec (29.530585 d); solar year: 365 d, 5 h, 48 min, 46 sec (365.242216 d); 12 lunations: 354 d, 8 h, 48 min, 34 sec (354.3671 d).

## Drift of the Vernal Equinox in the Julian Calendar

| Date | Julian year | Date | Julian year | Date | Julian year |
|---|---|---|---|---|---|
| March 21 | 325 A.D. | March 17 | 837 A.D. | March 13 | 1349 A.D. |
| March 20 | 453 A.D. | March 16 | 965 A.D. | March 12 | 1477 A.D. |
| March 19 | 581 A.D. | March 15 | 1093 A.D. | March 11 | 1605 A.D. |
| March 18 | 709 A.D. | March 14 | 1221 A.D. | | |

This rule eliminates three leap years in four centuries, making the calendar sufficiently correct for all ordinary purposes.

Unfortunately, all the Protestant princes in 1582 chose to ignore the papal bull; they continued with the Julian calendar. It was not until 1698 that the German professor Erhard Weigel persuaded the Protestant rulers of Germany and of the Netherlands to change to the new calendar. In England the shift took place in 1752, and in Russia it needed the revolution to introduce the Gregorian calendar in 1918.

The average year of the Gregorian calendar, in spite of the leap year rule, is about 26 seconds longer than the earth's orbital period. But this discrepancy will need 3,323 years to build up to a single day.

Modern proposals for calendar reform do not aim at a "better" calendar, but at one that is more convenient to use, especially for commercial purposes. A 365-day year cannot be divided into equal halves or quarters; the number of days per month is haphazard; the months begin or end in the middle of a week; a holiday fixed by date (e.g., the Fourth of July) will wander through a week; a holiday fixed in another manner (e.g., Easter) can fall on thirty-five possible dates. The Gregorian calendar, admittedly, keeps the calendar dates in reasonable unison with astronomical events, but it still is full of minor annoyances. Moreover, you need a calendar every year to look up dates; an ideal calendar should be one that you can memorize for one year and that is valid for all other years, too.

In 1834 an Italian priest, Marco Mastrofini, suggested taking one day out of every year. It would be made a holiday and *not* be given the name of a weekday. That would make every year begin with January 1 as a Sunday. The leap-year day would be treated the same way, so that in leap years there would be two unnamed holidays at the end of the year.

About a decade later the philosopher Auguste Comte also suggested a 364-day calendar with an extra day, which he called Year Day.

Since then there have been other unsuccessful attempts at calendar reform.

### Time and Calendar

The two natural cycles on which time measurements are based are the year and the day. The year is defined as the time required for the Earth to complete one revolution around the Sun, while the day is the time required for the Earth to complete one turn upon its axis. Unfortunately the Earth needs 365 days plus about six hours to go around the Sun once, so that the year does not consist of so and so many days; the fractional day has to be taken care of by an extra day every fourth year.

But because the Earth, while turning upon its axis, also moves around the Sun there are two kinds of days. A day may be defined as the interval between the highest point of the Sun in the sky on two successive days. This, averaged out over the year, produces the customary 24-hour day. But one might also define a day as the time interval between the moments when a certain point in the sky, say a conveniently located star, is directly overhead. This is called

*Sidereal time.* Astronomers use a point which they call the "vernal equinox" for the actual determination. Such a sidereal day is somewhat shorter than the "solar day," namely by about 3 minutes and 56 seconds of so-called "mean solar time."

*Apparent solar time* is the time based directly on the Sun's position in the sky. In ordinary life the day runs from midnight to midnight. It begins when the Sun is invisible by being 12 hours from its zenith. Astronomers use the so-called "Julian Day," which runs from noon to noon; the concept was invented by the astronomer Joseph Scaliger, who named it after his father Julius. To avoid the problems caused by leap-year days and so forth, Scaliger picked a conveniently remote date in the past and suggested just counting days without regard to weeks, months, and years. The Julian Day 2,440,-225.5 is Jan. 1, 1969. The reason for having the Julian Day run from noon to noon is the practical one that astronomical observations usually extend across the midnight hour, which would require a change in date (or in the Julian Day number) if the astronomical day, like the civil day, ran from midnight to midnight.

*Mean solar time,* rather than apparent solar time, is what is actually used most of the time. The mean solar time is based on the position of a fictitious "mean sun." The reason why this fictitious sun has to be introduced is the following: the Earth turns on its axis regularly; it needs the same number of seconds regardless of the season. But the movement of the Earth around the Sun is not regular because the Earth's orbit is an ellipse. This has the result (as explained in the section The Seasons) that the Earth moves faster in January and slower in July. Though it is the Earth that changes velocity, it looks to us as if the Sun did. In January, when the Earth moves faster, the *apparent* movement of the Sun looks faster. The "mean sun" of time measurements, then, is a sun that moves regularly all year round; the real Sun will be either ahead of or behind the "mean sun." The difference between the real Sun and the fictitious mean sun is called the *equation of time.*

When the real Sun is west of the mean sun we have the "sun fast" condition, with the real Sun crossing the meridian ahead of the mean sun. The opposite is the "sun slow" situation when the real Sun crosses the meridian after the mean sun. Of course, what is observed is the real Sun. The equation of time is needed to establish mean solar time, kept by the reference clocks.

But if all clocks were actually set by mean solar time we would be plagued by a welter of time differences that would be "correct" but a major nuisance. A clock on Long Island, correctly showing mean solar time for its location (this would be *local*

## The Names of the Days

| Latin | Saxon | English | Spanish | German |
|---|---|---|---|---|
| Dies Solis | Sun's Day | Sunday | domingo | Sonntag |
| Dies Lunae | Moon's Day | Monday | lunes | Montag |
| Dies Martis | Tiw's Day | Tuesday | martes | Dienstag |
| Dies Mercurii | Woden's Day | Wednesday | miércoles | Mittwoch |
| Dies Jovis | Thor's Day | Thursday | jueves | Donnerstag |
| Dies Veneris | Frigg's Day | Friday | viernes | Freitag |
| Dies Saturni | Seterne's Day | Saturday | sábado | Sonnabend |

NOTE: The Romans gave one day of the week to each planet known, the Sun and Moon being considered planets in this connection. The Saxon names are a kind of translation of the Roman names: Tiw was substituted for Mars, Woden (Wotan) for Mercury, Thor for Jupiter (Jove), Frigg for Venus, and Seterne for Saturn. The English names are adapted Saxon. The Spanish names, which are normally not capitalized, are adapted Latin. The German names follow the Saxon pattern with two exceptions: Wednesday is Mittwoch (Middle of the Week), and Saturday is Sonnabend (Sunday's Eve).

*civil time*), would be slightly ahead of a clock in Newark, N.J. The Newark clock would be slightly ahead of a clock in Trenton, N.J., which, in turn, would be ahead of a clock in Philadelphia. This condition actually prevailed in the past until 1883, when *standard time* was introduced. Standard time is the correct mean solar time for a designated meridian, and this time is used for a certain area to the east and west of this meridian. In the U.S. four meridians have been designated to supply standard times; they are 75°, 90°, 105°, and 120° west of Greenwich. The 75° meridian determines Eastern Standard Time. It happens to run through Camden, N.J., where standard time, therefore, is also mean solar time and local civil time. The 90° meridian (which happens to pass through the western part of Memphis, Tenn.) determines Central Standard Time, the 105° meridian (passing through Denver) determines Mountain Standard Time, and the 120° meridian (which runs through Lake Tahoe) determines Pacific Standard Time.

Canada, extending over more territory from west to east, adds one time zone on either side: Atlantic Standard Time (based on 60° west of Greenwich) for New Brunswick, Nova Scotia, and Quebec, and Yukon Standard Time (determined by the 135° meridian) for its extreme West. Alaska, extending still farther to the west, adds two more time zones, Alaska Standard Time (determined by the 150° meridian that passes through Anchorage) and Nome Standard Time, based on the 165° meridian just east of Nome.

In general the Earth is divided into 24 such time zones, which run one hour apart. For practical purposes the time zones sometimes show indentations, and there are a few "subzones" that differ from the neighboring zone by only half an hour, e.g., Newfoundland.

*The date line.* While the time zones are based on the natural event of the Sun crossing the meridian, the date must be an arbitrary decision. The meridians are traditionally counted from the meridian of the observatory of Greenwich in England, which is called the zero meridian. The logical place for changing the date is 12 hours, or 180° from Greenwich. Fortunately, the 180th meridian runs mostly through the open Pacific. The date line makes a zigzag in the north to incorporate the eastern tip of Siberia into the Siberian time system and then another one to incorporate a number of islands into the Alaska time system. In the south there is a similar zigzag for the purpose of tying a number of British-owned islands to the New Zealand time system. Otherwise the date line is the same as 180° from Greenwich. At points to the east of the date line the calendar is one day earlier than at points to the west of it. A traveller going eastward across the date line from one island to another would not have to re-set his watch because he would stay inside the time zone (provided he does so where the date line does *not* coincide with the 180° meridian), but it would be the same time of the previous day.

## The Seasons

The seasons are caused by the tilt of the Earth's axis (23½°) and not by the fact that the Earth's orbit around the Sun is an ellipse. The average distance of the Earth from the Sun is 93 million miles; the difference between aphelion (farthest away) and perihelion (closest to the Sun) is 3 million miles, so that perihelion is about 91½ million miles from the Sun. The Earth goes through the perihelion point a few days after New Year, just when the northern hemisphere has winter. Aphelion is

## The Names of the Months

**January:** named after Janus, protector of the gateway to heaven
**February:** named after Februalia, a time period when sacrifices were made to atone for sins
**March:** named after Mars, the god of war, presumably signifying that the campaigns interrupted by the winter could be resumed
**April:** from *aperire,* Latin for "to open" (buds)
**May:** named after Maia, the goddess of growth of plants
**June:** from *juvenis,* Latin for "youth."
**July:** named after Julius Caesar
**August:** named after Augustus, the first Roman Emperor
**September:** from *septem,* Latin for "seven"
**October:** from *octo,* Latin for "eight"
**November:** from *novem,* Latin for "nine"
**December:** from *decem,* Latin for "ten"

NOTE: The earliest Latin calendar was a 10-month one; thus September was the seventh month, October, the eighth, etc. July was originally called Quintilis, as the fifth month; August was originally called Sextilis, as the sixth month.

passed during the first days in July. This by itself shows that the distance from the Sun is not important within these limits. What is important is that when the Earth passes through perihelion, the northern end of the Earth's axis happens to tilt away from the Sun, so that the areas beyond the Tropic of Cancer receive only slanting rays from a Sun low in the sky.

The tilt of the Earth's axis is responsible for four lines you find on every globe. When, say, the North Pole is tilted away from the Sun as much as possible, the farthest points in the North which can still be reached by the Sun's rays are 23½° from the pole. This is the Arctic Circle. The Antarctic Circle is the corresponding limit 23½° from the South Pole; the Sun's rays cannot reach beyond this point when we have mid-summer in the North.

When the Sun is vertically above the equator, the day is of equal length all over the Earth. This happens twice a year, and these are the "equinoxes" in March and in September. After having been over the equator in March, the Sun will seem to move northward. The northernmost point where the Sun can be straight overhead is 23½° north of the equator. This is the Tropic of Cancer; the Sun can never be vertically overhead to the north of this line. Similarly the Sun cannot be vertically overhead to the south of a line 23½° south of the equator—the Tropic of Capricorn.

This explains the climatic zones. In the belt (the Greek word *zone* means "belt") between the Tropic of Cancer and the Tropic of Capricorn, the Sun can be straight overhead; this is the tropical zone. The two zones where the Sun cannot be overhead but will be above the horizon every day of the year are the two temperate zones; the two areas where the Sun will not rise at all for varying lengths of time are the two polar areas, Arctic and Antarctic.

# Holidays

## Religious and Secular, 1979

**New Year's Day,** Monday, Jan. 1. A legal holiday in all states and the District of Columbia, New Year's Day has its origin in Roman times, when sacrifices were offered to Janus, the two-faced Roman deity who looked back on the past and forward to the future.

**Epiphany,** Saturday, Jan. 6. Falls the twelfth day after Christmas and commemorates the manifestation of Jesus as the Son of God, as represented by the adoration of the Magi, the baptism of Jesus, and the miracle of the wine at the marriage feast at Cana. Epiphany originally marked the beginning of the carnival season preceding Lent, and the evening (sometimes the eve) is known as Twelfth Night.

**Lincoln's Birthday,** Monday, Feb. 12. A legal holiday in many states, this day was first formally observed in Washington, D.C., in 1866, when both houses of Congress gathered for a memorial address in honor of the late President.

**St. Valentine's Day,** Wednesday, Feb. 14. This day is the festival of two third-century martyrs, both named St. Valentine. It is not known why this day is associated with lovers. It may derive from an old pagan festival about this time of year, or it may have been inspired by the belief that birds mate on this day.

**Washington's Birthday,** Thursday, Feb. 22. The birthday of George Washington is celebrated as a legal holiday in almost every state of the Union, the District of Columbia, and all territories. The observance began in 1796.

**Shrove Tuesday,** Feb. 27. Falls the day before Ash Wednesday and marks the end of the carnival season, which once began on Epiphany but is now usually celebrated the last three days before Lent. In France, the day is known as Mardi Gras (Fat Tuesday), and Mardi Gras celebrations are also held in several American cities, particularly in New Orleans. The day is sometimes called Pancake Tuesday by the English because fats, which were prohibited during Lent, had to be used up.

**Ash Wednesday,** Feb. 28. The first day of the Lenten season, which lasts 40 days. Having its origin sometime before A.D. 1000, it is a day of public penance and is marked in the Roman Catholic Church by the burning of the palms blessed on the previous year's Palm Sunday. With his thumb, the priest then marks a cross upon the forehead of each worshipper. The Anglican Church and a few Protestant groups in the United States also observe the day, but generally without the use of ashes.

**Purim (Feast of Lots),** Tuesday, March 13 (14 Adar). A day of joy and feasting celebrating deliverance of the Jews from a massacre planned by the Persian Minister Haman. The Jewish Queen Esther interceded with her husband, King Ahasuerus, to spare the life of her uncle, Mordecai, and Haman was hanged on the same gallows he had built for Mordecai. The holiday is marked by the reading of the Book of Esther (megillah), and by the exchange of gifts, donations to the poor, and the presentation of Purim plays.

**St. Patrick's Day,** Saturday, March 17. St. Patrick, patron saint of Ireland, has been honored in America since the first days of the nation. There are many dinners and meetings but perhaps the most notable part of the observance is the annual St. Patrick's Day parade on Fifth Avenue in New York City.

**Palm Sunday,** April 8. Is observed the Sunday before Easter to commemorate the entry of Jesus into Jerusalem. The procession and the ceremonies introducing the benediction of palms probably had their origin in Jerusalem.

**First Day of Passover (Pesach),** Thursday, April 12 (15 Nisan). The Feast of the Passover, also called the Feast of Unleavened Bread, commemorates the escape of the Jews from Egypt. As the Jews fled they ate unleavened bread, and from that time the Jews have allowed no leavening in the houses during Passover, bread being replaced by matzoth.

**Good Friday,** April 13. This day commemorates the Crucifixion, which is retold during services from the Gospel according to St. John. A feature in Roman Catholic churches is the Liturgy of the Passion; there is no Consecration, the Host having been consecrated the previous day. The eating of hot cross buns on this day is said to have started in England.

**Easter Sunday,** April 15. Observed in all Christian churches, Easter commemorates the Resurrection of Jesus. It is celebrated on the first Sunday after the full moon which occurs on or next after March 21 and is therefore celebrated between March 22 and April 25 inclusive. This date was fixed by the Council of Nicaea in 325. The Orthodox Church celebrates Easter on April 22, 1979.

**Ascension Day,** Thursday, May 24. Took place in the presence of His apostles 40 days after the Resurrection of Jesus. It is traditionally held to have occurred on Mount Olivet in Bethany.

**Memorial Day,** Wednesday, May 30. Also known as Decoration Day, Memorial Day is a legal holiday in most of the states and in the territories, and is also observed by the armed forces. In 1868, General John A. Logan, Commander in Chief of the Grand Army of the Republic, issued an order designating the day as one in which the graves of soldiers would be decorated. The holiday was originally devoted to honoring the memory of those who fell in the Civil War, but is now also dedicated to the memory of all war dead.

**First Day of Shabuoth (Hebrew Pentecost),** Friday, June 1 (6 Sivan). This festival, sometimes called the Feast of Weeks, or of Harvest, or of the First Fruits, falls 50 days after Passover and originally celebrated the end of the seven-week grain harvesting season. In later tradition, it also celebrated the giving of the Law to Moses on Mt. Sinai.

**Pentecost (Whitsunday),** June 3. This day commemorates the descent of the Holy Ghost upon the apostles 50 days after the Resurrection. The sermon by the Apostle Peter, which led to the baptism of 3,000 who professed belief, originated the ceremonies that have since been followed. "Whitsunday" is believed to have come from "white Sunday" when, among the English, white robes were worn by those baptized on the day.

**Flag Day,** Thursday, June 14. This day commemorates the adoption by the Continental Congress on June 14, 1777, of the Stars and Stripes as the U.S. flag. Although it is a legal holiday only in Pennsylvania, President Truman, on Aug. 3, 1949, signed a bill requesting the President to call for its observance each year by proclamation.

**Independence Day,** Wednesday, July 4. The day of the adoption of the Declaration of Independence in 1776, celebrated in all states and territories. The observance began the next year in Philadelphia.

**Labor Day,** Monday, Sept. 3. Observed the first Monday in September in all states and territories, Labor Day was first celebrated in New York in 1882 under the sponsorship of the Central Labor Union, following the suggestion of Peter J. McGuire, of the Knights of Labor, that the day be set aside in honor of labor.

**First Day of Rosh Hashana (Jewish New Year),** Saturday, Sept. 22 (1 Tishri). This day marks the beginning of the Jewish year 5740 and opens the Ten Days of Penitence closing with Yom Kippur.

**Yom Kippur (Day of Atonement),** Monday, Oct. 1 (10 Tishri). This day marks the end of the Ten Days of Penitence that began with Rosh Hashana. It is described in *Leviticus* as a "Sabbath of rest," and synagogue services begin the preceding sundown, resume the following morning, and continue to sundown.

**First Day of Sukkoth (Feast of Tabernacles),** Saturday, Oct. 6 (15 Tishri). This festival, also known as the Feast of the Ingathering, originally celebrated the fruit harvest, and the name comes from the booths or tabernacles in which the Jews lived during the harvest, although one tradition traces it to the shelters used by the Jews in their wandering through the wilderness. During the festival many Jews build small huts in their back yards or on the roofs of their houses.

**Columbus Day,** Friday, Oct. 12. A legal holiday in many states, commemorating the discovery of America by Columbus in 1492. Quite likely the first celebration of Columbus Day was that organized in 1792 by the Society of St. Tammany, or Columbian Order, more widely known as Tammany Hall.

**Simhath Torah (Rejoicing of the Law),** Sunday, Oct. 14 (23 Tishri). This joyous holiday falls on the eighth day of Sukkoth. It marks the end of the year's reading of the Torah (Five Books of Moses) in the synagogue every Saturday and the beginning of the new cycle of reading.

**Halloween,** Wednesday, Oct. 31. Eve of All Saints' Day, formerly called All Hallows and Hallowmass. Halloween is traditionally associated in some countries with old customs such as bonfires, masquerading, and the telling of ghost stories. These are old Celtic practices that marked the beginning of winter.

**All Saints' Day,** Thursday, Nov. 1. A Roman Catholic and Anglican holiday celebrating all saints, known and unknown.

**Election Day,** (legal holiday in certain states), Tuesday, Nov. 6. Since 1845, by Act of Congress, the first Tuesday after the first Monday in November is the date for choosing Presidential electors. State elections are also generally held on this day.

**Veterans Day,** Sunday, Nov. 11. Armistice Day was established in 1926 to commemorate the signing in 1918 of the Armistice ending World War I. On June 1, 1954, the name was changed to Veterans Day to honor all men and women who have served America in its armed forces.

**Thanksgiving,** Thursday, Nov. 22. Observed nationally on the fourth Thursday in November by Act of Congress (1941), the first such national proclamation having been issued by President Lincoln in 1863, on the urging of Mrs. Sarah J. Hale, editor of *Godey's Lady's Book.* Most Americans believe that the holiday dates back to the day of thanks ordered by Governor Bradford of Plymouth Colony in New England in 1621 but scholars point out that days of thanks stem from ancient times.

**First Sunday of Advent,** Dec. 2. Advent is the season in which the faithful must prepare themselves for the advent of the Saviour on Christmas. The four Sundays before Christmas are marked by special church services.

**First Day of Hanukkah (Festival of Lights),** Saturday, Dec. 15 (25 Kislev). This festival was instituted by Judas Maccabaeus in 165 B.C. to celebrate the purification of the Temple of Jerusalem, which had been desecrated three years earlier by Antiochus Epiphanes, who set up a pagan altar and offered sacrifices to Zeus Olympius. In Jewish homes, a light is lighted on each night of the eight-day festival.

**Christmas (Feast of the Nativity),** Tuesday, Dec. 25. The most widely celebrated holiday of the Christian year, Christmas is observed as the anniversary of the birth of Jesus. Christmas customs are centuries old. The mistletoe, for example, comes from the Druids, who, in hanging the mistletoe, hoped for peace and good fortune. Use of such plants as holly comes from the ancient belief that such plants blossomed at Christmas. Comparatively recent is the Christmas tree, first set up in Germany in the 17th century, and the use of candles on trees developed from the belief that candles appeared by miracle on the trees at Christmas. Colonial Manhattan Islanders introduced the name Santa Claus, a corruption of the Dutch name for the 4th-century Asia Minor St. Nicholas.

## Legal Holidays in the 50 States, D.C., and Puerto Rico

### HOLIDAYS WIDELY OBSERVED

**January 1, New Year's Day:** All states, D.C., Puerto Rico.

**February 12, Lincoln's Birthday:** Alaska, California, Colorado, Connecticut, Illinois, Indiana, Iowa, Kansas, Kentucky, Maryland, Missouri, Montana, Nebraska, New Jersey, New Mexico, New York, Pennsylvania, Utah, Vermont, Washington, West Virginia.

**February (first Monday), Lincoln's Birthday:** Delaware, Oregon.

**February (third Monday), Washington's Birthday:** All states, D.C., Puerto Rico. Called **Washington Day** in Arizona. Called **President's Day** in Hawaii. Called **Founders Day** in Minnesota; **Washington-Lincoln Day** in Ohio, South Dakota, Wisconsin, Wyoming.

**May 30, Memorial Day:** Delaware, Illinois, Maryland, New Hampshire, New Mexico, New York, Vermont, West Virginia.

**May (last Monday), Memorial Day:** All states, D.C., and Puerto Rico except those listed above, and Alabama, Mississippi, South Carolina.

**July 4, Independence Day:** All states, D.C., Puerto Rico.

**September (1st Monday), Labor Day:** All states, D.C., Puerto Rico.

**October 12, Columbus Day:** Maryland.

**October (2nd Monday), Columbus Day:** All states, D.C., and Puerto Rico, except Alaska, Iowa, Maryland, Michigan, Mississippi, Nevada, North Carolina, North Dakota, Oregon, South Carolina, Washington. Also called **Fraternal Day** in Alabama. Called **Discoverers' Day** in Hawaii, **Farmers' Day** in Florida, **Pioneers' Day** in South Dakota.

**October (fourth Monday) Veterans' Day:** Arkansas, D.C.

**November (4th Thursday), Thanksgiving Day:** All states, D.C., Puerto Rico.

**November (first Tuesday after the first Monday), Election Day:** Arkansas, California, Colorado, D.C., Delaware, Florida, Hawaii, Idaho, Illinois, Indiana, Kentucky, Louisiana, Maryland, Missouri, Montana, New Hampshire, New Jersey, New York, Oklahoma, Pennsylvania, Rhode Island, South Carolina, Tennessee, Texas, Vermont, Virginia, West Virginia, Wisconsin, Wyoming, Puerto Rico.

**November 11, Veterans' Day:** All states and Puerto Rico, except those listed above for October (fourth Monday). Called **Armistice Day** and **Veterans' Day** in New Mexico.

**December 25, Christmas:** All states, D.C., Puerto Rico.

### OTHER HOLIDAYS

**January 6, Three Kings' Day:** Puerto Rico.

**January 8, Battle of New Orleans Day:** Louisiana.

**January 11, De Hostos' Birthday:** Puerto Rico.

**January 15, Martin Luther King Day:** D.C., Illinois, Kentucky, Maryland, Massachusetts, New Jersey.

**January 19, Robert E. Lee's Birthday:** Arkansas, Florida, Georgia, Kentucky, Louisiana, South Carolina. Called **Confederate Heroes Day** in Texas, also in honor of Jefferson Davis and other Confederate heroes.

**January (second Sunday), Martin Luther King Day:** Connecticut.

**January (third Sunday), Martin Luther King Day:** New York.

**January (third Monday), Martin Luther King Day:** Ohio.

**January (third Monday), Robert E. Lee's Birthday:** Alabama, Mississippi. **Lee-Jackson Day** in Virginia.

**January 30, F. D. Roosevelt's Birthday:** Kentucky.

**February or March (1 day before Ash Wednesday), Mardi Gras (Shrove Tuesday):** Alabama, Florida (in some counties), Louisiana (in some parishes).

**February 19, Robert E. Lee Day:** Kentucky.

**March (first Tuesday), Town Meeting Day:** Vermont.

**March 2, Texas Independence Day:** Texas.

**March 17, Evacuation Day:** Massachusetts (in Suffolk Co. only).

**March or April (2 days before Easter), Good Friday:** Connecticut, Delaware, Florida, Hawaii, Indiana, Louisiana, Maryland, New Jersey, North Dakota, Pennsylvania, Tennessee, Wisconsin (11 a.m.-3 p.m.),

**March or April (1 day after Easter), Easter Monday:** North Carolina.

**March 22, Abolition Day:** Puerto Rico.

**March 25, Maryland Day:** Maryland

**March 26, Kuhio Day:** Hawaii.

**March (last Monday), Seward's Day:** Alaska.

**April 13, Thomas Jefferson's Birthday:** Alabama, Oklahoma.

**April 16, De Diego's Birthday:** Puerto Rico.

**April (third Monday), Patriot's Day:** Maine, Mass.

**April 21, San Jacinto Day:** Texas.

**April 22, Arbor Day:** Nebraska.

**April 22, Oklahoma Day:** Oklahoma.

**April 26, Confederate Memorial Day:** Florida, Georgia.

**April (4th Monday), Fast Day:** New Hampshire.

**April (last Monday), Confederate Memorial Day:** Alabama, Mississippi.

**April (last Friday), Arbor Day:** Utah.
**May (1st Tuesday, after first Monday), Primary Election Day:** Indiana.
**May (2nd Sunday), Mother's Day:** Arizona, Oklahoma.
**May 4, Rhode Island Independence Day:** Rhode Island.
**May 8, Truman Day:** Missouri.
**May 10, Confederate Memorial Day:** S.C.
**May 20, Mecklenburg Independence Day:** N.C. **Lafayette Day** in Massachusetts.
**June (first Monday), Jefferson Davis' Birthday:** Alabama, Mississippi.
**June (second Sunday), Flag Day:** New York.
**June 3, Jefferson Davis' Birthday:** Florida, Georgia, South Carolina, also called **Confederate Memorial Day** in Kentucky and Louisiana.
**June 9, Senior Citizens Day:** Oklahoma.
**June 11, Kamehameha Day:** Hawaii.
**June 14, Flag Day:** Pennsylvania.
**June 15, Separation Day:** Delaware.
**June 17, Bunker Hill Day:** Massachusetts (in Suffolk Co. only).
**June 20, West Virginia Day:** West Virginia.
**July 17, Muñoz Rivera's Birthday:** Puerto Rico.
**July 24, Pioneer Day:** Utah.
**July 25, Constitution Day:** Puerto Rico.
**July 27, Barbosa's Birthday:** Puerto Rico.
**August (first Monday), Colorado Day:** Colo.
**August (second Monday), Victory Day:** R.I.
**August 16, Bennington Battle Day:** Vermont.
**August (third Friday), Admission Day:** Hawaii.
**August 27, Lyndon B. Johnson's Birthday:** Texas.
**August 30, Huey P. Long Day:** Louisiana.
**September 9, Admission Day:** California.
**September 12, Defenders' Day:** Maryland.
**September 16, Cherokee Strip Day:** Oklahoma.
**September (1st Saturday after full moon), Indian Day:** Oklahoma.
**October 10, Oklahoma Historical Day:** Oklahoma.
**October 18, Alaska Day:** Alaska.
**October 31, Nevada Day:** Nevada.
**November 4, Will Rogers Day:** Oklahoma.
**November 19, Discovery Day:** Puerto Rico.
**December 7, Delaware Day:** Delaware.

# Movable Holidays, 1979–1987

## CHRISTIAN AND SECULAR

| Year | Ash Wednesday | Easter | Pentecost | Labor Day | Election Day | Thanksgiving | 1st Sun. Advent |
|---|---|---|---|---|---|---|---|
| 1979 | Feb. 28 | April 15 | June 3 | Sept. 3 | Nov. 6 | Nov. 22 | Dec. 2 |
| 1980 | Feb. 20 | April 6 | May 25 | Sept. 1 | Nov. 4 | Nov. 27 | Nov. 30 |
| 1981 | Feb. 11 | March 29 | May 17 | Sept. 7 | Nov. 3 | Nov. 26 | Nov. 29 |
| 1982 | Feb. 24 | April 11 | May 30 | Sept. 6 | Nov. 2 | Nov. 25 | Nov. 28 |
| 1983 | Feb. 16 | April 3 | May 22 | Sept. 5 | Nov. 8 | Nov. 24 | Nov. 27 |
| 1984 | March 7 | April 22 | June 10 | Sept. 3 | Nov. 6 | Nov. 22 | Dec. 2 |
| 1985 | Feb. 20 | April 7 | May 26 | Sept. 2 | Nov. 5 | Nov. 28 | Dec. 1 |
| 1986 | Feb. 12 | March 30 | May 18 | Sept. 1 | Nov. 4 | Nov. 27 | Nov. 30 |
| 1987 | March 4 | April 19 | June 7 | Sept. 7 | Nov. 3 | Nov. 26 | Nov. 29 |

Shrove Tuesday: 1 day before Ash Wednesday
Palm Sunday: 7 days before Easter
Maundy Thursday: 3 days before Easter
Good Friday: 2 days before Easter
Holy Saturday: 1 day before Easter
Ascension Day: 10 days before Pentecost
Trinity Sunday: 7 days after Pentecost
Corpus Christi: 11 days after Pentecost

NOTE: Easter is celebrated on April 22, 1979, by the Orthodox Church.

## JEWISH

| Year | Purim[1] | 1st day Passover[2] | 1st day Shabuoth[3] | 1st day Rosh Hashana[4] | Yom Kippur[5] | 1st day Sukkoth[6] | Simhath Torah[7] | 1st day Hanukkah[8] |
|---|---|---|---|---|---|---|---|---|
| 1979 | March 13 | April 12 | June 1 | Sept. 22 | Oct. 1 | Oct. 6 | Oct. 14 | Dec. 15 |
| 1980 | March 2 | April 1 | May 21 | Sept. 11 | Sept. 20 | Sept. 25 | Oct. 3 | Dec. 3 |
| 1981 | March 20 | April 19 | June 8 | Sept. 29 | Oct. 8 | Oct. 13 | Oct. 21 | Dec. 21 |
| 1982 | March 9 | April 8 | May 28 | Sept. 18 | Sept. 27 | Oct. 2 | Oct. 10 | Dec. 11 |
| 1983 | Feb. 27 | March 29 | May 18 | Sept. 8 | Sept. 17 | Sept. 22 | Sept. 30 | Dec. 1 |
| 1984 | March 18 | April 17 | June 6 | Sept. 27 | Oct. 6 | Oct. 11 | Oct. 19 | Dec. 19 |
| 1985 | March 7 | April 6 | May 26 | Sept. 16 | Sept. 25 | Sept. 30 | Oct. 8 | Dec. 8 |
| 1986 | March 25 | April 24 | June 13 | Oct. 4 | Oct. 13 | Oct. 18 | Oct. 26 | Dec. 27 |
| 1987 | March 15 | April 14 | June 3 | Sept. 24 | Oct. 3 | Oct. 8 | Oct. 16 | Dec. 16 |

1. Feast of Lots. 2. Feast of Unleavened Bread. 3. Hebrew Pentecost; or Feast of Weeks, or of Harvest, or of First Fruits. 4. Jewish New Year. 5. Day of Atonement. 6. Feast of Tabernacles, or of the Ingathering. 7. Rejoicing of the Law. 8. Festival of Lights.

Length of Jewish holidays (O=Orthodox, C=Conservative, R=Reform):

Passover: O & C, 8 days (holy days: first 2 and last 2); R, 7 days (holy days: first and last)
Shabuoth: O & C, 2 days; R, 1 day
Rosh Hashana: O & C, 2 days; R, 1 day
Yom Kippur: All groups, 1 day
Sukkoth: All groups, 7 days (holy days: O & C, first 2; R, first only) O & C observe two additional days: Shemini Atsereth (Eighth Day of the Feast) and Simhath Torah R observes Shemini Atsereth but not Simhath Torah
Hanukkah: All groups, 8 days

NOTE: All holidays begin at sundown on the evening before the date given.

## National Holidays Around the World, 1979

| | | | | | |
|---|---|---|---|---|---|
| Afghanistan | July 17 | Guatemala | Sept. 15 | Panama | Nov. 3 |
| Albania | Nov. 29 | Guinea | Oct. 2 | Papua New Guinea | Sept. 16 |
| Algeria | Nov. 1 | Guinea-Bissau | Sept. 12 | Paraguay | May 14 |
| Angola | Nov. 11 | Guyana | Feb. 23 | Peru | July 28 |
| Argentina | May 25 | Haiti | Jan. 1 | Philippines | June 12 |
| Australia | Jan. 26 | Honduras | Sept. 15 | Poland | July 22 |
| Austria | Oct. 26 | Hungary | April 4 | Portugal | April 25 |
| Bahamas | July 10 | Iceland | June 17 | Qatar | Sept. 3 |
| Bahrain | Dec. 16 | India | Jan. 26 | Romania | Aug. 23 |
| Bangladesh | March 26 | Indonesia | Aug. 17 | Rwanda | July 1 |
| Barbados | Nov. 30 | Iran | Oct. 26 | São Tomé et Príncipe | July 12 |
| Belgium | July 21 | Iraq | July 14 | Saudi Arabia | Sept. 23 |
| Benin | Nov. 30 | Ireland | March 17 | Senegal | April 4 |
| Bhutan | Dec. 17 | Israel | May 2[1] | Sierra Leone | April 19 |
| Bolivia | Aug. 6 | Italy | June 2 | Singapore | Aug. 9 |
| Botswana | Sept. 30 | Ivory Coast | Dec. 7 | Somalia | Oct. 21 |
| Brazil | Sept. 7 | Jamaica | Aug. 6[2] | South Africa | May 31 |
| Bulgaria | Sept. 9 | Japan | April 29 | Spain | Oct. 12 |
| Burma | Jan. 4 | Jordan | May 25 | Sri Lanka | Feb. 4 |
| Burundi | July 1 | Kenya | Dec. 12 | Sudan | Jan. 1 |
| Cameroon | May 20 | Kuwait | Feb. 25 | Surinam | Nov. 25 |
| Canada | July 1 | Laos | Dec. 2 | Swaziland | Sept. 6 |
| Cape Verde | Sept. 12 | Lebanon | Nov. 22 | Sweden | April 30 |
| Central African Empire | Dec. 1 | Lesotho | Oct. 4 | Syria | April 17 |
| Chad | April 13 | Liberia | July 26 | Tanzania | April 26 |
| Chile | Sept. 18 | Libya | Sept. 1 | Thailand | Dec. 5 |
| China | Oct. 1 | Luxembourg | June 23 | Togo | April 27 |
| Colombia | July 20 | Madagascar | June 26 | Trinidad and Tobago | Aug. 31 |
| Congo | Aug. 15 | Malawi | July 6 | Tunisia | June 1 |
| Costa Rica | Sept. 15 | Malaysia | Aug. 31 | Turkey | Oct. 29 |
| Cuba | Jan. 1 | Maldives | March 29 | Uganda | Oct. 9 |
| Cyprus | Oct. 1 | Mali | Sept. 22 | U.S.S.R. | Nov. 7 |
| Czechoslovakia | May 9 | Malta | Dec. 13 | United Arab Emirates | Dec. 2 |
| Denmark | April 16 | Mauritania | Nov. 28 | United Kingdom | June 3 |
| Dominican Republic | Feb. 27 | Mauritius | March 12 | United States | July 4 |
| Ecuador | Aug. 10 | Mexico | Sept. 16 | Upper Volta | Dec. 11 |
| Egypt | July 23 | Mongolia | July 11 | Uruguay | Aug. 25 |
| El Salvador | Sept. 15 | Morocco | March 3 | Venezuela | July 5 |
| Equatorial Guinea | March 5 | Mozambique | June 25 | Vietnam | Sept. 2 |
| Ethiopia | Sept. 12 | Nepal | Dec. 28 | Western Samoa | Jan. 1 |
| Fiji | Oct. 10 | Netherlands | April 30 | Yemen (People's Dem. Rep.) | Oct. 14 |
| Finland | Dec. 6 | New Zealand | Feb. 6 | Yemen (Republic) | Sept. 26 |
| France | July 14 | Nicaragua | Sept. 15 | Yugoslavia | Nov. 29 |
| Gabon | Aug. 17 | Niger | Dec. 18 | Zaire | June 30 |
| Germany, East | Oct. 7 | Nigeria | Oct. 1 | Zambia | Oct. 24 |
| Ghana | March 6 | Norway | May 17 | | |
| Greece | March 25 | Oman | Nov. 18 | | |
| Grenada | Feb. 7 | Pakistan | March 23 | | |

1. Changes yearly according to Hebrew calendar. 2. Celebrated on first Monday in August. *Source:* United Nations.

## Arlington National Cemetery

Arlington National Cemetery occupies 578 acres in Virginia on the Potomac River, directly opposite Washington. This land was part of the estate of John Parke Custis, Martha Washington's son, who built the mansion which later became the home of Robert E. Lee. In 1864, Arlington became a military cemetery. Over 170,000 persons, including many thousands of soldiers as well as hundreds of distinguished Americans, are buried there. Expansion of the cemetery began in fiscal year 1965, using a 180-acre tract of land directly east of the present site.

In 1921, an Unknown American Soldier of World War I was buried in a temporary crypt in the cemetery; the completed Tomb was opened to the public without ceremony in 1932. Two additional Unknowns, one from World War II and one from the Korean War, were buried May 30, 1958. The inscription carved on the side of the Tomb, formerly the Tomb of the Unknown Soldier and now called The Tomb of the Unknown, reads:

HERE RESTS IN
HONORED GLORY
AN AMERICAN
SOLDIER
KNOWN BUT TO GOD

# RELIGION

## Estimated Membership of the Principal Religions of the World

Statistics of the world's religions are only very rough approximations. Aside from Christianity, few religions, if any, attempt to keep statistical records; and even Protestants and Catholics employ different methods of counting members. All persons of whatever age who have received baptism in the Catholic Church are counted as members, while in most Protestant Churches only those who "join" the church are numbered. The compiling of statistics is further complicated by the fact that in China one may be at the same time a Confucian, a Taoist, and a Buddhist. In Japan, one may be both a Buddhist and a Shintoist.

| Religion | North America[1] | South America | Europe | Asia | Africa | Oceania[2] | Total |
|---|---|---|---|---|---|---|---|
| Total Christian | 231,099,700 | 158,980,000 | 348,059,300 | 89,909,000 | 137,460,300 | 18,112,600 | 983,620,900 |
| Roman Catholic | 131,631,500 | 147,280,000 | 182,514,300 | 47,046,000 | 53,740,000 | 4,475,000 | 566,686,800 |
| Eastern Orthodox | 4,189,000 | 552,000 | 50,545,000 | 1,894,000 | 15,255,000 | 380,000 | 72,815,000 |
| Protestant | 95,279,200 | 11,148,000 | 115,000,000 | 40,969,000 | 68,465,300 | 13,257,600 | 344,119,100 |
| Jewish[3] | 6,641,118 | 727,000 | 4,082,400 | 3,203,460 | 294,400 | 84,000 | 15,032,378 |
| Moslem | 249,200 | 238,300 | 8,283,500 | 433,001,000 | 134,285,200 | 103,000 | 576,160,200 |
| Zoroastrian | 250 | 2,000 | 6,000 | 224,700 | 600 | — | 233,550 |
| Shinto | 60,000 | 92,000 | — | 55,004,000 | — | — | 55,156,000 |
| Taoist | 16,000 | 12,000 | — | 31,088,100 | — | — | 31,116,100 |
| Confucian | 96,100 | 85,150 | 25,000 | 173,940,250 | 500 | 42,200 | 174,189,200 |
| Buddhist | 155,250 | 195,300 | 200,000 | 260,117,000 | 2,000 | 16,000 | 260,685,550 |
| Hindu | 81,000 | 782,300 | 260,000 | 515,449,500 | 483,650 | 841,000 | 517,897,450 |
| **Total** | **238,398,618** | **161,114,050** | **360,916,200** | **1,561,937,010** | **272,526,650** | **19,198,800** | **2,614,091,328** |

1. Includes Central America and West Indies. 2. Includes Australia and New Zealand, as well as islands of the South Pacific. 3. Includes total Jewish population, whether or not related to the synagogue. NOTE: Because of war and persecution, there are about 18,000,000 refugees throughout the world who are not integrated into religious statistics of the land of their temporary residence. *Source: Britannica Book of the Year, 1978.*

## Major Religions of the World

### Judaism

The determining factors of Judaism are: descendance from Israel, the *Torah,* and Tradition.

The name Israel (Jacob, a patriarch) also signifies his descendants as a people. During the 15th–13th centuries B.C., Israelite tribes, coming from South and East, gradually settled in Palestine, then inhabited by Canaanites. They were held together by Moses, who gave them religious unity in the worship of *Jahweh,* the God who had chosen Israel to be his people.

Under Judges, the 12 tribes at first formed an amphictyonic covenant. Saul established kingship (circa 1050 B.C.), and under David, his successor (1000–960 B.C.), the State of Israel comprised all of Palestine with Jerusalem as religio-political center. A golden era followed under Solomon (965–926 B.C.), who built *Jahweh* a temple.

After Solomon's death, the kingdom separated into Israel in the North and Judah in the South. A period of conflicts ensued, which ended with the conquest of Israel by Assyria in 722 B.C. The Babylonians defeated Judah in 586 B.C., destroying Jerusalem and its temple, and deporting many to Babylon.

The era of the kings is significant also in that the great prophets worked in that time, emphasizing faith in *Jahweh* as both God of Israel and God of the universe, and stressing social justice.

When the Persians permitted the Jews to return from exile (539 B.C.), temple and cult were restored in Jerusalem. The Persian rulers were succeeded by the Seleucides. The Maccabaean revolt against these Hellenistic kings gave independence to the Jews in 128 B.C., which lasted till the Romans occupied the country.

Important groups that exerted influence during these times were the Sadducees, priests in the temple in Jerusalem; the Pharisees, teachers of the Law in the synagogues; Essenes, a religious order (from whom Dead Sea Scrolls, discovered in 1947, came); Apocalyptists, who were expecting the heavenly Messiah; and Zealots, who were prepared to fight for national independence.

When the latter turned against Rome in A.D. 66, Roman armies under Titus suppressed the revolt, destroying Jerusalem and its temple in A.D. 70. The Jews were scattered in the *diaspora* (Dispersion), subject to oppressions until the Age of the Enlightenment (18th century) brought their emancipation, although persecutions did not end entirely.

The fall of the Jerusalem temple was an important event in the religious life of the Jews, which now developed around *Torah* (Law) and synagogue. Around A.D. 100 the Sacred Scriptures were codified. Synagogue worship became central, with readings from *Torah* and prophets. Most important prayers are the *Shema* (Hear) and the Prayer of the 18 Benedictions.

Religious life is guided by the commandments contained in the *Torah:* circumcision and *Sabbath,* as well as other ethical and ceremonial commandments.

The *Talmud,* based on the *Mishnah* and its interpretations, took shape over many centuries in the Babylonian and Palestinian Schools. It was a strong binding force of Judaism in the Dispersion.

In the 12th century, Maimonides formulated his "13 Articles of Faith," which carried great authority. Fundamental in this creed are: belief in God and his oneness *(Shema)*, belief in the changeless *Torah*, in the words of Moses and the prophets, belief in reward and punishment, the coming of the Messiah, and the resurrection of the dead.

Judaism is divided into theological schools, the main divisions of which are Orthodox and Reform.

## Christianity

Christianity is founded upon Jesus Christ, to whose life the New Testament writings testify. Jesus, a Jew, was born in about 7 B.C. and assumed his public life, after his 30th year, in Galilee. The Gospels tell of many extraordinary deeds that accompanied his ministry. He proclaimed the Kingdom of God, a future reality that is at the same time already present. Nationalistic-Jewish expectations of the Messiah he rejected. Rather, he referred to himself as the "Son of Man," the Christ, who has power to forgive sins now and who shall also come as Judge at the end of time. Jesus set forth the religio-ethical demands for participation in the Kingdom of God as change of heart and love of God and neighbor.

At the Last Supper he signified his death as a sacrifice, which would inaugurate the New Covenant, by which many would be saved. Circa A.D. 30 he died on a cross in Jerusalem. The early Church carried on Jesus' proclamation, the apostle Paul emphasizing his death and resurrection.

The person of Jesus is fundamental to the Christian faith since it is believed that in his life, death, and resurrection, God's revelation became historically tangible. He is seen as the turning point in history, and man's relationship to God as determined by his attitude to Jesus.

Historically Christianity thus arose out of Judaism, claiming fulfillment of the promises of the Old Testament in Jesus. The early Church designated itself as "the true Israel," which expected the speedy return of Jesus. The mother church was at Jerusalem, but churches were soon founded in many other places. The apostle Paul was instrumental in founding and extending a Gentile Christianity that was free from Jewish legalism.

The new religion spread rapidly throughout the eastern and western parts of the Roman Empire. In coming to terms with other religious movements within the Empire, Christianity began to take definite shape as an organization in its doctrine, liturgy, and ministry circa A.D. 200. In the 4th century the Catholic Church had taken root in countries stretching from Spain in the West to Persia and India in the East. Christians had been repeatedly subject to persecution by the Roman state, but finally gained tolerance under Constantine the Great (A.D. 313). Since that time, the Church became favored under his successors and in 380 the Emperor Theodosius proclaimed Christianity the State religion. Paganism was suppressed and public life was gradually molded in accordance with Christian ethical demands.

It was in these years also that the Church was able to achieve a certain unity of doctrine. Due to differences of interpretation of basic doctrines concerning Christ, which threatened to divide the Catholic Church, a standard Christian Creed was formulated by bishops at successive Ecumenical Councils, the first of which was held in A.D. 325 (Nicaea). The chief doctrines formulated concerned the doctrine of the Trinity, i.e., that there is one God in three persons: Father, Son, and Holy Spirit (Constantinople, A.D. 381); and the nature of Christ as both divine and human (Chalcedon, A.D. 541).

Through differences and rivalry between East and West the unity of the Church was broken by schism in 1054. In 1517 a separation occurred in the Western Church with the Reformation. From the major Protestant denominations [Lutheran, Presbyterian, Anglican (Episcopalian)], many Free Churches separated themselves in an age of individualism.

In the 20th century, however, the direction is toward unity. The Ecumenical Movement led to the formation of the World Council of Churches in 1948 (Amsterdam), which has since been joined by many Protestant and Orthodox Churches.

Through its missionary activity Christianity has spread to most parts of the globe.

### Eastern Orthodoxy

Eastern Orthodoxy comprises the faith and practice of Churches stemming from ancient Churches in the Eastern part of the Roman Empire. The term covers Orthodox Churches in communion with the See of Constantinople, Uniate Churches in communion with Rome, and Nestorian and Monophysite Churches.

The Orthodox, Catholic, Apostolic Church is the direct descendant of the Byzantine State Church and consists of a series of independent national churches that are united by Doctrine, Liturgy, and Hierarchical organization (deacons and priests, who may either be married or be monks before ordination, and bishops, who must be celebates). The heads of these Churches are patriarchs or metropolitans; the Patriarch of Constantinople is only "first among equals." Rivalry between the Pope of Rome and the Patriarch of Constantinople, aided by differences and misunderstandings that existed for centuries between the Eastern and Western parts of the Empire, led to a schism in 1054. Repeated attempts at reunion have failed in past centuries. The mutual excommunication pronounced in that year was lifted in 1965, however, and because of greater interaction in theology between Orthodox Churches and those in the West, a climate of better understanding has been created in the 20th century. First contacts were with Anglicans and Old Catholics. Orthodox Churches belong to the World Council of Churches.

The Eastern Orthodox Churches recognize only the canons of the seven Ecumenical Councils (325–787) as binding for faith and they reject doctrines that have been added in the West.

The central worship service is called the Liturgy, which is understood as representation of God's acts of salvation. Its center is the celebration of the Eucharist, or Lord's Supper.

In their worship *icons* (sacred pictures) are used that have a sacramental meaning as representation. The Mother of Christ, angels, and saints are highly venerated.

The number of sacraments in the Orthodox Church is the same as in the Western Catholic Church.

Orthodox Churches are found in the Balkans and the Soviet Union also, since the 20th century, in Western Europe and other parts of the world, particularly in America.

Eastern Orthodoxy also includes the Uniate Churches that recognize the authority of the Pope but keep their own traditional liturgies and those Churches dating back to the 5th century that emancipated themselves from the Byzantine State Church: the Nestorian Church in the Near East and India with approximately half a million members and the Monophysite Churches with some 17 million members (Coptic, Ethiopian, Syrian, Armenian, and the Mar Thoma Church in India).

### Roman Catholicism

Roman Catholicism comprises the belief and practice of the Roman Catholic Church. The Church stands under the authority of the Bishop of Rome, the Pope, and is ruled by him and bishops who are held to be, through ordination, successors of Peter and the Apostles, respectively. Fundamental to the structure of the Church is the juridical aspect: doctrine and sacraments are bound to the power of jurisdiction and consecration of the hierarchy. The Pope, as the head of the hierarchy of archbishops, bishops, priests, and deacons, has full ecclesiastical power, granted him by Christ, through Peter. As successor to Peter, he is the Vicar of Christ. The powers that others in the hierarchy possess are delegated.

Roman Catholics believe their Church to be the one, holy, catholic, and apostolic Church, possessing all the properties of the one, true Church of Christ.

The faith of the Church is understood to be identical with that taught by Christ and his Apostles and contained in Bible and Tradition, i.e. the original deposit of faith, to which nothing new may be added. New definitions of doctrines, such as the Immaculate Conception of Mary (1854) and the bodily Assumption of Mary (1950), have been declared by Popes, however, in accordance with the principle of development (implicit-explicit doctrine).

At Vatican Council I (1870) the Pope was proclaimed "endowed with infallibility, *et cathedra,* i.e., when exercising the office of Pastor and Teacher of all Christians."

The center of Roman Catholic worship is the Sacrament of the Mass, which is the commemoration of Christ's sacrificial death and of his resurrection. Other sacraments are Baptism, Confirmation, Confession, Matrimony, Ordination, and Extreme Unction, seven in all. The Virgin Mary and saints, and their relics, are highly venerated and prayers are made to them to intercede with God, in whose presence they are believed to dwell.

The Roman Catholic Church is the largest Christian organization in the world, found in most countries. Some 8 million belong to the Uniate rites, the vast majority to the Latin rite.

Since Vatican Council II (1962–65), and the effort to "update" the Church, many interesting changes and developments have been taking place.

### Protestantism

Protestantism comprises the Christian churches that separated from Rome during the Reformation in the 16th century, initiated by an Augustinian monk, Martin Luther. "Protestant" was originally applied to followers of Luther, who protested at the Diet of Spires (1529) against the decree which prohibited all further ecclesiastical reforms. Subsequently, Protestantism came to mean rejection of attempts to tie God's revelation to earthly institutions, and a return to the Gospel and the Word of God as sole authority in matters of faith and practice. Central in the biblical message is the justification of the sinner by faith alone. The Church is understood as a fellowship and the priesthood of all believers stressed.

The Augsburg Confession (1530) was the principal statement of Lutheran faith and practice. It became a model for other Confessions of Faith, which in their turn had decisive influence on Church polity. Major Protestant denominations are the Lutheran, Reformed (Calvinist), Presbyterian, and Anglican (Episcopal). Smaller ones are the Mennonite. Schwenkfeldians, and Unitarians. In Great Britain and America there are the Congregationalists, Baptists, Quakers, Methodists, and other free church types of communities. (In regarding themselves as being faithful to original biblical Christianity, these Churches differ from such religious bodies as Unitarians, Mormons, Jehovah's Witnesses, and Christian Scientists, who either teach new doctrines or reject old ones.)

Since the latter part of the 19th century, national councils of churches have been established in many countries, e.g. the Federal Council of Churches of Christ in America in 1908. Denominations across countries joined in federations and world alliances, beginning with the Anglican Lambeth Conference in 1867.

Protestant missionary activity, particularly strong in the last century, resulted in the founding of many younger churches in Asia and Africa. The Ecumenical Movement, which originated with Protestant missions, aims at unity among Christians and churches.

## Islam

Islam is the religion founded in Arabia by Mohammed between 610 and 632. Its 400 million adherents are found in countries stretching from Morocco in the West to Indonesia in the East.

Mohammed was born in A.D. 570 at Mecca and belonged to the Quraysh tribe, which was active in caravan trade. At the age of 25 he joined the caravan trade from Mecca to Syria in the employment of a rich widow, Khadiji, whom he married. Critical of the idolatry of the inhabitants of Mecca, he began to lead a contemplative life in the deserts. There he received a series of revelations. Encouraged by Khadiji, he gradually became convinced that he was given a God-appointed task to devote himself to the reform of religion and society. Idolatry was to be abandoned.

The *Hegira (Hijra)* (migration) of Mohammed from Mecca, where he was not honored, to Medina, where he was well received, occurred in 622 and marks the beginning of the Muslim era. In 630 he marched on Mecca and conquered it. He died at Medina in 632. His grave there has since been a place of pilgrimage.

Mohammed's followers, called Moslems, revered him as the prophet of *Allah* (God), beside whom there is no other God. Although he had no close knowledge of Judaism and Christianity, he considered himself succeeding and completing them as the seal of the Prophets. Sources of the Islamic faith are the *Qur'an,* regarded as the uncreated, eternal Word of God, and Tradition *(hadith)* regarding sayings and deeds of the prophet.

Islam means surrender to the will of *Allah.* He is the all-powerful, whose will is supreme and determines man's fate. Good and evil deeds will be rewarded at the Last Judgment in paradise or in hell.

The Five Pillars, primary duties, of Islam are: witness; confessing the oneness of God and of Mohammed, his prophet; prayer, to be performed five times a day; almsgiving to the poor and the mosque (house of worship); fasting during daylight hours in the month of Ramadan; and pilgrimage to Mecca at least once in the Moslem's lifetime.

The practice of Holy War *(jihad),* at first responsible for the rapid growth of the new religion, could not be maintained. Mohammed curtailed the practice of polygamy by limiting it to four wives. In modern times the position of women has improved, due to Western influence. The eating of pork and drinking of intoxicants is forbidden.

Islam, upholding the law of brotherhood, succeeded in uniting an Arab world that had disintegrated into tribes and castes. Disagreements concerning the succession of the prophet caused a great division in Islam between *Sunnis* and *Shias.* Among these, other sects arose *(Wahhabi).* Doctrinal issues also led to the rise of different schools of thought in theology. Nevertheless, since Arab armies turned against Syria and Palestine in 635, Islam has expanded successfully under Mohammed's successors. Its rapid victorious conquests in Asia and Africa are unsurpassed in history. Turning against Europe, Moslems conquered Spain in 713. In 1453 Constantinople fell into their hands and in 1529 Moslem armies besieged Vienna. Since then, Islam has lost its foothold in Europe.

In modern times it has made great gains in Africa.

## Hinduism

In India alone there are more than 300 million adherents of Hinduism. In contrast to other religions, it has no founder. Considered the oldest religion in the world, it dates back, perhaps, to prehistoric times.

Hinduism is hard to define, there being no common creed, no one doctrine to bind Hindus together. Intellectually there is complete freedom of belief, and one can be monotheist, polytheist, or atheist. What matters is the social system: a Hindu is one born into a caste.

As a religion, Hinduism is founded on the sacred scriptures, written in Sanskrit and called the *Vedas* (*Veda*-knowledge). There are four Vedic books, among which the *Rig Veda* is the most important. It speaks of many gods and also deals with questions concerning the universe and creation. The dates of these works are unknown (1000 B.C.?).

The *Upanishads* (dated 1000–300 B.C.), commentaries on the Vedic texts, have philosophical speculations on the origin of the universe, the nature of deity, of *atman* (the human soul), and its relationship to *Brahman* (the universal soul).

*Brahman* is the principle and source of the universe who can be indicated only by negatives. As the divine intelligence, he is the ground of the visible world, a presence that pervades all beings. Thus the many Hindu deities came to be understood as manifestations of the one *Brahman* from whom everything proceeds and to whom everything ultimately returns. The religio-social system of Hinduism is based on the concept of reincarnation and transmigration in which all living beings, from plants below to gods above, are caught in a cosmic system that is an everlasting cycle of becoming and perishing.

Life is determined by the law of *karma,* according to which rebirth is dependent on moral behavior in a previous phase of existence. The doctrine of transmigration thus provides a rationale for the caste system. In this view, life on earth is regarded as transient *(maya)* and a burden. The goal of existence is liberation from the cycle of rebirth and redeath and entrance into the indescribable state of what in Buddhism is called *nirvana* (extinction of passion).

Further important sacred writings are the Epics *(puranas),* which contain legendary stories about gods and men. They are the *Mahabharata* (composed between 200 B.C. and A.D. 200) and the *Ramayana.* The former includes the *Bhagavad-Gita* (Song of the Lord), its most famous part, that tells of devotion to *Krishna* (Lord), who appears as an *avatar* (incarnation) of the god *Vishnu,* and of the duty of obeying caste rules. The work begins with a praise of the *yoga* (discipline) system.

The practice of Hinduism consists of rites and ceremonies, performed within the framework of the caste system and centering on the main socio-religious occasions of birth, marriage, and death. There are many Hindu temples, which are dwelling places of the deities and to which people bring offerings. There are also places of pilgrimages, the chief one being Benares on the Ganges, most sacred among the rivers in India.

In modern times work has been done to reform and revive Hinduism. One of the outstanding reformers was Ramakrishna (1836-86), who inspired many followers, one of whom founded the Ramakrishna mission, which seeks to convert others to its religion. The mission is active both in India and in other countries.

## Buddhism

Founded in the 6th century B.C. in northern India by Gautama Buddha, who was born in southern Nepal as son to a king. His birth is surrounded by many legends, but Western scholars agree that he lived from 563–483 B.C. Warned by a sage that his son would become an ascetic or a universal monarch, the king confined him to his home. He was able to escape and began the life of a homeless wanderer in search of peace, passing through many disappointments until he finally came to the Tree of Enlightenment, under which he lived in meditation till enlightenment came to him and he became a Buddha (enlightened one).

Now he understood the origin of suffering, summarized in the *Four Noble Truths,* which constitutes the foundation of Buddhism. The Four are the truth of suffering, which all living beings must endure; of the origin of suffering, which is craving and which leads to rebirth; that it can be destroyed; and of the way that leads to cessation of pain, i.e., the *Noble Eightfold Way,* which is the rule of practical Buddhism: right views, right intention, right speech, right action, right livelihood, right effort, right concentration, and right ecstasy.

*Nirvana* is the goal of all existence, the state of complete redemption, into which the redeemed enters. Buddha's insight can free every man from the law of reincarnation through complete emptying of the self.

The nucleus of Buddha's church or association was originally formed by monks and lay-brothers, whose houses gradually became monasteries used as places for religious instruction. The worship service consisted of a sermon, expounding of Scripture, meditation, and confession. At a later stage pilgrimages to the holy places associated with the Buddha came into being, as well as veneration of relics.

In the 3rd century B.C., King Ashoka made Buddhism the State religion of India but, as centuries passed, it gradually fell into decay through splits, persecutions, and the hostile Brahmans. Buddhism spread to countries outside India, however.

At the beginning of the Christian era, there occurred a split that gave rise to two main types: *Hinayana* (Little Vehicle), or southern Buddhism, and *Mahayana* (Great Vehicle), or northern Buddhism. The former type, more individualistic, survived in Ceylon and southern Asia. Hinayana retained more closely the original teachings of the Buddha, which did not know of a personal god or soul. *Mahayana,* more social, polytheistic, and developing a pluralistic pompous cult, was strong in the Himalayas, Tibet, Mongolia, China, Korea, and Japan.

In the present century, Buddhism has found believers also in the West and Buddhist associations have been established in Europe and the U.S.

## Confucianism

Confucius (K'ung Fu-tzu), born in the state of Lu (northern China), lived from 551–479 B.C. Tradition, exaggerating the importance of Confucius in life, has depicted him as a great statesman but, in fact, he seems to have been a private teacher. Anthologies of ancient Chinese classics, along with his own Analects *(Lun Yu),* became the basis of Confucianism. These Analects were transmitted as a collection of his sayings as recorded by his students, with whom he discussed ethical and social problems. They developed into men of high moral standing, who served the State as administrators.

In his teachings, Confucius emphasized the importance of an old Chinese concept *(li)* , which has the connotation of proper conduct. There is some disagreement as to the religious ideas of Confucius, but he held high the concepts handed down from centuries before him. Thus he believed in Heaven *(T'ien)* and sacrificed to his ancestors. Ancestor worship he indeed encouraged as an expression of filial piety, which he considered the loftiest of virtues.

Piety to Confucius was the foundation of the family as well as the State. The family is the nucleus of the State, and the "five relations," between king and subject, father and son, man and wife, older and younger brother, and friend and friend, are determined by the virtues of love of fellow men, righteousness, and respect.

An extension of ancestor worship may be seen in the worship of Confucius, which became official in the 2nd century B.C. when the emperor, in recognition of Confucius' teachings, as supporting the imperial rule, offered sacrifices at his tomb.

Mencius (Meng Tse), who lived around 400 B.C., did much to propagate and elaborate Confucianism in its concern with ordering society. Thus, for two millennia, Confucius' doctrine of State, with its emphasis on ethics and social morality, rooted in ancient Chinese tradition and developed and continued by his disciples, has been standard in China and the Far East.

With the revolution of 1911 in China, however, students, burning Confucius in effigy, called for the removel of "the old curiosity shop."

## Shintoism

Shinto, the Chinese term for the Japanese *Kami no Michi,* i.e., the Way of the Gods, comprises the religious ideas and cult indigenous to Japan. *Kami,* or gods, considered divine forces of nature that are worshipped, may reside in rivers, trees, rocks, mountains, certain animals, or, particularly, in the sun and moon. The worship of ancestors, heroes, and deceased emperors was incorporated later.

After Buddhism had come from Korea, Japan's native religion at first resisted it. Then there followed a period of compromise and amalgamation with Buddhist beliefs and ceremonies, resulting, since the 9th century A.D., in a syncretistic religion, a Twofold Shinto. Buddhist deities came to be regarded as manifestations of Japanese deities and Buddhist priests took over most of the Shinto shrines.

In modern times Shinto regained independence from Buddhism. Under the reign of the Emperor Meiji (1868–1912) it became the official State religion, in which loyalty to the emperor was emphasized. The line of succession of emperors is traced back to the first Emperor Jimmu (660 B.C.) and beyond him to the Sun-goddess *Amaterasuomikami.*

The centers of worship are the shrines and temples in which the deities are believed to dwell and believers approach them through *torii* (gateways). Most important among the shrines is the imperial shrine of the Sun-goddess at Ise, where state ceremonies were once held in June and December. The *Yasukuni* shrine of the war dead in Tokyo is also well known.

Acts of worship consist of prayers, clapping of hands, acts of purification, and offerings. On feast days processions and performances of music and dancing take place and priests read prayers before the gods in the shrines, asking for good harvest, the well-being of people and emperor, etc. In Japanese homes there is a god-shelf, a small wooden shrine that contains the tablets bearing the names of ancestors. Offerings are made and candles lit before it.

After World War II the Allied Command ordered the disestablishment of State Shinto. To be distinguished from State Shinto is Sect Shinto, consisting of 13 recognized sects. These have arisen in modern times, gaining large followings. Most important among them is *Tenrikyo* in Tenri City (Nara), in which healing by faith plays a central role.

## Taoism

Taoism, a religion of China, was, according to tradition, founded by Lao Tse, a Chinese philosopher, long considered one of the prominent religious leaders from the 6th century B.C.

Data about him are for the most part legendary, however, and the *Tao Te Ching* (the classic of the Way and of its Power), traditionally ascribed to him, is now believed by many scholars to have originated in the 3rd century B.C. The book is composed in short chapters, written in aphoristic rhymes. Central are the word *Tao,* which means way or path and, in a deeper sense, signifies the principle that underlies the reality of this world and manifests itself in nature and in the lives of men, and the word *Te* (power).

The virtuous man draws power from being absorbed in *Tao,* the ultimate reality within an ever-changing world. By non-action and keeping away from human striving it is possible for man to live in harmony with the principles that underlie and govern the universe. *Tao* cannot be comprehended by reason and knowledge, but only by inward quiet.

Besides the *Tao Te Ching,* dating from approximately the same period, are two Taoist works, written by Chuang Tse and Lieh Tse.

Theoretical Taoism of this classical philosophical movement of the 4th and 3rd centuries B.C. in China differed from popular Taoism, into which it gradually degenerated. The standard of theoretical Taoism was maintained in the classics, of course, and among the upper classes it continued to be alive until modern times.

Religious Taoism is a form of religion dealing with deities and spirits, magic and soothsaying. In the 2nd century A.D. it was organized with temples, cult, priests, and monasteries and was able to hold its own in the competition with Buddhism that came up at the same time.

After the 7th century A.D., however, Taoist religion further declined. Split into numerous sects which often operate like secret societies, it has become a syncretistic folk religion in which some of the old deities and saints live on.

## History of Leading Religious Groups in the United States

**(50,000 members or over)**

*Source: Yearbook of American and Canadian Churches, 1978.*

### BAPTIST

**American Baptist Association:** A group of independent Missionary Baptist Churches, mainly in the South, Southeast, and Southwest, organized in 1905. Members (1975): 1,071,000. Headquarters: 4605 N. State Line Ave., Texarkana, Tex. 75501.

**American Baptist Churches in the U.S.A.:** Formerly known as the Northern Baptist Convention and the American Baptist Convention, this body changed its name in 1973. Although national missionary organizational developments began in 1814 with the establishment of the American Baptist Foreign Mission Society, the Convention was not formed until 1907. Members (1976): 1,593,574. Headquarters: Valley Forge, Pa. 19481.

**Baptist General Conference:** Formerly known as the Swedish Baptist General Conference of America. It has operated as a general conference since 1879. Members (1976): 117,973. Headquarters: 1233 Central St., Evanston, Ill. 60201.

**Baptist Missionary Association of America:** Formerly called the North American Baptist Association. It was organized in 1950 in Little Rock, Ark. Members (1976): 216,471. Office of president: 7602 Breezeway, Houston, Tex. 77088.

**Conservative Baptist Association of America:** Organized in 1947. Adherents regard the Bible as infallible Local churches are independent, autonomous, and free from ecclesiastical or political authority. Members (1976): 300,000. Headquarters: Geneva Rd., Box 66, Wheaton, Ill. 60187.

**Free Will Baptists:** A body of evangelical Baptists, organized in 1727 in the South and 1780 in the North. Members (1976): 229,498. Headquarters: 1134 Murfreesboro Rd., Nashville, Tenn. 37217.

**General Association of Regular Baptist Churches:** Founded in 1932 in Chicago by a group of churches which had withdrawn from the Northern Baptist Convention (now the American Baptist Convention) because of doctrinal differences. Members (1977): 240,000. Headquarters: 1300 N. Meacham Rd., Schaumburg, Ill. 60185.

**General Baptists (General Association of):** An Arminian group of Baptists, organized in England in 1607 and transplanted to the colonies in 1714. It died out along the Seaboard, but revived in the Midwest in 1823. Members (1974): 70,000. Office of moderator: 1214 W. Hemphill Rd., Flint, Mich. 48507.

**National Baptist Convention, U.S.A., Inc.:** The older and parent convention of Black Baptists. This body is to be distinguished from the National Baptist Convention of America, usually referred to as the "unincorporated" body. Members (1958): 5,500,000. Office of president: 405 E. 31st St., Chicago, Ill. 60616.

**National Baptist Convention of America:** This is a body usually referred to as the "unincorporated" convention, not to be confused with the "incorporated" National Baptist Convention, U.S.A., Inc., from which this body withdrew. Organized in 1880. Members (1956): 2,668,799. Office of president: 1724 Jefferson St., Jacksonville, Fla. 32209.

**National Baptist Evangelical Life and Soul Saving Assembly of U.S.A.:** Organized in 1921 as a charitable, educational, and evangelical organization. Members (1951): 57,674. Headquarters: 441-61 Monroe Ave., Detroit, Mich. 48226

**National Primitive Baptist Convention, Inc.:** A group of Baptists having local associations and a National Convention. Organized in 1907. Members (1975): 250,000. Headquarters: Box 2355, Tallahassee, Fla.

**North American Baptist Association:** *See* Baptist Missionary Association of America.

**Primitive Baptists:** A large group of Baptists, largely through the South, who are opposed to all centralization and to modern missionary societies. Members (1950): 72,000. Headquarters: Cayce

## U. S. Church Membership

| Religious group | Members |
|---|---|
| Protestant bodies and others | 71,587,416 |
| Roman Catholics | 49,325,752 |
| Jewish congregations[1] | 6,115,000 |
| Eastern churches | 3,754,540 |
| Old Catholic, Polish National Catholic, Armenian churches | 846,166 |
| Buddhist Churches of America | 60,000 |
| Miscellaneous | 208,665 |
| **Total[2]** | **131,897,539** |

1. Includes Orthodox, Conservative, and Reform. 2. As reported in the *1978 Yearbook* from statistics furnished by 223 religious bodies in the United States.

Publishing Co., S. Second St., Thornton, Ariz., 71766.

**Progressive National Baptist Convention, Inc.:** A body that held its organizational meeting in Cincinnati in 1961 and its first annual session in Philadelphia in 1962. Members (1967): 521,692. Office of president: Second Baptist Church, 2412 Griffith Ave., Los Angeles, Calif., 90011.

**Southern Baptist Convention:** In 1845, Southern Baptists withdrew from the General Missionary Convention over the question of slavery and other matters and formed the Southern Baptist Convention. Members (1976): 12,917,992. Office of president: 515 McCullough, San Antonio, Tex. 78215.

**United Free Will Baptist Church:** A body which set up its organization in 1870. Members (1952): 100,000. Headquarters: Kinston College, 1000 University St., Kinston, N.C. 28501.

## CATHOLIC AND ORTHODOX

**American Carpatho-Russian Orthodox Greek Catholic Church:** This church is a self-governing diocese in communion with the Ecumenical Patriarchate of Constantinople. On Sept. 19, 1938, the late Patriarch Benjamin I canonized the diocese in the name of the Orthodox Church of Christ. Members (1976): 100,000. Headquarters: Johnstown, Pa. 15906.

**Antiochian Orthodox Christian Archdiocese of North America:** Formed in 1975 by merger of the Antiochian Orthodox Christian Archdiocese of New York and All North America (formerly the Syrian Antiochian Orthodox Archdiocese of New York and North America) and the Antiochian Orthodox Archdiocese of Toledo, Ohio, and Dependencies in North America. The new Archdiocese is under the jurisdiction of the Patriarch of Antioch. Members (1977): 152,000. Headquarters: 358 Mountain Rd., Englewood, N.J. 07631.

**Armenian Apostolic Church of America:** The Armenian Church divided into two separate dioceses in 1933 because of a dispute regarding the political activities of the prelate at that time, and because of the status of the church in Soviet Armenia. Since 1956, this diocese has been under the jurisdiction of the Holy See of Cilicia, Beirut, Lebanon. Members (1972): 125,000. Headquarters: 138 E. 39th St., New York, N.Y. 10016.

**Armenian Church of America, Diocese of the (including Diocese of California):** The American branch of the Ancient Church of Armenia. Established in the U. S. in 1889. Diocesan organization is under the jurisdiction of the Holy See of Etchmiadzin, Armenia, U.S.S.R. Members (1972): 372,000. Headquarters: St. Vartan Cathedral, 630 Second Ave., New York, N.Y. 10016.

**Bulgarian Eastern Orthodox Church (Diocese of North and South America and Australia):** A Synod of the Bulgarian Eastern Orthodox Church, established as the Bulgarian Orthodox Mission in 1909. Became a canonical metropolitan archdiocese in 1947. Members (1971): 86,000. Headquarters: 312 W. 101st St., New York, N.Y. 10025; 1953 Stockbridge Rd., Akron, Ohio, 44313.

**Greek Orthodox Archdiocese of North and South America:** Greek-speaking Orthodox Christians have parishes in the U. S., Canada, and South America. These are under the Ecumenical Patriarchate of Constantinople. Members (1977): 1,950,000. Headquarters: 8–10 E. 79th St., New York, N.Y. 10021.

**North American Old Roman Catholic Church:** A body with the doctrine of the Old Catholics; identical with the Roman Catholic Church in most worship and discipline. It is not under Papal jurisdiction. Members (1975): 60,124. Office of presiding bishop: 4200 N. Kedvale Ave., Chicago, Ill. 60641.

**Orthodox Church in America (The Russian Orthodox Greek Catholic Church of America):** This body entered Alaska in 1792. In 1872, its headquarters were moved from Sitka to San Francisco and, in 1905, to New York. Members (1975): 1,000,000. Office of primate: Box 675, Syosset, N.Y. 11791.

**Polish National Catholic Church of America:** After long dissatisfaction with Roman Catholic administration and ideology, this group was organized in 1897. Members (1960): 282,411. Headquarters: 529 E. Locust St., Scranton, Pa. 18505.

**Roman Catholic Church:** The largest single group of Christians in the U. S., the Roman Catholic Church is under the spiritual leadership of the Pope. This group dates back to the priests who accompanied Columbus on his second voyage to the New World. A settlement, later discontinued, was made at St. Augustine, Fla. The continuous history of this Church in the colonies began at St. Mary's in 1634, in Maryland. Members (1977): 49,325,752. National Conference of Catholic Bishops, 1312 Massachusetts Ave., N.W., Washington, D.C. 20005.

**Russian Orthodox Church in the U.S.A., Patriarchial Parishes of the:** This autonomous body is the direct canonical successor of the Orthodox Catholic mission established in Alaska by the Russian Orthodox Church in 1793. It is under the spiritual jurisdiction of the Patriarch of Moscow and all Russia, His Holiness Pimen. In 1962 an administration was established for the Orthodox Mission in Puerto Rico and the Spanish-speaking people in the United States. Members (1975): 51,500. Headquarters: St. Nicholas Patriarchal Cathedral, 15 E. 97th St., New York, N.Y. 10029.

**Russian Orthodox Church Outside Russia:** The governing body was set up in Constantinople. In 1950, it came to the U. S. Members (155): 55,000. Headquarters: 75 E. 93rd St., New York, N.Y. 10028.

**Serbian Eastern Orthodox Church for the U.S.A. and Canada:** This body of the Eastern Orthodox Church is autonomous. Members (1967): 65,000. Chancery: 5701 N. Redwood Dr., Chicago, Ill.

**Syrian Antiochian Orthodox Archdiocese of New York and North America:** *See* Antiochian Orthodox Christian Archdiocese of New York and All North America.

**Syrian Orthodox Church of Antioch (Archdiocese of the U.S.A. and Canada):** This group is in a direct ecclesiastical line of the Syrian Orthodox Church established in Antioch. There are 10 parishes in the U.S. and two in the Province of Quebec. Members (1972): 50,000. Headquarters: 293 Hamilton Pl., Hackensack, N.J. 07601.

**Ukrainian Orthodox Church in the U.S.A.:** This church was organized in the U.S. in 1919. Members (1966): 87,745.

**JEWISH**
Jews arrived in the colonies before 1650. The first congregation is recorded in 1654, in New York City, the Shearith Israel (Remnant of Israel). Members (1972): 6,115,000.

Following are the major Jewish organizations:
**Central Conference of American Rabbis:** 790 Madison Ave., New York, N.Y. 10021
**Rabbinical Alliance of America:** 156 Fifth Ave., New York, N.Y. 10011
**Rabbinical Assembly:** 3080 Broadway, New York, N.Y. 10027
**Rabbinical Council of America, Inc.:** 1250 Broadway, New York, N.Y. 10001
**Synagogue Council of America:** 432 Park Ave. South, New York, N.Y. 10016
**Union of American Hebrew Congregations:** 838 Fifth Ave., New York, N.Y. 10021
**Union of Orthodox Jewish Congregations of America:** 116 E. 27th St., New York, N.Y. 10016
**United Synagogue of America:** 155 Fifth Ave., New York, N.Y. 10010

**LUTHERAN**
**American Lutheran Church:** This church is the result of the merger in 1960 of the American Lutheran Church, the Evangelical Lutheran Church, and the United Evangelical Lutheran Church. In 1963, the Lutheran Free Church merged with The American Lutheran Church. Members (1976): 2,402,261. Headquarters: 422 S. Fifth St., Minneapolis, Minn. 55415.

**Evangelical Lutheran Churches, Association of:** Formed in 1976, this group is made up mainly of former affiliates of the Lutheran Church-Missouri Synod, plus some new and some formerly independent congregations. Its members have joined together to be in mission and ministry. Members (1977): 95,186. Headquarters: 12015 Manchester Rd., St. Louis, Mo. 63131.

**Lutheran Church—Missouri Synod:** This body, the largest constituent part of the Evangelical Lutheran Synodical Conference of North America, was organized in 1847. It is the leader in the conservative group among the Lutherans. Members (1976): 2,757,271. Headquarters: 500 N. Broadway, St. Louis, Mo. 63102.

**Lutheran Church in America:** This body was organized in 1962 by the consolidation of the American Evangelical Lutheran Church (1874), the Augustana Evangelical Lutheran Church (1860), the Finnish Evangelical Lutheran Church (1890), and the United Lutheran Church in America (1918). Members (1976): 2,974,749. Headquarters: 231 Madison Ave., New York, N.Y. 10016.

**Wisconsin Evangelical Lutheran Synod:** This body was organized in Wisconsin in 1850. Members (1976): 399,114. Office of president: 3512 W. North Ave., Milwaukee, Wis. 53208.

**METHODIST**
**African Methodist Episcopal Church:** This church began in 1787 in Philadelphia when persons in a Methodist Episcopal Church withdrew. In 1816, the denomination was started. Members (1951): 1,166,301. Office of senior bishop: 1002 Kirkwood Ave., Nashville, Tenn. 37203.

**African Methodist Episcopal Zion Church:** This group was organized in 1796, having withdrawn from the John Street Methodist Church, New York. Members (1973): 1,024,974. Office of president: 520 Red Cross St., Wilmington, N.C. 28401.

**Christian Methodist Episcopal Church:** In 1870, the General Conference of the M.E. Church, South, approved the request of its black membership for the formation of their conferences into a separate body. Members (1965): 466,718. Office of secretary: 664 Vance Ave., Memphis, Tenn. 38126.

**Free Methodist Church of North America:** This body, organized in 1860, grew out of a movement in the Genesee Conference of the Methodist Episcopal Church about 1850 towards a more original Methodism. Members (1976): 68,180. Headquarters: 901 College Ave., Winona Lake, Ind. 46590.

**United Methodist Church:** The United Methodist Church was formed in April, 1968, by the union of the Methodist Church and the Evangelical United Brethren Church. The two churches shared a common historical and spiritual heritage. The Methodist Church resulted in 1939 from the unification of three branches of Methodism—the Methodist Episcopal Church; the Methodist Episcopal Church South; and the Methodist Protestant Church. The Methodist movement began in 18th-century England under the preaching of John Wesley, but the so called Christmas Conference of 1784 in Baltimore is regarded as the date on which the organized Methodist Church was founded as an ecclesiastical organization. The Evangelical United Brethren Church was formed in 1946 with the merger of the Evangelical Church and the Church of the United Brethren in Christ, both of which had their beginnings in Pennsylvania in the evangelistic movement of the 18th and early 19th centuries. Members (1976): 9,861,028. Office of Secretary of General Conference, Perkins School of Theology, Southern Methodist University, Dallas, Tex. 75222.

**PRESBYTERIAN**
**Cumberland Presbyterian Church:** An outgrowth of the Great Revival of 1800, the Cumberland Presbytery was organized in 1810 in Tennessee. A union with the Presbyterian Church, U.S.A., in 1906, was only partially successful, and the Cumberland Presbyterian Church continued as a separate denomination. Members (1976): 92,995. Office of moderator: 3504 Villanova, Dallas, Tex. 75225.

**Presbyterian Church in America:** Formed in Birmingham, Ala., in 1973 after separating from the Presbyterian Church in the United States, this body believes the Bible is the only infallible rule of faith and practice. It is committed to the Reformed Faith as set forth in the Westminster Confession and Catechisms. Members (1976); 68,993. Office of moderator: 1107 E. Hernandez, Pensacola, Fla. 32503.

**Presbyterian Church in the United States:** This body is a branch of the Presbyterian Church established in separate existence in 1861. Members (1976): 877,664. Headquarters: 341 Ponce de Leon Ave., NE, Atlanta, Ga. 30308.

**United Presbyterian Church in the United States of America:** This group was formed in 1958 by a merger of the Presbyterian Church in the U.S.A. (dating from 1706) and the United Presbyterian Church of North America (established in 1858). Members (1976): 2,607,321. Headquarters: 475 Riverside Dr., New York, N.Y. 10027.

## OTHER RELIGIOUS BODIES

**Apostolic Overcoming Holy Church of God:** A black body incorporated in Alabama in 1919. It is evangelistic in purpose and emphasizes sanctification, holiness, and divine healing. Members (1956): 75,000. Office of secretary, 514 10th Ave., W., Birmingham, Ala. 35204.

**Assemblies of God:** A pentecostal, evangelical, missionary denomination which grew out of the spiritual revivals of the early 1900's. The organization is composed of self-governing churches. Founded in Arkansas in 1914. Members (1977): 1,302,318. Headquarters: 1445 Boonville Ave., Springfield, Mo. 65802.

**Bahá'í Faith:** Baháís are followers of Bahá'u'lláh (1817–1892), whose religion upholds the basic principle of progressive revelation, religious unity and a new world order. There is a spiritual and administrative world center in Haifa, Israel. Headquarters, 536 Sheridan Rd., Wilmette, Ill. 60091.

**Buddhist Churches of America:** Organized in 1914 as the Buddhist Mission of North America, this body was incorporated in 1942 under the present name and represents the Jodo Shinshu Sect of Buddhism in this country. Members (1975): 60,000. Headquarters: 1710 Octavia St., San Francisco, Calif. 94109.

**Christian and Missionary Alliance:** An evangelical, evangelistic, and missionary movement organized in 1887. It stresses "the deeper Christian life and consecration to the Lord's service." Members (1976): 150,492. Headquarters: 350 N. Highland Ave., Nyack, N.Y. 10960.

**Christian Congregation, Inc.:** Incorporated in 1887, denomination provides ministerial affiliation for independent clergymen. Members (1976): 79,230. Office of general superintendent: 804 W. Hemlock St., LaFollette, Tenn. 37766.

**Christian Church (Disciples of Christ):** In the revival period of the early nineteenth century, a movement resulted in the establishment of a fellowship called "Christians" or "Disciples." This movement calls for the reunion of the church on the basis of a return to New Testament faith and order. It is congregational in government. Members (1976): 1,278,734. Headquarters: 222 S. Downey Ave., Box 1986, Indianapolis, Ind. 46206.

**Christian Churches and Churches of Christ:** This fellowship, congregational in polity, has its origin in the movement to "restore the New Testament church in doctrine, ordinances and life." Members (1976): 1,040,856. North American Christian Convention, Box 39456, Cincinnati, Ohio 45231.

**Christian Reformed Church:** A group of Dutch Calvinists which dissented from the Reformed Church in America in 1857 and which was strengthened by later accessions from the same source and by immigration. Members (1976): 290,638. Office of stated clerk: William P. Brink, 2850 Kalamazoo Ave., S.E., Grand Rapids, Mich. 49508.

**Church of Christ, Scientist:** Founded by Mary Baker Eddy in 1879 to reinstate the healing power of original Christianity. As defined by Mrs. Eddy, her religion is the scientific system of divine healing.[1] Headquarters: Christian Science Church, Boston, Mass. 02115.

**Church of God:** Inaugurated by Bishop A. J. Tomlinson, who served as General Overseer 1903–43. Episcopal in administration. Members (1973): 75,890. Headquarters: 2504 Arrow Wood Dr., S.E., Huntsville, Ala. 35803.

**Church of God (Anderson, Ind.):** This group is one of the largest of the groups which have taken the name "Church of God." It originated about 1880 and emphasizes Christian unity. Members (1976): 170,285. Headquarters: Box 2420, Anderson, Ind. 46011.

**Church of God (Cleveland, Tenn.):** This church is one of the large groups which use the name "Church of God." Organized in 1886 in Tennessee as the Christian Union, it was reorganized in 1902 as the Holiness Church, and in 1907 under its present name. Members (1976): 365,124. Headquarters: Keith St. at 25th., N.W., Cleveland, Tenn. 37311.

**Church of God in Christ:** Organized in Arkansas in 1895, by C. P. Jones and C. H. Mason, who believed there was no salvation without holiness; incorporated 1897. Members (1965): 425,000. Headquarters: 938 Mason St., Memphis, Tenn. 38126.

**Church of God in Christ, International:** Organized in 1969 in Kansas City, Mo., by 14 bishops of the Church of God in Christ of Memphis, Tenn., after disagreement over polity and governmental authority. Church is Wesleyan in theology. Members (1971): 501,000. Headquarters: 1905 Columbia Ave., Philadelphia, Pa. 19121.

**Church of God of Prophecy:** Organized in 1903 at Murphy, N. C. Doctrine stresses justification by faith and the second coming of Christ. Members (1975): 65,801. Headquarters: Bible Place, Cleveland, Tenn. 37311.

**Church of the Brethren:** German pietists from Krefeld, Germany, under the leadership of Peter Becker, entered the colonies in 1719, and settled at Germantown, Philadelphia, Pa. They hold to the principles of nonviolence, temperance, and the expression of religion through the good life. Members (1976): 178,157. Headquarters: 1451 Dundee Ave., Elgin, Ill. 60120.

**Church of the Nazarene:** One of the larger holiness bodies, organized in Pilot Point, Tex., in 1908. It is in general accord with the early doctrines of Methodism and emphasizes entire sanctification. Members (1976): 449,205. Headquarters: 6401 The Paseo, Kansas City, Mo. 64131.

1. Membership figure not available. The manual of the church forbids "the numbering of people and the reporting of such statistics for publication."

**Churches of Christ:** This body is made up of a large group of churches, formerly reported with the Disciples of Christ but, since the religious census of 1906, reported separately. They are strictly congregational and have no organization larger than the local congregation. Members (1976): 2,500,000.

**Community Churches, National Council of:** This body was formed in 1946 by the merger of the Biennial Council of Community Churches, a black group, with white churches which had the name of the present Council. Its members are ecumenically minded, congregationally governed, non-creedal Protestant churches. Members (1977): 125,000. Headquarters: 89 E. Wilson Bridge Rd., Worthington, Ohio, 43085.

**Congregational Christian Churches:** *See* United Church of Christ.

**Congregational Christian Churches, National Association of:** Organized in Detroit, Mich., in 1955 to continue the Congregational way of faith and order in church life. It has no doctrinal requirements, and participation by member churches is voluntary. Members (1977): 90,000. Headquarters: Box 1620, Oak Creek, Wis. 53154.

**Disciples of Christ:** *See* Christian Church.

**Episcopal Church:** *See* Protestant Episcopal Church.

**Evangelical and Reformed Church:** *See* United Church of Christ.

**Evangelical Covenant Church of America:** This church has its roots in historical Christianity as it emerged in the Protestant Reformation in the biblical instruction of the Lutheran State Church of Sweden. Organized in 1885 in Chicago. Prior to 1957, it was known as the Evangelical Mission Covenant Church of America. Members (1976): 73,458. Headquarters: 5101 N. Francisco Ave., Chicago, Ill. 60625.

**Evangelical Free Church of America:** Organized in the 1880's in Boone, Iowa, as the Swedish Evangelical Free Mission. Later the name was changed to the Evangelical Free Church of America. In 1950, the Evangelical Free Church Association merged with this group. Members (1971): 70,490. Headquarters: 1515 E. 66th St., Minneapolis, Minn. 55423.

**Evangelical United Brethren Church:** *See* United Methodist Church under Methodist Churches.

**Friends United Meeting:** The Five Years Meeting of Friends was formed in 1902 by 11 Yearly Meetings entering into a loose confederation. Since then, two of the original Yearly Meetings have withdrawn (Kansas and Oregon) and two American and three Yearly Meetings outside the U. S. have joined. In 1965, the name was changed to Friends United Meeting. Members (1976): 65,585. Office of presiding clerk: 101 Quaker Hill Dr., Richmond, Ind. 47374.

**Independent Fundamental Churches of America:** Organized in 1930 by representatives of various independent churches. Members (1975): 87,582. Headquarters: 1860 Mannheim Rd., Westchester, Ill. 60153.

**International Church of the Foursquare Gospel:** An evangelistic missionary body organized by Aimee Semple McPherson in 1927. The parent church is Angelus Temple in Los Angeles. Members (1963): 89,215.

**Jehovah's Witnesses:** A group calling themselves primitive Christians. They believe that the Kingdom under Christ will replace all earthly governments. Members (1976): 577,362. Headquarters: 124 Columbia Heights, Brooklyn, N.Y. 11201.

**Latter-day Saints, Church of Jesus Christ of:** Organized in 1830. A group in which the Bible, the Book of Mormon, the Doctrine and Covenants, and the Pearl of Great Price are regarded as the word of God. Their belief is summed up in 13 Articles of Faith written by Joseph Smith. Members (1976): 2,391,892. Headquarters: 50 E. North Temple St., Salt Lake City, Utah, 84111.

**Latter-day Saints, Reorganized Church of Jesus Christ of:** A division among the Latter-day Saints (non-Mormon) occurred on the death of Joseph Smith in 1844. His son, Joseph Smith, became presiding officer of this group, which has headquarters at Independence, Mo. Members (1976): 185,839. Headquarters: Saints Auditorium, Independence, Mo. 64051.

**Mennonite Church:** The largest group of the Mennonites who began arriving in the U. S. in 1683, settling in Germantown, Pa. They derive their name from Menno Simons, born 1496. Members (1976): 96,092. Headquarters: 528 E. Madison St., Lombard, Ill. 60148.

**Moravian Church in America (Unitas Fratrum):** In 1735, Moravian missionaries of the pre-Reformation faith of John Hus came to Georgia, in 1740 to Pennsylvania, and in 1753 to North Carolina. Members (Northern Province, 1976): 32,765; (Southern Province, 1976): 21,288. Headquarters: 69 W. Church St., Box 1245, Bethlehem, Pa. 18018; 459 S. Church St., Winston-Salem, N.C. 27108.

**Pentecostal Church of God of America, Inc.:** Organized in 1919 at Chicago, Ill. The first convention was held in October, 1933. Members (1975): 135,000. Headquarters: Messenger Plaza, 221 Main St., Joplin, Mo. 64801.

**Pentecostal Holiness Church, Inc.:** This body grew out of the holiness movement in the South and Middle West from 1895 to 1900. Members (1972): 74,108. Headquarters: Box 12609, Oklahoma City, Okla. 73112.

**Plymouth Brethren:** This orthodox and evangelical movement began in Britain in the 1820s and has since become worldwide. It is made of up two groups—the smaller "exclusive" branch, which stresses the interdependency of congregations, and the "open" branch, in which each assembly is guided by local elders. Members (1976): 74,000.

**Protestant Episcopal Church:** This group entered the colonies with the earliest settlers as the Church of England. It became autonomous, adopted its present name in 1789. It is an integral part of the

Anglican Communion. In 1967, the General Convention adopted "The Episcopal Church" as an alternate name. Members (1976): 2,882,064. Headquarters: 815 Second Ave., New York, N.Y. 10017.

**Reformed Church in America:** This group was established by the earliest Dutch settlers of New York as the Reformed Protestant Dutch Church in 1628. Members (1976): 350,734. Headquarters: 475 Riverside Dr., New York, N.Y. 10027.

**Salvation Army:** An evangelistic organization, with a military government, first set up by General William Booth in England in 1865 and introduced into the U.S. in 1880. Members (1976): 380,618. Headquarters: 120–30 W. 14th St., New York, N.Y. 10011.

**Seventh-day Adventists:** This body developed out of an interdenominational movement in the early decades of the 19th century, but was not formally organized until 1863. Their two cardinal points of faith are belief in the personal, imminent, premillennial return of Christ and observance of the seventh day as the Sabbath. Members (1976): 509,792. Headquarters: 6840 Eastern Ave., N.W., Washington, D.C. 20012.

**Triumph the Church and Kingdom of God in Christ (International):** Organized by Elder E. D. Smith in Georgia in 1902. This group emphasizes the sanctification and the Second Coming of Christ. Members (1972): 54,307. Headquarters: 213 Farrington Ave., Atlanta, Ga. 30318.

**Unitarian Universalist Association:** This association is the result of a merger in 1961 of the American Unitarian Association, formed in 1825, and the Universalist Church in America, organized in the 1770's. Members (1976): 184,552. Headquarters, 25 Beacon St., Boston, Mass. 02108.

**United Church of Christ:** A merger in 1961 of the Evangelical and Reformed Church and the Congregational Christian Churches. Members (1976): 1,801,241. Headquarters: 297 Park Ave. S., New York, N.Y. 10010.

**United Pentecostal Church International:** Pentecostal Church, Inc., and Pentecostal Assemblies of Jesus Christ merged in 1945 at St. Louis. Members (1977): 405,000. Headquarters: 8855 Dunn Rd., Hazlewood, Mo. 63042.

**Wesleyan Church:** Originated through the uniting of the Pilgrim Holiness Church (1897) and the Wesleyan Methodist Church of America (1843) in 1968. Members (1976): 96,337. Headquarters: Box 2000, Marion, Ind. 46952.

## Other Religious Groups
**(1,000–50,000 members)**

Advent Christian Church (1976: 30,997)
African Orthodox Church (1957: 6,000)
Albanian Orthodox Archdiocese in America (1974: 40,000)
Albanian Orthodox Diocese of America (1977: 5,235)
Anglican Orthodox Church (1972: 2,630)
Apostolic Christian Church (Nazarean) (1975: 4,711)
Apostolic Christian Churches of America (1977: 17,888)
Apostolic Faith (1975: 4,100)
Apostolic Lutheran Church of America (1974: 9,384)
Associate Reformed Presbyterian Church (General Synod) (1976: 31,854)
Beachy Amish Mennonite Church (1977: 4,297)
Berean Fundamental Church (1972: 2,350)
Bethel Ministerial Association (1971: 4,000)
Bible Church of Christ, (1977: 1,800)
Bible Way Church of Our Lord Jesus Christ World Wide, Inc. (1970: 30,000)
Brethren Church (Ashland, Ohio) (1976: 15,920)
Brethren in Christ Church (1976: 11,375)
Christ Catholic Church (Diocese of Boston) (1976: 1,368)
Christadelphians (1964: 15,800)
Christian Catholic Church (1975: 2,000)
Christian Church of North America, General Council (1977: 8,500)
Christian Nation Church U.S.A. (1976: 2,000)
Christian Union (1976: 4,590)
Church of Christ (1972: 2,400)
Church of Christ (Holiness) U.S.A. (1972: 9,289)
Church of God General Conference (Oregon, Ill.) (1976: 7,620)
Church of God (Seventh Day) (1960: 2,000)
Church of God (Seventh Day), Denver (1976: 8,000)
Church of God and Saints of Christ (1959: 38,217)
Church of God by Faith (1973: 4,500)
Church of God in Christ (Mennonite) (1971: 6,204)
Church of God of the Mountain Assembly (1973: 3,500)
Church of Illumination (1963: 9,000)
Church of Jesus Christ (Bickertonites) (1976: 2,444)
Church of Our Lord Jesus Christ of the Apostolic Faith, Inc. (1954: 45,000)
Church of the Living God (1964: 45,320)
Church of the Lutheran Brethren of America (1973: 9,000)
Church of the Lutheran Confession (1976: 9,817)
Churches of Christ in Christian Union (1976: 10,177)
Churches of God, General Conference (1975: 36,016)
Congregational Holiness Church (1966: 4,859)
Conservative Congregational Christian Conference (1976: 21,977)
Coptic Orthodox Church (1976: 40,000)
Duck River (and Kindred) Association of Baptists (1975: 8,632)
Elim Fellowship (1973: 5,000)
Ethical Culture Movement (1976: 5,000)
Evangelical Church of North America (1976: 11,502)
Evangelical Congregational Church (1977: 28,840)
Evangelical Friends Alliance (1975: 25,531)
Evangelical Lutheran Church in America (Eielsen Synod) (1957: 2,500)
Evangelical Lutheran Synod (1976: 19,571)
Evangelical Mennonite Brethren Conference (1972: 3,874)
Evangelical Mennonite Church, Inc. (1977: 3,484)
Evangelical Methodist Church (1974: 10,502)
Free Christian Zion Church of Christ (1956: 22,260)
Free Lutheran Congregations, Association of (1977: 13,946)
Friends General Conference (1974: 26,184)
General Church of the New Jerusalem (1971: 2,143)
General Conference of Mennonite Brethren Churches (1976: 16,956)
General Convention, The Swedenborgian Church (1975: 3,500)
General Council of the Evangelical Baptist Churches, Inc. (1952: 2,200)
Grace Brethren Churches, Fellowship of (1975: 37,727)
Grace Gospel Fellowship (1976: 3,200)
Holy Ukrainian Autocephalic Orthodox Church in Exile (1965: 4,800)
House of God, Which Is the Church of the Living God, the Pillar and Ground of the Truth, Inc. (1956: 2,350)
Hungarian Reformed Church in America (1975: 11,679)
Hutterian Bretheren (1976: 3,500)
International Pentecostal Assemblies (1971: 10,000)
Latvian Evangelical Lutheran Church in America (1976: 13,247)
Liberal Catholic Church—Province of the United States of America (1973: 2,393)
Mennonite Church, The General Conference (1976: 36,397)

Metropolitan Community Churches, Universal Fellowship of (1977: 23,012)
Missionary Church, The (1972: 20,078)
National Spiritual Alliance of the U.S.A., The (1971: 3,230)
National Spiritualist Association of Churches (1976: 5,168)
Netherlands Reformed Congregations (1975: 4,878)
New Apostolic Church of North America (1976: 24,361)
North American Baptist Conference (1976: 42,277)
North American Old Roman Catholic Church (1976: 1,675)
Old German Baptist Brethren (1975: 4,810)
Old Order Amish Church (1972: 14,720)
Old Order (Wisler) Mennonite (1972: 8,000)
Open Bible Standard Churches, Inc. (1975: 2,500)
(Original) Church of God, Inc., The (1971: 20,000)
Orthodox Presbyterian Church, The (1976: 15,306)
Pentecostal Assemblies of the World, Inc. (1960: 4,500)
Pentecostal Church of Christ (1975: 1,659)
Pentecostal Free-Will Baptist Church (1976: 15,000)
Pillar of Fire (1949: 5,100)
Primitive Methodist Church, U.S.A. (1977: 10,519)
Protestant Conference (Lutheran), The (1976: 2,660)
Protestant Reformed Churches in America (1977: 3,871)
Reformed Church in the United States (1976: 3,861)
Reformed Episcopal Church (1972: 6,532)
Reformed Methodist Union Episcopal Church (1976: 3,800)
Reformed Presbyterian Church, Evangelical Synod (1976: 24,248)
Reformed Presbyterian Church of North America (1974: 5,445)
Reformed Zion Union Apostolic Church (1965: 16,000)
Religious Society of Friends (Conservative) (1976: 1,728)
Religious Society of Friends (Unaffiliated Meetings) (1975: 5,696)
Romanian Orthodox Episcopate of America, The (1976: 40,000)
Schwenkfelder Church, The (1976: 2,748)
Second Cumberland Presbyterian Church in U.S. (1959: 30,000)
Separate Baptists in Christ (1962: 7,496)
Seventh-Day Baptist General Conference (1976: 5,139)
Social Brethren (1975: 1,784)
Southern Methodist Church (1977: 11,000)
Ukrainian Orthodox Church in America (Ecumenical Patriarchate) (1976: 27,000)
United Brethren in Christ (1976: 28,035)
United Holy Church of America (1960: 28,980)
Unity of the Brethren (1964: 6,142)
Vedanta Society of New York (1976: 1,000)
Volunteers of America (1976: 35,640)

## Roman Catholic Pontiffs

St. Peter, of Bethsaida in Galilee, Prince of the Apostles, was the first Pope. He lived first in Antioch and then in Rome for 25 years. In AD 64 or 67, he was martyred. St. Linus became the second Pope.

| | | Reigned | |
|---|---|---|---|
| **Name** | **Birthplace** | **From** | **To** |
| St. Linus | Tuscia | 67 | 76 |
| St. Anacletus (Cletus) | Rome | 76 | 88 |
| St. Clement | Rome | 88 | 97 |
| St. Evaristus | Greece | 97 | 105 |
| St. Alexander I | Rome | 105 | 115 |
| St. Sixtus I | Rome | 115 | 125 |
| St. Telesphorus | Greece | 125 | 136 |
| St. Hyginus | Greece | 136 | 140 |
| St. Pius I | Aquilcia | 140 | 155 |
| St. Anicetus | Syria | 155 | 166 |
| St. Soter | Campania | 166 | 175 |
| St. Eleutherius | Epirus | 175 | 189 |
| St. Victor I | Africa | 189 | 199 |
| St. Zephyrinus | Rome | 199 | 217 |
| St. Callistus I | Rome | 217 | 222 |
| St. Urban I | Rome | 222 | 230 |
| St. Pontian | Rome | 230 | 235 |
| St. Anterus | Greece | 235 | 236 |
| St. Fabian | Rome | 236 | 250 |
| St. Cornelius | Rome | 251 | 253 |
| St. Lucius I | Rome | 253 | 254 |
| St. Stephen I | Rome | 254 | 257 |
| St. Sixtus II | Greece | 257 | 258 |
| St. Dionysius | Unknown | 259 | 268 |
| St. Felix I | Rome | 269 | 274 |
| St. Eutychian | Luni | 275 | 283 |
| St. Caius | Dalmatia | 283 | 296 |
| St. Marcellinus | Rome | 296 | 304 |
| St. Marcellus I | Rome | 308 | 309 |
| St. Eusebius | Greece | 309[1] | 309[1] |
| St. Meltiades | Africa | 311 | 314 |
| St. Sylvester I | Rome | 314 | 335 |
| St. Marcus | Rome | 336 | 336 |
| St. Julius I | Rome | 337 | 352 |
| Liberius | Rome | 352 | 366 |
| St. Damasus I | Spain | 366 | 384 |
| St. Siricius | Rome | 384 | 399 |
| St. Anastasius I | Rome | 399 | 401 |
| St. Innocent I | Albano | 401 | 417 |
| St. Zozimus | Greece | 417 | 418 |
| St. Boniface I | Rome | 418 | 422 |
| St. Celestine I | Campania | 422 | 432 |
| St. Sixtus III | Rome | 432 | 440 |
| St. Leo I (the Great) | Tuscany | 440 | 461 |
| St. Hilary | Sardinia | 461 | 468 |
| St. Simplicius | Tivoli | 468 | 483 |
| St. Felix III (II)[2] | Rome | 483 | 492 |
| St. Gelasius I | Africa | 492 | 496 |
| Anastasius II | Rome | 496 | 498 |
| St. Symmachus | Sardinia | 498 | 514 |
| St. Hormisdas | Frosinone | 514 | 523 |
| St. John I | Tuscany | 523 | 526 |
| St. Felix IV (III) | Samnium | 526 | 530 |
| Boniface II | Rome | 530 | 532 |
| John II | Rome | 533 | 535 |
| St. Agapitus I | Rome | 535 | 536 |
| St. Silverius | Campania | 536 | 537 |
| Vigilius | Rome | 537 | 555 |
| Pelagius I | Rome | 556 | 561 |
| John III | Rome | 561 | 574 |
| Benedict I | Rome | 575 | 579 |
| Pelagius II | Rome | 579 | 590 |
| St. Gregory I (the Great) | Rome | 590 | 604 |
| Sabinianus | Tuscany | 604 | 606 |
| Boniface III | Rome | 607 | 607 |
| St. Boniface IV | Marsi | 608 | 615 |
| St. Deusdedit (Adeodatus I) | Rome | 615 | 618 |
| Boniface V | Naples | 619 | 625 |
| Honorius I | Campania | 625 | 638 |
| Severinus | Rome | 640 | 640 |
| John IV | Dalmatia | 640 | 642 |
| Theodore I | Greece | 642 | 649 |
| St. Martin I | Todi | 649 | 655 |
| St. Eugene I[3] | Rome | 654 | 657 |
| St. Vitalian | Segni | 657 | 672 |
| Adeodatus II | Rome | 672 | 676 |

| Name | Birthplace | Reigned From | To |
|---|---|---|---|
| Donus | Rome | 676 | 678 |
| St. Agatho | Sicily | 678 | 681 |
| St. Leo II | Sicily | 682 | 683 |
| St. Benedict II | Rome | 684 | 685 |
| John V | Syria | 685 | 686 |
| Conon | Unknown | 686 | 687 |
| St. Sergius I | Syria | 687 | 701 |
| John VI | Greece | 701 | 705 |
| John VII | Greece | 705 | 707 |
| Sisinnius | Syria | 708 | 708 |
| Constantine | Syria | 708 | 715 |
| St. Gregory II | Rome | 715 | 731 |
| St. Gregory III | Syria | 731 | 741 |
| St. Zachary | Greece | 741 | 752 |
| Stephen II (III)[4] | Rome | 752 | 757 |
| St. Paul I | Rome | 757 | 767 |
| Stephen III (IV) | Sicily | 768 | 772 |
| Adrian I | Rome | 772 | 795 |
| St. Leo III | Rome | 795 | 816 |
| Stephen IV (V) | Rome | 816 | 817 |
| St. Paschal I | Rome | 817 | 824 |
| Eugene II | Rome | 824 | 827 |
| Valentine | Rome | 827 | 827 |
| Gregory IV | Rome | 827 | 844 |
| Sergius II | Rome | 844 | 847 |
| St. Leo IV | Rome | 847 | 855 |
| Benedict III | Rome | 855 | 858 |
| St. Nicholas I (the Great) | Rome | 858 | 867 |
| Adrian II | Rome | 867 | 872 |
| John VIII | Rome | 872 | 882 |
| Marinus I | Gallese | 882 | 884 |
| St. Adrian III | Rome | 884 | 885 |
| Stephen V (VI) | Rome | 885 | 891 |
| Formosus | Portus | 891 | 896 |
| Boniface VI | Rome | 896 | 896 |
| Stephen VI (VII) | Rome | 896 | 897 |
| Romanus | Gallese | 897 | 897 |
| Theodore II | Rome | 897 | 897 |
| John IX | Tivoli | 898 | 900 |
| Benedict IV | Rome | 900 | 903 |
| Leo V | Ardea | 903 | 903 |
| Sergius III | Rome | 904 | 911 |
| Anastasius III | Rome | 911 | 913 |
| Landus | Sabina | 913 | 914 |
| John X | Tossignano | 914 | 928 |
| Leo VI | Rome | 928 | 928 |
| Stephen VII (VIII) | Rome | 928 | 931 |
| John XI | Rome | 931 | 935 |
| Leo VII | Rome | 936 | 939 |
| Stephen VIII (IX) | Rome | 939 | 942 |
| Marinus II | Rome | 942 | 946 |
| Agapitus II | Rome | 946 | 955 |
| John XII | Tusculum | 955 | 964 |
| Leo VIII[5] | Rome | 963 | 965 |
| Benedict V[5] | Rome | 964 | 966 |
| John XIII | Rome | 965 | 972 |
| Benedict VI | Rome | 973 | 974 |
| Benedict VII | Rome | 974 | 983 |
| John XIV | Pavia | 983 | 984 |
| John XV | Rome | 985 | 996 |
| Gregory V | Saxony | 996 | 999 |
| Sylvester II | Auvergne | 999 | 1003 |
| John XVII | Rome | 1003 | 1003 |
| John XVIII | Rome | 1004 | 1009 |
| Sergius IV | Rome | 1009 | 1012 |
| Benedict VIII | Tusculum | 1012 | 1024 |
| John XIX | Tusculum | 1024 | 1032 |
| Benedict IX[6] | Tusculum | 1032 | 1044 |
| Sylvester III | Rome | 1045 | 1045 |

| Name | Birthplace | Reigned From | To |
|---|---|---|---|
| Benedict IX (2nd time) | — | 1045 | 1045 |
| Gregory VI | Rome | 1045 | 1046 |
| Clement II | Saxony | 1046 | 1047 |
| Benedict IX (3rd time) | — | 1047 | 1048 |
| Damasus II | Bavaria | 1048 | 1048 |
| St. Leo IX | Alsace | 1049 | 1054 |
| Victor II | Germany | 1055 | 1057 |
| Stephen IX (X) | Lorraine | 1057 | 1058 |
| Nicholas II | Burgundy | 1059 | 1061 |
| Alexander II | Milan | 1061 | 1073 |
| St. Gregory VII | Tuscany | 1073 | 1085 |
| Bl. Victor III | Benevento | 1086 | 1087 |
| Bl. Urban II | France | 1088 | 1099 |
| Paschal II | Ravenna | 1099 | 1118 |
| Gelasius II | Gaeta | 1118 | 1119 |
| Callistus II | Burgundy | 1119 | 1124 |
| Honorius II | Fiagnano | 1124 | 1130 |
| Innocent II | Rome | 1130 | 1143 |
| Celestine II | Città di Castello | 1143 | 1144 |
| Lucius II | Bologna | 1144 | 1145 |
| Bl. Eugene III | Pisa | 1145 | 1153 |
| Anastasius IV | Rome | 1153 | 1154 |
| Adrian IV | England | 1154 | 1159 |
| Alexander III | Siena | 1159 | 1181 |
| Lucius III | Lucca | 1181 | 1185 |
| Urban III | Milan | 1185 | 1187 |
| Gregory VIII | Benevento | 1187 | 1187 |
| Clement III | Rome | 1187 | 1191 |
| Celestine III | Rome | 1191 | 1198 |
| Innocent III | Anagni | 1198 | 1216 |
| Honorius III | Rome | 1216 | 1227 |
| Gregory IX | Anagni | 1227 | 1241 |
| Celestine IV | Milan | 1241 | 1241 |
| Innocent IV | Genoa | 1243 | 1254 |
| Alexander IV | Anagni | 1254 | 1261 |
| Urban IV | Troyes | 1261 | 1264 |
| Clement IV | France | 1265 | 1268 |
| Bl. Gregory X | Piacenza | 1271 | 1276 |
| Bl. Innocent V | Savoy | 1276 | 1276 |
| Adrian V | Genoa | 1276 | 1276 |
| John XXI[7] | Portugal | 1276 | 1277 |
| Nicholas III | Rome | 1277 | 1280 |
| Martin IV[8] | France | 1281 | 1285 |
| Honorius IV | Rome | 1285 | 1287 |
| Nicholas IV | Ascoli | 1288 | 1292 |
| St. Celestine V | Isernia | 1294 | 1294 |
| Boniface VIII | Anagni | 1294 | 1303 |
| Bl. Benedict XI | Treviso | 1303 | 1304 |
| Clement V | France | 1305 | 1314 |
| John XXII | Cahors | 1316 | 1334 |
| Benedict XII | France | 1334 | 1342 |
| Clement VI | France | 1342 | 1352 |
| Innocent VI | France | 1352 | 1362 |
| Bl. Urban V | France | 1362 | 1370 |
| Gregory XI | France | 1370 | 1378 |
| Urban VI | Naples | 1378 | 1389 |
| Boniface IX | Naples | 1389 | 1404 |
| Innocent VII | Sulmona | 1404 | 1406 |
| Gregory XII | Venice | 1406 | 1415 |
| Martin V | Rome | 1417 | 1431 |
| Eugene IV | Venice | 1431 | 1447 |
| Nicholas V | Sarzana | 1447 | 1455 |
| Callistus III | Jativa | 1455 | 1458 |
| Pius II | Siena | 1458 | 1464 |
| Paul II | Venice | 1464 | 1471 |
| Sixtus IV | Savona | 1471 | 1484 |
| Innocent VIII | Genoa | 1484 | 1492 |

| Name | Birthplace | Reigned From | To | Name | Birthplace | Reigned From | To |
|---|---|---|---|---|---|---|---|
| Alexander VI | Jativa | 1492 | 1503 | Clement X | Rome | 1670 | 1676 |
| Pius III | Siena | 1503 | 1503 | Bl. Innocent XI | Como | 1676 | 1689 |
| Julius II | Savona | 1503 | 1513 | Alexander VIII | Venice | 1689 | 1691 |
| Leo X | Florence | 1513 | 1521 | Innocent XII | Spinazzola | 1691 | 1700 |
| Adrian VI | Utrecht | 1522 | 1523 | Clement XI | Urbino | 1700 | 1721 |
| Clement VII | Florence | 1523 | 1534 | Innocent XIII | Rome | 1721 | 1724 |
| Paul III | Rome | 1534 | 1549 | Benedict XIII | Gravina | 1724 | 1730 |
| Julius III | Rome | 1550 | 1555 | Clement XII | Florence | 1730 | 1740 |
| Marcellus II | Montepulciano | 1555 | 1555 | Benedict XIV | Bologna | 1740 | 1758 |
| Paul IV | Naples | 1555 | 1559 | Clement XIII | Venice | 1758 | 1769 |
| Pius IV | Milan | 1559 | 1565 | Clement XIV | Rimini | 1769 | 1774 |
| St. Pius V | Bosco | 1566 | 1572 | Pius VI | Cesena | 1775 | 1799 |
| Gregory XIII | Bologna | 1572 | 1585 | Pius VII | Cesena | 1800 | 1823 |
| Sixtus V | Grottammare | 1585 | 1590 | Leo XII | Genga | 1823 | 1829 |
| Urban VII | Rome | 1590 | 1590 | Pius VIII | Cingoli | 1829 | 1830 |
| Gregory XIV | Cremona | 1590 | 1591 | Gregory XVI | Belluno | 1831 | 1846 |
| Innocent IX | Bologna | 1591 | 1591 | Pius IX | Senegallia | 1846 | 1878 |
| Clement VIII | Florence | 1592 | 1605 | Leo XIII | Carpineto | 1878 | 1903 |
| Leo XI | Florence | 1605 | 1605 | St. Pius X | Riese | 1903 | 1914 |
| Paul V | Rome | 1605 | 1621 | Benedict XV | Genoa | 1914 | 1922 |
| Gregory XV | Bologna | 1621 | 1623 | Pius XI | Desio | 1922 | 1939 |
| Urban VIII | Florence | 1623 | 1644 | Pius XII | Rome | 1939 | 1958 |
| Innocent X | Rome | 1644 | 1655 | John XXIII | Sotto il Monte | 1958 | 1963 |
| Alexander VII | Siena | 1655 | 1667 | Paul VI | Concesio | 1963 | 1978 |
| Clement IX | Pistoia | 1667 | 1669 | John Paul I | Forno di Canale | 1978 | |

1. Or 310. 2. He should be called Felix II, and his successors of the same name should be numbered accordingly. The discrepancy was caused by the erroneous insertion in some lists of the name of St. Felix of Rome, Martyr. 3. He was elected during the exile of St. Martin I, who endorsed him as Pope. 4. After St. Zachary died, a Roman priest named Stephen was elected but died before his consecration as Bishop of Rome. His name is not included in all lists for this reason. In view of this historical confusion, the *National Catholic Almanac* lists the true Stephen II as Stephen II (III), the true Stephen III as Stephen III (IV), etc. 5. Confusion exists concerning the legitimacy of claims. If the deposition of John was invalid, Leo was an antipope until after the end of Benedict's reign. If the deposition of John was valid, Leo was the legitimate Pope and Benedict an antipope. 6. If the triple removal of Benedict IX was not valid, Sylvester III, Gregory VI, and Clement II were antipopes. 7. Elimination was made of the name of John XX in an effort to rectify the numerical designation of Popes named John. The error dates back to the time of John XV. 8. The names of Marinus I and Marinus II were construed as Martin. In view of these two pontificates and the earlier reign of St. Martin I, this pontiff was called Martin IV. *Source: National Catholic Almanac, from Annuario Pontificio*

## Antipopes

Antipopes were those who falsely claimed Papal Sovereignty. The dates and, in some cases, Roman numerals after the names account for occasional discrepancies in the succession of the Popes.

| Name | Alleged reign | Name | Alleged reign | Name | Alleged reign |
|---|---|---|---|---|---|
| St. Hippolytus | 217–235 | Christopher | 903–904 | Victor IV | 1138 |
| Novatian | 251 | Boniface VII | 974; 984–985 | Victor IV[1] | 1159–1164 |
| Felix II | 355–365 | John XVI | 997–998 | Paschal III | 1164–1168 |
| Ursinus | 366–367 | Gregory | ended 1012 | Callistus III | 1168–1178 |
| Eulalius | 418–419 | Benedict X | 1058–1059 | Innocent III | 1179–1180 |
| Lawrence | 498; 501–505 | Honorius II | 1061–1072 | Nicholas V | 1328–1330 |
| Dioscorus | 530 | Clement III | 1080–1100 | Clement VII | 1378–1394 |
| Theodore | ended 687 | Theodoric | ended 1100 | Benedict XIII | 1394–1423 |
| Paschal | ended 687 | Albert | ended 1102 | Alexander V | 1409–1410 |
| Constantine | 767–769 | Sylvester IV | 1105–1111 | John XXIII | 1410–1415 |
| Philip | 768 | Gregory VIII | 1118–1121 | Felix V | 1439–1449 |
| John | ended 844 | Celestine II | ended 1124 | | |
| Anastasius | 855 | Anacletus II | 1130–1138 | | |

1. Did not recognize his predecessor of 1138, who, only two months after claiming the Papacy, submitted to the rightful Pope, Innocent II.

# U.S. SOCIETIES & ASSOCIATIONS

*Source: Information Please* questionnaires to organizations.

Names are listed alphabetically according to key word in title; figure in parentheses is year of founding; other figure is membership.

**Abortion Federation, National** (1976): 110 E. 59th St., New York, N.Y. 10022. Judith Widdicombe, President.

**Aeronautic Association, National** (1922): 821 15th St., N.W., Washington, D.C. 20005. 160,000; Vic Powell, Executive Director.

**Aeronautics and Astronautics, American Institute of** (1932): 1290 Avenue of the Americas, New York, N.Y. 10019. 26,750; James J. Harford, Executive Secretary.

**African-American Institute, The** (1953): 833 United Nations Plaza, New York, N.Y. 10017. M. Sandra Sennett, Assistant to the President.

**Air Pollution Control Association** (1907): P.O. Box 2861, Pittsburgh, Pa. 15230. 6,700; Lewis H. Rogers, Executive Vice President.

**Alcoholics Anonymous** (1935): P.O. Box 459, Grand Central Station, New York, N.Y. 10017. 1,000,000. Address communications to Secretary.

**America-Mideast Educational and Training Services, Inc.** (1951): 1717 Massachusetts Ave., N.W., Washington, D.C. 20036. 500; Virgil C. Crippin, President.

**American Federation of Labor and Congress of Industrial Organizations (AFL-CIO)** (1955): 815 16th St., N.W., Washington, D.C. 20006. 13,600,000; Albert J. Zack, Director of Public Relations.

**American Friends Service Committee** (1917): 1501 Cherry St., Philadelphia, Pa. 19102. Marjorie Seeley, Information Associate.

**American Legion** (1919): P.O. Box 1055, Indianapolis, Ind. 46206. 2,500,000; Frank C. Momsen, National Adjutant.

**American Legion Auxiliary** (1919): 777 N. Meridian St., Indianapolis, Ind. 46204. 940,000; Doris Anderson, National Secretary.

**Americans for Democratic Action** (1947): 1411 K St., N.W., Washington D.C. 20005. 75,000; Leon Shull, National Director.

**Animals, American Society for the Prevention of Cruelty to** (1866): 441 E. 92nd St., New York, N.Y. 10028. 3,000; Louis F. Bishop, Jr., Chairman.

**Anti-Vivisection Society, The American** (1883): 1903 Chestnut St., Philadelphia, Pa. 19103. 15,000; Owen B. Hunt, President.

**Arbitration Association, American** (1926): 140 W. 51st St., New York, N.Y. 10020. 4,310; E. W. Dippold, Corporate Secretary.

**Arthritis Foundation** (1948): 3400 Peachtree Rd., N.E., Atlanta, Ga. 30326. 73 local chapters; Clifford M. Clarke, President.

**Arts and Letters, American Academy and Institute of** (1904): 633 W. 155th St., New York, N.Y. 10032. 250; Margaret M. Mills, Executive Director.

**Astronomical Society, American** (1899): Leander-McCormick Observatory, Box 3818, University Station, Charlottesville, Va. 22903. 3,500; Laurence W. Fredrick, Secretary.

**Athletic Union of the U.S., Amateur** (1888): 3400 W. 86th St., Indianapolis, Ind. 46268. 372,000 registered athletes; Ollan Cassell, Executive Director.

**Audubon Society, National** (1905): 950 Third Ave., New York, N.Y. 10022. 365,000; Andrew Bihun, Environmental Information.

**Authors League of America** (1912): 234 W. 44th St., New York, N.Y. 10036. 7,500.

**Automobile Association, American** (1902): 8111 Gatehouse Rd., Falls Church, Va. 22042. 19,500,000; J. B. Creal, President.

**Bible Society, American** (1816): 1865 Broadway, New York, N.Y. 10023. 514,000; Charles W. Baas, John D. Erickson, General Officers.

**Big Brothers/Big Sisters of America** (1977): 220 Suburban Station Bldg., Philadelphia, Pa. 19103. Caroline Meline, Information Services Coordinator.

**Blind, National Federation of the** (1940): 212 Dupont Circle Bldg., 1346 Connecticut Ave., N.W., Washington, D.C. 20036. 50,000; Ralph Sanders, President.

**Blindness, National Society for the Prevention of** (1908): 79 Madison Ave., New York, N.Y. 10016. 327; Virginia Boyce, Executive Director.

**Blue Shield Association** (1946): 211 E. Chicago Ave., Chicago, Ill. 60611. 70 affiliates; Tom K. Mura, Vice President, Public Relations and Advertising.

**B'nai B'rith** (1843): 1640 Rhode Island Ave., N.W., Washington, D.C. 20036. 500,000; Hank Siegel, Director of Communications.

**B'nai B'rith, Anti-Defamation League of** (1913): 315 Lexington Ave., New York, N.Y. 10016. Benjamin R. Epstein, National Director.

**Boy Scouts of America** (1910): North Brunswick, N.J. 08902. 4,884,082.

**Boys' Clubs of America** (1906): 771 First Ave., New York, N.Y. 10017. 1,000,000; Joan R. Licursi, Director of Communications Services.

**Brookings Institution, The** (1927): 1775 Massachusetts Ave., N.W., Washington, D.C. 20036. James D. Farrell, Information Editor.

**Camp Fire Girls, Inc.** (1910): 4601 Madison Ave., Kansas City, Mo. 64112. 750,000; Dr. Hester Turner, National Executive Director.

**Camping Association, The American** (1910): Bradford Woods, Martinsville, Ind. 46151. 6,000; Armand Ball, Executive Vice President.

**Cancer Society, American** (1913): 777 Third Ave., New York, N.Y. 10017. 2,300,000; Lane W. Adams, Executive Vice President.

**CARE (Cooperative for American Relief Everywhere)** (1945): 660 First Ave., New York, N.Y. 10016. 24 agencies; Frank Goffio, Executive Director.

**Catholic Bishops, National Conference of** (1966): 1312 Massachusetts Ave., N.W., Washington, D.C. 20005. 340; Most Rev. John R. Quinn, President.

**Catholic Charities, National Conference of** (1910): 1346 Connecticut Ave., N.W., Washington, D.C. 20036. 3,000; Rev. Msgr. Lawrence Corcoran, Executive Director.

**Catholic Conference, United States** (1966): 1312 Massachusetts Ave., N.W., Washington, D.C. 20005. Bishop Thomas C. Kelly, O.P., General Secretary.

**Catholic Daughters of America** (1903): 10 W. 71st St., New York, N.Y. 10023. 180,000; Lorraine McMahon, Executive Secretary.

**Catholic War Veterans of the U.S.A.** (1935): 2 Massachusetts Ave., N.W., Washington, D.C. 20001. 75,000; Henry W. Woyach, National Commander.

**Cerebral Palsy Associations, Inc., United** (1949): 66 E. 34th St., New York, N.Y. 10016. 250 affiliates; Earl H. Cunerd, Executive Director.

**Chamber of Commerce of the U.S.** (1912): 1615 H St., N.W., Washington, D.C. 20006. 74,000; Richard L. Lesher, President.

**Chemical Society, American** (1876): 1155 16th St., N.W., Washington, D.C. 20036. 111,000; Raymond P. Mariella, Executive Director.

**Child Study Association of America/Wel Met, Inc.** (1900): 50 Madison Ave., New York, N.Y. 10010. Harriet Dronska, Executive Director.

**Christians and Jews, National Conference of** (1928): 43 W. 57th St., New York, N.Y. 10019. 200,000; David Hyatt, President.

**Churches, National Council of** (1950): 475 Riverside Drive, New York, N.Y. 10027. 31 Protestant and Orthodox communions; Claire Randall, General Secretary.

**Civil Liberties Union, American** (1920): 22 E. 40th St., New York, N.Y. 10016. 200,000; Alan Reitman, Associate Director.

**Colored Women's Clubs, National Association of** (1896): 5808 16th St., N.W., Washington, D.C. 20011. 50,000; Mrs. Inez W. Tinsley, National President.

**Common Cause** (1970): 2030 M St., N.W., Washington, D.C. 20036. 255,000; Nan Waterman, Chairwoman.

**Composers, Authors, and Publishers, American Society of (ASCAP)** (1914): One Lincoln Plaza, New York, N.Y. 10023. 23,400; Stanley Adams, President.

**Congress of Racial Equality (CORE)** (1942): 1916–38 Park Ave., New York, N.Y. 10035. Nationwide network of chapters; Roy Innis, National Director.

**Conscientious Objectors, Central Committee for** (1948): 2016 Walnut St., Philadelphia, Pa. 19103.

**Contract Bridge League, American** (1927): 2200 Democrat Rd., Memphis, Tenn. 38116. 200,000; Richard L. Goldberg, Executive Secretary.

**Cooperative League of the U.S.A.** (1916): 1828 L St., N.W., Washington, D.C. 20036. 30,000,000 families; Glenn M. Anderson, President.

**Country Music Association** (1958): 7 Music Circle North, Nashville, Tenn. 37203. 5,000; Jo Walker, Executive Director.

**Crime and Delinquency, National Council on** (1907): Continental Plaza, Hackensack, N.J. 07601. Nationwide membership; Milton G. Rector, President.

**Daughters of the American Revolution, National Society** (1890): 1776 D St., N.W., Washington, D.C. 20006. 206,000; Mrs. George Upham Baylies, President General.

**Daughters of the Confederacy, United** (1894): 328 N. Boulevard, Richmond, Va. 23220. 26,000; Mrs. Charlotte P. Crippen, Executive Secretary.

**Democratic Club, National** (1834): Chemists Club, 52 E. 41st St., New York, N.Y. 10017. 500; James Driscoll, Secretary.

**Dental Association, American** (1859): 211 E. Chicago Ave., Chicago, Ill. 60611. 131,066; C. Gordon Watson, Executive Director.

**Diabetes Association, American** (1940): 600 Fifth Ave., New York, N.Y. 10020. John L. Dugan, Jr., Executive Vice President.

**Dignity** (1969): 3719 Sixth Ave., San Diego, Calif. 92103. 6,000; Carla Kaesbauer, Acting President.

**Disabled American Veterans** (1922): P.O. Box 14301, Cincinnati, Ohio 45214. 550,000; Richard M. Wilson, Assistant Adjutant for Public Relations.

**Eagles, Fraternal Order of** (1898): 2401 W. Wisconsin Ave., Milwaukee, Wis. 53233. 850,000; Art Ehrmann, Publications Editor.

**Easter Seal Society for Crippled Children and Adults, The National** (1921): 2023 W. Ogden Ave., Chicago, Ill. 60612. 52 affiliated state societies; Donald W. Ullman, Acting Executive Director.

**Eastern Star, Order of the, General Grand Chapter** (1876): 1618 New Hampshire Ave., N.W., Washington, D.C. 20009. 3,000,000; Mabel L. Mackereth, Most Worthy Grand Matron.

**Education Association, National** (1857): 1201 16th St., N.W., Washington, D.C. 20036. 1,600,000; Terry Herndon, Executive Director.

**Electrochemical Society, Inc., The** (1902): P.O. Box 2071, Princeton, N.J. 08540. 4,476; V. H. Branneky, Executive Secretary.

**Elks of the U.S.A., Benevolent and Protective Order of the** (1868): 2750 Lake View Ave., Chicago, Ill. 60614. 1,630,000; Stanley F. Kocur, Grand Secretary.

**English-Speaking Union of the United States** (1920): 16 E. 69th St., New York, N.Y. 10021. 32,000; Charles P. Dennison, Executive Director.

**Exploration Geophysicists, Society of** (1930): P.O. Box 3098, Tulsa, Okla. 74101. 11,200; H. R. Breck, Executive Director.

**Family Service Association of America** (1911): 44 E. 23rd St., New York, N.Y. 10010. 290 member agencies; W. Keith Daugherty, General Director.

**Farm Bureau Federation, American** (1919): 225 Touhy Ave., Park Ridge, Ill. 60068. 2,800,000 member families; J. Patrick Batts, Director of Information.

**Fleet Reserve Association** (1924): 1303 New Hampshire Ave., N.W., Washington, D.C. 20036. 140,000; Robert W. Nolan, National Executive Secretary.

**Foreign Policy Association** (1918): 345 E. 46th St., New York, N.Y. 10017. Thetis Reavis, Director of Public Programs.

**Foreign Relations, Inc., Council on** (1921): 58 E. 68th St., New York, N.Y. 10021. 1,796; Winston Lord, President.

**Foster Parents Plan International** (1937): Box 400, Warwick, R.I. 02887. 103,000; George W. Ross, International Executive Director.

**4-H Program** (early 1900s): SEA-Extension, U.S. Department of Agriculture, Washington, D.C. 20250. 5,500,000; E. Dean Vaughan, Director.

**Geographic Society, National** (1888): 17th and M Sts., N.W., Washington, D.C. 20036. 10,000,000; Gilbert M. Grosvenor, Editor.

**Geriatrics Society, American** (1942): 10 Columbus Circle, New York, N.Y. 10019. 9,000; Kathryn S. Henderson, Executive Director.

**Gideons International, The** (1899): 2900 Lebanon Rd., Nashville, Tenn. 37214. 55,000; M.A. Henderson, Executive Director.

**Girl Scouts of the U.S.A., Inc.** (1912): 830 Third Ave., New York, N.Y. 10022. 3,140,000; Richard G. Knox, Director of Public Relations.

**Girls Clubs of America** (1945): 205 Lexington Ave., New York, N.Y. 10016. 215,000; Edith B. Phelps, National Executive Director.

**Hadassah, The Women's Zionist Organization of America** (1912): 50 W. 58th St., New York, N.Y. 10019. 360,000; Aline Kaplan, Executive Director.

**Health, Physical Education and Recreation, American Alliance for** (1885): 1201 16th St., N.W., Washington, D.C. 20036. 50,000; George F. Anderson, Executive Director.

**Hearing and Speech Action, National Association for** (1919): 814 Thayer Ave., Silver Spring, Md. 20910. 153 agencies.

**Heart Association, Inc., American** (1924): 7320 Greenville Ave., Dallas, Tex. 75231. 115,000; William W. Moore, Executive Vice President.

**Hemispheric Affairs, Council on** (1975): 1735 New Hampshire Ave., N.W., Washington, D.C. 20009. Laurence R. Birns, Director.

**Home Economics Association, American** (1909): 2010 Massachusetts Ave., N.W., Washington, D.C. 20036. 52,000; Kinsey Green, Executive Director.

**Horticultural Society, American** (1922): Mt. Vernon, Va. 22121. 35,000; Thomas W. Richards, Executive Vice President.

**Hospital Association, American** (1898): 840 N. Lake Shore Dr., Chicago, Ill. 60611. 6,300 institutions; J. Alexander McMahon, President.

**Humane Association, American** (1877): 5351 S. Roslyn St., Englewood, Colo. 80110. Milton C. Searle, Executive Director.

**Imperial Council of Ancient Arabic Order of Nobles of the Mystic Shrine** (1872): 323 N. Michigan Ave., Chicago, Ill. 60601. 937,712; Charles Cumpstone, Executive Secretary.

**Indian Rights Association** (1882): 1505 Race St., Philadelphia, Pa. 19102. 2,400; Sandra L. Cadwalader, Executive Director.

**Intercollegiate Athletics, National Association of** (1940): 1221 Baltimore St., Kansas City, Mo. 64105. 515; Harry Fritz, Executive Director.

**Intercollegiate (Big Ten) Conference** (1896): 1111 Plaza Dr., Schaumburg, Ill. 60195. Jeff Elliott, Service Bureau Director.

**Interfraternity Conference, National** (1909): 3901 W. 86th St., Indianapolis, Ind. 46268. 48; Jack L. Anson, Executive Director.

**Jewish Appeal Inc., United** (1939): 1290 Avenue of the Americas, New York, N.Y. 10019. Irving Bernstein, Executive Vice Chairman.

**Jewish Committee, American** (1906): 165 E. 56th St., New York, N.Y. 10022. 40,000; Morton Yarmon, Director of Public Relations.

**Jewish Community Centers, World Confederation of** (1946): 15 E. 26th St., New York, N.Y. 10010. Herbert Millman, Executive Director.

**Jewish War Veterans of the U.S.A.** (1896): 1712 New Hampshire Ave., N.W., Washington, D.C. 20009.

**Jewish Women, National Council of** (1893): 15 E. 26th St., New York, N.Y. 10010. Esther R. Landa, National President.

**John Birch Society** (1958): 395 Concord Ave., Belmont, Mass. 02178. 100,000; Ellen Sproul, Clerk of Corporation.

**Judaism, American Council for** (1943): 307 Fifth Ave., New York, N.Y. 10016. 10,000; Clarence L. Coleman, Jr., President.

**Junior Achievement, Inc.** (1919): 550 Summer St., Stamford, Conn. 06901. 300,000; Glenn V. Gardinier, National Public Relations Director.

**Junior Leagues, Inc., Association of** (1921): 825 Third Ave., New York, N.Y. 10022. 130,000.

**Kennel Club, American** (1884): 51 Madison Ave., New York, N.Y. 10010. 406 member clubs; Mark T. Mooty, Secretary.

**Kiwanis International** (1915): 101 E. Erie, Chicago, Ill. 60611. 293,000; R. P. Merridew, Secretary.

**Knights of Columbus** (1882): One Columbus Plaza, New Haven, Conn. 06507. 1,280,859; Virgil Dechant, Supreme Knight.

**Knights of Pythias, Supreme Lodge** (1864): 47 N. Grant St., Stockton, Calif. 95202. 145,326; Jule O. Pritchard, Supreme Secretary.

**Knights Templar, Grand Encampment of** (1816): 14 E. Jackson Blvd., Suite 1700, Chicago, Ill. 60604. 365,000; Paul C. Rodenhauser, Grand Recorder.

**Library Association, American** (1876): 50 E. Huron St., Chicago, Ill. 60611. 33,767; Robert Wedgeworth, Executive Director.

**Lions Clubs, The International Association of** (1917): 300 22nd St., Oak Brook, Ill. 60570. 1,225,000; Roy Schaetzel, Executive Administrator.

**Management Associations, American** (1923): 135 W. 50th St., New York, N.Y. 10020. 65,000; Joseph P. Keyes, Vice President of Public Relations.

**Manufacturers, National Association of** (1895): 1776 F St., N.W., Washington, D.C. 20006. 13,000; Edmund W. Haskins, Secretary.

**March of Dimes—National Foundation** (1938): 1275 Mamaroneck Ave., White Plains, N.Y. 10605. 1,400 chapters; Arthur A. Gallway, Vice President.

**Marine Corps League** (1923): 933 N. Kenmore St., Arlington, Va. 22201. 20,000; F. B. Starr, National Adjutant Paymaster.

**Masons, Ancient and Accepted Scottish Rite, Northern Masonic Jurisdiction, Supreme Council 33°** (1867): 33 Marrett Rd., Lexington, Mass. 02173. 511,687; Winthrop L. Hall, Executive Secretary.

**Masons, Ancient and Accepted Scottish Rite, Southern Jurisdiction, Supreme Council** (1801): 1733 16th St., N.W., Washington, D.C. 20009. 653,000; C. Fred Kleinknecht, Grand Secretary General.

**Mayflower Descendants, General Society of** (1897): 4 Winslow St., P.O. Box 297, Plymouth, Mass. 02360. 17,500; Mrs. Lester A. Hall, Historian General.

**Medical Association, American** (1847): 535 N. Dearborn St., Chicago, Ill. 60610.

**Mental Health Association** (1909): 1800 N. Kent St., Arlington, Va. 22209. 1,000,000; William Perry, Jr., Director of Communications.

**Modern Language Association of America** (1883): 62 Fifth Ave., New York, N.Y. 10011. 30,000; Jeffrey Howitt, Promotion and Production Manager.

**Moose, Loyal Order of** (1888): Mooseheart, Ill. 60539. 1,624,221; Carl A. Weis, Supreme Secretary.

**Multiple Sclerosis Society, National** (1946). 205 E. 42nd St., New York, N.Y. 10017. Sylvia Lawry, Executive Director.

**Museums, American Association of** (1906): 1055 Thomas Jefferson St., N.W., Washington, D.C. 20007. 6,406; Lawrence Reger, Director.

**National Association for the Advancement of Colored People** (1909): 1790 Broadway, New York, N.Y. 10019. 450,000; Benjamin L. Hooks, Executive Director.

**National Grange, The** (1867): 1616 H St., N.W., Washington, D.C. 20006. 600,000; John Scott, Master.

**Negro College Fund, Inc., United** (1944): 500 E. 62nd St., New York, N.Y. 10021. 41 colleges; Christopher F. Edley, Executive Director.

**Newspaper Publishers Association, American** (1887): P.O. Box 17407, Dulles International Airport, Washington, D.C. 20041. 1,291; Jerry W. Friedheim, Executive Vice President and General Manager.

**Nurses' Association, American** (1896): 2420 Pershing Rd., Kansas City, Mo. 64108. 200,000.

**Odd Fellows, Independent Order of** (1819): 16 W. Chase St., Baltimore, Md. 21201. 1,200,000; Edward T. Rogers, Sovereign Grand Secretary.

**Olympic Committee, United States** (1921): 1760 Boulder St., Colorado Springs, Colo. 80909. Bob Paul, Director of Communications.

**Organization of American States** (1890): 17th

Street and Constitution Avenue, N.W., Washington, D.C. 20006. 26 member nations.

**Parents and Teachers, National Congress of** (1897): 700 N. Rush St., Chicago, Ill. 60611. 6,328,348; Becky Schergens, Executive Director.

**Parks and Conservation Association, National** (1919): 1701 18th St., N.W., Washington, D.C. 20009. 45,000; Anthony Wayne Smith, President.

**Philatelic Society, American** (1886): P.O. Box 800, State College, Pa. 16801. 44,000; James DeVoss, Executive Secretary.

**Philosophical Society, American** (1743): 104 S. 5th St., Philadelphia, Pa. 19106. 600; W. J. Bell, Jr., Executive Officer.

**Photographic Society of America** (1933): 2005 Walnut St., Philadelphia, Pa. 19103. 18,600; Philip Katcher, Executive Secretary.

**Physical Society, American** (1899): 335 E. 45th St., New York, N.Y. 10017. 29,000; W. W. Havens, Jr., Executive Secretary.

**Planned Parenthood Federation of America** (1916): 810 Seventh Ave., New York, N.Y. 10019. 191 affiliates; Robin Elliott, Public Information Director.

**Political Science, Academy of** (1880): 2852 Broadway, New York, N.Y. 10025. 11,000; Robert H. Connery, President.

**Psychiatric Association, American** (1844): 1700 18th St., N.W., Washington, D.C. 20009. 22,000; Jules Masserman, M.D., President.

**Public Health Association, American** (1872): 1015 18th St., N.W., Washington, D.C. 20036. 29,000; William H. McBeath, M.D., Executive Director.

**Red Cross, American** (1881): 17th and D Sts., N.W., Washington, D.C. 20006. George M. Elsey, President.

**Retarded Citizens, National Association for** (1950): 2709 Avenue E East, Arlington, Tex. 76011. 1,800 units; Philip Roos, Executive Director.

**Retired Federal Employees, National Association of** (1914): 1533 New Hampshire Ave., N.W., Washington, D.C. 20036. 285,029; John F. McClelland, President.

**Retired Persons, American Association of** (1958): 1909 K St., N.W., Washington, D.C. 20049. 12,000,000; Cyril F. Brickfield, Executive Director.

**Rifle Association of America, National** (1871): 1600 Rhode Island Ave., N.W., Washington, D.C. 20036. 1,100,000; Harlon B. Carter, Executive Vice President.

**Rotary International** (1905): 1600 Ridge Ave., Evanston, Ill. 60201. 818,000; Harry A. Stewart, General Secretary.

**Safety Council, National** (1913): 444 N. Michigan Ave., Chicago, Ill. 60611. James C. Shaffer, Director of Public Relations.

**Salvation Army** (1865): 120 W. 14th St., New York, N.Y. 10011. 380,618; Col. Orval Taylor, National Chief Secretary.

**Science, American Association for the Advancement of** (1848): 1515 Massachusetts Ave., N.W., Washington, D.C. 20005. 125,000; Carol L. Rogers, Public Information.

**Screen Actors Guild** (1933): 7750 Sunset Blvd., Hollywood, Calif. 90046. 36,000; Judith Rheiner, Information Director.

**Seeing Eye** (1929): Morristown, N.J. 07960. 25,000; Stuart Grout, Executive Vice President.

**Sierra Club** (1892): 530 Bush St., San Francisco, Calif. 94108. 180,000; Michael McCloskey, Executive Director.

**Social Welfare, National Conference on** (1873): 22 W. Gay St., Columbus, Ohio 43215. 8,500; Margaret E. Berry, Executive Director.

**Social Workers, Inc., National Association of** (1955): 1425 H St., N.W., Washington, D.C. 20005. 70,000; Chauncey A. Alexander, Executive Director.

**Sons of Italy in America, Order** (1905): 1520 Locust St., Philadelphia, Pa. 19102. 2,300 lodges; Frank J. Montemuro, Supreme Venerable.

**Sons of the American Revolution, National Society of the** (1889): 2412 Massachusetts Ave., N.W., Washington, D.C. 20008. 22,000; Dr. Warren S. Woodward, Executive Secretary.

**Soroptimist International of the Americas** (1921): 1616 Walnut St., Philadelphia, Pa. 19103. 31,000; Valerie F. Levitan, Executive Director.

**Southern Christian Leadership Conference** (1957): 334 Auburn Ave., N.E., Atlanta, Ga. 30303. 1,000,000; 350 chapters, 260 affiliated organizations; Dr. Joseph E. Lowery, President.

**Speech and Hearing Association, American** (1925): 10801 Rockville Pike, Rockville, Md. 20852. 27,500; Kenneth Johnson, Executive Secretary.

**Sports Car Club of America** (1944): P.O. Box 22476, Denver, Colo. 80222. 23,000; Brian Van-Dercook, Director of Public Relations.

**Teachers, American Federation of** (1916): 11 Dupont Circle, N.W., Washington, D.C. 20036. 475,000; Albert Shanker, President.

**Travel Agents, Inc., American Society of (ASTA)** (1931): 711 Fifth Ave., New York, N.Y. 10022. 16,000; Richard P. Ramaglia, Executive Vice President.

**Travelers Aid Society of New York** (1905): 204 E. 39th St., New York, N.Y. 10016. 3,253; Elizabeth P. Anderson, General Director.

**University Women, American Association of** (1882): 2401 Virginia Ave., N.W., Washington, D.C. 20037. 190,000; Helen B. Wolfe, General Director.

**Urban League, National** (1910): 500 E. 62nd St.,

New York, N.Y. 10021. 107; James D. Williams, Director of Communications.

**Veterans Committee, American (AVC)** (1944): 1333 Connecticut Ave., N.W., Washington, D.C. 20036. 25,000; June A. Willenz, Executive Director.

**Veterans of Foreign Wars of the U.S.** (1899): V.F.W. Bldg., 34th and Broadway, Kansas City, Mo. 64111. V.F.W. and Auxiliary, 2,375,000; Julian Dickenson, Adjutant General.

**Veterinary Medical Association, American** (1863): 930 N. Meacham Rd., Schaumburg, Ill. 60196. 29,000; Dr. D. A. Price, Executive Vice President.

**Women Voters of the U.S., League of** (1920): 1730 M St., N.W., Washington, D.C. 20036. 137,000; Peggy Lampl, Executive Director.

**Women's American ORT** (1927): 1250 Broadway, New York, N.Y. 10001. 135,000; Nathan Gould, National Executive Director.

**Women's Clubs, General Federation of** (1890): 1734 N St., N.W., Washington, D.C. 20036. 600,000; Mrs. W. Ed Hamilton, Administrative Assistant.

**Young Men's Christian Associations, National Council of** (1844): 291 Broadway, New York, N.Y. 10007. 8,900,000; Robert W. Harlan, Executive Director.

**Young Women's Christian Association of the U.S.A.** (1858 in U.S.A., 1855 in England): 600 Lexington Ave., New York, N.Y. 10022. 2,471,000; Kit Kolchin, Public Relations Consultant.

**Youth Hostels, Inc., American** (1934): National Campus, Delaplane, Va. 22025. 70,000.

**Zionist Organization of America** (1897): ZOA House, 4 E. 34th St., New York, N.Y. 10016. 120,000; Leon Ilutovich, National Executive Director.

## Selected CB 10-Codes

| | | | | | |
|---|---|---|---|---|---|
| 10–1 | Receiving poorly | 10–21 | Call by phone | 10–51 | Wrecker needed at . . . |
| 10–2 | Receiving well | 10–23 | Stand by | 10–52 | Ambulance needed at . . . |
| 10–3 | Stop transmitting | 10–25 | Can you contact? | 10–53 | Road blocked |
| 10–4 | OK, message received | 10–26 | Disregard last information | 10–59 | Convoy or escort |
| 10–5 | Relay message | 10–27 | I am moving to channel . . . | 10–62 | Unable to copy, use phone |
| 10–6 | Stand by | 10–28 | Identify your station | 10–66 | Message cancellation |
| 10–7 | Out of service | 10–29 | I am leaving this location | 10–70 | Fire at . . . |
| 10–8 | In service | 10–30 | Does not conform to FCC rules | 10–73 | Speed Trap at . . . |
| 10–9 | Repeat message | 10–32 | Radio check | 10–75 | You are causing interference |
| 10–10 | Transmission completed, standing by | 10–33 | Emergency traffic at this station | 10–77 | ETA (estimated time of arrival |
| 10–11 | Speak more slowly | 10–34 | Trouble here, help needed | 10–82 | Reserve lodging |
| 10–12 | Visitors present | 10–36 | Correct time is . . . | 10–91 | Talk closer to mike |
| 10–13 | Report road conditions, weather | 10–39 | Your message delivered | 10–92 | Have your transmitter checked |
| 10–17 | Urgent business | 10–44 | I have a message for . . . | 10–93 | Check my frequency |
| 10–20 | Location . . . | 10–45 | All units please report | 10–94 | Give me a long count |
| | | 10–46 | Assist motorist | 10–200 | Police needed at . . . |
| | | 10–50 | Accident at . . . | | |

## Vending Machines

There is one vending machine for every 53 people in the U.S. The approximately 4 million machines produced sales of about $9.8 billion in 1976, or about $40 per person.

## Sunspots Influence Droughts?

A study of a 262-year period through tree rings reported in 1977 suggests that prolonged droughts of at least three years occur every 20–22 years, coinciding approximately with the double sunspot cycle. Droughts occurred two years after the low point of the sunspot cycle.

## Lightning Caused by Cosmic Rays

Cosmic rays from space probably provide the extra electric potential that triggers a lightning stroke, reported Johns Hopkins scientists in 1977. Such rays, very high-energy particles moving at almost the speed of light, hit the upper atmosphere as an "air shower." When such a shower passes through a thunderhead, it releases electrons from oxygen and nitrogen atoms through ionization of the air. The free electrons are accelerated by the electric field already existing within the cloud, concentrating enough negative electric charge at the bottom of the cloud to generate a lightning stroke. The first stroke generated is a preliminary "leader stroke" of low luminosity. It travels the zigzag path of least electrical resistance to the ground. When the leader stroke is about 50 yards above the ground, an electric charge leaps up to meet it. These strokes complete the circuit between the cloud and the ground, clearing the way for the powerful return stroke, usually the first lightning seen. Often other strokes follow so quickly that they may seem to be one single stroke.

# POSTAL REGULATIONS

## Domestic Mail Service

### First Class

First-class mail consists of letters and written and sealed matter. The rate is 15¢ for the first oz; 13¢ for each additional oz, or fraction of an oz, up to 12 oz. Pieces over 12 oz are subject to priority-mail (heavy pieces) rates. Single postcards, 10¢; double postcards, 20¢ (10¢ for each half). The post office sells prestamped single and double postal cards. Consult your postmaster for information on business-reply mail and presort rates.

The weight limit for first-class mail is 70 lb, and the maximum size is 100 in. in combined length and girth.

| Weight | Rates |
|---|---|
| First oz | $ .15 |
| Over 1 oz, but not over 2 | .28 |
| Over 2 oz, but not over 3 | .41 |
| Over 3 oz, but not over 4 | .54 |
| Over 4 oz, but not over 5 | .67 |
| Over 5 oz, but not over 6 | .80 |
| Over 6 oz, but not over 7 | .93 |
| Over 7 oz, but not over 8 | 1.06 |
| Over 8 oz, but not over 9 | 1.19 |
| Over 9 oz, but not over 10 | 1.32 |
| Over 10 oz, but not over 11 | 1.45 |
| Over 11 oz, but not over 12 | 1.58 |
| Over 12 oz, *see* Priority Mail | |

### Priority Mail (over 12 oz to 70 lb)

The zone rate applies to mailable matter over 12 oz of any class carried by air. Such matter shall not exceed 100 in. in length and girth combined. Your local post office will supply free official zone tables appropriate to your location. *See* the priority-mail table for rates for units up to 25 lb.

### Airmail

First-class and priority mail receive airmail service.

### Second Class

Second-class mail is used primarily by newspapers, magazines, and other periodicals with second-class mail privileges. Copies mailed by the public are 10¢ for the first 2 oz, 6¢ for each additional oz or fraction, or the applicable fourth-class rate, whichever is lower.

### Third Class (under 16 oz)

Third-class mail is used for circulars, books, printed matter, and all other mailable matter not in first or second class. There are two rate structures for this class, a single-piece and a bulk rate.

Many community organizations, as well as businesses, find it economical to use this service. Because of the number of categories of third-class mail, you should consult your postmaster for the one best suited to your needs.

**Third-Class, Single-Piece Rates**

| Weight | Rates | Weight | Rates |
|---|---|---|---|
| 0 to 2 oz | 20¢ | Over 8 oz to 10 oz | $ .79 |
| Over 2 oz to 4 oz | 40¢ | Over 10 oz to 12 oz | .92 |
| Over 4 oz to 6 oz | 53¢ | Over 12 oz to 14 oz | 1.05 |
| Over 6 oz to 8 oz | 66¢ | Over 14 oz to 15.99 oz | 1.18 |

1. Fourth-class zone rate is charged if it is lower.

### Fourth Class (Parcel Post— 16 oz and over)

Fourth-class mail is used for merchandise, books, printed matter, and all other mailable matter not in first, second, or third class.

The zone rates apply to fourth-class matter, except certain books, library books, publications or records for the blind, and certain controlled-circulation publications. *See* the table for fourth-class rates. Consult your postmaster for weight and size limits.

### Special Fourth-Class Rate

The special fourth-class rate is restricted specifically to books; 16-mm or narrower width films and catalogs of such films (except when mailed to or from commercial theaters); printed music, printed objective-test materials, sound recordings, and playscripts and manuscripts for books, periodicals, and music; printed educational reference charts permanently processed for preservation; looseleaf pages, and binders therefor, consisting of medical information for distribution to doctors, hospitals, medical schools, and medical students. The rate is 36¢ for the first lb or fraction, plus 14¢ for each additional lb or fraction through 7 lb, 10¢ for each additional lb or fraction over 7 lb.

Consult your postmaster for information on the Library Rate which allows certain restricted educational materials to be sent at a lower rate if mailed by or to certain educational institutions.

### Special Services

**Registered Mail.** When you use registered mail service, you are buying security—the safest way to send valuables. The full value of your mailing must be declared when mailed. You receive a receipt and the movement of your mail is controlled throughout the postal system. For an additional fee, a return receipt showing to whom, when, and where delivered may be obtained.

| Value | | | Fees (in addition to postage): For articles not covered by commercial or other insurance | For articles also covered by commercial or other insurance |
|---|---|---|---|---|
| 0.00 | to | $ 100 | $ 3.00 | $ 3.00 |
| 100.01 | to | 200 | 3.30 | 3.30 |
| 200.01 | to | 400 | 3.70 | 3.70 |
| 400.01 | to | 600 | 4.10 | 4.10 |
| 600.01 | to | 800 | 4.50 | 4.50 |
| 800.01 | to | 1,000 | 4.90 | 4.90 |
| 1,000.01 | to | 2,000 | 5.30 | $4.90 plus handling charge of 35¢ per $1,000 or fraction over first $1,000 |
| 2,000.01 | to | 3,000 | 5.70 | |
| 3,000.01 | to | 4,000 | 6.10 | |
| 4,000.01 | to | 5,000 | 6.50 | |
| 5,000.01 | to | 6,000 | 6.90 | |
| 6,000.01 | to | 7,000 | 7.30 | |
| 7,000.01 | to | 8,000 | 7.70 | |
| 8,000.01 | to | 9,000 | 8.10 | |
| 9,000.01 | to | 10,000[1] | 8.50 | |

1. Consult your postmaster for registry fees for values over $10,000.

**Certified Mail.** Certified mail service provides for a receipt to the sender and a record of delivery at the post office of address. No record is kept at the post office where mailed. It is handled in the ordinary mails and no insurance coverage is provided.

Any mail prepaid at the first class rate having no intrinsic value will be accepted as certified mail. Return-receipt service, requested at the time of mailing only, and special-delivery service are available.

Fee in addition to postage, 80¢; restricted delivery (additional fee), 80¢.

**Return Receipts.** Requested at time of mailing:

| | |
|---|---|
| Showing to whom and date delivered | $ .45 |
| Showing to whom, date, and address where delivered | .55 |

Requested after mailing:

| | |
|---|---|
| Showing to whom and date delivered | 2.10 |

**C.O.D. Mail.** Consult your postmaster for fees and conditions of mailing.

**Insured Mail.** Fees, in addition to postage, for coverage against loss or damage:

| Liability | | | Fees |
|---|---|---|---|
| $ .01 | to | $15 | $ .50 |
| $ 15.01 | to | $50 | .85 |
| $ 50.01 | to | $100 | 1.10 |
| $100.01 | to | $150 | 1.40 |
| $150.01 | to | $200 | 1.75 |
| $200.01 | to | $300 | 2.25 |
| $300.01 | to | $400[1] | 2.75 |

1. Liability for insured mail is limited to $400.

**Special Delivery.** The payment of the special-delivery fee entitles mail to the most expeditious transportation and delivery. The fee is in addition to the regular postage.

| Class of mail | Weight/Fees: Not more than 2 lb | More than 2 lb but not more than 10 lb | More than 10 lb |
|---|---|---|---|
| First-class and priority mail | $2.00 | $2.25 | $2.85 |
| All other classes | 2.25 | 2.85 | 3.25 |

**Special Handling.** Payment of the special-handling fee entitles third- and fourth-class matter to the most expeditious handling and transportation, but not special delivery. The fee is in addition to the regular postage.

| Weight | Fees |
|---|---|
| Not more than 10 lb | $ .70 |
| More than 10 lb | 1.25 |

**Money Orders.** Money orders are used for the safe transmission of money.

| Amount of money order | | | Fees |
|---|---|---|---|
| $ .01 | to | $10 | $ .55 |
| $10.01 | to | $50 | .80 |
| $50.01 | to | $400 | 1.10 |

## New Minimum Mail Sizes

Effective Nov. 30, 1978, all mail must be at least 0.007 in. thick and mail that is 1/4 in. or less in thickness must be at least 3 1/2 in. in height, at least 5 in. long, and rectangular in shape.

## Adhesive Stamps Available

| Purpose | Form | Denomination and prices |
|---|---|---|
| Ordinary postage | Single or sheet | 1, 2, 3, 4, 5, 9, 10, 11, 12, 13, 14, 15, 16, 18, 20, 21, 24, 25, 29, 30, 40, and 50¢; $1 and $5. |
| | Book | 8–15¢ = $1.20; 24–15¢ = $3.60 |
| | Coils of 100[1] | 13 and 15¢ |
| | Coils of 500 | 1, 2, 3, 5, 9, 10, 13, 15, and 16¢ and $1 |
| | Coils of 3,000 | 1, 2, 3, 5, 9, 10, 13, 15, 16, and 25¢ |
| International airmail postage | Single or sheet | 21, 25, 26, and 31¢ |

1. Dispenser to hold coil of 100 stamps may be purchased for 5¢.

# International Mail Service

## Canada and Mexico—Surface Rates

| Weight | Letter mail | Printed matter and small packets |
|---|---|---|
| 1 oz | $ .15 | — |
| 2 oz | .28 | $ .20 |
| 3 oz | .41 | — |
| 4 oz | .54 | .40 |
| 5 oz | .67 | — |
| 6 oz | .80 | .53 |
| 7 oz | .93 | — |
| 8 oz | 1.06 | .66 |
| 9 oz | 1.19 | — |
| 10 oz | 1.32 | .79 |
| 11 oz | 1.45 | — |
| 12 oz | 1.58 | .92 |
| 14 oz | — | 1.05 |
| 16 oz | 2.25 | 1.18 |
| Postcards | .10 | — |

Consult your postmaster for rates for heavier items.

## International Airmail

| Destination | Letters and letter packages[1] | Post-cards | Air letter sheets[2] |
|---|---|---|---|
| Central America Colombia, Venezuela, Caribbean Islands, Bahamas, Bermuda, St. Pierre and Miquelon | 25¢ per half oz through 2 oz 21¢ each additional half oz or fraction | 21¢ | 22¢ |
| All other countries | 31¢ per half oz through 2 oz 26¢ each additional half oz or fraction | 21¢ | 22¢ |

1. Weight limit, 4 lb. 2. No enclosures permitted.

For Canada and Mexico, *see* Surface Rates.

## International Money Order Fees

| Amount of money order | Fees |
|---|---|
| $ .01 to $10 | $ .90 |
| $10.01 to $50 | 1.10 |
| $50.01 to $300 | 1.40 |

## Countries Other Than Canada and Mexico—Surface Rates

| Ounces | Letter mail | Printed matter | Small packets |
|---|---|---|---|
| 1 | $ .20 | $ .20 | $ .20 |
| 2 | .36 | .20 | .20 |
| 4 | .48 | .40 | .40 |
| 8 | .96 | .66 | .66 |
| 16 | 1.84 | 1.05 | 1.05 |
| 32 | 3.20 | 1.26 | 1.26 |
| 64 | 5.20 | 1.68 | — |
| Each additional 32 oz | — | 0.84 | — |

## International Surface Parcel Post

| Weight through lb | Canada, Mexico, Central America, Caribbean Islands, Bahamas, Bermuda, St. Pierre and Miquelon | All other countries |
|---|---|---|
| 2 | $2.19 | $2.34 |
| 3 | 2.71 | 2.93 |
| 4 | 3.23 | 3.52 |
| 5 | 3.75 | 4.11 |
| 6 | 4.27 | 4.70 |
| 7 | 4.79 | 5.29 |
| 8 | 5.31 | 5.88 |
| 9 | 5.83 | 6.47 |
| 10 | 6.35 | 7.06 |
| | 52¢ each additional lb or fraction | 59¢ each additional lb or fraction |

Consult your postmaster for weight and size limits.

For other international services and rates consult your local postmaster.

## United Nations Stamps

United Nations stamps in U.S. denominations are sold for postage only if mailed at the U.N. Post Office, U.N. Headquarters, New York, N.Y. Stamps in Swiss denominations are valid for postage only if mailed at the Palais des Nations, Geneva, Switzerland. They may be purchased over the counter, by mail, or by opening a Customer Deposit Account. They are sold at face value subject to stock being available.

| 1978 | Subject | Price |
|---|---|---|
| Jan. 27 | Definitives | 1¢, 25¢, $1 |
| March 31 | Global Eradication of Smallpox | 13¢, 31¢ |
| May 5 | Namibia: Liberation, Justice, Cooperation | 13¢, 18¢ |
| June 12 | ICAO: Safety in the Air | 13¢, 25¢ |
| Sept. 15 | General Assembly | 13¢, 18¢ |
| Nov. 17 | Technical Cooperation Among Developing Countries | 13¢, 31¢ |

## Fourth Class (Parcel Post) Zone Rates

| Not exceeding (lb) | Local | Zones 1, 2 | Zone 3 | Zone 4 | Zone 5 | Zone 6 | Zone 7 | Zone 8 |
|---|---|---|---|---|---|---|---|---|
| 2 | $1.15 | $1.35 | $1.39 | $1.56 | $1.72 | $1.84 | $1.98 | $2.22 |
| 3 | 1.23 | 1.45 | 1.53 | 1.73 | 1.86 | 2.04 | 2.24 | 2.61 |
| 4 | 1.29 | 1.56 | 1.65 | 1.82 | 2.00 | 2.23 | 2.50 | 3.00 |
| 5 | 1.36 | 1.66 | 1.77 | 1.92 | 2.14 | 2.43 | 2.77 | 3.39 |
| 6 | 1.42 | 1.71 | 1.84 | 2.01 | 2.28 | 2.62 | 3.03 | 3.78 |
| 7 | 1.47 | 1.76 | 1.90 | 2.11 | 2.41 | 2.82 | 3.29 | 4.17 |
| 8 | 1.51 | 1.80 | 1.97 | 2.20 | 2.55 | 3.02 | 3.56 | 4.56 |
| 9 | 1.54 | 1.85 | 2.03 | 2.29 | 2.69 | 3.21 | 3.82 | 4.95 |
| 10 | 1.57 | 1.89 | 2.10 | 2.39 | 2.83 | 3.41 | 4.08 | 5.34 |
| 11 | 1.60 | 1.94 | 2.17 | 2.50 | 3.00 | 3.65 | 4.42 | 5.73 |
| 12 | 1.64 | 1.98 | 2.22 | 2.56 | 3.09 | 3.77 | 4.57 | 6.12 |
| 13 | 1.67 | 2.02 | 2.27 | 2.63 | 3.17 | 3.89 | 4.72 | 6.41 |
| 14 | 1.70 | 2.05 | 2.32 | 2.69 | 3.25 | 3.99 | 4.86 | 6.62 |
| 15 | 1.73 | 2.09 | 2.36 | 2.74 | 3.33 | 4.09 | 4.99 | 6.80 |
| 16 | 1.76 | 2.13 | 2.41 | 2.80 | 3.40 | 4.19 | 5.11 | 6.98 |
| 17 | 1.79 | 2.16 | 2.45 | 2.85 | 3.47 | 4.28 | 5.23 | 7.15 |
| 18 | 1.82 | 2.20 | 2.49 | 2.91 | 3.54 | 4.37 | 5.34 | 7.31 |
| 19 | 1.86 | 2.23 | 2.53 | 2.96 | 3.61 | 4.46 | 5.45 | 7.47 |
| 20 | 1.89 | 2.27 | 2.58 | 3.01 | 3.67 | 4.54 | 5.55 | 7.62 |
| 21 | 1.92 | 2.30 | 2.62 | 3.06 | 3.74 | 4.62 | 5.66 | 7.76 |
| 22 | 1.95 | 2.34 | 2.66 | 3.14 | 3.85 | 4.78 | 5.80 | 7.90 |
| 23 | 1.98 | 2.37 | 2.72 | 3.25 | 3.99 | 4.96 | 6.02 | 8.03 |
| 24 | 2.01 | 2.44 | 2.80 | 3.35 | 4.12 | 5.13 | 6.24 | 8.16 |
| 25 | 2.04 | 2.51 | 2.89 | 3.46 | 4.26 | 5.31 | 6.46 | 8.28 |
| 26 | 2.07 | 2.58 | 2.97 | 3.56 | 4.39 | 5.48 | 6.68 | 8.40 |
| 27 | 2.11 | 2.65 | 3.06 | 3.67 | 4.53 | 5.66 | 6.90 | 8.52 |
| 28 | 2.14 | 2.72 | 3.14 | 3.77 | 4.66 | 5.83 | 7.12 | 8.63 |
| 29 | 2.17 | 2.79 | 3.23 | 3.88 | 4.80 | 6.01 | 7.34 | 8.75 |
| 30 | 2.20 | 2.86 | 3.31 | 3.98 | 4.93 | 6.18 | 7.56 | 8.85 |
| 31 | 2.68 | 3.09 | 3.46 | 4.09 | 5.07 | 6.30 | 7.78 | 9.41 |
| 32 | 2.71 | 3.12 | 3.49 | 4.19 | 5.20 | 6.53 | 8.00 | 9.51 |
| 33 | 2.74 | 3.16 | 3.57 | 4.30 | 5.34 | 6.71 | 8.22 | 9.61 |
| 34 | 2.77 | 3.19 | 3.65 | 4.40 | 5.47 | 6.88 | 8.44 | 9.80 |
| 35 | 2.80 | 3.22 | 3.74 | 4.51 | 5.61 | 7.06 | 8.66 | 10.06 |
| 36 | 2.83 | 3.28 | 3.82 | 4.61 | 5.74 | 7.23 | 8.89 | 10.32 |
| 37 | 2.86 | 3.35 | 3.91 | 4.72 | 5.88 | 7.41 | 9.10 | 10.58 |
| 38 | 2.89 | 3.42 | 3.99 | 4.82 | 6.01 | 7.58 | 9.32 | 10.84 |
| 39 | 2.93 | 3.49 | 4.08 | 4.93 | 6.15 | 7.76 | 9.54 | 11.10 |
| 40 | 2.96 | 3.56 | 4.16 | 5.03 | 6.28 | 7.93 | 9.76 | 11.36 |
| 41 | 2.99 | 3.63 | 4.25 | 5.14 | 6.42 | 8.11 | 9.98 | 11.62 |
| 42 | 3.02 | 3.70 | 4.33 | 5.24 | 6.55 | 8.28 | 10.20 | 11.88 |
| 43 | 3.05 | 3.77 | 4.42 | 5.35 | 6.69 | 8.46 | 10.42 | 12.14 |
| 44 | 3.08 | 3.84 | 4.50 | 5.45 | 6.82 | 8.63 | 10.64 | 12.40 |
| 45 | 3.11 | 3.91 | 4.59 | 5.56 | 6.96 | 8.81 | 10.86 | 12.66 |
| 46 | 3.14 | 3.98 | 4.67 | 5.66 | 7.09 | 8.98 | 11.08 | 12.92 |
| 47 | 3.17 | 4.05 | 4.76 | 5.77 | 7.23 | 9.16 | 11.30 | 13.18 |
| 48 | 3.20 | 4.12 | 4.84 | 5.87 | 7.36 | 9.33 | 11.52 | 13.44 |
| 49 | 3.23 | 4.19 | 4.93 | 5.98 | 7.50 | 9.51 | 11.74 | 13.70 |
| 50 | 3.27 | 4.26 | 5.01 | 6.08 | 7.63 | 9.68 | 11.96 | 13.96 |
| 51 | 3.30 | 4.33 | 5.10 | 6.19 | 7.77 | 9.86 | 12.18 | 14.22 |
| 52 | 3.33 | 4.40 | 5.18 | 6.29 | 7.90 | 10.03 | 12.40 | 14.48 |
| 53 | 3.36 | 4.47 | 5.27 | 6.40 | 8.04 | 10.21 | 12.62 | 14.74 |
| 54 | 3.39 | 4.54 | 5.35 | 6.50 | 8.17 | 10.38 | 12.84 | 15.00 |
| 55 | 3.42 | 4.61 | 5.44 | 6.61 | 8.31 | 10.56 | 13.06 | 15.26 |
| 56 | 3.45 | 4.68 | 5.52 | 6.71 | 8.44 | 10.73 | 13.28 | 15.52 |
| 57 | 3.48 | 4.75 | 5.61 | 6.82 | 8.58 | 10.91 | 13.50 | 15.78 |
| 58 | 3.51 | 4.82 | 5.69 | 6.92 | 8.71 | 11.08 | 13.72 | 16.04 |
| 59 | 3.54 | 4.89 | 5.78 | 7.03 | 8.85 | 11.26 | 13.94 | 16.30 |
| 60 | 3.57 | 4.96 | 5.86 | 7.13 | 8.98 | 11.43 | 14.16 | 16.56 |
| 61 | 3.60 | 5.03 | 5.95 | 7.24 | 9.12 | 11.61 | 14.38 | 16.82 |
| 62 | 3.64 | 5.10 | 6.03 | 7.34 | 9.25 | 11.78 | 14.60 | 17.08 |
| 63 | 3.67 | 5.17 | 6.12 | 7.45 | 9.39 | 11.96 | 14.82 | 17.34 |
| 64 | 3.70 | 5.24 | 6.20 | 7.55 | 9.52 | 12.13 | 15.04 | 17.60 |
| 65 | 3.73 | 5.31 | 6.29 | 7.66 | 9.66 | 12.31 | 15.26 | 17.86 |

NOTES: Zone rates are determined from an official zone table, available free from your local post office. Exception: Parcels weighing less than 15 lb, and measuring over 84 in. but not exceeding 100 in. in length and girth combined, are chargeable with a minimum rate equal to that for a 15-lb parcel for the zone to which addressed.

## Priority Mail (Heavy Pieces)

| Weight over 12 oz and not exceeding (lb) | Rate | | | | | |
|---|---|---|---|---|---|---|
| | Local zones 1, 2, and 3 | Zone 4 | Zone 5 | Zone 6 | Zone 7 | Zone 8 |
| 1.0 | $1.71 | $1.81 | $1.88 | $1.97 | $2.06 | $2.25 |
| 1.5 | 1.86 | 1.96 | 2.07 | 2.21 | 2.34 | 2.50 |
| 2.0 | 1.99 | 2.12 | 2.27 | 2.44 | 2.61 | 2.83 |
| 2.5 | 2.11 | 2.27 | 2.46 | 2.68 | 2.89 | 3.16 |
| 3.0 | 2.23 | 2.42 | 2.65 | 2.91 | 3.17 | 3.50 |
| 3.5 | 2.35 | 2.58 | 2.84 | 3.15 | 3.45 | 3.83 |
| 4.0 | 2.47 | 2.73 | 3.03 | 3.38 | 3.73 | 4.16 |
| 4.5 | 2.59 | 2.89 | 3.22 | 3.62 | 4.01 | 4.50 |
| 5 | 2.72 | 3.04 | 3.42 | 3.85 | 4.29 | 4.83 |
| 6 | 2.96 | 3.35 | 3.80 | 4.32 | 4.84 | 5.50 |
| 7 | 3.20 | 3.66 | 4.18 | 4.79 | 5.40 | 6.16 |
| 8 | 3.44 | 3.96 | 4.56 | 5.26 | 5.96 | 6.83 |
| 9 | 3.69 | 4.27 | 4.95 | 5.73 | 6.51 | 7.49 |
| 10 | 3.93 | 4.58 | 5.33 | 6.20 | 7.07 | 8.16 |
| 11 | 4.17 | 4.89 | 5.71 | 6.67 | 7.63 | 8.83 |
| 12 | 4.42 | 5.20 | 6.10 | 7.14 | 8.18 | 9.49 |
| 13 | 4.66 | 5.50 | 6.48 | 7.61 | 8.74 | 10.16 |
| 14 | 4.90 | 5.81 | 6.86 | 8.08 | 9.30 | 10.82 |
| 15 | 5.15 | 6.12 | 7.25 | 8.55 | 9.86 | 11.49 |
| 16 | 5.39 | 6.43 | 7.63 | 9.02 | 10.41 | 12.16 |
| 17 | 5.63 | 6.74 | 8.01 | 9.49 | 10.97 | 12.82 |
| 18 | 5.87 | 7.04 | 8.39 | 9.96 | 11.53 | 13.49 |
| 19 | 6.12 | 7.35 | 8.78 | 10.43 | 12.08 | 14.15 |
| 20 | 6.36 | 7.66 | 9.16 | 10.90 | 12.64 | 14.82 |
| 21 | 6.60 | 7.97 | 9.54 | 11.37 | 13.20 | 15.49 |
| 22 | 6.85 | 8.28 | 9.93 | 11.84 | 13.75 | 16.15 |
| 23 | 7.09 | 8.58 | 10.31 | 12.31 | 14.31 | 16.82 |
| 24 | 7.33 | 8.89 | 10.69 | 12.78 | 14.87 | 17.48 |
| 25 | 7.58 | 9.20 | 11.08 | 13.25 | 15.43 | 18.15 |

NOTE: Consult your postmaster for rates for heavier pieces. Exception: Parcels weighing less than 15 lb, measuring over 84 in. but not exceeding 100 in. in length and girth combined, are chargeable with a minimum rate equal to that for a 15-lb parcel for the zone to which addressed.

## Authorized 2-Letter State Abbreviations

When the Post Office instituted the ZIP Code for mail in 1963, it also drew up a list of two-letter abbreviations for the states which would gradually replace the traditional ones in use. Following is the official list, including the District of Columbia, Guam, Puerto Rico, and the Virgin Islands (note that only capital letters are used):

| | | | | | |
|---|---|---|---|---|---|
| Alabama | AL | Kentucky | KY | Ohio | OH |
| Alaska | AK | Louisiana | LA | Oklahoma | OK |
| Arizona | AZ | Maine | ME | Oregon | OR |
| Arkansas | AR | Maryland | MD | Pennsylvania | PA |
| California | CA | Massachusetts | MA | Puerto Rico | PR |
| Colorado | CO | Michigan | MI | Rhode Island | RI |
| Connecticut | CT | Minnesota | MN | South Carolina | SC |
| Delaware | DE | Mississippi | MS | South Dakota | SD |
| Dist. of Columbia | DC | Missouri | MO | Tennessee | TN |
| Florida | FL | Montana | MT | Texas | TX |
| Georgia | GA | Nebraska | NE | Utah | UT |
| Guam | GU | Nevada | NV | Vermont | VT |
| Hawaii | HI | New Hampshire | NH | Virginia | VA |
| Idaho | ID | New Jersey | NJ | Virgin Islands | VI |
| Illinois | IL | New Mexico | NM | Washington | WA |
| Indiana | IN | New York | NY | West Virginia | WV |
| Iowa | IA | North Carolina | NC | Wisconsin | WI |
| Kansas | KS | North Dakota | ND | Wyoming | WY |

## Famous Firsts in Aviation

**1782** **First balloon flight.** Jacques and Joseph Montgolfier of Annonay, France, sent up a small smoke-filled balloon about mid-November.

**1783** **First hydrogen-filled balloon flight.** Jacques A. C. Charles, Paris physicist, supervised construction by A. J. and M. N. Robert of a 13-ft diameter balloon that was filled with hydrogen. It got up to about 3,000 ft and traveled about 16 mi. in a 45-min flight (Aug. 27).

**First human balloon flights.** A Frenchman, Jean Pilâtre de Rozier, made the first captive-balloon ascension (Oct. 15). With the Marquis d'Arlandes, Pilâtre de Rozier made the first free flight, reaching a peak altitude of about 500 ft, and traveling about 5½ mi. in 20 min (Nov. 21).

**1784** **First powered balloon.** Gen. Jean Baptiste Marie Meusnier developed the first propeller-driven and elliptically-shaped balloon—the crew cranking three propellors on a common shaft to give the craft a speed of about 3 mph.

**First woman to fly.** Mme. Thible, a French opera singer (June 4).

**1793** **First balloon flight in America.** Jean Pierre Blanchard, a French pilot, made it from Philadelphia to near Woodbury, Gloucester County, N.J., in a little over 45 min (Jan. 9).

**1794** **First military use of the balloon.** Jean Marie Coutelle, using a balloon built for the French Army, made two 4-hr observation ascents. The military purpose of the ascents seems to have been to damage the enemy's morale.

**1797** **First parachute jump.** André-Jacques Garnerin dropped from about 6,500 ft over Monceau Park in Paris in a 23-ft diameter parachute made of white canvas with a basket attached (Oct. 22).

**1843** **First air transport company.** In London, William S. Henson and John Stringfellow filed articles of incorporation for the Aerial Transit Company (March 24). It failed

**1852** **First dirigible.** Henri Giffard, a French engineer, flew in a controllable (more or less) steam-engine powered balloon, 144 ft long and 39 ft in diameter, inflated with 88,000 cu ft of coal gas. It reached 6.7 mph on a flight from Paris to Trappe (Sept. 24).

**1860** **First aerial photographers.** Samuel Archer King and William Black made two photos of Boston, still in existence.

**1872** **First gas-engine powered dirigible.** Paul Haenlein, a German engineer, flew in a semi-rigid-frame dirigible, powered by a 4-cylinder internal-combustion engine running on coal gas drawn from the supporting bag.

**1873** **First transatlantic attempt.** *The New York Daily Graphic* sponsored the attempt with a 400,000 cu ft balloon carrying a lifeboat. A rip in the bag during inflation brought collapse of the balloon and the project.

**1897** **First successful metal dirigible.** An all-metal dirigible, designed by David Schwarz, a Hungarian, took off from Berlin's Tempelhof Field and, powered by a 16-hp Daimler engine, got several miles before leaking gas caused it to crash (Nov. 13).

**1900** **First Zeppelin flight.** Germany's Count Ferdinand von Zeppelin flew the first of his long series of rigid-frame airships. It attained a speed of 18 mi. per h and got 3½ mi. before its steering gear failed (July 2).

**1903** **First successful heavier-than-air machine flight.** Aviation was really born on the sand dunes at Kitty Hawk, N.C., when Orville Wright crawled to his prone position between the wings of the biplane he and his brother Wilbur had built, opened the throttle of their homemade 12-hp engine and took to the air. He covered 120 ft in 12 sec. Later that day, in one of four flights, Wilbur stayed up 59 sec and covered 852 ft (Dec. 17).

**1904** **First airplane maneuvers.** Orville Wright made the first turn with an airplane (Sept. 15); 5 days later his brother Wilbur made the first complete circle.

**1905** **First airplane flight over half an hour.** Orville Wright kept his craft up 33 min 17 sec (Oct. 4).

**1906** **First European airplane flight.** Alberto Santos-Dumont, a Brazilian, flew a heavier-than-air machine at Bagatelle Field, Paris (Sept. 13).

**1908** **First airplane fatality.** Lt. Thomas E. Selfridge, U.S. Army Signal Corps, was in a group of officers evaluating the Wright plane at Fort Myer, Va. He was up about 75 ft with Orville Wright when the propeller hit a bracing wire and was broken, throwing the plane out of control, killing Selfridge and seriously injuring Wright (Sept. 17).

**1910** **First licensed woman pilot.** Baroness Raymonde de la Roche of France, who learned to fly in 1909, received ticket No. 36 on March 8.

**First flight from shipboard.** Lt. Eugene Ely, USN, took a Curtiss plane off from the deck of cruiser *Birmingham* at Hampton Roads, Va., and flew to Norfolk (Nov. 14). The following January, he reversed the process, flying from Camp Selfridge to the deck of the armored cruiser *Pennsylvania* in San Francisco Bay (Jan. 18).

**1911** **First U.S. woman pilot.** Harriet Quimby, a magazine writer, who got ticket No. 37.

1913 **First multi-engined aircraft.** Built and flown by Igor Ivan Sikorsky while still in his native Russia.

1914 **First aerial combat.** In August, Allied and German pilots and observers started shooting at each other with pistols and rifles—with negligible results.

1915 **First air raids on England.** German Zeppelins started dropping bombs on four English communities (Jan. 19).

1918 **First U.S. air squadron.** The U.S. Army Air Corps made its first independent raids over enemy lines, in DH-4 planes (British-designed) powered with 400-hp American-designed Liberty engines (April 8).

**First regular airmail service.** Operated for the Post Office Department by the Army, the first regular service was inaugurated with one round trip a day (except Sunday) between Washington, D.C., and New York City (May 15).

1919 **First transatlantic flight.** The NC-4, one of four Curtiss flying boats commanded by Lt. Comdr. Albert C. Read, reached Lisbon, Portugal, (May 27) after hops from Trepassy Bay, Newfoundland, to Horta, Azores (May 16–17), to Ponta Delgada (May 20). The Liberty-powered craft was piloted by Walter Hinton.

**First nonstop transatlantic flight.** Capt. John Alcock and Lt. Arthur Whitten Brown, British World War I flyers, made the 1,900 mi. from St. John's, Newfoundland, to Clifden, Ireland, in 16 h 12 min in a Vickers-Vimy bomber with two 350-hp Rolls-Royce engines (June 15–16).

**First lighter-than-air transatlantic flight.** The British dirigible R-34, commanded by Maj. George H. Scott, left Firth of Forth, Scotland, (July 2) and touched down at Mineola, L.I., 108 h later. The eastbound trip was made in 75 h (completed July 13).

**First scheduled passenger service (using airplanes).** Aircraft Travel and Transport inaugurated London-Paris service (Aug. 25). Later the company started the first trans-channel mail service on the same route (Nov. 10).

1921 **First naval vessel sunk by aircraft.** Two battleships being scrapped by treaty were sunk by bombs dropped from Army planes in demonstration put on by Brig. Gen. William S. Mitchell (July 21).

**First helium balloon.** The C-7, non-rigid Navy dirigible was first to use non-inflammable helium as lifting gas, making a flight from Hampton Roads, Va., to Washington, D.C. (Dec. 1).

1922 **First member of Caterpillar Club.** Lt. (later Maj. Gen.) Harold Harris bailed out of a crippled plane he was testing at McCook Field, Dayton, Ohio (Oct. 20), and became the first man to join the Caterpillar Club—those whose lives have been saved by parachute.

1923 **First nonstop transcontinental flight.** Lts. John A. Macready and Oakley Kelly flew a single-engine Fokker T-2 nonstop from New York to San Diego, a distance of just over 2,500 mi. in 26 h 50 min (May 2–3).

**First autogyro flight.** Juan de la Cierva, a brilliant Spanish mathematician, made the first successful flight in a rotary wing aircraft in Madrid (June 9).

1924 **First round-the-world flight.** Four Douglas Cruiser biplanes of the U.S. Army Air Corps took off from Seattle under command of Maj. Frederick Martin (April 6). 175 days later, two of the planes (Lt. Lowell Smith's and Lt. Erik Nelson's) landed in Seattle after a circuitous route—one source saying 26,345 mi., another saying 27,553 mi.

1926 **First polar flight.** Then-Lt. Cmdr. Richard E. Byrd, acting as navigator, and Floyd Bennett as pilot, flew a trimotor Fokker from Kings Bay, Spitsbergen, over the North Pole and back in 15½ h (May 8–9).

1927 **First solo transatlantic flight.** Charles Augustus Lindbergh lifted his Wright-powered Ryan monoplane, *Spirit of St. Louis,* from Roosevelt Field, L.I., to stay aloft 33 h 39 min and travel 3,600 mi. to Le Bourget Field outside Paris (May 20–21).

**First transatlantic passenger.** Charles A. Levine was piloted by Clarence D. Chamberlin from Roosevelt Field, L.I., to Eisleben, Germany, in a Wright-powered Bellanca (June 4–5).

1928 **First east-west transatlantic crossing.** Baron Guenther von Huenefeld, piloted by German Capt. Hermann Koehl and Irish Capt. James Fitzmaurice, left Dublin for New York City (April 12) in a single-engine all-metal Junkers monoplane. Some 37 h later, they crashed on Greely Island, Labrador. Rescued.

**First U.S.-Australia flight.** Sir Charles Kingsford-Smith and Capt. Charles T. P. Ulm, Australians, and two American navigators, Harry W. Lyon and James Warner, crossed the Pacific from Oakland to Brisbane. They went via Hawaii and the Fiji Islands in a trimotor Fokker (May 31–June 8).

**First transarctic flight.** Sir Hubert Wilkins, an Australian explorer and Carl Ben Eielson, who served as pilot, flew from Point Barrow, Alaska, to Spitsbergen (mid-April).

1929 **First of the endurance records.** With Air Corps Maj. Carl Spaatz in command and Capt. Ira Eaker as chief pilot, an Army Fokker, aided by refueling in the air, remained aloft 150 h 40 min at Los Angeles (Jan. 1–7).

**First blind flight.** James H. Doolittle proved the feasibility of instrument-guided flying when he took off and landed entirely on instruments (Sept. 24).

**First rocket-engine flight.** Fritz von Opel, a German auto maker, stayed aloft in his small rocket-powered craft for 75 sec, covering nearly 2 mi. (Sept. 30).

**First South Pole flight.** Comdr. Richard E. Byrd, with Bernt Balchen as pilot, Harold I. June, radio operator, and Capt. A. C. McKinley, photographer, flew a trimotor Fokker from the Bay of Whales, Little America, over the South Pole and back (Nov. 28–29).

1930 **First Paris–New York nonstop flight.** Dieudonné Coste and Maurice Bellonte, French pilots, flew a Hispano-powered Breguet biplane from Le Bourget Field to Valley Stream, L.I., in 37 h 18 min. (Sept. 2–3).

1931 **First flight into the stratosphere.** Auguste Piccard, a Swiss physicist, and Charles Knipfer, ascended in a balloon from Augsburg, Germany, and reached a height of 51,793 ft in a 17-h flight that terminated on a glacier near Innsbruck, Austria (May 27).

**First nonstop transpacific flight.** Hugh Herndon and Clyde Pangborn took off from Sabishiro Beach, Japan, dropped their landing gear, and flew 4,860 mi. to near Wenatchee, Wash., in 41 h 13 min. (Oct. 4–5).

1932 **First woman's transatlantic solo.** Amelia Earhart, flying a Pratt & Whitney Wasp-powered Lockheed Vega, flew alone from Harbor Grace, Newfoundland, to Ireland in approximately 15 h (May 20–21).

**First westbound transatlantic solo.** James A. Mollison, a British pilot, took a de Havilland Puss Moth from Portmarnock, Ireland, to Pennfield, N.B. (Aug. 18).

**First woman airline pilot.** Ruth Rowland Nichols, first woman to hold three international records at the same time—speed, distance, altitude—was employed by N.Y.-New England Airways.

1933 **First round-the-world solo.** Wiley Post took a Lockheed Vega, *Winnie Mae,* 15,596 mi. around the world in 7 d 18 h 49½ min (July 15–22).

1937 **First successful helicopter.** Hanna Reitsch, a German pilot, flew Dr. Heinrich Focke's FW-61 in free, fully-controlled flight at Bremen (July 4).

1939 **First turbojet flight.** Just before their invasion of Poland, the Germans flew a Heinkel He-178 plane powered by a Heinkel S3B turbojet (Aug. 27).

1942 **First American jet plane flight.** Robert Stanley, chief pilot for Bell Aircraft Corp., flew the Bell XP-59 *Airacomet* at Muroc Army Base, Calif. (Oct. 1).

1947 **First piloted supersonic flight in an airplane.** Capt. Charles E. Yeager, U.S. Air Force, flew the X-1 rocket-powered research plane built by Bell Aircraft Corp., faster than the speed of sound at Muroc Air Force Base, California (Oct. 14).

1949 **First round-the-world nonstop flight.** Capt. James Gallagher and USAF crew of 13 flew a Boeing B-50A Superfortress around the world nonstop from Ft. Worth, returning to same point: 23,452 mi. in 94 h 1 min, with 4 aerial refuelings enroute (Feb. 27–March 2).

1950 **First nonstop transatlantic jet flight.** Col. David C. Schilling (USAF) flew 3,300 mi. from England to Limestone, Maine, in 10 h 1 min (Sept. 22).

1951 **First solo across North Pole.** Charles F. Blair, Jr., flew a converted P-51 (May 29).

1952 **First jetliner service.** De Havilland Comet flight inaugurated by BOAC between London and Johannesburg, South Africa (May 2). Flight, including stops, took 23 h 38 min.

**First transatlantic helicopter flight.** Capt. Vincent H. McGovern and 1st Lt. Harold W. Moore piloted 2 Sikorsky H-19s from Westover, Mass., to Prestwick, Scotland (3,410 mi.). Trip was made in 5 steps, with flying time of 42 h 25 min (July 15–31).

**First transatlantic round trip in same day.** British Canberra twin-jet bomber flew from Aldergrove, Northern Ireland, to Gander, Newfoundland, and back in 7 h 59 min flying time (Aug. 26).

1955 **First transcontinental round trip in same day.** Lt. John M. Conroy piloted F-86 Sabrejet across U.S. (Los Angeles–New York) and back—5,085 mi.—in 11 h 33 min 27 sec (May 21).

1957 **First round-the-world, nonstop jet plane flight.** Maj. Gen. Archie J. Old, Jr., USAF, led a flight of 3 Boeing B-52 bombers, powered with 8 10,000-lb thrust Pratt & Whitney Aircraft J57 engines around the world in 45 h 19 min; distance 24,325 mi.; average speed 525 mph. (Completed Jan. 18.)

1958 **First transatlantic jet passenger service.** BOAC, New York to London (Oct. 4). Pan American started daily service, N.Y. to Paris (Oct. 26).

**First domestic jet passenger service.** National Airlines inaugurated service between New York and Miami (Dec. 10).

1976 **First regularly-scheduled commercial supersonic transport (SST) flights begin.** Air France and British Airways inaugurate service (January 21). Air France flies the Paris-Rio de Janeiro route; B.A., the London-Bahraine. Both airlines begin SST service to Washington, D.C. (May 24).

1977 **First successful man-powered aircraft.** Paul MacCready, an aeronautical engineer from Pasadena, Calif., was awarded the Kremer Prize for creating the world's first successful man-powered aircraft. The *Gossamer Condor* was flown by Bryan Allen over the required 3-mile course on Aug. 23.

1978 **First successful transatlantic balloon flight.** Three Albuquerque, N.M., men, Ben Abruzzo, Larry Newman, and Maxie Anderson, completed the crossing (Aug. 16. Landed, Aug. 17) in their hot air balloon, *Double Eagle II.*

## Aircraft Accidents

The number of American air carrier accidents recorded in 1977 was the lowest in history, but the collision of two jumbo jets in the Canary Islands put the total number of fatalities at a record 654, according to the National Transportation Safety Board. The Board's report, issued Jan. 6, 1978, said there were 26 air carrier accidents in 1977, 2 fewer than in 1976. However, 1976 was the record-low year for fatalities, with only 45 killed in accidents involving American carriers. The Canary Islands accident on March 27, 1977, killed 573 persons. Other fatal air carrier accidents in 1977 resulted in 70 deaths in a Southern Airways DC-9 crash at New Hope, Georgia; 5 deaths in a helicopter accident atop the Pan Am Building in New York City; 3 deaths in the United Airlines Cargo Jet that crashed in December near Kayesville, Utah; and 3 deaths in the crash of a Fleming International Airways plane at St. Louis.

## U.S. Scheduled Airlines, 1977

| Airline | Certificated route mileage | Revenue passenger-miles, (thousands)[1] |
|---|---|---|
| **DOMESTIC**[2] | | |
| Airlift[3] | 10,656 | — |
| Air Midwest | 896 | 18,383 |
| Air New England | 797 | 59,041 |
| Alaska[2] | 4,906[4] | 672,391 |
| Allegheny | 8,291[5] | 3,642,868 |
| Aloha | 494 | 330,290 |
| American | 42,884[5] | 21,432,339 |
| Aspen | 112 | 15,057 |
| Braniff | 23,269 | 5,956,848 |
| Continental | 27,673 | 7,093,427 |
| Delta | 46,327[5] | 18,655,431 |
| Eastern | 41,549[5] | 16,782,323 |
| Flying Tiger[3] | 3,950 | — |
| Frontier | 20,387[5] | 1,887,439 |
| Hawaiian | 400 | 431,863 |
| Helicopter (Chicago) | 42[6] | — |
| Helicopter (New York) | 139[6] | 4,625 |
| Hughes Airwest | 9,880[5] | 2,035,773 |
| National | 8,425 | 5,569,721 |
| North Central | 7,562[5] | 1,281,075 |
| Northwest | 30,927[5] | 8,168,010 |
| Ozark | 6,195 | 1,221,210 |
| Pan American | 23,941 | 1,918,431 |
| Piedmont | 3,909 | 1,261,415 |
| Southern | 9,541[5] | 1,044,818 |
| Texas International | 6,964[5] | 1,167,060 |
| Trans World | 28,099 | 16,112,571 |
| United | 48,685[5] | 31,743,702 |
| Western | 27,054[5] | 7,843,469 |
| Wright | 215 | 7,559 |
| **Total** | **444,169** | **156,357,139** |
| **INTERNATIONAL** | | |
| Airlift[3] | — | — |
| Air Micronesia | 14,561 | — |
| American | 21,855 | 3,201,611 |
| Braniff | 31,850[5] | 1,554,670 |
| Continental | 14,561 | 111,398 |
| Delta | 8,855 | 464,221 |
| Eastern | 23,569 | 3,829,971 |
| Flying Tiger[3] | 14,206 | — |
| National | 9,125 | 651,311 |
| Northwest | 23,588 | 2,932,398 |
| Pan American | 242,752 | 15,588,275 |
| Seaboard World[3] | 16,293 | — |
| Trans World | 78,444 | 7,743,673 |
| Western | 6,642 | 532,042 |
| **Total** | **506,301** | **36,609,570** |

1. Scheduled service. 2. Excluding intra-Alaska carrier. 3. All-cargo carriers. 4. Includes Alaska-Washington State mileage. 5. Includes small amounts of trans-border mileage. 6. Flight pattern. *Source:* Civil Aeronautics Board, Bureau of Accounts and Statistics.

## Active Pilot Certificates Held

(as of January 1)

| Year | Total[1] | Airline transport | Commercial | Private |
|---|---|---|---|---|
| 1965 | 431,041 | 21,572 | 108,428 | 175,574 |
| 1966 | 479,770 | 22,440 | 116,665 | 196,393 |
| 1967 | 548,757 | 23,917 | 131,539 | 222,427 |
| 1968 | 617,931 | 25,817 | 150,135 | 254,069 |
| 1969 | 691,695 | 28,607 | 164,458 | 281,728 |
| 1970 | 720,028 | 31,442 | 176,585 | 299,491 |
| 1971 | 732,729 | 34,430 | 186,821 | 303,779 |
| 1972 | 741,009 | 35,949 | 192,409 | 312,656 |
| 1973 | 750,869 | 37,714 | 196,228 | 321,413 |
| 1974 | 714,607 | 38,139 | 182,444 | 298,921 |
| 1975 | 733,728 | 41,002 | 192,425 | 305,848 |
| 1976 | 728,187 | 45,592 | 189,342 | 305,863 |
| 1977 | 744,246 | 45,072 | 187,801 | 309,005 |
| 1978 | 783,932 | 50,149 | 188,763 | 327,424 |

1. Includes other pilot categories—helicopter, glider and lighter-than-air (1978: 14,086); and students (1978: 203,510). *Source:* Department of Transportation, Federal Aviation Administration.

## Helicopter Records

*Source:* National Aeronautic Association.

**Distance in Straight Line**
International: 2,213.04 mi., 3,561.55 km.
Robert G. Ferry (U.S.) in Hughes YOH-6A helicopter powered by Allison T-63-A-5 engine; from Culver City, Calif., to Daytona Beach, Fla., April 6–7, 1966.

**Distance, Closed Circuit**
International: 1,739.96 mi; 2,800.20 km.
Jack Schweibold (U.S.) in Hughes YOH-6A helicopter powered by Allison T-62-A-5 engine; Edwards Air Force Base, Calif., March 26, 1966.

**Altitude**
International: 40,820 ft; 12,442 m.
Jean Boulet (France) in Alouette SA 315-001 "Lama" powered by Artouste IIIB 735 KW engine; Istres, France, June 21, 1972.

**Maximum Speed**
International: 220.889 mph; 355.485 kph.
Kurt F. Cannon (U.S.) in Sikorsky S-67 helicopter powered by 2 G.E. T-58 turbine engines; Stratford, Conn., Dec. 19, 1970.

**Speed for 100 Km (Closed Circuit)**
International: 211.35 mph; 340.15 kph.
Boris Galitsky (U.S.S.R.) in MI-6 helicopter powered by 2 TB-2BM turbine engines; Podmoskovnoe, U.S.S.R., Aug. 26, 1964.

**Speed for 500 Km (Closed Circuit)**
International: 205.688 mph; 331.023 kph.
Galina Rastorgoueva (U.S.S.R.) in A-10 helicopter powered by 2 TV2 117A engines; Ramenskoye, U.S.S.R., Aug. 1, 1975.

**Speed for 1,000 Km (Closed Circuit)**
International: 200.48 mph; 322.646 kph.
Galina Rastorgoueva (U.S.S.R.) in A-10 helicopter powered by 2 TV2 117A engines; Aug. 13, 1975.

**Speed for 2,000 Km (Closed Circuit)**
International: 146.09 mph; 235.119 kph.
Inna Kopets (U.S.S.R.) in MI-8 helicopter; Sept. 14, 1967.

## U. S. Airlines Transport Planes

| Manufacturer | Type | Number of passengers | Maximum speed, mph | Typical gross weight, lbs | Wingspan, ft | Maximum length, ft |
|---|---|---|---|---|---|---|
| **4-ENGINE** | | | | | | |
| Boeing | 707–120 | 100–181 | 600 | 258,000 | 130.9 | 145.1 |
| Boeing | 707–120B | 100–181 | 600+ | 258,000 | 130.9 | 145.1 |
| Boeing | 707–320/Intercontinental | 108–189 | 600+ | 316,000 | 142.4 | 152.9 |
| Boeing | 707–320B/Intercontinental | 189 | 600+ | 336,000 | 145.8 | 152.9 |
| Boeing | 707–320C/Intercontinental | 189 | 600+ | 336,000 | 145.8 | 152.9 |
| Boeing | 707–420/Intercontinental | 108–189 | 600+ | 316,000 | 142.4 | 152.9 |
| Boeing | 720 | 88–167 | 600 | 230,000 | 130.9 | 136.7 |
| Boeing | 720B | 167 | 600+ | 235,000 | 130.9 | 136.7 |
| Boeing | 747–100B/Superjet | 442 | 640 | 738,000 | 195.7 | 231.9 |
| Boeing | 747–200B/Superjet | 442 | 640 | 788,000 | 195.7 | 231.9 |
| Boeing | 747–200C/Superjet | 442 | 640 | 788,000 | 195.7 | 231.9 |
| Boeing | 747–SR/Superjet | 516 | 640 | 603,000 | 195.7 | 231.9 |
| Boeing | 747–SP/Superjet | 321 | 640 | 696,000 | 195.7 | 184.7 |
| McDonnell Douglas | DC–8/Series 10 | 116–176 | 580 | 273,000 | 142.3 | 150.5 |
| McDonnell Douglas | DC–8/Series 20 | 116–176 | 600 | 276,000 | 142.3 | 150.5 |
| McDonnell Douglas | DC–8/Series 30 | 116–176 | 600 | 315,000 | 142.3 | 150.5 |
| McDonnell Douglas | DC–8/Series 40 | 116–176 | 600 | 315,000 | 142.3 | 150.5 |
| McDonnell Douglas | DC–8/Series 50 | 116–189 | 600 | 325,000 | 142.3 | 150.5 |
| McDonnell Douglas | DC–8/Super 61 | 259 | 600 | 325,000 | 142.3 | 187.4 |
| McDonnell Douglas | DC–8/Super 62 | 189 | 600 | 335,000 | 148.4 | 157.4 |
| McDonnell Douglas | DC–8/Super 63 | 259 | 600 | 350,000 | 148.4 | 187.4 |
| General Dynamics | 990/Coronado | 96–146 | 621 | 255,000 | 120.0 | 139.2 |
| **3-ENGINE** | | | | | | |
| Boeing | 727–100 | 70–131 | 600+ | 170,000 | 108.0 | 133.1 |
| Boeing | 727–200/Advanced | 134–189 | 600+ | 191,500 | 108.0 | 153.1 |
| McDonnell Douglas | DC–10/Series 10 | 250–380 | 600+ | 455,000 | 155.3 | 182.3 |
| McDonnell Douglas | DC–10/Series 30 | 250–380 | 600+ | 572,000 | 165.3 | 181.6 |
| McDonnell Douglas | DC–10/Series 40 | 250–380 | 600+ | 572,000 | 165.3 | 182.3 |
| Lockheed | L–1011–1/TriStar | 250–400 | 620 | 430,000 | 155.3 | 177.7 |
| Lockheed | L–1011–100/TriStar | 250–400 | 620 | 466,000 | 155.3 | 177.7 |
| Lockheed | L–1011–200/TriStar | 250–400 | 620 | 466,000 | 155.3 | 177.7 |
| Lockheed | L–1011–250/TriStar | 250–400 | 620 | 496,000 | 155.3 | 177.7 |
| Lockheed | L–1011–500/TriStar | 230–330 | 620 | 496,000 | 155.3 | 164.2 |
| **2-ENGINE** | | | | | | |
| Beech | B–99 | 15 | 285 | 10,900 | 45.8 | 44.6 |
| Boeing | 737–100 | 112 | 586 | 111,000 | 93.0 | 94.0 |
| Boeing | 737–200/Advanced | 115–130 | 586 | 117,500 | 93.0 | 100.0 |
| Fairchild | F–27/Friendship | 40–48 | 275 | 40,500 | 95.2 | 77.2 |
| Fairchild | F–27A/Friendship | 40–48 | 300 | 42,000 | 95.2 | 77.2 |
| Fairchild | F–27B/Friendship | 40–48 | 275 | 40,500 | 95.2 | 77.2 |
| Fairchild | F–27J/Friendship | 40–48 | 300 | 42,000 | 95.2 | 77.2 |
| Fairchild | FH–227 | 44–52 | 300 | 43,500 | 95.2 | 83.1 |
| Fairchild | FH–227B | 44–52 | 300 | 45,500 | 95.2 | 83.1 |
| Fairchild | FH–227C | 44–52 | 300 | 43,500 | 95.2 | 83.1 |
| Fairchild | FH–227D | 44–52 | 300 | 45,500 | 95.2 | 83.1 |
| Fairchild | FH–227E | 44–52 | 300 | 43,500 | 95.2 | 83.1 |
| General Dynamics | 580 | 53 | — | 54,600 | 105.3 | 81.5 |
| McDonnell Douglas | DC–9/Series 10 | 90 | 576 | 90,700 | 89.4 | 104.4 |
| McDonnell Douglas | DC–9/Series 20 | 90 | 576 | 98,000 | 93.3 | 104.4 |
| McDonnell Douglas | DC–9/Series 30 | 115 | 586 | 121,000 | 93.3 | 119.3 |
| McDonnell Douglas | DC–9/Series 40 | 125 | 586 | 121,000 | 93.3 | 125.6 |
| McDonnell Douglas | DC–9/Series 50 | 139 | 586 | 122,200 | 93.3 | 133.5 |
| McDonnell Douglas | DC–90/Super 80 | 167 | 576 | 140,000 | 107.8 | 149.9 |
| Swearingen | SA–226TC | 20 | 300 | 12,500 | 46.4 | 59.4 |

*Source: Aviation Week & Space Technology*

## Dangerous Fun

In 1973-75, hang gliding—the most dangerous sport per participant—caused 81 deaths and 2,000 injuries. In 1977, about 60,000 people tried hang gliding.

# Important American Aircraft Types (U.S. Air Force)

Abbreviations: GA—Garrett AiResearch; All—Detroit Diesel Allison Div. of General Motors; Con—Continental; GD—General Dynamics; GE—General Electric; Lyc—Lycoming; RI—Rockwell International; P&W—Pratt & Whitney; PWC—Pratt & Whitney Aircraft of Canada, Ltd; Wr—Curtiss Wright; kt—knots.

| Type | Manufacturer | Popular name | Power plant | Crew | Wing-span, ft/in. | Length, ft/in. | Height, ft/in. | Gross weight, lb | Speed, mph |
|---|---|---|---|---|---|---|---|---|---|
| **ATTACK** | | | | | | | | | |
| A-7D | Vought Corp. | Corsair 2 | 1 All TF41-A-1 | 1 | 38/7 | 46/1 | 16/0 | 42,000 | 620 |
| A-10 | Fairchild Rep. | Thunderbolt II | 2 GE TF34-GE-100 | 1 | 57/5 | 53/3 | 14/6 | 46,038 | 400 kt |
| A-37B | Cessna | Dragonfly | 2 GE J85-GE-17A | 1 | 35/8 | 29/3 | 8/9 | 14,000 | 425 kt |
| **BOMBERS** | | | | | | | | | |
| B-1 | R1/B-1 Division | — | 4 GE F101-GE-F100 | 4 | 137/0[3] | 150/0 | 34/0 | 388,000 | Mach 2+ |
| B-52G | Boeing | Stratofortress | 8 P&W J57-P-43W | 6 | 185/0 | 161/11 | 40/8 | 488,000 | 650 |
| B-52H | Boeing | Stratofortress | 8 P&W TF33-P-3 | 6 | 185/0 | 159/3 | 40/8 | 488,000 | 650 |
| FB-111A | GD/Ft. Worth | — | 2 P&W TF30-P-7 | 2 | 70/0[4] | 73/6 | 17/0 | 114,000 | Mach 2+ |
| **FIGHTERS** | | | | | | | | | |
| F-4E | McDonnell Douglas | Phantom 2 | 2 GE J79-GE-17 | 2 | 38/6 | 63/0 | 16/5 | 58,000 | Mach 2.2 |
| F-15A | McDonnell Douglas | Eagle | 2 P&W F100-PW-100 | 1 | 42/8 | 63/8 | 18/6 | 41,000 | Mach 2.5 |
| F-16 | GD/Ft. Worth | — | 1 P&W F100-PW-100 | 1 | 31/0 | 47/6 | 16/4 | 22,000 | Mach 2 |
| F-106A | GD/Convair | Delta Dart | 1 P&W J75-P-17 | 1 | 38/3 | 70/8 | 20/3 | 36,000 | Mach 2 |
| F-111F | GD/Ft. Worth | — | 2 P&W TF30-P-100 | 2 | 63/0[5] | 73/6 | 17/0 | 100,000 | Mach 2.5 |
| YF-17 | Northrop | — | 2 GE YJ101-GE-100 | 1 | 35/0 | 56/0 | 14/6 | 23,000 | Mach 2 |
| **RECONNAISSANCE** | | | | | | | | | |
| RF-4C | McDonnell Douglas | Phantom 2 | 2 GE J79-GE-15 | 2 | 38/4 | 62/9 | 16/5 | 58,000 | Mach 2.2 |
| RWB-57F | GD/Ft. Worth | Canberra | 2 P&W TF33-P-11 | 2 | 122/0 | 69/0 | 19/0 | 50,000 | — |
| SR-71 | Lockheed/Calif. | — | 2 P&W J58 | 2 | 55/6 | 107/4 | 18/5 | — | Mach 3 |
| U/WU-2 | Lockheed/Calif. | — | 1 P &W J75 | 1–2 | 80/0 | 49/6 | 13/0 | 17,000 | 400 kt |
| **OBSERVATION** | | | | | | | | | |
| 0-2A | Cessna | Skymaster | 2 Con 10-360-D | 1 | 38/0 | 29/2 | 9/5 | 4,850 | 192 kt |
| OV-10A[1] | RI/Columbus | Bronco | 2 A&R T76-G-416/417 | 1 | 40/0 | 39/7 | 15/1 | 14,466 | 350 kt |
| **EARLY WARNING COMMAND, CONTROL AND COMMUNICATIONS** | | | | | | | | | |
| E-3A | Boeing | AWACS | 4 P&W TF33-P-100A | 17 | 145/9 | 152/1 | 42/0 | 325,000 | 473 |
| E-4A/B | Boeing | — | 4 GE CF6-50E | 5 | 195/7 | 231/3 | 63/5 | 803,000 | — |
| **CARGO/TRANSPORT** | | | | | | | | | |
| C-5A | Lockhead/Georgia | Galaxy | 4 GE TF39 | 7 | 222/8 | 245/9 | 65/1 | 764,500 | 550 |
| C-9A | McDonnell Douglas | Nightingale | 2 P&W JT8D-9 | 2–7 | 93/3 | 119/3 | 27/5 | 108,000 | 570 |
| C-12A[2] | Beech | King Air | 2 PWC PT6A-38 | 2 | 54/5 | 43/6 | 14/6 | 12,500 | 260 kt |
| C-130E/H | Lockheed/Georgia | Hercules | 4 All T56-A-7/-15(H) | 5 | 132/6 | 99/5 | 38/4 | 155,000 | 360 |
| C-140A | Lockheed/Georgia | Jetstar | 4 P&W J60-P-5 | 5 | 54/4 | 60/4 | 20/4 | 40,921 | 525 |
| C-141A | Lockheed/Georgia | Starlifter | 4 P&W TF33-P-7 | 4–9 | 160/7 | 145/0 | 39/3 | 325,000 | 505 |
| HC-130H | Lockheed/Georgia | Hercules | 4 All T56-A-15 | 8 | 132/6 | 100/5 | 38/4 | 155,000 | 360 |
| KC-135A | Boeing | Stratotanker | 4 P&W J57-P-59W | 4 | 130/9 | 136/3 | 38/4 | 297,000 | 530 |
| VC-6B | Beech | — | 2 PWC PT6A-20 | 1–2 | 50/2 | 35/5 | 14/7 | 9,650 | 280 |
| VC-137C | Boeing | — | 4 P&W JT3D-3B | 4 | 145/9 | 152/9 | 42/5 | 328,000 | Mach 0.84 |
| YC-14 | Boeing | — | 2 GE CF6-50 | 3 | 129/0 | 131/0 | 48/0 | — | 460 |
| YC-15 | McDonnell Douglas | — | 4 P&W JT8D-17 | 3 | 110/3 | 124/3 | 43/3 | 216,680 | 460 |
| CT-39 | RI/General Aviation | Sabreliner | 2 P&W J60-P-3 | 2 | 44/5 | 43/8 | 15/9 | 18,650 | Mach 0.75 |
| **TRAINERS** | | | | | | | | | |
| T-33A | Lockheed/Calif. | T-Bird | 1 All J33-A-35 | 2 | 38/9 | 37/7 | 11/7 | 15,100 | 505 |
| T-37B | Cessna | Tweet | 2 CAE J69-T-25 | 2 | 33/8 | 29/3 | 9/2 | 6,575 | 425 |
| T-38A | Northrop | Talon | 2 GE J85-5 | 2 | 25/3 | 46/4 | 12/1 | 12,500 | Mach 1.2 |
| T-41A/D | Cessna | Mescalero | 1 Con I0-360H-1 | 2 | 36/2 | 26/5 | 8/9 | 2,550 | 142 |
| T-43A | Boeing | — | 2 P&W JT8D-9 | 2 | 93/0 | 100/0 | 37/0 | 115,500 | — |
| **UTILITY** | | | | | | | | | |
| AU-23A | Fairchild | Peacemaker | 1 GA TPE 331-1-101F | 1–3 | 49/7 | 36/8 | 12/3 | 6,100 | 174 |
| AU-24A | Helio/Gen. Aircraft | Stallion | 1 PWC PT6A-27 | 1–3 | 41/0 | 39/9 | 9/3 | 6,300 | 216 |
| U-4B | RI/Gen. Aviation | Aero Commander | 2 Lyc GSO-480-A1A6 | 1 | 35/5 | 34/2 | 14/5 | 7,000 | 244 |
| U-5A | Helio/Gen. Aircraft | H-500 Twin | 2 Lyc 0-540 | 1 | 41/0 | 32/0 | 8/8 | 5,400 | 185 |
| U-10A/D | Helio/Gen. Aircraft | Courier | 1 Lyc GO-480-G1D6 | | 39/0 | 31/0 | 8/8 | 3,850 | 167 |

1. Air Force/Marines. 2. Air Force/Army. 3. Wing extended. 4. Wing extended; 34 ft fully swept. 5. Wing extended; 31.11 ft fully swept. *Source:* Department of the Air Force.

# Official World Airplane Records

*Source:* National Aeronautic Association.

## Speed Over Measured Straightaway Course

| Speed (mph) | Date | Type plane | Pilot | Place |
|---|---|---|---|---|
| 314.32 | Dec. 25, 1934 | Caudron | Raymond Delmotte (France) | Istres, France |
| 352.39 | Sept. 13, 1935 | Hughes Special | Howard Hughes (U.S.) | Santa Ana, Calif. |
| 379.63 | Nov. 11, 1937 | BF-113R | Herman Wurster (Germany) | Augsburg, Germany |
| 469.22 | April 26, 1939 | ME-109R | Fritz Wendel (Germany) | Augsburg, Germany |
| 606.25 | Nov. 7, 1945 | Gloster Meteor IV | Group Capt. H. Wilson (U.K.) | Herne Bay, England |
| 615.78 | Sept. 7, 1946 | Gloster Meteor | Group Capt. E. M. Donalson (U.K.) | Littlehampton, England |
| 650.80 | Aug. 25, 1947 | Douglas D-558 | Maj. Marion Carl, USMC | Muroc AFB, Calif. |
| 670.98 | Sept. 15, 1948 | North American F-86A | Maj. R. L. Johnson (USAF) | Muroc AFB, Calif. |
| 698.51 | Nov. 19, 1952 | North American F-86D | Capt. James S. Nash (USAF) | Salton Sea, Calif. |
| 755.14 | Oct. 29, 1953 | North American YF | Lt. Col. F. K. Everest, Jr. (USAF) | Salton Sea, Calif. |
| 822.27 | Aug. 20, 1955 | North American F-100C | Col. Horace A. Hanes (U.S.) | Palmdale, Calif. |
| 1,132.14 | March 10, 1956 | Fairey Delta 2 | L. Peter Twiss, D.S.C. (U.K.) | Ford-Chichester, England |
| 1,207.60 | Dec. 12, 1957 | McDonnell F-101A | Maj. Adrian E. Drew (USAF) | Edwards AFB, Calif. |
| 1,404.09 | May 16, 1958 | Lockheed F104 | Capt. Walter W. Irwin (USAF) | Edwards AFB, Calif. |
| 1,483.85 | Oct. 31, 1959 | Sukhoi S-66 | G. Mossolov (U.S.S.R.) | U.S.S.R. |
| 1,525.96 | Dec. 15, 1959 | F-106A Delta Wing Monoplane | Maj. Joseph W. Rogers (USAF) | Edwards AFB, Calif. |
| 1,606.32 | Nov. 22, 1961 | McDonnell F4H | Lt. Col. R. B. Robinson (USMC) | Edwards AFB, Calif. |
| 1,665.89 | July 7, 1962 | E-166 Jet | G. Mossolov (U.S.S.R.) | U.S.S.R. |
| 2,070.101 | May 1, 1965 | Lockheed YF-12A Jet | Col. R. L. Stephens (USAF) | Edwards AFB, Calif. |
| 2,196.17 | July 28, 1976 | Lockheed SR-71 | Capt. Eldon W. Joersz (USAF) | Beale AFB, Calif. |

Fastest U.S. continental: Capt. Robert G. Sowers (USAF)—Convair B-58 "Hustler"—from Long Beach, Calif., to Kennedy International Airport, N.Y.—2,458.58 statute miles—2 h 0 min 58.71 sec—average speed, 1,214.65 mph—March 5, 1962.

## Distance, Straight Line

| Distance (mi.) | Date | Crew | From | To |
|---|---|---|---|---|
| 4,911.93 | Sept. 27–29, 1929 | Costes & Bellonte (France) | Le Bourget, France | Manchuria |
| 5,011.35 | July 28–30, 1931 | Russel N. Boardman, John Polando (U.S.) | New York | Istanbul |
| 5,656.93 | Aug. 5–7, 1933 | Maurice Rossi, Paul Codos (France) | New York | Ryack, Syria |
| 6,305.66 | July 12–14, 1937 | Gromov, Youmachev, Daniline (U.S.S.R.) | Moscow | San Jacinto, Calif. |
| 7,158.44 | Nov. 5–7, 1938 | Sqd. Ldr. R. Kellett (U.K.) | Ismailia, Egypt | Darwin, Australia |
| 7,916.00 | Nov. 19–20, 1945 | Col. C. S. Irvine & Lt. Col. G. R. Stanley (U.S.) | Guam | Washington, D. C. |
| 11,235.60 | Sept. 29–Oct. 1, 1946 | Comdr. Thomas D. Davies, Comdrs. Eugene P. Rankin, Walter S. Reid, Lt. Comdr. Ray A. Tabeling (USN) | Perth, Australia | Columbus, Ohio |
| 12,532.28 | Jan. 10–11, 1962 | Maj. Clyde P. Evely (USAF) | Kadena, Okinawa | Madrid |

Longest light airplane (3,858–6,614 lb) distance: Maximillian A. Conrad—U. S. Piper Comanche 250, Lycoming 0-540-AIAS (250 hp), from Casablanca, Morocco, to Los Angeles, 7,668.48 mi.—June 2–4, 1959.

## Distance, Closed Course

| Distance (mi.) | Date | Crew | Place |
|---|---|---|---|
| 6,587.441 | March 23–26, 1932 | Bossoutrot & Rossi (France) | Oran |
| 7,239.588 | May 13–15, 1938 | Comdr. Fujita & Sgt. Maj. Takahashi (Japan) | Kisarasu, Japan |
| 8,037.899 | July 30–Aug. 1, 1939 | Angelo Tondi, Roberto Dagasso, Ferrucio Vignoli (Italy) | Rome |
| 8,854.308 | Aug. 1–2, 1947 | Lt. Col. O. F. Lassiter (U.S.) Capt. W. J. Valentine (U.S.) | Tampa, Fla. |
| 10,078.84 | Dec. 13–14, 1960 | Lt. Col. J. R. Grissom (USAF) | Edwards AFB, Calif. |
| 11,336.92 | June 6–7, 1962 | Capt. William Stevenson (USAF) | Seymour-Johnson, N.C. |

## Altitude

| Height (ft) | Date | Crew | Place |
|---|---|---|---|
| 44,819 | Sept. 28, 1933 | G. Lemoine (France) | Villacoublay, France |
| 47,352 | April 11, 1934 | Comdr. Renato Donati (Italy) | Rome |
| 49,944 | Sept. 28, 1936 | Sqd. Ldr. F. R. D. Swain (U.K.) | South Farnborough, England |
| 53,937 | June 30, 1937 | Fl. Lt. M. J. Adam (U.K.) | Farnborough, England |
| 56,046 | Oct. 22, 1938 | Col. Mario Pezzi (Italy) | Montecelio |

**Altitude**

| Height (ft) | Date | Crew | Place |
|---|---|---|---|
| 59,445[1] | March 23, 1948 | John Cunningham (U.K.) | Hatfield, England |
| 63,668[1] | May 4, 1953 | Walter F. Gibb (U.K.) | Bristol, England |
| 65,889[1] | Aug. 29, 1955 | Walter F. Gibb (U.K.) | Bristol, England |
| 70,308[1] | Aug. 28, 1957 | Michael Randrup (U.K.) | Luton, England |
| 91,243[1] | May 7, 1958 | Maj. H. C. Johnson (USAF) | Palmdale, Calif. |
| 103,389[1] | Nov. 14, 1959 | Capt. Joe B. Jordan (USAF) | Edwards AFB, Calif. |
| 314,750[2] | July 17, 1962 | Maj. Robert M. White (USAF) | Edwards AFB, Calif. |
| 118,898 | July 25, 1973 | Alexander Fedotov (U.S.S.R.) | U.S.S.R. |
| 123,524 | Aug. 31, 1977 | Alexander Fedotov (U.S.S.R.) | U.S.S.R. |

1. Jet-propelled aircraft. 2. X-15-1-rocket plane.

## Passenger Traffic of Leading U.S. Airports, 1977

| Airport | Passengers[1] |
|---|---|
| O'Hare; Chicago | 44.2 |
| Hartsfield International; Atlanta | 29.9 |
| International; Los Angeles | 28.4 |
| Kennedy; New York City | 22.7 |
| International; San Francisco | 20.2 |
| International; Honolulu | 18.1 |
| Dallas–Ft. Worth | 17.3 |
| Stapleton International; Denver | 15.3 |
| La Guardia; New York City | 15.2 |
| International; Miami | 13.3 |
| National; Washington, D.C. | 13.2 |
| Logan; Boston | 12.1 |
| Metro Wayne; Detroit | 9.0 |
| Pittsburgh | 8.8 |
| International; Philadelphia | 8.6 |
| Intercontinental; Houston | 8.0 |
| Las Vegas; Nev. | 8.0 |
| International; Newark, N.J. | 7.4 |
| Seattle–Tacoma; Seattle, Wash. | 7.3 |
| International; St. Louis | 6.9 |
| Hopkins; Cleveland | 6.4 |
| International; Tampa, Fla. | 5.9 |
| International; New Orleans | 5.4 |
| International; San Diego, Calif. | 5.4 |
| P.R. International; San Juan, P.R. | 5.3 |
| Memphis, Tenn. | 5.1 |
| Sky Harbor International; Phoenix | 5.0 |
| International; Kansas City, Mo. | 4.8 |
| International; Orlando, Fla. | 4.2 |
| International; Portland, Ore. | 3.7 |
| Baltimore–Washington | 3.2 |
| International; Greater Buffalo, N.Y. | 3.1 |
| San Jose; Calif. | 3.1 |
| Anchorage; Alaska | 2.9 |
| Dulles; Washington, D.C. | 2.9 |
| Charlotte; N.C. | 2.8 |
| Cincinnati | 2.8 |
| Kahului; Hawaii | 2.8 |
| Milwaukee | 2.8 |
| Weir Cook Municipal; Indianapolis | 2.8 |
| Oakland; Calif. | 2.5 |
| Sacramento; Calif. | 2.5 |
| San Antonio | 2.5 |

1. Enplaned, deplaned, and transfer, in millions. *Source:* Airport Operators Council International.

## Disposition of Hijackers of Aircraft in U.S. Commerce, 1930–78[1]

| Disposition of case | Number |
|---|---|
| Convictions[2] | 100 |
| United States | 91 |
| Foreign | 9 |
| Acquittals | 3 |
| Committed to mental institution | 22 |
| Cases dismissed | 6 |
| No prosecution | 5 |
| Killed or Suicide | 19 |
| Cases pending | 11 |
| Fugitives[3] | 94 |
| **Total** | **260** |

1. Through January 1, 1978. 2. Foreign convictions include 1 in Mexico, 1 in Lebanon, 1 in Italy, 2 in Argentina, 1 in the Dominican Republic, and 3 in Cuba. 3. Includes a number of passive companions indicted along with hijackers. *Source:* Department of Transportation, Federal Aviation Administration.

## World Airplane Hijackings and Attempts

| | Place of flight origin | | |
|---|---|---|---|
| Years | U.S. | Foreign | Total |
| 1930–67 | 12 | 67 | 79 |
| 1968 | 22 | 13 | 35 |
| 1969 | 40 | 47 | 87 |
| 1970 | 27 | 56 | 83 |
| 1971 | 27 | 31 | 58 |
| 1972 | 31 | 31 | 62 |
| 1973 | 2 | 20 | 22 |
| 1974 | 7 | 19 | 26 |
| 1975 | 12 | 13 | 25 |
| 1976 | 4 | 14 | 18 |
| 1977 | 6 | 26 | 32 |
| **Total** | **190** | **337** | **527** |

*Source:* Department of Transportation, Federal Aviation Administration.

## Average Hours and Earnings in Aircraft Industries

| Hours and earnings | 1976 | 1975 | 1974 | 1970 | 1965 | 1960 | 1955 | 1950 |
|---|---|---|---|---|---|---|---|---|
| Average weekly hours | | | | | | | | |
| Aircraft industries | 41.6 | 40.4 | 39.4 | 41.0 | 41.2 | 40.6 | 41.4 | 41.4 |
| Engines and parts industries | 41.0 | 41.4 | 41.2 | 40.5 | 42.1 | 41.1 | 40.6 | 41.7 |
| Average weekly earnings | | | | | | | | |
| Aircraft industries | $283 | $250 | $219 | $171 | $130 | $110 | $90 | $67 |
| Engines and parts industries | $281 | $249 | $224 | $166 | $133 | $112 | $86 | $69 |
| Average hourly earnings | | | | | | | | |
| Aircraft industries | $6.81 | $6.20 | $5.57 | $4.17 | $3.16 | $2.71 | $2.17 | $1.62 |
| Engines and parts industries | $6.86 | $6.03 | $5.43 | $4.10 | $3.17 | $2.73 | $2.13 | $1.66 |

NOTE: Figures are latest available. *Source:* Department of Transportation, Federal Aviation Administration.

## Foreign Words and Phrases

(The English meanings given are not necessarily literal translations.)

**ab ovo:** from the beginning
**à bon marché:** good bargain; cheap
**à deux:** for two; between two
**a priori:** from something previous
**à votre santé:** to your health
**ad infinitum:** to infinity; with no end
**ad valorem:** according to its value
**al fresco:** outdoors
**alma mater:** one's college or school
**alter ego:** other self
**amicus curiae:** friend of the court
**ancien regime:** the old order
**anno Domini:** year of our Lord
**ante bellum:** before the war
**au contraire:** on the contrary
**au courant:** current; up-to-date
**auf Wiedersehen:** goodbye
**bête noire:** particular nemesis
**bienvenue:** welcome
**bon mot:** a funny or witty saying
**bon vivant:** a gourmet, an epicure
**bona fide:** in good faith; genuine; honest
**carpe diem:** enjoy today; seize the day
**carte blanche:** unlimited authority
**cause célèbre:** a cause that generates wide interest
**caveat emptor:** buy at your own risk; let the buyer beware
**circa:** about; approximately
**chacun à son goût:** each to his own taste
**combien:** how much?
**corpus delicti:** fundamental fact or facts about the commission of a crime
**coup de grâce:** finishing blow
**cum grano salis:** with a grain of salt
**d'accord:** in accord; agreement
**de facto:** as a matter of fact; actual
**de profundis:** out of the depths
**Deo gratias:** thanks be to God
**Deo volente:** God willing
**dernier cri:** the last word
**deus ex machina:** artificially produced to bring a solution to some extreme difficulty
**dramatis personae:** characters in a play
**ecce homo:** this is the man
**en masse:** all together
**en passant:** in passing
**fait accompli:** an accomplished fact
**faux pas:** a false step; a mistake
**flagrante delicto:** caught in the act
**Gesundheit:** good health (God bless you)
**habeas corpus:** common-law writ to bring a person before a court or judge
**hoi polloi:** the common people
**honi soit qui mal y pense:** evil to him who thinks evil of it
**hors d'oeuvre:** appetizer
**idée fixe:** fixed idea; obsession
**in loco parentis:** in place of a parent
**ipso facto:** by the very fact
**je ne sais quoi:** I don't know what; an elusive quality
**jeunesse dorée:** gilded youth
**laissez faire:** noninterference
**l'chaim:** to life
**maven:** an expert; connoisseur
**mea culpa:** I am to blame
**mirabile dictu:** wonderful to relate
**modus operandi:** method of operation; way of working
**nom de plume:** pen name
**non compos mentis:** not of sound mind
**non sequitur:** it does not follow
**O tempora! O mores!:** What sad times and customs
**omnia vincit amor:** love conquers all
**per annum:** by the year
**per capita:** by the head; individually
**per diem:** by the day; daily
**persona non grata:** an unwelcome or unacceptable person
**plus ça change, plus c'est le même chose:** the more things change, the more they remain the same
**post mortem:** after death
**pro bono publico:** for the public good
**pro tempore (pro tem):** for the time being; temporary
**quid pro quo:** something done or given in exchange for something else
**repondez s'il vous plait:** please reply; please answer (abbr. R.S.V.P.)
**requiescat in pace:** rest in peace
**sans souci:** without worry or care
**savoir faire:** know-how; manners for all occasions
**semper fidelis:** always faithful
**shalom:** peace
**sic transit gloria mundi:** so passes the glory of the world
**s'il vous plait:** if you please; please
**sine die:** with no day set for the next meeting
**sine qua non:** indispensable
**status (in) quo:** state in which anything is
**sui generis:** in a class by itself
**tempus fugit:** time flies
**tout de suite:** immediately
**veni, vidi, vici:** I came, I saw, I conquered
**vis-à-vis:** face-to-face

# WHERE TO FIND OUT MORE

## Reference Books And Other Sources

This cannot be a complete record of all the thousands of available sources of information. Nevertheless, these selected references will enable the reader to locate additional facts about many subjects covered in the *Information Please Almanac.* The editors have chosen sources that they believe will be most helpful to the general reader.

### General References

**Encyclopedias** are a unique category, since they attempt to cover most subjects quite thoroughly. Two most valuable multivolume encyclopedias are the **Encyclopaedia Britannica** and the **Encyclopedia Americana.** Useful one-volume encyclopedias are the **New Columbia Encyclopedia** and the **Random House Encyclopedia.**

**Dictionaries** and similar "word books" are also unique: **Webster's New International Dictionary** (third edition, unabridged). **Random House Dictionary. Merriam Webster's Collegiate Dictionary** (eighth edition, abridged). **Oxford English Dictionary. Bartlett's Familiar Quotations. Roget's Thesaurus. Modern American Usage.**

There are a number of useful **atlases: New York Times Atlas of the World,** a number of historical atlases (Penguin Books), **Oxford Economic Atlas of the World, Atlas of the Universe** (Rand McNally), **Atlas of the Historical Geography of the U.S.** (Carnegie Institution of Washington and the American Geographical Society), and contemporary road atlases of the U.S. (Rand McNally).

A source of information on virtually all subjects is the United States Government Printing Office. For information write: Superintendent of Documents, Washington, D.C. 20402.

For help on any subject, consult: **Subject Guide to Books in Print, The New York Times Index,** and the **Reader's Guide to Periodical Literature** in your library.

### Specific References

**America Votes** (Congressional Quarterly, Inc.)
**American Indian, Reference Encyclopedia of the** (Todd Publications)
**Amphibians of the World, Living** (Doubleday)
**Animal Life Encyclopedia** (Van Nostrand Reinhold)
**Antiques, Collectors Encyclopedia of** (Crown)
**Architecture, World** (McGraw-Hill)
**Art, Encyclopedia of World** (McGraw-Hill)
**Art, History of** (Prentice-Hall)
**Art, Oxford Companion to** (Oxford University Press)
**Art, Who's Who in American** (R.R. Bowker)
**Art Directory, American** (R.R. Bowker)
**Authors, 1000–1900, European** (H.W. Wilson)
**Authors, 1600–1900, American** (H.W. Wilson)
**Authors, Twentieth Century** (H.W. Wilson)
**Authors Before 1800** (H.W. Wilson)
**Authors of the Nineteenth Century, British** (H.W. Wilson)
**Auto Racing, The New York Times Complete Guide to** (Quadrangle)
**Banking and Finance, Encyclopedia of** (Bankers Publishing Co.)
**Baseball Encyclopedia** (Information Concepts/Macmillan)
(Baseball) **World Series Records** (The Sporting News)
**Basketball, Modern Encyclopedia of** (Four Winds Press)
**Biographical Dictionary, Chambers** (St. Martin's Press)
**Biographical Dictionary, Webster's** (G. & C. Merriam)
**Biography Yearbook, Current** (H.W. Wilson)
**Birds of America** (Audubon)
**Book Review Digest, 1905—** (H.W. Wilson)
**Business Almanac, Dow Jones-Irwin** (Dow Jones-Irwin)
**Catholic Encyclopedia, New** (Publishers Guild/McGraw-Hill)
**Chemistry, Encyclopedia of** (Van Nostrand Reinhold)
**Chemistry and Physics, Handbook of** (Chemical Rubber Co.)
**Christian Church, Oxford Dictionary of the** (Oxford University Press)
**Church Annual, Episcopal** (Morehouse-Barlow)
**Churches, Yearbook of American and Canadian** (Abingdon Press)
**Climate and Man** (U.S. Department of Agriculture)
**Communist Affairs, Yearbook on International** (Hoover Institution Press)
**Composers, Great, 1300–1900; A Biographical and Critical Guide** (H.W. Wilson)
**Composers Since 1900; A Biographical and Critical Guide** (H.W. Wilson)
**Congressional Quarterly Directory** (Congressional Quarterly, Inc.)
**Consumer Sourcebook** (Gale Research Co.)
**Consumer Reports** (Consumers Union)
**Dance Encyclopedia** (Simon & Schuster)
**Drama, Crowell's Handbook of Classical** (Crowell)
**Ecology Information and Organizations, Guide to** (H.W. Wilson)
**Energy, Encyclopedia of** (McGraw-Hill)
**Environmental Quality Report** (Council on Environmental Quality)
**Environmental Science, Encyclopedia of** (McGraw-Hill)
**Europa Year Book** (Europa Publications)
**Facts, Famous First** (H.W. Wilson)
**Facts on File** (Facts on File, Inc.)
**Film, Oxford Companion to** (Oxford University Press)
**Filmgoer's Companion** (Hill & Wang)
**Fishing Encyclopedia, New Standard** (Holt, Rinehart & Winston)
**Football, Encyclopedia of** (A.S. Barnes & Co.)
**Foreign Terms, Dictionary of** (Crowell)
**Foundation Directory** (Columbia University Press, dist.)
**Game, Rules of the** (Bantam Books)
**Geographical Dictionary, Webster's New** (G. & C. Merriam)

**Geography, Dictionary of** (Penguin Books)
**Government Manual, U.S.** (U.S. Office of the Federal Register)
**History, Album of American** (Charles Scribner's)
**History, Atlas of American** (Oxford University Press)
**History, Dictionary of American** (Charles Scribner's)
**History, Documents of American** (Appleton-Century-Crofts)
**History, Encyclopedia of Latin American** (Bobbs-Merrill)
**History, Encyclopedia of World** (Houghton-Mifflin)
**History, Timetables of** (Simon & Schuster)
**History and Literature, Oxford Companion to Canadian** (Oxford University Press)
**Ice Hockey, Complete Encyclopedia of** (Prentice-Hall)
**Investments, American and Foreign, Manual of** (Moody's Investors Service)
**Jazz in the Seventies, Encyclopedia of** (Horizon)
**Judaica, Encyclopaedia** (Macmillan)
**Libraries, World Guide to** (R.R. Bowker)
**Library Directory, American** (R.R. Bowker)
**Literary History of the United States** (Macmillan)
**Literature, Oxford Companion to American** (Oxford University Press)
**Literature, Oxford Companion to Classical** (Oxford University Press)
**Literature, Oxford Companion to English** (Oxford University Press)
**Literature, Reader's Adviser to the Best in** (R.R. Bowker)
**Literature, Reader's Encyclopedia of American** (Crowell)
**Medical Adviser, Modern Home** (Doubleday)
**Museums, Directory of World** (Columbia University Press)
**Music, Handbook of American** (Free Press, Div. of Macmillan)
(Music) **ASCAP. Biographical Dictionary** (American Society of Authors, Composers, and Publishers)
**Music, Concise Oxford Dictionary of** (Oxford University Press)
**Music, Harvard Dictionary of** (Harvard University Press)
**Music and Musicians, Grove's Dictionary of** (St. Martin's Press)
**Musical Terms, Dictionary of** (Gordon Press)
**Mythology, (Larousse) World** (G.P. Putnam's Sons)
**Nations, Handbook of New** (Crowell)
**Nations, Worldmark Encyclopedia of the** (Harper & Row)
**Negro Reference Book, American** (Prentice-Hall)
**Newspapers and Periodicals, Ayer Directory of** (Ayer Press)
**Opera Book, Kobbe's Complete** (G.P. Putnam's)
**Periodicals Directory, International** (Ulrich's)
**Physics and Electronics, International Dictionary of** (Van Nostrand Reinhold)
**Pocket Data Book, U.S.A.** (Bureau of Census)
**Poetry, Granger's Index to** (Columbia University Press)
**Politics, Almanac of American** (Gambit, Inc.)
**Politics, Who's Who in American** (R.R. Bowker)
**Private Schools, Handbook of** (Porter Sargent)
**Robert's Rules of Order** (Morrow & Co.)
**Science, American Men and Women of** (R.R. Bowker)
**Science and Technology, Asimov's Biographical Encyclopedia of** (Doubleday)
**Scientific Encyclopedia, Van Nostrand's** (Van Nostrand Reinhold)
**Scientific Terms, McGraw-Hill Dictionary of** (McGraw-Hill)
**Space, Encyclopedia of** (McGraw-Hill)
**Sports Dictionary, Webster's** (G. & C. Merriam Co.)
**Sports, Encyclopedia of** (A.S. Barnes & Co.)
**States, Book of** (Council of State Governments)
**Statesman's Yearbook** (Burke's Peerage, Ltd.)
**Tennis, Encyclopedia of** (Viking Press)
**Theater, Oxford Companion to the** (Oxford University Press)
**Theater, Who's Who in the** (Gale Research Co.)
**Trotting and Pacing Guide** (U.S. Trotting Association)
**United Nations, Demographic Yearbook** (U.N. Publishing Service)
**United States, Historical Statistics of the** (U.S. Department of Commerce)
**United States, Statistical Abstract of the** (Government Printing Office)
**United Nations, Statistical Yearbook of the** (U.N. Publishing Service)
**Washington Information Directory** (Congressional Quarterly, Inc.)
**Way Things Work** (Simon & Schuster)
**Weather Almanac** (Gale Research Co.)
**Wildlife, Atlas of World** (Rand McNally)
**Women, Notable American, 1607–1950** (Belknap Press)
**Women's Movement, Practical Guide to the** (Women's Action Alliance, Inc.)
**Who's Who (British),** (St. Martin's Press)
**Who's Who in America** (Marquis)
**World, Harper Encyclopedia of the Modern** (Harper & Row)

See the full range of publications of Dun & Bradstreet and Standard & Poor's for corporate financial and stockholder information.

For detailed information on American colleges and universities, see the many publications of the **American Council on Education.**

Also see the many specialized **Who's Who** volumes issued by Marquis for biographies of famous contemporaries in many fields.

## Birthstones

| Month | Stone | Month | Stone |
|---|---|---|---|
| January | Garnet | July | Ruby or Star Ruby |
| February | Amethyst | August | Peridot or Sardonyx |
| March | Aquamarine or Bloodstone | September | Sapphire or Star Sapphire |
| April | Diamond | October | Opal or Tourmaline |
| May | Emerald | November | Topaz |
| June | Pearl, Alexandrite, or Moonstone | December | Turquoise or Zircon |

*Source:* Jewelry Industry Council.

# Rules for Correct Punctuation, Capitalization, Abbreviation

*Blanche Ormont*

## Punctuation

**Period (.)** Use a period: (1) After a statement or command: *Panama is roughly the size of South Carolina. Go to the head of the line.*

(2) After most abbreviations: C.O.D., Ms., U.S. (In familiar abbreviations, where the letters themselves are usually spoken, the period is often omitted: *CIO, NBC, SPCA.* )

(3) With decimals and in dollars and cents: *.05, 22.5, $12.95.* Do not use a period after *percent,* as in *twenty percent;* if cents is written out or the cents sign is used, as in *27 cents, 27¢;* or after Roman numerals, *XXIII, Act III,* except when numbering or listing.

**Question Mark (?)** Use the question mark after a direct question: *Do you know why the world's climate is changing?* Do not use the question mark after an indirect question or request: *The teacher asked him if he knew the capital of South Dakota. Will you please return this book as soon as possible.*

**Exclamation Point (!)** Use an exclamation point after an emphatic statement or after a sentence, phrase, or word expressing strong feeling: *You're absolutely wrong! Ouch! That hurts!*

**Comma (,)** The comma is the most commonly used (and misused) punctuation mark. It indicates a slight separation between words or groups of words and should serve primarily to make the writer's meaning clear. Too many commas may cause the reader to separate words that should be grouped together, or they may unnecessarily slow the movement of a sentence. Too few commas, or misplaced commas, may seriously distort the writer's meaning. Although one should always use good judgment in deciding when and where to use commas, the following rules are generally applicable. Use a comma:

(1) To separate words, phrases, or clauses (a clause is a group of words that has a subject and a predicate) in a series of three or more items: *Tuition, board, lodging, and medical and dental care are provided.* (Note that the comma before the second *and* has been omitted because *medical and dental care* is considered a single unit. However, in some cases it is necessary to insert the comma before *and* to avoid misreading: *The course includes navigation, electricity, ship construction, marine biology, and engineering.* )

Commas are used between two or more adjectives preceding a noun if each separately could modify the noun and if switching the order of the adjectives does not alter the sense: *It was a cold, bleak, rainy day.* Do not use commas if the first adjective qualifies the entire expression following it: *Their constitution established a strong central government.*

Use a comma after *etc.* (abbreviation of *et cetera* ) when it is the last of a series within a sentence: *Books, papers, cartons, etc., lay scattered about the room.*

(2) Between independent clauses (clauses that could stand alone as complete sentences) joined by *and, but, for, or, nor: Pluto has the most eccentric orbit in the solar system, and at times it comes closer to the sun than Neptune. A huge fireball appeared in the sky, but the natives were not afraid.* In a short compound sentence—a sentence made up of two or more independent clauses—the comma is often omitted: *The canoe turned over and everyone fell into the water*

(3) To set off introductory words, phrases, or clauses: *Outraged, he slammed the door behind him. During the wars that followed the French Revolution, Belgium was occupied and later annexed to France. Because Bolivia has no access to the sea, foreign trade must pass through free ports in Chile and river ports on the Amazon.*

If the introductory phrase or clause is very short, or if it is the subject of the sentence, do not use a comma: *Because of its beaches the state is a popular resort area. To cross the sea in ancient times was an extraordinary feat.*

Such introductory transitional words as *yes, no, still, nevertheless, moreover, however, therefore, besides, furthermore,* and weak exclamations like *well, oh,* and *why* should be followed by a comma: *No, I cannot go with you. Well, that's a long story. Why, how nice!*

(4) To set off nonessential elements—words, phrases, or clauses that are not closely related to the rest of the sentence and could be left out without drastically changing its meaning: *Hinduism dates back, perhaps, to prehistoric times. The emperor, in recognition of Confucius' teachings, offered sacrifices at his tomb. Gold, which was responsible for California's settlement boom, is still found in that state.*

To determine whether a modifying expression is restrictive or nonrestrictive (essential or nonessential), see if it can be omitted without significantly changing the meaning. If it is essential to the meaning of the sentence, commas are not used: *Delhi residents who would not limit their families were denied government assistance.* The clause "who would not limit their families" is clearly restrictive; if it were removed, the sentence would indicate that *all* Delhi residents were denied government assistance.

Use the comma before *for, although, though, as, since,* and *because* when these words introduce nonrestrictive clauses or phrases: *The Age of Enlightenment brought about the Jews' emancipation, although persecutions did not end entirely.* But: *The famous Dutch dikes are requisite to the use of much land because half of the country's area is below sea level.* (No comma before *because,* which introduces a restrictive clause.)

Appositives are words or phrases that directly follow a noun or pronoun and identify or explain it. If an appositive is nonrestrictive, it is set off by commas: *The fur-bearing chinchilla, a native of the colder plateau regions, is also raised.* If it is restrictive, no commas are used: *The phrase "hot line" refers to the emergency communications link between Washington and Moscow.*

Contrasting expressions introduced by such words and phrases as *not, but not,* and *though not* are usually nonrestrictive and are therefore set off by commas: *Venus, not Mars, is Earth's nearest neighbor.*

When nonrestrictive words, phrases, or clauses occur within a sentence, they must be set off by *two* commas—one before the expression and one after.

(5) In certain conventional places: (a) To separate items in addresses and dates: *He wrote to his aunt at 94 Birch Road, Omaha, Nebraska, on June 12, 1924.* (b) With numbers greater than three figures: *1,422, 12,498,620.* (c) In letters, after salutations (in informal letters) and after the complimentary close: *Dear Aunt Mary, Sincerely yours,.* (d) To set off the name of a person addressed: *John, please close the door. Listen carefully, Sarah, because this is important.* (e) To separate degrees and titles from names: *Margaret Harrison, M.D., Ph.D. Frank Simmons, Treasurer.* (f) To set off direct quotations: *"Happiness," someone said, "is a warm puppy."* With exclamations or very short quotations, no comma is necessary: *"Hi there!" she called. He constantly said "like" and "you know."*

(6) Whenever necessary to avoid misunderstanding: *Several months after, he saw his father.* (Without the comma the sentence changes meaning, turning into the clause *Several months after he saw his father.)*

**Semicolon (;)** The semicolon is a mark of separation that functions like a weak period or a strong comma. Use a semicolon:

(1) Between two independent clauses which are not joined by a conjunction: *The soil is generally poor; high crop yields are dependent upon large-scale use of fertilizers.*

(2) Between two independent clauses containing one or more commas even if a conjunction is used: *After members of the committee have debated the bill, a vote is taken; and if the vote is favorable, the bill is sent back to the floor of the house.*

(3) Between two main clauses linked by such connecting words as *therefore, however, finally, thus, otherwise, nevertheless,* and by such phrases as *for example, in fact, on the contrary: The first game of lawn tennis in the United States was played in 1874; however, it was not until 1880 that standard measurements for the court were established.*

(4) Between items in a series if one or more are subdivided by commas: *Among the great libraries of the world are the British Museum, with more than 6,000,000 printed volumes; the National Diet Library in Tokyo, containing more than 4,100,000 volumes; and, of course, the United States Library of Congress, whose extensive collections total over 72,466,000 volumes.*

**Colon (:)** The colon is a mark of anticipation introducing material that follows it. Use a colon:

(1) To introduce a long quotation, explanatory statement, or question: *The Declaration of Independence states: "We hold these truths to be self-evident, that all men are created equal, that they are endowed by their Creator with certain unalienable Rights, that among these are Life, Liberty, and the Pursuit of Happiness." In 1976, the World Health Organization accomplished a major goal: It virtually eliminated one of mankind's most ancient enemies—smallpox. The question we discussed was: What are the real differences between Socialism and Communism?*

(2) To introduce a list of items. The colon here is frequently, though not always, preceded by such phrases as *the following* or *as follows: Among the great Gothic structures of Europe are the following: Chartres Cathedral, Notre Dame de Paris, Milan Cathedral, and Cologne Cathedral.*

(3) In these customary places: (Note preceding use of colon.) After a formal salutation in a letter: *Dear Sir:;* between hours and minutes: *10:15 a.m.;* between volume and page in formal footnotes and bibliography: *The Dictionary of Dates 2:120–142;* between chapter and verse in the Bible: *Genesis 1:10;* between numerical elements in ratios: *4:2;* after the name of a speaker in a play: *Lady Macbeth: Out, damned spot!*

**Quotation Marks (" ")** Use quotation marks:

(1) To enclose a direct quotation: *"Life," said Julia Ward Howe, who lived to be ninety-one, "is like a cup of tea; the sugar is all at the bottom."*

Quotation marks are always used in *pairs,* before the quoted material and after it. However, if you quote two or more paragraphs, place quotation marks at the beginning of each paragraph and at the end of the entire quotation.

Single marks are used to enclose a quotation within a quotation. *"His constant use of such words as 'cool' and 'far out' has become very tiresome," the teacher remarked.*

(2) To enclose the title of a short literary work—a chapter, article, essay, poem, or short story—and titles of paintings, short musical compositions, and radio and television programs. The titles of longer works should be italicized. (Joyce's collection of short stories *Dubliners* includes the famous story "The Dead.")

(3) To enclose all words or phrases that are borrowed, that the writer does not wish to claim as his own, or that he uses ironically: *The term "the chain of being" was for centuries a descriptive name for the universe. For many of the world's poor, "home" is a tarpaper shack or a large oil pipe.*

(4) To enclose words or phrases which themselves are being discussed: *Many women now prefer the term "feminism" to the earlier phrase "women's lib."*

(5) When quotation marks are used with other punctuation, they appear as follows:

*Outside* a comma or period. *"I'm tired," she said. "It's been a long day."*

*Inside* the semicolon or colon: *A foreign phrase commonly misused to describe aristocracy is "hoi polloi"; actually, it means "the common people."*

*Outside* a question mark or exclamation point if either is part of the quotation—otherwise, inside. *"Get out of here!" she shrieked. Who wrote "The Unfinished Symphony"?*

**Apostrophe (')** Use an apostrophe:

(1) In contractions to indicate the omission of a letter: *haven't.*

(2) Before an *s* to form the plural of figures and

letters: *Two size 12's. Cross your t's and dot your i's.*

(3) To form possessives: *Mary's house, men's clothing.* If a plural ends in *s*, add only the apostrophe: *girls' sports, hostesses' duties.* If a singular ends in *s*, add the apostrophe and *s*: *James's car.* However, the second *s* may be omitted, especially if the word would become more difficult to pronounce: *Socrates' teachings.* Be sure never to use the apostrophe with the possessive pronouns *his, hers, its, yours, ours, theirs.*

**Hyphen (-)** Use a hyphen:

(1) To link many compound words—two or more words considered as a single unit: *secretary-treasurer, bull's-eye, heavy-hearted, cease-fire.* Do not use a hyphen if a compound modifier follows the noun: *This scientist is well known.* (But note use of hyphen in *a well-known scientist.*) Do not use a hyphen in a compound modifier that includes an adverb ending in *-ly* even if it precedes the noun: *richly deserved praise.*

(2) With certain prefixes and suffixes: *self-support, ex-wife, anti-American, co-worker, president-elect, husband-to-be.* When the parts have become merged in general use, the hyphen may be unnecessary: *midsummer, prehistoric, nonaligned.* (Since usage here is often inconsistent, it is wise, when in doubt, to consult a dictionary.)

(3) In compound numbers from twenty-one to ninety-nine and in fractions: *twenty-five, one-third.*

(4) To divide a word *between syllables* at the end of a line.

(5) Wherever misreading might occur, as in *a navy-blue uniform,* or if a prefix ends with a vowel and the root word begins with the same vowel: *re-elected, anti-inflationary, semi-independent.*

**Dash (—)** The dash indicates greater separation than a comma but lesser separation than parentheses. Use the dash:

(1) To indicate a sudden change in thought or sentence structure: *We rescheduled the picnic for the following Sunday—we hoped it would be a nice day—but it rained again.*

(2) To emphasize parenthetic, appositive, or explanatory matter. *Imagine a device that is only a cubic foot in size—the size of a hat box—containing 40,000 electronic parts!*

(3) To set off a parenthetic or appositive expression that is itself broken by commas: *She was beset by fears—of heights, open spaces, animals, traffic, strangers—and, as a result, she never left her home.*

**Parentheses (())** Generally speaking, dashes add emphasis to the material they enclose, while parentheses tend to subordinate it. Use parentheses:

(1) To enclose incidental or explanatory material that may be relevant but is not strictly necessary: *The rivers, lakes, and surrounding seas (except the Black Sea) are rich in fish. During the reign of Henry VIII (1509–47), the Church of England asserted its independence from the Roman Catholic Church.*

(2) Around figures or letters to enumerate items in a series: *Three qualities of good writing are (1) clarity, (2) consistency, and (3) coherence.*

Parenthetical statements within a sentence begin with a small letter and have no end punctuation, except a question mark or exclamation point if needed. If a comma, semicolon, or colon are necessary after the parenthetical material within a sentence, they are placed outside the closing curve. A complete parenthetic sentence within a paragraph but not within another sentence has an initial capital and end punctuation placed within the closing curve: *Although Nigeria was the world's sixth largest oil producer (its 1974 oil revenues totaled $8 billion), the country's per capita income was only $120 per year. (Even so, it remained black Africa's wealthiest nation.) This problem contributed to continuing government instability.*

**Brackets ([])** Use brackets to enclose parenthetic comments inserted in a quotation by the person using the quotation: *In his Nobel Lecture, Martin Luther King said, "In a dark, confused world [where war, poverty, and racism exist] the kingdom of God may yet reign in the hearts of men."*

## Capitalization

The use of capital letters is quite standardized in general English. Avoid unnecessary capitals, and when in doubt consult a dictionary. As a rule, capitalize the following:

(1) The first word of a complete sentence: *The modern museum originated during the Renaissance.*; of a quoted sentence: *Freud said, "What does a woman want?"*; of each line of poetry:

*Had we but world enough, and time,*
*This coyness, lady, were no crime.*—Andrew Marvell

(2) Proper names. A proper name is the name of a *particular* person, place, or thing. Capitalize all proper names including adjectives and abbreviations derived from proper names. Among the proper names to be capitalized are the names of specific persons or places: *John F. Kennedy, Vermont, China, Central Park;* organizations, institutions, buildings, and monuments: *the Republican Party, the Bank of America, Harvard University, the Museum of Modern Art, the Lincoln Memorial;* peoples, languages, religions, and political groups: *Africans, Indians, French, Caucasian, Methodist, Communist;* days of the week, months, holidays: *Tuesday, August, New Year's Day, Easter;* historical periods, events, or documents: *the Dark Ages, the Renaissance, the Holocaust, the Civil War, the Magna Carta, the Social Security Act;* geographical names and regions: *Yellowstone National Park, Lake Huron, the South Pole, the Northeast* (when words like *south* and *north* refer to directions rather than regions, they are not capitalized); names of departments of government and of institutions: *Department of Commerce, Police Department, the City Council, the English Department, the Graduate School;* stars, planets, constellations, satellites, except the sun, earth, and moon: *Sirius, Venus, Orion, Viking I, Halley's Comet;* words referring to the Deity, the Bible, and other sacred writings: *Jehovah, the Messiah, the Virgin, Genesis, Lamentations, the Koran.*

(3) Titles preceding proper names and titles of high rank used without the name: *Professor Cohen, Mayor Daley, Sergeant Jones, Aunt Ellen, the Pope, the President, the Secretary of State, the Queen Mother.*

(4) First and last words and all other words, except the articles *a, an, the,* conjunctions, and prepositions in titles of books, plays, poems, articles, movies, etc.: *Wild Animals of the World, Ode to the West Wind, All in the Family, Porgy and Bess.*

(5) The pronoun *I* and the exclamation *O*: *If I forget thee, O Jerusalem, let my right hand forget her cunning.*—Psalms

## Abbreviations

Abbreviations are useful and appropriate in notetaking, in reference works, in statistical tables, and in certain other situations where speed and space-saving are important. In general writing, however, abbreviations should be avoided. A few standard abbreviations that are correct in all writing are the following:

(1) Titles and names: *Mr., Messrs., Mrs., Dr., Esq., Sr., Jr., Ph.D., M.D., LL.D.* Do not use a title both before and after a name: *Mr. James T. Smith* or *James T. Smith, Ph.D.,* not *Mr. James T. Smith, Ph.D.*

Do not abbreviate civil, professional (except *Dr.* ), military, or political titles, except when the person's first name or initials are used: *Professor Downey* or *Prof. Charles Downey, General Marshall* or *Gen. G. C. Marshall,* never *Prof. Downey* or *Gen. Marshall.*

First names should, as a rule, be spelled out: *William Shakespeare,* not *Wm. Shakespeare.*

(2) Certain units of measurements: *a.m., p.m.,* A.D., B.C., *mph,* when used with figures, as in *50 mph; No.* with numbers expressed in figures, as in *No. 8.* Write out other expressions for time, weight, and size, as in *three ounces, two miles, four hours,* unless such expressions appear in directions, recipes, or technical writing: *½ tsp salt, 10 ft 2 in.*

(3) Names of organizations, governmental agencies, scientific words, trade names, and other expressions that are familiar to most people and are frequently referred to by their initials: *YMCA, AFL-CIO, FCC, CIA, FBI, NASA, DDT, DNA, CBS, MGM.* Generally no period is used. (Exceptions: *C.O.D., F.O.B.* ) Abbreviations like *Co., Inc., Ltd.,* or *Corp.* are correct when they are part of the company name: *Information Please Publishing, Inc.*

(4) Certain literary abbreviations: *i.e.* (that is); *e.g.* (for example); *ibid.* (in the same place); *etc.* (and so forth).

In ordinary usage, write out: names of states, countries, months, days of the week; words like *street, road, square* when they are used as part of a proper name: *Maple Street;* and numbers that can be expressed in not more than one or two words: *twenty books, four hundred miles* (but *$3,560.23, 60,211 miles* ).

These are "general" rules of punctuation, capitalization, and abbreviation designed to make writing as clear and "correct" as possible. There are no absolutes. Many publications have modifications of these basic rules that reflect their own special needs.

## Traditional Wedding Anniversary Gift List

| Anniversary | Gift | Anniversary | Gift | Anniversary | Gift |
|---|---|---|---|---|---|
| 1st | Paper | 9th | Pottery, willow | 25th | Silver |
| 2nd | Cotton | 10th | Tin, aluminum | 30th | Pearl |
| 3rd | Leather | 11th | Steel | 35th | Coral |
| 4th | Fruit, flowers | 12th | Silk, linen | 40th | Ruby |
| 5th | Wood | 13th | Lace | 50th | Gold |
| 6th | Candy, iron | 14th | Ivory | 55th | Emerald |
| 7th | Wool, copper | 15th | Crystal | 60th | Diamond |
| 8th | Bronze, pottery | 20th | China | 75th | Diamond |

*Source:* Jewelry Industry Council.

## Modern Wedding Anniversary Gift List

| Anniversary | Gift | Anniversary | Gift | Anniversary | Gift |
|---|---|---|---|---|---|
| 1st | Clock | 10th | Diamond jewelry | 19th | Bronze |
| 2nd | China | 11th | Fashion jewelry and accessories | 20th | Platinum |
| 3rd | Crystal, glass | | | 25th | Sterling Silver Jubilee |
| 4th | Electrical Appliances | 12th | Pearls or colored gems | 30th | Diamond |
| 5th | Silverware | 13th | Textiles, furs | 35th | Jade |
| 6th | Wood | 14th | Gold jewelry | 40th | Ruby |
| 7th | Desk sets, pen and pencil sets | 15th | Watches | 45th | Sapphire |
| | | 16th | Silver holloware | 50th | Golden Jubilee |
| 8th | Linens, laces | 17th | Furniture | 55th | Emerald |
| 9th | Leather | 18th | Porcelain | 60th | Diamond Jubilee |

*Source:* Jewelry Industry Council

# Forms of Address [1]



**Abbot.** *Address:* The Right Reverend ______ ______, O.S.B. (or other initials of the order), Abbot of ______; *or* The Right Rev. Abbot ______. *Begin:* Right Reverend and dear Father.

**Ambassador (American).** *Address:* His Excellency, The American Ambassador; *or* The Honorable ______ ______, American Ambassador; *or* His Excellency, ______ ______, Ambassador of Brazil at ______. *Begin:* Sir; *or* Excellency.

**Archbishop.** *Address:* The Most Reverend ______ ______, D.D., Archbishop of ______. *Begin:* Your Excellency.

**Archdeacon.** *Address:* The Venerable The Archdeacon of ______; *or* The Venerable ______ ______, Archdeacon of ______. *Begin:* Venerable Sir.

**Assemblyman.** *Address:* The Honorable ______ ______, Member of Assembly; *or* Assemblyman ______. *Begin:* Sir; *or* Dear Sir; *or* My dear Mr. ______.

**Associate Justice (Supreme Court).** *Address:* The Honorable ______ ______, United States Supreme Court; *or* Mr. Justice ______, The Supreme Court. *Begin:* My dear Mr. Justice; *or* Dear Justice ______.

**Bishop (Episcopal).** *Address:* To the Right Reverend ______ ______, Bishop of ______. *Begin:* Right Reverend and Dear Sir; *or* Dear Bishop ______; *or* My dear Bishop ______.

**Bishop (Methodist).** *Address:* The Reverend ______ ______, D.D. *Begin:* Reverend Sir; *or* Dear Sir; *or* Dear Bishop ______; *or* My dear Bishop ______.

**Bishop (Roman Catholic).** *Address:* The Most Reverend ______ ______, Bishop of ______. *Begin:* Your Excellency.

**Brother of a Religious Order.** *Address:* Brother ______ (followed by the initials of the order). *Begin:* Dear Brother ______.

**Cabinet Officer (U.S.).** *Address:* The Honorable the Secretary of State (*or* Defense, Agriculture, etc.); *or* The Honorable ______ ______, Secretary of State, The Attorney General, etc. *Begin:* Sir; *or* Dear Sir; *or* My dear Mr. Secretary; *or* My dear Mr. Attorney General.

**Cardinal.** *Address:* His Eminence John Cardinal Doe. *Begin:* Your Eminence.

**Chargé d'Affaires.** *Address:* The Chargé d'Affaires of ______; *or* ______ ______, Esq., Chargé d'Affaires; *or* Mr. ______ ______, Chargé d'Affaires. *Begin:* Dear Sir; *or* Sir; *or* My dear Mr. ______.

**Chief Justice of the U.S.** *Address:* The Chief Justice of the United States; *or* The Chief Justice, The Supreme Court. *Begin:* Sir; *or* My dear Mr. Chief Justice.

**Clergyman.** *Address:* The Reverend ______ ______; *or* (if a Doctor of Divinity) The Rev. Dr. ______ ______; *or* The Reverend ______ ______, D.D. *Begin:* Dear Sir; *or* Reverend Sir; *or* My dear Mr. (*or* Dr.) ______; *or* Dear Mr. (*or* Dr.) ______.

**Commissioner of a Department or Bureau.** *Address:* The Honorable ______ ______, Commissioner of ______. *Begin:* Sir; *or* Dear Sir.

**Congressman.** *Address:* The Honorable ______ ______, House of Representatives; or Honorable ______ ______, Representative in Congress, Springfield, Mass. *Begin:* Sir; *or* Dear Sir; *or* My dear Mr. ______.

**Consul.** *Address:* To the American Consul at ______; *or* ______ ______, Esq., American Consul at ______; *or* Mr. ______ ______, United States Consul at ______. *Begin:* Dear Sir.

**Deacon.** *Address:* The Reverend Deacon ______. *Begin:* Reverend Sir.

**Dean (of a Cathedral).** *Address:* The Very Reverend the Dean of ______. *Begin:* Very Reverend Sir; *or* Sir.

**Dean (of a College or Graduate School).** *Address:* Dean ______ ______. *Begin:* Dear Sir (*or* Madam); *or* Dear Dean ______.

**Divorced Woman.** *Address:* Ordinarily use *Mrs.* with her maiden name as a prename. Some divorced women prefer to resume the *Miss.*

**Doctor of Divinity.** *Address:* ______ ______, D.D.; *or* Dr. ______ ______; *or* Rev. Dr. ______. *Begin:* Dear Sir; *or* My dear Dr. ______; *or* Dear Dr. ______; *or* Reverend and Dear Sir; *or* Reverend Doctor.

**Doctor of Philosophy, Laws, Medicine, etc.** *Address:* ______ ______, Ph.D. (LL.D.) (M.D.) (D.D.S.) (D.V.M.). *Begin:* Dear Sir; *or* My dear Dr. ______; *or* Dear Dr. ______.

**Envoy.** Same as Minister (Diplomatic).

**Esquire.** *Address:* ______ ______, Esq. *Begin:* Sir: *or* Dear Sir; *or* Dear Mr. ______. (*Esq.* is never used if the person is addressed by any other title, even *Mr.* ).

**Governor.** *Address:* (in most states) The Honorable the Governor of ______; *or* The Honorable ______ ______, Governor of ______. *Begin:* Sir; *or* Dear Sir.

**Governor-General of Canada.** *Address:* His Excellency The Right Honourable ______ ______ (plus personal rank or title, if any). *Begin:* My Lord; *or* Sir (according to rank).

**Governor-General's Wife.** *Address:* Her Excellency ______ ______ (plus personal rank or title if any). *Begin:* Madam.

**Judge (in U.S.).** *Address:* The Honorable ______ ______, United States District Judge (or Chief Judge of the Court of Appeals, etc.). *Begin:* Dear Sir; *or* My dear Judge ______.

**King.** *Address:* The King's Most Excellent Majesty; *or* His Most Gracious Majesty, King ______. *Begin:* Sir; *or* May it please your Majesty.

**Lieutenant Governor.** *Address:* The Honorable ______ ______, Lieutenant Governor of ______. *Begin:* Sir; *or* Dear Sir.

**Mayor (in Canadian Cities and Towns, and English Boroughs and Cities).** *Address:* The Right Worshipful the Mayor of ______(English cities only); His Worship, The Mayor of ______ (other). *Begin:* Sir.

**Mayor (in U.S.).** *Address:* The Honorable ______ ______, Mayor of ______; *or* The Mayor of the City of ______. *Begin:* Sir; *or* Dear Sir; *or* Dear Mr. Mayor; *or* My dear Mr. Mayor.

**Member of Parliament** (or of a Legislative Council). The ordinary form of address followed by M.P. (*or* M.L.C.).

**Minister (Diplomatic).** *Address:* The Honorable ______ ______, Minister of ______. *Begin:* Sir.

**Minister of Religion.** See *Clergyman, Priest, Rabbi.*

**Monsignor.** *Address:* The Right Reverend Monsignor ______ ______, Domestic Prelate (or D.P.). *Begin:* Right Reverend Monsignor; *or* Dear Monsignor ______.

**Mother Superior of a Sisterhood.** *Address:* The Reverend Mother Superior, Convent of ______; *or* Reverend Mother ______, O.S.F. (or other initials of her order); *or* Mother ______, Superior, Convent of ______. *Begin:* Reverend Mother; *or* Dear Madam; *or* Dear Reverend Mother; *or* My dear Reverend Mother ______.

**Naval Officer.** *Address:* The Admiral of the Navy of the United States; or Admiral ______, Commanding United States Navy; Captain ______ ______, U.S.N. *Begin:* Sir; *or* My dear Admiral ______; Dear Commander ______; for officers below the rank of commander, Dear Mr. ______.

**Nun.** See *Sister of a Religious Order.*

**Papal Nuncio or Internuncio or Apostolic Delegate.** *Address:* His Excellency, The Papal Nuncio (*or* Internuncio *or* Apostolic Delegate) to ______. *Begin:* Your Excellency.

**Patriarch (Eastern Church).** *Address:* His Beatitude the Patriarch of ______; *or* His Beatitude the Lord ______, Patriarch of ______. *Begin:* Most Reverend Lord; *or* Your Beatitude.

**Pope.** *Address:* To His Holiness Pope ______. *Begin:* Most Holy Father; *or* Your Holiness.

**President of a College or University.** *Address:* ______ ______, LL.D. (or highest other degree), President of ______ University; *or* President, ______ University; if a clergyman, Reverend ______ ______, LL.D., President of ______ University. *Begin:* Dear Sir; *or* Dear President ______.

**President of a Theological Seminary.** *Address:* The Reverend President ______ ______. *Begin:* Dear Sir; *or* Dear President ______.

**President of State Senate.** *Address:* The Honorable ______ ______, President of the Senate of ______. *Begin:* Sir.

**President of the Senate of the U.S.** *Address:* The Honorable, The President of the Senate of the United States; *or* The Honorable ______ ______, President of the Senate. *Begin:* Sir.

**President of the U.S.** *Address:* The President, The White House. *Begin:* Mr. President; *or* The President; *or* My Dear Mr. President.

**Priest (Roman Catholic).** *Address:* Reverend ______ ______, O.S.M. (or other initials of his order). *Begin:* Dear Father ______ (religious name).

**Prime Minister of Canada.** *Address:* The Right Honourable ______ ______, P.C., Prime Minister of Canada. *Begin:* Sir.

**Privy Councillor (of Canada).** *Address:* The Honourable ______ ______. *Begin:* Sir.

**Professor in a College or University.** *Address:* Professor ______ ______; *or* ______ ______, Ph.D. (or LL.D., M.D., etc., using only his highest degree, if degrees are in same field), Professor of ______. *Begin:* Dear Sir; *or* My dear Professor ______; *or* Dear Professor ______; *or* My dear Professor.

**Queen.** *Address:* The Queen's Most Excellent Majesty; *or* Her Gracious Majesty, The Queen. *Begin:* Madam; *or* May it please your Majesty.

**Rabbi.** *Address:* Rabbi ______ ______; *or* Rev. ______ ______. *Begin:* Reverend Sir; *or* Dear Sir; *or* My dear Rabbi ______; *or* Dear Rabbi ______ (if he holds a D.D., Dr. may be substituted for Rabbi).

**Rector of a Religious House or of a Seminary.** *Address:* The Very Reverend ______ ______, O.S.B. (or other initials of his order), Rector, Brothers of St. Francis. *Begin:* Very Reverend and dear Father.

**Representative (State).** See *Congressman.*

**Representative (U.S.).** See *Congressman.*

**Secretary-General of the U.N.** *Address:* His Excellency ______ ______, Secretary-General of the United Nations. *Begin:* Excellency; *or* Dear Mr. Secretary-General; *or* Dear Mr. ______.

**Senator (State).** *Address:* The Honorable ______ ______, The State Senate, State Capitol. *Begin:* Dear Sir; *or* My dear Senator.

**Senator (U.S.).** *Address:* The Honorable ______ ______, The United States Senate. *Begin:* Dear Sir; *or* My dear Senator.

**Sister of a Religious Order.** *Address:* Sister ______ (followed by the intials of the order). *Begin:* Dear Sister; *or* My dear Sister; *or* Dear Sister ______; *or* My dear Sister ______.

**Speaker of the House of Commons (Canada).** *Address:* The Honourable ______ ______, The Speaker of the House of Commons. *Begin:* Dear Mr. Speaker.

**Speaker of the House of Representatives (U.S.).** *Address:* The Honorable ______ ______, Speaker of the House of Representatives. *Begin:* Sir; *or* Mr. Speaker; *or* My dear Mr. Speaker.

**Superior General of a Religious Community of Priests.** *Address:* The Most Reverend Father ______ (followed by the initials of the order), Superior General of the ______ Fathers. *Begin:* Most Reverend Father General.

**Superior General of a Religious Order (Female).** *Address:* The Reverend Mother ______ (followed by the initials of the order), Superior General of ______. *Begin:* Reverend Mother.

**Undersecretary of State (U.S.).** *Address:* The Undersecretary of State; *or* The Honorable ______ ______, Undersecretary of State. *Begin:* Sir; *or* Dear Sir; *or* Dear Mr. ______.

**United Nations Representative (Foreign Ambassador).** *Address:* His Excellency ______ ______, Representative of ______ to the United Nations. *Begin:* Excellency; *or* Sir; *or* My dear Mr. Ambassador.

**United Nations Representative (U.S.).** *Address:* The Honorable ______ ______, United States Representative to the United Nations. *Begin:* Sir: *or* My dear Mr. ______.

**Vice President.** *Address:* The Vice President; *or* The Honorable, The Vice President of the United States; *or* The Honorable ______ ______, Vice President of the United States. *Begin:* Mr. Vice President; *or* Sir; *or* My dear Mr. Vice President.

**Widow.** Ordinarily addressed by her former title; as, Mrs. John Doe, not Mrs. Jane Doe, unless the latter form is preferred by the person herself.

1. When two salutations are given, the formal one precedes the informal. In salutations where the addressee is a woman, the formal address Madam is to be substituted for Sir and, in informal address, Mrs., Miss, or Ms. may be substituted for Mr. NOTE: Forms of Address for foreign dignitaries may be obtained from their United Nations missions in New York City.

# Copyrights

*Source:* Library of Congress, Copyright Office.

The copyright law (Title 17 of the United States Code) has been amended by the enactment of a statute for its general revision, Public Law 94-553 (90 Stat. 2541), which was signed by the President on October 19, 1976. The new law superseded the copyright act of 1909, as amended, which remained effective until the new enactment took effect on January 1, 1978.

Under the new law, all copyrightable works, whether published or unpublished, are subject to a single system of statutory protection which gives a copyright owner the exclusive right to reproduce the copyrighted work in copies or phonorecords and distribute them to the public by sale, rental, lease, or lending. Among the other rights given to the owner of a copyright are the exclusive rights to prepare derivative works based upon the copyrighted work, to perform the work publicly if it be literary, musical, dramatic, choreographic, a pantomime, motion picture, or other audiovisual work, and in the case of literary, musical, dramatic, and choreographic works, pantomimes, and pictorial, graphic, or sculptural works, including the individual images of a motion picture or other audiovisual work, to display the copyrighted work publicly. All of these rights are subject to certain exceptions, including the principle of "fair use" which the new statute specifically recognizes.

Special provisions are included which permit compulsory licensing for the recording of musical compositions, noncommercial transmissions by public broadcasters of published musical and graphic works, performances of copyrighted music by jukeboxes, and the secondary transmission of copyrighted works on cable television systems.

Copyright protection under the new law extends to original works of authorship fixed in any tangible medium of expression, now known or later developed, from which they can be perceived, reproduced, or otherwise communicated, either directly or with the aid of a machine or device. Works of authorship include books, periodicals and other literary works, musical compositions with accompanying lyrics, dramas and dramatico-musical compositions, pantomimes and choreographic works, motion pictures and other audiovisual works, and sound recordings.

As a mandatory condition of copyright protection under the law in effect before 1978, all published copies of a work were required to bear a copyright notice. The 1976 Act provides for a notice on published copies, but omission or errors will not immediately result in forfeiture of the copyright, and can be corrected within certain time limits. Innocent infringers misled by the omission or error will be shielded from liability.

Registration in the Copyright Office is not a condition of copyright protection but will be a prerequisite to bringing an action in a court of law for infringement. With certain exceptions, the remedies of statutory damages and attorney's fees will not be available for infringements occurring before registration. Copies or phonorecords published in the United States with notice of copyright are required to be deposited for the collections of the Library of Congress, not as a condition of copyright protection, but under provisions of the law subjecting the copyright owner to certain penalties for failure to deposit after a demand by the Register of Copyrights. Registration is permissive, but may be made either at the time the depository requirements are satisfied or at any other time during the subsistence of the copyright.

For works already under statutory protection, the new law retains the present term of copyright of 28 years from first publication (or from registration in some cases), renewable by certain persons for a second period of protection, but it increases the length of the second period to 47 years. Copyrights in their first term on January 1, 1978, must still be renewed during the last (28th) year of the original copyright term to receive the maximum statutory term of 75 years (a first term of 28 years plus a renewal term of 47 years).

Copyrights in their second term on January 1, 1978, are automatically extended up to a maximum of 75 years, without the need for further renewal. Unpublished works that are already in existence on January 1, 1978, but are not protected by statutory copyright and have not yet gone into the public domain, will generally obtain automatic Federal copyright protection for the author's life, plus an additional 50 years after the author's death, but in any event, for a minimal term of 25 years (that is, until December 31, 2002), and if the work is published before that date, then for an additional term of 25 years, through the end of 2027.

For works created on or after January 1, 1978, the new law provides a term lasting for the author's life, plus an additional 50 years after the author's death. For works made for hire, and for anonymous and pseudonymous works (unless the author's identity is revealed in Copyright Office records), the new term will be 75 years from publication or 100 years from creation, whichever is shorter. The new law provides that all terms of copyright will run through the end of the calendar year in which they would otherwise expire. This will not only affect the duration of copyrights, but also the time-limits for renewal registrations.

Works already in the public domain cannot be protected under the new law. The 1976 Act provides no procedure for restoring protection to works in which copyright has been lost for any reason. In general, works published before September 19, 1906, are not under copyright protection in the United States, at least insofar as any version published before that date is concerned.

The new law requires that all visually perceptible copies published in the United States or elsewhere bear a notice of copyright affixed in such manner and location as to give reasonable notice of the claim of copyright. The notice consists of the symbol © (the letter C in a circle), the word "Copyright," or the abbreviation "Copr.," and the year of first publication of the work, and the name of the owner of copyright in the work. EXAMPLE: © *1978 John Doe.*

The notice of copyright prescribed for sound recordings consists of the symbol Ⓟ (the letter P in a circle), the year of first publication of the sound recording, and the name of the owner of copyright in the sound recording, placed on the surface of the phonorecord, or on the phonorecord label or container, in such manner and location as to give reasonable notice of the claim of copyright. EXAMPLE: Ⓟ *1978 Doe Records, Inc.*

A work by a U.S. citizen may obtain copyright protection in all countries that are members of the Universal Copyright Convention (UCC), provided the copyright notice appearing on all copies from the date of first publication includes the symbol ©, together with the name of the copyright owner and the year date of publication. EXAMPLE: © *John Doe 1978.*

Further information and application forms may be obtained free of charge upon request from the Copyright Office, Library of Congress, Washington, D.C. 20559.

## Patents

*Source:* Department of Commerce, Patent and Trademark Office.

A patent, in the most general sense, is a document issued by a government, conferring some special right or privilege. The term is now restricted mainly to patents for inventions; occasionally, land patents.

The grant of a patent for an invention gives the inventor the privilege, for a limited period of time, of excluding others from practicing a certain art or from making, using, or selling a certain article. However, it does not give him the right to make, use, or sell his own invention if it is an improvement on some unexpired patent whose claims are infringed thereby.

In the U.S., the law provides that a patent may be granted, for a term of 17 years, to any person who has invented or discovered any new and useful art, machine, manufacture, or composition of matter, as well as any new and useful improvements thereof. A patent may also be granted to a person who has invented or discovered and asexually reproduced a new and distinct variety of plant (other than a tuber-propagated one) or has invented a new, original and ornamental design for an article of manufacture.

A patent is granted only upon a regularly filed application, complete in all respects; upon payment of the fees; and upon determination that the disclosure is complete and that the invention is new, useful, and, in view of the prior art, unobvious to one skilled in the art. The disclosure must be of such nature as to enable others to reproduce the invention.

A complete application, which must be addressed to the Commissioner of Patents and Trademarks, Washington, D.C. 20231, consists of a specification with one or more claims; oath or declaration; drawing (whenever the nature of the case admits of it); and a basic filing fee of $65, plus certain additional charges for claims. The filing fee is not returned to the applicant if the patent is refused. If the patent is allowed, another fee of $100, plus additional printing charges, is required before the patent is issued. The fees for design patents vary.

Applications are ordinarily considered in the order in which they are received. Patents are not granted for printed matter, for methods of doing business, or for devices for which claims contrary to natural laws are made. Applications for a perpetual-motion machine have been made from time to time, but until a working model is presented that actually fulfills the claim, no patent will be issued.

## Trademarks

*Source:* Department of Commerce, Patent and Trademark Office.

A trademark may be defined as a word, letter, device, or symbol, as well as some combination of these, which is used in connection with merchandise and which points distinctly to the origin of the goods.

Certificates of registration of trademarks are issued under the seal of the Patent and Trademark Office and may be registered by the owner if he is engaged in interstate or foreign commerce, since any Federal jurisdiction over trademarks arises under the commerce clause of the Constitution. Trademarks may be registered by foreign owners who comply with our law, as well as by citizens of foreign countries with which the U.S. has treaties relating to trademarks. American citizens may register trademarks in foreign countries by complying with the laws of those countries. The right to registration and protection of trademarks in many foreign countries is guaranteed by treaties.

General jurisdiction in trademark cases involving Federal Registrations is given to Federal courts. Adverse decisions of examiners on applications for registration are appealable to the Trademark Trial and Appeal Board, whose affirmances, and decisions in *inter partes* proceedings, are subject to court review. Before adopting a trademark, a person should make a search of prior marks to avoid infringing unwittingly upon them.

The duration of a trademark registration is 20 years, but it may be renewed indefinitely for 20-year periods, provided the trademark is still in use at the time of expiration.

### Labors of Hercules

Hercules, hero and strong man, was the son of Zeus and Alcmene. He performed twelve labors or deeds to be free from bondage under Eurystheus. After his death, he became immortal. His twelve mythological labors were: (1) killing the Nemean lion; (2) killing the Lernaean Hydra; (3) capturing the Erymanthian boar; (4) capturing the Cerynean hind; (5) killing the man-eating Stymphalian birds; (6) procuring the girdle of Hippolyte; (7) cleaning the Augean stables; (8) capturing the Cretan bull; (9) capturing the man-eating horses of Diomedes; (10) capturing the cattle of Geryon; (11) procuring the golden apples of Hesperides; (12) bringing Cerberus up from Hades.

# GREAT DISASTERS

(For later disasters, see Current Events of 1978).

## Earthquakes and Volcanic Eruptions

A.D. 79 **Aug. 24, Italy:** eruption of Mt. Vesuvius buried cities of Pompeii and Herculaneum, killing thousands.

1556 **Jan. 24, Shensi Province, China:** most deadly earthquake in history; 830,000 killed.

1755 **Nov. 1, Portugal:** one of the most severe of recorded earthquakes leveled Lisbon and was felt as far away as southern France and North Africa; 10,000–20,000 killed in Lisbon.

1883 **Aug. 26–28, Netherlands Indies:** eruption of Krakatoa; violent explosions destroyed two thirds of island. Sea waves occurred as far away as Cape Horn, and possibly England. Estimated 36,000 dead.

1902 **May 8, Martinique, West Indies:** Mt. Pelée erupted and wiped out city of St. Pierre; 40,000 dead.

1906 **April 18, San Francisco:** earthquake accompanied by fire razed more than 4 sq mi.; more than 500 dead or missing; property damage about $250–300 million.

1908 **Dec. 28, Messina, Sicily:** about 85,000 killed and city totally destroyed.

1920 **Dec. 16, Kansu Province, China:** earthquake killed 200,000.

1923 **Sept. 1, Japan:** earthquake destroyed third of Tokyo and most of Yokohama; more than 140,000 killed.

1935 **May 31, India:** earthquake at Quetta killed an estimated 50,000.

1939 **Jan. 24, Chile:** earthquake razed 50,000 sq mi.; about 30,000 killed.
**Dec. 27, Northern Turkey:** severe quakes destroyed city of Erzingan; about 100,000 casualties.

1949 **Aug. 5, Ecuador:** earthquake killed about 6,000 and razed 50 towns.

1950 **Aug. 15, India:** earthquake affected 30,000 sq mi. in Assam; 20,000–30,000 believed killed.

1960 **May 21–22, 27–29, Chile:** 5,700 dead in earthquakes.

1962 **Sept. 1, Northwest Iran:** more than 10,000 killed in earthquakes.

1963 **July 26, Skoplje, Yugoslavia:** four fifths of city destroyed; 1,011 dead, 3,350 injured.

1964 **March 27, Alaska:** strongest earthquake ever to strike North America hits 80 miles east of Anchorage; followed by seismic wave 50 feet high that traveled 8,445 miles at 450 miles per hour; 131 killed and damage in Alaska and West Coast $500–750 million.

1970 **May 31, Peru:** earthquake left 50,000 dead, 17,000 missing.

1971 **Feb. 9, Los Angeles:** earthquake rocked San Fernando Valley. Death toll 64. damage $1 billion.

1972 **April 10, Iran:** 5,000 killed in earthquake 600 miles south of Teheran.
**Dec. 22, Managua, Nicaragua:** earthquake devastated city, leaving up to 12,000 dead.

1974 **Dec. 28, Pattan, Pakistan:** earthquake affecting 1,000 sq mi. in northern section killed over 5,000.

1976 **Feb. 4, Guatemala:** earthquake left over 23,000 dead.
**June 26, Irian-Jaya, Indonesia:** earthquake and landslides killed over 3,000, with another 3,000 missing.
**July 28, Tangshan, China:** earthquake devastated 20-sq-mi. area of city leaving estimated 655,000 dead.
**Aug. 17, Mindanao, Philippines:** earthquake and tidal wave left up to 8,000 dead or missing.

1977 **March 4, Bucharest:** earthquake razed most of downtown Bucharest; 1,541 reported dead, over 11,000 injured.

## Floods, Avalanches, and Tidal Waves

1228 **Holland:** 100,000 persons reputedly drowned by sea flood in Friesland.

1642 **China:** rebels destroyed Kaifeng seawall; 300,000 drowned.

1887 **China:** hundreds of thousands of lives lost in Honan province in overflow of Hwang Ho River.

1889 **Pennsylvania:** more than 2,000 died in Johnstown flood.

1896 **Japan:** earthquake and tidal wave at Sanriku killed 27,000.

1913 **Ohio and Indiana:** floods of Ohio and Indiana rivers took 730 lives.

1927 **Mississippi Valley:** floods inundated 20,000 sq mi.; 700,000 left homeless.

1939 **China:** floods in north; casualties estimated at 10 million homeless, starved, or drowned.

1950 **China:** floods in eastern and southern China left 1 million homeless and killed 500.

1953 **Northwest Europe:** storm followed by floods devastated North Sea coastal areas. Netherlands was hardest hit with 1,794 dead.

1955 **Northern California and Oregon:** rains caused $150 million damage, 74 deaths.

1959 **Dec. 2, Fréjus, France:** flood caused by collapse of Malpasset Dam left 412 dead.

1960 **Agadir, Morocco:** 10,000–12,000 dead as earthquake set off tidal wave and fire, destroying most of city.

1962 **Jan. 10, Peru:** avalanche down Huascaran, extinct Andean volcano, killed more than 3,000 persons.

1963 **Oct. 9, Italy:** landslide collapsed Valont Dam; flood killed about 2,000.

1966 **Oct. 21, Aberfan, Wales:** avalanche of coal, waste, mud, and rocks killed 144 persons, including 116 children in school.

1969 **Jan. 18–26, Southern California:** floods and mudslides from heavy rains caused widespread property damage; at least 100 dead. Another downpour (Feb. 23–26) caused further floods and mudslides; at least 18 dead.

1970 **Nov. 13, East Pakistan:** 200,000 killed by cyclone-driven tidal wave from Bay of Bengal. Over 100,000 missing.

1971 **Sept. 29, Orissa State, India:** cyclone and tidal wave off Bay of Bengal killed as many as 10,000.

1972 **Feb. 26, Man, W. Va.:** more than 118 died when slag-pile dam collapsed under pressure of torrential rains and flooded 17-mile valley.
**June 9–10, Rapid City, S.D.:** flash flood caused 237 deaths and $160 million in damage.
**June 20, Eastern Seaboard:** tropical storm Agnes, in 10-day rampage, caused widespread flash floods. Death toll was 129, 115,000 were left homeless, and damage estimated at $3.5 billion.

1976 **Aug. 1, Loveland, Colo.:** Flash flood along Route 34 in Big Thompson Canyon left 139 dead.

1977 **Nov. 6, Toccoa, Ga.:** rupture of Kelly Barnes Dam left 39 dead.
**Nov. 19, Andhra Pradesh State, India:** cyclone and flood from Bay of Bengal left 7,000–10,000 dead.

## Storms and Weather

(For U. S. tornadoes and hurricanes, see Index)

1864 **Oct. 5, India:** most of Calcutta denuded by cyclone; 70,000 killed.

1876 **Oct. 31, India:** cyclone and tidal wave swept 3,000 sq mi.; 215,000 killed.

1882 **June 6, India:** cyclone and tidal wave killed 100,000 in Bombay.

1906 **China:** typhoon at Hong Kong killed about 10,000.

1930 **Sept. 3. Santo Domingo:** hurricane killed about 2,000 and injured 6,000.

1934 **Sept. 21, Japan:** hurricane killed more than 4,000 on Honshu.

1942 **Oct. 16, India:** cyclone devastated Bengal; about 40,000 lives lost.

1963 **May 28–29, East Pakistan:** cyclone killed about 22,000 along coast.
**Oct. 2–7, Caribbean:** Hurricane Flora killed up to 7,000 in Haiti and Cuba.

1965 **May 11–12 and June 1–2, East Pakistan:** cyclones killed about 47,000.
**Dec. 15, Karachi, Pakistan:** cyclone killed about 10,000.

1974 **Sept. 20, Honduras:** Hurricane Fifi strikes northern section of country, leaving 8,000 dead, 100,000 homeless.
**Dec. 25, Darwin, Australia:** cyclone destroys nearly the entire city, causing mass evacuation.

## Fires and Explosions

1666 **Sept. 2, England:** "Great Fire of London" destroyed St. Paul's Church, etc. Damage £10 million.

1812 **Sept. 14, Russia:** fire started by Russians in Moscow after French occupation destroyed 30,800 houses.

1835 **Dec. 16, New York City:** 530 buildings destroyed by fire.

1871 **Oct. 8, Chicago:** the "Chicago Fire" burned 17,450 buildings, killed 250 persons; $196 million damage.
**Oct. 8. Peshtigo, Wis.:** over 1,200 lives lost; 2 billion trees burned.

1872 **Nov. 9, Boston:** fire destroyed 800 buildings; $75-million damage.

1876 **Dec. 5, New York City:** fire in Brooklyn Theater killed more than 300.

1881 **Dec. 8, Vienna:** at least 620 died in fire at Ring Theatre.

1900 **May 1, Scofield, Utah:** explosion of blasting powder in coal mine killed 1,200.

1903 **Dec. 30, Chicago:** Iroquois Theatre fire killed 602.

1904 **Feb. 7, Baltimore:** business section burned; estimated $125-million damage.

1906 **March 10, France:** explosion in coal mine in Courrières killed 1,060.

1909 **Nov. 13, Cherry, Ill.:** explosion in coal mine killed 259.

1911 **March 25, New York City:** fire in Triangle Shirtwaist Factory fatal to 145.

1913 **Oct. 22, Dawson, N.M.**: coal mine explosion left 263 dead.

1917 **Dec. 6, Canada**: explosion and fire at Halifax when ammunition ship collided with a vessel; 1,500 dead.

1930 **April 21, Columbus, Ohio**: fire in Ohio State Penitentiary killed 322 convicts.

1937 **March 18, New London, Tex.**: explosion destroyed schoolhouse; 294 killed.

1942 **April 26, Manchuria**: explosion in Honkeiko Colliery killed 1,549.
**Nov. 28, Boston**: Cocoanut Grove nightclub fire killed 498.

1944 **July 6, Hartford, Conn.**: fire and ensuing stampede in main tent of Ringling Brothers Circus killed 168, injured 487.
**July 17, Port Chicago, Calif.**: 300 killed as ammunition ships explode.

1946 **Dec. 7, Atlanta**: fire in Winecoff Hotel killed 119.

1947 **April 16–18, Texas City, Tex.**: most of city destroyed, 516 dead following explosion on ship.

1949 **Sept. 2, China**: fire on Chungking waterfront killed 1,700.

1953 **Oct. 16, Boston**: explosion and fire aboard U.S.S. *Leyte* killed 37.

1954 **May 26, off Quonset Point, R.I.**: explosion and fire aboard aircraft *Bennington* killed 103 crewmen.

1955 **June 11, France**: crash and explosion of racing car into crowd during Grand Prix race, Le Mans, killed 82.

1956 **Aug. 7, Colombia**: about 1,100 reported killed when seven army ammunition trucks exploded at Cali.
**Aug. 8, Belgium**: 262 died in coal mine fire at Marcinelle.

1958 **Dec. 1, Chicago**: fire at Our Lady of the Angels school killed 96.

1960 **Jan. 21, Coalbrook, South Africa**: coal mine explosion killed 437.
**Nov. 13, Syria**: 152 children killed in moviehouse fire.
**Dec. 19. Brooklyn, N.Y.**: blaze on aircraft carrier *Constellation* killed 49 workmen.

1961 **Dec. 17, Niteroi, Brazil**: circus fire fatal to 323.

1962 **Feb. 7, Saarland, West Germany**: coal mine gas explosion killed 298.

1963 **Nov. 9, Japan**: explosion in coal mine at Omuta killed 447.

1965 **May 28, India**: coal mine fire in state of Bihar killed 375.
**June 1, near Fukuoka, Japan**: coal mine explosion killed 236.

1966 **Oct. 17, New York City**: 12 firemen were killed in sudden collapse of burning building.
**Oct. 26, off South Vietnam**: fire on U.S. carrier *Oriskany* killed 43.

1967 **May 22, Brussels**: fire in L'Innovation, major department store, left 322 dead.
**July 29, off North Vietnam**: fire on U.S. carrier *Forrestal* killed 134.

1969 **Jan. 14, Pearl Harbor, Hawaii**: nuclear aircraft carrier *Enterprise* ripped by explosions; 27 dead, 82 injured.
**April 6, New Orleans**: Taiwanese freighter and string of oil-loaded barges collided in fiery explosion on Mississippi River; 25 dead.

1970 **Nov. 1, Saint-Laurent-du-Pont, France**: fire in dance hall killed 146 young people.
**Dec. 30, Wooten, Ky.**: coal-dust explosion in coal mine killed 38.

1972 **May 2, Kellogg, Idaho**: fire in Sunshine silver mine killed 91 miners; two men survived.
**May 13, Osaka, Japan**: 118 people died in fire in nightclub on top floor of Sennichi department store.
**June 6, Wankie, Rhodesia**: explosion in coal mine killed 427.

1973 **Nov. 29, Kumamoto, Japan**: fire in Taiyo department store killed 101.

1974 **Feb. 1, Sao Paulo, Brazil**: fire in upper stories of bank building killed 189 persons, many of whom leaped to death.

1975 **Dec. 27, Dhanbad, India**: explosion in coal mine followed by flooding from nearby reservoir left 372 dead.

1977 **Feb. 25, Moscow**: fire in 6,000-bed Hotel Rossiya fatal to at least 45 guests.
**May 28, Southgate, Ky.**: fire in Beverly Hills Supper Club; 167 dead.
**June 26, Columbia, Tenn.**: fire believed set by inmate is fatal to 42 prisoners and visitors at Maury County Jail.
**Dec. 22, Westwego, La.**: explosion destroyed Continental Grain Company plant, killing 35.

## Shipwrecks

1833 **May 11, *Lady of the Lake:*** bound from England to Quebec, struck iceberg; 215 perished.

1853 **Sept. 29 *Annie Jane:*** emigrant vessel off coast of Scotland; 348 died.

1865 **April 27, *Sultana:*** boiler explosion on Mississippi River steamboat near Memphis, 1,450 killed.

1898 **Nov. 26, *City of Portland:*** Loss of 157 off Cape Cod.

1904 **June 15, *General Slocum:*** excursion steamer burned in New York Harbor; 1,021 perished.

1912 **March 5, *Principe de Asturias:*** Spanish steamer struck rock off Sebastien Point; 500 drowned.
**April 15, *Titanic:*** sank after colliding with iceberg; 1,513 died.

1914 **May 29, *Empress of Ireland:*** sank after collision in St. Lawrence River; 1,024 perished.

1915 **July 24, *Eastland:*** Great Lakes excursion steamer overturned in Chicago River; 812 died.

**1928** **Nov. 12, *Vestris:*** British steamer sank in gale off Virginia; 110 died.

**1931** **June 14:** French excursion steamer overturned in gale off St. Nazaire; approximately 450 died.

**1934** **Sept. 8, *Morro Castle:*** about 130 killed in fire off Asbury Park, N.J.

**1939** **May 23, *Squalus:*** submarine with 59 men sank off Hampton Beach, N.H.; 33 saved.
**June 1, Submarine *Thetis:*** sank in Liverpool Bay, England; 99 perished.

**1942** **Oct. 2, *Queen Mary:*** rammed and sank a British cruiser; 338 aboard the cruiser died.

**1945** **April 9:** U.S. ship, loaded with aerial bombs, exploded at Bari, Italy; at least 360 killed.

**1948** **Dec. 3, *Kiangya:*** Chinese refugee ship wrecked in explosion; about 1,000 believed dead.

**1949** **Sept. 17, *Noronic:*** Canadian Great Lakes cruise ship burned at Toronto dock; about 130 died.

**1951** **April 16, *Affray:*** British submarine sank in English Channel; 75 dead.

**1952** **April 26, *Hobson:*** minesweeper collided with aircraft carrier *Wasp* and sank during night maneuvers in mid-Atlantic, 176 persons lost.

**1953** **Jan. 9, *Chang Tyong-Ho:*** South Korean ferry foundered off Pusan; 249 reported dead.
**Jan. 31, *Princess Victoria:*** British ferry sank in Irish Sea; 133 lost.

**1956** **July 25, *Andrea Doria:*** Italian liner collided with Swedish liner *Stockholm* off Nantucket Island, Mass., sinking next day; 52, mostly passengers on Italian ship, dead or unaccounted for; over 1,600 rescued.

**1962** **April 8, *Dara,*** British liner, exploded and sank in Persian Gulf; 236 persons dead. Caused by time bomb.

**1963** **April 10, *Thresher:*** atomic-powered submarine sank in North Atlantic; 129 dead.
**May 4:** U.A.R. ferry capsized and sank in upper Nile; over 200 died.

**1964** **Nov. 26, *Shalom:*** Israeli liner collided with Norwegian tanker *Stolt Dagali* off New Jersey coast; 19 of tanker's crew dead.

**1965** **Nov. 13, *Yarmouth Castle:*** cruise ship burned and sank 60 miles northeast of Nassau en route from Miami to Bahamas; 90 dead.

**1968** **Late May, *Scorpion:*** nuclear submarine sank in Atlantic 400 miles S.W. of Azores; 99 dead. (Located Oct. 31.)

**1970** **Aug. 1:** ferry between Basseterre, St. Kitts, and Charlestown, Nevis, capsized in Caribbean; 125 believed lost.
**Dec. 15:** ferry in Korean Strait capsized; 261 lost.

**1976** **Oct. 20, Luling, La.: *George Prince,*** Mississippi River ferry, rammed by Norwegian tanker *Frosta;* 77 dead.

## Aircraft Accidents

**1921** **Aug. 24, England:** *ZR-2* British dirigible, broke in two on trial trip near Hull; 62 died.

**1925** **Sept. 3, Caldwell, Ohio:** U.S. dirigible *Shenandoah* broke apart; 14 dead.

**1933** **April 4, New Jersey Coast:** U.S. dirigible *Akron* crashed; 73 died.

**1937** **May 6, Lakehurst, N.J.:** German zeppelin *Hindenburg* destroyed by fire at tower mooring; 36 killed.

**1945** **July 28, New York City:** U.S. Army bomber crashed into Empire State Building; 13 dead.

**1946** **May 20, New York City:** U.S. Army plane crashed into Manhattan Company building; five dead.

**1949** **Nov. 1, Washington, D.C.:** fighter plane rammed airliner, killing 55.

**1951** **Dec. 16, Elizabeth, N.J.:** nonscheduled airliner crash killed 56.

**1952** **Jan. 22, Elizabeth, N.J.:** 29 killed, including former Secretary of War Robert P. Patterson, when airliner hit apartments; seven of dead were on ground.
**Feb. 11, Elizabeth, N.J.:** third major air disaster in Elizabeth within two months fatally injured 33.

**1953** **June 18, near Tokyo:** crash of U.S. Air Force "Globemaster" killed 129 servicemen.

**1955** **Nov. 1, near Longmont, Colo.:** time bomb hidden in luggage destroyed airliner in flight, killing 44.

**1956** **June 30, Grand Canyon, Ariz.:** 128 died in collision of TWA Super Constellation and United Airlines DC-7.

**1957** **March 17, near Cebu City, Philippines:** President Ramón Magsaysay and 24 others killed in crash.

**1959** **Feb. 3, New York City:** American Airlines Lockheed Electra turboprop plane crashed in East River; 65 dead.

**1960** **Feb. 25, Rio de Janeiro:** U.S. Navy plane, flying Navy musicians to perform at dinner given by visiting President Eisenhower, collided with Brazilian airliner, killing 61.
**Sept. 19, near Guam:** crash shortly after take-off of World Airways plane took 78 lives.
**Oct. 4, Boston Harbor:** Eastern Airlines plane sank; 61 dead.
**Dec. 16, New York City:** United and Trans World planes collided in fog, crashed in two boroughs, killing 134 in air and on ground.

**1961** **Feb. 15, near Brussels:** 72 on board and farmer on ground killed in crash of Sabena plane; U.S. figure skating team wiped out.

**1962** **March 1, New York City:** American Airlines jetliner crashed into Jamaica Bay, near Idlewild Airport, killing all 95 on board.
**June 3, Paris:** chartered Air France Boeing Jet 707 crashed at Orly Airport; 130 dead.
**June 22, Grande-Teree Island, Guadeloupe:** Air France Boeing 707 crashed, killing all 113 aboard.

1965 **Feb. 8, New York City:** Eastern Airlines DC-7B went down in Atlantic shortly after take-off from Kennedy International Airport; 84 dead.

1966 **Jan. 24, Mont Blanc:** Indian airliner crashed into mountain in fog; 117 dead.
**March 5, Japan:** British airliner caught fire and crashed into Mt. Fuji; 124 dead.
**Dec. 24, Binh Thai, South Vietnam:** crash of military-chartered plane into village killed 129.

1967 **April 20, Nicosia, Cyprus:** crash of chartered Swiss Turboprop killed 126.
**July 19, near Hendersonville, N.C.:** Piedmont Airlines Boeing 727 collided with private plane; 82 dead.

1968 **May 3, near Dawson, Tex.:** Braniff airliner crashed; 85 dead.

1969 **March 16, Maracaibo, Venezuela:** Venezuelan jetliner crashed and exploded; 84 crew members and passengers died and 71 were killed on ground.
**Sept. 9, Shelbyville, Ind.:** Allegheny Airlines jetliner and single-engine plane flown by student pilot collided in air and crashed; 83 dead.
**Dec. 8, Keratea, Greece:** rain and hurricane winds caused Greek airliner to crash into 2,000-foot mountain while approaching Athens; 90 dead.

1970 **Feb. 15, Santo Domingo, Dominican Republic:** Dominican Republic jetliner plunged into Caribbean on takeoff; 102 dead.
**July 4, Arbucias, Spain:** British Comet crashed into mountains while coming in for landing at Barcelona; 112 dead.
**July 5, Toronto:** Canadian jetliner crashed on landing approach; 109 dead.
**Aug. 9, Cuzco, Peru:** Peruvian turboprop, with 51 teen-age U.S. students among passengers, crashed shortly after takeoff; 99 dead.
**Nov. 13, Huntington, W. Va.:** chartered plane carrying 43 players and coaches of Marshall University football team crashed; 75 dead.

1971 **June 6, near Los Angeles:** Air West DC-9 and Navy F-4 fighter collided over San Gabriel Canyon; 49 killed; one Navy crewman parachuted to safety.
**July 30, Morioka, Japan:** Japanese Boeing 727 and F-86 fighter collided in mid-air; toll was 162.
**Sept. 4, near Juneau, Alaska:** Alaska Airlines Boeing 727 crashed into Chilkoot Mountains; 109 killed.

1972 **May 5, Palermo, Sicily:** Alitalia DC-8 hit mountain, killing 115.
**June 18, London:** B.E.A. Trident jetliner plunged into field minutes after take-off from Heathrow Airport; all 118 aboard dead.
**Aug. 14, East Berlin, East Germany:** Soviet-built East German Ilyushin plane crashed, killing 156.
**Oct. 13, Moscow:** 176 died when Soviet Ilyushin airliner crashed.
**Dec. 3, Santa Cruz de Tenerife, Canary Islands:** Spanish charter jet carrying West German tourists crashed on take-off; all 155 aboard killed.
**Dec. 30, Miami, Fla.:** Eastern Airlines Lockheed 1011 TriStar Jumbo jet crashed into Everglades; 101 killed, 75 survived.

1973 **Jan. 22, Kano, Nigeria:** 171 Nigerian Moslems returning from Mecca and five crewmen died in crash.
**April 10, Hochwald, Switzerland:** British airliner carrying tourists to Swiss fair crashed in blizzard; 106 dead.
**July 11, Paris:** Boeing 707 of Varig Airlines, en route to Rio de Janeiro, crashed near airport, killing 122 of 134 passengers.
**July 31, Boston:** Delta Airlines jet crashed in heavy fog in landing at Logan International Airport killing 88 of 89 aboard.

1974 **Jan. 31, Pago Pago, Samoa:** Pan American 707 crashed while landing; 97 of 101 persons aboard killed.
**March 3, Paris:** Turkish DC-10 jumbo jet crashed in forest shortly after take-off; all 346 passengers and crew killed in worst single-plane disaster to date.
**Dec. 1, Upperville, Va.:** all 92 aboard killed in crash of TWA 727 into wooded area.
**Dec. 4, Colombo, Sri Lanka:** Dutch DC-8 carrying Moslems to Mecca crashed on landing approach, killing all 191 persons aboard.

1975 **April 4, near Saigon, Vietnam:** Air Force Galaxy C-58 crashed after take-off, killing 172, mostly Vietnamese children.
**June 24, New York City:** Eastern Airlines Boeing 727, arriving from New Orleans, crashed at Kennedy International Airport, killing 113 in highest single-aircraft toll in U.S. to date.
**Aug. 3, Agadir, Morocco:** Chartered Boeing 707, returning Moroccan workers home after vacation in France, plunged into mountainside; all 188 aboard killed.
**Aug. 20, Damascus, Syria:** Czech airliner crashed while landing, killing 126 of 128 persons aboard.

1976 **Sept. 10, Zagreb, Yugoslavia:** midair collision between British Airways Trident and Yugoslav charter DC-9 fatal to all 176 persons aboard; worst mid-air collision on record.

1977 **March 27, Santa Cruz de Tenerife, Canary Islands:** Pan American and KLM Boeing 747s collided on runway. All 249 on KLM plane and 333 of 394 aboard Pan Am jet killed. Total of 582 is highest for any type of aviation disaster.

1978 **Jan. 1, Bombay:** Air India 747 with 213 aboard explodes and plunges into sea minutes after takeoff.

## Railroad Accidents

1864 **June 29, near Beloeil, Canada:** about 90 killed when train ran through open switch.

1879 **Dec. 28, Dundee, Scotland:** train blown off Tay bridge; 73 drowned.

1881 **June 24, near Cuartla, Mexico:** about 200 died when train fell into river.

1882 **July 13, near Tcherny, Russia:** more than 150 killed in derailment.

1891 **June 14, near Basel, Switzerland:** about 100 killed in collision.

1915 **May 22, Gretna, Scotland:** two passenger trains and troop train collided; 227 killed.

**1917** **Dec. 12, Modane, France:** nearly 550 killed in derailment of troop train near mouth of Mt. Cenis tunnel.

**1939** **Dec. 22, near Magdeburg, Germany:** more than 125 killed in collision; 99 killed in another wreck near Friedrichshafen.

**1943** **Dec. 16, near Rennert, N.C.:** 72 killed in derailment and collision of two Atlantic Coast Line trains.

**1944** **March 2, near Salerno, Italy:** 521 suffocated when Italian train stalled in tunnel.
**Dec. 31, near Ogden, Utah:** 48 killed in collision of two sections of Southern Pacific's Pacific Limited.

**1946** **April 25, Naperville, Ill.:** at least 47 killed in collision of two trains of Burlington Railroad.

**1949** **Oct. 22, near Nowy Dwor, Poland:** more than 200 reported killed in derailment of Danzig-Warsaw express.

**1950** **Feb. 17, Rockville Centre, N.Y.:** head-on crash of two Long Island R.R. commuter trains killed 30.
**Nov. 22, Richmond Hill, N.Y.:** 79 died when one Long Island Rail Road commuter train crashed into rear of another.

**1951** **Feb. 6, Woodbridge, N.J.:** 85 died when Pennsylvania Railroad commuter train plunged through temporary overpass.

**1952** **Oct. 8, Harrow-Wealdstone, England:** two express trains crashed into commuter train; 112 dead.

**1953** **Dec. 24, near Sakvice, Czechoslovakia:** two trains crashed; over 100 dead.

**1956** **Sept. 2, near Mahbubnagar, India:** at least 120 killed when bridge collapsed under train.

**1957** **Sept. 1, near Kendal, Jamaica:** about 175 killed when train plunged into ravine.
**Sept. 29, near Montgomery, West Pakistan:** express train crashed into standing oil train; nearly 300 killed.
**Dec. 4, St. John's, England:** 92 killed, 187 injured as one commuter train crashed into another in fog.

**1958** **Sept. 15, near Bayonne, N.J.:** over 40 killed when Central Railroad of New Jersey train went through open drawbridge.

**1960** **Nov. 14, Pardubice, Czechoslovakia:** two trains collided; 110 dead, 106 injured.

**1962** **May 3, near Tokyo:** 163 killed and 400 injured when train crashed into wreckage of collision between inbound freight train and outbound commuter train.

**1963** **Nov. 9, near Yokohama, Japan:** two passenger trains crashed into derailed freight, killing 162.

**1964** **July 26, Custoias, Portugal:** passenger train derailed; 94 dead.

**1970** **Feb. 4, near Buenos Aires:** 236 killed when express train crashed into standing commuter train.

**1972** **July 21, Seville, Spain:** head-on crash of two passenger trains killed 76.
**Oct. 6, near Saltillo, Mexico:** train carrying religious pilgrims derailed and caught fire, killing 204 and injuring over 1,000.
**Oct. 30, Chicago:** two Illinois Central commuter trains collided during morning rush hour; 45 dead and over 200 injured.

**1974** **Aug. 30, Zagreb, Yugoslavia:** train entering station derailed, killing 153 and injuring over 60.

**1977** **Feb. 4, Chicago:** 11 killed and over 180 injured when elevated train hit rear of another, sending two cars to street.

## Freedom of Information

The Freedom of Information Act of 1966 established that Americans have a "right to know" much of the information in their government's files. In 1974, Congress amended the FOIA, providing for even more disclosure, and also passed the Privacy Act, which is intended to assist individuals to obtain information about themselves.

The Freedom of Information Act applies to documents held by administrative agencies of the executive branch of the federal government—for example, surveys of food and drugs, automobile safety, nursing homes, consumer products, etc. The Privacy Act applies to personal records maintained by the executive branch—for example, by the Armed Services, the FBI, VA, etc.

Records that will *not* be supplied fall under specific categories, such as those classified under national defense and foreign policy, confidential business information, etc.

*A Citizen's Guide on How to Use the Freedom of Information Act and the Privacy Act in Requesting Government Documents* is available from the Superintendent of Documents, U.S. Government Printing Office, Washington, D.C. 20402 for 35¢ (Stock No. 052–071–00540–4).

## How Old Is Man?

Paleoanthropologists (anthropologists who specialize in the study of fossil man) disagree on when humans first were differentiated from their pre-human ancestors. Estimates range from 2 to 3.8 million years ago, based on such criteria as brain size, knee joints indicating an ability to walk on two legs, and tool-making ability.

The old concept of a single line of development from ape to man has been replaced by the generally accepted theory that there were at least three different forms of early man and near man in Africa, where most scientists agree humans first emerged.

# GEOGRAPHY

## World Geography

### Explorations and Discoveries

**(All years are A.D. unless B.C. is specified.)**

| Country or place | Event | Explorer or discoverer | Date |
|---|---|---|---|
| **AFRICA** | | | |
| Sierra Leone | Visited | Hanno, Carthaginian seaman | c. 520 B.C. |
| Congo River | Mouth discovered | Diogo Cão, Protuguese | c. 1484 |
| Cape of Good Hope | Rounded | Bartholomeu Diaz, Portuguese | 1488 |
| Gambia River | Explored | Mungo Park, Scottish explorer | 1795 |
| Sahara Desert | Crossed | Dixon Denham and Hugh Clapperton, English explorers | 1822–23 |
| Zambezi River | Discovered | Davis Livingstone, Scottish explorer | 1851 |
| Sudan | Explored | Heinrich Barth, German explorer | 1852–55 |
| Victoria Falls | Discovered | Livingstone | 1855 |
| Lake Tanganyika | Discovered | Richard Burton and John Speke, British explorers | 1858 |
| Congo River | Traced | Sir Henry M. Stanley, British explorer | 1877 |
| **ASIA** | | | |
| Punjab (India) | Visited | Alexander the Great | 327 B.C. |
| China | Visited | Marco Polo, Italian traveler | c. 1272 |
| Tibet | Visited | Odoric of Pordenone, Italian monk | c. 1325 |
| Southern China | Explored | Niccolò dei Conti, Venetian traveler | c. 1440 |
| India | Visited (Cape route) | Vasco da Gama, Portuguese navigator | 1498 |
| Japan | Visited | St. Francis Xavier of Spain | 1549 |
| Arabia | Explored | Carsten Niebuhr, German explorer | 1762 |
| China | Explored | Ferdinand Richthofen, German scientist | 1868 |
| Mongolia | Explored | Nikolai M. Przhevalsky, Russian explorer | 1870–73 |
| Central Asia | Explored | Sven Hedin, Swedish scientist | 1890–1908 |
| **EUROPE** | | | |
| Shetland Islands | Visited | Pytheas of Massilia (Marseille) | c. 325 B.C. |
| North Cape | Rounded | Ottar, Norwegian explorer | c. 870 |
| Iceland | Colonized | Norwegian noblemen | c. 890–900 |
| **NORTH AMERICA** | | | |
| Greenland | Colonized | Eric the Red, Norwegian | c. 985 |
| Labrador; Nova Scotia (?) | Discovered | Leif Ericson, Norse explorer | 1000 |
| West Indies | Discovered | Christopher Columbus, Italian | 1492 |
| North America | Coast discovered | Giovanni Caboto (John Cabot), for British | 1497 |
| Pacific Ocean | Discovered | Vasco Núñez de Balboa, Spanish explorer | 1513 |
| Florida | Explored | Ponce de León, Spanish explorer | 1513 |
| Mexico | Conquered | Hernando Cortés, Spanish adventurer | 1519–21 |
| St. Lawrence River | Discovered | Jacques Cartier, French navigator | 1534 |
| Southwest U. S. | Explored | Francisco Coronado, Spanish explorer | 1540–42 |
| Colorado River | Discovered | Hernando de Alarcón, Spanish explorer | 1540 |
| Mississippi River | Discovered | Hernando de Soto, Spanish explorer | 1541 |
| Frobisher Bay | Discovered | Martin Frobisher, English seaman | 1576 |

| Country or place | Event | Explorer or discoverer | Date |
|---|---|---|---|
| Maine Coast | Explored | Samuel de Champlain, French explorer | 1604 |
| Jamestown, Va. | Settled | John Smith, English colonist | 1607 |
| Hudson River | Explored | Henry Hudson, English navigator | 1609 |
| Hudson Bay (Canada) | Discovered | Henry Hudson | 1610 |
| Baffin Bay | Discovered | William Baffin, English navigator | 1616 |
| Lake Michigan | Navigated | Jean Nicolet, French explorer | 1634 |
| Arkansas River | Discovered | Jacques Marquette and Louis Jolliet, French explorers | 1673 |
| Mississippi River | Explored | Sieur de La Salle, French explorer | 1682 |
| Bering Strait | Discovered | Vitus Bering, Danish explorer | 1728 |
| Alaska | Discovered | Vitus Bering | 1741 |
| Mackenzie River (Canada) | Discovered | Sir Alexander Mackenzie, Scottish-Canadian explorer | 1789 |
| Northwest U. S. | Explored | Meriwether Lewis and William Clark | 1804–06 |
| Northeast Passage (Arctic Ocean) | Navigated | Nils Nordenskjöld, Swedish explorer | 1879 |
| Greenland | Explored | Robert Peary, American explorer | 1892 |
| Northwest Passage | Navigated | Roald Amundsen, Norwegian explorer | 1906 |
| **SOUTH AMERICA** | | | |
| Continent | Visited | Columbus, Italian | 1498 |
| Brazil | Discovered | Pedro Alvarez Cabral, Portuguese | 1500 |
| Peru | Conquered | Francisco Pizarro, Spanish explorer | 1532–33 |
| Amazon River | Explored | Francisco Orellana, Spanish explorer | 1541 |
| Cape Horn | Discovered | Willem C. Schouten, Dutch navigator | 1615 |
| **OCEANIA** | | | |
| New Guinea | Visited | Jorge de Menezes, Portuguese explorer | 1526 |
| Australia | Visited } | Abel Janszoon Tasman, Dutch navigator | 1642 |
| Tasmania | Discovered } | | |
| Australia | Explored | John McDouall Stuart, English explorer | 1828 |
| Australia | Explored | Robert Burke and William Wills, Australian explorers | 1861 |
| New Zealand | Sighted (and named) | Abel Janszoon Tasman | 1642 |
| New Zealand | Visited | James Cook, English navigator | 1769 |
| **ARCTIC, ANTARCTIC, AND MISCELLANEOUS** | | | |
| Ocean exploration | Expedition | Magellan's ships circled globe | 1519–22 |
| Galápagos Islands | Visited | Diego de Rivadeneira, Spanish captain | 1535 |
| Spitsbergen | Visited | Willem Barents, Dutch navigator | 1596 |
| Antarctic Circle | Crossed | James Cook, English navigator | 1773 |
| Antarctica | Discovered | Nathaniel Palmer, U. S. whaler (archipelago) and Fabian Gottlieb von Bellingshausen, Russian admiral (mainland) | 1820–21 |
| Antarctica | Explored | Charles Wilkes, American explorer | 1840 |
| North Pole | Reached | Robert E. Peary, American explorer | 1909 |
| South Pole | Reached | Roald Amundsen, Norwegian explorer | 1911 |

## The Continents

A continent is defined as a large unbroken land mass completely surrounded by water, although in some cases continents are (or were in part) connected by land bridges.

The hypothesis first suggested late in the 19th century was that the continents consist of lighter rocks that rest on heavier crustal material in about the same manner that icebergs float on water. That the rocks forming the continents are lighter than the material below them and under the ocean bottoms is now established. As a consequence of this fact, Alfred Wegener (for the first time in 1912) suggested that the continents are slowly moving, at a rate of about one yard per century, so that their relative positions are not rigidly fixed. Many geologists that were originally skeptical have come to accept this theory of Continental Drift.

When describing a continent, it is important to remember that there is a fundamental difference between a deep ocean, like the Atlantic, and shallow seas, like the Baltic and most of the North Sea, which are merely flooded portions of a continent. Another and entirely different point to remember is that political considerations have often overridden geographical facts when it came to naming continents.

Geographically speaking, Europe, including the British Isles, is a large western peninsula of the continent of Asia; and many geographers, when referring to Europe and Asia, speak of the Eurasian Continent. But traditionally, Europe is counted as a separate continent, with the Ural and the Caucasus mountains forming the line of demarcation between Europe and Asia.

To the south of Europe, Asia has an odd-shaped peninsula jutting westward, which has a large number of political subdivisions. The northern section is taken up by Turkey; to the south of Turkey there are Syria, Iraq, Israel, Jordan, Saudi Arabia, and a number of smaller Arab countries. All this is part of Asia. Traditionally, the island of Cyprus in the Mediterranean is also considered to be part of Asia, while the island of Crete is counted as European.

The large islands of Java, Borneo, and Sumatra and the smaller islands near them are counted as part of "tropical Asia," while New Guinea is counted as related to Australia. In the case of the Americas, the problem arises as to whether they should be considered one or two continents. There are good arguments on both sides, but since there is now a land bridge between North and South America (in the past it was often flooded) and since no part of the sea east of the land bridge is deep ocean, it is more logical to consider the Americas as one continent.

Politically, based mainly on history, the Americas are divided into North America (from the Arctic to the Mexican border), Central America (from Mexico to Panama, with the Caribbean islands), and South America. Greenland is considered a section of North America, while Iceland is traditionally counted as a European island because of its political ties with the Scandinavian countries.

The island groups in the Pacific are often called "Oceania," but this name does *not* imply that scientists consider them the remains of a continent.

# Volcanoes of the World

About 500 volcanoes have had recorded eruptions within historical times. Almost two thirds of these are in the Northern Hemisphere. Most volcanoes occur at the boundaries of the earth's crustal plates, such as the famous "Ring of Fire" that surrounds the Pacific Ocean plate. Of the world's active volcanoes, about 60% are along the perimeter of the Pacific, about 17% on mid-oceanic islands, about 14% in an arc along the south of the Indonesian islands, and about 9% in the Mediterranean area, Africa, and Asia Minor. Many of the world's volcanoes are submarine and have unrecorded eruptions.

## Pacific "Ring of Fire"

### NORTHWEST

**Japan:** At least 33 active vents.

Aso (5,223 ft; 1,592 m), on Kyūshū, has one of the largest craters in the world.

Asama (over 8,300 ft; 2,530 m), on Honshū, is continuously active; violent eruption in 1783.

Azuma (nearly 7,700 ft; 2,347 m), on Honshū, erupted in 1900.

Chōkai (7,300 ft; 2,225 m), on Honshū, erupted in 1974 after having been quiescent since 1861.

Fujiyama (Fujisan) (12,385 ft; 3,775 m), on Honshū, southwest of Tokyo. Symmetrical in outline, snow-covered. Regarded as a sacred mountain.

On-take (3,668 ft; 1,118 m), on peninsula of Kyūshū. Strong smoke emissions and explosions began November 1973 and continued through 1974.

**U.S.S.R.:** Kamchatka peninsula, 14–18 active volcanoes. Klyuchevskaya (Kluchev) (15,500 ft; 4,724 m) reported active in 1974.

Kuril Islands: At least 13 active volcanoes and several submarine outbreaks.

### SOUTHWEST

**New Zealand:** Mount Tarawera (3,645 ft; 1,112 m), on North Island, had a severe eruption in 1886 that destroyed the famous Pink and White sinter terraces of Rotomahana, a hot lake.

Ngauruhoe (7,515 ft; 2,291 m), on North Island, emits steam and vapor constantly. Erupted 1974.

**Papua New Guinea:** Karkar Island (4,920 ft; 1,500 m). Mild eruptions 1974.

**Philippine Islands:** About 100 eruptive centers; Hibok Hibok, on Camiguin, erupted September 1950 and again in December 1951, when about 750 were reported killed or missing; eruptions continued during 1952–53.

Taal (4,752 ft; 1,448 m), on Luzon. Major eruption in 1965 killed 190; erupted again, 1968.

**Volcano Islands:** Mount Suribachi (546 ft; 166 m), on Iwo Jima. A sulfurous steaming volcano. Raising of U.S. flag over Mount Suribachi was one of the dramatic episodes of World War II.

### NORTHEAST

**Alaska:** Mount Wrangell (14,163 ft; 4,317 m) and Mount Katmai (about 6,700 ft; 2,042 m). On June 6, 1912, a violent eruption (Nova Rupta) of Mount Katmai occurred, during which the "Valley of Ten Thousand Smokes" was formed.

**Aleutian Islands:** There are 32 active vents known and numerous inactive cones. Akutan Island (over 4,000 ft; 1,220 m) erupted in 1974, with ash and debris rising over 300 ft.

Great Sitkin (5,741 ft; 1,750 m). Explosive activity February-September 1974, accompanied by earthquake originating at volcano that registered 2.3 on Richter scale.

**California, Oregon, Washington:** Lassen Peak (10,453 ft; 3,186 m) in California is the only observed active volcano in the U.S. outside Alaska and Hawaii. The last period of activity was 1914–17. Other mountains of volcanic origin include Mount Shasta (California), Mount Hood (Oregon), Mount Mazama (Oregon)—the mountain continaing Crater Lake, Mount Rainier (Washington), and Mount Baker (Washington), which has been steaming since October 1975, but gives no sign of an impending eruption.

### SOUTHEAST

**Chile and Argentina:** About 25 active or potentially active.

**Colombia:** Huila (nearly 18,900 ft; 5,760 m), a vapor-emitting volcano, and Tolima (nearly 18,500 ft; 5,640 m). Eruption of Puracé (15,600 ft; 4,755 m) in 1949 killed 17 people.

**Ecuador:** Cayambe (nearly 19,000 ft; 5,791 m). Almost on the equator.

Cotopaxi (19,344 ft; 5,896 m). Perhaps highest active volcano in the world. Possesses a beautifully formed cone.

Reventador (11,434 ft; 3,485 m). Observed in active state in late 1973.

**El Salvador:** Izalco ("beacon of Central America") (7,830 ft; 2,387 m) first appeared in 1770 and is still growing (erupted in 1950, 1956; last erupted in October-November 1966). San Salvador (6,187 ft; 1,886 m) had a violent eruption in 1923. Conchagua (about 4100 ft; 1250 m) erupted with considerable damage early in 1947.

**Guatemala:** Santa Maria Quezaltenango (12,361 ft; 3,768 m). Frequent activity between 1902–08 and 1922–28 after centuries of quiescence. Most dangerously active vent of Central America. Other volcanoes include Tajumulco (13,814 ft; 4,211 m) and Atitlán (11,633 ft; 3,546 m).

**Mexico:** Boquerón ("Big Mouth"), on San Benedicto, about 250 mi. south of Lower California. Newest volcano in Western Hemisphere, discovered September 1952.

Colima (about 14,000 ft; 4,270 m), in group that has had frequent eruptions.

Orizaba (Citlaltépetl) (18,701 ft; 5,700 m).

Parícutin (7,450 ft; 2,270 m). First appeared in February 1943. In less than a week, a cone over 140 ft high developed with a crater one quarter mile in circumference. Cone grew more than 1,500 ft (457 m) in 1943. Erupted 1952.

Popocatépetl (17,887 ft; 5,452 m). Large, deep, bell-shaped crater. Not entirely extinct; steam still escapes.

**Nicaragua:** Volcanoes include Telica, Coseguina, and Momotombo. Between Momotombo on the west shore of Lake Managua and Coseguina overlooking the Gulf of Fonseca, there is a string of more than 20 cones, many still active. One of these, Cerro Negro, erupted in July 1947, with considerable damage and loss of life, and again in 1971.

Concepción (5,100 ft; 1,555 m). Ash eruptions 1973–74.

## Mid-oceanic Islands

**Canary Islands:** Pico de Teide (12,192 ft; 3,716 m), on Tenerife.

**Cape Verde Islands:** Fogo (nearly 9,300 ft; 2,835 m). Severe eruption in 1857; quiescent until 1951.

**Caribbean:** La Soufrière (4,869 ft; 1,484 m), on Guadeloupe. Violent activity in July-August 1976 caused evacuation of 73,000 people.

**Comoro Islands:** One volcano, Karthala (nearly 8,000 ft; 2,440 m), is visible for over 100 miles. Last erupted in 1904.

**Hawaii:** Mauna Loa ("Long Mountain") (13,680 ft; 4,170 m), on Hawaii, discharges from its high side vents more lava than any other volcano. Largest volcanic mountain in the world in cubic content. Area of crater is 3.7 sq mi. Violent eruption in June 1950, with lava pouring 25 miles into the ocean. Last major eruption in July 1975.

Mauna Kea (13,796 ft; 4,205 m), on Hawaii. Highest mountain in state.

Kilauea (4,090 ft; 1,247 m) is a vent in the side of Mauna Loa, but its eruptions are apparently independent. One of the most spectacular and active craters. Crater has an area of 4.14 sq mi. Earthquake in July 1975 caused major eruption. Eruptions began in September 1977 and reached a height of 980 ft (300 m). Activity ended Oct. 1.

**Iceland:** At least 25 volcanoes active in historical times. Very similar to Hawaiian volcanoes. Askja (over 4,700 ft; 1,433 m) is the largest.

**Lesser Antilles (West Indian Islands):** Mount Pelée (over 4,500 ft; 1,370 m), northwestern Martinique. Eruption in 1902 destroyed town of St. Pierre and killed approximately 40,000 people.

**Réunion Island (east of Madagascar):** Piton de la Fournaise (Le Volcan) (8,610 ft; 2,624 m). Large lava flows. Last erupted in 1972.

**Samoan archipelago:** Savai'i Island had an eruption in 1905 that caused considerable damage. Niuafoo (Tin Can), in the Tonga Islands, has a crater that extends 6,000 feet below and 600 feet above water.

## Indonesia

**Sumatra:** Ninety volcanoes have been discovered; 12 are now active. The most famous, Krakatau, is a small volcanic island in the Sunda Strait. Numerous volcanic discharges occurred in 1883. One extremely violent explosion caused the disappearance of the highest peak and the northern part of the island. Fine dust was carried around the world in the upper atmosphere. Over 36,000 persons lost their lives in resultant tidal waves that were felt as far away as Cape Horn. Active in 1972.

## Mediterranean Area

**Italy:** Mount Etna (10,902 ft; 3,323 m), eastern Sicily. Two new craters formed in eruptions of February-March 1947. Worst eruption in 50 years occurred November 1950-Jaunary 1951. Erupted again in 1974, 1975, and 1977.

Stromboli (about 3,000 ft; 914 m), Lipari Islands (north of Sicily). Called "Lighthouse of the Mediterranean." Reported active in 1971.

Mount Vesuvius (4,200 ft; 1,280 m), southeast of Naples. Only active volcano on European mainland. Pompeii buried by an eruption, A.D. 79.

# Highest Mountain Peaks of the World

**(For U.S. peaks, see Index)**

| Mountain peak | Range | Location | Height feet | Height meters |
|---|---|---|---|---|
| Everest[1] | Himalayas | Nepal-Tibet | 29,028 | 8,848 |
| Godwin Austen (K-2) | Karakoram | India | 28,741 | 8,750 |
| Kanchenjunga | Himalayas | Nepal-Sikkim | 28,208 | 8,598 |
| Lhotse | Himalayas | Nepal-Tibet | 27,890 | 8,501 |

| Mountain peak | Range | Location | Height | |
|---|---|---|---|---|
| | | | feet | meters |
| Makalu | Himalayas | Tibet-Nepal | 27,790 | 8,470 |
| Dhaulagiri I | Himalayas | Nepal | 26,810 | 8,172 |
| Manaslu | Himalayas | Nepal | 26,760 | 8,156 |
| Cho Oyu | Himalayas | Nepal | 26,750 | 8,153 |
| Nanga Parbat | Himalayas | India | 26,660 | 8,126 |
| Annapurna I | Himalayas | Nepal | 26,504 | 8,078 |
| Gasherbrum I | Karakoram | India | 26,470 | 8,068 |
| Broad Peak | Karakoram | India | 26,400 | 8,047 |
| Gasherbrum II | Karakoram | India | 26,360 | 8,033 |
| Gosainthan | Himalayas | Tibet | 26,291 | 8,013 |
| Gasherbrum III | Karakoram | India | 26,090 | 7,952 |
| Annapurna II | Himalayas | Nepal | 26,041 | 7,937 |
| Gasherbrum IV | Karakoram | India | 26,000 | 7,925 |
| Kangbachen | Himalayas | Nepal | 25,925 | 7,902 |
| Gyachung Kang | Himalayas | Nepal | 25,910 | 7,897 |
| Himal Chuli | Himalayas | Nepal | 25,895 | 7,893 |
| Disteghil Sar | Karakoram | India | 25,868 | 7,885 |
| Nuptse | Himalayas | Nepal | 25,850 | 7,829 |
| Kunyang Kish | Karakoram | India | 25,760 | 7,852 |
| Dakum (Peak 29) | Himalayas | Nepal | 25,760 | 7,852 |
| Masherbrum | Karakoram | India | 25,660 | 7,821 |
| Nanda Devi | Himalayas | India | 25,645 | 7,817 |
| Chomolonzo | Himalayas | Nepal-Tibet | 25,640 | 7,815 |
| Rakaposhi | Karakoram | India | 25,550 | 7,788 |
| Batura | Karakoram | India | 25,540 | 7,785 |
| Kanjut Sar | Karakoram | India | 25,460 | 7,760 |
| Kamet | Himalayas | India-Tibet | 25,447 | 7,756 |
| Namche Barwa | Himalayas | Tibet | 25,445 | 7,756 |
| Dhaulagiri II | Himalayas | Nepal | 25,427 | 7,750 |
| Saltoro Kangri | Karakoram | India | 25,400 | 7,742 |
| Gurla Mandhata | Himalayas | Tibet | 25,355 | 7,728 |
| Ulugh Muztagh | Kunlun | Tibet | 25,341 | 7,724 |
| Trivor | Karakoram | India | 25,330 | 7,721 |
| Jannu | Himalayas | Nepal | 25,294 | 7,710 |
| Saser Kangri | Karakoram | India | 25,170 | 7,672 |
| Makalu II | Himalayas | Nepal | 25,130 | 7,660 |
| Chogolisa | Karakoram | India | 25,110 | 7,654 |
| Dhaulagiri IV | Himalayas | Nepal | 25,064 | 7,639 |
| Fang | Himalayas | Nepal | 25,013 | 7,624 |
| Kula Gangri | Himalayas | Tibet | 24,783 | 7,554 |
| Changtse | Himalayas | Tibet | 24,780 | 7,553 |
| Muztagh Ata | Muztagh Ata | China | 24,757 | 7,546 |
| Skyang Kangri | Himalayas | Kashmir | 24,750 | 7,544 |
| Communism Peak | Pamir | U.S.S.R. | 24,547 | 7,482 |
| Victory Peak | Pamir | U.S.S.R. | 24,406 | 7,439 |
| Sia Kangri | Himalayas | Kashmir | 24,340 | 7,419 |
| Chamlang | Himalayas | Nepal | 24,012 | 7,319 |
| Alung Gangri | Himalayas | Tibet | 23,999 | 7,315 |
| Chomo Lhari | Himalayas | Tibet-Bhutan | 23,996 | 7,314 |
| Muztagh (K-5) | Kunlun | China | 23,891 | 7,282 |
| Amne Machin | Kunlun | China | 23,490 | 7,160 |
| Gaurisankar | Himalayas | Nepal-Tibet | 23,440 | 7,145 |
| Lenin Peak | Pamir | U.S.S.R. | 23,405 | 7,134 |
| Korzhenevski Peak | Pamir | U.S.S.R. | 23,310 | 7,105 |
| Kangto | Himalayas | Tibet | 23,260 | 7,090 |
| Dunagiri | Himalayas | India | 23,184 | 7,066 |
| Pauhunri | Himalayas | India-Tibet | 23,180 | 7,065 |
| Aconcagua | Andes | Argentina-Chile | 23,034 | 7,021 |
| Revolution Peak | Pamir | U.S.S.R. | 22,880 | 6,974 |
| Kangchenjhan | Himalayas | India | 22,700 | 6,919 |
| Siniolchu | Himalayas | India | 22,620 | 6,895 |
| Ojos des Salado | Andes | Argentina-Chile | 22,588 | 6,885 |
| Bonete | Andes | Argentina-Chile | 22,546 | 6,872 |
| Simvuo | Himalayas | India | 22,346 | 6,811 |
| Tup | Andes | Argentina | 22,309 | 6,800 |
| Kungpu | Himalayas | Bhutan | 22,300 | 6,797 |
| Falso-Azufre | Andes | Argentina-Chile | 22,277 | 6,790 |
| Moscow Peak | Pamir | U.S.S.R. | 22,260 | 6,785 |
| Veladero | Andes | Argentina | 22,244 | 6,780 |
| Pissis | Andes | Argentina | 22,241 | 6,779 |

| Mountain peak | Range | Location | Height feet | Height meters |
|---|---|---|---|---|
| Mercedario | Andes | Argentina-Chile | 22,211 | 6,770 |
| Huascarán | Andes | Peru | 22,198 | 6,766 |
| Tocorpuri | Andes | Bolivia-Chile | 22,162 | 6,755 |
| Karl Marx Peak | Pamir | U.S.S.R. | 22,067 | 6,726 |
| Llullaillaco | Andes | Argentina-Chile | 22,057 | 6,723 |
| Libertador | Andes | Argentina | 22,047 | 6,720 |
| Kailas | Himalayas | Tibet | 22,027 | 6,714 |
| Lingtren | Himalayas | Nepal-Tibet | 21,972 | 6,697 |
| Incahuasi | Andes | Argentina-Chile | 21,719 | 6,620 |
| Carnicero | Andes | Peru | 21,689 | 6,611 |
| Kurumda | Pamir | U.S.S.R. | 21,686 | 6,610 |
| Garmo Peak | Pamir | U.S.S.R. | 21,637 | 6,595 |
| Sajama | Andes | Bolivia | 21,555 | 6,570 |
| Ancohuma | Andes | Bolivia | 21,490 | 6,550 |
| El Muerto | Andes | Argentina-Chile | 21,456 | 6,540 |
| Nacimiento | Andes | Argentina | 21,302 | 6,493 |
| Illimani | Andes | Bolivia | 21,184 | 6,457 |
| Antofalla | Andes | Argentina-Chile | 21,129 | 6,440 |
| Coropuña | Andes | Peru | 21,079 | 6,425 |
| Cuzco (Ausangate) | Andes | Peru | 20,995 | 6,399 |
| Toro | Andes | Argentina-Chile | 20,932 | 6,380 |
| Parinacota | Andes | Bolivia-Chile | 20,768 | 6,330 |
| Chimboraso | Andes | Ecuador | 20,702 | 6,310 |
| Salcantay | Andes | Peru | 20,575 | 6,271 |
| General Manuel Belgrano | Andes | Argentina | 20,505 | 6,250 |
| Chañi | Andes | Argentina | 20,341 | 6,200 |
| Caca Aca | Andes | Bolivia | 20,328 | 6,196 |
| McKinley | Alaska | Alaska | 20,320 | 6,194 |
| Vudor Peak | Pamir | U.S.S.R. | 20,118 | 6,132 |
| Condoriri | Andes | Bolivia | 20,095 | 6,125 |
| Solimana | Andes | Peru | 20,069 | 6,117 |
| Nevada | Andes | Argentina | 20,023 | 6,103 |

1. The U. S. Air Force Planning Charts list the height of Mt. Everest as 29,141 ft.

## World's Greatest Man-Made Lakes[1]

| Name of dam | Location | Millions of cubic meters | Thousands of acre-feet | Year completed |
|---|---|---|---|---|
| Owen Falls | Uganda | 204,800 | 166,000 | 1954 |
| Bratsk | U.S.S.R. | 169,270 | 137,220 | 1964 |
| High Aswān | Egypt | 169,000 | 137,000 | 1970 |
| Kariba | Rhodesia-Zambia | 160,368 | 130,000 | 1958 |
| Akosombo | Ghana | 148,000 | 120,000 | 1965 |
| Daniel Johnson | Canada | 141,852 | 115,000 | 1968 |
| Krasnoyarsk | U.S.S.R. | 73,300 | 59,425 | 1972 |
| W. A. C. Bennett | Canada | 70,309 | 57,006 | 1967 |
| Zeya | U.S.S.R. | 68,400 | 55,452 | 1975 |
| Cabora Bassa | Mozambique | 64,000 | 51,900 | 1974 |
| Ust-Ilim | U.S.S.R. | 59,300 | 48,100 | UC |
| Volga-V. I. Lenin | U.S.S.R. | 58,000 | 47,020 | 1955 |
| LaGrande | Canada | 55,000 | 44,589 | UC |
| Bukhtarma | U.S.S.R. | 53,000 | 42,970 | 1960 |
| Irkutsk | U.S.S.R. | 46,000 | 37,290 | 1956 |
| Hoover | Nevada-Arizona | 36,703 | 29,755 | 1936 |
| Vilyui | U.S.S.R. | 35,900 | 29,104 | 1967 |
| Sobradinho | Brazil | 34,200 | 27,700 | UC |
| Volgograd-22nd Congress | U.S.S.R. | 33,500 | 27,160 | 1958 |
| Glen Canyon | Arizona | 33,305 | 27,000 | 1964 |
| Sayano-Shushenskaya | U.S.S.R. | 31,300 | 25,353 | UC |
| Keban | Turkey | 31,000 | 25,110 | 1974 |
| Garrison | North Dakota | 30,000 | 24,321 | 1956 |
| Iroquois | U.S.-Canada | 29,960 | 24,288 | 1958 |
| Oahe | South Dakota | 29,100 | 23,591 | 1963 |

1. Formed by construction of dams. NOTE: UC means under construction in 1977. *Source:* Department of the Interior, Bureau of Reclamation.

## Oceans and Seas

| Name | Area sq mi. | Area sq km | Average depth feet | Average depth meters | Greatest known depth feet | Greatest known depth meters | Place greatest known depth |
|---|---|---|---|---|---|---|---|
| Pacific Ocean | 64,000,000 | 165,760,000 | 13,215 | 4,028 | 37,782 | 11,516 | Mindanao Deep |
| Atlantic Ocean | 31,815,000 | 82,400,000 | 12,880 | 3,926 | 30,246 | 9,219 | Puerto Rico Trough |
| Indian Ocean | 25,300,000 | 65,526,700 | 13,002 | 3,963 | 24,460 | 7,455 | Sunda Trench |
| Arctic Ocean | 5,440,200 | 14,090,000 | 3,953 | 1,205 | 18,456 | 5,625 | 77° 45′ N; 175° W |
| Mediterranean Sea[1] | 1,145,100 | 2,965,800 | 4,688 | 1,429 | 15,197 | 4,632 | Off Cape Matapan, Greece |
| Caribbean Sea | 1,049,500 | 2,718,200 | 8,685 | 2,647 | 22,788 | 6,946 | Off Cayman Islands |
| South China Sea | 895,400 | 2,319,000 | 5,419 | 1,652 | 16,456 | 5,016 | West of Luzon |
| Bering Sea | 884,900 | 2,291,900 | 5,075 | 1,547 | 15,659 | 4,773 | Off Buldir Island |
| Gulf of Mexico | 615,000 | 1,592,800 | 4,874 | 1,486 | 12,425 | 3,787 | Sigsbee Deep |
| Okhotsk Sea | 613,800 | 1,589,700 | 2,749 | 838 | 12,001 | 3,658 | 146° 10′ E; 46° 50′ N |
| East China Sea | 482,300 | 1,249,200 | 617 | 188 | 9,126 | 2,782 | 25° 16′ N; 125° E |
| Hudson Bay | 475,800 | 1,232,300 | 420 | 128 | 600 | 183 | Near entrance |
| Japan Sea | 389,100 | 1,007,800 | 4,429 | 1,350 | 12,276 | 3,742 | Central Basin |
| Andaman Sea | 308,100 | 797,700 | 2,854 | 870 | 12,392 | 3,777 | Off Car Nicobar Island |
| North Sea | 222,100 | 575,200 | 308 | 94 | 2,165 | 660 | Skagerrak |
| Red Sea | 169,100 | 438,000 | 1,611 | 491 | 7,254 | 2,211 | Off Port Sudan |
| Baltic Sea | 163,000 | 422,200 | 180 | 55 | 1,380 | 421 | Off Gotland |

1. Includes Black Sea and Sea of Azov. NOTE: For Caspian Sea, *see* Large Lakes of World elsewhere in this section.

## Large Lakes of the World

| Name and location | Area sq mi. | Area sq km | Length mi. | Length km | Maximum depth feet | Maximum depth meters |
|---|---|---|---|---|---|---|
| Caspian Sea, U.S.S.R.-Iran[1] | 152,239 | 394,299 | 745 | 1,199 | 3,104 | 946 |
| Superior, U.S.-Canada | 31,820 | 82,414 | 383 | 616 | 1,333 | 406 |
| Victoria, Tanzania–Uganda | 26,828 | 69,485 | 200 | 322 | 270 | 82 |
| Aral, U.S.S.R. | 25,659 | 66,457 | 266 | 428 | 223 | 68 |
| Huron, U.S.-Canada | 23,010 | 59,596 | 247 | 397 | 750 | 229 |
| Michigan, U.S. | 22,400 | 58,016 | 321 | 517 | 923 | 281 |
| Tanganyika, Tanzania-Zaire | 12,700 | 32,893 | 420 | 676 | 4,708 | 1,435 |
| Baikal, U.S.S.R. | 12,162 | 31,500 | 395 | 636 | 5,712 | 1,741 |
| Great Bear, Canada | 12,000 | 31,080 | 232 | 373 | 270 | 82 |
| Nyasa, Malawi-Mozambique-Tanzania | 11,600 | 30,044 | 360 | 579 | 2,316 | 706 |
| Great Slave, Canada | 11,170 | 28,930 | 298 | 480 | 2,015 | 614 |
| Chad,[2] Chad-Niger-Nigeria | 9,946 | 25,760 | — | — | 23 | 7 |
| Erie, U.S.-Canada | 9,930 | 25,719 | 241 | 388 | 210 | 64 |
| Winnipeg, Canada | 9,094 | 23,553 | 264 | 425 | 204 | 62 |
| Ontario, U.S.-Canada | 7,520 | 19,477 | 193 | 311 | 778 | 237 |
| Balkash, U.S.S.R. | 7,115 | 18,428 | 376 | 605 | 87 | 27 |
| Ladoga, U.S.S.R. | 7,000 | 18,130 | 124 | 200 | 738 | 225 |
| Onega, U.S.S.R. | 3,819 | 9,891 | 154 | 248 | 361 | 110 |
| Titicaca, Bolivia-Peru | 3,141 | 8,135 | 110 | 177 | 1,214 | 370 |
| Nicaragua, Nicaragua | 3,089 | 8,001 | 110 | 177 | 230 | 70 |
| Athabaska, Canada | 3,058 | 7,920 | 208 | 335 | 407 | 124 |
| Rudolf, Kenya | 2,473 | 6,405 | 154 | 248 | — | — |
| Reindeer, Canada | 2,444 | 6,330 | 152 | 245 | — | — |
| Eyre, South Australia | 2,400[3] | 6,216 | 130 | 209 | varies | varies |
| Issyk-Kul, U.S.S.R. | 2,394 | 6,200 | 113 | 182 | 2,297 | 700 |
| Urmia,[2] Iran | 2,317 | 6,001 | 81 | 130 | 49 | 15 |
| Torrens, South Australia | 2,200 | 5,698 | 130 | 209 | — | — |
| Vänern, Sweden | 2,141 | 5,545 | 87 | 140 | 322 | 98 |
| Winnipegosis, Canada | 2,086 | 5,403 | 152 | 245 | 59 | 18 |
| Mobutu Sese Seko, Uganda | 2,046 | 5,299 | 100 | 161 | 180 | 55 |
| Nettilling, Baffin Island, Canada | 1,950 | 5,051 | 70 | 113 | — | — |
| Nipigon, Canada | 1,870 | 4,843 | 72 | 116 | — | — |
| Manitoba, Canada | 1,817 | 4,706 | 140 | 225 | 22 | 7 |
| Great Salt, U.S. | 1,800 | 4,662 | 75 | 121 | 15/25 | 5/8 |
| Kioga, Uganda | 1,700 | 4,403 | 50 | 80 | about 30 | 9 |
| Koko-Nor, China | 1,630 | 4,222 | 66 | 106 | — | — |

1. The Caspian Sea is called "sea" because the Romans, finding it salty, named it *Mare Caspium.* Many geographers, however, consider it a lake because it is land-locked. 2. Figures represent high-water data. 3. Varies with the rainfall of the wet season. It has been reported to dry up almost completely on occasion.

## Principal Rivers of the World

(For other U.S. rivers, see Index)

| River | Source | Outflow | Approx. length miles | km |
|---|---|---|---|---|
| Nile | Tributaries of Lake Victoria, Africa | Mediterranean Sea | 4,180 | 6,690 |
| Amazon | Glacier-fed lakes, Peru | Atlantic Ocean | 3,912 | 6,296 |
| Mississippi-Missouri-Red Rock | Source of Red Rock, Montana | Gulf of Mexico | 3,741 | 6,020 |
| Yangtze Kiang | Tibetan plateau, China | China Sea | 3,602 | 5,797 |
| Ob | Altai Mts., U.S.S.R. | Gulf of Ob | 3,459 | 5,567 |
| Yellow (Hwang Ho) | Eastern part of Kunlan Mts., west China | Gulf of Chihli | 2,900 | 4,667 |
| Yenisei | Tannu-Ola Mts., western Tuva, U.S.S.R. | Arctic Ocean | 2,800 | 4,506 |
| Paraná | Confluence of Paranaiba and Grande rivers | Río de la Plata | 2,795 | 4,498 |
| Irtish | Altai Mts., U.S.S.R. | Ob River | 2,758 | 4,438 |
| Congo | Confluence of Lualaba and Luapula rivers, Zaire | Atlantic Ocean | 2,716 | 4,371 |
| Amur | Confluence of Shilka (U.S.S.R.) and Argun (Manchuria) rivers | Tatar Strait | 2,704 | 4,352 |
| Lena | Baikal Mts., U.S.S.R. | Arctic Ocean | 2,652 | 4,268 |
| Mackenzie | Head of Finlay River, British Columbia, Canada | Beaufort Sea (Arctic Ocean) | 2,635 | 4,241 |
| Niger | Guinea | Gulf of Guinea | 2,600 | 4,184 |
| Mekong | Tibetan highlands | South China Sea | 2,500 | 4,023 |
| Mississippi | Lake Itasca, Minnesota | Gulf of Mexico | 2,348 | 3,779 |
| Missouri | Confluence of Jefferson, Gallatin, and Madison rivers, Montana | Mississippi River | 2,315 | 3,726 |
| Volga | Valdai plateau, U.S.S.R. | Caspian Sea | 2,291 | 3,687 |
| Madeira | Confluence of Beni and Maumoré rivers, Bolivia-Brazil boundary | Amazon River | 2,012 | 3,238 |
| Purus | Peruvian Andes | Amazon River | 1,993 | 3,207 |
| São Francisco | Southwest Minas Gerais, Brazil | Atlantic Ocean | 1,987 | 3,198 |
| St. Lawrence | Lake Ontario | Gulf of St. Lawrence | 1,900 | 3,058 |
| Yukon | Junction of Lewes and Pelly rivers, Yukon Territory, Canada | Bering Sea | 1,900 | 3,058 |
| Rio Grande | San Juan Mts., Colorado | Gulf of Mexico | 1,885 | 3,034 |
| Brahmaputra | Himalayas | Ganges River | 1,800 | 2,897 |
| Indus | Himalayas | Arabian Sea | 1,800 | 2,897 |
| Danube | Black Forest, W. Germany | Black Sea | 1,766 | 2,842 |
| Euphrates | Confluence of Murat Nehri and Kara Su rivers, Turkey | Shatt-al-Arab | 1,739 | 2,799 |
| Darling | Central part of Eastern Highlands, Australia | Murray River | 1,702 | 2,739 |
| Zambezi | 11°21'S, 24°22'E, Zambia | Mozambique Channel | 1,700 | 2,736 |
| Tocantins | Goiás, Brazil | Pará River | 1,677 | 2,699 |
| Murray | Australian Alps, New South Wales | Indian Ocean | 1,609 | 2,589 |
| Nelson | Head of Bow River, western Alberta, Canada | Hudson Bay | 1,600 | 2,575 |
| Paraguay | Mato Grosso, Brazil | Paraná River | 1,584 | 2,549 |
| Ural | Southern Ural Mts., U.S.S.R. | Caspian Sea | 1,574 | 2,533 |
| Ganges | Himalayas | Bay of Bengal | 1,557 | 2,506 |
| Amu Darya (Oxus) | Nicholas Range, Pamir Mts., U.S.S.R. | Aral Sea | 1,500 | 2,414 |

| River | Source | Outflow | Approx. length miles | Approx. length km |
|---|---|---|---|---|
| Japurá | Andes, Colombia | Amazon River | 1,500 | 2,414 |
| Salween | Tibet, south of Kunlun Mts. | Gulf of Martaban | 1,500 | 2,414 |
| Arkansas | Central Colorado | Mississippi River | 1,450 | 2,333 |
| Colorado | Grand County, Colorado | Gulf of California | 1,450 | 2,333 |
| Dnieper | Valdai Hills, U.S.S.R. | Black Sea | 1,419 | 2,284 |
| Ohio-Allegheny | Potter County, Pennsylvania | Mississippi River | 1,306 | 2,102 |
| Irrawaddy | Confluence of Nmai and Mali rivers, northeast Burma | Bay of Bengal | 1,300 | 2,092 |
| Orange | Lesotho | Atlantic Ocean | 1,300 | 2,092 |
| Orinoco | Serra Parima Mts., Venezuela | Atlantic Ocean | 1,281 | 2,062 |
| Pilcomayo | Andes Mts., Bolivia | Paraguay River | 1,242 | 1,999 |
| Hsi | Eastern Yunnan Province, China | China Sea | 1,236 | 1,989 |
| Columbia | Columbia Lake, British Columbia, Canada | Pacific Ocean | 1,232 | 1,983 |
| Don | Tula, R.S.F.S.R., U.S.S.R. | Sea of Azov | 1,223 | 1,968 |
| Sungari | China-North Korea boundary | Amur River | 1,215 | 1,955 |
| Saskatchewan | Canadian Rocky Mts. | Lake Winnipeg | 1,205 | 1,939 |
| Peace | Stikine Mts., British Columbia, Canada | Great Slave River | 1,195 | 1,923 |
| Tigris | Taurus Mts., Turkey | Shatt-al-Arab | 1,180 | 1,899 |

# Table of Geological Periods

It is now generally assumed that planets are formed by the accretion of gas and dust in a cosmic cloud, but there is no way of estimating the length of this process. Our earth acquired its present size, more or less, between 4,000 and 5,000 million years ago. Life on earth originated about 2,000 million years ago, but there are no good fossil remains from periods earlier than the Cambrian, which began about 550 million years ago. The largely unknown past before the Cambrian Period is referred to as the Pre-Cambrian and is subdivided into the Lower (or older) and Upper (or younger) Pre-Cambrian—also called the Archaeozoic and Proterozoic Eras.

The known geological history of the earth since the beginning of the Cambrian Period is subdivided into three "eras," each of which comprises a number of "periods." They, in turn, are subdivided into "subperiods." In a subperiod, a certain section may be especially well known because of rich fossil finds. Such a section is called a "formation," and it is usually identified by a place name.

## Paleozoic Era

This era began 550 million years ago and lasted for 355 million years. The name was compounded from Greek *palaios* (old) and *zoön* (animal).

| Period | Duration[1] | Subperiods | Events |
|---|---|---|---|
| Cambrian (from *Cambria,* Latin name for Wales) | 70 | Lower Cambrian<br>Middle Cambrian<br>Upper Cambrian | Invertebrate sea life of many types, proliferating during this and the following period |
| Ordovician (from Latin *Ordovices,* people of early Britain) | 85 | Lower Ordovician<br>Upper Ordovician | |
| Silurian (from Latin *Silures,* people of early Wales) | 40 | Lower Silurian<br>Upper Silurian | First known fishes; gigantic sea scorpions |
| Devonian (from Devonshire in England) | 50 | Lower Devonian<br>Upper Devonian | Proliferation of fishes and other forms of sea life; land still largely lifeless |
| Carboniferous (from Latin *carbo* = coal + *fero* = to bear) | 85 | Lower or Mississippian<br>Upper or Pennsylvanian | Period of maximum coal formation in swampy forests; early insects and first known amphibians |
| Permian (from district of Perm in Russia) | 25 | Lower Permian<br>Upper Permian | Early reptiles and mammals; earliest form of turtles |

## Mesozoic Era

This era began 195 million years ago and lasted for 135 million years. The name was compounded from Greek *mesos* (middle) and *zoön* (animal). Popular name: Age of Reptiles.

| Period | Duration[1] | Subperiods | Events |
|---|---|---|---|
| Triassic (from *trias* = triad) | 35 | Lower or Buntsandstein (from German *bunt* = colorful + *Sandstein* = sandstone)<br>Middle or Muschelkalk (from German *Muschel* = clam + *Kalk* = limestone)<br>Upper or Keuper (old miners' term) | Early saurians |
| Jurassic (from Jura Mountains) | 35 | Lower or Black Jurassic, or Lias (from French *liais* = hard stone)<br>Middle or Brown Jurassic, or Dogger (old provincial English for ironstone)<br>Upper or White Jurassic, or Malm (Middle English for sand) | Many sea-going reptiles; early large dinosaurs; somewhat later, flying reptiles (pterosaurs), earliest known birds |
| Cretaceous (from Latin *creta* = chalk) | 65 | Lower Cretaceous<br>Upper Cretaceous | Maximum development of dinosaurs; birds proliferating; oppossum-like mammals |

## Cenozoic Era

This era began 60 million years ago and includes the geological present. The name was compounded from Greek *kainos* (new) and *zoön* (animal). Popular name: Age of Mammals.

| Period | Duration[1] | Subperiods | Events |
|---|---|---|---|
| Tertiary (originally thought to be the third of only three periods) | c. 60 | Paleocene (from Greek *palaios* = old + *kainos* = new) | First mammals other than marsupials |
| | | Eocene (from Greek *eos* = dawn + *kainos* = new) | Formation of amber; rich insect fauna; early bats |
| | | Oligocene (from Greek *oligos* = few + *kainos* = new)<br>Miocene (from Greek *meios* = less + *kainos* = new) | Steady increase of large mammals |
| | | Pliocene (from Greek *pleios* = more + *kainos* = new) | Mammals closely resembling present types; protohumans |
| Pleistocene (from Greek *pleistos* = most + *kainos* = new) (popular name: Ice Age) | 1 | Four major glaciations, named Günz, Mindel, Riss, and Würm, originally the names of rivers. Last glaciation ended 10,000 to 15,000 years ago | Various forms of early man |
| Holocene (from Greek *holos* = entire + *kainos* = new) | | The present | The last 3,000 years are called "history" |

1. In millions of years.

## Highest Waterfalls of the World

| Waterfall | Location | River | Height feet | Height meters |
|---|---|---|---|---|
| Angel | Venezuela | Tributary of Caroní | 3,281 | 1,000 |
| Tugela | Natal, South Africa | Tugela | 3,000 | 914 |
| Cuquenán | Venezuela | Cuquenán | 2,000 | 610 |
| Sutnerland | South Island, N.Z. | Arthur | 1,904 | 580 |
| Takkakaw | British Columbia | Tributary of Yoho | 1,650 | 503 |

| Waterfall | Location | River | Height feet | Height meters |
|---|---|---|---|---|
| Ribbon (Yosemite) | California | Creek flowing into Yosemite | 1,612 | 491 |
| Upper Yosemite | California | Yosemite Creek, tributary of Merced | 1,430 | 436 |
| Gavarnie | Southwest France | Gave de Pau | 1,384 | 422 |
| Vettisfoss | Norway | Mörkedola | 1,200 | 366 |
| Widows' Tears (Yosemite) | California | Tributary of Merced | 1,170 | 357 |
| Staubbach | Switzerland | Staubbach (Lauterbrunnen Valley) | 984 | 300 |
| Middle Cascade (Yosemite) | California | Yosemite Creek, tributary of Merced | 909 | 277 |
| King Edward VIII | Guyana | Courantyne | 850 | 259 |
| Gersoppa | India | Sharavati | 829 | 253 |
| Kaieteur | Guyana | Potaro | 822 | 251 |
| Skykje | Norway | In Skykjedal (valley of Inner Hardinger Fjord) | 820 | 250 |
| Kalambo | Tanzania-Zambia | — | 720 | 219 |
| Fairy (Mount Rainier Park) | Washington | Stevens Creek | 700 | 213 |
| Trummelbach | Switzerland | Trummelbach (Lauterbrunnen Valley) | 700 | 213 |
| Aniene (Teverone) | Italy | Tiber | 680 | 207 |
| Cascata delle Marmore | Italy | Velino, tributary of Nera | 650 | 198 |
| Maradalsfos | Norway | Stream flowing into Ejkisdalsvand (lake) | 643 | 196 |
| Feather | California | Fall River | 640 | 195 |
| Maletsunyane | Lesotho | Maletsunyane | 630 | 192 |
| Bridalveil (Yosemite) | California | Yosemite Creek | 620 | 189 |
| Multnomah | Oregon | Multnomah Creek, tributary of Columbia | 620 | 189 |
| Vøringsfos | Norway | Bjoreia | 597 | 182 |
| Nevada (Yosemite) | California | Merced | 594 | 181 |
| Skjeggedal | Norway | Tysso | 525 | 160 |
| Marina | Guyana | Tributary of Kuribrong, tributary of Potaro | 500 | 152 |
| Tequendama | Colombia | Funza, tributary of Magdalena | 425 | 130 |
| King George's | Cape of Good Hope, South Africa | Orange | 400 | 122 |
| Illilouette (Yosemite) | California | Illilouette Creek, tributary of Merced | 370 | 113 |
| Victoria | Rhodesia-Zambia boundary | Zambezi | 355 | 108 |
| Handöl | Sweden | Handöl Creek | 345 | 105 |
| Lower Yosemite | California | Yosemite | 320 | 98 |
| Comet (Mount Rainier Park) | Washington | Van Trump Creek | 320 | 98 |
| Vernal (Yosemite) | California | Merced | 317 | 97 |
| Virginia | Northwest Territories, Canada | South Nahanni, tributary of Mackenzie | 315 | 96 |
| Lower Yellowstone | Wyoming | Yellowstone | 310 | 94 |

NOTE: Niagara Falls (New York-Ontario), though of great volume, has parallel drops of only 158 and 167 feet.

## Interesting Caves and Caverns of the World

**Aggtelek.** In village of same name, northern Hungary. Large stalactitic cavern about 5 miles long.

**Altamira Cave.** Near Santander, Spain. Contains animal paintings (Old Stone Age art) on roof and walls.

**Antiparos.** On island of same name in the Grecian Archipelago. Some stalactites are 20 ft long. Brilliant colors and fantastic shapes.

**Blue Grotto.** On island of Capri, Italy. Cavern hollowed out in limestone by constant wave action. Now half filled with water because of sinking coast. Name derived from unusual blue light permeating the cave. Source of light is a submerged opening, light passing through the water.

**Carlsbad Caverns.** Southeast New Mexico. Largest underground labyrinth yet discovered. Three levels: 754,900, and 1,320 ft below the surface.

**Fingal's Cave.** On island of Staffa off coast of western Scotland. Penetrates about 200 ft inland. Contains basaltic columns almost 40 ft high.

**Ice Cave.** Near Dobsina, Czechoslovakia. Noted for its beautiful crystal effects.

**Jenolan Caves.** In Blue Mountain plateau, New South Wales, Australia. Beautiful stalactitic formations.

**Kent's Cavern.** Near Torquay, England. Source of much information on Paleolithic man.

**Luray Cavern.** Near Luray, Va. Has large stalactitic and stalagmitic columns of many colors.

**Mammoth Cave.** Limestone cavern in central Kentucky. Cave area is about 10 miles in diameter but has at least 150 miles of irregular subterranean passageways at various levels. Temperature remains fairly constant at 54°F.

**Peak Cavern** or **Devil's Hole.** Derbyshire, England. About 2,250 ft into a mountain. Lowest part is about 600 ft below the surface.

**Postojna (Postumia) Grotto.** Near Postumia in Julian Alps, about 25 miles northeast of Trieste. Stalactitic cavern, largest in Europe. Piuca (Pivka) River flows through part of it. Caves have numerous beautiful stalactites.

**Singing Cave.** Iceland. A lava cave; name derived from echoes of people singing in it.

**Wind Cave.** In Black Hills of South Dakota. Limestone caverns with stalactites and stalagmites almost entirely missing. Variety of crystal formations called "boxwork."

**Wyandotte Cave.** In Crawford County, southern Indiana. A limestone cavern with five levels of passages; one of the largest in North America. "Monumental Mountain," approximately 135 ft high, is believed to be one of the world's largest underground "mountains."

## Large Islands of the World

| Island | Location and status | Area sq mi. | Area sq km |
|---|---|---|---|
| Greenland | North Atlantic (Danish) | 839,999 | 2,175,597 |
| New Guinea | Southwest Pacific (Irian Jaya, Indonesian, west part; Papua New Guinea, east part) | 316,615 | 820,033 |
| Borneo | West mid-Pacific (Indonesian, south part; British protectorate, and Malaysian, north part) | 286,914 | 743,107 |
| Madagascar | Indian Ocean (Malagasy Republic) | 226,657 | 587,042 |
| Baffin | North Atlantic (Canadian) | 183,810 | 476,068 |
| Sumatra | Northeast Indian Ocean (Indonesian) | 182,859 | 473,605 |
| Honshu | Sea of Japan-Pacific (Japanese) | 88,925 | 230,316 |
| Great Britain | Off coast of NW Europe (England, Scotland, and Wales) | 88,758 | 229,883 |
| Ellesmere | Arctic Ocean (Canadian) | 82,119 | 212,688 |
| Victoria | Arctic Ocean (Canadian) | 81,930 | 212,199 |
| Celebes | West mid-Pacific (Indonesian) | 72,986 | 189,034 |
| South Island | South Pacafic (New Zealand) | 58,093 | 150,461 |
| Java | Indian Ocean (Indonesian) | 48,990 | 126,884 |
| North Island | South Pacific (New Zealand) | 44,281 | 114,688 |
| Cuba | Caribbean Sea (republic) | 44,218 | 114,525 |
| Newfoundland | North Atlantic (Canadian) | 42,734 | 110,681 |
| Luzon | West mid-Pacific (Philippines) | 40,420 | 104,688 |
| Iceland | North Atlantic (republic) | 39,768 | 102,999 |
| Mindanao | West mid-Pacific (Philippines) | 36,537 | 94,631 |
| Ireland | West of Great Britain (republic, south part; United Kingdom, north part) | 32,597 | 84,426 |
| Hokkaido | Sea of Japan—Pacific (Japanese) | 30,372 | 78,663 |
| Hispaniola | Caribbean Sea (Dominican Republic, east part; Haiti, west part) | 29,355 | 76,029 |
| Tasmania | South of Australia (Australian) | 26,215 | 67,897 |
| Sri Lanka (Ceylon) | Indian Ocean (republic) | 25,332 | 65,610 |
| Sakhalin (Karafuto) | North of Japan (U.S.S.R.) | 24,560 | 63,610 |
| Banks | Arctic Ocean (Canadian) | 23,230 | 60,166 |
| Devon | Arctic Ocean (Canadian) | 20,861 | 54,030 |
| Tierra del Fuego | Southern tip of South America (Argentinian, east part; Chilean, west part) | 18,605 | 48,187 |
| Kyushu | Sea of Japan—Pacific (Japanese) | 16,223 | 42,018 |
| Melville | Arctic Ocean (Canadian) | 16,141 | 41,805 |
| Axel Heiberg | Arctic Ocean (Canadian) | 15,779 | 40,868 |
| Southampton | Hudson Bay (Canadian) | 15,700 | 40,663 |

## The Continental Divide

The Continental Divide is a ridge of high ground which runs irregularly north and south through the Rocky Mountains and separates eastward-flowing from westward-flowing streams. The waters which flow eastward empty into the Atlantic Ocean, chiefly by way of the Gulf of Mexico; those which flow westward empty into the Pacific.

## Principal Deserts of the World

| Desert | Location | Approximate size | Approx. elevation, ft |
|---|---|---|---|
| Atacama | North Chile | 400 mi. long | 7,000–13,500 |
| Black Rock | Northwest Nevada | About 1,000 sq mi. | 2,000–8,500 |
| Colorado | Southeast California from San Gorgonio Pass to Gulf of California | 200 mi. long and a maximum width of 50 mi. | Few feet above to 250 below sea level |
| Dasht-e-Kavír | Southeast of Caspian Sea, Iran | — | 2,000 |
| Dasht-e-Lūt | Northeast of Kerman, Iran | — | 1,000 |
| Gobi (Shamo) | Covers most of Mongolia | 500,000 sq mi. | 3,000–5,000 |
| Great Arabian | Most of Arabia | 1,500 mi. long | — |
| An Nafud (Red Desert) | South of Jauf | 400 mi. by avg of 140 mi. | 3,000 |
| Dahna | Northeast of Nejd | 400 mi. by 30 mi. | — |
| Rub' al-Khali | South portion of Nejd | Over 200,000 sq mi. | — |
| Syrian (Al-Hamad) | North of lat. 30°N | — | 1,850 |
| Great Australian | Western portion of Australia | About one half the continent | 600–1,000 |
| Great Salt Lake | West of Great Salt Lake to Nevada–Utah boundary | About 110 mi. by 50 mi. | 4,500 |
| Kalahari | South Africa—South-West Africa | About 120,000 sq mi. | Over 3,000 |
| Kara Kum (Desert of Kiva) | Southwest Turkmen, U.S.S.R. | 115,000 sq mi. | — |
| Kyzyl Kum | Uzbek and Kazakh, U.S.S.R. | Over 100,000 sq mi. | 160 near Lake Aral to 2,000 in southeast |
| Libyan | Libya, Egypt, Sudan | Over 500,000 sq mi. | — |
| Mojave | North of Colorado Desert and south of Death Valley, southeast California | 15,000 sq mi. | 2,000 |
| Nubian | From Red Sea to great west bend of the Nile, Sudan | — | 2,500 |
| Painted Desert | Northeast Arizona | Over 7,000 sq mi. | High plateau, 5,000 |
| Sahara | North Africa to about lat. 15°N and from Red Sea to Atlantic Ocean | 3,200 mi. greatest length along lat. 20°N; area over 3,500,000 sq mi. | 440 below sea level to 11,000 above; avg elevation, 1,400–1,600 |
| Takla Makan | South central Sinkiang, China | Over 100,000 sq mi. | — |
| Thar (Indian) | Pakistan-India | Nearly 100,000 sq mi. | Over 1,000 |

# U.S. Geography

## Miscellaneous Data for the United States

*Source:* Department of the Interior, U.S. Geological Survey.

| | |
|---|---|
| Highest point: Mount McKinley, Alaska | 20,320 ft (6,193 m) |
| Lowest point: Death Valley, Calif. | 282 ft (86 m) below sea level |
| Approximate mean altitude | 2,500 ft (762 m) |
| Points farthest apart (50 states): | |
| Log Point, Elliot Key, Fla., and Kure Island, Hawaii | 5,852 mi. (9,418 km) |
| Geographic center (50 states): | |
| In Butte County, S.D. (west of Castle Rock) | 44° 58′ N. lat. 103° 46′ W. long. |
| Geographic center (48 conterminous states): | |
| In Smith County, Kan. (near Lebanon) | 39° 50′ N. lat. 98° 35′ W. long. |
| Boundaries: | |
| Between Alaska and Canada | 1,538 mi. (2,475 km) |
| Between the 48 conterminous states and Canada (incl. Great Lakes) | 3,987 mi. (6,416 km) |
| Between the United States and Mexico | 1,933 mi. (3,111 km) |

## Highest, Lowest, and Mean Altitudes in the United States

| State | Altitude, ft[1] | Highest point | Altitude, ft | Lowest point | Altitude, ft |
|---|---|---|---|---|---|
| Alabama | 500 | Cheaha Mountain | 2,407 | Gulf of Mexico | Sea level |
| Alaska | 1,900 | Mount McKinley | 20,320 | Pacific Ocean | Sea level |
| Arizona | 4,100 | Humphreys Peak | 12,633 | Colorado River | 70 |
| Arkansas | 650 | Magazine Mountain | 2,753 | Ouachita River | 55 |
| California | 2,900 | Mount Whitney | 14,494 | Death Valley | 282[2] |
| Colorado | 6,800 | Mount Elbert | 14,433 | Arkansas River | 3,350 |
| Connecticut | 500 | Mount Frissell, on south slope | 2,380 | Long Island Sound | Sea level |
| Delaware | 60 | On Ebright Road | 442 | Atlantic Ocean | Sea level |
| D. C. | 150 | Tenleytown, northwest part | 410 | Potomac River | 1 |
| Florida | 100 | Sec. 30, T6N, R20W[3] | 345 | Atlantic Ocean | Sea level |
| Georgia | 600 | Brasstown Bald | 4,784 | Atlantic Ocean | Sea level |
| Hawaii | 3,030 | Mauna Kea | 13,796 | Pacific Ocean | Sea level |
| Idaho | 5,000 | Borah Peak | 12,662 | Snake River | 710 |
| Illinois | 600 | Charles Mound | 1,235 | Mississippi River | 279 |
| Indiana | 700 | Franklin Township, Wayne County | 1,257 | Ohio River | 320 |
| Iowa | 1,100 | Sec. 29, T100N, R41W[4] | 1,670 | Mississippi River | 480 |
| Kansas | 2,000 | Mount Sunflower | 4,039 | Verdigris River | 680 |
| Kentucky | 750 | Black Mountain | 4,145 | Mississippi River | 257 |
| Louisiana | 100 | Driskill Mountain | 535 | New Orleans | 5[2] |
| Maine | 600 | Mount Katahdin | 5,268 | Atlantic Ocean | Sea level |
| Maryland | 350 | Backbone Mountain | 3,360 | Atlantic Ocean | Sea level |
| Massachusetts | 500 | Mount Greylock | 3,491 | Atlantic Ocean | Sea level |
| Michigan | 900 | Mount Curwood | 1,980 | Lake Erie | 572 |
| Minnesota | 1,200 | Eagle Mountain | 2,301 | Lake Superior | 602 |
| Mississippi | 300 | Woodall Mountain | 806 | Gulf of Mexico | Sea level |
| Missouri | 800 | Taum Sauk Mountain | 1,772 | St. Francis River | 230 |
| Montana | 3,400 | Granite Peak | 12,799 | Kootenai River | 1,800 |
| Nebraska | 2,600 | Johnson Township, Kimball County | 5,426 | Southeast corner of state | 840 |
| Nevada | 5,500 | Boundary Peak | 13,143 | Colorado River | 470 |
| New Hampshire | 1,000 | Mount Washington | 6,288 | Atlantic Ocean | Sea level |
| New Jersey | 250 | High Point | 1,803 | Atlantic Ocean | Sea level |
| New Mexico | 5,700 | Wheeler Peak | 13,161 | Red Bluff Reservoir | 2,817 |
| New York | 1,000 | Mount Marcy | 5,344 | Atlantic Ocean | Sea level |
| North Carolina | 700 | Mount Mitchell | 6,684 | Atlantic Ocean | Sea level |
| North Dakota | 1,900 | White Butte | 3,506 | Red River | 750 |
| Ohio | 850 | Campbell Hill | 1,550 | Ohio River | 433 |
| Oklahoma | 1,300 | Black Mesa | 4,973 | Little River | 287 |
| Oregon | 3,300 | Mount Hood | 11,235 | Pacific Ocean | Sea level |
| Pennsylvania | 1,100 | Mount Davis | 3,213 | Delaware River | Sea level |
| Rhode Island | 200 | Jerimoth Hill | 812 | Atlantic Ocean | Sea level |
| South Carolina | 350 | Sassafras Mountain | 3,560 | Atlantic Ocean | Sea level |
| South Dakota | 2,200 | Harney Peak | 7,242 | Big Stone Lake | 962 |
| Tennessee | 900 | Clingmans Dome | 6,643 | Mississippi River | 182 |
| Texas | 1,700 | Guadalupe Peak | 8,751 | Gulf of Mexico | Sea level |
| Utah | 6,100 | Kings Peak | 13,528 | Beaverdam Creek | 2,000 |
| Vermont | 1,000 | Mount Mansfield | 4,393 | Lake Champlain | 95 |
| Virginia | 950 | Mount Rogers | 5,729 | Atlantic Ocean | Sea level |
| Washington | 1,700 | Mount Rainier | 14,410 | Pacific Ocean | Sea level |
| West Virginia | 1,500 | Spruce Knob | 4,863 | Potomac River | 240 |
| Wisconsin | 1,050 | Timms Hill | 1,952 | Lake Michigan | 581 |
| Wyoming | 6,700 | Gannett Peak | 13,804 | Belle Fourche River | 3,100 |
| United States | 2,500 | Mount McKinley (Alaska) | 20,320 | Death Valley (California) | 282[2] |

1. Approximate mean altitude. 2. Below sea level. 3. Walton County. 4. Osceola County. *Source:* Department of the Interior, U.S. Geological Survey.

## Mason and Dixon's Line

Mason and Dixon's Line (often called the Mason-Dixon Line) is the boundary between Pennsylvania and Maryland, running at a north latitude of 39°43′19.11″. The greater part of it was surveyed from 1763–67 by Charles Mason and Jeremiah Dixon, English astronomers who had been appointed to settle a dispute between the colonies. As the line was partly the boundary between the free and the slave states it has come to signify the division between the North and the South.

## Extreme Points of the United States (50 States)

| Extreme point | Latitude | Longitude | Distance[1] mi. | Distance[1] km |
|---|---|---|---|---|
| Northernmost point: Point Barrow, Alaska | 71°23′ N | 156°29′ W | 2,502 | 4,027 |
| Easternmost point: West Quoddy Head, Me. | 44°49′ N | 66°57′ W | 1,785 | 2,873 |
| Southernmost point: Ka Lae (South Cape), Hawaii | 18°56′ N | 155°41′ W | 3,456 | 5,562 |
| Westernmost point: Cape Wrangell, Alaska (Attu Island) | 52°55′ N | 172°27′ E | 3,620 | 5,826 |

1. From geographic center of United States (incl. Alaska and Hawaii), west of Castle Rock, S.D., 44°58′ N. lat., 103°46′ W long.

## Coastline of the United States
### Fourth (April 1, 1961) Edition

| State | Lengths, statute miles: General coastline[1] | Lengths, statute miles: Tidal shoreline[2] |
|---|---|---|
| Atlantic Coast: | | |
| Maine | 228 | 3,478 |
| New Hampshire | 13 | 131 |
| Massachusetts | 192 | 1,519 |
| Rhode Island | 40 | 384 |
| Connecticut | — | 618 |
| New York | 127 | 1,850 |
| New Jersey | 130 | 1,792 |
| Pennsylvania | — | 89 |
| Delaware | 28 | 381 |
| Maryland | 31 | 3,190 |
| Virginia | 112 | 3,315 |
| North Carolina | 301 | 3,375 |
| South Carolina | 187 | 2,876 |
| Georgia | 100 | 2,344 |
| Florida (Atlantic) | 580 | 3,331 |
| Total Atlantic coast | 2,069 | 28,673 |
| Gulf Coast: | | |
| Florida (Gulf) | 770 | 5,095 |
| Alabama | 53 | 607 |
| Mississippi | 44 | 359 |
| Louisiana | 397 | 7,721 |
| Texas | 367 | 3,359 |
| Total Gulf coast | 1,631 | 17,141 |
| Pacific Coast: | | |
| California | 840 | 3,427 |
| Oregon | 296 | 1,410 |
| Washington | 157 | 3,026 |
| Hawaii | 750 | 1,052 |
| Alaska (Pacific) | 5,580 | 31,383 |
| Total Pacific coast | 7,623 | 40,298 |
| Arctic Coast: | | |
| Alaska (Arctic) | 1,060 | 2,521 |
| Total Arctic coast | 1,060 | 2,521 |
| **States Total** | **12,383** | **88,633** |

1. Figures are lengths of general outline of seacoast. Measurements made with unit measure of 30 minutes of latitude on charts as near scale of 1:1,200,000 as possible. Coastline of bays and sounds is included to point where they narrow to width of unit measure, and distance across at such point is included. 2. Figures obtained in 1939–40 with recording instrument on largest-scale maps and charts then available. Shoreline of outer coast, offshore islands, sounds, bays, rivers, and creeks is included to head of tidewater, or to point where tidal waters narrow to width of 100 feet. *Source:* Department of Commerce, National Oceanic and Atmospheric Administration, National Ocean Survey.

## Rivers of the United States
### (350 or more miles long)

**Alabama** (735 mi.; 1,183 km): From junction of Tallapoosa R. and Coosa R. in Alabama to Mobile R.
**Altamaha-Ocmulgee** (392 mi.; 631 km): From junction of Yellow R. and South R., Newton Co. in Georgia to Atlantic Ocean.
**Apalachicola-Chattahoochee** (524 mi.; 843 km): From Towns Co. in Georgia to Gulf of Mexico in Florida.
**Arkansas** (1,459 mi.; 2,348 km): From Lake Co. in Colorado to Mississippi R. in Arkansas.
**Brazos** (870 mi.; 1,400 km): From junction of Salt Fork and Double Mountain Fork in Texas to Gulf of Mexico.
**Canadian** (906 mi.; 1,458 km): From Las Animas Co. in Colorado to Arkansas R. in Oklahoma.
**Cimarron** (600 mi.; 966 km): From Colfax Co. in New Mexico to Arkansas R. in Oklahoma.
**Clark Fork-Pend Oreille** (505 mi.; 813 km): From Silver Bow Co. in Montana to Columbia R. in British Columbia.
**Colorado** (1,450 mi.; 2,333 km): From Rocky Mountain National Park in Colorado to Gulf of California in Mexico.
**Colorado** (840 mi.; 1,352 km): From Borden Co. in Texas to Matagorda Bay.
**Columbia** (1,243 mi.; 2,000 km): From Columbia Lake in British Columbia to Pacific Ocean (entering between Oregon and Washington).
**Colville** (350 mi.; 563 km): From Brooks Range in Alaska to Beaufort Sea.
**Connecticut** (407 mi.; 655 km): From Third Connecticut Lake in New Hampshire to Long Island Sound in Connecticut.
**Cumberland** (720 mi.; 1,159 km): From junction of Poor and Clover Forks in Harlan Co. in Kentucky to Ohio R.

**Delaware** (390 mi.; 628 km): From Schoharie County in New York to Liston Point, Delaware Bay.
**Gila** (630 mi.; 1,014 km): From Catron Co. in New Mexico to Colorado R. in Arizona.
**Green** (360 mi.; 579 km): From Lincoln Co. in Kentucky to Ohio R. in Kentucky.
**Green** (730 mi.; 1,175 km): From Sublette Co. in Wyoming to Colorado R. in Utah.
**Humboldt** (390 mi.; 628 km): From Wells, Nevada, to Humboldt Lake in Nevada.
**Illinois** (420 mi.; 676 km): From St. Joseph Co. in Indiana to Mississippi R. at Grafton in Illinois.
**James** (sometimes called *Dakota*) (710 mi.; 1,143 km): From Wells Co. in North Dakota to Missouri R. in South Dakota.
**Kanawha-New** (352 mi.; 566 km): From junction of North and South Forks of New R. in North Carolina to Ohio R.
**Koyukuk** (470 mi.; 756 km): From Brooks Range in Alaska to Yukon R.
**Kuskokwim** (680 mi.; 1,094 km): From Alaska Range in Alaska to Kuskokwim Bay.
**Licking** (350 mi.; 563 km): From Magoffin Co. in Kentucky to Ohio R. at Cincinnati in Ohio.
**Little Missouri** (560 mi.; 901 km): From Crook Co. in Wyoming to Missouri R. in North Dakota.
**Milk** (625 mi.; 1,006 km): From junction of forks in Alberta Province to Missouri R.
**Mississippi** (2,348 mi.; 3,779 km): From Lake Itasca in Minnesota to mouth of Southwest Pass.
**Mississippi-Missouri-Red Rock** (3,710 mi.; 5,971 km): From source of Red Rock R. in Montana to mouth of Southwest Pass in Louisiana.
**Missouri** (2,315 mi.; 3,726 km): From junction of Jefferson R., Gallatin R., and Madison R. in Montana to Mississippi R. near St. Louis.
**Missouri-Red Rock** (2,533 mi.; 4,076 km): From source of Red Rock R. in Montana to Mississippi R. near St. Louis.
**Mobile-Alabama-Coosa** (780 mi.; 1,255 km): From junction of Etowah R. and Oostanaula R. in Georgia to Mobile Bay.
**Neosho** (460 mi.; 740 km): From Morris Co. in Kansas to Arkansas R. in Oklahoma.
**Niobrara** (431 mi.; 694 km): From Niobrara Co. in Wyoming to Missouri R. in Nebraska.
**Noatak** (350 mi.; 563 km): From Brooks Range in Alaska to Kotzebue Sound.
**North Canadian** (760 mi.; 1,223 km): From Union Co. in New Mexico to Canadian R. in Oklahoma.
**North Platte** (618 mi.; 995 km): From Jackson Co. in Colorado to junction with So. Platte R. in Nebraska to form Platte R.
**Ohio** (981 mi.; 1,579 km): From junction of Allegheny R. and Monongahela R. at Pittsburgh to Mississippi R. between Illinois and Kentucky.
**Ohio-Allegheny** (1,306 mi.; 2,102 km): From Potter Co. in Pennsylvania to Mississippi R. at Cairo in Illinois.
**Osage** (500 mi.; 805 km): From east-central Kansas to Missouri R. near Jefferson City in Missouri.
**Ouachita** (605 mi.; 974 km): From Polk Co. in Arkansas to Red R. in Louisiana.
**Pearl** (411 mi.; 661 km): From Neshoba County in Mississippi to Gulf of Mexico (Mississippi-Louisiana).
**Pecos** (735 mi.; 1,183 km): From Mora Co. in New Mexico to Rio Grande in Texas.
**Pee Dee-Yadkin** (435 mi.; 700 km): From Watauga Co. in North Carolina to Winyah Bay in South Carolina.
**Pend Oreille** (490 mi.; 789 km): Near Butte in Montana to Columbia R. on Washington-Canada border.
**Porcupine** (460 mi.; 740 km): From Yukon Territory, Canada, to Yukon R. in Alaska.
**Potomac** (383 mi.; 616 km): From Garrett Co. in Maryland to Chesapeake Bay at Point Lookout in Maryland.
**Powder** (375 mi.; 603 km): From junction of forks in Johnson Co. in Wyoming to Yellowstone R. in Montana.
**Red** (1,270 mi.; 2,044 km): From junction of forks in Harmon Co. in Oklahoma to Mississippi R. in Louisiana.
**Red** (officially called *Red River of the North*) (545 mi.; 877 km): From junction of Otter Tail R. and Bois de Sioux R. in Minnesota to Lake Winnipeg in Manitoba.
**Republican** (445 mi.; 716 km): From junction of North Fork and Arikaree R. in Nebraska to junction with Smoky Hill R. in Kansas to form Kansas R.
**Rio Grande** (1,885 mi.; 3,034 km): From San Juan Co. in Colorado to Gulf of Mexico.
**Roanoke** (380 mi.; 612 km): From junction of forks in Montgomery Co. in Virginia to Albemarle Sound in North Carolina.
**Sabine** (380 mi.; 612 km): From junction of forks in Hunt Co. in Texas to Sabine Lake between Texas and Louisiana.
**Sacramento** (377 mi.; 607 km): From Siskiyou Co. in California to Suisun Bay.
**Saint Francis** (425 mi.; 684 km): From Iron Co. in Missouri to Mississippi R. in Arkansas.
**Salmon** (420 mi.; 676 km): From Custer Co. in Idaho to Snake R.
**San Joaquin** (350 mi.; 563 km): From junction of forks in Madera Co. in California to Suisun Bay.
**San Juan** (360 mi.; 579 km): From Archuleta Co. in Colorado to Colorado R. in Utah.
**Santee-Wateree-Catawba** (538 mi.; 866 km): From McDowell Co. in North Carolina to Atlantic Ocean in South Carolina.
**Smoky Hill** (540 mi.; 869 km): From Cheyenne Co in Colorado to junction with Republican R. in Kansas to form Kansas R.
**Snake** (1,038 mi.; 1,670 km): From Ocean Plateau in Wyoming to Columbia R. in Washington.
**South Platte** (424 mi.; 682 km): From Park Co. in Colorado to junction with North Platte R. in Nebraska to form Platte R.
**Susquehanna** (444 mi.; 715 km): From Otsego Lake in New York to Chesapeake Bay in Maryland.
**Tanana** (620 mi.; 998 km): From Wrangell Mts. in Yukon Territory, Canada, to Yukon R. in Alaska.
**Tennessee** (652 mi.; 1,049 km): From junction of Holston R. and French Broad R. in Tennessee to Ohio R. in Kentucky.
**Tennessee-French Broad** (900 mi.; 1,448 km): From Bland Co. in Virginia to Ohio R. at Paducah in Kentucky.
**Tombigbee** (525 mi.; 845 km): From junction of forks in Itawamba Co. in Mississippi to Mobile R. in Alabama.
**Trinity** (360 mi.; 579 km): From junction of forks in Dallas Co. in Texas to Galveston Bay.
**Wabash** (529 mi.; 851 km): From Darke Co. in Ohio to Ohio R. between Illinois and Indiana.
**Washita** (500 mi.; 805 km): From Hemphill Co. in Texas to Red R. in Oklahoma.
**White** (720 mi.; 1,159 km): From Madison Co. in Arkansas to Mississippi R.
**Wisconsin** (430 mi.; 692 km): From Vilas Co. in Wisconsin to Mississippi R.
**Yellowstone** (671 mi.; 1,080 km): From Park Co. in Wyoming to Missouri R. in North Dakota.
**Yukon** (1,770 mi.; 2,848 km): From junction of Lewes R. and Pelly R. in Yukon Territory, Canada, to Bering Sea in Alaska.

## Named Summits in the U. S. Over 14,000 Feet Above Sea Level

| Name | State | Height | Name | State | Height | Name | State | Height |
|---|---|---|---|---|---|---|---|---|
| Mt. McKinley | Alaska | 20,320 | Mt. Antero | Colo. | 14,269 | Windom Peak | Colo. | 14,087 |
| Mt. St. Elias | Alaska | 18,008 | Torreys Peak | Colo. | 14,267 | Mt. Russell | Calif. | 14,086 |
| Mt. Foraker | Alaska | 17,400 | Castle Peak | Colo. | 14,265 | Mt. Eolus | Colo. | 14,084 |
| Mt. Bona | Alaska | 16,421 | Quandary Peak | Colo. | 14,265 | Mt. Columbia | Colo. | 14,073 |
| Mt. Blackburn | Alaska | 16,390 | Mt. Evans | Colo. | 14,264 | Mt. Augusta | Alaska | 14,070 |
| Mt. Sanford | Alaska | 16,237 | Longs Peak | Colo. | 14,255 | Missouri Mtn. | Colo. | 14,067 |
| South Buttress | Alaska | 15,885 | Mt. Wilson | Colo. | 14,246 | Humboldt Peak | Colo. | 14,064 |
| Mt. Vancouver | Alaska | 15,700 | White Mtn. | Calif. | 14,246 | Mt. Bierstadt | Colo. | 14,060 |
| Mt. Churchill | Alaska | 15,638 | North Palisade | Calif. | 14,242 | Sunlight Peak | Colo. | 14,059 |
| Mt. Fairweather | Alaska | 15,300 | Shavano Peak | Colo. | 14,229 | Split Mtn. | Calif. | 14,058 |
| Mt. Hubbard | Alaska | 15,015 | Crestone Needle | Colo. | 14,197 | Handies Peak | Colo. | 14,048 |
| Mt. Bear | Alaska | 14,831 | Mt. Belford | Colo. | 14,197 | Culebra Peak | Colo. | 14,047 |
| East Buttress | Alaska | 14,730 | Mt. Princeton | Colo. | 14,197 | Mt. Lindsey | Colo. | 14,042 |
| Mt. Hunter | Alaska | 14,573 | Mt. Yale | Colo. | 14,196 | Middle Palisade | Calif. | 14,040 |
| Mt. Alverstone | Alaska | 14,565 | Mt. Bross | Colo. | 14,172 | Little Bear Peak | Colo. | 14,037 |
| Browne Tower | Alaska | 14,530 | Kit Carson Mtn. | Colo. | 14,165 | Mt. Sherman | Colo. | 14,036 |
| Mt. Whitney | Calif. | 14,494 | Mt. Wrangell | Alaska | 14,163 | Redcloud Peak | Colo. | 14,034 |
| Mt. Elbert | Colo. | 14,433 | Mt. Shasta | Calif. | 14,162 | Mt. Langley | Calif. | 14,028 |
| Mt. Massive | Colo. | 14,421 | Mt. Sill | Calif. | 14,162 | Mt. Tyndall | Calif. | 14,018 |
| Mt. Harvard | Colo. | 14,420 | El Diente Peak | Colo. | 14,159 | Pyramid Peak | Colo. | 14,018 |
| Mt. Rainier | Wash. | 14,410 | Maroon Peak | Colo. | 14,156 | Wilson Peak | Colo. | 14,017 |
| Mt. Williamson | Calif. | 14,375 | Tabeguache Mtn. | Colo. | 14,155 | Mt. Muir | Calif. | 14,015 |
| Blanca Peak | Colo. | 14,345 | Mt. Oxford | Colo. | 14,153 | Wetterhorn Peak | Colo. | 14,015 |
| La Plata Peak | Colo. | 14,336 | Mt. Sneffels | Colo. | 14,150 | No. Maroon Pk. | Colo. | 14,014 |
| Uncompahgre Pk. | Colo. | 14,309 | Mt. Democrat | Colo. | 14,148 | San Luis Peak | Colo. | 14,014 |
| Crestone Peak | Colo. | 14,294 | Capitol Peak | Colo. | 14,130 | Huron Peak | Colo. | 14,005 |
| Mt. Lincoln | Colo. | 14,286 | Pikes Peak | Colo. | 14,110 | Mt. of Holy Cross | Colo. | 14,005 |
| Grays Peak | Colo. | 14,270 | Snowmass Mtn. | Colo. | 14,092 | Sunshine Peak | Colo. | 14,001 |

*Source:* Department of the Interior, U.S. Geological Survey.

# MAPS

*Prepared by Vaughn Gray and Dyno Lowenstein*

*"Quick Maps" by Dyno Lowenstein*

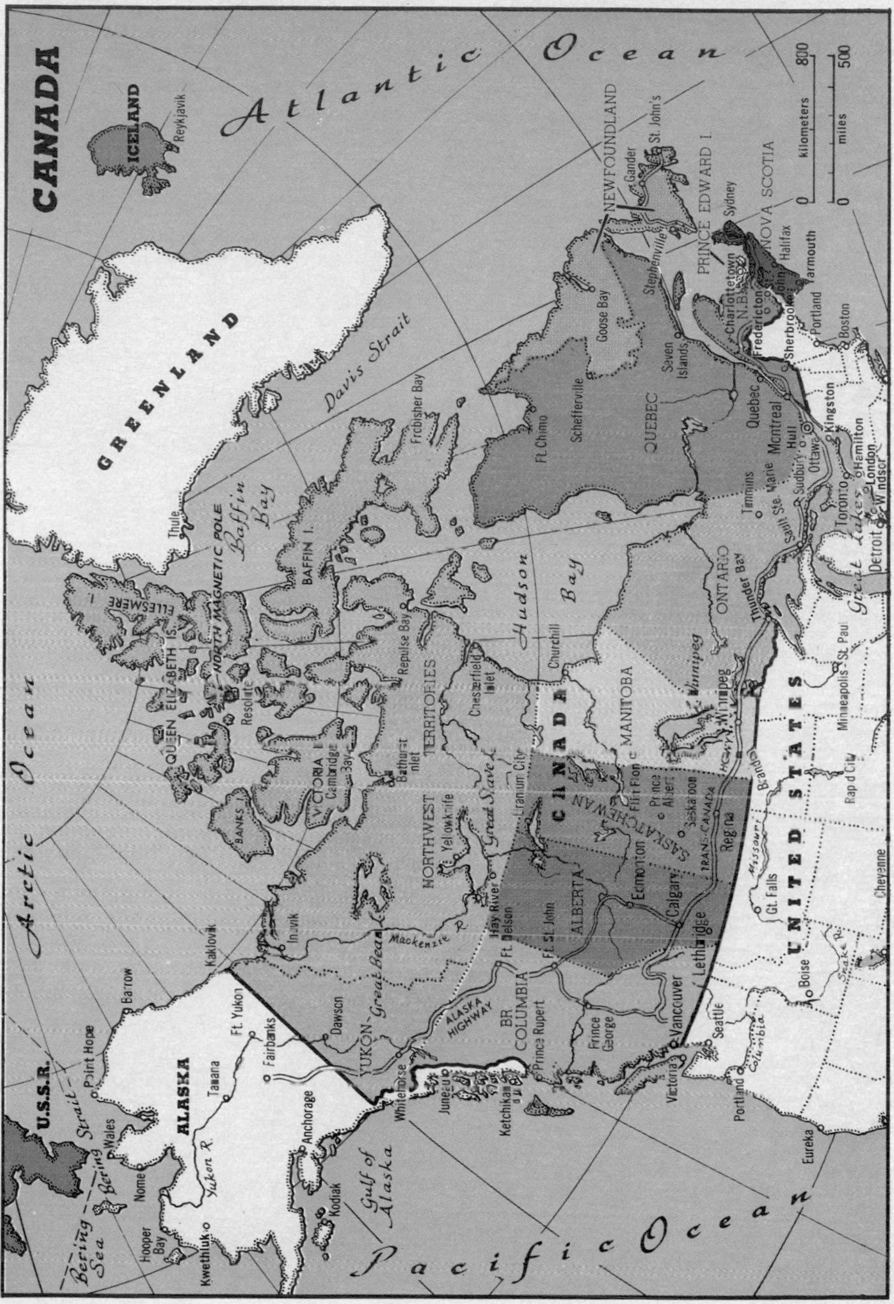
CANADA
ICELAND
Reykjavik
Atlantic Ocean
Arctic Ocean
Pacific Ocean
GREENLAND
Davis Strait
Baffin Bay
Hudson Bay
Thule
NORTH MAGNETIC POLE
ELLESMERE I.
QUEEN ELIZABETH IS.
BAFFIN I.
Frobisher Bay
Resolute
BANKS I.
VICTORIA I.
Cambridge Bay
Bathurst Inlet
Repulse Bay
Chesterfield Inlet
NORTHWEST TERRITORIES
Yellowknife
Great Slave L.
Great Bear L.
Mackenzie R.
Inuvik
Kaklovik
Hay River
Ft. Nelson
Ft. St. John
Uranium City
YUKON
Dawson
Whitehorse
ALASKA HIGHWAY
BR. COLUMBIA
Prince Rupert
Prince George
Vancouver
Victoria
ALBERTA
Edmonton
Calgary
Lethbridge
SASKATCHEWAN
Saskatoon
Prince Albert
Regina
Flin Flon
TRANS-CANADA HGWY.
MANITOBA
Churchill
L. Winnipeg
Winnipeg
Brandon
ONTARIO
Thunder Bay
Sault Ste. Marie
Timmins
Sudbury
Ottawa
Toronto
Hamilton
London
Windsor
Kingston
Great Lakes
Detroit
QUEBEC
Ft. Chimo
Schefferville
Seven Islands
Quebec
Montreal
Hull
Sherbrooke
Goose Bay
NEWFOUNDLAND
Gander
St. John's
Stephenville
PRINCE EDWARD I.
Charlottetown
N.B.
Fredericton
St. John
NOVA SCOTIA
Sydney
Halifax
Yarmouth
Portland
Boston
kilometers
miles
0
800
500
U.S.S.R.
ALASKA
Bering Strait
Bering Sea
Point Hope
Barrow
Wales
Nome
Hooper Bay
Kwethluk
Tanana
Fairbanks
Ft. Yukon
Anchorage
Yukon R.
Kodiak
Gulf of Alaska
Juneau
Ketchikan
UNITED STATES
Seattle
Portland
Columbia
Eureka
Boise
Snake R.
Gt. Falls
Missouri
Cheyenne
Rapid City
Minneapolis-St. Paul

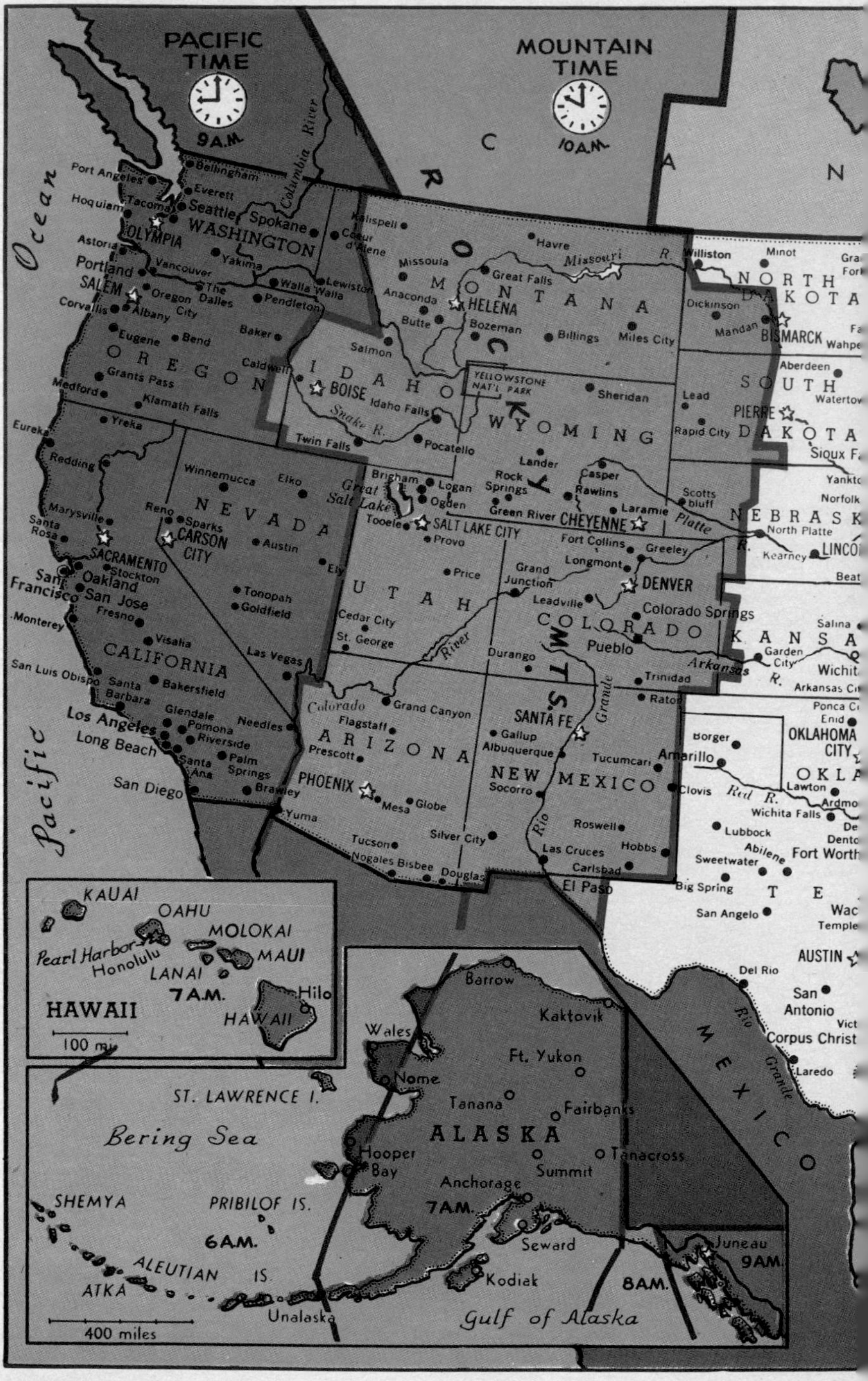
PACIFIC TIME
9A.M.
MOUNTAIN TIME
10A.M.
Pacific Ocean
Columbia River
Port Angeles
Bellingham
Everett
Hoquiam
Tacoma
Seattle
Spokane
OLYMPIA
WASHINGTON
Yakima
Astoria
Portland
Vancouver
SALEM
The Dalles
Walla Walla
Lewiston
Oregon City
Pendleton
Corvallis
Albany
Eugene
Bend
Baker
OREGON
Caldwell
Grants Pass
Medford
Klamath Falls
Kalispell
Coeur d'Alene
Missoula
Anaconda
Butte
HELENA
Bozeman
Great Falls
Havre
Missouri R.
MONTANA
Billings
Miles City
Salmon
IDAHO
BOISE
Idaho Falls
Snake R.
Twin Falls
Pocatello
YELLOWSTONE NAT'L PARK
WYOMING
Sheridan
Lander
Casper
Rock Springs
Rawlins
Green River
CHEYENNE
Laramie
Platte
ROCKY MTS.
Williston
Minot
NORTH DAKOTA
Dickinson
Mandan
BISMARCK
Aberdeen
SOUTH DAKOTA
Lead
PIERRE
Rapid City
Scotts bluff
NEBRASKA
North Platte
Kearney
Yreka
Eureka
Redding
Winnemucca
Elko
NEVADA
Reno
Sparks
CARSON CITY
Austin
Ely
Tonopah
Goldfield
Las Vegas
Marysville
Santa Rosa
SACRAMENTO
Stockton
San Francisco
Oakland
San Jose
Fresno
Monterey
Visalia
CALIFORNIA
San Luis Obispo
Santa Barbara
Bakersfield
Los Angeles
Glendale
Pomona
Riverside
Long Beach
Santa Ana
Palm Springs
San Diego
Needles
Brawley
Yuma
Brigham
Logan
Ogden
Great Salt Lake
Tooele
SALT LAKE CITY
Provo
Price
UTAH
Cedar City
St. George
Colorado River
Grand Canyon
Flagstaff
ARIZONA
Prescott
PHOENIX
Mesa
Globe
Tucson
Nogales
Bisbee
Douglas
Silver City
Fort Collins
Greeley
Longmont
Grand Junction
DENVER
Leadville
COLORADO
Colorado Springs
Pueblo
Durango
Trinidad
Raton
Arkansas R.
Garden City
KANSAS
SANTA FE
Gallup
Albuquerque
NEW MEXICO
Socorro
Tucumcari
Rio Grande
Roswell
Las Cruces
Hobbs
Carlsbad
El Paso
Clovis
Borger
Amarillo
OKLAHOMA CITY
Red R.
Lawton
Wichita Falls
Lubbock
Abilene
Sweetwater
Fort Worth
Big Spring
San Angelo
AUSTIN
Del Rio
San Antonio
Corpus Christi
Laredo
MEXICO
KAUAI
OAHU
MOLOKAI
Pearl Harbor
Honolulu
MAUI
LANAI
7A.M.
Hilo
HAWAII
HAWAII
100 mi.
Barrow
Kaktovik
Wales
Ft. Yukon
Nome
ST. LAWRENCE I.
Tanana
Fairbanks
Bering Sea
ALASKA
Hooper Bay
Summit
Tanacross
Anchorage
7A.M.
SHEMYA
PRIBILOF IS.
6A.M.
Seward
Juneau
9A.M.
ALEUTIAN IS.
ATKA
Kodiak
8A.M.
Unalaska
Gulf of Alaska
400 miles

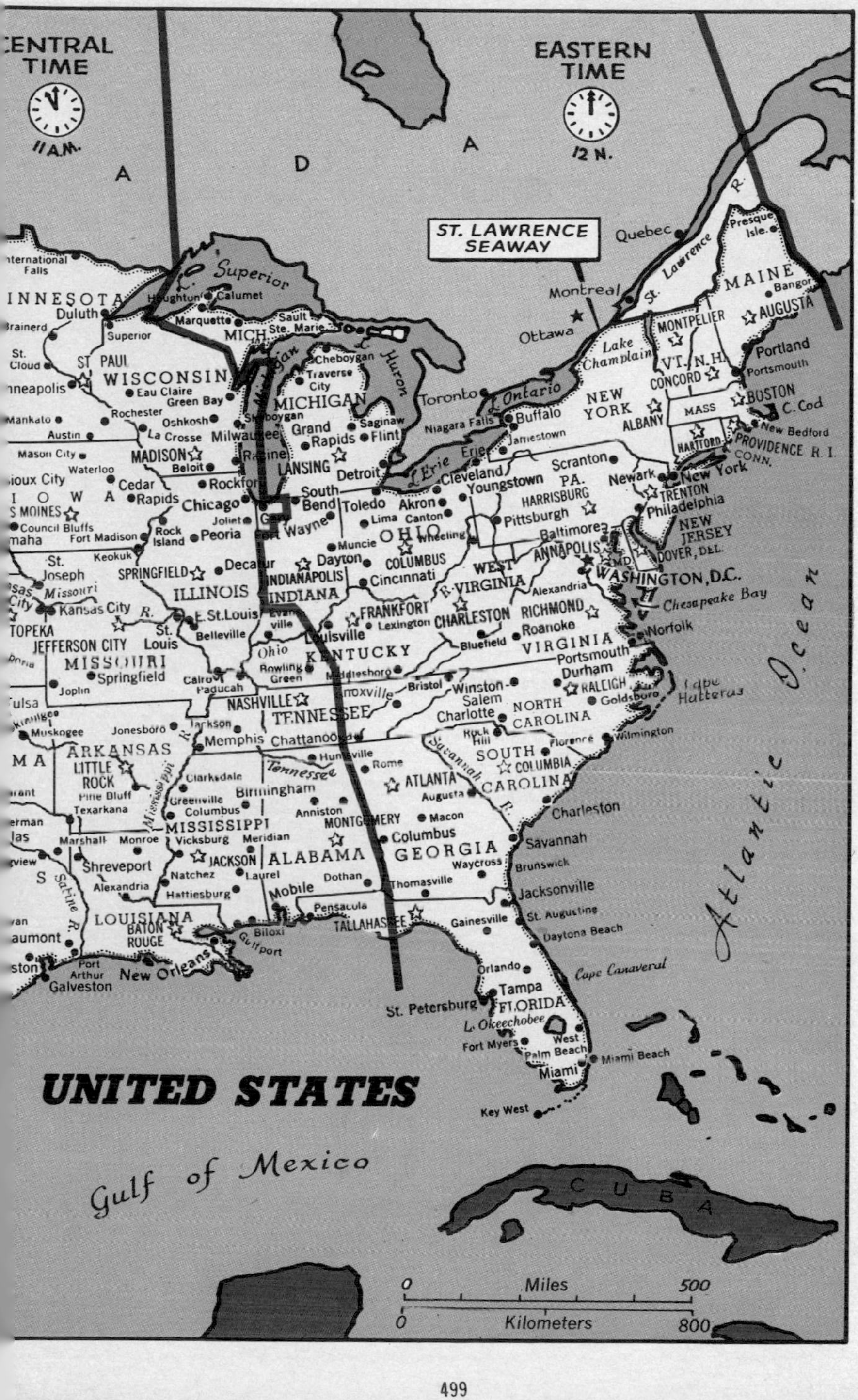
CENTRAL TIME
11 A.M.
EASTERN TIME
12 N.
C A N A D A
ST. LAWRENCE SEAWAY
Quebec
Montreal
Ottawa
St. Lawrence R.
Presque Isle
MAINE
Bangor
AUGUSTA
Portland
Portsmouth
MONTPELIER
VT.
N.H.
CONCORD
BOSTON
MASS
C. Cod
New Bedford
HARTFORD
PROVIDENCE R. I.
CONN.
Lake Champlain
NEW YORK
ALBANY
Toronto
L. Ontario
Buffalo
Niagara Falls
Jamestown
L. Erie
Erie
Scranton
PA.
HARRISBURG
Newark
New York
TRENTON
Philadelphia
NEW JERSEY
Baltimore
ANNAPOLIS
MD.
DOVER, DEL.
WASHINGTON, D.C.
Chesapeake Bay
Norfolk
Alexandria
RICHMOND
VIRGINIA
Roanoke
WEST VIRGINIA
CHARLESTON
Bluefield
Portsmouth
Durham
RALEIGH
Goldsboro
Cape Hatteras
Winston-Salem
NORTH CAROLINA
Charlotte
Wilmington
Rock Hill
Florence
SOUTH CAROLINA
COLUMBIA
Charleston
Savannah R.
Augusta
ATLANTA
Rome
GEORGIA
Macon
Columbus
Savannah
Brunswick
Waycross
Thomasville
Jacksonville
St. Augustine
Daytona Beach
Gainesville
Cape Canaveral
Orlando
Tampa
St. Petersburg
FLORIDA
L. Okeechobee
Fort Myers
West Palm Beach
Miami Beach
Miami
Key West
Atlantic Ocean
Superior
L. Superior
Houghton
Calumet
Marquette
Sault Ste. Marie
MICH.
L. Michigan
L. Huron
Cheboygan
Traverse City
MICHIGAN
Saginaw
Flint
Grand Rapids
LANSING
Detroit
Sheboygan
Milwaukee
Racine
Cleveland
Youngstown
Pittsburgh
Toledo
Akron
Canton
Lima
South Bend
Gary
Fort Wayne
OHIO
Wheeling
Muncie
Dayton
COLUMBUS
Cincinnati
INDIANAPOLIS
INDIANA
Evansville
FRANKFORT
Lexington
Louisville
KENTUCKY
Ohio
Bowling Green
Middlesboro
Knoxville
Bristol
NASHVILLE
TENNESSEE
Chattanooga
Jackson
Memphis
Huntsville
Tennessee
Birmingham
Anniston
MONTGOMERY
ALABAMA
Dothan
Mobile
Pensacola
TALLAHASSEE
International Falls
MINNESOTA
Duluth
Brainerd
Superior
St. Cloud
ST. PAUL
Minneapolis
WISCONSIN
Eau Claire
Green Bay
Oshkosh
Mankato
Rochester
La Crosse
Austin
Mason City
MADISON
Beloit
Waterloo
Sioux City
Cedar Rapids
Rockford
Chicago
IOWA
DES MOINES
Council Bluffs
Omaha
Fort Madison
Joliet
Rock Island
Peoria
Keokuk
St. Joseph
SPRINGFIELD
Decatur
ILLINOIS
Missouri
Kansas City
R.
E. St. Louis
St. Louis
Belleville
TOPEKA
JEFFERSON CITY
MISSOURI
Springfield
Joplin
Cairo
Paducah
Tulsa
Muskogee
Jonesboro
ARKANSAS
LITTLE ROCK
Pine Bluff
Texarkana
Mississippi R.
Clarksdale
Greenville
Columbus
MISSISSIPPI
Vicksburg
Meridian
JACKSON
Laurel
Natchez
Hattiesburg
Marshall
Monroe
Shreveport
Alexandria
Sabine R.
LOUISIANA
BATON ROUGE
Biloxi
Gulfport
New Orleans
Beaumont
Port Arthur
Galveston
UNITED STATES
Gulf of Mexico
CUBA
0 Miles 500
0 Kilometers 800

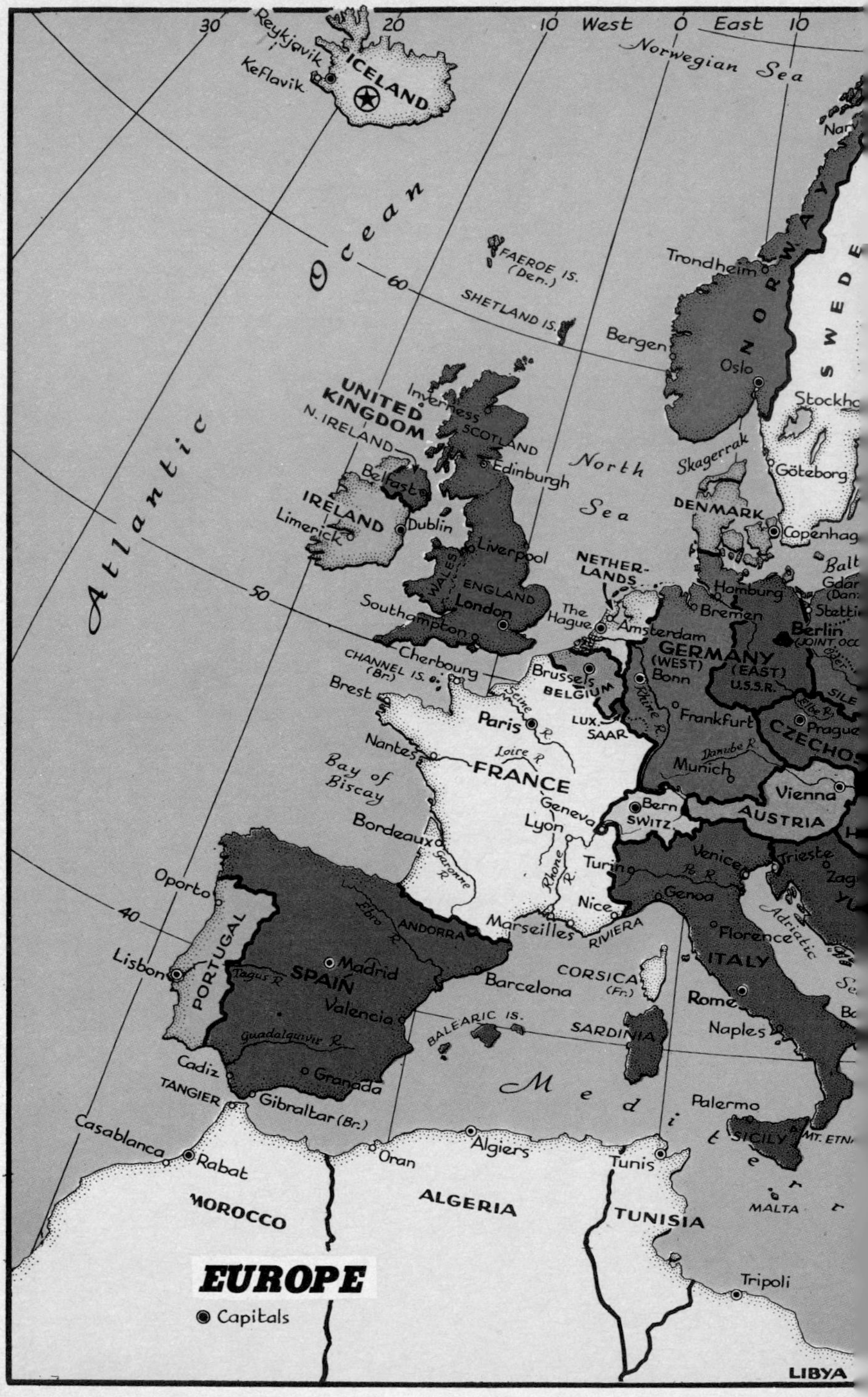
EUROPE
Capitals
Atlantic Ocean
Norwegian Sea
North Sea
Bay of Biscay
Mediterranean
ICELAND
Reykjavik
Keflavik
FAEROE IS. (Den.)
SHETLAND IS.
UNITED KINGDOM
N. IRELAND
SCOTLAND
WALES
ENGLAND
Inverness
Edinburgh
Belfast
Liverpool
London
Southampton
IRELAND
Dublin
Limerick
NORWAY
Trondheim
Bergen
Oslo
SWEDEN
Stockholm
Göteborg
Skagerrak
DENMARK
Copenhagen
NETHERLANDS
The Hague
Amsterdam
BELGIUM
Brussels
LUX.
SAAR
GERMANY (WEST)
GERMANY (EAST) U.S.S.R.
Hamburg
Bremen
Bonn
Frankfurt
Munich
Berlin
Rhine R.
Danube R.
Elbe R.
Prague
Vienna
AUSTRIA
SWITZ.
Bern
Geneva
FRANCE
Paris
Seine R.
Loire R.
Rhone R.
Garonne R.
Nantes
Brest
Cherbourg
CHANNEL IS. (Br.)
Bordeaux
Lyon
Marseilles
Nice
RIVIERA
ANDORRA
SPAIN
Madrid
Barcelona
Valencia
Granada
Cadiz
Tagus R.
Ebro R.
Guadalquivir R.
PORTUGAL
Lisbon
Oporto
Gibraltar (Br.)
TANGIER
BALEARIC IS.
CORSICA (Fr.)
SARDINIA
ITALY
Turin
Venice
Trieste
Genoa
Po R.
Florence
Rome
Naples
Palermo
SICILY
MT. ETNA
MALTA
Adriatic
MOROCCO
Casablanca
Rabat
ALGERIA
Oran
Algiers
TUNISIA
Tunis
Tripoli
LIBYA
30
20
10
West
0
East
10
60
50
40

Kilometers
0
800
Miles
0
500
40
50
Kirkenes
Murmansk
White Sea
Archangel
N. Dvina R.
FINLAND
Lulea
Vaasa
L. Onega
L. Ladoga
Leningrad
Helsinki
Tallinn
ESTONIA
Riga
LATVIA
LITHUANIA
Warsaw
URAL MTS.
Sverdlovsk
UNION OF SOVIET SOCIALIST REPUBLICS
Magnitogorsk
Kama R.
Volga R.
Moscow
Oka R.
Kuibyshev
Ural R.
Dvina R.
Smolensk
Saratov
Don R.
Volgograd
1938 BORDER
Kiev
Dnieper R.
Kharkov
Donetsk
UKRAINE
Dnepropetrovsk
Dniester R.
Rostov
Astrakhan
Caspian Sea
Prut R.
Odessa
Sea of Azov
RUMANIA
CRIMEA
Sevastopol
Yalta
CAUCASUS
Tbilisi
Baku
Bucharest
Danube R.
Black Sea
Batum
BULGARIA
Sofia
Istanbul
Bosporus
Erivan
Tabriz
AZERBAIJAN
L. Urmia
Teheran
THRACE
L. Van
Ankara
TURKEY
Dardanelles
Aegean Sea
Mosul
Tigris R.
IRAN
GREECE
Izmir
Adana
Athens
Aleppo
SYRIA
Baghdad
RHODES
CYPRUS
LEBANON
Damascus
IRAQ
Euphrates R.
CRETE
Beirut
Basra
KUWAIT
ISRAEL
Tel Aviv
Jerusalem
Amman
Dead Sea
JORDAN
Persian Gulf
Alexandria
SUEZ CANAL
HELD BY ISRAEL
SAUDI ARABIA
EGYPT
Cairo

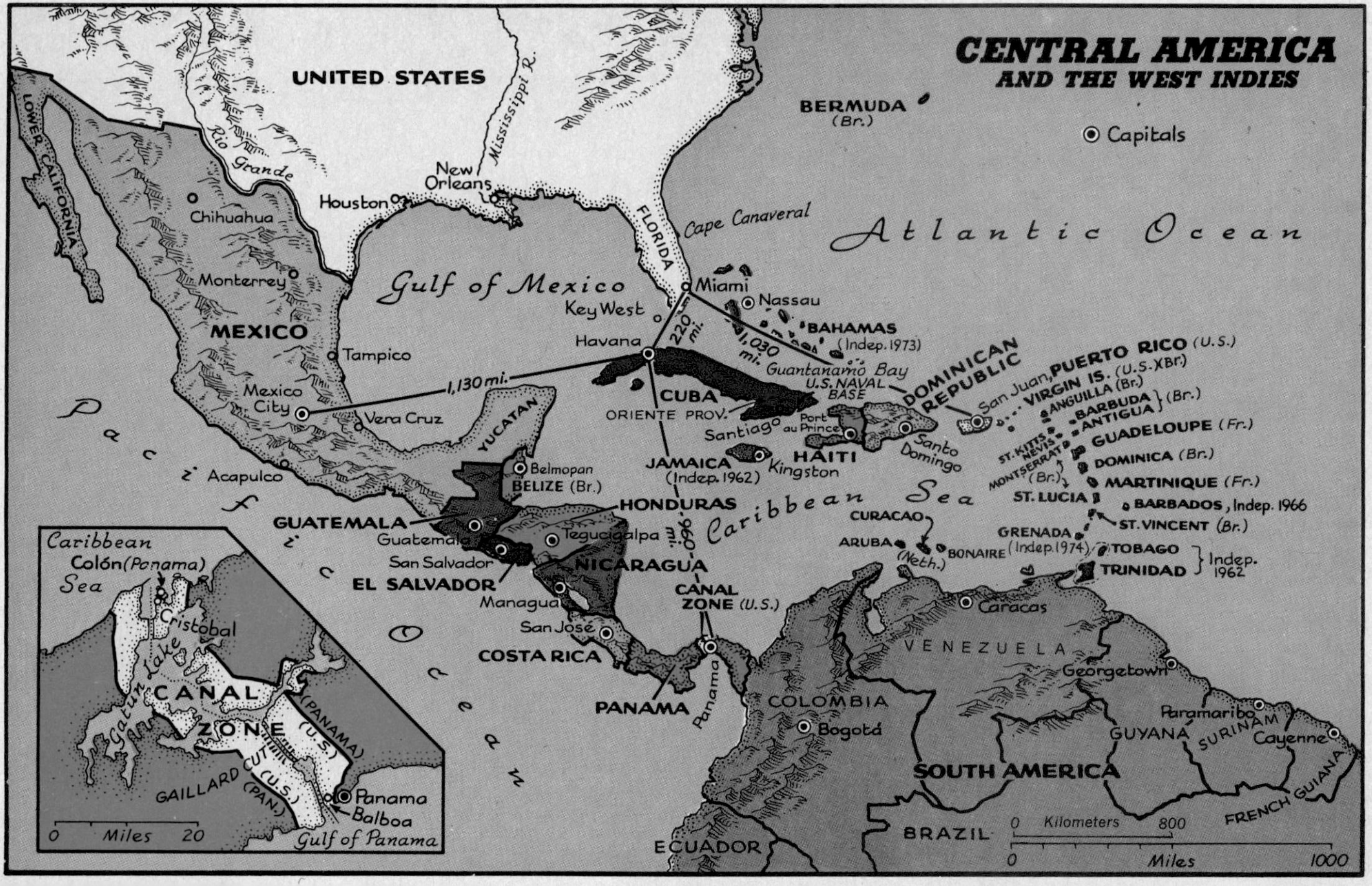
CENTRAL AMERICA
AND THE WEST INDIES
Capitals
UNITED STATES
Mississippi R.
Rio Grande
LOWER CALIFORNIA
Chihuahua
Monterrey
MEXICO
Tampico
Mexico City
Vera Cruz
Acapulco
Houston
New Orleans
FLORIDA
Cape Canaveral
Miami
Key West
Gulf of Mexico
1,130 mi.
220 mi.
1,030 mi.
Havana
Nassau
BAHAMAS
(Indep. 1973)
Guantanamo Bay
U.S. NAVAL BASE
CUBA
ORIENTE PROV.
Santiago
Port au Prince
HAITI
DOMINICAN REPUBLIC
Santo Domingo
San Juan, PUERTO RICO (U.S.)
VIRGIN IS. (U.S.)(Br.)
ANGUILLA (Br.)
BARBUDA
ANTIGUA
(Br.)
ST. KITTS
NEVIS
MONTSERRAT
(Br.)
GUADELOUPE (Fr.)
DOMINICA (Br.)
MARTINIQUE (Fr.)
ST. LUCIA
BARBADOS, Indep. 1966
ST. VINCENT (Br.)
GRENADA
(Indep. 1974)
TOBAGO
TRINIDAD
Indep. 1962
CURACAO
ARUBA
BONAIRE
(Neth.)
BERMUDA
(Br.)
Atlantic Ocean
JAMAICA
(Indep. 1962)
Kingston
Caribbean Sea
Belmopan
BELIZE (Br.)
YUCATAN
GUATEMALA
Guatemala
San Salvador
EL SALVADOR
HONDURAS
Tegucigalpa
960 mi.
NICARAGUA
Managua
San José
COSTA RICA
CANAL ZONE (U.S.)
PANAMA
Panama
Pacific Ocean
COLOMBIA
Bogotá
VENEZUELA
Caracas
Georgetown
GUYANA
Paramaribo
SURINAM
Cayenne
FRENCH GUIANA
SOUTH AMERICA
BRAZIL
ECUADOR
0 Kilometers 800
0 Miles 1000
Caribbean Sea
Colón (Panama)
Cristobal
Gatun Lake
CANAL ZONE
(PANAMA)
(U.S.)
GAILLARD CUT
(U.S.)
(PAN.)
Panama
Balboa
Gulf of Panama
0 Miles 20

SOUTH AMERICA
Miles 0 1000
Kilometers 0 1,600
CURAÇAO
WEST INDIES
Maracaibo
Caracas
TRINIDAD & TOBAGO
PANAMA CANAL
VENEZUELA
Orinoco
Ciudad Bolívar
ANGEL FALLS
GUYANA
Georgetown
Paramaribo
Cayenne
SURINAM
FR. GUIANA
Magdalena
Bogotá
COLOMBIA
Quito
ECUADOR
Guayaquil
Iquitos
Negro
Branco
Manaus
Amazon R.
Belém
Fortaleza
Natal
Recife
Marañon
Ucayali
Juruá
Madeira
Tapajos
Xingu
Araguaia
Parnaiba
São Francisco
B R A Z I L
PERU
Lima
Callao
MATO GROSSO
Arequipa
La Paz
BOLIVIA
Sucre
Brasília
FEDERAL DISTRICT
Salvador
Corumbá
Belo Horizonte
Paraná
Campinas
São Paulo
Rio de Janeiro
PARAGUAY
Antofagasta
Asunción
Tucumán
Salado
Paraguay
Uruguay
CHILE
Pôrto Alegre
MT. ACONCAGUA 22,835 ft.
Córdoba
Rosario
Rio Grande
URUGUAY
Valparaíso
Santiago
Buenos Aires
Montevideo
Rio de la Plata
PAMPAS
ARGENTINA
Colorado
Negro
Bahia Blanca
PATAGONIA
Punta Arenas
TIERRA DEL FUEGO
Strait of Magellan
Cape Horn
Pacific Ocean
Atlantic Ocean
CLIMATE
Tropical Rainforest
Savanna
Highland
Subtropical
Desert and Steppe
Marine
OIL
IRON
STEEL
TUNGSTEN
MANGANESE
TIN
COPPER
NITRATES
BAUXITE
COAL
DIAMONDS
RUBBER
COFFEE
COCOA
CATTLE
SHEEP

Black Sea
Sinope
Istanbul (Constantinople)
Bosporus
Zonguldak
Uskudar (Scutari)
Samsun
Sea of Marmara
Gallipoli
Izmit
Kizil R.
Dardanelles
Bursa
Ankara
LIMNOS
Eskisehir
Sivas
MITILINI
T U R
CHIOS
Smyrna (Izmir)
Afyon
Kayseri
A N A T O L I A
Malat
SAMOS
Konia
Isparta
Milas
TAURUS
KOS
Adana
Antalya
Tarsus
Alexandretta
RHODES
GREECE
Aegean Sea
Aleppo
CARPATHOS
CRETE
Latakia
SY
Lefka
Nicosia
Famagusta
Baniyas
Hama
CYPRUS
Homs
Limasol
Tripoli
Paln
LEBANON
Beirut
Mediterranean Sea
Sidon
Damascus
MT. HERMON
U.N. BUFFER ZONE
GOLAN HGTS.
Haifa
ISRAEL
Irbid
Jordan
Tel Aviv-Jaffa
Amman
Sidi Barrani
Alexandria
Gaza
Jerusalem
Matruh
Port Said
Dead Sea
El Alamein
Tanta
SUEZ
NEGEV
JORDAN
CANAL
BUFFER ZONE (U.N. TROOPS)
QATTARA DEPRESSION
Bitter Lake
Cairo
Suez
Ma'an
Siwa Oasis
Elath
Aqaba
SINAI PENINSULA
EGYPT
Gulf of Suez
AREAS TAKEN BY ISRAEL JUNE '67
G. of Aqaba
WESTERN DESERT
EASTERN DESERT
El Minya
TIRAN
HEJAZ
Nile R.
Red Sea
Qena
Luxor
El Kharga

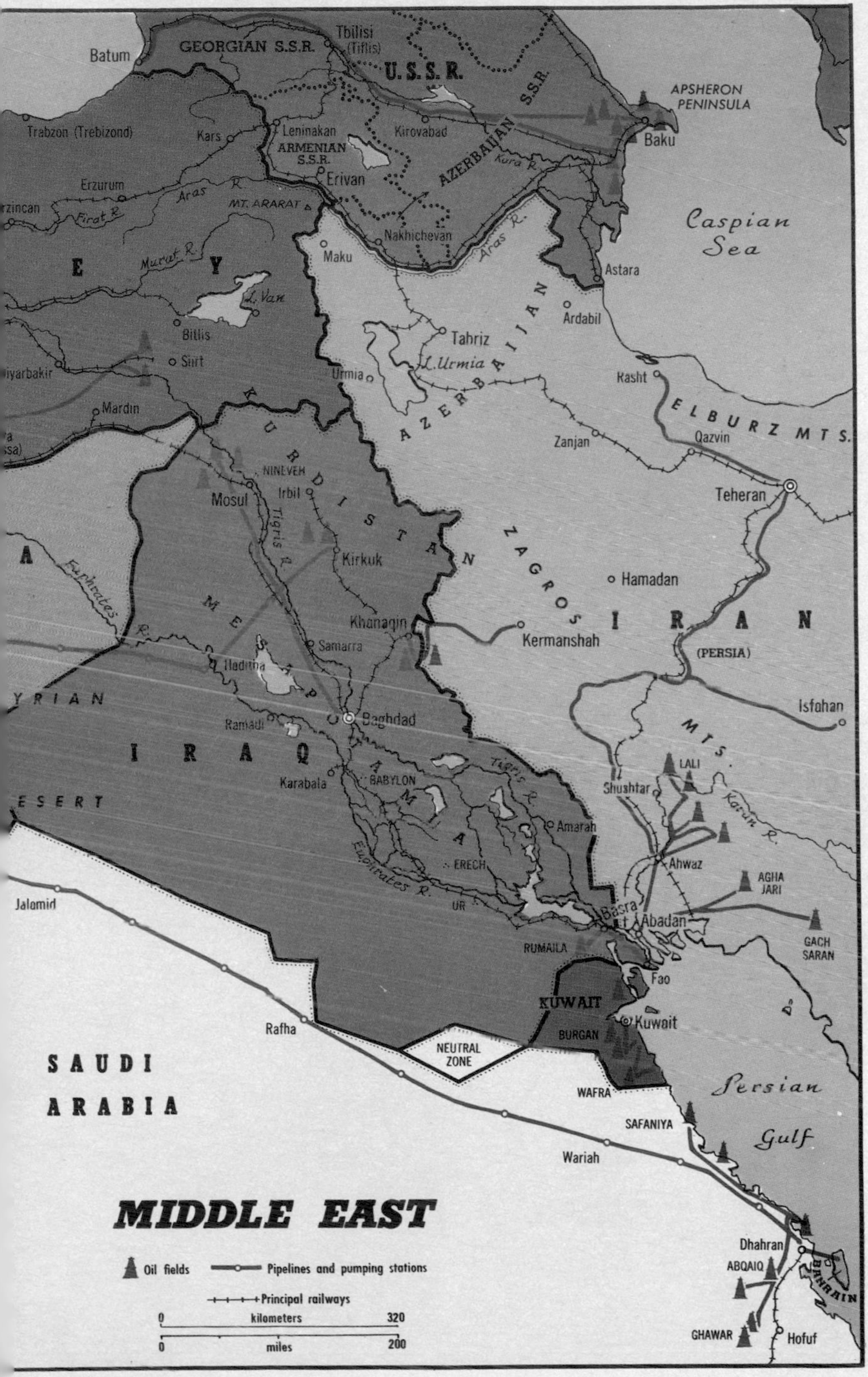
MIDDLE EAST
Oil fields
Pipelines and pumping stations
Principal railways
kilometers
miles
0
320
0
200
Batum
GEORGIAN S.S.R.
Tbilisi (Tiflis)
U.S.S.R.
AZERBAIJAN S.S.R.
APSHERON PENINSULA
Baku
Trabzon (Trebizond)
Kars
Leninakan
Kirovabad
ARMENIAN S.S.R.
Erivan
Kura R.
Erzurum
Aras R.
MT. ARARAT
Firat R.
Nakhichevan
Aras R.
Maku
Caspian Sea
Astara
Murat R.
L. Van
Bitlis
Siirt
Mardin
Ardabil
Tabriz
L. Urmia
Urmia
Rasht
AZERBAIJAN
ELBURZ MTS.
Qazvin
Zanjan
Teheran
KURDISTAN
NINEVEH
Irbil
Mosul
Tigris R.
Kirkuk
Euphrates R.
MESOPOTAMIA
ZAGROS MTS.
Hamadan
IRAN
(PERSIA)
Khanaqin
Kermanshah
Samarra
Haditha
SYRIAN DESERT
Baghdad
Ramadi
Isfahan
IRAQ
Karabala
BABYLON
Tigris R.
LALI
Shushtar
Karun R.
Amarah
ERECH
Ahwaz
AGHA JARI
UR
Basra
Abadan
GACH SARAN
RUMAILA
Fao
Jalamid
KUWAIT
Kuwait
BURGAN
Rafha
NEUTRAL ZONE
SAUDI ARABIA
WAFRA
Persian Gulf
SAFANIYA
Wariah
Dhahran
ABQAIQ
BAHRAIN
GHAWAR
Hofuf

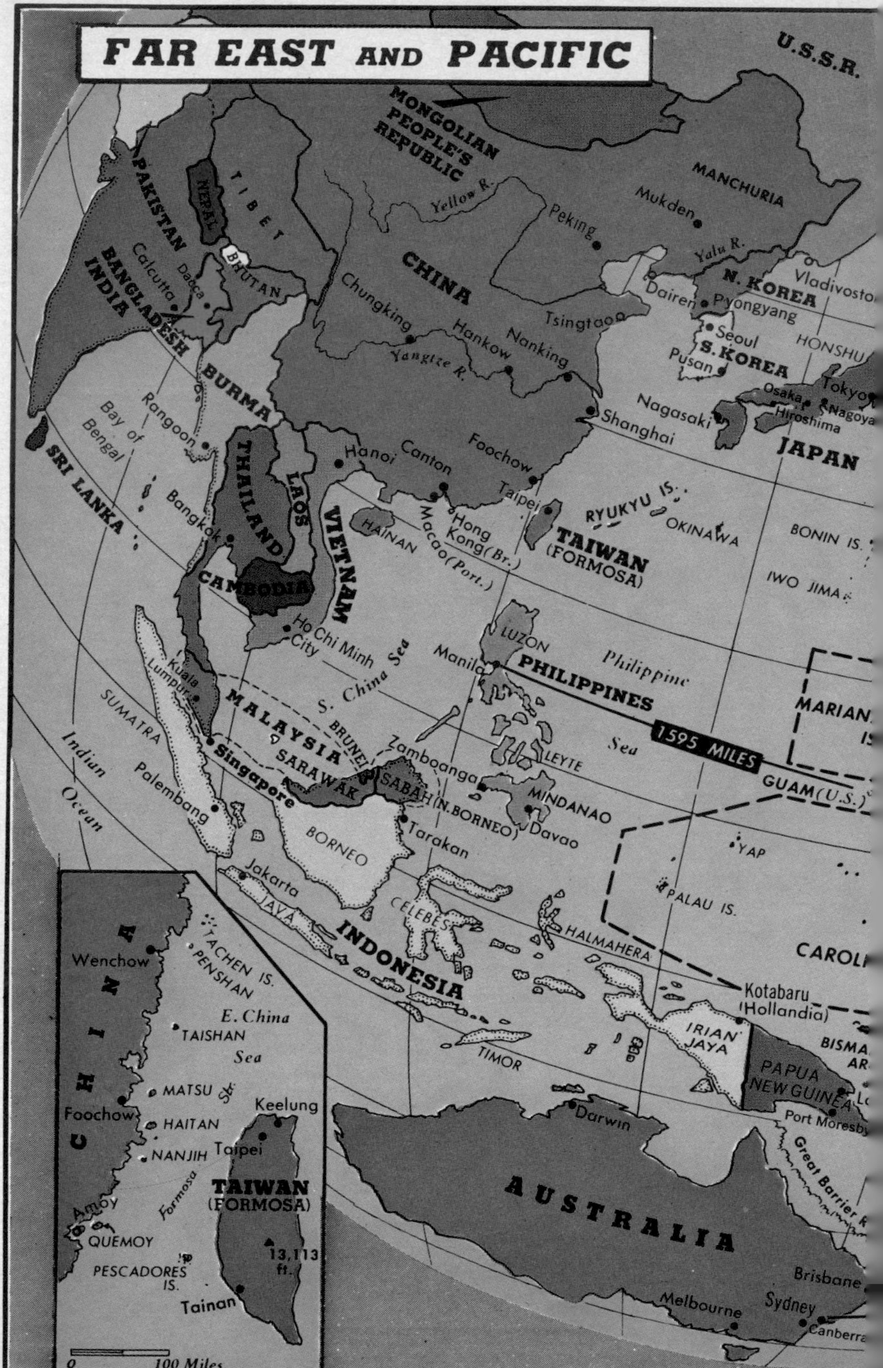
FAR EAST AND PACIFIC
U.S.S.R.
MONGOLIAN PEOPLE'S REPUBLIC
MANCHURIA
Mukden
Yellow R.
Peking
Yalu R.
Vladivostok
N. KOREA
Pyongyang
Dairen
Tsingtao
S. KOREA
Seoul
Pusan
HONSHU
Tokyo
Osaka
Nagoya
Hiroshima
Nagasaki
JAPAN
CHINA
Chungking
Hankow
Nanking
Yangtze R.
Shanghai
Foochow
Canton
Taipei
TIBET
NEPAL
BHUTAN
PAKISTAN
BANGLADESH
INDIA
Calcutta
Dacca
BURMA
Rangoon
Bay of Bengal
SRI LANKA
THAILAND
Bangkok
LAOS
VIETNAM
Hanoi
CAMBODIA
Ho Chi Minh City
HAINAN
Hong Kong (Br.)
Macao (Port.)
RYUKYU IS.
OKINAWA
TAIWAN (FORMOSA)
BONIN IS.
IWO JIMA
LUZON
Manila
PHILIPPINES
Philippine Sea
1595 MILES
MARIANA IS.
GUAM (U.S.)
S. China Sea
Kuala Lumpur
MALAYSIA
BRUNEI
SARAWAK
SABAH (N. BORNEO)
Singapore
Zamboanga
LEYTE
MINDANAO
Davao
YAP
PALAU IS.
SUMATRA
Palembang
Indian Ocean
BORNEO
Tarakan
Jakarta
JAVA
CELEBES
HALMAHERA
INDONESIA
CAROLINE
Kotabaru (Hollandia)
IRIAN JAYA
PAPUA NEW GUINEA
Port Moresby
TIMOR
Darwin
AUSTRALIA
Great Barrier Reef
Brisbane
Sydney
Melbourne
Canberra
CHINA
Wenchow
TACHEN IS.
PENSHAN
E. China Sea
TAISHAN
MATSU
Foochow
HAITAN
NANJIH
Keelung
Taipei
Formosa Str.
TAIWAN (FORMOSA)
Amoy
QUEMOY
13,113 ft.
PESCADORES IS.
Tainan
0 100 Miles

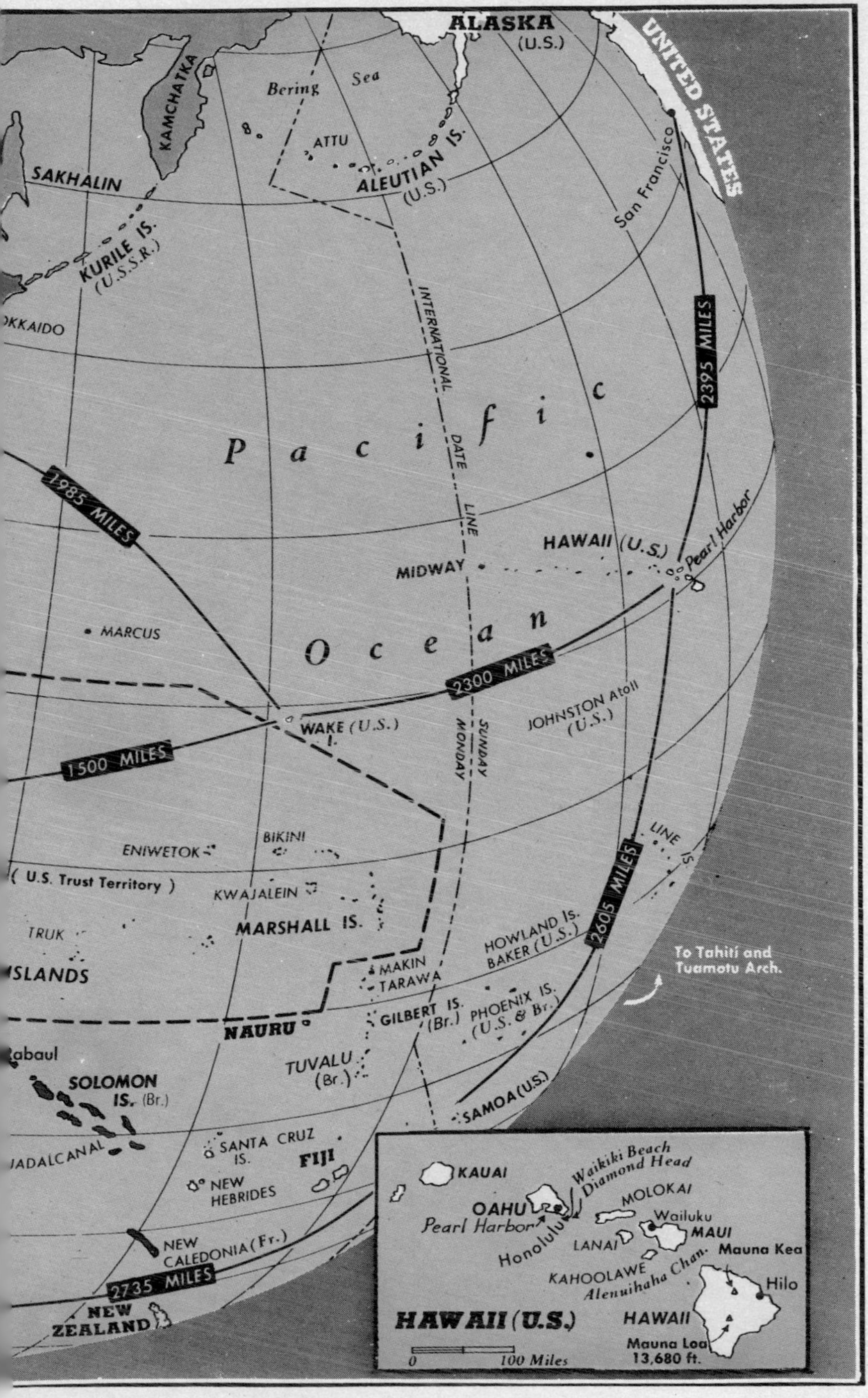

ALASKA (U.S.)
UNITED STATES
Bering Sea
KAMCHATKA
ATTU
ALEUTIAN IS. (U.S.)
SAKHALIN
KURILE IS. (U.S.S.R.)
San Francisco
INTERNATIONAL DATE LINE
2395 MILES
Pacific Ocean
1985 MILES
HAWAII (U.S.)
Pearl Harbor
MIDWAY
MARCUS
2300 MILES
WAKE (U.S.) I.
JOHNSTON Atoll (U.S.)
SUNDAY
MONDAY
1500 MILES
BIKINI
ENIWETOK
LINE IS.
2605 MILES
( U.S. Trust Territory )
KWAJALEIN
MARSHALL IS.
TRUK
HOWLAND IS.
BAKER (U.S.)
To Tahiti and Tuamotu Arch.
MAKIN
TARAWA
GILBERT IS. (Br.)
PHOENIX IS. (U.S. & Br.)
NAURU
Rabaul
TUVALU (Br.)
SOLOMON IS. (Br.)
SAMOA (U.S.)
SANTA CRUZ IS.
FIJI
NEW HEBRIDES
NEW CALEDONIA (Fr.)
2735 MILES
NEW ZEALAND
KAUAI
Waikiki Beach
Diamond Head
OAHU
MOLOKAI
Pearl Harbor
Wailuku
MAUI
LANAI
Honolulu
Mauna Kea
KAHOOLAWE
Alenuihaha Chan.
Hilo
HAWAII (U.S.)
HAWAII
0 100 Miles
Mauna Loa 13,680 ft.

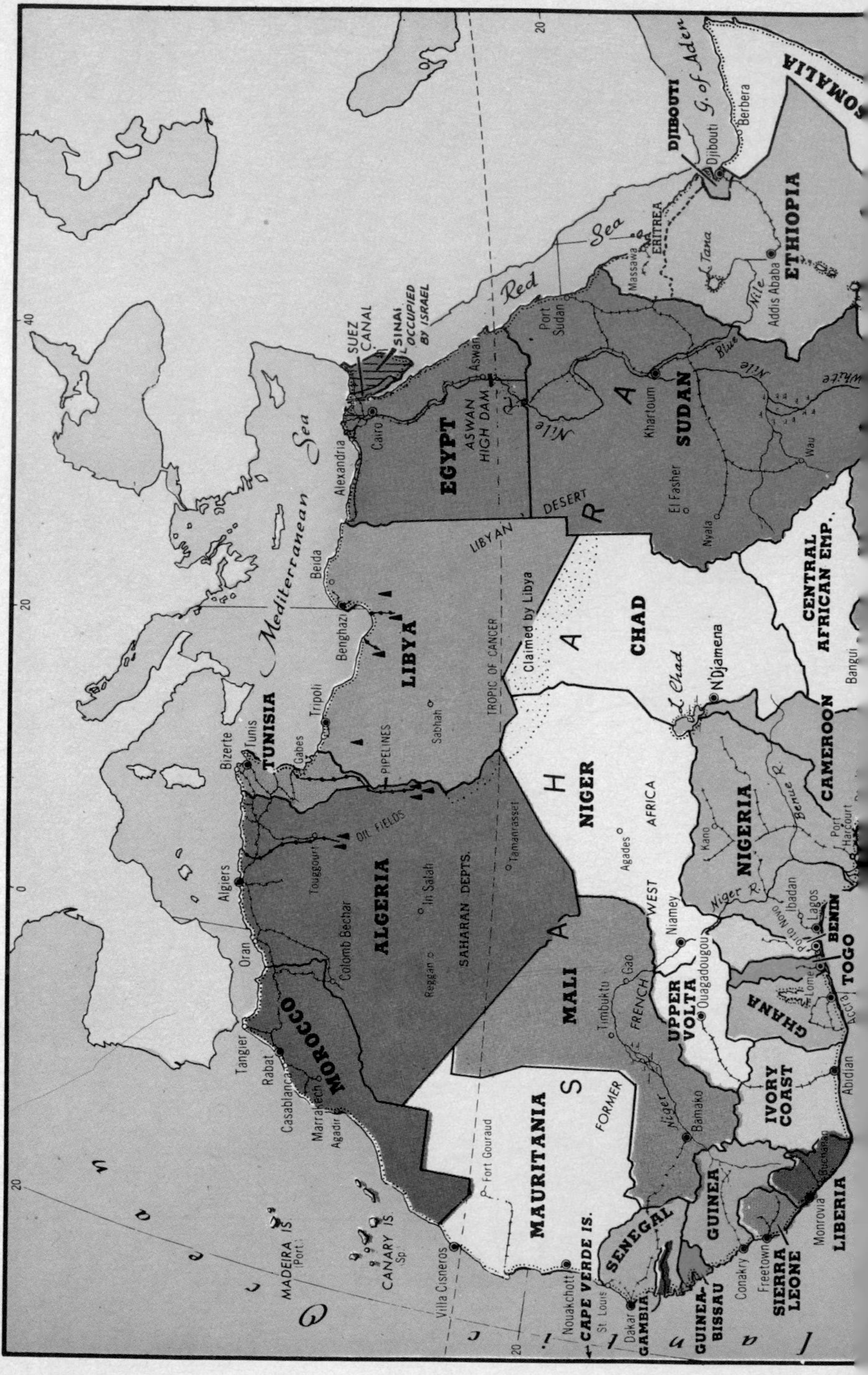
Mediterranean Sea
Red Sea
G. of Aden
MADEIRA IS. (Port.)
CANARY IS. (Sp.)
CAPE VERDE IS.
MOROCCO
ALGERIA
TUNISIA
LIBYA
EGYPT
SUEZ CANAL
SINAI OCCUPIED BY ISRAEL
ASWAN HIGH DAM
SUDAN
ETHIOPIA
ERITREA
DJIBOUTI
SOMALIA
CHAD
NIGER
MALI
MAURITANIA
SENEGAL
GAMBIA
GUINEA-BISSAU
GUINEA
SIERRA LEONE
LIBERIA
IVORY COAST
UPPER VOLTA
GHANA
TOGO
BENIN
NIGERIA
CAMEROON
CENTRAL AFRICAN EMP.
SAHARAN DEPTS.
OIL FIELDS
PIPELINES
TROPIC OF CANCER
LIBYAN DESERT
Claimed by Libya
SAHARA
FORMER FRENCH WEST AFRICA
Tangier
Rabat
Casablanca
Marrakech
Agadir
Oran
Algiers
Colomb Bechar
Touggourt
In Salah
Reggan
Tamanrasset
Bizerte
Tunis
Gabes
Tripoli
Benghazi
Beida
Sabhah
Alexandria
Cairo
Aswan
Port Sudan
Khartoum
El Fasher
Nyala
Wau
Massawa
Addis Ababa
Djibouti
Berbera
L. Tana
Blue Nile
White Nile
Nile
N'Djamena
L. Chad
Bangui
Agades
Kano
Ibadan
Lagos
Porto Novo
Port Harcourt
Benue R.
Niger R.
Niamey
Gao
Timbuktu
Ouagadougou
Bamako
Lomé
Accra
Abidjan
Monrovia
Freetown
Conakry
Buchanan
Dakar
St. Louis
Nouakchott
Fort Gouraud
Villa Cisneros
0
20
40

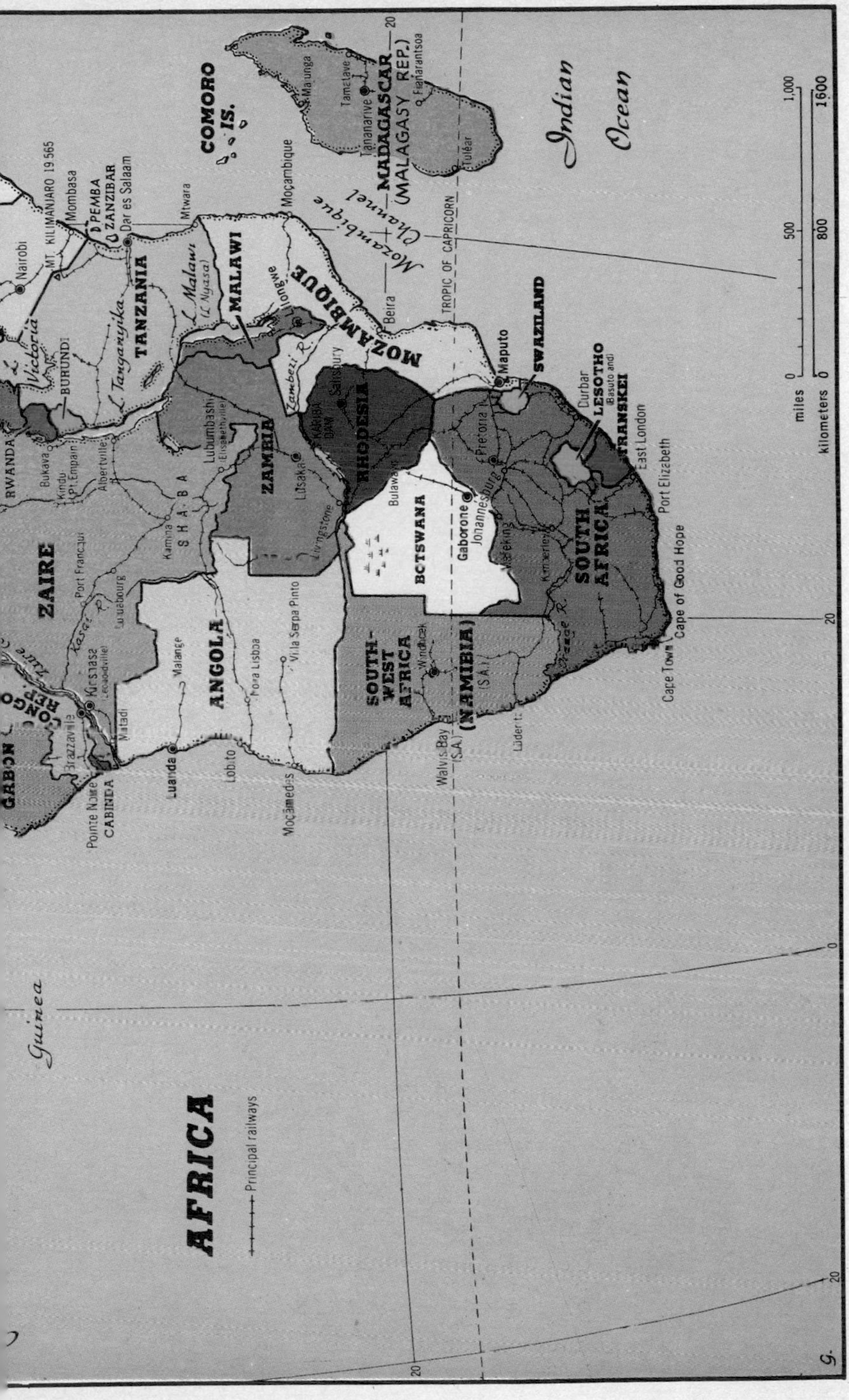
AFRICA
Principal railways
Guinea
GABON
CONGO REP.
ZAIRE
ANGOLA
ZAMBIA
RHODESIA
MOZAMBIQUE
MALAWI
TANZANIA
BURUNDI
RWANDA
BOTSWANA
SOUTH-WEST AFRICA
(NAMIBIA)
SOUTH AFRICA
SWAZILAND
LESOTHO
(Basuto and)
TRANSKEI
COMORO IS.
MADAGASCAR
(MALAGASY REP.)
PEMBA
ZANZIBAR
Mozambique Channel
Indian Ocean
TROPIC OF CAPRICORN
MT. KILIMANJARO 19,565
Nairobi
Mombasa
Dar es Salaam
Mtwara
Moçambique
Beira
Maputo
Salisbury
KARIBA DAM
Bulawayo
Lusaka
Livingstone
Lubumbashi
(Elisabethville)
SHABA
Kamina
Albertville
Kindu
Bukavu
Port Francqui
Luluabourg
Kinshasa
(Léopoldville)
Brazzaville
Matadi
Pointe Noire
CABINDA
Luanda
Lobito
Moçâmedes
Malange
Nova Lisboa
Vila Serpa Pinto
Windhoek
Walvis Bay
(S.A.)
Lüderitz
Gaboronе
Johannesburg
Pretoria
Kimberley
Cape Town
Cape of Good Hope
Port Elizabeth
East London
Durban
Lilongwe
Tananarive
Tamatave
Majunga
Fianarantsoa
Tuléar
L. Victoria
L. Tanganyika
L. Malawi
(L. Nyasa)
Zambezi R.
Kasai R.
Orange R.
miles
kilometers
0
500
1,000
800
1600
20
0

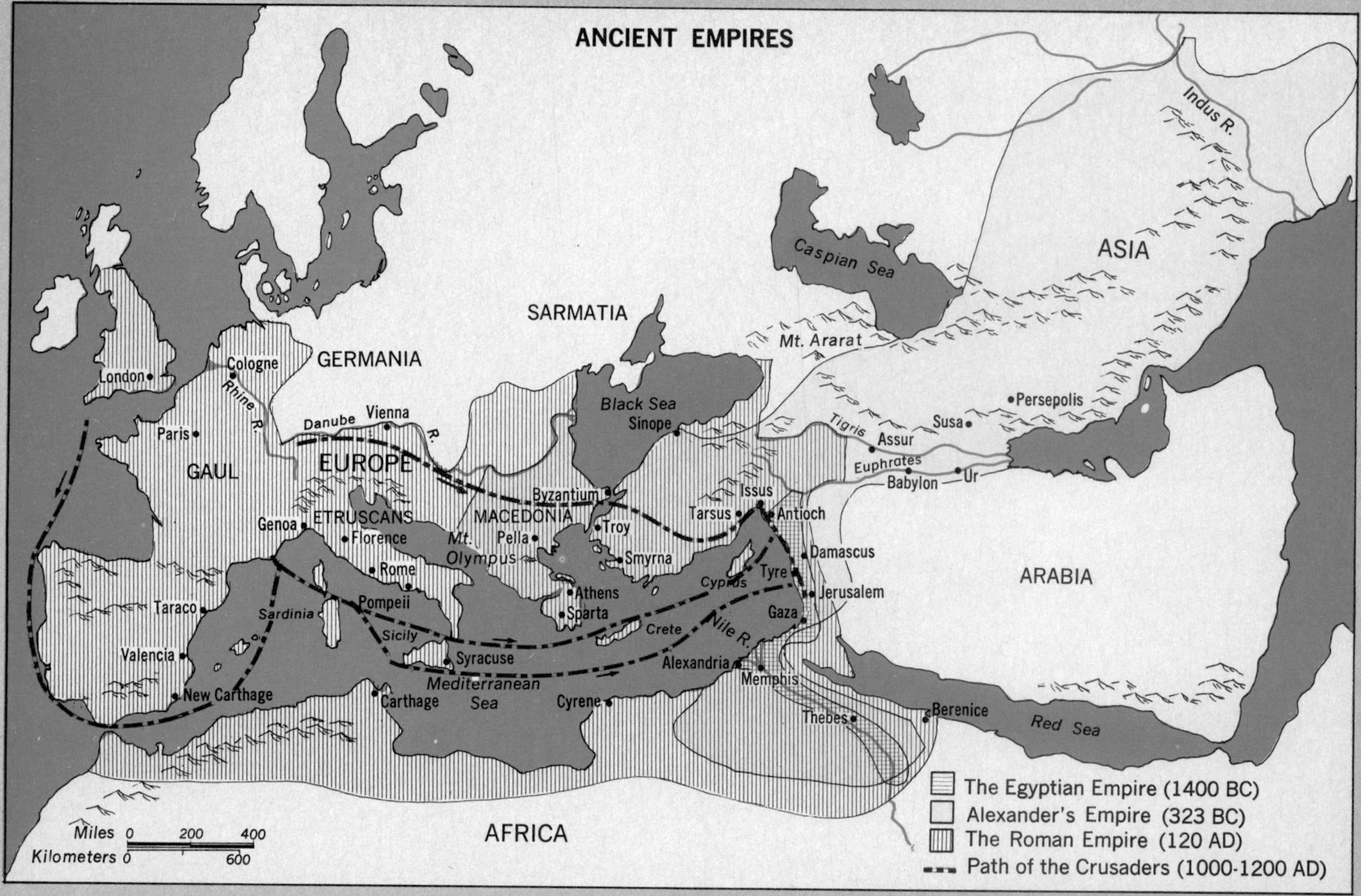
ANCIENT EMPIRES
SARMATIA
GERMANIA
ASIA
Caspian Sea
Mt. Ararat
Indus R.
London
Cologne
Rhine R.
Paris
GAUL
Danube
Vienna
R.
EUROPE
Black Sea
Sinope
Persepolis
Susa
Tigris
Assur
Euphrates
Babylon
Ur
Byzantium
Issus
Tarsus
Antioch
Genoa
ETRUSCANS
MACEDONIA
Troy
Florence
Mt.
Olympus
Pella
Smyrna
Damascus
Rome
Athens
Sparta
Cyprus
Tyre
Jerusalem
ARABIA
Taraco
Sardinia
Pompeii
Crete
Gaza
Nile R.
Sicily
Valencia
Syracuse
Alexandria
Memphis
New Carthage
Carthage
Mediterranean
Sea
Cyrene
Thebes
Berenice
Red Sea
AFRICA
Miles 0 200 400
Kilometers 0 600
The Egyptian Empire (1400 BC)
Alexander's Empire (323 BC)
The Roman Empire (120 AD)
Path of the Crusaders (1000-1200 AD)

## THE MIDDLE EAST

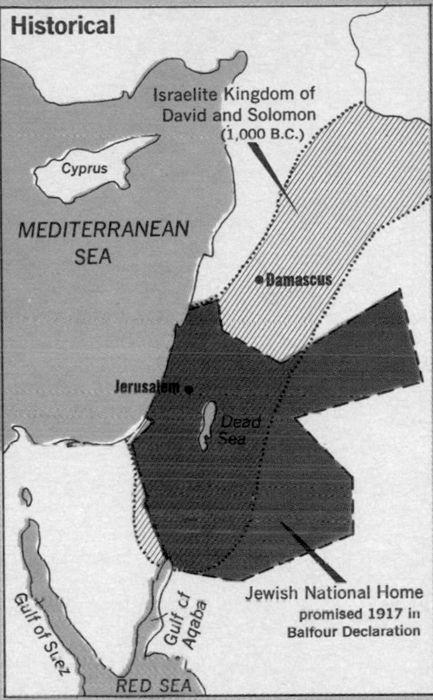
Historical
Israelite Kingdom of David and Solomon (1,000 B.C.)
Cyprus
MEDITERRANEAN SEA
Damascus
Jerusalem
Dead Sea
Jewish National Home promised 1917 in Balfour Declaration
Gulf of Suez
Gulf of Aqaba
RED SEA

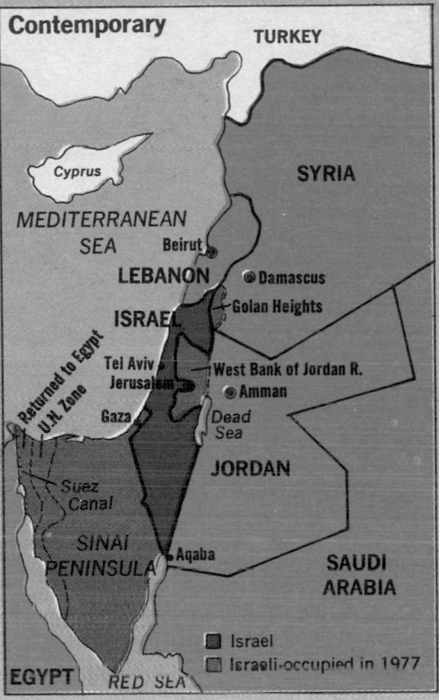
Contemporary
TURKEY
Cyprus
SYRIA
MEDITERRANEAN SEA
Beirut
LEBANON
Damascus
Golan Heights
ISRAEL
Returned to Egypt
U.N. Zone
Tel Aviv
Jerusalem
West Bank of Jordan R.
Amman
Gaza
Dead Sea
JORDAN
Suez Canal
SINAI PENINSULA
Aqaba
SAUDI ARABIA
Israel
Israeli-occupied in 1977
EGYPT
RED SEA

## MAJOR OIL PRODUCING COUNTRIES

CANADA
UNITED STATES
MEXICO
BELIZE
GUATEMALA
NICARAGUA
HONDURAS
VENEZUELA
COLOMBIA
ECUADOR
PERU
BOLIVIA
NORWAY
BRITAIN
ROMANIA
U.S.S.R.
CHINA
SOUTH KOREA
JAPAN
IRAQ
IRAN
KUWAIT
LIBYA
ALGERIA
SAUDI ARABIA
QATAR
VIETNAM
NIGERIA
GABON
ANGOLA
INDONESIA
AUSTRALIA
OPEC countries
Major non-OPEC producers
Recent oil finds
New explorations

# AFRICAN CLOSEUP

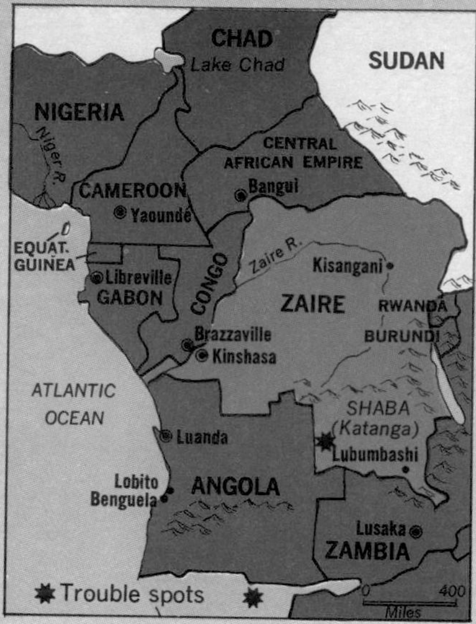

CHAD
Lake Chad
SUDAN
NIGERIA
Niger R.
CENTRAL AFRICAN EMPIRE
CAMEROON
Yaoundé
Bangui
EQUAT. GUINEA
Libreville
GABON
CONGO
Zaire R.
Kisangani
ZAIRE
RWANDA
BURUNDI
Brazzaville
Kinshasa
ATLANTIC OCEAN
SHABA (Katanga)
Luanda
Lubumbashi
Lobito
Benguela
ANGOLA
Lusaka
ZAMBIA
Trouble spots
0 400 Miles

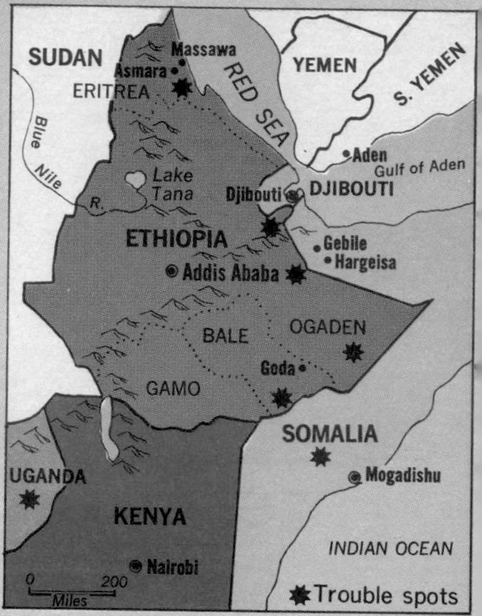

SUDAN
Massawa
Asmara
ERITREA
RED SEA
YEMEN
S. YEMEN
Blue Nile R.
Lake Tana
Aden
Gulf of Aden
Djibouti
DJIBOUTI
ETHIOPIA
Gebile
Hargeisa
Addis Ababa
BALE
OGADEN
Goda
GAMO
SOMALIA
UGANDA
Mogadishu
KENYA
INDIAN OCEAN
Nairobi
0 200 Miles
Trouble spots

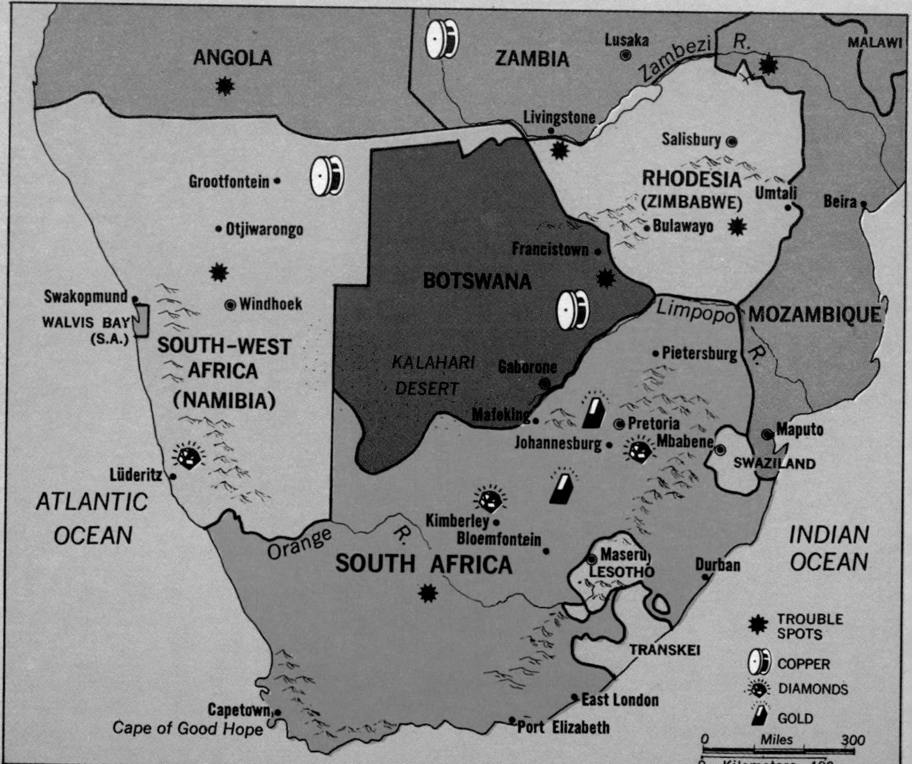

ANGOLA
ZAMBIA
Lusaka
Zambezi R.
MALAWI
Livingstone
Salisbury
Grootfontein
RHODESIA (ZIMBABWE)
Umtali
Beira
Otjiwarongo
Bulawayo
Francistown
BOTSWANA
Swakopmund
Windhoek
WALVIS BAY (S.A.)
Limpopo
MOZAMBIQUE
SOUTH-WEST AFRICA (NAMIBIA)
Pietersburg
R.
KALAHARI DESERT
Gaborone
Mafeking
Pretoria
Johannesburg
Mbabene
Maputo
SWAZILAND
Lüderitz
ATLANTIC OCEAN
Kimberley
Bloemfontein
Orange R.
INDIAN OCEAN
SOUTH AFRICA
Maseru
LESOTHO
Durban
TRANSKEI
TROUBLE SPOTS
COPPER
DIAMONDS
GOLD
East London
Capetown
Cape of Good Hope
Port Elizabeth
0 Miles 300
0 Kilometers 400

## Longitude and Latitude of Foreign Cities

(and time corresponding to 12:00 noon, eastern standard time)

| City | Long. ° | ′ | | Lat. ° | ′ | | Time |
|---|---|---|---|---|---|---|---|
| Aberdeen, Scotland | 2 | 9 | w | 57 | 9 | n | 5:00 p.m. |
| Adelaide, Australia | 138 | 36 | e | 34 | 55 | s | 2:30 a.m.[1] |
| Algiers | 3 | 0 | e | 36 | 50 | n | 6:00 p.m. |
| Amsterdam | 4 | 53 | e | 52 | 22 | n | 6:00 p.m. |
| Ankara, Turkey | 32 | 55 | e | 39 | 55 | n | 7:00 p.m. |
| Asunción, Paraguay | 57 | 40 | w | 25 | 15 | s | 1:00 p.m. |
| Athens | 23 | 43 | e | 37 | 58 | n | 7:00 p.m. |
| Auckland, New Zealand | 174 | 45 | e | 36 | 52 | s | 5:00 a.m.[1] |
| Bangkok, Thailand | 100 | 30 | e | 13 | 45 | n | midnight[1] |
| Barcelona | 2 | 9 | e | 41 | 23 | n | 6:00 p.m. |
| Belém, Brazil | 48 | 29 | w | 1 | 28 | s | 2:00 p.m. |
| Belfast, Northern Ireland | 5 | 56 | w | 54 | 37 | n | 5:00 p.m. |
| Belgrade, Yugoslavia | 20 | 32 | e | 44 | 52 | n | 6:00 p.m. |
| Berlin | 13 | 25 | e | 52 | 30 | n | 6:00 p.m. |
| Birmingham, England | 1 | 55 | w | 52 | 25 | n | 5:00 p.m. |
| Bogotá, Colombia | 74 | 15 | w | 4 | 32 | n | 12:00 noon |
| Bombay | 72 | 48 | e | 19 | 0 | n | 10:30 p.m. |
| Bordeaux, France | 0 | 31 | w | 44 | 50 | n | 6:00 p.m. |
| Bremen, West Germany | 8 | 49 | e | 53 | 5 | n | 6:00 p.m. |
| Brisbane, Australia | 153 | 8 | e | 27 | 29 | s | 3:00 a.m.[1] |
| Bristol, England | 2 | 35 | w | 51 | 28 | n | 5:00 p.m. |
| Brussels | 4 | 22 | e | 50 | 52 | n | 6:00 p.m. |
| Bucharest | 26 | 7 | e | 44 | 25 | n | 7:00 p.m. |
| Budapest | 19 | 5 | e | 47 | 30 | n | 6:00 p.m. |
| Buenos Aires | 58 | 22 | w | 34 | 35 | s | 2:00 p.m. |
| Cairo | 31 | 21 | e | 30 | 2 | n | 7:00 p.m. |
| Calcutta | 88 | 24 | e | 22 | 34 | n | 10:30 p.m. |
| Canton, China | 113 | 15 | e | 23 | 7 | n | 1:00 a.m.[1] |
| Cape Town, South Africa | 18 | 22 | e | 33 | 55 | s | 7:00 p.m. |
| Caracas, Venezuela | 67 | 2 | w | 10 | 28 | n | 12:30 p.m. |
| Cayenne, French Guiana | 52 | 18 | w | 4 | 49 | n | 1:00 p.m. |
| Chihuahua, Mexico | 106 | 5 | w | 28 | 37 | n | 11:00 a.m. |
| Chungking, China | 106 | 34 | e | 29 | 46 | n | 1:00 a.m.[1] |
| Copenhagen | 12 | 34 | e | 55 | 40 | n | 6:00 p.m. |
| Córdoba, Argentina | 64 | 10 | w | 31 | 28 | s | 2:00 p.m. |
| Dakar, Senegal | 17 | 28 | w | 14 | 40 | n | 5:00 p.m. |
| Darwin, Australia | 130 | 51 | e | 12 | 28 | s | 2:30 a.m.[1] |
| Djibouti | 43 | 3 | e | 11 | 30 | n | 8:00 p.m. |
| Dublin | 6 | 15 | w | 53 | 20 | n | 5:00 p.m. |
| Durban, South Africa | 30 | 53 | e | 29 | 53 | s | 7:00 p.m. |
| Edinburgh, Scotland | 3 | 10 | w | 55 | 55 | n | 5:00 p.m. |
| Frankfurt | 8 | 41 | e | 50 | 7 | n | 6:00 p.m. |
| Georgetown, Guyana | 58 | 15 | w | 6 | 45 | n | 1:15 p.m. |
| Glasgow, Scotland | 4 | 15 | w | 55 | 50 | n | 5:00 p.m. |
| Guatemala City, Guatemala | 90 | 31 | w | 14 | 37 | n | 11:00 a.m. |
| Guayaquil, Ecuador | 79 | 56 | w | 2 | 10 | s | 12:00 noon |
| Hamburg | 10 | 2 | e | 53 | 33 | n | 6:00 p.m. |
| Hammerfest, Norway | 23 | 38 | e | 70 | 38 | n | 6:00 p.m. |
| Havana | 82 | 23 | w | 23 | 8 | n | 12:00 noon |
| Helsinki, Finland | 25 | 0 | e | 60 | 10 | n | 7:00 p.m. |
| Hobart, Tasmania | 147 | 19 | e | 42 | 52 | s | 3:00 a.m.[1] |
| Iquique, Chile | 70 | 7 | w | 20 | 10 | s | 1:00 p.m. |
| Irkutsk, U.S.S.R. | 104 | 20 | e | 52 | 30 | n | 1:00 a.m.[1] |
| Jakarta, Indonesia | 106 | 48 | e | 6 | 16 | s | 0:30 a.m.[1] |
| Johannesburg, South Africa | 28 | 4 | e | 26 | 12 | s | 7:00 p.m. |
| Kingston, Jamaica | 76 | 49 | w | 17 | 59 | n | 12:00 noon |
| Kinshasa, Zaire | 15 | 17 | e | 4 | 18 | s | 6:00 p.m. |
| La Paz, Bolivia | 68 | 22 | w | 16 | 27 | s | 1:00 p.m. |
| Leeds, England | 1 | 30 | w | 53 | 45 | n | 5:00 p.m. |
| Leningrad | 30 | 18 | e | 59 | 56 | n | 8:00 p.m. |
| Lima, Peru | 77 | 2 | w | 12 | 0 | s | 12:00 noon |
| Lisbon | 9 | 9 | w | 38 | 44 | n | 5:00 p.m. |
| Liverpool, England | 3 | 0 | w | 53 | 25 | n | 5:00 p.m. |
| London | 0 | 5 | w | 51 | 32 | n | 5:00 p.m. |
| Lyons, France | 4 | 50 | e | 45 | 45 | n | 6:00 p.m. |
| Madrid | 3 | 42 | w | 40 | 26 | n | 6:00 p.m. |
| Manchester, England | 2 | 15 | w | 53 | 30 | n | 5:00 p.m. |
| Manila | 120 | 57 | e | 14 | 35 | n | 1:00 a.m.[1] |
| Marseilles, France | 5 | 20 | e | 43 | 20 | n | 6:00 p.m. |
| Mazatlán, Mexico | 106 | 25 | w | 23 | 12 | n | 10:00 a.m. |
| Mecca, Saudi Arabia | 39 | 45 | e | 21 | 29 | n | 8:00 p.m. |
| Melbourne | 144 | 58 | e | 37 | 47 | s | 3:00 a.m.[1] |
| Mexico City | 99 | 7 | w | 19 | 26 | n | 11:00 a.m. |
| Milan, Italy | 9 | 10 | e | 45 | 27 | n | 6:00 p.m. |
| Montevideo, Uruguay | 56 | 10 | w | 34 | 53 | s | 2:00 p.m. |
| Moscow | 37 | 36 | e | 55 | 45 | n | 8:00 p.m. |
| Munich, Germany | 11 | 35 | e | 48 | 8 | n | 6:00 p.m. |
| Nagasaki, Japan | 129 | 57 | e | 32 | 48 | n | 2:00 a.m.[1] |
| Nagoya, Japan | 136 | 56 | e | 35 | 7 | n | 2:00 a.m.[1] |
| Nairobi, Kenya | 36 | 55 | s | 1 | 25 | s | 8:00 p.m. |
| Nanking, China | 118 | 53 | e | 32 | 3 | n | 1:00 a.m.[1] |
| Naples, Italy | 14 | 15 | e | 40 | 50 | n | 6:00 p.m. |
| Newcastle-on-Tyne, Eng. | 1 | 37 | w | 54 | 58 | n | 5:00 p.m. |
| Odessa, U.S.S.R. | 30 | 48 | e | 46 | 27 | n | 8:00 p.m. |
| Osaka, Japan | 135 | 30 | e | 34 | 32 | n | 2:00 a.m.[1] |
| Oslo | 10 | 42 | e | 59 | 57 | n | 6:00 p.m. |
| Panama City, Panama | 79 | 32 | w | 8 | 58 | n | 12:00 noon |
| Paramaribo, Surinam | 55 | 15 | w | 5 | 46 | n | 1:30 p.m. |
| Paris | 2 | 20 | e | 48 | 48 | n | 6:00 p.m. |
| Peking | 116 | 25 | e | 39 | 55 | n | 1:00 a.m.[1] |
| Perth, Australia | 115 | 52 | e | 31 | 57 | s | 1:00 a.m.[1] |
| Plymouth, England | 4 | 5 | w | 50 | 25 | n | 5:00 p.m. |
| Port Moresby, Papua New Guinea | 147 | 8 | e | 9 | 25 | s | 3:00 a.m.[1] |
| Prague | 14 | 26 | e | 50 | 5 | n | 6:00 p.m. |
| Rangoon, Burma | 96 | 0 | e | 16 | 50 | n | 11:30 p.m. |
| Reykjavik, Iceland | 21 | 58 | w | 64 | 4 | n | 4:00 p.m. |
| Rio de Janeiro | 43 | 12 | w | 22 | 57 | s | 2:00 p.m. |
| Rome | 12 | 27 | e | 41 | 54 | n | 6:00 p.m. |
| Salvador, Brazil | 38 | 27 | w | 12 | 56 | s | 2:00 p.m. |
| Santiago, Chile | 70 | 45 | w | 33 | 28 | s | 1:00 p.m. |
| São Paulo, Brazil | 46 | 31 | w | 23 | 31 | s | 2:00 p.m. |
| Shanghai, China | 121 | 28 | e | 31 | 10 | n | 1:00 a.m.[1] |
| Singapore | 103 | 55 | e | 1 | 14 | n | 0:30 a.m.[1] |
| Sofia, Bulgaria | 23 | 20 | e | 42 | 40 | n | 7:00 p.m. |
| Stockholm | 18 | 3 | e | 59 | 17 | n | 6:00 p.m. |
| Sydney, Australia | 151 | 0 | e | 34 | 0 | s | 3:00 a.m.[1] |
| Tananarive, Madagascar | 47 | 33 | e | 18 | 50 | s | 8:00 p.m. |
| Teheran, Iran | 51 | 45 | e | 35 | 45 | n | 8:30 p.m. |
| Tokyo | 139 | 45 | e | 35 | 40 | n | 2:00 a.m.[1] |
| Tripoli, Libya | 13 | 12 | e | 32 | 57 | n | 7:00 p.m. |
| Venice | 12 | 20 | e | 45 | 26 | n | 6:00 p.m. |
| Veracruz, Mexico | 96 | 10 | w | 19 | 10 | n | 11:00 a.m. |
| Vienna | 16 | 20 | e | 48 | 14 | n | 6:00 p.m. |
| Vladivostok, U.S.S.R. | 132 | 0 | e | 43 | 10 | n | 3:00 a.m.[1] |
| Warsaw | 21 | 0 | e | 52 | 14 | n | 6:00 p.m. |
| Wellington, New Zealand | 174 | 47 | e | 41 | 17 | s | 5:00 a.m.[1] |
| Zürich | 8 | 31 | e | 47 | 21 | n | 6:00 p.m. |

1. On the following day.

## Longitude and Latitude of U.S. and Canadian Cities

**(and time corresponding to 12:00 noon, eastern standard time)**

| City | Long. w ° | Long. w ′ | Lat. n ° | Lat. n ′ | Time |
|---|---|---|---|---|---|
| Albany, N.Y. | 73 | 45 | 42 | 40 | 12:00 noon |
| Amarillo, Tex. | 101 | 50 | 35 | 11 | 11:00 a.m. |
| Anchorage, Alaska | 149 | 54 | 61 | 13 | 7:00 a.m. |
| Atlanta | 84 | 23 | 33 | 45 | 12:00 noon |
| Atlantic City, N.J. | 74 | 25 | 39 | 22 | 12:00 noon |
| Austin, Nev. | 117 | 4 | 39 | 29 | 9:00 a.m. |
| Baker, Ore. | 117 | 50 | 44 | 47 | 9:00 a.m. |
| Baltimore | 76 | 38 | 39 | 18 | 12:00 noon |
| Bangor, Me. | 68 | 47 | 44 | 48 | 12:00 noon |
| Birmingham, Ala. | 86 | 50 | 33 | 30 | 11:00 a.m. |
| Bismarck, N.D. | 100 | 47 | 46 | 48 | 11:00 a.m. |
| Boise, Idaho | 116 | 13 | 43 | 36 | 10:00 a.m. |
| Boston | 71 | 5 | 42 | 21 | 12:00 noon |
| Buffalo, N.Y. | 78 | 50 | 42 | 55 | 12:00 noon |
| Calgary, Alberta | 114 | 1 | 51 | 1 | 10:00 a.m. |
| Carlsbad, N.M. | 104 | 15 | 32 | 26 | 10:00 a.m. |
| Charleston, S.C. | 79 | 56 | 32 | 47 | 12:00 noon |
| Charleston, W.Va. | 81 | 38 | 38 | 21 | 12:00 noon |
| Charlotte, N.C. | 80 | 50 | 35 | 14 | 12:00 noon |
| Cheyenne, Wyo. | 104 | 52 | 41 | 9 | 10:00 a.m. |
| Chicago | 87 | 37 | 41 | 50 | 11:00 a.m. |
| Cincinnati | 84 | 30 | 39 | 8 | 12:00 noon |
| Cleveland | 81 | 37 | 41 | 28 | 12:00 noon |
| Columbia, S.C. | 81 | 2 | 34 | 0 | 12:00 noon |
| Columbus, Ohio | 83 | 1 | 40 | 0 | 12:00 noon |
| Dallas | 96 | 46 | 32 | 46 | 11:00 a.m. |
| Denver | 105 | 0 | 39 | 45 | 10:00 a.m. |
| Des Moines, Iowa | 93 | 37 | 41 | 35 | 11:00 a.m. |
| Detroit | 83 | 3 | 42 | 20 | 12:00 noon |
| Dubuque, Iowa | 90 | 40 | 42 | 31 | 11:00 a.m. |
| Duluth, Minn. | 92 | 5 | 46 | 49 | 11:00 a.m. |
| Eastport, Me. | 67 | 0 | 44 | 54 | 12:00 noon |
| El Centro, Calif. | 115 | 33 | 32 | 38 | 9:00 a.m. |
| El Paso | 106 | 29 | 31 | 46 | 11:00 a.m. |
| Eugene, Ore. | 123 | 5 | 44 | 3 | 9:00 a.m. |
| Fargo, N.D. | 96 | 48 | 46 | 52 | 11:00 a.m. |
| Flagstaff, Ariz. | 111 | 41 | 35 | 13 | 10:00 a.m. |
| Fresno, Calif. | 119 | 48 | 36 | 44 | 9:00 a.m. |
| Garden City, Kan. | 100 | 53 | 37 | 58 | 10:00 a.m. |
| Grand Junction, Colo. | 108 | 33 | 39 | 5 | 10:00 a.m. |
| Grand Rapids, Mich. | 85 | 40 | 42 | 58 | 12:00 noon |
| Havre, Mont. | 109 | 43 | 48 | 33 | 10:00 a.m. |
| Helena, Mont. | 112 | 2 | 46 | 35 | 10:00 a.m. |
| Honolulu | 157 | 50 | 21 | 18 | 7:00 a.m. |
| Hoquiam, Wash. | 123 | 54 | 46 | 59 | 9:00 a.m. |
| Hot Springs, Ark. | 93 | 3 | 34 | 31 | 11:00 a.m. |
| Idaho Falls, Idaho | 112 | 1 | 43 | 30 | 10:00 a.m. |
| Indianapolis | 86 | 10 | 39 | 46 | 12:00 noon |
| Jackson, Miss. | 90 | 12 | 32 | 20 | 11:00 a.m. |
| Jacksonville, Fla. | 81 | 40 | 30 | 22 | 12:00 noon |
| Juneau, Alaska | 134 | 24 | 58 | 18 | 9:00 a.m. |
| Kansas City, Mo. | 94 | 35 | 39 | 6 | 11:00 a.m. |
| Key West, Fla. | 81 | 48 | 24 | 33 | 12:00 noon |
| Kingston, Ont. | 76 | 30 | 44 | 15 | 12:00 noon |
| Klamath Falls, Ore. | 121 | 44 | 42 | 10 | 9:00 a.m. |
| Knoxville, Tenn. | 83 | 56 | 35 | 57 | 12:00 noon |
| Lander, Wyo. | 108 | 40 | 42 | 50 | 10:00 a.m. |
| Las Vegas, Nev. | 115 | 12 | 36 | 10 | 9:00 a.m. |
| Lewiston, Idaho | 117 | 2 | 46 | 24 | 9:00 a.m. |
| Lincoln, Neb. | 96 | 40 | 40 | 50 | 11:00 a.m. |
| London, Ont. | 81 | 34 | 43 | 2 | 12:00 noon |
| Los Angeles | 118 | 15 | 34 | 3 | 9:00 a.m. |
| Louisville, Ky. | 85 | 46 | 38 | 15 | 12:00 noon |
| Manchester, N.H. | 71 | 30 | 43 | 0 | 12:00 noon |
| Memphis, Tenn | 90 | 3 | 35 | 9 | 11:00 a.m. |
| Miami, Fla. | 80 | 12 | 25 | 46 | 12:00 noon |
| Milwaukee | 87 | 55 | 43 | 2 | 11:00 a.m. |
| Minneapolis | 93 | 14 | 44 | 59 | 11:00 a.m. |
| Mobile, Ala. | 88 | 3 | 30 | 42 | 11:00 a.m. |
| Montgomery, Ala. | 86 | 18 | 32 | 21 | 11:00 a.m. |
| Montpelier, Vt. | 72 | 32 | 44 | 15 | 12:00 noon |
| Montreal, Que. | 73 | 35 | 45 | 30 | 12:00 noon |
| Moose Jaw, Sask. | 105 | 31 | 50 | 37 | 10:00 a.m. |
| Nashville, Tenn. | 86 | 47 | 36 | 10 | 11:00 a.m. |
| Needles, Calif. | 114 | 36 | 34 | 50 | 9:00 a.m. |
| Nelson, B.C. | 117 | 17 | 49 | 30 | 9:00 a.m. |
| New Haven, Conn. | 72 | 55 | 41 | 19 | 12:00 noon |
| New Orleans | 90 | 4 | 29 | 57 | 11:00 a.m. |
| New York | 73 | 58 | 40 | 47 | 12:00 noon |
| Nogales, Ariz. | 110 | 56 | 31 | 21 | 10:00 a.m. |
| Nome, Alaska | 165 | 30 | 64 | 25 | 6:00 a.m. |
| North Platte, Neb. | 100 | 46 | 41 | 8 | 11:00 a.m. |
| Oklahoma City | 97 | 28 | 35 | 26 | 11:00 a.m. |
| Ottawa, Ont. | 75 | 43 | 45 | 24 | 12:00 noon |
| Philadelphia | 75 | 10 | 39 | 57 | 12:00 noon |
| Phoenix, Ariz. | 112 | 4 | 33 | 29 | 10:00 a.m. |
| Pierre, S.D. | 100 | 21 | 44 | 22 | 11:00 a.m. |
| Pittsburgh | 79 | 57 | 40 | 27 | 12:00 noon |
| Port Arthur, Ont. | 89 | 17 | 48 | 30 | 12:00 noon |
| Portland, Me. | 70 | 15 | 43 | 40 | 12:00 noon |
| Portland, Ore. | 122 | 41 | 45 | 31 | 9:00 a.m. |
| Providence, R.I. | 71 | 24 | 41 | 50 | 12:00 noon |
| Quebec, Que. | 71 | 11 | 46 | 49 | 12:00 noon |
| Raleigh, N.C. | 78 | 39 | 35 | 46 | 12:00 noon |
| Reno, Nev. | 119 | 49 | 39 | 30 | 9:00 a.m. |
| Richfield, Utah | 112 | 5 | 38 | 46 | 10:00 a.m. |
| Richmond, Va. | 77 | 29 | 37 | 33 | 12:00 noon |
| Roanoke, Va. | 79 | 57 | 37 | 17 | 12:00 noon |
| Sacramento, Calif. | 121 | 30 | 38 | 35 | 9:00 a.m. |
| St. John, N.B. | 66 | 10 | 45 | 18 | 1:00 p.m. |
| St. Louis | 90 | 12 | 38 | 35 | 11:00 a.m. |
| Salmon, Idaho | 113 | 54 | 45 | 11 | 10:00 a.m. |
| Salt Lake City, Utah | 111 | 54 | 40 | 46 | 10:00 a.m. |
| San Antonio | 98 | 33 | 29 | 23 | 11:00 a.m. |
| San Diego, Calif. | 117 | 10 | 32 | 42 | 9:00 a.m. |
| San Francisco | 122 | 26 | 37 | 47 | 9:00 a.m. |
| San Juan, P.R. | 66 | 10 | 18 | 30 | 1:00 p.m. |
| Santa Fe, N.M. | 105 | 57 | 35 | 41 | 10:00 a.m. |
| Sault Ste. Marie, Mich. | 84 | 21 | 46 | 30 | 11:00 a.m. |
| Savannah, Ga. | 81 | 5 | 32 | 5 | 12:00 noon |
| Scranton, Pa. | 75 | 39 | 41 | 24 | 12:00 noon |
| Seattle | 122 | 20 | 47 | 37 | 9:00 a.m. |
| Shreveport, La. | 93 | 42 | 32 | 28 | 11:00 a.m. |
| Sioux Falls, S.D. | 96 | 44 | 43 | 33 | 11:00 a.m. |
| Sitka, Alaska | 135 | 15 | 57 | 10 | 9:00 a.m. |
| Spokane, Wash. | 117 | 26 | 47 | 40 | 9:00 a.m. |
| Springfield, Ill. | 89 | 38 | 39 | 48 | 11:00 a.m. |
| Springfield, Mass. | 72 | 34 | 42 | 6 | 12:00 noon |
| Springfield, Mo. | 93 | 17 | 37 | 13 | 11:00 a.m. |
| Syracuse, N.Y. | 76 | 8 | 43 | 2 | 12:00 noon |
| Tampa, Fla. | 82 | 27 | 27 | 57 | 12:00 noon |
| Toronto, Ont. | 79 | 24 | 43 | 40 | 12:00 noon |
| Trinidad, Colo. | 104 | 30 | 37 | 10 | 10:00 a.m. |
| Victoria, B.C. | 123 | 21 | 48 | 25 | 9:00 a.m. |
| Watertown, N.Y. | 75 | 55 | 43 | 58 | 12:00 noon |
| Wichita, Kan. | 97 | 17 | 37 | 43 | 11:00 a.m. |
| Wilmington, N.C. | 77 | 57 | 34 | 14 | 12:00 noon |
| Winnipeg, Man. | 97 | 7 | 49 | 54 | 11:00 a.m. |

## World Population, Land Areas, and Elevations

| Area | Estimated population, in thousands, 1976 | Approximate land area, in thousands of sq mi. | Percent of total land area | Population density per sq mi. | Elevation, feet: Higest | Elevation, feet: Lowest | Dimensions, miles: East–West | Dimensions, miles: North–South |
|---|---|---|---|---|---|---|---|---|
| **WORLD** | 4,044,000 | 58,473 | 100.0 | 77.1[1] | Mt. Everest, Asia, 29,028 | Dead Sea, Asia, 1,290 below sea level | 24,902 | 24,860 |
| **ASIA**, incl. Phillippines, Indonesia, and European and Asiatic Turkey; excl. Asiatic U.S.S.R. | 2,304,000 | 10,678 | 18.2 | 215.8 | Mt. Everest, Tibet-Nepal, 29,028 | Dead Sea, Israel-Jordan, 1,290 below sea level | 5,400[2] | 5,300[2] |
| **AFRICA** | 412,000 | 11,707 | 20.0 | 35.2 | Mt. Kilimanjaro, Tanzania, 19,340 | Qattara Depression, Egypt, 440 below sea level | 4,600 | 5,000 |
| **NORTH AMERICA**, including Hawaii, Central America, and Caribbean region | 348,000 | 9,362 | 16.0 | 37.2 | Mt. McKinley, Alaska, 20,320 | Death Valley, Calif., 282 below sea level | 3,200[5] | 4,000[5] |
| **SOUTH AMERICA** | 224,000 | 6,885 | 11.8 | 32.5 | Mt. Aconcagua, Arg.-Chile, 23,034 | Sea level | 3,200 | 4,600 |
| **ANTARCTICA** | — | 6,000 | 10.3 | — | Vinson Massif, Sentinel Range, 16,863 | Sea level | — | — |
| **EUROPE**, incl. Iceland; excl. European U.S.S.R. and European Turkey | 476,000 | 1,906 | 3.3 | 249.7 | Mont Blanc, France, 15,781 | Sea level | 3,300[3] | 2,400[3] |
| **OCENIA**, incl. Australia, New Zealand, Melanesia, Micronesia, and Polynesia[4] | 21,700 | 3,286 | 5.6 | 6.6 | Mauna Kea, Hawaii, 13,796 | Lake Eyre, Australia, 38 below sea level | — | — |
| **U.S.S.R.**, both European and Asiatic | 258,000 | 8,649 | 14.8 | 29.8 | Communism Peak, Pamir, 24,547 | Caspian Sea, 96 below sea level | 5,000 | 2,500 |

1. In computing density per square mile, the area of Antarctica is omitted. 2. Including Asiatic U.S.S.R. 3. Including European U.S.S.R. 4. Although Hawaii is geographically part of Oceania, its population is included in the population figure for North America. 5. Excludes Hawaii.

## Some Countries With High Population Densities (per square mile)

| | | | | | | | |
|---|---|---|---|---|---|---|---|
| Monaco | 41,095.9 | South Korea | 973.1 | Lebanon | 788.3 | El Salvador | 534.2 |
| Singapore | 10,354.0 | Netherlands | 887.3 | West Germany | 630.4 | India | 506.6 |
| Bangladesh | 1,483.9 | Belgium | 835.7 | United Kingdom | 587.8 | Italy | 487.3 |
| China, Rep. of | 1,200.5 | Japan | 799.0 | Sri Lanka | 560.0 | Israel | 461.4 |

# AWARDS

## Nobel Prizes

The Nobel prizes are awarded under the will of Alfred Bernhard Nobel, Swedish chemist and engineer, who died in 1896. The interest of the fund is divided annually among the persons who have made the most outstanding contributions in the fields of physics, chemistry, and physiology of medicine, who have produced the most distinguished literary work of an idealist tendency, and who have contributed most toward world peace.

In 1968, a Nobel Prize of economic sciences was established by Riksbank, the Swedish bank, in celebration of its 300th anniversary. The prize was awarded for the first time in 1969.

The prizes for physics and chemistry are awarded by the Swedish Academy of Science in Stockholm, the one for physiology or medicine by the Caroline Medical Institute in Stockholm, that for literature by the academy in Stockholm, and that for peace by a committee of five elected by the Norwegian Storting. The distribution of prizes was begun on December 10, 1901, the anniversary of Nobel's death. The amount of each prize varies with the income from the fund and currently is about $145,000. No Nobel prizes were awarded for 1940, 1941, and 1942; prizes for Literature were not awarded for 1914, 1918, and 1943.

### PEACE

**1901** Henri Dunant (Switzerland); Frederick Passy (France)
**1902** Elie Ducommun and Albert Gobat (Switzerland)
**1903** Sir William R. Cremer (England)
**1904** Institut de Droit International (Belgium)
**1905** Bertha von Suttner (Austria)
**1906** Theodore Roosevelt (U.S.)
**1907** Ernesto T. Moneta (Italy) and Louis Renault (France)
**1908** Klas P. Arnoldson (Sweden) and Frederik Bajer (Denmark)
**1909** Auguste M. F. Beernaert (Belgium) and Baron Paul H. B. B. d'Estournelles de Constant de Rebecque (France)
**1910** Bureau International Permanent de la Paix (Switzerland)
**1911** Tobias M. C. Asser (Holland) and Alfred H. Fried (Austria)
**1912** Elihu Root (U.S.)
**1913** Henri La Fontaine (Belgium)
**1915** No award
**1916** No award
**1917** International Red Cross
**1919** Woodrow Wilson (U.S.)
**1920** Léon Bourgeois (France)
**1921** Karl H. Branting (Sweden) and Christian L. Lange (Norway)
**1922** Fridtjof Nansen (Norway)
**1923** No award
**1924** No award
**1925** Sir Austen Chamberlain (England) and Charles G. Dawes (U.S.)
**1926** Aristide Briand (France) and Gustav Stresemann (Germany)
**1927** Ferdinand Buisson (France) and Ludwig Quidde (Germany)
**1928** No award
**1929** Frank B. Kellogg (U.S.)
**1930** Lars O. J. Söderblom (Sweden)
**1931** Jane Addams and Nicholas M. Butler (U.S.)
**1932** No award
**1933** Sir Norman Angell (England)
**1934** Arthur Henderson (England)
**1935** Karl von Ossietzky (Germany)
**1936** Carlos de S. Lamas (Argentina)
**1937** Lord Cecil of Chelwood (England)
**1938** Office International Nansen pour les Réfugiés (Switzerland)
**1939** No award
**1944** International Red Cross
**1945** Cordell Hull (U.S.)
**1946** Emily G. Balch and John R. Mott (U.S.)
**1947** American Friends Service Committee (U.S.) and British Society of Friends' Service Council (England)
**1948** No award
**1949** Lord John Boyd Orr (Scotland)
**1950** Ralph J. Bunche (U.S.)
**1951** Léon Jouhaux (France)
**1952** Albert Schweitzer (French Equatorial Africa)
**1953** George C. Marshall (U.S.)
**1954** Office of U.N. High Commissioner for Refugees
**1955** No award
**1956** No award
**1957** Lester B. Pearson (Canada)
**1958** Rev. Dominique Georges Henri Pire (Belgium)
**1959** Philip John Noel-Baker (England)
**1960** Albert John Luthuli (South Africa)
**1961** Dag Hammarskjöld (Sweden)
**1962** Linus Pauling (U.S.)
**1963** Intl. Comm. of Red Cross; League of Red Cross Societies (both Geneva)
**1964** Rev. Dr. Martin Luther King, Jr. (U.S.)
**1965** UNICEF (United Nations Children's Fund)
**1966** No award
**1967** No award
**1968** René Cassin (France)
**1969** International Labour Organization
**1970** Norman E. Borlaug (U.S.)
**1971** Willy Brandt (West Germany)
**1972** No award
**1973** Henry A. Kissinger (U.S.); Le Duc Tho (North Vietnam)[1]
**1974** Eisaku Sato (Japan); Sean MacBride (Ireland)
**1975** Andrei D. Sakharov (U.S.S.R.)
**1976** Mairead Corrigan and Betty Williams (both Northern Ireland)
**1977** Amnesty International

1. Le Duc Tho refused prize, charging that peace had not yet been really established in South Vietnam.

## LITERATURE

1901 René F. A. Sully Prudhomme (France)
1902 Theodor Mommsen (Germany)
1903 Björnstjerne Björnson (Norway)
1904 Frédéric Mistral (France) and José Echegaray (Spain)
1905 Henryk Sienkiewicz (Poland)
1906 Giosuè Carducci (Italy)
1907 Rudyard Kipling (England)
1908 Rudolf Eucken (Germany)
1909 Selma Lagerlöf (Sweden)
1910 Paul von Heyse (Germany)
1911 Maurice Maeterlinck (Belgium)
1912 Gerhart Hauptmann (Germany)
1913 Rabindranath Tagore (India)
1915 Romain Rolland (France)
1916 Verner von Heidenstam (Sweden)
1917 Karl Gjellerup (Denmark) and Henrik Pontoppidan (Denmark)
1919 Carl Spitteler (Switzerland)
1920 Knut Hamsun (Norway)
1921 Anatole France (France)
1922 Jacinto Benavente (Spain)
1923 William B. Yeats (Ireland)
1924 Wladyslaw Reymont (Poland)
1925 George Bernard Shaw (England)
1926 Grazia Deledda (Italy)
1927 Henri Bergson (France)
1928 Sigrid Undset (Norway)
1929 Thomas Mann (Germany)
1930 Sinclair Lewis (U.S.)
1931 Erik A. Karlfeldt (Sweden)
1932 John Galsworthy (England)
1933 Ivan G. Bunin (Russia)
1934 Luigi Pirandello (Italy)
1935 No award
1936 Eugene O'Neill (U.S.)
1937 Roger Martin du Gard (France)
1938 Pearl S. Buck (U.S.)
1939 Frans Eemil Sillanpää (Finland)
1944 Johannes V. Jensen (Denmark)
1945 Gabriela Mistral (Chile)
1946 Hermann Hesse (Switzerland)
1947 André Gide (France)
1948 Thomas Stearns Eliot (England)
1949 William Faulkner (U.S.)
1950 Bertrand Russell (England)
1951 Pär Lagerkvist (Sweden)
1952 Francois Mauriac (France)
1953 Sir Winston Churchill (England)
1954 Ernest Hemingway (U.S.)
1955 Halldór Kiljan Laxness (Iceland)
1956 Juan Ramón Jiménez (Spain)
1957 Albert Camus (France)
1958 Boris Pasternak (U.S.S.R.) (declined)
1959 Salvatore Quasimodo (Italy)
1960 St.-John Perse (Alexis St.-Léger Léger) (France)
1961 Ivo Andric (Yugoslavia)
1962 John Steinbeck (U.S.)
1963 Giorgios Seferis (Seferiades) (Greece)
1964 Jean-Paul Sartre (France) (declined)
1965 Mikhail Sholokhov (U.S.S.R.)
1966 Shmuel Yosef Agnon (Israel) and Nelly Sachs (Sweden)
1967 Miguel Angel Asturias (Guatemala)
1968 Yasunari Kawabata (Japan)
1969 Samuel Beckett (France)
1970 Aleksandr Solzhenitsyn (U.S.S.R.)
1971 Pablo Neruda (Chile)
1972 Heinrich Böll (Germany)
1973 Patrick White (Australia)
1974 Eyvind Johnson and Harry Martinson (both Sweden)
1975 Eugenio Montale (Italy)
1976 Saul Bellow (U.S.)
1977 Vicente Aleixandre (Spain)

## PHYSICS

1901 Wilhelm K. Roentgen (Germany), for discovery of Roentgen rays
1902 Hendrik A. Lorentz and Pieter Zeeman (Netherlands), for work on influence of magnetism upon radiation
1903 A. Henri Becquerel (France), for work on spontaneous radioactivity; and Pierre and Marie Curie (France), for study of radiation
1904 John Strutt (Lord Rayleigh) (England), for discovery of argon in investigating gas density
1905 Philipp Lenard (Germany), for work with cathode rays
1906 Sir Joseph Thomson (England), for investigations on passage of electricity through gases
1907 Albert A. Michelson (U.S.), for spectroscopic and metrologic investigations
1908 Gabriel Lippmann (France), for method of reproducing colors by photography
1909 Guglielmo Marconi (Italy) and Ferdinand Braun (Germany), for development of wireless
1910 Johannes D. van der Waals (Netherlands), for work with the equation of state for gases and liquids
1911 Wilhelm Wien (Germany), for his laws governing the radiation of heat
1912 Gustaf Dalén (Sweden), for discovery of automatic regulators used in lighting lighthouses and light buoys
1913 Heike Kamerlingh-Onnes (Netherlands), for work leading to production of liquid helium
1914 Max von Laue (Germany), for discovery of diffraction of Roentgen rays passing through crystals
1915 Sir William Bragg and William L. Bragg (England), for analysis of crystal structure by X rays
1916 No award
1917 Charles G. Barkla (England), for discovery of Roentgen radiation of the elements
1918 Max Planck (Germany), discoveries in connection with quantum theory
1919 Johannes Stark (Germany), discovery of Doppler effect in Canal rays and decomposition of spectrum lines by electric fields
1920 Charles E. Guillaume (Switzerland), for discoveries of anomalies in nickel steel alloys
1921 Albert Einstein (Germany), for discovery of the law of the photoelectric effect
1922 Niels Bohr (Denmark), for investigation of structure of atoms and radiations emanating from them
1923 Robert A. Millikan (U.S.), for work on elementary charge of electricity and photoelectric phenomena
1924 Karl M. G. Siegbahn (Sweden), for investigations in X-ray spectroscopy
1925 James Franck and Gustav Hertz (Germany), for discovery of laws governing impact of electrons upon atoms
1926 Jean B. Perrin (France), for work on discontinuous structure of matter and discovery of the equilibrium of sedimentation
1927 Arthur H. Compton (U.S.), for discovery of Compton phenomenon; and Charles T. R. Wilson (England), for method of perceiving paths taken by electrically charged particles
1928 In 1929, the 1928 prize was awarded to Sir Owen Richardson (England), for work on the phenomenon of thermionics and discovery of the Richardson Law

**1929** Prince Louis Victor de Broglie (France), for discovery of the wave character of electrons
**1930** Sir Chandrasekhara Raman (India), for work on diffusion of light and discovery of the Raman effect
**1931** No award
**1932** In 1933, the prize for 1932 was awarded to Werner Heisenberg (Germany), for creation of the quantum mechanics
**1933** Erwin Schrödinger (Austria) and Paul A. M. Dirac (England), for discovery of new fertile forms of the atomic theory
**1934** No award
**1935** James Chadwick (England), for discovery of the neutron
**1936** Victor F. Hess (Austria), for discovery of cosmic radiation; and Carl D. Anderson (U.S.), for discovery of the positron
**1937** Clinton J. Davisson (U.S.) and George P. Thomson (England), for discovery of diffraction of electrons by crystals
**1938** Enrico Fermi (Italy), for identification of new radioactivity elements and discovery of nuclear reactions effected by slow neutrons
**1939** Ernest Orlando Lawrence (U.S.), for development of the cyclotron
**1943** Otto Stern (U.S.), for detection of magnetic momentum of protons
**1944** Isidor Isaac Rabi (U.S.), for work on magnetic movements of atomic particles
**1945** Wolfgang Pauli (Austria), for work on atomic fissions
**1946** Percy Williams Bridgman (U.S.), for studies and inventions in high-pressure physics
**1947** Sir Edward Appleton (England), for discovery of layer which reflects radio short waves in the ionosphere
**1948** Patrick M. S. Blackett (England), for improvement on Wilson chamber and discoveries in cosmic radiation
**1949** Hideki Yukawa (Japan), for mathematical prediction, in 1935, of the meson
**1950** Cecil Frank Powell (England), for method of photographic study of atom nucleus, and for discoveries about mesons
**1951** Sir John Douglas Cockcroft (England) and Ernest T. S. Walton (Ireland), for work in 1932 on transmutation of atomic nuclei
**1952** Edward Mills Purcell and Felix Bloch (U.S.), for work in measurement of magnetic fields in atomic nuclei
**1953** Fritz Zernike (Netherlands), for development of "phase contrast" microscope
**1954** Max Born (England), for work in quantum mechanics; and Walther Bothe (Germany), for work in cosmic radiation
**1955** Polykarp Kusch and Willis E. Lamb, Jr. (U.S.), for atomic measurements
**1956** William Shockley, Walter H. Brattain, and John Bardeen (U.S.), for developing electronic transistor
**1957** Tsung Dao Lee and Chen Ning Yang (China), for disproving principle of conservation of parity
**1958** Pavel A. Cherenkov, Ilya M. Frank, and Igor E. Tamm (U.S.S.R.), for work resulting in development of cosmic-ray counter
**1959** Emilio Segre and Owen Chamberlain (U.S.), for demonstrating the existence of the anti-proton
**1960** Donald A. Glaser (U.S.), for invention of "bubble chamber" to study subatomic particles
**1961** Robert Hofstadter (U.S.), for determination of shape and size of atomic nucleus; Rudolf Mössbauer (Germany), for method of producing and measuring recoil-free gamma rays
**1962** Lev D. Landau (U.S.S.R.), for his theories about condensed matter
**1963** Eugene Paul Wigner, Maria Goeppert Mayer (both U.S.), and J. Hans D. Jensen (Germany), for research on structure of atom and its nucleus
**1964** Charles Hard Townes (U.S.), Nikolai G. Basov, and Aleksandr M. Prochorov (both U.S.S.R.), for developing maser and laser principle of producing high-intensity radiation
**1965** Richard P. Feynman, Julian S. Schwinger (both U.S.) and Shinichero Tomonaga (Japan), for research in quantum electrodynamics
**1966** Alfred Kastler (France), for work on energy levels inside atom
**1967** Hans A. Bethe (U.S.), for work on energy production of stars
**1968** Luis Walter Alvarez (U.S.), for study of subatomic particles
**1969** Murray Gell-Mann (U.S.), for study of subatomic particles
**1970** Hannes Alfvén (Sweden), for theories in plasma physics; and Louis Néel (France), for discoveries in antiferromagnetism and ferrimagnetism
**1971** Dennis Gabor (England), for invention of holographic method of three-dimensional imagery
**1972** John Bardeen, Leon N. Cooper, and John Robert Schrieffer (all U.S.), for theory of superconductivity, where electrical resistance in certain metals vanishes above absolute zero temperature
**1973** Ivar Giaever (U.S.), Leo Esaki (Japan), and Brian D. Josephson (U.K.), for theories that have advanced and expanded the field of miniature electronics
**1974** Antony Hewish (England), for discovery of pulsars; Martin Ryle (England), for using radiotelescopes to probe outer space with high degree of precision
**1975** James Rainwater (U.S.) and Ben Mottelson and Aage N. Bohr (both Denmark), for showing that the atomic nucleus is asymmetrical
**1976** Burton Richter and Samuel C.C. Ting (U.S.), for discovery of subatomic particles known as J and psi
**1977** Philip W. Anderson and John H. Van Vleck (both U.S.), and Nevill F. Mott (U.K.), for work underlying computer memories and electronic devices

## CHEMISTRY

**1901** Jacobus H. van't Hoff (Netherlands), for laws of chemical dynamics and osmotic pressure in solutions
**1902** Emil Fischer (Germany), for experiments in sugar and purin groups of substances
**1903** Svante A. Arrhenius (Sweden), for his electrolytic theory of dissociation
**1904** Sir William Ramsay (England), for discovery and determination of place of inert gaseous elements in air
**1905** Adolf von Baeyer (Germany), for work on organic dyes and hydroaromatic combinations
**1906** Henri Moissan (France), for isolation of fluorine, and introduction of electric furnace
**1907** Eduard Buchner (Germany), discovery of cell-less fermentation and investigations in biological chemistry
**1908** Sir Ernest Rutherford (England), for investigations into disintegration of elements
**1909** Wilhelm Ostwald (Germany), for work on catalysis and investigations into chemical equilibri-

um and reaction rates
1910 Otto Wallach (Germany), for work in the field of alicyclic compounds
1911 Marie Curie (France), for discovery of elements radium and polonium
1912 Victor Grignard (France), for reagent discovered by him; and Paul Sabatier (France), for methods of hydrogenating organic compounds
1913 Alfred Werner (Switzerland), for linking up atoms within the molecule
1914 Theodore W. Richards (U.S.), for determining atomic weight of many chemical elements
1915 Richard Willstätter (Germany), for research into coloring matter of plants, especially chlorophyll
1916 No award
1917 No award
1918 Fritz Haber (Germany), for synthetic production of ammonia
1919 No award
1920 Walther Nernst (Germany), for work in thermochemistry
1921 Frederick Soddy (England), for investigations into origin and nature of isotopes
1922 Francis W. Aston (England), for discovery of isotopes in nonradioactive elements and for discovery of the whole number rule
1923 Fritz Pregl (Austria), for method of microanalysis of organic substances discovered by him
1924 No award
1925 In 1926, the 1925 prize was awarded to Richard Zsigmondy (Germany), for work on the heterogeneous nature of colloid solutions
1926 Theodor Svedberg (Sweden), for work on disperse systems
1927 In 1928 the 1927 prize was awarded to Heinrich Wieland (Germany), for investigations of bile acids and kindred substances
1928 Adolf Windaus (Germany), for investigations on constitution of the sterols and their connection with vitamins
1929 Sir Arthur Harden (England) and Hans K. A. S. von Euler-Chelpin (Sweden), for research of fermentation of sugars
1930 Hans Fischer (Germany), for work on coloring matter of blood and leaves and for his synthesis of hemin
1931 Karl Bosch and Friedrich Bergius (Germany), for invention and development of chemical high-pressure methods
1932 Irving Langmuir (U.S.), for work in realm of surface chemistry
1933 No award
1934 Harold C. Urey (U.S.), for discovery of heavy hydrogen
1935 Frédéric and Irène Joliot-Curie (France), for synthesis of new radioactive elements
1936 Peter J. W. Debye (Netherlands), for investigations on dipole moments and diffraction of X rays and electrons in gases
1937 Walter N. Haworth (England), for research on carbohydrates and Vitamin C; and Paul Karrer (Switzerland), for work on carotenoids, flavins, and Vitamins A and B
1938 Richard Kuhn (Germany), for carotinoid study and vitamin research (declined the prize)
1939 Adolf Butenandt (Germany), for work on sexual hormones (declined the prize); and Leopold Ružička (Switzerland), for work with polymethylenes
1943 Georg Hevesy De Heves (Hungary), for work on use of isotopes as indicators
1944 Otto Hahn (Germany), for work on atomic fission
1945 Artturi Ilmari Virtanen (Finland), for research in the field of conservation of fodder
1946 James B. Sumner (U.S.), for crystallizing enzymes; John H. Northrop and Wendell M. Stanley (U.S.), for preparing enzymes and virus proteins in pure form
1947 Sir Robert Robinson (England), for research in plant substances
1948 Arne Tiselius (Sweden), for biochemical discoveries and isolation of mouse paralysis virus
1949 William Francis Giauque (U.S.), for research in thermodynamics, especially effects of low temperature
1950 Otto Diels and Kurt Alder (Germany), for discovery of diene synthesis enabling scientists to study structure of organic matter
1951 Glenn T. Seaborg and Edwin H. McMillan (U.S.), for discovery of plutonium
1952 Archer John Porter Martin and Richard Laurence Millington Synge (England), for development of partition chromatography
1953 Hermann Staudinger (Germany), for research in giant molecules
1954 Linus C. Pauling (U.S.), for study of forces holding together protein and other molecules
1955 Vincent du Vigneaud (U.S.), for work on pituitary hormones
1956 Sir Cyril Hinshelwood (England) and Nikolai N. Semenov (U.S.S.R.), for parallel research on chemical reaction kinetics
1957 Sir Alexander Todd (England), for research with chemical compounds that are factors in heredity
1958 Frederick Sanger (England), for determining molecular structure of insulin
1959 Jaroslav Heyrovsky (Czechoslovakia), for development of polarography, an electrochemical method of analysis
1960 Willard F. Libby (U.S.), for "atomic time clock" to measure age of objects by measuring their radioactivity
1961 Melvin Calvin (U.S.), for establishing chemical steps during photosynthesis
1962 Max F. Perutz and John C. Kendrew (England), for mapping protein molecules with X rays
1963 Carl Ziegler (Germany) and Giulio Natta (Italy), for work in uniting simple hydrocarbons into large molecule substances
1964 Dorothy Mary Crowfoot Hodgkin (England), for determining structure of compounds needed in combating pernicious anemia
1965 Robert B. Woodward (U.S.), for work in synthesizing complicated organic compounds
1966 Robert Sanderson Mulliken (U.S.), for research on bond holding atoms together in molecule
1967 Manfred Eigen (Germany), Ronald G. W. Norrish, and George Porter (both England), for work in high-speed chemical reactions
1968 Lars Onsager (U.S.), for development of system of equations in thermodynamics
1969 Derek H. R. Barton (England) and Odd Hassel (Norway), for study of organic molecules
1970 Luis F. Leloir (Argentina), for discovery of sugar nucleotides and their role in biosynthesis of carbohydrates
1971 Gerhard Herzberg (Canada), for contributions to knowledge of electronic structure and geometry of molecules, particularly free radicals
1972 Christian Boehmer Anfinsen, Stanford Moore, and William Howard Stein (all U.S.), for pioneering studies in enzymes
1973 Ernst Otto Fischer (W. Germany) and Geoffrey

Wilkinson (U.K.), for work that could solve problem of automobile exhaust pollution

**1974** Paul J. Flory (U.S.), for developing analytic methods to study properties and molecular structure of long-chain molecules

**1975** John W. Cornforth (Australia) and Vladimir Prelog (Switzerland), for research on structure of biological molecules such as antibiotics and cholesterol

**1976** William N. Lipscomb, Jr. (U.S.), for work on the structure and bonding mechanisms of boranes

**1977** Ilya Prigogine (Belgium), for contributions to nonequilibrium thermodynamics, particularly the theory of dissipative structures

## PHYSIOLOGY OR MEDICINE

**1901** Emil A. von Behring (Germany), for work on serum therapy against diphtheria

**1902** Sir Ronald Ross (England), for work on malaria

**1903** Niels R. Finsen (Denmark), for his treatment of lupus vulgaris with concentrated light rays

**1904** Ivan P. Pavlov (U.S.S.R.), for work on the physiology of digestion

**1905** Robert Koch (Germany), for work on tuberculosis

**1906** Camillo Golgi (Italy) and Santiago Ramón y Cajal (Spain), for work on structure of the nervous system

**1907** Charles L. A. Laveran (France), for work with protozoa in the generation of disease

**1908** Paul Ehrlich (Germany), and Elie Metchnikoff (U.S.S.R.), for work on immunity

**1909** Theodor Kocher (Switzerland), for work on the thyroid gland

**1910** Albrecht Kossel (Germany), for achievements in the chemistry of the cell

**1911** Allvar Gullstrand (Sweden), for work on the dioptrics of the eye

**1912** Alexis Carrel (France), for work on vascular ligature and grafting of blood vessels and organs

**1913** Charles Richet (France), for work on anaphylaxy

**1914** Robert Bárány (Austria), for work on physiology and pathology of the vestibular system

**1915** No award

**1916** No award

**1917** No award

**1918** No award

**1919** Jules Bordet (Belgium), for discoveries in connection with immunity

**1920** August Krogh (Denmark), for discovery of regulation of capillaries' motor mechanism

**1921** No award

**1922** In 1923, the 1922 prize was shared by Archibald V. Hill (England), for discovery relating to heat-production in muscles; and Otto Meyerhof (Germany), for correlation between consumption of oxygen and production of lactic acid in muscles

**1923** Sir Frederick Banting (Canada) and John J. R. Macleod (Scotland), for discovery of insulin

**1924** Willem Einthoven (Netherlands), for discovery of the mechanism of the electrocardiogram

**1925** No award

**1926** Johannes Fibiger (Denmark), for discovery of the Spiroptera carcinoma

**1927** Julius Wagner-Jauregg (Austria), for use of malaria inoculation in treatment of dementia paralytica

**1928** Charles Nicolle (France), for work on typhus exanthematicus

**1929** Christiaan Eijkman (Netherlands), for discovery of the antineuritic vitamins; and Sir Frederick Hopkins (England), for discovery of growth-promoting vitamins

**1930** Karl Landsteiner (U.S.), for discovery of human blood groups

**1931** Otto H. Warburg (Germany), for discovery of the character and mode of action of the respiratory ferment

**1932** Sir Charles Sherrington (England) and Edgar D. Adrian (U.S.), for discoveries of the function of the neuron

**1933** Thomas H. Morgan (U.S.), for discoveries on hereditary function of the chromosomes

**1934** George H. Whipple, George R. Minot, and William P. Murphy (U.S.), for discovery of liver therapy against anemias

**1935** Hans Spemann (Germany), for discovery of the organizer-effect in embryonic development

**1936** Sir Henry Dale (England) and Otto Loewi (Germany), for discoveries on chemical transmission of nerve impulses

**1937** Albert Szent-Györgyi von Nagyrapolt (Hungary), for discoveries on biological combustion

**1938** Corneille Heymans (Belgium), for determining importance of sinus and aorta mechanisms in the regulation of respiration

**1939** Gerhard Domagk (Germany), for antibacterial effect of prontocilate

**1943** Henrik Dam (Denmark) and Edward A. Doisy (U.S.), for analysis of Vitamin K

**1944** Joseph Erlanger and Herbert Spencer Gasser (U.S.), for work on functions of the nerve threads

**1945** Sir Alexander Fleming, Ernst Boris Chain, and Sir Howard Florey (England), for discovery of penicillin

**1946** Herman J. Muller (U.S.), for hereditary effects of X rays on genes

**1947** Carl F. and Gerty T. Cori (U.S.), for work on animal starch metabolism; Bernardo A. Houssay (Argentina), for study of pituitary

**1948** Paul Mueller (Switzerland), for discovery of insect-killing properties of DDT

**1949** Walter Rudolf Hess (Switzerland), for research on brain control of body; and Antonio Caetano de Abreu Freire Egas Moniz (Portugal), for development of brain operation

**1950** Philip S. Hench, Edward C. Kendall (both U.S.), and Tadeus Reichstein (Switzerland), for discoveries about hormones of adrenal cortex

**1951** Max Theiler (South Africa), for development of anti-yellow-fever vaccine

**1952** Selman A. Waksman (U.S.), for co-discovery of streptomycin

**1953** Fritz A. Lipmann (Germany-U.S.) and Hans Adolph Krebs (Germany-England), for studies of living cells

**1954** John F. Enders, Thomas H. Weller, and Frederick C. Robbins (U.S.), for work with cultivation of polio virus

**1955** Hugo Theorell (Sweden), for work on oxidation enzymes

**1956** Dickinson W. Richards, Jr., André F. Cournand (both U.S.), and Werner Forssmann (Germany), for new techniques in treating heart disease

**1957** Daniel Bovet (Italy), for development of drugs to relieve allergies and relax muscles during surgery

**1958** Joshua Lederberg (U.S.), for work with genetic mechanisms; George W. Beadle and Edward L. Tatum (U.S.), for discovering how genes transmit hereditary characteristics

**1959** Severo Ochoa and Arthur Kornberg (U.S.), for discoveries related to compounds within chromosomes, which play a vital role in heredity

**1960** Sir Macfarlane Burnet (Australia) and Peter Brian Medawar (England), for discovery of acquired immunological tolerance

**1961** Georg von Bekesy (U.S.), for discoveries about physical mechanisms of stimulation within cochlea

**1962** James D. Watson (U.S.), Maurice H. F. Wilkins, and Francis H. C. Crick (England), for determining structure of deoxyribonucleic acid (DNA)

**1963** Alan Lloyd Hodgkin, Andrew Fielding Huxley (both England), and Sir John Carew Eccles (Australia), for research on nerve cells

**1964** Konrad E. Bloch (U.S.) and Feodor Lynen (Germany), for research on mechanism and regulation of cholesterol and fatty acid metabolism

**1965** François Jacob, André Lwolff, and Jacques Monod (France), for study of regulatory activities in body cells

**1966** Charles Brenton Huggins (U.S.), for studies in hormone treatment of cancer of prostate; Francis Peyton Rous (U.S.), for discovery of tumor-producing viruses

**1967** Haldan K. Hartline, George Wald, and Ragnar Granit (U.S.), for work on human eye

**1968** Robert W. Holley, Har Gobind Khorana, and Marshall W. Nirenberg (U.S.), for studies of genetic code

**1969** Max Delbruck, Alfred D. Hershey, and Salvador E. Luria (U.S.), for study of mechanism of virus infection in living cells

**1970** Julius Axelrod (U.S.), Ulf S. von Euler (Sweden), and Sir Bernard Katz (England), for studies of how nerve impulses are transmitted within the body

**1971** Earl W. Sutherland, Jr., (U.S.), for research on how hormones work

**1972** Gerald M. Edelman (U.S.), and Rodney R. Porter (U.K.), for research on the chemical structure and nature of antibodies

**1973** Karl von Frisch and Konrad Lorenz (Austria), and Nikolaas Tinbergen (Netherlands), for their studies of individual and social behavior patterns

**1974** George E. Palade and Christian de Duve (both U.S.) and Albert Claude (Belgium), for contributions to understanding inner workings of living cells

**1975** David Baltimore, Howard M. Temin and Renato Dulbecco (all U.S.), for work in interaction between tumor viruses and genetic material of the cell

**1976** Baruch S. Blumberg and D. Carleton Gajdusek (U.S.), for discoveries concerning new mechanisms for the origin and dissemination of infectious diseases

**1977** Rosalyn S. Yalow, Roger C. L. Guillemin, and Andrew V. Schally (all U.S.), for research in role of hormones in chemistry of the body

### ECONOMIC SCIENCE

**1969** Ragnar Frisch (Norway) and Jan Tinbergen (Netherlands), for work in econometrics (application of mathematics and statistical methods to economic theories and problems)

**1970** Paul A. Samuelson (U.S.), for efforts to raise the level of scientific analysis in economic theory

**1971** Simon Kuznets (U.S.), for developing concept of using a country's gross national product to determine its economic growth

**1972** Kenneth J. Arrow (U.S.) and Sir John R. Hicks (U.K.), for theories that help to assess business risk and government economic and welfare policies

**1973** Wassily Leontief (U.S.), for devising the input-output technique to determine how different sectors of an economy interact

**1974** Gunnar Myrdal (Sweden) and Friedrich A. von Hayek (Austria), for pioneering analysis of the interdependence of economic, social and institutional phenomena

**1975** Leonid V. Kantorovich (U.S.S.R.) and Tjalling C. Koopmans (U.S.), for work on the theory of optimum allocation of resources

**1976** Milton Friedman (U.S.), for work in consumption analysis and monetary history and theory, and for demonstration of complexity of stabilization policy

**1977** Bertil Ohlin (Sweden) and James E. Meade (U.K.), for contributions to theory of international trade and international capital movements

## Enrico Fermi Award

Named in honor of Enrico Fermi, the atomic pioneer, the $25,000 award is given in recognition of "exceptional and altogether outstanding" scientific and technical achievement in atomic energy.

1954 Enrico Fermi
1956 John von Neumann
1957 Ernest O. Lawrence
1958 Eugene P. Wigner
1959 Glenn T. Seaborg
1961 Hans A. Bethe
1962 Edward Teller
1963 J. Robert Oppenheimer
1964 Hyman G. Rickover
1966 Otto Hahn, Lise Meitner, and Fritz Strassman
1968 John A. Wheeler
1969 Walter H. Zinn
1970 Norris E. Bradbury
1971 Shields Warren and Stafford L. Warren
1972 Manson Benedict
1976 William L. Russell

## Poets Laureate of England

| | |
|---|---|
| Edmund Spenser | 1591–1599 |
| Samuel Daniel | 1599–1619 |
| Ben Jonson | 1619–1637 |
| William Davenant | 1638–1668 |
| John Dryden[1] | 1670–1689 |
| Thomas Shadwell | 1689–1692 |
| Nahum Tate | 1692–1715 |
| Nicholas Rowe | 1715–1718 |
| Laurence Eusden | 1718–1730 |
| Colley Cibber | 1730–1757 |
| William Whitehead | 1757–1785 |
| Thomas Warton | 1785–1790 |
| Henry James Pye | 1790–1813 |
| Robert Southey | 1813–1843 |
| William Wordsworth | 1843–1850 |
| Alfred Lord Tennyson | 1850–1892 |
| Alfred Austin | 1896–1913 |
| Robert Bridges | 1913–1930 |
| John Masefield | 1930–1967 |
| C. Day Lewis | 1967–1972 |
| Sir John Betjeman | 1972– |

1. First to bear the title officially. *Source: Encyclopaedia Britannica.*

# Pulitzer Prize Awards

**(For years not listed, no award was made.)**

*Source:* Columbia University.

## Pulitzer Prizes in Journalism

### MERITORIOUS PUBLIC SERVICE

**1918** *New York Times;* also special award to Minna Lewinson and Henry Beetle Hough
**1919** *Milwaukee Journal*
**1921** *Boston Post*
**1922** *New York World*
**1923** *Memphis Commercial Appeal*
**1924** *New York World*
**1926** *Columbus* (Ga.) *Enquirer Sun*
**1927** *Canton* (Ohio) *Daily News*
**1928** *Indianapolis Times*
**1929** *New York Evening World*
**1931** *Atlanta Constitution*
**1932** *Indianapolis News*
**1933** *New York World-Telegram*
**1934** *Medford* (Ore.) *Mail Tribune*
**1935** *Sacramento Bee*
**1936** *Cedar Rapids* (Iowa) *Gazette*
**1937** *St. Louis Post-Dispatch*
**1938** *Bismarck* (N.D.) *Tribune*
**1939** *Miami Daily News*
**1940** *Waterbury* (Conn.) *Republican* and *American*
**1941** *St. Louis Post-Dispatch*
**1942** *Los Angeles Times*
**1943** *Omaha World-Herald*
**1944** *New York Times*
**1945** *Detroit Free Press*
**1946** *Scranton* (Pa.) *Times*
**1947** *Baltimore Sun*
**1948** *St. Louis Post-Dispatch*
**1949** (Lincoln) *Nebraska State Journal*
**1950** *Chicago Daily News;* and *St. Louis Post-Dispatch*
**1951** *Miami Herald;* and *Brooklyn Eagle*
**1952** *St. Louis Post-Dispatch*
**1953** *Whiteville* (N.C.) *News Reporter;* and *Tabor City* (N.C.) *Tribune*
**1954** *Newsday* (Garden City, L.I.)
**1955** *Columbus* (Ga.) *Ledger* and *Sunday Ledger-Enquirer*
**1956** *Watsonville* (Calif.) *Register-Pajaronian*
**1957** *Chicago Daily News*
**1958** (Little Rock) *Arkansas Gazette*
**1959** *Utica* (N.Y.) *Observer Dispatch* and *Utica Daily Press*
**1960** *Los Angeles Times*
**1961** *Amarillo* (Tex.) *Globe-Times*
**1962** *Panama City* (Fla.) *News-Herald*
**1963** *Chicago Daily News*
**1964** *St. Petersburg* (Fla.) *Times*
**1965** *Hutchinson* (Kan.) *News*
**1966** *Boston Globe*
**1967** *Louisville Courier-Journal* and *Milwaukee Journal*
**1968** *Riverside* (Calif.) *Press-Enterprise*
**1969** *Los Angeles Times*
**1970** *Newsday* (Garden City, L.I.)
**1971** *Winston-Salem* (N.C.) *Journal and Sentinel*
**1972** *New York Times*
**1973** *Washington Post*
**1974** *Newsday* (Garden City, L.I.)
**1975** *Boston Globe*
**1976** *Anchorage* (Alaska) *Daily News*
**1977** *Lufkin* (Tex.) *News*
**1978** *Philadelphia Inquirer*

### EDITORIAL

**1917** *New York Tribune*
**1918** *Louisville Courier-Journal*
**1920** Harvey E. Newbranch *(Omaha Evening World-Herald)*
**1922** Frank M. O'Brien *(New York Herald)*
**1923** William Allen White *(Emporia* [Kan.] *Gazette)*
**1924** *Boston Hearld* (Frank Buxton); special prize; Frank I. Cobb *(New York World)*
**1925** *Charleston* (S.C.) *News and Courier*
**1926** *New York Times* (Edward M. Kingsbury)
**1927** *Boston Hearld* (F. Lauriston Bullard)
**1928** Grover Cleveland Hall *(Montgomery* [Ala.] *Advertiser)*
**1929** Louis Isaac Jaffe *(Norfolk Virginian-Pilot)*
**1931** Charles S. Ryckman *(Fremont* [Neb.] *Tribune)*
**1933** *Kansas City* (Mo.) *Star*
**1934** E. P. Chase *(Atlantic* [Iowa] *News Telegraph)*
**1936** Felix Morley *(Washington Post);* George B. Parker (Scripps-Howard Newspapers)
**1937** John W. Owens *(Baltimore Sun)*
**1938** W. W. Waymack *(Des Moines Register and Tribune)*
**1939** Ronald G. Callvert *(Portland Oregonian)*
**1940** Bart Howard *(St. Louis Post-Dispatch)*
**1941** Reuben Maury *(New York Daily News)*
**1942** Geoffrey Parsons *(New York Hearld Tribune)*
**1943** Forrest W. Seymour *(Des Moines Register and Tribune)*
**1944** *Kansas City* (Mo.) *Star* (Henry J. Haskell)
**1945** George W. Potter *(Providence* [R.I.] *Journal-Bulletin)*
**1946** Hodding Carter ([Greenville, Miss.] *Delta Democrat-Times* )
**1947** William H. Grimes *(Wall Street Journal)*
**1948** Virginius Dabney *(Richmond Times-Dispatch)*
**1949** John H. Crider *(Boston Herald);* Herbert Elliston *(Washington Post)*
**1950** Carl M. Saunders *(Jackson* [Mich.] *Citizen Patriot)*
**1951** William H. Fitzpatrick *(New Orleans States)*
**1952** Louis LaCoss *(St. Louis Globe-Democrat)*
**1953** Vermont C. Royster *(Wall Street Journal)*
**1954** *Boston Herald* (Don Murray)
**1955** *Detroit Free Press* (Royce Howes)
**1956** Lauren K. Soth *(Des Moines Register and Tribune)*
**1957** Buford Boone *Tuscaloosa (* [Ala.] *News)*
**1958** Harry S. Ashmore *(Arkansas Gazette)*
**1959** Ralph McGill *(Atlanta Constitution)*
**1960** Lenoir Chambers *(Virginian-Pilot)*
**1961** William J. Dorvillier *(San Juan* [P.R.] *Star)*
**1962** Thomas M. Storke *(Santa Barbara* [Calif.] *News-Press)*
**1963** Ira B. Harkey, Jr. *(Pascagoula* [Miss.] *Chronicle)*
**1964** Hazel Brannon Smith *(Lexington* [Miss.] *Advertiser)*
**1965** John R. Harrison *(Gainesville* [Fla.] *Daily Sun)*
**1966** Robert Lasch *(St. Louis Post-Dispatch)*
**1967** Eugene Patterson *(Atlanta Constitution)*
**1968** John S. Knight (Knight Newspapers)

**1969** Paul Greenberg *(Pine Bluff* [Ark.] *Commercial)*
**1970** Philip L. Geyelin *(Washington Post)*
**1971** Horance G. Davis, Jr. *(Gainesville* [Fla.] *Sun)*
**1972** John Strohmeyer *(Bethlehem* [Pa.] *Globe Times)*
**1973** Roger Bourne Linscott *(Berkshire Eagle* [Pittsfield, Mass.])
**1974** F. Gilman Spencer *(Trenton* [N.J.] *Trentonian)*
**1975** John Daniell Maurice *(Charleston* [W. Va] *Daily Mail)*
**1976** Philip P. Kerby *(Los Angeles Times)*
**1977** Warren L. Lerude, Foster Church and Norman F. Cardoza *(Reno* [Nev.] *Gazette* and *Nevada State Journal)*
**1978** Meg Greenfield *(Washington Post)*

### CORRESPONDENCE

**1929** Paul Scott Mowrer *(Chicago Daily News)*
**1930** Leland Stowe *(New York Herald Tribune)*
**1931** H. R. Knickerbocker *(Philadelphia Public Ledger* and *New York Evening Post)*
**1932** Walter Duranty *(New York Times);* Charles G. Ross *(St. Louis Post-Dispatch)*
**1933** Edgar Ansel Mowrer *(Chicago Daily News)*
**1934** Frederick T. Birchall *(New York Times)*
**1935** Arthur Krock *(New York Times)*
**1936** Wilfred C. Barber *(Chicago Tribune)*
**1937** Anne O'Hare McCormick *(New York Times)*
**1938** Arthur Krock *(New York Times)*
**1939** Louis P. Lochner (Associated Press)
**1940** Otto D. Tolischus *(New York Times)*
**1941** Group award[1]
**1942** Carlos P. Romulo *(Philippines Herald)*
**1943** Hanson W. Baldwin *(New York Times)*
**1944** Ernie Pyle (Scripps-Howard Newspaper Alliance)
**1945** Harold V. (Hal) Boyle (Associated Press)
**1946** Arnaldo Cortesi *(New York Times)*
**1947** Brooks Atkinson *(New York Times)*
**1948** Discontinued

### CARTOON

**1922** Rollin Kirby *(New York World)*
**1924** Jay Norwood Darling *(New York Tribune)*
**1925** Rollin Kirby *(New York World)*
**1926** D. R. Fitzpatrick *(St. Louis Post-Dispatch)*
**1927** Nelson Harding *(Brooklyn Eagle)*
**1928** Nelson Harding *(Brooklyn Eagle)*
**1929** Rollin Kirby *(New York World)*
**1930** Charles R. Macauley *(Brooklyn Eagle)*
**1931** Edmund Duffy *(Baltimore Sun)*
**1932** John T. McCutcheon *(Chicago Tribune)*
**1933** H. M. Talburt *(Washington Daily News)*
**1934** Edmund Duffy *(Baltimore Sun)*
**1935** Ross A. Lewis *(Milwaukee Journal)*
**1937** C. D. Batchelor *(New York Daily News)*
**1938** Vaughn Shoemaker *(Chicago Daily News)*
**1939** Charles G. Werner *(Daily Oklahoman* [Oklahoma City])
**1940** Edmund Duffy *(Baltimore Sun)*
**1941** Jacob Burck *(Chicago Times)*
**1942** Herbert L. Block (NEA Service)
**1943** Jay Norwood Darling *(New York Herald Tribune)*
**1944** Clifford K. Berryman *(Washington Evening Star)*
**1945** Bill Mauldin (United Features Syndicate)
**1946** Bruce Alexander Russell *(Los Angeles Times)*
**1947** Vaughn Shoemaker *(Chicago Daily News)*
**1948** Reuben L. Goldberg *(New York Sun)*
**1949** Lute Pease *(Newark Evening News)*
**1950** James T. Berryman *(Washington Evening Star)*
**1951** Reg (Reginald W.) Manning *(Arizona Republic* [Phoenix])
**1952** Fred L. Packer *(New York Mirror)*
**1953** Edward D. Kuekes *(Cleveland Plain Dealer)*
**1954** Herbert L. Block *(Washington Post* and *Times-Herald)*
**1955** Daniel R. Fitzpatrick *(St. Louis Post-Dispatch)*
**1956** Robert York *(Louisville Times)*
**1957** Tom Little *(Nashville Tennessean)*
**1958** Bruce M. Shanks *(Buffalo Evening News)*
**1959** Bill Mauldin *(St. Louis Post-Dispatch)*
**1961** Carey Orr *(Chicago Tribune)*
**1962** Edmund S. Valtman *(Hartford Times)*
**1963** Frank Miller *(Des Moines Register)*
**1964** Paul Conrad (formerly of *Denver Post,* later on *Los Angeles Times* )
**1966** Don Wright *(Miami News)*
**1967** Patrick B. Oliphant *(Denver Post)*
**1968** Eugene Gray Payne *(Charlotte* [N.C.] *Observer)*
**1969** John Fischetti *(Chicago Daily News)*
**1970** Thomas F. Darcy *(Newsday* [Garden City, L.I.])
**1971** Paul Conrad *(Los Angeles Times)*
**1972** Jeffrey K. MacNelly *(Richmond* [Va.] *News Leader)*
**1974** Paul Szep *(Boston Globe)*
**1975** Garry Trudeau (Universal Press Syndicate)
**1976** Tony Auth *(Philadelphia Inquirer)*
**1977** Paul Szep *(Boston Globe)*
**1978** Jeffrey K. MacNelly *(Richmond [Va.] News Leader)*

### NEWS PHOTOGRAPHY

**1942** Milton Brooks *(Detroit News)*
**1943** Frank Noel (Associated Press)
**1944** Frank Filan (Associated Press), Earle L. Bunker *(Omaha World-Herald)*
**1945** Joe Rosenthal (Associated Press)
**1947** Arnold Hardy
**1948** Frank Cushing *(Boston Traveler)*
**1949** Nat Fein *(New York Herald Tribune)*
**1950** Bill Crouch *(Oakland Tribune)*
**1951** Max Desfor (Associated Press)
**1952** John Robinson and Don Ultang *(Des Moines Register & Tribune)*
**1953** William M. Gallagher *(Flint* [Mich.] *Journal)*
**1954** Mrs. Walter M. Schau
**1955** John L. Gaunt, Jr. *(Los Angeles Times)*
**1956** *New York Daily News*
**1957** Harry A. Trask *(Boston Traveler)*
**1958** William C. Beall *(Washington Daily News)*
**1959** William Seaman *(Minneapolis Star)*
**1960** Andrew Lopez (United Press International)
**1961** Yasushi Nagao (Mainichi Newspapers, Tokyo)
**1962** Paul Vathis (Harrisburg [Pa.] bureau of Associated Press)
**1963** Hector Rondon (*La Republica,* Caracas, Venezuela)
**1964** Robert H. Jackson *(Dallas Times Herald)*
**1965** Horst Faas (Associated Press)
**1966** Kyoichi Sawada (United Press International)
**1967** Jack R. Thornell (Associated Press)
**1968** News: Rocco Morabito *(Jacksonville* [Fla.] *Journal);* features: Toshio Sakai (United Press International)
**1969** Spot news: Edward T. Adams (Associated Press); features: Moneta Sleet, Jr.
**1970** Spot news: Steve Starr (Associated Press); features: Dallas Kinney *(Palm Beach Post)*
**1971** Spot news: John Paul Filo (*Valley Daily News*

1. For the public services and the individual achievements of American news reporters in the war zones.

*and Daily Dispatch* [Tarentum and New Kensington, Pa.]); features: Jack Dykinga *(Chicago Sun-Times)*
1972 Spot news: Horst Faas and Michel Laurent (Associated Press); features: Dave Kennerly (United Press International)
1973 Spot News: Huynh Cong Ut *(Associated Press);* features: Brian Lanker *(Topeka Capital-Journal)*
1974 Spot news: Anthony K. Roberts (Associated Press); features: Slava Veder (Associated Press)
1975 Spot news: Gerald H. Gay *(Seattle Times);* features: Matthew Lewis *(Washington Post)*
1976 Spot news: Stanley J. Forman *(Boston Herald-American);* features: photographic staff of *Louisville Courier-Journal* and *Times)*
1977 Spot news: Neal Ulevich (Associated Press) and Stanley J. Forman *(Boston Herald-American);* features: Robin Hood *(Chattanooga News-Free Press)*
1978 Spot news: John Blair, freelance, Evansville, Ind.; features: J. Ross Baughman (Associated Press)

### NATIONAL TELEGRAPHIC REPORTING

1942 Louis Stark *(New York Times)*
1944 Dewey L. Fleming *(Baltimore Sun)*
1945 James Reston *(New York Times)*
1946 Edward A. Harris *(St. Louis Post-Dispatch)*
1947 Edward T. Folliard *(Washington Post)*

### NATIONAL REPORTING

1948 Bert Andrews *(New York Herald Tribune);* Nat S. Finney *(Minneapolis Tribune)*
1949 C. P. Trussel *(New York Times)*
1950 Edwin O. Guthman *(Seattle Times)*
1952 Anthony Leviero *(New York Times)*
1953 Don Whitehead (Associated Press)
1954 Richard Wilson (Cowles Newspapers)
1955 Anthony Lewis *(Washington Daily News)*
1956 Charles L. Bartlett *(Chattanooga Times)*
1957 James Reston *(New York Times)*
1958 Relman Morin (Associated Press) and Clark Mollenhoff *(Des Moines Register & Tribune)*
1959 Howard Van Smith *(Miami News)*
1960 Vance Trimble (Scripps-Howard Newspaper Alliance)
1961 Edward R. Cony *(Wall Street Journal)*
1962 Nathan G. Caldwell and Gene S. Graham *(Nashville Tennessean)*
1963 Anthony Lewis *(New York Times)*
1964 Merriman Smith (United Press International)
1965 Louis M. Kohlmeier *(Wall Street Journal)*
1966 Haynes Johnson *(Washington Evening Star)*
1967 Stanley Penn and Monroe Karmin *(Wall Street Journal)*
1968 Howard James *(Christian Science Monitor);* Nathan K. (Nick) Kotz *(Des Moines Register* and *Minneapolis Tribune)*
1969 Robert Cahn *(Christian Science Monitor)*
1970 William J. Eaton *(Chicago Daily News)*
1971 Lucinda Franks and Thomas Powers (United Press International)
1972 Jack Anderson *(United Feature Syndicate)*
1973 Robert Boyd and Clark Hoyt *(Knight Newspapers)*
1974 Jack White *(Providence* [R.I.] *Journal-Bulletin);* and James R. Polk *(Washington Star-News)*
1975 Donald L. Barlett and James B. Steele *(Philadelphia Inquirer)*
1976 James Risser *(Des Moines Register)*
1977 Walter Mears (Associated Press)
1978 Gaylord D. Shaw *(Los Angeles Times)*

### INTERNATIONAL TELEGRAPHIC REPORTING

1942 Laurence Edmund Allen (Associated Press)
1943 Ira Wolfert (North American Newspaper Alliance, Inc.)
1944 Daniel De Luce (Associated Press)
1945 Mark S. Watson *(Baltimore Sun)*
1946 Homer W. Bigart *(New York Herald Tribune)*
1947 Eddy Gilmore (Associated Press)

### INTERNATIONAL REPORTING

1948 Paul W. Ward *(Baltimore Sun)*
1949 Price Day *(Baltimore Sun)*
1950 Edmund Stevens *(Christian Science Monitor)*
1951 Keyes Beech and Fred Sparks *(Chicago Daily News);* Homer Bigart and Marguerite Higgins *(New York Herald Tribune);* Relman Morin and Don Whitehead (Associated Press)
1952 John M. Hightower (Associated Press)
1953 Austin C. Wehrwein *(Milwaukee Journal)*
1954 Jim G. Lucas (Scripps-Howard Newspapers)
1955 Harrison E. Salisbury *(New York Times)*
1956 William Randolph Hearst, Jr., and Frank Conniff (Hearst newspapers) and Kingsbury Smith (INS)
1957 Russell Jones (United Press)
1958 *New York Times*
1959 Joseph Martin and Philip Santora *(New York Daily News)*
1960 A. M. Rosenthal *(New York Times)*
1961 Lynn Heinzerling (Associated Press)
1962 Walter Lippmann (New York Herald Tribune Syndicate)
1963 Hal Hendrix *(Miami News)*
1964 Malcolm W. Browne (Associated Press) and David Halberstam *(New York Times)*
1965 J. A. Livingston *(Philadelphia Bulletin)*
1966 Peter Arnett (Associated Press)
1967 R. John Hughes *(Christian Science Monitor)*
1968 Alfred Friendly *(Washington Post)*
1969 William Tuohy *(Los Angeles Times)*
1970 Seymour M. Hersh (Dispatch News Service)
1971 Jimmie Lee Hoagland *(Washington Post)*
1972 Peter R. Kann *(Wall Street Journal)*
1973 Max Frankel *(New York Times)*
1974 Hedrick Smith *(New York Times)*
1975 William Mullen and Ovie Carter *(Chicago Tribune)*
1976 Sydney H. Schanberg *(New York Times)*
1978 Henry Kamm *(New York Times)*

### REPORTING

1917 Herbert B. Swope *(New York World)*
1918 Harold A. Littledale *(New York Evening Post)*
1920 John J. Leary, Jr. *(New York World)*
1921 Louis Seibold *(New York World)*
1922 Kirke L. Simpson (Associated Press)
1923 Alva Johnston *(New York Times)*
1924 Magner White *(San Diego Sun)*
1925 James W. Mulroy and Alvin H. Goldstein *(Chicago Daily News)*
1926 William Burke Miller *(Louisville Courier-Journal)*
1927 John T. Rogers *(St. Louis Post-Dispatch)*
1929 Paul Y. Anderson *(St. Louis Post-Dispatch)*
1930 Russell D. Owen *(New York Times);* special award: W. O. Dapping *(Auburn* [N.Y.] *Citizen)*
1931 A. B. MacDonald *(Kansas City* [Mo.] *Star)*
1932 W. C. Richards, D. D. Martin, J. S. Pooler, F. D. Webb, J. N. W. Sloan (all of *Detroit Free Press)*
1933 Francis A. Jamieson (Associated Press)
1934 Royce Brier *(San Francisco Chronicle)*
1935 William H. Taylor *(New York Herald Tribune)*

1936 Lauren D. Lyman *(New York Times)*
1937 John J. O'Neill *(New York Herald Tribune)*, William Leonard Laurence *(New York Times)*, Howard W. Blakeslee (Associated Press), Gobind Behari Lal (Universal Service), David Dietz (Scripps-Howard Newspapers)
1938 Raymond Sprigle *(Pittsburg Post-Gazette)*
1939 Thomas L. Stokes *(New York World-Telegram)*
1940 S. Burton Heath *(New York World-Telegram)*
1941 Westbrook Pegler *(New York World-Telegram)*
1942 Stanton Delaplane *(San Francisco Chronicle)*
1943 George Weller *(Chicago Daily News)*
1944 Paul Schoenstein and associates *(New York Journal-American)*
1945 Jack S. McDowell *(San Francisco Call-Bulletin)*
1946 William Leonard Laurence *(New York Times)*
1947 Frederick Woltman *(New York World-Telegram)*
1948 George E. Goodwin *(Atlanta Journal)*
1949 Malcolm Johnson *(New York Sun)*
1950 Meyer Berger *(New York Times)*
1951 Edward S. Montgomery *(San Francisco Examiner)*
1952 George de Carvalho *(San Francisco Chronicle)*
1953 Editorial staff *(Providence Journal and Evening Bulletin)*;[1] Edward J. Mowery *(New York World-Telegram and Sun)*[2]
1954 *Vicksburg* (Miss.) *Sunday Post-Herald*;[1] Alvin Scott McCoy *(Kansas City* [Mo.] *Star)*[2]
1955 Mrs. Caro Brown *(Alice* [Tex.] *Daily Echo)*;[1] Roland Kenneth Towery *(Cuero* [Tex.] *Record)*[2]
1956 Lee Hills *(Detroit Free Press)*;[1] Arthur Daley *(New York Times)*[2]
1957 *Salt Lake Tribune*;[1] Wallace Turner and William Lambert *(Portland Oregonian)*[2]
1958 *Fargo* [N.D.] *Forum*;[1] George Beveridge *(Washington* [D.C.] *Evening Star)*[2]
1959 Mary Lou Werner *(Washington* [D.C.] *Evening Star)*;[1] John Harold Brislin *(Scranton* [Pa.] *Tribune & Scrantonian)*[2]
1960 Jack Nelson *(Atlanta Constitution)*;[1] Miriam Ottenberg *(Washington Evening Star)*[2]
1961 Sanche de Gramont *(New York Herald Tribune)*;[1] Edgar May *(Buffalo Evening News)*[2]
1962 Robert D. Mullins (*Deseret News*, Salt Lake City);[1] George Bliss *(Chicago Tribune)*[2]
1963 Sylvan Fox, Anthony Shannon, and William Longgood *(New York World Telegram and Sun)*;[1] Oscar Griffin, Jr. (former editor of *Pecos* [Tex.] *Independent and Enterprise*, now on staff of *Houston Chronicle)*[2]

### GENERAL LOCAL REPORTING

1964 Norman C. Miller *(Wall Street Journal)*
1965 Melvin H. Ruder (*Hungry Horse News*, Columbia Falls, Mont.)
1966 Staff of *Los Angeles Times*
1967 Robert V. Cox *(Chambersburg* [Pa.] *Public Opinion)*
1968 Staff of *Detroit Free Press*
1969 John Fetterman *(Louisville Times* and *Courier-Journal)*
1970 Thomas Fitzpatrick *(Chicago Sun-Times)*
1971 Staff of *Akron* (Ohio) *Beacon*
1972 Richard Cooper and John Machacek *(Rochester* [N.Y.] *Times-Union)*
1973 *Chicago Tribune*
1974 Arthur M. Petacque and Hugh F. Hough *(Chicago Sun-Times)*
1975 *Xenia* (Ohio) *Daily Gazette*
1976 Gene Miller *(Miami Herald)*
1977 Margo Huston *(Milwaukee Journal)*
1978 Richard Whitt *Louisville Courier-Journal)*

### SPECIAL LOCAL REPORTING

1964 James V. Magee, Albert V. Gaudiosi, and Frederick A. Meyer *(Philadelphia Bulletin)*
1965 Gene Goltz *(Houston Post)*
1966 John A. Frasca *(Tampa Tribune)*
1967 Gene Miller *(Miami Herald)*
1968 J. Anthony Lukas *(New York Times)*
1969 Albert L. Delugach and Denny Walsh *(St. Louis Globe-Democrat)*
1970 Harold Eugene Martin *(Montgomery Advertiser)*
1971 William Hugh Jones *(Chicago Tribune)*
1972 Timothy Leland, Gerard N. O'Neill, Stephen A. Kurkjian, and Ann DeSantis *(Boston Globe)*
1973 Sun Newspapers of Omaha, Neb.
1974 William Sherman *(New York Daily News)*
1975 *Indianapolis Star*
1976 *Chicago Tribune*
1977 Acel Moore and Wendell Rawls, Jr. *(Philadelphia Inquirer)*
1978 Anthony R. Dolan *(Stamford* [Conn.] *Advocate)*

### COMMENTARY

1970 Marquis W. Childs *(St. Louis Post-Dispatch)*
1971 William A. Caldwell (*Record* [Hackensack, N.J.])
1972 Mike Royko *(Chicago Daily News)*
1973 David S. Broder *(Washington Post)*
1974 Edwin A. Roberts, Jr. *(National Observer)*
1975 Mary McGrory *(Washington Star)*
1976 Walter W. (Red) Smith *(New York Times)*
1977 George F. Will (*Washington Post* Writers Group)
1978 William Safire *(New York Times)*

### CRITICISM

1970 Ada Louise Huxtable *(New York Times)*
1971 Harold C. Schonberg *(New York Times)*
1972 Frank Peters, Jr. *(St. Louis Post-Dispatch)*
1973 Ronald Powers *(Chicago Sun-Times)*
1974 Emily Genauer (Newsday Syndicate)
1975 Roger Ebert *(Chicago Sun-Times)*
1976 Alan M. Kriegsman *(Washington Post)*
1977 William McPherson *(Washington Post)*
1978 Walter Kerr *(New York Times)*

### SPECIAL CITATIONS

1938 *Edmonton* (Alberta) *Journal*, special bronze plaque for editorial leadership in defense of freedom of press in Province of Alberta.
1941 *New York Times* for the public educational value of its foreign news report.
1944 Byron Price, Director of the Office of Censorship, for the creation and administration of the newspaper and radio codes. Mrs. William Allen White, for her husband's interest and services during the past seven years as a member of the Advisory Board of the Graduate School of Journalism, Columbia University. Richard Rodgers and Oscar Hammerstein II for their musical *Oklahoma!*
1945 The cartographers of the American press for their war maps.
1947 (Pulitzer centennial year.) Columbia University and the Graduate School of

1. Reporting under pressure of edition deadlines. 2. Reporting not under pressure of edition deadlines.

Journalism, for their efforts to maintain and advance the high standards governing the Pulitzer Prize awards. The *St. Louis Post-Dispatch,* for its unswerving adherence to the public and professional ideals of its founder and its leadership in American journalism.

1948 Dr. Frank D. Fackenthal, for his interest and service.

1951 Cyrus L. Sulzberger *(New York Times)* for his exclusive interview with Archbishop Stepinac in a Yugoslav prison.

1952 *Kansas City Star* for coverage of 1951 floods; Max Kase *(New York Journal-American)* for exposures of bribery in college basketball.

1953 *New York Times* for its 17-year publication of "News of the Week in Review"; and Lester Markel, its founder.

1957 Kenneth Roberts for his historical novels.

1958 Walter Lippmann *(New York Herald Tribune)* for his "wisdom, perception and high sense of responsibility" in his commentary on national and international affairs.

1960 Garrett Mattingly, for *The Armada.*

1961 *American Heritage Picture History of the Civil War,* as distinguished example of American book publishing.

1964 Gannett Newspapers, Rochester, N.Y.

1973 James Thomas Flexner for his biography *George Washington.*

1974 Roger Sessions, for his "life's work in music."

1976 John Hohenberg for "services for 22 years as administrator of the Pulitzer Prizes." Scott Joplin for his contributions to American music.

1977 Alex Haley for his novel, *Roots*

1978 E.B.White of *New Yorker* magazine and Richard L. Strout of *Christian Science Monitor*

## Pulitzer Prizes in Letters

### FICTION[1]

1918 *His Family.* Ernest Poole
1919 *The Magnificent Ambersons.* Booth Tarkington
1921 *The Age of Innocence.* Edith Wharton
1922 *Alice Adams.* Booth Tarkington
1923 *One of Ours.* Willa Cather
1924 *The Able McLaughlins.* Margaret Wilson
1925 *So Big.* Edna Ferber
1926 *Arrowsmith.* Sinclair Lewis
1927 *Early Autumn.* Louis Bromfield
1928 *The Bridge of San Luis Rey.* Thornton Wilder
1929 *Scarlet Sister Mary.* Julia Peterkin
1930 *Laughing Boy.* Oliver La Farge
1931 *Years of Grace.* Margaret Ayer Barnes
1932 *The Good Earth.* Pearl S. Buck
1933 *The Store.* T. S. Stribling
1934 *Lamb in His Bosom.* Caroline Miller
1935 *Now in November.* Josephine Winslow Johnson
1936 *Honey in the Horn.* Harold L. Davis
1937 *Gone with the Wind.* Margaret Mitchell
1938 *The Late George Apley.* John Phillips Marquand
1939 *The Yearling.* Marjorie Kinnan Rawlings
1940 *The Grapes of Wrath.* John Steinbeck
1942 *In This Our Life.* Ellen Glasgow
1943 *Dragon's Teeth.* Upton Sinclair
1944 *Journey in the Dark.* Martin Flavin
1945 *A Bell for Adano.* John Hersey
1947 *All the King's Men.* Robert Penn Warren
1948 *Tales of the South Pacific.* James A. Michener
1949 *Guard of Honor.* James Gould Cozzens
1950 *The Way West.* A. B. Guthrie, Jr.
1951 *The Town.* Conrad Richter
1952 *The Caine Mutiny.* Herman Wouk
1953 *The Old Man and the Sea.* Ernest Hemingway
1955 *A Fable.* William Faulkner
1956 *Andersonville.* MacKinlay Kantor
1958 *A Death in the Family.* James Agee
1959 *The Travels of Jaimie McPheeters.* Robert Lewis Taylor
1960 *Advise and Consent.* Allen Drury
1961 *To Kill a Mockingbird.* Harper Lee
1962 *The Edge of Sadness.* Edwin O'Connor
1963 *The Reivers.* William Faulkner
1965 *The Keepers of the House.* Shirley Ann Grau
1966 *Collected Stories of Katherine Anne Porter.* Katherine Anne Porter
1967 *The Fixer.* Bernard Malamud
1968 *The Confessions of Nat Turner.* William Styron
1969 *House Made of Dawn.* N. Scott Momaday
1970 *Collected Stories.* Jean Stafford
1972 *Angle of Repose.* Wallace Stegner
1973 *The Optimist's Daughter.* Eudora Welty
1975 *The Killer Angels.* Michael Shaara
1976 *Humboldt's Gift.* Saul Bellow
1978 *Elbow Room.* James Alan McPherson

1. Before 1948, award was for novels only.

### DRAMA

1918 *Why Marry?* Jesse Lynch Williams
1920 *Beyond the Horizon.* Eugene O'Neill
1921 *Miss Lulu Bett.* Zona Gale
1922 *Anna Christie.* Eugene O'Neill
1923 *Icebound.* Owen Davis
1924 *Hell-Bent Fer Heaven.* Hatcher Hughes
1925 *They Knew What They Wanted.* Sidney Howard
1926 *Craig's Wife.* George Kelly
1927 *In Abraham's Bosom.* Paul Green
1928 *Strange Interlude.* Eugene O'Neill
1929 *Street Scene.* Elmer L. Rice
1930 *The Green Pastures.* Marc Connelly
1931 *Alison's House.* Susan Glaspell
1932 *Of Thee I Sing.* George S. Kaufman, Morrie Ryskind, and Ira Gershwin
1933 *Both Your Houses.* Maxwell Anderson
1934 *Men in White.* Sidney Kingsley
1935 *The Old Maid.* Zöe Akins
1936 *Idiot's Delight.* Robert E. Sherwood
1937 *You Can't Take It with You.* Moss Hart and George S. Kaufman
1938 *Our Town.* Thornton Wilder
1939 *Abe Lincoln in Illinois.* Robert E. Sherwood
1940 *The Time of Your Life.* William Saroyan
1941 *There Shall Be No Night.* Robert E. Sherwood
1943 *The Skin of Our Teeth.* Thornton Wilder
1945 *Harvey.* Mary Chase
1946 *State of the Union.* Russel Crouse and

Howard Lindsay
1948 *A Streetcar Named Desire.* Tennessee Williams
1949 *Death of a Salesman.* Arthur Miller
1950 *South Pacific.* Richard Rodgers, Oscar Hammerstein II, and Joshua Logan
1952 *The Shrike.* Joseph Kramm
1953 *Picnic.* By William Inge
1954 *The Teahouse of the August Moon.* John Patrick
1955 *Cat on a Hot Tin Roof.* Tennessee Williams
1956 *The Diary of Anne Frank.* Frances Goodrich and Albert Hackett
1957 *Long Day's Journey Into Night.* Eugene O'Neill
1958 *Look Homeward, Angel.* Ketti Frings
1959 *J.B.* Archibald MacLeish
1960 *Fiorello!* George Abbott, Jerome Weidman, Jerry Bock, and Sheldon Harnick
1961 *All the Way Home.* Tad Mosel
1962 *How to Succeed in Business Without Really Trying.* Frank Loesser and Abe Burrows
1965 *The Subject Was Roses.* Frank D. Gilroy
1967 *A Delicate Balance.* Edward Albee
1969 *The Great White Hope.* Howard Sackler
1970 *No Place to Be Somebody.* Charles Gordone
1971 *The Effect of Gamma Rays on Man-in-the-Moon Marigolds.* Paul Zindel
1973 *That Championship Season.* Jason Miller
1975 *Seascape.* Edward Albee
1976 *A Chorus Line.* Conceived by Michael Bennett
1977 *The Shadow Box.* Michael Cristofer
1978 *The Gin Game.* Donald L. Coburn

## HISTORY OF UNITED STATES

1917 *With Americans of Past and Present Days.* J. J. Jusserand, Ambassador of France to United States
1918 *A History of the Civil War, 1861–1865.* James Ford Rhodes
1920 *The War with Mexico.* Justin H. Smith
1921 *The Victory at Sea.* William Sowden Sims in collaboration with Burton J. Hendrick
1922 *The Founding of New England.* James Truslow Adams
1923 *The Supreme Court in United States History.* Charles Warren
1924 *The American Revolution—A Constitutional Interpretation.* Charles Howard McIlwain
1925 *A History of the American Frontier.* Frederic L. Paxson
1926 *The History of the United States.* Edward Channing
1927 *Pinckney's Treaty.* Samuel Flagg Bemis
1928 *Main Currents in American Thought.* Vernon Louis Parrington
1929 *The Organization and Administration of the Union Army, 1861–1865.* Fred Albert Shannon
1930 *The War of Independence.* Claude H. Van Tyne
1931 *The Coming of the War: 1914.* Bernadotte E. Schmitt
1932 *My Experiences in the World War.* John J. Pershing
1933 *The Significance of Sections in American History.* Frederick J. Turner
1934 *The People's Choice.* Herbert Agar
1935 *The Colonial Period of American History.* Charles McLean Andrews
1936 *The Constitutional History of the United States.* Andrew C. McLaughlin
1937 *The Flowering of New England.* Van Wyck Brooks
1938 *The Road to Reunion, 1865–1900.* Paul Herman Buck
1939 *A History of American Magazines.* Frank Luther Mott
1940 *Abraham Lincoln: The War Years.* Carl Sandburg
1941 *The Atlantic Migration, 1607–1860.* Marcus Lee Hansen
1942 *Reveille in Washington.* Margaret Leech
1943 *Paul Revere and the World He Lived In.* Esther Forbes
1944 *The Growth of American Thought.* Merle Curti
1945 *Unfinished Business.* Stephen Bonsal
1946 *The Age of Jackson.* Arthur M. Schlesinger, Jr.
1947 *Scientists Against Time.* James Phinney Baxter, 3rd
1948 *Across the Wide Missouri.* Bernard DeVoto
1949 *The Disruption of American Democracy.* Roy Franklin Nichols
1950 *Art and Life in America.* Oliver W. Larkin
1951 *The Old Northwest, Pioneer Period 1815–1840.* R. Carlyle Buley
1952 *The Uprooted.* Oscar Handlin
1953 *The Era of Good Feelings.* George Dangerfield
1954 *A Stillness at Appomattox.* Bruce Catton
1955 *Great River: The Rio Grande in North American History.* Paul Horgan
1956 *The Age of Reform.* Richard Hofstadter
1957 *Russia Leaves the War: Soviet-American Relations, 1917–1920.* George F. Kennan
1958 *Banks and Politics in America: From the Revolution to the Civil War.* Bray Hammond
1959 *The Republican Era: 1869–1901.* Leonard D. White, assisted by Jean Schneider
1960 *In the Days of McKinley.* Margaret Leech
1961 *Between War and Peace: The Potsdam Conference.* Herbert Feis
1962 *The Triumphant Empire, Thunder-Clouds Gather in the West.* Lawrence H. Gipson
1963 *Washington, Village and Capital, 1800–1878.* Constance McLaughlin Green
1964 *Puritan Village: The Formation of a New England Town.* Sumner Chilton Powell
1965 *The Greenback Era.* Irwin Unger
1966 *Life of the Mind in America.* Perry Miller
1967 *Exploration and Empire: The Explorer and Scientist in the Winning of the American West.* William H. Goetzmann
1968 *The Ideological Origins of the American Revolution.* Bernard Bailyn
1969 *Origins of the Fifth Amendment.* Leonard W. Levy
1970 *Present at the Creation: My Years in the State Department.* Dean Acheson
1971 *Roosevelt: The Soldier of Freedom.* James McGregor Burns
1972 *Neither Black Nor White. Slavery and Race Relations in Brazil and the United States.* Carl N. Degler
1973 *People of Paradox: An Inquiry Concerning the Origin of American Civilization.* Michael Kammen
1974 *The Americans: The Democratic Experience, Vol. 3.* Daniel J. Boorstin
1975 *Jefferson and His Time.* Dumas Malone
1976 *Lamy of Santa Fe.* Paul Horgan
1977 *The Impending Crisis: 1841–1861.* David M. Potter (posth)
1978 *The Invisible Hand: The Managerial Revolution in American Business.* Alfred D. Chandler Jr.

## BIOGRAPHY OR AUTOBIOGRAPHY

1917 *Julia Ward Howe.* Laura E. Richards and Maude Howe Elliott, assisted by Florence Howe Hall
1918 *Benjamin Franklin, Self-Revealed.* William Cabell Bruce
1919 *The Education of Henry Adams.* Henry Adams
1920 *The Life of John Marshall.* Albert J. Beveridge
1921 *The Americanization of Edward Bok.* Edward Bok
1922 *A Daughter of the Middle Border.* Hamlin Garland
1923 *The Life and Letters of Walter H. Page.* Burton J. Hendrick
1924 *From Immigrant to Inventor.* Michael Idvorsky Pupin
1925 *Barrett Wendell and His Letters.* M. A. DeWolfe Howe
1926 *The Life of Sir William Osler.* Harvey Cushing
1927 *Whitman.* Emory Holloway
1928 *The American Orchestra and Theodore Thomas. Charles Edward Russell*
1929 *The Training of an American. The Earlier Life and Letters of Walter H. Page.* Burton J. Hendrick
1930 *The Raven.* Marquis James
1931 *Charles W. Eliot.* Henry James
1932 *Theodore Roosevelt.* Henry F. Pringle
1933 *Grover Cleveland.* Allan Nevins
1934 *John Hay.* Tyler Dennett
1935 *R. E. Lee.* Douglas S. Freeman
1936 *The Thought and Character of William James.* Ralph Barton Perry
1937 *Hamilton Fish.* Allan Nevins
1938 *Pedlar's Progress.* Odell Shepard. *Andrew Jackson.* Marquis James
1939 *Benjamin Franklin.* Carl Van Doren
1940 *Woodrow Wilson. Life and Letters,* Vols. VII and VIII. Ray Stannard Baker
1941 *Jonathan Edwards.* Ola E. Winslow
1942 *Crusader in Crinoline.* Forrest Wilson
1943 *Admiral of the Ocean Sea.* Samuel Eliot Morison
1944 *The American Leonardo: The Life of Samuel F. B. Morse.* Carleton Mabee
1945 *George Bancroft: Brahmin Rebel.* Russel Blaine Nye
1946 *Son of the Wilderness.* Linnie Marsh Wolfe
1947 *The Autobiography of William Allen White*
1948 *Forgotten First Citizen: John Bigelow.* Margaret Clapp
1949 *Roosevelt and Hopkins.* Robert E. Sherwood
1950 *John Quincy Adams and the Foundations of American Foreign Policy.* Samuel Flagg Bemis
1951 *John C. Calhoun: American Portrait.* Margaret Louise Coit
1952 *Charles Evans Hughes.* Merlo J. Pusey
1953 *Edmund Pendleton 1721–1803.* David J. Mays
1954 *The Spirit of St. Louis.* Charles A. Lindbergh
1955 *The Taft Story.* William S. White
1956 *Benjamin Henry Latrobe.* Talbot F. Hamlin
1957 *Profiles in Courage.* John F. Kennedy
1958 *George Washington.* Douglas Southall Freeman (Vols. 1–6) and John Alexander Carroll and Mary Wells Ashworth (Vol. 7)
1959 *Woodrow Wilson, American Prophet.* Arthur Walworth
1960 *John Paul Jones.* Samuel Eliot Morison
1961 *Charles Sumner and the Coming of the Civil War.* David Donald
1963 *Henry James: Vol. II, The Conquest of London, 1870–1881; Vol. III, The Middle Years, 1881–1895.* Leon Edel
1964 *John Keats.* Walter Jackson Bate
1965 *Henry Adams* (3 vols.). Ernest Samuels
1966 *A Thousand Days.* Arthur M. Schlesinger, Jr.
1967 *Mr. Clemens and Mark Twain.* Justin Kaplan
1968 *Memoirs, 1925–1950.* George F. Kennan
1969 *The Man from New York.* B. L. Reid
1970 *Huey Long.* T. Harry Williams
1971 *Robert Frost: The Years of Triumph, 1915–1938.* Lawrance Thompson
1972 *Eleanor and Franklin: The Story of Their Relationship Based on Eleanor Roosevelt's Private Papers.* Joseph P. Lash
1973 *Luce and His Empire.* W. A. Swanberg
1974 *O'Neill, Son and Artist.* Louis Sheaffer
1975 *The Power Broker: Robert Moses and the Fall of New York.* Robert A. Caro
1976 *Edith Wharton: A Biography.* Richard W. B. Lewis
1977 *A Prince of Our Disorder.* John E. Mack
1978 *Samuel Johnson.* Walter Jackson Bate

## POETRY[1]

1918 *Love Songs.* Sara Teasdale
1919 *Old Road to Paradise.* Margaret Widdemer; *Corn Huskers.* Carl Sandburg
1922 *Collected Poems.* Edwin Arlington Robinson
1923 *The Ballad of the Harp-Weaver; A Few Figs from Thistles;* eight sonnets in *American Poetry, 1922, A Miscellany.* Edna St. Vincent Millay
1924 *New Hampshire: A Poem with Notes and Grace Notes.* Robert Frost
1925 *The Man Who Died Twice.* Edwin Arlington Robinson
1926 *What's O'Clock.* Amy Lowell
1927 *Fiddler's Farewell.* Leonora Speyer
1928 *Tristram.* Edwin Arlington Robinson
1929 *John Brown's Body.* Stephen Vincent Benét
1930 *Selected Poems.* Conrad Aiken
1931 *Collected Poems.* Robert Frost
1932 *The Flowering Stone.* George Dillon
1933 *Conquistador.* Archibald MacLeish
1934 *Collected Verse.* Robert Hillyer
1935 *Bright Ambush.* Audrey Wurdemann
1936 *Strange Holiness.* Robert P. T. Coffin
1937 *A Further Range.* Robert Frost
1938 *Cold Morning Sky.* Marya Zaturenska
1939 *Selected Poems.* John Gould Fletcher
1940 *Collected Poems.* Mark Van Doren
1941 *Sunderland Capture.* Leonard Bacon
1942 *The Dust Which Is God.* William Rose Benét
1943 *A Witness Tree.* Robert Frost
1944 *Western Star.* Stephen Vincent Benét
1945 *V-Letter and Other Poems.* Karl Shapiro
1947 *Lord Weary's Castle.* Robert Lowell
1948 *The Age of Anxiety.* W. H. Auden
1949 *Terror and Decorum.* Peter Viereck
1950 *Annie Allen.* Gwendolyn Brooks
1951 *Complete Poems.* Carl Sandburg
1952 *Collected Poems.* Marianne Moore
1953 *Collected Poems 1917–1952.* Archibald MacLeish
1954 *The Waking.* Theodore Roethke
1955 *Collected Poems.* Wallace Stevens
1956 *Poems—North & South.* Elizabeth Bishop
1957 *Things of This World.* Richard Wilbur
1958 *Promises: Poems 1954–1956.* Robert Penn Warren

1. This prize was established in 1922. The 1918 and 1919 awards were made from gifts provided by the Poetry Society.

1959 *Selected Poems, 1928–1958.* Stanley Kunitz
1960 *Heart's Needle.* William Snodgrass
1961 *Times Three: Selected Verse from Three Decades.* Phyllis McGinley
1962 *Poems.* Alan Dugan
1963 *Pictures from Breughel.* William Carlos Williams
1964 *At the End of the Open Road.* Louis Simpson
1965 *77 Dream Songs.* John Berryman
1966 *Selected Poems.* Richard Eberhart
1967 *Live or Die.* Anne Sexton
1968 *The Hard Hours.* Anthony Hecht
1969 *Of Being Numerous.* George Oppen
1970 *Untitled Subjects.* Richard Howard
1971 *The Carrier of Ladders.* William S. Merwin
1972 *Collected Poems.* James Wright
1973 *Up Country.* Maxine Winokur Kumin
1974 *The Dolphin.* Robert Lowell
1975 *Turtle Island.* Gary Snyder
1976 *Self-Portrait in a Convex Mirror.* John Ashbery
1977 *Divine Comedies.* James Merrill
1978 *Collected Poems.* Howard Nemerov

**GENERAL NONFICTION**

1962 *The Making of the President 1960.* Theodore H. White
1963 *The Guns of August.* Barbara W. Tuchman
1964 *Anti-intellectualism in American Life.* Richard Hofstadter
1965 *O Strange New World.* Howard Mumford Jones
1966 *Wandering Through Winter.* Edwin Way Teale
1967 *The Problem of Slavery in Western Culture.* David Brion Davis
1968 *Rousseau and Revolution.* Will and Ariel Durant
1969 *So Human an Animal.* Rene Jules Dubos
*The Armies of the Night.* Norman Mailer
1970 *Gandhi's Truth.* Erik H. Erikson
1971 *The Rising Sun.* John Toland
1972 *Stilwell and the American Experience in China, 1911–1945.* Barbara W. Tuchman
1973 *Fire in the Lake: The Vietnamese and the Americans in Vietnam.* Frances FitzGerald; and *Children of Crisis* (Vols. 1 and 2). Robert M. Coles
1974 *The Denial of Death.* Ernest Becker
1975 *Pilgrim at Tinker Creek.* Annie Dillard
1976 *Why Survive? Being Old in America.* Robert N. Butler
1977 *Beautiful Swimmers: Watermen, Crabs and the Chesapeake Bay.* William W. Warner
1978 *The Dragons of Eden.* Carl Sagan

## Pulitzer Prizes in Music

1943 *Secular Cantata No. 2, A Free Song.* William Schuman
1944 *Symphony No. 4* (Op. 34). Howard Hanson
1945 *Appalachian Spring.* Aaron Copland
1946 *The Canticle of the Sun.* Leo Sowerby
1947 *Symphony No. 3.* Charles Ives
1948 *Symphony No. 3.* Walter Piston
1949 *Louisiana Story* music. Virgil Thomson
1950 *The Consul.* Gian Carlo Menotti
1951 Music for opera *Giants in the Earth.* Douglas Stuart Moore
1952 *Symphony Concertante.* Gail Kubik
1954 *Concerto for Two Pianos and Orchestra.* Quincy Porter
1955 *The Saint of Bleecker Street.* Gian Carlo Menotti
1956 *Symphony No. 3.* Ernst Toch
1957 *Meditations on Ecclesiastes.* Norman Dello Joio
1958 *Vanessa.* Samuel Barber
1959 *Concerto for Piano and Orchestra.* John La Montaine
1960 *Second String Quartet.* Elliott Carter
1961 *Symphony No. 7.* Walter Piston
1962 *The Crucible.* Robert Ward
1963 *Piano Concerto No. 1.* Samuel Barber
1966 *Variations for Orchestra.* Leslie Bassett
1967 *Quartet No. 3.* Leon Kirchner
1968 *Echoes of Time and the River.* George Crumb
1969 *String Quartet No. 3.* Karel Husa
1970 *Time's Encomium.* Charles Wuorinen
1971 *Synchronisms No. 6 for Piano and Electronic Sound.* Mario Davidowsky
1972 *Windows.* Jacob Druckman
1973 *String Quartet No. 3.* Elliott Carter
1974 *Notturno.* Donald Martino
1975 *From the Diary of Virginia Woolf.* Dominick Argento
1976 *Air Music.* Ned Rorem
1977 *Visions of Terror and Wonder.* Richard Wernick
1978 *Déjà Vu for Percussion Quartet and Orchestra.* Michael Colgrass

# Sigma Delta Chi Journalism Awards, 1977

**General Reporting:** Fredric Tulsky and David Phelps, Jackson (Miss.) *Clarion-Ledger*
**Editorial Writing:** Desmond Stone, Rochester (N.Y.) *Democrat & Chronicle*
**Washington Correspondence:** Gaylord Shaw, Los Angeles *Times*
**Foreign Correspondence:** Robert Toth, Los Angeles *Times*
**News Photography:** Eddie Adams, The Associated Press
**Editorial Cartoon:** Don Wright, Miami *News*
**Public Service (newspaper):** Philadelphia *Inquirer*
**Magazine Reporting:** John Conroy, Chicago, free-lance
**Public Service (magazine):** *Mother Jones*
**Radio Reporting:** Paul McGonigle, KOY, Phoenix, Ariz.
**Public Service (radio):** WSGN-AM News, Birmingham, Ala.
**Editorializing on Radio:** Jay Lewis, Alabama Information Network
**TV Reporting:** KPIX Eyewitness News Team, San Francisco
**Public Service (TV):** KOOL, Phoenix, Ariz.
**Editorializing on TV:** Rich Adams, WTOP, Washington
**Research in Journalism:** Peter Braestrup
**Public Service (Special Award):** Investigative Reporters and Editors, Inc.

## Motion Picture Academy Awards (Oscars)

| | Picture | Director | Actress |
|---|---|---|---|
| 1928 | *Wings,* Paramount | Frank Borzage, *Seventh Heaven;* Lewis Milestone, *Two Arabian Nights* | Janet Gaynor, *Seventh Heaven, Street Angel, Sunrise* |
| 1929 | *The Broadway Melody,* M-G-M | Frank Lloyd, *The Divine Lady* | Mary Pickford, *Coquette* |
| 1930 | *All Quiet on the Western Front,* Universal | Lewis Milestone, *All Quiet on the Western Front* | Norma Shearer, *The Divorcee* |
| 1931 | *Cimarron,* RKO Radio | Norman Taurog, *Skippy* | Marie Dressler, *Min and Bill* |
| 1932 | *Grand Hotel,* M-G-M | Frank Borzage, *Bad Girl* | Helen Hayes, *The Sin of Madelon Claudet* |
| 1933 | *Cavalcade,* Fox | Frank Lloyd, *Cavalcade* | Katharine Hepburn, *Morning Glory* |
| 1934 | *It Happened One Night,* Columbia | Frank Capra, *It Happened One Night* | Claudette Colbert *It Happened One Night* |
| 1935 | *Mutiny on the Bounty,* M-G-M | John Ford, *The Informer* | Bette Davis, *Dangerous* |
| 1936 | *The Great Ziegfeld,* M-G-M | Frank Capra, *Mr. Deeds Goes to Town* | Luise Rainer, *The Great Ziegfeld* |
| 1937 | *The Life of Emile Zola,* Warner Bros. | Leo McCarey, *The Awful Truth* | Luise Rainer, *The Good Earth* |
| 1938 | *You Can't Take It with You,* Columbia | Frank Capra, *You Can't Take It with You* | Bette Davis, *Jezebel* |
| 1939 | *Gone with the Wind,* Selznick-M-G-M | Victor Fleming, *Gone with the Wind* | Vivien Leigh, *Gone with the Wind* |
| 1940 | *Rebecca,* Selznick-UA | John Ford, *The Grapes of Wrath* | Ginger Rogers, *Kitty Foyle* |
| 1941 | *How Green Was My Valley,* 20th Century-Fox | John Ford, *How Green Was My Valley* | Joan Fontaine, *Suspicion* |
| 1942 | *Mrs. Miniver,* M-G-M | William Wyler, *Mrs. Miniver* | Greer Garson, *Mrs. Miniver* |
| 1943 | *Casablanca,* Warner Bros. | Michael Curtiz, *Casablanca* | Jennifer Jones, *The Song of Bernadette* |
| 1944 | *Going My Way,* Paramount | Leo McCarey, *Going My Way* | Ingrid Bergman, *Gaslight* |
| 1945 | *The Lost Weekend,* Paramount | Billy Wilder, *The Lost Weekend* | Joan Crawford, *Mildred Pierce* |
| 1946 | *The Best Years of Our Lives,* Goldwyn-RKO Radio | William Wyler, *The Best Years of Our Lives* | Olivia de Havilland, *To Each His Own* |
| 1947 | *Gentleman's Agreement,* 20th Century-Fox | Elia Kazan, *Gentleman's Agreement* | Loretta Young, *The Farmer's Daughter* |
| 1948 | *Hamlet,* Rank-Two Cities-U-I | John Houston, *Treasure of Sierra Madre* | Jane Wyman, *Johnny Belinda* |
| 1949 | *All the King's Men,* Rossen-Columbia | Joseph L. Mankiewicz, *A Letter to Three Wives* | Olivia de Havilland, *The Heiress* |
| 1950 | *All About Eve,* 20th Century-Fox | Joseph L. Mankiewicz, *All About Eve* | Judy Holliday, *Born Yesterday* |
| 1951 | *An American in Paris,* M-G-M | George Stevens, *A Place in the Sun* | Vivien Leigh, *A Streetcar Named Desire* |
| 1952 | *The Greatest Show on Earth,* DeMille-Paramount | John Ford, *The Quiet Man* | Shirley Booth, *Come Back, Little Sheba* |
| 1953 | *From Here to Eternity,* Columbia | Fred Zinnemann, *From Here to Eternity* | Audrey Hepburn, *Roman Holiday* |
| 1954 | *On the Waterfront,* Horizon-American Corp., Columbia | Elia Kazan, *On the Waterfront* | Grace Kelley, *The Country Girl* |
| 1955 | *Marty,* Hecht and Lancaster, United Artists | Delbert Mann, *Marty* | Anna Magnani, *The Rose Tattoo* |
| 1956 | *Around the World in 80 Days,* Michael Todd Co., Inc.-UA | George Stevens, *Giant* | Ingrid Bergman, *Anastasia* |
| 1957 | *The Bridge on the River Kwai,* Horizon Picture, Columbia | David Lean, *The Bridge on the River Kwai* | Joanne Woodward, *The Three Faces of Eve* |
| 1958 | *Gigi,* Arthur Freed Productions, Inc., M-G-M | Vincente Minnelli, *Gigi* | Susan Hayward, *I Want to Live!* |
| 1959 | *Ben-Hur,* M-G-M | William Wyler, *Ben-Hur* | Simone Signoret, *Room at the Top* |
| 1960 | *The Apartment,* Mirisch Co., Inc., United Artists | Billy Wilder, *The Apartment* | Elizabeth Taylor, *Butterfield 8* |
| 1961 | *West Side Story,* Mirisch Pictures, Inc., and B and P Enterprises, Inc., United Artists | Robert Wise and Jerome Robbins, *West Side Story* | Sophia Loren, *Two Women* |

| Actor | Supporting Actress | Supporting Actor | |
|---|---|---|---|
| Emil Jannings, *The Way of All Flesh, The Last Command* | — | — | 1928 |
| Warner Baxter, *In Old Arizona* | — | — | 1929 |
| George Arliss, *Disraeli* | — | — | 1930 |
| Lionel Barrymore, *A Free Soul* | — | — | 1931 |
| Frederic March, *Dr. Jekyll and Mr. Hyde*, and Wallace Beery, *The Champ* | — | — | 1932 |
| Charles Laughton, *The Private Life of Henry VIII* | — | — | 1933 |
| Clark Gable, *It Happened One Night* | — | — | 1934 |
| Victor McLaglen, *The Informer* | — | — | 1935 |
| Paul Muni, *The Story of Louis Pasteur* | Gale Sondergaard, *Anthony Adverse* | Walter Brennan, *Come and Get It* | 1936 |
| Spencer Tracy, *Captains Courageous* | Alice Brady, *In Old Chicago* | Joseph Schildkraut, *The Life of Emile Zola* | 1937 |
| Spencer Tracy, *Boys Town* | Fay Bainter, *Jezebel* | Walter Brennan, *Kentucky* | 1938 |
| Robert Donat, *Goodbye, Mr. Chips* | Hattie McDaniel, *Gone with the Wind* | Thomas Mitchell, *Stagecoach* | 1939 |
| James Stewart, *The Philadelphia Story* | Jane Darwell, *The Grapes of Wrath* | Walter Brennan, *The Westerner* | 1940 |
| Gary Cooper, *Sergeant York* | Mary Astor, *The Great Lie* | Donald Crisp, *How Green Was My Valley* | 1941 |
| James Cagney, *Yankee Doodle Dandy* | Teresa Wright, *Mrs. Minivor* | Van Heflin, *Johnny Eager* | 1942 |
| Paul Lukas, *Watch on the Rhine* | Katina Paxinou, *For Whom the Bell Tolls* | Charles Coburn, *The More the Merrier* | 1943 |
| Bing Crosby, *Going My Way* | Ethel Barrymore, *None But the Lonely Heart* | Barry Fitzgerald, *Going My Way* | 1944 |
| Ray Milland, *The Lost Weekend* | Anne Revere, *National Velvet* | James Dunn, *A Tree Grows in Brooklyn* | 1945 |
| Fredric March, *The Best Years of Our Lives* | Anne Baxter, *The Razor's Edge* | Harold Russell, *The Best Years of Our Lives* | 1946 |
| Ronald Colman, *A Double Life* | Celeste Holm, *Gentleman's Agreement* | Edmund Gwenn, *Miracle on 34th Street* | 1947 |
| Laurence Olivier, *Hamlet* | Claire Trevor, *Key Largo* | Walter Huston, *Treasure of Sierra Madre* | 1948 |
| Broderick Crawford, *All the King's Men* | Mercedes McCambridge, *All the King's Men* | Dean Jagger, *Twelve O'Clock High* | 1949 |
| José Ferrer, *Cyrano de Bergerac* | Josephine Hull, *Harvey* | George Sanders, *All About Eve* | 1950 |
| Humphrey Bogart, *The African Queen* | Kim Hunter, *A Streetcar Named Desire* | Karl Malden, *A Streetcar Named Desire* | 1951 |
| Gary Cooper, *High Noon* | Gloria Grahame, *The Bad and the Beautiful* | Anthony Quinn, *Viva Zapata!* | 1952 |
| William Holden, *Stalag 17* | Donna Reed, *From Here to Eternity* | Frank Sinatra, *From Here to Eternity* | 1953 |
| Marlon Brando, *On the Waterfront* | Eva Marie Saint, *On the Waterfront* | Edmond O'Brien, *The Barefoot Contessa* | 1954 |
| Ernest Borgnine, *Marty* | Jo Van Fleet, *East of Eden* | Jack Lemmon, *Mister Roberts* | 1955 |
| Yul Brynner, *The King and I* | Dorothy Malone, *Written on the Wind* | Anthony Quinn, *Lust for Life* | 1956 |
| Alec Guinness, *The Bridge on the River Kwai* | Miyoshi Umeki, *Sayonara* | Red Buttons, *Sayonara* | 1957 |
| David Niven, *Separate Tables* | Wendy Hiller, *Separate Tables* | Burl Ives, *The Big Country* | 1958 |
| Charlton Heston, *Ben-Hur* | Shelley Winters, *The Diary of Anne Frank* | Hugh Griffith, *Ben-Hur* | 1959 |
| Burt Lancaster, *Elmer Gantry* | Shirley Jones, *Elmer Gantry* | Peter Ustinov, *Spartacus* | 1960 |
| Maximilian Schell, *Judgment at Nuremberg* | Rita Moreno, *West Side Story* | George Chakiris, *West Side Story* | 1961 |

| | Picture | Director | Actress |
|---|---|---|---|
| 1962 | *Lawrence of Arabia,* Horizon Pictures, Ltd.-Columbia | David Lean, *Lawrence of Arabia* | Anne Bancroft, *The Miracle Worker* |
| 1963 | *Tom Jones,* A Woodfall Production, UA-Lopert Pictures | Tony Richardson, *Tom Jones* | Patricia Neal, *Hud* |
| 1964 | *My Fair Lady,* Warner Bros. | George Cukor, *My Fair Lady* | Julie Andrews, *Mary Poppins* |
| 1965 | *The Sound of Music,* Argyle Enterprises Production, 20th Century-Fox | Robert Wise, *The Sound of Music* | Julie Christie, *Darling* |
| 1966 | *A Man for All Seasons,* Highland Films, Ltd., Production, Columbia | Fred Zinnemann, *A Man for All Seasons* | Elizabeth Taylor, *Who's Afraid of Virginia Woolf?* |
| 1967 | *In the Heat of the Night,* Mirisch Corp. Production, United Artists | Mike Nichols, *The Graduate* | Katharine Hepburn, *Guess Who's Coming to Dinner* |
| 1968 | *Oliver!,* Columbia Pictures | Sir Carol Reed, *Oliver!* | Katharine Hepburn, *The Lion in Winter, and Barbara Streisand, Funny Girl* |
| 1969 | *Midnight Cowboy,* Jerome Hellman-John Schlesinger Production, United Artists | John Schlesinger, *Midnight Cowboy* | Maggie Smith, *The Prime of Miss Jean Brodie* |
| 1970 | *Patton,* Frank McCarthy-Franklin J. Schaffner Production, 20th Century-Fox | Franklin J. Schaffner, *Patton* | Glenda Jackson, *Women in Love* |
| 1971 | *The French Connection,* D'Antoni Productions, 20th Century-Fox | William Friedkin, *The French Connection* | Jane Fonda, *Klute* |
| 1972 | *The Godfather,* Albert S. Ruddy Production, Paramount | Bob Fosse, *Cabaret* | Liza Minnelli, *Cabaret* |
| 1973 | *The Sting,* Universal-Bill-Phillips-George Roy Hill Production, Universal | George Roy Hill, *The Sting* | Glenda Jackson, *A Touch of Class* |
| 1974 | *The Godfather, Part II,* Coppola Co. Production, Paramount | Francis Ford Coppola, *The Godfather, Part II* | Ellen Burstyn, *Alice Doesn't Live Here Anymore* |
| 1975 | *One Flew Over the Cuckoo's Nest,* Fantasy Films Production, United Artists | Milos Forman, *One Flew Over the Cuckoo's Nest* | Louise Fletcher, *One Flew Over the Cuckoo's Nest* |
| 1976 | *Rocky,* Robert Chartoff-Irwin Winkler Production, United Artists | John G. Avildsen, *Rocky* | Faye Dunaway *Network* |
| 1977 | *Annie Hall,* Jack Rollins-Charles H. Joffe Production, United Artists | Woody Allen, *Annie Hall* | Diane Keaton, *Annie Hall* |

## Other Academy Awards for 1977

**Art Direction:** John Barry, Norman Reynolds and Leslie Dilley, *Star Wars;* set decoration: Roger Christian, *Star Wars*

**Cinematography:** Vilmos Zsigmond, *Close Encounters of the Third Kind*

**Costume design:** John Mollo, *Star Wars*

**Documentary (feature):** *Who Are the DeBolts? And Where Did They Get Nineteen Kids?*

**Documentary (short subject):** *Gravity Is My Enemy*

**Editing:** Paul Hirsch, Marcia Lucas and Richard Chew, *Star Wars*

**Foreign-language film:** *Madame Rosa*

**Music (original score):** John Williams, *Star Wars*

**Scoring (adaptation):** Jonathan Tunick, *A Little Night Music*

**Screenplay (original):** Woody Allen and Marshall Brickman, *Annie Hall*

**Screenplay (adaptation):** Alvin Sargent, *Julia*

**Short subject (animated):** *Sand Castle*

**Short subject (live):** *I'll Find a Way*

**Song:** "You Light Up My Life," by Joseph Brooks, for film of the same name

**Sound:** Don MacDougall, Ray West, Bob Minkler and Derek Ball, *Star Wars*

**Visual effects:** John Stears, John Dykstra, Richard Edlund, Grant McCune and Robert Blalack, *Star Wars*

**SPECIAL AWARDS**

**Irving G. Thalberg Memorial Award:** Walter Mirisch

**Jean Hersholt Humanitarian Award:** Charlton Heston

**Honorary award:** Maggie Booth, film editor

**Sound effects editing:** Frank Warner, *Close Encounters of the Third Kind*

**Science and technical award:** Cinema Products, for the Steadycam

**For creation of alien creature and robot voices in** *Star Wars:* Benjamin Burtt, Jr.

## "Oscar"

In 1928, the Academy of Motion Picture Arts and Sciences began the annual presentation of its awards for motion picture excellence. The "Oscar" was originally sketched by Cedric Gibbons. The statue is 10 inches tall, weighs 7 pounds, and is made of gold plate over bronze. When Margaret Harrick, the Academy's first executive director, saw the statue, she remarked that it looked like her Uncle Oscar. The nickname stuck, and today the "Oscar" is the most important and sought after of film awards.

| Actor | Supporting Actress | Supporting Actor | |
|---|---|---|---|
| Gregory Peck, *To Kill a Mockingbird* | Patty Duke, *The Miracle Worker* | Ed Begley, *Sweet Bird of Youth* | 1962 |
| Sidney Poitier, *Lilies of the Field* | Margaret Rutherford, *The V.I.P.s* | Melvyn Douglas, *Hud* | 1963 |
| Rex Harrison, *My Fair Lady* | Lila Kedrova, *Zorba the Greek* | Peter Ustinov, *Topkapi* | 1964 |
| Lee Marvin, *Cat Ballou* | Shelley Winters, *A Patch of Blue* | Martin Balsam, *A Thousand Clowns* | 1965 |
| Paul Scofield, *A Man for All Seasons* | Sandy Dennis, *Who's Afraid of Virginia Woolf?* | Walter Matthau, *The Fortune Cookie* | 1966 |
| Rod Steiger, *In the Heat of the Night* | Estelle Parsons, *Bonnie and Clyde* | George Kennedy, *Cool Hand Luke* | 1967 |
| Cliff Robertson, *Charly* | Ruth Gordon, *Rosemary's Baby* | Jack Albertson, *The Subject Was Roses* | 1968 |
| John Wayne, *True Grit* | Goldie Hawn, *Cactus Flower* | Gig Young, *They Shoot Horses, Don't They?* | 1969 |
| George C. Scott, *Patton* | Helen Hayes, *Airport* | John Mills, *Ryan's Daughter* | 1970 |
| Gene Hackman, *The French Connection* | Cloris Leachman, *The Last Picture Show* | Ben Johnson, *The Last Picture Show* | 1971 |
| Marlon Brando, *The Godfather* | Eileen Heckart, *Butterflies Are Free* | Joel Grey, *Cabaret* | 1972 |
| Jack Lemmon, *Save the Tiger* | Tatum O'Neal, *Paper Moon* | John Houseman, *The Paper Chase* | 1973 |
| Art Carney, *Harry and Tonto* | Ingrid Bergman, *Murder on the Orient Express* | Robert De Niro, *The Godfather, Part II* | 1974 |
| Jack Nicholson, *One Flew Over the Cuckoo's Nest* | Lee Grant, *Shampoo* | George Burns, *The Sunshine Boys* | 1975 |
| Peter Finch, *Network* | Beatrice Straight, *Network* | Jason Robards, *All the President's Men* | 1976 |
| Richard Dreyfuss, *The Goodbye Girl* | Vanessa Redgrave, *Julia* | Jason Robards, *Julia* | 1977 |

## New York Drama Critics' Circle Awards

**1935–36**
*Winterset,* Maxwell Anderson
**1936–37**
*High Tor,* Maxwell Anderson
**1937–38**
*Of Mice and Men,* John Steinbeck
*Shadow and Substance,* Paul Vincent Carroll[1]
**1938–39**
(No award) *The White Steed,* Paul Vincent Carroll[1]
**1939–40**
*The Time of Your Life,* William Saroyan
**1940–41**
*Watch on the Rhine,* Lillian Hellman
*The Corn Is Green,* Emlyn Williams[1]
**1941–42**
(No award) *Blithe Spirit,* Noel Coward[1]
**1942–43**
*The Patriots,* Sidney Kingsley
**1943–44**
(No award) *Jacobowsky and the Colonel.* Franz Werfel and S. N. Behrman[1]
**1944–45**
*The Glass Menagerie,* Tennessee Williams
**1945–46**
(No award) *Carousel,* Richard Rodgers and Oscar Hammerstein II[2]
**1946–47**
*All My Sons,* Arthur Miller
*No Exit,* Jean-Paul Sartre[1]
*Brigadoon,* Alan Jay Lerner and Frederick Loewe[2]
**1947–48**
*A Streetcar Named Desire,* Tennessee Williams
*The Winslow Boy,* Terence Rattigan[1]
**1948–49**
*Death of a Salesman,* Arthur Miller
*The Madwoman of Chaillot,* Jean Giraudoux and Maurice Valency[1]
*South Pacific,* Richard Rodgers, Oscar Hammerstein II, and Joshua Logan[2]
**1949–50**
*The Member of the Wedding,* Carson McCullers
*The Cocktail Party,* T. S. Eliot[1]
*The Consul,* Gian-Carlo Menotti[2]
**1950–51**
*Darkness at Noon,* Sidney Kingsley[3]
*The Lady's Not for Burning,* Christopher Fry[1]
*Guys and Dolls,* Abe Burrows, Jo Swerling and Frank Loesser[2]

**1951–52**
*I Am a Camera,* John Van Druten[4]
*Venus Observed,* Christopher Fry[1]
*Pal Joey,* Richard Rodgers, Lorenz Hart, and John O'Hara[2]
*Don Juan in Hell,* George B. Shaw[5]

**1952–53**
*Picnic,* William Inge
*The Love of Four Colonels,* by Peter Ustinov[1]
*Wonderful Town,* Joseph Fields, Jerome Chodorov, Betty Comden, Adolph Green, and Leonard Bernstein[2]

**1953–54**
*The Teahouse of the August Moon,* John Patrick
*Ondine,* Jean Giraudoux[1]
*The Golden Apple,* John Latouche and Jerome Moross[2]

**1954–55**
*Cat on a Hot Tin Roof,* Tennessee Williams
*Witness for the Prosecution,* Agatha Christie[1]
*The Saint of Bleecker Street,* Gian-Carlo Menotti[2]

**1955-56**
*The Diary of Anne Frank,* Frances Goodrich and Albert Hackett
*Tiger at the Gates,* Jean Giraudoux and Christopher Fry[1]
*My Fair Lady,* Frederick Loewe and Alan Jay Lerner[2]

**1956–57**
*Long Day's Journey Into Night,* Eugene O'Neill
*Waltz of the Toreadors,* Jean Anouilh[1]
*The Most Happy Fella,* Frank Loesser[2, 6]

**1957–58**
*Look Homeward, Angel,* Ketti Frings[7]
*Look Back in Anger,* John Osborne[1]
*The Music Man,* Meredith Willson[2]

**1958–59**
*A Raisin in the Sun,* Lorraine Hansberry
*The Visit,* Friedrich Duerrenmatt–Maurice Valency[1]
*La Plume de ma Tante,* Robert Dhery and Gerard Calvi[2]

**1959–60**
*Toys in the Attic,* Lillian Hellman
*Five Finger Exercise,* Peter Shaffer[1]
*Fiorello!,* Jerome Weidman, George Abbott, Jerry Bock, and Sheldon Harnick[2]

**1960–61**
*All the Way Home,* Tad Mosel[8]
*A Taste of Honey,* Shelagh Delaney[1]
*Carnival,* Michael Stewart[2]

**1961–62**
*The Night of the Iguana,* Tennessee Williams
*A Man for All Seasons,* Robert Bolt[1]
*How to Succeed in Business Without Really Trying,* Abe Burrows, Jack Weinstock, Willie Gilbert, and Frank Loesser[2, 9]

**1962–63**
*Who's Afraid of Virginia Woolf?,* Edward Albee
*Beyond the Fringe,* Alan Bennett, Peter Cook, Jonathan Miller, and Dudley Moore[10]

**1963–64**
*Luther,* John Osborne
*Hello, Dolly!* Michael Stewart and Jerry Herman[2, 11]
*The Trojan Women,* Euripides[10, 12]

**1964–65**
*The Subject Was Roses,* Frank D. Gilroy
*Fiddler on the Roof,* Joseph Stein, Jerry Bock, and Sheldon Harnick[2, 13]

**1965–66**
*The Persecution and Assassination of Marat as Performed by the Inmates of the Asylum of Charenton under the Direction of the Marquis de Sade,* Peter Weiss
*The Man of La Mancha,* Dale Wasserman, Mitch Leigh, and Joe Darion

**1966–67**
*The Homecoming,* Harold Pinter
*Cabaret,* Joe Masteroff, John Kander, and Fred Ebb[2, 14]

**1967–68**
*Rosencrantz and Guilderstern Are Dead,* Tom Stoppard
*Your Own Thing,* Donald Driver, Hal Hester, and Danny Apolinar[2]

**1968–69**
*The Great White Hope,* Howard Sackler
*1776,* Sherman Edwards and Peter Stone[2]

**1969–70**
*Borstal Boy,* Frank McMahon[15]
*The Effect of Gamma Rays on Man-in-the-Moon Marigolds,* Paul Zindel[16]
*Company,* George Furth and Stephen Sondheim[2]

**1970–71**
*Home,* David Storey
*The House of Blue Leaves,* John Guare[16]
*Follies,* James Goldman and Stephen Sondheim[2]

**1971–72**
*That Championship Season,* Jason Miller
*Two Gentlemen of Verona,* adapted by John Guare and Mel Shapiro[2]
*The Screens,* Jean Genet[1]

**1972–73**
*The Changing Room,* David Storey
*The Hot l Baltimore,* by Lanford Wilson[16]
*A Little Night Music,* Hugh Wheeler and Stephen Sondheim[2]

**1973–74**
*The Contractors,* David Storey
*Short Eyes,* Miguel Piñero[16]
*Candide,* Leonard Bernstein, Hugh Wheeler, and Richard Wilbur[2]

**1974–75**
*Equus,* Peter Shaffer
*The Taking of Miss Janie,* Ed Bullins[16]
*A Chorus Line,* James Kirkwood and Nicholas Dante[2]

**1975–76**
*Travesties,* Tom Stoppard
*Streamers,* David Rabe[16]
*Pacific Overtures,* Stephen Sondheim, John Weidman, and Hugh Wheeler[2]

**1976–77**
*Otherwise Engaged,* Simon Gray
*American Buffalo,* David Mamet[6]
*Annie,* Thomas Meehan, Charles Strouse, and Martin Charnin[2]

**1977–78**
*Da,* Hugh Leonard
*Ain't Misbehavin',* conceived by Richard Maltby, Jr.[2]

1. Citation for best foreign play. 2. Citation for best musical. 3. Based on a novel by Arthur Koestler. 4. Based on Christopher Isherwood's *Berlin Stories.* 5. For "distinguished and original contribution to the theater." 6. Based on Sidney Howard's *They Knew What They Wanted.* 7. Based on a novel by Thomas Wolfe. 8. Based on James Agee's *A Death in the Family.* 9. Based on a book by Shepherd Mead. 10. Special citation. 11. Based on Thornton Wilder's *The Matchmaker.* 12. Translated by Edith Hamilton. 13. Based on Sholem Aleichem's Tevye stories, translated by Arnold Perl. 14. Based on John Van Druten's *I Am a Camera,* which won the award for the best play in 1951–52. 15. Based on Brendan Behan's autobiography. 16. Citation for best American play.

# Presidential Medal of Freedom

The nation's highest civilian award, the Presidential Medal of Freedom, was established in 1963 by President John F. Kennedy to continue and expand Presidential recognition of meritorious service which, since 1945, had been granted as the Medal of Freedom.

## AWARDED BY PRESIDENT KENNEDY

| | |
|---|---|
| Marian Anderson (contralto) | 1963 |
| Ralph J. Bunche (statesman) | 1963 |
| Ellsworth Bunker (diplomat) | 1963 |
| Pablo Casals (cellist) | 1963 |
| Genevieve Caulfield (educator) | 1963 |
| James B. Conant (educator) | 1963 |
| John F. Enders (bacteriologist) | 1963 |
| Felix Frankfurter (jurist) | 1963 |
| Karl Horton (youth authority) | 1963 |
| John XXIII (Pope) | 1963* |
| Robert J. Kiphuth (athletic director) | 1963 |
| Edwin H. Land (inventor) | 1963 |
| Herbert H. Lehman (statesman) | 1963* |
| Robert A. Lovett (statesman) | 1963 |
| J. Clifford MacDonald (educator) | 1963* |
| John J. McCloy (banker and statesman) | 1963 |
| George Meany (labor leader) | 1963 |
| Alexander Meiklejohn (philosopher) | 1963 |
| Ludwig Mies van der Rohe (architect) | 1963 |
| Jean Monnet (European statesman) | 1963 |
| Luis Muñoz-Marín (Governor of Puerto Rico) | 1963 |
| Clarence B. Randall (industrialist) | 1963 |
| Rudolf Serkin (pianist) | 1963 |
| Edward Steichen (photographer) | 1963 |
| George W. Taylor (educator) | 1963 |
| Alan T. Waterman (scientist) | 1963 |
| Mark S. Watson (journalist) | 1963 |
| Annie D. Wauneka (public health worker) | 1963 |
| E. B. White (author) | 1963 |
| Thornton N. Wilder (author) | 1963 |
| Edmund Wilson (author and critic) | 1963 |
| Andrew Wyeth (artist) | 1963 |

## AWARDED BY PRESIDENT JOHNSON

| | |
|---|---|
| Dean G. Acheson (statesman) | 1964 |
| Eugene R. Black (banker) | 1969 |
| Detlev W. Bronk (neurophysiologist) | 1964 |
| McGeorge Bundy (government service) | 1969 |
| Ellsworth Bunker (diplomat) | 1968 |
| Clark Clifford (statesman) | 1969 |
| Aaron Copland (composer) | 1964 |
| Michael E. DeBakey (surgeon) | 1969 |
| Willem de Kooning (artist) | 1964 |
| Walt Disney (cartoon film producer) | 1964 |
| J. Frank Dobie (author) | 1964 |
| David Dubinsky (labor leader) | 1969 |
| Lena F. Edwards (physician and humanitarian) | 1964 |
| Thomas Stearns Eliot (poet) | 1964 |
| Ralph Ellison (author) | 1969 |
| Lynn Fontanne (actress) | 1964 |
| Henry Ford II (industrialist) | 1969 |
| John W. Gardner (educator) | 1964 |
| W. Averell Harriman (statesman) | 1969 |
| Rev. Theodore M. Hesburgh (educator) | 1964 |
| Bob Hope (comedian) | 1969 |
| Clarence L. Johnson (aircraft engineer) | 1964 |
| Edgar F. Kaiser (industrialist) | 1969 |
| Frederick R. Kappel (telecommunications executive) | 1964 |
| Helen A. Keller (educator) | 1964 |
| John Fitzgerald Kennedy (U.S. President) | 1963* |
| Robert W. Komer (government service) | 1968 |
| Mary Lasker (philanthropist) | 1969 |
| John L. Lewis (labor leader) | 1964 |
| Walter Lippmann (journalist) | 1964 |
| Eugene M. Locke (diplomat) | 1968 |
| Alfred Lunt (actor) | 1964 |
| John W. Macy, Jr. (government service) | 1969 |
| Ralph McGill (journalist) | 1964 |
| Robert S. McNamara (government service) | 1968 |
| Samuel Eliot Morison (historian) | 1964 |
| Lewis Mumford (urban planner and critic) | 1964 |
| Edward R. Murrow (radio-TV commentator) | 1964 |
| Reinhold Niebuhr (theologian) | 1964 |
| Gregory Peck (actor) | 1969 |
| Leontyne Price (soprano) | 1964 |
| A. Philip Randolph (labor leader) | 1964 |
| Laurance S. Rockefeller (conservationist) | 1969 |
| Walt Whitman Rostow (government service) | 1969 |
| Deak Rusk (statesman) | 1969 |
| Carl Sandburg (poet and biographer) | 1964 |
| Merriman Smith (journalist) | 1969 |
| John Steinbeck (author) | 1964 |
| Helen B. Taussig (pediatrician) | 1964 |
| Cyrus R. Vance (government service) | 1969 |
| Carl Vinson (legislator) | 1964 |
| Thomas J. Watson, Jr. (industrialist) | 1964 |
| James E. Webb (NASA administrator) | 1968 |
| Paul Dudley White (physician) | 1964 |
| William S. White (journalist) | 1969 |
| Roy Wilkins (social welfare executive) | 1969 |
| Whitney M. Young, Jr. (social welfare executive) | 1969 |

*Awarded posthumously.

## AWARDED BY PRESIDENT NIXON

| | |
|---|---|
| Edwin E. Aldrin (astronaut) | 1969 |
| Apollo 13 Mission Operations Team | 1970 |
| Neil A. Armstrong (astronaut) | 1969 |
| Earl Charles Behrens (journalist) | 1970 |
| Manlio Brosio (NATO secretary general) | 1971 |
| Michael Collins (astronaut) | 1969 |
| Edward K. "Duke" Ellington (musician) | 1969 |
| Edward T. Folliard (journalist) | 1970 |
| John Ford (film director) | 1973 |
| Samuel Goldwyn (film producer) | 1971 |
| Fred Wallace Haise, Jr. (astronaut) | 1970 |
| William M. Henry (journalist) | 1970* |
| Paul G. Hoffman (statesman) | 1974 |
| William J. Hopkins (White House service) | 1971 |
| Arthur Krock (journalist) | 1970 |
| Melvin R. Laird (government service) | 1974 |
| David Lawrence (journalist) | 1970 |
| George Gould Lincoln (journalist) | 1970 |
| James A. Lovell, Jr. (astronaut) | 1970 |
| Dr. Charles L. Lowman (orthopedist) | 1974 |
| Raymond Moley (journalist) | 1970 |
| Eugene Ormandy (conductor) | 1970 |
| William P. Rogers (diplomat) | 1973 |
| Adela Rogers St. Johns (journalist) | 1970 |
| John Leonard Swigert, Jr. (astronaut) | 1970 |
| John Paul Vann (adviser, Vietnam war) | 1972* |
| DeWitt and Lila Wallace (founders, *Reader's Digest*) | 1972 |

## AWARDED BY PRESIDENT FORD

| | |
|---|---|
| I. W. Abel (labor leader) | 1977 |
| John Bardeen (physicist) | 1977 |
| Irving Berlin (composer) | 1977 |
| Norman Borlaug (agricultural scientist) | 1977 |
| Omar N. Bradley (national security) | 1977 |

David K. E. Bruce (diplomat) 1976
Arleigh Burke (national security) 1977
Alexander Calder (sculptor) 1977*
Bruce Catton (historian) 1977
Joseph P. DiMaggio (baseball star) 1977
Ariel Durant (author) 1977
Will Durant (author) 1977
Arthur Fiedler (conductor) 1977
Henry J. Friendly (jurist) 1977
Martha Graham (dancer-choreographer) 1976
Claudia "Lady Bird" Johnson (service to U.S. scenic beauty) 1977
Henry A. Kissinger (statesman) 1977
Archibald MacLeish (poet) 1977
James A. Michener (author) 1977
Georgia O'Keeffe (artist) 1977
Jesse Owens (track champion) 1976
Nelson A. Rockefeller (government service) 1977
Norman Rockwell (illustrator) 1977
Artur Rubinstein (pianist) 1976
Donald H. Rumsfeld (government service) 1977
Katherine Filene Shouse (service to the performing arts) 1977
Lowell Thomas (radio-TV commentator) 1977
James D. Watson (biochemist) 1977

**AWARDED BY PRESIDENT CARTER**

Rev. Dr. Martin Luther King, Jr. (civil rights leader) 1977*
Jonas Salk (medical research) 1977
Arthur J. Goldberg (government service) 1978

## Antoinette Perry (Tony) Awards, 1978

**Dramatic play:** *Da,* by Hugh Leonard
**Musical:** *Ain't Misbehavin',* music by Fats Waller
**Most innovative production of a revival:** *Dracula*
**Actress (play):** Jessica Tandy, *The Gin Game*
**Actor (play):** Barnard Hughes, *Da*
**Actress (musical):** Liza Minelli, *The Act*
**Actor (musical):** John Cullum, *On the Twentieth Century*
**Actress, featured (play):** Ann Wedgeworth, *Chapter Two*
**Actor, featured (play):** Lester Rawlins, *Da*
**Actress, featured (musical):** Nell Carter, *Ain't Misbehavin'*
**Actor, featured (musical):** Kevin Kline, *On the Twentieth Century*
**Director (play):** Melvin Bernhardt, *Da*
**Director (musical):** Richard Maltby, Jr., *Ain't Misbehavin'*
**Score:** Cy Coleman (music), Betty Comden and Adolph Green (lyrics), *On the Twentieth Century*
**Book:** Betty Comden and Adolph Green, *On the Twentieth Century*
**Choreography:** Bob Fosse, *Dancin'*
**Scenic design:** Robin Wagner, *On the Twentieth Century*
**Costumes:** Edward Gorey, *Dracula*
**Lighting:** Jules Fisher, *Dancin'*
**Lawrence Langer Award for distinguished lifetime achievement:** Irving Berlin
**Special award:** Long Wharf Theater, New Haven, Conn.

## George Foster Peabody Awards for Broadcasting, 1977

**WXYZ, Detroit:** *Winter's Fear: The Children, the Killer, the Search*
**Paul Hume, WGMS, Rockville, Md.:** *A Variable Feast*
**WHA, Madison, Wis.:** *EARPLAY*
**KSJN, St. Paul:** *The Prairie Was Quiet*
**KPFA, Berkeley, Calif.:** *Science Story*
**National Public Radio, Washington, D.C.:** *CROSSROADS: Sea Island Sketches*
**WHLN, Harlan, Ky.:** Coverage of April 1977 floods in Harlan area
**KABC-TV, Los Angeles:** *Police Accountability,* a part of *Eyewitness News*
**KCMO-TV, Kansas City, Mo.:** *Where Have All the Flood Cars Gone?,* a part of *Eyewitness News*
**WNBC-TV, New York:** *F.I.N.D. Investigative Reports,* a part of *NewsCenter 4*
**WNET/13, New York, and WETA, Arlington, Va.:** *The MacNeil/Lehrer Report*
**WBTV, Charlotte, N.C.:** *The Rowe String Quartet Plays on Your Imagination*
**Lorimar Productions, Los Angeles:** *Green Eyes,* an *ABC Theatre* presentation
**David Wolper and ABC-TV:** *Roots*
**Norman Lear:** *All in the Family*
**London Weekend Television, London:** *Upstairs, Downstairs*
**MTM Productions, Los Angeles:** *The Mary Tyler Moore Show*
**Steve Allen, KCET, Los Angeles:** *Meeting of Minds*
**NBC-TV:** *Tut: The Boy King*
**Metropolitan Opera Association, New York:** *Live From the Met* series, as exemplified by *La Bohème* and *Rigoletto*
**WNET/13, New York:** *A Good Dissonance Like a Man*
**Multimedia Program Productions, Cincinnati:** *Joshua's Confusion*
**NBC-TV:** Arthur Rankin and Jules Bass, *The Hobbit*
**WCBS-TV, New York:** *Camera Three*
**WPIX, New York:** *The Lifer's Group—I Am My Brother's Keeper,* a part of WPIX Editorial Report
**WNBC-TV, New York:** *Buyline: Betty Furness*
**WNET/13, New York:** *Police Tapes*

## American Library Association Awards for Children's Books

**Newbery Medal for best book:** *Bridge to Terabitha,* by Katherine Paterson (Thomas Y. Crowell)
**Caldecott Medal for best illustration:** *Noah's Ark,* by Peter Spier (Doubleday)

## Major Grammy Awards for Recording in 1977

**Album:** "Rumours," Fleetwood Mac (Warner Bros.)
**Record:** "Hotel California," Eagles (Asylum)
**Song:** Love Theme From *A Star Is Born* ("Evergreen"), Barbra Streisand and Paul Williams; and "You Light Up My Life," Joe Brooks
**New Artist:** Debby Boone (Warner Bros./Curb)
**Jazz Vocalist:** Al Jarreau, "Look To the Rainbow" (Warner Bros.)
**Jazz Soloist:** Oscar Peterson, "The Giants" (Pablo)
**Jazz Group:** Phil Woods, "The Phil Woods Six—Live From the Showboat" (RCA)
**Jazz Big Band:** Count Basie, "Prime Time" (Pablo)
**Pop Vocalists:** Barbra Streisand, Love Theme From *A Star Is Born* ("Evergreen") (Columbia); James Taylor, "Handy Man" (Columbia)
**Pop Group:** Bee Gees, "How Deep Is Your Love" (RSO)
**Pop Instrumental Recording:** London Symphony Orchestra, "Star Wars," John Williams (20th Century-Fox)
**Rhythm and Blues Vocalists:** Lou Rawls, "Unmistakably Lou" (Philadelphia International); Thelma Houston, "Don't Leave Me This Way" (Motown)
**Rhythm and Blues Instrumentalists:** Brothers Johnson, "Q" (A&M)
**Rhythm and Blues Song:** "You Make Me Feel Like Dancing," Leo Sayer and Vini Poncia
**Country Vocalists:** Crystal Gayle, "Don't It Make My Brown Eyes Blue" (United Artists); Kenny Rogers, "Lucille" (United Artists)
**Country Group:** The Kendalls, "Heaven's Just a Sin Away" (Ovation)
**Country Instrumentalist:** Hargus (Pig) Robbins, "Country Instrumentalist of the Year" (Elcctra)
**Country Song:** "Don't It Make My Brown Eyes Blue," Richard Leigh
**Gospel, Contemporary or Inspirational:** Imperials, "Sail On" (Dayspring/Word)
**Gospel, Traditional:** Oak Ridge Boys, "Have a Little Walk With Jesus" (Rockland Road)
**Soul Gospel, Contemporary:** Edwin Hawkins and the Edwin Hawkins Singers, "Wonderful" (Birthright)
**Soul Gospel, Traditional:** James Cleveland, "James Cleveland Live at Carnegie Hall" (Savoy)
**Inspirational Performance:** B.J. Thomas, "Home Where I Belong" (Myrrh/Word)
**Latin Recording:** "Dawn," Mongo Santamaria (Vaya)
**Children's Recording:** "Aren't You Glad You're You," Sesame Street cast (Sesame Street)
**Comedy:** Steve Martin, "Let's Get Small" (Warner Bros.)
**Spoken Word:** Julie Harris, "The Belle of Amherst" (Credo)
**Instrumental Composition:** Main Title Theme From "Star Wars," John Williams
**Motion Picture Score:** "Star Wars," John Williams (20th Century-Fox)
**Cast Show Album:** "Annie," Charles Strouse and Martin Charnin (Columbia)
**Classical Album:** "Concert of the Century," recorded live at Carnegie Hall (Columbia)
**Classical Orchestra Performance:** Carlo Maria Giulini leading Chicago Symphony Orchestra in Mahler's Ninth Symphony (Deutsche Grammophon)
**Opera Recording:** "Porgy and Bess," Houston Grand Opera (RCA)
**Classical Soloist With Orchestra:** Itzhak Perlman, violinist, in Vivaldi's "The Four Seasons" with London Philharmonic Orchestra (Angel)
**Classical Soloist Without Orchestra:** Arthur Rubinstein, Beethoven's Sonata for Piano No. 18 and Schumann's "Fantasiestücke" (RCA)
**Classical Vocalist:** Janet Baker, Bach arias (Angel)

## National Book Awards, 1978

**Biography and Autobiography:** *Samuel Johnson,* by W. Jackson Bate (Harcourt Brace Jovanovich)
**Children's Literature:** *The View From the Oak: The Private Worlds of Other Creatures,* by Judith and Herbert Kohl (Sierra Club/Scribner's)
**Contemporary Thought:** *Winners & Losers: Battles, Retreats, Gains, Losses and Ruins From a Long War,* by Gloria Emerson (Random House)
**Fiction:** *Blood Tie,* by Mary Lee Settle (Houghton Mifflin)
**History:** *The Path Between the Seas: The Creation of the Panama Canal, 1870-1914,* by David McCullough (Simon & Schuster)
**Poetry:** *The Collected Poems,* by Howard Nemerov (University of Chicago Press)
**Translation:** Richard and Clara Winston for *In the Deserts of This Earth* by Uwe George (Harcourt Brace Jovanovich)

## Winners of Bollingen Prize in Poetry, 1949–1977

($5,000 award is currently given biennially)

1949 Ezra Pound
1950 Wallace Stevens
1951 John Crowe Ransom
1952 Marianne Moore
1953 Archibald MacLeish and William Carlos Williams
1954 W. H. Auden
1955 Léonie Adams and Louise Bogan
1956 Conrad Aiken
1957 Allen Tate
1958 E.E. Cummings
1959 Theodore Roethke
1960 Delmore Schwartz
1961 Yvor Winters
1962 John Hall Wheelock and Richard Eberhart
1963 Robert Frost
1965 Horace Gregory
1967 Robert Penn Warren
1969 John Berryman and Karl Shapiro
1971 Richard Wilbur and Mona Van Duyn
1973 James Merrill
1975 Archie Randolph Ammons
1977 David Ignatow

# PEOPLE

Many public figures not listed here may be found elsewhere in the *Information Please Almanac.*



A name in parentheses is the original name or form of name. Localities are places of birth. Dates of birth appear as day/month/year. **Boldface** years in parentheses are dates of **(birth-death).**
Information has been gathered from many sources, including the individuals themselves. However, the *Information Please Almanac* cannot guarantee the accuracy of every individual item.

## A

**Aalto,** Alvar (architect); Kuortane, Finland **(1898–1976)**
**Abbott,** Bud (William) (comedian); Asbury Park, N.J. **(1898–1974)**
**Abbott,** George (stage producer); Forestville, N.Y., 6/25/1889
**Abel,** Walter (actor); St. Paul, 6/6/1898
**Abernathy,** Ralph (civil rights leader); Linden, Ala., 3/11/1926
**Acheson,** Dean (statesman); Middletown, Conn. **(1893–1971)**
**Acuff,** Roy (musician); nr. Maynardsville, Tenn. 9/15/1903
**Adams,** Charles Francis (diplomat); Boston **(1807–1886)**
**Adams,** Don (actor); New York City, 4/19/1927
**Adams,** Edie (actress); Kingston, Pa., 4/16/1929
**Adams,** Franklin Pierce (columnist and author); Chicago **(1881–1960)**
**Adams,** Henry Brooks (historian); Boston **(1838–1918)**
**Adams,** Joey (comedian); New York City, 1/6/1911
**Adams,** Maude (Maude Kiskadden) (actress); Salt Lake City, Utah **(1872–1953)**
**Adams,** Samuel (American Revolutionary patriot); Boston **(1722–1803)**
**Adamson,** Joy (naturalist); Troppau (Czechoslovakia) 1/20/1910
**Addams,** Charles (cartoonist); Westfield, N.J., 1/7/1912
**Addams,** Jane (social worker); Cedarville, Ill. **(1860–1935)**
**Adderley,** Julian "Cannonball" (jazz saxophonist); Tampa, Fla. **(1928–1975)**
**Ade,** George (humorist); Kentland, Ind. **(1866–1944)**
**Adenauer,** Konrad (statesman); Cologne, Germany **(1876–1967)**
**Adler,** Alfred (psychoanalyst); Vienna **(1870–1937)**
**Adler,** Larry (musician); Baltimore, 2/10/1914
**Adler,** Richard (songwriter); New York City, 8/3/1921
**Adoree,** Renée (Renée La Fonte) (actress); Lille, France **(1898–1933)**
**Aeschylus** (dramatist); Eleusis (Greece) **(525–456 B.C.)**
**Aesop** (fabulist); birthplace unknown **(lived c. 600 B.C.)**
**Aherne,** Brian (actor); King's Norton, England, 5/2/1902
**Aiken,** Conrad (poet); Savannah, Ga. **(1889–1973)**
**Ailey,** Alvin (choreographer); Rogers, Tex., 1/5/1931
**Aimee,** Anouk (actress); Paris, 4/27/1934
**Albanese,** Licia (operatic soprano); Bari, Italy, 7/22/1913
**Albee,** Edward (playwright); Washington, D.C., 3/12/1928
**Albers,** Josef (painter); Bottrop, Germany **(1888–1976)**
**Albert,** Eddie (Edward Albert Heimberger) (actor); Rock Island, Ill., 4/22/1908
**Albertson,** Jack (actor); Malden, Mass., 6/16/1910(?)
**Albright,** Lola (actress); Akron, Ohio, 7/20/1925
**Alcott,** Louisa May (novelist); Germantown, Pa. **(1832–1888)**
**Alda,** Alan (actor); New York City, 1/28/1936
**Alda,** Robert (Alphonso d'Abruzzo) (actor); New York City, 2/26/1914
**Alden,** John (American Pilgrim); England **(1599?–1687)**
**Alexander the Great** (monarch and conqueror); Pella (Greece) **(356–323 B.C.)**
**Alger,** Horatio (author); Revere, Mass. **(1834–1899)**
**Algren,** Nelson (novelist); Detroit, 3/28/1909
**Allen,** Ethan (American Revolutionary soldier); Litchfield, Conn. **(1738–1789)**
**Allen,** Fred (John Florence Sullivan) (comedian); Cambridge, Mass. **(1894–1956)**
**Allen,** Gracie (Grace Ethel Cecile Rosalie Allen) (comedienne); San Francisco **(1906–1964)**
**Allen,** Mel (Melvin Israel) (sportscaster); Birmingham, Ala., 2/14/1913
**Allen,** Steve (TV entertainer); New York City, 12/26/1921
**Allen,** Woody (Allen Stewart Konigsberg) (comedian, writer, and director); Brooklyn, N.Y., 12/1/1935
**Allison,** Fran (actress); LaPorte City, Iowa, 1924(?)
**Allman,** Gregg (singer); Nashville, Tenn., 12/8/1947
**Allyson,** June (Jan Allyson) (actress); New York City, 10/7/1923
**Alonso,** Alicia (ballerina); Havana, 12/21/1921(?)
**Alpert,** Herb (band leader); Los Angeles, 3/31/1935(?)
**Alsop,** Joseph W., Jr. (journalist); Avon, Conn., 10/11/1910
**Alsop,** Stewart (journalist); Avon, Conn. **(1914–1974)**
**Altman,** Robert (film director); Kansas City, Mo., 2/20/1925
**Ambler,** Eric (suspense writer); London, 6/28/1909
**Ameche,** Don (Dominic Amici) (actor); Kenosha, Wis., 5/31/1908
**Amis,** Kingsley (novelist); London, 4/16/1922
**Amory,** Cleveland (writer and conservationist); Nahant, Mass., 9/2/1917
**Amos** (Freeman F. Gosden) (radio comedian); Richmond, Va., 5/5/1899
**Amsterdam,** Morey (actor); Chicago, 12/14/1914
**Andersen,** Hans Christian (author of fairy-tales); Odense, Denmark **(1805–1875)**
**Anderson,** Eddie. *See* Rochester
**Anderson,** Jack (journalist); Long Beach, Calif., 10/19/1922
**Anderson,** Dame Judith (actress); Adelaide, Australia, 2/10/1898
**Anderson,** Lindsay (Gordon) (director); Bangalore, India, 4/17/1923
**Anderson,** Lynn (singer); Grand Forks, N.D., 9/26/1947
**Anderson,** Marian (contralto); Philadelphia, 2/17/1902
**Anderson,** Maxwell (dramatist); Atlantic, Pa. **(1888–1959)**
**Anderson,** Robert (playwright); New York City, 4/28/1917
**Andersson,** Bibi (actress); Stockholm, 11/11/1935
**Andress,** Ursula (actress); Switzerland, 3/19/1938
**Andrews,** Dana (actor); Collins, Miss., 1/1/1909
**Andrews,** Julie (Julia Wells) (actress and singer); Walton-on-Thames, England, 10/1/1935
**Andrews,** La Verne (singer); Minneapolis **(1916–1967)**
**Andrews,** Maxene (singer); Minneapolis, 1/3/1918
**Andrews,** Patti (singer); Minneapolis, 2/16/1920
**Andy** (Charles J. Correll) (radio comedian); Peoria, Ill. **(1890–1972)**
**Angeles,** Victoria de los (Victoria Gamez Cima) (operatic soprano); Barcelona, 11/1/1924
**Anka,** Paul (singer and composer); Ottawa, 7/30/1941
**Ann-Margret** (Ann-Margret Olsson) (actress); Valsjobyn, Sweden, 4/28/1941
**Annabella** (actress); Paris, 1912
**Anouilh,** Jean (playwright); Bordeaux, France, 6/23/1910
**Anthony,** Susan Brownell (woman suffragist); Adams, Mass. **(1820–1906)**
**Antonioni,** Michelangelo (director); Ferrara, Italy, 9/29/1912
**Antony,** Mark (Marcus Antonius) (statesman); Rome **(83?–30 B.C.)**
**Anuszkiewicz,** Richard (painter); Erie, Pa., 5/23/1930
**Aquinas,** St. Thomas (philosopher); nr. Aquino (Italy) **(1225? –1274)**
**Arbuckle,** Roscoe "Fatty" (actor and director); San Jose, Calif. **(1887–1933)**
**Archimedes** (physicist and mathematician); Syracuse (Italy) **(287?–212 B.C.)**
**Archipenko,** Alexandre (sculptor); Kiev, Russia **(1887–1964)**
**Arden,** Elizabeth (Florence Nightingale Graham) (cosmetics executive); Woodbridge, Canada **(1891–1966)**
**Arden,** Eve (Eunice Quedens) (actress); Mill Valley, Calif., 4/30/1912
**Arendt,** Hannah (historian); Hannover, Germany **(1906–1975)**
**Aristophanes** (dramatist); Athens **448?–380 B.C.)**
**Aristotle** (philosopher); Stagira (Greece) **(384–322 B.C.)**
**Arkin,** Alan (actor and director); New York City, 3/26/1934
**Arledge,** Roone (TV executive); Forest Hills, N.Y., 7/8/1931
**Arlen,** Harold (Hyman Arluck) (composer); Buffalo, N.Y., 2/15/1905
**Arlen,** Richard (actor); Charlottesville, Va. **(1900–1976)**
**Arliss,** George (actor); London **(1868–1946)**
**Armstrong,** Louis ("Satchmo") (musician); New Orleans **(1900–1971)**

Armstrong-Jones, Anthony, Earl of Snowden (ex-husband of Princess Margaret); London, 3/7/1930
Arnaz, Desi (Desiderio) (actor and producer); Santiago, Cuba, 3/2/1917
Arnaz, Desi, Jr. (actor); Los Angeles, 1953
Arnaz, Lucie (actress); Hollywood, Calif., 1951
Arness, James (James Aurness) (TV actor); Minneapolis, 5/26/1923
Arno, Peter (cartoonist); New York City **(1904–1968)**
Arnold, Benedict (American Revolutionary War General, convicted of treason); Norwich, Conn. **(1741–1801)**
Arnold, Eddy (singer); Henderson, Tenn., 5/15/1918
Arnold, Edward (actor); New York City **(1890–1956)**
Arnold, Matthew (poet and critic); Laleham, England **(1822–1888)**
Arp, Jean (sculptor and painter); Strasbourg (France) **(1887–1966)**
Arquette, Cliff ("Charley Weaver") (actor); Toledo, Ohio **(1905–1974)**
Arrau, Claudio (pianist); Chillán, Chile, 2/6/1903
Arthur, Bea (Bernice Frankel) (actress); New York City, 5/13/1926(?)
Arthur, Jean (Gladys Greene) (actress); New York City, 10/17/1908
Asch, Sholem (novelist); Kutno, Poland **(1880–1957)**
Ashkenazy, Vladimir (concert pianist); Gorki, U.S.S.R., 7/6/1937
Ashley, Elizabeth (actress); Ocala, Fla., 8/30/1939
Asimov, Isaac (author); Petrovichi, Russia, 1/2/1920
Asner, Edward (actor); Kansas City, Kan., 11/15/1929
Astaire, Fred (Frederick Austerlitz) (dancer and actor); Omaha, Neb., 5/10/1899
Astor, John Jacob (financier); Waldorf (Germany) **(1763–1848)**
Astor, Mary (Lucile Langhanke) (actress); Quincy, Ill., 5/3/1906
Atkins, Chet (guitarist); nr. Luttrell, Tenn., 6/20/1924
Atkinson, Brooks (drama critic); Melrose, Mass., 11/28/1894
Attenborough, Richard (actor); Cambridge, England, 8/29/1923
Attila (King of Huns, called "Scourge of God") **(406?–453)**
Attlee, Clement Richard (statesman); London **(1883–1967)**
Auden, W. H. (poet); York, England **(1907–1973)**
Audubon, John James (naturalist and painter); Haiti **(1785–1851)**
Auer, Leopold (violinist and teacher); Veszprém, Hungary **(1845–1930)**
Auer, Mischa (actor); St. Petersburg, Russia **(1905–1967)**
Augustine, Saint (Aurelius Augustinus) (philosopher); Numidia (Algeria) **(354–430)**
Augustus (Gaius Octavius) (Roman emperor); Rome **(63 B.C.-A.D. 14)**
Aumont, Jean-Pierre (actor); Paris, 1/5/1913
Austen, Jane (novelist); Steventon, England **(1775–1817)**
Autry, Gene (singer and actor); Tioga, Tex., 9/29/1907
Avalon, Frankie (singer); Philadelphia, 9/18/1940
Avedon, Richard (photographer); New York City, 5/15/1923
Avery, Milton (painter); Altmar, N.Y. **(1893–1965)**
Axelrod, George (playwright); New York City, 6/9/1922
Ayres, Lew (actor); Minneapolis, 12/28/1908

# B

Bacall, Lauren (Betty Joan Perske) (actress); New York City, 9/16/1924
Bach, Johann Sebastian (composer); Eisenach (Germany) **(1685–1750)**
Bacharach, Burt (songwriter); Kansas City, Mo., 5/12/1929
Backus, Jim (actor); Cleveland, 2/25/1913
Bacon, Francis (painter); Dublin, 1910
Bacon, Francis (philosopher and essayist); London **(1561–1626)**
Bacon, Roger (philosopher and scientist); Ilchester, England **(1214?–1294)**
Baedeker, Karl (travel-guidebook publisher); Essen (Germany) **1801–1859)**
Baez, Joan (folk singer); Staten Island, N.Y., 1/9/1941
Bagnold, Enid (novelist); Rochester, England, 12/27/1889
Bailey, F. Lee (lawyer); Waltham, Mass., 6/10/1933
Bailey, Pearl (singer); Newport News, Va., 3/29/1918
Bainter, Fay (actress); Los Angeles **(1891–1968)**
Baird, Bil (William B.) (puppeteer); Grand Island, Neb., 8/15/1904
Baker, Belle (actress); New York City **(1895–1957)**
Baker, Carroll (actress); Johnstown, Pa., 5/28/1935
Baker, Josephine (singer and dancer); St. Louis **(1906–1975)**
Baker, Kenny (singer and actor); Monrovia, Calif., 9/30/1912
Balanchine, George (choreographer); St. Petersburg, Russia, 1/9/1904
Balboa, Vasco Nuñez de (explorer); Jerez de los Caballeros (Spain) **(1475–1517)**
Baldwin, Faith (novelist); New Rochelle, N.Y. **(1893–1978)**
Baldwin, James (novelist); New York City, 8/2/1924
Balenciaga, Cristóbal (fashion designer); Guetaria, Spain **(1895–1972)**
Ball, Lucille (Dianne Belmont) (actress and producer); Celoran, N.Y., 8/6/1911
Ballard, Kaye (Catherine Gloria Balotta) (actress); Cleveland, 11/20/1926
Balmain, Pierre (fashion designer); St.-Jean-de-Maurienne, France, 5/18/1914
Balsam, Martin (actor); New York City, 11/4/1919
Balzac, Honoré de (novelist); Tours, France **(1799–1850)**
Bancroft, Anne (Annemarie Italiano) (actress); New York City, 9/17/1931
Bancroft, George (actor); Philadelphia **(1882–1956)**
Bankhead, Tallulah (actress); Huntsville, Ala. **(1903–1968)**
Banneker, Benjamin (almanacker and mathematician-astronomer on District of Columbia site survey), Ellicott, Md. **(1731–1806)**
Bara, Theda (Theodosia Goodman) (actress); Cincinnati **(1890–1955)**
Barber, Red (Walter Lanier) (sportscaster); Columbus, Miss., 2/17/1908
Barber, Samuel (composer); West Chester, Pa., 3/9/1910
Bardot, Brigitte (actress); Paris, 1935
Barenboim, Daniel (concert pianist and conductor); Buenos Aires, 11/15/1942
Barnard, Christiaan N. (heart surgeon); Beauford West, South Africa, 1923
Barnum, Phineas Taylor (showman); Bethel, Conn. **(1810–1891)**
Barrie, Sir James Matthew (author); Kirriemuir, Scotland **(1860–1937)**
Barrie, Wendy (actress); Hong Kong **(1913–1978)**
Barry, Gene (Eugene Klass) (actor); New York City, 6/4/1922
Barrymore, Diana (actress); New York City **(1921–1960)**
Barrymore, Ethel (Ethel Blythe) (actress); Philadelphia **(1879–1959)**
Barrymore, Georgiana Drew (actress); Philadelphia **(1856–1893)**
Barrymore, John (John Blythe) (actor); Philadelphia **(1882–1942)**
Barrymore, John, Jr. (John Drew Barrymore) (actor); Beverly Hills, Calif., 1932
Barrymore, Lionel (Lionel Blythe) (actor); Philadelphia **(1878-1954)**
Barrymore, Maurice (Herbert Blythe) (actor and playwright); Agra, India **(1847–1905)**
Barthelme, Donald (novelist); Philadelphia, 4/7/1931
Barthelmess, Richard (actor); New York City **(1897–1963)**
Bartholomew, Freddie (actor); London, 3/28/1924
Bartók, Béla (composer); Nagyszentmiklos (Romania) **(1881–1945)**
Barton, Clara (founder of American Red Cross); Oxford, Mass. **(1821–1912)**
Baruch, Bernard Mannes (statesman); Camden, S.C. **(1870–1965)**
Baryshnikov, Mikhail Nikolayevich (ballet dancer); Riga, Latvia, 1/27/1948
Basehart, Richard (actor); Zanesville, Ohio, 8/31/1919
Basie, Count (William) (band leader); Red Bank, N.J., 8/21/1904
Bassey, Shirley (singer); Cardiff, Wales, 1/8/1937
Batchelor, Clarence Daniel (political cartoonist); Osage City, Kan., 4/1/1888
Bates, Alan (actor); Allestree, England, 2/17/1934
Baudelaire, Charles Pierre (poet); Paris **(1821–1867)**
Baudouin (King); Palace of Laeken, Belgium, 9/7/1930
Baxter, Anne (actress); Michigan City, Ind., 5/7/1923
Baxter, Warner (actor); Columbus, Ohio **(1891–1951)**
Bean, Orson (Dallas Frederick Burrows) (actor); Burlington, Vt., 7/22/1928
Beardsley, Aubrey Vincent (illustrator); Brighton, England **(1872–1898)**
Beaton, Cecil (photographer and designer); London, 1/14/1904
Beatty, Warren (actor and producer); Richmond, Va., 3/30/1937
Becket, Thomas à (Archbishop of Canterbury); London **(1118? 1170)**
Beckett, Samuel (playwright); Dublin, 4/13/1906
Beckmann, Max (painter); Leipzig, Germany **(1884–1950)**
Bede, Saint ("The Venerable Bede") (scholar); Monkwearmouth, England **(673–735)**
Beecham, Sir Thomas (conductor); St. Helens, England **(1879–1961)**
Beecher, Henry Ward (clergyman); Litchfield, Conn. **(1813–1887)**
Beerbohm, Sir Max (author); London **(1872–1956)**
Beery, Noah, Jr. (actor); New York City, 8/10/1916
Beery, Wallace (actor); Kansas City, Mo. **(1886–1949)**
Beethoven, Ludwig van (composer); Bonn (Germany) **(1770–1827)**
Begley, Ed (actor); Hartford, Conn. **(1901–1970)**
Belafonte, Harry (singer and actor); New York City, 3/1/1927
Belasco, David (dramatist and producer); San Francisco **(1854–1931)**
Bell, Alexander Graham (inventor); Edinburgh, Scotland **(1847–1922)**
Bellamy, Edward (author); Chicopee Falls, Mass. **(1850–1898)**
Bellamy, Ralph (actor); Chicago, 6/17/1904
Bellini, Giovanni (painter); Venice **(c.1430–1516)**
Bellow, Saul (novelist); Lachine, Quebec, Canada, 7/10/1915
Bellows, George Wesley (painter and lithographer); Columbus, Ohio **(1882–1925)**
Belmondo, Jean-Paul (actor); Neuilly-sur-Seine, France, 4/9/1933
Benchley, Peter Bradford (novelist); New York City, 5/8/1940
Benchley, Robert Charles (humorist); Worcester, Mass. **(1889–1945)**
Bendix, William (actor); New York City **(1906–1964)**
Benes, Eduard (statesman); Kozlany (Czechoslovakia) **(1884–1948)**
Benét, Stephen Vincent (poet and story writer); Bethlehem, Pa. **(1898–1943)**
Benét, William Rose (poet and novelist); Ft. Hamilton, Brooklyn, N.Y. **(1886–1950)**
Ben-Gurion, David (David Green) (statesman); Plónsk (Poland) **(1886–1973)**
Benjamin, Richard (actor); New York City, 5/22/1938
Bennett, Constance (actress); New York City **(1905–1965)**
Bennett, Enoch Arnold (novelist and dramatist); Hanley, England **(1867–1931)**

**Bennett,** James Gordon (editor); Keith, Scotland **(1795–1872)**
**Bennett,** Joan (actress); Palisades, N.J., 2/27/1910
**Bennett,** Robert Russell (composer); Kansas City, Mo., 6/15/1894
**Bennett,** Tony (Anthony Benedetto) (singer); Astoria, Queens, N.Y., 8/3/1926
**Benny,** Jack (Benjamin Kubelsky) (comedian); Chicago **(1894–1974)**
**Benton,** Thomas Hart (painter); Neosho, Mo. **(1889–1975)**
**Berg,** Gertrude (writer, actress); New York City **(1899–1966)**
**Bergen,** Candice (actress); Beverly Hills, Calif., 5/9/1946
**Bergen,** Edgar (ventriloquist); Chicago, 2/16/1903
**Bergen,** Polly (actress and singer); Knoxville, Tenn., 7/14/1930
**Bergman,** Ingmar (film director); Uppsala, Sweden, 7/14/1918
**Bergman,** Ingrid (actress); Stockholm, 8/29/1917
**Berle,** Milton (Milton Berlinger) (comedian); New York City, 7/12/1908
**Berlin,** Irving (Israel Baline) (songwriter); Temum, Russia, 5/11/1888
**Berlioz,** Louis Hector (composer); La Côte-Saint-André, France **(1803–1869)**
**Berman,** Lazar (concert pianist); Leningrad, 1930.
**Berman,** Shelley (Sheldon) (comedian); Chicago, 2/3/1926
**Bernardi,** Herschel (actor); New York City, 1923
**Bernhardt,** Sarah (Rosine Bernard) (actress); Paris **(1844–1923)**
**Bernini,** Gian Lorenzo (sculptor and painter); Naples (Italy) **(1598–1680)**
**Bernstein,** Leonard (conductor); Lawrence, Mass., 8/25/1918
**Berry,** Chuck (Charles Edward Berry) (singer); San Jose, Calif., 1/15/1926
**Betjeman,** Sir John (Poet Laureate); London, 8/28/1906
**Bickford,** Charles (actor); Cambridge, Mass. **(1889-1967)**
**Bierce,** Ambrose Gwinnett (journalist); Meigs County, Ohio **(1842–1914?)**
**Bikel,** Theodore (actor and folk singer); Vienna, 5/2/1924
**Bing,** Sir Rudolf (opera manager); Vienna, 1/9/1902
**Bingham,** George Caleb (painter); Augusta Co., Va. **(1811–1879)**
**Bishop,** Joey (Joseph Gottlieb) (comedian); New York City, 2/3/1919
**Bismarck-Schonhausen,** Prince Otto Eduard Leopold von (statesman); Schönhausen (Germany) **(1815–1898)**
**Bisset,** Jacqueline (actress); Weybridge, England, 9/13/1944
**Bixby,** Bill (actor); San Francisco 1/22/1934
**Bizet,** Georges (Alexandre César Léopold Bizet) (composer); Paris **(1838–1875)**
**Black,** Cilla (singer and actress); Liverpool, England, 5/27/1943
**Black,** Hugo La Fayette (jurist); Harlan, Ala. **(1886–1971)**
**Black,** Karen (actress); Park Ridge, Ill., 7/1/1942
**Black,** Shirley Temple (former actress); Santa Monica, Calif., 4/23/1927
**Blackman,** Honor (actress); London, 8/22/1929
**Blackmer,** Sidney (actor); Salisbury, N.C. **(1898–1973)**
**Blackstone,** Sir William (jurist); London **(1723–1780)**
**Blaine,** Vivian (actress and singer); Newark, N.J., 11/21/1924
**Blair,** Janet (actress); Altoona, Pa., 4/23/1921
**Blake,** Amanda (Beverly Louise Neill) (actress); Buffalo, N.Y., 1931
**Blake,** Eubie (James Hubert) (pianist); Baltimore, 2/7/1883
**Blake,** Robert (Michael Gubitosi) (actor); Nutley, N.J., 9/18/1933
**Blake,** William (poet and artist); London **(1757–1827)**
**Blanc,** Mel(vin Jerome) (actor and voice specialist); San Francisco, 5/30/1908
**Blass,** Bill (fashion designer); Fort Wayne, Ind., 6/22/1922
**Bloch,** Ernest (composer); Geneva **(1880–1959)**
**Blondell,** Joan (actress); New York City, 8/30/1912
**Bloom,** Claire (actress); London, 2/15/1931
**Bloomgarden,** Kermit (producer); Brooklyn, N.Y. **(1904–1976)**
**Blue,** Monte (actor); Indianapolis **(1890–1963)**
**Blyth,** Ann (actress); New York City, 8/16/1928
**Boccaccio,** Giovanni (author); Paris **(1313–1375)**
**Boccioni,** Umberto (painter and sculptor); Reggio di Calabria, Italy **(1882–1916)**
**Bogarde,** Dirk (Derek Van den Bogaerde) (film actor and director); London, 3/28/1921
**Bogart,** Humphrey DeForest (actor); New York City **(1899–1957)**
**Bogdanovich,** Peter (producer and director); Kingston, N.Y., 7/30/1939
**Bohlen,** Charles E. (diplomat); Clayton, N.Y. **(1904–1974)**
**Bohr,** Niels (atomic physicist); Copenhagen **(1885–1962)**
**Bolger,** Ray (dancer and actor); Dorchester, Mass., 1/10/1904
**Bolivar,** Simón (South American liberator); Caracas, Venezuela **(1783–1830)**
**Bologna,** Giovanni da (sculptor); Douai (France) **(1529–1608)**
**Bond,** Julian (Georgia legislator); Nashville, Tenn., 1/14/1940
**Bondi,** Beulah (actress); Chicago, 1892
**Bonnard,** Pierre (painter); Fontenayaux-Roses, France **(1867–1947)**
**Bono,** Sonny (Salvatore) (singer); Detroit, 2/16/1935
**Boone,** Daniel (frontiersman); nr. Reading, Pa. **(1734–1820)**
**Boone,** Pat (Charles) (singer); Jacksonville, Fla., 6/1/1934
**Boone,** Richard (actor); Los Angeles, 6/18/1917
**Booth,** Edwin Thomas (actor); Bel Air, Md. **(1833–1893)**
**Booth,** Evangeline Cory (religious leader); London **(1865–1950)**
**Booth,** John Wilkes (actor; assassin of Lincoln); Harford County, Md. **(1838–1865)**
**Booth,** Shirley (Thelma Booth Ford) (actress); New York City, 8/30/1909
**Bordoni,** Irene (actress); Ajaccio (France) **(1895–1953)**
**Borge,** Victor (pianist and comedian); Copenhagen, 1/3/1909
**Borgia,** Cesare (nobleman and soldier); Rome **(1475?–1507)**
**Borgia,** Lucrezia (Duchess of Ferrara); Rome **(1480–1519)**
**Borgnine,** Ernest (actor); Hamden, Conn., 1/24/1917
**Borromini,** Francesco (architect); Bissone (Italy) **(1599–1667)**
**Bosch,** Hieronymus (Hieronymus van Aeken) (painter); Hertogenbosch (Netherlands) **(c.1450–1516)**
**Bosley,** Tom (actor); Chicago, 10/1/1927
**Boswell,** Connee (singer); New Orleans **(1907–1976)**
**Boswell,** James (diarist and biographer); Edinburgh, Scotland **(1740–1795)**
**Botticelli,** Sandro (Alessandro di Mariano dei Filipepi) (painter); Florence (Italy) **(1444?–1510)**
**Boulez,** Pierre (conductor); Montbrison, France, 3/26/1925
**Bouton,** Jim (James Alan) (sportscaster); Newark, N.J., 3/8/1939
**Bow,** Clara (actress); Brooklyn, N.Y. **(1905–1965)**
**Bowen,** Catherine Drinker (biographer); Haverford, Pa. **(1897–1973)**
**Bowie,** David (David Jones) (actor and musician); London, 1/8/1947(?)
**Bowie,** James (soldier); Burke County, Ga. **(1799–1836)**
**Bowles,** Chester (diplomat); Springfield, Mass., 4/5/1901
**Bowman,** Lee (actor); Cincinnati, 12/28/1914
**Boyd,** Bill (William) ("Hopalong Cassidy") (actor); Cambridge, Ohio **(1898–1972)**
**Boyd,** Stephen (actor); Belfast, Northern Ireland **(1928–1977)**
**Boyer,** Charles (actor); Figeac, France **(1899–1978)**
**Bracken,** Eddie (actor); Astoria, Queens, N.Y., 2/7/1920
**Bradbury,** Ray Douglas (science-fiction writer); Waukegan, Ill., 8/22/1920
**Bradlee,** Benjamin C. (editor); Boston, 8/26/1921
**Bradley,** Omar N. (5-star general); Clark, Mo., 2/12/1893
**Bradley,** Thomas (Mayor of Los Angeles); Calvert, Tex., 12/29/1917
**Brady,** Scott (actor); Brooklyn, N.Y., 9/13/1924
**Brahms,** Johannes (composer); Hamburg **(1833–1897)**
**Braille,** Louis (teacher of blind); Coupvray, France **(1809–1862)**
**Brailowsky,** Alexander (pianist); Kiev, Russia **(1896–1976)**
**Bramante,** Donato D'Agnolo (architect); Monte Asdrualdo (now Fermignano) (Italy) **(1444–1514)**
**Brancusi,** Constantin (sculptor); Pestisansi, Romania **(1876–1957)**
**Brandeis,** Louis Dembitz (jurist); Louisville, Ky. **(1856–1941)**
**Brando,** Marlon (actor); Omaha, Neb., 4/3/1924
**Brandt,** Willy (Herbert Frahm) (ex-Chancellor); Lübeck, Germany, 12/18/1913
**Braque,** Georges (painter); Argenteuil, France **(1882–1963)**
**Brasselle,** Keefe (actor); Elyria, Ohio, 2/7/1923
**Braun,** Wernher von (rocket scientist); Wirsitz, Germany **(1912–1977)**
**Brazzi,** Rossano (actor); Bologna, Italy, 9/18/1916
**Brecht,** Bertolt (dramatist and poet); Augsburg (Germany) **(1898–1956)**
**Brel,** Jacques (singer and composer); Brussels, 4/8/1929
**Brennan,** Walter (actor); Lynn, Mass. **(1894–1974)**
**Brent,** George (actor); Dublin, 3/15/1904
**Breslin,** Jimmy (journalist); Jamaica, Queens, N.Y., 10/17/1930
**Breuer,** Marcel (architect and designer); Pécs (Hungary), 5/21/1902
**Brewer,** Teresa (singer); Toledo, Ohio, 5/7/1931
**Brewster,** Kingman, Jr. (ex-president of Yale); Longmeadow, Mass., 6/17/1919
**Brezhnev,** Leonid I. (Communist Party Secretary); Dneprodzerzhinsk, Ukraine, 12/19/1906
**Brice,** Fanny (Fannie Borach) (comedienne); New York City **(1892–1951)**
**Bridges,** Beau (actor); Los Angeles, 12/9/1941
**Bridges,** Lloyd (actor); San Leandro, Calif., 1/15/1913
**Brinkley,** David (TV newscaster); Wilmington, N.C., 7/10/1920
**Britt,** May (Maybritt Wilkins) (actress); Sweden, 3/22/1936
**Britten,** Benjamin (composer); Lowestoft, England **(1913–1976)**
**Britton,** Barbara (actress); Long Beach, Calif., 1923
**Bromfield,** Louis (novelist); Mansfield, Ohio **(1896–1956)**
**Bronson,** Charles (Charles Buchinsky) (actor); Ehrenfield, Pa., 11/3/1922(?)
**Bronte,** Charlotte (novelist); Thornton, England **(1816–1855)**
**Bronte,** Emily Jane (novelist); Thornton, England **(1818–1848)**
**Bronzino,** Agnolo (painter); Monticelli (Italy) **(1503–1572)**
**Brook,** Peter (director); London, 3/21/1925
**Brooke,** Rupert (poet); Rugby, England **(1887–1915)**
**Brooks,** Geraldine (Geraldine Stroock) (actress); New York City **(1925–1977)**
**Brooks,** Gwendolyn (poet); Topeka, Kan., 6/7/1917
**Brooks,** Mel (Melvin Kaminsky) (writer and film director); Brooklyn, N.Y., 1926(?)
**Broun,** Matthew Heywood Campbell (journalist); Brooklyn, N.Y. **(1888–1939)**
**Brown,** Helen Gurley (author); Green Forest, Ark., 2/18/1922
**Brown,** James (singer); Augusta, Ga., 5/3/1934
**Brown,** Joe E. (comedian); Holgate, Ohio **(1892–1973)**
**Brown,** John (abolitionist); Torrington, Conn. **(1800–1859)**
**Brown,** John Mason (critic); Louisville, Ky. **(1900–1969)**
**Brown,** Les (band leader); Reinerton, Pa., 1912
**Brown,** Pamela (actress); London **(1918–1975)**

Brown, Vanessa (Smylla Brind) (actress); Vienna, 3/24/1928
Browne, Jackson (singer and guitarist); Heidelberg, Germany, 10/9/late 1940's
Browning, Elizabeth Barrett (poet); Durham, England **(1806–1861)**
Browning, Robert (poet); London **(1812–1889)**
Brubeck, Dave (musician); Concord, Calif., 12/6/1920
Bruce, Lenny (comedian); Long Island, N.Y. **(1926–1966)**
Brueghel, Pieter (painter); nr. Breda (Netherlands) **(1520?–1569)**
Bruhn, Erik (Belton Evers) (ballet dancer); Copenhagen, 10/3/1928
Brunelleschi, Filippo (architect); Florence (Italy) **(1377–1446)**
Brutus, Marcus Junius (Roman politician); **(85?–42 B.C.)**
Bryan, William Jennings (orator and politician); Salem, Ill. **(1860–1925)**
Bryant, Anita (singer); Barnsdall, Okla., 3/25/1940
Bryant, William Cullen (poet and editor); Cummington, Mass. **(1794–1878)**
Brynner, Yul (Taidje Khan) (actor); Sakhalin Island, Russia, 7/11/1920
Brzezinski, Zbigniew (presidential adviser); Warsaw, 3/28/1928
Buber, Martin (philosopher and theologian); Vienna **(1878–1965)**
Buchanan, Edgar (actor); Humansville, Mo., 1903
Buchholz, Horst (actor); Berlin, 12/4/1933
Buchwald, Art (Arthur) (columnist); Mount Vernon, N.Y., 10/20/1925
Buck, Pearl S(ydenstricker) (author); Hillsboro, W. Va. **(1892–1973)**
Buckley, William F., Jr. (journalist); New York City, 11/24/1925
Buddha. *See* Gautama Buddha
Buffalo Bill (William Frederick Cody) (scout); Scott County, Iowa **(1846–1917)**
Bujold, Genevieve (actress); Montreal, 7/1/1942
Bujones, Fernando (ballet dancer); Miami, Fla., 3/9/1955
Bullins, Ed (playwright); Philadelphia, 7/2/1935
Bumbry, Grace (mezzo-soprano); St. Louis, 1/4/1937
Bunche, Ralph J. (statesman); Detroit **(1904–1971)**
Bundy, McGeorge (Ford Foundation president); Boston, 3/30/1919
Bundy, William Putnam (editor); Washington, D.C., 9/24/1917
Buñuel, Luis (film director); Calanda, Spain, 2/22/1900
Bunyan, John (preacher and author); Elstow, England **(1628–1688)**
Burbank, Luther (horticulturist); Lancaster, Mass. **(1849–1926)**
Burke, Adm. Arleigh A. (ex-Chief of Naval Operations); Boulder, Colo., 10/19/1901
Burke, Billie (comedienne); Washington, D.C. **(1885–1970)**
Burke, Edmund (statesman); Dublin **(1729–1797)**
Burne-Jones, Edward Coley (painter); Birmingham, England **(1833–1898)**
Burnett, Carol (comedienne); San Antonio, 4/26/1936
Burns, George (Nathan Birnbaum) (comedian); New York City, 1/20/1896
Burns, Robert (poet); Alloway, Scotland **(1759–1796)**
Burr, Aaron (political leader); Newark, N.J. **(1756–1836)**
Burr, Raymond (William Stacey Burr) (actor); New Westminster, British Columbia, Canada, 5/21/1917
Burroughs, Edgar Rice (novelist); Chicago **(1875–1950)**
Burrows, Abe (playwright, director); New York City, 12/18/1910
Burstyn, Ellen (Edna Rae Gillooly) (actress); Detroit, 12/7/1932
Burton, Richard (Richard Jenkins) (actor); Pontrhydfen, Wales, 11/10/1925
Busch, Mae (actress); Melbourne **(1891–1946)**
Bush, Vannevar (scientist); Everett, Mass. **(1890–1974)**
Bushman, Francis X. (actor); Baltimore **(1883–1966)**
Butler, Samuel (author); Langar, England **(1835–1902)**
Buttons, Red (Aaron Chwatt) (actor); New York City, 2/5/1919
Buzzi, Ruth (comedienne); Wequetequock, Conn., 7/24/1936
Byrd, Richard Evelyn (polar explorer); Winchester, Va. **(1888–1957)**
Byron, George Gordon (6th Baron Byron) (poet); London **(1788–1824)**

# C

Caan, James (actor); The Bronx, N.Y., 3/26/1939
Cabot, John (Giovanni Caboto) (navigator); Genoa **(1450–1498)**
Cabot, Sebastian (navigator); Venice **(1476?–1557)**
Cadmus, Paul (painter and etcher); New York City, 12/17/1904
Caesar, Gaius Julius (statesman); Rome **(100?–44 B.C.)**
Caesar, Sid (comedian); Yonkers, N.Y., 9/8/1922
Cagney, James (actor); New York City, 7/17/1900
Cahn, Sammy (songwriter); New York City, 6/18/1913
Caine, Michael (Maurice J. Micklewhite) (actor); London, 3/14/1933
Calder, Alexander (sculptor); Lawnton, Pa. **(1898–1976)**
Caldwell, Erskine (novelist); White Oak, Ga., 12/17/1903
Caldwell, Sarah (opera director, conductor); Maryville, Mo., 1928
Caldwell, Taylor (novelist); Manchester, England, 9/7/1900
Caldwell, Zoe (actress); Hawthorn, Australia, 9/14/1933
Calhern, Louis (Carl Henry Vogt) (actor); Brooklyn, N.Y. **(1895–1956)**
Calhoun, John Caldwell (statesman); nr. Calhoun Mills, S.C. **(1782–1850)**
Calhoun, Rory (actor); Los Angeles, Calif., 1922
Calisher, Hortense (novelist); New York City, 12/20/1911
Callas, Maria (Maria Calogeropoulos) (dramatic soprano); New York City **(1923–1977)**
Calloway, Cab (Cabell) (band leader); Rochester, N.Y., 12/25/1907
Calvet, Corinne (actress); Paris, 4/30/1926
Calvin, John (Jean Chauvin) (religious reformer); Noyon (France) **(1509–1564)**
Cambridge, Godfrey (comedian); New York City **(1933–1976)**
Cameron, Rod (Rod Cox) (actor); Calgary, Alberta, Canada, 12/7/1912
Campbell, Glen (singer); nr. Delight, Ark., 4/22/1938
Camus, Albert (author); Mondovi, Algeria **(1913–1960)**
Caniff, Milton (cartoonist); Hillsboro, Ohio, 2/28/1907
Cannon, Dyan (actress); Tacoma, Wash., 1/4/1937
Canova, Judy (comedienne); Jacksonville, Fla., 11/20/1916
Cantinflas (Mario Moreno) (comedian); Mexico City, 8/12/1911
Cantor, Eddie (Edward Iskowitz) (actor); New York City **(1892–1964)**
Cantrell, Lana (singer); Sydney, Australia, 1944
Capote, Truman (novelist); New Orleans, 9/30/1924
Capp, Al (Alfred Gerald Caplin) (cartoonist); New Haven, Conn., 9/28/1909
Capra, Frank (film producer, director); Palermo, Italy, 5/18/1897
Caravaggio, Michelangelo Merisi da (painter); Caravaggio (Italy) **(1573–1610)**
Cardin, Pierre (fashion designer); nr. Venice, 7/7/1922
Cardinale, Claudia (actress); Tunis, Tunisia, 1939
Cardozo, Benjamin Nathan (jurist); New York City **(1870–1938)**
Carey, Harry (actor); New York City **(1878–1947)**
Carey, Macdonald (actor); Sioux City, Iowa, 3/15/1913
Carlisle, Kitty (singer and actress); New Orleans, 9/3/1915
Carlson, Richard (actor); Albert Lea, Minn., **(1912–1977)**
Carlyle, Thomas (essayist and historian); Ecclefechan, Scotland **(1795–1881)**
Carmichael, Hoagy (Hoagland Howard) (songwriter); Bloomington, Ind., 11/22/1899
Carne, Judy (Joyce Botterill) (singer): Northampton, England, 1939
Carnegie, Andrew (industrialist); Dunfermline, Scotland **(1835–1919)**
Carney, Art (actor); Mt. Vernon, N.Y., 11/4/1918
Carnovsky, Morris (actor); St. Louis, 9/5/1897
Caron, Leslie (actress); Paris, 7/1/1931
Carr, Vikki (singer); El Paso, 7/19/1942
Carracci, Annibale (painter); Bologna (Italy) **(1560–1609)**
Carracci, Lodovico (painter); Bologna (Italy) **(1555–1619)**
Carradine, David (actor); Hollywood, Calif., 12/8/1936
Carradine, John (actor); New York City, 2/5/1906
Carrillo, Leo (actor); Los Angeles **(1881–1961)**
Carroll, Diahann (Carol Diahann Johnson) (singer and actress); Bronx, N.Y., 7/17/1935
Carroll, Leo G. (actor); Weedon, England **(1892–1972)**
Carroll, Lewis (Charles Lutwidge Dodgson) (author and mathematician); Daresbury, England **(1832–1898)**
Carroll, Madeleine (actress); West Bromwich, England, 2/26/1906
Carroll, Pat (comedienne); Shreveport, La., 5/5/1927
Carson, Johnny (TV entertainer); Corning, Iowa, 10/23/1925
Carson, Kit (Christopher) (scout); Madison County, Ky. **(1809–1868)**
Carson, Rachel (biologist and author); Springdale, Pa. **(1907–1964)**
Carter, (Bessie) Lillian (President's mother); Richland, Ga., 8/15/1898
Carter, Jack (comedian); New York City, 1923
Cartier-Brisson, Henri (photographer); Chanteloup, France, 8/22/1908
Caruso, Enrico (Errico) (tenor); Naples, Italy **(1873–1921)**
Carver, George Washington (botanist); Missouri **(1864–1943)**
Cary, Arthur Joyce Lunel (novelist); Londonderry, Ireland **(1888–1957)**
Casals, Pablo (cellist); Vendrell, Spain **(1876–1973)**
Casanova de Seingalt, Giovanni Jacopo (adventurer); Venice **(1725–1798)**
Cash, Johnny (singer); nr. Kingsland, Ark., 2/26/1932
Cass, Peggy (comedienne); Boston, 5/21/1926
Cassatt, Mary (painter); Allegheny, Pa. **(1844–1926)**
Cassavetes, John (actor and director); New York City, 12/9/1929
Cassidy, David (singer); New York City, 4/12/1950
Cassidy, Jack (actor); Richmond Hill, Queens, N.Y. **(1927–1976)**
Cassini, Oleg (Oleg Lolewski-Cassini) (fashion designer); Paris, 4/11/1913
Castagno, Andrea del (painter); San Martino a Corella (Italy) **(c.1421–1457)**
Castellano, Richard (actor); New York City, 9/2/1934
Castle, Irene (Irene Foote) (actress and dancer); New Rochelle, N.Y. **(1893–1969)**
Castle, Vernon Blythe (dancer and aviator); Norwich, England **(1887–1918)**
Castro Ruz, Fidel (Premier); Mayari, Oriente, Cuba, 8/13/1926
Cather, Willa Sibert (novelist); Winchester, Va. **(1876–1947)**
Cato, Marcus Porcius (called Cato the Elder) (statesman); Tusculum (Italy) **(234–149 B.C.)**
Catt, Carrie Chapman Lane (woman suffragist); Ripon, Wis. **(1859–1947)**
Catton, Bruce (historian); Petoskey, Mich. **(1899–1978)**
Cavallaro, Carmen (band leader); New York City, 1913
Cavett, Dick (Richard) (TV entertainer); Gibbon, Neb., 11/19/1936
Cellini, Benvenuto (goldsmith and sculptor); Florence (Italy) **(1500–1571)**
Cervantes Saavedra, Miguel de (novelist); Alcalá de Henares, Spain **(1547–1616)**
Cézanne, Paul (painter); Aix-en-Provence, France **(1839–1906)**

Chagall, Marc (painter); Vitebsk, Russia, 7/7/1887
Chaliapin, Feodor Ivanovitch (operatic basso); Kazan, Russia (1873–1938)
Chamberlain, Arthur Neville (statesman) Edgbaston, England (1869–1940)
Chamberlain, Richard (actor); Los Angeles, 3/31/1935(?)
Champion, Gower (choreographer); Geneva, Ill., 6/22/1921
Champion, Marge (actress and dancer); Los Angeles, 9/2/1923
Champlain, Samuel de (explorer); nr. Rochefort, France (1567?–1635)
Chancellor, John (TV commentator); Chicago, 7/14/1927
Chandler, Raymond (writer); Chicago (1888–1959)
Chanel, "Coco" (Gabriel Bonheur) (fashion designer); Issoire, France (1883–1971)
Chaney, Lon (actor); Colorado Springs, Colo. (1883–1930)
Channing, Carol (actress); Seattle, 1/31/1923
Chaplin, Geraldine (actress); Santa Monica, Calif., 1944
Chaplin, Sir Charles (actor); London (1889–1977)
Chaplin, Sydney (actor); Cape Town, South Africa (1885–1956)
Chaplin, Sydney (actor); Los Angeles, 3/31/1926
Charisse, Cyd (Tula Finklea) (dancer and actress); Amarillo, Tex., 3/8/1923
Charlemagne (Holy Roman Emperor); birthplace unknown (742–814)
Charles, Ray (Ray Charles Robinson) (pianist, singer, and songwriter); Albany Ga., 9/23/1932
Chase, Chevy (comedian); New York City, 1944
Chase, Ilka (author and actress); New York City (1905–1978)
Chase, Lucia (ballet company manager); Waterbury, Conn., 3/24/1907
Chatterton, Ruth (actress); New York City (1893–1961)
Chaucer, Geoffrey (poet); London (1340?–1400)
Chávez, Carlos (composer); nr. Mexico City, (1899–1978)
Chavez, Cesar (labor leader); nr. Yuma, Ariz., 3/31/1927
Chayefsky, Paddy (Sidney) (playwright); New York City, 1/29/1923
Checker, Chubby (performer); Philadelphia, 10/3/1941
Cheever, John (novelist); Quincy, Mass., 5/27/1912
Chekhov, Anton Pavlovich (dramatist and short-story writer); Taganrog, Russia (1860–1904)
Cher (Cherilyn LaPiere) (singer); El Centro, Calif., 5/20/1946
Chesterton, Gilbert Keith (author); Kensington, England (1874–1936)
Chevalier, Maurice (entertainer); Paris (1888–1972)
Chiang Ch'ing (political leader); Chucheng, China, 1913(?)
Chiang Kai-shek (Chief of State); Feng-hwa, China (1887–1975)
Child, Julia (food expert); Pasadena, Calif., 8/15/1912
Chippendale, Thomas (cabinet-maker); Otley, England (1718?–1779)
Chirico, Giorgio de (painter); Vólos, Greece, 7/10/1888
Chisholm, Shirley (congresswoman); Brooklyn, N.Y., 11/30/1924
Chopin, Frédéric François (composer); nr. Warsaw (1810–1849)
Chou En-lai (Premier); Hualyin, China (1898–1976)
Christian, Linda (Blanca Rosa Welter) (actress); Tampico, Mexico, 11/13/1924
Christie, Agatha (mystery writer); Torquay, England, (1890–1976)
Christie, Julie (actress); Chukua, India, 4/14/1941
Christopher, Jordon (actor, musician); Youngstown, Ohio, 1941
Christy, June (singer); Springfield, Ill., 1925
Churchill, Sarah (actress); London, 10/7/1914
Churchill, Sir Winston Leonard Spencer (statesman); Blenheim Palace, Oxfordshire, England (1874–1965)
Cicero, Marcus Tullius (orator and statesman); Arpinum (Italy) (106–43 B.C.)
Cilento, Diane (actress); Queensland, Australia, 10/5/1933
Cimabue, Giovanni (painter); Florence (Italy) (c.1240–c.1302)
Clair, René (René Chomette (film director); Paris, 11/11/1898
Claire, Ina (Ina Fagan) (actress); Washington, D.C., 10/15/1895
Clapton, Eric (singer and guitarist); Ripley, England, 3/30/1945
Clark, Dane (Barney Zanville) (actor); New York City, 2/18/1915
Clark, Dick (TV personality); Mt. Vernon, N.Y., 11/30/1929
Clark, Petula (singer); Epsom, England, 11/15/1934
Clark, Roy (country music artist); Meherrin, Va., 4/15/1933
Clark, William (explorer); Caroline County, Va. (1770–1838)
Claude Lorrain (Claude Gellée) (painter); Champagne, France (1600–1682)
Clay, Henry (statesman); Hanover County, Va. (1777–1852)
Clay, Lucius D. (banker, ex-general); Marietta, Ga. (1897–1978)
Clemenceau, Georges (statesman); Mouilleron-en-Pareds, Vendée, France (1841–1929)
Clemens, Samuel L. *See* Mark Twain
Cleopatra (Queen of Egypt); Alexandria, Egypt (69–30 B.C.)
Cliburn, Van (Harvey Lavan Cliburn, Jr.) (concert pianist); Shreveport, La., 7/12/1934
Clifford, Clark M. (ex-Secretary of Defense); Ft. Scott, Kan., 12/25/1906
Clift, Montgomery (actor); Omaha, Neb. (1920–1966)
Clooney, Rosemary (singer); Maysville, Ky., 5/23/1928
Clurman, Harold (stage producer); New York City, 9/18/1901
Cobb, Irvin Shrewsbury (humorist); Paducah, Ky. (1876–1944)
Cobb, Lee J. (Leo Jacob) (actor); New York City (1911–1976)
Coburn, Charles Douville (actor); Savannah, Ga. (1877–1961)
Coburn, James (actor): Laurel, Neb., 8/31/1928
Coca, Imogene (comedienne); Philadelphia, 1914(?)
Cocker, Joe (John Robert Cocker) (singer); Sheffield, England 5/20/1944
Coco, James (actor); New York City, 3/21/1929
Cocteau, Jean (author); Maison-Lafitte, France (1891–1963)
Cody, W. F. *See* Buffalo Bill
Cohan, George Michael (actor and dramatist); Providence, R.I. (1878–1942)
Cohen, Leonard (singer and songwriter); Montreal, 1935
Colbert, Claudette (Lily Chauchoin) (actress); Paris, 9/13/1905
Colby, William E. (ex-Director of CIA); St. Paul, 1/4/1920
Cole, Nat "King" (singer); Montgomery, Ala. (1919–1965)
Cole, Natalie (singer); Los Angeles, 2/6/1950
Cole, Thomas (painter); Lancashire, England (1801–1848)
Coleridge, Samuel Taylor (poet); Ottery St. Mary, England (1772–1834)
Colette (Sidonie-Gabrielle Colette) (novelist); St.-Sauveur, France (c.1873–1954)
Collingwood, Charles (TV commentator); Three Rivers, Mich., 6/4/1917
Collins, Dorothy (Marjorie Chandler) (singer); Windsor, Ontario, Canada, 11/18/1926
Collins, Joan (actress); London, 1933
Collins, Judy (singer); Seattle, 5/1/1939
Colman, Ronald (actor); Richmond, England (1891–1958)
Colonna, Jerry (comedian); Boston, 1905
Columbus, Christopher (Cristoforo Colombo) (discoverer of America); Genoa (Italy) (1451–1506)
Comden, Betty (writer); New York City, 5/3/1919
Commager, Henry Steele (historian); Pittsburgh, 10/25/1902
Como, Perry (Pierino) (singer); Canonsburg, Pa., 5/18/1913
Compton, Karl Taylor (physicist); Wooster, Ohio (1887–1954)
Conant, James B. (educator and statesman); Dorchester, Mass. (1893–1978)
Condon, Eddie (jazz musician); Goodland, Ind. (1905–1973)
Confucius (K'ung Fu-tzu) (philosopher); Shantung province, China (c.551–479 B.C.)
Congreve, William (dramatist); nr. Leeds, England (1670–1729)
Connelly, Marc (playwright); McKeesport, Pa., 12/13/1890
Connery, Sean (actor); Edinburgh, Scotland, 8/25/1930
Conniff, Ray (band leader); Attleboro, Mass., 1916
Connors, Chuck (actor); Brooklyn, N.Y., 4/10/1921
Connors, Mike (Krekor Ohanian) (actor); Fresno, Calif., 8/15/1925
Conrad, Joseph (Teodor Jozef Konrad Korzeniowski) (novelist); Berdichev, Ukraine (1857–1924)
Conrad, Robert (actor); Chicago, 1935
Conrad, William (actor); Louisville, Ky., 9/27/1920
Conried, Hans (Frank Foster) (actor); Baltimore, 1917
Constable, John (painter); East Bergholt, Suffolk, England (1776–1837)
Constantine II (ex-king); Athens, 6/2/1940
Conte, Richard (actor); New York City (1916–1975)
Converse, Frank (actor); St. Louis, Mo., 1938
Conway, Tim (actor); Chagrin Falls, Ohio, 1933
Coogan, Jackie (actor); Los Angeles, 10/26/1914
Cooke, Alistair (Alfred Alistair); (TV narrator and journalist); Manchester, England, 11/20/1908
Cooley, Denton A(rthur) (heart surgeon); Houston, Tex., 8/22/1920
Coolidge, Rita (singer); Nashville, Tenn., 1944
Cooper, Alice (Vincent Furnier) (rock musician); Detroit, 2/4/1948
Cooper, Gary (Frank James Cooper) (actor); Helena, Mont. (1901–1961)
Cooper, Jackie (actor and director); Los Angeles, 9/15/1922
Cooper, James Fenimore (novelist); Burlington, N.J. (1789–1851)
Cooper, Peter (industrialist and philanthropist); New York City (1791–1883)
Copernicus, Nicolaus (Mikolaj Kopernik) (astronomer); Thorn, Poland (1473–1543)
Copland, Aaron (composer); Brooklyn, N.Y., 11/14/1900
Copley, John Singleton (painter); Boston, Mass. (1738–1815)
Corelli, Franco (operatic tenor); Ancona, Italy, 4/8/1923
Corneille, Pierre (dramatist); Rouen, France (1606–1684)
Cornell, Katharine (actress); Berlin (1893–1974)
Corot, Jean Baptiste Camille (painter); Paris (1796–1875)
Correggio, Antonio Allegri da (painter); Correggio (Italy) (1494–1534)
Corsaro, Frank (opera director); New York harbor, 12/22/1924
Cortés (or Cortez), Hernando (explorer); Medellín, Spain (1485–1547)
Cosby, Bill (actor); Philadelphia, 7/12/1937
Cosell, Howard (Howard Cohen) (sportscaster); Winston-Salem, N.C., 3/25/1920
Costa-Gavras, Henri (Kostantinos Gavras) (film director); Athens, 1933
Costello, Lou (comedian); Paterson, N.J. (1908–1959)
Cotten, Joseph (actor); Petersburg, Va., 5/15/1905
Courbet, Gustave (painter); Ornans, France (1819–1877)
Courrèges, André (fashion designer); Pau, France, 3/9/1923
Courtenay, Tom (actor); Hull, England, 2/25/1937
Cousins, Norman (publisher); Union Hill, N.J., 6/24/1915
Cousteau, Jacques-Yves (marine explorer); St. André-de-Cubzac, France, 6/11/1910
Coward, Sir Noel (playwright and actor); Teddington, England (1899–1973)

**Cowles**, Gardner (newspaper publisher); Algona, Iowa, 1/31/1903
**Cowper**, William (poet); Great Berkhamstead, England **(1731–1800)**
**Cozzens**, James Gould (novelist); Chicago **(1903–1978)**
**Crabbe**, Buster (Clarence) (actor); Oakland, Calif., 2/7/1908
**Crain**, Jeanne (actress); Barstow, Calif., 5/25/1925
**Cranach**, Lucas, the elder (painter); Kronach (Germany) **(1472–1553)**
**Crane**, Stephen (novelist, poet); Newark, N.J. **(1871–1900)**
**Crawford**, Broderick (actor); Philadelphia, 12/9/1911
**Crawford**, Cheryl (stage producer); Akron, Ohio, 9/24/1902
**Crawford**, Joan (Lucille LeSueur) (actress and business executive); San Antonio **(1908–1977)**
**Crenna**, Richard (actor); Los Angeles, 11/30/1927
**Crichton**, (John) Michael (novelist); Chicago, 10/23/1942
**Crisp**, Donald (actor); London **(1880–1974)**
**Croce**, Benedetto (philosopher); Pescasseroli, Aquila, Italy **(1866–1952)**
**Croce**, Jim (singer); Philadelphia **(1942–1973)**
**Crockett**, Davy (David) (frontiersman); Greene County, Tenn. **(1786–1836)**
**Cromwell**, Oliver (statesman); Huntingdon, England **(1599–1658)**
**Cronin**, A. J. (Archibald J. Cronin) (novelist); Cardross, Scotland, 7/19/1896
**Cronkite**, Walter (TV newscaster); St. Joseph, Mo., 11/4/1916
**Cronyn**, Hume (actor); London, Ontario, Canada, 7/18/1911
**Crosby**, Bing (Harry Lillis) (singer, actor); Tacoma, Wash. **(1901–1977)**
**Crosby**, Bob (musician); Spokane, Wash., 8/23/1913
**Crosby**, David (singer); Los Angeles, 8/14/1941
**Cross**, Milton (opera commentator); New York City **(1897–1975)**
**Crouse**, Russel (playwright); Findlay, Ohio **(1893–1966)**
**Cugat**, Xavier (band leader); Barcelona, Spain, 1/1/1900
**Cukor**, George (film director); New York City, 7/7/1899
**Cullen**, Bill (William Lawrence Cullen) (radio and TV entertainer); Pittsburgh, 2/18/1920
**Culp**, Robert (actor); Berkeley, Calif., 8/16/1931
**Cummings**, E. E. (Edward Estlin Cummings) (poet); Cambridge, Mass. **(1894–1962)**
**Cummings**, Robert (actor); Joplin, Mo., 6/9/1910
**Curie**, Marie (Marja Sklodowska) (physical chemist); Warsaw **(1867–1934)**
**Curtin**, Phyllis (soprano); Clarksburg, W.Va., 12/3/1927
**Curtis**, Tony (Bernard Schwartz) (actor); Bronx, N.Y., 6/3/1925
**Curzon**, Clifford (concert pianist); London, 5/18/1907
**Custer**, George Armstrong (army officer); New Rumley, Ohio **(1839–1876)**

# D

**Dache**, Lilly (fashion designer); Bègles, France
**Dahl**, Arlene (actress); Minneapolis, 8/11/1928
**Dailey**, Dan (actor and dancer); New York City, 12/14/1917
**Daley**, Richard J. (Mayor of Chicago); Chicago **(1902–1976)**
**Dali**, Salvador (painter); Figueras, Spain, 5/11/1904
**Daly**, James (actor); Wisconsin Rapids, Wis. **(1918–1978)**
**Daly**, John (radio and TV news analyst); Johannesburg, South Africa, 2/20/1914
**d'Amboise**, Jacques (ballet dancer); Dedham, Mass., 7/28/1934
**Damone**, Vic (Vito Farinola) (singer); Brooklyn, N.Y., 6/12/1928
**Damrosch**, Walter Johannes (orchestra conductor); Breslau (Poland) **(1862–1950)**
**Dana**, Charles Anderson (editor); b. Hinsdale, N.H. **(1819–1897)**
**Dandridge**, Dorothy (actress); Cleveland **(1923–1965)**
**Dangerfield**, Rodney (comedian); Babylon, L.I., N.Y., 1921
**Daniels**, Bebe (Virginia Daniels) (actress); Dallas **(1901–1971)**
**Danilova**, Alexandra (ballerina); Peterhof, Russia, 1/20/1904
**D'Annunzio**, Gabriele (soldier and author); Francaville al Mare, Pescara, Italy **(1863–1938)**
**Dante** (or **Durante**) **Alighieri** (poet); Florence (Italy) **(1265–1321)**
**Danton**, Georges Jacques (French Revolutionary leader); Arcis-sur-Aube, France **(1759–1794)**
**Darnell**, Linda (actress); Dallas **(1921–1965)**
**Darren**, James (actor); Philadelphia, 6/8/1936
**Darrieux**, Danielle (actress); Bordeaux, France, 5/1/1917
**Darrow**, Clarence Seward (lawyer); Kinsman, Ohio **(1857–1938)**
**Darwin**, Charles Robert (naturalist); Shrewsbury, England **(1809–1882)**
**daSilva**, Howard (actor); Cleveland, 5/4/1909
**Dassin**, Jules (film director); Middletown, Conn., 12/18/1911
**Daumier**, Honoré (caricaturist); Marseilles, France **(1808–1879)**
**Dauphin**, Claude (actor); Corbeil, France, 8/19/1903
**David**, Jacques-Louis (painter); Paris **(1748–1825)**
**David** (King of Israel and Judah) **(died c. 973 B.C.)**
**Davidson**, John (singer and actor); Pittsburgh, 12/13/1941
**Davies**, Marion (Marion Douras) (actress); New York City **(1898?–1961)**
**da Vinci**, Leonardo (painter and scientist); Vinci, Tuscany (Italy) **(1452–1519)**
**Davis**, Bette (actress); Lowell, Mass., 4/5/1908
**Davis**, Elmer Holmes (radio commentator); Aurora, Ind. **(1890–1958)**
**Davis**, Jefferson (President of the Confederacy); Christian (now Todd) County, Ky. **(1808–1889)**
**Davis**, Mac (singer); Lubbock, Tex.
**Davis**, Miles (jazz trumpeter); Alton, Ill., 5/25/1926
**Davis**, Ossie (actor and writer); Cogdell, Ga., 12/18/1917
**Davis**, Sammy, Jr. (actor); New York City, 12/8/1925
**Davis**, Skeeter (Mary Francis Penick) (singer); Dry Ridge, Ky., 12/30/1931
**Davis**, Stuart (painter); Philadelphia **(1894–1964)**
**Day**, Dennis (singer); New York City, 5/21/1917
**Day**, Doris (Doris von Kappelhoff) (singer and actress); Cincinnati, 4/3/1924
**Day**, Laraine (La Raine Johnson) (actress); Roosevelt, Utah, 10/13/1920
**Dayan**, Moshe (Defense Minister of Israel); Dagania, Palestine (Jordan), 5/20/1915
**Dean**, James (actor); Marion, Ind. **(1931–1955)**
**Dean**, Jimmy (singer); Seth Ward, nr. Plainview, Tex., 8/10/1928
**De Bakey**, Michael E. (heart surgeon); Lake Charles, La., 9/7/1908
**de Beauvoir**, Simone (novelist and philosopher); Paris, 1/9/1908
**Debs**, Eugene Victor (Socialist leader); Terre Haute, Ind. **(1855–1926)**
**Debussy**, Claude Achille (composer); St. Germain-en-Laye, France **(1862–1918)**
**De Carlo**, Yvonne (Peggy Yvonne Middleton) (actress); Vancouver, B.C., Canada, 9/1/1924
**de Chirico**, Giorgio (painter); Volos, Greece, 7/10/1888
**Dee**, Ruby (Ruby Ann Wallace) (actress); Cleveland, 10/27/1924(?)
**Dee**, Sandra (Alexandra Zuck) (actress); Bayonne, N.J., 4/23/1942
**Defoe**, Daniel (novelist); London **(1659?–1731)**
**Degas**, Hilaire Germain Edgar (painter); Paris **(1834–1917)**
**De Gaulle**, Charles André Joseph Marie (soldier and statesman); Lille, France **(1890–1970)**
**DeHaven**, Gloria (actress); Los Angeles, 7/23/1925
**De Havilland**, Olivia (actress); Tokyo, 7/1/1916
**Dekker**, Albert (actor); Brooklyn, N.Y. **(1904–1968)**
**De Kooning**, Willem (painter); Rotterdam, 4/24/1904
**Delacroix**, Eugène (painter); Charenton-St. Maurice, France **(1798–1863)**
**de la Renta**, Oscar (fashion designer); Santo Domingo, Dominican Republic, 7/22/1932
**Delaunay**, Robert (painter); Paris **(1885–1941)**
**De Laurentiis**, Dino (film producer); Torre Annunziata, Bay of Naples, Italy, 8/8/1919
**Delon**, Alain (actor); Sceaux, France, 11/8/1935
**Del Rio**, Dolores (actress); Durango, Mexico, 8/3/1905
**DeLuise**, Dom (comedian); Brooklyn, N.Y., 1933
**Demarest**, William (actor); St. Paul, 2/27/1892
**de Mille**, Agnes (choreographer); New York City
**De Mille**, Cecil Blount (film director); Ashfield, Mass. **(1881–1959)**
**Demosthenes** (orator); Athens **(385?–322 B.C.)**
**Deneuve**, Catherine (actress); Paris, 10/22/1943
**De Niro**, Robert (actor); New York City, 8/17/1943
**Dennis**, Sandy (actress); Hastings, Neb., 4/27/1937
**Denver**, John (Henry John Deutschendorf, Jr.) (singer); Roswell, N.M., 12/31/1943
**Derain**, André (painter); Chatou, Seine-et-Oise, France **(1880–1954)**
**Descartes**, René (philosopher and mathematician); La Haye, France **(1596–1650)**
**De Seversky**, Alexander P. (aviator); Tiflis, Russia **(1894–1974)**
**De Sica**, Vittorio (film director); Sora, Italy **(1901–1974)**
**Desmond**, Johnny (composer); Detroit, 11/14/1921
**Desmond**, William (actor); Dublin **(1878–1949)**
**De Soto**, Hernando (explorer); Barcarrota, Spain **(1500?–1542)**
**De Valera**, Eamon (ex-President of Ireland); New York City **(1882–1975)**
**Devine**, Andy (actor); Flagstaff, Ariz. **(1905–1977)**
**De Vries**, Peter (novelist); Chicago, 2/27/1910
**Dewey**, George (admiral); Montpelier, Vt. **(1837–1917)**
**Dewey**, John (philosopher and educator); Burlington, Vt. **(1859–1952)**
**Dewey**, Thomas E. (politician); Owosso, Mich. **(1902–1971)**
**Dewhurst**, Colleen (actress); Montreal, 1926(?)
**Diamond**, Neil (singer); Brooklyn, N.Y., 1/24/1941
**Dickens**, Charles John Huffam (novelist); Portsea, England **(1812–1870)**
**Dickey**, James (poet); Atlanta, 2/2/1923
**Dickinson**, Angie (Angeline Brown) (actress); Kulm, N.D., 9/30/1931
**Dickinson**, Emily Elizabeth (poet); Amherst, Mass. **(1830–1886)**
**Diddley**, Bo (Elias McDaniel) (guitarist); McComb, Miss., 12/30/1928
**Diefenbaker**, John G. (ex-Prime Minister); Grey County, Ontario, Canada, 9/18/1895
**Dietrich**, Marlene (Maria Magdalena von Losch) (actress); Berlin, 12/27/1901
**Diggs**, Dudley (actor); Dublin **(1879–1947)**
**Diller**, Phyllis (Phyllis Driver) (comedienne); Lima, Ohio, 7/17/1917
**Dillinger**, John (American bank robber); prob. Indianapolis **(1902–1934)**
**Dillman**, Bradford (actor); San Francisco, 4/14/1930
**Dine**, Jim (painter); Cincinnati, 6/16/1935
**Diogenes** (philosopher); Sinope (Turkey) **(412?–323 B.C.)**

Dion (Dion DiMucci) (singer); Bronx, N.Y., 7/18/1939
Dior, Christian (fashion designer); Granville, France (1905–1957)
Disney, Walt(er) Elias (film animator and producer); Chicago (1901–1966)
Disraeli, Benjamin (Earl of Beaconsfield) (statesman); London (1804–1881)
Dix, Dorothea (civil rights reformer); Hampden, Me. (1802–1887)
Dix, Richard (Ernest Carlton Brimmer) (actor); St. Paul (1894–1949)
Dixon, Jeane (Jeane Pinckert) (seer); Medford, Wis., 1918
Doctorow, E.L. (Edgar Laurence) (novelist); New York City, 1/6/1931
Dodgson, C. L. *See* Carroll, Lewis.
Dolin, Anton (dancer); Slinfold, England, 7/27/1904
Domingo, Placido (tenor); Madrid, 1/21/1941
Domino, Fats (Antoine) (musician); New Orleans, 2/26/1928
Donahue, Troy (actor); New York City, 1/27/1938
Donat, Robert (actor); Withington, England (1905–1958)
Donatello (Donato Niccolò di Betto Bardi) (sculptor); Florence (Italy) (c.1386–1466)
Donne, John (poet); London (1573–1631)
Donovan (Donovan Leitch) (singer and songwriter); Glasgow, Scotland 2/10/1946
Doolittle, James H. (ex-Air Force general); Alameda, Calif., 12/14/1896
Dorati, Antal (orchestra conductor); Budapest, 4/9/1906
Dors, Diana (Diana Fluck) (actress); Swondon, England, 10/23/1931
Dos Passos, John (author); Chicago (1896–1970)
Dostoevski, Fyodor Mikhailovich (novelist); Moscow (1821–1881)
Douglas, Helen Gahagan (ex-Representative); Boonton, N.J., 11/25/1900
Douglas, Kirk (Issur Danielovitch) (actor); Amsterdam, N.Y., 12/9/1916
Douglas, Melvyn (Melvyn Hesselberg) (actor); Macon, Ga., 4/5/1901
Douglas, Mike (Michael D. Dowd, Jr.) (TV personality); Chicago, 8/11/1920
Douglas, Paul (actor); Philadelphia (1907–1959)
Douglas, Stephen Arnold (politician); Brandon, Vt. (1813–1861)
Dowling, Eddie (Edward Goucher) (actor and stage producer); Woonsocket, R.I., (1894–1976)
Downs, Hugh (TV entertainer); Akron, Ohio, 2/14/1921
Doyle, Sir Arthur Conan (novelist and spiritualist); Edinburgh, Scotland (1859–1930)
Drake, Alfred (singer and actor); New York City, 10/7/1914
Drake, Sir Francis (navigator); Tavistock, England (1545–1596)
Dreiser, Theodore (writer); Terre Haute, Ind. (1871–1945)
Dressler, Marie (Leila Koeber) (actress); Cobourg, Ontario, Canada (1869–1934)
Dreyfus, Alfred (French army officer); Mulhouse (France) (1859–1935)
Dreyfuss, Richard (actor); Brooklyn, N.Y., 10/29/1947
Drury, Allen (novelist); Houston, 9/2/1918
Dryden, John (poet); Northamptonshire, England (1631–1700)
Dubček, Alexander (ex-President of Czechoslovakia); Uhroved (Czechoslovakia), 11/27/1921
Dubinsky, David (David Dobnievski) (labor leader); Brest-Litovsk (U.S.S.R.) 2/22/1892
Duchamp, Marcel (painter); Blainville, France (1887–1968)
Duchin, Peter (pianist and band leader); New York City, 7/28/1937
Duff, Howard (actor); Bremerton, Wash., 1917
Dufy, Raoul (painter); Le Havre, France (1877–1953)
Duke, James B. (industrialist); nr. Durham, N.C. (1856–1925)
Duke, Patty (Anna Marie Duke) (actress); New York City, 12/14/1946
Dullea, Keir (actor); Cleveland, 5/30/1936(?)
Dulles, Allen Welsh (ex-Director of CIA); Watertown, N.Y. (1893-1969)
Dulles, John Foster (statesman); Washington, D.C. (1888–1959)
Dumas, Alexandre (called Dumas fils) (novelist); Paris (1824–1895)
Dumas, Alexandre (called Dumas père) (novelist); Villers-Cotterets, France (1802–1870)
Du Maurier, Daphne (novelist); London, 5/13/1907
Du Maurier, George Louis Palmella Busson (novelist); Paris (1834–1896)
Dumont, Margaret (actress); (1889–1965)
Dunaway, Faye (actress); Bascom, Fla., 1/14/1941
Duncan, Isadora (dancer); San Francisco (1878–1927)
Duncan, Sandy (actress); Henderson, Tex., 1946
Dunn, James (actor); Santa Monica, Calif. (1905–1967)
Dunne, Irene (actress); Louisville, Ky., 12/20/1904
Dunnock, Mildred (actress); Baltimore, 1/25/(?)
Du Pont, Pierre S. (economist); Paris (1739–1817)
Durante, Jimmy (comedian); New York City, 2/10/1893
Durbin, Deanna (Edna Mae) (actress); Winnipeg, Canada, 12/4/1922
Dürer, Albrecht (painter and engraver); Nürnberg (Germany) (1471–1528)
Durrell, Lawrence George (novelist); Julundur, India, 2/27/1912
Duse, Eleonora (actress); Chioggia, Italy (1859–1924)
Duvalier, Jean-Claude (President; son of "Papa Doc"); Port-au-Prince, Haiti, 7/3/1951
Duvall, Robert (actor); San Diego, Calif., 1931.
Dvořák, Antonín (composer); Nelahozeves (Czechoslovakia) (1841–1904)
Dylan, Bob (Robert Zimmerman) (folk singer and composer); Duluth, Minn., 5/24/1941

# E

Eagels, Jeanne (actress); Kansas City, Mo. (1894–1929)
Eakins, Thomas (painter & sculptor); Philadelphia, (1844–1916)
Earhart, Amelia (aviator); Atchison, Kan. (1898–1937)
Eastman, George (inventor); Waterville, N.Y. (1854–1932)
Eastwood, Clint (actor); San Francisco, 5/31/1931(?)
Ebsen, Buddy (Christian Ebsen, Jr.) (actor); Belleville, Ill., 4/2/1908
Eckstine, Billy (singer); Pittsburgh, 7/8/1914
Eddy, Duane (band leader); Corning, N.Y., 4/26/1938
Eddy, Mary Baker (founder of Christian Science Church); Bow, N.H. (1821–1910)
Eddy, Nelson (baritone and actor); Providence, R.I. (1901–1967)
Eden, Sir Anthony (Earl of Avon) (ex-Prime Minister); Durham, England (1897–1977)
Eden, Barbara (Barbara Huffman) (actress); Tucson, Ariz., 1934
Edison, Thomas Alva (inventor); Milan, Ohio (1847–1931)
Edwards, Ralph (TV and radio producer); Merino, Colo., 1913
Edwards, Vincent (actor); Brooklyn, N.Y., 7/7/1928
Egan, Richard (actor); San Francisco, 7/29/1923
Eggar, Samantha (actress); London, 5/3/1939
Eglevsky, André (ballet dancer); Moscow (1917–1977)
Ehrlich, Paul (bacteriologist); Strzelin (Poland) (1854–1915)
Einstein, Albert (physicist); Ulm, Germany (1879–1955)
Eisenhower, Mamie Doud (President's widow); Boone, Iowa, 11/14/1896
Eisenhower, Milton S. (educator); Abilene, Kan., 9/15/1899
Eisenstaedt, Alfred (photographer and photojournalist); Dirschau (Poland), 12/6/1898
Ekberg, Anita (actress); Malmö, Sweden, 9/29/1931
Eldridge, Florence (Florence McKechnie) (actress); Brooklyn, N.Y., 9/5/1901
Elgar, Sir Edward (composer); Worcester, England (1857–1934)
Elgart, Larry (band leader); New London, Conn., 3/20/1922
El Greco (Domenicos Theotocopoulos) (painter); Candia (Greece) (c.1541–1614)
Eliot, George (Mary Ann Evans) (novelist); Chilvers Coton, England (1819–1880)
Eliot, Thomas Stearns (poet); St. Louis (1888–1965)
Ellington, Duke (Edward Kennedy) (jazz musician); Washington, D.C. (1899–1974)
Elliot, "Mama" Cass (Ellen Naomi Cohen) (singer); Baltimore (1941–1974)
Elman, Mischa (violinist); Stalnoye, Ukraine (1891–1967)
Emerson, Ralph Waldo (philosopher and poet); Boston (1803–1882)
Enesco, Georges (composer); Dorohoi, Romania (1881–1955)
Engels, Friedrich (Socialist writer); Barmen (Germany) (1820–1895)
Entremont, Philippe (concert pianist); Rheims, France, 6/7/1934.
Epicurus (philosopher); Samos (Greece) (341–270 B.C.)
Epstein, Sir Jacob (sculptor); New York City (1880–1959)
Erasmus, Desiderius (Gerhard Gerhards) (scholar); Rotterdam (1466?–1536)
Erhard, Ludwig (ex-Chancellor); Furth, Germany (1897–1977)
Erickson, Leif (actor); Alameda, Calif., 10/27/1911
Ericson, Leif (navigator); (c. 10th century A.D.)
Erikson, Erik H. (psychoanalyst); Frankfurt, Germany, 6/15/1902
Ernst, Max (painter); Bruhl, Germany (1891–1976)
Euclid (mathematician); Megara (Greece) (c. 300 B.C.)
Euripides (dramatist); Salamis (Greece) (c.484–407 B.C.)
Evans, Dale (Frances Butts) (actress and singer); Uvalde, Tex., 10/31/1912
Evans, Dame Edith (actress); London (1888–1976)
Evans, Maurice (actor); Dorchester, England, 6/3/1901
Everett, Chad (actor); South Bend, Ind., 1937
Evers, Charles (civil rights leader); Decatur, Miss., 9/14/1923(?)
Evers, Medgar (civil rights leader); Decatur, Miss. (1925–1963)
Ewell, Tom (Yewell Tompkins) (actor); Owensboro, Ky., 4/29/1909

# F

Fabian (Fabian Anthony Forte) (singer); Philadelphia, 2/6/1943
Fabray, Nanette (Nanette Fabarés) (actress); San Diego, Calif., 10/27/1922
Fadiman, Clifton (literary critic); Brooklyn, N.Y., 5/15/1904
Fairbanks, Douglas (Julius Ullman) (actor); Denver (1883–1939)
Fairbanks, Douglas, Jr. (actor); New York City, 12/9/1909
Faith, Percy (conductor); Toronto (1908–1976)
Falk, Peter (actor); New York City, 9/16/1927
Falla, Manuel de (composer); Cadiz, Spain (1876–1946)
Faraday, Michael (physicist); Newington, England (1791–1867)
Farber, Barry (radio broadcaster); Baltimore, Md., 1930
Farentino, James (actor); Brooklyn, N.Y., 2/24/1938
Farmer, James (civil rights leader); Marshall, Tex., 1/12/1920
Farnum, William (actor); Boston (1876–1953)

**Farrell**, Charles (actor); Onset Bay, Mass., 1901
**Farrell**, Eileen (soprano); Willimantic, Conn., 2/13/1920
**Farrell**, Glenda (actress); Enid, Okla. **(1904–1971)**
**Farrell**, James T. (novelist); Chicago, 2/27/1904
**Farrell**, Suzanne (ballerina); Cincinnati, 8/16/1945
**Farrow**, Mia (actress); Los Angeles, 2/9/1946
**Fasanella**, Ralph (painter); New York City, 9/2/1914
**Fassbinder**, Rainer Werner (film and stage director); Bad Worishofen, West Germany, 5/31/1946
**Fast**, Howard (novelist); New York City, 11/11/1914
**Faulkner**, William (novelist); New Albany, Miss. **(1897–1962)**
**Fawcett-Majors**, Farrah (actress); Corpus Christi, Tex., 2/2/1947(?)
**Faye**, Alice (Ann Leppert) (actress); New York City, 5/5/1915
**Feiffer**, Jules (cartoonist); New York City, 1/26/1929
**Feininger**, Lyonel (painter); New York City **(1871–1956)**
**Feldon**, Barbara (actress); Pittsburgh, 3/12/1941
**Feliciano**, José (singer); Larez, Puerto Rico, 9/10/1945
**Felker**, Clay S. (editor and publisher); St. Louis, 10/2/1925(?)
**Fellini**, Federico (film director); Rimini, Italy, 1/20/1920
**Fender**, Freddie (Baldemar Huerta) (singer); San Benito, Tex., 1937
**Ferber**, Edna (novelist); Kalamazoo, Mich. **(1885–1968)**
**Fermi**, Enrico (atomic physicist); Rome **(1901–1954)**
**Fernandel** (Fernand Joseph Desire Contandin) (actor); Marseilles, France **(1903–1971)**
**Ferrer**, José (actor and director); Santurce, Puerto Rico, 1/8/1912
**Ferrer**, Mel (actor); Elberon, N.J., 8/25/1917
**Fetchit**, Stepin (comedian); Key West, Fla., 1902
**Fiedler**, Arthur (conductor); Boston, 12/17/1894
**Field**, Eugene (poet); St. Louis **(1850–1895)**
**Field**, Marshall (merchant); nr. Conway, Mass. **(1834–1906)**
**Field**, Sally (actress); Pasadena, Calif., 11/6/1946
**Fielding**, Henry (novelist); nr. Glastonbury, England **(1707–1754)**
**Fields**, Gracie (comedienne); Rochdale, England, 1/9/1898
**Fields**, Totie (comedienne); Hartford, Conn. **(1931–1978)**
**Fields**, W. C. (William Claude Dukenfield) (comedian); Philadelphia **(1880–1946)**
**Filene**, Edward A. (merchant); **(1860–1937)**
**Finch**, Peter (actor); Kensington, England **(1916–1977)**
**Finney**, Albert (actor); Salford, England, 5/9/1936
**Firkusny**, Rudolf (pianist); Napajedia (Czechoslovakia), 2/11/1912
**Fischer-Dieskau**, Dietrich (baritone); Berlin, 5/28/1925
**Fisher**, Eddie (Edwin) (singer); Philadelphia, 8/10/1928
**Fitzgerald**, Barry (William Joseph Shields) (actor); Dublin **(1888–1961)**
**Fitzgerald**, Edward (radio broadcaster); Troy, N.Y., 1898(?)
**Fitzgerald**, Ella (singer); Newport News, Va., 4/25/1918
**Fitzgerald**, F. Scott (Francis Scott Key) (novelist); St. Paul, Minn. **(1896–1940)**
**Fitzgerald**, Geraldine (actress); Dublin, 11/24/1914
**Fitzgerald**, Pegeen (radio broadcaster); Norcatur, Kan., 1910
**Flack**, Roberta (singer); Black Mountain, N.C., 2/10/1940
**Flagstad**, Kirsten (Wagnerian soprano); Hamar, Norway **(1895–1962)**
**Flatt**, Lester Raymond (bluegrass musician); Overton County, Tenn., 6/19/1914
**Flaubert**, Gustave (novelist); Rouen, France **(1821–1880)**
**Fleming**, Sir Alexander (bacteriologist); Lochfield, Scotland **(1881–1955)**
**Fleming**, Rhonda (Marilyn Louis) (actress); Los Angeles, 8/10/1923
**Flynn**, Errol (actor); Hobart, Tasmania **(1909–1959)**
**Foch**, Nina (actress); Leyden, Netherlands, 4/20/1924
**Fodor**, Eugene (violinist); Turkey Creek, Colo., 3/5/1950
**Fonda**, Henry (actor); Grand Island, Neb., 5/16/1905
**Fonda**, Jane (actress); New York City, 12/21/1937
**Fonda**, Peter (actor); New York City, 2/23/1939
**Fontaine**, Frank (singer and comedian); Cambridge, Mass., 1920
**Fontaine**, Joan (Joan de Havilland) (actress); Tokyo, 10/22/1917
**Fontanne**, Lynn (actress); London, 12/6/1887(?)
**Fonteyn**, Dame Margot (Margaret Hookham) (ballerina); Reigate, England, 5/18/1919
**Forbes**, Malcolm S(tevenson) (publisher and sportsman); Brooklyn, N.Y., 8/19/1919
**Ford**, Glenn (Gwyllyn Ford) (actor); Quebec, 5/1/1916
**Ford**, Henry (industrialist); Greenfield, Mich. **(1863–1947)**
**Ford**, Henry, II (auto maker); Detroit, 9/4/1917
**Ford**, John (film director); Cape Elizabeth, Me. **(1895–1973)**
**Ford**, Paul (actor); Baltimore **(1901–1976)**
**Ford**, Tennessee Ernie (Ernie Jennings Ford) (singer); Bristol, Tenn., 2/13/1919
**Forsythe**, John (actor); Carney's Point, N.J., 1/29/1918
**Fosdick**, Harry Emerson (clergyman); Buffalo, N.Y. **(1878–1968)**
**Fosse**, Bob (Robert Louis) (choreographer and director); Chicago, 6/23/1927
**Foster**, Jodie (actress); Los Angeles, 1962
**Foster**, Stephen Collins (composer); nr. Pittsburgh **(1826–1864)**
**Foxx**, Redd (John Elroy Sanford) (actor and comedian); St. Louis 12/9/1922
**Foy**, Eddie, Jr. (dancer and actor); New Rochelle, N.Y., 2/4/1905
**Fra Angelico** (Giovanni da Fiesole) (painter); Vicchio in the Mugello, Tuscany (Italy) **(c.1387–1455)**
**Fracci**, Carla (ballerina); Milan, Italy, 8/20/1936
**Fragonard**, Jean Honoré (painter); Grasse, France **(1732–1806)**
**Frampton**, Peter (rock musician); Beckenham, England, 4/20/1950
**France**, Anatole (Jacques Anatole François Thibault) (author); Paris **(1844–1924)**
**Francescatti**, Zino (violinist); Marseilles, France, 8/9/1905
**Franciosa**, Anthony (Anthony Papaleo) (actor); New York City, 10/25/1928
**Francis**, Arlene (Arlene Francis Kazanjian) (actress); Boston, 10/20/1908
**Francis**, Connie (Concetta Franconero) (singer); Newark, N.J., 12/12/1938
**Francis**, Kay (Katherine Edwina Gibbs) (actress); Oklahoma City **(1903–1968)**
**Franciscus**, James (actor); Clayton, Mo., 1/31/1934
**Franck**, César Auguste (composer); Liège (Belgium) **(1822–1890)**
**Franco Bahamonde**, Francisco (Chief of State); El Ferrol, Spain **(1892–1975)**
**Franklin**, Aretha (singer); Memphis, Tenn., 3/25/1942
**Franklin**, Benjamin (statesman and scientist); Boston **(1706–1790)**
**Frazer**, Sir James George (anthropologist); Glasgow, Scotland **(1854–1941)**
**Freud**, Sigmund (psychoanalyst); Moravia (Czechoslovakia) **(1856–1939)**
**Friedan**, Betty (Betty Noami Goldstein) (feminist); Peoria, Ill., 2/4/1921
**Fromm**, Erich (psychoanalyst); Frankfurt-am-Main, Germany, 3/23/1900
**Frost**, David (TV entertainer); Tenterden, England, 4/7/1939
**Frost**, Robert Lee (poet); San Francisco **(1874–1963)**
**Fry**, Christopher (playwright); Bristol, England, 12/18/1907
**Frye**, David (impressionist); Brooklyn, N.Y., 1934
**Fuller**, R(ichard) Buckminster (Jr.) (architect and educator); Milton, Mass., 7/12/1895
**Fulton**, Robert (inventor); Lancaster County, Pa. **(1765–1815)**
**Funt**, Allen (TV producer); Brooklyn, N.Y., 9/16/1914
**Furness**, Betty (Elizabeth) (ex-actress and consumer advocate); New York City, 1/3/1916

# G

**Gabel**, Martin (actor and producer); Philadelphia, 1912
**Gabin**, Jean (actor); Paris **(1904–1976)**
**Gable**, (William) Clark (actor); Cadiz, Ohio **(1901–1960)**
**Gabo**, Naum (sculptor); Briansk, Russia **(1890–1977)**
**Gabor**, Eva (actress); Budapest, 2/11/1926(?)
**Gabor**, Zsa Zsa (Sari) (actress); Budapest, 2/6/1923
**Gainsborough**, Thomas (painter); Sudbury, Suffolk, England **(1727–1788)**
**Galbraith**, John Kenneth (economist); Iona Station, Ontario, Canada, 10/15/1908
**Galilei**, Galileo (astronomer and physicist); Pisa (Italy) **(1564–1642)**
**Gallico**, Paul (novelist); New York City **(1897–1976)**
**Gallup**, George H. (poll taker); Jefferson, Iowa, 11/18/1901
**Galsworthy**, John (novelist and dramatist); Coombe, England **(1867–1933)**
**Gambling**, John A. (radio broadcaster); New York City, 1930
**Gandhi**, Indira (Indira Nehru) (ex-Prime Minister); Allahabad, India, 11/19/1917
**Gandhi**, Mohandas Karamchand (called Mahatma Gandhi) (Hindu leader); Porbandar, India **(1869–1948)**
**Gannett**, Frank E. (editor and publisher); **(1876–1957)**
**Garagiola**, Joe (Joseph Henry) (sportscaster); St. Louis, 2/12/1926
**Garbo**, Greta (Greta Gustafsson) (actress); Stockholm, 9/18/1905
**Gardner**, Ava (Lucy Johnson) (actress); Smithfield, N.C., 12/24/1922
**Gardner**, Erle Stanley (novelist); Malden, Mass. **(1889–1970)**
**Garfield**, John (Jules Garfinkle) (actor); New York City **(1913–1952)**
**Garfunkel**, Art (Arthur) (singer); Newark, N.J., 11/5/1941
**Gargan**, William (actor); Brooklyn, N.Y., 7/17/1905
**Garibaldi**, Giuseppe (Italian nationalist leader); Nice, France **(1807–1882)**
**Garland**, Judy (Frances Gumm) (actress and singer); Grand Rapids, Mich. **(1922–1969)**
**Garner**, Erroll (jazz pianist); Pittsburgh **(1921–1977)**
**Garner**, James (James Bumgarner) (actor); Norman, Okla., 4/7/1928
**Garner**, Peggy Ann (actress); Canton, Ohio, 2/3/1932
**Garrett**, Betty (actress); St. Joseph, Mo., 5/23/1919
**Garrick**, David (actor); Hereford, England **(1717–1779)**
**Garrison**, William Lloyd (abolitionist); Newburyport, Mass. **(1805–1879)**
**Garroway**, Dave (TV host); Schenectady, N.Y., 7/13/1913
**Garson**, Greer (actress); County Down, Northern Ireland, 9/29/1912(?)
**Gary**, John (singer); Watertown, N.Y., 11/29/1932
**Gassman**, Vittorio (film actor and director); Genoa, Italy, 9/1/1922
**Gaudí**, Antonio (architect); Reus, Spain **(1852–1926)**
**Gauguin**, Eugène Henri Paul (painter); Paris **(1848-1903)**
**Gautama Buddha** (Prince Siddhartha) (philosopher); Kapilavastu (India) **(563?–?483 B.C.)**
**Gavin**, John (actor); Los Angeles, 4/8/1935

**Gayle,** Crystal (Brenda Gayle Webb) (singer); Paintsville, Ky., 1951
**Gaynor,** Janet (actress); Philadelphia, 10/6/1906
**Gaynor,** Mitzi (Francesca Mitzi Marlene de Czanyi von Gerber) (actress); Chicago, 9/4/1931
**Gazzara,** Ben (Biago Anthony Gazzara) (actor); New York City, 8/28/1930
**Gebel-Williams,** Gunther (animal trainer); Schweidnitz (Poland), 1934
**Geddes,** Barbara Bel (actress); New York City, 10/31/1922
**Genghis Khan** (Temujin) (conqueror); nr. Lake Baikal (U.S.S.R.) **(1162–1227)**
**Genn,** Leo (actor); London **(1905–1978)**
**Gentry,** Bobbie (Roberta Streeter) (singer); Chickasaw Co., Miss., 7/27/1944
**Gericault,** Jean Louis (painter); Rouen, France **(1791–1824)**
**Gernreich,** Rudi (fashion designer); Vienna, 8/8/1922
**Geronimo** (Goyathlay) (Apache chieftain); Arizona **(1829–1909)**
**Gershwin,** George (composer); Brooklyn, N.Y. **(1898–1937)**
**Gershwin,** Ira (lyricist); New York City, 12/6/1896
**Getty,** J. Paul (oil executive); Minneapolis **(1892–1976)**
**Getz,** Stan (saxophonist); Philadelphia, 2/2/1927
**Ghiberti,** Lorenzo (goldsmith and sculptor); Florence **(1378–1455)**
**Giacometti,** Alberto (sculptor); Switzerland **(1901–1966)**
**Gibbon,** Edward (historian); Putney, England **(1737–1794)**
**Gibson,** Charles Dana (illustrator); Roxbury, Mass. **(1867–1944)**
**Gibson,** Hoot (Edward) (actor); Tememah, Neb. **(1892–1962)**
**Gide,** André (author); Paris **(1869–1951)**
**Gielgud,** Sir John (actor); London, 4/14/1904
**Gilbert,** John (movie actor); Logan, Utah **(1897–1936)**
**Gilbert,** Sir William Schwenck (librettist); London **(1836–1911)**
**Gilels,** Emil (concert pianist); Odessa, Ukraine, 1916
**Gillespie,** Dizzy (John Birks Gillespie) (jazz trumpeter); Cheraw, S.C., 10/21/1917
**Gimbel,** Bernard F. (merchant); Vincennes, Ind. **(1885–1966)**
**Gingold,** Hermione (actress and comedienne); London, 12/9/1897
**Ginsberg,** Allen (poet); Newark, N.J., 6/3/1926
**Giorgione** (painter); Castelfranco, (Italy) **(c.1477–1510)**
**Giotto di Bondone** (painter); Vespignamo (Italy) **(c.1266–1337)**
**Giovanni,** Nikki (poet); Knoxville, Tenn., 6/7/1943
**Giroud,** Françoise (French government official); Geneva, 9/21/1916
**Gish,** Dorothy (actress); Massillon, Ohio **(1898–1968)**
**Gish,** Lillian (actress); Springfield, Ohio, 10/14/1896
**Givenchy,** Hubert (fashion designer); Beauvais, France, 2/21/1927
**Gladstone,** William Ewart (statesman); Liverpool, England **(1809–1898)**
**Glaser,** Paul Michel (actor); Cambridge, Mass., 3/25/(?)
**Gleason,** Jackie (comedian); Brooklyn, N.Y., 2/26/1916
**Gleason,** James (actor); New York City **(1886–1959)**
**Glenn,** John Herschel, Jr. (Senator and former astronaut); Cambridge, Ohio, 7/18/1921
**Gluck,** Christoph Willibald (composer); Erasbach (Germany) **(1714–1787)**
**Gobel,** George (comedian); Chicago, 5/20/1920
**Godard,** Jean Luc (film director); Paris, 12/3/1930
**Goddard,** Paulette (Marion Levy) (actress); Great Neck, N.Y., 6/3/1911
**Godfrey,** Arthur (entertainer); New York City, 8/31/1903
**Goebbels,** Joseph Paul (Nazi leader); Rheydt, Germany **(1897–1945)**
**Goering,** Hermann (Nazi leader); Rosenheim, Germany **(1893–1946)**
**Goethals,** George Washington (engineer); Brooklyn, N.Y. **(1858–1928)**
**Goethe,** Johann Wolfgang von (poet); Frankfurt am Main, Germany **(1749–1832)**
**Gogol,** Nikolai Vasilievich (novelist); nr. Mirgorod, Ukraine **(1809–1852)**
**Goldberg,** Rube (cartoonist); San Francisco **(1883–1970)**
**Golden,** Harry (Harry Goldhurst) (author); New York City, 5/6/1902
**Goldsmith,** Oliver (dramatist and poet); County Longford, Ireland **(1728–1774)**
**Goldwyn,** Samuel (Samuel Goldfish) (film producer); Warsaw **(1882–1974)**
**Golenpaul,** Dan (creator of Information Please radio show and editor of almanac of same name); New York City **(1900–1974)**
**Gompers,** Samuel (labor leader); London **(1850–1924)**
**Goodall,** Jane (Baroness van Lawick-Goodall) (ethologist); London, 4/3/1934
**Goodman,** Benny (clarinetist); Chicago, 5/30/1909
**Goodyear,** Charles (inventor); New Haven, Conn. **(1800–1860)**
**Gordon,** Max (stage producer); New York City; 1892
**Gordon,** Ruth (actress); Wollaston, Mass., 10/30/1896
**Gordy,** Berry, Jr. (record company executive); Detroit, 11/28/1929
**Gore,** Lesley (singer); Tenafly, N.J., 1946
**Goren,** Charles H. (bridge expert); Philadelphia, 3/4/1901
**Gorki,** Maxim (Alexei Maximovich Peshkov) (author); Nizhni Novgorod, Russia **(1868–1936)**
**Gorky,** Arshile (painter); Armenia **(1904–1948)**
**Gormé,** Eydie (singer); Bronx, N.Y., 8/16/1932
**Gorshin,** Frank (actor); Pittsburgh, 4/5/1934
**Gosden,** Freeman F. *See* Amos
**Gould,** Chester (cartoonist); Pawnee, Okla., 11/20/1900
**Gould,** Elliott (actor); Brooklyn, N.Y., 8/29/1938
**Gould,** Glenn (concert pianist); Toronto, 9/25/1932
**Gould,** Morton (composer); Richmond Hill, Queens, N.Y., 12/10/1913
**Goulet,** Robert (singer); Lawrence, Mass., 11/26/1933
**Gounod,** Charles François (composer); Paris **(1818–1893)**
**Goya y Lucientes,** Francisco José de (painter); Fuendetodos, Spain **(1746–1828)**
**Grable,** Betty (actress); St. Louis **(1916–1973)**
**Graham,** Bill (Wolfgang Grajonca) (rock impressario); Berlin, 1931
**Graham,** Billy (William F.) (evangelist); Charlotte, N.C., 11/7/1918
**Graham,** Katharine Meyer (newspaper publisher); New York City, 6/16/1917
**Graham,** Martha (choreographer); Pittsburgh, 5/11/1894(?)
**Grahame,** Gloria (Gloria Hallwood) (actress); Los Angeles, 11/28/1929
**Gramm,** Donald (bass-baritone); Milwaukee, 2/26/1927
**Granger,** Farley (actor); San Jose, Calif., 7/1/1925
**Granger,** Stewart (James Stewart) (actor); London, 5/6/1913
**Grant,** Cary (Alexander Archibald Leach) (actor); Bristol, England, 1/18/1904
**Grant,** Kathryn (actress); Houston, Tex., 1933
**Grant,** Lee (Lyova Haskell Rosenthal) (actress); New York City, 10/31/1930
**Granville,** Bonita (actress and producer); New York City, 1923
**Grass,** Günter (novelist); Danzig (Poland), 10/16/1927
**Grauer,** Ben (radio and TV announcer); New York City **(1908–1977)**
**Graves,** Peter (Peter Arness) (actor); Minneapolis, 3/18/1926
**Graves,** Robert (poet); London, 7/24/1895
**Gray,** Barry (Bernard Yaroslaw) (radio interviewer); Atlantic City, N.J., 7/2/1916
**Gray,** Dolores (singer and actress); Chicago, 6/7/1930
**Gray,** Thomas (poet); London **(1716–1771)**
**Grayson,** Kathryn (Zelma Hednick) (singer and actress); Winston-Salem, N.C., 2/9/1923
**Greco,** Buddy (singer); Philadelphia, 8/14/1926
**Greco,** José (dancer); Montorio nei Frentani, Italy, 12/23/1918
**Greeley,** Horace (journalist and politician); Amherst, N.H. **(1811–1872)**
**Green,** Adolph (actor and lyricist); New York City, 12/2/1915
**Green,** Al (singer); Forrest City, Ark., 4/13/1946
**Greene,** Graham (novelist); Berkhamsted, England, 10/2/1904
**Greene,** Lorne (actor); Ottowa, 2/12/1915
**Greene,** Martyn (actor); London **(1899–1975)**
**Greenstreet,** Sydney (actor); Sandwich, England **(1879–1954)**
**Greenwood,** Joan (actress, director); London, 3/4/1921
**Greer,** Germaine (feminist); Melbourne, 1/29/1939
**Gregory,** Dick (comedian); St. Louis, 1932
**Greuze,** Jean-Baptiste (painter); Tournus, France **(1725–1805)**
**Grey,** Joel (Joel Katz) (actor); Cleveland, 4/11/1932
**Grey,** Zane (author); Zanesville, Ohio **(1875–1939)**
**Grieg,** Edvard Hagerup (composer); Bergen, Norway **(1843–1907)**
**Grier,** Roosevelt (entertainer and former athlete); Cuthbert, Ga., 7/14/1932
**Griffin,** Merv (TV entertainer); San Mateo, Calif., 7/6/1925
**Griffith,** Andy (actor); Mount Airy, N.C., 6/1/1926
**Griffith,** David Lewelyn Wark (film producer); La Grange, Ky. **(1875–1948)**
**Grigorovich,** Yuri (choreographer); Leningrad, 1/1/1927
**Grimes,** Tammy (actress); Lynn, Mass., 1/30/1934
**Grimm,** Jacob (author of fairy tales); Hanau (Germany) **(1785–1863)**
**Grimm,** Wilhelm (author of fairy tales); Hanau (Germany) **(1786–1859)**
**Gris,** Juan (painter); Madrid **(1887–1927)**
**Grizzard,** George (actor); Roanoke Rapids, N.C., 4/1/1928
**Gromyko,** Andrei A. (diplomat); Starye Gromyki, Russia, 7/5/1909
**Gropius,** Walter (architect); Berlin **(1883–1969)**
**Gropper,** William (painter, illustrator); New York City **(1897–1977)**
**Grosz,** George (painter); Germany **(1893–1959)**
**Guardino,** Harry (actor); New York City, 12/23/1925
**Guggenheim,** Meyer (capitalist); Langnau, Switzerland **(1828–1905)**
**Guinness,** Sir Alec (actor); London, 4/2/1914
**Guitry,** Sacha (Alexandre) (actor and film director); St. Petersburg, Russia **(1885–1957)**
**Gunther,** John (author); Chicago **(1901–1970)**
**Gutenberg,** Johann (printer); Mainz (Germany) **(1400?–?1468)**
**Guthrie,** Arlo (singer); New York City, 7/10/1947
**Guthrie,** Woody (folk singer and composer); Okemah, Okla. **(1912–1967)**
**Gwenn,** Edmund (actor); London **(1875–1959)**

# H

**Hackett,** Bobby (trumpeter); Providence, R.I. **(1915–1976)**
**Hackett,** Buddy (Leonard Hacker) (comedian and actor); Brooklyn, N.Y., 8/31/1924
**Hackman,** Gene (actor); San Bernardino, Calif., 1/30/1931
**Hagen,** Uta (actress); Göttingen, Germany, 6/12/1919
**Haggard,** Merle (songwriter); Bakersfield, Calif., 4/6/1937
**Haig,** Alexander Meigs, Jr. (general); Bala-Cynwyd, Pa., 12/2/1924

**Haile Selassie** (Ras Tafari Makonnen) (ex-Emperor); Ethiopia **(1892–1975)**
**Hailey,** Arthur (novelist); Luton, England, 4/5/1920
**Halberstam,** David (journalist); New York City, 4/10/1934
**Hale,** Edward Everett (clergyman and author); Boston **(1822–1909)**
**Hale,** Nathan (American Revolutionary officer); Coventry, Conn. **(1755–1776)**
**Haley,** Alex (writer); Ithaca, N.Y., 8/11/1921
**Hall,** Monty (TV personality); Winnipeg, Canada, 1923
**Hals,** Frans (painter); Antwerp (Netherlands) **(1580?–1666)**
**Halsey,** William Frederick Jr. (naval officer); Elizabeth, N.J. **(1882–1959)**
**Hamill,** Pete (journalist); Brooklyn, N.Y., 6/24/1935
**Hamilton,** Alexander (statesman); Nevis I. (West Indies Associated States) **(1757?–1804)**
**Hamilton,** George (actor); Memphis, Tenn., 8/12/1939
**Hamilton,** Margaret (actress); Cleveland, Ohio, 9/12/1902
**Hamlisch,** Marvin (composer and pianist); New York City, 6/2/1944
**Hammarskjøld,** Dag (U.N. Secretary-General); Jönköping, Sweden **(1905–1961)**
**Hammerstein,** Oscar, II (librettist and stage producer); New York City **(1895–1960)**
**Hampden,** Walter (Walter Hampden Dougherty) (actor); Brooklyn, N.Y. **(1879–1955)**
**Hampton,** James (actor); Oklahoma City, 7/9/1936
**Hampton,** Lionel (vibraharpist and band leader); Birmingham, Ala., 4/20/1914
**Hancock,** John (statesman); Braintree, Mass. **(1737–1793)**
**Hand,** Learned (jurist); Albany, N.Y. **(1872–1961)**
**Handel,** George Frederick (Georg Friedrich Händel) (composer); Halle (Germany) **(1685–1759)**
**Handy,** William Christopher (blues composer); Florence, Ala. **(1873–1958)**
**Hannibal** (Carthaginian general) **(247–183 B.C.)**
**Hanson,** Howard (conductor); Wahoo, Neb., 10/28/1896
**Harburg,** E. Y. "Yip" (songwriter); New York City, 4/8/1896
**Harding,** Ann (actress); San Antonio, Tex., 8/7/1902
**Hardwicke,** Sir Cedric (actor); Stourbridge, England **(1893–1964)**
**Hardy,** Oliver (comedian); Atlanta **(1892–1957)**
**Hardy,** Thomas (novelist); Dorsetshire, England **(1840–1928)**
**Harkness,** Edward S. (capitalist); Cleveland **(1874–1940)**
**Harlow,** Jean (Harlean Carpentier) (actress); Kansas City, Mo. **(1911–1937)**
**Harnick,** Sheldon (songwriter); Chicago, 4/30/1924
**Harper,** Valerie (actress); Suffern, N.Y., 8/22/1940(?)
**Harriman,** W. (William) Averell (ex-Governor of New York); New York City, 11/15/1891
**Harris,** Barbara (actress); Evanston, Ill., 1935
**Harris,** Emmylou (singer); Birmingham, Ala., 1949
**Harris,** Julie (actress); Grosse Pointe Park, Mich., 12/2/1925
**Harris,** Phil (actor and band leader); Linton, Ind., 6/24/1906
**Harris,** Richard (actor); Limerick, Ireland, 10/1/1933
**Harris,** Rosemary (actress); Ashby, England, 9/19/1930
**Harris,** Roy (composer); Lincoln County, Olka., 2/12/1898
**Harrison,** George (singer); Liverpool, England, 2/25/1943
**Harrison,** Noel (singer and actor); London, 1/29/1936
**Harrison,** Rex (Reginald Carey) (actor); Huyton, England, 3/5/1908
**Hart,** Moss (playwright); New York City **(1904–1961)**
**Hart,** William S. (actor); Newburgh, N.Y. **(1862–1946)**
**Harte,** Bret (Francis Brett Harte) (author); Albany, N.Y. **(1836–1902)**
**Hartford,** Huntington (George Huntington Hartford II) (A.&P. heir); New York City, 4/18/1911
**Hartford,** John (singer and banjoist); New York City, 12/30/1937
**Hartman,** Elizabeth (actress); Youngstown, Ohio, 12/23/1941
**Harvey,** Laurence (Larushka Skikne) (actor); Joniskis, Lithuania **(1928–1973)**
**Harvey,** William (physician); Folkestone, England **(1578–1657)**
**Hasso,** Signe (actress); Stockholm, 8/15/1915
**Haver,** June (actress); Rock Island, Ill., 6/10/1926
**Havoc,** June (June Hovick) (actress); Seattle, 1916
**Hawkins,** Jack (actor); London **(1910–1973)**
**Hawn,** Goldie (actress); Washington, D.C., 11/21/1945
**Haworth,** Jill (actress); Sussex, England, 1945
**Hawthorne,** Nathaniel (novelist); Salem, Mass. **(1804–1864)**
**Hay,** John Milton (statesman); Salem, Ind. **(1838–1905)**
**Hayakawa,** S(amuel I(chiye) (Senator and semanticist); Vancouver, B.C., Canada, 7/18/1906
**Hayakawa,** Sessue (actor); Honshu, Japan **(1890–1973)**
**Hayden,** Melissa (ballerina); Toronto, 4/25/1928
**Hayden,** Sterling (Sterling Relyea Walter) (actor and writer); Montclair, N.J., 3/26/1916
**Haydn,** Franz Joseph (composer); Rohrau (Austria) **(1732–1809)**
**Hayes,** Helen (Helen Hayes Brown) (actress); Washington, D.C., 10/10/1900
**Hayes,** Isaac (composer); Covington, Tenn., 8/20/1942
**Hayward,** Louis (actor); Johannesburg, South Africa, 1909
**Hayward,** Susan (Edythe Marrener) (actress). Brooklyn, N.Y. **(1919?–1975)**
**Hayworth,** Rita (Margarita Cansino) (actress); New York City, 10/17/1918
**Head,** Edith (costume designer); Los Angeles, 10/28/1907
**Hearst,** William Randolph (publisher); San Francisco **(1863–1951)**
**Hearst,** William Randolph, Jr. (publisher); New York City, 1/27/1908
**Heath,** Edward (ex-Prime Minister); Broadstairs, England, 7/9/1916
**Heatherton,** Joey (actress); Rockville Centre, N.Y., 9/14/1944
**Hecht,** Ben (author); New York City **(1894–1964)**
**Heckart,** Eileen (actress); Columbus, Ohio, 3/29/1919
**Heflin,** Van (Emmet Evan Heflin) (actor); Walters, Okla. **(1910–1971)**
**Hefner,** Hugh (publisher); Chicago, 4/9/1926
**Hegel,** Georg Wilhelm Friedrich (philosopher); Stuttgart (Germany) **(1770–1831)**
**Heifetz,** Jascha (concert violinist); Vilna, Russia, 2/2/1901
**Heine,** Heinrich (Harry) (poet); Düsseldorf (Germany) **(1797–1856)**
**Heinemann,** Gustav (ex-President of Germany); Schweim, Germany **(1899–1976)**
**Heller,** Joseph (novelist); Brooklyn, N.Y., 5/1/1923
**Hellman,** Lillian (playwright); New Orleans, 6/20/1905
**Hemingway,** Ernest Miller (novelist); Oak Park, Ill. **(1899–1961)**
**Hemmings,** David (actor); Guilford, England, 1941
**Henderson,** Florence (actress); Dale, Ind., 2/14/1934
**Henderson,** Skitch (Lyle Russell Cedric) (conductor and pianist); Birmingham, England(?), 1/27/1918
**Hendrix,** Jimi (James Marshall Hendrix) (guitarist); Seattle **(1942–1970)**
**Henning,** Doug (magician; actor); Winnipeg, Canada, 1947(?)
**Henreid,** Paul (actor); Trieste, 1/10/1908
**Henri,** Robert (painter); Cincinnati **(1865–1926)**
**Henry,** O. (William Sydney Porter) (story writer); Greensboro, N.C. **(1862–1910)**
**Henry,** Patrick (statesman); Hanover County, Va. **(1736–1799)**
**Henson,** Jim (puppeteer); Greenville, Miss., 9/24/1936
**Hepburn,** Audrey (actress); Brussels, Belgium, 5/4/1929
**Hepburn,** Katharine (actress); Hartford, Conn., 11/8/1909
**Hepplewhite,** George (furniture designer); England **(?–1786)**
**Hepworth,** Barbara (sculptor); Wakefield, England **(1903–1975)**
**Herbert,** Victor (composer); Dublin **(1859–1924)**
**Herblock** (Herbert L. Block) (political cartoonist); Chicago, 10/13/1909
**Herman,** Woody (Woodrow Charles) (band leader); Milwaukee, 5/16/1913
**Herod** (Herodes) (called Herod the Great) (King of Judea) **(73?–4 B.C.)**
**Herodotus** (historian); Halicarnassus (Turkey) **(c. 484–425 B.C.)**
**Hershfield,** Harry (humorist and raconteur); Cedar Rapids, Iowa **(1885–1974)**
**Hersholt,** Jean (actor); Copenhagen **(1886–1956)**
**Heston,** Charlton (actor); Evanston, Ill., 10/4/1924
**Heyerdahl,** Thor (ethnologist and explorer); Larvik, Norway, 10/6/1914
**Hildegarde** (Hildegarde Loretta Sell) (singer); Adell, Wis., 2/1/1906
**Hill,** Arthur (actor); Melfort, Canada, 8/1/1922
**Hillary,** Sir Edmund (mountain climber); New Zealand, 7/20/1919
**Hiller,** Wendy (actress); Bramhall, England, 8/15/1912
**Hilliard,** Harriet. *See* Nelson, Harriet
**Hindemith,** Paul (composer); Hanau, Germany **(1895–1963)**
**Hindenburg,** Paul von (statesman); Posen (Poland) **(1847–1934)**
**Hines,** Earl "Fatha" (jazz pianist); Duquesne, Pa., 12/28/1905
**Hines,** Jerome (Jerome Heinz) (basso); Los Angeles, 11/8/1921
**Hingle,** Pat (actor); Denver, 7/19/1924
**Hippocrates** (physician); Kos (Turkey) **(460?–?377 B.C.)**
**Hirohito** (Emperor); Tokyo, 4/29/1901
**Hirschfeld,** Al (Albert) (cartoonist); St. Louis, 6/21/1903
**Hirschhorn,** Joseph Herman (financier, speculator, and art collector); Mitau, Latvia, 8/11/1899
**Hirt,** Al (trumpeter); New Orleans, 11/7/1922
**Hitchcock,** Alfred J. (film director); London, 8/13/1899
**Hitler,** Adolf (Adolf Schicklgruber) (German dictator); Braunau, Austria **(1889–1945)**
**Hitzig,** William Maxwell (physician); Austria, 12/15/1904
**Hobson,** Laura Z. (Laura K. Zametkin) (novelist); New York City, 1900(?)
**Hodges,** Eddie (actor); Hattiesburg, Miss., 3/5/1947
**Hoffa** James R(iddle) (labor leader); Brazil, Ind., 2/14/1913 (presumed dead, **1977**)
**Hoffman,** Dustin (film actor and director); Los Angeles, 8/8/1937
**Hofmann,** Hans (painter); Germany **(1880–1966)**
**Hogarth,** William (painter and engraver); London **(1697–1764)**
**Holbein,** Hans (the Elder) (painter); Augsburg (Germany) **(1465?–1524)**
**Holbein,** Hans (the Younger) (painter); Augsburg (Germany) **(1497?–1543)**
**Holbrook,** Hal (actor); Cleveland, 2/17/1925
**Holden,** William (William Franklin Beedle, Jr.) (actor); O'Fallon, Ill., 4/17/1918
**Holder,** Geoffrey (dancer); Port-of-Spain, Trinidad, 8/1/1930
**Holliday,** Judy (Judith Tuvim) (comedienne); New York City **(1922–1965)**
**Holloway,** Stanley (actor); London, 10/1/1890

**Holloway,** Sterling (actor); Cedartown, Ga., 1905
**Holm,** Celeste (actress); New York City, 4/29/1919
**Holmes,** Oliver Wendell (author); Cambridge, Mass. **(1809–1894)**
**Holmes,** Oliver Wendell (jurist); Boston **(1841–1935)**
**Holt,** Jack (actor); Winchester, Va. **(1888–1951)**
**Holtz,** Lou (comedian); San Francisco, 4/11/1898
**Home,** Lord (Alexander Frederick Douglas-Home) (diplomat); London, 7/2/1903
**Homeier,** Skip (actor); Chicago, 1930
**Homer,** Winslow (painter); Boston, Mass. **(1836–1910)**
**Homer** (Greek poet) **(c.850 B.C.?)**
**Homolka,** Oscar (actor); Vienna **(1898–1978)**
**Honegger,** Arthur (composer); Le Havre, France **(1892–1955)**
**Hook,** Sidney (philosopher); New York City, 12/20/1902
**Hoover,** J. Edgar (FBI director); Washington, D.C. **(1895–1972)**
**Hope,** Bob (Leslie Townes Hope) (comedian); London, 5/29/1903
**Hopkins,** Anthony (actor); Port Talbot, Wales, 12/31/1937
**Hopkins,** Johns (financier); Anne Arundel County, Md. **(1795–1873)**
**Hopkins,** Miriam (actress); Bainbridge, Ga. **(1902–1973)**
**Hopper,** Dennis (actor); Dodge City, Kan., 5/17/1936
**Hopper,** Edward (painter); Nyack, N.Y. **(1882–1967)**
**Horace** (Quintus Horatius Flaccus) (poet); Venosa (Italy) **(65–8 B.C.)**
**Horne,** Lena (singer); Brooklyn, N.Y., 6/30/1917
**Horne,** Marilyn (mezzo-soprano); Bradford, Pa., 1/16/1934
**Horowitz,** Vladimir (pianist); Kiev, Russia, 10/1/1904
**Horton,** Edward Everett (comedian); Brooklyn, N.Y. **(1887–1970)**
**Houdini,** Harry (Ehrich Weiss) (magician); Appleton, Wis. **(1874–1926)**
**Houseman,** John (John Haussmann) (producer, director, and actor); Bucharest, 9/22/1902
**Housman,** Alfred Edward (poet); Fockburg, England **(1859–1936)**
**Houston,** Samuel (political leader); Rockbridge County, Va. **(1793–1863)**
**Howard,** Leslie (Leslie Stainer) (actor); London **(1893–1943)**
**Howard,** Trevor (actor); Kent, England, 9/29/1916
**Howe,** Elias (inventor); Spencer, Mass. **(1819–1867)**
**Howe,** Irving (literary critic); New York City, 6/11/1920
**Howe,** Julia Ward (poet and reformer); New York City **(1819–1910)**
**Howes,** Sally Ann (actress); London, 7/20/1934
**Hudson,** Henry (English navigator) **(?–1611)**
**Hudson,** Rock (born Roy Scherer, Jr.; took Roy Fitzgerald as legal name) (actor); Winnetka, Ill., 11/17/1925
**Hughes,** Charles Evans (jurist); Glens Falls, N.Y. **(1862–1948)**
**Hughes,** Howard (industrialist and film producer); Houston **(1905–1976)**
**Hugo,** Victor Marie (author); Besançon, France **(1802–1885)**
**Hume,** David (philosopher); Edinburgh, Scotland **(1711–1776)**
**Humperdinck,** Engelbert (Arnold Dorsey) (singer); Madras, India, 5/2/1936
**Humperdinck,** Engelbert (composer); Siegburg (Germany) **(1854–1921)**
**Hunt,** H. L. (industrialist); nr. Vandalia, Ill. **(1889–1974)**
**Hunt,** Marsha (actress); Chicago, 10/17/1917
**Hunter,** Kim (Janet Cole) (actress); Detroit, 11/12/1922
**Hunter,** Tab (Arthur Andrew Gelien) (actor); New York City, 7/11/1931
**Huntley,** Chet (TV newscaster); Cardwell, Mont. **(1911–1974)**
**Hurok,** Sol (Solomon) (impressario); Pogar, Russia **(1884–1974)**
**Hurst,** Fannie (novelist); Hamilton, Ohio **(1889–1968)**
**Hussein I** (King); Jordan, 5/2/1935
**Huston,** John (film director and writer); Nevada, Mo., 8/5/1906
**Huston,** Walter (Walter Houghston) (actor); Toronto **(1884–1950)**
**Hutchins,** Robert M. (educator); Brooklyn, N.Y. **(1899–1977)**
**Hutton,** Barbara (Woolworth heiress); New York City, 11/14/1912
**Hutton,** Betty (Betty Thornburg) (actress); Battle Creek, Mich., 2/26/1921
**Hutton,** Lauren (model and actress); Charleston, S.C., 1944
**Huxley,** Aldous (author); Godalming, England **(1894–1963)**
**Huxley,** Sir Julian S. (biologist and author); London **(1887–1975)**
**Huxley,** Thomas Henry (biologist); Ealing, England **(1825–1895)**

# I

**Ian,** Janis (singer); New York City, 5/7/1951
**Ibsen,** Henrik (dramatist); Skien, Norway **(1828–1906)**
**Inge,** William (playwright); Independence, Kan. **(1913–1973)**
**Ingres,** Jean Auguste Dominique (painter); Montauban, France **(1780–1867)**
**Inness,** George (painter); nr. Newburgh, N.Y. **(1825–1894)**
**Ionesco,** Eugéne (playwright); Slatina, Romania, 11/26/1912
**Ireland,** John (actor); Vancouver, B.C., Canada, 1/30/1915
**Irving,** Washington (author); New York City **(1783–1859)**
**Isherwood,** Christopher (novelist and playwright); nr. Dilsey and High Lane, England, 8/26/1904
**Iturbi,** José (concert pianist); Valencia, Spain, 11/28/1895
**Ives,** Burl (Icle Ivanhoe) (singer); Hunt, Ill., 6/14/1909
**Ives,** Charles E(dward) (composer); Danbury, Conn. **(1874–1954)**

# J

**Jackson,** Anne (actress); Allegheny, Pa., 9/3/1926
**Jackson,** Glenda (actress); Hoylake, England, 1937(?)
**Jackson,** Rev. Jesse (civil rights leader); Greenville, N.C., 10/8/1941
**Jackson,** Kate (actress); Alabama, 1949
**Jackson,** Mahalia (gospel singer); New Orleans **(1912–1972)**
**Jackson,** Thomas Jonathan ("Stonewall") (general); Clarksburg, Va. (now W. Va.) **(1824–1863)**
**Jacobi,** Lou (actor); Toronto, 12/28/1913
**Jacobs,** Jane (urbanologist); Scranton, Pa., 5/1/1916.
**Jaffe,** Sam (actor); New York City, 3/8/1898
**Jagger,** Dean (actor); Lima, Ohio, 11/7/1903
**Jagger,** Mick (Michael Philip) (singer); Dartford, England, 7/26/1944
**James,** Harry (trumpeter); Albany, Ga., 3/15/1916
**James,** Henry (novelist); New York City **(1843–1916)**
**James,** Jesse Woodson (outlaw); Clay County, Mo. **(1847–1882)**
**James,** William (psychologist); New York City **(1842–1910)**
**Jameson,** (Margaret) Storm (novelist); Whitby, England, 1897
**Janis,** Byron (pianist); McKeesport, Pa., 3/24/1928
**Jannings,** Emil (actor); Brooklyn, N.Y. **(1886–1950)**
**Janssen,** David (David Meyer) (actor); Naponee, Neb., 3/27/1930
**Jay,** John (statesman, jurist); New York City **(1745–1829)**
**Jeanmaire,** Renée (dancer); Paris, 4/29/1924
**Jenner,** Edward (physician); Berkeley, England **(1749–1823)**
**Jennings,** Waylon (singer); Littlefield, Tex., 1937
**Jessel,** George (entertainer); New York City, 4/3/1898
**Jessup,** Philip C. (jurist); New York City, 1/5/1897
**Joan of Arc** (Jeanne d'Arc) (saint and patriot); Domremy-la-Pucelle, France **(1412–1431)**
**Joffrey,** Robert (Abdullah Jaffa Bey Khan) (choreographer); Seattle, 12/24/1930
**John,** Elton (Reginald Kenneth Dwight) (singer and pianist); Pinner, England, 3/25/1947
**Johns,** Glynis (actress); Pretoria, South Africa, 10/5/1923
**Johns,** Jasper (painter and sculptor); Augusta, Ga., 5/15/1930
**Johnson,** Philip Cortelyou (architect); Cleveland, Ohio, 7/8/1906
**Johnson,** Samuel (lexicographer and author); Lichfield, England **(1709–1784)**
**Johnson,** Van (actor); Newport, R.I., 8/20/1916
**Joliot-Curie,** Frédéric (physicist); Paris **(1900–1958)**
**Joliot-Curie,** Irène (Irène Curie) (physicist); France **(1897–1956)**
**Jolliet** (or **Joliet**), Louis (explorer); Beaupré, Canada **(1645–1700)**
**Jolson,** Al (Asa Yoelson) (actor and singer); St. Petersburg, Russia **(1886–1950)**
**Jones,** Carolyn (singer and actress); Amarillo, Tex., 4/28/1933
**Jones,** Dean (actor); Morgan County, Ala., 1/25/1935
**Jones,** George (singer); Saratoga, Tex., 9/12/1931
**Jones,** Inigo (architect); London **(1573–1652)**
**Jones,** James (novelist); Robinson, Ill. **(1921–1977)**
**Jones,** James Earl (actor); Arkabutla, Miss., 1/17/1931
**Jones,** Jennifer (Phyllis Isley) (actress); Tulsa, Okla., 3/2/1919
**Jones,** John Paul (John Paul) (naval officer); Scotland **(1747–1792)**
**Jones,** Quincy (composer); Chicago, 3/14/1933
**Jones,** Shirley (singer and actress); Smithtown, Pa., 3/31/1934
**Jones,** Tom (Thomas Jones Woodward) (singer); Pontypridd, Wales, 6/7/1940
**Jong,** Erica (writer); New York City, 3/26/1942
**Jonson,** Ben (Benjamin) (poet and dramatist); Westminster, England **(1572–1637)**
**Joplin,** Janis (singer); Port Arthur, Tex. **(1943–1970)**
**Jordan,** Barbara (congresswoman); Houston, 2/21/1936
**Jory,** Victor (actor); Dawson City, Yukon, Canada, 11/23/1903
**Jourdan,** Louis (Louis Gendre) (actor); Marseilles, France, 6/19/1920
**Joyce,** James (novelist); Dublin **(1882–1941)**
**Juárez,** Benito Pablo (statesman); Guelatao, Mexico **(1806–1872)**
**Juliana** (Queen); The Hague, Netherlands, 4/30/1909
**Jung,** Carl Gustav (psychoanalyst); Basel, Switzerland **(1875–1961)**
**Jurado,** Katy (actress); Guadalajara, Mexico, 1927

# K

**Kabalevsky,** Dmitri (composer); St. Petersburg, Russia, 12/30/1904
**Kádár,** János (Communist Party leader); Hungary, 1912
**Kahn,** Louis I. (architect); Oesel Island, Estonia **(1901–1974)**
**Kahn,** Madeline (actress); Boston, 9/29/1942
**Kaminska,** Ida (actress); Odessa, Russia, 9/4/1899
**Kandinsky,** Wassily (painter); Moscow **(1866–1944)**
**Kanin,** Garson (playwright); Rochester, N.Y., 11/24/1912
**Kant,** Immanuel (philosopher); Königsberg (Germany) **(1724–1804)**
**Kantor,** MacKinlay (novelist); Webster City, Iowa **(1904–1977)**

**Kaplan,** Gabe (actor); Brooklyn, N.Y., 1945
**Karloff,** Boris (William Henry Pratt) (actor); London **(1887–1969)**
**Kaufman,** George S. (playwright); Pittsburgh **(1889–1961)**
**Kaye,** Danny (David Daniel Kominski) (comedian); Brooklyn, N.Y., 1/18/1913
**Kaye,** Sammy (band leader); Cleveland, 3/13/1910
**Kazan,** Elia (director); Constantinople, Turkey, 9/7/1909
**Kazan,** Lainie (singer); New York City, 1940
**Keach,** Stacy (actor); Savannah, Ga., 6/2/1941
**Keaton,** Buster (Joseph Frank Keaton) (comedian); Piqua, Kan. **(1896–1966)**
**Keaton,** Diane (actress); Los Angeles, 1/5/1946
**Keats,** John (poet); London **(1795–1821)**
**Keel,** Howard (singer and actor); Gillespie, Ill., 4/13/1919
**Keeler,** Ruby (Lehy Keeler) (actress and dancer); Halifax, Nova Scotia, Canada, 8/25/1910
**Kefauver,** Estes (legislator); Madisonville, Tenn. **(1903–1963)**
**Keith,** Brian (actor); Bayonne, N.J., 11/14/1921
**Keller,** Helen Adams (author and educator); Tuscumbia, Ala. **(1880–1968)**
**Kellerman,** Sally (actress); Long Beach, Calif., 6/2/1938
**Kelly,** Emmett (clown); Sedan, Kan., 12/9/1898
**Kelly,** Gene (dancer and actor); Pittsburgh, 8/23/1912
**Kelly,** Grace (Princess Grace of Monaco) (former actress); Philadelphia, 11/12/1929
**Kelly,** Patsy (actress and comedienne); Brooklyn, N.Y., 1/12/1910
**Kelly,** Walt (cartoonist); Philadelphia **(1913–1973)**
**Kemal Ataturk** (Mustafa Kemal) (statesman); Salonika (Greece) **(1881–1938)**
**Kennan,** George F. (diplomat); Milwaukee, 2/16/1904
**Kennedy,** Arthur (actor); Worcester, Mass., 2/17/1914
**Kennedy,** Edward M. (U.S. Senator); Boston, Mass., 2/22/1932
**Kennedy,** George (actor); New York City, 2/18/1925
**Kennedy,** Jacqueline. *See* Onassis, Jacqueline
**Kennedy,** Joseph P. (financier); Boston **(1888–1969)**
**Kennedy,** Robert Francis (legislator); Brookline, Mass. **(1925–1968)**
**Kennedy,** Rose Fitzgerald (President's mother); Boston, 7/22/1890
**Kent,** Rockwell (painter); Tarrytown Heights, N.Y. **(1882–1971)**
**Kenton,** Stan (Stanley Newcomb) (jazz musician); Wichita, Kan., 2/19/1912
**Kepler,** Johannes (astronomer); Weil (Germany) **(1571–1630)**
**Kerensky,** Alexander Fedorovich (statesman); Simbirks, Russia **(1881–1970)**
**Kern,** Jerome David (composer); New York City **(1885–1945)**
**Kerr,** Deborah (actress); Helensburgh, Scotland, 9/30/1921
**Kesey,** Ken (novelist); La Junta, Colo., 9/17/1935
**Kettering,** Charles F. (engineer and inventor); nr. Loudonville, Ohio **(1876–1958)**
**Key,** Francis Scott (lawyer and author of national anthem); Frederick (now Carroll) County, Md. **(1779–1843)**
**Keyes,** Frances Parkinson (novelist); Charlottesville, Va., 7/21/1885
**Keynes** (1st Baron of Tilton) (John Maynard Keynes) (economist); Cambridge, England **(1883–1946)**
**Khachaturian,** Aram (composer); Tiflis, Russia **(1903–1978)**
**Khrushchev,** Nikita S. (Soviet leader); Kalinovka, nr. Kursk, Ukraine **(1894–1971)**
**Kibbee,** Guy (actor); El Paso **(1886–1956)**
**Kidd,** Michael (choreographer); Brooklyn, N.Y., 1917
**Kidd,** William (called Captain Kidd) (pirate); Greenock, Scotland **(1645?–1701)**
**Kieran,** John (writer); New York City, 8/2/1892
**Kiesinger,** Kurt Georg (diplomat); Ebingen, Germany, 4/6/1904
**Kiley,** Richard (actor and singer); Chicago, 3/31/1922
**Kilmer,** Alfred Joyce (poet); New Brunswick, N.J. **(1886–1918)**
**King,** Alan (Irwin Alan Kniberg) (entertainer); Brooklyn, N.Y., 12/26/1927
**King,** B.B. (Riley King) (guitarist); Itta Bena, Miss., 9/16/1925
**King,** Carole (singer and songwriter); Brooklyn, N.Y., 2/9/1941
**King,** Coretta Scott (civil rights leader); Marion, Ala., 4/27/1927
**King,** Martin Luther, Jr. (civil rights leader); Atlanta **(1929–1968)**
**King,** Pee Wee (Frank) (singer); Abrams, Wis., 2/18/1914
**Kingsley,** Sidney (Sidney Kirschner) (playwright); New York City, 10/18/1906
**Kipling,** Rudyard (author); Bombay **(1865–1936)**
**Kipnis,** Alexander (basso); Ukraine, **(1891–1978)**
**Kirby,** George (comedian); Chicago, 1923(?)
**Kirk,** Grayson (educator); Jeffersonville, Ohio, 10/12/1903
**Kirk,** Lisa (actress and singer); Charleroi, Pa., 1925
**Kirk,** Phyllis (actress); Plainfield, N.J., 9/18/1930
**Kirkland,** Gelsey (ballerina); Bethelhem, Pa., 12/29/1952
**Kirkpatrick,** Ralph (harpsichordist); Leominster, Mass., 6/10/1911
**Kirkwood,** James (actor); Grand Rapids, Mich. **(1883–1963)**
**Kirsten,** Dorothy (soprano); Montclair, N.J., 7/6/1919
**Kissinger,** Henry (Heinz Alfred Kissinger) (ex-Secretary of State); Furth, Germany, 5/27/1923
**Kitt,** Eartha (singer); North, S.C., 1/26/1928
**Klee,** Paul (painter); Münchenbuchsee, nr. Bern, Switzerland **(1879–1940)**
**Klein,** Robert (comedian); Bronx, N.Y., 2/8/1942
**Klemperer,** Otto (conductor); Breslau (Poland) **(1885–1973)**
**Klemperer,** Werner (actor); Cologne, Germany, 3/22/1920
**Klugman,** Jack (actor); Philadelphia, 1922
**Knievel,** Evel (Robert Craig) (daredevil motorcyclist); Butte, Mont., 10/17/1938
**Knight,** Gladys (singer); Atlanta, 5/28/1944
**Knight,** John S. (publisher); Bluefield, W. Va. 10/26/1894
**Knopf,** Alfred A. (publisher); New York City, 9/12/1892
**Knotts,** Don (actor); Morgantown, W.Va., 7/21/1924
**Knox,** John (religious reformer); Haddington, East Lothian, Scotland **(1505–1572)**
**Koch,** Robert (physician); Klausthal (Germany) **(1843–1910)**
**Koestler,** Arthur (novelist); Budapest, 9/5/1905
**Kokoschka,** Oskar (painter); Póchlarn Austria, 3/1/1886
**Kooper,** Al (singer and pianist); Brooklyn, N.Y., 2/5/1944
**Korman,** Harvey (actor); Chicago, 2/15/1927
**Kosciusko,** Thaddeus (Tadeusz Andrzej Bonawentura Kosciuszko) (military officer); Grand Duchy of Lithuania **(1746–1817)**
**Kostelanetz,** André (orchestra conductor); St. Petersburg, Russia, 12/22/1901
**Kosygin,** Aleksei N. (Premier); St. Petersburg, Russia, 2/20/1904
**Koussevitzky,** Serge (Sergei) Alexandrovitch (orchestra conductor); Vishni Volochek, Tver, Russia **(1874–1951)**
**Kovacs,** Ernie (comedian); Trenton, N.J. **(1919–1962)**
**Kramer,** Stanley E. (film producer and director); New York City, 9/29/1913
**Kraus,** Lili (pianist); Budapest, 3/4/1905(?)
**Kreisler,** Fritz (violinist and composer); Vienna **(1875–1962)**
**Kresge,** S. S. (merchant); Bald Mount, Pa. **(1867–1966)**
**Krips,** Josef (orchestra conductor); Vienna **(1902–1974)**
**Kristofferson,** Kris (singer); Brownsville, Tex., 6/22/1936
**Kruger,** Otto (actor); Toledo, Ohio **(1885–1974)**
**Krupa,** Gene (drummer); Chicago **(1909–1973)**
**Kubelik,** Rafael (conductor); Bychory (Czechoslovakia), 6/29/1914
**Kublai Khan** (Mongol conqueror) **(1216–1294)**
**Kubrick,** Stanley (producer and director); New York City, 7/26/1928
**Kuralt,** Charles (TV journalist); North Carolina, 1934
**Kurosawa,** Akira (film director); Tokyo, 3/23/1910
**Kurtz,** Efrem (conductor); St. Petersburg, Russia, 11/7/1900
**Ky,** Nguyen Cao (ex-Vice President of South Vietnam); Son Tay (Vietnam), 9/8/1930

# L

**Ladd,** Alan (actor); Hot Springs, Ark. **(1913–1964)**
**Ladd,** Cheryl (actress); Huron, S.D., 4/2/(?)
**Lafayette,** Marquis de (Marie Joseph Paul Yves Roch Gilbert du Motier) (military officer); Auvergne, France **(1757–1834)**
**La Follette,** Robert Marin (politician); Primrose, Wis. **(1855–1925)**
**La Guardia,** Fiorello Henry (Mayor of New York); New York City **(1882–1947)**
**Lahr,** Bert (Irving Lahrheim) (comedian); New York City **(1895–1967)**
**Laine,** Frankie (Frank Paul LoVecchio) (singer); Chicago, 3/30/1913
**Laird,** Melvin (ex-Secretary of Defense); Omaha, Neb., 9/1/1922
**Lamarck,** Chevalier de (Jean Baptiste Pierre Antoine de Monet) (naturalist); Bazantin, France **(1744–1829)**
**Lamarr,** Hedy (Hedwig Kiesler) (actress); Vienna, 1915
**Lamas,** Fernando (actor); Buenos Aires, 1/9/1915
**Lamb,** Charles (essayist); London **(1775–1834)**
**Lamour,** Dorothy (Dorothy Kaumeyer) (actress); New Orleans, 10/10/1914
**Lancaster,** Burt (actor); New York City, 11/2/1913
**Lanchester,** Elsa (Elsa Sullivan) (actress); London, 10/28/1902
**Landau,** Martin (actor); Brooklyn, N.Y. 1925(?)
**Landers,** Ann (columnist); Sioux City, Iowa, 7/14/1918
**Landon,** Michael (Michael Orowitz) (actor); Forest Hills, Queens, N.Y., 10/31/1936(?)
**Lane,** Abbe (singer); New York City, 1933
**Lang,** Fritz (film director); Vienna **(1890–1976)**
**Lang,** Paul Henry (music critic); Budapest, 8/28/1901
**Lange,** Hope (actress); Redding Ridge, Conn., 11/28/1933
**Langella,** Frank (actor); Bayonne, N.J., 1940
**Langford,** Frances (singer); Lakeland, Fla., 4/4/1913
**Langmuir,** Irving (chemist); Brooklyn, N.Y. **(1881–1957)**
**Langtry,** Lily (Emily Le Breton) (actress); Island of Jersey **(1852–1929)**
**Lansbury,** Angela (actress); London, 10/16/1925
**Lansing,** Robert (actor); San Diego, Calif., 6/5/1929
**Lanza,** Mario (Alfred Arnold Cocozza) (singer and actor); Philadelphia **(1925–1959)**
**Lao-Tzu** (or **Lao-Tse**) (Li Erh) (philosopher); Honan Province, China **(c. 604–531** B.C.**)**
**Lardner,** Ring (Ringgold Wilmer Lardner) (story writer); Niles, Mich. **(1885–1933)**

**La Salle**, Sieur de (Robert Cavelier) (explorer); Rouen, France **(1643–1687)**
**Lasser**, Louise (actress); New York City, 1940(?)
**Lauder**, Sir Harry (Harry MacLennan) (singer); Portobello, Scotland **(1870–1950)**
**Laughton**, Charles (actor); Scarborough, England **(1899–1962)**
**Laurel**, Stan (Arthur Jefferson) (comedian); Ulverston, England **(1890–1965)**
**Laurents**, Arthur (playwright); New York City, 7/14/1918
**Laurie**, Piper (actress); Detroit, 1/22/1932
**Lavoisier**, Antoine-Laurent (chemist); Paris **(1743–1794)**
**Lawford**, Peter (actor); London, 9/7/1923
**Lawrence**, Carol (Carol Maria Laraia) (dancer and actress); Melrose Park, Ill., 9/5/1932
**Lawrence**, David Herbert (novelist); Nottingham, England **(1885–1930)**
**Lawrence**, Gertrude (Gertrud Klasen) (actress); London **(1900–1952)**
**Lawrence**, Marjorie (singer); Deans Marsh, Australia, 2/17/1909
**Lawrence**, Steve (Sidney Leibowitz) (singer); Brooklyn, N.Y., 7/8/1935
**Lawrence**, Vicki (actress); Inglewood, Calif., 1949
**Lawrence of Arabia** (Thomas Edward Lawrence, later changed to Shaw) (author and soldier); Tremadoc, Wales **(1888–1935)**
**Leachman**, Cloris (actress); Des Moines, Iowa, 4/30/1926(?)
**Lean**, David (film director); Croydon, England, 3/25/1908
**Lear**, Edward (nonsense poet); London **(1812–1888)**
**Le Carré**, John (David John Moore Cornwell) (novelist); Poole, England, 10/19/1931
**Le Corbusier** (Charles Edouard Jeanneret) (architect); La Chaux-de-Fonds, Switzerland **(1887–1965)**
**Lederer**, Francis (actor); Prague, 11/6/1906
**Lee**, Christopher (actor); London, 5/27/1922
**Lee**, Gypsy Rose (Rose Louise Hovick) (entertainer); Seattle **(1919–1970)**
**Lee**, Peggy (Norma Engstrom) (singer); Jamestown, N.D., 5/26/1920
**Lee**, Robert Edward (Confederate general); Stratford Estate, Va. **(1807–1870)**
**Leek**, Sybil (Sybil Falk) (astrologer); Staffordshire, England, 1923
**Le Gallienne**, Eva (actress); London, 1/11/1899
**Léhar**, Franz (composer); Komárom (Czechoslovakia) **(1870–1948)**
**Lehman**, Herbert H. (Governor and Senator); New York City **(1878–1963)**
**Lehmann**, Lotte (soprano); Perleberg (Germany) **(1888–1976)**
**Leigh**, Janet (Jeanette Morrison) (actress); Merced, Calif., 7/6/1927
**Leigh**, Vivien (Vivien Mary Hartley) (actress); Darjeeling, India **(1913–1967)**
**Leighton**, Margaret (actress); nr. Birmingham, England **(1922–1976)**
**Leinsdorf**, Erich (conductor); Vienna, 2/4/1912
**Lemmon**, Jack (actor); Boston, 2/8/1925
**Lenin**, Nicolai (Vladimir Ilich Ulyanov) (Soviet leader); Simbirsk, Russia **(1870–1924)**
**Lennon**, John (singer and songwriter); Liverpool, England, 10/9/1940
**Lenya**, Lotte (Karoline Balmauer) (singer and actress); Hitzing, Austria, 1905
**Leonard**, Sheldon (actor and director); New York City, 2/22/1907
**Lerner**, Alan Jay (lyricist); New York City, 8/31/1918
**Lerner**, Max (columnist); Minsk, Russia, 12/20/190?
**Le Roy**, Mervyn (film producer); San Francisco, 10/15/1900
**Leslie**, Joan (actress); Detroit, 1/26/1925
**Lessing**, Doris (novelist); Kermanshah, Iran, 10/22/1919
**Lester**, Mark (actor); Richmond, England, 1958
**Levant**, Oscar (pianist); Pittsburgh **(1906–1972)**
**Levene**, Sam (actor); New York City, 8/28/1905
**Levenson**, Sam (humorist); New York City, 12/28/1911
**Levi**, Carlo (novelist); Turin, Italy **(1902–1975)**
**Levine**, James (music director, Metropolitan Opera); Cincinnati, 6/23/1943
**Lewis**, Jerry (Joseph Levitch) (comedian and film director); Newark, N.J., 3/16/1926
**Lewis**, Jerry Lee (singer); Ferriday, La., 9/?/1935
**Lewis**, John Llewellyn (labor leader); Lucas, Iowa **(1880–1969)**
**Lewis**, Meriwether (explorer); Albemarle Co., Va. **(1774–1809)**
**Lewis**, Shari (Shari Hurwitz) (puppeteer); New York City, 1/17/1934
**Lewis**, Sinclair (novelist); Sauk Centre, Minn. **(1885–1951)**
**Lewis**, Ted (entertainer); Circleville, Ohio **(1891–1971)**
**Ley**, Willy (science writer); Berlin **(1906–1969)**
**Liberace** (Wladziu Liberace) (pianist); West Allis, Wis., 5/16/1919
**Lichtenstein**, Roy (painter); New York City, 10/27/1923
**Lie**, Trygve Halvdan (first U.N. Secretary-General); Oslo **(1896–1968)**
**Lightfoot**, Gordon (singer and songwriter); Orillia, Ontario, Canada, 11/17/1938
**Lillie**, Beatrice (Lady Peel) (actress and comedienne); Toronto, 5/29/1898
**Lin Yutang** (author); Changchow, China **(1895–1976)**
**Lind**, Jenny (Johanna Maria Lind) (soprano); Stockholm **(1820–1887)**
**Lindbergh**, Anne Morrow (author); Englewood, N.J., 6/22/1906
**Lindbergh**, Charles A. (aviator); Detroit **(1902–1974)**
**Linden**, Hal (actor); New York City, 3/20/1931
**Lindfors**, Viveca (actress); Uppsala, Sweden, 12/29/1920
**Lindsay**, Howard (dramatist); Waterford, N.Y. **(1889–1968)**
**Lindsay**, John Vliet (ex-Mayor of New York City); New York City, 11/24/1921
**Lindstrom**, Pia (TV newscaster); Stockholm, 11/?/1938
**Linkletter**, Art (radio-TV personality); Moose Jaw, Saskatchewan, Canada, 7/17/1912
**Lipchitz**, Jacques (sculptor); Druskieniki, Latvia **(1891–1973)**
**Lippmann**, Walter (columnist, author, and political analyst); New York City **(1889–1974)**
**Lister**, (1st Baron of Lyme Regis) (Joseph Lister) (surgeon); Upton, England **(1827–1912)**
**Liszt**, Franz (composer and pianist); Raiding (Hungary) **(1811–1886)**
**Little**, Cleavon (actor and comedian); Chickasha, Okla., 6/1/1939
**Little**, Rich (impressionist); Ottawa, 11/26/1938
**Livesey**, Roger (actor); Barry, Wales **(1906–1976)**
**Livingstone**, David (missionary and explorer); Lanarkshire, Scotland **(1813–1873)**
**Livingstone**, Mary (Sadye Marks) (comedienne); Seattle, 1909
**Llewellyn**, Richard (novelist); St. David's, Wales
**Lloyd**, Harold (comedian); Burchard, Neb. **(1894–1971)**
**Lloyd George**, David (Earl of Dwyfor) (statesman); Manchester, England **(1863–1945)**
**Locke**, John (philosopher); Somersetshire, England **(1632–1704)**
**Lockhart**, Gene (actor); London, Ontario, Canada **(1891–1957)**
**Lockhart**, June (actress); New York City, 6/25/1925
**Lockwood**, Margaret (actress); Karachi (Pakistan), 9/15/1916
**Lodge**, Henry Cabot (legislator); Boston **(1850–1924)**
**Lodge**, Henry Cabot, Jr. (diplomat); Nahant, Mass., 7/5/1902
**Loesser**, Frank (composer); New York City **(1910–1969)**
**Loewe**, Frederick (composer); Vienna, 6/10/1904
**Logan**, Joshua (director and producer); Texarkana, Tex., 10/5/1908
**Lollobrigida**, Gina (actress); Subiaco, Italy, 1928
**Lombard**, Carole (Carol Jane Peters) (actress); Ft. Wayne, Ind. **(1908–1942)**
**Lombardo**, Guy (band leader); London, Ontario, Canada **(1902–1977)**
**London**, George (baritone); Montreal, 5/30/1920
**London**, Jack (John Griffith London) (novelist); San Francisco **(1876–1916)**
**London**, Julie (Julie Peck) (singer and actress); Santa Rosa, Calif., 9/26/1926
**Long**, Huey Pierce (politician); Winnfield, La. **(1893–1935)**
**Longfellow**, Henry Wadsworth (poet); Portland, Me. **(1807–1882)**
**Longworth**, Alice Roosevelt (social figure); New York City, 2/12/1884
**Loos**, Anita (novelist); Sissons, Calif., 4/26/1893
**Lopez**, Trini (Trinidad Lopez III) (singer); Dallas, 5/15/1937
**Lopez**, Vincent (band leader); Brooklyn, N.Y. **(1895–1975)**
**Lord**, Jack (actor); New York City, 12/30/1930
**Loren**, Sophia (Sofia Scicolone) (actress); Rome, 9/20/1934
**Lorre**, Peter (Laszlo Löewenstein) (actor); Rosenberg (Czechoslovakia) **(1904–1964)**
**Louise**, Tina (actress); New York City, 2/11/1937
**Lowell**, Amy (poet); Brookline, Mass. **(1874–1925)**
**Lowell**, James Russell (poet); Cambridge, Mass. **(1819–1891)**
**Lowell**, Robert (poet); Boston **(1917–1977)**
**Loy**, Myrna (Myrna Williams) (actress); nr. Helena, Mont., 8/2/1905
**Loyola**, St. Ignatius of (Iñigo de Oñez y Loyola) (founder of Jesuits); Gúipuzcoa Province, Spain **(1491–1556)**
**Lubitsch**, Ernst (film director); Berlin **(1892–1947)**
**Luce**, Clare Boothe (playwright and former Ambassador); New York City, 4/10/1903
**Luce**, Henry Robinson (editor and publisher); Tengchow, China **(1898–1967)**
**Lugosi**, Bela (Bela Lugosi Blasko) (actor); Logos, Hungary **(1888–1956)**
**Lukas**, Paul (actor); Budapest **(1895–1971)**
**Lumet**, Sidney (film and TV director); Philadelphia, 6/25/1924
**Lunt**, Alfred (actor); Milwaukee **(1892–1977)**
**Lupino**, Ida (actress and director); London, 2/4/1918
**Luther**, Martin (religious reformer); Eisleben (Germany) **(1483–1546)**
**Lynde**, Paul (comedian); Mt. Vernon, Ohio, 6/13/1926
**Lynley**, Carol (actress); New York City, 2/13/1942
**Lynn**, Jeffrey (actor); Auburn, Mass., 1909
**Lynn**, Loretta (singer); Butcher's Hollow, Ky., 4/14/1935

# M

**Maazel**, Lorin (conductor); Neuilly, France, 3/5/1930
**MacArthur**, Douglas (five-star general); Little Rock Barracks, Ark. **(1880–1964)**
**MacArthur**, James (actor); Los Angeles, 12/8/1937
**Macaulay**, Thomas Babington (author); Rothley Temple, England **(1800–1859)**
**MacDermot**, Galt (composer); Montreal, 12/19/1928

**MacDonald**, James Ramsay (statesman); Lossiemouth, Scotland (1866–1937)
**MacDonald**, Jeanette (actress, soprano); Philadelphia (1907–1965)
**MacDowell**, Edward Alexander (composer); New York City (1861–1908)
**Macfadden**, Bernarr (physical culturist); nr. Mill Spring, Mo. (1868–1955)
**MacGraw**, Ali (actress); New York City, 4/1/1939
**Machiavelli**, Niccolò (political philosopher); Florence (Italy) (1469–1527)
**Mack**, Ted (TV personality); Greeley, Colo. (1904–1976)
**MacKenzie**, Gisele (Marie Marguerite Louise Gisele LaFleche) (singer and actress); Winnipeg, Manitoba, Canada, 1/10/1927
**MacLaine**, Shirley (Shirley MacLean Beaty) (actress); Richmond, Va., 4/24/1934
**MacLeish**, Archibald (poet); Glencoe, Ill., 5/7/1892
**MacMahon**, Ed (TV personality); Detroit, 3/6/1923
**Macmillan**, Harold (ex-Prime Minister); London, 2/10/1894
**MacMurray**, Fred (actor); Kankakee, Ill., 8/30/1908
**MacNeil**, Cornell (baritone); Minneapolis, 1925
**MacRae**, Gordon (singer); East Orange, N.J., 3/12/1921
**MacRae**, Sheila (comedienne); London, 9/24/1924
**Madison**, Guy (Robert Moseley) (actor); Bakersfield, Calif., 1/19/1922
**Maeterlinck**, Count Maurice (author); Ghent, Belgium (1862–1949)
**Magellan**, Ferdinand (Fernando de Magalhaes) (navigator); Sabrosa, Portugal (1480?–1521)
**Magnani**, Anna (actress); Rome (1908–1973)
**Magritte**, René (painter); Belgium (1898–1967)
**Magsaysay**, Ramón (statesman); Iba, Luzon, Philippines (1907–1957)
**Mahan**, Alfred Thayer (naval historian); West Point, N.Y. (1840–1914)
**Mahler**, Gustav (composer and conductor); Kalischt (Czechoslovakia) (1860–1911)
**Mailer**, Norman (novelist); Long Branch, N.J., 1/31/1923
**Maillol**, Aristide (sculptor); Banyuls-sur-Mer, Rousillon, France (1861–1944)
**Main**, Marjorie (Mary Tomlinson Krebs) (actress); Acton, Ind. (1890–1975)
**Mainbocher** (Main Rousseau Bocher) (fashion designer); Chicago (1891–1976)
**Majors**, Lee (actor); Wyandotte, Mich., 1942
**Makarova**, Natalia (ballerina); Leningrad, 11/21/1940
**Makeba**, Miriam (singer); Johannesburg, South Africa, 3/4/1932
**Malamud**, Bernard (novelist); Brooklyn, N.Y., 4/26/1914
**Malden**, Karl (Mladon Sekulovich) (actor); Chicago, 3/22/1914
**Malone**, Dorothy (actress), Chicago, 1/30/1925
**Malraux**, André (author); Paris (1901–1976)
**Manchester**, Melissa (singer); Bronx, N.Y., 2/15/1951
**Manchester**, William (writer), Attleboro, Mass., 4/1/1922
**Mancini**, Henry (composer and conductor); Cleveland, 4/16/1924
**Manet**, Edouard (painter); Paris (1832–1883)
**Mangano**, Silvana (actress); Rome, 4/21/1930
**Manilow**, Barry (singer); Brooklyn, N.Y., 6/17/1946
**Mankiewicz**, Frank F. (columnist); New York City, 5/16/1924
**Mankiewicz**, Joseph L. (film writer and director); Wilkes-Barre, Pa., 2/11/1909
**Mann**, Horace (educator); Franklin, Mass. (1796–1859)
**Mann**, Thomas (novelist); Lübeck, Germany (1875–1955)
**Mannes**, Marya (writer); New York City, 11/14/1904
**Mansfield**, Jayne (Jayne Palmer) (actress); Bryn Mawr, Pa. (1932–1967)
**Mansfield**, Katherine (story writer); Wellington, New Zealand (1888–1923)
**Mantovani**, Annunzio (conductor); Venice, 1905
**Mao Tse-tung** (Chinese leader); Shao Shan, China (1893–1976)
**Marat**, Jean Paul (French revolutionist); Boudry, Neuchâtel, Switzerland (1743–1793)
**Marceau**, Marcel (mime); Strasbourg, France, 3/22/1923
**March**, Fredric (Frederick Bickel) (actor); Racine, Wis. (1897–1975)
**Marconi**, Guglielmo (inventor); Bologna, Italy (1874–1937)
**Marcus Aurelius** (Marcus Annius Verus) (Roman emperor); Rome (121–180)
**Marcuse**, Herbert (philosopher); Berlin, 7/19/1898
**Margaret Rose** (Princess); Glamis Castle, Angus, Scotland, 8/21/1930
**Margrethe II** (Queen); Copenhagen, 4/16/1940
**Marie Antoinette** (Josèphe Jeanne Marie Antoinette) (Queen of France); Vienna (1755–1793)
**Marisol** (sculptor); Venezuela, 1930
**Markham**, Edwin (poet); Oregon City, Ore. (1852–1940)
**Markova**, Dame Alicia (ballerina); London, 12/1/1910
**Marley**, Bob (reggae singer and songwriter); Kingston, Jamaica, c.1946
**Marlowe**, Christopher (dramatist); Canterbury, England (1564–1593)
**Marlowe**, Julia (Sarah Frances Frost) (actress); Cumberlandshire, England (1866–1950)
**Marquand**, John Phillips (novelist); Wilmington, Del. (1893–1960)
**Marquette**, Jacques (missionary and explorer); Laon, France (1637–1675)
**Marsh**, Jean (actress); Stoke Newington, England, 7/1/1934
**Marshall**, E.G. (actor); Owatonna, Minn., 6/18/1910
**Marshall**, George Catlett (general); Uniontown, Pa. (1880–1959)
**Marshall**, Herbert (actor); London (1890–1968)
**Marshall**, John (jurist); nr. Germantown, Va. (1755–1835)
**Marshall**, Penny (actress); New York City, 10/15/(?)
**Martin**, Dean (Dino Crocetti) (singer and actor); Steubenville, Ohio, 6/17/1917
**Martin**, Dick (actor and comedian); Battle Creek, Mich., 1/30/1922
**Martin**, Mary (singer and actress); Weatherford, Tex., 12/1/1914
**Martin**, Tony (Alvin Morris) (singer); San Francisco, 12/25/1914
**Martin**, William McChesney, Jr. (ex-chairman of Federal Reserve Board); St. Louis, 12/17/1906
**Martinelli**, Giovanni (tenor); Montagnana, Italy (1885–1969)
**Marvin**, Lee (actor); New York City, 2/19/1924
**Marx**, Chico (Leonard) (comedian); New York City (1891–1961)
**Marx**, Groucho (Julius) (comedian); New York City (1890–1977)
**Marx**, Harpo (Arthur) (comedian); New York City (1893–1964)
**Marx**, Karl (Socialist writer); Treves (Germany) (1818–1883)
**Marx**, Zeppo (Herbert) (comedian); New York City, 2/25/1901
**Mary Stuart** (Queen of Scotland); Linlithgow, Scotland (1542–1587)
**Masaryk**, Jan Garrigue (statesman); Prague (Czechoslovakia) (1886–1948)
**Masaryk**, Thomas Garrigue (statesman); Hodonin (Czechoslovakia) (1850–1937)
**Masefield**, John (poet); Ledbury, England (1878–1967)
**Masekela**, Hugh (trumpeter); Wilbank, South Africa, 4/4/1939
**Mason**, James (actor); Huddersfield, England, 5/15/1909
**Massenet**, Jules Emile Frédéric (composer); Montaud, France (1842–1912)
**Massey**, Raymond (actor); Toronto, 8/30/1896
**Massine**, Léonide (choreographer); Moscow, 8/9/1896
**Masters**, Edgar Lee (poet); Garnett, Kan. (1869–1950)
**Mastroianni**, Marcello (actor); Fontana Liri, Italy, 9/28/1924
**Mathis**, Johnny (singer); San Francisco, 9/30/1935
**Matisse**, Henri (painter); Le Cateau, France (1869–1954)
**Matthau**, Walter (Walter Matuschanskayasky) (actor); New York City, 10/1/1920
**Mature**, Victor (actor); Louisville, Ky., 1/19/1916
**Maugham**, (William) Somerset (author); Paris (1874–1965)
**Mauldin**, Bill (political cartoonist); Mountain Park, N.M., 10/29/1921
**Maupassant**, Henri René Albert Guy de (story writer); Normandy, France (1850–1893)
**Maurois**, André (Emile Herzog) (author); Elbeuf, France (1885–1967)
**Maximilian** (Ferdinand Maximilian Joseph) (Emperor of Mexico); Vienna (1832–1867)
**Maxwell**, James Clerk (physicist); Edinburgh, Scotland (1831–1879)
**May**, Elaine (entertainer); Philadelphia, 1932
**May**, Rollo (psychologist); Ada, Ohio, 4/21/1909
**Mayall**, John (singer and songwriter); Manchester, England, 11/29/1933
**Mayo**, Charles H. (surgeon); Rochester, Minn. (1865–1939)
**Mayo**, Charles W. (surgeon); Rochester, Minn. (1898–1968)
**Mayo**, Virginia (actress); St. Louis, 1920
**Mayo**, William J. (surgeon); Le Sueur, Minn. (1861–1939)
**McBride**, Mary Margaret (radio personality); Paris, Mo. (1899–1976)
**McBride**, Patricia (ballerina); Teaneck, N.J., 8/23/1942
**McCallum**, David (actor); Glasgow, Scotland, 9/19/1933
**McCambridge**, Mercedes (actress); Joliet, Ill., 3/17/1918
**McCarthy**, Eugene J. (ex-Senator); Watkins, Minn., 3/29/1916
**McCarthy**, Joseph Raymond (Senator); Grand Chute, Wis. (1908–1957)
**McCarthy**, Kevin (actor); Seattle, 1915
**McCarthy**, Mary (novelist); Seattle, 6/21/1912
**McCartney**, Paul (singer and songwriter); Liverpool, England, 6/18/1942
**McClellan**, George Brinton (general); Philadelphia (1826–1885)
**McCloy**, John J. (lawyer and banker); Philadelphia, 3/31/1895
**McClure**, Doug (actor); Glendale, Calif., 5/11/1938
**McCormack**, John (tenor); Athlone, Ireland (1884–1945)
**McCormack**, John W. (ex-Speaker of House), Boston, 12/21/1891
**McCormack**, Patty (actress); New York City, 8/21/1945
**McCormick**, Cyrus Hall (inventor); Rockbridge County, Va. (1809–1884)
**McCoy**, Tim (actor); Saginaw, Mich. (1891–1978)
**McCracken**, James (dramatic tenor); Gary, Ind., 12/16/1926
**McCrea**, Joel (actor); Los Angeles, 11/5/1906
**McCullers**, Carson (novelist); Columbus, Ga. (1917–1967)
**McDowall**, Roddy (actor); London, 9/17/1928
**McDowell**, Malcolm (actor); Leeds, England, 6/19/1943
**McGavin**, Darren (actor); San Joaquin, Calif., 5/7/1922
**McGinley**, Phyllis (poet and writer); Ontario, Ore. (1905–1978)
**McGoohan**, Patrick (actor); Astoria, Queens, N.Y., 1928
**McGuire**, Dorothy (actress); Omaha, Neb., 6/14/1919
**McKenna**, Siobhan (actress); Belfast, Northern Ireland, 5/24/1923
**McKuen**, Rod (singer and composer); Oakland, Calif., 4/29/1933
**McLaglen**, Victor (actor); Tunbridge Wells, Kent, England (1886–1959)
**McLaughlin**, John (guitarist); Yorkshire, England, 1942
**McLean**, Don (singer, songwriter); New Rochelle, N.Y., 10/2/1945
**McLuhan**, Marshall (Herbert Marshall) (communications writer); Edmonton, Canada, 7/21/1911
**McMahon**, Ed (TV personality); Detroit, 3/6/1923

**McNamara,** Robert S. (president of World Bank); San Francisco, 6/9/1916
**McQueen,** Steve (Terence Stephen McQueen) (actor); Indianapolis, 3/24/1930(?)
**Mead,** Margaret (anthropologist); Philadelphia, 12/16/1901
**Meadows,** Audrey (actress); Wu Chang, China, 1922(?)
**Meadows,** Jayne (actress); Wu Chang, China 9/27/1926
**Meany,** George (labor leader); New York City, 8/16/1894
**Meara,** Anne (actress); New York City, 1929
**Medici,** Lorenzo de' (called Lorenzo the Magnificent) (Florentine ruler); Florence (Italy) **(1449–1492)**
**Meeker,** Ralph (Ralph Rathgeber) (actor); Minneapolis, 11/21/1920
**Mehta,** Zubin (conductor); Bombay, 4/29/1936
**Meir,** Golda (Golda Myerson, nee Mabovitz) (ex-Premier of Israel); Kiev, Russia, 5/3/1898
**Melanie** (Melanie Safka) (singer and songwriter); New York City, 2/3/1947
**Melba,** Dame Nellie (Helen Porter Mitchell) (soprano); nr. Melbourne **(1861–1931)**
**Melchior,** Lauritz (Lebrecht Hommel) (heroic tenor); Copenhagen **(1890–1973)**
**Mellon,** Andrew William (financier); Pittsburgh **(1855–1937)**
**Melville,** Herman (novelist); New York City **(1819–1891)**
**Mencken,** Henry Louis (writer); Baltimore **(1880–1956)**
**Mendel,** Gregor Johann (botanist); Heinzendorf, Austria, Silesia **(1822–1884)**
**Mendeleyev,** Dmitri Ivanovich (chemist); Tobolsk, Russia **(1834–1907)**
**Mendelssohn-Bartholdy,** Jakob Ludwig Felix (composer); Hamburg **(1809–1847)**
**Mendès-France,** Pierre (ex-Premier); Paris, 1/11/1905
**Menjou,** Adolphe (actor); Pittsburgh **(1890–1963)**
**Mennin,** Peter (Peter Mennini) (composer); Erie, Pa., 5/17/1923
**Menninger,** William C. (psychiatrist); Topeka, Kan. **(1899–1966)**
**Menotti,** Gian Carlo (composer); Cadegliano, Italy, 7/7/1911
**Menuhin,** Yehudi (violinist, conductor); New York City, 4/22/1916
**Menzies,** Robert Gordon (ex-Prime Minister); Jeparit, Australia **(1894–1978)**
**Mercer,** Johnny (songwriter); Savannah, Ga. **(1909–1976)**
**Mercer,** Mabel (singer); Burton-on-Trent, England, 1/?/1900
**Mercouri,** Melina (actress); Athens, 10/18/1925
**Meredith,** Burgess (actor); Cleveland, 11/16/1908
**Merkel,** Una (actress); Covington, Ky., 12/10/1903
**Merman,** Ethel (Ethel Zimmerman) (singer and actress); Astoria, Queens, N.Y., 1/16/1909
**Merrick,** David (David Margulois) (stage producer); St. Louis, 11/27/1912
**Merrill,** Dina (actress); New York City, 12/9/1925
**Merrill,** Gary (actor); Hartford, Conn., 8/2/1914
**Merrill,** Robert (baritone); Brooklyn, N.Y., 6/4/1919
**Merton,** Thomas (clergyman and writer); France **(1915–1968)**
**Mesmer,** Franz Anton (physician); Itzmang, nr. Constance (Germany) **(1733–1815)**
**Mesta,** Perle (social figure); Sturgis, Mich. **(1889–1975)**
**Metternich,** Prince Klemens Wenzel Nepomuk Lothar von (statesman); Coblenz (Germany) **(1773–1859)**
**Michelangelo Buonarroti** (painter, sculptor, architect); Caprese (Italy) **(1475–1564)**
**Michener,** James A. (novelist); New York City, 2/3/1907
**Midler,** Bette (singer); Honolulu, 1945(?)
**Mielziner,** Jo (stage designer); Paris **(1901–1976)**
**Mies van der Rohe,** Ludwig (architect & designer); Aachen, Germany **(1886–1969)**
**Mikoyan,** Anastas I. (diplomat); Sanain, Armenia, 11/25/1895
**Miles,** Sarah (actress); Essex, England, 12/31/1943
**Miles,** Sylvia (actress); New York City, 9/9/1932
**Miles,** Vera (Vera Ralston) (actress); nr. Boise City, Okla., 8/23/1929
**Milhaud,** Darius (composer); Aix-en-Provence, France **(1892–1974)**
**Mill,** John Stuart (philosopher); London, **(1806–1873)**
**Milland,** Ray (Reginald Truscott-Jones) (actor); Neath, Wales, 1/3/1907
**Millay,** Edna St. Vincent (poet); Rockland, Me. **(1892–1950)**
**Miller,** Ann (Lucy Ann Collier) (dancer and actress); Chireno, Tex., 4/12/1919
**Miller,** Arthur (playwright); New York City, 10/17/1915
**Miller,** Glenn (band leader); Clarinda, Iowa **(1909?–1944)**
**Miller,** Henry (novelist); New York City, 12/26/1891
**Miller,** Jason (John Miller) (playwright); New York City, 1939(?)
**Miller,** Mitch (Mitchell) (musician); Rochester, N.Y., 7/4/1911
**Miller,** Roger (singer); Fort Worth, 1/2/1936
**Millet,** Jean François (painter); Gruchy, France **(1814–1875)**
**Millett,** Kate (feminist); St. Paul, 9/14/1934
**Mills,** Hayley (actress); London, 4/18/1946
**Mills,** John (actor); Felixstowe, England, 2/22/1908
**Milne,** A(lan) A(lexander) (author); London **(1882–1956)**
**Milstein,** Nathan (concert violinist); Odessa, Russia, 12/31/1904
**Milton,** John (poet); London **(1608–1674)**
**Mimieux,** Yvette (actress); Hollywood, Calif., 1/8/1941
**Mineo,** Sal (actor); New York City **(1939–1976)**
**Minnelli,** Liza (singer and actress); Hollywood, Calif., 3/12/1946
**Minnelli,** Vincente (film director); Chicago, 2/28/1913
**Minuit,** Peter (Governor of New Amsterdam); Wesel (Germany) **(1580–1638)**
**Miranda,** Carmen (Maria do Carmo da Cunha) (singer and dancer); Lisbon **(1913–1955)**
**Miró,** Joan (painter); Barcelona, 4/20/1893
**Mitchell,** Cameron (actor); Dallastown, Pa., 4/11/1918
**Mitchell,** Guy (actor); Detroit, 2/27/1927
**Mitchell,** John N. (former Attorney General); Detroit, 9/15/1913
**Mitchell,** Joni (Roberta Joan Anderson) (singer and songwriter); Ft. MacCleod, Canada, 11/7/1943
**Mitchell,** Margaret (novelist); Atlanta **(1900–1949)**
**Mitchum,** Robert (actor); Bridgeport, Conn., 8/6/1917
**Mitropoulos,** Dimitri (orchestra conductor); Athens **(1896–1960)**
**Mix,** Tom (actor); Mix Run, Pa. **(1880–1940)**
**Modigliani,** Amedeo (painter); Leghorn, Italy **(1884–1920)**
**Moffo,** Anna (soprano); Wayne, Pa., 6/27/1934
**Mohammed** (prophet); Mecca (Saudi Arabia) **(570–632)**
**Molière** (Jean Baptiste Poquelin) (dramatist); Paris **(1622–1673)**
**Molnar,** Ferenc (dramatist); Budapest **(1878–1952)**
**Molotov,** Vyacheslav M. (V. M. Skryabin) (diplomat); Kukarka, Russia, 3/9/1890
**Mondrian,** Piet (painter); Amersfoort, Netherlands **(1872–1944)**
**Monet,** Claude (painter); Paris **(1840–1926)**
**Monk,** Thelonious (pianist); Rocky Mount, N.C., 10/10/1918
**Monroe,** Marilyn (Norma Jean Mortenson or Baker) (actress); Los Angeles **(1926–1962)**
**Monroe,** Vaughn (Wilton) (band leader); Akron, Ohio **(1912–1973)**
**Monsarrat,** Nicholas (novelist); Liverpool, England, 3/22/1910
**Montaigne,** Michel Eyquem de (essayist); nr. Bordeaux, France **(1533–1592)**
**Montalban,** Ricardo (actor); Mexico City, 11/25/1920
**Montand,** Yves (Yves Montand Livi) (actor and singer); Mansummano, Italy, 10/13/1921
**Montez,** Maria (actress); Dominican Republic **(1918–1951)**
**Montezuma II** (Aztec emperor); Mexico **(1480?–1520)**
**Montgomery,** Elizabeth (actress); Hollywood, Calif., 4/15/1933
**Montgomery,** George (George Letz) (actor); Brady, Mont., 1929
**Montgomery,** Robert (Henry, Jr.) (actor); Beacon, N.Y., 5/21/1904
**Montgomery of Alamein,** 1st Viscount of Hindhead (Sir Bernard Law Montgomery) (military leader); London **(1887–1976)**
**Montoya,** Carlos (guitarist); Madrid, 12/13/1903
**Moore,** Clement Clarke (author); New York City **(1779–1863)**
**Moore,** Garry (Thomas Garrison Morfit) (TV personality); Baltimore, 1/31/1915
**Moore,** Grace (soprano); Jellico, Tenn. **(1901–1947)**
**Moore,** Henry (sculptor); Castleford, England, 7/30/1898
**Moore,** Marianne (poet); Kirkwood, Mo. **(1887–1972)**
**Moore,** Mary Tyler (actress); Brooklyn, N.Y., 12/29/1937
**Moore,** Melba (Beatrice) (singer and actress); New York City, 10/27/1945
**Moore,** Roger (actor); London, 10/14/1927(?)
**Moore,** Thomas (poet); Dublin **(1779–1852)**
**Moore,** Victor (actor); Hammonton, N.J. **(1876–1962)**
**Moorehead,** Agnes (actress); Clinton, Mass. **(1906–1974)**
**More,** Sir Thomas (statesman and author); London **(1478–1535)**
**Moreau,** Jeanne (actress); Paris, 1/23/1928
**Moreno,** Rita (Rosita Dolores Alverio) (actress); Humacao, Puerto Rico, 12/11/1931
**Morgan,** Dennis (actor); Prentice, Wis., 12/10/1920
**Morgan,** Helen (singer); Danville, Ohio **(1900?–1941)**
**Morgan,** Henry (comedian); New York City, 3/31/1915
**Morgan,** Jane (Florence Currier) (singer); Boston, 1920
**Morgan,** John Pierpont (financier); Hartford, Conn. **(1837–1913)**
**Moriarty,** Michael (actor); Detroit, 4/5/1941
**Morini,** Erica (concert violinist); Vienna, 1/5/1910
**Morison,** Samuel Eliot (historian); Boston **(1887–1976)**
**Morley,** Christopher Darlington (novelist); Haverford, Pa. **(1890–1957)**
**Morley,** Robert (actor); Semley, England, 5/26/1908
**Morrison,** Jim (James Douglas Morrison) (singer, songwriter); Melbourne, Fla. **(1943–1971)**
**Morse,** Marston (mathematician); Waterville, Me. **(1892–1977)**
**Morse,** Robert (actor); Newton, Mass., 5/18/1931
**Morse,** Samuel Finley Breese (painter and inventor); Charlestown, Mass. **(1791–1872)**
**Morse,** Wayne L. (Senator); Madison, Wis. **(1900–1974)**
**Moses,** Grandma (Mrs. Anna Mary Robertson Moses) (painter); Greenwich, N.Y. **(1860–1961)**
**Moses,** Robert (urban planner); New Haven, Conn., 12/18/1888
**Mostel,** Zero (Samuel Joel Mostel) (actor); Brooklyn, N.Y. **(1915–1977)**
**Moussorgsky,** Modest Petrovich (composer); Karev, Russia **(1839–1881)**
**Moyers,** Bill D. (Billy Don) (journalist); Hugo, Okla., 6/5/1934

**Moynihan,** Daniel Patrick (New York Senator); Tulsa, Okla., 3/16/1927
**Mozart,** Wolfgang Amadeus (Johannes Chrysostomus Wolfgangus Theophilus Mozart) (composer); Salzburg (Austria) **(1756–1791)**
**Mudd,** Roger (TV newscaster); Washington, D.C., 2/9/1928
**Muggeridge,** Malcolm (Thomas) (writer); Croydon, England, 3/24/1903
**Muhammad,** Elijah (Elijah Poole) (religious leader); Sandersville, Ga. **(1897–1975)**
**Mulhare,** Edward (actor); Ireland, 1923
**Mumford,** Lewis (cultural historian and city planner); Flushing, Queens, N.Y., 10/19/1895
**Munch,** Edvard (painter); Löten, Norway **(1863–1944)**
**Muni,** Paul (Muni Weisenfreund) (actor); Lemburg (Ukraine) **(1895–1967)**
**Munsel,** Patrice (soprano); Spokane, Wash., 5/14/1925
**Murdoch,** Rupert (publisher); Melbourne, 3/11/1931
**Murillo,** Bartolomé Esteban (painter); Seville, Spain **(1617–1682)**
**Murphy,** Audie (actor and war hero); Kingston, Tex. **(1924–1971)**
**Murphy,** George (actor, dancer, and ex-Senator); New Haven, Conn., 7/4/1902
**Murray,** Arthur (dance teacher); New York City, 4/4/1895
**Murray,** Kathryn (dance teacher); Jersey City, N.J., 1906
**Murray,** Ken (Don Court) (producer); New York City, 7/14/1903
**Murray,** Mae (Marie Adrienne Koenig) (actress); Portsmouth, Va. **(1890–1965)**
**Murrow,** Edward R. (commentator and government official); Greensboro, N.C. **(1908–1965)**
**Mussolini,** Benito (Italian dictator); Dovia, Forli, Italy **(1883–1945)**
**Myerson,** Bess (consumer advocate); Bronx, N.Y., 1924
**Myrdal,** Gunnar (sociologist and economist); Gustaf Parish, Sweden, 12/6/1898

# N

**Nabokov,** Vladimir (novelist); St. Petersburg, Russia **(1899–1977)**
**Nabors,** Jim (actor and singer); Sylacauga, Ala., 6/12/1932
**Nader,** Ralph (consumer advocate); Winsted, Conn., 2/27/1934
**Nagel,** Conrad (actor); Keokuk, Iowa **(1897–1970)**
**Naish,** J. Carrol (actor); New York City **(1900–1973)**
**Naldi,** Nita (Anita Donna Dooley) (actress); New York City **(1899–1961)**
**Napoleon Bonaparte** (Emperor of the French); Ajaccio, Corsica (France) **(1769–1821)**
**Nash,** Graham (singer); Blackpool, England, 1942
**Nash,** Ogden (poet); Rye, N.Y. **(1902–1971)**
**Nasser,** Gamal Abdel (statesman); Beni Mor, Egypt **(1918–1970)**
**Nast,** Thomas (cartoonist); Landau (Germany) **(1840–1902)**
**Nation,** Carry Amelia (temperance leader); Garrard County, Ky. **(1846–1911)**
**Natwick,** Mildred (actress); Baltimore, 6/19/1908
**Nazimova,** Alla (actress); Yalta, Crimea, Russia **(1879–1945)**
**Neagle,** Anna (Marjorie Robertson) (actress); London, 10/20/1908
**Neal,** Patricia (actress); Packard, Ky., 1/20/1926
**Neff,** Hildegarde (actress); Ulm, Germany, 12/28/1925
**Negri,** Pola (Appolina Chapulez) (actress); Bromberg (Poland), c. 1897
**Nehru,** Jawaharlal (First Prime Minister of India); Allahabad, India **(1889–1964)**
**Nelson,** Barry (actor); San Francisco, 1920
**Nelson,** David (actor); New York City, 10/24/1936
**Nelson,** Harriet Hilliard (Peggy Lou Snyder) (actress); Des Moines, Iowa, 1914
**Nelson,** Ozzie (Oswald) (actor); Jersey City, N.J. **(1907–1975)**
**Nelson,** Ricky (Eric) (singer and actor); Teaneck, N.J., 5/8/1940
**Nelson,** Viscount Horatio (naval officer); Burnham Thorpe, England **(1758–1805)**
**Nenni,** Pietro (Socialist leader); Faenza, Italy, 2/9/1891
**Nero** (Nero Claudius Caesar Drusus Germanicus) (Roman emperor); Antium (Italy) **(37–68)**
**Nero,** Peter (pianist); New York City, 5/22/1934
**Nesbit,** Cathleen (actress); Cheshire, England, 1889
**Nevelson,** Louise (sculptor); Kiev, Russia, 9/23/1900
**Newhart,** Bob (entertainer); Chicago, 9/5/1929
**Newhouse,** Samuel I. (publisher); New York City, 5/24/1895
**Newley,** Anthony (actor and song writer); London, 9/24/1931
**Newman,** Edwin (news commentator); New York City, 1/25/1919
**Newman,** Paul (actor and director); Cleveland, 1/26/1925
**Newman,** Randy (singer); Los Angeles, 11/28/1943
**Newton,** Huey (black activist); New Orleans, 2/17/1942
**Newton,** Sir Isaac (mathematician and scientist); nr. Grantham, England **(1642–1727)**
**Newton,** Wayne (singer); Norfolk, Va., 4/3/1942
**Newton-John,** Olivia (singer); Cambridge, England, 9/26/1947
**Nichols,** Mike (Michael Peschkowsky) (stage and film director); Berlin, 11/6/1931
**Nicholson,** Jack (actor); Neptune, N.J., 4/22/1937
**Nietzsche,** Friedrich Wilhelm (philosopher); nr. Lützen (Germany) **(1844–1900)**
**Nightingale,** Florence (nurse); Florence (Italy) **(1820–1910)**
**Nijinsky,** Waslaw (ballet dancer); Warsaw **(1890–1950)**
**Nilsson,** Harry (singer and songwriter); Brooklyn, N.Y., 6/15/1941
**Nilsson,** Birgit (soprano); West Karup, Sweden, 5/17/1923
**Nimitz,** Chester W. (naval officer); Fredericksburg, Tex. **(1885–1966)**
**Nimoy,** Leonard (actor); Boston, 3/26/1931
**Nin,** Anaïs (author and diarist); Neuilly, France **(1903–1977)**
**Niven,** David (actor); Kirriemuir, Scotland, 3/1/1910
**Nizer,** Louis (lawyer and author); London, 2/6/1902
**Nobel,** Alfred Bernhard (industrialist); Stockholm **(1833–1896)**
**Noguchi,** Isamu (sculptor); Los Angeles, 11/7/1904
**Nolan,** Lloyd (actor); San Francisco, 8/11/1902
**Nolte,** Nick (actor); Omaha, Neb., 1940
**Norell,** Norman (Norman Levinson) (fashion designer); Noblesville, Ind. **(1900–1972)**
**Norstad,** Gen. Lauris (ex-commander of NATO forces); Minneapolis, 3/24/1907
**North,** John Ringling (circus director); Baraboo, Wis., 8/14/1903
**North,** Sheree (actress); Los Angeles, 1/17/1933
**Norton,** Eleanor Holmes (New York City government official, lawyer); Washington, D.C., 6/13/1937
**Nostradamus** (Michel de Notredame) (astrologer); St. Rémy, France **(1503–1566)**
**Novaes,** Guiomar (pianist); Sao João de Boa Vista, Brazil, 2/28/1895
**Novak,** Kim (Marilyn Novak) (actress); Chicago, 2/13/1933
**Novarro,** Ramon (Ramon Samaniegoes) (actor); Durango, Mexico **(1899–1968)**
**Nugent,** Elliott (actor and director); Dover, Ohio, 9/20/1899
**Nureyev,** Rudolf (ballet dancer); U.S.S.R., 3/17/1938
**Nuyen,** France (actress); Marseilles, France, 7/31/1939
**Nyro,** Laura (singer and songwriter); Bronx, N.Y., 1947

# O

**Oakie,** Jack (actor); Sedalia, Mo. **(1903–1978)**
**Oates,** Joyce Carol (novelist); Lockport, N.Y., 6/16/1938
**Oberon,** Merle (Estelle Merle O'Brien Thompson) (actress); Tasmania, 2/19/1911
**O'Brian,** Hugh (Hugh J. Krampe) (actor); Rochester, N.Y., 4/19/1930
**O'Brien,** Edmond (actor); New York City, 9/10/1915
**O'Brien,** Lawrence F. (commissioner of National Basketball Association); Springfield, Mass., 7/7/1917
**O'Brien,** Margaret (Angela Maxine O'Brien) (actress); San Diego, Calif., 1/15/1937
**O'Brien,** Pat (William Joseph O'Brien, Jr.) (actor); Milwaukee, 11/11/1899
**O'Casey,** Sean (playwright); Dublin **(1881–1964)**
**Ochs,** Adolph Simon (publisher); Cincinnati **(1858–1935)**
**O'Connor,** Carroll (actor); New York City, 8/2/1924
**O'Connor,** Donald (actor); Chicago, 8/28/1925
**Odets,** Clifford (playwright); Philadelphia **(1906–1963)**
**Odetta** (Odetta Holmes) (folk singer and actress); Brimingham, Ala., 12/31/1930
**Offenbach,** Jacques (composer); Cologne, Germany **(1819–1880)**
**O'Hara,** John (novelist); Pottsville, Pa. **(1905–1970)**
**O'Hara,** Maureen (Maureen FitzSimons) (actress); Dublin, 8/17/1921
**Oistrakh,** David (concert violinist); Odessa, Russia **(1908–1974)**
**O'Keeffe,** Georgia (painter); Sun Prairie, Wis., 11/15/1887
**Oland,** Warner (actor); Umea, Sweden **(1880–1938)**
**Olav V** (King of Norway); Sandringham, England, 7/2/1903
**Oldenburg,** Claes (painter); Stockholm, Sweden, 1/28/1929
**Olivier,** Lord (Laurence) (actor); Dorking, England, 5/22/1907
**Olmsted,** Frederick Law (landscape architect); Hartford, Conn. **(1822–1903)**
**Olsen,** Ole (John Sigvard Olsen) (comedian); Peru, Ind. **(1892–1963)**
**Omar Khayyam** (poet and astronomer); Nishapur (Iran) **(died c. 1123)**
**Onassis,** Aristotle (shipping executive); Smyrna, Turkey **(1906–1975)**
**Onassis,** Christina (shipping executive); New York City, 12/11/1950
**Onassis,** Jacqueline Kennedy (Jacqueline Bouvier) (President's widow); Southampton, N.Y., 7/28/1929
**O'Neal,** Ryan (Patrick) (actor); Los Angeles, 4/20/1941
**O'Neal,** Tatum (actress); Los Angeles, Calif., 1963
**O'Neill,** Eugene Gladstone (playwright); New York City **(1888–1953)**
**O'Neill,** Jennifer (actress); Rio de Janeiro, 2/20/1949
**Oppenheimer,** J. Robert (nuclear physicist); New York City **(1904–1967)**
**Orff,** Carl (composer); Munich, Germany, 7/10/1895
**Orlando,** Tony (singer); New York City, 1944
**Ormandy,** Eugene (conductor); Budapest, 11/18/1899
**Orozco,** José Clemente (painter); Zapotlán, Jalisco, Mexico **(1883–1949)**
**Osborn,** Paul (playwright); Evansville, Ind., 9/4/1901
**Osborne,** John (playwright); London, 12/12/1929
**Osler,** Sir William (physician); Bondhead, Ontario, Canada **(1849–1919)**
**Osmond,** Donny (singer); Ogden, Utah, 12/9/1957
**Osmond,** Marie (singer); Ogden, Utah, 1959

**O'Sullivan,** Maureen (actress); County Roscommon, Ireland, 5/17/1911
**Otis,** Elisha (inventor); Halifax, Vt. **(1811–1861)**
**O'Toole,** Peter (actor); Connemara, Ireland, 8/2/1933
**Ovid** (Publius Ovidius Naso) (poet); Sulmona (Italy) **(43 B.C.–? A.D. 17)**
**Owens,** Buck (Alvis Edgar Owens) (singer); Sherman, Tex., 8/12/1929

# P

**Paar,** Jack (TV performer); Canton, Ohio, 5/1/1918
**Pacino,** Al (Alfred) (actor); New York City, 4/25/1940
**Packard,** Vance (author); Granville Summit, Pa., 5/22/1914
**Paderewski,** Ignace Jan (pianist and statesman); Kurylowka, Russian Podolia **(1860–1941)**
**Paganini,** Nicolò (violinist); Genoa (Italy) **(1782–1840)**
**Page,** Geraldine (actress); Kirksville, Mo., 11/22/1924
**Page,** Patti (Clara Ann Fowler) (singer and entertainer); Claremore, Okla., 11/8/1927
**Paige,** Janis (actress); Tacoma, Wash., 9/16/1922
**Paine,** Thomas (political philosopher); Thetford, England **(1737–1809)**
**Palance,** Jack (Walter Palanuik) (actor); Lattimer, Pa., 2/18/1920
**Paley,** William S. (broadcasting executive); Chicago, 9/28/1901
**Palladio,** Andrea (architect); Padua or Vicenza (Italy) **(1508–1580)**
**Palmer,** Betsy (actress); East Chicago, Ind., 1929
**Palmer,** Lilli (actress); Posen (Poland), 5/24/1914
**Palmerston,** Henry John Templeton (3rd Viscount) (statesman); Broadlands, England **(1784–1865)**
**Papanicolaou,** George N. (physician); Coumi, Greece **(1883–1962)**
**Papas,** Irene (actress); Chiliomodion, Greece, 1929
**Papp,** Joseph (Joseph Papirofsky) (stage producer and director); Brooklyn, N.Y., 6/22/1921
**Park,** Chung Hee (President of South Korea); Sangmo-ri, Korea, 9/30/1917
**Parker,** Dorothy (Dorothy Rothschild) (author); West End, N.J. **(1893–1967)**
**Parker,** Eleanor (actress); Cedarville, Ohio, 6/26/1922
**Parker,** Fess (actor); Fort Worth, Tex., 1925
**Parker,** Suzy (model and actress); San Antonio, 10/28/1933
**Parkinson,** C. (Cyril) Northcote (historian); Durham, England, 7/30/1909
**Parks,** Bert (Bert Jacobson) (entertainer); Atlanta, 12/30/1914
**Parks,** Gordon (film director); Ft. Scott, Kan., 11/30/1912
**Parnell,** Charles Stewart (statesman); Avondale, Ireland **(1846–1891)**
**Parnis,** Mollie (Mollie Parnis Livingston) (fashion designer); New York City, 3/18/1905
**Parsons,** Estelle (actress); Marblehead, Mass., 11/20/1927
**Parton,** Dolly (singer); Locust Ridge, Tenn. 1/19/1946
**Pascal,** Blaise (philosopher); Clermont, France **(1623–1662)**
**Pasternak,** Boris Leonidovich (author); Moscow **(1890–1960)**
**Pasternak,** Joseph (film producer); Silagy-Somlyo, Romania, 9/19/1901
**Pasteur,** Louis (chemist); Dôle, France **(1822–1895)**
**Patton,** George Smith, Jr. (general); San Gabriel, Calif., **(1885–1945)**
**Paul,** Les (Lester William Polfus) (guitarist); Waukesha, Wis. 6/9/1915
**Paul VI** (Giovanni Battista Montini) (Pope); Concesio, nr. Brescia, Italy **(1897–1978)**
**Pauling,** Linus Carl (chemist); Portland, Ore., 2/28/1901
**Pavarotti,** Luciano (tenor); Modena, Italy, 10/12/1935
**Pavlov,** Ivan Petrovich (physiologist); Ryazan district, Russia **(1849–1936)**
**Pavlova,** Anna (ballerina); St. Petersburg, Russia **(1885–1931)**
**Payne,** John (actor); Roanoke, Va., 1912
**Peale,** Norman Vincent (clergyman); Bowersville, Ohio, 5/31/1898
**Pearl,** Minnie (Sarah Ophelia Colley Cannon) (comedienne and singer); Centerville, Tenn., 10/25/1912
**Pears,** Peter (tenor); Farnham, England, 6/22/1910
**Pearson,** Drew (Andrew Russel Pearson) (columnist); Evanston, Ill. **(1897–1969)**
**Pearson,** Lester B. (statesman); Toronto, **(1897–1972)**
**Peary,** Robert Edwin (explorer); Cresson, Pa. **(1856–1920)**
**Peck,** Gregory (actor); La Jolla, Calif., 4/5/1916
**Peckinpah,** Sam (film director); Fresno, Calif., 2/21/1925
**Peerce,** Jan (tenor); New York City, 1904
**Pegler,** (James) Westbrook (columnist); Minneapolis, **(1894–1969)**
**Pei,** I. M. (architect); Canton, China, 4/26/1917
**Penn,** Arthur (stage and film director); Philadelphia, 9/27/1922
**Penn,** William (American colonist); London **(1644–1718)**
**Penney,** James C. (merchant); Hamilton, Mo. **(1875–1971)**
**Peppard,** George (actor); Detroit, 10/1/1933
**Pepys,** Samuel (diarist); Bampton, England **(1633–1703)**
**Perelman,** S. J. (Sidney J.) (humorist); Brooklyn, N.Y., 2/1/1904
**Pericles** (statesman); Athens **(died 429 B.C.)**
**Perkins,** Osgood (actor); West Newton, Mass. **(1892–1937)**
**Perkins,** Tony (Anthony) (actor); New York City, 4/14/1932
**Perlman,** Itzhak (violinist); Tel Aviv (Israel), 8/31/1945
**Perón,** Isabel (María Estela Martínez Cartas) (former chief of state); La Riója, Argentina, 2/4/1931
**Perón,** Juan D. (statesman); nr. Lobos, Argentina **(1895–1974)**
**Perón,** Maria Eva Duarte de (political leader); Los Toldos, Argentina **(1919–1952)**
**Perrine,** Valerie (actress and dancer); Galveston, Tex., 9/3/1943
**Pershing,** John Joseph (general); Linn County, Mo. **(1860–1948)**
**Peters,** Bernadette (actress); New York City, 1944
**Peters,** Jean (actress); Canton, Ohio, 10/15/1926
**Peters,** Roberta (Roberta Peterman) (soprano); New York City, 5/4/1930
**Petrarch** (Francesco Petrarca) (poet); Arezzo (Italy) **(1304–1374)**
**Philip** (Philip Mountbatten) (Duke of Edinburgh); Corfu, Greece, 6/10/1921
**Piaf,** Edith (Edith Gassion) (chanteuse); Paris **(1916–1963)**
**Piatigorsky,** Gregor (cellist); Ekaterinoslav, Russia **(1903–1976)**
**Piazza,** Ben (actor); Little Rock, Ark., 7/30/1934
**Piazza,** Marguerite (soprano); New Orleans, 5/6/1926
**Picasso,** Pablo (painter and sculptor); Málaga, Spain **(1881–1973)**
**Pickford,** Jack (Jack Smith) (actor); Toronto **(1896–1933)**
**Pickford,** Mary (Gladys Mary Smith) (actress); Toronto, 4/8/1893
**Picon,** Molly (actress); New York City, 6/1/1898
**Pidgeon,** Walter (actor); East St. John, New Brunswick, Canada, 9/23/1898
**Pinter,** Harold (playwright); London, 10/10/1930
**Pinza,** Ezio (basso); Rome **(1892–1957)**
**Pirandello,** Luigi (dramatist and novelist); nr. Girgenti, Italy **(1867–1936)**
**Pissaro,** Camille Jacob (painter); St. Thomas (U.S. Virgin Islands) **(1830–1903)**
**Piston,** Walter (composer); Rockland, Me. **(1894–1976)**
**Pitt,** William ("Younger Pitt") (statesman); nr. Bromley, England **(1759–1806)**
**Pitts,** ZaSu (actress); Parsons, Kan. **(1898–1963)**
**Pius XII** (Eugenio Pacelli) (Pope); Rome **(1876–1958)**
**Pizarro,** Francisco (explorer); Trujillo, Spain **(1470?–1541)**
**Plato** (Aristocles) (philosopher); Athens (?) **(427?–347 B.C.)**
**Pleasence,** Donald (actor); Worksop, England, 10/5/1919
**Pleshette,** Suzanne (actress); New York City, 1/31/1937
**Plimpton,** George (author); New York City, 3/18/1927
**Plisetskaya,** Maya (ballerina); Moscow, 11/20/1925
**Plowright,** Joan (actress); Brigg, England, 10/28/1929
**Plummer,** Christopher (actor); Toronto, 12/13/1929
**Plutarch** (biographer); Chaeronea (Greece) **(46?–?120)**
**Pocahontas** (Matoaka) (American Indian princess); Virginia (?) **(1595?–1617)**
**Podhoretz,** Norman (author); Brooklyn, N.Y., 1/16/1930
**Poe,** Edgar Allan (poet and story writer); Boston, Mass. **(1809–1849)**
**Poitier,** Sidney (film actor and director); Miami, Fla., 2/20/1924
**Polanski,** Roman (film director); Paris, 8/18/1933
**Pollard,** Michael J. (actor); Passaic, N.J., 5/30/1939
**Pollock,** Jackson (painter); Cody, Wyo. **(1912–1956)**
**Polo,** Marco (traveler); Venice **(1254?–?1324)**
**Pompey** (Gnaeus Pompeius Magnus) (general); Rome (?) **(106–48 B.C.)**
**Ponce de León,** Juan (explorer); Servas, Spain **(1460?–1521)**
**Pons,** Lily (coloratura soprano); Cannes, France **(1904–1976)**
**Ponti,** Carlo (director); Milan, Italy, 1913
**Pope,** Alexander (poet); London **(1688–1744)**
**Porter,** Cole (songwriter); Peru, Ind. **(1892–1964)**
**Porter,** Katherine Anne (novelist); Indian Creek, Tex., 5/15/1890
**Post,** Wiley (aviator); Grand Plain, Tex. **(1900–1935)**
**Poston,** Tom (actor); Columbus, Ohio, 10/17/1927
**Potok,** Chaim (author); New York City, 2/17/1929
**Pound,** Ezra (poet); Hailey, Idaho **(1885–1972)**
**Powell,** Adam Clayton, Jr. (congressman); New Haven, Conn. **(1908–1972)**
**Powell,** Dick (actor); Mt. View, Ark. **(1904–1963)**
**Powell,** Eleanor (actress); Springfield, Mass., 11/21/1912
**Powell,** Jane (Suzanne Burce) (actress and singer); Portland, Ore., 4/1/1929
**Powell,** William (actor); Pittsburgh, 7/29/1892
**Power,** Tyrone (actor); Cincinnati, Ohio **(1914–1958)**
**Powers,** Stephanie (Taffy Paul) (actress); Hollywood, Calif., 11/12/1942
**Praxiteles** (sculptor); Athens **(c.370–c.330 B.C.)**
**Preminger,** Otto (film director and producer); Vienna, 12/5/1906
**Prentiss,** Paula (Paula Ragusa) (actress); San Antonio, 1939
**Presley,** Elvis (singer and actor); Tupelo, Miss. **(1935–1977)**
**Preston,** Robert (Robert Preston Meservey) (actor); Newton Highlands, Mass., 6/8/1918
**Previn,** André (conductor); Berlin, 4/6/1929
**Previn,** Dory (singer); Rahway, N.J., 10/22/1929(?)
**Price,** Leontyne (Mary) (soprano); Laurel, Miss., 2/10/1927
**Price,** Ray (country music artist); Perryville, Tex., 1/12/1926
**Price,** Vincent (actor); St. Louis, 5/27/1911
**Pride,** Charley (singer); Sledge, Miss., 3/18/1938(?)
**Priestley,** J. B. (John B.) (author); Bradford, England, 9/13/1894
**Priestley,** Joseph (chemist); nr. Leeds, England **(1733–1804)**
**Primrose,** William (violist); Glasgow, Scotland, 8/23/1904
**Prince,** Harold (stage producer); New York City, 1/30/1928

**Prinze**, Freddie (actor); New York City **(1954–1977)**
**Pritchett**, V.S. (Victor Sawdon) (literary critic); Ipswich, England, 12/16/1900
**Procter**, William (scientist); Cincinnati, Ohio **(1872–1951)**
**Prokofieff**, Sergei Sergeevich (composer); St. Petersburg, Russia **(1891–1953)**
**Proust**, Marcel (novelist); Paris **(1871–1922)**
**Provine**, Dorothy (actress); Deadwood, S. Dak., 1/20/1937
**Prowse**, Juliet (actress); Bombay, 9/25/1936
**Pryor**, Richard (comedian); Peoria, Ill., 12/1/1940
**Ptolemy** (Claudius Ptolemaeus) (astronomer and geographer); Ptolemais Hermii (Egypt) **(2nd century** A.D.**)**
**Pucci**, Emilio (Marchese di Barsento) (fashion designer); Naples, Italy, 11/20/1914
**Puccini**, Giacomo (composer); Lucca, Italy **(1858–1924)**
**Puente**, Tito (band leader); New York City, 4/20/1923
**Pulitzer**, Joseph (publisher); Makó (Hungary) **(1847–1911)**
**Pullman**, George (inventor); Brockton, N.Y. **(1831–1897)**
**Pusey**, Nathan M. (educator); Council Bluffs, Iowa, 4/4/1907
**Pushkin**, Alexander Sergeevich (poet and dramatist); Moscow **(1799–1837)**
**Puzo**, Mario (novelist); New York City, 10/15/1921
**Pyle**, Ernest Taylor (journalist); Dana, Ind. **(1900–1945)**
**Pythagoras** (mathematician and philosopher); Samos (Greece) **(6th century** B.C.**)**

# Q

**Quayle**, Anthony (actor); Ainsdale, England, 9/7/1913
**Queen**, Ellery: pen name of Frederic Dannay and the late Manfred B. Lee.
**Quinn**, Anthony (actor); Chihuahua, Mexico, 4/21/1916

# R

**Rabe**, David (playwright); Dubuque, Iowa, 3/10/1940
**Rabelais**, François (satirist); nr. Chinon, France **(1494?–1553)**
**Rabi**, I. I. (Isidor Isaac) (physicist); Rymanow (Poland), 7/29/1898
**Rachmaninoff**, Sergei Wassilievitch (pianist and composer); Oneg Estate, Novgorod, Russia **(1873–1943)**
**Racine**, Jean Baptiste (dramatist); La Ferté-Milon, France **(1639–1699)**
**Raft**, George (actor); New York City, 9/27/1896
**Rainer**, Luise (actress); Vienna, 1912
**Raines**, Ella (actress); Snoqualmie Falls, Wash., 1921
**Rainier III** (Prince); Monaco, 5/31/1923
**Rains**, Claude (actor); London **(1889–1967)**
**Raitt**, Bonnie (singer); Los Angeles, 1950
**Raleigh**, Sir Walter (courtier and navigator); London **(1552?–1618)**
**Randall**, Tony (actor); Tulsa, Okla., 2/26/1924
**Randolph**, Asa Philip (labor leader); Crescent City, Fla., 4/15/1889
**Raphael** (Raffaello Santi) (painter and architect); Urbino (Italy) **(1483–1520)**
**Rasputin**, Grigori Efimovich (monk); Tobolsk Province, Russia **(1871?–1916)**
**Rathbone**, Basil (actor); Johannesburg, South Africa **(1892–1967)**
**Rather**, Dan (TV newscaster); Wharton, Tex., 10/31/1931
**Ratoff**, Gregory (film director); St. Petersburg, Russia **(1897–1960)**
**Rattigan**, Terence (playwright); London, **(1911–1978)**
**Rauschenberg**, Robert (painter); Port Arthur, Tex., 1925
**Ravel**, Maurice Joseph (composer); Ciboure, France **(1875–1937)**
**Rawls**, Lou (singer); Chicago, 12/1/1936
**Ray**, Man (painter); Philadelphia **(1890–1976)**
**Ray**, Satyajat (film director); Calcutta, 5/2/1922
**Rayburn**, Gene (TV personality); Christopher, Ill., 12/22/1917
**Raye**, Martha (Margie Yvonne Reed) (comedienne and actress); Butte, Mont., 8/27/1916
**Raymond**, Gene (actor); New York City, 8/13/1908
**Reagan**, Ronald (actor, ex-Gov. California); Tampico, Ill., 2/6/1911
**Reasoner**, Harry (TV commentator); Dakota City, Iowa, 4/17/1923
**Redding**, Otis (singer); Dawson, Ga. **(1941–1967)**
**Reddy**, Helen (singer); Melbourne, 10/25/1941
**Redford**, Robert (Charles Robert Redford, Jr.) (actor); Santa Monica, Calif., 8/18/1937
**Redgrave**, Lynn (actress); London, 3/8/1943
**Redgrave**, Sir Michael (actor); Bristol, England, 3/20/1908
**Redgrave**, Vanessa (actress); London, 1/30/1937
**Reed**, Donna (actress); Denison, Iowa, 1/27/1921
**Reed**, Rex (critic); Ft. Worth, 10/2/1940
**Reed**, Walter (army surgeon); Belroi, Va. **(1851–1902)**
**Reese**, Della (Deloreese Patricia Early) (singer); Detroit, 7/6/1932
**Reeves**, Jim (singer); Panola County, Tex. **(1923–1964)**
**Reid**, Wallace (actor); St. Louis **(1891–1923)**
**Reiner**, Carl (actor); New York City, 3/20/1922
**Reiner**, Fritz (conductor); Budapest **(1888–1963)**
**Reiner**, Robert (actor); Bronx, N.Y., 1945
**Reinhardt**, Max (Max Goldmann) (theater producer); nr. Vienna **(1873–1943)**
**Remarque**, Erich Maria (novelist); Osnabruk, Germany **(1898–1970)**
**Rembrandt** (Rembrandt Harmensz van Rijn) (painter); Leyden (Netherlands) **(1606–1669)**
**Remick**, Lee (Ann) (actress); Boston, 12/14/1935
**Rennert**, Günther (opera director and producer); Essen, Germany, 4/1/1911
**Rennie**, Michael (actor); Bradford, England **(1909–1971)**
**Renoir**, Jean (film director and writer); Paris, 9/15/1894
**Renoir**, Pierre Auguste (painter); Limoges, France **(1841–1919)**
**Resnais**, Alain (film director); Vannes, France, 6/3/1922
**Resnik**, Regina (mezzo-soprano); New York City, 8/30/1922
**Respighi**, Ottorino (composer); Bologna, Italy **(1879–1936)**
**Reston**, James (journalist); Clydebank, Scotland, 11/3/1909
**Reuther**, Walter (labor leader); Wheeling, W. Va. **(1907–1970)**
**Revere**, Paul (silversmith and hero of famous ride); Boston **(1735–1818)**
**Revson**, Charles (business executive); Boston **(1906–1975)**
**Reynolds**, Burt (actor); Waycross, Ga., 2/11/1936
**Renolds**, Debbie (Marie Frances Reynolds) (actress); El Paso, 4/1/1932
**Reynolds**, Sir Joshua (painter); nr. Plymouth, England **(1723–1792)**
**Rhodes**, Cecil John (South African statesman); Bishop Stortford, England **(1853–1902)**
**Rice**, Elmer (playwright); New York City **(1892–1967)**
**Rice**, Grantland (sports writer); Murfreesboro, Tenn. **(1880–1954)**
**Rich**, Buddy (Bernard) (drummer); Brooklyn, N.Y., 6/30/1917
**Rich**, Charlie (singer); Colt, Ark., 12/14/1934
**Richardson**, Elliot L. (ex-Cabinet member); Boston, 7/20/1920
**Richardson**, Sir Ralph (actor); Cheltenham, England, 12/19/1902
**Richardson**, Tony (director); Shipley, England, 6/5/1928
**Richelieu**, Duc de (Armand Jean du Plessis) (cardinal); Paris **(1585–1642)**
**Richter**, Charles Francis (seismologist); Hamilton, Canada, 4/26/1900
**Richter**, Sviatoslav (pianist); Zhitomir, Ukraine, 3/20/1914
**Rickenbacker**, Edward V. (aviator); Columbus, Ohio **(1890–1973)**
**Rickles**, Don (comedian); New York City, 5/8/1926
**Rickover**, Vice Admiral Hyman G. (atomic energy expert); Russia, 1/27/1900
**Riddle**, Nelson (composer); Hackensack, N.J., 6/1/1921
**Ridgway**, General Matthew B. (ex-Army Chief of Staff); Ft. Monroe, Va., 3/3/1895
**Rigg**, Diana (actress); Doncaster, England, 7/20/1938
**Riley**, James Whitcomb (poet); Greenfield, Ind. **(1849–1916)**
**Rimsky-Korsakov**, Nikolai Andreevich (composer); Tikhvin, Russia **(1844–1908)**
**Rinehart**, Mary (née Roberts) (novelist); Pittsburgh **(1876–1958)**
**Ritchard**, Cyril (actor and director); Sydney, Australia **(1898–1977)**
**Ritter**, Tex (Woodward Maurice Ritter) (singer) Panola County, Tex., **(1905–1973)**
**Ritz**, Al (Al Joachim) (comedian); Newark, N.J. **(1901–1965)**
**Rivera**, Diego (painter); Guanajuato, Mexico **(1886–1957)**
**Rivera**, Geraldo (Miguel) (TV newscaster); New York City, 7/3/1943
**Rivers**, Joan (comedienne); Brooklyn, N.Y., 1935(?)
**Rivers**, Larry (Yitzroch Loiza Grossberg) (painter); New York City, 8/17/1923
**Robards**, Jason, Jr. (actor); Chicago, 7/26/1922
**Robards**, Jason, Sr. (actor); Hillsdale, Mich. **(1892–1963)**
**Robbins**, Harold (novelist); New York City, 5/21/1916
**Robbins**, Jerome (Jerome Rabinowitz) (choreographer); New York City, 10/11/1918
**Robbins**, Marty (singer); Glendale, Ariz., 12/26/1925
**Roberts**, (Granville) Oral, Rev. (evangelist and publisher); nr. Ada, Okla., 1/24/1918
**Robertson**, Cliff (actor); La Jolla, Calif., 9/9/1925
**Robertson**, Dale (actor); Oklahoma City, 1923
**Robeson**, Paul (singer and actor); Princeton, N.J., **(1898–1976)**
**Robespierre**, Maximilien François Marie Isidore de (French Revolutionist); Arras, France **(1758–1794)**
**Robinson**, Bill "Bojangles" (Luther) (dancer); Richmond, Va. **(1878–1949)**
**Robinson**, Edward G. (Emanuel Goldenberg) (actor); Bucharest **(1893–1973)**
**Robinson**, Edwin Arlington (poet); Head Tide, Me. **(1869–1935)**
**Robson**, Dame Flora (actress); South Shields, England, 3/28/1902
**Rochester** (Eddie Anderson) (actor); Oakland, Calif. **(1905–1977)**
**Rockefeller**, David (banker); New York City, 6/12/1915
**Rockefeller**, John Davison (capitalist); Richford, N.Y. **(1839–1937)**
**Rockefeller**, John Davison, Jr. (industrialist); Cleveland **(1874–1960)**
**Rockefeller**, John D., 3rd (philanthropist); New York City **(1906–1978)**
**Rockefeller**, Laurance S. (conservationist); New York City, 5/26/1910
**Rockwell**, Norman (painter and illustrator); New York City, 2/3/1894
**Rodgers**, Jimmie (singer); Meridian, Miss. **(1897–1933)**
**Rodgers**, Richard (composer); New York City, 6/28/1902
**Rodin**, François Auguste René (sculptor); Paris **(1840–1917)**
**Roentgen**, Wilhelm Konrad (physicist); Lennep, Prussia **(1845–1923)**

**Rogers,** Buddy (Charles) (actor); Olathe, Kan., 8/13/1904
**Rogers,** Ginger (Virginia McMath) (dancer and actress); Independence, Mo., 7/16/1911
**Rogers,** Roy (Leonard Slye) (actor); Cincinnati, 11/5/1912
**Rogers,** Will (William Penn Adair Rogers) (humorist); Oologah, Okla. **(1879–1935)**
**Rogers,** Will, Jr. (actor); New York City, 10/20/1911
**Rogers,** William P. (ex-Secretary of State); Norfolk, N.Y., 6/23/1913
**Roland,** Gilbert (actor); Juarez, Mexico, 12/11/1905
**Rolland,** Romain (author); Clamecy, France **(1866–1944)**
**Rollins,** Sonny (saxophonist); New York City, 9/7/1930
**Romberg,** Sigmund (composer); Szeged (Hungary) **(1887–1951)**
**Rome,** Harold (composer); Hartford, Conn., 5/27/1908
**Romero,** Cesar (actor); New York City, 2/15/1907
**Romney,** George W. (ex-Secretary of HUD); Chihuahua, Mexico, 7/8/1907
**Romulo,** Carlos P. (diplomat and educator); Manila, 1/14/1899
**Ronstadt,** Linda (singer); Tucson, Ariz., 7/30/1946
**Rooney,** Mickey (Joe Yule, Jr.) (actor); Brooklyn, N.Y., 9/23/1920
**Roosevelt,** Anna Eleanor (reformer and humanitarian); New York City **(1884–1962)**
**Rose,** Billy (showman); New York City **(1899–1966)**
**Rose,** Leonard, (concert cellist); Washington, D.C., 7/27/1918
**Ross,** Diana (singer); Detroit, 3/26/1944
**Ross,** Katharine (actress); Hollywood, Calif., 1/29/1943
**Rossellini,** Roberto (film director); Rome **(1906–1977)**
**Rossetti,** Dante Gabriel (painter and poet); London, **(1828–1882)**
**Rossini,** Gioacchino Antonio (composer); Pesaro (Italy) **(1792–1868)**
**Rostand,** Edmond (dramatist); Marseilles, France **(1868–1918)**
**Rostow,** Walt Whitman (economist); New York City, 10/7/1916
**Rostropovich,** Mstislav (cellist and conductor); Baku, U.S.S.R., 8/12/1927
**Roth,** Lillian (singer); Boston, 12/13/1910
**Roth,** Philip (novelist); Newark, N.J., 3/19/1933
**Rothko,** Mark (Marcus Rothkovich) (painter); Russia **(1903–1970)**
**Rouault,** Georges (painter); Paris, France **(1871–1958)**
**Roundtree,** Richard (actor); New Rochelle, N.Y., 9/7/1942
**Rousseau,** Henri (painter); Laval, France **(1844–1910)**
**Rousseau,** Jean Jacques (philosopher); Geneva **(1712–1778)**
**Rovere,** Richard H. (journalist); Jersey City, N.J., 5/5/1915
**Rowan,** Dan (comedian); Beggs, Okla., 7/2/1922
**Rowlands,** Gena (actress); Cambria, Wis., 6/19/1936(?)
**Rubens,** Sir Peter Paul (painter); Siegen (Germany) **(1577–1640)**
**Rubenstein,** Artur (concert pianist); Lódz (Poland), 1/28/1887
**Rubinstein,** Helena (cosmetics executive); Kraków (Poland) **(1882?–1965)**
**Rudel,** Julius (conductor); Vienna, 3/6/1921
**Ruggles,** Charles (actor); Los Angeles **(1892–1970)**
**Rule,** Janice (actress); Norwood, Ohio, 8/15/1931
**Runyon,** (Alfred) Damon (journalist); Manhattan, Kan. **(1884–1946)**
**Rusk,** Dean (ex-Sec. of State); Cherokee County, Ga., 2/9/1909
**Ruskin,** John (art critic); London **(1819–1900)**
**Russell,** Lord Bertrand (Arthur William) (mathematician and philosopher); Trelleck, Wales **(1872–1970)**
**Russell,** Jane (actress); Bemidji, Minn., 6/21/1921
**Russell,** Leon (pianist and singer); Lawton, Okla., 4/2/1941
**Russell,** Lillian (Helen Louise Leonard) (soprano); Clinton, Iowa **(1861–1922)**
**Russell,** Nipsy (comedian); Atlanta, 1924(?)
**Russell,** Rosalind (actress); Waterbury, Conn. **(1912–1976)**
**Rustin,** Bayard (civil rights leader); West Chester, Pa., 1910
**Rutherford,** Dame Margaret (actress); London, England **(1892–1972)**
**Ryan,** Robert (actor); Chicago **(1909–1973)**
**Rydell,** Bobby (singer); Philadelphia, 1942
**Rysanek,** Leonie (dramatic soprano); Vienna, 11/14/1928

# S

**Saarinen,** Eero (architect); Finland **(1910–1961)**
**Sabin,** Albert B. (polio researcher); Bialystok (Poland), 8/26/1906
**Sadat,** Anwar el- (President); Egypt, 12/25/1918
**Sagan,** Françoise (novelist); Cajarc, France, 6/21/1935
**Sahl,** Mort (Morton Lyon Sahl) (comedian); Montreal, 5/11/1927
**Saint,** Eva Marie (actress); Newark, N.J., 7/4/1924
**Saint-Gaudens,** Augustus (sculptor); Dublin **(1848–1907)**
**St. James,** Susan (actress); Los Angeles, 1946
**St. John,** Jill (actress); Los Angeles, 8/19/1940
**St. Johns,** Adela Rogers (journalist and author); Los Angeles, 5/20/1894
**Saint-Laurent,** Yves (Henri Donat Mathieu) (fashion designer); Oran, Algeria, 8/1/1936
**Saint-Saens,** Charles Camille (composer); Paris **(1835–1921)**
**Sainte-Marie,** Buffy (Beverly) (folk singer); Craven, Canada. 2/20/1942(?)
**Salinger,** J. D. (Jerome David) (novelist); New York City, 1/1/1919
**Salisbury,** Harrison E. (journalist); Minneapolis, 11/14/1908
**Salk,** Jonas (polio researcher); New York City, 10/28/1914
**Sand,** George (Amandine Lucille Aurore Dudevant, née Dupin) (novelist); Paris **(1804–1876)**
**Sandburg,** Carl (poet and biographer); Galesburg, Ill. **(1878–1967)**
**Sanders,** George (actor); St. Petersburg, Russia **(1906–1972)**
**Sands,** Tommy (singer); Chicago, 8/27/1937
**Sanger,** Margaret (birth control leader); Corning, N.Y. **(1883–1966)**
**Santayana,** George (philosopher); Madrid **(1863–1952)**
**Sappho** (poet); Lesbos (Greece) **(lived c. 600** B.C.**)**
**Sargent,** John Singer (painter); Florence, Italy **(1856–1925)**
**Sarnoff,** David (radio executive); Minsk, Russia **(1891–1971)**
**Saroyan,** William (novelist); Fresno, Calif., 8/31/1908
**Sarrazin,** Michael (actor); Quebec, 5/22/1940
**Sarto,** Andrea del (Andrea Domenico d'Agnolo di Francesco) (painter); Florence (Italy) **(1486–1531)**
**Sartre,** Jean-Paul (existentialist writer); Paris, 6/21/1905
**Sassoon,** Vidal (hair stylist); London, 1/(?)/1928
**Saul** (King of Israel) **(11th century** B.C.**)**
**Savalas,** Telly (Aristoteles) (actor); Garden City, N.Y., 1/21/1924(?)
**Sayao,** Bidú (soprano); Rio de Janeiro, 5/11/1906
**Scaasi,** Arnold (Arnold Isaacs) (fashion designer); Montreal
**Schary,** Dore (producer and writer); Newark, N.J., 8/31/1905
**Schell,** Maria (actress); Vienna, 1/15/1926
**Schell,** Maximilian (actor); Vienna, 12/8/1930
**Schiaparelli,** Elsa (fashion designer); Rome **(1890?–1973)**
**Schiff,** Dorothy (newspaper publisher); New York City, 3/11/1903
**Schildkraut,** Joseph (actor); Vienna **(1896–1964)**
**Schiller,** Johann Christoph Friedrich von (dramatist and poet); Marbach (Germany) **(1759–1805)**
**Schippers,** Thomas (conductor); Kalamazoo, Mich. **(1930–1977)**
**Schlesinger,** Arthur M., Jr. (historian); Columbus, Ohio, 10/15/1917
**Schneider,** Romy (Rose-Marie Albach) (actress); Vienna, 9/23/1938
**Schönberg,** Arnold (composer); Vienna **(1874–1951)**
**Schopenhauer,** Arthur (philosopher); Danzig (Poland) **(1788–1860)**
**Schubert,** Franz Peter (composer); Vienna **(1797–1828)**
**Schulberg,** Budd (novelist); New York City, 3/27/1914
**Schulz,** Charles M. (cartoonist); Minneapolis, 11/26/1922
**Schuman,** Robert (statesman); Luxembourg **(1886–1963)**
**Schuman,** William (composer); New York City, 8/4/1910
**Schumann,** Robert Alexander (composer); Zwickau (Germany) **(1810–1856)**
**Schwartz,** Maurice (actor); Russia **(1891–1960)**
**Schwarzkopf,** Elisabeth (soprano); Jarotschin, Poznán (Poland), 12/9/1915
**Schweitzer,** Albert (humanitarian); Kaysersburg, Upper Alsace **(1875–1965)**
**Scofield,** Paul (actor); Hurstpierpoint, England, 1/21/1922
**Scott,** George C. (actor); Wise, Va., 10/18/1927
**Scott,** Lizabeth (Emma Matzo) (actress); Scranton, Pa., 1923
**Scott,** Martha (actress); Jamesport, Mo., 9/22/1914
**Scott,** Randolph (Randolph Crane) (actor); Orange County, Va., 1/23/1903
**Scott,** Robert Falcon (explorer); Devonport, England **(1868–1912)**
**Scott,** Sir Walter (novelist); Edinburgh, Scotland **(1771–1832)**
**Scott,** Zachary (actor); Austin, Tex. **(1914–1965)**
**Scruggs,** Earl Eugene (bluegrass musician); Cleveland County, N.C., 1/6/1924
**Sebastian,** John (composer); New York City, 3/17/1944
**Seberg,** Jean (actress); Marshalltown, Iowa, 11/13/1938
**Sedaka,** Neil (singer); Brooklyn, N.Y., 3/13/1939
**Seeger,** Pete (folk singer); New York City, 5/3/1919
**Segal,** Erich (novelist); Brooklyn, N.Y., 6/16/1937
**Segal,** George (actor); New York City, 2/13/1936
**Segovia,** Andrés (guitarist); Linares, Spain, 2/21/1893
**Sellers,** Peter (actor); Southsea, England, 9/8/1925
**Selye,** Hans (physician); Vienna, 1/26/1907
**Selznick,** David O. (film producer); Pittsburgh **(1902–1965)**
**Sendak,** Maurice (Bernard) (children's book author and illustrator); Brooklyn, N.Y., 6/10/1928
**Sennett,** Mack (Michael Sinnott) (film producer); Richmond, Quebec, Canada **(1880–1960)**
**Serkin,** Rudolf (pianist); Eger (Hungary), 3/28/1903
**Serling,** Rod (story writer); Syracuse, N.Y. **(1924–1975)**
**Sessions,** Roger (composer); Brooklyn, N.Y., 12/28/1896
**Seurat,** Georges (painter); b. Paris **(1859–1891)**
**Seuss,** Dr. (Theodor Seuss Geisel) (author and illustrator); Springfield, Mass., 3/2/1904
**Sevareid,** Eric (TV commentator); Velva, N.D., 11/26/1912
**Severinsen,** Doc (band leader); Arlington, Ore., 1927
**Sexton,** Anne (poet); Newton, Mass. **(1928–1974)**
**Shahn,** Ben(jamin) (painter); Kaunas, Lithuania **(1898–1969)**
**Shakespeare,** William (dramatist); Stratford on Avon, England **(1564–1616)**
**Shankar,** Ravi (sitar player); Benares, India, 4/7/1920
**Shanker,** Albert (labor leader); New York City, 9/14/1928

**Sharif,** Omar (Michael Shalhoub) (actor); Alexandria, Egypt, 4/10/1932
**Shatner,** William (actor); Montreal, 3/22/1931
**Shaw,** Artie (Arthur Arshawsky) (band leader); New York City, 5/23/1910
**Shaw,** George Bernard (dramatist); Dublin, **(1856–1950)**
**Shaw,** Irwin (novelist); Brooklyn, N.Y., 2/27/1913
**Shaw,** Robert (actor); Lancashire, England, **(1927–1978)**
**Shaw,** Robert (chorale conductor); Red Bluff, Calif., 4/30/1916
**Shearer,** Moira (ballerina); Dunfermline, Scotland, 1/17/1926
**Shearer,** Norma (actress); Montreal, 1904
**Shearing,** George (pianist); London, 8/13/1920
**Sheen,** Fulton J. (Roman Catholic bishop); El Paso, Ill., 5/8/1895
**Sheen,** Martin (Ramon Estevez) (actor); Dayton, Ohio, 8/3/1940
**Shelley,** Percy Bysshe (poet); nr. Horsham, England **(1792–1822)**
**Sheraton,** Thomas (furniture designer); Stockton-on-Tees, England **(1751–1806)**
**Sheridan,** Ann (actress); Denton, Tex. **(1915–1967)**
**Sheridan,** Philip (army officer); Albany, N.Y. **(1831–1888)**
**Sheridan,** Richard Brinsley (dramatist); Dublin, **(1751–1816)**
**Sherman,** William Tecumseh (army officer); Lancaster, Ohio **(1820–1891)**
**Sherwood,** Robert Emmet (playwright); New Rochelle, N.Y. **(1896–1955)**
**Shirer,** William L. (journalist and historian); Chicago, 2/23/1904
**Sholokhov,** Mikhail (novelist); Veshenskaya, Russia, 5/24/1905
**Shore,** Dinah (Frances Rose Shore) (singer); Winchester, Tenn., 3/1/1917(?)
**Short,** Bobby (Robert Waltrip Short) (singer and pianist); Danville, Ill., 9/15/1924
**Shostakovich,** Dmitri (composer); St. Petersburg, Russia **(1906–1975)**
**Shriver,** Sargent (Robert Sargent Shriver, Jr.) (business executive); Westminster, Md., 11/9/1915
**Shulman,** Max (novelist); St. Paul, 3/14/1919
**Sibelius,** Jean (Johann Julius Christian Sibelius) (composer); Tavastehus (Finland) **(1865–1957)**
**Sidney,** Sylvia (actress); New York City, 8/8/1910
**Siepi,** Cesare (basso); Milan, Italy, 2/14/1923
**Signoret,** Simone (Simone Kaminker) (actress); Wiesbaden, Germany, 3/25/1921
**Sikorsky,** Igor I. (inventor); Kiev, Russia **(1889–1972)**
**Sills,** Beverly (Belle Silverman) (soprano); Brooklyn, N.Y., 5/25/1929
**Silone,** Ignazio (Secondo Tranquilli) (novelist); Pescina del Marsi, Italy **(1900–1978)**
**Silvers,** Phil (Philip Silversmith) (comedian); Brooklyn, N.Y., 5/11/1912
**Sim,** Alastair (actor); Edinburgh, Scotland **(1900–1976)**
**Simenon,** Georges (Georges Sim) (mystery writer); Liège, Belgium, 2/13/1903
**Simmons,** Jean (actress); Crouch Hill, London, 1/31/1929
**Simon,** Carly (singer and songwriter); New York City, 6/25/1945
**Simon,** Neil (playwright); Bronx, N.Y., 7/4/1927
**Simon,** Norton (business executive); Portland, Ore., 2/5/1907
**Simon,** Paul (singer and songwriter); Newark, N.J., 11/5/1942
**Simon,** Simone (actress); Marseilles, France, 4/23/1914
**Simone,** Nina (Eunice Kathleen Waymon) (singer and pianist); Tryon, N.C., 2/21/1933
**Simpson,** Adele (Adele Smithline) (fashion designer); New York City, 12/8/1903
**Sinatra,** Frank (singer and actor); Hoboken, N.J., 12/12/1915
**Sinatra,** Frank, Jr. (singer); Jersey City, N.J., 1944
**Sinatra,** Nancy (singer); Jersey City, N.J., 6/8/1940
**Sinclair,** Upton Beall (novelist); Baltimore **(1878–1968)**
**Singer,** Isaac Bashevis (novelist); Radzymin (Poland), 7/14/1904
**Siqueiros,** David (painter); Chihuahua, Mexico **(1896–1974)**
**Sisley,** Alfred (painter); Paris **(1839–1899)**
**Sitting Bull** (Prairie Sioux Indian Chief); on Grand River, S.D. **(c. 1835–1890)**
**Skelton,** Red (Richard) (comedian); Vincennes, Ind., 7/18/1913
**Skinner,** B. F. (Burrhus Frederic) (psychologist); Susquehanna, Pa., 3/20/1904
**Skinner,** Cornelia Otis (writer and actress); Chicago, 5/30/1901
**Skinner,** Otis (actor); Cambridge, Mass. **(1858–1942)**
**Slezak,** Walter (actor); Vienna, 5/3/1902
**Sloan,** Alfred P., Jr. (industrialist); New Haven, Conn. **(1875–1966)**
**Sloan,** John (painter); Lock Haven, Pa. **(1871–1951)**
**Smetana,** Bedrich (composer); Litomysl (Czechoslovakia) (1824–1884)
**Smith,** Adam (economist); Kirkaldy, Scotland **(1723–1790)**
**Smith,** Alexis (actress); Penticon, Canada, 6/8/1921
**Smith,** Alfred Emanuel (politician); New York City **(1873–1944)**
**Smith,** David (sculptor); Decatur, Ind. **(1906–1965)**
**Smith,** H. Allen (humorist); McLeansboro, Ill. **(1907–1976)**
**Smith,** Howard K. (TV commentator); Ferriday, La., 5/12/1914
**Smith,** Jaclyn (actress); Houston, 10/26/(?)
**Smith,** John (American colonist); Willoughby, Lincolnshire, England **(1580–1631)**
**Smith,** Joseph (religious leader); Sharon, Vt. **(1805–1844)**
**Smith,** Kate (Kathryn) (singer); Greenville, Va., 5/1/1909
**Smith,** Maggie (actress); Ilford, England, 12/28/1934
**Smith,** Red (Walter) (sports columnist); Green Bay, Wis., 9/25/1905
**Smothers,** Dick (Richard) (comedian); Governors Island, New York City, 11/20/1939
**Smothers,** Tom (Thomas) (comedian); Governors Island, New York City, 2/2/1937
**Snow,** Lord (Charles Percy) (author); Leicester, England, 10/15/1905
**Socrates** (philosopher); Athens **(469–399 B.C.)**
**Solomon** (King of Israel); Jerusalem (?) **(died c. 933 B.C.)**
**Solon** (lawgiver); Salamis (Greece) **(638?–?559 B.C.)**
**Solti,** Sir Georg (conductor); Budapest, 10/21/1912
**Solzhenitsyn,** Aleksandr (novelist); Kislovodsk, Russia, 12/11/1918
**Sommer,** Elke (Elke Schletz) (actress); Berlin, 11/5/1942
**Sondheim,** Stephen (composer); New York City, 3/22/1930
**Sontag,** Susan (author and film director); New York City, 1/28/1933
**Sophocles** (dramatist); nr. Athens **(496?–406 B.C.)**
**Sothern,** Ann (Harriette Lake) (actress); Valley City, N.D., 1/22/1911
**Soul,** David (David Solberg) (actor); Chicago, 8/28/(?)
**Sousa,** John Philip (composer); Washington, D.C. **(1854–1932)**
**Soyer,** Raphael (painter); Borisoglebsk, Russia, 12/25/1899
**Spaak,** Paul-Henri (statesman); Brussels **(1899–1972)**
**Spacek,** Sissy (Mary Elizabeth) (actress); Quitman, Tex., 12/25/1949
**Spark,** Muriel (novelist); Edinburgh, Scotland, 2/1/1918
**Spector,** Phil (rock producer); Bronx, N.Y., 12/25/1940
**Spellman,** Francis Joseph (cardinal); Whitman, Mass. **(1889–1967)**
**Spencer,** Herbert (philosopher); Derby, England **(1820–1903)**
**Spender,** Stephen (poet); nr. London, 2/28/1909
**Spengler,** Oswald (philosopher); Blankenburg, Germany **(1880–1936)**
**Spenser,** Edmund (poet); London **(1552?–1599)**
**Spewack,** Bella (playwright); Hungary, 1899
**Spiegel,** Sam (producer); Jaroslaw (Poland), 11/11/1901
**Spillane,** Mickey (Frank Spillane) (mystery writer); Brooklyn, N.Y., 3/9/1918
**Spinoza,** Baruch (philosopher); Amsterdam (Netherlands) **(1632–1677)**
**Spivak,** Lawrence (TV producer); Brooklyn, N.Y., 1900
**Spock,** Benjamin (pediatrician); New Haven, Conn., 5/2/1903
**Springsteen,** Bruce (singer and songwriter); Freehold, N.J., 9/23/1949
**Sproul,** Robert G. (educator); San Francisco **(1891–1975)**
**Stack,** Robert (actor); Los Angeles, 1/13/1919
**Stafford,** Jo (singer); Coalinga, Calif., 1918
**Stalin,** Joseph Vissarionovich (Iosif V. Dzhugashvili) (Soviet leader); nr. Tiflis, Russia **(1879–1953)**
**Stalina,** Svetlana Alliluyeva (Stalin's daughter); Moscow, 2/28/1926
**Stallone,** Sylvester (actor and writer); New York City, 7/6/1946
**Stamp,** Terrence (actor); London, 1940
**Stang,** Arnold (comedian); Chelsea, Mass., 1925
**Stanislavski** (Konstantin Sergeevich Alekseev) (stage producer); Moscow **(1863–1938)**
**Stanley,** Sir Henry Morton (John Rowlands) (explorer); Denbigh, Wales **(1841–1904)**
**Stanley,** Kim (Patricia Reid) (actress); Tularosa, N.M., 2/11/1925
**Stans,** Maurice H. (ex-Secretary of Commerce); Shakope, Minn., 3/22/1908
**Stanton,** Frank (broadcasting executive); Muskegon, Mich., 3/20/1908
**Stanwyck,** Barbara (Ruby Stevens) (actress); Brooklyn, N.Y., 7/16/1907
**Stapleton,** Jean (Jeanne Murray) (actress); New York City, 1/19/1923
**Stapleton,** Maureen (actress); Troy, N.Y., 6/21/1925
**Starker,** János (cellist); Budapešt 7/5/1926
**Starr,** Kay (Starks) (singer); Dougherty, Okla., 7/21/1922
**Starr,** Ringo (Richard Starkey) (singer); Liverpool, England, 7/7/1940
**Stassen,** Harold E. (ex-government official); West St. Paul, Minn., 4/13/1907
**Steegmuller,** Francis (biographer); New Haven, Conn., 7/3/1906
**Steele,** Tommy (singer); London, 12/17/1936
**Stegner,** Wallace (Earle) (novelist and critic); Lake Mills, Iowa, 2/18/1909
**Steiger,** Rod (Rodney) (actor); Westhampton, N.Y., 4/14/1925
**Stein,** Gertrude (author); Allegheny, Pa. **(1874–1946)**
**Steinbeck,** John Ernst (novelist); Salinas, Calif. **(1902–1968)**
**Steinberg,** William (conductor); Cologne, Germany **(1899–1978)**
**Steinem,** Gloria (feminist); Toledo, Ohio, 3/25/1935(?)
**Steinmetz,** Charles (electrical engineer); Breslau (Poland) **(1865–1923)**
**Stendhal** (Marie Henri Beyle) (novelist); Grenoble, France **(1783–1842)**
**Sterling,** Jan (actress); New York City, 1923
**Stern,** Isaac (concert violinist); Kreminiecz, Russia, 7/21/1920
**Sterne,** Laurence (novelist); Clonmel, Ireland **(1713–1768)**
**Stevens,** Cat (Steven Georgiou) (singer and songwriter); London, 7/?/1947
**Stevens,** Connie (Concetta Ingolia) (singer); Brooklyn, N.Y., 8/8/1938
**Stevens,** George (film director); Oakland, Calif. **(1905–1975)**
**Stevens,** Risë (mezzo-soprano); New York City, 6/11/1913
**Stevens,** Stella (actress); Yazoo City, Miss., 10/1/1936
**Stevenson,** Adlai Ewing (statesman); Los Angeles **(1900–1965)**
**Stevenson,** Robert Louis Balfour (novelist and poet); Edinburgh, Scotland **(1850–1894)**
**Stewart,** James (actor); Indiana, Pa., 5/20/1908

**Stewart,** Rod (singer); London, 1/10/1945
**Stickney,** Dorothy (actress); Dickinson, N. Dak., 6/21/1903
**Stills,** Stephen (singer and songwriter); Dallas, 1/3/1945
**Stokes,** Carl (TV newscaster); Cleveland, 6/21/1927
**Stokowski,** Leopold (conductor); London **(1882–1977)**
**Stone,** Edward Durrell (architect); Fayetteville, Ark. **(1902–1978)**
**Stone,** Ezra (actor and producer); New Bedford, Mass., 12/2/1917
**Stone,** I. F. (Isidor Feinstein Stone) (journalist); Philadelphia, 12/24/1907
**Stone,** Irving (Irving Tennenbaum) (novelist); San Francisco, 7/14/1903
**Stone,** Lewis (actor); Worcester, Mass. **(1879–1953)**
**Stone,** Lucy (woman suffragist); nr. West Brookfield, Mass. **(1818–1893)**
**Stone,** Sly (Sylvester) (rock musician); 1944
**Storm,** Gale (actress); Bloomington, Tex., 1922
**Stout,** Rex (mystery writer); Noblesville, Ind. **(1886–1975)**
**Stowe,** Harriet Elizabeth Beecher (novelist); Litchfield, Conn. **(1811–1896)**
**Stradivari,** Antonio (violinmaker); Cremona (Italy) **(1644–1737)**
**Strasberg,** Lee (stage director); Budanov, Austria, 11/17/1901
**Strasberg,** Susan (actress); New York City, 5/22/1938
**Straus,** Oskar (composer); Vienna **(1870–1954)**
**Strauss,** Johann (composer); Vienna **(1825–1899)**
**Strauss,** Lewis L. (naval officer and scientist); Charleston, W. Va. **(1896–1974)**
**Strauss,** Richard (composer); Munich, Germany **(1864–1949)**
**Stravinsky,** Igor (composer); Orienbaum, Russia **(1882–1971)**
**Streisand,** Barbra (singer and actress); Brooklyn, N.Y., 4/24/1942
**Stritch,** Elaine (actress); Detroit, 2/2/1928
**Struthers,** Sally Ann (actress); Portland, Ore., 7/28/1948
**Stuart,** Gilbert Charles (painter); Rhode Island **(1755–1828)**
**Stuart,** James Ewell Brown (known as Jeb) (Confederate army officer); Patrick County, Va. **(1833–1864)**
**Stuyvesant,** Peter (Governor of New Amsterdam); West Friesland (Netherlands) **(1592–1672)**
**Styron,** William (William Clark Styron, Jr.) (novelist); Newport News, Va., 6/11/1925
**Sullavan,** Margaret Brooke (actress); Norfolk, Va. **(1911–1960)**
**Sullivan,** Sir Arthur Seymour (composer); London **(1842–1900)**
**Sullivan,** Barry (Patrick Barry) (actor); New York City, 8/29/1912
**Sullivan,** Ed (columnist and TV personality); New York City **(1901–1974)**
**Sullivan,** Francis Loftus (actor); London **(1903–1956)**
**Sullivan,** Frank (Francis John) (humorist); Saratoga Springs, N.Y. **(1892–1976)**
**Sullivan,** Louis Henry (architect); Boston, Mass. **(1856–1924)**
**Sulzberger,** Arthur Ochs (newspaper publisher); New York City, 2/5/1926
**Sumac,** Yma (singer); Ichocan, Peru, 9/10/1927
**Sun Yat-sen** (statesman); nr. Macao **(1866–1925)**
**Susann,** Jacqueline (novelist); Philadelphia **(1926?–1974)**
**Susskind,** David (TV producer); New York City, 12/19/1920
**Sutherland,** Joan (soprano); Sydney, Australia, 11/7/1926
**Suzman,** Janet (actress); Johannesburg, South Africa, 2/9/1939
**Suzuki,** Pat (actress); Cressey, Calif., 1931
**Swanson,** Gloria (Josephine Swenson) (actress); Chicago, 3/27/1899
**Swarthout,** Gladys (soprano); Deepwater, Mo. **(1904–1969)**
**Swayze,** John Cameron (news commentator); Wichita, Kan., 4/4/1906
**Swift,** Jonathan (satirist); Dublin **(1667–1745)**
**Swigert,** John L., Jr. (astronaut); Denver, 8/30/1931
**Swinburne,** Algernon Charles (poet); London **(1837–1909)**
**Swope,** Herbert Bayard (journalist); St. Louis **(1882–1958)**
**Sydow,** von, Max (Carl Adolf von Sydow) (actor); Lund, Sweden, 4/10/1929
**Synge,** John Millington (dramatist); nr. Dublin **(1871–1909)**
**Szilard,** Leo (physicist); Budapest **(1898–1964)**

# T

**Taft,** Robert Alphonso (legislator); Cincinnati **(1889–1953)**
**Tagore,** Sir Rabindranath (poet); Calcutta **(1861–1941)**
**Tallchief,** Maria (ballerina); Fairfax, Okla., 1/24/1925
**Talleyrand-Périgord,** Charles Maurice de (statesman); Paris **(1754–1838)**
**Talmadge,** Norma (actress); Niagara Falls, N.Y. **(1897–1957)**
**Tamerlane** (Timur) (Mongol conqueror); nr. Samarkand (U.S.S.R.) **(1336?–1405)**
**Tandy,** Jessica (actress); London, 6/7/1909
**Tarkington,** (Newton) Booth (novelist); Indianapolis **(1869–1946)**
**Tate,** Allen (John Orley) (poet and critic); Winchester, Ky., 11/19/1899
**Tate,** Sharon (actress); Dallas **(1943–1969)**
**Tati,** Jacques (Jacques Tatischeff) (actor); Pecq, France, 10/9/1908
**Taylor,** Elizabeth (actress); London, 2/27/1932
**Taylor,** Estelle (actress); Wilmington, Del. **(1899–1958)**
**Taylor,** Harold (educator); Toronto, 9/28/1914
**Taylor,** James (singer and songwriter); Boston, 3/12/1948
**Taylor,** (Joseph) Deems (composer); New York City **(1885–1966)**
**Taylor,** Laurette (Laurette Cooney) (actress); New York City **(1884–1946)**
**Taylor,** Gen. Maxwell D. (former Army Chief of Staff); Keytesville, Mo., 8/26/1901
**Taylor,** Robert (Spangler Arlington Brugh) (actor); Filley, Neb. **(1911–1969)**
**Taylor,** Rod (actor); Sydney, Australia, 1/11/1930
**Tchaikovsky,** Peter (Pëtr) Ilich (composer); Votkinsk, Russia **(1840–1893)**
**Teasdale,** Sara (poet); St. Louis **(1884–1933)**
**Tebaldi,** Renata (lyric soprano); Pesaro, Italy, 1/2/1922
**Tecumseh** (Shawnee Indian chief); nr. Springfield, Ohio **(1768?–1813)**
**Teller,** Edward (atomic physicist); Budapest, 1/15/1908
**Temple,** Shirley. *See* Black, Shirley Temple
**Tennyson,** Alfred (1st Baron Tennyson) (poet); Somersby, England **(1809–1892)**
**Terhune,** Albert Payson (novelist and journalist); Newark, N.J. **(1872–1942)**
**Terry,** Ellen Alicia (actress); Coventry, England **(1848–1928)**
**Terry-Thomas** (Thomas Terry Hoar Stevens) (actor); London, 7/14/1911
**Tesla,** Nikola (electrician and inventor); Smiljan (Yugoslavia) **(1856–1943)**
**Thackeray,** William Makepeace (novelist); Calcutta **(1811–1863)**
**Thant,** U (U.N. statesman); Pantanaw (Burma) **(1909–1974)**
**Tharp,** Twyla (dancer and choreographer); Portland, Ind., 7/1/1941(?)
**Thatcher,** Margaret (political leader); Grantham, England, 10/13/1925
**Thaxter,** Phyllis (actress); Portland, Me., 1921
**Thebom,** Blanche (mezzo-soprano); Monessen, Pa., 9/19/1919
**Theodorakis,** Mikis (composer); Chios, Greece, 7/29/1925
**Thieu,** Nguyen Van (ex-President of South Vietnam); Trithuy (Vietnam) 4/5/1923
**Thomas,** Danny (Amos Jacobs) (entertainer and TV producer); Deerfield, Mich., 1/6/1914
**Thomas,** Dylan Marlais (poet); Carmarthenshire, Wales **(1914–1953)**
**Thomas,** Lowell (explorer, commentator); Woodington, Ohio, 4/6/1892
**Thomas,** Marlo (actress); Detroit, 11/21/1943
**Thomas,** Michael Tilson (conductor); Hollywood, Calif., 12/21/1944
**Thomas,** Norman Mattoon (Socialist leader); Marion, Ohio **(1884–1968)**
**Thomas,** Richard (actor); New York City, 6/13/1951
**Thompson,** Dorothy (writer); Lancaster, N.Y. **(1894–1961)**
**Thompson,** Sada (actress); Des Moines, Iowa, 9/27/1929
**Thoreau,** Henry David (naturalist and author); Concord, Mass. **(1817–1862)**
**Thorndike,** Dame Sybil (actress); Gainsborough, England **(1882–1976)**
**Thurber,** James Grover (author and cartoonist); Columbus, Ohio **(1894–1961)**
**Tibbett,** Lawrence (baritone); Bakersfield, Calif. **(1896–1960)**
**Tierney,** Gene (actress); Brooklyn, N.Y., 11/20/1920
**Tiffin,** Pamela (actress); Oklahoma City, 10/13/1942
**Tillstrom,** Burr (puppeteer); Chicago, 10/13/1917
**Tintoretto,** Il (Jacopo Robusti) (painter); Venice **(1518–1594)**
**Tiny Tim** (Herbert Khaury) (entertainer); New York City, 1923(?)
**Tiomkin,** Dmitri (composer); Russia, 5/10/1899
**Titian** (Tiziano Vecelli) (painter); Pieve di Cadore (Italy) **(1477–1576)**
**Tito** (Josip Broz or Brozovich) (President of Yugoslavia); Croatia (Yugoslavia), 5/25/1892
**Tocqueville,** Alexis de (writer); Verneuil, France **(1805–1859)**
**Todd,** Thelma (actress); Lawrence, Mass. **(1905–1935)**
**Tolstoi,** Count Leo (Lev) Nikolaevich (novelist); Tula Province, Russia **(1828–1910)**
**Tomlin,** Lily (comedienne); Detroit, 1939(?)
**Tone,** Franchot (actor); Niagara Falls, N.Y. **(1905–1968)**
**Tormé,** Mel (Melvin) (singer); Chicago, 9/13/1925
**Torn,** Rip (Elmore Torn, Jr.) (actor and director); Temple, Tex., 2/6/1931
**Toscanini,** Arturo (orchestra conductor); Parma, Italy **(1867–1957)**
**Toulouse-Lautrec** (Henri Marie Raymond de Toulouse-Lautrec Monfa) (painter); Albi, France **(1864–1901)**
**Toynbee,** Arnold J. (historian); London **(1889–1975)**
**Tracy,** Spencer (actor); Milwaukee **(1900–1967)**
**Traubel,** Helen (Wagnerian soprano); St. Louis **(1903–1972)**
**Travolta,** John (actor); Englewood, N.J., 2/18/1954
**Treacher,** Arthur (actor); Brighton, England **(1894–1975)**
**Trevor,** Claire (actress); New York City, 1909
**Trigère,** Pauline (fashion designer); Paris, 11/4/1912
**Trilling,** Lionel (author and educator); New York City **(1905–1975)**
**Trotsky,** Leon (Lev Davidovich Bronstein) (statesman); Elisavetgrad, Russia **(1879–1940)**
**Trudeau,** Pierre Elliott (Prime Minister); Montreal, 10/18/1919
**Truffaut,** François (film director); Paris, 2/6/1932
**Trujillo y Molina,** Rafael Leonidas (Dominican Republic dictator); San Cristóbal, Dominican Republic **(1891–1961)**
**Truman,** Margaret (author); Independence, Mo., 2/17/1924
**Tryon,** Thomas (actor and novelist); Hartford, Conn., 1/14/1926
**Tucker,** Forrest (actor); Plainfield, Ind., 2/12/1919
**Tucker,** Richard (tenor); New York City **(1914–1975)**
**Tucker,** Sophie (Sophie Abuza) (singer); Boston **(1884?–1966)**
**Tudor,** Antony (choreographer); London, 4/4/1909

**Turgenev,** Ivan Sergeevich (novelist); Orel, Russia **(1818–1883)**
**Turner,** Ike (singer); Clarksdale, Miss., 11/?/1931
**Turner,** Joseph M.W. (painter); London **(1775–1851)**
**Turner,** Lana (Julia Jean Mildred Frances Turner) (actress); Wallace, Idaho, 2/8/1920
**Turner,** Nat (civil rights leader); Southampton County, Va. **(1800–1831)**
**Turner,** Tina (Annie Mae Bullock) (singer); Brownsville, Tex., 1939
**Turpin,** Ben (comedian); New Orleans **(1874–1940)**
**Tushingham,** Rita (actress); Liverpool, England, 3/14/1942
**Twain,** Mark (Samuel Langhorne Clemens) (author); Florida, Mo. **(1835–1910)**
**Tweed,** William Marcy (politician); New York City **(1823–1878)**
**Twiggy** (Leslie Hornby) (model); London, 9/19/1949
**Twining,** Gen. Nathan F. (former Air Force Chief of Staff); Monroe, Wis., 10/11/1897
**Twitty,** Conway (Harold Lloyd Jenkins) (singer and guitarist); Friars Point, Miss., 9/1/1933
**Tyson,** Cicely (actress); New York City, 12/19/1939(?)

# U

**Udall,** Stewart L. (ex-Secretary of the Interior); St. Johns, Ariz., 1/31/1920
**Uggams,** Leslie (singer and actress); New York City, 5/25/1943
**Ulanova,** Galina (ballerina); St. Petersburg, Russia, 1/10/1910
**Ullmann,** Liv (actress); Tokyo, 12/16/1939
**Ulric,** Lenore (actress); New Ulm, Minn. **(1894–1970)**
**Untermeyer,** Louis (anthologist and poet); New York City **(1885–1977)**
**Updike,** John (novelist); Shillington, Pa., 3/18/1932
**Urey,** Harold C. (physicist); Walkerton, Ind., 4/29/1893
**Uris,** Leon (novelist); Baltimore, 8/3/1924
**Ustinov,** Peter (actor, producer); London, 4/16/1921
**Utrillo,** Maurice (painter); Paris **(1883–1955)**

# V

**Vaccaro,** Brenda (actress); Brooklyn, N.Y., 11/18/1939
**Valentine,** Karen (actress); Santa Rosa, Calif., 1947
**Valentino,** Rudolph (Rodolpho d'Antonguolla) (actor); Castellaneta, Italy **(1895–1926)**
**Valentino** (Valentino Garavani) (fashion designer); nr. Milan, Italy, 5/11/1932
**Vallee,** Rudy (Hubert Vallée) (band leader and singer); Island Pond, Vt., 7/28/1901
**Van Allen,** James Alfred (space physicist); Mt. Pleasant, Iowa, 9/7/1914
**Van Buren,** Abigail (Mrs. Morton Phillips) (columnist); Sioux City, Iowa, 7/14/1918
**Vance,** Vivian (actress); Cherryvale, Kan., 1912
**Vandenberg,** Arthur Hendrick (legislator); Grand Rapids, Mich. **(1884–1951)**
**Vanderbilt,** Alfred G. (sportsman); London, 9/22/1912
**Vanderbilt,** Cornelius (financier); Port Richmond, N.Y. **(1794–1877)**
**Vanderbilt,** Gloria (artist and heiress); New York City, 2/20/1924
**Van Doren,** Carl (writer and educator); Hope, Ill. **(1885–1950)**
**Van Doren,** Mamie (actress); Rowena, S.D., 1933
**Van Dyke,** Dick (actor); West Plains, Mo., 12/13/1925
**Vandyke** (or Van Dyck), Sir Anthony (painter); Antwerp (Belgium) **(1599–1641)**
**Van Eyck,** Jan (painter); Maeseyck (Belgium) **(c.1390–1441)**
**van Gogh,** Vincent (painter); Groot Zundert, Brabant **(1853–1890)**
**Van Heusen,** Jimmy (Edward Chester Babcock) (songwriter); Syracuse, N.Y., 1/26/1913
**Van Peebles,** Melvin (playwright); Chicago, 9/21/1932
**Vaughan,** Sarah (singer); Newark, N.J., 3/27/1924
**Vaughan Williams,** Ralph (composer); Down Ampney, England **(1872–1958)**
**Vaughn,** Robert (actor); New York City, 11/22/1932
**Velázquez,** Diego Rodríguez de Silva y (painter); Seville, Spain **(1599–1660)**
**Velez,** Lupe (Guadelupe Velez de Villalobos) (actress); San Luis Potosi, Mexico **(1908–1944)**
**Venturi,** Robert (Charles) (architect); Philadelphia, 6/25/1925
**Verdi,** Giuseppe (composer); Roncole, (Italy) **(1813–1901)**
**Verdon,** Gwen (actress); Culver City, Calif., 1/13/1926
**Vereen,** Ben (actor and singer); Miami, Fla., 10/10/1946
**Vermeer,** Jan (or Jan van der Meer van Delft) (painter); Delft (Netherlands) **(1632–1675)**
**Verne,** Jules (author); Nantes, France **(1828–1905)**
**Verrazano,** Giovanni da (navigator); Florence (Italy) **(1485?–1528)**
**Verrett,** Shirley (mezzo-soprano); New Orleans, 5/31/1933
**Vespucci,** Amerigo (navigator); Florence (Italy) **(1454–1512)**
**Vickers,** Jon (tenor); Prince Albert, Sask., Canada, 10/29/1926
**Vidal,** Gore (novelist); West Point, N.Y., 10/3/1925
**Vidor,** King (film director and producer); Galveston, Tex., 2/8/1895
**Villa,** Pancho (Doroteo Arango) (bandit); Rio Grande, Mexico **(1877–1923)**
**Villella,** Edward (ballet dancer); Bayside, Queens, N.Y., 10/1/1936
**Villon,** François (François de Montcorbier) (poet); Paris **(1431–1463)**
**Vinton,** Bobby (singer); Canonsburg, Pa., 4/16/1935(?)
**Virgil** (or Vergil) (Publius Vergilius Maro) (poet); nr. Mantua (Italy) **(70–19 B.C.)**
**Vishnevskaya,** Galina (soprano); Leningrad, 10/25/1926
**Vlaminck,** Maurice de (painter); Paris **(1876–1958)**
**Voight,** Jon (actor); Yonkers, N.Y., 12/29/1938
**Voltaire** (François Marie Arouet) (author); Paris **(1694–1778)**
**Von Braun.** *See* Braun
**von Furstenberg,** Betsy (actress); Neiheim-Heusen, Germany, 8/16/1935
**von Fürstenberg,** Diane (Diane Simone Michelle Halfin) (fashion designer); Brussels, 12/31/1946
**von Karajan,** Herbert (conductor); Salzburg (Austria), 4/5/1908
**Vonnegut,** Kurt, Jr. (novelist); Indianapolis, 11/11/1922
**Von Stroheim,** Erich Oswald Hans Carl Maria von Nordenwall (film actor and director); Vienna **(1885–1957)**
**Vorster,** Balthazar Johannes (Prime Minister); Jamestown, Cape Province, South Africa, 12/13/1915
**Vreeland,** Diana (Dalziel) (fashion journalist and museum consultant); Paris, 1903(?)

# W

**Wagner,** Lindsay (actress); Los Angeles, 1949
**Wagner,** Robert (actor); Detroit, 2/10/1930
**Wagner,** Robert F. (ex-Mayor of New York City); New York City, 4/20/1910
**Wagner,** Wilhelm Richard (composer); Leipzig (Germany) **(1813–1883)**
**Waldheim,** Kurt (U.N. Secretary-General); St. Andrae Wörden, Austria, 12/21/1918
**Walker,** Clint (actor); Hartford, Ill., 5/30/1927
**Walker,** Nancy (Ann Myrtle Swoyer); (actress and comedienne); Philadelphia, 5/10/1922
**Wallace,** DeWitt (publisher); St. Paul, 11/12/1889
**Wallace,** George C. (Governor); Clio, Ala., 8/25/1919
**Wallace,** Henry Agard (statesman); Adair County, Iowa **(1888–1965)**
**Wallace,** Irving (novelist); Chicago, 3/19/1916
**Wallace,** Mike (Myron Wallace) (TV interviewer and commentator); Brookline, Mass., 5/9/1918
**Wallach,** Eli (actor); Brooklyn, N.Y., 12/7/1915
**Waller,** Thomas "Fats" (pianist); New York City **(1904–1943)**
**Wallis,** Hal (film producer); Chicago, 9/14/1899
**Waltari,** Mike (novelist); Helsinki, Finland, 9/19/1908
**Walter,** Bruno (Bruno Walter Schlesinger) (orchestra conductor); Berlin **(1876–1962)**
**Walters,** Barbara (TV commentator); Boston, 9/25/1931
**Walton,** Izaak (author); Stafford, England **(1593–1683)**
**Wanamaker,** John (merchant); Philadelphia **(1838–1922)**
**Ward,** Barbara (economist); York, England, 5/23/1914
**Warhol,** Andy (artist and producer); Cleveland, 8/8/1930(?)
**Waring,** Fred (band leader); Tyrone, Pa., 6/9/1900
**Warner,** H. B. (Henry Bryan Warner Lickford) (actor); London **(1876–1958)**
**Warren,** Earl (Chief Justice of the U.S.); Los Angeles **(1891–1974)**
**Warren,** Robert Penn (novelist); Guthrie, Ky., 4/24/1905
**Warwicke,** Dionne (singer); East Orange, N.J., 1941
**Washington,** Booker Taliaferro (educator); Franklin County, Va. **(1856–1915)**
**Waters,** Ethel (actress and singer); Chester, Pa. **(1896–1977)**
**Waters,** Muddy (McKinley Morganfield) (singer and guitarist); Rolling Fork, Miss., 4/4/1915
**Watson,** Thomas John (industrialist); Campbell, N.Y. **(1874–1956)**
**Watt,** James (inventor); Greenock, Scotland **(1736–1819)**
**Watteau,** Jean-Antoine (painter); Valenciennes, France **(1684–1721)**
**Watts,** André (concert pianist); Nuremberg, Germany, 6/20/1946
**Waugh,** Alex (Alexander Raban Waugh) (novelist); London, 7/8/1898
**Wayne,** Anthony (military officer); Waynesboro, Pa. **(1745–1796)**
**Wayne,** David (David McMeakan) (actor); Traverse City, Mich., 1/30/1914
**Wayne,** John (Marion Michael Morrison) (actor); Winterset, Iowa, 5/26/1907
**Weaver,** Dennis (actor); Joplin, Mo., 6/4/1925
**Weaver,** Fritz (actor); Pittsburgh, 1/19/1926
**Webb,** Clifton (Webb Parmelee Hollenbeck) (actor); Indianapolis **(1893–1966)**
**Webb,** Jack (film actor, producer); Santa Monica, Calif., 4/2/1920
**Weber,** Karl Maria Friedrich Ernst von (composer); nr. Lübeck (Germany) **(1786–1826)**
**Webster,** Daniel (statesman); Salisbury, N.H. **(1782–1852)**
**Webster,** Noah (lexicographer); West Hartford, Conn. **(1758–1843)**

**Weill**, Kurt (composer); Dessau, Germany **(1900–1950)**
**Weizmann**, Chaim (statesman); Grodno Province, Russia **(1874–1952)**
**Welch**, Raquel (Raquel Tejada) (actress); Chicago, 9/5/1942
**Weld**, Tuesday (Susan) (actress); New York City, 8/27/1943
**Welk**, Lawrence (band leader); Strasburg, N.D., 3/11/1903
**Welles**, Orson (actor and producer); Kenosha, Wis., 5/6/1915
**Wellington**, Duke of (Arthur Wellesley) (statesman); Ireland **(1769–1852)**
**Wells**, H(erbert) G(eorge) (author); Bromley, England **(1866–1946)**
**Welty**, Eudora (novelist); Jackson, Miss., 4/13/1909
**Werfel**, Franz (novelist); Prague **(1890–1945)**
**Werner**, Oskar (film actor and director); Vienna, 11/13/1922
**Wertmuller**, Lina (film director); Rome, 1926(?)
**Wesley**, John (religious leader); Epworth Rectory, Lincolnshire, England **(1703–1791)**
**West**, Jessamyn (novelist); nr. North Vernon, Ind., 7/18/1902
**West**, Mae (actress); Brooklyn, N.Y., 8/17/1893
**West**, Nathaniel (novelist); New York City **(1902–1940)**
**West**, Dame Rebecca (Cicily Fairchild) (novelist); County Kerry, Ireland, 12/25/1892
**Westinghouse**, George (inventor); Central Bridge, N.Y. **(1846–1914)**
**Westmoreland**, William Childs (ex-Army Chief of Staff); Saxon, S.C., 3/26/1914
**Wharton**, Edith Newbold (née Jones) (novelist); New York City **(1862–1937)**
**Wheeler**, Bert (Albert Jerome Wheeler) (comedian); Paterson, N.J. **(1895–1968)**
**Whistler**, James Abbott McNeill (painter and etcher); Lowell, Mass. **(1834–1903)**
**White**, E. B. (Elwyn Brooks White) (author); Mt. Vernon, N.Y., 7/11/1899
**White**, Stanford (architect); New York City **(1853–1906)**
**White**, Theodore H. (historian); Boston, 5/6/1915
**White**, William Allen (journalist); Emporia, Kan. **(1868–1944)**
**Whitehead**, Alfred North (mathematician and philosopher); Isle of Thanet, England **(1861–1947)**
**Whiteman**, Paul (band leader); Denver **(1891–1967)**
**Whitman**, Walt (Walter) (poet); West Hills, N.Y. **(1819–1892)**
**Whitmore**, James (actor); White Plains, N.Y., 10/1/1921
**Whitney**, Cornelius Vanderbilt (sportsman); New York City, 2/20/1899
**Whitney**, Eli (inventor); Westboro, Mass. **(1765–1825)**
**Whitney**, John Hay (publisher); Ellsworth, Me., 8/17/1904
**Whittier**, John Greenleaf (poet); Haverhill, Mass. **(1807–1892)**
**Widmark**, Richard (actor); Sunrise, Minn., 12/26/1914
**Wiesel**, Elie (Eliezer) (author); Sighet, Romania, 9/30/1928
**Wilbur**, Richard (poet); New York City, 3/1/1921
**Wilde**, Cornel (film actor and producer); New York City, 10/13/1918
**Wilde**, Oscar Fingal O'Flahertie Wills (author); Dublin **(1854–1900)**
**Wilder**, Billy (film producer and director); Vienna, 6/22/1906
**Wilder**, Gene (Jerome Silberman) (actor); Milwaukee, 6/11/1935(?)
**Wilder**, Thornton (author); Madison, Wis. **(1897–1975)**
**Wilding**, Michael (actor); Westcliff, England, 7/23/1912
**Wilkins**, Roy (civil rights leader); St. Louis, 8/30/1901
**Williams**, Andy (singer); Wall Lake, Iowa, 12/3/1930
**Williams**, Cindy (actress); Van Nuys, Calif., 8/22/(?)
**Williams**, Edward Bennett (lawyer); Hartford, Conn., 5/31/1920
**Williams**, Emlyn (actor, playwright); Mostyn, Wales, 11/26/1905
**Williams**, Esther (actress); Los Angeles, 8/8/1923
**Williams**, Gluyas (cartoonist); San Francisco, 7/23/1888
**Williams**, Hank, Sr. (Hiram King Williams) (singer); Georgiana, Ala. **(1923–1953)**
**Williams**, Roger (clergyman); London **(1603?–1683)**
**Williams**, Tennessee (Thomas L. Williams) (playwright); Columbus, Miss., 3/26/1911
**Willkie**, Wendell Lewis (lawyer); Elwood, Ind. **(1892–1944)**
**Willson**, Meredith (composer); Mason City, Iowa, 5/18/1902
**Wilson**, Don (radio and TV announcer); Lincoln, Neb., 1924
**Wilson**, Flip (Clerow) (comedian); Jersey City, N.J., 12/8/1933
**Wilson**, Harold (ex-Prime Minister); Huddersfield, England, 3/11/1916
**Wilson**, Nancy (singer); Chillicothe, Ohio, 2/20/1937
**Wilson**, Sloan (novelist); Norwalk, Conn., 5/8/1920
**Winchell**, Walter (columnist); New York City **(1897–1972)**
**Windsor**, Duchess of (Bessie Wallis Warfield); Blue Ridge Summit, Pa., 6/19/1896
**Windsor**, Duke of (formerly King Edward VIII of England); Richmond Park, England **(1894–1972)**
**Winkler**, Henry (actor); New York City, 10/30/1945
**Winter**, Johnny (guitarist); Leland, Miss., 2/23/1944
**Winters**, Jonathan (comedian); Dayton, Ohio, 11/11/1925
**Winters**, Shelley (Shirley Schrift) (actress); East St. Louis, Ill., 8/18/1922
**Winthrop**, John (first Governor, Massachusetts Bay Colony); Suffolk, England **(1588–1649)**
**Wise**, Stephen Samuel (rabbi); Budapest **(1874–1949)**
**Withers**, Jane (actress); Atlanta, 1927
**Wittgenstein**, Ludwig (Josef Johann) (philosopher); Vienna **(1889–1951)**
**Wodehouse**, P(elham) G(renville) (novelist); Guildford, England **(1881–1975)**
**Wolfe**, Thomas Clayton (novelist); Asheville, N.C. **(1900–1938)**
**Wolfe**, Tom (journalist); Richmond, Va., 3/2/1931
**Wolsey**, Thomas (prelate and statesman); Ipswich, England **(1475?–1530)**
**Wonder**, Stevie (Steveland Judkins, later Steveland Morris) (singer and songwriter); Saginaw, Mich., 5/13/1950
**Wong**, Anna May (Lu Tsong Wong) (actress); Los Angeles **(1907–1961)**
**Wood**, Grant (painter); Anamosa, Iowa **(1892–1942)**
**Wood**, Natalie (Natasha Gurdin) (film actress); San Francisco, 7/20/1938
**Woodward**, Joanne (film actress); Thomasville, Ga., 2/27/1930
**Woolf**, Adeline Virginia (née Stephens) (novelist); London **(1882–1941)**
**Woollcott**, Alexander (author); Phalanx, N.J. **(1887–1943)**
**Woolley**, Monty (Edgar Montillion Woolley) (actor); New York City **(1888–1963)**
**Woolworth**, Frank (merchant); Rodman, N.Y. **(1852–1919)**
**Wordsworth**, William (poet); Cockermouth, England **(1770–1850)**
**Worley**, Jo Anne (actress and singer); Lowell, Ind., 9/6/1937
**Wouk**, Herman (novelist); New York City, 5/27/1915
**Wray**, Fay (actress); Alberta, Canada, 1907
**Wren**, Sir Christopher (architect); East Knoyle, England **(1632–1723)**
**Wright**, Frank Lloyd (architect); Richland Center, Wis. **(1869–1959)**
**Wright**, Orville (inventor); Dayton, Ohio **(1871–1948)**
**Wright**, Richard (novelist); nr. Natchez, Miss. **(1908–1960)**
**Wright**, Teresa (actress); New York City, 10/27/1918
**Wright**, Wilbur (inventor); Millville, Ind. **(1867–1912)**
**Wyatt**, Jane (film actress); Campgaw, N.J., 8/12/1912
**Wyeth**, Andrew (painter); Chadds Ford, Pa., 7/12/1917
**Wyler**, William (film director); Mulhouse (France), 7/1/1902
**Wyman**, Jane (Sarah Jane Fulks) (actress); St. Joseph, Mo., 1/4/1914
**Wynette**, Tammy (Wynette Pugh) (singer); Tupelo, Miss. 5/5/1942
**Wynn**, Ed (Isaiah Edwin Leopold) (comedian); Philadelphia **(1886–1966)**
**Wynn**, Keenan (actor); New York City, 7/27/1916
**Wynter**, Dana (actress); London, 6/8/1930

# Y

**Yeats**, William Butler (poet); nr. Dublin **(1865–1939)**
**Yevtushenko**, Yevgeny (poet); Zima, U.S.S.R., 7/18/1933
**York**, Michael (actor); Fulmer, England, 3/27/1942
**York**, Susannah (Fletcher) (actress); London, 1/9/1942
**Yorty**, Samuel W. (ex-Mayor of Los Angeles); Lincoln, Neb., 10/1/1909
**Young**, Alan (actor); North Shield, England, 11/19/1919
**Young**, Brigham (religious leader); Whitingham, Vt. **(1801–1877)**
**Young**, Gig (Byron Barr) (actor); St. Cloud, Minn., 11/4/1917
**Young**, Loretta (Gretchen Young) (actress); Salt Lake City, Utah, 1/6/1913
**Young**, Neil (singer and songwriter); Toronto, 11/12/1945
**Young**, Robert (actor); Chicago, 2/22/1907
**Youngman**, Henny (comedian); England, 1906

# Z

**Zanuck**, Darryl F. (film producer); Wahoo, Neb., 9/5/1902
**Zappa**, Frank (Francis Vincent Zappa, Jr.) (singer and songwriter); Baltimore, 12/21/1940
**Zeffirelli**, Franco (director); Florence, Italy, 2/12/1923
**Ziegfeld**, Florenz (theatrical producer); Chicago **(1869–1932)**
**Zimbalist**, Efrem (concert violinist); Rostov-on-Don, Russia, 4/9/1889
**Zimbalist**, Efrem, Jr. (actor); New York City, 11/30/1923
**Zola**, Emile (novelist); Paris **(1840–1902)**
**Zoroaster** (religious leader); Persian Empire **(c. 6th century** B.C.**)**
**Zweig**, Stefan (author); Vienna **(1881–1942)**

## Art Prices

The five most expensive works of art ever sold at auction are: Velasquez's painting *Juan de Pareja,* purchased in 1970 for $5,544,000; Titian's painting, *Death of Actaeon,* purchased in 1971 for $4,065,600; enameled medallion (12th century, Rhineland), purchased in 1978 for $2,208,000; enameled arm-ornament (12th century, Rhineland), purchased in 1978 for $2,024,000; and a porcelain bowl (Chinese Ming dynasty), purchased in 1974 for $1,014,300.

# THE DECLARATION OF INDEPENDENCE

## In Congress, July 4, 1776

### The unanimous Declaration of the thirteen united States of America.

When in the Course of human events it becomes necessary for one people to dissolve the political bands which have connected them with another, and to assume among the powers of the earth, the separate and equal station to which the Laws of Nature and of Nature's God entitle them, a decent respect to the opinions of mankind requires that they should declare the causes which impel them to the separation.

We hold these truths to be self-evident, that all men are created equal, that they are endowed by their Creator with certain unalienable Rights, that among these are Life, Liberty and the pursuit of Happiness.—That to secure these rights, Governments are instituted among Men, deriving their just powers from the consent of the governed,—That whenever any Form of Government becomes destructive of these ends, it is the Right of the People to alter or to abolish it, and to institute new Government, laying its foundation on such principles and organizing its powers in such form, as to them shall seem most likely to effect their Safety and Happiness. Prudence, indeed, will dictate that Governments long established should not be changed for light and transient causes; and accordingly all experience hath shewn that mankind are more disposed to suffer, while evils are sufferable, than to right themselves by abolishing the forms to which they are accustomed. But when a long train of abuses and usurpations, pursuing invariably the same Object evinces a design to reduce them under absolute Despotism, it is their right, it is their duty, to throw off such Government, and to provide new Guards for their future security.—Such has been the patient sufferance of these Colonies; and such is now the necessity which constrains them to alter their former Systems of Government. The history of the present King of Great Britain is a history of repeated injuries and usurpations, all having in direct object the establishment of an absolute Tyranny over these States. To prove this, let Facts be submitted to a candid world.

He has refused his Assent to Laws, the most wholesome and necessary for the public good.

He has forbidden his Governors to pass Laws of immediate and pressing importance, unless suspended in their operation till his Assent should be obtained; and when so suspended, he has utterly neglected to attend to them.

He has refused to pass other Laws for the accommodation of large districts of people, unless those people would relinquish the right of Representation in the Legislature, a right inestimable to them and formidable to tyrants only.

He has called together legislative bodies at places unusual, uncomfortable, and distant from the depository of their Public Records, for the sole purpose of fatiguing them into compliance with his measures.

He has dissolved Representative Houses repeatedly, for opposing with manly firmness his invasions on the rights of the people.

He has refused for a long time, after such dissolutions, to cause others to be elected; whereby the Legislative Powers, incapable of Annihilation, have returned to the People at large for their exercise; the State remaining in the mean time exposed to all the dangers of invasion from without, and convulsions within.

He has endeavoured to prevent the population of these States; for that purpose obstructing the Laws for Naturalization of Foreigners; refusing to pass others to encourage their migrations hither, and raising the conditions of new Appropriations of Lands.

He has obstructed the Administration of Justice, by refusing his Assent to Laws for establishing Judiciary Powers.

He has made Judges dependent on his Will alone, for the tenure of their offices, and the amount and payment of their salaries.

He has erected a multitude of New Offices, and sent hither swarms of Officers to harass our people, and eat out their substance.

He has kept among us, in times of peace, Standing Armies without the Consent of our legislatures.

He has affected to render the Military independent of and superior to the Civil Power.

He has combined with others to subject us to a jurisdiction foreign to our constitution, and unacknowledged by our laws; giving his Assent to their Acts of pretended Legislation:

For quartering large bodies of armed troops among us:

For protecting them, by a mock Trial, from punishment for any Murders which they should commit on the Inhabitants of these States:

For cutting off our Trade with all parts of the

NOTE: On April 12, 1776, the legislature of North Carolina authorized its delegates to the Continental Congress to join with others in a declaration of separation from Great Britain; the first colony to instruct its delegates to take the actual initiative was Virginia on May 15. On June 7, 1776, Richard Henry Lee of Virginia offered a resolution to the Congress to the effect "that these United Colonies are, and of right ought to be, free and independent States. . . ." A committee, consisting of Thomas Jefferson, John Adams, Benjamin Franklin, Robert R. Livingston, and Roger Sherman was organized to "prepare a declaration to the effect of the said first resolution." The Declaration of Independence was adopted on July 4, 1776.

Most delegates signed the Declaration August 2, but George Wythe (Va.) signed August 27; Richard Henry Lee (Va.), Elbridge Gerry (Mass.), and Oliver Wolcott (Conn.) in September; Matthew Thornton (N. H.), not a delegate until September, in November; and Thomas McKean (Del.), although present on July 4, not until 1781 by special permission, having served in the army in the interim.

world:

For imposing Taxes on us without our Consent:

For depriving us in many cases, of the benefits of Trial by Jury:

For transporting us beyond Seas to be tried for pretended offences:

For abolishing the free System of English Laws in a neighbouring Province, establishing therein an Arbitrary government, and enlarging its Boundaries so as to render it at once an example and fit instrument for introducing the same absolute rule into these Colonies:

For taking away our Charters, abolishing our most valuable Laws and altering fundamentally the Forms of our Governments:

For suspending our own Legislatures, and declaring themselves invested with power to legislate for us in all cases whatsoever.

He has abdicated Government here, by declaring us out of his Protection and waging War against us.

He has plundered our seas, ravaged our Coasts, burnt our towns, and destroyed the lives of our people.

He is at this time transporting large Armies of foreign Mercenaries to compleat the works of death, desolation, and tyranny, already begun with circumstances of Cruelty & Perfidy scarcely paralleled in the most barbarous ages, and totally unworthy the Head of a civilized nation.

He has constrained our fellow Citizens taken Captive on the high Seas to bear Arms against their Country, to become the executioners of their friends and Brethren, or to fall themselves by their Hands.

He has excited domestic insurrections amongst us, and has endeavoured to bring on the inhabitants of our frontiers, the merciless Indian Savages, whose known rule of warfare, is an undistinguished destruction of all ages, sexes and conditions.

In every stage of these Oppressions We have Petitioned for Redress in the most humble terms: Our repeated Petitions have been answered only by repeated injury. A Prince, whose character is thus marked by every act which may define a Tyrant, is unfit to be the ruler of a free people.

Nor have We been wanting in attentions to our Brittish brethren. We have warned them from time to time of attempts by their legislature to extend an unwarrantable jurisdiction over us. We have reminded them of the circumstances of our emigration and settlement here. We have appealed to their native justice and magnanimity, and we have conjured them by the ties of our common kindred to disavow these usurpations, which would inevitably interrupt our connections and correspondence. They too have been deaf to the voice of justice and of consanguinity. We must, therefore, acquiesce in the necessity, which denounces our Separation, and hold them, as we hold the rest of mankind, Enemies in War, in Peace Friends.

We, therefore, the Representatives of the United States of America, in General Congress, Assembled, appealing to the Supreme Judge of the world for the rectitude of our intentions, do, in the Name, and by Authority of the good People of these Colonies, solemnly publish and declare, That these United Colonies are, and of Right ought to be Free and Independent States; that they are Absolved from all Allegiance to the British Crown, and that all political connection between them and the State of Great Britain, is and ought to be totally dissolved; and that as Free and Independent States, they have full Power to levy War, conclude Peace, contract Alliances, establish Commerce, and to do all other Acts and Things which Independent States may of right do.—And for the support of this Declaration, with a firm reliance on the protection of Divine Providence, we mutually pledge to each other our Lives, our Fortunes and our sacred Honor.

John Hancock

*New Hampshire*
Josiah Bartlett
Wm. Whipple
Matthew Thornton

*Rhode Island*
Step. Hopkins
William Ellery

*Connecticut*
Roger Sherman
Sam'el Huntington
Wm. Williams
Oliver Wolcott

*New York*
Wm. Floyd
Phil. Livingston
Frans. Lewis
Lewis Morris

*New Jersey*
Richd. Stockton
Jno. Witherspoon
Fras. Hopkinson
John Hart
Abra. Clark

*Pennsylvania*
Robt. Morris
Benjamin Rush
Benj. Franklin
John Morton
Geo. Clymer
Jas. Smith
Geo. Taylor
James Wilson
Geo. Ross

*Massachusetts-Bay*
Saml. Adams
John Adams
Robt. Treat Paine
Elbridge Gerry

*Delaware*
Caesar Rodney
Geo. Read
Tho. M'Kean

*Maryland*
Samuel Chase
Wm. Paca
Thos. Stone
Charles Carroll of Carrollton

*Virginia*
George Wythe
Richard Henry Lee
Th. Jefferson
Benj. Harrison
Ths. Nelson, Jr.
Francis Lightfoot Lee
Carter Braxton

*North Carolina*
Wm. Hooper
Joseph Hewes
John Penn

*South Carolina*
Edward Rutledge
Thos. Heyward, Junr.
Thomas Lynch, Junr.
Arthur Middleton

*Georgia*
Button Gwinnett
Lyman Hall
Geo. Walton

# Constitution of the United States of America

(Historical text has been edited to conform to contemporary American usage. The bracketed words are designations for your convenience; they are not part of the Constitution.)

*The oldest federal constitution in existence was framed by a convention of delegates from twelve of the thirteen original states in Philadelphia in May, 1787, Rhode Island failing to send a delegate. George Washington presided over the session, which lasted until September 17, 1787. The draft (originally a preamble and seven Articles) was submitted to all thirteen states and was to become effective when ratified by nine states. It went into effect on the first Wednesday in March, 1789, having been ratified by New Hampshire, the ninth state to approve, on June 21, 1788. The states ratified the Constitution in the following order:*

| | | | |
|---|---|---|---|
| Delaware | December 7, 1787 | South Carolina | May 23, 1788 |
| Pennsylvania | December 12, 1787 | New Hampshire | June 21, 1788 |
| New Jersey | December 18, 1787 | Virginia | June 25, 1788 |
| Georgia | January 2, 1788 | New York | July 26, 1788 |
| Connecticut | January 9, 1788 | North Carolina | November 21, 1789 |
| Massachusetts | February 6, 1788 | Rhode Island | May 29, 1790 |
| Maryland | April 28, 1788 | | |

## [Preamble]

We the people of the United States, in order to form a more perfect Union, establish justice, insure domestic tranquility, provide for the common defence, promote the general welfare, and secure the blessings of liberty to ourselves and our posterity, do ordain and establish this Constitution for the United States of America.

## Article I

### Section 1

**[Legislative powers vested in Congress.]** All legislative powers herein granted shall be vested in a Congress of the United States, which shall consist of a Senate and House of Representatives.

### Section 2

**[Composition of the House of Representatives.—1.]** The House of Representatives shall be composed of members chosen every second year by the people of the several States, and the electors in each State shall have the qualifications requisite for electors of the most numerous branch of the State Legislature.

**[Qualifications of Representatives.—2.]** No Person shall be a Representative who shall not have attained to the age of twenty-five years, and been seven years a citizen of the United States, and who shall not, when elected, be an inhabitant of that State in which he shall be chosen.

**[Apportionment of Representatives and direct taxes—census.[1]—3.]** (Representatives and direct taxes shall be apportioned among the several States which may be included within this Union, according to their respective numbers, which shall be determined by adding to the whole number of free persons, including those bound to service for a term of years, and excluding Indians not taxed, three fifths of all other persons.) The actual enumeration shall be made within three years after the first meeting of the Congress of the United States, and within every subsequent term of ten years, in such manner as they shall by law direct. The number of Representatives shall not exceed one for every thirty thousand, but each State shall have at least one Representative; and until such enumeration shall be made, the State of New Hampshire shall be entitled to choose three, Massachusetts eight, Rhode-Island and Providence Plantations one, Connecticut five, New York six, New Jersey four, Pennsylvania eight, Delaware one, Maryland six, Virginia ten, North Carolina five, South Carolina five, and Georgia three.

**[Filling of vacancies in representation.—4.]** When vacancies happen in the representation from any State, the Executive Authority thereof shall issue writs of election to fill such vacancies.

**[Selection of officers; power of impeachment.—5.]** The House of Representatives shall choose their Speaker and other officers; and shall have the sole power of impeachment.

### Section 3[2]

**[The Senate.—1.]** The Senate of the United States shall be composed of two Senators from each State, chosen by the Legislature thereof, for six years; and each Senator shall have one vote.

**[Classification of Senators; filling of vacancies.—2.]** Immediately after they shall be assembled in consequence of the first election, they shall be divided as equally as may be into three classes. The seats of the Senators of the first class shall be vacated at the expiration of the second year, of the second class at the expiration of the fourth year, and of the third class at the expiration of the sixth year, so that one-third may be chosen every second year; and if vacancies happen by resignation, or otherwise, during the recess of the Legislature of any State, the Executive thereof may make temporary appointments (until the next meeting of the Legislature, which shall then fill such vacancies).

**[Qualification of Senators.—3.]** No person shall be a Senator who shall not have attained to the age of thirty years, and been nine years a citizen of the United States, and who shall not, when elected, be an inhabitant of that State for which he shall be chosen.

**[Vice President to be President of Senate.—4.]** The Vice President of the United States shall be President of the Senate, but shall have no vote, unless they be equally divided.

**[Selection of Senate officers; President pro tempore.—5.]** The Senate shall choose their other officers, and also a President pro tempore, in the absence of the Vice President, or when he shall exercise the office of President of the United States.

**[Senate to try impeachments.—6.]** The Senate

shall have the sole power to try all impeachments. When sitting for that purpose, they shall be on oath or affirmation. When the President of the United States is tried, the Chief Justice shall preside: and no person shall be convicted without the concurrence of two thirds of the members present.

**[Judgment in cases of Impeachment.—7.]** Judgment in cases of impeachment shall not extend further than to removal from office, and disqualification to hold and enjoy any office of honor, trust, or profit under the United States: but the party convicted shall nevertheless be liable and subject to indictment, trial, judgment and punishment, according to Law.

### Section 4

**[Control of congressional elections.—1.]** The times, places, and manner of holding elections for Senators and Representatives, shall be prescribed in each State by the Legislature thereof; but the Congress may at any time by law make or alter such regulations, except as to the places of choosing Senators.

**[Time for assembling of Congress.[3]—2.]** The Congress shall assemble at least once in every year, and such meeting shall be on the first Monday in December, unless they shall by law appoint a different day.

### Section 5

**[Each house to be the judge of the election and qualifications of its members; regulations as to quorum.—1.]** Each House shall be the judge of the elections, returns, and qualifications of its own members, and a majority of each shall constitute a quorum to do business; but a smaller number may adjourn from day to day, and may be authorized to compel the attendance of absent members, in such manner, and under such penalties as each House may provide.

**[Each house to determine its own rules.—2.]** Each House may determine the rules of its proceedings, punish its members for disorderly behavior, and, with the concurrence of two thirds, expel a member.

**[Journals and yeas and nays.—3.]** Each House shall keep a journal of its proceedings, and from time to time publish the same, excepting such parts as may in their judgment require secrecy; and the yeas and nays of the members of either House on any question shall, at the desire of one fifth of those present, be entered on the journal.

**[Adjournment.—4.]** Neither House, during the session of Congress, shall, without the consent of the other, adjourn for more than three days, nor to any other place than that in which the two Houses shall be sitting.

### Section 6

**[Compensation and privileges of members of Congress.—1.]** The Senators and Representatives shall receive a compensation for their services, to be ascertained by law, and paid out of the Treasury of the United States. They shall in all cases, except treason, felony, and breach of the peace, be privileged from arrest during their attendance at the session of their respective Houses, and in going to and returning from the same; and for any speech or debate in either House, they shall not be questioned in any other place.

**[Incompatible offices; exclusions.—2.]** No Senator or Representative shall, during the time for which he was elected, be appointed to any civil office under the authority of the United States, which shall have been created, or the emoluments whereof shall have been increased during such time; and no person holding any office under the United States shall be a member of either House during his continuance in office.

### Section 7

**[Revenue bills to originate in House.—1.]** All bills for raising revenue shall originate in the House of Representatives; but the Senate may propose or concur with amendments as on other bills.

**[Manner of passing bills; veto power of President.—2.]** Every bill which shall have passed the House of Representatives and the Senate, shall, before it becomes a law, be presented to the President of the United States; if he approve he shall sign it, but if not he shall return it, with his objections to that House in which it shall have originated, who shall enter the objections at large on their journal, and proceed to reconsider it. If after such reconsideration two thirds of that House shall agree to pass the bill, it shall be sent, together with the objections, to the other House, by which it shall likewise be reconsidered, and if approved by two thirds of that House, it shall become a law. But in all such cases the votes of both Houses shall be determined by yeas and nays, and the names of the persons voting for and against the bill shall be entered on the journal of each house, respectively. If any bill shall not be returned by the President within ten days (Sundays excepted) after it shall have been presented to him, the same shall be a law, in like manner as if he had signed it, unless the Congress by their adjournment prevent its return, in which case it shall not be a law.

**[Concurrent orders or resolutions, to be passed by President.—3.]** Every order, resolution, or vote to which the concurrence of the Senate and House of Representatives may be necessary (except on a question of adjournment) shall be presented to the President of the United States; and before the same shall take effect, shall be approved by him, or being disapproved by him, shall be repassed by two thirds of the Senate and House of Representatives, according to the rules and limitations prescribed in the case of a bill.

### Section 8

**[General powers of Congress.[4]]**

**[Taxes, duties, imposts, and excises.—1.]** The Congress shall have power to lay and collect taxes, duties, imposts and excises, to pay the debts and provide for the common defense and general welfare of the United States; but all duties, imposts and excises shall be uniform throughout the United States;

**[Borrowing of money.—2.]** To borrow money on the credit of the United States;

**[Regulation of commerce.—3.]** To regulate commerce with foreign nations, and among the several States, and with the Indian tribes;

**[Naturalization and bankruptcy.—4.]** To establish a uniform rule of naturalization, and uniform laws on the subject of bankruptcies throughout the United States;

**[Money, weights and measures.—5.]** To coin money, regulate the value thereof, and of foreign coin, and fix the standard of weights and measures;

**[Counterfeiting.—6.]** To provide for the punishment of counterfeiting the securities and current coin of the United States;

**[Post offices.—7.]** To establish post offices and post roads;

**[Patents and copyrights.—8.]** To promote the

progress of science and useful arts, by securing for limited times to authors and inventors the exclusive right to their respective writings and discoveries;

[**Inferior courts.—9.**] To constitute tribunals inferior to the Supreme Court;

[**Piracies and felonies.—10.**] To define and punish piracies and felonies commited on the high seas, and offences against the law of nations;

[**War; marque and reprisal.—11.**] To declare war, grant letters of marque and reprisal, and make rules concerning captures on land and water;

[**Armies.—12.**] To raise and support armies, but no appropriation of money to that use shall be for a longer term than two years;

[**Navy.—13.**] To provide and maintain a navy;

[**Land and naval forces.—14.**] To make rules for the government and regulation of the land and naval forces;

[**Calling out militia.—15.**] To provide for calling forth the militia to execute the laws of the Union, suppress insurrections, and repel invasions.

[**Organizing, arming, and disciplining militia.—16.**] To provide for organizing, arming, and disciplining, the militia, and for governing such part of them as may be employed in the service of the United States, reserving to the States, respectively, the appointment of the officers, and the authority of training the militia according to the discipline prescribed by Congress;

[**Exclusive legislation over District of Columbia.—17.**] To exercise exclusive legislation in all cases whatsoever, over such district (not exceeding ten miles square) as may, by cession of particular States, and the acceptance of Congress, become the seat of the Government of the United States, and to exercise like authority over all places purchased by the consent of the Legislature of the State in which the same shall be, for the erection of forts, magazines, arsenals, dock-yards, and other needful buildings; —And

[**To enact laws necessary to enforce Constitution.—18.**] To make all laws which shall be necessary and proper for carrying into execution the foregoing powers, and all other powers vested by this Constitution in the Government of the United States, or in any department or officer thereof.

### Section 9

[**Migration or importation of certain persons not to be prohibited before 1808.—1.**] The migration or importation of such persons as any of the States now existing shall think proper to admit, shall not be prohibited by the Congress prior to the year one thousand eight hundred and eight, but a tax or duty may be imposed on such importation, not exceeding ten dollars for each person.

[**Writ of habeas corpus not to be suspended; exception.—2.**] The privilege of the writ of habeas corpus shall not be suspended, unless when in cases of rebellion or invasion the public safety may require it.

[**Bills of attainder and ex post facto laws prohibited.—3.**] No bill of attainder or ex post facto law shall be passed.

[**Capitation and other direct taxes.—4.**] No capitation, or other direct, tax shall be laid, unless in proportion to the census or enumeration herein before directed to be taken.[5]

[**Exports not to be taxed.—5.**] No tax or duty shall be laid on articles exported from any State.

[**No preference to be given to ports of any State; interstate shipping.—6.**] No preference shall be given by any regulation of commerce or revenue to the ports of one State over those of another: nor shall vessels bound to, or from, one State, be obliged to enter, clear, or pay duties in another.

[**Money, how drawn from treasury; financial statements to be published.—7.**] No money shall be drawn from the Treasury, but in consequence of appropriations made by law; and a regular statement and account of the receipts and expenditures of all public money shall be published from time to time.

[**Titles of nobility not to be granted; acceptance by government officers of favors from foreign powers.—8.**] No title of nobility shall be granted by the United States: and no person holding any office of profit or trust under them, shall, without the consent of the Congress, accept of any present, emolument, office, or title, of any kind whatever, from any king, prince, or foreign state.

### Section 10

[**Limitations of the powers of the several States.—1.**] No State shall enter into any treaty, alliance, or confederation; grant letters of marque and reprisal; coin money; emit bills of credit; make any thing but gold and silver coin a tender in payment of debts; pass any bill of attainder, ex post facto law, or law impairing the obligation of contracts, or grant any title of nobility.

[**State imposts and duties.—2.**] No State shall, without the consent of the Congress, lay any imposts or duties on imports or exports, except what may be absolutely necessary for executing its inspection laws: and the net produce of all duties and imposts, laid by any State on imports or exports, shall be for the use of the Treasury of the United States; and all such laws shall be subject to the revision and control of the Congress.

[**Further restrictions on powers of States.—3.**] No State shall, without the consent of Congress, lay any duty of tonnage, keep troops, or ships of war in time of peace, enter into any agreement or compact with another state, or with a foreign power, or engage in war, unless actually invaded, or in such imminent danger as will not admit of delay.

## Article II

### Section 1

[**The President; the executive power.—1.**] The executive power shall be vested in a President of the United States of America. He shall hold his office during the term of four years, and, together with the Vice President, chosen for the same term, be elected, as follows

[**Appointment and qualifications of presidential electors.—2.**] Each State shall appoint, in such manner as the Legislature thereof may direct, a number of electors, equal to the whole number of Senators and Representatives to which the State may be entitled in the Congress: but no Senator or Representative, or person holding an office of trust or profit under the United States, shall be appointed an elector.

[**Original method of electing the President and Vice President.**[6]] (The electors shall meet in their respective States, and vote by ballot for two persons, of whom one at least shall not be an inhabitant of the same State with themselves. And they shall make a list of all the persons voted for, and of the number of votes for each; which list they shall sign and certify, and transmit sealed to the seat of the Government of the United States, directed to the President of the Senate. The President of the Senate shall, in the presence of the Senate and House of Representatives, open all the certificates, and the votes shall then be counted. The person having the greatest number of votes shall be the President, if such number be a majority of the whole number of electors appointed; and if there be more than one who have such majority, and have an equal number of votes, then the House of Representatives shall immediately choose by ballot one of them for President; and if no person have a majority, then from the five highest on the list the said House shall in like manner choose the President. But in choosing the President, the votes shall be taken by States, the representation from each State having one vote; A quorum for this purpose shall consist of a member or members from two thirds of the States, and a majority of all the states shall be necessary to a choice. In every case, after the choice of the President, the person having the greatest number of votes of the electors shall be the Vice President. But if there should remain two or more who have equal votes, the Senate should choose from them by ballot the Vice President.)

**[Congress may determine time of choosing electors and day for casting their votes.—3.]** The Congress may determine the time of choosing the electors, and the day on which they shall give their votes; which day shall be the same throughout the United States.

**[Qualifications for the office of President.[7]—4.]** No person except a natural born citizen, or a citizen of the United States, at the time of the adoption of this Constitution, shall be eligible to the office of President; neither shall any person be eligible to that office who shall not have attained to the age of thirty-five years, and been fourteen years a resident within the United States.

**[Filling vacancy in the office of President.[8]—5.]** In case of the removal of the President from office, or of his death, resignation, or inability to discharge the powers and duties of the said office, the same shall devolve on the Vice President, and the Congress may by law provide for the case of removal, death, resignation or inability, both of the President and Vice President, declaring what officer shall then act as President, and such officer shall act accordingly, until the disability be removed, or a President shall be elected.

**[Compensation of the President.—6.]** The President shall, at stated times, receive for his services, a compensation, which shall neither be increased nor diminished during the period for which he shall have been elected, and he shall not receive within that period any other emolument from the United States, or any of them.

**[Oath to be taken by the President.—7.]** Before he enter on the execution of his office, he shall take the following oath or affirmation:—"I do solemnly swear (or affirm) that I will faithfully excute the office of President of the United States, and will to the best of my ability, preserve, protect, and defend the Constitution of the United States."

### Section 2

**[The President to be commander in chief of army and navy and head of executive departments; may grant reprieves and pardons.—1.]** The President shall be Commander in Chief of the Army and Navy of the United States, and of the militia of the several States, when called into the actual service of the United States; he may require the opinion, in writing, of the principal officer in each of the executive departments, upon any subject relating to the duties of their respective offices, and he shall have power to grant reprieves and pardons for offences against the United States, except in cases of impeachment.

**[President may, with concurrence of Senate, make treaties, appoint ambassadors, etc.; appointment of inferior officers, authority of Congress over.—2.]** He shall have power, by and with the advice and consent of the Senate, to make treaties, provided two thirds of the Senators present concur; and he shall nominate, and by and with the advice and consent of the Senate, shall appoint ambassadors, other public ministers and consuls, judges of the Supreme Court, and all other officers of the United States, whose appointments are not herein otherwise provided for, and which shall be established by law: but the Congress may by law vest the appointment of such inferior officers, as they think proper, in the President alone, in the courts of law, or in the heads of departments.

**[President may fill vacancies in office during recess of Senate.—3.]** The President shall have power to fill up all vacancies that may happen during the recess of the Senate, by granting commissions which shall expire at the end of their session.

### Section 3

**[President to give advice to Congress; may convene or adjourn it on certain occasions; to receive ambassadors, etc.; have laws executed and commission all officers.]** He shall from time to time give to the Congress information of the state of the Union, and recommend to their consideration such measures as he shall judge necessary and expedient; he may, on extraordinary occasions, convene both Houses, or either of them, and in case of disagreement between them, with respect to the time of adjournment, he may adjourn them to such time as he shall think proper; he shall receive ambassadors and other public ministers: he shall take care that the laws be faithfully executed, and shall commission all the officers of the United States.

### Section 4

**[All civil officers removable by impeachment.]** The President, Vice President, and all civil officers of the United States shall be removed from office on impeachment for, and conviction of, treason, bribery, or other high crimes and misdemeanors.

## Article III

### Section 1

**[Judicial powers; how vested; term of office and compensation of judges.]** The judicial Power of the United States, shall be vested in one Supreme Court, and in such inferior courts as the Congress may from time to time ordain and establish. The judges, both of the supreme and inferior courts, shall hold their offices during good behavior, and shall, at stated times, receive for their services, a compensation, which shall not be diminished during their continuance in office.

### Section 2

**[Jurisdiction of Federal courts.[9]—1.]** The judicial power shall extend to all cases, in law and equity, arising under this Constitution, the laws of the United States, and treaties made, or which shall be made, under their authority; to all cases affecting ambassadors, other public ministers and consuls, to all cases of admiralty and maritime jurisdiction; to controversies to which the United States, shall be a party; to controversies between two or more States; between a State and citizens of another State; between citizens of different States, between citizens of the same State claiming lands under grants of different states, and between a State, or the citizens thereof, and foreign states, citizens, or subjects.

**[Original and appellate jurisdiction of Supreme Court.—2.]** In all cases affecting ambassadors, other public ministers and consuls, and those in which a State shall be party, the Supreme Court shall have original jurisdiction. In all the other cases before mentioned, the Supreme Court shall have appellate jurisdiction, both as to law and fact, with such exceptions, and under such regulations, as the Congress shall make.

**[Trial of all crimes, except impeachment, to be by jury.—3.]** The trial of all crimes, except in cases of impeachment, shall be by jury; and such trial shall be held in the State where the said crimes shall have been committed; but when not committed within any State, the trial shall be at such place or places as the Congress may by law have directed.

### Section 3

**[Treason defined; conviction of.—1.]** Treason against the United States, shall consist only in levying war against them, or, in adhering to their enemies, giving them aid and comfort. No person shall be convicted of treason unless on the testimony of two witnesses to the same overt act, or on confession in open court.

**[Congress to declare punishment for treason; proviso.—2.]** The Congress shall have power to declare the punishment of treason, but no attainder of treason shall work corruption of blood, or forfeiture except during the life of the person attainted.

## Article IV

### Section 1

**[Each State to give full faith and credit to the public acts and records of other States.]** Full faith and credit shall be given in each State to the public acts, records, and judicial proceedings of every other State. And the Congress may by general laws prescribe the manner in which such acts, records, and proceedings shall be proved, and the effect thereof.

### Section 2

**[Privileges of citizens.—1.]** The citizens of each State shall be entitled to all privileges and immunities of citizens in the several States.

**[Extradition between the several States.—2.]** A person charged in any State with treason, felony, or other crime, who shall flee from justice, and be found in another State, shall on demand of the Executive authority of the State from which he fled, be delivered up, to be removed to the State having jurisdiction of the crime.

**[Persons held to labor or service in one State, fleeing to another, to be returned.—3.]** No person held to service or labor in one State, under the laws thereof, escaping into another, shall, in consequence of any law or regulation therein, be discharged from such service or labor, but shall be delivered up on claim of the party to whom such service or labor may be due.

### Section 3

**[New States.—1.]** New States may be admitted by the Congress into this Union; but no new State shall be formed or erected within the jurisdiction of any other State; nor any State be formed by the junction of two or more States, or parts of States, without the consent of the Legislatures of the States concerned as well as of the Congress.

**[Regulations concerning territory.—2.]** The Congress shall have power to dispose of and make all needful rules and regulations respecting the territory or other property belonging to the United States; and nothing in this Constitution shall be so construed as to prejudice any claims of the United States, or of any particular State.

### Section 4

**[Republican form of government and protection guaranteed the several States.]** The United States shall guarantee to every State in this Union a Republican form of government, and shall protect each of them against invasion; and on application of the Legislature, or of the Executive (when the Legislature cannot be convened) against domestic violence.

## Article V

**[Ways in which the Constitution can be amended.]** The Congress, whenever two thirds of both Houses shall deem it necessary, shall propose amendments to this Constitution, or, on the application of the Legislatures of two thirds of the several States shall call a convention for proposing amendments, which, in either case, shall be valid to all intents and purposes, as part of this Constitution, when ratified by the Legislatures of three fourths of the several States, or by conventions in three fourths thereof, as the one or the other mode of ratification may be proposed by the Congress; provided that no amendment which may be made prior to the year one thousand eight hundred and eight shall in any manner affect the first and fourth clauses in the ninth Section of the first Article; and that no State, without its consent, shall be deprived of its equal suffrage in the Senate.

## Article VI

**[Debts contracted under the confederation secured.—1.]** All debts contracted and engagements entered into, before the adoption of this Constitution, shall be as valid against the United States under this Constitution, as under the Confederation.

**[Constitution, laws, and treaties of the United States to be supreme.—2.]** This Constituion, and the laws of the United States which shall be made in pursuance thereof; and all treaties made, or which shall be made, under the authority of the United States, shall be the supreme law of the land; and the judges in every State shall be bound thereby, any thing in the Constitution or laws of any State to the contrary notwithstanding.

**[Who shall take constitutional oath; no religious test as to official qualification.—3.]** The Senators and Representatives before mentioned, and the

1. The clause included in parentheses is amended by the 14th Amendment, Section 2. 2. The first paragraph of this section and the part of the second paragraph included in parentheses are amended by the 17th Amendment. 3. Amended by the 20th Amendment, Section 2. 4. By the 16th Amendment, Congress is given the power to lay and collect taxes on income. 5. See the 16th Amendment. 6. This clause has been superseded by the 12th Amendment. 7. For qualifications of the Vice President, see 12th Amendment. 8. Amended by the 20th Amendment, Sections 3 and 4. 9. This section is abridged by the 11th Amendment. 10. See the 13th Amendment.

members of the several State Legislatures, and all executive and judicial officers, both of the United States and of the several States, shall be bound by oath or affirmation, to support this Constitution; but no religious test shall ever be required as a qualification to any office or public trust under the United States.

## Article VII

**[Constitution to be considered adopted when ratified by nine States.]** The ratification of the conventions of nine States shall be sufficient for the establishment of this Constitution between the States so ratifying the same.

Done in convention by the unanimous consent of the States present the seventeenth day of September in the year of our Lord one thousand seven hundred and eighty seven and of the independence of the United States of America the Twelfth. In witness whereof we have hereunto subscribed our names.

GEORGE WASHINGTON
*President and Deputy from Virginia*

NEW HAMPSHIRE

John Langdon — Nicholas Gilman

MASSACHUSETTS

Nathaniel Gorham — Rufus King

CONNECTICUT

Wm. Saml. Johnson — Roger Sherman

NEW YORK

Alexander Hamilton

NEW JERSEY

Wil. Livingston — Wm. Paterson
David Brearley — Jona. Dayton

PENNSYLVANIA

B. Franklin — Thomas Mifflin
Robt. Morris — Geo. Clymer
Thos. FitzSimons — Jared Ingersoll
James Wilson — Gouv. Morris

DELAWARE

Geo. Read — Gunning Bedford Jun.
John Dickinson — Richard Bassett
Jaco. Broom

MARYLAND

James McHenry — Dan. of St. Thos. Jenifer
Danl. Carroll

VIRGINIA

John Blair — James Madison, Jr.

NORTH CAROLINA

Wm. Blount — Richd Dobbs Spaight
Hu. Williamson

SOUTH CAROLINA

J. Rutledge — Charles Cotesworth Pinckney
Charles Pinckney — Pierce Butler

GEORGIA

William Few — Abr. Baldwin

Attest: William Jackson, Secretary

# Amendments to the Constitution of the United States

(Amendments I to X inclusive, popularly known as the Bill of Rights, were proposed and sent to the states by the first session of the First Congress. They were ratified Dec. 15, 1791.)

## Article I

**[Freedom of religion, speech, of the press, and right of petition.]** Congress shall make no law respecting an establishment of religion, or prohibiting the free exercise thereof; or abridging the freedom of speech, or of the press; or the right of the people peaceably to assemble, and to petition the Government for a redress of grievances.

## Article II

**[Right of people to bear arms not to be infringed.]** A well regulated militia, being necessary to the security of a free State, the right of the people to keep and bear arms, shall not be infringed.

## Article III

**[Quartering of troops.]** No soldier shall, in time of peace be quartered in any house, without the consent of the owner, nor in time of war, but in a manner to be prescribed by law.

## Article IV

**[Persons and houses to be secure from unreasonable searches and seizures.]** The right of the people to be secure in their persons, houses, papers, and effects, against unreasonable searches and seizures, shall not be violated, and no warrants shall issue, but upon probable cause, supported by oath or affirmation, and particularly describing the place to be searched, and the persons or things to be seized.

## Article V

**[Trials for crimes; just compensation for private property taken for public use.]** No person shall be held to answer for a capital, or otherwise infamous crime, unless on a presentment or indictment of a Grand Jury, except in cases arising in the land or naval forces, or in the militia, when in actual service in time of war or public danger; nor shall any person be subject for the same offence to be twice put in jeopardy of life or limb; nor shall be compelled in any criminal case to be a witness, against himself, nor be deprived of life, liberty, or property, without due process of law; nor shall private property be taken for public use, without just compensation.

## Article VI

**[Civil rights in trials for crimes enumerated.]** In all criminal prosecutions, the accused shall enjoy the right to a speedy and public trial, by an impartial jury of the State and district wherein the crime shall have been committed, which district shall have been previously ascertained by law, and to be informed of the nature and cause of the accusation;

to be confronted with the witnesses against him; to have compulsory process for obtaining witnesses in his favor, and to have the assistance of counsel for his defense.

## Article VII

**[Civil rights in civil suits.]** In suits at common law, where the value in controversy shall exceed twenty dollars, the right of trial by jury shall be preserved, and no fact tried by a jury, shall be otherwise re-examined in any court of the United States, than according to the rules of the common law.

## Article VIII

**[Excessive bail, fines, and punishments prohibited.]** Excessive bail shall not be required, nor excessive fines imposed, nor cruel and unusual punishments inflicted.

## Article IX

**[Reserved rights of people.]** The enumeration in the Constitution, of certain rights, shall not be construed to deny or disparage others retained by the people.

## Article X

**[Powers not delegated, reserved to states and people respectively.]** The powers not delegated to the United States by the Constitution, nor prohibited by it to the States, are reserved to the States, respectively, or to the people.

## Article XI

(The proposed amendment was sent to the states Mar. 5, 1794, by the Third Congress. It was ratified Feb. 7, 1795.)

**[Judicial power of United States not to extend to suits against a State.]** The judicial power of the United States shall not be contrued to extend to any suit in law or equity, commenced or prosecuted against one of the United States by citizens of another State, or by citizens or subjects of any foreign state.

## Article XII

(The proposed amendment was sent to the states Dec. 12, 1803, by the Eighth Congress. It was ratified July 27, 1804.)

**[Present mode of electing President and Vice-President by electors.[1]]** The electors shall meet in their respective states, and vote by ballot for President and Vice President, one of whom, at least, shall not be an inhabitant of the same state with themselves; they shall name in their ballots the person voted for as President, and in distinct ballots the person voted for as Vice President, and they shall make distinct lists of all persons voted for as President, and of all persons voted for as Vice President, and of the number of votes for each, which lists they shall sign and certify, and transmit sealed to the seat of the government of the United States, directed to the President of the Senate; the President of the Senate shall, in the presence of the Senate and House of Representatives, open all the certificates and the votes shall then be counted; the person having the greatest number of votes for President, shall be the President, if such number be a majority of the whole number of electors appointed; and if no person have such majority, then from the persons having the highest numbers not exceeding three on the list of those voted for as President, the House of Representatives shall choose immediately, by ballot, the President. But in choosing the President, the votes shall be taken by states, the representation from each State having one vote; a quorum for this purpose shall consist of a member or members from two thirds of the states, and a majority of all the states shall be necessary to a choice. And if the House of Representatives shall not choose a President whenever the right of choice shall devolve upon them, before the fourth day of March next following, then the Vice President shall act as President, as in the case of the death or other constitutional disability of the President. The person having the greatest number of votes as Vice President, shall be the Vice President, if such number be a majority of the whole number of electors appointed, and if no person have a majority, then from the two highest numbers on the list, the Senate shall choose the Vice President; a quorum for the purpose shall consist of two thirds of the whole number of Senators, and a majority of the whole number shall be necessary to a choice. But no person constitutionally ineligible to the office of President shall be eligible to that of Vice President of the United States.

## Article XIII

(The proposed amendment was sent to the states Feb. 1, 1865, by the Thirty-eighth Congress. It was ratified Dec. 6, 1865.)

### Section 1

**[Slavery prohibited.]** Neither slavery nor involuntary servitude, except as a punishment for crime whereof the party shall have been duly convicted, shall exist within the United States, or any place subject to their jurisdiction.

### Section 2

**[Congress given power to enforce this article.]** Congress shall have power to enforce this article by appropriate legislation.

## Article XIV

(The proposed amendment was sent to the states June 16, 1866, by the Thirty-ninth Congress. It was ratified July 9, 1868.)

### Section 1

**[Citizenship defined; privileges of citizens.]** All persons born or naturalized in the United States, and subject to the jurisdiction thereof, are citizens of the United States and of the State wherein they reside. No State shall make or enforce any law which shall abridge the privileges or immunities of citizens of the United States; nor shall any State deprive any person of life, liberty, or property, without due process of law; nor deny to any person within its jurisdiction the equal protection of the laws.

### Section 2

**[Apportionment of Representatives.]** Representatives shall be apportioned among the several States according to their respective numbers, counting the whole number of persons in each State, excluding Indians not taxed. But when the right to vote at any election for the choice of electors for President and Vice President of the United

States, Representatives in Congress, the executive and judicial officers of a State, or the members of the Legislature thereof, is denied to any of the male inhabitants of such State, being twenty-one years of age, and citizens of the United States, or in any way abridged, except for participation in rebellion, or other crime, the basis of representation therein shall be reduced in the proportion which the number of such male citizens shall bear to the whole number of male citizens twenty-one years of age in such State.

### Section 3

**[Disqualification for office; removal of disability.]** No person shall be a Senator or Representative in Congress, or elector of President and Vice President, or hold any office, civil or military, under the United States, or under any State, who, having previously taken an oath, as a member of Congress, or as an officer of the United States, or as a member of any State Legislature, or as an executive or judicial officer of any State, to support the Constitution of the United States, shall have engaged in insurrection or rebellion against the same, or given aid or comfort to the enemies thereof. But Congress may by a vote of two thirds of each House, remove such disability.

### Section 4

**[Public debt not to be questioned; payment of debts and claims incurred in aid of rebellion forbidden.]** The validity of the public debt of the United States, authorized by law, including debts incurred for payment of pensions and bounties for services in suppressing insurrection or rebellion, shall not be questioned. But neither the United States nor any State shall assume or pay any debt or obligation incurred in aid of insurrection or rebellion against the United States, or any claim for the loss or emancipation of any slave; but all such debts, obligations, and claims shall be held illegal and void.

### Section 5

**[Congress given power to enforce this article.]** The Congress shall have power to enforce, by appropriate legislation, the provisions of this article.

## Article XV

(The proposed amendment was sent to the states Feb. 27, 1869, by the Fortieth Congress. It was ratified Feb. 3, 1870.)

### Section 1

**[Right of certain citizens to vote established.]** The right of citizens of the United States to vote shall not be denied or abridged by the United States or by any State on account of race, color, or previous condition of servitude.

### Section 2

**[Congress given power to enforce this article.]** The Congress shall have power to enforce this article by appropriate legislation.

## Article XVI

(The proposed amendment was sent to the states July 12, 1909, by the Sixty-first Congress. It was ratified Feb. 3, 1913.)

**[Taxes on income; Congress given power to lay and collect.]** The Congress shall have power to lay and collect taxes on incomes, from whatever source derived, without apportionment among the several States, and without regard to any census or enumeration.

## Article XVII

(The proposed amendment was sent to the states May 16, 1912, by the Sixty-second Congress. It was ratified April 8, 1913.)

**[Election of United States Senators; filling of vacancies; qualifications of electors.]**

The Senate of the United States shall be composed of two Senators from each State, elected by the people thereof, for six years; and each Senator shall have one vote. The electors in each State shall have the qualifications requisite for electors of the most numerous branch of the State Legislatures.

When vacancies happen in the representation of any State in the Senate, the executive authority of such State shall issue writs of election to fill such vacancies: Provided, that the legislature of any State may empower the executive thereof to make temporary appointment until the people fill the vacancies by election as the legislature may direct.

This amendment shall not be so construed as to affect the election or term of any Senator chosen before it becomes valid as part of the Constitution.

## Article XVIII[2]

(The proposed amendment was sent to the states Dec. 18, 1917, by the Sixty-fifth Congress. It was ratified by three quarters of the states by Jan. 16, 1919, and became effective Jan. 16, 1920.)

### Section 1

**[Manufacture, sale, or transportation of intoxicating liquors, for beverage purposes, prohibited.]** After one year from the ratification of this article the manufacture, sale, or transportation of intoxicating liquors within, the importation thereof into, or the exportation thereof from the United States and all territory subject to the jurisdiction thereof for beverage purposes is hereby prohibited.

### Section 2

**[Congress and the several States given concurrent power to pass appropriate legislation to enforce this article.]** The Congress and the several States shall have concurrent power to enforce this article by appropriate legislation.

### Section 3

**[Provisions of article to become operative, when adopted by three fourths of the States.]** This article shall be inoperative unless it shall have been ratified as an amendment to the Constitution by the legislatures of the several States, as provided in the Constitution, within seven years from the date of the submission hereof to the States by Congress.

## Article XIX

(The proposed amendment was sent to the states June 4, 1919, by the Sixty-sixth Congress. It was ratified Aug. 18, 1920.)

**[The right of citizens to vote shall not be denied because of sex.]** The right of citizens of the United States to vote shall not be denied or abridged by the United States or by any State on account of sex.

**[Congress given power to enforce this article.]** Congress shall have power to enforce this article by appropriate legislation.

## Article XX

(The proposed amendment, sometimes called the "Lame Duck Amendment," was sent to the states Mar. 3, 1932, by the Seventy-second Congress. It was ratified Jan. 23, 1933; but, in accordance with Section 5, Sections 1 and 2 did not go into effect until Oct. 15, 1933.)

### Section 1

**[Terms of President, Vice President, Senators, and Representatives.]** The terms of the President and Vice President shall end at noon on the twentieth day of January, and the terms of Senators and Representatives at noon on the third day of January, of the years in which such terms would have ended if this article had not been ratified; and the terms of their successors shall then begin.

### Section 2

**[Time of assembling Congress.]** The Congress shall assemble at least once in every year, and such meeting shall begin at noon on the third day of January, unless they shall by law appoint a different day.

### Section 3

**[Filling vacancy in office of President.]** If, at the time fixed for the beginning of the term of the President, the President-elect shall have died, the Vice President-elect shall become President. If a President shall not have been chosen before the time fixed for the beginning of his term, or if the President-elect shall have failed to qualify, then the Vice President shall have qualified; and the Congress may by law provide for the case wherein neither a President-elect nor a Vice President-elect shall have qualified, declaring who shall then act as President, or the manner in which one who is to act shall be selected, and such person shall act accordingly until a President or Vice President shall have qualified.

### Section 4

**[Power of Congress in Presidential succession.]** The Congress may by law provide for the case of the death of any of the persons from whom the House of Representatives may choose a President whenever the right of choice shall have devolved upon them, and for the case of the death of any of the persons from whom the Senate may choose a Vice President whenever the right of choice shall have devolved upon them.

### Section 5

**[Time of taking effect.]** Sections 1 and 2 shall take effect on the 15th day of October following the ratification of this article.

### Section 6

**[Ratification.]** This article shall be inoperative unless it shall have been ratified as an amendment to the Constitution by the legislatures of three fourths of the several States within seven years from the date of its submission.

## Article XXI

(The proposed amendment was sent to the states Feb. 20, 1933, by the Seventy-second Congress. It was ratified Dec. 5, 1933.)

### Section 1

**[Repeal of Prohibition Amendment.]** The eighteenth article of amendment to the Constitution of the United States is hereby repealed.

### Section 2

**[Transportation of intoxicating liquors.]** The transportation or importation into any State, territory, or possession of the United States for delivery or use therein of intoxicating liquors, in violation of the laws thereof, is hereby prohibited.

### Section 3

**[Ratification.]** This article shall be inoperative unless it shall have been ratified as an amendment to the Constitution by convention in the several States, as provided in the Constitution, within seven years from the date of the submission thereof to the States by the Congress.

## Article XXII

(The proposed amendment was sent to the states Mar. 21, 1947, by the Eightieth Congress. It was ratified Feb. 27, 1951.)

### Section 1

**[Limit to number of terms a President may serve.]** No person shall be elected to the office of the President more than twice, and no person who has held the office of President, or acted as President, for more than two years of a term to which some other person was elected President shall be elected to the office of the President more than once. But this article shall not apply to any person holding the office of President when this article was proposed by the Congress, and shall not prevent any person who may be holding the office of President, or acting as President, during the term within which this article becomes operative from holding the office of President or acting as President during the remainder of such term.

### Section 2

**[Ratification.]** This article shall be inoperative unless it shall have been ratified as an amendment to the Constitution by the legislatures of three fourths of the several States within seven years from the date of its submission to the States by the Congress.

## Article XXIII

(The proposed amendment was sent to the states June 16, 1960, by the Eighty-sixth Congress. It was ratified March 29, 1961.)

### Section 1

**[Electors for the District of Columbia.]** The District constituting the seat of Government of the United States shall appoint in such manner as the Congress may direct:

A number of electors of President and Vice President equal to the whole number of Senators and Representatives in Congress to which the District would be entitled if it were a State, but in no event more than the least populous State; they shall be in addition to those appointed by the States, but they shall be considered, for the purposes of the election of President and Vice President, to be electors appointed by a State; and they shall meet in the District and perform such duties as provided by the twelfth article of amendment.

### Section 2

**[Congress given power to enforce this article.]** The Congress shall have the power to enforce this article by appropriate legislation.

## Article XXIV

(The proposed amendment was sent to the states Aug. 27, 1962, by the Eighty-seventh Congress. It was ratified Jan. 23, 1964.)

### Section 1

**[Payment of poll tax or other taxes not to be prerequisite for voting in federal elections.]** The right of citizens of the United States to vote in any primary or other election for President of Vice President, for electors for President or Vice President, or for Senator or Representative in Congress, shall not be denied or abridged by the United States or any State by reasons of failure to pay any poll tax or other tax.

### Section 2

**[Congress given power to enforce this article.]** The Congress shall have the power to enforce this article by appropriate legislation.

## Article XXV

(The proposed amendment was sent to the states July 6, 1965, by the Eighty-ninth Congress. It was ratified Feb. 10, 1967.)

### Section 1

**[Succession of Vice President to Presidency.]** In case of the removal of the President from office or of his death or resignation, the Vice President shall become President.

### Section 2

**[Vacancy in office of Vice President.]** Whenever there is a vacancy in the office of the Vice President, the President shall nominate a Vice President who shall take office upon confirmation by a majority vote of both Houses of Congress.

### Section 3

**[Vice President as Acting President.]** Whenever the President transmits to the President pro tempore of the Senate and the Speaker of the House of Representatives his written declaration that he is unable to discharge the powers and duties of his office, and until he transmits to them a written declaration to the contrary, such powers and duties shall be discharged by the Vice President as Acting President.

### Section 4

**[Vice President as Acting President.]** Whenever the Vice President and a majority of either the principal officers of the executive departments or of such other body as Congress may by law provide, transmit to the President pro tempore of the Senate and the Speaker of the House of Representatives their written declaration that the President is unable to discharge the powers and duties of his office, the Vice President shall immediately assume the powers and duties of the office as Acting President.

Thereafter, when the President transmits to the President pro tempore of the Senate and the Speaker of the House of Representatives his written declaration that no inability exists, he shall resume the powers and duties of his office unless the Vice President and a majority of either the principal officers of the executive department or of such other body as Congress may by law provide, transmit within four days to the President pro tempore of the Senate and the Speaker of the House of Representatives their written declaration that the President is unable to discharge the powers and duties of his office. Thereupon Congress shall decide the issue, asssembling within forty-eight hours for that purpose if not in session. If the Congress, within twenty-one days after receipt of the latter written declaration, or, if Congress is not in session, within twenty-one days after Congress is required to assemble, determines by two thirds vote of both Houses that the President is unable to discharge the powers and duties of his office, the Vice President shall continue to discharge the same as Acting President; otherwise, the President shall resume the powers and duties of his office.

## Article XXVI

(The proposed amendment was sent to the states Mar. 23, 1971, by the Ninety-second Congress. It was ratified July 1, 1971.)

### Section 1

**[Voting for 18-year-olds.]** The right of citizens of the United States, who are 18 years of age or older, to vote shall not be denied or abridged by the United States or by any state on account of age.

### Section 2

**[Congress given power to enforce this article.]** The Congress shall have power to enforce this article by appropriate legislation.

1. Amended by the 20th Amendment, Sections 3 and 4. 2. Repealed by the 21st Amendment.

## The White House

*Source:* Department of the Interior, U.S. National Park Service.

The White House, the official residence of the President, is at 1600 Pennsylvania Avenue in Washington, D.C. The site, covering about 18 acres, was selected by President Washington and Pierre Charles L'Enfant, and the architect was James Hoban. The design of the residence is said to have been suggested by the Duke of Leinster's house in Ireland. The cornerstone was laid Oct. 13, 1792, and the first residents were President and Mrs. John Adams in November 1800. The building was fired by the British in 1814. The sandstone exterior was painted white during the course of the reconstruction.

From December 1948 to March 1952, the interior of the White House was rebuilt, and the outer walls were strengthened.

The rooms for public functions are on the first floor; on the second and third are the President's apartments. The most celebrated public room is the East Room, where formal receptions take place. Other public rooms are the Red Room, the Green Room, and the Blue Room. The State Dining Room is used for formal dinners. There are 132 rooms.

# The Mayflower Compact

On Sept. 6, 1620, the *Mayflower,* a sailing vessel of about 180 tons, started her memorable voyage from Plymouth, England, with about 100[1] pilgrims aboard, bound for Virginia to establish a private permanent colony in North America. Arriving at what is now Provincetown, Mass., on Nov. 11 (Nov. 21, new style calendar), 41 of the passengers signed the famous "Mayflower Compact" as the boat lay at anchor in that Cape Cod harbor. A small detail of the pilgrims, led by William Bradford, assigned to select a place for permanent settlement landed at what is now Plymouth, Mass., on Dec. 21 (n.s.).

The text of the compact follows:

> In the name of God, Amen. We, whose names are underwritten, the Loyal Subjects of our dread Sovereign Lord, King *James,* by the Grace of God, of *Great Britain, France* and *Ireland,* King, *Defender of the Faith,* &,
> Having undertaken for the Glory of God, and Advancement of the Christian Faith, and the Honour of our King and Country, a voyage to plant the first colony in the northern Parts of Virginia; do by these Presents, solemnly and mutually in the Presence of God and one of another, covenant and combine ourselves together into a civil Body Politick, for our better Ordering and Preservation, and Furtherance of the Ends aforesaid; And by Virtue hereof to enact, constitute, and frame, such just and equal Laws, Ordinances, Acts, Constitutions and Offices, from time to time, as shall be thought most meet and convenient for the General good of the Colony; unto which we promise all due Submission and Obedience.
> In Witness whereof we have hereunto subscribed our names at *Cape Cod* the eleventh of *November,* in the Reign of our Sovereign Lord, King *James* of *England, France* and *Ireland,* the eighteenth, and of *Scotland* the fifty-fourth. *Anno Domini,* 1620

John Carver
Digery Priest
William Brewster
Edmund Margesson
John Alden
George Soule
James Chilton
Francis Cooke
Moses Fletcher
John Ridgate
Christopher Martin
William Mullins
Thomas English
John Howland
Stephen Hopkins
Edward Winslow
Gilbert Winslow
Miles Standish
Richard Bitteridge
Francis Eaton
John Tilly
John Billington
Thomas Tinker
Samuel Fuller
Richard Clark
John Allerton
Richard Warren
Edward Liester
William Bradford
Thomas Williams
Isaac Allerton
Peter Brown
John Turner
Edward Tilly
John Craxton
Thomas Rogers
John Goodman
Edward Fuller
Richard Gardiner
William White
Edward Doten

1. Historians differ as to whether 100, 101, or 102 passengers were abroad.

# The Monroe Doctrine

The Monroe Doctrine was announced in President James Monroe's message to Congress, during his second term on Dec. 2, 1823, in part as follows:

"In the discussions to which this interest has given rise, and in the arrangements by which they may terminate, the occasion has been deemed proper for asserting as a principle in which rights and interests of the United States are involved, that the American continents, by the free and independent condition which they have assumed and maintain, are henceforth not to be considered as subjects for future colonization by any European power. . . . We owe it, therefore, to candor and to the amicable relations existing between the United States and those powers to declare that we should consider any attempt on their part to extend their system to any portion of this hemisphere as dangerous to our peace and safety. With the existing colonies or dependencies of any European power we have not interfered and shall not interfere. But with the governments who have declared their independence and maintain it, and whose independence we have, on great consideration and on just principles, acknowledged, we could not view any interposition for the purpose of oppressing them or controlling in any other manner their destiny by any European power in any other light than as the manifestation of an unfriendly disposition toward the United States."

## Order of Presidential Succession

1. The Vice President
2. Speaker of the House
3. President pro tempore of the Senate
4. Secretary of State
5. Secretary of the Treasury
6. Secretary of Defense
7. Attorney General
8. Secretary of the Interior
9. Secretary of Agriculture
10. Secretary of Commerce
11. Secretary of Labor
12. Secretary of Health, Education, and Welfare
13. Secretary of Housing and Urban Development
14. Secretary of Transportation
15. Secretary of Energy

NOTE: An official cannot succeed to the Presidency unless he meets the Constitutional requirements.

## The Early Congresses

At the urging of Massachusetts and Virginia, the First Continental Congress met in Philadelphia on Sept. 5, 1774, and was attended by representatives of all the colonies except Georgia. Patrick Henry of Virginia declared: "The distinctions between Pennsylvanians, New Yorkers and New Englanders are no more. I am not a Virginian but an American." This Congress, which adjourned Oct. 26, 1774, passed intercolonial resolutions calling for extensive boycott by the colonies against British trade.

The following year, most of the delegates from the colonies were chosen by popular election to attend the Second Continental Congress, which assembled in Philadelphia on May 10. As war had already begun between the colonies and England, the chief problems before the Congress were the procuring of military supplies, the establishment of an army and proper defenses, the issuing of continental bills of credit, etc. On June 15, 1775, George Washington was elected to command the Continental army. Congress adjourned Dec. 12, 1776.

Other Continental Congresses were held in Baltimore (1776–77), Philadelphia (1777), Lancaster, Pa. (1777), York, Pa. (1777–78), and Philadelphia (1778–81).

In 1781, the Articles of Confederation, although establishing a league of the thirteen states rather than a strong central government, provided for the continuance of Congress. Known thereafter as the Congress of the Confederation, it held sessions in Philadelphia (1781–83), Princeton, N.J. (1783), Annapolis, Md. (1783–84), and Trenton, N.J. (1784). Five sessions were held in New York City between the years 1785 and 1789.

The Congress of the United States, established by the ratification of the Constitution, held its first meeting on March 4, 1789, in New York City. Several sessions of Congress were held in Philadelphia, and the first meeting in Washington, D.C., was on Nov. 17, 1800.

## Presidents of the Continental Congresses

| Name | Elected | Born | Died |
|---|---|---|---|
| Peyton Randolph, Va. | Sept. 5, 1774 | c.1721 | 1775 |
| Henry Middleton, S.C. | Oct. 22, 1774 | 1717 | 1784 |
| Peyton Randolph, Va. | May 10, 1775 | c.1721 | 1775 |
| John Hancock, Mass. | May 24, 1775 | 1737 | 1793 |
| Henry Laurens, S.C. | Nov. 1, 1777 | 1724 | 1792 |
| John Jay, N.Y. | Dec. 10, 1778 | 1745 | 1829 |
| Samuel Huntington, Conn. | Sept. 28, 1779 | 1731 | 1796 |
| Thomas McKean, Del. | July 10, 1781 | 1734 | 1817 |
| John Hanson, Md. | Nov. 5, 1781 | 1715 | 1783 |
| Elias Boudinot, N.J. | Nov. 4, 1782 | 1740 | 1821 |
| Thomas Mifflin, Pa. | Nov. 3, 1783 | 1744 | 1800 |
| Richard Henry Lee, Va. | Nov. 30, 1784 | 1732 | 1794 |
| John Hancock, Mass.[1] | Nov. 23, 1785 | 1737 | 1793 |
| Nathaniel Gorham, Mass. | June 6, 1786 | 1738 | 1796 |
| Arthur St. Clair, Pa. | Feb. 2, 1787 | 1734 | 1818 |
| Cyrus Griffin, Va. | Jan. 22, 1788 | 1748 | 1810 |

1. Resigned May 29, 1786, never having served, because of continued illness.

## The Great Seal of the U.S.

On July 4, 1776, the Continental Congress appointed a committee consisting of Benjamin Franklin, John Adams, and Thomas Jefferson "to bring in a device for a seal of the United States of America." After many delays, a verbal description of a design by William Barton was finally approved by Congress on June 20, 1782. The seal shows an American bald eagle with a ribbon in its mouth bearing the device *E pluribus unum* (One out of many). In its talons are the arrows of war and an olive branch of peace.

## The Liberty Bell

The Liberty Bell was cast in England in 1752 for the Pennsylvania Statehouse (now named Independence Hall) in Philadelphia. It was recast in Philadelphia in 1753. It is inscribed with the words, "Proclaim liberty throughout all the land unto all the inhabitants thereof" (Lev. 25:10). The bell was rung on July 8, 1776, for the first public reading of the Declaration of Independence. Hidden in Allentown during the British occupation of Philadelphia, it was replaced in Independence Hall in 1778. The bell cracked on July 8, 1835, while tolling the death of Chief Justice John Marshall. In 1976 the Liberty Bell was moved to a special exhibition building near Independence Hall.

# The Star-Spangled Banner

*Francis Scott Key, 1814*

O say, can you see, by the dawn's early light,
What so proudly we hail'd at the twilight's last gleaming?
Whose broad stripes and bright stars, thro' the perilous fight,
O'er the ramparts we watch'd, were so gallantly streaming?
And the rockets' red glare, the bombs bursting in air,
Gave proof thro' the night that our flag was still there.
O say, does that star-spangled banner yet wave
O'er the land of the free and the home of the brave?

On the shore dimly seen thro' the mists of the deep,
Where the foe's haughty host in dread silence reposes,
What is that which the breeze, o'er the towering steep,
As it fitfully blows, half conceals, half discloses?
Now it catches the gleam of the morning's first beam,
In full glory reflected, now shines on the stream:
'T is the star-spangled banner: O, long may it wave
O'er the land of the free and the home of the brave!

And where is that band who so vauntingly swore
That the havoc of war and the battle's confusion,
A home and a country should leave us no more?
Their blood has wash'd out their foul footsteps' pollution.
No refuge could save the hireling and slave
From the terror of flight or the gloom of the grave:
And the star-spangled banner in triumph doth wave
O'er the land of the free and the home of the brave.

O thus be it ever when free-men shall stand
Between their lov'd home and the war's desolation;
Blest with vict'ry and peace, may the heav'n-rescued land
Praise the Pow'r that hath made and preserv'd us a nation!
Then conquer we must, when our cause it is just,
And this be our motto: "In God is our trust!"
And the star-spangled banner in triumph shall wave
O'er the land of the free and the home of the brave!

On Sept. 13, 1814, Francis Scott Key visited the British fleet in Chesapeake Bay to secure the release of Dr. William Beanes, who had been captured after the burning of Washington, D.C. The release was secured, but Key was detained on ship overnight during the shelling of Fort McHenry, one of the forts defending Baltimore. In the morning, he was so delighted to see the American flag still flying over the fort that he began a poem to commemorate the occasion. Entitled "The Star-Spangled Banner," the poem soon attained wide popularity as sung to the tune "To Anacreon in Heaven." The origin of this tune is obscure, but it may have been written by John Stafford Smith, a British composer born in 1750. "The Star-Spangled Banner" was officially made the National Anthem by Congress in 1931, although it had been already adopted as such by the Army and the Navy.

# The Emancipation Proclamation

**January 1, 1863**

By the President of the United States of America:

A Proclamation.

Whereas on the 22d day of September, A.D. 1862, a proclamation was issued by the President of the United States, containing, among other things, the following, to wit:

"That on the 1st day of January, A.D. 1863, all persons held as slaves within any State or designated part of a State the people whereof shall then be in rebellion against the United States shall be then, thenceforward, and forever free; and the executive government of the United States, including the military and naval authority thereof, will recognize and maintain the freedom of such persons and will do no act or acts to repress such persons, or any of them, in any efforts they may make for their actual freedom.

"That the executive will on the 1st day of January aforesaid, by proclamation, designate the States and parts of States, if any, in which the people thereof, respectively, shall then be in rebellion against the United States; and the fact that any State or the people thereof shall on that day be in good faith represented in the Congress of the United States by members chosen thereto at elections wherein a majority of the qualified voters of such States shall have participated shall, in the absence of strong countervailing testimony, be deemed conclusive evidence that such State and the people thereof are not then in rebellion against the United States."

Now, therefore, I, Abraham Lincoln, President

of the United States, by virtue of the power in me vested as Commander-in-Chief of the Army and Navy of the United States in time of actual armed rebellion against the authority and government of the United States, and as a fit and necessary war measure for suppressing said rebellion, do, on this 1st day of January, A.D. 1863, and in accordance with my purpose so to do, publicly proclaimed for the full period of one hundred days from the first day above mentioned, order and designate as the States and parts of States wherein the people thereof, respectively, are this day in rebellion against the United States the following, to wit:

Arkansas, Texas, Louisiana (except the parishes of St. Bernard, Plaquemines, Jefferson, St. John, St. Charles, St. James, Ascension, Assumption, Terrebonne, Lafourche, St. Mary, St. Martin, and Orleans, including the city of New Orleans), Mississippi, Alabama, Florida, Georgia, South Carolina, North Carolina, and Virginia (except the forty-eight counties designated as West Virginia, and also the counties of Berkeley, Accomac, Northhampton, Elizabeth City, York, Princess Anne, and Norfolk, including the cities of Norfolk and Portsmouth), and which excepted parts are for the present left precisely as if this proclamation were not issued.

And by virtue of the power and for the purpose aforesaid, I do order and declare that all persons held as slaves within said designated States and parts of States are, and henceforward shall be, free; and that the Executive Government of the United States, including the military and naval authorities thereof, will recognize and maintain the freedom of said persons.

And I hereby enjoin upon the people so declared to be free to abstain from all violence, unless in necessary self-defense; and I recommend to them that, in all cases when allowed, they labor faithfully for reasonable wages.

And I further declare and make known that such persons of suitable condition will be received into the armed service of the United States to garrison forts, positions, stations, and other places, and to man vessels of all sorts in said service.

And upon this act, sincerely believed to be an act of justice, warranted by the Constitution upon military necessity, I invoke the considerate judgment of mankind and the gracious favor of Almighty God.

## The Confederate States of America

| State | Seceded from Union | Readmitted to Union[1] |
|---|---|---|
| 1. South Carolina | Dec. 20, 1860 | July 9, 1868 |
| 2. Mississippi | Jan. 9, 1861 | Feb. 23, 1870 |
| 3. Florida | Jan. 10, 1861 | June 25, 1868 |
| 4. Alabama | Jan. 11, 1861 | July 13, 1868 |
| 5. Georgia | Jan. 19, 1861 | July 15, 1870[2] |
| 6. Louisiana | Jan. 26, 1861 | July 9, 1868 |
| 7. Texas | March 2, 1861 | March 30, 1870 |
| 8. Virginia | April 17, 1861 | Jan. 26, 1870 |
| 9. Arkansas | May 6, 1861 | June 22, 1868 |
| 10. North Carolina | May 20, 1861 | July 4, 1868 |
| 11. Tennessee | June 8, 1861 | July 24, 1866 |

1. Date of readmission to representation in U.S. House of Representatives. 2. Second readmission date. First date was July 21, 1868, but the representatives were unseated March 5, 1869. NOTE: Four other slave states—Delaware, Kentucky, Maryland, and Missouri—remained in the Union.

## Lincoln's Gettysburg Address

The Battle of Gettysburg, one of the most noted battles of the Civil War, was fought on July 1, 2, and 3, 1863. On Nov. 19, 1863, the field was dedicated as a national cemetery by President Lincoln in a two-minute speech that was to become immortal. At the time of its delivery the speech was relegated to the inside pages of the papers, while a two-hour address by Edward Everett, the leading orator of the time, caught the headlines.

The following is the text of the address revised by President Lincoln from his own notes:

Fourscore and seven years ago our fathers brought forth on this continent a new nation conceived in liberty and dedicated to the proposition that all men are created equal. Now we are engaged in a great civil war testing whether that nation, or any nation so conceived and so dedicated, can long endure. We are met on a great battlefield of that war. We have come to dedicate a portion of that field as a final resting-place for those who here gave their lives that that nation might live. It is altogether fitting and proper that we should do this. But, in a larger sense, we cannot dedicate, we cannot consecrate, we cannot hallow this ground. The brave men, living and dead, who struggled here have consecrated it far above our poor power to add or detract. The world will little note nor long remember what we say here, but it can never forget what they did here. It is for us the living rather to be dedicated here to the unfinished work which they who fought here have thus far so nobly advanced. It is rather for us to be here dedicated to the great task remaining before us—that from these honored dead we take increased devotion to that cause for which they gave the last full measure of devotion—that we here highly resolve that these dead shall not have died in vain, that this nation under God shall have a new birth of freedom, and that government of the people, by the people, for the people shall not perish from the earth.

# History of the Flag

*Source: Encyclopaedia Britannica.*

The first official American flag, the Continental or Grand Union flag, was displayed on Prospect Hill, Jan. 1, 1776, in the American lines besieging Boston. It had 13 alternate red and white stripes, with the British Union Jack in the upper left corner.

On June 14, 1777, the Continental Congress adopted the design for a new flag, which actually was the Continental flag with the red cross of St. George and the white cross of St. Andrew replaced on the blue field by 13 stars, one for each state. No rule was made as to the arrangement of the stars, and while they were usually shown in a circle, there were various other designs. It is uncertain when the new flag was first flown, but its first official announcement is believed to have been on Sept. 3, 1777.

The first public assertion that Betsy Ross made the first Stars and Stripes appeared in a paper read before the Historical Society of Pennsylvania on March 14, 1870, by William J. Canby, a grandson. However, Mr. Canby on later investigation found no official documents of any action by Congress on the flag before June 14, 1777. Betsy Ross's own story, according to her daughter, was that Washington, Robert Morris, and George Ross, as representatives of Congress, visited her in Philadelphia in June 1776, showing her a rough draft of the flag and asking her if she could make one. However, the only actual record of the manufacture of flags by Betsy Ross is a voucher in Harrisburg, Pa., for 14 pounds and some shillings for flags for the Pennsylvania navy.

On Jan. 13, 1794, Congress voted to add two stars and two stripes to the flag in recognition of the admission of Vermont and Kentucky to the Union. By 1818, there were 20 states in the Union, and as it was obvious that the flag would soon become unwieldly, Congress voted April 18 to return to the original 13 stripes and to indicate the admission of a new state simply by the addition of a star the following July 4. The 49th star, for Alaska, was added July 4, 1959; and the 50th star, for Hawaii, was added July 4, 1960.

The first Confederate flag, adopted in 1861 by the Confederate convention in Montgomery, Ala., was called the Stars and Bars; but because of its similarity in colors to the American flag, there was much confusion in the Battle of Bull Run. To remedy this situation, Gen. G. T. Beauregard suggested a battle flag, which was used by the Southern armies throughout the war. The flag consisted of a red field on which was placed a blue cross of St. Andrew separated from the field by a white fillet and adorned with 13[1] white stars for the Confederate states. In May 1863, at Richmond, an official flag was adopted by the Confederate Congress. This flag was white and twice as long as wide; the union, two-thirds the width of the flag, contained the battle flag designed for Gen. Beauregard. A broad transverse stripe of red was added Feb. 4, 1865, so that the flag might not be mistaken for a signal of truce.

1. 11 states formally seceded, and unofficial groups in Kentucky and Missouri adopted ordinances of secession. On this basis, these two states were admitted to the Confederacy, although the official state governments remained in the Union.

# Flag Etiquette (Public Law 829—77th Congress)

**Joint Resolution**

**Public Law 94–344, approved July 7, 1976: To amend the joint resolution entitled "Joint resolution to codify and emphasize existing rules and customs pertaining to the display and use of the flag of the United States of America."**

*Resolved by the Senate and House of Representatives of the United States of America in Congress Assembled,* That Public Law Numbered 623, approved June 22, 1942, entitled "Joint resolution to codify and emphasize existing rules and customs pertaining to the display and use of the flag of the United States of America," be, and the same is hereby amended to read as follows:

That the following codification of existing rules and customs pertaining to the display and use of the flag of the United States of America be, and it is hereby, established for the use of such civilians or civilian groups or organizations as may not be required to conform with regulations promulgated by one or more executive departments of the Government of the United States. The flag of the United States for the purpose of this chapter shall be defined according to title 4, United States Code, chapter 1, section 1 and section 2 and Executive Order 10834 issued pursuant thereto.

Sec. 2. *(a)* It is the universal custom to display the flag only from sunrise to sunset on buildings and on stationary flagstaffs in the open. However, when a patriotic effect is desired, the flag may be displayed twenty-four hours a day if properly illuminated during the hours of darkness.

*(b)* The flag should be hoisted briskly and lowered ceremoniously.

*(c)* The flag should not be displayed on days when the weather is inclement, except when an all-weather flag is displayed.

*(d)* The flag should be displayed on all days, especially on New Year's Day, January 1; Inauguration Day, January 20; Lincoln's Birthday, February 12; Washington's Birthday, third Monday in February; Easter Sunday (variable); Mother's Day, second Sunday in May; Armed Forces Day, third Saturday in May; Memorial Day (half-staff until noon), the last Monday in May; Flag Day, June 14; Independence Day, July 4; Labor Day, first Monday in September; Constitution Day, September 17; Columbus Day, second Monday in October; Navy Day, October 27; Veterans Day, November 11; Thanksgiving Day, fourth Thursday in November; Christmas Day, December 25; and such other days as may be proclaimed by the President of the

NOTE: On July 5, 1968, a law was enacted making it a federal crime to desecrate the U.S. flag by knowingly casting contempt on it, by publicly mutilating or burning it, etc. The offense is punishable by a $1,000 fine and/or a year in prison.

United States; the birthdays of States (date of admission); and on state holidays.

*(e)* The flag should be displayed daily on or near the main administration building of every public institution.

*(f)* The flag should be displayed in or near every polling place on election days.

*(g)* The flag should be displayed during school days in or near every schoolhouse.

Sec. 3. That the flag, when carried in a procession with another flag or flags, should be either on the marching right; that is, the flag's own right, or, if there is a line of other flags, in front of the center of that line.

*(a)* The flag should not be displayed on a float in a parade except from a staff, or as provided in subsection *(i)*.

*(b)* The flag should not be draped over the hood, top, sides, or back of a vehicle or of a railroad train or a boat. When the flag is displayed on a motorcar, the staff shall be fixed firmly to the chassis or clamped to the right fender.

*(c)* No other flag or pennant should be placed above or, if on the same level, to the right of the flag of the United States of America, except during church services conducted by naval chaplains at sea, when the church pennant may be flown above the flag during church services for the personnel of the Navy. No person shall display the flag of the United Nations or any other national or international flag equal, above, or in a position of superior prominence or honor to, or in place of, the flag of the United States at any place within the United States or any Territory or possession thereof: *Provided,* That nothing in this section shall make unlawful the continuance of the practice heretofore followed of displaying the flag of the United Nations in a position of superior prominence or honor, and other national flags in positions of equal prominence or honor, with that of the flag of the United States at the headquarters of the United Nations.[1]

*(d)* The flag of the United States of America, when it is displayed with another flag against a wall from crossed staffs, should be on the right, the flag's own right, and its staff should be in front of the staff of the other flag.

*(e)* The flag of the United States of America should be at the center and at the highest point of the group when a number of flags of States or localities or pennants of societies are grouped and displayed from staffs.

*(f)* When flags of States, cities, or localities, or pennants of societies are flown on the same halyard with the flag of the United States, the latter should always be at the peak. When the flags are flown from adjacent staffs, the flag of the United States should be hoisted first and lowered last. No such flag or pennant may be placed above the flag of the United States or to the United States flag's right.

*(g)* When flags of two or more nations are displayed, they are to be flown from separate staffs of the same height. The flags should be of approximately equal size. International usage forbids the display of the flag of one nation above that of another nation in time of peace.

*(h)* When the flag of the United States is displayed from a staff projecting horizontally or at an angle from the window sill, balcony, or front of a building, the union of the flag should be placed at the peak of the staff unless the flag is at half-staff. When the flag is suspended over a sidewalk from a rope extending from a house to a pole at the edge of the sidewalk, the flag should be hoisted out, union first, from the building.

*(i)* When displayed either horizontally or vertically against a wall, the union should be uppermost and to the flag's own right, that is, to the observer's left. When displayed in a window, the flag should be displayed in the same way, with the union or blue field to the left of the observer in the street.

*(j)* When the flag is displayed over the middle of the street, it should be suspended vertically with the union to the north in an east and west street or to the east in a north and south street.

*(k)* When used on a speaker's platform, the flag, if displayed flat, should be displayed above and behind the speaker. When displayed from a staff in a church or public auditorium, the flag of the United States of America should hold the position of superior prominence, in advance of the audience, and in the position of honor at the clergyman's or speaker's right as he faces the audience. Any other flag so displayed should be placed on the left of the clergyman or speaker or to the right of the audience.

*(l)* The flag should form a distinctive feature of the ceremony of unveiling a statue or monument, but it should never be used as the covering for the statue or monument.

*(m)* The flag, when flown at half-staff, should be first hoisted to the peak for an instant and then lowered to the half-staff position. The flag should be again raised to the peak before it is lowered for the day. On Memorial Day, the flag should be displayed at half-staff until noon only, then raised to the top of the staff. By order of the President, the flag shall be flown at half-staff upon the death of principal figures of the United States Government and the Governor of a State, territory, or possession, as a mark of respect to their memory. In the event of the death of other officials or foreign dignitaries, the flag is to be displayed at half-staff according to Presidential instructions or orders, or in accordance with recognized customs or practices not inconsistent with law. In the event of the death of a present or former official of the government of any State, territory, or possession of the United States, the Governor of that State, territory, or possession may proclaim that the National flag shall be flown at half-staff. The flag shall be flown at half-staff thirty days from the death of the President or a former President; ten days from the day of the death of the Vice President, the Chief Justice or a retired Chief Justice of the United States, or the Speaker of the House of Representatives; from the day of death until interment of an Associate Justice of the Supreme Court, a Secretary of an executive or military department, a former Vice President, or the Governor of a State, territory, or possession; and on the day of death and the following day for a Member of Congress.

*(n)* When the flag is used to cover a casket, it should be so placed that the union is at the head and over the left shoulder. The flag should not be lowered into the grave or allowed to touch the ground.

*(o)* When the flag is suspended across a corridor or lobby in a building with only one main entrance, it should be suspended vertically with the union of the flag to the observer's left upon entering. If the building has more than one main entrance, the flag should be suspended vertically near the center of the corridor or lobby with the union to the north,

1. Section 3 (c) was amended by Public Law 107, approved July 9, 1953, to designate the position of the United Nations flag.

when entrances are to the east and west or to the east when entrances are to the north and south. If there are entrances in more than two directions, the union should be to the east.

Sec. 4. That no disrespect should be shown to the flag of the United States of America, the flag should not be dipped to any person or thing. Regimental colors, State flags, and organization or institutional flags are to be dipped as a mark of honor.

*(a)* The flag should never be displayed with the union down, except as a signal of dire distress in instances of extreme danger to life or property.

*(b)* The flag should never touch anything beneath it, such as the ground, the floor, water, or merchandise.

*(c)* The flag should never be carried flat or horizontally, but always aloft and free.

*(d)* The flag should never be used as wearing apparel, bedding or drapery. It should never be festooned, drawn back, nor up, in folds, but always allowed to fall free. Bunting of blue, white and red, always arranged with the blue above, the white in the middle and the red below, should be used for covering a speaker's desk, draping the front of the platform and for decoration in general.

*(e)* The flag should never be fastened, displayed, used or stored in such a manner as to permit it to be easily torn, soiled or damaged in any way.

*(f)* The flag should never be used as a covering for a ceiling.

*(g)* The flag should never have placed upon it, nor on any part of it, nor attached to it any mark, insignia, letter, word, figure, design, picture, or drawing of any nature.

*(h)* The flag should never be used as a receptacle for receiving, holding, carrying, or delivering anything.

*(i)* The flag should never be used for advertising purposes in any manner whatsoever. It should not be embroidered on such articles as cushions or handkerchiefs and the like, printed or otherwise impressed on paper napkins or boxes or anything that is designed for temporary use and discard. Advertising signs should not be fastened to a staff or halyard from which the flag is flown.

*(j)* No part of the flag should ever be used as a costume or athletic uniform. However, a flag patch may be affixed to the uniform of military personnel, firemen, policemen and members of patriotic organizations. The flag represents a living country and is itself considered a living thing. Therefore, the lapel flag pin, being a replica, should be worn on the left lapel near the heart.

*(k)* The flag, when it is in such condition that it is no longer a fitting emblem for display, should be destroyed in a dignified way, preferably by burning.

Sec. 5. During the ceremony of hoisting or lowering the flag or when the flag is passing in a parade or in review, all persons present except those in uniform should face the flag and stand at attention with the right hand over the heart. Those present in uniform should render the military salute. When not in uniform, men should remove their headdress with their right hand and hold it at the left shoulder, the hand being over the heart. Aliens should stand at attention. The salute to the flag in a moving column should be rendered at the moment the flag passes.

Sec. 6. During rendition of the national anthem when the flag is displayed, all present except those in uniform should stand at attention facing the flag with the right hand over the heart. Men not in uniform should remove their headdress with their right hand and hold it at the left shoulder, the hand being over the heart. Persons in uniform should render the military salute at the first note of the anthem and retain this position until the last note. When the flag is not displayed, those present should face toward the music and act in the same manner they would if the flag were displayed there.

Sec. 7. The Pledge of Allegiance[1] to the Flag, "**I pledge allegiance to the Flag of the United States of America, and to the Republic for which it stands, one Nation under God,[2] indivisible, with liberty and justice for all.**", should be rendered by standing at attention facing the flag with the right hand over the heart. When not in uniform, men should remove their headdress with their right hand and hold it at the left shoulder, the hand being over the heart. Persons in uniform should remain silent, face the flag and render the military salute.

Sec. 8. Any rule or custom pertaining to the display of the flag of the United States of America, set forth herein, may be altered, modified or repealed, or additional rules with respect thereto may be prescribed by the Commander in Chief of the Armed Forces of the United States, whenever he deems it to be appropriate or desirable; and any such alteration or additional rule shall be set forth in a proclamation.

Approved, July 7, 1976.

1. The idea originated in 1892 with James B. Upham, an editor of *Youth's Companion.* The claim that Upham was also the author is disputed by some who credit Francis Bellamy. 2. The phrase "under God" was added to the pledge on June 14, 1954.

# Statistical History of The United States

There are many ways of looking at American history—at the growth of the United States, its people, and its economy. One of the most interesting is to examine certain aspects of American life "by the numbers." This "Statistical History" makes such an examination possible. The data below—stripped of the men and women, events, and technological changes that have shaped American society—reveal much that is often hidden in the complex folds of the fabric of history.

This section includes over 1,100 entries in over 100 categories, from population to the price of steak. Teachers, writers, and editors will find these data particularly useful as they seek to make events of a particular era more understandable.

History buffs should discover that this material can add significantly to their knowledge of the past. And browsers in *Information Please* will find that this "Statistical History" is a counterpoint to the "Headline History" that appears elsewhere in this book.

| Item | Unit | 1975 | 1970 | 1960 | 1950 | 1940 |
|---|---|---|---|---|---|---|
| 1. Population estimates[1] | thousands | 213,540 | 204,879 | 180,671[2] | 151, 684 | 132,122 |
| 2. Land area | sq miles | 3,536,855 | 3,536,855 | 3,540,911[2] | 2,974,726 | 2,977,128 |
| 3. Population per sq mile[3] | | 60.2 | 57.5 | 50.6[2] | 50.7 | 44.2 |
| 4. Median age of population | years | 28.8 | 28.1 | 29.5[2] | 30.2 | 29.0 |
| 5. Number of households | thousands | 71,120 | 63,401 | 52,799[2] | 43,554 | 34,949 |
| 6. Average household size | | 2.94 | 3.14 | 3.33[2] | 3.37 | 3.67 |
| 7. Homicides | | 21,310 | 16,848 | 8,464[2] | 7,942 | 8,329 |
| 8. Rate per 100,000 population | | 10.0 | 8.3 | 4.7[2] | 5.3 | 6.3 |
| 9. Suicides | | 27,063 | 23,480 | 19,041[2] | 17,145 | 18,907 |
| 10. Rate per 100,000 population | | 12.7 | 11.6 | 10.6[2] | 11.4 | 14.4 |
| 11. Number of immigrants | | 386,200 | 373,326 | 265,398 | 249,187 | 70,756 |
| Immigrants by selected occupations | | | | | | |
| 12. Professional[4] | | 38,500 | 46,151 | 21,940 | 20,502 | 6,802 |
| 13. Farmers[4] [5] | | 900 | 3,839 | 3,050 | 17,642 | 847 |
| 14. Skilled[4] [6] | | 38,500 | 46,622 | 34,135 | 41,450 | 5,710 |
| 15. Laborers[4] [7] | | 13,000 | 14,148 | 12,838 | 5,693 | 2,120 |
| 16. Total Gross National Product—Current prices | billion dollars | 1,516.3 | 977.1 | 503.7[2] | 284.8 | 99.7 |
| 17. Per capita Gross National Product—Current prices | dollars | 7,016 | 4,808 | 2,788[2] | 1,877 | 754 |
| Retail prices of selected foods in U.S. cities | | | | | | |
| 18. Flour—5 lb | ¢/unit shown | 99.5 | 58.9 | 55.4 | 49.1 | 21.5 |
| 19. Bread—1 lb | ¢/unit shown | 36.0 | 24.3 | 20.3 | 14.3 | 8.0 |
| 20. Round steak—1 lb | ¢/unit shown | 188.5 | 130.2 | 105.5 | 93.6 | 36.4 |
| 21. Butter—1 lb | ¢/unit shown | 102.5 | 86.6 | 74.9 | 72.9 | 36.0 |
| 22. Potatoes—10 lb | ¢/unit shown | 134.0 | 89.7 | 71.8 | 46.1 | 23.9 |
| 23. Sugar—5 lb | ¢/unit shown | 186.0 | 64.8 | 58.2 | 48.7 | 26.0 |
| 24. Total labor force[10] | thousands 16 years and over | 94,793 | 82,049 | 69,877[2] [11] | 59,643[11] | 53,011[11] |
| 25. Percent of population | | 61.8 | 59.0 | 56.1[2] [11] | 54.1[11] | 52.9[11] |
| 26. Percent of civilian labor force unemployed[13] | 10 years and over | 8.5 | 4.9 | 5.5[2] | 5.3 | 14.6 |
| Physical output of selected manufactured commodities | | | | | | |
| 27. Wheat flour | mil. bbl | — | 129.1 | 130.4 | 115.4 | 110.9 |
| 28. Beer | thou. bbl | 158,000 | 134,654 | 94,548 | 88,807 | 54,892 |
| 29. Cigarettes | millions | 627,000 | 562,154 | 506,127 | 391,956 | 189,373 |
| 30. Total raw steel | thou. short tons | 116,642 | 131,514 | 99,282 | 96,836 | 66,983 |
| 31. Total value of new construction put in place | mil. dollars | 132,043 | 94,855 | 54,738 | 33,575 | 8,682 |
| 32. Total concerns in business | thousands | 2,679 | 2,442 | 2,708 | 2,687 | 2,156 |
| 33. Business failure rate | per 10,000 listed enterprises | 43 | 44 | 57 | 34 | 63 |
| 34. Average annual earnings of employees | dollars | 10,434[17] | 7,564 | 4,743 | 2,992 | 1,299 |
| Average annual earnings per full time employee in selected industries | | | | | | |
| 35. Services[19] | current $ | 8,141[20] | 5,946 | 3,513 | 2,183 | 953 |
| 36. Agriculture, Forestry, and Fisheries | current $ | 5,756[20] | 3,063 | 1,658 | 1,282 | 407 |
| 37. Manufacturing | current $ | 10,834[20] | 8,150 | 5,352 | 3,302 | 1,432 |
| 38. Mining[21] | current $ | 12,935[20] | 9,262 | 5,676 | 3,460 | 1,388 |
| 39. Construction | current $ | 12,206[20] | 9,293 | 5,443 | 3,333 | 1,330 |
| 40. Transportation | current $ | 12,616[20] | 9,928 | 6,185 | 3,714 | 1,756 |
| 41. Communications and public utilities | current $ | 12,353[20] | 8,897 | 5,681 | 3,346 | 1,717 |
| 42. Wholesale and retail trade | current $ | 8,749[20] | 6,886 | 4,597 | 3,045 | 1,382 |
| 43. Finance, insurance, and real estate | current $ | 9,854[20] | 8,026 | 5,030 | 3,223 | 1,725 |
| 44. Government | current $ | 10,632[20] | 7,965 | 4,676 | 3,014 | 1,344 |
| 45. Total farm population | thousands | 8,864 | 9,712 | 15,635 | 23,048 | 30,547 |
| 46. Number of farms | thousands | 2,808 | 2,954 | 3,962 | 5,388 | 6,102 |
| 47. Total land in farms | mil. acres | 1,086.0 | 1,102.8 | 1,176.9 | 1,161.4 | 1,065.1 |
| 48. Total value of all farm property | mil. dollars | — | 265,744 | 167,564 | 101,117[22] | 41,829 |
| 49. Average value per farm of land and buildings | dollars | — | 70,485 | 32,854 | 14,005 | 5,532 |
| 50. Farm wages, per day, with room and board | dollars | 16.13[17] | 10.70 | 6.50 | 4.45 | 1.30 |

| 1930 | 1920 | 1910 | 1900 | 1890 | 1880 | 1870 | 1860 | 1850 | 1840 | |
|---|---|---|---|---|---|---|---|---|---|---|
| 123,188 | 106,461 | 92,407 | 76,094 | 63,056 | 50,262 | 39,905 | 31,513 | 23,261 | 17,120 | 1. |
| 2,977,128 | 2,969,451 | 2,969,565 | 2,969,834 | 2,969,640 | 2,969,640 | 2,969,640 | 2,969,640 | 2,940,042 | 1,749,462 | 2. |
| 41.2 | 35.6 | 31.0 | 25.6 | 21.2 | 16.9 | 13.4 | 10.6 | 7.9 | 9.8 | 3. |
| 26.5 | 25.3 | 24.1 | 22.9 | 22.0 | 20.9 | 20.2 | 19.4 | 18.9 | 17.8 | 4. |
| 29,905 | 24,352 | 20,256 | 15,964 | 12,690 | 9,946 | 7,579 | 5,211 | 3,598 | — | 5. |
| 4.11 | 4.34 | 4.54 | 4.76 | 4.93 | 5.04 | 5.09 | 5.28 | 5.55 | — | 6. |
| 10,331 | 5,815 | 2,161 | 230 | — | — | — | — | — | — | 7. |
| 8.8 | 6.8 | 4.6 | 1.2 | — | — | — | — | — | — | 8. |
| 18,323 | 8,790 | 7,283 | 2,036 | — | — | — | — | — | — | 9. |
| 15.6 | 10.2 | 15.3 | 10.2 | — | — | — | — | — | — | 10. |
| 241,700 | 430,001 | 1,041,570 | 448,572 | 455,302 | 457,257 | 387,203 | 179,691 | 315,337 | 92,207 | 11. |
| 8,585 | 10,540 | 9,689 | 2,392 | 3,236 | 1,773 | 1,831 | 792 | 918 | 481 | 12. |
| 8,375 | 12,192 | 11,793 | 5,433 | 29,296 | 47,204 | 35,656 | 21,742 | 42,873 | 18,476 | 13. |
| 32,474 | 55,991 | 121,847 | 54,793 | 44,540 | 49,929 | 35,698 | 19,342 | 26,369 | 10,811 | 14. |
| 18,080 | 83,496 | 216,909 | 164,261 | 139,365 | 105,012 | 84,577 | 31,268 | 46,640 | 9,640 | 15. |
| 90.4 | 91.5 | 35.3 | 18.7 | 13.1 | 11.2[8] | 7.4[9] | — | — | — | 16. |
| 734 | 860 | 382 | 246 | 208 | 205[8] | 170[9] | — | — | — | 17. |
| 23.0 | 40.5 | 18.0 | 12.5 | 14.5 | — | — | — | — | — | 18. |
| 8.6 | 11.5 | — | — | — | — | — | — | — | — | 19. |
| 42.6 | 39.5 | 17.4 | 13.2 | 12.3 | — | — | — | — | — | 20. |
| 46.4 | 70.1 | 35.9 | 26.1 | 25.5 | — | — | — | — | — | 21. |
| 36.0 | 63.0 | 17.0 | 14.0 | 16.0 | — | — | — | — | — | 22. |
| 30.5 | 97.0 | 30.0 | 30.5 | 34.5 | — | — | — | — | — | 23. |
| 48,830[12] | 41,614[12] | 38,167[12] | 29,073[12] | 23,318[12] | 17,392[12] | 12,506[12] | — | — | — | 24. |
| 49.5[12] | 50.3[12] | 53.3[12] | 50.2[12] | 49.2[12] | 47.3[12] | 44.3[12] | — | — | — | 25. |
| 8.7 | 5.2 | 5.9 | 5.0 | 4.0 | — | — | — | — | — | 26. |
| 120.6[14] | 130.4 | 107.2 | 105.8 | 83.3 | 64.3 | 47.9 | 39.8 | — | — | 27. |
| 3,681 | 9,200 | 50,500 | 39,500 | 27,000 | 18,300 | 6,600 | — | — | — | 28. |
| 124,193 | 48,091 | 9,782 | 3,870 | 2,505 | 533 | 16 | — | — | | 29 |
| 44,591 | 46,183 | 28,330 | 11,227 | — | — | — | — | — | — | 30. |
| 8,741 | 6,749 | 3,262 | — | — | — | — | — | — | — | 31. |
| 2,183 | 1,821 | 1,515 | 1,174 | 1,111 | 747 | 427 | 230[15] | — | — | 32. |
| 122[16] | 48 | 84 | 92 | 99 | 63 | 83 | 170[15] | — | — | 33. |
| 1,308 | 1,236[18] | 517[18] | 375[18] | — | — | — | — | — | — | 34. |
| 1,066 | 912 | 447 | 340 | — | — | — | — | — | — | 35. |
| 388 | 528 | 223 | 178 | — | — | — | — | — | — | 36. |
| 1,488 | 1,532 | 651 | 487 | — | — | — | — | — | — | 37. |
| 1,424 | 1,684 | 668 | 479 | — | — | — | — | — | — | 38. |
| 1,526 | 1,710 | 804 | 593 | — | — | — | — | — | — | 39. |
| 1,610 | 1,645 | 607 | 505 | — | — | — | — | — | — | 40. |
| 1,499 | 1,238 | 516 | 470 | — | — | — | — | — | — | 41. |
| 1,569 | 1,270 | 630 | 508 | — | — | — | — | — | — | 42. |
| 1,973 | 1,758 | 1,301 | 1,040 | — | — | — | — | — | — | 43. |
| 1,553 | 1,245 | 725 | 584 | — | — | — | — | — | — | 44. |
| 30,529 | 31,974 | 32,077 | 29,875 | 24,771 | 21,973 | — | — | — | — | 45. |
| 6,295 | 6,454 | 6,366 | 5,740 | 4,565 | 4,009 | 2,660 | 2,044 | 1,449 | — | 46. |
| 990.1 | 958.7 | 881.4 | 841.2 | 623.2 | 536.1 | 407.7 | 407.2 | 293.6 | — | 47. |
| 57,689 | 78,386 | 40,959 | 20,365 | 16,439 | 12,404 | 9,412 | 7,980 | 3,967 | — | 48. |
| 7,624 | 10,295 | 5,480 | 2,895 | 2,909 | 2,544 | 2,799 | 3,251 | 2,258 | — | 49. |
| 1.80 | 2.80 | 1.05 | .75[23] | .70 | .65 | .65[24] | — | — | — | 50. |

*(continued)*

| Item | Unit | 1830 | 1820 | 1810 | 1800 | 1790 |
|---|---|---|---|---|---|---|
| 1. Population estimates[1] | thousands | 12,901 | 9,618 | 7,224 | 5,297 | 3,929 |
| 2. Land area | sq miles | 1,749,462 | 1,749,462 | 1,681,828 | 864,746 | 864,746 |
| 3. Population per sq mile[3] | | 7.4 | 5.5 | 4.3 | 6.1 | 4.5 |
| 4. Median age of population | years | 17.2 | 16.7 | — | — | — |
| 5. Number of households | thousands | — | — | — | — | — |
| 6. Average household size | | — | — | — | — | 5.79 |
| 7. Homicides | | — | — | — | — | — |
| 8. Rate per 100,000 population | | — | — | — | — | — |
| 9. Suicides | | — | — | — | — | — |
| 10. Rate per 100,000 population | | — | — | — | — | — |
| 11. Number of immigrants | | 24,837 | 10,311 | — | — | — |
| Immigrants by selected occupations | | | | | | |
| 12. Professional[4] | | 136 | 105 | — | — | — |
| 13. Farmers[4 5] | | 1,424 | 874 | — | — | — |
| 14. Skilled[4 6] | | 1,745 | 1,090 | — | — | — |
| 15. Laborers[4 7] | | 720 | 334 | — | — | — |
| 16. Total Gross National Product—Current prices | billion dollars | — | — | — | — | — |
| 17. Per capita Gross National Product—Current prices | dollars | — | — | — | — | — |
| Retail prices of selected foods in U.S. cities | | | | | | |
| 18. Flour—5 lb | ¢/unit shown | — | — | — | — | — |
| 19. Bread—1 lb | ¢/unit shown | — | — | — | — | — |
| 20. Round steak—1 lb | ¢/unit shown | — | — | — | — | — |
| 21. Butter—1 lb | ¢/unit shown | — | — | — | — | — |
| 22. Potatoes—10 lb | ¢/unit shown | — | — | — | — | — |
| 23. Sugar—5 lb | ¢/unit shown | — | — | — | — | — |
| 24. Total labor force[10] | thousands 16 years and over | — | — | — | — | — |
| 25. Percent of population | | — | — | — | — | — |
| 26. Percent of civilian labor force unemployed[13] | 10 years and over | — | — | — | — | — |
| Physical output of selected manufactured commodities | | | | | | |
| 27. Wheat flour | mil. bbl | — | — | — | — | — |
| 28. Beer | thou. bbl | — | — | — | — | — |
| 29. Cigarettes | millions | — | — | — | — | — |
| 30. Total raw steel | thou. short tons | — | — | — | — | — |
| 31. Total value of new construction put in place | mil. dollars | — | — | — | — | — |
| 32. Total concerns in business | thousands | — | — | — | — | — |
| 33. Business failure rate | per 10,000 listed enterprises | — | — | — | — | — |
| 34. Average annual earnings of employees | dollars | — | — | — | — | — |
| Average annual earnings per full time employee in selected industries | | | | | | |
| 35. Services[19] | current $ | — | — | — | — | — |
| 36. Agriculture, Forestry, and Fisheries | current $ | — | — | — | — | — |
| 37. Manufacturing | current $ | — | — | — | — | — |
| 38. Mining[21] | current $ | — | — | — | — | — |
| 39. Construction | current $ | — | — | — | — | — |
| 40. Transportation | current $ | — | — | — | — | — |
| 41. Communications and public utilities | current $ | — | — | — | — | — |
| 42. Wholesale and retail trade | current $ | — | — | — | — | — |
| 43. Finance, insurance, and real estate | current $ | — | — | — | — | — |
| 44. Government | current $ | — | — | — | — | — |
| 45. Total farm population | thousands | — | — | — | — | — |
| 46. Number of farms | thousands | — | — | — | — | — |
| 47. Total land in farms | mil. acres | — | — | — | — | — |
| 48. Total value of all farm property | mil. dollars | — | — | — | — | — |
| 49. Average value per farm of land and buildings | dollars | — | — | — | — | — |
| 50. Farm wages, per day, with room and board | dollars | — | — | — | — | — |

| Item | Unit | 1975 | 1970 | 1960 | 1950 | 1940 |
|---|---|---|---|---|---|---|
| Farm Productivity | | | | | | |
| 51. Wheat—yield per acre | bushels | 31.0 | 31.0 | 25.2[25] | 17.3[26] | 17.1[27] |
| 52. Wheat—man-hours | 100 bushels | 9 | 9 | 12[25] | 27[26] | 44[27] |
| 53. Cotton—yield per acre | pounds | 473 | 438 | 475[25] | 296[26] | 260[27] |
| 54. Cotton—man-hours | bale | 23 | 26 | 47[25] | 107[26] | 182[27] |
| 55. Potatoes—yield per acre | cwt | 239.0 | 229.0 | 194.9[25] | 151.2[26] | 82.1[27] |
| 56. Potatoes—man-hours | ton | 4 | 4 | 5[25] | 8[26] | 17[27] |
| 57. Tobacco—yield per acre | pounds | 2,000 | 2,121 | 1,879[25] | 1,292[26] | 1,026[27] |
| 58. Tobacco—man-hours | 100 pounds | 14 | 23 | 26[25] | 36[26] | 43[27] |
| 59. Milk cows—milk per cow | pounds | 10,200.0 | 9,385.0 | 7,507.0[25] | 5,440.0[26] | 4,653.0[27] |
| 60. Milk cows—man-hours | cwt of milk | 0.6 | 0.7 | 1.2[25] | 2.2[26] | 3.1[27] |
| 61. Total use of electrical energy | mil. kwh | — | 1,641,731 | 848,723[2] | 396,346 | 181,706 |
| 62. Residential | mil. kwh | — | 453,015 | 196,296[2] | 72,200 | 24,068 |
| 63. Commercial | mil. kwh | — | 295,057 | 121,437[2] | 52,091 | 22,373 |
| 64. Industrial | mil. kwh | — | 685,693 | 415,699[2] | 194,835 | 92,390 |
| 65. Value of exports | mil. dollars | 107,591 | 43,265 | 20,603 | 10,816 | 4,030 |
| 66. Value of imports | mil. dollars | 96,940 | 40,189 | 15,046 | 9,125 | 7,433 |
| 67. Passenger car factory sales | thousands | 6,713.0 | 6,546.8 | 6,674.7 | 6,665.8 | 3,717.3 |
| 68. Total motor vehicle registrations | millions | 133.7 | 108.4 | 73.9 | 49.2 | 32.4 |
| 69. Miles of travel by motor vehicles | mil. miles | 1,300,100 | 1,120,705 | 718,845 | 458,246 | 302,188 |
| 70. Number of operating railroads | | 341[20] | 351 | 407[2] | 471 | 574 |
| 71. Railroad passengers | thousands | 275,000[20] | 289,469 | 327,172[2] | 488,019 | 456,088 |
| Air transportation | | | | | | |
| 72. Number of operators | | 30 | 33 | 42 | 52 | 19 |
| 73. Aircraft in service | | 2,267 | 2,437 | 1,594 | 960 | 369 |
| 74. Revenue passengers carried | thousands | 189,000[34] | 153,408[34] | 56,352[34] | 17,345[34] | 2,523[34] |
| 75. Total school enrollments—elementary and secondary | thousands | 50,562[20] | 51,319 | 41,762[2] | 28,492 | 28,045 |
| 76. High school graduates | thousands | 3,139[17] | 2,906 | 1,864 | 1,200 | 1,221 |
| 77. Percent of persons 17 years old | percent | 74.3[17] | 75.6 | 63.4 | 57.4 | 40.0 |
| 78. Total institutions of higher education | | 2,747 | 2,525 | 1,959[2] | 1,863 | 1,708 |
| 79. Bachelor's or first professional degrees conferred | | 944,000[17] | 827,234 | 389,183 | 432,058 | 186,500 |
| Radio and television | | | | | | |
| 80. Radio sets produced | thousands | — | 16,406 | 17,127 | 13,468 | 11,831 |
| 81. Households with radio sets | thousands | — | 62,000 | 50,193 | 40,700 | 28,500 |
| 82. Television sets produced | thousands | — | 4,852 | 5,708 | 7,464 | — |
| 83. Households with television sets | thousands | — | 59,550 | 45,750 | 3,875 | — |
| 84. Books published | | 39,372 | 36,071 | 15,012 | 11,022 | 11,328 |
| 85. Daily newspapers—number | | 1,756 | 1,748 | 1,763 | 1,772 | 1,878 |
| 86. Daily newspapers—circulation | thousands | 60,655 | 62,108 | 58,882 | 53,829 | 41,132 |
| 87. Telephones per 1,000 population | | 695.0 | 583.4 | 407.8 | 280.9 | 165.1 |
| 88. Average number of daily telephone conversations | thousands | 633,000 | 485,200 | 285,386 | 170,623 | 98,783 |
| 89. Patents issued for inventions | | 71,994 | 64,427 | 47,170 | 43,040 | 42,238 |
| 90. Currency in circulation | mil. dollars | 92,005.0 | 54,351.0 | 32,064.6 | 27,156.3 | 7,847.5 |
| 91. Total social welfare expenditures under public programs | mil. dollars | 286,547[38] | 145,893 | 52,293 | 23,508 | 8,795 |
| 92. Percent of GNP | percent | 19.9[38] | 15.3 | 10.6 | 8.9 | 9.2 |
| 93. Percent of all government expenditures | percent | 58.4[38] | 47.8 | 38.0 | 37.6 | 49.0 |
| 94. Per capita (actual prices) | dollars | 1,319[38] | 701 | 286 | 153 | 66 |
| 95. Per capita health expenditure | dollars | 484.73[20] | 343.44 | 146.30 | 81.86 | 29.62 |
| 96. Number of physicians | | 394,000[20] | 348,328 | 274,833[2] | 191,947 | 165,989 |
| 97. Rate per 100,000 population | | 186 | 166 | 148[2] | 128 | 126 |
| Summary of federal government finances | | | | | | |
| 98. Receipts | mil. dollars | 281,000.0 | 193,700.0 | 92,500.0 | 40,900.0 | 6,900.0 |
| 99. Outlays | mil. dollars | 324,600.0 | 196,600.0 | 92,200.0 | 43,100.0 | 9,600.0 |
| 100. Total public debt | mil. dollars | 533,200.0 | 370,918.7 | 286,300.8 | 257,357.4 | 42,967.5 |
| 101. Per capita public debt | dollars | 2,496 | 1,811 | 1,585 | 1,697 | 325 |
| 102. Paid civilian employees of the federal government | | 2,896,944 | 2,981,574 | 2,398,704 | 1,960,708 | 1,042,420 |
| 103. Military personnel on active duty[54] | | 2,127,000[55] | 3,066,294[55] | 2,476,435 | 1,460,261 | 458,365[56] |

*(continued)*

| Item | Unit | 1930 | 1920 | 1910 | 1900 |
|---|---|---|---|---|---|
| Farm Productivity | | | | | |
| 51. Wheat—yield per acre | bushels | 13.5[28] | 13.8[29] | 14.4[30] | 13.9 |
| 52. Wheat—man-hours | 100 bushels | 70[28] | 90[29] | 106[30] | 108 |
| 53. Cotton—yield per acre | pounds | 184[28] | 155[29] | 201[30] | 189 |
| 54. Cotton—man-hours | bale | 252[28] | 296[29] | 276[30] | 284 |
| 55. Potatoes—yield per acre | cwt | 64.6[28] | 64.6[29] | 59.8[30] | — |
| 56. Potatoes—man-hours | ton | 21[28] | 23[29] | 25[30] | — |
| 57. Tobacco—yield per acre | pounds | 784[28] | 773[29] | 816[30] | — |
| 58. Tobacco—man-hours | 100 pounds | 47[28] | 46[29] | 44[30] | — |
| 59. Milk cows—milk per cow | pounds | 4,289.0[28] | 4,000.0[29] | 3,842.0[30] | — |
| 60. Milk cows—man-hours | cwt of milk | 3.4[28] | 3.6[29] | 3.8[30] | — |
| 61. Total use of electrical energy | mil. kwh | 115,783 | 57,125 | 14,262[31] | 6,029[32] |
| 62. Residential | mil. kwh | 11,018 | 3,190 | — | — |
| 63. Commercial | mil. kwh | 13,944 | 6,150 | — | — |
| 64. Industrial | mil. kwh | 61,023 | 31,500 | — | — |
| 65. Value of exports | mil. dollars | 4,013 | 8,664 | 1,919 | 1,499 |
| 66. Value of imports | mil. dollars | 3,500 | 5,784 | 1,646 | 930 |
| 67. Passenger car factory sales | thousands | 2,787.4 | 1,905.5 | 181.0 | 4.1 |
| 68. Total motor vehicle registrations | millions | 26.7 | 9.2 | .5 | .008 |
| 69. Miles of travel by motor vehicles | mil. miles | 206,320 | 55,027[33] | — | — |
| 70. Number of operating railroads | | 775 | 1,085 | 1,306 | 1,224 |
| 71. Railroad passengers | thousands | 707,987 | 1,269,913 | 971,683 | 576,831 |
| Air transportation | | | | | |
| 72. Number of operators | | 43 | — | — | — |
| 73. Aircraft in service | | 497 | — | — | — |
| 74. Revenue passengers carried | thousands | 385[35] | — | — | — |
| 75. Total school enrollments—elementary and secondary | thousands | 28,329 | 23,278 | 19,372 | 16,885 |
| 76. High school graduates | thousands | 667 | 311 | 156 | 95 |
| 77. Percent of persons 17 years old | percent | 28.8 | 16.3 | 8.6 | 6.3 |
| 78. Total institutions of higher education | | 1,409 | 1,041 | 951 | 977 |
| 79. Bachelor's or first professional degrees conferred | | 122,484 | 48,622 | 37,199 | 27,410 |
| Radio and television | | | | | |
| 80. Radio sets produced | thousands | 3,789 | 100[37] | — | — |
| 81. Households with radio sets | thousands | 13,750 | 60[37] | — | — |
| 82. Television sets produced | thousands | — | — | — | — |
| 83. Households with television sets | thousands | — | — | — | — |
| 84. Books published | | 10,027 | 8,422 | 13,470 | 6,356 |
| 85. Daily newspapers—number | | 1,942 | 2,042 | — | — |
| 86. Daily newspapers—circulation | thousands | 39,589 | 27,791 | — | — |
| 87. Telephones per 1,000 population | | 162.6 | 123.4 | 82.0 | 17.6 |
| 88. Average number of daily telephone conversations | thousands | 83,520 | 51,814 | 36,161 | 7,882 |
| 89. Patents issued for inventions | | 45,226 | 37,060 | 35,141 | 24,644 |
| 90. Currency in circulation | mil. dollars | 4,521.0 | 5,467.6 | 3,148.7 | 2,081.2 |
| 91. Total social welfare expenditures under public programs | mil. dollars | 4,085 | — | 1,000[39] | — |
| 92. Percent of GNP | percent | 4.2 | — | 2.5[39] | — |
| 93. Percent of all government expenditures | percent | — | — | 34.0[39] | — |
| 94. Per capita (actual prices) | dollars | 33 | — | — | — |
| 95. Per capita health expenditure | dollars | 29.49[14] | — | — | — |
| 96. Number of physicians | | 153,803 | 144,977 | 151,132 | 132,002 |
| 97. Rate per 100,000 population | | 125 | 137 | 164 | 173 |
| Summary of federal government finances | | | | | |
| 98. Receipts | mil. dollars | 4,057.9 | 6,648.9 | 675.5 | 567.2 |
| 99. Outlays | mil. dollars | 3,320.2 | 6,357.7 | 693.6 | 520.9 |
| 100. Total public debt | mil. dollars | 16,185.3 | 24,299.3 | 1,146.9 | 1,263.4 |
| 101. Per capita public debt | dollars | 132 | 228 | 12 | 17 |
| 102. Paid civilian employees of the federal government | | 601,319 | 655,265 | 388,708 | 239,476[44] |
| 103. Military personnel on active duty[54] | | 255,648 | 343,302 | 139,344[57] | 125,923 |

| 1890 | 1880 | 1870 | 1860 | 1850 | 1840 | 1830 | 1820 | 1810 | 1800 | 1790 | |
|---|---|---|---|---|---|---|---|---|---|---|---|
| — | 13.2 | — | — | — | 15.0 | — | — | — | 15.0 | — | 51. |
| — | 152 | — | — | — | 233 | — | — | — | 373 | — | 52. |
| — | 188 | — | — | — | 147 | — | — | — | 147 | — | 53. |
| — | 303 | — | — | — | 438 | — | — | — | 601 | — | 54. |
| — | — | — | — | — | — | — | — | — | — | — | 55. |
| — | — | — | — | — | — | — | — | — | — | — | 56. |
| — | — | — | — | — | — | — | — | — | — | — | 57. |
| — | — | — | — | — | — | — | — | — | — | — | 58. |
| — | — | — | — | — | — | — | — | — | — | — | 59. |
| — | — | — | — | — | — | — | — | — | — | — | 60. |
| — | — | — | — | — | — | — | — | — | — | — | 61. |
| — | — | — | — | — | — | — | — | — | — | — | 62. |
| — | — | — | — | — | — | — | — | — | — | — | 63. |
| — | — | — | — | — | — | — | — | — | — | — | 64. |
| 910 | 853 | 451 | 400 | 152 | 132 | 74 | 70 | 67 | 71 | 20 | 65. |
| 823 | 761 | 462 | 362 | 178 | 107 | 71 | 74 | 85 | 91 | 23 | 66. |
| — | — | — | — | — | — | — | — | — | — | — | 67. |
| — | — | — | — | — | — | — | — | — | — | — | 68. |
| — | — | — | — | — | — | — | — | — | — | — | 69. |
| 1,013 | — | — | — | — | — | — | — | — | — | — | 70. |
| 492,431 | — | — | — | — | — | — | — | — | — | — | 71. |
| — | — | — | — | — | — | — | — | — | — | — | 72. |
| — | — | — | — | — | — | — | — | — | — | — | 73. |
| — | — | — | — | — | — | — | — | — | — | — | 74. |
| 14,479 | 9,868[36] | 6,872[36] | — | — | — | — | — | — | — | — | 75. |
| 44 | 24 | 16 | — | — | — | — | — | — | — | — | 76. |
| 3.5 | 2.5 | 2.0 | — | — | — | — | — | — | — | — | 77. |
| 998 | 811 | 503 | — | — | — | — | — | — | — | — | 78. |
| 15,539 | 12,896 | — | — | — | — | — | — | — | — | — | 79. |
| — | — | — | — | — | — | — | — | — | — | — | 80. |
| — | — | — | — | — | — | — | — | — | — | — | 81. |
| — | — | — | — | — | — | — | — | — | — | — | 82. |
| — | — | — | — | — | — | — | — | — | — | — | 83. |
| 4,559 | 2,076 | — | — | — | — | — | — | — | — | — | 84. |
| — | — | — | — | — | — | — | — | — | — | — | 85. |
| — | — | — | — | — | — | — | — | — | — | — | 86. |
| 3.6 | 0.9 | — | — | — | — | — | — | — | — | — | 87. |
| 1,448 | 239 | — | — | — | — | — | — | — | — | — | 88. |
| 25,313 | 12,903 | 12,137 | 4,357 | 883 | 458 | 544 | 155 | 223 | 41 | 3 | 89. |
| 1,429.3 | 973.4 | 775.0 | 435.4 | 278.8 | 186.3 | 87.3 | 67.1 | 55.0 | 26.5 | — | 90. |
| 318 | — | — | — | — | — | — | — | — | — | — | 91. |
| 2.4 | — | — | — | — | — | — | — | — | — | — | 92. |
| 38.0 | — | — | — | — | — | — | — | — | — | — | 93. |
| — | — | — | — | — | — | — | — | — | — | — | 94. |
| — | — | — | — | — | — | — | — | — | — | — | 95. |
| 104,805 | 85,671 | 64,414 | 55,055 | 40,755 | — | — | — | — | — | — | 96. |
| 166 | 171 | 162 | 175 | 176 | — | — | — | — | — | — | 97. |
| 403.1 | 333.5 | 411.3 | 56.1 | 43.6 | 19.5 | 24.8 | 17.9 | 9.4 | 10.8 | 4.4[41] | 98. |
| 318.0 | 267.6 | 309.7 | 63.1 | 39.5 | 24.3 | 15.1 | 18.3 | 8.2 | 10.8 | 4.3[41] | 99. |
| 1,222.4 | 2,090.9 | 2,436.5 | 64.8 | 63.5 | 3.6 | 48.6 | 91.0 | 53.2 | 83.0 | 75.5[42] | 100. |
| 18 | 42 | 61 | 2 | 3[43] | — | — | — | — | — | — | 101. |
| 157,442[45] | 100,020[46] | 51,020[47] | 36,672[48] | 26,274[49] | 18,038[50] | 11,491[51] | 6,914[52] | 4,837[53] | — | — | 102. |
| 38,666 | 37,894 | 50,348 | 27,958[58] | 20,824 | 21,616 | 11,942 | 15,113 | 11,554 | 7,108[59] | 718[60] | 103. |

### Statistical History Table—Footnotes

1. Total, including Armed Forces overseas, as of July 1. For population during Colonial years (1610–1780), *see* table of Colonial Population Estimates. 2. Beginning with 1960, figures include Alaska and Hawaii. 3. Based on resident population figures, excluding Armed Forces overseas. 4. Like occupations have been grouped as closely as possible to allow for changing definitions over the years. *See* source for definitions and further explanation. 5. For 1900–75, includes "Farmers and Farm Managers." 6. For 1900–75, includes craftsmen, foremen, operatives, and kindred workers; for 1820–90, includes those occupations requiring special training of a manual rather than mental nature. 7. For 1900–75, excludes farm and mine laborers. 8. Decade average; 1879–88. 9. Decade average; 1869–78. 10. 1940–75, includes Armed Forces. 11. Data for persons 14 years old and over. 12. Data for persons 10 years old and over reporting a gainful occupation. 13. Prior to 1950, figures are for persons 14 years old and over. Annual averages. Unemployment percentages for the Depression years are as follows: 1931, 15.9%; 1932, 23.6%; 1933, 24.9%; 1934, 21.7%; 1935, 20.1%; 1936, 16.9%; 1937, 14.3%; 1938, 19.0%; 1939, 17.2%. 14. Figure is for 1929. 15. Figure is for 1859. 16. In 1932, the rate reached a high of 154. 17. Estimate. 18. After deduction for unemployment. 19. Includes workers in personal, medical, and other health services, domestic, nonprofit, educational service industries. 20. Figure is for 1974. 21. Includes workers in anthracite coal, bituminous coal, and metal mining. 22. Figure is for 1949. 23. Figure is for 1899. 24. Figure is for 1869. 25. Figures are annual averages for 1960–64. 26. Figures are annual averages for 1950–54. 27. Figures are annual averages for 1940–44. 28. Figures are annual averages 1930–34. 29. Figures are annual averages for 1920–24. 30. Figures are annual averages for 1910–14. 31. Figure is for 1907. 32. Figure is for 1902. 33. Figure is for 1921. 34. Duplication has been eliminated where the same passengers were carried on more than one route of an air carrier, but still exists where the same passengers were carried by more than one air carrier. 35. Includes nonrevenue passengers. 36. Figure for public day schools only. 37. Figure is for 1922. 38. Preliminary figures. 39. Figure is for 1913. 40. Includes hospital care, professional services, drugs and sundries, eyeglasses and appliances, nursing home care, expenses for prepayment and administration, government public health activities, other health services, and research and medical facilities construction. 41. Figure is for 1789–91. 42. Figure is for 1791. 43. Figure is for 1851. 44. Figure is for 1901. 45. Figure is for 1891. 46. Figure is for 1881. 47. Figure is for 1871. 48. Figure is for 1861. 49. Figure is for 1851. 50. Figure is for 1841. 51. Figure is for 1831. 52. Figure is for 1821. 53. Figure is for 1816. 54. Excludes Coast Guard. 55. Estimated. 56. In 1945, 12,123,455 people were on active military duty. 57. In 1918, 2,897,167 people were on active military duty. 58. In 1865, 1,062,848 people were on active military duty. 59. Figure is for 1801. 60. Figure is for 1789.
*Source: Historical Statistics of the U.S.*, Department of Commerce, Bureau of the Census.

## Washington Monument

Construction of this magnificent Washington, D.C., monument, which draws some two million visitors a year, took nearly a century of planning, building, and controversy. Provision for a large equestrian statue of George Washington was made in the original city plan, but the project was soon dropped. After Washington's death it was taken up again, and a number of false starts and changes of design were made. Finally, in 1848, work was begun on the monument that stands today. The design, by architect Robert Mills, then featured an ornate base. In 1854, however, political squabbling and a lack of money brought construction to a halt. Work was resumed in 1880, and the monument was completed in 1884 and opened to the public in 1888. The tapered shaft, faced with white marble and rising from walls 15 feet thick (4.6 m) at the base was modeled after the obelisks of ancient Egypt. The monument, one of the tallest masonry constructions in the world, stands just over 555 feet (169 m). Memorial stones from the 50 States, foreign countries, and organizations line the interior walls. The top, reached only by elevator, commands a panoramic view of the city.

## U.S. Capitol

When the French architect and engineer Maj. Pierre L'Enfant first began to lay out the plans for a new Federal city (now Washington, D.C.), he noted that Jenkins' Hill, overlooking the area, seemed to be "a pedestal waiting for a monument." It was here that the U.S. Capitol would be built. The basic structure as we know it today evolved over a period of more than 150 years. In 1792 a competition was held for the design of a capitol building. Dr. William Thornton, a physician and amateur architect, submitted the winning plan, a simple, low-lying structure of classical proportions with a shallow dome. Later, internal modifications were made by Benjamin Henry Latrobe. After the building was burned by the British in 1814, Latrobe and architect Charles Bulfinch were responsible for its reconstruction. Finally, under Thomas Walter, who was Architect of the Capitol from 1851 to 1865, the House and Senate wings and the imposing cast iron dome topped with the Statue of Freedom were added, and the Capitol assumed the form we see today. It was in the old Senate chamber that Daniel Webster cried out, "Liberty and Union, now and forever, one and inseparable!" In Statuary Hall, which used to be the old House chamber, a small disk on the floor marks the spot where John Quincy Adams was fatally stricken after more than 50 years of service to his country. A whisper from one side of this room can be heard across the vast space of the hall. Visitors can see the original Supreme Court chamber a floor below the Rotunda.

In addition to its historical association, the Capitol Building is also a vast artistic treasure house. The works of such famous artists as Gilbert Stuart, Rembrandt Peale, and John Trumbull are displayed on the walls. The Great Rotunda, with its 180-foot- (54.9-m-) high dome, is decorated with a massive fresco by Constantino Brumidi, which extends some 300 feet (90 m) in circumference. Throughout the building are many paintings of events in U.S. history and sculptures of outstanding Americans. The Capitol itself is situated on a 68-acre (27.5-ha) park designed by the 19th-century landscape architect Frederick Law Olmsted. There are free guided tours of the Capitol, which include admission to the House and Senate galleries. Those who wish to visit the visitors' gallery in either wing without taking the tour may obtain passes from their Senators or Congressmen. Visitors may ride on the monorail subway that joins the House and Senate wings of the Capitol with the Congressional office buildings.

# Biographies of the Presidents

**GEORGE WASHINGTON** was born Feb. 22, 1732 (Feb. 11, 1731/2, old style) in Westmoreland County, Va. He early trained as a surveyor; but in 1752 he was appointed adjutant in the Virginia militia, and for the next three years he took an active part in the wars against the French and Indians, serving as General Braddock's aide in the disastrous campaign against Fort Duquesne. In 1759 he resigned from the militia, married Martha Dandridge Custis, a widow, and settled down as a gentleman farmer at Mount Vernon.

As a militiaman, he had been exposed to the arrogance of the British officers, and his experience as a planter with British commercial restrictions increased his anti-British sentiment. He opposed the Stamp Act of 1765 and after 1770 became increasingly prominent in organizing resistance. A delegate to the Continental Congress, Washington was selected as commander in chief of the Continental Army and took command at Cambridge, Mass., on July 3, 1775.

Inadequately supported and sometimes covertly sabotaged by the Congress, in charge of troops who were inexperienced, badly equipped, and impatient of discipline, Washington conducted the war on the policy of avoiding major engagements with the British and wearing them down by harassing tactics. His able generalship, along with the French alliance and the growing weariness within Britain, brought the war to a conclusion with the surrender of Cornwallis at Yorktown on Oct. 19, 1781.

The chaotic years under the Articles of Confederation led Washington to return to public life in the hope of promoting the formation of a strong central government. He presided over the Constitutional Convention and yielded to the universal demand that he serve as first President. In office, he sought to unite the nation in the service of establishing the authority of the new government at home and abroad. Greatly distressed by the emergence of the Hamilton-Jefferson rivalry, he worked to maintain neutrality but actually sympathized more with Hamilton. Following his unanimous re-election in 1792, his second term was dominated by the Federalists. His Farewell Address rebuked party spirit and warned against foreign entanglements.

He died at Mt. Vernon on Dec. 14, 1799. Tall, dignified and impressive, Washington gave a public impression of austerity, though he was capable of gaiety in private. His life was characterized by a strict sense of duty to his people.

**JOHN ADAMS** was born on Oct. 30 (Oct. 19, old style), 1735, at Braintree (now Quincy), Mass. A Harvard graduate, he considered teaching and the ministry but finally turned to law and was admitted to the bar in 1758. He opposed the Stamp Act, served as lawyer for patriots indicted by the British and, by the time of the Continental Congresses, was in the vanguard of the movement for independence. In 1778 he went to France as commissioner. Subsequently he helped negotiate the peace treaty with Britain, and in 1785 became the U. S. envoy to London. Resigning in 1788, he was elected Vice President under Washington and was re-elected in 1792.

Though a Federalist, Adams did not get along with Hamilton, who sought to prevent his election to the presidency in 1796 and thereafter intrigued against his administration. Adams was chosen with 71 electoral votes to 68 for his closest competitor, Thomas Jefferson, who became Vice President. In 1798 Adams's independent policy averted a war with France but completed the break with Hamilton and the right-wing Federalists while, at the same time, the enactment of the Alien and Sedition Acts, directed against foreigners and against critics of the government, exasperated the Jeffersonian opposition. The split between Adams and Hamilton elected Jefferson in 1800. Adams retired to his home in Quincy. He later corresponded with Jefferson and they died on the same day, July 4, 1826.

Stout, somewhat vain and irascible, Adams was honest, fearless, and essentially fair-minded. His *Defence of the Constitutions of Government of the United States* (1787) contains original and striking if conservative political ideas. He married Abigail Smith in 1764 and their life together was long and happy.

**THOMAS JEFFERSON** was born on April 13 (April 2, old style), 1743, at Shadwell in Goochland (now Albemarle) County, Va. A William and Mary graduate, he studied law but from the start showed an interest in science and philosophy. His literary skill and political clarity brought him to the forefront of the revolutionary movement in Virginia. As delegate to the Continental Congress, he drafted the Declaration of Independence. In 1776 he entered the Virginia House of Delegates and initiated a comprehensive reform program for the abolition of feudal survivals in land tenure and the separation of church and state.

In 1779 he became governor, but constitutional limitations on his power combined with his own lack of executive energy caused an unsatisfactory administration, culminating in Jefferson's virtual abdication when the British invaded Virginia in 1781. He now retired to his beautiful home at Monticello, to his wife, Martha Wayles Skelton, whom he had married in 1772 and who died in 1782, and to his children.

Jefferson's *Notes on Virginia* (1784–85) illustrate his many-faceted interests, his limitless intellectual curiosity, his deep faith in agrarian democracy. Sent to Congress in 1783, he helped lay down the decimal system and drafted basic reports on the organization of the western lands. In 1785 he was appointed minister to France, where the Anglo-Saxon liberalism he had drawn from Locke was stimulated by contact with the thought that would soon ferment in the French Revolution. In 1789 Washington appointed him Secretary of State. While favoring the Constitution and a strengthened central government, Jefferson came to believe that Hamilton contemplated the establishment of a monarchy. Growing differences resulted in Jefferson's resignation on Dec. 31, 1793.

Elected vice president in 1796, Jefferson continued to serve as spiritual leader of the opposition to Federalism, particularly to the repressive Alien and Sedition Acts. He was elected President in 1801 by the House of Representatives as a result of Hamilton's decision to throw the Federalist votes to him rather than to Aaron Burr, who had tied him in electoral votes. The purchase of Louisiana from France in 1803, though in violation of his earlier constitutional scruples, was the most notable act of his administration. Re-elected in 1804 with 162 electoral votes to 14 for the Federalist Charles C. Pinckney, Jefferson tried desperately during his second term to keep the United States out of the Napoleonic Wars in Europe, employing to this end the unpopular embargo policy.

After his retirement to Monticello in 1809, he developed his interest in education, founding the University of Virginia and watching its development with never-flagging interest. He died at Monticello on July 4, 1826. Tall, loose-jointed, a poor speaker, Jefferson had an enormous variety of interests and skills, ranging from education and science to architecture and music. Economically, his conception of democracy presupposed an essentially rural community of small freeholds; but his deep and abiding faith in the common man provides inspiration for future generations.

**JAMES MADISON** was born in Port Conway, Va., on March 16, 1751 (March 5, 1750/1, old style). A Princeton graduate, he joined the struggle for independence on his return to Virginia in 1771. In the seventies and eighties he was active both in state politics, where he championed the Jefferson reform program, and in the Continental Congress. He was influential in the Constitutional Convention as leader of the group favoring a strong central government and as recorder of the debates; and he subsequently wrote, in collaboration with Alexander Hamilton and John Jay, the *Federalist* papers to aid the campaign for the adoption of the Constitution.

Serving in the new Congress, Madison soon emerged as the leader in the House of the men who opposed Hamilton's financial program and his pro-British leanings in foreign policy. Retiring from Congress in 1797, he continued active in Virginia and drafted the Virginia Resolution protesting the Alien and Sedition Acts. His intimacy with Jefferson made him the natural choice for Secretary of State in 1801.

In 1809 Madison succeeded Jefferson as President, with 122 electoral votes to 47 for the Federalist Pinckney, and 6 scattering. His attractive wife, Dolley Payne Todd, whom he married in 1794, brought a new social sparkle to the executive mansion. In the meantime, increasing tension with Britain culminated in the War of 1812—a war for which the United States was unprepared and for which Madison lacked the executive talent to clear out incompetence and mobilize the nation's energies. Madison was re-elected in 1812, with 128 electoral votes to 89 for the Federalist De Witt Clinton. In 1814 the British actually captured Washington and forced Madison to flee to Virginia.

Madison's domestic program capitulated to the Hamiltonian policies that he had resisted twenty years before and he now signed bills to establish a United States Bank and a higher tariff.

Following his presidency, he remained in retirement in Virginia until his death on June 28, 1836. Small, wrinkled, unimpressive, Madison had an acute political intelligence but lacked executive force.

**JAMES MONROE** was born on April 28, 1758, in Westmoreland County, Va. A William and Mary graduate, he served in the army during the first years of the Revolution and was wounded at Trenton. He then entered Virginia politics and later national politics under the sponsorship of Jefferson. In 1786 he married Elizabeth (Eliza) Kortright.

Fearing centralization, Monroe opposed the adoption of the Constitution and, as senator from Virginia, was highly critical of the Hamiltonian program. In 1794 he was appointed minister to France where his ardent sympathies with the Revolution exceeded the wishes of the State Department. A troubled diplomatic career ended with his recall in 1796. From 1799 to 1802 he was governor of Virginia. In 1803 Jefferson sent him to France to help negotiate the Louisiana Purchase and for the next few years he was active in various continental negotiations.

In 1808 Monroe flirted with the radical wing of the Republican party, which opposed Madison's candidacy; but the presidential boom came to naught and, after a brief term as governor of Virginia in 1811, Monroe accepted Madison's offer of the State Department. During the war he vainly sought a field command and served as Secretary of War from September 1814 to March 1815.

Elected President in 1816 with 183 electoral votes to 34 for the Federalist Rufus King, and re-elected without opposition in 1820, Monroe, the last of the Virginia dynasty, pursued the course of systematic tranquilization that won for his administrations the name "the era of good feeling." He continued Madison's surrender to the Hamiltonian domestic program, signed the Missouri Compromise, acquired Florida and, with the able assistance of his Secretary of State, John Quincy Adams, promulgated the Monroe Doctrine in 1823, declaring against foreign colonization or intervention in the Americas. He died in New York City on July 4, 1831.

A sound man of medium abilities, Monroe possessed qualities of judgment rather than of leadership.

**JOHN QUINCY ADAMS** was born on July 11, 1767, at Braintree (now Quincy), Mass., the son of John Adams. He spent his early years in Europe with his father, graduated from Harvard, and entered law practice. His anti-Jeffersonian newspaper articles won him political attention. In 1794 he became minister to the Netherlands, the first of several diplomatic posts that occupied him until his return to Boston in 1801. In 1797 he married Louisa Catherine Johnson.

In 1803 he was elected to the Senate, nominally as a Federalist, but his repeated displays of independence on such issues as the Louisiana Purchase and the embargo caused his party to compel his resignation and ostracize him socially. In 1809 Madison rewarded him for his support of Jefferson by appointing him minister to St. Petersburg. He helped negotiate the Treaty of Ghent in 1814 and in 1815 became minister to London. In 1817 Monroe appointed him Secretary of State where he served with great distinction, gaining Florida from Spain without hostilities and playing an equal part with Monroe in formulating the Monroe Doctrine.

When no presidential candidate received a majority of electoral votes in 1824, Adams, with the support of Henry Clay, was elected by the House in 1825 over Andrew Jackson, who had the original plurality. Adams had ambitious plans of government activity to foster internal improvements and promote the arts and sciences; but congressional obstructionism combined with his own unwillingness or inability to play the role of a politician meant that little was accomplished. Retiring to Quincy after his defeat in 1828, he was elected to the House of Representatives in 1831 where, though nominally a Whig, he pursued as ever an independent course. He led the fight to force Congress to receive antislavery petitions and fathered the Smithsonian Institution.

Stricken on the floor of the House, he died on Feb. 23, 1848. Tactless, brusque, conscientious, a rough and savage debater, Adams spared neither himself nor his enemies. His long and detailed *Diary* gives a unique picture of the personalities and politics of the times.

**ANDREW JACKSON** was born on March 15, 1767, in what is now generally agreed to be Waxhaw, S.C. After a turbulent boyhood as an orphan and a British prisoner, he moved west to Tennessee where he soon qualified for law practice but found time for such frontier pleasures as horse racing, cockfighting, and dueling. His marriage to Rachel Donelson Robards in 1791 was complicated by subsequent legal uncertainties about the status of her divorce. During the 1790s Jackson served in the Tennessee constitutional convention, the federal House of Representatives, the federal Senate, and the Tennessee supreme court.

After some years as a country gentleman, living at the Hermitage near Nashville, Jackson in 1812 was given command of Tennessee troops sent against the Creeks. He defeated the Indians at Horseshoe Bend in 1814; subsequently he became a major general and won the Battle of New Orleans over veteran British troops, though after the treaty of peace had been signed at Ghent. In 1818 General Jackson invaded Florida, captured Pensacola, and hanged two Englishmen named Arbuthnot and Ambrister, creating an international incident. A presidential boom began for him in 1821 and in its service he returned to the Senate (1823–25). Though he won a plurality of electoral votes in 1824, he lost in the House when Clay threw his strength to Adams; he won easily in 1828 by an electoral vote of 178 to 83.

As President, Jackson greatly expanded the power and prestige of the presidential office and carried through an unexampled program of domestic reform, vetoing the bill to extend the United States Bank, moving toward a hard-money currency policy, and checking the program of federal internal improvements. He also vindicated federal authority against South Carolina with its doctrine of nullification and against France on the question of debts. The support given his policies by the workingmen of the East as well as by the farmers of the East, West, and South resulted in his triumphant re-election in 1832 over Clay by an electoral vote of 219 to 49, with 18 scattering and 2 not cast.

After watching the inauguration of his handpicked successor, Martin Van Buren, Jackson retired to the Hermitage, where he maintained a lively interest in national affairs until his death on June 8, 1845. A tall, dignified man with a drawn and wrinkled face, Jackson has been endowed by partisan historians with a violence and irascibility he appears not to have possessed. His great contribution was to adjust the presidential office and the democratic doctrines of Jefferson to the new situation created by the Industrial Revolution.

**MARTIN VAN BUREN** was born on Dec. 5, 1782, at Kinderhook, N.Y. After graduating from the village school, he became a law clerk, entered practice in 1803, and soon became active in state politics as state senator and attorney general. In 1821 he was elected to the United States Senate. He threw the support of his efficient political organization, known as the Albany Regency, to William H. Crawford in 1824 and to Jackson in 1828. After leading the opposition to Adams's administration in the Senate, he served briefly as governor of New York and resigned to become Jackson's Secretary of State. He soon became on close personal terms with Jackson and played an important part in turning the Jacksonian program from the lines intended by his original Western backers.

In 1832 Van Buren became vice president; in 1836, President, with an electoral vote of 170 against 124 scattered among four opponents. The Panic of 1837 overshadowed his term. He attributed it to the overexpansion of the credit and favored the establishment of an independent treasury as repository for the federal funds. In 1840 he established a ten-hour day on public works. Defeated by Harrison in 1840, he was the leading contender for the Democratic nomination in 1844 until he publicly opposed immediate annexation of Texas and was subsequently beaten by the Southern delegations at the Baltimore convention. This incident increased his growing misgivings about the slave power.

After working behind the scenes among the antislavery Democrats, Van Buren joined in the movement that led to the Free-Soil party and became its candidate for President in 1848. He subsequently returned to the Democratic party while continuing to object to its pro-Southern policy. He died in Kinderhook on July 24, 1862. His *Autobiography* throws valuable sidelights on the political history of the times.

Small, erect, dapper, Van Buren had a reputation for slick politicking that won him such sobriquets as the Little Magician and the Red Fox of Kinderhook; but, as his later career showed, he was capable of taking firm and unpopular stands on public issues. His wife Hannah Hoes, whom he married in 1807, died in 1819.

**WILLIAM HENRY HARRISON** was born in Charles City County, Va., on Feb. 9, 1773. Joining the army in 1791, he was active in Indian fighting in the Northwest, became secretary of the Northwest Territory in 1798 and governor of Indiana in 1800. He married Anna Symmes in 1795. Growing discontent over white encroachments on Indian lands led to the formation of an Indian alliance under Tecumseh to resist further aggressions. In 1811 Harrison won a nominal victory over the Indians at Tippecanoe and in 1813 a more decisive one at the Battle of the Thames, where Tecumseh was killed.

After resigning from the army in 1814, Harrison had an obscure career in politics and diplomacy, ending up in twenty years as a county recorder in Ohio. Nominated for President in 1835 as a military hero whom the conservative politicians hoped to be able to control, he ran surprisingly well against Van Buren in 1836. Four years later he defeated Van Buren by an electoral vote of 234 to 60, but caught pneumonia and died in Washington a month after his inauguration, April 4, 1841. Harrison's qualities were those of a soldier rather than of a statesman or political leader.

**JOHN TYLER** was born in Charles City County, Va., on March 29, 1790. A William and Mary graduate, he entered law practice and politics, serving in the House of Representatives (1816–21) and later as governor of Virginia (1825–27), and as senator. A thoroughgoing strict constructionist, he supported Crawford in 1824 and Jackson in 1828, but broke with Jackson over his Bank policy and became a member of the Southern state-rights group that cooperated with the Whigs. In 1836 he resigned from the Senate rather than follow instructions from the Virginia legislature to vote for a resolution expunging censure of Jackson from the Senate record.

Elected vice president on the Whig ticket in 1840, Tyler succeeded to the presidency on Harrison's death. His strict-constructionist views soon caused a split with the Henry Clay wing of the Whig party and a stalemate on domestic questions. Tyler's more considerable achievements were his support of the Webster-Ashburton Treaty with Britain and his success in bringing about the annexation of Texas.

After his presidency he lived in retirement in Virginia until the outbreak of the Civil War, when he emerged briefly as chairman of a peace convention and then as delegate to the provisional Congress of the Confederacy. He died on Jan. 18, 1862. He was married first to Letitia Christian in March 1813 and, two years after her death in 1842, to Julia Gardiner. Witty, amiable, courteous, Tyler was a Virginia gentleman whose presidency was hamstrung by the basic contradiction between his own ideas and those of the party that put him on the ticket as vice president.

**JAMES KNOX POLK** was born in Mecklenburg County, N.C., on Nov. 2, 1795. A graduate of the University of North Carolina, he moved west to Tennessee, was admitted to the bar, and soon became prominent in state politics. In 1825 he was elected to the House of Representatives where he opposed Adams and, after 1829, became Jackson's floor leader in the fight against the Bank. In 1835 he became Speaker of the House. In 1839 he was elected governor of Tennessee, but was beaten in tries for re-election in 1841 and 1843.

The supporters of Van Buren for the Democratic nomination in 1844 counted on Polk as his running mate; but, when Van Buren's stand on Texas alienated Southern support, the convention swung to Polk on the ninth ballot. He was elected over Henry Clay, the Whig candidate, by an electoral vote of 170 to 105. Rapidly disillusioning those who thought that he would not run his own administration, Polk proceeded steadily and precisely to achieve four major objectives—the acquisition of California, the settlement of the Oregon question, the reduction of the tariff, and the establishment of the independent treasury. He also enlarged the Monroe Doctrine to exclude all non-American intervention in American affairs, whether forcible or not, and he forced Mexico into a war that he waged to a successful conclusion. His wife Sarah Childress, whom he married in 1824, was a woman of charm and ability. Polk died in Nashville, Tenn., on June 15, 1849.

Serious, hardworking, lacking in color, Polk has long been underrated by historians who mistakenly regarded him as a slaveholders' puppet; in fact, few Presidents have so thoroughly controlled their own administration or have so ably accomplished the purposes they set for themselves. Polk's *Diary* reflects the mood and problems of his presidency.

**ZACHARY TAYLOR** was born at Montebello, Orange County, Va., on Nov. 24, 1784. Embarking on a military career in 1808, Taylor fought in the War of 1812, the Black Hawk War, and the Seminole War, holding in between garrison jobs on the frontier or desk jobs in Washington. A brigadier general as a result of his victory over the Seminoles at Lake Okeechobee (1837), Taylor held a succession of Southwestern commands and in 1846 established a base on the Rio Grande, where his forces engaged in hostilities that precipitated the war with Mexico. He captured Monterrey in September 1846 and, disregarding Polk's orders to stay on the defensive, defeated Santa Anna at Buena Vista in February 1847, ending the war in the northern provinces.

Though Taylor had never cast a vote for President, his party affiliations were Whiggish and his availability was increased by his difficulties with Polk. He was elected President over the Democrat Lewis Cass by an electoral vote of 163 to 127. During the revival of the slavery controversy, which was to result in the Compromise of 1850, Taylor began to take an increasingly firm stand against appeasing the South; but he died in Washington on July 9, 1850, in the midst of the fight over the Compromise. He married Margaret Mackall Smith in 1810. His bluff and simple soldierly qualities won him the name of Old Rough and Ready. During his brief term as President he displayed a growing insight into political questions.

**MILLARD FILLMORE** was born at Locke, Cayuga County, N.Y., on Jan. 7, 1800. A lawyer, he entered politics as an Antimason under the sponsorship of Thurlow Weed, editor and party boss, and subsequently followed Weed into the Whig party. He served in the House of Representatives (1833–35 and 1837–43) and played a leading role in writing the tariff of 1842. Defeated for governor of New York in 1844, he became comptroller in 1848, was put on the Whig ticket with Taylor as a concession to the Clay wing of the party, and became President upon Taylor's death in 1850.

As President, Fillmore broke with Weed and William H. Seward and associated himself with the pro-Southern Whigs, supporting the Compromise of 1850. Defeated for the Whig nomination in 1852, he ran for President in 1856 as candidate of the American or Know-Nothing party, which sought to unite the country against foreigners in the alleged hope of diverting it from the explosive slavery issue. Fillmore opposed Lincoln during the Civil War. He died in Buffalo on March 8, 1874. He was married in 1826 to Abigail Powers, who died in 1853, and in 1858 to Caroline Carmichael McIntosh. Urbane, gracious, colorless, and weak, Fillmore was an undistinguished President.

**FRANKLIN PIERCE** was born at Hillsboro, N.H., on Nov. 23, 1804. A Bowdoin graduate and lawyer, he won rapid political advancement in the Democratic party, in part because of the prestige of his father, Governor Benjamin Pierce. By 1831 he was Speaker of the New Hampshire House of Representatives; from 1833 to 1837 he served in the federal House and from 1837 to 1842 in the Senate. His wife, Jane Means Appleton, whom he had married in 1834, disliked Washington and the somewhat dissipated life led by Pierce; and in 1842 Pierce, resigning from the Senate, took up a successful law practice in Concord, N.H. During the Mexican War he was a brigadier general.

Thereafter Pierce continued to oppose antislavery tendencies within the Democratic party. As a result, he was the Southern choice to break the deadlock at the Democratic convention of 1852 and was nominated on the 49th ballot. Pierce rolled up 254 electoral votes to 42 for Winfield Scott, the Whig candidate.

As President, Pierce followed a course of appeasing the South at home and of playing with schemes of territorial expansion abroad. The failure of both his foreign and domestic policies prevented his renomination; and he died in Concord, N.H., on Oct. 8, 1869, in relative obscurity. A kindly and courteous person, Pierce was weak, unstable, and lacking in presidential qualities.

**JAMES BUCHANAN** was born near Mercersburg, Pa., on April 23, 1791. A Dickinson graduate and a lawyer, he entered Pennsylvania politics as a Federalist. With the disappearance of the Federalist party, he became a Jacksonian Democrat. He served with ability in the House (1821–31), as minister to St. Petersburg (1832–33), and in the Senate (1834–45), and in 1845 became Polk's Secretary of State. Disappointed in the presidential nomination in 1852, Buchanan became minister to Britain in 1853 where he participated with other American diplomats in Europe in drafting the expansionist Ostend Manifesto.

In 1856 Buchanan received the Democratic nomination and won the election, gaining 174 electoral votes to 114 for John C. Frémont, the Republican candidate, and 8 for Millard Fillmore, American party. The growing crisis over slavery presented Buchanan with problems he lacked the will to tackle. His appeasement of the South alienated the Stephen Douglas wing of the Democratic party without reducing Southern militancy on slavery issues. While denying the right of secession, Buchanan also denied that the federal government could do anything about it. He supported the administration during the Civil War and died in Lancaster, Pa., on June 1, 1868.

The only President to remain a bachelor throughout his term, Buchanan used his charming niece, Harriet Lane, as White House hostess. Legalistic, indecisive, and timorous as President, Buchanan filled his other public offices capably.

**ABRAHAM LINCOLN** was born in Hardin (now Larue) County, Ky., on Feb. 12, 1809. His family moved to Indiana and then to Illinois, and Lincoln gained what education he could along the way. While reading law, he worked in a store, managed a mill, surveyed, and split rails. In 1834 he went to the state legislature as a Whig and became the party's floor leader. For the next twenty years he remained in law practice in Springfield, except for a single term (1847–49) in Congress, where he denounced the Mexican War. In 1855 he was a candidate for senator and in 1856 he joined the new Republican party.

A leading but unsuccessful candidate for the vice-presidential nomination with Frémont, Lincoln gained national attention in 1858 when, as Republican candidate for senator from Illinois, he engaged in a series of debates with Stephen A. Douglas, the Democratic candidate. He lost the senatorial election, but continued to prepare the way for the 1860 Republican convention and was rewarded with the presidential nomination on the third ballot. He polled 180 electoral votes, as against the 123 of his three opponents, but had only a plurality of the popular vote.

From the start, Lincoln made clear that, unlike Buchanan, he believed the national government had the power to crush the rebellion. Not an abolitionist, he held the slavery issue subordinate to that of preserving the Union, but soon perceived that the war could not be brought to a successful conclusion without freeing the slaves. His administration was hampered by the incompetence of many Union generals, the inexperience of the troops, and the harassing political tactics both of the Republican Radicals, who favored a hard policy toward the South, and the Democratic Copperheads, who desired a negotiated peace. The Gettysburg Address of Nov. 19, 1863, marks the high point in the record of American eloquence. His patient search for a winning combination finally brought Generals Ulysses S. Grant and William T. Sherman to the top; and their series of victories in 1864 dispelled the mutterings from both Radicals and Peace Democrats that at one time seemed to threaten Lincoln's re-election. He received 212 electoral votes to 21 for George B. McClellan, the Democratic candidate. His inaugural address urged leniency toward the South: "With malice toward none, with charity for all . . . let us strive on to finish the work we are in; to bind up the nation's wounds. . . . " This policy aroused growing opposition on the part of the Republican Radicals, but Lincoln was shot by the actor John Wilkes Booth at Ford's Theater, Washington, on April 14, 1865, before the matter could be put to the test. He died the following day.

Lincoln's marriage to Mary Todd in 1842 was often unhappy and turbulent, in part because of his wife's pronounced instability. By his remarkable literary artistry, his essential patience and devotion, his profound sense of the importance of government by, for, and of the people, by the manner of his life and of his death, Lincoln has won a unique place in the hearts of Americans.

**ANDREW JOHNSON** was born at Raleigh, N.C., on Dec. 29, 1808. Self-educated, he became a tailor in Greeneville, Tenn., but soon went into politics, where he rose steadily. From 1843 to 1853 he served in the House of Representatives, 1853–57 as governor of Tennessee, and in 1857 was elected Senator. Politically he was a Jacksonian Democrat and his specialty was the fight for a more equitable land policy. Alone among the Southern Senators, he stood by the Union during the Civil War. In 1862 he became war governor of Tennessee and carried out a thankless and difficult job with great courage. Johnson became Lincoln's running mate in 1864 as a result of an attempt to give the ticket a nonpartisan and nonsectional character. Succeeding to the presidency on Lincoln's death, Johnson sought to carry out Lincoln's policy but without Lincoln's political skill. The result was a hopeless conflict with the Radical Republicans who dominated Congress, passed measures over Johnson's vetoes, and attempted to limit the power of the executive concerning appointments and removals. The conflict culminated with Johnson's impeachment for attempting to remove his disloyal Secretary of War in defiance of the Tenure of Office Act which required senatorial concurrence for such dismissals. The opposition failed by one vote to get the two thirds necessary for conviction.

After his presidency, Johnson maintained an interest in politics and in 1875 was elected to the Senate. He died near Carter Station, Tenn., on July 31, 1875. He married Eliza McCardle in 1827. An honest, courageous, and intelligent man, Johnson lacked the tact, patience, and self-control to be an effective President.

**ULYSSES SIMPSON GRANT** was born (as Hiram Ulysses Grant) at Point Pleasant, Ohio, on April 27, 1822. He finished West Point in 1843 and served without particular distinction in the Mexican War. In 1848 he married Julia Dent. He resigned from the army in 1854, following warnings from his commanding officer about his drinking habits, and for the next six years held a wide variety of jobs in the Middle West. With the outbreak of the Civil War, he sought a command and soon, to his surprise, was made a brigadier general. His continuing successes in the western theaters, culminating in the capture of Vicksburg in 1863, brought him national fame and soon the command of all the Union armies. His dogged, implacable policy of concentrating on dividing and destroying the Confederate armies brought the war to an end in 1865. In 1866 he was made full general.

Grant's relations with Johnson grew steadily worse; and in 1868, as Republican candidate for President, Grant was elected with 214 electoral votes to 80 for the Democrat, Horatio Seymour. From the start Grant showed his unfitness for the office. His cabinet was weak, his domestic policy was confused, many of his intimate associates were corrupt. The notable achievement in foreign affairs was the settlement of controversies with Great Britain in the Treaty of London (1871), negotiated by his able Secretary of State, Hamilton Fish.

Nominated for a second term, he defeated Horace Greeley, the Democratic and Liberal Republican candidate, 286 votes to 63. The Panic of 1873 created difficulties for his second term.

After retiring from office, Grant toured Europe for two years and returned in time to accede to a third-term boom, but was beaten in the convention of 1880. Illness and bad business judgment darkened his last years, but he worked steadily at the *Personal Memoirs,* which were to be so successful when published after his death at Mount McGregor, near Saratoga, N.Y., on July 23, 1885. Inarticulate, taciturn, loyal to his friends, he was an able general who should never have accepted the presidency.

**RUTHERFORD BIRCHARD HAYES** was born at Delaware, Ohio, on Oct. 4, 1822. A graduate of Kenyon College and the Harvard Law School, he practiced law in Lower Sandusky (now Fremont) and then in Cincinnati. In 1852 he married Lucy Webb. A Whig, he joined the Republican party in 1855. During the Civil War he rose to the rank of major general. He served in Congress from 1865 to 1867 and then confirmed a reputation for honesty and efficiency in two terms as governor of Ohio. His re-election as governor in 1875 made him the logical candidate for those Republicans who wished to stop James G. Blaine in 1876 and he was successfully nominated.

The result of the election was for some time in doubt and hinged upon disputed returns from South Carolina, Louisiana, Florida, and Oregon. Samuel J. Tilden, the Democratic candidate, had the larger popular vote but was adjudged by the strictly partisan decisions of the Electoral Commission to have one less electoral vote, 185 to 184. The national acceptance of this result was due in part to the general understanding that Hayes would pursue a conciliatory policy toward the South. He withdrew the troops from the South, took a conservative position on financial and labor issues, and urged civil service reform.

Hayes served only one term by his own wish and spent the rest of his life in various humanitarian endeavors. He died in Fremont on Jan. 17, 1893. A hard-working, conscientious, sensible man, Hayes represented the best type of Republican of his day.

**JAMES ABRAM GARFIELD,** the last President to be born in a log cabin, was born at Cuyahoga County, Ohio, on Nov. 19, 1831. A Williams graduate, he taught school for a time and entered Republican politics in Ohio. In 1858 he married Lucretia Rudolph. During the Civil War he had a promising career, rising to the rank of major general of volunteers; but in 1863 he was elected to the House of Representatives, where he served until 1880. His oratorical and parliamentary abilities soon made him the leading Republican in the House, though his record was marred by his unorthodox acceptance of a fee in the DeGolyer paving contract case and by suspicions of his complicity in the Crédit Mobilier scandal.

In 1880 Garfield was elected to the Senate, but instead became the presidential candidate on the 36th ballot as a result of a deadlock in the Republican convention. He gained 214 electoral votes to 155 for General Winfield Scott Hancock, the Democratic candidate. Garfield's administration was barely under way when he was shot by Charles J. Guiteau, a disappointed office seeker, in July. He died in Elberon, N.J., on Sept. 19, 1881. An attractive and eloquent man, he was much beloved in his day.

**CHESTER ALAN ARTHUR** was born at Fairfield, Vt., on Oct. 5, 1830. A graduate of Union College, he became a successful New York lawyer. In 1859 he married Ellen Herndon. During the Civil War he held administrative jobs in the Republican state administration and in 1871 was appointed collector of the Port of New York by Grant. This post gave him control over considerable patronage; and, though not personally corrupt, Arthur managed his power in the interests of the New York machine so openly that President Hayes in 1877 called for an investigation and in 1878 Arthur was suspended from his responsibilities.

In 1880 Arthur was nominated for vice president in the hope of conciliating the followers of Grant and the powerful New York machine. As President on Garfield's assassination, Arthur, stepping out of his familiar role as spoilsman, backed civil service reform, reorganized the cabinet, and prosecuted political associates accused of post office graft. Losing machine support and failing to gain the reformers, he was not renominated. He died in New York City on Nov. 18, 1886. A tall, handsome, dignified man with real administrative abilities, he was a better President than his previous record promised.

**STEPHEN GROVER CLEVELAND** was born at Caldwell, N.J., on March 18, 1837. He was admitted to the bar in Buffalo, N.Y., in 1859 and lived there as a lawyer, with occasional incursions into Democratic politics, for more than twenty years. He did not participate in the Civil War. As mayor of Buffalo in 1881, he carried through a reform program so ably that the Democrats ran him successfully for governor in 1882. In 1884 he won the Democratic nomination for President. The campaign contrasted Cleveland's spotless public career with the uncertain record of James G. Blaine, the Republican candidate, and Cleveland received enough Mugwump (independent Republican) support to win by 219 to 182 electoral votes.

As President, Cleveland pushed civil service reform, opposed the pension grab and attacked the high tariff rates. While in the White House he married Frances Folsom (1886). Renominated in 1888, Cleveland was defeated by Benjamin Harrison, polling more popular but fewer electoral votes. In 1892 he was re-elected over Harrison, 277 to 145, with 22 votes for James B. Weaver, the Populist candidate. When the Panic of 1893 burst upon the country, Cleveland's attempts to solve it by sound-money measures alienated the free-silver wing of the party, while his tariff policy alienated the protectionists. In 1894 he sent troops to break the Pullman strike. In foreign affairs his firmness caused Great Britain to back down in the Venezuela border dispute.

In his last years Cleveland was an active and much respected public figure. He died in Princeton, N.J., on June 24, 1908. An honest, stubborn, high-principled man, Cleveland was an old-fashioned liberal in the nineteenth-century sense who was baffled by the new problems of industrial society.

**BENJAMIN HARRISON** was born in North Bend, Ohio, on Aug. 20, 1833, the grandson of William Henry Harrison. A graduate of Miami University, he took up the law in Indiana and became active in Republican politics. In 1853 he married Caroline Lavinia Scott. During the Civil War he rose to the rank of brigadier general. A sound-money Republican, he was elected senator from Indiana in 1880 and in 1888 received the Republican nomination for President on the 8th ballot. Though behind on the popular vote, he won over Grover Cleveland in the electoral college by 233 to 168.

As President, Benjamin Harrison failed to please either the bosses or the reform element in the party. In foreign affairs he backed Secretary of State Blaine, whose policy foreshadowed later American imperialism. In 1892 Harrison was renominated, but Cleveland beat him in the election. His wife died in the White House in 1892 and Harrison married her niece, Mary Scott (Lord) Dimmick, in 1896. After his presidency, he resumed law practice. He died in Indianapolis on March 13, 1901. Harrison was an honest man of very medium abilities.

**WILLIAM McKINLEY** was born in Niles, Ohio, on Jan. 29, 1843. He taught school, then served in the Civil War, rising from the ranks to become a major. Subsequently he opened a law office in Canton, Ohio, and in 1871 married Ida Saxton. Elected to Congress in 1876, he served there steadily till 1891, except for 1883–85. His faithful advocacy of business interests culminated in the passage of the highly protective McKinley Tariff of 1890. With the support of Mark Hanna, a shrewd Cleveland businessman interested in safeguarding tariff protection, McKinley became governor of Ohio in 1892 and Republican presidential candidate in 1896. The business community, alarmed by the progressivism of William Jennings Bryan, the Democratic candidate, spent considerable money to assure McKinley's victory, which was by the margin of 271 to 176 in the electoral college.

The chief event of McKinley's administration was the war with Spain, which resulted in our acquisition of the Philippines and other islands. With imperialism as an issue, McKinley defeated Bryan again in the election of 1900 by 292 to 155. On Sept. 6, 1901, he was shot at Buffalo, N.Y., by Leon F. Czolgosz, an anarchist, and he died there on Sept. 14.

**THEODORE ROOSEVELT** was born in New York City on Oct. 27, 1858. A Harvard graduate, he was early interested in ranching, in politics, and in writing picturesque historical narratives. He was a Republican member of the New York Assembly in 1882–84, an unsuccessful candidate for mayor of New York in 1886, a U. S. Civil Service Commissioner under Harrison, Police Commissioner of New York City in 1895, and Assistant Secretary of the Navy under McKinley in 1897. He resigned in 1898 to help organize a volunteer regiment named the Rough Riders and take a more direct part in the war with Spain. He won the New York gubernatorial nomination in 1898 and the vice presidency in 1900, in spite of lack of enthusiasm on the part of the bosses.

Assuming the presidency of the assassinated McKinley in 1901, Roosevelt embarked on a wide-ranging program of government reform and conservation of natural resources. He ordered antitrust suits against several large corporations, threatened to intervene in the anthracite coal strike of 1902, which prompted the operators to accept arbitration, and, in general, championed the rights of the "little man" and fought the "malefactors of great wealth." He was also responsible for such progressive legislation as the Elkins Act of 1901, which outlawed freight rebates by railroads; the bill establishing the Department of Commerce and Labor; the Hepburn Act, which gave the I.C.C. greater control over the railroads; the Meat Inspection Act; and the Pure Food and Drug Act.

In foreign affairs he pursued a strong policy, permitting the instigation of a revolt in Panama to dispose of Colombian objections to the Panama Canal and helping to maintain the balance of power in the East by bringing the Russo-Japanese war to an end, for which he won the Nobel Peace Prize, the first American to achieve a Nobel prize in any category. In 1904 he decisively defeated Alton B. Parker, his conservative Democratic opponent, by an electoral margin of 336 to 140.

Roosevelt's increasing coldness toward Taft after he left the White House led him to overlook his earlier disclaimer of third-term ambitions and to re-enter politics. Defeated by the machine in the Republican convention of 1912, he organized the Progressive Party and polled more votes than Taft, though the split brought about the election of Wilson. From 1915 on, Roosevelt strongly favored intervention in the European war. He became deeply embittered at Wilson's refusal to allow him to raise a volunteer division. He died in Oyster Bay, N.Y., on Jan. 6, 1919. He was married twice: in 1880 to Alice Hathaway Lee, who died in 1884; and in 1886 to Edith Kermit Carow.

An advocate of the strenuous life and a man of spirit and vigor, Roosevelt captured the imagination of the American people.

**WILLIAM HOWARD TAFT** was born in Cincinnati on Sept. 15, 1857. A Yale graduate, he entered Ohio Republican politics in the eighteen eighties. In 1886 he married Helen Herron. From 1887 to 1890, he served on the Ohio superior court; 1890–92, as solicitor general of the United States; 1892–1900, on the federal circuit court. In 1900 McKinley appointed him president of the Philippine Commission and in 1901 governor general. Taft had great success in pacifying the Filipinos, solving the problem of the church lands, improving economic conditions, and establishing limited self-government. His period as Secretary of War (1904–08) further demonstrated his capacity as administrator and conciliator and he was Roosevelt's hand-picked successor in 1908. In the election he polled 321 electoral votes to 162 for William Jennings Bryan.

As President, though he carried on many of Roosevelt's policies, Taft got into increasing trouble with the progressive wing of the party and displayed mounting irritability and indecision. After his defeat in 1912, he became professor of constitutional law at Yale. In 1921 he was appointed Chief Justice of the United States. He died in Washington, D.C., on March 8, 1930. Enormously large, deliberate, and good-humored, Taft excelled as an administrator and judge, not as a political leader.

**THOMAS WOODROW WILSON** was born in Staunton, Va., on Dec. 28, 1856. A Princeton graduate, he turned from law practice to post-graduate work in political science at Johns Hopkins University, receiving his Ph.D. in 1886. He taught at Bryn Mawr, Wesleyan, and Princeton, and in 1902 was made president of Princeton. After an unsuccessful attempt to democratize the social life of Princeton, he welcomed an invitation in 1910 to be the Democratic gubernatorial candidate in New Jersey. His success in fighting the machine and putting through a reform program attracted national attention.

In 1912, after a protracted contest at Baltimore, Wilson won the Democratic nomination on the 46th ballot. In the election he received 435 electoral votes to 88 for Roosevelt and 8 for Taft. During his first term Wilson proceeded under the standard of the New Freedom to enact a program of domestic reform, including the Federal Reserve Act, the Clayton Antitrust Act, the establishment of the Federal Trade Commission, and other measures designed to restore competition in the face of the great monopolies. In foreign affairs, while privately sympathetic with the Allies, he strove to maintain neutrality in the European war and warned both sides against encroachments on American interests.

Re-elected in 1916 as a peace candidate, he tried to mediate between the warring nations; but when the Germans resumed unrestricted submarine warfare in 1917 Wilson brought the United States into what he now believed was a war to make the world safe for democracy. He supplied the classic formulations of Allied war aims and the armistice of November 1918 was negotiated on the basis of Wilson's Fourteen Points. In 1919 he strove at Versailles to lay the foundations for enduring peace. He accepted the imperfections of the Versailles Treaty in the expectation that they could be remedied by action within the League of Nations. He probably could have secured ratification of the treaty if he had adopted a more conciliatory attitude toward the mild reservationists; but his insistence on all or nothing eventually caused the diehard isolationists and diehard Wilsonites to unite in rejecting a compromise.

In September 1919 Wilson suffered a paralytic stroke that limited his future activity. After the presidency he lived on in retirement in Washington, D.C., dying Feb. 3, 1924. He was married twice—in 1885 to Ellen Louise Axson, who died in 1914, and in 1915 to Edith Bolling Galt. A man of high principle, inspiring eloquence, and great intellectual ability, Wilson was the first leader to fire the imagination of the masses of the world with the vision of world peace.

**WARREN GAMALIEL HARDING** was born in Morrow County, Ohio, on Nov. 2, 1865. After attending Ohio Central College, Harding became interested in journalism and in 1884 bought the *Marion* (Ohio) *Star*. In 1891 he married a wealthy widow, Florence Kling De Wolfe. As his paper prospered, he entered Republican politics, serving as state senator (1899–1903) and as lieutenant governor (1904–06). In 1910 he was defeated for governor, but in 1914 was elected to the Senate. His reputation as orator made him keynoter in the 1916 convention.

When the 1920 Republican convention was deadlocked between Leonard Wood and Frank O. Lowden, Harding was made the dark-horse nominee on his solemn affirmation that there was no reason in his past that he should not be. Straddling the League question, Harding was elected easily with 404 electoral votes to 127 for James M. Cox, his Democratic opponent. His Cabinet contained some able men, but also some manifestly unfit for public office. Harding's own intimates were mediocre when they were not corrupt. The impending disclosure of scandals in the Interior and Justice departments and in the Veterans' Bureau, as well as political setbacks, profoundly worried him. On his return from Alaska in 1923, he died suddenly at San Francisco on Aug. 2. A handsome and genial man, undiscriminating in his associates, lacking in political ideas or fortitude, Harding was totally unfitted for the presidency.

**JOHN CALVIN COOLIDGE** was born in Plymouth, Vt., on July 4, 1872. An Amherst graduate, he went into law practice at Northampton, Mass., in 1897. He married Grace Anna Goodhue in 1905. He entered Republican state politics, becoming successively mayor of Northampton, state senator, lieutenant governor and, in 1919, governor. His conduct in regard to the Boston police strike in 1919 won him a somewhat undeserved reputation for decisive action and brought him the Republican vice-presidential nomination in 1920. After Harding's death Coolidge handled the Washington scandals with care and finally managed to save the Republican party from public blame for the widespread corruption.

In 1924 Coolidge won re-election without difficulty, getting 382 electoral votes to 136 for the Democrat, John W. Davis, and 13 for Robert M. La Follette running on the Progressive ticket. His second term, like his first, was characterized by a general satisfaction with the existing economic order. He stated that he did not choose to run in 1928.

After his presidency, Coolidge lived quietly in Northampton, writing an unilluminating *Autobiography* and conducting a syndicated column. He died there on Jan. 5, 1933. His dry, Yankee humor and his frugality and glumness made him a paradoxically popular President in the boom period.

**HERBERT CLARK HOOVER** was born at West Branch, Iowa, on Aug. 10, 1874. A Stanford graduate, he worked from 1895 to 1913 as a mining engineer and consultant in North America, Europe, Asia, Africa, and Australia. In 1899 he married Lou Henry. During the First World War he served with distinction as chairman of the American Relief Committee in London, as chairman of the Commission for Relief in Belgium, and as U.S. Food Administrator. His political affiliations were still sufficiently indeterminate for him to be mentioned as a possibility for both Republican and Democratic nominations in 1920, but after the election he served both Harding and Coolidge as Secretary of Commerce.

In the election of 1928 Hoover received 444 electoral votes to 87 for Alfred E. Smith, the Democratic candidate. He soon faced the worst depression in the nation's history, but his attacks upon it were hampered by his devotion to the theory that the forces that brought the crisis would soon bring the revival and then by his belief that in too many areas the federal government had no power to act.

In a succession of vetoes he struck down measures proposing a national employment system or national relief, he reduced income tax rates, and only at the end of his term did he yield to popular pressure and set up agencies such as the Reconstruction Finance Corporation to make emergency loans to assist business.

After his 1932 defeat, Hoover returned to private business. In 1946 President Truman charged him with various world food missions; and from 1947 to 1949 and again from 1953 to 1955 he was head of the Commission on Organization of the Executive Branch of the Government. He died in New York City on Oct. 20, 1964.

**FRANKLIN DELANO ROOSEVELT** was born in Hyde Park, N.Y., on Jan. 30, 1882. A Harvard graduate, he attended Columbia Law School and was admitted to the New York bar. In 1910 he was elected to the New York state senate as a Democrat. Reelected in 1912, he was appointed Assistant Secretary of the Navy by Woodrow Wilson in 1913. In 1920 his radiant personality and his war services resulted in his nomination for vice president as James M. Cox's running mate. After his defeat, he returned to law practice in New York. In August 1921 Roosevelt was stricken with infantile paralysis while at Campobello, New Brunswick. After a long and gallant fight against the disease he recovered partial use of his legs. In 1924 and 1928 he led the fight at the Democratic national conventions for the nomination of Gov. Alfred E. Smith of New York and in 1928 Roosevelt was himself induced to run for governor of New York. He was elected and was re-elected in 1930.

In 1932 Roosevelt received the Democratic nomination for President and immediately launched a campaign which brought new spirit to a weary and discouraged nation. He won the election over Herbert Hoover by a margin of 472 to 59 in the electoral college. His first term was characterized by an unfolding of the New Deal program, with greater benefits for labor, the farmers, and the unemployed, and the progressive estrangement of most of the business community.

At an early stage Roosevelt became aware of the menace to world peace involved in the existence of totalitarian fascism, and from 1937 on he tried to focus public attention on the trend of events in Europe and Asia. As a result he was widely denounced as a warmonger. He was re-elected in 1936 over Alfred M. Landon by the overwhelming electoral margin of 523 to 8 and the gathering international crisis caused him to decide to run again in 1940. He defeated Wendell L. Willkie by a vote of 449 to 82.

Roosevelt's program to bring maximum aid to Britain and, after June 1941, to Russia was opposed, until the Japanese attack on Pearl Harbor restored national unity. During the war Roosevelt shelved the New Deal in the interests of conciliating the business community, both in order to get full production during the war and to prepare the way for a united acceptance of the peace settlements after the war. A series of conferences with Winston Churchill and Joseph Stalin laid down the bases for the postwar world. In 1944 he was elected to a fourth term, running against Thomas E. Dewey.

On April 12, 1945, Roosevelt died at Warm Springs, Ga., shortly after his return from the Yalta Conference. His wife, Anna Eleanor Roosevelt, whom he married in 1905, was a woman of great ability who made significant contributions to her husband's policies.

**HARRY S. TRUMAN** was born on a farm near Lamar, Mo., on May 8, 1884. During the First World War he served in France with the 129th Field Artillery. He married Bess Wallace in 1919. After engaging briefly and unsuccessfully in the haberdashery business in Kansas City, Mo., Truman entered local politics. Under the sponsorship of Thomas Pendergast, Democratic boss of Missouri, he held a number of local offices, preserving his personal honesty in the midst of a notoriously corrupt political machine. In 1934 he was elected to the Senate and was re-elected in 1940. During his first term he was a loyal but quiet supporter of the New Deal, but in the course of his second term an appointment as head of a Senate committee to investigate war production brought out his special qualities of honesty, common sense, and hard work, and he won widespread respect.

Elected vice president in 1944, Truman became President upon Roosevelt's sudden death in April 1945 and was immediately faced with the problems of winding down the war against the Axis and preparing the nation for postwar adjustment.

The years 1947–48 were distinguished by civil rights proposals, the Truman Doctrine to contain the spread of Communism, and the Marshall Plan to aid in the economic reconstruction of war-ravaged nations. Truman's general record, highlighted by a vigorous Fair Deal campaign, brought about his unexpected election in 1948 over the heavily favored Thomas E. Dewey.

Truman's second term was primarily concerned with the Cold War with the Soviet Union, the implementing of the North Atlantic Pact, the United Nations police action in Korea, and the vast rearmament program with its accompanying problems of economic stabilization.

On March 29, 1952, Truman announced that he would not run again for the presidency. After leaving the White House, he returned to his home in Independence, Mo., to write his memoirs. He further busied himself with the Harry S. Truman Library there. He died in Kansas City, Mo., on Dec. 26, 1972.

**DWIGHT DAVID EISENHOWER** was born in Denison, Tex., on Oct. 14, 1890. His ancestors lived in Germany and emigrated to America, settling in Pennsylvania, early in the 18th century. His father, David, had a general store in Hope, Kan., which failed. After a brief time in Texas, the family moved to Abilene, Kan.

After graduating from Abilene High School in 1909, Dwight Eisenhower did odd jobs for almost two years. He won an appointment to the Naval Academy at Annapolis, but it turned out that he was too old for admittance. Then he received an appointment in 1910 to West Point. He was graduated a second lieutenant in 1915.

He did not see service in World War I, having been assigned to the 19th Infantry at Fort Sam Houston, Tex. There he met Mamie Geneva Doud, whom he married in Denver on July 1, 1916, and by whom he had two sons: Doud Dwight (died in infancy) and John Sheldon Doud.

Eisenhower served in the Philippines from 193 to 1939 with Gen. Douglas MacArthur. Afterwar Gen. George C. Marshall brought him into the W Department's General Staff and in 1942 put hi command of the invasion of North Africa. In he was made Supreme Allied Commander for the invasion of Europe.

After the war, Eisenhower served as Army Chief of Staff from November 1945 until February 1948, when he was appointed president of Columbia University.

In December 1950, President Truman recalled Eisenhower to active duty to command the North Atlantic Treaty Organization forces in Europe. He held this post until the end of May 1952.

At the Republican Convention of July 1952 in Chicago, Eisenhower won the presidential nomination on the first ballot in a close race with Senator Robert A. Taft of Ohio. In November he won the election, defeating Gov. Adlai E. Stevenson of Illinois by an electoral vote of 442 to 89.

Through two terms, Eisenhower hewed to moderate domestic policies. He quested for peace through Free World strength in an era of new nationalisms, nuclear rockets, and space exploration. He fostered alliances pledging the United States to resist Red aggression in Europe, Asia, and Latin America. The Eisenhower Doctrine of 1957 extended commitments to the Middle East.

At home, the popular President lacked G.O.P. Congressional majorities after 1954, but he was reelected in 1956 by 457 electoral votes to 73 for Adlai E. Stevenson.

While retaining most Fair Deal programs, he stressed "fiscal responsibility" in domestic affairs. A moderate in civil rights, he sent troops to Little Rock, Ark., to enforce court-ordered school integration.

With his wartime rank restored by Congress, Eisenhower returned to private life and the role of elder statesman with his vigor hardly impaired by a heart attack, an ileitis operation, and a mild stroke suffered while in office. He died in Washington, D.C., on March 28, 1969.

**JOHN FITZGERALD KENNEDY** was born in Brookline, Mass., on May 29, 1917. His father, Joseph P. Kennedy, was U. S. Ambassador to Great Britain from 1937 to 1940.

Kennedy was graduated from Harvard University in 1940 and joined the Navy in 1941. He became skipper of a PT boat that was sunk in the Pacific by a Japanese destroyer. Although given up for lost, he swam to a safe island, towing an injured enlisted man.

After recovering from a war-aggravated spinal injury, Kennedy entered politics in 1946 and was elected to Congress. In 1952 he ran against Senator Henry Cabot Lodge, Jr., of Massachusetts, and won.

Kennedy was married on Sept. 12, 1953, to Jacqueline Lee Bouvier, by whom he had three children: Caroline, John Fitzgerald, Jr., and Patrick Bouvier (died in infancy).

In 1957 Kennedy won the Pulitzer Prize for a book he had written earlier, *Profiles in Courage.*

After strenuous primary battles Kennedy won the Democratic presidential nomination on the first ballot at the 1960 Los Angeles convention. With a plurality of only 118,574 votes, he carried the November election with an electoral vote of 303 to Vice President Richard M. Nixon's 219, becoming the first Roman Catholic President.

Kennedy brought to the White House the dy-amic idea of a "New Frontier" approach in deal- with problems at home, abroad, and in the ensions of space. Out of his leadership in his few months in office came the 10-year Alliance for Progress to aid Latin America, the Peace Corps, and accelerated programs that brought the first Americans into orbit in the race in space.

Failure of the U. S.-supported Cuban invasion in April 1961 led to the entrenchment of the Communist-backed Castro regime, only 90 miles from United States soil. When it became known that Soviet offensive missiles were being installed in Cuba in 1962, the President ordered a naval "quarantine" of the island and moved troops into position to eliminate this threat to U. S. security. The world seemed on the brink of a nuclear war until Khrushchev ordered the removal of the missiles.

A sudden "thaw," or the appearance of one, in the cold war came with the agreement with the Soviet Union on a limited test-ban treaty signed in Moscow on Aug. 6, 1963.

In his domestic policies Kennedy's proposals for medical care for the aged, expanded area redevelopment, and aid to education were defeated, but on minimum wage, trade legislation, and other measures he won important victories.

Widespread racial disorders and demonstrations led to Kennedy's proposing sweeping civil rights legislation. As his third year in office drew to a close, he also recommended an $11-billion tax cut to bolster the economy. Both measures were pending in Congress when Kennedy, looking forward to a second term, journeyed to Texas for a series of speeches.

While riding in a procession in Dallas on Nov. 22, 1963, he was shot to death by an assassin firing from an upper floor of a building. The alleged assassin, Lee Harvey Oswald, was killed two days later in the Dallas city jail by Jack Ruby, owner of a strip-tease place.

At 46 years of age, Kennedy became the fourth President to be assassinated and the eighth to die in office.

**LYNDON BAINES JOHNSON** was born in Stonewall, Tex., on Aug. 27, 1908. On both sides of his family he had a political heritage mingled with a Baptist background of preachers and teachers. Both his father and his paternal grandfather served in the Texas House of Representatives.

After having been graduated from Southwest Texas State Teachers College, Johnson taught school for two years. He went to Washington in 1932 as secretary to Rep. Richard M. Kleberg. During this time he married Claudia Alta Taylor, known as "Lady Bird." They had two children: Lynda Bird (Robb) and Luci Baines (Nugent).

In 1935, Johnson became Texas administrator for the National Youth Administration. Two years later he was elected to Congress as an all-out supporter of Franklin D. Roosevelt. He was the first member of Congress to enlist in the armed forces after the attack on Pearl Harbor. He served in the Navy in the Pacific and won a Silver Star.

Johnson lost his first bid for a Senate seat in 1941, but won in 1948 after he had captured the Democratic nomination by only 87 votes. He was 40 years old. He became the Senate Democratic leader in 1953. A heart attack in 1955 threatened the end of his active political career, but he recovered fully and resumed his duties.

At the height of his power as Senate leader, Johnson sought the Democratic nomination for President in 1960. When he lost to John F. Kennedy he surprised even some of his closest associates by accepting second place on the ticket.

Johnson was riding in another car in the motorcade when Kennedy was assassinated in Dallas on Nov. 22, 1963. He took the oath of office in the presidential jet on the Dallas airfield.

With Johnson's insistent backing, Congress finally adopted a far-reaching civil rights bill, a voting rights bill, a Medicare program for the aged, and measures to improve education and conservation. Congress also began what Johnson described as "an all-out war" on poverty.

Reaching a record-breaking majority of nearly 16 million votes, Johnson was elected President in his own right in 1964. His electoral vote was 486 to 52 for his Republican opponent, Barry M. Goldwater.

The double tragedy of a war in Asia and urban riots at home marked Johnson's last two years in office. Faced with disunity in the nation and challenges within his own party, Johnson surprised the country on Mar. 31, 1968, with the announcement that he would not be a candidate for re-election. He died of a heart attack on Jan. 22, 1973.

**RICHARD MILHOUS NIXON** was born in Yorba Linda, Calif., on Jan. 9, 1913, to Midwestern-bred parents, Francis A. and Hannah Milhous Nixon, who raised their five sons as Quakers.

Nixon was a high school debater and was undergraduate president at Whittier College in California, where he was graduated in 1934. As a scholarship student at Duke University Law School in North Carolina, he graduated third in his class in 1937.

After five years as a lawyer, Nixon joined the Navy in August 1942. He was an air transport officer in the South Pacific and a legal officer stateside before his discharge in 1946 as a lieutenant commander.

Running for Congress as a Republican in 1946, Nixon defeated Rep. Jerry Voorhis (D-Calif.). On the House Un-American Activities Committee, he made a name as an investigator of Alger Hiss, who was later jailed for perjury. In 1950 Nixon defeated Rep. Helen Gahagan Douglas, a Democrat, for a vacant California Senate seat. He was criticized for portraying her as a Communist dupe.

Nixon's anti-Communism, his Western base and his youth figured in his selection in 1952 to run for vice president on the ticket headed by Dwight D. Eisenhower. Demands for Nixon's withdrawal followed disclosure that California businessmen had paid some of his Senate office expenses. He televised rebuttal, known as "the Checkers speech" (named for a cocker spaniel given to the Nixons), brought him support from the public and from Eisenhower. The ticket won easily in 1952 and again in 1956.

Eisenhower gave Nixon substantive assignments, including missions to 56 foreign countries. In Moscow in 1959, Nixon won acclaim for his defense of U.S. interests in an impromptu "kitchen debate" with Soviet Premier Nikita S. Khrushchev.

Nixon won the 1960 GOP Presidential nomination, but lost the election to Democratic Senator John F. Kennedy by 118,574 votes out of 68,838,-219. The electoral vote was 303 to 219.

In 1962 Nixon failed in a bid for California's governorship and seemed to be finished as a national candidate. He became a Wall Street lawyer, but kept his old party ties and developed new ones through constant travels to speak for Republicans.

Nixon won the 1968 GOP presidential nomination after a shrewd primary campaign, then made Maryland Governor Spiro T. Agnew his surprise choice for vice president. In the election, they edged out the Democratic ticket headed by Vice President Hubert H. Humphrey by 510,314 votes out of 73,212,065. The electoral vote was 301 to 191.

Committed to wind down the U.S. role in the Vietnam war, Nixon pursued "Vietnamization"—training and equipping South Vietnamese to do their own fighting. American ground combat forces in Vietnam fell steadily from 540,000 when Nixon took office to none in 1973 when the military draft was ended. But there was heavy continuing use of U.S. air power.

Nixon improved relations with Moscow and reopened the long-closed door to mainland China with a good-will trip there in February 1972. In May of that year, he visited Moscow and signed agreements on arms limitation and trade expansion and approved plans for a joint U.S.-Soviet space mission in 1975.

Inflation was a campaign issue for Nixon, but he failed to master it as President. On Aug. 15, 1971, with unemployment edging up, Nixon abruptly announced a new economic policy: A 90-day wage-price freeze, stimulative tax cuts, a temporary 10% tariff, spending cuts. A second phase, imposing guidelines on wage, price and rent boosts, was announced October 7.

The economy responded in time for the 1972 campaign, in which Nixon played up his foreign-policy achievements. Played down was the burglary on June 17, 1972, of Democratic national headquarters in the Washington, D.C., Watergate apartment complex. The Nixon-Agnew re-election campaign cost a record $60 million and swamped the Democratic ticket headed by Sen. George S. McGovern of South Dakota with a plurality of 17,-999,528 out of 77,718,554 votes. Only Massachusetts, with 14 electoral votes, and the District of Columbia, with 3, went for McGovern.

In January 1973 hints of a cover-up emerged at the trial of six men found guilty of the Watergate burglary. With a Senate investigation under way, Nixon announced on April 30 the resignations of his top aides, H. R. Haldeman and John D. Ehrlichman, and the dismissal of White House counsel John Dean III. Dean was the star witness at televised Senate hearings that exposed both a White House cover-up of Watergate and massive illegalities in GOP fund-raising in 1972.

The hearings also disclosed that Nixon had routinely tape-recorded his office meetings and telephone conversations.

On Oct. 10, 1973, Agnew resigned as vice president, then pleaded no-contest to a negotiated federal charge of evading income taxes on alleged bribes. Two days later Nixon nominated the House minority leader, Rep. Gerald R. Ford of Michigan, as the new vice president. Congress confirmed Ford Dec. 6, 1973.

In June 1974 Nixon visited Israel and four Arab nations. In July he met in Moscow with Soviet leader Leonid I. Brezhnev and reached preliminary nuclear arms limitation agreements.

But, in the month after his return, Watergate ended the Nixon regime. On July 24 the Supreme Court ordered Nixon to surrender subpoenaed tapes. On July 30 the Judiciary Committee referred three impeachment articles to the House. On August 5, Nixon bowed to the Supreme Court and released tapes showing he halted an FBI probe of the Watergate burglary six days after it occurred. It was in effect an admission of obstruction of justice and impeachment appeared inevitable.

Nixon resigned Aug. 9, 1974, the first President ever to do so. A month later, President Ford issued an unconditional pardon for any offenses Nixon might have committed as President, thus forestalling possible prosecution.

In 1940, Nixon married Thelma Catherine (Pat) Ryan. They had two daughters, Patricia (Tricia) Cox and Julie, who married Dwight David Eisenhower II, grandson of the former President.

**GERALD RUDOLPH FORD** was born in Omaha, Neb., on July 14, 1913, the only child of Leslie and Dorothy Gardner King. His parents were divorced in 1915. His mother moved to Grand Rapids, Mich., and married Gerald R. Ford. The boy was renamed for his stepfather.

Ford captained his high school football team in Grand Rapids and a football scholarship took him to the University of Michigan, where he starred as varsity center before his graduation in 1935. A job as assistant football coach at Yale gave him an opportunity to attend Yale Law School, where he graduated in the top third of his class in 1941.

He returned to Grand Rapids to practice law, but entered the Navy in April 1942. He saw wartime service in the Pacific on the light aircraft carrier *Monterey* and was a lieutenant commander when he returned to Grand Rapids early in 1946 to resume law practice and dabble in politics.

Ford got to Congress in 1948 by scoring a primary victory over Republican Rep. Bartel J. Jonkman, a conservative isolationist, and then winning the first of 13 elections to the House. He was soon assigned to the influential Appropriations Committee and rose to become the ranking Republican on the subcommittee on Defense Department appropriations and an expert in the field.

As a legislator, Ford described himself as "a moderate on domestic issues, a conservative in fiscal affairs, and a dyed-in-the-wool internationalist." He carried the ball for Pentagon appropriations, was a hawk on Vietnam, and kept a low profile on civil rights issues.

He was also dependable and hard-working and popular with his colleagues. In 1963 he was elected chairman of the House Republican Conference. He served in 1963–64 as a member of the Warren Commission that investigated the assassination of President John F. Kennedy. A revolt by dissatisfied younger Republicans in 1965 made him minority leader.

Ford shelved his hopes for the Speakership on Oct. 12, 1973, when Nixon nominated him to fill the vice presidency left vacant by Agnew's resignation under fire. It was the first use of the procedures for filling vacancies in the vice presidency laid down in the 25th Amendment to the Constitution, which Ford had helped enact.

Congress confirmed Ford as vice president on Dec. 6, 1973. Once in office, he said in speeches he did not believe Nixon was involved in the Watergate scandals, but criticized the President's stubborn court battle against releasing tape recordings of Watergate-related conversations for use as evidence.

The scandals led to Nixon's unprecedented resignation and Ford was sworn in immediately as the 38th President, the first to enter the White House without winning a national election.

Ford assured the nation when he took office that "our long national nightmare is over" and pledged "openness and candor" in all his actions. He won a warm response from the Democratic 93rd Congress when he said he wanted "a good marriage" rather than a honeymoon with his former colleagues. In December 1974 Congressional majorities backed his choice of former New York Governor Nelson A. Rockefeller as his successor in the again-vacant vice presidency.

The cordiality was chilled by Ford's announcement on Sept. 8, 1974, that he had granted an unconditional pardon to Nixon for any crimes he might have committed as President. Although no formal charges were pending, Ford said he feared "ugly passions" would be aroused if Nixon were brought to trial. The pardon was widely criticized.

To fight inflation, the new President first proposed fiscal restraints and spending curbs and a 5% tax surcharge that got nowhere in Congress. But rising unemployment led him early in 1975 to propose a broad tax-reduction program and energy-conservation measures that were expected to produce a record peacetime budget deficit of at least $60 billion in fiscal year 1976. Congress was slow to respond.

Congress rebuffed Ford in the spring of 1975 when he appealed for emergency military aid to help the governments of South Vietnam and Cambodia resist massive Communist offensives.

In November 1974 Ford visited Japan, South Korea, and the Soviet Union, where he and Soviet leader Leonid I. Brezhnev conferred in Vladivostok and reached a tentative agreement to limit the number of strategic offensive nuclear weapons. It was Ford's first meeting as President with Brezhnev, who planned a return visit to Washington in the fall of 1975.

Politically, Ford's fortunes improved steadily in the first half of 1975. Badly divided Democrats in Congress were unable to muster votes to override his vetoes of spending bills that exceeded his budget. He faced some right-wing opposition in his own party, but moved to pre-empt it with an early announcement—on July 8, 1975—of his intention to be a candidate in 1976.

Early state primaries in 1976 suggested an easy victory for Ford despite Ronald Reagan's bitter attacks on administration foreign policy and defense programs. But later Reagan primary successes threatened the President's lead. At the Kansas City convention in August, Ford was nominated by the narrow margin of 1,187 to 1,070. But Reagan had moved the party to the right and Ford himself was regarded as a caretaker President lacking in strength and vision. He was defeated in the November election by Jimmy Carter.

In 1948, Ford married Elizabeth Anne (Betty) Bloomer. They had four children, Michael Gerald, John Gardner, Steven Meigs, and Susan Elizabeth.

**JAMES EARL CARTER, JR.** was born in the village of Plains, Ga., Oct. 1, 1924, and grew up on the family farm at nearby Archery. Both parents were fifth-generation Georgians. His father, James Earl Carter, who died in 1953, was known as a segregationist, yet treated his black and white farm workers equally and was known for his lenient credit policies to the black families who made up most of the customers of his store in Archery. His mother, Lillian Gordy, was a matriarchal presence in the family and community and opposed the then-prevailing code of racial inequality.

In 1942 Carter was graduated from the U.S. Naval Academy at Annapolis and entered the nuclear-submarine program, working for Adm. Hyman G. Rickover. In 1946 he married Rosalynn Smith, daughter of a neighboring family. Their first child,

John William, was born a year later in Portsmouth, Va. Their other children are James Earl III, born in Honolulu in 1950; Donnel Jeffrey, born in New London, Conn., in 1952; and Amy Lynn, born in Plains, Ga., in 1967.

In 1954, after his father's death, Carter resigned from the Navy to take over the family business, which became one of the most flourishing agricultural enterprises in Georgia.

Carter's political career began in earnest with his election to the Georgia Senate in 1962. In 1966 he ran for governor and was defeated. In 1970 he ran again, successfully. During his term as governor, state government reorganization sharply reduced the number of state agencies. New social programs, judicial reform, and law-enforcement and highway programs were introduced, with no general tax increase.

In 1972, Carter decided to run for President. In 1974 he became chairman of the Democratic Campaign Committee, working to support congressional and gubernatorial candidates while building a base for himself. He crisscrossed the fifty states, tirelessly calling for revival and reform and gradually building support.

Throughout, he explained his position in a soft Southern drawl and faced down with his electric-blue stare the skeptics who mocked his campaign with gibes about "Jimmy who?" Even while phrasing his positions in a way to win most support with least offense, he pressed them with single-minded fervor. In July 1976 his mother said, "Jimmy always had big ideas. But they were never bigger than his willingness to work for them and make them happen."

Carter is a Southern Baptist, a "born again" Christian in a conservative and evangelical church. Despite the major influence of religion in his life, he has repeatedly stressed his commitment to separation of church and state. He is a serious reader of such innovative theologians as Niebuhr and Kierkegaard.

One campaign problem was Carter's image as the typical Southern white. This was erased when in 1975 he won the support of most of the old Southern civil rights coalition after endorsement by Rep. Andrew Young, a Black Democrat from Atlanta, who was a close aide to the late Dr. Martin Luther King, Jr. At his 1971 inauguration as governor, Carter demanded an end to all racial discrimination and later hung a portrait of Dr. King in the state capitol.

In the spring of 1976 Carter won 19 of the 31 primaries with a broad appeal to conservatives and liberals, black and white, poor and well-to-do.

After a closely fought primary campaign, Carter was nominated at the 3,000-delegate 37th Democratic National Convention at New York's Madison Square Garden, chosen on the first roll-call vote after the convention adopted a platform bearing his imprint. His choice of Sen. Walter F. Mondale of Minnesota as his vice president was endorsed enthusiastically by the convention.

Public-opinion polls reflected a gradual drop in Carter's popularity to the point that the election outcome was viewed as a toss-up. However, Carter won the Bicentennial year election with a bare electoral majority, 297 to 241, and a popular plurality of 1,743,866.

## Presidents

| Name and (party)[1] | Term | State of birth | Born | Died | Religion | Age at inaug. | Age at death |
|---|---|---|---|---|---|---|---|
| 1. Washington (F)[2] | 1789–1797 | Va. | 2/22/1732 | 12/14/1799 | Episcopalian | 57 | 67 |
| 2. J. Adams (F) | 1797–1801 | Mass. | 10/30/1735 | 7/4/1826 | Unitarian | 61 | 90 |
| 3. Jefferson (DR) | 1801–1809 | Va. | 4/13/1743 | 7/4/1826 | Deist | 57 | 83 |
| 4. Madison (DR) | 1809–1817 | Va. | 3/16/1751 | 6/28/1836 | Episcopalian | 57 | 85 |
| 5. Monroe (DR) | 1817–1825 | Va. | 4/28/1758 | 7/4/1831 | Episcopalian | 58 | 73 |
| 6. J. Q. Adams (DR) | 1825–1829 | Mass. | 7/11/1767 | 2/23/1848 | Unitarian | 57 | 80 |
| 7. Jackson (D) | 1829–1837 | S.C. | 3/15/1767 | 6/8/1845 | Presbyterian | 61 | 78 |
| 8. Van Buren (D) | 1837–1841 | N.Y. | 12/5/1782 | 7/24/1862 | Reformed Dutch | 54 | 79 |
| 9. W. H. Harrison (W)[3] | 1841 | Va. | 2/9/1773 | 4/4/1841 | Episcopalian | 68 | 68 |
| 10. Tyler (W) | 1841–1845 | Va. | 3/29/1790 | 1/18/1862 | Episcopalian | 51 | 71 |
| 11. Polk (D) | 1845–1849 | N.C. | 11/2/1795 | 6/15/1849 | Methodist | 49 | 53 |
| 12. Taylor (W)[3] | 1849–1850 | Va. | 11/24/1784 | 7/9/1850 | Episcopalian | 64 | 65 |
| 13. Fillmore (W) | 1850–1853 | N.Y. | 1/7/1800 | 3/8/1874 | Unitarian | 50 | 74 |
| 14. Pierce (D) | 1853–1857 | N.H. | 11/23/1804 | 10/8/1869 | Episcopalian | 48 | 64 |
| 15. Buchanan (D) | 1857–1861 | Pa. | 4/23/1791 | 6/1/1868 | Presbyterian | 65 | 77 |
| 16. Lincoln (R)[4] | 1861–1865 | Ky. | 2/12/1809 | 4/15/1865 | Liberal | 52 | 56 |
| 17. A. Johnson (U)[5] | 1865–1869 | N.C. | 12/29/1808 | 7/31/1875 | (6) | 56 | 66 |
| 18. Grant (R) | 1869–1877 | Ohio | 4/27/1822 | 7/23/1885 | Methodist | 46 | 63 |
| 19. Hayes (R) | 1877–1881 | Ohio | 10/4/1822 | 1/17/1893 | Methodist | 54 | 70 |
| 20. Garfield (R)[4] | 1881 | Ohio | 11/19/1831 | 9/19/1881 | Disciples of Christ | 49 | 49 |
| 21. Arthur (R) | 1881–1885 | Vt. | 10/5/1830 | 11/18/1886 | Episcopalian | 50 | 56 |
| 22. Cleveland (D) | 1885–1889 | N.J. | 3/18/1837 | 6/24/1908 | Presbyterian | 47 | 71 |
| 23. B. Harrison (R) | 1889–1893 | Ohio | 8/20/1833 | 3/13/1901 | Presbyterian | 55 | 67 |
| 24. Cleveland (D)[7] | 1893–1897 | — | — | — | — | 55 | — |
| 25. McKinley (R)[4] | 1897–1901 | Ohio | 1/29/1843 | 9/14/1901 | Methodist | 54 | 58 |
| 26. T. Roosevelt (R) | 1901–1909 | N.Y. | 10/27/1858 | 1/6/1919 | Reformed Dutch | 42 | 60 |
| 27. Taft (R) | 1909–1913 | Ohio | 9/15/1857 | 3/8/1930 | Unitarian | 51 | 72 |
| 28. Wilson (D) | 1913–1921 | Va. | 12/28/1856 | 2/3/1924 | Presbyterian | 56 | 67 |

| Name and (party)[1] | Term | State of birth | Born | Died | Religion | Age at inaug. | Age at death |
|---|---|---|---|---|---|---|---|
| 29. Harding (R)[3] | 1921–1923 | Ohio | 11/2/1865 | 8/2/1923 | Baptist | 55 | 57 |
| 30. Coolidge (R) | 1923–1929 | Vt. | 7/4/1872 | 1/5/1933 | Congregationalist | 51 | 60 |
| 31. Hoover (R) | 1929–1933 | Iowa | 8/10/1874 | 10/20/1964 | Quaker | 54 | 90 |
| 32. F. D. Roosevelt (D)[3] | 1933–1945 | N.Y. | 1/30/1882 | 4/12/1945 | Episcopalian | 51 | 63 |
| 33. Truman (D) | 1945–1953 | Mo. | 5/8/1884 | 12/26/1972 | Baptist | 60 | 88 |
| 34. Eisenhower (R) | 1953–1961 | Tex. | 10/14/1890 | 3/28/1969 | Presbyterian | 62 | 78 |
| 35. Kennedy (D)[4] | 1961–1963 | Mass. | 5/29/1917 | 11/22/1963 | Roman Catholic | 43 | 46 |
| 36. L. B. Johnson (D) | 1963–1969 | Tex. | 8/27/1908 | 1/22/1973 | Disciples of Christ | 55 | 64 |
| 37. Nixon (R)[8] | 1969–1974 | Calif. | 1/9/1913 | — | Quaker | 56 | — |
| 38. Ford (R) | 1974–1977 | Neb. | 7/14/1913 | — | Episcopalian | 61 | — |
| 39. Carter (D) | 1977– | Ga. | 10/14/1924 | — | Southern Baptist | 52 | — |

1. F—Federalist; DR—Democratic-Republican; D—Democratic; W—Whig; R—Republican; U—Union. 2. No party for first election. The party system in the U.S. made its appearance during Washington's first term. 3. Died in office. 4. Assassinated in office. 5. The Republican National Convention of 1864 adopted the name Union Party. It renominated Lincoln for President; for Vice President it nominated Johnson, a War Democrat. Although frequently listed as a Republican Vice President and President, Johnson undoubtedly considered himself strictly a member of the Union Party. When that party broke apart after 1868, he returned to the Democratic Party. 6. Johnson was not a professed church member; however, he admired the Baptist principles of church government. 7. Second nonconsecutive term. 8. Resigned Aug. 9, 1974.

## Burial Places of the Presidents

| President | Burial place | President | Burial place |
|---|---|---|---|
| Washington | Mt. Vernon, Va. | Grant | New York City |
| J. Adams | Quincy, Mass. | Hayes | Fremont, Ohio |
| Jefferson | Charlottesville, Va. | Garfield | Cleveland, Ohio |
| Madison | Montpelier Station, Va. | Arthur | Albany, N.Y. |
| Monroe | Richmond, Va. | Cleveland | Princeton, N.J. |
| J. Q. Adams | Quincy, Mass. | B. Harrison | Indianapolis, Ind. |
| Jackson | The Hermitage, nr. Nashville, Tenn. | McKinley | Canton, Ohio |
| | | T. Roosevelt | Oyster Bay, N.Y. |
| Van Buren | Kinderhook, N.Y. | Taft | Arlington National Cemetery |
| W. H. Harrison | North Bend, Ohio | Wilson | Washington National Cathedral |
| Tyler | Richmond, Va. | Harding | Marion, Ohio |
| Polk | Nashville, Tenn. | Coolidge | Plymouth, Vt. |
| Taylor | Louisville, Ky. | Hoover | West Branch, Iowa |
| Fillmore | Buffalo, N.Y. | F. D. Roosevelt | Hyde Park, N.Y. |
| Pierce | Concord, N.H. | Truman | Independence, Mo. |
| Buchanan | Lancaster, Pa. | Eisenhower | Abilene, Kan. |
| Lincoln | Springfield, Ill. | Kennedy | Arlington National Cemetery |
| A. Johnson | Greeneville, Tenn. | L. B. Johnson | Stonewall, Tex. |

## Wives and Children of the Presidents

| President | Wife's name | Year and place of wife's birth | Married | Wife died | Children of President[1] | |
|---|---|---|---|---|---|---|
| | | | | | Sons | Daughters |
| Washington | Mrs. Martha Dandridge Custis | 1732, Va. | 1759 | 1802 | — | — |
| John Adams | Abigail Smith | 1744, Mass. | 1764 | 1818 | 3 | 2 |
| Jefferson | Mrs. Martha Wayles Skelton | 1748, Va. | 1772 | 1782 | 1 | 5 |
| Madison | Mrs. Dorothy "Dolley" Payne Todd | 1768, N.C. | 1794 | 1849 | — | — |
| Monroe | Elizabeth "Eliza" Kortright | 1768, N.Y. | 1786 | 1830 | — | 2 |
| J. Q. Adams | Louisa Catherine Johnson | 1775, England | 1797 | 1852 | 3 | 1 |
| Jackson | Mrs. Rachel Donelson Robards | 1767, Va. | 1791 | 1828 | — | — |
| Van Buren | Hannah Hoes | 1788, N.Y. | 1807 | 1819 | 4 | — |
| W. H. Harrison | Anna Symmes | 1775, N.J. | 1795 | 1864 | 6 | 4 |
| Tyler | Letitia Christian | 1790, Va. | 1813 | 1842 | 3 | 4 |
| | Julia Gardiner | 1820, N.Y. | 1844 | 1889 | 5 | 2 |
| Polk | Sarah Childress | 1803, Tenn. | 1824 | 1891 | — | — |
| Taylor | Margaret Smith | 1788, Md. | 1810 | 1852 | 1 | 5 |
| Fillmore | Abigail Powers | 1798, N.Y. | 1826 | 1853 | 1 | 1 |
| | Mrs. Caroline Carmichael McIntosh | 1813, N.J. | 1858 | 1881 | — | — |
| Pierce | Jane Means Appleton | 1806, N.H. | 1834 | 1863 | 3 | — |

| President | Wife's name | Year and place of wife's birth | Married | Wife died | Children of President[1] | |
|---|---|---|---|---|---|---|
| | | | | | Sons | Daughters |
| Buchanan | (Unmarried) | — | — | — | — | — |
| Lincoln | Mary Todd | 1818, Ky. | 1842 | 1882 | 4 | — |
| A. Johnson | Eliza McCardle | 1810, Tenn. | 1827 | 1876 | 3 | 2 |
| Grant | Julia Dent | 1826, Mo. | 1848 | 1902 | 3 | 1 |
| Hayes | Lucy Ware Webb | 1831, Ohio | 1852 | 1889 | 7 | 1 |
| Garfield | Lucretia Rudolph | 1832, Ohio | 1858 | 1918 | 5 | 2 |
| Arthur | Ellen Lewis Herndon | 1837, Va. | 1859 | 1880 | 2 | 1 |
| Cleveland | Frances Folsom | 1864, N.Y. | 1886 | 1947 | 2 | 3 |
| B. Harrison | Caroline Lavinia Scott | 1832, Ohio | 1853 | 1892 | 1 | 1 |
| | Mrs. Mary Scott Lord Dimmick | 1858, Pa. | 1896 | 1948 | — | 1 |
| McKinley | Ida Saxton | 1847, Ohio | 1871 | 1907 | — | 2 |
| T. Roosevelt | Alice Hathaway Lee | 1861, Mass. | 1880 | 1884 | — | 1 |
| | Edith Kermit Carow | 1861, Conn. | 1886 | 1948 | 4 | 1 |
| Taft | Helen Herron | 1861, Ohio | 1886 | 1943 | 2 | 1 |
| Wilson | Ellen Louise Axson | 1860, Ga. | 1885 | 1914 | — | 3 |
| | Mrs. Edith Bolling Galt | 1872, Va. | 1915 | 1961 | — | — |
| Harding | Mrs. Florence Kling DeWolfe | 1860, Ohio | 1891 | 1924 | — | — |
| Coolidge | Grace Anna Goodhue | 1879, Vt. | 1905 | 1957 | 2 | — |
| Hoover | Lou Henry | 1875, Iowa | 1899 | 1944 | 2 | — |
| F. D. Roosevelt | Anna Eleanor Roosevelt | 1884, N.Y. | 1905 | 1962 | 5 | 1 |
| Truman | Bess Wallace | 1885, Mo. | 1919 | — | — | 1 |
| Eisenhower | Mamie Geneva Doud | 1896, Iowa | 1916 | — | 2 | — |
| Kennedy | Jacqueline Lee Bouvier | 1929, N.Y. | 1953 | — | 2[1] | 1 |
| L. B. Johnson | Claudia Alta Taylor | 1912, Tex. | 1934 | — | — | 2 |
| Nixon | Thelma Catherine "Patricia" Ryan | 1912, Nev. | 1940 | — | — | 2 |
| Ford | Mrs. Elizabeth "Betty" Bloomer Warren | 1918, Ill. | 1948 | — | 3 | 1 |
| Carter | Rosalynn Smith | 1928, Ga. | 1946 | — | 3 | 1 |

1. Includes children who died in infancy.

## Vice Presidents

| Name and (party)[1] | Term | State of birth | Birth and death dates | President served under |
|---|---|---|---|---|
| 1. John Adams (F)[2] | 1789–1797 | Massachusetts | 1735–1826 | Washington |
| 2. Thomas Jefferson (DR) | 1797–1801 | Virginia | 1743–1826 | J. Adams |
| 3. Aaron Burr (DR) | 1801–1805 | New Jersey | 1756–1836 | Jefferson |
| 4. George Clinton (DR)[3] | 1805–1812 | New York | 1739–1812 | Jefferson and Madison |
| 5. Elbridge Gerry (DR)[3] | 1813–1814 | Massachusetts | 1744–1814 | Madison |
| 6. Daniel D. Tompkins (DR) | 1817–1825 | New York | 1774–1825 | Monroe |
| 7. John C. Calhoun[4] | 1825–1832 | South Carolina | 1782–1850 | J. Q. Adams and Jackson |
| 8. Martin Van Buren (D) | 1833–1837 | New York | 1782–1862 | Jackson |
| 9. Richard M. Johnson (D) | 1837–1841 | Kentucky | 1780–1850 | Van Buren |
| 10. John Tyler (W)[5] | 1841 | Virginia | 1790–1862 | W. H. Harrison |
| 11. George M. Dallas (D) | 1845–1849 | Pennsylvania | 1792–1864 | Polk |
| 12. Millard Fillmore (W)[5] | 1849–1850 | New York | 1800–1874 | Taylor |
| 13. William R. King (D)[3] | 1853 | North Carolina | 1786–1853 | Pierce |
| 14. John C. Breckinridge (D) | 1857–1861 | Kentucky | 1821–1875 | Buchanan |
| 15. Hannibal Hamlin (R) | 1861–1865 | Maine | 1809–1891 | Lincoln |
| 16. Andrew Johnson (U)[5] | 1865 | North Carolina | 1808–1875 | Lincoln |
| 17. Schuyler Colfax (R) | 1869–1873 | New York | 1823–1885 | Grant |
| 18. Henry Wilson (R)[3] | 1873–1875 | New Hampshire | 1812–1875 | Grant |
| 19. William A. Wheeler (R) | 1877–1881 | New York | 1819–1887 | Hayes |
| 20. Chester A. Arthur(R)[5] | 1881 | Vermont | 1830–1886 | Garfield |
| 21. Thomas A. Hendricks (D)[3] | 1885 | Ohio | 1819–1885 | Cleveland |
| 22. Levi P. Morton (R) | 1889–1893 | Vermont | 1824–1920 | B. Harrison |
| 23. Adlai E. Stevenson (D) | 1893–1897 | Kentucky | 1835–1914 | Cleveland |
| 24. Garrett A. Hobart (R)[3] | 1897–1899 | New Jersey | 1844–1899 | McKinley |
| 25. Theodore Roosevelt (R)[5] | 1901 | New York | 1858–1919 | McKinley |
| 26. Charles W. Fairbanks (R) | 1905–1909 | Ohio | 1852–1918 | T. Roosevelt |
| 27. James S. Sherman (R)[3] | 1909–1912 | New York | 1855–1912 | Taft |
| 28. Thomas R. Marshall (D) | 1913–1921 | Indiana | 1854–1925 | Wilson |
| 29. Calvin Coolidge (R)[5] | 1921–1923 | Vermont | 1872–1933 | Harding |
| 30. Charles G. Dawes (R)– | 1925–1929 | Ohio | 1865–1951 | Coolidge |
| 31. Charles Curtis (R) | 1929–1933 | Kansas | 1860–1936 | Hoover |
| 32. John N. Garner (D) | 1933–1941 | Texas | 1868–1967 | F. D. Roosevelt |
| 33. Henry A. Wallace (D) | 1941–1945 | Iowa | 1888–1965 | F. D. Roosevelt |

| Name and (party)[1] | Term | State of birth | Birth and death dates | President served under |
|---|---|---|---|---|
| 34. Harry S. Truman (D)[5] | 1945 | Missouri | 1884–1972 | F. D. Roosevelt |
| 35. Alben W. Barkley (D) | 1949–1953 | Kentucky | 1877–1956 | Truman |
| 36. Richard M. Nixon (R) | 1953–1961 | California | 1913– | Eisenhower |
| 37. Lyndon B. Johnson (D)[5] | 1961–1963 | Texas | 1908–1973 | Kennedy |
| 38. Hubert H. Humphrey (D) | 1965–1969 | South Dakota | 1911–1978 | Johnson |
| 39. Spiro T. Agnew (R)[6] | 1969–1973 | Maryland | 1918– | Nixon |
| 40. Gerald R. Ford (R)[7] | 1973–1974 | Nebraska | 1913– | Nixon |
| 41. Nelson A. Rockefeller (R)[8] | 1974–1977 | Maine | 1908– | Ford |
| 42. Walter F. Mondale (D) | 1977– | Minnesota | 1928– | Carter |

1. F—Federalist; DR—Democratic-Republican; D—Democratic; W—Whig; R—Republican; U—Union. 2. No party for first election. The party system in the U.S. made its appearance during Washington's first term as President. 3. Died in office. 4. Democratic-Republican with J. Q. Adams; Democratic with Jackson. Calhoun resigned in 1832 to become a U.S. Senator. 5. Succeeded to presidency on death of President. 6. Resigned Oct. 10, 1973, after pleading no contest to Federal income tax evasion charges. 7. Nominated by Nixon on Oct. 12, 1973, under provisions of 25th Amendment. Confirmed by Congress on Dec. 6, 1973, and was sworn in same day. He became President Aug. 9, 1974, upon Nixon's resignation. 8. Nominated by Ford Aug. 20, 1974; confirmed by Congress on Dec. 19, 1974, and was sworn in same day.

# Elections

## How a President Is Nominated and Elected

The National Conventions of both major parties are held sometime during the summer of a presidential-election year. Earlier, each party selects delegates by primaries, conventions, committees, etc.

For their 1976 National Convention, the Republicans allowed each state a base of 6 delegates at large; the District of Columbia, 14; Puerto Rico, 8; Guam and the Virgin Islands, 4 each. In addition, each state received 3 district delegates for each of its Representatives in the House. This did not apply to the District of Columbia, Puerto Rico, Guam, and the Virgin Islands.

Each state was awarded additional delegates at large on the basis of having elected a Republican candidate for President in 1972 and electing Republican candidates for Senator, Governor, and U.S. Representative in the 1972 and 1974 elections.

The number of delegates at the 1976 convention, held in Kansas City, was 2,259. Following is the apportionment of delegates by state:

| | | | | | | | | | | | |
|---|---|---|---|---|---|---|---|---|---|---|---|
| Ala. | 37 | Fla. | 66 | Ky. | 37 | Mont. | 20 | Ohio | 97 | Tex. | 100 |
| Alaska | 19 | Ga. | 48 | La. | 41 | Neb. | 25 | Okla. | 36 | Utah | 20 |
| Ariz. | 29 | Guam | 4 | Me. | 20 | Nev. | 18 | Ore. | 30 | Vt. | 18 |
| Ark. | 27 | Hawaii | 19 | Md. | 43 | N.H. | 21 | Pa. | 103 | Va. | 51 |
| Calif | 167 | Idaho | 21 | Mass. | 43 | N.J. | 67 | P.R. | 8 | V.I. | 4 |
| Colo. | 31 | Ill. | 101 | Mich. | 84 | N.M. | 21 | R.I. | 19 | Wash. | 38 |
| Conn. | 35 | Ind. | 54 | Minn. | 42 | N.Y. | 154 | S.C. | 36 | W.Va. | 28 |
| Del. | 17 | Iowa | 36 | Miss. | 30 | N.C. | 54 | S.D. | 20 | Wis. | 45 |
| D.C. | 14 | Kan. | 34 | Mo. | 49 | N.D. | 18 | Tenn. | 43 | Wyo. | 17 |

The Democrats also based the number of delegates on a state's showing in a recent election, taking into account party enrollment as of Jan. 1, 1976, and total population. Thus, there were 3,048 delegates casting 3,008[1] votes, at the convention which was held in New York City. Following is the apportionment of votes by states:

| | | | | | | | | | | | |
|---|---|---|---|---|---|---|---|---|---|---|---|
| Ala. | 35 | D.C. | 17 | Kan. | 34 | Mo. | 71 | N.D. | 13 | Tenn. | 46 |
| Alaska | 10 | Fla. | 81 | Ky. | 46 | Mont. | 17 | Ohio | 152 | Tex. | 130 |
| Ariz. | 25 | Ga. | 50 | La. | 41 | Neb. | 23 | Okla. | 37 | Utah | 18 |
| Ark. | 26 | Guam | 3 | Me. | 20 | Nev. | 11 | Ore. | 34 | Vt. | 12 |
| alif. | 280 | Hawaii | 17 | Md. | 53 | N.H. | 17 | Pa. | 178 | V.I. | 3 |
| nal Zone | 3 | Idaho | 16 | Mass. | 104 | N.J. | 108 | P.R. | 22 | Va. | 54 |
| o. | 35 | Ill. | 169 | Mich. | 133 | N.M. | 18 | R.I. | 22 | Wash. | 53 |
| n. | 51 | Ind. | 75 | Minn. | 65 | N.Y. | 274 | S.C. | 31 | W.Va. | 33 |
| | 12 | Iowa | 47 | Miss. | 24 | N.C. | 61 | S.D. | 17 | Wis. | 68 |
| | | | | | | | | | | Wyo. | 10 |

## The Conventions

At each convention, a temporary chairman is chosen. After a credentials committee seats the delegates, a permanent chairman is elected. The convention then votes on a platform, drawn up by the platform committee.

By the third or fourth day, presidential nominations begin. The chairman calls the roll of states alphabetically. A state may place a candidate in nomination or yield to another state.

Voting, again alphabetically by roll call of states, begins after all nominations have been made and seconded. A simple majority is required in each party, although this may require many ballots.

Finally, the vice-presidential candidate is selected. Although there is no law saying that the candidates *must* come from different states, it is, practically, necessary for this to be the case. Otherwise, according to the Constitution (*see* Amendment XII), electors from that state could vote for only one of the candidates and would have to cast their other vote for some person of another state. This could result in a presidential candidate's receiving a majority electoral vote and his running mate's failing to.

## The Electoral College

The next step in the process is the nomination of electors in each state, according to its laws. These electors must not be Federal office holders. In the November election, the voters cast their votes for electors, not for President. In some states, the ballots include only the names of the presidential and vice-presidential candidates; in others, they include only names of the electors. Nowadays, it is rare for electors to be split between parties. The last such occurrence was in North Carolina in 1968[2]; the last before that, in Tennessee in 1948. On three occasions (1824, 1876, and 1888), the presidential candidate with the largest popular vote failed to obtain an electoral-vote majority.

Each state has as many electors as it has Senators and Representatives. For the 1976 election, the total electors were 538, based on 100 Senators, 435 Representatives, plus 3 electoral votes from the District of Columbia as a result of the 23rd Amendment to the Constitution.

On the first Monday after the second Wednesday in December, the electors cast their votes in their respective state capitols. Constitutionally they may vote for someone other than the party candidate but usually they do not since they are pledged to one party and its candidate on the ballot. Should the presidential or vice-presidential candidate die between the November election and the December meetings, the electors pledged to vote for him could vote for whomever they pleased. However, it seems certain that the national committee would attempt to get an agreement among the state party leaders for a replacement candidate.

The votes of the electors, certified by the states, are sent to Congress, where the president of the Senate opens the certificates and has them counted in the presence of both Houses on January 6. The new President is inaugurated at noon on January 20.

Should no candidate receive a majority of the electoral vote for President, the House of Representatives chooses a President from among the three highest candidates, voting, not as individuals, but as states, with a majority (now 26) needed to elect. Should no vice-presidential candidate obtain the majority, the Senate, voting as individuals, chooses from the highest two.

1. Includes 3 votes for Democrats abroad. 2. In 1956, 1 of Alabama's 11 electoral votes was cast for Walter B. Jones. In 1960, 6 of Alabama's 11 electoral votes and 1 of Oklahoma's 8 electoral votes were cast for Harry Flood Byrd. (Byrd also received all 8 of Mississippi's electoral votes.)

# Qualifications for Voting

The Supreme Court decision of March 21, 1972, declared lengthy requirements for voting in state and local elections unconstitutional and suggested that 30 days was an ample period. Most of the states have changed or eliminated their durational residency requirements to comply with the ruling, as shown.

**NO DURATIONAL RESIDENCY REQUIREMENT**

Alabama, Arkansas,[12] California, Connecticut, District of Columbia,[2] Georgia,[2] Hawaii, Idaho, Iowa,[6] Louisiana, Maine, Maryland, Massachusetts,[8] Nebraska,[9] New Hampshire, New Mexico,[7] North Carolina, Oklahoma, South Carolina,[2] South Dakota,[10] Tennessee, Texas, Virginia, West Virginia,[2] Wyoming[2]

**30-DAY RESIDENCY REQUIREMENT**

Alaska, Arizona,[11] Illinois, Indiana, Kentucky,[2] Michigan, Mississippi, Montana, Nevada, New Jersey, New York, North Dakota,[3] Ohio, Oregon, Pennsylvania, Rhode Island, Utah, Washington

**OTHER**

Colorado,[1] Delaware,[13] Florida,[5] Kansas, Minnesota, 20 days; Missouri,[4] 6 months; Vermont, 17 days; Wisconsin, 10 days

1. 29-day for Presidential elections, 32 for all other. 2. 30-day registration requirement. 3. 10-day for Presidential electio 4. 28 days in St. Louis County, 4th Wednesday prior to elections in rest of state. 5. 30-day for Presidential elections, 45 all other. 6. 10-day registration requirement. 7. 42-day registration requirement. 8. Registration deadline 28 days pri primary or state elections. 9. Registration requirement, 2nd Friday prior to elections. 10. 15-day registration require 11. 50-day for state. 12. 20-day registration requirement. 13. 1-year in state; 3-mo. in county, 30-day in election d
*Source: Information Please* questionnaires to the states.

# Presidential Elections, 1789 to 1976

For the original method of electing the President and the Vice President (elections of 1789, 1792, 1796, and 1800), see Article II, Section 1, of the Constitution. The election of 1804 was the first one in which the electors voted for President and Vice President on separate ballots. (See Amendment XII to the Constitution.)

| Year | Presidential candidates | Party | Electoral vote |
|---|---|---|---|
| 1789[1] | George Washington | (no party) | 69 |
| | John Adams | (no party) | 34 |
| | Scattering | (no party) | 35 |
| | Votes not cast | | 8 |
| 1792 | George Washington | Federalist | 132 |
| | John Adams | Federalist | 77 |
| | George Clinton | Anti-Federalist | 50 |
| | Thomas Jefferson | Anti-Federalist | 4 |
| | Aaron Burr | Anti-Federalist | 1 |
| | Votes not cast | | 6 |
| 1796 | John Adams | Federalist | 71 |
| | Thomas Jefferson | Dem.-Rep. | 68 |
| | Thomas Pinckney | Federalist | 59 |
| | Aaron Burr | Dem.-Rep. | 30 |
| | Scattering | | 48 |
| 1800[2] | Thomas Jefferson | Dem.-Rep. | 73 |
| | Aaron Burr | Dem.-Rep. | 73 |
| | John Adams | Federalist | 65 |
| | Charles C. Pinckney | Federalist | 64 |
| | John Jay | Federalist | 1 |

| Year | Presidential candidates | Party | Electoral vote | Vice-presidential candidates | Party | Electoral vote |
|---|---|---|---|---|---|---|
| 1804 | Thomas Jefferson | Dem.-Rep. | 162 | George Clinton | Dem.-Rep. | 162 |
| | Charles C. Pinckney | Federalist | 14 | Rufus King | Federalist | 14 |
| 1808 | James Madison | Dem.-Rep. | 122 | George Clinton | Dem.-Rep. | 113 |
| | Charles C. Pinckney | Federalist | 47 | Rufus King | Federalist | 47 |
| | George Clinton | Dem.-Rep. | 6 | John Langdon | Ind. (no party) | 9 |
| | Votes not cast | | 1 | James Madison | Dem.-Rep. | 3 |
| | | | | James Monroe | Dem.-Rep. | 3 |
| | | | | Votes not cast | | 1 |
| 1812 | James Madison | Dem.-Rep. | 128 | Elbridge Gerry | Dem.-Rep. | 131 |
| | De Witt Clinton | Federalist | 89 | Jared Ingersoll | Federalist | 86 |
| | Votes not cast | | 1 | Votes not cast | | 1 |
| 1816 | James Monroe | Dem.-Rep. | 183 | Daniel D. Tompkins | Dem.-Rep. | 183 |
| | Rufus King | Federalist | 34 | John E. Howard | Federalist | 22 |
| | Votes not cast | | 4 | James Ross | Ind. (no party) | 5 |
| | | | | John Marshall | Federalist | 4 |
| | | | | Robert G. Harper | Ind. (no party) | 3 |
| | | | | Votes not cast | | 4 |
| 1820 | James Monroe | Dem-Rep | 231 | Daniel D. Tompkins | Dem.-Rep. | 218 |
| | John Quincy Adams | Ind. (no party) | 1 | Richard Stockton | Ind. (no party) | 8 |
| | Votes not cast | | 3 | Daniel Rodney | Ind. (no party) | 4 |
| | | | | Richard Rush | Ind. (no party) | 1 |
| | | | | Robert G. Harper | Ind. (no party) | 1 |
| | | | | Votes not cast | | 3 |
| 1824[3] | John Quincy Adams | (no party) | 84 | John C. Calhoun | (no party) | 182 |
| | Andrew Jackson | (no party) | 99 | Nathan Sanford | (no party) | 30 |
| | William H. Crawford | (no party) | 41 | Nathaniel Macon | (no party) | 24 |
| | Henry Clay | (no party) | 37 | Andrew Jackson | (no party) | 13 |
| | | | | Martin Van Buren | (no party) | 9 |
| | | | | Henry Clay | (no party) | 2 |
| | | | | Votes not cast | | 1 |
| 1828 | Andrew Jackson | Democratic | 178 | John C. Calhoun | Democratic | 171 |
| | John Quincy Adams | Natl. Rep. | 83 | Richard Rush | Natl. Rep. | 83 |
| | | | | William Smith | Democratic | 7 |
| 1832 | Andrew Jackson | Democratic | 219 | Martin Van Buren | Democratic | 189 |
| | Henry Clay | Natl. Rep. | 49 | John Sergeant | Natl. Rep. | 49 |
| | John Floyd | Ind. (no party) | 11 | Henry Lee | Ind. (no party) | 11 |
| | William Wirt | Antimasonic[4] | 7 | Amos Ellmaker | Antimasonic | 7 |
| | Votes not cast | | 2 | William Wilkins | Ind. (no party) | 30 |
| | | | | Votes not cast | | 2 |

| Year | Presidential candidates | Party | Electoral vote | Vice-presidential candidates | Party | Electoral vote |
|---|---|---|---|---|---|---|
| 1836 | Martin Van Buren | Democratic | 170 | Richard M. Johnson[5] | Democratic | 147 |
| | William H. Harrison | Whig | 73 | Francis Granger | Whig | 77 |
| | Hugh L. White | Whig | 26 | John Tyler | Whig | 47 |
| | Daniel Webster | Whig | 14 | William Smith | Ind. (no party) | 23 |
| | W. P. Mangum | Ind. (no party) | 11 | | | |
| 1840 | William H. Harrison[6] | Whig | 234 | John Tyler | Whig | 234 |
| | Martin Van Buren | Democratic | 60 | Richard M. Johnson | Democratic | 48 |
| | | | | L. W. Tazewell | Ind. (no party) | 11 |
| | | | | James K. Polk | Democratic | 1 |
| 1844 | James K. Polk | Democratic | 170 | George M. Dallas | Democratic | 170 |
| | Henry Clay | Whig | 105 | Theo. Frelinghuysen | Whig | 105 |
| 1848 | Zachary Taylor[7] | Whig | 163 | Millard Fillmore | Whig | 163 |
| | Lewis Cass | Democratic | 127 | William O. Butler | Democratic | 127 |
| 1852 | Franklin Pierce | Democratic | 254 | William R. King | Democratic | 254 |
| | Winfield Scott | Whig | 42 | William A. Graham | Whig | 42 |
| 1856 | James Buchanan | Democratic | 174 | John C. Breckinridge | Democratic | 174 |
| | John C. Frémont | Republican | 114 | William L. Dayton | Republican | 114 |
| | Millard Fillmore | American[8] | 8 | A. J. Donelson | American[8] | 8 |
| 1860 | Abraham Lincoln | Republican | 180 | Hannibal Hamlin | Republican | 180 |
| | John C. Breckinridge | Democratic | 72 | Joseph Lane | Democratic | 72 |
| | John Bell | Const. Union | 39 | Edward Everett | Const. Union | 39 |
| | Stephen A. Douglas | Democratic | 12 | H. V. Johnson | Democratic | 12 |
| 1864 | Abraham Lincoln[9] | Union[10] | 212 | Andrew Johnson | Union[15] | 212 |
| | George B. McClellan | Democratic | 21 | G. H. Pendleton | Democratic | 21 |
| 1868 | Ulysses S. Grant | Republican | 214 | Schuyler Colfax | Republican | 214 |
| | Horatio Seymour | Democratic | 80 | Francis P. Blair, Jr. | Democratic | 80 |
| | Votes not counted[11] | | 23 | Votes not counted[11] | | 23 |

| Year | Presidential candidates | Party | Electoral vote | Popular vote | Vice-presidential candidates and party |
|---|---|---|---|---|---|
| 1872 | Ulysses S. Grant | Republican | 286 | 3,597,132 | Henry Wilson—R |
| | Horace Greeley | Dem., Liberal Rep. | ([12]) | 2,834,125 | B. Gratz Brown—D, LR—(47) |
| | Thomas A. Hendricks | Democratic | 42 | | Scattering—(19) |
| | B. Gratz Brown | Dem., Liberal Rep. | 18 | | Votes not counted—(14) |
| | Charles J. Jenkins | Democratic | 2 | | |
| | David Davis | Democratic | 1 | | |
| | Votes not counted | | 17 | | |
| 1876[13] | Rutherford B. Hayes | Republican | 185 | 4,033,768 | William A. Wheeler—R |
| | Samuel J. Tilden | Democratic | 184 | 4,285,992 | Thomas A. Hendricks—D |
| | Peter Cooper | Greenback | 0 | 81,737 | Samuel F. Cary—G |
| 1880 | James A. Garfield[14] | Republican | 214 | 4,449,053 | Chester A. Arthur—R |
| | Winfield S. Hancock | Democratic | 155 | 4,442,035 | William H. English—D |
| | James B. Weaver | Greenback | 0 | 308,578 | B. J. Chambers—G |
| 1884 | Grover Cleveland | Democratic | 219 | 4,911,017 | Thomas A. Hendricks—D |
| | James G. Blaine | Republican | 182 | 4,848,334 | John A. Logan—R |
| | Benjamin F. Butler | Greenback | 0 | 175,370 | A. M. West—G |
| | John P. St. John | Prohibition | 0 | 150,369 | William Daniel—P |
| 1888 | Benjamin Harrison | Republican | 233 | 5,440,216 | Levi P. Morton—R |
| | Grover Cleveland | Democratic | 168 | 5,538,233 | A. G. Thurman—D |
| | Clinton B. Fisk | Prohibition | 0 | 249,506 | John A. Brooks—P |
| | Alson J. Streeter | Union Labor | 0 | 146,935 | Charles E. Cunningham—UL |
| 1892 | Grover Cleveland | Democratic | 277 | 5,556,918 | Adlai E. Stevenson—D |
| | Benjamin Harrison | Republican | 145 | 5,176,108 | Whitelaw Reid—R |
| | James B. Weaver | People's[15] | 22 | 1,041,028 | James G. Field—Peo |
| | John Bidwell | Prohibition | 0 | 264,133 | James B. Cranfill—P |

| Year | Presidential candidates | Party | Electoral vote | Popular vote | Vice-presidential candidates and party |
|---|---|---|---|---|---|
| 1896 | William McKinley | Republican | 271 | 7,035,638 | Garret A. Hobart—R |
| | William J. Bryan | Dem., People's[15] | 176 | 6,467,946 | Arthur Sewall—D—(149) |
| | | | | | Thomas E. Watson—Peo—(27) |
| | John M. Palmer | Natl. Dem. | 0 | 133,148 | Simon B. Buckner—ND |
| | Joshua Levering | Prohibition | 0 | 132,007 | Hale Johnson—P |
| 1900 | William McKinley[16] | Republican | 292 | 7,219,530 | Theodore Roosevelt—R |
| | William J. Bryan | Dem., People's[15] | 155 | 6,358,071 | Adlai E. Stevenson—D, Peo |
| | Eugene V. Debs | Social Democratic | 0 | 94,768 | Job Harriman—SD |
| 1904 | Theodore Roosevelt | Republican | 336 | 7,628,834 | Charles W. Fairbanks—R |
| | Alton B. Parker | Democratic | 140 | 5,084,491 | Henry G. Davis—D |
| | Eugene V. Debs | Socialist | 0 | 402,400 | Benjamin Hanford—S |
| 1908 | William H. Taft | Republican | 321 | 7,679,006 | James S. Sherman—R |
| | William J. Bryan | Democratic | 162 | 6,409,106 | John W. Kern—D |
| | Eugene V. Debs | Socialist | 0 | 402,820 | Benjamin Hanford—S |
| 1912 | Woodrow Wilson | Democratic | 435 | 6,286,214 | Thomas R. Marshall—D |
| | Theodore Roosevelt | Progressive | 88 | 4,126,020 | Hiram Johnson—Prog |
| | William H. Taft | Republican | 8 | 3,483,922 | Nicholas M. Butler—R[17] |
| | Eugene V. Debs | Socialist | 0 | 897,011 | Emil Seidel—S |
| 1916 | Woodrow Wilson | Democratic | 277 | 9,129,606 | Thomas R. Marshall—D |
| | Charles E. Hughes | Republican | 254 | 8,538,221 | Charles W. Fairbanks—R |
| | A. L. Benson | Socialist | 0 | 585,113 | G. R. Kirkpatrick—S |
| 1920 | Warren G. Harding[18] | Republican | 404 | 16,152,200 | Calvin Coolidge—R |
| | James M. Cox | Democratic | 127 | 9,147,353 | Franklin D. Roosevelt—D |
| | Eugene V. Debs | Socialist | 0 | 917,799 | Seymour Stedman—S |
| 1924 | Calvin Coolidge | Republican | 382 | 15,725,016 | Charles G. Dawes—R |
| | John W. Davis | Democratic | 136 | 8,385,586 | Charles W. Bryan—D |
| | Robert M. LaFollette | Progressive, Socialist | 13 | 4,822,856 | Burton K. Wheeler—Prog S |
| 1928 | Herbert Hoover | Republican | 444 | 21,392,190 | Charles Curtis—R |
| | Alfred E. Smith | Democratic | 87 | 15,016,443 | Joseph T. Robinson—D |
| | Norman Thomas | Socialist | 0 | 267,420 | James H. Maurer—S |
| 1932 | Franklin D. Roosevelt | Democratic | 472 | 22,821,857 | John N. Garner—D |
| | Herbert Hoover | Republican | 59 | 15,761,841 | Charles Curtis—R |
| | Norman Thomas | Socialist | 0 | 884,781 | James H. Maurer—S |
| 1936 | Franklin D. Roosevelt | Democratic | 523 | 27,751,597 | John N. Garner—D |
| | Alfred M. Landon | Republican | 8 | 16,679,583 | Frank Knox—R |
| | Norman Thomas | Socialist | 0 | 187,720 | George Nelson—S |
| 1940 | Franklin D. Roosevelt | Democratic | 449 | 27,244,160 | Henry A. Wallace—D |
| | Wendell L. Willkie | Republican | 82 | 22,305,198 | Charles L. McNary—R |
| | Norman Thomas | Socialist | 0 | 99,557 | Maynard C. Krueger—S |
| 1944 | Franklin D. Roosevelt[19] | Democratic | 432 | 25,602,504 | Harry S. Truman—D |
| | Thomas E. Dewey | Republican | 99 | 22,006,285 | John W. Bricker—R |
| | Norman Thomas | Socialist | 0 | 80,518 | Darlington Hoopes—S |
| 1948 | Harry S. Truman | Democratic | 303 | 24,179,345 | Alben W. Barkley—D |
| | Thomas E. Dewey | Republican | 189 | 21,991,291 | Earl Warren—R |
| | J. Strom Thurmond | States' Rights Dem. | 39 | 1,176,125 | Fielding L. Wright—SR |
| | Henry A. Wallace | Progressive | 0 | 1,157,326 | Glen Taylor—Prog |
| | Norman Thomas | Socialist | 0 | 139,572 | Tucker P. Smith—S |
| 1952 | Dwight D. Eisenhower | Republican | 442 | 33,936,234 | Richard M. Nixon—R |
| | Adlai E. Stevenson | Democratic | 89 | 27,314,992 | John J. Sparkman—D |
| 1956[20] | Dwight D. Eisenhower | Republican | 457 | 35,590,472 | Richard M. Nixon—R |
| | Adlai E. Stevenson | Democratic | 73 | 26,022,752 | Estes Kefauver—D |
| | John F. Kennedy[22] | Democratic | 303 | 34,226,731 | Lyndon B. Johnson—D |
| | Richard M. Nixon | Republican | 219 | 34,108,157 | Henry Cabot Lodge—R |

| Year | Presidential candidates | Party | Electoral vote | Popular vote | Vice-presidential candidates and party |
|---|---|---|---|---|---|
| 1964 | Lyndon B. Johnson | Democratic | 486 | 43,129,484 | Hubert H. Humphrey—D |
| | Barry M. Goldwater | Republican | 52 | 27,178,188 | William E. Miller—R |
| 1968 | Richard M. Nixon | Republican | 301 | 31,785,480 | Spiro T. Agnew—R |
| | Hubert H. Humphrey | Democratic | 191 | 31,275,166 | Edmund S. Muskie—D |
| | George C. Wallace | American Independent | 46 | 9,906,473 | Curtis F. LeMay—AI |
| 1972 | Richard M. Nixon[23] | Republican | 520[24] | 47,169,911 | Spiro T. Agnew—R |
| | George McGovern | Democratic | 17 | 29,170,383 | Sargent Shriver—D |
| | John G. Schmitz | American | 0 | 1,099,482 | Thomas J. Anderson—A |
| 1976 | Jimmy Carter | Democrat | 297 | 40,828,657 | Walter F. Mondale—D |
| | Gerald R. Ford | Republican | 240[25] | 39,145,520 | Robert J. Dole—R |
| | Eugene J. McCarthy | Independent | 0 | 756,605 | None |

1. Only 10 states participated in the election. The New York legislature chose no electors, and North Carolina and Rhode Island had not yet ratified the Constitution. 2. As Jefferson and Burr were tied, the House of Representatives chose the President. In a vote by states, 10 votes were cast for Jefferson, 4 for Burr; 2 votes were not cast. 3. As no candidate had an electoral-vote majority, the House of Representatives chose the President from the first three. In a vote by states, 13 votes were cast for Adams, 7 for Jackson, and 4 for Crawford. 4. The Antimasonic Party on Sept. 26, 1831, was the first party to hold a nominating convention to choose candidates for President and Vice-President. 5. As Johnson did not have an electoral-vote majority, the Senate chose him 33–14 over Granger, the others being legally out of the race. 6. Harrison died April 4, 1841, and Tyler succeeded him April 6. 7. Taylor died July 9, 1850, and Fillmore succeeded him July 10. 8. Also known as the Know-Nothing Party. 9. Lincoln died April 15, 1865, and Johnson succeeded him the same day. 10. Name adopted by the Republican National Convention of 1864. Johnson was a War Democrat. 11. 23 Southern electoral votes were excluded. 12. See Election of 1872 in *Unusual Voting Results* under Elections, Presidential, in Index. 13. See Election of 1876 in *Unusual Voting Results* under Elections, Presidential, in Index. 14. Garfield died Sept. 19, 1881, and Arthur succeeded him Sept. 20. 15. Members of People's Party were called Populists. 16. McKinley died Sept. 14, 1901, and Roosevelt succeeded him the same day. 17. James S. Sherman, Republican candidate for Vice President, died Oct. 30, 1912, and the Republican electoral votes were cast for Butler. 18. Harding died Aug. 2, 1923, and Coolidge succeeded him Aug. 3. 19. Roosevelt died April 12, 1945, and Truman succeeded him the same day. 20. One electoral vote from Alabama was cast for Walter B. Jones. 21. Sen. Harry F. Byrd received 15 electoral votes. 22. Kennedy died Nov. 22, 1963, and Johnson succeeded him the same day. 23. Nixon resigned Aug. 9, 1974, and Gerald R. Ford succeeded him the same day. 24. One electoral vote from Virginia was cast for John Hospers, Libertarian Party. 25. One electoral vote from Washington was cast for Ronald Reagan.

## Estimated Population of Voting Age, 1976

**(in thousands)**

| | 18–24 years | 25–44 years | 45–64 years | 65 years and over | Total |
|---|---|---|---|---|---|
| Alabama | 470 | 922 | 720 | 390 | 2,501 |
| Alaska | 65 | 104 | 52 | 9 | 231 |
| Arizona | 301 | 575 | 441 | 238 | 1,555 |
| Arkansas | 257 | 534 | 434 | 278 | 1,503 |
| Calif. | 2,918 | 5,856 | 4,400 | 2,119 | 15,294 |
| Colorado | 380 | 711 | 467 | 215 | 1,773 |
| Conn. | 388 | 814 | 682 | 328 | 2,211 |
| Delaware | 84 | 153 | 115 | 52 | 403 |
| D.C. | 102 | 202 | 139 | 71 | 514 |
| Florida | 1,020 | 2,008 | 1,861 | 1,436 | 6,326 |
| Georgia | 672 | 1,343 | 914 | 445 | 3,375 |
| Hawaii | 142 | 230 | 168 | 61 | 600 |
| Idaho | 110 | 210 | 165 | 82 | 567 |
| Illinois | 1,427 | 2,845 | 2,282 | 1,163 | 7,718 |
| Indiana | 695 | 1,368 | 1,038 | 538 | 3,640 |
| Iowa | 355 | 707 | 582 | 366 | 2,010 |
| Kansas | 307 | 561 | 455 | 287 | 1,610 |
| Kentucky | 445 | 875 | 679 | 375 | 2,374 |
| Louisiana | 522 | 958 | 697 | 355 | 2,532 |
| Maine | 132 | 263 | 218 | 128 | 741 |
| Maryland | 563 | 1,121 | 831 | 348 | 2,863 |
| Mass. | 771 | 1,498 | 1,225 | 679 | 4,173 |
| Michigan | 1,260 | 2,385 | 1,795 | 828 | 6,268 |
| Minnesota | 534 | 1,011 | 730 | 446 | 2,721 |
| Miss. | 308 | 557 | 420 | 260 | 1,544 |
| Missouri | 607 | 1,190 | 943 | 608 | 3,348 |
| Montana | 98 | 188 | 156 | 76 | 518 |
| Nebraska | 204 | 380 | 300 | 196 | 1,080 |
| Nevada | 78 | 169 | 130 | 48 | 424 |
| N.H. | 101 | 223 | 161 | 89 | 574 |
| N.J. | 853 | 1,862 | 1,657 | 783 | 5,154 |
| N.M. | 166 | 294 | 216 | 95 | 771 |
| New York | 2,175 | 4,709 | 3,982 | 2,043 | 12,910 |
| N.C. | 764 | 1,480 | 1,091 | 512 | 3,847 |
| N.D. | 86 | 147 | 125 | 74 | 432 |
| Ohio | 1,417 | 2,769 | 2,195 | 1,078 | 7,459 |
| Oklahoma | 348 | 697 | 553 | 340 | 1,937 |
| Oregon | 295 | 613 | 478 | 266 | 1,653 |
| Pa. | 1,430 | 2,897 | 2,714 | 1,400 | 8,441 |
| R.I. | 112 | 220 | 201 | 115 | 648 |
| S.C. | 411 | 750 | 533 | 239 | 1,933 |
| S.D. | 91 | 154 | 138 | 86 | 469 |
| Tenn. | 532 | 1,122 | 850 | 455 | 2,958 |
| Texas | 1,702 | 3,257 | 2,349 | 1,195 | 8,503 |
| Utah | 190 | 299 | 200 | 94 | 783 |
| Vermont | 61 | 127 | 86 | 53 | 327 |
| Virginia | 738 | 1,356 | 998 | 436 | 3,528 |
| Wash. | 485 | 975 | 700 | 375 | 2,53[illegible] |
| W.Va. | 209 | 452 | 406 | 214 | 1,[illegible] |
| Wis. | 617 | 1,163 | 911 | 519 | 3[illegible] |
| Wyoming | 53 | 99 | 80 | 34 | [illegible] |
| **Total** | **28,055** | **55,403** | **43,664** | **22,918** | **1[illegible]** |

NOTE: Resident population; includes aliens. *Source:* Department of Commerce, Bureau of the Census.

# Presidential Election of 1964

**Principal Candidates for President and Vice President**
**Democratic: Lyndon B. Johnson; Hubert H. Humphrey**
**Republican: Barry M. Goldwater; William E. Miller**

| State | Total | Johnson Dem. | Goldwater Rep. | Plurality | Electoral Vote D | Electoral Vote R | Votes at Natl. Convs. Dem. | Votes at Natl. Convs. Rep. |
|---|---|---|---|---|---|---|---|---|
| Alabama | 689,818 | ([1]) | 479,085 | 268,353 R[2] | — | 10 | 38 | 20 |
| Alaska | 67,259 | 44,329 | 22,930 | 21,399 D | 3 | — | 12 | 12 |
| Arizona | 480,770 | 237,753 | 242,535 | 4,782 R | — | 5 | 19 | 16 |
| Arkansas | 560,246 | 314,197 | 243,264 | 70,933 D | 6 | — | 32 | 12 |
| California | 7,057,586 | 4,171,877 | 2,879,108 | 1,292,769 D | 40 | — | 154 | 86 |
| Colorado | 776,986 | 476,024 | 296,767 | 179,257 D | 6 | — | 23 | 18 |
| Connecticut | 1,218,578 | 826,269 | 390,996 | 435,273 D | 8 | — | 43 | 16 |
| Delaware | 201,320 | 122,704 | 78,078 | 44,626 D | 3 | — | 22 | 12 |
| D. C. | 198,597 | 169,796 | 28,801 | 140,995 D | 3 | — | 16 | 9 |
| Florida | 1,854,481 | 948,540 | 905,941 | 42,599 D | 14 | — | 51 | 34 |
| Georgia | 1,139,335 | 522,556 | 616,584 | 94,028 R | — | 12 | 53 | 24 |
| Hawaii | 207,271 | 163,249 | 44,022 | 119,227 D | 4 | — | 25 | 8 |
| Idaho | 292,477 | 148,920 | 143,557 | 5,363 D | 4 | — | 15 | 14 |
| Illinois | 4,702,841 | 2,796,883 | 1,905,946 | 890,887 D | 26 | — | 114 | 58 |
| Indiana | 2,091,606 | 1,170,848 | 911,118 | 259,730 D | 13 | — | 51 | 32 |
| Iowa | 1,184,539 | 733,030 | 449,148 | 283,882 D | 9 | — | 35 | 24 |
| Kansas | 857,901 | 464,028 | 386,579 | 77,449 D | 7 | — | 27 | 20 |
| Kentucky | 1,046,105 | 669,659 | 372,977 | 296,682 D | 9 | — | 34 | 24 |
| Louisiana | 896,293 | 387,068 | 509,225 | 122,157 R | — | 10 | 46 | 20 |
| Maine | 380,965 | 262,264 | 118,701 | 143,563 D | 4 | — | 16 | 14 |
| Maryland | 1,116,547 | 730,912 | 385,495 | 345,417 D | 10 | — | 48 | 20 |
| Massachusetts | 2,344,798 | 1,786,422 | 549,727 | 1,236,695 D | 14 | — | 69 | 34 |
| Michigan | 3,203,102 | 2,136,615 | 1,060,152 | 1,076,463 D | 21 | — | 92 | 48 |
| Minnesota | 1,554,462 | 991,117 | 559,624 | 431,493 D | 10 | — | 50 | 26 |
| Mississippi | 409,146 | 52,618 | 356,528 | 303,910 R | — | 7 | 24 | 13 |
| Missouri | 1,817,879 | 1,164,344 | 653,535 | 510,809 D | 12 | — | 58 | 24 |
| Montana | 278,628 | 164,246 | 113,032 | 51,214 D | 4 | — | 17 | 14 |
| Nebraska | 584,154 | 307,307 | 276,847 | 30,460 D | 5 | — | 19 | 16 |
| Nevada | 135,433 | 79,339 | 56,094 | 23,245 D | 3 | — | 22 | 6 |
| New Hampshire | 288,093 | 184,064 | 104,029 | 80,035 D | 4 | — | 15 | 14 |
| New Jersey | 2,847,663 | 1,868,231 | 964,174 | 904,057 D | 17 | — | 77 | 40 |
| New Mexico | 328,645 | 194,015 | 132,838 | 61,177 D | 4 | — | 26 | 14 |
| New York | 7,166,275 | 4,913,102[3] | 2,243,559 | 2,669,543 D | 43 | — | 179 | 92 |
| North Carolina | 1,424,983 | 800,139 | 624,844 | 175,295 D | 13 | — | 58 | 26 |
| North Dakota | 258,389 | 149,784 | 108,207 | 41,577 D | 4 | — | 15 | 14 |
| Ohio | 3,969,196 | 2,498,331 | 1,470,865 | 1,207,466 D | 26 | — | 99 | 58 |
| Oklahoma | 932,499 | 519,834 | 412,665 | 107,169 D | 8 | — | 30 | 22 |
| Oregon | 786,305 | 501,017 | 282,779 | 218,238 D | 6 | — | 24 | 18 |
| Pennsylvania | 4,822,690 | 3,130,954 | 1,673,657 | 1,457,297 D | 29 | — | 125 | 64 |
| Rhode Island | 390,091 | 315,463 | 74,615 | 240,848 D | 4 | — | 27 | 14 |
| South Carolina | 524,779 | 215,723 | 309,048 | 93,325 R | — | 8 | 38 | 16 |
| South Dakota | 293,118 | 163,010 | 130,108 | 32,902 D | 4 | — | 15 | 14 |
| Tennessee | 1,144,046 | 635,047 | 508,965 | 126,082 D | 11 | — | 40 | 28 |
| Texas | 2,626,811 | 1,663,185 | 958,566 | 704,619 D | 25 | — | 99 | 56 |
| Utah | 401,413 | 219,628 | 181,785 | 37,843 D | 4 | — | 16 | 14 |
| Vermont | 163,809 | 108,127 | 54,942 | 53,185 D | 3 | — | 12 | 12 |
| Virginia | 1,042,267 | 558,038 | 481,334 | 76,704 D | 12 | — | 42 | 30 |
| Washington | 1,258,374 | 779,699 | 470,366 | 309,333 D | 9 | — | 35 | 24 |
| West Virginia | 792,040 | 538,087 | 253,953 | 284,134 D | 7 | — | 37 | 14 |
| Wisconsin | 1,691,815 | 1,050,424 | 638,495 | 411,929 D | 12 | — | 46 | 30 |
| Wyoming | 142,716 | 80,718 | 61,998 | 18,720 D | 3 | — | 15 | 12 |
| **Total** | **70,644,510** | **43,129,484** | **27,178,188** | **15,951,296 D** | **486** | **52** | **2,316[4]** | **1,308[5]** |

1. The Alabama Democratic elector slate was unpledged; thus no specific Johnson vote was obtainable. 2. Plurality over 10,732 unpledged Democratic votes. 3. Contains 4,570,670 Democratic and 342,432 Liberal votes. 4. Includes 21 votes allocated to U. S. territories. 5. Includes 8 votes allocated to U. S. territories.

OTHER CANDIDATES FOR PRESIDENT: Constitution Party, Joseph B. Lightburn; National States' Rights Party. John Kasper; Prohibition Party, E. Harold Munn; Socialist Labor Party, Eric Hass; Socialist Workers Party, Clifton DeBerry; Universal Party, s Hensley.

NATIONAL TOTALS OF OTHER VOTES: Socialist Labor, 45,219; Socialist Workers, 32,720; Prohibition, 23,267; National Rights, 6,953; Constitution, 5,060; Universal, 19; unpledged Democratic elector ticket (Alabama), 210,732; scattered,

*America at the Polls,* compiled and edited by Richard M. Scammon.

# Presidential Election of 1968

**Principal Candidates for President and Vice President**
**Republican: Richard M. Nixon; Spiro T. Agnew**
**Democratic: Hubert H. Humphrey; Edmund S. Muskie**
**American Independent Party: George C. Wallace; Curtis E. LeMay**

| | | Nixon | Humphrey | Wallace | | Electoral Vote | | | Votes at Natl. Convs. | |
|---|---|---|---|---|---|---|---|---|---|---|
| State | Total | Rep. | Dem. | Am. Ind. | Plurality | R | D | A | Dem. | Rep. |
| Alabama | 1,049,922 | 146,923 | 196,579[1] | 691,425[2] | 494,846 A | — | — | 10 | 32 | 26 |
| Alaska | 83,035 | 37,600 | 35,411 | 10,024 | 2,189 R | 3 | — | — | 22 | 12 |
| Arizona | 486,936 | 266,721 | 170,514 | 46,573 | 96,207 R | 5 | — | — | 19 | 16 |
| Arkansas | 619,969 | 190,759 | 188,228 | 240,982 | 50,223 A | — | — | 6 | 33 | 18 |
| California | 7,251,587 | 3,467,664 | 3,244,318 | 487,270 | 223,346 R | 40 | — | — | 174 | 86 |
| Colorado | 811,199 | 409,345 | 335,174 | 60,813 | 74,171 R | 6 | — | — | 35 | 18 |
| Connecticut | 1,256,232 | 556,721 | 621,561 | 76,650 | 64,840 D | — | 8 | — | 44 | 16 |
| Delaware | 214,367 | 96,714 | 89,194 | 28,459 | 7,520 R | 3 | — | — | 22 | 12 |
| D.C. | 170,578 | 31,012 | 139,566 | — | 108,554 D | — | 3 | — | 23 | 9 |
| Florida | 2,187,805 | 886,804 | 676,794 | 624,207 | 210,010 R | 14 | — | — | 63 | 34 |
| Georgia | 1,250,266 | 380,111 | 334,440 | 535,550 | 155,439 A | — | — | 12 | 43 | 30 |
| Hawaii | 236,218 | 91,425 | 141,324 | 3,469 | 49,899 D | — | 4 | — | 26 | 14 |
| Idaho | 291,183 | 165,369 | 89,273 | 36,541 | 76,096 R | 4 | — | — | 25 | 14 |
| Illinois | 4,619,749 | 2,174,774 | 2,039,814 | 390,958 | 134,960 R | 26 | — | — | 118 | 58 |
| Indiana | 2,123,597 | 1,067,885 | 806,659 | 243,108 | 261,226 R | 13 | — | — | 63 | 26 |
| Iowa | 1,167,931 | 619,106 | 476,699 | 66,422 | 142,407 R | 9 | — | — | 46 | 24 |
| Kansas | 872,783 | 478,674 | 302,996 | 88,921 | 175,678 R | 7 | — | — | 38 | 20 |
| Kentucky | 1,055,893 | 462,411 | 397,541 | 193,098 | 64,870 R | 9 | — | — | 46 | 24 |
| Louisiana | 1,097,450 | 257,535 | 309,615 | 530,300 | 220,685 A | — | — | 10 | 36 | 26 |
| Maine | 392,936 | 169,254 | 217,312 | 6,370 | 48,058 D | — | 4 | — | 27 | 14 |
| Maryland | 1,235,039 | 517,995 | 538,310 | 178,734 | 20,315 D | — | 10 | — | 49 | 26 |
| Massachusetts | 2,331,752 | 766,844 | 1,469,218 | 87,088 | 702,374 D | — | 14 | — | 72 | 34 |
| Michigan | 3,306,250 | 1,370,665 | 1,593,082 | 331,968 | 222,417 D | — | 21 | — | 96 | 48 |
| Minnesota | 1,588,506 | 658,643 | 857,738 | 68,931 | 199,095 D | — | 10 | — | 52 | 26 |
| Mississippi | 654,509 | 88,516 | 150,644 | 415,349 | 264,705 A | — | — | 7 | 24 | 20 |
| Missouri | 1,809,502 | 811,932 | 791,444 | 206,126 | 20,488 R | 12 | — | — | 60 | 24 |
| Montana | 274,404 | 138,835 | 114,117 | 20,015 | 24,718 R | 4 | — | — | 26 | 14 |
| Nebraska | 536,851 | 321,163 | 170,784 | 44,904 | 150,379 R | 5 | — | — | 30 | 16 |
| Nevada | 154,218 | 73,188 | 60,598 | 20,432 | 12,590 R | 3 | — | — | 22 | 12 |
| New Hampshire | 297,298 | 154,903 | 130,589 | 11,173 | 24,314 R | 4 | — | — | 26 | 8 |
| New Jersey | 2,875,395 | 1,325,467 | 1,264,206 | 262,187 | 61,261 R | 17 | — | — | 82 | 40 |
| New Mexico | 327,350 | 169,692 | 130,081 | 25,737 | 39,611 R | 4 | — | — | 26 | 14 |
| New York | 6,791,688 | 3,007,932 | 3,378,470[3] | 358,864 | 370,538 D | — | 43 | — | 190 | 92 |
| North Carolina | 1,587,493 | 627,192 | 464,113 | 496,188 | 131,004 R | 12 | — | 1 | 59 | 26 |
| North Dakota | 247,882 | 138,669 | 94,769 | 14,244 | 43,900 R | 4 | — | — | 25 | 8 |
| Ohio | 3,959,698 | 1,791,014 | 1,700,586 | 467,495 | 90,428 R | 26 | — | — | 115 | 58 |
| Oklahoma | 943,086 | 449,697 | 301,658 | 191,731 | 148,039 R | 8 | — | — | 41 | 22 |
| Oregon | 819,622 | 408,433 | 358,866 | 49,683 | 49,567 R | 6 | — | — | 35 | 18 |
| Pennsylvania | 4,747,928 | 2,090,017 | 2,259,405 | 378,582 | 169,388 D | — | 29 | — | 130 | 64 |
| Rhode Island | 385,000 | 122,359 | 246,518 | 15,678 | 124,159 D | — | 4 | — | 27 | 14 |
| South Carolina | 666,978 | 254,062 | 197,486 | 215,430 | 38,632 R | 8 | — | — | 28 | 22 |
| South Dakota | 281,264 | 149,841 | 118,023 | 13,400 | 31,818 R | 4 | — | — | 26 | 14 |
| Tennessee | 1,248,617 | 472,592 | 351,233 | 424,792 | 47,800 R | 11 | — | — | 51 | 28 |
| Texas | 3,079,406 | 1,227,844 | 1,266,804 | 584,269 | 38,960 D | — | 25 | — | 104 | 56 |
| Utah | 422,568 | 238,728 | 156,665 | 26,906 | 82,063 R | 4 | — | — | 26 | 8 |
| Vermont | 161,404 | 85,142 | 70,255 | 5,104 | 14,887 R | 3 | — | — | 22 | 12 |
| Virginia | 1,361,491 | 590,319 | 442,387 | 321,833 | 147,932 R | 12 | — | — | 54 | 24 |
| Washington | 1,304,281 | 588,510 | 616,037 | 96,990 | 27,527 D | — | 9 | — | 47 | 24 |
| West Virginia | 754,206 | 307,555 | 374,091 | 72,560 | 66,536 D | — | 7 | — | 38 | 14 |
| Wisconsin | 1,691,538 | 809,997 | 748,804 | 127,835 | 61,193 R | 12 | — | — | 59 | 30 |
| Wyoming | 127,205 | 70,927 | 45,173 | 11,105 | 25,754 R | 3 | — | — | 22 | 12 |
| **Total** | **73,212,065** | **31,785,480** | **31,275,166** | **9,906,473** | **510,314 R** | **301** | **191** | **46** | **2,622[4]** | **1,333[5]** |

1. This vote, cast for Humphrey, is a combination of National Democratic (54,144) and Independent Democratic (142,435).
2. This vote for Wallace was cast as Democratic in Alabama. 3. Contains 3,066,848 Democratic and 311,622 Liberal votes.
4. Includes 23 votes allocated to U.S. territories. 5. Includes 8 votes allocated to U.S. territories.
OTHER CANDIDATES FOR PRESIDENT: New Party, Dick Gregory; Peace and Freedom Party, Eldridge Cleaver; Prohibition Party, E. Harold Munn; Socialist Labor Party, Hennings Blomen; Socialist Workers Party, Fred Halstead.
NATIONAL TOTAL OF OTHER VOTES: 244,946, from 30 states.
*Source: America Votes,* compiled and edited by Richard M. Scammon.

# Presidential Election of 1972

**Principal Candidates for President and Vice President**
**Republican: Richard M. Nixon; Spiro T. Agnew**
**Democratic: George McGovern; Sargent Shriver**
**American Party[1]: John G. Schmitz; Thomas J. Anderson**

| State | Total | Nixon Republican | McGovern Democratic | Schmitz American | Plurality | Electoral vote R | Electoral vote D | Electoral vote A | Votes at Natl. Convs. Dem. | Votes at Natl. Convs. Rep. |
|---|---|---|---|---|---|---|---|---|---|---|
| Alabama | 1,006,111 | 728,701 | 256,923 | 11,928 | 471,778 R | 9 | — | — | 37 | 17 |
| Alaska | 95,219 | 55,349 | 32,967 | 6,903 | 22,382 R | 3 | — | — | 10 | 12 |
| Arizona | 622,926 | 402,812 | 198,540 | 21,208 | 204,272 R | 6 | — | — | 25 | 18 |
| Arkansas | 651,320 | 448,541 | 199,892 | 2,887 | 248,649 R | 6 | — | — | 27 | 18 |
| California | 8,367,862 | 4,602,096 | 3,475,847 | 232,554 | 1,126,249 R | 45 | — | — | 271 | 96 |
| Colorado | 953,884 | 597,189 | 329,980 | 17,269 | 267,209 R | 7 | — | — | 36 | 20 |
| Connecticut | 1,384,277 | 810,763 | 555,498 | 17,239 | 255,265 R | 8 | — | — | 51 | 22 |
| Delaware | 235,516 | 140,357 | 92,283 | 2,638 | 48,074 R | 3 | — | — | 13 | 12 |
| D.C. | 163,421 | 35,226 | 127,627 | — | 92,401 D | — | 3 | — | 15 | 9 |
| Florida | 2,583,283 | 1,857,759 | 718,117 | — | 1,139,642 R | 17 | — | — | 81 | 40 |
| Georgia | 1,174,772 | 881,496 | 289,529 | 812 | 591,967 R | 12 | — | — | 53 | 24 |
| Hawaii | 270,274 | 168,865 | 101,409 | — | 67,456 R | 4 | — | — | 17 | 14 |
| Idaho | 310,379 | 199,384 | 80,826 | 28,869 | 118,558 R | 4 | — | — | 17 | 14 |
| Illinois | 4,723,236 | 2,788,179 | 1,913,472 | 2,471 | 874,707 R | 26 | — | — | 170 | 58 |
| Indiana | 2,125,529 | 1,405,154 | 708,568 | — | 696,586 R | 13 | — | — | 76 | 32 |
| Iowa | 1,225,944 | 706,207 | 496,206 | 22,056 | 210,001 R | 8 | — | — | 46 | 20 |
| Kansas | 916,095 | 619,812 | 270,287 | 21,808 | 349,525 R | 7 | — | — | 35 | 24 |
| Kentucky | 1,067,499 | 676,446 | 371,159 | 17,627 | 305,287 R | 9 | — | — | 47 | 20 |
| Louisiana | 1,051,491 | 686,852 | 298,142 | 52,099 | 388,710 R | 10 | — | — | 44 | 8 |
| Maine | 417,042 | 256,458 | 160,584 | — | 95,874 R | 4 | — | — | 20 | 26 |
| Maryland | 1,353,812 | 829,305 | 505,781 | 18,726 | 323,524 R | 10 | — | — | 53 | 34 |
| Massachusetts | 2,458,756 | 1,112,078 | 1,332,540 | 2,877 | 220,462 D | — | 14 | — | 102 | 48 |
| Michigan | 3,489,727 | 1,961,721 | 1,459,435 | 63,321 | 502,286 R | 21 | — | — | 132 | 26 |
| Minnesota | 1,741,652 | 898,269 | 802,346 | 31,407 | 95,923 R | 10 | — | — | 64 | 26 |
| Mississippi | 645,963 | 505,125 | 126,782 | 11,598 | 378,343 R | 7 | — | — | 25 | 13 |
| Missouri | 1,855,803 | 1,153,852 | 697,147 | — | 456,705 R | 12 | — | — | 73 | 30 |
| Montana | 317,603 | 183,976 | 120,197 | 13,430 | 63,779 R | 4 | — | — | 17 | 14 |
| Nebraska | 576,289 | 406,298 | 169,991 | — | 236,307 R | 5 | — | — | 24 | 16 |
| Nevada | 181,766 | 115,750 | 66,016 | — | 49,734 R | 3 | — | — | 11 | 12 |
| New Hampshire | 334,055 | 213,724 | 116,435 | 3,386 | 97,289 R | 4 | — | — | 18 | 14 |
| New Jersey | 2,997,229 | 1,845,502 | 1,102,211 | 34,378 | 743,291 R | 17 | — | — | 109 | 40 |
| New Mexico | 386,241 | 235,606 | 141,084 | 8,767 | 94,522 R | 4 | — | — | 18 | 14 |
| New York | 7,165,919 | 4,192,778 | 2,951,084 | — | 1,241,694 R | 41 | — | — | 278 | 88 |
| North Carolina | 1,518,612 | 1,054,889 | 438,705 | 25,018 | 616,184 R | 13 | — | — | 64 | 32 |
| North Dakota | 280,514 | 174,109 | 100,384 | 5,646 | 73,725 R | 3 | — | — | 14 | 12 |
| Ohio | 4,094,787 | 2,441,827 | 1,558,889 | 80,067 | 882,938 R | 25 | — | — | 153 | 56 |
| Oklahoma | 1,029,900 | 759,025 | 247,147 | 23,728 | 511,878 R | 8 | — | — | 39 | 22 |
| Oregon | 927,946 | 486,686 | 392,760 | 46,211 | 93,926 R | 6 | — | — | 34 | 18 |
| Pennsylvania | 4,592,106 | 2,714,521 | 1,796,951 | 70,593 | 917,570 R | 27 | — | — | 182 | 60 |
| Rhode Island | 415,808 | 220,383 | 194,645 | 25 | 25,738 R | 4 | — | — | 22 | 8 |
| South Carolina | 673,960 | 477,044 | 186,824 | 10,075 | 290,220 R | 8 | — | — | 32 | 22 |
| South Dakota | 307,415 | 166,476 | 139,945 | — | 26,531 R | 4 | — | — | 17 | 14 |
| Tennessee | 1,201,182 | 813,147 | 357,293 | 30,373 | 455,854 R | 10 | — | — | 49 | 26 |
| Texas | 3,471,281 | 2,298,896 | 1,154,289 | 6,039 | 1,144,607 R | 26 | — | — | 130 | 52 |
| Utah | 478,476 | 323,643 | 126,284 | 28,549 | 197,359 R | 4 | — | — | 19 | 14 |
| Vermont | 186,947 | 117,149 | 68,174 | — | 48,975 R | 3 | — | — | 12 | 12 |
| Virginia | 1,457,019 | 988,493 | 438,887 | 19,721 | 549,606 R | 11[2] | — | — | 53 | 30 |
| Washington | 1,470,847 | 837,135 | 568,334 | 58,906 | 268,801 R | 9 | — | — | 52 | 24 |
| West Virginia | 762,399 | 484,964 | 277,435 | — | 207,529 R | 6 | — | — | 35 | 18 |
| Wisconsin | 1,852,890 | 989,430 | 810,174 | 47,525 | 179,256 R | 11 | — | — | 67 | 18 |
| Wyoming | 145,570 | 100,464 | 44,358 | 748 | 56,106 R | 3 | — | — | 11 | 12 |
| **Total** | **77,718,554** | **47,169,911** | **29,170,383** | **1,099,482** | **17,999,528 R** | **520** | **17** | **0** | **3,016[3]** | **1,346[4]** |

1. Known as American Independent Party and by other names in some states. 2. One Virginia elector cast vote for Libertarian Party. 3. Includes 16 votes allocated to U.S. territories. 4. Includes 11 votes allocated to U.S. territories.

OTHER CANDIDATES FOR PRESIDENT: Communist, Gus Hall, Libertarian Party, John Hospers; People's Party, Benjamin Spock; Prohibition Party, Earle H. Munn; Socialist Labor Party, Louis Fisher; Socialist Workers Party, Linda Jenness.

NATIONAL TOTALS OF OTHER VOTES: People's, 78,756; Social Workers, 66,677; Socialist Labor, 53,814; Communist, [illegible].595; Prohibition, 13,505; others and scattered, 40,431.

Source: *America Votes 10*, compiled and edited by Richard M. Scammon.

# Presidential Election of 1976

**Principal Candidates for President and Vice President**
**Democratic: Jimmy Carter; Walter F. Mondale**
**Republican: Gerald R. Ford; Robert J. Dole**
**Independent: Eugene J. McCarthy**

| | | Carter | Ford | McCarthy | | Electoral vote | | Votes at Natl. Convs. | |
|---|---|---|---|---|---|---|---|---|---|
| State | Total | Dem. | Rep. | Ind. | Plurality | D | R | Dem. | Rep. |
| Alabama | 1,182,850 | 659,170 | 504,070 | 99 | 155,100 D | 9 | | 35 | 37 |
| Alaska | 123,574 | 44,058 | 71,555 | — | 27,497 R | | 3 | 10 | 19 |
| Arizona | 742,719 | 295,602 | 418,642 | 19,229 | 123,040 R | | 6 | 25 | 29 |
| Arkansas | 767,535 | 498,604 | 267,903 | 639 | 230,701 D | 6 | | 26 | 27 |
| California | 7,867,117 | 3,742,284 | 3,882,244 | 58,412 | 139,960 R | | 45 | 280 | 167 |
| Colorado | 1,081,554 | 460,801 | 584,278 | 26,047 | 123,477 R | | 7 | 35 | 31 |
| Connecticut | 1,381,526 | 647,895 | 719,261 | 3,759 | 71,366 R | | 8 | 51 | 35 |
| Delaware | 235,834 | 122,596 | 109,831 | 2,437 | 12,765 D | 3 | | 12 | 17 |
| D.C. | 168,830 | 137,818 | 27,873 | — | 109,945 D | 3 | | 17 | 14 |
| Florida | 3,150,631 | 1,636,000 | 1,469,531 | 23,643 | 166,469 D | 17 | | 81 | 66 |
| Georgia | 1,467,458 | 979,409 | 483,743 | 991 | 495,666 D | 12 | | 50 | 48 |
| Hawaii | 291,301 | 147,375 | 140,003 | — | 7,372 D | 4 | | 17 | 19 |
| Idaho | 344,071 | 126,549 | 204,151 | 1,194 | 77,602 R | | 4 | 16 | 21 |
| Illinois | 4,718,914 | 2,271,295 | 2,364,269 | 55,939 | 92,974 R | | 26 | 169 | 101 |
| Indiana | 2,220,362 | 1,014,714 | 1,183,958 | — | 169,244 R | | 13 | 75 | 54 |
| Iowa | 1,279,306 | 619,931 | 632,863 | 20,051 | 12,932 R | | 8 | 47 | 36 |
| Kansas | 957,845 | 430,421 | 502,752 | 13,185 | 72,331 R | | 7 | 34 | 34 |
| Kentucky | 1,167,142 | 615,717 | 531,852 | 6,837 | 83,865 D | 9 | | 46 | 37 |
| Louisiana | 1,278,439 | 661,365 | 587,446 | 6,588 | 73,919 D | 10 | | 41 | 41 |
| Maine | 483,216 | 232,279 | 236,320 | 10,874 | 4,041 R | | 4 | 20 | 20 |
| Maryland | 1,439,897 | 759,612 | 672,661 | 4,541 | 86,951 D | 10 | | 53 | 43 |
| Massachusetts | 2,547,558 | 1,429,475 | 1,030,276 | 65,637 | 399,199 D | 14 | | 104 | 43 |
| Michigan | 3,653,749 | 1,696,714 | 1,893,742 | 47,905 | 197,028 R | | 21 | 133 | 84 |
| Minnesota | 1,949,931 | 1,070,440 | 819,395 | 35,490 | 251,045 D | 10 | | 65 | 42 |
| Mississippi | 769,361 | 381,309 | 366,846 | 4,074 | 14,463 D | 7 | | 24 | 30 |
| Missouri | 1,953,600 | 998,387 | 927,443 | 24,029 | 70,944 D | 12 | | 71 | 49 |
| Montana | 328,734 | 149,259 | 173,703 | — | 24,444 R | | 4 | 17 | 20 |
| Nebraska | 607,668 | 233,293 | 359,219 | 9,409 | 125,926 R | | 5 | 23 | 25 |
| Nevada | 201,876 | 92,479 | 101,273 | — | 8,794 R | | 3 | 11 | 18 |
| New Hampshire | 339,618 | 147,645 | 185,935 | 4,095 | 38,290 R | | 4 | 17 | 21 |
| New Jersey | 3,014,472 | 1,444,653 | 1,509,688 | 32,717 | 65,035 R | | 17 | 108 | 67 |
| New Mexico | 418,409 | 201,148 | 211,419 | 1,161 | 10,271 R | | 4 | 18 | 21 |
| New York | 6,534,170 | 3,389,558 | 3,100,791 | 4,303 | 288,767 D | 41 | | 274 | 154 |
| North Carolina | 1,678,914 | 927,365 | 741,960 | 780 | 185,405 D | 13 | | 61 | 54 |
| North Dakota | 297,188 | 136,078 | 153,470 | 2,952 | 17,392 R | | 3 | 13 | 18 |
| Ohio | 4,111,873 | 2,011,621 | 2,000,505 | 58,258 | 11,116 D | 25 | | 152 | 97 |
| Oklahoma | 1,092,251 | 532,442 | 545,708 | 14,101 | 13,266 R | | 8 | 37 | 36 |
| Oregon | 1,029,876 | 490,407 | 492,120 | 40,207 | 1,713 R | | 6 | 34 | 30 |
| Pennsylvania | 4,620,787 | 2,328,677 | 2,205,604 | 50,584 | 123,073 D | 27 | | 178 | 103 |
| Rhode Island | 411,170 | 227,636 | 181,249 | 479 | 46,387 D | 4 | | 22 | 19 |
| South Carolina | 802,583 | 450,807 | 346,149 | 289 | 104,658 D | 8 | | 31 | 36 |
| South Dakota | 300,678 | 147,068 | 151,505 | — | 4,437 R | | 4 | 17 | 20 |
| Tennessee | 1,476,345 | 825,879 | 633,969 | 5,004 | 191,910 D | 10 | | 46 | 43 |
| Texas | 4,071,884 | 2,082,319 | 1,953,300 | 20,118 | 129,019 D | 26 | | 130 | 100 |
| Utah | 541,198 | 182,110 | 337,908 | 3,907 | 155,798 R | | 4 | 18 | 20 |
| Vermont | 187,765 | 78,789 | 100,387 | 4,001 | 21,598 R | | 3 | 12 | 18 |
| Virginia | 1,697,094 | 813,896 | 836,554 | — | 22,658 R | | 12 | 54 | 51 |
| Washington | 1,555,534 | 717,323 | 777,732 | 36,986 | 60,409 R | | 8[1] | 53 | 38 |
| West Virginia | 750,964 | 435,914 | 314,760 | 113 | 121,154 D | 6 | | 33 | 28 |
| Wisconsin | 2,104,175 | 1,040,232 | 1,004,987 | 34,943 | 35,245 D | 11 | | 68 | 45 |
| Wyoming | 156,343 | 62,239 | 92,717 | 624 | 30,478 R | | 3 | 10 | 17 |
| **Total** | **81,555,889** | **40,830,763** | **39,147,793** | **756,631** | **1,682,970D** | **297** | **240** | **3,008[2]** | **2,259[3]** |

1. Ninth Washington elector cast vote for Ronald Reagan. 2. Includes 34 votes allocated to U.S. territories and Democrat abroad. 3. Includes 16 votes allocated to U.S. territories.

OTHER CANDIDATES FOR PRESIDENT: Roger L. MacBride, Libertarian; Lester G. Maddox, American Independent; Thoma Anderson, American; Peter Camejo, Socialist Workers; Gus Hall, Communist; Margaret Wright, People's; Lyndon LaRou United States Labor; Benjamin C. Bubar, Prohibition; Julius Levin, Socialist Labor; Frank P. Zeidler, Socialist.

NATIONAL TOTALS OF OTHER VOTES: Libertarian, 173,011; American Independent, 170,531; American, 160,773; Sc Workers, 91,314; Communist, 58,992; People's, 49,024; United States Labor, 40,043; Prohibition, 15,934; Socialist 9,616; Socialist, 6,038; others and scattered, 45,366.

*Source: America Votes 12,* compiled and edited by Richard M. Scammon and Alice V. McGillivray.

## Electoral Vote for President

(For electoral votes by state from 1964 to 1976, see pages 608–611)

| | 1960 | | 1956 | | 1952 | | 1948 | | | 1944 | | 1940 | | 1936 | | 1932 | | 1928 | | 1924 | | |
|---|---|---|---|---|---|---|---|---|---|---|---|---|---|---|---|---|---|---|---|---|---|---|
| States | Kennedy, Dem. | Nixon, Rep. | Eisenhower, Rep. | Stevenson, Dem. | Eisenhower, Rep. | Stevenson, Dem. | Truman, Dem. | Dewey, Rep. | Thurmond, Sts. Rgts. | Roosevelt, Dem. | Dewey, Rep. | Roosevelt, Dem. | Willkie, Rep. | Roosevelt, Dem. | Landon, Rep. | Roosevelt, Dem. | Hoover, Rep. | Hoover, Rep. | Smith, Dem. | Coolidge, Rep. | Davis, Dem. | LaFollette, Prog. |
| Alabama | 5 | — | — | 10 | — | 11 | — | — | 11 | 11 | — | 11 | — | 11 | — | 11 | — | — | 12 | — | 12 | — |
| Alaska | — | 3 | — | — | — | — | — | — | — | — | — | — | — | — | — | — | — | — | — | — | — | — |
| Arizona | — | 4 | 4 | — | 4 | — | 4 | — | — | 4 | — | 3 | — | 3 | — | 3 | — | 3 | — | 3 | — | — |
| Arkansas | 8 | — | — | 8 | — | 8 | 9 | — | — | 9 | — | 9 | — | 9 | — | 9 | — | — | 9 | — | 9 | — |
| California | — | 32 | 32 | — | 32 | — | 25 | — | — | 25 | — | 22 | — | 22 | — | 22 | — | 13 | — | 13 | — | — |
| Colorado | — | 6 | 6 | — | 6 | — | 6 | — | — | — | 6 | — | 6 | 6 | — | 6 | — | 6 | — | 6 | — | — |
| Connecticut | 8 | — | 8 | — | 8 | — | — | 8 | — | 8 | — | 8 | — | 8 | — | — | 8 | 7 | — | 7 | — | — |
| Delaware | 3 | — | 3 | — | 3 | — | — | 3 | — | 3 | — | 3 | — | 3 | — | — | 3 | 3 | — | 3 | — | — |
| Florida | — | 10 | 10 | — | 10 | — | 8 | — | — | 8 | — | 7 | — | 7 | — | 7 | — | 6 | — | — | 6 | — |
| Georgia | 12 | — | — | 12 | — | 12 | 12 | — | — | 12 | — | 12 | — | 12 | — | 12 | — | — | 14 | — | 14 | — |
| Hawaii | 3 | — | — | — | — | — | — | — | — | — | — | — | — | — | — | — | — | — | — | — | — | — |
| Idaho | — | 4 | 4 | — | 4 | — | 4 | — | — | 4 | — | 4 | — | 4 | — | 4 | — | 4 | — | 4 | — | — |
| Illinois | 27 | — | 27 | — | 27 | — | 28 | — | — | 28 | — | 29 | — | 29 | — | 29 | — | 29 | — | 29 | — | — |
| Indiana | — | 13 | 13 | — | 13 | — | — | 13 | — | — | 13 | — | 14 | 14 | — | 14 | — | 15 | — | 15 | — | — |
| Iowa | — | 10 | 10 | — | 10 | — | 10 | — | — | — | 10 | — | 11 | 11 | — | 11 | — | 13 | — | 13 | — | — |
| Kansas | — | 8 | 8 | — | 8 | — | — | 8 | — | — | 8 | — | 9 | 9 | — | 9 | — | 10 | — | 10 | — | — |
| Kentucky | — | 10 | 10 | — | — | 10 | 11 | — | — | 11 | — | 11 | — | 11 | — | 11 | — | 13 | — | 13 | — | — |
| Louisiana | 10 | — | 10 | — | — | 10 | — | — | 10 | 10 | — | 10 | — | 10 | — | 10 | — | — | 10 | — | 10 | — |
| Maine | — | 5 | 5 | — | 5 | — | — | 5 | — | — | 5 | — | 5 | — | 5 | — | 5 | 6 | — | 6 | — | — |
| Maryland | 9 | — | 9 | — | 9 | — | — | 8 | — | 8 | — | 8 | — | 8 | — | 8 | — | 8 | — | 8 | — | — |
| Massachusetts | 16 | — | 16 | — | 16 | — | 16 | — | — | 16 | — | 17 | — | 17 | — | 17 | — | — | 18 | 18 | — | — |
| Michigan | 20 | — | 20 | — | 20 | — | — | 19 | — | 19 | — | — | 19 | 19 | — | 19 | — | 15 | — | 15 | — | — |
| Minnesota | 11 | — | 11 | — | 11 | — | 11 | — | — | 11 | — | 11 | — | 11 | — | 11 | — | 12 | — | 12 | — | — |
| Mississippi | — | — | — | 8 | — | 8 | — | — | 9 | 9 | — | 9 | — | 9 | — | 9 | — | — | 10 | — | 10 | — |
| Missouri | 13 | — | — | 13 | 13 | — | 15 | — | — | 15 | — | 15 | — | 15 | — | 15 | — | 18 | — | 18 | — | — |
| Montana | — | 4 | 4 | — | 4 | — | 4 | — | — | 4 | — | 4 | — | 4 | — | 4 | — | 4 | — | 4 | — | — |
| Nebraska | — | 6 | 6 | — | 6 | — | — | 6 | — | — | 6 | — | 7 | 7 | — | 7 | — | 8 | — | 8 | — | — |
| Nevada | 3 | — | 3 | — | 3 | — | 3 | — | — | 3 | — | 3 | — | 3 | — | 3 | — | 3 | — | 3 | — | — |
| New Hampshire | — | 4 | 4 | — | 4 | — | — | 4 | — | 4 | — | 4 | — | 4 | — | — | 4 | 4 | — | 4 | — | — |
| New Jersey | 16 | — | 16 | — | 16 | — | — | 16 | — | 16 | — | 16 | — | 16 | — | 16 | — | 14 | — | 14 | — | — |
| New Mexico | 4 | — | 4 | — | 4 | — | 4 | — | — | 4 | — | 3 | — | 3 | — | 3 | — | 3 | — | 3 | — | — |
| New York | 45 | — | 45 | — | 45 | — | — | 47 | — | 47 | — | 47 | — | 47 | — | 47 | — | 45 | — | 45 | — | — |
| North Carolina | 14 | — | — | 14 | — | 14 | 14 | — | — | 14 | — | 13 | — | 13 | — | 13 | — | 12 | — | — | 12 | — |
| North Dakota | — | 4 | 4 | — | 4 | — | — | 4 | — | — | 4 | — | 4 | 4 | — | 4 | — | 5 | — | 5 | — | — |
| Ohio | — | 25 | 25 | — | 25 | — | 25 | — | — | — | 25 | 26 | — | 26 | — | 26 | — | 24 | — | 24 | — | — |
| Oklahoma | — | 7 | 8 | — | 8 | — | 10 | — | — | 10 | — | 11 | — | 11 | — | 11 | — | 10 | — | — | 10 | — |
| Oregon | — | 6 | 6 | — | 6 | — | — | 6 | — | 6 | — | 5 | — | 5 | — | 5 | — | 5 | — | 5 | — | — |
| Pennsylvania | 32 | — | 32 | — | 32 | — | — | 35 | — | 35 | — | 36 | — | 36 | — | — | 36 | 38 | — | 38 | — | — |
| Rhode Island | 4 | — | 4 | — | 4 | — | 4 | — | — | 4 | — | 4 | — | 4 | — | 4 | — | — | 5 | 5 | — | — |
| South Carolina | 8 | — | — | 8 | — | 8 | — | — | 8 | 8 | — | 8 | — | 8 | — | 8 | — | — | 9 | — | 9 | — |
| South Dakota | — | 4 | 4 | — | 4 | — | — | 4 | — | — | 4 | — | 4 | 4 | — | 4 | — | 5 | — | 5 | — | — |
| Tennessee | — | 11 | 11 | — | 11 | — | 11 | — | 1 | 12 | — | 11 | — | 11 | — | 11 | — | 12 | — | — | 12 | — |
| Texas | 24 | — | 24 | — | 24 | — | 23 | — | — | 23 | — | 23 | — | 23 | — | 23 | — | 20 | — | — | 20 | — |
| Utah | — | 4 | 4 | — | 4 | — | 4 | — | — | 4 | — | 4 | — | 4 | — | 4 | — | 4 | — | 4 | — | — |
| Vermont | — | 3 | 3 | — | 3 | — | — | 3 | — | — | 3 | — | 3 | — | 3 | — | 3 | 4 | — | 4 | — | — |
| Virginia | — | 12 | 12 | — | 12 | — | 11 | — | — | 11 | — | 11 | — | 11 | — | 11 | — | 12 | — | — | 12 | — |
| Washington | — | 9 | 9 | — | 9 | — | 8 | — | — | 8 | — | 8 | — | 8 | — | 8 | — | 7 | — | 7 | — | — |
| West Virginia | 8 | — | 8 | — | — | 8 | 8 | — | — | 8 | — | 8 | — | 8 | — | 8 | — | 8 | — | 8 | — | — |
| Wisconsin | — | 12 | 12 | — | 12 | — | 12 | — | — | — | 12 | 12 | — | 12 | — | 12 | — | 13 | — | — | — | 13 |
| Wyoming | — | 3 | 3 | — | 3 | — | 3 | — | — | — | 3 | 3 | — | 3 | — | 3 | — | 3 | — | 3 | — | — |
| Total | 303 | 219 | 457 | 73 | 442 | 89 | 303 | 189 | 39 | 432 | 99 | 449 | 82 | 523 | 8 | 472 | 59 | 444 | 87 | 382 | 136 | 13 |

## Characteristics of Voters in 1976 Presidential Election
(in millions)

| Characteristic | Persons of voting age | Persons reporting they voted: Total | Persons reporting they voted: Percent | Persons reporting they did not vote |
|---|---|---|---|---|
| Male | 69.0 | 41.1 | 59.6 | 40.4 |
| Female | 77.6 | 45.6 | 58.8 | 41.2 |
| White | 129.3 | 78.8 | 60.9 | 39.1 |
| Black | 14.9 | 7.3 | 48.7 | 51.3 |
| Spanish origin[1] | 6.6 | 2.1 | 31.8 | 68.2 |
| Age: 18–20 | 12.1 | 4.6 | 38.0 | 62.0 |
| 21–24 | 14.8 | 6.8 | 45.6 | 54.4 |
| 25–34 | 31.5 | 17.5 | 55.4 | 44.6 |
| 35–44 | 22.8 | 14.4 | 63.3 | 36.7 |
| 45–64 | 43.3 | 29.8 | 68.7 | 31.3 |
| 65 and over | 22.0 | 13.7 | 62.2 | 37.8 |
| Median age | 41.5 | 45.1 | — | — |
| Residence: | | | | |
| Metropolitan | 99.6 | 58.9 | 59.2 | 40.8 |
| Nonmetropolitan | 47.0 | 27.8 | 59.1 | 40.9 |
| North and West | 99.4 | 60.8 | 61.2 | 38.8 |
| South | 47.1 | 25.9 | 54.9 | 45.1 |
| Education: | | | | |
| 8 years or less | 24.9 | 11.0 | 44.1 | 55.9 |
| 9–11 years | 22.2 | 10.5 | 47.2 | 52.8 |
| 12 years | 55.7 | 33.1 | 59.4 | 40.6 |
| More than 12 | 43.7 | 32.2 | 73.5 | 26.5 |
| Employed | 86.0 | 53.3 | 62.0 | 38.0 |
| Unemployed | 6.4 | 2.8 | 43.7 | 56.3 |
| Not in labor force | 54.1 | 30.6 | 56.5 | 43.5 |
| **Total** | **146.5** | **86.7** | **59.2** | **40.8** |

1. Persons of Spanish origin may be of any race. *Source:* Department of Commerce, Bureau of the Census.

# Unusual Voting Results

## Election of 1872

The presidential and vice-presidential candidates of the Liberal Republicans and the northern Democrats in 1872 were Horace Greeley and B. Gratz Brown. Greeley died Nov. 29, 1872, before his 66 electors voted. In the electoral balloting for President, 63 of Greeley's votes were scattered among four other men, including Brown.

## Election of 1876

In the election of 1876 Samuel J. Tilden, the Democratic candidate, received a popular majority but lacked one undisputed electoral vote to carry a clear majority of the electoral college. The crux of the problem was in the 22 electoral votes which were in dispute because Florida, Louisiana, South Carolina, and Oregon each sent in two sets of election returns. In the three southern states, Republican election boards threw out enough Democratic votes to certify the Republican candidate, Hayes. In Oregon, the Democratic governor disqualified a Republican elector, replacing him with a Democrat. Since the Senate was Republican and the House of Representatives Democratic, it seemed useless to refer the disputed returns to the two houses for solution. Instead Congress appointed an Electoral Commission with five representatives each from the Senate, the House, and the Supreme Court. All but one Justice was named, giving the Commission seven Republican and seven Democratic members. The naming of the fifth Justice was left to the other four. He was a Republican who first favored Tilden but, under pressure from his party, switched to Hayes, ensuring his election by the Commission voting 8 to 7 on party lines.

## Minority Presidents

Fifteen candidates have become President of the United States with a popular vote less than 50% of the total cast. It should be noted, however, that in elections before 1872, presidential electors were not chosen by popular vote in all states. Adams' election in 1824 was by the House of Representatives, which chose him over Jackson, who had a plurality of both electoral and popular votes, but not a majority in the electoral college.

Besides Jackson in 1824, only two other candidates receiving the largest popular vote have failed to gain a majority in the electoral college—Samuel J. Tilden (D) in 1876 and Grover Cleveland (D) in 1888.

The "minority" Presidents follow:

### Vote Received by Minority Presidents

| Year | President | Electoral Percent | Popular vote Percent |
|---|---|---|---|
| 1824 | John Q. Adams | 31.8 | 29.8 |
| 1844 | James K. Polk (D) | 61.8 | 49.3 |
| 1848 | Zachary Taylor (W) | 56.2 | 47.3 |
| 1856 | James Buchanan (D) | 58.7 | 45.3 |
| 1860 | Abraham Lincoln (R) | 59.4 | 39.9 |
| 1876 | Rutherford B. Hayes (R) | 50.1 | 47.9 |
| 1880 | James A. Garfield (R) | 57.9 | 48.3 |
| 1884 | Grover Cleveland (D) | 54.6 | 48.8 |
| 1888 | Benjamin Harrison (R) | 58.1 | 47.8 |
| 1892 | Grover Cleveland (D) | 62.4 | 46.0 |
| 1912 | Woodrow Wilson (D) | 81.9 | 41.8 |
| 1916 | Woodrow Wilson (D) | 52.1 | 49.3 |
| 1948 | Harry S. Truman (D) | 57.1 | 49.5 |
| 1960 | John F. Kennedy (D) | 56.4 | 49.7 |
| 1968 | Richard M. Nixon (R) | 56.1 | 43.4 |

## National Political Conventions Since 1856

| Opening date | Party | Where held | Presidential nominee | Vote |
|---|---|---|---|---|
| June 17, 1856 | Republican | Philadelphia | John C. Frémont | 520 |
| June 2, 1856 | Democratic | Cincinnati | James Buchanan | 296 |
| May 16, 1860 | Republican | Chicago | Abraham Lincoln | 364 |
| April 23, 1860 | Democratic | Charleston and Baltimore | S. A. Douglas | 181 |
| June 7, 1864 | Republican[1] | Baltimore | Abraham Lincoln | Unanimous |
| Aug. 29, 1864 | Democratic | Chicago | Geo. B. McClellan | 202½ |
| May 20, 1868 | Republican | Chicago | U. S. Grant | Unanimous |
| July 4, 1868 | Democratic | New York City | Horatio Seymour | Unanimous |
| June 5, 1872 | Republican | Philadelphia | U. S. Grant | Unanimous |
| June 9, 1872 | Democratic | Baltimore | Horace Greeley | 688 |
| June 14, 1876 | Republican | Cincinnati | R. B. Hayes | 384 |
| June 28, 1876 | Democratic | St. Louis | S. J. Tilden | 508 |
| June 2, 1880 | Republican | Chicago | J. A. Garfield | 399 |
| June 23, 1880 | Democratic | Cincinnati | W. S. Hancock | 705 |
| June 3, 1884 | Republican | Chicago | J. G. Blaine | 541 |
| July 11, 1884 | Democratic | Chicago | Grover Cleveland | 683 |
| June 19, 1888 | Republican | Chicago | Benjamin Harrison | 544 |
| June 6, 1888 | Democratic | St. Louis | Grover Cleveland | By acclamation |
| June 7, 1892 | Republican | Minneapolis | Benjamin Harrison | 535 1/6 |
| June 21, 1892 | Democratic | Chicago | Grover Cleveland | 617½ |
| June 16, 1896 | Republican | St. Louis | William McKinley | 661½ |
| July 7, 1896 | Democratic | Chicago | William J. Bryan | 500 |
| June 19, 1900 | Republican | Philadelphia | William McKinley | Unanimous |
| July 4, 1900 | Democratic | Kansas City | William J. Bryan | By acclamation |
| June 21, 1904 | Republican | Chicago | Theodore Roosevelt | Unanimous |
| July 6, 1904 | Democratic | St. Louis | Alton B. Parker | 678 |
| June 16, 1908 | Republican | Chicago | William H. Taft | 702 |
| July 7, 1908 | Democratic | Denver | William J. Bryan | 892½ |
| June 18, 1912 | Republican | Chicago | William H. Taft | 561 |
| June 25, 1912 | Democratic | Baltimore | Woodrow Wilson | 990 |
| June 7, 1916 | Republican | Chicago | Charles E. Hughes | 949½ |
| June 14, 1916 | Democratic | St. Louis | Woodrow Wilson | By acclamation |
| June 8, 1920 | Republican | Chicago | Warren G. Harding | 692 1/5 |
| June 28, 1920 | Democratic | San Francisco | James M. Cox | 732½ |
| June 10, 1924 | Republican | Cleveland | Calvin Coolidge | 1,065 |
| June 24, 1924[2] | Democratic | New York City | John W. Davis | 839[3] |
| June 12, 1928 | Republican | Kansas City | Herbert Hoover | 837 |
| June 26, 1928 | Democratic | Houston | Alfred E. Smith | 849½ |
| June 14, 1932 | Republican | Chicago | Herbert Hoover | 1,126½ |
| June 27, 1932 | Democratic | Chicago | F. D. Roosevelt | 945 |
| June 9, 1936 | Republican | Cleveland | Alfred M. Landon | 984 |
| June 23, 1936 | Democratic | Philadelphia | F. D. Roosevelt | By acclamation |
| June 24, 1940 | Republican | Philadelphia | Wendell L. Willkie | Unanimous |
| July 15, 1940 | Democratic | Chicago | F. D. Roosevelt | Unanimous |
| June 26, 1944 | Republican | Chicago | Thomas E. Dewey | 1,056 |
| July 19, 1944 | Democratic | Chicago | F. D. Roosevelt | 1,086–90 |
| June 21, 1948 | Republican | Philadelphia | Thomas E. Dewey | 1,094–0 |
| July 12, 1948 | Democratic | Philadelphia | Harry S. Truman | 947½–263½ |
| July 17, 1948 | (4) | Birmingham | J. Strom Thurmond | By acclamation |
| July 22, 1948 | Progressive | Philadelphia | Henry A. Wallace | By acclamation |
| July 7, 1952 | Republican | Chicago | Dwight D. Eisenhower | 845–361 |
| July 21, 1952 | Democratic | Chicago | Adlai E. Stevenson | By acclamation |
| Aug. 20, 1956 | Republican | San Francisco | Dwight D. Eisenhower | Unanimous |
| Aug. 13, 1956 | Democratic | Chicago | Adlai E. Stevenson | By acclamation |
| July 25, 1960 | Republican | Chicago | Richard M. Nixon | Unanimous |
| July 11, 1960 | Democratic | Los Angeles | John F. Kennedy | Unanimous |
| July 13, 1964 | Republican | San Francisco | Barry M. Goldwater | Unanimous |
| Aug. 24, 1964 | Democratic | Atlantic City | Lyndon B. Johnson | By acclamation |
| Aug. 5, 1968 | Republican | Miami Beach | Richard M. Nixon | Unanimous |
| Aug. 26, 1968 | Democratic | Chicago | Hubert H. Humphrey | Unanimous |
| July 10, 1972 | Democratic | Miami Beach | George McGovern | 1,618 |
| Aug. 21, 1972 | Republican | Miami Beach | Richard M. Nixon | 1,347–1 |
| July 12, 1976 | Democratic | New York City | Jimmy Carter | 2,238½–769½ |
| Aug. 16, 1976 | Republican | Kansas City, Mo. | Gerald R. Ford | 1,187–1,070 |

1. The Convention adopted name Union party to attract War Democrats and others favoring prosecution of war. 2. In session July 10, 1924. 3. 103d ballot. 4. States' Rights delegates from 13 Southern states.

## National Committee Chairmen Since 1932

| Chairman and (state) | Term |
|---|---|
| **REPUBLICAN** | |
| Everett Sanders (Ind.) | 1932–34 |
| Henry P. Fletcher (Pa.) | 1934–36 |
| John Hamilton (Kan.) | 1936–40 |
| Joseph W. Martin, Jr. (Mass.) | 1940–42 |
| Harrison E. Spangler (Iowa) | 1942–44 |
| Herbert Brownell, Jr. (N.Y.) | 1944–46 |
| Carroll Reece (Tenn.) | 1946–48 |
| Hugh D. Scott, Jr. (Pa.) | 1948–49 |
| Guy G. Gabrielson (N.J.) | 1949–52 |
| Arthur E. Summerfield (Mich.) | 1952–53 |
| Wesley Roberts (Kan.) | 1953 |
| Leonard W. Hall (N.Y.) | 1953–57 |
| Meade Alcorn (Conn.) | 1957–59 |
| Thruston B. Morton (Ky.) | 1959–61 |
| William E. Miller (N.Y.) | 1961–64 |
| Dean Burch (Ariz.) | 1964–65 |
| Ray C. Bliss (Ohio) | 1965–69 |
| Rogers C. B. Morton (Md.) | 1969–71 |
| Robert Dole (Kan.) | 1971–73 |
| George H. Bush (Tex.) | 1973–74 |
| Mary Louise Smith (Iowa) | 1974–77 |
| William E. Brock III (Tenn.) | 1977– |

| Chairman and (state) | Term |
|---|---|
| **DEMOCRATIC** | |
| James A. Farley (N.Y.) | 1932–40 |
| Edward J. Flynn (N.Y.) | 1940–43 |
| Frank C. Walker (Mont.) | 1943–44 |
| Robert E. Hannegan (Mo.) | 1944–47 |
| J. Howard McGrath (R.I.) | 1947–49 |
| William M. Boyle, Jr. (Mo.) | 1949–51 |
| Frank E. McKinney (Ind.) | 1951–52 |
| Stephen A. Mitchell (Ill.) | 1952–54 |
| Paul M. Butler (Ind.) | 1955–60 |
| Henry M. Jackson (Wash.) | 1960–61 |
| John M. Bailey (Conn.) | 1961–68 |
| Lawrence F. O'Brien (Mass.) | 1968–69 |
| Fred R. Harris (Okla.) | 1969–70 |
| Lawrence F. O'Brien (Mass.) | 1970–72 |
| Jean Westwood (Utah) | 1972 |
| Robert S. Strauss (Tex.) | 1972–77 |
| Kenneth M. Curtis (Me.) | 1977 |
| John C. White (Tex.) | 1977– |

*Republican National Committee:* 310 First St., S.E., Washington, D. C. 20003.
*Democratic National Committee:* 1625 Massachusetts Ave., N.W., Washington, D. C. 20036.

## Facts About Elections

**Candidate with highest popular vote:** Nixon (1972), 47,169,911.

**Candidate with highest electoral vote:** F. D. Roosevelt (1936), 523.

**Candidate carrying most states:** Nixon (1972), 49.

**Candidate running most times:** Norman Thomas, 6 (1928, 1932, 1936, 1940, 1944, 1948).

**Candidate elected, defeated, then reelected:** Cleveland (1884, 1888, 1892).

## How a Bill Becomes a Law

When a Senator or a Representative introduces a bill, he sends it to the clerk of his house, who gives it a number and title. This is the *first reading,* and the bill is referred to the proper committee.

The committee may decide the bill is unwise or unnecessary and *table* it, thus killing it at once. Or it may decide the bill is worthwhile and hold hearings to listen to facts and opinions presented by experts and other interested persons. After members of the committee have debated the bill and perhaps offered amendments, a vote is taken; and if the vote is favorable, the bill is sent back to the floor of the house.

The clerk reads the bill sentence by sentence to the house, and this is known as the *second reading.* Members may then debate the bill and offer amendments. In the House of Representatives, the time for debate is limited by a *cloture rule,* but there is no such restriction in the Senate for cloture, where 60 votes are required. This makes possible a *filibuster,* in which one or more opponents hold the floor to defeat the bill.

The *third reading* is by title only, and the bill is put to a vote, which may be by voice or roll call, depending on the circumstances and parliamentary rules. Members who must be absent at the time but who wish to record their vote may be paired if each negative vote has a balancing affirmative one.

The bill then goes to the other house of Congress, where it may be defeated, or passed with or without amendments. If the bill is defeated, it dies. If it is passed with amendments, a joint Congressional committee must be appointed by both houses to iron out the differences.

After its final passage by both houses, the bill is sent to the President. If he approves, he signs it, and the bill becomes a law. However, if he disapproves, he *vetoes* the bill by refusing to sign it and sending it back to the house of origin with his reasons for the veto. The objections are read and debated, and a roll-call vote is taken. If the bill receives less than a two-thirds vote, it is defeated and goes no farther. But if it receives a two-third vote or greater, it is sent to the other house for vote. If that house also passes it by a two-thir vote, the President's veto is *overridden,* and the becomes a law.

Should the President desire neither to sign veto the bill, he may retain it for ten days, Su excepted, after which time it autom becomes a law without signature. However gress has adjourned within those ten day is automatically killed, that process of i jection being known as a *pocket veto.*

# Government Officials

## U.S. Cabinet Members With Dates of Appointment

Although the Constitution made no provision for a President's advisory group, the heads of the three executive departments (State, Treasury, and War) and the Attorney General were organized by Washington into such a group; and by about 1793, the name "Cabinet" was applied to it. With the exception of the Attorney General up to 1870 and the Postmaster General from 1829 to 1872, Cabinet members have been heads of executive departments.

A Cabinet member is appointed by the President, subject to the confirmation of the Senate; and as his term is not fixed, he may be replaced at any time by the President. At a change in Administration, it is customary for him to tender his resignation, but he remains in office until a successor is appointed.

The table of Cabinet members lists only those members who actually served after being duly commissioned.

The dates shown are those of appointment. "Cont." indicates that the term continued from the previous Administration for a substantial amount of time.

With the creation of the Department of Transportation in 1966, the Cabinet consisted of 12 members. This figure was reduced to 11 when the Post Office Department became an independent agency in 1970 but, with the establishment in 1977 of a Department of Energy, became 12 again.

**WASHINGTON**

| | |
|---|---|
| *Secretary of State* | Thomas Jefferson 1789 |
| | Edmund Randolph 1794 |
| | Timothy Pickering 1795 |
| *Secretary of the Treasury* | Alexander Hamilton 1789 |
| | Oliver Wolcott, Jr. 1795 |
| *Secretary of War* | Henry Knox 1789 |
| | Timothy Pickering 1795 |
| | James McHenry 1796 |
| *Attorney General* | Edmund Randolph 1789 |
| | William Bradford 1794 |
| | Charles Lee 1795 |

**J. ADAMS**

| | |
|---|---|
| *Secretary of State* | Timothy Pickering (Cont.) |
| | John Marshall 1800 |
| *Secretary of the Treasury* | Oliver Wolcott, Jr. (Cont.) |
| | Samuel Dexter 1801 |
| *Secretary of War* | James McHenry (Cont.) |
| | Samuel Dexter 1800 |
| *Attorney General* | Charles Lee (Cont.) |
| *Secretary of the Navy* | Benjamin Stoddert 1798 |

**JEFFERSON**

| | |
|---|---|
| *Secretary of State* | James Madison 1801 |
| *Secretary of the Treasury* | Samuel Dexter (Cont.) |
| | Albert Gallatin 1801 |
| *Secretary of War* | Henry Dearborn 1801 |
| *Attorney General* | Levi Lincoln 1801 |
| | Robert Smith 1805 |
| | John Breckinridge 1805 |
| | Caesar A. Rodney 1807 |
| *Secretary of the Navy* | Benjamin Stoddert (Cont.) |
| | Robert Smith 1801 |

**MADISON**

| | |
|---|---|
| *Secretary of State* | Robert Smith 1809 |
| | James Monroe 1811 |
| *Secretary of the Treasury* | Albert Gallatin (Cont.) |
| | George W. Campbell 1814 |
| | Alexander J. Dallas 1814 |
| | William H. Crawford 1816 |
| *Secretary of War* | William Eustis 1809 |
| | John Armstrong 1813 |
| | James Monroe 1814 |
| | William H. Crawford 1815 |
| *…ney General* | Caesar A. Rodney (Cont.) |
| | William Pinckney 1811 |
| | Richard Rush 1814 |
| *… of the Navy* | Paul Hamilton 1809 |
| | William Jones 1813 |
| | B. W. Crowninshield 1814 |

| | |
|---|---|
| *…ate* | John Quincy Adams 1817 |
| *Secretary of the Treasury* | William H. Crawford (Cont.) |
| *Secretary of War* | John C. Calhoun 1817 |
| *Attorney General* | Richard Rush (Cont.) |
| | William Wirt 1817 |
| *Secretary of the Navy* | B. W. Crowninshield (Cont.) |
| | Smith Thompson 1818 |
| | Samuel L. Southard 1823 |

**J. Q. ADAMS**

| | |
|---|---|
| *Secretary of State* | Henry Clay 1825 |
| *Secretary of the Treasury* | Richard Rush 1825 |
| *Secretary of War* | James Barbour 1825 |
| | Peter B. Porter 1828 |
| *Attorney General* | William Wirt (Cont.) |
| *Secretary of the Navy* | Samuel L. Southard (Cont.) |

**JACKSON**

| | |
|---|---|
| *Secretary of State* | Martin Van Buren 1829 |
| | Edward Livingston 1831 |
| | Louis McLane 1833 |
| | John Forsyth 1834 |
| *Secretary of the Treasury* | Samuel D. Ingham 1829 |
| | Louis McLane 1831 |
| | William J. Duane 1833 |
| | Roger B. Taney[3] 1833 |
| | Levi Woodbury 1834 |
| *Secretary of War* | John H. Eaton 1829 |
| | Lewis Cass 1831 |
| *Attorney General* | John M. Berrien 1829 |
| | Roger B. Taney 1831 |
| | Benjamin F. Butler 1833 |
| *Postmaster General[1]* | William T. Barry 1829 |
| | Amos Kendall 1835 |
| *Secretary of the Navy* | John Branch 1829 |
| | Levi Woodbury 1831 |
| | Mahlon Dickerson 1834 |

**VAN BUREN**

| | |
|---|---|
| *Secretary of State* | John Forsyth (Cont.) |
| *Secretary of the Treasury* | Levi Woodbury (Cont.) |
| *Secretary of War* | Joel R. Poinsett 1837 |
| *Attorney General* | Benjamin F. Butler (Cont.) |
| | Felix Grundy 1838 |
| | Henry D. Gilpin 1840 |
| *Postmaster General* | Amos Kendall (Cont.) |
| | John M. Niles 1840 |
| *Secretary of the Navy* | Mahlon Dickerson (Cont.) |
| | James K. Paulding 1838 |

**W. H. HARRISON**

| | |
|---|---|
| *Secretary of State* | Daniel Webster 1841 |
| *Secretary of the Treasury* | Thomas Ewing 1841 |
| *Secretary of War* | John Bell 1841 |
| *Attorney General* | John J. Crittenden 1841 |
| *Postmaster General* | Francis Granger 1841 |
| *Secretary of the Navy* | George E. Badger 1841 |

## TYLER

| | |
|---|---|
| *Secretary of State* | Daniel Webster (Cont.) |
| | Abel P. Upshur 1843 |
| | John C. Calhoun 1844 |
| *Secretary of the Treasury* | Thomas Ewing (Cont.) |
| | Walter Forward 1841 |
| | John C. Spencer[3] 1843 |
| | George M. Bibb 1844 |
| *Secretary of War* | John Bell (Cont.) |
| | John C. Spencer 1841 |
| | James M. Porter[3] 1843 |
| | William Wilkins 1844 |
| *Attorney General* | John J. Crittenden (Cont.) |
| | Hugh S. Legaré 1841 |
| | John Nelson 1843 |
| *Postmaster General* | Francis Granger (Cont.) |
| | Charles A. Wickliffe 1841 |
| *Secretary of the Navy* | George E. Badger (Cont.) |
| | Abel P. Upshur 1841 |
| | David Henshaw[3] 1843 |
| | Thomas W. Gilmer 1844 |
| | John Y. Mason 1844 |

## POLK

| | |
|---|---|
| *Secretary of State* | James Buchanan 1845 |
| *Secretary of the Treasury* | Robert J. Walker 1845 |
| *Secretary of War* | William L. Marcy 1845 |
| *Attorney General* | John Y. Mason 1845 |
| | Nathan Clifford 1846 |
| | Isaac Toucey 1848 |
| *Postmaster General* | Cave Johnson 1845 |
| *Secretary of the Navy* | George Bancroft 1845 |
| | John Y. Mason 1846 |

## TAYLOR

| | |
|---|---|
| *Secretary of State* | John M. Clayton 1849 |
| *Secretary of the Treasury* | William M. Meredith 1849 |
| *Secretary of War* | George W. Crawford 1849 |
| *Attorney General* | Reverdy Johnson 1849 |
| *Postmaster General* | Jacob Collamer 1849 |
| *Secretary of the Navy* | William B. Preston 1849 |
| *Secretary of the Interior* | Thomas Ewing 1849 |

## FILLMORE

| | |
|---|---|
| *Secretary of State* | Daniel Webster 1850 |
| | Edward Everett 1852 |
| *Secretary of the Treasury* | Thomas Corwin 1850 |
| *Secretary of War* | Charles M. Conrad 1850 |
| *Attorney General* | John J. Crittenden 1850 |
| *Postmaster General* | Nathan K. Hall 1850 |
| | Samuel D. Hubbard 1852 |
| *Secretary of the Navy* | William A. Graham 1850 |
| | John P. Kennedy 1852 |
| *Secretary of the Interior* | Thos. M. T. McKennan 1850 |
| | Alex. H. H. Stuart 1850 |

## PIERCE

| | |
|---|---|
| *Secretary of State* | William L. Marcy 1853 |
| *Secretary of the Treasury* | James Guthrie 1853 |
| *Secretary of War* | Jefferson Davis 1853 |
| *Attorney General* | Caleb Cushing 1853 |
| *Postmaster General* | James Campbell 1853 |
| *Secretary of the Navy* | James C. Dobbin 1853 |
| *Secretary of the Interior* | Robert McClelland 1853 |

## BUCHANAN

| | |
|---|---|
| *Secretary of State* | Lewis Cass 1857 |
| | Jeremiah S. Black 1860 |
| *Secretary of the Treasury* | Howell Cobb 1857 |
| | Philip F. Thomas 1860 |
| | John A. Dix 1861 |
| *Secretary of War* | John B. Floyd 1857 |
| | Joseph Holt 1861 |
| *Attorney General* | Jeremiah S. Black 1857 |
| | Edwin M. Stanton 1860 |
| *Postmaster General* | Aaron V. Brown 1857 |
| | Joseph Holt 1859 |
| | Horatio King 1861 |
| *Secretary of the Navy* | Isaac Toucey 1857 |
| *Secretary of the Interior* | Jacob Thompson 1857 |

## LINCOLN

| | |
|---|---|
| *Secretary of State* | William H. Seward 1861 |
| *Secretary of the Treasury* | Salmon P. Chase 1861 |
| | William P. Fessenden 1864 |
| | Hugh McCulloch 1865 |
| *Secretary of War* | Simon Cameron 1861 |
| | Edwin M. Stanton 1862 |
| *Attorney General* | Edward Bates 1861 |
| | James Speed 1864 |
| *Postmaster General* | Montgomery Blair 1861 |
| | William Dennison 1864 |
| *Secretary of the Navy* | Gideon Welles 1861 |
| *Secretary of the Interior* | Caleb B. Smith 1861 |
| | John P. Usher 1863 |

## A. JOHNSON

| | |
|---|---|
| *Secretary of State* | William H. Seward (Cont.) |
| *Secretary of the Treasury* | Hugh McCulloch (Cont.) |
| *Secretary of War* | Edwin M. Stanton (Cont.) |
| | John M. Schofield 1868 |
| *Attorney General* | James Speed (Cont.) |
| | Henry Stanbery 1866 |
| | William M. Evarts 1868 |
| *Postmaster General* | William Dennison (Cont.) |
| | Alexander W. Randall 1866 |
| *Secretary of the Navy* | Gideon Welles (Cont.) |
| *Secretary of the Interior* | John P. Usher (Cont.) |
| | James Harlan 1865 |
| | Orville H. Browning 1866 |

## GRANT

| | |
|---|---|
| *Secretary of State* | Elihu B. Washburne 1869 |
| | Hamilton Fish 1869 |
| *Secretary of the Treasury* | George S. Boutwell 1869 |
| | William A. Richardson 1873 |
| | Benjamin H. Bristow 1874 |
| | Lot M. Morrill 1876 |
| *Secretary of War* | John A. Rawlins 1869 |
| | William W. Belknap 1869 |
| | Alphonso Taft 1876 |
| | James D. Cameron 1876 |
| *Attorney General* | Ebenezer R. Hoar 1869 |
| | Amos T. Akerman 1870 |
| | George H. Williams 1871 |
| | Edwards Pierrepont 1875 |
| | Alphonso Taft 1876 |
| *Postmaster General* | John A. J. Creswell 1869 |
| | Marshall Jewell 1874 |
| | James N. Tyner 1876 |
| *Secretary of the Navy* | Adolph E. Borie 1869 |
| | George M. Robeson 1869 |
| *Secretary of the Interior* | Jacob D. Cox 1869 |
| | Columbus Delano 1870 |
| | Zachariah Chandler 1875 |

## HAYES

| | |
|---|---|
| *Secretary of State* | William M. Evarts 1877 |
| *Secretary of the Treasury* | John Sherman 1877 |
| *Secretary of War* | George W. McCrary 1877 |
| | Alexander Ramsey 1879 |
| *Attorney General* | Charles Devens 1877 |
| *Postmaster General* | David M. Key 1877 |
| | Horace Maynard 1880 |
| *Secretary of the Navy* | Richard W. Thompson 1877 |
| | Nathan Goff, Jr. 1881 |
| *Secretary of the Interior* | Carl Schurz 1877 |

## GARFIELD

| | |
|---|---|
| *Secretary of State* | James G. Blaine 1881 |
| *Secretary of the Treasury* | William Windom 1881 |
| *Secretary of War* | Robert T. Lincoln 1881 |
| *Attorney General* | Wayne MacVeagh 1881 |
| *Postmaster General* | Thomas L. James 1881 |
| *Secretary of the Navy* | William H. Hunt 1881 |
| *Secretary of the Interior* | Samuel J. Kirkwood 1881 |

## ARTHUR

| | |
|---|---|
| *Secretary of State* | James G. Blaine (Cont.) |
| | F. T. Frelinghuysen 1881 |
| *Secretary of the Treasury* | William Windom (Cont.) |
| | Charles J. Folger 1881 |
| | Walter Q. Gresham 18 |

| | |
|---|---|
| | Hugh McCulloch 1884 |
| *Secretary of War* | Robert T. Lincoln (Cont.) |
| *Attorney General* | Wayne MacVeagh (Cont.) |
| | Benjamin H. Brewster 1881 |
| *Postmaster General* | Thomas L. James (Cont.) |
| | Timothy O. Howe 1881 |
| | Walter Q. Gresham 1883 |
| | Frank Hatton 1884 |
| *Secretary of the Navy* | William H. Hunt (Cont.) |
| | William E. Chandler 1882 |
| *Secretary of the Interior* | Samuel J. Kirkwood (Cont.) |
| | Henry M. Teller 1882 |

**CLEVELAND**

| | |
|---|---|
| *Secretary of State* | Thomas F. Bayard 1885 |
| *Secretary of the Treasury* | Daniel Manning 1885 |
| | Charles S. Fairchild 1887 |
| *Secretary of War* | William C. Endicott 1885 |
| *Attorney General* | Augustus H. Garland 1885 |
| *Postmaster General* | William F. Vilas 1885 |
| | Don M. Dickinson 1888 |
| *Secretary of the Navy* | William C. Whitney 1885 |
| *Secretary of the Interior* | Lucius Q. C. Lamar 1885 |
| | William F. Vilas 1888 |
| *Secretary of Agriculture* | Norman J. Colman 1889 |

**B. HARRISON**

| | |
|---|---|
| *Secretary of State* | James G. Blaine 1889 |
| | John W. Foster 1892 |
| *Secretary of the Treasury* | William Windom 1889 |
| | Charles Foster 1891 |
| *Secretary of War* | Redfield Proctor 1889 |
| | Stephen B. Elkins 1891 |
| *Attorney General* | William H. H. Miller 1889 |
| *Postmaster General* | John Wanamaker 1889 |
| *Secretary of the Navy* | Benjamin F. Tracy 1889 |
| *Secretary of the Interior* | John W. Noble 1889 |
| *Secretary of Agriculture* | Jeremiah M. Rusk 1889 |

**CLEVELAND**

| | |
|---|---|
| *Secretary of State* | Walter Q. Gresham 1893 |
| | Richard Olney 1895 |
| *Secretary of the Treasury* | John G. Carlisle 1893 |
| *Secretary of War* | Daniel S. Lamont 1893 |
| *Attorney General* | Richard Olney 1893 |
| | Judson Harmon 1895 |
| *Postmaster General* | Wilson S. Bissell 1893 |
| | William L. Wilson 1895 |
| *Secretary of the Navy* | Hilary A. Herbert 1893 |
| *Secretary of the Interior* | Hoke Smith 1893 |
| | David R. Francis 1896 |
| *Secretary of Agriculture* | Julius Sterling Morton 1893 |

**McKINLEY**

| | |
|---|---|
| *Secretary of State* | John Sherman 1897 |
| | William R. Day 1898 |
| | John Hay 1898 |
| *Secretary of the Treasury* | Lyman J. Gage 1897 |
| *Secretary of War* | Russell A. Alger 1897 |
| | Elihu Root 1899 |
| *Attorney General* | Joseph McKenna 1897 |
| | John W. Griggs 1898 |
| | Philander C. Knox 1901 |
| *Postmaster General* | James A. Gary 1897 |
| | Charles E. Smith 1898 |
| *Secretary of the Navy* | John D. Long 1897 |
| *Secretary of the Interior* | Cornelius N. Bliss 1897 |
| | Ethan A. Hitchcock 1898 |
| *Secretary of Agriculture* | James Wilson 1897 |

**T. ROOSEVELT**

| | |
|---|---|
| *Secretary of State* | John Hay (Cont.) |
| | Elihu Root 1905 |
| | Robert Bacon 1909 |
| *retary of the Treasury* | Lyman J. Gage (Cont.) |
| | Leslie M. Shaw 1902 |
| | George B. Cortelyou 1907 |
| *ary of War* | Elihu Root (Cont.) |
| | William H. Taft 1904 |
| | Luke E. Wright 1908 |
| *General* | Philander C. Knox (Cont.) |
| | William H. Moody 1904 |
| | Charles J. Bonaparte 1906 |
| *Postmaster General* | Charles E. Smith (Cont.) |
| | Henry C. Payne 1902 |
| | Robert J. Wynne 1904 |
| | George B. Cortelyou 1905 |
| | George von L. Meyer 1907 |
| *Secretary of the Navy* | John D. Long (Cont.) |
| | William H. Moody 1902 |
| | Paul Morton 1904 |
| | Charles J. Bonaparte 1905 |
| | Victor H. Metcalf 1906 |
| | Truman H. Newberry 1908 |
| *Secretary of the Interior* | Ethan A. Hitchcock (Cont.) |
| | James R. Garfield 1907 |
| *Secretary of Agriculture* | James Wilson (Cont.) |
| *Secretary of Commerce and Labor* | George B. Cortelyou 1903 |
| | Victor H. Metcalf 1904 |
| | Oscar S. Straus 1906 |

**TAFT**

| | |
|---|---|
| *Secretary of State* | Philander C. Knox 1909 |
| *Secretary of the Treasury* | Franklin MacVeagh 1909 |
| *Secretary of War* | Jacob M. Dickinson 1909 |
| | Henry L. Stimson 1911 |
| *Attorney General* | George W. Wickersham 1909 |
| *Postmaster General* | Frank H. Hitchcock 1909 |
| *Secretary of the Navy* | George von L. Meyer 1909 |
| *Secretary of the Interior* | Richard A. Ballinger 1909 |
| | Walter L. Fisher 1911 |
| *Secretary of Agriculture* | James Wilson (Cont.) |
| *Secretary of Commerce and Labor* | Charles Nagel 1909 |

**WILSON**

| | |
|---|---|
| *Secretary of State* | William J. Bryan 1913 |
| | Robert Lansing 1915 |
| | Bainbridge Colby 1920 |
| *Secretary of the Treasury* | William G. McAdoo 1913 |
| | Carter Glass 1918 |
| | David F. Houston 1920 |
| *Secretary of War* | Lindley M. Garrison 1913 |
| | Newton D. Baker 1916 |
| *Attorney General* | James C. McReynolds 1913 |
| | Thomas W. Gregory 1914 |
| | A. Mitchell Palmer 1919 |
| *Postmaster General* | Albert S. Burleson 1913 |
| *Secretary of the Navy* | Josephus Daniels 1913 |
| *Secretary of the Interior* | Franklin K. Lane 1913 |
| | John B. Payne 1920 |
| *Secretary of Agriculture* | David F. Houston 1913 |
| | Edwin T. Meredith 1920 |
| *Secretary of Commerce* | William C. Redfield 1913 |
| | Joshua W. Alexander 1919 |
| *Secretary of Labor* | William B. Wilson 1913 |

**HARDING**

| | |
|---|---|
| *Secretary of State* | Charles E. Hughes 1921 |
| *Secretary of the Treasury* | Andrew W. Mellon 1921 |
| *Secretary of War* | John W. Weeks 1921 |
| *Attorney General* | Harry M. Daugherty 1921 |
| *Postmaster General* | Will H. Hays 1921 |
| | Hubert Work 1922 |
| | Harry S. New 1923 |
| *Secretary of the Navy* | Edwin Denby 1921 |
| *Secretary of the Interior* | Albert B. Fall 1921 |
| | Hubert Work 1923 |
| *Secretary of Agriculture* | Henry C. Wallace 1921 |
| *Secretary of Commerce* | Herbert Hoover 1921 |
| *Secretary of Labor* | James J. Davis 1921 |

**COOLIDGE**

| | |
|---|---|
| *Secretary of State* | Charles E. Hughes (Cont.) |
| | Frank B. Kellogg 1925 |
| *Secretary of the Treasury* | Andrew W. Mellon (Cont.) |
| *Secretary of War* | John W. Weeks (Cont.) |
| | Dwight F. Davis 1925 |
| *Attorney General* | Harry M. Daugherty (Cont.) |
| | Harlan F. Stone 1924 |
| | John G. Sargent 1925 |
| *Postmaster General* | Harry S. New (Cont.) |
| *Secretary of the Navy* | Edwin Denby (Cont.) |
| | Curtis D. Wilbur 1924 |
| *Secretary of the Interior* | Hubert Work (Cont.) |
| | Roy O. West 1928 |

| | |
|---|---|
| *Secretary of Agriculture* | Henry C. Wallace (Cont.) |
| | Howard M. Gore 1924 |
| | William M. Jardine 1925 |
| *Secretary of Commerce* | Herbert Hoover (Cont.) |
| | William F. Whiting 1928 |
| *Secretary of Labor* | James J. Davis (Cont.) |

**HOOVER**

| | |
|---|---|
| *Secretary of State* | Frank B. Kellogg (Cont.) |
| | Henry L. Stimson 1929 |
| *Secretary of the Treasury* | Andrew W. Mellon (Cont.) |
| | Ogden L. Mills 1932 |
| *Secretary of War* | James W. Good 1929 |
| | Patrick J. Hurley 1929 |
| *Attorney General* | William D. Mitchell 1929 |
| *Postmaster General* | Walter F. Brown 1929 |
| *Secretary of the Navy* | Charles F. Adams 1929 |
| *Secretary of the Interior* | Ray Lyman Wilbur 1929 |
| *Secretary of Agriculture* | Arthur M. Hyde 1929 |
| *Secretary of Commerce* | Robert P. Lamont 1929 |
| | Roy D. Chapin 1932 |
| *Secretary of Labor* | James J. Davis (Cont.) |
| | William N. Doak 1930 |

**F. D. ROOSEVELT**

| | |
|---|---|
| *Secretary of State* | Cordell Hull 1933 |
| | E. R. Stettinius, Jr. 1944 |
| *Secretary of the Treasury* | William H. Woodin 1933 |
| | Henry Morgenthau, Jr. 1934 |
| *Secretary of War* | George H. Dern 1933 |
| | Harry H. Woodring 1936 |
| | Henry L. Stimson 1940 |
| *Attorney General* | Homer S. Cummings 1933 |
| | Frank Murphy 1939 |
| | Robert H. Jackson 1940 |
| | Francis Biddle 1941 |
| *Postmaster General* | James A. Farley 1933 |
| | Frank C. Walker 1940 |
| *Secretary of the Navy* | Claude A. Swanson 1933 |
| | Charles Edison 1940 |
| | Frank Knox 1940 |
| | James Forrestal 1944 |
| *Secretary of the Interior* | Harold L. Ickes 1933 |
| *Secretary of Agriculture* | Henry A. Wallace 1933 |
| | Claude R. Wickard 1940 |
| *Secretary of Commerce* | Daniel C. Roper 1933 |
| | Harry L. Hopkins 1938 |
| | Jesse H. Jones 1940 |
| | Henry A. Wallace 1945 |
| *Secretary of Labor* | Frances Perkins 1933 |

**TRUMAN**

| | |
|---|---|
| *Secretary of State* | E. R. Stettinius, Jr. (Cont.) |
| | James F. Byrnes 1945 |
| | George C. Marshall 1947 |
| | Dean Acheson 1949 |
| *Secretary of the Treasury* | Henry Morgenthau, Jr. (Cont.) |
| | Frederick M. Vinson 1945 |
| | John W. Snyder 1946 |
| *Secretary of Defense* | James Forrestal 1947 |
| | Louis A. Johnson 1949 |
| | George C. Marshall 1950 |
| | Robert A. Lovett 1951 |
| *Attorney General* | Francis Biddle (Cont.) |
| | Tom C. Clark 1945 |
| | J. Howard McGrath 1949 |
| | James P. McGranery 1952 |
| *Postmaster General* | Frank C. Walker (Cont.) |
| | Robert E. Hannegan 1945 |
| | Jesse M. Donaldson 1947 |
| *Secretary of the Interior* | Harold L. Ickes (Cont.) |
| | Julius A. Krug 1946 |
| | Oscar L. Chapman 1949 |
| *Secretary of Agriculture* | Claude R. Wickard (Cont.) |
| | Clinton P. Anderson 1945 |
| | Charles F. Brannan 1948 |
| *Secretary of Commerce* | Henry A. Wallace (Cont.) |
| | W. Averell Harriman 1946 |
| | Charles Sawyer 1948 |
| *Secretary of Labor* | Frances Perkins (Cont.) |
| | Lewis B. Schwellenbach 1945 |
| | Maurice J. Tobin 1948 |
| *Secretary of War*[2] | Henry L. Stimson (Cont.) |
| | Robert P. Patterson 1945 |
| | Kenneth C. Royall 1947 |
| *Secretary of the Navy*[2] | James E. Forrestal (Cont.) |

**EISENHOWER**

| | |
|---|---|
| *Secretary of State* | John Foster Dulles 1953 |
| | Christian A. Herter 1959 |
| *Secretary of the Treasury* | George M. Humphrey 1953 |
| | Robert B. Anderson 1957 |
| *Secretary of Defense* | Charles E. Wilson 1953 |
| | Neil H. McElroy 1957 |
| | Thomas S. Gates, Jr. 1959 |
| *Attorney General* | Herbert Brownell, Jr. 1953 |
| | William P. Rogers 1958 |
| *Postmaster General* | Arthur E. Summerfield 1953 |
| *Secretary of the Interior* | Douglas McKay 1953 |
| | Frederick A. Seaton 1956 |
| *Secretary of Agriculture* | Ezra Taft Benson 1953 |
| *Secretary of Commerce* | Sinclair Weeks 1953 |
| | Lewis L. Strauss[3] 1958 |
| | Frederick H. Mueller 1959 |
| *Secretary of Labor* | Martin P. Durkin 1953 |
| | James P. Mitchell 1953 |
| *Secretary of Health, Education, and Welfare* | Oveta Culp Hobby 1953 |
| | Marion B. Folsom 1955 |
| | Arthur S. Flemming 1958 |

**KENNEDY**

| | |
|---|---|
| *Secretary of State* | Dean Rusk 1961 |
| *Secretary of the Treasury* | C. Douglas Dillon 1961 |
| *Secretary of Defense* | Robert S. McNamara 1961 |
| *Attorney General* | Robert F. Kennedy 1961 |
| *Postmaster General* | J. Edward Day 1961 |
| | John A. Gronouski 1963 |
| *Secretary of the Interior* | Stewart L. Udall 1961 |
| *Secretary of Agriculture* | Orville L. Freeman 1961 |
| *Secretary of Commerce* | Luther H. Hodges 1961 |
| *Secretary of Labor* | Arthur J. Goldberg 1961 |
| | W. Willard Wirtz 1962 |
| *Secretary of Health, Education, and Welfare* | Abraham A. Ribicoff 1961 |
| | Anthony J. Celebrezze 1962 |

**L. B. JOHNSON**

| | |
|---|---|
| *Secretary of State* | Dean Rusk (Cont.) |
| *Secretary of the Treasury* | C. Douglas Dillon (Cont.) |
| | Henry H. Fowler 1965 |
| | Joseph W. Barr[4] 1968 |
| *Secretary of Defense* | Robert S. McNamara (Cont.) |
| | Clark M. Clifford 1968 |
| *Attorney General* | Robert F. Kennedy (Cont.) |
| | N. de B. Katzenbach 1965 |
| | Ramsey Clark 1967 |
| *Postmaster General* | John A. Gronouski (Cont.) |
| | Lawrence F. O'Brien 1965 |
| | W. Marvin Watson 1968 |
| *Secretary of the Interior* | Stewart L. Udall (Cont.) |
| *Secretary of Agriculture* | Orville L. Freeman (Cont.) |
| *Secretary of Commerce* | Luther H. Hodges (Cont.) |
| | John T. Connor 1964 |
| | A. B. Trowbridge 1967 |
| | C. R. Smith 1968 |
| *Secretary of Labor* | W. Willard Wirtz (Cont.) |
| *Secretary of Health, Education, and Welfare* | Anthony J. Celebrezze (Cont.) |
| | John W. Gardner 1965 |
| | Wilbur J. Cohen 1968 |
| *Secretary of Housing and Urban Development* | Robert C. Weaver 1966 |
| | Robert C. Wood[4] 1969 |
| *Secretary of Transportation* | Alan S. Boyd 1966 |

**NIXON**

| | |
|---|---|
| *Secretary of State* | William P. Rogers 19 |
| | Henry A. Kissinger |
| *Secretary of the Treasury* | David M. Kennedy |
| | John B. Connally |
| | George P. Shultz |
| | William E. Simo |

| | |
|---|---|
| *Secretary of Defense* | Melvin R. Laird 1969 |
| | Elliot L. Richardson 1973 |
| | James R. Schlesinger 1973 |
| *Attorney General* | John N. Mitchell 1969 |
| | Richard G. Kleindienst 1972 |
| | Elliot L. Richardson 1973 |
| | William B. Saxbe 1974 |
| *Postmaster General*[5] | William M. Blount 1969 |
| *Secretary of the Interior* | Walter J. Hickel 1969 |
| | Rogers C. B. Morton 1971 |
| *Secretary of Agriculture* | Clifford M. Hardin 1969 |
| | Earl L. Butz 1971 |
| *Secretary of Commerce* | Maurice H. Stans 1969 |
| | Peter G. Peterson 1972 |
| | Frederick B. Dent 1973 |
| *Secretary of Labor* | George P. Shultz 1969 |
| | James D. Hodgson 1970 |
| | Peter J. Brennan 1973 |
| *Secretary of Health, Education, and Welfare* | Robert H. Finch 1969 |
| | Elliot L. Richardson 1970 |
| | Caspar W. Weinberger 1973 |
| *Secretary of Housing and Urban Development* | George Romney 1969 |
| | James T. Lynn 1973 |
| *Secretary of Transportation* | John A. Volpe 1969 |
| | Claude S. Brinegar 1973 |

**FORD**

| | |
|---|---|
| *Secretary of State* | Henry A. Kissinger (Cont.) |
| *Secretary of the Treasury* | William E. Simon (Cont.) |
| *Secretary of Defense* | James R. Schlesinger (Cont.) |
| | Donald H. Rumsfeld 1975 |
| *Attorney General* | William B. Saxbe (Cont.) |
| | Edward H. Levi 1975 |
| *Secretary of the Interior* | Rogers C. B. Morton (Cont.) |
| | Stanley K. Hathaway 1975 |
| | Thomas S. Kleppe 1975 |
| *Secretary of Agriculture* | Earl L. Butz 1976 |
| *Secretary of Commerce* | Frederick B. Dent (Cont.) |
| | Rogers C. B. Morton 1975 |
| | Elliot L. Richardson 1976 |
| *Secretary of Labor* | Peter J. Brennan (Cont.) |
| | John T. Dunlop 1975 |
| | William J. Usery, Jr. 1976 |
| *Secretary of Health, Education and Welfare* | Caspar W. Weinberger (Cont.) |
| | F. David Mathews 1975 |
| *Secretary of Housing and Urban Development* | James T. Lynn (Cont.) |
| | Carla A. Hills 1975 |
| *Secretary of Transportation* | Claude S. Brinegar (Cont.) |
| | William T. Coleman, Jr. 1975 |

**CARTER**

| | |
|---|---|
| *Secretary of State* | Cyrus R. Vance 1977 |
| *Secretary of the Treasury* | W. Michael Blumenthal 1977 |
| *Secretary of Defense* | Harold Brown 1977 |
| *Attorney General* | Griffin B. Bell 1977 |
| *Secretary of the Interior* | Cecil D. Andrus 1977 |
| *Secretary of Agriculture* | Bob S. Bergland 1977 |
| *Secretary of Commerce* | Juanita M. Kreps 1977 |
| *Secretary of Labor* | F. Ray Marshall 1977 |
| *Secretary of Health, Education and Welfare* | Joseph A. Califano, Jr. 1977 |
| *Secretary of Housing and Urban Development* | Patricia Roberts Harris 1977 |
| *Secretary of Transportation* | Brock Adams 1977 |
| *Secretary of Energy* | James R. Schlesinger 1977 |

1. The Postmaster General did not become a Cabinet member until 1829. Earlier Postmasters General were: Samuel Osgood (1789), Timothy Pickering (1791), Joseph Habersham (1795), Gideon Granger (1801), Return J. Meigs, Jr. (1814), and John McLean (1823). 2. On July 26, 1947, the Departments of War and of the Navy were incorporated into the Department of Defense. 3. Not confirmed by the Senate. 4. Recess appointment. 5. The Postmaster General is no longer a Cabinet member.

## Plurality and Majority

In order to win a plurality, a candidate must receive a greater number of votes than anyone running against him. If he receives 50 votes, for example, and two other candidates receive 49 and 2, he will have a plurality of one vote over his closest opponent.

However, a candidate does not have a majority unless he receives more than 50% of the total votes cast. In the example above, the candidate does not have a majority, because his 50 votes are less than 50% of the 101 votes cast.

## The Statue of Liberty

The Statue of Liberty ("Liberty Enlightening the World") is a 225-ton, steel-reinforced copper female figure, 152 ft in height, facing the ocean from Liberty[1] Island in New York Harbor. The right hand holds aloft a torch, and the left hand carries a tablet upon which is inscribed: "July IV MDCCLXXVI."

The statue was designed by Fredéric Auguste Bartholdi of Alsace as a gift to the United States from the people of France to memorialize the alliance of the two countries in the American Revolution and their abiding friendship. The French people contributed the $250,000 cost.

The 150-foot pedestal was designed by Richard Hunt and built by Gen. Charles P. Stone, both ericans. It contains steel underpinnings de- ed by Alexander Eiffel of France to support the . The $270,000 cost was borne by popular iption in this country. President Grover nd accepted the statue for the United Oct. 28, 1886.

. 26, 1972, President Richard M. Nixon dedicated the American Museum of Immigration, housed in structural additions to the base of the statue. Some 200 exhibits memorialize the flow of immigrants into the United States, including as many as 5,000 a day on nearby Ellis Island.

On a tablet inside the pedestal is engraved the following sonnet, written by Emma Lazarus (1849–1887):

### The New Colossus

Not like the brazen giant of Greek fame,
With conquering limbs astride from land to land;
Here at our sea-washed, sunset gates shall stand
A mighty woman with a torch, whose flame
Is the imprisoned lightning, and her name
Mother of Exiles. From her beacon-hand
Glows world-wide welcome; her mild eyes command
The air-bridged harbor that twin cities frame.
"Keep, ancient lands, your storied pomp!" cries she
With silent lips. "Give me your tired, your poor,
Your huddled masses yearning to breathe free,
The wretched refuse of your teeming shore.
Send these, the homeless, tempest-tost to me,
I lift my lamp beside the golden door!"

oe's Island prior to 1956.

# Members of the Supreme Court of the United States

| Name | Birth Place | Birth Date | Religious affiliation (*Source:* Library of Congress) | Appointment From | Appointment President | Oath taken Date | Oath taken Age | Service terminated Date | Service terminated Cause | Years served | Service terminated Age | Death Date | Death Age |
|---|---|---|---|---|---|---|---|---|---|---|---|---|---|
| **CHIEF JUSTICES** | | | | | | | | | | | | | |
| John Jay | N.Y. | 1745 | Episcopal | N.Y. | Washington | 1789 | 44 | 1795 | resigned | 5 | 49 | 1829 | 83 |
| John Rutledge | S.C. | 1739 | Church of England | S.C. | Washington | 1795 | 55 | 1795 | rejected | 0 | 56 | 1800 | 60 |
| Oliver Ellsworth | Conn. | 1745 | Congregational | Conn. | Washington | 1796 | 50 | 1800 | resigned | 4 | 55 | 1807 | 62 |
| John Marshall | Va. | 1755 | Episcopal | Va. | J. Adams | 1801 | 45 | 1835 | death | 34 | 79 | 1835 | 79 |
| Roger B. Taney | Md. | 1777 | Roman Catholic | Md. | Jackson | 1836 | 59 | 1864 | death | 28 | 87 | 1864 | 87 |
| Salmon P. Chase | N.H. | 1808 | Episcopal | Ohio | Lincoln | 1864 | 56 | 1873 | death | 8 | 65 | 1873 | 65 |
| Morrison R. Waite | Conn | 1816 | Episcopal | Ohio | Grant | 1874 | 57 | 1888 | death | 14 | 71 | 1888 | 71 |
| Melville W. Fuller | Me. | 1833 | Episcopal | Ill. | Cleveland | 1888 | 55 | 1910 | death | 21 | 77 | 1910 | 77 |
| Edward D. White | La. | 1845 | Roman Catholic | La. | Taft | 1910 | 65 | 1921 | death | 10 | 75 | 1921 | 75 |
| William H. Taft | Ohio | 1857 | Unitarian | Conn. | Harding | 1921 | 63 | 1930 | retired | 8 | 72 | 1930 | 72 |
| Charles E. Hughes | N.Y. | 1862 | Baptist | N.Y. | Hoover | 1930 | 67 | 1941 | retired | 11 | 79 | 1948 | 86 |
| Harlan F. Stone | N.H. | 1872 | Episcopal | N.Y. | F. Roosevelt | 1941 | 68 | 1946 | death | 4 | 73 | 1946 | 73 |
| Frederick M. Vinson | Ky. | 1890 | Methodist | Ky. | Truman | 1946 | 56 | 1953 | death | 7 | 63 | 1953 | 63 |
| Earl Warren | Calif. | 1891 | Protestant | Calif. | Eisenhower | 1953 | 62 | 1969 | retired | 15 | 78 | 1974 | 83 |
| Warren E. Burger | Minn. | 1907 | Presbyterian | Va. | Nixon | 1969 | 61 | — | — | — | — | — | — |
| **ASSOCIATE JUSTICES** | | | | | | | | | | | | | |
| James Wilson | Scotland | 1742 | Episcopal | Pa. | Washington | 1789 | 47 | 1798 | death | 8 | 55 | 1798 | 55 |
| John Rutledge | S.C. | 1739 | Church of England | S.C. | Washington | 1790 | 50 | 1791 | resigned | 1 | 51 | 1800 | 60 |
| William Cushing | Mass. | 1732 | Unitarian | Mass. | Washington | 1790 | 57 | 1810 | death | 20 | 78 | 1810 | 78 |
| John Blair | Va. | 1732 | Presbyterian | Va. | Washington | 1790 | 58 | 1796 | resigned | 5 | 64 | 1800 | 68 |
| James Iredell | England | 1751 | Episcopal | N.C. | Washington | 1790 | 38 | 1799 | death | 9 | 48 | 1799 | 48 |
| Thomas Johnson | Md. | 1732 | Episcopal | Md. | Washington | 1792 | 59 | 1793 | resigned | 0 | 60 | 1819 | 86 |
| William Paterson | Ireland | 1745 | Protestant | N.J. | Washington | 1793 | 47 | 1806 | death | 13 | 60 | 1806 | 60 |
| Samuel Chase | Md. | 1741 | Episcopal | Md. | Washington | 1796 | 54 | 1811 | death | 15 | 70 | 1811 | 70 |
| Bushrod Washington | Va. | 1762 | Episcopal | Va. | J. Adams | 1799 | 36 | 1829 | death | 30 | 67 | 1829 | 67 |
| Alfred Moore | N.C. | 1755 | Episcopal | N.C. | J. Adams | 1800 | 45 | 1804 | resigned | 3 | 48 | 1810 | 55 |
| William Johnson | S.C. | 1771 | Presbyterian | S.C. | Jefferson | 1804 | 32 | 1834 | death | 30 | 62 | 1834 | 62 |
| Brockholst Livingston | N.Y. | 1757 | Presbyterian | N.Y. | Jefferson | 1807 | 49 | 1823 | death | 16 | 65 | 1823 | 65 |
| Thomas Todd | Va. | 1765 | Presbyterian | Ky. | Jefferson | 1807 | 42 | 1826 | death | 18 | 61 | 1826 | 61 |
| Gabriel Duval | Md. | 1752 | French Protestant | Md. | Madison | 1811 | 58 | 1835 | resigned | 23 | 82 | 1844 | 91 |
| Joseph Story | Mass. | 1779 | Unitarian | Mass. | Madison | 1812 | 32 | 1845 | death | 33 | 65 | 1845 | 65 |
| Smith Thompson | N.Y. | 1768 | Presbyterian | N.Y. | Monroe | 1823 | 55 | 1843 | death | 20 | 75 | 1843 | 75 |
| Robert Trimble | Va. | 1777 | Protestant | Ky. | J. Q. Adams | 1826 | 49 | 1828 | death | 2 | 51 | 1828 | 51 |
| John McLean | N.J. | 1785 | Methodist-Epis. | Ohio | Jackson | 1830 | 44 | 1861 | death | 31 | 76 | 1861 | 76 |
| [illegible]ry Baldwin | Conn. | 1780 | Trinity Church | Pa. | Jackson | 1830 | 50 | 1844 | death | 14 | 64 | 1844 | 64 |
| [illegible] Wayne | Ga. | 1790 | Protestant | Ga. | Jackson | 1835 | 45 | 1867 | death | 32 | 77 | 1867 | 77 |
| [illegible]ur | Va. | 1783 | Episcopal | Va. | Jackson | 1836 | 52 | 1841 | death | 4 | 57 | 1841 | 57 |
| [illegible] | Pa. | 1786 | Presbyterian | Tenn. | Jackson | 1837 | 51 | 1865 | death | 28 | 79 | 1865 | 79 |

| Name | Birth | | Religious affiliation (Source: Library of Congress) | Appointment | | Oath taken | | Service terminated | | | | Death | |
|---|---|---|---|---|---|---|---|---|---|---|---|---|---|
| | Place | Date | | From | President | Date | Age | Date | Cause | Years served | Age | Date | Age |
| John McKinley | Va | 1780 | Protestant | Ala. | Van Buren | 1837 | 57 | 1852 | death | 14 | 72 | 1852 | 72 |
| Peter V. Daniel | Va. | 1784 | Episcopal | Va. | Van Buren | 1841 | 57 | 1860 | death | 18 | 76 | 1860 | 76 |
| Samuel Nelson | N.Y. | 1792 | Protestant | N.Y. | Tyler | 1845 | 52 | 1872 | retired | 27 | 80 | 1873 | 81 |
| Levi Woodbury | N.H. | 1789 | Protestant | N.H. | Polk | 1845 | 55 | 1851 | death | 5 | 61 | 1851 | 61 |
| Robert C. Grier | Pa. | 1794 | Presbyterian | Pa. | Polk | 1846 | 52 | 1870 | retired | 23 | 75 | 1870 | 76 |
| Benjamin R. Curtis | Mass. | 1809 | (2) | Mass. | Fillmore | 1851 | 41 | 1857 | resigned | 5 | 47 | 1874 | 64 |
| John A. Campbell | Ga. | 1811 | Episcopal | Ala. | Pierce | 1853 | 41 | 1861 | resigned | 8 | 49 | 1889 | 77 |
| Nathan Clifford | N.H. | 1803 | (1) | Maine | Buchanan | 1858 | 54 | 1881 | death | 23 | 77 | 1881 | 77 |
| Noah H. Swayne | Va. | 1804 | Quaker | Ohio | Lincoln | 1862 | 57 | 1881 | retired | 18 | 76 | 1884 | 79 |
| Samuel F. Miller | Ky. | 1816 | Unitarian | Iowa | Lincoln | 1862 | 46 | 1890 | death | 28 | 74 | 1890 | 74 |
| David Davis | Md. | 1815 | (4) | Ill. | Lincoln | 1862 | 47 | 1877 | resigned | 14 | 61 | 1886 | 71 |
| Stephen J. Field | Conn. | 1816 | Episcopal | Calif. | Lincoln | 1863 | 46 | 1897 | retired | 34 | 81 | 1899 | 82 |
| William Strong | Conn. | 1808 | Presbyterian | Pa. | Grant | 1870 | 61 | 1880 | retired | 10 | 72 | 1895 | 87 |
| Joseph P. Bradley | N.Y. | 1813 | Presbyterian | N.J. | Grant | 1870 | 57 | 1892 | death | 21 | 78 | 1892 | 78 |
| Ward Hunt | N.Y. | 1810 | Episcopal | N.Y. | Grant | 1872 | 62 | 1882 | disabled | 9 | 71 | 1886 | 75 |
| John M. Harlan | Ky. | 1833 | Presbyterian | Ky. | Hayes | 1877 | 44 | 1911 | death | 33 | 78 | 1911 | 78 |
| William B. Woods | Ohio | 1824 | Protestant | Ga. | Hayes | 1880 | 56 | 1887 | death | 6 | 62 | 1887 | 62 |
| Stanley Matthews | Ohio | 1824 | Presbyterian | Ohio | Garfield | 1881 | 56 | 1889 | death | 7 | 64 | 1889 | 64 |
| Horace Gray | Mass. | 1828 | (3) | Mass. | Arthur | 1882 | 53 | 1902 | death | 20 | 74 | 1902 | 74 |
| Samuel Blatchford | N.Y. | 1820 | Presbyterian | N.Y. | Arthur | 1882 | 62 | 1893 | death | 11 | 73 | 1893 | 73 |
| Lucius Q. C. Lamar | Ga. | 1825 | Methodist | Miss. | Cleveland | 1888 | 62 | 1893 | death | 5 | 67 | 1893 | 67 |
| David J. Brewer | Asia Minor | 1837 | Protestant | Kan. | Harrison | 1889 | 52 | 1910 | death | 20 | 72 | 1910 | 72 |
| Henry B. Brown | Mass. | 1836 | Protestant | Mich. | Harrison | 1890 | 54 | 1906 | retired | 15 | 70 | 1913 | 77 |
| George Shiras, Jr. | Pa. | 1832 | Presbyterian | Pa. | Harrison | 1892 | 60 | 1903 | retired | 10 | 71 | 1924 | 92 |
| Howell E. Jackson | Tenn. | 1832 | Baptist | Tenn. | Harrison | 1893 | 60 | 1895 | death | 2 | 63 | 1895 | 63 |
| Edward D. White | La. | 1845 | Roman Catholic | La. | Cleveland | 1894 | 48 | 1910 | promoted | 16 | 65 | 1921 | 75 |
| Rufus W. Peckham | N.Y. | 1838 | Episcopal | N.Y. | Cleveland | 1895 | 57 | 1909 | death | 13 | 70 | 1909 | 70 |
| Joseph McKenna | Pa. | 1843 | Roman Catholic | Calif. | McKinley | 1898 | 54 | 1925 | retired | 26 | 81 | 1926 | 83 |
| Oliver W. Holmes | Mass. | 1841 | Unitarian | Mass. | T. Roosevelt | 1902 | 61 | 1932 | retired | 29 | 90 | 1935 | 93 |
| William R. Day | Ohio | 1849 | Protestant | Ohio | T. Roosevelt | 1903 | 53 | 1922 | retired | 19 | 73 | 1923 | 74 |
| William H. Moody | Mass. | 1853 | Episcopal | Mass. | T. Roosevelt | 1906 | 52 | 1910 | disabled | 3 | 56 | 1917 | 63 |
| Horace H. Lurton | Ky. | 1844 | Episcopal | Tenn. | Taft | 1909 | 65 | 1914 | death | 4 | 70 | 1914 | 70 |
| Charles E. Hughes | N.Y. | 1862 | Baptist | N.Y. | Taft | 1910 | 48 | 1916 | resigned | 5 | 54 | 1948 | 86 |
| Willis Van Devanter | Ind. | 1859 | Episcopal | Wyo. | Taft | 1910 | 51 | 1937 | retired | 26 | 78 | 1941 | 81 |
| Joseph R. Lamar | Ga. | 1857 | Ch. of Disciples | Ga. | Taft | 1910 | 53 | 1916 | death | 4 | 58 | 1916 | 58 |
| Mahlon Pitney | N.J. | 1858 | Presbyterian | N.J. | Taft | 1912 | 54 | 1922 | disabled | 10 | 64 | 1924 | 66 |
| James C. McReynolds | Ky. | 1862 | Disciples of Christ | Tenn. | Wilson | 1914 | 52 | 1941 | retired | 26 | 78 | 1946 | 84 |
| Louis D. Brandeis | Ky. | 1856 | Jewish | Mass. | Wilson | 1916 | 59 | 1939 | retired | 22 | 82 | 1941 | 84 |
| John H. Clarke | Ohio | 1857 | Protestant | Ohio | Wilson | 1916 | 59 | 1922 | resigned | 5 | 65 | 1945 | 87 |
| George Sutherland | England | 1862 | Episcopal | Utah | Harding | 1922 | 60 | 1938 | retired | 15 | 75 | 1942 | 80 |
| Pierce Butler | Minn. | 1866 | Roman Catholic | Minn. | Harding | 1923 | 56 | 1939 | death | 16 | 73 | 1939 | 73 |
| Edward T. Sanford | Tenn. | 1865 | Episcopal | Tenn. | Harding | 1923 | 57 | 1930 | death | 7 | 64 | 1930 | 64 |

| | | | | | | | | | | | | | |
|---|---|---|---|---|---|---|---|---|---|---|---|---|---|
| Harlan F. Stone | N.H. | 1872 | Episcopal | N.Y. | Coolidge | 1925 | 52 | 1941 | promoted | 16 | 68 | 1946 | 73 |
| Owen J. Roberts | Pa. | 1875 | Episcopal | Pa. | Hoover | 1930 | 55 | 1945 | resigned | 15 | 70 | 1955 | 80 |
| Benjamin N. Cardozo | N.Y. | 1870 | Jewish | N.Y. | Hoover | 1932 | 61 | 1938 | death | 6 | 68 | 1938 | 68 |
| Hugo L. Black | Ala. | 1886 | Baptist | Ala. | F. Roosevelt | 1937 | 51 | 1971 | retired | 34 | 85 | 1971 | 85 |
| Stanley F. Reed | Ky. | 1884 | Protestant | Ky. | F. Roosevelt | 1938 | 53 | 1957 | retired | 19 | 72 | — | — |
| Felix Frankfurter | Austria | 1882 | Jewish | Mass. | F. Roosevelt | 1939 | 56 | 1962 | retired | 23 | 79 | 1965 | 82 |
| William O. Douglas | Minn. | 1898 | Presbyterian | Conn. | F. Roosevelt | 1939 | 40 | 1975 | retired | 36 | 77 | — | — |
| Frank Murphy | Mich. | 1890 | Roman Catholic | Mich. | F. Roosevelt | 1940 | 49 | 1949 | death | 9 | 59 | 1949 | 59 |
| James F. Byrnes | S.C. | 1879 | Episcopal | S.C. | F. Roosevelt | 1941 | 62 | 1942 | resigned | 1 | 63 | 1972 | 92 |
| Robert H. Jackson | N.Y. | 1892 | Episcopal | Pa. | F. Roosevelt | 1941 | 49 | 1954 | death | 13 | 62 | 1954 | 62 |
| Wiley B. Rutledge | Ky. | 1894 | Unitarian | Iowa | F. Roosevelt | 1943 | 48 | 1949 | death | 6 | 55 | 1949 | 55 |
| Harold H. Burton | Mass. | 1888 | Unitarian | Ohio | Truman | 1945 | 57 | 1958 | retired | 13 | 70 | 1964 | 76 |
| Tom C. Clark | Tex. | 1899 | Presbyterian | Tex. | Truman | 1949 | 49 | 1967 | retired | 17 | 67 | 1977 | 78 |
| Sherman Minton | Ind. | 1890 | Roman Catholic | Ind. | Truman | 1949 | 58 | 1956 | retired | 7 | 65 | 1965 | 74 |
| John M. Harlan | Ill. | 1899 | Presbyterian | N.Y. | Eisenhower | 1955 | 55 | 1971 | retired | 16 | 72 | 1971 | 72 |
| William J. Brennan, Jr. | N.J. | 1906 | Roman Catholic | N.J. | Eisenhower | 1956 | 50 | — | — | — | — | — | — |
| Charles E. Whittaker | Kan. | 1901 | Methodist | Mo. | Eisenhower | 1957 | 56 | 1962 | disabled | 5 | 61 | 1973 | 73 |
| Potter Stewart | Mich. | 1915 | Episcopal | Ohio | Eisenhower | 1958 | 43 | — | — | — | — | — | — |
| Byron R. White | Colo. | 1917 | Episcopal | Colo. | Kennedy | 1962 | 44 | — | — | — | — | — | — |
| Arthur J. Goldberg | Ill. | 1908 | Jewish | Ill. | Kennedy | 1962 | 54 | 1965 | resigned | 2 | 56 | — | — |
| Abe Fortas | Tenn. | 1910 | Jewish | Tenn. | Johnson | 1965 | 55 | 1969 | resigned | 3 | 58 | — | — |
| Thurgood Marshall | Md. | 1908 | Episcopalian | N.Y. | Johnson | 1967 | 59 | — | — | — | — | — | — |
| Harry A. Blackmun | Ill. | 1908 | Methodist | Minn. | Nixon | 1970 | 61 | — | — | — | — | — | — |
| Lewis F. Powell, Jr. | Va. | 1907 | Presbyterian | Va. | Nixon | 1972 | 64 | — | — | — | — | — | — |
| William H. Rehnquist | Minn. | 1924 | Lutheran | Wis. | Nixon | 1972 | 47 | — | — | — | — | — | — |
| John Paul Stevens | Ill. | 1920 | Protestant | Ill. | Ford | 1975 | 55 | — | — | — | — | — | — |

1. Congregationalist; later Unitarian. 2. Unitarian; then Episcopal. 3. Unitarian or Congregational. 4. Not a member of any church.

## Impeachments of Federal Officials

*Source: Congressional Directory*

The procedure for the impeachment of Federal officials is detailed in Article I, Section 3, of the Constitution. See Index.

The Senate has sat as a court of impeachment in the following cases:

**William Blount,** Senator from Tennessee; charges dismissed for want of jurisdiction, January 14, 1799.

**John Pickering,** Judge of the U.S. District Court for [illegible] Hampshire; removed from office March 12, [illegible] Associate Justice of the Supreme Court; acquitted March 1, 1805.

**James H. Peck,** Judge of the U.S. District Court for Missouri; acquitted Jan. 31, 1831.

**West H. Humphreys,** Judge of the U.S. District Court for the middle, eastern, and western districts of Tennessee; removed from office June 26, 1862.

**Andrew Johnson,** President of the United States; acquitted May 26, 1868.

**William W. Belknap,** Secretary of War; acquitted Aug. 1, 1876.

**Charles Swayne,** Judge of the U.S. District Court for the northern district of Florida; acquitted Feb. 27, 1905.

**Robert W. Archbald,** Associate Judge, U.S. Commerce Court; removed Jan. 13, 1913.

**George W. English,** Judge of the U.S. District Court for eastern district of Illinois; resigned Nov. 4, 1926; proceedings dismissed.

**Harold Louderback,** Judge of the U.S. District Court for the northern district of California; acquitted May 24, 1933.

**Halsted L. Ritter,** Judge of the U.S. District Court for the southern district of Florida; removed from office April 17, 1936.

# Federal Judiciary

*Source:* Administrative Office of the United States Courts.

## SUPREME COURT OF THE U.S.

*(Washington, D.C. 20543)*

**Chief Justice:** Warren E. Burger

**Associate Justices:**
William J. Brennan, Jr.
Potter Stewart
Byron R. White
Thurgood Marshall
Harry A. Blackmun
Lewis F. Powell, Jr.
William H. Rehnquist
John Paul Stevens

## U.S. COURTS OF APPEALS

*(CJ indicates Chief Judge)*

**District of Columbia:** David L. Bazelon, CJ, J. Skelly Wright, Carl McGowan, Edward Allen Tamm, Harold Leventhal, Spottswood W. Robinson III, Roger Robb, George E. MacKinnon, Malcolm R. Wilkey, all Washington.

**First Circuit (Me., Mass., N.H., R.I., Puerto Rico):** Frank M. Coffin, CJ, Portland, Me.; Levin H. Campbell, Boston; Hugh H. Bownes, Concord, Mass.

**Second Circuit (Conn., N.Y., Vt.):** Irving R. Kaufman, CJ, Wilfred Feinberg, Walter R. Mansfield, William H. Mulligan, Murray I. Gurfein, all New York City; Ellsworth A. Van Graafeiland, Rochester, N.Y.; James L. Oakes, Brattleboro, Vt.; William H. Timbers, Bridgeport, Conn.; Thomas J. Meskill, Hartford, Conn.

**Third Circuit (Del., N.J., Pa., Virgin Is.):** Collins J. Seitz, CJ, Wilmington, Del.; Arlin M. Adams, Philadelphia; Ruggero J. Aldisert, Joseph F. Weis, Jr., both Pittsburgh; John J. Gibbons, Leonard I. Garth, both Newark, N.J.; Max Rosenn, Wilkes-Barre, Pa.; James Hunter, III, Camden, N.J.; A. Leon Higginbotham, Jr., Philadelphia.

**Fourth Circuit (Md., N.C., S.C., Va., W. Va.):** Clement F. Haynsworth, Jr., CJ, Greenville, S.C.; Harrison L. Winter, Baltimore; John D. Butzner, Jr., Richmond, Va.; Donald Stuart Russell, Spartanburg, S.C.; H. Emory Widener, Jr., Abingdon, Va.; Kenneth K. Hall, Charleston, W. Va.

**Fifth Circuit (Ala., Fla., Ga., La., Miss., Tex., Canal Zone):** John R. Brown, CJ, Houston; Homer Thornberry, Robert A. Ainsworth, Jr., Alvin B. Rubin, all New Orleans; Thomas G. Gee, Austin, Tex.; James P. Coleman, Ackerman, Miss.; Irving L. Goldberg, Dallas; John C. Godbold, Montgomery, Ala.; Lewis R. Morgan, Newman, Ga.; Charles Clark, Jackson, Miss.; Paul H. Roney, St. Petersburg, Fla.; Gerald B. Tjoflat, Jacksonville, Fla.; James C. Hill, Atlanta; Peter T. Fay, Miami, Fla.; Robert S. Vance, Birmingham, Ala.

**Sixth Circuit (Ky., Mich., Ohio, Tenn.):** Harry Phillips, CJ, Gilbert S. Merritt, both Nashville, Tenn.; Paul C. Weick, Akron, Ohio; George Clifton Edwards, Jr., John W. Peck, both Cincinnati; Anthony J. Celebrezze, Cleveland; Albert J. Engel, Grand Rapids, Mich.; Pierce Lively, Danville, Ky.; Damon J. Keith, Detroit.

**Seventh Circuit (Ill., Ind., Wis.):** Thomas E. Fairchild, CJ, Luther M. Swygert, Walter J. Cummings, Wilbur F. Pell, Jr., Robert A. Sprecher, Philip W. Tone, William J. Bauer, Harlington Wood, Jr., all Chicago.

**Eighth Circuit (Ark., Iowa, Minn., Mo., Neb., N.D., S.D.):** Floyd R. Gibson, CJ, Kansas City, Mo.; Donald P. Lay, Donald R. Ross, both Omaha, Neb.; Gerald W. Heaney, Duluth, Minn.; Myron H. Bright, Fargo, N.D.; Roy L. Stephenson, Des Moines, Iowa; J. Smith Henley, Harrison, Ark.

**Ninth Circuit (Ariz., Calif., Idaho, Mont., Nev., Ore., Wash., Alaska, Hawaii, Guam):** James R. Browning, CJ, Joseph T. Sneed, both San Francisco; Walter Ely, Shirley M. Hufstedler, both Los Angeles; J. Clifford Wallace, San Diego, Calif.; Eugene A. Wright, Seattle; Ozell M. Trask, Thomas Tang, both Phoenix, Ariz.; Herbert Y. C. Choy, Honolulu; Alfred T. Goodwin, Portland, Ore.; Anthony M. Kennedy, Sacramento, Calif., J. Blaine Anderson, Boise, Idaho; Procter Hug, Jr., Reno, Nev.

**Tenth Circuit (Colo., Kan., N.M., Okla., Utah, Wyo.):** Oliver Seth, CJ, Santa Fe, N.M.; William J. Holloway, Jr., Oklahoma City; Robert H. McWilliams, William E. Doyle, both Denver; James E. Barrett, Cheyenne, Wyo.; James K. Logan, Kansas City, Kan.

## U.S. COURT OF CLAIMS

*(Washington, D.C. 20005)*

**Chief Judge:** Daniel M. Friedman.

**Associate Judges:** Oscar H. Davis, Philip Nichols, Jr., Shiro Kashiwa, Robert L. Kunzig, Marion T. Bennett.

## U.S. COURT OF CUSTOMS AND PATENT APPEALS

*(Washington, D.C. 20439)*

**Chief Judge:** Howard T. Markey.

**Associate Judges:** Giles S. Rich, Phillip B. Baldwin, Donald E. Lane, Jack R. Miller.

## U.S. CUSTOMS COURT

*(One Federal Plaza, New York, N.Y. 10007)*

**Chief Judge:** Edward D. Re.

**Judges:** Paul P. Rao, Morgan Ford, Scovel Richardson, Frederick Landis, James L. Watson, Herbert N. Maletz, Bernard Newman, Nils A. Boe.

## U.S. TAX COURT

*(Washington, D.C. 20217)*

**Chief Judge:** Howard A. Dawson, Jr.

**Judges:** Arnold Raum, Bruce M. Forrester, William Miller Drennen, Irene Feagin Scott, William M. Fay, Theodore Tannenwald, Jr., Charles R. Simpson, C. Moxley Featherston, Leo H. Irwin, Samuel B. Sterrett, William H. Quealy, William A. Goffe, Cynthia Holcomb Hall, Darrell D. Wiles, Richard C. Wilbur, John Gregory Bruce, Norman O. Tietjens.

# Annual Salaries of Federal Officials

| | | | |
|---|---|---|---|
| President of the U.S. | $200,000[1] | Secretaries of the Army, Navy, Air Force | $57,500 |
| Vice President of the U.S. | 75,000[2] | Senators and Representatives | 57,500 |
| Cabinet members | 66,000 | President Pro Tempore of Senate | 65,000 |
| Under secretaries of executive departments | 52,500 | Speaker of the House | 75,000 |
| Deputy Secretaries of State, Defense, Treasury | 57,500 | Majority and Minority Leader of the Senate | 65,000 |
| eputy Attorney General | 57,500 | Majority and Minority Leader of the House | 65,000 |
| der Secretary of Transportation | 57,500 | Chief Justice of the United States | 75,000 |
| | | Associate Justices of the Supreme Court | 72,000 |

s taxable $50,000 for expenses and a nontaxable sum (not to exceed $40,000 a year) for travel expenses. 2. Plus taxable 00 for expenses. NOTE: All salaries shown above are taxable.

# The Ninety-Fifth Congress

## Members of 94th and 95th Congresses

| | 94th Congress | | | | | | 95th Congress | | | | | |
|---|---|---|---|---|---|---|---|---|---|---|---|---|
| | Dem. | Rep. | Male | Female | White | Black and other | Dem. | Rep. | Male | Female | White | Black and other |
| Senate | 68[1] | 32[2] | 100 | 0 | 97 | 3 | 62[1] | 38 | 98 | 2 | 96 | 4 |
| House | 286 | 145 | 412 | 19 | 415 | 16 | 287[3] | 146 | 415 | 18 | 418 | 15 |

1. Includes one Independent (Byrd of Virginia). 2. Includes one Conservative-Republican (Buckley of New York). 3. Two vacancies (California and Tennessee). *Source: Congressional Directory.*

## The Senate

Senior Senator is listed first. The dates in the first column indicate period of service. The date given in parentheses after the Senator's name is year of birth. All terms are for six years and expire in January. Mailing address of Senators: The Senate, Washington, D.C. 20510.

**ALABAMA**
1946–79 John J. Sparkman, D (1899)
1978–79 Maryon Allen, D[1] (1925)
**ALASKA**
1968–79 Ted Stevens, R[2] (1923)
1969–81 Mike Gravel, D (1930)
**ARIZONA**
1969–81 Barry Goldwater, R (1909)
1977–83 Dennis DeConcini, D (1937)
**ARKANSAS**
1975–81 Dale Bumpers, D (1925)
1977–79 Kaneaster Hodges, Jr., D (1938)
**CALIFORNIA**
1969–81 Alan Cranston, D[3] (1914)
1977–83 S. I. Hayakawa, R (1906)
**COLORADO**
1973–79 Floyd K. Haskell, D (1916)
1975–81 Gary W. Hart, D (1937)
**CONNECTICUT**
1963–81 Abraham A. Ribicoff, D (1910)
1971–83 Lowell P. Weicker, Jr., R (1931)
**DELAWARE**
1971–83 William V. Roth, Jr., R (1921)
1973–79 Joseph R. Biden, Jr., D (1942)
**FLORIDA**
1971–83 Lawton Chiles, D (1930)
1975–81 Richard Stone, D (1928)
**GEORGIA**
1957–81 Herman E. Talmadge, D (1913)
1973–79 Sam Nunn, D (1938)
**HAWAII**
1963–81 Daniel K. Inouye, D (1924)
1977–83 Spark M. Matsunaga, D (1916)
**IDAHO**
1957–81 Frank Church, D (1924)
1973–79 James A. McClure, R (1924)
**ILLINOIS**
1967–79 Charles H. Percy, R (1919)
1971–81 Adlai E. Stevenson, D (1930)
**INDIANA**
1963–81 Birch Bayh, D (1928)
1977–83 Richard G. Lugar, R (1932)
**IOWA**
1973–79 Dick Clark, D (1929)
1975–81 John C. Culver, D (1932)
**KANSAS**
1962–79 James B. Pearson, R (1920)
1969–81 Robert J. Dole, R (1923)
**KENTUCKY**
1973–79 Walter Huddleston, D (1926)
1975–81 Wendell H. Ford, D (1924)
**LOUISIANA**
1948–81 Russell B. Long, D (1918)
1973–79 J. Bennett Johnston, Jr., D (1932)
**MAINE**
1959–83 Edmund S. Muskie, D (1914)
1973–79 William D. Hathaway, D (1924)
**MARYLAND**
1969–81 Charles McC. Mathias, Jr., R (1922)
1977–83 Paul S. Sarbanes, D (1933)
**MASSACHUSETTS**
1962–83 Edward M. Kennedy, D (1932)
1967–79 Edward W. Brooke, R (1919)
**MICHIGAN**
1966–79 Robert P. Griffin, R (1923)
1977–83 Donald W. Riegle, Jr., D (1938)

## LATEST ELECTION RETURNS

Readers may obtain a complete listing of members of the 96th Congress, reflecting the final electio returns of November 1978. Write Election, Information Please, 57 West 57th St., New York, New Yo 10019, enclosing a self-addressed, stamped envelope. There will be no charge for this information.

**MINNESOTA**
1977–79 Wendell R. Anderson, D (1933)
1978–79 Muriel Humphrey, D[1] (1912)
**MISSISSIPPI**
1943–79 James O. Eastland, D[4] (1904)
1947–83 John C. Stennis, D (1901)
**MISSOURI**
1968–81 Thomas F. Eagleton, D (1929)
1977–83 John C. Danforth, R (1936)
**MONTANA**
1977–83 John Melcher, D (1924)
1978–79 Paul G. Hatfield, D (1928)
**NEBRASKA**
1955–79 Carl T. Curtis, R (1905)
1977–83 Edward Zorinsky, D (1928)
**NEVADA**
1959–83 Howard W. Cannon, D (1912)
1975–81 Paul D. Laxalt, R (1922)
**NEW HAMPSHIRE**
1962–79 Thomas J. McIntyre, D (1915)
1975–81 John A. Durkin, D (1936)
**NEW JERSEY**
1955–79 Clifford P. Case, R (1904)
1959–83 Harrison A. Williams, Jr., D (1919)
**NEW MEXICO**
1973–79 Pete V. Domenici, R (1932)
1977–83 Harrison H. Schmitt, R (1935)
**NEW YORK**
1957–81 Jacob K. Javits, R (1904)
1977–83 Daniel P. Moynihan, D (1927)
**NORTH CAROLINA**
1973–79 Jesse A. Helms, R (1921)
1975–81 Robert B. Morgan, D (1925)
**NORTH DAKOTA**
1945–81 Milton R. Young, R (1897)
1960–83 Quentin N. Burdick, D (1908)
**OHIO**
1975–81 John H. Glenn, Jr., D (1921)
1977–83 Howard M. Metzenbaum, D (1917)
**OKLAHOMA**
1969–81 Henry L. Bellmon, R (1921)
1973–79 Dewey F. Bartlett, R (1919)
**OREGON**
1967–79 Mark O. Hatfield, R (1922)
1969–81 Bob Packwood, R (1932)
**PENNSYLVANIA**
1969–81 Richard S. Schweiker, R (1926)
1977–83 H. John Heinz III, R (1938)
**RHODE ISLAND**
1961–79 Claiborne Pell, D (1918)
1977–83 John H. Chafee, R (1922)
**SOUTH CAROLINA**
1956–79 Strom Thurmond, R (1902)
1966–81 Ernest F. Hollings, D (1922)
**SOUTH DAKOTA**
1963–81 George McGovern, D (1922)
1973–79 James G. Abourezk, D (1931)
**TENNESSEE**
1967–79 Howard H. Baker, Jr., R[5] (1925)
1977–83 James R. Sasser, D (1936)
**TEXAS**
1961–79 John G. Tower, R (1925)
1971–83 Lloyd M. Bentsen, D (1921)
**UTAH**
1975–81 E. J. (Jake) Garn, R (1932)
1977–83 Orrin G. Hatch, R (1934)
**VERMONT**
1971–83 Robert T. Stafford, R (1913)
1975–81 Patrick J. Leahy, D (1940)
**VIRGINIA**
1965–83 Harry F. Byrd, Jr., I (1914)
1973–79 William L. Scott, R (1915)
**WASHINGTON**
1944–81 Warren G. Magnuson, D (1905)
1953–83 Henry M. Jackson, D (1912)
**WEST VIRGINIA**
1958–79 Jennings Randolph, D (1902)
1959–83 Robert C. Byrd, D[6] (1918)
**WISCONSIN**
1957–83 William Proxmire, D (1915)
1963–81 Gaylord Nelson, D (1916)
**WYOMING**
1967–79 Clifford P. Hansen, R (1912)
1977–83 Malcolm Wallop, R (1933)

1. Appointed to fill late husband's seat. 2. Assistant minority leader (whip). 3. Assistant majority leader (whip). 4. President pro tem. 5. Minority leader. 6. Majority leader.

## The House of Representatives

The numerals indicate the Congressional Districts of the states; the designation AL means At-Large. All terms end January 1979. Mailing address of Representatives: House of Representatives, Washington, D.C. 20515.

**ALABAMA**
*(7 Representatives)*
1. Jack Edwards, R
2. William L. Dickinson, R
3. William Nichols, D
4. Tom Bevill, D
5. Ronnie G. Flippo, D
6. John H. Buchanan, R
7. Walter Flowers, D

**ASKA**
*Representative)*
on E. Young, R

**ARIZONA**
*(4 Representatives)*
1. John J. Rhodes, R[1]
2. Morris K. Udall, D
3. Bob Stump, D
4. Eldon Rudd, R

**ARKANSAS**
*(4 Representatives)*
1. Bill Alexander, D
2. Jim Guy Tucker, D
3. John P. Hammerschmidt, R
4. Ray Thornton, D

**CALIFORNIA**
*(43 Representatives)*
1. Harold T. Johnson, D
2. Don H. Clausen, R
3. John E. Moss, D
4. Robert L. Leggett, D
5. John L. Burton, D
6. Phillip Burton, D
7. George Miller, D
8. Ronald V. Dellums, D
9. Fortney H. Stark, Jr., D
10. Don Edwards, D
11. Leo J. Ryan, D

12. Paul N. McCloskey, Jr., R
13. Norman Y. Mineta, D
14. John J. McFall, D
15. B. F. Sisk, D
16. Leon E. Panetta, D
17. John H. Krebs, D
18. (Vacant)
19. Robert J. Lagomarsino, R
20. Barry M. Goldwater, Jr., R
21. James C. Corman, D
22. Carlos J. Moorhead, R
23. Anthony C. Beilenson, D
24. Henry A. Waxman, D
25. Edward R. Roybal, D
26. John H. Rousselot, R
27. Robert K. Dornan, R
28. Yvonne B. Burke, D
29. Augustus F. Hawkins, D
30. George E. Danielson, D
31. Charles H. Wilson, D
32. Glenn M. Anderson, D
33. Del Clawson, R
34. Mark W. Hannaford, D
35. James F. Lloyd, D
36. George E. Brown, Jr., D
37. Shirley N. Pettis, R
38. Jerry M. Patterson, D
39. Charles E. Wiggins, R
40. Robert E. Badham, R
41. Bob Wilson, R
42. Lionel Van Deerlin, D
43. Clair W. Burgener, R

**COLORADO**
*(5 Representatives)*
1. Patricia Schroeder, D
2. Timothy E. Wirth, D
3. Frank E. Evans, D
4. James P. Johnson, R
5. William L. Armstrong, R

**CONNECTICUT**
*(6 Representatives)*
1. William R. Cotter, D
2. Christopher J. Dodd, D
3. Robert N. Giaimo, D
4. Stewart B. McKinney, R
5. Ronald A. Sarasin, R
6. Toby Moffett, D

**DELAWARE**
*(1 Representative)*
AL Thomas B. Evans, Jr., R

**FLORIDA**
*(15 Representatives)*
1. Robert L. F. Sikes, D
2. Don Fuqua, D
3. Charles E. Bennett, D
4. William V. Chappell, Jr., D
5. Richard Kelly, R
6. C. W. Bill Young, R
7. Sam M. Gibbons, D
8. Andrew P. Ireland, D
9. Lou Frey, Jr., R
10. L. A. Bafalis, R
11. Paul G. Rogers, D
12. J. Herbert Burke, R
13. William Lehman, D
14. Claude D. Pepper, D
15. Dante B. Fascell, D

**GEORGIA**
*(10 Representatives)*
1. Ronald B. Ginn, D
2. Dawson Mathis, D
3. Jack T. Brinkley, D
4. Elliott H. Levitas, D
5. Wyche F. Fowler, Jr., D
6. John J. Flynt, Jr., D
7. Lawrence P. McDonald, D
8. Billy Lee Evans, D
9. Edgar L. Jenkins, D
10. D. Douglas Barnard, Jr., D

**HAWAII**
*(2 Representatives)*
1. Cecil Heftel, D
2. Daniel K. Akaka, D

**IDAHO**
*(2 Representatives)*
1. Steven D. Symms, R
2. George V. Hansen, R

**ILLINOIS**
*(24 Representatives)*
1. Ralph H. Metcalfe, D
2. Morgan F. Murphy, D
3. Martin A. Russo, D
4. Edward J. Derwinski, R
5. John G. Fary, D
6. Henry J. Hyde, R
7. Cardiss Collins, D
8. Dan Rostenkowski, D
9. Sidney R. Yates, D
10. Abner J. Mikva, D
11. Frank Annunzio, D
12. Philip M. Crane, R
13. Robert McClory, R
14. John N. Erlenborn, R
15. Tom Corcoran, R
16. John B. Anderson, R
17. George M. O'Brien, R
18. Robert H. Michel, R[2]
19. Tom Railsback, R
20. Paul Findley, R
21. Edward R. Madigan, R
22. George E. Shipley, D
23. Melvin Price, D
24. Paul Simon, D

**INDIANA**
*(11 Representatives)*
1. Adam Benjamin, Jr., D
2. Floyd J. Fithian, D
3. John Brademas, D[3]
4. J. Danforth Quayle, R
5. Elwood H. Hillis, R
6. David W. Evans, D
7. John T. Myers, R
8. David L. Cornwell, D
9. Lee H. Hamilton, D
10. Philip R. Sharp, D
11. Andrew Jacobs, Jr., D

**IOWA**
*(6 Representatives)*
1. James A. S. Leach, R
2. Michael T. Blouin, D
3. Charles E. Grassley, R
4. Neal Smith, D
5. Thomas R. Harkin, D
6. Berkley W. Bedell, D

**KANSAS**
*(5 Representatives)*
1. Keith G. Sebelius, R
2. Martha E. Keys, D
3. Larry Winn, Jr., R
4. Dan Glickman, D
5. Joe Skubitz, R

**KENTUCKY**
*(7 Representatives)*
1. Carroll Hubbard, Jr., D
2. William H. Natcher, D
3. Romano L. Mazzoli, D
4. M. G. (Gene) Snyder, R
5. Tim Lee Carter, R
6. John B. Breckinridge, D
7. Carl D. Perkins, D

**LOUISIANA**
*(8 Representatives)*
1. Robert L. Livingston, Jr., R
2. Corinne (Lindy) Boggs, D
3. David C. Treen, R
4. Joe D. Waggonner, Jr., D
5. Jerry Huckaby, D
6. W. Henson Moore, R
7. John B. Breaux, D
8. Gillis W. Long, D

**MAINE**
*(2 Representatives)*
1. David F. Emery, R
2. William S. Cohen, R

**MARYLAND**
*(8 Representatives)*
1. Robert E. Bauman, R
2. Clarence D. Long, D
3. Barbara A. Mikulski, D
4. Marjorie S. Holt, R
5. Gladys N. Spellman, D
6. Goodloe E. Byron, D
7. Parren J. Mitchell, D[4]
8. Newton I. Steers, Jr., R

**MASSACHUSETTS**
*(12 Representatives)*
1. Silvio O. Conte, R
2. Edward P. Boland, D
3. Joseph D. Early, D
4. Robert F. Drinan, D
5. Paul E. Tsongas, D
6. Michael J. Harrington, D
7. Edward J. Markey, D
8. Thomas P. O'Neill, Jr., D[5]
9. John J. Moakley, D
10. Margaret M. Heckler, R
11. James A. Burke, D
12. Gerry E. Studds, D

**MICHIGAN**
*(19 Representatives)*
1. John Conyers, Jr., D
2. Carl D. Pursell, R
3. Garry Brown, R
4. David A. Stockman, R
5. Harold S. Sawyer, R
6. M. Robert Carr, D
7. Dale E. Kildee, D
8. Bob Traxler, D
9. Guy Vander Jagt, R
10. Elford A. Cederberg, R
11. Philip E. Ruppe, R

12. David E. Bonior, D
13. Charles C. Diggs, Jr., D
14. Lucien N. Nedzi, D
15. William D. Ford, D
16. John D. Dingell, D
17. William M. Brodhead, D
18. James J. Blanchard, D
19. William S. Broomfield, R

**MINNESOTA**
*(8 Representatives)*
1. Albert H. Quie, R
2. Thomas M. Hagedorn, R
3. Bill Frenzel, R
4. Bruce F. Vento, D
5. Donald M. Fraser, D
6. Richard M. Nolan, D
7. Arlan Stangeland, R
8. James L. Oberstar, D

**MISSISSIPPI**
*(5 Representatives)*
1. Jamie L. Whitten, D
2. David R. Bowen, D
3. G. V. (Sonny) Montgomery, D
4. Thad Cochran, R
5. Trent Lott, R

**MISSOURI**
*(10 Representatives)*
1. William L. Clay, D
2. Robert A. Young, D
3. Richard A. Gephardt, D
4. Ike Skelton, D
5. Richard Bolling, D
6. E. Thomas Coleman, R
7. Gene Taylor, R
8. Richard H. Ichord, D
9. Harold L. Volkmer, D
10. Bill D. Burlison, D

**MONTANA**
*(2 Representatives)*
1. Max Baucus, D
2. Ron Marlenee, R

**NEBRASKA**
*(3 Representatives)*
1. Charles Thone, R
2. John J. Cavanaugh, D
3. Virginia Smith, R

**NEVADA**
*(1 Representative)*
AL James D. Santini, D

**NEW HAMPSHIRE**
*(2 Representatives)*
1. Norman E. D'Amours, D
2. James C. Cleveland, R

**NEW JERSEY**
*(15 Representatives)*
1. James J. Florio, D
2. William J. Hughes, D
3. James J. Howard, D
4. Frank Thompson, Jr., D
Millicent Fenwick, R
Edwin B. Forsythe, R
ndrew Maguire, D
obert A. Roe, D
rold C. Hollenbeck, R
er W. Rodino, Jr., D
ph G. Minish, D

12. Matthew J. Rinaldo, R
13. Helen S. Meyner, D
14. Joseph A. LeFante, D
15. Edward J. Patten, D

**NEW MEXICO**
*(2 Representatives)*
1. Manuel Lujan, Jr., R
2. Harold Runnels, D

**NEW YORK**
*(39 Representatives)*
1. Otis G. Pike, D
2. Thomas J. Downey, D
3. Jerome A. Ambro, D
4. Norman F. Lent, R
5. John W. Wydler, R
6. Lester L. Wolff, D
7. Joseph P. Addabbo, D
8. Benjamin S. Rosenthal, D
9. James J. Delaney, D
10. Mario Biaggi, D
11. James H. Scheuer, D
12. Shirley Chisholm, D
13. Stephen J. Solarz, D
14. Frederick W. Richmond, D
15. Leo C. Zeferetti, D
16. Elizabeth Holtzman, D
17. John M. Murphy, D
18. S. William Green, R
19. Charles B. Rangel, D
20. Theodore S. Weiss, D
21. Robert Garcia, D
22. Jonathan B. Bingham, D
23. Bruce F. Caputo, R
24. Richard L. Ottinger, D
25. Hamilton Fish, Jr., R
26. Benjamin A. Gilman, R
27. Matthew F. McHugh, D
28. Samuel S. Stratton, D
29. Edward W. Pattison, D
30. Robert C. McEwen, R
31. Donald J. Mitchell, R
32. James M. Hanley, D
33. William F. Walsh, R
34. Frank Horton, R
35. Barber B. Conable, Jr., R
36. John J. LaFalce, D
37. Henry J. Nowak, D
38. Jack Kemp, R
39. Stanley N. Lundine, D

**NORTH CAROLINA**
*(11 Representatives)*
1. Walter B. Jones, D
2. L. H. Fountain, D
3. Charles O. Whitley, Sr., D
4. Ike F. Andrews, D
5. Stephen L. Neal, D
6. Richardson Preyer, D
7. Charles Rose, D
8. W. G. Hefner, D
9. James G. Martin, R
10. James T. Broyhill, R
11. Lamar Gudger, D

**NORTH DAKOTA**
*(1 Representative)*
AL Mark Andrews, R

**OHIO**
*(23 Representatives)*
1. Willis D. Gradison, Jr., R
2. Thomas A. Luken, D
3. Charles W. Whalen, Jr., R
4. Tennyson Guyer, R
5. Delbert L. Latta, R
6. William H. Harsha, R
7. Clarence J. Brown, R
8. Thomas N. Kindness, R
9. Thomas L. Ashley, D
10. Clarence E. Miller, R
11. J. William Stanton, R
12. Samuel L. Devine, R
13. Donald J. Pease, D
14. John F. Seiberling, D
15. Chalmers P. Wylie, R
16. Ralph S. Regula, R
17. John M. Ashbrook, R
18. Douglas Applegate, D
19. Charles J. Carney, D
20. Mary Rose Oakar, D
21. Louis Stokes, D
22. Charles A. Vanik, D
23. Ronald M. Mottl, D

**OKLAHOMA**
*(6 Representatives)*
1. James R. Jones, D
2. Ted Risenhoover, D
3. Wesley W. Watkins, D
4. Tom Steed, D
5. Mickey Edwards, R
6. Glenn English, D

**OREGON**
*(4 Representatives)*
1. Les AuCoin, D
2. Al Ullman, D
3. Robert B. Duncan, D
4. James H. Weaver, D

**PENNSYLVANIA**
*(25 Representatives)*
1. Michael O. Myers, D
2. Robert N. C. Nix, D
3. Raymond F. Lederer, D
4. Joshua Eilberg, D
5. Richard T. Schulze, R
6. Gus Yatron, D
7. Robert W. Edgar, D
8. Peter H. Kostmayer, D
9. E. G. (Bud) Shuster, R
10. Joseph M. McDade, R
11. Daniel J. Flood, D
12. John P. Murtha, D
13. Lawrence Coughlin, R
14. William S. Moorhead, D
15. Fred B. Rooney, D
16. Robert S. Walker, R
17. Allen E. Ertel, D
18. Doug Walgren, D
19. William F. Goodling, R
20. Joseph M. Gaydos, D
21. John H. Dent, D
22. Austin J. Murphy, D
23. Joseph S. Ammerman, D
24. Marc L. Marks, R
25. Gary A. Myers, R

**RHODE ISLAND**
*(2 Representatives)*
1. Fernand J. St. Germain, D
2. Edward P. Beard, D

**SOUTH CAROLINA**
*(6 Representatives)*
1. Mendel J. Davis, D

2. Floyd D. Spence, R
3. Butler C. Derrick, Jr., D
4. James R. Mann, D
5. Kenneth L. Holland, D
6. John W. Jenrette, Jr., D

**SOUTH DAKOTA**
*(2 Representatives)*
1. Larry Pressler, R
2. James Abdnor, R

**TENNESSEE**
*(8 Representatives)*
1. James H. Quillen, R
2. John J. Duncan, R
3. Marilyn L. Lloyd, D
4. Albert Gore, Jr., D
5. (Vacant)
6. Robin L. Beard, R
7. Ed Jones, D
8. Harold E. Ford, D

**TEXAS**
*(24 Representatives)*
1. Sam B. Hall, Jr., D
2. Charles Wilson, D
3. James M. Collins, R
4. Ray Roberts, D
5. James A. Mattox, D
6. Olin E. Teague, D
7. Bill Archer, R
8. Bob Eckhardt, D
9. Jack Brooks, D
10. J. J. (Jake) Pickle, D
11. W. R. Poage, D
12. Jim Wright D[6]
13. Jack E. Hightower, D
14. John Young, D
15. Eligio de la Garza, D
16. Richard C. White, D
17. Omar Burleson, D
18. Barbara C. Jordan, D
19. George H. Mahon, D
20. Henry B. Gonzalez, D
21. Robert C. Krueger, D
22. Robert A. Gammage, D
23. Abraham Kazen, Jr., D
24. Dale Milford, D

**UTAH**
*(2 Representatives)*
1. K. Gunn McKay, D
2. David D. Marriott, R

**VERMONT**
*(1 Representative)*
AL James M. Jeffords, R

**VIRGINIA**
*(10 Representatives)*
1. Paul S. Trible, Jr., R
2. G. William Whitehurst, R
3. David E. Satterfield III, D
4. Robert W. Daniel, Jr., R
5. W. C. (Dan) Daniel, D
6. M. Caldwell Butler, R
7. J. Kenneth Robinson, R
8. Herbert E. Harris II, D
9. William C. Wampler, R
10. Joseph L. Fisher, D

**WASHINGTON**
*(7 Representatives)*
1. Joel Pritchard, R
2. Lloyd Meeds, D
3. Don Bonker, D
4. Mike McCormack, D
5. Thomas S. Foley, D
6. Norman D. Dicks, D
7. Jack Cunningham, R

**WEST VIRGINIA**
*(4 Representatives)*
1. Robert H. Mollohan, D
2. Harley O. Staggers, D
3. John Slack, D
4. Nick J. Rahall II, D

**WISCONSIN**
*(9 Representatives)*
1. Les Aspin, D
2. Robert W. Kastenmeier, D
3. Alvin J. Baldus, D
4. Clement J. Zablocki, D
5. Henry S. Reuss, D
6. William A. Steiger, R
7. David R. Obey, D
8. Robert J. Cornell, D
9. Robert W. Kasten, Jr., R

**WYOMING**
*(1 Representative)*
AL Teno Roncalio, D

1. Minority leader. 2. Assistant minority leader (whip). 3. Assistant majority leader (whip). 4. Head of Black Caucus. 5. Speaker. 6. Majority Leader. NOTE: The District of Columbia is represented by a nonvoting delegate (Walter E. Fauntroy, D). Puerto Rico has a resident commissioner in the House.

# Congressional Standing Committees

(Based on organization of 95th Congress. Subject to changes when 96th Congress convenes in January 1979.)

## Committees of the Senate

**Agriculture, Nutrition, and Forestry** (18 members)
*Chairman:* Herman E. Talmadge (Ga.)
*Ranking Repub.:* Robert J. Dole (Kan.)
**Appropriations** (25 members)
*Chairman:* Warren G. Magnuson (Wash.)
*Ranking Repub.:* Milton R. Young (N.D.)
**Armed Services** (18 members)
*Chairman:* John C. Stennis (Miss.)
*Ranking Repub.:* John G. Tower (Tex.)
**Banking, Housing, and Urban Affairs** (15 members)
*Chairman:* William Proxmire (Wis.)
*Ranking Repub.:* Edward W. Brooke (Mass.)
**Budget** (16 members)
*Chairman:* Edmund S. Muskie (Me.)
*Ranking Repub.:* Henry Bellmon (Okla.)
**Commerce, Science, and Transportation** (17 members)
*Chairman:* Howard W. Cannon (Nev.)
*Ranking Repub.:* James B. Pearson (Kan.)
**Energy and Natural Resources** (19 members)
*Chairman:* Henry M. Jackson (Wash.)
*Ranking Repub.:* Clifford P. Hansen (Wyo.)
**Environment and Public Works** (15 members)
*Chairman:* Jennings Randolph (W.Va.)
*Ranking Repub.:* Robert T. Stafford (Vt.)
**Finance** (18 members)
*Chairman:* Russell B. Long (La.)
*Ranking Repub.:* Carl T. Curtis (Neb.)
**Foreign Relations** (16 members)
*Chairman:* John Sparkman (Ala.)
*Ranking Repub.:* Clifford P. Case (N.J.)
**Governmental Affairs** (16 members)
*Chairman:* Abraham A. Ribicoff (Conn.)
*Ranking Repub.:* Charles H. Percy (Ill.)
**Human Resources** (15 members)
*Chairman:* Harrison A. Williams (N.J.)
*Ranking Repub.:* Jacob K. Javits (N.Y.)
**Judiciary** (17 members)
*Chairman:* James O. Eastland (Miss.)
*Ranking Repub.:* Strom Thurmond (S.C.)
**Rules and Administration** (9 members)
*Chairman:* Claiborne Pell (R.I.)
*Ranking Repub.:* Mark O. Hatfield (Ore.)
**Veterans' Affairs** (9 members)
*Chairman:* Alan Cranston (Calif.)
*Ranking Repub.:* Strom Thurmond (S.C.)

## Select and Special Committees

**Aging** (9 members)
*Chairman:* Frank Church (Idaho)
*Ranking Repub.:* Pete V. Domenici (N.M.)
**Ethics** (6 members)
*Chairman:* Adlai E. Stevenson III (Ill.)
*Ranking Repub.:* Harrison Schmitt (N.M.)
**Indian Affairs** (5 members)
*Chairman:* James Abourezk (S.D.)
*Ranking Repub.:* Dewey F. Bartlett (Okla.)
**Intelligence** (17 members)
*Chairman:* Birch Bayh (Ind.)
*Ranking Repub.:* Barry Goldwater (Ariz.)
**Small Business** (9 members)
*Chairman:* Gaylord Nelson (Wis.)
*Ranking Repub.:* Lowell P. Weicker, Jr. (Conn.)

## Committees of the House

**Agriculture** (46 members)
*Chairman:* Thomas S. Foley (Wash.)
*Ranking Repub.:* William C. Wampler (Va.)
**Appropriations** (55 members)
*Chairman:* George H. Mahon (Tex.)
*Ranking Repub.:* Elford A. Cederberg (Mich.)
**Armed Services** (41 members)
*Chairman:* Melvin Price (Ill.)
*Ranking Repub.:* Bob Wilson (Calif.)
**Banking, Finance, and Urban Affairs** (48 members)
*Chairman:* Henry S. Reuss (Wis.)
*Ranking Repub.:* J. William Stanton (Ohio)
**Budget** (25 members)
*Chairman:* Robert N. Giaimo (Conn.)
*Ranking Repub.:* Delbert L. Latta (Ohio)
**District of Columbia** (20 members)
*Chairman:* Charles C. Diggs, Jr. (Mich.)
*Ranking Repub.:* Stewart B. McKinney (Conn.)
**Education and Labor** (37 members)
*Chairman:* Carl D. Perkins (Ky.)
*Ranking Repub.:* Albert H. Quie (Minn.)
**Government Operations** (43 members)
*Chairman:* Jack Brooks (Tex.)
*Ranking Repub.:* Frank Horton (N.Y.)
**House Administration** (25 members)
*Chairman:* Frank Thompson, Jr. (N.J.)
*Ranking Repub.:* William L. Dickinson (Ala.)
**Interior and Insular Affairs** (46 members)
*Chairman:* Morris K. Udall (Ariz.)
*Ranking Repub.:* Joe Skubitz (Kan.)
**International Relations** (37 members)
*Chairman:* Clement J. Zablocki (Wis.)
*Ranking Repub.:* William S. Broomfield (Mich.)
**Interstate and Foreign Commerce** (43 members)
*Chairman:* Harley O. Staggers (W. Va.)
*Ranking Repub.:* Samuel L. Devine (Ohio)
**Judiciary** (34 members)
*Chairman:* Peter W. Rodino, Jr. (N.J.)
*Ranking Repub.:* Robert McClory (Ill.)
**Merchant Marine and Fisheries** (41 members)
*Chairman:* John M. Murphy (N.Y.)
*Ranking Repub.:* Philip E. Ruppe (Mich.)
**Post Office and Civil Service** (25 members)
*Chairman:* Robert N. C. Nix (Pa.)
*Ranking Repub.:* Edward J. Derwinski (Ill.)
**Public Works and Transportation** (44 members)
*Chairman:* Harold T. Johnson (Calif.)
*Ranking Repub.:* William H. Harsha (Ohio)
**Rules** (16 members)
*Chairman:* James J. Delaney (N.Y.)
*Ranking Repub.:* James H. Quillen (Tenn.)
**Science and Technology** (40 members)
*Chairman:* Olin E. Teague (Tex.)
*Ranking Repub.:* John W. Wydler (N.Y.)
**Small Business** (37 members)
*Chairman:* Neal Smith (Iowa)
*Ranking Repub.:* Silvio O. Conte (Mass.)
**Standards of Official Conduct** (12 members)
*Chairman:* John J. Flynt, Jr. (Ga.)
*Ranking Repub.:* Floyd D. Spence (S.C.)
**Veterans' Affairs** (28 members)
*Chairman:* Ray Roberts (Tex.)
*Ranking Repub.:* John P. Hammerschmidt (Ark.)
**Ways and Means** (37 members)
*Chairman:* Al Ullman (Ore.)
*Ranking Repub.:* Barber B. Conable, Jr. (N.Y.)

## Floor Leaders of the Senate

| Democratic | Republican |
|---|---|
| Gilbert M. Hitchcock, Neb. (Min. 1919–20) | Charles Curtis, Kan. (Maj. 1925–29) |
| Oscar W. Underwood, Ala. (Min. 1920–23) | James E. Watson, Ind. (Maj. 1929–33) |
| Joseph T. Robinson, Ark. (Min. 1923–33, Maj. 1933–37) | Charles L. McNary, Ore. (Min. 1933–44) |
| Alben W. Barkley, Ky. (Maj. 1937–46, Min. 1947–48) | Wallace H. White, Jr., Me. (Min. 1944–47, Maj. 1947–48) |
| Scott W. Lucas, Ill. (Maj. 1949–50) | Kenneth S. Wherry, Neb. (Min. 1949–51) |
| Ernest W. McFarland, Ariz. (Maj. 1951–52) | Styles Bridges, N. H. (Min. 1951–52) |
| Lyndon B. Johnson, Tex. (Min. 1953–54, Maj. 1955–60) | Robert A. Taft, Ohio (Maj. 1953) |
| Mike Mansfield, Mont. (Maj. 1961–1977) | William F. Knowland, Calif. (Maj. 1953–54, Min. 1955–58) |
| Robert C. Byrd, W. Va. (Maj. 1977– ) | Everett M. Dirksen, Ill. (Min. 1959–69) |
| | Hugh Scott, Pa. (Min. 1969–1977) |
| | Howard H. Baker, Jr., Tenn. (Min. 1977– ) |

NOTE: Min. = Minority Leader; Maj. = Majority Leader. *Source:* United States Senate, Secretary for the Majority.

## "In God We Trust"

"In God We Trust" first appeared on U.S. coins after April 22, 1864, when Congress passed an act authorizing the coinage of a 2-cent piece bearing this motto. Thereafter, Congress extended its use to other coins. On July 30, 1956, it became the national motto.

## Speakers of the House of Representatives

| Dates served | Congress | Name and state |
|---|---|---|
| 1789–1791 | 1 | Frederick A. C. Muhlenberg (Pa.) |
| 1791–1793 | 2 | Jonathan Trumbull (Conn.) |
| 1793–1795 | 3 | Frederick A. C. Muhlenberg (Pa.) |
| 1795–1799 | 4–5 | Jonathan Dayton (N.J.)[1] |
| 1799–1801 | 6 | Theodore Sedgwick (Mass.) |
| 1801–1807 | 7–9 | Nathaniel Macon (N.C.) |
| 1807–1811 | 10–11 | Joseph B. Varnum (Mass.) |
| 1811–1814 | 12–13 | Henry Clay (Ky.)[2] |
| 1814–1815 | 13 | Langdon Cheves (S.C.) |
| 1815–1820 | 14–16 | Henry Clay (Ky.)[3] |
| 1820–1821 | 16 | John W. Taylor (N.Y.) |
| 1821–1823 | 17 | Philip P. Barbour (Va.) |
| 1823–1825 | 18 | Henry Clay (Ky.) |
| 1825–1827 | 19 | John W. Taylor (N.Y.) |
| 1827–1834 | 20–23 | Andrew Stevenson (Va.)[4] |
| 1834–1835 | 23 | John Bell (Tenn.) |
| 1835–1839 | 24–25 | James K. Polk (Tenn.) |
| 1839–1841 | 26 | Robert M. T. Hunter (Va.) |
| 1841–1843 | 27 | John White (Ky.) |
| 1843–1845 | 28 | John W. Jones (Va.) |
| 1845–1847 | 29 | John W. Davis (Ind.) |
| 1847–1849 | 30 | Robert C. Winthrop (Mass.) |
| 1849–1851 | 31 | Howell Cobb (Ga.) |
| 1851–1855 | 32–33 | Linn Boyd (Ky.) |
| 1855–1857 | 34 | Nathaniel P. Banks (Mass.) |
| 1857–1859 | 35 | James L. Orr (S.C.) |
| 1859–1861 | 36 | Wm. Pennington (N.J.) |
| 1861–1863 | 37 | Galusha A. Grow (Pa.) |
| 1863–1869 | 38–40 | Schuyler Colfax (Ind.) |
| 1869–1869 | 40 | Theodore M. Pomeroy (N.Y.)[5] |
| 1869–1875 | 41–43 | James G. Blaine (Me.) |
| 1875–1876 | 44 | Michael C. Kerr (Ind.)[6] |
| 1876–1881 | 44–46 | Samuel J. Randall (Pa.) |
| 1881–1883 | 47 | J. Warren Keifer (Ohio) |
| 1883–1889 | 48–50 | John G. Carlisle (Ky.) |
| 1889–1891 | 51 | Thomas B. Reed (Me.) |
| 1891–1895 | 52–53 | Charles F. Crisp (Ga.) |
| 1895–1899 | 54–55 | Thomas B. Reed (Me.) |
| 1899–1903 | 56–57 | David B. Henderson (Iowa) |
| 1903–1911 | 58–61 | Joseph G. Cannon (Ill.) |
| 1911–1919 | 62–65 | Champ Clark (Mo.) |
| 1919–1925 | 66–68 | Frederick H. Gillett (Mass.) |
| 1925–1931 | 69–71 | Nicholas Longworth (Ohio) |
| 1931–1933 | 72 | John N. Garner (Tex.) |
| 1933–1934 | 73 | Henry T. Rainey (Ill.)[7] |
| 1935–1936 | 74 | Joseph W. Byrns (Tenn.)[8] |
| 1936–1940 | 74–76 | William B. Bankhead (Ala.)[9] |
| 1940–1947 | 76–79 | Sam Rayburn (Tex.) |
| 1947–1949 | 80 | Joseph W. Martin, Jr. (Mass.) |
| 1949–1953 | 81–82 | Sam Rayburn (Tex.) |
| 1953–1955 | 83 | Joseph W. Martin, Jr. (Mass.) |
| 1955–1961 | 84–87 | Sam Rayburn (Tex.)[10] |
| 1962–1971 | 87–91 | John W. McCormack (Mass.)[11] |
| 1971–1977 | 92–94 | Carl Albert (Okla.)[12] |
| 1977– | 95– | Thomas P. O'Neill, Jr. (Mass.) |

1. George Dent (Md.) was elected Speaker pro tempore for April 20 and May 28, 1798. 2. Resigned during second session of 13th Congress. 3. Resigned between first and second sessions of 16th Congress. 4. Resigned during first session of 23rd Congress. 5. Elected Speaker and served the day of adjournment. 6. Died between first and second sessions of 44th Congress. During first session, there were two Speakers pro tempore: Samuel S. Cox (N.Y.), appointed for Feb. 17, May 12, and June 19, 1876, and Milton Sayler (Ohio), appointed for June 4, 1876. 7. Died in 1934 after adjournment of second session of 73rd Congress. 8. Died during second session of 74th Congress. 9. Died during third session of 76th Congress. 10. Died between first and second sessions of 87th Congress. 11. Not a candidate in 1970 election. 12. Not a candidate in 1976 election. *Source:* Congressional Directory.

## Executive Departments and Agencies

*Source: U.S. Government Organization Manual.*

Unless otherwise indicated, addresses shown are in Washington, D.C.

### Executive Office of the President

**THE WHITE HOUSE OFFICE**

*1600 Pennsylvania Ave., N.W. (20500).*

**Counsel to the President:** Robert J. Lipshutz. **Deputy Counsel:** Margaret A. McKenna. **Senior Associate Counsel:** Michael H. Cardozo V, Douglas B. Huron. **Associate Counsel:** Patrick Apodaca. **Counsellor to the President on Aging:** Nelson Cruikshank.

**Assistants to the President:** Hamilton Jordan. *For National Security Affairs:* Zbigniew Brzezinski. *For Domestic Affairs* and *Policy:* Stuart E. Eizenstat. *For Intergovernmental Affairs:* Jack H. Watson, Jr. *For Congressional Liaison:* Frank B. Moore. *For Reorganization:* Richard A. Pettigrew.

**Special Assistants to the President:** Joseph W. Aragon. *For Intergovernmental Affairs:* Jack H. Watson, Jr. *For Administration:* Hugh A. Carter, Jr. *For Information Management:* Richard M. Harden. *For Media and Public Affairs:* Barry Jagoda. *For Appointments:* Timothy E. Kraft. *For Special Projects:* Martha M. Mitchell. *For Consumer Affairs:* Esther Peterson.

**Deputy Assistants to the President:** Landon Butler, S. Stephen Selig III. *For National Security Affairs:* David L. Aaron. *For Intergovernmental Affairs:* Lawrence A. Bailey. *For Public Liaison:* Seymour Wishman. *For Domestic Affairs* and *Policy:* David M. Rubenstein. *For Research:* Elizabeth A. Rainwater. *For Policy Analysis:* Mark A. Siegel. *For Congressional Liaison:* William H. Cable, Danny C. Tate.

**Press Secretary:** Joseph L. Powell. **Deputy Press Secretary:** Walter W. Wurfel, Rex L. Granum. **Associate Press Secretaries:** Patricia Y. Bario, Jerrold Schecter, Claudia M. Townsend, Marc T. Henderson.

**Personal Assistant/Secretary to the President:** Susan S. Clough.

**Secretary to the Cabinet:** Jack H. Watson, **Deputy Secretary:** Jane L. Frank.

**Director Research Office:** Stephen M. Travi

**Staff Secretary:** Richard G. Hutcheson III.
**Associates:** Bruce Kirschenbaum, Lawrence D. Gilson.
**Special Assistants:** Leslie C. Francis, James C. Free, Valerie F. Pinson, Robert K. Russell, Jr., Robert Thomson.
**Director, White House Operations:** Valerio L. Giannini.
**Director of Presidential Personnel Office:** James F. Gammill, Jr.
**Chief Speechwriter:** James M. Fallows. **Speechwriters:** Jerome H. Doolittle, Achsah P. Nesmith, Griffin Smith, Jr.
**Director, White House Projects:** Gregory S. Schneiders.
**Director of Scheduling:** Frances M. Voorde.
**Social Secretary:** Gretchen Poston.
**Press Secretary to the First Lady:** Mary Finch Hoyt.
**Personal Assistant to the First Lady:** Madeline F. MacBean.
**Director of Projects, Issues, Research for First Lady:** Kathryn E. Cade.
**Appointments Secretary to the First Lady:** Jane S. Fenderson.
**Editor, News Summary:** Patricia E. Bauer.
**Director, White House Military Office:** Marvin L. Beaman, Jr.
**Director, Visitors Office:** Nancy A. Willing.
**Director of Advance:** Ellis A. Woodward.
**Physician to the President:** Rear Adm. William M. Lukash, USN.
**Chief Executive Clerk:** Robert D. Linder.
**Chief Usher:** Rex W. Scouten.

### CENTRAL INTELLIGENCE AGENCY (CIA)
*Washington, D.C. (20505)*
**Established:** 1947.
**Director:** Adm. Stansfield Turner.
**Activities:** Coordinates intelligence activities of certain government departments and agencies by making recommendations to the National Security Council; correlates and evaluates intelligence and disseminates the results; performs certain additional services for existing intelligence agencies when the National Security Council determines that these can be more efficiently accomplished centrally.

### COUNCIL OF ECONOMIC ADVISERS (CEA)
*Executive Office Bldg. (20506).*
**Members:** 3.
**Established:** Feb. 20, 1946.
**Chairman:** Charles L. Schultze.
**Activities:** Assists President in preparation of economic reports to Congress; studies economic trends; appraises government activities on nation's economy; recommends economic policies.

### COUNCIL ON ENVIRONMENTAL QUALITY
*722 Jackson Pl., N.W. (20006).*
**Members:** 3.
**Established:** 1969.
**Chairman:** Charles H. Warren.
**Activities:** Develops and recommends to President national policies that promote environmental quality.

### COUNCIL ON WAGE AND PRICE STABILITY
*Jackson Place, N.W. (20506).*
**Members:** 8.
**Established:** Aug. 24, 1974.
**Chairman:** Charles L. Schultze.
**Director:** Robert W. Crandall (acting).
**Activities:** Monitors wages and prices and provides guidance on broad terms to labor and management.

### DOMESTIC POLICY STAFF
*1600 Pennsylvania Ave., N.W. (20500).*
**Members:** 19.
**Established:** July 1, 1970.
**Executive Director:** Stuart E. Eizenstat.
**Activities:** Formulates and coordinates domestic policy recommendations to President. Endeavors to resolve federal-state-local problems.

### NATIONAL SECURITY COUNCIL (NSC)
*Executive Office Bldg. (20506).*
**Members:** 4.
**Established:** July 26, 1947.
**Chairman:** President of U.S.
**Other members:** Vice President; Secretary of State; Secretary of Defense.
**Activities:** Assesses and appraises objectives, commitments and risks of United States in relation to our actual and potential military power.

### OFFICE OF ADMINISTRATION
*Old Executive Office Building (20500).*
**Established:** Dec. 12, 1977.
**Director:** Richard M. Harden.
**Activities:** Provides the common services for the Executive Office of the President such as mail, payroll, dataprocessing and messengers.

### OFFICE OF MANAGEMENT AND BUDGET
*Executive Office Bldg. (20503).*
**Established:** July 1, 1970.
**Director:** James T. McIntyre, Jr.
**Activities:** Assists President in preparing budget and formulating fiscal program; supervises administration of budget; coordinates advice on proposed legislation; plans improvements in statistical services; keeps President informed of progress of activities by government agencies so that Congressional appropriations are spent most economically.

### OFFICE OF SCIENCE AND TECHNOLOGY POLICY
*Executive Office Building (20500).*
**Established:** June 8, 1962.
**Director:** Frank Press.
**Activities:** Advises the President on scientific, engineering and technological aspects of issues requiring his attention.

### OFFICE OF THE SPECIAL REPRESENTATIVE FOR TRADE NEGOTIATIONS
*1800 G St., N.W. (20506).*
**Established:** Jan. 15, 1963.
**Special Representative:** Robert S. Strauss.
**Activities:** Advises the President on the administration and carrying out of the trade agreements program and on non-tariff barriers to international trade and international commodity agreements; chairs the Trade Expansion Act Advisory Committee.

## Executive Departments

### DEPARTMENT OF STATE

*2201 C St., N.W. (20520).*

**Established:** 1781 as Department of Foreign Affairs; reconstituted, 1789, following adoption of Constitution; name changed to Department of State Sept. 15, 1789.

**Secretary:** Cyrus R. Vance.

**Deputy Secretary:** Warren M. Christopher.

**Activities:** Determines government policy in relation to international problems; formulates measures for promoting friendship with other countries; develops policies and programs for U.S. participation in U.N. and other international organizations; conducts correspondence with our representatives abroad and accredited foreign representatives here; administers Foreign Service, Agency for International Development.

### DEPARTMENT OF THE TREASURY

*15th St. & Pennsylvania Ave., N.W. (20220).*

**Established:** Sept. 2, 1789.

**Secretary:** W. Michael Blumenthal.

**Deputy Secretary:** Robert Carswell.

**Treasurer of the U.S.:** Mrs. Azie T. Morton.

**Comptroller of the Currency:** John G. Heimann.

**Activities:** Manages national finances; grants warrants for money drawn from Treasury pursuant to legal appropriations; handles collection of revenue; keeps and renders public accounts; prepares plans for improvement of revenue and for support of public credit; controls coinage and printing of money; administers Secret Service, Customs Service, Internal Revenue Service, Bureau of Engraving and Printing, Bureau of the Mint, Bureau of Alcohol, Tobacco and Firearms, Office of Law Enforcement, Federal Law Enforcement Training Center.

### DEPARTMENT OF DEFENSE

*The Pentagon (20301).*

**Established:** July 26, 1947, as National Department Establishment; name changed to Department of Defense on Aug. 10, 1949. Subordinate to Secretary of Defense are Secretaries of Army, Navy, Air Force.

**Secretary:** Harold Brown.

**Deputy Secretary:** Charles W. Duncan, Jr.

**Secretary of Army:** Clifford L. Alexander, Jr.

**Secretary of Navy:** W. Graham Claytor, Jr.

**Secretary of Air Force:** John C. Stetsen.

**Commandant of Marine Corps:** Gen. Louis H. Wilson.

**Joint Chiefs of Staff:**[1] Gen. David C. Jones, Chairman; Adm. Thomas B. Hayward, Jr., Navy; Gen. Lew Allen, Jr., Air Force: Gen. Bernard W. Rogers, Army; Gen. Louis H. Wilson, Marine Corps.

**Activities:** Provides for security of U.S. by establishing integrated policies and procedures; co-ordinates and directs the activities of three separately administered military departments (Army, Navy, and Air Force).

1. Consisting of chairman and chiefs of each service.

### DEPARTMENT OF JUSTICE

*Constitution Ave. between 9th & 10th Sts., N.W. (20530).*

**Established:** Office of Attorney General was created Sept. 24, 1789. Although he was one of original Cabinet members, he was not executive department head until June 22, 1870, when Department of Justice was established.

**Attorney General:** Griffin B. Bell.

**Deputy Attorney General:** Benjamin R. Civiletti.

**Solicitor General:** Wade H. McCree, Jr.

**Director of FBI:** William H. Webster.

**Activities:** Provides means for enforcing Federal laws; investigates and detects violations; represents U.S. in legal matters generally and gives advice and opinions when requested by President or heads of executive departments; directs FBI, Bureau of Prisons, Immigration and Naturalization Service, Drug Enforcement Administration, Law Enforcement Assistance Administration, Marshals Service.

### DEPARTMENT OF THE INTERIOR

*C St. between 18th & 19th Sts., N.W. (20240).*

**Established:** March 3, 1849.

**Secretary:** Cecil D. Andrus.

**Under Secretary:** James A. Joseph.

**Activities:** Develops and conserves natural resources of U.S. and territories; supervises public business relating to such offices as Bureau of Land Management, Geological Survey, Bureau of Indian Affairs, National Park Service, Bureau of Mines, Fish and Wildlife Service, Bureau of Outdoor Recreation, Office of Water Research and Technology, Office of Minerals Policy and Research Analysis, Ocean Mining Administration.

### DEPARTMENT OF AGRICULTURE

*Independence Ave. between 12th & 14th Sts., S.W. (20250).*

**Established:** May 15, 1862. Administered by Commissioner of Agriculture until 1889, when it was made executive department.

**Secretary:** Bob Bergland.

**Deputy Secretary:** (Vacant).

**Activities:** Conducts comprehensive research and educational program relating to agriculture; provides crop reports, commodity standards, meat inspection and other marketing services; administers national forests; aids in flood control; administers price-support and production-adjustment programs; makes loans to farmers; supervises Farmers Home Administration, Rural Development Service, Rural Electrification Administration, Federal Grain Inspection Service, Food Safety and Quality Service, Commodity Credit Corporation.

### DEPARTMENT OF COMMERCE

*14th St. between Constitution Ave. & E St., N.W. (20230).*

**Established:** Department of Commerce and Labor was created Feb. 14, 1903. On March 4, 1913, all labor activities were transferred out of Department of Commerce and Labor and it was renamed Department of Commerce.

**Secretary:** Juanita Morris Kreps.

**Under Secretary:** Sidney L. Harman.

**Activities:** Fosters and develops foreign and domestic commerce of U.S.; maintains Bureau of the Census, Domestic and International Business Administration, Economic Development Administration, Bureau of Economic Analysis, Office of Minority Business Enterprise, Patent and Trademark Office, National Oceanic and Atmospheric Administration (including National Weather Se vice), National Technical Information Service, National Telecommunications and Information Administration, Travel Service, Maritime Administration, National Bureau of Standards, National Fire Prevention and Control Administration.

**DEPARTMENT OF LABOR**
*200 Constitution Ave., N.W. (20210).*
**Established:** Bureau of Labor was created in 1884 under Department of the Interior; later became independent department without executive rank. Returned to bureau status in Department of Commerce and Labor, but on March 4, 1913, became independent executive department under its present name.
**Secretary:** F. Ray Marshall.
**Under Secretary:** Robert J. Brown.
**Activities:** Promotes welfare of wage earners of U.S., improving working conditions and advancing opportunities for profitable employment; directs collection and collation of statistics concerning labor conditions; promulgates and enforces certain maximum-hour, minimum-wage, child-labor, safety and health standards. Maintains Employment and Training Administration, Labor-Management Services Administration, Employment Standards Administration, Occupational Safety and Health Administration, Bureau of Labor Statistics.

**DEPARTMENT OF HEALTH, EDUCATION AND WELFARE**
*330 Independence Ave., S.W. (20201).*
**Established:** April 11, 1953, replacing Federal Security Agency created in 1939.
**Secretary:** Joseph A. Califano, Jr.
**Under Secretary:** Hale Champion.
**Activities:** Supervises and coordinates various organizations within the department. Organizations are: Food and Drug Administration, Office of Human Development, Office of Education, Public Health Service, Social Security Administration, Alcohol, Drug Abuse and Mental Health Administration, National Institutes of Health, Center for Disease Control, Health Care Financing Administration, Office of Child Support Enforcement, Office on Smoking and Health.

**DEPARTMENT OF HOUSING AND URBAN DEVELOPMENT**
*451 7th St., S.W. (20410).*
**Established:** 1965, replacing Housing and Home Finance Agency created in 1947.
**Secretary:** Patricia Roberts Harris.
**Under Secretary:** Jay Janis.
**Activities:** Supervises and coordinates New Community Development Corporation, Federal Disaster Assistance Administration, Federal Insurance Administration, Government National Mortgage Association, Office of Consumer Affairs and Regulatory Functions.

**DEPARTMENT OF TRANSPORTATION**
*400 7th St., S.W. (20590).*
**Established:** Oct. 15, 1966, as result of Department of Transportation Act, which became effective April 1, 1967.
**Secretary:** Brock Adams.
**Deputy Secretary:** Alan A. Butchman.
**Activities:** Supervises and coordinates activities of Coast Guard, Federal Aviation Administration, Federal Highway Administration, Federal Railroad Administration, St. Lawrence Seaway Development Corporation, National Highway Traffic Safety Administration, Urban Mass Transportation Administration, Materials Transportation Bureau.

**DEPARTMENT OF ENERGY**
*Washington, D.C. 20314.*
**Established:** August 1977.
**Secretary:** James R. Schlesinger.
**Deputy Secretary:** John F. O'Leary.
**Activities:** Takes over the Federal Energy Administration, the Federal Power Commission, the Energy Research and Development Administration, and functions of other government agencies concerned with energy. Has management responsibility for such projects as Bonneville dam, an Energy Information Administration to develop reliable energy statistics, and an Energy Regulatory Administration to audit and police energy companies.

## Independent Agencies

(Titles and addresses of independent agencies not described below follow on pages 636–37.)

**ACTION**
*806 Connecticut Ave., N.W. (20525).*
**Established:** July 1, 1971.
**Director:** Sam Brown.
**Activities:** Coordinates a system of volunteer services to people in need at home and abroad; administers Peace Corps and VISTA (Volunteers in Service to America).

**CIVIL AERONAUTICS BOARD (CAB)**
*1825 Connecticut Ave., N.W. (20428)*
**Members:** 5.
**Established:** June 30, 1940.
**Chairman:** Alfred E. Kahn.
**Activities:** Regulates economic aspects of U.S. air carrier operation; assists in development of international air transportation; promotes safety in civil aviation.

**COMMUNITY SERVICES ADMINISTRATION**
*1200 19th St., N.W. (20506).*
**Established:** 1974.
**Director:** Graciela Olivarez.
**Activities:** Assists low-income individuals and persons of limited English-speaking ability to attain the skills, knowledge and opportunities to become self-sufficient.

**ENVIRONMENTAL PROTECTION AGENCY (EPA)**
*401 M St., S.W. (20460).*
**Established:** Dec. 2, 1970.
**Administrator:** Douglas M. Costle.
**Activities:** Coordinates governmental action to assure protection of the environment by abating and controlling pollution.

**FARM CREDIT ADMINISTRATION (FCA)**
*490 L'Enfant Plaza East, S.W. (20578).*
**Established:** July 17, 1916.
**Members:** 13.

**Chairman of Federal Farm Credit Board:** E. Riddell Lage.
**Activities:** Supervises and coordinates cooperative credit system for agriculture; provides long- and short-term credit to farmers and their cooperative marketing, purchasing, and business service organizations.

### FEDERAL COMMUNICATIONS COMMISSION (FCC)
*1919 M St., N.W. (20554).*
**Members:** 7.
**Established:** 1934.
**Chairman:** Charles D. Ferris.
**Activities:** Regulates interstate and foreign communications by wire and radio, including amateur radio and TV; regulates operator's licenses; classifies radio stations and prescribes their services.

### FEDERAL ELECTION COMMISSION (FEC)
*1325 K St., N.W. (20463).*
**Members:** 6.
**Established:** 1975.
**Chairman:** Thomas E. Harris.
**Activities:** Certifies distribution of public funding of federal elections; regulates compliance with Federal Election Campaign Act; makes available to the public copies of reports filed with the commission.

### FEDERAL MARITIME COMMISSION
*1100 L St., N.W. (20573).*
**Members:** 5.
**Established:** Aug. 12, 1961.
**Chairman:** Richard J. Daschbach.
**Activities:** Regulates waterborne shipping in foreign and domestic offshore commerce of U.S.

### FEDERAL MEDIATION AND CONCILIATION SERVICE (FMCS)
*2100 K St., N.W. (20427).*
**Established:** 1947.
**Director:** Wayne L. Horvitz.
**Activities:** Assists in labor-management disputes in industries affecting interstate commerce to reach settlements by mediation or conciliation.

### FEDERAL RESERVE SYSTEM (FRS), BOARD OF GOVERNORS OF
*20th St. & Constitution Ave., N.W. (20551).*
**Members:** 7.
**Established:** Dec. 23, 1913.
**Chairman:** G. William Miller.
**Activities:** Supervises the 12 Federal Reserve banks, 24 branches and member commercial banks; determines country's monetary policy, including setting maximum interest paid by member banks, amount of credit extended for purchase of securities and discount rates charged by members; handles Government deposits and debt issue; regulates open-market operations; issues Federal Reserve notes.

### FEDERAL TRADE COMMISSION (FTC)
*Pennsylvania Ave. at 6th St., N.W. (20580).*
**Members:** 5.
**Established:** Sept. 26, 1914.
**Chairman:** Michael Pertschuk.
**Activities:** Prevents unfair competition, deceptive practices, false advertising, price discrimination, monopolies.

### GENERAL SERVICES ADMINISTRATION (GSA)
*18th and F Sts., N.W. (20405).*
**Established:** July 1, 1949.
**Administrator:** Joel W. (Jay) Solomon.
**Activities:** Establishes policy and provides efficient system for management of the government's property and records, including construction and operation of buildings, procurement and distribution of supplies, stockpiling of strategic materials and utilization and disposal of property. Directs National Archives and Records Service, Federal Supply Service, Public Buildings Service, Federal Preparedness Agency, Automated Data and Telecommunications Service.

### INTERSTATE COMMERCE COMMISSION (ICC)
*12th St. & Constitution Ave., N.W. (20423).*
**Members:** 11.
**Established:** Feb. 4, 1887.
**Chairman:** A. Daniel O'Neal.
**Activities:** Regulates railroads, motor carriers, water carriers and freight forwarders as to rates, through-routes, services and bills of lading; authorizes mergers or consolidations; authorizes issue of securities by carriers.

### NATIONAL AERONAUTICS AND SPACE ADMINISTRATION (NASA)
*400 Maryland Ave., S.W. (20546).*
**Established:** 1958.
**Administrator:** Robert A. Frosch.
**Activities:** Conducts research into problems of flight within and outside earth's atmosphere.

### NATIONAL FOUNDATION ON THE ARTS AND THE HUMANITIES
*806 15th St., N.W. (20506).*
**Established:** 1965.
**Chairman:** National Endowment for the Arts, Livingston L. Biddle, Jr.; National Endowment for the Humanities, Joseph D. Duffey.
**Activities:** Encourages and supports national progress in the humanities and the arts. Also includes National Councils on the Arts and the Humanities, which coordinates activities of the two endowments and related programs of other agencies.

### NATIONAL LABOR RELATIONS BOARD (NLRB)
*1717 Pennsylvania Ave., N.W. (20570).*
**Members:** 5.
**Established:** July 5, 1935.
**Chairman:** John H. Fanning.
**Activities:** Prevents unfair labor practices by employers or labor organizations; conducts secret ballots among employees to determine bargaining representatives.

### NATIONAL SCIENCE FOUNDATION (NSF)
*1800 G St., N.W. (20550).*
**Established:** 1950.

**Chairman:** Norman Hackerman.
**Activities:** Awards grants and contracts to support research in the sciences. Encourages research in areas that can lead to improvements in economic growth, productivity and environmental quality. Administered by 25-member National Science Board.

### NATIONAL TRANSPORTATION SAFETY BOARD

*800 Independence Ave., S.W. (20594).*
**Members:** 5.
**Established:** April 1, 1975.
**Chairman:** Kay Bailey (acting).
**Activities:** Conducts investigations into accidents, assesses techniques of accident investigation and recommends safety-improvement measures.

### NUCLEAR REGULATORY COMMISSION (NRC)

*1717 H St., N.W. (20555) and Bethesda, Md. (20014).*
**Members:** 5.
**Established:** Jan. 19, 1975.
**Chairman:** Joseph M. Hendrie.
**Activities:** Regulates civilian nuclear facilities to assure protection of public health and safety and the environment, and safeguarding of nuclear materials and facilities.

### SECURITIES AND EXCHANGE COMMISSION (SEC)

*500 N. Capitol St., N.W. (20549).*
**Members:** 5.
**Established:** June 6, 1934.
**Chairman:** Harold M. Williams.
**Activities:** Registers and issues regulations for securities and exchanges; registers securities offered for public sale; penalizes violators of regulations subject to appeal to U.S. Court of Appeals.

### SMALL BUSINESS ADMINISTRATION (SBA)

*1441 L St., N.W. (20416).*
**Established:** July 30, 1953.
**Administrator:** A. Vernon Weaver, Jr.
**Activities:** Aids and assists the interests of small business firms to insure a fair share of total government contracts; makes loans to small firms and victims of flood and disaster.

### TENNESSEE VALLEY AUTHORITY (TVA)

*Commercial Realty Management Bldg., Knoxville, Tenn. (37902). Washington office: Woodward Bldg., 15th & H Sts., N.W. (20444).*
**Members of Board of Directors:** 3.
**Established:** May 18, 1933.
**Chairman:** S. David Freeman.
**Activities:** Provides navigable channel and flood control of Tennessee River and some of its larger tributaries; disposes of surplus electric power, improves, increases and cheapens fertilizer production.

### U.S. ARMS CONTROL AND DISARMAMENT AGENCY

*Department of State Building (20451).*
**Established:** Sept. 26, 1961.
**Director:** Paul C. Warnke.
**Activities:** Conducts studies and provides advice relating to arms control and disarmament policy fomulation; prepares for and manages U.S. participation in international negotiations in arms control and disarmament; prepares for, operates, or as needed, directs U.S. participation in international control systems.

### U.S. CIVIL SERVICE COMMISSION (CSC)

*1900 E St., N.W. (20415).*
**Members:** 3.
**Established:** Jan. 16, 1883.
**Chairman:** Alan K. Campbell.
**Activities:** Provides examinations to test fitness of applicants for positions in competitive service; provides personnel in response to requests from appointing officers; investigates applicants for national security purposes; classifies positions; provides leadership to Federal agencies in personnel matters.

### U.S. INFORMATION AGENCY (USIA)

*1750 Pennsylvania Ave., N.W. (20547).*
**Established:** Aug. 1, 1953.
**Director:** John E. Reinhardt.
**Activities:** Directs information to foreign peoples, such as explanation of policies of U.S. Government and delineation of U.S. life and culture.

### U.S. INTERNATIONAL TRADE COMMISSION

*701 E St., N.W. (20436).*
**Members:** 6.
**Established:** Sept. 8, 1916.
**Chairman:** Daniel Minchew.
**Activities:** Investigates customs laws, unfair competition and foreign and domestic manufacturing costs; advises the President on duty rates.

### U.S. POSTAL SERVICE

*475 L'Enfant Plaza West, S.W. (20260).*
**Established:** Office of Postmaster General and temporary post office system created in 1789. Act of Feb. 20, 1792, made detailed provisions for Post Office Department. Postmaster General became Cabinet member in 1829, and Department received executive status in 1872. In 1970 became independent agency headed by 11-member board of governors. Postmaster General, no longer Cabinet member, is chosen by nine governors, who, with Postmaster General, choose Deputy Postmaster General.
**Postmaster General:** William F. Bolger.
**Deputy Postmaster General:** James V.P. Conway.
**Activities:** Maintains Postal system of U.S.

### VETERANS ADMINISTRATION (VA)

*810 Vermont Ave., N.W. (20420).*
**Established:** July 21, 1930.
**Administrator:** Max Cleland.
**Activities:** Administers laws authorizing benefits for veterans and dependents or beneficiaries. Included are hospitals, pensions, insurance, loans, education, etc.

## Other Independent Agencies

#### Executive Department

**Administrative Conference of the United States**—2120 L St., N.W. (20037).
**American Battle Monuments Commission**—Forres-

tal Bldg. (20314).
**Appalachian Regional Commission**—1666 Connecticut Ave., N.W. (20235).
**Board for International Broadcasting**—1030 15th St., N.W. (20005).
**Canal Zone Government**—312 Pennsylvania Bldg. (20004).
**Commission of Fine Arts**—708 Jackson Place, N.W. (20006).
**Commission on Civil Rights**—1121 Vermont Ave., N.W. (20425).
**Commodity Futures Trading Commission**—2033 K St., N.W. (20581).
**Consumer Product Safety Commission**—1111 18th St., N.W. (20207).
**District of Columbia**—District Bldg., 1358 E St., N.W. (20004).
**Equal Employment Opportunity Commission**—2401 E St., N.W. (20506).
**Export-Import Bank of the United States**—811 Vermont Ave., N.W. (20571).
**Federal Deposit Insurance Corporation**—550 17th St., N.W. (20429).
**Federal Home Loan Bank Board**—320 First St., N.W. (20552).
**Foreign Claims Settlement Commission of the U.S.**—1111 20th St., N.W. (20579).
**Indian Claims Commission**—1730 K St., N.W. (20006).
**Inter-American Foundation**—1515 Wilson Blvd., Rosslyn, Va. (22209).
**National Center for the Prevention and Control of Rape**—5600 Fishers Lane, Rockville, Md. (20875).
**National Center for Productivity and Quality of Working Life**—2000 M St. (20036).
**National Commission on Libraries and Information Science**—1717 K St. (20036).
**National Credit Union Administration**—2025 M St., N.W. (20456).
**National Mediation Board**—1425 K St., N.W. (20572).
**Occupational Safety and Health Review Commission**—1825 K St., N.W. (20006).
**Overseas Private Investment Corporation**—1129 20th St., N.W. (20527).
**Panama Canal Company**—312 Pennsylvania Bldg. (20004).
**Pension Benefit Guaranty Corporation**—2020 K St., N.W. (20006).
**Postal Rate Commission**—2000 L St., N.W. (20268).
**President's Committee on Employment of the Handicapped**—Vanguard Bldg. (20210).
**President's Council on Physical Fitness and Sports**—400 6th St., S.W. (20201).
**Railroad Retirement Board (RRB)**—844 Rush St., Chicago, Ill. (60611). Washington Liaison Office: Room 444, 425 13th St., N.W. (20004).
**Renegotiation Board**—2000 M St., N.W. (20446).
**Selective Service System**—National Headquarters, 600 E St., N.W. (20435).

### Legislative Department

#### ARCHITECT OF THE CAPITOL
*U.S. Capitol Building (20515).*
**Established:** First Architect of the Capitol was appointed in 1793; office has been continuous since 1851.
**Architect of Capitol:** George M. White.
**Activities:** Architect of the Capitol has charge of structural and mechanical care of Capitol Building and various other government buildings in Washington.

#### GENERAL ACCOUNTING OFFICE
*441 G Street, N.W. (20548).*
**Established:** 1921.
**Comptroller General:** Elmer B. Staats.
**Deputy Comptroller General:** Robert F. Keller.
**Activities:** Assists Congress in providing legislative control over receipt, disbursement, and application of public funds.

#### GOVERNMENT PRINTING OFFICE (GPO)
*North Capitol & H Sts., N.W. (20401).*
**Established:** June 23, 1860.
**Public Printer:** John J. Boyle.
**Superintendent of Documents:** Carl A. LaBarre.
**Activities:** Executes printing and binding orders for Congress and Federal agencies; distributes government publications.

#### LIBRARY OF CONGRESS
*10 First St., S.E. (20540).*
**Established:** April 24, 1800.
**Librarian of Congress:** Daniel J. Boorstin.
**Activities:** Extends services to members of government and offers facilities for persons engaged in scholarly research.

#### UNITED STATES BOTANIC GARDEN
*Office of Director, 245 First St., S.W. (20024).*
**Established:** 1820.
**Director:** George M. White (acting).
**Activities:** Collects, cultivates, and grows various vegetable products for exhibition and study.

### Quasi-Official Agencies

**American National Red Cross**—17th & D Sts., N.W. (20006).
**National Academy of Sciences, National Academy of Engineering, National Research Council, Institute of Medicine**—2101 Constitution Ave., N.W. (20418).
**National Railroad Passenger Corporation (Amtrak)**—400 N. Capitol St., N.W. (20001).
**Smithsonian Institution**—1000 Jefferson Dr., S.W. (20560).

## IRS Informers

In the year ending Sept. 30, 1977, the Internal Revenue Service paid out $360,304 to 483 informers (an average of $745.97 per informant) for tips on which were based $14.9 million worth of tax assessments.

According to the Office of Management and Budget, the total hours spent by the American people filling out federal forms was 784,862,000 per year (as of March 1978). This is down from the 870,420,000 hours in the year ending the month after President Carter took office.

## Major U.S. Daily Newspapers[1]

| City and newspaper | Net paid circulation: Morning[2] | Evening[2] | Sunday |
|---|---|---|---|
| Akron, Ohio: *Beacon Journal* | — | 167,040 | 215,559 |
| Albany, N.Y.: *Times-Union* (M & S); *Knickerbocker News* (E) | 79,177 | 58,059[3] | 139,980 |
| Albuquerque, N.M.: *Journal* (M & S); *Tribune* (E) | 79,256[4] | 38,733[4] | 117,941[4] |
| Allentown, Pa.: *Call* (M); *Chronicle* (E); *Call-Chronicle* (S) | 103,071[3] | 22,386[3] | 157,359 |
| Asbury Park, N.J.: *Press* | — | 96,749 | 126,834 |
| Atlanta: *Constitution* (M); *Journal* (E); *Journal and Constitution* (S) | 216,532 | 221,292 | 544,444 |
| Austin, Tex.: *American* (M); *Statesman* (E); *American-Statesman* (S) | 83,230[3] | 36,517[3] | 127,961 |
| Baltimore: *Sun* | 174,013[3] | 174,542[3] | 368,675 |
| *News-American* | — | 163,187[3] | 245,650 |
| Baton Rouge, La.: *Advocate* (M & S); *State-Times* (E) | 69,436 | 43,665 | 106,653 |
| Bergen County, N.J.: *Record* (E); *Sunday Record* (Hackensack) | — | 154,677[4] | 206,726[4] |
| Birmingham, Ala.: *Post-Herald* (M); *News* (E & S) | 69,169[3] | 179,008[3] | 226,045 |
| Boston: *Globe* | 306,114[3] | 160,569[3] | 660,428 |
| *Herald American* | 273,716[3] | — | 388,255 |
| *Christian Science Monitor* | 175,179[3] | — | — |
| Buffalo, N.Y.: *Courier-Express* | 124,061 | — | 261,398 |
| *News* | — | 273,535[3] | 164,131 |
| Camden, N.J.: *Courier-Post* | — | 123,755[4] | — |
| Charleston, W.Va.: *Gazette* (M); *Daily Mail* (E); *Gazette-Mail* (S) | 56,248 | 56,734 | 105,715 |
| Charlotte, N.C.: *Observer* (M & S); *News* (E) | 171,952 | 55,696 | 240,777 |
| Chicago: *Tribune* | 762,810[3] [5] | — | 1,155,687 |
| *Sun-Times* | 611,135[3] | — | 704,358 |
| *Wall Street Journal* (Midwest edition) | 458,106[6] | — | — |
| Cincinnati: *Enquirer* (M & S); *Post* (E) | 185,523 | 187,096 | 288,831 |
| Cleveland: *Plain Dealer* (M & S); *Press* (E) | 379,615 | 320,346 | 453,840 |
| Columbia, S.C.: *State* (M & S); *Record* (E) | 103,694 | 33,333 | 120,777 |
| Columbus, Ohio: *Dispatch* (E & S); *Citizen-Journal* (M) | 111,042 | 202,474 | 338,447 |
| Dallas: *News* | 282,751 | — | 352,257 |
| *Times-Herald* | — | 250,505[3] | 344,601 |
| *Wall Street Journal* (Southwest edition) | 167,392[6] | — | — |
| Dayton, Ohio: *News* (E & S); *Journal Herald* (M) | 100,746 | 149,323 | 222,552 |
| Denver: *Post* | — | 262,952[3] | 347,466 |
| *Rocky Mountain News* | 255,270 | — | 275,487 |
| Des Moines, Iowa: *Register* (M & S); *Tribune* (E) | 224,393 | 89,972 | 423,241 |
| Detroit: *News* | — | 633,708[3] | 826,111 |
| *Free Press* | 608,987[3] | — | 716,107 |
| Evansville, Ind.: *Courier* (M); *Press* (E); *Courier & Press* (S) | 63,597 | 45,688 | 118,419 |
| Flint, Mich.: *Journal* | — | 105,903[4] | 105,983[4] |
| Fort Lauderdale, Fla.: *News* (E); *News and Sun-Sentinel* (Sat. & Sun.) | 153,105[7] | 112,787[3] | 167,310 |
| Fort Wayne, Ind.: *Journal-Gazette* (M & S); *News-Sentinel* (E) | 60,779[4] | 72,294[4] | 101,419[4] |
| Fort Worth: *Star-Telegram* | 87,989 | 142,355 | 233,464 |
| Fresno, Calif.: *Bee* | 125,548 | — | 144,999 |
| Grand Rapids, Mich.: *Press* | — | 125,055[4] | 139,922[4] |
| Greensboro, N.C.: *News* (M & S); *Record* (E) | 82,509 | 33,266 | 114,431 |
| Greenville, S.C.: *News* (M); *Piedmont* (E); *News Piedmont* (S) | 84,853[3] | 23,745[3] | 103,409 |
| Harrisburg, Pa.: *Patriot* (M); *Evening News* (E); *Patriot-News* (S) | 47,855[3] | 65,714[3] | 159,208 |
| Hartford, Conn.: *Courant* | 211,016 | — | 281,890 |
| Honolulu: *Advertiser* (M); *Star-Bulletin* (E); *Star-Bulletin & Advertiser* (S) | 81,420 | 120,258 | 198,046 |

| City and newspaper | Net paid circulation: Morning[2] | Evening[2] | Sunday |
|---|---|---|---|
| Houston: *Chronicle* | — | 322,762 | 413,934 |
| *Post* | 303,447 | — | 360,603 |
| Indianapolis: *Star* (M & S); *News* (E) | 214,979[4] | 154,648[4] | 354,602[4] |
| Jackson, Miss.: *Clarion-Ledger* (M); *Daily News* (E); *Clarion-Ledger-News* (S) | 61,092 | 40,750 | 112,172 |
| Jacksonville, Fla.: *Florida Times-Union* (M & S); *Journal* (E) | 151,235[3] | 52,533[3] | 188,736 |
| Kansas City, Mo.: *Star* (E & S); *Times* (M) | 322,800 | 295,606 | 403,851 |
| Knoxville, Tenn.: *News-Sentinel* (E & S); *Journal* (M) | 58,064 | 103,666 | 157,882 |
| Lancaster, Pa.: *Intelligencer-Journal* (M); *New Era* (E); *News* (S) | 39,931[4] | 59,939[4] | 133,367[4] |
| Lexington, Ky.: *Herald* (M); *Leader* (E); *Herald-Leader* (S) | 63,835[3] | 33,926[3] | 103,292 |
| Little Rock, Ark.: *Arkansas Gazette* | 129,725[3] | — | 153,790 |
| *Arkansas Democrat* | — | 55,520[3] | 101,550 |
| Long Beach, Calif.: *Independent* (M); *Press* (E); *Independent Press-Telegram* (S) | 64,593[3] | 80,318[3] | 138,079 |
| Long Island (Garden City, N.Y.); *Newsday* | — | 478,354 | 506,821 |
| Los Angeles: *Times* | 1,020,208 | — | 1,315,051 |
| *Herald-Examiner* | — | 322,143[3] | 325,426 |
| Louisville, Ky.: *Courier-Journal* (M); *Times* (E); *Courier-Journal & Times* (S) | 205,430 | 160,637 | 348,667 |
| Madison, Wis.: *State Journal* (M & S); *Capital Times* (E) | 73,435 | 35,959 | 119,643 |
| Memphis, Tenn.: *Commercial Appeal* (M & S); *Press-Scimitar* (E) | 208,971 | 105,092 | 287,994 |
| Miami, Fla.: *Herald* (M & S); *News* (E) | 447,057 | 71,743 | 551,593 |
| Milwaukee: *Journal* (E & S); *Sentinel* (M) | 161,310 | 334,167 | 532,692 |
| Minneapolis: *Tribune* (M & S); *Star* (E) | 227,378[3] | 236,634[3] | 607,194 |
| New Haven, Conn.: *Register* (E & S); *Journal-Courier* (M) | 32,018[6] | 101,911 | 139,428 |
| New Orleans: *Times-Picayune* (M & S); *States-Item* (E) | 213,275[4] | 117,582[3 4] | 318,132[4] |
| New York City: *News* | 1,824,836[3] | — | 2,656,981 |
| *Times* | 878,714[3] | — | 1,486,662 |
| *Post* | — | 621,564[3] | 457,007[7] |
| *Wall Street Journal* (Eastern edition) | 605,793[6] | — | — |
| Newark, N.J.: *Star-Ledger* | 406,282[3 4] | — | 572,847[4] |
| Norfolk-Portsmouth-Virginia Beach-Chesapeake, Va.: *Virginian-Pilot* (M & S); *Ledger-Star* (E) | 126,523[4] | 96,658[4] | 196,603[4] |
| Oakland, Calif.: *Tribune* | — | 164,525[3] | 190,763 |
| Oklahoma City: *Daily Oklahoman* (M); *Times* (E); *Sunday Oklahoman* | 181,562[3] | 91,512[3] | 290,083 |
| Omaha, Neb.: *World-Herald* | 124,900[3] | 112,238[3] | 282,093 |
| Orange County (Santa Ana), Calif.: *Register* | 96,792[3] | 111,606[3] | 237,680 |
| Orlando, Fla.: *Sentinel Star* | 192,868[3 5] | — | 219,438 |
| Palo Alto, Calif.: *Wall Street Journal* (M) (Western edition); *Times* (E) | 288,514[6] | 45,090 | — |
| Peoria, Ill.: *Journal-Star* | 104,992[5] | — | 121,136 |
| Philadelphia: *Inquirer* | 413,200[3] | — | 842,119 |
| *Bulletin* | — | 516,872[3] | 610,898 |
| *Daily News* | — | 230,663[3] | |
| Phoenix, Ariz.: *Arizona Republic* (M & S); *Gazette* (E) | 251,055[4] | 112,247[4] | 377,363[4] |
| Pittsburgh: *Press* (E & S); *Post-Gazette* (M) | 190,812[3] | 266,077[3] | 675,356 |
| Portland, Me.: *Press Herald* (M); *Express* (E); *Maine Sunday Telegram* | 52,710 | 30,085 | 112,270 |
| Portland, Ore.: *Oregonian* (M & S); *Oregon Journal* (S) | 241,264 | 106,628[3] | 413,229 |
| Providence, R.I.: *Journal* (M & S); *Bulletin* (E) | 69,280[3] | 142,501[3] | 218,873 |
| Raleigh, N.C.: *News & Observer* (M & S); *Times* (E) | 128,887[4] | 33,239[4] | 162,640[4] |
| Richmond, Va.: *Times-Dispatch* (M & S); *News-Leader* (E) | 136,266 | 116,234 | 214,092 |
| Riverside, Calif.: *Enterprise* (M); *Press* (E); *Press-Enterprise* (S) | 63,551[6] | 34,299[6] | 103,367 |
| Roanoke, Va.: *Times* (M); *World-News* (E); *Times & World-News* (S) | 65,412[3] | 49,594[3] | 115,703 |
| Rochester, N.Y.: *Democrat & Chronicle* (M & S); *Times-Union* (E) | 125,601 | 126,035 | 229,149 |

| City and newspaper | Net paid circulation Morning[2] | Evening[2] | Sunday |
|---|---|---|---|
| Sacramento, Calif.: *Bee* | — | 186,300[3] | 216,048 |
| *Union* | 94,401[3] | — | 95,020 |
| St. Louis: *Post Dispatch* | — | 262,707[3] | 452,169 |
| *Globe-Democrat* | 271,755[3] | — | 270,801[8] |
| St. Paul: *Pioneer Press* (M & S); *Dispatch* (E) | 100,439[3] | 117,985[3] | 240,696 |
| St. Petersburg, Fla.: *Times* (M & S); *Independent* (E) | 210,835 | 39,923 | 260,187 |
| Salt Lake City, Utah: *Tribune* (M & S); *Deseret News* (E) | 110,945 | 76,908 | 181,110 |
| San Antonio: *Express* (M); *News* (E); *Express-News* (S) | 82,511[3] | 75,971[3] | 176,057 |
| *Light* | — | 124,091[3] | 180,976 |
| San Diego, Calif.: *Union* (M & S); *Tribune* (E) | 198,351[4] | 131,374[4] | 325,055[4] |
| San Francisco: *Chronicle* (M); *Examiner* (E); *Examiner & Chronicle* (S) | 488,782[3] | 156,083[3] | 668,550 |
| San Jose, Calif.: *Mercury* (M); *News* (E); *Mercury-News* (S) | 144,745[3,6] | 67,859[3,6] | 252,966 |
| Seattle: *Times* | — | 245,614[3] | 327,818 |
| *Post-Intelligencer* | 187,015[3] | — | 233,404 |
| Shreveport, La.: *Times* (M & S); *Journal* (E) | 91,528[4] | 38,010[4] | 127,730[4] |
| South Bend-Mishawaka, Ind.: *Tribune* | — | 109,630 | 126,134 |
| Spokane, Wash.: *Spokesman-Review* (M & S); *Chronicle* (E) | 73,468 | 62,631 | 123,077 |
| Springfield, Mass.: *Union* (M); *News* (E); *Republican* (S) | 73,770 | 77,689 | 143,709 |
| Syracuse, N.Y.: *Post-Standard* (M); *Herald-Journal* (E); *Herald-American* (S) | 84,854 | 121,876 | 236,465 |
| Tacoma, Wash.: *News-Tribune* (E); *News-Tribune & Ledger* (S) | — | 103,417 | 107,863 |
| Tampa, Fla.: *Tribune* (M); *Times* (E); *Tribune & Times* (S) | 187,947 | 24,758 | 217,287 |
| Toledo, Ohio: *Blade* | — | 170,107 | 209,663 |
| Tucson, Ariz.: *Daily Star* (M & S); *Citizen* (E) | 70,833[4] | 64,798[4] | 128,091[4] |
| Tulsa, Okla.: *World* (M & S); *Tribune* (E) | 122,560[4] | 77,272[4] | 209,586[4] |
| Washington, D.C.: *Post* | 561,640[3] | — | 801,035 |
| *Star* | — | 329,147[3] | 315,763 |
| West Palm Beach, Fla.: *Post* (M); *Times* (E); *Post-Times* (S) | 83,076[3] | 31,510[3] | 125,002 |
| Wichita, Kan.: *Eagle* (M); *Beacon* (E); *Eagle and Beacon* | 125,288 | 43,699 | 179,683 |
| Wilmington, Del.: *News* (M); *Journal* (E); *News Journal* (Sat. & hldys.) | 47,387[3,4] | 85,070[3,4] | 118,761[4,9] |
| Worcester, Mass.: *Telegram* (M & S); *Gazette* (E) | 52,765[4] | 88,763[4] | 107,329[4] |
| Youngstown, Ohio: *Vindicator* | — | 101,325[4] | 150,951[4] |

1. Listing is of cities in which any one edition of a newspaper exceeds an average circulation of 100,000; newspapers of smaller circulation in those cities are also included. 2. Unless otherwise indicated, figures are average Monday-through-Saturday circulation for six-month period ending March 31, 1978. 3. Average Monday-through-Friday circulation. 4. Three-month average for period ending March 31, 1978. 5. All-day edition. 6. Not published on Saturday. 7. Saturday morning only. 8. Week-end edition. 9. Published Saturday and holidays; average circulation of Sunday paper, *Sunday News Journal,* is 92,001.

# Leading Magazines: United States and Canada

| Magazine | Circulation[1] |
|---|---|
| A.D. | 296,440 |
| American Girl | 602,984 |
| American Home | 2,217,510 |
| American Journal of Nursing | 327,701 |
| American Legion Magazine | 2,616,027 |
| Americana | 264,877 |
| Apartment Life | 809,457 |
| Architectural Digest | 329,589 |
| Atlantic Monthly | 333,655 |
| Better Homes & Gardens | 8,056,355 |
| Bon Appetit | 656,418 |
| Book Digest | 749,787 |
| Boy's Life | 1,529,252 |
| Business Week | 761,295 |
| Business Week/Industrial | 313,649 |
| Camping Journal | 280,106 |
| Capper's Weekly | 423,409 |
| Car Craft | 331,592 |
| Car & Driver | 749,426 |
| Carte Blanche | 574,139 |
| Catholic Digest | 550,682 |
| Chatelaine | 1,001,535 |
| Chatelaine (French Language Edition) | 277,964 |
| Club | 620,936 |
| Co-ed | 830,598 |
| Cosmopolitan | 2,581,157 |

| Magazine | Circulation[1] |
|---|---|
| Cue | 277,343 |
| Cycle | 433,598 |
| Cycle World | 286,851 |
| Decorating & Craft Ideas | 684,806 |
| Discovery | 928,178 |
| Eagle | 666,688 |
| Easyriders | 285,639 |
| Ebony | 1,255,077 |
| Elks Magazine | 1,609,220 |
| Esquire | 1,007,101 |
| Essence | 550,264 |
| Exploring | 376,931 |
| Family Circle | 8,498,517 |
| Family Handyman | 706,712 |
| Family Health | 926,450 |
| Farm Journal | 1,422,909 |
| Farmer-Stockman, The | 299,124 |
| Field & Stream | 2,033,135 |
| Flower & Garden Magazine | 576,956 |
| Flying | 420,060 |
| Forbes | 658,828 |
| Fortune | 629,046 |
| Gallery | 740,041 |
| Genesis | 406,989 |
| Gentlemen's Quarterly | 327,479 |
| Glamour | 1,755,775 |
| Golf (incl. Golfing) | 670,134 |
| Golf Digest | 877,217 |
| Good Housekeeping | 5,170,007 |
| Gourmet | 650,169 |
| Grit | 1,145,340 |
| Guns & Ammo (incl. Guns & Hunting) | 452,023 |
| Harper's Bazaar | 571,629 |
| Harper's Magazine | 304,369 |
| Harvest Farm Unit | 421,492 |
| High Fidelity | 340,472 |
| High Times | 338,726 |
| Holiday | 403,349[3] |
| Hot Rod Magazine (incl. Rod & Custom) | 810,545 |
| House Beautiful | 804,717 |
| House & Garden | 1,042,078 |
| Hustler | 1,799,650 |
| Jet | 633,536 |
| Junior Scholastic | 962,589 |
| Kiwanis Magazine, The | 273,551 |
| Ladies' Home Journal | 6,004,334 |
| Legion Magazine | 474,331 |
| Lion Magazine, The | 660,658 |
| Lutheran, The | 562,311 |
| Maclean's | 666,383 |
| Mademoiselle | 882,645 |
| McCalls | 6,512,186 |
| Mechanix Illustrated | 1,640,116 |
| Michigan Living-AAA Motor News | 791,536 |
| Midnight Globe | 1,706,746 |
| Modern Photography | 555,845 |
| Modern Romances | 373,707 |
| Modern Screen | 466,070 |
| Money | 708,572 |
| Moneysworth | 861,428 |
| Mother Earth News | 491,948 |
| Motor Trend (incl. Car Life, Sports Graphic, & Wheels Afield) | 733,311 |
| Ms. Magazine | 514,095 |
| National Enquirer | 5,208,375 |
| National Future Farmer | 495,574 |
| National Geographic, The | 9,756,312 |
| National Lampoon | 631,996 |
| National Observer | 434,516[3] |
| Nation's Business | 1,155,620 |
| Natural History | 439,970 |
| New Times | 354,639 |
| New West | 313,515 |
| New Woman | 840,741 |
| New York Magazine | 383,194 |
| New Yorker, The | 494,127 |
| Newsweek | 2,947,406 |
| Nursing '77 | 503,722 |
| 1,001 Decorating Ideas | 750,400 |
| Oui | 1,001,329 |
| Our Sunday Visitor | 332,916[3] |
| Outdoor Life | 1,795,598 |
| Parent's Magazine | 1,511,065 |
| Penthouse | 4,606,134 |
| Penthouse Forum | 737,657 |
| People | 2,394,979 |
| Photoplay (incl. TV Mirror) | 949,104 |
| Playboy | 4,970,753 |
| Playgirl | 755,166 |
| Popular Electronics | 401,233 |
| Popular Hot Rodding | 290,627 |
| Popular Mechanics | 1,661,568 |
| Popular Photography | 784,121 |
| Popular Science | 1,828,600 |
| Progressive Farmer | 935,701 |
| Psychology Today | 1,163,248 |
| Reader's Digest | 18,371,000 |
| Reader's Digest (Canadian English & Canadian French Editions) | 1,543,761 |
| Redbook Magazine | 4,613,908 |
| Road & Track | 529,080 |
| Rolling Stone | 553,650 |
| Rona Barrett's Gossip | 341,242 |
| Rona Barrett's Hollywood | 376,737 |
| Rotarian, The | 450,045 |
| Saturday Evening Post, The | 467,473 |
| Saturday Review | 528,834 |
| Scholastic Magazines | 3,889,097 |
| Scientific American | 680,724 |
| Scouting | 951,729 |
| Selection du Reader's Digest | 309,582 |
| Senior Scholastic Unit | 2,927,108 |
| Seventeen | 1,496,676 |
| Simplicity Home Catalog | 560,871 |
| Signature | 630,979 |
| Ski (incl. Ski Life) | 444,029 |
| Skiing Magazine | 474,606 |
| Smithsonian | 1,585,318 |
| Soap Opera Digest | 499,378 |
| Southern Living | 1,433,620 |
| Sphere Magazine | 649,582 |
| Sport | 1,305,429 |
| Sporting News, The | 355,793 |
| Sports Afield | 652,610 |
| Sports Illustrated | 2,263,148 |
| Star, The | 2,708,495 |
| Stereo Review | 465,278 |
| Successful Farming | 766,232 |
| Sunset, The Magazine of Western Living | 1,365,509 |
| 'Teen | 961,733 |
| Teen Beat | 326,675 |
| Tennis Magazine | 417,035 |
| Tiger Beat | 570,135 |
| Time, The Weekly Newsmagazine | 4,273,962 |
| Time Atlantic | 485,953 |
| Time in Canada | 309,372 |
| Time Pacific | 336,347 |
| Time Worldwide | 5,533,983 |
| Today's Education | 1,666,689 |
| Trailer Life | 306,587 |
| True Confessions | 332,268 |
| True Story | 1,797,127 |
| TV Guide | 19,412,819 |
| TV Guide (Canada) | 1,030,435 |

| Magazine | Circulation[1] | Magazine | Circulation[1] |
|---|---|---|---|
| T.V. Hebdo | 348,871 | Weight Watchers Magazine | 773,271 |
| TV Mirror | 735,324[3] | Westways | 447,773 |
| United Church Observer, The | 312,304[2] | Woman's Day | 8,404,618 |
| U.S. News & World Report | 2,040,589 | Woodall's Trailer Travel | 274,086 |
| V.F.W. Magazine | 1,793,529 | Workbasket, The | 1,731,647 |
| Viva | 392,148 | Workbench | 520,238 |
| Vogue (incorp. Vanity Fair) | 925,451 | World Tennis | 321,550 |
| Vogue Patterns | 386,536 | Yankee | 735,527 |

1. Average total paid circulation for the six-month period ending December 31, 1977. The table lists magazines of over 260,000 circulation. 2. Religious publication using congregation-wide subscription plan. 3. December 31, 1976 figure. *Source:* Audit Bureau of Circulations. Publishers' Statements for six-month period ending December 31, 1977.

## English Language Daily and Sunday U. S. Newspapers

**(number of newspapers as of March 30, 1978; circulation as reported for Sept. 30, 1977)**

| State | Morning papers and circulation | | Evening papers and circulation | | Total M and E and circulation | | Sunday papers and circulation | |
|---|---|---|---|---|---|---|---|---|
| Alabama | 7 | 202,761 | 18 | 529,337 | 25 | 732,098 | 17 | 671,390 |
| Alaska | 1 | 14,172 | 6 | 74,536 | 7 | 88,708 | 1 | 49,311 |
| Arizona | 2 | 282,705 | 15 | 280,827 | 17 | 563,532 | 5 | 480,097 |
| Arkansas[1] | 5 | 70,766 | 30 | 289,420 | 33 | 360,186 | 16 | 455,310 |
| California[1] | 2 | 3,126,820 | 100 | 2,955,020 | 125 | 6,081,840 | 44 | 5,139,437 |
| Colorado[1] | 4 | 345,065 | 24 | 490,889 | 27 | 835,954 | 9 | 837,976 |
| Connecticut | 6 | 351,953 | 20 | 537,825 | 26 | 889,778 | 7 | 650,998 |
| Delaware | 1 | 49,477 | 2 | 111,747 | 3 | 161,224 | 2 | 148,833 |
| District of Columbia | 1 | 541,074 | 1 | 349,475 | 2 | 890,549 | 2 | 1,099,505 |
| Florida[1] | 18 | 1,562,544 | 34 | 849,288 | 51 | 2,411,832 | 34 | 2,398,479 |
| Georgia | 7 | 438,548 | 30 | 604,150 | 37 | 1,042,698 | 14 | 1,020,709 |
| Hawaii | 1 | 77,597 | 4 | 233,746 | 5 | 311,343 | 2 | 210,841 |
| Idaho | 4 | 87,810 | 11 | 113,260 | 15 | 201,070 | 6 | 165,645 |
| Illinois[1] | 22 | 1,761,212 | 71 | 1,481,826 | 88 | 3,243,038 | 23 | 2,741,523 |
| Indiana | 7 | 444,379 | 72 | 1,220,147 | 79 | 1,664,526 | 18 | 1,172,860 |
| Iowa[1] | 4 | 324,611 | 37 | 576,433 | 40 | 901,044 | 9 | 766,514 |
| Kansas[1] | 5 | 226,823 | 47 | 420,268 | 51 | 647,091 | 14 | 446,879 |
| Kentucky | 5 | 320,939 | 22 | 459,937 | 27 | 780,876 | 13 | 616,031 |
| Louisiana | 5 | 407,158 | 21 | 452,847 | 26 | 860,005 | 14 | 775,749 |
| Maine | 5 | 209,246 | 4 | 69,433 | 9 | 278,679 | 1 | 112,902 |
| Maryland | 5 | 232,507 | 8 | 467,321 | 13 | 699,828 | 4 | 673,927 |
| Massachusetts | 5 | 899,764 | 41 | 1,116,352 | 46 | 2,016,116 | 8 | 1,457,034 |
| Michigan | 2 | 629,287 | 50 | 1,827,922 | 52 | 2,457,209 | 14 | 2,237,415 |
| Minnesota[1] | 6 | 407,717 | 28 | 701,829 | 30 | 1,109,546 | 12 | 1,069,555 |
| Mississippi | 5 | 123,557 | 20 | 271,868 | 25 | 395,425 | 10 | 289,837 |
| Missouri | 9 | 726,517 | 45 | 956,897 | 54 | 1,682,814 | 16 | 1,140,459 |
| Montana | 4 | 149,612 | 7 | 45,433 | 11 | 195,045 | 7 | 190,553 |
| Nebraska | 3 | 172,159 | 16 | 320,364 | 19 | 492,523 | 4 | 369,720 |
| Nevada | 3 | 79,878 | 6 | 109,740 | 9 | 189,618 | 4 | 170,265 |
| New Hampshire[1] | 1 | 32,682 | 9 | 145,272 | 9 | 177,954 | 2 | 70,079 |
| New Jersey[1] | 7 | 648,633 | 21 | 1,073,385 | 27 | 1,722,018 | 13 | 1,349,920 |
| New Mexico | 1 | 76,662 | 20 | 179,457 | 21 | 256,119 | 12 | 227,583 |
| New York[1] | 20 | 4,190,261 | 58 | 2,619,552 | 76 | 6,809,813 | 32 | 6,295,360 |
| North Carolina | 10 | 602,727 | 41 | 719,993 | 51 | 1,322,720 | 22 | 1,069,762 |
| North Dakota[1] | 2 | 22,564 | 9 | 122,296 | 10 | 144,860 | 2 | 49,984 |
| Ohio | 8 | 860,344 | 89 | 2,545,257 | 96 | 3,405,601 | 23 | 2,414,030 |
| Oklahoma | 9 | 420,238 | 45 | 442,808 | 54 | 863,046 | 46 | 898,756 |
| Oregon | 3 | 285,078 | 19 | 379,766 | 22 | 664,844 | 5 | 568,919 |
| Pennsylvania[1] | 31 | 1,273,401 | 80 | 2,613,125 | 106 | 3,886,526 | 14 | 3,057,795 |
| Rhode Island | 1 | 68,818 | 6 | 293,826 | 7 | 362,644 | 2 | 221,425 |
| South Carolina | 8 | 390,855 | 12 | 196,028 | 20 | 586,883 | 8 | 469,255 |
| South Dakota | 1 | 3,364 | 12 | 173,919 | 13 | 177,283 | 3 | 101,798 |
| Tennessee | 9 | 524,970 | 26 | 652,738 | 34 | 1,177,702 | 14 | 980,210 |
| Texas | 25 | 1,582,725 | 89 | 1,833,658 | 112 | 3,416,383 | 87 | 3,589,840 |
| Utah | 1 | 108,491 | 4 | 162,396 | 5 | 270,887 | 4 | 264,438 |
| Vermont | 2 | 68,729 | 8 | 56,450 | 8 | 125,179 | 4 | 73,487 |
| Virginia | 11 | 481,848 | 23 | 585,515 | 33 | 1,067,363 | 14 | 820,282 |
| Washington[1] | 5 | 306,739 | 19 | 776,701 | 23 | 1,083,440 | 13 | 1,050,731 |

| State | Morning papers and circulation | | Evening papers and circulation | | Total M and E and circulation | | Sunday papers and circulation | |
|---|---|---|---|---|---|---|---|---|
| West Virginia | 9 | 206,075 | 19 | 263,015 | 28 | 469,090 | 9 | 382,587 |
| Wisconsin | 4 | 256,211 | 32 | 971,568 | 36 | 1,227,779 | 6 | 851,493 |
| Wyoming | 6 | 64,245 | 4 | 28,566 | 10 | 92,811 | 3 | 61,746 |
| **Total** | **352** | **26,742,318** | **1,435** | **34,752,822** | **1,753** | **61,495,140** | **668** | **52,429,234** |
| Total U.S., Sept. 30, 1976 | 346 | 25,858,386 | 1,435 | 35,118,625 | 1,762 | 60,977,011 | 650 | 51,565,334 |
| Total U.S., Sept. 30, 1975 | 339 | 25,490,186 | 1,436 | 35,165,245 | 1,756 | 60,655,431 | 639 | 51,096,323 |
| Total U.S. Sept. 30, 1974 | 340 | 26,144,966 | 1,449 | 35,732,231 | 1,768 | 61,877,197 | 641 | 51,678,726 |
| Total U.S., Sept. 30, 1973 | 343 | 26,524,140 | 1,451 | 36,623,140 | 1,774 | 63,147,280 | 634 | 51,717,465 |
| Total U.S., Sept. 30, 1972 | 337 | 26,078,386 | 1,441 | 36,431,856 | 1,761 | 62,510,242 | 605 | 50,000,669 |
| Total U.S., Sept. 30, 1971 | 339 | 26,116,131 | 1,425 | 36,115,127 | 1,749 | 62,231,258 | 590 | 49,664,643 |
| Total U.S., Sept. 30, 1970 | 334 | 25,933,783 | 1,429 | 36,173,744 | 1,748 | 62,107,527 | 586 | 49,216,602 |

1. "All-day" newspapers are listed in morning and evening columns, and their circulations are divided between morning and evening figures. Adjustments have been made in state and U.S. total figures. *Source: Editor and Publisher Yearbook.*

## World's Largest Newspapers[1]

**(over 1 million circulation in any one edition)**

| Newspaper | Circulation |
|---|---|
| *Pravda* (U.S.S.R.[2]) | 10,000,000 (d&S) |
| *Komsomolskaya Pravda* (Moscow) | 10,000,000 (d) |
| *Izvestia* (U.S.S.R.[2]) | 9,000,000 (d) |
| *Asahi Shimbun* (5 cities, Japan) | 6,853,045 (d) |
| *Selskaya Zhizn* (U.S.S.R.[2]) | 6,700,000 (d) |
| *Yomiuri Shimbun* (5 cities, Japan) | 6,690,000 (d) |
| *Trud* (U.S.S.R.[2]) | 5,000,000 (d) |
| *Mainichi Shimbun* (5 cities, Japan) | 4,408,000 (d) |
| *Sunday Express* (London) | 3,436,000 (S) |
| *Renmin Ribao* (Peking) | 3,400,000 (d&S) |
| *Sovetskaya Rossia* (Moscow[3]) | 3,230,000 (d) |
| *News* (New York) | 2,759,000 (S) |
| *Chunichi Shimbun* (3 cities, Japan) | 2,663,000 (d) |
| *Daily Express* (London) | 2,608,000 (d) |
| *Bild Am Sonntag* (Hamburg) | 2,583,000 (S) |
| *Krasnaya Zvezda* (Moscow) | 2,400,000 (d) |
| *Sankei Shimbun* (2 cities, Japan) | 1,964,000 (d) |
| *Daily Mail* (London) | 1,739,000 (d) |
| *Nihon Keizai Shimbun* (4 cities, Japan) | 1,645,000 (d) |
| *Scinteia* (Bucharest) | 1,600,000 (d&S) |
| *Wall Street Journal* (4 regions, U.S.) | 1,408,000 (d) |
| *Times* (New York) | 1,407,000 (S) |
| *Sunday Times* (London) | 1,374,000 (S) |
| *Daily Telegraph* (London) | 1,315,000 (d) |
| *Westdeutsche Allgemeine Waz* (Essen, W. Germany) | 1,314,000 (d) |
| *Times* (Los Angeles) | 1,266,000 (S) |
| *Akhbar Al Yom* (Cairo) | 1,200,000 (d) |
| *Tribune* (Chicago) | 1,114,000 (S) |
| *Jenmin Jih Pao* (Peking) | 1,000,000 (d) |
| *Rude Pravo* (Prague) | 1,000,000 (d) |

1. *See also* U.S. daily newspapers. 2. National dailies are printed simultaneously in 20–45 U.S.S.R. cities. 3. Printed simultaneously in 16 Russian S.F.S.R. cities. NOTE: (d) = daily edition; (S) = Sunday edition. *Source: Editor and Publisher Yearbook, 1977.*

*See* **the Entertainment and Culture section for additional Media information.**

## State Lotteries

State lotteries continue to grow in popularity as a way for states to raise extra revenue. In the latest fiscal year, the 13 states sponsoring lotteries raised $639 million, up 15% from the previous year. However, the lotteries are criticized as being inefficient; states now spend about 60¢ for every dollar raised in the lotteries.

# TAXES

*Alfred L. Whinston, Touche Ross & Co., formerly*
*District Director, Internal Revenue Service*

## History of the Income Tax in the United States

The nation had few taxes in its early history. From 1791 to 1802, the United States Government was supported by internal taxes on distilled spirits, carriages, refined sugar, tobacco and snuff, property sold at auction, corporate bonds, and slaves. The high cost of the War of 1812 brought about the nation's first sales taxes on gold, silverware, jewelry, and watches. In 1817, however, Congress did away with all internal taxes, relying on tariffs on imported goods to provide sufficient funds for running the Government.

In 1862, in order to support the Civil War effort, Congress enacted the nation's first income tax law. It was a forerunner of our modern income tax in that it was based on the principles of graduated, or progressive, taxation and of withholding income at the source. During the Civil War, a person earning from $600 to $10,000 per year paid tax at the rate of 3%. Those with incomes of more than $10,000 paid taxes at a higher rate. Additional sales and excise taxes were added, and an "inheritance" tax also made its debut. In 1866, internal revenue collections reached their highest point in the nation's 90-year history—more than $310 million, an amount not reached again until 1911.

The Act of 1862 established the office of Commissioner of Internal Revenue. The Commissioner was given the power to assess, levy, and collect taxes, and the right to enforce the tax laws through seizure of property and income and through prosecution. His powers and authority remain very much the same today.

In 1868, Congress again focused its taxation efforts on tobacco and distilled spirits and eliminated the income tax in 1872. It had a short-lived revival in 1894 and 1895. In the latter year, the U.S. Supreme Court decided that the income tax was unconstitutional because it was not apportioned among the states in conformity with the Constitution.

By 1913, with the 16th Amendment to the Constitution, the income tax had become a permanent fixture of the U.S. tax system. The amendment gave Congress legal authority to tax income and resulted in a revenue law that taxed incomes of both individuals and corporations. In fiscal year 1918, annual internal revenue collections for the first time passed the billion-dollar mark, rising to $5.4 billion by 1920. With the advent of World War II, employment increased, as did tax collections—to $7.3 billion. The withholding tax on wages was introduced in 1943 and was instrumental in increasing the number of taxpayers to 60 million and tax collections to $43 billion by 1945.

## Internal Revenue Service

The Internal Revenue Service (IRS), a bureau of the U.S. Treasury Department, is the federal agency charged with the administration of the tax laws passed by Congress. The IRS functions through a national office in Washington, 7 regional offices, 58 district offices, and 10 service centers.

Operations involving most taxpayers are carried out in the district offices and service centers. District offices are organized into Administration, Audit, Collection, Taxpayer Service, and Intelligence Divisions. All tax returns are filed with the service centers, where the IRS computer operations are located.

### Auditing Tax Returns

Most taxpayers' contacts with IRS arise through the auditing of their tax returns. The service has been empowered by Congress to inquire about all persons who may be liable for any tax and to obtain for review the books and/or records pertinent to those taxpayers' returns. A wide-ranging audit operation is carried out in the 58 district offices by some 14,000 field agents and 5,000 office auditors.

### Selecting Returns for Audit

The primary method used by the IRS in selecting returns for audits is a computer program that measures the probability of tax error in each return. The data base (established by an in-depth audit of randomly selected returns in various income categories) consists of approximately 200–250 individual items of information taken from each return. These 200–250 variables individually or in combination are weighted as relative indicators of potential tax change. Returns are then scored according to the weights given the combinations of variables as they appear on each return. The higher the score, the greater the tax change potential. Other returns are selected for examination on the basis of claims for refund, multi-year audits, related return audits, and other audits initiated by the IRS as a result of informants' information, special compliance programs, and the information document matching program.

### The Appeals Process

The IRS attempts to resolve tax disputes through an administrative appeals system. Taxpayers who, after audit of their tax returns, disagree with a proposed change in their tax liabilities are entitled to an independent review of their cases. A recent change in IRS procedures has reduced the administrative levels of appeals from two to one—the appellate division of the regional office. Proceed-

## Internal Revenue Service

| | 1977 | 1976 | 1975 | 1970 | 1960 | 1950 |
|---|---|---|---|---|---|---|
| U.S. population (in thousands) | 217,329 | 215,118 | 213,540 | 204,878 | 180,671 | 152,271 |
| Number of IRS employees | 84,414 | 85,712 | 82,266 | 68,098 | 50,199 | 55,551 |
| Cost to govt. of collecting $100 in taxes | $0.51 | $0.56 | $0.54 | $0.45 | $0.40 | $0.59 |
| Tax per capita | $1,648 | $1,406.30 | $1,375.96 | $955.31 | $507.96 | $255.84 |
| Collections by principal sources (in thousands of dollars) | | | | | | |
| Total IRS collections | $358,139,416 | $302,519,792 | $293,822,726 | $195,722,096 | $91,744,803 | $38,957,132 |
| Income and profits taxes | | | | | | |
| Individual | 186,755,263 | 158,968,797 | 156,399,437 | 103,651,585 | 44,945,711 | 17,153,308 |
| Corporation | 60,049,804 | 46,782,956 | 45,746,660 | 35,036,983 | 22,179,414 | 10,854,351 |
| Employment taxes | 86,076,316 | 74,202,853 | 70,140,809 | 37,449,188 | 11,158,589 | 2,644,575 |
| Estate and gift taxes | 7,425,325 | 5,307,466 | 4,688,079 | 3,680,076 | 1,626,348 | 706,227 |
| Alcohol taxes | 5,406,633 | 5,427,722 | 5,350,858 | 4,746,382 | 3,193,714 | 2,219,202 |
| Tobacco taxes | 2,398,501 | 2,487,894 | 2,315,090 | 2,094,212 | 1,931,504 | 1,328,464 |
| Manufacturers' excise taxes | 6,068,682 | 5,486,106 | 5,516,611 | 6,683,061 | 4,735,129 | 1,836,053 |
| All other taxes | 3,958,893 | 3,855,998 | 3,665,182 | 2,380,609 | 2,004,394 | 2,214,951 |

ings are informal at this level of appeal. A written protest to the examining officer's findings does not have to be submitted unless the amount of tax involved in the dispute is more than $2,500. Taxpayers may represent themselves or be represented by an attorney, accountant, or any other advisor authorized to practice before the IRS. In 97% of the cases, the administrative appeal results in a mutually acceptable basis for resolving the disputo. However, the taxpayer at any point may bypass the administrative appeals procedure and appeal directly to the Tax Court. Claims for refunds may be appealed to the U.S. District Court or the Court of Claims. In 1976, 56,004 cases were disposed of by agreement through the administrative process. The Tax Court tried 1,407 cases, and the U.S. District Courts and the Court of Claims tried 344 cases.

## Federal Individual Income Tax

The Federal individual income tax is levied on the taxable incomes of both citizens and non-citizens who earn income from U.S. sources. A new term, "tax table income," was introduced by the Tax Reduction and Simplification Act of 1977. For a non-itemizer, "tax table income" is adjusted gross income (*see* below) since the tax tables have been simplified to account for both the standard and itemized deductions and exemptions. Because the standard deduction is built into the tax tables, an individual whose itemized deductions exceed his standard deduction deducts his itemized deductions only to the extent they exceed the standard deduction. Commencing with 1977 returns, the vast majority of taxpayers will use the tax tables to compute tax liability. Taxpayers whose incomes exceed those in the tax tables will be required to compute their tax liabilities in the traditional manner. For this purpose, tax rates are graduated from a minimum of 14% on the first $1,000 of taxable income above $3,200 (for joint returns) to a maximum of 70% of taxable income above $203,200. The maximum rate on earned income, however, is 50%.

### Who Must File a Return

| You must file a return if you are: | and your gross income is at least: |
|---|---|
| Single (legally separated, divorced, or married living apart from spouse with dependent child) and are under 65 | $2,950 |
| Single (legally separated, divorced, or married living apart from spouse with dependent child) and are 65 or older | $3,700 |
| A person who can be claimed as a dependent on your parent's return, and who has taxable dividends, interest, or other unearned income | $ 750 |
| A qualifying widow(er) with a dependent child and are 65 or older | $4,700 |
| Married, filing jointly, living together at end of year (or at date of death of spouse), and both are under 65 | $4,700 |
| Married, filing jointly, living together at end of year (or at date of death of spouse), and one is 65 or older | $5,450 |
| Married, filing jointly, living together at end of year (or at date of death of spouse), and both are 65 or older | $6,200 |
| Married, filing separate return, or married but not living together at end of year | $ 750 |
| A person with income from sources within U.S. possessions | $ 750 |
| Self-employed and your net earnings from self-employment were at least $400 | |

### Adjusted Gross Income

*Gross income* consists of wages and salaries, tips and gratuities, interest, dividends, annuities, rents and royalties, and certain other types of income. Among the items excluded from gross income, and thus not subject to tax, are social security payments, unemployment and workmen's compensation benefits, public assistance benefits, interest on exempt securities (mostly state and local bonds), the first $100 of dividends received, and one half of net long-term capital gains. *Adjusted gross income* is determined by subtracting from gross income those business-type expenses considered necessary in earning income. Job-related moving expenses and alimony may also be deducted in arriving at adjusted gross income.

## Deductions

Taxpayers may itemize deductions or use one of two forms of the standard deduction. In itemizing deductions, the following are the major items that may be deducted (with limits, in some instances); interest payments; state and local general sales, income, property, and gasoline taxes; medical expenses; charitable contributions; and casualty losses. The Tax Reduction and Simplification Act of 1977 simplified the use of the standard deduction by eliminating the minimum percentage and maximum standard deduction and replaces them with what is, in effect, a standard deduction of $2,200 for single persons, $3,200 for married individuals filing joint returns, and $1,600 for married individuals filing separate returns.

## Personal Exemptions

Personal exemptions are available to the taxpayer, his spouse, and his dependents. The amount is $750 for each individual. Additional exemptions of $750 each are granted for persons 65 and over and for the blind.

A minimum tax is imposed on certain tax preference items that result from special deductions and deferrals of tax liability (*e.g.*, the excluded portion of capital gains). The tax is imposed at 15% on preference items, reduced by a $10,000 exemption or by one half the regular income tax for the year.

## Credits

A temporary provision of the law allows a general tax credit of $35 for each personal exemption claimed on a return, or 2% of taxable income with a maximum of $180, whichever is greater. Another temporary provision grants a refundable earned income credit for lower-income households with dependent children, with a maximum credit of $400 phased out as adjusted gross income rises from $4,000 to $8,000. The Tax Reform Act of 1976 provided for a credit for child or dependent care expense of 20% of employment-related expenses incurred by the taxpayer up to $2,000 for one qualifying individual in the taxpayer's household and up to $4,000 if there are two or more qualifying individuals.

The Tax Reform Act of 1976 also provided for a new expanded and simplified credit for the elderly. A credit (a reduction of tax owed) of as much as $375 (if single) or $562.50 (if married and filing jointly) may be claimed by persons 65 or older (or persons under age 65 and retired under a public retirement system) who have retirement income. This credit, however, phases out for married couples with adjusted gross income over $10,000 and single persons with adjusted gross income over $7,500.

## Recent Legislation

**Tax Reform Act of 1976.** A major portion of the Tax Reform Act of 1976 was directed toward minimizing the widespread use of tax shelters to avoid payment of tax by high-bracket taxpayers. The principal method for doing this was by providing that investors' deductions were limited to amounts "at risk" in the investment. Other provisions of this law (1) limit deductions for non-business interest to $10,000 for the year plus the amount of a taxpayer's net investment income, (2) increase to $2,000 in 1977 and $3,000 in 1978 and subsequent years the amount by which capital losses could offset ordinary income, (3) substantially curb the deductions that may be taken related to renting vacation homes, (4) allow a taxpayer to deduct only expenses attributable to the use of a portion of his home for business purposes if it is used "exclusively" on a regular basis, (5) repeal the sick pay exclusion and substitute a maximum annual exclusion of $5,200 a year for retirees under age 65 who retired on a disability and who were permanently and totally disabled, and (6) place restrictions on claiming deductions for attending conventions outside of North America.

**The Tax Reduction and Simplification Act of 1977.** The principal purpose of this law was to simplify the preparation of individual income tax returns.

Another feature of this new law provides impetus for employers to create new jobs. It provides for a jobs credit against tax due for the years 1977 and 1978. The credit applies to individual-, partnership-, and corporation-owned businesses. The maximum credit is $2,100 (50% of the first $4,200 paid to net new employees). The credit is based on the first $4,200 of an employee's wages paid by an employer during a year in excess of 102% of Federal Unemployment Tax Act wages paid during the preceding year. The law also provides for certain limitations and safeguards against abuse.

The tables that will be used by most taxpayers to compute their tax liabilities for 1978 will be based on "tax table" income and the number of exemptions. For taxpayers using the standard deduction, tax table income is adjusted gross income. The personal exemptions, the standard deduction, and the general tax credit are built into the tables.

## Results of Criminal Action in Tax Fraud Cases

**Internal Revenue Service**

| | Number of Defendants | | | | | |
|---|---|---|---|---|---|---|
| Action | 1977 | 1976 | 1975 | 1974 | 1973 | 1972 |
| Plea of guilty nolo contendere | 1,229 | 977 | 1,046 | 1,062 | 914 | 733 |
| Convicted after trial | 247 | 216 | 173 | 191 | 190 | 113 |
| Acquitted | 55 | 77 | 83 | 97 | 55 | 40 |
| Nol-prossed or dismissed | 110 | 71 | 168 | 115 | 112 | 151 |
| Total disposals | 1,641 | 1,341 | 1,470 | 1,465 | 1,271 | 1,037 |
| Indictments and Informations | 1,636 | 1,331 | 1,495 | 1,441 | 1,186 | 1,085 |

# Federal Individual Income Tax Rates
# Effective January 1, 1977

## MARRIED INDIVIDUALS FILING JOINT RETURNS AND SURVIVING SPOUSES:

| *If the taxable income is:* | *The tax is:* |
|---|---|
| Not over $3,200 | No tax. |
| Over $3,200 but not over $4,200 | 14% of the excess over $3,200. |
| Over $4,200 but not over $5,200 | $140, plus 15% of excess over $4,200. |
| Over $5,200 but not over $6,200 | $290, plus 16% of excess over $5,200. |
| Over $6,200 but not over $7,200 | $450, plus 17% of excess over $6,200. |
| Over $7,200 but not over $11,200 | $620, plus 19% of excess over $7,200. |
| Over $11,200 but not over $15,200 | $1,380, plus 22% of excess over $11,200. |
| Over $15,200 but not over $19,200 | $2,260, plus 25% of excess over $15,200. |
| Over $19,200 but not over $23,200 | $3,260, plus 28% of excess over $19,200. |
| Over $23,200 but not over $27,200 | $4,380, plus 32% of excess over $23,200. |
| Over $27,200 but not over $31,200 | $5,660, plus 36% of excess over $27,200. |
| Over $31,200 but not over $35,200 | $7,100, plus 39% of excess over $31,200. |
| Over $35,200 but not over $39,200 | $8,660, plus 42% of excess over $35,200. |
| Over $39,200 but not over $43,200 | $10,340, plus 45% of excess over $39,200. |
| Over $43,200 but not over $47,200 | $12,140, plus 43% of excess over $43,200. |
| Over $47,200 but not over $55,200 | $14,060, plus 50% of excess over $47,200. |
| Over $55,200 but not over $67,200 | $18,060, plus 53% of excess over $55,200. |
| Over $67,200 but not over $79,200 | $24,420, plus 55% of excess over $67,200. |
| Over $79,200 but not over $91,200 | $31,020, plus 58% of excess over $79,200. |
| Over $91,200 but not over $103,200 | $37,980, plus 60% of excess over $91,200. |
| Over $103,200 but not over $123,200 | $45,180, plus 62% of excess over $103,200. |
| Over $123,200 but not over $143,200 | $57,580, plus 64% of excess over $123,200. |
| Over $143,200 but not over $163,200 | $70,380, plus 66% of excess over $143,200. |
| Over $163,200 but not over $183,200 | $83,580, plus 68% of excess over $163,200. |
| Over $183,200 but not over $203,200 | $97,180, plus 69% of excess over $183,200. |
| Over $203,200 | $110,980, plus 70% of excess over $203,200. |

## HEADS OF HOUSEHOLDS:

| *If the taxable income is:* | *The tax is:* |
|---|---|
| Not over $2,200 | No tax. |
| Over $2,200 but not over $3,200 | 14% of the excess over $2,200. |
| Over $3,200 but not over $4,200 | $140, plus 16% of excess over $3,200. |
| Over $4,200 but not over $6,200 | $300, plus 18% of excess over $4,200. |
| Over $6,200 but not over $8,200 | $660, plus 19% of excess over $6,200. |
| Over $8,200 but not over $10,200 | $1,040, plus 22% of excess over $8,200. |
| Over $10,200 but not over $12,200 | $1,480, plus 23% of excess over $10,200. |
| Over $12,200 but not over $14,200 | $1,940, plus 25% of excess over $12,200. |
| Over $14,200 but not over $16,200 | $2,440, plus 27% of excess over $14,200. |
| Over $16,200 but not over $18,200 | $2,980, plus 28% of excess over $16,200. |
| Over $18,200 but not over $20,200 | $3,540, plus 31% of excess over $18,200. |
| Over $20,200 but not over $22,200 | $4,160, plus 32% of excess over $20,200. |
| Over $22,200 but not over $24,200 | $4,800, plus 35% of excess over $22,200. |
| Over $24,200 but not over $26,200 | $5,500, plus 36% of excess over $24,200. |
| Over $26,200 but not over $28,200 | $6,220, plus 38% of excess over $26,200. |
| Over $28,200 but not over $30,200 | $6,980, plus 41% of excess over $28,200. |
| Over $30,200 but not over $34,200 | $7,800, plus 42% of excess over $30,200. |
| Over $34,200 but not over $38,200 | $9,480, plus 45% of excess over $34,200. |
| Over $38,200 but not over $40,200 | $11,280, plus 48% of excess over $38,200. |
| Over $40,200 but not over $42,200 | $12,240, plus 51% of excess over $40,200. |
| Over $42,200 but not over $46,200 | $13,260, plus 52% of excess over $42,200. |
| Over $46,200 but not over $52,200 | $15,340, plus 55% of excess over $46,200. |
| Over $52,200 but not over $54,200 | $18,640, plus 56% of excess over $52,200. |
| Over $54,200 but not over $66,200 | $19,760, plus 58% of excess over $54,200. |
| Over $66,200 but not over $72,200 | $26,720, plus 59% of excess over $66,200. |
| Over $72,200 but not over $78,200 | $30,260, plus 61% of excess over $72,200. |
| Over $78,200 but not over $82,200 | $33,920, plus 62% of excess over $78,200. |
| Over $82,200 but not over $90,200 | $36,400, plus 63% of excess over $82,200. |
| Over $90,200 but not over $102,200 | $41,440, plus 64% of excess over $90,200. |
| Over $102,200 but not over $122,200 | $49,120, plus 66% of excess over $102,200. |
| Over $122,200 but not over $142,200 | $62,320, plus 67% of excess over $122,200. |
| Over $142,200 but not over $162,200 | $75,720, plus 68% of excess over $142,200. |
| Over $162,200 but not over $182,200 | $89,320, plus 69% of excess over $162,200. |
| Over $182,200 | $103,120, plus 70% of excess over $182,200. |

**UNMARRIED INDIVIDUALS:**

| *If the taxable income is:* | *The tax is* |
|---|---|
| Not over $2,200 | No tax. |
| Over $2,200 but not over $2,700 | 14% of the excess over $2,200. |
| Over $2,700 but not over $3,200 | $70, plus 15% of excess over $2,700. |
| Over $3,200 but not over $3,700 | $145, plus 16% of excess over $3,200. |
| Over $3,700 but not over $4,200 | $225, plus 17% of excess over $3,700. |
| Over $4,200 but not over $6,200 | $310, plus 19% of excess over $4,200. |
| Over $6,200 but not over $8,200 | $690, plus 21% of excess over $6,200. |
| Over $8,200 but not over $10,200 | $1,110, plus 24% of excess over $8,200. |
| Over $10,200 but not over $12,200 | $1,590, plus 25% of excess over $10,200. |
| Over $12,200 but not over $14,200 | $2,000, plus 27% of excess over $12,200. |
| Over $14,200 but not over $16,200 | $2,630, plus 29% of excess over $14,200. |
| Over $16,200 but not over $18,200 | $3,210, plus 31% of excess over $16,200. |
| Over $18,200 but not over $20,200 | $3,830, plus 34% of excess over $18,200. |
| Over $20,200 but not over $22,200 | $4,510, plus 36% of excess over $20,200. |
| Over $22,200 but not over $24,200 | $5,230, plus 38% of excess over $22,200. |
| Over $24,200 but not over $28,200 | $5,990, plus 40% of excess over $24,200. |
| Over $28,200 but not over $34,200 | $7,590, plus 45% of excess over $28,200. |
| Over $34,200 but not over $40,200 | $10,290, plus 50% of excess over $34,200. |
| Over $40,200 but not over $46,200 | $13,290, plus 55% of excess over $40,200. |
| Over $46,200 but not over $52,200 | $16,590, plus 60% of excess over $46,200. |
| Over $52,200 but not over $62,200 | $20,190, plus 62% of excess over $52,200. |
| Over $62,200 but not over $72,200 | $26,390, plus 64% of excess over $62,200. |
| Over $72,200 but not over $82,200 | $32,790, plus 66% of excess over $72,200. |
| Over $82,200 but not over $92,200 | $39,390, plus 68% of excess over $82,200. |
| Over $92,200 but not over $102,200 | $46,190, plus 69% of excess over $92,200. |
| Over $102,200 | $53,090, plus 70% of excess over $102,200. |

**MARRIED INDIVIDUALS FILING SEPARATE RETURNS:**

| *If the taxable income is:* | *The tax is:* |
|---|---|
| Not over $1,600 | No tax. |
| Over $1,600 but not over $2,100 | 14% of the excess over $1,600. |
| Over $2,100 but not over $2,600 | $70, plus 15% of excess over $2,100. |
| Over $2,600 but not over $3,100 | $145, plus 16% of excess over $2,600. |
| Over $3,100 but not over $3,600 | $225, plus 17% of excess over $3,100. |
| Over $3,600 but not over $5,600 | $310, plus 19% of excess over $3,600. |
| Over $5,600 but not over $7,600 | $690, plus 22% of excess over $5,600. |
| Over $7,600 but not over $9,600 | $1,130, plus 25% of excess over $7,600. |
| Over $9,600 but not over $11,600 | $1,630, plus 28% of excess over $9,600. |
| Over $11,600 but not over $13,600 | $2,190, plus 32% of excess over $11,600. |
| Over $13,600 but not over $15,600 | $2,830, plus 36% of excess over $13,600. |
| Over $15,600 but not over $17,600 | $3,550, plus 39% of excess over $15,600. |
| Over $17,600 but not over $19,600 | $4,330, plus 42% of excess over $17,600. |
| Over $19,600 but not over $21,600 | $5,170, plus 45% of excess over $19,600. |
| Over $21,600 but not over $23,600 | $6,070, plus 48% of excess over $21,600. |
| Over $23,600 but not over $27,600 | $7,030, plus 50% of excess over $23,600. |
| Over $27,600 but not over $33,600 | $9,030, plus 53% of excess over $27,600. |
| Over $33,600 but not over $39,600 | $12,210, plus 55% of excess over $33,600. |
| Over $39,600 but not over $45,600 | $15,510, plus 58% of excess over $39,600. |
| Over $45,600 but not over $51,600 | $18,990, plus 60% of excess over $45,600. |
| Over $51,600 but not over $61,600 | $22,590, plus 62% of excess over $51,600. |
| Over $61,600 but not over $71,600 | $28,790, plus 64% of excess over $61,600. |
| Over $71,600 but not over $81,600 | $35,190, plus 66% of excess over $71,600. |
| Over $81,600 but not over $91,600 | $41,790, plus 68% of excess over $81,600. |
| Over $91,600 but not over $101,600 | $48,590, plus 69% of excess over $91,600. |
| Over $101,600 | $55,490, plus 70% of excess over $101,600. |

## Tax Errors

In 1978, taxpayers made fewer errors on their tax returns. For the 1040A short form, the error rate was 4.3%, down from 11.3% in 1977. For the 1040 return, the error rate was 5.5%, down from 8.5% in the year before.

## Taxes, Taxes, Taxes

The Internal Revenue Service mailed out about 45.5 million 1040 forms and 37.7 million 1040-A forms and instructions for the 1977 tax year. The 83.2 million total is about 2.9 million more than the number mailed the year before.

# Federal Income Tax Comparisons

### Taxes at Selected Brackets After Standard Deductions

| Adjusted gross income | Single return listing no dependents | | | | Joint return listing 2 dependents | | | |
|---|---|---|---|---|---|---|---|---|
| | 1977[1] | 1976[1] | 1972[2] | 1967 | 1977[1] | 1976[1] | 1972[2] | 1967 |
| $ 3,000 | $ 0 | $ 44 | $ 141 | $ 333 | $–300[3] | $–300[3] | $ 0 | $ 4 |
| 5,000 | 271[4] | 366 | 495 | 667 | –300[3] | –300[3] | 102 | 286 |
| 10,000 | 1,227[4] | 1,337 | 1,545 | 1,742 | 517[4] | 656 | 901 | 1,114 |
| 15,000 | 2,472[4] | 2,416 | 2,703 | 3,334 | 1,356[4] | 1,558 | 1,820 | 2,172 |
| 20,000 | 4,016[4] | 3,948 | 4,255 | 5,350 | 2,526[4] | 2,736 | 3,010 | 3,428 |
| 25,000 | 5,830[4] | 5,753 | 6,090 | 7,730 | 3,871[4] | 3,983 | 4,380 | 4,892 |

1. Includes $35 general tax credit per exemption or 2% of taxable income, whichever is greater. 2. A 2.5% surcharge was in effect. 3. Refund based on Earned Income Credit for families with dependent children ($400 maximum), earning up to $8,000 adjusted gross income. 4. Tax is approximate; tax tables not available.

# Returns Filed, Examined, and Audited

### Internal Revenue Service

| Category | Returns filed for calendar year 1976 | Returns examined 1977 | Percent audited |
|---|---|---|---|
| Individual, total | 82,537,199 | 1,742,056 | 2.11 |
| Form 1040—Standard | 28,459,841 | 193,566 | .68 |
| Under $10,000 (non–business) | 12,236,251 | 421,712 | 3.45 |
| $10,000–$50,000 (non–business) | 31,166,880 | 748,122 | 2.40 |
| $50,000 and over (non–business) | 642,020 | 72,841 | 11.35 |
| Under $10,000 (business) | 4,467,807 | 139,256 | 3.12 |
| $10,000–$30,000 (business) | 4,588,019 | 94,744 | 2.07 |
| $30,000 and over (business) | 976,381 | 71,815 | 7.36 |
| Fiduciary | 1,621,163 | 10,881 | .67 |
| Corporation, total | 1,769,334 | 167,689 | 9.48 |
| Assets not reported | 119,387 | 6,850 | 5.74 |
| Under $100,000 | 909,855 | 33,841 | 3.72 |
| $100,000–$1 million | 606,138 | 71,793 | 11.84 |
| $1–$10 million | 109,180 | 42,101 | 38.56 |
| $10–$100 million | 20,979 | 10,247 | 48.84 |
| $100 million and over | 3,795 | 2,857 | 75.28 |
| Estate | 253,505 | 42,320 | 16.69 |
| Gift | 322,115 | 11,484 | 3.57 |
| Income, Estate, and Gift, Total | 86,503,316 | 1,974,430 | 2.28[1] |
| Service Center Examination— Income, Estate, and Gift | — | 150,730 | .17[1] |
| **Income, Estate, and Gift, Grand Total** | — | **2,125,160** | **2.46[1]** |

1. Does not add due to rounding.

# National Average Deductions Claimed

| Deductions | Adjusted gross income (in thousands of dollars) | | | | | | | |
|---|---|---|---|---|---|---|---|---|
| | 9–10 | 10–15 | 15–20 | 20–25 | 25–30 | 30–50 | 50–100 | 100 up |
| Medical expenses | $896 | $655 | $586 | $487 | $442 | $523 | $700 | $1,095 |
| Taxes | 958 | 1,129 | 1,503 | 1,869 | 2,262 | 3,050 | 5,383 | 13,296 |
| Contributions | 441 | 414 | 472 | 542 | 646 | 939 | 2,015 | 9,902 |
| Interest | | | | | | | | |
| Home mortgage | 1,122 | 1,148 | 1,341 | 1,434 | 1,575 | 1,862 | 2,568 | 3,310 |
| **Total** | **1,268** | **1,378** | **1,690** | **1,836** | **1,977** | **2,366** | **3,954** | **9,249** |

NOTE: Based on 1976 returns.

## Federal Corporation Taxes

The tax on net income of corporations is 20% on the first $25,000, 22% of the next $25,000, and 48% on net income above $50,000. These rates were first enacted by the Tax Reduction Act of 1975 to apply to 1976 tax years only. The Tax Reform Act of 1976 extended these rates through Dec. 31, 1977, and the Tax Reduction and Simplification Act of 1977 further extended the applicability of these rates to Dec. 31, 1978.

The Tax Reform Act of 1976 also made other changes affecting the taxation of corporations. Foreign tax breaks are denied to companies that participate in international boycotts. The foreign tax credit, deferral of earnings of foreign subsidiaries, and benefits derived through Domestic International Sales Corporations (DISC) are denied in proportion to income attributable to boycott activity. The amount of any illegal payment to a foreign official may not be deducted. DISCs are exempt from all federal taxes, but DISC shareholders were deemed to have received as a dividend 50% of the corporation's net income every taxable year. Thus, use of a DISC permitted deferral of tax on one-half of the DISC's income. The 1976 Tax Reform Act reduces this deferral and permits DISC benefits only to the extent that export gross receipts exceed 67% of the average for a four-year base (initially 1972–75). The base moves forward one year for each year beyond 1979. Full DISC benefits are retained for those having taxable income of $100,000 or less for a taxable year, but phase out at $150,000.

Tax law provides for a credit against tax liabilities for investments in depreciable personal property. The Tax Reduction Act of 1975 increased this credit from 7% to 10% for the period Jan. 22, 1975, through Dec. 31, 1976. Also provided was an additional 1% credit if the employer established an Employee Stock Ownership Plan (ESOP) meeting specified criteria. The Tax Reform Act of 1976 extended the 10% and 11% credits through Dec. 31, 1980, and provided an additional ½% credit if employee contributions to an ESOP matched the ½%. Unused credits may be carried over seven years against tax liabilities in those years.

The Tax Reduction and Simplification Act of 1977 provides a new jobs tax credit for corporations (and for individuals and partnerships engaged in business) effective in 1977 and through Dec. 31, 1978. The credit is equal to 50% of the increase in each employer's wage base ($4,200) under the Federal Unemployment Tax Act (FUTA), above 102% of that base in the previous year, or up to $2,100 per new employee hired. The maximum total credit an employer may take each year is $100,000. An additional 10% credit is allowed for the first $4,200 of wages paid to newly-hired handicapped individuals, including disabled veterans, who were first paid FUTA wages by the employer during 1977 and 1978 and who have begun or recently completed vocational rehabilitation programs. The $100,000 limitations on the jobs credit does not apply to the additional credit for handicapped employees.

## State Corporation Income and Franchise Taxes

All states but Nevada, South Dakota, Texas, Washington, and Wyoming impose a tax on corporation net income. The majority of states impose the tax at flat rates ranging from 3% to 12%. Several states have adopted a graduated basis of rates for corporations.

Nearly all states follow the federal law in defining net income. However, many states provide for varying exclusions and adjustments.

A state is empowered to tax all of the net income of its domestic corporations. With regard to nonresident corporations, however, it may only tax the net income on business carried on within its boundaries. Corporations are, therefore, required to apportion their incomes among the states where they do business and pay a tax to each of these states. Nearly all states provide an apportionment to their domestic corporations, too, in order that they not be unduly burdened.

Several states tax unincorporated businesses separately.

## Federal Estate and Gift Taxes

A Federal Estate Tax Return must be filed for the estate of every U.S. citizen or resident whose gross estate, if the decedent died in 1978, exceeds $134,000. The size of the estate required for filing increases each year until 1981. The phased-in filing requirements are $134,000 for persons dying in 1978, $147,333 in 1979, $161,563 in 1980, and $175,625 in 1981 and later years. An estate tax return must also be filed for the estate of a nonresident, not a citizen, if the value of his gross estate in the U.S. is more than $30,000 at the date of death. The estate tax return is due nine months after the date of death of the decedent, but reasonable extension of time to file may be obtained for good reason. Tax due is to be paid when the return is filed. The executor of an estate with an interest in closely held business may pay estate tax attributable to the business in from two to ten equal annual installments. To be eligible for this treatment, the interest in the closely held business (or businesses) must represent at least 35% of the gross estate or 50% of the taxable estate. A 15-year extension for the payment of estate taxes may be exercised for that portion of the tax attributable to a business whose value constitutes more than 65% of the decedent's adjusted gross estate.

Under the unified federal estate and gift tax structure, a gift tax return is required to be filed on a quarterly basis only when the sum of (1) the taxable gifts made during the calendar quarter plus (2) all other gifts made during the calendar year exceeds $25,000. If a return is required, it should be filed no later than one and one half months after the end of a calendar quarter. The gift tax is due at the same time the return is required to be filed.

The Tax Reform Act of 1976 replaced the old $30,000 gift tax exemption and $60,000 estate tax exemption with a unified credit. This credit is used for both estate and gift taxes. Any part of the credit used to offset gift taxes is not available to offset estate taxes. As a result, although they are still taxable as gifts, lifetime transfers no longer cushion the impact of progressive estate tax rates. Lifetime transfers and transfers made at death are cumulated for estate tax rate purposes. Gift taxes are computed by applying the uniform rate schedule to lifetime taxable transfers (after deducting the unified credit) and subtracting the taxes payable for prior taxable periods. In general, estate taxes are computed by applying the uniform rate schedule to cumulated transfers and subtracting the gift taxes paid. An appropriate adjustment is made for taxes on lifetime transfers—such as gifts within three years of death—in a decedent's estate.

Among the deductions allowed in computing the amount of the estate subject to tax are funeral expenditures, administrative costs, claims and bequests to religious, charitable, and fraternal organizations or government welfare agencies, and state inheritance taxes. A marital deduction is also allowable for both estates and gifts. The Tax Reform Act of 1976 provides a maximum estate marital deduction of the greater of $250,000 or one-half of the decedent's adjusted gross estate. As a result, a decedent utilizing the maximum marital deduction will have no estate tax in 1978 if his estate is less than $384,000. The amount phases up to $425,625 for death occurring in 1981 and thereafter. The Tax Reform Act of 1976 provides for a gift marital deduction of $100,000 for the first $100,000 of lifetime gifts made to a spouse, no deduction for the next $100,000 of such gifts, and thereafter a deduction for one half of the aggregate lifetime gifts made to a spouse in excess of $200,000. An annual gift tax exclusion is provided that permits tax-free gifts to each donee of $3,000 for each year.

## Unified Credit—Estate & Gift Taxes

| Year | Credit |
|---|---|
| 1977 | $30,000 |
| 1978 | 34,000 |
| 1979 | 38,000 |
| 1980 | 42,500 |
| 1981 & after | 47,000 |

## Federal Estate and Gift Taxes

### Unified Rate Schedule[1]

| If the net amount is: From | To | Tentative tax is: Tax | + % | On excess over |
|---|---|---|---|---|
| $ 0 | $ 10,000 | $ 0 | 18 | $ 0 |
| 10,000 | 20,000 | 1,800 | 20 | 10,000 |
| 20,000 | 40,000 | 3,800 | 22 | 20,000 |
| 40,000 | 60,000 | 8,200 | 24 | 40,000 |
| 60,000 | 80,000 | 13,000 | 26 | 60,000 |
| 80,000 | 100,000 | 18,200 | 28 | 80,000 |
| 100,000 | 150,000 | 23,800 | 30 | 100,000 |
| 150,000 | 250,000 | 38,800 | 32 | 150,000 |
| 250,000 | 500,000 | 70,800 | 34 | 250,000 |
| 500,000 | 750,000 | 155,800 | 37 | 500,000 |
| 750,000 | 1,000,000 | 248,300 | 39 | 750,000 |
| 1,000,000 | 1,250,000 | 345,800 | 41 | 1,000,000 |
| 1,250,000 | 1,500,000 | 448,300 | 43 | 1,250,000 |
| 1,500,000 | 2,000,000 | 555,800 | 45 | 1,500,000 |
| 2,000,000 | 2,500,000 | 780,800 | 49 | 2,000,000 |
| 2,500,000 | 3,000,000 | 1,025,800 | 53 | 2,500,000 |
| 3,000,000 | 3,500,000 | 1,290,800 | 57 | 3,000,000 |
| 3,500,000 | 4,000,000 | 1,575,800 | 61 | 3,500,000 |
| 4,000,000 | 4,500,000 | 1,880,800 | 65 | 4,000,000 |
| 4,500,000 | 5,000,000 | 2,205,800 | 69 | 4,500,000 |
| 5,000,000 | — | 2,550,800 | 70 | 5,000,000 |

1. The estate and gift tax rates are combined in the single rate schedule effective for the estates of decedents dying, and for gifts made, after Dec. 31, 1976.

## State Individual Income Taxes for 1977

### Comparison at Selected Incomes After Standard Deductions and Joint Returns of Married Persons with Two Dependents

| State | Adjusted gross income | | | | | | | | | | | |
|---|---|---|---|---|---|---|---|---|---|---|---|---|
| | Single returns | | | | | | Joint returns | | | | | |
| | $7,500 | $10,000 | $15,000 | $20,000 | $30,000 | $50,000 | $7,500 | $10,000 | $15,000 | $20,000 | $30,000 | $50,000 |
| Alabama | 145 | 229 | 417 | 590 | 887 | 1381 | 80 | 173 | 366 | 559 | 915 | 1487 |
| Alaska[1] | 248 | 380 | 700 | 1098 | 2047 | 4214 | 217 | 311 | 533 | 800 | 1455 | 3179 |
| Arizona[2] | 220 | 347 | 673 | 940 | 1425 | 2215 | 73 | 162 | 366 | 642 | 1211 | 2127 |
| Arkansas[3] | 115 | 194 | 419 | 705 | 1342 | 2742 | 86 | 165 | 390 | 676 | 1313 | 2713 |
| California[4] | 130 | 265 | 655 | 1190 | 2290 | 4490 | 0 | 0 | 144 | 514 | 1294 | 3464 |
| Colorado[5] | 190 | 282 | 543 | 820 | 1295 | 2085 | 121 | 178 | 452 | 758 | 1327 | 2243 |
| Connecticut[6] | — | — | — | — | — | — | — | — | — | — | — | — |
| Delaware | 226 | 399 | 839 | 1279 | 2199 | 4685 | 132 | 236 | 644 | 1094 | 2010 | 4408 |
| District of Columbia | 270 | 428 | 770 | 1175 | 2088 | 4068 | 128 | 270 | 590 | 970 | 1850 | 3820 |
| Florida[7] | — | — | — | — | — | — | — | — | — | — | — | — |
| Georgia | 121 | 230 | 500 | 800 | 1400 | 2600 | 46 | 83 | 270 | 456 | 1156 | 2356 |
| Hawaii[8] | 351 | 551 | 1024 | 1520 | 2561 | 4753 | 35 | 214 | 641 | 1090 | 2000 | 4020 |
| Idaho | 211 | 398 | 721 | 944 | 1864 | 3194 | 0 | 82 | 345 | 685 | 1435 | 2935 |
| Illinois | 163 | 225 | 350 | 475 | 725 | 1225 | 88 | 150 | 275 | 400 | 650 | 1150 |
| Indiana[9] | 130 | 180 | 280 | 380 | 580 | 980 | 90 | 140 | 240 | 340 | 540 | 940 |
| Iowa | 170 | 269 | 513 | 755 | 1330 | 2194 | 166 | 276 | 624 | 838 | 1443 | 2624 |
| Kansas[10] | 128 | 221 | 409 | 681 | 1108 | 1550 | 48 | 97 | 239 | 394 | 820 | 1668 |
| Kentucky | 166 | 268 | 494 | 704 | 1118 | 1650 | 41 | 251 | 499 | 729 | 1156 | 1843 |
| Louisiana | 70 | 104 | 215 | 349 | 605 | 981 | 6 | 55 | 138 | 212 | 418 | 898 |
| Maine | 93 | 220 | 530 | 942 | 1866 | 3860 | 14 | 39 | 145 | 351 | 1056 | 2788 |
| Maryland[11] | 372 | 560 | 938 | 1313 | 2063 | 3563 | 192 | 380 | 720 | 1095 | 1845 | 3335 |
| Massachusetts[12] | 296 | 430 | 699 | 968 | 1505 | 2580 | 199 | 333 | 602 | 871 | 1408 | 2483 |
| Michigan[13] | 276 | 391 | 621 | 851 | 1311 | 2231 | 69 | 184 | 414 | 644 | 1104 | 2024 |
| Minnesota[14] | 365 | 567 | 1012 | 1484 | 2325 | 3806 | 363 | 578 | 1089 | 1628 | 2660 | 4376 |
| Mississippi | 68 | 143 | 340 | 540 | 940 | 1740 | 0 | 38 | 200 | 400 | 800 | 1600 |
| Missouri[15] | 18 | 65 | 208 | 399 | 755 | 1347 | 0 | 0 | 192 | 253 | 675 | 1361 |
| Montana | 276 | 451 | 878 | 1372 | 2459 | 4811 | 152 | 279 | 662 | 1129 | 2199 | 4510 |
| Nebraska | 124 | 224 | 355 | 732 | 1464 | 3287 | −29 | 25 | 200 | 407 | 926 | 2466 |
| Nevada[7] | — | — | — | — | — | — | — | — | — | — | — | — |
| New Hampshire[16] | — | — | — | — | — | — | — | — | — | — | — | — |
| New Jersey[17] | 120 | 180 | 280 | 380 | 625 | 1125 | 60 | 120 | 220 | 320 | 550 | 1050 |
| New Mexico[18] | 45 | 92 | 226 | 440 | 960 | 2080 | 0 | 0 | 58 | 286 | 763 | 1883 |
| New York | 196 | 317 | 628 | 1099 | 2413 | 5413 | 111 | 205 | 478 | 900 | 2120 | 5120 |
| North Carolina[24] | 240 | 390 | 725 | 1075 | 1775 | 3175 | 132 | 258 | 571 | 921 | 1621 | 3021 |

| State | Single returns $7,500 | $10,000 | $15,000 | $20,000 | $30,000 | $50,000 | Joint returns $7,500 | $10,000 | $15,000 | $20,000 | $30,000 | $50,000 |
|---|---|---|---|---|---|---|---|---|---|---|---|---|
| | Adjusted gross income | | | | | | | | | | | |
| North Dakota | 90 | 177 | 449 | 795 | 1388 | 2376 | 37 | 94 | 333 | 677 | 1389 | 2533 |
| Ohio | 44 | 69 | 162 | 284 | 581 | 1227 | 25 | 49 | 123 | 235 | 522 | 1159 |
| Oklahoma[19] | 106 | 181 | 445 | 639 | 1327 | 2497 | 23 | 50 | 149 | 359 | 945 | 2118 |
| Oregon[20] | 343 | 519 | 873 | 1223 | 2120 | 4120 | 76 | 299 | 611 | 988 | 1740 | 3740 |
| Pennsylvania | 150 | 200 | 300 | 400 | 600 | 1000 | 150 | 200 | 300 | 400 | 600 | 1000 |
| Rhode Island | 21 | 207 | 418 | 680 | 1371 | 3092 | 7 | 75 | 234 | 429 | 919 | 2374 |
| South Carolina | 190 | 332 | 659 | 1009 | 1709 | 3109 | 87 | 172 | 456 | 806 | 1506 | 2906 |
| South Dakota[7] | — | — | — | — | — | — | — | — | — | — | — | — |
| Tennessee[21] | — | — | — | — | — | — | — | — | — | — | — | — |
| Texas | — | — | — | — | — | — | — | — | — | — | — | — |
| Utah | 190 | 332 | 659 | 1009 | 1709 | 3109 | 87 | 172 | 456 | 806 | 1506 | 2906 |
| Vermont[22] | 178 | 304 | 614 | 1000 | 2016 | 4548 | 10 | 110 | 344 | 631 | 1352 | 3491 |
| Virginia | 150 | 265 | 493 | 781 | 1356 | 2506 | 84 | 175 | 400 | 677 | 1252 | 2402 |
| Washington[7] | — | — | — | — | — | — | — | — | — | — | — | — |
| West Virginia | 150 | 224 | 424 | 676 | 1282 | 2686 | 93 | 145 | 280 | 437 | 882 | 1923 |
| Wisconsin[23] | 255 | 425 | 850 | 1417 | 2557 | 4837 | 108 | 342 | 790 | 1357 | 2497 | 4777 |
| Wyoming[7] | — | — | — | — | — | — | — | — | — | — | — | — |

1. Add $10 School Tax for each taxpayer over 19 years of age employed or self-employed in Alaska. 2. Property tax credit allowed to taxpayers over 65 years of age. Tax credit for renters is allowed for 10% of rent paid or $50, whichever is lesser. 3. Credit against tax of up to $400 is allowed to persons 65 years of age or older with household incomes of less than $8,000 for taxes paid on homesteads. 4. Credit against the tax of $37 is allowed to qualified renters. Solar Energy Tax Credit of 55% of the cost of solar energy devices with a maximum credit of $3,000 is allowed. 5. 2% surtax on dividend, interest, partnership, fiduciary and undistributed subchapter "S" Income where net income is over $5,000. A food tax credit of from $16 to $7 depending on income is allowed for each exemption. A credit against the tax for up to $100 of general property tax or 20% of rent is allowed to qualified elderly taxpayers. 6. A graduated tax of from 1% to 9% is applicable to dividends if Federal Adjusted Gross Income is $20,000 or more. A tax of 7% is levied against capital gains. 7. No income tax imposed. 8. A credit against the tax of 10% of the cost of installing solar energy devices is allowed. 9. Taxpayers over 65 years of age with income below $5,000 allowed property tax credit of from 10% to 75% (maximum $500). A County Tax is added at various rates. 13.3% of retirement income credit claimed on federal return is allowed as credit. 10. Taxpayers acquiring, leasing, or using a new business facility are allowed a credit for new employees added to payroll. Credit is $50 per new employee and $50 per $100,000 of additional investment not to exceed 50% of net income from new business facility. Taxpayers installing a solar energy system in their dwelling are entitled to a credit of 25% of the cost of the system or $1,000, whichever is less. Solar energy systems installed in a business facility result in a credit of 25% of the cost of the system or $3,000, whichever is less, not to exceed tax liability. Excess credit may be carried over for succeeding 4 years. 11. A County Tax of 50% of State Tax has been added. 19 of 24 counties in Maryland add 50% on to State Tax on the State Tax Return. The rates for the other 5 counties range from 20% to 40%. 12. Interest, dividends, and capital gains are taxed at a 10% rate. Salaries and other types of income are taxed at a 5% rate. This example uses 5%. 13. Property taxes of up to $1,200 are allowed as a credit against the tax to taxpayers 65 years of age or older. 14. A portion of property taxes paid is allowed as a credit against the tax. A credit of 5% of the cost of installation of pollution control equipment is also allowed. 15. Property taxes of up to $500 are allowed as a credit against the tax to taxpayers 65 years of age or older whose income is $7,500 or less. 16. An income tax of 4¼% is levied on interest income in excess of $600 and dividend income in excess of $600. An income tax of 4% of Federal Taxable Income in excess of $2,000 is levied against residents earning income outside the state. However if this income is taxed outside the state, no tax is due. 17. Qualified residential tenants are entitled to a credit against the tax of $65. The credit for persons 65 years of age or over is $100. 18. A credit against the tax of 25% of the cost of installing solar energy equipment not to exceed $1,000 may be claimed. A credit of up to $360 is allowed for elderly property owners with incomes up to $16,000. 19. A credit against the tax of up to $200 is allowed to persons 65 years of age or older with income of not more than $6,000 for property taxes paid. 20. A credit against the tax of up to $655 is allowed to persons with $16,000 or less of income for property taxes paid. 21. Interest income is subject to tax at the rate of 6%. Dividend income from non-resident corporations is taxable at 6% from resident corporations at 4%. 22. Taxpayers 65 years of age or older are allowed a credit against the tax for property taxes or 20% of rent paid in excess of a sliding scale of percentage of household income. 23. A credit against the tax for property taxes or 25% of rent paid up to $535 is allowed to persons with household incomes of $9,300 or less. 24. Credits up to $100 are allowed for installation of insulation and up to $1,000 for installation of solar heating devices.

## California and New York Average Federal Deductions

| Deductions | Adjusted gross income (in thousands of dollars) 15–20 N.Y. | 15–20 Calif. | 20–25 N.Y. | 20–25 Calif. | 25–50 N.Y. | 25–50 Calif. | 50–100 N.Y. | 50–100 Calif. |
|---|---|---|---|---|---|---|---|---|
| Medical expenses | $ 641 | $ 597 | $ 548 | $ 480 | $ 614 | $ 506 | $1,005 | $ 773 |
| Taxes | 2,032 | 1,559 | 2,573 | 1,926 | 4,064 | 2,883 | 9,867 | 7,340 |
| Contributions | 409 | 456 | 458 | 486 | 735 | 686 | 1,945 | 1,798 |
| Interest | | | | | | | | |
| Home mortgage | 950 | 1,478 | 992 | 1,518 | 1,224 | 1,916 | 1,906 | 3,030 |
| **Total** | **1,031** | **1,824** | **1,167** | **1,941** | **1,511** | **2,468** | **3,119** | **4,808** |

NOTE: Based on 1976 returns.

## State General Sales and Use Taxes[1]
(as of August 1, 1978)

| State | Percent rate | State | Percent rate | State | Percent rate |
|---|---|---|---|---|---|
| Alabama | 4 | Kentucky | 5 | Ohio | 4 |
| Arizona | 4 | Louisiana | 3 | Oklahoma | 2 |
| Arkansas | 3 | Maine | 5 | Pennsylvania | 6 |
| California | 4.75 | Maryland | 5 | Rhode Island | 6 |
| Colorado | 3 | Massachusetts | 5 | South Carolina | 4 |
| Connecticut | 7 | Michigan | 4 | South Dakota[2] | 4 |
| D.C. | 5 | Minnesota | 4 | Tennessee[3] | 4.5 |
| Florida | 4 | Mississippi | 5 | Texas | 4 |
| Georgia | 3 | Missouri | 3.125 | Utah | 4 |
| Hawaii | 4 | Nebraska | 3 | Vermont | 3 |
| Idaho | 3 | Nevada | 3 | Virginia | 3 |
| Illinois | 4 | New Jersey | 5 | Washington | 4.6 |
| Indiana | 4 | New Mexico | 4 | West Virginia | 3 |
| Iowa | 3 | New York | 4 | Wisconsin | 4 |
| Kansas | 3 | North Carolina | 3 | Wyoming | 3 |
| | | North Dakota | 3 | | |

1. Local and county taxes, if any, are additional. 2. Scheduled to rise to 5% on July 1, 1979. 3. Scheduled to drop to 3% on July 1, 1979. NOTE: Alaska, Delaware, Montana, New Hampshire and Oregon have no statewide sales and use taxes.

## Sales Tax Rates in Selected Cities[1]

| City | Percent rate | City | Percent rate | City | Percent rate |
|---|---|---|---|---|---|
| Amarillo, Tex. | 1 | Ithaca, N.Y.[2] | 3 | Richmond, Va. | 1 |
| Anaheim, Calif.[2] | 1.25 | Jefferson City, Mo. | 1 | Roanoke, Va. | 1 |
| Austin, Tex. | 1 | Lincoln, Neb. | 1 | Sacramento, Calif.[2] | 1.25 |
| Baton Rouge, La.[3] | 3 | Los Angeles[2] | 1.25 | St. Louis | 1 |
| Berkeley, Calif.[2,4] | 1.75 | Lynchburg, Va. | 1 | San Antonio, Tex. | 1 |
| Birmingham, Ala. | 1 | Mobile, Ala. | 2 | San Diego, Calif.[2] | 1.25 |
| Boulder, Colo. | 2 | Montgomery, Ala. | 2 | San Francisco[2,4] | 1.75 |
| Chicago[2] | 2 | New Orleans[3] | 3 | Seattle[2] | 0.925 |
| Dallas | 1 | New York | 4 | Shreveport, La.[3] | 2 |
| Denver | 3 | Nome, Alaska | 3 | Spokane, Wash.[2] | 0.925 |
| Duluth, Minn. | 1 | Norfolk, Va. | 1 | Springfield, Ill.[2] | 2 |
| El Paso | 1 | Oakland, Calif.[2,4] | 1.75 | Topeka, Kan. | 0.5 |
| Fort Worth | 1 | Oklahoma City | 2 | Troy, N.Y.[2] | 3 |
| Fresno, Calif.[2] | 1.25 | Omaha, Neb. | 1 | Tucson, Ariz. | 2 |
| Glendale, Calif.[2] | 1.25 | Pasadena, Calif.[2] | 1.25 | Tulsa, Okla. | 2 |
| Houston | 1 | Phoenix, Ariz. | 1 | Washington, D.C. | 5 |
| Huntsville, Ala. | 2 | Rapid City, S.D. | 1.5 | Yonkers, N.Y.[2] | 4 |

1. Excludes state and county sales taxes unless otherwise indicated. 2. Combined city and county rate. 3. Includes Parish School Board tax. 4. Includes 0.5% imposed by San Francisco Bay Area Rapid Transit District.

## Income Tax Rates in Selected Cities
(Population exceeding 50,000)

| City | Percent rate | Year begun |
|---|---|---|
| Akron, Ohio | 1.5 | 1962 |
| Allentown, Pa. | 1 | 1958 |
| Altoona, Pa. | 1 | 1948 |
| Baltimore | (1) | 1966 |
| Bethlehem, Pa. | 1 | 1957 |
| Birmingham, Ala. | 1 | 1970 |
| Canton, Ohio | 1.5 | 1954 |
| Chester, Pa. | 1 | 1956 |
| Cincinnati | 2 | 1954 |
| Cleveland | 1 | 1967 |
| Cleveland Heights, Ohio | 1.5 | 1968 |
| Columbus, Ohio | 1.5 | 1947 |
| Covington, Ky. | 1.5 | 1956 |
| Dayton, Ohio | 1.75 | 1949 |
| Detroit | 2 | 1965 |
| District of Columbia | 2–11 | 1947 |
| Elyria, Ohio | 1.5 | 1969 |
| Erie, Pa. | 1 | 1948 |
| Euclid, Ohio | 1 | 1967 |
| Flint, Mich. | 1 | 1965 |
| Gadsden, Ala. | 2 | 1956 |
| Grand Rapids, Mich. | 1 | 1967 |
| Hamilton, Ohio | 1.5 | 1960 |
| Harrisburg, Pa. | 1 | 1966 |
| Kansas City, Mo. | 1 | 1964 |
| Kettering, Ohio | 1 | 1968 |
| Lakewood, Ohio | 1 | 1968 |
| Lancaster, Pa. | 0.5 | 1959 |
| Lansing, Mich. | 1 | 1968 |
| Lexington, Ky. | 2 | 1952 |
| Lima, Ohio | 1 | 1959 |
| Lorain, Ohio | 1 | 1967 |
| Louisville, Ky. | 2 | 1948 |
| Mansfield, Ohio | 1 | 1966 |
| New York | 0.9–4.3 | 1966 |
| Owensboro, Ky. | 1 | 1960 |
| Parma, Ohio | 1 | 1967 |
| Philadelphia | 4.3125 | 1939 |
| Pontiac, Mich. | 1 | 1968 |
| Reading, Pa. | 1 | 1969 |
| Saginaw, Mich. | 1 | 1965 |
| St. Louis | 1 | 1948 |
| Scranton, Pa. | 2 | 1948 |
| Springfield, Ohio | 2 | 1948 |
| Toledo, Ohio | 1.5 | 1946 |
| Warren, Ohio | 1 | 1952 |
| Wilkes-Barre, Pa. | 1 | 1966 |
| Wilmington, Del. | 1.25 | 1970 |
| York, Pa. | 1 | 1965 |
| Youngstown, Ohio | 1.5 | 1948 |

1. Tax is 50% of state income tax. NOTE: Rates are for residents only, except in Kentucky, Ohio, and Pennsylvania cities, where non-resident rate is the same. *Source:* Tax Foundation, Inc.

## Books of the Bible

**OLD TESTAMENT — STANDARD VERSIONS**

Genesis
Exodus
Leviticus
Numbers
Deuteronomy
Joshua
Judges
Ruth
I Samuel
II Samuel
I Kings
II Kings
I Chronicles
II Chronicles
Ezra
Nehemiah
Tobit
Judith
Esther
1 Maccabees
2 Maccabees
Job
Psalms
Proverbs
Ecclesiastes
Song of Solomon
Wisdom
Ecclesiasticus
Isaiah
Jeremiah
Lamentations
Baruch
Ezekiel
Daniel
Hosea
Joel
Amos
Obadiah
Jonah
Micah
Nahum
Habakkuk
Zephaniah
Haggai
Zechariah
Malachi

**NEW TESTAMENT — STANDARD VERSIONS**

Matthew
Mark
Luke
John
Acts
Romans
Corinthians
Galatians
Ephesians
Philippians
Colossians
Thessalonians
Timothy
Titus
Philemon
Hebrews
James
Peter
John
Jude
Revelation

**OLD TESTAMENT — DOUAY VERSION[1]**

Genesis
Exodus
Leviticus
Numbers
Deuteronomy
Josue
Judges
Ruth
I Kings
II Kings
III Kings
IV Kings
I Paralipomenon
II Paralipomenon
I Esdras
II Esdras
Tobias
Judith
Esther
Job
Psalms
Proverbs
Ecclesiastes
Canticle of Canticles
Wisdom
Ecclesiasticus
Isaias
Jeremias
Lamentations
Baruch
Ezechiel
Daniel
Osee
Joel
Amos
Abdias
Jonas
Micheas
Nahum
Habacuc
Sophonias
Aggeus
Zacharias
Malachias
I Machabees
II Machabees

1. In the Douay Version of the Bible, the books of the New Testament are the same as those of the Authorized (King James) Version, except that the Revelation of St. John is called the Apocalypse of St. John in the Douay Version.

# GUIDE TO GROWING OLDER

*American Association of Retired Persons*

Once regarded as the country of the young, the United States is rapidly becoming middle-aged through a demographic sea change some have called "the graying of America."

The reasons are simple. More people than ever before are living longer than ever before. And they are having fewer children.

While the demographic shift—portending immense political, social and economic impacts—appears to have suddenly gripped the nation's interest, the change itself has not been sudden at all. It has developed gradually—and relatively slowly—over nearly three-quarters of a century. What was sudden was our realization during the past decade that the change had occurred.

In 1900, the average life expectancy at birth was only 49 years; today, it is 72.5, due primarily to childhood diseases being controlled. At the turn of the century, medical science was more interested in reducing infant and child mortality than in extending the later years of life. In the process, however, improved health care lengthened the average individual lifespan by at least 20 years.

A person who reaches age 65 in reasonably good health today has a fair chance of living another 15 years—13 for men, and 18 for women. While this is just about the same as in 1900, many more people are now reaching 65 and continuing onward. Nearly nine million Americans today have celebrated their 75th birthday, compared to less than a million at the turn of the century.

When the century began, only three million Americans were over 65, a mere 4% of the population; today, there are 24 million, comprising 11%. More significant, however, is the fact that, while the total population has nearly tripled since 1900, there are now seven times as many people over age 65 than there were then.

Beyond the increase in life expectancy, the other major reason for the disproportionate growth of the older population segment is that, with the exception of the post-World War II "baby boom," people started having fewer babies. This decline became most evident during the so-called "baby bust" of the last few years as the United States' birth rate dropped to an all-time low.

With fewer babies being born to provide balance to the population distribution, the middle-aged and older segments will continue to expand even further. This trend is expected to peak around the year 2020, when the "boom babies" of the late 1940s and early 1950s start turning 65.

During the last few years, there has been a slight, but nonetheless noticeable rise in the birthrate among married couples in their mid-to-late 30s and early 40s. The additional births, however, are being offset by the mortality rate falling faster than had been anticipated, resulting in expectations of an even larger elderly population by the turn of the century.

Does this mean that the land of the young is turning into the home of the frail and the feeble? Hardly!

Today's older Americans are far "younger" in many ways than their counterparts of the past. And they are growing progressively younger as the composition of the 65-plus population continues to change while constantly expanding.

In the United States each day, approximately 5,000 people turn 65 while 3,600 who are 65 or over die; the result is a net increase in the 65-plus population of about 1,400 persons daily, or 500,000 yearly. These new older Americans are generally healthier, more vigorous and active, better educated, and more outspoken than their predecessors.

And, contrary to the widespread misconception that all older people act and think alike, older Americans are—and, for that matter, always have been—as different from each other in their later years as they were when younger. Frequently, the only thing that many of them have in common is being old.

With the nation's older population continuing to expand, gerontologists and demographers have begun to redefine this unprecedented expansion of the human lifespan.

According to the newly developed definitions, middle age begins in the mid-to-late 30s and lasts until 55. People between 55 and 75 are considered

With more than 12 million members, the American Association of Retired Persons is the nation's—and possibly the world's—largest membership organization of older persons. Founded in 1958, AARP is a nonprofit, nonpartisan association providing a wide range of membership programs and services including legislative representation at federal and state levels.

## U.S. Population by Age
(in millions)

| Age | | 2000[1] | Percent | 1978 | Percent | 1900 | Percent |
|---|---|---|---|---|---|---|---|
| Under 19 | | 100.9 | 35 | 71.8 | 33 | 33.7 | 44 |
| 20–34 | | 55.6 | 19 | 54.4 | 25 | 19.4 | 26 |
| 35–44 | Middle age | 41.3 | 14 | 24.4 | 11 | 9.2 | 12 |
| 45–54 | Middle age | 35.8 | 12 | 23.2 | 11 | 6.4 | 8 |
| 55–64 | Young-old | 22.9 | 8 | 20.7 | 9 | 4.0 | 5 |
| 65–74 | Young-old | 17.1 | 6 | 14.9 | 7 | 2.2 | 3 |
| 75 & over | Old-old | 13.5 | 5 | 9.0 | 4 | .9[2] | 1 |

1. Projected. 2. 899,000. NOTE: Percentages are approximate and because of rounding may not add to 100%.

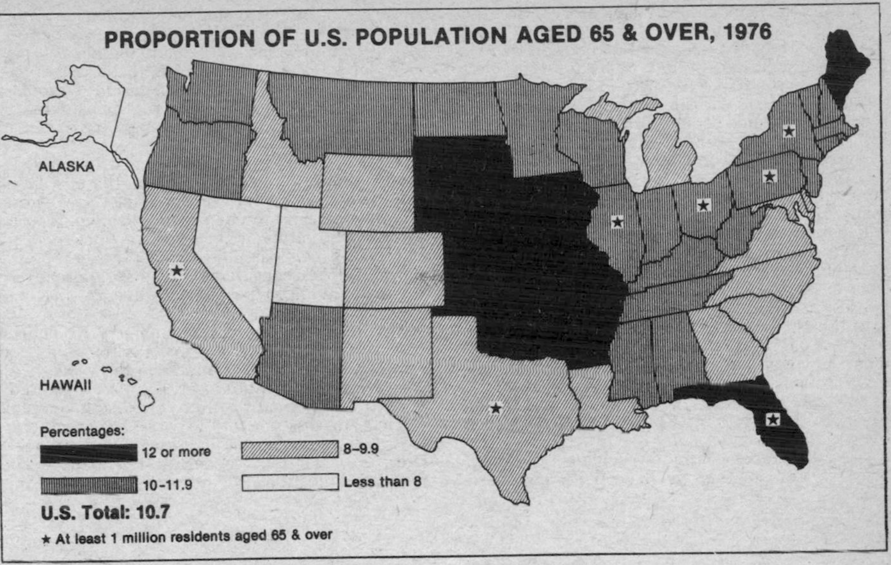


to be the "young-old," while those 75 or older are the "old-old."

Out of this has evolved "the new middle age," encompassing the years from about 40 to 60 or 65. Where the 40s and 50s were once regarded as the beginning of the end—a momentary preface to a brief old age—they are now being viewed as a potential-filled time for new beginnings.

Take age 49. At the turn of the century, it was the average life expectancy, making anyone who reached it seem even older than the age alone implied. Today, a 49-year-old man or woman is regarded as being in the prime of both life and middle age.

For many, middle age is a period of life in which personal relationships begin to change. It sometimes brings freedom to pursue anew dreams abandoned in order to provide for children, now grown and independent. Marriages take on whole new dimensions, achieving maturity, or—as a climbing divorce rate among older couples indicates—dissolving as one or both partners explore new ways of life.

It is a time also when people see their work begin to reach fruition. Or, as is happening with increasing frequency, they switch away from long-held jobs or long-pursued careers to embark upon whole new ventures. Women, after years of staying home to tend nests now suddenly empty, are moving into the world of work—many for the first time.

An indication of how widespread these practices are becoming is to be found in the informal network of support groups springing up to aid and encourage career changers and new work force members. Across the country, colleges are offering "second career" counseling services—and, at some schools, entire courses of study are now available for those caught up in this burgeoning trend.

For the first time, large numbers of people are living long enough to be able to watch their children growing old along with them. To many middle-aged and older people, this means the assumption of simultaneous responsibility for two generations—their parents and their own children. Earlier generations had already lost both parents by the time their own children were approaching adulthood, but it is no longer unusual for today's 65-and-over retirees to have one or both parents still living.

While this can be—and frequently is—a joyful and rewarding experience for all concerned, it is often accompanied by the distressing intimations of one's own mortality that stem from seeing a parent grown suddenly old. To many in the middle years, it signals a first awareness of their own aging—and the realization that they, too, are approaching the unexplored terrain of old age.

For anyone unprepared to cope with this new situation, few experiences can be more upsetting than having to deal with a family crisis involving one's own parents. Yet, dealing with these crises—however disturbing they may be—can bring the knowledge, experience, and insight necessary to comprehend them when they become intensely personal a few years later.

Thus, the greatest value of the new middle age may lie in the opportunities it offers people to prepare for their own old age—and the problems and potentials that accompany it. The aged, after all, are the only minority group to which we shall all eventually belong.

As is the case with any minority, there are questions of where this growing population fits into the big social picture, what roles its members are to play, and what their relationship is to be to the rest of society. No matter what one's age, these questions apply to—and will ultimately affect—each and every one of us as individuals.

Since such questions rarely result in a single answer that is right for all concerned, the last decade or so has begun to see the development of trends offering broader options for older Americans.

Even as the elimination of mandatory retirement is finally being considered seriously, the number of workers opting for voluntary early retirement is growing steadily and rapidly. Some are still in their 50s, and most are covered by pension plans which will provide them with an adequate, if not affluent, retirement income should they choose to live the rest of their lives in total leisure.

Many, however, find new employment, which may be either a part-time job with few demands or an endeavor as demanding—but different from—their former work. One area of commerce into which many retirees of all ages are moving is entrepreneurship, using their savings to invest in a new or franchised business while relying on their pensions or Social Security to provide their living expenses.

At the same time, many retirees have found personal satisfaction (and, in some cases, extra pocket money) by working for the good of their communities through such volunteer programs as Foster Grandparents, Senior Companions, the Peace Corps, and the Service Corps of Retired Executives.

The importance of finding fulfillment through volunteer or income-producing activity is frequently stressed in retirement preparation programs, such as those offered by Action for Independent Maturity, which encourages anticipation and planning for retirement as least ten to 15 years in advance. Change, however, is a constant factor that must be taken into consideration in planning for one's later years. Lately, the changes have been for the better.

Where breakthroughs in pediatric medicine saved children's lives years ago—thereby laying the foundation for the current aging boom—geriatric medicine is just coming into its own, focusing intensive attention on the special medical needs of old age. By at least alleviating the symptoms of chronic illness, considerable progress is already being made in improving the daily lives of older people.

Further advances will undoubtedly result from research under way at university gerontology centers across the country and from the work of the new National Institute on Aging, part of the government's National Institutes on Health complex.

Thus, in almost every aspect of contemporary existence, aging in America is beginning to come of age. Yet, it is still in its comparative infancy—and, from all indications, the best may be yet to come.

## The Facts of Later Life

### Income

Most economists estimate that for retirees to maintain their pre-retirement lifestyle within reasonable limits, they need a retirement income equal to 60–70% of their earnings immediately preceding retirement, plus occasional adjustments for inflation.

Even with recent improvements in Social Security benefits, this is a goal beyond the reach of most older Americans who, on average, have half the income of their younger counterparts.

One-seventh of the over-65 population now lives below the poverty level—an improvement over 1970 when a full quarter of all older Americans did.

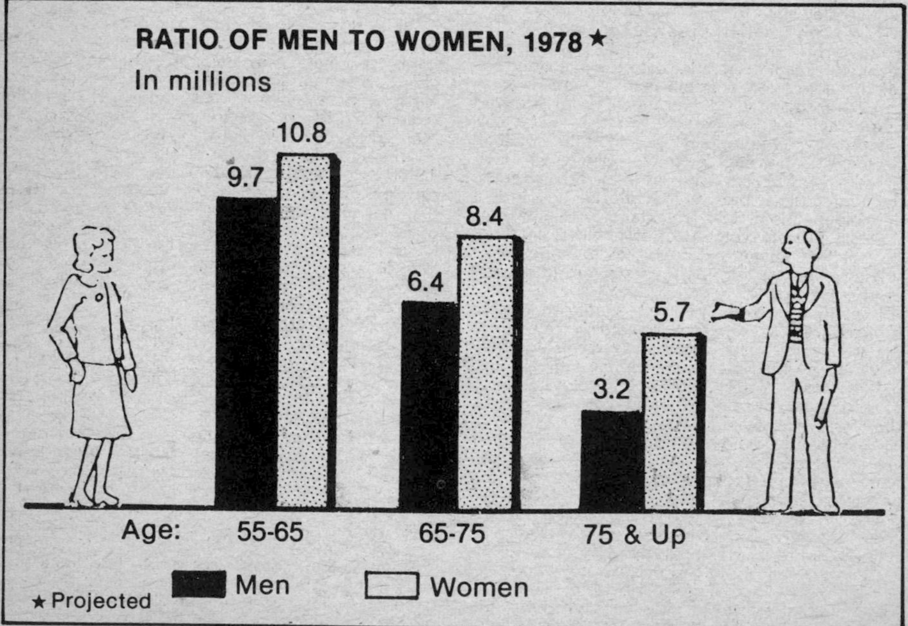

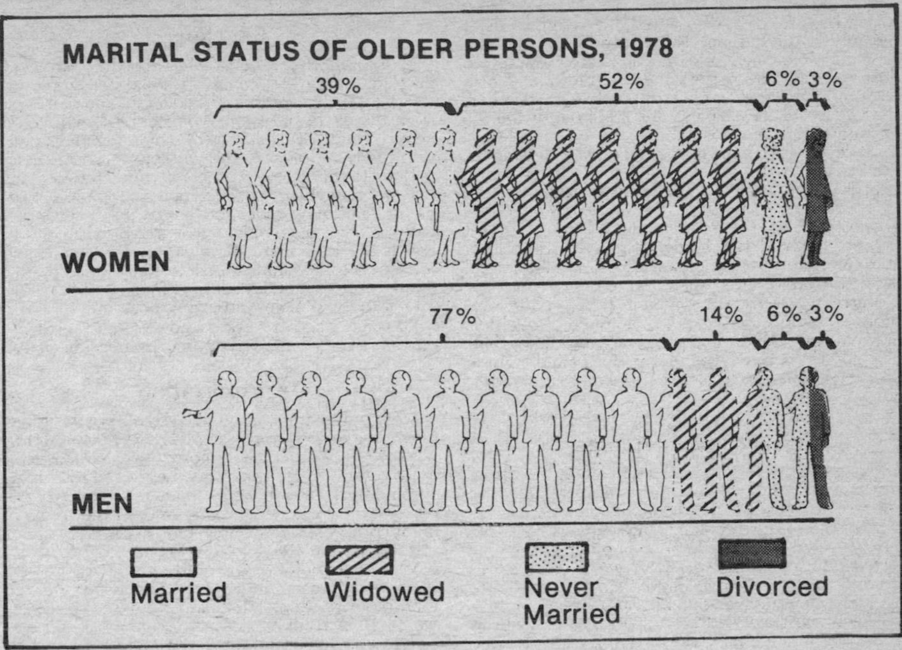


Poverty most often afflicts women and minority aged. While there are, of course, many well-off older persons, most tend to fall economically somewhere between poverty and affluence.

Most of the aged poor did not become poor until they retired, and their income dropped by 50–66%. These are essentially middle-class working people, and it is probably harder for them to cope with their newfound poverty than it is for people who have been poor all their lives.

The economic situation of almost all older Americans, however, is complicated by years of continually escalating inflation, which steadily saps the purchasing power of people living on fixed incomes. Since the elderly do not generally possess the ability to increase their income in response to inflationary pressures, they are perenially attempting to cut back and catch up with little hope of ever breaking even again.

Even with annual Social Security increments, which are supposed to offset inflation, retirees continue to fall farther and farther behind. This is due to the increments coming at least a year after the fact of a cost-of-living increase and thus never compensating fully for inflation's inroads.

## Health

Although generally healthier than previous generations of elders, today's older people are still more subject to chronic illness and disability than younger persons. On average, they visit physicians 50% more often, and have health care and medication costs nearly four times those of younger individuals.

Comprising only 11% of the nation's population, older people account for 29% of total personal health care expenditures ($34.9 billion out of $120.4 billion). Yet, most older Americans regard themselves as being comparatively healthy and capable of caring for themselves well enough to continue living independently.

In a 1975 survey, 69% of the older persons questioned described their health as good or excellent in comparison with others of their own age, and 22% said their health was fair. Those describing their health as being chronically poor reported suffering from arthritis (38%), hearing loss (29%), and vision impairment, hypertension, and heart disease (20% each). Many suffered from several of these conditions simultaneously.

A 1973–74 study found that 83% of the older persons polled had not been hospitalized during the previous year. And most persons entering nursing homes returned later to their own residences.

## Employment

In 1900, 67% of men and 8% of women over 65 were actively working. By 1977, only 20% of older men remained employed, while the percentage of women in the workforce had slipped back to eight after rising to ten in 1974. In general, they are working today at part-time jobs, agricultural labor, or self-employment.

Once unemployed, however, older workers usually experience greater difficulty finding new jobs and have longer average periods of unemployment than younger workers. This tendency begins in the mid-to-late 40s and increases with the worker's age.

## Marital Status

In 1977, 77% of all older men were married. Among older women, 52% were widows, a figure which rises to 70% after age 75. It is almost predictable: If the husband is five years younger than his wife, the chances of widowhood are 50%; if the husband and wife are the same age, the chances are two out of three; if the husband is five years older than his wife, the chances are three out of four.

Widows outnumber widowers by 5.5 to 1. Men, however, experience greater difficulty adjusting to the loss of a mate—most likely because they don't expect their wives to die before they do.

In 1975, there were 21,300 brides and 40,100 grooms over 65. For approximately 1,200 of these older brides and 1,800 older grooms, it was a first marriage. For the rest, remarriage came mostly after widowhood rather than divorce.

Marriage rates for older men in 1975 were seven times those for older women. The number of older men entering into first marriages was 2.5 times that of older women, while the number of older men remarrying was 8.6 times greater than that of older women.

## Living Arrangements

While most older persons live in a family setting —with a husband, wife or other relatives—this frequently decreases with advancing age.

More than a third of older Americans—41% of all older women, but only 17% of all older men—live alone or with non-relatives. One reason for this disparity is that women live longer than men, and thus eventually outnumber them in later life.

The majority of older women are widows or divorcees (or, in some cases, both) without adequate means of support and little, if any, preparation for living alone—a circumstance which may in time give rise to new forms of communal living.

## Pensions

The newer the retiree, the greater the chances of participation in a company or union pension—and the greater the likelihood of collecting on that pension, thanks to the Employee Retirement Income Security Act (ERISA) of 1974 which regulates pension plans and insures the worker's stake in them.

Prior to that, many workers participated in plans but were unable to collect pensions upon retirement. Thus, most older retirees do not receive private pension payments, but live instead solely on Social Security and whatever savings they have managed to accumulate; some must also depend upon Supplemental Security Income (SSI) payments to assist them in making ends meet.

Of today's active workers, however, it is estimated that nearly half are covered by pension plans.

## Transportation

Most public transportation systems are designed primarily to satisfy the needs of the commuting worker. Older people (whose needs are usually quite different) are thus forced either to rely upon automobiles—which are becoming increasingly expensive to own and maintain—or to surrender their mobility and settle for whatever is within walking distance, no matter how inferior it may be.

Some communities have attempted to provide special transportation services at reduced rates for their older residents, but many of these subsidized systems have fallen victim to their own success. The more they are utilized, the more they cost to operate, and the growing cost often exceeds a community's ability to sustain them. In this age of energy scarcity, this looms large as a major problem.

**LIVING ARRANGEMENTS, 1977**
(Noninstitutional Population)

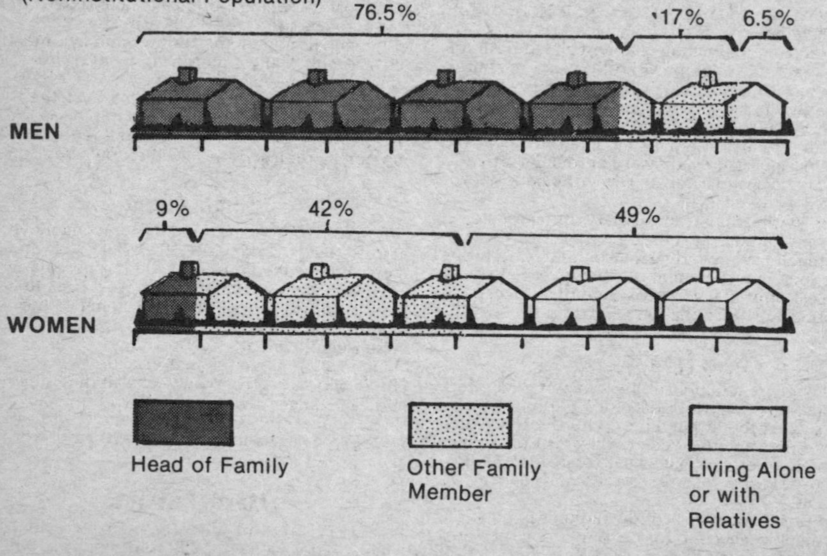

## Crime

While violent crimes against the elderly have been increasing lately and have thus received the most news coverage, they are not nearly as prevalent as "bunco" offenses, in which the victim is defrauded of whatever savings he or she may have managed to accumulate over the course of a lifetime.

Older victims tend to suffer more intensely. A younger victim can recoup a monetary loss by accumulating future earnings, but older victims no longer have that opportunity. Similarly, older victims wounded in crimes of violence require longer to heal, leading to prolonged loss of mobility and the increased possibility of medical complications.

## Voting Patterns

An indication of the political impact of America's older population is the existence of the Special Committee on Aging in the Senate and the Select Committee on Aging in the House of Representatives.

Equally significant is the fact that a larger percentage of older people vote in comparison to the rest of the population. While they make up approximately 15% of the eligible electorate, older people comprise 17% of the actual voting population in 1974 and 16% in 1976.

On both occasions, they cast their ballots pretty much along the same lines as the entire electorate. So much for the great myth about all older people leaning in one political direction!

# The Coming End of Mandatory Retirement

Although it is still too early for there to be any apparent indication of the immediate effects of the new law restricting mandatory retirement policies and practices, a discernable pattern of long-term change has already begun to emerge—and the world of work may never be quite the same.

While not totally prohibiting mandatory retirement, the new law (in actuality, a series of amendments to the Age Discrimination in Employment Act) has dealt it a severe blow by making it illegal to force most workers into retirement before age 70, and abolishing mandatory retirement altogether for almost all federal government employees.

In addition, there is the distinct possibility that the upper age limit could be raised again in a few more years, and perhaps ultimately eliminated entirely. It is quite likely, however, that before too many years have passed, it will no longer be necessary to prohibit mandatory retirement at any age because it will have been abandoned out of necessity.

With the nation's work force shrinking as a result of the lowered birthrate, it is possible that the turn of the century will see employers offering productive older workers incentives to stay on the job instead of retiring. Many employers are currently recruiting the services of retirees and other older people on a part-time or temporary basis to fill staffing gaps in their organizations.

Even as Congress was debating the ADEA amendments, many companies were already abandoning mandatory retirement practices, and still more were considering doing so. Most, however, have adopted a wait-and-see attitude toward adapting to the rapidly changing situation in the world of work.

Public opposition to mandatory retirement grew out of the realization that many of the socio-economic, medical, and psychological problems afflicting the elderly stem almost directly from being driven from the workplace and forced into a form of exile in the very midst of one of the world's most work-oriented cultures.

In the United States and much of the western world, a person's identity and self-esteem are frequently determined by the individual's work role—what he, or increasingly she, does for a living. Whether these values are right or wrong is, of course, debatable, but they nonetheless prevail.

When older people are forced out of the world of work, they are essentially being banished from society's mainstream. Deprived of their work roles, they are figuratively—and perhaps even literally—being stripped of their personal public identities.

Ask an active worker for a self-description, and he or she will usually respond: "I am an accountant" or whatever that particular person does for a living. Ask a retiree (especially an involuntary one), and the response will all too often be: "I *was* an accountant"—as if that person no longer possesses an identity worth describing.

There is, however, increasing evidence that people who choose to retire—sometimes at relatively early ages—and who prepare for this newest phase of life experience less difficulty in adjusting to a new lifestyle than workers who have been contractually coerced into the extended unemployment euphemistically termed "retirement."

By late 1977, public opposition to mandatory retirement—among people of all ages—had coalesced to such a degree that the ADEA amendments were able to pass both houses of Congress almost unanimously and then be signed into law by President Carter in April 1978.

Defenders of mandatory retirement had argued that the continuing presence of older workers in high-salaried, upper-level positions would tend to discourage ambitious younger workers. They also contended that if older employees do not leave the workforce, there will not be enough jobs for younger workers and that pension systems, based on mandatory retirement standards, would be actuarially disrupted by not having to pay out benefits as soon as had been anticipated.

These claims were disputed by many labor economists who maintain that there is no direct relationship between mandatory retirement and the number of jobs available to younger workers. In fact, there are also indications that the number of totally new jobs created in the economy each year is greater than the number of older workers who would continue to work beyond age 65.

At the same time, there are also indications that —even without mandatory retirement—most workers would continue to retire at about 65 or earlier *by personal choice*, and that the percentage of workers who would choose to continue working beyond 65 grows smaller as they grow older.

Even so, the curtailing of mandatory retirement —and the promised potential of its eventual elimination—should help to alleviate some of the burden being placed on younger workers by the changing dependency ratio. To a great extent, this is what Social Security's current fiscal problems are all about, and many economists feel it will not be long before the same pressures are also felt by private pension plans.

As recently as 1955, there were seven workers for each person collecting Social Security benefits. By 1960, there were four. The ratio is now in the area of three-to-one, and it has been estimated that by shortly after the year 2000 it will be reduced to no more than two-to-one.

Couple this with the smaller future work force mentioned earlier, plus the growing tendency of many workers to opt for early retirement (frequently while still in their 50s), and you have the basis for the development of new work-life patterns.

Up to now, virtually all education was concentrated at the start of life, with work dominating the early adult and middle years, and most leisure being postponed until retirement. This is what is known as "the three boxes of life," and there is a growing determination to open the boxes and redistribute their timely contents.

Labor economists and sociologists are now investigating such innovative concepts as extended work sabbaticals with income-support provisions (for recreation or study), job sharing for those interested in part-time employment, extended leaves of absence, time-income tradeoffs, and long-term work scheduling options. Some of these are already being explored in Europe, and increasing interest is emerging in this country as well.

Thus, the coming end of mandatory retirement may be the beginning of massive changes in the distribution of work, education, and leisure throughout the human lifespan.

# Coping

## When You Need Help or Information

Whether your concern is for your own later years or for someone you know with problems, the basic approaches to seeking help or information are essentially the same. In general, your primary sources of information are your local telephone directory, your community's public library, and *Your Retirement Information Guide,* a helpful booklet published by the American Association of Retired Persons and its affiliate, the National Retired Teachers Association. Single copies are available free from AARP-NRTA, P.O. Box 2400, Long Beach, Calif. 90801.

A good way to begin is to take stock of your resources relating to the problem. This doesn't necessarily mean financial resources, although they can be undeniably important. There are, however, other resources which you may have built up over a lifetime of activity without really being aware of them.

Did you, for instance, serve in the nation's military services? If so, check with the Veterans Administration (listed in the phonebook under "U.S. Government") to see if it can help.

Are you a union member? Then, contact your nearest local and find out if the union has any programs to help retirees with your particular problem. This also applies to any civic or fraternal organizations to which you may belong.

Don't forget the many local and national organizations for older people; being a member of one or more of them can prove helpful. These are the major national ones:

American Association of Retired Persons/National Retired Teachers Association (AARP/NRTA), 1909 K Street N.W., Washington, D.C. 20049

National Council of Senior Citizens (NCSC), 1511 K Street N.W., Washington, D.C. 20005

National Association of Retired Federal Employees (NARFE), 1533 New Hampshire Avenue N.W., Washington, D.C. 20036

Gray Panthers, c/o Tabernacle Church, 38th & Chestnut Streets, Philadelphia, Pa. 19104

Older Women Rights Committee, and Alliance for Displaced Homemakers, both of the National Organization for Women (NOW), 3800 Harrison Street, Oakland, Calif. 94611

For ages 50–64:

Action for Independent Maturity (AIM), 1909 K Street N.W., Washington, D.C. 20049

There are also organizations of professionals who work with and on behalf of the elderly: National Council on the Aging (NCOA), 1828 L Street N.W., Washington, D.C. 20036; The Gerontological Society, 1835 K Street N.W., Washington, D.C. 20006; American Geriatric Society, 10 Columbus Circle, New York, N.Y. 10019.

## When You Have a Problem . . .

For just about every problem today, there is a private public service organization or government program trying to solve it. The trick is for you to get in touch with the right one.

In this *Almanac (see* Index), there is a listing of U.S. Societies and Associations in which you might find the name of an organization dealing with your particular problem. Look in your telephone directory to see if there is a branch office in your area; if not, contact the organization's national headquarters at the address given.

To find government agencies that might be able to help, start with your local government (city, town, or village) and move on to county, state, and federal levels only as necessary. Often, the agency nearest home will be the most help. Again, your telephone directory can be your best source of information; if you can't find exactly what you're looking for there, try phoning the municipal or country clerk's office for more specific guidance.

## Keys to Finding Help

A few of the sources of assistance or information to which you might turn when dealing with a specific problem are given below. (Unless an address is given, look in your phonebook for the key-word indicated.)

**Aging.** Administration on Aging, U.S. Department of Health, Education & Welfare, Washington, D.C. 20201. Locally, try state **Offices, Commissions, Departments,** or **Bureaus** on **Aging** or **Senior**

**Citizens Affairs**; look for county or municipal agencies with similar titles, and for regional **Area Agencies on Aging.**

**Career Considerations:** If you're unhappy in your present work situation, and are trying to decide whether to stick with it until you can retire gracefully or to attempt to start anew in middle age, these books might provide some helpful insights. *Overcoming Executive Mid-Life Crisis* by Homer R. Figler; *Second Chance: Blueprints for Change* by Herbert B. Livesey; *Where Do I Go From Here With My Life?* by John C. Crystal and Richard N. Bolles; and *What Color Is Your Parachute?* by Richard N. Bolles.

**Federal Government.** Your tie-line and guide to the federal bureaucracy is the **Federal Information Center,** listed in the phonebook under "U.S. Government." If nothing else works, try phoning your Congressional representative's local office; his or her staff can sometimes cut through a lot of red tape.

## Aging: Myths and Truths

**Myth:** You can't teach an old dog new tricks.
**Truth:** A smart dog can learn new tricks at any age, and so can most people. Research has shown that older people do not necessarily lose their ability to learn, but sometimes learn differently than when younger. Their speed of comprehension, for instance, may decrease somewhat, but their retention and interpretation of new information may improve. Contrary to common belief, senility is not a state of mind that invariably accompanies old age. Rather, it is a serious and complex illness which, in many cases, can be alleviated through proper medical diagnosis and treatment.

**Myth:** Sex doesn't exist after age 60, and anyone who thinks it does is a "dirty old man" (or woman).
**Truth:** Normal sexual activity continues well into later life—sometimes even into the 90s—although frequency may decrease somewhat over the years.

**Myth:** When you grow old, you end up in a nursing home or some other institution.
**Truth:** Less than 5% of people 65 and over are institutionalized; the rest maintain their independence in a variety of residential situations. The majority of people who enter nursing homes usually do so following a period of hospitalization and eventually return to their homes.

**Myth:** Like birds in winter, people head south as soon as they retire.
**Truth:** While some do move south, most don't. Approximately 80% of the 65-plus population still live in the same house in which they lived before retiring. Of those who have moved, most moved a relatively short distance—frequently to a smaller residence more suited to their needs—while only 4% moved to different states, such as Florida, Arizona, and Nevada.

**Food.** The key words here are **Food Stamps, Meals on Wheels, National Nutrition Program for the Elderly.** If none of these is listed in your phonebook, check with the agencies listed under Aging.

**Health Care.** Don't overlook your local **health department.** If your problem involves a hospital, there is probably a staff social worker to whom you can turn. Also, try local medical and dental societies and schools—the latter frequently provide quality care at relatively low cost. For information about health care at home, contact the National Council for Homemaker-Home Health Aide Service, 67 Irving Place, New York, N.Y. 10003.

**Housing.** The key agency here is the U.S. Department of Housing and Urban Development; check your phonebook for a local office, or write to HUD, Washington, D.C. 20410. If you live in a rural area, contact your agricultural extension agent or write directly to Farmers Home Administration, U.S. Department of Agriculture, 14th Street and Independence Avenue S.W., Washington, D.C. 20250. Your local **housing authority** can also prove helpful.

**Legal Problems.** Many communities have special legal counseling programs for older residents. Try your local **Aging** agency, or write to National Senior Citizens Law Center, 1709 West 8th Street, Los Angeles, Calif. 90017. Information is also available from the National Resource Center for Consumers of Legal Services, 1302 18th Street N.W., Washington, D.C. 20036.

**Middle Age.** The processes, problems, and potentials of adult development in the middle years are explored in authoritative depth in two new books, *The Seasons of a Man's Life* by Daniel Levinson and *Transformations* by Roger Gould. The original research and theories of both of these psychiatrists served as a basis for Gail Sheehy's best-selling *Passages.*

**Money.** Information about **Social Security** and **Supplemental Security Income** may be found in this *Almanac* or from the **Social Security Administration** office nearest you. Also helpful in special circumstances are the U.S. Civil Service Commission, Bureau of Retirement, 1900 E Street N.W., Washington, D.C. 20415; and the U.S. Railroad Retirement Board, Headquarters office, 844 Rush Street, Chicago, Ill. 60611.

**Nursing Homes.** Check with your local **health department,** hospital social worker, or the nearest branches of the American Nursing Home Association and the American Association of Homes for the Aging. Some state **Aging** agencies have a **Nursing Home Ombudsman.** Write for the free pamphlet *Thinking About a Nursing Home* to the American Health Care Association, 1200 15th Street N.W., Washington, D.C. 20005.

**Parents.** Two excellent books for middle-aged-and-over people with elderly parents are: *You and Your Aging Parent* by Barbara Silverstone and Helen Kandel Hyman and *When Your Parents Grow Old* by Jane Otten and Florence D. Shelley.

**Research.** If you want to read more about growing older, look in your local library catalog under **aging, gerontology, geriatrics, retirement.**

**Volunteering.** If you're interested in working as a volunteer, check with your local **hospitals, nonprof-**

**it nursing homes, social service agencies,** and **civic organizations.** Or write to: National Center for Voluntary Action, 1785 Massachusetts Avenue N.W., Washington, D.C. 20036; ACTION, Older Americans Volunteer Programs, Washington, D.C. 20525; Service Corps of Retired Executives (SCORE), Small Business Administration, 1441 L Street N.W., Washington, D.C. 20416.

## Characteristics of Persons 65 Years Old and Over

(in percentages)

| Characteristic | 1976 Male | 1976 Female | 1975 Male | 1975 Female | 1970 Male | 1970 Female | 1965 Male | 1965 Female |
|---|---|---|---|---|---|---|---|---|
| Marital status:[1] | | | | | | | | |
| Single | 4.4 | 5.9 | 4.7 | 5.8 | 7.5 | 7.7 | 6.6 | 7.7 |
| Married | 79.1 | 38.5 | 79.3 | 39.1 | 73.1 | 35.6 | 71.3 | 36.0 |
| Spouse present | 76.5 | 36.7 | 77.3 | 37.6 | 69.9 | 33.9 | 67.9 | 34.1 |
| Spouse absent | 2.6 | 1.8 | 2.0 | 1.5 | 3.2 | 1.7 | 3.4 | 1.9 |
| Widowed | 13.8 | 52.8 | 13.6 | 52.5 | 17.1 | 54.4 | 19.5 | 54.4 |
| Divorced | 2.7 | 2.8 | 2.5 | 2.6 | 2.3 | 2.3 | 2.6 | 1.9 |
| Family status:[1] | | | | | | | | |
| In families | 83.4 | 57.9 | 83.3 | 59.3 | 79.2 | 58.5 | 80.3 | 62.9 |
| Primary individuals | 15.7 | 41.2 | 15.4 | 39.4 | 14.9 | 35.2 | 13.9 | 30.6 |
| Secondary individuals | .9 | .9 | 1.2 | 1.3 | 2.4 | 1.9 | 2.3 | 2.2 |
| Inmates of institutions[1] | n.a. | n.a. | n.a. | n.a. | 3.6 | 4.4 | 3.5 | 4.3 |
| Labor force participation: | | | | | | | | |
| Employed | 19.0 | 8.0 | 21.1 | 7.8 | 26.2 | 10.0 | 26.8 | 10.2 |
| Unemployed | 1.4 | .5 | 1.2 | .4 | 1.0 | .3 | 1.3 | .4 |
| Not in labor force | 79.6 | 91.5 | 77.7 | 91.8 | 72.8 | 89.7 | 71.9 | 89.5 |
| Living arrangements:[1] | | | | | | | | |
| Living in household | 99.9 | 99.8 | 99.8 | 99.8 | 95.5 | 95.0 | 96.2 | 95.3 |
| Living alone | 14.9 | 40.3 | 14.8 | 38.0 | 14.1 | 33.8 | 13.1 | 28.6 |
| Spouse present | 76.5 | 36.7 | 77.3 | 37.6 | 69.9 | 33.9 | 67.9 | 34.1 |
| Living with someone else | 8.5 | 22.8 | 7.7 | 24.2 | 11.5 | 27.4 | 15.2 | 32.6 |
| Not in household[2] | .1 | .2 | .2 | .2 | 4.5 | 5.0 | 3.8 | 4.7 |

1. Resident population as of March of year indicated. 2. In institutions and other group quarters. NOTE: n.a. = not available. *Source:* Department of Commerce, Bureau of the Census.

# Social Security

(For details of the Medicare program, see page 668.)

The original Social Security Act was passed in 1935 and amended in 1939, 1946, 1950, 1952, 1954, 1956, 1958, 1960, 1961, 1965, 1967, 1969, 1972, and 1974.

The act is administered by the Social Security Administration, part of the Department of Health, Education, and Welfare.

For purposes of clarity, the explanations given below will describe the provisions of the act as amended.

## Who Is Covered?

Practically everyone who works fairly regularly is covered by social security. Many state and local government employees are covered under voluntary agreements between states and the Secretary of Health, Education, and Welfare. Workers not covered include most federal civilian employees, career railroad workers, and a few other exceptions.

Cash tips count for social security if they amount to $20 or more in a month from employment with a single employer.

To qualify for benefits or make payments possible for your survivors, you must be in work covered by the law for a certain number of "quarters of coverage." Before 1978, a quarter of coverage was earned if a worker was paid $50 or more wages in a 3-month calendar quarter. A self-employed person got 4 "quarters of coverage" for a year in which his net earnings were $400 or more.

Starting with 1978, a worker, whether employed or self-employed, receives one quarter of coverage for each $250 of covered annual earnings up to a maximum of four for a year. The $250 measure will increase automatically to keep pace with increases in average wages. The number of quarters needed differs for different persons and depends on the date of your birth; in general, it is related to the number of years after 1950, or after the year you reach 21, if later, and up to the year you reach 62, become disabled, or die. One "quarter of coverage" is required for each such year in order for you or your family to get benefits. No one will need more than 40 quarters. Your local social security office can tell you how long you need to work.

## Who Pays for the Insurance?

Both workers and their employers pay for the workers' insurance. Self-employed persons pay their own social security contributions annually along with their income tax. The rates include the cost of Medicare hospital insurance. The contribution and benefit base is $22,900 for 1979, and will

## Social Security Contribution and Rate Schedule
(percent of covered earnings)

| Year | Retirement, survivors, and disability insurance | Hospital insurance | Total |
|---|---|---|---|
| EMPLOYERS AND EMPLOYEES | | | |
| 1978 | 4.95% | 1.10% | 6.05% |
| 1979–80 | 5.08 | 1.05 | 6.13 |
| 1981 | 5.35 | 1.30 | 6.65 |
| 1982–84 | 5.40 | 1.30 | 6.70 |
| 1985 | 5.70 | 1.35 | 7.05 |
| 1986–89 | 5.70 | 1.45 | 7.15 |
| 1990 & later | 6.20 | 1.45 | 7.65 |
| SELF-EMPLOYED | | | |
| 1978 | 7.00% | 1.10% | 8.10% |
| 1979–80 | 7.05 | 1.05 | 8.10 |
| 1981 | 8.00 | 1.30 | 9.30 |
| 1982–84 | 8.05 | 1.30 | 9.35 |
| 1985 | 8.55 | 1.35 | 9.90 |
| 1986 89 | 8.55 | 1.45 | 10.00 |
| 1990 & later | 9.30 | 1.45 | 10.75 |

increase automatically in future years as earnings levels rise. The contribution rate schedules under present law are shown in a table in this section.

The separate payroll contribution to finance hospital insurance is placed in a separate trust fund in the U.S. Treasury. In addition, the medical insurance premiums, currently $8.20 a month, and the government's shares go into another separate trust fund.

## How to Apply for Benefits

You apply for benefits by filing a claim either in person, by mail, or by telephone at any social security office. You can get the address either from the post office or from the phone book under the listing, United States Government—Department of Health, Education, and Welfare—Social Security Administration. You will need certain kinds of proof, depending upon the type of benefit you are claiming. If it is a retirement benefit, you should provide a birth or baptismal certificate. If you are unable to get these documents, other old documents showing your age or date of birth—such as census records, school records, early naturalization certificate, etc.—may be acceptable. A widow 60 or older who is claiming widow's benefits based on her husband's earnings should have both proof of age and a copy of the marriage certificate. If formal proof is not available, the social security office will tell you what kinds of information will be acceptable.

## What Does Social Security Offer?

The social security contribution you pay gives you four different kinds of protection: (1) retirement benefits, (2) survivors' benefits, (3) disability benefits, and (4) Medicare health insurance benefits.

**Retirement benefits** A worker becomes eligible for the full amount of his retirement benefit at age 65, if he has retired under the definition in the law. A worker may retire at 62 and get 80% of his full benefit. The closer he is to age 65 when he starts collecting his benefit, the larger is the fraction of his full benefit that he will get.

The amount of the retirement benefit you are entitled to at 65 is the key to all other benefits under the program. The retirement benefit is based on covered earnings, generally those after 1950.

A worker who doesn't get any benefits before 65 and who delays his retirement past age 65 will get a special credit that can mean a larger benefit. The credit adds to a worker's benefits 1% (3% starting in 1982) for each year (1/12 of 1% for each month) from age 65 to age 72 for which he did not get benefits.

The law provides a special minimum benefit at retirement for people who worked under social security more than 20 years. This provision will help people who had low incomes, but above a specific level, in their working years. The amount of the special minimum depends on the number of years of coverage. For a worker retiring at 65 in 1979 with 30 or more years of coverage, the minimum would be $230. These benefits are reduced if a worker is under 65.

Using the table as a guide, you will see that average monthly earnings of $500 ($6,000 a year) would give you a benefit of $388.20 a month when you retire at 65.

If your wife is also 65, then she will get a wife's benefit that is equal to half your benefit. So if your benefit is $388.20, your wife gets $194.10.

If your wife is between ages 62 and 65, she can draw a reduced benefit; the amount depends on the number of months before 65 that she starts getting checks. If she draws her benefit when she is 62, she will get about ⅜ of your basic benefit, or $145.60. (She will get this amount for the rest of her life, unless you should die first; then she can start getting widow's benefit, described below.)

If your wife is entitled to a worker's retirement benefit on her own earnings, she can draw whichever—the worker's or the wife's—is larger.

If you have children under 18 or a child in school aged 18 up to 22 or a son or daughter who became totally disabled prior to reaching age 22, when you retire they will get a benefit equal to half your full retirement benefits (subject to maximum payments that can be made to a family). If your wife is caring for a child who is under 18 or who became disabled before 22 (and getting benefits too), she is eligible for benefits, even if she is under 62.

In general, the highest retirement check that can be paid to a worker who is 65 in 1978 is about $489.70 a month. Maximum payment to the family of a retired worker is about $856.50. When your children reach age 18, their benefits will stop except for children in school aged 18 up to 22, and except for a benefit that is going to a son or daughter who became totally disabled before attaining age 22. Such a person can continue to get his benefits as long as his disability meets the definition in the law.

If you are a woman worker entitled to a retirement benefit and you have a husband aged 62 or over, he may draw a benefit similar to a wife's benefit at 62.

**Survivor benefits.** This feature of the social security program gives your family valuable life insurance protection—in some cases benefits to a family could amount to $100,000 or more over a period of years. The amount of protection is again geared to what the worker would be entitled to at 65. If you

## Examples of Monthly Social Security Payments
(effective June 1978)

| Benefits can be paid to: | Average yearly earnings after 1950 covered by social security | | | | | | |
|---|---|---|---|---|---|---|---|
| | $923 or less | $3,000 | $4,000 | $5,000 | $6,000 | $8,000 | $10,000[1] |
| Retired worker at 65 | 121.80 | 251.80 | 296.20 | 343.50 | 388.20 | 482.60 | 534.70 |
| Worker under 65 and disabled | 121.80 | 251.80 | 296.20 | 343.50 | 388.20 | 482.60 | 534.70 |
| Retired worker at 62 | 97.50 | 201.50 | 237.00 | 274.80 | 310.60 | 386.10 | 427.80 |
| Wife or husband at 65 | 60.90 | 125.90 | 148.10 | 171.80 | 194.10 | 241.30 | 267.40 |
| Wife or husband at 62 | 45.70 | 94.50 | 111.10 | 128.90 | 145.60 | 181.00 | 200.60 |
| Wife under 65 with one child in her care | 61.00 | 133.20 | 210.00 | 290.40 | 324.00 | 362.00 | 401.00 |
| Widow or widower at 65 if worker never received reduced benefits | 121.80 | 251.80 | 296.20 | 343.50 | 388.20 | 482.60 | 534.70 |
| Widow or widower at 60 if sole survivor | 87.10 | 180.10 | 211.80 | 245.70 | 277.60 | 345.10 | 382.40 |
| Widow or widower at 50 and disabled if sole survivor | 61.00 | 126.00 | 148.20 | 171.90 | 194.10 | 241.40 | 267.50 |
| Widow or widower with one child in care | 182.80 | 377.80 | 444.40 | 515.40 | 582.40 | 724.00 | 802.20 |
| Maximum family payment | 182.70 | 384.90 | 506.20 | 633.80 | 712.10 | 844.50 | 935.70 |

1. Maximum earnings covered by social security were lower in past years and must be included in figuring your average earnings. This average determines your payment amount. Therefore, amounts shown in the last column generally won't be payable until future years. The maximum retirement benefit generally payable to a worker who is 65 in 1978 is $489.70. *Source:* Department of Health, Education, and Welfare, Social Security Administration.

can estimate from the table what your basic monthly benefit would be at 65, this is what your survivors would get:

1. A cash payment to help cover your burial expenses. This "lump-sum death payment" is $255.

2. A benefit for each child until he reaches 18, or 22 if the child is in school, or at any age if disabled before 22. Each eligible child receives 75% of the basic benefit (subject to reduction for the family maximum). (A disabled child can continue to collect benefits after age 22.) If certain conditions are met, dependent grandchildren of insured workers can receive survivor or dependent benefits.

3. A benefit for your widow, or widower, if she has children under 18 or disabled in her care. Her benefit is also 75% of the basic benefit. She can collect this as long as she has a child under 18 or disabled in her care. Payments stop then (they will start again upon application when she is 60 at a slightly lower amount).

Total family survivor benefits can go to as high as $1,159.80 a month in 1978.

4. If there are no children either under 18 or disabled, your wife can get a widow's benefit starting at age 60. This would come to 71½% of the basic amount at age 60. A widow who first becomes entitled at 65 or later may get 100% of her deceased husband's basic amount (provided neither he nor she ever drew reduced benefits).

5. Dependent parents can sometimes collect survivors' benefits. They are usually eligible if: (a) they were getting at least half their support from the deceased worker when he died, (b) they have reached 62, and (c) they are not eligible for a greater retirement benefit based on their own earnings. A single surviving parent can then get 82½% of the basic benefit. If two parents are eligible, each would get 75%.

A woman worker can provide survivors' benefits for any of these dependents: (1) her children under age 18, or for children in school up to age 22, (2) her disabled child after 18, if the child is unmarried and was disabled before 22, (3) her widowed husband at age 60, if he hasn't remarried, or (4) her parents if they meet the tests in paragraph 5 above. Also, a widowed father can get benefits on the same basis as a widowed mother.

*Here is an example of survivors' benefits in one family situation:* John Jones dies, leaving a wife and two children aged one and three. His average monthly earnings were $450. Family survivors benefits would include: (1) a cash lump-sum death payment of $255.00, and (2) a total monthly benefit of $673.40 for the family. When the children reach 18, their benefits stop unless they are attending school full-time, in which case payments continue up to age 22. When the older child no longer collects benefits, the widow and younger child continue to receive $541.20 a month until that child is 18. If he continues in school, he will get $270.60 a month, but Mrs. Jones' checks will stop. When Mrs. Jones becomes 60 (assuming she has not remarried), she will be paid $258.00 a month if she so chooses. If she waits until age 65, the monthly check will be $360.80.

**Disability benefits.** Disability benefits are paid to three groups of people:

1. An insured worker under age 65 with a severe disability can collect the same amount as if he were 65. Eligible dependents of disabled workers will receive the usual benefits. To be eligible for disability benefits, a person must: (a) have worked in employment (or self-employment) covered by social security long enough and recently enough (any social security office can tell you exactly); (b) be suff-

ering from a physical or mental disability that is expected to last for at least 12 months; and (c) be so disabled that he can't work, or at least "engage in any substantial gainful activity." If he meets those tests, his benefits will start after a 5-month waiting period.

The applicant is referred to the state vocational rehabilitation agency and, if rehabilitation services are offered and the applicant refuses them without good cause, his disability benefit will be withheld.

2. The permanently disabled son or daughter of a worker who is receiving retirement or disability benefits or who has died can collect benefits after age 18 (when children's benefits are ordinarily cut off). If the child is eligible, his mother can also get a benefit if the child is in her care. The child must be unmarried and have been disabled before age 22 (but he need not have been drawing benefits before 22). The child's benefit would be 50% of a retired or disabled parent's or 75% of a deceased parent's basic benefit, and his mother would get the same amount.

The benefit for an adult disabled since childhood can actually be paid to adults if the above tests are met. For example, an unmarried person, aged 40, who was born blind and is dependent on his father for support, can collect a benefit as soon as his father starts drawing a retirement or disability benefit or dies.

3. The disabled widow, widower, or (under certain conditions) the surviving divorced wife of a worker who worked long enough under social security, may be able to get benefits as early as age 50 if he or she is disabled. The benefit is reduced (50% of the worker's benefit if the widow starts getting checks at 50). A widow (or widower or surviving divorced wife) needs no work credits of her own. She is considered disabled only if she has an impairment that is so severe that it would ordinarily prevent a person from working and that is expected to last at least 12 months. Vocational factors cannot be considered. In general, a widow cannot get these benefits unless her disability starts before her spouse's death or within seven years after his death. However, a widow who received benefits as a mother can be eligible if she becomes disabled before those payments end or within seven years after they end. There is a 5-month waiting period before benefits can start. If in addition to your social security benefit as a wife, husband, widow, or widower you receive a pension based on your work in public employment not covered by social security, your benefit as a dependent or survivor will be reduced by the amount of that pension. Under an exception in the law, your government pension will not affect your dependent's or survivor's benefit if you become eligible for that pension before December 1982 and if, at the time you apply or become entitled to your social security benefit as a dependent or survivor, you could have qualified for that benefit if the law as in effect in January 1977 had remained in effect. (At that time, men had to prove they were dependent upon their wives for their support to be eligible for benefits as a dependent or survivor.) Your government pension, however, will not affect any social security benefit based on your own work covered by social security.

**Medicare.** Most people 65 and over and many under 65 who have been entitled to disability checks for at least 2 years have Medicare protection. So do insured people and their dependents who need a kidney transplant or dialysis treatment because of permanent kidney failure.

The hospital insurance part of Medicare helps pay the cost of inpatient hospital care and certain kinds of follow-up care. The medical insurance part helps pay for the cost of doctors' services, outpatient hospital services, and for certain other medical items and services.

A person who is eligible for monthly benefits at 65 gets hospital insurance automatically and does not have to pay a premium. He does pay a monthly premium for medical insurance.

## You Can Earn Income Without Losing Benefits

If you are 72 or over, you can earn any amount and still get all your benefits. If you are under 72, you can receive all benefits if your earnings do not exceed the annual exempt amount. The annual amount for 1978 is $4,000 for people 65 or over and $3,240 for people under 65. (The 1977 annual limit was $3,000 for everyone.)

If your earnings go over the annual amount, $1 in benefits is withheld for each $2 of earnings above the limit.

The monthly measure used for 1977 and earlier years to determine whether benefits could be paid for any month during which they earned 1/12 or less of the annual exempt amount and did no substantial work in their business has been eliminated. Starting in January 1978, a person will be able to use the monthly test only in the first year that he or she has a month in which earnings do not exceed 1/12 of the annual amount or does not perform substantial services in self-employment. If such a month occurs in 1978, a benefit can be paid for any month in which you earn $334 or less (if 65 or older) or $270 (if under 65) and don't perform substantial services in self-employment even though your total yearly earnings exceed the annual amount.

For people 65 or over, the annual exempt amount will increase to $4,500 for 1979, to $5,000 in 1980, to $5,500 for 1981, and to $6,000 for 1982. After that, the limit will increase automatically as the level of average wages rises. The limit for people under 65 will also continue to increase.

If a widow with young children loses her benefits by working, the children will continue to get theirs.

Anyone earning over the annual exempt amount a year while receiving benefits (and under age 72) must report these earnings to the Social Security Administration. If you continue to work after you have applied for social security, your additional earnings may increase the amount of your monthly payment. This will be done automatically by the Social Security Administration. You need not ask for it.

**Supplemental Security Income.** The supplemental security income program started January 1974. These federal payments assure a minimum level of income for aged, blind, and disabled people who have limited income and resources.

The new program is administered by the Social Security Administration, but it is financed from general revenues, not from social security contributions. Before 1974, payments to these people were made by state and local public assistance agencies.

Payments of up to $189.40 a month for an individual and up to $284.10 for a couple can be made. Further information is available from any social security office.

## How to Protect Your Social Security Record

*Always show your social security card when you start a new job.* In that way you will be sure that your earnings will be credited to *your* social security record and not someone else's. If you lose your social security card, apply for a new one at any social security office. When a woman marries, she should apply for a new card showing her married name (and the same number).

## Public Assistance

The Federal government makes grants to the states to help them provide financial assistance, medical care, and social services to certain persons in need, including children dependent because of the death, absence from home, incapacity, or (in some states) unemployment of a parent. In addition, in all states some help is provided from only state and/or local funds to some other needy persons.

Under the Social Security Act, federal sharing in state assistance costs is based on each state's average monthly payment times the number of recipients in each program. The act fixes maximums on the amount of payment to be shared, and sets the ratio of federal contributions. Administrative costs in all the programs are shared equally by the federal and state governments.

Within these and other general patterns set by the requirements of the Social Security Act and their administrative interpretations, each state initiates and administers its own public assistance programs, including the determination of who is eligible to receive assistance, and how much can be granted and under what conditions. Assistance is in the form of cash payments made to recipients, except for payments for medical care. Other social services are provided, in some instances, to help assistance recipients increase their capacity for self-care and self-support or to strengthen family life.

In the medical assistance Medicaid program, federal funds pay 50% to 83% of the costs for medical care. If it is to a state's benefit, it may use the Medicaid formula for federal sharing for its money payment programs, ignoring the maximum on dollar amounts per recipient.

The federal government pays 75% of the cost for services that help recipients become personally and financially self-sufficient.

# Medicare Program

The Medicare program is a federal health-insurance program for persons 65 and over. Most disabled people under 65 who have been entitled to social security disability benefits at least 24 consecutive months, and insured workers and their dependents who need dialysis treatment or a kidney transplant because of permanent kidney failure, also are eligible for Medicare protection.

Enacted under the Social Security Amendments of 1965, Medicare's official name is Title XVIII of the Social Security Act. These amendments also carried Title XIX, providing federal assistance to state medical-aid programs, which has come to be known as Medicaid.

## Medicare

It will be helpful to your understanding of the Medicare program if you keep the following points in mind:

- The federal health-insurance program does not of itself offer medical services. It helps pay hospital, doctor, and other medical bills. You choose your own doctor, who prescribes your treatment and place of treatment.
- There are two parts of the program:
  (1) The hospital insurance part for the payment of most of the cost of covered care provided by participating hospitals, skilled nursing facilities, and home health agencies.
  (2) The medical insurance part which helps pay doctors' bills and certain other expenses.
- Another important point to remember: While Medicare pays the major share of the costs of many illnesses requiring hospitalization, it does not offer adequate protection for long-term illness or mental illness.
- Therefore, it may be advisable not to cancel any private health insurance you now carry. You may wish to cancel a policy whose benefits are duplicated by the federal program, and consider a new policy that will provide for the payment of costs not covered by the federal program. Private insurance companies offer policies supplementing the protection offered by the federal program.

## Do You Qualify for Hospital Insurance?

If you're entitled to monthly social security or railroad retirement checks (as a worker, dependent, or survivor), you have hospital insurance protection automatically when you're 65. Disabled people will have hospital insurance automatically after they have been entitled to social security disability benefits for 24 consecutive months. (Disabled people who get railroad annuities must meet special requirements.) People 65 or older who are not entitled to monthly benefits need credit for some work under social security to get hospital insurance without paying a monthly premium. If they do not have enough work, they can buy hospital insurance. The premium was $54 a month through June 30, 1978. It increased to $63 a month for the 12-month period starting July 1, 1978.

To be sure your protection will start the month you reach 65, apply for Medicare insurance 3 months before reaching 65, even if you don't plan to retire.

## Do You Qualify for Voluntary Medical Insurance?

The voluntary medical insurance plan is a vital supplement to the hospital plan. It helps pay for doctors' and other medical services. Many people have not been able to obtain such insurance because they could not afford it or because of their medical histories.

One difference between the hospital insurance plan and the medical insurance plan is that you do not have to be under the social security or railroad retirement systems to enroll in the medical plan. Anyone who is 65 or older or who is eligible for hospital insurance can enroll in medical insurance.

People who get social security benefits or retirement benefits under the railroad retirement system and who live in one of the 50 States or the District of Columbia will be enrolled automatically for medical insurance—unless they say they don't want it—when they become entitled to hospital insurance. People who have medical insurance pay a monthly premium covering part of the cost of this protection. The other part is paid from general federal revenues. The basic premium for enrollees was $7.70 a month through June 30, 1978. It increased to $8.20 a month for the 12-month period starting July 1, 1978.

### Is Other Insurance Necessary?

As already indicated, Medicare provides only partial reimbursement. Therefore, you should know how much medical cost you can bear and perhaps arrange for other insurance.

For the first 60 days of inpatient hospital care in each benefit period, hospital insurance pays for all covered services except for the first $144. For the 61st through 90th day of a covered inpatient hospital stay, hospital insurance pays for all covered services except for $36 a day. People who need to be in a hospital for more than 90 days in a benefit period can use their 60 inpatient hospital reserve days. Hospital insurance pays for all covered services except for $72 a day for each reserve day used. Hospital insurance also does not pay the full cost of an inpatient stay in a skilled nursing facility.

Under medical insurance, the patient must meet an annual deductible of $60. After the patient has $60 in reasonable charges for covered services each year, medical insurance generally pays 80% of the reasonable charges for any additional covered services the patient receives during the rest of the year.

### How You Obtain Coverage

If you are receiving social security or railroad retirement monthly benefits, you will receive from the government information concerning Medicare about 3 months before you become entitled to hospital insurance.

If you are not receiving benefits or are not covered under social security, contact any social security office to find out how you can get Medicare. People who have permanent kidney failure also should contact a social security office to apply for Medicare.

## Unemployment Insurance

Unemployment insurance is managed jointly by the states and the federal government. Most states began paying benefits in 1938 and 1939.

### Under What Conditions Can the Worker Collect?

The laws vary from state to state. In general, a waiting period of one week is required after a claim is filed before collecting unemployment insurance; the worker must be able to work, must not have quit without good cause or have been discharged for misconduct; he must not be involved in a labor dispute; above all, he must be ready and willing to work. He may be disqualified if he refuses, without good cause, to accept a job which is suitable for him in terms of his qualifications and experience, unless the wages, hours and working conditions offered are substantially less favorable than those prevailing for similar jobs in the community.

The unemployed worker must go to the local state employment security office and register for work. If that office has a suitable opening available, he must accept it or lose his unemployment payments, unless he has good cause for the refusal. If a worker moves out of his own state, he can still collect at his new residence; the state in which he is now located will act as agent for the other state, which will pay his benefits.

Benefits are paid only to unemployed workers who have had at least a certain amount of recent past employment or earnings in a job covered by the state law. The amount of employment or earnings, and the period used to measure them, vary from state to state, but the intent of the various laws is to limit benefits to workers whose recent records indicate that they are members of the labor force. The amount of benefits an unemployed worker may receive for any week is also determined by application to his past wages of a formula specified in the law. The general objective is to provide a weekly benefit which is about half the worker's customary weekly wages, up to a maximum set by the law (see table). In a majority of states, the total benefits a worker may receive in a 12-month period is limited to a fraction of his total wages in a prior 12-month period, as well as to a stated number of weeks. Thus, not all workers in a state are entitled to benefits for the number of weeks shown in the table.

### Who Pays for the Insurance?

The total cost is borne by the employer in all but three states. Each state has a sliding scale of rates. The standard rate is set at 2.7% of taxable payroll in most states. But employers with records of less unemployment (that is, with fewer unemployment benefits paid to their former workers) are rewarded with rates lower than the standard 2.7%. The estimated average rate for employers in 1978 was 2.9% of taxable wages or 1.4% of total wages. As of Jan. 1, 1978, taxes are payable on the first $6,000 of a worker's pay, except that the limit for 1978 is $6,100 in N.M., $6,200 in N.J., $6,500 in Iowa, $6,600 in Ala., $6,900 in Nev., $7,500 in Minn., $8,000 in Ore., $8,400 in Wash., $9,600 in Idaho and Utah, $9,800 in Hawaii, and $10,000 in Alaska. For 1979, the limit will be $8,000 in Minn., $9,000 in Ore., and $10,300 in Utah. Employees as well as employers pay a tax in Alaska ranging from 0.3% to 0.8% in accordance with their employer's tax; in N.J., employees pay 0.5% for unemployment insurance. In Ala., employees pay contributions of 0.5% only when the fund is below a specified amount.

Employers pay an additional unemployment tax to the federal government—0.7% of the first $6,000 paid to each employee. This money is used for the federal and state costs of administering the employment security program, including both unemployment insurance and the employment service. Any amount over these costs, up to the greater of $550 million or 0.125% of total wages subject to contributions under the state unemployment compensation laws for the calendar year, is put in a special fund on which the states draw when the benefit payment funds are low. Any remaining excess is distributed to the states in proportion to their taxable payrolls. These excess funds may be used for benefit payments, or may be used for administrative expenses if so appropriated by the state legislature.

Requirements vary from state to state, but all states cover firms having at least one employee for 20 weeks or a quarterly payroll of $1,500 in the current or preceding calendar year. In some states, firms with one employee at any time are covered. Certain classes of workers are specifically excluded under some or all state laws—members of the employer's family, insurance agents on commission, student nurses, internes, casual labor, and the self-employed.

During periods of high unemployment on either a state or national level, federal-state extended benefits are available to workers who have exhausted their regular benefits. An unemployed worker may receive benefits equal to the weekly benefit he received under the state program for one half the weeks of his basic entitlement to benefits up to a maximum (including regular benefits) of 39 weeks.

## Federal Unemployment Insurance Programs

Amendments to the Social Security Act provided unemployment insurance for Federal civilian employees (1954) and for ex-servicemen (1958). Benefits under these programs are paid by state employment security agencies as agents of the federal government under agreements with the Secretary of Labor. Eligibility for benefits and the amount of benefits paid are determined according to the terms and conditions of the applicable state unemployment insurance law. Thus, federal civilian employees and ex-servicemen are subject to the same eligibility, disqualification, and benefit payment provisions as are claimants for benefits under the state unemployment insurance system.

## Railroad Workers

These are covered by the federal Railroad Retirement Act which provides retirement and survivor annuities and lump-sum death benefits for aged or disabled employees and their families. Railroad workers are also covered by the Railroad Unemployment Insurance Act, which provides unemployment and sickness benefits as well as a placement service. Both acts are administered by the U.S. Railroad Retirement Board. Those covered by the railroad retirement system also participate in the health insurance program (Medicare) provided by the Social Security Act.

## State Unemployment Compensation Maximums, Jan. 2, 1978

| State | Weekly benefit[1] | Maximum duration, weeks | State | Weekly benefit[1] | Maximum duration, weeks |
|---|---|---|---|---|---|
| Alabama | $90 | 26 | Montana | $104 | 26 |
| Alaska | 90–120 | 28 | Nebraska | 90 | 26 |
| Arizona | 85 | 26 | Nevada | 100 | 26 |
| Arkansas | 100 | 26 | New Hampshire | 102 | 26 |
| California | 104 | 26 | New Jersey | 110 | 26 |
| Colorado | 122 | 26 | New Mexico | 90 | 30 |
| Connecticut | 122–183 | 26 | New York | 115 | 26 |
| Delaware | 140 | 26 | North Carolina | 112 | 26 |
| D. C. | 160 | 34 | North Dakota | 115 | 26 |
| Florida | 82 | 26 | Ohio | 111–175 | 26 |
| Georgia | 90 | 26 | Oklahoma | 101 | 26 |
| Hawaii | 126 | 26 | Oregon | 112 | 26 |
| Idaho | 110 | 26 | Pennsylvania | 143–151 | 30 |
| Illinois | 116–138 | 26 | Puerto Rico | 64 | 20 |
| Indiana | 74–124 | 26 | Rhode Island | 106–126 | 26 |
| Iowa | 124 | 39 | South Carolina | 111 | 26 |
| Kansas | 109 | 26 | South Dakota | 96 | 26 |
| Kentucky | 94 | 26 | Tennessee | 95 | 26 |
| Louisiana | 130 | 28 | Texas | 84 | 26 |
| Maine | 86–129 | 26 | Utah | 128 | 36 |
| Maryland | 89 | 26 | Vermont | 102 | 26 |
| Massachusetts | 115–173 | 30 | Virginia | 110 | 26 |
| Michigan | 97–136 | 26 | Washington | 119 | 30 |
| Minnesota | 122 | 26 | West Virginia | 139 | 26 |
| Mississippi | 80 | 26 | Wisconsin | 135 | 34 |
| Missouri | 85 | 26 | Wyoming | 111 | 26 |

1. Maximum amounts. When two amounts are shown, higher includes dependents' allowances. *Source:* Department of Labor, Employment and Training Administration.

## Medicaid Services by State

**(as of December 1, 1977[1])**

Basic required Medicaid services: Every Medicaid program must cover at least these services for at least everyone receiving federally supported financial assistance: inpatient hospital care; outpatient hospital services; other laboratory and X-ray services; skilled nursing facility services and home health services for individuals 21 and older; early and periodic screening, diagnosis, and treatment for individuals under 21; family planning; and physician services. Federal financial participation is also available to states electing to expand their Medicaid programs by covering additional services and/or by including people eligible for medical but not for financial assistance. For the latter group, states may offer the services required for financial assistance recipients or may substitute a combination of seven services. Services provided only under the Medicare buy-in or the screening and treatment program for individuals under 21 are not shown on this chart. Definitions and limitations on eligibility and services vary from state to state. Details are available from local welfare offices and state Medicaid agencies.

NOTE: O = Offered for people receiving federally supported financial assistance. X = Offered also for people in public assistance[2] and SSI[3] categories who are financially eligible for medical but not for financial assistance.

| | | Additional services for which federal financial participation is available to states under Medicaid | | | | | | | | | | | | | | | | |
|---|---|---|---|---|---|---|---|---|---|---|---|---|---|---|---|---|---|---|
| States | Basic required Medicaid services | Clinic services | Prescribed drugs | Dental services | Prosthetic devices | Eyeglasses | Private-duty nursing | Physical therapy and related services | Other diagnostic, screening, preventive and rehabilitative services | Emergency hospital services | Skilled nursing facility services for patients under 21 | Optometrists' services | Podiatrists' services | Chiropractors' services | Care for patients 65 or older in institutions for mental diseases | Care for patients 65 or older in institutions for tuberculosis | Care for patients under 21 in psychiatric hospitals | Institutional services in intermediate care facilities |
| Alabama | 0 | — | 0 | — | 0 | 0 | — | — | — | 0 | 0 | 0 | — | — | — | 0 | 0 | 0[4] |
| Alaska | 0 | 0 | — | — | — | 0 | — | — | — | 0 | 0 | 0 | — | — | 0 | — | 0 | 0[4] |
| Arizona | | — | — | — | — | — | — | — | — | — | — | — | — | — | — | — | — | — |
| Arkansas | X | X | X | X | X | X | — | — | — | X | 0 | X | — | X | X | X | X | 0[4] |
| California | X | X | X | X | X | X | — | X | X | X | X | X | X | X | X | X | X | X[4] |
| Colorado | 0 | — | 0 | — | 0 | — | — | 0 | — | 0 | 0 | — | 0 | — | 0 | — | 0 | 0[4] |
| Connecticut | X | X | X | X | X | X | X | X | X | — | X | X | X | X | X | — | X | X[4] |
| Delaware | 0 | 0 | 0 | — | — | — | — | 0 | — | — | — | — | 0 | — | 0 | — | 0 | 0[4] |
| D.C. | X | X | X | — | X | X | — | X | X | X | X | X | X | — | X | X | X | X[4] |
| Florida | 0 | — | 0 | — | — | — | — | — | — | 0 | — | — | — | — | 0 | 0 | 0 | 0[4] |
| Georgia | 0 | 0 | 0 | — | 0 | — | — | — | — | — | 0 | — | 0 | — | 0 | 0 | — | 0[4] |
| Guam | X | X | X | X | X | X | — | X | — | X | X | X | — | — | — | — | — | — |
| Hawaii | X | X | X | X | X | X | — | X | X | X | X | X | — | — | — | — | — | X |
| Idaho | 0 | 0 | 0 | — | — | — | — | — | — | 0 | 0 | 0 | 0 | 0 | — | — | — | 0[4] |
| Illinois | X | X | X | X | X | X | X | X | X | X | X | X | X | X | X | X | X | X[4] |
| Indiana | 0 | 0 | 0 | 0 | 0 | 0 | 0 | 0 | 0 | 0 | 0 | 0 | 0 | 0 | 0 | — | 0 | 0[4] |
| Iowa | 0 | — | 0 | 0 | 0 | 0 | — | 0 | 0 | 0 | 0 | 0 | 0 | 0 | — | — | — | 0[4] |
| Kansas | X | X | X | X | X | X | X | X | — | X | X | X | X | X | X | X | X | X[4] |
| Kentucky | X | X | X | X | X | — | — | X | — | X | X | — | — | — | X | X | X | X[4] |
| Louisiana | X | X | X | — | X | — | — | — | — | X | 0 | — | — | X | 0 | 0 | 0 | 0[4] |
| Maine | X | 0 | X | — | X | — | — | X | X | 0 | X | — | X | X | X | — | X | 0[4] |
| Maryland | X | X | X | — | X | X | — | — | — | X | — | X | X | — | X | X | — | 0[4] |
| Massachusetts | X | X | X | X | X | X | X | X | X | X | X | X | X | — | X | X | — | X[4] |
| Michigan | X | X | X | X | X | X | — | X | — | X | X | X | X | X | X | — | X | X[4] |
| Minnesota | X | X | X | X | X | X | X | X | X | X | X | X | X | X | X | X | X | X[4] |
| Mississippi | 0 | — | 0 | 0 | — | — | — | — | — | — | 0 | — | — | — | 0 | 0 | — | 0[4] |
| Missouri | 0 | — | 0 | 0 | — | — | — | — | — | 0 | — | 0 | — | — | 0 | 0 | — | 0[4] |
| Montana | X | X | X | X | X | X | X | X | X | X | X | X | X | — | X | — | X | X[4] |
| Nebraska | X | X | X | X | X | X | X | X | — | X | X | X | X | X | X | X | — | X[4] |
| Nevada | 0 | 0 | 0 | 0 | 0 | 0 | 0 | 0 | — | 0 | 0 | 0 | 0 | 0 | — | — | — | 0 |
| New Hampshire | X | X | X | — | X | X | X | X | X | X | X | X | X | X | X | — | — | 0[4] |
| New Jersey | 0 | 0 | 0 | 0 | 0 | 0 | — | 0 | 0 | 0 | 0 | 0 | 0 | 0 | 0 | 0 | 0 | 0[4] |
| New Mexico | 0 | 0 | 0 | 0 | 0 | 0 | 0 | 0 | — | 0 | 0 | 0 | 0 | — | — | — | — | 0[4] |
| New York | X | X | X | X | X | X | — | X | X | X | X | X | — | — | X | X | X | X[4] |
| North Carolina | X | X | X | — | — | X | — | — | X | — | X | X | X | X | X | X | X | X[4] |
| North Dakota | X | — | X | X | X | X | X | X | X | X | X | X | X | X | X | — | X | X |
| Ohio | 0 | 0 | 0 | 0 | 0 | 0 | 0 | 0 | — | 0 | 0 | 0 | 0 | 0 | 0 | — | 0 | 0[4] |
| Oklahoma | X | — | X | X | X | — | — | — | — | — | — | — | X | — | X | — | X | X[4] |
| Oregon | 0 | 0 | 0 | 0 | 0 | 0 | 0 | — | 0 | 0 | 0 | 0 | 0 | 0 | 0 | — | 0 | 0[4] |
| Pennsylvania | X | X | 0 | 0 | 0 | — | — | — | — | X | X | X | 0 | X | X | — | X | X[4] |
| Puerto Rico | X | X | X | X | — | — | — | X | X | X | — | — | — | — | — | X | — | — |

| States | Basic required Medicaid services | Additional services for which federal financial participation is available to states under Medicaid: Clinic services | Prescribed drugs | Dental services | Prosthetic devices | Eyeglasses | Private duty nursing | Physical therapy and related services | Other diagnostic, screening, preventive and rehabilitative services | Emergency hospital services | Skilled nursing facility services for patients under 21 | Optometrists' services | Podiatrists' services | Chiropractors' services | Care for patients 65 or older in institutions for mental diseases | Care for patients 65 or older in institutions for tuberculosis | Care for patients under 21 in psychiatric hospitals | Institutional services in intermediate care facilities |
|---|---|---|---|---|---|---|---|---|---|---|---|---|---|---|---|---|---|---|
| Rhode Island | X | — | X | X | X | X | — | — | — | — | X | X | X | — | X | — | — | 0[4] |
| South Carolina | 0 | 0 | 0 | 0 | 0 | — | — | — | — | 0 | 0 | — | — | 0 | 0 | 0 | 0 | 0[4] |
| South Dakota | 0 | 0 | 0 | 0 | 0 | — | — | 0 | — | 0 | 0 | — | — | 0 | — | — | — | 0[4] |
| Tennessee | X | X | X | — | X | — | — | — | — | X | — | — | — | — | X | X | X | X[4] |
| Texas | 0 | — | 0 | — | 0 | 0 | — | — | — | 0 | — | 0 | 0 | 0 | — | 0 | — | 0[4] |
| Utah | X | X | X | X | X | X | X | X | — | X | X | X | X | X | X | — | X | X[4] |
| Vermont | X | X | X | — | X | — | — | — | — | X | X | — | X | — | X | — | X | X[4] |
| Virgin Islands | X | X | X | X | X | X | — | — | — | — | — | — | — | — | — | — | — | — |
| Virginia | X | X | X | — | — | X | — | X | — | X | X | X | X | — | X | X | — | X[4] |
| Washington | X | X | X | X | X | X | X | X | X | X | X | X | X | X | X | X | X | X[4] |
| West Virginia | X | X | X | — | X | X | X | X | — | — | X | X | X | X | X | X | — | X |
| Wisconsin | X | X | X | X | X | X | X | X | X | X | X | X | X | X | X | X | X | X[4] |
| Wyoming | 0 | — | — | — | — | — | — | — | — | — | 0 | 0 | — | — | — | — | — | 0 |

1. Data from Regional Office reports of characteristics of state programs and state plan amendments. 2. People qualifying as members of families with dependent children (usually families with at least one parent absent or incapacitated). 3. People qualifying as aged, blind, or disabled under the Supplemental Security Income program. 4. Including intermediate care facilities services in institutions for the mentally retarded. *Source:* Department of Health, Education, and Welfare, Health Care Financing Administration.

## Doctors-to-Be

Medical schools accepted a record 15,774 new students in the 1976-77 academic year, up from 15,365 the year before, acccording to figures supplied by the Association of American Medical Colleges. These students were picked from 42,155 applicants. The average number of applications sent out by each individual reached a record 8.8, about twice as many as each student filed in the mid-1960s. Total enrollment in 116 medical and basic science schools offering curricula leading to a medical degree reached 58,266 in 1976, an increase of more than 2,000 from the previous academic year. The number of minority students enrolled increased slightly, but continued to constitute 8.2% of total enrollment. About 46% of the would-be doctors had an "A" average for their pre-med college education.

## Doctor's Fees

From 1950 to 1977, the cost of physicians' services rose 273%, compared to 150% for all other items in the Consumer Products Index.

## Portraits and Designs of U.S. Paper Currency[1]

| Currency | Portrait | Design on back | Currency | Portrait | Design on back |
|---|---|---|---|---|---|
| $1 | Washington | ONE between obverse and reverse of Great Seal of U.S. | $50 | Grant | U.S. Capitol |
| | | | $100 | Franklin | Independence Hall |
| $2[2] | Jefferson | Monticello | $500 | McKinley | Ornate FIVE HUNDRED |
| $2[3] | Jefferson | "The Signing of the Declaration of Independence" | $1,000 | Cleveland | Ornate ONE THOUSAND |
| | | | $5,000 | Madison | Ornate FIVE THOUSAND |
| $5 | Lincoln | Lincoln Memorial | $10,000 | Chase | Ornate TEN THOUSAND |
| $10 | Hamilton | U.S. Treasury Building | $100,000[4] | Wilson | Ornate ONE HUNDRED THOUSAND |
| $20 | Jackson | White House | | | |

1. Denominations of $500 and higher were discontinued in 1969. 2. Discontinued in 1966. 3. New issue, April 13, 1976. 4. For use only in transactions between Federal Reserve System and Treasury Department.

# U.S. STATES & CITIES

## States and Territories

State flower, bird, etc., are official unless otherwise indicated; dates in parentheses are those of adoption. Largest cities include incorporated places only. Land areas for 1970 are revised figures. For secession and readmission dates of the former Confederate states, *see* Index. For lists of Governors and Senators, *see* Index. For additional state information, *see* the sections on "Business and the Economy," "Taxes," and "U.S. Statistics."

### ALABAMA

**Capital:** Montgomery
**Governor:** George C. Wallace, D (to Jan. 1979)
**Lieut. Governor:** Jere Beasley, D (to Jan. 1979)
**Secy. of State:** Agnes Baggett, D (to Jan. 1979)
**Controller:** George C. Dean, Jr
**Atty. General:** William J. Baxley, D (to Jan. 1979)
**Organized as territory:** March 3, 1817
**Entered Union & (rank):** Dec. 14, 1819 (22)
**Present constitution adopted:** 1901
**Motto:** *Audemus jura nostra defendere* (We dare defend our rights)
**State flower:** Camellia (1959)
**State bird:** Yellowhammer (1927)
**State song:** "Alabama" (1931)
**State tree:** Southern pine (longleaf) (1949)
**Nickname:** Yellowhammer State
**Origin of name:** May come from Choctaw meaning "thicket-clearers" or "vegetation-gatherers"
**1970 population & (rank):** 3,444,165 (21)
**1977 est. population & (rank):** 3,690,000 (21)
**1970 land area & (rank):** 50,708 sq mi. (131,334 sq km) (28)
**Geographic center:** In Chilton Co., 12 mi. SW of Clanton
**Number of counties:** 67
**Largest cities (1975 est.):** Birmingham (276,273); Mobile (196,441); Montgomery (153,343); Huntsville (136,419); Tuscaloosa (69,425)
**State forests:** 8 (14,248.58 ac.)
**State parks:** 39 (41,959.35 ac.)
**Gross receipts (1976–77):** $4,883,395,308
**Net receipts (1976–77):** $3,555,422,921
**Net disbursements (1976–77):** $3,501,105,161

Spanish explorers are believed to have arrived at Mobile Bay in 1519, and the territory was visited in 1540 by the explorer Hernando de Soto. The first permanent European settlement in Alabama was founded by the French at Fort Louis in 1702. The British gained control of the area in 1763 by the Treaty of Paris, but had to cede almost all the Alabama region to the U.S. after the American Revolution. The Confederacy was founded at Montgomery in February 1861 and, for a time, the city was the Confederate capital.

During the last part of the 19th century, the economy of the state slowly improved. At Tuskegee Institute, founded in 1881 by Booker T. Washington, Dr. George Washington Carver carried out his famous agricultural research.

In the 1950s and '60s, Alabama was the site of such landmark civil-rights actions as the bus boycott in Montgomery (1955–56) and the "Freedom March" from Selma to Birmingham (1965).

Today, Alabama is the leading heavy-industry state in the South. Textiles, iron, and steel lead its manufacturing, which centers around Birmingham, the "Pittsburgh of the South." Industry is growing rapidly in other areas, including the Tennessee River Valley, with its great Muscle Shoals power plant. Manufacturing also includes cement, feed, fertilizer, chemical, rubber, and aluminum products. The state ranks high in the output of poultry, cotton, cattle, hogs, corn, potatoes, peanuts, and fruit.

Points of interest include the George C. Marshall Space Flight Center at Huntsville, Russell Cave National Monument near Bridgeport, and the White House of the Confederacy in Montgomery.

### ALASKA

**Capital:** Juneau
**Governor:** Jay S. Hammond, R (to Dec. 1978)
**Lieut. Governor:** Lowell Thomas, Jr., R (to Dec. 1978)
**Commissioner of Administration:** R. R. Allen
**Atty. General:** Avrum M. Gross (apptd. by Governor)
**Organized as territory:** 1912
**Entered Union & (rank):** Jan. 3, 1959 (49)
**Constitution ratified:** April 24, 1956
**Motto:** North to the Future
**State flower:** Forget-me-not
**State tree:** Sitka spruce
**State bird:** Willow ptarmigan
**State fish:** King salmon
**State song:** "Alaska's Flag"
**Nickname:** The state is commonly called "The Last Frontier" or "Land of the Midnight Sun"
**Origin of name:** Corruption of Aleut word meaning "great land" or "that which the sea breaks against"
**1970 population & (rank):** 302,173 (50)
**1977 est. population & (rank):** 407,000 (49)
**1970 land area & (rank):** 566,432 sq mi. (1,467,059 sq km) (1)
**Geographic center:** 60 mi. NW of Mt. McKinley
**Number of boroughs:** 12
**Largest cities (1975 est.):** Anchorage, city and borough (161,018); Fairbanks (29,920); Juneau, city and borough (16,749); Ketchikan (7,527); Sitka, city and borough (6,073)
**State forests:** None
**State parks:** 4; 59 waysides and areas (1.5 million ac.)
**General funds (1976–77):** $865,200,000
**General Expenditure (1976–77):** $728,100,000

Vitus Bering, a Dane working for the Russians, and Alexei Chirikov discovered the Alaskan mainland and the Aleutian Islands in 1741. The tremendous land mass of Alaska—equal to one fifth of the continental U.S.—was unexplored in 1867 when

Secretary of State William Seward arranged for its purchase from the Russians for $7,200,000. The transfer of the territory took place on Oct. 18, 1867. Despite a price of about two cents an acre, the purchase was widely ridiculed as "Seward's Folly." The first official census (1880) reported a total of 33,426 Alaskans, all but 430 being of aboriginal stock. The Gold Rush of 1898 resulted in a mass influx of more than 30,000 people. Since then, Alaska has returned billions of dollars' worth of products to the U.S.

In 1968, a large oil and gas reservoir near Prudhoe Bay on the Arctic Coast was found. The Prudhoe Bay reservoir, with an estimated recoverable 10 billion barrels of oil and 27 trillion cubic feet of gas, is twice as large as any other oil field in North America. The Trans-Alaska pipeline was completed in 1977 at a cost of $7.7 billion. On June 20, oil started flowing through the 800-mile-long pipeline from Prudhoe Bay to the port of Valdez.

Other industries important to Alaska's economy are fisheries, wood and wood products, and furs.

Mount McKinley National Park and Mendenhall Glacier in North Tongass National Forest are of interest, as is the large totem pole collection at Sitka National Historical Park. The Katmai National Monument includes the "Valley of Ten Thousand Smokes," an area of active volcanoes.

## ARIZONA

**Capital:** Phoenix
**Governor:** Bruce Babbitt, D (to Jan. 1979)
**Secy. of State:** Rose Mofford, D (to Jan. 1979)
**Atty. General:** Jack LaSota, R (to Jan. 1979)
**State Treasurer:** Bartlett S. Fleming, R (to Jan. 1979)
**Organized as territory:** Feb. 24, 1863
**Entered Union & (rank):** Feb. 14, 1912 (48)
**Present constitution adopted:** 1911
**Motto:** *Ditat Deus* (God enriches)
**State flower:** Flower of saguaro cactus (1931)
**State bird:** Cactus wren (1931)
**State colors:** Blue and old gold (1915)
**State song:** "Arizona," a march song (1919)
**State tree:** Paloverde (1957)
**Nickname:** Grand Canyon State
**Origin of name:** From the Indian "Arizonac," meaning "little spring"
**1970 population & (rank):** 1,772,482 (33)
**1977 est. population & (rank):** 2,296,000 (32)
**1970 land area & (rank):** 113,417 sq mi. (293,750 sq km) (6)
**Geographic center:** In Yavapai Co., 55 mi. ESE of Prescott
**Number of counties:** 14
**Largest cities (1975 est.):** Phoenix (664,721); Tucson (296,457); Mesa (99,043); Tempe (84,072); Scottsdale (77,529); Glendale (65,671); Flagstaff (31,127)
**State forests:** None
**State parks:** 10
**State revenue (1976):** $2,591,200,000
**State expenditure (1976):** $2,610,600,000

Marcos de Niza, a Spanish Franciscan friar, was the first European to explore Arizona. He entered the area in 1539 in search of the mythical Seven Cities of Gold. Although he was followed a year later by another gold seeker, Francisco Vásquez de Coronado, most of the early settlement was for missionary purposes. In 1776 the Spanish established Fort Tucson. In 1848, after the Mexican War, most of the Arizona territory became part of the U.S., and the southern portion of the territory was added by the Gadsden Purchase in 1853.

In 1973 the world's biggest dam, the New Cornelia Tailings, was completed near Ajo.

Arizona history is rich in legends of America's Old West. It was here that the great Indian chiefs Geronimo and Cochise led their people against the frontiersmen. Tombstone, Ariz., was the site of the West's most famous shoot-out—the gunfight at the O.K. Corral. Today, Arizona has the largest U.S. Indian population; more than 14 tribes are represented on 19 reservations.

Manufacturing has become Arizona's most important industry. Principal products include electrical, communications, and aeronautical items. The state produces over half the country's copper. Agriculture is also important to the state's economy.

State attractions include such famous scenery as the Grand Canyon, the Petrified Forest, and the Painted Desert. Hoover Dam, Lake Mead, Fort Apache, and the reconstructed London Bridge at Lake Havasu City are of particular interest.

## ARKANSAS

**Capital:** Little Rock
**Governor:** David Pryor, D (to Jan. 1979)
**Lieut. Governor:** Joe Purcell, D (to Jan. 1979)
**Secy. of State:** Winston Bryant, D (to Jan. 1979)
**Atty. General:** Bill Clinton (to Jan. 1979)
**Auditor of State:** Jimmie "Red" Jones (to Jan. 1979)
**Treasurer of State:** Mrs. Nancy Hall, D (to Jan. 1979)
**Land Commissioner:** Sam Jones, D (to Jan. 1979)
**Organized as territory:** March 2, 1819
**Entered Union & (rank):** June 15, 1836 (25)
**Present constitution adopted:** 1874
**Motto:** *Regnat populus* (The people rule)
**State flower:** Apple Blossom (1901)
**State tree:** Pine (1939)
**State bird:** Mockingbird (1929)
**State insect:** Honeybee
**State song:** "Arkansas" (1963)
**Nickname:** Land of Opportunity
**Origin of name:** From the Quapaw Indians
**1970 population & (rank):** 1,923,295 (32)
**1977 est. population & (rank):** 2,144,000 (33)
**1970 land area & (rank):** 51,945 sq mi. (134,538 sq km) (27)
**Geographic center:** In Pulaski Co., 12 mi. NW of Little Rock
**Number of counties:** 75
**Largest cities (1975 est.):** Little Rock (141,143); Fort Smith (64,734); North Little Rock (61,768); Pine Bluff (54,631); Hot Springs (38,207)
**State forests:** None
**State parks:** 36
**State tax receipts (1977):** $843,309,412
**Taxes from all sources (1977):** $1,513,370,649
**State general expenditure (1977):** $1,485,672,791

Hernando de Soto, in 1541, was among the early European explorers to visit the territory. It was a Frenchman, Henri de Tonty, who in 1686 founded the first permanent white settlement—the Arkansas Post. In 1803 the area was acquired by the U.S. as part of the Louisiana Purchase.

Food products are the state's largest employing sector, with lumber and wood products a close second. Arkansas is also a leader in the production of cotton, rice, and soybeans. The state produces 97% of the nation's high-grade domestic bauxite ore—the source of aluminum. It also has the country's only active diamond mine; located near Murfreesboro, it is operated as a tourist attraction.

Hot Springs National Park is a major state attraction. Its 47 curative springs flow at an average temperature of 147°F year round. Blanchard Springs Caverns, the Arkansas Territorial Capitol Restoration at Little Rock, and Dogpatch U.S.A. near Harrison are of interest. There are two large national forests in Arkansas—the Ouachita and the Ozark—and one of the nation's smallest—the St. Francis.

## CALIFORNIA

**Capital:** Sacramento
**Governor:** Edmund G. Brown, Jr., D (to Jan. 1979)
**Lieut. Governor:** Mervin M. Dymally, D (to Jan. 1979)
**Secy. of State:** March Fong Eu, D (to Jan. 1979)
**Controller:** Ken Cory, D (to Jan. 1979)
**Atty. General:** Evelle J. Younger, R (to Jan. 1979)
**Treasurer:** Jesse M. Unruh (to Jan. 1979)
**Entered Union & (rank):** Sept. 9, 1850 (31)
**Present constitution adopted:** 1879
**Motto:** *Eureka* (I have found it)
**State flower:** Golden poppy (1903)
**State tree:** California redwoods *(Sequoia sempervirens & Sequoia gigantea)* (1937 & 1953)
**State bird:** California valley quail (1931)
**State animal:** California grizzly bear (1953)
**State fish:** California golden trout (1947)
**State insect:** California dog-face butterfly (unofficial)
**State colors:** Blue and gold (1951)
**State song:** "I Love You, California" (1951)
**Nickname:** Golden State
**Origin of name:** From a book, *Las Sergas de Esplandián,* by García Ordóñez de Montalvo, c. 1500
**1970 population & (rank):** 19,953,134 (1)
**1977 est. population & (rank):** 21,896,000 (1)
**1970 land area & (rank):** 156,361 sq mi. (404,975 sq km) (3)
**Geographic center:** In Madera Co., 35 mi. NE of Madera
**Number of counties:** 58
**Largest cities (1975 est.):** Los Angeles (2,727,399); San Diego (773,996); San Francisco (664,520); San Jose (555,707); Long Beach (335,602)
**State forests:** 8 (70,283 ac.)
**State parks and beaches:** 180 (723,000 ac.)
**State general revenue (1976–77):** $13,260,024,889
**State general expenditure (1976–77):** $12,519,984,699

Although California was sighted by Spanish navigator Juan Rodríguez Cabrillo in 1542, its first Spanish mission (at San Diego) was not established until 1769. California became a U.S. Territory in 1847 when Mexico surrendered it to John C. Frémont. On Jan. 24, 1848, James W. Marshall discovered gold at Sutter's Mill, starting the California Gold Rush and bringing settlers to the state in large numbers.

In 1964, the U.S. Census Bureau estimated that California had become the most populous state, surpassing New York. California also leads the country in personal income and consumer expenditures.

Leading industries include manufacturing (transportation equipment, machinery, and electronic equipment), agriculture, and fishing. Principal natural resources include petroleum, cement, and natural gas.

The Bank of America National Trust and Savings Association, founded by the Giannini family, ranks first or second in the world.

Death Valley, in the southeast, is 282 feet below sea level, the lowest point in the nation; and Mt. Whitney (14,495 ft) is the highest point in the contiguous 48 states. Lassen Peak is the only active U.S. volcano outside of Alaska and Hawaii; its last eruptions were recorded in 1917. The General Sherman Tree in Sequoia National Park is estimated to be about 3,500 years old and a stand of bristlecone pine trees in the White Mountains may be over 4,000 years old.

Other points of interest include Yosemite National Park, Disneyland, Hollywood, the Golden Gate bridge, San Simeon State Park, and Point Reyes National Seashore.

## COLORADO

**Capital:** Denver
**Governor:** Richard D. Lamm, D (to Jan. 1979)
**Lieut. Governor:** George Brown, D (to Jan. 1979)
**Secy. of State:** Mary Estill Buchanan, R (to Jan. 1979)
**Treasurer:** Roy Romer
**Controller:** Dan S. Whittemore
**Atty. General:** J. D. MacFarlane (to Jan. 1979)
**Organized as territory:** Feb. 28, 1861
**Entered Union & (rank):** Aug. 1, 1876 (38)
**Present constitution adopted:** 1876
**Motto:** *Nil sine Numine* (Nothing without Providence)
**State flower:** Rocky Mountain columbine (1899)
**State tree:** Colorado blue spruce (1939)
**State bird:** Lark bunting (1931)
**State animal:** Rocky Mountain bighorn sheep
**State colors:** Blue and white (1911)
**State gemstone:** Aquamarine (1971)
**State song:** "Where the Columbines Grow" (1915)
**Nickname:** Centennial State
**Origin of name:** From the Spanish, meaning "ruddy" or "red"
**1970 population & (rank):** 2,207,259 (30)
**1977 est. population & (rank):** 2,619,000 (28)
**1970 land area & (rank):** 103,766 sq mi. (268,754 sq km) (8)
**Geographic center:** In Park Co., 30 mi. NW of Pikes Peak
**Number of counties:** 63
**Largest cities (1975 est.):** Denver (484,531); Colorado Springs (179,584); Lakewood (120,350); Aurora (118,060), Pueblo (105,312); Boulder (78,560)
**State forests:** 1 (71,000 ac.)
**Total state revenue (1976–77):** $2,135,758,000
**Total state expenditure (1976–77):** $2,063,378,000

First visited by Spanish explorers in the 1500s, the territory was claimed for Spain by Juan de Ulibarri in 1706. The U.S. obtained eastern Colorado as part of the Louisiana Purchase in 1803, the central portion in 1845 with the admission of Texas as a state, and the western part in 1848 as a result of the Mexican War.

Colorado has the highest mean elevation of any state, with more than 1,000 Rocky Mountain peaks over 10,000 feet high and 54 towering above 14,000 feet. Pikes Peak, the most famous of these mountains, was found by U.S. Army Lieut. Zebulon M. Pike in 1806.

Gold was first discovered near present-day Denver in 1858 and at Cripple Creek in 1891. Rich silver deposits were also found in 1875.

Once primarily a mining and agricultural state, today Colorado draws the largest segment of its income from manufacturing. Denver is a leader in electronics and space-age industry. Pueblo, the "Pittsburgh of the West," makes iron, steel, brick, tile, and foundry products.

Rich in natural resources, Colorado now produces most of the world's molybdenum. Uranium, vanadium, gold, silver, lead, tin, zinc, and other minerals are also mined. Colorado's highly developed irrigation system promotes farming of wheat, hay, beans, sugar beets, corn, potatoes, barley, and truck vegetables. Cattle and sheep raising is also important.

Tourism has developed into a major industry largely because of Colorado's magnificent scenery. Among the major attractions are Rocky Mountain National Park, Garden of the Gods, Great Sand Dunes and Dinosaur National Monuments, Pikes Peak and Mt. Evans Highways, and Mesa Verde National Park (prehistoric cliff dwellings).

Colorado Springs, with the nearby U.S. Air Force Academy, is probably the most popular tourist center in the Rocky Mountains, while Aspen and Vail have become leading ski resorts.

## CONNECTICUT

**Capital:** Hartford
**Governor:** Ella T. Grasso, D (to Jan. 1979)
**Lieut. Governor:** Robert K. Killian, D (to Jan. 1979)
**Secy. of State:** Gloria Schaffer, D (to Jan. 1979)
**Comptroller:** J. Edward Caldwell, D (to Jan. 1979)
**Treasurer:** Henry E. Parker, D (to Jan. 1979)
**Atty. General:** Carl R. Ajello, D (to Jan. 1979)
**Entered Union & (rank):** Jan. 9, 1788 (5)
**Present constitution adopted:** Dec. 30, 1965
**Motto:** *Qui transtulit sustinet* (He who transplanted still sustains)
**State flower:** Mountain laurel (1907)
**State tree:** White Oak (1947)
**State animal:** Sperm whale (1975)
**State bird:** American robin (1943)
**State insect:** Praying mantis (1977)
**State mineral:** Garnet (1977)
**State song:** "Yankee Doodle" (1978)
**Official designation:** *Constitution State* (1959)
**Nickname:** Nutmeg State
**Origin of name:** From an Indian word (Quinnehtukqut) meaning "beside the long tidal river"
**1970 population & (rank):** 3,032,217 (24)
**1977 est. population & (rank):** 3,108,000 (24)
**1970 land area & (rank):** 4,862 sq mi. (12,593 sq km) (48)
**Geographic center:** In Hartford Co., at East Berlin
**Number of counties:** 8
**Largest cities (1975 est.):** Bridgeport (142,960); Hartford (138,152); New Haven (126,845); Waterbury (107,065); Stamford (105,151); New Britain (78,556)
**State forests:** 30 (134,461 ac.)
**State parks:** 88 (30,316 ac.)
**State and local general revenue (1976–77):** $3,296,000,000
**State and local general expenditure (1976–77):** $3,226,000,000

The Dutch navigator, Adriaen Block, was the first European of record to explore the area, sailing up the Connecticut River in 1614. In 1633, Dutch colonists built a fort and trading post near present-day Hartford, but soon lost control to English Puritans migrating south from the Massachusetts Bay Colony.

English settlements, established in the 1630s at Windsor, Wethersfield, and Hartford, united in 1639 to form the Connecticut Colony and adopted the *Fundamental Orders,* considered the world's first written constitution.

The colony's royal charter of 1682 was exceptionally liberal. When Gov. Edmund Andros tried to seize it in 1687, it was hidden in the Hartford Oak, commemorated in Charter Oak Place.

Connecticut played a prominent role in the Revolutionary War, serving as the Continental Army's major supplier. Sometimes called the "Arsenal of the Nation," the state became one of the most industrialized in the nation. Its early business and industrial pioneers included Eli Whitney, Samuel Colt, and Charles Goodyear.

Today, Connecticut factories produce weapons, sewing machines, jet engines, helicopters, motors, hardware and tools, cutlery, clocks, locks, ball bearings, silverware, and submarines. Hartford, which has the oldest U.S. newspaper still being published —the *Courant,* established 1764— is the insurance capital of the nation.

Poultry, fruit, and dairy products account for the largest portion of farm income, and Connecticut shade-grown tobacco is acknowledged to be the nation's most valuable crop, per acre.

Connecticut is a popular resort area with its 250-mile Long Island Sound shoreline and many inland lakes. Among the major points of interest are the American Shakespeare Theatre in Stratford, Yale University's Gallery of Fine Arts and Peabody Museum. Other famous museums include the P.T. Barnum, Winchester Gun, and American Clock and Watch. The town of Mystic features a recreated 19th-century New England seaport and the Mystic Marinelife Aquarium.

## DELAWARE

**Capital:** Dover
**Governor:** Pierre S. du Pont IV, R (to Jan. 1981)
**Lieut. Governor:** James D. McGinnis, D (to Jan. 1981)
**Secy. of State:** Glenn C. Kenton, R (Pleasure of Governor)
**State Treasurer:** Thomas R. Carper, D (to Jan. 1979)
**Atty. General:** Richard R. Wier, Jr., D (to Jan. 1979)
**Entered Union & (rank):** Dec. 7, 1787 (1)
**Present constitution adopted:** 1897
**Motto:** Liberty and independence
**State colors:** Colonial blue and buff
**State flower:** Peach blossom
**State tree:** American holly
**State bird:** Blue Hen chicken
**State insect:** Ladybug
**State song:** "Our Delaware"
**Nicknames:** Diamond State; First State
**Origin of name:** From Delaware River and Bay; named in turn for Sir Thomas West, Lord De La Warr
**1970 population & (rank):** 548,104 (46)
**1977 est. population & (rank):** 582,000 (47)
**1970 land area & (rank):** 1,982 sq mi. (5,133 sq km) (49)
**Geographic center:** In Kent Co., 11 mi. S of Dover
**Number of counties:** 3
**Largest cities (1975 est.):** Wilmington (76,152); Newark (26,645); Dover (22,480); Elsmere (8,809); Seaford (5,587); Milford (5,411)
**State forests:** 2 (6,200 ac.)
**State parks:** 9
**State receipts (1977):** $442,616,365
**State disbursements (1977):** $454,052,761

Henry Hudson, sailing under the Dutch flag, is credited with Delaware's discovery in 1609. The following year, Capt. Samuel Argall of Virginia named Delaware for his colony's governor, Thomas West, Baron De La Warr. An attempted Dutch settlement failed in 1631. Swedish colonization began at Fort Christina (now Wilmington) in 1638, but New Sweden fell to Dutch forces led by New Netherlands' Gov. Peter Stuyvesant in 1655.

England took over the area in 1664 and it was transferred to William Penn as the southern Three Counties in 1682. Semiautonomous after 1704, Delaware fought as a separate state in the American Revolution and became the first state to ratify the constitution in 1787.

During the Civil War, although a slave state, Delaware did not secede from the Union.

In 1802, Éleuthère Irénée du Pont established a gunpowder mill near Wilmington that laid the foundation for Delaware's huge chemical industry. Delaware's manufactured products now also include vulcanized fiber, glazed kid and morocco leathers, textiles, paper, dental supplies, metal products, machinery, machine tools, and automobiles.

Delaware also grows a great variety of fruits and vegetables and is a U.S. pioneer in the food-canning industry. Corn, soybeans, potatoes, and hay are important crops. Delaware's broiler chicken farms supply the big Eastern markets, and fishing is another major industry.

Points of interest include the Fort Christina Monument, Hagley Museum, Holy Trinity Church (erected in 1698, the oldest Protestant church in the United States still in use), and Winterthur Museum, in and near Wilmington; central New Castle, an almost unchanged late 18th-century capital; and the Delaware Museum of Natural History.

Popular recreation areas include Cape Henlopen, Delaware Seashore, Trapp Pond State Park, and Rehoboth Beach.

## DISTRICT OF COLUMBIA

See listing at end of *50 Largest Cities of the United States.*

## FLORIDA

**Capital:** Tallahassee
**Governor:** Reubin Askew, D (to Jan. 1979)
**Lieut. Governor:** J. H. Williams, D (to Jan. 1979)
**Secy. of State:** Jesse J. McCrary, Jr., D (to Jan. 1979)
**Comptroller:** Gerald Lewis (to Jan. 1979)
**Commissioner of Agriculture:** Doyle Conner
**Atty. General:** Robert L. Shevin (to Jan. 1979)
**Organized as territory:** March 30, 1822
**Entered Union & (rank):** March 3, 1845 (27)
**Present constitution adopted:** 1969
**Motto:** In God we trust (1868)
**State flower:** Orange blossom (1909)
**State bird:** Mockingbird (1927)
**State song:** "Suwannee River" (1935)
**Nickname:** Sunshine State (1970)
**Origin of name:** From the Spanish, meaning "feast of flowers" (Easter)
**1970 population & (rank):** 6,789,443 (9)
**1977 est. population & (rank):** 8,452,000 (8)
**1970 land area & (rank):** 54,090 sq mi. (140,093 sq km) (26)
**Geographic center:** In Hernando Co., 12 mi. NNW of Brooksville
**Number of counties:** 67
**Largest cities (1975 est.):** Jacksonville (535,030); Miami (365,082); Tampa (280,340); St. Petersburg (234,389); Fort Lauderdale (152,959); Hollywood (119,002)
**State forests:** 4 (306,881 ac.)
**State parks:** 68 (187,763 ac.)
**State tax receipts (1976–77):** $3,587,643,747
**Other state revenue (1976–77):** $6,704,318,938
**State expenditures (1976–77):** $10,192,163,407

In 1513, Ponce de Leon, seeking the mythical "Fountain of Youth," named Florida and claimed it for Spain. Later, Florida would be held at different times by Spain, France, and England until Spain finally sold it to the United States in 1819.

Florida's early 19th-century history as a U.S. territory was scarred by savage wars with the Seminole Indians that did not end until 1842.

One of the nation's fastest-growing states, Florida's population has gone from 2.8 million in 1950 to more than 9 million today.

Florida's economy rests on a solid base of tourism, manufacturing, and agriculture. The state entertained more than 27 million visitors, who spent about $9 billion, in 1975.

Oranges and grapefruit lead Florida's crop list, followed by sugarcane, tomatoes, beans, celery, potatoes, field corn, honey, watermelons, limes, and mangoes. Forestry, truck gardening, commercial fishing, and cattle raising are leading industries. Deep-sea fishing for sport is a leading tourist industry.

Florida is expanding in all industrial areas with the greatest development taking place in the research-oriented Space Age manufacturing. The state produces 80% of the nation's phosphate.

Major tourist attractions are Miami Beach, Palm Beach, St. Augustine (founded in 1565 and the oldest city in the U.S.), Daytona Beach, and Fort Lauderdale)—all on the East Coast. West Coast resorts include Sarasota, Tampa, Key West, and St. Petersburg. Disney World, located on a 27,000-acre site near Orlando, is the state's newest attraction.

The John F. Kennedy Space Center at Cape Canaveral, and Everglades National Park, a 5,000-square-mile preserve, also draw many visitors.

## GEORGIA

**Capital:** Atlanta
**Governor:** George Busbee, D (to Jan. 1979)
**Lieut. Governor:** Zell Miller, D (to Jan. 1979)
**Secy. of State:** Ben Forston, D (to Jan. 1979)
**Comptroller General:** Johnnie Caldwell, D (to Jan. 1979)
**Atty. General:** Arthur K. Bolton, D (to Jan. 1979)
**Entered Union & (rank):** Jan. 2, 1788 (4)
**Present constitution adopted:** 1977
**Motto:** Wisdom, justice, and moderation
**State flower:** Cherokee rose (1916)
**State tree:** Live oak (1937)
**State bird:** Brown thrasher (1935)
**State song:** "Georgia" (1922)
**Nicknames:** Peach State, Empire State of the South
**Origin of name:** In honor of George II of England
**1970 population & (rank):** 4,589,575 (15)
**1977 est. population & (rank):** 5,048,000 (14)
**1970 land area & (rank):** 58,073 sq mi. (150,409 sq km) (21)
**Geographic center:** In Twiggs Co., 18 mi. SE of Macon
**Number of counties:** 159
**Largest cities (1975 est.):** Atlanta (436,057); Columbus (159,352); Macon (121,157); Savannah (110,348); Albany (73,373); Augusta (54,019)
**State forests:** 25,258,000 ac. (67% of total state area)
**State parks:** 53 (42,600 ac.)
**State revenue receipts (1977):** $1,890,095,530
**State revenue distribution (1977):** $1,890,095,530

Hernando de Soto, the Spanish explorer, first traveled parts of Georgia in 1540. British claims later conflicted with those of Spain. After obtaining a royal charter, Gen. James Oglethorpe established the first permanent settlement in Georgia in 1733 as a refuge for English debtors. In 1742, Oglethorpe defeated Spanish invaders in the Battle of Bloody Marsh.

A Confederate stronghold, Georgia was the scene of extensive military action during the Civil War. Union General William T. Sherman burned

Atlanta and destroyed a 60-mile wide path to the coast where he captured Savannah in 1864.

The largest state east of the Mississippi, Georgia is typical of the changing South with an ever-increasing industrial development. Atlanta, largest city in the state, is the communications and transportation center for the Southeast and the area's chief distributor of goods.

Georgia leads the nation in the production of paper and board, tufted textile products, and processed chicken. Other major manufactured products are transportation equipment, food products, apparel, and chemicals.

Important agricultural products are corn, cotton, tobacco, soybeans, eggs, and peaches. Georgia produces twice as many peanuts as the next leading state. From its vast stands of pine come more than half the world's resins and turpentine and 74.4% of the U.S. supply. Georgia is also a leader in the production of marble, kaolin, barite, and bauxite.

Principal tourist attractions in Georgia include the Okefenokee National Wildlife Refuge, Andersonville Prison Park and National Cemetery, Chickamauga and Chattanooga National Military Park, the Little White House at Warm Springs where Pres. Franklin D. Roosevelt died in 1945, Sea Island, the enormous Confederate Memorial at Stone Mountain, Kennesaw Mountain National Battlefield Park, and Cumberland Island National Seashore.

## HAWAII

**Capital:** Honolulu (on Oahu)
**Governor:** George R. Ariyoshi, D (to Dec. 1978)
**Lieut. Governor:** Nelson K. Doi, D (to Dec. 1978)
**Comptroller:** Hideo Murakami, D (to Dec. 1978)
**Atty. General:** Ronald Y. Amemiya, D (to Dec. 1978)
**Organized as territory:** 1900
**Entered Union & (rank):** Aug. 21, 1959 (50)
**Motto:** *Ua Mau Ke Ea O Ka Aina I Ka Pono* (The life of the land is perpetuated in righteousness)
**State flower:** Hibiscus
**State song:** "Hawaii Ponoi"
**State bird:** Nene (Hawaiian goose)
**Nickname:** Aloha State
**Origin of name:** Uncertain. The islands may have been named by Hawaii Loa, their traditional discoverer. Or they may have been named after Hawaii or Hawaiki, the traditional home of the Polynesians.
**1970 population & (rank):** 769,913 (40)
**1977 est. population & (rank):** 895,000 (40)
**1970 land area & (rank):** 6,425 sq mi. (16,641 sq km) (47)
**Geographic center:** In Hawaii Co., off Maui Island
**Number of counties:** 4
**Largest cities (1975 est.):** Honolulu (705,381); **(1970):** Hilo (26,353)[1]
**State parks and historic sites:** 47
**Total state government revenues (1977):** $1,290,133,895
**Total state government expenditures (1977):** $1,315,069,143

First settled by Polynesians sailing from other Pacific islands in the 6th century, Hawaii was visited in 1778 by British Captain James Cook who called the group the Sandwich Islands.

Hawaii was a native kingdom throughout most of the 19th century when the expansion of vital sugar and pineapple industries meant increasing U.S. business and political involvement. In 1893, Queen Liliuokalani was deposed and a year later the Republic of Hawaii was established with Sanford B. Dole as president. Then, following its annexation in 1898, Hawaii became a U.S. Territory in 1900.

The Japanese attack on the naval base at Pearl Harbor on Dec. 7, 1941, was directly responsible for U.S. entry into World War II.

Hawaii, 2,100 miles west-southwest of San Francisco, is a 1,600-mile chain of islets and eight main islands—Hawaii, Kahoolawe, Maui, Lanai, Molokai, Oahu, Kauai, and Niihau. Kure (Ocean) Island, an uninhabited islet in the Leeward Islands, is administratively part of Hawaii.

The temperature is mild and Hawaii's soil is fertile for tropical fruits and vegetables. Cane sugar and pineapple are the chief products, approximately 35% of the world's canned pineapple being produced in the islands. Hawaii also grows coffee, rice, bananas, nuts, and potatoes. The tourist business is one of Hawaii's largest sources of income.

Hawaii's highest peak is Mauna Kea (13,796 ft.). Mauna Loa (13,680 ft.) is the largest volcanic mountain in the world in cubic content.

Among the major points of interest are Hawaii Volcanoes National Park (Hawaii), Haleakala National Park (Maui), City of Refuge National Historical Park (Hawaii), Polynesian Cultural Center (Oahu), the U.S.S. *Arizona* Memorial at Pearl Harbor, and Iolani Palace (the only royal palace in the U.S.), Bishop Museum, and Waikiki Beach (all in Honolulu).

1. Honolulu and Hilo have legally established limits and are therefore treated as incorporated places. All other places are unincorporated.

## IDAHO

**Capital:** Boise
**Governor:** John V. Evans, D (to Jan. 1979)
**Lieut. Governor:** William J. Murphy (to Jan. 1979)
**Secy. of State:** Pete T. Cenarrusa, R (to Jan. 1979)
**State Auditor:** Joe R. Williams, D (to Jan. 1979)
**Atty. General:** Wayne Kidwell, R (to Jan. 1979)
**Organized as territory:** March 3, 1863
**Entered Union & (rank):** July 3, 1890 (43)
**Present constitution adopted:** 1890
**Motto:** *Esto perpetua* (May you last forever)
**State flower:** Syringa (1931)
**State tree:** White pine (1935)
**State bird:** Mountain bluebird (1931)
**State horse:** Appaloosa (1975)
**State gem:** Star garnet (1967)
**State song:** "Here We Have Idaho"
**Nicknames:** Gem State; Spud State; Panhandle State
**Origin of name:** Means "Gem of the Mountains"
**1970 population & (rank):** 713,008 (42)
**1977 est. population & (rank):** 857,000 (41)
**1970 land area & (rank):** 82,677 sq mi. (214,133 sq km) (11)
**Geographic center:** In Custer Co., at Custer, SW of Challis
**Number of counties:** 44, plus small part of Yellowstone National Park
**Largest cities (1975 est.):** Boise (99,771); Pocatello (40,980); Idaho Falls (37,042); Lewiston (26,547); Nampa (23,940); Twin Falls (23,709)
**State forests:** 981,200 ac.
**State parks:** 18 (21,838 ac.)
**State revenue (1976–77):** $285,033,573
**State expenditure (1976–77):** $118,533,902

After its acquisition by the U.S. as part of the Louisiana Purchase in 1803, the region was explored by Meriwether Lewis and William Clark in 1805–06. Northwest boundary disputes with Great Britain were settled by the Oregon Treaty in 1846 and the first permanent U.S. settlement in Idaho was established by the Mormons at Franklin in 1860.

After gold was discovered on Orofino Creek in 1860, prospectors swarmed into the territory, but left little more than a number of ghost towns.

In the 1870s, growing white occupation of Indian lands led to a series of battles between U.S. forces and the Nez Percé, Bannock, and Sheepeater tribes.

Mining, lumbering, and irrigation farming have been important for years. Idaho produces more than one third of all the silver mined in the U.S. It also ranks high among the states in antimony, lead, cobalt, garnet, phosphate rock, vanadium, zinc, and mercury.

Idaho's most impressive growth began when World War II military needs made processing agricultural products a big industry, particularly the dehydrating and freezing of potatoes. The state produces about one fourth of the nation's potato crop, as well as wheat, apples, corn, barley, sugar beets, and hops. More money is made from livestock in the state than from all agricultural products.

With the growth of winter sports, tourism now outranks mining in dollar revenue. Idaho's many streams and lakes provide fishing, camping, and boating sites. The nation's largest elk herds draw hunters from all over the world and the famed Sun Valley resort attracts thousands of visitors to its swimming and skiing facilities.

Other points of interest are the Craters of the Moon National Monument, Nez Percé National Historic Park, which includes many sites visited by Lewis and Clark; and the State Historical Museum in Boise.

## ILLINOIS

**Capital:** Springfield
**Governor:** James R. Thompson, R (to Jan. 1979)
**Lieut. Governor:** Dave O'Neal, R (to Jan. 1979)
**Secy. of State:** Alan J. Dixon, D (to Jan. 1979)
**Comptroller:** Michael J. Bakalis, D (to Jan. 1979)
**Atty. General:** William J. Scott, R (to Jan. 1979)
**Treasurer:** Donald R. Smith, D (to Jan. 1979)
**Organized as territory:** Feb. 3, 1809
**Entered Union & (rank):** Dec. 3, 1818 (21)
**Present constitution adopted:** 1970
**Motto:** State sovereignty, national union
**State flower:** Violet (1908)
**State tree:** White oak (1973)
**State bird:** Cardinal (1929)
**State insect:** Monarch butterfly
**State song:** "Illinois" (1925)
**State slogan:** Land of Lincoln
**State mineral:** Fluorite (1965)
**Nickname:** Prairie State
**Origin of name:** From an Indian word and French suffix meaning "tribe of superior men"
**1950 population & (rank):** 8,712,176 (4)
**1977 est. population & (rank):** 11,245,000 (5)
**1970 land area & (rank):** 56,400 sq mi. (146,076 sq km) (23)
**Geographic center:** In St. Clair County near Mascoutah
**Number of counties:** 102
**Largest cities (1975 est.):** Chicago (3,099,391); Rockford (145,459); Peoria (125,983); Decatur (89,604); Springfield (87,418); Aurora (76,955); Joliet (74,401)
**Public use areas:** 187 (275,000 ac.), incl. state parks, memorials, forests and conservation areas
**State revenue (1976):** $7,975,676,000
**State expenditure (1976):** $8,037,489,000

French explorers Marquette and Joliet, in 1673, were the first Europeans of record to visit the region. In 1699 French settlers established the first permanent settlement at Cahokia, near present-day East St. Louis.

Great Britain obtained the region at the end of the French and Indian War in 1763. The area figured prominently in frontier struggles during the Revolutionary War and in Indian wars during the early 19th century.

Significant episodes in the state's early history include the growing migration of Eastern settlers following the opening of the Erie Canal in 1825; the Black Hawk War, which virtually ended the Indian troubles in the area; and the rise of Abraham Lincoln from farm laborer to President-elect.

Today, Illinois stands high in manufacturing, coal mining, agriculture, and oil production. The sprawling Chicago district (including a slice of Indiana) is a great iron and steel producer, meat packer, grain exchange, and railroad center. Chicago is also famous as a busy long-flight airport city and Great Lakes port.

Illinois ranks first in the nation in export of agricultural products and second in hog production. An important dairying state, Illinois is also a leader in corn, oats, wheat, barley, rye, truck vegetables, and nursery products.

The state manufactures a great variety of industrial and consumer products: railroad cars, clothing, furniture, tractors, liquor, watches, and farm implements are just some of the items made in its factories and plants.

Central Illinois is noted for shrines and memorials associated with the life of Abraham Lincoln. In Springfield are the Lincoln Home, the Lincoln Tomb, and the restored Old State Capitol. Other points of interest are the home of Mormon leader Joseph Smith in Nauvoo and, in Chicago: the Art Institute, Field Museum, Museum of Science and Industry, Shedd Aquarium, Adler Planetarium, Merchandise Mart, and Chicago Portage National Historic Site.

## INDIANA

**Capital:** Indianapolis
**Governor:** Dr. Otis R. Bowen, R (to Jan. 1981)
**Lieut. Governor:** Robert D. Orr, R (to Jan. 1981)
**Secy. of State:** Larry A. Conrad, D (to Dec. 1978)
**Treasurer:** Jack L. New, D (to Feb. 1979)
**Atty. General:** Theodore L. Sendak, R (to Jan. 1981)
**Auditor:** Mary Aikins Currie, D (to Dec. 1978)
**Organized as territory:** May 7, 1800
**Entered Union & (rank):** Dec. 11, 1816 (19)
**Present constitution adopted:** 1851
**Motto:** The Crossroads of America
**State flower:** Peony (1957)
**State tree:** Tulip tree (1931)
**State bird:** Cardinal (1933)
**State song:** "On the Banks of the Wabash, Far Away" (1913)
**Nickname:** Hoosier State
**Origin of name:** Meaning "land of Indians"
**1970 population & (rank):** 5,193,669 (11)
**1977 est. population & (rank):** 5,330,000 (12)
**1970 land area & (rank):** 36,097 sq mi. (93,491 sq km) (38)
**Geographic center:** In Boone Co., 14 mi. NNW of Indianapolis
**Number of Counties:** 92
**Largest cities (1975 est.):** Indianapolis (714,878); Fort Wayne (185,299); Gary (167,546); Evansville (133,566); South Bend (117,478); Hammond (104,892)

**State parks:** 22 (66,186 ac.)
**State memorials:** 19 (931 ac.)
**State general revenue (1975–76):** $3,117,312,000
**State general expenditure (1975–76):** $3,096,367,000

First explored for France by La Salle in 1679–80, the region figured importantly in the Franco-British struggle for North America that culminated with British victory in 1763.

George Rogers Clark led American forces against the British in the area during the Revolutionary War and, prior to becoming a state, Indiana was the scene of frequent Indian uprisings until the victory of Gen. William Henry Harrison at Tippecanoe in 1811.

Indiana's 41-mile Lake Michigan waterfront—one of the world's great industrial centers—turns out iron, steel, and oil products. Products include automobile parts and accessories, mobile homes and recreational vehicles, truck and bus bodies, aircraft engines, farm machinery, and fabricated structural steel. Phonograph records, wood office furniture, and pharmaceuticals are also manufactured.

The state is a leader in agriculture with corn the principal crop. Hogs, soybeans, wheat, oats, rye, tomatoes, onions, and poultry also contribute heavily to Indiana's agricultural output. Much of the building limestone used in the U.S. is quarried in Indiana which is also a large producer of coal.

Wyandotte Cave, one of the largest in the U.S., is located in Crawford County in southern Indiana and West Baden and French Lick are well known for their mineral springs. Other attractions include Indiana Dunes National Lakeshore, Indianapolis Motor Speedway, Lincoln Boyhood National Memorial, and the George Rogers Clark National Historical Park.

## IOWA

**Capital:** Des Moines
**Governor:** Robert D. Ray, R (to Jan. 1979)
**Lieut. Governor:** Arthur A. Neu, R (to Jan. 1979)
**Secy. of State:** Melvin D. Synhorst, R (to Jan. 1979)
**Treasurer:** Maurice E. Baringer, R (to Jan. 1979)
**Atty. General:** Richard Turner, R (to Jan. 1979)
**Organized as territory:** June 12, 1838
**Entered Union & (rank):** Dec. 28, 1846 (29)
**Present constitution adopted:** 1857
**Motto:** Our liberties we prize and our rights we will maintain
**State flower:** Wild rose (1897)
**State bird:** Eastern goldfinch (1933)
**State colors:** Red, white, and blue (in state flag)
**State song:** "Song of Iowa"
**Nickname:** Hawkeye State
**Origin of name:** Probably from an Indian word meaning "I-o-w-a, this is the place," or "The Beautiful Land"
**1970 population & (rank):** 2,825,041 (25)
**1977 est. population & (rank):** 2,879,000 (25)
**1970 land area & (rank):** 55,491 sq mi. (144,887 sq km) (24)
**Geographic center:** In Story Co., 5 mi. NE of Ames
**Number of counties:** 99
**Largest cities (1975 est.):** Des Moines (194,168); Cedar Rapids (108,998); Davenport (99,941); Sioux City (85,719); Waterloo (77,681); Dubuque (61,754); Council Bluffs (58,660)
**State forests:** 5 (28,000 ac.)
**State parks:** 95 (49,237)
**Total revenue (1975):** $2,941,000,000
**Total expenditures (1975):** $2,864,000,000

The first Europeans to visit the area were the French explorers, Father Jacques Marquette and Louis Jolliet in 1673. The U.S. obtained control of the area in 1803 as part of the Louisiana Purchase.

During the first half of the 19th century, there was heavy fighting between white settlers and Indians. Lands were taken from the Indians after the Black Hawk War in 1832 and again in 1836 and 1837.

When Iowa became a state in 1846, its capital was Iowa City; the more centrally located Des Moines became the new capital in 1857. At that time, the state's present boundaries were also drawn.

Although Iowa produces a tenth of the nation's food supply, the value of Iowa's manufactured products is almost 2½ times that of its agriculture. Major industries are food and associated products, non-electrical machinery, electrical equipment, printing and publishing, and fabricated products.

Iowa stands in a class by itself as an agricultural state. Its farms sell over $7 billion worth of crops and livestock annually. Iowa leads the nation in all livestock and hog marketings, with about 22% of the pork supply and 13% of the grain-fed cattle. Iowa's forests produce hardwood lumber, particularly walnut, and its mineral products include cement, limestone, sand, gravel, gypsum, and coal.

Tourist attractions include the Herbert Hoover birthplace and library near West Branch; the Amana Colonies; Fort Dodge Historical Museum, Fort, and Stockade; the Iowa State Fair at Des Moines in August; and the Effigy Mounds National Monument at Marquette, a prehistoric Indian burial site.

## KANSAS

**Capital:** Topeka
**Governor:** Robert F. Bennett, R (to Jan. 1979)
**Lieut. Governor:** Shelby Smith, R (to Jan. 1979)
**Secy. of State:** Elwill Shanahan, R (to Jan. 1979)
**Treasurer:** Joan Finney, D (to Jan. 1979)
**Atty. General:** Curt Schneider, D (to Jan. 1979)
**Organized as territory:** May 30, 1854
**Entered Union & (rank):** Jan. 29, 1861 (34)
**Present constitution adopted:** 1859
**Motto:** *Ad astra per aspera* (To the stars through difficulties)
**State flower:** Sunflower (1903)
**State tree:** Cottonwood (1937)
**State bird:** Western meadow lark (1937)
**State animal:** Buffalo (1955)
**State song:** "Home on the Range" (1947)
**State march:** "The Kansas March" (1935)
**Nicknames:** Sunflower State; Jayhawk State
**Origin of name:** From a Siouan word meaning "people of the south wind"
**1970 population & (rank):** 2,249,071 (28)
**1977 est. population & (rank):** 2,326,000 (31)
**1970 land area & (rank):** 81,787 sq mi. (211,828 sq km) (13)
**Geographic center:** In Barton Co., 15 mi. NE of Great Bend
**Number of counties:** 105
**Largest cities (1975 est.):** Wichita (264,901); Kansas City (168,153); Topeka (119,203); Overland Park (81,013); Lawrence (50,887); Hutchinson (40,925); Salina (38,960)
**State parks:** 22 (14,394 ac.)
**State operating revenue (1976–77):** $1,719,200,000
**State operating expenditure (1976–77):** $1,723,000,000

Spanish explorer Francisco de Coronado, in 1541, is considered the first European to have traveled this region. La Salle's extensive land claims for France (1682) included present-day Kansas. Ceded to Spain by France in 1763, the territory reverted back to France in 1800 and was sold to the U.S. as part of the Louisiana Purchase in 1803.

Lewis and Clark, Zebulon Pike, and Stephen H. Long explored the region between 1803 and 1819. The first permanent settlements in Kansas were outposts—Fort Leavenworth (1827), Fort Scott (1842), and Fort Riley (1853)—established to protect travelers along the Santa Fe and Oregon Trails.

Just before the Civil War, the conflict between the pro- and anti-slavery forces earned the region the grim title "Bleeding Kansas."

Today, wheat fields, oil well derricks, herds of cattle, and grain storage elevators are chief features of the Kansas landscape. A leading wheat-growing state, Kansas also raises corn, sorghums, oats, barley, soy beans, and potatoes. Kansas stands high in petroleum production and mines zinc, coal, salt, and lead. It is also the nation's leading producer of helium.

Wichita is one of the nation's leading aircraft manufacturing centers, ranking first in production of private aircraft. Kansas City is an important transportation, milling, and meat-packing center.

Points of interest include the Kansas State Historical Society Museum at Topeka, the Eisenhower boyhood home and the new Eisenhower Memorial Museum and Presidential Library at Abilene, John Brown's cabin at Osawatomie, recreated Front Street in Dodge City, Fort Larned (once the most important military post on the Santa Fe Trail), and Fort Leavenworth and Fort Riley, still active military posts.

## KENTUCKY

**Capital:** Frankfort
**Governor:** Julian M. Carroll, D (to Dec. 1979)
**Lieut. Governor:** Thelma L. Stovall, D (to Dec. 1979)
**Secy. of State:** Drexell Davis, D (to Jan. 1980)
**State Treasurer:** Francis Jones Mills, D (to Jan. 1980)
**State Auditor:** George Atkins, D (to Jan. 1980)
**Atty. General:** Robert Stephens, D (to Jan. 1980)
**Entered Union & (rank):** June 1, 1792 (15)
**Present constitution adopted:** 1891
**Motto:** United we stand, divided we fall
**State tree:** Coffeetree
**State flower:** Goldenrod
**State bird:** Kentucky cardinal
**State song:** "My Old Kentucky Home"
**Nickname:** Bluegrass State
**Origin of name:** From an Iroquoian word "Ken-tah-ten" meaning "land of tomorrow"
**1970 population & (rank):** 3,219,311 (23)
**1977 est. population & (rank):** 3,458,000 (23)
**1970 land area & (rank):** 39,650 sq mi. (102,694 sq km) (37)
**Geographic center:** In Marion Co., 3 mi. NNW of Lebanon
**Number of counties:** 120
**Largest cities (1975 est.):** Louisville (335,954); Lexington-Fayette (186,048); Owensboro (50,788); Covington (44,467); Bowling Green (36,082)
**State forests:** 9 (44,173 ac.)
**State parks:** 43 (40,574 ac.)
**Total state revenue (1976–77):** $2,962,412,217
**Total state expenditure (1976–77):** $2,704,621,670

Kentucky was the first region west of the Allegheny Mountains settled by American pioneers. James Harrod established the first permanent settlement at Harrodsburg in 1774; the following year Daniel Boone, who had explored the area in 1767, blazed the Wilderness Trail and founded Boonesboro.

Politically, the Kentucky region was originally part of Virginia, but early statehood was gained in 1792.

During the Civil War, as a slaveholding state with a considerable abolitionist population, Kentucky was caught in the middle of the conflict, supplying both Union and Confederate forces with thousands of troops.

In recent years, manufacturing has shown important gains, but agriculture and mining are still vital to Kentucky's economy. Kentucky prides itself on producing some of the nation's best tobacco, horses, and whiskey. Corn, soybeans, wheat, fruit, hogs, cattle, and dairy farming are also important.

Among the manufactured items produced in the state are furniture, aluminum ware, brooms, shoes, lumber products, machinery, textiles, and iron and steel products. Kentucky also produces significant amounts of petroleum, natural gas, fluorspar, clay, and stone. However, coal accounts for 90% of the total mineral income.

Louisville, the largest city, famed for the Kentucky Derby at Churchill Downs, is also the location of a large state university, whiskey distilleries, and cigarette factories. The Bluegrass country around Lexington is the home of some of the world's finest race horses. Other attractions are Mammoth Cave, the George S. Patton, Jr., Military Museum at Fort Knox, and Old Fort Harrod State Park.

## LOUISIANA

**Capital:** Baton Rouge
**Governor:** Edwin W. Edwards, D (to March 1980)
**Lieut. Governor:** James F. Fitzmorris, Jr., D (to March 1980)
**Secy. of State:** Paul J. Hardy, D (to March 1980)
**Comptroller:** S. E. Vines, Jr., D (to March 1980)
**Atty. General:** William J. Guste, Jr., D (to March 1980)
**Organized as territory:** March 26, 1804
**Entered Union & (rank):** April 30, 1812 (18)
**Present constitution adopted:** 1974
**Motto:** Union, justice, and confidence
**State flower:** Magnolia (1900)
**State tree:** Bald cypress
**State bird:** Pelican
**State song:** "Give Me Louisiana," and "You Are My Sunshine"
**Nicknames:** Pelican State; Sportsman's Paradise; Creole State; Sugar State
**Origin of name:** In honor of Louis XIV of France
**1970 population & (rank):** 3,643,180 (20)
**1977 est. population & (rank):** 3,921,000 (20)
**1970 land area & (rank):** 44,930 sq mi. (116,369 sq km) (33)
**Geographic center:** In Avoyelles Parish, 3 mi. SE of Marksville
**Number of parishes (counties):** 64
**Largest cities (1975 est.):** New Orleans (559,770); Metropolitan Baton Rouge (294,394); Shreveport (185,711); Lake Charles (76,087); Lafayette (75,430)
**State forests:** 1 (8,000 ac.)
**State parks:** 31 (14,360 ac.)
**State general revenue (1977–78):** $2,710,344,481 Federal grants: $1,032,112,524
**State general expenditure (1977–78):** $3,732,257,018

Louisiana has a rich, colorful historical background. Early Spanish explorers were Piñeda,

1519; Cabeza de Vaca, 1528; and de Soto in 1541. La Salle reached the mouth of the Mississippi and claimed all the land drained by it and its tributaries for Louis XIV of France in 1682.

Louisiana became a French crown colony in 1731, was ceded to Spain in 1763, returned to France in 1800, and sold by Napoleon to the U.S. as part of the Louisiana Purchase (with large territories to the north and northwest) in 1803.

In 1815, Gen. Andrew Jackson's troops defeated a larger British army in the Battle of New Orleans, neither side aware that the treaty ending the War of 1812 had been signed.

As to total value of its mineral output, Louisiana is a leader in natural gas, salt, petroleum, and sulfur production. Much of the oil and sulfur comes from offshore deposits. The state also produces large crops of sweet potatoes, rice, sugarcane, pecans, soybeans, corn, and cotton.

Leading manufactures include chemicals, processed food, petroleum and coal products, paper, lumber and wood products, transportation equipment, and apparel.

Louisiana marshes supply most of the nation's muskrat fur as well as that of opossum, raccoon, mink, and otter, and large numbers of game birds.

Major points of interest include New Orleans with its French Quarter and Superdome, plantation homes near Natchitoches and New Iberia, Cajun country in the Mississippi delta region, Chalmette National Historical Park, and the state capital at Baton Rouge.

## MAINE

**Capital:** Augusta
**Governor:** James B. Longley, Ind. (to Jan. 1979)
**Secy. of State:** Markham L. Gartley, D (to Jan. 1979)
**Controller:** Richard A. Dieffenbach (term indefinite)
**Atty. General:** Joseph E. Brennan, D (to Jan. 1979)
**Entered Union & (rank):** March 15, 1820 (23)
**Present constitution adopted:** 1820
**Motto:** *Dirigo* (I direct)
**State flower:** White pine cone and tassel (1895)
**State tree:** White pine tree (1945)
**State bird:** Chickadee (1927)
**State fish:** Landlocked salmon (1969)
**State mineral:** Tourmaline (1971)
**State song:** "State of Maine Song" (1937)
**Nickname:** Pine Tree State
**Origin of name:** First used to distinguish the mainland from the offshore islands. It has been considered a compliment to Henrietta Maria, Queen of Charles I of England. She was said to have owned the province of Mayne in France.
**1970 population & (rank):** 993,663 (38)
**1977 est. population & (rank):** 1,085,000 (38)
**1970 land area & (rank):** 30,920 sq mi. (80,083 sq km) (39)
**Geographic center:** In Piscataquis Co., 18 mi. N of Dover-Foxcroft
**Number of counties:** 16
**Largest cities (est. 1975):** Portland (59,857); Lewiston (41,045); Bangor (32,262); Auburn (23,304); South Portland (22,677)
**State forests:** 1 (21,000 ac.)
**State parks:** 26 (247,627 ac.)
**State historic sites:** 18 (403 ac.)
**State general revenue (1977 est.):** $825,098,727
**State general expenditure (1977 est.):** $964,402,510

John Cabot and his son, Sebastian, are believed to have visited the Maine coast in 1498. However, the first permanent English settlements were not established until more than a century later, in 1623.

The first naval action of the Revolutionary War occurred in 1775 when colonials captured the British sloop *Margaretta* off Machias on the Maine coast. In that same year, the British burned Falmouth (now Portland).

Long governed by Massachusetts, Maine became the 23rd state as part of the Missouri Compromise in 1820.

Maine produces one out of every nine potatoes raised in the U.S. and 95% of the nation's low-bush blueberries. Farm income is also dervied from apples, sweet corn, peas, and beans, with poultry and eggs the largest items.

The state is one of the world's largest pulp-paper producers. It ranks fifth in boot-and-shoe manufacturing. With more than 80% of its area forested, Maine turns out wood products from boats to toothpicks.

Maine leads the world in the production of the familiar flat tins of sardines, producing more than 100 million of them annually. Lobstermen normally catch 80–90% of the nation's true total of lobsters.

A scenic seacoast, beaches, lakes, mountains, and resorts make Maine a popular vacationland. There are more than 2,500 lakes and 5,000 streams, plus 26 state parks, to attract hunters, fishermen, skiers, and campers.

Major points of interest are: Bar Harbor, Allagash National Wilderness Waterway, the Wadsworth-Longfellow House in Portland, Roosevelt Campobello International Park, and the St. Croix Island National Monument.

## MARYLAND

**Capital:** Annapolis
**Governor:** Blair Lee III (acting), D (to Jan. 1979)
**Lieut. Gov.:** Vacant
**Secy. of State:** Fred L. Wineland, D (appointed by governor)
**Comptroller of the Treasury:** Louis L. Goldstein, D (to Jan. 1979)
**Treasurer:** William S. James, D (to Jan. 1979)
**Atty. General:** Francis B. Burch, D (to Jan. 1979)
**Entered Union & (rank):** April 28, 1788 (7)
**Present constitution adopted:** 1867
**Motto:** *Fatti maschii, parole femine* (Manly deeds, womanly words)
**State flower:** Black-eyed susan (1918)
**State tree:** White oak (1941)
**State bird:** Baltimore oriole (1947)
**State dog:** Chesapeake Bay retriever (1964)
**State fish:** Rockfish (1965)
**State insect:** Baltimore checkerspot butterfly (1973)
**State sport:** Jousting (1962)
**State song:** "Maryland! My Maryland!" (1939)
**Nicknames:** Free State; Old Line State
**Origin of name:** In honor of Henrietta Maria (Queen of Charles I of England)
**1970 population & (rank):** 3,922,399 (18)
**1977 est. population & (rank):** 4,139,000 (18)
**1970 land area & (rank):** 9,891 sq mi. (25,618 sq km) (42)
**Geographic center:** In Prince Georges Co., 4½ mi. NW of Davidsonville
**Number of counties:** 23, and 1 independent city
**Largest cities (1975 est.):** Baltimore (851,698); Rockville (44,299); Bowie (37,323); Hagerstown (37,233); Annapolis (32,458); College Park (27,709)
**State forests:** 9 (116,213 ac.)
**State parks:** 42 (65,559 ac.)
**State general revenue (1977):** $5,007,068,597
**State general expenditure (1977):** $4,709,598,310

In 1608, Chesapeake Bay was explored by Capt. John Smith. Charles I granted a royal charter to Cecil Calvert, Lord Baltimore, in 1632 and English Roman Catholics landed on St. Clement's (now Blakistone Island) in 1634. Religious freedom, granted all Christians in the Toleration act passed by the Maryland assembly in 1649, was ended by a Puritan revolt, 1654–58.

In 1814, when the British unsuccessfully tried to capture Baltimore, the bombardment of Fort McHenry inspired Francis Scott Key to write *The Star Spangled Banner.*

Maryland is almost cut in two by the Chesapeake Bay, and the many estuaries and rivers create one of the longest waterfronts of any state. The Bay produces more seafood—oysters, crabs, clams, fin fish—than any comparable body of water. Important agricultural products, in order of cash value, are chickens, dairy products, corn, cattle, tobacco, and vegetables. Maryland is a leader in vegetable canning. Sand, gravel, lime and cement, stone, coal, and clay are the chief mineral products.

Manufacturing industries produce missiles, airplanes, steel, clothing, and chemicals. Baltimore, home of The Johns Hopkins University and Hospital, ranks as the nation's second port in foreign tonnage. Annapolis, site of the U.S. Naval Academy, has one of the earliest state houses (1772–79) still in regular use by a State government.

Among the popular attractions in Maryland are the Fort McHenry National Monument, Harpers Ferry and Chesapeake and Ohio Canal National Historical Parks, St. Marys City restoration near Leonardtown, USS *Constellation* at Baltimore, U.S. Naval Academy in Annapolis, Assateague Island National Seashore, and Catoctin Mountain and Piscataway parks.

## MASSACHUSETTS

**Capital:** Boston
**Governor:** Michael S. Dukakis, D (to Jan. 1979)
**Lieut. Governor:** Thomas P. O'Neill III, D (to Jan. 1979)
**Secy. of the Commonwealth:** Paul H. Guzzi, D (to Jan. 1979)
**Treasurer & Receiver-General:** Robert Q. Crane, D (to Jan. 1979)
**Auditor of the Commonwealth:** Thaddeus Buczko, D (to Jan. 1979)
**Atty. General:** Francis X. Bellotti (to Jan. 1979)
**Entered Union & (rank):** Feb. 6, 1788 (6)
**Motto:** *Ense petit placidam sub libertate quietem* (By the sword we seek peace, but peace only under liberty)
**State flower:** Mayflower (1918)
**State tree:** American elm (1941)
**State bird:** Chickadee (1941)
**State colors:** Blue and gold
**State song:** "All Hail to Massachusetts" (1966)
**State beverage:** Cranberry juice (1970)
**State horse:** Morgan horse (1970)
**State insect:** Ladybug (1974)
**Nicknames:** Bay State; Old Colony State
**Origin of name:** From two Indian words meaning "Great mountain place"
**1970 population & (rank):** 5,689,170 (10)
**1977 est. population & (rank):** 5,782,000 (10)
**1970 land area & (rank):** 7,826 sq mi. (20,269 sq km) (45)
**Geographic center:** In Worcester Co., in S part of city of Worcester
**Number of counties:** 14
**Largest cities (1975 est.):** Boston (636,725); Worcester (171,566); Springfield (170,790); Cambridge (102,420); Fall River (100,430); New Bedford (100,133)
**State forests and parks:** 123 (270,000 ac.)[1]
**State general revenue (1976–77):** $4,911,382,549
**State general expenditure (1976–77):** $5,142,999,230

Massachusetts has played a significant role in American history since the Pilgrims, seeking religious freedom, founded Plymouth Colony in 1620.

As one of the most important of the 13 colonies, Massachusetts became a leader in resisting British oppression. In 1773, the Boston Tea Party protested unjust taxation. The Minutemen started the American Revolution by battling British troops at Lexington and Concord on April 19, 1775.

During the 19th century, Massachusetts was famous for the vigorous intellectual activity of famous writers and educators and for its expanding commercial fishing, shipping, and manufacturing interests.

Massachusetts pioneered in the manufacture of textiles and shoes. Today, these industries have been replaced in importance by activity in the electronics and communications equipment fields.

The state's cranberry crop is the nation's largest. Also important are dairy and poultry products, nursery and greenhouse produce, vegetables, and fruit.

Tourism has become an important factor in the economy of the state because of its numerous recreational areas and historical landmarks.

Cape Cod has summer theaters, water sports, and an artists' colony at Provincetown. Tanglewood, in the Berkshires, features the summer concerts of the Boston Symphony.

Among the many other points of interest are Old Sturbridge Village, Minute Man National Historical Park between Lexington and Concord, and, in Boston: Old North Church, Old State House, Faneuil Hall, and the USS *Constitution.*

## MICHIGAN

**Capital:** Lansing
**Governor:** William G. Milliken, R (to Jan. 1979)
**Lieut. Governor:** James J. Damman, D (to Jan. 1979)
**Secy. of State:** Richard H. Austin, D (to Jan. 1979)
**Atty. General:** Frank J. Kelley, D (to Jan. 1979)
**Organized as territory:** Jan. 11, 1805
**Entered Union & (rank):** Jan. 26, 1837 (26)
**Present constitution adopted:** April 1, 1963, (effective Jan. 1, 1964)
**Motto:** *Si quaeris peninsulam amoenam circumspice* (If you seek a pleasant peninsula, look around you)
**State flower:** Apple blossom (1897)
**State bird:** Robin
**State fish:** Brook trout (1965)
**State gem:** Isle Royal Greenstone (Chlorastrolite) (1972)
**State stone:** Petoskey stone (1965)
**Nickname:** Wolverine State
**Origin of name:** From two Indian words meaning "great lake"
**1970 population & (rank):** 8,875,083 (7)
**1977 est. population & (rank):** 9,129,000 (7)
**1970 land area & (rank):** 56,817 sq mi. (147,156 sq km) (22)
**Geographic center:** In Wexford Co., 5 mi. NNW of Cadillac
**Number of counties:** 83
**Largest cities (1975 est.):** Detroit (1,335,085); Grand Rapids (187,946); Flint (174,218); Warren (172,755); Lansing (126,805); Livonia (114,881)

1. The Metropolitan District Commission, an agency of the Commonwealth serving municipalities in the Boston area, has about 14,000 acres of parkways and reservations under its jurisdiction.

**State forests:** 33 (3,762,184 ac.)
**State parks and recreation areas:** 92 (216,857 ac.)
**State general revenue (1976—15-month fiscal year):** $7,888,417,000
**State general expenditure (1976—15-month fiscal year):** $7,139,422,000

Indian tribes were living in the Michigan region when the first European, Etienne Brulé of France, arrived in 1618. Other French explorers, including Marquette, Jolliet, and La Salle, followed, and the first permanent settlement was established in 1668 at Sault Ste. Marie. France was ousted from the territory by Great Britain in 1763, following the French and Indian War.

After the Revolutionary War, the U.S. acquired most of the region, which remained the scene of constant conflict between the British and U.S. forces and their respective Indian allies through the War of 1812.

Bordering on four of the five Great Lakes, Michigan is divided into Upper and Lower Peninsulas by the Straits of Mackinac, which link Lakes Michigan and Huron. The two parts of the state are connected by the Mackinac Bridge, one of the world's longest suspension bridges. To the north, connecting Lakes Superior and Huron are the busy Sault Ste. Marie Canals.

While Michigan ranks first among the states in production of motor vehicles and parts, it is also a leader in many other manufacturing and processing lines including prepared cereals, machine tools, airplane parts, refrigerators, hardware, steel springs, and furniture.

The state produces important amounts of iron, copper, iodine, gypsum, bromine, salt, lime, gravel, and cement. Michigan's farms grow apples, cherries, pears, grapes, potatoes, and sugar beets and the annual value of its forest products is estimated at $2 billion. With over 36,000 miles of streams, some 11,000 lakes, and a 2,000 mile shoreline, Michigan is a prime area for both commercial and sport fishing.

Points of interest are the automobile plants in Dearborn, Detroit, Flint, Lansing, and Pontiac; Mackinac Island; Pictured Rocks and Sleeping Bear Dunes National Lakeshores, Greenfield Village near Dearborn; and the many summer resorts along both the inland and Great Lakes.

## MINNESOTA

**Capital:** St. Paul
**Governor:** Rudy G. Perpich, D (to Jan. 1979)
**Lieut. Governor:** Alec G. Olson, D (to Jan. 1979)
**Secy. of State:** Joan Grow (to Jan. 1979)
**State Auditor:** Robert W. Mattson (to Jan. 1979)
**Atty. General:** Warren Spannus, D (to Jan. 1979)
**State Treasurer:** Jim Lord (to Jan. 1979)
**Organized as territory:** March 3, 1849
**Entered Union & (rank):** May 11, 1858 (32)
**Present constitution adopted:** 1858
**Motto:** L'Etoile du Nord (The North Star)
**State flower:** Showy lady slipper (1902)
**State tree:** Red (or Norway) pine
**State bird:** Common loon (also called Great Northern Diver)
**State song:** "Hail Minnesota"
**Nicknames:** North Star State; Gopher State; Land of 10,000 Lakes
**Origin of name:** From a Dakota Indian word meaning "sky-tinted water"
**1970 population & (rank):** 3,805,069 (19)
**1977 est. population & (rank):** 3,975,000 (19)
**1970 land area & (rank):** 79,289 sq mi. (205,359 sq km) (14)
**Geographic center:** In Crow Wing Co., 10 mi. SW of Brainerd
**Number of counties:** 87
**Largest cities (1975 est.):** Minneapolis (378,112); St. Paul (279,535); Duluth (93,971); Bloomington (79,210); Rochester (56,211); Edina (47,989)
**State forests:** 55 (2,984,000 ac.)
**State parks:** 92 (202,205 ac.)
**Total revenue (fiscal 1975):** $3,601,778,924
**Total expenditures (fiscal 1975):** $3,389,554,666

Following the visits of several French explorers, fur traders, and missionaries, including Marquette and Jolliet and La Salle, the region was claimed for Louis XIV by Daniel Greysolon, Sieur Duluth, in 1679.

The U.S. acquired eastern Minnesota from Great Britain after the Revolutionary War and 20 years later bought the western part from France in the Louisiana Purchase of 1803. Much of the region was explored by U.S. Army Lt. Zebulon M. Pike before cession of the northern strip of Minnesota bordering Canada by Britain in 1818.

The state is rich in natural resources. A few square miles of land in the north in the Mesabi, Cuyuna, and Vermillion ranges, produce more than 60% of the nation's iron ore. The state's farms rank high in yields of corn, wheat, rye, alfalfa, and sugar beets. Other leading farm products include butter, eggs, milk, potatoes, green peas, barley, and livestock.

Minnesota's factory production includes nonelectrical machinery, fabricated metals, flour-mill products, plastics, electronic computers, scientific instruments, and processed foods.

Minneapolis is the trade center of the Northwest; St. Paul is the nation's biggest publisher of calendars and law books. These "twin cities" are the nation's third largest trucking center. Duluth has the nation's largest inland harbor and now handles a significant amount of foreign trade. Rochester is the home of the Mayo Clinic, an internationally famous medical center.

Today, tourism is a major revenue producer in Minnesota, with fishing, hunting, water sports, and winter sports bringing in millions of visitors each year.

Among the most popular attractions are the St. Paul Winter Carnival; the Tyrone Guthrie Theatre, the Institute of Arts, Walker Art Center, and Minnehaha Park, in Minneapolis; Voyageurs National Park; and North Shore Drive.

## MISSISSIPPI

**Capital:** Jackson
**Governor:** Charles C. (Cliff) Finch, D (to Jan. 1980)
**Lieut. Governor:** Evelyn Gandy, D (to Jan. 1980)
**Secy. of State:** Heber A. Ladner, D (to Jan. 1980)
**Treasurer:** Edwin Lloyd Pittman (to Jan. 1980)
**Atty. General:** A. F. Summer (to Jan. 1980)
**Organized as Territory:** April 7, 1798
**Entered Union & (rank):** Dec. 10, 1817 (20)
**Present constitution adopted:** 1890
**Motto:** *Virtute es armis* (By valor and arms)
**State flower:** Flower or bloom of the magnolia or evergreen magnolia (1952)
**State tree:** Magnolia (1938)
**State bird:** Mockingbird (1944)
**State song:** "Go, Mississippi" (1962)
**Nickname:** Magnolia State

**Origin of name:** From an Indian word meaning "Father of Waters"
**1970 population & (rank):** 2,216,912 (29)
**1977 est. population & (rank):** 2,389,000 (29)
**1970 land area & (rank):** 47,296 sq mi. (122,497 sq km) (31)
**Geographic center:** In Leake Co., 9 mi. WNW of Carthage
**Number of counties:** 82
**Largest cities (1975 est.):** Jackson (166,512); Biloxi (46,407); Meridian (46,256); Gulfport (43,126); Greenville (42,499); Hattiesburg (38,490); Pascagoula (30,403)
**State forests:** 1 (1,760 ac.)
**State parks:** 15 (16,220 ac.)
**State general and special revenue (1977):** $2,067,776,344
**State general and special expenditure (1977):** $2,020,694,858

First explored for Spain by Hernando de Soto who discovered the Mississippi River in 1540, the region was later claimed by France. In 1699, a French group under Sieur d'Iberville established the first permanent settlement near present-day Biloxi.

Great Britain took over the area in 1763 after the French and Indian War, ceding it to the U.S. in 1783 after the Revolution. Spain did not relinquish its claims until 1798, and in 1810 the U.S. annexed West Florida from Spain, including what is now southern Mississippi.

Mississippi, the stronghold of the Old South, has until the past decade been one of the least industrialized states, with more than half its population making a living from the soil. However, a recent industrialization program has attracted manufacturing industries such as lumber, furniture, paper, food processing, apparel, chemicals, transportation equipment, and machinery.

Cotton, nevertheless, is still king with the state ranking second to Texas in cotton production, though soybeans have become Mississippi's largest crop. Other important farm products are corn, peanuts, pecans, rice, sugarcane, sweet potatoes, and hay. Poultry and eggs are also important.

The state abounds in historical landmarks and is the home of the Vicksburg National Military Park where visitors may see the remains of forts, trenches, and other military relics used in the 1863 Union-army siege of the city. Other National Park Service areas are Brices Cross Roads National Battlefield Site, Tupelo National Battlefield, and part of Natchez Trace National Parkway. Pre-Civil War mansions are the special pride of Natchez, Oxford, Hattiesburg, and Jackson.

## MISSOURI

**Capital:** Jefferson City
**Governor:** Joseph P. Teasdale, D (to Jan. 1981)
**Lieut. Governor:** William C. Phelps, R (to Jan. 1981)
**Secy. of State:** James C. Kirkpatrick, D (to Jan. 1981)
**Auditor:** Thomas M. Keyes, D (to Jan. 1979)
**Treasurer:** James I. Spainhower, D (to Jan. 1981)
**Atty. General:** John D. Ashcroft, R (to Jan. 1981)
**Organized as territory:** June 4, 1812
**Entered Union & (rank):** Aug. 10, 1821 (24)
**Present constitution adopted:** 1945
**Motto:** *Salus populi suprema lex esto* (The welfare of the people shall be the supreme law)
**State flower:** Hawthorn (1923)
**State bird:** Bluebird (1927)
**State colors:** Red, white, and blue (1913)
**State song:** "Missouri Waltz" (1949)
**State rock:** Mozarkite (1967)
**State mineral:** Galena (1967)
**Nickname:** Show-me State
**Origin of name:** Named after a tribe called Missouri Indians. "Missouri" means "town of the large canoes."
**1970 population & (rank):** 4,677,399 (13)
**1977 est. population & (rank):** 4,801,000 (15)
**1970 land area & (rank):** 68,995 sq mi. (178,697 sq km) (18)
**Geographic center:** In Miller Co., 20 mi. SW of Jefferson City
**Number of counties:** 114, plus 1 independent city
**Largest cities (1975 est.):** St. Louis (524,964); Kansas City (472,529); Springfield (131,557); Independence (111,481); St. Joseph (77,679); Florissant (70,465)
**State forests and Tower sites:** 125 (210,000 ac.)
**State parks:** 57 (79,059 ac.)[1]
**State cash receipts (1977):** $2,489,997,056
**State general expenditure (1977):** $2,414,053,223

De Soto visited the Missouri area in 1541. France's claim to the entire region was based on La Salle's travels in 1682. French fur traders established Ste. Genevieve in 1735 and St. Louis was first settled in 1764.

The U.S. gained Missouri from France as part of the Louisiana Purchase in 1803, and the territory was admitted as a state following the Missouri Compromise of 1820. Throughout the pre-Civil War period and during the war, Missourians were sharply divided in their opinions about slavery and in their allegiances, supplying both Union and Confederate forces with troops. However, the state itself remained in the Union.

Historically, Missouri played a leading role as a gateway to the West, St. Joseph being the eastern starting point of the Pony Express, while the much-traveled Santa Fe and Oregon Trails began in Independence. Now a popular vacationland, Missouri has 11 major lakes and numerous fishing streams, springs, and caves. Bagnell Dam, across the Osage River in the Ozarks, completed in 1931, created one of the largest man-made lakes in the world, covering 65,000 acres of surface area.

Manufacturing, paced by the aerospace industry, provides more income and jobs than any other segment of the economy. Missouri is also a leading producer of transportation equipment, shoes, lead, and beer. Among the major crops are corn, soybeans, wheat, oats, barley, potatoes, tobacco, and cotton.

Points of interest include Mark Twain's boyhood home and Mark Twain Cave (Hannibal), the Harry S. Truman Library and Museum (Independence), the house where Jesse James was killed in St. Joseph, Jefferson National Expansion Memorial (St. Louis), and the Ozark National Scenic Riverway.

## MONTANA

**Capital:** Helena
**Governor:** Thomas L. Judge, D (to Jan. 1981)
**Lieut. Governor:** Theodore Schwinden, D (to Jan. 1981)
**Secy. of State:** Frank Murray, D (to Jan. 1981)
**Auditor:** E. V. "Sonny" Omholt, R (to Jan. 1981)
**Atty. General:** Michael Greely, D (to Jan. 1981)
**Organized as territory:** May 26, 1864
**Entered Union & (rank):** Nov. 8, 1889 (41)
**Present constitution adopted:** 1972
**Motto:** *Oro y plata* (Gold and silver)
**State flower:** Bitterroot (1895)
**State tree:** Ponderosa pine (1949)

1. Includes 19 historic sites and 1 archaeological site.

**State stones:** Sapphire and agate (1969)
**State bird:** Western meadow lark (1931)
**State song:** "Montana" (1945)
**Nickname:** Treasure State
**Origin of name:** Chosen from Latin dictionary by J. M. Ashley. It is a Latinized Spanish word.
**1970 population & (rank):** 694,409 (43)
**1977 est. population & (rank):** 761,000 (43)
**1970 land area & (rank):** 145,587 sq mi. (377,070 sq km) (4)
**Geographic center:** In Fergus Co., 12 mi. W of Lewistown
**Number of counties:** 56, plus small part of Yellowstone National Park
**Largest cities (1975 est.):** Billings (68,987); Great Falls (60,868); Missoula (29,569); Helena (26,251); Butte (23,476); Bozeman (19,847)
**State forests:** 7 (214,000 ac.)
**State parks and recreation areas:** 68 (18,273 ac.)
**State general revenue (1976–77):** $172,204,872
**State general expenditure (1976–77):** $155,613,552

First explored for France by François and Louis-Joseph Verendrye in the early 1740s, much of the region was acquired by the U.S. from France as part of the Louisiana Purchase in 1803. Before western Montana was obtained from Great Britain in the Oregon Treaty of 1846, American trading posts and forts had been established in the territory.

The major Indian wars (1867–1877) included the famous 1876 Battle of the Little Big Horn, better known as "Custer's Last Stand," in which Cheyennes and Sioux killed George A. Custer and more than 200 of his men in southeastern Montana.

Much of Montana's early history was concerned with mining with copper, lead, zinc, silver, coal, and oil as principal products.

Butte, sitting on the "richest hill in the world," is the center of the area that once supplied half of the U.S. copper.

Fields of grain cover much of Montana's plains; it ranks high among the states in wheat and barley, with rye, oats, flaxseed, sugar beets, and potatoes other important crops. Sheep and cattle raising make significant contributions to the state's economy.

Tourist attractions include hunting, fishing, skiing, and dude ranching. Glacier National Park, on the Continental Divide, is a scenic and vacation wonderland with 60 glaciers, 200 lakes, and many streams with good trout fishing.

Other major points of interest include the Custer Battlefield National Monument, Virginia City, Yellowstone National Park, Museum of the Plains Indians at Browning, and the Fort Union Trading Post and Grant-Kohr's Ranch National Historic Sites.

## NEBRASKA

**Capital:** Lincoln
**Governor:** J. James Exon, D (to Jan. 1979)
**Lieut. Governor:** Gerald T. Whelan, R (to Jan. 1979)
**Secy. of State:** Allen J. Beermann, R (to Jan. 1979)
**Atty. General:** Paul L. Douglas (to Jan. 1979)
**Auditor:** Ray A. C. Johnson (to Jan. 1979)
**Treasurer:** Frank Marsh, R (to Jan. 1979)
**Organized as territory:** May 30, 1854
**Entered Union & (rank):** March 1, 1867 (37)
**Present constitution adopted:** Nov. 1, 1875 (extensively amended 1919–20)
**Motto:** Equality before the law
**State flower:** Goldenrod (1895)
**State tree:** Cottonwood (1972)
**State bird:** Western meadow lark (1929)
**State insect:** Honeybee
**State gem stone:** Blue agate (1967)
**State rock:** Prairie agate (1967)
**State fossil:** Mammoth (1967)
**State song:** "Beautiful Nebraska" (1967)
**Nicknames:** Cornhusker State; Beef State; Tree Planters State
**Origin of name:** From an Oto Indian word meaning "flat water"
**1970 population & (rank):** 1,483,791 (35)
**1977 est. population & (rank):** 1,561,000 (35)
**1970 land area & (rank):** 76,483 sq mi. (198,091 sq km) (15)
**Geographic center:** In Custer Co., 10 mi. NW of Broken Bow
**Number of counties:** 93
**Largest cities (1975 est.):** Omaha (371,455); Lincoln (163,112); Grand Island (33,304); Fremont (23,953); Hastings (22,633); Kearney (19,333)
**State forests:** None
**State parks:** 93 areas, 4 categories, 5 major areas
**State general revenue (1976–77):** $444,424,708
**State general expenditure (1976–77):** $440,103,331

French fur traders first visited Nebraska in the early 1700s. Part of the Louisiana Purchase in 1803, Nebraska was explored by Lewis and Clark in 1804–06.

Robert Stuart pioneered the Oregon Trail across Nebraska in 1812–13 and the first permanent settlement was established at Bellevue in 1823. Western Nebraska was acquired by treaty following the Mexican War in 1848. The Union Pacific began its transcontinental railroad at Omaha in 1865. In 1937, Nebraska became the only state in the Union to have a unicameral (one-house) legislature. Members are elected to it without party designation.

Nebraska is a leading grain-producer with bumper crops of rye, corn, and wheat. More varieties of grass, valuable for forage, grow in this state than in any other in the nation.

The state's sizable cattle and hog industries make Omaha with its surrounding area the nation's largest meat-packing center and the second-largest cattle market in the world.

Manufacturing has become diversified in Nebraska, strengthening the state's economic base. Firms making electronic components, auto accessories, pharmaceuticals, and mobile homes have joined such older industries as clothing, farm machinery, chemicals, and transportation equipment. Oil was discovered in 1939 and natural gas in 1949.

Among the principal attractions are Agate Fossil Beds, Homestead, and Scotts Bluff National Monuments; Chimney Rock National Historic Site; a recreated pioneer village at Minden; the Union stockyards in Omaha; the Stuhr Museum of the Prairie Pioneer with 57 original 19th-century buildings near Grand Island; and the Sheldon Memorial Art Gallery at the University of Nebraska in Lincoln.

## NEVADA

**Capital:** Carson City
**Governor:** Mike O'Callaghan, D (to Jan. 1979)
**Lieut. Governor:** Robert Rose, D (to Jan. 1979)
**Secy. of State:** William D. Swackhamer (to Jan. 1979)
**State Treasurer:** Michael Mirabelli, D (to Jan. 1979)
**Controller:** Wilson McGowan (to Jan. 1979)
**Atty. General:** Robert List (to Jan. 1979)
**Organized as territory:** March 2, 1861
**Entered Union & (rank):** Oct. 31, 1864 (36)

**Present constitution adopted:** 1864
**Motto:** All for Our Country
**State flower:** Sagebrush (1967)
**State tree:** Single-leaf pinon (1953)
**State bird:** Mountain bluebird (1967)
**State animal:** Desert bighorn sheep (1973)
**State colors:** Silver and blue (unofficial)
**State song:** "Home Means Nevada" (1933)
**Nicknames:** Sagebrush State; Silver State; Battle-born State
**Origin of name:** Spanish: "snowcapped"
**1970 population & (rank):** 488,738 (47)
**1977 est. population & (rank):** 633,000 (46)
**1970 land area & (rank):** 109,889 sq mi. (284,613 sq km) (7)
**Geographic center:** In Lander Co., 26 mi. SE of Austin
**Number of counties:** 16, plus 1 independent city
**Largest cities (1975 est.):** Las Vegas (146,030); Reno (78,097); North Las Vegas (37,476); Sparks (31,639); Carson City (24,928)
**State forests:** None
**State parks:** 13 (104,255 ac., including leased lands)
**General fund revenue (1977–78):** $220,961,039
**General fund expenditure (1977–78):** $223,079,510

Trappers and traders, including Jedediah Smith and Peter Skene Ogden, entered the Nevada area in the 1820s. In 1843–45, John C. Fremont and Kit Carson explored the Great Basin and Sierra Nevada.

In 1848 following the Mexican War, the U.S. obtained the region and the first permanent settlement was a Mormon trading post near present-day Genoa.

The driest state in the nation with an average annual rainfall of only 3.73 inches, much of Nevada is uninhabited, sagebrush-covered desert.

Nevada was made famous by the discovery of the fabulous Comstock Lode in 1859 and its mines have produced large quantities of gold, silver, copper, lead, zinc, mercury, barite, and tungsten. Oil was discovered in 1954. Copper now far exceeds all other minerals in value of production.

In 1931, the state created two industries, divorce and gambling. For many years, Reno and Las Vegas were the "divorce capitals of the nation." More liberal divorce laws in many states have ended this distinction, but Nevada is the gambling and entertainment capital of the U.S. State gambling taxes account for 45% of tax revenues. Although Nevada leads the nation in per capita gambling revenue, it ranks only fourth in total gambling revenue.

Near Las Vegas, on the Colorado River, stands Hoover Dam, which impounds the waters of Lake Mead, one of the world's largest artificial lakes.

The state's agricultural crop consists mainly of hay, alfalfa seed, barley, and wheat.

Nevada manufactures gaming devices, chemicals, forest products, suntan lotion, and stone-clay-glass products.

Major resort areas flourish in Lake Tahoe, Reno, and Las Vegas. Recreation areas include those at Pyramid Lake, Lake Tahoe, and Lake Mead and Lake Mohave, both in Lake Mead National Recreation Area. Among the other attractions are Hoover Dam, Virginia City, and Lehman Caves National Monument.

## NEW HAMPSHIRE

**Capital:** Concord
**Governor:** Meldrim Thomson, Jr., R (to Jan. 1979)
**Secy. of State:** William M. Gardner, D (to Jan. 1979)
**Comptroller:** Arthur H. Fowler
**Atty. General:** Thomas Rath
**Entered Union & (rank):** June 21, 1788 (9)
**Present constitution adopted:** 1784
**Motto:** Live free or die
**State flower:** Purple lilac (1919)
**State tree:** White birch (1947)
**State bird:** Purple finch (1957)
**State songs:** "Old New Hampshire" (1949) and "New Hampshire, My New Hampshire" (1963)
**Nickname:** Granite State
**Origin of name:** From the English county of Hampshire
**1970 population & (rank):** 737,681 (41)
**1977 est. population & (rank):** 849,000 (42)
**1970 land area & (rank):** 9,027 sq mi. (23,380 sq km) (44)
**Geographic center:** In Belknap Co., 3 mi. E of Ashland
**Number of counties:** 10
**Largest cities (1975 est.):** Manchester (83,417); Nashua (61,002); Concord (29,321); Portsmouth (24,780); Dover (21,431); Keene (21,107)
**State forests & parks:** 175 (96,975 ac.)
**State revenue (1977):** $416,331,673
**State expenditure (1977):** $450,865,038

Under an English land grant, Capt. John Smith sent settlers to establish a fishing colony at the mouth of the Piscataqua River, near present-day Rye and Dover, in 1623. Capt. John Mason, who participated in the founding of Portsmouth in 1630, gave New Hampshire its name.

After a 38-year period of union with Massachusetts, New Hampshire was made a separate royal colony in 1679. As leaders in the revolutionary cause, New Hampshire delegates received the honor of being the first to vote for the Declaration of Independence on July 4, 1776. New Hampshire is the only state that ever played host at the formal conclusion of a foreign war when, in 1905, Portsmouth was the scene of the treaty ending the Russo-Japanese War.

Abundant water power early turned New Hampshire into an industrial state and manufacturing is the principal source of income in the state. The most important industrial products are leather goods, electrical and other machinery, textiles, and pulp and paper products.

Dairy and poultry farming and growing fruit, truck vegetables, corn, potatoes, and hay are the major agricultural pursuits.

Tourism, because of New Hampshire's scenic and recreational resources, now brings over $400 million into the state annually.

Vacation attractions include Lake Winnipesaukee, largest of 1,300 lakes and ponds; the 724,000-acre White Mountain National Forest; Daniel Webster's birthplace near Franklin; Strawberry Banke, restored building of the original settlement at Portsmouth; and the famous "Old Man of the Mountain" granite head profile, the state's official emblem, at Franconia.

## NEW JERSEY

**Capital:** Trenton
**Governor:** Brendan T. Byrne, D (to Jan. 1982)
**Secy. of State:** Donald Lan (to Jan. 1982) (apptd. by Governor)
**Treasurer:** Clifford A. Goldman, D (to Jan. 1982) (apptd. by Governor)
**Atty. General:** John J. Degnan, D (to Jan. 1982)
**Entered Union & (rank):** Dec. 18, 1787 (3)
**Present constitution adopted:** 1947
**Motto:** Liberty and prosperity

**State flower:** Purple violet (1913)
**State bird:** Eastern goldfinch (1935)
**State insect:** Honeybee
**State tree:** Red oak (1950)
**State animal:** Horse (1977)
**State colors:** Buff and blue (1965)
**State song:** None
**Nickname:** Garden State
**Origin of name:** From the Channel Isle of Jersey
**1970 population & (rank):** 7,168,164 (8)
**1977 est. population & (rank):** 7,329,000 (9)
**1970 land area & (rank):** 7,521 sq mi. (19,479 sq km) (46)
**Geographic center:** In Mercer Co., 5 mi. SE of Trenton
**Number of counties:** 21
**Largest cities (1975 est.):** Newark (339,568); Jersey City (243,756); Paterson (136,098); Elizabeth (104,405); Trenton (101,365); Camden (89,214)
**State forests:** 11
**State parks:** 40 (73,483 ac.)
**State general revenue (1977):** $6,465,716,449
**State appropriations (1977):** $6,345,894,392

New Jersey's early colonial history was involved with that of New York (New Netherlands), of which it was a part. One year after the Dutch surrender to England in 1664, New Jersey was organized as an English colony under Gov. Philip Carteret.

In the late 1600s the colony was divided between Carteret and William Penn; later it would be administered by the royal governor of New York. Finally, in 1738, New Jersey was separated from New York under its own royal governor, Lewis Morris.

Because of its key location between New York City and Philadelphia, New Jersey saw much fighting during the American Revolution.

Today, New Jersey, an area of wide industrial diversification, is known as the Crossroads of the East. Products from over 15,000 factories can be delivered overnight to almost 60 million people, representing 12 states and the District of Columbia. The greatest single industry is chemicals and New Jersey is one of the foremost research centers in the world. Many large oil refineries are located in northern New Jersey and other important manufactures are pharmaceuticals, instruments, machinery, electrical goods, and apparel.

Of the total land area, 43% is forested and about 24% is devoted to agriculture. The state ranks high in production of almost all garden vegetables. Tomatoes, asparagus, corn, and blueberries are important crops, and poultry farming and dairying make significant contributions to the state's economy.

Tourism is the second largest industry in New Jersey. The state has numerous resort areas on 127 miles of Atlantic coastline. In 1977, New Jersey voters approved legislation allowing legalized casino gambling in Atlantic City. Points of interest include the Walt Whitman House in Camden, the Delaware Water Gap, the Edison National Historic Site in West Orange, and Princeton University.

## NEW MEXICO

**Capital:** Santa Fe
**Governor:** Jerry Apodaca, D (to Jan. 1979)
**Lieut. Governor:** Robert E. Ferguson, D (to Jan. 1979)
**Secy. of State:** Ernestine D. Evans, D (to Jan. 1979)
**Atty. General:** Toney Anaya, D (to Jan. 1979)
**State Auditor:** Max Sanchez, D (to Jan. 1979)
**State Treasurer:** Edward M. Murphy, D (to Jan. 1979)
**Commissioner of Public Lands:** Phil R. Lucero (to Jan. 1979)
**Organized as territory:** Sept. 9, 1850
**Entered Union & (rank):** Jan. 6, 1912 (47)
**Present constitution adopted:** 1911
**Motto:** *Crescit eundo* (It grows as it goes)
**State flower:** Yucca (1927)
**State tree:** Pinon (1949)
**State animal:** Black bear (1963)
**State bird:** Roadrunner (1949)
**State fish:** Cutthroat trout (1955)
**State vegetables:** Chile and frijol (1965)
**State gem:** Turquoise (1967)
**State colors:** Red and yellow of old Spain (1925)
**State song:** "O Fair New Mexico" (1917)
**Spanish language state song:** "Asi Es Nuevo Mejico" (1971)
**Nicknames:** Land of Enchantment; Sunshine State
**Origin of name:** From the country of Mexico
**1970 population & (rank):** 1,016,000 (37)
**1977 est. population & (rank):** 1,190,000 (37)
**1970 land area & (rank):** 121,412 sq mi. (314,457 sq km) (5)
**Geographic center:** In Torrance Co., 12 mi. SSW of Willard
**Number of counties:** 32
**Largest cities (1975 est.):** Albuquerque (279,401); Santa Fe (44,937); Las Cruces (40,336); Roswell (37,980); Clovis (31,734); Farmington (27,802)
**State-owned forested land:** 933,000 ac.
**State parks:** 29 (105,012 ac.)
**State general revenue (1976):** $1,118,997,000
**State general expenditure (1976):** $990,343,000

Francisco Vásquez de Coronado, Spanish explorer searching for gold, traveled the region that became New Mexico in 1540–42. In 1598 the first Spanish settlement was established on the Rio Grande River by Juan de Onate and in 1610 Santa Fe was founded and made the capital of New Mexico.

The U.S. acquired most of New Mexico in 1848, as a result of the Mexican War, and the remainder in the 1853 Gadsden Purchase. Union troops captured the territory from the Confederates during the Civil War. With the surrender of Geronimo in 1886, the Apache Wars and most of the Indian troubles in the area were ended.

Since 1945, New Mexico has been a leader in energy research and development with extensive experiments conducted at Los Alamos Scientific Laboratory and Sandia Laboratories in the nuclear, solar, and geothermal areas.

Minerals are the state's richest natural resource and New Mexico leads the U.S. in output of uranium and potassium salts. Petroleum, natural gas, copper, gold, silver, zinc, lead, and molybdenum also contribute heavily to the state's income.

The principal manufacturing industries include food products, chemicals, transportation equipment, lumber, electrical machinery, and stone-clay-glass products. More than two thirds of New Mexico's farm income comes from livestock products, especially sheep. Cotton, pecans, and sorghum are the most important field crops. Corn, peanuts, beans, onions, and lettuce are also grown.

Tourist attractions in New Mexico include the Carlsbad Caverns National Park, Inscription Rock at El Morro National Monument, the ruins at Fort Union, Billy the Kid mementos at Lincoln, and the White Sands and Gila Cliff Dwellings National Monuments.

## NEW YORK

**Capital:** Albany
**Governor:** Hugh L. Carey, D (to Jan. 1979)
**Lieut. Governor:** Mary Anne Krupsak, D (to Jan. 1979)
**Secy. of State:** Mario M. Cuomo, D (to Jan. 1979)
**Comptroller:** Arthur Levitt, D (to Jan. 1979)
**Atty. General:** Louis J. Lefkowitz, R (to Jan. 1979)
**Entered Union & (rank):** July 26, 1788 (11)
**Present constitution adopted:** 1777 (last revised 1938)
**Motto:** *Excelsior* (Ever upward)
**State animal:** Beaver (1975)
**State fish:** Brook trout (1975)
**State gem:** Garnet (1969)
**State flower:** Rose (1955)
**State tree:** Sugar maple (1956)
**State bird:** Bluebird
**State song:** None
**Nickname:** Empire State
**Origin of name:** In honor of the English Duke of York
**1970 population & (rank):** 18,241,266 (2)
**1977 est. population & (rank):** 17,924,000 (2)
**1970 land area & (rank):** 47,931 sq mi. (123,882 sq km) (30)
**Geographic center:** In Madison Co., 12 mi. S of Oneida and 26 mi. SW of Utica
**Number of counties:** 62
**Largest cities (1975 est.):** New York (7,481,613); Buffalo (407,160); Rochester (267,173); Yonkers (192,509); Syracuse (182,543); Albany, (110,311)
**State forest preserves:** Adirondacks, 2,500,000 ac., Catskills, 250,000 ac.
**State parks:** 145 (more than 220,000 ac.)
**State general fund income (1977–78):** $11,302,000,000
**State general fund outgo (1977–78):** $11,301,000,000

Giovanni da Verrazano, Italian-born navigator sailing for France, discovered New York Bay in 1524. Henry Hudson, an Englishman employed by the Dutch, reached the bay and sailed up the river now bearing his name in 1609, the same year that northern New York was explored and claimed for France by Samuel de Champlain.

In 1624 the first permanent Dutch settlement was established at Fort Orange (now Albany); one year later Peter Minuit is said to have purchased Manhattan Island from the Indians for trinkets worth about $24 and founded the Dutch colony of New Amsterdam (now New York City), which was surrendered to the English in 1664.

For a short time, New York City was the U.S. capital and George Washington was inaugurated there as first President on April 30, 1789.

New York's extremely rapid commercial growth may be partly attributed to Governor De Witt Clinton, who pushed through the construction of the Erie Canal (Buffalo to Albany), which was opened in 1825. Today, the 559-mile Governor Thomas E. Dewey Thruway connects New York City with Buffalo and with Connecticut, Massachusetts, and Pennsylvania express highways. Two toll-free superhighways, the Adirondack Northway (linking Albany with the Canadian border) and the North-South-Expressway (crossing central New York from the Pennsylvania border to the Thousand Islands) have been opened.

New York, with the great metropolis of New York City, is the spectacular nerve center of the nation. It leads in manufacturing, foreign trade, commercial and financial transactions, book and magazine publishing, and theatrical production.

New York City is not only a national but an international leader. A leading seaport, its John F. Kennedy International Airport is one of the busiest airports in the world. The largest manufacturing center in the country, it had, in 1972, over 24,000 manufacturing establishments employing 757,300 persons and reported $11.6 billion of value added by manufacture. The apparel industry is the city's largest manufacturing employer, with printing and publishing second.

Nearly all the rest of the state's manufacturing is done on Long Island, along the Hudson River north to Albany and through the Mohawk Valley, Central New York, and Southern Tier regions to Buffalo. The St. Lawrence seaway and power projects have opened the North Country to industrial expansion and have given the state a second seacoast. In 1962, the Niagara power development was completed, giving the state the largest hydroelectric installation in the free world.

The state is the nation's manufacturing leader, with 1,711,500 employees and second with $33.6 billion in value added by manufacture in 1973. The principal industries are machinery, printing and publishing, instruments, apparel, and food.

The convention and tourist business is one of the state's most important sources of income.

New York farms are famous for dairying, truck gardening, and the raising of potatoes, onions, cabbage, fruits, and poultry. The state is a leading wine producer.

Among the major points of interest are Castle Clinton, Fort Stanwix, and Statue of Liberty National Monuments; Niagara Falls; U.S. Military Academy at West Point; National Historic Sites that include homes of Franklin D. Roosevelt at Hyde Park and Theodore Roosevelt in Oyster Bay and New York City; National Memorials, including Grant's Tomb and Federal Hall in New York City; Fort Ticonderoga; the Baseball Hall of Fame in Cooperstown; and the United Nations, skyscrapers, museums, theaters, and parks in New York City.

## NORTH CAROLINA

**Capital:** Raleigh
**Governor:** James B. Hunt, Jr., D (to Jan. 1981)
**Lieut. Governor:** James C. Greene (to Jan. 1981)
**Secy. of State:** Thad Eure, D (to Jan. 1981)
**Treasurer:** Harlan E. Boyles (to Jan. 1981)
**Auditor:** Henry L. Bridges, D (to Jan. 1981)
**Atty. General:** Rufus Edmisten, D (to Jan. 1981)
**Entered Union & (rank):** Nov. 21, 1789 (12)
**Present constitution adopted:** 1971
**Motto:** *Esse quam videri* (To be rather than to seem)
**State flower:** Dogwood (1941)
**State tree:** Pine (1963)
**State bird:** Cardinal (1943)
**State mammal:** Gray Squirrel (1969)
**State insect:** Honeybee (1973)
**State gem stone:** Emerald (1973)
**State shell:** Scotch bonnet (1965)
**State song:** "The Old North State" (1927)
**State colors:** Red and blue (1945)
**Nickname:** Tar Heel State
**Origin of name:** In honor of Charles I of England
**1970 population & (rank):** 5,082,059 (12)
**1977 est. population & (rank):** 5,525,000 (11)
**1970 land area & (rank):** 48,798 sq mi. (126,387 sq km) (29)
**Geographic center:** In Chatham Co., 10 mi. NW of Sanford
**Number of counties:** 100
**Largest cities (1975 est.):** Charolotte (281,417); Greensboro (155,848); Winston-Salem (141,018); Raleigh (134,231); Durham (101,224); Fayetteville (65,915)
**State forests:** 1

**State parks:** 26 (115,051 ac.)
**State revenues (1976–77):** $2,422,617,190[1]
**State expenditure (1976–77):** $3,634,885,020[2]

English colonists, sent by Sir Walter Raleigh, unsuccessfully attempted to settle Roanoke Island in 1585 and 1587. Virginia Dare, born there in 1587, was the first child of English parentage born in America.

In 1653 the first permanent settlements were established by English colonists from Virginia near the Roanoke and Chowan Rivers.

The region was established as an English proprietary colony in 1663–65 and its early history was the scene of Culpepper's Rebellion (1677), the Quaker-led Cary Rebellion of 1708, the Tuscarora Indian War in 1711–13, and many pirate raids.

During the American Revolution, there was relatively little fighting within the state, but many North Carolinians saw action elsewhere. Despite considerable pro-Union, anti-slavery sentiment, North Carolina joined the Confederacy.

North Carolina is the nation's largest furniture, tobacco, brick, and textile producer. It holds second place in the Southeast in population and first place in the value of its industrial and agricultural production. This production is highly diversified, with metalworking, chemicals, and paper constituting enormous industries. Tobacco, corn, cotton, hay, peanuts, and truck and vegetable crops are of major importance. It is the country's leading producer of mica and lithium.

Tourism is also important, with travelers and vacationers spending more than $1 billion annually in North Carolina. Sports include year-round golfing, skiing at mountain resorts, both fresh and salt water fishing, and hunting.

Among the major attractions are the Great Smoky Mountains, the Blue Ridge National Parkway, the Cape Hatteras and Cape Lookout National Seashores, the Wright Brothers National Memorial at Kitty Hawk, Guilford Courthouse and Moores Creek National Military Parks, Carl Sandburg's home near Hendersonville, and the Old Salem Restoration in Winston-Salem.

## NORTH DAKOTA

**Capital:** Bismarck
**Governor:** Arthur A. Link, D (to Jan. 1981)
**Lieut. Governor:** Wayne Sanstead, D (to Jan. 1981)
**Secy. of State:** Ben Meier, R (to Jan. 1981)
**Auditor:** Robert W. Peterson, R (to Jan. 1981)
**Atty. General:** Allen I. Olson, R (to Jan. 1981)
**Organized as territory:** March 2, 1861
**Entered Union & (rank):** Nov. 2, 1889 (39)
**Present constitution adopted:** 1889
**Motto:** Liberty and union, now and forever: one and inseparable
**State tree:** American Elm (1947)
**State bird:** Western meadow lark (1947)
**State song:** "North Dakota Hymn" (1947)
**Nickname:** Sioux State; Flickertail State
**Origin of name:** From the Dakotah tribe, meaning "allies"
**1970 population & (rank):** 617,761 (45)
**1977 est. population & (rank):** 653,000 (45)
**1970 land area & (rank):** 69,273 sq mi (179,417 sq km) (17)
**Geographic center:** In Sheridan Co., 5 mi. SW of McClusky
**Number of counties:** 53

1. Excludes Federal revenues to state. 2. All expenditures: operating, and capital improvements.

**Largest cities (1975 est.):** Fargo (56,058); Grand Forks (41,909); Bismarck (38,378); Minot (32,790); Jamestown (15,330); Mandan (12,560)
**State forests:** None
**State parks:** 5 (2,981 ac.)
**Total state collections (1976):** $721,165,761
**Total state disbursements (1976):** $701,545,888

North Dakota was explored in 1738–40 by French Canadians led by Vérendrye. In 1803, the U.S. acquired most of North Dakota from France in the Louisiana Purchase. Lewis and Clark explored the region in 1804–06 and the first settlements were made at Pembina in 1812 by Scottish and Irish families while this area was still in dispute between the U.S. and Great Britian.

In 1818, the U.S. obtained the northeastern part of North Dakota by treaty with Great Britain and took possession of Pembina in 1823.

North Dakota is the most rural of all the states, with farms covering more than 90% of the land. Only Kansas produces more wheat and the state's coal and oil reserves are plentiful.

Other agricultural products include barley, rye, oats and flaxseed, sugar beets, and hay; beef cattle, sheep, and hogs are also important to the state's economy.

Recently, manufacturing industries have grown, especially food processing and farm equipment. The state also produces natural gas, lignite, salt, clay, sand, and gravel.

The Garrison Dam on the Missouri River provides extensive irrigation and produces 400,000 kilowatts of electricity for the Missouri Basin areas.

Known for its waterfowl, grouse, and deer hunting and bass, trout, and northern pike fishing, North Dakota has 20 state parks and recreation areas. Points of interest include the International Peace Garden near Dunseith, Fort Union Trading Post National Historic Site, the State Capitol at Bismarck, the Badlands, and Fort Lincoln, now a state park, from which Gen. George Custer set out on his last campaign in 1876.

## OHIO

**Capital:** Columbus
**Governor:** James A. Rhodes, R (to Jan. 1979)
**Lieut. Governor:** Richard F. Celeste, D (to Jan. 1979)
**Secy. of State:** Ted W. Brown, R (to Jan. 1979)
**Auditor:** Thomas E. Ferguson (to Jan. 1979)
**Treasurer:** Gertrude W. Donahey, D (to Jan. 1979)
**Atty. General:** William J. Brown, D (to Jan. 1979)
**Entered Union & (rank):** March 1, 1807 (17)
**Present constitution adopted:** 1851
**Motto:** With God, all things are possible
**State flower:** Scarlet carnation (1904)
**State tree:** Buckeye (1953)
**State bird:** Cardinal (1933)
**State insect:** Ladybug (1975)
**State gem stone:** Flint (1965)
**State song:** "Beautiful Ohio"
**State drink:** Tomato juice (1965)
**Nickname:** Buckeye State
**Origin of name:** From an Iroquoian word meaning "great river"
**1970 population & (rank):** 10,652,017 (6)
**1977 est. population & (rank):** 10,701,000 (6)
**1970 land area & (rank):** 40,975 sq mi. (106,125 sq km) (35)
**Geographic center:** In Delaware Co., 25 mi. NNE of Columbus
**Number of counties:** 88

**Largest cities (1975 est.):** Cleveland (638,793); Columbus (535,610); Cincinnati (412,564); Toledo (367,650); Akron (251,747); Dayton (205,986)
**State forests:** 18 (163,972 ac.)
**State parks:** 64 (199,351 ac.)
**State actual revenue (fiscal 1977):** $6,081,694,446
**State actual expenditure (fiscal 1977):** $6,443,281,407

First explored for France by La Salle in 1669, the Ohio region became British property after the French and Indian War. Ohio was acquired by the U.S. after the Revolutionary War in 1783 and, in 1788, the first permanent settlement was established at Marietta, capital of the Northwest Territory.

The 1790s saw severe fighting with the Indians in Ohio; a major battle was won by Maj. Gen. Anthony Wayne at Fallen Timbers in 1794. In the War of 1812, Commodore Oliver H. Perry defeated the British in the Battle of Lake Erie on Sept. 10, 1813.

Ohio is one of the nation's industrial leaders, ranking third in the value of manufactured products. Important manufacturing centers are located in or near Ohio's major cities. Akron is known for rubber; Canton for roller bearings; Cincinnati for jet engines and machine tools; Cleveland for auto assembly and parts, refining, and steel; Dayton for office machines, refrigeration, and heating and auto equipment; Youngstown and Steubenville for steel; and Toledo for glass and auto parts.

The state's thousands of factories almost overshadow its importance in agriculture and mining. Its fertile soil produces soybeans, corn, oats, grapes, and clover. More than half of Ohio's farm receipts come from dairying and sheep and hog raising. Ohio is the top state in lime production and among the leaders in coal, clay, salt, sand, and gravel. Petroleum, gypsum, cement, and natural gas are also important.

Tourism is a valuable revenue producer, bringing in over $3 billion annually. Attractions include the Indian burial grounds at Mound City Group National Monument, Perry's Victory International Peace Memorial, the Pro Football Hall of Fame at Canton, and the homes of Presidents Grant, Taft, Hayes, Harding, and Garfield.

## OKLAHOMA

**Capital:** Oklahoma City
**Governor:** David L. Boren, D (to Jan. 1979)
**Lieut. Governor:** George Nigh, D (to Jan. 1979)
**Secy. of State:** Jerome W. Byrd, D (to Jan. 1979)
**Treasurer:** Leo Winters, D (to Jan. 1979)
**Atty. General:** Larry Derryberry, D (to Jan. 1979)
**Organized as territory:** May 2, 1890
**Entered Union & (rank):** Nov. 16, 1907 (46)
**Present constitution adopted:** 1907
**Motto:** *Labor omnia vinci* (Labor conquers all things)
**State flower:** Mistletoe (1893)
**State tree:** Redbud (1937)
**State bird:** Scissor-tailed flycatcher (1951)
**State animal:** Bison (1972)
**State reptile:** Mountain boomer lizard (1969)
**State stone:** Rose Rock (barite rose) (1968)
**State colors:** Green and white (1915)
**State song:** "Oklahoma" (1953)
**Nickname:** Sooner State
**Origin of name:** From two Choctaw Indian words meaning "red people"
**1970 population & (rank):** 2,559,253 (27)
**1977 est. population & (rank):** 2,811,000 (27)
**1970 land area & (rank):** 68,782 sq mi. (178,145 sq km) (19)
**Geographic center:** In Oklahoma Co., 8 mi. N of Oklahoma City
**Number of counties:** 77
**Largest cities (1975 est.):** Oklahoma City (365,916); Tulsa (331,726); Lawton (76,421); Norman (59,948); Midwest City (50,105); Enid (48,030)
**State forests:** None
**State parks:** 28 (88,959 ac.)
**Total state revenue (1977):** $2,200,794,053
**Total state expenditure (1977):** $2,196,476,052

Francisco Vásquez de Coronado first explored the region for Spain in 1541. The U.S. acquired most of Oklahoma in 1803 in the Louisiana Purchase from France; the Western Panhandle region became U.S. territory with the annexation of Texas in 1845.

In 1834, Oklahoma was set aside as Indian Territory. It remained so until April 22, 1889, when it was opened to homestead settlement. On that one day 50,000 people swarmed in and the term "Sooners" was applied to those who tried to beat the noon starting gun. Other Oklahoma "Land Rushes" took place through 1901.

Oil has made Oklahoma a rich state and Tulsa one of the world's wealthiest cities per capita. Oil refining, meat packing, food processing, and machinery manufacturing (especially construction and oil equipment) are important industries.

Other minerals produced in Oklahoma include natural gas, helium, gypsum, zinc, cement, coal, copper, and silver.

Oklahoma's rich plains produce bumper yields of wheat, as well as large crops of sorghum, corn, cotton, and peanuts. Its beef cattle herd is among the largest in the nation; more than half of Oklahoma's annual farm receipts are contributed by livestock products.

Tourist attractions include the National Cowboy Hall of Fame in Oklahoma City, the Will Rogers Memorial in Claremore, the Cherokee Cultural Center with a restored Cherokee village, the restored Fort Gibson Stockade near Muskogee, and the Lake Texoma recreation area.

## OREGON

**Capital:** Salem
**Governor:** Robert W. Straub, D (to Jan. 1979)
**Secy. of State:** Norma Paulus, R (to Jan. 1981)
**Treasurer:** Clay Myers, R (to Jan. 1981)
**Atty. General:** James A. Redden, D (to Jan. 1981)
**Organized as territory:** Aug. 14, 1848
**Entered Union & (rank):** Feb. 14, 1859 (33)
**Present constitution adopted:** 1859
**Motto:** The Union (1957)
**State flower:** Oregon grape (1899)
**State tree:** Douglas fir (1939)
**State animal:** Beaver (1969)
**State bird:** Western meadow lark (1927)
**State fish:** Chinook salmon (1961)
**State rock:** Thunderegg (1965)
**State colors:** Navy blue and gold (1959)
**State song:** "Oregon, My Oregon" (1927)
**Nickname:** Beaver State
**Origin of name:** Unknown. However, it is generally accepted that the name, first used by Jonathan Carver in 1778, was taken from the writings of Maj. Robert Rogers, an English army officer.
**1970 population & (rank):** 2,091,385 (31)
**1977 est. population & (rank):** 2,376,000 (30)
**1970 land area & (rank):** 96,184 sq mi. (249,117 sq km) (10)
**Geographic center:** In Crook Co., 25 mi. SSE of Princevilleu

**Number of counties:** 36
**Largest cities (1975 est.):** Portland (356,732); Eugene (92,451); Salem (78,168); Corvallis (38,502); Springfield (33,432); Medford (32,577); Gresham (23,249)
**State forests:** 785,062 ac.
**State parks:** 237 (95,800 ac.)
**State general revenue (1977–79):** $2,164,233,514
**State general expenditure (1977–79):** $2,126,840,878

Spanish and English sailors are believed to have sighted the Oregon coast in the 1500s and 1600s. Capt. James Cook, seeking the Northwest Passage, charted some of the coastline in 1778. In 1792, Capt. Robert Gray, in the *Columbia*, discovered the river named after his ship and claimed the area for the U.S.

In 1805 the Lewis and Clark expedition explored the area and John Jacob Astor's fur depot, Astoria, was founded in 1811. Disputes for control of Oregon between American settlers and the Hudson Bay Company were finally resolved in the 1846 Oregon Treaty in which Great Britain gave up claims to the region.

Oregon, with the greatest U.S. reserve of standing timber, has a billion-dollar wood processing industry. Its salmon-fishing industry, centered at Astoria at the mouth of the Columbia, is one of the world's largest.

In agriculture, the state leads in growing peppermint, holly, lily bulbs, cranberries, filberts, Blue Lake beans, and cover seed crops, and also raises strawberries, hops, wheat and other grains, sugar beets, potatoes, green peas, fiber flax, dairy products, livestock and poultry, apples, pears, and cherries. Oregon is the source of all the nickel produced in the U.S.

With the low-cost electric power provided by Bonneville Dam, McNary Dam, and other dams in the Pacific Northwest, Oregon has developed steadily as a manufacturing state. Leading manufactures are lumber and plywood, metalwork, machinery, aluminum, chemicals, paper, food packing, and electronic equipment.

Crater Lake National Park, Mount Hood, and Bonneville Dam on the Columbia are major tourist attractions. Oregon Dunes National Recreation Area has been established near Florence. Other points of interest include the Oregon Caves National Monument, Cape Perpetua in Siuslaw National Forest, Columbia River Gorge between The Dalles and Troutdale, and Hells Canyon.

## PENNSYLVANIA

**Capital:** Harrisburg
**Governor:** Milton J. Shapp, D (to Jan. 1979)
**Lieut. Governor:** Ernest P. Kline, D (to Jan. 1979)
**Secy. of the Commonwealth:** Barton A. Fields, D (term indefinite)
**Auditor General:** Al Benedict, D (to Jan. 1979)
**Atty. General:** Robert Kane, D (to Jan. 1979)
**Entered Union & (rank):** Dec. 12, 1787 (2)
**Present constitution adopted:** 1874
**Motto:** Virtue, liberty, and independence
**State flower:** Mountain laurel (1933)
**State tree:** Hemlock (1931)
**State bird:** Ruffed grouse (1931)
**State insect:** Firefly
**State dog:** Great Dane (1965)
**State colors:** Blue and gold
**State song:** None
**Nickname:** Keystone State
**Origin of name:** In honor of Adm. Sir. William Penn, father of William Penn. It means "Penn's Woodland."
**1970 population & (rank):** 11,793,909 (3)
**1977 est. population & (rank):** 11,785,000 (4)
**1970 land area & (rank):** 44,966 sq mi. (116,462 sq km) (32)
**Geographic center:** In Centre Co., 2½ mi. SW of Bellefonte
**Number of counties:** 67
**Largest cities (1975 est.):** Philadelphia (1,815,808); Pittsburgh (458,651); Erie (127,895); Allentown (106,624); Scranton (95,884); Reading (81,592)
**State forests:** 1,930,108 ac.
**State parks:** 120 (297,438 ac.)
**Total estimated revenue subject to general appropriations (1978–79):** $5,777,455,000
**Total approved appropriations (1978–79):** $5,777,044,000

Rich in historic lore, Pennsylvania territory was disputed in the early 1600s among the Dutch, the Swedes, and the English. England acquired the region in 1664 with the capture of New York and in 1681 Pennsylvania was granted to William Penn, a Quaker, by King Charles II.

Philadelphia was the seat of the federal government almost continuously from 1776 to 1800; there the Declaration of Independence was signed in 1776 and the U.S. Constitution drawn up in 1787. Valley Forge, of Revolutionary War fame, and Gettysburg, the turning-point of the Civil War, are both in Pennsylvania. The Liberty Bell is located in Independence Hall in Philadelphia.

Approximately 23% of all American pig iron steel is made in Pennsylvania, which ranks first among the states in steel wire and structural metal production. Other manufactures include machinery, chemicals, storage batteries, motor vehicles and trailers, computers, textiles and apparel, shoes, plastics, and explosives. Pennsylvania produces almost all the nation's anthracite coal. Also important are bituminous coal, cement, stone, petroleum, natural gas, lime, clays, zinc, and iron.

Prosperous farms brought in total receipts of more than $1.3 billion in 1973. The state ranked high in milk cows, chickens, and turkeys. Agricultural products include apples, peaches, potatoes, corn, wheat, barley, buckwheat, and mushrooms.

Tourists now spend approximately $6 billion in Pennsylvania annually. Among the chief attractions: the Gettysburg National Military Park, Valley Forge National Historical Park, Independence National Historical Park in Philadelphia, the Pennsylvania Dutch region, the Eisenhower farm near Gettysburg, and the Delaware Water Gap National Recreation Area.

## RHODE ISLAND

**Capital:** Providence
**Governor:** J. Joseph Garrahy, D (to Jan. 1979)
**Lieut. Governor:** Thomas R. Di Luglio, D (to Jan. 1979)
**Secy. of State:** Robert F. Burns, D (to Jan. 1979)
**Controller:** James A. Carter (civil service)
**Atty. General:** Julius C. Michaelson, D (to Jan. 1979)
**Entered Union & (rank):** May 29, 1790 (13)
**Present constitution adopted:** 1843
**Motto:** Hope
**State flower:** Violet (unofficial)
**State tree:** Red maple (official)
**State bird:** Rhode Island Red (official)
**State colors:** Blue, white, and gold (in state flag)
**State song:** "Rhode Island" (1946)
**Nickname:** The Ocean State
**Origin of name:** From the Greek island of Rhodes
**1970 population & (rank):** 949,723 (39)

**1977 est. population & (rank):** 935,000 (39)
**1970 land area & (rank):** 1,049 sq mi. (2,717 sq km) (50)
**Geographic center:** In Kent Co., 1 mi. SSW of Crompton
**Number of counties:** 5
**Largest cities (1975 est.):** Providence (167,724); Warwick (85,875); Cranston (74,381); Pawtucket (72,024); East Providence (49,636); Woonsocket (46,888)
**State forests:** 11 (20,900 ac.)
**State parks:** 17 (8,200 ac.)
**State general revenue (1976–77):** $728,191,718
**State general expenditure (1976–77):** $714,663,866

From its beginnings, Rhode Island has been distinguished by its support for freedom of conscience and action, started by Roger Williams, exiled by the Massachusetts Bay Colony Puritans in 1636, and the founder of the present state capital, Providence. Williams was followed by other religious exiles who founded Pocasset, now Portsmouth, in 1638 and Newport in 1639.

The first Baptist church in the U.S. was established in Providence in 1638 and Rhode Island provided a haven for Quakers in 1657 and for Jews from Holland in 1659.

Rhode Island's rebellious, authority-defying nature was further demonstrated by the burnings of the British revenue cutters *Liberty* and *Gaspee* prior to the Revolution, by its early declaration of independence from Great Britain in May 1776, its refusal to participate actively in the War of 1812, and by Dorr's Rebellion of 1842, which protested property requirements for voting.

Rhode Island, smallest of the 50 states, is densely populated and highly industrialized. The state pioneered in the manufacture of jewelry and silverware and still retains first place in the U.S. Other leading industries are primary metal processing, metal products, machinery, rubber and plastics, food processing, chemicals, and apparel.

With more than eight tenths of the population living in urban areas, adjacent areas of the state are involved in dairying and poultry and truck farming. Nursery and greenhouse products, potatoes, corn, apples, oats, and hay lead the crop list.

Newport became famous as the summer capital of society in the mid-19th century. Touro Synagogue (1763) is the oldest in the U.S. Other points of interest include the Roger Williams National Memorial in Providence, Samuel Slater's Mill in Pawtucket, the General Nathaniel Greene Homestead in Coventry, Block Island, and Narragansett Pier.

## SOUTH CAROLINA

**Capital:** Columbia
**Governor:** James B. Edwards, R (to Jan. 1979)
**Lieut. Governor:** W. Brantley Harvey, D (to Jan. 1979)
**Secy. of State:** O. Frank Thornton, D (to Jan. 1979)
**Comptroller General:** Earl E. Morris, Jr. (to Jan. 1979)
**Atty. General:** Daniel R. McLeod, D (to Jan. 1979)
**Entered Union & (rank):** May 23, 1788 (8)
**Present constitution adopted:** 1895
**Mottoes:** *Animis opibusque parati* (Prepared in mind and resources) and *Dum spiro spero* (While I breathe, I hope)
**State flower:** Carolina yellow jessamine (1924)
**State tree:** Palmetto tree (1939)
**State bird:** Carolina wren (1948)
**State song:** "Carolina" (1911)
**Nickname:** Palmetto State
**Origin of name:** In honor of Charles I of England
**1977 est. population & (rank):** 2,876,000 (26)
**1970 land area & (rank):** 30,225 sq mi. (78,283 sq km) (40)
**Geographic center:** In Richland Co., 13 mi. SE of Columbia
**Number of counties:** 46
**Largest cities (1975 est.):** Columbia (111,616); North Charleston (58,544); Greenville (58,518); Charleston (57,470); Spartanburg (46,929); Rock Hill (35,346)
**State forests:** 4 (124,052 ac.)
**State parks:** 50 (61,726 ac.)
**State general fund revenue (1976–77):** $1,077,197,025[1]
**State general expenditures (1976–77):** $1,047,320,041[1]

Following exploration of the coast in 1521 by De Gordillo, the Spanish tried unsuccessfully to establish a colony near present-day Georgetown in 1526 and the French also failed to colonize Parris Island near Fort Royal in 1562.

The first English settlement was made in 1670 at Albemarle Point on the Ashley River, but poor conditions drove the settlers to the site of Charleston (originally called Charles Town). South Carolina, officially separated from North Carolina in 1729, was the scene of extensive military action during the Revolution and again during the Civil War. The Civil War began in 1861 as South Carolina troops fired on federal Fort Sumter in Charleston Harbor and the state was the first to secede from the Union.

Once primarily agricultural, South Carolina has built so many large textile and other mills that today its factories produce eight times the output of its farms in cash value. Charleston makes asbestos, wood, pulp, and steel products; chemicals, machinery, and apparel are also important.

Farms have become fewer but larger in recent years. South Carolina grows more peaches than any other state except California; it ranks fourth in tobacco. Other farm products include cotton, peanuts, sweet potatoes, soybeans, corn, and oats. Poultry and dairy products are also important revenue producers.

Points of interest include Fort Sumter National Monument, Fort Moultrie, Fort Johnson, and aircraft carrier USS *Yorktown* in Charleston Harbor; the Middleton, Magnolia, and Cypress Gardens in Charleston; Cowpens National Battlefield; and the Hilton Head resorts.

## SOUTH DAKOTA

**Capital:** Pierre
**Governor:** Richard F. Kneip, D (to Jan. 1979)
**Lieut. Governor:** Harvey Wollman, D (to Jan. 1979)
**Atty. General:** William Janklow, R (to Jan. 1979)
**Secy. of State:** Lorna B. Herseth, D (to Jan. 1979)
**State Auditor:** Alice Kundert, R (to Jan. 1979)
**State Treasurer:** David L. Volk, R (to Jan. 1979)
**Organized as territory:** March 2, 1861
**Entered Union & (rank):** Nov. 2, 1889 (40)
**Present constitution adopted:** 1889
**Motto:** Under God the people rule
**State flower:** American pasqueflower (1903)
**State grass:** Western wheat grass (1970)
**State tree:** Black Hills spruce (1947)
**State bird:** Ring-necked pheasant (1943)
**State insect:** Honeybee (1978)
**State animal:** Coyote (1949)
**State mineral stone:** Rose quartz (1966)
**State gem stone:** Fairburn agate (1966)
**State colors:** Blue and gold (in state flag)
**State song:** "Hail! South Dakota" (1943)
**Nicknames:** Sunshine State; Coyote State
**Origin of name:** Same as for North Dakota

1. Highway Department has separate funding and expenditures.

**1970 population & (rank):** 666,257 (44)
**1977 est. population & (rank):** 689,000 (44)
**1970 land area & (rank):** 75,955 sq mi. (196,723 sq km) (16)
**Geographic center:** In Hughes Co., 8 mi. NE of Pierre
**Number of counties:** 67 (64 county governments)
**Largest cities (1975 est.):** Sioux Falls (73,925); Rapid City (48,156); Aberdeen (26,628); Watertown (14,402); Brookings (13,860); Mitchell (13,696)
**State forests:** None[1]
**State parks:** 12 plus 31 recreational areas (87,269 ac.)[2]
**State general revenue (1977–78):** $440,312,409[3]
**State general expenditure (1977–78):** $382,417,059[3]

Exploration of this area began in 1743 when Louis-Joseph and François Verendrye came from France in search of a route to the Pacific.

The U.S. acquired the region as part of the Louisiana Purchase in 1803 and it was explored by Lewis and Clark in 1804–06. Fort Pierre, the first permanent settlement, was established in 1817 and, in 1831, the first Missouri River steamboat reached the fort.

Settlement of South Dakota did not begin in earnest until the arrival of the railroad in 1873 and the discovery of gold in the Black Hills the following year.

Agriculture is South Dakota's basic industry today. It normally ranks first in the U.S. in the size of its rye crop and high in spring wheat, flaxseed, oats, and barley. In 1974 South Dakota had 5 million cattle, almost a million sheep, and 2 million hogs.

South Dakota is the nation's second leading producer of gold (Nevada ranks first) and the Homestake Mine is the richest in the U.S. Other minerals produced include berylium, bentonite, granite, silver, petroleum, and uranium.

Processing of foods produced by farms and ranches is the largest South Dakota manufacturing industry, followed by lumber, wood products, and machinery, including farm equipment.

The Black Hills, a great tourist attraction, are the highest mountains east of the Rockies. Mt. Rushmore, in this group, is famous for the likenesses of Washington, Jefferson, Lincoln, and Theodore Roosevelt, which were carved in granite by Gutzon Borglum. The Badlands offer scenic masses of bare rock and clay unrelieved by any vegetation. Other points of interest are Deadwood, where Wild Bill Hickok was killed in 1876; the Crazy Horse Memorial near Custer; and the Corn Palace in Mitchell.

## TENNESSEE

**Capital:** Nashville
**Governor:** Ray Blanton, D (Jan. 1979)
**Lieut. Governor:** John S. Wilder, D (to Jan. 1981)
**Secy. of State:** Gentry Crowell, D (to Jan. 1981)
**Atty. General:** Brooks McLemore, D (to Sept. 1982)
**State Treasurer:** Harlan Matthews, D (to Jan. 1979)
**Entered Union & (rank):** June 1, 1796 (16)
**Present constitution adopted:** 1870; amended 1953, 1960, 1965 and 1973
**Motto:** "Tennessee—America at its best" (1965)
**State flower:** Iris (1933)
**State tree:** Tulip poplar (1947)
**State bird:** Mockingbird (1933)
**State horse:** Tennessee walking horse

1. No designated state forests; about 13,000 ac. of state land is forest land. 2. Acreage includes 31 recreation areas and 80 roadside parks, in addition to 12 state parks. 3. Includes Federal funds.

**State animal:** Raccoon
**State wild flower:** Passion flower
**State song:** "Tennessee Waltz" (1965)
**Nickname:** Volunteer State
**Origin of name:** Of Cherokee origin; the exact meaning is unknown
**1970 population & (rank):** 3,924,164 (17)
**1977 est. population & (rank):** 4,299,000 (17)
**1970 land area & (rank):** 41,328 sq mi. (107,040 sq km) (34)
**Geographic center:** In Rutherford Co., 5 mi. NE of Murfreesboro
**Number of counties:** 95
**Largest cities (1975 est.):** Memphis (661,319); Nashville-Davidson (423,426); Knoxville (183,383); Chattanooga (161,978); Clarksville (51,910); Jackson (43,357)
**State forests:** 14 (155,752 ac.)
**State parks:** 21 (130,000 ac.)
**State general revenue (1976):** $2,300,555,000
**State general expenditure (1976):** $2,807,698,000

First visited by the Spanish explorer de Soto in 1541, the Tennessee area would later be claimed by both France and England as a result of the 1670s and 1680s explorations of Marquette and Jolliet, La Salle, and the Englishmen James Needham and Gabriel Arthur.

Great Britain obtained the region following the French and Indian War in 1763 and it was rapidly occupied by settlers moving in from Virginia and the Carolinas.

During 1784–87, the settlers formed the "state" of Franklin, which was disbanded when the region was allowed to send representatives to the North Carolina legislature. In 1790 Congress organized the territory south of the Ohio River and Tennessee joined the Union in 1796.

Although Tennessee joined the Confederacy during the Civil War, there was much pro-Union sentiment in the state, which was the scene of extensive military action.

The state is now predominantly industrial; in 1970, 58.8% of its population lived in urban areas. Among the most important products are chemicals, textiles, apparel, electrical machinery, furniture, and leather goods. Other lines include food processing, lumber, primary metals, and metal products. The state is known as the U.S. hardwood-flooring center and ranks first in the production of marble, zinc, pyrite, and ball clay.

Tennessee is one of the leading tobacco-producing states in the nation and its farming income is also derived from livestock and dairy products as well as corn, cotton, and soybeans.

With six other states, Tennessee shares the extensive federal reservoir developments on the Tennessee and Cumberland River systems. The Tennessee Valley Authority operates a number of dams and reservoirs in the state.

Among the major points of interest: the Andrew Johnson National Historic Site at Greenville, American Museum of Atomic Energy at Oak Ridge, Great Smoky Mountains National Park, The Hermitage (home of Andrew Jackson near Nashville), Rock City Gardens near Chattanooga, and three National Military Parks.

## TEXAS

**Capital:** Austin
**Governor:** Dolph Briscoe, D (to Jan. 1979)
**Lieut. Governor:** William P. Hobby, D (to Jan. 1979)

**Secy. of State:** Steve Oaks, D (to Jan. 1979)
**Comptroller:** Bob Bullock (to Jan. 1979)
**Atty. General:** John L. Hill, D (to Jan. 1979)
**Entered Union & (rank):** Dec. 29, 1845 (28)
**Present constitution adopted:** 1876
**Motto:** Friendship
**State flower:** Bluebonnet (1901)
**State tree:** Pecan (1919)
**State bird:** Mockingbird (1927)
**State song:** "Texas, Our Texas" (1930)
**Nickname:** Lone Star State
**Origin of name:** From an Indian word meaning "friends"
**1970 population & (rank):** 11,196,730 (4)
**1977 est. population & (rank):** 12,830,000 (3)
**1970 land area & (rank):** 262,134 sq mi. (678,927 sq km) (2)
**Geographic center:** In McCulloch Co., 15 mi. NE of Brady
**Number of counties:** 254
**Largest cities (1975 est.):** Houston (1,357,394); Dallas (812,797); San Antonio (773,248); El Paso (385,691); Fort Worth (358,364); Austin (301,147)
**State forests:** 4 (6,306 ac.)
**State parks:** 83 (64 developed)
**State revenue receipts (1976–77):** $7,390,734,138
**State government cost (1976–77):** $6,620,440,594

Spanish explorers, including Cabeza de Vaca and Coronado, were the first to visit the region in the 16th and 17th centuries, settling at Ysleta near present-day El Paso in 1682. In 1685, La Salle established a short-lived French colony at Matagorda Bay.

Americans, led by Stephen F. Austin, began to settle along the Brazos River in 1821 when Texas was controlled by Mexico, recently independent from Spain. In 1836, following a brief war between the American settlers in Texas and the Mexican government, and famous for the battles of the Alamo and San Jacinto, the Independent Republic of Texas was proclaimed with Sam Houston as president.

After Texas became the 28th U.S. state in 1845, border disputes led to the Mexican War of 1846–48.

Today, Texas, second only to Alaska in land area, leads all other states in such categories as oil, cattle, sheep, and cotton. Possessing enormous natural resources, Texas is a major agricultural state and an industrial giant.

Sulfur, salt, helium asphalt, graphite, bromine, natural gas, cement, and clays give Texas first place in mineral production—nearly $8 billion in 1973. Chemicals, oil refining, food processing, machinery, and transportation equipment are among the major Texas manfacturing industries.

Texas ranches and farms produce beef cattle, poultry, rice, pecans, peanuts, sorghum, and an extensive variety of fruits and vegetables.

Millions of tourists spend well over $2 billion annually visiting more than 70 state parks, recreations areas, and points of interest such as the Gulf Coast resort area, the Lyndon B. Johnson Space Center in Houston, the Alamo in San Antonio, the state capital in Austin, and the Big Bend and Guadalupe Mountains National Parks.

## UTAH

**Capital:** Salt Lake City
**Governor:** Scott M. Matheson, D (to Jan. 1981)
**Lieut. Governor/Secretary of State:** David S. Monson, R (to Jan. 1981)
**Atty. General:** Robert B. Hansen, R (to Jan. 1981)
**Organized as territory:** Sept. 9, 1850
**Entered Union & (rank):** Jan. 4, 1896 (45)
**Present constitution adopted:** 1896
**Motto:** Industry
**State flower:** Sego lily (1911)
**State tree:** Blue spruce (1933)
**State bird:** Seagull (1955)
**State emblem:** Beehive
**State song:** "Utah, We Love Thee"
**Nickname:** Beehive State
**Origin of name:** From the Ute tribe, meaning "people of the mountains"
**1970 population & (rank):** 1,059,273 (36)
**1977 est. population & (rank):** 1,268,000 (36)
**1970 land area & (rank):** 82,096 sq mi. (212,629 sq km) (12)
**Geographic center:** In Sanpete Co., 3 mi. N. of Manti
**Number of counties:** 29
**Largest cities (1975 est.):** Salt Lake City (169,917); Ogden (68,978); Provo (55,593); Orem (35,584); Bountiful (30,358); Logan (23,810)
**State forests:** None
**State parks:** 35 (64,097 ac.)
**Total state receipt (1976–77):** $960,844,421
**Total state disbursements (1976–77):** $982,026,152
**Cash balance (1976–77):** $16,600,000

The region was first explored for Spain by Franciscan friars, Escalante and Dominguez in 1776. In 1824 the famous American frontiersman Jim Bridger discovered the Great Salt Lake.

Fleeing the religious persecution encountered in eastern and middle-western states, the Mormons reached the Great Salt Lake in 1847 and began to build Salt Lake City. The U.S. acquired the Utah region in the treaty ending the Mexican War in 1848 and the first transcontinental railroad was completed with the driving of a golden spike at Promontory Point in 1869.

Mormon difficulties with the federal government about polygamy did not end until the Mormon Church renounced the practice in 1890, six years before Utah became a state.

In recent years, manufacturing has become Utah's most important industry, ahead of mining, agriculture, and tourism. The state's factories produce transportation equipment, food products, machinery, metal products, and electrical equipment. Utah has also become an important aerospace research and production center and is a leading warehousing and distribution point for much of the western U.S.

Rich in natural resources, Utah has long been a leading producer of copper, gold, silver, lead, zinc, and molybdenum. Oil has also become a major product; with Colorado and Wyoming, Utah shares what have been called the world's richest oil shale deposits.

Ranked eighth among the states in number of sheep in 1973, Utah also produces large crops of apricots and cherries as well as sugar beets, potatoes, onions, alfalfa, winter wheat, and beans. Utah's farmlands and crops require extensive irrigation.

Utah is a great vacationland with 11,000 miles of fishing streams and 147,000 acres of lakes and reservoirs. Among the many tourist attractions are Arches, Bryce Canyon, Canyonlands, Capitol Reef, and Zion National Parks; Dinosaur, Natural Bridges, and Rainbow Bridge National Monuments; the Mormon Tabernacle in Salt Lake City; and Monument Valley.

## VERMONT

**Capital:** Montpelier
**Governor:** Richard A. Snelling, R (to Jan. 1979)
**Lieut. Governor:** T. Garry Buckley, R (to Jan. 1979)
**Secy. of State:** James A. Guest, D (to Jan. 1979)
**Treasurer:** Emory A. Hebard, R (to Jan. 1979)
**Auditor of Accounts:** Alexander V. Acebo (to Jan. 1979)
**Atty. General:** M. Jerome Diamond (to Jan. 1979)
**Entered Union & (rank):** March 4, 1791 (14)
**Present constitution adopted:** 1793
**Motto:** Vermont, Freedom, and Unity
**State flower:** Red clover (1894)
**State tree:** Sugar maple (1949)
**State bird:** Hermit thrush (1941)
**State animal:** Morgan horse (1961)
**State insect:** Honeybee (1978)
**State song:** "Hail, Vermont!" (1938)
**Nickname:** Green Mountain State
**Origin of name:** From the French "vert mont," meaning "green mountain"
**1970 population & (rank):** 444,732 (48)
**1977 est. population & (rank):** 483,000 (48)
**1970 land area & (rank):** 9,276 sq mi. (24,025 sq km) (43)
**Geographic center:** In Washington Co., 3 mi. E of Roxbury
**Number of counties:** 14
**Largest cities (1975 est.):** Burlington (37,133); Rutland (19,010); South Burlington (11,090); Barre (9,805); Montpelier (8,217); St. Albans (7,413)
**State forests:** 34 (113,953 ac.)
**State parks:** 45 (31,325 ac.)
**State receipts (1976–77):** $446,527,055
**State disbursements (1976–77):** $444,270,960

The Vermont region was explored and claimed for France by Samuel de Champlain in 1609 and the first French settlement was established at Fort Ste. Anne in 1666. The first English settlers moved into the area in 1724 and built Fort Drummer on the site of present-day Brattleboro. England gained control of the area in 1763 after the French and Indian War.

First organized to drive settlers from New York out of Vermont, the Green Mountain Boys, led by Ethan Allen, won fame by capturing Fort Ticonderoga from the British on May 10, 1775, in the early days of the Revolution.

In 1777 Vermont adopted its first constitution abolishing slavery and providing for universal male suffrage without property qualifications. In 1791 Vermont became the first state after the original 13 to join the Union.

Vermont leads the nation in the production of monument granite, marble, and maple syrup. It is also a leader in the production of asbestos and talc.

In ratio to population, Vermont keeps more dairy cows than any other state. Vermont's soil is devoted to dairying, truck farming, and fruit growing because the rugged, rocky terrain discourages extensive farming.

Principal manufactured goods are machine tools, computer components, stone and clay products, lumber, furniture, and paper.

Tourism is a major industry in Vermont. Vermont's many famous ski areas include Stowe, Killington, Mt. Snow, Bromley, Jay Peak, and Sugarbush. Hunting and fishing also attract many visitors to Vermont each year. Among the many points of interest are the Green Mountain National Forest, Bennington Battle Monument, the Calvin Coolidge Homestead at Plymouth, and the Marble Exhibit in Proctor.

## VIRGINIA

**Capital:** Richmond
**Governor:** John N. Dalton, R (to Jan. 1982)
**Lieut. Governor:** Charles S. Robb, D (to Jan. 1982)
**Secy. of the Commonwealth:** Frederick T. Gray, D (apptd. by Governor)
**Acting Comptroller:** Vincent Pross, Jr. (apptd. by Governor)
**Atty. General:** J. Marshall Coleman, R (to Jan. 1982)
**Entered Union & (rank):** June 25, 1788 (10)
**Present constitution adopted:** 1970
**Motto:** *Sic semper tyrannis* (Thus always to tyrants)
**State flower:** American dogwood (1918)
**State bird:** Cardinal (1950)
**State dog:** American foxhound (1966)
**State shell:** Oyster shell
**State song:** "Carry Me Back to Old Virginia" (1940)
**Nicknames:** The Old Dominion; Mother of Presidents
**Origin of name:** In honor of Elizabeth, "Virgin Queen" of England
**1970 population & (rank):** 4,648,494 (14)
**1977 est. population & (rank):** 5,135,000 (13)
**1970 land area & (rank):** 39,780 sq mi. (103,030 sq km) (36)
**Geographic center:** In Buckingham Co., 5 mi. SW of Buckingham
**Number of counties:** 95, plus 41 independent cities
**Largest cities (1975 est.):** Norfolk (286,694); Richmond (232,652); Virginia Beach (213,954); Newport News (138,760); Hampton (125,013)
**State forests:** 8 (49,566 ac.)
**State parks and recreational parks:** 19, plus 7 in process of acquisition and/or development (42,722 ac.)[1]
**State revenue (1976–77):** $4,079,607,819
**State expenditure (1976–77):** $3,864,633,453

The history of America is closely tied to that of Virginia, particularly in the Colonial period. Jamestown, founded in 1607, was the first permanent English settlement in North America and slavery was introduced there in 1619. The surrenders ending both the American Revolution (Yorktown) and the Civil War (Appomattox) occurred in Virginia. The state is called the "Mother of Presidents" because eight chief executives of the United States were born there.

Today, Virginia has a large number of diversified manufacturing industries including chemicals, textiles, food products, and clothing. Other important lines are lumber, paper, furniture, cigarettes, electrical machinery, transportation equipment, and stone-glass-clay products.

Agriculture remains an important sector in the Virginia economy and the state ranks among the leaders in the U.S. in tobacco, peanuts, apples, and sweet potatoes. Other crops include corn, vegetables, barley, and peaches. Famous for its turkeys and Smithfield hams, Virginia also has a large dairy industry.

Coal mining accounts for roughly 70% of Virginia's mineral output, and lime, zinc, and stone are also mined.

Points of interest include Mt. Vernon and other places associated with George Washington; Monticello, home of Thomas Jefferson; Stratford, home of the Lees; Richmond, capital of the Confederacy and of Virginia; and Williamsburg, the restored Colonial capital.

Other attractions are the Shenandoah National Park, Fredericksburg and Spotsylvania National

1. Does not include portion of Breaks Interstate Park (Va.-Ky., 1,200 ac.) which lies in Virginia.

Military Park, the Booker T. Washington birthplace near Roanoke, Arlington House (the Robert E. Lee Memorial), the Skyline Drive, and the Blue Ridge National Parkway.

## WASHINGTON

**Capital:** Olympia
**Governor:** Dixy Lee Ray, D (to Jan. 1981)
**Lieut. Governor:** John A. Cherbert, D (to Jan. 1981)
**Secy. of State:** Bruce K. Chapman, R (to Jan. 1981)
**State Treasurer:** Robert S. O'Brien, D (to Jan. 1981)
**Atty. General:** Slade Gorton, R (to Jan. 1981)
**Organized as territory:** March 2, 1853
**Entered Union & (rank):** Nov. 11, 1889 (42)
**Present constitution adopted:** 1889
**Motto:** *Al-Ki* (Indian word meaning "by and by")
**State flower:** Rhododrendron (1949)
**State tree:** Western hemlock (1947)
**State bird:** Willow goldfinch (1951)
**State gem:** Petrified wood (1975)
**State colors:** Green and gold (1925)
**State song:** "Washington, My Home" (1959)
**Nicknames:** Evergreen State; Chinook State
**Origin of name:** In honor of George Washington
**1970 population & (rank):** 3,409,169 (22)
**1977 est. population & (rank):** 3,658,000 (22)
**1970 land area & (rank):** 66,570 sq mi (172,416 sq km) (20)
**Geographic center:** In Chelan Co., 10 mi. WSW of Wenatchee
**Number of counties:** 39
**Largest cities (1975 est.):** Seattle (487,091), Spokane (173,698); Tacoma (151,267); Bellevue (65,365); Everett (48,371); Vancouver (47,742)
**State forest lands:** 1,843,020 ac.
**State parks:** 173 (79,212 ac.)
**State revenue (all funds, 1977–79—projected):** $8,210,200,000
**State expenditure (all funds, 1977–79—budget):** $8,459,300,000

As part of the vast Oregon Country, Washington territory was visited by Spanish, American, and British explorers—Bruno Heceta for Spain in 1775, the American Capt. Robert Gray in 1792, and Capt. George Vancouver for Britain in 1792–94. Lewis and Clark explored the Columbia River region and coastal areas for the U.S. in 1805–06.

Rival American and British settlers and conflicting territorial claims threatened war in the early 1840s. However, in 1846 the Oregon Treaty set the boundary at the 49th parallel and war was averted.

Washington is a leading lumber producer. Its rugged surface is rich in stands of Douglas fir, hemlock, ponderosa and white pine, spruce, larch, and cedar. The state holds first place in apples, blueberries, hops, and red raspberries and it ranks high in potatoes, winter wheat, pears, grapes, apricots, and strawberries. Livestock and livestock products make important contributions to total farm revenue and the commercial fishing catch of salmon, halibut, and bottomfish makes a significant contribution to the state's economy.

Manufacturing industries in Washington include aircraft and missiles, shipbuilding and other transportation equipment, lumber, food processing, metals and metal products, chemicals, and machinery.

The Columbia River contains one third of the potential water power in the U.S., harnessed by such dams as the Grand Coulee, one of the greatest power producers in the world. Washington has 90 dams throughout the state built for irrigation, power, flood control, and water storage. Its abundance of electrical power makes Washington the nation's largest producer of refined aluminum.

Among the major points of interest: Mt. Rainier, Olympic, and North Cascades National Parks; Whitman Mission and Fort Vancouver National Historic Sites; and the Pacific Science Center and Space Needle in Seattle.

## WEST VIRGINIA

**Capital:** Charleston
**Governor:** John D. Rockefeller IV, D (to Jan. 1981)
**Secy. of State:** James A. Manchin, D (to Jan. 1981)
**State Auditor:** Glen Gainer (to Jan. 1981)
**Atty. General:** Chauncey H. Browning, Jr., D (to Jan. 1981)
**Entered Union & (rank):** June 20, 1863 (35)
**Present constitution adopted:** 1872
**Motto:** *Montani semper liberi* (Mountaineers are always free)
**State flower:** Rhododendron (1903)
**State tree:** Sugar maple (1949)
**State bird:** Cardinal (1949)
**State animal:** Black bear
**State colors:** Blue and gold (unofficial)
**State songs:** "West Virginia, My Home Sweet Home," "The West Virginia Hills," and "This Is My West Virginia" (adopted by Legislature in 1947, 1961 and 1963 as official state songs)
**Nickname:** Mountain State
**Origin of name:** Same as for Virginia
**1970 population & (rank):** 1,744,237 (34)
**1977 est. population & (rank):** 1,859,000 (34)
**1970 land area & (rank):** 24,070 sq mi. (62,341 sq km) (41)
**Geographic center:** In Braxton Co., 4 mi. E of Sutton
**Number of counties:** 55
**Largest cities (1975 est.):** Huntington (68,811); Charleston (67,348); Wheeling (44,369); Parkersburg (38,882); Morgantown (30,318); Fairmont (26,000)
**State forests:** 9 (77,000 ac.)
**State parks:** 34 (65,861 ac.)
**Total state revenue (1976–77):** $1,792,111,849
**Total state expenditure (1976–77):** $1,862,238,389

West Virginia's early history from 1609 until 1863 is largely shared with Virginia, of which it was a part until Virginia seceded from the Union in 1861. Then the delegates of 40 western counties formed their own government, which was granted statehood in 1863.

First permanent settlement dates from 1731 when Morgan Morgan founded Mill Creek. In 1742 coal was discovered on the Coal River, an event that would be of great significance in determining West Virginia's future.

The state usually ranks first in bituminous coal production with about 20% of the U.S. total. It also is a leader in steel, glass, aluminum, and chemical manufactures; natural gas, oil, quarry products, and hardwood lumber.

Poultry, dairy products, cattle, and sheep account for the major portion of farm receipts. Apples, peaches, wheat, corn, and hay are profitable crops. More than 75% of West Virginia is covered with forests.

Tourism is increasingly popular in mountainous West Virginia and visitors spend over $750 million annually. More than a million acres have been set aside in 34 state parks and recreation areas and in 9 state forests.

Major points of interest include Harpers Ferry

and Chesapeake and Ohio Canal National Historical Parks, White Sulphur Springs and Berkeley Springs resorts, the scenic railroad at Cass, and the historic homes at Charles Town.

## WISCONSIN

**Capital:** Madison
**Governor:** Martin J. Schreiber, D (to Jan. 1979)
**Lieut. Governor:** Vacant
**Secy. of State:** Douglas J. LaFollette, D (to Jan. 1979)
**State Treasurer:** Charles P. Smith, D (to Jan. 1979)
**Atty. General:** Bronson C. La Follette (to Jan. 1979)
**Organized as territory:** July 4, 1836
**Entered Union & (rank):** May 29, 1848 (30)
**Present constitution adopted:** 1848
**Motto:** Forward
**State flower:** Wood violet
**State tree:** Sugar maple
**State bird:** Robin
**State animal:** Badger; "wild life" animal: white-tailed deer; "domestic" animal; dairy cow
**State insect:** Honeybee (1977)
**State fish:** Musky (Muskellunge)
**State song:** "On Wisconsin"
**State mineral:** Galena (1971)
**State rock:** Red Granite (1971)
**Nickname:** Badger State
**Origin of name:** French corruption of an Indian word meaning "gathering of waters"
**1970 population & (rank):** 4,417,933 (16)
**1977 est. population & (rank):** 4,651,000 (16)
**1970 land area & (rank):** 54,464 sq mi. (141,062 sq km) (25)
**Geographic center:** In Wood Co., 9 mi. SE of Marshfield
**Number of counties:** 72
**Largest cities (1975 est.):** Milwaukee (665,796); Madison (168,196); Racine (94,744); Green Bay (91,189); Kenosha (80,727); West Allis (69,084)
**State forests:** 8 (449,486 ac.)
**State parks & scenic trails:** 55 parks, 8 trails (61,340 ac.)
**State total net revenue (all funds, 1976–77):** $5,694,897,754
**State total net expenditure (all funds, 1976–77):** $5,089,321,662

The Wisconsin region was first explored for France by Jean Nicolet who landed at Green Bay in 1634. In 1660 a French trading post and Roman Catholic mission were established near present-day Ashland.

Great Britain obtained the region in settlement of the French and Indian War in 1763; the U.S. acquired it in 1783 after the Revolutionary War. However, Great Britain retained actual control until after the War of 1812. The region was successively governed as part of the territories of Indiana, Illinois, and Michigan between 1800 and 1836, when it became a separate territory.

Wisconsin leads the nation in milk and cheese production. In 1975, the state ranked first in the number of milk cows (1,812,000), and produced 16% of the nation's total output of milk. Other important farm products are peas, beets, corn, potatoes, cabbage, maple sugar, and cranberries.

The chief industrial products of the state are automobiles, machinery, furniture, paper, beer, and processed foods. Wisconsin ranks second among the 47 paper-producing states. Tourism also ranks among the major industries.

Wisconsin pioneered in social legislation, providing pensions for the blind (1907), aid to dependent children (1913), and old-age assistance (1925). In 1932 it was the first state to enact an unemployment compensation law. In labor legislation, the state has also pioneered in important laws, among them the first workmen's compensation law actually to take effect. Wisconsin had the first state-wide primary-election law and the first successful income-tax law.

The state has over 8,500 lakes, of which Winnebago is the largest. Water sports, ice-boating, and fishing are popular, as are skiing and hunting. Public parks and forests take up one seventh of the land, with 49 state parks, 9 state forests, and 2 national forests.

Among the many points of interest are the Apostle Islands National Lakeshore; Ice Age National Scientific Reserve; the Circus World Museum at Baraboo; the Wolf, St. Croix, and Lower St. Croix national scenic riverways; and the Wisconsin Dells.

## WYOMING

**Capital:** Cheyenne
**Governor:** Ed Herschler, D (to Jan. 1979)
**Secy. of State:** Thyra G. Thomson, R (to Jan. 1979)
**Auditor:** James B. Griffith, Jr., R (to Jan. 1979)
**Treasurer:** Edwin J. Witzenburger, R (to Jan. 1979)
**Atty. General:** V. Frank Mendicino, D (apptd. by Governor)
**Organized as territory:** May 19, 1869
**Entered Union & (rank):** July 10, 1890 (44)
**Present constitution adopted:** 1890
**Motto:** Equal rights (1955)
**State flower:** Indian paintbrush (1917)
**State tree:** Cottonwood (1947)
**State bird:** Meadow lark (1927)
**State gemstone:** Jade (1967)
**State insignia:** Bucking horse (unofficial)
**State song:** "Wyoming" (1955)
**Nickname:** Equality State
**Origin of name:** From the Indian, meaning "mountains and valleys alternating"; named after the Wyoming Valley in Pennsylvania
**1970 population & (rank):** 332,416 (49)
**1977 est. population & (rank):** 406,000 (50)
**1970 land area & (rank):** 97,203 sq mi. (251,756 sq km) (9)
**Geographic center:** In Fremont Co., 58 mi. ENE of Lander
**Number of counties:** 23, plus Yellowstone National Park
**Largest cities (1975 est.):** Cheyenne (46,677); Casper (41,192); Laramie (23,421); Rock Springs (17,773); Sheridan (11,617); Rawlins (9,592)
**State forests:** None
**State parks:** 9 (44,732 ac.)
**Estimated income (1978–80):** $555,717,562
**Estimated expenditure (1978–80):** $341,718,137

The U.S. acquired the territory from France as part of the Louisiana Purchase in 1803. John Colter, a fur-trapper, is the first white man known to have entered present Wyoming. In 1807 he explored the Yellowstone area and brought back news of its geysers and hot springs.

Robert Stuart pioneered the Oregon Trail across Wyoming in 1812–13 and, in 1834, Fort Laramie, the first permanent trading post in Wyoming, was built. Western Wyoming was obtained by the U.S. in the 1846 Oregon Treaty with Great Britain and as a result of the treaty ending the Mexican War in 1848.

When the Wyoming Territory was organized in 1869 Wyoming women became the first in the nation to obtain the right to vote. In 1925 Mrs. Nellie Tayloe Ross was elected first woman governor in the United States.

Wyoming's towering mountains and vast plains provide spectacular scenery, grazing lands for sheep and cattle, and rich mineral deposits.

Mining, particularly oil and natural gas, is the most important industry. In 1973, Wyoming led the nation in sodium carbonate production and was second in uranium.

Wyoming ranks second among the states in wool production. In 1974 its sheep numbered 1.5 million, exceeded only by Texas; it also had 1.6 million cattle. Principal crops include wheat, oats, sugar beets, corn, potatoes, barley, and alfalfa.

Second in mean elevation to Colorado, Wyoming has many attractions for the tourist trade, notably Yellowstone National Park. Cheyenne is famous for its annual "Frontier Days" celebration. Flaming Gorge, the Fort Laramie National Historic Site, and Devils Tower and Fossil Butte National Monuments are other points of interest.

# Self-Governing Areas

## PUERTO RICO

**Capital:** San Juan
**Governor:** Carlos Romero Barceló, New Progressive Party (to Jan. 1981)
**Song:** "La Borinqueña"
**1970 population:** 2,712,033
**1976 est. population:** 3,196,000
**1970 land area:** 3,421 sq mi. (8,860 sq km)
**Largest cities (1970):** San Juan (452,749); Ponce (128,233); Bayamón (147,552); Carolina (94,271); Mayagüez (68,872)

Puerto Rico is an island about 100 miles long and 35 miles wide at the northeastern end of the Caribbean Sea. It is a self-governing Commonwealth freely and voluntarily associated with the U.S. Under its Constitution, a Governor and a Legislative Assembly are elected by direct vote for a four-year period. The judiciary is vested in a Supreme Court and lower courts established by law. The people elect a Resident Commissioner to the U.S. House of Representatives, where he has a voice but no vote. The island was formerly an unincorporated territory of the U.S. after being ceded by Spain as a result of the Spanish-American War.

The Commonwealth, established in 1952, has one of the highest standards of living in Latin America. Featuring Puerto Rican economic development is Operation Bootstrap. This program has established over 2,300 new factories and has greatly increased agricultural production, transportation and communications facilities, electric power, housing, and other industries.

The island's chief exports are chemicals, textiles, fish products and petroleum products.

Columbus discovered the island on his second voyage to America in 1493.

## GUAM

**Capital:** Agaña
**Governor:** Ricardo J. Bordallo
**1950 population:** 59,498
**1960 population:** 67,044
**1970 population:** 84,996
**1970 land area:** 212 sq mi. (549 sq km)

Guam, the largest of the Mariana Islands, is independent of the trusteeship assigned to the U.S. in 1947. It was acquired by the U.S. from Spain in 1898 (occupied 1899) and was placed under the Navy Department.

In World War II, Guam was seized by the Japanese on Dec. 11, 1941; but on July 21, 1944, it was once more in U. S. hands.

On Aug. 1, 1950, President Truman signed a bill which granted U.S. citizenship to the people of Guam and established self-government. However, the people do not vote in national elections. In 1972 Guam elected its first delegate to the U.S. Congress. The Executive Branch of the Guam government is under the general supervision of the U.S. Secretary of the Interior. In November 1970, Guam elected its first Governor.

Military installations and tourism are important factors in Guam's economy.

# Non-Self-Governing Territories

## AMERICAN SAMOA

**Capital:** Pago Pago (on Tutuila Island)
**Governor:** Peter Tali Coleman
**Lieut. Governor:** Tufele Liá
**1950 population:** 18,937
**1960 population:** 20,051
**1977 est. population:** 31,000
**1970 land area:** 76 sq mi. (197 sq km)

American Samoa, a group of five volcanic islands and two coral atolls located some 2,400 miles south of Hawaii in the South Pacific Ocean, is an unincorporated, unorganized territory of the U.S., administered by the Department of the Interior.

By the Treaty of Berlin, signed Dec. 2, 1899, and ratified Feb. 16, 1900, the U.S. was internationally acknowledged to have rights extending over all the islands of the Samoa group east of longitude 171° west of Greenwich. On April 17, 1900, the chiefs of Tutuila and Aunu'u ceded those islands to the U.S. In 1904, the King and chiefs of Manu'a ceded the islands of Ofu, Olosega and Tau (composing the Manu'a group) to the U.S. Swains Island, some 200 miles north of Samoa, was included as part of the territory by Act of Congress March 4, 1925; and on Feb. 20, 1929, Congress formally accepted sovereignty over the entire group and placed the responsibility for administration in the hands of the President. From 1900 to 1951, by Presidential direction, the Department of the Navy governed the territory. On July 1, 1951, administration was transferred to the Department of the Interior. The first Constitution for the territory was signed on April 27, 1960, and became effective on Oct. 17, 1960. It was revised in 1967 and 1973.

The principal products are canned tuna, pet food, fish meal, mats, handicrafts, and ginger.

## BAKER, HOWLAND, AND JARVIS ISLANDS

These Pacific islands were not to play a role in the extraterritorial plans of the U.S. until May 13, 1936. President F. D. Roosevelt, at that time, placed them under the control of and jurisdiction by the Secretary of the Interior for administration purposes.

Baker Island is a saucer-shaped atoll with an area of approximately one square mile. It is about 1,650 miles from Hawaii.

Howland Island, 36 miles to the northeast, is approximately one and a half miles long and half a mile wide.

Jarvis Island is several hundred miles to the east and is approximately two miles long by one and an eighth miles wide.

Baker, Howland, and Jarvis have been uninhabited since 1942. In 1974, these islands became part of the National Wildlife Refuge System.

## CANAL ZONE

**Headquarters:** Balboa Heights, C. Z.; 4400 Dauphine St., New Orleans, La. 70146; 425 Thirteenth St., N.W., Washington, D.C. 20004
**Governor-President:** H. R. Parfitt
**1950 population:** 52,822
**1960 population:** 42,122
**1970 population:** 44,198
**1970 land area:** 553 sq mi. (1,432 sq km)

The Canal Zone is a 50-mile strip between the Atlantic and Pacific Oceans which was granted to the U.S. in perpetuity by the Republic of Panama by treaty in 1903 (ratified Feb. 26, 1904) for the purpose of building, maintaining, protecting, and operating a canal. The zone extends roughly five miles on either side of the center line of the Panama Canal.

The 1903 treaty empowered the U.S. to act as sovereign within the zone to the exclusion of the exercise of any such sovereign rights by the Republic. The treaty was unpopular in Panama from the start.

In return for the perpetual sovereign grant, the U.S. guaranteed the independence of the Republic and agreed to pay $10,000,000 to Panama upon ratification of the treaty and $250,000 in gold annually, beginning nine years after ratification. The annual payments were increased to $430,000 after the U.S. went off the gold standard. The annuity was increased by the 1955 treaty and is currently $2,328,200.

The history of the Canal goes back to 1534, when King Charles V of Spain ordered a survey made. In 1876 a concession to construct a Panama Canal was granted by Colombia to an American citizen, Anthony de Gogorza. A revised concession was granted in 1878 to St. Lucien N. B. Wyse, who represented a French company. Construction of the waterway was formally inaugurated in January, 1880, by the French Canal Company. Twenty years later, the French gave up their efforts to build a canal and sold their canal rights and properties to the U.S. for $40,000,000, the transfer being made May 4, 1904, in Panama City. The construction of the canal was completed 10 years later.

The Canal is 40.27 miles from shore line to shore line and 50.72 miles from deep water in the Caribbean to deep water in the Pacific. The Panama Railroad, completed in 1855 by private U. S. enterprise, is owned by the Panama Canal Company. It roughly parallels the Canal channel, running 47.64 miles from Colon to Panama City and is the oldest transcontinental railroad in the Americas.

The Panama Canal Locks lift or lower ships 85 feet between sea level and Gatún Lake level in three steps on each side of the Isthmus. On the Atlantic side the three steps are at Gatún Locks. On the Pacific side there are two steps at Miraflores Locks and one step at the Pedro Miguel Locks. Each of the twin chambers in every flight of locks has a nominal length of 1,000 feet, a width of 110 feet, and a minimum depth of water of 40 feet.

The Canal Zone is, in effect, a U. S. government reservation, and in general no private enterprise is permitted except that relating directly to the operation of the waterway. The Governor, who is appointed by the U. S. President, administers the Canal Zone Government, which is responsible for such civil functions as health, sanitation, and protection of the Zone. The Governor is also ex-officio President of the Panama Canal Company, which is a corporate agency of the U.S. charged with the operation of the Canal and its related activities.

In 1936, President Roosevelt agreed to a treaty that reduced some of the tensions caused by terms of the original treaty, which Panamanians found "humiliating." In 1955, President Eisenhower agreed to a new treaty that increased Panama's annuity and granted other concessions.

In 1964, riots in Panama led President Johnson to agree to negotiations which would examine the eventual transfer of the Canal to Panama. Through different administrations, with changing negotiators and various treaty drafts, negotiations continued. They reached a definitive point in August 1977, when the U.S. and the Republic of Panama announced agreement in principle on the basic issues of a new treaty that would restore the Canal Zone to Panamanian jurisdiction by the year 2000.

On September 7, President Carter and General Torrijos signed the treaties in Washington. After tense debate in the Senate a treaty guaranteeing the neutrality of the Canal was ratified on March 16, 1978, and the Panama Canal treaty itself was ratified on April 18. These treaties turn over control of the Canal to Panama by the year 2000 and provide for the premanent neutrality of the Canal thereafter.

## CANTON AND ENDERBURY ISLANDS

Canton and Enderbury islands, the largest of the Phoenix group, are jointly administered by the U.S. and Great Britain after an agreement signed April 6, 1939.

Canton is triangular in shape and the largest of the eight islands of this group. It lies about 1,600 miles southwest of Hawaii and was discovered at the turn of the 18th century by U.S. whalers. After World War II it served as an aviation support facility, and later as a missile tracking station. Since 1967, the island has been utilized by the U.S. Air Force Space and Missile Test Center.

Enderbury is rectangular in shape and is 3.5 miles long by 1.5 miles wide. It is unpopulated and lies about 32 miles southeast of Canton.

## JOHNSTON ATOLL

Johnston is a coral atoll about 700 miles southwest of Hawaii. It consists of four small islands—Johnston Island, Sand Island, Hikina Island, and Akau Island—which are surrounded by a reef about

12 miles in circumference.

The atoll was discovered by Capt. Charles James Johnston of *H.M.S. Cornwallis* in 1807. In 1858 it was claimed by Hawaii, and later became a U.S. possession.

Johnston Atoll is under the administrative control of the Air Force.

## KINGMAN REEF

Kingman Reef, located about 1,000 miles south of Hawaii, was discovered by Capt. E. Fanning in 1798, but named for Capt. W. E. Kingman, who rediscovered it in 1853. It is about 9.5 miles long and 5 miles wide within the 100-fathom curve. It dries at low water on its northeastern, eastern, and southeastern edges. A small islet, 3 feet high, lies on its eastern side.

## MIDWAY ISLAND

Midway, lying about 1,200 miles west-northwest of Hawaii, was discovered by Captain N. C. Brooks of the Hawaiian bark *Gambia* on July 5, 1859, in the name of the United States. It was formally declared a U.S. possession in 1867, and in 1903 Theodore Roosevelt made it a naval reservation.

Sand and Eastern Islands, with 850 acres and 328 acres respectively, are its largest individual islands. The circular atoll enclosing the islands is 6 miles in diameter.

The total group comprises an area of two square miles and has no native population. The Navy Department maintains an installation and has jurisdiction over the atoll.

## SWAN ISLANDS

The Swan Islands are two small islands, Great Swan and Little Swan, in the Caribbean Sea, 98 miles north of Honduras. They were claimed by the U.S. in 1863, but Honduras also claimed them on the basis of their discovery by the Spanish. After years of dispute, the U.S. in 1971 signed a treaty recognizing Honduran sovereignty over the islands. The treaty ratifications were exchanged on Sept. 1, 1972.

## U.S. VIRGIN ISLANDS

**Capital:** Charlotte Amalie (on St. Thomas)
**Governor:** Juan Luis
**1950 population:** 26,665
**1960 population:** 32,099
**1970 population:** 62,468 (St. Thomas, 28,960; St. Croix, 31,779; St. John, 1,729)
**1978 est. population:** 101,130 (St. Croix, 51,570; St. Thomas, 47,260; St. John, 2,300)
**1970 land area:** 132 sq mi. (342 sq km) (St. Croix, 82 [212 sq km]; St. Thomas, 32 [83 sq km]; St. John, 20 [52 sq km])

The Virgin Islands, consisting of nine main islands and some 75 islets, were discovered by Columbus in 1493. Since 1666, England has held six of the main islands; the other three (St. Croix, St. Thomas, and St. John), as well as about 50 of the islets, were eventually acquired by Denmark, which named them the Danish West Indies. In 1917, these islands were purchased by the U.S. from Denmark for $25 million.

Congress granted U.S. citizenship to Virgin Islanders in 1927; and, in 1931, administration was transferred from the Navy to the Department of the Interior. Universal suffrage was given in 1936 to all persons who could read and write the English language. The Governor was elected by popular vote for the first time in 1970; previously he had been appointed by the President of the U.S. A unicameral 15-man legislature serves the Virgin Islands, and recent Congressional legislation gave the islands a non-voting Representative in Congress.

About 80% of the population is black, and there is limited farming, fishing, and cattle raising. Industrial products include rum, watches, costume jewelry, clothing, alumina, pharmaceuticals, and petroleum products. Tourism is the principal industry.

## WAKE ISLAND

Wake Island, about halfway between Midway and Guam, is an atoll comprising the three islets of Wilkes, Peale, and Wake. They were discovered by the British in 1796 and annexed by the U.S. in 1898. The entire area comprises 3 square miles and has no native population. In 1938, Pan American Airways established a seaplane base and Wake Island has been used as a commercial base since then. On Dec. 8, 1941, it was attacked by the Japanese, who finally took possession on Dec. 23. It was surrendered by the Japanese on Sept. 4, 1945.

The Federal Aviation Administration maintained a station on Wake Island until June 1972, when civil administration of the island was taken over by the U.S. Air Force. In 1962, the area was placed under the jurisdiction of the Department of the Interior.

# Trust Territory of the Pacific Islands (Micronesia)

In 1885, Germany assumed a protectorate over the Marshall Islands; and, in 1899, she purchased the Northern Mariana and Caroline Islands from Spain. These islands were occupied by the Japanese in 1914 and were mandated to Japan by the League of Nations in 1919. On April 2, 1947, the U. N. Security Council approved a trusteeship agreement proposed by the U.S. under which the Northern Mariana, Caroline, and Marshall Islands became a Strategic Trust Territory under the administration of the U.S. The measure was approved by the President, with the agreement of Congress, on July 18, 1947. Administration was transferred from the Navy to the Department of the Interior on July 1, 1951. However, during 1953, administration of the islands of the Northern Marianas, except

Rota, was transferred back to the Navy. The Department of the Interior again took over administration of these islands in July, 1962.

In February 1975 a covenant was signed by the U.S. and the Marianas Political Status Commission that would make the 17 islands in the Northern Marianas a commonwealth under American sovereignty. The covenant was overwhelmingly ratified by the people of the islands and was approved by President Ford on March 24, 1976.

On April 10, 1978, in Hilo, Hawaii, the heads of the three Micronesian political status commissions and the U.S. negotiator signed a statement of agreed principles which are intended to form the basis of a free association relationship between the U.S. and Micronesia. Negotiations now continue on these aspects. It is the U.S.'s objective to end the trusteeship in 1981.

The entire group comprises more than 2,000 islands, but the total land area is only 717 square miles, many of the islands being only tiny coral reefs. The Micronesians are the main ethnic group; however, the inhabitants of two outlying islands, Kapingamarangi and Nukuoro, are Polynesian. The population of the Trust Territory in 1974 was 114,973.

## MARIANA ISLANDS

The Mariana Islands, east of the Philippines and south of Japan, include the islands of Guam, Rota, Saipan, Tinian, Pagan, Guguan, Agrihan, and Aguijan. Guam, the largest, is independent of the trusteeship, having been acquired by the U.S. from Spain in 1898. (For more information, *see* the entry on Guam in this section.)

Chief crops are copra and fresh fruits and vegetables.

## CAROLINE ISLANDS

The Caroline Islands, east of the Philippines and south of the Marianas, include the Yap, Truk, and the Palau groups and the islands of Ponape and Kusaie, as well as many coral atolls.

The islands are composed chiefly of volcanic rock, and their peaks rise 2,000 to 3,000 feet above sea level. Chief exports of the islands are copra, fish products, and handicrafts.

## MARSHALL ISLANDS

The Marshall Islands, east of the Carolines, are divided into two chains: the western or Ralik group, including the atolls Jaluit, Kwajalein, Wotho, Bikini, and Eniwetok; and the eastern or Ratak group, including the atolls Mili, Majuro, Maloelap, Wotje, and Likiep.

The islands are of the coral-reef type and rise only a few feet above sea level. The chief crop is coconuts; exports include copra, tortoise shell, mother-of-pearl, etc.

Bikini and Eniwetok were the scene of several atom-bomb tests after World War II. Eniwetok was returned to Trust Territory administration in August 1976. In April 1977, some 75 original inhabitants, the forerunner of 450 returnees, were resettled after an absence of 30 years.

# The Governors of the Fifty States

| State | Governor | Year of birth | Current term | State | Governor | Year of birth | Current term |
|---|---|---|---|---|---|---|---|
| Ala. | George C. Wallace, D | 1919 | 1975–79 | Mont. | Thomas L. Judge, D | 1934 | 1977–81 |
| Alaska | Jay S. Hammond, R | 1922 | 1974–78[1] | Neb. | J. James Exon, D | 1921 | 1975–79 |
| Ariz. | Bruce E. Babbitt, D | 1938 | 1977–79 | Nev. | Mike O'Callaghan, D | 1930 | 1975–79 |
| Ark. | David Pryor, D | 1934 | 1977–79 | N.H. | Meldrim Thomson, Jr., R | 1912 | 1977–79 |
| Calif. | Edmund G. Brown, Jr., D | 1938 | 1975–79 | N.J. | Brendan T. Byrne, D | 1924 | 1978–82 |
| Colo. | Richard D. Lamm, D | 1935 | 1975–79 | N.M. | Jerry Apodaca, D | 1934 | 1975–79 |
| Conn. | Ella T. Grasso, D. | 1919 | 1975–79 | N.Y. | Hugh L. Carey, D | 1919 | 1975–79 |
| Del. | Pierre S. du Pont, IV, R | 1935 | 1977–81 | N.C. | James B. Hunt, Jr., D | 1937 | 1977–81 |
| Fla. | Reubin Askew, D | 1928 | 1975–79 | N.D. | Arthur A. Link, D | 1914 | 1977–81 |
| Ga. | George Busbee, D | 1927 | 1975–79 | Ohio | James A. Rhodes, R | 1909 | 1975–79 |
| Hawaii | George R. Ariyoshi, D | 1926 | 1974–78[1] | Okla. | David L. Boren, D | 1941 | 1975–79 |
| Idaho | John V. Evans, D | 1925 | 1977–79 | Ore. | Robert W. Straub, D | 1920 | 1975–79 |
| Ill. | James R. Thompson, R | 1936 | 1977–79 | Pa. | Milton J. Shapp, D | 1912 | 1975–79 |
| Ind. | Otis R. Bowen, R | 1918 | 1977–81 | R.I. | J. Joseph Garrahy, D | 1931 | 1977–79 |
| Iowa | Robert D. Ray, R | 1928 | 1975–79 | S.C. | James B. Edwards, R | 1927 | 1975–79 |
| Kan. | Robert F. Bennett, R | 1927 | 1975–79 | S.D. | Richard F. Kneip, D | 1933 | 1975–79 |
| Ky. | Julian M. Carroll, D | 1931 | 1975–79[1] | Tenn. | Ray Blanton, D | 1930 | 1975–79 |
| La. | Edwin W. Edwards, D | 1927 | 1976–80[2] | Tex. | Dolph Briscoe, D | 1923 | 1975–79 |
| Me. | James B. Longley, I | 1924 | 1975–79 | Utah | Scott M. Matheson, D | 1929 | 1977–81 |
| Md. | Blair Lee III, D[3] | 1916 | 1977–79 | Vt. | Richard A. Snelling, R | 1928 | 1977–79 |
| Mass. | Michael S. Dukakis, D | 1934 | 1975–79 | Va. | John N. Dalton, R | 1931 | 1978–82 |
| Mich. | William G. Milliken, R | 1922 | 1975–79 | Wash. | Dixy Lee Ray, D | 1914 | 1977–81 |
| Minn. | Rudolph G. Perpich, D | 1928 | 1976–79 | W.Va. | John D. Rockefeller IV | 1937 | 1977–81 |
| Miss. | Cliff Finch, D | 1927 | 1976–80 | Wis. | Martin J. Schreiber, D | 1939 | 1977–79 |
| Mo. | Joseph P. Teasdale, D | 1936 | 1977–81 | Wyo. | Ed C. Herschler, D | 1918 | 1975–79 |

1. December. 2. March. 3. Acting; serving pending appeal of Marvin Mandel, convicted of Federal corruption charges in August 1977. NOTE: Except when indicated, all terms begin in January.

# Tabulated Data on State Governments

| | Governor | | Legislature[1] | | | | | Highest Court[2] | | |
|---|---|---|---|---|---|---|---|---|---|---|
| State | Term, years | Annual salary | Membership U[3] | Membership L[4] | Term, yrs. U[3] | Term, yrs. L[4] | Salaries of members[5] | Mem-bers | Term, years | Annual salary[6] |
| Alabama | 4[10] | $25,000[16] | 35 | 106 | 4 | 4 | $3,600 per annum[16] | 9 | 6 | $33,500 |
| Alaska | 4 | 50,000 | 20 | 40 | 4 | 2 | 9,000 per annum | 5 | ([8]) | 52,992 |
| Arizona | 4 | 35,000 | 30 | 60 | 2 | 2 | 6,000 per annum | 5 | 6 | 32,000 |
| Arkansas | 2 | 35,000 | 35 | 100 | 4 | 2 | 7,200 per annum | 8 | 8 | 34,024 |
| California | 4 | 49,100 | 40 | 80 | 4 | 2 | 23,232 per annum | 7 | 12 | 51,615 |
| Colorado | 4 | 40,000 | 35 | 65 | 4 | 2 | 12,000 per annum | 7 | 10 | 40,000 |
| Connecticut | 4 | 42,000 | 36 | 151 | 2 | 2 | 8,500 per biennium[24] | 6 | 8 | 36,000 |
| Delaware | 4[9] | 35,000 | 21 | 41 | 4 | 2 | 9,000 per annum | 3 | 12 | 42,000 |
| Florida | 4[10] | 50,000 | 40 | 120 | 4 | 2 | 12,000 per annum | 7 | 6 | 40,000 |
| Georgia | 4[9] | 50,000 | 56 | 180 | 2 | 2 | 7,200 per annum[5] | 7 | 6 | 46,000 |
| Hawaii | 4 | 50,000 | 25 | 51 | 4 | 2 | 12,000 per session | 5 | 10 | 45,000 |
| Idaho | 4 | 40,000 | 35 | 70 | 2 | 2 | 3,000 per annum | 5 | 6 | 38,000 |
| Illinois | 4 | 50,000 | 59 | 177 | 4–2 | 2 | 20,000 per annum | 7 | 10 | 50,000 |
| Indiana | 4[10] | 36,000 | 50 | 100 | 4 | 2 | 8,000 per annum | 5 | 6 | 38,100 |
| Iowa | 4 | 55,000 | 50 | 100 | 4 | 2 | 8,000 per annum | 9 | 8 | 45,000 |
| Kansas | 4 | 45,000 | 40 | 125 | 4 | 2 | 35 per diem[25] | 7 | 6 | 43,000 |
| Kentucky | 4[7] | 45,000[27] | 38 | 100 | 4 | 2 | 50 per diem[25] | 7 | 8 | 39,000 |
| Louisiana | 4 | 50,000 | 39 | 105 | 4 | 4 | 50 per diem[23] | 7 | 10 | 37,500 |
| Maine | 4 | 35,000 | 33 | 151 | 2 | 2 | 7,000 per biennium[16] | 6 | 7 | 26,000 |
| Maryland | 4[10] | 60,000 | 47 | 141 | 4 | 4 | 16,000 per annum | 7 | 15 | 46,400 |
| Massachusetts | 4 | 40,000 | 40 | 240 | 2 | 2 | 16,073 per annum | 7 | Life | 43,079 |
| Michigan | 4 | 58,000 | 38 | 110 | 4 | 2 | 22,500 per annum | 7 | 8 | 50,000 |
| Minnesota | 4 | 58,000 | 67 | 134 | 4 | 2 | 16,500 per annum | 9 | 6 | 49,000 |
| Mississippi | 4[7] | 43,000 | 52 | 122 | 4 | 4 | 8,100 per session | 9 | 8 | 34,000 |
| Missouri | 4[10] | 37,500 | 34 | 163 | 4 | 2 | 15,000 per annum[5] | 7 | 12 | 50,000 |
| Montana | 4 | 35,000 | 50 | 100 | 4 | 2 | 40 per diem | 5 | 8 | 36,000 |
| Nebraska | 4[10] | 40,000 | 49[11] | — | 4[11] | — | 4,800 per annum | 7 | 6 | 39,750 |
| Nevada | 4 | 50,000 | 20 | 40 | 4 | 2 | 4,800 per biennium | 5 | 6 | 47,250 |
| New Hampshire | 2 | 34,070 | 24 | ([12]) | 2 | 2 | 200 per biennium | 5 | ([13]) | 34,268 |
| New Jersey | 4[10] | 65,000 | 40 | 80 | 4[14] | 2 | 10,000 per annum | 7 | 7[15] | 56,000 |
| New Mexico | 4[7] | 40,000 | 42 | 70 | 4 | 2 | 40 per diem | 5 | 8 | 38,165 |
| New York | 4 | 85,000 | 60 | 150 | 2 | 2 | 23,500 per annum | 7 | 14 | 60,575 |
| North Carolina | 4[7] | 45,000 | 50 | 120 | 2 | 2 | 4,800 per annum | 7 | 8 | 43,408 |
| North Dakota | 4 | 42,000 | 50 | 100 | 4 | 2 | 5 per diem[16 26] | 5 | 10 | 36,800 |
| Ohio | 4 | 50,000 | 33 | 99 | 4 | 2 | 17,500 per annum | 7 | 6 | 40,000 |
| Oklahoma | 4 | 42,500 | 48 | 101 | 4 | 2 | 12,948 per annum | ([19]) | 6 | 38,000 |
| Oregon | 4[10] | 50,372 | 30 | 60 | 4 | 2 | 7,848 per annum | 7 | 6 | 45,707 |
| Pennsylvania | 4 | 66,000 | 50 | 203 | 4 | 2 | 18,720 per annum | 7 | 10 | 55,000 |
| Rhode Island | 2 | 42,500 | 50 | 100 | 2 | 2 | 5 per diem[17] | 5 | ([18]) | 38,350 |
| South Carolina | 4[7] | 39,000 | 46 | 124 | 4 | 2 | 7,000 per annum | 5 | 10 | 45,000 |
| South Dakota | 4[10] | 37,000 | 35 | 70 | 2 | 2 | 6,000 per biennium | 5 | 8 | 35,000 |
| Tennessee | 4 | 50,000 | 33 | 99 | 4 | 2 | 7,800 per annum | 5 | 8 | 54,590 |
| Texas | 4 | 71,400 | 31 | 150 | 4 | 2 | 7,200 per annum | ([20]) | 6 | 50,300 |
| Utah | 4 | 40,000 | 29 | 77 | 4 | 2 | 25 per diem | 5 | 10 | 35,000 |
| Vermont | 2 | 39,000 | 30 | 150 | 2 | 2 | 200 per week[21] | 5 | 6 | 31,750 |
| Virginia | 4[7] | 60,000 | 40 | 100 | 4 | 2 | 8,000 per annum | 7 | 12 | 51,000 |
| Washington | 4 | 55,000 | 49 | 98 | 4 | 2 | 9,800 per annum | 9 | 6 | 45,000 |
| West Virginia | 4 | 50,000 | 34 | 100 | 4 | 2 | 4,800 per annum | 5 | 12 | 35,000 |
| Wisconsin | 4 | 65,800 | 33 | 99 | 4 | 2 | 19,767[22] per annum | 7 | 10 | 46,368[28] |
| Wyoming | 4 | 37,500 | 30 | 62 | 4 | 2 | 66 per diem | 5 | 8 | 32,500 |

1. General Assembly in Ark., Colo., Conn., Del., Ga., Ind., Ky., Md., Mo., N.C., Ohio, Pa., R.I., S.C., Tenn., Vt., Va., Legislative Assembly in N.D., Ore.; General Court in Mass., N.H.; Legislature in other states. Meets biennially in Calif., Ky., Me., Mont., Nev., N.H., N.J., N.C., N.D., Ore., Pa., Texas, Wash. and Wyo.; meets annually in other states. 2. Court of Appeals in Ky., Md., N.Y., Supreme Court of Virginia in Va., Supreme Judicial Court in Me., Mass.; Supreme Court in other states. 3. Upper house: Senate in all states. 4. Lower house: Assembly in Calif., Nev., N.Y., Wis.; House of Delegates in Md., Va., W.Va.; General Assembly in N.J.; House of Representatives in other states. 5. Does not include additional payments for expenses, mileage, special sessions, etc., or additional per diem payments beyond salary shown. 6. In some states, Chief Justice receives a higher salary. 7. Cannot succeed himself. 8. Appointed for 3 years; thereafter elected popularly for 10-year term. 9. May serve only 2 terms, consecutive or otherwise. 10. May not serve 3rd consecutive term. 11. Unicameral legislature. 12. Constitutional number: 375–400. 13. Until 70 years old. 14. When term begins in Jan. of 2nd year following U.S. census, term shall be 2 years. 15. 2nd term receive tenure, mandatory retirement at 70. 16. Plus additional expenses. 17. For 60 days only. 18. Term of good behavior. 19. 9 members in Supreme Court, highest in civil cases; 3 in Court of Criminal Appeals. 20. 9 members in Supreme Court, highest in civil cases; 5 in Court of Criminal Appeals. 21. To limit of $6,750 per biennium. 22. Commencing in 1979, except for Senate holdovers. 23. $500 per month when not in session. 24. $6,500 for second year, plus $1,000 per year expenses, plus mileage. 25. When in session. 26. Plus $150 per month. 27. As of Dec. 1979. 28. $48,919 upon replacement or reelection of any justice after July 1, 1978. *Source: Information Please* questionnaires to the states.

# 50 Largest Cities of the United States

Source of population and land area: U.S. Census Bureau. Television households apply to county or counties in which a city is located, except for independent cities; source: A. C. Nielsen Co. Telephones; source: American Telephone & Telegraph Co. Other data were supplied by the cities in response to *Information Please* questionnaires.

## ATLANTA, GA.

**Incorporated as city:** 1847
**Mayor:** Maynard Jackson (to Jan. 1982)
**1970 population & (rank):** 495,039 (27)
**1975 est. population & (rank):** 436,057 (29)
**1970–75 population change:** −11.9%
**1976 city land area:** 136.0 sq mi.
**Altitude:** Highest, 1050 ft; lowest, 940
**Location:** In northwest central part of state, near Chattahoochee River
**Counties:** Fulton and De Kalb
**Churches (5-county area):** 1,500
**City-owned parks and parkways:** 164 (2,802 ac.)
**Telephones (Jan. 1, 1977):** 863,622
**Television households (Jan. 1978):** 359,600 (98%)
**Radio stations (15-county area):** AM, 22; FM, 9; educational, 5
**Television stations (15-county area):** 6 commercial; 2 educational
**Gross assessed valuation (City, 1975):** $2,857,119,676
**City tax rate (1975):** $48.79 per $1,000
**Total bonded debt (1975):** $169,207,014.25
**Revenue (1977, incl. General Fund, Airport Revenue, Water/Sewer Fund):** $182,630,297
**Expenditures (1977):** $154,078,229
**Chamber of Commerce:** Atlanta Chamber of Commerce, 1300 N Omni International, Atlanta, Ga. 30303

Information is gathered on 3 geographic areas: City of Atlanta, 5-county metro area, 15-county SMSA

## AUSTIN, TEX.

**Incorporated as city:** 1839
**Mayor:** Carole McClellan (to May, 1979)
**1970 population & (rank):** 225,869 (56)
**1975 est. population & (rank):** 301,147 (46)
**1970–75 population change:** +17.7%
**1976 city land area:** 118.99 sq mi.
**Altitude:** Highest, 425 ft
**Location:** In south central part of state, on the Colorado River
**County:** Seat of Travis Co.
**Churches:** Protestant, 230; Roman Catholic, 19; Jewish, 2
**City-owned parks and parkways:** 73
**Telephones (Jan. 1, 1977):** 296,905
**Television households (Jan. 1978):** 122,600 (97%)
**Radio stations:** AM, 5; FM, 7
**Television stations:** 3 commercial; 1 educational
**Assessed valuation (1977):** $2,742,144,830
**City tax rate (1977):** $12.40 per $1,000
**Bonded debt (1977–78):** $562,905,000
**Revenue (1977–78):** $265,117,508
**Expenditures (1977–78):** $263,138,116
**Chamber of Commerce:** Austin Chamber of Commerce, 901 W Riverside Dr., Austin, Tex. 78701

## BALTIMORE, MD.

**Incorporated as city:** 1797
**Mayor:** William D. Schaefer (to Dec. 1979)
**1970 population & (rank):** 905,787 (7)
**1975 est. population & (rank):** 851,698 (7)
**1970–75 population change:** −6.0%
**1970 land area:** 78.3 sq mi.
**Altitude:** Highest, 490 ft; lowest, sea level
**Location:** On Patapsco River, about 12 mi. from Chesapeake Bay
**County:** Baltimore
**Churches:** Roman Catholic, 68; Jewish, 50; Protestant and others, 356
**City-owned parks:** 347 park areas and tracts (6,314 ac.)
**Telephones (Jan. 1, 1977):** 1,251,557
**Television households (Jan. 1978):** 504,600 (99%)
**Radio stations:** AM, 11; FM, 9
**Television stations:** 5
**Assessed valuation (1978):** $2,633,163,000
**City tax rate (1977–78):** $59.90 per $1,000
**Net bonded debt (June 30, 1977):** $484,916,200
**Revenue (1978):** $1,238,344,774
**Expenditures (1978):** $1,257,363,476
**Chamber of Commerce:** Greater Baltimore Committee, 900 Mercantile Building, Baltimore, Md. 21201

## BOSTON, MASS.

**Incorporated as city:** 1822
**Mayor:** Kevin H. White (to Jan. 1980)
**1970 population & (rank):** 641,071 (16)
**1975 est. population & (rank):** 636,725 (19)
**1970–75 population change:** −0.7%
**1970 land area:** 46.0 sq mi.
**Altitude:** Highest, 330 ft; lowest, sea level
**Location:** On Massachusetts Bay, at mouths of Charles and Mystic Rivers
**County:** Seat of Suffolk Co.
**Churches:** Protestant, 187; Roman Catholic, 73; Jewish, 28; others, 100
**City-owned parks, playgrounds, etc.:** 2,276.36 ac.
**Telephones (Jan. 1, 1977):** 493,875
**Television households (Jan. 1978):** 262,300 (96%)
**Radio Stations:** AM, 9; FM, 8
**Television stations:** 7
**Assessed valuation (1977–78):** $1,783,002,014
**City tax rate (1977–78):** $252.90 per $1,000
**Net bonded debt (June 30, 1977):** $471,980,000
**Revenue (1976–77):** $928,842,687
**Expenditures (1976–77):** $920,572,968
**Chamber of Commerce:** Boston Chamber of Commerce, 125 High St., Boston, Mass. 02110

## BUFFALO, N.Y.

**Incorporated as city:** 1832
**Mayor:** James Griffin (to Dec. 1981)
**1970 population & (rank):** 462,768 (28)
**1975 est. population & (rank):** 407,160 (32)
**1970–75 population change:** −12.0%
**1970 land area:** 41.3 sq mi.
**Altitude:** Highest, 698 ft; lowest, 571
**Location:** At east end of Lake Erie, on Niagara River
**County:** Seat of Erie Co.
**Churches:** 60 denominations, with over 400 churches

City-owned parks: 10 public parks (3,000 ac.)
Telephones (Jan. 1, 1977): 428,459
Television households (Jan. 1978): 369,000 (98%)
Radio stations: AM, 12; FM, 13
Television stations: 5 (plus reception from 3 Canadian stations)
Assessed valuation (1977–78): $1,033,049,000
City tax rate (1977–78): $121.12 per $1,000
Total funded debt (long-term, June 30, 1977): $132,207,000
Revenue (general fund, 1976–77): $192,644,670
Expenditures (1976–77): $160,282,883
Chamber of Commerce: Buffalo Area Chamber of Commerce, 107 Delaware Ave., Buffalo, N.Y. 14202

## CHARLOTTE, N.C.

**Incorporated as city:** 1768
**Mayor:** Kenneth R. Harris (to Nov. 1979)
**1970 population & (rank):** 274,640 (53)
**1975 est. population & (rank):** 281,417 (49)
**1970–75 population change:** +2.5%
**1977 city land area:** 29.3 sq mi.
**Altitude:** 765 ft
**Location:** In the southern part of state near the border of South Carolina
**County:** Seat of Mecklenburg Co.
**Churches:** Protestant, over 400; Roman Catholic, 8; Jewish, 3
**City-owned parks and parkways:** 67
**Telephones (Jan. 1, 1977):** 332,442
**Television households (Jan. 1978):** 129,200 (98%)
**Radio stations:** AM, 8; FM, 6
**Television stations:** 4 commercial; 2 educational
**Assessed valuation (1977–78):** $5,191,652,742
**City tax rate (includes county, 1977–78):** $16.80 per $1,000
**Bonded debt (1977–78):** $125,744,000
**Revenue (1977–78):** $139,535,057
**Expenditures (1977–78):** $139,535,057
**Chamber of Commerce:** Greater Charlotte Chamber of Commerce, P.O. Box 1867, Charlotte, N.C., 28233

## CHICAGO, ILL.

**Incorporated as city:** 1837
**Mayor:** Michael A. Bilandic (to April 1979)
**1970 population & (rank):** 3,369,359 (2)
**1975 est. population & (rank):** 3,099,391 (2)
**1970–75 population change:** −8.0%
**1975 land area:** 228,124 sq mi.
**Altitude:** Highest, 672 ft; lowest, 578.5
**Location:** On lower west shore of Lake Michigan
**County:** Seat of Cook Co.
**Churches:** Protestant, 850; Roman Catholic, 278; Jewish, 66
**City-owned parks:** 577
**Telephones (Jan. 1, 1977):** 2,540,611
**Television households (Jan. 1978):** 1,902,700 (98%)
**Radio stations:** AM, 16; FM, 18
**Television stations:** 8
**Assessed valuation (1976):** $12,569,904,506
**Total Chicago Tax rate (1976):** $87.85 per $1,000
**Total gross bonded debt (1976):** $1,096,320,000
**Revenue (1978):** $1, 328,179,082
**Expenditures (1978):** $1,297,300,917
**Chamber of Commerce:** Chicago Association of Commerce & Industry, 130 S Michigan Ave., Chicago, Ill. 60603

## CINCINNATI, OHIO

**Incorporated as city:** 1819
**Mayor:** Mrs. Bobbie Sterne (to Dec. 1979)
**City Manager:** William V. Donaldson
**1970 population & (rank):** 451,410 (30)
**1975 est. population & (rank):** 412,564 (31)
**1970–75 population change:** −9.0%
**1970 land area:** 78.1 sq mi.
**Altitude:** Highest, 960 ft; lowest, 441
**Location:** In southwestern corner of state on Ohio River
**County:** Seat of Hamilton Co.
**Churches:** 850
**City-owned parks:** 96 (3,879 ac.)
**Telephones (Jan. 1, 1977):** 727,700
**Television households (Jan. 1978):** 310,100 (98%)
**Radio stations:** AM, 9; FM, 12 (Greater Cincinnati)
**Television stations:** 5
**Assessed valuation (1977):** $2,055,325,660
**City tax rate (1977):** $11.40 per $1,000
**Bonded debt (1977):** $203,854,023
**Revenue (general fund, 1977):** $98,332,978
**Expenditures (general fund, 1977):** $95,077,075
**Chamber of Commerce:** Cincinnati Chamber of Commerce, 120 W Fifth St., Cincinnati, Ohio 45202

## CLEVELAND, OHIO

**Incorporated as city:** 1836
**Mayor:** Dennis J. Kucinich (to Dec. 1979)
**1970 population & (rank):** 750,879 (10)
**1975 est. population & (rank):** 638,793 (18)
**1970–75 population change:** −14.9%
**1970 land area:** 75.9 sq mi.
**Altitude:** Highest, 865 ft.; lowest, 573
**Location:** On Lake Erie at mouth of Cuyahoga River
**County:** Seat of Cuyahoga Co.
**Churches:** [1] Protestant, 717; Roman Catholic, 162; Jewish, 23; Eastern Orthodox, 18
**City-owned parks:** 341 (2,130 ac.)
**Telephones (Jan. 1, 1977):** 902,453
**Television households (Jan. 1978):** 549,700 (99%)
**Radio stations:** AM, 13; FM, 14
**Television stations:** 7
**Assessed valuation (1978):** $3,056,309,908
**City tax rate (1978):** $68 per $1,000
**Bonded debt (March 31, 1978):** $455,871,000
**Revenue (est. 1978):** $336,024,849
**Expenditures (est. 1978):** $336,024,849
**Chamber of Commerce:** Greater Cleveland Growth Association, 690 Union Commerce Building, Cleveland, Ohio 44115

1. 100-mile area.

## COLUMBUS, OHIO

**Incorporated as city:** 1834
**Mayor:** Tom Moody (to Jan. 1980)
**1970 population & (rank):** 540,025 (21)
**1975 est. population & (rank):** 535,610 (22)
**1970–75 population change:** −0.8%
**1977 land area:** 174.1 sq. mi.
**Altitude:** Highest, 902 ft; lowest, 702
**Location:** In central part of state, on Scioto River
**County:** Seat of Franklin Co.
**Churches:** Protestant, 412; Roman Catholic, 43; Jewish, 5
**City-owned parks:** 135 (10,931 ac.)
**Telephones (Jan. 1, 1977):** 467,362
**Television households (Jan. 1978):** 297,200 (99%)
**Radio stations:** AM, 8; FM, 6
**Television stations:** 3 commercial, 2 educational
**Assessed valuation (1978):** $3,153,937,894
**City tax rate (1978):** $41.70 per $1,000
**Bonded debt (Dec. 31, 1977):** $268,214,446
**Revenue (1977):** $604,432,987
**Expenditures (1977):** $597,999,526
**Chamber of Commerce:** Columbus Area Chamber of Commerce, P.O. Box 1527, Columbus, Ohio 43216

## DALLAS, TEX.

**Incorporated as city:** 1856
**Mayor:** Bob Folsom (to April 1979)
**City Manager:** George Schrader (apptd. Dec. 1972)
**1970 population & (rank):** 844,401 (8)
**1975 est. population & (rank):** 812,797 (8)
**1970–75 population change:** −3.7%
**1970 land area:** 265.6 sq mi.
**Altitude:** Highest, 750 ft; lowest, 375
**Location:** In northeastern part of state, on Trinity River
**County:** Seat of Dallas Co.
**Churches:** 1,200 (in Dallas Co.)
**City-owned parks:** 256 (20,982 ac.)
**Telephones (Jan. 1, 1977):** 788,693
**Television households (Jan. 1978):** 495,000 (98%)
**Radio stations:** AM, 14; FM, 15
**Television stations:** 7
**Assessed valuation (1977):** $8,704,976,035
**City tax rate (1977–78):** $13.50 per $1,000
**Net revenue bond debt (Sept. 30, 1977):** $149,816,000
**Net tax supported debt (Sept. 30, 1977):** $287,978,000
**Revenue (est. 1977–78):** $333,075,567
**Expenditures (est. 1977–78):** $325,460,979
**Chamber of Commerce:** Dallas Chamber of Commerce. 1507 Pacific, Dallas, Tex. 75201

## DENVER, COLO.

**Incorporated as city:** 1861
**Mayor:** William H. McNichols, Jr. (to July 1, 1979)
**1970 population & (rank):** 514,678 (25)
**1975 est. population & (rank):** 484,531 (26)
**1970–75 population change:** −5.9%
**1975 land area:** 115.08 sq mi.
**Altitude:** Highest, 5,470 ft; lowest, 5,130
**Location:** In northeast central part of state, on South Platte River
**County:** Coextensive with Denver Co.
**Churches:** Protestant, 815; Roman Catholic, 63; Jewish, 13[1]
**City-owned parks:** 155 (3,600 ac.)
**City-owned mountain parks:** 40 (13,448 ac.)
**Telephones (Jan. 1, 1977):** 1,146,866
**Television households (Jan. 1978):** 191,100 (97%)
**Radio stations:** AM, 18; FM, 13[1]
**Television stations:** 5
**Assessed valuation (1977):** $2,023,198,170
**City tax rate (1977):** $28.05 per $1,000[2]
**Bonded debt (1977):** $345,389,000[2]
**Revenue (1977):** $643,230,440[2]
**Expenditures (1977):** $587,051,082[2]
**Chamber of Commerce:** Denver Chamber of Commerce, 1301 Welton, Denver, Colo. 80204

1. Metropolitan area. 2. Excluding school district.

## DETROIT, MICH.

**Incorporated as city:** 1815
**Mayor:** Coleman A. Young (to Jan. 1982)
**1970 population & (rank):** 1,514,063 (5)
**1975 est. population & (rank):** 1,335,085 (6)
**1970–75 population change:** −11.8%
**1970 land area:** 143.3 sq mi.
**Altitude:** Highest, 685 ft; lowest, 574
**Location:** In southeastern part of state, on Detroit River
**County:** Seat of Wayne Co.
**Churches:** [1] Protestant, 2,204; Roman Catholic, 357; Jewish, 39
**City-owned parks:** 60 parks (3,843 ac.); 388 sites (5,838 ac.)
**Telephones (Jan. 1, 1977):** 1,492,384
**Television households (Jan. 1978):** 848,300 (99%)
**Radio stations:** AM, 13; FM, 20[1]
**Television stations:** 10 (incl. Windsor, Ontario, Canada)[1]
**Assessed valuation (1977):** $4,930,166,730
**City tax rate (1977–78):** $33.17 per $1,000[2]
**Net bonded debt (April 1, 1978):** General obligations, $376,890,090; revenue and self-supporting debt, $356,922,335
**Revenue (1977–78):** $1,222,872,242[3]
**Expenditures (1977–78):** $1,222,872,242[3]
**Chamber of Commerce:** Greater Detroit Chamber of Commerce, 150 Michigan Ave., Detroit, Mich. 48226

1. Six-county metropolitan area. 2. Excludes school system. 3. Includes utilities.

## EL PASO, TEX.

**Incorporated as city:** 1873
**Mayor:** Ray Salazar (to April 1979)
**1970 population & (rank):** 322,261 (45)
**1975 est. population & (rank):** 385,691 (33)
**1970–75 population change:** +19.7%
**1976 land area:** 161.01 sq mi.
**Altitude:** 4,000 ft
**Location:** In far western part of state, on Rio Grande
**County:** Seat of El Paso Co.
**Churches:** Protestant, 212; Roman Catholic, 36; Jewish, 2; others, 13
**City-owned parks:** 82 (1,419.8 ac.)
**Telephones (Jan. 1, 1977):** 251,488
**Television households (Jan. 1978):** 126,600 (98%)
**Radio stations:** AM, 9; FM, 5
**Television stations:** 3
**Assessed valuation (1976):** $1,995,943,930
**City tax rate (1977):** $11.50 per $1,000 city, $15.20 per $1,000 El Paso Independent School District
**Bonded debt (1977):** $36,180,000
**Revenue (1977–78):** $55,199,415
**Expenditures (1977–78):** $53,097,045
**Chamber of Commerce:** El Paso Chamber of Commerce, 10 Civic Center Plaza, El Paso, Tex. 79944

## FORT WORTH, TEX.

**Incorporated as city:** 1873
**Mayor:** Hugh Q. Parmer (to April 1979)
**City Manager:** Morris C. Matson
**1970 population & (rank):** 393,476 (33)
**1975 est. population & (rank):** 358,364 (39)
**1970–75 population change:** −8.9%
**1977 land area:** 242.059 sq mi.
**Altitude:** Highest, 780 ft; lowest, 520
**Location:** In north central part of state, on Trinity River
**County:** Seat of Tarrant Co.
**Churches:** Protestant, 392; Roman Catholic, 16; Jewish, 2
**City-owned parks:** 126 (7,817 ac.; 3,500 ac. in Nature Center)
**Telephones (Jan. 1, 1977):** 336,027
**Television households (Jan. 1978):** 254,800 (98%)
**Radio stations:** AM, 7; FM, 6
**Television stations:** 6 (2 local)
**Assessed valuation (1977–78):** $2,161,150,180
**City tax rate (1978):** $16.55 per $1,000
**Bonded debt (Sept. 30, 1977):** $195,754,000
**Revenue (1977–78 tax supported funds):** $81,275,180
**Expenditures (1977–78 tax supported funds):** $81,275,180
**Chamber of Commerce:** Fort Worth Chamber of Commerce, 700 Throckmorton, Fort Worth, Tex. 76102

## HONOLULU, HAWAII

**Incorporated as city and county:** 1907

Mayor: Frank F. Fasi (to Jan. 1981)
**1970 population & (rank):** 324,871 (44)
**1975 est. population & (rank):** 705,381[1] (12)
**1974 land area of city:** 604 sq mi.
Altitude: Highest, 4,025 ft; lowest, sea level
Location: The city and county government's jurisdiction includes the entire island of Oahu
Churches: Roman Catholic, 33; Buddhist, 32; Jewish, 2; Protestant and others, 320
City-owned parks: 4,556 ac.
Telephones (Jan. 1, 1977): 347,806
Television households (Sept. 1976): 204,200 (97%)
Radio stations: AM, 18; FM, 6
Television stations: 5
Assessed valuation (June 1977): $7,805,949,576 (60% of market value.)
City and county tax rate (1977): $15.37 per $1,000
Bonded debt (June 1977): $206,423,000
Net revenue (1976–77): $273,752,578
Net expenditures (1976–77): $234,778,378; capital improvement budget, $14,443,976
Chamber of Commerce: Chamber of Commerce of Hawaii, 735 Bishop St., Honolulu, Hawaii 96813

1. City and County area.

## HOUSTON, TEX.

Incorporated as city: 1837
Mayor: Jim McConn (to Jan. 1980)
**1970 population & (rank):** 1,233,535 (6)
**1975 est. population & (rank):** 1,357,394 (5)
**1970–75 population change:** +10%
**1976 land area:** 507.64 sq mi.
Altitude: Highest, 120 ft; lowest, sea level
Location: In southeastern part of state, near Gulf of Mexico
County: Seat of Harris Co.
Churches: 1,750[1]
City-owned parks: 259 (5,742 ac., not including parkways)
Telephones (Jan. 1, 1977): 1,299,450
Television households (Jan. 1978): 709,900 (98%)
Radio stations: AM, 14; FM, 16[1]
Television stations: 6
Assessed valuation (1977): $10,624,560,450
City tax rate (1977): $15.80 per $1,000
Bonded debt (1977): $1,189,768,000
Revenue (1977): $309,251,143
Expenditures (1977): $304,101,292
Chamber of Commerce: Houston Chamber of Commerce, 1100 Milam Building, Houston, Tex. 77002

1. Metropolitan area (Harris County).

## INDIANAPOLIS, IND.

Incorporated as city: 1832 (reincorporated 1838)
Mayor: William H. Hudnut III (to Jan. 1980)
**1970 population & (rank):** 742,925 (11)
**1975 est. population & (rank):** 714,878 (11)
**1970–75 population change:** −2.0%
**1970 land area:** 379.4 sq mi.
Altitude: Highest, 840 ft; lowest, 700
Location: In central part of the state, on West Fork of White River
County: Seat of Marion Co.
Churches: 988[1]
City-owned parks: 188 (9,154 ac.)
Telephones (Jan. 1, 1977): 648,041
Television households (Jan. 1978): 267,300 (98%)
Radio Stations: AM, 9; FM, 13[1]
Television Stations: 6[1]
Assessed valuation (1977): (consolidated city), $2,148,598,480; (Marion County) $2,291,779,140
City tax rate (Center Township, 1977): $126.94 per $1,000
Gross debt (consolidated city, Dec. 31, 1976): $262,681,180
Revenue (1976): $169,146,104
Expenditures (1976): $162,511,404
Chamber of Commerce: Indianapolis Chamber of Commerce, 320 N Meridian St., Indianapolis, Ind. 46202

1. Marion County.

## JACKSONVILLE, FLA.

Incorporated as City: 1822
Mayor: Hans G. Tanzler, Jr. (to July 1, 1979)
**1970 population & (rank):** 528,865 (23)
**1975 est. population & (rank):** 535,030 (23)
**1970–75 population change:** +6.1%
**1970 land area:** 766.0 sq mi.
Altitude: Highest, 71 ft; lowest, sea level
Location: On St. Johns River, 20 miles from Atlantic Ocean
County: Duval
Churches: Protestant, 612; Roman Catholic, 23; Jewish, 4, others, 10
City-owned parks and playgrounds: 136 (1,475 ac.)
Telephones (Jan. 1, 1977): 409,591
Television households (Jan. 1978): 198,100 (98%)
Radio stations: AM, 15; FM, 9
Television stations: 3 commercial, 1 educational
Assessed valuation (1977): $5,965,814,449
City tax rate (1977–78): $19.27 per $1,000 (old city area); $18.16 (old county area)
Bonded debt (1977): $51,624,223
Revenue (1977–78): $721,302,459
Expenditures (1977–78): $721,302,459
Chamber of Commerce: Jacksonville Area Chamber of Commerce, Jacksonville, Fla. 32202

## KANSAS CITY, MO.

Incorporated as city: 1850
Mayor: Dr. Charles B. Wheeler, Jr. (to April 1979)
City Manager: Robert A. Kipp (apptd. Jan. 1974)
**1970 population & (rank):** 507,330 (26)
**1975 est. population & (rank):** 472,529 (27)
**1970–75 population change:** −6.9%
**1970 land area:** 316.33 sq mi.
Altitude: Highest, 1,014 ft; lowest, 722
Location: In western part of state, at juncture of Missouri and Kansas Rivers
County: Located in Jackson, Clay, and Platte Co.
Churches: 1,100 churches of all denominations
City-owned parks and playgrounds: 144 (7,233 ac.)
Telephones (Jan. 1, 1977): 337,326
Television households (Jan. 1978): 301,000 (98%)
Radio stations: AM, 14; FM, 15[1]
Television Stations: 6[1]
Assessed valuation (1976–77): $1,637,987,206
City tax rate (1976–77): $15.20 per $1,000
Bonded debt (1977): $92,311,000[2]
Revenue (1976–77): $219,169,241
Expenditures (1976–77): $209,238,438
Budget (gross total, 1977–78): $245,800,000
Chamber of Commerce: Chamber of Commerce of Greater Kansas City, 920 Main St., Kansas City, Mo. 64105

1. Metropolitan area. 2. Operating and debt.

## LONG BEACH, CALIF.

Founded: 1881
Mayor: Dr. Thomas J. Clark (to July 1981)
City Manager: John E. Dever (Jan. 1, 1977)

**1970 population & (rank):** 359,879 (40)
**1975 est. population & (rank):** 335,602 (43)
**1970–75 population change:** −7.1%
**1970 land area:** 50 sq mi.
**Altitude:** Highest, 170 ft; lowest, sea level
**Location:** On San Pedro Bay, south of Los Angeles
**County:** In Los Angeles Co.
**Churches:** 236
**City-owned parks:** 43 (1,620 ac.)
**Telephones:** (included in Los Angeles area)
**Television households:** (included in Los Angeles area)
**Radio stations:** AM, 2; FM, 6
**Television stations:** 1 (cable)
**Assessed valuation (1976–77):** $1,304,085,108
**City tax rate (1976–77):** $21.81 per $1,000
**Bonded debt (June 1976):** $9,053,594
**Revenue (1976–77):** $232,555,260[1]
**Expenditures (1976–77):** $285,860,652
**Chamber of Commerce:** Long Beach Chamber of Commerce, 121 Linden Ave., Long Beach, Calif. 90802

1. Does not include 1976–77 beginning surplus of $53,305,392.

## LOS ANGELES, CALIF.

**Incorporated as city:** 1850
**Mayor:** Tom Bradley (to June 1981)
**1970 population & (rank):** 2,811,801 (3)
**1975 est. population & (rank):** 2,727,399 (3)
**1970–75 population change:** −3.0%
**1976 land area:** 463.9 sq mi.
**Altitude:** Highest, 5,081 ft; lowest, sea level
**Location:** In southwestern part of state, on Pacific Ocean
**County:** Seat of Los Angeles Co.
**Churches:** 1,928 of all denominations
**City-owned parks:** 273 (13,786 ac.)
**Telephones (extended area, Jan. 1, 1977):** 5,640,361[1]
**Television households (Jan. 1978):** 2,636,500 (97%)[1]
**Radio stations:** AM, 32; FM, 40
**Television stations:** 18
**Assessed valuation (1977–78):** $10,368,046,000
**City tax rate (1977–78):** $28.81 per $1,000
**Gross debt (June 30, 1977):** general obligation bonds, $135,795,000; revenue bonds, $2,149,264,000
**Revenue (est. 1977–78):** $2,312,554,401
**Expenditures (est. 1977–78):** $2,312,554,401
**Chamber of Commerce:** Los Angeles Chamber of Commerce, 404 S Bixel St., Los Angeles, Calif. 90017

1. Includes Long Beach, Calif.

## LOUISVILLE, KY.

**Incorporated as city:** 1828
**Mayor:** William B. Stansbury (to Dec. 1981)
**1970 population & (rank):** 361,706 (38)
**1975 est. population & (rank):** 335,954 (42)
**1970–75 population change:** −7.1%
**1970 land area:** 65.2 sq mi.
**Altitude:** Highest, 565 ft; lowest, 477
**Location:** In north central part of state, on Ohio River
**County:** Seat of Jefferson Co.
**Churches:** 678[1]
**City-owned parks and playgrounds:** 166 (over 7,000 ac.)
**Telephones (Jan. 1, 1977):** 540,401[1]
**Television households (Jan. 1978):** 235,700 (99%)
**Radio stations:** 16
**Television stations:** 5
**Assessed valuation (1977):** $2,204,702,664
**City tax rate (1975–76):** $5.66 per $1,000 (city purposes only; exclusive of schools)
**Net bonded debt (Jan. 1, 1978):** $44,317,000
**Revenue (1976–77):** $85,898,000
**Expenditures (1976–77):** $83,334,000
**Chamber of Commerce:** Louisville Area Chamber of Commerce, 300 W Liberty St., Louisville, Ky. 40202

1. Metropolitan area.

## MEMPHIS, TENN.

**Incorporated as city:** 1826
**Mayor:** Wyeth Chandler (to Jan. 1980)
**1970 population & (rank):** 623,530 (17)
**1975 est. population & (rank):** 661,319 (17)
**1970–75 population change:** +0.7%
**1970 land area:** 280.89 sq mi.
**Altitude:** Highest, 331 ft
**Location:** In southwestern corner of state, on Mississippi River
**County:** Seat of Shelby Co
**Churches:** 800
**Parks and playgrounds:** 117 (5,565 ac.)
**Telephones (Jan. 1, 1977):** 574,196
**Television households (Jan. 1978):** 246,600 (98%)
**Radio stations:** AM, 12; FM, 9
**Television stations:** 4
**Assessed valuation (1976):** $1,957,915,069
**City tax rate (1977–78):** $37.40 per $1,000[1]
**Bonded debt (1978):** $407,599,726
**Revenue (1977–78):** $227,954,033
**Expenditures (1977–78):** $227,954,033
**Chamber of Commerce:** Memphis Area Chamber of Commerce, P.O. Box 224, Memphis, Tenn. 38103

1. Includes school indebtedness.

## MIAMI, FLA.

**Incorporated as city:** 1896
**Mayor:** Maurice A. Ferre (to Nov. 1979)
**City manager:** Joseph R. Grassie (apptd. May 1976)
**1970 population & (rank):** 334,859 (42)
**1975 est. population & (rank):** 365,082 (38)
**1970–75 population change:** +9.0%
**1970 land area:** 34.3 sq mi.
**Altitude:** Average, 12 ft
**Location:** In southeastern part of state, on Biscayne Bay
**County:** Seat of Dade Co.
**Churches:** Protestant, 592; Roman Catholic, 53; Jewish, 48
**City-owned parks:** 90 (1,110 ac.)
**Telephones (Jan. 1, 1977):** 980,834
**Television households (Jan. 1978):** 551,100 (98%)
**Radio stations:** AM, 18; FM, 20; educational, 1
**Television stations:** 5 commercial, 2 educational, 2 closed-circuit
**Assessed valuation (1977–78):** $3,828,183,022
**City tax rate (1977–78):** $13.20 per $1,000
**Bonded debt (1977–78):** $137,445,000
**Revenue (1977–78):** $139,056,232
**Expenditures (1977–78):** $140,056,232
**Chamber of Commerce:** Greater Miami Chamber of Commerce, 1200 Biscayne Blvd., Miami, Fla. 33132

## MILWAUKEE, WIS.

**Incorporated as city:** 1846
**Mayor:** Henry W. Maier (to April 1980)
**1970 population & (rank):** 717,372 (12)
**1975 est. population & (rank):** 665,796 (14)
**1970–75 population change:** −7.2%
**1970 land area:** 95.0 sq mi.
**Altitude:** 580.60 ft
**Location:** In southeastern part of state, on Lake Michigan
**County:** Seat of Milwaukee Co.
**Churches:** 769

County-owned parks: 14,061 ac.
Telephones (Jan. 1, 1977): 828,572
Television households (Jan. 1978): 362,500 (98%)
Radio stations: AM, 8; FM, 10
Television stations: 6
Assessed valuation (1978): $5,860,569,932
City tax rate (1978): $45.93 per $1,000
Gross debt (1977): $163,114,275
Revenue (1977): $336,534,655
Expenditures (1977): $314,225,598
Chamber of Commerce: Metropolitan Milwaukee Association of Commerce, 828 N. Broadway, Milwaukee, Wis. 53202

## MINNEAPOLIS, MINN.

**Incorporated as city:** 1867
**Mayor:** Albert J. Hofstede (to Jan. 1980)
**1970 population & (rank):** 434,400 (32)
**1975 est. population & (rank):** 378,112 (34)
**1970–75 population change:** −13.0%
**1970 land area:** 55.1 sq mi.
**Altitude:** Highest, 945 ft; lowest, 695
**Location:** In southeast central part of state, on Mississippi River
**County:** Seat of Hennepin Co.
**Churches:** 419
**City-owned parks:** 153
**Telephones (incl. St. Paul, Jan. 1, 1977):** 1,546,100
**Television households (Jan. 1978):** 327,300 (98%)
**Radio stations:** AM, 17; FM, 15 (metro area)
**Television stations:** 6 (metro area)
**Assessed valuation (1977):** $1,489,639,752[1]
**City tax rate (1978):** $130.09 per $1,000
**Net debt (Dec. 1977):** $245,920,000
**Revenue (1977):** $181,800,858
**Expenditures (1977):** $181,800,858
**Chamber of Commerce:** Greater Minneapolis Chamber of Commerce, 15 S Fifth Street, Minneapolis, Minn. 55402

1. Assessed valuations on majority of properties now range from 25% (homesteads) to 43% (commercial, industrial) of actual market value.

## NASHVILLE, TENN.

**Incorporated as city:** 1806
**Mayor:** Richard H. Fulton (to Sept. 1979)
**1970 population & (rank):** 447,877 (31)
**1975 est. population & (rank):** 423,426 (30)
**1970–75 population change:** −0.6%
**1970 land area:** 507.8 sq mi.
**Altitude:** Highest, 1,100 ft; lowest, approx. 400 ft
**Location:** In north central part of state, on Cumberland River
**County:** Davidson
**Churches:** Protestant, 702; Roman Catholic, 15; Jewish, 3
**City-owned parks:** 47 (6,200 ac.)
**Telephones (Jan. 1, 1977):** 387,298
**Television households (Jan. 1978):** 162,100 (99%)
**Radio stations:** AM, 14; FM, 11
**Television stations:** 5
**Assessed valuation (1977):** $1,753,194,214
**City tax rate (1974):** $60 per $1,000
**Bonded debt (June 1976):** $261,631,720
**Revenue (1977):** $233,786,508
**Expenditures (1977):** $230,082,075
**Chamber of Commerce:** Nashville Area Chamber of Commerce, 161 Fourth Ave. North, Nashville, Tenn. 37219

## NEW ORLEANS, LA.

**Incorporated as city:** 1805
**Mayor:** Ernest N. Morial (to May 1982)
**1970 population & (rank):** 593,471 (19)
**1975 est. population & (rank):** 559,770 (20)
**1970–75 population change:** −5.7%
**1970 land area:** 197.1 sq mi.
**Altitude:** Highest, 15 ft; lowest, −4
**Location:** In southeastern part of state, between Mississippi River and Lake Ponchartrain
**Parish:** Seat of Orleans Parish
**Churches:** 644
**City-owned parks:** 69 (21,000 ac.)
**Telephones (Jan. 1, 1977):** 698,428
**Television households (Jan. 1978):** 201,600 (98%)
**Radio stations:** AM, 12; FM, 5
**Television stations:** 5
**Assessed valuation (1978):** $755,000,000
**City tax rate (1978):** $84.35 per $1,000
**Bonded debt (1977):** $178,583,000
**Revenue (1978):** $214,700,000
**Expenditures (1978):** $214,700,000
**Chamber of Commerce:** Chamber of Commerce of the New Orleans Area, 301 Camp Street, New Orleans, La. 70130.

## NEW YORK, N.Y.

**Chartered as "Greater New York':** 1898
**Mayor:** Edward Koch (to Dec. 31, 1981)
**Borough Presidents:** Bronx, Robert Abrams; Brooklyn, Howard Golden; Manhattan, Andrew Stein; Queens, Donald R. Manes; Staten Island, Anthony Gaeta
**1970 population & (rank):** 7,895,563 (1)[1]
**1975 est. population & (rank):** 7,481,613 (1)[1]
**1970–75 population change:** −5.2%
**1970 land area:** 303.7 sq mi. (Queens, 109.6; Brooklyn, 72.8; Staten Island, 55.8; Bronx, 42.5; Manhattan, 23.0)
**Altitude:** Highest, 410 ft; lowest, sea level
**Location:** In south of state, at mouth of Hudson River (also known as the North River as it passes Manhattan)
**Counties:** Consists of 5 counties: Bronx, Kings (Brooklyn), New York (Manhattan), Queens, Richmond (Staten Island)
**Churches:** Protestant, 1,766; Jewish, 1,256; Roman Catholic 437; Orthodox, 66
**City-owned parks:** 1,588 (37,372 ac.)
**Telephones (Jan. 1, 1977):** 5,945,045
**Television households (Jan. 1978):** 2,935,200 (97%)
**Radio stations:** AM and FM, 7; AM only, 10; FM only, 12
**Television stations:** 6 commercial
**Assessed valuation (1976–77):** $38,827,124,989[2]
**City tax rate: (1976–77):** $87.95 per $1,000
**Total funded debt (Jan. 31, 1976):** $7,674,445,960
**Revenue (1978):** $13,800,199,631
**Expenditures (1978):** $13,800,199,631
**Chamber of Commerce:** New York Chamber of Commerce and Industry, 65 Liberty St., New York, N.Y. 10005

1. For population of boroughs, *see* Index. 2. Taxable property only.

## NEWARK, N.J.

**Incorporated as city:** 1836
**Mayor:** Kenneth A. Gibson (to July 1982)
**1970 population & (rank):** 381,930 (35)
**1975 est. population & (rank):** 339,568 (41)
**1970–75 population change:** −11.1%
**1970 land area:** 23.5 sq mi.
**Altitude:** Highest, 273.4 ft; lowest, sea level
**Location:** In northeastern part of state, on Passaic River and Newark Bay
**County:** Seat of Essex Co.
**Churches:** Roman Catholic, 32; Jewish, 4; Protestant and others, 250
**City-owned parks:** 40 (and 20 mini parks); (39.3 ac.)
**County-governed parks in city:** 7 (743.97 ac.)

Telephones (Jan. 1, 1977): 316,942
Television households (Jan. 1978): 307,800 (98%)
Radio stations: AM, 2; FM, 4
Television stations: UHF, 1; VHF, 1
Assessed valuation (1977): $1,146,793,800
City tax rate (1977): $92.50 per $1,000
Net bonded debt (1977): $52,913,559
Revenue (1977): $245,483,870
Expenditures (1977): $245,483,870
Chamber of Commerce: Greater Newark Chamber of Commerce, 1180 Raymond Blvd., Newark, N.J. 07102

## NORFOLK, VA.

**Incorporated as city:** 1845
**Mayor:** Vincent J. Thomas (to May 1980)
**1970 population & (rank):** 307,951 (47)
**1975 est. population & (rank):** 286,694 (48)
**1970–75 population change:** −6.9%
**1970 land area:** 52.6 sq mi.
**Location:** In southeastern part of state, on Elizabeth River and Hampton Roads
**County:** Norfolk
**Churches:** 236
**Telephones (Jan. 1, 1977):** 436,057[1]
**Television households (Jan. 1978):** 155,500 (98%)
**Radio stations:** AM, 12; FM, 9
**Television stations:** 5
**Assessed valuation (April 30, 1977):** $2,000,000,000
**City tax rate (1977–78):** Real, $16.20 per $1,000 at 100% of fair market value; personal, $40 per $1,000; machinery, $16 per $1,000
**Bonded debt (April 30, 1977):** $98,000,000
**Revenue (1977–78):** $170,000,000
**Expenditures (1977–78):** $166,000,000
**Chamber of Commerce:** Norfolk Chamber of Commerce, 475 Saint Paul's Blvd., Norfolk, Va. 23510

1. Metropolitan area.

## OAKLAND, CALIF.

**Incorporated as city:** 1854
**Mayor:** Lionel J. Wilson (to June 30, 1981)
**Acting City Manager:** David A. Self (appt. April 1978)
**1970 population & (rank):** 361,561 (39)
**1975 est. population & (rank):** 330,651 (45)
**1970–75 population change:** −8.5%
**1970 land area:** 53.4 sq mi.
**Altitude:** Highest, 1,700 ft; lowest, sea level
**Location:** In west central part of state, on east side of San Francisco Bay
**County:** Seat of Alameda Co.
**Churches:** 374, representing over 78 denominations in the City; over 500 churches in Alameda County
**City-owned parks:** 2,196 ac.
**Telephones (Jan. 1, 1977):** 562,354[1]
**Television households (Jan. 1978):** 404,900 (96%)
**Radio Stations:** AM, 3; FM, 2
**Television stations:** 9 commercial; 3 educational
**Assessed valuation (1977–78):** $1,505,155,227
**City tax rate (1977–78):** $27.30 per $1,000
**Bonded debt (est. June 1978):** $7,350,000
**Revenue (all funds, 1977–78):** $98,151,000
**Expenditures (all funds, 1977–78):** $105,588,758
**Chamber of Commerce:** Oakland Chamber of Commerce, 1939 Harrison St., Suite 400, Oakland, Calif. 94612

1. Included in East Bay Exchange.

## OKLAHOMA CITY, OKLA.

**Incorporated as city:** 1890
**Mayor:** Mrs. Patience Latting (to April 1979)
**City Manager:** James J. Cook (apptd. April 3, 1976)
**1970 population & (rank):** 368,164 (37)
**1975 est. population & (rank):** 365,916 (37)
**1970–75 population change:** −0.6%
**1975 land area:** 648.5 sq mi.
**Altitude:** Highest, 1,320 ft; lowest, 1,140
**Location:** In central part of state, on North Canadian River
**County:** Seat of Oklahoma Co.
**Churches:** Roman Catholic, 15; Jewish, 2; Protestant and others, 741
**City-owned parks:** 130 (3,701 ac.)
**Telephones (Jan. 1, 1977):** 575,581
**Television households (Jan. 1978):** 200,300 (98%)
**Radio stations:** AM, 10; FM, 14
**Assessed valuation (1977–78):** $806,031,656
**City tax rate (1977–78):** $31.50 per $1,000
**Bonded debt (1977–78):** $229.966,700
**Revenue (general fund, 1977–78):** $78,793,000
**Expenditures (general fund, 1977–78):** $78,793,000
**Chamber of Commerce:** Oklahoma City Chamber of Commerce, 1 Santa Fe Plaza, Oklahoma City, Okla. 73102

## OMAHA, NEB.

**Incorporated as city:** 1857
**Mayor:** Al Veys (to June, 1981)
**1970 population & (rank):** 354,389 (41)
**1975 est. population & (rank):** 371,455 (35)
**1970–75 population change:** +3.6%
**1970 land area:** 76.6 sq mi.
**Altitude:** Highest, 1,270 ft
**Location:** In eastern part of state, on Missouri River
**County:** Seat of Douglas Co.
**Churches:** Protestant, 246; Roman Catholic, 44; Jewish, 4
**City-owned parks:** 99 (3,671.6 ac.)
**Telephones (Jan. 1, 1977):** 422,300
**Television households (Jan. 1978):** 139,500 (98%)
**Radio stations:** AM, 7; FM, 6
**Television stations:** 4
**Assessed valuation (1977):** $1,177,438,734
**City tax rate (1978):** $27.10 per $1,000
**Bonded debt (1978):** $65,895,500
**Revenue (1976):** $97,822,797
**Expenditures (1976):** $96,445,531
**Chamber of Commerce:** Omaha Chamber of Commerce, 1620 Dodge St., Omaha, Neb. 68102

## PHILADELPHIA, PA.

**First charter as city:** 1701
**Mayor:** Frank L. Rizzo (to Jan. 1980)
**1970 population & (rank):** 1,949,996 (4)
**1975 est. population & (rank):** 1,815,808 (4)
**1970–75 population change:** −6.9%
**1970 land area:** 129.7 sq mi.
**Altitude:** Highest, 440 ft; lowest, sea level
**Location:** In southeastern part of state, at junction of Schuylkill and Delaware Rivers
**County:** Seat of Philadelphia Co. (coterminous)
**Churches:** Roman Catholic, 139; Jewish, 70; Protestant and others, 830
**City-owned parks:** 219 (9,160 ac.)
**Telephones (Jan. 1, 1977):** 1,675,541
**Television households (Jan. 1978):** 639,000 (98%)
**Radio stations:** AM, 20; FM, 22
**Television stations:** 8
**Assessed valuation (Jan. 1978):** $5,626,346,990
**City and school district tax rate (1977):** $61.75 per $1,000
**Net bonded debt (June 30, 1977):** $1,402,538,000 (incl. bond anticipation notes of $75,000,000 for tax-supported projects); revenue bonds of $181,588,547 for water and sewer; $110,352,456 for gas works

**Revenue (1977):** $904,676,000
**Expenditures (1977):** $840,259,000
**Chamber of Commerce:** Greater Philadelphia Chamber of Commerce, 1617 John F. Kennedy Blvd., Philadelphia, Pa. 19103

## PHOENIX, ARIZ.

**Incorporated as city:** 1881
**Mayor:** Margaret T. Hance (to Jan. 1980)
**City Manager:** Marvin A. Andrews (appt. Oct. 1976)
**1970 population & (rank):** 587,213 (20)
**1975 est. population & (rank):** 664,721 (15)
**1970–75 population change:** +12.9%
**1977 land area:** 276.6 sq mi.
**Altitude:** Highest, 2,740 ft.; lowest, 1,017
**Location:** In center of state, on Salt River
**County:** Seat of Maricopa Co.
**City-owned parks:** 133 major areas (25,145 ac.)
**Telephones (Jan. 1, 1977):** 872,105
**Television households (Jan. 1978):** 436,700 (98%)
**Radio stations:** AM, 20; FM, 14
**Television stations:** 5 commercial; 1 educational
**Assessed valuation (1977–78):** $1,594,225,457
**City tax rate (1977–78):** $18.90 per $1,000
**Bonded debt (Dec. 1977):** $120,275,000
**Resources (est. 1978–79):** $298,014,673
**Expenditures (est. 1978–79):** $242,257,439
**Chamber of Commerce:** Phoenix Chamber of Commerce, 805 N Second St., Phoenix, Ariz. 85004

## PITTSBURGH, PA.

**Incorporated as city:** 1816
**Mayor:** Richard S. Caliguiri (to Jan. 1982)
**1970 population & (rank):** 520,089 (24)
**1975 est. population & (rank):** 458,651 (28)
**1970–75 population change:** −11.8%
**1970 land area:** 55 sq mi.
**Altitude:** Highest, 1,240 ft; lowest, 715
**Location:** In southwestern part of state, at beginning of Ohio River
**County:** Seat of Allegheny Co.
**Churches:** Protestant, 348; Roman Catholic, 86; Jewish, 28; Orthodox, 26
**City-owned parks and playgrounds:** 88 (2,471 ac.)
**Telephones (Jan. 1, 1977):** 802,937
**Television households (Jan. 1978):** 525,100 (98%)
**Radio stations:** AM, 18; FM, 9
**Television stations:** 4
**Assessed valuation (1978):** land, $383,817,000; buildings, $1,022,842,000
**City tax rate (1976):** Land, $49.50 per $1,000; buildings, $24.75 per $1,000
**Net bonded debt (March 31, 1977):** $217,573,786.11
**Revenue (1977):** $119,141,198
**Expenditures (1977):** $132,064,125
**Chamber of Commerce:** The Chamber of Commerce of Greater Pittsburgh, 411 Seventh Ave., Pittsburgh, Pa. 15222

## PORTLAND, ORE.

**Incorporated as city:** 1851
**Mayor:** Neil Goldschmidt (to Jan. 1981)
**1970 population & (rank):** 379,967 (36)
**1975 est. population & (rank):** 356,732 (40)
**1970–75 population change:** −6.7%
**1970 land area:** 89.1 sq mi.
**Altitude:** Highest, 1,073 ft; lowest, sea level
**Location:** In northwestern part of state, on Willamette River
**County:** Seat of Multnomah Co.
**Churches:** Protestant, 332; Roman Catholic, 27; Jewish, 4; Buddhist, 4; Vedanta Society, 1
**City-owned parks:** 160 (7,233 ac.)
**Telephones (Jan. 1, 1977):** 472,249
**Television households (Jan. 1978):** 205,800 (95%)
**Radio stations:** AM, 12; FM, 12
**Television stations:** 5
**Assessed valuation (1977–78):** $6,180,595,371 (at 100% of cash value)
**City tax rate (1977–78):** $7.92 per $1,000
**Bonded debt (July 1, 1979):** $43,560,455
**Revenue (budgeted 1979):** $207,244,774
**Expenditures (budgeted 1978–79):** $203,538,357
**Chamber of Commerce:** Portland Chamber of Commerce, 824 SW Fifth Ave., Portland, Ore. 97204

## ST. LOUIS, MO.

**Incorporated as city:** 1822
**Mayor:** James F. Conway (to April 1981)
**1970 population & (rank):** 622,236 (18)
**1975 est. population & (rank):** 524,964 (24)
**1970–75 population change:** −15.6%
**1970 land area:** 61.2 sq mi.
**Altitude:** Highest, 616 ft; lowest, 413
**Location:** In east central part of state, on Mississippi River
**County:** St. Louis
**Churches:** 900[1]
**City-owned parks:** 89 (2,639 ac.)
**Telephones (Jan. 1, 1977):** 569,676
**Television households (Jan. 1978):** 492,300 (98%)
**Radio stations:** AM, 18; FM, 20[1]
**Television stations:** 5 commercial; 1 educational
**Assessed valuation (1977):** $1,370,506,818
**City tax rate (1977):** $64.20 per $1,000
**Bonded debt (general obligation, 1977–78):** $82,414,766
**Revenue (1977–78):** $190,452,564
**Expenditures (1977–78):** $209,082,414
**Chamber of Commerce:** St. Louis Regional Commerce and Growth Association, 10 Broadway, St. Louis, Mo. 63102.

1. Metropolitan area.

## SAN ANTONIO, TEX.

**Incorporated as city:** 1837
**Mayor:** Mrs. Lila Cockrell (to May 1979)
**City Manager:** Thomas E. Huebner (apptd. Jan. 1977)
**1970 population & (rank):** 707,503 (14)
**1975 est. population & (rank):** 773,248 (10)
**1970–75 population change:** +9.1%
**1970 land area:** 184 sq mi.
**Altitude:** 700 ft
**Location:** In south central part of state, on San Antonio River
**County:** Seat of Bexar Co.
**City-owned parks:** Approximately 5,265 ac.
**Telephones (Jan. 1, 1977):** 399,796
**Television households, (Jan. 1978):** 278,400 (97%)
**Radio stations:** AM, 13; FM, 12
**Television stations:** 5
**Assessed valuation (1977):** $2,524,933,415
**City tax rate (1977):** $16.50 per $1,000
**Net funded debt (1977):** $118,619,007
**Revenue (est. 1977–78):** $178,268,459
**Expenditures (est. 1977–78):** $175,071,464
**Chamber of Commerce:** Greater San Antonio Chamber of Commerce, P.O. Box 1628, 602 E Commerce, San Antonio, Tex. 78296

## SAN DIEGO, CALIF.

**Incorporated as city:** 1850
**Mayor:** Pete Wilson (to Dec. 1979)
**City Manager:** Hugh McKinley (apptd. April 1975)
**1970 population & (rank):** 697,027 (15)
**1975 est. population & (rank):** 773,996 (9)
**1970–75 population change:** +11.0%
**1975 land area:** 319.5 sq mi.
**Altitude:** Highest, 1,591 ft; lowest, sea level
**Location:** In southwesternmost part of state, on San Diego Bay
**County:** Seat of San Diego Co.
**Churches:** Roman Catholic, 80; Jewish, 8; Protestant 334; Eastern Orthodox, 7; other, 6
**City park & recreation facilities:** 200 (15,063 ac.)
**Telephones (Jan. 1, 1977):** 989,465[1]
**Television households (Jan. 1978):** 594,200 (96%)
**Radio stations:** AM, 10; FM, 19
**Television stations:** 4
**Assessed valuation (1978):** $3,560,284,164
**City tax rate (1978):** $13.57 per $1,000
**Bonded debt (1978):** $39,138,000
**Revenue (1978):** $263,248,873
**Expenditures (1978):** $263,248,873
**Chamber of Commerce:** San Diego Chamber of Commerce, 233 A Street, San Diego, Calif. 92101

1. Metropolitan area.

## SAN FRANCISCO, CALIF.

**Incorporated as city:** 1850
**Mayor:** George R. Moscone (to Jan. 1980)
**1970 population & (rank):** 715,674 (13)
**1975 est. population & (rank):** 664,520 (16)
**1970–75 population change:** −7.1%
**1970 land area:** 46.6 sq mi.
**Altitude:** Highest, 925 ft; lowest, sea level
**Location:** In northern part of state between Pacific Ocean and San Francisco Bay
**County:** Coextensive with San Francisco Co.
**Churches:** 540 of all denominations
**City-owned parks and squares:** 120
**Telephones (Jan. 1, 1977):** 794,464
**Television households (Jan. 1978):** 276,700 (92%)
**Radio stations:** 22
**Television stations:** 7
**Assessed valuation (1977–78):** $3,867,668,374
**City and county tax rate (1977–78):** $117 per $1,000
**Bonded debt (June 30, 1977):** $586,476,000
**Revenue (1976–77):** $910,456,871
**Expenditures (1976–77):** $767,393,645
**Chamber of Commerce:** Greater San Francisco Chamber of Commerce, 465 California St., San Francisco, Calif. 94104

## SAN JOSE, CALIF.

**Incorporated as city:** 1897
**Mayor:** Janet Gray Hayes (to Dec. 31, 1978)
**1970 population & (rank):** 459,913 (29)
**1975 est. population & (rank):** 555,707 (21)
**1970–75 population change:** +20.5%
**1975 land area:** 150 sq mi.
**Altitude:** 80 ft
**Location:** In northern part of state, on south San Francisco Bay, 50 miles from San Francisco
**County:** Santa Clara
**Churches:** Protestant, 151; Roman Catholic, 24; Jewish, 4; others, 28
**City-owned parks and playgrounds:** 128 (2,339 ac.)
**Telephones (Jan. 1, 1977):** 564,498
**Television households (Jan. 1978):** 401,200 (97%)[1]
**Radio stations:** AM, 5; FM, 3
**Television stations:** 2 commercial; 1 educational
**Assessed valuation (1977–78):** $2,412,045,956
**City tax rate (1977–78):** $13.63 per $1,000
**Bonded debt (June 1978):** $51,989,000
**Revenue (1977–78):** $253,316,200[2]
**Expenditures (1977–78):** $253,316,200[2]
**Chamber of Commerce:** San Jose Chamber of Commerce, One Paseo de San Antonio, San Jose, Calif. 95113

1. County total. 2. Per 1977–78 adopted budget.

## SEATTLE, WASH.

**Incorporated as city:** 1869
**Mayor:** Wes Uhlman (to Nov. 1980)
**1970 population & (rank):** 530,831 (22)
**1975 est. population & (rank):** 487,091 (25)
**1970–75 population change:** −8.2%
**1970 land area:** 83.6 sq mi.
**Altitude:** Highest, 540 ft; lowest, sea level
**Location:** In west central part of state, on Puget Sound
**County:** Seat of King Co.
**Churches:** Roman Catholic, 36; Jewish, 13; Protestant and others, 535
**City-owned parks, playgrounds, etc.:** 278 (4,773.4 ac.)
**Telephones (Jan. 1, 1977):** 605,917
**Television households (Jan. 1978):** 435,700 (96%)
**Radio stations:** AM, 26; FM, 25; AM-FM, 10
**Television stations:** 4 commercial; 2 educational
**Assessed valuation (1977):** $7,734,784,281
**City tax rate (1978):** $17.14 per $1,000
**Bonded debt (1976):** $168,820,000
**Revenue (1977):** $120,300,000
**Expenditures (1977):** $112,100,000
**Chamber of Commerce:** Seattle Chamber of Commerce, 215 Columbia Street, Seattle, Wash. 98104

## TAMPA, FLA.

**Incorporated as city:** 1855
**Mayor:** William F. Poe (to Sept. 30, 1979)
**1970 population & (rank):** 277,714 (50)
**1975 est. population & (rank):** 280,340 (50)
**1970–75 population change:** +0.9%
**1970 land area:** 84.5 sq mi.
**Altitude:** Highest, 84 ft; lowest, sea level
**Location:** In west central part of state, on Tampa Bay
**County:** Seat of Hillsborough Co.
**City-owned parks:** 68 (25 major parks)
**Telephones (Jan. 1, 1977):** 374,801
**Television households (Jan. 1978):** 213,700 (98%)
**Radio stations:** AM, 8; FM, 4
**Television stations:** 7
**Assessed valuation (Sept. 1976):** $2,210,042,392
**City tax rate (1977–78):** $9.80 per $1,000
**Bonded debt (1977–78):** $149,968,000
**Revenue (1977–78):** $172,750,377
**Expenditures (1977–78):** $172,750,377
**Chamber of Commerce:** Greater Tampa Chamber of Commerce, 801 E Kennedy Blvd., Tampa, Fla. 33601

## TOLEDO, OHIO

**Incorporated as city:** 1837
**Mayor:** Doug DeGood (to Dec. 1979)
**City Manager:** Walter Kane (apptd. April 1977)
**1970 population & (rank):** 383,062 (30)
**1975 est. population & (rank):** 367,650 (36)
**1970–75 population change:** −4.0%
**1976 land area:** 84.16 sq mi.
**Altitude:** 630 ft

**Location:** In northwestern part of state, on Maumee River at Lake Erie
**County:** Seat of Lucas Co.
**Churches:** Protestant, 301; Roman Catholic, 55; Jewish, 4; others, 98
**City-owned parks & playgrounds:** 134 (2,650.90 ac.)
**Telephones (Jan. 1, 1977):** 302,513
**Television households (Jan. 1978):** 164,100 (99%)
**Radio stations:** AM, 8; FM, 8
**Television stations:** 4
**Assessed valuation (1978):** $2,069,575,070
**City tax rate (1978):** $51.75 per $1,000
**Bonded debt (1978):** $132,311,025
**Revenue (1977):** $107,816,705
**Expenditures (1977):** $101,982,102
**Chamber of Commerce:** Toledo Area Chamber of Commerce, 218 Huron St., Toledo, Ohio 43604

## TUCSON, ARIZ.

**Incorporated as city:** 1877
**Mayor:** Lewis C. Murphy (to Dec. 1979)
**1970 population & (rank):** 267,418 (54)
**1975 est. population & (rank):** 296,457 (47)
**1970–75 population change:** +10.9%
**1977 city land area:** 91.87 sq mi.
**Altitude:** 2,500 ft
**Location:** In southeastern part of state, on the Santa Cruz River
**County:** Seat of Pima Co.
**Churches:** Protestant, 181; Roman Catholic, 24; Other, 136
**City-owned parks and parkways:** (2,001.75 ac.)
**Telephones (Jan. 1, 1977):** 293,737
**Television households (Jan. 1978):** 161,000 (97%)
**Radio stations:** AM, 12; FM, 6
**Television stations:** 3 commercial; 1 educational; 1 other
**Assessed valuation (1978):** $653,798,524
**City tax rate (1978):** $12.50 per $1,000
**Net bonded debt (1978):** $134,357,676
**Revenue (1978):** $236,995,824
**Expenditures (1978):** $236,995,242
**Chamber of Commerce:** Tucson Chamber of Commerce, P.O. Box 991, Tucson, Arizona, 85702

## TULSA, OKLA.

**Incorporated as city:** 1898
**Mayor:** James Inhofe (to May 1980)
**1970 population & (rank):** 330,350 (43)
**1975 est. population & (rank):** 331,726 (44)
**1970–75 population change:** +0.4%
**1975 land area:** 181.14 sq mi.
**Altitude:** 674 ft
**Location:** In northeastern part of state, on Arkansas River
**County:** Seat of Tulsa Co.
**Churches:** Protestant, 593; Roman Catholic, 32; Jewish, 2; others, 4
**City parks and playgrounds:** 107 (4,811 ac.)
**Telephones (Jan. 1, 1977):** 382,944
**Television households (Jan. 1978):** 154,100. (98%)
**Radio stations:** AM, 9; FM, 6
**Television stations:** 3 commercial; 1 educational; 1 cable
**Assessed valuation (1977–78):** $935,823,698
**City tax rate (1977–78):** $81.03 per $1,000
**Bonded debt (June 1977):** $122,896,000
**Revenue (1976–77):** $125,559,672[1]
**Expenditures (1976–77):** $116,935,362[1]
**Chamber of Commerce:** Metropolitan Tulsa Chamber of Commerce, 616 S Boston, Tulsa, Okla. 74119

1. Does not include bond fund proceeds or expenditures.

## WASHINGTON, D.C.

**Land ceded to Congress:** 1788 by Maryland; 1789 by Virginia (retroceded to Virginia Sept. 7, 1846)
**Seat of government transferred to D. C.:** Dec. 1, 1800
**Created municipal corporation:** Feb. 21, 1871
**Mayor:** Walter E. Washington (to Jan. 1979)[1]
**Motto:** *Justitia omnibus* (Justice to all)
**Flower:** American beauty rose
**Tree:** Scarlet oak
**Origin of name:** In honor of Columbus
**1970 population & (rank):** 756,668 (9)
**1976 est. population & (rank):** 702,000 (13)
**1970–75 population change:** −7.3%
**1970 land area:** 68 sq mi.
**Geographic center:** Near corner of Fourth and L Sts., NW
**Altitude:** Highest, 420 ft; lowest, sea level
**Location:** Between Virginia and Maryland, on Potomac River
**Churches:** Protestant, 446; Roman Catholic, 23; Jewish, 10; others, 23
**City parks:** 753 (7,725 ac.)
**Telephones (Jan. 1, 1977):** 1,020,944
**Television households (Jan. 1978):** 279,800 (97%)
**Radio stations:** AM, 15; FM, 16
**Television stations:** 6 (including 2 UHF stations)
**Assessed valuation (1978):** $9,125,140,126[2]
**City tax rate (1977–78):** $18.30 per $1,000
**Bonded debt:** None
**Revenue (est. 1978):** $1,254,432,000
**Expenditures (est. 1978):** $1,237,084,200
**Chamber of Commerce:** D.C. Chamber of Commerce, 1319 F St., NW, Washington, D.C. 20004

The District of Columbia—identical with the City of Washington—is the capital of the United States and the first carefully planned capital in the world.

D.C. history began in 1790 when Congress directed selection of a new capital site, 10 miles square, along the Potomac. When the site was determined, it included 30.75 square miles on the Virginia side of the river. In 1846, however, Congress returned that area to Virginia.

The city was planned and partly laid out by Major Pierre Charles L'Enfant, a French engineer. This work was perfected and completed by Major Andrew Ellicott. In 1814, during the War of 1812, a British force fired the capital, and it was from the white paint applied to cover fire damage that the President's home was called the White House.

Until November 3, 1967, the District of Columbia was administered by three commissioners appointed by the President. On that day, a government consisting of a mayor-commissioner and a 9-member Council, all appointed by the President with the approval of the Senate, took office. On May 7, 1974, the citizens of the District of Columbia approved the Home Rule Charter, giving them their first form of elected government in over 100 years. The District also has one non-voting member in the House of Representatives.

On Aug. 22, 1978, the Senate passed a proposed constitutional amendment to give Washington, D.C., voting representation in the Congress. The House had approved the legislation in the spring. The amendment must be ratified by at least 38 state legislatures within the next seven years to become effective.

1. Elected in November 1974, took office January 2, 1975, becoming the capital's first elected mayor in over a century.
2. On taxable property only. More than 50% of all land in District of Columbia is owned by the Federal government and tax-exempt organizations, and therefore is nontaxable.

# Tabulated Data on City Governments

| City | Mayor: Term, years | Mayor: Salary[1] | City manager's salary[2] | Council or Commission: Name | Members | Term, years | Salary[3] |
|---|---|---|---|---|---|---|---|
| Atlanta | 4 | $40,000 | — | Council | 19 | 4 | $ 8,800 |
| Austin, Tex. | 2 | 12,000 | $52,179 | Council | 6 | 2 | 12,000 |
| Baltimore | 4 | 40,000 | — | Council | 19 | 4 | 16,000 |
| Boston | 4 | 40,000 | — | Council | 9 | 2 | 20,000 |
| Buffalo, N.Y. | 4 | 40,500 | — | Council | 15 | 2[4] | 20,000 |
| Charlotte, N.C. | 2 | — | 45,000 | Council | 11 | 2 | 5,700 |
| Chicago | 4 | 60,000 | — | Council | 50 | 4 | 17,500 |
| Cincinnati | 2 | 22,624 | 51,678 | Council | 9 | 2 | 19,124 |
| Cleveland | 2 | 50,000 | — | Council | 33 | 2 | 18,000 |
| Columbus, Ohio | 4 | 40,000 | — | Council | 7 | 4 | 10,000 |
| Dallas | 2 | 50[6] | 64,250 | Council | 11 | 2 | 50[6] |
| Denver | 4 | 40,000 | — | Council | 13 | 4 | 12,500 |
| Detroit | 4 | 61,950 | — | Council | 9 | 4 | 33,600 |
| El Paso | 2 | 9,600 | — | Council | 7[7] | 2 | 4,800 |
| Fort Worth | 2 | 10[8] | 48,500 | Council | 9 | 2 | 10[8] |
| Honolulu | 4 | 40,000 | 39,720 | Council | 9 | 4 | 17,500[9] |
| Houston | 2 | 72,000 | — | Council | 8 | 2 | 19,120 |
| Indianapolis | 4 | 34,000 | — | Council | 29 | 4 | 10[10] |
| Jacksonville, Fla. | 4 | 30,000 | — | Council | 19 | 4 | 8,400 |
| Kansas City, Mo. | 4 | 25,000 | 46,380 | Council | 13[7] | 4 | 4,800 |
| Long Beach, Calif. | 4 | 583[11] | 55,486 | Council | 9[12] | — | 583[11] |
| Los Angeles | 4 | 57,750 | 64,352[13] | Council | 15 | 4 | 34,650 |
| Louisville, Ky. | 4 | 27,950 | — | Board of Aldermen | 12 | 2 | 7,738 |
| Memphis, Tenn. | 4 | 35,000 | 30,300 | Council | 13 | 4 | 6,000 |
| Miami, Fla. | 2 | 5,000[14] | 48,730 | Commission | 5 | 4 | 5,000 |
| Milwaukee | 4 | 46,332 | — | Council | 16 | 4 | 19,349 |
| Minneapolis | 2 | 36,250 | 52,000 | Council | 13 | 2 | 25,383 |
| Nashville, Tenn. | 4 | 25,000 | — | Council | 41 | 4 | 3,600 |
| New Orleans | 4 | 59,868 | — | Council | 7 | 4 | 15,000 |
| New York | 4 | 60,000 | 49,894[15] | Council | 43 | 4 | 20,000 |
| Newark, N.J. | 4 | 38,588 | 38,588[16] | Council | 9 | 4 | 16,538 |
| Norfolk, Va. | 2 | 7,200 | 45,800 | Council | 7 | 4 | 4,800 |
| Oakland, Calif. | 4 | 15,000 | 52,680 | Council | 9[7] | 4 | ([17]) |
| Oklahoma City | 4 | 2,000 | 45,000 | Council | 8 | 4 | 20[18] |
| Omaha, Neb. | 4 | 36,000 | — | Council | 7 | 4 | 9,600 |
| Philadelphia | 4 | 55,000 | 42,000[19] | Council | 17 | 4 | 25,000 |
| Phoenix, Ariz. | 2 | 15,000 | 54,294 | Council | 7[7] | 2 | 7,500 |
| Pittsburgh | 4 | 45,000 | — | Council | 9 | 4 | ([20]) |
| Portland, Ore. | 4 | 43,264 | — | Commission | 4 | 4 | 34,715 |
| St. Louis | 4 | 25,000 | — | Board of Aldermen | 29 | 4 | 12,500 |
| San Antonio | 2 | 3,000[21] | 50,000 | Council | 8[7] | 4 | 20[22] |
| San Diego, Calif. | 4 | 25,000 | 45,205 | Council | 8 | 4 | 17,000 |
| San Francisco | 4 | 55,496 | 54,131[23] | Board of Supervisors | 11 | 4 | 9,600 |
| San Jose, Calif. | 4 | 7,200 | 50,820 | Council | 7 | 4 | 4,800 |
| Seattle | 4 | 56,652 | — | Council | 9 | 4 | 37,380 |
| Tampa, Fla. | 4 | 45,000 | — | Council | 7 | 4 | 9,600 |
| Toledo, Ohio | 2 | 23,350 | 41,000 | Council | 9[12] | 2 | 7,800 |
| Tucson, Ariz. | 4 | 14,000 | 45,000 | Council | 7 | 4 | 7,200 |
| Tulsa, Okla. | 2 | 37,500 | — | Commission | 4 | 2 | 28,125 |
| Washington, D.C. | 4 | 52,500 | 50,000 | Council | 13 | 4 | 28,444[24] |

1. Annual salary unless otherwise indicated. 2. Annual salary. City Manager's term is indefinite and at will of Council. 3. Annual salary unless otherwise indicated. In some cities, President of Council receives a higher salary. 4. For 9 District Councilmen; 4 years for 5 Councilmen-at-Large. 5. Plus $100 monthly for expenses. 6. Per Council meeting; not over $2,600 per year. 7. Including Mayor. 8. Per week and per Council meeting. 9. Managing Director appointed by Mayor; no Council approval required. 10. Plus $50 per meeting for two meetings a month. 11. Per month. 12. Including Mayor and Vice-Mayor. 13. City Administrative Officer appointed by Mayor; approved by Council. 14. Plus annual expense account of $2,500. 15. At present, no City Manager; salary is for Deputy Mayor. 16. Business Administrator, appointed by Mayor and confirmed by Council. 17. Flat $500 per month, or $6,000 annually. 18. Per Council meeting; not to exceed 5 meetings a month. 19. Appointed by Mayor, with title of Managing Director. 20. 4 members at $22,500; 5 members at &$20,000. 21. Plus Council pay. 22. Per Council meeting; not over $1,040 per year. 23. Chief Administrative Officer; appointed by Mayor for 10-year term. 24. $10,000 additional for Chairman. *Source: Information Please* questionnaires to the cities.

# Firsts in America

**This selection is based on our editorial judgment. Other sources may list different firsts.**

**Admiral in U.S. Navy:** David Glasgow Farragut, 1866.

**Air-mail route,** first transcontinental: Between New York City and San Francisco, 1920.

**Assembly, representative:** House of Burgesses, founded in Virginia, 1619.

**Bank established:** Bank of North America, Philadelphia, 1781.

**Birth in America to English parents:** Virginia Dare, born Roanoke Island, N.C., 1587.

**Botanic garden:** Established by John Bartram in Philadelphia, 1728. (Oldest still existing was established in Cambridge, Mass., in 1807.)

**Cartoon, colored:** "The Yellow Kid," by Richard Outcault, in *New York World,* 1895.

**College:** Harvard, founded 1636.

**College to confer degrees on women:** Oberlin (Ohio) College, 1841.

**College to establish coeducation:** Oberlin (Ohio) College, 1833.

**Electrocution of a criminal:** William Kemmler in Auburn Prison, Auburn, N.Y., Aug. 6, 1890.

**Five and Ten Cents Store:** Founded by Frank Woolworth, Utica, N.Y., 1879 (moved to Lancaster, Pa., same year).

**Fraternity:** Phi Beta Kappa; founded Dec. 5, 1776, at College of William and Mary.

**Law to be declared unconstitutional by U.S. Supreme Court:** Judiciary Act of 1789. Case: *Marbury* v. *Madison,* 1803.

**Library, circulating:** Philadelphia, 1731.

**Newspaper, illustrated daily:** *New York Daily Graphic,* 1873.

**Newspaper published daily:** *Pennsylvania Packet and General Advertiser,* Philadelphia, Sept., 1784.

**Newspaper published over a continuous period:** *The Boston News-Letter,* April, 1704.

**Newsreel:** Pathé Frères of Paris, in 1910, circulated a weekly issue of their *Pathé Journal.*

**Oil well, commercial:** Titusville, Pa., 1859.

**Panel quiz show on radio:** *Information Please,* May 17, 1938.

**Postage stamps issued:** 1847.

**Railroad, transcontinental:** Central Pacific and Union Pacific railroads, joined at Promontory, Utah, May 10, 1869.

**Savings bank:** The Provident Institute for Savings, Boston, 1816.

**Science museum:** Founded by Charleston (S.C.) Library Society, 1773.

**Skyscraper:** Home Insurance Co., Chicago, 1885 (10 floors, 2 added later).

**Slaves brought into America:** At Jamestown, Va., 1619, from a Dutch ship.

**Sorority:** Kappa Alpha Theta, at De Pauw University, 1870.

**State to abolish capital punishment:** Michigan, 1847.

**State to enter Union after original 13:** Vermont, 1791.

**Steam-heated building:** Eastern Hotel, Boston, 1845.

**Steam railroad (carried passengers and freight):** Baltimore & Ohio, 1830.

**Strike on record by union:** Journeymen Printers, New York City, 1776.

**Subway:** Opened in Boston, 1897.

**"Tabloid" picture newspaper:** *The Illustrated Daily News* (now *The Daily News*), New York City, 1919.

**Vaudeville theater:** Gaiety Museum, Boston, 1883.

**Woman cabinet member:** Frances Perkins, Secretary of Labor, 1933.

**Woman candidate for President:** Victoria Claflin Woodhull, nominated by National Woman's Suffrage Assn. on ticket of Nation Radical Reformers, 1872.

**Woman doctor of medicine:** Elizabeth Blackwell; M.D. from Geneva Medical College of Western New York, 1849.

**Woman elected governor of a state:** Mrs. Nellie Tayloe Ross, Wyoming, 1925.

**Woman elected to U.S. Senate:** Mrs. Hattie Caraway, Arkansas; elected Nov., 1932.

**Woman graduate of law school:** Mrs. Ada H. Kepley, Union College of Law, Chicago, 1870.

**Woman member of U.S. House of Representatives:** Jeannette Rankin; elected Nov., 1916.

**Woman member of U.S. Senate:** Mrs. Rebecca Latimer Felton of Georgia; appointed Oct. 3, 1922.

**Woman suffrage granted:** Wyoming Territory, 1869.

**Written constitution:** *Fundamental Orders of Connecticut,* 1639.

## Figures and Legends in American Folklore

**Appleseed, Johnny** (John Chapman, 1774–1847): Massachusetts-born nurseryman; reputed to have spread seeds and seedlings from which rose orchards of the Midwest.

**Billy the Kid** (William H. Bonney, 1859–1881): New York-born desperado; killed his first man before he reached his teens; after short life of crime in Wild West, was gunned down by Sheriff Pat Garrett; symbol of lawless West.

**Boone, Daniel** (1734–1820): Frontiersman and Indian fighter, about whom legends of early America have been built; figured in Byron's *Don Juan*.

**Brodie, Steve** (1863–1901): Reputed to have dived off Brooklyn Bridge on July 23, 1886. (Whether he actually did so has never been proved.)

**Buffalo Bill** (William F. Cody, 1846–1917): Buffalo hunter and Indian scout; much of legend about him and Wild West stems from his own Wild West show, which he operated in late 19th century.

**Bunyan, Paul:** Mythical lumberjack; subject of tall tales throughout timber country (that he dug Grand Canyon, for example).

**Crockett, David** (1786–1836): Frontiersman and member of U.S. Congress, about whom legends have been built of heroic feats; died in defense of Alamo.

**Fritchie (or Frietchie), Barbara:** Symbol of patriotism; in ballad by John Greenleaf Whittier, 90-year-old Barbara Fritchie defiantly waves Stars and Stripes as "Stonewall" Jackson's Confederate troops march through Frederick, Md.

**James, Jesse** (1847–1882): Bank and train robber; folklore has given him quality of American Robin Hood.

**Jones, Casey** (John Luther Jones, 1863–1900): Example of heroic locomotive engineer given to feats of prowess; died in wreck with his hand on brake lever when his Illinois Central "Cannonball" express hit freight train at Vaughan, Miss.

**Ross, Betsy** (1752–1836): Member of Philadelphia flag-making family; reported to have designed and sewn first American flag. (Report is without confirmation.)

**Uncle Sam:** Personification of United States and its people; origin uncertain; may be based on inspector of government supplies in Revolutionary War and War of 1812.

## Assassinations and Attempts in U. S. Since 1865

**Cermak, Anton J. (Mayor of Chicago):** Shot Feb. 15, 1933, in Miami by Giuseppe Zangara, who attempted to assassinate Franklin D. Roosevelt; Cermak died March 6.

**Ford, Gerald R. (President of U.S.):** Escaped assassination attempt Sept. 5, 1975, in Sacramento, Calif., by Lynette Alice (Squeaky) Fromm, who pointed but did not fire .45-caliber pistol.

**Ford, Gerald R. (President of U.S.):** Escaped assassination attempt in San Francisco, Calif., Sept. 22, 1975, by Sara Jane Moore, who fired one shot from a .38-caliber pistol that was deflected.

**Garfield, James A. (President of U.S.):** Shot July 2, 1881, in Washington, D.C., by Charles J. Guiteau; died Sept. 19.

**Kennedy, John F. (President of U.S.):** Shot Nov. 22, 1963, in Dallas, Tex., allegedly by Lee Harvey Oswald; died same day. Injured was Gov. John B. Connally of Texas. Oswald was shot and killed two days later by Jack Ruby.

**Kennedy, Robert F. (U.S. Senator from New York):** Shot June 5, 1968, in Los Angeles by Sirhan Bishara Sirhan; died June 6.

**King, Martin Luther, Jr. (civil rights leader):** Shot April 4, 1968, in Memphis by James Earl Ray; died same day.

**Lincoln, Abraham (President of U.S.):** Shot April 14, 1865, in Washington, D.C., by John Wilkes Booth; died April 15.

**Long, Huey P. (U.S. Senator from Louisiana):** Shot Sept. 8, 1935, in Baton Rouge by Dr. Carl A. Weiss; died Sept. 10.

**McKinley, William (President of U.S.):** Shot Sept. 6, 1901, in Buffalo by Leon Czolgosz; died Sept. 14.

**Roosevelt, Franklin D. (President-elect of U.S.):** Escaped assassination unhurt Feb. 15, 1933, in Miami. *See* Cermak.

**Roosevelt, Theodore (ex-President of U.S.):** Escaped assassination (though shot) Oct. 14, 1912, in Milwaukee while campaigning for President.

**Seward, William H. (Secretary of State):** Escaped assassination (though injured) April 14, 1865, in Washington, D.C., by Lewis Powell (or Paine), accomplice of John Wilkes Booth.

**Truman, Harry S. (President of U.S.):** Escaped assassination unhurt Nov. 1, 1950, in Washington, D.C., as 2 Puerto Rican nationalists attempted to shoot their way into Blair House.

**Wallace, George C. (Governor of Alabama):** Shot and critically wounded in assassination attempt May 15, 1972, at Laurel, Md., by Arthur Herman Bremer.

## Environmental Glossary

*Source:* Environmental Protection Agency

**abatement:** the reduction in degree or intensity of pollution.
**acclimation:** the physiological and behavioral adjustments of an organism to changes in the environment.
**adaptation:** a change in structure or habit of an organism that produces better adjustment to its surroundings.
**adulterants:** chemical impurities or substances that by law do not belong in a food, plant, animal, or pesticide formulation.
**aeration:** to circulate oxygen through a substance, as in waste water treatment where it aids in purification.
**agricultural pollution:** the liquid and solid wastes from farming, including: runoff from pesticides, fertilizers, and feedlots; erosion and dust from plowing; animal manure and carcasses, crop residues, and debris.
**air pollution:** the presence of contaminant substances in the air that do not disperse properly and interfere with human health.
**air quality standards:** the level of pollutants prescribed by law that cannot be exceeded during a specified time in a defined area.
**ambient air:** any unconfined portion of the atmosphere; open air.
**asbestos:** a mineral fiber that can pollute air or water and cause cancer if inhaled or ingested.
**A-scale sound level:** a measurement of sound approximating the sensitivity of the human ear, used to note the intensity or annoyance of sounds.
**attractant:** a chemical or agent that lures insects or other pests by stimulating their sense of smell.
**biodegradable:** any substance that decomposes quickly through the action of microorganisms.
**breeder:** a nuclear reactor that produces more fuel than it consumes.
**carcinogenic:** cancer producing.
**catalytic converter:** an air pollution abatement device that removes organic contaminants by oxidizing them into carbon dioxide and water.
**chilling effect:** the lowering of the earth's temperature because of increased particles in the air blocking the sun's rays.
**chlorination:** the application of chlorine to drinking water, sewage, or industrial waste to disinfect or oxidize undesirable compounds.
**combined sewers:** a system that carries both sewage and storm water runoff. In dry weather all flow goes to the waste treatment plant. During a storm, only part of the flow is intercepted due to overloading. The remaining mixture of sewage and storm water overflows untreated into the receiving stream.
**desalinization:** removing salt from ocean or brackish water.
**ecological impact:** the total effect of an environmental change, natural or man-made, on the community of living things.
**ecology:** the relationships of living things to one another and to their environment, or the study of such relationships.
**effluent:** treated or untreated waste material discharged into the environment. Generally refers to water pollution.
**emission standard:** the maximum amount of discharge legally allowed from a single source, mobile or stationary.
**environment:** the sum of all external conditions affecting the life, development, and survival of an organism.
**fluorocarbons:** a gas used as a propellant in aerosols, thought to be modifying the ozone layer in the stratosphere, thereby allowing more harmful solar radiation to reach the earth's surface.
**fossil fuels:** combustibles—like coal, oil, and natural gas—derived from the remains of ancient plants and animals.
**greenhouse effect:** the warming of our atmosphere caused by build-up of carbon dioxide, which allows light from the sun's rays to heat the earth, but prevents loss of the heat.
**groundwater:** the supply of fresh water under the earth's surface that forms a natural reservoir.
**habitat:** the sum of environmental conditions in a specific place that is occupied by an organism, population, or community.
**herbicide:** a chemical that controls or destroys undesirable plants.
**inversion:** an atmospheric condition caused by a layer of warm air preventing the rise of cool air trapped beneath it. This holds down pollutants that might otherwise be dispersed, and can cause an air pollution episode.
**nuclear power plant:** a device that converts atomic energy into usable power; heat produced by a reactor makes steam to drive electricity-generating turbines.
**oil spill:** accidental discharge into bodies of water, can be controlled by chemical dispersion, combustion, mechanical containment, and absorption.
**organic:** referring to or derived from living organisms. In chemistry, any compound containing carbon.
**pesticide:** any substance used to control pests ranging from rats, weeds, and insects to algae and fungi. Pesticides can accumulate in the food chain and can contaminate the environment if misused.
**pollutant:** any introduced substance that adversely affects the usefulness of a resource.
**pollution:** the presence of matter or energy whose nature, location, or quantity produces undesired environmental effects.
**radiation:** the emission of particles or rays by the nucleus of an atom.
**radiation standards:** regulations that govern exposure to permissible concentrations of and transportation of radioactive materials.
**radioactive:** substances that emit rays either naturally or as a result of scientific manipulation.
**recycling:** converting solid waste into new products by using the resources contained in discarded materials.
**refuge, wildlife:** an area designated for the protection of wild animals, within which hunting and

fishing are either prohibited or strictly controlled.
**runoff:** water from rain, snow melt, or irrigation that flows over the ground surface and returns to streams. It can collect pollutants from air or land and carry them to the receiving waters.
**sanitary landfill, landfilling:** protecting the environment when disposing of solid waste. Waste is spread in thin layers, compacted by heavy machinery, and covered with soil daily.
**sewage:** the organic waste and waste water produced by residential and commercial establishments.
**solar energy:** power collected from sunlight, used most often for heating purposes but occasionally to generate electricity.
**strip mining:** a process that uses machines to scrape soil or rock away from mineral deposits just under the earth's surface.
**thermal pollution:** discharge of heated water from industrial processes that can affect the life processes of aquatic plants and animals.
**toxicity:** the degree of danger posed by a substance to animal or plant life.
**waste:** unwanted materials left over from manufacturing processes, refuse from places of human or animal habitation.
**water pollution:** the addition of enough harmful or objectionable material to damage water quality.
**water quality criteria:** the levels of pollutants that affect use of water for drinking, swimming, raising fish, farming, or industrial use.

## Some Endangered Species of the World

| Common name | Scientific name | Range |
|---|---|---|
| **MAMMALS** | | |
| Anteater, scaly | *Manis temmincki* | Africa |
| Bear, brown | *Ursus arctos pruinosus* | China (Tibet) |
| Bear, brown or grizzly | *Ursus arctos horribilis* | U.S. |
| Cat, leopard | *Felis bengalensis bengalensis* | Eastern Asia |
| Cat, tiger | *Felis tigrina* | Costa Rica to northern South America |
| Cheetah | *Acinonyx jubatus* | Africa to India |
| Chimpanzee | *Pan troglodytes* | Western and central Africa |
| Chinchilla | *Chinchilla brevicaudata boliviana* | Bolivia |
| Deer, Columbian white-tailed | *Odocoileus virginianus leucurus* | U.S. (Ore., Wash.) |
| Deer, marsh | *Blastocerus dichotomus* | Argentina, Uruguay, Paraguay, Brazil |
| Deer, musk | *Moschus moschiferus moschiferus* | Southcentral Asia |
| Elephant, Asian | *Elephas maximus* | India, Burma, Thailand, Cambodia, Laos, Malaysia, Sri Lanka, Vietnam |
| Gazelle, Clark's (Dibatag) | *Ammordorcas clarki* | Somalia, Ethiopia |
| Gazelle, slender-horned (Rhim) | *Gazella leptoceros* | Sudan, Algeria, Egypt, Libya |
| Gorilla | *Gorilla gorilla* | Central and western Africa |
| Ibex, Walia | *Capra walie* | Ethiopia |
| Jaguar | *Panthera onca* | Central and South America |
| Kangaroo, red | *Megaleia rufa* | Australia |
| Leopard | *Panthera pardus* | Africa, Asia |
| Leopard, snow | *Panthera uncia* | Central Asia |
| Lion, Asiatic | *Panthera leo persica* | India |
| Mandrill | *Papio sphinx* | Central west Africa |
| Monkey, black howler | *Alouatta pigra* | Mexico, Guatemala, Belize |
| Ocelot | *Felis pardalis* | Central and South America |
| Orangutan | *Pongo pygmaeus* | Indonesia, Malaysia, Brunei |
| Otter, Southern Sea | *Enhydra lutris nereis* | U.S. (Calif.) |
| Panther, Florida | *Felis concolor coryi* | U.S. (Fla.) |
| Prairie Dog, Utah | *Synomys parvidens* | U.S. (Utah) |
| Pronghorn, Sonoran | *Antilocapra americana sonoriensis* | U.S. (Ariz.), Mexico |
| Rat, Morro Bay kangaroo | *Dipodomys heermanni morroensis* | U.S. (Calif.) |
| Rhinoceros, great Indian | *Rhinoceros unicornis* | India, Nepal |
| Sloth, Brazilian three-toed | *Bradypus torquatus* | Brazil |
| Tiger | *Panthera tigris* | Temperate and tropical Asia |
| Whale, humpback | *Megaptera novaeangliae* | Oceanic |
| Wolf, gray | *Canis lupus* | U.S., Mexico |
| Zebra, mountain | *Equus zebra zebra* | Southern Africa |
| **BIRDS** | | |
| Albatross, short-tailed | *Diomedea albatrus* | North Pacific Ocean |
| Condor, Andean | *Vultur gryphus* | Colombia to Chile and Argentina |
| Eagle, bald | *Haliaeetus leucocephalus* | U.S. |
| Falcon, peregrine | *Falco peregrinus peregrinus* | Europe, U.S.S.R. |
| Parakeet, paradise | *Psephotus pulcherrimus* | Australia |

| Common name | Scientific name | Range |
|---|---|---|
| Pelican, brown | *Pelecanus occidentalis* | U.S., West Indies, Central and South America |
| Penguin, Galápagos | *Spheniscus mendiculus* | Ecuador (Galápagos Islands) |
| Stork, white oriental | *Ciconia ciconia boyciana* | China, Japan, Korea, U.S.S.R. |
| **REPTILES** | | |
| Alligator, American | *Alligator mississippiensis* | U.S. (Fla., Ga., La., Tex., S.C.) |
| Crocodile, American | *Crocodylus acutus* | U.S. (Fla.), Central and South America |
| Iguana, Anegada ground | *Cyclura pinquis* | Virgin Islands |
| Python, Indian | *Python molurus molurus* | Sri Lanka, India |
| Snake, Atlantic salt-marsh | *Nerodia fasciata taeniata* | U.S. (Fla.) |
| Tortoise, Indian flap-shell | *Lissemys punctata punctata* | India, Pakistan, Bangladesh |
| **AMPHIBIANS** | | |
| Frog, Israel painted | *Discoglossus nigriventer* | Israel |
| Toads, African viviparous | *Nectophrynoides* sps. | Tanzania, Guinea |
| Treefrog, Pine Barrens | *Hyla andersonii* | U.S. (Fla.) |
| **FISH** | | |
| Catfish, giant | *Pangasianodon gigas* | Thailand |
| Pike, blue | *Stizostedion vitreum glaucum* | U.S. (Lakes Erie and Ontario) |
| Trout, greenback cutthroat | *Salmo clarki stomias* | U.S. (Colo.) |

*Source:* Department of the Interior, Fish and Wildlife Service.

# 1978 Environmental Quality Index

*Source:* Copyright 1978 by the National Wildlife Federation.
Reprinted from the February-March issue of *National Wildlife* Magazine.

*National Wildlife* 's annual Environmental Quality (EQ) Index is a subjective analysis of the state of the nation's natural resources. The judgments on resource trends represent the collective thinking of the editors and the National Wildlife Federation staff, based on extensive consultation with government experts, private specialists, and academic researchers.

**Wildlife:** Bad weather and loss of habitat continued a downward trend, but there were some breakthroughs. Many acres of wetlands were saved—but about 600,000 other acres were drained. The federal government spent millions to preserve habitat —and billions to destory it. Congress labored to pass tough new environmental laws—then worked just as hard to weaken old ones. The new Administration began by championing wildlife causes—then would up compromising on some of them. Partly as a result of these contradictory policies, wildlife's prospects for a turnaround dropped again in 1977.

**Air:** EQ Trend for air has not changed. Although three of the nation's worst pollutants have been reduced by as much as a third, and the Council on Environmental Quality predicts that the air in most urban areas will meet health standards within a decade, the clean-air push hasn't even come close to its ambitious original goal: healthful air all over the country by 1977. Congress granted car makers a fourth delay—until 1982—to meet emission standards. The "Biggest Needs" in the area of air, according to the EQ are better automobile emission control devices; mandatory emission inspection systems for all cars on the road, as well as assembly-line testing of new cars; and a major crackdown on polluting industries and power plants.

**Minerals:** The EQ Trend for minerals is down. However, at long last, the U.S. seemed ready to confront the realities of scarcity, cost, and the environment, and to start moving toward the establishment of a national energy program. Perhaps the single most important change was the growing willingness of Congress and, to a lesser extent, the public to accept the need for higher energy prices. This willingness was linked in turn to a growing recognition that the U.S. wastes energy on a grand scale. Homeowners were insulating dwellings at a rate that outstripped supply. But there has been little progress in reducing the country's appalling waste of resources.

**Water:** EQ Trend for water is down again. The U.S. got its first national standard for drinking water quality last year. All 40,000 of the country's community water systems are now under strict federal supervision. As efforts to monitor water quality continue to improve, the seriousness of the nation's pollution problems becomes even more apparent. Even if every industry and every city stopped polluting tomorrow, the nation still would not have clean water. The reason: urban and agricultural runoffs, together with natural drainage, remain the largest uncontrolled sources of water pollution.

**Forests:** EQ Trend for forests is up slightly. Over all, the U.S. is continuing to grow more trees than it's cutting—but not on national forestlands, where the annual sawtimber harvest now exceeds growth by about 30%. However, new weapons have been developed in the war against insects, disease, and fire that claim about 15 billion board feet of sawtimber each year. Nobody is willing to concede that industry's pressure on national forests is easing very dramatically. As the demand for wood mounts, so, too, will the battle over who and what forests are for.

**Soil:** EQ Trend for soil is down again. Four billion tons of soil were lost to erosion again last year, but the amount of cropland protected by grass may increase. Two persistent soil conservation problems continue—the continuing loss of soil to erosion, and the runoff into streams and lakes of chemicals from pesticides and fertilizers. To complicate matters further, 1977 saw renewed encroachment on prime farmland by development and suburban sprawl. But two bright spots partially offset the damage. First, millions of acres of farmland may be retired from crop production; second, 42 states now have laws designed to save farmland.

**Living Space:** EQ Trend for living space is down. America is more crowded than ever, and land-use planning remains more wish than reality. Right now, more than 70% of all Americans live on less than 2% of the land. And while nonmetropolitan areas are now growing faster than metropolitan areas, 53% of the population lives within 50 miles of a coastline. Result: Growing pressure on coastal-area resources and ecosystems that are more sensitive to modification than inland plains, forests, and croplands. The "Biggest Needs" in this area are a concerted national effort to develop truly effective land-use plans and, at the local level, a broader commitment by more Americans to minimize their personal impact on the environment.

## Federal Funds for Environmental Protection and Enhancement[1]

(in millions of dollars)

| | Budget Authority | | | | | Outlays | | | | |
|---|---|---|---|---|---|---|---|---|---|---|
| Activity | 1979[2] | 1978[2] | 1977 | 1976[2] | 1975 | 1979[2] | 1978[2] | 1977 | 1976 | 1975 |
| Aid to state and local governments | 918 | 890 | 799 | 489 | 473 | 832 | 650 | 426 | 392 | 403 |
| City recreation | 392 | 308 | 399 | 144 | 152 | 360 | 306 | 205 | 99 | 110 |
| Preservation and protection[3] | ([4]) | ([4]) | — | 2 | ([4]) | ([4]) | ([4]) | — | 2 | ([4]) |
| Noncity general recreation | 311 | 286 | 178 | 156 | 156 | 257 | 182 | 145 | 143 | 151 |
| Sport fish and wildlife | 6 | 7 | 7 | 110 | 98 | 6 | 8 | 7 | 85 | 90 |
| Historic preservation and rehabilitation | 101 | 89 | 63 | 20 | 20 | 74 | 75 | 47 | 14 | 11 |
| Other | 107 | 200 | 152 | 57 | 47 | 136 | 79 | 22 | 50 | 41 |
| Direct federal activities | 1,702 | 1,527 | 1,337 | 812 | 776 | 1,573 | 1,456 | 1,073 | 902 | 725 |
| City recreation | 194 | 145 | 130 | 129 | 155 | 182 | 172 | 113 | 139 | 145 |
| Preservation and protection[3] | 439 | 394 | 486 | 222 | 155 | 414 | 417 | 303 | 245 | 164 |
| Noncity general recreation | 420 | 421 | 355 | 191 | 188 | 399 | 380 | 325 | 264 | 189 |
| Sport fish and wildlife | 321 | 247 | 156 | 144 | 138 | 260 | 219 | 163 | 160 | 128 |
| Historic preservation and rehabilitation | 121 | 97 | 98 | 45 | 65 | 112 | 102 | 73 | 39 | 60 |
| Other | 207 | 223 | 113 | 81 | 75 | 207 | 166 | 95 | 55 | 39 |
| **Total** | **2,620** | **2,417** | **2,137** | **1,301** | **1,248** | **2,405** | **2,106** | **1,499** | **1,294** | **1,128** |

1. Covers purchase, development, and operations. 2. Estimated. 3. Unique natural areas and endangered species. 4. Less than $500,000. NOTE: Due to rounding, figures may not total. *Source:* U.S. Office of Management and Budget, *Special Analyses, Budget of the United States Government,* 1979.

## Water Supply of the World[1]

The Antarctic Icecap is the largest supply of fresh water, nearly 2 percent of the world's total of fresh and salt water. As can be seen from the table below, the amount of water in our atmosphere is over ten times as large as the water in all the rivers taken together. The fresh water actually available for human use in lakes and rivers and the accessible ground water amounts to only about one third of one percent of the total.

| | Surface area (square miles) | Volume (cubic miles) | Percentage of total |
|---|---|---|---|
| Salt Water | | | |
| The oceans | 139,500,000 | 317,000,000 | 97.2 |
| Inland seas and saline lakes | 270,000 | 25,000 | 0.008 |
| Fresh Water | | | |
| Freshwater lakes | 330,000 | 30,000 | 0.009 |
| All rivers (average level) | — | 300 | 0.0001 |
| Antarctic Icecap | 6,000,000 | 6,300,000 | 1.9 |
| Arctic Icecap and glaciers | 900,000 | 680,000 | 0.15 |
| Water in the atmosphere | 197,000,000 | 3,100 | 0.001 |
| Ground water within half a mile from surface | — | 1,000,000 | 0.31 |
| Deep-lying ground water | — | 1,000,000 | 0.31 |
| **Total (rounded)** | — | **326,000,000** | **100.00** |

1. All figures are estimated. *Source:* Department of the Interior, Geological Survey.

## Polluting Incidents in and Around U.S. Waters, 1976

| Item | Number | Volume: Gallons (thousands) | Volume: Liters (thousands) |
|---|---|---|---|
| Source | | | |
| Vessels | 3,296 | 11,192 | 42,365 |
| Tank ships | 623 | 8,930 | 33,803 |
| Tank barges | 976 | 1,953 | 7,393 |
| Other | 1,697 | 309 | 1,170 |
| Land vehicles | 464 | 614 | 2,324 |
| Onshore facilities | 708 | 6,435 | 24,358 |
| Offshore facilities | 1,358 | 275 | 1,041 |
| Other facilities | 1,055 | 9,760 | 36,945 |
| Pipelines | 653 | 4,530 | 17,147 |
| Marine facilities | 560 | 377 | 1,427 |
| Land facilities | 182 | 443 | 1,677 |
| Misc./unknown | 4,379 | 227 | 859 |

| Item | Number | Volume: Gallons (thousands) | Volume: Liters (thousands) |
|---|---|---|---|
| Selected type of pollutant | | | |
| Crude oil | 2,667 | 4,991 | 18,892 |
| Fuel oil | 909 | 9,781 | 37,024 |
| Asphalt or residual fuel oil | 132 | 4,982 | 18,858 |
| Liquid chemical | 296 | 2,110 | 7,987 |
| Locations | | | |
| Atlantic coast | 2,627 | 8,876 | 33,598 |
| Gulf coast | 4,482 | 7,640 | 28,920 |
| Pacific coast | 2,237 | 1,443 | 5,462 |
| Great Lakes | 973 | 8,757 | 33,148 |
| Inland U.S. | 2,336 | 7,136 | 27,012 |
| Total discharges, 1976 | 12,655 | 33,852 | 128,140 |
| Total discharges, 1975 | 12,057 | 14,968 | 56,658 |
| Total discharges, 1970 | 3,711 | 15,253 | 57,737 |

*Source:* Department of Transportation, U.S. Coast Guard.

## Air Pollutant Emissions, by Source

(estimates)

| Year and pollutant | Total emissions[1] | Controllable emissions[1]: Transportation: Total | Transportation: Road vehicles | Fuel combustion[2]: Total | Fuel combustion[2]: Electric utilities | Industrial processes | Solid waste disposal | Misc. uncontrollable[1] |
|---|---|---|---|---|---|---|---|---|
| 1970 | | | | | | | | |
| Carbon monoxide | 113.7 | 88.0 | 77.4 | 1.5 | .2 | 11.5 | 6.8 | 5.9 |
| Sulfur oxides | 32.3 | .7 | .3 | 24.8 | 17.4 | 6.6 | .1 | .1 |
| Hydrocarbons | 33.9 | 14.1 | 12.3 | 1.6 | .1 | 3.6 | 1.9 | 12.7 |
| Particulates[3] | 26.8 | 1.3 | .8 | 9.7 | 4.5 | 13.6 | 1.2 | 1.0 |
| Nitrogen oxides | 22.7 | 9.3 | 7.0 | 12.3 | 5.7 | .6 | .3 | .2 |
| 1973 | | | | | | | | |
| Carbon monoxide | 111.5 | 90.3 | 80.0 | 1.4 | .3 | 11.5 | 4.0 | 4.3 |
| Sulfur oxides | 32.5 | .7 | .4 | 25.2 | 19.2 | 6.4 | .1 | .1 |
| Hydrocarbons | 34.0 | 13.7 | 11.8 | 1.7 | .1 | 3.7 | 1.1 | 13.8 |
| Particulates[3] | 21.9 | 1.3 | .9 | 7.5 | 3.7 | 11.7 | .7 | .7 |
| Nitrogen oxides | 25.7 | 10.9 | 8.1 | 13.7 | 7.0 | .7 | .2 | .2 |
| 1974 | | | | | | | | |
| Carbon monoxide | 104.2 | 83.0 | 73.7 | 1.4 | .3 | 11.0 | 3.5 | 5.3 |
| Sulfur oxides | 31.7 | .8 | .4 | 24.7 | 19.0 | 6.0 | .1 | .1 |
| Hydrocarbons | 32.5 | 12.6 | 10.9 | 1.7 | .1 | 3.7 | 1.0 | 13.5 |
| Particulates[3] | 20.3 | 1.3 | .9 | 7.0 | 3.4 | 10.6 | .6 | .8 |
| Nitrogen oxides | 25.0 | 10.6 | 8.1 | 13.3 | 6.9 | .7 | .2 | .2 |
| 1975 | | | | | | | | |
| Carbon monoxide | 96.2 | 77.4 | 67.8 | 1.2 | .3 | 9.4 | 3.3 | 4.9 |
| Sulfur oxides | 32.9 | .8 | .4 | 26.3 | 21.0 | 5.7 | (4) | .1 |
| Hydrocarbons | 30.9 | 11.7 | 10.0 | 1.4 | .1 | 3.5 | .9 | 13.4 |
| Particulates[3] | 18.0 | 1.3 | .9 | 6.6 | 3.5 | 8.7 | .6 | .8 |
| Nitrogen oxides | 24.2 | 10.7 | 8.2 | 12.4 | 6.8 | .7 | .2 | .2 |

1. In millions of tons. 2. Stationary. 3. Suspended particulate matter (particles of smoke or dust, fumes, and droplets of viscous liquid remaining in the air for varying periods of time and ranging from less than 1 micron [1/25,000 in.] to 100 microns). 4. Less than 50,000 tons. *Source:* Environmental Protection Agency.

## Ocean Dumping of Waste Materials
(in thousands of tons)

| Type of waste | 1977 Atlantic | 1977 Gulf | 1977 Pacific | 1975 Atlantic | 1975 Gulf | 1975 Pacific | 1973 Atlantic | 1973 Gulf | 1973 Pacific |
|---|---|---|---|---|---|---|---|---|---|
| Industrial | 1,783.6 | 60.2 | 0 | 3,322.3 | 119.6 | 0 | 3,642.8 | 1,408.0 | 0 |
| Sewage sludge | 1,534.0 | 0 | 0 | 5,039.6 | 0 | 0 | 4,898.9 | 0 | 0 |
| Construction and demolition debris | 379.0 | 0 | 0 | 395.9 | 0 | 0 | 973.7 | 0 | 0 |
| Solid | .1 | 0 | 0 | 0 | 0 | 0 | 0 | 0 | .2 |
| Explosives | 0 | 0 | 0 | 0 | 0 | 0 | 0 | 0 | 0 |
| Incinerated (wood) | 15.1 | 0 | 0 | 6.2 | 0 | 0 | 10.8 | 0 | 0 |
| Incinerated (chemicals) | 0 | 17.6 | 12.1 | 0 | 4.1 | 0 | 0 | 0 | 0 |
| Total | 7,311.7 | 77.8 | 12.1 | 8,764.0 | 123.7 | 0 | 9,526.2 | 1,408.0 | .2 |

*Source:* Environmental Protection Agency, Office of Public Awareness.

## Speed of Animals

Most of the following measurements are for maximum speeds over approximate quarter-mile distances. Exceptions—which are included to give a wide range of animals—are the lion and elephant, whose speeds were clocked in the act of charging; the whippet, which was timed over a 200-yard course; the cheetah over a 100-yard distance; man for a 15-yard segment of a 100-yard run; and the black mamba, six-lined race runner, spider, giant tortoise, three-toed sloth, and garden snail, which were measured over various small distances.

| Animal | Speed mph |
|---|---|
| Cheetah | 70 |
| Pronghorn antelope | 61 |
| Wildebeest | 50 |
| Lion | 50 |
| Thomson's gazelle | 50 |
| Quarter horse | 47.5 |
| Elk | 45 |
| Cape hunting dog | 45 |
| Coyote | 43 |
| Gray fox | 42 |
| Hyena | 40 |
| Zebra | 40 |
| Mongolian wild ass | 40 |
| Greyhound | 39.35 |
| Whippet | 35.5 |
| Rabbit (domestic) | 35 |
| Mule deer | 35 |
| Jackal | 35 |
| Reindeer | 32 |
| Giraffe | 32 |
| White-tailed deer | 30 |
| Wart hog | 30 |
| Grizzly bear | 30 |
| Cat (domestic) | 30 |
| Man | 27.89 |
| Elephant | 25 |
| Black mamba snake | 20 |
| Six-line race runner | 18 |
| Squirrel | 12 |
| Pig (domestic) | 11 |
| Chicken | 9 |
| Spider (Tegenearia atrica) | 1.17 |
| Giant tortoise | 0.17 |
| Three-toed sloth | 0.15 |
| Garden snail | 0.03 |

*Source: Natural History* Magazine, March 1974, copyright 1974, The American Museum of Natural History; and James Doherty, Curator of Mammals, N.Y. Zoological Society.

## Animal Names: Male, Female, and Young

| Animal | Male | Female | Young |
|---|---|---|---|
| Ass | Jack | Jenny | Foal |
| Bear | He-bear | She-bear | Cub |
| Cat | Tom | Queen | Kitten |
| Cattle | Bull | Cow | Calf |
| Chicken | Rooster | Hen | Chick |
| Deer | Buck | Doe | Fawn |
| Dog | Dog | Bitch | Pup |
| Duck | Drake | Duck | Duckling |
| Elephant | Bull | Cow | Calf |
| Fox | Dog | Vixen | Cub |
| Goose | Gander | Goose | Gosling |
| Horse | Stallion | Mare | Foal |
| Lion | Lion | Lioness | Cub |
| Rabbit | Buck | Doe | Bunny |
| Sheep | Ram | Ewe | Lamb |
| Swan | Cob | Pen | Cygnet |
| Swine | Boar | Sow | Piglet |
| Tiger | Tiger | Tigress | Cub |
| Whale | Bull | Cow | Calf |
| Wolf | Dog | Bitch | Pup |

*Source:* James Doherty, Curator of Mammals, N.Y. Zoological Society.

## Animal Group Terminology

*Source:* James Doherty, Curator of Mammals, N.Y. Zoological Society, and *Information Please* data.

**ants:** colony
**bears:** sleuth, sloth
**bees:** grist, hive, swarm
**birds:** flight, volery
**cattle:** drove
**cats:** clutter, clowder
**chicks:** brood, clutch
**clams:** bed
**cranes:** sedge, seige
**crows:** murder
**doves:** dule
**ducks:** brace, team
**elephants:** herd
**elks:** gang
**finches:** charm
**fish:** school, shoal, draught
**foxes:** leash, skulk
**geese:** flock, gaggle, skein
**gnats:** cloud, horde
**goats:** trip
**gorillas:** band
**hares:** down, husk
**hawks:** cast
**hens:** brood
**hogs:** drift
**horses:** pair, team
**hounds:** cry, mute, pack
**kangaroos:** troop
**kittens:** kindle
**larks:** exaltation
**leopards:** leap
**lions:** pride
**locusts:** plague
**magpies:** tidings
**mules:** span
**nightingales:** watch
**oxen:** yoke
**oysters:** bed
**parrots:** company
**partridges:** covey
**peacocks:** muster, ostentation
**pheasants:** nest, bouquet
**pigs:** litter
**ponies:** string
**quail:** bevy, covey
**rabbits:** nest
**seals:** pod
**sheep:** drove, flock
**sparrows:** host
**storks:** mustering
**swans:** bevy, wedge
**swine:** sounder
**toads:** knot
**turkeys:** rafter
**turtles:** bale
**vipers:** nest
**whales:** gam, pod
**wolves:** pack, route
**woodcocks:** fall

## Gestation, Incubation, and Longevity of Certain Animals

| Animal | Gestation or incubation, in days & (average) | Longevity, in years & (record exceptions) |
|---|---|---|
| Ass | 365 | 18–20 (63) |
| Bear | 180–240[1] | 15–30 (47) |
| Cat | 52–69 (63) | 10–12 (26+) |
| Chicken | 22 | 7–8 (14) |
| Cow | c. 280 | 9–12 (25) |
| Deer | 197–300[1] | 10–15 (26) |
| Dog | 53–71 (63) | 10–12 (24) |
| Duck | 21–35[1] (28) | 10 (15) |
| Elephant | 510–730 (624)[1] | 30–40 (71) |
| Fox | 51–63[1] | 8–10 (14) |
| Goat | 136–160 (151) | 12 (17) |
| Groundhog | 31–32 | 4–9 |
| Guinea pig | 58–75 (68) | 3 (6) |
| Hamster, golden | 15–17 | 2 (8) |
| Hippopotamus | 220–255 (240) | 30 (49+) |

| Animal | Gestation or incubation, in days & (average) | Longevity, in years & (record exceptions) |
|---|---|---|
| Horse | 264–420 (336)[2] | 20–25 (50+) |
| Kangaroo | 32–39[1] | 4–6 (23) |
| Lion | 105–113 (108) | 10 (29) |
| Man | 253–303 | ([3]) |
| Monkey | 139–270[1] | 12–15[1] (29) |
| Mouse | 19–31[1] | 1–3 (4) |
| Parakeet (Budgerigar) | 17–20 (18) | 8 (12+) |
| Pig | 101–130 (115) | 10 (22) |
| Pigeon | 11–19 | 10–12 (39) |
| Rabbit | 30–35 (31) | 6–8 (15) |
| Rat | 21 | 3 (5) |
| Sheep | 144–152 (151)[1] | 12 (16) |
| Squirrel | 44 | 8–9 (15) |
| Whale | 365–547[1] | |
| Wolf | 60–63 | 10–12 (16) |

1. Depending on kind. 2. Horse has the greatest variation of gestation period of any species. This is caused by seasonal or feed factors. 3. For life expectancy charts, *see* Index. *Source:* James Doherty, Curator of Mammals, N.Y. Zoological Society.

## Zoological Gardens

North America has more than 30 major zoos, in the United States, Canada, and Mexico. The *Quebec Zoological Society's* collection is made up of Canadian species; Toronto has many exotic species.

The first zoological garden in the United States was established in Philadelphia in 1874. Since that time nearly every large city in the country has acquired a zoo. Among the largest are San Diego's on the West Coast; Chicago's Brookfield Zoo and those of St. Louis and Kansas City in the Middle West; and, in the East, the New York Zoological Society's park in the Bronx. The *National Zoological Park* in Washington, D.C., in a beautiful setting of hills, woods, and streams, was established in 1890 by an act of Congress. The major U.S. zoos now have created large natural-habitat areas for their collections.

In Europe, zoological gardens have long been popular public institutions. The *Jardin d'Acclimatation,* in the Bois de Boulogne, Paris, is the oldest and largest. Others are located at Clères, Ermenonville, Lyons, Marseilles, Maubeuge, Mulhouse, and Nancy.

Germany had about 20 zoological gardens, many of which were developed in the peacetime years between World Wars I and II. Large zoos were located in Berlin and Frankfurt am Main. In Munich, the animals were grouped according to the continent of their origin. At Stellingen near Hamburg, the *Hagenback Garden* became an outstanding show place and distributing center for animals.

The *Schönbrunn* at Vienna is one of the oldest zoos in Europe. The Budapest zoological gardens house a fine collection of European birds. At Antwerp, the *Royal Zoological Society* founded a large menagerie in 1843. It was seriously damaged by German bombs during World War II.

In the British Isles, a popular zoo is in the garden of the *London Zoological Society* in Regent's Park. Although this zoo received a number of direct bomb hits in 1940–41 and again in 1944, it remained open throughout World War II; visitors during this period numbered 6,500,000. Manchester and Clifton have smaller gardens, and the one at Edinburgh is famous for its collection of penguins. The *Dublin Zoo* is noted for its lions, many of which were born there.

The Amsterdam zoo, with its East Indian collection and its aquarium, and the Rotterdam gardens are the two best known in the Netherlands. Built on a high elevation, the *Skansen Zoo* in Stockholm exhibits north European specimens. The most important gardens in the U.S.S.R. are found in Moscow, where northern as well as exotic species are collected. The zoo at Rome has part of its collection confined in barless pits. At Lisbon there is a small zoological garden, and in Madrid a part of the original royal menagerie.

## Notable American Zoos

*Source: Information Please* questionnaires to the zoos.

**Atlanta Zoological Park:** 800 Cherokee Ave., S.E., Atlanta, Ga. 30315

**Audubon Park Zoo and Odenheimer Aquarium:** St. Charles Ave. between Walnut and Exposition Blvd., New Orleans, La. 70118

**Baltimore Zoo:** Druid Hill Park, Baltimore, Md. 21217

**Belle Isle Aquarium and Children's Zoo:** Detroit, Mich. Mailing address: Royal Oak, Mich. 48068

**Boston Zoo and Children's Zoo:** Franklin Park Zoological Gardens, Boston, Mass. 02121

**Bronx Zoo.** *See* New York Zoological Park

**Buffalo Zoological Gardens:** Delaware Park, Buffalo, N.Y. 14214

**Burnet Park Zoo:** Coleridge and Wilbur Ave., Syracuse, N.Y. 13204

**Central Park Zoo:** 830 Fifth Ave. at 64th St., New York, N.Y. 10021

**Cheyenne Mountain Zoological Park:** Cheyenne Mountain Hgwy., P.O. Box 158, Colorado Springs, Colo. 80901

**Chicago Zoological Park (Brookfield Zoo):** First Ave. and 31st St., Brookfield, Ill. 60513

**Cincinnati, Zoological Society of:** 3400 Vine St., Cincinnati, Ohio 45220

**Cleveland Metroparks Zoo:** Brookside Park, Cleveland, Ohio 44109

**Columbus Zoo:** 9990 Riverside Drive, Powell, Ohio 43065

**Dallas Zoo:** 621 East Clarendon Drive, Dallas, Tex. 75203

**Denver Zoological Gardens:** City Park, Denver, Colo. 80205

**Detroit Zoological Park:** Woodward and Ten Mile Road, Royal Oak, Mich. 48068

**El Paso Zoological Park:** Evergreen and Paisano, El Paso, Tex. 79905

**Fort Worth Zoological Park:** 2727 Zoological Park Drive, Fort Worth, Tex. 76110

**Hogle Zoological Gardens:** 2600 East Sunnyside Ave., Salt Lake City, Utah 84108

**Houston Zoological Gardens:** Hermann Park, P.O. Box 1562, Houston, Tex. 77001

**Jacksonville Zoological Park:** 8605 Zoo Road, Jacksonville, Fla. 32218

**Kansas City Zoo:** Swope Park, Kansas City, Mo. 64132

**Lincoln Municipal Zoo:** 1300 South 27th St., Lincoln, Neb. 68502

**Lincoln Park Zoological Gardens:** 2200 N. Cannon Drive, Chicago, Ill. 60614

**Los Angeles Zoo:** 5333 Zoo Drive, Los Angeles, Calif. 90027

**Memphis Zoo and Aquarium:** Overton Park, Memphis, Tenn. 38112

**Mesker Park Zoo:** Bement Ave., Evansville, Ind. 47712

**Milwaukee County Zoo:** 10001 West Bluemound Road, Milwaukee, Wis. 53226

**National Zoological Park:** 3000 block of Connecticut Ave. N.W., Washington, D.C. 20008

**New York Zoological Park (Bronx Zoo):** Southern Blvd. and 185th St., Bronx, N.Y. 10460

**Oakland Zoo:** Golf Links Road, off Freeway 580, Oakland, Calif. 94605

**Oklahoma City Zoo:** N.E. 50th and N. Eastern Ave., Oklahoma City, Okla. 73111

**Philadelphia Zoo:** 34th St. and Girard Ave., Philadelphia, Pa. 19104

**Pittsburgh Zoo:** Highland Park, Pittsburgh, Pa. 15206

**Rio Grande Zoological Park:** 903 Tenth St., S.W., Albuquerque, N.M. 87102

**St. Louis Zoological Park:** Forest Park, St. Louis, Mo. 63110

**St. Paul's Como Zoo:** Midway Pkwy. and Kaufman Drive, St. Paul, Minn. 55103

**San Diego Zoological Garden:** Park Blvd. and Zoo Place, San Diego, Calif. 92112

**San Francisco Zoological Gardens:** Zoo Road and Skyline Blvd., San Francisco, Calif., 94132

**Seneca Park Zoo:** 2222 St. Paul St., Rochester, N.Y. 14621

**Staten Island Zoo:** Barrett Park, W. Brighton, Staten Island, New York 10310

**Toledo Zoological Gardens:** 2700 Broadway, Toledo, Ohio 43609

**Washington Park Zoo:** 4001 S.W. Canyon Road, Portland, Ore. 97221

**Woodland Park Zoological Gardens:** 5500 Phinney Ave. N., Seattle, Wash. 98103

# The National Park System

*Source:* Department of the Interior, National Park Service.

The National Park System of the United States is administered by the National Park Service, a bureau of the Department of the Interior. Started with the establishment of Yellowstone National Park in 1872, the system includes not only the most extraordinary and spectacular scenic exhibits in the United States but also a large number of sites distinguished either for their historic or prehistoric importance or scientific interest, or for their superior recreational assets. The number and extent of the various types of areas that make up the system follow.

| Type of area | Number | Total acreage[1] |
|---|---|---|
| National Parks | 37 | 15,657,644.28 |
| National Monuments | 82 | 9,881,118.24 |
| National Battlefield Parks | 3 | 6,762.38 |
| National Battlefields | 8 | 6,658.27 |
| National Battlefield Sites | 2 | 1,812.36 |
| National Military Parks | 11 | 34,654.53 |
| National Historical Parks | 18 | 78,584.70 |
| National Historical Sites | 53 | 15,016.60 |
| National Memorials | 22 | 6,019.08 |
| National Memorial Park | 1 | 70,408.64 |
| National Seashores | 10 | 595,168.86 |
| National Lakeshores | 4 | 196,455.98 |
| National Scenic Riverways | 6 | 373,684.91 |
| National Recreation Areas | 16 | 3,493,655.32 |
| National Parkways | 4 | 160,838.66 |
| National Scenic Trail | 1 | 52,034.25 |
| Other Parks[2] | 10 | 31,916.34 |
| National Preserves | 2 | 654,550.00 |
| White House | 1 | 18.01 |
| National Mall | 1 | 146.35 |
| National Visitor Center | 1 | 0.00 |
| National Capital Parks[3] | 1 | 6,470.59 |
| **Total** | **294** | **31,323,618.41** |

1. Acreage as of December 31, 1977, for most areas. New areas reflect data available at time of authorization. Ten national cemeteries administered by the National Park Service are administered in conjunction with associated historical units and are not listed separately. 2. Parks without national designation. 3. Comprises 346 units within the District of Columbia, Maryland, and Virginia.

## National Parks

| Name, location, and year established | Acreage | Outstanding characteristics |
|---|---|---|
| Acadia (Maine), 1919 | 38,521.91 | Rugged seashore on Mt. Desert Island and adjacent mainland |
| Arches (Utah), 1971 | 73,378.98 | Unusual stone arches, windows, pedestals caused by erosion |
| Big Bend (Tex.), 1935 | 708,118.40 | Mountains and desert bordering the Rio Grande |
| Bryce Canyon (Utah), 1924 | 38,835.08 | Area of grotesque eroded rocks brilliantly colored |
| Canyonlands (Utah), 1964 | 377,570.43 | Colorful wilderness with impressive red-rock canyons, spires, arches |
| Capitol Reef (Utah), 1971 | 241,874.29 | Highly colored sedimentary rock formations in high, narrow gorges |
| Carlsbad Caverns (N.M.), 1930 | 46,755.33 | The world's largest known caves |
| Crater Lake (Ore.), 1902 | 160,290.33 | Deep blue lake in heart of inactive volcano |
| Everglades (Fla.), 1934 | 1,398,800.00 | Subtropical area with abundant bird and animal life |
| Glacier (Mont.), 1910 | 1,013,594.67 | Rocky Mountain scenery with many glaciers and lakes |
| Grand Canyon (Ariz.), 1919 | 1,218,375.24 | Mile-deep gorge, 4 to 18 miles wide, 217 miles long |
| Grand Teton (Wyo.), 1929 | 310,515.94 | Picturesque range of high mountain peaks |
| Great Smoky Mts. (N.C.-Tenn), 1926 | 517,368.15 | Highest mountain range east of Black Hills; luxuriant plant life |
| Guadalupe Mountains (Tex.), 1966 | 76,293,06 | Contains highest point in Texas: Guadalupe Peak (8,751 ft) |
| Haleakala (Hawaii), 1960 | 28,660.39 | World-famous 10,023-ft Haleakala volcano (dormant) |
| Hawaii Volcanoes (Hawaii), 1916 | 229,177.03 | Spectacular volcanic area; luxuriant vegetation at lower levels |
| Hot Springs (Ark.), 1921 | 5,800.69 | 47 mineral hot springs said to have therapeutic value |
| Isle Royale (Mich.), 1931 | 571,796.18 | Largest wilderness island in Lake Superior; moose, wolves, lakes |
| Kings Canyon (Calif.), 1940 | 460,136.20 | Huge canyons; high mountains; giant sequoias |
| Lassen Volcanic (Calif.), 1916 | 106,372.36 | Exhibits of impressive volcanic phenomena |
| Mammoth Cave (Ky.), 1926 | 52,128.92 | Vast limestone labyrinth with underground river |
| Mesa Verde (Colo.), 1906 | 52,036.24 | Best-preserved prehistoric cliff dwellings in United States |
| Mount McKinley (Alaska), 1917 | 1,939,492.80 | Highest mountain in North America; spectacular wildlife |
| Mount Rainier (Wash.), 1899 | 235,404,00 | Single-peak glacial system; dense forests, flowered meadows |
| North Cascades (Wash.), 1968 | 504,780.34 | Roadless Alpine landscape; jagged peaks; mountain lakes; glaciers |
| Olympic (Wash.), 1938 | 908,692.46 | Finest Pacific Northwest rain forest; scenic mountain park |
| Petrified Forest (Ariz.), 1962 | 93,492.57 | Extensive natural exhibit of petrified wood |
| Redwood (Calif.), 1968 | 62,210.57 | Coastal redwood forests; contains world's tallest known tree (369.2 ft) |

| Name, location, and year established | Acreage | Outstanding characteristics |
|---|---|---|
| Rocky Mountain (Colo.), 1915 | 263,793.14 | Section of the Rocky Mountains; 107 named peaks over 10,000 ft |
| Sequoia (Calif.), 1890 | 386,823.00 | Giant sequoias; magnificent High Sierra scenery, including Mt. Whitney |
| Shenandoah (Va.), 1926 | 190,590.82 | Tree-covered mountains; scenic Skyline Drive |
| Virgin Islands (U.S. V.I.), 1956 | 14,490.01 | Beaches; lush hills; prehistoric Carib Indian relics |
| Voyageurs (Minn.), 1971 | 219,128.00 | Wildlife, canoeing, fishing, and hiking |
| Wind Cave (S.D.), 1903 | 28,060.03 | Limestone caverns in Black Hills; buffalo herd |
| Yellowstone (Wyo.-Mont.-Idaho), 1872 | 2,219,822.70 | World's greatest geyser area; abundant falls, wildlife, and canyons |
| Yosemite (Calif.), 1890 | 760,917.05 | Mountains; inspiring gorges and waterfalls; giant sequoias |
| Zion (Utah), 1919 | 146,546.97 | Multicolored gorge in heart of southern Utah desert |

## NATIONAL HISTORICAL PARKS

| *Name and location* | *Total acreage* |
|---|---|
| Appomattox Court House (Va.) | 1,318.70 |
| Boston (Mass.) | 34.74 |
| Chalmette (La.) | 142.85 |
| Chesapeake and Ohio Canal (Md.-W.Va.-D.C.) | 20,239.00 |
| City of Refuge (Hawaii) | 181.80 |
| Colonial (Va.) | 9,833.58 |
| Cumberland Gap (Ky.-Tenn.-Va.) | 20,273.57 |
| George Rogers Clark (Ind.) | 24.30 |
| Harpers Ferry (W.Va.-Md.) | 1,909.47 |
| Independence (Pa.) | 36.66 |
| Klondike Goldrush (Alaska) | 13,270.49 |
| Minute Man (Mass.) | 745.37 |
| Morristown (N.J.) | 1,676.63 |
| Nez Perce (Idaho) | 2,113.78 |
| San Juan Island (Wash.) | 1,751.99 |
| Saratoga (N.Y.) | 2,455.11 |
| Sitka (Alaska) | 107.71 |
| Valley Forge (Pa.) | 2,466.04 |

## NATIONAL MONUMENTS

| *Name and location* | *Total acreage* |
|---|---|
| Agate Fossil Beds (Neb.) | 3,054.43 |
| Alibates Flint Quarries (Tex.) | 92.56 |
| Aztec Ruins (N.M.) | 27.14 |
| Badlands (S.D.) | 243,302.33 |
| Bandelier (N.M.) | 36,971.20 |
| Biscayne (Fla.) | 103,642.65 |
| Black Canyon (Colo.) | 13,672.13 |
| Booker T. Washington (Va.) | 223.92 |
| Buck Island Reef (U.S. V.I.) | 880.00 |
| Cabrillo (Calif.) | 143.94 |
| Canyon de Chelly (Ariz.) | 83,840.00 |
| Capulin Mountain (N.M.) | 775.38 |
| Casa Grande Ruins (Ariz.) | 472.50 |
| Castillo de San Marcos (Fla.) | 20.49 |
| Castle Clinton (N.Y.) | 1.00 |
| Cedar Breaks (Utah) | 6,154.60 |
| Chaco Canyon (N.M.) | 21,509.40 |
| Channel Islands (Calif.) | 18,388.07 |
| Chiricahua (Ariz.) | 10,648.25 |
| Colorado (Colo.) | 20,445.47 |
| Congaree Swamp (S.C.) | 15,200.00 |
| Craters of the Moon (Idaho) | 53,545.05 |
| Custer Battlefield (Mont.) | 765.34 |
| Death Valley (Calif.-Nev.) | 2,067,795.06 |
| Devils Postpile (Calif.) | 798.46 |
| Devils Tower (Wyo.) | 1,346.91 |
| Dinosaur (Utah-Colo.) | 211,050.70 |
| Effigy Mounds (Iowa) | 1,474.63 |
| El Morro (N.M.) | 1,278.72 |
| Florissant Fossil Beds (Colo.) | 5,992.32 |
| Fort Frederica (Ga.) | 214.52 |
| Fort Jefferson (Fla.) | 47,125.00 |
| Fort Matanzas (Fla.) | 298.51 |
| Fort McHenry (Md.) | 43.26 |
| Fort Pulaski (Ga.) | 5,615.50 |
| Fort Stanwix (N.Y.) | 15.52 |
| Fort Sumter (S.C.) | 64.27 |
| Fort Union (N.M.) | 720.60 |
| Fossil Butte (Wyo.) | 8,178.00 |
| George Washington Birthplace (Va.) | 455.98 |
| George Washington Carver (Mo.) | 210.00 |
| Gila Cliff Dwellings (N.M.) | 533.13 |
| Glacier Bay (Alaska) | 2,805,269.49 |
| Gran Quivira (N.M.) | 610.94 |
| Grand Portage (Minn.) | 709.97 |
| Great Sand Dunes (Colo.) | 36,826.50 |
| Hohokam Pima (Ariz.) | 1,690.00 |
| Homestead (Neb.) | 194.57 |
| Hovenweep (Utah-Colo.) | 785.43 |
| Jewel Cave (S.D.) | 1,274.56 |
| John Day Fossil Beds (Ore.) | 14,402.00 |
| Joshua Tree (Calif.) | 559,959.79 |
| Katmai (Alaska) | 2,792,150.74 |
| Lava Beds (Calif.) | 46,821.33 |
| Lehman Caves (Nev.) | 640.00 |
| Montezuma Castle (Ariz.) | 841.75 |
| Mound City Group (Ohio) | 67.50 |
| Muir Woods (Calif.) | 553.55 |
| Natural Bridges (Utah) | 7,779.14 |
| Navajo (Ariz.) | 360.00 |
| Ocmulgee (Ga.) | 683.48 |
| Oregon Caves (Ore.) | 465.80 |
| Organ Pipe Cactus (Ariz.) | 330,688.86 |
| Pecos (N.M.) | 364.80 |
| Pinnacles (Calif.) | 16,215.67 |
| Pipe Spring (Ariz.) | 40.00 |
| Pipestone (Minn.) | 281.78 |
| Rainbow Bridge (Utah) | 160.00 |
| Russell Cave (Ala.) | 310.45 |
| Saguaro (Ariz.) | 83,576.07 |
| St. Croix Island (Me.) | 35.39 |
| Scotts Bluff (Neb.) | 2,987.97 |
| Statue of Liberty (N.Y.-N.J.) | 58.38 |
| Sunset Crater (Ariz.) | 3,040.00 |
| Timpanogos Cave (Utah) | 250.00 |
| Tonto (Ariz.) | 1,120.00 |
| Tumacacori (Ariz.) | 10.15 |
| Tuzigoot (Ariz.) | 57.78 |
| Walnut Canyon (Ariz.) | 2,249.46 |
| White Sands (N.M.) | 145,334.76 |
| Wupatki (Ariz.) | 35,253.24 |
| Yucca House (Colo.) | 10.00 |

## NATIONAL PRESERVES

| | |
|---|---|
| Big Cypress (Fla.) | 570,000.00 |
| Big Thicket (Tex.) | 84,550.00 |

## NATIONAL MILITARY PARKS

| | |
|---|---|
| Chickamauga and Chattanooga (Ga.-Tenn.) | 8,095.41 |
| Fort Donelson (Tenn.) | 543.65 |

| Name and location | Total acreage |
|---|---|
| Fredericksburg and Spotsylvania (Va.) | 5,886.68 |
| Gettysburg (Pa.) | 3,861.80 |
| Guilford Courthouse (N.C.) | 220.44 |
| Horseshoe Bend (Ala.) | 2,040.00 |
| Kings Mountain (S.C.) | 3,945.29 |
| Moores Creek (N.C.) | 84.38 |
| Pea Ridge (Ark.) | 4,300.35 |
| Shiloh (Tenn.) | 3,761.50 |
| Vicksburg (Miss.) | 1,740.78 |

### NATIONAL MEMORIAL PARK

| | |
|---|---|
| Theodore Roosevelt (N.D.) | 70,408.64 |

### NATIONAL BATTLEFIELDS

| | |
|---|---|
| Big Hole (Mont.) | 655.61 |
| Cowpens (S.C.) | 842.54 |
| Fort Necessity (Pa.) | 900.97 |
| Monocacy (Md.) | 633.31 |
| Petersburg (Va.) | 1,515.26 |
| Stones River (Tenn.) | 330.86 |
| Tupelo (Miss.) | 1.00 |
| Wilson's Creek (Mo.) | 1,749.91 |

### NATIONAL BATTLEFIELD PARKS

| | |
|---|---|
| Kennesaw Mountain (Ga.) | 2,884.38 |
| Manassas (Va.) | 3,108.87 |
| Richmond (Va.) | 769.13 |

### NATIONAL BATTLEFIELD SITES

| | |
|---|---|
| Antietam (Md.) | 1,800.00 |
| Brices Crossroads (Miss.) | 1.00 |

### NATIONAL HISTORIC SITES

| | |
|---|---|
| Abraham Lincoln Birthplace (Ky.) | 116.50 |
| Adams (Mass.) | 8.45 |
| Allegheny Portage Railroad (Pa.) | 760.21 |
| Andersonville (Ga.) | 478.03 |
| Andrew Johnson (Tenn.) | 16.68 |
| Bent's Old Fort (Colo.) | 178.00 |
| Carl Sandburg Home (N.C.) | 247.37 |
| Christiansted (V.I.) | 27.15 |
| Clara Barton (Md.) | 8.59 |
| Edison (N.J.) | 21.35 |
| Eisenhower (Pa.) | 492.54 |
| Eleanor Roosevelt (N.Y.) | 174.86 |
| Ford's Theatre (Lincoln Museum) (D.C.) | 0.29 |
| Fort Bowie (Ariz.) | 1,000.00 |
| Fort Davis (Tex.) | 460.00 |
| Fort Laramie (Wyo.) | 571.30 |
| Fort Larned (Kan.) | 718.39 |
| Fort Point (Calif.) | 29.00 |
| Fort Raleigh (N.C.) | 160.40 |
| Fort Smith (Ark.-Okla.) | 63.04 |
| Fort Union Trading Post (N.D.-Mont.) | 398.45 |
| Fort Vancouver (Wash.) | 208.89 |
| Golden Spike (Utah) | 2,203.20 |
| Grant-Kohrs Ranch (Mont.) | 1,527.69 |
| Hampton (Md.) | 45.42 |
| Herbert Hoover (Iowa) | 186.80 |
| Home of F. D. Roosevelt (N.Y.) | 263.89 |
| Hopewell Village (Pa.) | 848.06 |
| Hubbell Trading Post (Ariz.) | 160.09 |
| Jefferson National Expansion Memorial (Mo.) | 90.96 |
| John F. Kennedy (Mass.) | 0.09 |
| John Muir (Calif.) | 8.90 |
| Knife River Indian Villages (N.D.) | 1,291.48 |
| Lincoln Home (Ill.) | 12.28 |
| Longfellow (Mass.) | 1.98 |
| Lyndon B. Johnson (Tex.) | 240.81 |
| Mar-a-Lago (Fla.) | 17.17 |
| Martin Van Buren (N.Y.) | 40.25 |
| Ninety Six (S.C.) | 1,115.08 |
| Puukohola Heiau (Hawaii) | 76.57 |
| Sagamore Hill (N.Y.) | 85.00 |
| Saint-Gaudens (N.H.) | 149.31 |
| Salem Maritime (Mass.) | 8.80 |
| San Juan (P.R.) | 53.20 |
| Saugus Iron Works (Mass.) | 8.51 |
| Sewall-Belmont House (D.C.) | 0.35 |
| Springfield Armory (Mass.) | 55.00 |
| Theodore Roosevelt Birthplace (N.Y.) | 0.11 |
| Theodore Roosevelt Inaugural (N.Y.) | 1.03 |
| Tuskegee Institute (Ala.) | 74.39 |
| Vanderbilt Mansion (N.Y.) | 211.65 |
| Whitman Mission (Wash.) | 98.15 |
| William Howard Taft (Ohio) | 0.83 |

### NATIONAL MEMORIALS

| | |
|---|---|
| Arkansas Post (Ark.) | 389.18 |
| Chamizal (Tex.) | 54.90 |
| Coronado (Ariz.) | 2,834.16 |
| Desoto (Fla.) | 30.00 |
| Federal Hall (N.Y.) | 0.45 |
| Fort Caroline (Fla.) | 128.88 |
| Fort Clatsop (Ore.) | 124.97 |
| General Grant (N.Y.) | 0.76 |
| Hamilton Grange (N.Y.) | 0.71 |
| John F. Kennedy Center for Performing Arts (D.C.) | 17.50 |
| Johnstown Flood (Pa.) | 106.40 |
| Lincoln Boyhood (Ind.) | 197.60 |
| Lincoln Memorial (D.C.) | 163.63 |
| Lyndon Baines Johnson Memorial Grove on the Potomac (D.C.) | 17.00 |
| Mount Rushmore (S.D.) | 1,278.45 |
| Perry's Victory and International Peace Memorial (Ohio) | 25.64 |
| Roger Williams (R.I.) | 4.56 |
| Thaddeus Kosciuszko (Pa.) | 0.02 |
| Theodore Roosevelt Island (D.C.) | 88.50 |
| Thomas Jefferson Memorial (D.C.) | 18.36 |
| Washington Monument (D.C.) | 106.01 |
| Wright Brothers (N.C.) | 431.40 |

### NATIONAL CEMETERIES[1]

| | |
|---|---|
| Antietam (Md.) | 11.36 |
| Battleground (D.C.) | 1.03 |
| Fort Donelson (Tenn.) | 15.34 |
| Fredericksburg (Va.) | 12.00 |
| Gettysburg (Pa.) | 20.58 |
| Poplar Grove (Va.) | 8.72 |
| Shiloh (Tenn.) | 10.05 |
| Stones River (Tenn.) | 20.09 |
| Vicksburg (Miss.) | 116.28 |
| Yorktown (Va.) | 2.91 |

### NATIONAL SEASHORES

| | |
|---|---|
| Assateague Island (Md.-Va.) | 39,630.93 |
| Canaveral (Fla.) | 57,627.07 |
| Cape Cod (Mass.) | 44,600.00 |
| Cape Hatteras (N.C.) | 30,318.63 |
| Cape Lookout (N.C.) | 28,400.00 |
| Cumberland Island (Ga.) | 36,878.44 |
| Fire Island (N.Y.) | 19,356.55 |
| Gulf Islands (Fla.-Miss.) | 139,175.46 |
| Padre Island (Tex.) | 133,918.72 |
| Point Reyes (Calif.) | 65,263.06 |

### NATIONAL PARKWAYS

| | |
|---|---|
| Blue Ridge (Va.-N.C.-Ga.) | 81,578.07 |
| George Washington Memorial (Va.-Md.) | 7,141.63 |

1. The National Cemeteries are not independent areas of the National Park System; each is part of the military park, battlefield, etc., with which it is related. Their acreage is kept separately. Arlington National Cemetery is under the Department of the Army. *See* Index.

| *Name and location* | *Total acreage* |
|---|---|
| John D. Rockefeller, Jr., Memorial (Wyo.) | 23,777.22 |
| Natchez Trace (Miss.-Tenn.-Ala.) | 48,341.74 |
| **NATIONAL LAKESHORES** | |
| Apostle Islands (Wis.) | 42,009.20 |
| Indiana Dunes (Ind.) | 12,534.82 |
| Pictured Rocks (Mich.) | 70,807.19 |
| Sleeping Bear Dunes (Mich.) | 71,104.77 |
| **NATIONAL SCENIC RIVERS AND RIVERWAYS** | |
| Big South Fork National River & Recreation Area (Ky.-Tenn.) | 122,960.00 |
| Buffalo (Ark.) | 94,146.00 |
| Lower St. Croix (Minn.-Wis.) | 7,845.00 |
| Obed Wild & Scenic River (Tenn.) | 6,451.00 |
| Ozark (Mo.) | 79,587.00 |
| St. Croix (Minn.-Wis.) | 62,695.91 |
| **NATIONAL CAPITAL PARKS** | |
| National Capital Parks (D.C.-Va.-Md.) | 6,469.56 |
| **WHITE HOUSE** | |
| White House (D.C.) | 18.07 |
| **OTHER PARKS** | |
| Arlington House, the Robert E. Lee Memorial (Va.) | 27.91 |
| Catoctin Mountain (Md.) | 5,768.90 |
| Fort Benton (Mont.) | 0.0 |
| Fort Washington Park (Md.) | 341.00 |
| Frederick Douglass Home (D.C.) | 8.08 |
| Greenbelt Park (Md.) | 1,096.72 |
| Piscataway (Md.) | 4,217.53 |
| Prince William Forest (Va.) | 18,571.55 |
| Rock Creek Park (D.C.) | 1,754.37 |
| Wolf Trap Farm Park for the Performing Arts (Va.) | 130.28 |
| **NATIONAL RECREATION AREAS** | |
| Amistad (Tex.) | 62,451.74 |
| Bighorn Canyon (Wyo.-Mont.) | 120,157.88 |
| Chickasaw (Okla.) | 9,655.59 |
| Coulee Dam (Wash.) | 100,059.00 |
| Curecanti (Colo.) | 42,114.47 |
| Cuyahoga Valley (Ohio) | 30,020.19 |
| Delaware Water Gap (Pa.-N.J.) | 47,676.38 |

| *Name and location* | *Total acreage* |
|---|---|
| Gateway (N.Y.-N.J.) | 26,172.00 |
| Glen Canyon (Ariz.-Utah) | 1,236,880.00 |
| Golden Gate (Calif.) | 34,938.29 |
| Lake Chelan (Wash.) | 61,889.84 |
| Lake Mead (Ariz.-Nev.) | 1,496,600.52 |
| Lake Meredith (Tex.) | 45,964.30 |
| Ross Lake (Wash.) | 117,574.09 |
| Shadow Mountain (Colo.) | 19,003.58 |
| Whiskeytown-Shasta-Trinity (Calif.) | 42,497.45 |
| **NATIONAL SCENIC TRAIL** | |
| Appalachian (Maine, N.H. Vt., Mass., Conn., N.Y., N.J., Pa., Md., W.Va., Va., N.C., Tenn., Ga.) | 52,034.25 |
| **NATIONAL MALL** | |
| National Mall (D.C.) | 146.35 |
| **NATIONAL VISITOR CENTER** | |
| National Visitor Center (D.C.) | 0.00 |
| **AFFILIATED AREAS** | |
| (National Historic Sites unless otherwise noted.) | |
| Benjamin Franklin (Pa.)[1] | 0.00 |
| Cherokee Strip Living Museum (Kan.) | 6.00 |
| Chicago Portage (Ill.) | 91.20 |
| Chimney Rock (Neb.) | 83.36 |
| Dorchester Heights (Mass.) | 5.43 |
| Eugene O'Neill (Calif.) | 14.00 |
| Father Marquette (Mich.) | 52.00 |
| Fort Scott Historic Area (Kan.) | 6.69 |
| Gloria Dei Church (Pa.) | 3.71 |
| Ice Age (Wis.)[2] | 32,500.00 |
| International Peace Garden (N.D.) | 2,330.30 |
| Jamestown (Va.) | 20.63 |
| McLoughlin House (Ore.) | 0.63 |
| Pennsylvania Avenue (D.C.) | 0.00 |
| Roosevelt-Campobello International Park (Canada) | 2,721.50 |
| St. Paul's Church (N.Y.) | 6.09 |
| St. Thomas (V.I.) | 0.00 |
| San Jose Mission (Tex.) | 4.13 |
| Touro Synagogue (R.I.) | 0.23 |

1. National Memorial. 2. National Scientific Reserve.

## Sources of Information

*Source:* Brooklyn Botanic Garden, *Handbook on The Environment and The Home Gardener.*

Advice on various aspects of conservation programs and problems is available from national, state, and local organizations. Dr. Richard H. Pough, President of the Natural Area Council, has compiled a list of membership organizations that are happy to help smaller groups get started on worthwhile projects in conservation.

**America the Beautiful Fund, Inc.,** 145 East 52nd St., Rm. 601, New York, N.Y. 10022

**American Forestry Association,** 1319 18th St., N.W., Washington, D.C. 20036

**Defenders of Wildlife,** 1244 19th St., N.W., Washington, D.C. 20036

**Environmental Defense Fund, Inc.,** 475 Park Ave. South, New York, N.Y. 10016

**Friends of the Earth,** 72 Jane St., New York, N.Y. 10014

**Izaak Walton League of America,** 1800 N. Kent St., Suite 806, Arlington, Va. 22209

**National Audubon Society,** 950 Third Ave., New York, N.Y. 10022

**National Park and Conservation Association,** 1701 18th St., N.W., Washington, D.C. 20009

**National Trust for Historic Preservation,** 748 Jackson Place, N.W., Washington, D.C. 20006

**National Wildlife Federation,** 1412 16th St., N.W., Washington, D.C. 20036

**Natural Science for Youth Foundation,** 763 Silvermine Rd., New Canaan, Conn. 06840

**The Nature Conservancy,** 1800 N. Kent St., Suite 800, Arlington, Va. 22209

**Open Space Institute, Inc.,** 45 Rockefeller Plaza, Room 2350, New York, N.Y. 10020

**Sierra Club,** 530 Bush St., San Francisco, Calif. 94108

**The Wilderness Society,** 1901 Pennsylvania Ave., N.W., Washington, D.C. 20006

**World Wildlife Fund,** 1319 18th St., N.W., Washington, D.C. 20036

# FIRST AID

The following material was compiled from information provided by the American Red Cross, the American Heart Association, and Edumed, Inc.

First aid is the rendering of prompt and knowledgeable treatment to a person who has been injured or suddenly taken ill and for whom no immediate medical attention is available. Depending on circumstances, effective first aid can mean the difference between life and death or between temporary and permanent disability. Most accidents occur in and about the home and usually involve burns, choking, cuts or serious bleeding, poisons, and heart attacks. Artificial respiration and treatment for shock that sets in after a serious accident are also important factors in the success of first aid. The best course of action to follow after taking emergency measures is to summon assistance from the local police or fire department or from the nearest available doctor.

## Burns

Burns are classified according to first degree (reddened skin), second degree (blisters develop), and third degree (deep tissue damage). Face, feet, and hands are critical areas. For first-degree and small second-degree burns, submerge affected area in cold water until pain subsides. Or else apply a thick, dry sterile dressing and bandage firmly to keep air out. *Do not break blisters.* For third-degree burns, bandage as above, elevate the extremities, and obtain medical help immediately.

**Eye burns:** For burns of the eye, wash thoroughly with water for 15 minutes—hold the eyelid open and pour the water from the inside corner out. Put a clean pad over closed eyelid, bandage, and get medical help.

## Poisons

Speed and a clear head are vital in first aid for poison intake. If the victim loses consciousness, call for an emergency squad and give artificial respiration or cardiopulmonary resuscitation (CPR) if needed to keep the airway open. If the victim is conscious and not in convulsions, dilute the swallowed poison with a glass of water or milk, but stop at signs of nausea.

Next, call your physician or local poison-control center. Be ready to supply information on what poison, and how much of it, was taken and the weight and age of the victim, and to take down instructions for treatment and antidotes. (Antidotes suggested on a poison-container label should not be given without approval by your physician or poison-control center.)

If vomiting occurs, save a vomit specimen along with the container label for the attending physician.

## Shock

Shock is caused by many types of severe injuries and severe illnesses—poisoning, damage to the respiratory system, and loss of body fluids resulting from vomiting, dysentery, or burns. It is prudent to give shock care to all seriously injured individuals.

The symptoms are: pale or bluish skin that is cold to the touch (in the case of dark-skinned persons, examine the color of the mucous membranes inside the mouth or under the eyelids, or of the nail beds); moist or clammy skin; weakness of the injured person; rapid pulse; increased rate of breathing, which may be shallow, possibly deep, and irregular; severe thirst; vomiting or retching from nausea.

With possible neck or back injury, a victim should not be moved. Otherwise, a person in shock should be kept lying down and covered only enough to keep him from losing body heat. (*Do not* add extra heat, because raising the body's surface temperature is harmful.)

A patient with severe injuries of the lower face and jaw or who is unconscious should be placed on the side, with care taken to prevent suffocation from vomit and blood. When in doubt about the proper position, keep the person lying flat, making sure the head is not lower than the rest of the body. Fluids may be given by mouth only when medical help is not available. But fluids *should not* be given to persons who are unconscious, are vomiting, or are having convulsions.

## Cardiac Pulmonary Resuscitation (CPR) for Cardiac Arrest[1]

The most common signal of a heart attack is uncomfortable pressure, squeezing, fullness, or pain in the center of the chest behind the breastbone; others may be sweating, nausea, shortness of breath or a feeling of weakness. These signals may subside and return.

**Airway:** Determine if the collapsed person is conscious by shaking his shoulder and shouting "Are you all right?". If there is no response, you must open his airway. Be sure he is lying flat on his back. If you have to roll him over, move his entire body as a total unit.

To open the airway, lift up his neck (or chin) gently with one hand while pushing down on the forehead with the other to tilt the head back. Place your ear close to the victim's mouth. Look at his chest and stomach for movement. Listen for sounds of breathing. Feel for breath on your cheek.

If none of these signs is present, the victim is not breathing.

**Breathing:** Use the mouth-to-mouth technique. Turn the hand on the victim's forehead and pinch his nose shut while maintaining the head tilt with the heel of the hand. The other hand should remain under the victim's neck (or chin), lifting up.

Immediately give four quick, full breaths in rapid succession.

**Check Pulse:** After giving four quick breaths, locate the victim's carotid pulse to see if his heart is beating. Take the hand that is under the victim's neck and locate the voice box. Slide the tips of your index and middle fingers into the groove beside the voice box. Feel for the pulse.

If you cannot find the pulse, you must provide artificial circulation in addition to rescue breathing.

**Cardiac Compression:** To perform external cardiac compression, kneel at the victim's side near his chest. Locate the lowest portion of the sternum (breastbone). Place the heel of one hand about 1 to 1½ inches from that tip and the other on top of the first. Be sure to keep the fingers off the chest wall. You may find it easier to do by interlocking the fingers.

Bring your shoulders directly over the victim's sternum as you compress downward, keeping your arms straight. Depress the sternum about 1½ to 2 inches for an adult victim. Relaxation must follow compression immediately and be of equal time. Do *not* remove your hands from the sternum.

If you are the only rescuer, you must provide both rescue breathing and cardiac compression at the ratio of 15 chest compressions to 2 quick breaths. You must compress at the rate of 80 times per minute, since you will lose compressions when you take time to interpose these breaths.

If there is another rescuer, position yourselves on opposite sides of the victim. One should interpose a breath after every fifth compression; the other should compress the chest at a rate of 60 compressions per minute.

**For Infants and Small Children:** Do not exaggerate the backward position of the head tilt because it might block breathing passages.

Do not try to pinch off the nose. Cover both the mouth and nose if the victim is not breathing. Use small breaths with less volume to inflate the lungs. Give one small breath every 3 seconds.

Only one hand is used for compression. The other is slipped under the child to provide a firm support for his back.

For infants, use only the *tips* of the index and middle fingers to compress the chest at mid-sternum, depressing between ½ to ¾ inch at a rate of 80 to 100 times per minute.

For small children, use only the *heel* of one hand to compress the chest at midsternum, depressing between ¾ and 1½ inches, depending on the size of the child. The rate should be 80 to 100 times per minute.

For both infants and small children, breaths should be interposed after every fifth chest compression.

**Neck Fracture:** If the victim is injured in a diving or automobile accident, the possibility of a neck fracture should be considered. The airway should be opened by using a modified jaw thrust, keeping the victim's head in a fixed, neutral position.

## The Heimlich Maneuver[2]

Food-choking is caused by a piece of food lodging in the throat creating a blockage of the airway, making it impossible for the victim to breathe or speak. The victim will die of strangulation in four minutes if you do not act to save him.

Using the Heimlich Maneuver, you exert pressure that forces the diaphragm upward, compresses the air in the lungs, and expels the object blocking the breathing passage.

The victim should see a physician immediately after the rescue. Performing the Maneuver could result in injury to the victim. However, he will survive only if his airway is quickly cleared.

If no help is at hand, victims should attempt to perform the Heimlich Maneuver on themselves by pressing their own fists upward into the abdomen as described.

**What to Look for:** The victim of food-choking: (1) Cannot speak or breathe, (2) turns blue, (3) collapses.

**Performing the Heimlich Maneuver with the rescuer standing and the victim standing or sitting:** Stand behind the victim and wrap your arms around his waist.

Place your fist thumb side against the victim's abdomen, slightly above the navel and below the rib cage.

Grasp your fist with your other hand and press into the victim's abdomen with a **quick upward thrust.**

(When the victim is sitting, the rescuer stands behind the victim's chair and performs the Maneuver in the same manner.)

**With the rescuer kneeling and the victim lying face up:** Facing the victim, kneel astride his hips.

With one of your hands on top of the other, place the heel of your bottom hand on the abdomen slightly above the navel and below the rib cage.

Press into the victim's abdomen with a **quick upward thrust.**

Repeat several times if necessary.

 Teaching slides, posters, wallet cards, and other instructional materials on the Heimlich Maneuver are now available. To obtain these send a self-addressed, stamped envelope to: Edumed, Inc., Box 52, Cincinnati, Ohio 45201.

## Automobile Expense

The American Automobile Association says the cost of owning and operating the average 1978 intermediate-size car is 19.6¢ per mile ($1,957 a year), down from 20.2¢ for the 1977-model car.

## Increasing Foreign Investment in the U.S.

Foreign investment activity in the U.S. from October 1977 to April 1978 was the highest for any comparable period since the Conference Board has been compiling such data.

The United Kingdom and West Germany accounted for nearly half (39) of the first-quarter 1978 investments. Following were Canada (10), Japan (7), and France and Switzerland (6 each).

California attracted 11 foreign manufacturing investments during the first quarter of 1978, leading all other states. Following were New York (8), Georgia, New Jersey, and South Carolina (6 each), and Michigan (5).

The foreign investment trend was fueled by the acquisition of U.S. firms rather than by construction of new plants here. The most favored industries for foreign buyers were industrial machinery and chemical firms, along with food, soft drink, and publishing companies.

# The Year in Education

*William W. Turnbull*
*President, Educational Testing Service*

Perhaps the most important trend in education, and one of the most heartening, in the 1970s is the gradual emergence of the individual as the arbiter of the critical choices that affect his or her life. As young people face an enormously expanded array of choices about education, careers, and "lifestyle," they are assuming responsibility for self-management at markedly younger ages than their parents. Increasingly, the main job of the schools is seen as helping to develop self-sufficient individuals, and the consequent pressures on educators and teachers have greatly multiplied.

## Accountability

Not the least of those pressures in 1978 is the increased demand from parents and students for accountability by all segments of the educational community. As students struggle through the labyrinth of critical choices, they want good teachers and reasonable discipline policies. They want fair tests, they want options, and they want diverse course offerings. Concurrently, parents want to make certain that their tax dollars have at least enabled children to read, write, and compute at levels sufficient to meet their needs.

The insistent call for accountability has, in turn, important effects on the educational community. Perhaps the most notable result, and the one that distinguished 1978 from other periods in education, is the widespread concern with the results of the educational process—the outcome as measured by student ability to *perform*.

## A Return to Basics

For instance, parents and educators alike were dismayed when the College Board revealed that the scores of the Scholastic Aptitude Test (SAT) that measures verbal and mathematical abilities had declined steadily over the past 14 years. In an intensive inquiry into the reasons for the decline, an advisory panel found complex causes. They included too much television watching, lowering of educational standards in reading and writing, a decrease in emphasis on "home learning," and years of "national disillusionment" created by the Vietnam War and Watergate. Also, the group taking the tests included many students of limited academic ability—students who, a generation ago, might not have remained in school through grade 12, and who would not then have taken an SAT in the first place.

One response by the public to the decline in scores was a loud and clear call for a return to basics in the schools. Today, children are being given drills on punctuation, vocabulary, and math tables—tasks that might well have been avoided by their older brothers and sisters. It is apparent, however, that a narrow interpretation of basic-skill teaching, which emphasizes "fundamentals" to the exclusion of broad-scale reading and writing, may not provide the hoped-for improvement in student performance.

From some of the rhetoric surrounding the new emphasis on teaching basic skills, one might conclude there had been no serious teaching in the United States since the disappearance of the McGuffey readers. While such rhetoric does the educational community a disservice, the decline in reading, writing, and math proficiency cannot be ignored. As a result, we see now, not only changes in curriculum, but also a new and concentrated commitment to testing minimum competency in the schools. No longer can students count on automatic promotion and graduation from high school, regardless of accomplishment. Nearly every state in the country has adopted some kind of minimum competency requirement, and many colleges have instituted freshman competency tests in reading, writing, and math.

Some change in student performance is already indicated. By mid-1978, the College Board reported that scores were roughly on a par with those of the previous year, perhaps a sign that the downward trend has been arrested.

## Difficult Choices—Difficult Times

Questions raised by the swing back to basics involve difficult choices. What courses should be eliminated in high school curricula to make room for more basics? Will the arts suffer? Or personal development? Or physical education?

For school boards and administrators, this is an introspective period, a time of self-evaluation in response to demands for accountability. As teaching jobs become more scarce, teachers are subjected to greater scrutiny than in previous years. Hiring practices are being redefined; tenured teachers are being evaluated and pressured to improve where needed. They respond by voicing greater demands for job security and protection from arbitrary decisions. Administrators also face new challenges. As taxpayers oppose higher taxes, curricula must sometimes be trimmed. In some states, schools are depending more on the income tax for support than on the property tax, thus reducing the inequity between wealthy and poor districts.

Standardized testing itself is the subject of heated controversy. Students and consumer groups question the value, validity, and reliability of tests. Even as testing becomes more widespread through new minimum competency programs, responsible test-makers are cautioning schools to use the tests as only one measure of student ability and not to emphasize test scores to the exclusion of other evidence of student performance.

Assessment, however, is a valuable aid for pinpointing student problems. It enables both the school district and the individual to evaluate and strengthen areas where weaknesses are indicated. If testing begins when children are young and remedial work is prescribed when indicated, both students and schools will benefit from the test programs.

## Special Education

Nineteen seventy-eight was a year when both educators and the federal government seemed especially preoccupied with helping children whose needs are extraordinary. James Bryant Conant (whose death in February 1978 marked the end of a brilliant educational career) was a man of vision who, as far back as the early 1950s, urged that the public school system in the United States become more responsive to the needs of the diverse population of this country—the blacks, the poor, the ethnic groups who contribute so much to the nation's strength. His ideas continue to influence the educational community.

For instance, the federal government has moved firmly to aid elementary and secondary school children in poor areas by extending financial support to help meet the enormous problems created by extreme poverty. In a related area, desegregation efforts continue, although progress, while evident in some cities, is negligible in others. Also, the special needs of the Spanish-speaking child are being addressed in a number of states by bilingual programs and by recruiting qualified teachers proficient in both languages.

One federal program resulted in changes in school facilities. A new law now protects the rights of the handicapped and brings them into the mainstream of education. Whenever possible, handicapped students are now placed in regular classrooms of the public schools. To make this possible, all schools and colleges were ordered to provide appropriate facilities, such as wheelchair ramps.

Special education continues to grow. Children with learning disabilities are identified in increasing numbers, each requiring tutorial help outside regular classes. The principle of "mainstreaming" these children, so they can interact on a daily basis with their peers, keeps only the most severely disabled in special classrooms.

Gifted children, too—those who display extraordinary academic or creative talents—are gaining recognition as individuals with special needs. The schools seek new ways to challenge their minds and their creativity to insure full development of their potential. Thus, special education—whether for the gifted or the handicapped—represents a major breakthrough for the individual in the schools.

## The Cost of Education

The cost of higher education is increasing dramatically. Many institutions, facing greatly increased costs of fuel and other necessities and a concurrent drop in student enrollment, respond with tuition increases that have their greatest impact on the middle-income family. As the cost of higher education rises, both federal and state governments are debating the need for adopting tuition aid in the form of tax relief.

## The Bakke Case

In higher education, concern over the celebrated case of Alan Bakke is nationwide. Bakke, who is white, was twice refused admission to the University of California medical school at Davis. He then sued the school, citing the equal protection clause of the U.S. Constitution, on grounds that giving preference to blacks, who he said were less qualified than he, violated his constitutional rights. The University of California claimed, in its defense, that the students who were admitted with lower scores and grades than Bakke demonstrated other qualities that justified their acceptance. The U.S. Supreme Court in its decision in June, while deciding the issue on narrow grounds that insured further challenges to the practice, found enough evidence in favor of Mr. Bakke to compel colleges and professional schools to re-examine admissions policies and make them more equitable. Alan Bakke clearly demonstrated that an individual can challenge, and even change, institutional policies in a way seldom seen before in education.

## Lifelong Education

Although education has traditionally been the province of the young, the emergence of learning as a lifelong pursuit constitutes a major development in education today. Adult needs are changing. Men and women are making mid-life career choices, or discovering a need to keep current with new technologies, or simply enriching their lives. Many church groups and senior organizations now sponsor informal late-in-life educational programs. Learning is no longer restricted by time and age.

For those desiring college credits, there are more degree-granting programs. Many institutions are also increasingly willing to give credit for non-traditional learning—for what has been learned in life. For others, college credit may not be important, but the pursuit of continuing education, to fill gaps in professional careers or open the way to new interests, may be.

Such pursuits illustrate the realization of one American dream: that men and women can enjoy learning unfettered by grade-seeking and other pressures that traditionally have accompanied education. Learning for its own sake must, in the final analysis, provide the greatest potential for individual growth.

# What Do Those Scores Mean?

How scores on standardized tests are interpreted and used is critically important. Although testing can provide much valuable information about student achievement and ability, administrators and teachers need to make responsible judgments about how the test results are used. For instance, scores should not be the sole basis for determining college or graduate school admissions, nor should tests be used alone in any final determinations about grade placement or instructional needs. Rather, they give the most accurate picture when combined with other information, such as grades and personal observations.

Among the types of tests young people are most likely to encounter are college admissions tests, such as the Scholastic Aptitude Test (SAT) and the American College Testing (ACT) Program, and achievement tests administered by their schools. Recently, tests determining minimum competency in the basic skills—reading, writing, and math—

have attracted a great deal of national attention.

Test-makers distinguish between types of achievement tests by dividing them into two tongue-twisting categories—*criterion-referenced* tests and *norm-referenced* tests. In simple terms, criterion-referenced tests measure a student's mastery of a certain skill, or knowledge of a field of subject matter, but no attempt is made to compare the student's proficiency with that of other students. Either the skill is mastered or it is not. Minimum compentency tests and most teacher-made tests are examples of criterion-referenced tests.

Norm-referenced tests not only measure student achievement or aptitude—how much the student has learned—but also compare his/her performance on the test with others who have taken the test or others in the same grade across the country. Of the millions of achievement tests administered in elementary and secondary schools each year, most are norm-referenced tests.

For parents and students alike, interpreting test scores can be a chore. Perhaps a brief glossary of terms will help:

**Score Scale.** The range of scores given on any test. For instance, the College Board Admissions Testing Program, the Law School Admission Test, and the Graduate Management Admission Test use score scales ranging from a low of 200 to a high of 800.

**Raw Score.** A score based on the number of correct answers or, in some tests, the number of correct responses minus a fraction of the incorrect ones.

**Percentile Rank.** A number indicating where the student placed in relation to others. A percentile rank of 75 means that the student did as well or better than 75% of some other specified group of students and not as well as 25% of it. The comparisons may be made with others taking the same test or with others in the same age group or grade across the country.

**Standard Error of Measurement.** An estimate of the range of scores that might be expected if one individual took the test several times. Test-makers give the standard error for each test as a reminder to the public that tests are not perfect and should not be regarded as perfect or unchangeable. The smaller the standard error of measurement, the more confidence a test-taker can have in an actual score.

**Grade-Equivalent Score.** A numerical designation used to describe a student's achievement level in terms of grade and month. For instance, a sixth-grade student may be scored as reading on an 8.2 level, meaning on the level expected of an eighth grader in the second month of school. Although widely used in elementary and secondary school tests, grade-equivalent scores can be misleading if they are used to describe achievement above or below the student's actual grade.

## A Testing Dictionary

In recent years, increasing attention has been paid to *testing*—for admission to schools, for employment, and for increased self-awareness. This listing of established, frequently used achievement, intelligence, and psychological tests from a broad range of test publishers was compiled by the Educational Testing Service. It briefly describes what these tests measure, and how they are used.

**Advanced Placement Program Act.** These tests are designed to measure advanced student achievement in a variety of subject areas. They are generally taken by the student in grades 10–12 who is entering college and who wishes to receive credit for college-level work completed during high school. Most colleges in the United States give credit or advanced-placement standing or both for college-level courses taken in the student's own high school.

**American College Testing Program (ACT).** A series of measures in English, mathematics, social sciences, and natural sciences, which is designed to measure the academic development of the college-bound student who takes these tests in grades 11–13. Scores are reported to the individual student, as well as to the secondary school and designated colleges. Results provide information helpful in formulating educational plans.

**Basic Skills Assessment Program.** This program for students in grades 8–12 measures student mastery of basic skills in reading, writing, and mathematics. By determining the competency of each student, this program assists the teacher in identifying the need for additional educational assistance.

**California Achievement Tests.** The tests of this series may be administered by the classroom teacher to measure the achievement growth of pupils at various levels, from kindergarten through high school. The subject areas include: pre-reading, reading, spelling, language, mathematics, and reference skills. Scores indicate both achievement level and mastery of curriculum goals. Score reports are furnished for the individual student and for the teacher as class lists.

**California Psychological Inventory.** The purpose of this test is to measure specific personality characteristics considered important for social living. Essentially self-administered, the test may be used in schools, colleges, businesses, or counseling agencies. Test results are reported as profiles representing the degree to which individuals exhibit each trait.

**CIRCUS.** CIRCUS assesses the skills of young children (pre-school to second grade) in language, mathematics, perception, information processing, attitudes and interests, and divergent production. Results aid in determining the child's readiness for academic instruction and in identifying particular needs. Scores are reported to the teacher numerically and in sentence format.

**College Board Achievement Tests.** A series of achievement tests that measure knowledge in each of fifteen subject areas. They are designed for the college-bound student and are administered in group sessions. The number of tests taken is decided by the student, and scores are reported to designated colleges.

**College-Level Examination Program (CLEP).** CLEP enables people of all ages to earn college credit by successful achievement on examinations. Two types of tests are offered—General Examinations and Subject Examinations. The General Examinations are based on materials covered in the first two years of college and focus on achievement in five basic areas of the liberal arts: English composition, humanities, mathematics, natural sciences, and social sciences-history. The 47 Subject Examinations measure achievement in specific college courses and are essentially end-of-course tests.

**Comprehensive Tests of Basic Skills (CTBS).** CTBS measures basic academic skills as well as the ability to apply knowledge to everyday living from kindergarten through high school. The general areas of assessment include reading, language, arithmetic, and study skills. Test results may prove useful to school administrators for educational planning and guidance and for determining minimum competency in necessary life-skills.

**Differential Aptitude Tests.** The purpose of this test battery is to measure student potential in each of eight areas. Test results may be used as a basis for educational or vocational planning. It is administered in group sessions, and scores, reported separately for each area, yield a profile of relative strengths and weaknesses for each student.

**Edwards Personal Preference Schedule.** Administered primarily for personal counseling or guidance, this test is used to measure the basic motivations and needs of the individual. The responses may be hand- or machine-scored, and are plotted on an individual profile depicting which of fifteen possible needs are most characteristic of that individual.

**Flanagan Aptitude Classification Tests.** A series of separate tests for senior high school students and adults that may be used in various combinations to evaluate the potential for success in specific careers. Each test measures a different job-related skill and may be self-scored. Tests are generally administered in the course of vocational counseling or to job applicants.

**General Aptitude Test Battery.** This battery of tests is available only for use by State Employment Service offices or approved organizations. Each test measures a specific ability associated with a number of occupations. Test scores provide a basis upon which vocational plans may be made.

**Graduate Management Admission Test.** This test is specifically intended for students who are interested in attending graduate business schools. Verbal, quantitative, and total scores are reported for each student and may be used by the school in screening applicants. Test questions are designed to measure the general abilities associated with success in business and management studies.

**Graduate Record Examinations (GRE).** The purpose of these tests is to determine the scholastic ability of college seniors who wish to continue their education beyond the college level. The scores are typically used by graduate schools to screen applicants. There is a test of general aptitude, which covers verbal, quantitative, and analytical skills. There are also advanced tests available to measure ability in each of twenty specific subject areas. Some of these tests offer subscores that may be used for guidance and placement by the graduate school.

**Henmon-Nelson Tests of Mental Ability.** This series is designed for students from kindergarten through high school to provide an evaluation of the abilities considered important for academic success. Appropriate for classroom testing, the scores are reported as group lists. Individual student scores may prove helpful to parents and teachers as indications of future progress.

**Kuder Preference Record.** To assist high school students and adults in choosing a suitable profession, this test measures the individual's preference for the types of social situations that may influence vocational choice. It is scored by hand, and test results are reported as profiles depicting relative preference for group activities, familiar situations, working with ideas, avoiding conflict, and directing others.

**Kuhlmann-Anderson Intelligence Test, Seventh Edition.** Designed to measure the mental capacities of the student in grades K–12 as an indication of academic potential. Verbal and quantitative abilities are measured in tests for grade 7 and above. All tests may be administered and scored by the school teacher. Student score-reports depict an intelligence quotient, as well as the student's standing in relation to others of the same age.

**Law School Admission Test.** This examination is given to college seniors who are considering application to law school. A general measure of the academic skills related to success in the study of law, score reports are made available to the student and to the schools under consideration. They may be used by law schools in the selection and counseling of applicants for admission.

**Medical College Admission Test.** College seniors wishing to study medicine take this examination to fulfill admissions requirements. Scores are reported to the schools in biology, chemistry, physics, science problems, and skills analysis—reading and quantitative skills.

**Metropolitan Achievement Tests.** This battery of tests is intended to measure academic achievement from kindergarten through junior high. Areas of assessment include: reading, mathematics, word knowledge, language, spelling, science, and social studies. The test may be administered by the teacher to student groups. Score reports are made to each pupil, and group lists are provided to assist teachers and school administrators.

**Minnesota Multiphasic Personality Inventory.** This test is designed for ages 16 through adult to evaluate the personality characteristics that affect social and personal adjustment. It may be used, in conjunction with other measures, in personnel selection or in clinical therapy. It is required, however, that the test administrator have training and experience in testing. A tape-recorded version of the test is available for use with semiliterate and disabled persons.

**National Teachers Examination.** Designed for college students who have completed degree programs in teaching, the tests measure general knowledge within the field of education and readiness for the profession of teaching. Some 26 subject area tests are also available to measure knowledge within specialized fields. Scores are used by school boards in the selection of teaching staff and by states for certification.

**Otis-Lennon Mental Ability Tests.** A test of general mental ability or scholastic aptitude that may be administered to groups by the classroom teacher. There are various levels appropriate for use from kindergarten through high school. The score for each student is reported within a group list, which indicates an intelligence quotient, as well as the student's relative status by age and grade.

**Preliminary Scholastic Aptitude Test (PSAT)/National Merit Scholarship Qualifying Tests.** As an abbreviated version of the *Scholastic Aptitude Test,* this examination is designed to provide sophomores, juniors, or seniors in high school with an indication of their ability to handle college work. Consisting of general verbal and mathematical measures, a third score is also reported that is considered for National Merit Scholarship Programs. Scores are reported to the student, the school principal, and/or the school system.

**Rorschach Technique.** This well-known test is primarily used in clinical therapy for ages 3-up, and may be interpreted only by an experienced examiner. It is designed to identify aspects of the individual's personality through responses to each of a series of inkblots.

**Scholastic Aptitude Test (SAT).** Designed to measure scholastic ability, the SAT is generally required for admission to college. As an indication of the student's readiness for college curricula, verbal and mathematical reasoning skills are assessed. Scores are reported to each student and to designated college admissions offices, where they are used for selecting applicants.

**Stanford Achievement Tests.** This achievement battery is useful for assessing the academic performance of students within the classroom (grades 1–9) or within the entire school system. Skills are measured in the areas of reading comprehension, language, science, social science, and auditory proficiency. The scoring system allows for both individual and group reporting.

**Stanford-Binet Intelligence Scale.** An individually administered test of intelligence that consists of different performance tasks for ages 2-up. Responses may only be recorded and interpreted by an experienced examiner. The test results are reported as an intelligence quotient, which takes into consideration both the age and the performance of the individual being tested.

**STEP III.** The Sequential Tests of Educational Progress are achievement tests for grades 3–12 that measure the extent of student learning in reading, mathematics computation and concepts, writing skills, listening, study skills, science, and social studies. The tests are designed for out-of-level testing within a single classroom.

**The Strong-Campbell Interest Inventory.** A test used to determine the occupational interests of students 16 years and older and adults. Feelings about specific occupations, occupational activities, hobbies, amusements, school subjects, and types of people are analyzed to produce an individual profile. Scores are reported on each of 23 basic Interest Scales, as well as each of 125 Occupational Scales to demonstrate the over-all orientation of the individual.

**Tests of General Educational Development (GED).** These tests measure the educational competency of adults who have not graduated from high school. They provide a means of demonstrating abilities comparable to those of a high school graduate. Measures of language, usage, mathematics, and reading interpretation are available in English, Spanish, and French.

**Wechsler Intelligence Scale for Children.** This test measures general intelligence. The subtests focus on performance tasks and verbal responses. Appropriate for both children and adolescents, the test is administered individually by persons with extensive training in psychological measurement. Analysis of responses yields an intelligence quotient for the individual tested.

**Wonderlic Personnel Test.** In the process of gathering information, a business or industrial personnel office may use this brief test to determine the general mental ability of job applicants. It may be administered either on an individual basis or in groups, and the final score is determined by the number of questions answered correctly. Actual score interpretation is limited to those persons who are experienced in psychological testing procedures.

## Selected Degree Abbreviations

*Source:* This material has been taken from *American Universities and Colleges,* 10th and 11th editions, published by the American Council on Education.

**A.B.** Bachelor of Arts
**Ae.E.** Aeronautical Engineer
**A.M.** Master of Arts
**A.M.T.** Master of Arts in Teaching
**B.A.** Bachelor of Arts
**B.A.E.** Bachelor of Arts in Education, or Bachelor of Art Education, Aeronautical Engineering, Agricultural Engineering, or Architectural Engineering
**B.Ag.** Bachelor of Agriculture
**B.Arch.** Bachelor of Architecture
**B.B.A.** Bachelor of Business Administration
**B.C.E.** Bachelor of Civil Engineering or Bachelor of Christian Education
**B.Ch.E.** Bachelor of Chemical Engineering
**B.D.** Bachelor of Divinity
**B.E.** Bachelor of Education or Bachelor of Engineering
**B.E.E.** Bachelor of Electrical Engineering
**B.F.** Bachelor of Forestry
**B.F.A.** Bachelor of Fine Arts
**B.J.** Bachelor of Journalism
**B.L.S.** Bachelor of Liberal Studies or Bachelor of Library Science
**B.Litt.** Bachelor of Literature
**B.M.** Bachelor of Medicine or Bachelor of Music
**B.Mus.** Bachelor of Music

**B.N.** Bachelor of Nursing
**B.Pharm.** Bachelor of Pharmacy
**B.R.E.** Bachelor of Religious Education
**B.S.** Bachelor of Science
**B.S.Ed.** Bachelor of Science in Education
**C.E.** Civil Engineer
**Chem.E.** Chemical Engineer
**D.B.A.** Doctor of Business Administration
**D.D.** Doctor of Divinity[1]
**D.D.S.** Doctor of Dental Surgery or Doctor of Dental Science
**D.L.S.** Doctor of Library Science
**D.M.D.** Doctor of Dental Medicine
**D.O.** Doctor of Osteopathy
**D.M.S.** Doctor of Medical Science
**D.P.A.** Doctor of Public Administration[2]
**D.P.H.** Doctor of Public Health
**D.R.E.** Doctor of Religious Education
**D.S.W.** Doctor of Social Welfare or Doctor of Social Work
**D.Sc.** Doctor of Science[3]
**D.V.M.** Doctor of Veterinary Medicine
**Ed.D.** Doctor of Education[2]
**Ed.S.** Education Specialist
**E.E.** Electrical Engineer
**E.M.** Engineer of Mines or Mining Engineer
**E.Met.** Engineer of Metallurgy
**I.E.** Industrial Engineer
**J.D.** Doctor of Jurisprudence[2]
**J.S.D.** Doctor of the Science of Law
**L.H.D.** Doctor of Humane Letters[3]
**Litt.M.** Master of Letters[4]
**LL.B.** Bachelor of Laws
**LL.D.** Doctor of Laws[3]
**LL.M.** Master of Laws
**M.A.** Master of Arts
**M.Aero.E.** Master of Aeronautical Engineering
**M.B.A.** Master of Business Administration
**M.C.E.** Master of Christian Education or Master of Civil Engineering
**M.C.S.** Master of Commercial Science or Master of Computer Science
**M.D.** Doctor of Medicine
**M.Div.** Master of Divinity
**M.E.** Master of Engineering
**M.Ed.** Master of Education
**M.Eng.** Master of Engineering
**M.F.** Master of Forestry
**M.F.A.** Master of Fine Arts
**M.L.S.** Master of Library Science
**M.M.** Master of Music
**M.M.E.** Master of Mechanical Engineering or Master of Music Education
**M.Mus.** Master of Music
**M.Nurs.** Master of Nursing
**M.R.E.** Master of Religious Education
**M.S.** Master of Science
**M.S.W.** Master of Social Work
**M.Th.** Master of Theology
**Nuc.E.** Nuclear Engineer
**O.D.** Doctor of Optometry
**Pharm.D.** Doctor of Pharmacy[2]
**Ph.B.** Bachelor of Philosophy
**Ph.D.** Doctor of Philosophy
**S.B.** Bachelor of Science
**Sc.D.** Doctor of Science[3]
**S.J.D.** Doctor of Juridical Science or Doctor of the Science of Law
**S.Sc.D.** Doctor of Social Science
**S.T.B.** Bachelor of Sacred Theology
**S.T.D.** Doctor of Sacred Theology[2]
**S.T.M.** Master of Sacred Theology
**Th.B.** Bachelor of Theology
**Th.D.** Doctor of Theology
**Th.M.** Master of Theology

1. Honorary. 2. Earned and honorary. 3. Usually honorary. 4. Sometimes honorary.

## Academic Costume: Colors Associated With Fields

| Field | Color | Field | Color |
|---|---|---|---|
| Agriculture | Maize | Medicine | Green |
| Arts, Letters, Humanities | White | Music | Pink |
| Commerce, Accountancy, Business | Drab | Nursing | Apricot |
| Dentistry | Lilac | Oratory (Speech) | Silver gray |
| Economics | Copper | Pharmacy | Olive green |
| Education | Light Blue | Philosophy | Dark blue |
| Engineering | Orange | Physical Education | Sage green |
| Fine Arts, Architecture | Brown | Public Admin. including Foreign Service | Peacock blue |
| Forestry | Russet | Public Health | Salmon pink |
| Journalism | Crimson | Science | Golden yellow |
| Law | Purple | Social Work | Citron |
| Library Science | Lemon | Theology | Scarlet |
| | | Veterinary Science | Gray |

## Enrollment Trends

The Census Bureau reported the following enrollment trends:

Kindergarten enrollments showed the greatest decline in history, dropping from 3.5 million to 3.2 million in the 1977-78 school year. The drop almost entirely reflected the fall in the birth rate five years earlier.

Nursery school enrollments in the 1977-78 school year rose to 1.7 million, from 1.5 million the year before.

Elementary school enrollments dropped to 29.2 million in 1977-78, from 29.8 million the year earlier. Private schools enrolled 11% of all elementary school pupils in 1977.

High school enrollment in October 1977 was about the same as a year earlier, 16.7 million.

# Universities—Medieval and Modern

Universities, in the modern sense of the term, sprang up in the 12th and 13th centuries in response to the resurgence of learning that preceded the Renaissance in Europe. Procedure at the early universities was informal, with students gathering at some place in a city to listen to a preeminent teacher. There were no campuses, buildings, or endowments. Actually, the term "university" once meant a guild or corporation; there were, in the medieval period, "universities" of bootmakers, weavers, etc. Thus the university of learning was similar in organization to the guilds. The students filled the role of apprentices, and the teachers were the masters.

The first European university was that of *Salerno* in the 9th century, when it was known as a school of medicine. By the 11th century, it had become one of the most famous medical schools of Europe.

*University of Bologna.* Originated in the 12th century as student guilds for protection against the merchants and citizens of Bologna who had raised prices of food and lodging, it was famous for its legal scholars. The students were organized into two guilds and exercised a great deal of authority over the administration.

Other Italian universities famed in the Middle Ages included those at *Arezzo, Ferrara, Florence, Modena, Naples, Padua, Pavia, Perugia, Siena,* and *Vicenza.*

*University of Paris.* Originated between 1150 and 1170 in a cathedral school on the Île de la Cité, it was later moved to the left (south) bank of the Seine, although it remained under the authority of the chancellor of Notre Dame. It developed into the most famous continental center of learning of its day. Its four principal schools were theology, medicine, law, and arts. By the 14th century, the university had some 40 colleges, of which the *Sorbonne* became the most celebrated.

The universities of Paris and Bologna had a marked influence in the subsequent creation of other university centers. About 1167–68 there was a migration of students from Paris to *Oxford* (founded in the 12th century) and about 1210, from Oxford to *Cambridge* (also founded in the 12th century).

Other famous universities of the Middle Ages include the *University of Toulouse* (1233), *Salamanca* (1243), *Seville* (1254), *Orléans* (1305), *Valladolid* (1346), *Prague* (1347), *Kraków* (1364), *Vienna* (1364), *Erfurt* (1379), *Heidelberg* (1385), *Cologne* (1388), *Leipziq* (1409), *Rostock* (1419), and *Louvain* (1426).

## The Renaissance

The Renaissance gave fresh impetus to the universities of Europe. In France three of importance arose in the 15th century—the *University of Aix* (1409, Provence), the *University of Poitiers* (1431), and the *University of Caen* (1437).

Other French institutions of note that arose in this era were at *Bordeaux* (1441), *Valence* (1452), *Nantes* (1463), and *Bourges* (1465). New European universities were also founded at *Trier* (1450), *Freiburg* (1455), *Ingolstadt* (1469), *Basel* (1460), *Budapest* (1475), *Mainz* (1476), *Uppsala* (1477), *Tübingen* (1477), *Copenhagen* (1479), *Wittenberg* (1502), *Frankfurt an der Oder* (1506), and *Coimbra* (1537).

*St. Andrews,* founded in 1411, was the first university in Scotland. Others were the *University of Glasgow* (1453) and the *University of Aberdeen* (1494). The *University of Edinburgh* was established as a college in the post-Reformation period (1582). In Ireland, *Trinity College* was founded in Dublin in 1591. The earliest Dutch university, *Leyden,* was founded in 1575.

## Reformation and Post-Reformation

Until the Reformation, most of the institutions of higher learning in Europe were under the tutelage of the Catholic Church. After 1520, however, many established universities declared their independence of the Church. Cromwell's rule brought about new scholastic methods at both Oxford and Cambridge and the establishment of new colleges thoroughly imbued with Protestantism.

But the first Protestant university was that of *Marburg,* Germany, founded in 1527. Other Protestant universities were *Königsberg* (1544), *Jena* (1558), *Helmstedt* (1575), *Altdorf* (1575), *Giessen* (1607), *Strasbourg* (1621), and *Halle* (1693).

## 18th, 19th, and 20th Centuries

Among the more famous institutions in this era was *Göttingen* (1736), whose school of history became celebrated throughout Europe. Others were *Erlangen* (1743), *Berlin* (1809), *Lemberg* (Lwów) (1816), *Bonn* (1818), *Helsingfors* (1828), the *National University* at Athens (1837), *Bucharest* (1864), *Tokyo* (1877), *Sofia* (1888), and *Kyoto* (1897).

Among the more famous British universities established in the 19th and 20th centuries were the *University of London* (1828), *Manchester* (1851), the *Mason University College* in Birmingham, later *Birmingham University* (1900), *Liverpool* (1903), *Leeds* (1904), and the *University of Sheffield* (1905). The *University of Wales* (1893) is composed of the colleges of Aberystwyth, Bangor, Cardiff, and Swansea.

There are many large and important universities in the British Commonwealth. In Canada, the famous *McGill University* in Montreal was founded in 1821. Others are the *University of Toronto* (1827), *Queens University* at Kingston, Ont. (1841), *Laval University,* Quebec (1852), *Dalhousie,* Halifax (1818), and *Montreal University* (1878).

The early universities in India were patterned after London University, rather than on the Oxford-Cambridge style, and were purely examining institutions. *Calcutta, Bombay,* and *Madras* universities were founded in 1857 as examining bodies.

In Australia, the state plays an important role in the development of universities. The *University of Melbourne* (1853) has the largest enrollment. Among the others are *Adelaide* (1874), *Tasmania* (1890), *Queensland* (1909), *Sydney* (1850), and *Western Australia* (1911).

There are also many well-endowed universities in New Zealand and other parts of the Commonwealth.

By 1800, Russia had only three universities—*Vilna* (1578), *Dorpat* (1632), and *Moscow* (1755). Other institutions developed later were the *University of Kharkov* (1804), *Kazan* (1804), *Warsaw,* now Polish (originally established 1816, but closed 1832–69), *St. Petersburg* (1819), *St. Vladimir* in Kiev (1835), *Odessa* (1865), and *Tomsk,* in Siberia (1888). The building of universities after the Revolution of 1917 was spurred by the Soviet government.

In China, the growth of universities was hampered by the chaotic state of the government in the 1900s, the recurring civil wars, and the conflict with Japan.

## The United States

Universities in the United States marched in step with the progress of the nation. The early settlers brought a heritage of European culture, which they planted in New England soil. The first university in the country was started as *Harvard College* in 1636, with an endowment totaling 800 pounds. Harvard was to become probably the most famous of the American universities.

The *College of William and Mary* (1693) was the second institution of higher learning established in the colonies. Others started during the colonial period (current names only) are *Yale* (1701, *University of Pennsylvania* (1740), *Princeton* (1746), *Washington and Lee* (1749), *Columbia* (1754), *Brown* (1764), *Rutgers* (1766), and *Dartmouth* (1769).

After the Revolution of 1776, the state tax-supported university was established. The *University of Virginia* (1819) was a notable early example of this type.

Colleges that until the 1970s were designed only for women grew up in the second quarter of the 19th century. Among these are *Mt. Holyoke* (1837), *Elmira* (1855), *Vassar* (1861), *Wells* (1868), *Hunter* (1870), *Wellesley* (1870), *Smith* (1871), and *Bryn Mawr (1885).*

After the middle of the 19th century, under the Morrill acts, Congress began making appropriations for support of agricultural and mechanical-arts colleges on land granted to individual states by the federal government. These now greatly expanded land-grant universities today offer the full range of curricula, but still also confer 99% of the advanced degrees in agriculture and two fifths of all the engineering degrees in the U.S.

In the latter part of the 19th century, universities established by private endowments arose. Typical of these are *Cornell* (1865), which is also a land-grant institution; *Johns Hopkins* (1876); *Stanford* (1885); and the *University of Chicago* (1891).

## School Enrollment, October 1977
**(in thousands)**

| Age | White Enrolled | White Percent | Black Enrolled | Black Percent | Spanish origin[1] Enrolled | Spanish origin[1] Percent | All races Enrolled | All races Percent |
|---|---|---|---|---|---|---|---|---|
| 3 and 4 years | 1,541 | 31.1 | 328 | 35.2 | 89 | 19.5 | 1,935 | 32.0 |
| 5 and 6 years | 5,282 | 95.6 | 997 | 96.5 | 446 | 93.7 | 6,433 | 95.8 |
| 7 to 9 years | 8,571 | 99.5 | 1,505 | 99.3 | 668 | 99.0 | 10,285 | 99.5 |
| 10 to 13 years | 12,325 | 99.4 | 2,162 | 99.0 | 873 | 99.3 | 14,767 | 99.4 |
| 14 and 15 years | 6,839 | 98.5 | 1,148 | 98.8 | 485 | 97.6 | 8,130 | 98.5 |
| 16 and 17 years | 6,222 | 88.5 | 1,056 | 90.8 | 430 | 83.6 | 7,399 | 88.9 |
| 18 and 19 years | 3,159 | 45.5 | 517 | 48.3 | 209 | 40.6 | 3,762 | 46.2 |
| 20 and 21 years | 2,172 | 31.8 | 296 | 29.5 | 108 | 23.1 | 2,540 | 31.8 |
| 22 to 24 years | 1,571 | 16.3 | 200 | 15.2 | 68 | 10.8 | 1,850 | 16.5 |
| 25 to 29 years | 1,595 | 10.6 | 216 | 11.3 | 89 | 9.3 | 1,869 | 10.8 |
| 30 to 34 years | 872 | 6.6 | 139 | 9.0 | 51 | 6.0 | 1,043 | 6.9 |
| Total | 50,149 | 51.6 | 8,564 | 57.7 | 3,516 | 50.8 | 60,013 | 52.5 |

1. Persons of Spanish origin may be of any race. NOTE: Figures include persons enrolled in nursery school, kindergarten, elementary school, high school, and college. *Source:* Department of Commerce, Bureau of the Census.

## Statistics of State School Systems

| Years | Enrollment: Total | Enrollment: Kindergarten through Grade 8 | Enrollment: Grades 9 through 12 and postgraduate | High school graduates[1]: Total | High school graduates[1]: Boys | High school graduates[1]: Girls | Total expenditures (in thousands) | Current expenditure per pupil in average daily attendance |
|---|---|---|---|---|---|---|---|---|
| 1963–64 | 41,025,000 | 29,907,000 | 11,118,000 | 2,290,000 | 1,121,000 | 1,169,000 | $21,324,993 | $ 460 |
| 1965–66 | 42,835,000 | 31,177,000 | 11,658,000 | 2,632,000 | 1,308,000 | 1,324,000 | 26,248,026 | 537 |
| 1967–68[2] | 45,076,000 | 32,495,000 | 12,581,000 | 2,702,000 | 1,341,000 | 1,361,000 | 32,977,182 | 658 |
| 1969–70[2] | 46,531,000 | 33,249,000 | 13,282,000 | 2,896,000 | 1,433,000 | 1,463,000 | 40,683,429 | 816 |
| 1971–72[2] | 47,002,000 | 32,910,000 | 14,092,000 | 3,006,000 | 1,490,000 | 1,516,000 | 48,050,283 | 990 |
| 1973–74[2] | 46,317,000 | 31,960,000 | 14,357,000 | 3,080,000 | 1,515,000 | 1,565,000 | 56,970,355 | 1,207 |
| 1975–76 | 45,735,000 | 31,156,000 | 14,580,000 | 3,153,000[3] | 1,572,000 | 1,581,000 | 70,829,345 | 1,509 |
| 1976–77 | 45,222,000 | 30,612,000 | 14,610,000 | n.a. | n.a. | n.a. | 74,801,266[4] | 1,578 |

1. Regular day school programs. 2. Estimated from fall data. 3. Preliminary data. 4. Estimated. n.a. = not available. *Source:* Department of Health, Education, and Welfare, National Center for Educational Statistics.

## School Enrollment by Grade, Control, and Race

(in thousands)

| Grade level and type of control | White Oct. 1977 | White Oct. 1976 | White Oct. 1970 | Black Oct. 1977 | Black Oct. 1976 | Black Oct. 1970 | All races[1] Oct. 1977 | All races[1] Oct. 1976 | All races[1] Oct. 1970 |
|---|---|---|---|---|---|---|---|---|---|
| Nursery school: Public | 372 | 318 | 198 | 171 | 146 | 129 | 562 | 476 | 333 |
| Private | 942 | 929 | 695 | 78 | 80 | 49 | 1,056 | 1,050 | 763 |
| Kindergarten: Public | 2,153 | 2,423 | 2,233 | 447 | 482 | 374 | 2,665 | 2,962 | 2,647 |
| Private | 458 | 457 | 473 | 50 | 60 | 53 | 526 | 528 | 536 |
| Grades 1–8: Public | 21,312 | 21,947 | 24,923 | 4,166 | 4,256 | 4,668 | 25,983 | 26,698 | 30,001 |
| Private | 2,950 | 2,829 | 3,715 | 221 | 175 | 200 | 3,251 | 3,075 | 3,949 |
| Grades 9–12: Public | 11,980 | 12,093 | 11,599 | 2,269 | 2,187 | 1,794 | 14,505 | 14,541 | 13,545 |
| Private | 1,172 | 1,121 | 1,124 | 59 | 71 | 41 | 1,248 | 1,201 | 1,170 |
| College: Public | 6,743 | 6,657 | 5,168 | 916 | 887 | 422 | 7,925 | 7,739 | 5,699 |
| Private | 2,069 | 1,987 | 1,591 | 187 | 175 | 100 | 2,292 | 2,211 | 1,714 |
| Total: Public | 42,560 | 43,438 | 44,121 | 7,969 | 7,958 | 7,387 | 51,640 | 52,416 | 52,225 |
| Private | 7,591 | 7,323 | 7,598 | 595 | 561 | 443 | 8,373 | 8,065 | 8,132 |
| **Grand total** | 50,151 | 50,761 | 51,719 | 8,564 | 8,519 | 7,830 | 60,013 | 60,481 | 60,357 |

1. Includes persons of Spanish origin. *Source:* Department of Commerce, Bureau of the Census.

## Federal Grants and Loans for Education, Fiscal Year 1978

| Type of support, level, and program area | Amount in millions[1] |
|---|---|
| Grants, total | $17,959.3 |
| Elementary-secondary education | 5,578.7 |
| School assistance in federally affected areas | 490.0 |
| Economic opportunity programs | 3,351.0 |
| Supporting services | 363.4 |
| Teacher corps | 18.5 |
| Vocational education | 390.0 |
| Dependents' schools abroad | 321.5 |
| Public lands revenue for schools | 198.1 |
| Assistance in special areas | 118.8 |
| Veterans' education | 84.2 |
| Emergency school assistance | 200.3 |
| Other | 36.8 |
| Higher education | 8,002.4 |
| Basic research | 1,483.0[2] |
| Research facilities | 326.0[2] |
| Training grants, fellowships and traineeships | $834.1 |
| Facilities and equipment | 157.3 |
| Other institutional support | 472.5 |
| Other student assistance | 4,729.5 |
| Vocational-technical and continuing education | 4,378.1 |
| Vocational-technical & work training | 3,501.0 |
| Veterans' education | 605.6 |
| General continuing education | 189.9 |
| Training state and local personnel | 81.7 |
| Loans, total (higher education) | 486.8 |
| Student loan program, National Defense Education Act | 382.0 |
| College facilities loans | 104.8 |
| **Total grants and loans** | 18,446.0 |

1. Estimated outlay for fiscal year 1978. 2. 1977 data. NOTE: The table lists the federal funds that support education in educational institutions. Excluded are certain other federal funds for education and related activities. n.a. = not available. *Source:* Department of Health, Education, and Welfare, National Center for Educational Statistics.

## Persons Not Enrolled in School, October 1977

(in thousands)

| Age | Population | Total not enrolled Number | Total not enrolled Percent | High school graduate Number | High school graduate Percent | Not high school graduate (dropouts)[1] Number | Not high school graduate (dropouts)[1] Percent |
|---|---|---|---|---|---|---|---|
| 14 and 15 years | 8,255 | 125 | 1.5 | 8 | 0.1 | 117 | 1.4 |
| 16 and 17 years | 8,327 | 928 | 11.1 | 209 | 2.5 | 718 | 8.6 |
| 18 and 19 years | 8,151 | 4,389 | 53.8 | 3,034 | 37.2 | 1,355 | 16.6 |
| 20 and 21 years | 7,990 | 5,450 | 68.2 | 4,198 | 52.5 | 1,252 | 15.7 |
| 22 to 24 years | 11,190 | 9,340 | 83.5 | 7,634 | 68.2 | 1,706 | 15.2 |

1. Persons who are not enrolled in school and who are not high school graduates are considered dropouts. *Source:* Department of Commerce, Bureau of the Census.

## State Compulsory School Attendance Laws

| State | Enactment[1] | Age limits | State | Enactment[1] | Age limits |
|---|---|---|---|---|---|
| Alabama | 1915 | 7–16 | Montana | 1883 | 7–16 |
| Alaska | 1929 | 7–16 | Nebraska | 1887 | 7–16 |
| Arizona | 1899 | 8–16 | Nevada | 1873 | 7–17 |
| Arkansas | 1909 | 7–15 | New Hampshire | 1871 | 6–16 |
| California | 1874 | 6–16 | New Jersey | 1875 | 6–16 |
| Colorado | 1889 | 7–16 | New Mexico | 1891 | 6–17 |
| Connecticut | 1872 | 7–16 | New York | 1874 | 6–16 |
| Delaware | 1907 | 6–16 | North Carolina | 1907 | 7–16 |
| D. C. | 1864 | 7–16 | North Dakota | 1883 | 7–16 |
| Florida | 1915 | 7–16 | Ohio | 1877 | 6–18 |
| Georgia | 1916 | 7–16 | Oklahoma | 1907 | 8–16 |
| Hawaii | 1896 | 6–18 | Oregon | 1889 | 7–18 |
| Idaho | 1887 | 7–16 | Pennsylvania | 1895 | 8–17 |
| Illinois | 1883 | 7–16 | Rhode Island | 1883 | 7–16 |
| Indiana | 1897 | 7–16 | South Carolina | 1915 | 7–16 |
| Iowa | 1902 | 7–16 | South Dakota | 1883 | 7–16 |
| Kansas | 1874 | 7–16 | Tennessee | 1905 | 7–16 |
| Kentucky | 1896 | 7–16 | Texas | 1915[2] | 7–17 |
| Louisiana | 1910 | 7–15 | Utah | 1890 | 6–18 |
| Maine | 1875 | 7–15 | Vermont | 1867 | 7–16 |
| Maryland | 1902 | 6–16 | Virginia | 1908 | 6–17 |
| Massachusetts | 1852 | 6–16 | Washington | 1871 | 8–15 |
| Michigan | 1871 | 6–16 | West Virginia | 1897 | 7–16 |
| Minnesota | 1885 | 7–16 | Wisconsin | 1879 | 6–16 |
| Mississippi | 1918 | 7–13 | Wyoming | 1876 | 7–16 |
| Missouri | 1905 | 7–16 | | | |

1. Date of enactment of first compulsory attendance law. 2. A compulsory school attendance law was contained in a law of 1873 establishing free public schools. However, the provision was omitted in superseding legislation passed in 1876. *Source:* Department of Health, Education, and Welfare, National Center for Educational Statistics.

## High School and College Graduates

**(Public and private schools; beginning in 1959–60, Alaska and Hawaii are included.)**

| Year of graduation | High School | | | College[1] | | |
|---|---|---|---|---|---|---|
| | Men | Women | Total | Men | Women | Total |
| 1900 | 38,075 | 56,808 | 94,883 | 22,173 | 5,237 | 27,410 |
| 1910 | 63,676 | 92,753 | 156,429 | 28,762 | 8,437 | 37,199 |
| 1920 | 123,684 | 187,582 | 311,266 | 31,980 | 16,642 | 48,622 |
| 1929–30 | 300,376 | 366,528 | 666,904 | 73,615 | 48,869 | 122,484 |
| 1939–40 | 578,718 | 642,757 | 1,221,475 | 109,546 | 76,954 | 186,500 |
| 1949–50 | 570,700 | 629,000 | 1,199,700 | 328,841 | 103,217 | 432,058 |
| 1957–58 | 727,500 | 780,400 | 1,505,900 | 241,560 | 121,942 | 363,502 |
| 1959–60 | 898,000 | 966,000 | 1,864,000 | 254,063 | 138,377 | 392,440 |
| 1960–61 | 958,000 | 1,013,000 | 1,971,000 | 254,215 | 144,495 | 398,710 |
| 1961–62 | 941,000 | 984,000 | 1,925,000 | 260,531 | 157,315 | 417,846 |
| 1962–63 | 959,000 | 991,000 | 1,950,000 | 273,169 | 174,453 | 447,622 |
| 1963–64 | 1,121,000 | 1,169,000 | 2,290,000 | 296,676 | 197,477 | 494,153 |
| 1964–65 | 1,314,000 | 1,351,000 | 2,665,000 | 316,286 | 213,717 | 530,003 |
| 1965–66 | 1,308,000 | 1,324,000 | 2,632,000 | 328,853 | 222,194 | 551,047 |
| 1966–67 | 1,332,000 | 1,348,000 | 2,679,000 | 353,349 | 237,198 | 590,547 |
| 1967–68 | 1,341,000 | 1,361,000 | 2,702,000 | 390,507 | 276,203 | 666,710 |
| 1968–69 | 1,402,000 | 1,427,000 | 2,829,000 | 444,380 | 319,805 | 764,185 |
| 1969–70 | 1,433,000 | 1,463,000 | 2,896,000 | 484,174 | 343,060 | 827,234 |
| 1970–71 | 1,456,000 | 1,487,000 | 2,943,000 | 511,138 | 366,538 | 877,676 |
| 1971–72 | 1,490,000 | 1,516,000 | 3,006,000 | 541,313 | 389,371 | 930,684 |
| 1972–73 | 1,501,000 | 1,536,000 | 3,037,000 | 564,680 | 407,700 | 972,380 |
| 1973–74 | 1,515,000 | 1,565,000 | 3,080,000 | 575,843 | 423,749 | 999,592 |
| 1974–75 | 1,541,000 | 1,599,000 | 3,140,000 | 533,797 | 425,052 | 978,849 |
| 1975–76 | 1,572,000[2] | 1,581,000[2] | 3,153,000[2] | 557,817 | 430,578 | 988,395 |

1. Includes bachelor's and first-professional degrees. 2. Preliminary data. NOTE: Because of rounding, details may not add to totals. *Source:* Department of Health, Education, and Welfare, National Center for Education Statistics.

# Elementary and Secondary Public School Statistics, 1975–76

| State | Number of elementary and secondary schools | Pupils enrolled: Elementary: Kindergarten through grade 8[1] | Pupils enrolled: Secondary: Grades 9–12 and postgraduate[1] | Classroom teachers[1] | Pupil/teacher ratio | Annual expenditure[2] (thousands) | Annual expenditure per pupil | Average annual salary of classroom teachers[3] |
|---|---|---|---|---|---|---|---|---|
| Alabama | 812 | 503,000 | 238,000 | 37,000 | 20.0 | $ 912,406 | $1,195 | $ 9,503 |
| Alaska | 334 | 64,000 | 26,000 | 4,440 | 20.3 | 308,629 | 3,710 | 16,906 |
| Arizona | 851 | 348,000 | 147,000 | 23,320 | 21.2 | 788,146 | 1,753 | 11,168 |
| Arkansas | 1,185 | 313,000 | 141,000 | 21,670 | 21.0 | 517,757 | 1,161 | 9,021 |
| California | 7,044 | 2,885,000 | 1,431,000 | 202,610 | 21.3 | 8,114,784 | 1,721 | 14,915 |
| Colorado | 1,246 | 378,000 | 184,000 | 28,260 | 19.9 | 970,500 | 1,605 | 11,554 |
| Connecticut | 1,104 | 426,000 | 200,000 | 36,050 | 17.4 | 1,189,762 | 1,687 | 12,051 |
| Delaware | 189 | 78,000 | 42,000 | 6,190 | 19.4 | 233,000 | 1,871 | 12,110 |
| D.C. | 185 | 88,000 | 36,000 | 6,020 | 20.6 | 246,053 | 2,125 | 14,716 |
| Florida | 1,889 | 1,023,000 | 492,000 | 73,000 | 20.8 | 2,341,173 | 1,576 | 10,780 |
| Georgia | 1,724 | 754,000 | 325,000 | 46,130 | 23.4 | 1,283,701 | 1,323 | 10,641 |
| Hawaii | 212 | 116,000 | 56,000 | 7,860 | 21.9 | 310,791 | 1,817 | 13,665 |
| Idaho | 548 | 133,000 | 64,000 | 9,210 | 21.4 | 288,974 | 1,368 | 9,573 |
| Illinois | 4,506 | 1,478,000 | 727,000 | 109,740 | 20.1 | 4,616,331 | 1,848 | 13,469 |
| Indiana | 2,057 | 770,000 | 376,000 | 52,730 | 21.7 | 1,676,000 | 1,446 | 11,358 |
| Iowa | 1,875 | 392,000 | 204,000 | 33,110 | 18.0 | 1,054,355 | 1,653 | 10,598 |
| Kansas | 1,662 | 285,000 | 145,000 | 25,460 | 16.9 | 707,883 | 1,538 | 9,770 |
| Kentucky | 1,400 | 468,000 | 216,000 | 32,080 | 21.3 | 810,140 | 1,122 | 9,240 |
| Louisiana | 1,265 | 571,000 | 256,000 | 40,150 | 20.6 | 1,063,700 | 1,391 | 9,800 |
| Maine | 825 | 167,000 | 78,000 | 13,140 | 18.6 | 338,300 | 1,406 | 13,202 |
| Maryland | 1,308 | 576,000 | 272,000 | 42,600 | 19.9 | 1,485,947 | 2,054 | 13,282 |
| Massachusetts | 2,417 | 772,000 | 380,000 | 64,240[4] | 17.9 | 2,313,296 | 2,059 | 12,468 |
| Michigan | 3,960 | 1,361,000 | 645,000 | 87,400 | 23.0 | 3,858,736 | 1,902 | 14,224 |
| Minnesota | 1,743 | 544,000 | 306,000 | 44,720 | 19.0 | 1,793,332 | 1,911 | 12,852 |
| Mississippi | 1,069 | 347,000 | 156,000 | 23,970 | 21.0 | 549,000 | 1,072 | 8,338 |
| Missouri | 2,288 | 619,000 | 317,000 | 48,230 | 19.4 | 1,246,624 | 1,389 | 10,257 |
| Montana | 816 | 111,000 | 57,000 | 9,510 | 17.7 | 301,400 | 1,745 | 10,160 |
| Nebraska | 1,804 | 202,000 | 105,000 | 17,730 | 17.3 | 476,850 | 1,477 | 9,715 |
| Nevada | 238 | 94,000 | 46,000 | 5,950 | 23.5 | 212,600 | 1,617 | 12,854 |
| New Hampshire | 475 | 118,000 | 66,000 | 9,560 | 18.1 | 223,232 | 1,493 | 10,010 |
| New Jersey | 2,409 | 943,000 | 463,000 | 79,460 | 17.7 | 2,957,000 | 2,122 | n.a. |
| New Mexico | 610 | 189,000 | 92,000 | 12,800 | 22.0 | 448,908 | 1,509 | 10,200 |
| New York | 4,223 | 2,195,000 | 1,135,000 | 177,260 | 18.8 | 7,824,200 | 2,580 | 15,000 |
| North Carolina | 1,921 | 810,000 | 364,000 | 52,540 | 22.3 | 1,738,623 | 1,394 | 11,275 |
| North Dakota | 765 | 80,000 | 47,000 | 7,500 | 16.9 | 190,925 | 1,408 | 9,176 |
| Ohio | 4,160 | 1,476,000 | 741,000 | 104,870 | 21.1 | 3,363,000 | 1,481 | 11,100 |
| Oklahoma | 1,887 | 399,000 | 190,000 | 30,200 | 19.5 | 792,000 | 1,278 | 9,208 |
| Oregon | 1,282 | 311,000 | 157,000 | 23,780 | 19.7 | 792,000 | 1,995 | 10,958 |
| Pennsylvania | 3,973 | 1,414,000 | 748,000 | 113,530 | 19.0 | 4,526,300 | 1,914 | 12,200 |
| Rhode Island | 343 | 115,000 | 55,000 | 9,100 | 18.7 | 293,413 | 1,722 | 12,885 |
| South Carolina | 1,136 | 417,000 | 195,000 | 30,710 | 19.9 | 782,500 | 1,278 | 9,770 |
| South Dakota | 825 | 96,000 | 50,000 | 8,110 | 18.0 | 210,059 | 1,445 | 8,860 |
| Tennessee | 1,568 | 593,000 | 237,000 | 39,860 | 20.8 | 1,143,529 | 1,214 | 9,878 |
| Texas | 5,283 | 1,962,000 | 819,000 | 42,110 | 19.6 | 3,502,136 | 1,487 | 10,136 |
| Utah | 535 | 212,000 | 98,000 | 12,860 | 24.1 | 484,543 | 1,471 | 10,150 |
| Vermont | 388 | 71,000 | 32,000 | 6,270 | 16.4 | 165,707 | 1,504 | 9,206 |
| Virginia | 1,703 | 739,000 | 346,000 | 59,130 | 18.3 | 1,660,867 | 1,488 | 11,279 |
| Washington | 1,619 | 514,000 | 255,000 | 33,460 | 23.0 | 1,338,549 | 1,684 | 12,538 |
| West Virginia | 1,254 | 280,000 | 119,000 | 20,040 | 20.0 | 561,918 | 1,382 | 9,124 |
| Wisconsin | 2,253 | 592,000 | 340,000 | 49,030 | 19.0 | 1,601,287 | 1,792 | 13,046 |
| Wyoming | 328 | 61,000 | 28,000 | 4,960 | 18.0 | 190,400 | 2,142 | 10,350 |
| **Total** | **85,496** | **29,453,000** | **14,234,000** | **2,178,000** | **20.5** | **74,801,266** | **1,699** | **12,070** |

1. Fall 1977 estimated. 2. 1976–77 estimated. 3. 1974–75 figures estimated. 4. Fall 1976 figure. n.a. = not available.
*Source:* Department of Health, Education, and Welfare, National Center for Education Statistics.

## Women Up in the Air

In 1978, over 50 women were flying in the cockpits of commercial airliners in the U.S. There were none in 1972. Most were flight engineers or second officers; one reached captain's rank. About 30,000 pilots now are flying commercial domestic routes.

## Enrollment in Educational Institutions

| Level of instruction by type of school | Fall, 1975 | Fall, 1969 | 1959–60 | 1949–1950 | 1939–1940 | 1929–1930 |
|---|---|---|---|---|---|---|
| Kindergarten: Public[2] | 2,944,757 | 2,601,242 | 1,922,712 | 1,034,203 | 594,647 | 723,443 |
| Nonpublic[2] | 200,000[1] | 200,000[1] | 354,000 | 133,000 | 57,341 | 54,456 |
| Residential schools for exceptional children | 6,000[1] | 7,000[1] | 4,800 | 4,459[3] | 5,777 | 5,164[4] |
| Other | 12,854 | 12,971 | 11,980 | 3,650 | 3,144 | 3,400 |
| Total kindergarten | 3,163,611 | 2,821,213 | 2,293,492 | 1,175,312 | 660,909 | 786,463 |
| Grades 1–8 inclusive: Public[2] | 27,541,830 | 29,995,626 | 25,679,190 | 18,352,603 | 18,237,451 | 20,555,150 |
| Nonpublic[2] | 3,400,000[1] | 4,000,000[1] | 4,285,696 | 2,574,777 | 2,095,938 | 2,255,430 |
| Residential schools for exceptional children | 83,000[1] | 87,000[1] | 59,400 | 48,894[3] | 55,954 | 124,153[4] |
| Other | 92,690 | 107,551[1] | 94,488 | 55,655 | 76,769 | 18,644 |
| Total grades 1–8 | 31,117,520 | 34,190,177 | 30,118,774 | 21,031,929 | 20,466,112 | 22,953,377 |
| Total kindergarten through grade 8 | 34,281,131 | 37,011,390 | 32,412,266 | 22,207,241 | 21,127,021 | 23,739,840 |
| Grades 9–12: Public high schools[2] | 14,304,359 | 13,021,710 | 8,484,869 | 5,724,621 | 6,601,444 | 4,339,422 |
| Nonpublic high schools[2] | 1,400,000[1] | 1,300,000[1] | 1,035,274 | 672,362 | 457,768 | 341,158 |
| Residential schools for exceptional children | 41,000[1] | 37,000[1] | 23,800 | 9,784[3] | 9,727 | 4,388[4] |
| Other | 58,739 | 59,591[1] | 55,894 | 46,242 | 61,040 | 66,832 |
| Total grades 9–12[5] | 15,804,098 | 14,418,301 | 9,599,810 | 6,453,009 | 7,129,979 | 4,811,800 |
| Total kindergarten through grade 12[5] | 50,085,229 | 51,429,691 | 412,012,076 | 28,660,250 | 28,257,000 | 28,551,640 |
| Higher education: Publicly controlled | 7,425,772 | 5,111,837 | 1,831,782 | 1,354,902 | 796,531 | 532,647 |
| Privately controlled | 2,305,659 | 2,024,238 | 1,383,762 | 1,304,119 | 697,672 | 568,090 |
| Total higher education | 9,731,431 | 7,136,075 | 3,215,544 | 2,659,021 | 1,494,203 | 1,100,737 |
| **Total all levels** | **59,816,660** | **58,565,766** | **45,227,620** | **31,319,271** | **29,751,203** | **29,652,377** |

1. Estimated. 2. Does not include subcollegiate departments of institutions of higher education. 3. 1945–46. 4. 1926–27. 5. And postgraduate. *Source:* Department of Health, Education, and Welfare, National Center for Education Statistics.

## Institutions of Higher Education—Faculty and Enrollment Characteristics and Projections to 1985

**(in thousands except for institutions)**

| Item | 1985 | 1980 | 1975 | 1974 | 1973 | 1972 | 1971 | 1970 | 1965 | 1960 |
|---|---|---|---|---|---|---|---|---|---|---|
| Institutions | n.a. | n.a. | 2,765 | 2,747 | 2,720 | 2,665 | 2,606 | 2,556 | 2,230 | 1,968 |
| 4-year | n.a. | n.a. | 1,767 | 1,744 | 1,717 | 1,701 | 1,675 | 1,665 | 1,551 | 1,447 |
| 2-year | n.a. | n.a. | 998 | 1,003 | 1,003 | 964 | 931 | 891 | 679 | 521 |
| Resident instructional staff | 696 | 730 | 670 | 622 | 599 | 590 | 590 | 573 | 412 | 276 |
| **ENROLLMENT** | | | | | | | | | | |
| Degree credit | 11,000 | 11,142 | 9,731 | 9,023 | 8,518 | 8,265 | 8,116 | 7,920 | 5,526 | 3,583 |
| Male | 5,621 | 5,876 | 5,321 | 4,969 | 4,771 | 4,701 | 4,717 | 4,637 | 3,375 | 2,257 |
| Female | 5,379 | 5,266 | 4,410 | 4,055 | 3,747 | 3,564 | 3,399 | 3,284 | 2,152 | 1,326 |
| 4-year institutions | 7,530 | 7,896 | 7,223 | 6,825 | 6,597 | 6,473 | 6,391 | 6,290 | 4,685 | 3,131 |
| 2-year institutions | 3,470 | 3,246 | 2,508 | 2,198 | 1,921 | 1,792 | 1,725 | 1,630 | 841 | 451 |
| Full-time | 6,139 | 6,585 | 6,147 | 5,817 | 5,683 | 5,647 | 5,676 | 5,489 | 3,910 | 2,466 |
| Part-time | 4,861 | 4,557 | 3,584 | 3,206 | 2,835 | 2,618 | 2,440 | 2,431 | 1,616 | 1,117 |
| Public | 8,756 | 8,721 | 7,426 | 6,838 | 6,389 | 6,159 | 6,014 | 5,800 | 3,624 | 2,116 |
| Private | 2,244 | 2,421 | 2,306 | 2,185 | 2,130 | 2,106 | 2,102 | 2,120 | 1,902 | 1,467 |
| Graduate | 1,456 | 1,468 | 1,263 | 1,190 | 1,123 | 1,066 | 1,012 | 1,031 | 697 | 356[1] |
| Undergraduate[2] | 9,544 | 9,674 | 8,468 | 7,833 | 7,395 | 7,199 | 7,104 | 6,889 | 4,829 | 3,227 |
| percent of persons 18-21 years | 62.4 | 56.7 | 51.2 | 48.4 | 46.6 | 46.4 | 47.0 | 46.6 | 39.0 | 33.2 |
| Male | 4,915 | 5,114 | 4,621 | 4,306 | 4,124 | 4,074 | 4,102 | 4,005 | 2,910 | 2,004 |
| Female | 4,629 | 4,560 | 3,847 | 3,527 | 3,271 | 3,125 | 3,002 | 2,884 | 1,919 | 1,223 |
| 4-year institutions | 6,074 | 6,428 | 5,960 | 5,635 | 5,474 | 5,407 | 5,379 | 5,259 | 3,988 | 2,776 |
| Full-time | 4,421 | 4,830 | 4,619 | 4,429 | 4,350 | 4,350 | 4,358 | 4,234 | 3,159 | 2,077 |
| Part-time | 1,653 | 1,598 | 1,341 | 1,206 | 1,124 | 1,057 | 1,021 | 1,025 | 829 | 699 |
| 2-year institutions | 3,470 | 3,246 | 2,508 | 2,198 | 1,921 | 1,792 | 1,725 | 1,630 | 841 | 451 |
| Public | 7,704 | 7,663 | 6,520 | 5,986 | 5,589 | 5,401 | 5,302 | 5,076 | 3,184 | 1,929 |
| Private | 1,840 | 2,011 | 1,948 | 1,847 | 1,806 | 1,799 | 1,802 | 1,813 | 1,645 | 1,298 |
| 1st time enrolled | 1,709 | 1,936 | 1,910 | 1,854 | 1,757 | 1,740 | 1,766 | 1,780 | 1,442 | 923 |
| Nondegree credit | 2,360 | 2,072 | 1,453 | 1,200 | 1,084 | 950 | 833 | 661 | 395 | 206 |
| **Total** | **13,360** | **13,214** | **11,184** | **10,223** | **9,602** | **9,215** | **8,949** | **7,951** | **5,921** | **3,789** |

1. Includes resident only. 2. Includes first-professional enrollment. NOTE: As of fall. Covers universities, colleges, professional schools, junior and teachers colleges, and normal schools, both publicly and privately controlled, regular session. n.a.- not available. *Source:* Department of Health, Education, and Welfare, National Center for Educational Statistics.

## Median Salaries of Staffs at 4-Year Colleges and Universities

| Position | 1973–74 | 1971–72 | 1969–70 | 1967–68 | 1965–66 | 1963–64 | 1959–60 |
|---|---|---|---|---|---|---|---|
| Instructional staff | | | | | | | |
| All ranks | $14,373 | $12,932 | $11,745 | $10,235 | $ 9,081 | $ 8,163 | $ 6,711 |
| Professors | 19,897 | 18,091 | 16,799 | 14,713 | 12,953 | 11,312 | 9,107 |
| Associate professors | 15,331 | 13,958 | 12,985 | 11,393 | 10,058 | 8,969 | 7,332 |
| Assistant professors | 12,644 | 11,511 | 10,698 | 9,472 | 8,417 | 7,539 | 6,231 |
| Instructors and lecturers | 10,211 | 9,347 | 8,416 | 7,496 | 6,761 | 6,114 | 5,095 |
| Administrative officers | | | | | | | |
| President | 31,342 | 29,750 | 25,979 | 22,303 | 19,638 | 17,330 | 13,827 |
| Vice president | 27,667 | 26,313 | 23,250 | 21,458 | 19,012 | 17,130 | 14,154 |
| Dean of the college | 22,000 | 19,975 | 19,125 | 16,141 | 15,703 | 13,644 | 10,723 |
| Dean of students | 19,117 | 17,830 | 16,050 | 14,086 | 12,027 | 10,694 | 8,796 |
| Dean of admissions | 15,773 | 14,280 | 12,983 | 11,446 | 10,364 | 9,572 | 7,680 |
| Registrar | 14,443 | 13,108 | 11,743 | 10,366 | 9,123 | 8,142 | 6,340 |
| Chief librarian | 16,417 | 14,891 | 13,439 | 11,817 | 10,225 | 8,883 | 7,078 |
| Director of athletics | 17,515 | 15,821 | 14,311 | 12,470 | 11,125 | 9,871 | 8,104 |
| Head football coach | 16,159 | 14,591 | 13,395 | 11,488 | 10,716 | 9,321 | 7,824 |
| Head basketball coach | 14,700 | 13,208 | 11,779 | 10,485 | 9,383 | 8,542 | 6,888 |

NOTE: Salaries of instructional staff are for 9 months of full-time teaching; salaries of administrative officers are usually for 11 or 12 months. From: "Economic Status of the Teaching Profession, 1972–73" and "Summary of Salaries Paid in Higher Education, 1973–74." 
*Source:* Department of Health, Education, and Welfare, National Center for Education Statistics.

## College and University Endowments, 1976–77
(in millions)

| Institution | Endowment (market value) | Voluntary support[1] | Expenditures[2] |
|---|---|---|---|
| Harvard U | $1,456.3 | $65.0 | n.a. |
| Yale U | 555.4 | 28.6 | 190.5 |
| Stanford U | 467.0 | 56.1 | 216.2 |
| Princeton U | 433.6 | 23.1 | 73.1 |
| Massachusetts Inst. of Tech. | 422.4 | 29.4 | 178.2 |
| U of California | 367.3 | 56.2 | 154.6 |
| U of Rochester | 366.0 | 13.1 | 107.9 |
| Columbia U | 287.6 | 32.6 | 225.0 |
| U of Chicago | 278.5 | 33.1 | 369.7 |
| Cornell U | 271.5 | 27.1 | 234.5 |
| Northwestern U | 268.6 | 21.2 | 130.2 |
| New York U | 243.5 | 22.3 | 274.0 |
| Rice U | 242.6 | 9.4 | 30.5 |
| Washington U (St. Louis) | 231.3 | 15.9 | 122.7 |
| Rockefeller U | 185.4 | 9.8 | 31.1 |
| Johns Hopkins U | 177.2 | 21.7 | 147.7 |
| U of Pennsylvania | 167.5 | 31.0 | 262.2 |
| Emory U | 164.2 | 10.1 | 65.2 |
| Dartmouth C | 157.5 | 12.7 | 54.8 |
| California Inst. of Tech. | 155.5 | 15.2 | 65.7 |
| U of Virginia | 139.8 | 16.3 | 96.1 |
| Duke U | 121.9 | 20.8 | 108.3 |
| U of Michigan | 117.6 | 27.0 | 294.1 |
| Vanderbilt U | 115.6 | 11.5 | 68.9 |
| Carnegie-Mellon U | 112.5 | 5.4 | 48.6 |
| Wellesley C | 109.6 | 7.1 | 16.3 |
| Wesleyan U | 107.9 | 1.4 | 20.6 |
| Delaware U | 104.9 | 3.7 | 70.2 |
| U of So. California | 103.8 | 37.1 | 180.8 |
| Case Western Reserve U | 101.9 | 27.3 | 82.5 |
| U of Notre Dame | $100.8 | $12.8 | $46.1 |
| Brown U | 96.6 | 8.9 | 49.6 |
| U of Pittsburgh | 88.2 | 5.2 | 158.5 |
| U of Minnesota | 87.2 | 33.9 | 334.0 |
| Oberlin C | 85.7 | 4.9 | 19.4 |
| Rensselaer Poly. Inst. | 85.6 | 4.0 | 34.5 |
| Smith C | 83.1 | 9.2 | 20.3 |
| Claremont Colleges | 80.8 | 20.0 | 31.4 |
| Trinity U | 79.6 | 2.5 | 14.0 |
| Amherst C | 77.6 | 2.6 | 12.7 |
| U of Kansas | 76.9 | 8.3 | 151.1 |
| Williams C | 73.5 | 7.4 | 13.0 |
| U of Washington | 73.4 | 12.4 | 237.3 |
| Berea C | 71.7 | 5.0 | 7.1 |
| Vassar C | 68.7 | 4.9 | 14.0 |
| Swarthmore C | 63.8 | 3.3 | 9.4 |
| Ohio State U | 61.8 | 11.4 | 251.5 |
| Southern Methodist U | 59.7 | 11.0 | 38.5 |
| U of Richmond | 59.2 | 3.2 | 11.4 |
| U of Wisconsin (Madison) | 58.7 | 23.2 | 269.6 |
| St. Louis U | 57.0 | 5.8 | 48.6 |
| Lehigh U | 56.6 | 7.4 | 30.2 |
| Syracuse U | 55.6 | 5.6 | 89.7 |
| Brandeis U | 53.6 | 11.5 | 33.2 |
| Baylor U | 50.2 | 9.1 | 20.9 |
| Thomas Jefferson U | 49.1 | 4.8 | 31.4 |
| Mount Holyoke C | 48.9 | 5.2 | 10.8 |
| Buffalo State U | 48.7 | 1.3 | 117.0 |
| Lafayette C | 48.4 | 2.3 | 10.3 |
| Stevens Inst. of Tech. | 47.8 | 1.9 | 14.5 |

1. Gifts from business, alumni, religious denominations, and others. 2. Figure represents about 80% of typical operating budget. Does not include auxiliary enterprises and capital outlays. NOTE: C—College; U—University; n.a.—not available. *Source:* Council for Financial Aid to Education.

## Degrees Conferred by Institutions of Higher Education, 1975–1976

| Field of study | Bachelor's[1] | Master's | Doctorate |
|---|---|---|---|
| Agriculture and natural resources | 19,402 | 3,340 | 928 |
| Architecture and environmental design | 9,146 | 3,215 | 82 |
| Area studies | 3,079 | 945 | 182 |
| Biological sciences | 54,275 | 6,582 | 3,392 |
| Business and management | 143,436 | 42,620 | 956 |
| Communications | 21,282 | 3,126 | 204 |
| Computer and information sciences | 5,652 | 2,603 | 244 |
| Education | 154,758 | 127,948 | 7,769 |
| Engineering | 46,331 | 16,342 | 2,821 |
| Fine and applied arts | 42,138 | 8,817 | 620 |
| Foreign languages | 15,471 | 3,531 | 864 |
| Health professions | 53,958 | 12,556 | 577 |
| Home economics | 17,409 | 2,179 | 178 |
| Letters | 51,515 | 11,293 | 2,447 |
| Library sciences | 843 | 8,037 | 71 |
| Mathematics | 15,984 | 3,857 | 856 |
| Military sciences | 1,177 | — | — |
| Physical sciences | 21,465 | 5,466 | 3,431 |
| Psychology | 49,908 | 7,811 | 2,581 |
| Public affairs and services | 33,238 | 17,106 | 319 |
| Social sciences | 126,785 | 15,874 | 4,160 |
| Total, all fields | 925,746 | 311,771 | 34,064 |
| Dentistry (D.D.S. or D.M.D.) | 5,425 | — | — |
| Law, (LL.B. or J.D.) | 32,293 | — | — |
| Medicine (M.D.) | 13,426 | — | — |
| Theological professions (B.D., M.Div., Rabbi) | 5,706 | — | — |
| Total, professional | 62,649 | — | — |
| **Total** | **988,395** | **311,771** | **34,064** |

1. Includes Bachelor of Arts, Bachelor of Science, and first-professional degrees. *Source:* Department of Health, Education, and Welfare, National Center for Educational Statistics.

## Major U.S. College and University Libraries
(over 1.75 million volumes)

| Institution | Volumes | Microforms[1] |
|---|---|---|
| Harvard | 9,547,576 | 1,501,444 |
| Yale | 6,884,604 | 992,994 |
| U of Illinois | 5,828,980 | 1,358,993 |
| U of Michigan | 4,917,381 | 1,406,214 |
| U of California, Berkeley | 4,917,330 | 1,084,450 |
| Columbia | 4,730,492 | 1,707,474 |
| Indiana | 4,399,020 | 1,271,750 |
| Stanford | 4,363,593 | 1,630,598 |
| U of Texas | 4,053,715 | 1,621,400 |
| Cornell | 3,979,581 | 1,632,462 |
| U of California, Los Angeles | 3,908,053 | 1,513,356 |
| U of Chicago | 3,886,130 | 572,833 |
| U of Minnesota | 3,363,576 | 941,976 |
| Ohio State | 3,257,759 | 1,145,094 |
| U of Wisconsin | 3,238,152 | 1,339,646 |
| U of Washington | 3,236,944 | 2,397,288 |
| Princeton | 2,910,461 | 1,095,090 |
| Duke | 2,869,558 | 273,712 |
| U of Pennsylvania | 2,784,260 | 1,037,125 |
| Northwestern | 2,594,777 | 669,946 |
| New York University | 2,501,672 | 1,126,567 |
| Michigan State | 2,325,795 | 973,852 |
| U of North Carolina | 2,274,173 | 1,198,980 |
| U of Pittsburgh | 2,174,868 | 938,931 |
| U of Virginia | 2,143,226 | 1,931,786 |
| Johns Hopkins | 2,101,525 | 993,789 |
| U of Iowa | 2,055,581 | 1,085,982 |
| Rutgers | 1,995,278 | 1,136,954 |
| U of Kansas | 1,962,539 | 737,245 |
| Pennsylvania State | 1,957,276 | 1,804,111 |
| U of Arizona | 1,955,196 | 933,925 |
| U of Missouri | 1,882,394 | 1,778,760 |
| U of Florida | 1,852,841 | 927,500 |
| U of Southern California | 1,792,782 | 994,927 |

1. Includes reels of microfilm and number of microcards, microprint sheets, and microfiches. *Source:* Association of Research Libraries.

## Education of U.S. Adults, 1977
(in thousands)

| Age group | Total population | Less than 4 years high school | High school, 4 years | College, 1 year or more | Median years of school completed |
|---|---|---|---|---|---|
| **WHITE** | | | | | |
| 18 and 19 years | 6,977 | 2,461 | 3,643 | 874 | 12.3 |
| 20 to 24 years | 16,544 | 2,463 | 7,276 | 6,806 | 12.8 |
| 25 to 29 years | 15,191 | 2,006 | 6,031 | 7,154 | 12.9 |
| 30 to 34 years | 12,981 | 2,259 | 5,168 | 5,553 | 12.8 |

| Age group | Total population | Less than 4 years high school | High school, 4 years | College, 1 year or more | Median years of school completed |
|---|---|---|---|---|---|
| 35 to 39 years | 10,491 | 2,435 | 4,450 | 3,606 | 12.6 |
| 40 to 44 years | 9,704 | 2,463 | 4,213 | 3,027 | 12.6 |
| 45 to 49 years | 10,131 | 3,113 | 4,149 | 2,871 | 12.5 |
| 50 to 54 years | 10,555 | 3,620 | 4,289 | 2,646 | 12.4 |
| 55 to 59 years | 9,775 | 3,682 | 3,873 | 2,220 | 12.3 |
| 60 to 64 years | 8,368 | 3,711 | 3,008 | 1,648 | 12.2 |
| 65 to 69 years | 7,373 | 3,853 | 2,072 | 1,448 | 11.4 |
| 70 to 74 years | 5,383 | 3,210 | 1,231 | 942 | 10.0 |
| 75 years and over | 7,264 | 5,013 | 1,227 | 1,025 | 8.8 |
| **BLACK** | | | | | |
| 18 and 19 years | 1,057 | 593 | 367 | 96 | 11.8 |
| 20 to 24 years | 2,322 | 573 | 1,014 | 735 | 12.6 |
| 25 to 29 years | 1,899 | 486 | 823 | 589 | 12.6 |
| 30 to 34 years | 1,501 | 492 | 624 | 385 | 12.4 |
| 35 to 39 years | 1,265 | 507 | 483 | 275 | 12.3 |
| 40 to 44 years | 1,196 | 584 | 405 | 207 | 12.0 |
| 45 to 49 years | 1,151 | 754 | 259 | 137 | 10.6 |
| 50 to 54 years | 1,105 | 701 | 265 | 139 | 10.3 |
| 55 to 59 years | 923 | 634 | 185 | 102 | 9.2 |
| 60 to 64 years | 807 | 644 | 121 | 42 | 8.4 |
| 65 to 69 years | 790 | 663 | 76 | 50 | 8.0 |
| 70 to 74 years | 445 | 385 | 42 | 19 | 6.3 |
| 75 years and over | 618 | 532 | 43 | 43 | 5.8 |
| **SPANISH ORIGIN[1]** | | | | | |
| 18 and 19 years | 497 | 292 | 163 | 43 | 11.7 |
| 20 to 24 years | 1,085 | 418 | 392 | 274 | 12.3 |
| 25 to 29 years | 915 | 385 | 313 | 219 | 12.2 |
| 30 to 34 years | 792 | 404 | 233 | 155 | 11.8 |
| 35 to 39 years | 679 | 378 | 185 | 117 | 11.0 |
| 40 to 44 years | 586 | 366 | 150 | 71 | 10.0 |
| 45 to 49 years | 521 | 324 | 118 | 78 | 9.2 |
| 50 to 54 years | 398 | 292 | 67 | 41 | 8.2 |
| 55 to 59 years | 317 | 240 | 54 | 23 | 7.8 |
| 60 to 64 years | 243 | 195 | 35 | 16 | 7.9 |
| 65 to 69 years | 192 | 155 | 24 | 15 | 6.7 |
| 70 to 74 years | 127 | 112 | 10 | 4 | 4.0 |
| 75 years and over | 146 | 123 | 13 | 11 | 4.5 |

1. Persons of Spanish origin may be of any race. *Source:* Department of Commerce, Bureau of the Census.

## Earned Degrees by Sex of Student

| Degree level | 1975–76 | 1974–75 | 1973–74 | 1972–73 | 1971–72 | 1970–71 | 1965–66 |
|---|---|---|---|---|---|---|---|
| Bachelor's | 925,746 | 922,933 | 945,776 | 922,362 | 887,273 | 839,730 | 520,248 |
| Men | 504,925 | 504,841 | 527,313 | 518,191 | 500,590 | 475,594 | 299,196 |
| Women | 420,821 | 418,092 | 418,463 | 404,171 | 386,683 | 364,136 | 221,052 |
| First professional[1] | 62,649 | 55,916 | 53,816 | 50,018 | 43,411 | 37,946 | 30,799 |
| Men | 52,892 | 48,956 | 48,530 | 46,489 | 40,723 | 35,544 | 29,657 |
| Women | 9,757 | 6,960 | 5,286 | 3,529 | 2,688 | 2,402 | 1,142 |
| Master's | 311,771 | 292,450 | 277,033 | 263,371 | 251,633 | 230,509 | 140,508 |
| Men | 167,248 | 161,570 | 157,842 | 154,468 | 149,550 | 138,146 | 93,063 |
| Women | 144,523 | 130,880 | 119,191 | 108,903 | 102,083 | 92,363 | 47,485 |
| Doctorate | 34,064 | 34,083 | 33,816 | 34,777 | 33,363 | 32,107 | 18,237 |
| Men | 26,267 | 26,817 | 27,365 | 28,571 | 28,090 | 27,530 | 16,121 |
| Women | 7,797 | 7,266 | 6,451 | 6,206 | 5,273 | 4,577 | 2,116 |

1. Includes degrees in medicine, dentistry, law, theology, veterinary medicine, chiropody or podiatry, optometry, osteopathy, and pharmacy. *Source:* Department of Health, Education, and Welfare, National Center for Education Statistics.

# Community, Junior, and Technical Colleges

An asterisk indicates tuition and required fees of $600 or less for the full academic year 1977–78; where applicable, the costs are for students living within the state and within the institutional district.

## ALABAMA

*Publicly controlled*

Alabama Aviation and Tech. College* — Ozark
Alabama Technical College* — East Gadsden
Alexander City State Junior College* — Alexander City
Bessemer State Technical College* — Bessemer
Brewer State Junior College* — Fayette
Chattahoochee Valley State Comm. Coll.* — Phenix City
Enterprise State Junior College* — Enterprise
Gadsden State Junior College* — East Gadsden
George C. Wallace State Comm. College* — Dothan
George C. Wallace State Comm. College* — Hanceville
George Corley Wallace St. Comm. Coll. — Selma
Harry M. Ayers State Tech. College* — Anniston
Hobson State Technical College* — Thomasville
J. F. Drake State Technical College* — Huntsville
James H. Faulkner State Junior College* — Bay Minette
Jefferson Davis State Junior College* — Brewton
Jefferson State Junior College* — Birmingham
John C. Calhoun State Comm. College* — Decatur
John M. Patterson State Tech. College* — Montgomery
Lawson State Community College* — Birmingham
Lurleen B. Wallace State Junior College* — Andalusia
Northeast Alabama State Junior College* — Rainsville
Northwest Alabama State Junior College* — Phil Campbell
Northwest Alabama State Tech. College* — Hamilton
Patrick Henry State Junior College* — Monroeville
Reid State Technical College* — Evergreen
S. D. Bishop State Junior College* — Mobile
Shelton State Technical College* — Tuscaloosa
Snead State Junior College* — Boaz
Southern Union State Junior College* — Wadley
Southwest State Technical College — Mobile
Trenholm State Technical College — Montgomery

*Privately controlled*

Alabama Christian College — Montgomery
Alabama Lutheran College—Academy — Selma
Marion Military Institute — Marion
Selma University — Selma
Walker College — Jasper

## ALASKA

*Publicly controlled*

Univ. of Alaska Community Colleges — College
- Anchorage Community College* — Anchorage
- Juneau-Douglas Community College* — Juneau
- Kenai Peninsula Community College* — Soldotna
- Ketchikan Community College* — Ketchikan
- Kodiak Community College — Kodiak
- Kuskokwim Community College* — Bethel
- Matanuska Susitna Community College — Palmer
- Northwest Community College* — Nome
- Sitka Community College* — Sitka
- Tanana Valley Community College* — Fairbanks

*Privately controlled*

Sheldon Jackson College — Sitka

## AMERICAN SAMOA

*Publicly controlled*

American Samoa Community College* — Pago Pago

## ARIZONA

*Publicly controlled*

Arizona Western College* — Yuma
Cochise College* — Douglas
Eastern Arizona College* — Thatcher
Maricopa County Comm. Coll. District — Phoenix
- Glendale Community College* — Glendale
- Maricopa Technical Community Coll.* — Phoenix
- Mesa Community College* — Mesa
- Phoenix College* — Phoenix
- Scottsdale Community College* — Scottsdale

Mohave Community College* — Kingman
Navajo Community College — Chinle
Northland Pioneer College* — Holbrook
Pima Community College* — Tucson
- Community Campus* — Tucson
- Downtown Campus* — Tucson
- West Campus* — Tucson

Pinal County Community College District — Coolidge
- Arizona College of Technology* — Winkleman
- Central Arizona College* — Coolidge

Yavapai College* — Prescott

*Privately controlled*

Ganado, College of — Ganado

## ARKANSAS

*Publicly controlled*

Arkansas State Univ.—Beebe Branch* — Beebe
East Arkansas Community College* — Forrest City
Garland County Community College* — Hot Springs
Mississippi County Community College* — Blytheville
North Arkansas Community College* — Harrison
Phillips County Community College* — Helena
Southern Arkansas University — Magnolia
- El Dorado Branch* — El Dorado
- Technical Branch* — East Camden

Westark Community College* — Fort Smith

*Privately controlled*

Central Baptist College* — Conway
Crowley's Ridge College* — Paragould
Shorter College — North Little Rock
Southern Baptist College — Walnut Ridge

## CALIFORNIA

*Publicly controlled*

Allan Hancock College* — Santa Maria
Antelope Valley College* — Lancaster
Barstow Community College* — Barstow
Butte College* — Oroville
Cabrillo College* — Aptos
Canyons, College of the* — Valencia
Cerritos College — Norwalk
Chabot College — Hayward
Chaffey College — Alta Loma
Citrus College* — Azusa
Coast Community College District — Costa Mesa
- Coastline Community College — Fountain Valley
- Golden West College* — Huntington Beach
- Orange Coast College* — Costa Mesa

Compton Community College* — Compton
Contra Costa Community Coll. District — Martinez
- Contra Costa College — San Pablo
- Diablo Valley College — Pleasant Hill
- Los Medanos College* — Pittsburg

Cuesta College — San Luis Obispo
Desert, College of the* — Palm Desert
El Camino College — Via Torrance
Foothill-Deanza Comm. Coll. District — Los Altos Hills

| | |
|---|---|
| De Anza College* | Cupertino |
| Foothill College* | Los Altos Hills |
| Gavilan College* | Gilroy |
| Glendale Community College | Glendale |
| Grossmont Community College District | El Cajon |
| Grossmont College | El Cajon |
| Hartnell College | Salinas |
| Imperial Valley College | Imperial |
| Kern Community College District | Bakersfield |
| Bakersfield College* | Bakersfield |
| Cerro Coso Community College* | Ridgecrest |
| Porterville College* | Porterville |
| Lake Tahoe Community College* | South Lake Tahoe |
| Lassen College* | Susanville |
| Long Beach City College | Long Beach |
| Los Angeles Community College District | Los Angeles |
| East Los Angeles College | Monterey Park |
| Los Angeles City College | Los Angeles |
| Los Angeles Harbor College | Wilmington |
| Los Angeles Mission College | San Fernando |
| Los Angeles Pierce College* | Woodland Hills |
| Los Angeles Southwest College | Los Angeles |
| Los Angeles Trade-Technical College | Los Angeles |
| Los Angeles Valley College | Van Nuys |
| West Los Angeles College | Culver City |
| Los Rios Community College District | Sacramento |
| American River College | Sacramento |
| Cosumnes River College | Sacramento |
| Sacramento City College | Sacramento |
| Marin County Community Coll. District | Kentfield |
| Indian Valley Colleges | Novato |
| Marin, College of | Kentfield |
| Mendocino College* | Ukiah |
| Merced College | Merced |
| Mira Costa College* | Oceanside |
| Monterey Peninsula College* | Monterey |
| Mt. San Antonio College* | Walnut |
| Mt. San Jacinto College | San Jacinto |
| Napa College | Napa |
| North Orange County Comm. Coll. District | Fullerton |
| Cypress College* | Cypress |
| Fullerton College* | Fullerton |
| Ohlone College | Fremont |
| Palo Verde College* | Blythe |
| Palomar College* | San Marcos |
| Pasadena City College | Pasadena |
| Peralta Community College District | Oakland |
| Alameda, College of* | Alameda |
| Feather River College* | Quincy |
| Laney College* | Oakland |
| Merritt College* | Oakland |
| Peralta Coll. for Nontraditional Study | Berkeley |
| Redwoods, College of the | Eureka |
| Rio Hondo College | Whittier |
| Riverside City College* | Riverside |
| Saddleback College* | Mission Viejo |
| San Bernardino Community Coll. District | San Bernardino |
| Crafton Hills College* | Yucaipa |
| San Bernardino Valley College | San Bernardino |
| San Diego Community College District | San Diego |
| San Diego City College* | San Diego |
| San Diego Evening College | San Diego |
| San Diego Mesa College* | San Diego |
| San Diego Miramar College* | San Diego |
| San Francisco Community Coll. District | San Francisco |
| San Francisco, City College of | San Francisco |
| San Joaquin Delta College* | Stockton |
| San Jose Community College District | San Jose |
| Evergreen Valley College* | San Jose |
| San Jose City College* | San Jose |
| San Mateo County Comm. Coll. District | San Mateo |
| Canada College* | Redwood City |
| San Mateo, College of* | San Mateo |
| Skyline College* | San Bruno |
| Santa Ana College* | Santa Ana |
| Santa Barbara City College | Santa Barbara |
| Santa Monica College* | Santa Monica |
| Santa Rosa Junior College* | Santa Rosa |
| Shasta College* | Redding |
| Sequoias, College of the* | Visalia |
| Sierra College* | Rocklin |
| Siskiyous, College of the* | Weed |
| Solano Community College | Suisun City |
| Southwestern College | Chula Vista |
| State Center Community College District | Fresno |
| Fresno City College* | Fresno |
| Reedley College* | Reedley |
| Taft College | Taft |
| Ventura County Community Coll. District | Ventura |
| Moorpark College* | Moorpark |
| Oxnard College | Oxnard |
| Ventura College* | Ventura |
| Victor Valley College* | Victorville |
| West Hills Community College* | Coalinga |
| West Valley Joint Comm. Coll. District* | Saratoga |
| Mission College* | Santa Clara |
| West Valley College* | Saratoga |
| Yosemite Community College District | Modesto |
| Columbia Junior College* | Columbia |
| Modesto Junior College* | Modesto |
| Yuba College* | Marysville |

*Privately controlled*

| | |
|---|---|
| Deep Springs College | Via Dyer, Nevada |
| Don Bosco Technical Institute | Rosemead |
| Humphreys College | Stockton |
| Marymount Palos Verdes College | Rancho Palos Verdes |
| Menlo College | Menlo Park |
| Nairobi College | East Palo Alto |

## CANAL ZONE

*Publicly controlled*

| | |
|---|---|
| Canal Zone College* | Balboa |

## COLORADO

*Publicly controlled*

| | |
|---|---|
| Aims Community College* | Greeley |
| Arapahoe Community College* | Littleton |
| Colorado Mountain College* | Glenwood Springs |
| East Campus | Leadville |
| West Campus | Glenwood Springs |
| Colorado Northwestern Comm. College* | Rangely |
| Community College of Denver | Denver |
| Auraria Campus* | Denver |
| North Campus* | Westminster |
| Red Rocks Campus* | Golden |
| El Paso Community College* | Colorado Springs |
| Lamar Community College* | Lamar |
| Morgan Community College* | Fort Morgan |
| Northeastern Junior College* | Sterling |
| Otero Junior College* | La Junta |
| Trinidad State Junior College* | Trinidad |
| U.S.C.—Coll. for Community Services* | Pueblo |

## CONNECTICUT

*Publicly controlled*

| | |
|---|---|
| Asnuntuck Community College* | Enfield |
| Greater Hartford Community College* | Hartford |
| Greater New Haven State Tech. Coll.* | Hamden |
| Hartford State Technical College* | Hartford |
| Housatonic Community College* | Bridgeport |
| Manchester Community College* | Manchester |
| Mattatuck Community College* | Waterbury |

| | |
|---|---|
| Middlesex Community College* | Middletown |
| Mohegan Community College* | Norwich |
| Northwestern Connecticut Comm. College* | Winsted |
| Norwalk Community College* | Norwalk |
| Norwalk State Technical College* | Norwalk |
| Quinebaug Valley Community College* | Danielson |
| South Central Community College* | New Haven |
| Thames Valley State Technical College* | Norwich |
| Tunxis Community College* | Farmington |
| Waterbury State Technical College* | Waterbury |
| *Privately controlled* | |
| Hartford College for Women | Hartford |
| Mitchell College | New London |
| Mount Sacred Heart College | Hamden |
| Post College | Waterbury |
| St. Thomas Seminary Junior College | Bloomfield |

## DELAWARE

| | |
|---|---|
| *Publicly controlled* | |
| Delaware Technical and Comm. College | Dover |
| Southern Campus* | Georgetown |
| Stanton Campus* | Newark |
| Terry Campus* | Dover |
| Wilmington Campus* | Wilmington |
| *Privately controlled* | |
| Brandywine College | Wilmington |
| Goldey Beacom College | Wilmington |
| Wesley College | Dover |

## DISTRICT OF COLUMBIA

| | |
|---|---|
| *Privately controlled* | |
| Immaculata College of Washington | Washington |
| Mount Vernon College | Washington |

## FLORIDA

| | |
|---|---|
| *Publicly controlled* | |
| Brevard Community College* | Cocoa |
| Broward Community College* | Ft. Lauderdale |
| Central Florida Community College* | Ocala |
| Chipola Junior College* | Marianna |
| Daytona Beach Community College* | Daytona Beach |
| Edison Community College* | Ft. Myers |
| Florida Junior Coll. at Jacksonville* | Jacksonville |
| Downtown Campus | Jacksonville |
| Fred H. Kent Campus | Jacksonville |
| North Campus | Jacksonville |
| South Campus | Jacksonville |
| Florida Keys Community College* | Key West |
| Gulf Coast Community College* | Panama City |
| Hillsborough Community College* | Tampa |
| Indian River Community College* | Ft. Pierce |
| Lake City Community College* | Lake City |
| Lake-Sumter Community College* | Leesburg |
| Manatee Junior College* | Bradenton |
| Miami-Dade Community College* | Miami |
| Medical Center Campus* | Miami |
| New World Center Campus* | Miami |
| North Campus* | Miami |
| South Campus* | Miami |
| North Florida Junior College* | Madison |
| Okaloosa-Walton Junior College* | Niceville |
| Palm Beach Junior College* | Lake Worth |
| Pasco-Hernando Community College* | Dade City |
| Pensacola Junior College* | Pensacola |
| Polk Community College* | Winter Haven |
| St. Johns River Community College* | Palatka |
| St. Petersburg Junior College* | St. Petersburg |
| Santa Fe Community College* | Gainesville |
| Seminole Community College* | Sanford |
| South Florida Junior College* | Avon Park |
| Tallahassee Community College* | Tallahassee |
| Valencia Community College* | Orlando |
| *Privately controlled* | |
| Florida College | Temple Terrace |
| St. John Vianney Junior College | Miami |
| Webber College | Babson Park |

## GEORGIA

| | |
|---|---|
| *Publicly controlled* | |
| Abraham Baldwin Agriculture College* | Tifton |
| Albany Junior College* | Albany |
| Atlanta Junior College* | Atlanta |
| Bainbridge Junior College* | Bainbridge |
| Brunswick Junior College* | Brunswick |
| Clayton Junior College* | Morrow |
| Dalton Junior College* | Dalton |
| DeKalb Community College* | Clarkston |
| Emanuel County Junior College* | Swainsboro |
| Floyd Junior College* | Rome |
| Gainesville Junior College* | Gainesville |
| Georgia Military College | Milledgeville |
| Gordon Junior College* | Barnesville |
| Kennesaw College* | Marietta |
| Macon Junior College* | Macon |
| Middle Georgia College* | Cochran |
| South Georgia College* | Douglas |
| Waycross Junior College* | Waycross |
| *Privately controlled* | |
| Andrew College | Cuthbert |
| Brewton-Parker College | Mt. Vernon |
| Emmanuel College* | Franklin Springs |
| Oxford College of Emory University | Oxford |
| Reinhardt College | Waleska |
| Truett-McConnell College | Cleveland |
| Young Harris College | Young Harris |

## HAWAII

| | |
|---|---|
| *Publicly controlled* | |
| Univ. of Hawaii Community Coll. System* | Honolulu |
| Hawaii Community College* | Hilo |
| Honolulu Community College* | Honolulu |
| Kapiolani Community College* | Honolulu |
| Kauai Community College* | Lihue Kauai |
| Leeward Community College* | Pearl City |
| Maui Community College* | Kahului |
| Windward Community College* | Kaneohe |

## IDAHO

| | |
|---|---|
| *Publicly controlled* | |
| North Idaho College* | Coeur d'Alene |
| Southern Idaho, College of* | Twin Falls |
| *Privately controlled* | |
| Ricks College | Rexburg |
| St. Gertrude, College of | Cottonwood |

## ILLINOIS

| | |
|---|---|
| *Publicly controlled* | |
| Belleville Area College* | Belleville |
| Black Hawk College | Moline |
| East Campus* | Kewanee |
| Quad Cities Campus* | Moline |
| Carl Sandburg College* | Galesburg |
| Chicago, City Colleges of | Chicago |
| Chicago City-Wide College* | Chicago |
| Chicago Urban Skills Institute* | Chicago |
| Kennedy-King College* | Chicago |
| Loop College, The* | Chicago |
| Malcolm X College* | Chicago |
| Olive Harvey College* | Chicago |
| Richard J. Daley College* | Chicago |
| Truman College* | Chicago |
| Wilbur Wright College* | Chicago |
| Danville Junior College* | Danville |
| DuPage, College of* | Glen Ellyn |
| Elgin Community College* | Elgin |
| Highland Community College* | Freeport |
| Illinois Central College* | East Peoria |

| | |
|---|---|
| Illinois Eastern Community Colleges | Olney |
| Continuing Education, College of* | Fairfield |
| Lincoln Trail College* | Robinson |
| Olney Central College* | Olney |
| Wabash Valley College* | Mt. Carmel |
| Illinois Valley Community College* | Oglesby |
| John A. Logan College* | Carterville |
| John Wood Community College* | Quincy |
| Joliet Junior College* | Joliet |
| Kankakee Community College* | Kankakee |
| Kaskaskia College* | Centralia |
| Kishwaukee College* | Malta |
| Lake County, College of* | Grayslake |
| Lake Land College* | Mattoon |
| Lewis and Clark Community College* | Godfrey |
| Lincoln Land Community College* | Springfield |
| McHenry County College* | Crystal Lake |
| Moraine Valley Community College* | Palos Hills |
| Morton College* | Cicero |
| Oakton Community College* | Morton Grove |
| Parkland College* | Champaign |
| Prairie State College* | Chicago Heights |
| Rend Lake College* | Ina |
| Richland Community College* | Decatur |
| Rock Valley College* | Rockford |
| Sauk Valley College* | Dixon |
| Shawnee Community College* | Ullin |
| Southeastern Illinois College* | Harrisburg |
| Spoon River College* | Canton |
| State Comm. College of East St. Louis* | East St. Louis |
| Thornton Community College* | South Holland |
| Triton College* | River Grove |
| Waubonsee Community College* | Sugar Grove |
| William Rainey Harper College* | Palatine |
| *Privately controlled* | |
| Central YMCA Community College | Chicago |
| Felician College | Chicago |
| Kendall College | Evanston |
| Lincoln College | Lincoln |
| MacCormac College | Chicago |
| Mallinckrodt College | Wilmette |
| Springfield College in Illinois | Springfield |

## INDIANA

| | |
|---|---|
| *Publicly controlled* | |
| Indiana Vocational Technical College | Indianapolis |
| Columbus Campus | Columbus |
| Evansville Campus | Evansville |
| Fort Wayne Campus | Fort Wayne |
| Indianapolis Campus* | Indianapolis |
| Kokomo Campus* | Kokomo |
| Lafayette Campus | Lafayette |
| Northwest Campus | Gary |
| Muncie Campus | Muncie |
| Richmond Campus | Richmond |
| South Bend Campus* | South Bend |
| South Central Campus | Sellersburg |
| Southeast Campus | Madison |
| Terre Haute Campus | Terre Haute |
| Vincennes University | Vincennes |
| *Privately controlled* | |
| Ancilla College | Donaldson |
| Holy Cross Junior College | Notre Dame |

## IOWA

| | |
|---|---|
| *Publicly controlled* | |
| Des Moines Area Community College* | Ankeny |
| Ankeny Campus | Ankeny |
| Boone Campus | Boone |
| Eastern Iowa Community Coll. District | Davenport |
| Clinton Community College* | Clinton |
| Muscatine Community College* | Muscatine |
| Scott Community College | Bettendorf |
| Hawkeye Institute of Technology* | Waterloo |
| Indian Hills Community College* | Ottumwa |
| Centerville Campus | Centerville |
| Ottumwa Campus | Ottumwa |
| Iowa Central Community College* | Fort Dodge |
| Eagle Grove Center | Eagle Grove |
| Fort Dodge Center | Fort Dodge |
| Webster City Center | Webster City |
| Iowa Lakes Community College* | Estherville |
| North Attendance Center | Estherville |
| South Attendance Center | Emmetsburg |
| Iowa Valley Community Coll. District | Marshalltown |
| Ellsworth Community College* | Iowa Falls |
| Marshalltown Community College* | Marshalltown |
| Iowa Western Community College* | Council Bluffs |
| Clarinda Campus | Clarinda |
| Council Bluffs Campus | Council Bluffs |
| Kirkwood Community College* | Cedar Rapids |
| North Iowa Area Community College* | Mason City |
| Northeast Area One Voc.-Tech. School* | Calmar |
| North Center* | Calmar |
| South Center* | Dubuque |
| Northwest Iowa Technical College* | Sheldon |
| Southeastern Community College* | West Burlington |
| North Campus* | West Burlington |
| South Campus* | Keokuk |
| Southwestern Community College* | Creston |
| Western Iowa Tech. Community College* | Sioux City |
| *Privately controlled* | |
| Mount St. Clare College | Clinton |
| Ottumwa Heights College | Ottumwa |
| Palmer Junior College | Davenport |
| Sioux Empire College | Hawarden |
| Waldorf College | Forest City |

## KANSAS

| | |
|---|---|
| *Publicly controlled* | |
| Allen County Community Junior College* | Iola |
| Barton County Community Junior Coll.* | Great Bend |
| Butler County Community Junior Coll.* | El Dorado |
| Cloud County Community Junior College* | Concordia |
| Coffeyville Community Junior College* | Coffeyville |
| Colby Community Junior College* | Colby |
| Cowley County Community Junior Coll.* | Arkansas City |
| Dodge City Community Junior College* | Dodge City |
| Fort Scott Community Junior College* | Fort Scott |
| Garden City Community Junior College* | Garden City |
| Haskell Indian Junior College | Lawrence |
| Highland Community Junior College* | Highland |
| Hutchinson Community Junior College* | Hutchinson |
| Independence Community Junior Coll.* | Independence |
| Johnson County Community Junior Coll.* | Overland Park |
| Kansas City, Kan., Community Jr. Coll.* | Kansas City |
| Kansas Technical Institute* | Salina |
| Labette Community Junior College* | Parsons |
| Neosho County Community Junior Coll.* | Chanute |
| Pratt Community Junior College* | Pratt |
| Seward County Community Junior Coll.* | Liberal |
| *Privately controlled* | |
| Central College | McPherson |
| Donnelly College | Kansas City |
| Hesston College | Hesston |
| St. John's College | Winfield |

## KENTUCKY

| | |
|---|---|
| *Publicly controlled* | |
| Bowling Green Community College* | Bowling Green |
| Eastern Kentucky Univ.—Office of Community College Programs* | Richmond |
| Kentucky, Univ. of, Comm. Coll. System | Lexington |
| Ashland Community College* | Ashland |
| Elizabethtown Community College* | Elizabethtown |

| | |
|---|---|
| Hazard Community College* | Hazard |
| Henderson Community College* | Henderson |
| Hopkinsville Community College* | Hopkinsville |
| Jefferson Community College* | Louisville |
| Lexington Technical Institute* | Lexington |
| Madisonville Community College* | Madisonville |
| Maysville Community College* | Maysville |
| Paducah Community College* | Paducah |
| Prestonsburg Community College* | Prestonsburg |
| Somerset Community College* | Somerset |
| Southeast Community College* | Cumberland |
| *Privately controlled* | |
| Alice Lloyd College | Pippa Passes |
| Lees Junior College | Jackson |
| Lindsey Wilson College | Columbia |
| Midway College | Midway |
| St. Catharine College | St. Catharine |
| Southeastern Christian College | Winchester |
| Sue Bennett College | London |

## LOUISIANA

| | |
|---|---|
| *Publicly controlled* | |
| Bossier Parish Community College* | Bossier City |
| Delgado College* | New Orleans |
| Louisiana State University | Baton Rouge |
| Alexandria Campus* | Alexandria |
| Eunice Campus* | Eunice |
| St. Bernard Parish Community College* | Chalmette |
| Southern University at Shreveport* | Shreveport |

## MAINE

| | |
|---|---|
| *Publicly controlled* | |
| Central Maine Vocational Tech. Inst.* | Auburn |
| Eastern Maine Vocational Tech. Inst.* | Bangor |
| Kennebec Valley Vocational Tech. Inst.* | Waterville |
| Maine, University of | Bangor |
| Augusta Branch | Augusta |
| Bangor Community College | Bangor |
| Northern Maine Vocational Tech. Inst.* | Presque Isle |
| Southern Maine Vocational Tech. Inst.* | South Portland |
| Washington County Voc. Tech. Inst. | Calais |
| *Privately controlled* | |
| Westbrook College | Portland |

## MARYLAND

| | |
|---|---|
| *Publicly controlled* | |
| Allegany Community College* | Cumberland |
| Anne Arundel Community College* | Arnold |
| Catonsville Community College* | Baltimore |
| Cecil Community College* | North East |
| Charles County Community College* | La Plata |
| Chesapeake College* | Wye Mills |
| Community College of Baltimore* | Baltimore |
| Dundalk Community College* | Dundalk |
| Essex Community College* | Baltimore Co. |
| Frederick Community College* | Frederick |
| Garrett Community College* | McHenry |
| Hagerstown Junior College* | Hagerstown |
| Harford Community College* | Bel Air |
| Howard Community College* | Columbia |
| Montgomery College | Rockville |
| Germantown Campus | Gaithersburg |
| Rockville Campus | Rockville |
| Takoma Park Campus | Takoma Park |
| Prince George's Community College* | Largo |
| Wor-Wic Tech. Community College* | Salisbury |
| *Privately controlled* | |
| Bay College of Maryland | Baltimore |
| Villa Julie College | Stevenson |

## MASSACHUSETTS

| | |
|---|---|
| *Publicly controlled* | |
| Berkshire Community College* | Pittsfield |
| Blue Hills Regional Tech. Institute* | Canton |
| Bristol Community College* | Fall River |
| Bunker Hill Community College* | Charlestown |
| Cape Cod Community College* | W. Barnstable |
| Franklin Institute of Boston | Boston |
| Greenfield Community College* | Greenfield |
| Holyoke Community College* | Holyoke |
| Massachusetts Bay Community College* | Wellesley Hills |
| Massasoit Community College* | Brockton |
| Middlesex Community College* | Bedford |
| Mount Wachusett Community College* | Gardner |
| North Shore Community College* | Beverly |
| Northern Essex Community College* | Haverhill |
| Quincy Junior College | Quincy |
| Quinsigamond Community College* | Worcester |
| Roxbury Community College* | Roxbury |
| Springfield Technical Community Coll.* | Springfield |
| *Privately controlled* | |
| Aquinas Junior College | Milton |
| Bay Path Junior College | Longmeadow |
| Becker Junior College | Worcester |
| Leicester Campus | Leicester |
| Chamberlayne Junior College | Boston |
| Dean Junior College | Franklin |
| Endicott College | Beverly |
| Fisher Junior College | Boston |
| Grahm Junior College | Boston |
| Laboure Junior College | Boston |
| Lasell Junior College | Newton |
| Mount Ida Junior College | Newton Centre |
| Newbury Junior College | Boston |
| Pine Manor College | Chestnut Hill |
| Worcester Junior College | Worcester |

## MICHIGAN

| | |
|---|---|
| *Publicly controlled* | |
| Alpena Community College* | Alpena |
| Bay de Noc Community College* | Escanaba |
| Charles Stewart Mott Community Coll.* | Flint |
| Delta College* | University Center |
| Glen Oaks Community College* | Centreville |
| Gogebic Community College* | Ironwood |
| Grand Rapids Community College* | Grand Rapids |
| Henry Ford Community College* | Dearborn |
| Highland Park Community College* | Highland Park |
| Jackson Community College* | Jackson |
| Kalamazoo Valley Community College* | Kalamazoo |
| Kellogg Community College* | Battle Creek |
| Kirtland Community College* | Roscommon |
| Lake Michigan College | Benton Harbor |
| Lansing Community College* | Lansing |
| Macomb County Community College* | Warren |
| Center Campus | Mt. Clemens |
| South Campus | Warren |
| Mid Michigan Community College* | Harrison |
| Monroe County Community College* | Monroe |
| Montcalm Community College* | Sidney |
| Muskegon Community College* | Muskegon |
| North Central Michigan College* | Petoskey |
| Northwestern Michigan College* | Traverse City |
| Oakland Community College* | Bloomfield Hills |
| Auburn Hills Campus | Auburn Heights |
| Highland Lakes Campus | Union Lake |
| Orchard Ridge Campus | Farmington |
| Southeast Campus | Oak Park |
| St. Clair County Community College* | Port Huron |
| Schoolcraft College* | Livonia |
| Southwestern Michigan College* | Dowagiac |
| Washtenaw Community College* | Ann Arbor |
| Wayne County Community College* | Detroit |
| West Shore Community College* | Scottville |
| *Privately controlled* | |
| Davenport College of Business | Grand Rapids |
| Michigan Christian Junior College | Rochester |

| | |
|---|---|
| Suomi College | Hancock |

## MINNESOTA

*Publicly controlled*

| | |
|---|---|
| Anoka-Ramsey Community College* | Coon Rapids |
| Austin Community College* | Austin |
| Brainerd Community College* | Brainerd |
| Fergus Falls Community College* | Fergus Falls |
| Hibbing Community College* | Hibbing |
| Inver Hills Community College* | Inver Grove Heights |
| Itaska Community College* | Grand Rapids |
| Lakewood Community College* | White Bear Lake |
| Mesabi Community College* | Virginia |
| Metropolitan Community College* | Minneapolis |
| Minnesota, Univ. of, Technical Coll. | Minneapolis |
| Crookston Campus | Crookston |
| Waseca Campus | Waseca |
| Normandale Community College* | Bloomington |
| North Hennepin Community College* | Brooklyn Park |
| Northland Community College* | Thief River Falls |
| Rainy River Community College* | International Falls |
| Rochester Community College* | Rochester |
| Vermilion Community College* | Ely |
| Willmar Community College* | Willmar |
| Worthington Community College* | Worthington |

*Privately controlled*

| | |
|---|---|
| Bethany Lutheran College | Mankato |
| Crosier Seminary Junior College | Onamia |
| Golden Valley Lutheran College | Minneapolis |
| St. Mary's Junior College | Minneapolis |

## MISSISSIPPI

*Publicly controlled*

| | |
|---|---|
| Coahoma Junior College* | Clarksdale |
| Copiah-Lincoln Junior College* | Wesson |
| East Central Junior College* | Decatur |
| East Mississippi Junior College* | Scooba |
| Hinds Junior College* | Raymond |
| Holmes Junior College* | Goodman |
| Itawamba Junior College* | Fulton |
| Jones County Junior College* | Ellisville |
| Meridian Junior College* | Meridian |
| Mississippi Delta Junior College* | Moorhead |
| Mississippi Gulf Coast Junior College | Perkinston |
| Jackson County Campus* | Gautier |
| Jefferson Davis Campus* | Gulfport |
| Perkinston Campus* | Perkinston |
| Northeast Mississippi Junior College* | Booneville |
| Northwest Mississippi Junior College* | Senatobia |
| Pearl River Junior College* | Poplarville |
| Southwest Mississippi Junior College* | Summit |
| Utica Junior College* | Utica |

*Privately controlled*

| | |
|---|---|
| Clarke College | Newton |
| Mary Holmes College | West Point |
| Wood Junior College | Mathiston |

## MISSOURI

*Publicly controlled*

| | |
|---|---|
| Crowder College* | Neosho |
| East Central Junior College* | Union |
| Jefferson College* | Hillsboro |
| Metropolitan Community Colleges, The | Kansas City |
| Longview Community College* | Lee's Summit |
| Maple Woods Community College* | Kansas City |
| Penn Valley Community College* | Kansas City |
| Pioneer Community College* | Kansas City |
| Mineral Area College* | Flat River |
| Moberly Junior College* | Moberly |
| St. Louis Community College | St. Louis |
| Florissant Valley Campus* | St. Louis |
| Forest Park Campus* | St. Louis |
| Meramec Campus* | St. Louis |
| State Fair Community College* | Sedalia |
| Three Rivers Community College* | Poplar Bluff |
| Trenton Junior College* | Trenton |

*Privately controlled*

| | |
|---|---|
| Cottey College | Nevada |
| Kemper Military School and College | Boonville |
| St. Mary's College of O'Fallon | O'Fallon |
| St. Paul's College | Concordia |
| Wentworth Military Academy | Lexington |

## MONTANA

*Publicly controlled*

| | |
|---|---|
| Dawson College* | Glendive |
| Flathead Valley Community College* | Kalispell |
| Miles Community College* | Miles City |

## NEBRASKA

*Publicly controlled*

| | |
|---|---|
| Central Technical Comm. Coll. Area | Grand Island |
| Central Technical Community Coll.* | Hastings |
| Platte Technical Community Coll.* | Columbus |
| Metropolitan Technical Community Coll. | Omaha |
| Mid-Plains Technical Comm. Coll. Area | North Platte |
| McCook Community College* | McCook |
| Mid-Plains Community College* | North Platte |
| Nebraska, Univ. of, Sch. of Tech. Agri.* | Curtis |
| Northeast Technical Community College* | Norfolk |
| Southeast Community College | Lincoln |
| Fairbury Campus* | Fairbury |
| Lincoln Campus* | Lincoln |
| Milford Campus* | Milford |
| Western Technical Comm. Coll. Area | Scottsbluff |
| Nebraska Western College* | Scottsbluff |
| Western Nebraska Technical Coll.* | Sidney |

*Privately controlled*

| | |
|---|---|
| York College | York |

## NEVADA

*Publicly controlled*

| | |
|---|---|
| Nevada, Univ. of, Comm. Coll. System | Reno |
| Clark County Community College* | North Las Vegas |
| Northern Nevada Community College* | Elko |
| Western Nevada Community College* | Carson City |
| North Campus* | Reno |
| South Campus* | Carson City |

## NEW HAMPSHIRE

*Publicly controlled*

| | |
|---|---|
| New Hampshire Technical Institute* | Concord |
| New Hampshire Vocational Technical Coll. | |
| Berlin Campus* | Berlin |
| Claremont Campus* | Claremont |
| Laconia Campus* | Laconia |
| Manchester Campus* | Manchester |
| Nashua Campus* | Nashua |
| Portsmouth Campus* | Portsmouth |

*Privately controlled*

| | |
|---|---|
| Colby-Sawyer College | New London |
| Daniel Webster College | Nashua |
| White Pines College | Chester |

## NEW JERSEY

*Publicly controlled*

| | |
|---|---|
| Atlantic Community College* | Mays Landing |
| Bergen Community College* | Paramus |
| Brookdale Community College* | Lincroft |
| Burlington County College* | Pemberton |
| Camden County College* | Blackwood |
| Cumberland County College* | Vineland |
| Essex County College* | Newark |

| | |
|---|---|
| Gloucester County College* | Sewell |
| Hudson County Community College* | North Bergen |
| Mercer County Community College* | Trenton |
| Middlesex County College* | Edison |
| Morris, County College of* | Dover |
| Ocean County College* | Toms River |
| Passaic County Community College* | Paterson |
| Salem Community College* | Penns Grove |
| Somerset County College* | Somerville |
| *Privately controlled* | |
| Edward Williams College | Hackensack |
| Luther College of Bible & Liberal Arts | Teaneck |
| Union College* | Cranford |

## NEW MEXICO

| | |
|---|---|
| *Publicly controlled* | |
| Eastern New Mexico University | Portales |
| Clovis Campus | Clovis |
| Roswell Campus* | Roswell |
| Luna Vocational Technical Institute* | Las Vegas |
| New Mexico, University of | Albuquerque |
| Gallup Campus* | Gallup |
| New Mexico Junior College* | Hobbs |
| New Mexico Military Institute | Roswell |
| New Mexico State University | Las Cruces |
| Alamogordo Campus* | Alamogordo |
| Carlsbad Campus* | Carlsbad |
| Dona Ana Occupational Ed. Branch* | Las Cruces |
| Grants Campus* | Grants |
| San Juan Campus* | Farmington |
| Northern New Mexico Community Coll.* | El Rito |

## NEW YORK

| | |
|---|---|
| *Publicly controlled* | |
| Adirondack Community College | Glens Falls |
| Borough of Manhattan Community Coll. | New York |
| Bronx Community College | Bronx |
| Broome Community College | Binghamton |
| Cayuga County Community College | Auburn |
| Clinton Community College | Plattsburgh |
| Columbia-Greene Community College* | Hudson |
| Corning Community College | Corning |
| Dutchess Community College | Poughkeepsie |
| Erie Community College | Buffalo |
| City Campus | Buffalo |
| North Campus | Williamsville |
| South Campus | Orchard Park |
| Fashion Institute of Technology | New York |
| Finger Lakes, Community College of the | Canandaigua |
| Fulton-Montgomery Community College | Johnstown |
| Genesee Community College | Batavia |
| Herkimer County Community College | Herkimer |
| Hostos Community College | Bronx |
| Hudson Valley Community College | Troy |
| Jamestown Community College | Jamestown |
| Jefferson Community College | Watertown |
| Kingsborough Community College | Brooklyn |
| Laguardia Community College | Long Island City |
| Mohawk Valley Community College | Utica |
| Monroe Community College | Rochester |
| Nassau Community College | Garden City |
| New York City Community College | Brooklyn |
| Niagara County Community College | Sanborn |
| North Country Community College | Saranac Lake |
| Onondaga Community College | Syracuse |
| Orange County Community College | Middletown |
| Queensborough Community College | Bayside |
| Rockland Community College* | Suffern |
| Schenectady County Community College | Schenectady |
| SUNY Agricultural & Technical Colleges | |
| Alfred Campus | Alfred |
| Canton Campus | Canton |
| Cobleskill Campus | Cobleskill |
| Delhi Campus | Delhi |
| Farmingdale Campus | Farmingdale |
| Morrisville Campus | Morrisville |
| Suffolk County Community College | Selden |
| Sullivan County Community College | Loch Sheldrake |
| Tompkins-Cortland Community College | Dryden |
| Ulster County Community College | Stoneridge |
| Westchester Community College | Valhalla |
| *Privately controlled* | |
| Aeronautics, Academy of | Flushing |
| Albany, Junior College of | Albany |
| Bennett College | Millbrook |
| Cazenovia College | Cazenovia |
| Elizabeth Seton College | Yonkers |
| Five Towns College | Merrick |
| Harriman College | Harriman |
| Hilbert College | Hamburg |
| Human Services, College for | New York |
| Maria College | Albany |
| Maria Regina College | Syracuse |
| Mater Dei College | Ogdensburg |
| Paul Smith's Coll. of Arts & Science | Paul Smiths |
| Trocaire College | Buffalo |
| Villa Maria College of Buffalo | Buffalo |

## NORTH CAROLINA

| | |
|---|---|
| *Publicly controlled* | |
| Alamance, Technical Institute of* | Haw River |
| Albemarle, College of the* | Elizabeth City |
| Anson Technical Institute* | Ansonville |
| Asheville-Buncombe Technical Institute* | Asheville |
| Beaufort County Technical Institute* | Washington |
| Bladen Technical Institute* | Dublin |
| Caldwell Comm. Coll. and Tech. Inst.* | Hudson |
| Cape Fear Technical Institute* | Wilmington |
| Carteret Technical Institute* | Morehead City |
| Catawba Valley Technical Institute* | Hickory |
| Central Carolina Technical Institute* | Sanford |
| Central Piedmont Community College* | Charlotte |
| Cleveland County Technical Institute* | Shelby |
| Coastal Carolina Community College* | Jacksonville |
| Craven Community College | New Bern |
| Davidson County Community College* | Lexington |
| Durham Technical Institute* | Durham |
| Edgecombe Technical Institute* | Tarboro |
| Fayetteville Technical Institute* | Fayetteville |
| Forsyth Technical Institute* | Winston-Salem |
| Gaston College* | Dallas |
| Guilford Technical Institute* | Jamestown |
| Halifax Community College* | Weldon |
| Haywood Technical Institute* | Clyde |
| Isothermal Community College* | Spindale |
| James Sprunt Institute* | Kenansville |
| Johnston Technical Institute* | Smithfield |
| Lenoir Community College* | Kinston |
| Martin Community College* | Williamston |
| Mayland Technical Institute* | Spruce Pine |
| McDowell Technical Institute* | Marion |
| Mitchell Community College* | Statesville |
| Montgomery Technical Institute* | Troy |
| Nash Technical Institute* | Rocky Mount |
| Pamlico Technical Institute* | Grantsboro |
| Piedmont Technical Institute* | Roxboro |
| Pitt Technical Institute* | Greenville |
| Randolph Technical Institute* | Asheboro |
| Richmond Technical Institute* | Hamlet |
| Roanoke-Chowan Technical Institute* | Ahoskie |
| Robeson Technical Institute* | Lumberton |
| Rockingham Community College* | Wentworth |
| Rowan Technical Institute* | Salisbury |
| Sampson Technical Institute* | Clinton |
| Sandhills Community College* | Carthage |
| Southeastern Community College* | Whiteville |
| Southwestern Technical Institute* | Sylva |

| | |
|---|---|
| Stanly Technical Institute* | Albemarle |
| Surry Community College* | Dobson |
| Tri-County Technical Institute* | Murphy |
| Vance-Granville Community College* | Henderson |
| Wake Technical Institute* | Raleigh |
| Wayne Community College* | Goldsboro |
| Western Piedmont Community College* | Morganton |
| Wilkes Community College* | Wilkesboro |
| Wilson County Technical Institute* | Wilson |
| *Privately controlled* | |
| Blue Ridge Technical Institute* | Flat Rock |
| Brevard College | Brevard |
| Chowan College | Murfreesboro |
| Durham College | Durham |
| Lees-McRae College | Banner Elk |
| Louisburg College | Louisburg |
| Montreat-Anderson College | Montreat |
| Mount Olive College | Mount Olive |
| Peace College | Raleigh |
| St. Mary's College | Raleigh |
| Wingate College | Wingate |

**NORTH DAKOTA**

| | |
|---|---|
| *Publicly controlled* | |
| Bismarck Junior College* | Bismarck |
| Lake Region Junior College | Devils Lake |
| North Dakota, Univ. of—Williston* | Williston |
| North Dakota State School of Science* | Wahpeton |
| North Dakota State Univ.—Bottineau* | Bottineau |

**OHIO**

| | |
|---|---|
| *Publicly controlled* | |
| Akron, Univ. of, Comm. and Tech. Coll. | Akron |
| Belmont Technical College | St. Clairsville |
| Bowling Green Univ.–Firelands Campus | Huron |
| Central Ohio Technical College | Newark |
| Cincinnati, University of | Cincinnati |
| Clermont General & Technical Coll. | Batavia |
| Ohio College of Applied Science | Cincinnati |
| Raymond Walters Gen. & Tech. Coll. | Cincinnati |
| University College | Cincinnati |
| Cincinnati Technical College | Cincinnati |
| Clark Technical College | Springfield |
| Columbus Technical Institute | Columbus |
| Cuyahoga Community College District | Cleveland |
| Eastern Campus* | Warrensville Twnsp. |
| Metropolitan Campus* | Cleveland |
| Western Campus* | Parma |
| Edison State Community College | Piqua |
| Hocking Technical College | Nelsonville |
| Jefferson Technical College* | Steubenville |
| Kent State University | Kent |
| Ashtabula Campus | Ashtabula |
| East Liverpool Regional Campus | East Liverpool |
| Salem Campus | Salem |
| Stark Regional Campus* | Canton |
| Trumbull Campus | Warren |
| Tuscarawas Campus | New Philadelphia |
| Lakeland Community College* | Mentor |
| Lima Technical College* | Lima |
| Lorain County Community College* | Elyria |
| Marion Technical College | Marion |
| Miami University | Oxford |
| Hamilton Campus | Hamilton |
| Middletown Campus | Middletown |
| Michael J. Owens Technical College | Toledo |
| Muskingum Area Technical College* | Zanesville |
| North Central Technical College | Mansfield |
| Northwest Technical College | Archbold |
| Ohio State University | Columbus |
| Agricultural Technical Institute | Wooster |
| Lima Campus* | Lima |
| Mansfield Campus | Mansfield |
| Marion Campus | Marion |
| Newark Campus | Newark |
| Ohio University | Athens |
| Belmont County Campus* | St. Clairsville |
| Ironton Campus | Ironton |
| Chillicothe Campus | Chillicothe |
| Lancaster Campus* | Lancaster |
| Zanesville Campus | Zanesville |
| Rio Grande Community College* | Rio Grande |
| Shawnee State Community College | Portsmouth |
| Sinclair Community College* | Dayton |
| Southern State Community College | Wilmington |
| Stark Technical College* | Canton |
| Terra Technical College* | Fremont |
| Toledo, Univ. of, Comm. & Tech. Coll. | Toledo |
| Washington Technical College* | Marietta |
| Wright State Univ.–Western Branch | Celina |
| Youngstown State U.–Coll. of Applied Sci. | Youngstown |
| *Privately controlled* | |
| Chatfield College | St. Martin |
| Franklin Univ., Junior College of* | Columbus |
| Kettering College of Medical Arts | Kettering |
| Lourdes College | Sylvania |

**OKLAHOMA**

| | |
|---|---|
| *Publicly controlled* | |
| Carl Albert Junior College* | Poteau |
| Claremore Junior College* | Claremore |
| Connors State College* | Warner |
| Eastern Oklahoma State College | Wilburton |
| El Reno Junior College* | El Reno |
| Murray State College* | Tishomingo |
| Northeastern Oklahoma A&M College* | Miami |
| Northern Oklahoma College* | Tonkawa |
| Oklahoma State U. Technical Institute* | Oklahoma City |
| Oscar Rose Junior College* | Midwest City |
| Sayre Junior College* | Sayre |
| Seminole Junior College* | Seminole |
| South Oklahoma City Junior College* | Oklahoma City |
| Tulsa Junior College* | Tulsa |
| Western Oklahoma State College* | Altus |
| *Privately controlled* | |
| Bacone College | Muskogee |
| Oklahoma City Southwestern College* | Oklahoma City |
| St. Gregory's College | Shawnee |

**OREGON**

| | |
|---|---|
| *Publicly controlled* | |
| Blue Mountain Community College* | Pendleton |
| Central Oregon Community College* | Bend |
| Chemeketa Community College* | Salem |
| Clackamas Community College* | Oregon City |
| Clatsop Community College* | Astoria |
| Lane Community College* | Eugene |
| Linn-Benton Community College* | Albany |
| Mt. Hood Community College* | Gresham |
| Portland Community College* | Portland |
| Rogue Community College* | Grants Pass |
| Southwestern Oregon Community Coll.* | Coos Bay |
| Treasure Valley Community College* | Ontario |
| Umpqua Community College* | Roseburg |
| *Privately controlled* | |
| Concordia College | Portland |
| Judson Baptist College | Portland |

**PENNSYLVANIA**

| | |
|---|---|
| *Publicly controlled* | |
| Allegheny County, Community Coll. of | Pittsburgh |
| Allegheny Campus* | Pittsburgh |
| Boyce Campus* | Monroeville |
| College Center-North* | Pittsburgh |
| South Campus* | West Mifflin |
| Beaver County, Community College of* | Monaca |

| | |
|---|---|
| Bucks County Community College* | Newtown |
| Butler County Community College | Butler |
| Delaware County Community College* | Media |
| Harrisburg Area Community College* | Harrisburg |
| Lehigh County Community College | Schnecksville |
| Luzerne County Community College* | Nanticoke |
| Montgomery County Community College* | Blue Bell |
| Northhampton County Area Comm. Coll.* | Bethlehem |
| Philadelphia, Community College of* | Philadelphia |
| Reading Area Community College* | Reading |
| Westmoreland County Community Coll.* | Youngwood |
| Williamsport Area Community College | Williamsport |

*Privately controlled*

| | |
|---|---|
| Cushing Junior College | Bryn Mawr |
| Harcum Junior College | Bryn Mawr |
| Keystone Junior College | La Plume |
| Lackawanna Junior College | Scranton |
| Manor Junior College | Jenkintown |
| Mount Aloysius Junior College | Cresson |
| Northeastern Christian Junior College | Villanova |
| Peirce Junior College | Philadelphia |
| Pennsylvania Junior Coll. of Medical Arts | Harrisburg |
| Pinebrook Junior College | Coopersburg |
| United Wesleyan College | Allentown |
| Valley Forge Military Junior College | Wayne |

## PUERTO RICO

*Publicly controlled*

| | |
|---|---|
| Puerto Rico, Univ. of, Regional Colleges | Rio Piedras |
| Aguadilla Regional College* | Aguadilla |
| Arecibo Regional College* | Arecibo |
| Bayamon Regional College* | Bayamon |
| Carolina Regional College* | Carolina |
| Ponce Regional College* | Ponce |

*Privately controlled*

| | |
|---|---|
| Catholic University of Puerto Rico | Ponce |
| Aguadilla Center | Aguadilla |
| Arecibo Center | Arecibo |
| Guayama Center | Guayama |
| Ponce Center | Ponce |
| College of the Sacred Heart Junior Coll. | Santurce |
| Interamerican University of Puerto Rico | San Juan |
| Aguadilla Regional College | Aguadilla |
| Arecibo Regional College | Arecibo |
| Barranquitas Regional College | Barranquitas |
| Bayamon Regional College | Bayamon |
| Fajardo Regional Campus | San Juan |
| Guayama Regional College | Guayama |
| Ponce Regional College | Ponce |
| Puerto Rico Junior College | Rio Piedras |

## RHODE ISLAND

*Publicly controlled*

| | |
|---|---|
| Rhode Island Junior College* | Warwick |

*Privately controlled*

| | |
|---|---|
| Johnson and Wales College | Providence |

## SOUTH CAROLINA

*Publicly controlled*

| | |
|---|---|
| State System of Technical Colleges: | Columbia |
| Aiken Technical College* | Aiken |
| Beaufort Technical Education Center* | Beaufort |
| Chesterfield-Marlboro Technical Coll.* | Cheraw |
| Denmark Technical Education Center | Denmark |
| Florence-Darlington Technical Coll.* | Florence |
| Greenville Technical College* | Greenville |
| Horry-Georgetown Technical College* | Conway |
| Midlands Technical College | Columbia |
| Airport Campus | West Columbia |
| Beltline Campus | Columbia |
| Orangeburg-Calhoun Technical College* | Orangeburg |
| Piedmont Technical College* | Greenwood |
| South Carolina, University of | Columbia |
| Beaufort Regional Campus | Beaufort |
| Lancaster Regional Campus | Lancaster |
| Salkehatchie Regional Campus* | Allendale |
| Sumter Regional Campus | Sumter |
| Union Regional Campus* | Union |
| Spartanburg Technical College* | Spartanburg |
| Sumter Area Technical College* | Sumter |
| Tri-County Technical College* | Pendleton |
| Trident Technical College* | No. Charleston |
| North Campus* | No. Charleston |
| Palmer Campus* | Charleston |
| Williamsburg Tech. Education Center* | Kingstree |
| York Technical College* | Rock Hill |

*Privately controlled*

| | |
|---|---|
| Anderson College | Anderson |
| Clinton Junior College | Rock Hill |
| Friendship Junior College* | Rock Hill |
| North Greenville College | Tigerville |
| Spartanburg Methodist College | Spartanburg |

## SOUTH DAKOTA

*Publicly controlled*

| | |
|---|---|
| Black Hills State College | Spearfish |
| Junior College Division | Spearfish |
| Oglala Sioux Community College* | Pine Ridge |

*Privately controlled*

| | |
|---|---|
| Freeman Junior College | Freeman |
| Presentation College | Aberdeen |
| Sinte Glaska College Center | Rosebud |

## TENNESSEE

*Publicly controlled*

| | |
|---|---|
| Chattanooga State Tech. Comm. Coll.* | Chattanooga |
| Cleveland State Community College* | Cleveland |
| Columbia State Community College* | Columbia |
| Dyersburg State Community College* | Dyersburg |
| Jackson State Community College* | Jackson |
| Motlow State Community College* | Tullahoma |
| Nashville State Technical Institute* | Nashville |
| Roane State Community College* | Harriman |
| Shelby State Community College* | Memphis |
| State Technical Inst. at Knoxville* | Knoxville |
| State Technical Inst. at Memphis | Memphis |
| Volunteer State Community College* | Gallatin |
| Walters State Community College* | Morristown |

*Privately controlled*

| | |
|---|---|
| Aquinas Junior College | Nashville |
| Cumberland College of Tennessee | Lebanon |
| Hiwassee College | Madisonville |
| John A. Gupton College | Nashville |
| Martin College | Pulaski |
| Morristown College | Morristown |
| Tomlinson College | Cleveland |

## TEXAS

*Publicly controlled*

| | |
|---|---|
| Air Force, Community College of the | Lackland AFB |
| Alvin Community College* | Alvin |
| Amarillo College* | Amarillo |
| Angelina College* | Lufkin |
| Austin Community College* | Austin |
| Bee County College* | Beeville |
| Blinn College* | Brenham |
| Brazosport College* | Lake Jackson |
| Central Texas College* | Killeen |
| Cisco Junior College* | Cisco |
| Clarendon College* | Clarendon |
| Cooke County College* | Gainesville |
| Dallas County Community Coll. District | Dallas |
| Cedar Valley College* | Lancaster |
| Eastfield College* | Mesquite |
| El Centro College* | Dallas |
| Mountain View College* | Dallas |
| North Lake College* | Irving |
| Richland College* | Dallas |

| | |
|---|---|
| Del Mar College* | Corpus Christi |
| El Paso Community College* | El Paso |
| Frank Phillips College* | Borger |
| Galveston College | Galveston |
| Grayson County Junior College* | Denison |
| Henderson County Junior College* | Athens |
| Hill Junior College* | Hillsboro |
| Houston Community College* | Houston |
| Howard College at Big Spring* | Big Spring |
| Kilgore College* | Kilgore |
| Lamar University | Beaumont |
| Orange County Center* | Orange |
| Port Arthur Branch | Port Arthur |
| Laredo Junior College* | Laredo |
| Lee College* | Baytown |
| Mainland, College of the* | Texas City |
| McLennan Community College* | Waco |
| Midland College* | Midland |
| Navarro College* | Corsicana |
| North Harris County College* | Houston |
| Odessa College* | Odessa |
| Panola Junior College* | Carthage |
| Paris Junior College* | Paris |
| Ranger Junior College* | Ranger |
| San Antonio Union Junior Coll. District | San Antonio |
| St. Philip's College* | San Antonio |
| San Antonio College* | San Antonio |
| San Jacinto College | Pasadena |
| Central Campus* | Pasadena |
| North Campus* | Houston |
| South Plains College* | Levelland |
| Southwest Texas Junior College* | Uvalde |
| Tarrant County Junior Coll. District | Fort Worth |
| Northeast Campus* | Hurst |
| Northwest Campus* | Fort Worth |
| South Campus* | Fort Worth |
| Temple Junior College* | Temple |
| Texarkana Community College* | Texarkana |
| Texas Southmost College* | Brownsville |
| Texas State Technical Institute | Waco |
| James Connally Campus* | Waco |
| Mid-Continent Campus* | Amarillo |
| Rio Grande Campus* | Harlingen |
| Rolling Plains Campus* | Sweetwater |
| Tyler Junior College* | Tyler |
| Vernon Regional Junior College* | Vernon |
| Victoria College* | Victoria |
| Weatherford College* | Weatherford |
| Western Texas College* | Snyder |
| Wharton County Junior College* | Wharton |

*Privately controlled*

| | |
|---|---|
| Concordia Lutheran College | Austin |
| Jacksonville College | Jacksonville |
| Lon Morris College | Jacksonville |
| Schreiner College | Kerrville |
| Southern Bible College* | Houston |
| Southwestern Christian College | Terrell |
| Southwestern Junior College | Waxahachie |

## UTAH

*Publicly controlled*

| | |
|---|---|
| Dixie College* | St. George |
| Eastern Utah, College of* | Price |
| Snow College* | Ephraim |
| Utah Technical College at Provo | Provo |
| Utah Technical Coll. at Salt Lake | Salt Lake City |

## VERMONT

*Publicly controlled*

| | |
|---|---|
| Vermont, Community College of | Montpelier |
| Vermont Technical College | Randolph Center |

*Privately controlled*

| | |
|---|---|
| Champlain College | Burlington |
| Ethan Allen Community College* | Manchester Center |
| Green Mountain College | Poultney |
| Vermont College of Norwich University | Montpelier |
| Vermont Inst. of Community Involvement | Burlington |

## VIRGINIA

*Publicly controlled*

| | |
|---|---|
| Blue Ridge Community College* | Weyers Cave |
| Central Virginia Community College* | Lynchburg |
| Dabney S. Lancaster Community Coll.* | Clifton Forge |
| Danville Community College* | Danville |
| Eastern Shore Community College* | Melfa |
| Germanna Community College* | Locust Grove |
| J. Sargeant Reynolds Community Coll.* | Richmond |
| Downtown Campus | Richmond |
| Parham Road Campus | Richmond |
| John Tyler Community College* | Chester |
| Lord Fairfax Community College* | Middletown |
| Mountain Empire Community College* | Big Stone Gap |
| New River Community College* | Dublin |
| Northern Virginia Community College* | Annandale |
| Alexandria Campus | Alexandria |
| Annandale Campus | Annandale |
| Loudoun Campus | Sterling |
| Manassas Campus | Manassas |
| Woodbridge Campus | Woodbridge |
| Patrick Henry Community College* | Martinsville |
| Paul D. Camp Community College* | Franklin |
| Piedmont Virginia Community College* | Charlottesville |
| Rappahannock Community College* | Glenns |
| North Campus* | Warsaw |
| South Campus* | Glenns |
| Richard Bland College* | Petersburg |
| Southside Virginia Community College* | Alberta |
| Christanna Campus | Alberta |
| John H. Daniel Campus | Keysville |
| Southwest Virginia Community College* | Richlands |
| Thomas Nelson Community College* | Hampton |
| Tidewater Community College | Portsmouth |
| Chesapeake Campus* | Chesapeake |
| Frederick Campus* | Portsmouth |
| Virginia Beach Campus* | Virginia Beach |
| Virginia Highlands Community College* | Abingdon |
| Virginia Western Community College* | Roanoke |
| Wytheville Community College* | Wytheville |

*Privately controlled*

| | |
|---|---|
| Ferrum College | Ferrum |
| Southern Seminary Junior College | Buena Vista |

## WASHINGTON

*Publicly controlled*

| | |
|---|---|
| Bellevue Community College* | Bellevue |
| Big Bend Community College* | Moses Lake |
| Centralia Community College* | Centralia |
| Clark Community College* | Vancouver |
| Columbia Basin College* | Pasco |
| Community College District V | Everett |
| Edmonds Community College* | Lynnwood |
| Everett Community College* | Everett |
| Community College District VI | Seattle |
| North Seattle Community College* | Seattle |
| Seattle Central Community College* | Seattle |
| South Seattle Community College* | Seattle |
| Community College District XVII | Spokane |
| Spokane Community College* | Spokane |
| Spokane Falls Community College* | Spokane |
| Fort Steilacoom Community College* | Tacoma |
| Grays Harbor College* | Aberdeen |
| Green River Community College* | Auburn |
| Highline Community College* | Midway |
| Lower Columbia College* | Longview |
| Olympia Technical Community College* | Olympia |
| Olympic College* | Bremerton |

| | |
|---|---|
| Peninsula College* | Port Angeles |
| Shoreline Community College* | Seattle |
| Skagit Valley College* | Mount Vernon |
| Tacoma Community College* | Tacoma |
| Walla Walla Community College* | Walla Walla |
| Wenatchee Valley College* | Wenatchee |
| Whatcom Community College* | Bellingham |
| Yakima Valley College* | Yakima |

## WEST VIRGINIA

*Publicly controlled*

| | |
|---|---|
| Fairmont Community College* | Fairmont |
| Marshall Univ. Community College | Huntington |
| Parkersburg Community College* | Parkersburg |
| Shepherd College—Community College Component* | Shepherdstown |
| Southern West Virginia Comm. College | Logan |
| Logan Campus* | Logan |
| Williamson Campus* | Williamson |
| West Virginia Institute of Technology—Community and Technical College* | Montgomery |
| West Virginia Northern Comm. College* | Wheeling |
| Weirton Campus | Weirton |
| Wheeling Campus | Wheeling |
| West Virginia University—Potomac State College* | Keyser |

*Privately controlled*

| | |
|---|---|
| Beckley College | Beckley |
| Ohio Valley College | Parkersburg |

## WISCONSIN

*Publicly controlled*

| | |
|---|---|
| University Center System | Madison |
| Baraboo-Sauk County Campus | Baraboo |
| Barron County Campus | Rice Lake |
| Fond du Lac Campus | Fond du Lac |
| Fox Valley Campus | Menasha |
| Manitowoc County Campus | Manitowoc |
| Marathon County Campus | Wausau |
| Marinette County Campus | Marinette |
| Marshfield-Wood County Campus | Marshfield |
| Medford Campus | Medford |
| Richland Campus | Richland Center |
| Rock County Campus | Janesville |
| Sheboygan Campus | Sheboygan |
| Washington County Campus | West Bend |
| Waukesha County Campus | Waukesha |
| Vocational Tech. & Adult Education Sys.: | Madison |
| Blackhawk Technical Institute* | Janesville |
| Beloit Campus | Beloit |
| Central Campus | Janesville |
| Decatur Campus | Brodhead |
| District One Technical Institute* | Eau Claire |
| VTAE District Four | Madison |
| Fort Atkinson Voc.-Tech. School | Madison |
| Madison Area Technical College* | Madison |
| Watertown Center | Watertown |
| Fox Valley Technical Institute* | Appleton |
| Appleton Campus | Appleton |
| Oshkosh Campus | Oshkosh |
| Gateway Technical Institute | Kenosha |
| Elkhorn Campus* | Elkhorn |
| Kenosha Campus* | Kenosha |
| Racine Campus* | Racine |
| Lakeshore Technical Institute* | Cleveland |
| Mid-State Technical Institute* | Wisconsin Rapids |
| Marshfield Campus | Marshfield |
| Stevens Point Campus | Stevens Point |
| Wisconsin Rapids Campus | Wisconsin Rapids |
| Milwaukee Area Technical College | Milwaukee |
| Central Campus* | Milwaukee |
| North Campus* | Mequon |
| South Campus* | Oak Creek |
| West Campus* | West Allis |
| Moraine Park Technical Institute* | Fond du Lac |
| Beaver Dam Campus | Beaver Dam |
| Fond du Lac Campus | Fond du Lac |
| West Bend Campus | West Bend |
| Nicolet College and Tech. Institute* | Rhinelander |
| North Central Technical Institute* | Wausau |
| Wausau Campus | Wausau |
| Antigo Campus | Antigo |
| Northeast Wisconsin Technical Inst.* | Green Bay |
| Green Bay Campus | Green Bay |
| Marinette Campus | Marinette |
| Sturgeon Bay Campus | Sturgeon Bay |
| Southwest Wisconsin Technical Inst.* | Fennimore |
| Waukesha County Technical Institute* | Pewaukee |
| Western Wisconsin Technical Institute* | La Crosse |
| Wisconsin Indianhead VTAE District | Shell Lake |
| Ashland Campus | Ashland |
| Grantsburg Campus | Grantsburg |
| New Richmond Campus | New Richmond |
| Rice Lake Campus | Rice Lake |
| Superior Campus | Superior |

*Privately controlled*

| | |
|---|---|
| Concordia College | Milwaukee |
| Milwaukee School of Engineering | Milwaukee |

## WYOMING

*Publicly controlled*

| | |
|---|---|
| Casper College* | Casper |
| Central Wyoming College* | Riverton |
| Eastern Wyoming College* | Torrington |
| Laramie County Community College* | Cheyenne |
| Northern Wyoming Community College* | Sheridan |
| Northwest Community College* | Powell |
| Western Wyoming Community College* | Rock Springs |

## CANADA

*Publicly controlled*

| | |
|---|---|
| Fraser Valley College* | Chilliwack, B.C. |
| Grant McEwan Community College* | Edmonton, Albta. |
| Lambton College* | Sarnia, Ont. |
| Lethbridge Community College* | Lethbridge, Albta. |
| Malaspina College* | Nanaimo, B.C. |
| Medicine Hat College* | Medicine Hat, Albta. |
| Mount Royal College* | Calgary, Albta. |

## OTHER COUNTRIES

*Privately controlled*

| | |
|---|---|
| American College of Switzerland | Leysin, Switz. |
| Franklin College | Lugano, Switz. |
| Schiller College | Heidelberg, W. Ger. |
| St. Johns College* | Belize |

## Stock Traders

In 1976, financial institutions and intermediaries accounted for 70.3% of the value of all shares traded on the Big Board. Individuals accounted for only 29.7%.

# Accredited U.S. Senior Colleges and Universities, Spring 1978

*Source: Information Please* questionnaires to Colleges and Universities.

Only four-year schools, offering at least a Bachelor's degree, that are fully accredited by one of the institutional and professional accrediting associations recognized by the Council on Postsecondary Accreditation are listed. The number of students is for matriculated undergraduate and graduate students who are working for a degree.

Tuition, room, and board listed are average annual figures, subject to fluctuation, covering two semesters, two out of three trimesters, or three out of four quarters, depending on school calendar.

For further information, write to the Registrar of the school concerned.

**Abbreviations used for controls:**

| | |
|---|---|
| **AC** | Advent Christian |
| **AG** | Assembly of God |
| **AL** | American Lutheran |
| **AME** | African Methodist Episcopal |
| **B** | Baptist |
| **CB** | Church of Brethren |
| **CC** | Church of Christ |
| **CG** | Church of God |
| **CMA** | Christian & Missionary Alliance |
| **Cong** | Congregational |
| **CP** | Cumberland Presbyterian |
| **CR** | Christian Reformed |
| **DC** | Disciples of Christ |
| **E** | Episcopalian |
| **EC** | Evangelical Covenant |
| **F** | Federal |
| **FM** | Free Methodist |
| **GO** | Greek Orthodox |
| **ID** | Interdenominational |
| **Ind** | Independent |
| **J** | Jewish |
| **L** | Lutheran |
| **LCA** | Lutheran Church of America |
| **LDS** | Latter-day Saints |
| **M** | Methodist |
| **MB** | Mennonite Brethren |
| **MC** | Missionary Church |
| **Men** | Mennonite |
| **Mun** | Municipal |
| **Naz** | Nazarene |
| **ND** | Non-denominational |
| **P** | Private |
| **Pres** | Presbyterian |
| **Pub** | Public |
| **PUS** | Presbyterian, U.S. |
| **RC** | Roman Catholic |
| **RCA** | Reformed Church in America |
| **RP** | Reformed Presybyterian |
| **S** | State |
| **SB** | Southern Baptist |
| **SDA** | Seventh Day Adventist |
| **SOF** | Society of Friends |
| **UCC** | United Church of Christ |
| **UM** | United Methodist |
| **UP** | United Presbyterian |
| **W** | Wesleyan |

| Institution and location | Enrollment | | Faculty | Control | Tuition | | Rm/Bd |
|---|---|---|---|---|---|---|---|
| | Male | Female | | | Res. | Nonres. | |
| Abilene Christian University; Abilene, Tex. 79601 | 1,508[1] | 1,449[1] | 152 | P | $1410 | $1410 | $1094 |
| Academy of Art College; San Francisco, Calif. 94102 | 750[2] | | n.a. | P/CC | 1500[2] | n.a. | 1100[2] |
| Adams State College; Alamosa, Colo. 81102 | 1,173[1] | 1,239[1] | 125 | S | 604 | 1934 | 1434 |
| Adelphi University; Garden City, N.Y. 11530 | 10,500[2] | | n.a. | P | 2940[2] | n.a. | 1495[2] |
| Adrian College; Adrian, Mich. 49221 | 431[1] | 481[1] | 54 | P/UM | 3060 | ([3]) | 1566 |
| Agnes Scott College; Decatur, Ga. 30030 | — | 523 | 67 | P | 3200 | 3200 | 1500 |
| Akron, The University of; Akron, Ohio 44325 | 12,028[1] | 11,093[1] | 817 | S | 940 | 1900 | 1551 |
| Alabama, The University of; University, Ala. 35486 | 7,436[1] | 6,192[1] | 774 | S | 667 | 1412 | 1178 |
| Alabama, The Univ. of, in Birmingham; Birmingham, Ala. 35294 | 3,677[1] | 3,827[1] | 1198 | S | 630 | 1260 | — |
| Alabama, The Univ. of, in Huntsville; Huntsville, Ala. 35807 | 1,215[1] | 1,143[1] | 193 | S | 645 | 645 | 1046 |
| Alabama A&M University; Normal, Ala. 35762 | 1,992[1] | 1,609[1] | 242 | S | 490 | 715 | 1138 |
| Alabama State University; Montgomery, Ala. 36101 | 1,935 | 2,596 | 238 | S | 495 | 825 | 975 |
| Alaska, University of; Fairbanks, Alaska 99701 | | | | | | | |
| Northern Region; Fairbanks, Alaska 99701 | 2,532[2] | | n.a. | S | 320 | n.a. | 1864[2] |
| South Central Region; Anchorage, Alaska 99504 | 11,246[2] | | n.a. | S | 334[2] | n.a. | n.a. |
| Albany College of Pharmacy. *See* Union University | | | | | | | |
| Albany Law School. *See* Union University | | | | | | | |
| Albany Medical College. *See* Union University | | | | | | | |
| Albany State College; Albany, Ga. 31705 | 2,190[2] | | n.a. | S | 732[2] | n.a. | 1504[2] |
| Albertus Magnus College; New Haven, Conn. 06511 | 12[1] | 528[1] | 32 | P/RC | 2950[4] | 2950[4] | 1850 |
| Albion College; Albion, Mich. 49224 | 894 | 730 | 106 | P/UM | 3432 | 3432 | 1664 |
| Albright College; Reading, Pa. 19604 | 570 | 585 | 82 | P | 3350 | 3350 | 1500 |
| Albuquerque, University of; Albuquerque, N.M. 87140 | 686 | 580 | 96 | P | 1500 | 1500 | 1547 |
| Alcorn State University; Lorman, Miss. 39096 | 1,312 | 1,738 | 122 | S | 588 | 1288 | 912 |
| Alderson–Broaddus College; Philippi, W. Va. 26416 | 740[2] | | n.a. | P/B | 2200[2] | n.a. | 1182[2] |
| Alfred University[5]; Alfred, N.Y. 14802 | 1,090 | 1,005 | 172 | P | 4090 | 4090 | 1725 |
| Allegheny College; Meadville, Pa. 16335 | 947 | 851 | 120 | P | 3300 | 3300 | 1280 |
| Allentown College of St. Francis de Sales; Center Valley, Pa. 18034 | 283 | 275 | 38 | P/RC | 2800 | 2800 | 1700 |
| Alliance College; Cambridge Springs, Pa. 16403 | 121 | 82 | 23 | P | 1950 | 1950 | 1400 |
| Alma College; Alma, Mich. 48801 | 548 | 549 | 70 | P | 3348 | 3348 | 1560 |
| Alvernia College; Reading, Pa. 19607 | 167 | 155 | 18 | P/RC | 1650 | 1650 | 1400 |
| Alverno College; Milwaukee, Wis. 53215 | 12[1] | 1,089[1] | 69 | P | 2350 | 2350 | 1160 |
| American Baptist College; Nashville, Tenn. 37207 | 103 | 8 | 5 | P/B | 400 | 400 | 750 |

| Institution and location | Enrollment | | Faculty | Control | Tuition | | |
|---|---|---|---|---|---|---|---|
| | Male | Female | | | Res. | Nonres. | Rm/Bd |
| American College in Paris; Paris, France 75007 | 209[1] | 327[1] | 17 | P | $2800 | $2800 | $3150 |
| American Conservatory of Music; Chicago, Ill. 60603 | 98 | 102 | 30 | P | 2000 | 2000 | — |
| American Grad. School of Intl. Mgt.; Glendale, Ariz. 85306 | 661 | 209 | 57 | P | 2970 | 2970 | 1450 |
| American International College; Springfield, Mass. 01109 | 795[1] | 448[1] | 70 | P | 2370 | 2370 | 1507 |
| American Technological University; Killeen, Tex. 76541 | 620 | 77 | 7[6] | P | 865 | 865 | 1260 |
| American University, The; Washington, D.C. 20016 | 3,667[1] | 3,076[1] | 360 | P/M | 3690[4] | 3690[4] | 1892 |
| Americas, University of the; Puebla, Mexico | 802 | 405 | 47 | P | 3375 | 4219 | 1700 |
| Amherst College; Amherst, Mass. 01002 | 1,087 | 395 | 150 | P | 4550[4] | 4550[4] | 1800[4] |
| Ana G. Méndez Educational Foundation; Rio Piedras, P.R. 00928 | 1,903[7] | 2,808[7] | n.a. | P | n.a. | n.a. | n.a. |
| Turabo University College; Caguas, P.R. 00625 | 4,366[2] | | n.a. | P | n.a. | n.a. | n.a. |
| Anderson College; Anderson, Ind. 46011 | 772 | 923 | 89 | P/CG | 2600 | 2600 | 1120 |
| Andrews University; Berrien Springs, Mich. 49104 | 1,384[1] | 1,035[1] | 191 | P/SDA | 3171 | 3171 | 1665 |
| Angelo State University; San Angelo, Tex. 76901 | 2,077 | 1,820 | 190 | S | 386 | 1466 | 1230 |
| Anna Maria College; Paxton, Mass. 01612 | 600[2] | | n.a. | P/RC | 2100[2] | n.a. | 1650[2] |
| Annhurst College; Woodstock, Conn. 06281 | 55 | 228 | 36 | P/RC | 2526 | 2526 | 1936 |
| Antioch College; Yellow Springs, Ohio 45387 | 1,450 | 2,000 | 230 | P | n.a. | n.a. | n.a. |
| Appalachian Bible Institute; Bradley, W. Va. 25818 | 128 | 92 | 12 | P | 1174 | 1174 | 1225 |
| Appalachian State Univ. *See* North Carolina, Univ. System of | | | | | | | |
| Aquinas College; Grand Rapids, Mich. 49506 | 1,009[2] | | n.a. | P/RC | 2260[2] | n.a. | 1400[2] |
| Arizona, University of; Tucson, Ariz. 85721 | 11,902 | 10,139 | 1579 | S | 450 | 1640 | 1370 |
| Arizona State University; Tempe, Ariz. 85281 | 18,222 | 15,510 | 1267 | S | 450 | 1640 | 1070 |
| Arkansas, University of; Fayetteville, Ark. 72701 | 6,103 | 4,069 | 629 | S | 460 | 1090 | 1295 |
| Univ. of Arkansas at Little Rock; Little Rock, Ark. 72204 | 9,297[7] | | n.a. | S | 400[7] | n.a. | n.a. |
| Univ. of Arkansas at Monticello; Monticello, Ark. 71655 | 901 | 916 | 103 | S | 488 | 888 | 1096 |
| Univ. of Arkansas at Pine Bluff; Pine Bluff, Ark. 71601 | 1,426 | 1,751 | 184 | S | 400 | 700 | 1064 |
| Arkansas College; Batesville, Ark. 72501 | 195 | 275 | 20 | P/PUS | 1750 | 1750 | 1250 |
| Arkansas State University; State University, Ark. 72467 | 2,763[1] | 2,702[1] | 350 | S | 460 | 760 | 910 |
| Arkansas Tech University; Russellville, Ark. 72801 | 1,312 | 1,078 | 120 | S | 490 | 840 | 1040 |
| Armstrong College; Berkeley, Calif. 94704 | 623[2] | | n.a. | P | 2004[2] | n.a. | n.a. |
| Armstrong State College; Savannah, Ga. 31406 | 1,528 | 1,672 | 182 | S | 504 | 1215 | — |
| Art Academy of Cincinnati; Cincinnati, Ohio 45202 | 63 | 68 | 9 | P | 1750 | 1750 | — |
| Art Center College of Design; Pasadena, Calif. 91103 | 680 | 340 | 130 | P | 2800 | 2800 | — |
| Art Institute of Boston, The; Boston, Mass. 02215 | 160 | 218 | 48 | P | 1850 | 1850 | 2500 |
| Asbury College; Wilmore, Ky. 40390 | 597 | 595 | 93 | P/ND | 2230 | 2230 | 1338 |
| Ashland College; Ashland, Ohio 44805 | 1,240 | 813 | 105 | P/CB | 3430 | 3430 | 1500 |
| Assumption College; Worcester, Mass. 01609 | 660 | 635 | 70 | P | 3000 | 3000 | 1625 |
| Athens State College; Athens, Ala. 35611 | 426 | 277 | 40 | S | 480 | 480 | 1100 |
| Atlanta Christian College; East Point, Ga. 30344 | 116 | 68 | 13 | P/CC | 960 | 960 | 1000 |
| Atlanta College of Art; Atlanta, Ga. 30309 | 235[2] | | n.a. | P | 2150[2] | n.a. | n.a. |
| Atlanta University; Atlanta, Ga. 30314 | 362 | 544 | 112 | P | 1700 | 1700 | 550[8] |
| Atlantic, College of the; Bar Harbor, Me. 04609 | 48 | 61 | 10 | P | 3200 | 3200 | 810 |
| Atlantic Christian College; Wilson, N.C. 27893 | 553[1] | 992[1] | 88 | P/DC | 1510 | 1510 | 1020 |
| Atlantic Union College; South Lancaster, Mass. 01561 | 273 | 339 | 55 | P/SDA | 3192 | 3192 | 1500 |
| Auburn University; Auburn, Ala. 36830 | 10,620 | 7,357 | 1013 | S | 600 | 1200 | 1275 |
| Auburn University at Montgomery; Montgomery, Ala. 36117 | 3,800[2] | | n.a. | S | 525[2] | n.a. | n.a. |
| Augsburg College; Minneapolis, Minn. 55454 | 749[1] | 846[1] | 100 | P/AL | 3100[4] | 3100[4] | 1500 |
| Augusta College; Augusta, Ga. 30904 | 1,811 | 2,055 | 141 | S | 496 | 1210 | — |
| Augustana College; Rock Island, Ill. 61201 | 1,084[9] | 1,104[9] | 119 | P/LCA | 2610 | 2610 | 1422 |
| Augustana College; Sioux Falls, S.D. 57102 | 2,263[7] | | n.a. | P | 2475[10] | n.a. | 1150[10] |
| Aurora College; Aurora, Ill. 60507 | 613[1] | 329[1] | 38[1] | P | 2700 | 2700 | 1590 |
| Austin College; Sherman, Tex. 75090 | 688[1] | 510[1] | 88 | P/PUS | 2950 | 2950 | 1385 |
| Austin Peay State University; Clarksville, Tenn. 37040 | 2,424[1] | 2,448[1] | 186 | S | 402 | 1740 | 1245 |
| Averett College; Danville, Va. 24541 | 262 | 552 | 45 | P/B | 3600[11] | | — |
| Avila College; Kansas City, Mo. 64145 | 191 | 634 | 59 | P/RC | 1950 | 1950 | 1250 |
| Azusa Pacific College; Azusa, Calif. 91702 | 596 | 699 | 84 | P/ID | 2760 | 2760 | 1540 |
| Babson College; Babson Park, Mass. 02157 | 1,041[1] | 298[1] | 79 | P | 3600 | 3600 | 1650 |
| Baker University; Baldwin City, Kan. 66006 | 469 | 434 | 53 | P/M | 2150 | 2150 | 1260 |
| Baldwin-Wallace College; Berea, Ohio 44017 | 1,007[1] | 837[1] | 133 | P | 3132 | 3132 | 1479 |
| Ball State University; Muncie, Ind. 47306 | 6,241 | 6,496 | 868 | S | 840 | 1800 | 1224 |
| Baltimore, University of; Baltimore, Md. 21201 | 3,932[1] | 1,542[1] | 115 | S | 700 | 1600 | — |
| Baltimore Hebrew College; Baltimore, Md. 21215 | 84 | 125 | 16 | P | 850 | 850 | — |
| Bank Street College of Education; New York, N.Y. 10025 | 20 | 132 | 35 | P | 4820 | 4820 | — |
| Baptist Bible Coll. of Pennsylvania; Clarks Summit, Pa. 18411 | 513 | 375 | 41 | P/B | 1760 | 1760 | 1406 |
| Baptist College at Charleston; Charleston, S.C. 29411 | 545[1] | 740[1] | 91 | P/B | 1175 | 1175 | 785 |

| Institution and location | Enrollment | | Faculty | Control | Tuition | | Rm/Bd |
|---|---|---|---|---|---|---|---|
| | Male | Female | | | Res. | Nonres. | |
| Barat College; Lake Forest, Ill. 60045 | — | 479[1] | 44 | P/RC | $2790 | $2790 | $1680 |
| Barber–Scotia College; Concord, N.C. 28025 | 155 | 260 | 22 | P/UP | 1050 | 1050 | 1129 |
| Bard College; Annandale–on–Hudson, N.Y. 12504 | 661[10] | | n.a. | P | 4430[10] | n.a. | 1780[10] |
| Barnard College. *See* Columbia University | | | | | | | |
| Barrington College; Barrington, R.I. 02806 | 203 | 273 | 35 | P/ND | 2822 | 2822 | 1770 |
| Barry College; Miami, Fla. 33161 | 266 | 1,230 | 70 | P/RC | 2600 | 2600 | 1460 |
| Bates College; Lewiston, Me. 04240 | 736[9] | 593[9] | 115 | P | 5360 | 5360 | 1400 |
| Bayamón Central University; Bayamón, P.R. 00619 | 1,163 | 1,276 | 60 | P/RC | 2633 | — | — |
| Baylor College of Dentistry; Dallas, Tex. 75246 | 394 | 109 | 103 | P | 500 | 1500 | — |
| Baylor College of Medicine; Houston, Tex. 77025 | 860[2] | | n.a. | P | n.a. | n.a. | n.a. |
| Baylor University; Waco, Tex. 76703 | 3,862 | 3,913 | 381 | P/SB | 1760 | 1760 | 1370 |
| Beaver College; Glenside, Pa. 19038 | 76[1] | 531[1] | 56 | P | 3600 | 3600 | 1900 |
| Behrend College. *See* Pennsylvania State University | | | | | | | |
| Belhaven College; Jackson, Miss. 39202 | 192 | 279 | 31 | P/Pres | 1850 | 1850 | 1100 |
| Bellarmine College; Louisville, Ky. 40205 | 906[1] | 876[1] | 92 | P/RC | 2050 | 2050 | 1200 |
| Bellevue College; Bellevue, Neb., 68005 | 318 | 178 | 23 | P | 960 | 960 | — |
| Belmont Abbey College; Belmont, N.C. 28012 | 429 | 212 | 29 | P/RC | 2063 | 2063 | 1420 |
| Belmont College; Nashville, Tenn. 37203 | 628[1] | 639[1] | 69 | P/B | 1700 | 1700 | 1090 |
| Beloit College; Beloit, Wis. 53511 | 502[1] | 522[1] | 80 | P | 3900 | 3900 | 1460 |
| Bemidji State Univ. *See* Minnesota State College System | | | | | | | |
| Benedict College; Columbia, S.C. 29204 | 665 | 1,193 | 96 | P | 1800 | 1800 | 1200 |
| Benedictine College; Atchison, Kan. 66002 | 427[1] | 418[1] | 61 | P | 2200[4] | 2200[4] | 1475 |
| Bennett College; Greensboro, N.C. 27420 | — | 618[2] | n.a. | P/M | 1565[2] | n.a. | 935[2] |
| Bennington College; Bennington, Vt. 05201 | 195 | 377 | 70 | P | 6100 | 6100 | 1440 |
| Bentley College; Waltham, Mass. 02154 | 2,317[1] | 816 | 111 | P | 3225 | 3225 | 2100 |
| Berea College; Berea, Ky. 40403 | 592[1] | 799[1] | 110 | P | — | — | 1197 |
| Berklee College of Music; Boston, Mass. 02215 | 2,263[1] | 271[1] | 165 | P | 2580 | 2580 | 1750 |
| Berkshire Christian College; Lenox, Mass. 01240 | 60 | 69 | 13 | P/AC | 1990 | 1990 | 1150 |
| Bernard M. Baruch College. *See* New York, City University of | | | | | | | |
| Berry College; Mount Berry, Ga. 30149 | 496 | 698 | 83 | P | 1800 | 1800 | 1395 |
| Bethany Bible College; Santa Cruz, Calif. 95066 | 261[1] | 199[1] | 31 | P/AG | 1460 | 1460 | 1192 |
| Bethany College, Bethany, W. Va. 26032 | 542 | 376 | 63 | P/DC | 3200 | 3200 | 1335 |
| Bethany College; Lindsborg, Kan. 67456 | 370[1] | 352[1] | 45 | P/LCA | 1885 | 1885 | 1135 |
| Bethany Nazarene College; Bethany, Okla. 73008 | 626[1] | 698[1] | 64 | Naz | 1400 | 1400 | 1240 |
| Bethel College; McKenzie, Tenn. 38201 | 135 | 130 | 19 | P/CP | 1500 | 1500 | 1260 |
| Bethel College; Mishawaka, Ind. 46544 | 218 | 194 | 31 | P | 2000 | 2000 | 1150 |
| Bethel College; North Newton, Kan. 67117 | 289 | 225 | 39 | P/Men | 2028 | 2028 | 168 |
| Bethel College; St. Paul, Minn. 55112 | 826[9] | 1,041[9] | 76 | P/B | 2500 | 2500 | 1150 |
| Bethune–Cookman College; Daytona Beach, Fla. 32015 | 1,465[2] | | n.a. | P/M | 1550[2] | n.a. | 1316[2] |
| Biola College; La Mirada, Calif. 90639 | 2,282[7] | | n.a. | P/ID | 2400[2] | n.a. | 1450[2] |
| Birmingham–Southern College; Birmingham, Ala. 35204 | 634[1] | 568[1] | 65 | P/M | 2000 | 2000 | 1300 |
| Biscayne College; Miami, Fla. 33054 | 937 | 686 | 50 | P/RC | 2475 | 2475 | 2000 |
| Bishop College; Dallas, Tex. 75241 | 1,733[7] | | n.a. | P/B | 1500[2] | n.a. | 1265[2] |
| Black Hills State College; Spearfish, S.D. 57783 | 685 | 872 | 87 | S | 563 | 1187 | 1043 |
| Blackburn College; Carlinville, Ill. 62626 | 252 | 295 | 38 | P | 2200[4] | 2200[4] | 500 |
| Bloomfield College; Bloomfield, N.J. 07003 | 1,097[1] | 612[1] | 54 | P | 2670 | 2670 | 1680 |
| Bloomsburg State College; Bloomsburg, Pa. 17815 | 2,229[1] | 2,838[1] | 281 | S | 950 | 1780 | 1000 |
| Blue Mountain College; Blue Mountain, Miss. 38610 | 64 | 195 | 25 | P/SB | 1100 | 1100 | 1100 |
| Bluefield State College; Bluefield, W. Va. 24701 | 1,426[9] | 1,297[9] | 65 | S | 320 | 1220 | — |
| Bluffton College; Bluffton, Ohio 45817 | 289[1] | 291[1] | 47 | P/Men | 2700 | 2700 | 1130 |
| Boise State University; Boise, Idaho 83725 | 2,578 | 2,059 | 332 | S | 369 | 1409 | 1270 |
| Borromeo College of Ohio; Wickliffe, Ohio 44092 | 85 | — | 20 | P/RC | 2375 | — | 1200 |
| Boston College; Chestnut Hill, Mass. 02167 | 4,100 | 4,400 | 540 | P/RC | 3645 | 3645 | 2000 |
| Boston Conservatory of Music; Boston, Mass. 02215 | 168[1] | 338[1] | 55 | P | 2900 | 2900 | 1800 |
| Boston State College; Boston, Mass. 02115 | 3,064[1] | 2,559[1] | 290 | S | 500 | 1250 | — |
| Boston University; Boston, Mass. 02215 | 7,768 | 7,966 | 1330 | P | 4230 | 4230 | 2050 |
| Bowdoin College; Brunswick, Me. 04011 | 791 | 488 | 100 | P | 4600 | 4600 | 1880 |
| Bowie State College; Bowie, Md. 20715 | 671[1] | 649[1] | 97[1] | S | 750 | 1700 | 660 |
| Bowling Green State University; Bowling Green, Ohio 43403 | 7,308 | 9,352 | 721 | S | 945 | 2145 | 1368 |
| Bradford College; Bradford, Mass. 01830 | 114[1] | 233[1] | 19[13] | P | 3650 | 3650 | 2050 |
| Bradley University; Peoria, Ill. 61625 | 2,576[1] | 2,474[1] | 270 | P | 3020 | 3020 | 1420 |
| Brandeis University; Waltham, Mass. 02154 | 1,513[1] | 1,430[1] | 349 | P | 4650[4] | 4650[4] | 2093 |
| Brenau College; Gainesville, Ga. 30501 | 165 | 630 | 42 | P | 2016 | ([14]) | 1784 |
| Brescia College; Owensboro, Ky. 42301 | 221[1] | 322[1] | 50 | P | 1590 | 1590 | 1125 |
| Briar Cliff College; Sioux City, Iowa 51104 | 244 | 440 | 55 | P/RC | 2190 | 2190 | 1145 |
| Bridgeport, University of; Bridgeport, Conn. 06602 | 1,296 | 1,668 | 346 | P | 3660 | 3660 | 1200 |
| Bridgeport Engineering Institute; Bridgeport, Conn. 06606 | 370 | 18 | 80[15] | P | 1240 | 1240 | — |
| Bridgewater College; Bridgewater, Va. 22812 | 427[1] | 388[1] | 55 | P | 2215 | 2215 | 1400 |
| Bridgewater State College; Bridgewater, Mass. 02324 | 1,279 | 2,373 | 218 | S | 500 | 1250 | 1300 |

| Institution and location | Enrollment | | | | Tuition | | |
|---|---|---|---|---|---|---|---|
| | Male | Female | Faculty | Control | Res. | Nonres. | Rm/Bd |
| Brigham Young University; Provo, Utah 84601 | 11,902[16] | 9,966[16] | 1075 | P/LDS | $840 | $1260 | $1280 |
| Hawaii Campus; Laie, Hawaii 96762 | 639 | 867 | 90 | P | 320 | 380 | 580 |
| Brooklyn College. *See* New York, City University of | | | | | | | |
| Brooklyn Coll. of Pharmacy. *See* Long Island Univ., Arnold & Marie Schwartz Coll. of Pharmacy & Health Sciences | | | | | | | |
| Brooklyn Law School; Brooklyn, N.Y. 11201 | 633 | 364 | 26 | P | 3000 | 3000 | — |
| Brooks Institute; Santa Barbara, Calif. 93108 | 663 | 120 | 25 | P | 2730 | 2730 | — |
| Brown University; Providence, R.I. 02912 | 3,710 | 2,703 | 464 | P | 5050 | 5050 | 2090 |
| Bryan College; Dayton, Tenn. 37321 | 276 | 272 | 31 | P | 1750 | 1750 | 1500 |
| Bryant College; Smithfield, R.I. 02917 | 1,752[1] | 1,017[1] | 115 | P | 2550 | 2550 | 1525 |
| Bryn Mawr College; Bryn Mawr, Pa. 19010 | 105[1] | 1,180[1] | 154 | P | 4625 | 4625 | 1990 |
| Bucknell University; Lewisburg, Pa. 17837 | 1,671 | 1,338 | 225 | P | 4425 | 4425 | 1500 |
| Buena Vista College; Storm Lake, Iowa 50588 | 489 | 376 | 50 | P/Pres | 2650 | 2650 | 1130 |
| Butler University; Indianapolis, Ind. 46208 | 1,031 | 1,156 | 164 | P | 2720 | 2720 | 675 |
| Cabrini College; Radnor, Pa. 19087 | 58 | 289 | 30 | P/RC | 2350 | 2350 | 1750 |
| Caldwell College; Caldwell, N.J. 07006 | 504[7] | | n.a. | P/RC | 2100[2] | n.a. | n.a. |
| California, New College of; San Francisco, Calif. 94110 | 75 | 85 | 7 | P | 2400 | 2400 | 2000 |
| California, University of; Berkeley, Calif. 94720 | 67,288[1] | 50,824[1] | 7853 | S | 710 | 2620 | 2600 |
| UC, Berkeley; Berkeley, Calif. 94720 | 16,718[1] | 10,852[1] | 1652 | S | 709 | 2614 | 3500 |
| UC, Davis; Davis, Calif. 95616 | 8,388[1] | 7,106[1] | 1037 | S | 685 | 2595 | 2270 |
| UC, Irvine; Irvine, Calif. 92717 | 4,721[1] | 3,717[1] | 450 | S | 735 | 2640 | 2165 |
| UC, Los Angeles; Los Angeles, Calif. 90024 | 15,125[1] | 12,824[1] | 2070 | S | 702 | 1905 | 1515 |
| UC, Riverside; Riverside, Calif. 92502 | 2,754[1] | 2,102[1] | 531 | S | 717 | 2622 | 1500 |
| UC, San Diego; La Jolla, Calif. 92093 | 5,439[1] | 3,827[1] | 800 | S | 723 | 2628 | 2300 |
| UC, San Francisco; San Francisco, Calif. 94143 | 2,123[1] | 1,444[1] | n.a. | S | 710 | 2620 | 2600 |
| UC, Santa Barbara; Santa Barbara, Calif. 93106 | 7,443[1] | 7,145[1] | 725 | S | 715 | 2620 | 1680 |
| UC, Santa Cruz; Santa Cruz, Calif. 95064 | 3,016[1] | 3,081[1] | 352 | S | — | 1905 | 1700 |
| California Baptist College; Riverside, Calif. 92504 | 306 | 282 | 36 | P/SB | 1650 | 1650 | 1100 |
| California Coll. of Arts and Crafts; Oakland, Calif. | 337[1] | 538[1] | 33 | P | 3130 | 3130 | 1900 |
| California Coll. of Podiatric Medicine; San Francisco, Calif. 94120 | 345 | 35 | 18 | P | 5800 | 5800 | — |
| California Inst. of Technology; Pasadena, Calif. 91125 | 1,484[1] | 183[1] | 340 | P | 3939 | 3939 | 2050 |
| California Institute of the Arts; Valencia, Calif. 91355 | 407 | 231 | 64 | P | 3750 | — | 1860 |
| California Lutheran College; Thousand Oaks, Calif. 91360 | 2,502[2] | | n.a. | P | 2600[2] | n.a. | 1500[2] |
| California Maritime Academy; Vallejo, Calif. 94590 | 388[7] | 14[7] | n.a. | S | n.a. | n.a. | n.a. |
| California Polytech. St. Univ.; San Luis Obispo, Calif. 93407 | 9,157 | 5,784 | 778 | S | 271 | 2100 | n.a. |
| California School of Professional Psychology—Fresno; Fresno, 93721 | 89 | 24 | — | P | 4230 | — | 2880 |
| California School of Professional Psychology—Los Angeles; Los Angeles, Calif. 90004 | 100 | 135 | 5 | P | 4230 | 4230 | 5000 |
| California School of Professional Psychology—San Diego; San Diego, Calif. 92121 | 140 | 85 | 21 | P | 4230 | 4230 | 3225 |
| California School of Professional Psychology—San Francisco; San Francisco, Calif. 94110 | 109[7] | 116[7] | n.a. | P | n.a. | n.a. | n.a. |
| California State College; Bakersfield, Calif. 93309 | 1,549[1] | 1,681[1] | 142 | S | 172 | 1710 | 1500 |
| California State College; California, Pa. 15419 | 2,378 | 2,260 | 331 | S | 950 | 1780 | 1024 |
| California St. Coll., Dominguez Hills; Carson, Calif. 90747 | 2,114 | 2,111 | 305 | S | 190 | 1765 | 3450 |
| California State Coll., San Bernardino; San Bernardino, Calif. 92407 | 1,536 | 1,524 | 173 | S | 201 | 1710 | 1350 |
| California State Coll., Sonoma. *See* Sonoma State Coll. | | | | | | | |
| California State Coll., Stanislaus; Turlock, Calif. 95380 | 1,719 | 1,729 | 161 | S | 200 | 1912 | 1503 |
| California State Polytechnic Univ.; Pomona, Calif. 91768 | 8,201[1] | 4,646[1] | 600 | S | 200 | 1775 | 1600 |
| California State Univ., Chico; Chico, Calif. 95929 | 6,764 | 6,520 | 800 | S | 211 | 1575 | 1620 |
| California State Univ., Fresno; Fresno, Calif. 93740 | 5,417 | 5,015 | 780 | S | 208 | 1783 | 1650 |
| California State Univ., Fullerton; Fullerton, Calif. 92634 | 5,670 | 5,500 | 725 | S | 200 | 1910 | 1700 |
| California State Univ., Hayward; Hayward, Calif. 94542 | 4,943 | 5,127 | 509 | S | 193 | 1903 | — |
| California State Univ., Long Beach; Long Beach, Calif. 90840 | 7,875 | 8,344 | 1025 | S | 100 | 600 | 1500 |
| California State Univ., Los Angeles; Los Angeles, Calif. 90032 | 5,293[1] | 5,644[1] | 555 | S | 200 | 1575 | — |
| California State Univ., Northridge; Northridge, Calif. 91330 | 6,997 | 6,793 | 1300 | S | 200 | 1910 | — |
| California State Univ., Sacramento; Sacramento, Calif. 95819 | 8,463[1] | 7,931[1] | 907 | S | 232 | 1532 | 1650 |
| California Western School of Law; San Diego, Calif. 92101 | 517 | 135 | 18 | P | 3630 | 3630 | — |
| Calumet College; Whiting, Ind. 46394 | 290[1] | 274[1] | 37 | RC | 1080 | 1080 | n.a. |
| Calvary Bible College; Kansas City, Mo. 64111 | 148 | 124 | 15 | P/ND | 1280 | 1280 | 1104 |

| Institution and location | Enrollment Male | Enrollment Female | Faculty | Control | Tuition Res. | Tuition Nonres. | Rm/Bd |
|---|---|---|---|---|---|---|---|
| Calvin College; Grand Rapids, Mich. 49506 | 1,880[1] | 1,921[1] | 199 | P/CR | $2230 | $2230 | $1170 |
| Cameron University; Lawton, Okla. 73505 | 1,407 | 1,287 | 197 | S | 464 | 1231 | 1062 |
| Campbell College; Buie's Creek, N.C. 27506 | 1,184[1] | 1,033[1] | 145 | P/SB | 2226 | 2226 | 1233 |
| Campbellsville College; Campbellsville, Ky. 42718 | 281 | 367 | 45 | P/SB | 1780 | 1780 | 1420 |
| Canisius College; Buffalo, N.Y. 14208 | 2,432[1] | 1,594[1] | 162 | P | 2650 | 2650 | 1400 |
| Capital University; Columbus, Ohio 43209 | 1,069[1] | 1,032[1] | 155 | P/AL | 3540 | — | 1555 |
| Capitol Institute of Technology; Kensington, Md. 20795 | 378 | 11 | 9 | P | — | 2600 | — |
| Cardinal Stritch College; Milwaukee, Wis. 53217 | 232[1] | 941[1] | 47 | P/RC | 2200 | 2200 | 1200 |
| Caribbean Center for Advanced Studies; Santurce, P.R. 00940 | 52 | 68 | 6 | P | n.a. | 1510 | n.a. |
| Carleton College; Northfield, Minn. 55057 | 888 | 773 | 135 | P | 3660 | 3660 | 1575 |
| Carlow College; Pittsburgh, Pa. 15213 | 25 | 750 | 47 | P/RC | 3100 | 3100 | 1650 |
| Carnegie–Mellon University; Pittsburgh, Pa. 15213 | 3,013 | 1,212 | 414 | P | 3400 | 3400 | 1750 |
| Carroll College; Helena, Mont. 59601 | 500[1] | 592[1] | 85 | P/RC | 1790 | 1790 | 1290 |
| Carroll College; Waukesha, Wis. 53186 | 573[1] | 559[1] | 76 | P | 3480 | — | 1270 |
| Carson–Newman College; Jefferson City, Tenn. 37760 | 730[1] | 749[1] | 94 | P/B | 1700 | 1800 | 1100 |
| Carthage College; Kenosha, Wis. 53141 | 590[1] | 625[1] | 88 | P/L | 2700 | 2700 | 1255 |
| Case Western Reserve University; Cleveland, Ohio 44106 | 3,803 | 2,097 | 601 | P | 3900 | 3900 | 1900 |
| Castleton State College; Castleton, Vt. 05735 | 700 | 500 | 100 | S | 670 | 2100 | 1445 |
| Catawba College; Salisbury, N.C. 28144 | 533 | 385 | 77 | P/UCC | 2257 | 2257 | 1124 |
| Cathedral Coll. of the Immac. Concep.; Douglaston, N.Y. 11362 | 195 | — | 40 | RC | 2350 | — | 2000 |
| Catholic University of America, The; Washington, D.C. 20064 | 3,641[1] | 3,596[1] | 382 | P/RC | 3200 | 3200 | 2000 |
| Cayey University College. *See* Puerto Rico, University of | | | | | | | |
| Cedar Crest College; Allentown, Pa. 18104 | — | 638[1] | 59 | P | 3300 | 3300 | 1500 |
| Cedarville College; Cedarville, Ohio 45314 | 610 | 640 | 52 | P/B | 1860 | 1860 | 1425 |
| Centenary College for Women; Hackettstown, N.J. 07840 | — | 550 | 41 | P | 2750 | 2750 | 2300 |
| Centenary College of Louisiana; Shreveport, La. 71104 | 359 | 316 | 75 | P/UM | 1800 | 1800 | 1500 |
| Center for Creative Studies—College of Art & Design; Detroit, Mich. 48202 | 266[1] | 186[1] | 40 | P | 2650 | 2650 | n.a. |
| Central Arkansas, University of; Conway, Ark. 72032 | 2,125 | 3,065 | 254 | S | 480 | 1020 | 1120 |
| Central Bible College; Springfield, Mo. 65802 | 684 | 450 | 38 | P/AG | 1140 | 1140 | 1288 |
| Central College. *See* Central University of Iowa | | | | | | | |
| Central Connecticut State College; New Britain, Conn. 06050 | 3,607 | 3,519 | 493 | S | 390 | 1030 | 1198 |
| Central Methodist College; Fayette, Mo. 65248 | 260 | 264 | 55 | M | 2350 | — | 1000 |
| Central Michigan University; Mt. Pleasant, Mich. 48859 | 5,926 | 6,878 | 649 | S | 720 | 1860 | 1460 |
| Central Missouri State University; Warrensburg, Mo. 64093 | 4,099[1] | 3,968[1] | 435 | S | 390 | 990 | 960 |
| Central State University; Edmond, Okla. 73034 | 3,641[1] | 3,515[1] | 338 | S | 430 | 1010 | 910 |
| Central State University; Wilberforce, Ohio 45384 | 1,080 | 976 | 108 | S | 2361 | 2991 | 1533 |
| Central University of Iowa; Pella, Iowa 50219 | 643[1] | 729[1] | 77 | P/RCA | 2828 | 2826 | 1074 |
| Central Washington University; Ellensburg, Wash. 98926 | 3,495 | 3,980 | 319 | S | 591 | 1983 | 1500 |
| Central Wesleyan College; Central, S.C. 29630 | 325[2] | | n.a. | P/W | 2150[2] | n.a. | 900[2] |
| Centre College of Kentucky; Danville, Ky. 40422 | 421 | 327 | 79 | P | 3300 | 3300 | 1600 |
| Chadron State College; Chadron, Neb. 69337 | 738 | 839 | 92 | S | 510 | 900 | 1088 |
| Chaminade University of Honolulu; Honolulu, Hawaii 96816 | 1,524 | 705 | 51 | P | 1700 | 1700 | 1850 |
| Chapman College; Orange, Calif. 92666 | 541 | 507 | 97 | P | 3400 | 3400 | 1740 |
| Charleston, College of; Charleston, S.C. 29401 | 1,617[1] | 2,109[1] | 191 | S | 550 | 1450 | 1400 |
| Chatham College; Pittsburgh, Pa. 15232 | 1 | 483 | 51 | P | 3450 | 3450 | 1740 |
| Chestnut Hill College; Philadelphia, Pa. 19118 | — | 630[1] | 50 | P/RC | 2000 | 2000 | 1500 |
| Cheyney State College; Cheyney, Pa. 19319 | 1,556 | 1,431 | 205 | S | 2234 | n.a. | 2232 |
| Chicago, The School of the Art Institute of; Chicago, Ill. 60604 | 414 | 550 | 70 | P | 3096 | 3096 | 2250 |
| Chicago, The University of; Chicago, Ill. 60637 | 6,016[1] | 3,099[1] | 1039 | P | 3720 | 3720 | 2275 |
| Chicago Coll. of Osteopathic Medicine; Chicago, Ill. 60615 | 334 | 47 | 90 | P | 4600 | — | — |
| Chicago Conservatory College; Chicago, Ill. 60605 | 80 | 40 | 57 | P | 2000 | 2000 | n.a. |
| Chicago State University; Chicago, Ill. 60628 | 1,291 | 2,201 | 266 | S | 510 | 1530 | — |
| Christian Brothers College; Memphis, Tenn. 38104 | 647 | 306 | 60 | P/RC | 2190 | 2190 | 1680 |
| Christopher Newport College; Newport News, Va. 23606 | 770 | 770 | 108 | S | ([17]) | 780 | n.a. |
| Cincinnati, University of; Cincinnati, Ohio 45221 | 13,765[1] | 10,112[1] | 1781 | S | 960 | 2280 | 1764 |
| Cincinnati Bible Seminary; Cincinnati, Ohio 45204 | 548 | 341 | 18 | P/CC | 1024 | 1024 | 1260 |
| Circleville Bible College; Circleville, Ohio 43113 | 106 | 86 | 14 | P | 1350 | 1350 | 690 |
| Citadel, The; Charleston, S.C. 29409 | 2100 | — | 156 | S | 3200[11] | 4060[11] | — |
| City College (NYC). *See* New York, City University of | | | | | | | |
| Claflin College; Orangeburg, S.C. 29115 | 320[1] | 580[1] | 50 | P/UM | 700 | 700 | 100 |
| Claremont Colleges: | | | | | | | |
| Claremont Graduate School; Claremont, Calif. 91711 | 606 | 309 | 78 | P | 2900 | 2900 | n.a. |
| Claremont Men's College; Claremont, Calif. 91711 | 684 | 121 | 95 | P | 4300 | n.a. | 2100 |

| Institution and location | Enrollment | | | | Tuition | | |
|---|---|---|---|---|---|---|---|
| | Male | Female | Faculty | Control | Res. | Nonres. | Rm/Bd |
| Harvey Mudd College; Claremont, Calif. 91711 | 414[1] | 62[1] | 60 | P | $4186 | $4186 | $1951 |
| Pitzer College; Claremont, Calif. 91711 | 290 | 490 | 80 | P | 4380 | 4380 | 1760 |
| Pomona College; Claremont, Calif. 91711 | 725[1] | 600[1] | 130 | P | 4400 | 4400 | 1900 |
| Scripps College; Claremont, Calif. 91771 | — | 598 | 48 | P | 3950 | 3950 | 1950 |
| Clarion State College; Clarion, Pa. 16214 | 2,118 | 2,289 | 307 | S | 1050 | 1880 | 1008 |
| Clark College; Atlanta, Ga. 30314 | 632[1] | 1,164[1] | 114 | P/UM | 1800 | 1800 | 1225 |
| Clark University; Worcester, Mass. 01610 | 1,021 | 934 | 128 | P | 3875 | 3875 | 1655 |
| Clarke College; Dubuque, Iowa 52001 | 24 | 614 | 55 | P/RC | 2500 | 2500 | 650 |
| Clarkson College of Technology; Potsdam, N.Y. 13676 | 2,669 | 439 | 219 | P | 7150 | 7150 | 3460 |
| Cleary College; Ypsilanti, Mich. 48197 | 148[1] | 313[1] | 32 | P | 1515 | 1515 | n.a. |
| Clemson University; Clemson, S.C. 29631 | 6,101[1] | 3,616[1] | 632 | S | 830 | 1780 | 1260 |
| Cleveland Institute of Art; Cleveland, Ohio 44106 | 227[1] | 308[1] | 65 | P | 2300 | 2300 | 1970 |
| Cleveland State University, The; Cleveland, Ohio 44115 | 5,640[1] | 3,920[1] | 565 | S | 900 | 1800 | 1785 |
| Clinch Valley College. *See* University of Virginia | | | | | | | |
| Coe College; Cedar Rapids, Iowa 52402 | 538 | 496 | 67 | P | 3240 | 3240 | 1300 |
| Cogswell College; San Francisco, Calif. 94108 | 281 | 15 | 14 | P | 1650 | 1650 | 2250 |
| Coker College; Hartsville, S.C. 29550 | 99[1] | 183[1] | 32 | P | 1041 | 1041 | 640 |
| Colby College; Waterville, Me. 04901 | 872 | 702 | 135 | P | 4300 | 4300 | 1670 |
| Colby–Sawyer College; New London, N.H. 03257 | 2 | 652 | 43 | P | 3470 | 3470 | 1500 |
| Colgate University; Hamilton, N.Y. 13346 | 1,700[1] | 800[1] | 165 | P | 4390 | 4390 | 1760 |
| College Misericordia; Dallas, Pa. 18612 | 89[1] | 714[1] | 79 | P/RC | 2550 | 2550 | 1600 |
| Colorado, University of; Boulder, Colo. 80302 | | | | | | | |
| U. of Colorado at Boulder; Boulder, Colo. 80309 | 11,176[1] | 8,028[1] | 988 | S | 816 | 2659 | 720 |
| U. of Colo. at Colo. Springs; Colorado Springs, Colo. 80907 | 1,337 | 1,199 | 156 | S | 450 | 1804 | n.a. |
| U. of Colorado at Denver; Denver, Colo. 80202 | 4,449 | 3,823 | 566 | S | 464 | 1852 | n.a. |
| Colorado College, The; Colorado Springs, Colo. 80903 | 1,021[1] | 921[1] | 171 | P | 3600 | 3600 | 1400 |
| Colorado School of Mines; Golden, Colo. 80227 | 2,267[2] | | n.a. | S | 290[2] | n.a. | 1135[2] |
| Colorado State University; Fort Collins, Colo. 80523 | 8,926[1] | 7,348[1] | 1150 | S | 727 | 2275 | 1510 |
| Colorado Women's College; Denver, Colo. 80220 | — | 416[1] | 40 | P | 3450 | 3450 | 1865 |
| Columbia Bible College; Columbia, S.C. 29203 | 419 | 294 | 34 | P[18] | 1575 | 1575 | 1395 |
| Columbia Christian College; Portland, Ore. 97220 | 132[1] | 127[1] | 12 | P/CC | 1872 | 1872 | 1365 |
| Columbia College; Chicago, Ill. 60605 | 1,300 | 1,200 | 20 | P | 1045 | 1045 | n.a. |
| Columbia College; Columbia, Mo. 65201 | 418 | 572 | 51 | P | 2750 | 2750 | 1500 |
| Columbia College; Columbia, S.C. 29203 | 5[19] | 910 | 56 | P/M | 2150 | 2150 | 1600 |
| Columbia Union College; Takoma Park, Md. 20012 | 360[1] | 634[1] | 35 | SDA | 2985 | 2985 | 1500 |
| Columbia University; New York, N.Y. 10027 | 8,942[1] | 4,316[1] | 1525 | P | 4900 | — | 2400 |
| Barnard College; New York, N.Y. 10027 | — | 1,990 | 138 | P | 2060 | 2060 | 850 |
| Teachers College; New York, N.Y. 10027 | 685[1] | 1265[1] | 191 | P | ([20]) | ([20]) | 2500 |
| Columbus College; Columbus, Ga. 31907 | 1,106 | 1,121 | 215 | S | 503 | 1217 | n.a. |
| Columbus College of Art and Design, The; Columbus, Ohio 43215 | 338[1] | 298[1] | 34 | P | 2610 | n.a. | 1410 |
| Concord College; Athens, W. Va. 24712 | 802 | 928 | 88 | S | 344 | 1244 | 1570 |
| Concordia College; Ann Arbor, Mich. 48105 | 353 | 262 | 41 | P/L[21] | 1205 | 1205 | 1235 |
| Concordia College; Bronxville, N.Y. 10708 | 189[1] | 224[1] | 46 | P/L[21] | 1995 | 1995 | 1510 |
| Concordia College; Moorhead, Minn. 56560 | 1,094 | 1,438 | 149 | P/AL | 2960 | 2960 | 1145 |
| Concordia College; St. Paul, Minn. 55104 | 307[1] | 316[1] | 54 | P/L | 2160 | 2160 | 1215 |
| Concordia Teachers College; River Forest, Ill. 60305 | 411 | 681 | 78 | P/L[21] | 1968 | 1968 | 1335 |
| Concordia Teachers College; Seward, Neb. 68434 | 502[1] | 629[1] | 91 | P/L[21] | 2080 | 2080 | 1230 |
| Connecticut, The University of; Storrs, Conn. 06268 | 9,914 | 7,743 | 1150 | S | 540 | 1230 | 1350 |
| Connecticut College; New London, Conn. 06320 | 701[1] | 1,010[1] | 140 | P | 4710 | 4710 | 1740 |
| Conservatory of Music; Hato Rey, P.R. 00936 | 77[1] | 151[1] | 27 | S | 150 | 150 | — |
| Converse College; Spartanburg, S.C. 29301 | 7[19] | 775 | 77 | P | 4950[11] | 3250[11] | — |
| Cooper Union; New York, N.Y. 10003 | 712 | 218 | 52 | P | — | — | — |
| Coppin State College; Baltimore, Md. 21216 | 545 | 1,482 | 140 | S | 700 | 1600 | — |
| Cornell College; Mt. Vernon, Iowa 52314 | 438[1] | 413[1] | 72 | P/M | 3580 | — | 1410 |
| Cornell University[78]; Ithaca, N.Y. 14853 | 10,181 | 6,159 | 1,481 | P | 4800 | 4800 | 2100 |
| Cornish Institute of Allied Arts; Seattle, Wash. 98102 | 134 | 158 | 18 | P | 1610 | 1610 | n.a. |
| Covenant College; Lookout Mountain, Tenn./Ga. 37350 | 287[1] | 266[1] | 32 | RP | 2600 | 2600 | 1270 |
| Cranbrook Academy of Art; Bloomfield Hills, Mich. 48013 | 97[1] | 59[1] | 10 | P | 2700 | 2700 | 2150 |
| Creighton University, The; Omaha, Neb. 68178 | 2,806[1] | 1,551[1] | 419 | P | 2840 | 2840 | 1380 |
| Culver–Stockton College; Canton, Mo. 63435 | 217 | 189 | 37 | P | 2530 | 2530 | 1470 |
| Cumberland College; Williamsburg, Ky. 40769 | 783[1] | 888[1] | 95 | P/B | 1400 | 1400 | 1000 |
| Curry College; Milton, Mass. 02186 | 368 | 292 | 54 | P | 3585 | 3585 | 2082 |
| Daemen College; Amherst, N.Y. 14226 | 273[1] | 731[1] | 69 | P | 2675 | 2675 | 1500 |
| Dakota State College; Madison, S.D. 57042 | 419[1] | 483[1] | 47 | S | 528 | 1152 | 1120 |
| Dakota Wesleyan University; Mitchell, S.D. 57301 | 200 | 287 | 32 | P/UM | 1865 | 1865 | 1235 |
| Dallas, University of; Irving, Tex. 75061 | 761[1] | 406[1] | 77 | P/RC | 2370 | 2370 | 1390 |
| Dallas Baptist College; Dallas, Tex. 75211 | 599[1] | 469[1] | 63 | P/SB | 1650 | 1650 | 1250 |

| Institution and location | Enrollment | | Faculty | Control | Tuition | | |
|---|---|---|---|---|---|---|---|
| | Male | Female | | | Res. | Nonres. | Rm/Bd |
| Dallas Bible College; Dallas, Tex. 75228 | 122 | 43 | 14 | P | $1500 | $1500 | $1250 |
| Dana College; Balir, Neb. 68008 | 200 | 203 | 34 | P/AL | 2485 | 2485 | 1215 |
| Dartmouth College; Hanover, N.H. 03755 | 3,005 | 1,112 | 500 | P | 6040 | 6040 | 2872 |
| David Lipscomb College; Nashville, Tenn. 37203 | 1,048 | 1,000 | 96 | P/CC | 1460 | 1460 | 1350 |
| Davidson College; Davidson, N.C. 28036 | 898 | 396 | 98 | P/Pres | 4665[11] | 4665[11] | — |
| Davis and Elkins College; Elkins, W. Va. 26241 | 934[7] | | n.a. | Pres | 2850[2] | n.a. | 1300[2] |
| Dayton, University of; Dayton, Ohio 45469 | 5,939[1] | 3,672[1] | 338 | P/RC | 2400 | 2400 | 1256 |
| Defiance College, The; Defiance, Ohio 43512 | 350[1] | 294[1] | 50 | P/UCC | 3170 | 3170 | 1385 |
| Delaware, University of; Newark, Del. 19711 | 5,937 | 6,311 | 810 | S[22] | 1000 | 2170 | 1712 |
| Delaware Law School of Widener College; Wilmington, Del. 19802 | 296[7] | 41[7] | n.a. | P | n.a. | n.a. | n.a. |
| Delaware State College; Dover, Del. 19901 | 1,114 | 1,014 | 120 | S | — | 660 | 1,100 |
| Delaware Valley Coll. of Sci. & Agri.; Doylestown, Pa. 18901 | 946 | 405 | 70 | P | 2516 | 2516 | 1141 |
| Delta State University; Cleveland, Miss. 38733 | 1,011 | 1,183 | 157 | S | 554 | 1329 | 912 |
| Denison University; Granville, Ohio 43023 | 1,088 | 1,038 | 149 | P | 3995 | 3995 | 1565 |
| Denver, University of; Denver, Colo. 80208 | 2,375 | 1,985 | 450 | P | 4170 | 4170 | 1735 |
| DePaul University; Chicago, Ill. 60604 | 11,052[2] | | n.a. | P/RC | 2445[2] | n.a. | 1590[2] |
| DePauw University; Greencastle, Ind. 46135 | 1,069[1] | 1,178[1] | 145 | P/M | 3692 | 3692 | 1590 |
| Detroit, University of; Detroit, Mich. 48221 | 5,121[1] | 3,242[1] | 270 | P | 3000 | 3000 | 1800 |
| Detroit Bible College; Detroit, Mich. 48034 | 64 | 25 | 14 | P/ND | 675 | 675 | n.a. |
| Detroit College of Business; Dearborn, Mich. 48126 | 705[1] | 732[1] | 19 | P | 1665 | 1665 | — |
| Detroit College of Law; Detroit, Mich. 48201 | 950 | | 19 | P | 2400 | — | — |
| Detroit Institute of Technology, The; Detroit, Mich. 48201 | 1,400[2] | | n.a. | P | ([23]) | n.a. | n.a. |
| DeVry Institute of Technology; Atlanta, Ga. 30308 | 682[1] | 21[1] | 17 | P | 1965 | 1965 | — |
| DeVry Institute of Technology; Chicago, Ill. 60618 | 2,275[1] | 95[1] | 40 | P | 1965 | 1965 | — |
| DeVry Institute of Technology; Dallas, Tex. 75235 | 724[1] | 30[1] | 15 | P | 1965 | 1965 | — |
| DeVry Institute of Technology; Phoenix, Ariz. 85016 | 2,256[1] | 118[1] | 34 | P | 1965 | 1965 | — |
| Dickinson College; Carlisle, Pa. 17013 | 815 | 820 | 127 | P | 3780 | 3780 | 1740 |
| Dickinson School of Law; Carlisle, Pa. 17013 | 316 | 124 | 15 | P | 2050 | 2350 | 1425 |
| Dickinson State College; Dickinson, N.D. 58601 | 1,026[2] | | n.a. | S | 480[2] | n.a. | 900[2] |
| Dillard University; New Orleans, La. 70122 | 1,186[2] | | n.a. | P | 1900[2] | n.a. | 1150[2] |
| District of Columbia, University of the; Washington, D.C. 20008 | | | | | | | |
| Georgia Ave.–Harvard St. Campus; Washington, D.C. 20009 | 270[1] | 854[1] | 131 | Mun/S | 135 | 1157 | — |
| Mount Vernon Square Campus; Washington, D.C. 20005 | 3,384[1] | 4,398[1] | 371 | Mun/S | 135 | 1157 | |
| Van Ness Campus; Washington, D.C. 20008 | 2,403[1] | 1,983[1] | 184 | Mun/S | 135 | 1157 | — |
| Divine Word College; Epworth, Iowa 52045 | 94 | — | 20 | P/RC | 2000 | 2000 | 1000 |
| Doane College; Crete, Neb. 68333 | 331 | 301 | 42 | P | 2335 | 2335 | 1130 |
| Dominican College of Blauvelt; Orangeburg, N.Y. 10962 | 319 | 811 | 35 | P/Ind | — | 1500 | — |
| Dominican College of San Rafael; San Rafael, Calif. 94901 | 76[1] | 291[1] | 40 | P/RC | 2200 | 2200 | 1550 |
| Dordt College; Sioux Center, Iowa 51250 | 479[1] | 608[1] | 61 | P/CR | 2370 | 2370 | 1000 |
| Dowling College; Oakdale, N.Y. 11769 | 2,224[2] | | n.a. | P | 2850[2] | n.a. | 1200[2] |
| Drake University; Des Moines, Iowa 50311 | 2,559[1] | 1,998[1] | 345 | P | 3150 | 3150 | 1580 |
| Drew University; Madison, N.J. 07940 | 1,135[1] | 1,026[1] | 131 | P | 3700 | 3700 | 1585 |
| Drexel University; Philadelphia, Pa. 19104 | 4,833 | 1,768 | 278 | P | 3000 | 3000 | 1609 |
| Dropsie University, The; Philadelphia, Pa. 19132 | 49 | 3 | 12 | P | — | 3500 | — |
| Drury College; Springfield, Mo. 65802 | 1,205 | 1,013 | 59 | P/UCC | 2175 | 2175 | 1407 |
| Dubuque, University of; Dubuque, Iowa 52001 | 425 | 380 | 42 | P/Pres | 2275 | 2275 | 1200 |
| Duke University; Durham, N.C. 27706 | 5,576 | 3,853 | 551 | P | 3830 | — | 2025 |
| Duns Scotus College; Southfield, Mich. 48075 | 33 | — | 7 | P/RC | 1500 | 1500 | 1000 |
| Duquesne University; Pittsburgh, Pa. 15219 | 3,758 | 3,131 | 296 | P/RC | 3090 | 3090 | 805 |
| D'Youville College; Buffalo, N.Y. 14201 | 111 | 950 | 71 | P/RC | 2600 | 2600 | 1400 |
| Earlham College; Richmond, Ind. 47374 | 504[1] | 556[1] | 79 | P/SOF | 4050 | 4050 | 1550 |
| East Carolina Univ. *See* North Carolina, Univ. System of | | | | | | | |
| East Central Oklahoma State University; Ada, Okla. 74820 | 995[1] | 1,229[1] | 125 | S | 450 | 625 | 825 |
| East Stroudsburg State College; East Stroudsburg, Pa. 18301 | 1,755[1] | 2,268[1] | 228 | S | 522 | 938 | 504 |
| East Tennessee State University; Johnson City, Tenn. 37601 | 4,763 | 4,377 | 520 | S | 462 | 1398 | 1100 |
| East Texas Baptist College; Marshall, Tex. 75670 | 398 | 315 | 42 | P/SB | 1260 | — | 1164 |
| East Texas State University; Commerce, Tex. 75428 | 10,092[7] | | n.a. | S | 462[2] | n.a. | 1000[2] |
| Eastern College; St. Davids, Pa. 19087 | 406 | 235 | 50 | P | 2720 | 2720 | 1270 |
| Eastern Connecticut State College; Willimantic, Conn. 06226 | 898 | 1,115 | 120 | S | 195 | 515 | 1200 |
| Eastern Illinois University; Charleston, Ill. 61920 | 4,341[1] | 5,043[1] | 522 | S | 510 | 1530 | 1312 |
| Eastern Kentucky University; Richmond, Ky. 40475 | 6,439[1] | 7,240[1] | 571 | S | 480 | 1200 | 1110 |
| Eastern Mennonite College; Harrisonburg, Va. 22801 | 365 | 581 | 64 | P | 2562 | 2562 | 1185 |

| Institution and location | Enrollment | | Faculty | Control | Tuition | | Rm/Bd |
|---|---|---|---|---|---|---|---|
| | Male | Female | | | Res. | Nonres. | |
| Eastern Michigan University; Ypsilanti, Mich. 48197 | 4,800[1] | 5,300[1] | 590 | S | $735 | $1800 | $1600 |
| Eastern Montana College; Billings, Mont. 59101 | 890 | 1,285 | 147 | S | 692 | 1491 | 1450 |
| Eastern Nazarene College; Quincy, Mass. 02170 | 326 | 416 | 46 | P/Naz | 1920 | — | 1274 |
| Eastern New Mexico University; Portales, N.M. 88130 | 2,148 | 2,118 | 161 | S | 500 | 1207 | 1100 |
| Eastern Oregon State College; La Grande, Ore. 97850 | 701[1] | 602[1] | 80 | S | 928 | 928 | 2025 |
| Eastern Virginia Medical School; Norfolk, Va. 23501 | 128 | 48 | 93 | P | 4000 | 5300 | 3400 |
| Eastern Washington University; Cheney, Wash. 99004 | 3,358 | 3,936 | 355 | S | 591 | 1983 | 1245 |
| Eckerd College; St. Petersburg, Fla. 33733 | 466 | 353 | 63 | P | 3670 | 3670 | 1457 |
| Edgecliff College; Cincinnati, Ohio 45206 | 912[2] | | n.a. | P/RC | 2016[2] | n.a. | 1420[2] |
| Edgewood College; Madison, Wis. 53711 | 100 | 300 | 40 | P/RC | 2400 | 2400 | 1350 |
| Edinboro State College; Edinboro, Pa. 16444 | 2,662 | 3,010 | 359 | S | 2100 | 1200 | 900 |
| Eisenhower College; Seneca Falls, N.Y. 13148 | 202 | 189 | 51 | P | 3100 | 3100 | 1650 |
| Elizabeth City State Univ. *See* North Carolina, Univ. System of | | | | | | | |
| Elizabethtown College; Elizabethtown, Pa. 17022 | 644[1] | 797[1] | 103 | P/CB | 2997 | 2997 | 1415 |
| Elmhurst College; Elmhurst, Ill. 60126 | 856[1] | 891[1] | 92 | P/UCC | 2910 | 2910 | 1560 |
| Elmira College; Elmira, N.Y. 14901 | 490 | 495 | 62 | P | 3500 | 3500 | 1500 |
| Elon College; Elon College, N.C. 27244 | 1189[1] | 861[1] | 83 | P | 1884 | 1884 | 1116 |
| Embry–Riddle Aeronautical Univ.; Daytona Beach, Fla. 32014 | 2,598[1] | 103[1] | 160 | P | 3000 | 3000 | 1500 |
| Emerson College; Boston, Mass. 02116 | 718[1] | 855[1] | 84 | P | 3400 | 3400 | 2140 |
| Emmanuel College; Boston, Mass. 02115 | — | 580[1] | 62 | P/RC | 2960 | 2960 | 1575 |
| Emory and Henry College; Emory, Va. 24327 | 413 | 374 | 55 | P/UM | 2145 | 2145 | 1155 |
| Emory University; Atlanta, Ga. 30322 | 4,278[1] | 2,696[1] | 917 | P | 3450 | 3450 | 2415 |
| Emporia Kansas State College; Emporia, Kan. 66801 | 2,870[1] | 3,516[1] | 224 | S | 528 | 1128 | 1300 |
| Erskine College; Due West, S.C. 29639 | 312[1] | 336[1] | 46 | P/RP | 2200 | 2200 | 1180 |
| Eureka College; Eureka, Ill. 61530 | 210 | 165 | 30 | P/DC | 2800 | 2800 | 1550 |
| Evangel College; Springfield, Mo. 65802 | 534[1] | 757[1] | 65 | P/AG | 1700 | 1700 | 1400 |
| Evansville, University of; Evansville, Ind. 47702 | 1,285[1] | 1,633[1] | 192 | P/UM | 2625 | — | 1455 |
| Evergreen State College, The; Olympia, Wash. 98505 | 1,267[1] | 1,277[1] | 120 | S | 591 | 1983 | 1576 |
| Fairfield University; Fairfield, Conn. 06430 | 1,441[1] | 1,282[1] | 152 | P/RC | 3200 | 3200 | 1800 |
| Fairleigh Dickinson University; Rutherford, N.J. 07070 | 11,535 | 7,450 | 546 | P | — | — | — |
| Florham–Madison Campus; Madison, N.J. 07940 | 1,064[1] | 1,009[1] | 111 | P | 2912 | 2912 | 1750 |
| Rutherford Campus; Rutherford, N.J. 07070 | 826[1] | 831[1] | 127 | P | 2912 | 2912 | 1750 |
| Teaneck–Hackensack Campus; Teaneck, N.J. 07666 | 2,162[1] | 1,317[1] | 319 | P | 2912 | 2912 | 1750 |
| Fairmont State College; Fairmont, W. Va. 26554 | 1,404[1] | 1,542[1] | 178 | S | 320 | 1224 | 1550 |
| Faith Baptist Bible College; Ankeny, Iowa 50021 | 281[1] | 251[1] | 31 | P/B | 1400 | 1400 | 1400 |
| Fashion Institute of Technology[24]; New York, N.Y. 10001 | 29[25] | 157[25] | — | S/Mun | 660 | 1310 | 1995 |
| Fayetteville State U. *See* North Carolina, U. System of | | | | | | | |
| Federal City College, D.C. *See* District of Columbia, Univ. of | | | | | | | |
| Felician College; Lodi, N.J. 07644 | 1 | 425 | 50 | P/RC | 1760 | 1760 | 600 |
| Ferris State College; Big Rapids, Mich. 49307 | 6,198[1] | 3,774[1] | 510 | S | 696 | 1680 | 1608 |
| Ferrum College; Ferrum, Va. 24088 | 943[1] | 568[1] | 60 | UM | 1590 | 1590 | 1470 |
| Findlay College; Findlay, Ohio 45840 | 378 | 318 | 50 | P/CG | 2790 | 2790 | 1260 |
| Fisk University; Nashville, Tenn. 37203 | 423[1] | 702[1] | 64 | P | 2350 | 2350 | 1385 |
| Fitchburg State College; Fitchburg, Mass. 01420 | 6,629[7] | | n.a. | S | 500[2] | n.a. | 1292[2] |
| Flagler College; St. Augustine, Fla. 32084 | 301 | 413 | 34 | P | 1900 | 1900 | 1265 |
| Florida, University of; Gainesville, Fla. 32611 | 15,966 | 10,255 | 2662 | S | 705 | 1740 | 1710 |
| Florida A.&M. University; Tallahassee, Fla. 32307 | 2,460 | 2,447 | 320 | S | 675 | 1710 | 573 |
| Florida Atlantic University; Boca Raton, Fla. 33431 | 1,813 | 1,508 | 280 | S | 775 | 2350 | 1575 |
| Florida Institute of Technology; Melbourne, Fla. 32901 | 4,287[7] | | n.a. | P | 2256[2] | n.a. | 1440[2] |
| Florida International University; Miami, Fla. 33199 | 5,543 | 5,284 | 338 | S | ([26]) | ([27]) | — |
| Florida Memorial College; Miami, Fla. 33054 | 400 | 432 | 44 | P/B | 1440 | 1440 | 1320 |
| Florida Southern College; Lakeland, Fla. 33802 | 774[1] | 820[1] | 73 | P/UM | 2080 | 2080 | 1660 |
| Florida State University; Tallahassee, Fla. 32306 | 8,319[1] | 8,710[1] | 1020 | S | 700 | 1950 | 1720 |
| Florida Technological University; Orlando, Fla. 32816 | 5,889 | 4,716 | 464 | S | 742 | 2317 | 1350 |
| Fontbonne College; St. Louis, Mo. 63105 | 92[1] | 804[1] | 58 | P | 2660 | 2660 | 1600 |
| Fordham University; Bronx, N.Y. 10458 | 4,701[1] | 3,606[1] | 489 | P | 2800 | 2800 | 1790 |
| Fort Hays State College; Hays, Kan. 67601 | 2,598[1] | 3,080[1] | 291 | S | 622 | 1222 | 1244 |
| Fort Lauderdale Coll. of Business and Finance; Fort Lauderdale, Fla. 33301 | 1,084[7] | | n.a. | P | 1440[2] | n.a. | 2000[2] |
| Fort Lewis College; Durango, Colo. 81301 | 1,529[1] | 1,258[1] | 142 | S | 405 | 1620 | 1220 |
| Fort Valley State College, The; Fort Valley, Ga. 31030 | 832[1] | 865[1] | 150 | S | 564 | 714 | 1110 |
| Fort Wayne Bible College; Fort Wayne, Ind. 46807 | 226 | 221 | 32 | P/MC | 1792 | 1792 | 1300 |
| Fort Wright College; Spokane, Wash. 99204 | 127[1] | 402[1] | 41 | P/RC | 2050 | 2050 | 1500 |
| Framingham State College; Framingham, Mass. 01701 | 927 | 2,190 | 157 | S | 500 | 1320 | 1400 |
| Francis Marion College; Florence, S.C. 29501 | 846 | 697 | 96 | S | 500 | 1000 | — |
| Franklin and Marshall College; Lancaster, Pa. 17604 | 1,260 | 675 | 124 | P | 3780 | 3780 | 1465 |

| Institution and location | Enrollment | | Faculty | Control | Tuition | | |
|---|---|---|---|---|---|---|---|
| | Male | Female | | | Res. | Nonres. | Rm/Bd |
| Franklin College of Indiana; Franklin, Ind. 46131 | 338 | 281 | 60 | P | $3170 | $3170 | $1400 |
| Franklin Pierce College; Rindge, N.H. 03461 | 592 | 336 | 46 | P | 3325 | — | 1700 |
| Franklin University; Columbus, Ohio 43215 | 2,605[1] | 1,584[1] | 42 | P | (28) | (28) | — |
| Free Will Baptist Bible College; Nashville, Tenn. 37205 | 272 | 213 | 28 | P/B | (29) | (29) | 2478 |
| Freed-Hardeman College; Henderson, Tenn. 38340 | 579 | 633 | 64 | P/CC | 785 | 785 | 587 |
| Fresno Pacific College[30]; Fresno, Calif. 93702 | 542[7] | | n.a. | P/MB | 1800[2] | n.a. | 1215[2] |
| Friends Bible College; Haviland, Kan. 67059 | 52[1] | 66[1] | 10 | P/SOF | 1400 | 1400 | 1280 |
| Friends University; Wichita, Kan. 67213 | 352 | 315 | 44 | P | 2100 | 2100 | 1150 |
| Frostburg State College; Frostburg, Md. 21532 | 1800[1] | 1706[1] | 181 | S | 620 | 1520 | 1474 |
| Furman University; Greenville, S.C. 29613 | 1,100 | 912 | 131 | P/B | 2592 | 2592 | 1612 |
| Gallaudet College; Washington, D.C. 20002 | 494 | 658 | 193 | P | 618 | 618 | 1525 |
| Gannon College; Erie, Pa. 16501 | 1300[1] | 829[1] | 117 | P/RC | 2330 | 2330 | 1240 |
| Gardner–Webb College; Boiling Springs, N.C. 28017 | 668[1] | 540[1] | 72 | SB | 2200 | 2200 | 1332 |
| General Motors Institute; Flint, Mich. 48502 | 1,741[1] | 617[1] | 143 | P | 1000 | 1000 | 880[31] |
| Geneva College; Beaver Falls, Pa. 15010 | 605 | 504 | 65 | P/RP | 2524 | 2524 | 1310 |
| George Fox College; Newberg, Ore. 97132 | 313[1] | 394[1] | 38 | P/SOF | 2500 | 2500 | 1360 |
| George Mason University; Fairfax, Va. 22030 | 4,212[1] | 5,398[1] | 340 | S | 768 | 1488 | 1963 |
| George Peabody College for Teachers; Nashville, Tenn. 37203 | 1,900[7] | | n.a. | P | 1950[7] | n.a. | 1050[7] |
| George Washington University, The; Washington, D.C. 20052 | 4,363 | 3,089 | 998 | P | 3000 | 3000 | 2100 |
| George Williams College; Downers Grove, Ill. 60515 | 267 | 462 | 100 | P | 2730 | — | 1437 |
| Georgetown College; Georgetown, Ky. 40324 | 432 | 390 | 64 | P/SB | 2090 | 2190 | 1270 |
| Georgetown University; Washington, D.C. 20057 | 11,327[7] | | n.a. | P/RC | 3500[2] | n.a. | 2000[2] |
| Georgia, University of; Athens, Ga. 30602 | 11,673[1] | 9,984[1] | 2263 | S | 702 | 1653 | 1182 |
| Georgia College; Milledgeville, Ga. 31061 | 1,622[1] | 1,977[1] | 140 | S | 519 | 1233 | 993 |
| Georgia Institute of Technology; Atlanta, Ga. 30332 | 8,079[1] | 1,482[1] | 625 | S | 693 | 1860 | 1539 |
| Southern Technical Institute; Marietta, Ga. 30060 | 2,000[1] | 150[1] | 100 | S | 512 | 1250 | 1300 |
| Georgia Southern College; Statesboro, Ga. 30458 | 2,871 | 3,613 | 207 | S | 435 | 1149 | 1053 |
| Georgia Southwestern College; Americus, Ga. 31709 | 809 | 1,569 | 107 | S | 516 | 1230 | 1596 |
| Georgia State University; Atlanta, Ga. 30303 | 9,470[1] | 11,216[1] | 654 | S | 570 | 1695 | — |
| Georgian Court College; Lakewood, N.J. 08701 | 12 | 674 | 68 | P/RC | 2050 | 2050 | 1250 |
| Gettysburg College; Gettysburg, Pa. 17325 | 1,002[1] | 912[1] | 138 | P/L | 3620 | 3620 | 1250 |
| Glassboro State College; Glassboro, N.J. 08028 | 4,434 | 6,227 | 377 | S | 660 | 1320 | 1250 |
| Glenville State College; Glenville, W. Va. 26351 | 640 | 671 | 84 | S | 310 | 1210 | 1200 |
| Goddard College; Plainfield, Vt. 05667 | 1,699 | | n.a. | P | 4187[11] | — | — |
| Golden Gate University; San Francisco, Calif. 94105 | 9,400 | | 47 | P | (32) | (32) | — |
| Gonzaga University; Spokane, Wash. 99258 | 2,183 | 1,062 | 143 | P/RC | 2850 | 2850 | 1536 |
| Gordon College; Wenham, Mass. 01984 | 438 | 547 | 55 | P | 2895 | — | 1425 |
| Goshen College; Goshen, Ind. 46526 | 432 | 649 | 78 | P/Men | 2735 | 2735 | 1260 |
| Goucher College; Towson, Baltimore, Md. 21204 | — | 855[1] | 70 | P | 3700 | 3700 | 2100 |
| Governors State University; Park Forest South, Ill. 60466 | 1,747[1] | 2,067[1] | 155 | S | 510 | 1530 | — |
| Grace Bible College; Grand Rapids, Mich. 49509 | 91[1] | 71[1] | 9 | P/Ind | 880 | 880 | 1350 |
| Grace College; Winona Lake, Ind. 46590 | 297[1] | 330[1] | 35 | UP | 2240 | 2240 | 1470 |
| Grace College of the Bible; Omaha, Neb. 68108 | 269 | 213 | 28 | P/ID | 1500 | 1500 | 1150 |
| Graceland College; Lamoni, Iowa 50140 | 565[1] | 672[1] | 80 | P | 2455 | 2455 | 1210 |
| Grad. Sch. & Univ. Ctr. (NYC). *See* New York, City Univ. of | | | | | | | |
| Grambling State University; Grambling, La. 71245 | 1,681 | 1,888 | 189 | S | 340 | 690 | 1106 |
| Grand Canyon College; Phoenix, Ariz. 85017 | 652[1] | 548[1] | 46 | P/SB | 1728 | 1728 | 2260 |
| Grand Rapids Baptist College; Grand Rapids, Mich. 49505 | 407 | 440 | 31 | P/B | | — | — |
| Grand Valley State Colleges; Allendale, Mich. 49401 | 2,318[1] | 2,220[1] | 253 | S | 810 | 1845 | 1530 |
| Gratz College; Philadelphia, Pa. 19141 | 70 | 106 | 18 | P/J | 250 | 250 | — |
| Great Falls, College of; Great Falls, Mont. 59405 | 240 | 252 | 42 | P/RC | (33) | (33) | 1190 |
| Greensboro College; Greensboro, N.C. 27420 | 222 | 397 | 31 | P/M | 3350 | 2130 | 1220 |
| Greenville College; Greenville, Ill. 62246 | 340 | 366 | 45 | P/FM | 2871 | 2871 | 1390 |
| Grinnell College; Grinnell, Iowa 50112 | 667 | 507 | 101 | P | 4280 | 4280 | 1255 |
| Grove City College; Grove City, Pa. 16127 | 1,163 | 1,033 | 100 | P/UP | 1740 | 1740 | 1180 |
| Guam, University of; Agana, Guam 96910 | 1,791 | 1,046 | 180 | S | 240 | 600 | 2400 |
| Guilford College; Greensboro, N.C. 27410 | 715 | 485 | 74 | P/SOF | 2325 | 2625 | 1350 |
| Gustavus Adolphus College; St. Peter, Minn. 56082 | 964 | 1,234 | 130 | P/LCA | 3500 | 3500 | 1200 |
| Gwynedd–Mercy College; Gwynedd Valley, Pa. 19437 | 47 | 614 | 64 | P/RC | 1900[34] | 1900 | 1500 |
| Hamilton College; Clinton, N.Y. 13323 | 960 | — | 93 | P | 4625 | 4625 | 1800 |
| Hamline University; St. Paul, Minn. 55104 | 1,816[2] | | n.a. | P/UM | 3150[2] | n.a. | 1400[2] |
| Hampden–Sydney College; Hampden–Sydney, Va. 23943 | 682 | — | 49 | P/Pres | 2850 | 2850 | 1225 |
| Hampshire College; Amherst, Mass. 01002 | 720 | 795 | 70 | P | 5150 | 5150 | 1700 |
| Hampton Institute; Hampton, Va. 23668 | 869 | 1,284 | 238 | P | 2390 | 2390 | 1210 |
| Hanover College; Hanover, Ind. 47243 | 500 | 400 | 66 | P/Pus | 2315 | 2315 | 1220 |

| Institution and location | Enrollment | | Faculty | Control | Tuition | | Rm/Bd |
|---|---|---|---|---|---|---|---|
| | Male | Female | | | Res. | Nonres. | |
| Hardin–Simmons University; Abilene, Tex. 79601 | 575 | 629 | 88 | P/SB | $1710 | $1710 | $1200 |
| Harding College; Searcy, Ark. 72143 | 1,318 | 1,359 | 160 | P | 2000 | — | 1200 |
| Harris–Stowe College; St. Louis, Mo. 63103 | 384 | 897 | 47 | Mun | ([35]) | ([36]) | — |
| Hartford, University of; West Hartford, Conn. 06117 | 2,426[1] | 1,831[1] | 280 | P | 3000 | — | 1994 |
| The Hartford Graduate Center[37]; Hartford, Conn. 06120 | 34 | 5 | 12 | P | ([38]) | ([38]) | — |
| Hartwick College; Oneonta, N.Y. 13820 | 655[1] | 859[1] | 107 | P | 4100 | 4100 | 1750 |
| Harvard University; Cambridge, Mass. 02138 | 10,625 | 4,646 | 1,408 | P | 4850 | 4850 | 2655 |
| Radcliffe College; Cambridge, Mass. 02138 | — | 1,988[7] | n.a. | P | 4450[2] | n.a. | 2550[2] |
| Harvey Mudd College. *See* Claremont Colleges | | | | | | | |
| Hastings College; Hastings, Neb. 68901 | 329[1] | 407[1] | 54 | P/Pres | 2400 | 2400 | 1350 |
| Haverford College; Haverford, Pa. 19041 | 863 | 18 | 57 | P | 4930 | 4930 | 1950 |
| Hawaii, University of, at Hilo; Hilo, Hawaii 96720 | 1,344[1] | 1,054[1] | n.a. | S | 300 | 900 | 1080 |
| Hawaii, University of, at Manoa; Honolulu, Hawaii 96822 | 8,098 | 7,693 | 980 | S | 450 | 1125 | 1076 |
| Hawaii Loa College; Kaneohe, Hawaii 96744 | 91[1] | 101[1] | 17 | P | 1700 | 1700 | 1800 |
| Hawaii Pacific College; Honolulu, Hawaii 96813 | 1,351[7] | | n.a. | P | 1550[7] | n.a. | n.a. |
| Hebrew College; Brookline, Mass. 02146 | 20[1] | 31[1] | 9 | P | 600 | 600 | n.a. |
| Heidelberg College; Tiffin, Ohio 44883 | 412 | 409 | 83 | P | 3600 | 3600 | 1450 |
| Hellenic College; Brookline, Mass. 02146 | 139 | 23 | 19 | P/GO | 2077 | 1900 | 1500 |
| Henderson State University; Arkadelphia, Ark. 71923 | 1,150 | 1,447 | 180 | S | 480 | 880 | 1200 |
| Hendrix College; Conway, Ark. 72032 | 520[1] | 439[1] | 53 | P/UM | 1950 | 1950 | 1077 |
| Herbert H. Lehman College. *See* New York, City University of | | | | | | | |
| High Point College; High Point, N.C. 27262 | 529[1] | 475[1] | 57 | P/M | 1450 | 1450 | 1090 |
| Hillsdale College; Hillsdale, Mich. 49242 | 548 | 454 | 67 | P | 3090 | 3090 | 1560 |
| Hiram College; Hiram, Ohio 44234 | 564 | 502 | 78 | P | 3337 | 3337 | 1164 |
| Hobart and William Smith Colleges; Geneva, N.Y. 14456 | 1.098[1] | 709[1] | 135 | P | 3870 | 3870 | 930 |
| Hofstra University; Hempstead, N.Y. 11550 | 3,287 | 2,447 | 337 | P | 3000 | 3000 | 2200 |
| Hollins College; Hollins College, Va. 24020 | 9[39] | 896 | 71 | P | 4000 | 4000 | 1700 |
| Holy Cross, College of the; Worcester, Mass. 01610 | 1,495[1] | 1,070[1] | 164 | P/RC | 3875 | 3875 | 5625 |
| Holy Family College; Mission San Jose, Calif. 94538 | — | 98[7] | n.a. | P/RC | n.a. | n.a. | n.a. |
| Holy Family College; Philadelphia, Pa. 19114 | 1,103[2] | | n.a. | P/RC | 1850[2] | n.a. | n.a. |
| Holy Names College; Oakland, Calif. 94619 | 67 | 244 | 43 | P | 2600 | 2600 | 1725 |
| Holy Redeemer College; Waterford, Wis. 53185 | 47 | — | 20 | RC | 1375 | 1375 | 850 |
| Hood College; Frederick, Md. 21701 | 25 | 916 | 142 | P | 3270 | 3270 | 1700 |
| Hope College; Holland, Mich. 49423 | 2,161[2] | | 130 | P/LCA | 2825[10] | n.a. | 1345[10] |
| Houghton College; Houghton, N.Y. 14744 | 541[1] | 675[1] | 81 | P/W | 2420 | 2420 | 1350 |
| Houston, University of; Houston, Tex. 77004 | 9,412[1] | 6,772[1] | 990 | S | 352 | 1212 | 1575 |
| Houston, Univ. of, at Clear Lake City; Houston, Tex. 77058 | 535 | 675 | 156 | S | 165 | 1500 | — |
| Houston Baptist University; Houston, Tex. 77074 | 758[1] | 1,036[1] | 95 | P/B | 2310 | 2310 | 1380 |
| Howard Payne University; Brownwood, Tex. 76801 | 591[1] | 531[1] | 82 | SB | ([36]) | ([36]) | 1290 |
| Howard University; Washington, D.C. 20059 | 4,249 | 4,088 | 1086 | P | 1715 | 1715 | 1765 |
| Humacao College. *See* Puerto Rico, University of | | | | | | | |
| Humboldt State University; Arcata, Calif. 95521 | 4,400 | 3,200 | 450 | S | 190 | 2280 | 1810 |
| Hunter College. *See* New York, City University of | | | | | | | |
| Huntingdon College; Montgomery, Ala. 36106 | 263[1] | 360[1] | 34 | UM | 1850 | 1850 | 1550 |
| Huntington College; Huntington, Ind. 46750 | 304 | 226 | 60 | P/RC | 1309 | — | 3834 |
| Huron College; Huron, S.D. 57350 | 170 | 145 | 26 | P | 2175 | 1240 | — |
| Husson College; Bangor, Me. 04401 | 592 | 509 | 36 | P | 2600 | 2600 | 1550 |
| Huston–Tillotson College; Austin, Tex. 78702 | 432 | 280 | 40 | P/UM | 1100 | 1100 | 1335 |
| Idaho, The College of; Caldwell, Idaho 83605 | 348[1] | 235[1] | 40 | P | 2950 | 2950 | 1300 |
| Idaho, University of; Moscow, Idaho 83843 | 4,297[1] | 2,332[1] | 400 | S | — | 1200 | 1290 |
| Idaho State University; Pocatello, Idaho 83209 | 2,987 | 2,463 | 316 | S | 460 | 850 | 1260 |
| Illinois, University of; Urbana, Ill. 61801 | | | | | | | |
| Univ. of Illinois at Chicago Circle; Chicago, Ill. 60680 | 7,785 | 2,333 | — | S | 789 | 1959 | — |
| Univ. of Illinois at the Medical Center; Chicago, Ill. 60612 | 2,568[1] | 2,046[1] | 1206 | S | 311 | 701 | 2000 |
| Univ. of Illinois at Urbana–Champaign; Urbana, Ill. 61801 | 19,099 | 12,597 | 9,834[7] | S | 586 | 1758 | 1628 |
| Illinois Benedictine College; Lisle, Ill. 60532 | 1,405[2] | | n.a. | P/RC | 2500[2] | n.a. | 1500[2] |
| Illinois College; Jacksonville, Ill. 62650 | 398[1] | 318[1] | 45 | P | 2125 | 2125 | 1275 |
| Illinois College of Optometry; Chicago, Ill. 60616 | 510[1] | 74[1] | 35 | P | 3975 | 3975 | 1971 |
| Illinois College of Podiatric Medicine; Chicago, Ill. 60610 | 614[2] | | n.a. | P | 4000[2] | n.a. | n.a. |
| Illinois Institute of Technology; Chicago, Ill. 60616 | 2,239[1] | 410[1] | 286 | P | 3300 | — | 1620 |
| Illinois State University; Normal, Ill. 61761 | 6,408 | 8,303 | 868 | S | 500 | 1500 | 1344 |
| Illinois Wesleyan University; Bloomington, Ill. 61701 | 749[1] | 932[1] | 125 | P/M | 3730 | 3730 | 1635 |
| Immaculata College; Immaculata, Pa. 19345 | — | 500 | 51 | P/RC | 2100 | — | 1550 |
| Immaculate Heart College; Los Angeles, Calif. 90027 | 73 | 260 | 37 | P | 1380 | — | — |
| Incarnate Word College; San Antonio, Tex. 78209 | 194 | 845 | 76 | P/RC | 1920 | 1920 | 1264 |

| Institution and location | Enrollment Male | Enrollment Female | Faculty | Control | Tuition Res. | Tuition Nonres. | Rm/Bd |
|---|---|---|---|---|---|---|---|
| Indiana Central College; Indianapolis, Ind. 46227 | 473 | 638 | 96 | P/UM | $2640 | $2640 | $1350 |
| Indiana Institute of Technology; Fort Wayne, Ind. 46803 | 376 | 44 | n.a. | P | 2205 | 2205 | 1545 |
| Indiana State University; Terre Haute, Ind. 47809 | 4,522[1] | 4,156[1] | 693 | S | 795 | 1635 | 1173 |
| Evansville Campus; Evansville, Ind. 47712 | 1,007[1] | 788[1] | 91 | S | 729 | 1148 | — |
| Indiana University; Bloomington, Ind. 47401 | | | | | | | |
| Indiana Univ. at Bloomington; Bloomington, Ind. 47401 | 17,160[1] | 15,116[1] | 1550 | S | 870 | 2100 | 1350 |
| Indiana Univ. at Kokomo; Kokomo, Ind. 46901 | 2,562[7] | | n.a. | S | 640[7] | n.a. | n.a. |
| Indiana Univ. at South Bend; South Bend, Ind. 46615 | 857 | 878 | 145 | S | ([40]) | ([36]) | — |
| Indiana University Northwest; Gary, Ind. 46408 | 630 | 1,150 | 120 | S | 750 | 1500 | — |
| Indiana University Southeast; New Albany, Ind. 47150 | 770 | 740 | 75 | S | 440 | 920 | — |
| I.U.–Purdue U. at Fort Wayne; Fort Wayne, Ind. 46805 | 4,500[1] | 4,857[1] | 320 | S | 800 | 1600 | 1150 |
| I.U.–Purdue U. at Indianapolis; Indianapolis, Ind. 46202 | 4,390 | 3,765 | 869 | S | ([41]) | ([14]) | — |
| Indiana University of Pennsylvania; Indiana, Pa. 15701 | 4,233[1] | 5,881[1] | 656 | S | 950 | 1780 | 1088 |
| Instituto Tecnológico; Monterrey, Mexico | 7,500 | 1,500 | 250 | P | 1450 | 1450 | — |
| Insurance, The College of; New York, N.Y. 10038 | 212[1] | 55[1] | 125 | P | 2800[42] | — | 1000 |
| International Fine Arts College; Miami, Fla. 33132 | 225[1] | | 10 | P | 4785 | 4785 | 1575 |
| International Training, The School for; Brattleboro, Vt. 05301 | 298 | | 43 | P | 4000 | 4000 | ([43]) |
| Iona College; New Rochelle, N.Y. 10801 | 2,103[1] | 1,057[1] | 170 | P | 2560 | — | 1650 |
| Iowa, University of; Iowa City, Iowa 52242 | 10,131[1] | 7,895[1] | 1445 | S | 750 | 1710 | 1438 |
| Iowa State University; Ames, Iowa 50011 | 12,373[1] | 7,748[1] | 1414 | S | 858 | 1701 | 1284 |
| Iowa Wesleyan College; Mount Pleasant, Iowa 52641 | 248 | 372 | 46 | P/UM | 2860 | 2860 | 1165 |
| Ithaca College; Ithaca, N.Y. 14850 | 2,030[1] | 2,391[1] | 279 | P | 4052 | 4052 | 1810 |
| Jackson College for Women. *See* Tufts University | | | | | | | |
| Jackson State University; Jackson, Miss. 39217 | 3,617[1] | 4,180[1] | 268 | S | 532 | 750 | 2321 |
| Jacksonville State University; Jacksonville, Ala. 36265 | 3,646[1] | 3,365[1] | 277 | S | 500 | 500 | 1100 |
| Jacksonville University; Jacksonville, Fla. 32211 | 1,212 | 951 | 104 | P | 2400 | 2400 | 1600 |
| James Madison University, Harrisonburg, Va. 22801 | 3,488 | 4,147 | 391 | S | 850 | 1400 | 1526 |
| Jamestown College; Jamestown, N.D. 58401 | 252 | 267 | 40 | P/Pres | 1341 | 1341 | 1375 |
| Jarvis Christian College; Hawkins, Tex. 75765 | 252 | 276 | 46 | P/DC | ([44]) | ([44]) | 1107 |
| Jersey City State College; Jersey City, N.J. 07305 | 2,139 | 2,097 | 250 | S | 916 | 1620 | 650 |
| John Brown University; Siloam Springs, Ark. 72761 | 335[1] | 298[1] | 47 | P/ID | 1600 | 1600 | 1150 |
| John Carroll University; Cleveland, Ohio 44118 | 1,592 | 780 | 172 | P/RC | 2000 | — | 1200 |
| John F. Kennedy University; Orinda, Calif. 94598 | 402 | 478 | 5 | P | 1500 | 1500 | — |
| John Jay Coll. of Criminal Justice. *See* New York, City Univ. of | | | | | | | |
| John Marshall Law School, The; Chicago, Ill. 60604 | 1,227[1] | 261[1] | 43 | P | ([45]) | ([45]) | — |
| Johns Hopkins University, The; Baltimore, Md. 21218 | 3,132 | 1,523 | 1176 | P | 4050 | 4050 | 2200 |
| Johnson and Wales College; Providence, R.I. 02903 | 1,440[1] | 960[1] | 90 | P | 2205 | 2205 | 1410 |
| Johnson C. Smith University; Charlotte, N.C. 28216 | 713 | 740 | 69 | P | 1446 | 1446 | 1200 |
| Johnson State College; Johnson, Vt. 05656 | 1,189[7] | | n.a. | S | 670[7] | n.a. | 1400[7] |
| Johnston College, Univ. of Redlands; Redlands, Calif. 92373 | 195[2] | | n.a. | P | 3425[2] | n.a. | 1340[2] |
| Jones College; Jacksonville, Fla. 32211 | 1,368[7] | | n.a. | P | 1210[2] | n.a. | n.a. |
| Jones College; Orlando, Fla. 32803 | 975 | 325 | 11 | P | 1093 | — | — |
| Judge Advocate General's School, U.S. Army; Charlottesville, Va. 22901 | 125[7] | 3[7] | n.a. | Pub/F | n.a. | n.a. | n.a. |
| Judson College; Elgin, Ill. 60120 | 169[1] | 212[1] | 20 | P/B | 2808 | 2808 | 2220 |
| Judson College; Marion, Ala. 36756 | — | 292[7] | n.a. | P/B | 1200[46] | n.a. | 1400[46] |
| Juilliard School, The; New York, N.Y. 10023 | 445[1] | 339[1] | 125 | P | 3000 | 3000 | 2600 |
| Juniata College; Huntingdon, Pa. 16652 | 610 | 419 | 73 | P | 3375 | 3375 | 1530 |
| Kalamazoo College; Kalamazoo, Mich. 49007 | 795 | 646 | 86 | P/B | 2907 | 2907 | 1599 |
| Kansas, University of; Lawrence, Kan. 66045 | 12,744 | 10,702 | 1286 | S | 688 | 1678 | 1300 |
| Kansas City Art Institute; Kansas City, Mo. 64111 | 274 | 230 | 42 | P | 3250 | 3250 | 800 |
| Kansas City Coll. of Osteopathic Med.; Kansas City, Mo. 64124 | 546 | 59 | 50 | P | 6250 | 6250 | 720 |
| Kansas Newman College; Wichita, Kan. 67213 | 310 | 281 | 36 | P/RC | 1890 | 1890 | 1190 |
| Kansas State College of Pittsburg; Pittsburg, Kan. 66762 | 5,284[7] | | n.a. | S | 510[2] | n.a. | 1400[2] |
| Kansas State University; Manhattan, Kan. 66506 | 18,220[7] | | n.a. | S | 680[2] | n.a. | 1200[2] |
| Kansas Wesleyan University; Salina, Kan. 67401 | 199 | 170 | 32 | P/UM | 1960 | 1960 | 1310 |
| Kean College of New Jersey; Union, N.J. 07083 | 12,450[7] | | n.a. | S | ([47]) | n.a. | n.a. |
| Kearney State College; Kearney, Neb. 68847 | 1,752 | 2,158 | 220 | S | ([48]) | ([49]) | 1038 |
| Keene State College; Keene, N.H. 03431 | 1,017[7] | 1,544[7] | n.a. | S | 617[46] | n.a. | 1175[46] |
| Kent State University; Kent, Ohio 44242 | 9,461[1] | 9,892[1] | 1050 | S | 930 | 2130 | 1320 |
| Kentucky, University of; Lexington, Ky. 40506 | 8,331 | 6,438 | — | S | 550 | 1650 | 1636 |
| Kentucky Christian College; Grayson, Ky. 41143 | 504[2] | | n.a. | P/CC | 1000[2] | n.a. | 1050[2] |
| Kentucky State University; Frankfort, Ky. 40601 | 775[1] | 585[1] | 130 | S | 500 | 1220 | 1054 |
| Kentucky Wesleyan College; Owensboro, Ky. 42301 | 377[1] | 429[1] | 43 | P/UM | 1920 | 1920 | 1260 |

| Institution and location | Enrollment | | Faculty | Control | Tuition | | |
|---|---|---|---|---|---|---|---|
| | Male | Female | | | Res. | Nonres. | Rm/Bd |
| Kenyon College; Gambier, Ohio 43022 | 874[1] | 583[1] | 106 | P | $4040 | $4040 | $1855 |
| Keuka College; Keuka Park, N.Y. 14478 | 3[1] | 540[1] | 49 | P | 3920 | 3920 | 1340 |
| King College; Bristol, Tenn. 37620 | 153 | 111 | 29 | P/Pres | 2469 | 2469 | 1300 |
| King of Prussia Grad. Center. *See* Pennsylvania State Univ. | | | | | | | |
| King's College; Wilkes-Barre, Pa. 18711 | 993 | 557 | 100 | P | 2400 | 2400 | 730 |
| King's College, The; Briarcliff Manor, N.Y. 10510 | 343 | 469 | 45 | P | 2775 | 2775 | 1375 |
| Kirkland College; Clinton, N.Y. 13323 | — | 629[7] | n.a. | P | 4150[10] | n.a. | 1700[10] |
| Kirksville Coll. of Osteopathic Medicine; Kirksville, Mo. 63501 | 424 | 69 | 67 | P | 7500 | 7500 | 2925 |
| Knox College; Galesburg, Ill. 61401 | 575[1] | 446[1] | 88 | P | 3795 | 3795 | 1395 |
| Knoxville College; Knoxville, Tenn. 37921 | 386 | 349 | 56 | P | 1580 | — | 1170 |
| Kutztown State College; Kutztown, Pa. 19530 | 5,322[7] | | n.a. | S | 800[2] | n.a. | 956[2] |
| Ladycliff College; Highland Falls, N.Y. 10928 | 73 | 415 | 29 | P | 2300 | 2300 | 1650 |
| Lafayette College; Easton, Pa. 18042 | 1,404 | 642 | 158 | P | 4100 | 4100 | 1635 |
| LaGrange College; LaGrange, Ga. 30240 | 289 | 381 | 46 | P/M | 1890 | 1890 | 1065 |
| Lake Erie College; Painesville, Ohio 44077 | 334 | 653 | 52 | P | 3900 | 3100 | 1600 |
| Lake Forest College; Lake Forest, Ill. 60045 | 547 | 479 | — | P | 4265 | 4265 | 1570 |
| Lake Superior State College; Sault Ste. Marie, Mich. 49783 | 1,028[1] | 805[1] | 109 | S | 684 | 1404 | 1550 |
| Lakeland College; Sheboygan, Wis. 53081 | 302[1] | 221[1] | 28 | P/UCC | 2645 | 2645 | 1575 |
| Lamar University; Beaumont, Tex. 77710 | 6,241 | 5,973 | 475 | S | 306 | 1166 | 1254 |
| Lambuth College; Jackson, Tenn. 38301 | 344[1] | 463[1] | 62 | P/UM | 2000 | 2000 | 1150 |
| Lander College; Greenwood, S.C. 29646 | 570[1] | 823[1] | 84 | S | 600 | 1250 | 1200 |
| Lane College; Jackson, Tenn. 38301 | 323 | 309 | 42 | P | 1600 | 1600 | 1260 |
| Langston University; Langston, Okla. 73050 | 521 | 415 | 79 | S | 467[50] | 1065[50] | 1197 |
| La Roche College; Pittsburgh, Pa. 15237 | 957[2] | | n.a. | P/RC | 1970[2] | n.a. | 1550[2] |
| La Salle College; Philadelphia, Pa. 19141 | 1,870 | 1,004 | 184 | P/RC | 2830 | 2830 | 1530 |
| La Verne, University of[51]; La Verne, Calif. 91750 | 1,204[1] | 701[1] | 74 | P | 3165 | 3165 | 1650 |
| Lawrence Institute of Technology; Southfield, Mich. 48075 | 3,839 | 441 | 60 | P | 1380 | 1380 | — |
| Lawrence University; Appleton, Wis. 54911 | 580[1] | 608[1] | 125 | P | 4022 | — | 1278 |
| Lebanon Valley College; Annville, Pa. 17003 | 477 | 450 | 78 | P/UM | 3020 | 3020 | 1500 |
| Lee College; Cleveland, Tenn. 37311 | 594 | 532 | 65 | P/CG | 2653 | 2653 | 1200 |
| Lehigh University; Bethlehem, Pa. 18015 | 3,337[1] | 1,013[1] | 327 | P | 3825 | 3825 | 1675 |
| Le Moyne College; Syracuse, N.Y. 13214 | 1,011[1] | 703[1] | 97 | P | 2770 | 2770 | 1550 |
| LeMoyne-Owen College; Memphis, Tenn. 38126 | 1,040[2] | | n.a. | P | 1350[2] | n.a. | n.a. |
| Lenoir-Rhyne College; Hickory, N.C. 28601 | 515[1] | 674[1] | 94 | P/LCA | 2275 | 2275 | 1025 |
| Lesley College; Cambridge, Mass. 02138 | 2,490[52] | | n.a. | P | 3250[2] | n.a. | 2030[2] |
| LeTourneau College; Longview, Tex. 75601 | 755 | 85 | 52 | P/ND | 2100 | 2100 | 1258 |
| Lewis and Clark College; Portland, Ore. 97219 | 2,976[7] | | n.a. | P | 3391[10] | n.a. | 1380[10] |
| Lewis-Clark State College; Lewiston, Idaho 83501 | 600[1] | 500[1] | 105 | S | 334 | 1084 | 1400 |
| Lewis University; Lockport, Ill. 60441 | 2,345 | 1,230 | 122 | P/RC | 2560 | 2560 | 1340 |
| Limestone College; Gaffney, S.C. 29340 | 409[1] | 272[1] | 33 | P | 2225 | 2225 | 1375 |
| Lincoln Christian College; Lincoln, Ill. 62656 | 201 | 227 | 30 | P/CC | 1580 | 1580 | 965 |
| Lincoln Memorial University; Harrogate, Tenn. 37752 | 385 | 437 | 38 | P | 1550 | 1550 | 1145 |
| Lincoln University; Jefferson City, Mo. 65101 | 637 | 658 | 155 | S | 785 | 985 | 525 |
| Lincoln University; Lincoln University, Pa. 19352 | 574 | 530 | 68 | S | 1068 | 1768 | 1350 |
| Lindenwood Colleges, The; St. Charles, Mo. 63301 | 290[1] | 514[1] | 54 | P | 2775 | 2775 | 1875 |
| Linfield College; McMinnville, Ore. 97128 | 537 | 618 | 70 | P | 3170 | 3170 | 1725 |
| Livingston University; Livingston, Ala. 35470 | 638 | 468 | — | S | 600 | 600 | 1050 |
| Livingstone College; Salisbury, N.C. 28144 | 538 | 451 | 43 | P/AME | 1600 | 1600 | 1350 |
| Lock Haven State College; Lock Haven, Pa. 17745 | 936 | 1,073 | 197 | S | 525 | 890 | 522 |
| Loma Linda Univ.; Loma Linda, Calif. 92354 | 2,270[1] | 2,184[1] | 578[2] | SDA | 2995 | 2995 | 1446 |
| Lone Mountain College; San Francisco, Calif. 94118 | 937[2] | | n.a. | P/RC | 2600[2] | n.a. | 1670[2] |
| Long Island University System; Greenvale, N.Y. 11548 | | | | | | | |
| Arnold and Marie Schwartz Coll. of Pharmacy and Health Sciences[53]; Brooklyn, N.Y. 11201 | 1,000[2] | | n.a. | P | 2900[2] | n.a. | 1500[2] |
| Brooklyn Center; Brooklyn, N.Y. 11201 | 1,285[1] | 1,828[1] | 300 | P | 3200 | 3200 | 1791 |
| C.W. Post Center; Greenvale, N.Y. 11548 | 2,808 | 2,523 | 351 | P | 4986 | 3060 | 1926 |
| Southampton College; Southampton, N.Y. 11968 | 751[1] | 534[1] | 65 | P | 3150 | 3150 | 1950 |
| Longwood College; Farmville, Va. 23901 | 2,232[2] | | n.a. | S | 675[2] | n.a. | 1360[2] |
| Loras College; Dubuque, Iowa 52001 | 872[1] | 468[1] | 96 | P | 2275 | 2275 | 1220 |
| Loretto Heights College; Denver, Colo. 80236 | 750[2] | | n.a. | P | 3150[2] | n.a. | 1750[2] |
| Los Angeles Baptist College; Newhall, Calif. 91322 | 173[1] | 170[1] | 25 | P/B | 2160 | 2160 | 1350 |
| Los Angeles College of Chiropractic; Glendale, Calif., 91205 | 554 | 111 | 37 | P | 2850 | 2850 | — |
| Louisiana College; Pineville, La. 71360 | 449 | 463 | 59 | P/B | 900 | 900 | 1040 |
| Louisiana State Univ. System; Baton Rouge, La. 70803 | 19,820[1] | 15,496[1] | 2374 | S | — | — | — |
| LSU-Baton Rouge; Baton Rouge, La. 70803 | 11,439[1] | 8,479[1] | 952 | S | 445 | 1275 | 1089 |

| Institution and location | Enrollment Male | Enrollment Female | Faculty | Control | Tuition Res. | Tuition Nonres. | Rm/Bd |
|---|---|---|---|---|---|---|---|
| LSU in Shreveport; Shreveport, La. 71105 | 885[1] | 853[1] | 110 | S | $380 | $1210 | — |
| LSU Medical Center; New Orleans, La. 70112 | 1,341[1] | 833[1] | 555 | S | 800 | 2300 | — |
| Louisiana Tech University; Ruston, La. 71272 | 8,197[1] | | 400 | S | 460 | 1090 | $1050 |
| Louisville, University of; Louisville, Ky. 40208 | 6,837 | 4,138 | — | S | 550 | 1980 | 1275 |
| Lowell, University of; Lowell, Mass. 01854 | 4,300 | 2,500 | 402 | S | 525 | 1450 | 1600 |
| Loyola College; Baltimore, Md. 21210 | 1,056[1] | 746[1] | 114 | P/RC | 2350 | 2350 | 1400 |
| Loyola Marymount University; Los Angeles, Calif. 90045 | 2,470 | 2,059 | 193 | P/RC | 3000 | 3000 | 1504 |
| Loyola University, New Orleans; New Orleans, La. 70118 | 1,109 | 1,097 | — | P/RC | 2250 | 2250 | 1750 |
| Loyola University of Chicago; Chicago, Ill. 60611 | 2,759 | 2,816 | 654 | P/RC | 2600 | 2600 | 1550 |
| Lubbock Christian College; Lubbock, Tex. 79407 | 483 | 464 | 60 | P/CC | 1530 | 1530 | 1000 |
| Luther College; Decorah, Iowa 52101 | 848 | 1,023 | 124 | P/AL | 3160 | 3160 | 1075 |
| Lycoming College; Williamsport, Pa. 17701 | 679 | 454 | 72 | P/UM | 2700 | 2700 | 1300 |
| Lynchburg College; Lynchburg, Va. 24501 | 2,200[2] | | n.a. | P/DC | 4050[11] | — | — |
| Lyndon State College; Lyndonville, Vt. 05851 | 515 | 420 | 63 | S | 720 | 2300 | 1600 |
| Macalester College; St. Paul, Minn. 55105 | 821[1] | 832[1] | 122 | P | 3600 | 3600 | 1400 |
| MacMurray College; Jacksonville, Ill. 62650 | 247 | 470 | 53 | P/UM | 3160 | 3160 | 1350 |
| Madonna College; Livonia, Mich. 48150 | 759 | 1830 | 62 | P | 1268 | 1268 | 1515 |
| Maine, Univ. of, at Farmington; Farmington, Me. 04938 | 447[1] | 1,159[1] | 82 | S | 770 | 2284 | 1475 |
| Maine, Univ. of, at Fort Kent; Fort Kent, Me. 04743 | 221 | 135 | 24 | S | 770 | 2350 | 1445 |
| Maine, Univ. of, at Machias; Machias, Me. 04654 | 325 | 327 | 48 | S | 880 | 2350 | 1500 |
| Maine, Univ. of, at Orono; Orono, Me. 04473 | 5,286 | 3,980 | 550 | S | 785 | 2263 | 1605 |
| Maine, Univ. of, at Portland–Gorham; Gorham, Me. 04038 | 3,574 | 3,861 | 255 | S | 749 | 1037 | 1440 |
| Maine, Univ. of, at Presque Isle; Presque Isle, Me. 04769 | 465[1] | 501[1] | n.a. | S | 770 | 2285 | 1500 |
| Maine Maritime Academy; Castine, Me. 04421 | 612 | 4 | 46 | S | 1200 | 2325 | 1600 |
| Malone College; Canton, Ohio 44709 | 402[1] | 448[1] | 40 | P/SOF | 2542 | 2542 | 1350 |
| Manchester College; North Manchester, Ind. 46962 | 504 | 457 | 70 | P/CB | 2370 | 2370 | 1220 |
| Manhattan Christian College; Manhattan, Kan. 66502 | 111 | 88 | 12 | P/CC | 1200 | 1200 | 800 |
| Manhattan College; Riverdale, Bronx, N.Y. 10471 | 1,033 | 98 | 300 | P | 4470 | 2750 | 1720 |
| Manhattan School of Music; New York, N.Y. 10027 | 349 | 323 | 25 | P | 2950 | 2950 | — |
| Manhattanville College; Purchase, N.Y. 10577 | 191[1] | 639[1] | 73 | P | 3800 | 3800 | 1975 |
| Mankato State Univ. *See* Minnesota State College System | | | | | | | |
| Mannes College of Music; New York, N.Y. 10021 | 202[2] | | n.a. | P | 2750[7] | n.a. | n.a. |
| Mansfield State College, Mansfield, Pa. 16933 | 1,140[1] | 1,510[1] | 200 | S | 950 | 1780 | 1042 |
| Marian College; Indianapolis, Ind. 46222 | 229[10] | 358[10] | 54 | P/RC | 2080 | 2080 | 1280 |
| Marian College of Fond du Lac; Fond du Lac, Wis. 54935 | 68[1] | 401[1] | 38 | P/RC | 1950 | 1950 | 612 |
| Marietta College; Marietta, Ohio 45750 | 921[1] | 490[1] | 88 | P | 3600 | 3600 | 1350 |
| Marion College; Marion, Ind. 46952 | 338[1] | 542[1] | 49 | P/W | 2194 | 2194 | 1275 |
| Marist College; Poughkeepsie, N.Y. 12601 | 1,881[2] | | n.a. | P | 2670[2] | n.a. | 1575[2] |
| Marlboro College; Marlboro, Vt. 05344 | 91 | 100 | 22 | P | 6170 | 4180 | 1905 |
| Marquette University; Milwaukee, Wis. 53233 | 5,907[1] | 4,020[1] | 485 | P/RC | 3100 | 3100 | 1475 |
| Mars Hill College; Mars Hill, N.C. 28754 | 693[1] | 915[1] | 95 | P/SB | 2360 | 2360 | 1060 |
| Marshall University; Huntington, W. Va. 25701 | 3,287[1] | 3,235[1] | 373 | S | 350 | 1300 | 1700 |
| Mary Baldwin College; Staunton, Va. 24401 | 10 | 657 | 53 | P | 5470[11] | 5470[11] | — |
| Mary College; Bismarck, N.D. 58501 | 231[1] | 529[1] | 100 | P/RC | 1698 | 1698 | 1145 |
| Mary Hardin–Baylor College; Belton, Tex. 76513 | 372 | 671 | 65 | B | 1670 | 1670 | 1260 |
| Mary Washington College; Fredericksburg, Va. 22401 | 2,292[7] | | n.a. | S | 788[2] | n.a. | 1440[2] |
| Marycrest College; Davenport, Iowa 52804 | 99[1] | 648[1] | 70 | P | 3940 | 2550 | 1390 |
| Marygrove College; Detroit, Mich. 48221 | 128[1] | 683[1] | 48 | P/RC | 2190 | — | 1450 |
| Maryland, University of (System); College Park, Md. 20742 | 19,920[1] | 17,946[1] | 1,566 | S | — | — | — |
| UM at Baltimore (UMAB); Baltimore, Md. 21201 | 4,353[2] | | n.a. | S | 620[2] | n.a. | 679[8] |
| UM, Baltimore County (UMBC); Catonsville, Md. 21228 | 1,993 | 2,161 | 300 | S | 758 | 2148 | 1530 |
| UM at College Park (UMCP); College Park, Md. 20742 | 36,761[7] | | n.a. | S | 784[2] | n.a. | 1738[2] |
| UM Eastern Shore (UMES); Princess Anne, Md. 21853 | 432[1] | 390[1] | 69 | S | 550 | 995 | 1330 |
| UM University College (UMUC); College Park, Md. 20742 | 29,073[7] | | n.a. | S | ([29]) | n.a. | n.a. |
| Maryland Institute, College of Art; Baltimore, Md. 21217 | 997[2] | | n.a. | P | 2850[2] | n.a. | 2700[2] |
| Marylhurst Education Center; Marylhurst, Ore. 90736 | 771[1] | | 23 | P | — | 1500 | — |
| Marymount College; Tarrytown, N.Y. 10591 | — | 922[2] | n.a. | P | 2925[2] | n.a. | 2025[2] |
| Marymount College of Kansas; Salina, Kan. 67401 | 406 | 237 | 45 | P/RC | 1900 | 1900 | 1240 |
| Marymount College of Virginia; Arlington, Va. 22207 | 5 | 815 | 52 | P | 2475 | 2475 | 1625 |
| Marymount Manhattan College; New York, N.Y. 10021 | — | 700 | 45 | P | 2550 | 2550 | — |
| Maryville College; Maryville, Tenn. 37801 | 301 | 249 | 45 | P/PUS | 2305 | 2305 | 1135 |
| Maryville College; St. Louis, Mo. 63141 | 150 | 455 | 55 | P | 2650 | 2650 | 1500 |
| Marywood College; Scranton, Pa. 18509 | 231 | 1,629 | 135 | P/RC | ([54]) | ([54]) | 1600 |
| Massachusetts at Amherst, Univ. of; Amherst, Mass. 01002 | 11,926[1] | 9,049[1] | 1214 | S | 525 | 1550 | 1631 |
| Massachusetts at Boston, Univ. of; Boston, Mass. 02125 | 3,750[7] | 3,264[7] | n.a. | S | 300[46] | n.a. | n.a. |

| Institution and location | Enrollment | | Faculty | Control | Tuition | | Rm/Bd |
|---|---|---|---|---|---|---|---|
| | Male | Female | | | Res. | Nonres. | |
| Massachusetts College of Art; Boston, Mass. 02215 | 376[1] | 718[1] | 67 | S | $500 | $1200 | — |
| Massachusetts College of Pharmacy; Boston, Mass. 02115 | 1,480[2] | | n.a. | P | 2310[2] | n.a. | $2100[2] |
| Massachusetts Institute of Technology; Cambridge, Mass. 02139 | 7,330[1] | 1,382[1] | 969 | P | 4700 | — | 2735 |
| Massachusetts Maritime Academy; Buzzards Bay, Mass. 02532 | 844 | 6 | 47 | S | 500 | — | 1750 |
| Mayo Medical School[55]; Rochester, Minn. 55901 | 126[7] | 35[7] | n.a. | P | n.a. | n.a. | n.a. |
| Mayville State College; Mayville, N.D. 58257 | 288 | 388 | 46 | S | 372 | 933 | 1080 |
| McKendree College; Lebanon, Ill. 62254 | 515 | 301 | 39 | P/UM | 2496 | 2496 | 1300 |
| McMurray College; Abilene, Tex. 79605 | 355 | 296 | 55 | P/UM | 1620 | 1620 | 1000 |
| McNeese State University; Lake Charles, La. 70609 | 2,046 | 2,104 | 260 | S | 436 | 1066 | 1080 |
| McPherson College; McPherson, Kan. 67460 | 286[10] | 218[10] | 30 | P/CB | 2070 | 2070 | 2230 |
| Medaille College; Buffalo, N.Y. 14214 | 207 | 385 | 25 | P | 1950 | 1950 | — |
| Medical College of Georgia; Augusta, Ga. 30901 | 942[1] | 1,025[1] | 469 | S | 555 | 1506 | 450 |
| Meharry Medical College; Nashville, Tenn. 37208 | 599[1] | 411[1] | 237 | P | 4000 | 4000 | 3000 |
| Memphis Academy of Arts, The; Memphis, Tenn. 38112 | 92[1] | 98[1] | 17 | P | 1550 | 1550 | 800 |
| Memphis State University; Memphis, Tenn. 38152 | 5,720 | 5,423 | 800 | S | 448 | 1384 | 475[8] |
| Menlo College; Menlo Park, Calif. 94025 | 457[1] | 160[1] | 40 | P | 3600 | — | 1980 |
| Mercer University; Macon, Ga. 31207 | 2,101[1] | 1,484[1] | 150 | P/B | 2175 | 2829 | 1422 |
| Mercer University in Atlanta; Atlanta, Ga. 30341 | 582[1] | 500[1] | 42 | P/B | 1821 | — | — |
| Mercer U. Southern School of Pharmacy; Atlanta, Ga. 30312 | 235 | 109 | 35 | P/B | 2700 | — | — |
| Mercy College; Dobbs Ferry, N.Y. 10522 | 3,321 | 3,733 | 124 | P | 1800 | — | — |
| Mercy College of Detroit; Detroit, Mich. 48219 | 646 | 1,127 | 80 | P/RC | 2180 | 2180 | 680[8] |
| Mercyhurst College; Erie, Pa. 16501 | 550 | 650 | 80 | P | 2580 | 2580 | 1330 |
| Meredith College; Raleigh, N.C. 27611 | — | 1,280 | 63 | P/B | 2100 | 2100 | 1100 |
| Merrimack College; North Andover, Mass. 01845 | 1,232 | 782 | 149 | P/RC | 3059 | 3059 | 2084 |
| Mesa College; Grand Junction, Colo. 81501 | 1,362[1] | 1,083[1] | 142 | S | 423 | 1695 | 1377 |
| Messiah College; Grantham, Pa. 17027 | 398 | 594 | 48 | P | 2660 | 2660 | 1430 |
| Methodist College; Fayetteville, N.C. 28301 | 325 | 329 | 47 | P | 1500 | 1500 | 1240 |
| Metropolitan State College; Denver, Colo. 80204 | 13,000[2] | | n.a. | S | 402[2] | n.a. | n.a. |
| Metropolitan State Univ., Minn. *See* Minnesota State Univ. System | | | | | | | |
| Miami, University of; Coral Gables, Fla. 33124 | 9,481 | 6,630 | 1306 | P | 3700 | — | — |
| Miami Christian College; Miami, Fla. 33167 | 99 | 81 | 10 | P | 1700 | 1700 | 1500 |
| Miami University; Oxford, Ohio 45056 | 8,243 | 8,887 | 664 | S | 1220 | 2620 | 1560 |
| Michigan, The University of; Ann Arbor, Mich. 48109 | 18,448[1] | 12,196[1] | 2227 | S | 1200 | 3560 | 1638 |
| U. of Michigan—Dearborn; Dearborn, Mich. 48128 | 5,023[56] | | n.a. | S | 676[2] | n.a. | n.a. |
| U. of Michigan—Flint; Flint, Mich. 48503 | 3,685[7] | | n.a. | S | 676[2] | n.a. | n.a. |
| Michigan State University; East Lansing, Mich. 48824 | 20,949 | 18,948 | 2781 | S | 1043 | 2144 | 1488 |
| Michigan Technological University; Houghton, Mich. 49931 | 4,926[1] | 1,361[1] | 346 | S | 861 | 2001 | 1630 |
| Mid-America Nazarene College; Olathe, Kan. 66061 | 333 | 384 | 39 | P/Naz | 1512 | — | 1180 |
| Mid-South Bible College; Memphis, Tenn. 38112 | 51 | 18 | 9 | P/ND | 1368 | 1368 | 1340 |
| Middle Tennessee State Univ.; Murfreesboro, Tenn. 37132 | 4,057[1] | 3,829[1] | 480 | S | 442 | 1378 | 760 |
| Middlebury College; Middlebury, Vt. 05753 | 989 | 890 | 140 | P | 5750[11] | — | — |
| Midland Lutheran College; Fremont, Neb. 68025 | 279 | 401 | 48 | P/L | 2370 | 2370 | 1130 |
| Midwestern State University; Wichita Falls, Tex. 76308 | 2,350 | 2,290 | 150 | S | ([57]) | ([58]) | 1040 |
| Miles College; Birmingham, Ala. 35208 | 467 | 579 | 91 | P | ([59]) | ([59]) | 550 |
| Millersville State College; Millersville, Pa. 17551 | 2,594 | 3,588 | 304 | S | 950 | 1780 | 1168 |
| Milligan College; Milligan College, Tenn. 37682 | 379 | 407 | 45 | P/CC | 1692 | 1692 | 1454 |
| Millikin University; Decatur, Ill. 62522 | 850 | 650 | 100 | P/Pres | 3300 | 3300 | 1425 |
| Mills College; Oakland, Calif. 94613 | 25[1] | 883[1] | 63 | P | 3770 | 3770 | 3770 |
| Millsaps College; Jackson, Miss. 39210 | 488 | 414 | 60 | P/UM | 2270 | 2270 | 1136 |
| Milton College; Milton, Wis. 53563 | 400 | 200 | 29 | P | 2350 | 2350 | 1150 |
| Milton S. Hershey Medical Ctr. *See* Pennsylvania State Univ. | | | | | | | |
| Milwaukee School of Engineering; Milwaukee, Wis. 53201 | 1,311[7] | | n.a. | P | 2625[2] | n.a. | 1305[2] |
| Minneapolis College of Art & Design; Minneapolis, Minn. 55404 | 328 | 341 | 62 | P | 2460 | 2460 | 750[8] |
| Minnesota, The University of; Minneapolis, Minn. 55455 | 22,496 | 17,249 | 4340 | S | 930 | 2340 | 1640 |
| Univ. of Minnesota, Duluth; Duluth, Minn. 55812 | 3,383[1] | 2,716[1] | 404 | S | 264 | 754 | 520 |
| Univ. of Minnesota, Morris; Morris, Minn. 56267 | 883[1] | 678[1] | 107 | S | 2172 | — | 1260 |
| Minnesota Bible College; Rochester, Minn. 55901 | 72[1] | 63[1] | 10 | P/CC | 900 | 900 | 1170 |
| Minnesota State University System; St. Paul, Minn. 55101 | | | | | | | |
| Bemidji State University; Bemidji, Minn. 56601 | 2,166[1] | 1,900[1] | 254 | S | 511 | 1015 | 1183 |
| Mankato State University; Mankato, Minn. 56001 | 3,906[1] | 3,831[1] | 500 | S | ([60]) | ([60]) | 1148 |
| Metropolitan State University; St. Paul, Minn. 55101 | 954[1] | 1,073[1] | 15 | S | 600 | 1200 | — |
| Moorhead State University; Moorhead, Minn. 56560 | 2,374 | 2,484 | — | S | 575 | 710 | 1158 |
| St. Cloud State University; St. Cloud, Minn. 56301 | 4,155 | 3,999 | 461 | S | 492 | 972 | 1200 |
| Southwest State University; Marshall, Minn. 56258 | 910 | 649 | 106 | S | 465 | 950 | 1200 |

| Institution and location | Enrollment: Male | Female | Faculty | Control | Tuition: Res. | Nonres. | Rm/Bd |
|---|---|---|---|---|---|---|---|
| Winona State University; Winona, Minn. 55987 | 2,000 | 2,500 | 220 | S | $500 | $1000 | $1200 |
| Minot State College; Minot, N.D. 58701 | 800 | 1,442 | 110 | S | 468 | 1029 | 1100 |
| Mississippi, The University of; University, Miss. 38677 | 5,420 | 4,150 | 500 | S | 703 | 1503 | 1200 |
| Mississippi College; Clinton, Miss. 39058 | 3,088[7] | | n.a. | P/B | 1300[2] | n.a. | 1020[2] |
| Mississippi State University; Mississippi State, Miss. 39762 | 5,159 | 3,164 | 665 | S | 672 | 1472 | 1600 |
| Mississippi University for Women; Columbus, Miss. 39701 | — | 2,862[1] | 161 | S | 574 | 1374 | 1174 |
| Mississippi Valley State University; Itta Bena, Miss. 38941 | 1,181 | 1,435 | 160 | S | 577 | 1327 | 888 |
| Missouri, University of; Columbia, Mo. 65201 | | | | | | | |
| Univ. of Missouri—Columbia; Columbia, Mo. 65201 | 23,325[1] | | n.a. | S | 600[2] | n.a. | 1220[2] |
| Univ. of Missouri—Kansas City; Kansas City, Mo. 64110 | 3,597[1] | 2,519[1] | 650 | S | 670 | 1870 | 1485 |
| Univ. of Missouri—Rolla; Rolla, Mo. 65401 | 3,716[1] | 614[1] | 324 | S | 791 | 2147 | 1500 |
| Univ. of Missouri—St. Louis; St. Louis, Mo. 63121 | 6,301[1] | 5,073[1] | 416 | S | 678 | 1356 | — |
| Missouri Institute of Technology[61]; Kansas City, Mo. 64114 | 641[1] | 20[1] | 11 | P | 1965 | 1965 | — |
| Missouri Southern State College; Joplin, Mo. 64801 | 2,045[1] | 1,729[1] | 177 | S | 350 | 740 | 980 |
| Missouri Valley College; Marshall, Mo. 65340 | 237[1] | 159[1] | 32 | P/Pres | 1960 | 1960 | 1394 |
| Missouri Western State College; St. Joseph, Mo. 64507 | 1,898 | 1,729 | 160 | S | 201 | 391 | 970 |
| Mobile College; Mobile, Ala. 36613 | 378[1] | 584[1] | 45 | P/B | 1600 | 1600 | 1350 |
| Molloy College; Rockville Centre, N.Y. 11570 | 17 | 907 | 95 | P/RC | 2600 | — | — |
| Monmouth College; Monmouth, Ill. 61462 | 370 | 260 | 55 | P | 3045 | 3045 | 1410 |
| Monmouth College; West Long Branch, N.J. 07764 | 1,054[1] | 934[1] | 156 | Ind | 3180 | 3180 | 1700 |
| Montana, University of; Missoula, Mont. 59812 | 4,870 | 3,461 | 450 | S | 613 | 1981 | 1659 |
| Montana College of Mineral Science & Technology; Butte, Mont. 59701 | 680[1] | 242[1] | 61 | S | 460 | 1468 | 1285 |
| Montana State University; Bozeman, Mont. 59715 | 9,400[7] | | n.a. | S | 525[2] | n.a. | 1225[2] |
| Montclair State College; Upper Montclair, N.J. 07043 | 3,105 | 4,657 | 587 | S | ([62]) | ([63]) | 764 |
| Monterey Institute of Foreign Studies; Monterey, Calif. 93940 | 470[7] | | n.a. | P | 2700[2] | n.a. | n.a. |
| Montevallo, University of; Montevallo, Ala. 35115 | 1,241 | 1,771 | 250 | S | 1500 | 400 | 1000 |
| Moody Bible Institute; Chicago, Ill. 60610 | 717 | 573 | 88 | P/ID | — | — | 1800 |
| Moore College of Art; Philadelphia, Pa. 19103 | — | 500 | 45 | P | 3500 | — | 1550 |
| Moorhead State Univ. *See* Minnesota State College System | | | | | | | |
| Moravian College; Bethlehem, Pa. 18018 | 605 | 548 | 78 | P | 4725 | 3310 | 1415 |
| Morehead State University; Morehead, Ky. 40351 | 2,286[1] | 2,462[1] | 311 | S | 480 | 1200 | 320[8] |
| Morehouse College; Atlanta, Ga. 30314 | 1,455 | — | 100 | P | 2214 | 2214 | 1540 |
| Morgan State University; Baltimore, Md. 21239 | 2,819 | 3,668 | 400 | S | 830 | 1730 | 835 |
| Morningside College; Sioux City, Iowa 51106 | 521 | 573 | 84 | P/M | 2660 | 2660 | 990 |
| Morris Brown College; Atlanta, Ga. 30314 | 782 | 979 | 112 | P/AME | 1950 | 1950 | 1340 |
| Morris Harvey College; Charleston, W. Va. 25304 | 387 | 492 | 78 | P | 1700 | 1700 | 1250 |
| Mount Holyoke College; South Hadley, Mass. 01075 | — | 1,850 | 175 | P | 4250 | 4250 | 2050 |
| Mount Marty College; Yankton, S.D. 57078 | 131 | 328 | 51 | P/RC | 960 | 960 | 1150 |
| Mount Mary College; Milwaukee, Wis. 53222 | — | 787 | 73 | P/RC | 2100 | — | 1300 |
| Mount Mercy College; Cedar Rapids, Iowa 52402 | 143[1] | 468[1] | 65 | P/RC | 2385 | 2385 | 740 |
| Mount St. Joseph on the Ohio, College of; Mt. St. Joseph, Ohio 45051 | 23[10] | 772[10] | 68 | P/RC | 2368 | 2368 | 1548 |
| Mount Saint Mary College; Hooksett, N.H. 03106 | — | 210[2] | n.a. | P/RC | 2000[2] | n.a. | 1500[2] |
| Mount Saint Mary College; Newburg, N.Y. 12550 | 119 | 896 | 58 | P/RC | 2520 | 2520 | 1540 |
| Mount Saint Mary's College; Emmitsburg, Md. 21727 | 727 | 545 | 93 | P/RC | 2500 | 2500 | 1425 |
| Mount St. Mary's College; Los Angeles, Calif. 90049 | 12[1] | 809[1] | 67 | P/RC | 2700 | 2700 | 1596 |
| Mount Saint Vincent, College of; Riverdale, N.Y. 10471 | 50 | 775 | 70 | P | 2600 | 2600 | 1800 |
| Mount Senario College; Ladysmith, Wis. 54848 | 164[1] | 116[1] | 24 | P | 2350 | 2350 | 1380 |
| Mount Sinai Sch. of Medicine. *See* New York, City Univ. of | | | | | | | |
| Mount Union College; Alliance, Ohio 44601 | 613 | 458 | 76 | P/UM | 3030 | — | 1290 |
| Mount Vernon College; Washington, D.C. 20007 | — | 447 | 22 | P | 3150 | 3150 | 2300 |
| Mount Vernon Nazarene College; Mount Vernon, Ohio 43050 | 390[1] | 466[1] | 53 | P/Naz | 1975 | 1975 | 1230 |
| Muhlenberg College; Allentown, Pa. 18104 | 860[1] | 606[1] | 92 | P/L | 3315 | 3315 | 1350 |
| Multnomah School of the Bible; Portland, Ore. 97220 | 433 | 283 | 40 | P | 2040 | 2040 | 1200 |
| Mundelein College; Chicago, Ill. 60660 | 31[1] | 792[1] | 67 | P | 2670 | 2670 | 1425 |
| Murray State University; Murray, Ky. 42071 | 2,724[1] | 2,955[1] | 350 | S | 500 | 1270 | — |
| Museum Art School; Portland, Ore. 97205 | 61 | 76 | 13 | P | 2090 | 2090 | n.a. |
| Museum of Fine Arts, School of the; Boston, Mass. 02115 | 497 | | 66 | P | 2650[10] | n.a. | n.a. |
| Muskingum College; New Concord, Ohio 43762 | 534 | 432 | 85 | P | 3250 | — | 1411 |
| Nasson College; Springvale, Me. 04083 | 298 | 182 | 43 | P | 3340 | 3340 | 1550 |

| Institution and location | Enrollment | | Faculty | Control | Tuition | | Rm/Bd |
|---|---|---|---|---|---|---|---|
| | Male | Female | | | Res. | Nonres. | |
| Nathaniel Hawthorne College; Antrim, N.H. 03440 | 350 | 198 | 28 | Mun | $3350 | $3350 | $1100 |
| National College of Business; Rapid City, S.D. 57709 | 3,500[2] | | n.a. | P | 1950[2] | n.a. | 1750[2] |
| National College of Chiropractic; Lombard, Ill. 60148 | 780[1] | 90[1] | 48 | P | 2370 | 2370 | — |
| National College of Education; Evanston, Ill. 60201 | 45 | 355 | 55 | P | 3390 | 3390 | 1875 |
| Chicago Branch, Chicago, Ill. 60603 | 75 | 275 | — | P | 2700 | 2700 | — |
| National University; San Diego, Calif. 92018 | 1,865 | 589 | — | P | 2500 | 2500 | — |
| Naval Postgraduate School; Monterey, Calif. 93940 | 954 | 16 | 180 | F | — | — | — |
| Nazareth College at Kalamazoo; Nazareth, Mich. 49074 | 93 | 447 | 31 | P/RC | 2800 | 2800 | 1490 |
| Nazareth College of Rochester; Rochester, N.Y. 14610 | 2,409[2] | | n.a. | P | 2700[2] | n.a. | 1800[2] |
| Nebraska, University of; Lincoln, Neb. 68588 | 12,236 | 8,934 | 1244 | S | 750 | 900 | 1365 |
| Univ. of Nebraska at Omaha; Omaha, Neb. 68101 | 14,150[52] | | n.a. | S | 600[2] | n.a. | n.a. |
| Nebraska Wesleyan University; Lincoln, Neb. 68504 | 582[1] | 526[1] | 75 | P | 2310 | 2310 | 1260 |
| Nevada, University of; Reno, Nev. 89557 | 4,834[1] | 4,347[1] | — | S | — | — | — |
| University of Nevada, Las Vegas; Las Vegas, Nev. 89154 | 2,321[1] | 1,640[1] | 419 | S | 660 | 2160 | 1700 |
| University of Nevada, Reno; Reno, Nev. 89557 | 2,543[1] | 2,027[1] | 398 | S | 704 | 2204 | 1404 |
| New England College; Henniker, N.H. 03242 | 1,482[2] | | n.a. | P | 3300[2] | n.a. | 1520[2] |
| New England College of Optometry; Boston, Mass. 02115 | 298[1] | 62[1] | 35 | P | 4200 | — | 3000 |
| New England Conservatory of Music; Boston, Mass. 02115 | 250 | 500 | 55 | P | 3900 | 3900 | 2550 |
| New England School of Law; Boston, Mass. 02116 | 685 | 210 | 20 | P | 2700 | 2700 | — |
| New Hampshire, University of; Durham, N.H. 03824 | 5,048 | 4,922 | 540 | S | 1000 | 3250 | 1500 |
| New Hampshire College; Manchester, N.H. 03104 | 1,968 | 690 | 42 | P | 2836 | 2836 | 1700 |
| New Haven, University of; West Haven, Conn. 06516 | 6,607[7] | | n.a. | P | 2572[10] | n.a. | 1615[10] |
| New Jersey Institute of Technology; Newark, N.J. 07102 | 5,665[7] | | n.a. | S | 760[2] | n.a. | n.a. |
| New Mexico, The University of; Albuquerque, N.M. 87131 | 7,966[1] | 6,786[1] | 741 | S | 576 | 1716 | 1400 |
| New Mexico Highlands University; Las Vegas, N.M. 87701 | 973 | 973 | 119 | S | 376 | 1184 | 1095 |
| New Mexico Inst. of Mining & Technology; Socorro, N.M. 87801 | 568[1] | 173[1] | 75 | S | 301 | 1436 | 1390 |
| New Mexico State University; Las Cruces, N.M. 88003 | 5,476[1] | 3,523[1] | 528 | S | 608 | 1744 | 1336 |
| New Orleans, University of[64]; New Orleans, La. 70122 | 4,709[1] | 4,218[1] | 401 | S | 424 | 1254 | 1386 |
| New Rochelle, College of; New Rochelle, N.Y. 10801 | 494 | 3,089 | 75 | P | 2600 | 2600 | 1800 |
| New School for Social Research; New York, N.Y. 10011 | 900 | 1,300 | 100 | P | 3000 | — | 2200 |
| Parsons School of Design; New York, N.Y. 10011 | 358[7] | 769[7] | n.a. | P | n.a. | n.a. | n.a. |
| New School of Music, The; Philadelphia, Pa. 19103 | 21 | 63 | 6 | P | 2500 | — | 2000 |
| New York, City University of; New York, N.Y. 10021 | 115,805[1] | | 4773 | Mun | — | — | — |
| Bernard M. Baruch College; New York, N.Y. 10010 | 8,400 | 7,000 | 550 | Mun | 387[50] | 712 | — |
| Brooklyn College; Brooklyn, N.Y. 11210 | 6,060 | 7,099 | 900 | Mun | 775[50] | 1425 | — |
| City College; New York, N.Y. 10031 | 8,211 | 6,309 | 712 | Mun | 850 | 1425 | — |
| Coll. of Staten Island; Staten Island, N.Y. 10301 | 3,852[1] | 2,305[1] | 423 | Mun | 800 | 1400 | — |
| Graduate School & University Center; New York, N.Y. 10036 | 1,189 | 1,002 | 1316 | Mun | ([65]) | ([66]) | — |
| Herbert H. Lehman College; Bronx, N.Y. 10468 | 2,344 | 3,756 | 408 | Mun | 775[50] | 1425 | — |
| Hunter College; New York, N.Y. 10021 | 2,493 | 7,200 | 651 | Mun | 775[50] | 1425 | — |
| John Jay College of Criminal Justice; New York, N.Y. 10019 | 2,719 | 1,738 | 240 | Mun | 775[50] | 1425 | — |
| Mount Sinai School of Medicine, New York, N.Y. 10029 | 383[2] | | n.a. | P | 5000[2] | n.a. | 2500[2] |
| Queens College; Flushing, N.Y. 11367 | 5,761 | 6,810 | 993 | Mun | 900 | 1400 | — |
| York College; Jamaica, N.Y. 11451 | 1,231 | 1,772 | 137 | Mun | 387[50] | 712 | — |
| New York, Polytechnic Institute of; Brooklyn, N.Y. 11201 | 4,570[2] | | n.a. | P | 3200[2] | n.a. | n.a. |
| New York, State University of; Albany, N.Y. 12246 | 169,711[1] | 174,235 | 14148[1] | S | — | — | — |
| SUNY at Albany; Albany, N.Y. 12222 | 7,377[1] | 7,302[1] | 729[1] | S | 825 | 1350 | 1480 |
| SUNY at Binghamton; Binghamton, N.Y. 13901 | 5,184[1] | 4,732[1] | 448[1] | S | 825 | 1350 | 1550 |
| SUNY at Buffalo; Buffalo, N.Y. 14260 | 12,629[1] | 8,482[1] | 936[1] | S | 750[50] | 1200[50] | 1600 |
| SUNY at Stony Brook; Stony Brook, N.Y. 14214 | 8,184[1] | 6,822[1] | 637[1] | S | 750[50] | 1200[50] | 1565 |
| SUNY College at Brockport; Brockport, N.Y. 14420 | 4,752[1] | 5,281[1] | 509[1] | S | 800 | 1200 | 1600 |
| SUNY College at Buffalo; N.Y. 14222 | 4,881[1] | 6,379[1] | 571[1] | S | 750[50] | 1200[50] | 1750 |
| SUNY College at Cortland; Cortland, N.Y. 13045 | 2,204[1] | 3,411[1] | 312[1] | S | 750[50] | 1200[50] | 1434 |
| SUNY College at Fredonia; Fredonia, N.Y. 14063 | 2,358[1] | 2,619[1] | 258[1] | S | 750[50] | 1200[50] | 1400 |
| SUNY College at Geneseo; Geneseo, N.Y. 14454 | 1,717[1] | 3,436[1] | 303[1] | S | 750[50] | 1200[50] | 1500 |
| SUNY College at New Paltz; New Paltz, N.Y. 12561 | 3,240[1] | 4,303[1] | 362[1] | S | 750[50] | 1200[50] | 1650 |
| SUNY Coll. at Old Westbury; Old Westbury, N.Y. 11568 | 895[1] | 1,357[1] | 79[1] | S | 750[50] | 1200[50] | 1590 |
| SUNY College at Oneonta; Oneonta, N.Y. 13820 | 2,533[1] | 3,894[1] | 347[1] | S | 750[50] | 1200[50] | 1590 |
| SUNY College at Oswego; Oswego, N.Y. 13126 | 4,283[1] | 3,989[1] | 401[1] | S | 750[50] | 1200[50] | 1590 |
| SUNY College at Plattsburgh; Plattsburgh, N.Y. 12901 | 2,670[1] | 3,397[1] | 296[1] | S | 750[50] | 1200[50] | 1500 |
| SUNY College at Potsdam; Potsdam, N.Y. 13676 | 2,116[1] | 2,848[1] | 263[1] | S | 750[50] | 1200[50] | 1600 |
| SUNY Coll. at Purchase; Purchase, N.Y. 10577 | 1,015[1] | 1,531[1] | 107[1] | S | 750[50] | 1200[50] | 1590 |
| SUNY Coll. of Environmental Sci. & Forestry; Syracuse, N.Y. 13210 | 1,622[1] | 525[1] | 107[1] | S | 750[50] | 1200[50] | 2000 |

| Institution and location | Enrollment: Male | Enrollment: Female | Faculty | Control | Tuition: Res. | Tuition: Nonres. | Rm/Bd |
|---|---|---|---|---|---|---|---|
| SUNY Coll. of Optometry; New York, N.Y. 10010 | 143[1] | 47[1] | 43[1] | S | $3000 | $4400 | $2280 |
| SUNY Downstate Medical Center; Brooklyn, N.Y. 11203 | 813[1] | 634[1] | 454[1] | S | 3000 | 4400 | 2000 |
| SUNY Empire State College; Saratoga Springs, N.Y. 12866 | 1,473[1] | 1,637[1] | 94[1] | S | 1163 | 1838 | — |
| SUNY Maritime College; Fort Schuyler, Bronx, N.Y. 10465 | 1,045[1] | 40[1] | 74[1] | S | 750[50] | 1200[50] | — |
| SUNY Upstate Medical Center; Syracuse, N.Y. 13210 | 532[1] | 334[1] | 274[1] | S | 3000 | 4400 | — |
| New York, Univ. of the State of, Regents External Degree Program; Albany, N.Y. 12230 | 7,138 | 5,561 | — | S | 125 | — | — |
| New York College of Podiatric Medicine; New York, N.Y. 10035 | 349 | 34 | 20 | P | 4600 | 4600 | — |
| New York Institute of Technology; Old Westbury, N.Y. 11568 | 5,512[1] | 1,244[1] | 161 | P | 1205 | 1205 | 1967 |
| New York Law School; New York, N.Y. 10013 | 633 | 245 | 40 | P | 1600 | 1600 | — |
| New York Medical College; New York, N.Y. 10029 | 807[2] | | n.a. | P | 6850[2] | n.a. | 3300[2] |
| New York University; New York, N.Y. 10003 | 12,228 | 15,029 | — | P | 4000 | — | 2225 |
| Newberry College; Newberry, S.C. 29108 | 508[1] | 302[1] | 50 | P/LCA | 2675 | 2675 | 1055 |
| Newcomb College. *See* Tulane University | | | | | | | |
| Niagara University; Niagara Falls, N.Y. 14109 | 1,502 | 1,610 | 184 | P/RC | 2700 | 2700 | 1700 |
| Nicholls State University; Thibodaux, La. 70301 | 2,909 | 3,281 | 206 | S | 422 | 1052 | 1040 |
| Nichols College; Dudley, Mass. 01570 | 542 | 91 | 33 | P | 4672 | 2904 | 1768 |
| Norfolk State College; Norfolk, Va. 23504 | 6,956[2] | | n.a. | S | 530[2] | n.a. | 1144[2] |
| North Adams State College; North Adams, Mass. 01247 | 1,146 | 1,120 | 105 | S | 500 | 1250 | 1800 |
| North Alabama, University of; Florence, Ala. 35630 | 2,428[1] | 2,801[1] | 183 | S | 580 | 580 | 1090 |
| North Carolina, University System of; Chapel Hill, N.C. 27514 | | | | | | | |
| Appalachian State University; Boone, N.C. 28608 | 3,407 | 3,695 | 455 | S | 531 | 2179 | 1090 |
| East Carolina University; Greenville, N.C. 27834 | 4,445[1] | 5,221[1] | 714 | S | 310 | 2030 | 1432 |
| Elizabeth City State University; Elizabeth City, N.C. 27909 | 705[1] | 915[1] | 95 | S | 250 | 1734 | 1140 |
| Fayetteville State University; Fayetteville, N.C. 28301 | 827 | 1,204 | 157 | S | 590 | 2092 | 1087 |
| North Carolina Agri. & Tech. St. U.; Greensboro, N.C. 27411 | 2,886[1] | 2,725[1] | 349 | S | 595 | 2300 | 1029 |
| North Carolina Central University; Durham, N.C. 27707 | 1,776[1] | 2,691[1] | 275 | S | 310 | 2048 | 1255 |
| North Carolina Sch. of the Arts; Winston-Salem, N.C. 27107 | 234 | 193 | 70 | S | 568 | 2020 | 1421 |
| N.C. State Univ. at Raleigh; Raleigh, N.C. 27607 | 10,091 | 4,524 | 1215 | S | 558 | 2270 | 1470 |
| Pembroke State University; Pembroke, N.C. 28372 | 1,030 | 1,304 | 127 | S | 470 | 1960 | 920 |
| Univ. of N.C. at Asheville; Asheville, N.C. 28804 | 494 | 521 | 70 | S | 436 | 2130 | 980 |
| Univ. of N.C. at Chapel Hill; Chapel Hill, N.C. 27514 | 10,203[1] | 9,959[1] | 1813 | S | 524 | 2234 | 1572 |
| Univ. of N.C. at Charlotte; Charlotte, N.C. 28223 | 2,855 | 2,238 | 378 | S | 505 | 2235 | 1090 |
| Univ. of N.C. at Greensboro; Greensboro, N.C. 27412 | 3,123[1] | 6,841[1] | 617 | S | 508 | 2226 | 1298 |
| Univ. of N.C. at Wilmington; Wilmington, N.C. 28401 | 1,396 | 1,185 | — | S | 245 | 2000 | 1330 |
| Western Carolina University; Cullowhee, N.C. 28723 | 2,853[1] | 2,626[1] | 311 | S | 544 | 2282 | 1010 |
| Winston-Salem State Univ.; Winston-Salem, N.C. 27105 | 413 | 1,026 | 160 | S | 270 | 1799 | 1410 |
| North Carolina Wesleyan College; Rocky Mount, N.C. 27801 | 329 | 295 | 30 | P | 1870 | 1870 | 1220 |
| North Central Bible College; Minneapolis, Minn. 55404 | 290 | 209 | 21 | P/AG | 1248 | 1248 | 1243 |
| North Central College; Naperville, Ill. 60540 | 549 | 331 | 54 | P/UM | 3120 | 3120 | 1500 |
| North Dakota, University of; Grand Forks, N.D. 58202 | 5,180[1] | 4,183[1] | 420 | S | 545 | 1313 | 1250 |
| North Dakota State University; Fargo, N.D. 58102 | 4,455 | 3,121 | 381 | S | 522 | 1290 | 1250 |
| North Florida, University of; Jacksonville, Fla. 32216 | 2,300[10] | 2,200[10] | — | S | 742 | 2317 | — |
| North Georgia College; Dahlonega, Ga. 30533 | 700 | 757 | 99 | S | 435 | 1149 | 1200 |
| North Park College; Chicago, Ill. 60625 | 1,177[2] | | n.a. | P/EC | 2851[2] | n.a. | 1365[2] |
| North Texas State University; Denton, Tex. 76203 | 8,837[1] | 8,314[1] | 685 | S | 393 | 1473 | 2074 |
| Northeast Louisiana University; Monroe, La. 71209 | 2,926 | 3,296 | 359 | S | 450 | 1100 | 1300 |
| Northeast Missouri State University; Kirksville, Mo. 63501 | 2,130[1] | 2,534[1] | 249 | S | 310 | 760 | 980 |
| Northeastern Bible College; Essex Fells, N.J. 07021 | 424[2] | | n.a. | P | 1858[2] | n.a. | 1312[2] |
| Northeastern Illinois University; Chicago, Ill. 60625 | 2,228[1] | 2,766[1] | 341[1] | S | 510 | 1530 | — |
| Northeastern Oklahoma State Univ.; Tahlequah, Okla. 74464 | 5,662[2] | | n.a. | S | 390[2] | n.a. | 1080[2] |
| Northeastern University; Boston, Mass. 02115 | 12,054[1] | 6,862[1] | 750 | P | 2500 | — | — |
| Northern Arizona University; Flagstaff, Ariz. 86011 | 7,000 | 6,000 | 625 | S | 200 | 700 | 1100 |
| Northern Colorado, University of; Greeley, Colo. 80639 | 4,685[1] | 6,363[1] | 732 | S | 432 | 1720 | 1400 |
| Northern Illinois University; DeKalb, Ill. 60115 | 7,443[1] | 8,194[1] | 1046 | S | 729 | 1729 | 1460 |
| Northern Iowa, University of; Cedar Falls, Iowa 50613 | 3,618[1] | 4,487[1] | 622 | S | 700 | 1300 | 1175 |
| Northern Kentucky University; Highland Heights, Ky. 41076 | 1,797 | 1,552 | 234 | S | 480 | 1200 | — |
| Northern Michigan University; Marquette, Mich. 49855 | 3,208 | 2,881 | 309 | S | 800 | 1760 | 1526 |

| Institution and location | Enrollment | | Faculty | Control | Tuition | | |
|---|---|---|---|---|---|---|---|
| | Male | Female | | | Res. | Nonres. | Rm/Bd |
| Northern Montana College; Havre, Mont. 59501 | 650 | 500 | 71 | S | $459 | $1450 | $1290 |
| Northern State College; Aberdeen, S.D. 57401 | 1,000[1] | 1,000[1] | 112 | S | 547 | 1187 | 1250 |
| Northland College; Ashland, Wis. 54806 | 372 | 265 | 43 | P | 2750 | 2750 | 1525 |
| Northrop University; Inglewood, Calif. 90306 | 891 | | 28 | P | 2430 | 2430 | 1665 |
| Northwest Bible College; Minot, N.D. 58701 | 176[2] | | n.a. | P/CC | 800[2] | n.a. | 1200[2] |
| Northwest Christian College; Eugene, Ore. 97401 | 220 | 151 | 15 | P | 1440 | 1440 | 1410 |
| Northwest College; Kirkland, Wash. 98033 | 316 | 221 | 20 | AG | 1260 | 1260 | 1200 |
| Northwest Missouri State University; Maryville, Mo. 64468 | 1,483 | 1,690 | 250 | S | 380 | 770 | 1040 |
| Northwest Nazarene College; Nampa, Idaho 83651 | 553 | 696 | 65 | P/Naz | 1890 | 1890 | 1350 |
| Northwestern College; Orange City, Iowa 51041 | 328[1] | 348[1] | 45 | P/RCA | 1087 | 1087 | 482 |
| Northwestern Coll. of Chiropractic; St. Paul, Minn. 55116 | 320 | 30 | 13 | P | 2710 | — | — |
| Northwestern Oklahoma State University; Alva, Okla. 73717 | 888[1] | 868[1] | 73 | S | 414 | 1046 | 960 |
| Northwestern State Univ. of Louisiana; Natchitoches, La. 71457 | 1,400 | 2,133 | 272 | S | 463 | 1090 | 1070 |
| Northwestern University; Evanston, Ill. 60201 | 6,968 | 4,541 | 1200 | P | 5025 | 5025 | 1800 |
| Northwood Institute; Midland, Mich. 48640 | 960 | 445 | 52 | P | 2310 | 2310 | 1200 |
| Norwich University; Northfield, Vt. 05663 | 1,114 | 142 | 114 | P | 5250[11] | — | — |
| Vermont College; Montpelier, Vt. 05602 | 49 | 330 | — | P | 4790[11] | — | — |
| Notre Dame, College of; Belmont, Calif. 94002 | 197 | 321 | 59 | P/RC | 2500 | — | 1650 |
| Notre Dame, University of; Notre Dame, Ind. 46556 | 6,268[1] | 1,979[1] | 798 | P/RC | 3480 | 3480 | 1400 |
| Notre Dame College; Manchester, N.H. 03104 | 38[10] | 428[10] | 34 | P/RC | 2000 | 2000 | 450 |
| Notre Dame of Maryland, College of; Baltimore, Md. 21210 | 121[56] | 476[56] | 55 | P/RC | 2500 | 2500 | 1600 |
| Notre Dame of Ohio, College of; Cleveland, Ohio 44121 | — | 374 | 34 | P/RC | 2060 | 2060 | 1250 |
| Nova University; Ft. Lauderdale, Fla. 33314 | 6,305[2] | | n.a. | P | 2500[2] | n.a. | n.a. |
| Nyack College; Nyack, N.Y. 10960 | 324 | 277 | — | P/CMA | 2240 | 2240 | 1340 |
| Oakland City College; Oakland City, Ind. 47660 | 356[7] | 108[7] | n.a. | P/B | n.a. | n.a. | n.a. |
| Oakland University; Rochester, Mich. 48063 | 4,138 | 6,075 | 338 | S | 776 | 2032 | 1548 |
| Oakwood College; Huntsville, Ala. 35806 | 592[1] | 742[1] | 64 | P/SDA | 2100 | 2100 | 1395 |
| Oberlin College; Oberlin, Ohio 44074 | 1,391 | 1,359 | 226 | P | 4300 | 4300 | 1800 |
| Occidental College; Los Angeles, Calif. 90041 | 862[1] | 811[1] | 112 | P | 4000 | 4000 | 1800 |
| Oglethorpe University; Atlanta, Ga. 30319 | 561 | | 38 | P | 2386 | 2386 | 1200 |
| Ohio, Medical College of, at Toledo; Toledo, Ohio 43699 | 269[1] | 91[1] | 195 | S | 2660 | 3260 | — |
| Ohio College of Podiatric Medicine; Cleveland, Ohio 44106 | 496[1] | 40[1] | 20 | P | 5000 | — | — |
| Ohio Dominican College; Columbus, Ohio 43219 | 366[1] | 544[1] | 45 | P/RC | 2730 | 2730 | 1540 |
| Ohio Institute of Technology[61]; Columbus, Ohio 43209 | 2,448[1] | 76[1] | 47 | P | 1965 | 1965 | — |
| Ohio Northern University; Ada, Ohio 45810 | 1,799 | 863 | 159 | P/UM | 2736 | — | 1350 |
| Ohio State University, The; Columbus, Ohio 43210 | 30,887[1] | 24,656[1] | 3533 | S | — | — | — |
| Columbus Campus; Columbus, Ohio 43210 | 25,817[1] | 18,947[1] | 3138 | S | 915 | 2025 | 1698 |
| Lima Campus; Lima, Ohio 45804 | 376[1] | 369[1] | 36 | S | 870 | 1980 | — |
| Mansfield Campus; Mansfield, Ohio 44906 | 388[1] | 452[1] | 44 | S | 870 | 1980 | — |
| Marion Campus; Marion, Ohio 43302 | 297[1] | 275[1] | 28 | S | 870 | 1980 | — |
| Newark Campus; Newark, Ohio 43055 | 377[1] | 321[1] | 31 | S | 870 | 1980 | — |
| Ohio University; Athens, Ohio 45701 | 6,745[1] | 4,783[1] | 685 | S | 1056 | 2400 | 1629 |
| Ohio Wesleyan University; Delaware, Ohio 43015 | 1,172 | 1,042 | 156 | P/M | 3625 | 3625 | 1555 |
| Oklahoma, University of; Norman, Okla. 73019 | 9,060[1] | 5,754[1] | 743 | S | 524 | 1518 | 1213 |
| Oklahoma, Univ. of Science and Arts of; Chickasha, Okla. 73018 | 1,200[2] | | n.a. | S | 500[2] | n.a. | 1500[2] |
| Oklahoma Baptist University; Shawnee, Okla. 74801 | 694 | 805 | 99 | P/B | 1400 | 1500 | 1015 |
| Oklahoma Christian College; Oklahoma City, Okla. 73111 | 673[1] | 823[1] | 50 | P/CC | 1480 | 1480 | 1100 |
| Oklahoma City University; Oklahoma City, Okla. 73106 | 1,102 | 577 | 122 | P/UM | 1760 | 1760 | 1350 |
| Oklahoma Coll. of Osteopathic Med. & Surgery; Tulsa, Okla. 74101 | 268[2] | | n.a. | S | 1599[2] | n.a. | n.a. |
| Oklahoma Panhandle State University; Goodwell, Okla. 73939 | 1,022[2] | | n.a. | S | 1398[2] | n.a. | 750[2] |
| Oklahoma State University; Stillwater, Okla. 74074 | 21,129[2] | | n.a. | S | 540[2] | n.a. | 1100[2] |
| Old Dominion University; Norfolk, Va. 23508 | 7,263[1] | 6,925 | 653 | S | 720 | 1320 | 1450 |
| Olivet College; Olivet, Mich. 49076 | 426 | 284 | 52 | P | 3100 | 3100 | 7500 |
| Olivet Nazarene College; Kankakee, Ill. 60901 | 696[1] | 952[1] | 85 | P/Naz | 1940 | 1940 | 1265 |
| Oral Roberts University; Tulsa, Okla. 74171 | 3,500[2] | | n.a. | P | 1600[2] | n.a. | 1600[2] |
| Oregon, University of; Eugene, Ore. 97403 | 9,035 | 7,666 | 1031 | S | 739 | 2488 | 1484 |
| Oregon College of Education; Monmouth, Ore. 97361 | 1,291 | 1,921 | 245 | S | 750 | 2250 | 1300 |
| Oregon Graduate Center; Beaverton, Ore. 97005 | 32[2] | | n.a. | P | ([67]) | n.a. | n.a. |
| Oregon Institute of Technology; Klamath Falls, Ore. 97601 | 1,575[1] | 661[1] | — | S | 726 | 2475 | 1400 |
| Oregon State University; Corvallis, Ore. 97331 | 9,896[1] | 6,605[1] | 1122 | S | 728 | 2487 | 1450 |
| Osteopathic Med. & Surgery, Coll. of; Des Moines, Iowa 50312 | 442 | 81 | 54 | P | 4450 | 7000 | 3000 |
| Otis Art Inst. of Los Angeles County; Los Angeles, Calif. 90057 | 94 | 106 | 15 | Mun | — | 1300 | 2300 |

| Institution and location | Enrollment | | Faculty | Control | Tuition | | |
|---|---|---|---|---|---|---|---|
| | Male | Female | | | Res. | Nonres. | Rm/Bd |
| Ottawa University; Ottawa, Kan. 66067 | 294[1] | 286[1] | 36 | P | $2160 | $2160 | $1230 |
| Otterbein College; Westerville, Ohio 43081 | 521 | 617 | 79 | P | 3696 | — | 1422 |
| Ouachita Baptist University; Arkadelphia, Ark. 71923 | 791 | 902 | 105 | P | 1470 | 1470 | 1100 |
| Our Lady of Angels College; Aston, Pa. 19014 | 90 | 552 | 32 | P/RC | 1700 | — | — |
| Our Lady of Holy Cross College; New Orleans, La. 70114 | 74 | 147 | 39 | P/RC | 1500 | 1500 | — |
| Our Lady of the Elms, College of; Chicopee, Mass. 01013 | — | 440[1] | 70 | P/RC | 2450 | 2450 | 1400 |
| Our Lady of the Lake University of San Antonio; San Antonio, Tex. 78285 | 439 | 818 | 91 | P/RC | 1920 | 1920 | 1310 |
| Ozarks, The College of the; Clarksville, Ark. 72830 | 259 | 219 | 28 | P/Pres | 850 | — | 1000 |
| Ozarks, The School of the; Point Lookout, Mo. 65726 | 451[1] | 513[1] | 81 | P | ([68]) | ([68]) | ([68]) |
| Pace University; New York, N.Y. 10038 | 1,893[1] | 1,639[1] | 178 | P | 2720 | 2720 | 1884 |
| College of White Plains; White Plains, N.Y. 10603 | 143[1] | 284[1] | 21 | P | 2720 | 2720 | 1800 |
| Pleasantville/Briarcliff Campus; Pleasantville, N.Y. 10570 | 1,160[1] | 1,386[1] | 127 | P | 2720 | 2720 | 1884 |
| Pacific, University of the; Stockton, Calif. 95211 | 3,603 | 2,500 | 369 | P | 4216 | 4216 | 1956 |
| Pacific Christian College; Fullerton, Calif. 92631 | 191 | 139 | 19 | P/CC | 1650 | 1650 | 1300 |
| Pacific Coll. of Fresno, Calif. *See* Fresno Pacific Coll. | | | | | | | |
| Pacific Lutheran University; Tacoma, Wash. 98447 | 1,043 | 1,401 | — | P/L | 2944 | 2944 | 1265 |
| Pacific Oaks College; Pasadena, Calif. 91103 | 25 | 330 | 27 | P | ([69]) | ([69]) | — |
| Pacific Union College; Angwin, Calif. 94508 | 994[1] | 1,002[1] | 104 | P/SDA | 2955 | 2955 | 1440 |
| Pacific University; Forest Grove, Ore. 97116 | 676 | 344 | 78 | P/UCC | 2975[10] | 2975[10] | 1368 |
| Paine College; Augusta, Ga. 30901 | 224 | 469 | 69 | P/M | 1500 | 1500 | 1150 |
| Palm Beach Atlantic College; West Palm Beach, Fla. 33401 | 397 | 105 | 36 | P/B | 700 | — | 800 |
| Pan American University; Edinburg, Tex. 78539 | 2,745[1] | 2,707[1] | 289 | S | 265 | 1345 | 1100 |
| Paper Chemistry, The Institute of; Appleton, Wis. 54911 | 73 | 7 | 41 | P | 3000 | 3000 | 1250 |
| Park College; Parkville, Mo. 64152 | 2,034 | 1,785 | — | P/LDS | 2620 | 2620 | 1300 |
| Parks College of St. Louis University; Cahokia, Ill. 62206 | 689 | 51 | 44 | P/RC | 2050 | 2050 | 1425 |
| Parsons School of Design. *See* New School for Social Research | | | | | | | |
| Paul Quinn College; Waco, Tex. 76704 | 537[2] | | n.a. | P/AME | 1350[2] | n.a. | 1600[2] |
| Peabody Conservatory of Music; Baltimore, Md. 21202 | 508[2] | | n.a. | P | 3400[2] | n.a. | 1050[8] |
| Pembroke State Univ. *See* North Carolina, Univ. System of | | | | | | | |
| Pennsylvania, Medical College of; Philadelphia, Pa. 19129 | 389[7] | | n.a. | P | 5000[7] | n.a. | n.a. |
| Pennsylvania, University of; Philadelphia, Pa. 19104 | 9,073 | 5,512 | 1534 | P | — | — | 1600 |
| Pennsylvania College of Optometry; Philadelphia, Pa. 19141 | 545[2] | | n.a. | P | 8200[2] | n.a. | 2500[2] |
| Pennsylvania Coll. of Podiatric Med.; Philadelphia, Pa. 19107 | 466[2] | | n.a. | P | 5320[2] | n.a. | 3500[2] |
| Pennsylvania State University, The; University Park, Pa. 16802 | 30,697[1] | 18,089[1] | 3026 | S | 1368 | 2748 | 1566 |
| Behrend College; Erie, Pa. 16510 | 1,700[56] | | n.a. | S | 1056[2] | n.a. | 1473[2] |
| Capitol Campus; Middletown, Pa. 17057 | 1,593 | 733 | 130 | S | 1233 | 2748 | 1509 |
| King of Prussia Graduate Center; King of Prussia, Pa. 19406 | 13[7] | 1[7] | n.a. | S | n.a. | n.a. | n.a. |
| The Milton S. Hershey Medical Center; Hershey, Pa. 17033 | 345[7] | 103[7] | n.a. | S | n.a. | n.a. | n.a. |
| Pepperdine University; Malibu, Calif. 90265 | | | | | | | |
| Pepperdine Univ.—Los Angeles; Los Angeles, Calif. 90044 | 1,645[1] | 808[1] | 90 | P/CC | 2160 | 2160 | — |
| Pepperdine Univ.—Malibu; Malibu, Calif. 90265 | 953[1] | 921[1] | 66 | P/CC | 4192 | 4192 | 2040 |
| Pepperdine Univ. School of Law; Malibu, Calif. 90265 | 345[1] | 62[1] | 16 | P/CC | 4200 | 4200 | — |
| Peru State College; Peru, Neb. 68421 | 281 | 276 | 48 | S | 510 | 900 | 1240 |
| Pfeiffer College; Misenheimer, N.C. 28109 | 450[1] | 440[1] | 56 | P/UM | 1870 | 1870 | 1300 |
| Philadelphia College of Art; Philadelphia, Pa. 19102 | 482 | 678 | 80 | P | 6296 | 5246 | 1650 |
| Philadelphia College of Bible; Philadelphia, Pa. 19103 | 296 | 254 | 34 | P/ND | 3230 | 1850 | 1380 |
| Philadelphia Coll. of Osteopathic Med.; Philadelphia, Pa. 19131 | 796[1] | 119[1] | 98 | P | 4706 | 5006 | 3015 |
| Philadelphia Coll. of Pharmacy & Sci.; Philadelphia, Pa. 19104 | 659 | 430 | 67 | P | 2800 | 2800 | 1675 |
| Philadelphia Coll. of Textiles & Science; Philadelphia, Pa. 19144 | 782[1] | 660[1] | 79 | P | 2600 | 2600 | 1775 |
| Philadelphia College of the Performing Arts; Philadelphia, Pa. 19102 | 208 | 121 | 14 | P | — | 2800 | — |
| Philander Smith College; Little Rock, Ark. 72203 | 467 | 360 | 30 | P/UM | 750 | 750 | 1125 |
| Phillips University; Enid, Okla. 73701 | 528[1] | 444[1] | 78 | P/DC | 1800 | 1800 | 1340 |
| Piedmont Bible College; Winston-Salem, N.C. 27101 | 231[1] | 149[1] | 18 | P/B | 700 | 700 | 1000 |
| Piedmont College; Demorest, Ga. 30535 | 500[2] | | n.a. | P/Cong | 1215[2] | n.a. | 1787[2] |
| Pikeville College; Pikeville, Ky. 41501 | 237 | 190 | 48 | P/Pres | 1395 | 1395 | 1365 |
| Pine Manor College; Chestnut Hill, Mass. 02167 | — | 400 | 50 | P | 4000 | — | 2500 |

| Institution and location | Enrollment | | Faculty | Control | Tuition | | Rm/Bd |
|---|---|---|---|---|---|---|---|
| | Male | Female | | | Res. | Nonres. | |
| Pittsburgh, University of; Pittsburgh, Pa. 15260 | 16,011[1] | 13,732[1] | 2267 | P | $1410 | $2820 | $1650 |
| U. of Pittsburgh at Greensburg; Greensburg, Pa. 15601 | 585[1] | 416[1] | 27 | P | 1295 | 2225 | — |
| U. of Pittsburgh at Johnstown; Johnstown, Pa. 15904 | 1,301 | 889 | 150 | P | 1410 | 2820 | 1440 |
| Pitzer College. *See* Claremont Colleges | | | | | | | |
| Plymouth State College; Plymouth, N.H. 03264 | 1,351[1] | 1,277[1] | 133 | S | 700 | 2050 | 1320 |
| Point Loma College; San Diego, Calif. 92106 | 823[1] | 1,082[1] | 86 | P/Naz | 2544 | 2544 | 1200 |
| Point Park College; Pittsburgh, Pa. 15222 | 745[1] | 562[1] | 84 | P | 2800 | 2800 | 1430 |
| Pomona College. *See* Claremont Colleges | | | | | | | |
| Portland, University of; Portland, Ore. 97203 | 2,318[2] | | 110 | P | 2840 | 2840 | 1370 |
| Portland State University; Portland, Ore. 97207 | 8,039[1] | 7,849[1] | 551 | S | 726 | 2475 | — |
| Prairie View A&M University; Prairie View, Tex. 77445 | 2,478[1] | 2,602[1] | 278 | S | 1800 | 3000 | 1200 |
| Pratt Institute; Brooklyn, N.Y. 11205 | 1,852 | 1,335 | 150 | P | 3604 | 3604 | 1200 |
| Presbyterian College; Clinton, S.C. 29325 | 830[2] | | n.a. | Pres | 2450[2] | n.a. | 1265[2] |
| Princeton University; Princeton, N.J. 08540 | 3,185 | 1,987 | 675 | P | 5100 | 5100 | 2117 |
| Principia College; Elsah, Ill. 62028 | 392 | 459 | 72 | P | 3708 | 3708 | 1998 |
| Providence College; Providence, R.I. 02918 | 5,435[2] | | n.a. | P | 2852[10] | n.a. | 1780[10] |
| Puerto Rico, Catholic University of; Ponce, P.R. 00731 | 2,935[1] | 5,490[1] | 426 | P/RC | 1350 | — | 400 |
| Puerto Rico, Inter American Univ. of; San Germán, P.R. 00753 | | | | | | | |
| San Germán Campus; San Germán, P.R. 00753 | 6,597[1] | | 134 | P | 1290 | 1290 | 1140 |
| San Juan Campus; San Juan, P.R. 00919 | 7,050[1] | | 138 | P | 1290 | 1290 | — |
| School of Law; Santurce, P.R. 00910 | 1,000[2] | | n.a. | P | 2550[2] | n.a. | n.a. |
| Puerto Rico, University of; Río Piedras, P.R. 00931 | 50,225[2] | | n.a. | S | n.a. | n.a. | n.a. |
| Cayey University College; Cayey, P.R. 00633 | 2,600 | | 117 | S | 200 | 2000 | 1200 |
| Humacao College; Humacao, P.R. 00661 | n.a. | n.a. | n.a. | S | n.a. | n.a. | n.a. |
| Mayaguez Campus; Mayaguez, P.R. 00708 | 4,412 | 2,664 | 724 | S | 216 | 2060 | 1200 |
| Medical Sciences Campus; San Juan, P.R. 00936 | 2,120[7] | | n.a. | S | n.a. | n.a. | n.a. |
| Río Piedras Campus; Río Piedras, P.R. 00931 | 6,257[1] | 10,279[1] | 1211 | S | 200 | 1000 | 1200 |
| Puget Sound, University of; Tacoma, Wash. 98416 | 2,800[2] | | n.a. | P | 3150[2] | n.a. | 1500[2] |
| Purdue University; West Lafayette, Ind. 47907 | 18,626[1] | 11,677 | 1780 | S | 870 | 2100 | 1610 |
| Calumet Campus; Hammond, Ind. 46323 | 3,481 | 2,872 | 187 | S | 840 | 1440 | — |
| Indiana U.–Purdue U. at Indianapolis. *See* Indiana Univ. | | | | | | | |
| Queens College; Charlotte, N.C. 28274 | 15 | 555 | 37 | P | 3000 | 3000 | 1785 |
| Queens College (NYC). *See* New York, City University of | | | | | | | |
| Quincy College; Quincy, Ill. 62301 | 1,550[7] | | n.a. | P/RC | 2300[2] | n.a. | 1350[2] |
| Quinnipiac College; Hamden, Conn. 06518 | 823 | 1,283 | 168 | P | 2950 | 2950 | 1670 |
| Radcliffe College. *See* Harvard University | | | | | | | |
| Radford College; Radford, Va. 24142 | 1,498 | 3,608 | 277 | S | 2454 | 3054 | 1,587 |
| Ramapo College of New Jersey; Mahwah, N.J. 07430 | 1,452 | 993 | 155 | S | 352 | 704 | 940[8] |
| Randolph–Macon College; Ashland, Va. 23005 | 569 | 358 | 58 | P | 2940 | 2940 | 1120 |
| Randolph–Macon Woman's College; Lynchburg, Va. 24503 | 2 | 763 | 63 | P | 3600 | 3600 | 1900 |
| Redlands, University of; Redlands, Calif. 92373 | 81 | 84 | 16 | P | 4100 | 4100 | 1735 |
| Reed College; Portland, Ore. 97202 | 696 | 477 | 77 | P | 4430 | 4430 | 1750 |
| Reformed Bible College; Grand Rapids, Mich. 49506 | 85 | 91 | 13 | P | 1300 | 1300 | 1050 |
| Regis College; Denver, Colo. 80221 | 537 | 316 | 69 | P/RC | 2880 | 2880 | 1636 |
| Regis College; Weston, Mass. 02193 | — | 703 | 56 | P | 2750 | 2750 | 1870 |
| Rensselaer Polytechnic Institute; Troy, N.Y. 12181 | 4,686 | 740 | 343 | P | 4025 | 4025 | 1620 |
| Rhode Island, University of; Kingston, R.I. 02881 | 5,516 | 4,762 | 900 | S | — | 1145 | 1891 |
| Rhode Island College; Providence, R.I. 02908 | 8,714[7] | | n.a. | S | 625[7] | n.a. | 1410[7] |
| Rhode Island School of Design; Providence, R.I. 02903 | 631 | 730 | 97 | P | 4250 | 4250 | 1850 |
| Rice University; Houston, Tex. 77001 | 2,399 | 1,209 | 476 | P | 2500 | 2500 | 1940 |
| Richmond, University of; Richmond, Va. 23173 | 2,390 | 1,571 | 193 | P | 3065 | 3065 | 1515 |
| Ricker College; Houlton, Me. 04730 | 710[2] | | n.a. | P | 2500[2] | n.a. | 1380[2] |
| Rider College; Lawrenceville, N.J. 08648 | 1,990[1] | 1,453[1] | 198 | P | 2750 | 2750 | 1560 |
| Rio Grande College; Rio Grande, Ohio 45674 | 540[1] | 545[1] | 47 | P | 600 | 765 | 1555 |
| Ripon College; Ripon, Wis. 54971 | 540 | 400 | 72 | P | 3755 | 3755 | 1385 |
| Rivier College; Nashua, N.H. 03060 | — | 1,455[2] | n.a. | P/RC | 1900[2] | n.a. | 1320[2] |
| Roanoke College; Salem, Va. 24153 | 506[1] | 540[1] | 65 | P | 2875 | 2875 | 1475 |
| Robert Morris College; Coraopolis, Pa. 15108 | 1,265[1] | 1,119[1] | 101 | P | 1920 | 1920 | 1300 |
| Roberts Wesleyan College; Rochester, N.Y. 14624 | 171 | 385 | 42 | P/FM | 2635 | 2635 | 1525 |
| Rochester, The University of; Rochester, N.Y. 14627 | 3,773 | 2,224 | 1259 | P | 4400 | 4400 | 2077 |
| Rochester Institute of Technology; Rochester, N.Y. 14623 | 12,192[7] | | n.a. | P | 3096[2] | n.a. | 1872[2] |
| Rockford College; Rockford, Ill. 61101 | 268[1] | 318[1] | 55 | P | 3000 | 3000 | 1600 |
| Rockhurst College; Kansas City, Mo. 64110 | 672 | 420 | 78 | P/RC | 2500 | 2500 | 1480 |
| Rocky Mountain College; Billings, Mont. 59102 | 254 | 237 | 25 | ([70]) | 1850 | 1850 | 1275 |
| Roger Williams College; Bristol, R.I. 02809 | 1,021 | 680 | 75 | P | 2590 | — | 1650 |
| Rollins College; Winter Park, Fla. 32789 | 644 | 615 | — | P | 3200 | 3200 | 1600 |

| Institution and location | Enrollment | | Faculty | Control | Tuition | | Rm/Bd |
|---|---|---|---|---|---|---|---|
| | Male | Female | | | Res. | Nonres. | |
| Roosevelt University; Chicago, Ill. 60605 | 2,081[1] | 2,250[1] | 263 | P | $2460 | $2460 | $1800 |
| Rosary College; River Forest, Ill. 60305 | 222 | 797 | 86 | P/RC | 2700 | 2700 | 1690 |
| Rose–Hulman Institute of Technology; Terre Haute, Ind. 47803 | 1,060 | — | 79 | P | 3000 | 3000 | 1250 |
| Rosemead Grad. School of Psychology; La Mirada, Calif. 90639 | 65 | 33 | 14 | P | 3700 | 3700 | 1000 |
| Rosemont College; Rosemont, Pa. 19010 | — | 590 | 43 | P/RC | 3150 | 3150 | 1900 |
| Rush University; Chicago, Ill. 60612 | 377[1] | 472[1] | 241 | P | 4800 | — | — |
| Russell Sage College; Troy, N.Y. 12180 | — | 1,449 | 114 | P | 2900 | 2900 | 1800 |
| Rust College; Holly Springs, Miss. 38635 | 230 | 456 | 33 | P/UM | 2125 | 2125 | 1089 |
| Rutgers University; New Brunswick, N.J. 08903 | 25,853[1] | 23,192[1] | 2523 | S | 760 | 1520 | 1650 |
| Sacred Heart, Univ. of the; Santurce, P.R. 09914 | 1,926[1] | 3,125[1] | 81 | P/RC | 1100 | 1000 | 800 |
| Sacred Heart College; Belmont, N.C. 28012 | 17[1] | 217[1] | 21 | P/RC | 1650 | 1650 | 1400 |
| Sacred Heart University; Bridgeport, Conn. 06606 | 528 | 528 | 75 | P/RC | 1175 | 1175 | — |
| Saginaw Valley State College; University Center, Mich. 48710 | 1,716[1] | 1,813[1] | 100 | S | 720 | 1800 | 1580 |
| St. Ambrose College; Davenport, Iowa 52803 | 1,014 | 612 | 65 | P/RC | 2460 | 2460 | 1350 |
| St. Andrews Presbyterian College; Laurinburg, N.C. 28352 | 321[1] | 242[1] | 50 | P/Pres | 2450 | 2450 | 1285 |
| St. Anselm's College; Manchester, N.H. 03102 | 1,157[1] | 727[1] | — | P/RC | 2900 | — | 1600 |
| St. Augustine's College; Raleigh, N.C. 27611 | 752[1] | 1,023[1] | 76 | P | 1200 | 1200 | 1000 |
| St. Benedict, College of; St. Joseph, Minn. 56374 | 27 | 1,965 | 100 | RC | 3175 | 3175 | 1300 |
| St. Bonaventure University; St. Bonaventure, N.Y. 14778 | 1,222[1] | 956[1] | 140 | P | 2900 | 2900 | 1690 |
| St. Catherine, The College of; St. Paul, Minn. 55105 | — | 1,869 | 104 | P/RC | 2620 | 2620 | 1480 |
| St. Cloud State Univ. *See* Minnesota State College System | | | | | | | |
| St. Edward's University; Austin, Tex. 78704 | 836 | 492 | 53 | P/RC | 875 | — | 1558 |
| St. Elizabeth, College of; Convent Station, N.J. 07961 | — | 518[1] | 48 | P/RC | 2550 | 2550 | 1550 |
| St. Fidelis College; Herman, Pa. 16039 | 28[1] | — | 5 | P/RC | 1200 | 1200 | 700 |
| St. Francis, College of; Joliet, Ill. 60435 | 196 | 323 | 34 | P/RC | 2340 | 2340 | 1490 |
| St. Francis College; Biddeford, Me. 04005 | 239 | 121 | 25 | P | 2830 | 2830 | 1675 |
| St. Francis College; Brooklyn, N.Y. 11201 | 1,198 | 705 | 63 | P | 2400 | 2400 | — |
| St. Francis College; Fort Wayne, Ind. 46808 | 174[1] | 291[1] | 38 | P/RC | 1440 | 1440 | 1450 |
| St. Francis College; Loretto, Pa. 15940 | 688[1] | 429[1] | 64 | P/RC | 2400 | 2400 | 1500 |
| St. Francis de Sales College; Milwaukee, Wis. 53207 | 64 | — | 11 | P/RC | 1050 | 1050 | 800 |
| St. John Fisher College; Rochester, N.Y. 14618 | 931[1] | 542[1] | 75 | P | 3165 | 3165 | 1765 |
| St. John's College; Annapolis, Md. 21404 | 208 | 163 | 54 | P | 4000 | — | 1475 |
| St. John's College; Santa Fe, N.M. 87501 | 139 | 113 | 30 | P | 4275 | 4275 | 1600 |
| St. John's University; Jamaica, N.Y. 11439 | 6,411[1] | 3,689[1] | 489 | P/RC | 2730 | 2730 | — |
| St. Joseph College; West Hartford, Conn. 06117 | 30 | 746 | 80 | P/RC | 2800 | 2800 | 1750 |
| St. Joseph the Provider, College of; Rutland, Vt. 05701 | 26[1] | 133[1] | 10 | P | 2190 | 2190 | 1450 |
| St. Joseph's College; Brooklyn, N.Y. 11205 | 144[1] | 598[1] | 55 | P | — | 2000 | — |
| St. Joseph's College; North Windham, Me. 04062 | 136 | 372 | 30 | P/RC | 2250 | 2250 | 1400 |
| St. Joseph's College; Philadelphia, Pa. 19131 | 1,695 | 888 | 125 | P/RC | 2625 | 2625 | 1830 |
| St. Joseph's College; Rensselaer, Ind. 47978 | 643 | 389 | 55 | P/RC | 2370 | 2370 | 1330 |
| St. Lawrence University; Canton, N.Y. 13617 | 1,154 | 1,029 | 145 | P | 4090 | 4090 | 1695 |
| St. Leo College; St. Leo, Fla. 33574 | 600 | 400 | 43 | P/RC | 2400 | 2400 | 1200 |
| St. Louis College of Pharmacy; St. Louis, Mo. 63110 | 452 | 251 | 35 | P | 2450 | 2450 | 1600 |
| St. Louis Conservatory of Music; St. Louis, Mo. 63130 | 25 | 17 | 3 | P | 2500 | 2500 | — |
| St. Louis University; St. Louis, Mo. 63103 | 10,000[7] | | n.a. | P/RC | 2800[2] | n.a. | 1500[2] |
| St. Martin's College; Olympia, Wash. 98503 | 185[7] | 145[7] | 42 | P/RC | 2550 | 2550 | 1450 |
| St. Mary, College of; Omaha, Neb. 68124 | 31 | 387 | 48 | P/RC | (71) | (71) | 1225 |
| St. Mary College; Leavenworth, Kan. 66048 | — | 800[2] | n.a. | P/RC | 1450[2] | n.a. | 1150[2] |
| St. Mary of the Plains College; Dodge City, Kan. 67801 | 210 | 283 | 45 | RC | 2000 | 2000 | 1200 |
| St. Mary–of–the–Woods College; St.–Mary–of–the–Woods, Ind. 47876 | — | 666 | 46 | P/RC | 2525 | 2525 | 1370 |
| St. Mary's College; Notre Dame, Ind. 46556 | 9 | 1,763 | 117 | P/RC | 3150 | 3150 | 1770 |
| St. Mary's College; Orchard Lake, Mich. 48033 | 70 | 35 | 21 | P/RC | 1400 | 1400 | 1000 |
| St. Mary's College; Winona, Minn. 55987 | 1,185[7] | | n.a. | P/RC | 2600[2] | n.a. | 1350[2] |
| St. Mary's College of California; Moraga, Calif. 94575 | 1,500[2] | | n.a. | P/RC | 2660[2] | n.a. | 1500[2] |
| St. Mary's College of Maryland; St. Mary's City, Md. 20686 | 459[1] | 483[1] | 67 | S | 600 | 1500 | 1185 |
| St. Mary's Dominican College; New Orleans, La. 70118 | — | 820[2] | n.a. | P/RC | 1850[2] | n.a. | 1450[2] |
| St. Mary's University; San Antonio, Tex. 78284 | 1,796 | 970 | 133 | P/RC | 1920 | 1920 | 1300 |
| St. Michael's College; Winooski, Vt. 05404 | 1,021[1] | 595[1] | 87 | P | 3000 | — | 4575 |
| St. Norbert College; De Pere, Wis. 54115 | 868 | 658 | 83 | P/RC | 2650 | 2650 | 1400 |
| St. Olaf College; Northfield, Minn. 55057 | 1,383 | 1,411 | 180 | P/AL | 3325 | 3325 | 1375 |
| St. Patrick's College; Mountain View, Calif. 94042 | 48[1] | — | 11 | P/RC | 1300 | 1300 | 700 |
| St. Paul's College; Lawrenceville, Va. 23868 | 312 | 315 | 43 | P/E | 1725 | 1725 | 1275 |
| St. Peter's College; Jersey City, N.J. 07306 | 1,565[1] | 1,036[1] | 134 | P | 2240 | — | — |

| Institution and location | Enrollment | | Faculty | Control | Tuition | | Rm/Bd |
|---|---|---|---|---|---|---|---|
| | Male | Female | | | Res. | Nonres. | |
| St. Rose, The College of; Albany, N.Y. 12203 | 209[1] | 858[1] | 100 | Ind | $2310 | $2310 | $1440 |
| St. Scholastica, College of; Duluth, Minn. 55811 | 217[1] | 931[1] | 75 | P | 2685 | 2685 | 1431 |
| St. Teresa, College of; Winona, Minn. 55987 | — | 1,051[2] | n.a. | P/RC | 2535[2] | n.a. | 1341[2] |
| St. Thomas, College of; St. Paul, Minn. 55105 | 3,035 | 948 | 137 | P | 2650 | 2650 | 1400 |
| St. Thomas, University of; Houston, Tex. 77006 | 669[1] | 1,070[1] | — | P/RC | 1620 | 1620 | 1080 |
| St. Thomas Aquinas College; Sparkill, N.Y. 10976 | 232[1] | 364[1] | 50 | P | 1700 | 1700 | 750 |
| St. Vincent College; Latrobe, Pa. 15650 | 817 | — | 51 | P/RC | 2280 | 2280 | 1300 |
| St. Xavier College; Chicago, Ill. 60655 | 315 | 779 | 91 | P/RC | 2430 | 2430 | 1480 |
| Salem College; Salem, W. Va. 26426 | 500[56] | 400[56] | 50 | P | 2350 | 2350 | 1310 |
| Salem College; Winston-Salem, N.C. 27108 | 3 | 544 | 57 | P | 2950 | 2950 | 1800 |
| Salem State College; Salem, Mass. 01970 | 1,838 | 2,793 | 275 | S | 500 | 1250 | 1460 |
| Salisbury State College; Salisbury, Md. 21801 | 1,262 | 1,373 | 161 | S | 570 | 1470 | 1310 |
| Salvé Regina College; Newport, R.I. 02840 | 130[1] | 658[1] | 59 | P/RC | 2700 | — | 1700 |
| Sam Houston State University; Huntsville, Tex. 77340 | 3,762 | 3,755 | 403 | S | 386 | 1344 | 1200 |
| Samford University; Birmingham, Ala. 35209 | 2,072[1] | 1,878[1] | 195 | P/B | 1920 | 2016 | 1210 |
| San Diego, University of; San Diego, Calif. 92110 | 1,224[1] | 1,356[1] | 150 | P/RC | 3250 | 3250 | 1700 |
| San Diego State University; San Diego, Calif. 92182 | 8,871 | 8,590 | 1500 | S | — | 1600 | 1300 |
| San Francisco, University of; San Francisco, Calif. 94117 | 2,235[1] | 2,231[1] | 245 | P/RC | 2860 | 2860 | 1650 |
| San Francisco Art Institute; San Francisco, Calif. 94133 | 356[1] | 228[1] | 29 | P | 2860 | 2860 | — |
| San Francisco Conserv. of Music, The; San Francisco, Calif. 94122 | 100[1] | 54[1] | 12 | P | 3200 | 3200 | — |
| San Francisco State University; San Francisco, Calif. 94132 | 5,364 | 5,787 | 719 | S | 182 | n.a. | n.a. |
| San Jose Bible College; San Jose, Calif. 95108 | 256 | | 8 | P/ND | 1344 | 1344 | 855 |
| San Jose State University; San Jose, Calif. 95192 | 7,327 | 7,278 | 910 | S | 97 | 1575 | 1662 |
| Sangamon State University; Springfield, Ill. 62708 | 1,023 | 757 | — | S | 500 | 1500 | 2000 |
| Santa Clara, University of; Santa Clara, Calif. 95053 | 2,932[1] | 1,803[1] | 238 | P/RC | 3216 | 3216 | 1851 |
| Santa Fe, College of; Santa Fe, N.M. 87501 | 615 | 668 | 54 | P/RC | 1900 | 1900 | 1800 |
| Sarah Lawrence College; Bronxville, N.Y. 10708 | 180 | 609 | 76 | P | 5050 | 5050 | 2350 |
| Savannah State College; Savannah, Ga. 31404 | 2,508[2] | | n.a. | S | 546[2] | n.a. | 990[2] |
| Scranton, University of; Scranton, Pa. 18509 | 1,660 | 896 | 145 | P/RC | 2400 | 2400 | 1600 |
| Scripps College. *See* Claremont Colleges | | | | | | | |
| Seattle Pacific College; Seattle, Wash. 98119 | 829[1] | 1,447[1] | 127 | P/FM | 2790 | 2790 | 1542 |
| Seattle University; Seattle, Wash. 98122 | 1,844 | 1,802 | 174 | P/RC | ([72]) | ([72]) | 1513 |
| Seton Hill College; Greensburg, Pa. 15601 | — | 734 | 51 | P/RC | 2560 | 2560 | 1400 |
| Seton Hall University; South Orange, N.J. 07079 | 9,000[2] | | n.a. | RC | 2500[2] | n.a. | 1400[2] |
| Shaw University; Raleigh, N.C. 27611 | 660 | 548 | 73 | P | 1620 | 1620 | 509 |
| Shepherd College; Shepherdstown, W. Va. 25443 | 1,098 | 1,266 | 105 | S | 342 | 1242 | 1340 |
| Sherwood Music School; Chicago, Ill. 60605 | 30[73] | | — | P | 1700 | — | 1500 |
| Shimer College; Mt. Carroll, Ill. 61053 | 65 | 50 | 16 | P | 2700 | 2700 | 1700 |
| Shippensburg State College; Shippensburg, Pa. 17257 | 2,982[1] | 3,039[1] | 304 | S | 950 | 1750 | 1004 |
| Shorter College; Rome, Ga. 30161 | 397[1] | 464[1] | 47 | P/B | 2325 | 2925 | 1150 |
| Siena College; Loudonville, N.Y. 12211 | 1,315 | 723 | 108 | P | 2700 | 2700 | 1710 |
| Siena Heights College; Adrian, Mich. 49221 | 208 | 351 | 46 | P/RC | 2040 | 2040 | 1402 |
| Sierra Nevada College; Incline Village, Nev. 89450 | 80 | 100 | 23 | P | 1250 | 1250 | 2175 |
| Silver Lake College; Manitowoc, Wis. 54220 | 40 | 146 | — | P/RC | 1850 | — | — |
| Simmons College; Boston, Mass. 02115 | 164[1] | 2,434[1] | 140 | P | 4128 | 4128 | 2110 |
| Simon's Rock Early College; Great Barrington, Mass. 01230 | 88 | 152 | — | P | 4100 | 4100 | 1600 |
| Simpson College; Indianola, Iowa 50125 | 421[1] | 323[1] | 57 | P | 3140 | — | 1190 |
| Simpson College; San Francisco, Calif. 94134 | 136 | 130 | 24 | P | 1650 | 1650 | 1220[8] |
| Sioux Falls College; Sioux Falls, S.D. 57101 | 238 | 281 | 25 | P/B | 2000 | 2000 | 1329 |
| Skidmore College; Saratoga Springs, N.Y. 12866 | 328[1] | 1,674[1] | 164 | P | 4660 | — | 2200 |
| Slippery Rock State College; Slippery Rock, Pa. 16057 | 2,193 | 2,513 | 338 | S | 970 | 1800 | 1096 |
| Smith College; Northampton, Mass. 01063 | 4 | 2,530 | 260 | P | 4100 | 4100 | 1800 |
| Sonoma State College; Rohnert Park, Calif. 94928 | 1,700 | 1,835 | 279 | S | 170 | 1575 | 2000 |
| South, The University of the; Sewanee, Tenn. 37375 | 655 | 416 | 87 | P/E | 3200 | 3200 | 1310 |
| South Alabama, University of; Mobile, Ala. 36688 | 3,565[1] | 3,392[1] | 381 | S | 771 | — | 1392 |
| South Carolina, Medical University of; Charleston, S.C. 29403 | 2,303[2] | | n.a. | S | 1200[2] | n.a. | 1450[2] |
| South Carolina, University of; Columbia, S.C. 29208 | 12,294[1] | 11,259[1] | 891 | S | 732 | 1692 | 1115 |
| U of SC at Coastal Carolina; Conway, S.C. 29526 | 941[1] | 677[1] | 125 | S | 630 | 1540 | — |
| U of SC at Spartanburg; Spartanburg, S.C. 29303 | 660[1] | 523[1] | 89 | S | 630 | 1540 | — |
| South Carolina State College; Orangeburg, S.C. 29117 | 1,317 | 1,722 | 245 | S | 600 | 1300 | 2472 |
| South Dakota, University of; Vermillion, S.D. 57069 | 3,188[1] | 2,624[1] | 400 | S | 653 | 1358 | 1080 |
| Univ. of South Dakota at Springfield; Springfield, S.D. 57062 | 575 | 165 | 63 | S | 528 | 1152 | 1060 |
| South Dakota School of Mines & Tech.; Rapid City, S.D. 57701 | 1,400[1] | 412[1] | 96 | S | 632 | 1430 | 1000 |
| South Dakota State University; Brookings, S.D. 57007 | 3,656 | 2,833 | 301 | S | 595 | 1347 | 980 |

| Institution and location | Enrollment | | Faculty | Control | Tuition | | |
|---|---|---|---|---|---|---|---|
| | Male | Female | | | Res. | Nonres. | Rm/Bd |
| South Florida, The University of; Tampa, Fla. 33620 | 11,656[1] | 11,156[1] | 879 | S | $567 | $1611 | $1266 |
| New College Campus; Sarasota, Fla. 33580 | 260[1] | 250[1] | 40 | S | 950 | 2900 | 685[8] |
| South Texas College of Law; Houston, Tex. 77002 | 880 | 223 | 16 | P | 2380 | 2380 | — |
| Southeast Missouri State Univ.; Cape Girardeau, Mo. 63701 | 3,371 | 3,397 | 352 | S | 300 | 800 | 1028 |
| Southeastern Bible College; Birmingham, Ala. 35205 | 145[7] | 72[7] | 15 | P | 1550 | 1550 | 1400 |
| Southeastern Coll. of the Assemblies; Lakeland, Fla. 33801 | 1,153[7] | | 34 | P/AG | 1025 | — | 960 |
| Southeastern Louisiana University; Hammond, La. 70402 | 3,013 | 3,741 | 240 | S | 478 | 1108 | 1140 |
| Southeastern Massachusetts U.; North Dartmouth, Mass. 02747 | 2,826[1] | 2,372[1] | 300 | S | 651 | 1426 | 2200 |
| Southeastern Oklahoma State Univ.; Durant, Okla. 74701 | 2,150 | 1,950 | 139 | S | 400 | 1000 | 1200 |
| Southern Arkansas University; Magnolia, Ark. 71753 | 853[1] | 1,038[1] | 103 | S | 460 | 730 | 1040 |
| Southern Benedictine College; St. Bernard, Ala. 35138 | 222[1] | 162[1] | 27 | P/RC | 1500 | 1500 | 1516 |
| Southern Bible College; Houston, Tex. 77015 | 89 | 56 | 8 | P/CG | ([74]) | ([74]) | 1365 |
| Southern California, University of; Los Angeles, Calif. 90007 | 9,889 | 6,180 | 2000 | P | 4200 | 4200 | 2100 |
| Southern California College; Costa Mesa, Calif. 92626 | 311 | 227 | 36 | P/AG | 1830 | 1830 | 1450 |
| Southern California Coll. of Optometry; Fullerton, Calif. 92631 | 350 | 47 | 38 | P | 3660 | 3660 | — |
| Southern College of Optometry; Memphis, Tenn. 38104 | 541 | 46 | 49 | P | 2750 | 6000 | — |
| Southern Colorado, University of; Pueblo, Colo. 81001 | 3,084 | 2,313 | 255 | S | 438 | 1750 | 1330 |
| Southern Connecticut State College; New Haven, Conn. 06515 | 2,262 | 3,857 | 440 | S | 678 | 1668 | 1316 |
| Southern Illinois University; Carbondale, Ill. 62901 | 14,024[1] | 8,513[1] | 1668 | S | 524 | 1572 | 1520 |
| Southern Illinois University–Edwardsville; Edwardsville, Ill. 62026 | 11,327[2] | | n.a. | S | 690[2] | n.a. | 1450[2] |
| Southern Methodist University; Dallas, Tex. 75275 | 3,259 | 2,757 | 460 | P | 2760 | 2760 | 1580 |
| Southern Missionary College; Collegedale, Tenn. 37315 | 699 | 810 | 125 | P/SDA | 2880 | 2880 | 1300 |
| Southern Mississippi, University of; Hattiesburg, Miss. 39401 | 4,733 | 5,073 | 590 | S | 660 | 1460 | 920 |
| Southern Oregon State College; Ashland, Ore. 97520 | 2,097[1] | 2,178[1] | 203 | S | 732 | 2,157 | 1400 |
| Southern Technical Inst. *See* Georgia Inst. of Tech. | | | | | | | |
| Southern University and A&M College; Baton Rouge, La. 70813 | 3,570 | 4,683 | 461 | S | 446 | 1076 | 1650 |
| Southern Univ. in New Orleans; New Orleans, La. 70126 | 980 | 1,642 | 111 | S | 195 | 315 | — |
| Southern Utah State College; Cedar City, Utah 84720 | 883[1] | 699[1] | 72 | S | 534 | 1119 | 1236 |
| Southwest Baptist College; Bolivar, Mo. 65613 | 639 | 721 | 80 | P | 1850 | 1850 | 1110 |
| Southwest Minnesota State Univ. *See* Minnesota State Coll. System | | | | | | | |
| Southwest Missouri State University; Springfield, Mo. 65802 | 4,615 | 4,484 | 453 | S | 400 | 900 | 1020 |
| Southwest Texas State University; San Marcos, Tex. 78666 | 7,378[1] | 7,292[1] | 528 | S | 396 | 1476 | 1230 |
| Southwestern Adventist College; Keene, Tex. 76059 | 326 | 300 | 52 | P/SDA | 2878 | 2878 | 1450 |
| Southwestern Assemblies of God College; Waxahachie, Tex. 75165 | 382 | 303 | 17 | P/AG | 1042 | 1042 | 1368 |
| Southwestern at Memphis; Memphis, Tenn. 38112 | 974[2] | | n.a. | P/Pres | 3050[2] | n.a. | 1595[2] |
| Southwestern College; Winfield, Kan. 67156 | 280 | 258 | 45 | P/UM | 2075 | 2075 | 1200 |
| Southwestern Louisiana, University of; Lafayette, La. 70504 | 4,975 | 4,516 | 544 | S | 438 | 1068 | 912 |
| Southwestern Oklahoma State Univ.; Weatherford, Okla. 73096 | 1,970[1] | 1,976[1] | 238 | S | 410 | 920 | 900 |
| Southwestern Union Coll. *See* Southwestern Adventist Coll. | | | | | | | |
| Southwestern University; Georgetown, Tex. 78626 | 410 | 490 | 66 | P/M | 2250 | 2250 | 1430 |
| Southwestern Univ. School of Law; Los Angeles, Calif. 90005 | 1,100[1] | 600[1] | 75 | P | 3300 | — | — |
| Spalding College; Louisville, Ky. 40203 | 58 | 458 | 59 | P/RC | 2000 | 2000 | 1520 |
| Spelman College; Atlanta, Ga. 30314 | — | 1276 | 94 | P | 1800 | 1800 | 1600 |
| Spertus College of Judaica; Chicago, Ill. 60605 | 143[1] | 161[1] | 11 | P | ([74]) | — | — |
| Spring Arbor College; Spring Arbor, Mich. 49283 | 316 | 359 | 40 | P/FM | 2550 | 2550 | 1300 |
| Spring Garden College; Philadelphia, Pa. 19118 | 874[1] | 103[1] | 60 | P | — | — | — |
| Spring Hill College; Mobile, Ala. 36608 | 420[1] | 391[1] | 49 | P/RC | 2400 | 2400 | 1609 |
| Springfield College; Springfield, Mass. 01109 | 1,044 | 964 | 126 | P | 2607 | — | 1491 |
| Stanford University; Stanford, Calif. 94305 | 13,043[7] | | n.a. | P | 4695[10] | n.a. | 1970[10] |
| Staten Island, Coll. of (NYC). *See* New York, City Univ. of | | | | | | | |
| Steed College; Johnson City, Tenn. 37601 | 600 | 253 | 12 | P | 1440 | 1440 | — |

| Institution and location | Enrollment | | Faculty | Control | Tuition | | Rm/Bd |
|---|---|---|---|---|---|---|---|
| | Male | Female | | | Res. | Nonres. | |
| Stephen F. Austin State University; Nacogdoches, Tex. 75961 | 5,169[1] | 5,587[1] | 441 | S | $112 | $400 | $1310 |
| Stephens College; Columbia, Mo. 65201 | 52[1] | 1,593[1] | 142 | P | 4875 | — | — |
| Sterling College; Sterling, Kan. 67579 | 220 | 241 | 40 | P | 2274 | 2274 | 1175 |
| Stetson University; DeLand, Fla. 32720 | 1,875[2] | | n.a. | P/SB | 2750[2] | n.a. | 1395[2] |
| Stetson College of Law; St. Petersburg, Fla. 33707 | 345 | 134 | 18 | P | 3000 | 3000 | 600[8] |
| Steubenville, The College of; Steubenville, Ohio 43952 | 300[1] | 300[1] | 45 | P | 2350 | 2350 | 1550 |
| Stevens Institute of Technology; Hoboken, N.J. 07030 | 1,225 | 130 | 130 | P | 3950 | 3950 | 1730 |
| Stillman College; Tuscaloosa, Ala. 35401 | 813[2] | | n.a. | P/PUS | 1400[2] | n.a. | 1100[2] |
| Stockton State College; Pomona, N.J. 08239 | 2,079[7] | 1,175[7] | n.a. | S | n.a. | n.a. | n.a. |
| Stonehill College; North Easton, Mass. 02356 | 860[1] | 860[1] | 80 | P/RC | 3010 | 3010 | 1805 |
| Suffolk University; Boston, Mass. 02114 | 1,445[1] | 922[1] | 131 | P | 2340 | — | — |
| Sul Ross State University; Alpine, Tex. 79830 | 1,321 | 936 | 78 | S | 128 | 1280 | 1392 |
| Susquehanna University; Selinsgrove, Pa. 17870 | 781 | 579 | 99 | P/LCA | 3156 | 3156 | 1346 |
| Swarthmore College; Swarthmore, Pa. 19081 | 690[1] | 599[1] | 137 | P | 4250 | 4250 | 1920 |
| Sweet Briar College; Sweet Briar, Va. 24595 | — | 682 | 71 | P | 4165 | 4165 | 1560 |
| Syracuse University; Syracuse, N.Y. 13210 | 10,676[1] | 8,789[1] | 895 | P | 2075 | — | 2000 |
| Tabor College; Hillsboro, Kan. 67063 | 238[1] | 292[1] | 28 | P/MB | 2520 | 2520 | 1445 |
| Talladega College; Talladega, Ala. 35160 | 184 | 372 | 40 | P | 1250 | 1250 | 1360 |
| Tampa, The University of; Tampa, Fla. 33606 | 1,288 | 1,008 | 90 | P | 3200 | 3200 | 1900 |
| Tampa College; Tampa, Fla. 33607 | 735 | 130 | 21 | P | 1215 | 1215 | — |
| Tarkio College; Tarkio, Mo. 64491 | 241 | 145 | 31 | P/UP | 2425 | 2425 | 1275 |
| Tarleton State College[75]; Stephenville, Tex. 76402 | 3,189[2] | | n.a. | S | 120[2] | n.a. | 1180[2] |
| Taylor University; Upland, Ind. 46989 | 685 | 758 | 83 | ID | 2778 | 2778 | 1497 |
| Temple University; Philadelphia, Pa. 19122 | 11,026[1] | 8,854[1] | 1713 | S | 1450 | 2650 | 1850 |
| Tennessee State University; Nashville, Tenn. 37203 | 2,465 | 2,779 | 281 | S | 462 | 1398 | 1060 |
| Tennessee System, University of; Knoxville, Tenn. 37916 | | | | | | | |
| U. of Tennessee at Chattanooga; Chattanooga, Tenn. 37401 | 1,862 | 1,764 | 245 | S | 512 | 900 | 1425 |
| U. of Tennessee at Knoxville; Knoxville, Tenn. 37916 | 16,909[1] | 13,559[1] | 1281 | S | 450 | 936 | 1350 |
| U. of Tennessee at Martin; Martin, Tenn. 38238 | 2,102 | 1,995 | 201 | S | 549 | 1461 | 1245 |
| U. of Tennessee at Nashville; Nashville, Tenn. 37203 | 1,292[1] | 1,276[1] | 144 | S | 600 | 1848 | — |
| U. of Tennessee Center for the Health Sciences; Memphis, Tenn. 38163 | 1,373[1] | 716[1] | 550 | S | 1760 | 3380 | 2470 |
| Tennessee Technological University; Cookeville, Tenn. 38501 | 3,369[1] | 2,106[1] | 390 | S | 1208 | 1852 | 1260 |
| Tennessee Wesleyan College; Athens, Tenn. 37303 | 445[2] | | n.a. | P/M | 1440[2] | n.a. | 1320[2] |
| Texas, U. of, Health Sci. Ctr. at Dallas; Dallas, Tex. 75235 | 1,217[2] | | n.a. | S | 400[2] | n.a. | 3600[2] |
| Texas, U. of, Health Sci. Ctr. at Houston; Houston, Tex. 77025 | 1,837[52] | | n.a. | S | 1301[2] | n.a. | n.a. |
| Texas, U. of, Health Science Center at San Antonio, San Antonio, Tex. 78284 | 947 | 804 | — | S | 400 | 1200 | — |
| Texas, University of, Medical Branch; Galveston, Tex. 77550 | 802[1] | 668[1] | 483 | S | 400 | 1200 | 2500 |
| Texas, Univ. of, of the Permian Basin; Odessa, Tex. 79762 | 828 | 747 | 60 | S | 130 | 1300 | 400[8] |
| Texas A&I University at Corpus Christi; Corpus Christi 78411 | 449 | 398 | 89 | S | 150 | 1290 | — |
| Texas A&I University at Laredo; Laredo, Tex. 78040 | 884[7] | | n.a. | S | 160[7] | n.a. | 1600[7] |
| Texas A&I University in Kingsville; Kingsville, Tex. 78363 | 3,237 | 3,114 | 254 | S | 328 | 1408 | 1200 |
| Texas A&M University; College Station, Tex. 77843 | 17,701 | 8,647 | 913 | S | 124 | 1240 | 1400 |
| Texas Chiropractic College; Pasadena, Texas 77505 | 215[7] | 28[7] | n.a. | P | n.a. | n.a. | n.a. |
| Texas Christian University; Fort World, Tex. 76129 | 3,009[1] | 3,150[1] | 318 | P/DC | 2816 | 2816 | 1565 |
| Texas College; Tyler, Tex. 75701 | 607[2] | | n.a. | P/M | 1350[2] | n.a. | 1300[2] |
| Texas College of Osteopathic Medicine; Fort Worth, Tex. 76107 | 236 | 37 | 176 | S | 400 | 1200 | — |
| Texas Eastern University; Tyler, Tex. 75701 | 824 | 1,014 | 77 | S | 345 | 1425 | — |
| Texas Lutheran College; Seguin, Tex. 78155 | 501 | 433 | 57 | P/AL | 2045 | 2045 | 1125 |
| Texas Southern University; Houston, Tex. 77004 | 9,170[2] | | n.a. | S | 425[2] | n.a. | 1300[2] |
| Texas System, University of; Austin, Tex. 78701 | | | | | | | |
| Univ. of Texas at Arlington; Arlington, Tex. 76019 | 7,048[1] | 4,227[1] | 550 | S | 370 | 1450 | 1785 |
| Univ. of Texas at Austin; Austin, Tex. 78712 | 23,382[1] | 18,278[1] | 1504 | S | 100 | 960 | 1657 |
| Univ. of Texas at Dallas; Dallas, Tex. 75080 | 4,469[2] | | n.a. | S | 334[2] | n.a. | n.a. |
| Univ. of Texas at El Paso; El Paso, Tex. 79968 | 8,832[1] | 7,004[1] | 449 | S | 380 | 1460 | 1200 |
| Univ. of Texas at San Antonio; San Antonio, Tex. 78285 | 3,962 | 3,732 | 236 | S | 525 | 1200 | 1280 |
| Texas Tech University; Lubbock, Tex. 79409 | 12,612[1] | 9,746[1] | 984 | S | 378 | 1458 | 1269 |
| Texas Wesleyan College; Fort Worth, Tex. 76105 | 835[1] | 753[1] | 100 | P/UM | ([76]) | ([76]) | 621 |
| Texas Woman's University; Denton, Tex. 76204 | 508 | 8,515 | 485 | S | 128 | 1280 | 1750 |
| Thiel College; Greenville, Pa. 16125 | 513 | 434 | 61 | P | 4697 | 3143 | 1546 |

| Institution and location | Enrollment | | Faculty | Control | Tuition | | Rm/Bd |
|---|---|---|---|---|---|---|---|
| | Male | Female | | | Res. | Nonres. | |
| Thomas A. Edison College; Princeton, N.J. 08540 | 1,488[7] | | n.a. | Pub/S | n.a. | n.a. | n.a. |
| Thomas College; Waterville, Me. 04901 | 212[1] | 224[1] | 25 | P | $2650 | $2650 | $1700 |
| Thomas Jefferson University; Philadelphia, Pa. 19107 | 870[1] | 929[1] | 369 | P | n.a. | — | — |
| Thomas M. Cooley Law School; Lansing, Mich. 48933 | 739 | 259 | 19 | P | 2250 | 2550 | — |
| Thomas More College; Fort Mitchell, Ky. 41017 | 420 | 280 | 60 | P/RC | 1584 | 1584 | 1280 |
| Tiffin University; Tiffin, Ohio 44883 | 293 | 102 | 15 | P | 1700 | 1700 | 1120 |
| Tift College; Forsyth, Ga. 31029 | 30[1] | 470[1] | 34 | P/B | 440 | 440 | 425 |
| Toccoa Falls College; Toccoa Falls, Ga. 30577 | 213[1] | 212[1] | 33 | P | 1600 | 1600 | 1300 |
| Toledo, The University of; Toledo, Ohio 43606 | 9,104[1] | 6,885[1] | 682 | S | 720 | 2100 | 1644 |
| Tougaloo College; Tougaloo, Miss. 39174 | 317 | 465 | 53 | P | 1600 | 1600 | 1004 |
| Touro College; New York, N.Y. 10036 | 624[1] | 1,040[1] | 50 | P | 2835 | — | 2000 |
| Towson State College; Towson, Md. 21204 | 5,994 | 8,169 | 449 | S | 774 | 1674 | 1450 |
| Transylvania University; Lexington, Ky. 40508 | 321 | 336 | 53 | P | 2800 | 2800 | 1475 |
| Trenton State College; Trenton, N.J. 08625 | 2,558 | 3,518 | 393 | S | 900 | 1600 | 1475 |
| Trevecca Nazarene College; Nashville, Tenn. 37210 | 360 | 347 | 45 | P/Naz | 1725 | 1725 | 1050 |
| Trinity Christian College; Palos Heights, Ill. 60463 | 154[7] | 165[7] | n.a. | P/CR | n.a. | n.a. | n.a. |
| Trinity College; Burlington, Vt. 05401 | 46 | 400 | 33 | P/RC | 2580 | 2580 | 1460 |
| Trinity College; Deerfield, Ill. 60015 | 338 | 395 | 37 | P | 2800 | 2800 | 1450 |
| Trinity College; Hartford, Conn. 06106 | 900 | 640 | 133 | P | 4300 | 4300 | 1790 |
| Trinity College; Washington, D.C. 20017 | 20[1] | 586[1] | 44 | P/RC | 3100 | 3100 | 1800 |
| Trinity University; San Antonio, Tex. 78284 | 3,570[2] | | n.a. | P/UP | 2352[2] | n.a. | 1476[2] |
| Tri-State College; Angola, Ind. 46703 | 1,130 | 247 | 74 | P | 2520 | 2520 | 1440 |
| Troy State University; Troy, Ala. 36081 | 2,826 | 2,294 | 251 | S | 555 | 780 | 660 |
| Tufts University; Medford, Mass. 02155 | 1,681 | — | 277 | P | 4500 | 4500 | 5760 |
| Jackson College for Women; Medford, Mass. 02155 | — | 1,810 | — | P | 4500 | 4500 | 5760 |
| Tulane University; New Orleans, La. 70118 | 4,956[1] | 2,611[1] | 760 | P | 3940 | 3940 | 1755 |
| Newcomb College; New Orleans, La. 70118 | — | 1,548[1] | 137 | P | 3340 | 3340 | 1260 |
| Tulsa, The University of; Tulsa, Okla. 74104 | 2,321 | 1,680 | 314 | P | 1900 | 1900 | 1230 |
| Turabo University College. *See* Ana G. Méndez Educational Foundation | | | | | | | |
| Tusculum College; Greeneville, Tenn. 37743 | 233[1] | 190[1] | 25 | P | 640 | 640 | 1182 |
| Tuskegee Institute; Tuskegee Institute, Ala. 36088 | 1,594 | 1,716 | 325 | P | 1850 | — | 1300 |
| Union College; Barbourville, Ky 40906 | 1,151[7] | | n.a. | P/UM | 1710[2] | n.a. | 920[2] |
| Union College; Lincoln, Neb. 68506 | 341[1] | 406[1] | — | P/SDA | 2960 | 2960 | 1300 |
| Union College; Schenectady, N.Y. 12308 | 2,256[1] | 924[1] | 167 | P | 4600 | 4600 | 1850 |
| Union University; Albany, N.Y. 12208 | | | | | | | |
| Albany College of Pharmacy; Albany, N.Y. 12208 | 300 | 300 | 26 | P | 1750 | 1750 | 1600 |
| Albany Law School; Albany, N.Y. 12208 | 543[7] | 196[7] | n.a. | P | n.a. | n.a. | n.a. |
| Albany Medical College; Albany, N.Y. 12208 | 366 | 129 | 250 | P | 7100 | 7100 | — |
| Union University; Jackson, Tenn. 38301 | 332 | 462 | 58 | P/SB | 1620 | 1620 | 355 |
| U.S. Air Force Academy; USAF Academy, Colo. 80840 | 4,046 | 231 | 560 | F | — | — | — |
| U.S. Army Command and General Staff College; Fort Leavenworth, Kan. 66027 | 997[7] | 8[7] | n.a. | F | n.a. | n.a. | n.a. |
| U.S. Coast Guard Academy; New London, Conn. 06320 | 855 | 54 | 124 | F | — | — | — |
| U.S. International University; San Diego, Calif. 92131 | 1,551 | 951 | 73 | P | 3069 | 3069 | 3165 |
| U.S. Merchant Marine Academy; Kings Point, N.Y. 11024 | 1,012 | 55 | 85 | F | — | | — |
| U.S. Military Academy; West Point, N.Y. 10996 | 3,900 | 130 | 600 | F | — | — | — |
| U.S. Naval Academy; Annapolis, Md. 21402 | 4,094 | 144 | 550 | F | — | — | — |
| United Wesleyan College; Allentown, Pa. 18103 | 126 | 86 | 13 | P/W | 1660 | 1660 | 1480 |
| Unity College; Unity, Me. 04988 | 195 | 53 | 30 | P | 2045 | 2045 | 1650 |
| Upper Iowa University; Fayette, Iowa 52142 | 282 | 168 | 31 | P | 3080 | 3080 | 1220 |
| Upsala College; East Orange, N.J. 07019 | 637 | 531 | 65 | P/L | 3120 | 3120 | 1820 |
| Urbana College; Urbana, Ohio 43078 | 432[1] | 134[1] | 19 | P | 2100 | 2100 | 1590 |
| Ursinus College; Collegeville, Pa. 19426 | 613[1] | 443[1] | 82 | P | 3300 | 3300 | 1450 |
| Ursuline College; Cleveland, Ohio 44124 | 9 | 471 | 43 | P | 2170 | 2170 | 1400 |
| Utah, University of; Salt Lake City, Utah 84112 | 13,270[1] | 8,610[1] | 1316 | S | 589 | 1474 | 1400 |
| Utah State University; Logan, Utah 84322 | 5,610[10] | 3,826[10] | 463 | S | 462 | 1431 | 1300 |
| Valdosta State College; Valdosta, Ga. 31601 | 2,284[1] | 2,844[1] | 250 | S | 546 | 1260 | 1500 |
| Valley City State College; Valley City, N.D. 58072 | 357[1] | 437[1] | 53 | S | 487 | 1048 | 1035 |
| Valparaiso University; Valparaiso, Ind. 46383 | 1,752[1] | 1,828[1] | 260 | P/L | 2860 | 2860 | 1520 |
| Vanderbilt University; Nashville, Tenn. 37240 | 4,311 | 2,958 | 1165 | P | 3950 | — | 2000 |
| VanderCook College of Music; Chicago, Ill. 60616 | 75 | 20 | 12 | P | 2300 | 2300 | 1540 |
| Vassar College; Poughkeepsie, N.Y. 12601 | 794[1] | 1,430[1] | 119 | P | 3875 | 3875 | 1825 |
| Vennard College; University Park, Iowa 52595 | 126 | 132 | 15 | P/ID | 1216 | 1216 | 1276 |
| Vermont, University of; Burlington, Vt. 05401 | 3,436[1] | 4,245[1] | 709 | S | 1300 | 3735 | 1734 |
| Vermont College. *See* Norwich University | | | | | | | |
| Vermont Law School; South Royalton, Vt. 05068 | 247[1] | 73[1] | 15 | P | 3400 | 3400 | 2610 |
| Villa Maria College; Erie, Pa. 16505 | 7[1] | 458[1] | 50 | P/RC | 2500 | 2500 | 1600 |

| Institution and location | Enrollment | | Faculty | Control | Tuition | | Rm/Bd |
|---|---|---|---|---|---|---|---|
| | Male | Female | | | Res. | Nonres. | |
| Villanova University; Villanova, Pa. 19085 | 3,518 | 2,167 | 417 | P/RC | $3200 | $3200 | $2000 |
| Virgin Islands, College of the; St. Thomas, V.I. 00801 | 169 | 391 | 58 | S | 300 | 900 | 1230 |
| Virginia, University of; Charlottesville, Va. 22903 | 8,423[1] | 6,090[1] | 1534 | S | 694 | 1619 | 1475 |
| Clinch Valley College; Wise, Va. 24293 | 340[1] | 403[1] | 49 | S | 550 | 800 | 448[8] |
| Virginia Commonwealth University; Richmond, Va. 23284 | 6,445 | 8,663 | 662 | S | 730 | 1460 | 1450 |
| Virginia Intermont College; Bristol, Va. 24201 | 40[1] | 479[1] | 39 | P/SB | 2250 | 2250 | 1570 |
| Virginia Military Institute; Lexington, Va. 24450 | 1,314[1] | 28[1] | 92 | S | 550 | 1700 | 1020 |
| Virginia Polytechnic Inst. & State Univ.; Blacksburg, Va. 24061 | 19,314[7] | | n.a. | S | 570[2] | n.a. | 1038[2] |
| Virginia State College; Petersburg, Va. 23803 | 2,168[1] | 2,684[1] | 229 | S | 790 | 1250 | 928 |
| Virginia Union University; Richmond, Va. 23220 | 734[1] | 751[1] | 80 | P/B | 1950 | 1950 | 1315 |
| Virginia Wesleyan College; Norfolk, Va. 23502 | 389 | 332 | 36 | P/UM | 2750 | 2750 | 1350 |
| Viterbo College; La Crosse, Wis. 54601 | 149[1] | 702[1] | 90 | P | 2790 | 2790 | 1237 |
| Voorhees College; Denmark, S.C. 29042 | 1,050[7] | | n.a. | P/E | 1500[2] | n.a. | 1170[2] |
| Wabash College; Crawfordsville, Ind. 47933 | 818 | — | 69 | P | 3400 | 3400 | 1585 |
| Wagner College; Staten Island, N.Y. 10301 | 806 | 1,059 | 104 | P | 3025 | 3025 | 1750 |
| Wake Forest University; Winston–Salem, N.C. 27109 | 2,807[1] | 1,323[1] | 544 | P/B | 3000 | 3000 | 1350 |
| Walla Walla College; College Place, Wash. 99324 | 945[1] | 919[1] | 136 | P/SDA | 3330 | 3330 | 1400 |
| Walsh College; Canton, Ohio 44720 | 210 | 170 | 52 | P/RC | 2400 | 2400 | 1400 |
| Walsh Coll. of Accountancy & Business Admin.; Troy, Mich. 48084 | 152 | 85 | 5 | P | 1350 | — | — |
| Warner Pacific College; Portland, Ore. 97215 | 225 | 229 | 34 | CG | 825 | 825 | 1470 |
| Warren Wilson College; Swannanoa, N.C. 28778 | 252 | 299 | 36 | P/UP | 2400 | 2400 | 1200 |
| Wartburg College; Waverly, Iowa 50677 | 525[1] | 590[1] | 76 | P/AL | 2833 | — | 1275 |
| Washburn University of Topeka; Topeka, Kan. 66621 | 1,931[1] | 1,431[1] | 150 | Mun | 710 | 1220 | 1425 |
| Washington, University of; Seattle, Wash. 98195 | 18,021 | 13,951 | 2208 | S | 687 | 2394 | 1650 |
| Washington and Jefferson College; Washington, Pa. 15301 | 657 | 287 | 90 | P | 3725 | 3725 | 1525 |
| Washington and Lee University; Lexington, Va. 24450 | 1,636[1] | 56[1] | 155 | P | 3350 | 3350 | 1475 |
| Washington Bible College; Lanham, Md. 20801 | 210 | 140 | 18 | P/ND | 1628 | 1628 | 1594 |
| Washington College; Chestertown, Md. 21620 | 368[1] | 324[1] | 65 | P | 3000 | 3000 | 1400 |
| Washington State University; Pullman, Wash. 99164 | 9,550[1] | 7,115[1] | 704 | S | 686 | 2394 | 1620 |
| Washington University; St. Louis, Mo. 63130 | 5,241[1] | 3,128[1] | 1234 | P | 3950[1] | 3950[1] | 1900[1] |
| Wayland Baptist College; Plainview, Tex. 79072 | 731[1] | 417[1] | 52 | P/SB | 1480 | 1480 | 1236 |
| Wayne State College; Wayne, Neb. 68787 | 842[1] | 958[1] | 91 | S | 646 | 1062 | 1218 |
| Wayne State University; Detroit, Mich. 48202 | 18,740[1] | 15,649[1] | 1600 | S | 1020 | 2767 | — |
| Waynesburg College; Waynesburg, Pa. 15370 | 451 | 273 | 49 | P | 2950 | 2950 | 1420 |
| Webb Institute of Naval Architecture; Glen Cove, N.Y. 11542 | 69 | 4 | 12 | P | — | — | 1600 |
| Weber State College; Ogden, Utah 84408 | 5,818 | 3,943 | 425 | S | 558 | 1176 | 1075 |
| Webster College; St. Louis, Mo. 63119 | 375[1] | 646[1] | 75 | P | 2600 | 2600 | 2500 |
| Wellesley College; Wellesley, Mass. 02181 | 5[1] | 1,985[1] | 195 | P | 4300 | 3050 | 2250 |
| Wells College; Aurora, N.Y. 13026 | — | 462 | 60 | P | 3720 | 3720 | 1830 |
| Wentworth Institute of Technology; Boston, Mass. 02115 | 1,659[7] | 53[7] | n.a. | P | n.a. | n.a. | n.a. |
| Wesleyan College; Macon, Ga. 31201 | — | 510 | 45 | P | 2700 | 1845 | 1420 |
| Wesleyan University; Middletown, Conn. 06457 | 1,483 | 1,285 | 274 | P | 4720 | 4720 | 950 |
| West Chester State College; West Chester, Pa. 19380 | 2,352 | 3,256 | 485 | S | 950 | 1780 | 1012 |
| West Coast University; Los Angeles, Calif. 90020 | 1,133[1] | 167[1] | 4 | P | 1710 | 1710 | — |
| West Florida, The University of; Pensacola, Fla. 32504 | 1,545 | 1,191 | 225 | S | 742 | 2317 | 1575 |
| West Georgia College; Carrollton, Ga. 30117 | 2,263 | 3,076 | 280 | S | 540 | 1254 | 480 |
| West Liberty State College; West Liberty, W. Va. 26074 | 1,102[1] | 1,092[1] | 147 | S | 332 | 1232 | 1350 |
| West Texas State University; Canyon, Tex. 79016 | 2,281[1] | 2,320[1] | 229 | S | 120 | 1200 | 1040 |
| West Virginia College of Grad. Studies; Institute, W. Va. 25112 | 2,463[7] | | n.a. | S | 250[2] | n.a. | n.a. |
| West Virginia Inst. of Technology; Montgomery, W. Va. 25136 | 1,390 | 559 | 137 | S | 360 | 1260 | 1540 |
| West Virginia Sch. of Osteopathic Med.; Lewisburg, W. Va. 24901 | 203 | | — | S | 526 | 1612 | — |
| West Virginia State College; Institute, W. Va. 25112 | 1,050[1] | 971[1] | 136 | S | 315 | 1215 | 1600 |
| West Virginia University; Morgantown, W. Va. 26506 | 13,000 | 9,000 | 1193 | S | 425 | 1405 | 1650 |
| West Virginia Wesleyan College; Buckhannon, W. Va. 26201 | 715[1] | 986[1] | 118 | P/UM | 2240 | 2240 | 1430 |
| Westbrook College; Portland, Me. 04103 | 22[1] | 486[1] | 54 | P | 3050 | — | 1670 |
| Western Baptist Bible College; Salem, Ore. 97302 | 237[1] | 202[1] | 20 | P/B | 2115 | 2115 | 1353 |
| Western Bible Institute; Morrison, Colo. 80209 | 122 | 70 | 10 | P | 1216 | 1216 | 1070 |
| Western Carolina Univ. *See* North Carolina, Univ. System of | | | | | | | |
| Western Connecticut State College; Danbury, Conn. 06810 | 1,240[1] | 1,595[1] | 172 | S | 540 | 1530 | 800 |
| Western Illinois University; Macomb, Ill. 61455 | 7,548[1] | 6,333[1] | 747 | S | 510 | 1530 | 1349 |
| Western Kentucky University; Bowling Green, Ky. 42101 | 6,382[1] | 7,108[1] | 468 | S | 500 | 1270 | 1540 |

| Institution and location | Enrollment Male | Enrollment Female | Faculty | Control | Tuition Res. | Tuition Nonres. | Rm/Bd |
|---|---|---|---|---|---|---|---|
| Western Maryland College; Westminster, Md. 21157 | 655[1] | 708[1] | 100 | P | $3175 | $3175 | $1450 |
| Western Michigan University; Kalamazoo, Mich. 49008 | 8,006[1] | 6,994[1] | 940 | S | 765 | 1725 | 1490 |
| Western Montana College; Dillon, Mont. 59725 | 244[1] | 229[1] | 39 | S | 504 | 1515 | 1255 |
| Western New England College; Springfield, Mass. 01119 | 1,197[1] | 449[1] | 76 | P | 2730 | 1290 | 1440 |
| Western New Mexico University; Silver City, N.M. 88061 | 527[1] | 441[1] | 60 | S | 375 | 1178 | 1200 |
| Western State College; Gunnison, Colo. 81230 | 1,653 | 1,105 | 160 | S | 340 | 1348 | 1500 |
| Western State University College of Law of Orange County; Fullerton, Calif. 92631 | 1,229[1] | 371[1] | 48 | P | 2053 | 2053 | — |
| Western State University Coll. of Law of San Diego; San Diego, Calif. 92101 | 1,188[2] | | 14 | P | ([77]) | ([77]) | — |
| Western Washington State College; Bellingham, Wash. 98225 | 4,137[1] | 3,991[1] | 394 | S | 618 | 1983 | 1550 |
| Westfield State College; Westfield, Mass. 01085 | 978 | 1478 | 155 | S | 500 | 1200 | 1280 |
| Westmar College; LeMars, Iowa 51031 | 319 | 271 | 37 | P/UM | 2250 | 2250 | 1175 |
| Westminster Choir College; Princeton, N.J. 08540 | 218[1] | 258[1] | 36 | P | 3145 | 3145 | 1530 |
| Westminster College; Fulton, Mo. 65251 | 610 | — | 54 | P | 2800 | — | 1290 |
| Westminster College; New Wilmington, Pa. 16142 | 782 | 813 | 108 | P/UP | 2950 | 2950 | 1360 |
| Westminster College; Salt Lake City, Utah 84105 | 433[1] | 453[1] | 53 | P | 1700 | 1700 | 1210 |
| Westmont College; Santa Barbara, Calif. 93108 | 392 | 497 | 54 | P/ND | 3125 | 3125 | 1460 |
| Wheaton College; Norton, Mass. 02766 | 1 | 1132 | 84 | P | 4815 | — | 1920 |
| Wheaton College; Wheaton, Ill. 60187 | 1,144[1] | 1,045[1] | 157 | P | 2766 | 2766 | 1572 |
| Wheeling College; Wheeling, W. Va. 26003 | 1,041[7] | | n.a. | P | 2280[2] | n.a. | 1500[2] |
| Wheelock College; Boston, Mass. 02215 | 14 | 563 | 52 | P | 3500 | 3500 | 1900 |
| Whitman College; Walla Walla, Wash. 99362 | 1,090[2] | | n.a. | P | 3110[2] | n.a. | 1350[2] |
| Whittier College; Whittier, Calif. 90608 | 580 | 608 | 85 | P | 3500 | 3500 | 1660 |
| Whitworth College; Spokane, Wash. 99251 | 511 | 645 | 61 | P/Pres | 3325 | 3325 | 1525 |
| Wichita State University; Wichita, Kan. 67208 | 3,850[1] | 3,282[1] | 572 | S | 723 | 1713 | 1350 |
| Widener College; Chester, Pa. 19013 | 978 | 690 | 134 | P | 3500 | 3500 | 1675 |
| Wilberforce University; Wilberforce, Ohio 45384 | 1123 | | 80 | P/AME | — | — | — |
| Wiley College; Marshall, Tex. 75670 | 544[2] | | n.a. | P/UM | ([44]) | n.a. | 1369[2] |
| Wilkes College; Wilkes-Barre, Pa, 18703 | 1,156[1] | 960[1] | 142 | P | 2950 | 2950 | 1600 |
| Willamette University; Salem, Ore. 97301 | 1,032[1] | 684[1] | 105 | P | 3370 | 3370 | 1563 |
| William and Mary in Virginia, Coll. of; Williamsburg, Va. 23185 | 2,635[1] | 2,649[1] | 359 | S | 1076 | 2524 | 1510 |
| William Carey College; Hattiesburg, Miss. 39401 | 430[1] | 517[1] | 70 | P/SB | 1470 | 1470 | 1030 |
| William Jewell College; Liberty, Mo 64068 | 618[1] | 699[1] | 85 | P | 2210 | 2210 | 1140 |
| William Mitchell College of Law; St. Paul, Minn. 55105 | 779 | 346 | 22 | P | 1750 | 1750 | — |
| William Paterson College of New Jersey; Wayne, N.J. 07470 | 3,000 | 3,500 | 393 | S | 660 | 1320 | 940[8] |
| William Penn College, Oskaloosa, Iowa 52577 | 365 | 207 | 55 | P/SOF | 2800 | 2800 | 1310 |
| William Smith College. *See* Hobart & William Smith Colleges | | | | | | | |
| William Woods College; Fulton, Mo. 65251 | — | 907[10] | — | P | 3095 | 3095 | 1530 |
| Williams College; Williamstown, Mass. 01267 | 1,162[1] | 808[1] | 167 | P | 4100 | 4100 | 1855 |
| Wilmington College; New Castle, Del. 19720 | 720[2] | | 12 | P | — | 1900 | — |
| Wilmington College; Wilmington, Ohio 45177 | 398 | 202 | 55 | P | 2340[10] | 2340[10] | 1410[10] |
| Wilson College; Chambersburg, Pa. 17201 | — | 235[1] | 48 | P/Pres | 3385 | 3385 | 1575 |
| Windham College; Putney, Vt. 05346 | 106 | 67 | 18 | P | 1600 | 3150 | 1300 |
| Winona State University. *See* Minnesota State College System | | | | | | | |
| Winston-Salem State U. *See* North Carolina, Univ. System of | | | | | | | |
| Winthrop College; Rock Hill, S.C. 29733 | 747 | 2,083 | 239 | S | 815 | 1515 | 1042 |
| Wisconsin, The Medical College of; Milwaukee, Wis. 53233 | 443 | 101 | 390 | P | 4950 | 5620 | 1710 |
| Wisconsin, University of; Madison, Wis. 53706 | | | | | | | |
| U. of Wisconsin—Eau Claire; Eau Claire, Wis. 54701 | 3,625 | 4,512 | 441 | S | 739[10] | 2470[10] | 1270[10] |
| U. of Wisconsin—Green Bay; Green Bay, Wis. 54302 | 1,209[1] | 1,042[1] | 162 | S | 765 | 2650 | 1550 |
| U. of Wisconsin—La Crosse; La Crosse, Wis. 54601 | 3,164 | 3,516 | 460 | S | 735 | 2467 | 1226 |
| U. of Wisconsin—Madison; Madison, Wis. 53706 | 21,652[1] | 17,370[1] | 2357 | S | 812 | 2946 | 1690 |
| U. of Wisconsin—Milwaukee; Milwaukee, Wis. 53211 | 24,686[7] | | n.a. | S | 675[2] | n.a. | 1600[2] |
| U. of Wisconsin—Oshkosh; Oshkosh, Wis. 54901 | 5,069[1] | 4,999[1] | 608 | S | 723 | 2454 | 1414 |
| U. of Wisconsin—Parkside; Kenosha, Wis. 53140 | 2,869[1] | 2,314[1] | 175 | S | 750 | 1750 | 1800 |
| U. of Wisconsin—Platteville; Platteville, Wis. 53818 | 2,946 | 1,674 | — | S | 780 | 2660 | 1370 |
| U. of Wisconsin—River Falls; River Falls, Wis. 54022 | 2,400 | 2,182 | 260 | S | 760 | 2500 | 1400 |
| U. of Wisconsin—Stevens Point; Stevens Point, Wis. 54481 | 3,910 | 3,541 | — | S | 730 | 2462 | 1280 |
| U. of Wisconsin—Stout; Menomonie, Wis. 54751 | 2,965[1] | 2,791[1] | 450 | S | 726 | 2458 | 1330 |
| U. of Wisconsin—Superior; Superior, Wis. 54880 | 961 | 603 | 189 | S | 927 | 3115 | 1685 |
| U. of Wisconsin—Whitewater; Whitewater, Wis. 53190 | 4,882[1] | 4,707[1] | — | S | 810 | 2700 | 1500 |
| Wittenberg University; Springfield, Ohio 45501 | 1,125[1] | 1,183[1] | 136 | P/LCA | 3372 | 3372 | 1560 |

| Institution and location | Enrollment Male | Female | Faculty | Control | Tuition Res. | Nonres. | Rm/Bd |
|---|---|---|---|---|---|---|---|
| Wofford College; Spartanburg, S.C. 29301 | 851[1] | 124[1] | 58 | P/UM | $2715 | $2715 | $1505 |
| Woodbury University; Los Angeles, Calif. 90017 | 661 | 533 | 42 | P | 2268 | 2268 | — |
| Wooster, The College of; Wooster, Ohio 44691 | 980 | 820 | 130 | P | 5240[11] | — | — |
| Worcester Art Museum, School of the; Worcester, Mass. 01608 | 35 | 75 | 11 | P | — | 1950 | — |
| Worcester Polytechnic Institute; Worcester, Mass. 01609 | 2,053[1] | 242[1] | 154 | P | 3700 | — | 1782 |
| Worcester State College; Worcester, Mass. 01602 | 1,206 | 1,742 | 188 | S | 500 | 1300 | 1929 |
| Wright Institute; Berkeley, Calif. 94704 | 74[1] | 69[1] | — | P | 3150 | — | — |
| Wright State University; Dayton, Ohio 45435 | 3,764[1] | 3,508[1] | 561 | S | 870 | 1860 | 1575 |
| Wyoming, University of; Laramie, Wyo. 82071 | 4,681[1] | 3,115[1] | 708 | S | 434 | 1400 | 1466 |
| Xavier University; Cincinnati, Ohio 45207 | 1,459[1] | 839[1] | 175 | P | 2400 | 2400 | 1570 |
| Xavier University of Louisiana; New Orleans, La. 70125 | 626 | 930 | 120 | P | 1800 | 1800 | 620 |
| Yale University; New Haven, Conn. 06520 | 3,140 | 1,936 | 835 | P | 4750[10] | 4750[10] | 2200[10] |
| Yankton College; Yankton, S.D. 57078 | 123 | 106 | 29 | P/UCC | 2660 | 2660 | 1250 |
| Yeshiva University; New York, N.Y. 10033 | 3,287[1] | 1,891[1] | 1260 | P | 3000 | 3000 | 1700 |
| York College (NYC). *See* New York, City University of | | | | | | | |
| York College of Pennsylvania; York, Pa. 17405 | 976[1] | 883[1] | 88 | P | 1880 | 1880 | 1358 |
| Youngstown State University; Youngstown, Ohio 44555 | 8,423[1] | 7,273[1] | 729 | S | 738 | 1398 | 1165 |

1. Fall 1977. 2. Spring 1977. 3. $75 per credit hour. 4. 1978–79. 5. Includes SUNY College of Ceramics at Alfred University. 6. Part-time, 40. 7. 1976. 8. Room only. 9. Fall 1978. 10. 1977–78. 11. Comprehensive fee including room and board. 12. $55 per hour. 13. Part-time, 23. 14. $42 per credit hour. 15. Part-time. 16. Winter 1978. 17. $26 per semester hour. 18. Protestant, not affiliated. 19. Males no longer admitted. 20. $129 per credit. 21. Missouri Synod. 22. Tax oriented. 23. $59 per credit hour. 24. Part of SUNY System. 25. Upper Division. 26. $16.50 per quarter hour. 27. $51.50 per quarter hour. 28. $45 per semester hour. 29. $34 per semester hour. 30. Formerly Pacific College of Fresno. 31. Board only. 32. $54 per unit. 33. $60 per semester hour. 34. Nursing tuition, $2300. 35. $175 per semester. 36. $50 per credit hour. 37. Affiliated with Rensselaer Polytechnic Institute. 38. $135 per credit hour. 39. At graduate level. 40. $23 per credit hour. 41. $21 per credit hour. 42. Two thirds tuition paid in co-op program. 43. $44 per week. 44. $50 per semester hour. 45. $100 per semester hour. 46. 1975. 47. $22 per semester hour. 48. $17 per hour. 49. $30 per hour. 50. Lower Division. 51. Formerly La Verne College. 52. Winter 1977. 53. Formerly Brooklyn College of Pharmacy. 54. $60 per credit. 55. Affiliated academically with the University of Minnesota. 56. Winter 1977. 57. $4 per hour. 58. $40 per hour. 59. $38 per hour. 60. $10 per credit hour. 61. Part of De Vry Institute of Technology. 62. $22 per credit hour. 63. $44 per credit hour. 64. Part of Louisiana State University System. 65. $125–$750. 66. $170–$1,000. 67. Tuition remission. 68. Students work for tuition, room, and board. 69. $105 per unit. 70. UCC/UM/PUS. 71. $84 per credit hour. 72. $61 per credit hour. 73. Spring 1975. 74. $35 per credit hour. 75. Member Texas A&M System. 76. $54 per credit hour. 77. $70 per unit. 78. Includes SUNY statutory colleges. NOTE: A dash means the information does not apply; n.a. = not available.

## Purposes of Institutional Accreditation

Institutional accreditation of the postsecondary level is a means used by the accrediting commissions for the purposes of: fostering excellence in postsecondary education through the development of criteria and guidelines for assessing educational effectiveness; encouraging institutional improvement of educational endeavors through continuous self-study and evaluation; assuring the educational community, the general public, and other agencies or organizations that an institution has clearly defined and appropriate objectives, has established conditions under which their achievement can reasonably be expected, appears in fact to be accomplishing them substantially, and is so organized, staffed, and supported that it can be expected to continue to do so; providing counsel and assistance to established and developing institutions; protecting institutions against encroachments which might jeopardize their educational effectiveness or academic freedom.

Accreditation is attained through a process of evaluation and periodic review of total institutions conducted by the commission in accord with policies and procedures approved by the Council on Postsecondary Accreditation.

## Living Alone

In 1977, 45% of women aged 20 to 24 had never married, up from 28% in 1960, reported the U.S. Department of Commerce. The median age at first marriage climbed in 1977 to 24 for men and 21.6 for women.

At the same time, divorces have increased. By 1977, there was 84 people divorced for every 1,000 persons married and living with a spouse. The divorce rate increased 79% between 1970 and 1977.

In 1977, more than 17 million people maintained their own households or lived with people unrelated to them.

# U.S. STATISTICS

## Population

### Colonial Population Estimates (round numbers)

| Year | Population | Year | Population | Year | Population | Year | Population |
|---|---|---|---|---|---|---|---|
| 1610 | 350 | 1660 | 75,100 | 1710 | 331,700 | 1760 | 1,593,600 |
| 1620 | 2,300 | 1670 | 111,900 | 1720 | 466,200 | 1770 | 2,148,100 |
| 1630 | 4,600 | 1680 | 151,500 | 1730 | 629,400 | 1780 | 2,780,400 |
| 1640 | 26,600 | 1690 | 210,400 | 1740 | 905,600 | | |
| 1650 | 50,400 | 1700 | 250,900 | 1750 | 1,170,800 | | |

### National Censuses[1]

| Year | Resident population[2] | Land area, sq. mi. | Pop. per sq. mi. | Year | Resident population[2] | Land area, sq. mi. | Pop. per sq. mi. |
|---|---|---|---|---|---|---|---|
| 1790 | 3,929,214 | 864,746 | 4.5 | 1890 | 62,947,714 | 2,969,640 | 21.2 |
| 1800 | 5,308,483 | 864,746 | 6.1 | 1900 | 75,994,575 | 2,969,834 | 25.6 |
| 1810 | 7,239,881 | 1,681,828 | 4.3 | 1910 | 91,972,266 | 2,969,565 | 31.0 |
| 1820 | 9,638,453 | 1,749,462 | 5.5 | 1920 | 105,710,620 | 2,969,451 | 35.6 |
| 1830 | 12,866,020 | 1,749,462 | 7.4 | 1930 | 122,775,046 | 2,977,128 | 41.2 |
| 1840 | 17,069,453 | 1,749,462 | 9.8 | 1940 | 131,669,275 | 2,977,128 | 44.2 |
| 1850 | 23,191,876 | 2,940,042 | 7.9 | 1950 | 150,697,361 | 2,974,726 | 50.7 |
| 1860 | 31,443,321 | 2,969,640 | 10.6 | 1960 | 170,323,175 | 3,540,911 | 50.6 |
| 1870 | 39,818,449 | 2,969,640 | 13.4 | 1970 | 203,235,298 | 3,536,855 | 57.5 |
| 1880 | 50,155,783 | 2,969,640 | 16.9 | | | | |

1. Beginning with 1960, figures include Alaska and Hawaii. 2. Excludes armed forces overseas. *Source:* Department of Commerce, Bureau of the Census.

### Population Projections, 1980–2000[1]
(in millions)

| Race, sex, age group | 1980 | 1982 | 1984 | 1986 | 1988 | 1990 | 1995 | 2000 |
|---|---|---|---|---|---|---|---|---|
| **MALE, WHITE** | 93.6 | 95.1 | 96.7 | 98.2 | 99.8 | 101.2 | 104.4 | 106.9 |
| Up to 19 years | 29.9 | 29.5 | 29.3 | 29.5 | 29.9 | 30.3 | 31.6 | 32.3 |
| 20 to 39 years | 30.8 | 32.1 | 33.0 | 33.5 | 33.2 | 33.1 | 31.6 | 29.6 |
| 40 to 59 years | 19.7 | 19.8 | 20.3 | 20.6 | 21.8 | 22.7 | 26.0 | 29.6 |
| 60 to 79 years | 11.7 | 12.2 | 12.6 | 12.9 | 13.1 | 13.2 | 13.2 | 13.2 |
| 80 years and over | 1.5 | 1.6 | 1.6 | 1.7 | 1.8 | 1.9 | 2.1 | 2.3 |
| **FEMALE, WHITE** | 98.0 | 99.5 | 101.2 | 102.8 | 104.5 | 106.0 | 109.4 | 112.0 |
| Up to 19 years | 29.0 | 28.2 | 28.0 | 28.1 | 28.5 | 28.8 | 30.0 | 30.7 |
| 20 to 39 years | 30.5 | 31.8 | 32.6 | 33.2 | 32.9 | 32.8 | 31.3 | 29.3 |
| 40 to 59 years | 20.7 | 20.8 | 21.2 | 21.4 | 22.5 | 23.5 | 26.8 | 30.4 |
| 60 to 79 years | 15.0 | 15.6 | 16.1 | 16.5 | 16.7 | 16.8 | 16.7 | 16.6 |
| 80 years and over | 3.1 | 3.3 | 3.4 | 3.6 | 3.8 | 4.0 | 4.5 | 4.9 |
| **MALE, BLACK** | 12.5 | 12.8 | 13.2 | 13.5 | 13.9 | 14.2 | 15.0 | 15.6 |
| Up to 19 years | 5.2 | 5.2 | 5.2 | 5.2 | 5.3 | 5.3 | 5.4 | 5.5 |
| 20 to 39 years | 3.9 | 4.1 | 4.3 | 4.6 | 4.7 | 4.7 | 4.8 | 4.7 |
| 40 to 59 years | 2.1 | 2.2 | 2.3 | 2.3 | 2.4 | 2.6 | 3.1 | 3.7 |
| 60 to 79 years | 1.1 | 1.2 | 1.2 | 1.3 | 1.3 | 1.4 | 1.4 | 1.5 |
| 80 years and over | 0.1 | 0.1 | 0.1 | 0.1 | 0.2 | 0.2 | 0.2 | 0.2 |

| Race, sex, age group | 1980 | 1982 | 1984 | 1986 | 1988 | 1990 | 1995 | 2000 |
|---|---|---|---|---|---|---|---|---|
| **FEMALE, BLACK** | 13.7 | 14.1 | 14.5 | 14.9 | 15.2 | 15.6 | 16.5 | 17.2 |
| Up to 19 years | 5.1 | 5.1 | 5.1 | 5.2 | 5.1 | 5.2 | 5.2 | 5.3 |
| 20 to 39 years | 4.4 | 4.7 | 4.9 | 5.1 | 5.3 | 5.4 | 5.4 | 5.3 |
| 40 to 59 years | 2.5 | 2.5 | 2.6 | 2.7 | 2.8 | 3.0 | 3.6 | 4.3 |
| 60 to 79 years | 1.4 | 1.5 | 1.6 | 1.7 | 1.7 | 1.8 | 1.9 | 2.0 |
| 80 years and over | 0.3 | 0.3 | 0.3 | 0.3 | 0.3 | 0.3 | 0.4 | 0.4 |
| Total white | 191.6 | 194.6 | 197.8 | 201.1 | 204.2 | 207.3 | 213.8 | 218.9 |
| Total black | 26.2 | 26.9 | 27.6 | 28.4 | 29.1 | 29.8 | 31.4 | 32.8 |
| **Total United States[2]** | **222.2** | **226.3** | **230.7** | **235.1** | **239.4** | **243.5** | **252.8** | **260.4** |
| Median age | 30.2 | 30.7 | 31.2 | 31.7 | 32.3 | 32.8 | 34.2 | 35.5 |

1. Based on average of 2.1 lifetime births per woman. 2. Includes all races. *Source:* Department of Commerce, Bureau of the Census.

## Population of Large Metropolitan Areas

(in thousands)

| Standard metropolitan statistical area | Population: July 1, 1975 Total | July 1, 1975 Rank | April 1970 | April 1960 | Population change 1970–1975: Number | 1970–1975: Per-cent | 1970–1975: Net migration | 1960–1970: Number | 1960–1970: per cent | 1960–1970: Net migration |
|---|---|---|---|---|---|---|---|---|---|---|
| Akron, Ohio | 667 | 55 | 679 | 605 | —12 | —1.8 | —36 | 74 | 12.2 | 1 |
| Albany-Schenectady-Troy, N.Y. | 798 | 44 | 778 | 715 | 20 | 2.6 | 6 | 63 | 8.8 | 9 |
| Albuquerque, N.M. | 385 | 93 | 333 | 276 | 51 | 15.4 | 29 | 57 | 20.6 | 17 |
| Allentown-Bethlehem-Easton, Pa.-N.J. | 624 | 59 | 594 | 545 | 29 | 4.9 | 21 | 49 | 9.0 | 16 |
| Anaheim-Santa Ana-Garden Grove, Calif. | 1,700 | 19 | 1,421 | 704 | 278 | 19.6 | 200 | 717 | 101.9 | 553 |
| Ann Arbor, Mich. | 245 | 144 | 234 | 172 | 11 | 4.5 | —3 | 62 | 35.8 | 32 |
| Appleton-Oshkosh, Wis. | 284 | 124 | 277 | 232 | 7 | 2.4 | —4 | 45 | 19.4 | 9 |
| Atlanta | 1,790 | 18 | 1,596 | 1,169 | 195 | 12.2 | 100 | 426 | 36.5 | 233 |
| Augusta, Ga.-S.C. | 280 | 125 | 276 | 230 | 4 | 1.4 | —11 | 46 | 19.9 | 12 |
| Austin, Tex. | 397 | 90 | 323 | 232 | 74 | 22.8 | 52 | 91 | 39.3 | 51 |
| Bakersfield, Calif. | 350 | 102 | 330 | 292 | 20 | 6.0 | 3 | 38 | 13.1 | —5 |
| Baltimore | 2,148 | 14 | 2,071 | 1,804 | 77 | 3.7 | 22 | 267 | 14.8 | 54 |
| Baton Rouge, La. | 412 | 86 | 376 | 300 | 36 | 9.6 | 12 | 76 | 25.3 | 21 |
| Beaumont, Port Arthur-Orange, Tex. | 351 | 101 | 348 | 331 | 3 | 0.9 | —10 | 17 | 5.1 | —25 |
| Binghamton, N.Y.-Pa. | 304 | 114 | 303 | 284 | 1 | 0.5 | —7 | 19 | 6.7 | —12 |
| Birmingham, Ala. | 791 | 45 | 767 | 747 | 24 | 3.1 | (1) | 21 | 2.8 | —52 |
| Boston | 2,890 | 8 | 2,899 | 2,688 | —9 | —.3 | —63 | 211 | 7.9 | n.a. |
| Boston-Lowell-Brockton-Lawrence-Haverhill, Mass.-N.H.[2] | 3.914 | — | 3,849 | 3,457 | 65 | 1.7 | —16 | 392 | 11.3 | 61 |
| Bridgeport, Conn. | 395 | 91 | 402 | 350 | —5 | —1.1 | —14 | 52 | 14.7 | n.a. |
| Bridgeport-Stamford-Norwalk-Danbury, Conn.[2] | 799 | — | 793 | 654 | 7 | 0.8 | —11 | 139 | 21.3 | 72 |
| Buffalo, N.Y. | 1,327 | 27 | 1,349 | 1,307 | —22 | —1.7 | —49 | 42 | 3.2 | —82 |
| Canton, Ohio | 400 | 89 | 394 | 361 | 7 | 1.7 | —6 | 33 | 9.0 | —3 |
| Charleston-North Charleston, S.C. | 371 | 97 | 336 | 279 | 35 | 10.5 | 12 | 57 | 20.5 | —1 |
| Charleston, W.Va. | 256 | 139 | 257 | 276 | —1 | —.5 | —8 | —19 | —7.0 | —46 |
| Charlotte-Gastonia, N.C. | 593 | 61 | 558 | 444 | 35 | 6.3 | 6 | 114 | 25.7 | 45 |
| Chattanooga, Tenn.-Ga. | 392 | 92 | 371 | 340 | 21 | 5.7 | 5 | 31 | 9.1 | —7 |
| Chicago | 7,015 | 2 | 6,978 | 6,221 | 38 | 0.5 | —225 | 757 | 12.2 | 18 |
| Cincinnati, Ohio-Ky.-Ind. | 1,381 | 25 | 1,385 | 1,268 | —6 | —0.4 | —55 | 117 | 9.2 | —34 |
| Cleveland | 1,967 | 17 | 2,064 | 1,909 | —97 | —4.7 | —152 | 154 | 8.1 | —44 |
| Colorado Springs, Colo. | 287 | 121 | 239 | 146 | 47 | 19.8 | 26 | 93 | 63.6 | 62 |
| Columbia, S.C. | 365 | 99 | 323 | 261 | 42 | 13.1 | 23 | 62 | 23.8 | 24 |
| Columbus, Ga.-Ala. | 222 | 154 | 239 | 218 | —17 | —6.9 | —31 | 21 | 9.5 | —22 |
| Columbus, Ohio | 1,069 | 35 | 1,018 | 845 | 51 | 5.0 | 1 | 173 | 20.4 | 52 |
| Corpus Christi, Tex. | 299 | 117 | 285 | 267 | 14 | 4.9 | —9 | 18 | 6.8 | —33 |
| Dallas-Ft. Worth | 2,527 | 10 | 2,378 | 1,738 | 150 | 6.3 | 17 | 640 | 36.8 | 368 |
| Davenport-Rock Island-Moline, Iowa-Ill. | 370 | 98 | 363 | 319 | 8 | 2.1 | —5 | 43 | 13.5 | 6 |
| Dayton, Ohio | 836 | 43 | 853 | 727 | —17 | —2.0 | —53 | 125 | 17.2 | 27 |
| Denver-Boulder, Colo. | 1,413 | 22 | 1,239 | 935 | 174 | 14.0 | 112 | 305 | 32.6 | 165 |
| Des Moines, Iowa | 328 | 110 | 314 | 287 | 15 | 4.7 | 2 | 26 | 9.2 | —8 |
| Detroit | 4,424 | 5 | 4,435 | 3,950 | —11 | —0.2 | —192 | 485 | 12.3 | —17 |
| Duluth-Superior, Minn.-Wis. | 261 | 138 | 265 | 277 | —5 | —1.8 | —8 | —11 | —4.1 | —30 |

| Standard metropolitan statistical area | Population | | | | Population Change | | | | | |
|---|---|---|---|---|---|---|---|---|---|---|
| | July 1, 1975 | | April 1970 | April 1960 | 1970–1975 | | | 1960–1970 | | |
| | Total | Rank | | | Number | Percent | Net migration | Number | Per cent | Net migration |
| El Paso | 424 | 83 | 359 | 314 | 65 | 18.1 | 28 | 45 | 14.4 | —29 |
| Erie, Pa. | 273 | 130 | 264 | 251 | 10 | 3.7 | (1) | 13 | 5.2 | —13 |
| Eugene-Springfield, Ore. | 238 | 145 | 215 | 163 | 23 | 10.5 | 13 | 53 | 32.2 | 29 |
| Evansville, Ind.-Ky. | 288 | 119 | 285 | 272 | 3 | 1.0 | —4 | 13 | 4.7 | —9 |
| Fayetteville, N.C. | 226 | 151 | 212 | 148 | 14 | 6.7 | —7 | 64 | 42.9 | 21 |
| Flint, Mich. | 519 | 71 | 509 | 428 | 10 | 2.0 | —19 | 81 | 18.9 | 6 |
| Fort Lauderdale-Hollywood, Fla. | 848 | 42 | 620 | 334 | 228 | 36.8 | 222 | 286 | 85.7 | 257 |
| Fort Wayne, Ind. | 373 | 96 | 362 | 306 | 11 | 3.1 | —8 | 56 | 18.2 | 12 |
| Fresno, Calif. | 446 | 77 | 413 | 366 | 32 | 7.8 | 12 | 47 | 12.9 | —3 |
| Gary-Hammond-East Chicago, Ind. | 643 | 57 | 633 | 574 | 10 | 1.5 | —22 | 60 | 10.4 | —24 |
| Grand Rapids, Mich. | 564 | 67 | 539 | 462 | 25 | 4.6 | (1) | 77 | 16.7 | 11 |
| Greensboro-Winston-Salem-High Point, N.C. | 764 | 49 | 724 | 622 | 40 | 5.5 | 11 | 102 | 16.4 | 20 |
| Greenville-Spartanburg, S.C. | 525 | 70 | 473 | 413 | 52 | 11.0 | 30 | 61 | 14.7 | 7 |
| Hamilton-Middletown, Ohio | 245 | 143 | 226 | 199 | 18 | 8.1 | 7 | 27 | 13.6 | 1 |
| Harrisburg, Pa. | 427 | 82 | 411 | 372 | 16 | 3.9 | 6 | 39 | 10.5 | 7 |
| Hartford, Conn. | 732 | 52 | 721 | 588 | 11 | 0.2 | —10 | 132 | 22.5 | n.a. |
| Hartford-New Britain-Bristol, Conn.[2] | 1,063 | — | 1,035 | 847 | 27 | 2.6 | —2 | 188 | 22.2 | 83 |
| Honolulu | 705 | 53 | 631 | 500 | 75 | 11.9 | 24 | 130 | 26.0 | 18 |
| Houston | 2,286 | 13 | 1,999 | 1,430 | 287 | 14.4 | 152 | 569 | 39.8 | 317 |
| Huntington-Ashland, W.Va.-Ky.-Ohio | 290 | 118 | 287 | 284 | 3 | 1.0 | —6 | 3 | 1.0 | —24 |
| Huntsville, Ala. | 286 | 122 | 282 | 202 | 3 | 1.1 | —11 | 81 | 39.9 | 38 |
| Indianapolis | 1,139 | 32 | 1,111 | 944 | 27 | 2.5 | —24 | 167 | 17.7 | 38 |
| Jackson, Miss. | 285 | 123 | 259 | 221 | 26 | 10.2 | 11 | 38 | 17.0 | (1) |
| Jacksonville, Fla. | 693 | 54 | 622 | 530 | 71 | 11.4 | 39 | 92 | 17.4 | 13 |
| Jersey City, N.J. | 578 | 65 | 608 | 611 | 30 | —5.0 | —41 | —3 | —0.5 | —46 |
| Johnson City-Kingsport-Bristol, Tenn.-Va. | 401 | 88 | 374 | 347 | 27 | 7.2 | 13 | 26 | 7.6 | —11 |
| Johnstown, Pa. | 267 | 138 | 263 | 281 | 4 | 1.4 | —1 | —18 | —6.4 | —33 |
| Kalamazoo-Portage, Mich. | 263 | 137 | 258 | 218 | 5 | 2.1 | —6 | 40 | 18.2 | 12 |
| Kansas City, Mo.-Kan. | 1,290 | 28 | 1,274 | 1,109 | 16 | 1.3 | —36 | 165 | 14.9 | 31 |
| Killeen-Temple, Tex. | 201 | 159 | 160 | 118 | 42 | 26.0 | 23 | 42 | 35.4 | 15 |
| Knoxville, Tenn. | 435 | 81 | 409 | 377 | 26 | 6.4 | 13 | 33 | 8.7 | —7 |
| Lakeland-Winter Haven, Fla. | 274 | 129 | 229 | 195 | 45 | 19.9 | 37 | 33 | 17.1 | 12 |
| Lancaster, Pa. | 343 | 107 | 320 | 278 | 23 | 7.1 | 11 | 42 | 15.0 | 11 |
| Lansing-East Lansing, Mich. | 445 | 78 | 424 | 342 | 21 | 4.9 | —2 | 82 | 24.0 | 28 |
| Las Vegas, Nev. | 331 | 109 | 273 | 127 | 57 | 21.0 | 39 | 146 | 115.2 | 110 |
| Lawrence-Haverhill, Mass.-N.H. | 270 | 132 | 259 | 218 | 12 | 4.5 | 6 | 40 | 18.4 | n.a. |
| Lexington-Fayette, Ky. | 287 | 120 | 267 | 212 | 21 | 7.8 | 8 | 55 | 25.8 | 26 |
| Lima, Ohio | 212 | 156 | 210 | 197 | 1 | 0.7 | —7 | 13 | 6.6 | —10 |
| Little Rock-North Little Rock, Ark. | 348 | 104 | 323 | 272 | 25 | 7.8 | 6 | 51 | 18.9 | 12 |
| Long Branch-Asbury Park, N.J. | 492 | 73 | 462 | 334 | 30 | 6.5 | 17 | 127 | 38.1 | 89 |
| Lorain-Elyria, Ohio | 269 | 134 | 257 | 218 | 12 | 4.6 | —2 | 39 | 18.1 | 6 |
| Los Angeles-Long Beach, Calif. | 6,987 | 3 | 7,042 | 6,039 | —55 | —0.8 | —321 | 1,003 | 16.6 | 269 |
| Louisville, Ky.-Ind. | 888 | 39 | 867 | 754 | 21 | 2.4 | —14 | 113 | 15.0 | 21 |
| Macon, Ga. | 237 | 146 | 227 | 197 | 11 | 4.7 | —1 | 30 | 15.2 | (1) |
| Madison, Wis. | 302 | 115 | 290 | 222 | 11 | 3.9 | —1 | 68 | 30.7 | 29 |
| McAllen-Pharr-Edinburg, Tex. | 228 | 449 | 182 | 181 | 46 | 25.5 | 22 | 1 | 0.4 | —43 |
| Melbourne-Titusville-Cocoa, Fla. | 232 | 148 | 230 | 111 | 2 | 0.8 | —6 | 119 | 106.4 | 87 |
| Memphis, Tenn.-Ark.-Miss. | 867 | 41 | 834 | 727 | 33 | 3.9 | —10 | 107 | 14.7 | —4 |
| Miami, Fla. | 1,439 | 21 | 1,268 | 935 | 172 | 13.5 | 150 | 333 | 35.6 | 255 |
| Milwaukee | 1,409 | 23 | 1,404 | 1,279 | 5 | 0.4 | —41 | 125 | 9.8 | —37 |
| Minneapolis-St. Paul | 2,011 | 15 | 1,965 | 1,598 | 45 | 2.3 | —40 | 368 | 23.0 | 118 |
| Mobile, Ala. | 403 | 87 | 377 | 363 | 27 | 7.1 | 7 | 13 | 3.7 | 42 |
| Modesto, Calif. | 224 | 153 | 195 | 157 | 29 | 15.0 | 21 | 37 | 23.7 | 19 |
| Montgomery, Ala. | 250 | 141 | 226 | 218 | 24 | 10.8 | 14 | 7 | 3.4 | —18 |
| Nashville-Davidson, Tenn. | 748 | 50 | 699 | 597 | 59 | 7.0 | 21 | 102 | 17.2 | 30 |
| Nassau-Suffolk, N.Y. | 2,657 | 9 | 2,556 | 1,967 | 101 | 4.0 | 35 | 589 | 29.9 | 359 |
| Newark, N.J. | 1,999 | 16 | 2,057 | 1,833 | —58 | —2.8 | —107 | 224 | 12.2 | 47 |
| New Bedford-Fall River, Mass.[2] | 464 | — | 444 | 398 | 20 | 4.4 | 9 | 46 | 11.5 | 15 |
| New Brunswick-Perth Amboy-Sayreville, N.J. | 593 | 60 | 584 | 434 | 9 | 1.5 | —11 | 150 | 34.6 | 87 |
| New Haven-West Haven, Conn | 414 | 85 | 411 | 359 | 3 | 0.8 | —5 | 52 | 14.4 | n.a. |
| New Haven-West Haven-Waterbury-Meriden, Conn.[2] | 760 | — | 745 | 660 | 15 | 2.1 | —2 | 85 | 12.8 | 20 |
| New London-Norwich, Conn.-R.I. | 252 | 140 | 242 | 196 | 10 | 4.0 | 1 | 46 | 23.2 | n.a. |
| New London-Norwich, Conn.[2] | 242 | — | 231 | 186 | 11 | 4.9 | 2 | 45 | 24.2 | 15 |

| Standard metropolitan statistical area | Population | | | | Population Change | | | | | |
|---|---|---|---|---|---|---|---|---|---|---|
| | July 1, 1975 | | April | April | 1970–1975 | | | 1960–1970 | | |
| | Total | Rank | 1970 | 1960 | Number | Per-cent | Net migration | Number | Per cent | Net migration |
| New Orleans | 1,094 | 33 | 1,046 | 907 | 48 | 4.6 | —2 | 139 | 15.4 | 11 |
| Newport News-Hampton, Va. | 347 | 106 | 333 | 255 | 14 | 4.2 | —5 | 78 | 30.8 | 31 |
| New York, N.Y.-N.J. | 9,561 | 1 | 9,974 | 9,540 | —413 | —4.1 | —609 | 434 | 4.5 | —319 |
| Norfolk-Virginia Beach-Portsmouth, Va.-N.C. | 773 | 48 | 733 | 629 | 40 | 5.5 | 1 | 104 | 16.5 | —2 |
| Northeast Pa. | 635 | 58 | 622 | 621 | 13 | 2.1 | 15 | 1 | 0.1 | —13 |
| Oklahoma City | 746 | 51 | 699 | 566 | 47 | 6.8 | 11 | 133 | 23.5 | 54 |
| Omaha, Neb.-Iowa | 573 | 66 | 543 | 458 | 31 | 5.7 | 2 | 85 | 18.5 | 9 |
| Orlando, Fla. | 583 | 64 | 453 | 338 | 129 | 28.6 | 108 | 116 | 34.3 | 70 |
| Oxnard-Simi Valley-Ventura, Calif. | 438 | 80 | 378 | 199 | 59 | 15.7 | 36 | 179 | 90.1 | 134 |
| Paterson-Clifton-Passaic, N.J. | 452 | 76 | 461 | 407 | —8 | —1.8 | —23 | 54 | 13.3 | 13 |
| Pensacola, Fla. | 269 | 133 | 243 | 203 | 26 | 10.8 | 11 | 40 | 19.5 | ([1]) |
| Peoria, Ill. | 354 | 100 | 342 | 313 | 12 | 3.5 | —2 | 29 | 9.1 | —8 |
| Philadelphia, Pa.-N.J. | 4,807 | 4 | 4,824 | 4,343 | —17 | —0.4 | —131 | 481 | 11.1 | 57 |
| Phoenix, Ariz. | 1,221 | 30 | 969 | 664 | 250 | 25.8 | 192 | 306 | 46.1 | 190 |
| Pittsburgh | 2,322 | 12 | 2,401 | 2,405 | —79 | —3.3 | —103 | —4 | —0.2 | —166 |
| Portland, Me.[2] | 228 | — | 216 | 206 | 12 | 5.8 | 6 | 10 | 5.1 | —9 |
| Portland, Ore.-Wash. | 1,083 | 34 | 1,007 | 822 | 76 | 7.5 | 47 | 185 | 22.5 | 117 |
| Poughkeepsie, N.Y. | 235 | 147 | 222 | 176 | 12 | 5.5 | 5 | 46 | 26.3 | 26 |
| Providence-Warwick-Pawtucket, R.I.-Mass. | 904 | 38 | 909 | 821 | —5 | —0.6 | —23 | 88 | 10.7 | n.a. |
| Providence-Warwick-Pawtucket, R.I.[2] | 853 | — | 855 | 778 | —3 | —0.3 | —19 | 78 | 10.0 | 12 |
| Raleigh-Durham, N.C. | 469 | 74 | 419 | 324 | 49 | 11.8 | 31 | 95 | 29.4 | 49 |
| Reading, Pa. | 305 | 113 | 296 | 275 | 9 | 2.9 | 5 | 21 | 7.6 | 6 |
| Richmond, Va. | 585 | 63 | 542 | 457 | 38 | 6.9 | 21 | 85 | 18.5 | 34 |
| Riverside-San Bernardino-Ontario, Calif. | 1,226 | 29 | 1,141 | 810 | 87 | 7.6 | 42 | 332 | 40.9 | 216 |
| Roanoke, Va. | 212 | 155 | 203 | 179 | 9 | 4.4 | 4 | 24 | 13.6 | 9 |
| Rochester, N.Y. | 971 | 37 | 962 | 801 | 10 | 10.3 | —22 | 161 | 20.1 | 68 |
| Rockford, Ill. | 272 | 131 | 272 | 230 | ([1]) | —0.2 | —14 | 42 | 18.2 | 8 |
| Sacramento, Calif. | 880 | 40 | 804 | 626 | 76 | 9.5 | 45 | 178 | 28.5 | 89 |
| Saginaw, Mich. | 227 | 150 | 220 | 191 | 7 | 3.2 | —5 | 29 | 15.2 | 2 |
| Salem, Ore. | 206 | 157 | 189 | 147 | 19 | 10.3 | 14 | 39 | 26.6 | 26 |
| Salinas-Seaside-Monterey, Calif. | 268 | 135 | 247 | 198 | 20 | 8.2 | 5 | 49 | 24.8 | 16 |
| Salt Lake City, Utah | 783 | 46 | 705 | 576 | 77 | 11.0 | 10 | 129 | 22.4 | 8 |
| San Antonio | 982 | 36 | 888 | 736 | 93 | 10.5 | 29 | 152 | 20.7 | 18 |
| San Diego, Calif. | 1,585 | 20 | 1,358 | 1,033 | 227 | 16.7 | 165 | 325 | 31.4 | 169 |
| San Francisco-Oakland, Calif. | 3,140 | 6 | 3,109 | 2,649 | 31 | 1.0 | —44 | 460 | 17.4 | 184 |
| San Jose, Calif. | 1,174 | 31 | 1,065 | 642 | 109 | 10.2 | 53 | 423 | 65.9 | 285 |
| Santa Barbara-Santa Maria-Lompoc, Calif. | 280 | 126 | 264 | 169 | 15 | 5.8 | 6 | 95 | 56.4 | 65 |
| Santa Rosa, Calif. | 247 | 142 | 205 | 147 | 42 | 20.3 | 37 | 58 | 39.0 | 45 |
| Seattle-Everett, Wash. | 1,407 | 24 | 1,425 | 1,107 | —18 | —1.3 | —58 | 317 | 28.7 | 188 |
| Shreveport, La. | 349 | 103 | 334 | 321 | 13 | 3.9 | —4 | 13 | 3.9 | —32 |
| South Bend, Ind. | 279 | 127 | 280 | 271 | —1 | —0.5 | —10 | 9 | 3.3 | —18 |
| Spokane, Wash. | 306 | 112 | 287 | 278 | 19 | 6.6 | 9 | 9 | 3.3 | 14 |
| Springfield-Chicopee-Holyoke, Mass.-Conn. | 549 | 68 | 542 | 504 | 7 | 1.4 | —4 | 38 | 7.5 | n.a. |
| Springfield-Chicopee-Holyoke, Mass.[2] | 597 | — | 542 | 504 | 14 | 2.5 | 2 | 38 | 7.5 | n.a. |
| St. Louis, Mo.-Ill. | 2,367 | 11 | 2,411 | 2,144 | —44 | —1.8 | —122 | 266 | 12.4 | 24 |
| Stamford, Conn. | 203 | 158 | 206 | 178 | —3 | —1.7 | —6 | 28 | 15.7 | n.a. |
| Stockton, Calif. | 300 | 116 | 291 | 250 | 9 | 2.9 | —1 | 41 | 16.4 | 16 |
| Syracuse, N.Y. | 648 | 56 | 637 | 564 | 11 | 1.8 | —10 | 73 | 12.9 | 2 |
| Tacoma, Wash. | 416 | 84 | 412 | 322 | 3 | 0.8 | —15 | 91 | 28.2 | 46 |
| Tampa-St. Petersburg, Fla. | 1,348 | 26 | 1,089 | 809 | 259 | 23.8 | 263 | 279 | 34.5 | 253 |
| Toledo, Ohio-Mich. | 779 | 47 | 763 | 695 | 16 | 2.1 | —15 | 67 | 9.7 | —8 |
| Trenton, N.J. | 318 | 111 | 304 | 266 | 14 | 4.7 | 6 | 38 | 14.2 | 12 |
| Tucson, Ariz. | 444 | 79 | 352 | 266 | 92 | 26.2 | 73 | 86 | 32.3 | 48 |
| Tulsa, Okla. | 586 | 62 | 549 | 475 | 37 | 6.7 | 15 | 74 | 15.5 | 25 |
| Utica-Rome, N.Y. | 334 | 108 | 341 | 331 | —6 | —1.9 | —14 | 10 | 3.0 | —21 |
| Vallejo-Fairfield-Napa, Calif. | 277 | 128 | 251 | 200 | 26 | 10.5 | 15 | 51 | 25.3 | 20 |
| Washington, D.C.-Md.-Va. | 3,022 | 7 | 2,910 | 2,097 | 112 | 3.8 | —27 | 813 | 38.8 | 427 |
| Waterbury, Conn. | 226 | 152 | 217 | 191 | 9 | 4.3 | 4 | 26 | 13.7 | n.a. |
| West Palm Beach-Boca Raton, Fla. | 455 | 75 | 349 | 228 | 106 | 30.5 | 103 | 121 | 53.0 | 101 |
| Wichita, Kan. | 385 | 94 | 389 | 382 | —4 | —1.1 | —22 | 8 | 2.0 | —46 |
| Wilmington, Del.-N.J.-Md. | 518 | 72 | 499 | 415 | 18 | 3.7 | ([1]) | 85 | 20.5 | 28 |
| Worcester, Mass. | 378 | 95 | 372 | 354 | 6 | 1.6 | —1 | 18 | 5.1 | n.a. |
| Worcester-Fitchburg-Leominster, Mass.[2] | 648 | — | 637 | 583 | 11 | 1.7 | —2 | 54 | 9.2 | 4 |

| Standard metropolitan statistical area | Population | | | | Population Change | | | | | |
|---|---|---|---|---|---|---|---|---|---|---|
| | July 1, 1975 | | April 1970 | April 1960 | 1970–1975 | | | 1960–1970 | | |
| | Total | Rank | | | Number | Percent | Net migration | Number | Per cent | Net migration |
| York, Pa. | 348 | 105 | 330 | 290 | 18 | 5.5 | 7 | 39 | 13.5 | 10 |
| Youngstown-Warren, Ohio | 549 | 69 | 537 | 509 | 11 | 2.1 | —4 | 28 | 5.5 | —18 |
| **STANDARD CONSOLIDATED STATISTICAL AREA** | | | | | | | | | | |
| Boston-Lawrence-Lowell, Mass.-N.H. | 3,553 | 7 | 3,526 | 3,169 | 27 | 0.8 | —45 | 357 | 11.3 | n.a. |
| Chicago-Gary, Ill.-Ind. | 7,658 | 3 | 7,611 | 6,794 | 48 | 0.6 | —248 | 817 | 12.0 | —6 |
| Cincinnati-Hamilton, Ohio-Ky.-Ind. | 1,626 | 12 | 1,611 | 1,468 | 12 | 0.8 | —48 | 141 | 9.8 | —33 |
| Cleveland-Akron-Lorain, Ohio | 2,902 | 8 | 3,000 | 2,732 | —97 | —3.3 | —191 | 267 | 9.8 | —36 |
| Detroit-Ann Arbor, Mich. | 4,669 | 5 | 4,669 | 4,122 | (1) | (1) | —195 | 547 | 13.3 | 14 |
| Houston-Galveston, Tex.[3] | 2,469 | 9 | 2,169 | 1,571 | 300 | 13.9 | 158 | 598 | 38.1 | 328 |
| Los Angeles-Long Beach-Anaheim, Calif.[4] | 10,350 | 2 | 9,983 | 7,752 | 370 | 3.7 | —43 | 2,231 | 28.8 | 1,172 |
| Miami-Fort Lauderdale, Fla. | 2,288 | 10 | 1,888 | 1,269 | 400 | 21.2 | 373 | 619 | 48.8 | 512 |
| Milwaukee-Racine, Wis. | 1,585 | 13 | 1,575 | 1,421 | 10 | 0.7 | —43 | 154 | 10.9 | —29 |
| New York-Newark-Jersey City, N.Y.-N.J.-Conn.[5] | 16,662 | 1 | 17,035 | 15,405 | —373 | —2.2 | —748 | 1,631 | 10.6 | 265 |
| Philadelphia-Wilmington-Trenton, Pa.-Del.-Md.-N.J. | 5,643 | 4 | 5,628 | 5,024 | 16 | 0.3 | —124 | 604 | 12.0 | 98 |
| San Francisco-Oakland-San Jose, Calif.[6] | 4,592 | 6 | 4,423 | 3,492 | 166 | 3.8 | 25 | 932 | 26.7 | 487 |
| Seattle-Tacoma, Wash. | 1,822 | 11 | 1,837 | 1,429 | —14 | —0.8 | —73 | 408 | 28.6 | 235 |

1. Less than 500 or .05 percent. 2. New England County Metropolitan Area; not included in rank. 3. Includes Galveston-Texas City SMSA. 4. Includes Oxnard-Simi Valley-Ventura SMSA and Riverside-San Bernardino-Ontario SMSA. 5. Includes Nassau-Suffolk SMSA, Long Branch-Asbury Park SMSA, New Brunswick-Perth Amboy-Sayreville SMSA, Patterson-Clifton-Passaic SMSA, and Stamford and Norwalk SMSAs. 6. Includes Vallejo-Fairfield-Napa SMSA. NOTE: Covers 159 large SMSAs with estimated population of 200,000 or more as of July 1, 1975. Rank based on unrounded figures. *Source:* Department of Commerce, Bureau of the Census

## Population by Age, Sex, and Race, 1977
(in thousands)

| Age | White | | Black | | Other races | | All persons | |
|---|---|---|---|---|---|---|---|---|
| | Male | Female | Male | Female | Male | Female | Male | Female |
| Under 5 | 6,424 | 6,111 | 1,172 | 1,144 | 194 | 190 | 7,790 | 7,446 |
| Under 1 | 1,345 | 1,276 | 235 | 228 | 40 | 38 | 1,620 | 1,542 |
| 1-4 | 5,079 | 4,835 | 937 | 916 | 155 | 152 | 6,170 | 5,904 |
| 5-9 | 7,293 | 6,958 | 1,278 | 1,264 | 190 | 187 | 8,760 | 8,409 |
| 10-14 | 8,200 | 7,843 | 1,411 | 1,394 | 179 | 174 | 9,790 | 9,411 |
| 15-19 | 9,106 | 8,787 | 1,450 | 1,446 | 193 | 185 | 10,749 | 10,418 |
| 20-24 | 8,692 | 8,476 | 1,216 | 1,297 | 197 | 197 | 10,104 | 9,969 |
| 25-29 | 7,725 | 7,636 | 929 | 1,060 | 173 | 210 | 8,827 | 8,906 |
| 30-34 | 6,750 | 6,738 | 729 | 859 | 158 | 181 | 7,637 | 7,778 |
| 35-39 | 5,318 | 5,450 | 609 | 736 | 103 | 126 | 6,030 | 6,311 |
| 40-44 | 4,818 | 4,956 | 555 | 665 | 92 | 115 | 5,466 | 5,736 |
| 45-49 | 4,977 | 5,164 | 546 | 622 | 91 | 111 | 5,614 | 5,897 |
| 50-54 | 5,115 | 5,475 | 519 | 599 | 79 | 92 | 5,713 | 6,166 |
| 55–59 | 4,759 | 5,181 | 451 | 520 | 60 | 64 | 5,269 | 5,765 |
| 60-64 | 3,979 | 4,500 | 357 | 438 | 45 | 43 | 4,381 | 4,981 |
| 65-69 | 3,342 | 4,201 | 358 | 476 | 39 | 31 | 3,739 | 4,708 |
| 70-74 | 2,365 | 3,259 | 199 | 251 | 33 | 29 | 2,597 | 3,540 |
| 75-79 | 1,448 | 2,296 | 113 | 155 | 28 | 28 | 1,589 | 2,479 |
| 80-84 | 897 | 1,633 | 78 | 124 | 15 | 16 | 989 | 1,774 |
| 85 and over | 583 | 1,292 | 60 | 119 | 12 | 13 | 655 | 1,424 |
| All ages | 91,791 | 95,957 | 12,030 | 13,169 | 1,878 | 1,993 | 105,699 | 111,119 |
| 14 and over | 71,651 | 76,745 | 8,470 | 9,663 | 1,351 | 1,476 | 81,471 | 87,883 |
| 18 and over | 64,436 | 69,833 | 7,279 | 8,490 | 1,201 | 1,332 | 72,916 | 79,655 |
| 21 and over | 58,885 | 64,439 | 6,436 | 7,631 | 1,080 | 1,220 | 66,400 | 73,290 |
| 65 and over | 8,635 | 12,681 | 808 | 1,125 | 126 | 118 | 9,569 | 13,925 |
| Median age | 29.0 | 31.6 | 22.9 | 25.2 | 24.7 | 26.5 | 28.2 | 30.6 |

NOTE: Figures represent resident population of the 50 states and Armed Forces overseas. *Source:* Department of Commerce, Bureau of the Census.

## Population by State

| State | 1970 | Percent change, 1960–70 | Pop. per sq mi., 1970 | Pop. rank, 1970 | 1960 | 1950 | 1900 | 1790 |
|---|---|---|---|---|---|---|---|---|
| Alabama | 3,444,165 | 5.4 | 67.9 | 21 | 3,266,740 | 3,061,743 | 1,828,697 | — |
| Alaska | 302,173 | 33.6 | 0.5 | 50 | 226,167 | 128,643 | 63,592 | — |
| Arizona | 1,772,482 | 36.1 | 15.6 | 33 | 1,302,161 | 749,587 | 122,931 | — |
| Arkansas | 1,923,295 | 7.7 | 37.0 | 32 | 1,786,272 | 1,909,511 | 1,311,564 | — |
| California | 19,953,134 | 27.0 | 127.6 | 1 | 15,717,204 | 10,586,223 | 1,485,053 | — |
| Colorado | 2,207,259 | 25.8 | 21.3 | 30 | 1,753,947 | 1,325,089 | 539,700 | — |
| Connecticut | 3,032,217 | 19.6 | 623.7 | 24 | 2,535,234 | 2,007,280 | 908,420 | 237,946 |
| Delaware | 548,104 | 22.8 | 276.5 | 46 | 446,292 | 318,085 | 184,735 | 59,096 |
| D.C. | 756,510 | −1.0 | 12,401.8 | — | 763,956 | 802,178 | 278,718 | — |
| Florida | 6,789,443 | 37.1 | 125.5 | 9 | 4,951,560 | 2,771,305 | 528,542 | — |
| Georgia | 4,589,575 | 16.4 | 79.0 | 15 | 3,943,116 | 3,444,578 | 2,216,331 | 82,548 |
| Hawaii | 769,913 | 21.7 | 119.8 | 40 | 632,772 | 499,794 | 154,001 | — |
| Idaho | 713,008 | 6.9 | 8.6 | 42 | 667,191 | 588,637 | 161,772 | — |
| Illinois | 11,113,976 | 10.2 | 199.4 | 5 | 10,081,158 | 8,712,176 | 4,821,550 | — |
| Indiana | 5,193,669 | 11.4 | 143.9 | 11 | 4,662,498 | 3,934,224 | 2,516,462 | — |
| Iowa | 2,825,041 | 2.4 | 50.5 | 25 | 2,757,537 | 2,621,073 | 2,231,853 | — |
| Kansas | 2,249,071 | 3.2 | 27.5 | 28 | 2,178,611 | 1,905,299 | 1,470,495 | — |
| Kentucky | 3,219,311 | 6.0 | 81.2 | 23 | 3,038,156 | 2,944,806 | 2,147,174 | 73,677 |
| Louisiana | 3,643,180 | 11.9 | 81.1 | 20 | 3,257,022 | 2,683,516 | 1,381,625 | — |
| Maine | 993,663 | 2.5 | 32.1 | 38 | 969,265 | 913,774 | 694,466 | 96,540 |
| Maryland | 3,922,399 | 26.5 | 396.6 | 18 | 3,100,689 | 2,343,001 | 1,188,044 | 319,728 |
| Massachusetts | 5,689,170 | 10.5 | 727.0 | 10 | 5,148,578 | 4,690,514 | 2,805,346 | 378,787 |
| Michigan | 8,875,083 | 13.4 | 156.2 | 7 | 7,823,194 | 6,371,766 | 2,420,982 | — |
| Minnesota | 3,805,069 | 11.5 | 48.0 | 19 | 3,413,864 | 2,982,483 | 1,751,394 | — |
| Mississippi | 2,216,912 | 1.8 | 46.9 | 29 | 2,178,141 | 2,178,914 | 1,551,270 | — |
| Missouri | 4,677,399 | 8.3 | 67.8 | 13 | 4,319,813 | 3,954,653 | 3,106,665 | — |
| Montana | 694,409 | 2.9 | 4.8 | 43 | 674,767 | 591,024 | 243,329 | — |
| Nebraska | 1,483,791 | 5.1 | 19.4 | 35 | 1,411,330 | 1,325,510 | 1,066,300 | — |
| Nevada | 488,738 | 71.3 | 4.4 | 47 | 285,278 | 160,083 | 42,335 | — |
| New Hampshire | 737,681 | 21.5 | 81.7 | 41 | 606,921 | 533,242 | 411,588 | 141,885 |
| New Jersey | 7,168,164 | 18.2 | 953.1 | 8 | 6,066,782 | 4,835,329 | 1,883,669 | 184,139 |
| New Mexico | 1,016,000 | 6.8 | 8.4 | 37 | 951,023 | 681,187 | 195,310 | — |
| New York | 18,241,266 | 8.4 | 381.3 | 2 | 16,782,304 | 14,830,192 | 7,268,894 | 340,120 |
| North Carolina | 5,082,059 | 11.5 | 104.1 | 12 | 4,556,155 | 4,061,929 | 1,893,810 | 393,751 |
| North Dakota | 617,761 | −2.3 | 8.9 | 45 | 632,446 | 619,636 | 319,146 | — |
| Ohio | 10,652,017 | 9.7 | 260.0 | 6 | 9,706,397 | 7,946,627 | 4,157,545 | — |
| Oklahoma | 2,559,253 | 9.9 | 37.2 | 27 | 2,328,284 | 2,233,351 | 790,391[1] | — |
| Oregon | 2,091,385 | 18.2 | 21.7 | 31 | 1,768,687 | 1,521,341 | 413,536 | — |
| Pennsylvania | 11,793,909 | 4.2 | 262.3 | 3 | 11,319,366 | 10,498,012 | 6,302,115 | 434,373 |
| Rhode Island | 949,723 | 10.5 | 905.4 | 39 | 859,488 | 791,896 | 428,556 | 68,825 |
| South Carolina | 2,590,516 | 8.7 | 85.7 | 26 | 2,382,594 | 2,117,027 | 1,340,316 | 249,073 |
| South Dakota | 666,257 | −2.2 | 8.8 | 44 | 680,514 | 652,740 | 401,570 | — |
| Tennessee | 3,924,164 | 10.0 | 95.0 | 17 | 3,567,089 | 3,291,718 | 2,020,616 | 35,691 |
| Texas | 11,196,730 | 16.9 | 42.7 | 4 | 9,579,677 | 7,711,194 | 3,048,710 | — |
| Utah | 1,059,273 | 18.9 | 12.9 | 36 | 890,627 | 688,862 | 276,749 | — |
| Vermont | 444,732 | 14.1 | 48.0 | 48 | 389,881 | 377,747 | 343,641 | 85,425 |
| Virginia | 4,648,494 | 17.2 | 116.9 | 14 | 3,966,949 | 3,318,680 | 1,854,184 | 747,610 |
| Washington | 3,409,169 | 19.5 | 51.2 | 22 | 2,853,214 | 2,378,963 | 518,103 | — |
| West Virginia | 1,744,237 | −6.2 | 72.5 | 34 | 1,860,421 | 2,005,552 | 958,800 | — |
| Wisconsin | 4,417,933 | 11.8 | 81.1 | 16 | 3,951,777 | 3,434,575 | 2,069,042 | — |
| Wyoming | 332,416 | 0.7 | 3.4 | 49 | 330,066 | 290,529 | 92,531 | — |
| **Total U.S.** | **203,235,298** | **13.3** | **57.4** | — | **179,323,175** | **151,325,798** | **76,212,168** | **3,929,214** |

1. Includes population of Indian Territory: 1900, 392,960. NOTE: In April 1973, the Census Bureau reported that it had overlooked 5,300,000 people in the 1970 Census. However, by law, the total figure listed above is official. For estimated 1977 population and rank, *see* the individual states. *Source:* Department of Commerce, Bureau of the Census.

## Population Shifts

From 1970 to 1975, the population in *non*-metropolitan areas climbed from 53.5 million to 57 million. During this period, about 400,000 Americans left the larger cities to live in rural areas. By 1978, non-metro areas contained 28% of the U.S. population, according to the Conference Board.

The return to the country is not a stampede, but it does represent a significant shift from the 1960s, when the primary flow was from rural to metropolitan areas.

Although the rate of growth has slowed considerably since 1970, the most rapid population gains continue to be in the suburbs and areas ringing metropolitan areas.

# Population of Cities over 50,000

Asterisk denotes more than one ZIP code for a city and refers to general delivery. To find the ZIP code for a particular address, consult the ZIP code directory available in every post office. NOTE: U = unincorporated area; T = town. For latest population figures of many cities, see listing for individual states in The United States section.

| City and major ZIP code | 1970 census | 1970 rank | 1960 census | % change 1960–70 | 1940 census | 1920 census |
|---|---|---|---|---|---|---|
| Abilene, Tex. (79604*) | 89,653 | 181 | 90,368 | −0.8 | 26,612 | 10,274 |
| Akron, Ohio (44309*) | 275,425 | 52 | 290,351 | −5.1 | 244,791 | 208,435 |
| Alameda, Calif. (94501) | 70,968 | 260 | 63,855 | 11.1 | 36,256 | 28,806 |
| Albany, Ga. (31706*) | 72,263 | 249 | 55,890 | 29.9 | 19,055 | 11,555 |
| Albany, N.Y. (12201*) | 115,781 | 127 | 129,726 | −10.8 | 130,577 | 113,344 |
| Albuquerque, N.M. (87101*) | 243,751 | 59 | 201,189 | 21.2 | 35,449 | 15,157 |
| Alexandria, Va. (22313*) | 110,927 | 134 | 91,023 | 21.9 | 33,523 | 18,060 |
| Alhambra, Calif. (91802*) | 62,125 | 310 | 54,807 | 13.4 | 38,935 | 9,096 |
| Allentown, Pa. (18105*) | 109,871 | 139 | 108,347 | 1.4 | 96,904 | 73,502 |
| Altoona, Pa. (16603*) | 63,115 | 305 | 69,407 | −9.1 | 80,214 | 60,331 |
| Amarillo, Tex. (79105*) | 127,010 | 116 | 137,969 | −7.9 | 51,686 | 15,494 |
| Anaheim, Calif. (92803*) | 166,408 | 82 | 104,184 | 59.7 | 11,031 | 5,526 |
| Anderson, Ind. (46011*) | 70,787 | 261 | 49,061 | 44.3 | 41,572 | 29,767 |
| Ann Arbor, Mich. (48106*) | 100,035 | 157 | 67,340 | 48.5 | 29,815 | 19,516 |
| Appleton, Wis. (54911) | 57,143 | 342 | 48,411 | 18.0 | 28,436 | 19,561 |
| Arden, Calif. (U) (95825) | 82,492 | 209 | 73,352 | 12.5 | — | — |
| Arlington, Tex. (76010*) | 90,032 | 180 | 44,775 | 101.0 | 4,240 | 3,031 |
| Arlington, Va. (U) (22210*) | 174,284 | 78 | 163,401 | 6.9 | 26,615 | — |
| Arlington Heights, Ill. (60004*) | 64,884 | 294 | 27,878 | 132.7 | 5,668 | 2,250 |
| Asheville, N.C. (28801*) | 57,681 | 336 | 60,192 | −4.2 | 51,310 | 28,504 |
| Atlanta, Ga. (30301*) | 495,039 | 27 | 487,455 | 1.6 | 302,288 | 200,616 |
| Augusta, Ga. (30903*) | 59,864 | 344 | 70,626 | −15.2 | 65,919 | 52,548 |
| Aurora, Colo. (80010*) | 74,974 | 237 | 48,548 | 54.5 | 3,437 | 983 |
| Aurora, Ill. (60507*) | 74,182 | 241 | 63,715 | 16.4 | 47,710 | 36,397 |
| Austin, Tex. (78767*) | 251,808 | 57 | 186,545 | 35.0 | 87,930 | 34,876 |
| Bakersfield, Calif. (93302*) | 69,515 | 268 | 56,848 | 22.3 | 29,252 | 18,638 |
| Baltimore, Md. (21233*) | 905,787 | 7 | 939,024 | −3.5 | 859,100 | 733,826 |
| Baton Rouge, La. (70821*) | 165,921 | 83 | 152,419 | 8.9 | 34,719 | 21,782 |
| Bayonne, N.J. (07002) | 72,743 | 245 | 74,215 | −2.0 | 79,198 | 76,754 |
| Beaumont, Tex. (77704*) | 117,548 | 125 | 119,175 | −1.4 | 59,061 | 40,422 |
| Bellevue, Wash. (98009*) | 61,102 | 317 | 12,809 | 377.0 | — | — |
| Bellflower, Calif. (90706) | 51,454 | 380 | 45,909 | 12.1 | — | — |
| Berkeley, Calif. (94701*) | 114,091 | 128 | 111,268 | 2.5 | 85,547 | 56,036 |
| Berwyn, Ill. (60402) | 52,502 | 376 | 54,224 | −3.2 | 48,451 | 14,150 |
| Bethesda, Md. (U) (20014) | 71,621 | 255 | 56,527 | 26.7 | — | — |
| Bethlehem, Pa. (18015*) | 72,686 | 247 | 75,408 | −3.6 | 58,490 | 50,358 |
| Billings, Mont. (59101*) | 61,581 | 314 | 52,851 | 16.5 | 23,261 | 15,100 |
| Binghamton, N.Y. (13902*) | 64,123 | 297 | 75,941 | −15.6 | 78,309 | 66,800 |
| Birmingham, Ala. (35203*) | 300,910 | 48 | 340,887 | −11.7 | 267,583 | 178,806 |
| Bloomington, Minn. (55420) | 81,970 | 211 | 50,498 | 62.3 | — | — |
| Boise, Idaho (83701*) | 74,990 | 236 | 34,481 | 117.5 | 26,130 | 21,393 |
| Boston, Mass. (02109*) | 641,071 | 16 | 697,197 | −8.1 | 770,816 | 748,060 |
| Boulder, Colo. (80302*) | 66,870 | 287 | 37,718 | 77.3 | 12,958 | 11,006 |
| Bridgeport, Conn. (06601*) | 156,542 | 88 | 156,748 | −0.1 | 147,121 | 143,555 |
| Bristol, Conn. (06010) | 55,487 | 355 | 45,499 | 22.0 | 30,167 | 20,620 |
| Brockton, Mass. (02403) | 89,040 | 184 | 72,813 | 22.3 | 62,343 | 66,254 |
| Brownsville, Tex. (78520*) | 52,522 | 375 | 48,040 | 9.3 | 22,083 | 11,791 |
| Buena Park, Calif. (90622*) | 63,646 | 301 | 46,401 | 37.2 | — | — |
| Buffalo, N.Y. (14240*) | 462,768 | 28 | 532,759 | −13.1 | 575,901 | 506,775 |
| Burbank, Calif. (91505*) | 88,871 | 185 | 90,155 | −1.4 | 34,337 | 2,913 |
| Cambridge, Mass. (02138*) | 100,361 | 155 | 107,716 | −6.8 | 110,879 | 109,694 |
| Camden, N.J. (08101*) | 102,551 | 150 | 117,159 | −12.5 | 117,536 | 116,309 |
| Canton, Ohio (44711*) | 110,053 | 137 | 113,631 | −3.1 | 108,401 | 87,091 |
| Carson, Calif. (90745*) | 71,150 | 259 | 38,059 | 89.6 | — | — |
| Cedar Rapids, Iowa (52401*) | 110,642 | 135 | 92,035 | 20.2 | 62,120 | 45,566 |
| Champaign, Ill. (61820) | 56,532 | 346 | 49,583 | 14.0 | 23,302 | 15,873 |
| Charleston, S.C. (29401*) | 66,945 | 284 | 65,925 | 1.5 | 71,275 | 67,957 |
| Charleston, W. Va. (25301*) | 71,505 | 257 | 85,796 | −16.7 | 67,914 | 39,608 |
| Charlotte, N.C. (28202*) | 274,640 | 53 | 201,564 | 36.2 | 100,899 | 46,338 |
| Chattanooga, Tenn. (37401*) | 141,904 | 97 | 130,009 | 9.1 | 128,163 | 57,895 |
| Chesapeake, Va. (23320*) | 89,580 | 182 | — | — | — | — |
| Chester, Pa. (19013*) | 56,331 | 348 | 63,658 | −11.5 | 59.285 | 58,030 |
| Chicago, Ill. (60607*) | 3,369,359 | 2 | 3,550,404 | −5.1 | 3,396,808 | 2,701,705 |
| Chicopee, Mass. (01021*) | 66,676 | 288 | 61,553 | 8.3 | 41,664 | 36,214 |
| Chula Vista, Calif. (92010*) | 67,901 | 280 | 42,034 | 61.5 | 5,138 | 1,718 |

| City and major ZIP code | 1970 census | 1970 rank | 1960 census | % change 1960–70 | 1940 census | 1920 census |
|---|---|---|---|---|---|---|
| Cicero, Ill. (60650) | 67,058 | 283 | 69,130 | −3.0 | 64,712 | 44,995 |
| Cincinnati, Ohio (45202*) | 451,410 | 30 | 502,550 | −10.1 | 455,610 | 401,247 |
| Clearwater, Fla. (33515*) | 52,074 | 379 | 34,653 | 50.3 | 10,136 | 2,427 |
| Cleveland, Ohio (44101*) | 750,879 | 10 | 876,050 | −14.3 | 878,336 | 796,841 |
| Cleveland Heights, Ohio (44118) | 60,767 | 318 | 61,813 | −1.7 | 54,992 | 15,236 |
| Clifton, N.J. (07015*) | 82,437 | 210 | 82,084 | 0.4 | 48,827 | 26,470 |
| Colorado Springs, Colo. (80901*) | 135,060 | 107 | 70,194 | 92.4 | 36,789 | 30,105 |
| Columbia, Mo. (65201) | 58,804 | 330 | 36,650 | 60.4 | 18,399 | 10,392 |
| Columbia, S.C. (29201*) | 113,542 | 129 | 97,433 | 16.5 | 62,396 | 37,524 |
| Columbus, Ga. (31908*) | 155,028 | 90 | 116,779 | 32.7 | 53,280 | 31,125 |
| Columbus, Ohio (43215*) | 540,025 | 21 | 471,316 | 14.6 | 306,087 | 237,031 |
| Compton, Calif. (90220*) | 78,611 | 223 | 71,812 | 9.5 | 16,198 | 1,478 |
| Concord, Calif. (94520*) | 85,164 | 205 | 36,000 | 136.5 | 1,373 | 912 |
| Corpus Christi, Tex. (78408*) | 204,525 | 62 | 167,690 | 22.0 | 57,301 | 10,522 |
| Costa Mesa, Calif. (92626*) | 72,660 | 248 | 37,550 | 93.5 | — | — |
| Council Bluffs, Iowa (51501) | 60,348 | 320 | 55,641 | 8.5 | 41,439 | 36,162 |
| Covington, Ky. (41011*) | 52,535 | 374 | 60,376 | −13.0 | 62,018 | 57,121 |
| Cranston, R.I. (02910) | 74,287 | 240 | 66,766 | 11.3 | 47,085 | 29,407 |
| Dallas, Tex. (75221*) | 844,401 | 8 | 679,684 | 24.2 | 294,734 | 158,976 |
| Daly City, Calif. (94015*) | 66,922 | 285 | 44,791 | 49.4 | 9,625 | 3,779 |
| Danbury, Conn. (06810) | 50,781 | 384 | 22,928 | 121.5 | 22,339 | 18,943 |
| Davenport, Iowa (52802*) | 98,469 | 160 | 88,981 | 10.7 | 66,039 | 56,727 |
| Dayton, Ohio (45401*) | 242,917 | 60 | 262,332 | −7.4 | 210,718 | 152,559 |
| Dearborn, Mich. (48120*) | 104,199 | 148 | 112,007 | −7.0 | 63,584 | 2,470 |
| Dearborn Heights, Mich. (48127) | 80,069 | 215 | — | — | — | — |
| Decatur, Ill. (62521*) | 90,397 | 177 | 78,004 | 15.9 | 59,305 | 43,818 |
| Denver, Colo (80201*) | 514,678 | 25 | 493,887 | 4.2 | 322,412 | 256,491 |
| Des Moines, Iowa (50318*) | 201,404 | 64 | 208,982 | −3.9 | 159,819 | 126,468 |
| Des Plaines, Ill. (60018*) | 57,239 | 341 | 34,886 | 64.1 | 9,518 | 3,451 |
| Detroit, Mich. (48226*) | 1,514,063 | 5 | 1,670,144 | −9.4 | 1,623,452 | 993,678 |
| Downey, Calif. (90241*) | 88,445 | 187 | 82,505 | 7.2 | — | — |
| Duluth, Minn. (55806*) | 100,578 | 154 | 106,884 | −5.9 | 101,065 | 98,917 |
| Dundalk, Md. (U) (21222) | 85,377 | 203 | 82,428 | 3.6 | — | — |
| Durham, N.C. (27701*) | 95,438 | 165 | 78,302 | 21.9 | 60,195 | 21,719 |
| East Los Angeles, Calif. (U) (90022) | 105,033 | 146 | 104,270 | 0.7 | — | — |
| East Orange, N.J. (07019*) | 75,471 | 234 | 77,259 | −2.3 | 68,945 | 50,710 |
| East St. Louis, Ill. (62201*) | 69,996 | 266 | 81,712 | −14.3 | 75,609 | 66,767 |
| El Cajon, Calif. (92020*) | 52,273 | 377 | 37,618 | 39.0 | 1,471 | 469 |
| El Monte, Calif. (91734*) | 69,852 | 267 | 13,163 | 430.7 | 4,746 | 1,283 |
| El Paso, Tex. (79940*) | 322,261 | 45 | 276,687 | 16.5 | 96,810 | 77,560 |
| Elgin, Ill. (60120) | 55,691 | 353 | 49,447 | 12.6 | 38,333 | 27,454 |
| Elizabeth, N.J. (07207*) | 112,654 | 131 | 107,698 | 4.6 | 109,912 | 95,783 |
| Elyria, Ohio (44035*) | 53,427 | 367 | 43,782 | 22.0 | 25,120 | 20,474 |
| Erie, Pa. (16501*) | 129,231 | 114 | 138,440 | −6.7 | 116,955 | 93,372 |
| Euclid, Ohio (44117) | 71,552 | 256 | 62,998 | 13.6 | 17,866 | 3,363 |
| Eugene, Ore. (97401*) | 78,389 | 224 | 50,977 | 53.8 | 20,838 | 10,593 |
| Evanston, Ill. (60204*) | 79,808 | 216 | 79,283 | 0.7 | 65,389 | 37,234 |
| Evansville, Ind. (47708*) | 138,764 | 103 | 141,543 | −2.0 | 97,062 | 85,264 |
| Everett, Wash. (98201*) | 53,622 | 365 | 40,304 | 33.0 | 30,224 | 27,644 |
| Fall River, Mass. (02722*) | 96,898 | 162 | 99,942 | −3.0 | 115,428 | 120,485 |
| Fargo, N.D. (58102) | 53,365 | 368 | 46,662 | 14.4 | 32,580 | 21,961 |
| Fayetteville, N.C. (28302*) | 53,510 | 366 | 47,106 | 13.6 | 17,428 | 8,877 |
| Flint, Mich. (48502*) | 193,317 | 67 | 196,940 | −1.8 | 151,543 | 91,599 |
| Florissant, Mo. (63033*) | 65,908 | 290 | 38,166 | 72.7 | 1,369 | 682 |
| Fort Lauderdale, Fla. (33310*) | 139,590 | 101 | 83,648 | 66.9 | 17,996 | 2,065 |
| Fort Smith, Ark. (72901*) | 62,802 | 308 | 52,991 | 18.5 | 36,584 | 28,870 |
| Fort Wayne, Ind. (46802*) | 178,021 | 74 | 161,776 | 10.0 | 118,410 | 86,549 |
| Fort Worth, Tex. (76101*) | 393,476 | 33 | 356,268 | 10.4 | 177,662 | 106,482 |
| Framingham, Mass. (T) (01701) | 64,048 | 299 | 44,526 | 43.8 | 23,214 | 17,033 |
| Fremont, Calif. (94538*) | 100,869 | 153 | 43,790 | 130.3 | — | — |
| Fresno, Calif. (93706*) | 165,655 | 84 | 133,929 | 23.6 | 60,685 | 45,086 |
| Fullerton, Calif. (92631*) | 85,987 | 199 | 56,180 | 53.1 | 10,442 | 4,415 |
| Gadsden, Ala. (35901*) | 53,928 | 362 | 58,088 | −7.2 | 36,975 | 14,737 |
| Gainesville, Fla. (32601*) | 64,510 | 295 | 29,701 | 117.2 | 13,757 | 6,860 |
| Galveston, Tex (77553*) | 61,809 | 311 | 67,175 | −8.0 | 60,862 | 44,255 |
| Garden Grove, Calif. (92640*) | 121,155 | 121 | 84,238 | 43.8 | — | — |
| Garland, Tex. (75040*) | 81,437 | 213 | 38,501 | 111.5 | 2,233 | 1,421 |
| Gary, Ind. (46401*) | 188,398 | 69 | 178,320 | 5.6 | 111,719 | 55,378 |
| Glendale, Calif. (91209*) | 132,664 | 111 | 119,442 | 11.1 | 82,582 | 13,536 |
| Grand Prairie, Tex. (75051*) | 50,904 | 382 | 30,386 | 67.5 | 14,595 | 1,595 |
| Grand Rapids, Mich. (49501*) | 197,649 | 65 | 177,313 | 11.5 | 164,292 | 137,634 |

| City and major ZIP code | 1970 census | 1970 rank | 1960 census | % change 1960–70 | 1940 census | 1920 census |
|---|---|---|---|---|---|---|
| Great Falls, Mont. (59401*) | 60,091 | 321 | 55,244 | 8.8 | 29,928 | 24,121 |
| Green Bay, Wis. (54305*) | 87,809 | 191 | 62,888 | 39.6 | 46,235 | 31,017 |
| Greensboro, N.C. (27420*) | 144,076 | 96 | 119,574 | 20.5 | 59,319 | 19,861 |
| Greenville, S.C. (29602*) | 61,436 | 315 | 66,188 | −7.2 | 34,734 | 23,127 |
| Hamilton, Ohio (45012*) | 67,865 | 281 | 72,354 | −6.2 | 50,592 | 39,675 |
| Hammond, Ind. (46320*) | 107,983 | 143 | 111,698 | −3.3 | 70,184 | 36,004 |
| Hampton, Va. (23669*) | 120,779 | 122 | 89,258 | 35.3 | 5,898 | 6,138 |
| Harrisburg, Pa. (17105*) | 68,061 | 277 | 79,697 | −14.6 | 83,893 | 75,917 |
| Hartford, Conn. (06101*) | 158,017 | 87 | 162,178 | −2.6 | 166,207 | 138,036 |
| Hawthorne, Calif. (90250) | 53,304 | 369 | 33,035 | 61.4 | 8,263 | — |
| Hayward, Calif. (94544*) | 93,058 | 169 | 72,700 | 28.0 | 6,736 | 3,487 |
| Hialeah, Fla. (33010*) | 102,452 | 151 | 66,972 | 52.9 | 3,958 | — |
| High Point, N.C. (27260*) | 63,259 | 304 | 62,063 | 4.2 | 38,495 | 14,302 |
| Hollywood, Fla. (33022*) | 106,873 | 144 | 35,237 | 203.3 | 6,239 | — |
| Holyoke, Mass. (01040) | 50,112 | 390 | 52,689 | −4.9 | 53,750 | 60,203 |
| Honolulu, Hawaii (96820*) | 324,871 | 44 | 294,194 | 10.4 | 179,326 | 83,327 |
| Houston, Tex. (77052*) | 1,233,535 | 6 | 938,219 | 31.5 | 384,514 | 138,276 |
| Huntington, W. Va. (25701*) | 74,315 | 239 | 83,627 | −11.1 | 78,836 | 50,177 |
| Huntington Beach, Calif. (92647*) | 115,960 | 126 | 11,492 | 909.0 | 3,738 | 1,687 |
| Huntsville, Ala. (35804*) | 139,282 | 102 | 72,365 | 90.9 | 13,050 | 8,018 |
| Independence, Mo. (64050*) | 111,630 | 132 | 62,328 | 79.2 | 16,066 | 11,686 |
| Indianapolis, Ind. (46204*) | 742,925 | 11 | 476,258 | 55.9 | 386,972 | 314,194 |
| Inglewood, Calif. (90306*) | 89,985 | 179 | 63,390 | 42.0 | 30,114 | 3,286 |
| Irving, Tex. (75061*) | 98,961 | 159 | 45,985 | 115.2 | 1,089 | 357 |
| Jackson, Miss. (39205*) | 162,380 | 86 | 144,422 | 12.4 | 62,107 | 22,817 |
| Jacksonville, Fla. (32201*) | 528,865 | 23 | 201,030 | 163.1 | 173,065 | 91,558 |
| Jersey City, N.J. (07303*) | 260,350 | 55 | 276,101 | −5.7 | 301,173 | 298,103 |
| Joliet, Ill. (60431*) | 78,887 | 221 | 66,780 | 18.0 | 42,365 | 38,442 |
| Kalamazoo, Mich. (49003*) | 85,555 | 202 | 82,089 | 4.2 | 54,097 | 48,487 |
| Kansas City, Kan. (66110*) | 178,561 | 73 | 121,901 | 46.4 | 121,458 | 101,177 |
| Kansas City, Mo. (64108*) | 507,330 | 26 | 475,539 | 6.7 | 399,178 | 324,410 |
| Kenosha, Wis. (53141*) | 78,805 | 222 | 67,899 | 16.1 | 48,765 | 40,472 |
| Kettering, Ohio (45429) | 71,864 | 252 | 54,462 | 32.0 | — | — |
| Knoxville, Tenn. (37901*) | 174,587 | 77 | 111,827 | 56.1 | 111,580 | 77,818 |
| La Crosse, Wis. (54601) | 51,153 | 381 | 47,575 | 7.5 | 42,707 | 30,421 |
| Lafayette, La. (70502*) | 68,908 | 273 | 40,400 | 70.6 | 19,210 | 7,855 |
| Lake Charles, La. (70601*) | 77,998 | 228 | 63,392 | 23.0 | 21,207 | 13,088 |
| Lakewood, Calif. (90714*) | 82,973 | 208 | 67,126 | 23.6 | — | — |
| Lakewood, Colo. (80215) | 92,743 | 170 | 19,338 | 379.8 | — | — |
| Lakewood, Ohio (44107) | 70,173 | 264 | 66,154 | 6.1 | 69,160 | 41,732 |
| Lancaster, Pa. (17604*) | 57,690 | 335 | 61,055 | −5.5 | 61,345 | 53,150 |
| Lansing, Mich. (48924*) | 131,403 | 113 | 107,807 | 21.8 | 78,753 | 57,327 |
| Laredo, Tex. (78040*) | 69,024 | 272 | 60,678 | 13.8 | 39,274 | 22,710 |
| Las Vegas, Nev. (89114*) | 125,787 | 118 | 64,405 | 95.3 | 8,422 | 2,304 |
| Lawrence, Mass. (01842*) | 66,915 | 286 | 70,933 | −5.7 | 84,323 | 94,270 |
| Lawton, Okla. (73501*) | 74,470 | 238 | 61,697 | 20.7 | 18,055 | 8,930 |
| Lexington, Ky. (40507*) | 108,137 | 141 | 62,810 | 72.2 | 49,304 | 41,534 |
| Lima, Ohio (45801*) | 53,734 | 364 | 51,037 | 5.3 | 44,711 | 41,326 |
| Lincoln, Neb. (68501*) | 149,518 | 92 | 128,521 | 16.3 | 81,984 | 54,948 |
| Lincoln Park, Mich. (48146) | 52,984 | 372 | 53,933 | −1.8 | 15,236 | — |
| Little Rock, Ark. (72201*) | 132,483 | 112 | 107,813 | 22.9 | 88,039 | 65,142 |
| Livonia, Mich. (48150*) | 110,109 | 136 | 66,702 | 65.1 | 8,728 | — |
| Long Beach, Calif. (90801*) | 358,879 | 40 | 344,168 | 4.3 | 164,271 | 55,593 |
| Lorain, Ohio (44052*) | 78,185 | 226 | 68,932 | 13.4 | 44,125 | 37,295 |
| Los Angeles, Calif. (90055*) | 2,811,801 | 3 | 2,479,015 | 13.4 | 1,504,277 | 576,673 |
| Louisville, Ky. (40202*) | 361,706 | 38 | 390,639 | −7.4 | 319,077 | 234,891 |
| Lowell, Mass. (01853*) | 94,239 | 168 | 92,107 | 2.3 | 101,389 | 112,759 |
| Lubbock, Tex. (79408*) | 149,101 | 93 | 128,691 | 15.9 | 31,853 | 4,051 |
| Lynchburg, Va. (24505*) | 54,083 | 361 | 54,790 | −1.3 | 44,541 | 30,070 |
| Lynn, Mass. (01901*) | 90,294 | 178 | 94,478 | −4.4 | 98,123 | 99,148 |
| Macon, Ga. (31201*) | 122,423 | 120 | 69,764 | 75.5 | 57,865 | 52,995 |
| Madison, Wis. (53714*) | 171,809 | 80 | 126,706 | 35.6 | 67,447 | 38,378 |
| Malden, Mass. (02148) | 56,127 | 350 | 57,676 | −2.7 | 58,010 | 49,103 |
| Manchester, N.H. (03103*) | 87,754 | 192 | 88,282 | −0.6 | 77,685 | 78,384 |
| Mansfield, Ohio (44901) | 55,047 | 358 | 47,325 | 16.3 | 37,154 | 27,824 |
| Medford, Mass. (02155) | 64,397 | 296 | 64,971 | −0.9 | 63,083 | 39,038 |
| Memphis, Tenn. (38101*) | 623,530 | 17 | 497,524 | 25.3 | 292,942 | 162,351 |
| Meriden, Conn. (06450) | 55,959 | 351 | 51,850 | 7.9 | 39,494 | 29,867 |
| Mesa, Ariz. (85201*) | 62,853 | 307 | 33,772 | 86.1 | 7,222 | 3,036 |
| Mesquite, Tex. (75149*) | 55,131 | 356 | 27,526 | 100.3 | 1,045 | 674 |
| Metairie, La. (U) (70002*) | 136,477 | 106 | — | — | — | — |

| City and major ZIP code | 1970 census | 1970 rank | 1960 census | % change 1960–70 | 1940 census | 1920 census |
|---|---|---|---|---|---|---|
| Miami, Fla. (33101*) | 334,859 | 42 | 291,688 | 14.8 | 172,172 | 29,571 |
| Miami Beach, Fla. (33139) | 87,072 | 196 | 63,145 | 37.9 | 28,012 | 644 |
| Midland, Tex. (79702*) | 59,463 | 327 | 62,625 | −5.0 | 9,352 | 1,795 |
| Milford, Conn. (06460) | 50,858 | 383 | 41,662 | 22.1 | — | — |
| Milwaukee, Wis. (53201*) | 717,372 | 12 | 741,324 | −3.2 | 587,472 | 457,147 |
| Minneapolis, Minn. (55440*) | 434,400 | 32 | 482,872 | −10.0 | 492,370 | 380,582 |
| Mobile, Ala. (36601*) | 190,026 | 68 | 194,856 | −2.5 | 78,720 | 60,777 |
| Modesto, Calif. (95350*) | 61,712 | 312 | 36,585 | 68.7 | 16,379 | 9,241 |
| Monroe, La. (71201*) | 56,374 | 347 | 52,219 | 8.0 | 28,309 | 12,675 |
| Monterey Park, Calif. (91754) | 49,166 | 395 | 37,821 | 30.0 | 8,531 | 4,108 |
| Montgomery, Ala. (36104*) | 140,102 | 99 | 134,393 | 4.2 | 78,084 | 43,464 |
| Mount Vernon, N.Y. (10551*) | 72,778 | 244 | 76,010 | −4.3 | 67,632 | 42,726 |
| Mountain View, Calif. (94042*) | 54,206 | 359 | 30,889 | 75.5 | 3,946 | 1,888 |
| Muncie, Ind. (47302*) | 69,082 | 271 | 68,603 | 0.7 | 49,720 | 36,524 |
| Nashua, N.H. (03060) | 55,820 | 352 | 39,096 | 42.8 | 32,927 | 23,379 |
| Nashville, Tenn. (37202*) | 447,877 | 31 | 170,874 | 162.1 | 167,402 | 118,342 |
| New Bedford, Mass. (02741*) | 101,777 | 152 | 102,477 | −0.7 | 110,341 | 121,217 |
| New Britain, Conn. (06050*) | 83,441 | 207 | 82,201 | 1.5 | 68,685 | 59,316 |
| New Haven, Conn. (06510*) | 137,707 | 105 | 152,048 | −9.4 | 160,605 | 162,537 |
| New Orleans, La. (70140*) | 593,471 | 19 | 627,525 | −5.4 | 494,537 | 387,219 |
| New Rochelle, N.Y. (10802*) | 75,385 | 235 | 76,812 | −1.9 | 58,408 | 36,213 |
| New York, N.Y. | 7,895,563 | 1 | 7,781,984 | 1.1 | 7,454,995 | 5,620,048 |
| Bronx borough (10451*) | 1,471,701 | — | 1,424,815 | 3.3 | 1,394,711 | 732,016 |
| Brooklyn borough (11201*) | 2,602,012 | — | 2,627,319 | −1.0 | 2,698,285 | 2,018,356 |
| Manhattan borough (10001*) | 1,539,233 | — | 1,698,281 | 10.2 | 1,889,924 | 2,284,103 |
| Queens borough[1] | 1,987,174 | — | 1,809,578 | 9.1 | 1,297,634 | 469,042 |
| Staten Island borough (10314) | 295,443 | — | 221,991 | 33.1 | 174,441 | 116,531 |
| Newark, N.J. (07101*) | 381,930 | 35 | 405,220 | −5.7 | 429,760 | 414,524 |
| Newport News, Va. (23607*) | 138,177 | 104 | 113,662 | 21.6 | 37,067 | 35,596 |
| Newton, Mass. (02158) | 91,263 | 176 | 92,384 | −1.2 | 69,873 | 46,054 |
| Niagara Falls, N.Y. (14302*) | 85,615 | 201 | 102,394 | −16.4 | 78,029 | 50,760 |
| Norfolk, Va. (23501*) | 307,951 | 47 | 304,869 | 1.0 | 144,332 | 115,777 |
| Norman, Okla. (73070*) | 52,117 | 378 | 33,412 | 56.0 | 11,429 | 5,004 |
| North Little Rock, Ark. (72114*) | 60,040 | 322 | 58,032 | 3.5 | 21,137 | 14,048 |
| Norwalk, Calif. (90650) | 91,827 | 173 | 88,739 | 3.5 | — | — |
| Norwalk, Conn. (06856*) | 79,113 | 217 | 67,775 | 16.7 | 39,849 | 27,743 |
| Oak Park, Ill. (60303*) | 62,511 | 309 | 61,093 | 2.3 | 66,015 | 39,858 |
| Oakland, Calif. (94617*) | 361,561 | 39 | 367,548 | −1.6 | 302,163 | 216,261 |
| Odessa, Tex. (79760*) | 78,380 | 225 | 80,338 | −2.4 | 9,573 | — |
| Ogden, Utah (84401*) | 69,478 | 269 | 70,197 | −1.0 | 43,688 | 32,804 |
| Oklahoma City, Okla. (73125*) | 368,164 | 37 | 324,253 | 13.5 | 204,424 | 91,295 |
| Omaha, Neb. (68108*) | 354,389 | 41 | 301,598 | 17.5 | 223,844 | 191,601 |
| Ontario, Calif. (91761*) | 64,118 | 298 | 46,617 | 37.5 | 14,197 | 7,280 |
| Orange, Calif. (92667*) | 77,365 | 231 | 26,444 | 192.6 | 7,901 | 4,884 |
| Orlando, Fla. (32802*) | 99,006 | 158 | 88,135 | 12.3 | 36,736 | 9,282 |
| Oshkosh, Wis. (54901) | 53,221 | 370 | 45,110 | 18.0 | 39,089 | 33,162 |
| Overland Park, Kan. (66204) | 79,034 | 219 | 21,110 | 274.4 | — | — |
| Owensboro, Ky. (42301) | 50,329 | 387 | 42,471 | 18.5 | 30,245 | 17,424 |
| Oxnard, Calif. (93030) | 71,225 | 258 | 40,265 | 76.9 | 8,519 | 4,417 |
| Palo Alto, Calif. (94302*) | 56,181 | 349 | 52,287 | 7.4 | 16,774 | 5,900 |
| Parma, Ohio (44129) | 100,216 | 156 | 82,845 | 21.0 | 16,365 | — |
| Pasadena, Calif. (91109*) | 112,951 | 130 | 116,407 | −2.9 | 81,864 | 45,354 |
| Pasadena, Tex. (77501*) | 89,277 | 183 | 58,737 | 52.0 | 3,436 | — |
| Passaic, N.J. (07055*) | 55,124 | 357 | 53,963 | 2.2 | 61,394 | 63,841 |
| Paterson, N.J. (07510*) | 144,824 | 95 | 143,663 | 0.8 | 139,656 | 135,875 |
| Pawtucket, R.I. (02860*) | 76,984 | 232 | 81,001 | −5.0 | 75,797 | 64,248 |
| Pensacola, Fla. (32502*) | 59,507 | 326 | 56,752 | 4.9 | 37,449 | 31,035 |
| Peoria, Ill. (61601*) | 126,963 | 117 | 103,162 | 23.1 | 105,087 | 76,121 |
| Philadelphia, Pa. (19104*) | 1,949,996 | 4 | 2,002,512 | −2.6 | 1,931,334 | 1,823,779 |
| Phoenix, Ariz. (85026*) | 587,213 | 20 | 439,170 | 33.7 | 65,414 | 29,053 |
| Pico Rivera, Calif. (90660) | 54,170 | 360 | 49,150 | 10.2 | — | — |
| Pine Bluff, Ark. (71601*) | 57,389 | 338 | 44,037 | 30.3 | 21,290 | 19,280 |
| Pittsburgh, Pa. (15230*) | 520,089 | 24 | 604,332 | −13.9 | 671,659 | 588,343 |
| Pittsfield, Mass. (01201) | 57,020 | 343 | 57,879 | −1.5 | 49,684 | 41,763 |
| Pomona, Calif. (91766*) | 87,384 | 195 | 67,157 | 30.1 | 23,539 | 13,505 |
| Pontiac, Mich. (48056*) | 85,279 | 204 | 82,233 | 3.7 | 66,626 | 34,273 |
| Port Arthur, Tex. (77640) | 57,371 | 340 | 66,676 | −14.0 | 46,140 | 22,251 |
| Portland, Me (04101*) | 65,116 | 293 | 72,566 | −10.3 | 73,643 | 69,272 |
| Portland, Ore. (97208*) | 379,967 | 36 | 372,676 | 1.9 | 305,394 | 258,288 |
| Portsmouth, Va. (23705*) | 110,963 | 133 | 114,773 | −3.3 | 50,745 | 54,387 |
| Providence, R.I. (02940*) | 179,116 | 72 | 207,498 | −13.6 | 253,504 | 237,595 |

| City and major ZIP code | 1970 census | 1970 rank | 1960 census | % change 1960–70 | 1940 census | 1920 census |
|---|---|---|---|---|---|---|
| Provo, Utah (84601) | 53,131 | 371 | 36,047 | 47.4 | 18,071 | 10,303 |
| Pueblo, Colo. (81002*) | 97,774 | 160 | 91,181 | 7.2 | 52,162 | 43,050 |
| Quincy, Mass. (02169) | 87,966 | 190 | 87,409 | 0.6 | 75,810 | 47,876 |
| Racine, Wis. (53401*) | 95,162 | 167 | 89,144 | 6.8 | 67,195 | 58,593 |
| Raleigh, N.C. (27611*) | 123,793 | 119 | 93,931 | 31.7 | 46,897 | 24,418 |
| Reading, Pa. (19603*) | 87,643 | 194 | 98,177 | −10.7 | 110,568 | 107,784 |
| Redondo Beach, Calif. (90277*) | 57,425 | 337 | 46,986 | 22.2 | 13,092 | 4,913 |
| Redwood City, Calif. (94063*) | 55,686 | 354 | 46,290 | 20.3 | 12,453 | 4,020 |
| Reno, Nev. (89501*) | 72,863 | 242 | 51,470 | 41.6 | 21.317 | 12,016 |
| Richmond, Calif. (94802*) | 79,043 | 218 | 71,854 | 10.0 | 23,642 | 16,843 |
| Richmond, Va. (23232*) | 249,431 | 58 | 219,958 | 13.4 | 193,042 | 171,667 |
| Riverside, Calif. (92502*) | 140,089 | 100 | 84,332 | 66.1 | 34,696 | 19,341 |
| Roanoke, Va. (24001*) | 92,115 | 171 | 97,110 | −5.1 | 69,287 | 50,842 |
| Rochester, Minn. (55901*) | 53,766 | 363 | 40,663 | 32.2 | 26,312 | 13,722 |
| Rochester, N.Y. (14603*) | 295,011 | 49 | 318,611 | −7.4 | 324,925 | 295,750 |
| Rock Island, Ill. (61201) | 50,166 | 388 | 51,863 | −3.3 | 42,775 | 35,177 |
| Rockford, Ill. (61125*) | 147,370 | 94 | 126,706 | 16.3 | 84,637 | 65,651 |
| Rome, N.Y. (13440) | 50,148 | 389 | 51,646 | −2.9 | 34,214 | 26,341 |
| Roseville, Mich. (48066) | 60,529 | 319 | 50,195 | 20.6 | 9,023 | — |
| Royal Oak, Mich. (48067*) | 86,238 | 198 | 80,612 | 7.0 | 25,087 | 6,007 |
| Sacramento, Calif. (95814*) | 257,105 | 56 | 191,667 | 34.1 | 105,958 | 65,908 |
| Saginaw, Mich. (48605*) | 91,849 | 172 | 98,265 | −6.5 | 82,794 | 61,903 |
| St. Clair Shores, Mich. (48083*) | 88,093 | 189 | 76,657 | 14.9 | 10,405 | — |
| St. Joseph, Mo. (64501*) | 72,691 | 246 | 79,673 | −8.8 | 75,711 | 77,939 |
| St. Louis, Mo. (63166*) | 622,236 | 18 | 750,026 | −17.0 | 816,048 | 772,897 |
| St. Paul, Minn. (55101*) | 309,866 | 46 | 313,411 | −1.1 | 287,736 | 234,698 |
| St. Petersburg, Fla. (33733*) | 216,159 | 61 | 181,298 | 19.3 | 60,812 | 14,237 |
| Salem, Ore. (97301*) | 68,856 | 274 | 49,142 | 40.1 | 30,908 | 17,679 |
| Salinas, Calif. (93901*) | 58,896 | 328 | 28,957 | 103.4 | 11,586 | 4,308 |
| Salt Lake City, Utah (84101*) | 175,885 | 76 | 189,454 | −7.2 | 149,934 | 118,110 |
| San Angelo, Tex. (76902*) | 63,884 | 300 | 58,815 | 8.6 | 25,802 | 10,050 |
| San Antonio, Tex. (78205*) | 707,503 | 14 | 587,718 | 20.3 | 253,854 | 161,379 |
| San Bernadino Calif. (92401*) | 106,869 | 145 | 91,922 | 16.2 | 43,646 | 18,721 |
| San Diego, Calif. (92101*) | 697,027 | 15 | 573,224 | 21.6 | 203,341 | 74,361 |
| San Francisco, Calif. (94101*) | 715,674 | 13 | 740,316 | −3.3 | 634,536 | 506,676 |
| San Jose, Calif. (95113*) | 459,913 | 29 | 204,196 | 124.7 | 68,457 | 39,642 |
| San Leandro, Calif. (94577*) | 68,608 | 275 | 65,962 | 4.1 | 14,601 | 5,703 |
| San Mateo, Calif. (94402*) | 78,991 | 220 | 69,870 | 13.1 | 19,403 | 5,979 |
| Santa Ana, Calif. (92711*) | 155,710 | 89 | 100,350 | 55.1 | 31,921 | 15,485 |
| Santa Barbara, Calif. (93102*) | 70,215 | 263 | 58,768 | 19.5 | 34,958 | 19,441 |
| Santa Clara, Calif. (95050) | 87,717 | 193 | 58,880 | 49.0 | 6,650 | 5220 |
| Santa Monica, Calif. (90406*) | 88,289 | 188 | 83,249 | 6.1 | 53,500 | 15,252 |
| Santa Rosa, Calif. (95402*) | 50,006 | 391 | 31,027 | 61.2 | 12,605 | 8,758 |
| Savannah, Ga. (31402*) | 118,349 | 124 | 149,245 | −20.7 | 95,996 | 83,252 |
| Schenectady, N.Y. (12305*) | 77,958 | 229 | 81,682 | −4.6 | 87,549 | 88,723 |
| Scottsdale, Ariz. (85251*) | 67,823 | 282 | 10,026 | 576.5 | — | — |
| Scranton, Pa. (18501*) | 103,564 | 149 | 111,443 | −7.1 | 140,404 | 137,783 |
| Seattle, Wash. (98101*) | 530,831 | 22 | 557,087 | −4.7 | 368,302 | 315,312 |
| Shreveport, La. (71101*) | 182,064 | 70 | 164,372 | 10.8 | 98,167 | 43,874 |
| Silver Spring, Md. (U) (20907*) | 77,496 | 230 | 66,348 | 16.8 | — | — |
| Simi Valley, Calif. (93065*) | 59,832 | 325 | — | — | — | — |
| Sioux City, Iowa (51101*) | 85,925 | 200 | 89,159 | −3.6 | 82,364 | 71,227 |
| Sioux Falls, S.D. (57101*) | 72,488 | 251 | 65,466 | 10.7 | 40,832 | 25,202 |
| Skokie, Ill. (60076) | 68,627 | 276 | 59,364 | 15.6 | 7,172 | 763 |
| Somerville, Mass. (02143) | 88,779 | 186 | 94,697 | −6.2 | 102,177 | 93,091 |
| South Bend, Ind. (46624*) | 127,328 | 115 | 132,445 | −3.8 | 101,268 | 70,983 |
| South Gate, Calif. (90280) | 56,909 | 344 | 53,831 | 5.7 | 26,945 | — |
| Southfield, Mich. (48037*) | 69,285 | 270 | 31,501 | 119.9 | — | — |
| Spokane, Wash. (90210*) | 170,516 | 81 | 181,608 | −6.1 | 122,001 | 104,437 |
| Springfield, Ill. (62708*) | 91,753 | 174 | 83,271 | 10.2 | 75,503 | 59,183 |
| Springfield, Mass. (01101*) | 163,905 | 85 | 174,463 | −6.1 | 149,554 | 129,614 |
| Springfield, Mo. (65801*) | 120,096 | 123 | 95,865 | 25.3 | 61,238 | 39,631 |
| Springfield, Ohio (45501*) | 81,941 | 212 | 82,723 | −1.0 | 70,662 | 60,840 |
| Stamford, Conn. (06904*) | 108,798 | 140 | 92,713 | 17.3 | 47,938 | 35,096 |
| Sterling Heights, Mich. (48077) | 61,365 | 316 | — | — | — | — |
| Stockton, Calif. (95208*) | 109,963 | 138 | 86,321 | 27.4 | 54,714 | 40,296 |
| Sunnyvale, Calif. (94088*) | 95,976 | 164 | 52,898 | 81.4 | 4,373 | 1,675 |
| Syracuse, N.Y. (13201*) | 197,297 | 66 | 216,038 | −8.7 | 205,967 | 171,717 |
| Tacoma, Wash. (98402*) | 154,407 | 91 | 147,979 | 4.3 | 109,408 | 96,965 |
| Tallahassee, Fla. (32301*) | 72,586 | 250 | 48,174 | 50.1 | 16,240 | 5,637 |
| Tampa, Fla. (33602*) | 277,714 | 50 | 274,970 | 1.0 | 108,391 | 51,608 |

| City and major ZIP code | 1970 census | 1970 rank | 1960 census | % change 1960–70 | 1940 census | 1920 census |
|---|---|---|---|---|---|---|
| Taylor, Mich. (48180) | 70,020 | 265 | — | — | — | — |
| Tempe, Ariz. (85282*) | 63,550 | 302 | 24,897 | 155.3 | 2,906 | 1,963 |
| Terre Haute, Ind. (47808*) | 70,335 | 262 | 72,500 | −3.1 | 62,693 | 66,083 |
| Toledo, Ohio (43601*) | 383,062 | 34 | 318,003 | 20.4 | 282,349 | 243,164 |
| Topeka, Kan. (66601*) | 132,952 | 110 | 119,484 | 11.2 | 67,833 | 50,022 |
| Torrance, Calif. (90510*) | 134,968 | 108 | 100,991 | 33.3 | 9,950 | — |
| Towson, Md. (21204) | 77,999 | 227 | 19,090 | 307.6 | — | — |
| Trenton, N.J. (08608*) | 104,786 | 147 | 114,167 | −8.2 | 124,697 | 119,289 |
| Troy, N.Y. (12180*) | 62,918 | 306 | 67,492 | −6.8 | 70,304 | 71,996 |
| Tucson, Ariz. (85702*) | 265,799 | 54 | 212,892 | 24.8 | 35,752 | 20,292 |
| Tulsa, Okla. (74101*) | 330,350 | 43 | 261,685 | 26.2 | 142,157 | 72,075 |
| Tuscaloosa, Ala. (35401*) | 65,773 | 291 | 63,370 | 3.8 | 27,493 | 11,996 |
| Tyler, Tex. (75702*) | 57,770 | 334 | 51,230 | 12.8 | 28,279 | 12,085 |
| Union City, N.J. (07087) | 58,537 | 332 | 52,180 | 12.2 | 56,173 | 20,651 |
| Utica, N.Y. (13503*) | 91,611 | 175 | 100,410 | −8.8 | 100,518 | 94,156 |
| Vallejo, Calif. (94590*) | 71,710 | 253 | 60,877 | 17.8 | 20,072 | 21,107 |
| Ventura, Calif. (93001*) | 57,964 | 333 | 29,114 | 99.0 | — | — |
| Virginia Beach, Va. (23458*) | 172,106 | 78 | 8,091 | 1.000+ | 2,600 | 846 |
| Waco, Tex. (76703*) | 95,326 | 166 | 97,808 | −2.5 | 55,982 | 38,500 |
| Waltham, Mass. (02154) | 61,582 | 313 | 55,413 | 11.1 | 40,020 | 30,915 |
| Warren, Mich. (48089*) | 179,260 | 71 | 89,246 | 100.9 | 582 | — |
| Warren, Ohio (44482*) | 63,494 | 303 | 59,648 | 6.4 | 42,837 | 27,500 |
| Warwick, R.I. (02887*) | 83,694 | 206 | 68,504 | 22.2 | 28,757 | 13,481 |
| Washington, D.C. (20013*) | 756,668 | 9 | 763,956 | −1.0 | 663,091 | 437,571 |
| Waterbury, Conn. (06720*) | 108,033 | 142 | 107,130 | 0.8 | 99,314 | 91,715 |
| Waterloo, Iowa (50701*) | 75,533 | 233 | 71,755 | 5.3 | 51,743 | 36,230 |
| Waukegan, Ill. (60085*) | 65,269 | 292 | 55,719 | 17.1 | 34,241 | 19,226 |
| Wauwatosa, Wis. (53213) | 58,676 | 331 | 56,923 | 3.1 | 27,769 | 5,818 |
| West Allis, Wis. (53214) | 71,649 | 254 | 68,157 | 5.1 | 36,364 | 13,745 |
| West Covina, Calif. (91793*) | 68,034 | 278 | 50,645 | 34.3 | 1,072 | — |
| West Hartford, Conn. (T) (06107) | 68,031 | 279 | 62,382 | 9.1 | 33,776 | 8,854 |
| West Haven, Conn. (06516) | 52,851 | 373 | — | — | — | — |
| West Palm Beach, Fla. (33401*) | 57,375 | 339 | 56,208 | 2.1 | 33,693 | 8,659 |
| Westland, Mich. (48185) | 86,749 | 197 | — | — | — | — |
| Westminster, Calif. (92683) | 59,874 | 323 | 25,750 | 132.5 | — | — |
| Wheaton, Md. (U) (20902) | 66,247 | 289 | 54,635 | 21.3 | — | — |
| White Plains, N.Y. (10602*) | 50,346 | 385 | 50,485 | −0.3 | 40,327 | 21,031 |
| Whittier, Calif. (90605*) | 72,863 | 243 | 33,663 | 116.4 | 16,115 | 7,995 |
| Wichita, Kan. (67209*) | 276,554 | 51 | 254,698 | 8.6 | 114,966 | 72,217 |
| Wichita Falls, Tex. (76307*) | 96,265 | 163 | 101,724 | −5.3 | 45,112 | 40,079 |
| Wilkes-Barre, Pa. (18703*) | 58,856 | 329 | 63,551 | −7.4 | 86,236 | 73,833 |
| Wilmington, Del. (19899*) | 80,386 | 214 | 95,827 | −16.1 | 112,504 | 110,168 |
| Winston-Salem, N.C. (27102*) | 133,683 | 109 | 111,135 | 21.2 | 79,815 | 48,395 |
| Worcester, Mass. (01613*) | 176,572 | 75 | 186,587 | −5.4 | 193,694 | 179,754 |
| Wyoming, Mich. (49509) | 56,560 | 345 | 45,829 | 23.4 | — | — |
| Yonkers, N.Y. (10701*) | 204,297 | 63 | 190,634 | 7.2 | 142,598 | 100,176 |
| York, Pa. (17405*) | 50,335 | 386 | 54,504 | −7.6 | 56,712 | 47,512 |
| Youngstown, Ohio (44501*) | 140,909 | 98 | 166,689 | −15.5 | 167,720 | 132,358 |

1. Queens has four major ZIP codes: 11690*—Far Rockaway; 11352*—Flushing; 11431*—Jamaica; 11101*—Long Island City. *Source:* Department of Commerce, Bureau of the Census.

## Income of Households by Age of Head, 1976

| Age of head | Household income | | | | | | |
|---|---|---|---|---|---|---|---|
| | Under $4,000 | $4,000 to $6,999 | $7,000 to $9,999 | $10,000 to $14,999 | $15,000 to $24,999 | $25,000 and over | Total |
| 14-24 years | 10.0 | 12.0 | 13.5 | 10.1 | 5.1 | 1.0 | 8.1 |
| 25-34 years | 11.3 | 14.9 | 22.8 | 29.2 | 27.8 | 16.1 | 21.8 |
| 35-44 years | 7.4 | 10.0 | 12.5 | 16.6 | 22.7 | 24.8 | 16.8 |
| 45-54 years | 8.9 | 9.6 | 12.4 | 15.3 | 21.2 | 32.3 | 17.4 |
| 55-64 years | 15.7 | 14.4 | 14.9 | 14.9 | 15.9 | 19.6 | 15.9 |
| 65 years and over | 46.7 | 39.0 | 23.9 | 13.9 | 7.3 | 6.2 | 20.0 |
| **Total** | **100%** | **100%** | **100%** | **100%** | **100%** | **100%** | **100%** |

*Source:* Department of Commerce, Bureau of the Census.

## Territorial Expansion

| Accession | Date | Area[1] |
|---|---|---|
| United States | — | 3,615,122 |
| Territory in 1790 | — | 888,685 |
| Louisiana Purchase | 1803 | 827,192 |
| Florida | 1819 | 58,560 |
| By treaty with Spain | 1819 | 13,443 |
| Texas | 1845 | 390,143 |
| Oregon | 1846 | 285,580 |
| Mexican Cession | 1848 | 529,017 |
| Gadsden Purchase | 1853 | 29,640 |
| Alaska | 1867 | 586,412 |
| Hawaii | 1898 | 6,450 |
| Other territory | — | 12,944 |
| Philippines | 1898 | 115,600[2] |
| Puerto Rico | 1899 | 3,435 |
| Guam | 1899 | 212 |
| American Samoa | 1900 | 76 |
| Canal Zone | 1904 | 553 |
| Corn Islands[3] | 1914 | 4 |
| Virgin Islands of U.S. | 1917 | 133 |
| Trust Territory of Pacific Islands | 1947 | 8,489 |
| All other | — | 42 |
| **Total, 1970** | — | **3,628,066** |

1. Total land and water area in square miles. 2. Became independent in 1946; area not included in total. 3. Leased from Nicaragua for 99 years in 1914, but returned April 25, 1971; area included in total. *Source:* Department of Commerce, Bureau of the Census.

## Total Population

| Area | 1940 | 1960 | 1970 |
|---|---|---|---|
| 50 states of U.S. | — | 179,323,175 | 203,235,298 |
| 48 coterminous | 131,669,275 | 178,464,236 | 202,163,212 |
| Alaska | 72,524 | 226,167 | 302,173 |
| Hawaii | 422,770 | 632,772 | 769,913 |
| American Samoa | 12,908 | 20,051 | 27,159 |
| Canal Zone | 51,827 | 42,122 | 44,198 |
| Canton Island | 40 | 320 | — |
| Corn Islands | 1,523 | 1,872 | (4) |
| Guam | 22,290 | 67,044 | 84,996 |
| Johnston Island | 69 | 156 | 1,007 |
| Midway | 437 | 2,356 | 2,220 |
| Philippines | 16,356,000 | — | — |
| Puerto Rico | 1,869,255 | 2,349,544 | 2,712,033 |
| Swan Islands | (1) | 28 | 22 |
| Trust Ter. of Pac. Is. | — | 70,724 | 90,940 |
| Virgin Is. of U.S. | 24,889 | 32,099 | 62,468 |
| Wake Island | (1) | 1,097 | 1,647 |
| Population abroad | 118,933 | 1,374,421 | 1,737,836 |
| Armed forces | (2) | 609,720 | 1,057,776 |
| Other[3] | 14 | — | — |
| Total | 150,622,754 | 183,285,009 | 207,999,824 |

1. Not enumerated. 2. Not available. 3. Includes Baker Island (3), Enderbury Island (4), Howland Island (4), and Jarvis Island (3); uninhabited in 1960 and 1970. 4. Returned to Nicaragua April 25, 1971. *Source:* Department of Commerce, Bureau of the Census.

## Estimated Population by Race, 1975
(in thousands)

| State | White | Black | Other |
|---|---|---|---|
| Alabama | 2,682.0 | 919.9 | (1) |
| Alaska | 287.2 | (1) | 66.8 |
| Arizona | 2,007.0 | 67.4 | 137.4 |
| Arkansas | 1,722.6 | 356.1 | 31.3[2] |
| California | 18,660.1 | 1,601.1 | 936.7[2] |
| Colorado | 2,421.9 | 86.8 | 32.6 |
| Connecticut | 2,896.2 | 187.9 | (1) |
| Delaware | 491.4 | 85.3 | (1) |
| D.C. | 189.8 | 511.4 | (1) |
| Florida | 7,045.4 | 1,179.0 | 53.0[2] |
| Georgia | 3,626.3 | 1,288.1 | (1) |
| Hawaii | 317.0 | (1) | 539.9 |
| Idaho | 799.0 | (1) | (1) |
| Illinois | 9,549.3 | 1,534.3 | 113.9 |
| Indiana | 4,908.1 | 388.6 | (1) |
| Iowa | 2,814.4 | 40.3 | (1) |
| Kansas | 2,151.7 | 107.7 | (1) |
| Kentucky | 3,133.9 | 244.3 | (1) |
| Louisiana | 2,655.7 | 1,134.0 | (1) |
| Maine | 1,051.0 | (1) | (1) |
| Maryland | 3,251.5 | 828.5 | 41.6 |
| Massachusetts | 5,564.1 | 211.2 | 39.0 |
| Michigan | 7,976.0 | 1,080.3 | 55.0 |
| Minnesota | 3,843.1 | 39.9 | 38.5 |
| Mississippi | 1,489.5 | 840.5 | (1) |
| Missouri | 4,234.7 | 507.3 | 25.2 |
| Montana | 710.5 | (1) | 33.7 |
| Nebraska | 1,484.2 | 46.3 | (1) |
| Nevada | 541.5 | 35.6 | (1) |
| New Hampshire | 805.9 | (1) | (1) |
| New Jersey | 6,392.8 | 870.5 | 69.7 |
| New Mexico | 1,032.1 | (1) | 90.9 |
| New York | 15,434.3 | 2,382.2 | 259.5 |
| North Carolina | 4,185.4 | 1,193.3 | 62.6 |
| North Dakota | 615.6 | (1) | (1) |
| Ohio | 9,655.8 | 1,033.6 | 45.9 |
| Oklahoma | 2,408.7 | 191.4 | 114.5 |
| Oregon | 2,215.0 | 30.7 | 38.6 |
| Pennsylvania | 10,739.0 | 1,049.2 | 71.5[2] |
| Rhode Island | 897.1 | 27.6 | (1) |
| South Carolina | 1,936.8 | 867.0 | (1) |
| South Dakota | 639.3 | (1) | 39.7 |
| Tennessee | 3,509.2 | 651.2 | (1) |
| Texas | 10,637.3 | 1,529.6 | 70.3 |
| Utah | 1,172.7 | (1) | (1) |
| Vermont | 468.5 | (1) | (1) |
| Virginia | 4,007.6 | 930.8 | 42.1 |
| Washington | 3,379.0 | 80.4 | 99.7 |
| West Virginia | 1,729.1 | 64.4 | (1) |
| Wisconsin | 4,410.8 | 143.5 | 34.3 |
| Wyoming | 364.0 | (1) | (1) |
| **Total** | **185,141.3** | **24,434.9** | **3,456.1** |

1. Less than 25,000. 2. Includes Vietnamese refugees in resettlement centers on July 1, 1975, as follows: Arkansas, 24,000; California, 18,000; Florida, 6,000; Pennsylvania, 17,000. *Source:* Department of Commerce, Bureau of the Census.

## Population Distribution by Age, Race, Nativity, and Sex

| Year | Total | Age: Under 5 | Age: 5–19 | Age: 20–44 | Age: 45–64 | Age: 65 and over | Race and nativity: White: Total | White: Native born | White: Foreign born | Nonwhite |
|---|---|---|---|---|---|---|---|---|---|---|
| **PERCENT DISTRIBUTION** | | | | | | | | | | |
| 1860[1] | 100.0 | 15.4 | 35.8 | 35.7 | 10.4 | 2.7 | 85.6 | 72.6 | 13.0 | 14.4 |
| 1870[1] | 100.0 | 14.3 | 35.4 | 35.4 | 11.9 | 3.0 | 87.1 | 72.9 | 14.2 | 12.9 |
| 1880[1] | 100.0 | 13.8 | 34.3 | 35.9 | 12.6 | 3.4 | 86.5 | 73.4 | 13.1 | 13.5 |
| 1890[2] | 100.0 | 12.2 | 33.9 | 36.9 | 13.1 | 3.9 | 87.5 | 73.0 | 14.5 | 12.5 |
| 1900 | 100.0 | 12.1 | 32.3 | 37.8 | 13.7 | 4.1 | 87.9 | 74.5 | 13.4 | 12.1 |
| 1910 | 100.0 | 11.6 | 30.4 | 39.1 | 14.6 | 4.3 | 88.9 | 74.4 | 14.5 | 11.1 |
| 1920 | 100.0 | 11.0 | 29.8 | 38.4 | 16.1 | 4.7 | 89.7 | 76.7 | 13.0 | 10.3 |
| 1930 | 100.0 | 9.3 | 29.5 | 38.3 | 17.5 | 5.4 | 89.8 | 78.4 | 11.4 | 10.2 |
| 1940 | 100.0 | 8.0 | 26.4 | 38.9 | 19.8 | 6.9 | 89.8 | 81.1 | 8.7 | 10.2 |
| 1950[3] | 100.0 | 10.7 | 23.2 | 37.7 | 20.3 | 8.1 | 89.5 | 82.8 | 6.7 | 10.5 |
| 1960[3] | 100.0 | 11.3 | 27.1 | 32.4 | 20.0 | 9.2 | 88.6 | 83.4 | 5.2 | 11.4 |
| 1970[3] | 100.0 | 8.4 | 29.4 | 31.7 | 20.6 | 9.9 | 87.7 | 83.4 | 4.3 | 12.3 |
| 1977[5] | 100.0 | 7.0 | 26.5 | 35.4 | 20.2 | 10.8 | 86.6 | (4) | (4) | 13.4 |
| **MALES PER 100 FEMALES** | | | | | | | | | | |
| 1860[1] | 104.7 | 102.4 | 101.2 | 107.9 | 111.5 | 98.3 | 105.3 | 103.7 | 115.1 | 101.2 |
| 1870[1] | 102.2 | 102.9 | 101.2 | 99.2 | 114.5 | 100.5 | 102.8 | 100.6 | 115.3 | 98.4 |
| 1880[1] | 103.6 | 103.0 | 101.3 | 104.0 | 110.2 | 101.4 | 104.0 | 102.1 | 115.9 | 100.7 |
| 1890[2] | 105.0 | 103.6 | 101.4 | 107.3 | 108.3 | 104.2 | 105.4 | 102.9 | 118.7 | 102.2 |
| 1900 | 104.4 | 102.1 | 100.9 | 105.8 | 110.7 | 102.0 | 104.9 | 102.8 | 117.4 | 101.0 |
| 1910 | 106.0 | 102.5 | 101.3 | 108.1 | 114.4 | 101.1 | 106.6 | 102.7 | 129.2 | 101.3 |
| 1920 | 104.0 | 102.5 | 100.8 | 102.8 | 115.2 | 101.3 | 104.4 | 101.7 | 121.7 | 100.9 |
| 1930 | 102.5 | 103.0 | 101.4 | 100.5 | 109.1 | 100.5 | 102.9 | 101.1 | 115.8 | 99.1 |
| 1940 | 100.7 | 103.2 | 102.0 | 98.1 | 105.2 | 95.5 | 101.2 | 100.1 | 111.1 | 96.7 |
| 1950[3] | 99.0 | 103.9 | 102.9 | 97.0 | 100.2 | 89.6 | 99.4 | 99.0 | 103.9 | 96.2 |
| 1960[3] | 97.1 | 103.4 | 103.0 | 96.9 | 95.8 | 82.9 | 97.9 | 97.5 | 94.2 | 95.1 |
| 1970[3] | 94.8 | 104.0 | 103.3 | 95.1 | 91.4 | 72.2 | 95.7 | 95.9 | 83.8 | (4) |
| 1977[5] | 95.1 | 104.6 | 103.8 | 98.4 | 92.0 | 68.7 | 95.7 | (4) | (4) | 91.7 |

1. Excludes Indians in Indian Territory and on Indian reservations. 2. The age figures exclude all persons residing on Indian reservations, whether white or nonwhite; these persons are included in the race and nativity distributions. 3. Data by age and race include, and data by nativity exclude, Armed Forces overseas and other persons abroad. 4. Not available. 5. Total population including Armed Forces overseas. NOTE: For 1860, the data in the census reports at ages 40–49 and 60–69 are published in 10-year age groupings; these were subdivided into 5-year age groupings by the author. *Sources:* Mortimer Spiegelman, *Introduction to Demography;* Department of Commerce, Bureau of the Census.

## Distribution of Population by Race

| Year[1] | White | Black | Indian | Japanese | Chinese | All other | Total nonwhite |
|---|---|---|---|---|---|---|---|
| 1850 | 19,553,068 | 3,638,808 | — | — | — | — | 3,638,808 |
| 1860 | 26,922,537 | 4,441,830 | 44,021 | — | 34,933 | — | 4,520,784 |
| 1870 | 33,589,377 | 4,880,009 | 25,731 | 55 | 63,199 | — | 4,968,994 |
| 1880 | 43,402,970 | 6,580,793 | 66,407 | 148 | 105,465 | — | 6,752,813 |
| 1890 | 55,101,258 | 7,488,676 | 248,253 | 2,039 | 107,488 | — | 7,846,456 |
| 1900 | 66,809,196 | 8,833,994 | 237,196 | 24,326 | 89,863 | — | 9,185,379 |
| 1910 | 81,731,957 | 9,827,763 | 265,683 | 72,157 | 71,531 | 3,175 | 10,240,309 |
| 1920 | 94,820,915 | 10,463,131 | 244,437 | 111,010 | 61,639 | 9,488 | 10,889,705 |
| 1930 | 110,286,740 | 11,891,143 | 332,397 | 138,834 | 74,954 | 50,978 | 12,488,306 |
| 1940 | 118,214,870 | 12,865,518 | 333,969 | 126,947 | 77,504 | 50,467 | 13,454,405 |
| 1950 | 134,942,028 | 15,042,286 | 343,410 | 141,768 | 117,629 | 110,240 | 15,755,333 |
| 1960 | 158,831,732 | 18,871,831 | 523,591 | 464,332 | 237,292 | 394,397 | 20,491,443 |
| 1970 | 177,748,975 | 22,580,289 | 792,730 | 591,290 | 435,062 | 1,063,580 | 25,462,951 |
| Urban | 128,773,240 | 18,367,318 | 355,738 | 523,651 | 418,779 | 886,204 | 20,551,690 |
| Rural | 48,975,735 | 4,212,971 | 436,992 | 67,639 | 16,283 | 177,376 | 4,911,261 |

1. Beginning with 1960, data include Alaska and Hawaii. *Source:* Department of Commerce, Bureau of the Census.

## Distribution of Population According to Size of Place

| Census year | Total population | Population distribution (total for year = 100%): Total urban | Places of 2,500 or more: 1,000,000 or more | Places of 2,500 or more: 100,000 to 1,000,000 | Places of 2,500 or more: Under 100,000 | Total rural | Number of places of 2,500 or more: 1,000,000 or more | Number of places of 2,500 or more: 100,000 to 1,000,000 | Number of places of 2,500 or more: Under 100,000 |
|---|---|---|---|---|---|---|---|---|---|
| 1790 | 3,929,214 | 5.1 | — | — | 5.1 | 94.9 | — | — | 24 |
| 1800 | 5,308,483 | 6.1 | — | — | 6.1 | 93.9 | — | — | 33 |
| 1810 | 7,239,881 | 7.3 | — | — | 7.3 | 92.7 | — | — | 46 |
| 1820 | 9,638,453 | 7.2 | — | 1.3 | 5.9 | 92.8 | — | 1 | 60 |
| 1830 | 12,866,020 | 8.8 | — | 1.6 | 7.2 | 91.2 | — | 1 | 89 |
| 1840 | 17,069,453 | 10.8 | — | 3.0 | 7.8 | 89.2 | — | 3 | 128 |
| 1850 | 23,191,876 | 15.3 | — | 5.1 | 10.2 | 84.7 | — | 6 | 230 |
| 1860 | 31,443,321 | 19.8 | — | 8.4 | 11.4 | 80.2 | — | 9 | 383 |
| 1870 | 39,818,449 | 25.7 | — | 10.7 | 15.0 | 74.3 | — | 14 | 649 |
| 1880 | 50,155,783 | 28.2 | 2.4 | 10.0 | 15.8 | 71.8 | 1 | 19 | 919 |
| 1890 | 62,947,714 | 35.1 | 5.8 | 9.6 | 19.7 | 64.9 | 3 | 25 | 1,320 |
| 1900 | 75,994,575 | 39.7 | 8.5 | 10.2 | 21.0 | 60.3 | 3 | 35 | 1,699 |
| 1910 | 91,972,266 | 45.7 | 9.2 | 12.9 | 23.6 | 54.3 | 3 | 47 | 2,212 |
| 1920 | 105,710,620 | 51.2 | 9.6 | 16.3 | 25.3 | 48.8 | 3 | 65 | 2,654 |
| 1930 | 122,775,046 | 56.2 | 12.3 | 17.3 | 26.6 | 43.8 | 5 | 88 | 3,072 |
| 1940 | 131,669,275 | 56.5 | 12.1 | 16.8 | 27.6 | 43.5 | 5 | 87 | 3,372 |
| 1950[1] | 150,697,361 | 59.0 | 11.5 | 18.0 | 29.5 | 41.0 | 5 | 102 | 3,916 |
| 1950[2] | 150,697,361 | 64.0 | 11.5 | 17.9 | 34.6 | 36.0 | 5 | 101 | 4,635 |
| 1960[2,3] | 179,323,175 | 69.9 | 9.8 | 18.7 | 41.4 | 30.1 | 5 | 127 | 5,909 |
| 1970[2,3] | 203,235,298 | 73.5 | 9.2 | 18.5 | 45.8 | 26.5 | 6 | 150 | 6,279 |

1. Old urban definition. 2. New urban definition. 3. Includes Alaska and Hawaii. *Source:* Department of Commerce, Bureau of the Census.

## Population of Races Other Than White or Black, 1970

| State | Indian | Japanese | Chinese | Filipino | All other[1] | State | Indian | Japanese | Chinese | Filipino | All other[1] |
|---|---|---|---|---|---|---|---|---|---|---|---|
| Alabama | 2,443 | 1,079 | 626 | 540 | 2,179 | Montana | 27,130 | 574 | 289 | 236 | 1,142 |
| Alaska | 16,276 | 916 | 228 | 1,498 | 35,786 | Nebraska | 6,624 | 1,314 | 551 | 324 | 1,902 |
| Arizona | 95,812 | 2,394 | 3,878 | 1,253 | 9,271 | Nevada | 7,933 | 1,087 | 955 | 817 | 2,007 |
| Arkansas | 2,014 | 587 | 743 | 289 | 1,302 | N.H. | 361 | 360 | 420 | 157 | 772 |
| Calif. | 91,018 | 213,280 | 170,131 | 138,859 | 178,671 | N.J. | 4,706 | 5,681 | 9,233 | 5,623 | 22,721 |
| Colorado | 8,836 | 7,831 | 1,489 | 1,068 | 9,272 | N.M. | 72,788 | 940 | 563 | 386 | 5,953 |
| Conn. | 2,222 | 1,621 | 2,209 | 2,177 | 6,845 | New York | 28,355 | 20,351 | 81,378 | 14,279 | 89,565 |
| Delaware | 656 | 359 | 559 | 392 | 1,403 | N.C. | 44,406 | 2,104 | 1,255 | 905 | 5,144 |
| D.C. | 956 | 651 | 2,582 | 1,662 | 3,675 | N.D. | 14,369 | 239 | 165 | 204 | 805 |
| Florida | 6,677 | 4,090 | 3,133 | 5,092 | 9,457 | Ohio | 6,654 | 5,555 | 5,305 | 3,490 | 13,539 |
| Georgia | 2,347 | 1,836 | 1,584 | 1,253 | 4,164 | Oklahoma | 98,468 | 1,408 | 999 | 612 | 5,488 |
| Hawaii | 1,126 | 217,307 | 52,039 | 93,915 | 98,441 | Oregon | 13,510 | 6,843 | 4,814 | 1,633 | 6,198 |
| Idaho | 6,687 | 2,255 | 498 | 206 | 1,989 | Pa. | 5,533 | 5,461 | 7,053 | 4,560 | 17,056 |
| Illinois | 11,413 | 17,299 | 14,474 | 12,654 | 32,081 | R.I. | 1,390 | 629 | 1,093 | 1,761 | 1,757 |
| Indiana | 3,887 | 2,279 | 2,115 | 1,365 | 6,235 | S.C. | 2,241 | 826 | 521 | 1,222 | 2,235 |
| Iowa | 2,992 | 1,009 | 993 | 614 | 3,410 | S.D. | 32,365 | 221 | 163 | 83 | 715 |
| Kansas | 8,672 | 1,584 | 1,233 | 758 | 5,286 | Tenn. | 2,276 | 1,160 | 1,610 | 846 | 2,604 |
| Kentucky | 1,531 | 1,095 | 558 | 612 | 2,351 | Texas | 17,957 | 6,537 | 7,635 | 3,442 | 45,026 |
| Louisiana | 5,294 | 1,123 | 1,340 | 1,249 | 3,970 | Utah | 11,273 | 4,713 | 1,281 | 392 | 3,071 |
| Maine | 2,195 | 348 | 206 | 453 | 770 | Vermont | 229 | 134 | 173 | 53 | 427 |
| Maryland | 4,239 | 3,733 | 6,520 | 5,170 | 8,370 | Va. | 4,853 | 3,500 | 2,805 | 7,496 | 6,958 |
| Mass. | 4,475 | 4,393 | 14,012 | 2,361 | 10,488 | Wash. | 33,386 | 20,335 | 9,201 | 11,462 | 12,422 |
| Michigan | 16,854 | 5,221 | 6,407 | 3,657 | 18,404 | W. Va. | 751 | 368 | 373 | 722 | 1,201 |
| Minnesota | 23,128 | 2,603 | 2,422 | 1,456 | 4,456 | Wisconsin | 18,924 | 2,648 | 2,700 | 1,209 | 5,067 |
| Miss. | 4,113 | 461 | 1,441 | 475 | 1,369 | Wyoming | 4,980 | 566 | 292 | 108 | 878 |
| Missouri | 5,405 | 2,382 | 2,815 | 2,010 | 6,222 | **Total** | **792,730** | **591,290** | **435,062** | **343,060** | **720,520** |

1. Aleuts, Asian Indians, Eskimos, Hawaiians, Indonesians, Koreans, Polynesians, and other races not shown separately. NOTE: As of April 1, resident popluation. *Source:* Department of Commerce, Bureau of the Census.

# Immigration to U.S. by Country of Origin

(Figures are totals, not annual averages, and were tabulated as follows: 1820–67, alien passengers arrived; 1868–91 and 1895–97, immigrant aliens arrived; 1892–94 and 1898 to present, immigrant aliens admitted. Data before 1906 relate to country whence alien came; since 1906, to country of last permanent residence.)

| Countries | 1977 | 1820–1977 | 1961–70 | 1951–60 | 1941–50 | 1931–40 | 1921–30 | 1820–1920 |
|---|---|---|---|---|---|---|---|---|
| Europe: Albania[1] | 51 | 2,515 | 98 | 59 | 85 | 2,040 | — | |
| Austria[2] | 459 | 4,314,512 | 20,621 | 67,106 | 24,860 | 3,563 | 32,868 | 3,626,110 |
| Belgium | 531 | 201,807 | 9,192 | 18,575 | 12,189 | 4,817 | 15,846 | 137,542 |
| Bulgaria[3] | 98 | 67,692 | 619 | 104 | 375 | 938 | 2,945 | 61,973 |
| Czechoslovakia[1] | 273 | 136,591 | 3,273 | 918 | 8,347 | 14,393 | 102,194 | 3,426 |
| Denmark | 403 | 363,761 | 9,201 | 10,984 | 5,393 | 2,559 | 32,430 | 300,036 |
| Estonia[1] | 1 | 1,122 | 163 | 185 | 212 | 506 | — | — |
| Finland[1] | 227 | 33,128 | 4,192 | 4,925 | 2,503 | 2,146 | 16,691 | 756 |
| France | 2,651 | 747,683 | 45,237 | 51,121 | 38,809 | 12,623 | 49,610 | 532,765 |
| Germany[2] | 7,414 | 6,970,176 | 190,796 | 477,765 | 226,578 | 114,058 | 412,202 | 5,495,691 |
| Great Britain: England | 12,579 | 3,163,576 | 174,452 | 156,171 | 112,252 | 21,756 | 157,420 | 2,462,015 |
| Scotland | 884 | 819,108 | 29,849 | 32,854 | 16,131 | 6,887 | 159,781 | 567,106 |
| Wales | 139 | 94,993 | 2,052 | 2,589 | 3,209 | 735 | 13,012 | 72,647 |
| Not specified[4] | 438 | 804,468 | 3,675 | 3,884 | — | — | — | 793,741 |
| Greece | 7,792 | 647,892 | 85,969 | 47,608 | 8,973 | 9,119 | 51,084 | 370,405 |
| Hungary[2] | 475 | — | 5,401 | 36,637 | 3,469 | 7,861 | 30,680 | 442,693 |
| Ireland | 967 | 4,722,621 | 37,461 | 57,332 | 26,967 | 13,167 | 220,591 | 4,358,350 |
| Italy | 7,369 | 5,287,386 | 214,111 | 185,491 | 57,661 | 68,028 | 455,315 | 4,195,880 |
| Latvia[1] | 8 | 2,539 | 510 | 352 | 361 | 1,192 | — | — |
| Lithuania[1] | 11 | 3,822 | 562 | 242 | 683 | 2,201 | — | — |
| Luxembourg[1] | 27 | 2,843 | 556 | 684 | 820 | 565 | — | — |
| Netherlands | 1,039 | 358,459 | 30,606 | 52,277 | 14,860 | 7,150 | 26,948 | 219,661 |
| Norway[5] | 344 | 856,046 | 15,484 | 22,935 | 10,100 | 4,740 | 68,531 | 731,584 |
| Poland[6] | 3,331 | 510,001 | 53,539 | 9,985 | 7,571 | 17,026 | 227,734 | 169,995 |
| Portugal | 9,977 | 434,837 | 76,065 | 19,588 | 7,423 | 3,329 | 29,994 | 222,721 |
| Romania[7] | 1,506 | 169,263 | 2,531 | 1,039 | 1,076 | 3,871 | 67,646 | 85,428 |
| Spain | 5,568 | 255,285 | 44,659 | 7,894 | 2,898 | 3,258 | 28,958 | 137,907 |
| Sweden[5] | 576 | 1,271,281 | 17,116 | 21,697 | 10,665 | 3,960 | 97,249 | 1,116,239 |
| Switzerland | 812 | 348,243 | 18,453 | 17,675 | 10,547 | 5,512 | 29,676 | 260,492 |
| U.S.S.R.[8] | 5,443 | 3,368,637 | 2,336 | 584 | 548 | 1,356 | 61,742 | 3,280,249 |
| Yugoslavia[3] | 2,315 | 111,322 | 20,381 | 8,225 | 1,576 | 5,835 | 49,064 | 1,888 |
| Other Europe | 340 | 55,198 | 4,203 | 8,155 | 3,983 | 2,361 | 22,983 | 10,716 |
| Total Europe | 74,048 | 36,126,807 | 1,123,363 | 1,325,640 | 621,124 | 347,552 | 2,463,194 | 29,658,016 |
| Asia: China[9] | 12,513 | 513,272 | 34,764 | 9,657 | 16,709 | 4,928 | 29,907 | 347,338 |
| India | 16,849 | 144,553 | 27,189 | 1,973 | 1,761 | 496 | 1,886 | 7,491 |
| Japan[10] | 4,545 | 401,938 | 39,988 | 46,250 | 1,555 | 1,948 | 33,462 | 242,181 |
| Turkey | 991 | 384,533 | 10,142 | 3,519 | 798 | 1,065 | 33,824 | 326,347 |
| Other Asia | 115,944 | 1,165,868 | 315,688 | 88,707 | 11,537 | 7,644 | 12,980 | 22,915 |
| Total Asia[11] | 150,842 | 2,610,164 | 427,771 | 150,106 | 32,360 | 16,081 | 112,059 | 946,272 |
| America: Canada and Newfoundland[12] | 18,003 | 4,081,362 | 413,310 | 377,952 | 171,718 | 108,527 | 924,515 | 1,972,686 |
| Central America | 16,892 | 292,382 | 101,330 | 44,751 | 21,665 | 5,861 | 15,769 | 27,524 |
| Mexico[13] | 44,645 | 2,031,045 | 453,937 | 299,811 | 60,589 | 22,319 | 459,287 | 296,649 |
| South America | 33,671 | 670,944 | 257,954 | 91,628 | 21,831 | 7,803 | 42,215 | 71,284 |
| West Indies | 109,959 | 1,599,084 | 470,213 | 123,091 | 49,725 | 15,502 | 74,899 | 356,570 |
| Other America[13] | 4 | 109,424 | 19,630 | 59,711 | 29,276 | 25 | 31 | — |
| Total America | 223,174 | 8,784,241 | 1,716,374 | 996,944 | 354,804 | 160,037 | 1,516,716 | 2,724,713 |
| **Africa** | 9,612 | 121,723 | 28,954 | 14,092 | 7,367 | 1,750 | 6,286 | 18,024 |
| **Australia and New Zealand** | 2,544 | 115,843 | 19,562 | 11,506 | 13,805 | 2,231 | 8,299 | 44,002 |
| Pacific Islands[14] | 195 | 24,434 | 1,769 | 4,698 | 5,437 | 780 | 427 | 9,938 |
| Countries not specified[15] | 1,900 | 280,311 | 3,884 | 12,493 | 142 | — | 228 | 253,838 |
| **Total all countries** | **462,315** | **48,063,523** | **3,321,677** | **2,515,479** | **1,135,039** | **528,431** | **4,107,209** | **33,654,803** |

1. Countries established since beginning of World War I are included with countries to which they belonged. 2. Data for Austria-Hungary not reported until 1861. Austria and Hungary recorded separately after 1905, Austria included with Germany 1938–45. 3. Bulgaria, Serbia, Montenegro first reported in 1899. Bulgaria reported separately since 1920. In 1920, separate enumeration for Kingdom of Serbs, Croats, Slovenes; since 1922, recorded as Yugoslavia. 4. United Kingdom not specified; for 1901–51, included in "Other Europe." 5. Norway included with Sweden 1820–68. 6. Included with Austria-Hungary, Germany, and Russia 1899–1919. 7. No record of immigration until 1880. 8. From 1931–63, the U.S.S.R. was broken down into European U.S.S.R. and Asian U.S.S.R. Since 1964, total U.S.S.R. has been reported in Europe. 9. Beginning in 1957, China includes Taiwan. 10. No record of immigration until 1861. 11. From 1952, Asia included Philippines. From 1934–51, Philippines were included in Pacific Islands; before 1934, recorded in separate tables as insular travel. 12. Includes all British North American possessions, 1820–98. 13. No record of immigration, 1886–93. 14. Included with "Countries not specified" prior to 1925. 15. Includes 32,897 persons returning in 1906 to their homes in U.S. *Source:* Department of Justice, Immigration and Naturalization Service.

## Population of Largest Indian Reservations, 1977

| | | | | | |
|---|---|---|---|---|---|
| Navajo (Ariz., N.M., Utah) | 154,748 | Papago (Ariz.) | 10,542 | Standing Rock (N.D., S.D.) | 6,957 |
| Creek (Okla.)[1] | 26,562 | Osage (Okla.)[1] | 10,499 | Chickasaw (Okla.)[1] | 6,800 |
| Cherokee (Okla.)[1] | 23,500 | Yakima (Wash.) | 9,802 | Wind River (Wyo.) | 6,742 |
| Southern Pueblos (N.M.) | 20,080 | Gila River (Ariz.) | 8,777 | Blackfeet (Mont.) | 6,269 |
| Choctaw (Okla.)[1] | 17,313 | Turtle Mountain (N.D.) | 7,850 | Zuni (N.M.) | 6,266 |
| Pine Ridge (S.D.) | 12,260 | Fort Apache (Ariz.) | 7,706 | San Carlos (N.M.) | 5,979 |
| Rosebud (S.D.) | 12,186 | Hopi (Ariz.) | 7,177 | | |

1. Includes Indians living in former reservation areas. NOTE: The Bureau of Indian Affairs lists 648,700 Indians residing on or near Federal reservations. *Source:* Department of the Interior, Bureau of Indian Affairs.

## Immigrant and Nonimmigrant Aliens Admitted to U.S.

| Period[1] | Immigrants | Non-immigrants | Total | Period[1] | Immigrants | Non-immigrants | Total |
|---|---|---|---|---|---|---|---|
| 1901–10 | 8,795,386 | 1,007,909 | 9,803,295 | 1971 | 370,478 | 4,403,761 | 4,774,239 |
| 1911–20 | 5,735,811 | 1,376,271 | 7,112,082 | 1972 | 384,685 | 5,171,460 | 5,556,145 |
| 1921–30 | 4,107,209 | 1,774,896 | 5,882,090 | 1973 | 400,063 | 5,977,324 | 6,377,387 |
| 1931–40 | 528,431 | 1,574,071 | 2,102,502 | 1974 | 394,861 | 6,908,708 | 7,303,569 |
| 1941–50 | 1,035,039 | 2,461,359 | 3,496,398 | 1975 | 386,194 | 7,083,937 | 7,470,131 |
| 1951–55 | 1,087,638 | 2,654,461 | 3,742,009 | 1976 | 398,613 | 7,654,491 | 8,053,104 |
| 1956–60 | 1,427,841 | 4,458,562 | 5,886,403 | 1976, TQ[2] | 103,676 | 2,673,652 | 2,777,328 |
| 1961–65 | 1,450,312 | 7,879,564 | 9,329,876 | 1977[3] | 462,315 | 8,036,916 | 8,499,231 |
| 1966–70 | 1,871,365 | 16,227,660 | 18,099,025 | | | | |

1. Fiscal year ending June 30, except as noted. 2. Transition Quarter, July–Sept. 1976. 3. Fiscal year, Oct. 1976–Sept. 1977. *Source:* Department of Justice, Immigration and Naturalization Service.

## Persons Naturalized Since 1907

| Period[1] | Civilian | Military | Total | Period[1] | Civilian | Military | Total |
|---|---|---|---|---|---|---|---|
| 1907–30 | 2,713,389 | 300,506 | 3,013,895 | 1973 | 112,944 | 7,796 | 120,740 |
| 1931–40 | 1,498,573 | 19,891 | 1,518,464 | 1974 | 124,807 | 6,848 | 131,655 |
| 1941–50 | 1,837,229 | 149,799 | 1,987,028 | 1975 | 135,323 | 6,214 | 141,537 |
| 1951–60 | 1,148,241 | 41,705 | 1,189,946 | 1976 | 136,873 | 5,631 | 142,504 |
| 1961–70 | 1,084,195 | 36,068 | 1,120,263 | 1976, TQ[2] | 46,705 | 1,513 | 48,218 |
| 1971 | 98,858 | 9,549 | 108,407 | 1977[3] | 154,568 | 5,305 | 159,873 |
| 1972 | 107,740 | 8,475 | 116,215 | 1907–77 | 9,199,445 | 599,300 | 9,798,745 |

1. Fiscal year ending June 30, except as noted. 2. Transition Quarter, July-Sept. 1976. 3. Fiscal year, Oct. 1976–Sept. 1977. *Source:* Department of Justice, Immigration and Naturalization Service.

# Marriage and Divorce

## Median Age at First Marriage

| Year | Males | Females | Year | Males | Females | Year | Males | Females | Year | Males | Females |
|---|---|---|---|---|---|---|---|---|---|---|---|
| 1890 | 26.1 | 22.0 | 1920 | 24.6 | 21.2 | 1950 | 22.8 | 20.3 | 1975 | 23.5 | 21.1 |
| 1900 | 25.9 | 21.9 | 1930 | 24.3 | 21.3 | 1960 | 22.8 | 20.3 | 1976 | 23.8 | 21.3 |
| 1910 | 25.1 | 21.6 | 1940 | 24.3 | 21.5 | 1970 | 23.1 | 20.8 | 1977 | 24.0 | 21.6 |

*Source:* Department of Commerce, Bureau of the Census.

## Marriage Information by State

| State | Legal minimum marriage age: With parental consent[3] M | With parental consent[3] F | Without parental consent M | Without parental consent F | Blood test required | Waiting period[1]: Before license | Waiting period[1]: After license | Marriages[2]: 1977[4] | Marriages[2]: 1976 |
|---|---|---|---|---|---|---|---|---|---|
| Alabama | 17 | 14 | 19 | 18 | yes | none | none | 45,392 | 47,639 |
| Alaska | 16 | 16 | 18 | 18 | yes | 3 d | none | 4,961 | 4,878 |
| Arizona | 18 | 18 | 18 | 18 | yes | none | none | 28,270 | 28,312 |
| Arkansas | 18 | 16 | 18 | 18 | yes | 3 d | none | 24,038 | 22,630 |
| California | 18 | 16 | 18 | 18 | yes | none | none | 151,346 | 150,654 |
| Colorado | 16[21] | 16[21] | 18 | 18 | yes[18] | none | none | 29,435 | 27,144 |
| Connecticut | 16 | 16 | 18 | 18 | yes | 4 d | none | 22,851 | 22,648 |
| Delaware | 18 | 16 | 18 | 18 | yes[11] | none | 24 h[5] | 3,999 | 3,941 |
| D. C. | — | 16–17 | 18 | 18 | yes[7] | 5 d[6] | none | 4,601 | 4,681 |
| Florida | 18 | 16 | 18 | 18 | yes | 3 d | none | 89,142 | 86,170 |
| Georgia | 16 | 16 | 18 | — | yes[23] | 3 d | none | 67,192 | 60,207 |
| Hawaii | 16 | 16 | 18 | 18 | yes | none | none | 10,274 | 9,750 |
| Idaho | 18 | 16 | 21 | 18 | yes | 3 d | none | 13,439 | 13,105 |
| Illinois | 16 | 16 | 18 | 18 | yes | none | none | 108,051 | 111,261 |
| Indiana | 17 | 17[22] | 18 | 18 | yes | 3 d | none | 56,290 | 56,359 |
| Iowa | 16 | 16 | 18 | 18 | yes | 3 d | none | 26,422 | 25,643 |
| Kansas | (25) | (25) | 18 | 18 | yes | 3 d | none | 23,556 | 23,416 |
| Kentucky | (19) | (19) | 18 | 18 | yes | 3 d | none | 34,030 | 34,807 |
| Louisiana | 18 | 16 | 18 | 18 | yes | none | 72 h | 38,343 | 39,050 |
| Maine | 16 | 16 | 18 | 18 | no | 5 d | none | 11,526 | 11,345 |
| Maryland | 16[15] | 16[15] | 18 | 18 | no | 48 h | none | 44,973 | 44,891 |
| Massachusetts | 14–17[12] | 12–15[12] | 18 | 18 | yes | 3 d | none | 39,728 | 40,928 |
| Michigan | 18 | 16[8] | 18 | 18 | yes | 3 d | none | 86,221 | 83,193 |
| Minnesota | 18 | 16 | 21 | 18 | no | 5 d | none | 31,593 | 33,198 |
| Mississippi | 17 | 15 | 21 | 21 | yes | 3 d | none | 26,481 | 26,450 |
| Missouri | 15[12] | 15[12] | 18 | 18 | yes | 3 d | none | 52,138 | 44,750 |
| Montana | 18 | 18 | 16[24] | 16[24] | yes | 5 d | 3 d | 7,532 | 7,328 |
| Nebraska | 17 | 17 | 19 | 19 | yes | 2 d | none | 12,978 | 13,386 |
| Nevada | 16 | 16 | 18 | 18 | no | none | none | 108,013 | 99,722 |
| New Hampshire | 14[12,15] | 13[12,15] | 18 | 18 | yes[11] | 5 d | none | 8,792 | 8,396 |
| New Jersey | 18 | 16 | 18 | 18 | yes | 72 h | none | 50,016 | 52,281 |
| New Mexico | 16 | 16 | 18 | 18 | yes | none | none | 12,445 | 12,393 |
| New York | 16 | 14[9] | 21 | 18 | yes | none | (10) | 131,611 | 136,694 |
| North Carolina | 16 | 16 | 18 | 18 | yes | none | none | 43,400 | 42,548 |
| North Dakota | 18 | 15 | 18 | 18 | yes | none | none | 5,672 | 5,638 |
| Ohio | 18 | 16 | 18 | 18 | yes | 5 d | none | 97,358 | 97,929 |
| Oklahoma | 16[17] | 16[17] | 18 | 18 | yes | none[14] | none | 41,440 | 40,677 |
| Oregon | 17 | 17 | 18 | 18 | yes | 7 d | none | 20,850 | 19,507 |
| Pennsylvania | 16 | 16 | 18 | 18 | yes | 3 d | none | 91,382 | 88,557 |
| Rhode Island | 18 | 16[9] | 18 | 18 | yes | none | none | 7,096 | 6,910 |
| South Carolina | 16 | 14 | 18 | 18 | no | 24 h | none | 51,157 | 50,028 |
| South Dakota | 16 | 16 | 18 | 18 | yes | none | none | 10,300 | 10,755 |
| Tennessee | 16 | 16 | 18 | 18 | yes | none[14] | none | 55,327 | 53,365 |
| Texas | 14[13] | 14[13] | 18 | 18 | yes | none | none | 161,331 | 156,479 |
| Utah | 14 | 14 | 16 | 16 | yes | none | none | 15,188 | 14,275 |
| Vermont | 16 | 16 | 18 | 18 | yes | none | 5 d[16] | 4,825 | 4,292 |
| Virginia | 16 | 16 | 18 | 18 | yes | none | none | 57,832 | 56,474 |
| Washington | 17 | 17 | 18 | 18 | no | 3 d | none | 41,308 | 40,684 |
| West Virginia | 18 | 16 | 18 | 18 | yes | 3 d | none | 17,522 | 17,145 |
| Wisconsin | 16 | 16 | 18 | 18 | yes | 5 d | none | 37,283 | 35,972 |
| Wyoming | 16[20] | 16[20] | 19[20] | 19[20] | yes | none | none | 5,909 | 5,763 |

1. In some states, waiting period may be waived or reduced by court order. 2. By place of occurrence. 3. In most states, persons younger than the age shown may be married by court permission. 4. Provisional figures; data represent marriages reported, marriage intentions filed, or marriage licenses issued. 5. 96 hours if nonresidents. 6. Day of application and day of pickup are included in 5-day waiting period. 7. No exceptions granted under this age. 8. Consent of one parent or guardian necessary for female only. 9. Females 14 to 16 years old must also have consent of judge of Family Court. 10. Marriage may not be solemnized within 10 days from date on which specimen was taken for serological test, and not until 24 hours after issuance of marriage license. Waiting period may be waived by court order. 11. Blood test may be waived by court order. 12. Need court order. 13. Parent must appear in person or provide doctor's affidavit of his or her illness. 14. 3 days if either party is under legal age. 15. If pregnant. 16. After date on which marriage application has been filed with town clerk, excluding date of filing. 17. Males under 18 and females under 15 only if female is pregnant. 18. Blood test for rubella and RH type not required of females over 45 years or found by physician to be incapable of bearing children. 19. No age limit. 20. If under 16 need court order. 21. Males and females under age of 16 may obtain a license with parental consent and judicial approval. 22. 15 for pregnancy or maternity. 23. Prior to issuance of license, a medical examination for rubella is required. 24. With judicial approval. 25. Under 18 with parental consent only. *Sources:* Legal information, *Information Please* questionnaires to states; marriage statistics, Department of Health, Education, and Welfare, National Center for Health Statistics.

# Divorce Information by State

| State | Residence for divorce | Period before parties may remarry: Plaintiff | Period before parties may remarry: Defendant | Divorces[1] 1977[2] | Divorces[1] 1976 |
|---|---|---|---|---|---|
| Alabama | 6 mo | 60 d | 60 d | 23,491 | 24,063 |
| Alaska | 1 yr | none | none | 3,839 | 3,207 |
| Arizona | 90 d | none | none | (3) | (3) |
| Arkansas | 90 d | none | none | 18,366 | 17,398 |
| California | 6 mo | none | none | 132,888 | 133,672 |
| Colorado | 90 d[20] | none | none | 20,250 | 17,424 |
| Connecticut | 1 yr | none | none | 11,859 | 10,546 |
| Delaware | 6 mo[20] | none[12] | none[12] | 3,044 | 3,235 |
| D.C. | 1 yr | 60 d | 60 d | 2,935 | 2,805 |
| Florida | 6 mo | none | none | 63,326 | 62,571 |
| Georgia | 6 mo | none | none | 30,096 | 28,625 |
| Hawaii | 6 mo | none | none | 4,653 | 4,714 |
| Idaho | 6 wk | none | none | 5,841 | 5,707 |
| Illinois | 1 yr | none | none | 50,553 | 50,043 |
| Indiana | 6 mo[4, 6] | none | none | (3) | (3) |
| Iowa | 1 yr[11] | 1 yr | 1 yr | 10,938 | 10,803 |
| Kansas | 60 d | 30 d | 30 d | 12,652 | 12,900 |
| Kentucky | 6 mo[4, 24] | none | none | 16,156 | 16,784 |
| Louisiana | 1 yr | none[8] | none[8] | (3) | (3) |
| Maine | 6 mo | none | none | 5,751 | 5,416 |
| Maryland | 1 yr[25] | none | none | 15,701 | 15,613 |
| Massachusetts | 1 yr | (23) | (23) | 16,040 | 16,407 |
| Michigan | 1 yr | none | none | 42,081 | 43,109 |
| Minnesota | 1 yr | 6 mo | 6 mo | 13,896 | 13,735 |
| Mississippi | 1 yr | (10) | (10) | 12,828 | 12,096 |
| Missouri | 90 d | none | none | 25,021 | 25,316 |
| Montana | 1 yr | none | none | 4,841 | 4,847 |
| Nebraska | 1 yr[5] | none | none | 6,258 | 5,929 |
| Nevada | 6 wk | none | none | 10,301 | 10,151 |
| New Hampshire | 1 yr | none | none | 4,256 | 4,803 |
| New Jersey | 1 yr | none | none | 26,351 | 17,866 |
| New Mexico | 6 mo[13] | none | none | 6,880 | 7,089 |
| New York | (14) | none | none | 50,171 | 53,866 |
| North Carolina | 6 mo | none | none | 25,065 | 24,443 |
| North Dakota | 1 yr | (9) | (9) | 1,982 | 1,864 |
| Ohio | 6 mo[6] | none | none | 55,552 | 61,036 |
| Oklahoma | 6 mo[22] | 6 mo[21] | 6 mo[21] | 21,450 | 21,755 |
| Oregon | 6 mo | 60 d | 60 d | 16,623 | 16,126 |
| Pennsylvania | 1 yr | none | none[15] | 37,675 | 35,695 |
| Rhode Island | 2 yr | none | none | 3,414 | 3,289 |
| South Carolina | 1 yr | none | none | 11,428 | 9,830 |
| South Dakota | (7) | none | none | (3) | 2,363 |
| Tennessee | 1 yr | none[16] | none[16] | 28,227 | 27,801 |
| Texas | 6 mo | 30 d[16] | 30 d[16] | 83,215 | 80,235 |
| Utah | 3 mo | 3 mo[12] | 3 mo[12] | 6,901 | 6,170 |
| Vermont | 6 mo[19] | none | none | 1,938 | 1,844 |
| Virginia | 6 mo | none | none | 21,577 | 21,468 |
| Washington | none[20] | none | none | 25,646 | 26,715 |
| West Virginia | 1 yr[17] | (18) | (18) | 9,552 | 9,092 |
| Wisconsin | 6 mo | 6 mo | 6 mo | 14,932 | 14,088 |
| Wyoming | 60 d | none | none | 3,074 | 2,825 |

1. By place of occurrence, including reported annulments. 2. Provisional. 3. Data not available. 4. Only one party must have resided in the state for 180 days. 5. Decree not final until 6 months after trial and decision. 6. 6-month residence in state; 90-day residence in county. 7. Physical presence plus intent to make state the place of residence. 8. In case of adultery, guilty party cannot marry correspondent. 9. At discretion of court. 10. Until court that grants the divorce is adjourned. 11. No time required if both parties are residents of state and intend to make state their place of residence. 12. 3 months between first and final judgment. 13. Servicemen acquire residence by being continuously stationed at military base in state for 6 months. 14. Action for divorce may be maintained only where (1) parties were married in the state and either has been a resident for one year preceding the action; (2) parties have resided in the state as husband and wife and either has been a resident for one year preceding the action; (3) cause for divorce occurred in the state and either party has been a resident for one year preceding the action; (4) cause for divorce occurred in the state and both parties are residents at time of the action; (5) either party is a resident for at least 2 years preceding the action. 15. Party guilty of adultery may not marry the correspondent during lifetime of former spouse. 16. Parties may remarry each other at any time. 17. 2 years if residence is acquired after cause of divorce action arose. 18. Court can lengthen waiting period if desired. 19. Court must find resumption of marital relations not reasonably probable. 20. Must be domiciled in state. 21. 30 days from date of judgment of appeal. 22. 5 years if on grounds of insanity and insane spouse is in institution. 23. 6-month wait between date decree is granted and date it becomes final. 24. No decree shall be entered until parties have lived apart for 60 days. 25. When cause for divorce occurred out of state. *Sources:* Legal information, *Information Please* questionnaires to states; divorce statistics, Department of Health, Education, and Welfare, National Center for Health Statistics.

## Grounds for Divorce

| State | Adultery | Cruelty | Desertion | Alcoholism | Impotence | Felony conviction | Neglect to provide | Insanity | Pregnancy at marriage[1] | Bigamy | Separation | Indignities | Drug addiction | Violence | Fraudulent contract | Others |
|---|---|---|---|---|---|---|---|---|---|---|---|---|---|---|---|---|
| Alabama | yes | yes | yes[2] | yes | yes | yes[16] | yes[3] | yes[6] | yes[1] | — | yes[3] | — | yes | yes | — | (27,29,34) |
| Alaska | yes | yes | yes[2] | yes | yes | yes | yes | yes[9] | — | — | — | yes | yes | yes | — | — |
| Arizona | — | — | — | — | — | — | — | — | — | — | — | — | — | — | — | (29) |
| Arkansas | yes | yes | yes[2] | yes | yes | yes | yes | yes | — | yes | yes[4] | yes | — | yes | yes | (12,31,48) |
| California | — | — | — | — | — | — | — | — | — | — | — | — | — | — | — | (28) |
| Colorado | — | — | — | — | — | — | — | — | — | — | — | — | — | — | — | (29,52) |
| Connecticut | yes | yes | yes[2] | yes | — | yes[20] | — | yes[6] | — | — | yes | — | — | yes | yes | (9,23,28,30,34,42,46) |
| Delaware | — | — | — | — | — | — | — | — | — | — | — | — | — | — | — | (29) |
| D.C. | yes[53] | yes[53] | — | — | — | — | — | — | — | — | yes[2] | — | — | — | — | (63) |
| Florida | — | — | — | — | — | — | — | — | — | — | — | — | — | — | — | (49,52) |
| Georgia | yes | yes | yes[2] | yes | yes | yes[15] | yes | yes | yes | yes | yes | yes | yes | yes | yes | (27,31,44,49) |
| Hawaii | — | — | — | — | — | — | — | — | — | — | yes[3] | — | — | — | — | (29) |
| Idaho | yes | yes | yes | — | — | yes | yes | yes[4] | — | yes | — | — | — | — | — | (26,28,42) |
| Illinois | yes | yes | yes[2] | yes[3] | yes | yes | — | — | — | yes | — | — | yes[3] | yes | — | (32,37,56) |
| Indiana | — | — | — | — | yes | — | — | yes[3] | — | — | — | — | — | — | — | (29,33,52) |
| Iowa | — | — | — | — | — | — | — | — | — | — | — | — | — | — | — | (49) |
| Kansas | yes | yes | yes[2] | yes | — | yes | yes | yes[6] | — | — | — | — | — | — | yes | (31,48) |
| Kentucky | — | — | — | — | — | — | — | — | — | — | — | — | — | — | — | (49) |
| Louisiana | yes | yes | yes | yes | — | yes | yes | — | — | yes | yes[3] | — | yes | yes | — | (37,58) |
| Maine | yes | yes | yes | yes | yes | yes[20] | yes | — | — | — | — | — | yes | — | — | (28) |
| Maryland[65] | yes | — | — | — | yes | yes[18] | — | yes[66] | — | — | yes[10] | — | — | — | — | (28,35,67) |
| Massachusetts | yes | yes | yes[2] | yes | yes | yes[19] | yes | — | — | — | — | — | yes | — | — | (29,35,49) |
| Michigan | — | — | — | — | — | — | — | — | — | — | — | — | — | — | — | (29) |
| Minnesota | yes | — | yes[2] | yes[2] | yes | yes | — | yes[4] | — | — | yes[3] | — | — | — | — | (36,49) |
| Mississippi | yes | yes | yes | yes | yes | yes[22] | — | yes[47] | yes | yes | yes[2] | — | yes | yes | — | (10,28,31,49) |
| Missouri | yes | yes | yes | yes | yes | yes | — | — | yes | yes | — | yes | | — | — | (10,30,32,52) |
| Montana | — | — | — | — | — | — | — | — | — | — | — | — | — | — | — | (29) |
| Nebraska | — | — | — | — | — | — | — | — | — | — | — | — | — | — | — | (49) |
| Nevada | — | — | — | — | — | — | — | yes[3] | — | — | yes[2] | — | — | — | — | (27) |
| New Hampshire | yes | yes | yes[3] | yes[3] | yes | yes[14] | yes[3] | — | — | — | — | — | — | yes | — | (25,28,40,57,60) |
| New Jersey | yes | yes | yes[2] | yes[2] | yes[51] | yes[44] | — | yes[3] | — | yes[51] | yes[9] | — | yes[2] | — | yes[51] | (34,49) |
| New Mexico | yes | yes | yes | — | — | — | — | — | — | — | — | — | — | — | — | (27) |
| New York | yes | yes | yes[2] | — | — | yes[17] | — | — | — | — | yes[2] | — | — | — | — | — |
| North Carolina | yes | — | — | — | yes | — | — | yes[6] | yes | — | yes[2] | — | — | — | — | (34) |
| North Dakota | yes | yes | yes[2] | yes[2] | — | yes | yes[2] | yes[6] | — | — | — | — | — | — | — | (28) |
| Ohio | yes | yes | yes | yes[4] | yes | yes | yes | yes[5] | — | yes | yes[2] | — | — | — | yes | (12,24,41,55) |
| Oklahoma | yes | yes | yes[2] | yes | yes | yes[21] | yes | yes[6] | yes | yes | — | — | — | — | yes | (27,41,55) |
| Oregon | — | — | — | — | — | — | — | — | — | — | — | — | — | — | — | (49) |
| Pennsylvania | yes | yes | yes[3] | — | yes[45] | yes[15] | — | yes | — | yes | — | yes | — | yes | yes | (31) |
| Rhode Island | yes | yes | yes[6] | yes | yes | yes[7] | yes[2] | yes[48] | — | yes | yes[3] | — | yes | yes | yes | (13,38) |
| South Carolina | yes | yes[39] | yes[2] | yes | — | — | — | — | — | — | yes[4] | — | yes | — | — | (50) |
| South Dakota | yes | yes | yes[2] | yes[2] | — | yes | yes[2] | yes[6] | — | yes[61] | — | — | — | — | yes[61] | — |
| Tennessee | yes | yes | yes[2] | yes[43] | yes | yes | yes | — | yes | yes | — | yes | — | — | — | (28,32,37,59) |
| Texas | yes | yes | yes[2] | — | — | yes[54] | — | yes[4] | — | — | yes[4] | yes | — | yes | — | (28) |
| Utah | yes | yes | yes[2] | yes | yes | yes | yes | yes | — | — | yes[4] | — | — | — | — | — |
| Vermont | yes | yes | yes[7] | — | — | yes[17] | yes | yes[6] | — | — | yes[8] | — | — | — | — | (29) |
| Virginia | yes | yes | yes[2] | — | — | yes | — | — | — | — | yes[2] | — | — | — | — | — |
| Washington | — | — | — | — | — | — | — | — | — | — | — | — | — | — | — | (29) |
| West Virginia | yes | yes | yes[2] | yes | — | yes | — | yes | — | — | yes[3] | — | yes | — | — | (62) |
| Wisconsin | — | — | — | — | — | — | — | — | — | — | — | — | — | — | — | (29,64) |
| Wyoming | yes | yes | yes[2] | yes | yes | yes | yes[2] | yes[3] | yes | — | yes[3] | yes | — | — | — | (11,25) |

1. If unknown to husband. 2. 1 year. 3. 2 years. 4. 3 years. 5. 4 years. 6. 5 years. 7. 7 years. 8. 6 months. 9. 18 months. 10. Absence of 1 year. 11. Absence of 1 year voluntarily, or under legal separation judgment. 12. Absence of 3 years. 13. Absence of one spouse; presumption of death. 14. With imprisonment of 1 year. 15. With imprisonment of 2 years. 16. With imprisonment of 2 years, sentence being for 7 years or more. 17. With imprisonen of 3 years. 18. With imprisonment of three years, twelve months of which have been served. 19. With imprisonment of 5 years. 20. With imprisonment for life. 21. Imprisonment of other party in state or federal penal institution under sentence thereto for commission of felony at time the petition is filed. 22. Unless pardoned before beginning sentence. 23. Noncohabitation for 18 months. 24. Court of Common Pleas may grant a dissolution of marriage—6 months residency required. 25. Noncohabitation for 2 years. 26. Noncohabitation for 5 years. 27. Incompatibility. 28. Irreconcilable differences. 29. Irretrievable breakdown of marriage relationship. 30. Irretrievably broken upon proof, decree of dissolution. 31. Relationship within prohibited degree. 32. Infamous crime. 33. Infamous crime subsequent to marriage. 34. Crime against nature. 35. Excessively vicious conduct; any cause which, by laws

(Footnotes continued on next page)

# Marriages and Divorces

| Year | Marriage Number | Marriage Rate[2] | Divorce[1] Number | Divorce[1] Rate[2] | Year | Marriage Number | Marriage Rate[2] | Divorce[1] Number | Divorce[1] Rate[2] |
|---|---|---|---|---|---|---|---|---|---|
| 1900 | 709,000 | 9.3 | 55,751 | .7 | 1955 | 1,531,000 | 9.3 | 377,000 | 2.3 |
| 1905 | 842,000 | 10.0 | 67,976 | .8 | 1956 | 1,585,000 | 9.5 | 382,000 | 2.3 |
| 1910 | 948,166 | 10.3 | 83,045 | .9 | 1957 | 1,518,000 | 8.9 | 381,000 | 2.2 |
| 1915 | 1,007,595 | 10.0 | 104,298 | 1.0 | 1958 | 1,451,000 | 8.4 | 368,000 | 2.1 |
| 1920 | 1,274,476 | 12.0 | 170,505 | 1.6 | 1959 | 1,494,000 | 8.5 | 395,000 | 2.2 |
| 1925 | 1,188,334 | 10.3 | 175,449 | 1.5 | 1960 | 1,523,000 | 8.5 | 393,000 | 2.2 |
| 1930 | 1,126,856 | 9.2 | 195,961 | 1.6 | 1961 | 1,548,000 | 8.5 | 414,000 | 2.3 |
| 1935 | 1,327,000 | 10.4 | 218,000 | 1.7 | 1962 | 1,577,000 | 8.5 | 413,000 | 2.2 |
| 1940 | 1,595,879 | 12.1 | 264,000 | 2.0 | 1963 | 1,654,000 | 8.8 | 428,000 | 2.3 |
| 1941 | 1,695,999 | 12.7 | 293,000 | 2.2 | 1964 | 1,725,000 | 9.0 | 450,000 | 2.4 |
| 1942 | 1,772,132 | 13.2 | 321,000 | 2.4 | 1965 | 1,800,000 | 9.3 | 479,000 | 2.5 |
| 1943 | 1,577,050 | 11.7 | 359,000 | 2.6 | 1966 | 1,857,000 | 9.5 | 499,000 | 2.5 |
| 1944 | 1,452,394 | 10.9 | 400,000 | 2.9 | 1967 | 1,927,000 | 9.7 | 523,000 | 2.6 |
| 1945 | 1,612,992 | 12.2 | 485,000 | 3.5 | 1968 | 2,069,258 | 10.4 | 584,000 | 2.9 |
| 1946 | 2,291,045 | 16.4 | 610,000 | 4.3 | 1969 | 2,145,438 | 10.6 | 639,000 | 3.2 |
| 1947 | 1,991,878 | 13.9 | 483,000 | 3.4 | 1970 | 2,158,802 | 10.6 | 708,000 | 3.5 |
| 1948 | 1,811,155 | 12.4 | 408,000 | 2.8 | 1971 | 2,190,481 | 10.6 | 773,000 | 3.7 |
| 1949 | 1,579,798 | 10.6 | 397,000 | 2.7 | 1972 | 2,282,154 | 11.0 | 845,000 | 4.1 |
| 1950 | 1,667,231 | 11.1 | 385,144 | 2.6 | 1973 | 2,284,108 | 10.9 | 915,000 | 4.4 |
| 1951 | 1,594,694 | 10.4 | 381,000 | 2.5 | 1974 | 2,229,667 | 10.5 | 977,000 | 4.6 |
| 1952 | 1,539,318 | 9.9 | 392,000 | 2.5 | 1975 | 2,152,662 | 10.1 | 1,036,000 | 4.9 |
| 1953 | 1,546,000 | 9.8 | 390,000 | 2.5 | 1976 | 2,133,000 | 9.9 | 1,083,000 | 5.0 |
| 1954 | 1,490,000 | 9.2 | 379,000 | 2.4 | 1977[3] | 2,176,000 | 10.1 | 1,097,000 | 5.1 |

1. Includes annulments. 2. Per 1,000 population. Divorce rates for 1941–46 are based on population including armed forces overseas. Marriage rates are based on population excluding armed forces overseas. 3. Provisional. NOTE: Marriage and divorce figures for most years include some estimated data. Alaska is included beginning 1959, Hawaii beginning 1960. *Source:* Department of Health, Education, and Welfare, National Center for Health Statistics.

# Percent of Population Ever Married

| Age group, years | 1977 | 1976 | 1970 | 1960 | 1950 | 1940 | 1930 | 1920 | 1910 | 1900 |
|---|---|---|---|---|---|---|---|---|---|---|
| Males: 14 to 19 | 2.4 | 3.0 | 2.6 | 3.3 | 2.9 | 1.5 | 1.5 | 1.8 | 1.0 | 0.9 |
| 20 to 24 | 36.3 | 37.9 | 45.3 | 46.9 | 41.0 | 27.8 | 29.0 | 29.1 | 24.7 | 22.2 |
| 25 to 29 | 73.9 | 75.1 | 80.9 | 79.2 | 76.2 | 64.0 | 63.2 | 60.5 | 57.1 | 54.1 |
| 30 to 34 | 87.9 | 87.8 | 90.6 | 88.1 | 86.8 | 79.3 | 78.8 | 75.8 | 73.9 | 72.3 |
| 35 to 44 | 92.9 | 92.7 | 93.3 | 91.9 | 90.4 | 86.0 | 85.7 | 83.8 | 83.3 | 83.0 |
| 45 to 54 | 94.4 | 94.4 | 92.5 | 92.6 | 91.5 | 88.9 | 88.6 | 88.0 | 88.8 | 89.7 |
| Females: 14 to 19 | 8.7 | 9.2 | 9.7 | 13.5 | 14.4 | 10.0 | 10.9 | 10.8 | 9.8 | 9.4 |
| 20 to 24 | 54.7 | 57.4 | 64.2 | 71.6 | 67.7 | 52.8 | 53.9 | 54.4 | 51.5 | 48.4 |
| 25 to 29 | 83.9 | 85.2 | 89.5 | 89.5 | 86.7 | 77.2 | 78.3 | 76.9 | 75.0 | 72.4 |
| 30 to 34 | 93.0 | 93.0 | 93.8 | 93.1 | 90.7 | 85.3 | 86.8 | 85.1 | 83.8 | 83.4 |
| 35 to 44 | 95.0 | 95.3 | 94.8 | 93.9 | 91.7 | 89.6 | 90.0 | 88.6 | 88.6 | 88.9 |
| 45 to 54 | 95.7 | 95.6 | 95.1 | 93.0 | 92.2 | 91.3 | 90.9 | 90.4 | 91.4 | 92.2 |

*Source:* Department of Commerce, Bureau of the Census.

### Footnote for Grounds for Divorce Table (cont.)

of state, renders marriage null and void at its inception. 36. A course of conduct detrimental to the marriage relationship of the party seeking the divorce. 37. Attempt by one party on life of other. 38. Any other gross misbehavior or wickedness. 39. Physical cruelty only. 40. Treatment such as to injure health or endanger reason. 41. Gross neglect of duty. 42. Habitual intemperance. 43. Habitual drunkenness contracted after marriage. 44 With imprisonment of 18 months. 45. If at time of marriage and incurable. 46. Involuntary commitment to mental institution for 1 year subsequent to marriage. 47. Incurable, regardless when it occurs. 48. Insanity at time of marriage. 49. No-fault divorce. 50. No-fault divorce after 3 years' separation. 51. Grounds for nullity. 52. The term divorce is no longer used. The term now used is Dissolution of Marriage. 53. Limited divorce; may be enlarged into absolute divorce after separation of 1 year. 54. Suit for divorce cannot be sustained until 12 months after final judgment of conviction. Divorce cannot be obtained if plaintiff's testimony contributed toward conviction. 55. Defendant obtained divorce from plaintiff in any other state or country. 56. Infected other party with communicable venereal disease. 57. Joining a religious cult disbelieving in marriage. 58. Public defamation. 59. Wife's refusal to remove with husband to this state and willfully absenting herself for 2 years. 60. Wife gone to reside outside state and absent 10 years. 61. Annulment. 62. Abuse of a child. 63. Modified "no-fault" law enacted April 6, 1977. 64. Voluntary noncohabitation for 1 year. 65. Maryland grants two types of divorce—vinculo and mensa. The information here applies to vinculo divorce. 66. Only after confined 3 years, plus other requirements. 67. Abandonment after 12 months, or living separately for 3 years. *Source: Information Please* questionnaires to the states.

## Marriage Prospects of Single Men and Women

| Age | Percent of population single[1] | | Percent who ever marry[2] | | Age | Percent of population single[1] | | Percent who ever marry[2] | |
|---|---|---|---|---|---|---|---|---|---|
| | Male | Female | Male | Female | | Male | Female | Male | Female |
| 15 | 99.4 | 97.6 | 95.8 | 97.4 | 33 | 10.9 | 6.3 | 63.5 | 49.7 |
| 16 | 99.0 | 94.3 | 95.9 | 97.4 | 34 | 10.3 | 6.4 | 60.2 | 46.0 |
| 17 | 98.1 | 87.9 | 96.0 | 97.3 | 35 | 9.9 | 6.4 | 57.2 | 42.9 |
| 18 | 94.6 | 75.5 | 96.0 | 97.0 | 36 | 9.0 | 6.1 | 54.1 | 40.0 |
| 19 | 87.3 | 59.6 | 95.9 | 96.4 | 37 | 8.7 | 6.0 | 51.0 | 37.3 |
| 20 | 75.8 | 45.8 | 95.6 | 95.5 | 38 | 8.1 | 5.7 | 48.0 | 34.7 |
| 21 | 63.3 | 35.1 | 95.0 | 94.2 | 39 | 8.1 | 6.2 | 45.1 | 32.2 |
| 22 | 51.4 | 25.8 | 94.1 | 92.2 | 40 | 7.6 | 6.1 | 42.3 | 29.9 |
| 23 | 40.5 | 19.4 | 92.8 | 89.4 | 41 | 7.5 | 6.0 | 39.7 | 27.6 |
| 24 | 33.5 | 15.6 | 91.1 | 86.1 | 42 | 6.9 | 5.9 | 37.2 | 25.5 |
| 25 | 27.8 | 13.1 | 89.1 | 82.5 | 43 | 7.1 | 6.0 | 34.8 | 23.6 |
| 26 | 23.9 | 11.5 | 86.6 | 78.4 | 44 | 7.4 | 6.5 | 32.7 | 21.7 |
| 27 | 19.6 | 9.9 | 83.6 | 74.2 | 45 | 7.1 | 6.1 | 30.6 | 20.0 |
| 28 | 17.3 | 9.3 | 80.3 | 70.3 | 50 | 7.6 | 7.4 | 21.6 | 12.8 |
| 29 | 15.9 | 8.7 | 77.3 | 65.7 | 55 | 7.9 | 7.9 | 13.9 | 7.7 |
| 30 | 14.2 | 7.9 | 73.8 | 61.2 | 60 | 8.0 | 7.8 | 8.2 | 4.4 |
| 31 | 12.9 | 7.2 | 70.4 | 57.3 | 65 and over | 7.7 | 8.5 | — | — |
| 32 | 11.7 | 6.6 | 67.1 | 53.3 | | | | | |

1. Per cent single within specified year of age in 1960, in 5% sample of population (latest available data). 2. Per cent of white persons single at beginning of year of age who marry during that year and all later years, based on data for 1958–60. NOTE: "Single" excludes widowed and divorced. *Source:* Department of Commerce, Bureau of the Census.

## Marital Status of the Population, 1976

| State | Males | | | | Females | | | |
|---|---|---|---|---|---|---|---|---|
| | Population 14 years old and over in thousands | Percent distribution[1] | | | Population 14 years old and over in thousands | Percent distribution[1] | | |
| | | Single | Married | Widowed or divorced | | Single | Married | Widowed or divorced |
| Alabama | 1,308 | 29.2 | 64.4 | 6.3 | 1,448 | 21.0 | 59.0 | 20.0 |
| Alaska | 131 | 35.1 | 58.8 | 6.1 | 119 | 25.2 | 63.0 | 10.9 |
| Arizona | 835 | 29.6 | 63.7 | 6.7 | 877 | 20.8 | 61.5 | 17.8 |
| Arkansas | 776 | 27.4 | 67.3 | 5.3 | 889 | 21.7 | 60.1 | 18.2 |
| California | 7,911 | 31.0 | 61.4 | 7.6 | 8,382 | 22.4 | 59.0 | 18.6 |
| Colorado | 948 | 31.2 | 62.8 | 6.1 | 997 | 25.4 | 60.0 | 14.6 |
| Connecticut | 1,162 | 33.2 | 61.9 | 4.8 | 1,235 | 25.0 | 59.6 | 15.5 |
| Delaware | 213 | 31.0 | 63.4 | 5.6 | 227 | 23.8 | 61.2 | 15.0 |
| D. C. | 254 | 43.7 | 47.2 | 9.1 | 296 | 36.8 | 41.9 | 21.3 |
| Florida | 3,226 | 27.2 | 65.1 | 7.7 | 3,595 | 20.4 | 58.4 | 21.2 |
| Georgia | 1,768 | 30.7 | 62.6 | 6.7 | 1,959 | 22.6 | 58.9 | 18.4 |
| Hawaii | 323 | 36.8 | 57.6 | 5.6 | 316 | 28.2 | 58.9 | 13.0 |
| Idaho | 306 | 28.1 | 66.3 | 5.9 | 311 | 19.9 | 65.6 | 14.5 |
| Illinois | 4,075 | 32.2 | 61.1 | 6.7 | 4,367 | 24.4 | 57.9 | 17.8 |
| Indiana | 1,929 | 27.6 | 66.4 | 6.0 | 2,079 | 21.0 | 62.2 | 16.8 |
| Iowa | 1,054 | 28.7 | 66.0 | 5.1 | 1,124 | 21.6 | 61.7 | 16.6 |
| Kansas | 838 | 27.6 | 66.5 | 6.0 | 907 | 20.7 | 61.7 | 17.5 |
| Kentucky | 1,231 | 28.4 | 64.7 | 6.8 | 1,359 | 22.4 | 59.5 | 18.2 |
| Louisiana | 1,340 | 32.8 | 62.2 | 5.0 | 1,471 | 25.2 | 58.5 | 16.2 |
| Maine | 390 | 29.0 | 64.1 | 6.9 | 423 | 22.0 | 59.6 | 18.4 |
| Maryland | 1,484 | 30.5 | 64.1 | 5.4 | 1,627 | 25.9 | 59.6 | 14.6 |
| Massachusetts | 2,155 | 35.7 | 58.6 | 5.7 | 2,319 | 27.6 | 56.4 | 16.0 |
| Michigan | 3,291 | 31.1 | 62.9 | 6.0 | 3,639 | 24.8 | 58.6 | 16.6 |
| Minnesota | 1,446 | 33.1 | 62.0 | 4.9 | 1,536 | 26.4 | 58.5 | 15.1 |
| Mississippi | 811 | 31.4 | 63.0 | 5.7 | 915 | 21.9 | 58.8 | 19.3 |
| Missouri | 1,744 | 27.6 | 65.1 | 7.3 | 1,919 | 21.3 | 59.9 | 18.8 |
| Montana | 283 | 31.4 | 62.2 | 6.0 | 292 | 23.6 | 61.0 | 15.4 |
| Nebraska | 559 | 29.2 | 65.1 | 5.7 | 613 | 24.0 | 60.0 | 16.0 |

| State | Males | | | | Females | | | |
|---|---|---|---|---|---|---|---|---|
| | Population 14 years old and over in thousands | Percent distribution[1] | | | Population 14 years old and over in thousands | Percent distribution[1] | | |
| | | Single | Married | Widowed or divorced | | Single | Married | Widowed or divorced |
| Nevada | 227 | 27.8 | 62.1 | 10.1 | 233 | 21.5 | 60.5 | 18.5 |
| New Hampshire | 302 | 28.8 | 64.9 | 6.3 | 324 | 23.1 | 60.8 | 16.0 |
| New Jersey | 2,676 | 31.3 | 63.4 | 5.3 | 2,939 | 25.5 | 59.3 | 15.2 |
| New Mexico | 413 | 31.2 | 62.5 | 6.3 | 446 | 25.6 | 59.0 | 15.7 |
| New York | 6,474 | 33.2 | 61.6 | 5.2 | 7,559 | 26.8 | 55.7 | 17.5 |
| North Carolina | 1,992 | 28.4 | 66.8 | 4.8 | 2,173 | 21.3 | 61.8 | 16.9 |
| North Dakota | 237 | 33.8 | 62.4 | 4.2 | 238 | 25.6 | 62.2 | 12.2 |
| Ohio | 3,852 | 29.4 | 64.9 | 5.8 | 4,214 | 23.0 | 60.1 | 16.9 |
| Oklahoma | 994 | 26.2 | 67.7 | 6.0 | 1,087 | 17.8 | 62.6 | 19.5 |
| Oregon | 843 | 27.8 | 65.4 | 6.9 | 931 | 22.7 | 60.0 | 17.3 |
| Pennsylvania | 4,302 | 32.1 | 62.3 | 5.6 | 4,821 | 25.1 | 57.1 | 17.8 |
| Rhode Island | 336 | 32.7 | 61.9 | 5.4 | 376 | 25.5 | 56.6 | 17.8 |
| South Carolina | 1,018 | 32.6 | 63.3 | 4.1 | 1,103 | 23.6 | 59.8 | 16.7 |
| South Dakota | 256 | 32.0 | 63.3 | 5.1 | 263 | 24.0 | 61.6 | 14.4 |
| Tennessee | 1,545 | 27.6 | 66.1 | 6.3 | 1,701 | 20.1 | 61.4 | 18.5 |
| Texas | 4,415 | 27.7 | 66.2 | 6.1 | 4,848 | 21.6 | 61.0 | 17.4 |
| Utah | 422 | 30.1 | 65.6 | 4.5 | 440 | 23.4 | 63.2 | 13.4 |
| Vermont | 173 | 31.2 | 63.0 | 5.8 | 186 | 23.7 | 59.7 | 16.7 |
| Virginia | 1,825 | 28.7 | 65.6 | 5.6 | 1,979 | 23.8 | 60.6 | 15.6 |
| Washington | 1,309 | 29.2 | 63.9 | 7.0 | 1,378 | 22.6 | 61.4 | 16.0 |
| West Virginia | 673 | 27.6 | 66.3 | 6.1 | 738 | 19.1 | 61.0 | 19.8 |
| Wisconsin | 1,710 | 33.1 | 61.8 | 5.1 | 1,827 | 27.1 | 58.8 | 14.0 |
| Wyoming | 143 | 28.7 | 65.0 | 6.3 | 145 | 21.4 | 64.8 | 14.5 |
| **Total U.S.** | **77,926** | **30.5** | **63.4** | **6.1** | **85,183** | **23.6** | **59.2** | **17.3** |

1. Total for ages 14 and over = 100%. *Source:* Department of Commerce, Bureau of the Census.

# Births

## Registered Live Births and Birth Rates

| State | 1977[1] Number | 1976[2] Number | 1976[2] Rate | State | 1977[1] Number | 1976[2] Number | 1976[2] Rate |
|---|---|---|---|---|---|---|---|
| Alabama | 60,905 | 57,974 | 15.8 | Montana | 13,004 | 12,600 | 16.7 |
| Alaska | 8,138 | 7,942 | 20.8 | Nebraska | 25,140 | 23,804 | 15.3 |
| Arizona | 41,591 | 39,969 | 17.6 | Nevada | 10,152 | 9,659 | 15.8 |
| Arkansas | 34,502 | 34,162 | 16.2 | New Hampshire | 12,064 | 11,217 | 13.6 |
| California | 338,716 | 332,256 | 15.4 | New Jersey | 90,981 | 90,800 | 12.4 |
| Colorado | 43,424 | 41,003 | 15.9 | New Mexico | 22,433 | 22,054 | 18.9 |
| Connecticut | 35,991 | 35,606 | 11.4 | New York | 237,894 | 235,688 | 13.0 |
| Delaware | 8,771 | 8,087 | 13.9 | North Carolina | 84,772 | 80,594 | 14.7 |
| D.C. | 21,322 | 18,983 | 13.8 | North Dakota | 12,228 | 10,692 | 16.6 |
| Florida | 111,414 | 104,655 | 12.4 | Ohio | 162,353 | 155,491 | 14.5 |
| Georgia | 85,138 | 79,258 | 15.9 | Oklahoma | 43,805 | 43,705 | 15.8 |
| Hawaii | 17,024 | 16,377 | 18.5 | Oregon | 38,398 | 34,863 | 15.0 |
| Idaho | 18,242 | 17,347 | 20.9 | Pennsylvania | 153,654 | 148,289 | 12.5 |
| Illinois | 173,945 | 170,257 | 15.2 | Rhode Island | 11,932 | 10,806 | 11.7 |
| Indiana | 85,425 | 80,713 | 15.2 | South Carolina | 48,419 | 47,788 | 16.8 |
| Iowa | 45,270 | 41,635 | 14.5 | South Dakota | 11,917 | 11,671 | 17.0 |
| Kansas | 34,820 | 35,419 | 15.3 | Tennessee | 70,032 | 62,582 | 14.9 |
| Kentucky | 60,532 | 55,198 | 16.1 | Texas | 235,791 | 218,746 | 17.5 |
| Louisiana | 76,155 | 69,754 | 18.2 | Utah | 38,237 | 35,273 | 28.7 |
| Maine | 15,695 | 15,012 | 14.0 | Vermont | 6,413 | 6,737 | 14.2 |
| Maryland | 47,909 | 52,714 | 12.7 | Virginia | 71,298 | 70,038 | 13.9 |
| Massachusetts | 71,049 | 66,012 | 11.4 | Washington | 55,038 | 52,987 | 14.7 |
| Michigan | 137,565 | 131,370 | 14.4 | West Virginia | 30,118 | 28,569 | 15.7 |
| Minnesota | 60,145 | 56,598 | 14.3 | Wisconsin | 68,561 | 64,915 | 14.1 |
| Mississippi | 46,850 | 42,943 | 18.2 | Wyoming | 7,530 | 7,380 | 18.9 |
| Missouri | 72,361 | 68,879 | 14.4 | **Total** | 3,315,063 | 3,167,788 | 14.8 |

1. Provisional. 2. Final. NOTE: Based on 100% of births in selected states and 50% sample in others. Rates are per 1,000 population. *Source:* Department of Health, Education, and Welfare, National Center for Health Statistics.

## Live Births and Birth Rates

| Year | Births[1] | Rate[2] | Year | Births[1] | Rate[2] | Year | Births[1] | Rate[2] |
|---|---|---|---|---|---|---|---|---|
| 1910 | 2,777,000 | 30.1 | 1946 | 3,411,000 | 24.1 | 1962[3] | 4,167,362 | 22.4 |
| 1915 | 2,965,000 | 29.5 | 1947 | 3,817,000 | 26.6 | 1963[3] | 4,098,020 | 21.7 |
| 1920 | 2,950,000 | 27.7 | 1948 | 3,637,000 | 24.9 | 1964[3] | 4,027,490 | 21.0 |
| 1925 | 2,909,000 | 25.1 | 1949 | 3,649,000 | 24.5 | 1965[3] | 3,760,358 | 19.4 |
| 1930 | 2,618,000 | 21.3 | 1950 | 3,632,000 | 24.1 | 1966[3] | 3,606,274 | 18.4 |
| 1935 | 2,377,000 | 18.7 | 1951[3] | 3,823,000 | 24.9 | 1967 | 3,520,959 | 17.8 |
| 1936 | 2,355,000 | 18.4 | 1952[3] | 3,913,000 | 25.1 | 1968 | 3,501,564 | 17.5 |
| 1937 | 2,413,000 | 18.7 | 1953[3] | 3,965,000 | 25.1 | 1969 | 3,600,206 | 17.8 |
| 1938 | 2,496,000 | 19.2 | 1954[3] | 4,078,000 | 25.3 | 1970 | 3,731,386 | 18.4 |
| 1939 | 2,466,000 | 18.8 | 1955 | 4,104,000 | 25.0 | 1971 | 3,555,970 | 17.2 |
| 1940 | 2,559,000 | 19.4 | 1956[3] | 4,218,000 | 25.2 | 1972 | 3,258,411 | 15.6 |
| 1941 | 2,703,000 | 20.3 | 1957[3] | 4,308,000 | 25.3 | 1973 | 3,136,965 | 14.9 |
| 1942 | 2,989,000 | 22.2 | 1958[3] | 4,255,000 | 24.5 | 1974 | 3,159,958 | 14.9 |
| 1943 | 3,104,000 | 22.7 | 1959[3] | 4,295,000 | 24.3 | 1975 | 3,144,198 | 14.8 |
| 1944 | 2,939,000 | 21.2 | 1960[3] | 4,257,850 | 23.7 | 1976 | 3,167,788 | 14.8 |
| 1945 | 2,858,000 | 20.4 | 1961[3] | 4,268,326 | 23.3 | 1977[4] | 3,313,000 | 15.3 |

1. Figures through 1959 include adjustment for underregistration; beginning 1960, figures represent number registered. For comparison, the 1959 registered count was 4,245,000. 2. Rates are per 1,000 population estimated as of July 1 for each year except 1940, 1950, 1960, and 1970, which are as of April 1, the census date; for 1941–46 based on population including armed forces overseas. 3. Based on 50% sample of births. 4. Provisional. NOTE: Alaska is included beginning 1959, Hawaii beginning 1960. Since 1972, based on 100% of births in selected states and on 50% sample in all other states. *Sources:* Department of Commerce, Bureau of the Census; and Department of Health, Education, and Welfare, Center for Health Statistics.

## Illegitimate Live Births

**(in thousands, except as indicated)**

| Age and race | 1976 | 1975 | 1970 | 1965 | 1960 | 1955 | 1950 | 1945 | 1940 |
|---|---|---|---|---|---|---|---|---|---|
| By age of mother: | | | | | | | | | |
| Under 15 years | 10.3 | 11.0 | 9.5 | 6.1 | 4.6 | 3.9 | 3.2 | 2.5 | 2.1 |
| 15–19 years | 225.0 | 222.5 | 190.4 | 123.1 | 87.1 | 68.9 | 56.0 | 49.2 | 40.5 |
| 20–24 years | 145.4 | 134.0 | 126.7 | 90.7 | 68.0 | 55.7 | 43.1 | 39.3 | 27.2 |
| 25–29 years | 55.4 | 50.2 | 40.6 | 36.8 | 32.1 | 28.0 | 20.9 | 14.1 | 10.5 |
| 30–34 years | 21.0 | 19.8 | 19.1 | 19.6 | 18.9 | 16.1 | 10.8 | 7.1 | 5.2 |
| 35–39 years | 8.6 | 8.1 | 9.4 | 11.4 | 10.6 | 8.3 | 6.0 | 4.0 | 3.0 |
| 40 years and over | 2.3 | 2.3 | 3.0 | 3.7 | 3.0 | 2.4 | 1.7 | 1.2 | 1.0 |
| By race: | | | | | | | | | |
| White | 197.1 | 186.4 | 175.1 | 123.7 | 82.5 | 64.2 | 53.5 | 56.4 | 40.3 |
| Black and other | 271.0 | 261.6 | 223.6 | 167.5 | 141.8 | 119.2 | 88.1 | 60.9 | 49.2 |
| Total illegitimate births | 468.1 | 447.9 | 398.7 | 291.2 | 224.3 | 183.4 | 141.6 | 117.3 | 89.5 |
| Percent of all births[1] | 14.8 | 14.2 | 10.7 | 7.7 | 5.3 | 4.5 | 3.9 | 4.1 | 3.5 |
| Rate[2] | 24.7 | 24.8 | 26.4 | 23.4 | 21.8 | 19.3 | 14.1 | 10.1 | 7.1 |

1. Through 1955, based on data adjusted for underregistration; thereafter, registered births. 2. Rate per 1,000 unmarried (never married, widowed, and divorced) women, 15–44 years old. NOTE: Figures are estimates based on 100% of births in 38 states and District of Columbia and on 50% sample of other states that report marital status of maternity cases. *Sources:* Department of Commerce, Bureau of the Census; and Department of Health, Education, and Welfare, National Center for Health Statistics.

## Live Births and Birth Rates by Race

| Race | Births 1976[1] | Rates 1976 | Rates 1950 | Rates 1940 | Race | Births 1976[1] | Rates 1976 | Rates 1950 | Rates 1940 |
|---|---|---|---|---|---|---|---|---|---|
| White | 2,567,614 | 13.8 | 23.0 | 18.6 | Chinese | 9,825 | n.a. | 43.9 | 14.5 |
| Black | 514,479 | 20.8 | 33.1 | 26.5 | Other | 38,911 | n.a. | 19.1 | 22.0 |
| Indian | 29,009 | n.a. | 45.8 | 42.0 | All races | 3,167,788 | 14.8 | 24.1 | 19.4 |
| Japanese | 7,950 | n.a. | 24.5 | 15.0 | | | | | |

1. Based on all births in selected states and on a 50% sample of births in all other states. 1976 figures include Alaska and Hawaii. NOTES: Rates per 1,000 population in each specified group. Rates for 1940 and 1950 based on births adjusted for under-registration; data for 1976, registered births. n.a. = not available. *Source:* Department of Health, Education, and Welfare, National Center for Health Statistics.

## Families in the U. S.

| State | 1976 | | | 1970 | | | 1960 | | |
|---|---|---|---|---|---|---|---|---|---|
| | Total families (in thousands) | Percent with own children under 18 | Percent increase, 1970–76 | Total families (in thousands) | Percent with own children under 18 | Percent increase, 1960–70 | Total families (in thousands) | Percent with own children under 18 | Percent increase 1950–60 |
| Alabama | 970 | 54 | 11.5 | 870 | 55 | 10.0 | 791 | 59 | 8.2 |
| Alaska | 82 | 66 | 24.2 | 66 | 67 | 41.1 | 47 | 69 | 96.9 |
| Arizona | 592 | 54 | 34.9 | 439 | 56 | 40.6 | 312 | 62 | 71.1 |
| Arkansas | 585 | 51 | 16.5 | 502 | 51 | 11.0 | 452 | 55 | −4.1 |
| California | 5,574 | 54 | 11.7 | 4,988 | 55 | 25.0 | 3,992 | 58 | 42.4 |
| Colorado | 660 | 57 | 21.1 | 545 | 58 | 24.3 | 439 | 60 | 30.2 |
| Connecticut | 820 | 53 | 6.9 | 767 | 55 | 17.3 | 654 | 57 | 26.0 |
| Delaware | 153 | 56 | 12.5 | 136 | 58 | 21.6 | 112 | 59 | 38.4 |
| D. C. | 158 | 51 | −3.1 | 163 | 51 | 6.4 | 174 | 46 | −11.5 |
| Florida | 2,361 | 47 | 30.7 | 1,806 | 47 | 39.3 | 1,297 | 52 | 79.9 |
| Georgia | 1,292 | 56 | 12.9 | 1,144 | 57 | 20.5 | 949 | 59 | 14.2 |
| Hawaii | 201 | 57 | 18.2 | 170 | 62 | 30.2 | 131 | 70 | 35.7 |
| Idaho | 222 | 55 | 24.0 | 179 | 57 | 7.9 | 166 | 63 | 12.1 |
| Illinois | 2,849 | 53 | 2.3 | 2,784 | 55 | 7.4 | 2,592 | 55 | 13.2 |
| Indiana | 1,422 | 56 | 7.9 | 1,318 | 56 | 10.0 | 1,198 | 57 | 13.4 |
| Iowa | 751 | 53 | 5.3 | 713 | 54 | .2 | 712 | 56 | 3.7 |
| Kansas | 619 | 50 | 6.9 | 579 | 53 | 1.8 | 569 | 56 | 11.0 |
| Kentucky | 909 | 54 | 10.7 | 821 | 54 | 9.1 | 753 | 56 | 5.3 |
| Louisiana | 944 | 57 | 8.8 | 868 | 58 | 12.5 | 771 | 59 | 18.7 |
| Maine | 279 | 54 | 13.4 | 246 | 54 | 2.2 | 240 | 57 | 7.4 |
| Maryland | 1,066 | 55 | 9.7 | 972 | 57 | 27.3 | 763 | 59 | 29.5 |
| Massachusetts | 1,483 | 52 | 6.8 | 1,388 | 54 | 7.4 | 1,292 | 55 | 9.9 |
| Michigan | 2,399 | 56 | 9.9 | 2,182 | 58 | 12.2 | 1,944 | 59 | 17.3 |
| Minnesota | 994 | 56 | 8.4 | 917 | 57 | 9.5 | 837 | 59 | 11.4 |
| Mississippi | 597 | 56 | 12.6 | 530 | 55 | 5.9 | 501 | 57 | −1.6 |
| Missouri | 1,276 | 51 | 6.3 | 1,200 | 52 | 5.9 | 1,133 | 52 | 7.8 |
| Montana | 193 | 53 | 13.5 | 170 | 57 | 2.0 | 166 | 61 | 13.7 |
| Nebraska | 401 | 54 | 7.8 | 372 | 54 | 1.8 | 366 | 58 | 5.3 |
| Nevada | 159 | 54 | 28.2 | 124 | 56 | 70.9 | 72 | 58 | 75.3 |
| New Hampshire | 218 | 66 | 19.1 | 183 | 55 | 10.8 | 153 | 56 | 11.8 |
| New Jersey | 1,927 | 53 | 5.1 | 1,833 | 55 | 16.0 | 1,581 | 56 | 24.8 |
| New Mexico | 297 | 59 | 22.7 | 242 | 62 | 9.0 | 222 | 67 | 39.3 |
| New York | 4,676 | 53 | 2.0 | 4,585 | 53 | 5.7 | 4,336 | 54 | 11.7 |
| North Carolina | 1,504 | 54 | 17.0 | 1,286 | 56 | 17.8 | 1,092 | 60 | 15.6 |
| North Dakota | 159 | 57 | 8.2 | 147 | 57 | 1.8 | 150 | 62 | 1.4 |
| Ohio | 2,833 | 54 | 5.6 | 2,683 | 56 | 8.8 | 2,465 | 57 | 16.9 |
| Oklahoma | 749 | 50 | 10.6 | 677 | 52 | 10.4 | 613 | 55 | 5.3 |
| Oregon | 615 | 52 | 13.5 | 542 | 53 | 17.8 | 460 | 57 | 12.0 |
| Pennsylvania | 3,076 | 49 | 2.6 | 2,999 | 53 | 3.3 | 2,903 | 55 | 9.1 |
| Rhode Island | 242 | 51 | 3.0 | 235 | 53 | 7.0 | 220 | 55 | 7.1 |
| South Carolina | 731 | 53 | 17.1 | 624 | 58 | 15.3 | 541 | 61 | 12.2 |
| South Dakota | 177 | 54 | 10.6 | 160 | 56 | 4.0 | 167 | 60 | 3.7 |
| Tennessee | 1,162 | 53 | 13.9 | 1,020 | 54 | 14.2 | 894 | 56 | 10.5 |
| Texas | 3,258 | 54 | 15.9 | 2,810 | 56 | 17.4 | 2,393 | 59 | 21.3 |
| Utah | 303 | 62 | 21.7 | 249 | 63 | 19.0 | 209 | 67 | 23.3 |
| Vermont | 122 | 59 | 15.1 | 106 | 56 | 12.7 | 94 | 57 | 2.9 |
| Virginia | 1,318 | 53 | 13.7 | 1,159 | 56 | 21.4 | 955 | 59 | 21.8 |
| Washington | 924 | 54 | 7.2 | 862 | 56 | 18.9 | 725 | 59 | 16.4 |
| West Virginia | 495 | 49 | 9.5 | 452 | 52 | 2.2 | 462 | 57 | −4.4 |
| Wisconsin | 1,182 | 54 | 10.3 | 1,072 | 56 | 8.7 | 987 | 57 | 12.3 |
| Wyoming | 100 | 54 | 19.0 | 84 | 57 | 0.8 | 84 | 63 | 16.5 |
| **United States** | **56,080** | **53** | **10.0** | **50,969** | **55** | **12.9** | **45,128** | **57** | **17.0** |

*Source:* Department of Commerce, Bureau of the Census.

## More Women Run Homes

The Census Bureau reports that, in 1978, about 11% of the country's 76 million households were headed by a woman, with no husband present. This represents an increase of 2.5 million woman-run households. The report also indicated that the average size of U.S. households declined from 3.1 persons in 1970 to 2.8 persons in 1978.

## Live Births by Age of Mother

| Year[1] and race | Total | Under 15 yr | 15–19 yr | 20–24 yr | 25–29 yr | 30–34 yr | 35–39 yr | 40–44 yr | 45 yr and over |
|---|---|---|---|---|---|---|---|---|---|
| 1940 | 2,558,647 | 3,865 | 332,667 | 799,537 | 693,268 | 431,468 | 222,015 | 68,269 | 7,558 |
| 1945 | 2,858,449 | 4,028 | 298,868 | 832,746 | 785,299 | 554,906 | 296,852 | 78,853 | 6,897 |
| 1950 | 3,631,512 | 5,413 | 432,911 | 1,155,167 | 1,041,360 | 610,816 | 302,780 | 77,743 | 5,322 |
| 1955 | 4,014,112 | 6,181 | 493,770 | 1,290,939 | 1,133,155 | 732,540 | 352,320 | 89,777 | 5,430 |
| 1960 | 4,257,850 | 6,780 | 586,966 | 1,426,912 | 1,092,816 | 687,722 | 359,908 | 91,564 | 5,182 |
| 1965 | 3,760,358 | 7,768 | 590,894 | 1,337,350 | 925,732 | 529,376 | 282,908 | 81,716 | 4,614 |
| 1970 | 3,731,386 | 11,752 | 644,708 | 1,418,874 | 994,904 | 427,806 | 180,244 | 49,952 | 3,146 |
| 1972 | 3,258,411 | 12,082 | 616,280 | 1,174,183 | 900,392 | 375,001 | 141,328 | 36,861 | 2,284 |
| 1974 | 3,159,958 | 12,529 | 595,449 | 1,108,051 | 923,318 | 372,907 | 118,115 | 27,878 | 1,711 |
| 1975 | 3,144,198 | 12,642 | 582,238 | 1,093,676 | 936,786 | 375,500 | 115,409 | 26,319 | 1,628 |
| 1976 | 3,167,788 | 11,928 | 558,744 | 1,091,602 | 972,130 | 391,896 | 115,662 | 24,383 | 1,443 |
| White | 2,567,614 | 5,054 | 393,275 | 888,219 | 835,398 | 332,359 | 93,229 | 19,014 | 1,066 |
| Black | 514,479 | 6,661 | 153,936 | 178,902 | 108,124 | 44,596 | 17,514 | 4,436 | 310 |
| Other | 85,695 | 213 | 11,533 | 24,481 | 28,608 | 14,941 | 4,919 | 933 | 67 |

1. Data for 1940–50 are adjusted for underregistration. Beginning 1960, registered births only are shown. Beginning 1955, figures are based on birth data from a 50% sampling. Beginning 1960, including Alaska and Hawaii. NOTE: Data refer only to births occurring within the U.S. Figures are shown to the last digit as computed for convenience in summation. They are not assumed to be accurate to the last digit. Figures for age of mother not stated are distributed. *Sources:* Department of Commerce, Bureau of the Census; and Department of Health, Education, and Welfare, National Center for Health Statistics.

## Live Births by Sex and Sex Ratio[1]

| | Total | | | White | | | Black | | |
|---|---|---|---|---|---|---|---|---|---|
| Year | Male | Female | Males per 1,000 females | Male | Female | Males per 1,000 females | Male | Female | Males per 1,000 females |
| 1970[2] | 1,915,378 | 1,816,008 | 1,055 | 1,590,140 | 1,501,124 | 1,059 | 290,508 | 281,854 | 1,031 |
| 1971[2] | 1,822,910 | 1,733,060 | 1,052 | 1,499,958 | 1,419,788 | 1,056 | 286,430 | 278,530 | 1,028 |
| 1972[3] | 1,669,927 | 1,588,484 | 1,051 | 1,364,578 | 1,290,980 | 1,057 | 268,842 | 262,487 | 1,024 |
| 1973[3] | 1,608,326 | 1,528,639 | 1,052 | 1,311,032 | 1,239,998 | 1,057 | 259,877 | 252,720 | 1,028 |
| 1974[3] | 1,622,114 | 1,537,844 | 1,055 | 1,325,019 | 1,250,773 | 1,059 | 257,277 | 249,885 | 1,030 |
| 1975[3] | 1,613,135 | 1,531,063 | 1,054 | 1,312,308 | 1,239,688 | 1,059 | 259,610 | 251,971 | 1,030 |
| 1976[3] | 1,624,436 | 1,543,352 | 1,053 | 1,319,717 | 1,247,897 | 1,058 | 260,661 | 253,818 | 1,027 |

1. Excludes births to nonresidents of U.S. 2. Based on 50% sample of births. 3. Based on 100% of births in selected states and 50% sample in all others. *Source:* Department of Health, Education, and Welfare, National Center for Health Statistics.

## Households, Families, and Married Couples

| | Households | | Families | | Married couples |
|---|---|---|---|---|---|
| Date | Number | Average population per household | Number | Average population per family | Number |
| June 1890 | 12,690,000 | 4.93 | — | — | — |
| April 1930 | 29,905,000 | 4.11 | — | — | 25,174,000 |
| April 1940 | 34,949,000 | 3.67 | 32,166,000 | 3.76 | 28,517,000 |
| March 1950 | 43,554,000 | 3.37 | 39,303,000 | 3.54 | 36,091,000 |
| March 1960[1] | 52,799,000 | 3.33 | 45,111,000 | 3.67 | 40,200,000 |
| March 1970 | 63,401,000 | 3.14 | 51,586,000 | 3.58 | 45,373,000 |
| March 1976 | 72,867,000 | 2.89 | 56,245,000 | 3.39 | 47,866,000 |
| March 1977 | 74,142,000 | 2.86 | 56,710,000 | 3.37 | 48,002,000 |

[1]First year in which figures for Alaska and Hawaii are included. *Source:* Department of Commerce, Bureau of the Census.

# Mortality

## Accidental Death Rates, 1970

**(per 100,000 population by place of residence)**

| State | Total accidents | Motor vehicle: Total | Motor vehicle: Pedestrian | Falls | Fires and flames | Drownings[1] | Firearms | All others |
|---|---|---|---|---|---|---|---|---|
| Alabama | 74.8 | 38.8 | 4.7 | 6.8 | 5.8 | 4.0 | 3.2 | 16.2 |
| Alaska | 117.2 | 34.7 | (2) | (2) | 10.3 | 8.6 | (2) | 63.6 |
| Arizona | 75.9 | 40.0 | 6.5 | 4.1 | 3.9 | 4.8 | 2.5 | 20.6 |
| Arkansas | 69.4 | 31.1 | 4.2 | 7.1 | 6.2 | 4.8 | 2.3 | 17.9 |
| California | 58.3 | 26.3 | 4.5 | 8.4 | 2.7 | 3.4 | 0.9 | 16.6 |
| Colorado | 58.3 | 29.4 | 3.0 | 9.4 | 2.1 | 2.5 | 1.3 | 13.6 |
| Connecticut | 37.1 | 15.8 | 3.3 | 7.2 | 2.2 | 2.4 | (2) | 9.5 |
| Delaware | 56.6 | 28.8 | 4.9 | 8.4 | (2) | (2) | (2) | 19.4 |
| D.C. | 69.3 | 22.6 | 8.5 | 11.8 | 7.5 | (2) | (2) | 27.4 |
| Florida | 65.1 | 31.1 | 5.5 | 7.7 | 3.3 | 6.8 | 1.6 | 14.6 |
| Georgia | 73.7 | 38.5 | 4.9 | 6.5 | 5.6 | 4.2 | 2.7 | 16.2 |
| Hawaii | 35.8 | 17.7 | 4.0 | 2.9 | (2) | 3.6 | (2) | 11.6 |
| Idaho | 82.9 | 43.9 | 4.6 | 7.2 | (2) | 5.0 | 2.8 | 24.0 |
| Illinois | 48.4 | 21.9 | 3.7 | 7.3 | 3.3 | 2.5 | 1.0 | 12.4 |
| Indiana | 56.4 | 29.9 | 4.0 | 8.5 | 3.0 | 2.5 | 1.1 | 11.4 |
| Iowa | 61.1 | 32.8 | 2.3 | 9.3 | 2.3 | 2.7 | (2) | 14.0 |
| Kansas | 61.0 | 30.1 | 2.0 | 10.0 | 2.7 | 3.3 | 1.2 | 13.6 |
| Kentucky | 68.5 | 32.5 | 4.8 | 10.5 | 3.6 | 3.0 | 1.7 | 17.2 |
| Louisiana | 68.0 | 32.2 | 4.2 | 6.4 | 4.7 | 5.7 | 2.4 | 16.6 |
| Maine | 56.7 | 24.0 | 4.0 | 9.4 | 4.4 | 3.2 | (2) | 15.7 |
| Maryland | 47.9 | 20.8 | 4.6 | 8.2 | 3.7 | 3.2 | 0.7 | 11.3 |
| Massachusetts | 46.3 | 17.2 | 4.5 | 13.1 | 2.9 | 2.6 | 0.4 | 10.1 |
| Michigan | 50.1 | 25.7 | 4.2 | 7.0 | 2.8 | 2.6 | 0.9 | 10.8 |
| Minnesota | 55.8 | 27.2 | 4.3 | 9.1 | 2.4 | 2.6 | 0.7 | 13.8 |
| Mississippi | 81.6 | 41.5 | 4.7 | 5.5 | 7.2 | 5.1 | 3.9 | 18.4 |
| Missouri | 64.2 | 30.6 | 3.8 | 11.8 | 3.5 | 2.6 | 1.5 | 14.2 |
| Montana | 81.1 | 42.6 | (2) | 11.2 | (2) | 4.3 | (2) | 22.8 |
| Nebraska | 65.4 | 30.1 | 2.7 | 11.9 | 2.8 | 3.0 | 1.7 | 15.9 |
| Nevada | 74.7 | 40.5 | 7.2 | 4.9 | (2) | 5.9 | (2) | 23.4 |
| New Hampshire | 54.1 | 27.0 | 3.8 | 9.5 | 4.6 | (2) | (2) | 13.0 |
| New Jersey | 41.8 | 18.3 | 4.4 | 8.5 | 2.7 | 1.8 | 0.4 | 10.1 |
| New Mexico | 89.1 | 46.9 | 8.4 | 7.7 | 5.8 | 4.5 | 2.9 | 21.3 |
| New York | 38.3 | 17.9 | 5.6 | 7.8 | 2.0 | 1.6 | 0.3 | 8.7 |
| North Carolina | 66.2 | 33.9 | 6.3 | 6.2 | 4.8 | 4.0 | 1.7 | 15.6 |
| North Dakota | 62.8 | 29.5 | (2) | 9.1 | (2) | 3.6 | (2) | 20.6 |
| Ohio | 51.8 | 24.5 | 3.8 | 10.9 | 2.8 | 2.3 | 0.7 | 10.6 |
| Oklahoma | 67.8 | 30.9 | 3.0 | 7.8 | 4.7 | 3.6 | 2.5 | 18.3 |
| Oregon | 66.4 | 34.8 | 4.4 | 8.0 | 3.3 | 4.4 | 1.0 | 14.9 |
| Pennsylvania | 46.9 | 20.4 | 4.3 | 8.8 | 3.1 | 1.7 | 0.6 | 12.3 |
| Rhode Island | 36.6 | 13.7 | 4.7 | 10.0 | 2.1 | (2) | (2) | 10.8 |
| South Carolina | 73.0 | 37.9 | 7.3 | 5.9 | 6.6 | 5.2 | 2.0 | 15.4 |
| South Dakota | 71.4 | 36.9 | (2) | 9.8 | (2) | 3.8 | (2) | 20.9 |
| Tennessee | 66.7 | 35.8 | 4.4 | 7.2 | 4.7 | 3.3 | 1.9 | 13.8 |
| Texas | 63.1 | 32.1 | 4.2 | 6.8 | 3.5 | 4.2 | 1.8 | 14.7 |
| Utah | 58.2 | 30.5 | 5.1 | 7.7 | (2) | 3.8 | (2) | 16.2 |
| Vermont | 49.5 | 21.1 | (2) | 9.7 | (2) | (2) | (2) | 18.7 |
| Virginia | 56.8 | 26.0 | 4.4 | 8.6 | 3.8 | 3.5 | 1.2 | 13.7 |
| Washington | 60.0 | 27.0 | 3.6 | 9.3 | 3.6 | 3.9 | 0.7 | 15.5 |
| West Virginia | 71.1 | 30.8 | 4.2 | 9.3 | 4.4 | 3.3 | 1.9 | 21.4 |
| Wisconsin | 52.8 | 24.7 | 3.3 | 8.8 | 2.8 | 2.9 | 1.1 | 12.5 |
| Wyoming | 100.2 | 51.1 | (2) | 9.0 | (2) | (2) | (2) | 40.1 |
| **United States** | **56.4** | **26.9** | **4.4** | **8.3** | **3.3** | **3.1** | **1.2** | **13.6** |

1. Exclusive of deaths in water transportation. 2. Fewer than 20 deaths; rate not computed. NOTE: Data are latest available. *Source:* Statistical Bureau, Metropolitan Life Insurance Company.

## Taxpayers

Taxpayers earning more than $30,000 made up 5% of the population, but paid 39% of the personal income taxes collected by the Internal Revenue Service in 1976.

## Accident Rates, 1977

(twelve accidental deaths every hour)

| Class of accident | | One every | Class of accident | | One every |
|---|---|---|---|---|---|
| All accidents | Deaths | 5 minutes | Workers off-job | Deaths | 13 minutes |
| | Injuries | 3 seconds | | Injuries | 10 seconds |
| Motor-vehicle | Deaths | 11 minutes | Home | Deaths | 22 minutes |
| | Injuries | 17 seconds | | Injuries | 9 seconds |
| Work | Deaths | 40 minutes | Public non-motor-vehicle | Deaths | 24 minutes |
| | Injuries | 14 seconds | | Injuries | 11 seconds |

*Source:* National Safety Council.

## Transportation-Accident Death Rates

| Kind of transportation | 1977 Passenger miles | 1977 Passenger deaths | 1977 Death rate[1] | 1975–77 average death rate[1] |
|---|---|---|---|---|
| Passenger automobiles and taxis[2] | 2,120,000,000,000 | 28,250 | 1.33 | 1.36 |
| Passenger automobiles on turnpikes[2] | 50,800,000,000 | 330 | 0.65 | 0.65 |
| Buses | 79,600,000,000 | 105 | 0.13 | 0.15 |
| Intercity buses | 16,600,000,000 | 6 | 0.04 | 0.02 |
| Railroad passenger trains[3] | 10,600,000,000 | 5 | 0.05 | 0.07 |
| Scheduled air transport planes (domestic) | 166,400,000,000 | 64 | 0.04 | 0.04 |

1. Per 100 million passenger miles. 2. Drivers of passenger automobiles are considered passengers. 3. 1977 data not available. Figures shown are for 1976 and 1974–76 averages. *Source:* National Safety Council.

## Motor-Vehicle Traffic Deaths

| State | 1977 Number | 1977 Rate[1] | 1976 Number | 1976 Rate[1] |
|---|---|---|---|---|
| Alabama | 1,121 | 4.0 | 1,033 | 3.8 |
| Alaska | 135 | 3.6 | 127 | 3.5 |
| Arizona | 931 | 5.1 | 739 | 4.4 |
| Arkansas | 556 | 3.6 | 536 | 3.7 |
| California | 4,942 | 3.4 | 4,489 | 3.2 |
| Colorado | 701 | 3.9 | 633 | 3.6 |
| Connecticut | 449 | 2.3 | 424 | 2.2 |
| Delaware | 124 | 3.1 | 122 | 3.2 |
| District of Columbia | 58 | 1.8 | 60 | 1.9 |
| Florida | 2,066 | 3.1 | 2,015 | 3.1 |
| Georgia | 1,460 | 3.4 | 1,292 | 3.1 |
| Hawaii | 154 | 3.4 | 149 | 3.5 |
| Idaho | 320 | 5.0 | 277 | 4.3 |
| Illinois | 2,170 | 3.3 | 2,073 | 3.2 |
| Indiana | 1,249 | 3.0 | 1,267 | 3.2 |
| Iowa | 639 | 3.1 | 785 | 3.8 |
| Kansas | 562 | 3.4 | 563 | 3.5 |
| Kentucky | 958 | 3.5 | 874 | 3.3 |
| Louisiana | 1,042 | 4.5 | 967 | 4.5 |
| Maine | 218 | 2.9 | 201 | 2.7 |
| Maryland | 674 | 2.5 | 678 | 2.6 |
| Massachusetts | 743 | 2.2 | 809 | 2.5 |
| Michigan | 1,950 | 3.1 | 1,955 | 3.2 |
| Minnesota | 856 | 3.1 | 809 | 3.0 |
| Mississippi | 690 | 4.3 | 677 | 4.4 |
| Missouri | 1,207 | 3.6 | 1,209 | 3.7 |
| Montana | 320 | 5.0 | 300 | 4.9 |
| Nebraska | 350 | 2.8 | 402 | 3.4 |
| Nevada | 255 | 5.1 | 222 | 4.7 |
| New Hampshire | 150 | 2.5 | 160 | 2.8 |
| New Jersey | 1,110 | 2.1 | 1,056 | 2.0 |
| New Mexico | 673 | 5.9 | 551 | 5.3 |
| New York | 2,440 | 3.6 | 2,359 | 3.5 |
| North Carolina | 1,441 | 3.5 | 1,531 | 4.0 |
| North Dakota | 180 | 3.7 | 183 | 3.8 |
| Ohio | 1,873 | 2.7 | 1,930 | 2.9 |
| Oklahoma | 860 | 3.2 | 838 | 3.4 |
| Oregon | 675 | 3.7 | 638 | 3.7 |
| Pennsylvania | 2,069 | 2.9 | 2,025 | 2.9 |
| Rhode Island | 136 | 2.2 | 121 | 2.1 |
| South Carolina | 949 | 4.1 | 820 | 3.7 |
| South Dakota | 211 | 3.7 | 224 | 4.1 |
| Tennessee | 1,218 | 3.4 | 1,146 | 3.3 |
| Texas | 3,698 | 3.9 | 3,230 | 3.6 |
| Utah | 356 | 3.9 | 254 | 3.0 |
| Vermont | 118 | 3.1 | 117 | 3.4 |
| Virginia | 1,145 | 3.0 | 1,020 | 2.8 |
| Washington | 926 | 3.4 | 825 | 3.2 |
| West Virginia | 527 | 4.3 | 497 | 4.4 |
| Wisconsin | 945 | 3.0 | 947 | 3.1 |
| Wyoming | 249 | 5.4 | 260 | 6.1 |
| **Total** | **48,849** | **3.4** | **46,419** | **3.3** |

1. Number of deaths per 100 million vehicle-miles. *Source:* National Safety Council.

## Deaths and Death Rates

| State | Total deaths 1977[1] number | Total deaths 1976 rate | Infant mortality 1977[1] number | Infant mortality 1976 rate |
|---|---|---|---|---|
| Alabama | 34,366 | 9.3 | 1,043 | 19.7 |
| Alaska | 1,707 | 4.2 | 120 | 16.2 |
| Arizona | 18,459 | 7.6 | 610 | 15.4 |
| Arkansas | 20,986 | 10.1 | 480 | 15.5 |
| California | 169,657 | 7.9 | 4,008 | 12.4 |
| Colorado | 18,494 | 7.0 | 577 | 13.0 |
| Connecticut | 25,779 | 8.4 | 464 | 14.2 |
| Delaware | 4,884 | 8.2 | 103 | 12.9 |
| District of Columbia | 7,295 | 10.4 | 435 | 25.3 |
| Florida | 93,559 | 10.6 | 1,702 | 15.1 |
| Georgia | 43,431 | 8.4 | 1,211 | 15.9 |
| Hawaii | 4,723 | 5.0 | 208 | 10.8 |
| Idaho | 6,146 | 8.0 | 164 | 13.1 |
| Illinois | 100,998 | 9.2 | 2,748 | 16.7 |
| Indiana | 46,852 | 8.8 | 1,122 | 14.6 |
| Iowa | 26,355 | 9.7 | 543 | 14.3 |
| Kansas | 20,661 | 9.5 | 417 | 14.1 |
| Kentucky | 34,035 | 9.4 | 812 | 14.7 |
| Louisiana | 34,837 | 9.0 | 1,390 | 17.8 |
| Maine | 10,176 | 9.8 | 135 | 11.0 |
| Maryland | 31,338 | 7.9 | 594 | 17.3 |
| Massachusetts | 52,623 | 9.3 | 683 | 12.1 |
| Michigan | 73,124 | 8.3 | 1,880 | 15.2 |
| Minnesota | 32,216 | 8.3 | 678 | 13.9 |
| Mississippi | 22,895 | 9.8 | 659 | 21.5 |
| Missouri | 42,270 | 10.3 | 1,162 | 15.3 |

| State | Total deaths 1977[1] number | Total deaths 1976 rate | Infant morality 1977[1] number | Infant morality 1976 rate |
|---|---|---|---|---|
| Montana | 6,304 | 9.0 | 163 | 16.5 |
| Nebraska | 14,390 | 9.4 | 295 | 14.2 |
| Nevada | 5,331 | 7.5 | 133 | 14.2 |
| New Hampshire | 7,147 | 9.0 | 109 | 11.5 |
| New Jersey | 64,339 | 8.9 | 1,209 | 15.0 |
| New Mexico | 8,193 | 7.0 | 309 | 15.5 |
| New York | 165,923 | 9.5 | 3,914 | 16.0 |
| North Carolina | 46,701 | 8.4 | 1,426 | 17.8 |
| North Dakota | 5,492 | 8.6 | 162 | 13.8 |
| Ohio | 96,238 | 9.0 | 2,270 | 14.9 |
| Oklahoma | 26,006 | 9.8 | 620 | 16.7 |
| Oregon | 20,710 | 8.8 | 480 | 12.7 |
| Pennsylvania | 119,689 | 10.2 | 2,136 | 15.4 |
| Rhode Island | 9,208 | 9.9 | 175 | 14.4 |
| South Carolina | 23,916 | 8.3 | 854 | 19.6 |
| South Dakota | 6,220 | 9.8 | 184 | 17.1 |
| Tennessee | 41,128 | 9.2 | 1,158 | 16.2 |
| Texas | 102,182 | 8.1 | 3,470 | 16.0 |
| Utah | 7,976 | 6.1 | 453 | 11.7 |
| Vermont | 4,345 | 9.0 | 64 | 12.6 |
| Virginia | 39,444 | 8.0 | 1,091 | 16.3 |
| Washington | 30,074 | 8.4 | 649 | 14.5 |
| West Virginia | 19,349 | 10.8 | 438 | 16.9 |
| Wisconsin | 39,301 | 8.7 | 741 | 12.5 |
| Wyoming | 2,953 | 8.1 | 79 | 16.5 |
| **United States** | **1,897,425** | **8.9** | **46,530** | **15.2** |

1. Provisional. By place of occurrence. NOTE: Data exclude fetal deaths. Rates for total deaths are per 1,000 population in each area, estimated as of December for each year. Infant mortality rates are deaths under 1 year per 1,000 live births in each area. *Source:* Department of Health, Education, and Welfare, National Center for Health Statistics.

## Death Rates

| Year | Rate |
|---|---|
| 1900 | 17.2 |
| 1905 | 15.9 |
| 1910 | 14.7 |
| 1915 | 13.2 |
| 1916 | 13.8 |
| 1917 | 14.0 |
| 1918 | 18.1 |
| 1919 | 12.9 |
| 1920 | 13.0 |
| 1921 | 11.5 |
| 1922 | 11.7 |
| 1923 | 12.1 |
| 1924 | 11.6 |
| 1925 | 11.7 |
| 1926 | 12.1 |
| 1927 | 11.3 |
| 1928 | 12.0 |
| 1929 | 11.9 |
| 1930 | 11.3 |
| 1931 | 11.1 |
| 1932 | 10.9 |
| 1933 | 10.7 |

| Year | Rate |
|---|---|
| 1934 | 11.1 |
| 1935 | 10.9 |
| 1936 | 11.6 |
| 1937 | 11.3 |
| 1938 | 10.6 |
| 1939 | 10.6 |
| 1940 | 10.8 |
| 1941 | 10.5 |
| 1942 | 10.3 |
| 1943 | 10.9 |
| 1944 | 10.6 |
| 1945 | 10.6 |
| 1946 | 10.0 |
| 1947 | 10.1 |
| 1948 | 9.9 |
| 1949 | 9.7 |
| 1950 | 9.6 |
| 1951 | 9.7 |
| 1952 | 9.6 |
| 1953 | 9.6 |
| 1954 | 9.2 |

| Year | Deaths | Rate |
|---|---|---|
| 1955 | 1,528,717 | 9.3 |
| 1956 | 1,564,476 | 9.4 |
| 1957 | 1,633,128 | 9.6 |
| 1958 | 1,647,886 | 9.5 |
| 1959 | 1,656,814 | 9.4 |
| 1960 | 1,711,982 | 9.5 |
| 1961 | 1,701,522 | 9.3 |
| 1962 | 1,756,720 | 9.5 |
| 1963 | 1,813,549 | 9.6 |
| 1964 | 1,798,051 | 9.4 |
| 1965 | 1,828,136 | 9.4 |
| 1966 | 1,863,149 | 9.5 |
| 1967 | 1,851,323 | 9.4 |
| 1968 | 1,930,082 | 9.7 |
| 1969 | 1,921,990 | 9.5 |
| 1970[1] | 1,921,031 | 9.5 |
| 1971 | 1,927,542 | 9.3 |
| 1972 | 1,963,944 | 9.4 |
| 1973 | 1,973,003 | 9.4 |
| 1974 | 1,934,388 | 9.2 |
| 1975 | 1,892,879 | 8.9 |
| 1976 | 1,909,440 | 8.9 |
| 1977[2] | 1,898,000 | 8.8 |

1. First year for which deaths of nonresidents are excluded. 2. Provisional. NOTE: Includes only deaths occurring within the registration area. Beginning with 1933, area includes entire U.S.; with 1959 includes Alaska, and with 1960 includes Hawaii. Excludes fetal deaths. Rates per 1,000 population residing in area, as of April 1 for 1940, 1950, 1960, and 1970, and estimated as of July 1 for all other years. *Sources:* Department of Commerce, Bureau of the Census; and Department of Health Education and Welfare, National Center for Health Statistics.

## Average of Annual Death Rates for Selected Causes

| Cause of death | 1977 | 1976 | 1950 | 1945–49 | 1940–44 | 1920–24 | 1900–04 |
|---|---|---|---|---|---|---|---|
| | Death rates per 100,000 | | | | | | |
| Typhoid fever | 0.0 | 0.0 | 0.1 | 0.2 | 0.6 | 7.3 | 26.7 |
| Communicable diseases of childhood | 0.0 | 0.0 | 1.3 | 2.3 | 4.6 | 33.8 | 65.2 |
| Measles | 0.0 | 0.0 | 0.3 | 0.6 | 1.1 | 7.3 | 10.0 |
| Scarlet fever | 0.0 | 0.0 | 0.2 | 0.1 | 0.4 | 4.0 | 11.8 |
| Whooping cough | 0.0 | 0.0 | 0.7 | 1.0 | 2.2 | 8.9 | 10.7 |
| Diphtheria | 0.0 | 0.0 | 0.3 | 0.7 | 1.0 | 13.7 | 32.7 |
| Gastritis, duodenitis, enteritis, and colitis | 0.7 | 0.9 | 5.1 | 6.5 | 9.8 | 42.8 | 115.3 |
| Pneumonia and influenza | 23.1 | 28.8 | 31.3 | 41.3 | 63.7 | 140.3 | 184.3 |
| Influenza | 0.5 | 3.7 | 4.4 | 5.0 | 13.0 | 34.8 | 22.8 |
| Pneumonia | 22.6 | 25.2 | 26.9 | 37.2 | 50.7 | 105.5 | 161.5 |
| Tuberculosis | 1.4 | 1.5 | 22.5 | 33.3 | 43.4 | 96.7 | 184.7 |
| Cancer | 178.4 | 175.8 | 139.8 | 134.0 | 123.1 | 86.9 | 67.7 |
| Diabetes melitus | 15.5 | 16.1 | 16.2 | 24.1 | 26.2 | 17.1 | 12.2 |
| Major cardiovascular diseases | 443.6 | 454.0 | 510.8 | 493.1 | 490.4 | 369.9 | 359.5 |
| Diseases of the heart | 331.6 | 337.2 | 356.8 | 325.1 | 303.2 | 169.8 | 153.0 |
| Cerebral hemorrhage | n.a. | 11.6 | 104.0 | 93.8 | 91.7 | 93.5 | 106.3 |
| Chronic nephritis | 3.8 | 4.0 | 16.4 | 48.4 | 72.1 | 81.5 | 84.3 |
| Syphilis | 0.1 | 0.1 | 5.0 | 8.4 | 12.7 | 17.6 | 12.9 |
| Appendicitis | n.a. | 0.4 | 2.0 | 3.5 | 7.2 | 14.0 | 9.4 |
| Accidents, all forms | 46.8 | 46.9 | 60.6 | 67.6 | 73.0 | 70.8 | 79.2 |
| Motor vehicle accidents | 22.3 | 21.9 | 23.1 | 22.3 | 22.7 | 12.9 | n.a. |
| Infant mortality[1] | 10.7 | 11.6 | 29.2 | 33.3 | 42.4 | 76.7 | n.a. |
| Neonatal mortality[1] | n.a. | n.a. | 20.5 | 22.9 | 26.2 | 39.7 | n.a. |
| Fetal mortality[1] | n.a. | n.a. | 22.9 | 24.3 | 28.5 | 39.2[2] | n.a. |
| Maternal mortality[1] | n.a. | 0.2 | 0.8 | 1.4 | 2.8 | 6.9 | n.a. |
| **All causes** | **877.5** | **889.6** | **963.8** | **1,003.3** | **1,062.0** | **1,196.6** | **1,621.6** |

1. Rates per 1,000 live births. 2. 1922–24. NOTE: Includes only deaths occurring within the registration areas. Beginning with 1940, area includes the entire United States; beginning with 1960, Alaska and Hawaii were included. Rates per 100,000 population residing in areas, enumerated as of April 1 for 1940 and 1950 and estimated as of July 1 for all other years. Average rates computed from 5-year totals of deaths occurring in area and corresponding population. Due to changes in statistical methods, death rates are not strictly comparable. n.a. = not available. *Source:* Department of Health, Education, and Welfare, National Center for Health Statistics.

## Motor-Vehicle Deaths by Type of Accident

| Year | Deaths from collisions with— Pedestrians | Other motor vehicles | Railroad trains | Street cars | Pedalcycles | Animal-drawn vehicle or animal | Fixed objects | Deaths from non-collision accidents | Total deaths[1] |
|---|---|---|---|---|---|---|---|---|---|
| 1937 | 15,500 | 10,320 | 1,810 | 264 | 700 | 200 | 1,160 | 9,690 | 39,643 |
| 1939 | 12,400 | 8,700 | 1,330 | 150 | 710 | 200 | 1,000 | 7,900 | 32,386 |
| 1941 | 13,550 | 12,500 | 1,840 | 118 | 910 | 250 | 1,350 | 9,450 | 39,969 |
| 1943 | 9,900 | 5,300 | 1,448 | 171 | 450 | 160 | 700 | 5,690 | 23,823 |
| 1945 | 11,000 | 7,150 | 1,703 | 163 | 500 | 130 | 800 | 6,600 | 28,076 |
| 1947 | 10,450 | 9,900 | 1,736 | 102 | 550 | 150 | 1,000 | 8,800 | 32,697 |
| 1949 | 8,800 | 10,500 | 1,452 | 56 | 550 | 140 | 1,100 | 9,100 | 31,701 |
| 1951 | 9,150 | 13,100 | 1,573 | 46 | 390 | 100 | 1,400 | 11,200 | 36,996 |
| 1953 | 8,750 | 13,400 | 1,506 | 26 | 420 | 120 | 1,500 | 12,200 | 37,955 |
| 1955 | 8,200 | 14,500 | 1,490 | 15 | 410 | 90 | 1,600 | 12,100 | 38,426 |
| 1957 | 7,850 | 15,400 | 1,376 | 13 | 460 | 80 | 1,700 | 11,800 | 38,702 |
| 1959 | 7,850 | 14,900 | 1,202 | 6 | 480 | 70 | 1,600 | 11,800 | 37,910 |
| 1961 | 7,650 | 14,700 | 1,267 | 5 | 490 | 80 | 1,700 | 12,200 | 38,091 |
| 1963 | 8,200 | 17,600 | 1,385 | 10 | 580 | 80 | 1,900 | 13,800 | 43,564 |
| 1965 | 8,900 | 20,800 | 1,556 | 5 | 680 | 120 | 2,200 | 14,900 | 49,163 |
| 1967 | 9,400 | 22,000 | 1,620 | 3 | 750 | 100 | 2,350 | 16,700 | 52,924 |
| 1969 | 10,100 | 23,700 | 1,495 | 2 | 800 | 100 | 3,900 | 15,700 | 55,791 |
| 1970 | 9,900 | 23,200 | 1,459 | 3 | 780 | 100 | 3,800 | 15,400 | 54,633 |
| 1971 | 9,900 | 23,100 | 1,378 | 2 | 800 | 100 | 3,800 | 15,300 | 54,381 |
| 1972 | 10,300 | 23,900 | 1,260 | 2 | 1,000 | 100 | 3,900 | 15,800 | 56,278 |

| Year | Deaths from collisions with— Pedestrians | Other motor vehicles | Railroad trains | Street cars | Pedalcycles | Animal-drawn vehicle or animal | Fixed objects | Deaths from non-collision accidents | Total deaths[1] |
|---|---|---|---|---|---|---|---|---|---|
| 1973 | 10,200 | 23,600 | 1,194 | 2 | 1,000 | 100 | 3,800 | 15,600 | 55,511 |
| 1974 | 8,500 | 19,700 | 1,209 | 1 | 1,000 | 100 | 3,100 | 12,800 | 46,402 |
| 1975 | 8,400 | 19,550 | 979 | 1 | 1,000 | 100 | 3,130 | 12,700 | 45,853 |
| 1976 | 8,300 | 20,100 | 1,200 | (2) | 900 | 100 | 3,200 | 12,900 | 46,700 |
| 1977 | 8,700 | 21,600 | 1,000 | (2) | 1,100 | 100 | 3,400 | 13,600 | 49,500 |

1. Yearly totals do not quite equal sums of various types because totals for most types are estimated, and these have been made to nearest 10 deaths for some types and to nearest 50 deaths for others. 2. No longer tabulated. *Source:* National Safety Council.

## Death Rates by Age, Color, and Sex

| Age[1] | 1976[2] | 1975[2] | 1970[2] | 1960 | 1940 | 1920 | 1976[2] | 1975[2] | 1970[2] | 1960 | 1940 | 1920 |
|---|---|---|---|---|---|---|---|---|---|---|---|---|
| | White males | | | | | | White females | | | | | |
| Under 1 | 15.1 | 15.9 | 21.1 | 26.9 | 56.7 | 98.1 | 11.9 | 12.2 | 16.1 | 20.1 | 43.6 | 76.1 |
| 1–4 | 0.7 | 0.7 | 0.8 | 1.0 | 2.8 | 9.8 | 0.6 | 0.6 | 0.8 | 0.9 | 2.4 | 9.0 |
| 5–14 | 0.4 | 0.4 | 0.5 | 0.5 | 1.1 | 2.7 | 0.3 | 0.3 | 0.3 | 0.3 | 0.8 | 2.3 |
| 15–24 | 1.6 | 1.7 | 1.7 | 1.4 | 2.0 | 4.2 | 0.5 | 0.6 | 0.6 | 0.5 | 1.4 | 4.3 |
| 25–34 | 1.6 | 1.7 | 1.8 | 1.6 | 2.8 | 5.9 | 0.7 | 0.7 | 0.8 | 0.9 | 2.2 | 6.5 |
| 35–44 | 2.8 | 3.0 | 3.4 | 3.3 | 5.1 | 7.7 | 1.6 | 1.6 | 1.9 | 1.9 | 3.7 | 7.3 |
| 45–54 | 7.7 | 7.9 | 8.8 | 9.3 | 11.4 | 12.0 | 4.1 | 4.1 | 4.6 | 4.6 | 7.5 | 10.9 |
| 55–64 | 19.2 | 19.5 | 22.0 | 22.3 | 25.2 | 24.2 | 9.4 | 9.4 | 10.1 | 10.8 | 16.8 | 21.7 |
| 65-74 | 42.8 | 43.6 | 48.1 | 48.5 | 54.0 | 54.2 | 21.1 | 21.5 | 24.7 | 27.8 | 41.5 | 49.9 |
| 75–84 | 96.0 | 96.1 | 101.0 | 103.0 | 122.0 | 122.5 | 59.8 | 60.3 | 67.0 | 77.0 | 104.8 | 116.4 |
| 85 and over | 187.7 | 182.0 | 185.5 | 217.5 | 251.4 | 253.6 | 148.2 | 144.9 | 159.8 | 194.8 | 235.0 | 247.0 |
| | All other males | | | | | | All other females | | | | | |
| Under 1 | 30.1 | 30.0 | 40.2 | 51.9 | 101.2 | 167.7 | 25.4 | 25.2 | 31.7 | 40.7 | 77.4 | 131.1 |
| 1–4 | 1.1 | 1.1 | 1.4 | 2.1 | 5.3 | 15.0 | 0.9 | 0.9 | 1.2 | 1.7 | 4.4 | 14.2 |
| 5–14 | 0.5 | 0.6 | 0.6 | 0.8 | 1.6 | 3.7 | 0.3 | 0.3 | 0.4 | 0.5 | 1.4 | 3.9 |
| 15–24 | 2.2 | 2.4 | 3.0 | 2.1 | 5.0 | 9.9 | 0.8 | 0.9 | 1.1 | 1.1 | 5.0 | 10.8 |
| 25–34 | 4.1 | 4.5 | 5.0 | 3.9 | 8.5 | 12.2 | 1.6 | 1.6 | 2.2 | 2.6 | 7.4 | 13.5 |
| 35–44 | 6.9 | 7.4 | 8.7 | 7.3 | 13.2 | 14.4 | 3.4 | 3.6 | 4.9 | 5.5 | 11.7 | 16.0 |
| 45–54 | 14.0 | 14.2 | 16.5 | 15.5 | 24.5 | 20.1 | 7.7 | 7.8 | 9.8 | 11.4 | 21.1 | 23.4 |
| 55–64 | 28.1 | 28.1 | 30.5 | 31.5 | 37.1[3] | 31.1 | 15.9 | 16.4 | 18.9 | 24.1 | 33.2[3] | 35.8 |
| 65–74 | 48.5 | 49.7 | 54.7 | 56.6 | 62.8[3] | 60.2 | 30.1 | 31.7 | 36.8 | 39.8 | 52.3[3] | 60.4 |
| 75–84 | 86.5 | 86.0 | 89.8 | 86.6 | 108.8 | 116.0 | 62.2 | 59.8 | 63.9 | 67.1 | 84.1 | 106.4 |
| 85 and over | 115.2 | 116.9 | 114.1 | 152.4 | 199.7 | 247.1 | 91.8 | 91.8 | 102.9 | 128.7 | 159.7 | 221.2 |

1. In years. 2. Excludes deaths of nonresidents of U.S. 3. Based on enumerated population adjusted for age bias in nonwhite population at ages 55–69 years. NOTE: For 1920, data are from only 10 selected states and the District of Columbia; for 1940, from D.C. and the former 48 states; for 1960, from D.C. and all 50 states. Excludes fetal deaths. Rates are per 1,000 population in each group, enumerated as of April 1 for 1940, 1950, and 1960, and estimated as of July 1 for all other years. *Sources:* Department of Commerce, Bureau of the Census; and Department of Health, Education, and Welfare, National Center for Health Statistics.

## Cigarette Smoking

In 1975, Americans smoked 603 billion cigarettes, 9 billion more than they did in 1974. The Federal Trade Commission reported that in 1975 an average of 11.2 cigarettes a day was produced for every person in the nation over 18 years of age. These figures do not include the number of cigarettes smoked by children *under* 18.

Each American over 18 smoked, on average, 4,095 cigarettes in 1975.

## Home Gardening Can Be Profitable

A backyard garden can produce as much as $300 worth of vegetables in a growing season for an investment of $20. The National Association for Gardening estimates that there are over 32 million home gardens in the U.S., and that translates into a possible $9.6 billion worth of home-grown vegetables.

# Law Enforcement and Crime

## Full-Time Law Enforcement Employees

| City | Officers | Civilians | Total | City | Officers | Civilians | Total |
|---|---|---|---|---|---|---|---|
| Atlanta | 1,251 | 335 | 1,586 | Minneapolis | 826 | 103 | 929 |
| Baltimore | 3,455 | 556 | 4,011 | New Orleans | 1,510 | 503 | 2,013 |
| Birmingham, Ala. | 619 | 110 | 729 | New York | 25,789 | 3,644 | 29,433 |
| Boston | 2,301 | 481 | 2,782 | Newark, N.J. | 1,507 | 133 | 1,640 |
| Buffalo, N.Y. | 1,181 | 244 | 1,425 | Norfolk, Va. | 612 | 115 | 727 |
| Chicago | 13,039 | 1,795 | 14,834 | Oakland, Calif. | 678 | 286 | 964 |
| Cincinnati | 1,111 | 193 | 1,304 | Oklahoma City | 620 | 120 | 740 |
| Cleveland | 2,031 | 111 | 2,142 | Omaha, Neb. | 544 | 131 | 675 |
| Columbus, Ohio | 1,080 | 239 | 1,319 | Philadelphia | 8,154 | 878 | 9,032 |
| Dallas | 2,014 | 549 | 2,563 | Phoenix, Ariz. | 1,559 | 364 | 1,923 |
| Denver | 1,359 | 297 | 1,656 | Pittsburgh | 1,398 | 26 | 1,424 |
| Detroit | 5,016 | 574 | 5,590 | Portland, Ore. | 683 | 166 | 849 |
| El Paso | 597 | 108 | 705 | Rochester, N.Y. | 627 | 123 | 750 |
| Fort Worth | 681 | 149 | 830 | St. Louis | 2,068 | 564 | 2,632 |
| Honolulu | 1,506 | 343 | 1,849 | St. Paul | 524 | 115 | 639 |
| Houston | 2,737 | 589 | 3,326 | San Antonio | 1,166 | 239 | 1,405 |
| Indianapolis | 1,082 | 278 | 1,360 | San Diego, Calif. | 1,067 | 298 | 1,365 |
| Jacksonville, Fla. | 982 | 572 | 1,554 | San Francisco | 1,667 | 428 | 2,095 |
| Kansas City, Mo. | 1,221 | 472 | 1,693 | San Jose, Calif. | 771 | 179 | 950 |
| Long Beach, Calif. | 637 | 271 | 908 | Seattle | 1,030 | 300 | 1,330 |
| Los Angeles | 7,296 | 2,761 | 10,057 | Tampa, Fla. | 628 | 132 | 760 |
| Louisville, Ky. | 729 | 325 | 1,054 | Toledo, Ohio | 704 | 107 | 811 |
| Memphis, Tenn. | 1,304 | 295 | 1,599 | Tucson, Ariz. | 510 | 184 | 694 |
| Miami, Fla. | 821 | 265 | 1,086 | Tulsa, Okla. | 673 | 113 | 786 |
| Milwaukee | 2,083 | 230 | 2,313 | Washington, D.C. | 4,340 | 606 | 4,946 |

NOTE: As of Oct. 31, 1976. *Source:* Department of Justice, Federal Bureau of Investigation, *Uniform Crime Reports for the United States, 1976.*

## Arrests by Race, 1976
(in thousands)

| Offense | White | Black | Other | Total |
|---|---|---|---|---|
| Serious Crimes | 1,064.0 | 561.9 | 34.7 | 1,660.7 |
| Murder[1] | 5.8 | 6.9 | 0.2 | 12.9 |
| Manslaughter by negligence | 1.9 | 0.6 | 0.1 | 2.6 |
| Forcible rape | 10.1 | 9.2 | 0.6 | 19.8 |
| Robbery | 35.2 | 53.7 | 2.4 | 90.6 |
| Aggravated assault | 98.2 | 70.9 | 6.0 | 172.6 |
| Burglary—breaking and entering | 260.1 | 110.1 | 12.5 | 376.7 |
| Larceny—theft | 582.5 | 284.7 | 31.9 | 886.6 |
| Motor vehicle theft | 70.2 | 25.8 | 2.7 | 98.8 |
| All Other | | | | |
| Other assaults | 214.7 | 114.4 | 9.4 | 335.8 |
| Arson | 10.7 | 2.7 | 0.2 | 13.6 |
| Forgery and counterfeiting | 34.7 | 17.6 | 0.7 | 52.8 |
| Fraud | 108.3 | 46.3 | 1.8 | 156.4 |
| Embezzlement | 5.3 | 2.4 | 0.1 | 7.8 |
| Stolen property—buying, receiving, possessing | 54.9 | 28.8 | 1.1 | 84.9 |
| Vandalism | 136.9 | 26.3 | 2.4 | 165.7 |
| Weapons—carrying, possessing, etc. | 66.2 | 46.1 | 2.1 | 114.4 |
| Prostitution and commercial vice | 23.6 | 26.8 | 0.8 | 51.3 |
| Sex offenses, except forcible rape and prostitution | 37.4 | 10.2 | 1.2 | 48.7 |
| Narcotic drug laws | 366.1 | 103.6 | 5.5 | 475.2 |
| Gambling | 26.2 | 34.4 | 1.9 | 62.5 |
| Offenses against family and children | 39.9 | 16.6 | 0.8 | 57.2 |
| Driving under the influence | 682.7 | 116.0 | 24.5 | 823.2 |
| Liquor laws | 260.7 | 28.1 | 8.9 | 297.8 |
| Drunkenness | 818.6 | 205.9 | 39.7 | 1,064.2 |
| Disorderly conduct | 371.2 | 128.3 | 14.2 | 513.7 |
| Vagrancy | 16.5 | 10.0 | 0.9 | 27.4 |
| All other offenses, except traffic | 773.3 | 292.0 | 23.3 | 1,088.6 |
| Curfew and loitering law violations | 61.8 | 24.3 | 1.7 | 87.9 |
| Runaways | 143.8 | 16.9 | 3.4 | 164.1 |
| **Total** | **5,336.9** | **1,870.2** | **176.9** | **7,384.0** |

1. Includes non-negligent manslaughter. NOTE: Figures represent arrests reported by 10,058 agencies with a total 1976 population of 173,488,000 as estimated by FBI. *Source:* Department of Justice, Federal Bureau of Investigation, *Uniform Crime Reports for the United States, 1976.*

## Number of Arrests by Sex and Age

| Offense | Male | | | | Female | | | |
|---|---|---|---|---|---|---|---|---|
| | Total | | Under 18 | | Total | | Under 18 | |
| | 1976 | 1970 | 1976 | 1970 | 1976 | 1970 | 1976 | 1970 |
| Serious Crimes | 1,260,300 | 925,951 | 543,622 | 435,171 | 325,139 | 196,642 | 125,158 | 88,506 |
| Murder[1] | 10,163 | 9,077 | 981 | 933 | 1,870 | 1,711 | 135 | 84 |
| Manslaughter by negligence | 2,179 | 2,174 | 229 | 179 | 228 | 274 | 29 | 22 |
| Forcible rape | 18,670 | 13,176 | 3,204 | 2,686 | 184 | 6 | 56 | 1 |
| Robbery | 80,969 | 70,432 | 25,630 | 23,656 | 6,303 | 4,672 | 1,970 | 1,823 |
| Aggravated assault | 141,712 | 96,181 | 23,184 | 15,574 | 21,663 | 14,125 | 4,523 | 2,554 |
| Burglary—breaking or entering | 338,219 | 234,839 | 177,920 | 123,512 | 19,122 | 11,448 | 9,902 | 5,858 |
| Larceny—theft | 580,693 | 394,336 | 265,201 | 208,028 | 268,904 | 158,784 | 104,490 | 74,776 |
| Motor vehicle theft | 87,695 | 105,736 | 47,273 | 60,603 | 6,865 | 5,622 | 4,053 | 3,388 |
| All Other | | | | | | | | |
| Other assaults | 273,180 | 219,402 | 49,396 | 36,147 | 44,714 | 33,038 | 12,876 | 9,151 |
| Arson | 11,534 | — | 6,352 | — | 1,446 | — | 652 | — |
| Forgery and counterfeiting | 34,179 | 30,689 | 4,154 | 3,148 | 14,709 | 9,627 | 1,866 | 1,143 |
| Fraud | 92,893 | 47,710 | 3,010 | 1,798 | 53,927 | 17,817 | 1,213 | 633 |
| Embezzlement | 5,155 | 5,793 | 413 | 253 | 2,445 | 1,917 | 89 | 88 |
| Stolen property—buying, receiving, possessing | 72,003 | 50,803 | 23,618 | 15,455 | 8,622 | 5,281 | 2,151 | 1,227 |
| Vandalism | 145,993 | — | 92,379 | — | 13,104 | — | 7,450 | — |
| Weapons—carrying, possessing, etc. | 98,438 | 81,624 | 16,482 | 13,854 | 8,939 | 5,929 | 1,099 | 591 |
| Prostitution and commercialized vice | 15,388 | 7,995 | 545 | 305 | 35,413 | 34,998 | 1,839 | 749 |
| Sex offenses, except forcible rape and prostitution | 42,706 | 36,942 | 7,978 | 7,060 | 4,354 | 5,332 | 940 | 1,894 |
| Narcotic drug laws | 386,371 | 249,883 | 91,431 | 53,158 | 62,549 | 47,608 | 18,128 | 15,555 |
| Gambling | 66,105 | 67,308 | 2,061 | 1,358 | 5,962 | 5,812 | 259 | 54 |
| Offenses against family and children | 48,173 | 44,004 | 2,719 | 515 | 5,760 | 4,362 | 1,280 | 245 |
| Driving under the influence | 709,297 | 340,873 | 14,839 | 3,850 | 59,610 | 24,394 | 1,270 | 199 |
| Liquor laws | 245,794 | 171,355 | 83,101 | 55,282 | 40,780 | 25,684 | 21,701 | 11,978 |
| Drunkenness | 933,259 | 1,279,657 | 32,057 | 30,523 | 71,518 | 97,049 | 4,957 | 4,592 |
| Disorderly conduct | 413,054 | 383,254 | 84,960 | 87,483 | 72,108 | 75,241 | 18,929 | 19,237 |
| Vagrancy | 22,426 | 75,481 | 3,503 | 9,459 | 4,153 | 18,797 | 649 | 1,653 |
| All other offenses, except traffic | 849,970 | 840,210 | 189,408 | 378,273 | 165,128 | 218,083 | 52,039 | 153,544 |
| Curfew and loitering law violations | 68,648 | — | 68,648 | — | 17,135 | — | 17,135 | — |
| Runaways | 66,748 | — | 66,748 | — | 88,942 | — | 88,942 | — |
| **Total** | **5,850,614** | **4,858,934** | **1,387,424** | **1,133,092** | **1,106,466** | **827,973** | **380,622** | **311,039** |

1. Includes non-negligent manslaughter. NOTE: 1976 figures represent arrests reported by 8,602 agencies with a total 1976 population of 162,700,000 as estimated by FBI. *Source:* Department of Justice, Federal Bureau of Investigation, *Uniform Crime Reports for the United States, 1976.*

## Domestic Production and Imports of Civilian Firearms
(in thousands)

| Item | 1976 | 1976, TQ[1] | 1975 | 1974 | 1973 | 1972 | 1971 | 1970 | 1965 | 1960 |
|---|---|---|---|---|---|---|---|---|---|---|
| Domestic production | 5,225 | 1,234 | 5,768 | 5,639 | 4,844 | n.a. | n.a. | n.a. | 2,355 | 1,508 |
| Handguns | 1,833 | 431 | 2,024 | 1,715 | 1,734 | n.a. | n.a. | n.a. | 666 | 475 |
| Rifles | 2,091 | 494 | 2,123 | 2,099 | 1,830 | n.a. | n.a. | n.a. | 790 | 469 |
| Shotguns | 1,301 | 309 | 1,621 | 1,825 | 1,280 | n.a. | n.a. | n.a. | 899 | 564 |
| Imports for consumption | 895 | 177 | 1,084 | 903 | 914 | 1,200 | 951 | 826 | 766 | 655 |
| Handguns | 270 | 86 | 462 | 259 | 299 | 468 | 301 | 227 | 347 | 128 |
| Rifles | 157 | 29 | 166 | 188 | 195 | 197 | 243 | 237 | 245 | 402 |
| Shotguns | 468 | 62 | 457 | 456 | 420 | 535 | 406 | 363 | 174 | 125 |
| **Total** | **6,120** | **1,411** | **6,852** | **6,542** | **5,758** | **n.a.** | **n.a.** | **n.a.** | **3,121** | **2,163** |

1. Transition quarter, July-September. NOTE: Beginning 1971, fiscal-year data. Includes firearms sold under civilian marksmanship program of Department of Defense. n.a.=not available. *Source:* 1960–1970, Department of Commerce, Bureau of the Census; beginning 1971, Department of the Treasury, Bureau of Alcohol, Tobacco, and Firearms.

## Crime Rates for Population Groups and Selected Cities, 1976

(offenses known to the police per 100,000 population)

| Group and city | Total all crimes[1] | Violent crime: Total | Violent crime: Murder | Violent crime: Forcible rape | Violent crime: Robbery | Violent crime: Aggravated assault | Property crime: Total | Property crime: Burglary—breaking or entering | Property crime: Larceny—theft | Property crime: Motor vehicle theft |
|---|---|---|---|---|---|---|---|---|---|---|
| 59 cities over 250,000 | 8,263 | 1,095 | 19.3 | 54.2 | 626 | 396 | 7,167 | 2,287 | 3,886 | 994 |
| 110 cities, 100,000 to 250,000 | 7,558 | 573 | 10.0 | 34.9 | 238 | 290 | 6,985 | 2,000 | 4,376 | 610 |
| 265 cities, 50,000 to 100,000 | 6,243 | 416 | 6.1 | 26.0 | 161 | 223 | 5,827 | 1,606 | 3,731 | 490 |
| 604 cities, 25,000 to 50,000 | 5,537 | 338 | 5.4 | 18.9 | 115 | 199 | 5,199 | 1,328 | 3,486 | 386 |
| 1,398 cities, 10,000 to 25,000 | 4,676 | 254 | 4.0 | 13.9 | 69 | 167 | 4,422 | 1,112 | 3,029 | 281 |
| 4,925 cities, under 10,000 | 3,988 | 216 | 3.6 | 11.1 | 38 | 163 | 3,772 | 929 | 2,644 | 199 |
| Total, 7,361 cities | 6,366 | 580 | 9.9 | 30.8 | 276 | 264 | 5,786 | 1,652 | 3,561 | 572 |
| Suburbs, 4,022 agencies[2] | 4,627 | 292 | 5.1 | 20.0 | 85 | 182 | 4,334 | 1,253 | 2,757 | 325 |
| Rural areas, 1,677 agencies | 2,215 | 174 | 7.5 | 13.3 | 21 | 133 | 2,041 | 826 | 1,103 | 112 |
| **Total, 9,512 agencies** | **5,525** | **488** | **9.1** | **27.9** | **213** | **238** | **5,038** | **1,502** | **3,064** | **472** |
| Selected cities: | | | | | | | | | | |
| New York | 8,740 | 1,781 | 21.5 | 45.1 | 1,144 | 570 | 6,958 | 2,593 | 3,082 | 1,284 |
| Chicago | 6,829 | 978 | 26.0 | 37.6 | 561 | 353 | 5,852 | 1,233 | 3,583 | 1,036 |
| Los Angeles | 8,057 | 1,167 | 18.3 | 74.7 | 519 | 554 | 6,890 | 2,403 | 3,341 | 1,146 |
| Philadelphia | 4,018 | 684 | 17.6 | 39.9 | 406 | 220 | 3,334 | 1,046 | 1,578 | 710 |
| Houston | 7,196 | 545 | 21.7 | 46.7 | 374 | 102 | 6,651 | 2,052 | 3,781 | 819 |
| Detroit | 11,512 | 2,226 | 49.7 | 92.2 | 1,590 | 494 | 9,286 | 3,347 | 3,847 | 2,093 |
| Dallas | 10,274 | 815 | 25.9 | 66.5 | 350 | 373 | 9,459 | 2,581 | 6,300 | 578 |
| Baltimore | 7,847 | 1,648 | 23.2 | 53.5 | 901 | 671 | 6,199 | 1,779 | 3,736 | 684 |
| San Diego | 8,092 | 532 | 7.6 | 30.1 | 294 | 201 | 7,559 | 2,049 | 4,706 | 804 |
| San Antonio | 8,172 | 436 | 15.8 | 34.9 | 168 | 218 | 7,736 | 2,759 | 4,484 | 493 |
| Cleveland | 8,274 | 1,323 | 36.7 | 78.0 | 849 | 359 | 6,951 | 2,047 | 2,940 | 1,964 |
| Washington, D.C. | 7,083 | 1,481 | 26.8 | 72.4 | 1,003 | 379 | 5,602 | 1,691 | 3,491 | 421 |
| Indianapolis | 7,877 | 838 | 13.7 | 70.0 | 478 | 276 | 7,040 | 2,093 | 4,135 | 811 |
| San Francisco | 11,622 | 1,618 | 19.7 | 93.1 | 997 | 508 | 10,004 | 3,307 | 5,165 | 1,532 |
| Milwaukee | 5,671 | 413 | 8.7 | 25.7 | 248 | 130 | 5,259 | 1,095 | 3,533 | 631 |
| **CRIME INDEX TRENDS (percent change, 1976–77)** | | | | | | | | | | |
| Cities over 1,000,000 (total population 18,132,000) | −6 | −7 | −3 | +13 | −11 | −2 | −6 | −7 | −6 | −3 |
| All cities over 25,000 (total population 97,154,000) | −5 | 0 | +2 | +11 | −5 | +4 | −5 | −3 | −8 | −1 |
| Suburban areas (total population 70,469,000) | −4 | +6 | −1 | +9 | +3 | +8 | −5 | −2 | −7 | +4 |
| Rural areas (total population 25,525,000) | −1 | +2 | −3 | +8 | 0 | +2 | −2 | 0 | −4 | +11 |
| All areas (total population 196,695) | −4 | +1 | +1 | +10 | −4 | +5 | −5 | −2 | −7 | 0 |

1. Includes manslaughter by negligence, not shown separately. 2. Agencies also included in other city groups. NOTE: Population in 1976 as estimated by FBI. *Source:* Department of Justice, Federal Bureau of Investigation, *Uniform Crime Reports for the United States, 1976.*

## National Crime, Rate, and Percent Change

| Crime index offenses | Estimated crime 1976: Number | Estimated crime 1976: Rate per 100,000 inhabitants | Percent change over 1975: Number | Percent change over 1975: Rate | Percent change over 1972: Number | Percent change over 1972: Rate | Percent change over 1967: Number | Percent change over 1967: Rate |
|---|---|---|---|---|---|---|---|---|
| Murder | 18,780 | 8.8 | −8.4 | −8.3 | +.6 | −2.2 | +53.4 | +41.9 |
| Forcible rape | 56,730 | 26.4 | +1.1 | +.4 | +21.1 | +17.3 | +105.4 | +88.6 |
| Robbery | 420,210 | 195.8 | −9.6 | −10.3 | +11.7 | +8.4 | +107.1 | +90.5 |
| Aggravated assault | 490,850 | 228.7 | +1.3 | +.6 | +24.9 | +21.1 | +90.9 | +75.7 |
| Burglary | 3,089,800 | 1,439.4 | −5.0 | −5.7 | +30.1 | +26.2 | +89.3 | +74.1 |
| Larceny-theft | 6.270,800 | 2,921.3 | +4.9 | +4.2 | +51.1 | +46.5 | +101.5 | +85.4 |
| Motor vehicle theft | 957,600 | 446.1 | −4.3 | −5.0 | +7.9 | +4.7 | +45.1 | +33.5 |
| Violent | 986,580 | 459.6 | −3.9 | −4.5 | +18.2 | +14.6 | +97.3 | +81.5 |
| Property | 10,318,200 | 4,806.8 | +.9 | +.1 | +39.2 | +35.0 | +91.0 | +75.7 |
| **Total** | **11,304,800** | **5,266.4** | +.4 | −.3 | **+37.0** | **+32.9** | **+91.5** | **+76.2** |

*Source:* Department of Justice, Federal Bureau of Investigation, *Uniform Crime Reports for the United States, 1976.*

## Total Estimated Arrests, 1976[1]

| | | | |
|---|---|---|---|
| Criminal homicide: | | Narcotic drug laws | 609,700 |
| Murder and nonnegligent manslaughter | 17,250 | Opium or cocaine and their derivatives | 60,200 |
| Manslaughter by negligence | 3,310 | Marijuana | 441,100 |
| Forcible rape | 26,400 | Synthetic or manufactured narcotics | 18,200 |
| Robbery | 132,930 | Other—dangerous nonnarcotic drugs | 90,200 |
| Aggravated assault | 235,050 | Gambling | 79,000 |
| Burglary—breaking or entering | 495,200 | Bookmaking | 17,900 |
| Larceny—theft | 1,117,300 | Numbers and lottery | 12,700 |
| Motor vehicle theft | 134,400 | All other gambling | 48,400 |
| Other assaults | 428,000 | Offenses against family and children | 72,400 |
| Arson | 17,700 | Driving under the influence | 1,029,300 |
| Forgery and counterfeiting | 68,000 | Liquor laws | 369,700 |
| Fraud | 199,300 | Drunkenness | 1,297,800 |
| Embezzlement | 10,000 | Disorderly conduct | 657,500 |
| Stolen property—buying, receiving, possessing | 111,600 | Vagrancy | 39,400 |
| Vandalism | 211,800 | All other offenses (except traffic) | 1,619,100 |
| Weapons; carrying, possessing, etc. | 147,100 | Suspicion (not included in total) | 37,600 |
| Prostitution and commercialized vice | 70,200 | Curfew and loitering law violations | 106,300 |
| Sex offenses (except forcible rape and prostitution) | 62,600 | Runaways | 202,600 |
| | | **Total** | **9,608,500** |

1. Arrest totals based on all reporting agencies and estimates for unreported areas. *Source:* Department of Justice, Federal Bureau of Investigation, *Uniform Crime Reports for the United States, 1976.*

## Methods of Execution[1]

| State | Method | State | Method |
|---|---|---|---|
| Alabama[2] | Electrocution | New Hampshire[2] | Hanging |
| Alaska | No death penalty | New Jersey[5] | No death penalty |
| Arizona[2] | Lethal gas | New Mexico | No death penalty |
| Arkansas[2] | Electrocution | New York[2] | Electrocution |
| California | Lethal gas | North Carolina[2] | Lethal gas |
| Colorado[2] | Lethal gas | North Dakota | No death penalty |
| Connecticut[2] | Electrocution | Ohio[2] | Electrocution |
| Delaware | Hanging | Oklahoma[5] | Electrocution or lethal injection |
| D.C. | No death penalty | Oregon | No death penalty |
| Florida | Electrocution | Pennsylvania[2] | Electrocution |
| Georgia[2] | Electrocution | Rhode Island[2] | ([3]) |
| Hawaii | No death penalty | South Carolina[2] | Electrocution |
| Idaho[2] | Hanging or lethal injection | South Dakota | Electrocution |
| Illinois | No death penalty | Tennessee[2] | Electrocution |
| Indiana[2] | Electrocution | Texas[2] | Lethal injection |
| Iowa | No death penalty | Utah[2] | Hanging or shooting |
| Kansas | Hanging | Vermont | Electrocution |
| Kentucky[2] | Electrocution | Virginia | Electrocution |
| Louisiana[2] | Electrocution | Washington[2] | Hanging |
| Maine | No death penalty | West Virginia | No death penalty |
| Maryland[2] | Lethal gas | Wisconsin | No death penalty |
| Massachusetts[5] | No death penalty | Wyoming | Lethal gas |
| Michigan | No death penalty | U.S. (Fed. Govt.) | ([4]) |
| Minnesota | No death penalty | American Samoa | Hanging |
| Mississippi[2] | Lethal gas | Canal Zone | Hanging |
| Missouri | Lethal gas | Guam | No death penalty |
| Montana[2] | Hanging | Puerto Rico | No death penalty |
| Nebraska[2] | Electrocution | Virgin Islands | No death penalty |
| Nevada[2] | Lethal gas | | |

1. On July 1, 1976, by a 7–2 decision, the U.S. Supreme Court upheld the death penalty as not being "cruel or unusual." However, in another ruling the same day, the Court, by a 5–4 vote, stated that states may not impose, "mandatory" capital punishment on every person convicted of murder. These decisions left uncertain the fate of condemned persons throughout the U.S. On Oct. 4, the Court refused to reconsider its July ruling, which allows some states to proceed with executions of condemned prisoners. The first execution in this country since 1967 was in Utah on January 17, 1977. Gary Mark Gilmore was executed by shooting. 2. Voted to restore death penalty after June 29, 1972, Supreme Court decision ruling capital punishment unconstitutional. 3. Person shall be executed by gas if he commits murder while serving a prison term. 4. Method shall be that used by state in which sentence is imposed. If state does not have death penalty, federal judge shall prescribe method for carrying out sentence. 5. New legislation pending. *Source: Information Please* questionnaires to the states.

## Prisoners Under Sentence of Death

| Characteristic | 1976 | 1975 | 1974 |
|---|---|---|---|
| White | 243 | 214 | 116 |
| Black and other | 201 | 265 | 138 |
| Under 20 years | 20 | 43 | 15 |
| 20–24 years | 133 | 139 | 80 |
| 25–34 years | 206 | 204 | 94 |
| 35–54 years | 79 | 83 | 58 |
| 55 years and over | 6 | 10 | 7 |
| Schooling completed | | | |
| 0–7 years | 49 | 71 | 48 |
| 8 years | 47 | 50 | 33 |
| 9–11 years | 145 | 167 | 88 |
| 12 years | 95 | 93 | 49 |
| More than 12 years | 26 | 21 | 11 |
| Unknown years | 82 | 77 | 25 |
| Marital status | | | |
| Never married | 206 | 217 | 107 |
| Married | 146 | 167 | 90 |
| Divorced or separated[1] | 92 | 95 | 57 |
| Time elapsed since sentencing | | | |
| 6 months or less | 85 | 166 | 101 |
| 7–12 months | 99 | 130 | 59 |
| 1–3 years | 256 | 155 | 39 |
| 4–8 years | 4 | 13 | 30 |
| More than 8 years | 0 | 15 | 25 |
| Legal status at arrest | | | |
| Not under sentence | 274 | 293 | 163 |
| On parole or probation | 50 | 51 | 32 |
| In prison or escaped | 22 | 27 | 19 |
| Unknown | 98 | 108 | 40 |
| **Total** | **444** | **479** | **254** |

1. Includes widows, widowers, and unknown. NOTE: As of Dec. 31, excludes prisoners under sentence of death confined in local correctional systems pending appeal or who had not been committed to prison. *Source:* Department of Justice, Law Enforcement Assistance Administration.

## Disposition of Persons Formally Charged by the Police, 1976

| Offense | Number of persons charged (held for prosecution) | Percent of charged[1] | | | |
|---|---|---|---|---|---|
| | | Guilty | | Acquitted or dismissed | Referred to juvenile court |
| | | Offense charged | Lesser offense | | |
| Serious Crimes | 265,526 | 40.1 | 4.2 | 16.1 | 39.6 |
| Criminal homicide: | | | | | |
| Murder and nonnegligent manslaughter | 1,377 | 44.5 | 13.3 | 35.1 | 7.1 |
| Manslaughter by negligence | 270 | 42.2 | 10.0 | 32.6 | 15.2 |
| Forcible rape | 2,418 | 33.0 | 7.4 | 40.0 | 19.7 |
| Robbery | 10,707 | 38.9 | 5.6 | 25.0 | 30.5 |
| Aggravated assault | 19,903 | 41.6 | 10.7 | 29.3 | 18.4 |
| Burglary—breaking or entering | 55,455 | 27.8 | 4.9 | 13.9 | 53.4 |
| Larceny—theft | 160,263 | 46.3 | 2.8 | 14.5 | 36.4 |
| Motor vehicle theft | 15,133 | 19.2 | 4.4 | 12.8 | 63.6 |
| Other assaults | 53,363 | 46.0 | 3.9 | 36.3 | 13.7 |
| Arson | 1,937 | 20.6 | 4.0 | 15.5 | 59.8 |
| Forgery and counterfeiting | 7,784 | 57.4 | 6.5 | 20.5 | 15.6 |
| Fraud | 18,755 | 60.2 | 2.6 | 33.1 | 4.1 |
| Embezzlement | 1,780 | 78.0 | 3.1 | 14.9 | 3.9 |
| Stolen property;—buying, receiving, possessing | 9,443 | 39.0 | 4.8 | 22.4 | 33.7 |
| Vandalism | 26,067 | 34.1 | 1.4 | 20.4 | 44.1 |
| Weapons;—carrying, possessing, etc. | 16,113 | 56.8 | 4.0 | 25.1 | 14.1 |
| Prostitution and commercialized vice | 7,718 | 44.6 | 1.6 | 48.7 | 5.1 |
| Sex offenses, except forcible rape and prostitution | 7,227 | 49.6 | 5.6 | 27.7 | 17.1 |
| Narcotic drug laws | 58,523 | 44.9 | 4.1 | 24.4 | 26.5 |
| Gambling | 6,259 | 75.5 | 3.3 | 18.5 | 2.7 |
| Offenses against family and children | 5,766 | 49.5 | 2.4 | 23.9 | 24.2 |
| Driving under the influence | 127,736 | 75.7 | 12.7 | 9.9 | 1.7 |
| Liquor laws | 72,264 | 68.3 | .7 | 9.2 | 21.8 |
| Drunkenness | 202,349 | 85.5 | .5 | 12.0 | 2.0 |
| Disorderly conduct | 122,652 | 70.4 | 1.3 | 19.3 | 9.0 |
| Vagrancy | 4,720 | 60.8 | .4 | 29.5 | 9.3 |
| All other offenses | 187,898 | 56.5 | 1.4 | 21.0 | 21.2 |
| **Total** | **1,203,880** | **60.3** | **3.4** | **17.7** | **18.7** |

1. Due to rounding, percentages may not add to 100%. NOTE: Figures based on reports furnished to FBI by 2,793 cities with 1976 estimated population of 34,415,000. *Source:* Department of Justice, Federal Bureau of Investigation, *Uniform Crime Reports for the United States, 1976.*

# Motor Vehicle Laws, 1978

| State | Date new license plates can be used | Age for driver's license[1] | | | State gasoline tax | Percent State tax[2] | Annual inspection required |
|---|---|---|---|---|---|---|---|
| | | Regular | Learner's | Restrictive | | | |
| Alabama | Oct. 1 | 16 | 15[5] | 14[15] | $.07 | 1½ | no[19] |
| Alaska | Jan. 1 | 18 | | 16[3] | .08 | — | no[19] |
| Arizona | On issue | 18 | 15 & 7 mos.[3,5] | 16[3] | .08 | 4 | no |
| Arkansas | On issue | 18 | ([5]) | 14[3] | .085 | 3 | yes |
| California | On issue | 18 | 15½[4,10] | 16[4] | .07 | 6 | no[19] |
| Colorado | On issue | 21 | 15½[5] | 16[4] | .07 | 3 | yes |
| Connecticut | On issue | 18 | | 16[4] | .11 | 7[6] | no[19] |
| Delaware | On issue | 18 | ([5]) | 16[4] | .11 | ([18]) | yes |
| D. C. | On issue | 18 | ([5]) | 16[3] | .10 | ([21]) | yes |
| Florida | 30 days before exp. of old | 18 | ([5]) | 15[3,4] | .08 | 4 | yes |
| Georgia | Jan. 1 | 18 | 15 | 16[3] | .075 | 3 | yes |
| Hawaii | On issue | 18 | ([5]) | 15[3] | ([8]) | ([9]) | yes[12] |
| Idaho | On issue | 16 | ([5]) | 14[4] | .095 | 3 | yes |
| Illinois | Dec. 1 | 18 | ([5]) | 16[3,4] | .075 | 4 | no |
| Indiana | On issue | 16½ | 15[20] | 16 & 1 mo.[4] | .08 | 4 | yes |
| Iowa | Dec. 1 | 18 | 14 | 16[4] | .07 | 3 | ([7,19]) |
| Kansas | On issue | 16 | ([5]) | 14 | .08 | 3 | no |
| Kentucky | Dec. 29 | 18 | ([5]) | 16[3] | .09 | 5[11] | yes |
| Louisiana | On issue | 17 | | 15 | .08 | 3 | yes |
| Maine | On issue | 17 | ([5]) | 15[4] | .09 | 5 | 6 mos. |
| Maryland | Mar. 1 | 18 | ([5]) | 16[3,4] | .09 | 5 | yes |
| Massachusetts | On issue | 18 | ([5]) | 16½[3,4] | .085 | 5 | 6 mos. |
| Michigan | Nov. 15 | 18 | | 16[3,4] | .09 | 4 | no[19] |
| Minnesota | On issue | 18 | ([5]) | 16[4] | .09 | 4 | no[19] |
| Mississippi | Nov. 1 | 15 | ([5]) | | .09 | 3 | yes |
| Missouri | On issue | 16 | | 15[4] | .07 | 3 | yes |
| Montana | On issue | 18 | ([5]) | 16[3,4] | .08 | 1½[13] | yes |
| Nebraska | On issue | 16 | 15[5] | 14 | .095 | 2½ | yes |
| Nevada | On issue | 18 | 15½[5] | 16[3] | .06 | 2[14] | no |
| New Hampshire | On issue | 18 | | 16[4] | .10 | — | 6 mos. |
| New Jersey | On issue | 17 | | 16 | .08 | 5 | yes |
| New Mexico | Dec. 15 | 16 | 15 | 15[4] | .07 | 2 | 6 mos. |
| New York | On issue | 18 | | 16[3] | .08 | 4 | yes |
| North Carolina | Jan. 1 | 18 | | 16[3,4] | .09 | 2[16] | yes |
| North Dakota | On issue | 16 | ([5]) | 14¾ | .08 | 3 | no[19] |
| Ohio | 1st day/mo. of exp. | 18 | 16[3,5] | 16[4] | .07 | 4 | no[19] |
| Oklahoma | Dec. 11 | 16 | | 15½[4] | .0658 | 2 | yes |
| Oregon | On issue | 16 | 15[5] | 14 | .07 | — | no[19] |
| Pennsylvania | On issue | 18 | ([5]) | 16[3] | .09 | 6 | 6 mos. |
| Rhode Island | Mar. 1 | 18 | ([5]) | 16[4] | .10 | 6 | 6 mos. |
| South Carolina | Oct. 4 | 16 | 15[10] | 15 | .09 | 4 | yes |
| South Dakota | Jan. 1 | 16 | ([5]) | 14 | .08 | 3[17] | yes |
| Tennessee | Mar. 1 | 16 | ([5]) | 14 | .07 | 4½ | no |
| Texas | On issue | 18 | 15 | 15[4] | .05 | 4 | yes |
| Utah | On issue | 16[4] | ([5]) | | .07 | 4¾ | yes |
| Vermont | On issue | 18 | 15[5] | 16 | .09 | 4 | 6 mos. |
| Virginia | On issue | 18 | 15 & 8 mos.[3,5] | 16[3,4] | .09 | 2 | 6 mos. |
| Washington | On issue | 18 | 15[20] | 16[4] | ([22]) | 4.6 | no[19] |
| West Virginia | On issue | 18 | ([5]) | 16[3] | .085 | 5 | yes |
| Wisconsin | On issue | 18 | ([5]) | 16[4] | .07 | 4 | no |
| Wyoming | Jan. 1 | 18 | 15[3,10] | 16[3] | .08 | 3 | no |

1. Full driving privileges at age given in "Regular" column. A license restricted or qualified in some manner may be obtained at age given in "Restricted" column. 2. Applicable to car sales (local and county sales taxes extra where applicable). 3. Guardian's or parent's consent required. 4. Must have completed approved Driver Education course. 5. Learner's Permit required. 6. Sales or use tax on first registration of new or used cars. 7. Prior to first registration and transfers. 8. 8.5–13.5¢ varies by county. 9. 4% on cars purchased out of state only. 10. Driver with Learner's Permit must be accompanied by locally licensed operator 18 years or older. 11. Use tax on 90% of original retail price. 12. If car is 10 years or older, every 6 months. 13. Periodic reductions for cars purchased later in year. 14. Plus 1% school support tax. 15. Restricted to Mopeds. 16. $120 maximum. 17. Tax on first registration. 18. Document fee of 2% of cost of car. 19. State troopers are authorized to inspect at their discretion. 20. Must be enrolled in a Driver Education course. 21. 4–7%, depending on weight of car. 22. Variable 9–12¢. Based on the average weighted retail sales price of fuel. NOTES: A driver's license is required in every state. The national speed limit is 55 miles per hour. All states have an *implied consent* Chemical Test Law for alcohol. *Source:* American Automobile Association.

## Total Arrests, by Age Groups, 1976[1]

| Age | Arrests | Age | Arrests | Age | Arrests | Age | Arrests | Age | Arrests |
|---|---|---|---|---|---|---|---|---|---|
| Under 15 | 665,781 | 18 | 469,471 | 22 | 317,932 | 30–34 | 614,456 | 50–54 | 269,675 |
| 15 | 392,526 | 19 | 429,657 | 23 | 290,842 | 35–39 | 467,418 | 55 & over | 366,955 |
| 16 | 465,308 | 20 | 386,792 | 24 | 266,519 | 40–44 | 390,036 | Not known | 5,303 |
| 17 | 449,639 | 21 | 355,572 | 25–29 | 974,405 | 45–49 | 334,061 | **Total** | **7,912,348** |

1. At press time, latest figures available. NOTE: Based on reports furnished to the FBI by 10,119 agencies covering an estimated population of 175,499,000. *Source:* Department of Justice, Federal Bureau of Investigation, *Uniform Crime Reports for the United States, 1976.*

## Law Enforcement Officers Killed in Line of Duty
(beginning 1972, includes Federal officers)

| Area | 1976 | 1975 | 1974 | 1973 | 1972 | 1971 | 1970 | 1969 | 1968 | 1965 | 1960 |
|---|---|---|---|---|---|---|---|---|---|---|---|
| New England | 4 | 4 | 2 | 7 | 2 | 5 | 2 | 3 | 3 | 3 | 3 |
| Middle Atlantic | 15 | 24 | 18 | 21 | 22 | 31 | 29 | 15 | 10 | 10 | 7 |
| East North Central | 19 | 32 | 43 | 21 | 23 | 32 | 38 | 31 | 19 | 10 | 9 |
| West North Central | 11 | 8 | 8 | 6 | 12 | 13 | 6 | 10 | 12 | 3 | 3 |
| South Atlantic | 34 | 31 | 42 | 37 | 38 | 28 | 23 | 15 | 34 | 15 | 13 |
| East South Central | 14 | 18 | 12 | 13 | 12 | 13 | 5 | 9 | 9 | 9 | 2 |
| West South Central | 21 | 22 | 23 | 30 | 27 | 23 | 15 | 19 | 15 | 14 | 6 |
| Mountain | 4 | 14 | 9 | 16 | 7 | 11 | 4 | 6 | 4 | 7 | 0 |
| Pacific | 13 | 22 | 18 | 21 | 12 | 22 | 24 | 17 | 17 | 12 | 5 |
| Puerto Rico | 4 | 8 | 4 | 4 | 2 | 3 | n.a. | n.a. | n.a. | n.a. | n.a. |
| **CAUSE** | | | | | | | | | | | |
| By felons | 111 | 129[1] | 132 | 134 | 116 | 129 | 100 | 86 | 64 | 53 | n.a. |
| In accidents | 29 | 56 | 47 | 42 | 41 | 52 | 46 | 39 | 59 | 30 | n.a. |
| **Total** | **140[2]** | **185[1]** | **179** | **176** | **157** | **181** | **146** | **125** | **123** | **83** | **48** |

1. Includes one officer each in Virgin Islands and Guam. 2. Includes one officer killed in Bogota, Colombia. NOTE: n.a. = not available. *Source:* Department of Justice, Federal Bureau of Investigation, *Uniform Crime Reports for the United States, 1976.*

## Minimum Legal Age for Purchase of Liquor, Wine, and Beer

| State | Liquor | Wine | Beer |
|---|---|---|---|
| Alabama | 19 | 19 | 19 |
| Alaska | 19 | 19 | 19 |
| Arizona | 19 | 19 | 19 |
| Arkansas | 21 | 21 | 21 |
| California | 21 | 21 | 21 |
| Colorado | 21 | 21 | 21[1] |
| Connecticut | 18 | 18 | 18 |
| Delaware | 20 | 20 | 20 |
| D.C. | 21 | 21[2] | 18 |
| Florida | 18 | 18 | 18 |
| Georgia | 18 | 18 | 18 |
| Hawaii | 18 | 18 | 18 |
| Idaho | 19 | 19 | 19 |
| Illinois | 21 | 19 | 19 |
| Indiana | 21 | 21 | 21 |
| Iowa | 18 | 18 | 18 |
| Kansas | 21 | 21 | 21[1] |
| Kentucky | 21 | 21 | 21 |
| Louisiana | 18 | 18 | 18 |
| Maine | 20 | 20 | 20 |
| Maryland | 21 | 21[2] | 18 |
| Massachusetts | 18 | 18 | 18 |
| Michigan | 19 | 19 | 19 |
| Minnesota | 19 | 19 | 19 |
| Mississippi | 21 | 21[2] | 21[3] |
| Missouri | 21 | 21 | 21 |
| Montana | 18 | 18 | 18 |
| Nebraska | 19 | 19 | 19 |
| Nevada | 21 | 21 | 21 |
| New Hampshire | 18 | 18 | 18 |
| New Jersey | 18 | 18 | 18 |
| New Mexico | 21 | 21 | 21 |
| New York | 18 | 18 | 18 |
| North Carolina | 21 | 21[2] | 18 |
| North Dakota | 21 | 21 | 21 |
| Ohio | 21 | 21 | 21[1] |
| Oklahoma | 21 | 21 | 21 |
| Oregon | 21 | 21 | 21 |
| Pennsylvania | 21 | 21 | 21 |
| Rhode Island | 18 | 18 | 18 |
| South Carolina | 21 | 18 | 18 |
| South Dakota | 21 | 21 | 21[1] |
| Tennessee | 18 | 18 | 18 |
| Texas | 18 | 18 | 18 |
| Utah | 21 | 21 | 21 |
| Vermont | 18 | 18 | 18 |
| Virginia | 21 | 21 | 18 |
| Washington | 21 | 21 | 21 |
| West Virginia | 18 | 18 | 18 |
| Wisconsin | 18 | 18 | 18 |
| Wyoming | 19 | 19 | 19 |

1. 3.2 beer: 18. 2. Light wine: 18. 3. Up to 4% alcohol by weight: 18. *Source:* Distilled Spirits Council of the United States.

## Murder Victims by Weapons Used

| Year | Murder victims, total | Weapons used or cause of death: Guns — Total | Guns — Percent | Cutting or stabbing | Blunt object[1] | Strangulations, beatings | Drownings, arson, etc. | All other[2] |
|---|---|---|---|---|---|---|---|---|
| 1965 | 8,773 | 5,015 | 57.2 | 2,021 | 505 | 894 | 226 | 112 |
| 1966 | 9,552 | 5,660 | 59.3 | 2,134 | 516 | 896 | 203 | 143 |
| 1967 | 11,114 | 6,998 | 63.0 | 2,200 | 589 | 957 | 211 | 159 |
| 1968 | 12,503 | 8,105 | 64.8 | 2,317 | 713 | 936 | 294 | 138 |
| 1969 | 13,575 | 8,876 | 65.4 | 2,534 | 613 | 1,039 | 322 | 191 |
| 1970 | 13,649 | 9,039 | 66.2 | 2,424 | 604 | 1,031 | 353 | 198 |
| 1971 | 16,183 | 10,712 | 66.2 | 3,017 | 645 | 1,295 | 314 | 200 |
| 1972 | 15,832 | 10,379 | 65.6 | 2,974 | 672 | 1,291 | 331 | 185 |
| 1973 | 17,123 | 11,249 | 65.7 | 2,985 | 848 | 1,445 | 173[3] | 423 |
| 1974 | 18,632 | 12,474 | 66.9 | 3,228 | 976 | 1,417 | 153[3] | 384 |
| 1975 | 18,642 | 12,061 | 64.7 | 3,245 | 1,001 | 1,646 | 193[3] | 496 |
| 1976 | 16,605 | 10,592 | 63.8 | 2,956 | 806 | 1,330 | 227[3] | 694 |

1. Refers to club, hammer, etc. 2. Includes poison, explosives, unknown, and not stated; for 1973 to 1976, includes drowning. 3. Arson only. *Source:* Department of Justice, Federal Bureau of Investigation, *Uniform Crime Reports for the United States, 1976.*

# Expectation of Life

## Expectation of Life in the United States

| Calendar period | Age 0 | 10 | 20 | 30 | 40 | 50 | 60 | 70 | 80 |
|---|---|---|---|---|---|---|---|---|---|
| **WHITE MALES** | | | | | | | | | |
| 1850[1] | 38.3 | 48.0 | 40.1 | 34.0 | 27.9 | 21.6 | 15.6 | 10.2 | 5.9 |
| 1890[1] | 42.50 | 48.45 | 40.66 | 34.05 | 27.37 | 20.72 | 14.73 | 9.35 | 5.40 |
| 1900–1902[2] | 48.23 | 50.59 | 42.19 | 34.88 | 27.74 | 20.76 | 14.35 | 9.03 | 5.10 |
| 1909–1911[2] | 50.23 | 51.32 | 42.71 | 34.87 | 27.43 | 20.39 | 13.98 | 8.83 | 5.09 |
| 1919–1921[3] | 56.34 | 54.15 | 45.60 | 37.65 | 29.86 | 22.22 | 15.25 | 9.51 | 5.47 |
| 1929–1931 | 59.12 | 54.96 | 46.02 | 37.54 | 29.22 | 21.51 | 14.72 | 9.20 | 5.26 |
| 1930–1939 | 60.62 | 55.86 | 46.77 | 38.06 | 29.57 | 21.71 | 14.86 | 9.29 | 5.30 |
| 1939–1941 | 62.81 | 57.03 | 47.76 | 38.80 | 30.03 | 21.96 | 15.05 | 9.42 | 5.38 |
| 1949–1951 | 66.31 | 58.98 | 49.52 | 40.29 | 31.17 | 22.83 | 15.76 | 10.07 | 5.88 |
| 1959–1961 | 67.55 | 59.78 | 50.25 | 40.98 | 31.73 | 23.22 | 16.01 | 10.29 | 5.89 |
| 1969–1971 | 67.94 | 59.69 | 50.22 | 41.07 | 31.87 | 23.34 | 16.07 | 10.38 | 6.18 |
| 1976 | 69.7 | 61.1 | 51.6 | 42.4 | 33.1 | 24.4 | 16.9 | 10.9 | 6.6 |
| **WHITE FEMALES** | | | | | | | | | |
| 1850[1] | 40.5 | 47.2 | 40.2 | 35.4 | 29.8 | 23.5 | 17.0 | 11.3 | 6.4 |
| 1890[1] | 44.46 | 49.62 | 42.03 | 35.36 | 28.76 | 22.09 | 15.70 | 10.15 | 5.75 |
| 1900–1902[2] | 51.08 | 52.15 | 43.77 | 36.42 | 29.17 | 21.89 | 15.23 | 9.59 | 5.50 |
| 1909–1911[2] | 53.62 | 53.57 | 44.88 | 36.96 | 29.26 | 21.74 | 14.92 | 9.38 | 5.35 |
| 1919–1921[3] | 58.53 | 55.17 | 46.46 | 38.72 | 30.94 | 23.12 | 15.93 | 9.94 | 5.70 |
| 1929–1931 | 62.67 | 57.65 | 48.52 | 39.99 | 31.52 | 23.41 | 16.05 | 9.98 | 5.63 |
| 1930–1939 | 64.52 | 58.98 | 49.71 | 40.90 | 32.24 | 23.96 | 16.44 | 10.19 | 5.76 |
| 1939–1941 | 67.29 | 60.85 | 51.38 | 42.21 | 33.25 | 24.72 | 17.00 | 10.50 | 5.88 |
| 1949–1951 | 72.03 | 64.26 | 54.56 | 45.00 | 35.64 | 26.76 | 18.64 | 11.68 | 6.59 |
| 1959–1961 | 74.19 | 66.05 | 56.29 | 46.63 | 37.13 | 28.08 | 19.69 | 12.38 | 6.67 |
| 1969–1971 | 75.49 | 66.97 | 57.24 | 47.60 | 38.12 | 29.11 | 20.79 | 13.37 | 7.59 |
| 1976 | 77.3 | 68.5 | 58.7 | 49.1 | 39.5 | 30.4 | 22.0 | 14.4 | 8.5 |
| **ALL OTHER MALES**[4] | | | | | | | | | |
| 1900–1902[2] | 32.54 | 41.90 | 35.11 | 29.25 | 23.12 | 17.34 | 12.62 | 8.33 | 5.12 |
| 1909–1911[2] | 34.05 | 40.65 | 33.46 | 27.33 | 21.57 | 16.21 | 11.67 | 8.00 | 5.53 |

| Calendar period | Age 0 | 10 | 20 | 30 | 40 | 50 | 60 | 70 | 80 |
|---|---|---|---|---|---|---|---|---|---|
| 1919–1921[3] | 47.14 | 45.99 | 38.36 | 32.51 | 26.53 | 20.47 | 14.74 | 9.58 | 5.83 |
| 1929–1931 | 47.55 | 44.27 | 35.95 | 29.45 | 23.36 | 17.92 | 13.15 | 8.78 | 5.42 |
| 1930–1939 | 50.06 | 46.56 | 38.05 | 31.11 | 24.65 | 18.98 | 14.13 | 9.53 | 6.01 |
| 1939–1941 | 52.26 | 48.34 | 39.52 | 32.05 | 25.06 | 19.06 | 14.37 | 10.11 | 6.58 |
| 1949–1951 | 58.91 | 52.96 | 43.73 | 35.31 | 27.29 | 20.25 | 14.91 | 10.74 | 7.07 |
| 1959–1961 | 61.48 | 55.19 | 45.78 | 37.05 | 28.72 | 21.28 | 15.29 | 10.81 | 6.87 |
| 1969–1971 | 60.98 | 53.67 | 44.37 | 36.20 | 28.29 | 21.24 | 15.35 | 10.68 | 7.57 |
| 1976 | 64.1 | 56.3 | 46.8 | 38.2 | 30.0 | 22.5 | 16.3 | 11.3 | 8.6 |
| **ALL OTHER FEMALES[4]** | | | | | | | | | |
| 1900–1902[2] | 35.04 | 43.02 | 36.89 | 30.70 | 24.37 | 18.67 | 13.60 | 9.62 | 6.48 |
| 1909–1911[2] | 37.67 | 42.84 | 36.14 | 29.61 | 23.34 | 17.65 | 12.78 | 9.22 | 6.05 |
| 1919–1921[3] | 46.92 | 44.54 | 37.15 | 31.48 | 25.60 | 19.76 | 14.69 | 10.25 | 6.58 |
| 1929–1931 | 49.51 | 45.33 | 37.22 | 30.67 | 24.30 | 18.60 | 14.22 | 10.38 | 6.90 |
| 1930–1939 | 52.62 | 48.29 | 39.90 | 32.88 | 26.11 | 20.09 | 15.28 | 10.88 | 7.18 |
| 1939–1941 | 55.56 | 50.75 | 42.04 | 34.40 | 27.19 | 20.95 | 16.10 | 11.82 | 8.02 |
| 1949–1951 | 62.70 | 56.17 | 46.77 | 38.02 | 29.82 | 22.67 | 16.95 | 12.29 | 8.15 |
| 1959–1961 | 66.47 | 59.72 | 50.07 | 40.83 | 32.16 | 24.31 | 17.83 | 12.46 | 7.66 |
| 1969–1971 | 69.05 | 61.49 | 51.85 | 42.61 | 33.87 | 25.97 | 19.02 | 13.30 | 9.01 |
| 1976 | 72.6 | 64.6 | 54.9 | 45.5 | 36.4 | 28.0 | 20.7 | 14.3 | 10.9 |

1. Massachusetts only; white and nonwhite combined, the latter being about one percent of the total. 2. Original Death Registration States. 3. Death Registration States of 1920. 4. Data for periods 1900–1902 to 1929–1931 and 1939–1941 relate to blacks only. *Sources:* Division of Vital Statistics, Metropolitan Life Insurance Company; Department of Health, Education and Welfare, National Center for Health Statistics; Department of Commerce, Bureau of the Census.

## Expectation of Life and Mortality Rates, 1976

| | Expectation of life in years | | | | | Mortality rate per 1,000 | | | | |
|---|---|---|---|---|---|---|---|---|---|---|
| | | White | | All other | | | White | | All other | |
| Age | Total persons | Male | Female | Male | Female | Total Persons | Male | Female | Male | Female |
| 0 | 72.8 | 69.7 | 77.3 | 64.1 | 72.6 | 15.4 | 14.9 | 11.8 | 25.9 | 21.7 |
| 1 | 72.9 | 69.8 | 77.2 | 64.9 | 73.3 | 0.9 | 1.0 | 0.7 | 1.3 | 1.1 |
| 2 | 72.0 | 68.9 | 76.3 | 63.9 | 72.3 | 0.7 | 0.8 | 0.6 | 1.1 | 0.9 |
| 3 | 71.0 | 67.9 | 75.3 | 63.0 | 71.4 | 0.6 | 0.6 | 0.5 | 0.9 | 0.7 |
| 4 | 70.1 | 67.0 | 74.4 | 62.1 | 70.5 | 0.5 | 0.5 | 0.4 | 0.8 | 0.6 |
| 5 | 69.1 | 66.0 | 73.4 | 61.1 | 69.5 | 0.4 | 0.4 | 0.3 | 0.7 | 0.5 |
| 6 | 68.1 | 65.0 | 72.4 | 60.2 | 68.5 | 0.4 | 0.4 | 0.3 | 0.6 | 0.4 |
| 7 | 67.2 | 64.0 | 71.5 | 59.2 | 67.6 | 0.3 | 0.4 | 0.3 | 0.5 | 0.3 |
| 8 | 66.2 | 63.1 | 70.5 | 58.2 | 66.6 | 0.3 | 0.4 | 0.2 | 0.5 | 0.3 |
| 9 | 65.2 | 62.1 | 69.5 | 57.3 | 65.6 | 0.3 | 0.3 | 0.2 | 0.4 | 0.3 |
| 10 | 64.2 | 61.1 | 68.5 | 56.3 | 64.6 | 0.2 | 0.3 | 0.2 | 0.4 | 0.3 |
| 11 | 63.2 | 60.1 | 67.5 | 55.3 | 63.6 | 0.2 | 0.3 | 0.2 | 0.4 | 0.3 |
| 12 | 62.3 | 59.1 | 66.5 | 54.3 | 62.6 | 0.3 | 0.3 | 0.2 | 0.4 | 0.3 |
| 13 | 61.3 | 58.2 | 65.5 | 53.3 | 61.7 | 0.4 | 0.5 | 0.3 | 0.6 | 0.3 |
| 14 | 60.3 | 57.2 | 64.6 | 52.4 | 60.7 | 0.6 | 0.7 | 0.3 | 0.8 | 0.4 |
| 15 | 59.3 | 56.2 | 63.6 | 51.4 | 59.7 | 0.7 | 1.0 | 0.4 | 1.0 | 0.4 |
| 16 | 58.4 | 55.3 | 62.6 | 50.5 | 58.7 | 0.9 | 1.2 | 0.5 | 1.2 | 0.5 |
| 17 | 57.4 | 54.4 | 61.6 | 49.5 | 57.8 | 1.0 | 1.4 | 0.5 | 1.5 | 0.6 |
| 18 | 56.5 | 53.4 | 60.7 | 48.6 | 56.8 | 1.1 | 1.6 | 0.6 | 1.8 | 0.7 |
| 19 | 55.5 | 52.5 | 59.7 | 47.7 | 55.8 | 1.2 | 1.7 | 0.6 | 2.1 | 0.8 |
| 20 | 54.6 | 51.6 | 58.7 | 46.8 | 54.9 | 1.2 | 1.8 | 0.6 | 2.5 | 0.9 |
| 21 | 53.7 | 50.7 | 57.8 | 45.9 | 53.9 | 1.3 | 1.8 | 0.6 | 2.8 | 1.0 |
| 22 | 52.7 | 49.8 | 56.8 | 45.0 | 53.0 | 1.3 | 1.9 | 0.6 | 3.1 | 1.1 |
| 23 | 51.8 | 48.9 | 55.8 | 44.2 | 52.0 | 1.4 | 1.9 | 0.6 | 3.3 | 1.2 |
| 24 | 50.9 | 48.0 | 54.9 | 43.3 | 51.1 | 1.3 | 1.8 | 0.6 | 3.5 | 1.2 |
| 25 | 50.0 | 47.1 | 53.9 | 42.5 | 50.2 | 1.3 | 1.7 | 0.6 | 3.6 | 1.3 |
| 26 | 49.0 | 46.1 | 52.9 | 41.6 | 49.2 | 1.3 | 1.6 | 0.6 | 3.8 | 1.3 |
| 27 | 48.1 | 45.2 | 52.0 | 50.8 | 48.3 | 1.3 | 1.6 | 0.6 | 3.9 | 1.4 |
| 28 | 47.1 | 44.3 | 51.0 | 39.9 | 47.3 | 1.3 | 1.5 | 0.6 | 4.0 | 1.5 |
| 29 | 46.2 | 43.3 | 50.0 | 39.1 | 46.4 | 1.3 | 1.5 | 0.7 | 4.1 | 1.5 |
| 30 | 45.3 | 42.4 | 49.1 | 38.2 | 45.5 | 1.3 | 1.6 | 0.7 | 4.1 | 1.6 |
| 31 | 44.3 | 41.5 | 48.1 | 37.4 | 44.6 | 1.4 | 1.6 | 0.8 | 4.2 | 1.7 |
| 32 | 43.4 | 40.5 | 47.1 | 36.6 | 43.6 | 1.4 | 1.6 | 0.8 | 4.3 | 1.8 |
| 33 | 42.4 | 39.6 | 46.2 | 35.7 | 42.7 | 1.5 | 1.7 | 0.9 | 4.5 | 1.9 |
| 34 | 41.5 | 38.7 | 45.2 | 34.9 | 41.8 | 1.6 | 1.8 | 0.9 | 4.8 | 2.0 |

| Age | Expectation of life in years | | | | | Mortality rate per 1,000 | | | | |
|---|---|---|---|---|---|---|---|---|---|---|
| | Total persons | White | | All other | | Total Persons | White | | All other | |
| | | Male | Female | Male | Female | | Male | Female | Male | Female |
| 35 | 40.6 | 37.7 | 44.2 | 34.0 | 40.9 | 1.7 | 1.9 | 1.0 | 5.1 | 2.2 |
| 36 | 39.6 | 36.8 | 43.3 | 33.2 | 40.0 | 1.8 | 2.0 | 1.1 | 5.4 | 2.3 |
| 37 | 38.7 | 35.9 | 42.3 | 32.4 | 39.1 | 1.9 | 2.2 | 1.2 | 5.8 | 2.6 |
| 38 | 37.8 | 35.0 | 41.4 | 31.6 | 38.2 | 2.1 | 2.3 | 1.3 | 6.2 | 2.8 |
| 39 | 36.9 | 34.0 | 40.4 | 30.8 | 37.3 | 2.3 | 2.6 | 1.4 | 6.6 | 3.2 |
| 40 | 35.9 | 33.1 | 39.5 | 30.0 | 36.4 | 2.6 | 2.8 | 1.6 | 7.0 | 3.5 |
| 41 | 35.0 | 32.2 | 38.6 | 29.2 | 35.5 | 2.8 | 3.1 | 1.7 | 7.5 | 3.9 |
| 42 | 34.1 | 31.3 | 37.6 | 28.4 | 34.6 | 3.1 | 3.5 | 1.9 | 8.1 | 4.3 |
| 43 | 33.2 | 30.4 | 36.7 | 27.6 | 33.8 | 3.4 | 3.8 | 2.1 | 8.6 | 4.6 |
| 44 | 32.4 | 29.5 | 35.8 | 26.8 | 32.9 | 3.7 | 4.3 | 2.3 | 9.2 | 5.0 |
| 45 | 31.5 | 28.7 | 34.9 | 26.1 | 32.1 | 4.1 | 4.7 | 2.6 | 9.8 | 5.3 |
| 46 | 30.6 | 27.8 | 33.9 | 25.3 | 31.3 | 4.5 | 5.3 | 2.9 | 10.4 | 5.7 |
| 47 | 29.7 | 26.9 | 33.0 | 24.6 | 30.5 | 4.9 | 5.8 | 3.2 | 11.2 | 6.2 |
| 48 | 28.9 | 26.1 | 32.1 | 23.9 | 29.6 | 5.4 | 6.4 | 3.5 | 12.1 | 6.7 |
| 49 | 28.0 | 25.3 | 31.3 | 23.2 | 28.8 | 5.9 | 7.0 | 3.8 | 13.2 | 7.3 |
| 50 | 27.2 | 24.4 | 30.4 | 22.5 | 28.0 | 6.4 | 7.7 | 4.1 | 14.4 | 7.9 |
| 51 | 26.4 | 23.6 | 29.5 | 21.8 | 27.3 | 7.0 | 8.5 | 4.4 | 15.6 | 8.6 |
| 52 | 25.6 | 22.8 | 28.6 | 21.1 | 26.5 | 7.6 | 9.3 | 4.8 | 16.8 | 9.3 |
| 53 | 24.7 | 22.0 | 27.8 | 20.5 | 25.7 | 8.3 | 10.2 | 5.3 | 17.9 | 9.9 |
| 54 | 24.0 | 21.3 | 26.9 | 19.8 | 25.0 | 9.0 | 11.2 | 5.7 | 19.1 | 10.6 |
| 55 | 23.2 | 20.5 | 26.1 | 19.2 | 24.3 | 9.8 | 12.2 | 6.2 | 20.3 | 11.3 |
| 56 | 22.4 | 19.7 | 25.2 | 18.6 | 23.5 | 10.6 | 13.4 | 6.8 | 21.5 | 12.0 |
| 57 | 21.6 | 19.0 | 24.4 | 18.0 | 22.8 | 11.6 | 14.7 | 7.4 | 23.0 | 12.9 |
| 58 | 20.9 | 18.3 | 23.6 | 17.4 | 22.1 | 12.7 | 16.3 | 8.1 | 24.9 | 14.0 |
| 59 | 20.1 | 17.6 | 22.8 | 16.9 | 21.4 | 14.0 | 18.0 | 8.9 | 27.0 | 15.3 |
| 60 | 19.4 | 16.9 | 22.0 | 16.3 | 20.7 | 15.4 | 19.9 | 9.8 | 29.6 | 17.0 |
| 61 | 18.7 | 16.2 | 21.2 | 15.8 | 20.1 | 16.9 | 21.9 | 10.7 | 32.1 | 18.6 |
| 62 | 18.0 | 15.6 | 20.4 | 15.3 | 19.6 | 18.3 | 24.0 | 11.6 | 34.1 | 19.7 |
| 63 | 17.3 | 14.9 | 19.6 | 14.8 | 18.8 | 19.5 | 25.9 | 12.4 | 35.2 | 20.1 |
| 64 | 16.7 | 14.3 | 18.9 | 14.3 | 18.2 | 20.6 | 27.9 | 13.1 | 35.6 | 19.9 |
| 65 | 16.0 | 13.7 | 18.1 | 13.8 | 17.6 | 21.8 | 30.0 | 13.9 | 35.6 | 19.3 |
| 66 | 15.4 | 13.1 | 17.4 | 13.3 | 16.9 | 23.1 | 32.2 | 14.9 | 35.9 | 19.1 |
| 67 | 14.7 | 12.6 | 16.6 | 12.8 | 16.2 | 24.8 | 34.7 | 16.1 | 37.3 | 20.3 |
| 68 | 14.1 | 12.0 | 15.9 | 12.0 | 15.6 | 27.0 | 37.6 | 17.7 | 40.8 | 23.6 |
| 69 | 13.5 | 11.4 | 15.2 | 11.8 | 14.9 | 29.6 | 40.8 | 19.8 | 45.0 | 28.6 |
| 70 | 12.9 | 10.9 | 14.4 | 11.3 | 14.3 | 32.4 | 44.2 | 21.6 | 51.9 | 34.3 |
| 71 | 12.3 | 10.4 | 13.8 | 10.9 | 13.8 | 35.3 | 47.8 | 23.8 | 57.9 | 39.9 |
| 72 | 11.7 | 9.9 | 13.1 | 10.6 | 13.4 | 38.7 | 51.9 | 26.5 | 63.6 | 45.0 |
| 73 | 11.2 | 9.4 | 12.4 | 10.3 | 13.0 | 42.4 | 56.6 | 29.7 | 68.2 | 49.1 |
| 74 | 10.6 | 8.9 | 11.8 | 10.0 | 12.7 | 46.4 | 61.8 | 33.5 | 71.7 | 52.1 |
| 75 | 10.1 | 8.5 | 11.2 | 9.7 | 12.3 | 50.9 | 67.5 | 37.6 | 74.7 | 54.7 |
| 76 | 9.6 | 8.1 | 10.6 | 9.5 | 12.0 | 55.6 | 73.5 | 42.0 | 77.7 | 57.2 |
| 77 | 9.2 | 7.7 | 10.0 | 9.2 | 11.7 | 60.5 | 79.9 | 46.6 | 81.1 | 59.9 |
| 78 | 8.7 | 7.3 | 9.5 | 9.0 | 11.4 | 65.7 | 86.5 | 51.5 | 85.1 | 63.0 |
| 79 | 8.3 | 7.0 | 9.0 | 8.8 | 11.2 | 71.0 | 93.4 | 56.6 | 89.2 | 66.0 |
| 80 | 7.9 | 6.6 | 8.5 | 8.6 | 10.9 | 76.6 | 100.3 | 62.2 | 92.9 | 68.3 |
| 81 | 7.5 | 6.3 | 8.0 | 8.4 | 10.7 | 82.2 | 107.2 | 68.2 | 94.7 | 68.9 |
| 82 | 7.2 | 6.0 | 7.6 | 8.2 | 10.4 | 87.9 | 113.8 | 74.8 | 93.0 | 66.6 |
| 83 | 6.8 | 5.7 | 7.2 | 8.0 | 10.1 | 93.5 | 119.8 | 82.4 | 85.1 | 59.6 |
| 84 | 6.4 | 5.4 | 6.8 | 7.7 | 9.7 | 98.8 | 124.4 | 91.1 | 67.7 | 46.1 |
| 85 | 6.1 | 5.1 | 6.4 | 7.2 | 9.1 | — | — | — | — | — |

*Sources:* Metropolitan Life Insurance Company, Division of Vital Statistics; Department of Health, Education, and Welfare, National Center for Health Statistics.

## Abortions

In 1975, there were three legal abortions for every ten live births, according to a Census Bureau 1978 report. Unmarried women had three out of four of these abortions. Nine out of ten abortions occurred in the first twelve weeks of pregnancy. The report also noted that there were 448,000 illegitimate children born in 1975, with teenage mothers accounting for more than half of these births.

## Vehicular Trivia

In 1977, 10,400,000 American cars of various model years were recalled, while only 9,300,000 new cars were sold.

# Poverty

Median income of all U.S. families was $16,009 in 1977, according to the Current Population Survey of March 1978, conducted by the Bureau of the Census. After adjusting for price increases, there was no statistically significant change in real median family income from 1976 to 1977.

The Survey indicated that there were about 24.7 million persons below the poverty level in 1977, or 11.6% of the U.S. population.

The "poverty level" classification is based on an index, adopted by the federal government, which reflects family consumption requirements based on size and composition, sex and age of family head, and farm-nonfarm residence. The poverty thresholds are updated to reflect changes in the Consumer Price Index.

In 1977, as in earlier years, Blacks, persons of Spanish origin, children under 18 years, elderly persons, and persons in families of female householders constituted larger proportions of the poverty population than of the general population. Of the 25 million poor in 1977, 31% were Black, 11% were Spanish, 13% were 65 years old and older, 41% were related children under 18 years of age, and 37% were in families of female householders with no husband present. In contrast, these same groups represented the following proportions of the total population: Blacks, 12%; Spanish, 6%; 65 years old and older, 11%; related children, 29%; and persons in families of female householders, 12%.

Although 66% of U.S. families lived in metropolitan areas in 1977, only 59% of poor families did so.

## Poverty Thresholds, 1977

| Size of family unit | Total | Non-farm Total | Farm Total |
|---|---|---|---|
| 1 person (unrelated individual) | $ 3,067 | $ 3,075 | $2,588 |
| 14 to 64 years | 3,147 | 3,152 | 2,709 |
| 65 years and over | 2,895 | 2,906 | 2,475 |
| 2 persons | 3,928 | 3,951 | 3,318 |
| Head 14 to 64 years | 4,054 | 4,072 | 3,466 |
| Head 65 years and over | 3,637 | 3,666 | 3,128 |
| 3 persons | 4,806 | 4,833 | 4,093 |
| 4 persons | 6,157 | 6,191 | 5,273 |
| 5 persons | 7,279 | 7,320 | 6,247 |
| 6 persons | 8,208 | 8,261 | 7,026 |
| 7 persons or more | 10,137 | 10,216 | 8,708 |

*Source:* Department of Commerce, Bureau of the Census.

## Selected Characteristics of the Poverty Population, 1977

| Characteristics | Number (thousands) | Percent |
|---|---|---|
| **PERSONS** | | |
| All persons[1] | 24,720 | 11.6 |
| Race and Spanish origin[2] | | |
| White | 16,416 | 8.9 |
| Black | 7,726 | 31.3 |
| Other races | 579 | 14.8 |
| Spanish origin | 2,700 | 22.4 |
| Age | | |
| Under 14 years | 7,856 | 16.9 |
| 14 to 21 years | 4,346 | 13.2 |
| 22 to 44 years | 5,780 | 8.5 |
| 45 to 54 years | 1,672 | 7.2 |
| 55 to 59 years | 944 | 8.6 |
| 60 to 64 years | 946 | 10.0 |
| 65 years and over | 3,177 | 14.1 |
| Related children under 18 years | 10,028 | 16.0 |
| Total, under 18 years | 10,228 | 16.2 |
| Related children 5 to 17 years | 7,249 | 15.2 |
| Total, 5 to 17 years | 7,449 | 15.5 |
| Metropolitan-nonmetropolitan residence | | |
| Inside metropolitan areas | 14,859 | 10.4 |
| Inside central cities | 9,203 | 15.4 |
| In poverty areas | 4,132 | 36.4 |
| Outside central cities | 5,657 | 6.8 |
| In poverty areas | 972 | 21.5 |
| Outside metropolitan areas | 9,861 | 13.9 |
| In poverty areas | 5,236 | 21.4 |
| **FAMILIES[1]** | | |
| Race and sex of head | | |
| All families | 5,311 | 9.3 |
| Male head | 2,701 | 5.5 |
| Female head | 2,610 | 31.7 |
| White families | 3,540 | 7.0 |
| Male head | 2,140 | 4.8 |
| Female head | 1,400 | 24.0 |
| Black families | 1,637 | 28.2 |
| Male head | 475 | 13.5 |
| Female head | 1,162 | 51.0 |
| Unrelated individuals[1] | | |
| All unrelated individuals | 5,216 | 22.6 |
| Male | 1,796 | 18.0 |
| Female | 3,419 | 26.1 |

1. As of March 1978. 2. Persons of Spanish origin may be of any race. *Source:* Department of Commerce, Bureau of the Census.

## Selected Family Characteristics

| Characteristics | 1977 Number (thousands) | 1977 Median income | 1976 Median income |
|---|---|---|---|
| **ALL RACES** | | | |
| All Families | 57,215 | $16,009 | $14,958 |
| Type of Residence | | | |
| Nonfarm | 55,042 | 16,140 | 15,065 |
| Farm | 2,172 | 12,637 | 11,663 |
| Inside Metropolitan Areas | 37,841 | 17,371 | 16,001 |
| 1,000,000 or more | 21,572 | 18,196 | 16,771 |
| Inside Central Cities | 7,993 | 14,677 | 13,700 |
| Outside Central Cities | 13,579 | 20,110 | 18,419 |
| Under 1,000,000 | 16,269 | 16,329 | 15,154 |
| Inside Central Cities | 7,367 | 15,192 | 14,198 |
| Outside Central Cities | 8,902 | 17,252 | 15,908 |
| Outside Metropolitan Areas | 19,374 | 13,789 | 12,831 |
| Region | | | |
| Northeast | 12,936 | 16,804 | 15,405 |
| North Central | 15,308 | 16,845 | 15,942 |
| South | 18,724 | 14,567 | 13,419 |
| West | 10,247 | 16,512 | 15,484 |
| Type of Family | | | |
| Male Head | 48,979 | 17,517 | 16,095 |
| Married, Wife Present | 47,385 | 17,616 | 16,203 |
| Wife in Paid Labor Force | 21,936 | 20,268 | 18,731 |
| Wife Not in Paid Labor Force | 25,449 | 15,063 | 13,931 |
| Other Marital Status | 1,594 | 14,518 | 12,860 |
| Female Head | 8,236 | 7,765 | 7,211 |
| Number of Earners[1] | 56,448 | 16,060 | 15,001 |
| No Earners | 7,083 | 6,019 | 5,689 |
| 1 Earner | 18,621 | 13,148 | 12,436 |
| 2 Earners | 22,414 | 18,704 | 17,341 |
| 3 Earners | 5,533 | 23,511 | 21,680 |
| 4 Earners or More | 2,797 | 27,236 | 25,696 |
| Size of Family | | | |
| 2 Persons | 22,033 | 12,890 | 12,091 |
| 3 Persons | 12,629 | 16,364 | 15,085 |
| 4 Persons | 11,774 | 18,723 | 17,315 |
| 5 Persons | 6,269 | 19,116 | 17,756 |
| 6 Persons | 2,649 | 19,256 | 17,760 |
| 7 Persons or More | 1,861 | 17,196 | 16,521 |
| Employment Status and Occupation of Head[2] | | | |
| Head in Civilian Labor Force | 44,122 | 18,262 | 16,853 |
| Head Employed | 42,277 | 18,582 | 17,194 |
| White-Collar Workers | 19,611 | 21,619 | 20,163 |
| Professional, Techincal, and Kindred Workers | 6,678 | 23,047 | 21,888 |
| Salaried | 5,963 | 22,566 | 21,423 |
| Self-Employed | 715 | 29,170 | 28,565 |
| Managers and Administrators, except Farm | 6,817 | 23,791 | 21,563 |
| Salaried | 5,547 | 25,152 | 22,747 |
| Self-Employed | 1,270 | 17,433 | 15,593 |
| Sales Workers | 2,545 | 20,988 | 18,898 |
| Clerical & Kind. Workers | 3,571 | 15,851 | 15,377 |
| Blue-Collar Workers | 17,787 | 17,161 | 15,928 |
| Craft and Kindred Workers | 8,739 | 18,658 | 17,419 |
| Operatives, Incl. Transport | 7,121 | 16,070 | 14,835 |
| Operatives, Exc. Transport | 4,800 | 15,509 | 14,447 |
| Transport Equip. Oper. | 2,321 | 17,457 | 15,714 |
| Laborers, except Farm | 1,926 | 14,737 | 13,455 |
| Service Workers | 3,420 | 12,570 | 11,999 |
| Private Household Workers | 157 | 5,571 | 4,937 |
| Service Workers, Exc. Private Household | 3,263 | 12,972 | 12,550 |

| Characteristics | 1977 Number (thousands) | 1977 Median income | 1976 Median income |
|---|---|---|---|
| Farm Workers | 1,459 | 10,637 | 9,951 |
| Farmers and Farm Managers | 1,077 | 10,865 | 10,580 |
| Farm Lab. and Supervisors | 382 | 10,416 | 8,754 |
| Head Unemployed | 1,845 | 10,334 | 10,120 |
| Head not in Civilian Labor Force | 13,093 | 8,289 | 7,850 |
| Tenure Status[3] | | | |
| Owner Occupied | 41,427 | 18,301 | 16,897 |
| Renter Occupied | 14,410 | 10,919 | 10,324 |
| Occupier Paid No Cash Rent | 1,121 | 10,883 | 9,999 |
| Total | 56,958 | 16,067 | 15,003 |
| Educational Attainment of Head | | | |
| Elementary | 10,228 | 9,606 | 9,223 |
| High School | 25,878 | 15,892 | 14,907 |
| College | 17,258 | 21,799 | 20,499 |
| 1 to 3 Years | 7,697 | 19,033 | 17,759 |
| 4 Years or More | 9,561 | 24,852 | 23,134 |
| 4 Years | 5,173 | 23,409 | 22,019 |
| 5 Years or More | 4,389 | 26,042 | 24,676 |
| Total, 25 Years and Over | 53,364 | 16,574 | 15,454 |
| **WHITE** | | | |
| All Families | 50,530 | 16,740 | 15,537 |
| Type of Residence | | | |
| Nonfarm | 48,467 | 16,892 | 15,646 |
| Farm | 2,063 | 13,082 | 12,129 |
| Inside Metropolitan Areas | 32,824 | 18,211 | 16,767 |
| 1,000,000 or More | 18,333 | 19,207 | 17,693 |
| Inside Central Cities | 5,694 | 16,255 | 15,083 |
| Outside Central Cities | 12,639 | 20,413 | 18,778 |
| Under 1,000,000 | 14,491 | 17,025 | 15,646 |
| Inside Central Cities | 6,123 | 16,315 | 15,089 |
| Outside Central Cities | 8,368 | 17,503 | 16,068 |
| Outside Metropolitan Areas | 17,706 | 14,403 | 13,318 |
| Region | | | |
| Northeast | 11,797 | 17,302 | 15,825 |
| North Central | 14,045 | 17,231 | 16,335 |
| South | 15,521 | 15,721 | 14,414 |
| West | 9,167 | 16,985 | 15,741 |
| Type of Family | | | |
| Male Head | 44,701 | 17,848 | 16,418 |
| Married, Wife Present | 43,423 | 17,916 | 16,501 |
| Wife in Paid Labor Force | 19,662 | 20,518 | 19,047 |
| Wife Not in Paid Labor Force | 23,761 | 15,389 | 14,288 |
| Other Marital Status | 1,278 | 15,630 | 13,530 |
| Female Head | 5,828 | 8,799 | 8,226 |
| Number of Earners[1] | 49,898 | 16,782 | 15,571 |
| No Earners | 5,959 | 6,608 | 6,184 |
| 1 Earner | 16,350 | 14,077 | 13,123 |
| 2 Earners | 20,086 | 19,019 | 17,643 |
| 3 Earners | 4,988 | 24,058 | 22,265 |
| 4 Earners or More | 2,514 | 27,689 | 25,986 |
| **BLACK** | | | |
| All Families | 5,806 | 9,563 | 9,242 |
| Type of Residence | | | |
| Nonfarm | 5,721 | 9,649 | 9,355 |
| Farm | 86 | 5,561 | 5,181 |
| Inside Metropolitan Areas | 4,358 | 10,431 | 9,984 |
| 1,000,000 or More | 2,821 | 10,796 | 10,501 |
| Inside Central Cities | 2,069 | 10,012 | 9,850 |
| Outside Central Cities | 751 | 13,104 | 12,343 |
| Under 1,000,000 | 1,537 | 9,910 | 9,085 |
| Inside Central Cities | 1,119 | 8,922 | 8,294 |
| Outside Central Cities | 418 | 12,858 | 11,414 |
| Outside Metropolitan Areas | 1,448 | 7,512 | 7,435 |
| Region | | | |
| Northeast | 1,035 | 10,285 | 9,727 |
| North Central | 1,152 | 10,690 | 10,883 |
| South | 3,067 | 8,962 | 8,526 |
| West | 552 | 9,917 | 9,853 |

| Characteristics | 1977 Number (thousands) | 1977 Median income | 1976 Median income |
|---|---|---|---|
| Type of Family | | | |
| Male Head | 3,529 | 13,443 | 12,873 |
| Married, Wife Present | 3,260 | 13,716 | 13,137 |
| Wife in Paid Labor Force | 1,892 | 17,008 | 15,703 |
| Wife not in Paid Labor Force | 1,368 | 9,697 | 9,219 |
| Other Marital Status | 269 | 10,296 | 10,277 |
| Female Head | 2,277 | 5,598 | 5,069 |
| Number of Earners[1] | 5,699 | 9,485 | 9,264 |
| No Earners | 1,053 | 3,669 | 3,699 |
| 1 Earner | 2,029 | 7,761 | 7,394 |
| 2 Earners | 1,948 | 14,984 | 14,275 |
| 3 Earners | 442 | 18,222 | 15,946 |
| 4 Earners or More | 228 | 20,629 | 18,933 |
| **SPANISH ORIGIN OF HEAD[4]** | | | |
| All Families | 2,764 | 11,421 | 10,259 |
| Type of Residence | | | |
| Nonfarm | 2,744 | 11,453 | 10,304 |
| Farm | 20 | — | — |
| Inside Metropolitan Areas | 2,359 | 11,578 | 10,603 |
| 1,000,000 or more | 1,535 | 11,651 | 10,775 |
| Inside Central Cities | 898 | 10,026 | 9,197 |
| Outside Central Cities | 637 | 14,301 | 13,187 |
| Under 1,000,000 | 824 | 11,455 | 10,298 |
| Inside Central Cities | 514 | 10,866 | 9,757 |
| Outside Central Cities | 310 | 12,273 | 11,084 |
| Outside Metropolitan Areas | 405 | 10,752 | 9,069 |
| Region | | | |
| Northeast | 572 | 8,304 | 8,057 |
| North Central | 234 | 15,584 | 12,679 |
| South | 836 | 10,956 | 10,138 |
| West | 1,122 | 12,210 | 11,220 |
| Type of Family | | | |
| Male Head | 2,203 | 13,037 | 11,820 |
| Married, Wife Present | 2,104 | 13,063 | 11,905 |
| Wife in Paid Labor Force | 927 | 16,106 | 14,898 |
| Wife not in Paid Labor Force | 1,177 | 11,031 | 9,908 |
| Other Marital Status | 99 | 12,628 | 9,350 |
| Female Head | 561 | 5,454 | 5,118 |
| Number of Earners[1] | 2,737 | 11,408 | 10,278 |
| No Earners | 380 | 4,351 | 3,946 |
| 1 Earner | 973 | 9,381 | 8,753 |
| 2 Earners | 1,020 | 14,571 | 13,692 |
| 3 Earners | 228 | 19,416 | 17,439 |
| 4 Earners or More | 137 | 22,256 | 17,860 |

1. Excludes families with members in Armed Forces. 2. Employment status and occupation of head as of March 1978. 3. Restricted to primary families. 4. Persons of Spanish origin may be of any race. *Source:* Department of Commerce, Bureau of the Census.

## Sales Costs

The cost of an industrial sales call rose to $96.79 in 1977, reports McGraw-Hill's Laboratory for Advertising Performance. In 1942, the comparable figure was only $9.02; by 1970 it had reached $57.71.

## Military Costs

In 1977, the world spent almost $1 million a minute on arms, according to the Stockholm International Peace Research Institute. Worldwide military expenditures totaled $400 billion. The U.S. and U.S.S.R. accounted for more than half of the world's total military spending.

# ENTERTAINMENT & CULTURE

## The Year in Classical Music

*Risë Stevens*

This has been a year of consolidation and refining in music; no new movements surfaced. Musicians seemed content with the innovations made in the first half of the twentieth century, and the austerity of those earlier musical statements and forms is now being mellowed by the inevitable maturation process.

This does not mean that today's composers are abandoning new musical forms, or that today's performers are compromising themselves. Rather, the music of Stravinsky, Schoenberg, Varèse, and Cage has been accepted—and no one is fighting at the barricades. Thus, composers and performers alike can be—and are—both less ideological and less austere. Interestingly, their increased flexibility has produced more lyrical, more romantic music.

Back at the turn of the century, performers took great liberties with the musical score. From World War I to the 1930s, performances became much more austere as artists revolted against earlier excesses and returned to a "purer" music. Today, more comfortable, the musicians perform the scores as written, but with a newly found and attractive lyricism. Audiences, once shocked by the strange rhythms and tone clusters of Stravinsky's *Rite of Spring*, now are pleasantly surprised by its newly perceived melodic lines. Performers, once mechanical, are becoming expressive and even passionate.

In terms of 1978 as a musical "happening," it was the year that a number of major American orchestras changed their conductors in an accelerated game of musical chairs. Zubin Mehta went to the New York Philharmonic, Carlo Maria Giulini to Los Angeles, Antal Dorati to Detroit, Mstislav Rostropovich to Washington, D.C., Edo de Waart to San Francisco, and Neville Marriner to Minneapolis. As new maestros bring different kinds of music to their new audiences, both listeners and musicians will be in for an exciting time.

Orchestral music took another interesting turn in 1978 when the Manchurian-born Japanese conductor of the Boston Symphony, Seiji Ozawa, toured China. He held master classes and re-introduced western music to Chinese musicians—a task not possible before the recent cultural thaw. Not as a matter of reciprocity, the Chinese Ballet and Orchestra toured the United States in 1978.

For performers, the year was mixed. Artur Rubinstein retired and Beverly Sills announced that she will retire in 1980. The fiftieth anniversary of Vladimir Horowitz's New York debut with the New York Philharmonic was widely celebrated. The great pianist's White House performance was televised around the world to universal critical acclaim. Another anniversary, Leonard Bernstein's sixtieth birthday, was celebrated in August, also with a televised concert.

As a matter of fact, 1978 was the year when music-on-television came of age. Mikhail Baryshnikov, the greatest Russian ballet dancer to defect since Rudolf Nureyev, danced before a nationwide television audience. Luciano Pavarotti, the great operatic tenor, gave an extraordinary television recital also. Several performances of the Metropolitan Opera were televised with fabulous success: *La Bohème, Cavalleria Rusticana, I Pagliacci,* and *Don Giovanni,* with many more to come before the television audiences in the future. All these events show the enormous progress and success music is enjoying in all phases.

Finally, the 1978 Pulitzer Prize for Music went to Michael Colgrass for his *Déjà Vu for Percussion Quartet and Orchestra.* Colgrass, a poet and percussionist as well as a composer, has become increasingly well known and honored for his music in recent years.

## The Year in Popular Music

*Clive Davis*

*President, Arista Records*

When a double-record set finds its way into more than 12 million American homes, one vocalist sells a combined total of 11 million copies of three albums in only 18 months, a British group that has been rolling for 15 years fills 60,000–70,000 seat arenas from one end of the U.S. to the other, and at the same time local club, concert, and cabaret scenes flourish as never before, we can see that 1978 was an unprecedented year for music. Categories are shattered and sales and attendance zoom cross all demographic lines as the audience for recorded and live music expands beyond the industry's expectations. Along with the historic block-busters—top LPs are now selling into the unheard-of eight-figure range and numerous others sell between 3 and 6 million—there are more new acts and a wider spectrum of music, both signs of a very healthy musical environment.

Records performed, composed, and produced by The Bee Gees dominated the singles charts for a good portion of the year; the group made a major tour of the United States, and their songs on the soundtrack of *Saturday Night Fever* helped that album become the most popular of all time. The enormous impact of *Fever* was just one instance of the increasingly close relationship between movies and music. Films like *The Last Waltz, Sgt. Pepper's Lonely Hearts Club Band, FM, Grease, The Wiz,*

*American Hot Wax*, and *The Buddy Holly Story* all generated hit LPs.

A number of rock music's pantheon figures made returns to disc and the stage during 1978. The Rolling Stones and Bob Dylan both released their first studio albums in more than two years and backed them up with big box-office tours, and the long-awaited fourth album by Bruce Springsteen came out in the early summer, also in conjunction with a string of personal appearances. Other significant rock LPs released in 1978 included new records by Jefferson Starship, Steely Dan, Boston, Bob Seger, Eric Clapton, Paul McCartney and Wings, The Alan Parsons Project, and The Who. Randy Newman achieved much-deserved mass acceptance, as did singer-songwriter Warren Zevon.

Also, 1978 was a year in which female performers continued to produce hit records of wide appeal, with success scored by Linda Ronstadt, Rita Coolidge, Heart, Patti Smith, Yvonne Elliman, Olivia Newton-John, Roberta Flack, Bonnie Tyler, Deniece Williams, Crystal Gayle, and Dolly Parton. The latter two singers, both initially established in the field of country music, represented the growing popularity of the idiom. Dolly and Crystal earned platinum albums for more than a million copies sold, as did country stars Waylon Jennings and Willie Nelson. Such "crossover" successes were not limited to country. Jazz artists like Chuck Mangione, R&B groups like Raydio, and disco acts like The Michael Zager Band all managed to span musical boundaries.

In a virtually trendless year, one tendency has certainly been the return of melody, the well-crafted popular song in the tradition of the Harold Arlens and Johnny Mercers. Barry Manilow's astounding accomplishments are part of that direction, as are the hit records by talented artists like The Bee Gees, Billy Joel, Barbra Streisand, Johnny Mathis—who had his first #1 single in a 21-year career in 1978—and George Benson. Carly Simon and Art Garfunkel, two other major figures who belong to this new melodic tradition, treated their many followers to rare concert and club tours during the year.

Music stops growing when it stops producing exciting young talent, and 1978 saw, particularly in rock and roll, a whole new breed of performer injecting vitality, conviction, and genuine energy onto the scene. With artists like Graham Parker, Elvis Costello, Ian Dury, The Dwight Twilley Band, Tom Petty, and David Johansen emerging, the rock scene is alive to an extent that it hasn't been for more than a decade.

## Artists of the Year, 1977

*Source: Billboard.* Copyright © Billboard Publications, Inc., 1977.

Based on combined singles and albums chart performance—through sales and radio play—during the year.

**Single of the Year:** Tonight's the Night (Gonna Be Alright), Rod Stewart
**Album of the Year:** Rumours, Fleetwood Mac
**Female Artist of the Year:** Linda Ronstadt
**Male Artist of the Year:** Stevie Wonder
**Group of the Year:** Fleetwood Mac
**New Artist of the Year:** Foreigner
**Soul Artist of the Year:** Stevie Wonder
**Country Artist of the Year:** Waylon Jennings
**Disco Artist of the Year:** Donna Summer
**Easy Listening Artist of the Year:** Barbra Streisand
**Jazz Artist of the Year:** George Benson
**Soundtrack of the Year:** A Star Is Born

## Top 10 Classical Albums, 1977

*Source: Billboard.* Copyright © Billboard Publications, Inc., 1977

**The Great Pavarotti,** Luciano Pavarotti
**Suite for Flute and Jazz Piano,** Jean-Pierre Rampal and Claude Bolling
**Holst: The Planets,** Isao Tomita
**Caruso: A Legendary Performer,** Enrico Caruso
**Concerto for Classic Guitar and Jazz Piano,** Claude Bolling and Lagoya
**Pachelbel Canon: Two Suites; Fasch: Two Symphonies,** Paillard Chamber Orchestra (Andre)
**Gershwin: Porgy & Bess,** Houston Opera Company
**Luciano Pavarotti: The World's Favorite Tenor Arias,** Luciano Pavarotti
**Beethoven: Symphony No. 5,** Vienna Philharmonic Orchestra (Kleiber)
**Ravel: Bolero,** Chicago Symphony Orchestra (Solti)

## Top 10 Pop Single Recordings, 1977

*Source: Billboard.* Copyright © Billboard Publications, Inc., 1977.

**Tonight's the Night (Gonna Be Alright),** Rod Stewart
**I Just Want to Be Your Everything,** Andy Gibb
**Best of My Love,** Emotions
**Love Theme From "A Star Is Born,"** Barbra Streisand
**Angel in Your Arms,** Hot
**I Like Dreamin',** Kenny Nolan
**Don't Leave Me This Way,** Thelma Houston
**(Your Love Has Lifted Me) Higher and Higher,** Rita Coolidge
**Undercover Angel,** Alan O'Day
**Torn Between Two Lovers,** Mary Macgregor

## Top 10 Country Single Recordings, 1977

*Source: Billboard.* Copyright © Billboard Publications, Inc., 1977.

**Luckenbach, Texas (Back to the Basics of Love),** Waylon Jennings
**Don't It Make My Brown Eyes Blue,** Crystal Gayle
**Lucille,** Kenny Rogers
**Heaven's Just a Sin Away,** Kendalls
**It Was Almost Like a Song,** Ronnie Milsap
**Rolling With the Flow,** Charlie Rich
**She's Pulling Me Back Again,** Mickey Gilley
**Southern Nights,** Glen Campbell
**Way Down/Pledging My Love,** Elvis Presley
**She's Got You,** Loretta Lynn

## Top 10 Pop Albums, 1977

*Source: Billboard.* Copyright © Billboard Publications, Inc., 1977.

**Rumours,** Fleetwood Mac
**Songs in the Key of Life,** Stevie Wonder
**A Star Is Born/Soundtrack,** Barbra Streisand, Kris Kristofferson
**Hotel California,** Eagles
**Boston,** Boston
**A New World Record,** Electric Light Orchestra
**Part 3,** K. C. & The Sunshine Band
**Silk Degrees,** Boz Scaggs
**Night Moves,** Bob Seger & The Silver Bullet Band
**Fleetwood Mac,** Fleetwood Mac

## Manufacturers' Dollar Sales of Phonograph Records
(in millions)

| | Singles | | Albums | |
|---|---|---|---|---|
| Year | Units | Dollars[1] | Units | Dollars[1] |
| 1977 | 190 | $245 | 344 | $2,195 |
| 1976 | 190 | 245 | 273 | 1,663 |
| 1975 | 164 | 212 | 257 | 1,485 |
| 1974 | 204 | 194 | 276 | 1,356 |
| 1973 | 228 | 190 | 280 | 1,246 |

1. List price value. *Source:* Recording Industry Association of America, Inc.

## Television Statistics for the United States, 1977

| Type of equipment | Number | Type of equipment | Number |
|---|---|---|---|
| TV sets in use | 138,200,000[1] | Monochrome | 6,090,000 |
| Color | 68,000,000[1] | TV sets sold[1] | 15,350,000 |
| Monochrome | 70,200,000[1] | Color | 9,398,000 |
| TV sets manufactured[1] | 15,431,000 | Monochrome | 5,952,000 |
| Color | 9,341,000 | | |

1. Includes imports. *Source:* Electronic Industries Association.

## Radio and Audio Statistics for the United States, 1977

| Type of equipment | Number | Type of equipment | Number |
|---|---|---|---|
| Radios in use | 444,000,000 | Portable | 26,599,000 |
| Auto radios | 106,000,000 | Automobile | 12,890,000 |
| Others | 338,000,000 | Radios sold | 54,353,000 |
| Radios manufactured[2] | 52,926,000 | Phonographs in use | 77,600,000[1] |
| Table | 1,990,000 | Phonographs manufactured | 4,362,000 |
| Clock | 11,447,000 | Phonographs sold | 4,387,000 |

1. Estimated. 2. Includes imports. *Source:* Electronic Industries Association.

## Radio and Television Networks

| | Radio Owned and operated | | Television Owned and operated |
|---|---|---|---|
| | AM | FM | |
| ABC—American Broadcasting Co.[1] | 7 | 7 | 5 |
| CBS—Columbia Broadcasting System[1] | 7 | 7 | 5 |
| NBC—National Broadcasting Co.[2] | 4 | 4 | 5 |

1. As of July 1, 1977. 2. As of Jan. 1, 1978.

## Number of Radio and Television Stations

| | Radio | | Television | |
|---|---|---|---|---|
| | AM | FM | VHF | UHF |
| Commercial | 4,525 | 3,046 | 516 | 210 |
| Educational | — | 956 | 102 | 158 |
| **Totals** | **4,525** | **4,002** | **618** | **368** |

*Source:* Federal Communications Commission.

## Audience Composition of Selected Prime Time Program Types
(in millions)[1]

| | General drama | Suspense and mystery drama | Situation comedy | Adventure | Variety | Feature films | All regular network programs 8–11 p.m.[2] |
|---|---|---|---|---|---|---|---|
| Women (18 years old and over) | 10.71 | 10.58 | 11.83 | 10.22 | 9.48 | 11.74 | 10.77 |
| Men (18 and over) | 6.86 | 8.37 | 8.74 | 9.07 | 7.38 | 9.30 | 8.57 |
| Teens (12–17) | 2.25 | 2.68 | 3.72 | 3.01 | 2.74 | 2.66 | 2.76 |
| Children (2–11) | 2.77 | 3.00 | 4.55 | 6.42 | 3.73 | 2.53 | 3.56 |
| **Total** | **22.59** | **24.63** | **28.84** | **28.72** | **23.33** | **26.23** | **25.66** |

1. All figures are estimates for the period October-December 1977. 2. 7–11 p.m. Sunday (EST). *Source:* A. C. Nielsen Company, Nielsen Television Index Audience Estimates.

## Top 15 Prime Time TV Programs of 1977

| Program name | Total percent of TV households |
|---|---|
| Laverne and Shirley | 32.1 |
| Happy Days | 31.4 |
| Three's Company | 27.6 |
| All in the Family | 25.2 |
| Charlie's Angels | 24.6 |
| 60 Minutes | 24.5 |
| Alice | 24.1 |
| Eight Is Enough | 22.9 |
| NBC Monday Night Movies | 22.8 |
| Little House on the Prairie | 22.8 |
| On Our Own | 22.4 |
| Rhoda | 21.9 |
| Soap | 21.7 |
| NFL Monday Night Football | 21.7 |
| One Day at a Time | 21.6 |
| **Total U.S. TV Households** | **72,900,000** |

NOTE: Percentages are calculated from average audience viewings, 15 minutes or longer and 4 or more telecasts. *Source:* A. C. Nielsen Company, Nielsen Television Index Audience Estimates.

## Syndicated Program Rankings by Households

| Rank | Program name | Rating (percent DMA)[1] |
|---|---|---|
| 1 | Lawrence Welk | 14.8 |
| 2 | Hee Haw | 14.5 |
| 3 | Muppets | 14.0 |
| 4 | Name That Tune | 13.9 |
| 5 | Price Is Right | 13.8 |
| 6 | Match Game PM | 13.7 |
| 7 | Hollywood Squares | 13.5 |
| 8 | Gong Show | 12.7 |
| 8 | Family Feud PM | 12.7 |
| 10 | $25,000 Pyramid | 12.4 |
| 11 | Wild Wild World—Animals | 12.2 |
| 12 | Candid Camera | 12.1 |
| 13 | Wild Kingdom | 11.7 |
| 14 | All Star—Anything Goes | 11.2 |
| 15 | Bowling for Dollars | 10.8 |
| 15 | Let's Go to the Races | 10.8 |

1. During November 1977. Ranked on the basis of the number of people viewing a program for 15 minutes or longer in a Designated Market Area (DMA). *Source:* A. C. Nielsen Company, Nielsen Television Index Audience Estimates.

## Weekly TV Viewing by Age
(in hours and minutes)

| | Time per week |
|---|---|
| Women 18–24 years old | 29 h 22 min |
| Women 25–54 | 29 h 44 min |
| Women 55 and over | 35 h 1 min |
| Men 18–24 | 20 h 12 min |
| Men 25–54 | 24 h 29 min |
| Men 55 and over | 31 h 57 min |
| Female Teens | 21 h 25 min |
| Male Teens | 22 h 42 min |
| Children 6–11 | 24 h 26 min |
| Children 2–5 | 27 h 35 min |
| **Total Persons** | **27 h 19 min** |

NOTE: All figures are estimates as of November 1977. *Source:* A. C. Nielsen Company, Nielsen Television Index Audience Estimates.

## Persons Viewing Nightly Prime Time TV[1]
(in millions)

| | Total persons[2] |
|---|---|
| Monday | 88.73 |
| Tuesday | 89.12 |
| Wednesday | 85.49 |
| Thursday | 83.69 |
| Friday | 81.79 |
| Saturday | 83.54 |
| Sunday | 98.39 |
| **Total average** | **87.75** |

1. Average minute audiences. 2. Estimated for the period October-December 1977. NOTE: Prime time is 8–11 p.m. (EST), except 7–11 p.m. Sunday. *Source:* A. C. Nielsen Company, Nielsen Television Index Audience Estimates.

## Average Hours of Household TV Usage
(in hours and minutes per day)

| | Yearly average | Jan. | July |
|---|---|---|---|
| 1977 | 6 h 10 min | 7 h 16 min | 5 h 13 min |
| 1973 | 6 h 15 min | 6 h 58 min | 5 h 29 min |
| 1969 | 5 h 48 min | 6 h 35 min | 5 h 7 min |
| 1965 | 5 h 30 min | 6 h 21 min | 4 h 25 min |

NOTE: Estimates are based on total U.S. TV households, excluding unusual days; January-December 1977 averages. *Source:* A. C. Nielsen Company, Nielsen Television Index Audience Estimates.

## Television Network Addresses

**American Broadcasting Companies (ABC)**
1330 Avenue of the Americas
New York, N.Y. 10019

**Canadian Broadcasting Corporation (CBC)**
1500 Bronson Ave.
Ottawa, Ontario, Canada K1G 3J5

**Columbia Broadcasting System (CBS)**
51 W. 52nd St.
New York, N.Y. 10019

**Metromedia, Inc. (WNEW)**
277 Park Ave.
New York, N.Y. 10017

**National Broadcasting Company (NBC)**
30 Rockefeller Plaza
New York, N.Y. 10020

**Public Broadcasting Service (PBS)**
15 W. 51st St.
New York, N.Y. 10020

**Westinghouse Broadcasting (Group W)**
90 Park Ave.
New York, N.Y. 10016

## Plays and Movies

### LONGEST BROADWAY RUNS[1]

| | |
|---|---|
| 1. Fiddler on the Roof (M) (1964–72) | 3,242 |
| 2. Life With Father (1939–47) | 3,224 |
| 3. Tobacco Road (1933–41) | 3,182 |
| 4. Hello, Dolly! (M) (1964–71) | 2,844 |
| 5. Grease (M) (1972–) | 2,720 |
| 6. My Fair Lady (M) (1956–62) | 2,717 |
| 7. Man of La Mancha (M) (1965–71) | 2,329 |
| 8. Abie's Irish Rose (1922–27) | 2,327 |
| 9. Oklahoma! (M) (1943–48) | 2,212 |
| 10. South Pacific (M) (1949–54) | 1,925 |
| 11. Pippin (M) (1972–77) | 1,908 |
| 12. Harvey (1944–49) | 1,775 |
| 13. The Magic Show (1974–) | 1,765 |
| 14. Hair (M) (1968–72) | 1,742 |
| 15. Born Yesterday (1946–49) | 1,642 |
| 16. Mary, Mary (1961–64) | 1,572 |
| 17. Voice of the Turtle (1943–48) | 1,557 |
| 18. Barefoot in the Park (1963–67) | 1,532 |
| 19. The Wiz (M) (1975–) | 1,512 |
| 20. Mame (M) (1966–70) | 1,503 |
| 21. Same Time, Next Year (1975–) | 1,455 |
| 22. Arsenic and Old Lace (1941–44) | 1,444 |
| 23. Sound of Music (M) (1959–63) | 1,443 |
| 24. How to Succeed in Business Without Really Trying (M) (1961–65) | 1,417 |
| 25. Hellzapoppin' (M) (1938–41) | 1,404 |

### TOP MONEY-MAKING FILMS[2]

| | |
|---|---|
| 1. Star Wars (1977) | $127,000,000 |
| 2. Jaws (1975) | 121,356,000 |
| 3. The Godfather (1972) | 86,112,947 |
| 4. The Exorcist (1973) | 82,200,000 |
| 5. The Sound of Music (1965) | 78,662,000 |
| 6. The Sting (1973) | 78,090,000 |
| 7. Gone With the Wind (1939) | 76,700,000 |
| 8. One Flew Over the Cuckoo's Nest (1975) | 58,300,000 |
| 9. Rocky (1976) | 54,000,000 |
| 10. Love Story (1970) | 50,000,000 |
| 11. Towering Inferno (1975) | 50,000,000 |
| 12. The Graduate (1968) | 49,078,000 |
| 13. American Graffiti (1973) | 47,308,000 |
| 14. Doctor Zhivago (1965) | 46,550,000 |
| 15. Butch Cassidy and the Sundance Kid (1969) | 46,039,000 |
| 16. Airport (1970) | 45,300,000 |
| 17. The Ten Commandments (1956) | 43,000,000 |
| 18. Mary Poppins (1964) | 42,250,000 |
| 19. The Poseidon Adventure (1972) | 42,000,000 |
| 20. Smokey and the Bandit (1977) | 39,744,000 |
| 21. A Star Is Born (1976) | 37,100,000 |
| 22. M*A*S*H (1970) | 36,720,000 |
| 23. Ben-Hur (1959) | 36,650,000 |
| 24. Earthquake (1974) | 36,094,000 |
| 25. King Kong (1976) | 35,851,283 |

1. As of Sept. 10, 1978. M = musical. Years are those of opening and closing. 2. Figures are rentals collected by film distributors in the U.S. and Canada as of Jan. 1, 1977. *Source: Variety.*

## Notable Books, 1977

This list has been compiled by the Notable Books Council of the American Library Association for use by the general reader and by librarians who work with adult readers. The titles were selected for their significant contribution to the expansion of knowledge or for the pleasure they can provide to adult readers. Criteria include wide general appeal and literary merit.

Ashbery, John. **Houseboat Days.** Viking Press.
Baryshnikov, Mikhail with photographs by Martha Swope. **Baryshnikov at Work.** Alfred A. Knopf, Inc.
Bate, Walter Jackson. **Samuel Johnson.**[1] Harcourt, Brace, Jovanovich, Inc.
Berlant, Anthony and Mary Hunt Kahlenberg. **Walk in Beauty: The Navajo and Their Blankets.** New York Graphic Society/Little, Brown and Co.
Berryman, John. **Henry's Fate & Other Poems, 1967–1972.** Farrar, Straus & Giroux, Inc.
Bishop, Elizabeth. **Geography III.** Farrar, Straus & Giroux, Inc.
Brain, Robert. **Kolonialagent.** Harper & Row.
Caputo, Philip. **A Rumor of War.** Holt, Rinehart and Winston.
Cooper, Patricia and Norma Bradley Buferd. **The Quilters: Women and Domestic Art.** Doubleday & Company, Inc.
Djilas, Milovan. **Wartime.** Harcourt, Brace, Jovanovich, Inc.
Drew, Elizabeth. **American Journal: The Events of 1976.** Random House, Inc.
Emerson, Gloria. **Winners and Losers: Battles, Retreats, Gains, Losses and Ruins from a Long War.** Random House, Inc.
Espy, Willard R. **Oysterville: Roads to Grandpa's Village.** Clarkson N. Potter, Inc.
French, Marilyn. **The Women's Room.** Summit Books Simon & Schuster, Inc.
Gardner, John. **The Life and Times of Chaucer.** Alfred A. Knopf, Inc.
Gavin, Thomas. **King-kill.** Random House, Inc.
Gibbons, Boyd. **Wye Island: Outsiders, Insiders and Resistance to Change.** The Johns Hopkins University Press.
Hanley, James. **A Dream Journey.** Horizon Press.
Harris, Marvin. **Cannibals and Kings: The Origins of Cultures.** Random House, Inc.
Hennig, Margaret and Anne Jardim. **The Managerial Woman.** Anchor Books.
Herr, Michael. **Dispatches.** Alfred A. Knopf, Inc.
Joyes, Claire. **Monet at Giverny.** Two Continents Publishing Group, Inc.
Leakey, Richard E. and Roger Lewin. **Origins.** E. P. Dutton & Co., Inc.
Lowell, Robert. **Day by Day.** Farrar, Straus & Giroux, Inc.
McCullough, David. **The Path Between the Seas: The Creation of the Panama Canal, 1870–1914.** Simon & Schuster, Inc.
McPhee, John. **Coming into the Country.** Farrar, Straus & Giroux, Inc.
Mitford, Jessica. **A Fine Old Conflict.** Alfred A. Knopf, Inc.
Morante, Elsa. **History: A Novel.** Alfred A. Knopf, Inc.
Morrison, Toni. **Song of Solomon.** Alfred A. Knopf, Inc.
Naipaul, V.S. **India: A Wounded Civilization.** Alfred A. Knopf, Inc.
Packard, Vance. **The People Shapers.** Little, Brown and Co.
Percy, Walker. **Lancelot.** Farrar, Straus & Giroux, Inc.
Sagan, Carl. **The Dragons of Eden: Speculations on the Evolution of Human Intelligence.** Random House, Inc.
Sampson, Anthony. **The Arms Bazaar: From Lebanon to Lockheed.** Viking Press.
Savage, Thomas. **I Heard My Sister Speak My Name.** Little, Brown and Co.
Scott, Paul. **Staying On.** William Morrow & Co., Inc.
Selzer, Richard. **Mortal Lessons: Notes on the Art of Surgery.** Simon & Schuster, Inc.
Shreve, Susan Richards. **A Woman Like That.** Atheneum Publishers.
Taylor, Peter. **In the Miro District and Other Stories.** Alfred A. Knopf, Inc.
Theroux, Paul. **The Consul's File.** Houghton Mifflin Company.
Vidal, Gore. **Matters of Fact and Fiction: Essays 1973–1976.** Random House, Inc.
White, E.B. **Essays of E.B. White.** Harper & Row.
Winn, Marie. **The Plug-in-Drug.** Grossman Publishers/Viking Press.
Wright, Richard. **American Hunger.** Harper & Row.

1. Won both the Pulitzer Prize and the National Book Award.

*Source:* Reprinted by permission of the American Library Association. Issued as a pamphlet by ALA, 50 E. Huron St., Chicago, Ill. 60611, annually in the spring for the preceding year.

## Major U.S. Symphony Orchestras and Their Conductors

*Source:* American Symphony Orchestra League.

**Atlanta Symphony:** Robert Shaw
**Baltimore Symphony:** Sergiu Comissiona
**Boston Symphony:** Seiji Ozawa
**Buffalo Philharmonic:** Michael Tilson Thomas
**Chicago Symphony:** Georg Solti
**Cincinnati Symphony:** Walter Susskind
**Cleveland Orchestra:** Lorin Maazel
**Dallas Symphony:** Eduardo Mata
**Denver Symphony:** Sixten Ehrling
**Detroit Symphony:** Antal Dorati
**Honolulu Symphony:** Robert LaMarchina
**Houston Symphony:** Lawrence Foster
**Indianapolis Symphony:** John Nelson
**Kansas City Philharmonic:** Maurice Peress
**Los Angeles Philharmonic:** Carlo Maria Giulini
**Milwaukee Symphony:** Kenneth Schermerhorn
**Minnesota Orchestra:** Stanislaw Skrowaczewski
**National Symphony** (Washington, D.C.): Mstislav Rostropovich
**New Jersey Symphony:** Thomas Michalak
**New York Philharmonic:** Zubin Mehta
**North Carolina Symphony:** John Gosling
**Philadelphia Orchestra:** Eugene Ormandy
**Pittsburgh Symphony:** André Previn
**Rochester Philharmonic:** David Zinman
**St. Louis Symphony:** Leonard Slatkin
**San Antonio Symphony:** François Huybrechts
**San Francisco Symphony:** Edo de Waart
**Seattle Symphony:** Rainer Miedel
**Syracuse Symphony:** Christopher Keene
**Utah Symphony:** Maurice Abravanel

## Major Public Libraries

| City (branches) | Volumes | Circulation | Budget (in millions) |
|---|---|---|---|
| Akron, Ohio (17) | 868,628 | 2,022,444 | $ 3.3 |
| Albuquerque, N.M. (8) | 350,000 | 1,350,000 | 1.7 |
| Annapolis, Md. (12) | 610,000 | 2,475,000 | 3.2 |
| Atlanta (28) | 996,226 | 2,281,018 | 4.4 |
| Austin, Tex. (14) | 568,000 | 2,422,599 | 3.9 |
| Baltimore (34) | 2,220,767 | 2,359,695 | 9.5 |
| Baton Rouge, La. (8) | 334,135 | 880,556 | 1.0 |
| Birmingham, Ala. (16) | 967,460 | 2,034,180 | 2.8 |
| Buffalo, N.Y. (60) | 3,072,063 | 4,646,907 | 9.6 |
| Charleston, W. Va. | 458,311 | 863,206 | 1.2 |
| Charlotte, N.C. (15) | 655,231 | 1,701,784 | 3.0 |
| Chicago (78) | 6,404,116 | 6,924,142 | 30.0 |
| Cincinnati, Ohio (36) | 3,188,959 | 5,438,253 | 7.8 |
| Cleveland (34) | 2,797,450 | 2,730,706 | 13.0 |
| Columbus, Ohio (21) | 1,154,423 | 2,871,442 | 6.2 |
| Dallas (17) | 2,458,398 | 3,822,643 | 7.0 |
| Dayton, Ohio (19) | 1,302,269 | 4,132,154 | 4.2 |
| Des Moines, Iowa (5) | 412,000 | 1,225,000 | 1.6 |
| Denver (21) | 1,561,033 | 2,969,651 | 6.9 |
| Detroit (26) | 2,404,074 | 2,307,388 | 14.5 |
| D.C. (28) | 2,118,000 | 1,662,712 | 8.7 |
| El Paso (8) | 391,651 | 965,837 | 1.3 |
| Erie, Pa. (6) | 397,202 | 1,017,016 | 1.2 |
| Evansville, Ind. (7) | 480,844 | 1,042,614 | 1.2 |
| Ft. Wayne, Ind. (11) | 1,511,995 | 1,250,762 | 3.1 |
| Ft. Worth (7) | 743,305 | 2,048,058 | 2.2 |
| Grand Rapids, Mich. (5) | 624,680 | 842,466 | 1.6 |
| Greenville, S.C. (10) | 513,120 | 1,092,644 | 2.1 |
| Honolulu (18) | 834,772 | 2,641,244 | 2.4 |
| Houston (30) | 1,874,092 | 5,149,175 | 9.8 |
| Independence, Mo. (24) | 1,037,714 | 2,791,027 | 3.6 |
| Indianapolis (21) | 1,297,887 | 3,625,727 | 6.1 |
| Jackson, Miss. (40) | 630,711 | 1,521,911 | 1.9 |
| Jacksonville, Fla. (10) | 1,022,735 | 2,017,035 | 2.4 |
| Kansas City, Mo. (13) | 1,200,000 | 800,000 | 2.9 |
| Knoxville, Tenn. (19) | 532,904 | 1,538,992 | 1.8 |
| Lincoln, Neb. (10) | 455,645 | 1,017,070 | 1.5 |
| Long Beach, Calif. (11) | 706,763 | 2,024,243 | 4.8 |
| Los Angeles (107) | 4,074,905 | 11,344,100 | 20.1 |
| Louisville, Ky. (24) | 979,143 | 1,592,367 | 3.6 |
| Madison, Wis. (7) | 492,840 | 1,803,911 | 2.5 |
| Memphis, Tenn. (19) | 1,448,281 | 2,615,332 | 4.8 |
| Miami, Fla. (19) | 1,238,352 | 2,659,312 | 10.4 |
| Milwaukee (12) | 2,366,716 | 3,388,905 | 7.9 |
| Minneapolis (15) | 1,454,462 | 2,515,399 | 6.9 |
| Nashville, Tenn. (15) | 502,106 | 1,512,362 | 2.9 |
| New Orleans (11) | 795,165 | 1,305,513 | 2.6 |
| New York City (83) | 3,527,968 | 9,259,666 | 23.6 |
| Research (0) | 5,697,863 | 0 | 17.9 |
| Brooklyn (58) | 3,770,154 | 6,361,954 | 12.7 |
| Queens (56) | 3,376,863 | 6,046,116 | 18.5 |
| Newark, N.J. (12) | 1,300,000 | 1,810,000 | 4.0 |
| Norfolk, Va. (10) | 601,539 | 1,154,146 | 1.6 |
| Oklahoma City (11) | 601,220 | 1,704,000 | 2.0 |
| Omaha, Neb. (9) | 522,352 | 1,700,855 | 1.9 |
| Philadelphia (50) | 3,040,254 | 5,613,971 | 17.3 |
| Phoenix, Ariz. (9) | 1,056,129 | 3,015,615 | 5.1 |
| Pittsburgh (21) | 2,029,904 | 3,070,460 | 6.3 |
| Portland, Ore. (16) | 1,107,579 | 2,807,697 | 4.2 |
| Providence, R.I. (8) | 616,514 | 706,505 | 1.7 |
| Richmond, Va. (6) | 565,810 | 1,018,773 | 1.4 |
| Rochester, N.Y. (11) | 885,214 | 1,539,385 | 4.2 |
| Sacramento, Calif. (28) | 1,016,050 | 4,069,475 | 5.1 |
| St. Louis (18) | 1,363,984 | 1,770,031 | 5.0 |
| St. Paul (10) | 746,371 | 1,996,297 | 2.6 |
| St. Petersburg, Fla. (3) | 388,279 | 1,210,483 | 1.1 |
| Salt Lake City, Utah (13) | 503,770 | 2,005,940 | 3.3 |
| San Antonio (8) | 954,825 | 2,297,850 | 2.6 |
| San Diego, Calif. (28) | 1,462,510 | 4,196,624 | 5.3 |
| San Francisco (26) | 1,615,044 | 2,691,636 | 7.5 |
| San Jose, Calif. (16) | 800,000 | 2,900,000 | 4.0 |
| Seattle (22) | 1,629,795 | 4,391,104 | 6.8 |
| Springfield, Mass. (8) | 650,000 | 1,029,820 | 2.2 |
| Tampa, Fla. (14) | 865,205 | 1,980,952 | 3.8 |
| Tucson, Ariz. (10) | 800,000 | 2,700,000 | 4.0 |
| Tulsa, Okla. (20) | 733,775 | 1,638,132 | 2.6 |
| Wichita, Kan. (7) | 359,813 | 1,116,043 | 1.5 |
| Winston-Salem, N.C. (8) | 310,000 | 1,140,000 | 1.5 |
| Worcester, Mass. (6) | 855,817 | 855,110 | 2.2 |
| Youngstown, Ohio (23) | 709,246 | 1,485,642 | 2.7 |

*Source: Information Please* questionnaires to the libraries.

## Glossary of Art Movements

**Abstract Expressionism.** American art movement of the 1940s that emphasized form and color within a nonrepresentational framework. Jackson Pollock initiated the revolutionary technique of splattering the paint directly on canvas to achieve the subconscious interpretation of the artist's inner vision of reality.

**Art Deco.** A 1920s style characterized by setbacks, zigzag forms, and the use of chrome and plastic ornamentation. New York's Chrysler Building is an architectural example of the style.

**Art Nouveau.** An 1890s style in architecture, graphic arts, and interior decoration characterized by writhing forms, curving lines, and asymmetrical organization. Some critics regard the style as the first stage of modern architecture.

**Ashcan School.** A group of New York realist artists, formed in 1908, who abandoned decorous subject matter and portrayed the more common as well as the sordid aspects of city life.

**Assemblage (Collage).** Forms of modern sculpture and painting utilizing readymades, found objects, and pasted fragments to form an abstract composition. Louise Nevelson's boxlike enclosures, each with its own composition of assembled objects, illustrate the style in sculpture. Pablo Picasso developed the technique of cutting and pasting natural or manufactured materials to a painted or unpainted surface.

**Barbizon School (Landscape Painting).** A group of painters who, around the middle of the 19th century, reacted against classical landscape and advocated a direct study of nature. They were influenced by English and Dutch landscape masters. Theodore Rousseau, one of the principal figures of the group, led the fight for outdoor painting. In this respect, the school was a forerunner of Impressionism.

**Baroque.** European art and architecture of the 17th and 18th centuries. Giovanni Bernini, a major exponent of the style, believed in the union of the arts of architecture, painting, and sculpture to overwhelm the spectator with ornate and highly dramatized themes. Although the style originated in Rome as the instrument of the Church, it spread throughout Europe in such monumental creations as the Palace of Versailles.

**Beaux Arts.** Elaborate and formal architectural style characterized by symmetry and an abundance of sculptured ornamentation. New York's old Custom House at Bowling Green is an example of the style.

**Black or Afro-American Art.** The work of American artists of African descent produced in various styles characterized by a mood of protest and a search for identity and historical roots.

**Classicism.** A form of art derived from the study of Greek and Roman styles characterized by harmony, balance, and serenity. In contrast, the Romantic Movement gave free rein to the artist's imagination and to the love of the exotic.

**Constructivism.** A form of sculpture using wood, metal, glass, and modern industrial materials expressing the technological society. The mobiles of Alexander Calder are examples of the movement.

**Cubism.** Early 20th-century French movement marked by a revolutionary departure from representational art. Pablo Picasso and Georges Bracque penetrated the surface of objects, stressing basic abstract geometric forms that presented the object from many angles simultaneously.

**Dada.** A product of the turbulent and cynical post-World War I period, this anti-art movement extolled the irrational, the absurd, the nihilistic, and the nonsensical. The reproduction of *Mona Lisa* adorned with a mustache is a famous example. The movement is regarded as a precursor of Surrealism. Some critics regard HAPPENINGS as a recent development of Dada. This movement incorporates environment and spectators as active and important ingredients in the production of random events.

**Expressionism.** A 20th-century European art movement that stresses the expression of emotion and the inner vision of the artist rather than the exact representation of nature. Distorted lines and shapes and exaggerated colors are used for emotional impact. Vincent Van Gogh is regarded as the precursor of this movement.

**Fauvism.** The name "wild beasts" was given to this group of early 20th-century French painters because their work was characterized by distortion and violent colors. Henri Matisse and Georges Rouault were leaders of this group.

**Futurism.** This early 20th-century movement originating in Italy glorified the machine age and attempted to represent machines and figures in motion. The aesthetics of Futurism affirmed the beauty of technological society.

**Genre.** This French word meaning "type" now refers to paintings that depict scenes of everyday life without any attempt at idealization. Genre paintings can be found in all ages, but the Dutch productions of peasant and tavern scenes are typical.

**Impressionism.** Late 19th-century French school dedicated to defining transitory visual impressions painted directly from nature, with light and color of primary importance. If the atmosphere changed, a totally different picture would emerge. It was not the object or event that counted but the visual impression as caught at a certain time of day under a certain light. Claude Monet and Camille Pissarro were leaders of the movement.

**Mannerism.** A 17th-century movement, Italian in origin, although El Greco was a major practitioner of the style. The human figure, distorted and elongated, was the most frequent subject.

**Neoclassicism.** An 18th-century reaction to the excesses of Baroque and Rococo, this European art movement tried to recreate the art of Greece and Rome by imitating the ancient classics both in style and subject matter.

**Op Art.** The 1960s movement known as Optical Painting is characterized by geometrical forms that create an optical illusion in which the eye is required to blend the colors at a certain distance.

**Pop Art.** In this return to representational art, the artist returns to the world of tangible objects in a reaction against abstraction. Materials are drawn from the everyday world of popular culture—comic strips, canned goods, and science fiction.

**Rococo.** A French style of interior decoration developed during the reign of Louis XV consisting mainly of asymmetrical arrangements of curves in paneling, porcelain, and gold and silver objects. The characteristics of ornate curves, prettiness, and gaiety can also be found in the painting and sculpture of the period.

**Surrealism.** A further development of Collage, Cubism, and Dada, this 20th-century movement stresses the weird, the fantastic, and the dreamworld of the subconscious. Salvador Dali's distorted timepiece in the desert is typical.

## Pet Cemeteries

About 500 pet cemeteries in the U.S. served more than 75,000 pets, from turtles to horses, in 1978. The pet-burial industry is big business; 1978 revenues were expected to reach $7.5 million. A funeral for an average-sized pet can cost as much as $600. Cremation, offered by most pet cemeteries, can cost as little as $20.

# Museums of the United States

*Source: Information Please* questionnaires to museums

## New York City

**American Academy and Institute of Arts and Letters:** 633 W. 155th St., NYC 10032. Open: Tues.-Sun. 1–4 during exhibitions (closed Mon. and natl. hldys.). Free.
*Annual exhibitions of work of members, recipients of awards and honors, Hassam and Speicher Fund Purchases.*

**American Museum of Natural History:** Central Park West at 79th St., NYC 10024. Open: Mon.-Sat. 10–4:45, Wed. till 9, Sun. and hldys. 11–5 (closed Thanksgiving, Dec. 25).
*All branches of natural sciences with exhibits including astronomy at American Museum-Hayden Planetarium.*

**Brooklyn Museum, The:** 188 Eastern Pkwy., Brooklyn, N.Y. 11238. Open: Wed.-Sat. 10–5, Sun. 12–5, hldys. 1–5 (closed Jan. 1, Dec. 25). Free.
*Egyptian and classical art, American and European paintings, decorative arts and period rooms, prints, drawings, costumes, and textiles. Arts of Africa, Oceania, Orient, Middle East, Islam, and New World. Two reference libraries, sculpture garden.*

**Cloisters, The:** Ft. Tryon Pk., NYC 10040. Open: wkdys. 10–4:45 (closed Mon.), Sun. and hldys. 1–4:45 (May-Sept. 12–4:45). Discretionary admission fee.
*Cloisters, chapel, chapter house, apse. The various cloisters are reconstituted from elements of 12–15th-century French cloisters. Apse has been relocated here in its entirety. Frescoes, polychromed statues, stained glass, tapestries, paintings, ivories, precious metalwork. Medieval branch of The Metropolitan Museum of Art.*

**Cooper-Hewitt Museum of Design and Decorative Arts, Smithsonian Institution:** 2 E. 91st St., NYC 10028. Open: Tues. 10–9, Wed.-Sat. 10–5, Sun. 12–5 (closed Mon.; also Jan. 1, July 4, Thanksgiving, Dec. 25). Adm. $1 (free on Tues.).
*Over 100,000 decorative arts objects and related library housed in 64-room Carnegie mansion.*

**Frick Collection:** 1 E. 70th St., NYC 10021. Open: Sept.-May—Tues.-Sat. 10–6, Sun. and most hldys. 1–6 (closed Mon.; also Jan. 1, Thanksgiving, Dec. 24–25); June-Aug.—Sun. 1–6, Wed.-Sat. 10–6 (closed Mon. and Tues.; also July 4). Adm. $1.
*Paintings, prints, drawings of 14th to 19th centuries, Italian Renaissance and French sculpture and furniture. Chinese and French porcelain. Concerts, lectures.*

**Guggenheim Museum, The Solomon R.:** 1071 Fifth Ave. at 88th St., NYC 10028. Open: Tues. 11–8; Wed.-Sun. and hldys. 11–5 (closed Mon., except hldys., and Dec. 25). Adm. $1.50 (children under 7, free). Tues. 5–8 free. College students with ID's, and senior citizens, 75¢; school children in groups of 10 with a teacher, 50¢.
*Works of leading 20th-century foreign and American painters and sculptors.*

**Hayden Planetarium.** *See* American Museum of Natural History.

**Hispanic Society of America, The (Museum and Library):** 613 W. 155th St., NYC 10032. Museum open: Tues.-Sat. 10–4:30, Sun. 1–4 (closed Mon.; also Jan. 1, Feb. 12, Feb. 22, Good Friday, Easter, May 30, July 4, Oct. 12, Thanksgiving, Dec. 24–25, 31). Library open: Tues.-Fri. 1–4:30, Sat. 10:30–4:30 (closed Sun., Mon.; also hldys., Good Friday, month of Aug., Dec. 24—Jan. 1 incl.). Free.
*Paintings, sculpture, decorative arts, manuscripts, and incunabula, representative of Hispanic culture. Works on Hispanic art, history, literature.*

**Jewish Museum:** 1109 Fifth Ave. at 92nd St., NYC 10028. Open: Mon.-Thurs., 12–5, Sun. 11–6 (closed Fri. and Sat., also Jewish hldys.). Adm. $1.75 (children 6–16 and students with ID's, $1). Members, free; senior citizens, pay what you wish.
*Former Warburg mansion and adjoining Albert A. List building house most extensive collection of Jewish ceremonial objects in U.S. Changing contemporary exhibits of sculpture, paintings, photography and architecture illuminate Jewish experience, culture, and tradition. Also children's programs.*

**Metropolitan Museum of Art, The:** Fifth Ave. at 82nd St., NYC 10028. Open: Tues. 10–8:45, Wed.-Sat. 10–4:45, Sun. and hldys. 11–4:45 (closed Mon.). Discretionary admission fee.
*Comprehensive collection of European paintings, drawings, sculpture, decorative arts, prints. Egyptian, Greek, Roman, Near and Far Eastern art. Musical instruments, arms and armor. European period rooms. Costumes and textiles.* See also *Cloisters.*

**Museum of the American Indian, Heye Foundation:** Broadway at 155th St., NYC 10032. Open: Tues.-Sun. 1–5 (closed Mon., also Jan. 1, Easter, July 4, Thanksgiving, Dec. 25). Adm. $1 (students and senior citizens, 50¢); Tues. 25¢ to all.
*Archeology, ethnology, and primitive-to-20th-century arts of North, Central, and South America. Objects of historical importance in Indian-white history. Largest collection of artifacts of the native peoples of the Western Hemisphere.*

**Museum of the City of New York:** 1220 Fifth Ave. at 103rd St., NYC 10029. Open: Tues.-Sat. 10–5, Sun. and hldys. 1–5 (closed Mon.; also Dec. 25). Free.
*History and life of New York City. Period costumes, furniture, miniature scenes, portraits, paintings, prints, manuscripts, theater and music collection, silver, dolls and doll houses.*

**Museum of Modern Art, The:** 11 W. 53rd St., NYC 10019. Open: Mon., Tues., Fri., Sat. and Sun. 11–6, Thurs. 11–9 (closed Wed.; also Dec. 25). Adm. $2 (full-time students with ID's, $1.25; children and senior citizens, 75¢; members, free). Tuesday, pay what you wish.
*Founded 1929 to help people enjoy and understand the art of our times. Changing exhibitions of contemporary painting, sculpture, drawings, prints, photography, architecture, industrial and graphic design, films.*

**National Academy of Design:** 1083 Fifth Ave. at 90th St., NYC 10028. Open: wkdys. and Sun. 1–5 (during exhibitions).
*Special annual exhibitions by selected organizations Oct. through May.*

**New-York Historical Society:** 170 Central Park West at 77th St., NYC 10024. Museum open; Tues.-Fri. 11–5, Sat. 10–5, Sun. 1–5. Library open to adults: Tues.-Sat. 10–5. (Both closed Mon.; also Jan. 1, July 4, Thanksgiving, Dec. 25). Library adm. $1 to nonmembers; museum, free.
*New York city and state historical exhibits. Early*

*American paintings and portraits. Period rooms. Audubon watercolors. Gallery of American silver.*

**Pierpont Morgan Library:** 29–33 E. 36th St. NYC 10016. Open: Tues.-Sat. 10:30–5, Sun. 1–5 (closed Mon.; also legal hldys., Sundays in July, and month of August).

*Medieval and Renaissance illuminated manuscripts, rare books, music and autograph manuscripts, old master drawings, bindings, early children's books, ancient written records.*

**Whitney Museum of American Art:** 945 Madison Ave. at 75th St., NYC 10021. Open: Wed.-Sat. 11–6, Tues. 11–9 (free 6–9), Sun. and hldys. 12–6 (closed Mon.; also Dec. 25). Adm. $1.50 (senior citizens and children under 12, free).

*Sculpture, paintings, watercolors, drawings, and prints by 20th-century American artists. Exhibitions of contemporary and historical American art. Daily film showings; occasional performing arts programs in spring.*

## Chicago

**Art Institute of Chicago, The:** Michigan Ave. at Adams St., Chicago, Ill. 60603. Open: Mon.-Wed. and Fri. 10:30–4:30, Thurs. 10:30–8, Sat. 10–5, Sun. and hldys. 12–5 (Closed Dec. 25). Voluntary admission fee, $2.

*Paintings, sculpture, prints, drawings, textiles, photography. Oriental arts; European, American decorative arts; primitive art. Thorne Miniature Rooms. Junior Museum. Goodman Theatre, School of Drama, School of Art.*

**Beverly Art Center:** 2153 W. 111th St., Chicago, Ill. 60643. Open: daily 9 a.m. 10 p.m.

*Exhibitions change monthly.*

**Chicago Academy of Sciences, Museum of Ecology:** Lincoln Park—2001 North Clark St., Chicago, Ill. 60614. Open: daily 10–5 (closed Dec. 25). Free.

*Exhibits of ecology of animal and plant life, minerals and fossils of Chicago region. Lectures, field trips, movies.*

**Chicago Historical Society:** Clark St. and North Ave., Chicago, Ill. 60614. Open: Mon.-Sat. 9:30–4:30, Sun. 12–5 (closed Jan. 1, Thanksgiving, Dec. 25). Adults, $1; children 6–17, 50¢; senior citizens, 25¢. Free admission Monday. Research collection open Tues.-Sat. 9:30–4:30.

*Exhibits and collections relating to Chicago and Illinois history, Illinois pioneer crafts, American history, Lincoln, Civil War.*

**Field Museum of Natural History:** Roosevelt Rd. at Lake Shore Dr., Chicago, Ill. 60605. Open: Daily at 9 a.m. to as early as 4 p.m. in winter and as late as 9 p.m. in summer (closed Jan. 1, Dec. 25). Adm: families, $3.50; adults, $1.50; children (6–17) and students with ID's, 50¢; senior citizens, 35¢. Free on Fri. (9–9).

*Dioramas of plants, animals and fossils, rocks and geological fragments, and artifacts of early civilizations.*

**Museum of Science and Industry:** 57th St. and Lake Shore Dr., Chicago, Ill. 60637. Open: May 1-Labor Day 9:30–5:30; rest of year, Mon.-Fri. 9:30–4, Sat., Sun. and hldys. 9:30–5:30 (closed Dec. 25). Free (small fee to four exhibits).

*Operating coal mine, captured German submarine, giant heart, Paul Bunyan house, Colleen Moore's Fairy Castle, The Farm, the Apollo 8 spacecraft, Sears' Cinema Circus, computerized "Food for Life," historic and advanced forms of planes, ships, trains, and cars.*

**Oriental Institute Museum of the University of Chicago:** 1155 E. 58th St., Chicago, Ill. 60637. Open: Tues.-Sat. 10–4, Sun. 12–4 (closed Mon. and hldys.). Free.

*Ancient Near Eastern objects, including 40-ton human-headed winged bull from Khorsabad in Assyria, 16-ft. statue of Tutankhamen from Egypt, colossal bull's head from Persepolis; glyptic, bronze, and ivory artifacts.*

**Vanderpoel (John H.) Memorial Art Gallery:** 2135 W. 111th St., Chicago, Ill. 60643. Open: Tues.-Fri. and Sun. 1–4 (closed Mon., Sat. and hldys.).

*Paintings, watercolors, etchings, scuplture contributed by the artists in tribute to Mr. Vanderpoel.*

## Washington, D.C.

**Anacostia Neighborhood Museum, Smithsonian Institution:** 2405 Martin Luther King, Jr., Ave. SE, Washington, D.C. 20020. Open: Mon.-Fri. 10–6, Sat. and Sun. 1–6 (closed Dec. 25). Free.

*Exhibits on Afro-American history, urban problems, art. Programs for children.*

**Arts and Industries Building, Smithsonian Institution:** 900 Jefferson Dr. SW, Washington, D.C. 20560. Open: daily 10–5:30; summer 10–9 (closed Dec. 25). Free.

*Constructed to house exhibits from 1876 Centennial Exhibition, building has been restored as nearly as possible to original appearance.*

**Corcoran Gallery of Art:** 17th St. and New York Ave. NW, Washington, D.C. 20006. Open: Tues.-Sun. 11–5 (closed Mon.; also Jan. 1, July 4, Thanksgiving, Dec. 25). Free Tues. and Wed.; $1.50 adm. Thurs.-Sun. (members free).

*Comprehensive collection of American paintings, sculpture, graphics. Choice selection of European art.*

**Freer Gallery of Art, Smithsonian Institution:** Jefferson Dr. at 12th St. SW, Washington, D.C. 20560. Open: daily 10–5:30 (closed Dec. 25). Free.

*Oriental paintings, sculpture, bronzes, pottery, metalwork, manuscripts. Largest extant Whistler collection.*

**Hirshhorn Museum and Sculpture Garden, Smithsonian Institution:** Eighth St. at Independence Ave. SW, Washington, D.C. 20560. Open: daily, 10–5:30; summer, 10–9 (closed Dec. 25). Free.

*Collection numbers 4,000 paintings and 2,000 sculptures, tracing development of modern art from 19th century to present. Rodin, Moore, Picasso, Calder, Miró, and Matisse among those represented.*

**National Air and Space Museum, Smithsonian Institution:** Independence Ave. bet. 5th and 7th Sts. SW, Washington, D.C. 20560. Open: daily 10–5:30, summer 10–9 (closed Dec. 25). Free.

*Exhibits on aviation and space age; Wright Brothers'* Kitty Hawk Flyer, *Lindbergh's* Spirit of St. Louis.

**National Collection of Fine Arts, Smithsonian Institution:** Eighth and G Sts. NW, Washington, D.C. 20560. Open: daily 10–5:30 (closed Dec. 25). Free.

*Collections survey 300 years of American art. Paintings, sculpture, graphic art. Large selection of contemporary art.*

**National Gallery of Art:** Constitution Ave. bet. 3rd and 7th Sts. NW, Washington, D.C. 20565. Open: Mon.-Sat. 10–5, Sun. 12–9[1] (closed Jan. 1, Dec. 25). Free.

*Paintings, sculpture, drawings, prints, decorative arts given by Mellon, Kress, Widener, Rosenwald, Dale, Harriman, and others. Index of American Design.*

**National Museum of History and Technology, Smith-**

**sonian Institution:** 12th St. and Constitution Ave. NW, Washington, D.C. 20560. Open: daily 10–5:30, summer 10–9 (closed Dec. 25). Free.
*Exhibits showing scientific, technological, and cultural development of U.S. Original Star-Spangled Banner. Costumes and furnishings. Gowns of First Ladies. Inventions. Stamps, coins, musical instruments, ceramics, and crafts.*

**National Museum of Natural History and National Museum of Man, Smithsonian Institution:** 10th St. and Constitution Ave. NW, Washington, D.C. 20560. Open: daily 10–5:30, summer 10–9. (closed Dec. 25). Free.
*Origin, development, and physical characteristics of man. Dioramas of peoples and animals in natural settings. Land and sea mammals, birds, fish, reptiles, and gems, minerals, meteorites, volcanoes, prehistoric animals. Hope Diamond. Insect Zoo.*

**National Portrait Gallery, Smithsonian Institution:** Eighth and F Sts. NW, Washington, D.C. 20560. Open: daily 10–5:30 (closed Dec. 25). Free.
*Only major museum in hemisphere devoted exclusively to portraiture. Exhibits likenesses of persons who have made significant contributions to U.S. history, development, and culture.*

**Renwick Gallery, Smithsonian Institution:** 17th St. and Pennsylvania Ave. NW, Washington, D.C. 20560. Open: daily 10–5:30 (closed Dec. 25). Free.
*American crafts, decorative arts, and design, housed in a mid-19th-century building restored to its original appearance.*

**Smithsonian Institution Building:** 1000 Jefferson Dr. SW, Washington, D.C. 20560. Open: daily 10–5:30, summer 10–9 (closed Dec. 25). Free.
*Information center and James Smithson's tomb are in original building. Institution maintains the museums and art galleries indicated above; also Cooper-Hewitt Museum of Design and Decorative Arts in New York City, National Zoological Park in Washington, D.C., and research facilities elsewhere.*

## Philadelphia

**Academy of Natural Sciences of Philadelphia:** 19th St. and the Parkway, Philadelphia, Pa. 19103. Natural History Museum open: daily 10–4 (closed Jan. 1, Thanksgiving, Dec. 25). Adm. $2 (students, $1.50; children $1.25).
*Exhibits on shells, extinct species. Animal habitat dioramas. Birds, gems. Live animal shows daily.*

**Franklin Institute, The:** 20th St. and the Parkway, Philadelphia, Pa. 19103. Open: Mon.-Sat. 10–5, Sun. 12–5 (closed Jan. 1, Thanksgiving, Dec. 24–25). Adm: $2.50 (senior citizens, $1.25; students 12-college, $2; children 5–11, $1.50; children under 5, 50¢).
*Nonprofit educational and research institution operating science museum, planetarium, library, and research laboratories.*

**Pennsylvania Academy of the Fine Arts:** Broad and Cherry Sts., Philadelphia, Pa. 19102. Open: Tues.-Sat. 10–5, Sun. 1–5 (closed Jan. 1, Dec. 25). Adm. $1 (children under 12, students and senior citizens, 50¢).
*Oldest art museum and school in U.S. Collection devoted to American art. Lectures, concerts.*

**Philadelphia Museum of Art:** 26th St. and the Parkway, Philadelphia, Pa. 19130. Open: daily 9–5 (closed major hldys.). Adm. $1.50 (children and senior citizens, 75¢), (free Sun. 9–1).
*Paintings, drawings, prints, from old masters to present. Sculpture, decorative arts, period rooms and armor. Oriental collections. New American Wing open. Rodin Museum at Parkway and 22nd St. Colonial Houses in Fairmont Park. Samuel S. Fleisher Art Memorial, 715–19 Catharine St.*

## Museums In Other Cities

**Addison Gallery of American Art:** Phillips Academy, Andover, Mass. 01810. Open: Tues.-Sat. 10–5, Sun. 2:30–5 (closed Mon.; also natl. hldys.). Free.
*Paintings, sculpture, graphics, photographs of 18th, 19th, and 20th centuries. Changing contemporary exhibitions.*

**Alabama, Museum of Natural History of:** Smith Hall, on campus of U. of Alabama, Tuscaloosa, Ala. 35486. Open: Mon.-Sat. 8–5, Sun. 1–5. Free.
*All phases of natural history.* See also *Mound State Monument Museum.*

**Albright-Knox Art Gallery:** 1285 Elmwood Ave., Buffalo, N.Y. 14222. Open: Tues.-Sat. 10–5; Sun. 12–5 (closed Mon.; also Jan. 1, Thanksgiving, Dec. 25). Voluntary admission fee.
*Comprehensive collection of contemporary paintings; 18th-19th-century English, French, and American paintings. Sculpture since 3000 B.C.*

**Atomic Energy, American Museum of:** 300 South Tulane, Oak Ridge, Tenn. 37830. Open: Sept.-May, Mon.-Sat. 9–5; Sun. 12:30–5; June-Aug., Mon.-Sat. 9–6; Sun. 12:30–6 (closed Jan. 1, Thanksgiving, Dec. 25). Free.
*Demonstrations, exhibits, motion pictures, models, etc., relating to atomic and other forms of energy. Traveling exhibits available free to qualified exhibitors in U.S.*[2]

**Baltimore Museum of Art:** Art Museum Dr., Baltimore, Md. 21218. Open: Tues.-Sat. 11–5, Thurs. evening 7–10 (except in summer). Sun. 1–5 (closed Mon.). Free.
*Paintings, sculpture, graphics, 2nd-6th-century mosaics from Antioch. Concerts, dance recitals, educational programs for all ages.*

**Baseball Hall of Fame and Museum, National:** Main St., Cooperstown, N.Y. 13326. Open: May-Oct. 9–9, Nov.-Apr. 9–5 (closed Jan. 1, Thanksgiving, Dec. 25). Adm. $2.50 (children 7–15, $1).
*Relics, pictures, documents of baseball history. Bronze plaques of game's immortals. Baseball movies shown daily.* See also *Hall of Fame in index.*

**Berkshire Museum, The:** 39 South St., Pittsfield, Mass. 01201. Open: Tues.-Sat. 10–5, Sun. 2–5 (closed Mon.; also Jan. 1, July 4, Thanksgiving, Dec. 25). Open Mon. in July and Aug. Free.
*Painting, sculpture, decorative arts—ancient to modern. Loan exhibits. Galleries on biology, birds, man, minerals, and American history. Live exhibits. Junior Department. Movies, lectures.*

**Birmingham Museum of Art:** 2000 Eighth Ave. North, Birmingham, Ala. 35203. Open: Mon.-Wed., Fri. and Sat. 10–5, Thurs. 10–9, Sun. 2–6 (closed Jan. 1, Dec. 25). Free.
*Kress Collection of Italian art; 17th-century Dutch, Flemish, and English paintings; modern American painting; silver, porcelain.*

**(Boston) Museum of Fine Arts:** Huntington Ave., Boston, Mass. 02115. Open: Wed.-Sun. 10–5, Tues. 10–9 (closed Mon.; also Jan. 1, July 4, Labor Day, Thanksgiving, and Dec. 24–25). Adm. $1.75 (Tues. 5–9, free; Sun. $1.25; free to senior citizens on Fri.; members and children under 16, free).
*European and American paintings, sculpture, furniture, interiors, tapestries, textiles, silver, costumes, musical instruments. Prints, drawings,*

*watercolors. Egyptian, Asiatic, contemporary collections.*

**Buffalo Museum of Science:** Humboldt Parkway, Buffalo, N.Y. 14211. Open: Mon.-Sat. 10–5 (Fri. 10–10, except July and Aug., 10–5), Sun. and hldys. 1:30–5:30 (closed Dec. 25). Free.
*Exhibits of astronomy, geology, zoology, botany, anthropology. Kellogg Observatory.*

**California Academy of Sciences:** Golden Gate Park, San Francisco, Calif. 94118. Open: daily 10–5. Adm. 50¢ (children 12–18, 25¢; under 12 and over 65, free). Free adm. first day of month.
*North American and African habitat groups. Astronomical exhibits, clocks, watches, lamps, minerals, fossils, plants. Steinhart Aquarium, Morrison Planetarium, Wattis Hall of Man.*

**California Palace of the Legion of Honor:** 34th Ave. and Clement St., Lincoln Park, San Francisco, Calif. 94121. Open: daily 10–5. Adm. 75¢ (youths 12–18, 25¢; under 12 and senior citizens, free). Free adm. first day of month.
*Devoted to arts of France: paintings, sculpture, and decorative arts; prints and drawings of all periods.*

**Carnegie Institute:** 4400 Forbes Ave., Pittsburgh, Pa. 15213. Open: Tues.-Sat. 10–5, Sun. 1–6 (closed Mon. and major hldys.). Suggested contributions: Adults, $1; children and students, 50¢. Sat. free.
*Museum of Art: European and American paintings, sculpture, and decorative arts. Carnegie Museum of Natural History: exhibits in natural history and science.*

**Cincinnati Art Museum:** Eden Park, Cincinnati, Ohio 45202. Open: wkdys. 10–5, Sun. and hldys. 1–5 (closed Mon. and major hldys.). Adm. $1 (children 12–18, 50¢; 11 and under, free). Free to everyone on Sat.
*European and American painting, prints, photographs, decorative arts, sculpture, costumes. Egyptian, Greco-Roman, Medieval, Near and Far Eastern arts. Ancient musical instruments.*

**Clark (Sterling and Francine) Art Institute:** Williamstown, Mass. 01267. Open: daily except Monday, 10–5 (closed Jan. 1, Thanksgiving, Dec. 25). Free.
*Paintings from 14th to 19th centuries, including works by Corot, Renoir, Degas, Toulouse-Lautrec, Homer; sculpture, antique silver, prints and drawings.*

**Cleveland Museum of Art:** 11150 East Boulevard, Cleveland, Ohio 44106. Open: Tues. 10–6, Wed. 10–10, Thurs. and Fri. 10–6, Sat. 9–5, Sun. 1–6 (closed Mon.; also Jan. 1, July 4, Thanksgiving, Dec. 25). Free.
*Paintings, sculpture, graphic arts, furniture, silver, gold, arms, armor, textiles, ceramics from all cultures and periods.*

**Cleveland Museum of Natural History:** Wade Oval, University Circle, Cleveland, Ohio 44106. Open: Mon.-Sat. 10–5, Sun. 1–5:30 (closed Jan. 1, Memorial Day, July 4, Labor Day, Thanksgiving, Dec. 25). Adm. $1.50 (children 6–18 and senior citizens, 50¢). Free Tues. after 1.
*Dinosaurs, area fossils, minerals, birds, mammals, insects, reptiles, plants. American Indian and Eskimo displays. Planetarium, observatory. Hall of Man's Ecology, Hall of Earth Science.*

**Colonial Williamsburg:** Williamsburg, Va. 23185. Open: daily. Tickets for one day, adults $7, children (6–12) $3.50; 2 days, adults, $10, children $5; 3 days, adults $13, children $6.50.
*Restored 18th-century capital of Virginia colony; 173 acres of colonial city with more than 30 exhibition homes, craft shops, and public buildings; 90 acres of gardens; outdoor events; colonial lodging and dining.*

**Colorado Springs Fine Arts Center:** 30 W. Dale St., Colorado Springs, Colo. 80903. Open: Wed., Fri., and Sat. 10–5; Tues. and Thurs. 10–9; Sun. 1:30–5 (closed Mon.; also Jan. 1, Thanksgiving, Dec. 25). Free.
*Art produced within limits of U.S. from prehistoric to contemporary, including decorative and fine arts. Survey of arts of world. Drama, dance, and music programs.*

**Columbus Gallery of Fine Arts:** 480 E. Broad St., Columbus, Ohio 43215. Open: Tues., Thurs., Fri., and Sun. 11–5; Wed. 11–8:30; Sat. 10–5 (closed Mon.). Adm. $1.50 (children 6–17, students, and senior citizens, 50¢). Tues. free.
*Renaissance, baroque and 19th- and 20th-century American and European paintings; lithographs and paintings of George Bellows. Decorative arts and prints.*

**Corning Glass Center:** Centerway, Corning, N.Y. 14830. Open daily 9–5 (closed Jan. 1, Thanksgiving, Dec. 24–25). Free.
*Museum has comprehensive collection of historical glass dating from 1500 B.C. Hall of Science and Industry shows modern methods of making and using glass. In Steuben factory, visitors may watch crystal hand-crafted and engraved.*

**Currier Gallery of Art:** 192 Orange St., Manchester, N.H. 03104. Open: Tues.-Sat. 10–4, Sun. 2–5 (closed major hldys.). Free.
*European and American paintings, 13th-20th century. American decorative arts, 18th-19th century, including New England furniture, silver, pewter, and early glass.*

**Davenport Museum:** *See* Putnam Museum.

**Delaware Art Museum, The:** 2301 Kentmere Pkwy., Wilmington, Del. 19806. Open: Mon.-Sat. 10–5, Sun. 1–5. Adm.: $1 (youths 12–18 and students, 50¢; children under 12, members, and senior citizens, free).
*English pre-Raphaelite; 19th- and 20th-century American art; complete set of John Sloan's graphic work; complete first folio of Audubon's* Birds of America. *Art reference library.*

**Denver Art Museum, The:** 100 W. 14th Ave. Parkway, Denver, Colo. 80204. Open: Tues.-Sat. 9–5, Sun. 1–5; also Wed. 6–9 p.m.
*Art from nearly every culture and period.*

**Denver Museum of Natural History:** City Park, Denver, Colo. 80205. Open: Mon.-Sat. 9–4:30, Sun. and hldys. 12–4:30 (closed Jan. 1, Thanksgiving, Dec. 24–25, Dec. 31). Free.
*Sixty life-size ecological habitat dioramas. Animals from three continents, earth-science exhibits, dinosaurs, displays of fossil mammals and historic native Americans. Planetarium (small charge).*

**Des Moines Art Center:** Greenwood Park, 45th St. and Grand Ave., Des Moines, Iowa 50312. Open: Tues.-Sat. 11–5, Sun. 12–5. Free.
*Permanent collection includes Calder, Rodin, Arp, Bellows, Johns, Hopper, Giacometti, David Smith, and Morris Louis, among others.*

**Detroit Historical Museum:** 5401 Woodward Ave., Detroit, Mich. 48202. Open: Tues., Thurs., Fri., Sat. 9:30–5; Wed. 1–9; Sun. 1–5 (closed Mon. and legal hldys.).
*Detroit-related industrial, transportation, social history, and ethnic exhibits. Detroit streets of 1840–50, 1870–80, 1895–1905. Urban history. Corridor of Costumes. Marine exhibits at Dossin Great Lakes Museum on Belle Isle; military history exhibits at Ft. Wayne, at the foot of Livernois.*

**Detroit Institute of Arts, The:** 5200 Woodward Ave., Detroit, Mich. 48202. Open: Tues.-Sun. 9:30–5:30

(closed Mon.; also natl. hldys.). Voluntary admission fee.

*Paintings, sculpture, decorative arts from ancient times to modern.*

**Dickson Mounds Museum:** off Route 97–78 near Lewistown, Ill. 61542. Open: Daily 8:30–5 (closed Jan. 1, Easter, Thanksgiving, Dec. 25). Free.

*Museum of prehistoric Indians. Branch of Illinois State Museum.*

**Farmers' Museum:** Lake Rd., Route 80, Cooperstown, N.Y. 13326. Open: summer season, daily. 9–5; winter season, Tues.-Sat. 9–5, Sun. 1–5 (closed Mon.; also Jan. 1, Thanksgiving, Dec. 25). Adm. $2.75[3] (children $1).

*Re-created village crossroads. Early farm and handicraft tools. School house, country store, smithy, print shop, doctor's and lawyer's offices, pharmacy, tavern, church, farm unit. Cardiff Giant. Operated by New York State Historical Association.*

**Fenimore House:** Lake Rd., Route 80, Cooperstown, N.Y. 13326. Open: summer season, daily 9–5; Nov., Dec., and April, Tues.-Sat. 9–5, Sun. 1–5 (closed Mon.; also Jan., Feb., March, Dec. 25). Adm: $2.25[3] (children $1).

*American portraits, genre paintings. Browere life masks of Founding Fathers. James Fenimore Cooper memorabilia. Folk art. Library. Operated by New York State Historical Association.*

**Florida State Museum, University of Florida:** Museum Road, Gainesville, Fla. 32611. Open: Mon.-Fri. 9–5, Sat. 9–5, Sun. 1–5 (closed Dec. 25). Free.

*State and University museum with research emphasis on natural and social history of Florida, southeastern United States, and Caribbean area.*

**Fogg Art Museum:** Harvard University, 32 Quincy St., Cambridge, Mass. 02138. Open: Mon.-Fri. 9–5, Sat. 10–5, Sun. 2–5 (closed weekends from July 1 to Labor Day; also natl. hldys.). Free.

*Collections illustrate evolution of Eastern and Western art from ancient to modern times. Chinese sculpture and bronzes; Romanesque sculpture; Italian primitives; French 19th-century paintings; European drawings and prints.*

**Gardner (Isabella Stewart) Museum:** 2 Palace Road, Boston, Mass. 02115. Open: Tues., 1–9:30, Wed.-Sun. 1–5:30. July-Aug., Tues.-Sun. 1–5:30 (closed natl. hldys., Sunday before Labor Day). Adm.: $1 preferred, lesser amount acceptable.

*Paintings, 14th-20th centuries, in building of Venetian palace style. Sculpture, tapestries, furniture. Flowering courtyard. Tours on Thursday at 2:30 p.m.*

**Getty (J. Paul) Museum, The:** 17985 Pacific Coast Hgwy., Malibu, Calif. 90265. Open: Mon.-Fri. 10–5 (June-Sept.), Tues.-Sat. 10–5 (Oct.-May), (closed Jan. 1, Feb. 22, Memorial Day, July 4, Labor Day, Thanksgiving, Dec. 25). Free. Reservations for free parking should be made a week in advance.

*Re-creation of Roman seaside villa destroyed by Vesuvius in 79 A.D. Greek and Roman antiquities, Western European paintings, 18th-century French decorative arts. Research library.*

**Heard Museum:** 22 East Monte Vista Rd., Phoenix, Ariz. 85004. Open: Mon.-Sat. 10–5, Sun. 1–5 (closed hldys.). Adm.: suggested donation, $1 for adults (students, 50¢).

*Anthropology and primitive arts, with emphasis on rich heritage of Southwest.*

**High Museum of Art, The:** 1280 Peachtree St. NE, Atlanta, Ga. 30309. Open: Mon.-Sat. 10–5, Sun. 12–5 (closed natl. hldys.). Free.

*Paintings and sculpture from 14th to 18th century in Samuel H. Kress Collection. Ralph K. Uhry Print Collection; decorative arts; Richman Collection of African Art; 18th-century European porcelains; photography, contemporary art.*

**(Houston) Museum of Fine Arts, The:** 1001 Bissonnet at Main, Houston, Tex. 77005. Open: Tues.-Sat. 10–5, Sun. 12–6 (closed Mon.; also July 4, Labor Day, Thanksgiving, Dec. 25). Free.

*American and European art through 20th century; Southwest American Indian art and artifacts; early American furniture and decorative arts; pre-Columbian and Far Eastern art; native arts from Africa, Australia, South Pacific. Impressionist and post-Impressionist paintings. 20th-century photography.*

**Huntington Library, Art Gallery, and Botanical Gardens:** 1151 Oxford Rd., San Marino, Calif. 91108. Open: Tues.-Sun. 1–4:30 (closed Mon.; also month of Oct., Jan. 1, Easter, Memorial Day, July 4, Labor Day, Thanksgiving, Dec. 25). Free.

*18th-century British paintings, including Gainsborough's "Blue Boy" and Lawrence's "Pinkie." Manuscript and rare-book exhibits include Gutenberg Bible, Franklin's* Autobiography *in his handwriting. Botanical gardens. Research library.*

**Illinois State Museum:** Spring and Edwards Sts., Springfield, Ill. 62706. Open: Mon.-Sat. 8:30–5, Sun. 1:30–5 (closed Jan. 1, Easter, Thanksgiving, Dec. 25). Free.

*Museum of natural science, anthropology, and art.*

**Indianapolis Museum of Art:** 1200 W. 38th St., Indianapolis, Ind. 46208. Krannert and Clowes Pavilions open: Tues.-Sun. and hldys. 11–5 (closed Mon.; also Dec. 25). Free. Lilly Pavilion of Decorative Arts open Tues.-Sun. 1–4 (closed Mon.; also Dec. 25). Free.

*Pre-Columbian through contemporary art in all media. British and American paintings of 19th century; J.M.W. Turner collection. Dutch and Flemish paintings of 17th century; textiles, decorative arts of 18th-century Germany, England, France, and Italy. Oriental collection. Clowes Fund Collection of old masters.*

**Los Angeles County Museum of Art:** 5905 Wilshire Blvd., Los Angeles, Calif. 90036. Open: Tues.-Fri. 10–5, Sat. 10–6, Sun. 10–6 (closed Mon.; also Thanksgiving, Dec. 25). Free.

*Ahmanson Gallery houses permanent collections covering entire range of history of art. Special Exhibitions Gallery (free for members, $1 for adult nonmembers, 50¢ for senior citizens and children to 18).*

**(Los Angeles County) Natural History Museum:** Exposition Park, 900 Exposition Blvd., Los Angeles, Calif. 90007. Open: Tues.-Sun. 10–5 (closed Mon.; also Jan. 1, Thanksgiving, Dec. 25). Free.

*Exhibits in Pre-Columbian archeology, Pacific Islands and African ethnology, Southern California botany, evolution of life, marine biology, insects, mineralogy. Dinosaur and Cenozoic fossil reconstructions. North American and African animal habitat groups. U.S., California, Western, Plains, and West Coast Indian history. Rancho La Brea tar pits, a designated natural history landmark, are at 5801 Wilshire Blvd., Hancock Park, with satellite George C. Page Museum of La Brea. Pleistocene fossil reconstructions. Open: same as parent museum. Free.*

**Milwaukee Art Center:** Milwaukee County War Memorial Bldg., 750 North Lincoln Memorial Dr., Milwaukee, Wis. 53202. Open: Tues.-Sun. 10–5 (closed Mon.). Adm. $1 (students, senior citizens, 50¢; children under 12, free).

*Paintings, sculpture, graphics, and decorative*

*arts from ancient to modern; Bradley Collection of 19th- and 20th-century American art. Villa Terrace, Branch Museum for Decorative Arts, 2220 North Terrace Ave.; seasonal hours.*

**Milwaukee Public Museum:** 800 W. Wells St., Milwaukee, Wis. 53233. Open: daily 9–5 (closed some major hldys.). Adm.: $1 (children under 18, 25¢) for Milwaukee County residents; $2 (children, 75¢) for nonresidents.

*American Indian and West African art, pre-Columbian collections. Natural history and history displays.*

**Mint Museum, Art Museum:** 501 Hempstead Pl., Charlotte, N.C. 28207. Open: Tues.-Fri. 10–5, Sat.-Sun. 2–5 (closed Mon. and hldys.). Free.

*Paintings, sculpture, decorative arts, prints (Renaissance-20th century), pre-Columbian Collection, Delhom Gallery and Institute for Study and Research in Ceramics. Coins and artifacts from 19th-century Charlotte branch of U.S. Mint.*

**Mound State Monument Archaeological Museum:** Rte. 69, Moundville, Ala. 35474. Open: daily 9–5 (closed Dec. 25). Adm. $2 (children $1).

*Indian artifacts, re-created temple and village of Moundville Indians. Trailer and tent campgrounds. Operated by Alabama Museum of Natural History, The University of Alabama.*

**Mystic Seaport:** Mystic, Conn. 06355. Open: daily. Dec.-March 10–4, April-Nov. 9–5 (closed Jan. 1, Dec. 25). Adm., Dec.-March $4.50 (children 6–12 $2.25); April-Nov. $5.50 (children $2.75). Two-day tickets and group rates available.

*Maritime museum emphasizing Age of Sail. Waterfront village.* Charles W. Morgan, *last of wooden whaleships. Smallcraft collection; craft demonstrations. Working shipyard. Planetarium.*

**Navaho Ceremonial Art, Museum of:** See Wheelwright Museum.

**Nelson (William Rockhill) Gallery—Atkins Museum of Fine Arts:** 4525 Oak St., Kansas City, Mo. 64111. Open: Tues.-Sat. 10–5, Sun. 2–6 (closed Mon.; also Jan. 1, Memorial Day, July 4, Thanksgiving, Dec. 25). Adm. 50¢ (children 6–12, 25¢). Free on Sun.

*Egyptian, Oriental, classic, and European art. American paintings and decorative arts; five Early American rooms. Pre-Columbian and Indian art. Children's Museum, lectures, films, musical programs.*

**New Mexico, Museum of:** Admin. bldg. at 113 Lincoln St., P.O. Box 2087, Santa Fe, N.M. 87503. Museum of Fine Arts, Museum of International Folk Art, Palace of the Governors. Open: daily 9–4:45 (closed Mon.; also Oct. 1-March 15). Laboratory of Anthropology. Open: Mon.-Fri. 8–12, 1–5 (closed Sat., Sun., and hldys.).

*Exhibits of fine arts, folk arts; history of Southwest and of American Indian; archeology; ethnology.*

**New Orleans Museum of Art:** Lelong Ave., City Park, New Orleans, La. 70179. Open: Tues., Wed., Fri., Sat., Sun. 10–5; Thurs. 1–9 (closed Mon.; also hldys., Mardi Gras, Good Friday).

*Old master paintings from 14th to 19th centuries, including Kress Collection of Italian Art; 20th-century European and American art; African, Oriental and pre-Columbian collections; Latin American Colonial painting and sculpture; prints and photographs.*

**New York State Historical Association;** Lake Rd., Rte. 80, Cooperstown, N.Y. 13326.

*Administers Farmers' Museum and Fenimore House.* See *those entries. Also, Cooperstown Graduate Program in American Folk Culture, History Museum Training and Art Conservation.*

**Newark Museum:** 43–49 Washington St., Newark, N.J. 07101. Open: daily 12–5, hldys. 1–5 (closed Jan. 1, July 4, Thanksgiving, Dec. 25). Free.

*Collections: American painting, sculpture; Tibetan, Chinese, Japanese arts; decorative arts, ancient glass and ceramics; natural science, ethnology. Planetarium. Ballantine House restoration. Fire Museum. Sculpture garden. Junior Museum.*

**Norton Simon Museum of Art at Pasadena:** Colorado Blvd. at Orange Grove, Pasadena, Calif. 91105. Open: Thurs.-Sun. 12–6. Adm. $1.50 (students and senior citizens, 50¢; children under 12, free).

*Paintings by old masters and from Italian Renaissance; Dutch 17th-century school; paintings and sculpture by Impressionist and early 20th-century masters; Southeast Asian stone sculptures and bronzes.*

**Putnam Museum:** 1717 W. 12th St., Davenport, Iowa 52804. Open: Tues.-Sat. 9–5, Sun. 1–5 (closed Mon.; also Jan. 1, Easter, Memorial Day, July 4, Labor Day, Thanksgiving, Dec. 25). Adm. 75¢ (children 25¢).

*Art, history and natural history collections from the Orient, Africa, and North, Central, and South America.*

**Ringling Museums:** P.O. Box 1838, Sarasota, Fla. 33578. John and Mable Ringling Museum of Art, Asolo Theater, Ringling Residence, Museum of the Circus. Open: Mon.-Fri. 9 a.m.-10 p.m., Sat. 9–5, Sun. 11–6. Adm.: $3.50 (groups, $3; children under 12, free).

*Extensive collection of Rubens and Baroque art. Asolo is only 18th-century Italian theater in America. Circus Museum contains gilded wagons and memorabilia.*

**Rosicrucian Egyptian Museum and Art Gallery:** Park and Naglee Aves., San Jose, Calif. 95191. Open: Tues.-Fri. 9–5, Sat.-Mon. 12–5 (closed Jan. 1, July 4, Aug. 2, Thanksgiving, Dec. 25). Free.

*Egyptian and Oriental antiquities. Mummies, statuary, jewelry, utensils, clothing. Reproduction of Egyptian rock tomb. Babylonian collection. Art gallery.*

**St. Louis Art Museum:** Forest Park, St. Louis, Mo. 63110. Open: Tues. 2:30–9:30, Wed.-Sun. 10–5 (closed Mon.; also Jan. 1, Dec. 25). Free.

*American, European, and Asian painting, sculpture, and decorative arts. African, Oceanic, pre-Columbian, and American Indian arts.*

**San Diego, Fine Arts Gallery of:** Balboa Park, San Diego, Calif. 92112. Open: Tues.-Sun. 10–5 (closed Mon.; also Jan. 1, Thanksgiving, Dec. 25). Free.

*European paintings of Renaissance and Baroque periods. American paintings; Oriental and modern art.*

**San Diego Museum of Man:** 1350 El Prado, Balboa Park, San Diego, Calif. 92101. Open: daily 10–4:45 (closed Jan. 1, Thanksgiving, Dec. 25). Adm. 75¢ (children 6–16, 10¢; under 6, free). Free adm. on Wed.

*Exhibits on Man of the Western Americas, early man, Indians' life style, and Mayan civilization.*

**San Diego Society of Natural History—Natural History Museum:** Balboa Park, San Diego, Calif. 92112. Open: wkdys. and Sun. 10–4:30 (closed Jan. 1, Dec. 25). Adm. $1 (children, free).

*Mammals, birds, fossils, shells, plants, insects, minerals, marine biology. Emphasis on Southwestern U.S., Sonora, and Lower California.*

**San Francisco, The Fine Arts Museums of, M.H. de**

**Young Memorial Museum:** Kennedy Dr. and Eighth Ave., Golden Gate Park, San Francisco, Calif. 94118. Open: Daily 10–5. Adm. 75¢ (children 12–18, 25¢; under 12 and over 65, free). Free adm. first day of month.

*Art of Europe, America, Ancient Egypt, Greece, and Rome; traditional arts of Africa, Oceania, and the Americas. Paintings, sculpture, and decorative arts.* See also *California Palace of the Legion of Honor.*

**San Francisco Museum of Modern Art:** Van Ness at McAllister, San Francisco, Calif. 94102. Open: Tues.-Fri. 10–10, Sat. and Sun. 10–5 (closed Mon.; also Jan. 1, Memorial Day, July 4, Labor Day, Thanksgiving, Dec. 25). Free ($1 adm. for changing exhibitions).

*Contemporary American and international paintings, sculpture, graphics, photography, and ceramics.*

**Seattle Art Museum:** Volunteer Park, Seattle, Wash. 98112. Open: Tues.-Sat. 10–5, Thurs. 7–10 p.m., Sun. 12–5 (closed Mon.; also Jan. 1, Thanksgiving, Dec. 25). Adm. $1 (50¢ for students and senior citizens; children under 12 with adult, free). Free on Thurs.

*Asian art and jade; Greek and Roman art; 14th-20th century European paintings; tribal art. Samuel H. Kress Collection of 14th-18th century. European painting and sculpture. Modern Art Pavilion is in Seattle Center.*

**Southwest Museum, Inc.:** Marmion Way at Museum Dr., Highland Pk., Los Angeles, Calif. 90065. Open: Tues.-Sun. 1–4:45 (closed mid-Aug.-mid-Sept., Mon., Jan. 1, July 4, Thanksgiving, Dec. 25). Free.

*American Indian exhibits, ancient and modern. Research library. Casa de Adobe, reproduction of adobe hacienda, at 4605 N. Figueroa St.; open Wed., Sat., and Sun. 1–4:45 (closed mid-Aug.-mid-Sept.).*

**Toledo Museum of Art, The:** Monroe St. at Scottwood Ave., Toledo, Ohio 43697. Open: wkdys. 9–5; Sun. and Mon. 1–5 (closed legal hldys.). Free.

*European and American paintings and decorative arts. Ancient and medieval art; books, manuscripts, prints, graphics. Ancient and American glass.*

**Virginia Museum of Fine Arts:** Boulevard and Grove Ave., Richmond, Va. 23221. Open: Tues.-Sat. 11–5, Sun. 1–5 (closed Mon.; also Jan. 1, July 4, Dec. 25). Adm. 50¢.

**Wadsworth Atheneum:** 600 Main St., Hartford, Conn. 06103. Open: Tues.-Fri. 11–3, Sat. and Sun. 11–5 (closed Mon.; also Jan. 1, July 4, Thanksgiving, Dec. 25). Suggested contribution: adults, $1; teenagers, 50¢ (children free).

*European and American paintings and drawings. Sculpture. Bronzes, silver, porcelain, American period furniture, firearms.*

**Walters Art Gallery:** 600 North Charles St., Baltimore, Md. 21201. Open: Mon. 1–5, Tues.-Sat. 11–5 (July-Aug. Mon. 1–4, Tues.-Sat. 11–4), Sun. and hldys. 2–5 (closed Jan. 1, July 4, Thanksgiving, Dec. 24–25). Free.

*Art from ancient empires through 19th-century Europe. Collections of paintings, sculpture, decorative arts, and manuscripts.*

**Wheelwright Museum, The:** 704 Camino Lejo, Santa Fe, N.M. 87501. Open: Tues.-Sat. 10–5, Sun. 2–5 (closed Mon.; also Jan. 1, Thanksgiving, Dec. 25). Free.

*Baskets, textiles, pottery, jewelry. Contemporary Indian painting. (Formerly the Museum of Navajo Ceremonial Art.)*

**Worcester Art Museum:** 55 Salisbury St., Worcester, Mass. 01608. Open: Tues.-Sat. 10–5, Sun. 2–5 (closed Mon.; also Jan. 1, July 4, Thanksgiving, Dec. 25). Adm. $1 (children under 14 and senior citizens, 50¢; children under 5, free).

*Art from Egyptian to modern times, with emphasis on painting and sculpture.*

1. Summer hours (April 1-Labor Day), Mon.-Sat. 10–9, Sun. 12–9. 2. Send inquiries to Museum Division, Oak Ridge Associated Universities, P.O. Box 117, Oak Ridge, Tenn. 37830. 3. Combination rates are available for Farmers' Museum and Fenimore House.

## Squeezing the Family Budget

The average U.S. family has had to boost it pretax income by at least two thirds to maintain a 1970 standard of living, according to The Conference Board.

The Consumer Price Index shot up by 56% between 1970 and 1977 and rose more than 6% in 1978. More than a dollar was needed in 1978 to purchase what 60¢ bought in 1970. Family earnings also increased, but the federal income tax took a larger share of high incomes. Social Security tax rates have also risen sharply since 1970.

As a result of these pressures, a family of four making $13,000-plus in 1970 needed more than $22,500 in 1978 to maintain the same standard of living. This was up from $21,000 in 1977.

Federal income and Social Security taxes siphoned off about $4,000 from the $22,500 household's 1978 income. Price hikes since 1970 consumed $7,500 of the $18,500 left.

Other income brackets have experienced similar drains. The $6,500 household in 1970 needed $11,000 in 1978 to ensure equivalent purchasing power, while the $20,000 family had to earn $34,000.

Across the country, the share of personal income going to state and local taxes has been rising. In 1977, state and local taxes (income, sales, and property) took an estimated 9% of total U.S. personal income, while federal taxes (income, Social Security, and excise) took about 14%.

The actual experience of the typical American family in the 1970s has been to just break even. The median income of U.S. households grew from around $10,000 in 1970 to some $16,000 in 1977. But after inflation and federal taxes, their actual purchasing power remained about the same.

# Buying Wisely

*Karl F. Lauby, Vice-President*
*The Better Business Bureau of Metropolitan New York, Inc.*

Know and exercise your rights in the marketplace. In addition to legal rights, by statute and in common law, you should expect a firm to comply with fair business practices. For example, you have rights to full information about the products or services, to courteous and honest treatment, to fair prices, and to effective services and efficient products that live up to maximum performance claims. When your complaint is valid, you are entitled to quick recourse and effective adjustment.

## The Consumer's Responsibility

You must also exercise responsibilities. You—not any government agency, consumer advocate, Better Business Bureau, retailer or manufacturer—are responsible for your own protection. Consumer protection laws and agencies, despite their names, cannot protect you against your own ignorance, timidity, impulse, or greed.

You do not need to know, and cannot possibly learn, everything about every gadget or service you want to buy. But when you make a major cash out lay, thoroughly gather and carefully evaluate information *before you buy.* Insist on receiving full value for every dollar you spend.

Consumer self-protection begins with your devoting some time, thought, and energy to developing knowledge. Armed with accurate and complete information, you will be in a position to trade hard-earned money for quality goods and services that enrich your life.

## Sources of Information

Finding the necessary information before you buy is not always easy. Where do you go? Two tips: Check several sources listed below. Don't be content with one. Second, don't be timid. Ask a lot of questions. It's your money.

**Better Business Bureaus** can give you reliability reports on a specific company and general advice on numerous subjects, from home insulation to dating services to business opportunities to buying a pet.

**Industry trade associations** often distribute consumer booklets which set forth standards for a product's minimum performance and a member's business practices. For the correct trade association, check a directory of associations at the reference desk of your local public library or look in the nearest big-city *Yellow Pages* under "Associations."

**The U.S. Government Printing Office** offers booklets free or at nominal cost. For a list of publications, write to Public Documents Department Distribution Center, Pueblo, Colo., 81002. Major cities have a local U.S. Government Printing Office retail bookstore, with many publications available.

**State university schools** of home economics or agriculture, or home service and consumers affairs departments of public utility companies may have booklets on a wide range of subjects.

**Government consumer agencies** at all levels—local, state, and national—distribute booklets on their specialities or on current topics of timely interest. You can usually find the agencies listed under the government section in your telephone directory.

Know the local and state laws and regulations that offer you protection. Your state attorney general, city or county consumer affairs department, or county district attorney may be able to mail you a summary of the basic laws. Often local or state laws cover such things as contract cancellation procedures, door-to-door sales, dating of perishables, unit pricing, refund and exchange policies, savings claims in advertising, and a host of common occurrences in the market place. Keep a copy handy to review from time to time.

You should expect **the retailer** or **the manufacturer** to be able to fully inform you about the product or service you are buying. Know enough about the product and your needs to ask intelligent questions at the time of sale. And do not be too timid to request references and challenge claims that do not make sense to you. If you do not get satisfactory answers to ALL your questions, do not buy!

## Product Performance Claims

Product performance tests and comparisons are reported in numerous publications, including *Consumer Reports,* published by the Consumers Union, 256 Washington St., Mount Vernon, N.Y. 10550. Your local public library probably has a subscription.

Ask a retailer or a manufacturer for test results to substantiate any advertised performance claim that you rely on. Don't be surprised if a salesman is taken aback by your question. Ask it again. You may not get substantiation because there may not be any. But learn that *before* you buy to determine if you still want to buy.

## Checking Out the Store and the Transaction

**1.** Get the full corporate, proprietorship, or partnership name and address, and the name of the owner or president. Find out how many years the firm has been in business at the same location.

**2.** Ask for references—a bank, trade creditors, suppliers, and names of satisfied customers who have had similar work done between six months and two years ago.

**3.** If you buy a product or service with a warranty, get the warranty in writing with terms and limitations clearly spelled out so that you understand them. Who pays for parts, labor, pick-up, and delivery?

**4.** If your product might require service, check the firm's service department. Is it conveniently located? When is it open? Is it well staffed and well equipped?

**5.** If you think you might want to exchange the item or might want a cash refund, get the firm's refund and exchange policy in writing before purchase. Understand the limitations.

**6.** If buying on credit, get written details of the interest charges calculated as an annual percentage rate. (Before you buy on credit, if you don't know how to calculate the annual percentage rate of interest, find out.)

**7.** Check the store's reliability with friends, neighbors, and fellow workers. Check with the BBB and the local licensing or consumer agency for confirmation of what you have learned. But one caution: Neither a license nor a complaint-free BBB report is a guarantee of satisfaction or recourse if you have a complaint.

Do comparison shopping *before* you buy, not after. Reduce the chances of suffering buyer's remorse—discovering too late that you could have bought the product for less money elsewhere or that you should not have bought it at all. In order to make competition work for you, you've got to shop the market!

## When You Have a Complaint

Go back to the seller and state your claim calmly and factually. If necessary, speak to the owner or manager.

If that does not work, put your complaint in writing—a short, factual letter to the store president or owner stating what adjustment you want and why you are entitled to it. Attach a photocopy—never an original—of a sales slip, receipt, warranty, or contract. Keep a copy of your letter for your records. Give a date by which you want an answer or action.

If the retailer won't help, try the manufacturer. Manufacturers have learned to listen to consumers more attentively in recent years. Customer service is often a corporate executive's primary responsibility. Many national trade associations representing major consumer industries operate advisory panels to assist consumers by mediating product problems involving their member companies.

Usually the manufacturer is responsible for providing warranty service. Make sure you hold him accountable. The manufacturer's name and address usually appear on the product's nameplate or in the owner's manual. If it does not, refer to the standard corporation directories available in local libraries: Dun and Bradstreet's **Million Dollar Directory** and Standard and Poor's **Register of Corporations, Directors and Executives.** You can also obtain corporate names and addresses from the **National Association of Manufacturers,** 1776 F St., N.W., Washington, D.C. 20006, or the **Chamber of Commerce of the United States,** 1615 H St., N.W., Washington, D.C. 20006.

If necessary, go to a third party, such as a BBB, government agency, industry-sponsored group, consumer organization, or small claims court.

## Where to Get Help

**Write a letter to the BBB.** Attach a copy of your letter to the company with a covering note telling the BBB you received no satisfaction to date. If your complaint appears valid, the BBB will get in touch with the firm. Many businesses prefer to adjust complaints quickly rather than amass an unfavorable customer experience record in BBB files and have it reported to inquirers.

If the BBB does not resolve the complaint for you, try **a city, county, or state consumer protection agency.** Usually they are listed in the telephone book among government agencies. Many agencies can mediate consumer complaints, issue summonses, hold hearings, assess fines, revoke licenses, and initiate suits for violations of regulations. In most states, the state consumer protection agency is an arm of either the attorney general's office or the office of the governor. Some have toll-free "800" telephone numbers for use by state residents.

Complaints that might involve local or state fraud or violations of other than purely local laws may be filed with the frauds division of the district attorney's office or the state attorney general.

Numerous national agencies are charged with protecting consumers. Foremost among them is the **Federal Trade Commission.** Any consumer may file a complaint with the FTC if the firm causing the problem is involved in interstate commerce. But the FTC is not primarily involved in the resolution of individual complaints. They are looking for widespread patterns of unfair or deceptive practices which adversely affect thousands if not millions of consumers. They attempt to correct these problems by issuing and enforcing trade rules and regulations. In the process, your individual complaint may be resolved.

The **U.S. Postal Inspection Service** investigates the fraudulent use of the mails and shares with the FTC the handling of mail-order complaints alleging non-delivery. The FBI looks into fraud by telephone. Product safety is the responsibility of the **Consumer Product Safety Commission,** but the safety and effectiveness of many drugs and medicines are the responsibilities of the **Food and Drug Administration.** Interstate moving firms are regulated by the **Interstate Commerce Commission** and the airlines by the **Civil Aeronautics Board.** As you can see, finding the proper agency is fundamental to complaining effectively. If the federal government maintains an information service in your city, use it. Otherwise, call your congressman to get the proper agency.

All these agencies feed potential criminal cases into the closest regional office of the **United States Attorney.** The odds are that your individual complaint will have little impact on an agency with a national obligation, but it may well be part of a pattern that provokes an investigation, litigation, or legislation.

**Voluntary Consumer Groups.** Throughout the country there are state and local voluntary consumer groups, many of which assist consumers with advice and serve as mediators of complaints. Typical organizations call themselves "consumer associations" or "consumer councils." More than 200 such groups are affiliated with the **Consumer Federation of America,** Suite 901, 1012 14th St., N.W., Washington, D.C. 20005. Write for the nearest consumer action group.

**Media.** Newspapers, radio, and TV stations have columns and programs to assist consumers. These carry such names as "Hot-Line," "Action Line," and "Help!" The prestige and local influence of the media, plus their extensive contacts in business and government, often produce results where an individual's efforts fail. Check local media to determine whether such services are available in your community. Also, don't forget that the media carrying an advertisement for the product or service that you are complaining about may have been the beginning of your problem. Send a copy of your letter to the newspaper's publisher or the TV or radio station's general manager asking how such an advertiser gets into their pages or onto their airwaves and what they are willing to do to help you with your complaint.

**Arbitration.** Most Better Business Bureaus in the United States now offer voluntary consumer-business arbitration as a no-cost alternative to expensive and lengthy court procedures. Both parties to the dispute must agree, not only to binding arbitration, but to the acceptability of the arbitrator. They submit their case to an impartial volunteer arbitrator, who, after an informal hearing and often after his own investigation, renders a final determination, known as an award. No attorneys are required, although some parties do use their attorneys' services. While BBBs administer these programs, they do not serve as arbitrators. In most states, courts of law will enforce the arbitrator's award without rehearing the case.

**Small Claims Courts.** Consumers and businesses in many localities may take their dispute to a small claims court, some of which will hear cases with dollar values as high as $1,000. As in BBB arbitration hearings, procedures are informal and attorneys are not necessary. Court fees are usually quite low, and these fees often are returned to the party winning the suit. Details on pre-hearing requirements and procedures are available from the clerk of the court. For addresses and phone numbers, check your telephone directory under municipal, county, or state headings.

Fair-minded businesses have always been responsible to the consumer for the products and services they provide. Today, consumers have many new ways to influence business and exercise their rights. Make sure you use them. Get full information before you buy, a fair price through comparative shopping, and satisfaction if you have a complaint.

## Federal Consumer Offices

The federal government publishes a *Directory of Federal Consumer Offices.* This directory lists the addresses and phone numbers of federal offices and agencies that deal with a variety of areas of interest to consumers. It is arranged by subject. A free copy of the complete directory may be obtained by writing to the Consumer Information Center, Pueblo, Colo. 81009. Following are some selected offices:

**Advertising:** Director, Bureau of Consumer Protection, Federal Trade Commission, Washington, D.C. 20580

**Air Travel—Routes and Service:** Director, Office of the Consumer Advocate, Civil Aeronautics Board, Washington, D.C. 20423

**Alcoholism, Drug Abuse, and Mental Illness:** Office of Public Affairs, Alcohol, Drug Abuse, and Mental Health Service, 5600 Fishers Lane, Rockville, Md. 20857

**Auto Safety and Highways:** Director, Office of Public and Consumer Affairs, Transportation Department, Washington, D.C. 20590, *and* National Highway Traffic Safety Administration, toll-free hotline, 800–424–9393

**Children and Youth:** Director of Public Information, Office of Human Development Services, Department of Health, Education, and Welfare, Washington, D.C. 20201

**Consumer Affairs—Complaints:** Director, Office of Consumer Affairs, Department of Health, Education, and Welfare, 621 Reporters Bldg., Washington, D.C. 20201. This office serves as a clearinghouse for complaints from consumers. Complaints not handled directly are referred to appropriate federal, state, or local offices.

**Credit:** Director, Bureau of Consumer Protection, Federal Trade Commission, Washington, D.C. 20850

**Crime Insurance:** Federal Crime Insurance, Department of Housing and Urban Development, P.O. Box 41033, Washington, D.C. 20014

**Drugs and Cosmetics:** Consumer Inquiry Section, Food and Drug Administration, 5600 Fishers Lane, Rockville, Md. 20852

**Energy:** Director for Consumer Affairs, Department of Energy, Washington, D.C. 20461

**Food:** Assistant Secretary for Food and Consumer Services, U.S. Department of Agriculture, Washington, D.C. 20205 *and* Consumer Inquiry Section, Food and Drug Administration, 5600 Fishers Lane, Rockville, Md. 20852

**Handicapped:** Director, Division of Public Information, Office of Human Development Services, Department of Health, Education, and Welfare, Washington, D.C. 20201

**Housing:** Assistant Secretary for Neighborhoods, Voluntary Associations, and Consumer Protection, Department of Housing and Urban Development, Washington, D.C. 20410.

**Mail:** Check with your local postal inspector about problems relating to mail fraud and undelivered merchandise, or contact the Chief Postal Inspector, U.S. Postal Service, Washington, D.C. 20260

**Medicaid-Medicare:** Health Care Financing Administration, Department of Health, Education, and Welfare, Washington, D.C. 20201

**Moving:** Interstate Commerce Commission, toll-free hotline, 800–424–9312

**Pensions:** Office of Communications, Pension Benefit Guaranty Corporation, 2020 K St., N.W., Washington, D.C. 20006 *and* Labor Management Standards Administration, Department of Labor, Washington, D.C. 20210

**Runaway Children:** The National Runaway Hotline, toll-free, 800–621–4000

**Travel Information:** U.S. Travel Service, Department of Commerce, Washington, D.C. 20230

**Wages and Working Conditions:** Employment Standards Administration, Department of Labor, Washington, D.C. 20210

# Consumer Credit

*Personal Credit Center, Chemical Bank*

## What Is A Credit Rating?

Your ability to open a charge account, get a new credit card, or take out a cash loan depends on your credit standing. A creditor can readily determine your credit-worthiness through voluminous dossiers available in the files of some 2,500 credit bureaus throughout the U.S. These bureaus process from 125 to 150 million consumer credit reports each year.

Credit bureaus, however, do not rate how good or bad a credit risk you are. They simply collect information from merchants with whom you have credit, public records, and other sources that can be used by banks and merchants to decide whether you meet their credit standards. The information may include your name, address, occupation, employer, earnings record, moving habits, repayment patterns on previous loans, and records of any court proceedings against you.

The guidelines for a good credit risk vary from lender to lender. A department store may be satisfied if you are in the habit of repaying charges within 30 to 60 days. A bank may require that you repay loan installments on the due dates. Or lenders sometimes summarize their rating policy in terms of the "Three C's" of credit: character, capacity, and capital.

## Basic Types and Maturities of Loans

There are two basic types of loans and three major maturities on loans. The types are the single-payment loan and the installment loan. You must repay a single-payment loan in one lump sum, whether upon demand or at the end of a fixed maturity date. A single-payment loan is usually made against collateral, such as stocks, bonds, insurance policies, or certain other valuable assets. You must repay an installment loan in specific amounts at periodic intervals. Usually you repay in equal amounts every month over a period of from 12 to 60 months.

The three major maturities are short-term, intermediate-term, and long-term loans. Short-term loans are most frequently used to buy goods and services. You are using short-term credit when you pledge to repay within 30 days to within three years. Intermediate-term credit is generally used to finance major improvements or repairs on your home. The mortgage is the best illustration of a long-term loan.

## Sources of Loans in Cash

| Source | Comments |
|---|---|
| Full Service Commercial Banks | Loans compare favorably with rates from most other sources and so do maturity terms. |
| Licensed Small Loan Companies | Smaller loans. Greater availability. Higher interest rates. |
| Credit Unions | May be an inexpensive borrowing source if you are a member. |
| Savings Bank or Savings and Loan Associations | Specialize in mortgage and home improvement loans, but have mobile home, education, and personal loans. Borrow own money with passbook loan at relatively modest rates. |
| Life Insurance Companies | May be your number-one source for money, if you have regular life insurance policy (not term coverage). Your insurance company will lend you the cash surrender value of your policy at a specified and relatively low interest rate. |
| Bank Credit Cards | Quick, easy, and convenient for the credit-worthy. Interest rates up to 18% a year. |
| Home Mortgages | If your home is worth more than your mortgage liability, you can raise money by refinancing or obtaining a second mortgage. Not necessarily inexpensive, especially if you are giving up a lower rate of interest. |

## Typical Statistics for Commercial Banks

Maximum amounts you may borrow, interest rates, and maximum maturities are so flexible and variable from year to year, loan to loan, and area to area that "typical" has little real meaning other than as a rough guide as to what you may expect. However, here are some "typical" statistics as of 1977:

### Maximums You May Borrow

Personal loan: up to $15,000
Auto loan: $5,000
Mortgage: $100,000
Home improvement: $10,000
Federal-state-guaranteed student loans: $2,500
Check loan: $5,000
Bank credit card: $500 to $5,000

### Annual Percentage Rates

Personal Loan: 10.5 to 13%
Automobile
  New car: 9 to 12%
  Used car: 11 to 14%

Check loan: 12 to 18%
Mortgage loan: 8 to 11%
Home improvement loan: 10 to 14%
Passbook loan: 9 to 13.5%
Secured loan: 10 to 13%
Federal-guaranteed student loan: 7%
Credit card loan: 12 to 18%
Education loan: 9 to 12%

**Maximum Maturities**

Personal, auto, secured: 3 to 4 years
Home improvement: 5 to 10 years
First mortgage: Up to 35 years
Second mortgage: 3 to 10 years
Refinancing mortgage: Up to 30 years
Student loans: Up to 10 years (after graduation)

## An Explanation of Percentage Rate Charges

The Truth in Lending law makes it mandatory for lenders or merchants to provide you with complete information about the cost of credit. The theory is that such information will put you in a position to shop around before you borrow. But to understand what you are looking for, you need to know a few terms:

When you know the *annual percentage rate* and the *finance charge*, you know the cost of borrowing money. The *annual percentage rate* (APR) is the key yardstick by which you can measure and compare the costs of all types of credit. It essentially relates the finance charge to the amount of credit you get and the amount of time you have to repay the money. The *finance charge* is the total of all charges you are asked to pay for credit. Among the charges are interest, loan fees, finder's fees, service charges, points, investigation fees, premiums for life insurance if it is required, and amount paid as a discount. Such costs as taxes, license fees, certain legal fees, and some real estate closing costs are not included in the finance charge.

Finance charges on bank credit cards and revolving credit accounts are usually expressed as a *percentage of the unpaid balance* per month, as of the billing date. This is a simple monthly rate, which is then multiplied by 12 to give you the annual percentage rate. For instance, a monthly rate of 1½% becomes an annual percentage rate of 18%. The rates on credit card accounts are higher than on a simple installment loan because the amounts are smaller and the monthly processing expenses are higher. However, because institutions vary in the way they charge, the law provides for an explanation on the revolving-credit agreement given to the customer before the account is used.

Mortgage rates are traditionally described in terms of simple annual interest rates. However, if points, a finder's fee, or certain other charges are required, these now—under the Truth in Lending law—must be included in the finance charge.

To compare the dollar cost of different ways of charging interest, take as an example a $500 loan to be repaid in 12 monthly installments. If the rates charged are:

- 1% per month on the unpaid balance, the dollar cost will be about $32
- 6% annual interest on the unpaid balance, the dollar cost will be about $16
- 6% annual interest "add-on," the dollar cost will be about $30

If the payments are spread over 18 months, each payment would be smaller, but the total dollar cost would be higher. For example, at 1% per month on the unpaid balance of a $500 loan, the cost over 18 months would be about $47 compared to $32 for 12 months.

If you repay a loan before the final maturity date, you are entitled by law to a proportionate rebate.

## New Consumer Aid

The second edition of the *Consumer Sourcebook* (Gale Research Co.) appeared in 1978. This comprehensive, two-volume compilation of consumer information covers governmental and other organizations, media services, sources of recourse, etc. It should be available in many libraries.

## Consumer Information Catalog

For a copy of the free *Consumer Information Catalog,* a listing of more than 200 selected federal consumer publications on such topics as child care, automobiles, health, employment, housing, energy, etc., send a postcard to the Consumer Information Center, Pueblo, Colo. 81009.

# The Economics of Used Cars

*Source:* The Hertz Corporation.

Second only to homes, automobiles are the most expensive items that most people buy. The following data point out that many Americans are continually searching for ways to hold auto costs down:

Nearly three out of four U.S. passenger cars bought for personal driving are second-hand. An average of 13.5 million used autos were sold annually from 1967 to 1976. Motorists spend more than $21.3 billion a year for used cars; new car dealers account for over $14 billion of this total.

For used cars from one to four years old, purchase prices ranged from 20 to 80 percent below new car outlays. Savings on running expenses ran 10 to 50 percent under typical new car expenses.

The greatest potential savings are realized if a used car is kept at least three years, at an assumed 10,000 miles per year of travel. A three-year-old used car driven 10,000 miles a year for another three years costs half as much to run as the same car purchased new and also driven for three years.

Only about 12 percent of all new U.S. cars sold are traded after one year; another 14 percent are sold at the end of two years. In the third year, nearly 17 percent of the cars are traded; another 14.5 percent are sold after four years of operation.

After ten years of operation, 40 to 45 percent of cars are still on the road.

# SPORTS

## Sports Personalities

A name in parentheses is the original name or form of name. Localities are places of birth. Dates of birth appear as month/day/year. **Boldface** years in parentheses are dates of **(birth-death).**
Information has been gathered from many sources, including the individuals themselves. However, the *Information Please Almanac* cannot guarantee the accuracy of every individual item.

**Aaron,** Hank (Henry) (baseball); Mobile, Ala., 2/5/1934
**Abdul-Jabbar,** Kareem (Lewis Ferdinand Alcindor, Jr.) (basketball); New York City, 4/16/1947
**Abel,** Sid (hockey); Melville, Saskatchewan, Canada, 2/22/1918
**Adderly,** Herbert A. (football); Philadelphia, 6/8/1939
**Alcindor,** Lew. *See* Abdul-Jabbar
**Ali,** Muhammad (Cassius Clay) (boxing); Louisville, Ky., 1/18/1942
**Allen,** Dick (Richard Anthony) (baseball); Wampum, Pa., 3/8/1942
**Allison,** Bobby (Robert Arthur) (auto racing); Hueytown, Ala., 12/3/1937
**Alston,** Walter (baseball); Butler County, Ohio, 12/1/1911
**Alworth,** Lance (football); Houston, 8/3/1940
**Anderson,** Dick (Richard P.) (football); Midland, Mich., 2/10/1946
**Anderson,** Donny (Gary Donny) (football); Brooklyn, N.Y., 4/3/1949
**Anderson,** Sparky (George) (baseball); Bridgewater, S.D., 2/22/1934
**Andretti,** Mario (auto racing); Montona, Trieste, Italy, 2/28/1940
**Arcaro,** Eddie (George Edward) (jockey); Cincinnati, 2/19/1916
**Archer,** George (golf); San Francisco, 10/1/1939
**Arfons,** Arthur Eugene (auto racing); Akron, Ohio, 2/3/1926
**Ashe,** Arthur (tennis); Richmond, Va., 7/10/1943
**Austin,** Tracy (tennis); Rolling Hills, Calif., 12/2/1962
**Axelrod,** Albert (fencing); New York City, 2/21/1921
**Babashoff,** Shirley (swimming); Whittier, Calif., 1/31/1957
**Baer,** Max (boxer); Omaha, Neb. **(1909–1959)**
**Bakken,** Jim (James Leroy) (football); Madison, Wis., 11/2/1940
**Ball,** Catherine (Catie) (swimming); Jacksonville, Fla., 9/30/1951
**Banks,** Ernie (baseball); Dallas, 1/31/1931
**Bannister,** Roger (runner); Harrow, England, 3/24/1929
**Barry,** Rick (Richard) (basketball); Elizabeth, N.J., 3/28/1944
**Bauer,** Hank (Henry) (baseball); East St. Louis, Ill., 7/31/1922
**Baugh,** Sammy (football); Temple, Tex., 3/17/1914
**Bayi,** Filbert (runner); Karratu, Tanganyika, 6/23/1953
**Baylor,** Elgin (basketball); Washington, D.C., 9/16/1934
**Beamon,** Bob (long jumper); New York City, 8/2/1946
**Beard,** Frank (golf); Dallas, 5/1/1939
**Beliveau,** Jean (hockey); Three Rivers, Quebec, Canada, 8/31/1931
**Bell,** Earl (track); Panama Canal Zone, 8/26/1955
**Beman,** Deane (golf); Washington, D.C., 4/22/1938
**Bench,** Johnny (Johnny Lee) (baseball); Oklahoma City, 12/7/1947
**Berg,** Patty (Patricia Jane) (golf); Minneapolis, 2/13/1918
**Berning,** Susie Maxwell (golf); Pasadena, Calif., 7/22/1941
**Berra,** Yogi (Lawrence) (baseball); St. Louis, 5/12/1925
**Biletnikoff,** Frederick (football); Erie, Pa., 2/23/1943
**Blaik,** Earl H. (football); Detroit, 2/15/1897
**Blanda,** George Frederick (football); Youngwood, Pa., 9/17/1927
**Blue,** Vida (baseball); Mansfield, La., 7/28/1949
**Boggs,** Phil (diving); Akron, Ohio, 12/20/1943
**Boozer,** Emerson (football); Augusta, Ga., 7/4/1943
**Borg,** Björn (tennis); Stockholm, 6/6/1956
**Boros,** Julius (golf); Fairfield, Conn., 3/3/1920
**Boston,** Ralph (long jumper); Laurel, Miss., 5/9/1939
**Bradley,** Bill (William Warren) (basketball); Crystal City, Mo., 7/28/1943
**Bradshaw,** Terry (football); Shreveport, La., 9/2/1948
**Breedlove,** Craig (Norman) (speed driving); Los Angeles, 3/23/1938
**Brock,** Louis Clark (baseball); El Dorado, Ark., 6/18/1939
**Brown,** Doris (runner); Tacoma, Wash., 9/17/1942
**Brown,** Jimmy (football); St. Simon Island, Ga., 2/17/1936
**Brown,** Larry (football); Clairton, Pa., 9/19/1947
**Brumel,** Valeri (high jumper); Tolbuzino, Siberia, 4/14/1942
**Brundage,** Avery (Olympics executive); Detroit **(1887–1975)**
**Bryant,** Rosalyn Evette (track); Chicago, 1/7/1956
**Burton,** Michael (swimming); Des Moines, Iowa, 7/3/1947
**Butkus,** Dick (Richard Marvin) (football); Chicago, 12/9/1942
**Campanella,** Roy (baseball); Homestead, Pa., 11/19/1921
**Caponi,** Donna Maria. *See* Young, Donna
**Cappelletti,** Gino (football); Keewatin, Minn., 3/26/1934
**Carew,** Rod (Rodney Cline) (baseball); Gatun, Panama, 10/1/1945
**Carlos,** John (sprinter); New York City, 6/5/1945
**Carner,** Joanne Gunderson (Mrs. Don) (golf); Kirkland, Wash., 3/4/1939
**Casals,** Rosemary (tennis); San Francisco, 9/16/1948
**Casper,** Billy (golf); San Diego, Calif., 6/24/1931
**Caulkins,** Tracy (swimming); Winona, Minn., 1/11/63
**Cauthen,** Steve (jockey); Covington, Ky., 5/1/1960
**Chamberlain,** Wilt (Wilton) (basketball); Philadelphia, 8/21/1936
**Chapot,** Frank (equestrian); Camden, N.J., 2/24/1934
**Clarke,** Bobby (Robert Earle) (hockey); Flin Flon, Manitoba, Canada, 8/13/1949
**Clay,** Cassius. *See* Ali, Muhammad
**Clemente,** Roberto Walker (baseball); Carolina, Puerto Rico **(1934–1972)**
**Cobb,** Tyrus Raymond (Ty) (baseball); Narrows, Ga. **(1886–1961)**
**Cochran,** Barbara Ann (skiing); Claremont, N.H., 1/4/1951
**Cochran,** Marilyn (skiing); Burlington, Vt., 2/7/1950
**Cochran,** Robert (skiing); Claremont, N.H., 12/11/1951
**Colavito,** Rocky (Rocco Domenico) (baseball); New York City, 8/10/1933
**Comaneci,** Nadia (gymnast); Onesti, Romania, 11/12/1961
**Connors,** Jimmy (James Scott) (tennis); East St. Louis, Ill., 9/2/1952
**Cordero,** Angel (jockey); Santurce, Puerto Rico, 5/8/1942
**Cournoyer,** Yvan Serge (hockey); Drummondville, Quebec, Canada, 11/22/1943
**Court,** Margaret Smith (tennis); Albury, New South Wales, Australia, 7/16/1942
**Cousy,** Bob (basketball); New York City, 8/9/1928
**Cronin,** Joe (baseball executive); San Francisco, 10/12/1906
**Csonka,** Larry (Lawrence Richard) (football); Stow, Ohio, 12/25/1946
**Dancer,** Stanley (harness racing); New Egypt, N.J., 7/25/1927
**Dark,** Alvin (baseball); Comanche, Okla., 1/7/1922
**Davenport,** Willie (track); Troy, Ala., 6/6/1943
**Davis,** Tommy (baseball); Brooklyn, N.Y., 3/21/1939
**Dawson,** Leonard Ray (football); Alliance, Ohio, 6/20/1935
**Dean,** Dizzy (Jay Hanna) (baseball player); Lucas, Ark. **(1911–1974)**
**DeBusschere,** Dave (basketball); Detroit, 10/16/1940
**Delvecchio,** Alex Peter (hockey); Fort William, Ontario, Canada, 12/4/1931
**Demaret,** Jim (golf); Houston, 5/10/1910
**Dempsey,** Jack (William H.) (boxing); Manassa, Colo., 6/24/1895
**DeVicenzo,** Roberto (golf); Buenos Aires, 4/14/1923
**Dibbs,** Edward George (tennis); Brooklyn, N.Y., 2/23/1951
**Dietz,** James W. (rowing); New York, N.Y., 1/12/1949
**DiMaggio,** Joe (baseball); Martinez, Calif., 11/25/1914
**Dionne,** Marcel (hockey); Drummondville, Quebec, Canada, 8/3/1951
**Dominguín,** Luis Miguel (matador); Madrid, 12/9/1926
**Douglass,** Bobby (football); Manhattan, Kan., 6/22/1947
**Dryden,** Kenneth (hockey); Hamilton, Ontario, Canada, 8/4/1947
**Drysdale,** Don (baseball); Van Nuys, Calif., 7/23/1936
**Durocher,** Leo (baseball); West Springfield, Mass., 7/27/1906
**Durr,** François (tennis); Algiers, Algeria, 12/25/1942
**El Cordobés,** (Manuel Benítez Pérez) (matador); Palma del Río, Córdoba, Spain, 5/4/1936(?)
**Elder,** Lee (golf); Dallas, 7/14/1934
**Elliott,** Michael (skiing); Durango, Colo., 4/3/1942
**Ellis,** Jimmy (equestrian); Louisville, Ky., 2/24/1940
**Emerson,** Roy (tennis); Kingsway, Australia, 11/3/1936
**Ender,** Kornelia (swimming); Plauen, East Germany, 10/25/1958
**Ervin,** Frank (harness racing); Pekin, Ill., 8/12/1904
**Erving,** Julius (Dr. J) (basketball); Roosevelt, N.Y., 2/22/1950
**Esposito,** Phil (Philip Anthony) (hockey); Sault Ste. Marie, Ontario, Canada, 2/20/1942
**Evans,** Lee (runner); Mandena, Calif., 2/25/1947
**Evert,** Chris (Christine Marie) (tennis); Fort Lauderdale, Fla., 12/21/1954
**Ewbank,** Weeb (football); Richmond, Ind., 5/6/1907
**Feller,** Robert (Bobby) (baseball); Van Meter, Iowa, 11/3/1918
**Ferrell,** Barbara (sprinter); Hattiesburg, Miss., 7/28/1947
**Feuerbach,** Allan Dean (track); Preston, Iowa, 1/12/1948
**Finley,** Charles O. (sportsman); Ensley, Ala., 2/22/1918
**Fischer,** Bobby (chess); Chicago, 3/9/1943
**Fittipaldi,** Emerson (auto racer); São Paulo, Brazil, 12/12/1946
**Fitzsimmons,** Bob (Robert Prometheus) (boxer); Cornwall, England **(1862–1917)**
**Fleming,** Peggy Gale (ice skating); San Jose, Calif., 7/27/1948
**Ford,** Whitey (Edward) (baseball); New York City, 10/28/1928
**Foreman,** Chuck (Walter Eugene) (football); Frederick, Md., 10/26/1950
**Foreman,** George (boxing); Marshall, Tex., 1/10/1949
**Fosbury,** Richard (high jumper); Portland, Ore., 3/6/1947

**Fox,** Nellie (Jacob Nelson) (baseball); St. Thomas, Pa. **(1927–1975)**
**Foxx,** James Emory (baseball); Sudlersville, Md., **(1907–1967)**
**Foyt,** A. J. (auto racing); Houston, 1/16/1935
**Francis,** Emile (hockey); North Battleford, Sask., 9/13/1926
**Frazier,** Joe (boxing); Beauford, S.C., 1/17/1944
**Frazier,** Walt (basketball); Atlanta, 3/29/1945
**Frick,** Ford C. (baseball); Wawaka, Ind., **(1894–1978)**
**Gable,** Dan (wrestling); Waterloo, Iowa; 10/25/1945
**Gabriel,** Roman (football); Wilmington, N.C., 8/5/1940
**Gallagher,** Michael Donald (skiing); Yonkers, N.Y., 10/3/1941
**Gehrig,** Lou (Henry Louis Gehrig) (baseball); New York City **(1903–1941)**
**Gehringer,** Charlie (baseball); Fowlerville, Mich., 5/11/1903
**Geoffrion,** Bernie (Boom Boom) (hockey); Montreal, 2/14/1931
**Gerulaitis,** Vitas (tennis); Brooklyn, N.Y., 7/26/1954
**Giacomin,** Ed (hockey); Sudbury, Ontario, Canada, 6/6/1939
**Gibson,** Bob (baseball); Omaha, Neb., 11/9/1935
**Gifford,** Frank (football); Santa Monica, Calif., 8/16/1930
**Gilbert,** Rod (Rodrique) (hockey); Montreal, 7/1/1941
**Giles,** Warren (baseball executive); Tiskilwa, Ill., 5/28/1896
**Gilmore,** Artis (basketball); Chipley, Fla., 9/21/1949
**Glance,** Harvey (track); Phenix City, Ala., 3/28/1957
**Gonzalez,** Pancho (tennis); Los Angeles, 5/9/1928
**Goodell,** Brian Stuart (swimming); Stockton, Calif., 4/2/1959
**Goodrich,** Gail (basketball); Los Angeles, 4/23/1943
**Goolagong Cawley,** Evonne (tennis); Griffith, Australia, 7/31/1951
**Gorman,** Tom (Thomas Warner) (tennis); Seattle, 1/19/1946
**Gottfried,** Brian (tennis); Baltimore, Md., 1/27/1952
**Graham,** Otto Everett (football); Waukegan, Ill., 12/6/1921
**Grange,** Red (Harold) (football); Forksville, Pa., 6/13/1904
**Green,** Hubert (golf); Birmingham, Ala., 12/28/1946
**Greene,** Charles E. (sprinter); Pine Bluff, Ark., 3/21/1945
**Griese,** Bob (Robert Allen) (football); Evansville, Ind., 2/3/1945
**Grove,** Lefty (Robert Moses) (baseball); Lonaconing, Md., **(1900–1975)**
**Groza,** Lou (football); Martins Ferry, Ohio, 1/25/1924
**Gunter,** Nancy Richey (tennis); San Angelo, Tex., 8/23/1942
**Hadl,** John Willard (football); Lawrence, Kan., 2/15/1940
**Halas,** George (football); Chicago, 2/2/1895
**Hall,** Albert W. (weight thrower); Manchester, N.H., 8/2/1934
**Hall,** Gary (swimming); Fayetteville, N.C., 8/7/1951
**Hamill,** Dorothy (figure skater); Chicago, 1956(?)
**Hammond,** Kathy (runner); Sacramento, Calif., 11/2/1951
**Harris,** Franco (football); Ft. Dix, N.J., 3/7/1950
**Hartack,** William, Jr. (jockey); Colver, Pa., 12/9/1932
**Harvey,** Doug (hockey); South Gate, Calif., 3/13/1930
**Haughton,** William (harness racing); Gloversville, N.Y., 11/2/1923
**Havlicek,** John (basketball); Martins Ferry, Ohio, 4/8/1940
**Hayes,** Elvin (basketball); Rayville, La., 11/17/1945
**Haynie,** Sandra (golf); Fort Worth, 6/4/1943
**Hencken,** John (swimming); Culver City, Calif., 5/29/1954
**Henie,** Sonja (ice skater); b. Oslo **(1912–1969)**
**Hickcox,** Charles (swimming); Phoenix, Ariz., 2/6/1947
**Hines,** James (sprinter); Dumas, Ark., 9/10/1946
**Hodges,** Gil (baseball); Princeton, Ind. **(1924–1972)**
**Hogan,** Ben (golf); Dublin, Tex., 8/13/1912
**Hornsby,** Rogers (baseball); Winters, Tex. **(1896–1963)**
**Hornung,** Paul (football); Louisville, Ky., 12/23/1935
**Hough,** Lawrence A. (rowing); Janesville, Wis., 4/4/1944
**Houk,** Ralph (baseball); Lawrence, Kan., 8/9/1919
**Howard,** Elston (baseball); St. Louis, 2/23/1930
**Howe,** Gordon (hockey); Floral, Sask., Canada, 3/31/1928
**Howell,** Jim Lee (football); Lonoke, Ark., 9/27/1914
**Hubbell,** Carl (baseball); Carthage, Mo., 6/22/1903
**Huff,** Sam (Robert Lee) (football); Morgantown, W. Va., 10/4/1934
**Hull,** Bobby (hockey); Point Anne, Ontario, Canada, 1/3/1939
**Hunter,** Jim (Catfish) (baseball); Hertford, N.C., 4/8/1946
**Huntley,** Joni (track); McMinnville, Ore., 8/4/1956
**Hutson,** Donald (football); Pine Bluff, Ark., 1/31/1913
**Insko,** Del (harness racing); Amboy, Minn., 7/10/1931
**Irwin,** Hale (golf); Joplin, Mo., 6/3/1945
**Jackson,** Reggie (baseball); Wyncote, Pa., 5/18/1946
**Jeffries,** James J. (boxer); Carroll, Ohio **(1875–1953)**
**Jenkins,** Ferguson Arthur (baseball); Chatham, Ontario, Canada, 12/13/1943
**Jenner,** (W.) Bruce (track); Mt. Kisco, N.Y., 10/28/1949
**Job,** Brian (swimming); Warren, Ohio, 11/29/1951
**Johnson,** Anthony (rowing); Washington, D.C., 11/16/1940
**Johnson,** Jack (John Arthur Johnson) (boxer); Galveston, Tex. **(1876–1946)**
**Johnson,** Rafer (decathlon); Hillsboro, Tex., 8/18/1935
**Jones,** Deacon (David) (football); Eatonville, Fla., 12/9/1938
**Juantoreno,** Alberto (track); Santiago, Cuba, 12/3/1951
**Jurgensen,** Sonny (football); Wilmington, N.C., 8/23/1934
**Kaline,** Al (Albert) (baseball); Baltimore, 12/19/1934
**Keino,** Kipchoge (runner); Kapchemoiymo, Kenya, 1/1940
**Kelly,** Leroy (football); Philadelphia, 5/20/1942
**Kelly,** Red (Leonard Patrick) (hockey); Simcoe, Ontario, Canada, 7/9/1927
**Kennedy,** James Walter (basketball); Stamford, Conn., **(1912–1977)**
**Killebrew,** Harmon (baseball); Payette, Idaho, 6/29/1936
**Killy,** Jean-Claude (skiing); Saint-Cloud, France, 8/30/1943
**Kilmer,** Bill (William Orland) (football); Topeka, Kan., 9/5/1939
**King,** Billie Jean (Billie Jean Moffitt) (tennis); Long Beach, Calif., 11/22/1943
**King,** Harriet (fencing); New York City, 9/22/1935
**King,** Micki (diving); Pontiac, Mich., 7/26/1944
**Kinsella,** John (swimming); Oak Park, Ill., 8/26/1952
**Kodes,** Jan (tennis); Prague, 3/1/1946
**Kolb,** Claudia (swimming); Hayward, Calif., 12/19/1949
**Koosman,** Jerry Martin (baseball); Appleton, Minn., 12/23/1942
**Korbut,** Olga (gymnast); Grodno, Byelorussia, U.S.S.R., 5/16/1955
**Koufax,** Sandy (Sanford) (baseball); Brooklyn, N.Y., 12/30/1935
**Kramer,** Jack (tennis); Las Vegas, Nev., 8/1/1921
**Kramer,** Jerry (football); Jordan, Mont., 1/23/1936
**Kuhn,** Bowie Kent (baseball); Takoma Park, Md., 10/28/1926
**Kwalik,** Ted (Thaddeus John) (football); McKees Rocks, Pa., 4/15/1947
**Lafleur,** Guy Damien (hockey); Thurson, Quebec, Canada, 8/20/1951
**Laird,** Ronald (walker); Louisville, Ky., 5/31/1935
**Lamonica,** Daryle (football); Fresno, Calif., 7/17/1941
**Landis,** Kenesaw Mountain (1st baseball commissioner); Millville, Ohio **(1866–1944)**
**Landry,** Tom (football); Mission, Tex., 9/11/1924
**Landy,** John (runner); Australia, 4/4/1930
**Larrieu,** Francie (track); Palo Alto, Calif., 11/28/1952
**Laver,** Rod (tennis); Rockhampton, Australia, 8/9/1938
**Leonard,** Benny (Benjamin Leiner) (boxer); New York City **(1896–1947)**
**Lilly,** Robert (football); Olney, Tex., 7/26/1939
**Liquori,** Marty (runner); Montclair, N.J., 9/11/1949
**Little,** Floyd Douglas (football); New Haven, Conn., 7/4/1942
**Little,** Lou (football); Leominster, Mass., 12/6/1893
**Littler,** Gene (golf); San Diego, Calif., 11/16/1920
**Lombardi,** Vince (football); Brooklyn, N.Y. **(1913–1970)**
**Longden,** Johnny (horse racing); Wakefield, England, 2/14/1907
**Lopez,** Al (baseball); Tampa, Fla., 8/20/1908
**Lopez,** Nancy (golf); Torrance, Calif., 1/6/1957
**Louis,** Joe (Joe Louis Barrow) (boxing); Lexington, Ala., 5/13/1914
**Lutz,** Robert Charles (tennis); Lancaster, Pa., 8/29/1947
**Lynn,** Janet (figure skating); Rockford, Ill., 4/6/1953
**Mack,** Connie (Cornelius Alexander McGillicuddy) (baseball executive); East Brookfield, Mass. **(1862–1956)**
**Mackey,** John (football); New York City, 9/24/1941
**Mahovlich,** Frank (Francis William) (hockey); Timmins, Ontario, Canada, 1/10/1938
**Mann,** Carol (golf); Buffalo, N.Y., 2/3/1941
**Manning,** Madeline (runner); Cleveland, 1/11/1948
**Mantle,** Mickey Charles (baseball); Spavinaw, Okla., 10/20/1931
**Marichal,** Juan (baseball); Laguna Verde, Montecristi, Dominican Republic, 10/20/1937
**Maris,** Roger (baseball); Hibbing, Minn., 9/10/1934
**Martin,** Billy (Alfred Manuel) (baseball); Berkeley, Calif., 5/16/1928
**Martin,** Rick (Richard Lionel) (hockey); Verdun, Quebec, Canada, 7/26/1951
**Mathews,** Ed (Edwin) (baseball); Texarkana, Tex., 10/13/1931
**Matson,** Randy (shot putter); Kilgore, Tex., 3/5/1945
**Maynard,** Don (football); Crosbyton, Tex., 1/25/1937
**Mays,** Willie (baseball); Westfield, Ala., 5/6/1931
**McAdoo,** Bob (basketball); Greensboro, N.C., 9/25/1951
**McCarthy,** Joe (Joseph Vincent) (baseball); Philadelphia **(1887–1978)**
**McCovey,** Willie Lee (baseball); Mobile, Ala., 1/10/1938
**McEnroe,** John Patrick, Jr. (tennis); Wiesbaden, Germany, 2/16/1959
**McGraw,** John Joseph (baseball); Truxton, N.Y. **(1873–1934)**
**McIngvale,** Cynthia Potter (diving); Houston, 8/27/1950
**McKinney,** Richard L. (archery); Decatur, Iowa, 10/12/1953
**McLain,** Dennis (baseball); Chicago, 3/24/1944
**McMillan,** Kathy Laverne (track); Raeford, N.C., 11/7/1957
**Merrill,** Janice (track); New London, Conn., 6/18/1962
**Metreveli,** Alexander (tennis); Tblisi, U.S.S.R., 11/2/1944
**Meyer,** Deborah (swimming); Haddonfield, N.J., 8/14/1952
**Middlecoff,** Cary (golf); Halls, Tenn., 1/6/1921
**Mikita,** Stan (hockey); Sokolce, Czechoslovakia, 5/20/1940
**Milburn,** Rodney, Jr. (hurdler); Opelousas, La., 5/18/1950
**Miller,** Johnny (golf); San Francisco, 4/29/1947
**Montgomery,** Jim (swimming); Madison, Wis., 1/24/1955
**Moore,** Archie (boxing); Benoit, Miss., 12/13/1916
**Morgan,** Joe Leonard (baseball); Bonham, Tex., 9/19/1943
**Morrall,** Earl (football); Muskegon, Mich., 5/17/1934
**Morris,** Mercury (Eugene) (football); Pittsburgh, 1/5/1947
**Morton,** Craig L. (football); Flint, Mich., 2/5/1943
**Mosconi,** Willie (pocket billiards); Philadelphia, 6/27/1913
**Moses,** Edward Corley (track); Dayton, Ohio, 8/31/1958
**Murphy,** Calvin (basketball), Norwalk, Conn., 5/9/1948
**Musial,** Stan (baseball); Donora, Pa., 11/21/1920
**Myers,** Linda (archery); York, Pa., 6/19/1947
**Naber,** John (swimming); Evanston, Ill., 1/20/1956
**Namath,** Joe (Joseph William) (football); Beaver Falls, Pa., 5/31/1943

**Nastase**, Ilie (tennis); Bucharest, 7/19/1946
**Navratilova**, Martina (tennis); Prague, 10/10/1956
**Newcombe**, John (tennis); Sydney, Australia, 5/23/1943
**Nicklaus**, Jack (golf); Columbus, Ohio, 1/21/1940
**North**, Lowell (yachting); Springfield, Mo., 12/2/1929
**Oerter**, Al (discus thrower); New York City, 9/19/1936
**Okker**, Tom (tennis); Amsterdam, 2/22/1944
**Oldfield**, Barney (racing driver); Fulton County, Ohio **(1878–1946)**
**Oliva**, Tony (Pedro) (baseball); Pinar Del Rio, Cuba, 7/20/1940
**Olsen**, Merlin Jay (football); Logan, Utah, 9/15/1940
**O'Malley**, Walter (baseball); New York City, 10/9/1903
**Orantes**, Manuel (tennis); Granada, Spain, 2/6/1949
**Orr**, Bobby (hockey); Parry Sound, Ontario, Canada, 3/20/1948
**Owens**, Jesse (sprinter); Decatur, Ala., 9/12/1918
**Pace**, Darrell (archery); Cincinnati, 10/23/1956
**Paige**, Satchel (Leroy) (baseball); Mobile, Ala., 7/7/1906
**Palmer**, Arnold (golf); Latrobe, Pa., 9/10/1929
**Palmer**, James Alvin (baseball); New York City, 10/15/1945
**Parent**, Bernard Marcel (hockey); Montreal, 4/3/1945
**Park**, Brad (Douglas Bradford) (hockey); Toronto, Ontario, Canada, 7/6/1948
**Parseghian**, Ara (football); Akron, Ohio, 5/21/1923
**Pasarell**, Charles (tennis); San Juan, Puerto Rico, 2/12/1944
**Patterson**, Floyd (boxing); Waco, N.C., 1/4/1935
**Pearson**, David Gene (auto racing); 12/22/1934
**Pelé** (Edson Arantes do Nascimento) (soccer); Tres Coracoes, Brazil, 10/23/1940
**Pennel**, John (pole vaulter); Memphis, Tenn., 7/25/1940
**Perry**, Gaylord (baseball); Williamston, N.C., 9/13/1938
**Pettit**, Bob (basketball); Baton Rouge, La., 12/12/1932
**Petty**, Richard Lee (auto racing); Randleman, N.C., 7/2/1937
**Pincay**, Laffit, Jr. (jockey); Panama City, Panama, 12/29/1946
**Plante**, Jacques (hockey); Shawinigan Falls, Quebec, Canada, 1/17/1929
**Player**, Gary (golf); Johannesburg, South Africa, 11/1/1935
**Plunkett**, Jim (football); San Jose, Calif., 12/5/1947
**Potter**, Cynthia. *See* McIngvale
**Potvin**, Denis Charles (hockey); Hull, Quebec, Canada, 10/29/1953
**Powell**, Boog (John) (baseball); Lakeland, Fla., 8/17/1941
**Prefontaine**, Steve Roland (runner); Coos Bay, Ore. **(1951–1975)**
**Proell**, Annemarie Moser (Alpine skier); Kleinarl, Austria, 3/27/1953
**Rallins**, Mamie (hurdler); Chicago, 7/8/1941
**Ralston**, Dennis (tennis); Bakersfield, Calif., 7/27/1942
**Ratelle**, Jean (Joseph Gilbert Yvon Jean) (hockey); St. Jean, Quebec, Canada, 10/29/1953
**Rawls**, Betsy (Elizabeth Earle) (golf); Spartanburg, S.C., 5/4/1928
**Reed**, Willis (basketball); Hico, La., 6/25/1942
**Reese**, Pee Wee (Harold) (baseball); Ekron, Ky., 7/23/1919
**Reid**, Kerry Melville (tennis); Mosman, Australia, 8/7/1947
**Richard**, Maurice (hockey); Montreal, 8/14/1924
**Richards**, Paul (baseball); Waxahachie, Tex., 11/21/1908
**Richey**, Cliff (George Clifford, Jr.) (tennis); San Angelo, Tex., 12/31/1946
**Riessen**, Martin (tennis); Hinsdale, Ill., 12/4/1941
**Rigney**, William (baseball); Alameda, Calif., 1/29/1918
**Rizzuto**, Phil (baseball); New York City, 9/25/1918
**Roark**, Helen Wills Moody (tennis); Centerville, Calif., 10/6/1922
**Robertson**, Oscar (basketball); Charlotte, Tenn., 11/24/1938
**Robinson**, Arnie (track); San Diego, Calif., 4/7/1948
**Robinson**, Brooks (baseball); Little Rock, Ark., 5/18/1937
**Robinson**, Frank (baseball); Beaumont, Tex., 8/31/1935
**Robinson**, Jackie (baseball); Cairo, Ga. **(1919–1972)**
**Robinson**, Larry Clark (hockey); Marvelville, Ontario, Canada, 6/2/1951
**Robinson**, (Sugar) Ray (boxing); Detroit, 5/3/1920
**Rockne**, Knute Kenneth (football); Voss, Norway **(1888–1931)**
**Rockwell**, Martha (skiing); Providence, R.I., 4/26/1944
**Rose**, Pete (Peter Edward) (baseball); Cincinnati, 4/14/1942
**Rosenbloom**, Maxie (boxing); New York City **(1904–1976)**
**Rosewall**, Ken (tennis); Sydney, Australia, 11/2/1934
**Rote**, Kyle (football); San Antonio, 10/27/1928
**Rothhammer**, Keena (swimming); Little Rock, Ark., 2/26/1957
**Rozelle**, Pete (Alvin Ray) (commissioner of National Football League); South Gate, Calif., 3/1/1926
**Rudolph**, Wilma Glodean (sprinter); St. Bethlehem, Tenn., 6/23/1940
**Russell**, Bill (basketball); Monroe, La., 2/12/1934
**Ruth**, Babe (George Herman Ruth) (baseball); Baltimore **(1895–1948)**
**Rutherford**, Johnny (auto racing); Fort Worth, 3/12/1938
**Ryan**, Nolan (Lynn Nolan, Jr.) (baseball); Refugio, Tex., 1/31/1947
**Ryon**, Luann (archery); Long Beach, Calif., 1/13/1953
**Ryun**, Jim (runner); Wichita, Kan., 4/29/1947
**Santana**, Manuel (Manuel Santana Martinez) (tennis); Chamartín, Spain, 5/10/1938
**Sayers**, Gale (football); Wichita, Kan., 5/30/1943
**Schoendienst**, Al (Albert) (baseball); Germantown, Ill., 2/2/1923
**Schollander**, Donald (swimming); Charlotte, N.C., 4/30/1946
**Seagren**, Bob (Robert Lloyd) (pole vaulter); Pomona, Calif., 10/17/1946
**Seaver**, Tom (baseball); Fresno, Calif., 11/17/1944
**Seidler**, Marem (track); Brooklyn, N.Y., 6/11/1962
**Sherman**, Allie (football); Brooklyn, N.Y., 2/10/1923
**Shoemaker**, Willie (jockey); Fabens, Tex., 8/19/1931
**Shorter**, Frank (runner); Munich, Germany, 10/31/1947
**Shula**, Don (Donald Francis) (football); Grand River, Ohio, 1/4/1930
**Silvester**, Jay (discus thrower); Tremonton, Utah, 2/27/1937
**Simpson**, O. J. (Orenthal James) (football); San Francisco, 7/9/1947
**Smith**, Bubba (Charles Aaron) (football); Orange, Tex., 2/28/1945
**Smith**, Ronnie Ray (sprinter); Los Angeles, 3/28/1949
**Smith**, Stanley Roger (tennis); Pasadena, Calif., 12/14/1946
**Smith**, Tommie (sprinter); Clarksville, Tex., 6/5/1944
**Smoke**, Marcia Jones (canoeing); Oklahoma City, 7/18/1941
**Snead**, Sam (golf); Hot Springs, Va., 5/27/1912
**Snell**, Matt (football); Garfield, Ga., 8/18/1941
**Sneva**, Tom (auto racing); Spokane, Wash., 6/1/1948
**Snider**, Duke (Edwin) (baseball); Los Angeles, 9/19/1926
**Solomon**, Harold (tennis); Washington, D.C., 9/17/1952
**Spahn**, Warren (baseball); Buffalo, N.Y., 4/23/1921
**Spassky**, Boris (chess); Leningrad, 1/30/1937
**Speaker**, Tristram (baseball); Hubbard City, Tex. **(1888–1958)**
**Spinks**, Leon (boxing); St. Louis, 7/11/1953
**Spitz**, Mark (swimming); Modesto, Calif., 2/10/1950
**Stabler**, Kenneth (football); Foley, Ala., 12/25/1945
**Stagg**, Amos Alonzo (football); West Orange, N.J. **(1862–1965)**
**Stapleton**, Pat (hockey); Sarnia, Ontario, Canada, 7/4/1940
**Stargell**, Willie (Wilver Dornell) (baseball); Earlsboro, Okla., 3/6/1941
**Starr**, Bart (football); Montgomery, Ala., 1/9/1934
**Staubach**, Roger (football); Cincinnati, 2/5/1942
**Stecher**, Renate (track); Suptitz, East Germany, 5/12/1950
**Steinkraus**, William C. (equestrian); Cleveland, 10/12/1925
**Stenerud**, Jan (football); Fetsund, Norway, 11/26/1942
**Stengel**, Casey (Charles Dillon) (baseball); Kansas City, Mo. **(1891–1975)**
**Stenmark**, Ingemar (Alpine skier); Tarnaby, Sweden, 3/18/1956
**Stockton**, Richard LaClede (tennis); New York City, 2/18/1951
**Stones**, Dwight Edwin (track); Los Angeles, 12/6/1953
**Sullivan**, John Lawrence (boxer); Boston **(1858–1918)**
**Sutton**, Don (Donald Howard) (baseball); Clio, Ala., 4/2/1945
**Tanner**, Leonard Roscoe III (tennis); Chattanooga, Tenn., 10/15/1951
**Tarkenton**, Fran (Francis) (football); Richmond, Va., 2/3/1940
**Tebbetts**, Birdie (George R.) (baseball); Nashua, N.H., 11/10/1914
**Thoeni**, Gustavo (Alpine skier); Trafoi, Italy, 2/28/1951
**Thompson**, David (basketball); Shelby, N.C., 7/13/1954
**Thorpe**, Jim (James Francis Thorpe) (all-around athlete); nr. Prague, Okla. **(1888–1953)**
**Tilden**, William Tatem II (tennis); Philadelphia **(1893–1953)**
**Tittle**, Y. A. (Yelberton Abraham) (football); Marshall, Tex., 10/24/1926
**Toomey**, William (decathlon); Philadelphia, 1/10/1939
**Trevino**, Lee (golf); Dallas, 12/1/1939
**Tunney**, Gene (James J.) (boxing); New York City, 5/25/1898
**Tyus**, Wyomia (runner); Griffin, Ga., 8/29/1945
**Unitas**, John (football); Pittsburgh, 5/7/1933
**Unser**, Al (auto racing); Albuquerque, N. Mex., 5/29/1939
**Unser**, Bobby (auto racing); Albuquerque N. Mex., 2/20/1934
**Van Brocklin**, Norm (football); Eagle Butte, S. Dak. 3/15/1926
**Vilas**, Guillermo (tennis); Mar del Plata, Argentina, 8/17/1952
**Viren**, Lasse (track); Myrskyla, Finland, 7/12/1949
**Wade**, Virginia (tennis); Bournemouth, England; 7/10/1945
**Wagner**, Honus (John Peter Honus) (baseball); Carnegie, Pa. **(1867–1955)**
**Walcott**, Jersey Joe (Arnold Cream) (boxing); Merchantville, N.J., 1/31/1914
**Walker**, Mickey (boxing); Elizabeth, N.J., 7/13/1901
**Walton**, Bill (basketball); La Mesa, Calif., 11/5/1952
**Watson**, Martha Rae (track); Long Beach, Calif., 8/19/1946
**Watson**, Tom (golf); Kansas City, Mo., 9/4/1944
**Weaver**, Earl (baseball); St. Louis, 8/14/1930
**Webster**, Alex (football); Kearny, N.J., 4/19/1931
**Weiskopf**, Tom (golf); Massillon, Ohio, 11/9/1942
**Weiss**, George (baseball executive); New Haven, Conn. **(1895–1972)**
**Weissmuller**, Johnny (swimmer and actor); Windber, Pa., 6/2/1904
**West**, Jerry (basketball); Cheylan, W. Va., 5/28/1938
**White**, Willye B. (long jumper); Money, Miss., 1/1/1936
**Whitworth**, Kathy (golf); Monahans, Tex., 9/27/1939
**Wilbur**, Doreen (archery); Jefferson, Iowa, 1/8/1930
**Wilkens**, Mac Maurice (track); Eugene, Ore., 11/15/1950
**Wilkins**, Lennie (basketball); 11/25/1937
**Wilkinson**, Bud (football); Minneapolis, 4/23/1916
**Williams**, Dick (baseball); St. Louis, 5/7/1929
**Williams**, Ted (baseball); San Diego, Calif., 8/30/1918
**Wills**, Maury (baseball); Washington, D.C., 10/2/1932
**Wohlhuter**, Richard C. (runner); Geneva, Ill. 12/23/1945
**Wottle**, David James (runner); Canton, Ohio, 8/7/1950
**Wright**, Mickey (Mary Kathryn) (golf); San Diego, Calif., 2/14/1935
**Yarborough**, Cale (William Caleb) (auto racing); Timmonsville, S.C., 3/27/1939
**Yastrzemski**, Carl (baseball); Southampton, N.Y., 8/22/1939
**Young**, Cy (Denton True Young) (baseball); Gilmore, Ohio **(1867–1955)**
**Young**, Donna Caponi (golf); Detroit, 1/29/1945
**Young**, Sheila (speed skater, bicycle racer); Detroit, 10/14/1950

# THE OLYMPIC GAMES

(W)—Site of Winter Games. (S)—Site of Summer Games

| | |
|---|---|
| 1896 | Athens |
| 1900 | Paris |
| 1904 | St. Louis |
| 1906 | Athens |
| 1908 | London |
| 1912 | Stockholm |
| 1920 | Antwerp |
| 1924 | Chamonix (W) |
| 1924 | Paris (S) |
| 1928 | St. Moritz (W) |
| 1928 | Amsterdam (S) |
| 1932 | Lake Placid (W) |
| 1932 | Los Angeles (S) |
| 1936 | Garmisch-Partenkirchen (W) |
| 1936 | Berlin (S) |
| 1948 | St. Moritz (W) |
| 1948 | London (S) |
| 1952 | Oslo (W) |
| 1952 | Helsinki (S) |
| 1956 | Cortina d'Ampezzo, Italy (W) |
| 1956 | Melbourne (S) |
| 1960 | Squaw Valley, Calif. (W) |
| 1960 | Rome (S) |
| 1964 | Innsbruck, Austria (W) |
| 1964 | Tokyo (S) |
| 1968 | Grenoble, France (W) |
| 1968 | Mexico City (S) |
| 1972 | Sapporo, Japan (W) |
| 1972 | Munich (S) |
| 1976 | Innsbruck, Austria (W) |
| 1976 | Montreal (S) |
| 1980 | Lake Placid (W) |
| 1980 | Moscow (S) |

The first Olympic Games of which there is record occurred in 776 B.C. and consisted of one event, a great foot race of about 200 yards held on a plain by the River Alpheus (now the Ruphia) just outside the little town of Olympia in Greece. It was from that date that the Greeks began to keep their calendar by "Olympiads," the four-year spans between the celebrations of the famous games.

The modern Olympic Games, which started in Athens in 1896, are the result of the devotion of a French educator, Baron Pierre de Coubertin, to the idea that, since young people and athletics have gone together down the ages, education and athletics might well go hand-in-hand toward a better international understanding.

At the top of the organization responsible for the Olympic movement and the staging of the Games every four years is the International Olympic Committee (IOC). Other important roles are played by National Olympic Committees in each participating country, international sports federations, and the Organizing Committee of the host city.

In 1978, the IOC consisted of 89 members, elected by the IOC itself. Its headquarters are in Lausanne, Switzerland. The president of the IOC is Lord Killanin of Ireland.

The Olympic motto is "Citius, Altius, Fortius"—"Faster, Higher, Stronger." The Olympic symbol is five interlocking circles colored blue, yellow, black, green, and red, on a white background, representing the five continents. At least one of these colors appears in the national flag of every country.

## Summer Games

### TRACK AND FIELD—MEN

#### 100-Meter Dash

| | | |
|---|---|---|
| 1896 | Thomas Burke, United States | 12s |
| 1900 | F. W. Jarvis, United States | 10.8s |
| 1904 | Archie Hahn, United States | 11s |
| 1906 | Archie Hahn, United States | 11.2s |
| 1908 | Reginald Walker, South Africa | 10.8s |
| 1912 | Ralph Craig, United States | 10.8s |
| 1920 | Charles Paddock, United States | 10.8s |
| 1924 | Harold Abrahams, Great Britain | 10.6s |
| 1928 | Percy Williams, Canada | 10.8s |
| 1932 | Eddie Tolan, United States | 10.3s |
| 1936 | Jesse Owens, United States | 10.3s[1] |
| 1948 | Harrison Dillard, United States | 10.3s |
| 1952 | Lindy Remigino, United States | 10.4s |
| 1956 | Bobby Morrow, United States | 10.5s |
| 1960 | Armin Hary, Germany | 10.2s |
| 1964 | Robert Hayes, United States | 10s |
| 1968 | James Hines, United States | 9.9s |
| 1972 | Valery Borzov, U.S.S.R. | 10.14s |
| 1976 | Hasely Crawford, Trinidad and Tobago | 10.06s |

1. Wind assisted.

#### 200-Meter Dash

| | | |
|---|---|---|
| 1900 | John Tewksbury, United States | 22.2s |
| 1904 | Archie Hahn, United States | 21.6s |
| 1908 | Robert Kerr, Canada | 22.6s |
| 1912 | Ralph Craig, United States | 21.7s |
| 1920 | Allan Woodring, United States | 22s |
| 1924 | Jackson Scholz, United States | 21.6s |
| 1928 | Percy Williams, Canada | 21.8s |
| 1932 | Eddie Tolan, United States | 21.2s |
| 1936 | Jesse Owens, United States | 20.7s |
| 1948 | Melvin E. Patton, United States | 21.1s |
| 1952 | Andrew Stanfield, United States | 20.7s |
| 1956 | Bobby Morrow, United States | 20.6s |
| 1960 | Livio Berruti, Italy | 20.5s |
| 1964 | Henry Carr, United States | 20.3s |
| 1968 | Tommie Smith, United States | 19.8s |
| 1972 | Valery Borzov, U.S.S.R. | 20s |
| 1976 | Don Quarrie, Jamaica | 20.23s |

#### 400-Meter Dash

| | | |
|---|---|---|
| 1896 | Thomas Burke, United States | 54.2s |
| 1900 | Maxey Long, United States | 49.4s |
| 1904 | Harry Hillman, United States | 49.2s |
| 1906 | Paul Pilgrim, United States | 53.2s |
| 1908 | Wyndham Halswelle, Great Britain (walkover) | 50s |
| 1912 | Charles Reidpath, United States | 48.2s |
| 1920 | Bevil Rudd, South Africa | 49.6s |
| 1924 | Eric Liddell, Great Britain | 47.6s |
| 1928 | Ray Barbuti, United States | 47.8s |
| 1932 | William Carr, United States | 46.2s |
| 1936 | Archie Williams, United States | 46.5s |
| 1948 | Arthur Wint, Jamaica, B.W.I. | 46.2s |
| 1952 | George Rhoden, Jamaica, B.W.I. | 45.9s |
| 1956 | Charles Jenkins, United States | 46.7s |
| 1960 | Otis Davis, United States | 44.9s |
| 1964 | Mike Larrabee, United States | 45.1s |
| 1968 | Lee Evans, United States | 43.8s |
| 1972 | Vincent Matthews, United States | 44.66s |
| 1976 | Alberto Juantorena, Cuba | 44.26s |

#### 800-Meter Run

| | | |
|---|---|---|
| 1896 | Edwin Flack, Australia | 2m11s |
| 1900 | Alfred Tysoe, Great Britain | 2m1.4s |
| 1904 | James Lightbody, United States | 1m56s |
| 1906 | Paul Pilgrim, United States | 2m1.2s |
| 1908 | Mel Sheppard, United States | 1m52.8s |
| 1912 | Ted Meredith, United States | 1m51.9s |
| 1920 | Albert Hill, Great Britain | 1m53.4s |
| 1924 | Douglas Lowe, Great Britain | 1m52.4s |
| 1928 | Douglas Lowe, Great Britain | 1m51.8s |

| | | |
|---|---|---|
| 1932 | Thomas Hampson, Great Britain | 1m49.8s |
| 1936 | John Woodruff, United States | 1m52.9s |
| 1948 | Malvin Whitfield, United States | 1m49.2s |
| 1952 | Malvin Whitfield, United States | 1m49.2s |
| 1956 | Tom Courtney, United States | 1m47.7s |
| 1960 | Peter Snell, New Zealand | 1m46.3s |
| 1964 | Peter Snell, New Zealand | 1m45.1s |
| 1968 | Ralph Doubell, Australia | 1m44.3s |
| 1972 | David Wottle, United States | 1m45.9s |
| 1976 | Alberto Juantorena, Cuba | 1m43.5s |

### 1,500-Meter Run

| | | |
|---|---|---|
| 1896 | Edwin Flack, Australia | 4m33.2s |
| 1900 | Charles Bennett, Great Britain | 4m6s |
| 1904 | James Lightbody, United States | 4m5.4s |
| 1906 | James Lightbody, United States | 4m12s |
| 1908 | Mel Sheppard, United States | 4m3.4s |
| 1912 | Arnold Jackson, Great Britain | 3m56.8s |
| 1920 | Albert Hill, Great Britain | 4m1.8s |
| 1924 | Paavo Nurmi, Finland | 3m53.6s |
| 1928 | Harry Larva, Finland | 3m53.2s |
| 1932 | Luigi Beccali, Italy | 3m51.2s |
| 1936 | Jack Lovelock, New Zealand | 3m47.8s |
| 1948 | Henri Eriksson, Sweden | 3m49.8s |
| 1952 | Joseph Barthel, Luxembourg | 3m45.2s |
| 1956 | Ron Delany, Ireland | 3m41.2s |
| 1960 | Herb Elliott, Australia | 3m35.6s |
| 1964 | Peter Snell, New Zealand | 3m38.1s |
| 1968 | Kipchoge Keino, Kenya | 3m34.9s |
| 1972 | Pekka Vasala, Finland | 3m36.3s |
| 1976 | John Walker, New Zealand | 3m39.17s |

### 5,000-Meter Run

| | | |
|---|---|---|
| 1912 | Hannes Kolehmainen, Finland | 14m36.6s |
| 1920 | Joseph Guillemot, France | 14m55.6s |
| 1924 | Paavo Nurmi, Finland | 14m31.2s |
| 1928 | Willie Ritola, Finland | 14m38s |
| 1932 | Lauri Lehtinen, Finland | 14m30s |
| 1936 | Gunnar Hockert, Finland | 14m22.2s |
| 1948 | Gaston Reiff, Belgium | 14m17.6s |
| 1952 | Emil Zatopek, Czechoslovakia | 14m6.6s |
| 1956 | Vladimir Kuts, U.S.S.R. | 13m39.6s |
| 1960 | Murray Halberg, New Zealand | 13m43.4s |
| 1964 | Bob Schul, United States | 13m48.8s |
| 1968 | Mohamed Gammoudi, Tunisia | 14m.05s |
| 1972 | Lasse Viren, Finland | 13m26.4s |
| 1976 | Lasse Viren, Finland | 13m24.76s |

### 5-Mile Run

| | | |
|---|---|---|
| 1906 | H. Hawtrey, Great Britain | 26m26.2s |
| 1908 | Emil Voigt, Great Britain | 25m11.2s |

### 10,000-Meter Run

| | | |
|---|---|---|
| 1912 | Hannes Kolehmainen, Finland | 31m20.8s |
| 1920 | Paavo Nurmi, Finland | 31m45.8s |
| 1924 | Willie Ritola, Finland | 30m23.2s |
| 1928 | Paavo Nurmi, Finland | 30m18.8s |
| 1932 | Janusz Kusocinski, Poland | 30m11.4s |
| 1936 | Ilmari Salminen, Finland | 30m15.4s |
| 1948 | Emil Zatopek, Czechoslovakia | 29m59.6s |
| 1952 | Emil Zatopek, Czechoslovakia | 29m17s |
| 1956 | Vladimir Kuts, U.S.S.R. | 28m45.6s |
| 1960 | Peter Bolotnikov, U.S.S.R. | 28m32.2s |
| 1964 | Billy Mills, United States | 28m24.4s |
| 1968 | Naftali Temu, Kenya | 29m27.4s |
| 1972 | Lasse Viren, Finland | 27m38.4s |
| 1976 | Lasse Viren, Finland | 27m40.38s |

### Marathon

| | | |
|---|---|---|
| 1896 | Spiridon Loues, Greece | 2h58m50s |
| 1900 | Michel Teato, France | 2h59m45s |
| 1904 | Thomas Hicks, United States | 3h28m53s |
| 1906 | W. J. Sherring, Canada | 2h51m23.65s |
| 1908 | John J. Hayes, United States | 2h55m18.4s |
| 1912 | Kenneth McArthur, South Africa | 2h36m54.8s |
| 1920 | Hannes Kolehmainen, Finland | 2h32m35.8s |
| 1924 | Albin Stenroos, Finland | 2h41m22.6s |
| 1928 | A. B. El Ouafi, France | 2h32m57s |
| 1932 | Juan Zabala, Argentina | 2h31m36s |
| 1936 | Kitei Son, Japan | 2h29m19.2s |
| 1948 | Delfo Cabrera, Argentina | 2h34m51.6s |
| 1952 | Emil Zatopek, Czechoslovakia | 2h23m3.2s |
| 1956 | Alain Mimoun, France | 2h25m |
| 1960 | Abebe Bikila, Ethiopia | 2h15m16.2s |
| 1964 | Abebe Bikila, Ethiopia | 2h12m11.2s |
| 1968 | Mamo Wold, Ethiopia | 2h20m26.4s |
| 1972 | Frank Shorter, United States | 2h12m19.8s |
| 1976 | Walter Cierpinski, East Germany | 2h09m55s |

### 110-Meter Hurdles

| | | |
|---|---|---|
| 1896 | Thomas Curtis, United States | 17.6s |
| 1900 | Alvin Kraenzlein, United States | 15.4s |
| 1904 | Frederick Schule, United States | 16s |
| 1906 | R. G. Leavitt, United States | 16.2s |
| 1908 | Forrest Smithson, United States | 15s |
| 1912 | Frederick Kelly, United States | 15.1s |
| 1920 | Earl Thomson, Canada | 14.8s |
| 1924 | Daniel Kinsey, United States | 15s |
| 1928 | Sydney Atkinson, South Africa | 14.8s |
| 1932 | George Saling, United States | 14.6s |
| 1936 | Forrest Towns, United States | 14.2s |
| 1948 | William Porter, United States | 13.9s |
| 1952 | Harrison Dillard, United States | 13.7s |
| 1956 | Lee Calhoun, United States | 13.5s |
| 1960 | Lee Calhoun, United States | 13.8s |
| 1964 | Hayes Jones, United States | 13.6s |
| 1968 | Willie Davenport, United States | 13.3s |
| 1972 | Rodney Milburn, United States | 13.24s |
| 1976 | Guy Drut, France | 13.30s |

### 200-Meter Hurdles

| | | |
|---|---|---|
| 1900 | Alvin Kraenzlein, United States | 25.4s |
| 1904 | Harry Hillman, United States | 24.6s |

### 400-Meter Hurdles

| | | |
|---|---|---|
| 1900 | John Tewksbury, United States | 57.6s |
| 1904 | Harry Hillman, United States | 53s |
| 1908 | Charles Bacon, United States | 55s |
| 1920 | Frank Loomis, United States | 54s |
| 1924 | F. Morgan Taylor, United States | 52.6s |
| 1928 | Lord David Burghley, Great Britain | 53.4s |
| 1932 | Robert Tisdall, Ireland | 51.8s[1] |
| 1936 | Glenn Hardin, United States | 52.4s |
| 1948 | Roy Cochran, United States | 51.1s |
| 1952 | Charles Moore, United States | 50.8s |
| 1956 | Glenn Davis, United States | 50.1s |
| 1960 | Glenn Davis, United States | 49.3s |
| 1964 | Rex Cawley, United States | 49.6s |
| 1968 | David Hemery, Great Britain | 48.1s |
| 1972 | John Akii-Bua, Uganda | 47.8s |
| 1976 | Edwin Moses, United States | 47.64 |

1. Record not allowed.

### 2,500-Meter Steeplechase

| | | |
|---|---|---|
| 1900 | George Orton, United States | 7m34s |
| 1904 | James Lightbody, United States | 7m39.6s |

### 3,000-Meter Steeplechase

| | | |
|---|---|---|
| 1920 | Percy Hodge, Great Britain | 10m0.4s |
| 1924 | Willie Ritola, Finland | 9m33.6s |
| 1928 | Toivo Loukola, Finland | 9m21.8s |
| 1932 | Volmari Iso-Hollo, Finland | 10m33.4s[1] |
| 1936 | Volmari Iso-Hollo, Finland | 9m3.8s |
| 1948 | Thure Sjoestrand, Sweden | 9m4.6s |
| 1952 | Horace Ashenfelter, United States | 8m45.4s |
| 1956 | Chris Brasher, Great Britain | 8m41.2s |

| | | |
|---|---|---|
| 1960 | Zdzislaw Krzyskowiak, Poland | 8m34.2s |
| 1964 | Gaston Roelants, Belgium | 8m30.8s |
| 1968 | Amos Biwott, Kenya | 8m51s |
| 1972 | Kipchoge Keino, Kenya | 8m23.6s |
| 1976 | Anders Gardervd, Sweden | 8m08.02s |

1. About 3,450 meters—extra lap by error.

### Cross-Country

| | | |
|---|---|---|
| 1912 | Hannes Kolehmainen, Finland (8,000 meters) | 45m11.6s |
| 1920 | Paavo Nurmi, Finland (10,000 meters) | 27m15s |
| 1924 | Paavo Nurmi, Finland (10,000 meters) | 32m54.8s |

### Cross-Country Team Races

| | | Pts. |
|---|---|---|
| 1912 | Sweden (8,000 meters) | 10 |
| 1920 | Finland (10,000 meters) | 10 |
| 1924 | Finland (10,000 meters) | 11 |

### 1,500-Meter Walk

| | | |
|---|---|---|
| 1906 | George V. Bonhag, United States | 7m12.6s |

### 3,000-Meter Walk

| | | |
|---|---|---|
| 1920 | Ugo Frigerio, Italy | 13m14.2s |

### 10,000-Meter Walk

| | | |
|---|---|---|
| 1912 | George Goulding, Canada | 46m28.4s |
| 1920 | Ugo Frigerio, Italy | 48m6.2s |
| 1924 | Ugo Frigerio, Italy | 47m49s |
| 1948 | John Mikaelsson, Sweden | 45m13.2s |
| 1952 | John Mikaelsson, Sweden | 45m2.8s |

### 20,000-Meter Walk

| | | |
|---|---|---|
| 1956 | Leonid Spirin, U.S.S.R. | 1h31m27.4s |
| 1960 | Vladimir Golubnichy, U.S.S.R. | 1h34m7.2s |
| 1964 | Ken Mathews, Great Britain | 1h29m34s |
| 1968 | Vladimir Golubnichy, U.S.S.R. | 1h33m58.4s |
| 1972 | Peter Frenkel, East Germany | 1h26m42.4s |
| 1976 | Daniel Bautista, Mexico | 1h24m40.6s |

### 50,000-Meter Walk

| | | |
|---|---|---|
| 1932 | Thomas W. Green, Great Britain | 4h50m10s |
| 1936 | Harold Whitlock, Great Britain | 4h30m41.1s |
| 1948 | John Ljunggren, Sweden | 4h41m52s |
| 1952 | Giuseppe Dordoni, Italy | 4h28m7.8s |
| 1956 | Norman Read, New Zealand | 4h30m42.8s |
| 1960 | Donald Thompson, Great Britain | 4h25m30s |
| 1964 | Abdon Pamich, Italy | 4h11m12.4s |
| 1968 | Christoph Hohne, East Germany | 4h20m13.6s |
| 1972 | Bern Kannernberg, West Germany | 3h56m11.6s |

### 400-Meter Relay (4 x 100)

| | | |
|---|---|---|
| 1912 | Great Britain | 42.4s |
| 1920 | United States | 42.2s |
| 1924 | United States | 41s |
| 1928 | United States | 41s |
| 1932 | United States | 40s |
| 1936 | United States | 39.8s |
| 1948 | United States | 40.6s |
| 1952 | United States | 40.1s |
| 1956 | United States | 39.5s |
| 1960 | Germany | 39.5s |
| 1964 | United States | 39s |
| 1968 | United States | 38.2s |
| 1972 | United States | 38.19s |
| 1976 | United States | 38.33s |

### 1,600-Meter Relay (200–200–400–800)

| | | |
|---|---|---|
| 1908 | United States | 3m29.4s |

### 1,600-Meter Relay (4 x 400)

| | | |
|---|---|---|
| 1912 | United States | 3m16.6s |
| 1920 | Great Britain | 3m22.2s |
| 1924 | United States | 3m16s |
| 1928 | United States | 3m14.2s |
| 1932 | United States | 3m8.2s |
| 1936 | Great Britain | 3m9s |
| 1948 | United States | 3m10.4s |
| 1952 | Jamaica, B.W.I. | 3m3.9s |
| 1956 | United States | 3m4.8s |
| 1960 | United States | 3m2.2s |
| 1964 | United States | 3m0.7s |
| 1968 | United States | 2m56.1s |
| 1972 | Kenya | 2m59.8s |
| 1976 | United States | 2m58.65s |

### Team Race

| | | Pts. |
|---|---|---|
| 1900 | Great Britain (5,000 meters) | 26 |
| 1904 | United States (4 miles) | 27 |
| 1908 | Great Britain (3 miles) | 6 |
| 1912 | United States (3,000 meters) | 9 |
| 1920 | United States (3,000 meters) | 10 |
| 1924 | Finland (3,000 meters) | 9 |

### Standing High Jump

| | | |
|---|---|---|
| 1900 | Ray Ewry, United States | 5 ft 5 in. |
| 1904 | Ray Ewry, United States | 4 ft 11 in. |
| 1906 | Ray Ewry, United States | 5 ft 1⅝ in. |
| 1908 | Ray Ewry, United States | 5 ft 2 in. |
| 1912 | Platt Adams, United States | 5 ft 4⅛ in. |

### Running High Jump

| | | |
|---|---|---|
| 1896 | Ellery Clark, United States | 5 ft 11¼ in. |
| 1900 | Irving Baxter, United States | 6 ft 2¾ in. |
| 1904 | Samuel Jones, United States | 5 ft 11 in. |
| 1906 | Con Leahy, Ireland | 5 ft 9⅞ in. |
| 1908 | Harry Porter, United States | 6 ft 3 in. |
| 1912 | Alma Richards, United States | 6 ft 4 in. |
| 1920 | Richmond Landon, United States | 6 ft 4¼ in. |
| 1924 | Harold Osborn, United States | 6 ft 5 15/16 in. |
| 1928 | Robert W. King, United States | 6 ft 4⅜ in. |
| 1932 | Duncan McNaughton, Canada | 6 ft 5⅝ in. |
| 1936 | Cornelius Johnson, United States | 6 ft 7 15/16 in. |
| 1948 | John Winter, Australia | 6 ft 6 in. |
| 1952 | Walter Davis, United States | 6 ft 8 5/16 in. |
| 1956 | Charles Dumas, United States | 6 ft 11¼ in. |
| 1960 | Robert Shavlakadze, U.S.S.R. | 7 ft 1 in. |
| 1964 | Valeri Brumel, U.S.S.R. | 7 ft 1¾ in. |
| 1968 | Dick Fosbury, United States | 7 ft 4¼ in. |
| 1972 | Yuri Tarmak, U.S.S.R. | 7 ft 3¾ in. |
| 1976 | Jacek Wszola, Poland | (2.25) 7 ft 4½ in. |

### Standing Long Jump

| | | |
|---|---|---|
| 1900 | Ray Ewry, United States | 10 ft 6⅖ in. |
| 1904 | Ray Ewry, United States | 11 ft 4⅞ in. |
| 1906 | Ray Ewry, United States | 10 ft 10 in. |
| 1908 | Ray Ewry, United States | 10 ft 11¼ in. |
| 1912 | Constantin Tsicilitiras, Greece | 11 ft ¼ in. |

### Long Jump

| | | |
|---|---|---|
| 1896 | Ellery Clark, United States | 20 ft 9¾ in. |
| 1900 | Alvin Kraenzlein, United States | 23 ft 6⅞ in. |
| 1904 | Myer Prinstein, United States | 24 ft 1 in. |
| 1906 | Myer Prinstein, United States | 23 ft 7½ in. |
| 1908 | Frank Irons, United States | 24 ft 6½ in. |
| 1912 | Albert Gutterson, United States | 24 ft 11¼ in. |
| 1920 | Wm. Pettersson, Sweden | 23 ft 5½ in. |
| 1924 | DeHart Hubbard, United States | 24 ft 5⅛ in. |
| 1928 | Edward B. Hamm, United States | 25 ft 4¾ in. |
| 1932 | Edward Gordon, United States | 25 ft ¾ in. |
| 1936 | Jesse Owens, United States | 26 ft 5 5/16 in. |
| 1948 | Willie Steele, United States | 25 ft 8 in. |
| 1952 | Jerome Biffle, United States | 24 ft 10 in. |
| 1956 | Gregory Bell, United States | 25 ft 8¼ in. |

| | | |
|---|---|---|
| 1960 | Ralph Boston, United States | 26 ft 7¾ in. |
| 1964 | Lynn Davies, Great Britain | 26 ft 5¾ in. |
| 1968 | Bob Beamon, United States | 29 ft 2½ in. |
| 1972 | Randy Williams, United States | 27 ft ½ in. |
| 1976 | Arnie Robinson, United States | (8.35) 24 ft 7¾ in. |

**Standing Triple Jump**

| | | |
|---|---|---|
| 1900 | Ray Ewry, United States | 34 ft 8½ in. |
| 1904 | Ray Ewry, United States | 34 ft 7¼ in. |

**Triple Jump**

| | | |
|---|---|---|
| 1896 | James B. Connolly, United States | 45 ft |
| 1900 | Myer Prinstein, United States | 47 ft 4¼ in. |
| 1904 | Myer Prinstein, United States | 47 ft |
| 1906 | P. G. O'Connor, Ireland | 46 ft 2 in. |
| 1908 | Timothy Ahearne, Great Britain | 48 ft 11¼ in. |
| 1912 | Gustaf Lindblom, Sweden | 48 ft 5⅛ in. |
| 1920 | Vilho Tuulos, Finland | 47 ft 6⅞ in. |
| 1924 | Archie Winter, Australia | 50 ft 11⅛ in. |
| 1928 | Mikio Oda, Japan | 49 ft 10¹³⁄₁₆ in. |
| 1932 | Chuhei Nambu, Japan | 51 ft 7 in. |
| 1936 | Naoto Tajima, Japan | 52 ft 5⅞ in. |
| 1948 | Arne Ahman, Sweden | 50 ft 6¼ in. |
| 1952 | Adhemar da Silva, Brazil | 53 ft 2½ in. |
| 1956 | Adhemar da Silva, Brazil | 53 ft 7½ in. |
| 1960 | Jozef Schmidt, Poland | 55 ft 1¾ in. |
| 1964 | Jozef Schmidt, Poland | 55 ft 3¼ in. |
| 1968 | Viktor Saneyev, U.S.S.R. | 57 ft ¾ in. |
| 1972 | Viktor Saneyev, U.S.S.R. | 56 ft 11 in. |
| 1976 | Viktor Saneyev, U.S.S.R. | (17.29) 56 ft 8¾ in. |

**Pole Vault**

| | | |
|---|---|---|
| 1896 | William Hoyt, United States | 10 ft 9¾ in. |
| 1900 | Irving Baxter, United States | 10 ft 9⅞ in. |
| 1904 | Charles Dvorak, United States | 11 ft 6 in. |
| 1906 | Fernand Gouder, France | 11 ft 6 in. |
| 1908 | A. C. Gilbert, United States, and Edward Cook, United States (tie) | 12 ft 2 in. |
| 1912 | Harry Babcock, United States | 12 ft 11½ in. |
| 1920 | Frank Foss, United States | 13 ft 5⁹⁄₁₆ in. |
| 1924 | Lee Barnes, United States | 12 ft 11½ in. |
| 1928 | Sabin W. Carr, United States | 13 ft 9⅜ in. |
| 1932 | William Miller, United States | 14 ft 1⅞ in. |
| 1936 | Earle Meadows, United States | 14 ft 3¼ in. |
| 1948 | Guinn Smith, United States | 14 ft 1¼ in. |
| 1952 | Robert Richards, United States | 14 ft 11⅛ in. |
| 1956 | Robert Richards, United States | 14 ft 11½ in. |
| 1960 | Don Bragg, United States | 15 ft 5⅛ in. |
| 1964 | Fred Hansen, United States | 16 ft 8¾ in. |
| 1968 | Bob Seagren, United States | 17 ft 8½ in. |
| 1972 | Wolfgang Nordwig, East Germany | 18 ft ½ in. |
| 1976 | Tadeusz Slusarski, Poland | (5.50) 18 ft ½ in. |

**16-lb Shot-Put**

| | | |
|---|---|---|
| 1896 | Robert Garrett, United States | 36 ft 9¾ in. |
| 1900 | Richard Sheldon, United States | 46 ft 3⅛ in. |
| 1904 | Ralph Rose, United States | 48 ft 7 in. |
| 1906 | Martin Sheridan, United States | 40 ft 4⅘ in. |
| 1908 | Ralph Rose, United States | 46 ft 7½ in. |
| 1912 | Pat McDonald, United States | 50 ft 4 in. |
| 1920 | Ville Porhola, Finland | 48 ft 7⅛ in. |
| 1924 | Clarence Houser, United States | 49 ft 2½ in. |
| 1928 | John Kuck, United States | 52 ft 11¹¹⁄₁₆ in. |
| 1932 | Leo Sexton, United States | 52 ft 6³⁄₁₆ in. |
| 1936 | Hans Woellke, Germany | 53 ft 1¾ in. |
| 1948 | Wilbur Thompson, United States | 56 ft 2 in. |
| 1952 | Parry O'Brien, United States | 57 ft 1½ in. |
| 1956 | Parry O'Brien, United States | 60 ft 11 in. |
| 1960 | Bill Nieder, United States | 64 ft 6¾ in. |
| 1964 | Dallas Long, United States | 66 ft 8¼ in. |
| 1968 | Randy Matson, United States | 67 ft 4¾ in. |
| 1972 | Wladyslaw Konar, Poland | 69 ft 6 in. |
| 1976 | Udo Beyer, East Germany | (21.05) 69 ft ¾ in. |

**16-lb Shot-Put (Both Hands)**

| | | |
|---|---|---|
| 1912 | Ralph Rose, United States | 90 ft 5⅜ in. |

**Discus Throw**

| | | |
|---|---|---|
| 1896 | Robert Garrett, United States | 95 ft 7½ in. |
| 1900 | Rudolf Bauer, Hungary | 118 ft 2⅞ in. |
| 1904 | Martin Sheridan, United States | 128 ft 10½ in. |
| 1906 | Martin Sheridan, United States | 136 ft ⅓ in. |
| 1908 | Martin Sheridan, United States | 134 ft 2 in. |
| 1912 | Armas Taipale, Finland | 145 ft ⁹⁄₁₆ in. |
| 1920 | Elmer Niklander, Finland | 146 ft 7 in. |
| 1924 | Clarence Houser, United States | 151 ft 5¼ in. |
| 1928 | Clarence Houser, United States | 155 ft 2⅘ in. |
| 1932 | John Anderson, United States | 162 ft 4⅞ in. |
| 1936 | Ken Carpenter, United States | 165 ft 7⅜ in. |
| 1948 | Adolfo Consolini, Italy | 173 ft 2 in. |
| 1952 | Simeon Iness, United States | 180 ft 6½ in. |
| 1956 | Al Oerter, United States | 184 ft 10½ in. |
| 1960 | Al Oerter, United States | 194 ft 2 in. |
| 1964 | Al Oerter, United States | 200 ft 1½ in. |
| 1968 | Al Oerter, United States | 212 ft 6 in. |
| 1972 | Ludvik Danek, Czechoslovakia | 211 ft 3 in. |
| 1976 | Mac Wilkins, United States | (67.5) 221 ft 5 in. |

**Discus Throw—Greek Style**

| | | |
|---|---|---|
| 1906 | Werner Jaervinen, Finland | 115 ft 4 in. |
| 1908 | Martin Sheridan, United States | 124 ft 8 in. |

**Discus Throw (Both Hands)**

| | | |
|---|---|---|
| 1912 | Armas Taipale, Finland | 271 ft 10⅛ in. |

**Javelin Throw**

| | | |
|---|---|---|
| 1906 | Eric Lemming, Sweden | 175 ft 6 in. |
| 1908 | Eric Lemming, Sweden | 179 ft 10½ in. |
| 1912 | Eric Lemming, Sweden | 198 ft 11¼ in. |
| 1920 | Jonni Myyra, Finland | 215 ft 9¾ in. |
| 1924 | Jonni Myyra, Finland | 206 ft 6¾ in. |
| 1928 | Eric Lundquist, Sweden | 218 ft 6⅛ in. |
| 1932 | Matti Jarvinen, Finland | 238 ft 7 in. |
| 1936 | Gerhard Stoeck, Germany | 235 ft 8⁵⁄₁₆ in. |
| 1948 | Kaj Rautavaara, Finland | 228 ft 10½ in. |
| 1952 | Cy Young, United States | 242 ft ¾ in. |
| 1956 | Egil Danielsen, Norway | 281 ft 2¼ in. |
| 1960 | Viktor Tsibulenko, U.S.S.R. | 277 ft 8⅜ in. |
| 1964 | Pauli Nevala, Finland | 271 ft 2¼ in. |
| 1968 | Janis Lusis, U.S.S.R. | 295 ft 7 in. |
| 1972 | Klaus Wolfermann, West Germany | 296 ft 10 in. |
| 1976 | Miklos Nemeth, Hungary | (94.58) 310 ft 4 in. |

**Javelin Throw—Free Style**

| | | |
|---|---|---|
| 1908 | Eric Lemming, Sweden | 178 ft 7½ in. |

**Javelin Throw (Both Hands)**

| | | |
|---|---|---|
| 1912 | Julius Saaristo, Finland | 358 ft 11½ in. |

**16-lb Hammer Throw**

| | | |
|---|---|---|
| 1900 | John Flanagan, United States | 167 ft 4 in. |
| 1904 | John Flanagan, United States | 168 ft 1 in. |
| 1908 | John Flanagan, United States | 170 ft 4¼ in. |
| 1912 | Matt McGrath, United States | 179 ft 7⅛ in. |
| 1920 | Pat Ryan, United States | 173 ft 5⅝ in. |
| 1924 | Fred Tootell, United States | 174 ft 10¼ in. |
| 1928 | Patrick O'Callaghan, Ireland | 168 ft 7½ in. |
| 1932 | Patrick O'Callaghan, Ireland | 176 ft 11⅛ in. |
| 1936 | Karl Hein, Germany | 185 ft 4 in. |
| 1948 | Imre Nemeth, Hungary | 183 ft 11½ in. |
| 1952 | Jozsef Csermak, Hungary | 197 ft 11⁹⁄₁₆ in. |
| 1956 | Harold Connolly, United States | 207 ft 2¾ in. |
| 1960 | Vasily Rudenkov, U.S.S.R. | 220 ft 1⅝ in. |
| 1964 | Romuald Klim, U.S.S.R. | 228 ft 9½ in. |
| 1968 | Gyula Zsivotzky, Hungary | 240 ft 8 in. |

| | | |
|---|---|---|
| 1972 | Anatoly Bondarchuk, U.S.S.R. | 247 ft 8½ in. |
| 1976 | Yuri Sedyh, U.S.S.R. | (77.52) 254 ft 4 in. |

### Throwing the Stone (14 lbs.)

| | | |
|---|---|---|
| 1906 | Nicolas Georgantas, Greece | 65 ft 4⅕ in. |

### 56-lb Weight Throw

| | | |
|---|---|---|
| 1904 | Etienne Desmarteau, Canada | 34 ft 4 in. |
| 1920 | Pat McDonald, United States | 36 ft 11⅝ in. |

### All-Around

| | | |
|---|---|---|
| 1904 | Thomas Kiely, Great Britain | 6,036 pts. |

### Pentathlon

| | | |
|---|---|---|
| 1906 | H. Mellander, Sweden | 24 pts. |
| 1912 | Ferdinand Bie, Norway | 21 pts. |
| 1920 | Eero Lehtonen, Finland | 14 pts. |
| 1924 | Eero Lehtonen, Finland | 16 pts. |

### Decathlon

| | | |
|---|---|---|
| 1912 | Hugo Wieslander, Sweden | 7,724.495 pts. |
| 1920 | Helge Lovland, Norway | 6,804.35 pts. |
| 1924 | Harold Osborn, United States | 7,710.775 pts. |
| 1928 | Paavo Yrjola, Finland | 8,053.29 pts. |
| 1932 | James Bausch, United States | 8,462.23 pts. |
| 1936 | Glenn Morris, United States | 7,900 pts.[1] |
| 1948 | Robert B. Mathias, United States | 7,139 pts. |
| 1952 | Robert B. Mathias, United States | 7,887 pts. |
| 1956 | Milton Campbell, United States | 7,937 pts. |
| 1960 | Rafer Johnson, United States | 8,392 pts. |
| 1964 | Willi Holdorf, Germany | 7,887 pts.[1] |
| 1968 | Bill Toomey, United States | 8,193 pts. |
| 1972 | Nikolai Avilov, U.S.S.R. | 8,454 pts. |
| 1976 | Bruce Jenner, United States | 8,618 pts. |

1. Point system revised.

### Tug of War

| | | | |
|---|---|---|---|
| 1904 | United States | 1912 | Sweden |
| 1906 | Germany | 1920 | Great Britain |
| 1908 | Great Britain | | |

## TRACK AND FIELD—WOMEN

### 100-Meter Dash

| | | |
|---|---|---|
| 1928 | Elizabeth Robinson, United States | 12.2s |
| 1932 | Stella Walsh, Poland | 11.9s |
| 1936 | Helen Stephens, United States | 11.5s |
| 1948 | Fanny Blankers-Koen, Netherlands | 11.9s |
| 1952 | Marjorie Jackson, Australia | 11.5s |
| 1956 | Betty Cuthbert, Australia | 11.5s |
| 1960 | Wilma Rudolph, United States | 11s |
| 1964 | Wyomia Tyus, United States | 11.4s |
| 1968 | Wyomia Tyus, United States | 11s |
| 1972 | Renate Stecher, East Germany | 11.07s |
| 1976 | Annegret Richter, West Germany | 11.08s |

### 200-Meter Dash

| | | |
|---|---|---|
| 1948 | Fanny Blankers-Koen, Netherlands | 24.4s |
| 1952 | Marjorie Jackson, Australia | 23.7s |
| 1956 | Betty Cuthbert, Australia | 23.4s |
| 1960 | Wilma Rudolph, United States | 24s |
| 1964 | Edith McGuire, United States | 23s |
| 1968 | Irena Szewinska, Poland | 22.5s |
| 1972 | Renate Stecher, East Germany | 22.4s |
| 1976 | Baerbel Eckert, East Germany | 22.37s |

### 400-Meter Dash

| | | |
|---|---|---|
| 1964 | Betty Cuthbert, Australia | 52s |
| 1968 | Colette Besson, France | 52s |
| 1972 | Monika Zehrt, East Germany | 51.08s |
| 1976 | Irena Szewinska, Poland | 49.29s |

### 800-Meter Run

| | | |
|---|---|---|
| 1928 | Lina Radke, Germany | 2m16.8s |
| 1960 | Ljudmila Shevcova, U.S.S.R. | 2m4.3s |
| 1964 | Ann Packer, Great Britain | 2m1.1s |
| 1968 | Madeline Manning, United States | 2m0.9s |
| 1972 | Hildegard Falck, West Germany | 1m58.6s |
| 1976 | Tatiana Kazankina, U.S.S.R. | 1m54.94s |

### 1,500-Meter Run

| | | |
|---|---|---|
| 1972 | Ludmila Bragina, U.S.S.R. | 4m01.4s |
| 1976 | Tatiana Kazankina, U.S.S.R. | 4m05.48s |

### 80-Meter Hurdles

| | | |
|---|---|---|
| 1932 | Mildred Didrikson, United States | 11.7s |
| 1936 | Trebisonda Valla, Italy | 11.7s |
| 1948 | Fanny Blankers-Koen, Netherlands | 11.2s |
| 1952 | Shirley S. de la Hunty, Australia | 10.9s |
| 1956 | Shirley S. de la Hunty, Australia | 10.7s |
| 1960 | Irina Press, U.S.S.R. | 10.8s |
| 1964 | Karin Balzer, Germany | 10.5s[1] |
| 1968 | Maureen Caird, Australia | 10.3s |

1. Wind assisted.

### 100-Meter Hurdles

| | | |
|---|---|---|
| 1972 | Annelie Ehrhardt, East Germany | 12.59s |
| 1976 | Johanna Schaller, East Germany | 12.77s |

### 400-Meter Relay

| | | |
|---|---|---|
| 1928 | Canada | 48.4s |
| 1932 | United States | 47s |
| 1936 | United States | 46.9s |
| 1948 | Netherlands | 47.5s |
| 1952 | United States | 45.9s |
| 1956 | Australia | 44.5s |
| 1960 | United States | 44.5s |
| 1964 | Poland | 43.6s |
| 1968 | United States | 42.8s |
| 1972 | West Germany | 42.81s |
| 1976 | East Germany | 42.55s |

### 1,600-Meter Relay

| | | |
|---|---|---|
| 1972 | East Germany | 3m23s |
| 1976 | East Germany | 3m19.23s |

### Running High Jump

| | | |
|---|---|---|
| 1928 | Ethel Catherwood, Canada | 5 ft 3 in. |
| 1932 | Jean Shiley, United States | 5 ft 5¼ in. |
| 1936 | Ibolya Csak, Hungary | 5 ft 3 in. |
| 1948 | Alice Coachman, United States | 5 ft 6⅛ in. |
| 1952 | Ester Brand, South Africa | 5 ft 5¾ in. |
| 1956 | Mildred McDaniel, United States | 5 ft 9¼ in. |
| 1960 | Iolanda Balas, Romania | 6 ft ¾ in. |
| 1964 | Iolanda Balas, U.S.S.R. | 6 ft 2¾ in. |
| 1968 | Miloslava Rezkova, Czechoslovakia | 5 ft 11¾ in. |
| 1972 | Ulrike Meyfarth, West Germany | 6 ft 3⅝ in. |
| 1976 | Rosemarie Ackerman, East Germany | (1.93) 6 ft 4 in. |

### Long Jump

| | | |
|---|---|---|
| 1948 | Olga Gyarmati, Hungary | 18 ft 8¼ in. |
| 1952 | Yvette Williams, New Zealand | 20 ft 5¾ in. |
| 1956 | Elzbieta Krzesinska, Poland | 20 ft 9¾ in. |
| 1960 | Vera Krepkina, U.S.S.R. | 20 ft 10¾ in. |
| 1964 | Mary Rand, Great Britain | 22 ft 2 in. |
| 1968 | Viorica Ciscopoleanu, Romania | 22 ft 4½ in. |
| 1972 | Heidemarie Rosendahl, West Germany | 22 ft 3 in. |
| 1976 | Angela Voigt, East Germany | (6.72) 22 ft ½ in. |

### Shot-Put

| | | |
|---|---|---|
| 1948 | Micheline Ostermeyer, France | 45 ft 1½ in. |
| 1952 | Galina Zybina, U.S.S.R. | 50 ft 1½ in. |
| 1956 | Tamara Tishkyevich, U.S.S.R. | 54 ft 5 in. |

| | | |
|---|---|---|
| 1960 | Tamara Press, U.S.S.R. | 56 ft 9⅞ in. |
| 1964 | Tamara Press, U.S.S.R. | 59 ft 6 in. |
| 1968 | Margita Gummel, East Germany | 64 ft 4 in. |
| 1972 | Nadezhda Chizhova, U.S.S.R. | 69 ft |
| 1976 | Ivanka Christova, Bulgaria | (21.16) 69 ft 5 in. |

**Discus Throw**

| | | |
|---|---|---|
| 1928 | Helena Konopacka, Poland | 129 ft 11⅞ in. |
| 1932 | Lillian Copeland, United States | 133 ft 2 in. |
| 1936 | Gisela Mauermayer, Germany | 156 ft 3 3/16 in. |
| 1948 | Micheline Ostermeyer, France | 137 ft 6½ in. |
| 1952 | Nina Romaschkova, U.S.S.R. | 168 ft 8 7/16 in. |
| 1956 | Olga Fikotova, Czechoslovakia | 176 ft 1½ in. |
| 1960 | Nina Ponomareva, U.S.S.R. | 180 ft 8¼ in. |
| 1964 | Tamara Press, U.S.S.R. | 187 ft 10¾ in. |
| 1968 | Lia Manoliu, Romania | 191 ft 2½ in. |
| 1972 | Faina Melnik, U.S.S.R. | 218 ft 7 in. |
| 1976 | Evelin Schlaak, East Germany | (69.0) 226 ft 4 in. |

**Javelin Throw**

| | | |
|---|---|---|
| 1932 | Mildred Didrikson, United States | 143 ft 4 in. |
| 1936 | Tilly Fleischer, Germany | 148 ft 2¾ in. |
| 1948 | Herma Bauma, Austria | 149 ft 6 in. |
| 1952 | Dana Zatopek, Czechoslovakia | 165 ft 7 in. |
| 1956 | Inessa Janzeme, U.S.S.R. | 176 ft 8 in. |
| 1960 | Elvira Ozolina, U.S.S.R. | 183 ft 8 in. |
| 1964 | Mihaela Penes, Romania | 198 ft 7½ in. |
| 1968 | Angela Nemeth, Hungary | 198 ft 0 in. |
| 1972 | Ruth Fuchs, East Germany | 209 ft 7 in. |
| 1976 | Ruth Fuchs, East Germany | (65.94) 216 ft 4 in. |

**Pentathlon**

| | | |
|---|---|---|
| 1964 | Irina Press, U.S.S.R. | 5,246 pts. |
| 1968 | Ingrid Becker, West Germany | 5,098 pts. |
| 1972 | Mary Peters, Britain | 4,801 pts. |
| 1976 | Siegrun Siegl, East Germany | 4,745 pts. |

## SWIMMING—MEN

### 50 Yards Freestyle

| | | |
|---|---|---|
| 1904 | Zoltan de Halmay, Hungary | 28s |

### 100 Meters Freestyle

| | | |
|---|---|---|
| 1896 | Alfred Hajos, Hungary | 1m22.2s |
| 1904 | Zoltan de Halmay, Hungary | 1m2.8s[1] |
| 1906 | Charles Daniels, United States | 1m13s |
| 1908 | Charles Daniels, United States | 1m5.6s |
| 1912 | Duke P. Kahanamoku, United States | 1m3.4s |
| 1920 | Duke P. Kahanamoku, United States | 1m1.4s |
| 1924 | John Weissmuller, United States | 59s |
| 1928 | John Weissmuller, United States | 58.6s |
| 1932 | Yasuji Miyazaki, Japan | 58.2s |
| 1936 | Ferenc Csik, Hungary | 57.6s |
| 1948 | Walter Ris, United States | 57.3s |
| 1952 | Clarke Scholes, United States | 57.4s |
| 1956 | Jon Henricks, Australia | 55.4s |
| 1960 | John Devitt, Australia | 55.2s |
| 1964 | Don Schollander, United States | 53.4s |
| 1968 | Michael Wenden, Australia | 52.2s |
| 1972 | Mark Spitz, United States | 51.22s |
| 1976 | Jim Montgomery, United States | 49.99s |

1. 100 yards.

### 200 Meters Freestyle

| | | |
|---|---|---|
| 1900 | Frederick Lane, Australia | 2m25.2s |
| 1904 | Charles Daniels, United States | 2m44.2s[1] |
| 1968 | Michael Wenden, Australia | 1m55.2s |
| 1972 | Mark Spitz, United States | 1m52.78s |
| 1976 | Bruce Furniss, United States | 1m50.29s |

1. 220 yards.

### 400 Meters Freestyle

| | | |
|---|---|---|
| 1896 | Paul Neumann, Austria | 8m12.6s[1] |
| 1904 | Charles Daniels, United States | 6m16.2s[2] |
| 1906 | Otto Sheff, Austria | 6m23.8s |
| 1908 | Henry Taylor, Great Britain | 5m36.8s |
| 1912 | George Hodgson, Canada | 5m24.4s |
| 1920 | Norman Ross, United States | 5m26.8s |
| 1924 | John Weissmuller, United States | 5m4.2s |
| 1928 | Albert Zorilla, Argentina | 5m1.6s |
| 1932 | Clarence Crabbe, United States | 4m48.4s |
| 1936 | Jack Medica, United States | 4m44.5s |
| 1948 | William Smith, United States | 4m41s |
| 1952 | Jean Boiteux, France | 4m30.7s |
| 1956 | Murray Rose, Australia | 4m27.3s |
| 1960 | Murray Rose, Australia | 4m18.3s |
| 1964 | Don Schollander, United States | 4m12.2s |
| 1968 | Mike Burton, United States | 4m9s |
| 1972 | Bradford Cooper, Australia[3] | 4m00.27s |
| 1976 | Brian Goodell, United States | 3m51.93s |

1. 500 meters. 2. 440 yards. 3. Rick DeMont, United States, won but was disqualified following day for medical reasons.

### 1,200 Meters Freestyle

| | | |
|---|---|---|
| 1896 | Alfred Hajos, Hungary | 18m22.2s |

### 1,500 Meters Freestyle

| | | |
|---|---|---|
| 1904 | Emil Rausch, Germany | 27m18.2s[1] |
| 1906 | Henry Taylor, Great Britain | 28m28s[2] |
| 1908 | Henry Taylor, Great Britain | 22m48.4s |
| 1912 | George Hodgson, Canada | 22m |
| 1920 | Norman Ross, United States | 22m23.2s |
| 1924 | Andrew Charlton, Australia | 20m6.6s |
| 1928 | Arne Borg, Sweden | 19m51.8s |
| 1932 | Kusuo Kitamura, Japan | 19m12.4s |
| 1936 | Noboru Terada, Japan | 19m13.7s |
| 1948 | James McLane, United States | 19m18.5s |
| 1952 | Ford Konno, United States | 18m30s |
| 1956 | Murray Rose, Australia | 17m58.9s |
| 1960 | Jon Konrads, Australia | 17m19.6s |
| 1964 | Robert Windle, Australia | 17m1.7s |
| 1968 | Michael Burton, United States | 16m38.9s |
| 1972 | Mike Burton, United States | 15m52.58s |
| 1976 | Brian Goodell, United States | 15m02.4s |

1. One mile. 2. 1,600 meters.

### 4,000 Meters Freestyle

| | | |
|---|---|---|
| 1900 | John Jarvis, Great Britain | 58m24s |

### 100-Meter Backstroke

| | | |
|---|---|---|
| 1904 | Walter Brack, Germany | 1m16.8s[1] |
| 1908 | Arno Bieberstein, Germany | 1m24.6s |
| 1912 | Harry Hebner, United States | 1m21.2s |
| 1920 | Warren Kealoha, United States | 1m15.2s |
| 1924 | Warren Kealoha, United States | 1m13.2s |
| 1928 | George Kojac, United States | 1m8.2s |
| 1932 | Masaji Kiyokawa, Japan | 1m8.6s |
| 1936 | Adolph Kiefer, United States | 1m5.9s |
| 1948 | Allen Stack, United States | 1m6.4s |
| 1952 | Yoshinobu Oyakawa, United States | 1m5.4s |
| 1956 | David Thiele, Australia | 1m2.2s |
| 1960 | David Thiele, Australia | 1m1.9s |
| 1968 | Roland Matthes, East Germany | 58.7s |
| 1972 | Roland Matthes, East Germany | 56.58s |
| 1976 | John Naber, United States | 55.49s |

1. 100 yards

### 200-Meter Backstroke

| | | |
|---|---|---|
| 1900 | Ernst Hoppenberg, Germany | 2m47s |
| 1964 | Jed Graef, United States | 2m10.3s |
| 1968 | Roland Matthes, East Germany | 2m9.6s |
| 1972 | Roland Matthes, East Germany | 2m2.82s |
| 1976 | John Naber, United States | 1m59.19s |

### 100-Meter Breaststroke

| | | |
|---|---|---|
| 1968 | Donald McKenzie, United States | 1m7.7s |

| | | |
|---|---|---|
| 1972 | Nobutaka Taguchi, Japan | 1m4.94s |
| 1976 | John Hencken, United States | 1m03.11s |

**200-Meter Breaststroke**

| | | |
|---|---|---|
| 1908 | Frederick Holman, Great Britain | 3m9.2s |
| 1912 | Walter Bathe, Germany | 3m1.8s |
| 1920 | Haken Malmroth, Sweden | 3m4.4s |
| 1924 | Robert Skelton, United States | 2m56.6s |
| 1928 | Yoshiyuki Tsuruta, Japan | 2m48.8s |
| 1932 | Yoshiyuki Tsuruta, Japan | 2m45.4s |
| 1936 | Tetsuo Hamuro, Japan | 2m41.5s |
| 1948 | Joseph Verdeur, United States | 2m39.3s |
| 1952 | John Davies, Australia | 2m34.4s |
| 1956 | Masura Furukawa, Japan | 2m34.7s |
| 1960 | Bill Mulliken, United States | 2m37.4s |
| 1964 | Ian O'Brien, Australia | 2m27.8s |
| 1968 | Felipe Munoz, Mexico | 2m28.7s |
| 1972 | John Hencken, United States | 2m21.55s |
| 1976 | David Willkie, Britain | 2m15.11s |

**400-Meter Breaststroke**

| | | |
|---|---|---|
| 1904 | Georg Zacharias, Germany | 7m23.6s[1] |
| 1912 | Walter Bathe, Germany | 6m29.6s |
| 1920 | Haken Malmroth, Sweden | 6m31.8s |

1. 440 yards

**100-Meter Butterfly**

| | | |
|---|---|---|
| 1968 | Douglas Russell, United States | 55.9s |
| 1972 | Mark Spitz, United States | 54.27s |
| 1976 | Matt Vogel, United States | 54.35s |

**200-Meter Butterfly**

| | | |
|---|---|---|
| 1956 | Bill Yorzyk, United States | 2m19.3s |
| 1960 | Mike Troy, United States | 2m12.8s |
| 1964 | Kevin Berry, Australia | 2m6.6s |
| 1968 | Carl Robie, United States | 2m8.7s |
| 1972 | Mark Spitz, United States | 2m00.7s |
| 1976 | Mike Bruner, United States | 1m59.23s |

**200-Meter Individual Medley**

| | | |
|---|---|---|
| 1968 | Charles Hickcox, United States | 2m12s |
| 1972 | Gunnar Larsson, Sweden | 2m7.17s |

**400-Meter Individual Medley**

| | | |
|---|---|---|
| 1964 | Dick Roth, United States | 4m45.4s |
| 1968 | Charles Hickcox, United States | 4m48.4s |
| 1972 | Gunnar Larsson, Sweden | 4m31.98s |
| 1976 | Rod Strachan, United States | 4m23.68s |

**60-Meter Underwater**

| | | |
|---|---|---|
| 1900 | de Vaudeville, France | 1m53.4s |

**200-Meter Obstacle**

| | | |
|---|---|---|
| 1900 | Frederick Lane, Australia | 2m38.4s |

**Relays**

| | | |
|---|---|---|
| 1900 | Germany (200 meters, 5 men) | 32 pts. |
| 1904 | United States (200 yards) | 2m4.6s |
| 1906 | Hungary (1,000 meters) | 16m52.4s |

**400-Meter Freestyle Relay**

| | | |
|---|---|---|
| 1964 | United States | 3m32.2s |
| 1968 | United States | 3m31.7s |
| 1972 | United States | 3m26.42s |

**800-Meter Freestyle Relay**

| | | |
|---|---|---|
| 1908 | Great Britain | 10m55.6s |
| 1912 | Australia | 10m11.2s |
| 1920 | United States | 10m4.4s |
| 1924 | United States | 9m53.4s |
| 1928 | United States | 9m36.2s |
| 1932 | Japan | 8m58.4s |
| 1936 | Japan | 8m51.5s |
| 1948 | United States | 8m46s |
| 1952 | United States | 8m31.1s |
| 1956 | Australia | 8m23.6s |
| 1960 | United States | 8m10.2s |
| 1964 | United States | 7m52.1s |
| 1968 | United States | 7m52.3s |
| 1972 | United States | 7m35.78s |
| 1976 | United States | 7m23.22s |

**400-Meter Medley Relay**

| | | |
|---|---|---|
| 1960 | United States | 4m5.4s |
| 1964 | United States | 3m58.4s |
| 1968 | United States | 3m54.9s |
| 1972 | United States | 3m48.16s |
| 1976 | United States | 3m42.22s |

**Springboard Dive**

| | | Points |
|---|---|---|
| 1908 | Albert Zuerner, Germany | 85.5 |
| 1912 | Paul Guenther, Germany | 79.23 |
| 1920 | Louis Kuehn, United States | 675 |
| 1924 | Albert White, United States | 696.4 |
| 1928 | Pete Desjardins, United States | 185.04 |
| 1932 | Michael Galitzen, United States | 161.38 |
| 1936 | Richard Degener, United States | 163.57 |
| 1948 | Bruce Harlan, United States | 163.64 |
| 1952 | David Browning, United States | 205.59 |
| 1956 | Robert Clotworthy, United States | 159.56 |
| 1960 | Gary Tobian, United States | 170.00 |
| 1964 | Ken Sitzberger, United States | 159.90 |
| 1968 | Bernard Wrightson, United States | 170.15 |
| 1972 | Vladimir Vasin, U.S.S.R. | 594.09 |
| 1976 | Phil Boggs, United States | 619.05 |

**Platform Dive**

| | | Points |
|---|---|---|
| 1904 | G. E. Sheldon, United States | 12.75 |
| 1906 | Gottlob Walz, Germany | 156 |
| 1908 | Hialmar Johansson, Sweden | 83.75 |
| 1912 | Erik Adlerz, Sweden | 73.94 |
| 1920 | Clarence Pinkston, United States | 100.67 |
| 1924 | Albert White, United States | 487.3 |
| 1928 | Pete Desjardins, United States | 98.74 |
| 1932 | Harold Smith, United States | 124.80 |
| 1936 | Marshall Wayne, United States | 113.58 |
| 1948 | Samuel Lee, United States | 130.05 |
| 1952 | Samuel Lee, United States | 156.28 |
| 1956 | Joaquin Capilla, Mexico | 152.44 |
| 1960 | Bob Webster, United States | 165.56 |
| 1964 | Bob Webster, United States | 148.58 |
| 1968 | Klaus Dibiasi, Italy | 164.18 |
| 1972 | Klaus Dibiasi, Italy | 504.12 |
| 1976 | Klaus Dibiasi, Italy | 600.51 |

**Plain High Dive**

| | | Points |
|---|---|---|
| 1912 | Erik Adlerz, Sweden | 40 |
| 1920 | Arvid Wallman, Sweden | 7 |
| 1924 | Richard Eve, Australia | 160 |

**Plunge for Distance**

| | | |
|---|---|---|
| 1904 | W. E. Dickey, United States | 62 ft 6 in. |

## SWIMMING—WOMEN

**100 Meters Freestyle**

| | | |
|---|---|---|
| 1912 | Fanny Durack, Australia | 1m22.2s |
| 1920 | Ethelda Bleibtrey, United States | 1m13.6s |
| 1924 | Ethel Lackie, United States | 1m12.4s |
| 1928 | Albina Osipowich, United States | 1m11s |

| | | |
|---|---|---|
| 1932 | Helene Madison, United States | 1m6.8s |
| 1936 | Hendrika Mastenbroek, Netherlands | 1m5.9s |
| 1948 | Greta Andersen, Denmark | 1m6.3s |
| 1952 | Katalin Szoke, Hungary | 1m6.8s |
| 1956 | Dawn Fraser, Australia | 1m2s |
| 1960 | Dawn Fraser, Australia | 1m1.2s |
| 1964 | Dawn Fraser, Australia | 59.5s |
| 1968 | Marge Jan Henne, United States | 1m |
| 1972 | Sandra Neilson, United States | 58.59s |
| 1976 | Kornelia Ender, East Germany | 55.65s |

### 200 Meters Freestyle

| | | |
|---|---|---|
| 1968 | Debbie Meyer, United States | 2m10.5s |
| 1972 | Shane Gould, Australia | 2m3.56s |
| 1976 | Kornelia Ender, East Germany | 1m59.26s |

### 400 Meters Freestyle

| | | |
|---|---|---|
| 1920 | Ethelda Bleibtrey, United States | 4m34s[1] |
| 1924 | Martha Norelius, United States | 6m2.2s |
| 1928 | Martha Norelius, United States | 5m42.8s |
| 1932 | Helene Madison, United States | 5m28.5s |
| 1936 | Hendrika Mastenbroek, Netherlands | 5m26.4s |
| 1948 | Ann Curtis, United States | 5m17.8s |
| 1952 | Valerie Gyenge, Hungary | 5m12.1s |
| 1956 | Lorraine Crapp, Australia | 4m54.6s |
| 1960 | Chris von Saltza, United States | 4m50.6s |
| 1964 | Ginny Duenkel, United States | 4m43.3s |
| 1968 | Debbie Meyer, United States | 4m31.8s |
| 1972 | Shane Gould, Australia | 4m19.04s |
| 1976 | Petra Thumer, East Germany | 4m09.89s |

1. 300 meters.

### 800 Meters Freestyle

| | | |
|---|---|---|
| 1968 | Debbie Meyer, United States | 9m24s |
| 1972 | Keena Rothhammer, United States | 8m53.68s |
| 1976 | Petra Thumer, East Germany | 8m37.14s |

### 100-Meter Backstroke

| | | |
|---|---|---|
| 1924 | Sybil Bauer, United States | 1m23.2s |
| 1928 | Marie Braun, Netherlands | 1m22s |
| 1932 | Eleanor Holm, United States | 1m19.4s |
| 1936 | Dina Senff, Netherlands | 1m18.9s |
| 1948 | Karen Harup, Denmark | 1m14.4s |
| 1952 | Joan Harrison, South Africa | 1m14.3s |
| 1956 | Judy Grinham, Great Britain | 1m12.9s |
| 1960 | Lynn Burke, United States | 1m9.3s |
| 1964 | Cathy Ferguson, United States | 1m7.7s |
| 1968 | Kaye Hall, United States | 1m6.2s |
| 1972 | Melissa Belote, United States | 1m5.78s |
| 1976 | Ulrike Richter, East Germany | 1m01.83s |

### 200-Meter Backstroke

| | | |
|---|---|---|
| 1968 | Pokey Watson, United States | 2m24.8s |
| 1972 | Melissa Belote, United States | 2m19.19s |
| 1976 | Ulrike Richter, East Germany | 2m13.43s |

### 100-Meter Breaststroke

| | | |
|---|---|---|
| 1968 | Djurdjica Bjedov, Yugoslavia | 1m15.8s |
| 1972 | Catherine Carr, United States | 1m13.58s |
| 1976 | Hannelore Anke, East Germany | 1m11.16s |

### 200-Meter Breaststroke

| | | |
|---|---|---|
| 1924 | Lucy Morton, Great Britain | 3m33.2s |
| 1928 | Hilde Schrader, Germany | 3m12.6s |
| 1932 | Clare Dennis, Australia | 3m6.3s |
| 1936 | Hideko Maehata, Japan | 3m3.6s |
| 1948 | Nel van Vliet, Netherlands | 2m57.2s |
| 1952 | Eva Szekely, Hungary | 2m51.7s |
| 1956 | Ursala Happe, Germany | 2m53.1s |
| 1960 | Anita Lonsbrough, Great Britain | 2m49.5s |
| 1964 | Galina Prozumenschikova, U.S.S.R. | 2m46.4s |
| 1968 | Sharon Wichman, United States | 2m44.4s |
| 1972 | Beverly Whitfield, Australia | 2m41.71s |
| 1976 | Marina Koshevaia, U.S.S.R. | 2m33.35s |

### 100-Meter Butterfly

| | | |
|---|---|---|
| 1956 | Shelley Mann, United States | 1m11s |
| 1960 | Carolyn Schuler, United States | 1m9.5s |
| 1964 | Sharon Stouder, United States | 1m4.7s |
| 1968 | Lynn McClements, Australia | 1m5.5s |
| 1972 | Mayumi Aoki, Japan | 1m3.34s |
| 1976 | Kornelia Ender, East Germany | 1m00.13s |

### 200-Meter Butterfly

| | | |
|---|---|---|
| 1968 | Ada Kok, Netherlands | 2m24.7s |
| 1972 | Karen Moe, United States | 2m15.57s |
| 1976 | Andrea Pollack, East Germany | 2m11.41s |

### 200-Meter Individual Medley

| | | |
|---|---|---|
| 1968 | Claudia Kolb, United States | 2m24.7s |
| 1972 | Shane Gould, Australia | 2m23.07s |

### 400-Meter Individual Medley

| | | |
|---|---|---|
| 1964 | Donna de Varona, United States | 5m18.7s |
| 1968 | Claudia Kolb, United States | 5m8.5s |
| 1972 | Gail Neall, Australia | 5m2.97s |
| 1976 | Ulrike Tauber, East Germany | 4m42.77s |

### 400-Meter Freestyle Relay

| | | |
|---|---|---|
| 1912 | Great Britain | 5m52.8s |
| 1920 | United States | 5m11.6s |
| 1924 | United States | 4m58.8s |
| 1928 | United States | 4m47.6s |
| 1932 | United States | 4m38s |
| 1936 | Netherlands | 4m36s |
| 1948 | United States | 4m29.2s |
| 1952 | Hungary | 4m24.4s |
| 1956 | Australia | 4m17.1s |
| 1960 | United States | 4m8.9s |
| 1964 | United States | 4m3.8s |
| 1968 | United States | 4m2.5s |
| 1972 | United States | 3m55.19s |
| 1976 | United States | 3m44.82s |

### 400-Meter Medley Relay

| | | |
|---|---|---|
| 1960 | United States | 4m41.1s |
| 1964 | United States | 4m33.9s |
| 1968 | United States | 4m28.3s |
| 1972 | United States | 4m20.75s |
| 1976 | East Germany | 4m07.95s |

### Springboard Dive

| | | Points |
|---|---|---|
| 1920 | Aileen Riggin, United States | 539.90 |
| 1924 | Elizabeth Becker, United States | 474.5 |
| 1928 | Helen Meany, United States | 78.62 |
| 1932 | Georgia Coleman, United States | 87.52 |
| 1936 | Marjorie Gestring, United States | 89.27 |
| 1948 | Victoria M. Draves, United States | 108.74 |
| 1952 | Patricia McCormick, United States | 147.30 |
| 1956 | Patricia McCormick, United States | 142.36 |
| 1960 | Ingrid Kramer, Germany | 155.81 |
| 1964 | Ingrid Kramer Engel, Germany | 145.00 |
| 1968 | Sue Gossick, United States | 150.77 |
| 1972 | Micki King, United States | 450.03 |
| 1976 | Jennifer Chandler, United States | 506.19 |

### Platform Dive

| | | Points |
|---|---|---|
| 1912 | Greta Johansson, Sweden | 39.9 |
| 1920 | Stefani Fryland, Denmark | 34.60 |
| 1924 | Caroline Smith, United States | 166 |
| 1928 | Elizabeth B. Pinkston, United States | 31.60 |

| | | |
|---|---|---|
| 1932 | Dorothy Poynton, United States | 40.26 |
| 1936 | Dorothy Poynton Hill, United States | 33.92 |
| 1948 | Victoria M. Draves, United States | 68.87 |
| 1952 | Patricia McCormick, United States | 79.37 |
| 1956 | Patricia McCormick, United States | 84.85 |
| 1960 | Ingrid Kramer, Germany | 91.28 |
| 1964 | Lesley Bush, United States | 99.80 |
| 1968 | Milena Duchkova, Czechoslovakia | 109.59 |
| 1972 | Ulrika Knape, Sweden | 390.00 |
| 1976 | Elena Vaytsekhovskaia, U.S.S.R. | 406.59 |

## BOXING

(U.S. winners only)

**Flyweight—112 Pounds (51 kilograms)**

1904 George V. Finnegan
1920 Frank De Genaro
1924 Fidel La Barba
1952 Nate Brooks
1976 Leo Randolph

**Bantamweight—119 pounds (54 kg)**

1904 O.L. Kirk

**Featherweight—126 pounds (57 kg)**

1904 O.L. Kirk
1924 Jackie Fields

**Lightweight—132 Pounds (60 kg)**

1904 H.J. Spanger
1920 Samuel Mosberg
1968 Ronnie Harris
1976 Howard Davis

**Light Welterweight—140 Pounds (63.5 kg)**

1952 Charles Adkins
1972 Ray Seales
1976 Ray Leonard

**Welterweight—148 Pounds (67 kg)**

1904 Al Young
1932 Edward Flynn

**Light Middleweight—157 Pounds (71 kg)**

1960 Wilbert McClure

**Middleweight—165 Pounds (75 kg)**

1904 Charles Mayer
1932 Carmen Barth
1952 Floyd Patterson
1960 Eddie Crook
1976 Mike Spinks

**Light Heavyweight—179 Pounds (81 kg)**

1920 Edward Eagan
1952 Norvel Lee
1956 James Boyd
1960 Cassius Clay
1976 Leon Spinks

**Heavyweight (unlimited)**

1904 Sam Berger
1952 Edward Sanders
1956 Pete Rademacher
1964 Joe Frazier
1968 George Foreman

## BASKETBALL—MEN

1904 United States
1936 United States
1948 United States
1952 United States
1956 United States
1960 United States
1964 United States
1968 United States
1972 U.S.S.R.
1976 United States

## BASKETBALL—WOMEN

1976 U.S.S.R.

# *Winter Games*

## FIGURE SKATING—MEN

1908 Ulrich Salchow, Sweden
1920 Gillis Grafstrom, Sweden
1924 Gillis Grafstrom, Sweden
1928 Gillis Grafstrom, Sweden
1932 Karl Schaefer, Austria
1936 Karl Schaefer, Austria
1948 Richard Button, United States
1952 Richard Button, United States
1956 Hayes Alan Jenkins, United States
1960 David Jenkins, United States
1964 Manfred Schnelldorfer, Germany
1968 Wolfgang Schwartz, Austria
1972 Ondrej Nepela, Czechoslovakia
1976 John Curry, Britain

## FIGURE SKATING—WOMEN

1908 Madge Syers, Britain
1920 Magda Mauroy, Sweden
1924 Herma Szabo-Planck, Austria
1928 Sonja Henie, Norway
1932 Sonja Henie, Norway
1936 Sonja Henie, Norway
1948 Barbara Ann Scott, Canada
1952 Jeannette Altwegg, Britain
1956 Tenley Albright, United States
1960 Carol Heiss, United States
1964 Sjoukje Dijkstra, Netherlands
1968 Peggy Fleming, United States
1972 Beatrix Schuba, Austria
1976 Dorothy Hamill, United States

## SPEED SKATING—MEN

(U.S. winners only)

**500 Meters**

1924 Charles Jewfraw
1932 John A. Shea
1952 Kenneth Henry
1964 Terrence McDermott

**1,000 Meters**

1976 Peter Mueller

**1,500 Meters**

1932 John A. Shea

**5,000 Meters**

1932 Irving Jaffee

**10,000 Meters**

1932 Irving Jaffee

## SPEED SKATING—WOMEN

**500 Meters**

1972 Anne Henning
1976 Sheila Young

**1,500 Meters**

1972 Dianne Holum

## SKIING, ALPINE—MEN

### Downhill

| | | |
|---|---|---|
| 1948 | Henry Oreiller, France | 2m55.0s |
| 1952 | Zeno Colo, Italy | 2m30.8s |
| 1956 | Anton Sailer, Austria | 2m52.2s |
| 1960 | Jean Vuarnet, France | 2m06.2s |
| 1964 | Egon Zimmermann, Austria | 2m18.16s |
| 1968 | Jean-Claude Killy, France | 1m59.85s |
| 1972 | Bernhard Russi, Switzerland | 1m51.43s |
| 1976 | Franz Klammer, Austria | 1m45.72s |

### Slalom

| | | |
|---|---|---|
| 1948 | Edi Reinalter, Switzerland | 2m10.3s |
| 1952 | Othmar Schneider, Austria | 2m00.0s |
| 1956 | Anton Sailer, Austria | 194.7 pts. |
| 1960 | Ernst Hinterseer, Austria | 2m08.9s |
| 1968 | Jean-Claude Killy, France | 1m39.73s |
| 1972 | Francisco Fernandez Ochoa, Spain | 1m49.27s |
| 1976 | Piero Gros, Italy | 2m03.29s |

### Giant Slalom

| | | |
|---|---|---|
| 1952 | Stein Eriksen, Norway | 2m25.0s |
| 1956 | Anton Sailer, Austria | 3m00.1s |
| 1960 | Roger Staub, Switzerland | 1m48.3s |
| 1964 | Francois Bonlieu, France | 1m46.71s |
| 1968 | Jean-Claude Killy, France | 3m29.28s |
| 1972 | Gustavo Thoeni, Italy | 3m09.52s |
| 1976 | Heini Hemmi, Switzerland | 3m26.97s |

## SKIING, ALPINE—WOMEN

### Downhill

| | | |
|---|---|---|
| 1948 | Hedi Schlunegger, Switzerland | 2m28.3s |
| 1952 | Trude Jochum-Beiser, Austria | 1m47.1s |
| 1956 | Madeleine Berthod, Switzerland | 1m40.1s |
| 1960 | Heidi Biebl, Germany | 1m37.6s |
| 1964 | Christl Haas, Austria | 1m55.39s |
| 1968 | Olga Pall, Austria | 1m40.87s |
| 1972 | Marie-Therese Nadig, Switzerland | 1m36.68s |
| 1976 | Rosi Mittermeier, West Germany | 1m46.16s |

### Slalom

| | | |
|---|---|---|
| 1948 | Gretchen Fraser, United States | 1m57.2s |
| 1952 | Andrea M. Lawrence, United States | 2m10.6s |
| 1956 | Renee Colliard, Switzerland | 112.3 pts. |
| 1960 | Anne Heggtveigt, Canada | 1m49.6s |
| 1964 | Christine Goitschel, France | 1m29.86s |
| 1968 | Marielle Goitschel, France | 1m25.86s |
| 1972 | Barbara Cochran, United States | 1m31.24s |
| 1976 | Rosi Mittermeier, West Germany | 1m30.54s |

### Giant Slalom

| | | |
|---|---|---|
| 1952 | Andrea M. Lawrence, United States | 2m06.8s |
| 1956 | Ossi Reichert, Germany | 1m56.5s |
| 1960 | Yvonne Ruegg, Switzerland | 1m39.9s |
| 1964 | Marielle Goitschel, France | 1m52.24s |
| 1968 | Nancy Greene, Canada | 1m51.97s |
| 1972 | Marie-Therese Nadig, Switzerland | 1m29.90s |
| 1976 | Kathy Kreiner, Canada | 1m29.13s |

## ICE HOCKEY

| | |
|---|---|
| 1920 | Canada |
| 1924 | Canada |
| 1928 | Canada |
| 1932 | Canada |
| 1936 | Britain |
| 1948 | Canada |
| 1952 | Canada |
| 1956 | U.S.S.R. |
| 1960 | United States |
| 1964 | U.S.S.R. |
| 1968 | U.S.S.R. |
| 1972 | U.S.S.R. |
| 1976 | U.S.S.R. |

## DISTRIBUTION OF MEDALS 1976 SUMMER GAMES

| | Gold | Silver | Bronze | Total |
|---|---|---|---|---|
| Soviet Union | 47 | 43 | 35 | 125 |
| East Germany | 40 | 25 | 25 | 90 |
| United States | 34 | 35 | 25 | 94 |
| West Germany | 10 | 12 | 17 | 39 |
| Japan | 9 | 6 | 10 | 25 |
| Poland | 8 | 6 | 11 | 25 |
| Bulgaria | 7 | 8 | 9 | 24 |
| Cuba | 6 | 4 | 3 | 13 |
| Romania | 4 | 9 | 14 | 27 |
| Hungary | 4 | 5 | 12 | 21 |
| Finland | 4 | 2 | 0 | 6 |
| Sweden | 4 | 1 | 0 | 5 |
| Britain | 3 | 5 | 5 | 13 |
| Italy | 2 | 7 | 4 | 13 |
| France | 2 | 2 | 5 | 9 |
| Yugoslavia | 2 | 3 | 3 | 8 |
| Czechoslovakia | 2 | 2 | 4 | 8 |
| New Zealand | 2 | 1 | 1 | 4 |
| South Korea | 1 | 1 | 4 | 6 |
| Switzerland | 1 | 1 | 2 | 4 |
| Jamaica | 1 | 1 | 0 | 2 |
| North Korea | 1 | 1 | 0 | 2 |
| Norway | 1 | 1 | 0 | 2 |
| Denmark | 1 | 0 | 2 | 3 |
| Mexico | 1 | 0 | 1 | 2 |
| Trinidad and Tobago | 1 | 0 | 0 | 1 |
| Canada | 0 | 5 | 6 | 11 |
| Belgium | 0 | 3 | 3 | 6 |
| Netherlands | 0 | 2 | 3 | 5 |
| Portugal | 0 | 2 | 0 | 2 |
| Spain | 0 | 2 | 0 | 2 |
| Austalia | 0 | 1 | 4 | 5 |
| Iran | 0 | 1 | 1 | 2 |
| Mongolia | 0 | 1 | 0 | 1 |
| Venezuela | 0 | 1 | 0 | 1 |
| Brazil | 0 | 0 | 2 | 2 |
| Austria | 0 | 0 | 1 | 1 |
| Bermuda | 0 | 0 | 1 | 1 |
| Pakistan | 0 | 0 | 1 | 1 |
| Puerto Rico | 0 | 0 | 1 | 1 |
| Thailand | 0 | 0 | 1 | 1 |

(all weight-lifting medals included)

## DISTRIBUTION OF MEDALS 1976 WINTER GAMES

| | Gold | Silver | Bronze | Total |
|---|---|---|---|---|
| U.S.S.R. | 13 | 6 | 8 | 27 |
| East Germany | 7 | 5 | 7 | 19 |
| United States | 3 | 3 | 4 | 10 |
| Norway | 3 | 3 | 1 | 7 |
| West Germany | 2 | 5 | 3 | 10 |
| Finland | 2 | 4 | 1 | 7 |
| Austria | 2 | 2 | 2 | 6 |
| Switzerland | 1 | 3 | 1 | 5 |
| Netherlands | 1 | 2 | 3 | 6 |
| Italy | 1 | 2 | 1 | 4 |
| Canada | 1 | 1 | 1 | 3 |
| Britain | 1 | 0 | 0 | 1 |
| Czechoslovakia | 0 | 1 | 0 | 1 |
| Liechtenstein | 0 | 0 | 2 | 2 |
| Sweden | 0 | 0 | 2 | 2 |
| France | 0 | 1 | 1 | 2 |

Total countries competing: 26.
Total athletes: 1,036
(788 men, 248 women).

## SKIING, NORDIC, JUMPING

### 90-Meter Hill

| | | |
|---|---|---|
| 1924 | Jacob T. Thams, Norway | 227.5 |
| 1928 | Alfred Andersen, Norway | 230.5 |
| 1932 | Birger Ruud, Norway | 228.0 |
| 1936 | Birger Ruud, Norway | 232.0 |
| 1948 | Peter Hugsted, Norway | 228.1 |
| 1952 | A. Bergmann, Norway | 226.0 |
| 1956 | Antti Hyvarinen, Finland | 227.0 |
| 1960 | Helmut Recknagel, Germany | 227.2 |
| 1964 | Toralf Engan, Norway | 230.7 |
| 1968 | Vladimir Beloussov, U.S.S.R. | 231.3 |
| 1972 | Wojciech Fortuna, Poland | 219.9 |
| 1976 | Karl Schnabl, Austria | 234.8 |

### Small Hill (70 meters)

| | | |
|---|---|---|
| 1964 | Veikko Kankkonen, Finland | 229.9 |
| 1968 | Jiri Raska, Czechoslovakia | 216.5 |
| 1972 | Yukio Kasaya, Japan | 244.2 |
| 1976 | Hans-Georg Aschenbach, East Germany | 252.0 |

# Other 1976 Olympic Games Champions

## SUMMER

### Archery
Men—Darrell Pace, United States
Women—Luann Ryon, United States

### Boxing
Light flyweight—Jorge Hernandez, Cuba
Bantamweight—Yong Jo Gu, North Korea
Featherweight—Angel Herrera, Cuba
Welterweight—Jochen Bachfield, E. Ger.
Light middleweight—Jerzy Rybicki, Poland
Heavyweight—Teofilo Stevenson, Cuba

### Canadian Canoeing
500 m—Aleksandr Rogov, U.S.S.R.
1,000 m—Matija Ljubek, Yugoslavia
500-m pairs—Sergei Petrenko–Aleksandr Vinogradov, U.S.S.R.
1,000-m pairs—Sergei Petrenko–Aleksandr Vinogradov, U.S.S.R.

### Kayak—Men
500 m—Vasile Diba, Romania
1,000 m—Rudiger Helm, E. Ger.
500-m pairs—Joachim Mattern–Bernd Olbricht, E. Ger.
1,000-m pairs—Sergei Nagorny—Vladimir Romanovsky, U.S.S.R.
1,000-m fours—U.S.S.R.

### Kayak—Women
500 m—Carola Zirzow, E. Ger.
500-m pairs—Nina Gopova–Galina Kreft, U.S.S.R.

### Cycling
1,000 m—Klaus-Jurgen Grunke, E. Ger.
Spring—Anton Tkac, Czechoslovakia
Pursuit—Gregor Braun, W. Ger.
Team pursuit—W. Ger.
Road race—Bernt Johansson, Sweden
Team road race—U.S.S.R.

### Equestrian
Dressage—Christine Stueckelberger, Switzerland
Dressage team—W. Ger.
Jumping—Alwin Schockemoehle, W. Ger.
Team jumping—France
3-Day event—Tad Coffin, Strafford, Vt.
Team 3-day event—United States (Tad Coffin, Mike Plumb, Mary Ann Tauskey, Bruce Davidson)

### Fencing
Foil—Fabio Dal Zotto, Italy
Team foil—W. Ger.
Epee—Alexander Pusch, W. Ger.
Team epee—Sweden
Saber—Victor Kropovskov, U.S.S.R.
Team saber—U.S.S.R.
Women's foil—Ildiko Schwarczenberger, Hungary
Women's team foil—U.S.S.R.

### Gymnastics—Men
All around—Nikolai Andrianov, U.S.S.R.
Floor exercises—Nikolai Andrianov, U.S.S.R.
Horizontal bar—Mitsuo Tsukahara, Japan
Long horse—Nikolai Andrianov, U.S.S.R.
Parallel bars—Sawao Kato, Japan
Rings—Nikolai Andrianov, U.S.S.R.
Side horse—Zoltan Magyar, Hungary
Team all-around—Japan

### Gymnastics—Women
All-around—Nadia Comaneci, Romania
Balance beam—Nadia Comaneci, Romania
Floor exercises—Nelli Kim, U.S.S.R.
Uneven bars—Nadia Comaneci, Romania
Vault—Nelli Kim, U.S.S.R.
Team all-around—U.S.S.R.

### Judo
Light middleweight—Vladimir Nevzorov, U.S.S.R.
Middleweight—Isamu Sonada, Japan
Light heavyweight—Kazuhir Ninomiya, Japan
Heavyweight—Sergi Novikov, U.S.S.R.
Open—Haruki Uemura, Japan
Lightweight—Hector Rodriguez, Cuba

### Modern Pentathlon
Individual—Janucz Pyciak-Peciak, Poland
Team—Britain

### Rowing—Men
Singles—Pertti Karppinen, Finland
Doubles—Frank and Alf Hansen, Norway
Pairs—Jorg and Bernd Landvoigt, E. Ger.
Pairs with coxswain—Harald Jahrling–Friedrich Ulrich–Georg Spohr, E. Ger.
Fours—E. Ger.
Fours with coxswains—U.S.S.R.
Quadruple sculls—E. Ger.
Eights—E. Ger.

### Rowing—Women
Singles—Christine Scheiblich, E. Ger.
Doubles—Svetla Otzetova–Zdravka Yoradanova, Bulgaria
Pairs—Siika Kelbetcheva–Stoyanka Grouitcheva, Bulgaria
Fours with coxswains—E. Ger.
Quadruple sculls—E. Ger.

### Shooting
Free pistol—Uwe Potteck, E. Ger.
Rapid fire pistol—Norbert Klaar, E. Ger.
Small-bore rifle, prone—Karlheinz Smieszek, W. Ger.
Small-bore rifle, 3 positions—Lanny Bassham, Bedford, Tex.
Rifle, running game target—Aleksandr Gazov, U.S.S.R.
Trap—Don Haldeman, Souderton, Pa.
Skeet—Josef Panacek, Czechoslovakia

### Weight Lifting
Feather—Nikolai Kolesnikov, U.S.S.R.
Fly—Aleksandr Voronin, U.S.S.R.
Bantam—Norair Nurikin, Bulgaria
Light—Zhigniev Kaesmarek, Poland
Middle—Yordan Mitkov, Bulgaria
Light heavy—Valery Shary, U.S.S.R.
Middle heavy—David Rigert, U.S.S.R.
Heavy—Valentin Khristov, Bulgaria
Super heavy—Vasily Alexyev, U.S.S.R.

### Wrestling—Freestyle
Paper—Khassan Issaev, Bulgaria
Fly—Yuji Takata, Japan
Bantam—Vladimir Umin, U.S.S.R.
Feather—Jung-Mo Jang, South Korea
Light—Pavel Pinigin, U.S.S.R.
Welter—Date Jiichiro, Japan
Middle—John Peterson, Comstock, Wis.
Light heavy—Levan Tediashvili, U.S.S.R.
Heavy—Ivan Yarygin, U.S.S.R.
Unlimited—Soslan Andiev, U.S.S.R.

### Wrestling—Greco-Roman
Paper—Alexei Schumakov, U.S.S.R.
Fly—Vitaly Konstantinov, U.S.S.R.
Bantam—Pertti Ukkola, Finland
Feather—Kazimier Lipien, Poland
Light—Suren Nalbandy, U.S.S.R.
Welter—Anatoly Bykov, U.S.S.R.
Middle—Momir Petkovic, Yugoslavia
Light heavy—Valery Kezantsev, U.S.S.R.
Heavy—Nikolai Bolboshin, U.S.S.R.
Super heavy—Aleksandr Kolchinski, U.S.S.R.

### Yachting

Finn—Jocken Schumann, E. Ger.
Flying Dutchman—Joerg Diesch, W. Ger.
470 Class—Frank Huebner, W. Ger.
Soling—Paul Jensen, Denmark
Tempest—John Albrechtson, Sweden
Tornado—Reginald White, Britain

### Team Champions

Field hockey—New Zealand
Handball (team), Men—U.S.S.R.
Handball (team), Women—U.S.S.R.
Soccer—East Germany
Volleyball, men—Poland
Volleyball, women—Japan
Water polo—Hungary

## WINTER

### Biathlon

Individual—Nikolai Kruglov, U.S.S.R.
Relay—U.S.S.R.

### Bobsledding

2-man—Meinhard Nehmer–Bernard Germeshausen, East Germany
4-man—East Germany

### Figure Skating

Men—John Curry, Britain
Women—Dorothy Hamill, Riverside, Conn.
Pairs—Irina Rodnina–Aleksandr Zaitsev, U.S.S.R.
Dance—Ludmilla Pakhomova–Aleksandr Gorschkov, U.S.S.R.

### Speed Skating—Men

500 m—Evgeni Kulikov, U.S.S.R.
1,000 m—Peter Mueller, Mequon, Wis.
1,500 m—Jan Egil Storhold, Norway
5,000 m—Sten Stensen, Norway
10,000 m—Piet Kleine, Netherlands

### Speed Skating—Women

500 m—Sheila Young, Detroit
1,000 m—Tatiana Averina, U.S.S.R.
1,500 m—Galina Stepanskaya, U.S.S.R.
3,000 m—Tatiana Averina, U.S.S.R.

### Hockey

Team—U.S.S.R.

### Luge

Men—Detlef Guenther, East Germany
Doubles—Hans Rinn–Norbert Hahn, East Germany
Women—Margit Schumann, East Germany

### Skiing, Nordic—Men

Combined—Ulrich Wehling, East Germany

### Cross-Country Skiing—Men

15 km—Nikola Bajukov, U.S.S.R.
30 km—Sergei Saveliev, U.S.S.R.
50 km—Ivar Formo, Norway
40-km relay—Finland

### Cross-Country Skiing—Women

5 km—Helena Takalo, Finland
10 km—Raisa Smetanina, U.S.S.R.

## JAMES E. SULLIVAN MEMORIAL AWARD WINNERS

(Amateur Athlete of Year Chosen in Amateur Athletic Union Poll)

| | | |
|---|---|---|
| 1930 | Robert T. Jones, Jr. | Golf |
| 1931 | Bernard E. Berlinger | Track and field |
| 1932 | James A. Bausch | Track and field |
| 1933 | Glenn Cunningham | Track and field |
| 1934 | William R. Bonthron | Track and field |
| 1935 | W. Lawson Little, Jr. | Golf |
| 1936 | Glenn Morris | Track and field |
| 1937 | J. Donald Budge | Tennis |
| 1938 | Donald R. Lash | Track and field |
| 1939 | Joseph W. Burk | Rowing |
| 1940 | J. Gregory Rice | Track and field |
| 1941 | Leslie MacMitchell | Track and field |
| 1942 | Cornelius Warmerdam | Track and field |
| 1943 | Gilbert L. Dodds | Track and field |
| 1944 | Ann Curtis | Swimming |
| 1945 | Felix (Doc) Blanchard | Football |
| 1946 | Y. Arnold Tucker | Football |
| 1947 | John B. Kelly, Jr. | Rowing |
| 1948 | Robert B. Mathias | Track and field |
| 1949 | Richard T. Button | Figure skating |
| 1950 | Fred Wilt | Track and field |
| 1951 | Robert E. Richards | Track and field |
| 1952 | Horace Ashenfelter | Track and field |
| 1953 | Major Sammy Lee | Diving |
| 1954 | Malvin Whitfield | Track and field |
| 1955 | Harrison Dillard | Track and field |
| 1956 | Patricia McCormick | Diving |
| 1957 | Bobby Morrow | Track and field |
| 1958 | Glenn Davis | Track and field |
| 1959 | Parry O'Brien | Track and field |
| 1960 | Rafer Johnson | Track and field |
| 1961 | Wilma Rudolph Ward | Track and field |
| 1962 | Jim Beatty | Track and field |
| 1963 | John Pennel | Track and field |
| 1964 | Don Schollander | Swimming |
| 1965 | Bill Bradley | Basketball |
| 1966 | Jim Ryun | Track and field |
| 1967 | Randy Matson | Track and field |
| 1968 | Debbie Meyer | Swimming |
| 1969 | Bill Toomey | Decathlon |
| 1970 | John Kinsella | Swimming |
| 1971 | Mark Spitz | Swimming |
| 1972 | Frank Shorter | Marathon |
| 1973 | Bill Walton | Basketball |
| 1974 | Rick Wohlhuter | Track |
| 1975 | Tim Shaw | Swimming |
| 1976 | Bruce Jenner | Track and Field |
| 1977 | John Naber | Swimming |

# Sports Terminology

This concise list does not contain words that most sports followers know, such as "double" in baseball or "touchdown" in football. Rather, it defines those middle-ground terms that somehow are neither simple nor technical—terms that are often used by sports writers and commentators.

**A (worn on shirt in hockey):** Alternate captain of team; has right to discuss issues with referee if captain is off ice.
**Ace (golf):** A hole-in-one shot; **(tennis):** Ball placed so well opponent cannot not get to it; if on service, it is a service ace.
**Add in, add out (tennis):** Score following first point after deuce. If won by server it is advantage, or add in; if won by receiver it is advantage, or add out.
**Aerial (skiing):** One of three events or disciplines in freestyle competition. The others are ballet and mogul. It involves acrobatic maneuvers such as backflips.
**All court press (basketball):** Close guarding by defense at all points, trying to force misplays.
**Anchor (relay racing):** Fourth and last runner or swimmer.
**Around-the-horn (baseball):** Double play initiated

by third baseman who throws to second where relay goes to first.
**At bats (baseball):** Times in which player bats officially. Does not include bases on balls, hits by pitched ball, sacrifices, sacrifice flies, or bases awarded for interference.
**Audible (football):** Quarterback's vocal signals at scrimmage line, changing play called in huddle.
**Axel (figure skating):** To jump from outer forward edge of one skate and land on outer backward edge of other skate after one and one half body turns in air.
**Back check (hockey):** Delaying or stopping player with puck by opponent in defensive zone.
**Back court (basketball):** Area between center line and basket which offensive team leaves as it moves toward own basket.
**Balanced line (football):** Offensive line with guard, tackle, and end on each side of center.
**Balk (baseball):** Illegal move by pitcher intended to deceive baserunner; runners allowed to advance one base.
**Ball control (basketball, football):** Prolonged possession of ball on attack, seeking good scoring chance.
**Ballet (skiing):** One of three disciplines or events in freestyle skiing. Like figure skating, it involves artistic concepts which are announced before performance and done to music.
**Baltimore chop (baseball):** Ball batted down into fair territory near plate that bounces high, usually allowing runner to reach first base before infielder's throw.
**Bean ball (baseball):** Pitched ball thrown near batter's head. Pitch is illegal and can cause pitcher's removal from game if judged deliberate.
**Blind side (football, hockey):** Side opposite direction player is looking.
**Blitz (football):** Concentrated charge, usually on passer, by linebackers and defensive backs.
**Board check (hockey):** Illegal knocking or riding of opponent into boards.
**Body check (hockey):** Blocking or hitting opponent with body; legal when opponent has puck or has just released it.
**Bogey (golf):** One stroke over par figure allotted to hole; **double bogey:** two strokes over par.
**Bomb (football):** Long pass to receiver speeding toward goal line; intended for quick score.
**Bonspiel (curling):** A tournament.
**Bonus free throw (basketball):** Second throw allowed if first is made on foul committed when team has exceeded limit for fouls in the period.
**Bootleg (football):** Quarterback's run to side opposite to direction blockers have moved, usually with ball held near hip in effort of concealment.
**Break point (tennis):** Point being contested that, if won by receiver, will win game and break service.
**Breakaway (football, hockey):** Play in which player gets free behind defense with good chance to score.
**Breather:** Game that appears to be an easy victory during hard schedule.
**Broken field runner (football):** Back who is adept at getting past widely spaced defensemen.
**Brush back (baseball):** A pitch intended to move batter from position close to plate.
**Buttonhook pass (football):** Receiver goes downfield and U-turns sharply to catch ball.
**Caber (Scotch games):** Tapered, heavy tree trunk thrown in competition. It is usually 16 to 20 feet long and weighs around 90 pounds.
**Check off (football):** *See* audible.
**Christie (skiing):** A Christiana or quick turn for stopping or changing direction.
**Clipping (football):** Throwing body across back of legs of non-ball-carrying opponent.
**Conversion (basketball):** Sinking of free-throw attempt; **(football):** score of point or points after touchdown.
**Corner kick (soccer):** Kick from corner of field at opponent's goal line awarded offensive team when ball is knocked over line at side of goal by defenders.
**Crab, catch a (rowing):** Dropping of oar into water on recovery from stroke; can cause injury to oarsman or throw him out of boat.
**Crack back (football):** Illegal blind-side block usually of defender in secondary by a pass receiver.
**Cripple (baseball):** Straightaway throw aimed at center of plate when pitcher is in danger of walking batter.
**Cross-checking (hockey):** Hitting of opponent with both hands on stick and no part of stick on ice; subject to penalty.
**Double dribble (basketball):** Starting to dribble again after grasping ball with both hands; a violation.
**Double fault (tennis):** Second failure to hit ball into service court on serve.
**Double-team:** Method of defense by which two defenders converge on one player, usually a top scorer.
**Draw (football):** Quarterback fakes as if to pass but hands ball off to another back for running play.
**Dribble (soccer):** Advancing ball by series of short taps with one or both feet.
**Dunking (basketball):** Reaching above rim and thrusting ball into basket.
**Duster (baseball):** Pitch that forces batter to drop to ground.
**Eagle (golf):** Two shots under par, **double eagle:** three shots under par.
**Elbowing (hockey):** Striking of opponent with elbow; subject to penalty.
**Encroachment (football):** Charging of player into neutral zone at line of scrimmage before ball is snapped.
**End-around (football):** Play in which end takes ball on handoff and races around other end.
**E.R.A. (baseball):** Earned run average of pitchers; earned run is one scored without errors, passed balls, wild pitches, or interference.
**Fair catch (football):** Signal, with upraised arm, by kick receiver for chance to make catch unmolested; he cannot advance ball, and a tackler is penalized.
**Fast break (basketball):** Attempt to get into scoring position before defensive team can regain back court posts.
**Fielder's choice (baseball):** Scorer's term to show how batter reached first base when batted ball is played to another base.
**Flanker (football):** Back stationed wide right or left as a pass receiver.
**Flare (football):** Pass to receiver swinging wide or flaring out of backfield.
**Fly pattern (football):** *See* Bomb.
**Fore checking (hockey):** Stopping or delaying opponent with puck in his own zone.
**Forwards (hockey):** Three players on front line, two wings and a center.
**Freestyle (skiing):** Style that is innovative and imaginative in the use of acrobatics, tricks, and fancy strides. It has three disciplines—aerials, moguls, and ballet.
**Freezing (hockey):** Pinning puck against boards with feet or stick to force face-off.

**Front court (basketball):** Area from center line to offensive team's basket where most of play occurs; area must be reached within 10 seconds after gaining possession of ball and play cannot go to back court unless ball is touched by opponent.
**Front four (football):** Tackles and ends of defensive line.
**Give-and-go (basketball):** Player passes to teammate and races for basket, anticipating return pass.
**Goal crease (hockey):** Area in front of goal cage, outlined by lines, which can be occupied only by goalkeeper.
**Goal tending (basketball):** Touching or knocking ball back when ball is above the basket.
**Grand slam (baseball):** A home run with the bases full; **(golf):** Winning of United States Amateur, United States Open, British Amateur, and British Open in same year. (Achieved by Bobby Jones in 1930.) **Pro golf:** Winning of United States Open, British Open, Professional Golfers' Association championship, and Masters in one season; **(tennis):** Winning of French, Wimbledon, United States, and Australian championships in one year.
**Hat trick (hockey):** Scoring of three goals in one game by one player is present conception of term. However, the National Hockey League Guide says that most accepted definition for term, which originated for bowlers in cricket, is the scoring of three successive goals with none scored in between by either team.
**Heading (soccer):** Method of passing, scoring, or controlling ball with the head.
**Held ball (basketball):** Each of opponents has firm hold on ball with neither in control.
**High post (basketball):** Position near outer circle of free-throw line.
**High-sticking (hockey):** Carrying of stick above shoulder level, sometimes for whacking opponent. It is always illegal and subject to penalty.
**Hit for cycle (baseball):** Player who hits single, double, triple, and home run in one game. Hits don't have to be in order.
**Hooking (hockey):** Holding or delaying opponent with blade of stick; subject to penalty.
**Hot-dogging (skiing):** *See* Freestyle skiing.
**Icing (hockey):** Shooting of puck from behind red line, or length of ice, into opponent's zone; it is illegal unless team is short-handed and play is restarted in zone where puck was hit.
**Illegal procedure (football):** Usually applies to backfield man in motion before ball was snapped. Calls for penalty.
**Infield fly (baseball):** Fair ball hit above infielders' territory with men on first and second or first, second, and third with less than two out. Umpire must declare it, saying so, and raising hand. The batter is automatically out.
**Interference (hockey):** Impeding of opponent who does not have puck; subject to penalty.
**Jump ball (basketball):** Ball put into play by tossing it up between two players in one of circles marked on floor, usually after held ball.
**Jump shot (basketball):** Field-goal attempt by player with both feet off floor, shooting over an opponent.
**Lateral (football):** Pass tossed parallel with goal line or back toward opponent's goal.
**Lay-up (basketball):** An easy shot, usually banked off backboard from side of basket. It is pushed up with one hand rather than thrown.
**Let (tennis):** Ball to be served over, usually a net ball, which hits top of net and falls into service court. Lets are called for any interference and are used in most other racquet games.
**Let-up pitch (baseball):** Ball that is thrown with less speed but usually with same motion as fast ball; a change of pace.
**Lob (tennis):** Ball stroked high, but not hard, in a loop; usually used as a defensive move to get opponent back from net; **(soccer):** high soft kick taken on the volley.
**Look-in pass (football):** Receiver breaks quickly downfield and turns at once to look over shoulder for pass.
**Love (tennis):** Term for zero, or nothing, in counting score.
**Low post (basketball):** Position at side of basket outside free-throw lane.
**Major penalty (hockey):** Five-minute penalty assessed for fighting or drawing blood in rough play that would normally be a minor.
**Man-to-man defense (basketball):** Player guards only the man he is assigned unless switch is called on cross-over plays.
**Match penalty (hockey):** Banning of player from remainder of game, often for unkind words to an official.
**Match play (golf):** Competition in which two players compete against each other on each hole. Victor is one who wins most holes, and match may end before 18 holes are played. A player ahead by three holes after 16, or two more to go, is winner 3 and 2.
**Medal play (golf):** Competition decided on fewest strokes taken among group of players for number of holes in tournament.
**Medalist (golf):** Player with lowest score in qualifying round for match-play tournament.
**Metric mile (track):** The 1,500-meter run, so called because it is the closest distance to the one-mile run (1,608.84 meters).
**Middle-distance races (track):** Races from 800 meters to 1,500 yards, or one mile.
**Minor penalty (hockey):** Penalty of two minutes given for most infractions.
**Misconduct penalty (hockey):** Ten-minute penalty assessed player for certain violations during which team can use a substitute; usually given for arguing too heatedly with official. Game misconduct is same as match penalty, assessed most often for being third man in fight.
**Moguls (skiing):** Bump skiing, one of three disciplines or events in freestyle, in which contestants must master difficult slopes covered with moguls (bumps made by turns).
**Nassau (golf):** Scoring system allowing one point for best score on first nine, one for best on second nine, and one for best on the 18 holes.
**Neutral corner (boxing):** One of two corners not being used by contestants between rounds. After knocking opponent down, boxer must go to one of neutral corners during count.
**Nose guard (football):** Defensive lineman, usually the middle guard in some formations. He plays opposite offensive center.
**Offside (football):** Movement of player over line of scrimmage or kicking line before ball is put into play; **(hockey):** illegal procedure of player with puck or by teammate in preceding puck across opponent's blue line; calls for face-off; **(soccer):** often when player gets between defender and goalkeeper before ball is played.
**One-two (boxing):** Left jab followed by straight right.
**Onside kick (football):** Short, usually angled kickoff, which kicking team hopes to recover after it travels required 10 yards.

**Option (football):** Choice of ball carrier to run, pass, or hand off.
**Overtime:** Game in which extra periods are played to dissolve tie existing at end of regular time; **Sudden death:** overtime play which ends as soon as score is made.
**Par (golf):** Score deemed proper for hole or round by good play.
**Pass rush (football):** Charge of lineman against passer.
**Pattern (football):** Manner in which receiver runs and maneuvers to gain position against defenders.
**Penalty kick (soccer):** Free kick allowed for flagrant violations from mark 12 yards from goal with only goalkeeper to defend.
**Penalty killer (hockey):** Player adept at defensive play, who is used when team is short-handed.
**Penalty shot (hockey):** Shot awarded player when checked illegally while going in alone on opposing goalie; he has only goalie to beat on shot as he skates in on goal from center.
**Pick (basketball):** Block of defender by player that sets up teammate for shot at basket.
**Pitch (cricket, soccer):** The field of play.
**Pitch-out (baseball):** Pitch thrown high or wide to enable catcher to make fast throw to second or third when it is thought baserunner might try to steal.
**Pivot, pivotman (basketball):** Player stationed at strategic point, low post or high post, who stands with back to basket and hands off or passes to others in motion about him, or pivots and uses hook shots to score.
**Pocket (football):** Small area amid blockers where passer stands while looking for receivers.
**Poke-check (hockey):** Poking of puck away from opponent with stick.
**Possession (football):** Player's holding of ball long enough to perform act common to game, such as completion of pass.
**Power play (hockey):** Offensive maneuver in effort to score when opponents have man in penalty box; usually four forwards and a good defenseman shooter are used.
**Prevent defense (football):** Stratagem of lessening front-line strength for deep defense, allowing short yardage but defending against long gain or score.
**Punt (football):** Ball dropped from hands by player and kicked before it strikes ground.
**Pursuit race (cycling):** A relay race by teams of four riders.
**Quarterback sneak (football):** Play in which quarterback carries ball himself, often through center for short gain to get first down.
**Rebound (basketball):** Carom of ball off basket after field goal attempt.
**Red dog (football):** *See* blitz.
**Red light (hockey):** Indication of score by goal judge who pushes button lighting goal light.
**Red shirt (football):** Designation for college player who is remaining out of competition during current season in order to have another year of eligibility. He may be working out with squad.
**Repechage (rowing):** Second chance heats to qualify for semifinals for oarsmen beaten in first heats of regatta.
**Reverse (football):** Running play in which ball is carried in direction opposite to that in which play started; **naked reverse:** play in which second carrier has no blockers in front of him.
**Roll-out (football):** Quarterback runs laterally behind blockers, keeping or passing.
**Roughing (hockey):** Scuffling or show of fists; subject to penalty.
**Running (basketball):** *See* traveling.
**Safety (football):** Occurrence in which ball becomes dead behind goal line of player in possession when impetus came from his own team.
**Salchow (figure skating):** Jump from inside back edge of one skate, landing on outside back edge of other skate after one body revolution.
**Save (hockey, soccer):** Shot on goal stopped by goalkeeper.
**Schuss (skiing):** Straight downhill run.
**Scratch (racing):** Individual or boat that has no handicap.
**Screen (basketball):** Legal action taken by player to delay opponent from reaching desired position.
**Screen pass (football):** Pass to receiver stationed behind wall of blockers as defenders harass passer.
**Service break (tennis):** Loss of game while serving.
**Set shot (basketball):** Field goal attempt taken with deliberation by player with both feet on floor.
**Setbacks (football):** Other backs lined up at side or to rear of quarterback.
**Skip (curling):** Captain of rink or team.
**Slalom (skiing):** A zigzag race through a series of gates (pairs of poles) so placed as to create sharp turns; **(canoeing):** race through pairs of poles set in water, some at sides of course, some in which the paddler comes in at reverse.
**Slant (football):** A play run obliquely into line.
**Slap-shot (hockey):** Hard shot hit with snap of wrists.
**Slashing (hockey):** Swinging of stick at opponent; subject to penalty.
**Slot back (football):** Player placed at least one yard behind line of scrimmage between wide receiver and interior lineman.
**Spearing (hockey):** Using butt-end of stick to jab opponent; subject to penalty.
**Spike (volleyball):** To hit ball down hard into opponent's court, often by a leap after ball is set up high for spiker by teammate.
**Steps (basketball):** *See* traveling.
**Stick-handling (hockey):** Moving of puck around the ice.
**Striker (soccer):** A central forward player whose responsibility is to score.
**Strong side (football):** Overbalance of linemen to one side of center.
**Stuffing (basketball):** *See* dunking.
**Sweep check (hockey):** Swinging of stick, low along ice, to dislodge puck from stick of opponent or to intercept pass.
**Sweeper (soccer):** Player who roams either in front or behind defender line to pick up stray passes.
**Swing pass (football):** *See* flare.
**Tackling (soccer):** Attempting to take ball away from opponent when both are playing ball with feet, sometimes by sliding under opponent.
**Ten-second rule (basketball):** Limit of time offensive team has to clear ball from from back court.
**Three-point goal (basketball):** Field goal from 25 feet out or farther used in certain leagues. It counts 3 points instead of 2.
**Three-point play (basketball):** Maximum score by player fouled while shooting field goal and who converts free throw.
**Three-second rule (basketball):** Limit of time an offensive player can stay in free-throw lane unless battling for rebound.
**Throw-in (basketball):** Method of putting ball into play after score or out of bounds; player must throw to teammate on court within five seconds.
**Tipoff (basketball):** Jump ball at center court that begins game and second half.

**Touchback (football):** Occurrence in which ball becomes dead behind goal line of team in possession when impetus came from other team, such as kick. There are no points for touchback.
**Touchdown (football):** Carrying of ball into, or gaining possession of ball in opponent's end zone.
**Trap (football):** Maneuver permitting defender into backfield to be blocked from side by another player.
**Traveling (basketball):** Extra steps taken by player with ball who is allowed one full step after receiving ball.
**Turnover:** Loss of ball or puck to opponents without scoring.
**Violations (basketball):** Rule infractions such as double-dribble, traveling, for which there is no free-throw penalty.
**Weak side (football):** Opposite strong side.
**Wide receiver (football):** Split end or flanker set wide of scrimmage line.
**Zone defense (basketball):** Method by which player guards an area instead of one man. It is barred in National Basketball Association play.

# FISHING

## WORLD ALL-TACKLE FISHING RECORDS

**Caught With Rod and Reel in Fresh Water**

*Source:* Mary Ball, *Field & Stream*

| Species | lb, oz | Length | Girth | Where caught | Year | Angler |
|---|---|---|---|---|---|---|
| Bass, Largemouth | 22–4 | 32½" | 28½" | Montgomery Lake, Ga. | 1932 | George W. Perry |
| Bass, Redeye | 8–3 | 23" | 16½" | Flint River, Ga. | 1977 | David A. Hubbard |
| Bass, Rock | 3 | 13½" | 10¾" | York River, Ontario | 1974 | Peter Guigin |
| Bass, Smallmouth | 11–15 | 27" | 21⅔" | Dale Hollow Lake, Ky. | 1955 | Billy Henderson |
| Bass, Spotted | 8–10½ | 23½" | 19⅞" | Smith Lake, Ala. | 1972 | Billy Henderson |
| Bass, White | 5–5 | 19½" | 17" | Ferguson Lake, Calif | 1972 | Norman W. Mize |
| Bass, Yellow | 2–4 | 16¼" | 12¾" | Lake Monroe, Ind. | 1977 | Donald L. Stalker |
| Bluegill | 1–12 | 15" | 18¼" | Ketona Lake, Ala. | 1950 | T. S. Hudson |
| Bowfin | 19–12 | 39" | — | Lake Marion, S.C. | 1972 | M. R. Webster |
| Buffalo, Bigmouth | 56 | 44¾" | 33" | Lock Loma Lake, Mo. | 1976 | W. J. Long |
| Buffalo, Smallmouth | 32–8 | 34½" | 29" | Sardia Reservoir, Miss. | 1977 | Eddie O'Daniel |
| Bullhead, Black | 8 | 24" | 17¾" | Lake Waccabuc, N.Y. | 1951 | Kani Evans |
| Carp | 55–5 | 42" | 31" | Clearwater Lake, Minn. | 1952 | Frank J. Ledwein |
| Catfish, Blue | 97 | 57" | 37" | Missouri River, S.D. | 1959 | Edward B. Elliott |
| Catfish, Channel | 58 | 47¼" | 29⅛" | Santee-Cooper Res., S.C. | 1964 | W. B. Whaley |
| Catfish, Flathead | 79–8 | 44" | 27" | White River, Indiana | 1966 | Glenn T. Simpson |
| Catfish, White | 10–5 | 25" | 17½" | Raritan River, N.J. | 1976 | L. W. Lomerson |
| Char, Arctic | 29–11 | 39¾" | 26" | Arctic River, N.W.T. | 1968 | Jeanne P. Branson |
| Crappie, Black | 5 | 19¼" | 18⅝" | Santee-Cooper Res., S.C. | 1957 | Paul E. Foust |
| Crappie, White | 5–3 | 21" | 19" | Enid Dam, Miss. | 1957 | Fred L. Bright |
| Dolly Varden | 32 | 40½" | 29¾" | Lake Pend Oreille, Idaho | 1949 | N. L. Higgins |
| Drum, Freshwater | 54–8 | 31½" | 29" | Nickajack Lake, Tenn. | 1972 | Benny E. Hull |
| Gar, Alligator | 279 | 93" | — | Rio Grande River, Tex. | 1951 | Bill Valverde |
| Gar, Longnose | 50–5 | 72¼" | 22½" | Trinity River, Tex. | 1954 | Townsend Miller |
| Grayling, American | 5–15 | 29⅞" | 15⅛" | Katseyedie River, N.W.T. | 1967 | Jeanne P. Branson |
| Kokanee | 6–9¾ | 24½" | 14½" | Priest Lake, Idaho | 1975 | Jerry Verge |
| Muskellunge | 69–15 | 64½" | 31¾" | St. Lawrence River, N.Y. | 1957 | Arthur Lawton |
| Perch, White | 4–12 | 19½" | 13" | Messalonskee Lake, Maine | 1949 | Mrs. Earl Small |
| Perch, Yellow | 4–3½ | — | — | Bordentown, N.J. | 1865 | Dr. C. C. Abbot |
| Pickerel, Eastern chain | 9–6 | 31" | 14" | Homerville, Ga. | 1961 | Baxley McQuaig, Jr. |
| Pike, Northern | 46–2 | 52½" | 25" | Sacandaga Reservoir, N.Y. | 1940 | Peter Dubuc |
| Redhorse, Silver | 4–2 | 20½" | 14" | Gasconade River, Mo. | 1974 | C. J. McKinney |
| Salmon, Atlantic | 79–2 | — | — | Tana River, Norway | 1928 | Henrik Henriksen |
| Salmon, Chinook | 93 | 50" | 39" | Kelp Bay, Alaska | 1977 | Howard C. Rider |
| Salmon, Chum | 27–3 | 39⅜" | 24½" | Raymond Cove, Alaska | 1977 | Robert A. Jahnke |
| Salmon Landlocked | 22–8 | 36" | — | Sebago Lake, Maine | 1907 | Edward Blakely |
| Salmon CoHo | 31 | — | — | Cowichan Bay, B.C. | 1947 | Mrs. Lee Hallberg |
| Sauger | 8–12 | 28" | 15" | Lake Sakakawea, N.D. | 1971 | Mike Fischer |
| Shad, American | 9–12 | 25" | 17½" | Enfield, Conn. | 1973 | Edward P. Nelson |
| Sturgeon, White | 360 | 111" | 86" | Snake River, Idaho | 1956 | Willard Cravens |
| Sunfish, Green | 2–2 | 14¾" | 14" | Stockton Lake, Mo. | 1971 | Paul M. Dilley |
| Sunfish, Refbreast | 1–8½ | 11" | 12⅝" | Suwannee River, Fla. | 1977 | Tommy D. Cason, Jr. |
| Sunfish, Redear | 4–8 | 16¼" | 17¾" | Chase City, Va. | 1970 | Maurice E. Ball |
| Trout, Brook | 14–8 | 31½" | 11½" | Nipigon River, Ontario | 1916 | Dr. W. J. Cook |
| Trout, Cutthroat | 41 | 39" | — | Pyramid Lake, Nev. | 1925 | John Skimmerhorn |
| Trout, Golden | 11 | 28" | 16" | Cook's Lake, Wyo. | 1948 | Charles S. Reed |
| Trout, Lake | 65 | 52" | 38" | Great Bear Lake, N.W.T. | 1970 | Larry Daunis |
| Trout, Rainbow or Steelhead | 42–2 | 43" | 23½" | Bell Island, Alaska | 1970 | David R. White |
| Trout, Sunapee | 11–8 | 33" | 17¼" | Lake Sunapee, N.H. | 1954 | Ernest Theoharis |

| Species | lb, oz | Length | Girth | Where caught | Year | Angler |
|---|---|---|---|---|---|---|
| Trout, Tiger | 17 | 31" | 21" | Lake Michigan, Wis. | 1977 | Edward Rudnicki |
| Walleye | 25 | 41" | 29" | Old Hickory Lake, Tenn. | 1960 | Mabry Harper |
| Warmouth | 2 | 12" | 12½" | Sylvania, Ga. | 1974 | Carlton Robbins |
| Whitefish, Lake | 13 | 32¼" | 19" | Great Bear Lake, N.W.T. | 1974 | Robert L. Stintsman |
| Whitefish, Mountain | 5 | 19" | 14" | Athabasca River, Alberta, Can. | 1963 | Orville Welch |

## Caught With Rod and Reed in Salt Water

*Source:* International Game Fish Association

| Species | lb, oz | Length | Girth | Where caught | Year | Angler |
|---|---|---|---|---|---|---|
| Albacore | 88–2 | — | — | Canary Islands | 1977 | Siegfried Dickemann |
| Amberjack | 149 | 71" | 41¾" | Bermuda | 1964 | Peter Simons |
| Barracuda | 83 | 72¼" | 29" | Lagos, Nigeria | 1952 | K. J. W. Hackett |
| Bass, Black Sea | 8 | 22" | 19" | Nantucket Sound, Mass. | 1951 | H. R. Rider |
| Bass, Giant Sea | 563/8 | 89" | 72" | Anacapa Is., Calif. | 1968 | J. D. McAdam, Jr. |
| Bass, Striped[1] | 73 | 60" | 30½" | Vineyard Sound, Mass. | 1913 | C. B. Church |
| Bass, Striped | 72 | 54½" | 31" | Cuttyhunk, Mass. | 1969 | Edward J. Kirker |
| Blackfish (Tautog) | 21–6 | 31½" | 23½" | Cape May, N.J. | 1954 | R. N. Sheafer |
| Bluefish | 31–12 | 47" | 23" | North Carolina | 1972 | James M. Hussey |
| Bonito, Pacific | 23–8 | 35¼" | 23¼" | Victoria, Mahe | 1975 | Mrs. Anne Cochain |
| Cod | 98–12 | 63" | 41" | Isle of Shoals, Mass. | 1969 | Alphonse Bielevich |
| Dolphin | 87 | 81⅔" | 28" | Papapagalio Gulf, Costa Rica | 1976 | Manual Salazar |
| Drum, Black | 113–1 | 53⅛" | 43½" | Lewes, Del. | 1975 | G. M. Townsend |
| Drum, Red | 90 | 55½" | 38¼" | Rodanthe, N.C. | 1973 | Elvin Hooper |
| Flounder | 30–12 | 38½" | 30½" | Chile | 1971 | Augusto Nunez Moreno |
| Jewfish | 680 | 85½" | 66" | Fernandina Beach, Fla. | 1961 | Lynn Joiner |
| Kawakawa | 21 | 34" | 22" | Kilauea, Kauai, Hawaii | 1975 | E. John O'Dell |
| Mackerel, King | 90 | — | — | Key West, Florida | 1976 | Norton I. Thomton |
| Marlin, Black | 1560 | 174" | 81" | Cabo Blanco, Peru | 1953 | A. C. Glassel, Jr. |
| Marlin, Atlantic Blue | 1,282 | 176" | 76½" | St. Thomas, Virgin Is. | 1977 | Larry Martin |
| Marlin, Pacific Blue | 1153 | 176" | 73" | Ritidian Point, Guam | 1969 | Greg G. Perez |
| Marlin, Striped | 417–8 | 139½" | 52½" | Cavalli Is., New Zealand | 1977 | Phillip Bryers |
| Marlin, White | 174–3 | 104⅓" | 35½" | Vitória, Brazil | 1975 | O. C. Reboucas |
| Permit | 50–8 | 44¾" | 33¼" | Key West, Fla. | 1971 | Marshal E. Earnest |
| Pollock | 46–7 | 50½" | 30" | Brielle, N.J. | 1975 | John T. Holton |
| Roosterfish | 114 | 64" | 33" | La Paz, Mexico | 1960 | Abe Sackheim |
| Runner, Rainbow | 33–10 | 55¼" | 22½" | Clarion Island, Mexico | 1976 | R. A. Mikkelsen |
| Sailfish, Atlantic | 128–1 | 106¼" | 34¼" | Luanda, Angola, Africa | 1974 | Harm Stevn |
| Sailfish, Pacific | 221 | 129" | — | Santa Cruz Is., Galapagos Is. | 1947 | C. W. Stewart |
| Seabass, White | 83–12 | 65½" | 34" | San Felipe, Mexico | 1953 | L. C. Baumgardner |
| Seatrout, Spotted | 16 | 32½" | 21¾" | Mason's Beach, Va. | 1977 | William G. Katko |
| Shark, Blue | 410 | 138" | 52" | Rockport, Mass. | 1960 | Richard C. Webster |
| | 410 | 134" | 52½" | Rockport, Mass. | 1967 | Martha C. Webster |
| Shark, Hammerhead | 703 | 172" | 63" | Jacksonville, Fla. | 1975 | H. B. Reasor |
| Shark, Mako | 1061 | 146" | 79½" | Mayor Island, N.Z. | 1970 | J. B. Penwarden |
| Shark, Porbeagle | 465 | 111" | 56" | Padstow, Cornwall, England | 1976 | Jorge Potier |
| Shark, Thresher | 739 | 106" | 68" | Tutukaka, N.Z. | 1975 | Brian Galvin |
| Shark, Tiger | 1780 | 166½" | 103" | Cherry Grove, S.C. | 1964 | Walter Maxwell |
| Shark, White | 2664 | 202" | 114" | South Australia | 1959 | Alfred Dean |
| Snook (Robalo) | 52–6 | 49½" | 26" | La Paz, Mexico | 1963 | Jane Haywood |
| Swordfish | 1182 | 179¼" | 78" | Iquique, Chile | 1953 | L. E. Marron |
| Tanguigue | 81 | 71½" | 29¼" | Karachi, Pakistan | 1960 | George E. Rusinak |
| Tarpon | 283 | 85⅗" | — | Lake Maracaibo, Venezuela | 1956 | M. Salazar |
| Tautog (See Blackfish) | | | | | | |
| Tuna, Alison (Yellowfin) | 308 | 84" | 57" | San Benedicto Is., Mex. | 1973 | Harold J. Tolson |
| Tuna, Altantic Bigeye | 375–8 | — | — | Ocean City, Md. | 1977 | Cecil Browne |
| Tuna, Blackfin | 39–8 | — | — | Commissioner's Pt., Bermuda | 1977 | Carlston Spencer |
| Tuna, Bluefin | 1200 | — | — | Chaleur Bay, New Brunswick, Can. | 1976 | Leslie Vibert |
| Tuna Dog-tooth | 153–8 | 68" | 44" | Cooktown, Australia | 1975 | William E. Chapman |
| Tuna, Longtail | 60 | 56" | 30" | Bermagui, N.S.W., Australia | 1975 | N. Noel Webster |
| Tuna, Pacific Big-Eyed | 435 | 93" | 63½" | Cabo Blanco, Peru | 1957 | R.V. A. Lee |
| Tuna, Skipjack | 39–15 | 39" | 28" | Walker City, Bahamas | 1952 | R. Drawley |
| | 40 | 38¾" | 27½" | Baie du Tambeau, Mauritius | 1971 | Joseph R. Cabache |
| Tuna, Southern Bluefin | 213–13 | 74" | 50" | Tasmania, Australia | 1977 | Gerald Harvey |
| Tunny, Little | 27 | 39" | 22" | Key Largo, Fla. | 1976 | William E. Allison |
| Weakfish | 19–8 | 37" | 23¾" | Trinidad, W.I. | 1962 | Dennis B. Hall |
| Yellowtail | 111 | 62" | 38" | Bay of Islands, N.Z. | 1961 | A. F. Plim |

1. Lines not tested.

# FOOTBALL

The pastime of kicking around a ball goes back beyond the limits of recorded history. Ancient savage tribes played football of a primitive kind. There was a ball-kicking game played by Athenians, Spartans, and Corinthians 2500 years ago, which the Greeks called *Episkuros*. The Romans had a somewhat similar game called *Harpastum* and are supposed to have carried the game with them when they invaded the British Isles in the First Century, B.C.

Undoubtedly the game known in the United Stated as Football traces directly to the English game of Rugby, though the modifications have been many. Informal football was played on college lawns well over a century ago, and an annual Freshman-Sophomore series of "scrimmages" began at Yale in 1840. The first formal intercollegiate football game was the Princeton-Rutgers contest at New Brunswick, N.J., on Nov. 6, 1869, with Rutgers winning by 6 goals to 4.

In those days, games were played with 25, 20, 15, or 11 men on a side. In 1880, there was a convention at which Walter Camp of Yale persuaded the delegates to agree to a rule calling for 11 players on a side. The game grew so rough that it was attacked as brutal, and some colleges abandoned the sport. Conditions were so bad in 1906 that President Theodore Roosevelt called a meeting of Yale, Harvard, and Princeton representatives at the White House in the hope of reforming and improving the game. The outcome was that the game, with the forward pass introduced and some other modifications of the rules inserted, became faster and cleaner.

The first professional game was played in 1895 at Latrobe, Pa. The National Football League was founded in 1921. The All-American Conference went into action in 1946. At the end of the 1949 season the two circuits merged, retaining the name of the older league. In 1960, the American Football League, began operations. In 1970, the leagues merged.

# College Football

## NATIONAL COLLEGE FOOTBALL CHAMPIONS

The "National Collegiate A. A. Football Guide" recognizes as unofficial national champion the team selected each year by press association polls. Where The Associated Press poll (of writers) does not agree with the United Press International poll (of coaches), the guide lists both teams selected.

| | |
|---|---|
| 1937 | Pittsburgh |
| 1938 | Texas Christian |
| 1939 | Texas A & M |
| 1940 | Minnesota |
| 1941 | Minnesota |
| 1942 | Ohio State |
| 1943 | Notre Dame |
| 1944 | Army |
| 1945 | Army |
| 1946 | Notre Dame |
| 1947 | Notre Dame |
| 1948 | Michigan |
| 1949 | Notre Dame |
| 1950 | Oklahoma |
| 1951 | Tennessee |
| 1952 | Michigan State |
| 1953 | Maryland |
| 1954 | Ohio State and U.C.L.A. |
| 1955 | Oklahoma |
| 1956 | Oklahoma |
| 1957 | Auburn and Ohio State |
| 1958 | Louisiana State |
| 1959 | Syracuse |
| 1960 | Minnesota |
| 1961 | Alabama |
| 1962 | So. California |
| 1963 | Texas |
| 1964 | Alabama |
| 1965 | Alabama and Michigan State |
| 1966 | Notre Dame |
| 1967 | So. California |
| 1968 | Ohio State |
| 1969 | Texas |
| 1970 | Texas and Nebraska |
| 1971 | Nebraska |
| 1972 | So. California |
| 1973 | Notre Dame |
| 1974 | Oklahoma and So. California |
| 1975 | Oklahoma |
| 1976 | Pittsburgh |
| 1977 | Notre Dame |

## ARMY-NAVY SERIES RECORD SINCE 1962

| | |
|---|---|
| 1962 | Navy 34, Army 14 |
| 1963 | Navy 21, Army 15 |
| 1964 | Army 11, Navy 8 |
| 1965 | Army 7, Navy 7 |
| 1966 | Army 20, Navy 7 |
| 1967 | Navy 19, Army 14 |
| 1968 | Army 21, Navy 14 |
| 1969 | Army 27, Navy 0 |
| 1970 | Navy 11, Army 7 |
| 1971 | Army 24, Navy 23 |
| 1972 | Army 23, Navy 15 |
| 1973 | Navy 51, Army 0 |
| 1974 | Navy 19, Army 0 |
| 1975 | Navy 30, Army 6 |
| 1976 | Navy 38, Army 10 |
| 1977 | Army 17, Navy 14 |

## RECORD OF ANNUAL MAJOR BOWL COLLEGE FOOTBALL GAMES

**Rose Bowl**

(At Pasadena, Calif.)

| | |
|---|---|
| 1902 | Michigan 49, Stanford 0 |
| 1916 | Washington State 14, Brown 0 |
| 1917 | Oregon 14, Pennsylvania 0 |
| 1918 | Mare Island Marines 19, Camp Lewis 7 |
| 1919 | Great Lakes 17, Mare Island Marines 0 |
| 1920 | Harvard 7, Oregon 6 |
| 1921 | California 28, Ohio State 0 |
| 1922 | Washington and Jefferson 0, California 0 |
| 1923 | So. California 14, Penn State 3 |
| 1924 | Navy 14, Washington 14 |
| 1925 | Notre Dame 27, Stanford 10 |
| 1926 | Alabama 20, Washington 19 |
| 1927 | Alabama 7, Stanford 7 |
| 1928 | Stanford 7, Pittsburgh 6 |
| 1929 | Georgia Tech 8, California 7 |
| 1930 | So. California 47, Pittsburgh 14 |
| 1931 | Alabama 24, Washington State 0 |
| 1932 | So. California 21, Tulane 12 |
| 1933 | So. California 35, Pittsburgh 0 |
| 1934 | Columbia 7, Stanford 0 |
| 1935 | Alabama 29, Stanford 13 |
| 1936 | Stanford 7, So. Methodist 0 |
| 1937 | Pittsburgh 21, Washington 0 |
| 1938 | California 13, Alabama 0 |
| 1939 | So. California 7, Duke 3 |
| 1940 | So. California 14, Tennessee 0 |
| 1941 | Stanford 21, Nebraska 13 |
| 1942 | Oregon State 20, Duke 16[1] |
| 1943 | Georgia 9, U.C.L.A. 0 |
| 1944 | So. California 29, Washington 0 |
| 1945 | So. California 25, Tennessee 0 |
| 1946 | Alabama 34, So. California 14 |
| 1947 | Illinois 45, U.C.L.A. 14 |
| 1948 | Michigan 49, So. California 0 |
| 1949 | Northwestern 20, California 14 |
| 1950 | Ohio State 17, California 14 |
| 1951 | Michigan 14, California 6 |
| 1952 | Illinois 40, Stanford 7 |
| 1953 | So. California 7, Wisconsin 0 |
| 1954 | Michigan State 28, U.C.L.A. 20 |
| 1955 | Ohio State 20, So. California 7 |
| 1956 | Michigan State 17, U.C.L.A. 14 |
| 1957 | Iowa 35, Oregon State 19 |
| 1958 | Ohio State 10, Oregon 7 |
| 1959 | Iowa 38, California 12 |
| 1960 | Washington 44, Wisconsin 8 |

1961 Washington 17, Minnesota 7
1962 Minnesota 21, U.C.L.A. 3
1963 So. California 42, Wisconsin 37
1964 Illinois 17, Washington 7
1965 Michigan 34, Oregon State 7
1966 U.C.L.A. 14, Michigan State 12
1967 Purdue 14, So. California 13
1968 So. California 14, Indiana 3
1969 Ohio State 27, So. California 16
1970 So. California 10, Michigan 3
1971 Stanford 27, Ohio State 17
1972 Stanford 13, Michigan 12
1973 So. California 42, Ohio State 17
1974 Ohio State 42, So. California 21
1975 So. California 18, Ohio State 17
1976 U.C.L.A. 23, Ohio State 10
1977 So. California 14, Michigan 6
1978 Washington 27, Michigan 20

1. Played at Durham, N.C.

### Orange Bowl

(At Miami)

1933 Miami (Fla.) 7, Manhattan 0
1934 Duquesne 33, Miami (Fla.) 7
1935 Bucknell 26, Miami (Fla.) 0
1936 Catholic 20, Mississippi 19
1937 Duquesne 13, Mississippi State 12
1938 Auburn 6, Michigan State 0
1939 Tennessee 17, Oklahoma 0
1940 Georgia Tech 21, Missouri 7
1941 Mississippi State 14, Georgetown 7
1942 Georgia 40, Texas Christian 26
1943 Alabama 37, Boston College 21
1944 Louisiana State 19, Texas A&M 14
1945 Tulsa 26, Georgia Tech 12
1946 Miami (Fla.) 13, Holy Cross 6
1947 Rice 8, Tennessee 0
1948 Georgia Tech 20, Kansas 14
1949 Texas 41, Georgia 28
1950 Santa Clara 21, Kentucky 13
1951 Clemson 15, Miami (Fla.) 14
1952 Georgia Tech 17, Baylor 14
1953 Alabama 61, Syracuse 6
1954 Oklahoma 7, Maryland 0
1955 Duke 34, Nebraska 7
1956 Oklahoma 20, Maryland 6
1957 Colorado 27, Clemson 21
1958 Oklahoma 48, Duke 21
1959 Oklahoma 21, Syracuse 6
1960 Georgia 14, Missouri 0
1961 Missouri 21, Navy 14
1962 Louisiana State 25, Colorado 7
1963 Alabama 17, Oklahoma 0
1964 Nebraska 13, Auburn 7
1965 Texas 21, Alabama 17
1966 Alabama 39, Nebraska 28
1967 Florida 27, Georgia Tech 12
1968 Oklahoma 26, Tennessee 24
1969 Penn State 15, Kansas 14
1970 Penn State 10, Missouri 3
1971 Nebraska 17, Louisiana State 12
1972 Nebraska 38, Alabama 6
1973 Nebraska 40, Notre Dame 6
1974 Penn State 16, Louisiana State 9
1975 Notre Dame 13, Alabama 11
1976 Oklahoma 14, Michigan 6
1977 Ohio State 27, Colorado 10
1978 Arkansas 31, Oklahoma 6

### Sugar Bowl

(At New Orleans)

1935 Tulane 20, Temple 14
1936 Texas Christian 3, Louisiana State 2
1937 Santa Clara 21, Louisiana State 14
1938 Santa Clara 6, Louisiana State 0
1939 Texas Christian 15, Carnegie Tech 7
1940 Texas A & M 14, Tulane 13
1941 Boston College 19, Tennessee 13
1942 Fordham 2, Missouri 0
1943 Tennessee 14, Tulsa 7
1944 Georgia Tech 20, Tulsa 18
1945 Duke 29, Alabama 26
1946 Oklahoma A & M 33, St. Mary's (Calif.) 13
1947 Georgia 20, North Carolina 10
1948 Texas 27, Alabama 7
1949 Oklahoma 14, North Carolina 6
1950 Oklahoma 35, Louisiana State 0
1951 Kentucky 13, Oklahoma 7
1952 Maryland 28, Tennessee 13
1953 Georgia Tech 24, Mississippi 7
1954 Georgia Tech 42, West Virginia 19
1955 Navy 21, Mississippi 0
1956 Georgia Tech 7, Pittsburgh 0
1957 Baylor 13, Tennessee 7
1958 Mississippi 39, Texas 7
1959 Louisiana State 7, Clemson 0
1960 Mississippi 21, Louisiana State 0
1961 Mississippi 14, Rice 6
1962 Alabama 10, Arkansas 3
1963 Mississippi 17, Arkansas 13
1964 Alabama 12, Mississippi 7
1965 Louisiana State 13, Syracuse 10
1966 Missouri 20, Florida 18
1967 Alabama 34, Nebraska 7
1968 Louisiana State 20, Wyoming 13
1969 Arkansas 16, Georgia 2
1970 Mississippi 27, Arkansas 22
1971 Tennessee 34, Air Force Academy 13
1972 Oklahoma 40, Auburn 22
1973 Oklahoma 14, Penn State 0
1974 Notre Dame 24, Alabama 23
1975 Nebraska 13, Florida 10
1976 Alabama 13, Penn State 6
1977 Pittsburgh 27, Georgia 3
1978 Alabama 35, Ohio State 6

### Cotton Bowl

(At Dallas)

1937 Texas Christian 16, Marquette 6
1938 Rice 28, Colorado 14
1939 St. Mary's (Calif.) 20, Texas Tech. 13
1940 Clemson 6, Boston College 3
1941 Texas A & M 13, Fordham 12
1942 Alabama 29, Texas A & M 21
1943 Texas 14, Georgia Tech 7
1944 Randolph Field 7, Texas 7
1945 Oklahoma A & M 34, Texas Christian 0
1946 Texas 40, Missouri 27
1947 Louisiana State 0, Arkansas 0
1948 So. Methodist 13, Penn State 13
1949 So. Methodist 21, Oregon 13
1950 Rice 27, North Carolina 13
1951 Tennessee 20, Texas 14
1952 Kentucky 20, Texas Christian 7
1953 Texas 16, Tennessee 0
1954 Rice 28, Alabama 6
1955 Georgia Tech 14, Arkansas 6
1956 Mississippi 14, Texas Christian 13
1957 Texas Christian 28, Syracuse 27
1958 Navy 20, Rice 7
1959 Air Force 0, Texas Christian 0
1960 Syracuse 23, Texas 14
1961 Duke 7, Arkansas 6
1962 Texas 12, Mississippi 7
1963 Louisiana State 13, Texas 0
1964 Texas 28, Navy 6
1965 Arkansas 10, Nebraska 7
1966 Louisiana State 14, Arkansas 7
1967 Georgia 24, So. Methodist 9
1968 Texas A & M 20, Alabama 16
1969 Texas 36, Tennessee 13
1970 Texas 21, Notre Dame 17
1971 Notre Dame 24, Texas 11
1972 Penn State 30, Texas 6
1973 Texas 17, Alabama 13
1974 Nebraska 19, Texas 3
1975 Penn State 41, Baylor 20
1976 Arkansas 31, Georgia 10
1977 Houston 30, Maryland 21
1978 Notre Dame 38, Texas 10

### Gator Bowl

(At Jacksonville, Fla. Played on Saturday nearest New Year's Day of year indicated)

1953 Florida 14, Tulsa 13
1954 Texas Tech 35, Auburn 13
1955 Auburn 33, Baylor 13
1956 Vanderbilt 25, Auburn 13
1957 Georgia Tech 21, Pittsburgh 14
1958 Tennessee 3, Texas A & M 0
1959 Mississippi 7, Florida 3
1960 Arkansas 14, Georgia Tech 7
1961 Florida 13, Baylor 12
1962 Penn State 30, Georgia Tech 15
1963 Florida 17, Penn State 7
1964 No. Carolina 35, Air Force 0
1965 Florida State 36, Oklahoma 19
1966 Georgia Tech 31, Texas Tech 21
1967 Tennessee 18, Syracuse 12
1968 Penn State 17, Florida State 17
1969 Missouri 35, Alabama 10
1970 Florida 14, Tennessee 13
1971 Auburn 35, Mississippi 28
1972 Georgia 7, North Carolina 3
1973 Auburn 24, Colorado 3
1974 Texas Tech 28, Tennessee 19
1975 Auburn 27, Texas 3
1976 Maryland 13, Florida 0
1977 Notre Dame 20, Penn State 9
1978 Pittsburgh 34, Clemson 3

## RESULTS OF OTHER 1977 SEASON BOWL GAMES

Astro-Bluebonnet (Houston)—Southern California 47, Texas A&M 28
Fiesta (Tempe, Ariz.)—Penn State 42, Arizona State 30
Hall of Fame (Birmingham, Ala.)—Maryland 17, Minnesota 7
Liberty (Memphis, Tenn.)—Nebraska 21, North Carolina 17
Independence (Shreveport, La.)—Louisiana Tech 24, Louisville 14
Peach (Atlanta)—North Carolina State 24, Iowa State 14
Sun (El Paso)—Stanford 24, Louisiana State 14
Tangerine (Orlando, Fla.)—Florida State 40, Texas Tech 17

## HEISMAN MEMORIAL TROPHY WINNERS

The Heisman Memorial Trophy is presented annually by the Downtown Athletic Club of New York City to the nation's outstanding college football player, as determined by a poll of sportswriters and sportscasters.

| | |
|---|---|
| 1935 | Jay Berwanger, Chicago |
| 1936 | Larry Kelley, Yale |
| 1937 | Clinton Frank, Yale |
| 1938 | Davey O'Brien, Texas Christian |
| 1939 | Nile Kinnick, Iowa |
| 1940 | Tom Harmon, Michigan |
| 1941 | Bruce Smith, Minnesota |
| 1942 | Frank Sinkwich, Georgia |
| 1943 | Angelo Bertelli, Notre Dame |
| 1944 | Leslie Horvath, Ohio State |
| 1945 | Felix Blanchard, Army |
| 1946 | Glenn Davis, Army |
| 1947 | Johnny Lujack, Notre Dame |
| 1948 | Doak Walker, So. Methodist |
| 1949 | Leon Hart, Notre Dame |
| 1950 | Vic Janowicz, Ohio State |
| 1951 | Dick Kazmaier, Princeton |
| 1952 | Billy Vessels, Oklahoma |
| 1953 | Johnny Lattner, Notre Dame |
| 1954 | Alan Ameche, Wisconsin |
| 1955 | Howard Cassady, Ohio State |
| 1956 | Paul Hornung, Notre Dame |
| 1957 | John Crow, Texas A & M |
| 1958 | Pete Dawkins, Army |
| 1959 | Billy Cannon, Louisiana State |
| 1960 | Joe Bellino, Navy |
| 1961 | Ernie Davis, Syracuse |
| 1962 | Terry Baker, Oregon State |
| 1963 | Roger Staubach, Navy |
| 1964 | John Huarte, Notre Dame |
| 1965 | Mike Garrett, Southern California |
| 1966 | Steve Spurrier, Florida |
| 1967 | Gary Beban, U.C.L.A. |
| 1968 | O. J. Simpson, Southern California |
| 1969 | Steve Owens, Oklahoma |
| 1970 | Jim Plunkett, Stanford |
| 1971 | Pat Sullivan, Auburn |
| 1972 | Johnny Rodgers, Nebraska |
| 1973 | John Cappelletti, Penn State |
| 1974–75 | Archie Griffin, Ohio State |
| 1976 | Tony Dorsett, Pittsburgh |
| 1977 | Earl Campbell, Texas |

## COLLEGE FOOTBALL HALL OF FAME

(Kings Island, Interstate 71, Kings Mills, Ohio)
(Date given is player's last year of competition)

### Players

Abell, Earl—Colgate, 1915
Agase, Alex—Purdue/Illinois, 1946
Agganis, Harry—Boston Univ., 1952
Albert, Frank—Stanford, 1941
Aldrich, Chas. (Ki)—T.C.U., 1938
Aldrich, Malcolm—Yale, 1921
Alexander, John—Syracuse, 1920
Ameche, Alan (Horse)—Wisconsin, 1954
Anderson, H. (Hunk)—Notre Dame, 1921
Bacon, C. Everett—Wesleyan, 1912
Bagnell, Francis (Reds)—Penn, 1950
Baker, Hobart (Hobey)—Princeton, 1913
Ballin, Harold—Princeton, 1914
Banker, Bill—Tulane, 1929
Barnes, Stanley—S. California, 1921
Barrett, Charles—Cornell, 1915
Baston, Bert—Minnesota, 1916
Battles, Cliff—W. Va. Wesleyan, 1931
Baugh, Sammy—Texas Christian U., 1936
Bausch, James—Kansas, 1930
Beckett, John—Oregon, 1913
Bednarik, Chuck—Pennsylvania, 1948
Bellini, Joe—Navy, 1960
Benbrook, A.—Michigan, 1911
Bertelli, A.—Notre Dame, 1943
Berwanger, John (Jay)—Chicago, 1935
Bettencourt, Larry—St. Mary's, 1927
Blanchard, Felix (Doc)—Army, 1946
Bock, Ed—Iowa State, 1938
Bomar, Lynn—Vanderbilt, 1924
Bomeisler, Doug (Bo)—Yale, 1913
Booth, Albie—Yale, 1931
Borries, Fred—Navy, 1934
Boynton, Ben—Williams, 1920
Brewer, Charles—Harvard, 1895
Brooke, George—Pennsylvania, 1895
Brown, Gordon—Yale, 1900
Brown, John, Jr.—Navy, 1913
Brown, Johnny Mack—Alabama, 1925
Bunker, Paul—Army, 1902
Butler, Robert—Wisconsin, 1912
Cafego, George—Tennessee, 1939
Cagle, Chris—SW La./Army, 1929
Cain, John—Alabama, 1932
Cameron, Eddie—Wash. & Lee, 1924
Campbell, David C.—Harvard, 1901
Cannon, Jack—Notre Dame, 1929
Carideo, Frank—Notre Dame, 1930
Carney, Charles—Illinois, 1921
Carpenter, C. Hunter—VPI, 1905
Carroll, Charles—Washington, 1928
Casey, Edward L.—Harvard, 1919
Chamberlain, Guy—Nebraska, 1915
Christman, Paul—Missouri, 1940
Clark, Earl (Dutch)—Colo. College, 1929
Clevenger, Zora—Indiana, 1903
Cochran, Gary—Princeton, 1895
Cody, Josh—Vanderbilt, 1920
Coleman, Don—Mich. State, 1951
Conerly, Chuck—Mississippi, 1947
Connor, George—Notre Dame, 1947
Corbin, W.—Yale, 1888
Corbus, William—Stanford, 1933
Cowan, Hector—Princeton, 1889
Coy, Edward H. (Tad)—Yale, 1909
Crawford, Fred—Duke, 1933
Crow, John D.—Texas A&M, 1957
Crowley, James—Notre Dame, 1924
Cutter, Slade—Navy, 1934
Czarobski, Ziggie—Notre Dame, 1947
Dalrymple, Gerald—Tulane, 1931
Daniell, James—Ohio State, 1941
Dawkins, Pete—Army, 1958
Dalton, John—Navy, 1912
Daly, Charles—Harvard/Army, 1902
Daniell, Averell—Pittsburgh, 1936
Davies, Tom—Pittsburgh, 1921
Davis, Glenn—Army, 1946
Davis, Robert T.—Georgia Tech, 1947
DesJardien, Paul—Chicago, 1914
Devine, Aubrey—Iowa, 1921
DeWitt, John—Princeton, 1903
Dodd, Bobby—Tennessee, 1930
Dougherty, Nathan—Tennessee, 1909
Driscoll, Paddy—Northwestern, 1917
Drury, Morley—So. California, 1927
Dudley, William (Bill)—Virginia, 1941
Eckersall, Walter—Chicago, 1906
Edwards, Turk—Washington State, 1931
Edwards, William—Princeton, 1900
Eichenlaub, R.—Notre Dame, 1913
Evans, Ray—Kansas, 1947
Exendine, Albert—Carlisle, 1908
Falaschi, Nello—Santa Clara, 1937
Fears, Tom—Santa Clara/UCLA, 1947
Feathers, Beattie—Tennessee, 1933
Fenimore, Robert—Oklahoma State, 1947
Fenton, G.E. (Doc)—La. State U., 1910
Ferraro, John—So. California, 1944
Fesler, Wesley—Ohio State, 1930
Fincher, Bill—Georgia Tech, 1920
Fish, Hamilton—Harvard, 1909
Fisher, Robert—Harvard, 1911
Flowers, Abe—Georgia Tech, 1920
Fortmann, Daniel—Colgate, 1935
Francis, Sam—Nebraska, 1936
Frank, Clint—Yale, 1937
Franz, Rodney—California, 1949
Friedman, Benny—Michigan, 1926
Garbisch, Edgar—Army, 1924
Gelbert, Charles—Pennsylvania, 1896
Geyer, Forest—Oklahoma, 1915
Giel, Paul—Minnesota, 1953
Gifford, Frank—So. California, 1951
Gilbert, Walter—Auburn, 1936
Gipp, George—Notre Dame, 1920
Gladchuk, Chet—Boston College, 1940
Goldberg, Marshall—Pittsburgh, 1938
Gordon, Walter—California, 1918
Graham, Otto—Northwestern, 1943
Grange, Harold (Red)—Illinois, 1925
Grayson, Robert—Stanford, 1935
Gulick, Merel—Hobart, 1929
Guyon, Joe—Georgia Tech, 1919
Hale, Edwin—Mississippi Col, 1921
Hamilton, Robert (Bones)—Stanford, 1935
Hamilton, Tom—Navy, 1925
Hanson, Vic—Syracuse, 1926
Hardwick, H. (Tack)—Harvard, 1914
Hare, T. Truxton—Pennsylvania, 1900
Harley, Chick—Ohio State, 1919
Harmon, Tom—Michigan, 1940
Harpster, Howard—Carnegie Tech, 1928
Hart, Edward J.—Princeton, 1911
Hart, Leon—Notre Dame, 1949
Hazel, Homer—Rutgers, 1924
Healey, Ed—Dartmouth, 1916
Heffelfinger, W. (Pudge)—Yale, 1891
Hein, Mel—Washington State, 1930
Henry, Wilber—Wash. & Jefferson, 1919
Herschberger, Clarence—Chicago, 1899
Herwig, Robert—California, 1937

Heston, Willie—Michigan, 1904
Hickman, Herman—Tennessee, 1931
Hickok, William—Yale, 1895
Hill, Dan—Duke, 1938
Hillebrand, A.R. (Doc)—Princeton, 1900
Hinkey, Frank—Yale, 1894
Hinkle, Carl—Vanderbilt, 1937
Hinkle, Clark—Bucknell, 1932
Hirsch, Elroy—Wis./Mich., 1943
Hitchcock, James—Auburn, 1932
Hoffman, Frank—Notre Dame, 1931
Hogan, James J.—Yale, 1904
Holland, Jerome (Brud)—Cornell, 1938
Hollenbeck, William—Penn., 1908
Horrell, Edwin—California, 1924
Horvath, Les—Ohio State, 1944
Howe, Arthur—Yale, 1911
Howell, Millard (Dixie)—Alabama, 1934
Hubbard, Cal—Centenary, 1926
Hubbard, John—Amherst, 1906
Hubert, Allison—Alabama, 1925
Humble, Weldon G.—Rice, 1946
Hunt, Joel—Texas A&M, 1927
Huntington, Ellery—Colgate, 1914
Hutson, Don—Alabama, 1934
Ingram, James—Navy, 1906
Isbell, Cecil—Purdue, 1937
Jablonsky, Harvey—Wash. U./Army, 1933
Janowicz, Vic—Ohio State, 1951
Jenkins, Darold—Missouri, 1941
Joesting, Herbert—Minnesota, 1927
Johnson, James—Carlisle, 1903
Jones, Gomer—Ohio State, 1935
Juhan, Frank—Univ. of South, 1910
Justice, Charlie—North Carolina, 1949
Kaer, Mort—So. California, 1926
Kavanaugh, Kenneth—La. State U., 1939
Kaw, Edgar—Cornell, 1922
Kazmaier, Richard—Princeton, 1951
Keck, James—Princeton, 1921
Kelley, Larry—Yale, 1936
Kelly, William—Montana, 1926
Ketcham, Henry—Yale, 1913
Killinger, William—Penn State, 1922
Kirkpatrick, John Reed—Yale, 1910
Kimbrough, John—Texas A&M, 1940
Kinard, Frank—Mississippi, 1937
King, Phillip—Princeton, 1893
Kinnick, Nile—Iowa, 1939
Kipke, Harry—Michigan, 1923
Kitzmiller, John—Oregon, 1929
Koch, Barton—Baylor, 1931
Kitner, Malcolm—Texas, 1942
Kramer, Ron—Michigan, 1956
Lane, Myles—Dartmouth, 1927
Lautenschlaeger—Tulane, 1925
Layden, Elmer—Notre Dame, 1924
Layne, Bobby—Texas, 1947
Lea, Langdon—Princeton, 1895
Leech, James—Va. Mil. Inst., 1920
Locke, Gordon—Iowa, 1922
Lourie, Don—Princeton, 1921
Luckman, Sid—Columbia, 1938
Lujack, John—Notre Dame, 1947
Lund, J.L. (Pug)—Minnesota, 1934
Macomber, Bart—Illinois, 1915
MacLeod, Robert—Dartmouth, 1938
Mahan, Edward W.—Harvard, 1915
Mallory, William—Yale, 1893
Mann, Gerald—So. Methodist, 1927
Markov, Vic—Washington, 1937
Marshall, Robert—Minnesota, 1907
Matson, Ollie—San Fran. U., 1952
Matthews, Ray—Texas Christ. U., 1928
Maulbetsch, John—Michigan, 1914
Mauthe, J.L. (Pete)—Penn State 1912
Maxwell, Robert—Chi./Swarthmore, 1906
McAfee, George—Duke, 1939
McColl, William F.—Stanford, 1951
McCormick, James B.—Princeton, 1907
McDowall, Jack—No. Car. State, 1927
McEver, Gene—Tennessee, 1931
McEwan, John—Minn./Army, 1916
McFadden, J.B.—Clemson, 1939
McClung, Thomas L.—Yale, 1891
McGovern, J.—Minnesota, 1910
McLaren, George—Pittsburgh, 1918
McMillan, Dan—U.S.C./Calif., 1922
McMillan, Bob—Centre, 1921
McWhorter, Robert—Georgia, 1913
Mercer, Leroy—Pennsylvania, 1912
Mickal, Abe—La. State U., 1935
Miller, Creighton—Notre Dame, 1943
Miller, Don—Notre Dame, 1925
Miller, Edgar (Rip)—Notre Dame, 1924
Miller, Eugene—Penn State, 1913
Milstead, Century—Wabash, Yale 1923
Minds, John—Pennsylvania, 1897
Moffatt, Alex—Princeton, 1884
Montgomery, Cliff—Columbia, 1933
Moomaw, Donn—U.C.L.A., 1952
Morley, William—Columbia, 1903
Morton, William—Dartmouth, 1931
Muller, Harold (Brick)—Calif., 1922
Nagurski, Bronko—Minnesota, 1929
Nevers, Ernie—Stanford, 1925
Newell, Marshall—Harvard, 1893
Newman, Harry—Michigan, 1932
Nomellini, Leo—Minnesota, 1949
Oberlander, Andrew—Dartmouth, 1925
O'Brien, Davey—Texas Christ. U., 1938
O'Dea, Pat—Wisconsin, 1899
O'Hearn, J.—Cornell, 1915
Oliphant, Elmer—Purdue/Army, 1917
Oosterbaan, Ben—Michigan, 1927
O'Rourke, Charles—Boston College, 1940
Osgood, W.D.—Cornell/Penn, 1895
Osmanski, William—Holy Cross, 1938
Parker, Clarence (Ace)—Duke, 1936
Parker, Jackie—Miss. State, 1953
Parker, James—Ohio State, 1956
Pazzetti, V.J.—Wes./Lehigh, 1912
Peabody, Endicott—Harvard, 1941
Peck, Robert—Pittsburgh, 1916
Pennock, Stanley B.—Harvard, 1914
Pfann, George—Cornell, 1923
Phillips, H.D.—U. of South, 1904
Pingel, John—Michigan State, 1938
Pihos, Pete—Indiana, 1945
Pinckert, Ernie—So. California, 1931
Poe, Arthur—Princeton, 1899
Pollard, Fritz—Brown, 1916
Poole, Barney—Miss./Army, 1947
Pund, Henry—Georgia Tech, 1928
Ramsey, Gerrard—Wm. & Mary, 1942
Reeds, Claude—Oklahoma, 1913
Reid, William—Harvard, 1900
Reynolds, Robert—Stanford, 1935
Rinehart, Charles—Lafayette, 1897
Rodgers, Ira—West Virginia, 1919
Rogers, Edward L.—Minnesota, 1903
Rosenberg, Aaron—So. California, 1934
Rote, Kyle—So. Methodist, 1950
Routt, Joe—Texas A&M., 1937
Salmon, Louis—Notre Dame, 1904
Sauer, George—Nebraska, 1933
Sayers, Gale—Kansas, 1964
Scarlett, Hunter—Pennsylvania, 1909
Schoonover, Wear—Arkansas, 1929
Schreiner, Dave—Wisconsin, 1942
Schultz, Adolf (Germany)—Mich., 1908
Schwab, Frank—Lafayette, 1922
Schwartz, Marchmont—Notre Dame, 1931
Schwegler, Paul—Washington, 1931
Scott, Clyde—Arkansas, 1949
Seibels, Henry—Sewanee, 1899
Shelton, Murray—Cornell, 1915
Shevlin, Tom—Yale, 1905
Simons, Claude—Tulane, 1934
Sington, Fred—Alabama, 1930
Sinkwich, Frank—Georgia, 1942
Skladany, Joe—Pittsburgh, 1933
Slater, F.F. (Duke)—Iowa, 1921
Smith, Bruce—Minnesota, 1941
Smith, Ernie—So. California, 1932
Smith, Harry—So. California, 1939
Smith, John (Clipper)—Notre Dame, 1927
Snow, Neil—Michigan, 1901
Spears, Clarence W.—Dartmouth, 1915
Spears, W.D.—Vanderbilt, 1927
Sprackling, William—Brown, 1911
Sprague, M. (Bud)—Texas/Army, 1928
Stafford, Harrison—Texas, 1932
Stagg, Amos Alonzo—Yale, 1889
Steffen, Walter—Chicago, 1908
Stein, Herbert—Pittsburgh, 1921
Steuber, Robert—Missouri, 1943
Stevens, Mal—Yale, 1923
Stinchcomb, Gaylord—Ohio State, 1920
Stevenson, Vincent—Pennsylvania, 1905
Strong, Ken—New York Univ., 1928
Strupper, George—Georgia Tech, 1917
Stuhldreher, Harry—Notre Dame, 1924
Stydahar, Joe—West Virginia, 1935
Suffridge, Robert—Tennessee, 1940
Sundstrom, Frank—Cornell, 1923
Swanson, Clarence—Nebraska, 1921
Swiacki, Bill—Holy Cross/Colombia. 1947
Thompson, Joe—Pittsburgh, 1907
Thorne, Samuel B.—Yale, 1906
Thorpe, Jim—Carlisle, 1912
Ticknor, Ben—Harvard, 1930
Tigert, John—Vanderbilt, 1904
Tinsley, Gaynell—La. State U., 1936
Tipton, Eric—Duke, 1938
Torrey, Robert—Pennsylvania, 1906
Travis, Ed Tarkio—Missouri, 1920
Trippi, Charles—Georgia, 1946
Tryon, J. Edward—Colgate, 1925
Utay, Joe—Texas A&M, 1907
Van Brocklin, Norm—Oregon, 1948
Van Sickel, Dale—Florida, 1929
Van Surdam, Henderson—Wesleyan, 1905
Very, Dexter—Penn State, 1912
Vessels, Billy—Oklahoma, 1931
Wagner, Huber—Pittsburgh, 1913
Walker, Doak—So. Methodist, 1949
Wallace, Bill—Rice, 1935
Walsh, Adam—Notre Dame, 1924
Warburton, I. (Cotton)—So. Calif., 1934
Warner, William—Cornell, 1903
Washington, Ken—U.C.L.A., 1939
Weekes, Harold—Columbia, 1902
Weir, Ed—Nebraska, 1925
Welch, Gus—Carlisle, 1914
Weller, John—Princeton, 1935
Wendell, Percy—Harvard, 1913
West, D. Belford—Colgate, 1919
Weyand, Alex—Army, 1915

Wharton, Charles—Pennsylvania, 1896
Wheeler, Arthur—Princeton, 1894
White, Byron (Whizzer)—Colorado, 1937
Whitmire, Don—Alabama/Navy, 1944
Wickhorst, Frank—Navy, 1926
Widseth, Ed—Minnesota, 1936
Wildung, Richard—Minnesota, 1942
Williams, James—Rice, 1949
Willis, William—Ohio State, 1945
Wilson, George—Washington, 1925
Wilson, Harry—Penn State/Army, 1923
Wistert, Albert A.—Michigan, 1942
Wistert, Frank (Whitey)—Mich., 1933
Wojciechowicz, Alex—Fordham, 1936
Wyant, Andrew—Bucknell/Chicago, 1894
Wyatt, Bowden—Tennessee, 1938
Wyckoff, Clint—Cornell, 1896
Young, Claude (Buddy)—Illinois, 1946
Young, Harry—Wash. & Lee, 1916
Zarnas, Gus—Ohio State, 1937

**Coaches**

Bill Alexander
Dr. Ed Anderson
Ike Armstrong
Matty Bell
Hugo Bezdek
Dana X. Bible
Bernie Bierman
Earl (Red) Blaik
Charles W. Caldwell
Walter Camp
Len Casanova
Frank Cavanaugh
Fritz Crisler
Gil Dobie
Michael Donohue
Gus Dorais
Charles (Rip) Engle
Don Faurot
Jake Gaither
Ernest Godfrey
Edward K. Hall
Richard Harlow
Jesse Harper
Percy Haughton
John W. Heisman
R. A. (Bob) Higgins
William Ingram
Morley Jennings
Howard Jones
L. (Biff) Jones
Thomas (Tad) Jones
Andy Kerr
Frank Leahy
George E. Little
Lou Little
El (Slip) Madigan
Herbert McCracken
Daniel McGugin
DeOrmond (Tuss) McLaughry
L. R. (Dutch) Meyer
Bernie Moore
Ray Morrison
George A. Munger
Clarence Munn
William Murray
Ed (Hooks) Mylin
Earle (Greasy) Neale
Jess Neely
Robert Neyland
Homer Norton
Frank (Buck) O'Neill
Bennie Owen
James Phalea
E. N. Robinson
Knute Rockne
E. L. (Dick) Romney
William W. Roper
George F. Sanford
Francis A. Schmidt
Clark Shaughnessy
Buck Shaw
Andrew L. Smith
Carl Snavely
Amos A. Stagg
Jock Sutherland
Frank W. Thomas
Wallace Wade
Lynn Waldorf
Glenn (Pop) Warner
E. E. (Tad) Wieman
John W. Wilce
Bud Wilkinson
Henry L. Williams
George W. Woodruff
Fielding H. Yost
Robert Zuppke

## MAJOR COLLEGE FOOTBALL RECORDS (1940–1977)

*Source:* National Collegiate Sports Services, compiled by Steve Boda, Jr.

### LONGEST PLAYS

**Rushing**

| | Yards |
|---|---|
| Kelsey Finch, Tennessee (Florida) 1977 | 99 |
| Ralph Thompson, W. Tex. State (Wichita State) 1970 | 99 |
| Max Anderson, Arizona State (Wyoming) 1967 | 99 |
| Gale Sayers, Kansas (Nebraska) 1963 | 99 |
| Granville Amos, Virginia M. I. (Wm. & Mary) 1964 | 98 |
| Jim Thacker, Davidson (George Washington) 1952 | 98 |
| Bill Powell, California (Oregon State) 1951 | 98 |
| Al Yannelli, Bucknell (Delaware) 1946 | 98 |
| Meredith Warner, Iowa State (Iowa Pre-Flight) 1943 | 98 |

**Passing**

| | Yards |
|---|---|
| Chris Collingsworth–Derrick Gaffney, Florida (Rice) 1977 | 99 |
| Terry Peel–Robert Ford, Houston (San Diego St.) 1972 | 99 |
| Terry Peel–Robert Ford, Houston (Syracuse) 1970 | 99 |
| Colin Clapton–Eddie Jenkins, Holy Cross (Boston U.) 1970 | 99 |
| Bo Burris–Warren McVea, Houston (Wash. St.) 1966 | 99 |
| Fred Owens–Jack Ford, Portland (St. Mary's) 1947 | 99 |
| Jeff Martin–Mark Flaker, Drake (N.M. State) 1976 | 98 |
| Pete Woods–Joe Stewart, Missouri (Nebraska) 1976 | 98 |
| Dan Hagemann–Jack Steptoe, Utah (New Mexico) 1976 | 98 |
| Bruce Shaw–Pat Kenny, N.C. State (Penn State) 1972 | 98 |
| Jerry Rhome–Jeff Jordan, Tulsa (Wichita State) 1963 | 98 |
| Bob Dean–Norman Dawson, Cornell (Navy) 1947 | 98 |

**Punt Returns**

| | Yards |
|---|---|
| Jimmy Campagna, Georgia (Vanderbilt) 1952 | 100 |
| Hugh McElhenny, Washington (So. Cal.) 1951 | 100 |
| Frank Brady, Navy (Maryland) 1951 | 100 |
| Bert Rechichar, Tennessee (Wash. & Lee) 1950 | 100 |
| Eddie Macon, Pacific (Boston U.) 1950 | 100 |
| Richie Luzzi, Clemson (Georgia) 1968 | 100[1] |
| Don Guest, California (Washington State) 1966 | 100[1] |

1. Return of a field goal attempt.

**Punts**

| | Yards |
|---|---|
| Pat Brady, Nevada (Loyola, L. A.) 1950 | 99 |
| George O'Brien, Wisconsin (Iowa) 1952 | 96 |
| John Hadl, Kansas (Oklahoma) 1959 | 94 |
| Carl Knox, Texas Christian (Oklahoma State) 1947 | 94 |
| Preston Johnson, SMU (Pittsburgh) 1940 | 94 |

**Field Goals**

| | Yards |
|---|---|
| Steve Little, Arkansas (Texas) 1977 | 67 |
| Russell Erxleben, Texas (Rice) 1977 | 67 |
| Tony Franklin, Texas A&M (Baylor) 1976 | 65 |
| Russell Erxleben, Texas (Oklahoma) 1977 | 64 |
| Tony Franklin, Texas A&M (Baylor) 1976 | 64 |
| Clark Kemble, Colorado State (Arizona) 1975 | 63 |
| Dan Christopulos, Wyoming (Colorado State) 1977 | 62 |
| Iseed Khoury, North Texas State (Richmond) 1977 | 62 |
| Dave Lawson, Air Force Academy (Iowa State) 1975 | 62 |
| Steve Little, Arkansas (Tulsa) 1976 | 61 |
| Wayne Latimer, Virginia Tech (Florida State) 1975 | 61 |
| Ray Guy, Southern Mississippi (Utah State) 1972 | 61 |
| Russell Erxleben, Texas (Texas Tech) 1977 | 60 |
| Bubba Hicks, Baylor (Rice) 1975 | 60 |
| Dave Lawson, Air Force Academy (Colorado) 1974 | 60 |
| Tony Di Rienzo, Oklahoma (Kansas) 1973 | 60 |
| Bill McClard, Arkansas (So. Methodist) 1970 | 60 |

**Kickoff Returns**

107 players have returned kickoffs 100 yards since 1941. The most recent:

| | |
|---|---|
| Bobby Weber, Minnesota (Ohio State) | 1977 |
| Larry Anderson, Louisiana Tech (Illinois State) | 1977 |
| Ron Harris, Colorado State (Brigham Young) | 1977 |
| Preston Brown, Vanderbilt (Mississippi) | 1977 |
| Ray Crisp, Marshall (Akron) | 1977 |

### BEST SINGLE-GAME PERFORMANCES

Most yards, rushing—350, Eric Allen, Michigan State (Purdue) 1971

Most yards, total offense—599, Virgil Carter, Brigham Young (Texas-El Paso) 1966

Most yards, passing—571, Marc Wilson, Brigham Young (Utah) 1977

Most yards, pass receiving—349, Chuck Hughes, Texas-El Paso (North Texas State) 1965

Most points scored—43, Jim Brown, Syracuse (Colgate) 1956

Most passes attempted—69, Chuck Hixson, Southern Methodist (Ohio State) 1968

Most passes completed—42, Bill Anderson, Tulsa (Southern Illinois) 1965

Most passes caught—22, Jay Miller, Brigham Young (New Mexico) 1973

### CAREER LEADERS

#### Rushing

| | Years | Plays | Yds | Avg |
|---|---|---|---|---|
| Tony Dorsett, Pittsburgh | 1973–76 | 1,074[1] | 6,082[1] | 5.66 |
| Archie Griffin, Ohio State | 1972–75 | 845 | 5,177 | 6.13 |
| Ed Marinaro, Cornell | 1969–71 | 918 | 4,715 | 5.14 |
| Terry Miller, Oklahoma State | 1974–77 | 847 | 4,582 | 5.41 |
| Earl Campbell, Texas | 1974–77 | 765 | 4,443 | 5.81 |
| Joe Washington, Oklahoma | 1972–75 | 656 | 3,995 | 6.09 |
| Mike Voight, North Carolina | 1973–76 | 826 | 3,971 | 4.81 |
| Ron Po James, New Mexico St. | 1968–71 | 818 | 3,884 | 4.75 |
| Sonny Collins, Kentucky | 1972–75 | 777 | 3,835 | 4.94 |

1. Record.

#### Passing

| | Years | Cmp | Pct | Yds | Td |
|---|---|---|---|---|---|
| Chuck Hixson, So. Methodist | 1968–70 | 642[1] | .576 | 7,179 | 40 |
| John Reaves, Florida | 1969–71 | 603 | .535 | 7,549[1] | 54 |
| Gene Swick, Toledo | 1972–75 | 556 | .593 | 7,267 | 44 |
| Jim Plunkett, Stanford | 1968–70 | 530 | .551 | 7,544 | 52 |
| Tommy Kramer, Rice | 1973–76 | 507 | .489 | 6,197 | 37 |
| Lynn Dickey, Kansas St. | 1968–70 | 501 | .504 | 6,208 | 29 |
| Steve Ramsey, North Texas St. | 1967–69 | 491 | .484 | 7,076 | 69[1] |

1. Record.

#### Total Offense

| | Years | Plays | Yds | Tdr[1] |
|---|---|---|---|---|
| Gene Swick, Toledo | 1972–75 | 1,579[2] | 8,074[2] | 63 |
| Jim Plunkett, Stanford | 1968–70 | 1,174 | 7,887 | 62 |
| John Reaves, Florida | 1969–71 | 1,258 | 7,283 | 58 |
| Chuck Hixson, So. Methodist | 1968–70 | 1,358 | 6,884 | 50 |
| Pat Sullivan, Auburn | 1969–71 | 968 | 6,884 | 71 |
| Tony Adams, Utah State | 1970–72 | 1,132 | 6,587 | 62 |
| Steve Ramsey, N. Tex. State | 1967–69 | 1,132 | 6,568 | 71 |
| Danny White, Arizona State | 1971–73 | 813 | 6,453 | 73[2] |

1. Touchdowns responsible for—scored or passed for. 2. Record.

#### Pass Receiving

| | Years | Rec | Yds | Td |
|---|---|---|---|---|
| Howard Twilley, Tulsa | 1963–65 | 261[1] | 3,343 | 32 |
| Ron Sellers, Florida State | 1966–68 | 212 | 3,598 | 23 |
| Phil Odle, Brig. Young | 1965–67 | 181 | 2,548 | 25 |
| Tim Delaney, San Diego St. | 1968–70 | 180 | 2,535 | 22 |
| Hugh Campbell, Washington State | 1960–62 | 176 | 2,453 | 22 |

1. Record.

#### Scoring

| | Years | Td | Pat | Fg | Pts |
|---|---|---|---|---|---|
| Tony Dorsett, Pittsburgh | 1973–76 | 59[1] | 2 | 0 | 356[1] |
| Glenn Davis, Army | 1943–46 | 59[1] | 0 | 0 | 354 |
| Art Luppino, Arizona | 1953–56 | 48[1] | 49 | 0 | 337 |
| Steve Owens, Oklahoma | 1967–69 | 56 | 0 | 0 | 336 |
| Wilford White, Arizona St. | 1947–50 | 48 | 27 | 4 | 327 |
| Ed Marinaro, Cornell | 1969–71 | 52 | 6 | 0 | 318 |
| Pete Johnson, Ohio State | 1973–76 | 53 | 0 | 0 | 318 |
| Eddie Talboom, Wyoming | 1948–50 | 34 | 99 | 0 | 303 |
| Anthony Davis, So. California | 1972–74 | 50 | 2 | 0 | 302 |

1. Record.

## N.C.A.A. DIVISION II AND III FOOTBALL RECORDS (1942–77)

### LONGEST PLAYS

#### Rushing

| | Yards |
|---|---|
| Fred Deutsch, Springfield (Wagner) 1977 | 99 |
| Sam Hallston, Albany State, N.Y. (Norwich) 1977 | 99 |
| Sammy Croom, San Diego (Azusa Pacific) 1972 | 99 |
| John Stenger, Swarthmore (Widener) 1970 | 99 |
| Jed Knuttila, Hamline (St. Thomas) 1968 | 99 |
| Dave Lanoha, Colorado College (Texas Lutheran) 1967 | 99 |
| Tom Pabst, Cal-Riverside (Cal. Tech) 1965 | 99 |
| George Phillips, Concord (Davis and Elkins) 1961 | 99 |
| Gerry White, Connecticut (Rhode Island) 1960 | 99 |
| Leo Williams, St. Augustine's (Morris) 1960 | 99 |
| George Phelps, Cornell College (Monmouth) 1959 | 99 |
| Mark Lydon, Tufts (Bowdoin) 1958 | 99 |
| David Wells, Tufts (Williams) 1956 | 99 |
| Jack Moskal, Western Reserve (Case Tech) 1954 | 99 |
| Lou Mariano, Kent State (Western Reserve) 1954 | 99 |
| Ron Temple, Chico State (Southern Oregon) 1963 | 99 |
| Ellis Horton, Eureka, (Rose-Hulman) 1952 | 99 |
| Pat Abbruzzi, Rhode Island (New Hampshire) 1951 | 99 |

#### Field Goals

| | |
|---|---|
| Joe Duren, Arkansas State (McNeese State) 1974 | 63 |
| Dom Antonini, Glassboro State (Salisbury State) 1976 | 62 |
| Mike Flater, Colorado Mines (Western State) 1973 | 62 |
| Duane Christian, Cameron (Southwestern Oklahoma) 1976 | 61 |
| Mike Wood, Southeast Missouri (Lincoln) 1975 | 61 |
| Bill Shear, Cortland State (Hobart) 1966 | 61 |

#### Passing

| | Yards |
|---|---|
| Rich Boling–Lewis Borsellino, DePauw (Valparaiso) 1976 | 99 |
| John Wicinski–Donnell Lipford, John Carroll (Allegheny) 1975 | 99 |
| Jack Berry–Mercer West, Wash. & Lee (Hampden-Sydney) 1974 | 99 |
| Gary Shope–Rick Rudolph, Juniata (Moravian) 1973 | 99 |
| Gary Dusenberg–Harvey King, North Park (Ill. Wesleyan) 1970 | 99 |
| John Williams–Bill Carter, N.M. Highlands (No. Colorado) 1964 | 99 |
| Bob Janesko–Frank Stankiewicz, Emporia (Pittsburg State) 1969 | 99 |
| Carl Meyers–Roger Sayers, Nebraska-Omaha (Drake) 1963 | 99 |

#### Punts

| | |
|---|---|
| Earl Hurst, Emporia State (Central Missouri) 1964 | 97 |
| Gary Frens, Hope (Olivet) 1966 | 96 |
| Jim Jarrett, North Dakota (South Dakota) 1957 | 96 |
| Elliot Mills, Carleton (Monmouth) 1970 | 93 |
| Kaspar Fitins, Taylor (Georgetown, Ky.) 1966 | 93 |
| Leeroy Sweeney, Pomona (Cal-Riverside) 1960 | 93 |

## CAREER LEADERS

### Rushing

| | Years | Plays | Yds | Avg |
|---|---|---|---|---|
| Jerry Linton, Panhandle State | 1959–62 | 648 | 4,839[1] | 7.47 |
| John VanWagner, Mich. Tech. | 1973–76 | 958 | 4,788 | 5.00 |
| Rich Kowalski, Hobart | 1972–75 | 907 | 4,631 | 5.11 |
| Don Aleksiewicz, Hobart | 1969–72 | 819 | 4,525 | 5.53 |
| Dale Mills, NE Missouri | 1957–60 | 751 | 4,502 | 5.99 |
| Leo Lewis, Lincoln (Mo.) | 1951–54 | 623 | 4,458 | 7.16 |
| Bernie Peeters, Luther | 1968–71 | 1,072 | 4,435 | 4.14 |
| Larry Schreiber, Tenn. Tech. | 1966–69 | 878 | 4,421 | 5.04 |
| Brad Rowland, McMurry | 1947–50 | 683 | 4,347 | 6.36 |
| Vincent Allen, Indiana State | 1973–77 | 832 | 4,335 | 5.21 |
| Bill Rhodes, Colorado Western | 1953–56 | 506 | 4,294 | 8.49[1] |
| Lem Harkey, Col. of Emporia | 1951–54 | 502 | 4,232 | 8.43 |

### Scoring

| | Years | Td | Pat | Fg | Pts |
|---|---|---|---|---|---|
| Walter Payton, Jackson State | 1971–74 | 66[1] | 53 | 5 | 464[1] |
| Dale Mills, NE Missouri | 1957–60 | 64 | 23 | 0 | 407 |
| Garney Henley, Huron | 1956–59 | 63 | 16 | 0 | 394 |
| Leo Lewis, Lincoln (Mo.) | 1951–54 | 64 | 0 | 0 | 384 |
| Billy Johnson, Widener | 1971–73 | 62 | 0 | 0 | 372 |
| Tank Younger, Grambling | 1945–48 | 60 | 9 | 0 | 369 |

### Passing

| | Years | Cmp | Pct | Yds | Td |
|---|---|---|---|---|---|
| Jim Lindsey, Abilene Chr. | 1967–70 | 642[1] | .519 | 8,521[1] | 61 |
| Bob Caress, Bradley | 1962–65 | 610 | .528 | 7,115 | 64 |
| Dan Miles, So. Oregon | 1964–67 | 577 | .662[1] | 6,531 | 52 |
| George Bork, N. Illinois | 1960–63 | 577 | .640 | 6,782 | 60 |
| Kim McQuilken, Lehigh | 1971–73 | 516 | .558 | 6,996 | 37 |
| Tim Von Dulm, Portland St. | 1969–70 | 500 | .541 | 5,967 | 51 |
| Doug Williams, Grambling | 1974–77 | 484 | .480 | 8,411 | 99[1] |
| Jerry Bishop, Austin | 1962–65 | 464 | .551 | 5,992 | 44 |

1. Record.

### Pass Receiving

| | Years | Rec | Yards | Td |
|---|---|---|---|---|
| Chris Myers, Kenyon | 1967–70 | 253[1] | 3,897 | 33 |
| Bruce Cerone, Yankton–Emporia St. | 1966–67<br>1968–1969 | 241 | 4,354[1] | 49[1] |
| Harold Roberts, Austin Peay | 1967–70 | 232 | 3,005 | 31 |
| Jerry Hendren, Idaho | 1967–69 | 230 | 3,435 | 27 |
| Terry Fredenberg, Wis.–Milwaukee | 1965–68 | 206 | 2,789 | 24 |
| Rick Fry, Occidental | 1974–77 | 200 | 3,073 | 18 |
| Bill Wick, Carroll (Wis.) | 1966–69 | 190 | 2,967 | 20 |
| Don Hutt, Boise State | 1971–73 | 187 | 2,716 | 30 |

1. Record

### Total Offense

| | Years | Plays | Yds |
|---|---|---|---|
| Jim Lindsey, Abilene Christian | 1967–70 | 1,510 | 8,385 |
| Doug Williams, Grambling | 1974–77 | 1,072 | 8,195 |
| Donald Smith, Langston | 1958–61 | 998 | 7,376 |
| Bruce Upstill, Coll. Emporia | 1960–63 | 922 | 7,122 |
| Kim McQuilken, Lehigh | 1971–73 | 991 | 6,878 |
| Bob Caress, Bradley | 1962–65 | 1,361 | 6,757 |
| Ken Anderson, Augustana (Ill.) | 1967–70 | 1,135 | 6,682 |
| Terry Bradshaw, La. Tech. | 1966–69 | 1,028 | 6,664 |

## MOST POINTS IN SEASON

| | Yards | Tds | PAT | Fg | Pts |
|---|---|---|---|---|---|
| Terry Metcalf, Long Beach St. | 1971 | 29[1] | 4 | 0 | 178 |
| Jim Switzer, Coll. Emporia | 1963 | 28 | 0 | 0 | 168 |
| Carl Herakovich, Rose Polytech | 1958 | 25 | 18 | 0 | 168 |
| Ted Scown, Sul Ross State | 1948 | 28 | 0 | 0 | 168 |
| Eddie McGovern, Rose Polytech | 1942 | 23 | 27 | 0 | 165 |
| Leon Burns, Long Beach State | 1969 | 27 | 2 | 0 | 164 |

1. Record.

## N.C.A.A. 1977 CHAMPIONSHIP PLAYOFFS

### DIVISION II

**First Round**

California–Davis 34, Bethune–Cookman 16
Lehigh 30, Massachusetts 23
North Dakota State 20, Northern Michigan 6
Jacksonville State 35, Northern Arizona 0

**Semifinals**

Knute Rockne Bowl—Lehigh 39, California–Davis 30
Grantland Rice Bowl—Jacksonville State 31, North Dakota State 7

**Championship**

Pioneer Bowl—Lehigh 33, Jacksonville State 0

### DIVISION III

**First Round**

Wabash 20, St. John's 9
Widener 19, Central (Iowa) 0
Minnesota–Morris 13, Albion 10
Albany State (N.Y.) 51, Hampden–Sydney 45

**Semifinals**

Wabash 37, Minnesota–Morris 21
Widener 33, Albany State (N.Y.) 15

**Championship**

Amos Alonzo Stagg Bowl—Widener 39, Wabash 36

## NATIONAL ASSOCIATION OF INTERCOLLEGIATE ATHLETICS CHAMPIONS, 1978

### DIVISION I

**Semifinals**

Abilene Christian 35, Wisconsin–Stevens Point 7
Southwest Oklahoma 21, Kearney State 7

**Championship**

Abilene Christian 24, Southwest Oklahoma 7

### DIVISION II

**Semifinals**

Westminster (Pa.) 14, Concord (W. Va.) 13
California Lutheran 29, Linfield (Ore.) 28

**Championship**

Westminster (Pa.) 17, California Lutheran 9

## N.C.A.A. SETS UP DIVISION 1-A AND 1-AA FOR FOOTBALL

The National Collegiate Athletic Association has divided Division I into two groups for football competition beginning in 1978. The schools had a choice to be in either group provided that they met certain requirements. A total of 139 schools chose Division 1-A, and 37 opted for 1-AA.

To be a member of Division 1-A, an institution must sponsor a minimum of eight varsity sports, including football, in Division I and schedule at least 60 percent of its football games against Division 1-A opponents; must have averaged better than 17,000 in paid attendance over the last four-year period and have a stadium that seats a minimum of 30,000; or must sponsor at least 12 varsity sports.

A Division 1-AA member is required to sponsor at least eight varsity sports and schedule more than 50 percent of its football games against Division 1-A or 1-AA opponents.

Membership of Division 1-A: conferences: Atlantic Coast, Big Eight, Big Ten, Ivy League, Mid-American, Missouri Valley, Pacific Coast Athletic Association, Pacific-10, Southeastern, Southern, Southland, Southwest, Western Athletic; independents: Air Force, Army, Boston College, Cincinnati, Colgate, East Carolina, East Tennessee State, Florida State, Georgia Tech, Hawaii, Holy Cross, Illinois State, Memphis State, Miami (Florida), Navy, Nevada–Las Vegas, North Texas State, Northeast Louisiana, Notre Dame, Penn State, Pittsburgh, Richmond, Rutgers, San Diego State, South Carolina, Southern Mississippi, Syracuse, Temple, Tulane, Utah State, Villanova, Virginia Tech, West Virginia, William and Mary.

Membership of Division 1-AA: conferences: Big Sky, Ohio Valley (except East Tennessee State), Southwestern, Yankee; independents: Florida A & M, Idaho, Northwestern Louisiana.

# Professional Football

## NATIONAL FOOTBALL LEAGUE FINAL STANDING 1977

### AMERICAN CONFERENCE

**Eastern Division**

| | W | L | T | Pct | Pts | OP |
|---|---|---|---|---|---|---|
| Baltimore | 10 | 4 | 0 | .714 | 295 | 221 |
| Miami | 10 | 4 | 0 | .714 | 313 | 197 |
| New England | 9 | 5 | 0 | .643 | 278 | 217 |
| New York Jets | 3 | 11 | 0 | .214 | 191 | 300 |
| Buffalo | 3 | 11 | 0 | .214 | 160 | 313 |
| **Central Division** | | | | | | |
| Pittsburgh | 9 | 5 | 0 | .643 | 283 | 243 |
| Houston | 8 | 6 | 0 | .571 | 299 | 230 |
| Cincinnati | 8 | 6 | 0 | .571 | 238 | 235 |
| Cleveland | 6 | 8 | 0 | .429 | 269 | 267 |
| **Western Division** | | | | | | |
| Denver | 12 | 2 | 0 | .857 | 274 | 148 |
| Oakland[1] | 11 | 3 | 0 | .786 | 351 | 230 |
| San Diego | 7 | 7 | 0 | .500 | 222 | 205 |
| Seattle | 5 | 9 | 0 | .357 | 282 | 373 |
| Kansas City | 2 | 12 | 0 | .143 | 225 | 349 |

1. Wild card qualifier for playoffs.

Playoffs: Denver 34, Pittsburgh 21; Oakland 37, Baltimore 31 (sudden death overtime)

Conference championship: Denver 20, Oakland 17

### NATIONAL CONFERENCE

**Eastern Division**

| | W | L | T | Pct | Pts | OP |
|---|---|---|---|---|---|---|
| Dallas | 12 | 2 | 0 | .857 | 345 | 212 |
| Washington | 9 | 5 | 0 | .643 | 196 | 189 |
| St. Louis | 7 | 7 | 0 | .500 | 272 | 287 |
| Philadelphia | 5 | 9 | 0 | .357 | 220 | 207 |
| New York Giants | 5 | 9 | 0 | .357 | 181 | 265 |
| **Central Division** | | | | | | |
| Minnesota | 9 | 5 | 0 | .643 | 231 | 227 |
| Chicago[1] | 9 | 5 | 0 | .643 | 255 | 253 |
| Detroit | 6 | 8 | 0 | .429 | 183 | 252 |
| Green Bay | 4 | 10 | 0 | .286 | 134 | 219 |
| Tampa Bay | 2 | 12 | 0 | .143 | 103 | 223 |
| **Western Division** | | | | | | |
| Los Angeles | 10 | 4 | 0 | .714 | 302 | 146 |
| Atlanta | 7 | 7 | 0 | .500 | 179 | 129 |
| San Francisco | 5 | 9 | 0 | .357 | 220 | 260 |
| New Orleans | 3 | 11 | 0 | .214 | 232 | 336 |

1. Wild card qualifier for playoffs.

Playoffs: Dallas 37, Chicago 7; Minnesota 14, Los Angeles 7

Conference championship: Dallas 23, Minnesota 6

## League Championship (Super Bowl XII, New Orleans, Jan. 15, 1978)

(At Louisiana Superdome; Attendance 75,583)

| | 1st Q | 2nd Q | 3rd Q | 4th Q | Final |
|---|---|---|---|---|---|
| Dallas Cowboys (NFC) | 10 | 3 | 7 | 7 | 27 |
| Denver Broncos (AFC) | 0 | 0 | 10 | 0 | 10 |

Scoring—Dallas: Touchdowns: Dorsett, 3-yard run; Johnson, 45-yard pass from Staubach; Richards, 29-yard pass from Newhouse. Conversions: Herrera 3 (kicks). Field goals: Herrera 35 and 43 yards. Denver: touchdowns: Lyle, 1-yard run. Conversion: Turner (kick); Field goal: Turner, 47 yards.

**Statistics of the Game**

| | Dallas | Denver |
|---|---|---|
| First downs | 17 | 11 |
| Yards gained rushing | 143 | 121 |
| Yards gained passing | 182 | 35 |
| Passes completed | 19 of 28 | 8 of 25 |
| Passes intercepted by | 4 | 0 |
| Punts | 5–41.6 | 4–38.2 |
| Ball lost, fumbles | 2 | 4 |
| Yards penalized | 94 | 60 |

Financial Summary—Gross receipts (including TV, radio, films): $6,923,141. Players' Share: $1,633,500. Each winning player's share: $18,000; each loser's share: $9,000.

## SUPER BOWLS V–XII (N.F.L. CHAMPIONSHIPS)

National Conference Champion vs. American Conference Champion

| Season | Site | Date | Attendance | Winner | Loser |
|---|---|---|---|---|---|
| 1970 | Orange Bowl, Miami | Jan. 17, 1971 | 79,204 | Baltimore Colts, A.C., 16 | Dallas Cowboys, N.C., 13 |
| 1971 | Tulane Stadium, New Orleans | Jan. 16, 1972 | 80,591 | Dallas Cowboys, N.C., 24 | Miami Dolphins, A.C., 3 |
| 1972 | Memorial Coliseum, Los Angeles | Jan. 14, 1973 | 90,182 | Miami Dolphins A.C., 14 | Wash. Redskins, N.C., 7 |
| 1973 | Rice Stadium, Houston | Jan. 13, 1974 | 68,142 | Miami Dolphins, A.C., 24 | Minnesota Vikings, N.C., 7 |
| 1974 | Tulane Stadium, New Orleans | Jan. 12, 1975 | 80,997 | Pittsburgh Steelers, A.C., 16 | Minnesota Vikings N.C., 6 |
| 1975 | Orange Bowl, Miami | Jan. 18, 1976 | 80,187 | Pittsburgh Steelers, A.C., 21 | Dallas Cowboys N.C., 17 |
| 1976 | Rose Bowl, Pasadena | Jan. 9, 1977 | 100,421 | Oakland Raiders, A.C., 32 | Minnesota Vikings, N.C. 14 |
| 1977 | Superdome, New Orleans | Jan. 15, 1978 | 75,583 | Dallas Cowboys, N.C. 27, | Denver Broncos, A.C. 10 |

## SUPER BOWLS I–IV (INTER-LEAGUE CHAMPIONSHIPS)

National League Champion vs. American League Champion

| | | | | | |
|---|---|---|---|---|---|
| 1966 | Memorial Coliseum, Los Angeles | Jan. 15, 1967 | 63,036 | Green Bay Packers, N.L., 35 | Kansas City Chiefs, A.L., 10 |
| 1967 | Orange Bowl, Miami | Jan. 14, 1968 | 75,546 | Green Bay Packers, N.L., 33 | Oakland Raiders, A.L., 14 |
| 1968 | Orange Bowl, Miami | Jan. 12, 1969 | 75,377 | New York Jets, A.L. 16 | Baltimore Colts, N.L. 7 |
| 1969 | Tulane Stadium, New Orleans | Jan. 11, 1970 | 80,562 | Kansas City Chiefs, A.L. 23 | Minnesota Vikings, N.L. 7 |

## NATIONAL LEAGUE CHAMPIONS

| Year | Champion (W-L-T) |
|---|---|
| 1921 | Chicago Bears (Staley's) (10–1–1) |
| 1922 | Canton Bulldogs (10–0–2) |
| 1923 | Canton Bulldogs (11–0–1) |
| 1924 | Cleveland Indians (7–1–1) |
| 1925 | Chicago Cardinals (11–2–1) |
| 1926 | Frankford Yellow Jackets (14–1–1) |
| 1927 | New York Giants (11–1–1) |
| 1928 | Providence Steamrollers (8–1–2) |
| 1929 | Green Bay Packers (12–0–1) |
| 1930 | Green Bay Packers (10–3–1) |
| 1931 | Green Bay Packers (12–2–0) |
| 1932 | Chicago Bears (7–1–6) |

| Year | Eastern Conference Winners (W-L-T) | Western Conference Winners (W-L-T) | League champion playoff results |
|---|---|---|---|
| 1933 | New York Giants (11–3–0) | Chicago Bears (10–2–1) | Chicago Bears 23, New York 21 |
| 1934 | New York Giants (8–5–0) | Chicago Bears (13–0–0) | New York 30, Chicago Bears 13 |
| 1935 | New York Giants (9–3–0) | Detroit Lions (7–3–2) | Detroit 26, New York 7 |
| 1936 | Boston Redskins (7–5–0) | Green Bay Packers (10–1–1) | Green Bay 21, Boston 6 |
| 1937 | Washington Redskins (8–3–0) | Chicago Bears (9–1–1) | Washington 28, Chicago Bears 21 |
| 1938 | New York Giants (8–2–1) | Green Bay Packers (8–3–0) | New York 23, Green Bay 17 |
| 1939 | New York Giants (9–1–1) | Green Bay Packers (9–2–0) | Green Bay 27, New York 0 |
| 1940 | Washington Redskins (9–2–0) | Chicago Bears (8–3–0) | Chicago Bears 73, Washington 0 |
| 1941 | New York Giants (8–3–0) | Chicago Bears (10–1–1)[2] | Chicago Bears 37, New York 9 |
| 1942 | Washington Redskins (10–1–1) | Chicago Bears (11–0–0) | Washington 14, Chicago Bears 6 |
| 1943 | Washington Redskins (6–3–1)[2] | Chicago Bears (8–1–1) | Chicago Bears 41, Washington 21 |
| 1944 | New York Giants (8–1–1) | Green Bay Packers (8–2–0) | Green Bay 14, New York 7 |
| 1945 | Washington Redskins (8–2–0) | Cleveland Rams (9–1–0) | Cleveland 15, Washington 14 |
| 1946 | New York Giants (7–3–1) | Chicago Bears (8–2–1) | Chicago Bears 24, New York 14 |
| 1947 | Philadelphia Eagles (8–4–0)[2] | Chicago Cardinals (9–3–0) | Chicago Cardinals 28, Philadelphia 21 |
| 1948 | Philadelphia Eagles (9–2–1) | Chicago Cardinals (11–1–0) | Philadelphia 7, Chicago Cardinals 0 |
| 1949 | Philadelphia Eagles (11–1–0) | Los Angeles Rams (8–2–2) | Philadelphia 14, Los Angeles 0 |
| 1950[1] | Cleveland Browns (10–2–0)[2] | Los Angeles Rams (9–3–0)[2] | Cleveland 30, Los Angeles 28 |
| 1951[1] | Cleveland Browns (11–1–0) | Los Angeles Rams (8–4–0) | Los Angeles 24, Cleveland 17 |
| 1952[1] | Cleveland Browns (8–4–0) | Detroit Lions (9–3–0)[2] | Detroit 17, Cleveland 7 |
| 1953 | Cleveland Browns (11–1–0) | Detroit Lions (10–2–0) | Detroit 17, Cleveland 16 |
| 1954 | Cleveland Browns (9–3–0) | Detroit Lions (9–2–1) | Cleveland 56, Detroit 10 |
| 1955 | Cleveland Browns (9–2–1) | Los Angeles Rams (8–3–1) | Cleveland 38, Los Angeles 14 |
| 1956 | New York Giants (8–3–1) | Chicago Bears (9–2–1) | New York 47, Chicago Bears 7 |
| 1957 | Cleveland Browns (9–2–1) | Detroit Lions (8–4–0)[3] | Detroit 59, Cleveland 14 |
| 1958 | New York Giants (9–3–0)[2] | Baltimore Colts (9–3–0) | Baltimore 23, New York 17[3] |
| 1959 | New York Giants (10–2–0) | Baltimore Colts (9–3–0) | Baltimore 31, New York 16 |
| 1960 | Philadelphia Eagles (10–2–0) | Green Bay Packers (8–4–0) | Philadelphia 17, Green Bay 13 |
| 1961 | New York Giants (10–3–1) | Green Bay Packers (11–3–0) | Green Bay 37, New York 0 |
| 1962 | New York Giants (12–2–0) | Green Bay Packers (13–1–0) | Green Bay 16, New York 7 |
| 1963 | New York Giants (11–3–0) | Chicago Bears (11–1–2) | Chicago 14, New York 10 |
| 1964 | Cleveland Browns (10–3–1) | Baltimore Colts (12–2–0) | Cleveland 27, Baltimore 0 |
| 1965 | Cleveland Browns (11–3–0) | Green Bay Packers (11–3–1)[2] | Green Bay 23, Cleveland 12 |
| 1966 | Dallas Cowboys (10–3–1) | Green Bay Packers (12–2–0) | Green Bay 34, Dallas 27 |
| 1967 | Dallas Cowboys (9–5–0)[2] | Green Bay Packers (9–4–1)[2] | Green Bay 21, Dallas 17 |
| 1968 | Cleveland Browns (10–4–0)[2] | Baltimore Colts (13–1–0)[2] | Baltimore 34, Cleveland 0 |
| 1969 | Cleveland Browns (10–3–1)[2] | Minnesota Vikings (12–2–0)[2] | Minnesota 27, Cleveland 7 |

1. League was divided into American and National Conferences, 1950–52 and again in 1970, when leagues merged. 2. Won divisional playoff. 3. Won at 8:15 of sudden death overtime period.

# TEAM NICKNAMES AND HOME FIELD STADIUM CAPACITIES

## AMERICAN CONFERENCE

### Eastern Division

| | | |
|---|---|---|
| Baltimore Colts | Memorial Stadium (G) | 60,020 |
| Buffalo Bills | Rich Stadium (AT) | 80,020 |
| Miami Dolphins | Orange Bowl (G) | 75,449 |
| New England Patriots | Schaefer Stadium (AT)[1] | 61,279 |
| New York Jets | Shea Stadium (G) | 60,000 |

1. At Foxboro, Mass.

### Central Division

| | | |
|---|---|---|
| Cincinnati Bengals | Riverfront Stadium (AT) | 56,200 |
| Cleveland Browns | Cleveland Stadium (G) | 80,356 |
| Houston Oilers | Astrodome (AT) | 50,000 |
| Pittsburgh Steelers | Three Rivers Stadium (TT) | 50,350 |

### Western Division

| | | |
|---|---|---|
| Denver Broncos | Mile High Stadium (G) | 75,087 |
| Kansas City Chiefs | Arrowhead Stadium (TT) | 78,198 |
| Oakland Raiders | County Coliseum (G) | 54,615 |
| San Diego Chargers | San Diego Stadium (G) | 52,552 |
| Seattle Seahawks | Kingdome (AT) | 64,752 |

NOTE: Stadium playing surfaces in parentheses: AT = AstroTurf; G = grass; TT = TartanTurf.

## NATIONAL CONFERENCE

### Eastern Division

| | | |
|---|---|---|
| Dallas Cowboys | Texas Stadium (TT) | 65,101 |
| New York Giants | Giants Stadium (AT)[2] | 76,500 |
| Philadelphia Eagles | Veterans Stadium (AT) | 66,052 |
| St. Louis Cardinals | Busch Mem. Stadium (AT) | 51,392 |
| Washington Redskins | R. F. Kennedy Stadium (G) | 55,031 |

2. At East Rutherford, N.J.

### Central Division

| | | |
|---|---|---|
| Chicago Bears | Soldier Field (AT) | 57,359 |
| Detroit Lions | Pontiac Silverdome (AT) | 80,638 |
| Green Bay Packers | Lambeau Field (G) | 56,267 |
| | Milwaukee Stadium (G) | 55,896 |
| Minnesota Vikings | Metropolitan Stadium (G) | 48,446 |
| Tampa Bay Buccaneers | Tampa Stadium (G) | 71,951 |

### Western Division

| | | |
|---|---|---|
| Atlanta Falcons | Atlanta-Fulton Stadium (G) | 60,489 |
| Los Angeles Rams | Memorial Coliseum (G) | 71,039 |
| New Orleans Saints | Louisiana Superdome (AT) | 71,330 |
| San Francisco 49ers | Candlestick Park (AT) | 61,246 |

## National Conference Champions

| Year | Eastern Division Winners | Central Division | Western Division | Champion |
|---|---|---|---|---|
| 1970 | Dallas Cowboys (10–4–0) | Minnesota Vikings (12–2–0) | San Francisco 49ers (10–3–1) | Dallas |
| 1971 | Dallas Cowboys (11–3–0) | Minnesota Vikings (11–3–0) | San Francisco 49ers (9–5–0) | Dallas |
| 1972 | Washington Redskins (11–3–0) | Green Bay Packers (10–4–0) | San Francisco 49ers (8–5–1) | Washington |
| 1973 | Dallas Cowboys (10–4–0) | Minnesota Vikings (12–2–0) | Los Angeles Rams (12–2–0) | Minnesota |
| 1974 | St. Louis Cardinals (10–4–0) | Minnesota Vikings (10–4–0) | Los Angeles Rams (10–4–0) | Minnesota |
| 1975 | St. Louis Cardinals (11–3–0) | Minnesota Vikings (12–2–0) | Los Angeles Rams (10–4–0) | Dallas |
| 1976 | Dallas Cowboys (11–3–0) | Minnesota Vikings ( (11–2–1) | Los Angeles Rams (10–3–1) | Minnesota |
| 1977 | Dallas Cowboys (12–2–0) | Minnesota Vikings (9–5–0) | Los Angeles Rams (10–4–0) | Dallas |

## American Conference Champions

| Year | Eastern Division Winners | Central Division | Western Division | Champion |
|---|---|---|---|---|
| 1970 | Baltimore Colts (11–2–1) | Cincinnati Bengals (8–6–0) | Oakland Raiders (8–4–2) | Baltimore |
| 1971 | Miami Dolphins (10–3–1) | Cleveland Browns (9–5–0) | Kansas City Chiefs (10–3–1) | Miami |
| 1972 | Miami Dolphins (14–0–0) | Pittsburgh Steelers (11–3–0) | Oakland Raiders (10–3–1) | Miami |
| 1973 | Miami Dolphins (12–2–0) | Cincinnati Bengals (10–4–0) | Oakland Raiders (9–4–1) | Miami |
| 1974 | Miami Dolphins (11–3–0) | Pittsburgh Steelers (10–3–1) | Oakland Raiders (12–2–0) | Pittsburgh |
| 1975 | Baltimore Colts (10–4–0) | Pittsburgh Steelers (12–2–0) | Oakland Raiders (12–2–0) | Pittsburgh |
| 1976 | Baltimore Colts (11–3–0) | Pittsburgh Steelers (10–4–0) | Oakland Raiders (13–1–0) | Oakland |
| 1977 | Baltimore Colts (10–4–0) | Pittsburgh Steelers (9–5–0) | Denver Broncos (12–2–0) | Denver |

## American League Champions

| Year | Eastern Division Winners (W-L-T) | Western Division Winners (W-L-T) | League champion, playoffs results |
|---|---|---|---|
| 1960 | Houston Oilers (10–4–0) | Los Angeles Chargers (10–4–0) | Houston 24, Los Angeles 16 |
| 1961 | Houston Oilers (10–3–1) | San Diego Chargers (12–2–0) | Houston 10, San Diego 3 |
| 1962 | Houston Oilers (11–3–0) | Dallas Texans (11–3–0) | Dallas 20, Houston 17[1] |
| 1963 | Boston Patriots (8–6–1)[2] | San Diego Chargers (11–3–0) | San Diego 51, Boston 10 |
| 1964 | Buffalo Bills (12–2–0) | San Diego Chargers (8–5–1) | Buffalo 20, San Diego 7 |
| 1965 | Buffalo Bills (10–3–1) | San Diego Chargers (9–2–3) | Buffalo 23, San Diego 0 |
| 1966 | Buffalo Bills (9–4–1) | Kansas City Chiefs (11–2–1) | Kansas City 31, Buffalo 7 |
| 1967 | Houston Oilers (9–4–1) | Oakland Raiders (13–1–0) | Oakland 40, Houston 7 |
| 1968 | New York Jets (11–3–0) | Oakland Raiders (12–2–0)[2] | New York 27, Oakland 23 |
| 1969 | New York Jets (10–4–0) | Oakland Raiders (12–1–1) | Kansas City 17, Oakland 7[3] |

1. Won at 2:45 of second sudden death overtime period. 2. Won divisional playoff. 3. Kansas City defeated New York, 13–6, and Oakland defeated Houston, 56–7, in interdivisional playoffs.

## PRO FOOTBALL HALL OF FAME

(National Football Museum, Canton, Ohio)

Teams named are those with which player is best identified; figures in parentheses indicate number of playing seasons.

Alworth, Lance, wide receiver, Chargers 1962–70
Battles, Cliff, back, Redskins (6) 1932–37
Baugh, Sammy, quarterback, Redskins (16) 1937–52
Bednarik, Chuck, center-lineback, Eagles (14) 1949–62
Bell, Bert, N.F.L. founder, owner Eagles and Steelers, N.F.L. Commissioner (13) 1946–59
Berry, Raymond, end, Colts (13) 1955–67
Bidwell, Charles W., owner Chi. Cardinals 1933–47
Brown, Jim, fullback, Browns (9) 1957–65
Brown, Paul E., coach, Browns (1946–62), Bengals (1968—) 1946–19—
Brown, Roosevelt, tackle, Giants (13) 1953–65
Canadeo, Tony, back, Packers (11) 1941–52
Carr, Joe, president N.F.L. (18) 1921–39
Chamberlin, Guy, end 4 teams (9) 1919–27
Christiansen, Jack, def. back, Lions (8) 1951–58
Clark, Earl (Dutch), Qback, Spartans, Lions (7) 1931–38
Connor, George, tackle, linebacker, Bears (8) 1948–55
Conzelman, Jimmy, Qback 5 teams (10), owner 1921–48
Donovan, Art, def. tackle, Colts (12) 1950–61
Driscoll, John (Paddy), Qback, Cards, Bears (11) 1919–29
Dudley, Bill, back, Steelers, Lions, Skins (9) 1942–53
Edwards, Albert (Turk), tackle, Redskins (9) 1932–40
Ewbank, Weeb, coach (20), Colts, Jets 1954–73
Fears, Tom, end, Rams (9) 1948–56
Flaherty, Ray, end 3 teams; coach, Redskins, N.Y. Yankees (22) 1928–49
Ford, Len, end, def. end, Browns (11) 1948–57
Fortmann, Daniel J., guard, Bears (8) 1936–43
George, Bill, linebacker, Bears, Rams (15) 1952–65
Gifford, Frank, back, Giants (11) 1952–64
Graham, Otto, quarterback, Browns (10) 1946–55
Grange, Harold (Red), back, Bears, Yankees (9) 1925–34
Gregg, Forrest, tackle, Packers (15) 1956–71
Groza, Lou, place-kicker, tackle, Browns (21) 1946–67
Guyon, Joe, back, 6 teams (8) 1919–27
Halas, George, N.F.L. founder, owner and coach Staleys and Bears, end (11) 1919——
Healey, Ed, tackle, Bears (8) 1920–27
Hein, Mel, center, Giants (15) 1931–45
Henry, Wilbur (Pete), tackle, Bulldogs (8) 1920–28
Herber, Arnie, Qback, Packers, Giants (13) 1930–45
Hewitt, Bill, end, Bears, Eagles (9) 1932–43
Hinkle, Clarke, fullback, Packers (10) 1932–41
Hirsch, Elroy (Crazy Legs), back, end, Rams (12) 1946–57
Hubbard, R. (Cal), tackle, Giants, Packers (9) 1927–36
Hunt, Lamar, Founder A.F.L., owner Texans, Chiefs 1959——
Hutson, Don, end, Packers (11) 1935–45
Kiesling, Walt, guard 6 teams (13) 1926–38
Kinard, Frank (Bruiser), tackle, Dodgers (9) 1938–47
Lambeau, Earl (Curly), N.F.L. founder, coach, end, back, Packers (11) 1919–53
Lane, Richard (Night Train), def. back, Cards, Lions, Steelers (14) 1948–62
Lavelli, Dante, end, Browns (11) 1946–56
Layne, Bobby, Qback, Lions, Steelers (15) 1948–62
Leemans, Alphonse (Tuffy), back, Giants (7) 1937–43
Lombardi, Vince, coach, Packers, Redskins 1959–70
Luckman, Sid, quarterback, Bears (12) 1939–50
Lyman, Roy (Link), tackle, Bulldogs (11) 1922–34
Mara, Tim, N.F.L. founder, owner Giants 1925–59
Marchetti, Gino, defensive end, Colts (14) 1952–66
Marshall, George P., N.F.L. founder, owner Redskins 1932–65
Matson, Ollie, back, Chi. Cards, Rams (14) 1952–66
McAfee, George, back, Bears (8) 1940–50
McElhenny, Hugh, back, 49ers (13) 1952–64
McNally, John (Blood), back, 7 teams (15) 1925–39
Michalske, August, guard, Yankees, Packers (11) 1926–37
Millner, Wayne, end, Redskins (7) 1936–45
Moore, Lenny, back, Colts (13) 1956–67
Motley, Marion, fullback, Browns (9) 1946–55
Nagurski, Bronko, fullback, Bears (9) 1930–37
Neale, Earle (Greasy), coach, Eagles 1941–50
Nevers, Ernie, fullback, Chi. Cards (5) 1926–31
Nitschke, Ray, linebacker, Packers (15) 1958–72
Nomellini, Leo, defensive tackle, 49ers (14) 1950–63
Owen, Steve, tackle Giants (9), coach Giants 1931–53
Parker, Clarence (Ace), Qback, Dodgers (7) 1937–46
Parker, Jim, guard, tackle, Colts (11) 1957–67
Perry, Joe, fullback, 49ers (16) 1948–62
Pihos, Pete, end, Eagles (9) 1947–55
Ray, Hugh (Shorty), N.F.L. adviser 1938–52
Reeves, Dan, owner Rams 1941–71
Robustelli, Andy, def. end, Rams, Giants (14) 1951–64
Rooney, Art, N.F.L. founder, owner Steelers 1933——
Sayers, Gale, back, Bears (7) 1965–71
Schmidt, Joe, linebacker, Lions (13) 1953–65
Starr, Bart, quarterback, Packers (16) 1956–71
Stautner, Ernie, def. tackle, Steelers (14) 1950–63
Strong, Ken, back, Giants (14) 1929–47
Stydahar, Joe, tackle, Bears (9) 1936–42
Taylor, Jim, fullback, Packers (10) 1958–67
Thorpe, Jim, back, 7 teams (12) 1919–28
Tittle, Y. A., Qback, Colts, 49ers, Giants (17) 1948–64
Trafton, George, center, Bears (13) 1920–32
Trippi, Charley, back, Chi. Cards (9) 1947–55
Tunnell, Emlen, def. back, Giants, Packers (14) 1948–61
Turner, Clyde (Bulldog), center, Bears (13) 1940–52
Van Brocklin, Norm, Qback, Rams, Eagles (12) 1949–57
Van Buren, Steve, back, Eagles (8) 1944–51
Waterfield, Bob, quarterback, Rams (8) 1945–52
Willis, Bill, Guard, Browns (8) 1946–53
Wojciechowicz, Alex, center, Lions, Eagles (13) 1938–50
Wilson, Larry, defensive back, Cardinals (13) 1960–72

## N.F.L. INDIVIDUAL LIFETIME, SEASON AND GAME RECORDS

(Through 1977 American Football League marks were incorporated in N.F.L. records after merger in 1970)

### All-Time Leading Scorers

| | Yrs | Td | Fg | PAT | Pts |
|---|---|---|---|---|---|
| George Blanda | 26 | 9 | 335 | 943 | 2,002 |
| Fred Cox | 15 | 0 | 282 | 519 | 1,365 |
| Lou Groza | 17 | 1 | 234 | 641 | 1,349 |
| Jim Bakken | 16 | 0 | 271 | 507 | 1,320 |
| Jim Turner | 14 | 1 | 280 | 458 | 1,304 |
| Gino Cappelletti | 11 | 42 | 176 | 350 | 1,130[1] |
| Jan Stenerud | 11 | 0 | 247 | 341 | 1,082 |
| Bruce Gossett | 11 | 0 | 219 | 374 | 1,031 |
| Sam Baker | 15 | 2 | 179 | 428 | 977 |
| Lou Michaels | 13 | 1 | 187 | 386 | 955[2] |

1. Includes four 2-point conversions. 2. Includes one safety.

### All-Time Leading Touchdown Scorers

| | Yrs | Rush | Pass Rec | Returns | Total Td |
|---|---|---|---|---|---|
| Jim Brown | 9 | 106 | 20 | 0 | 126 |
| Lenny Moore | 12 | 63 | 48 | 2 | 113 |
| Don Hutson | 11 | 3 | 99 | 3 | 105 |
| Jim Taylor | 10 | 83 | 10 | 0 | 93 |
| Bobby Mitchell | 11 | 18 | 65 | 8 | 91 |
| Leroy Kelly | 10 | 74 | 13 | 3 | 90 |
| Charley Taylor | 13 | 11 | 79 | 0 | 90 |
| Don Maynard | 15 | 0 | 88 | 0 | 88 |
| Lance Alworth | 11 | 2 | 85 | 0 | 87 |
| Paul Warfield | 13 | 0 | 85 | 1 | 86 |

### All-Time Leading Rushers

| | Yrs | Att | Yds | Avg |
|---|---|---|---|---|
| Jim Brown | 9 | 2,359 | 12,312 | 5.2 |
| O. J. Simpson | 9 | 2,138 | 10,183 | 4.8 |
| Jim Taylor | 10 | 1,941 | 8,597 | 4.4 |
| Joe Perry | 14 | 1,737 | 8,378 | 4.8 |
| Leroy Kelly | 10 | 1,727 | 7,274 | 4.2 |
| Larry Csonka | 9 | 1,580 | 6,933 | 4.4 |
| John Henry Johnson | 13 | 1,571 | 6,803 | 4.3 |
| Floyd Little | 9 | 1,641 | 6,323 | 3.9 |
| Franco Harris | 6 | 1,435 | 6,295 | 4.4 |
| Don Perkins | 8 | 1,500 | 6,217 | 4.1 |

### All-Time Leading Receivers

| | Yrs | Pass Rec | Yds | Avg |
|---|---|---|---|---|
| Charley Taylor | 13 | 649 | 9,110 | 14.0 |
| Don Maynard | 15 | 633 | 11,834 | 18.7 |
| Raymond Berry | 13 | 631 | 9,275 | 14.7 |
| Fred Biletnikoff | 13 | 569 | 8,689 | 15.3 |
| Lionel Taylor | 10 | 567 | 7,195 | 12.7 |
| Lance Alworth | 11 | 542 | 10,266 | 18.9 |
| Bobby Mitchell | 11 | 521 | 7,954 | 15.3 |
| Billy Howton | 12 | 503 | 8,459 | 16.8 |
| Tommy McDonald | 12 | 495 | 8,410 | 17.0 |
| Don Hutson | 11 | 488 | 7,991 | 16.4 |

### All-Time Leading Passers

| | Comp | Pct Comp | Yds | Td | Int | Rating |
|---|---|---|---|---|---|---|
| Ken Stabler | 945 | 59.9 | 12,519 | 108 | 91 | 83.6 |
| Sonny Jurgensen | 2,433 | 57.1 | 32,224 | 255 | 189 | 82.8 |
| Len Dawson | 2,136 | 57.1 | 28,711 | 239 | 183 | 82.6 |
| Ken Anderson | 1,208 | 56.8 | 15,471 | 99 | 69 | 82.1 |
| Fran Tarkenton | 3,341 | 56.7 | 43,535 | 317 | 234 | 81.5 |
| Roger Staubach | 1,187 | 57.0 | 15,924 | 101 | 82 | 81.2 |
| Bart Starr | 1,808 | 57.4 | 24,718 | 152 | 138 | 80.3 |
| Johnny Unitas | 2,830 | 54.6 | 40,239 | 290 | 253 | 78.2 |
| Otto Graham | 872 | 55.7 | 13,499 | 88 | 94 | 78.1 |
| Frank Ryan | 1,090 | 51.1 | 16,042 | 149 | 111 | 77.7 |

The passing ratings are based on performance standards established for completion percentage, interception percentage, touchdown percentage, and average gain. Passers are allocated points according to how their marks compare to these standards.

### Scoring

Most points scored, lifetime—2,002, George Blanda, Chicago Bears, 1949–58; Baltimore, 1950; Houston, 1960–66; Oakland, 1967–75 (9tds, 943 pat, 335 fgs).

Most points, season—176, Paul Hornung, Green Bay, 1960 (15 td, 41 pat, 15 fg).

Most points, game—40, Ernie Nevers, Chicago Cards, 1929 (6 td, 4 pat).

Most points, per quarter—29, Don Hutson, Green Bay, 1945 (4 td, 5 pat).

Most touchdowns, lifetime—126, Jim Brown, Cleveland, 1957–65.

Most touchdowns, season—23, O.J. Simpson, Buffalo, 1975.

Most touchdowns, game—6, Ernie Nevers, Chicago Cards; William Jones, Cleveland, 1929; Gale Sayers, Chicago Bears, 1965.

Most points after touchdown, lifetime—943, George Blanda, Chicago Bears, 1949–58; Baltimore, 1950; Houston, 1960–66; Oakland, 1967–75.

Most points after touchdown, game—9, Pat Harder, Chicago Cards, 1948; Bob Waterfield, Los Angeles, 1950; Charlie Gogolak, Washington, 1966.

Most consecutive points after touchdown—234, Tommy Davis, San Francisco, 1959–65.

Most points after touchdown, no misses, season—56, Danny Villanueva, Dallas, 1966.

Most field goals, lifetime—335, George Blanda, Chicago Bears 1949–58; Baltimore, 1950; Houston, 1960–66; Oakland, 1967–75.

Most field goals, season—34, Jim Turner, New York Jets, 1968.

Most field goals, game—7, Jim Bakken, St. Louis, 1967.

Longest field goal—63 yards, Tom Dempsey, New Orleans, 1970.

### Rushing

Most yards gained, lifetime—12,312, Jim Brown, Cleveland, 1957–65.

Most yards gained, season—2,003, O. J. Simpson, Buffalo, 1973.

Most yards gained, game—275, Walter Payton, Chicago, 1977.

Most touchdowns, lifetime—106, Jim Brown, Cleveland, 1957–65.

Most touchdowns, season—19, Jim Taylor, Green Bay, 1962.

Most touchdowns, game—6, Ernie Nevers, Chicago Cards, 1929.

Longest run from scrimmage—97 yards, Andy Uram, Green Bay, 1939; Bob Gage, Pittsburgh, 1949 (both for touchdowns).

### Passing

Most passes completed, lifetime—3,341, Fran Tarkenton, Minnesota, 1961–66, 72–77; N.Y. Giants, 1967–71.

Most passes completed, season—288, Sonny Jurgensen, Washington, 1967

Most passed completed, game—37, George Blanda, Houston, 1964 (68 attempts).

Most consecutive passes completed—17, Bert Jones, Baltimore, 1974.

Most yards gained, lifetime—43,535, Fran Tarkenton, Minnesota, 1961–66, 72–77; N.Y. Giants, 1967–71.

Most yards gained, season—4,007, Joe Namath, New York Jets, 1967.

Most yards gained, game—554, Norm Van Brocklin, Los Angeles, 1951

Most touchdown passes, lifetime—317, Fran Tarkenton, Minnesota, 1961–66, 72–77; N.Y. Giants, 1967–71.

Most touchdown passes, season—36, George Blanda, Houston, 1961; Y. A. Tittle, New York Giants, 1963.

Most touchdown passes, game—7, Sid Luckman, Chicago Bears, 1943; Adrian Burk, Philadelphia, 1954; George Blanda, Houston 1961; Y.A. Tittle, New York Giants, 1963; Joe Kapp, Minnesota, 1969.

Most consecutive games, touchdown passes—47, John Unitas, Baltimore.

Most consecutive passes attempted, none intercepted—294, Bart Starr, Green Bay, 1964–65.

Longest pass completion—99 yards, Frank Filchock (to Andy Farkas), Washington, 1939; George Izo (to Bob Mitchell), Washington, 1963; Karl Sweetan (to Pat Studstill), Detroit, 1966; Sonny Jurgensen (to Gerry Allen), Washington, 1968, (all for touchdowns).

Most pass receptions, lifetime—649, Charley Taylor, Washington, 1964–75, 1977.

Most pass receptions, season—101, Charley Hennigan, Houston, 1964.

Most pass receptions, game—18, Tom Fears, Los Angeles, 1950.

Most consecutive games, pass receptions—105, Dan Abramowicz, New Orleans, 1967–73; San Francisco, 1973–74.

Most yards gained, pass receptions, lifetime—11,834, Don Maynard, New York Giants, 1958; New York Jets, 1960–72; St. Louis, 1973.

Most yards gained receptions, season—1,746, Charley Hennigan, Houston, 1961.

Most yards gained receptions, game—303, Jim Benton, Cleveland Rams, 1945.

Most touchdown pass receptions, lifetime—99, Don Hutson, Green Bay, 1935–45.

Most touchdown pass receptions, season—17, Don Hutson,

Green Bay, 1942; Elroy Hirsch, Los Angeles, 1951; Bill Groman, Houston, 1961.
Most touchdown pass receptions, game—5, Bob Shaw, Chicago Cards, 1950.
Most consecutive games, touchdown pass receptions—11, Elroy Hirsch, Los Angeles, 1950–51; Buddy Dial, Pittsburgh, 1959–60.
Most pass interceptions, lifetime—79, Emlen Tunnell, New York Giants, 1948–58 (74); Green Bay, 1959–61 (5).
Most pass interceptions, season—14, Richard (Night Train) Lane, Los Angeles, 1952.
Most pass interceptions, game—4, by 14 players.
Longest pass interception return—102 yards, Bob Smith, Chicago Bears, 1949; Erich Barnes, New York Giants, 1961; Gary Barbaro, Kansas City, 1977.

### Kicking

Longest punt—98 yards, Steve O'Neal, New York Jets, 1969.
Highest average punting, lifetime—45.10 yards, Sammy Baugh, Washington, 1937–52.
Longest punt return—98 yards, Gil LeFebvre, Cincinnati Reds, 1933; Charlie West, Minnesota, 1968; Dennis Morgan, Dallas, 1974.
Longest kick-off return—106 yards, Al Carmichael, Green Bay, 1956; Noland Smith, Kansas City, 1967.

## NATIONAL FOOTBALL LEAGUE GOVERNMENT

**Commissioner's Office:** Pete Rozelle, commissioner; Don Weiss, executive director; Jan Van Duser, director of player personnel; Jim Heffernan, director of public relations; Fran Connors, public relations staff assistant; Val Pinchbeck, Jr., director of broadcasting.

**American Conference:** Lamar Hunt, president; Al Ward, assistant to the president; Joe Browne, director of information.

**National Conference:** George Halas, president; Joe Rhein, assistant to the president; Dick Maxwell, director of information.

# COLLEGE ATHLETIC CONFERENCES

**Atlantic Coast:** Clemson, Duke, Georgia Tech, Maryland, North Carolina, North Carolina State, Virginia, Wake Forest

**Big Eight:** Colorado, Iowa State, Kansas, Kansas State, Missouri, Nebraska, Oklahoma, Oklahoma State

**Big Ten:** Illinois, Indiana, Iowa, Michigan, Michigan State, Minnesota, Northwestern, Purdue, Ohio State, Wisconsin

**Ivy League:** Brown, Columbia, Cornell, Dartmouth, Harvard, Pennsylvania, Princeton, Yale

**Pacific Ten:** Arizona, Arizona State, California, Oregon, Oregon State, Stanford, California–Los Angeles (UCLA), Southern California (USC), Washington, Washington State

**Southeastern:** Alabama, Auburn, Georgia, Florida, Kentucky, Louisiana State, Mississippi, Mississippi State, Tennessee, Vanderbilt

**Southwest:** Arkansas, Baylor, Houston, Rice, Southern Methodist, Texas, Texas A&M, Texas Christian, Texas Tech

**Southwestern:** Alcorn State, Grambling, Jackson State, Mississippi Valley, Prairie View, Southern, Texas Southern

**Western Athletic:** Brigham Young, Colorado State, Hawaii, Nevada–Las Vegas, New Mexico, San Diego State, Texas–El Paso, Utah, Wyoming

# COLLEGE COLORS AND NICKNAMES

Abilene Christian—Purple, white; Wildcats
Adelphi—Brown, gold; Panthers
Air Force—Silver, blue; Falcons
Akron—Blue, gold; Zips
Alabama—Crimson, white; Crimson Tide
Alcorn State—Purple, gold; Braves
Alfred—Purple, gold; Saxons
Amherst—Purple, white; Lord Jeffs
Arizona—Red, navy blue; Wildcats
Arizona State—Maroon, gold; Sun Devils
Arkansas—Cardinal, white; Razorbacks
Army—Black, gold, gray; Cadets
Auburn—Orange, navy blue; Tigers
Bates—Garnet; Bobcats
Baylor—Green, gold; Bears
Boston Coll.—Maroon, gold; Eagles
Boston—Scarlet, white; Terriers
Bowdoin—White; Polar Bears
Bowling Green—Brown, orange; Falcons
Bradley—Cardinal, white; Braves
Brigham Young—Blue, white; Cougars
Brooklyn—Maroon, gold; Kingsmen
Brown—Brown, white; Bruins
Bucknell—Orange, blue; Bisons
Buffalo—Blue, white; Bulls
Butler—Blue, white; Bulldogs
California at Berkeley—Blue, gold; Golden Bears
Cal, Irvine—Blue, gold; Anteaters
Cal, Davis—Navy, gold; Cal Aggies
Cal, Northridge—Red, white; Matadors
Cal, San Diego—Royal blue, gold; Tritons
Cal, Santa Barbara—Blue, gold; Gauchos
Canisius—Blue, gold; Griffins
Carnegie-Mellon—Tartan plaid; Tartans
Catholic—Red, black; Cardinals
Centre—Gold, white; Colonels
Chicago—Maroon; Maroons
Chico State—Cardinal, white; Wildcats
Cincinnati—Red, black; Bearcats
Citadel—Blue, white; Bulldogs
City Coll. of N.Y.—Lavender; Beavers
Clemson—Purple, orange; Tigers
Coast Guard—Blue, white; Cadets
Colgate—Maroon; Red Raiders
Colorado—Silver, gold; Buffaloes
Colorado State—Green, gold; Rams
Columbia—Blue, white; Lions
Connecticut—Blue, white; Huskies
Cornell—Carnelian, white; Big Red
Cortland State—Red, white; Red Dragons
Creighton—White, blue; Blue Jays
C.W. Post—Green, gold; Pioneers
Dartmouth—Green; Big Green
Davidson—Red, black; Wildcats
Dayton—Red, blue; Flyers
Delaware—Blue, gold; Blue Hens
Denver—Red, gold; Pioneers
DePaul—Scarlet, blue; Blue Demons
Detroit—Cardinal, white; Titans
Drake—White, blue; Bulldogs
Duke—Blue, white; Blue Devils
Duquesne—Red, blue; Dukes
East Carolina—Purple, gold; Pirates
Eastern Kentucky—Maroon, white; Maroons
Fairleigh Dickinson—Maroon, white, blue; Knights
Florida—Orange, blue; Gators
Florida State—Garnet, gold; Seminoles
Fordham—Maroon; Rams
Franklin and Marshall—Blue, white; Diplomats
Fresno State—Cardinal, blue; Bulldogs
Fullerton State—Royal blue, orange; Titans
Furman—Purple, white; Paladines
Georgetown—Blue, gray; Hoyas
George Washington—Buff, blue; Colonials
Georgia—Red, black; Bulldogs
Georgia Tech—White, gold; Yellow Jackets
Gonzaga—Blue, white; Bulldogs
Grambling—Black, gold; Tigers
Hamilton—Buff, blue; Continentals
Hampden-Sydney—Garnet, gray; Tigers

Hardin-Simmons—Purple, gold; Cowboys
Harvard—Crimson; The Crimson
Hayward—Red, white, black; Pioneers
Hobart—Orange, purple; Statesmen
Hofstra—Blue, gold; Flying Dutchmen
Holy Cross—Purple; Crusaders
Houston—Scarlet, white; Cougars
Howard—Blue, white; Bisons
Hunter—Purple, white; Hawks
Idaho—Silver, gold; Vandals
Illinois—Orange, blue; Illini
Indiana—Cream, crimson; Hoosiers
Indiana State—Blue, white; Sycamores
Iowa—Gold, black; Hawkeyes
Iowa State—Cardinal, gold; Cyclones
Jackson State—Blue, white; Tigers
Johns Hopkins—Blue, black; Blue Jays
Kansas—Crimson, blue; Jayhawks
Kansas State—Purple, white; Wildcats
Kent State—Blue, gold; Golden Flashes
Kentucky—Blue, white; Wildcats
Lafayette—Maroon, white; Leopards
LaSalle—Blue, gold; Explorers
Lehigh—Brown, white; Engineers
Long Beach State—Brown, gold; 49ers
Los Angeles State—Black, gold; Diablos
Louisiana State—Purple, gold; Tigers
Louisville—Cardinal, black; Cardinals
Loyola (Ill.)—Maroon, gold; Ramblers
Maine—Blue, white; Black Bears
Manhattan—Green, white; Jaspers
Marquette—Blue, gold; Warriors
Maryland—Red, white; Terrapins
Massachusetts—Maroon, white; Redmen
Merchant Marine—Blue, gray; Mariners
Miami (Fla.)—Orange, green, white; Hurricanes
Miami (Ohio)—Red, white; Redskins
Michigan—Maize, blue; Wolverines
Michigan State—Green, white; Spartans
Mid Tennessee—Blue, white; Blue Raiders
Middlebury—Blue, white; Panthers
Minnesota—Maroon, gold; Gophers
Mississippi—Red, blue; Rebels
Mississippi State—Maroon, white; Maroons
Missouri—Black, gold; Tigers
M.I.T.—Cardinal, gray; Beavers
Montana—Copper, silver, gold; Grizzlies
Montana State—Gold, royal blue; Bobcats
Morgan State—Blue, orange; Bears
Navy—Blue, gold; Midshipmen
Nebraska—Scarlet, cream; Cornhuskers
Nevada—Silver, blue; Wolfpack
New Hampshire—Blue, white; Wildcats
New Mexico—Cherry, silver; Lobos
New York—Violet; Violets
Niagara—Purple, white; Purple Eagles
North Carolina—Blue, white; Tar Heels
North Carolina State—Scarlet, white; Wolfpack
North Dakota—Green, white; Sioux
North Texas State—Green, white; Eagles
Northeastern—Red, black; Huskies
Northwestern—Purple, white; Wildcats
Notre Dame—Blue, gold; Fighting Irish
Occidental—Orange, black; Bengals
Ohio State—Scarlet, gray; Buckeyes
Ohio—Green, white; Bobcats
Oklahoma—Maroon, white; Sooners
Okla. State—Orange, black; Cowboys
Omaha—Red, black; Indians
Oneonta State—Red, white; Red Dragons
Oregon—Yellow, green; Webfoots
Oregon State—Orange, black; Beavers
Penn State—Blue, white; Nittany Lions
Pennsylvania—Red, blue; Quakers
Pepperdine—Blue, orange, white; Waves
Pittsburgh—Blue, gold; Panthers
Princeton—Orange, black; Tigers
Providence—Black, white; Friars
Purdue—Gold, black; Boilermakers
Rhode Island—Blue, white; Rams
Rice—Blue, gray; Owls
Richmond—Red, blue; Spiders
Rider—Purple, gold; Braves
Rochester—Yellow; Yellowjackets
Rollins—Blue, gold; Tars
R.P.I.—Cherry, white; Engineers
Rutgers—Scarlet; The Scarlet
St. Bonaventure—Brown, white; Bonnies
St. Francis (N.Y.)—Red, blue; Terriers
St. John's (N.Y.)—Red, white; Redman
St. Joseph's (Pa.)—Crimson, gray; Hawks
St. Lawrence—Scarlet, brown; Larries
St. Louis—Blue, white; Billikens
St. Mary's (Calif.)—Red, blue; Gaels
San Diego State—Red, black; Aztecs
San Francisco—Green, gold; Dons
San Jose State—Gold, white; Spartans
Santa Clara—Cardinal, white; Broncos
Seattle—Maroon, white; Chieftains
Seton Hall—Blue, white; Pirates
Sewanee—Purple, gold; Tigers
So. Carolina—Garnet, black; Gamecocks
South Dakota—Scarlet, white; Coyotes
So. California—Cardinal, gold; Trojans
So. Illinois—Maroon, white; Salukis
So. Methodist—Red, blue; Mustangs
Southern—Blue, gold; Jaguars
Springfield—Maroon, white; Maroons
Stanford—Cardinal, white; Cardinals
Stony Brook—Scarlet, white; Patriots
Swarthmore—Garnet; Little Quakers
Syracuse—Orange; Orangemen
Temple—Cherry, white; Owls
Tennessee—Orange, white; Vols
Tennessee A. & I.—Blue, white; Tigers
Texas—Orange, white; Longhorns
Texas A. & M.—Maroon, white; Aggies
Texas Christian—Purple, white; Horned Frogs
Texas, El Paso—Orange, white; Miners
Texas Southern—Maroon, gray; Tigers
Texas Tech—Scarlet, black; Red Raiders
Toledo—Blue, gold; Rockets
Trinity (Conn.)—Blue, gold; Bantams
Tufts—Blue, brown; Jumbos
Tulane—Green, blue; Green Wave
Tulsa—Crimson, blue, gold; Golden Hurricane
Tuskegee—Gold, crimson; Golden Tigers
U.C.L.A.—Blue, gold; Bruins
Utah—Crimson, white; Utes
Utah State—Blue, white; Aggies
Vanderbilt—Gold, black; Commodores
Vermont—Green, gold; Catamounts
Villanova—Blue, white; Wildcats
Virginia—Blue, orange; Cavaliers
V.M.I.—Red, white, yellow; Keydets
V.P.I.—Orange, maroon; Gobblers
Wagner—Green, white; Seahawks
Wake Forest—Gold, black; Deacons
Washington & Lee—Blue, white; Generals
Washington (Mo.)—Myrtle, maroon; Bears
Washington (Wash.)—Purple, gold; Huskies
Washington State—Crimson, gray; Cougars
Wesleyan—Cardinal, black; Cardinals
Western Kentucky—Red, white; Hilltoppers
W. Virginia—Gold, blue; Mountaineers
Wichita—Black, gold; Wheatshockers
William and Mary—Green, gold, silver; Indians
Williams—Royal purple; Ephmen
Wisconsin—Cardinal; Badgers
Wyoming—Brown, yellow; Cowboys
Yale—Blue; Bulldogs, Elis

# BOBSLEDDING

## 1978 WORLD CHAMPIONSHIPS

(Mount Van Hoevenberg, Lake Placid, N.Y.)

2-man (Feb. 4–5)—Switzerland (Erich Scharer and Josef Benz) 4:22.89[1]
4-man (Feb. 11–12)—East Germany (Horst Schonau, driver) 4:17.50[1]

1. Time for four heats.

## 1978 A.A.U. NATIONAL CHAMPIONSHIPS

(Mount Van Hoevenberg, Lake Placid, N.Y.)

2-man (Feb. 18)—Bob Hickey and Joe LeClair (brakeman), Keene, N.Y. 4:32.68[1]
4-man (Feb. 25)—Wade Whitney (driver), Keene, N.Y. 2:11.13[2]

## 1978 NORTH AMERICAN CHAMPIONSHIPS

(Mount Van Hoevenberg, Lake Placid, N.Y.)

2-man (Feb. 19)—Paul Vincent (driver), Keene, N.Y. 4:29.83[1]
4-man (Feb. 26)—Wade Whitney (driver), Keene, N.Y. 4:21.33[1]

1. Time for four heats. 2. Racing cut to two heats because of hazardous course conditions.

# BASKETBALL

Basketball may be the one sport whose exact origin is definitely known. In the winter of 1891–92, Dr. James Naismith, an instructor in the Y.M.C.A. Training College (now Springfield College) at Springfield, Mass., deliberately invented the game of basketball in order to provide indoor exercise and competition for the students between the closing of the football season and the opening of the baseball season. He affixed peach baskets overhead on the walls at opposite ends of the gymnasium and organized teams to play his new game in which the purpose was to toss an association (soccer) ball into one basket and prevent the opponents from tossing the ball into the other basket. The game is fundamentally the same today, though there have been improvements in equipment and some changes in rules.

Because Dr. Naismith had eighteen available players when he invented the game, the first rule was: "There shall be nine players on each side." Later the number of players became optional, depending upon the size of the available court, but the five-player standard was adopted when the game spread over the country. United States soldiers brought basketball to Europe in World War I, and it soon became a world-wide sport.

## College Basketball

### NATIONAL COLLEGIATE A.A. CHAMPIONS

| | | | | | | | |
|---|---|---|---|---|---|---|---|
| 1939 | Oregon | 1948 | Kentucky | 1957 | North Carolina | 1966 | Texas Western |
| 1940 | Indiana | 1949 | Kentucky | 1958 | Kentucky | 1967–73 | U.C.L.A. |
| 1941 | Wisconsin | 1950 | C.C.N.Y. | 1959 | California | 1974 | No. Carolina State |
| 1942 | Stanford | 1951 | Kentucky | 1960 | Ohio State | 1975 | U.C.L.A. |
| 1943 | Wyoming | 1952 | Kansas | 1961 | Cincinnati | 1976 | Indiana |
| 1944 | Utah | 1953 | Indiana | 1962 | Cincinnati | 1977 | Marquette |
| 1945 | Oklahoma A & M | 1954 | La Salle | 1963 | Loyola (Chicago) | 1978 | Kentucky |
| 1946 | Oklahoma A & M | 1955 | San Francisco | 1964 | U.C.L.A. | | |
| 1947 | Holy Cross | 1956 | San Francisco | 1965 | U.C.L.A. | | |

### NATIONAL INVITATION TOURNAMENT (NIT) CHAMPIONS

| | | | | | | | |
|---|---|---|---|---|---|---|---|
| 1939 | Long Island U. | 1950 | C.C.N.Y. | 1960 | Bradley | 1970 | Marquette |
| 1940 | Colorado | 1951 | Brigham Young | 1961 | Providence | 1971 | North Carolina |
| 1941 | Long Island U. | 1952 | La Salle | 1962 | Dayton | 1972 | Maryland |
| 1942 | West Virginia | 1953 | Seton Hall | 1963 | Providence | 1973 | Virginia Tech |
| 1943–44 | St. John's (Bklyn.) | 1954 | Holy Cross | 1964 | Bradley | 1974 | Purdue |
| 1945 | DePaul | 1955 | Duquesne | 1965 | St. John's (Bklyn.) | 1975 | Princeton |
| 1946 | Kentucky | 1956 | Louisville | 1966 | Brigham Young | 1976 | Kentucky |
| 1947 | Utah | 1957 | Bradley | 1967 | So. Illinois | 1977 | St. Bonaventure |
| 1948 | St. Louis | 1958 | Xavier (Cincinnati) | 1968 | Dayton | 1978 | Texas |
| 1949 | San Francisco | 1959 | St. John's (Bklyn.) | 1969 | Temple | | |

### N.C.A.A. MAJOR COLLEGE INDIVIDUAL SCORING RECORDS

**Single Season Averages**

| Player, Team | Year | G | FG | FT | Pts | Avg |
|---|---|---|---|---|---|---|
| Pete Maravich, Louisiana State | 1969–70 | 31 | 522[1] | 337 | 1381[1] | 44.5[1] |
| Pete Maravich | 1968–69 | 26 | 433 | 282 | 1148 | 44.2 |
| Pete Maravich | 1967–68 | 26 | 432 | 274 | 1138 | 43.8 |
| Frank Selvy, Furman | 1953–54 | 29 | 427 | 355[1] | 1209 | 41.7 |
| Johnny Neumann, Mississippi | 1970–71 | 23 | 366 | 191 | 923 | 40.1 |
| Freeman Williams, Portland State | 1976–77 | 26 | 417 | 176 | 1010 | 38.8 |
| Billy McGill, Utah | 1961–62 | 26 | 394 | 221 | 1009 | 38.8 |
| Calvin Murphy, Niagara | 1967–68 | 24 | 337 | 242 | 916 | 38.2 |
| Austin Carr, Notre Dame | 1969–70 | 29 | 444 | 218 | 1106 | 38.1 |

1. Record.

### N.C.A.A. CAREER SCORING TOTALS

**Division I**

| Player, Team | Last year | G | FG | FT | Pts | Avg |
|---|---|---|---|---|---|---|
| Pete Maravich, Louisiana State | 1970 | 83 | 1387[1] | 893 | 3667[1] | 44.2[1] |
| Austin Carr, Notre Dame | 1971 | 74 | 1017 | 526 | 2560 | 34.6 |
| Oscar Robertson, Cincinnati | 1960 | 88 | 1052 | 869 | 2973 | 33.8 |
| Calvin Murphy, Niagara | 1970 | 77 | 947 | 654 | 2548 | 33.1 |
| Dwight Lanar[2] | 1973 | 57 | 768 | 326 | 1862 | 32.7 |
| Frank Selvy, Furman | 1954 | 78 | 922 | 694 | 2538 | 32.5 |

| Player, Team | Last year | G | FG | FT | Pts | Avg |
|---|---|---|---|---|---|---|
| Rick Mount, Purdue | 1970 | 72 | 910 | 503 | 2323 | 32.3 |
| Darrel Floyd, Furman | 1956 | 71 | 868 | 545 | 2281 | 32.1 |
| Dick Werkman, Seton Hall | 1964 | 71 | 812 | 640 | 2273 | 32.0 |

1. Record. 2. Also played two seasons in college division.

**Division II**

| | Last year | G | FG | FT | Pts | Avg |
|---|---|---|---|---|---|---|
| Travis Grant, Kentucky State | 1972 | 121 | 1760[1] | 525 | 4045[1] | 33.4[1] |
| John Rinka, Kenyon | 1970 | 99 | 1261 | 729 | 3251 | 32.8 |
| Florindo Vierira, Quinnipiac | 1957 | 69 | 671 | 741 | 2263 | 32.8 |
| Willie Shaw, Lane | 1964 | 76 | 960 | 459 | 2379 | 31.3 |
| Mike Davis, Virginia Union | 1969 | 89 | 1014 | 730 | 2758 | 31.0 |
| Willie Scott, Alabama State | 1969 | 103 | 1277 | 601 | 3155 | 30.6 |
| Gregg Northington, Alabama State | 1972 | 75 | 894 | 403 | 2191 | 29.2 |
| Bob Hopkins, Grambling | 1956 | 126 | 1403 | 953 | 3759 | 29.8 |

1. Record.

## TOP SINGLE-GAME SCORING MARKS

| Player, Team (Opponent) | Yr | Pts |
|---|---|---|
| Selvy, Furman (Newberry) | 1954 | 100[1] |
| Williams, Portland State (Rocky Mtn.) | | 81 |
| Mikvy, Temple (Wilkes) | 1951 | 73 |
| Williams, Portland State (So. Oregon) | 1977 | 71 |
| Maravich, LSU (Alabama) | 1970 | 69 |
| Murphy, Niagara (Syracuse) | 1969 | 68 |
| Floyd, Furman (Morehead) | 1955 | 67 |
| Maravich, LSU (Tulane) | 1969 | 66 |
| Handlan, W & L (Furman) | 1951 | 66 |
| Roberts, Oral Roberts (N.C. A&T) | 1977 | 66 |
| Williams, Portland State (Geo. Fox Coll.) | | 66 |
| Roberts, Oral Roberts (Oregon) | 1977 | 65 |

1. Record.

## NATIONAL COLLEGIATE ATHLETIC ASSOCIATION (N.C.A.A.), 1978

### DIVISION I

**First Round—East**

Duke 63, Rhode Island 62
Penn 92, St. Bonaventure 62
Indiana 63, Furman 62
Villanova 103, LaSalle 97

**First Round—Mideast**

Utah 86, Missouri 79
Notre Dame 100, Houston 77
DePaul 80, Creighton 78
Louisville 76, St. John's 68

**First Round—Midwest**

Miami (Ohio) 84, Marquette 81
Michigan State 77, Providence 63
Western Kentucky 87, Syracuse 86
Kentucky 85, Florida State 76

**First Round—West**

U.C.L.A. 83, Kansas 76
Arkansas 73, Weber State 52
San Francisco 68, North Carolina 64
California State–Fullerton 90, New Mexico 85

**Second Round**

Duke 84, Penn 80
Villanova 61, Indiana 60
Notre Dame 69, Utah 56
DePaul 90, Louisville 89
Michigan State 90, Western Kentucky 69
Kentucky 91, Miami 69
Arkansas 74, U.C.L.A. 70
Cal State–Fullerton 75, San Francisco 72

**Regional Championships**

Duke 90, Villanova 72
Notre Dame 84, DePaul 64
Kentucky 52, Michigan State 49
Arkansas 61, Cal State–Fullerton 58

**Semifinals**

(St. Louis, March 25)

Kentucky 64, Arkansas 59
Duke 90, Notre Dame 86

**Third Place**

Arkansas 71, Notre Dame 69

**Championship**

(St. Louis, March 27)

Kentucky 94, Duke 88

### N.C.A.A. CHAMPIONSHIP—1978

(At St. Louis Checkerdome)

| Kentucky (94) | FG | FT | Pts |
|---|---|---|---|
| Givens | 18 | 5–8 | 41 |
| Robey | 8 | 4–6 | 20 |
| Phillips (c) | 1 | 2–2 | 4 |
| Macy | 3 | 3–4 | 9 |
| Claytor | 3 | 2–4 | 8 |
| Lee | 4 | 0–0 | 8 |
| Shidler | 1 | 0–1 | 2 |
| Aleksinas | 0 | 0–0 | 0 |
| Williams | 1 | 0–0 | 2 |
| Casey | 0 | 0–0 | 0 |
| Total | 39 | 16–25 | 94 |

| Duke (88) | FG | FT | Pts |
|---|---|---|---|
| Banks | 6 | 10–12 | 22 |
| Dennard | 5 | 0–0 | 10 |
| Gminski (c) | 6 | 8–8 | 20 |
| Harrell | 2 | 0–0 | 4 |
| Spanarkel | 8 | 5–6 | 21 |
| Suddath | 1 | 2–3 | 4 |
| Bender | 1 | 5–5 | 7 |
| Goetsch | 0 | 0–0 | 0 |
| Total | 29 | 30–34 | 88 |

Halftime: Kentucky 45, Duke 38
Total fouls: Kentucky 26, Duke 22
Attendance: 18,721

### DIVISION II

#### Quarterfinals

Eastern Illinois 84, Elizabeth City 71
Florida Tech 77, San Diego University 77
Wisconsin–Green Bay 63, Lincoln (Mo.) 61
Cheyney State (Pa.) 59, Sacred Heart (Conn.) 57

#### Semifinals

Cheyney State 79, Florida Tech 63
Wisconsin–Green Bay 58, Eastern Illinois 43

#### Third Place

Eastern Illinois 77, Florida Tech 67

#### Championship

Cheyney State 47, Wisconsin–Green Bay 40

### DIVISION III

#### Quarterfinals

North Park (Ill.) 65, Humboldt State 62
Widener (Pa.) 55, Kean (N.J.) 49
Albion (Mich.) 78, Knoxville 77
Stony Brook (N.Y.) 98, Brandeis 84

#### Semifinals

Widener 48, Stony Brook 38
North Park 75, Albion 69

#### Third Place

Albion 87, Stony Brook 78

#### Championship

North Park 69, Widener 57

## NATIONAL ASSOCIATION OF INTERCOLLEGIATE ATHLETICS—1978

#### Round of 16

Kearney State 84, Wisconsin–Parkside 80 (overtime)
Missouri Southern 69, Ouchita Baptist 56
Central State (Ohio) 92, Westmont 91 (2 overtimes)
Winston-Salem 64, Briar Cliff (Iowa) 63
Quincy 85, Erskine 84 (overtime)
Drury 86, St. John's (Minn.) 79
East Texas State 78, Birmingham Southern 72
Grand Canyon 83, Hawaii–Hilo 67

#### Quarterfinals

Kearney State 89, Winston-Salem 76
Quincy 73, Missouri Southern 66
East Texas State 79, Drury 77
Grand Canyon 88, Central State (Ohio) 82 (5 overtimes)

#### Semifinals

Kearney State 76, Quincy 74
Grand Canyon 74, East Texas State 69

#### Third Place

Quincy 87, East Texas State 73

#### Championship

Grand Canyon 79, Kearney State 75

## LEADING SCORERS—1977–78

#### N.C.A.A.—Division I

| | FG | FT | Pts | Pct |
|---|---|---|---|---|
| Freeman Williams, Portland State | 410 | 149 | 969 | 35.9 |
| Larry Bird, Indiana State | 403 | 153 | 959 | 30.0 |
| Purvis Short, Jackson State | 285 | 80 | 650 | 29.5 |
| Oliver Mack, East Carolina | 292 | 115 | 699 | 28.0 |
| Roger Phegley, Bradley | 237 | 189 | 663 | 27.6 |
| Frankie Sanders, Southern Univ. | 316 | 108 | 740 | 27.4 |

#### N.C.A.A.—Division II

| | FG | FT | Pts | Pct |
|---|---|---|---|---|
| Harold Robertson, Lincoln (Mo.) | 408 | 149 | 965 | 34.5 |
| Barry Frazier, Dist. of Columbia | 235 | 103 | 573 | 31.8 |
| Ed Murphy, Merrimack | 362 | 114 | 838 | 31.0 |
| Larry Wilson, Nicholls State | 252 | 143 | 647 | 28.1 |
| Mike Epps, Pfeiffer | 261 | 148 | 670 | 26.8 |
| Jeff Covington, Youngstown State | 249 | 162 | 660 | 26.4 |

#### N.C.A.A.—Division III

| | FG | FT | Pts | Pct |
|---|---|---|---|---|
| John Atkins, Knoxville | 340 | 103 | 783 | 31.5 |
| Cam Brown, Maine–Farmington | 244 | 160 | 648 | 29.5 |
| Howard Kelsey, Principia | 240 | 72 | 552 | 29.1 |
| Lud Wurtz, Ripon | 283 | 131 | 697 | 27.9 |
| Curt Artis, Pace | 309 | 162 | 780 | 27.9 |
| Pat Ryan, Suffolk | 263 | 150 | 676 | 27.0 |

#### N.A.I.A.

| | FG | FT | Pts | Pct |
|---|---|---|---|---|
| Kirkley, East. New Mexico | 245 | 97 | 587 | 30.9 |
| Cam Brown, Maine-Farmington | 230 | 148 | 608 | 30.4 |
| Noll, Grace (Ind.) | 311 | 260 | 882 | 28.4 |
| Hall, Howard Payne | 292 | 96 | 680 | 27.2 |
| Mike Epps, Pfeiffer | 243 | 136 | 622 | 27.0 |
| Ron Herkley, Lee (Tenn.) | 267 | 85 | 619 | 26.9 |

## ASSOCIATION OF INTERCOLLEGIATE ATHLETICS FOR WOMEN (A.I.A.W.)—1978

### REGIONAL CHAMPIONSHIPS

#### East

Montclair State 75, Queens College (NY) 60

#### South

Maryland 93, Southern Connecticut 53

#### Central

Wayland Baptist 72, North Carolina State 55

#### West

U.C.L.A. 86, Stephen F. Austin 60

### SEMIFINALS

(Los Angeles, March 23)
U.C.L.A. 85, Montclair State 77
Maryland 90, Wayland Baptist 85

### THIRD PLACE

Montclair State 90, Wayland Baptist 88 (overtime)

### CHAMPIONSHIP

(Los Angeles, March 25)
U.C.L.A. 90, Maryland 74

## A.I.A.W. SMALL COLLEGE—1978

#### Championship

Southeastern Louisiana 99, Shorter (Georgia) 90
Berry (Georgia) 99, Biola (California) 79
High Point (N.C.) 92, South Carolina State 88 (overtime)

## A.A.U. CHAMPIONSHIP—MEN
(London, Ky., April 5–9, 1978)

**Quarterfinals**
Joliet (Ill.) Christian Youth Center 126, Quincy (Fla.) Rackley Raiders, 119
Federal Way (Wash.) Dynasties 93, Iowa City Airliner 86
Lexington (Ky.) Marathon Oil 90, Oklahoma City Angel Aire 78
Little Rock Carver YMCA 107, Los Angeles Capital Insulation 91

**Semifinals**
Joliet Christian Youth Center 106, Federal Way Dynasties 103
Little Rock YMCA 94, Lexington Marathon Oil 93

**Third Place**
Federal Way Dynasties 76, Lexington Marathon Oil 74

**Championship**
Joliet Christian Youth Center 108, Little Rock Carver YMCA 106
Most valuable player: Tim Bryant, Joliet

## A.A.U. CHAMPIONSHIP—WOMEN
(Allentown, Pa., March 28-April 1, 1978)

**Quarterfinals**
Allentown (Pa.) Crestettes 86, Roberto Clemente State Park (N.Y.) 73
Anna's Bananas (Los Angeles) 84, Grand Rapids (Mich.) Condors 61
New York Planters 82, Detroit Cobras 74
Sophisticated Ladies (Wash. D.C.) 107, Darlington, S.C., 98

**Semifinals**
Sophisticated Ladies 82, Allentown Crestettes 81
Anna's Bananas 80, New York Planters 67

**Third Place**
Allentown Crestettes 104, New York Planters 58

**Championship**
Anna's Bananas (Los Angeles) 100, Sophisticated Ladies (Wash. D.C.,) 95
Most valuable player: Monica Havelka, Anna's Bananas

## NATIONAL INVITATION TOURNAMENT—1978
(Madison Square Garden, New York)

**Third Place**
Rutgers 85, Georgetown 72

**Semifinals (March 18)**
North Carolina State 86, Georgetown 85
Texas 96, Rutgers 76

**Final (March 21)**
Texas 101, North Carolina State 93

## A.A.U. NATIONAL YOUTH CHAMPIONSHIPS—1978
(Jacksonville, Fla., July 9–12)

**Third Place**
Washington D.C. 97, Pittsburgh 74

**Semifinals**
Detroit 73, Washington, D.C. 69
Jersey City–Newark N.J. 103, Pittsburgh 91

**Final**
Jersey City–Newark, N.J. 86, Detroit 81

Most valuable player: Howard McNeil, Jersey City–Newark, N.J.

# *Professional Basketball*

## NATIONAL BASKETBALL ASSOCIATION CHAMPIONS

The National Basketball Association was originally the Basketball Association of America. It took its current name in 1949 when it merged with the National Basketball League.

| Season | Eastern Conference (W-L) | Western Conference (W-L) | Playoff Champions[1] |
|---|---|---|---|
| 1946–47 | Washington Capitols (49–11) | Chicago Stags (39–22) | Philadelphia Warriors |
| 1947–48 | Philadelphia Warriors (27–21) | St. Louis Bombers (29–19) | Baltimore Bullets |
| 1948–49 | Washington Capitols (38–22) | Rochester Royals (45–15) | Minneapolis Lakers |
| 1949–50 | Syracuse Nationals (51–13) | Indianapolis Olympians (39–25) | Minneapolis Lakers |
| 1950–51 | Philadelphia Warriors (40–26) | Minneapolis Lakers (44–24) | Rochester Royals |
| 1951–52 | Syracuse Nationals (40–26) | Rochester Royals (41–25) | Minneapolis Lakers |
| 1952–53 | New York Knickerbockers (47–23) | Minneapolis Lakers (48–22) | Minneapolis Lakers |
| 1953–54 | New York Knickerbockers (44–28) | Minneapolis Lakers (46–26) | Minneapolis Lakers |
| 1954–55 | Syracuse Nationals (43–29) | Ft. Wayne Pistons (43–29) | Syracuse Nationals |
| 1955–56 | Philadelphia Warriors (45–27) | Ft. Wayne Pistons (37–35) | Philadelphia Warriors |
| 1956–57 | Boston Celtics (44–28) | St. Louis Hawks (34–38) | Boston Celtics |
| 1957–58 | Boston Celtics (48–23) | St. Louis Hawks (41–31) | St. Louis Hawks |
| 1958–59 | Boston Celtics (52–20) | St. Louis Hawks (49–23) | Boston Celtics |
| 1959–60 | Boston Celtics (59–16) | St. Louis Hawks (46–29) | Boston Celtics |
| 1960–61 | Boston Celtics (57–22) | St. Louis Hawks (51–28) | Boston Celtics |
| 1961–62 | Boston Celtics (60–20) | Los Angeles Lakers (54–26) | Boston Celtics |
| 1962–63 | Boston Celtics (58–22) | Los Angeles Lakers (53–27) | Boston Celtics |
| 1963–64 | Boston Celtics (59–21) | San Francisco Warriors (48–32) | Boston Celtics |
| 1964–65 | Boston Celtics (62–18) | Los Angeles Lakers (49–31) | Boston Celtics |
| 1965–66 | Philadelphia 76ers (55–25) | Los Angeles Lakers (45–35) | Boston Celtics |
| 1966–67 | Philadelphia 76ers (68–13) | San Francisco Warriors (44–37) | Philadelphia 76ers |
| 1967–68 | Philadelphia 76ers (62–20) | St. Louis Hawks (56–26) | Boston Celtics |
| 1968–69 | Baltimore Bullets (57–25) | Los Angeles Lakers (55–27) | Boston Celtics |

*Source:* Matt Winick, Director of Media Information, National Basketball Association

| Season | Eastern Conference (W-L) | Western Conference (W-L) | Playoff Champions[1] |
|---|---|---|---|
| 1969–70 | New York Knickerbockers (60–22) | Atlanta Hawks (48–34) | New York Knicks |
| 1970–71 | Baltimore Bullets (42–40) | Milwaukee Bucks (66–16) | Milwaukee Bucks |
| 1971–72 | New York Knickerbockers (48–34) | Los Angeles Lakers (69–13) | Los Angeles Lakers |
| 1972–73 | New York Knickerbockers (57–25) | Los Angeles Lakers (69–22) | New York Knicks |
| 1973–74 | Boston Celtics (56–26) | Milwaukee Bucks (59–23) | Boston Celtics |
| 1974–75 | Washington Bullets (60–22) | Golden State Warriors (48–34) | Golden State Warriors |
| 1975–76 | Boston Celtics (54–28) | Phoenix Suns (42–40) | Boston Celtics |
| 1976–77 | Philadelphia 76ers (50–32) | Portland Trail Blazers (49–33) | Portland Trail Blazers |
| 1977–78 | Washington Bullets (44–38) | Seattle Super Sonics (47–35) | Washington Bullets |

1. Playoffs may involve teams other than conference winners.

## INDIVIDUAL N.B.A. SCORING CHAMPIONS

| Season | Player, Team | G | FG | FT | Pts | Avg |
|---|---|---|---|---|---|---|
| 1953–54 | Neil Johnston, Philadelphia Warriors | 72 | 591 | 577 | 1759 | 24.4 |
| 1954–55 | Neil Johnston, Philadelphia Warriors | 72 | 521 | 589 | 1631 | 22.7 |
| 1955–56 | Bob Pettit, St. Louis Hawks | 72 | 646 | 557 | 1849 | 25.7 |
| 1956–57 | Paul Arizin, Philadelphia Warriors | 71 | 613 | 591 | 1817 | 25.6 |
| 1957–58 | George Yardley, Detroit Pistons | 72 | 673 | 655 | 2001 | 27.8 |
| 1958–59 | Bob Pettit, St. Louis Hawks | 72 | 719 | 667 | 2105 | 29.2 |
| 1959–60 | Wilt Chamberlain, Philadelphia Warriors | 72 | 1065 | 577 | 2707 | 37.6 |
| 1960–61 | Wilt Chamberlain, Phildelphia Warriors | 79 | 1251 | 531 | 3033 | 38.4 |
| 1961–62 | Wilt Chamberlain, Philadelphia Warriors | 80 | 1597 | 835 | 4029 | 50.4 |
| 1962–63 | Wilt Chamberlain, San Francisco Warriors | 80 | 1463 | 660 | 3586 | 44.8 |
| 1963–64 | Wilt Chamberlain, San Francisco Warriors | 80 | 1204 | 540 | 2948 | 36.9 |
| 1964–65 | Wilt Chamberlain, San Francisco Warriors-Phila. 76ers | 73 | 1063 | 408 | 2534 | 34.7 |
| 1965–66 | Wilt Chamberlain, Philadelphia 76ers | 79 | 1074 | 501 | 2649 | 33.5 |
| 1966–67 | Rick Barry, San Francisco Warriors | 78 | 1011 | 753 | 2775 | 35.6 |
| 1967–68 | Dave Bing, Detroit Pistons | 79 | 835 | 472 | 2142 | 27.1 |
| 1968–69 | Elvin Hayes, San Diego Rockets | 82 | 930 | 467 | 2327 | 28.4 |
| 1969–70 | Jerry West, Los Angeles Lakers | 74 | 831 | 647 | 2309 | 31.2 |
| 1970–71 | Lew Alcindor,[1] Milwaukee Bucks | 82 | 1063 | 470 | 2596 | 31.7 |
| 1971–72 | Kareem Abdul-Jabbar, Milwaukee Bucks | 81 | 1159 | 504 | 2822 | 34.8 |
| 1972–73 | Nate Archibald, Kansas City-Omaha | 80 | 1028 | 663 | 2719 | 34.0 |
| 1973–74 | Bob McAdoo, Buffalo | 74 | 901 | 459 | 2261 | 30.8 |
| 1974–75 | Bob McAdoo, Buffalo | 82 | 1095 | 641 | 2831 | 34.5 |
| 1975–76 | Bob McAdoo, Buffalo | 78 | 934 | 559 | 2427 | 31.1 |
| 1976–77 | Pete Maravich, New Orleans | 73 | 886 | 501 | 2273 | 31.1 |
| 1977–78 | George Gervin, San Antonio | 82 | 864 | 504 | 2232 | 27.2 |

1. (Kareem Abdul-Jabbar).

## N.B.A. MOST VALUABLE PLAYERS

| | |
|---|---|
| 1956 | Bob Pettit |
| 1957 | Bob Cousy |
| 1958 | Bill Russell |
| 1959 | Bob Pettit |
| 1960 | Wilt Chamberlain |
| 1961–63 | Bill Russell |
| 1964 | Oscar Robertson |
| 1965 | Bill Russell |
| 1966–68 | Wilt Chamberlain |
| 1969 | Wes Unseld |
| 1970 | Willis Reed |
| 1971–72 | Lew Alcindor (Kareem Abdul-Jabbar) |
| 1973 | Dave Cowens |
| 1974 | Kareem Abdul-Jabbar, Milwaukee |
| 1975 | Bob McAdoo, Buffalo |
| 1976–77 | Kareem Abdul-Jabbar, Los Angeles |
| 1978 | Bill Walton, Portland |

## N.B.A. LIFETIME LEADERS

(Through June 1978)

### Scoring

| | Yrs | FG | FT | Pts |
|---|---|---|---|---|
| Wilt Chamberlain | 14 | 12,681 | 6,057 | 31,419 |
| Oscar Robertson | 14 | 9,508 | 7,694 | 26,710 |
| John Havlicek | 16 | 10,513 | 5,369 | 26,395 |
| Jerry West | 14 | 9,016 | 7,160 | 25,192 |
| Flgin Baylor | 14 | 8,693 | 5,763 | 23,149 |
| Hal Greer | 15 | 8,504 | 4,578 | 21,586 |
| Walt Bellamy | 14 | 7,914 | 5,113 | 20,941 |
| Bob Pettit | 11 | 7,349 | 6,182 | 20,880 |
| Kareem Abdul-Jabbar[1] | 9 | 8,367 | 3,504 | 20,238 |
| Elvin Hayes[1] | 10 | 7,810 | 3,540 | 19,460 |

### Scoring Average

(400 games or 10,000 points minimum)

| | Games | Pts | Avg |
|---|---|---|---|
| Wilt Chamberlain | 1,045 | 31,419 | 30.1 |
| Kareem Abdul-Jabbar[1] | 693 | 20,238 | 29.2 |
| Bob McAdoo[1] | 465 | 12,918 | 27.8 |
| Elgin Baylor | 846 | 23,149 | 27.4 |
| Jerry West | 932 | 25,192 | 27.0 |
| Bob Pettit | 792 | 20,880 | 26.4 |
| Oscar Robertson | 1,040 | 26,710 | 25.7 |
| Rick Barry[1] | 642 | 16,447 | 25.6 |
| Pete Maravich[1] | 566 | 14,254 | 25.2 |
| Nate Archibald[1] | 467 | 11,591 | 24.8 |

### Field Goal Percentage
(2,000 field goals minimum)

| | Att | FG | Pct |
|---|---|---|---|
| Kareem Abdul-Jabbar[1] | 15,253 | 8,367 | .549 |
| Wilt Chamberlain | 23,497 | 12,681 | .540 |
| Walt Bellamy | 15,340 | 7,914 | .516 |
| Bob McAdoo[1] | 10,005 | 5,069 | .507 |
| Terry Dischinger | 6,836 | 3,457 | .506 |
| Bob Lanier[1] | 10,813 | 5,468 | .506 |
| Paul Westphal[1] | 5,571 | 2,817 | .506 |
| Doug Collins[1] | 4,586 | 2,316 | .505 |
| Rudy Tomjanovich[1] | 8,699 | 4,377 | .503 |
| Wes Unseld[1] | 6,920 | 3,471 | .502 |

### Assists

| | | | |
|---|---|---|---|
| Oscar Robertson | 9,887 | John Havlicek | 6,114 |
| Lenny Wilkens | 7,211 | Dave Bing[1] | 5,397 |
| Bob Cousy | 6,955 | Norm Van Lier[1] | 5,059 |
| Guy Rodgers | 6,917 | Walt Frazier[1] | 5,000 |
| Jerry West | 6,238 | Wilt Chamberlain | 4,643 |

1. Active player.

### Free Throw Percentage
(1,200 free throws made minimum)

| | Att | FT | Pct |
|---|---|---|---|
| Rick Barry[1] | 3,921 | 3,515 | .896 |
| Bill Sharman | 3,557 | 3,143 | .884 |
| Calvin Murphy[1] | 2,822 | 2,484 | .880 |
| Mike Newlin[1] | 2,185 | 1,886 | .863 |
| Larry Siegfried | 1,945 | 1,662 | .854 |
| Flynn Robinson | 1,881 | 1,597 | .849 |
| Dolph Schayes | 8,273 | 6,979 | .844 |
| Jack Marin[1] | 2,852 | 2,405 | .843 |
| Larry Costello | 2,891 | 2,432 | .841 |
| Bill Bradley | 1,623 | 1,363 | .840 |

### Rebounds

| | | | |
|---|---|---|---|
| Wilt Chamberlain | 23,924 | Bob Pettit | 12,849 |
| Bill Russell | 21,620 | Elvin Hayes[1] | 11,977 |
| Nate Thurmond | 14,464 | Elgin Baylor | 11,463 |
| Walt Bellamy | 14,241 | Paul Silas[1] | 11,346 |
| Jerry Lucas | 12,942 | Dolph Schayes | 11,256 |

## N.B.A. INDIVIDUAL RECORDS

Most points, game—100, Wilt Chamberlain, Philadelphia vs. New York at Hershey, Pa., 1962
Most points, quarter—33, George Gervin, San Antonio, 1978
Most points, half—59, Wilt Chamberlain, Philadelphia, 1962
Most free throws, game—28, Wilt Chamberlain, Philadelphia, vs. New York at Hershey, Pa. 1962
Most free throws, quarter—13, David Thompson, Denver, 1978
Most free throws, half—19, Oscar Robertson, Cincinnati, 1964
Most field goals, game—28, Wilt Chamberlain, Philadelphia, 1962
Most consective field goals—18, Wilt Chamberlain, San Francisco, 1963; Wilt Chamberlain, Philadelphia, 1967
Most assists, game—29, Kevin Porter, New Jersey Nets, 1978
Most rebounds, game—55, Wilt Chamberlain, Philadelphia, 1963

## N.B.A. TEAM RECORDS

Most points, game—173, Boston vs. Minneapolis, 1959
Most points, quarter—58, Buffalo vs. Boston 1968
Most points, half—97, Atlanta vs. San Diego, 1970
Most points, overtime period—22, Detroit vs. Cleveland, 1973
Most field goals, game—72, Boston, 1959
Most field goals, quarter—23, Boston, 1959, 1972
Most field goals, half—40, Boston, 1959; Syracuse, 1963
Most assists, game—52, Chicago 1971
Most rebounds, game—112, Philadelphia, 1959
Most points, both teams, game—316 (Philadelphia 169, New York 147), Hershey, Pa. 1962; (Cincinnati 165, San Diego 151), Cincinnati, 1970
Most points, both teams, quarter—96 (Boston 52, Minneapolis 44), 1959; (Detroit 53, Cincinnati 43), 1972
Most points, both teams, half—170 (Philadelphia 90, Cincinnati 80), Philadelphia, 1971
Longest winning streak—33, Los Angeles, 1971–72
Longest losing streak—20, Philadelphia, 1973
Longest winning streak at home—36, Philadelphia, 1966–67
Most games won, season—69, Los Angeles, 1971–72
Most games lost, season—73, Philadelphia, 1972–73
Highest average points per game—125.4, Philadelphia, 1961–62

## NATIONAL BASKETBALL ASSOCIATION FINAL STANDING OF THE CLUBS

### EASTERN CONFERENCE
#### Atlantic Division

| | W | L | Pct | Scoring For | Scoring Agst |
|---|---|---|---|---|---|
| Philadelphia 76ers | 55 | 27 | .671 | 114.7 | 109.6 |
| New York Knicks | 43 | 39 | .524 | 113.4 | 114.0 |
| Boston Celtics | 32 | 50 | .390 | 105.7 | 107.7 |
| Buffalo Braves | 27 | 55 | .329 | 105.3 | 109.0 |
| New Jersey Nets | 24 | 58 | .293 | 106.7 | 112.5 |

#### Central Division

| | W | L | Pct | Scoring For | Scoring Agst |
|---|---|---|---|---|---|
| San Antonio Spurs | 52 | 30 | .634 | 114.5 | 111.1 |
| Washington Bullets | 44 | 38 | .537 | 110.3 | 109.4 |
| Cleveland Cavaliers | 43 | 39 | .524 | 104.4 | 103.9 |
| Atlanta Hawks | 41 | 41 | .500 | 103.7 | 103.9 |
| New Orleans Jazz | 39 | 43 | .476 | 107.6 | 109.5 |
| Houston Rockets | 28 | 54 | .341 | 103.8 | 107.8 |

### WESTERN CONFERENCE
#### Midwest Division

| | W | L | Pct | Scoring For | Scoring Agst |
|---|---|---|---|---|---|
| Denver Nuggets | 48 | 34 | .585 | 111.8 | 110.9 |
| Milwaukee Bucks | 44 | 38 | .537 | 112.4 | 113.0 |
| Chicago Bulls | 40 | 42 | .488 | 103.9 | 104.8 |
| Detroit Pistons | 38 | 44 | .463 | 109.0 | 110.2 |
| Indiana Pacers | 31 | 51 | .378 | 108.6 | 111.1 |
| Kansas City Kings | 31 | 51 | .378 | 109.5 | 111.4 |

#### Pacific Division

| | W | L | Pct | Scoring For | Scoring Agst |
|---|---|---|---|---|---|
| Portland Trail Blazers | 58 | 24 | .707 | 107.7 | 101.5 |
| Phoenix Suns | 49 | 33 | .598 | 112.3 | 108.6 |
| Seattle SuperSonics | 47 | 35 | .573 | 104.5 | 102.9 |
| Los Angeles Lakers | 45 | 37 | .549 | 110.3 | 107.6 |
| Golden State Warriors | 43 | 39 | .524 | 106.1 | 105.7 |

## PLAYOFFS

### EASTERN CONFERENCE

**First Round**

New York defeated Cleveland, 2 games to 0
Washington defeated Atlanta, 2 games to 0

**Semifinals**

Philadelphia defeated New York, 4 games to 0
Washington defeated San Antonio, 4 games to 2

**Conference Final**

Washington defeated Philadelphia, 4 games to 2
April 30—Washington 122, Philadelphia 117
May 3—Philadelphia 110, Washington 104
May 5—Washington 123, Philadelphia 108[1]
May 7—Washington 121, Philadelphia 105[1]
May 10—Philadelphia 107, Washington 94
May 12—Washington 101, Philadelphia 99[1]
1. At Landover, Md.

### WESTERN CONFERENCE

**First Round**

Milwaukee defeated Phoenix, 2 games to 0
Seattle defeated Los Angeles, 2 games to 1

**Semifinals**

Seattle defeated Portland, 4 games to 2
Denver defeated Milwaukee, 4 games to 3

**Conference Final**

Seattle defeated Denver, 4 games to 2
May 5[1]—Denver 116, Seattle 107
May 7[1]—Seattle 121, Denver 111
May 10—Seattle 105, Denver 91
May 12—Seattle 100, Denver 94
May 14[1]—Denver 123, Seattle 114
May 17—Seattle 123, Denver 108
1. At Denver.

### League Championship

Washington defeated Seattle, 4 games to 3
May 21—Seattle 106, Washington 102
May 25[1]—Washington 106, Seattle 98
May 28[1]—Seattle 93, Washington 92
May 30—Washington 120, Seattle 116
June 2—Seattle 98, Washington 94
June 4[1]—Washington 117, Seattle 82
June 7—Washington 105, Seattle 99
1. At Landover, Md.

## LEADING SCORERS

| | G | FG | FT | Pts | Pct |
|---|---|---|---|---|---|
| George Gervin, San Antonio | 82 | 864 | 504 | 2,232 | 27.21 |
| David Thompson, Denver | 80 | 826 | 520 | 2,172 | 27.15 |
| Bob McAdoo, New York | 79 | 814 | 469 | 2,097 | 26.5 |
| Kareem Abdul-Jabbar, Los Angeles | 62 | 663 | 274 | 1,600 | 25.8 |
| Calvin Murphy, Houston | 76 | 852 | 245 | 1,949 | 25.6 |
| Paul Westphal, Phoenix | 80 | 809 | 396 | 2,014 | 25.2 |
| Randy Smith, Buffalo | 82 | 789 | 443 | 2,021 | 24.6 |
| Bob Lanier, Detroit | 63 | 622 | 298 | 1,542 | 24.5 |
| Walter Davis, Phoenix | 81 | 786 | 387 | 1,959 | 24.2 |
| Bernard King, New Jersey | 79 | 798 | 313 | 1,909 | 24.2 |
| John Williamson, New Jersey | 75 | 723 | 331 | 1,777 | 23.7 |
| John Drew, Atlanta | 70 | 593 | 437 | 1,623 | 23.2 |
| Rick Barry, Golden State | 82 | 760 | 378 | 1,898 | 23.1 |
| Artis Gilmore, Chicago | 82 | 704 | 471 | 1,879 | 22.9 |
| Leonard Robinson, New Orleans | 82 | 748 | 366 | 1,862 | 22.7 |
| Adrian Dantley, Los Angeles | 79 | 578 | 541 | 1,697 | 21.5 |
| Dan Issel, Denver | 82 | 659 | 428 | 1,746 | 21.3 |
| Julius Erving, Philadelphia | 74 | 611 | 306 | 1,528 | 20.6 |
| Larry Kenon, San Antonio | 81 | 698 | 276 | 1,672 | 20.6 |
| George McGinnis, Philadelphia | 78 | 588 | 411 | 1,587 | 20.3 |

## ALL-STAR TEAM

| First Team | Pos. | Second Team |
|---|---|---|
| Leonard Robinson, New Orleans | F | Walter Davis, Phoenix |
| Julius Erving, Philadelphia | F | Maurice Lucas, Portland |
| Bill Walton, Portland | C | Kareem Abdul-Jabbar, Los Angeles |
| George Gervin, San Antonio | G | Paul Westphal, Phoenix |
| David Thompson, Denver | G | Pete Maravich, New Orleans |

## OTHER 1977–78 AWARDS

Most valuable player—Bill Walton, Portland
Rookie of the Year—Walter Davis, Phoenix
Most valuable in playoffs—Wes Unseld, Washington

## FIELD GOAL LEADERS

(Minimum of 300 FG made)

| | FG | Att | Pct |
|---|---|---|---|
| Bobby Jones, Denver | 440 | 761 | .578 |
| Darryl Dawkins, Philadelphia | 332 | 577 | .575 |
| Artis Gilmore, Chicago | 704 | 1260 | .559 |
| Kareem Abdul-Jabbar, Los Angeles | 663 | 1205 | .550 |
| Alex English, Milwaukee | 343 | 633 | .542 |
| Bob Lanier, Detroit | 622 | 1159 | .537 |
| George Gervin, San Antonio | 864 | 1611 | .536 |
| Bob Gross, Portland | 381 | 720 | .529 |
| Billy Paultz, San Antonio | 518 | 979 | .529 |
| Walter Davis, Phoenix | 786 | 1494 | .526 |

## FREE THROW LEADERS

(Minimum of 125 FT made)

| | FT | Att | Pct |
|---|---|---|---|
| Rick Barry, Golden State | 378 | 409 | .924 |
| Calvin Murphy, Houston | 245 | 267 | .918 |
| Fred Brown, Seattle | 176 | 196 | .898 |
| Mike Newlin, Houston | 152 | 174 | .874 |
| Scott Wedman, Kansas City | 221 | 254 | .870 |
| Pete Maravich, New Orleans | 240 | 276 | .870 |
| John Havlicek, Boston | 230 | 269 | .855 |
| Larry Kenon, San Antonio | 276 | 323 | .854 |
| Ron Boone, Kansas City | 322 | 377 | .854 |
| Walt Frazier, Cleveland | 153 | 180 | .850 |

### ASSISTS LEADERS

(Minimum 70 games or 400 assists)

| | G | No. | Avg |
|---|---|---|---|
| Kevin Porter, New Jersey | 82 | 837 | 10.2 |
| John Lucas, Houston | 82 | 768 | 9.4 |
| Ricky Sobers, Indianapolis | 79 | 584 | 7.4 |
| Norm Nixon, Los Angeles | 81 | 553 | 6.8 |
| Norm Van Lier, Chicago | 78 | 531 | 6.8 |
| Henry Bibby, Philadelphia | 82 | 464 | 5.7 |
| Clarence Walker, Cleveland | 81 | 453 | 5.6 |
| Randy Smith, Buffalo | 82 | 458 | 5.6 |
| Quinn Buckner, Milwaukee | 82 | 456 | 5.6 |
| Paul Westphal, Phoenix | 80 | 437 | 5.5 |

### REBOUND LEADERS

(Minimum 70 games or 800 rebounds)

| | G | Off | Def | Total | Avg |
|---|---|---|---|---|---|
| Leonard Robinson, New Orleans | 82 | 298 | 990 | 1288 | 15.7 |
| Moses Malone, Houston | 59 | 380 | 506 | 886 | 15.0 |
| Dave Cowens, Boston | 77 | 248 | 830 | 1078 | 14.0 |
| Elvin Hayes, Washington | 81 | 335 | 740 | 1075 | 13.3 |
| Swen Nater, Buffalo | 78 | 278 | 751 | 1029 | 13.2 |
| Artis Gilmore, Chicago | 82 | 318 | 753 | 1071 | 13.1 |
| Kareem Abdul-Jabbar, Los Angeles | 62 | 186 | 615 | 801 | 12.9 |
| Bob McAdoo, New York | 79 | 236 | 774 | 1010 | 12.8 |
| Marvin Webster, Seattle | 82 | 361 | 674 | 1035 | 12.6 |
| Wes Unseld, Washington | 80 | 286 | 669 | 955 | 11.9 |

### BLOCKED SHOTS LEADERS

(Minimum 70 games or 100 blocked shots)

| | G | No. | Avg |
|---|---|---|---|
| George Johnson, New Jersey | 81 | 274 | 3.38 |
| Kareem Abdul-Jabbar, Los Angeles | 62 | 185 | 2.98 |
| Wayne Rollins, Atlanta | 80 | 218 | 2.73 |
| Bill Walton, Portland | 58 | 146 | 2.52 |
| Billy Paultz, San Antonio | 80 | 194 | 2.43 |

### STEALS LEADERS

(Minimum 70 games or 125 steals)

| | G | No. | Avg |
|---|---|---|---|
| Ron Lee, Phoenix | 82 | 225 | 2.74 |
| Gus Williams, Seattle | 79 | 185 | 2.34 |
| Quinn Buckner, Milwaukee | 82 | 188 | 2.29 |
| Mike Gale, San Antonio | 70 | 159 | 2.27 |
| Don Buse, Phoenix | 82 | 185 | 2.26 |

### NATIONAL BASKETBALL ASSOCIATION GOVERNMENT

Commissioner's Office: Lawrence F. O'Brien. Commissioner; Simon P. Gourdine, Deputy Commissioner; Norman F. Drucker, Supervisor of Officials; Matt Winick, Director of Media Information.

### AMERICAN BASKETBALL ASSOCIATION CHAMPIONS

| Season | Eastern Division (W-L) | Western Division (W-L) | Playoff Champions |
|---|---|---|---|
| 1967–68 | Pittsburgh Pipers (54–24) | New Orleans Buccaneers (48–30) | Pittsburgh Pipers |
| 1968–69 | Indiana Pacers (44–34) | Oakland Oaks (60–18) | Oakland Oaks |
| 1969–70 | Indiana Pacers (59–25) | Denver Rockets (51–33) | Indiana Pacers |
| 1970–71 | Virginia Squires (55–29) | Indiana Pacers (58–26) | Utah Stars |
| 1971–72 | New York Nets (44–40)[1] | Indiana Pacers (47–37)[1] | Indiana Pacers |
| 1972–73 | Kentucky Colonels (56–28)[1] | Indiana Pacers (51–33)[1] | Indiana Pacers |
| 1973–74 | New York Nets (55–29)[1] | Utah Stars (51–33)[1] | New York Nets |
| 1974–75 | Kentucky Colonels (58–26) | Indiana Pacers (45–39)[1] | Kentucky Colonels |
| **Regular Season Winner**[2] | | **Playoff Finalist** | **Playoff Winner** |
| 1975–76 | Denver Nuggets (60–24)[3] | New York Nets | New York Nets |

1. Won division playoffs; 2. League reduced to one division; 3. Won final playoff berth.

### INDIVIDUAL A.B.A. SCORING CHAMPIONS

| Season | Player, Team | G | Field Goals 2 pt | 3 pt | FT | Pts | Avg |
|---|---|---|---|---|---|---|---|
| 1967–68 | Connie Hawkins, Pittsburgh Pipers | 70 | 633 | 2 | 603 | 1,875 | 26.8 |
| 1968–69 | Rick Barry, Oakland Oaks | 36 | 389 | 3 | 403 | 1,190 | 34.0 |
| 1969–70 | Spencer Haywood, Denver Rockets | 84 | 986 | 0 | 547 | 2,519 | 30.0 |
| 1970–71 | Dan Issel, Kentucky Colonels | 83 | 938 | 0 | 604 | 2,480 | 29.9 |
| 1971–72 | Charlie Scott, Virginia Squires | 73 | 927 | 29 | 525 | 2,524 | 34.5 |
| 1972–73 | Julius Erving, Virginia | 71 | 889 | 3 | 475 | 2,262 | 31.9 |
| 1973–74 | Julius Erving, New York Nets | 84 | 897 | 7 | 484 | 2,299 | 27.4 |
| 1974–75 | George McGinnis, Indiana Pacers | 79 | 811 | 62 | 545 | 2,353 | 29.8 |
| 1975–76 | Julius Erving, New York Nets | 84 | 915 | 34 | 530 | 2,462 | 29.3 |

## *TRAMPOLINE*

### A.A.U. NATIONAL CHAMPIONSHIPS

(New Brunswick, N.J., April 27–28, 1978)

Men—Stuart Ransom, Memphis, Tenn. 79.6
Women—Leigh Hennessey, Lafayette, La. 74.1
Men's Double-mini—Ron Merriott, Rockford, Ill. 28.2
Women's Double-mini—Leigh Hennessey 25.6
Men's Synchronized—Chris Eilertsen, Memphis, Tenn., and Jim Cartledge, Memphis, Tenn. 42.8
Women's Synchronized—Shelly Grant, Spring, Ohio, and Leigh Hennessey 42.1

# HOCKEY

Ice hockey, by birth and upbringing a Canadian game, is an offshoot of field hockey. Some historians say that the first ice hockey game was played in Montreal in December 1879 between two teams composed almost exclusively of McGill University students, but others assert that earlier hockey games took place in Kingston, Ontario, or Halifax, Nova Scotia. In the Montreal game of 1879, there were fifteen players on a side, who used an assortment of crude sticks to keep the puck in motion. Early rules allowed nine men on a side, but the number was reduced to seven in 1886 and later to six.

The first governing body of the sport was the Amateur Hockey Association of Canada, organized in 1887. In the winter of 1894–95, a group of college students from the United States visited Canada and saw hockey played. They became enthused over the game and introduced it as a winter sport when they returned home. The first professional league was the International Hockey League, which operated in northern Michigan in 1904–06.

Until 1910, professionals and amateurs were allowed to play together on "mixed teams," but this arrangement ended with the formation of the first "big league," the National Hockey Association, in eastern Canada in 1910. The Pacific Coast League was organized in 1911 for western Canadian hockey. The league included Seattle and later other American cities. The National Hockey League replaced the National Hockey Association in 1917. Boston, in 1924, was the first American city to join that circuit. The league expanded to include western cities in 1967. The Stanley Cup was competed for by "mixed teams" from 1894 to 1910, thereafter by professionals. It was awarded to the winner of the N.H.L. playoffs from 1926–67 and now to the league champion. The World Hockey Association was organized in October 1972 in opposition to the N.H.L.

## STANLEY CUP WINNERS

Emblematic of World Professional Championship; N.H.L. Championship after 1967

| | |
|---|---|
| 1894 | Montreal A.A.A. |
| 1895 | Montreal Victorias |
| 1896 | Winnipeg Victorias |
| 1897–99 | Montreal Victorias |
| 1900 | Montreal Shamrocks |
| 1901 | Winnipeg Victorias |
| 1902 | Montreal A.A.A. |
| 1903–05 | Ottawa Silver Seven |
| 1906 | Montreal Wanderers |
| 1907 | Kenora Thistles[1] |
| 1907 | Mont. Wanderers[2] |
| 1908 | Montreal Wanderers |
| 1909 | Ottawa Senators |
| 1910 | Montreal Wanderers |
| 1911 | Ottawa Senators |
| 1912–13 | Quebec Bulldogs |
| 1914 | Toronto |
| 1915 | Vancouver Millionaires |
| 1916 | Montreal Canadiens |
| 1917 | Seattle Metropolitans |
| 1918 | Toronto Arenas |
| 1919 | No champion |
| 1920–21 | Ottawa Senators |
| 1922 | Toronto St. Patricks |
| 1923 | Ottawa Senators |
| 1924 | Montreal Canadiens |
| 1925 | Victoria Cougars |
| 1926 | Montreal Maroons |
| 1927 | Ottawa Senators |
| 1928 | N.Y. Rangers |
| 1929 | Boston Bruins |
| 1930–31 | Montreal Canadiens |
| 1932 | Toronto Maple Leafs |
| 1933 | N.Y. Rangers |
| 1934 | Chicago Black Hawks |
| 1935 | Montreal Maroons |
| 1936–37 | Detroit Red Wings |
| 1938 | Chicago Black Hawks |
| 1939 | Boston Bruins |
| 1940 | N.Y. Rangers |
| 1941 | Boston Bruins |
| 1942 | Toronto Maple Leafs |
| 1943 | Detroit Red Wings |
| 1944 | Montreal Canadiens |
| 1945 | Toronto Maple Leafs |
| 1946 | Montreal Canadiens |
| 1947–49 | Toronto Maple Leafs |
| 1950 | Detroit Red Wings |
| 1951 | Toronto Maple Leafs |
| 1952 | Detroit Red Wings |
| 1953 | Montreal Canadiens |
| 1954–55 | Detroit Red Wings |
| 1956–60 | Montreal Canadiens |
| 1961 | Chicago Black Hawks |
| 1962–64 | Toronto Maple Leafs |
| 1965–66 | Montreal Canadiens |
| 1967 | Toronto Maple Leafs |
| 1968–69 | Montreal Canadiens |
| 1970 | Boston Bruins |
| 1971 | Montreal Canadiens |
| 1972 | Boston Bruins |
| 1973 | Montreal Canadiens |
| 1974–75 | Philadelphia Flyers |
| 1976–78 | Montreal Canadiens |

1. January. 2. March.

## NATIONAL HOCKEY LEAGUE YEARLY TROPHY WINNERS

### The Hart Trophy—Most Valuable Player

| | |
|---|---|
| 1924 | Frank Nighbor, Ottawa |
| 1925 | Billy Burch, Hamilton |
| 1926 | Nels Stewart, Montreal Maroons |
| 1927 | Herb Gardiner, Montreal Canadiens |
| 1928 | Howie Morenz, Montreal Canadiens |
| 1929 | Roy Worters, New York Americans |
| 1930 | Nels Stewart, Montreal Maroons |
| 1931–32 | Howie Morenz, Montreal Canadiens |
| 1933 | Eddie Shore, Boston |
| 1934 | Aurel Joliat, Montreal Canadiens |
| 1935–36 | Eddie Shore, Boston |
| 1937 | Babe Siebert, Montreal Canadiens |
| 1938 | Eddie Shore, Boston |
| 1939 | Toe Blake, Montreal Canadiens |
| 1940 | Ebbie Goodfellow, Detroit |
| 1941 | Bill Cowley, Boston |
| 1942 | Tom Anderson, New York Americans |
| 1943 | Bill Cowley, Boston |
| 1944 | Babe Pratt, Toronto |
| 1945 | Elmer Lach, Montreal Canadiens |
| 1946 | Max Bentley, Chicago |
| 1947 | Maurice Richard, Montreal Canadiens |
| 1948 | Buddy O'Connor, New York Rangers |
| 1949 | Sid Abel, Detroit |
| 1950 | Chuck Rayner, New York Rangers |
| 1951 | Milt Schmidt, Boston |
| 1952–53 | Gordon Howe, Detroit |
| 1954 | Al Rollins, Chicago |
| 1955 | Ted Kennedy, Toronto |
| 1956 | Jean Beliveau, Montreal Canadiens |
| 1957–58 | Gordon Howe, Detroit |
| 1959 | Andy Bathgate, New York Rangers |
| 1960 | Gordon Howe, Detroit |
| 1961 | Bernie Geoffrion, Montreal Canadiens |
| 1962 | Jacques Plante, Montreal Canadiens |
| 1963 | Gordon Howe, Detroit |
| 1964 | Jean Beliveau, Montreal Canadiens |
| 1965–66 | Bobby Hull, Chicago |
| 1967–68 | Stan Mikita, Chicago |

| | |
|---|---|
| 1969 | Phil Esposito, Boston |
| 1970–72 | Bobby Orr, Boston |
| 1973 | Bobby Clarke, Philadelphia |
| 1974 | Phil Esposito, Boston |
| 1975–76 | Bobby Clarke, Philadelphia |
| 1977–78 | Guy Lafleur, Montreal |

**Vezina Trophy—Leading Goalkeeper**

| | |
|---|---|
| 1956–60 | Jacques Plante, Montreal |
| 1961 | Johnny Bower, Toronto |
| 1962 | Jacques Plante, Montreal |
| 1963 | Glenn Hall, Chicago |
| 1964 | Charlie Hodge, Montreal |
| 1965 | Terry Sawchuk–Johnny Bower, Toronto |
| 1966 | Lorne Worsley–Charlie Hodge, Montreal |
| 1967 | Glenn Hall–Denis DeJordy, Chicago |
| 1968 | Lorne Worsley–Rogatien Vachon, Montreal |
| 1969 | Glenn Hall–Jacques Plante, St. Louis |
| 1970 | Tony Esposito, Chicago |
| 1971 | Ed Giacomin–Gilles Villemure, New York |
| 1972 | Tony Esposito–Gary Smith, Chicago |
| 1973 | Ken Dryden, Montreal |
| 1974 | Bernie Parent, Philadelphia, and Tony Esposito, Chicago |
| 1975 | Bernie Parent, Philadelphia |
| 1976 | Ken Dryden, Montreal |
| 1977–78 | Ken Dryden–Michel Larocque, Montreal |

**James Norris Trophy—Defenseman**

| | |
|---|---|
| 1954 | Red Kelly, Detroit |
| 1955–58 | Doug Harvey, Montreal |
| 1959 | Tom Johnson, Montreal |
| 1960–62 | Doug Harvey, Montreal, New York (62) |
| 1963–65 | Pierre Pilote, Chicago |
| 1966 | Jacques Laperriere, Montreal |
| 1967 | Harry Howell, New York |
| 1968–75 | Bobby Orr, Boston |
| 1976 | Denis Potvin, N.Y. Islanders |
| 1977 | Larry Robinson, Montreal |
| 1978 | Denis Potvin, N.Y. Islanders |

**Lady Byng Trophy—Sportsmanship**

| | |
|---|---|
| 1960 | Don McKenney, Boston |
| 1961 | Red Kelly, Detroit |
| 1962–63 | Dave Keon, Toronto |
| 1964 | Ken Wharram, Chicago |
| 1965 | Bobby Hull, Chicago |
| 1966 | Alex Delvecchio, Detroit |
| 1967–68 | Stan Mikita, Chicago |
| 1969 | Alex Delvecchio, Detroit |
| 1970 | Phil Goyette, St. Louis |
| 1971 | John Bucyk, Boston |
| 1972 | Jean Ratelle, New York |
| 1973 | Gil Perreault, Buffalo |
| 1974 | John Buyck, Boston |
| 1975 | Marcel Dionne, Detroit |
| 1976 | Jean Ratelle, N.Y. Rangers–Boston |
| 1977 | Marcel Dionne, Los Angeles |
| 1978 | Butch Goring, Los Angeles |

**Calder Trophy—Rookie**

| | |
|---|---|
| 1962 | Bobby Rousseau, Montreal |
| 1963 | Kent Douglas, Toronto |
| 1964 | Jacques Laperriere, Montreal |
| 1965 | Roger Crozier, Detroit |
| 1966 | Brit Selby, Toronto |
| 1967 | Bobby Orr, Boston |
| 1968 | Derek Sanderson, Boston |
| 1969 | Danny Grant, Minnesota |
| 1970 | Tony Esposito, Chicago |
| 1971 | Gilbert Perreault, Buffalo |
| 1972 | Ken Dryden, Montreal |
| 1973 | Steve Vickers, New York Rangers |
| 1974 | Denis Potvin, N.Y. Islanders |
| 1975 | Eric Vail, Atlanta |
| 1976 | Bryan Trottier, N.Y. Islanders |
| 1977 | Willi Plett, Atlanta |
| 1978 | Mike Bossy, N.Y. Islanders |

## N.H.L. CAREER SCORING LEADERS

(Listed in order of total points scored)

| | Yr | Games | G | A | Pts |
|---|---|---|---|---|---|
| Gordie Howe (1) | 25 | 1,687 | 786 | 1,023 | 1,809 |
| Phil Esposito (2)[1] | 15 | 1,081 | 634 | 780 | 1,414 |
| Stan Mikita (7)[1] | 19 | 1,312 | 520 | 885 | 1,405 |
| John Bucyk (4)[1] | 23 | 1,540 | 556 | 813 | 1,369 |
| Alex Delvecchio (10) | 23 | 1,549 | 456 | 825 | 1,281 |
| Norm Ullman (9) | 20 | 1,410 | 490 | 739 | 1,229 |
| Jean Beliveau (8) | 18 | 1,125 | 507 | 712 | 1,219 |
| Bobby Hull (3) | 15 | 1,036 | 604 | 549 | 1,153 |
| Frank Mahovlich (6) | 17 | 1,181 | 533 | 570 | 1,103 |
| Jean Ratelle (12)[1] | 16 | 1,087 | 425 | 660 | 1,085 |
| Henri Richard (18) | 20 | 1,256 | 358 | 688 | 1,046 |
| Rod Gilbert (13) | 16 | 1,065 | 406 | 615 | 1,021 |
| Andy Bathgate (19) | 16 | 1,069 | 349 | 624 | 973 |
| Maurice Richard (5) | 18 | 978 | 544 | 421 | 965 |
| Bobby Orr (21) | 11 | 651 | 268 | 643 | 911 |
| Dean Prentice (15) | 22 | 1,378 | 391 | 469 | 860 |
| Dave Keon (17) | 15 | 1,062 | 365 | 493 | 858 |
| Yvan Cournoyer (11)[1] | 14 | 953 | 426 | 430 | 856 |
| Ted Lindsay (16) | 17 | 1,068 | 379 | 472 | 851 |
| Red Kelly (20) | 20 | 1,316 | 281 | 542 | 823 |

1. Still active in N.H.L. (Figures in parentheses indicate ranking in goals scored).

**Art Ross Trophy—Leading scorer**

| | |
|---|---|
| 1955 | Bernie Geoffrion, Montreal |
| 1956 | Jean Beliveau, Montreal |
| 1957 | Gordie Howe, Detroit |
| 1958–59 | Dickie Moore, Montreal |
| 1960 | Bobby Hull, Chicago |
| 1961 | Bernie Geoffrion, Montreal |
| 1962 | Bobby Hull, Chicago |
| 1963 | Gordie Howe, Detroit |
| 1964–65 | Stan Mikita, Chicago |
| 1966 | Bobby Hull, Chicago |
| 1967–68 | Stan Mikita, Chicago |
| 1969 | Phil Esposito, Boston |
| 1970 | Bobby Orr, Boston |
| 1971–74 | Phil Esposito, Boston |
| 1975 | Bobby Orr, Boston |
| 1976–78 | Guy Lafleur, Montreal |

## N.H.L. CHAMPIONS

**Prince of Wales Trophy**

| | | | |
|---|---|---|---|
| 1939 | Boston | 1956 | Montreal |
| 1940 | Boston | 1957 | Detroit |
| 1941 | Boston | 1958–62 | Montreal |
| 1942 | New York | 1963 | Toronto |
| 1943 | Detroit | 1964 | Montreal |
| 1944–47 | Montreal | 1965 | Detroit |
| 1948 | Toronto | 1966 | Montreal |
| 1948–55 | Detroit | 1967 | Chicago |

**Eastern Division**

| | | | |
|---|---|---|---|
| 1968–69 | Montreal | 1972 | Boston |
| 1970 | Chicago | 1973 | Montreal |
| 1971 | Boston | 1974 | Boston |

**Prince of Wales Conference**

| | |
|---|---|
| 1975 | Buffalo |
| 1976–78 | Montreal |

## CAMPBELL BOWL

### Western Division

| | | | |
|---|---|---|---|
| 1968 | Philadelphia | 1971–73 | Chicago |
| 1969 | St. Louis | 1974 | Philadelphia |
| 1970 | St. Louis | | |

### Clarence Campbell Conference

| | |
|---|---|
| 1975 | Philadelphia |
| 1976–77 | Philadelphia |
| 1978 | N.Y. Islanders |

## WORLD HOCKEY ASSOCIATION YEARLY LEADERS

### Most Valuable Player

| | | | |
|---|---|---|---|
| 1973 | Bobby Hull, Winnipeg | 1976 | Marc Tardif, Quebec |
| 1974 | Gordie Howe, Houston | 1977 | Robbie Ftorek, Phoenix |
| 1975 | Bobby Hull, Winnipeg | 1978 | Marc Tardif, Quebec |

### Scoring Champion

| | | | |
|---|---|---|---|
| 1973 | Andre Lacroix, Philadelphia | 1975 | Andre Lacroix, San Diego |
| 1974 | Mike Walton, Minnesota | 1976 | Marc Tardif, Quebec |
| | | 1977 | Real Cloutier, Quebec |
| | | 1978 | Marc Tardif, Quebec |

### Best Defenseman

| | | | |
|---|---|---|---|
| 1973 | J. C. Tremblay, Quebec | 1976 | Paul Shmyr, Cleveland |
| 1974 | Pat Stapleton, Chicago | 1977 | Ron Plumb, Cincinnati |
| 1975 | J. C. Tremblay, Quebec | 1978 | Lars-Erik Sjoberg, Winnipeg |

### Best Goaltender

| | | | |
|---|---|---|---|
| 1973 | Gerry Cheevers, Cleveland | 1976 | Michel Dion, Indianapolis |
| 1974 | Don McLeod, Houston | 1977 | Ron Grahame, Houston |
| 1975 | Ron Grahame, Houston | 1978 | Al Smith, New England |

### Most Gentlemanly

| | | | |
|---|---|---|---|
| 1973 | Ted Hampson, Minnesota | 1976 | Vaclav Nedomansky, Toronto |
| 1974 | Ralph Backstrom, Chicago | 1977 | Dave Keon, New England |
| 1975 | Mike Rogers, Edmonton | 1978 | Dave Keon, New England |

## W.H.A. LEAGUE CHAMPIONS

### Winners of AVCO Trophy

| | | | |
|---|---|---|---|
| 1972–73 | New Eng. Whalers | 1975–76 | Winnipeg Jets |
| 1973–74 | Houston Aeros | 1976–77 | Quebec Nordiques |
| 1974–75 | Houston Aeros | 1977–78 | Winnipeg Jets |

## NATIONAL HOCKEY LEAGUE

*Source:* John Halligan, Publicity Director, New York Rangers

### Final Standing of the Clubs—1978

#### CLARENCE CAMPBELL CONFERENCE

**Patrick Division**

| | W | L | T | GF | GA | Pts |
|---|---|---|---|---|---|---|
| New York Islanders | 48 | 17 | 15 | 334 | 210 | 111 |
| Philadelphia Flyers | 45 | 20 | 15 | 295 | 200 | 105 |
| Atlanta Flames | 34 | 27 | 19 | 274 | 252 | 87 |
| New York Rangers | 30 | 37 | 13 | 279 | 280 | 73 |

**Smythe Division**

| | W | L | T | GF | GA | Pts |
|---|---|---|---|---|---|---|
| Chicago Black Hawks | 32 | 29 | 19 | 230 | 220 | 83 |
| Colorado Rockies | 19 | 40 | 21 | 257 | 305 | 59 |
| Vancouver Canucks | 20 | 43 | 17 | 239 | 320 | 57 |
| St. Louis Blues | 20 | 47 | 13 | 195 | 304 | 53 |
| Minnesota North Stars | 18 | 53 | 9 | 219 | 325 | 45 |

#### PRINCE OF WALES CONFERENCE

**Norris Division**

| | W | L | T | GF | GA | Pts |
|---|---|---|---|---|---|---|
| Montreal Canadiens | 59 | 10 | 11 | 359 | 183 | 129 |
| Detroit Red Wings | 32 | 34 | 14 | 252 | 266 | 78 |
| Los Angeles Kings | 31 | 34 | 15 | 243 | 245 | 77 |
| Pittsburgh Penguins | 25 | 37 | 18 | 254 | 321 | 68 |
| Washington Capitals | 17 | 49 | 14 | 195 | 321 | 48 |

**Adams Division**

| | W | L | T | GF | GA | Pts |
|---|---|---|---|---|---|---|
| Boston Bruins | 51 | 18 | 11 | 333 | 218 | 113 |
| Buffalo Sabres | 44 | 19 | 17 | 288 | 215 | 105 |
| Toronto Maple Leafs | 41 | 29 | 10 | 271 | 237 | 92 |
| Cleveland Barons | 22 | 45 | 13 | 230 | 325 | 57 |

### Stanley Cup Playoffs

**Preliminary Round**

Philadelphia defeated Colorado, 2 games to 0
Buffalo defeated New York Rangers, 2 games to 1
Toronto defeated Los Angeles, 2 games to 0
Detroit defeated Atlanta, 2 games to 0

**Quarterfinals**

Montreal defeated Detroit, 4 games to 1
Boston defeated Chicago, 4 games to 0
Toronto defeated New York Islanders, 4 games to 3
Philadelphia defeated Buffalo, 4 games to 1

**Semifinals**

Montreal defeated Toronto, 4 games to 0
May 2—Montreal 5, Toronto 3
May 4—Montreal 3, Toronto 2
May 6[1]—Montreal 6, Toronto 1
May 9[1]—Montreal 2, Toronto 0

Boston defeated Philadelphia, 4 games to 1
May 2[2]—Boston 3, Philadelphia 2
May 4[2]—Boston 7, Philadelphia 5
May 7—Philadelphia 3, Boston 1
May 9—Boston 4, Philadelphia 2
May 11[2]—Boston 6, Philadelphia 3

1. At Toronto. 2. At Boston.

### Championship

Montreal defeated Boston, 4 games to 2
May 13[1]—Montreal 4, Boston 1
May 16[1]—Montreal 3, Boston 2
May 18—Boston 4, Montreal 0
May 21—Boston 4, Montreal 3
May 23[1]—Montreal 4, Boston 1
May 25—Montreal 4, Boston 1
1. At Montreal

## N.H.L. LEADING SCORERS

| | GP | G | A | Pts |
|---|---|---|---|---|
| Guy Lafleur, Montreal | 78 | 60 | 72 | 132 |
| Bryan Trottier, Islanders | 77 | 46 | 77 | 123 |
| Darryl Sittler, Toronto | 80 | 45 | 72 | 117 |
| Jacques Lemaire, Montreal | 76 | 36 | 61 | 97 |
| Denis Potvin, Islanders | 80 | 30 | 64 | 94 |
| Mike Bossy, Islanders | 73 | 53 | 38 | 91 |
| Terry O'Reilly, Boston | 77 | 29 | 61 | 90 |
| Gilbert Perreault, Buffalo | 79 | 41 | 48 | 89 |
| Bobby Clarke, Philadelphia | 71 | 21 | 68 | 89 |
| Lanny McDonald, Toronto | 74 | 47 | 40 | 87 |
| Wilf Paiement, Colorado | 80 | 31 | 56 | 87 |
| Steve Shutt, Montreal | 80 | 49 | 37 | 86 |
| Clark Gillies, Islanders | 80 | 35 | 50 | 85 |
| Jean Ratelle, Boston | 80 | 25 | 59 | 84 |
| Phil Esposito, Rangers | 79 | 38 | 43 | 81 |
| Peter McNab, Boston | 79 | 41 | 39 | 80 |
| van Boldirev, Chicago | 80 | 35 | 45 | 80 |
| Marcel Dionne, Los Angeles | 70 | 36 | 43 | 79 |
| Brad Park, Boston | 80 | 22 | 57 | 79 |
| Danny Gare, Buffalo | 69 | 39 | 38 | 77 |

## N.H.L. LEADING GOALTENDERS

| | GP | Min | GA | Avg |
|---|---|---|---|---|
| Ken Dryden, Montreal | 52 | 3,071 | 105 | 2.05 |
| Bernie Parent, Philadelphia | 49 | 2,923 | 108 | 2.22 |
| Gilles Gilbert, Boston | 25 | 1,326 | 56 | 2.53 |
| Glenn Resch, N.Y. Islanders | 45 | 2,637 | 112 | 2.55 |
| Mike Velsor, Chicago | 12 | 720 | 31 | 2.58 |
| Tony Esposito, Chicago | 64 | 3,840 | 168 | 2.63 |
| Bill Smith, N.Y. Islanders | 38 | 2,154 | 95 | 2.65 |
| Gerry Cheevers, Boston | 21 | 1,086 | 48 | 2.65 |
| Michel Larocque, Montreal | 30 | 1,729 | 77 | 2.67 |
| Mike Palmateer, Toronto | 63 | 3,760 | 172 | 2.74 |

### Top Team Records

| | GP | Min | GA | Avg |
|---|---|---|---|---|
| Montreal (Dryden–Larocque) | 80 | 4,800 | 183 | 2.29 |
| Philadelphia (Parent–Stephenson–St. Croix) | 80 | 4,800 | 200 | 2.50 |
| N.Y. Islanders (Resch–Smith–Hogosta) | 80 | 4,800 | 210 | 2.63 |

## N.H.L. 1977–78 ALL-STAR TEAMS

| Pos. | First Team | Second Team |
|---|---|---|
| Goal | Ken Dryden, Montreal | Don Edwards, Buffalo |
| Defense | Denis Potvin, N.Y. Islanders | Larry Robinson, Montreal |
| Defense | Brad Park, Boston | Borje Salming, Toronto |
| Center | Bryan Trottier, N.Y. Islanders | Darryl Sittler, Toronto |
| Right Wing | Guy Lafleur, Montreal | Mike Bossy, N.Y. Islanders |
| Left Wing | Clark Gillies, N.Y. Islanders | Steve Shutt, Montreal |

## WORLD HOCKEY ASSOCIATION

### Final Standing of the Clubs—1978

| | W | L | T | GF | GA | Pts |
|---|---|---|---|---|---|---|
| Winnipeg Jets | 50 | 28 | 2 | 381 | 270 | 102 |
| New England Whalers | 44 | 31 | 5 | 335 | 269 | 93 |
| Houston Aeros | 42 | 34 | 4 | 296 | 302 | 88 |
| Quebec Nordiques | 40 | 37 | 3 | 349 | 347 | 83 |
| Edmonton Oilers | 38 | 39 | 3 | 309 | 307 | 79 |
| Birmingham Barons | 36 | 41 | 3 | 287 | 314 | 75 |
| Cincinnati Stingers | 35 | 42 | 3 | 298 | 332 | 73 |
| ndianapolis Racers | 24 | 51 | 5 | 267 | 353 | 53 |

### Avco Trophy Playoffs

#### Preliminary Round

Winnipeg defeated Birmingham, 4 games to 1
New England defeated Edmonton, 4 games to 1
Quebec defeated Houston, 4 games to 2

#### Semifinals

New England defeated Quebec, 4 games to 1
April 28—New England 5, Quebec 1
April 30—Quebec 3, New England 2
May 3[1]—New England 5, Quebec 4
May 5[1]—New England 7, Quebec 3
May 7—New England 6, Quebec 3
1. At Quebec.

#### Championship

Winnipeg defeated New England, 4 games to 0
May 12[1]—Winnipeg 4, New England 1
May 14[1]—Winnipeg 5, New England 2
May 19—Winnipeg 10, New England 2
May 22—Winnipeg 5, New England 3
1. At Springfield, Mass.

## W.H.A. LEADING SCORERS—1978

| | GP | G | A | Pts |
|---|---|---|---|---|
| Marc Tardif, Quebec | 73 | 65 | 89 | 154 |
| Real Cloutier, Quebec | 73 | 56 | 73 | 129 |
| Ulf Nilsson, Winnipeg | 73 | 37 | 89 | 126 |
| Anders Hedberg, Winnipeg | 77 | 63 | 59 | 122 |
| Bobby Hull, Winnipeg | 77 | 46 | 71 | 117 |
| Andre Lacroix, Houston | 78 | 36 | 77 | 113 |
| Robbie Ftorek, Cincinnati | 80 | 59 | 50 | 109 |
| Kent Nilsson, Winnipeg | 80 | 42 | 65 | 107 |
| Gordie Howe, New England | 76 | 34 | 62 | 96 |
| Mark Howe, New England | 78 | 30 | 61 | 91 |
| Ron Chipperfield, Edmonton | 80 | 33 | 53 | 85 |
| Rich Leduc, Indianapolis | 80 | 37 | 46 | 83 |
| Claude St. Sauveur, Indiana | 72 | 36 | 42 | 78 |
| Serge Bernier, Quebec | 58 | 26 | 52 | 78 |
| Ken Linseman, Birmingham | 71 | 38 | 38 | 76 |
| Morris Lukovich, Houston | 80 | 40 | 35 | 75 |

## W.H.A. LEADING GOALTENDERS—1978

| | GP | Min | GA | Avg |
|---|---|---|---|---|
| Al Smith, New England | 55 | 3,246 | 174 | 3.22 |
| Lewis Levasseur, New England | 27 | 1,655 | 91 | 3.30 |
| Joe Daley, Winnipeg | 37 | 2,075 | 114 | 3.30 |
| Gary Bromley, Winnipeg | 39 | 2,252 | 124 | 3.30 |
| Ernie Wakely, Houston | 57 | 3,371 | 192 | 3.42 |
| Dave Dryden, Edmonton | 48 | 2,578 | 150 | 3.49 |
| Michel Dion, Cincinnati | 45 | 2,356 | 140 | 3.57 |
| Richard Brodeur, Quebec | 36 | 1,962 | 122 | 3.73 |

## W.H.A. 1978 ALL-STAR TEAMS

| Position | First Team | Second Team |
|---|---|---|
| Goalie | Al Smith, New England | Ernie Wakely, Houston |
| Defense | Lars-Erik Sjoberg, Winnipeg | Rick Ley, New England |
| Defense | Al Hamilton, Edmonton | Barry Long, Winnipeg |
| Center | Ulf Nilsson, Winnipeg | Robbie Ftorek, Cincinnati |
| Left Wing | Marc Tardif, Quebec | Bobby Hull, Winnipeg |
| Right Wing | Anders Hedberg, Winnipeg | Real Cloutier, Quebec |

## AMATEUR CHAMPIONS—1978

World—U.S.S.R. defeated Czechoslovakia, 3–1, in final: Class B: Poland

N.C.C.A. (At Providence, R.I., March 23–25)—Final: Boston University defeated Boston College, 5–3. Third place: Bowling Green defeated Wisconsin, 4–3. Semifinals: Boston University defeated Wisconsin, 5–2; Boston College defeated Bowling Green, 6–2.

N.C.C.A. Division II—Merrimack defeated Lake Forest in final, 12–2. Third place: Mankato State defeated Elmira, 5–3. Semifinals: Merrimack defeated Mankato State, 6–1; Lake Forest defeated Elmira, 4–1.

E.C.A.C. Division I—Regular season: Boston University (21–1). Playoffs: Boston College defeated Providence in final, 4–2. In special playoff, Boston University defeated Providence, 5–3, for place in N.C.C.A. championships.

E.C.A.C. Division II—Bowdoin defeated Merrimack, 3–0, in playoffs.

E.C.A.C. Division III—Westfield State defeated Trinity, 4–3, in playoff final.

W.C.H.A.—Regular season: Denver (27–5). Playoffs: Colorado College defeated Denver 9–7 (two-game total goals); Wisconsin defeated Michigan Tech, 11–7 (two game totals).

C.C.H.A.—Regular season: Bowling Green.

W.C.H.A.-C.C.H.A. Playoff—Bowling Green defeated Colorado College, 5–3.

N.A.I.A.—Final: Augsburg (Minn.) defeated Bemidji State 4–3. Third place: St. Thomas (Minn.) defeated Wisconsin-River Falls, 7–6. Semifinals: Bemidji State defeated St. Thomas, 7–1; Augsburg defeated Wisconsin–River Falls, 10–2.

## MINOR LEAGUE HOCKEY CHAMPIONS
### American League—1978

**Northern Division**

| | W | L | T | PF | PA | Pts |
|---|---|---|---|---|---|---|
| Maine Mariners | 43 | 28 | 9 | 305 | 256 | 95 |
| Nova Scotia Voyageurs | 37 | 28 | 16 | 304 | 250 | 90 |
| Springfield Indians | 39 | 33 | 9 | 347 | 349 | 87 |
| Binghamton Dusters | 27 | 46 | 8 | 287 | 377 | 62 |

**Southern Division**

| | W | L | T | PF | PA | Pts |
|---|---|---|---|---|---|---|
| Rochester Americans | 43 | 31 | 7 | 332 | 296 | 93 |
| New Haven Nighthawks | 38 | 31 | 11 | 313 | 292 | 87 |
| Philadelphia Firebirds | 35 | 35 | 11 | 294 | 290 | 81 |
| Hershey Bears | 27 | 44 | 10 | 281 | 324 | 64 |
| Hampton Gulls[1] | 15 | 28 | 3 | 142 | 171 | 33 |

1. Disbanded Feb. 10.

**CALDER CUP PLAYOFFS**
**Quarterfinals**

Nova Scotia defeated Springfield, 3 games to 1
New Haven defeated Philadelphia, 3 games to 1

**Semifinals**

Maine defeated Nova Scotia, 4 games to 3
New Haven defeated Rochester, 4 games to 2

**Final**

Maine defeated New Haven, 4 games to 1

### Central League

| | W | L | T | PF | PA | Pts |
|---|---|---|---|---|---|---|
| Fort Worth Texans | 44 | 29 | 3 | 262 | 251 | 91 |
| Salt Lake City Golden Eagles | 42 | 31 | 3 | 283 | 238 | 87 |
| Dallas Black Hawks | 38 | 36 | 3 | 284 | 281 | 79 |
| Tulsa Oilers | 34 | 39 | 3 | 264 | 273 | 71 |
| Kansas City Red Wings | 33 | 40 | 3 | 266 | 257 | 69 |
| Phoenix Roadrunners[1] | 4 | 20 | 3 | 75 | 134 | 11 |

1. Disbanded Dec. 12, 1977

**ADAMS CUP PLAYOFFS**
**Semifinals**

Dallas defeated Salt Lake City, 4 games to 2
Fort Worth defeated Tulsa, 4 games to 3

**Final**

Fort Worth defeated Dallas, 4 games to 3

# PLATFORM TENNIS

United States Champions—1978

Men—Herb FitzGibbon, New York, and Hank Irvine, Millburn, N.J.

Women—Louise Gengler, Locust Valley, N.Y., and Hilary Hilton, New York

Mixed—Louise Gengler and Clark Graebner, Greens Farms, Conn.

Team (President's Cup)—Midwest

# STANDARD MEASUREMENTS IN SPORTS

## BASEBALL

**Home plate to pitcher's box:** 60 feet 6 inches.
**Plate to second base:** 127 feet 3³/₈ inches.
**Distance from base to base (home plate included):** 90 feet.
**Size of bases:** 15 inches by 15 inches.
**Pitcher's plate:** 24 inches by 6 inches.
**Batter's box:** 3 feet by 4 feet.
**Home plate:** 17 inches by 17 inches, cut to a point at rear.
**Home plate to backstop:** Not less than 60 feet (recommended).
**Weight of ball:** Not less than 5 ounces nor more than 5¹/₄ ounces.
**Circumference of ball:** Not less than 9 inches nor more than 9¹/₄ inches.
**Bat:** Must be round, not over 2³/₄ inches in diameter at thickest part, nor more than 42 inches in length, and of solid wood in one piece or laminated.

## FOOTBALL

**Length of field:** 120 yards. (including 10 yards of end zone at each end).
**Width of field:** 53¹/₃ yards (160 feet).
**Height of goal posts:** At least 20 feet.
**Height of crossbar:** 10 feet.
**Width of goal posts (above crossbar):** 23 feet 4 inches, inside to inside, and not more than 24 feet, outside to outside.
**Length of ball:** 11 to 11.25 inches (long axis).
**Circumference of ball:** 21.25 to 21.50 inches (middle); 28 to 28.5 inches (long axis).

## LAWN TENNIS

**Size of court:** Rectangle 78 feet long and 27 feet wide (singles); 78 feet long and 36 feet wide (doubles).
**Height of net:** 3 feet in center, gradually rising to reach 3-foot 6-inch posts at a point 3 feet outside each side of court.
**Ball:** Shall be more than 2¹/₂ inches and less than 2⁵/₈ inches in diameter and weigh more than 2 ounces and less than 2¹/₁₆ ounces.
**Service line:** 21 feet from net.

## HOCKEY

**Size of rink:** 200 feet long by 85 feet wide surrounded by a wooden wall not less than 40 inches and not more than 48 inches above level of ice.
**Size of goal:** 6 feet wide by 4 feet in height.
**Puck:** 1 inch thick and 3 inches in diameter; made of vulcanized rubber; weight 5¹/₂ to 6 ounces.
**Length of stick:** Not more than 55 inches from heel to end of shaft nor 12¹/₂ inches from heel to end of blade. Blade should not be more than 3 inches in width but not less than 2 inches, except goalkeeper's stick, which shall not exceed 3¹/₂ inches in width except at the heel, where it must not exceed 4¹/₂ inches.

## BOWLING

**Lane dimensions:** Overall length 62 feet 10³/₁₆ inches, measuring from foul line to pit (not including tail plank), with ¹/₂ inch tolerance permitted. Foul line to center of No. 1 pinspot 60 feet, with ¹/₂ inch tolerance permitted. Lane width, 41¹/₂ inches with a tolerance of ¹/₂ inch permitted. Approach, not less than 15 feet. Gutters, 9 ⁵/₁₆ inches wide with ³/₁₆ plus or ⁵/₁₆ minus tolerances permitted.
**Ball:** Circumference, not more than 27 inches. Weight, 16 pounds maximum.

## GOLF

**Weight of ball:** Not greater than 1.620 ounces avoirdupois.
**Size of ball:** Not less than 1.680 inches in diameter.
**Velocity of ball:** Not greater than 250 feet per second when tested on U.S.G.A. apparatus, with 2 percent tolerance.
**Hole:** 4¹/₄ inches in diamater and at least 4 inches deep.
**Clubs:** 14 is the maximum number permitted.

## BASKETBALL

(National Collegiate A. A. Rules)

**Playing court:** College: 94 feet long by 50 feet wide. High School: 84 feet long by 50 feet wide (maximum inside dimensions).
**Baskets:** Rings 18 inches in inside diameter, with white cord 12-mesh nets, 15 to 18 inches in length. Each ring is made of metal, is not more than ⁵/₈ of an inch in diameter and is bright orange in color.
**Height of basket ring:** 10 feet (upper edge).
**Weight of ball:** Not less than 20 ounces nor more than 22.
**Circumference of ball:** No greater than 30 inches and not less than 29¹/₂.
**Free-throw line:** 15 feet from the face of the backboard.

## BOXING

**Ring:** Professional matches take place in an area not less than 18 nor more than 24 feet square including apron. It is enclosed by four covered ropes, each not less than one inch in diameter. The floor has a 2-inch padding of Ensolite (or equivalent) underneath ring cover that extends at least 6 inches beyond the roped area in the case of elevated rings. For A.A.U. boxing, not less than 16 nor more than 25 feet square within the ropes. The floor must extend beyond the ring ropes not less than 2 feet. The ring posts shall not be nearer to the ring ropes than 18 inches and must be properly padded.
**Gloves:** In professional fights, not less than 8-ounce gloves generally are used. A.A.U., not less than 10 ounces for all divisions.

# LUGE

### 1978 WORLD CHAMPIONSHIPS

| | |
|---|---|
| Men—Paul Hildgartner, Italy | 1:22.26 |
| Women—Vera Sosulya, U.S.S.R. | 1:13.00 |

# TUMBLING

### A.A.U. NATIONAL CHAMPIONSHIPS

(New Brunswick, N.J., April 27–28, 1978)

Men—Steve Elliott, Amarillo, Tex. 62.40
Women—Nancy Quattrocki, Chicago 61.70

# FIGURE SKATING

## WORLD CHAMPIONS

**Men**

| | |
|---|---|
| 1960 | Alain Giletti, France |
| 1961 | No competition |
| 1962 | Donald Jackson, Canada |
| 1963 | Don McPherson, Canada |
| 1964 | Manfred Schnelldorfer, West Germany |
| 1965 | Alain Calmat, France |
| 1966–68 | Emmerich Danzer, Austria |
| 1969–70 | Tim Wood, United States |
| 1971–73 | Ondrej Nepela, Czechoslovakia |
| 1974 | Jan Hoffman, East Germany |
| 1975 | Sergei Yolkov, U.S.S.R. |
| 1976 | John Curry, Britain |
| 1977 | Vladimir Kovelov, U.S.S.R. |
| 1978 | Charles Tickner, United States |

**Women**

| | |
|---|---|
| 1956–60 | Carol Heiss, United States |
| 1961 | No competition |
| 1962–64 | Sjoukje Dijkstra, Netherlands |
| 1965 | Petra Burka, Canada |
| 1966–68 | Peggy Fleming, United States |
| 1969–70 | Gabriele Seyfert, East Germany |
| 1971–72 | Beatrix Schuba, Austria |
| 1973 | Karen Magnusson, Canada |
| 1974 | Christine Errath, East Germany |
| 1975 | Dianne de Leeuw, Netherlands |
| 1976 | Dorothy Hamill, United States |
| 1977 | Linda Fratianne, United States |
| 1978 | Anett Poetzsch, East Germany |

## U.S. CHAMPIONS

**Men**

| | |
|---|---|
| 1946–52 | Richard Button |
| 1953–56 | Hayes Jenkins |
| 1957–60 | David Jenkins |
| 1961 | Bradley Lord |
| 1962 | Monty Hoyt |
| 1963 | Tommy Litz |
| 1964 | Scott Allen |
| 1965 | Gary Visconti |
| 1966 | Scott Allen |
| 1967 | Gary Visconti |
| 1968–70 | Tim Wood |
| 1971 | John M. Petkevich |
| 1972 | Ken Shelley |
| 1973–75 | Gordon McKellen |
| 1976 | Terry Kubicka |
| 1977–78 | Charles Tickner |

**Women**

| | |
|---|---|
| 1943–48 | Gretchen Merrill |
| 1949–50 | Yvonne Sherman |
| 1951 | Sonya Klopfer |
| 1952–56 | Tenley Albright |
| 1957–60 | Carol Heiss |
| 1961 | Laurence Owen |
| 1962 | Barbara Roles Pursley |
| 1963 | Lorraine Hanlon |
| 1964–68 | Peggy Fleming |
| 1969–73 | Janet Lynn |
| 1974–76 | Dorothy Hamill |
| 1977–78 | Linda Fratianne |

## 1978 WORLD CHAMPIONSHIPS

(Ottawa, March 7-11)

Men's singles—Charles Tickner, Littleton, Colo.
Women's singles—Anett Poetzsch, East Germany
Pairs—Irina Rodnina and Aleksandr Zaitsev, U.S.S.R.
Dance—Nataliy Linichuk and Gennadij Karponosov, U.S.S.R.

## 1978 U.S. CHAMPIONSHIPS

(Portland, Ore., February 9-12)

Men's singles—Charles Tickner, Littleton, Colo.
Women's singles—Linda Fratianne, Northridge, Calif.
Pairs—Tai Babalonia, Mission Hills, Calif., and Randy Gardner, Los Angeles
Gold Dance—Stacey Smith and John Summers, Wilmington, Del.
Junior women—Jill Sawyer, Tacoma, Wash.

## 1978 WORLD JUNIOR CHAMPIONSHIPS

(Megève, France, March 22-28)

Men's singles—Dennis Col, Canada
Women's singles—Jill Sawyer, Tacoma, Wash.
Pairs—Barbara Underhill and Paul Martini, Canada
Dance—Tatiana Durasova and Sergei Panomarenko, U.S.S.R.

# BOWLING

## AMERICAN BOWLING CONGRESS CHAMPIONS

| Year | Singles | All-events |
|---|---|---|
| 1959 | Ed Lubanski | Ed Lubanski |
| 1960 | Paul Kulbaga | Vince Lucci |
| 1961 | Lyle Spooner | Luke Karen |
| 1962 | Andy Renaldo | Billy Young |
| 1963 | Fred Delello | Bus Owalt |
| 1964 | Jim Stefanich | Les Zikes, Jr. |
| 1965 | Ken Roeth | Tom Hathaway |
| 1966 | Don Chapman | John Wilcox |
| 1967 | Frank Perry | Gary Lewis |
| 1968 | Wayne Kowalski | Vince Mazzanti |
| 1969 | Greg Campbell | Eddie Jackson |
| 1970 | Jake Yoder | Mike Berlin |
| 1971 | Al Cohn | Al Cohn |
| 1972 | Bill Pointer | Mac Lowry |
| 1973 | Ed Thompson | Ron Woolet |
| 1974 | Gene Krause | Bob Hart |
| 1975 | Jim Setser | Bobby Meadows |
| 1976 | Mike Putzer | Jim Lindquist |
| 1977 | Frank Gadaleto | Bud Debenham |
| 1978 | Rich Mersek | Chris Cobus |

## BOWLING PROPRIETORS' ASSOCIATION OF AMERICA—MEN

**United States Open[1]**

| | |
|---|---|
| 1971 | Mike Lemongello |
| 1972 | Don Johnson |
| 1973 | Mike McGrath |
| 1974 | Larry Laub |
| 1975 | Steve Neff |
| 1976 | Paul Moser |
| 1977 | Johnny Petraglia |
| 1978 | Nelson Burton, Jr. |

1. Replaced All-Star tournament and is rolled as part of B.P.A. tour.

## PROFESSIONAL BOWLERS ASSOCIATION

**National Championship Tournament**

| | | | | | | | |
|---|---|---|---|---|---|---|---|
| 1960 | Don Carter | 1965 | Dave Davis | 1970 | Mike McGrath | 1975 | Earl Anthony |
| 1961 | Dave Soutar | 1966 | Wayne Zahn | 1971 | Mike Lemongello | 1976 | Paul Colwell |
| 1962 | Carmen Salvino | 1967 | Dave Davis | 1972 | Johnny Guenther | 1977 | Tommy Hudson |
| 1963 | Billy Hardwick | 1968 | Wayne Zahn | 1973 | Earl Anthony | | |
| 1964 | Bob Strampe | 1969 | Mike McGrath | 1974 | Earl Anthony | | |

## WOMEN'S INTERNATIONAL BOWLING CONGRESS CHAMPIONS

| Year | Singles | All-events | Year | Singles | All-events |
|---|---|---|---|---|---|
| 1959 | Mae Ploegman | Pat McBride | 1969 | Joan Bender | Helen Duval |
| 1960 | Marge McDaniels | Judy Roberts | 1970 | Dorothy Fothergill | Dorothy Fothergill |
| 1961 | Elaine Newton | Evelyn Teal | 1971 | Ginny Younginer | Lorrie Koch |
| 1962 | Martha Hoffman | Flossie Argent | 1972 | D. D. Jacobson | Mildred Martorella |
| 1963 | Dot Wilkinson | Helen Shablis | 1973 | Bobby Buffaloe | Toni Calvery |
| 1964 | Jean Havlish | Jean Havlish | 1974 | Shirley Garms | Judy C. Soutar |
| 1965 | Doris Rudell | Donna Zimmerman | 1975 | Barbara Leicht | Virginia Park |
| 1966 | Gloria Bouvia | Kate Helbig | 1976 | Bev Shonk | Betty Morris |
| 1967 | Gloria Paeth | Carol Miller | 1977 | Akiko Yamaga | Akiko Yamaga |
| 1968 | Norma Parks | Susie Reichley | 1978 | Mae Bolt | Annese Kelly |

## W.I.B.C. QUEENS TOURNAMENT CHAMPIONS

| | | | | | | | |
|---|---|---|---|---|---|---|---|
| 1961 | Janet Harman | 1966 | Judy Lee | 1971 | Mildred Martorella | 1976 | Pamela Rutherford |
| 1962 | Dorothy Wilkinson | 1967 | Mildred Martorella | 1972 | Dorothy Fothergill | 1977 | Dana Stewart |
| 1963 | Irene Monterosso | 1968 | Phyllis Massey | 1973 | Dorothy Fothergill | 1978 | Loa Boxberger |
| 1964 | D.D. Jacobson | 1969 | Ann Feigel | 1974 | Judy Soutar | | |
| 1965 | Betty Kuczynski | 1970 | Mildred Martorella | 1975 | Cindy Powell | | |

## BOWLING PROPRIETORS' ASSOCIATION OF AMERICA—WOMEN

**United States Open**[1]

| | | | | | | | |
|---|---|---|---|---|---|---|---|
| 1971 | Paula Carter | 1973 | Mildred Martorella | 1975 | Paula Carter | 1977 | Betty Morris |
| 1972 | Lorrie Nichols | 1974 | Pat Costello | 1976 | Pat Costello | 1978 | Donna Adamek |

1. Replaced All-Star tournament.

## AMERICAN BOWLING CONGRESS TOURNAMENT

(St. Louis, March–May 14, 1978)

**Regular Division**

Singles—Rich Mersek, Cleveland 739
Doubles—Bob Kulaszewicz and Don Gazzana, Milwaukee 1,352
All Events—Chris Cobus, Milwaukee 1,994
Team—Berlin's Pro Shop, Muscatine, Iowa 3,077

**Classic Division**

Singles—Bill Beach, Sharon, Pa. 701
Doubles—Steve Fehr and Dave Newrath, Cincinnati 1,300
All Events—Bill Beach 1,941

**Booster Division**

Team—Bush Pest Control, Austin, Tex. 2,741

**Collegiate**

(Association of College Unions-International)
All Events—Jeff Bellinger, South Carolina 2,374

## WOMEN'S INTERNATIONAL BOWLING CONGRESS

(Miami, April 6-June 6, 1978)

**Open Division**

Singles—Mae Bolt, Berwyn, Ill. 709
Doubles—Barbara Shelton, Jamaica, N.Y. and Annese Kelly, Brooklyn, N.Y. 1,211
All-events—Annese Kelly, Brooklyn, N.Y. 1,896
Team—Cook County Vending, Chicago 2,956

**Division I**

Singles—Norma Walker, Tacoma, Wash. 659
Doubles—Jeannie Hand, Fairview, Ill. and Judy Hart Canton, Ill. 1,201
All-events—Sandy Klingshirn, Boca Raton, Fla. 1,852
Team—Joyner Garden Center, Alexandria, Minn. 2,706

**Division II**

Singles—Faydra Austin, Miami, Fla. 618
Doubles—Margaret Thelander and Kris Ihlenfeldt, Arlington Heights, Ill. 1,049
All-events—Faydra Austin 1,798
Team—Dixie Doodles, Guntersville, Ala. 2,462

### QUEENS TOURNAMENT

(Miami, May 9–13, 1978)

Winner—Loa Boxberger, Russell, Kan. (defeated Cora Fiebig, Madison Heights, Mich., 197–176, in final one-game match.)

### COLLEGIATE

**Association of College Unions—International**

Singles—Lauren LaCost, Illinois State at Normal 585
Doubles—Sue Fulton, State of New York–Buffalo and Diane Johnson, Univ. of Montana 1,109
All-events—Nikki Gianulias, Solano (Calif.) C.C. 1,739

# SKIING

## ALPINE WORLD CUP OVERALL WINNERS

| | Men | Women | Team |
|---|---|---|---|
| 1967 | Jean-Claude Killy, France | Nancy Greene, Canada | France |
| 1968 | Jean-Claude Killy, France | Nancy Greene, Canada | France |
| 1969 | Karl Schranz, Austria | Gertrude Gabl, Austria | Austria |
| 1970 | Karl Schranz, Austria | Michel Jacot, France | France |
| 1971 | Gustavo Thoeni, Italy | Annemarie Proell, Austria | France |
| 1972 | Gustavo Thoeni, Italy | Annemarie Proell, Austria | France |
| 1973 | Gustavo Thoeni, Italy | Annemarie Proell Moser, Austria | Austria |
| 1974 | Piero Gros, Italy | Annemarie Proell Moser, Austria | Austria |
| 1975 | Gustavo Thoeni, Italy | Annemarie Proell Moser, Austria | Austria |
| 1976 | Ingemar Stenmark, Sweden | Rosi Mittermaier, West Germany | Austria |
| 1977 | Ingemar Stenmark, Sweden | Lise-Marie Morerod, Switzerland | Austria |
| 1978 | Ingemar Stenmark, Sweden | Hanni Wenzel, Liechtenstein | Austria |

## WORLD CHAMPIONSHIPS

### ALPINE

(Garmisch-Partenkirchen, West Germany, Jan. 28–Feb. 5, 1978)

**Men's Events**

| | |
|---|---|
| Downhill—Josef Walcher, Austria | 2:04.12 |
| Slalom—Ingemar Stenmark, Sweden | 1:39.54 |
| Giant slalom—Ingemar Stenmark | 3:02.52 |
| Combined—Andreas Wenzel, Liechtenstein | |

**Women's Events**

| | |
|---|---|
| Downhill—Annemarie Proell Moser, Austria | 1:48.31 |
| Slalom—Lea Soelkner, Austria | 1:24.85 |
| Giant slalom—Maria Epple, West Germany | 2:41.15 |
| Combined—Annemarie Proell Moser | |

### NORDIC

(Lahti, Finland, Feb. 14–26, 1978)

**Jumping**

| | |
|---|---|
| 70-meter—Matthias Buse, East Germany (84 and 86 meters) | 253.2 pts |
| 90-meter—Tapio Raisanen, Finland (102, 91 meters) | 256.6 pts |

**Combined**

| | |
|---|---|
| 70-meter jump—Rauno Miettinen, Finland | 232 pts |
| 15-km cross-country—Arne-Morton Granlien, Norway | 48:22.27 |
| Combined—Konrad Winkler, East Germany (2nd in jump, 6th in run) | 435.25 pts |

**Men's Cross-Country**

| | |
|---|---|
| 15 kilometers—Josef Lusczcek, Poland | 49:09.37 |
| 30 kilometers—Sergei Saveliev, U.S.S.R. | 1:32:56 |
| 50 kilometers—Ake Lundback, Sweden | 2:46:43.06 |
| 40-km relay—Sweden | 2:05:17.83 |

**Women's Cross-Country**

| | |
|---|---|
| 5 km—Helena Takalo, Finland | 18:53.50 |
| 10 km—Zinaida Amosova, U.S.S.R. | 37:01.72 |
| 15-km relay—Finland | 1:13:25.08 |

## UNITED STATES CHAMPIONSHIPS

### ALPINE

(Lake Placid, N.Y., Feb. 23–28, 1978)

**Men's Events**

| | |
|---|---|
| Downhill—Karl Anderson, Greene, Me. | 1:55.36 |
| Slalom—Phil Mahre, White Pass, Wash. | 1:34.17 |
| Giant slalom—Phil Mahre | 2:40.86 |
| Combined—Billy Taylor, Orchard Park, N.Y. | |

**Women's Events**

| | |
|---|---|
| Downhill—Cindy Nelson, Lutsen, Minn. | 1:47.14 |
| Slalom—Becky Dorsey, Wenham, Mass. | 1:13.56 |
| Giant slalom—Becky Dorsey | 2:34.18 |
| Combined—Cindy Nelson | |

### NORDIC

**Jumping**

(Leavenworth, Wash., Feb. 4, 1978)

| | |
|---|---|
| Class A—Mike Devecka, Bend, Ore. (93.5, 94.5 meters) | 227.7 pts |
| Veteran—Earl Murphy, Farmingdale, N.J. (79, 83 meters) | 168.3 pts |
| Junior—Jon Bassette, Quechee, Vt. (88.5, 84.5 meters) | 201.2 pts |

**Men's Cross-Country**

(Anchorage, Alaska, Dec. 31–Jan. 7, 1978)

| | |
|---|---|
| 15 km—Stan Dunklee, Brattleboro, Vt. | 43:46.18 |
| 30 km—Bob Treadwell, Amherst, N.H. | 1:32:23.98 |
| 50 km—Kevin Swigert, Ketchum, Idaho | 2:48:02.43 |
| Veterans, 10 km—Paul Sawyer, Northern Div. | 36:56.16 |
| Junior 10 km—Don Simoneu, Livermore Falls, Me. | 32:42.43 |
| Junior 20 km—Don Simoneu | 57:07.56 |
| 30-km relay—Eastern (Doug Peterson, Hanover, N.H., Stan Dunklee, Bob Treadwell) | 1:25:56.50 |
| Junior 30-km relay—Alaska #1 | 1:33:05.73 |

**Women's Cross-Country**

(Anchorage, Alaska, Dec. 31–Jan. 7, 1978)

| | |
|---|---|
| 7.5 km—Alison Spencer, Anchorage, Alaska | 24:40.59 |
| 10 km—Lynn VonderHeide, Anchorage, Alaska | 32:26.32 |
| 20 km—Alison Spencer | 1:04:28.64 |
| Junior 5 km—Beth Paxson, Charlotte, Vt. | 17:50.99 |
| Junior 10 km—Betsy Haines, Anchorage, Alaska | 32:59.23 |
| Veterans' 15 km—Virginia Moore, Anchorage, Alaska | 24:29.03 |
| 15-km relay—Alaska (Betsy Haines, Lynn VonderHeide, Alison Spencer) | 49:16.60 |
| Junior 15-km relay—Alaska | 53:39.66 |

## CANADIAN ALPINE CHAMPIONSHIPS

(Lake Louise, Alberta, Feb. 24, 1978)

**Men's Events**

| | |
|---|---|
| Downhill—Ken Read, Calgary, Alta. | 1:49.60 |
| Slalom—Pete Monod, Banff | 1:43.64 |

| | |
|---|---|
| Giant slalom—John Hilland, Calgary | 2:18.52 |
| Combined—Ken Read | |

**Women's Events**

| | |
|---|---|
| Downhill—Kathy Kreiner, Timmins, Ont. | 1:22.41 |
| Slalom—Vanita Haining, Calgary, Alta. | 1:38.26 |
| Giant slalom—Kathy Kreiner | 2:21.64 |
| Combined—Laurie Graham, Inglewood, Ont. | |

## CANADIAN NORDIC CHAMPIONSHIPS

(Sault Ste. Marie, Ont., March 2–7, 1978)

**Men's Cross-Country**

| | |
|---|---|
| 15 km—Pierre Vezina, Beaupre, Que. | 47:49.06 |
| 30 km—Pierre Vezina | 1:37:22.25 |
| 50 km—Doug Gudwer, Prince George, B.C. | 2:47:06.47 |
| Veterans' 30 km—Risto Santala, Whitby, Ont. | 1:50:29.32 |

**Women's Cross-Country**

| | |
|---|---|
| 5 km—Shirley Firth, Inuvik, N.W.T. | 19:15.04 |
| 10 km—Shirley Firth | 39:08.95 |
| 20 km—Shirley Firth | 1:20:47.39 |

## WORLD CUP, 1978

**Overall—Men**

| | Pts |
|---|---|
| Ingemar Stenmark, Sweden | 150 |
| Phil Mahre, White Pass, Wash. | 115 |
| Andreas Wenzel, Liechtenstein | 100 |
| Klaus Heidegger, Austria | 95 |
| Franz Klammer, Austria | 70 |
| Herbert Plank, Italy | 70 |
| T23—Steve Mahre, White Pass, Wash. | 25 |
| T36—Cary Adgate, Boyne City, Mich. | 13 |

**Overall—Women**

| | Pts |
|---|---|
| Hanni Wenzel, Liechtenstein | 154 |
| Annemarie Proell Moser, Austria | 147 |
| Lise-Marie Morerod, Switzerland | 135 |
| Fabienne Serrat, France | 105 |
| Cindy Nelson, Lutsen, Minn. | 97 |
| T13—Becky Dorsey, Wenham, Mass. | 45 |
| T15—Abbi Fisher, South Conway, N.H. | 27 |
| 18—Christin Cooper, Sun Valley, Idaho | 24 |
| 21—Viki Fleckenstein, Syracuse, N.Y. | 20 |
| 25—Kathy Kreiner, Timmins, Ont. | 11 |

**Event Leaders—Men**

| | |
|---|---|
| Downhill—Franz Klammer, Austria | 96 |
| 4. Ken Read, Calgary, Alta. | 56 |
| Slalom—Ingemar Stenmark, Sweden | 115 |
| 3. Phil Mahre, White Pass, Wash. | 66 |
| Giant Slalom—Ingemar Stenmark, Sweden | 120 |
| 3. Phil Mahre, White Pass, Wash. | 84 |

**Event Leaders—Women**

| | Pts |
|---|---|
| Downhill—Annemarie Proell Moser, Austria | 125 |
| 2. Cindy Nelson, Lutsen, Minn. | 91 |
| Slalom—Hanni Wenzel, Liechtenstein | 110 |
| 7. Christin Cooper, Sun Valley, Idaho | 23 |
| 9. Abbi Fisher, South Conway, N.H. | 18 |
| 10. Becky Dorsey, Wenham, Mass. | 17 |
| 13. Cindy Nelson, Lutsen, Minn. | 12 |
| 15. Viki Fleckenstein, Syracuse, N.Y. | 7 |
| Giant Slalom—Lise-Marie Morerod, Switzerland | 115 |
| T8. Becky Dorsey, Wenham, Mass. | 30 |
| T8. Cindy Nelson, Lutsen, Minn. | 30 |

## NATIONS CUP, 1978

| | Pts |
|---|---|
| Overall—Austria | 906 |
| Switzerland | 517 |
| United States | 411 |
| 9. Canada | 96 |
| Men's Events—Austria | 483 |
| 4. United States | 179 |
| 8. Canada | 85 |
| Women's Events—Austria | 423 |
| 4. United States | 232 |
| 7. Canada | 11 |

## NORTH AMERICAN TROPHY SERIES, 1978

**Men's Events**

| | Pts |
|---|---|
| Overall—Tie between Cory Murdock, Lake Tahoe, Calif., and Billy Taylor, Orchard Park, N.Y. | 81 |
| Slalom, East—Ikou Yamamoto, Japan | 50 |
| Giant slalom, East—John Morrissey, Stowe, Vt. | 50 |
| Combined, East—John Morrissey | 55 |
| Slalom, West—Mike Dorris, McCall, Idaho | 49 |
| Giant slalom, West—Ikou Yamamoto | 55 |

**Women's Events**

| | |
|---|---|
| Overall—Cindy Nelson, Lutsen, Minn. | 102 |
| Slalom, East—Joanne Hendy, Middlebury, Vt. | 42 |
| Giant slalom, East—Diane Berard, Hayward, Minn. | 55 |
| Combined, East—Diane Berard | 46 |
| Slalom, West—Rebecca Simming, Far West S.A. | 40 |
| Giant slalom, West—Betsy Devin, Winthrop, Wash. | 60 |

## U.S. AMATEUR

**Freestyle**

| | Pts |
|---|---|
| Men's overall—Peter Young, Rocky Mountain | 44.21 |
| Women's overall—Lita Hitchcock, Rocky Mountain | 32.27 |

# *HANDBALL*

## U.S.H.A. NATIONAL FOUR-WALL CHAMPIONS

**Singles**

| | |
|---|---|
| 1960 | Jimmy Jacobs |
| 1961 | John Sloan |
| 1962–63 | Oscar Obert |
| 1964–65 | Jimmy Jacobs |
| 1966–67 | Paul Haber |
| 1968 | Simon (Stuffy) Singer |
| 1969–71 | Paul Haber |
| 1972 | Fred Lewis |
| 1973 | Terry Muck |
| 1974 | Fred Lewis |
| 1975 | Jay Bilyeu |
| 1976 | Vern Roberts, Jr. |
| 1977 | Nary Alvarado |
| 1978 | Fred Lewis |

**Doubles**

| | |
|---|---|
| 1960 | Jimmy Jacobs-Dick Weisman |
| 1961 | John Sloan-Vic Hershkowitz |
| 1962–63 | Jimmy Jacobs-Marty Decatur |
| 1964 | John Sloan-Phil Elbert |
| 1965 | Jimmy Jacobs-Marty Decatur |
| 1966 | Pete Tyson-Bob Lindsay |
| 1967–68 | Jimmy Jacobs-Marty Decatur |
| 1969 | Lou Kramberg-Lou Russo |
| 1970 | Karl and Ruby Obert |
| 1971 | Ray Neveau-Simie Fein |
| 1972 | Kent Fusselman-Al Drews |
| 1973–74 | Ray Neveau-Simie Fein |
| 1975 | Marty Decatur-Steve Lott |
| 1976 | Gary Rohrer-Dan O'Connor |
| 1977 | Skip McDowell-Matt Kelly |
| 1978 | Stuffy Singer-Marty Decatur |

### U.S. HANDBALL ASSOCIATION—1978

**Four Wall**

(Tucson, Ariz., June 4–10)

Open singles—Fred Lewis, Miami, Fla.
Open doubles—Stuffy Singer, Los Angeles, and Marty Decatur, New York
Masters singles—Rene Zamorano, Tucson, Ariz.
Masters doubles—Pete Tyson and Dick Roberson, Austin, Tex.
Golden masters singles—Jack Briscoe, St. Louis
Golden masters doubles—Ken Schneider and Bud Perelman, Chicago
Super masters doubles—Al Klein and Reg Chapman, Las Vegas, Nev.
Challengers singles—Larry Vanderpool, Portland, Ore.

**National Masters**

(Minneapolis, April 6–9)

Masters (over 40)—Ken Crespi, Livonia, Mich.
Golden masters (over 50)—Wayne Stewart, Minneapolis
Super masters (over 60)—Dave Weinberg, Chicago

**Collegiate**

(Lake Forest, Ill., March 3–5)

A singles—Mike Lloyd, Memphis State
B singles—Greg Kenney, Lake Forest
Doubles—Dave Dohrman and Gary Stedman, Lake Forest
Team—Lake Forest (18½ pts)

# *RACQUETS*

### NATIONAL CHAMPIONSHIPS—1978

Open—William Surtees, New York
Amateur—William Surtees, New York

# *CANOE RACING*

### AMERICAN CANOE ASSOCIATION

*Source:* Marcia Smoke, Buchanan, Mich.

### NATIONAL FLATWATER CHAMPIONS—1978

(Syracuse, N.Y., August 26–27)

**Men's Kayak**

500 m—Steve Kelly, Inwood C.C., New York
1,000 m—Steve Kelly
10,000 m—Brent Turner, St. Charles (Ill.) C.C.
500–m tandem—Greg and Bruce Barton, Niles (Mich.) C.C.
1,000–m tandem—Brent Turner and Steve Kelly
10,000–m tandem—Paul and Ralph Lowenwirth, New York A.C.
1,000–m fours—Greg and Bruce Barton, Brent Turner, Steve Kelly
10,000–m fours—Jerry Welbourn, Potomac B.C., Washington, Paul Lowenwirth, Don Endrizzi, Bill Hanson, Sebago C.C., New York

**Women's Kayak**

500 m—Leslie Klein, Hadley, Mass.
5,000–m—Ann Turner, St. Charles (Ill.) C.C.
500–m tandem—Leslie Klein and Ann Turner
5,000–m tandem—Linda Dragan and Jackie Scribner, Washington C.C.
500–m fours—Washington Canoe Club (Linda Dragan, Teresa Dimarino, Nancy Leahy, Jackie Scribner)
5,000–m fours—Ann Turner, Leslie Klein, Connie Barton, Niles C.C., Jan Streib, St. Charles C.C.

**Men's Canoe**

500 m—Roland Muhlen, St. Charles (Ill.) C.C.
1,000 m—Jay Kearney, University of Kentucky
10,000 m—Kurt Doberstein, St. Charles C.C.
500–m tandem—Jay Kearney and Kurt Doberstein
1,000–m tandem—Jay Kearney and Kurt Doberstein
10,000–m tandem—Jay Kearney and Kurt Doberstein
1,000 m fours—St. Charles C.C. (Roland Muhlen, Dave Landenwitch, John and Rob Diebold)

### NATIONAL WHITEWATER CHAMPIONS—1978

Men's kayak—Eric Evans, Belchertown, Mass.
Women's kayak—Linda Harrison, Newark, Del.
Men's canoe—Angus Morrison, Wayzata, Minn.
Men's doubles—Ron Lugbill, Fairfax, Va., and David Hearn, Garrett Park, Md.
Mixed doubles—Linda Aponte and John Kennedy, Bryson City, N.C.

### NATIONAL WILDWATER CHAMPIONS—1978

Men's kayak—William Nutt, Etna, N.H.
Women's kayak—Leslie Klein, Hadley, Mass.
Men's canoe—Angus Morrison, Wayzata, Minn.
Men's canoe doubles—Ron Lugbill, Fairfax, Va., and David Hearn, Garrett Park, Md.
Mixed doubles canoe—Bern Collins and Margaret Osborne, Arlington, Va.

### NATIONAL LONG DISTANCE CHAMPIONS—1978

| | |
|---|---|
| Men's kayak (19 miles)—Cliff Taubes, Washington C.C. | 2:05.46 |
| Men's kayak tandem (19 miles)—Jerry Welbourn and Ken Stockin, Washington C.C. | 2:03.20 |
| Women's kayak (11 miles)—Ilana Effinger, Inwood C.C., New York | 1:20.18 |
| Women's kayak tandem (19 miles)—Nancy Leahy and Teresa DiMarino, Washington C.C. | 2:56.54 |
| Men's canoe (11 miles)—Ray Effinger, Inwood C.C., New York | 1:20.16 |

# *RACQUETBALL*

### NATIONAL CHAMPIONSHIPS

(Belleville, Mich., June 17–24, 1978)

**Men's Events**

Open singles—Jeff Bowman, San Diego, Calif. (defeated Bobby Bolan, Houston, 21–5, 12–21, 11–7, in final)
Open doubles—Mark Malowitz and Jeff Kwartler, Houston
Senior singles—Bill Schmidtke, Minneapolis
Senior doubles—Charlie Garfinkel and Bill King
Masters singles—Bud Muehleisen, San Diego, Calif.
Golden masters singles—Burt Morro, Los Angeles
Golden Masters doubles—Jim DiVito and Sam Rizzio, Chicago
Professional—Marty Hogan, St. Louis (defeated Charlie Brumfield, San Diego, Calif. 21–12, 21–20)

**Women's Events**

Open singles—Alicia Moore, Soquel, Calif. (defeated Linda Prefontaine, Portland, Ore., 21–18, 20–21, 11–7, in final)
Open doubles—Barb Tennesson and Ev Dillon, Minneapolis
Senior singles—Judy Thompson, Davenport, Iowa
Professional—Shannon Wright, San Diego, Calif. (defeated Jennifer Harding, 21–3, 21–8, in final)

# SPEED SKATING

## U.S. OUTDOOR CHAMPIONS

### Men

| | |
|---|---|
| 1959–60 | Ken Bartholomew |
| 1961 | Ed Rudolph |
| 1962 | Floyd Bedbury |
| 1963 | Tom Gray |
| 1964 | Neil Blatchford |
| 1965–66 | Rich Wurster |
| 1967 | Mike Passarella |
| 1968–70 | Peter Cefalu |
| 1971 | Jack Walters |
| 1972 | Barth Levy |
| 1973 | Mike Woods |
| 1974 | Leigh Barczewski, Mike Passarella |
| 1975 | Rich Wurster |
| 1976 | John Wurster |
| 1977 | Jim Chapin |
| 1978 | Bill Heinkel |

### Women

| | |
|---|---|
| 1960 | Mary Novak |
| 1961 | Jean Ashworth |
| 1962 | Jean Omelenchuk |
| 1963 | Jean Ashworth |
| 1964 | Diane White |
| 1965 | Jean Omelenchuk |
| 1966 | Diane White |
| 1967 | Jean Ashworth |
| 1968 | Helen Lutsch |
| 1969 | Sally Blatchford |
| 1970–71 | Sheila Young |
| 1972 | Ruth Moore, Nancy Thorne |
| 1973 | Nancy Class |
| 1974 | Kris Garbe |
| 1975 | Nancy Swider |
| 1976 | Connie Carpenter |
| 1977 | Liz Crowe |
| 1978 | Paula Class, Betsy Davis |

## WORLD SPEED SKATING RECORDS

### Men

| Distance | Time | Skater | Place | Year |
|---|---|---|---|---|
| 500 m | 0:37.00 | Evgeny Kulikov, U.S.S.R. | Medeo, U.S.S.R. | 1975 |
| 1,000 m | 1:14.99 | Eric Heiden, U.S. | Savalen, Norway | 1976 |
| 1,500 m | 1:55.18 | Jan Egil Storholt, Norway | Medeo, U.S.S.R. | 1977 |
| 3,000 m | 4:04.01 | Eric Heiden, U.S. | Inzell, Austria | 1978 |
| 5,000 m | 6:56.90 | Kay Arne Stenshjemmet, Norway | Medeo, U.S.S.R. | 1977 |
| 10,000 m | 14:34.33 | Viktor Leskin, U.S.S.R. | Medeo, U.S.S.R. | 1977 |

### Women

| Distance | Time | Skater | Place | Year |
|---|---|---|---|---|
| 500 m | 0:40.68 | Sheila Young, U.S. | Inzell, Austria | 1976 |
| 1,000 m | 1:23.46 | Tatiana Averina, U.S.S.R. | Medeo, U.S.S.R. | 1975 |
| 1,500 m | 2:07.18 | Holida Vorobieva, U.S.S.R. | Medeo, U.S.S.R. | 1978 |
| 3,000 m | 4:31.00 | Galina Stepanskaya, U.S.S.R. | Medeo, U.S.S.R | 1976 |

## 1978 WORLD CHAMPIONSHIPS

### Men

(Göteborg, Sweden, Feb. 25–26)

| | |
|---|---|
| Champion—Eric Heiden, Madison, Wis. | 169.016 pts |
| 500 m—Eric Heiden | 0:39.01 |
| 1,500 m—Eric Heiden | 2:00.22 |
| 5,000 m—Eric Heiden | 7:20.80 |
| 10,000 m—Sten Stensen, Norway | 15:06.57 |

### Women

(Helsinki, Finland, March 4–5)

| | |
|---|---|
| Champion—Tatiana Averina, U.S.S.R. | 186.891 pts |
| 500 m—Valentina Golovenkina, U.S.S.R. | 0:44.91 |
| 1,000 m—Tatiana Avernina | 1:29.56 |
| 1,500 m—Tatiana Averina | 2:21.44 |
| 3,000 m—Marion Dittmann, East Germany | 4:54.24 |

## 1978 SPRINTS

(Lake Placid, N.Y., Feb. 11–12)

### Men

| | |
|---|---|
| Champion—Erik Heiden, Madison, Wis. | 153.905 pts |
| 500 m (1st race)—Eric Heiden | 0:38.22 |
| 1,000 m (1st race)—Eric Heiden | 1:17.47 |
| 500 m (2nd race)—Frode Ronning, Norway | 0:38.52 |
| 1,000 m (2nd race)—Eric Heiden | 1:16.52 |

### Women

| | |
|---|---|
| Champion—Liubov Sadchikova, U.S.S.R. | 174.670 pts |
| 500 m (1st race)—Beth Heiden, Madison, Wis. | 0:42.97 |
| 1,000 m (1st race)—Kim Kostron, St. Paul, Minn. | 1:28.77 |
| 500 m (2nd race)—Liubov Sadchikova | 0:42.38 |
| 1,000 m (2nd race)—Liubov Sadchikova | 1:28.00 |

## NATIONAL CHAMPIONSHIPS

### Sprints

(West Allis, Wis., Jan. 6–8, 1978)

#### Men's Events

| | |
|---|---|
| 500 meters (1st race)—Eric Heiden, Madison, Wis. | 0:38.60 |
| 500 meters (2nd race)—Eric Heiden | 0:39.85 |
| 1,000 meters (1st race)—Eric Heiden | 1:17.19 |
| 1,000 meters (2nd race)—Eric Heiden | 1:21.29 |

#### Women's Events

| | |
|---|---|
| 500 meters (1st race)—Beth Heiden, Madison, Wis. | 0:43.17 |
| 500 meters (2nd race)—Beth Heiden, | 0:45.31 |
| 1,000 meters (1st race)—Beth Heiden | 1:28.29 |
| 1,000 meters (2nd race)—Beth Heiden | 1:21.29 |

### Outdoor

(St. Paul, Feb. 4–5, 1978)

#### Men's Events

| | |
|---|---|
| Champion—Bill Heinkel, Racine, Wis. | 21 pts |
| 300 meters—Bill Heinkel | 0:26.35 |
| 500 meters—Bill Heinkel | 0:42.93 |
| 1,000 meters—Bill Heinkel | 1:30.39 |
| 800 meters—Bill Heinkel | 1:13.67 |
| 1,500 meters—Jacko Mortell, Wilmette, Ill. | 3:06.94 |
| 5,000 meters—Jacko Mortell | |

#### Other Men's Champions

Intermediate: Jeff Bradley, Davenport, Iowa; junior: Kevin Johnson, Sterling Heights, Minn.; juvenile: Robert Kuspa, Milwaukee; Midget: Brian Tetzlaff, St. Paul

**Women's Events**

Champion—Tie between Paula Class, St. Paul, and Betsy Davis, Montclair, N.J. 16 pts
300 meters—Paula Class 0:31.50
500 meters—Debbie Carlstrom, Des Plaines, Ill. 0:50.36
800 meters—Debbie Carlstrom 1:39.03
1,000 meters—Betsy Davis 2:11.91
1,500 meters—Paula Class 3:16.33

**Other Women's Champions**

Intermediate: Valerie Raimann, Milwaukee; junior: Kelly Lunda, Madison, Wis.; juvenile: Sarah Doctor, Madison, Wis.; midget: Anne Hills, St. Paul

## Indoor

(Evanston, Ill, March 17–19, 1978)

**Men's Events**

Champion—Stan Wisniewski, Sierra Madre, Calif. 16 pts
400 meters—Jacko Mortell, Wilmette, Ill. 0:37.89
800 meters—Stan Wisniewski no time
1,000 meters—Allan Rattray, Anaheim, Calif. 1:39.38
1,500 meters—Jacko Mortell 2:32.49
3,000 meters—Stan Wisniewski 5:27.24

**Other Men's Champions**

Intermediate: Greg Morris, Long Beach, Calif.; junior: Nick Thometz, Minnetonka, Minn.; juvenile: Robert Kuspa, Milwaukee; midget: Martin Pierce, Milwaukee.

**Women's Events**

Champion—Debbie Carlstrom, Des Plaines, Ill. 14 pts
400 m—P. Lyman, Colorado no time
800 m—Peggy Hartrich, St. Louis 1:24.78
1,000 m—Debbie Carlstrom 1:48.25
1,500 m—Debbie Carlstrom no time

**Other Women's Champions**

Intermediate: Lydia Stephans, Northbrook, Ill.; junior: Deanna Prather, Champaign, Ill.; juvenile: Sarah Doctor, Madison, Wis.; midget: Lauri Glynn, Winchester, Mass.

## NORTH AMERICAN CHAMPIONSHIPS
## Outdoor

(West Allis, Wis., Feb. 11–12, 1978)

Men's champion—Jacko Mortell, Wilmette, Ill.
Women's champion—Debbie Carlstrom, Des Plaines, Ill.

## Indoor

(Scarborough, Ont., March 31; April 1–2, 1978)

Men's champion—Scott Drebes, Champaign, Ill.
Women's champion—Cathy Turnbull, Saskatchewan, Canada

## 1978 World Junior Championships

(Ottawa, Canada, March 7–11)

**Men's Events**

Champion—Eric Heiden, Madison Wis. 166.584 pts
(Eric Heiden won all four events)

**Women's Events**

Champion—Beth Heiden, Madison, Wis. 185.128 pts
(Beth Heiden won all four events)

# *CYCLING*

## NATIONAL AMATEUR CHAMPIONS

| | |
|---|---|
| 1951 | Gus Gatto |
| 1952 | Steve Hromjak |
| 1953 | Ronald Rhoads |
| 1954–58 | Jack Disney |
| 1959–63 | James Rossi |
| 1964 | Jack Simes, 3rd |
| 1965 | Jack Simes 3rd |
| 1966 | Jack Disney |
| 1967 | Jack Simes, 3rd |
| 1968 | Jack Disney |
| 1969 | Tim Mountford |
| 1970 | Harry Cutting |
| 1971–72 | Gary Campbell |
| 1973 | Roger Young |
| 1975–75 | Steve Woznick |
| 1976–78 | Leigh Barszewski |

## WORLD CHAMPIONSHIPS

**TRACK EVENTS**

(Munich, West Germany, Aug. 16–27, 1978)

**Amateur—Men**

Sprint—Anton Tkac, Czechoslovakia
Pursuit—Detlef Macha, East Germany
Team pursuit (4 km)—East Germany
Point race (50 km)—Noel deJonckheerre, Belgium 1:01:30.85
1,000-m time trial—Lothar Thoms, East Germany 1:05.23
Motor-pace (50 km)—Rainer Podlesch, W. Germany 42:09.72

**Amateur—Women**

Sprint—Galina Zareva, U.S.S.R.

**Professional**

Sprint—Koichi Nakano, Japan
Pursuit—Gregor Braun, West Germany

## NATIONAL CHAMPIONSHIPS

**U.S. CYCLING FEDERATION**
**Road Racing**

(Milwaukee, July 26–30, 1978)

Men (114 miles)—Dale Stetina, Indianapolis 4:30.24
Junior men (70 miles)—Jeff Bradley, Davenport, Iowa 2:50:48.45
Veterans (40 miles)—Michael Carnahan, Greece, N.Y. 1:36:06
Intermediate boys (22 miles)—Frank Kratzer, Reno, Nev. 0:56:43.52
Midget boys (12 miles)—Gordon Holterman, Jr. Petersburg, Va.
Women (40 miles)—Barbara Hintzen, Grosse Pointe Farms, Mich. 1:41:31.49
Junior women (28 miles)—Sherry Nelsen, St. Louis 1:03:51.37
Veteran women (15 miles)—Jeanne Omelenchuck, Warren, Mich. 0:40:26.83
Intermediate girls (15 miles)—Jacque Bradley, Davenport, Iowa
Midget girls (9 miles)—Elis Lobdell, Indianapolis 0:28:44

### Track Racing—Men

(Kenosha, Wis., Aug. 1-5, 1978)

| | |
|---|---|
| 4,000-m pursuit—Dave Grylls, Grosse Pointe, Mich. | 4:59.27 |
| Team pursuit—Illinois (Scott Holzrichter, Mike Cavanaugh, Danny Van Haute, Scott Andrews) | 4:59.72 |
| Sprint—Leigh Barczewski, West Allis, Wis. | |
| 1,000-m time trial—Jerry Ash, Burbank, Calif. | 1:08.69 |
| Points race—Ron Skarin, Van Nuys, Calif. | |
| Junior men—Eric Baltes, Madison, Wis. | 13 pts |
| Intermediate boys—Robert Krippendorf, Milwaukee | 21 pts |
| Midget boys—Gregg Foster, San Jose, Calif. | 19 pts |

### Track Racing—Women

| | |
|---|---|
| 3,000-m pursuit—Mary Jane Reoch, Philadelphia | 4:08.71 |
| Sprint—Sue Novara, Flint, Mich. | |
| Points race—Mary Jane Reoch | |
| Junior women—Connie Paraskevin, Detroit | 17 pts |
| Intermediate girls—Jacque Bradley, Davenport, Iowa | 19 pts |
| Midget girls—Beth Burger, Allentown, Pa. | 19 pts |

### Time Trials

(Port Washington, Wis., Aug. 1-5, 1978)
(All events 25 miles)

| | |
|---|---|
| Men—Andy Weaver, Coral Springs, Fla. | 56:06.94 |
| Junior men—Dean Meeker, Madison, Wis. | 59:02.44 |
| Veterans—Franz Hammer, Redmond, Wash. | 57:44.82 |
| Masters (50-54)—Milo Hadlock, Salt Lake City, Utah | 1:10:40.89 |
| Women—Esther Salmi, Chester, Conn. | 1:06:04.81 |
| Junior women—Tracy McConachie, Smithton, Ill. | 1:08:18.89 |
| Veterans—Joyce Sulanke, Boise, Idaho | 1:06:44.53 |

# BADMINTON

*Source:* Jack H. van Praag, U.S. Badminton Assn.

## U.S. BADMINTON ASSOCIATION CHAMPIONSHIPS

(Austin, Tex., March 22-25, 1978)

Men's singles—Mike Walker, Manhattan Beach, Calif.
Women's singles—Cheryl Carton, San Diego, Calif.
Men's doubles—John Britton, Scotland, Charles Coakley, Pasadena, Calif.
Women's doubles—Diana Osterhues and Janet Wilts, Pasadena, Calif.
Mixed doubles—Bruce Pontow, Chicago, and Pam Bristol, Flint, Mich.

### Seniors

Men's singles—Jim Poole, Manhattan Beach, Calif.
Men's doubles—Bill Goodman, Wellesley, Mass., and Tom Hed-en, Milwood, N.Y.
Women's doubles—Rosine Lemon, Longlak, N.Y., and Carlene Starkey, San Diego, Calif.
Mixed doubles—Carlono and Rod Starkey, San Diego, Calif.

### 18 and Under

(Austin, Tex., March 19, 1978)

Boys' singles—Geoff Stensland, Manhattan Beach, Calif.
Girls' singles—Lisa De Rousie, Manhattan Beach, Calif.
Boys' doubles—Gary Shelstad and David Collis, Manhattan Beach, Calif.
Girls' doubles—Lisa de Rousie and Anne French, Elmhurst, Ill.
Mixed doubles—David Collis and Tracy McDonald, Manhattan Beach, Calif.

## ALL-ENGLAND CHAMPIONSHIPS

(Wembley Arena, London, March 15-18, 1978)

Men's singles—Liem Swie King, Indonesia
Women's singles—Gillian Gilks, England
Men's doubles—Tjun-Tjun and Johan Wajudi, Indonesia
Women's doubles—Atsuko Tokuda and Mikiko Tokuda, Japan

## WORLD CHAMPIONSHIPS

(Kuala Lumpur, Malaysia, March 15-18, 1978)

Men's singles—Liem Swie King, Indonesia
Women's singles—S. Ng, Malaysia
Men's doubles—Tjun-Tjun and Johan Wahjudi, Indonesia
Women's doubles—Regina Masli and T. Widiastuti, Indonesia
Mixed doubles—Regina Masli-Christian, Indonesia

## WORLD WOMEN'S TEAM

(Auckland, New Zealand, May 13-30, 1978)

Final—Japan 5, Indonesia 2

# DUCKPIN BOWLING

## NATIONAL DUCKPIN BOWLING CONGRESS—1978

(Newington, Conn., April 1-May 7)

| | |
|---|---|
| Men's singles—Jim Simmons, Baltimore | 599 |
| Women's singles—Doris Gravelin, Jewett City, Conn. | 493 |
| Men's doubles—Don Lopardo and Nick Tronsky, Torrington, Conn. | 993 |
| Women's doubles—Chickey Balesano and Cathy Dyak, Manchester, Conn. | 838 |
| Men's team—Troc Pleasure Palace, Baltimore | 2,271 |
| Women's team—I.B.E.W. Local 42, Glastonbury, Conn. | 2,129 |
| Mixed team—Greenway #5, Glen Burnie, Md. | 2,161 |
| Men's booster team—Howie Price, Baltimore | 1,993 |
| Women's booster team—Northern Lites, Newington, Conn. | 1,770 |
| Mixed booster team—Cannon YMCA, Kannapolis, N.C. | 2,001 |

# PADDLE TENNIS

United States Champions—1978
Open doubles—Sol Hauptman and Jeff Fleitman, Brooklyn, N.Y.

# COURT TENNIS

United States Champions—1978
Amateur—Gene Scott, New York
Open—Jimmy Burke (professional), Philadelphia
Senior doubles—William J. Clothier and William T. Vogt, Philadelphia

# SQUASH TENNIS—1978

U.S. Open—Pedro Baccallao, New York

# SPORTS ORGANIZATIONS AND INFORMATION BUREAUS

**Amateur Athletic Union of the U.S.** 3400 West 86th St., Indianapolis, Indiana 46862
**Amateur Bicycle League of America.** *See* United States Cycling Federation
**Amateur Hockey Association of the U.S.** 10 Lake Circle, Colorado Springs, Colo. 80906
**Amateur Skating Union of the U.S.** 4423 West Deming Place, Chicago, Ill. 60639
**Amateur Softball Association.** 2801 N.E. 50th St., P.O. Box 11437, Oklahoma City, Okla. 73111
**Amateur Trapshooting Association of America.** Vandalia, Ohio 45377
**American Amateur Baseball Congress.** Box 4, Battle Creek, Mich. 49016
**American Association (baseball).** P.O. Box 382, Wichita, Kan. 67201
**American Bowling Congress.** 5301 South 76th St., Greendale, Wis. 53129
**American Canoe Association.** 4260 East Evans Ave., Denver, Colo. 80222
**American Casting Association.** P.O. Box 158, Jackson, Ky. 41339
**American Fencers League of America.** 249 Eton Place, Westfield, N.J. 07090
**American Hockey League.** P.O. Box 100, West Springfield, Mass. 01089
**American Horse Shows Association.** 527 Madison Ave., New York, N.Y. 10022
**American Kennel Club.** 51 Madison Ave., New York, N.Y. 10010
**American League (baseball).** 280 Park Ave., New York, N.Y. 10017
**American Motorcycle Association.** P.O. Box 141, Westerville, Ohio 43081
**American Power Boat Association.** 415 Burns Drive, Detroit, Mich. 48214
**American Water Ski Association.** State Route 550 at Carl Floyd Road, P.O. Box 191, Winter Haven, Fla. 33880
**Association of Intercollegiate Athletics for Women.** 1201 16th St. N.W., Washington, D.C.
**Baseball Commissioner.** 75 Rockefeller Plaza, New York, N.Y. 10019
**Baseball Hall of Fame.** Cooperstown, N.Y.
**Bowling Proprietors' Association of America.** P.O. Box 5802, Arlington, Texas 76011
**Central Hockey League.** 5740 Oakland Ave., St. Louis, Mo. 63110
**Eastern College Athletic Conference.** P.O. Box 3, Centerville, Mass. 02632
**Elias Sports Bureau.** 500 Fifth Ave., New York, N.Y. 10036
**Fish and Wildlife Service.** Department of the Interior, Washington, D.C. 20240
**Football Hall of Fame (college).** Kings Mills, Ohio 45034
**Football Hall of Fame (pro).** Canton, Ohio 44708
**International Amateur Athletic Federation.** Halton House, 23 Holborn, London, E. C. 1, England
**International Game Fish Association.** 3000 East Las Olas Blvd., Fort Lauderdale, Fla. 33316
**International League (baseball).** Box 608, Grove City, Ohio 43123
**International Motor Sports Association.** P.O. Box 805, Fairfield, Conn. 06430
**International Olympic Committee.** Chateau de Vidy, Lausanne, Switzerland
**The Jockey Club.** 300 Park Ave., New York, N.Y. 10022
**Ladies Professional Golf Association.** 919 Third Ave., New York, N.Y. 10022
**Little League Baseball.** Williamsport, Pa. 17701
**National Archery Association.** 1951 Geraldson Drive, Lancaster, Pa. 17601
**National Association for Girls and Women in Sports.** 1201 16th St. N.W., Washington, D.C.
**National Association of Amateur Oarsmen.** 4 Boathouse Row, Philadelphia, Pa. 19130
**National Association of Intercollegiate Athletics.** 1221 Baltimore St., Kansas City, Mo. 64105
**National Association of Professional Baseball Leagues (minors).** P.O. Box A, St. Petersburg, Fla. 33731
**National Association for Stock Car Auto Racing.** P.O. Box K, Daytona Beach, Fla. 32015
**National Baseball Congress.** Wichita, Kan. 67201
**National Basketball Association.** Olympic Tower, 645 Fifth Ave., New York, N.Y. 10022
**National Collegiate Athletic Association.** P.O. Box 1906, Shawnee Mission, Kan. 66222
**National Duck Pin Bowling Congress.** 711–14th St. N.W., Washington, D.C. 20005
**National Field Archery Association.** Rt. 2, Box 514, Redlands, Calif. 92373
**National Football Foundation.** 201 East 42nd St., New York, N.Y. 10017. *See also:* Football Hall of Fame (college)
**National Football League.** 410 Park Ave., New York, N.Y. 10022
**National Hockey League.** 922 Sun Life Bldg., Montreal, Que., Canada
**National Horseshoe Pitchers Association.** Route 5, Lucasville, Ohio 45648
**National Hot Rod Association.** P.O. Box 150, North Hollywood, Calif. 91603
**National Junior College Athletic Association.** P.O. Box 1586, Hutchinson, Kan. 67501
**National Lawn Tennis Hall of Fame.** Newport Casino, Newport, R.I., 02840
**National League (baseball).** 1 Rockefeller Plaza, New York, N.Y. 10019
**National Rifle Association of America.** 1600 Rhode Island Ave., N.W., Washington, D.C. 20036
**National Skeet Shooting Association.** P.O. Box 28188, San Antonio, Tex. 78228
**New York Racing Association.** P.O. Box 90, Jamaica, N.Y. 11417
**New York State Athletic Commission (boxing).** 226 W. 47th St., New York, N.Y. 10036
**National Shuffleboard Association.** 6815 Lake Ave., West Palm Beach, Fla. 33405
**North American Yacht Racing Union.** *See* United States Yacht Racing Union
**North American Soccer League.** 1133 Avenue of the Americas, New York, N.Y. 10036
**Pacific Coast League (baseball).** P.O. Box 530, Paoli, Pa. 19301
**Professional Bowlers Association.** 1720 Merriman Road, Akron, Ohio 44313
**Professional Golfers' Association of America.** Box 12458, Lake Park, Fla. 33403
**Rodeo Cowboys Association.** 2929 W. 19th Ave., Denver, Colo. 80204
**Roller Skating Rink Operators Association.** P.O. Box 81846, Lincoln, Neb. 68501
**Sports Car Club of America.** P.O. Box 22476, Denver, Colo. 80222

**Tennis Hall of Fame.** *See* National Lawn Tennis Hall of Fame
**Thoroughbred Racing Associations of the U.S.** 3000 Marcus Ave., Lake Success, N.Y. 11040
**Track and Field Hall of Fame.** Charleston, W.Va.
**United States of America Roller Skating Confederation.** 7700 "A" Street, Lincoln, Neb. 68501
**U.S. Auto Club.** 49 W. 16th St., Speedway, Ind. 46202
**United States Badminton Association.** 787 South Orange Grove Blvd., Unit 9, Pasadena, Calif. 91105
**U.S. Chess Federation.** 186 Route 9W, New Windsor, N.Y. 12550
**U.S. Cycling Federation.** Box 669, Wall Street Station, New York, N.Y. 10005
**U.S. Figure Skating Association.** 575 Boylston St., Boston, Mass. 02116
**U.S. Golf Association.** Far Hills, N.J. 07931
**U.S. Handball Association.** 4101 Dempster St., Skokie, Ill. 60077
**U.S. Men's Curling Association.** 2232 Vermillion Road, Duluth, Minn. 55803
**U.S. Olympic Committee.** 1750 East Boulder Street, Colorado Springs, Colo. 80909
**U.S. Olympic Training Center.** P.O. Box 4000, Colorado Springs, Colo. 80930
**U.S. Parachute Association.** 806-15th St. N.W., Washington, D.C. 20005
**U.S. Polo Association.** 1301 W. 22nd St., Oak Brook, Ill. 60521
**U.S. Ski Association.** 1726 Champa St., Denver, Colorado 80202
**U.S. Ski Team.** P.O. Box 100, Park City, Utah 84060
**U.S. Soccer Federation.** 350 Fifth Ave., New York, N.Y. 10001
**U.S. Squash Racquets Association.** 211 Ford Road, Bala-Cynwyd, Pa., 19004
**U.S. Table Tennis Association.** 3466 Bridgeland Drive, Bridgeland Square Building, St. Louis, Mo. 63044
**U.S. Tennis Association.** 51 E. 42nd St., New York, N.Y. 10017
**U.S. Trotting Association.** 750 Michigan Ave., Columbus, Ohio 43215
**U.S. Volleyball Association.** 557 Fourth Street, San Francisco, Calif. 94107
**U.S. Women's Curling Association.** 635 Chatham Road, Glenview, Ill. 60025
**U.S. Yacht Racing Union.** P.O. Box 209, Goat Island, Newport, R.I. 02840
**Women's International Bowling Congress.** 5301 S. 76th St., Greendale, Wis. 53129
**World Hockey Association.** One Financial Plaza, Hartford, Conn. 06103

# WEIGHT LIFTING

## A.A.U. NATIONAL CHAMPIONSHIPS

(York, Pa., June 10–11, 1978)

| | Snatch | C&J[1] | Total |
|---|---|---|---|
| 114½ lb—Ronald Crawley, Washington, D.C. | 165¼ | 220¼ | 385¾ |
| 123½ lb—Stewart Thornburgh, Charleston, Ill. | 209¼ | 275½ | 485 |
| 132¼ lb—Don Warner, York, Pa. | 242½ | 303 | 545½ |
| 148¾ lb—Don Abrahamson, Maitland, Fla | 253½ | 319½ | 573 |
| 165¼ lb—David Jones, Eastman, Ga. | 286½ | 363¾ | 650¼ |
| 181¾ lb—Michael Karchut, Sayre Park, Chicago | 330½ | 413¼ | 743¾ |
| 198¾ lb—Lee James, York, Pa. | 352½ | 429¾ | 782¼ |
| 220½ lb—Kurt Setterberg, Warren, Ohio | 336 | 424¼ | 760¼ |
| 242½ lb—Mark Cameron, York, Pa. | 352½ | 462¾ | 815¼ |
| Super heavyweight—Tom Stock, Belleville, Ill. | 363¾ | 468¼ | 832 |

1. Clean and jerk.

# WATER POLO

## WORLD CHAMPIONSHIPS

(West Berlin, Aug. 18–28, 1978)

Champion—Italy; 2, Hungary; 3, Yugoslavia

## A.A.U. National Champions—1978

Men's outdoor—Concord, Calif.
Women's outdoor—City of Commerce, Calif.
Women's indoor—Long Beach, Calif.

## COLLEGIATE

N.C.A.A. (November 1977)—California–Berkeley

# WATER SKIING

## NATIONAL CHAMPIONSHIPS—1978

(Brighton, Mich., Aug. 23–27)

### Men's Open

| | |
|---|---|
| Overall—Ricky McCormick, Winter Haven, Fla. | 2,663 pts |
| Slalom—Bob LaPoint, Castro Valley, Calif. | 55 buoys |
| Tricks—Cory Pickos, Eagle Lake, Fla. | 6,080 pts |
| Jumping—Robert Kempton, Tampa, Fla. | 162 ft |

### Women's Open

| | |
|---|---|
| Overall—Deena Brush, W. Sacramento, Calif. | 3,021 pts |
| Slalom—Deena Brush | 56 buoys |
| Tricks—Cyndi M. Benzel, Prior Lake, Minn. | 3,750 pts |
| Jumping—Deena Brush | 118 ft |

### Men's Division I

| | |
|---|---|
| Overall—David Golly, Naples, Fla. | 2,459 pts |
| Slalom—Bob Knoedler, Whitmore Lake, Mich. | 47 buoys |
| Tricks—Brad Wahl, Prior Lake, Minn. | 4,160 pts |
| Jumping—Tom Hinman, Pine Meadow, Conn. | 154 ft |

### Women's Division

| | |
|---|---|
| Overall—Lisa Nock, Englewood, Colo. | 2,734 pts |
| Slalom—Pam Zeigler, Parkman, Ohio | 46 buoys |
| Tricks—Gun Evans, Miami, Fla. | 2,990 pts |
| Jumping—Lisa Nock | 111 ft |

### Senior Men

| | |
|---|---|
| Overall—Ken White, Bynum, Tex. | 2,746 pts |
| Slalom—J.D. Morgan, Pensacola, Fla. | 51 buoys |
| Tricks—Robert Hurm, St. Mary's, Ohio | 4,640 pts |
| Jumping—J.D. Morgan | 127 ft |

### Senior Women

| | |
|---|---|
| Overall—Vicki Johndrow, Odessa, Fla. | 3,445 pts |
| Slalom—Vicki Johndrow | 44½ buoys |
| Tricks—Thelma Salmas, Canyon Lake, Calif. | 3,410 pts |
| Jumping—Vicki Johndrow | 111 ft |

**Veteran Men**

| | |
|---|---|
| Overall—Harry Price, Libertyville, Ill. | 2,749 pts |
| Slalom—Johnny Matranga, Sacramento, Calif. | 40 buoys |
| Tricks—Harry Price | 3,300 pts |
| Jumping—Lloyd Meredith, Reddick, Ill. | 116 ft |

**Other Divisions—Overall**

| | |
|---|---|
| Men's Division II—Frankie Dees, Lakeland, Fla. | 2,844 pts |
| Boys—Sammy Duvall, Greenville, S.C. | 3,253 pts |
| Girls—Karin Roberge, San Diego, Calif. | 2,733 pts |
| Junior boys—Billy Allen, San Mateo, Calif. | 2,458 pts |
| Junior girls—Nathalie Roberge, San Diego, Calif. | 3,516 pts |

### Masters Tournament—1978
(Callaway Gardens, Ga., July 8–9)

**Men's Division**

| | |
|---|---|
| Overall—Mike Hazelwood, England | 3,038 pts |
| Slalom—Mike Hazelwood | 55¼ buoys |
| Tricks—Patrice Martin, Graslin, France | 6,090 pts |
| Jumping—Lucky Lowe, Birmingham, Ala. | 178 ft |

**Women's Division**

| | |
|---|---|
| Overall—Cindy Todd, Pierson, Fla. | 2,447 pts |
| Slalom—Patsy Messner, Ottawa, Canada | 50 buoys |
| Tricks—Pam Folsom, Boynton Beach, Fla. | 4,360 pts |
| Jumping—Deena Brush, W. Sacramento, Calif. | 117 ft |

# TRAPSHOOTING

### 1978 GRAND AMERICAN TOURNAMENT
(Vandalia, Ohio, Aug. 12–19)

**Grand American Handicap**

| | |
|---|---|
| Men—Reg Jachimowski, Antioch, Ill. (27-yd handicap) | 100 |
| Women—Frieda Summer, Washington, Ind. (21) | 98 |
| Junior—Tie between Dave Durant, Waukesha, Wis. (22) and Gary Guydosh, Bloomingdale, Ohio (19) | 98 |
| Veteran—Carl Fritz, Cincinnati (20½) | 98 |
| Sub junior—Scott Baxter, Fort Wayne, Ind. (17) | 97 |

**All-Around**

| | |
|---|---|
| Men—Leo Harrison 3rd, Hannibal, Mo. | 396 |
| Women—Loral I. Delaney, Anoka, Minn. | 376 |
| Junior—Dave Durant, Waukesha, Wis. | 384 |

**Overall**

| | |
|---|---|
| Men—Dan Bonillas, Los Banos, Calif. | 979 |
| Women—Loral I. Delaney, Anoka, Minn. | 942 |
| Junior—Dave Durant, Waukesha, Wis. | 956 |

**Doubles**

| | |
|---|---|
| Men—Leo Harrison 3rd, Hannibal, Mo. | 100 |
| Women—Barbara Yochem, Glendora, Calif. | 93 |
| Junior—Storm Mitchell, Murray, Utah | 98 |

# SKEET SHOOTING

### NATIONAL SKEET SHOOTING ASSOCIATION WORLD CHAMPIONSHIPS—1978
(San Antonio, Tex., July 31–Aug. 6)

**High Overall**

| | |
|---|---|
| Men—Walter Badorek, Klamath Falls, Ore. | 550 |
| Women—Ila Hill, Birmingham, Mich. | 543 |
| Senior—Tom Hanzel, San Antonio, Tex. | 535 |
| Veteran—Tom Sanfilipo, Fairfield, Calif. | 532 |
| Junior—John R. Dail, Anderson, S.C. | 546 |
| Junior women—Kathryn Drennan, Ada, Okla. | 539 |
| Collegiate—Chip Youngblood, Fort Lauderdale, Fla. | 546 |

**Individual Gun**

| | |
|---|---|
| 12-gauge, men—Chip Youngblood | 250 |
| 12-gauge, women—Gena Clark, Del Mar, Calif. | 250 |
| 20-gauge, men—John R. Dail | 100 |
| 20-gauge, women—Ila Hill | 99 |
| 28-gauge, men—John R. Dail | 100 |
| 28-gauge, women—Virginia Schmidt, Prior Lake, Minn. | 100 |
| 410-gauge, men—Walter Badorek | 100 |
| 410-gauge, women—Susan Pockmire, Pinehurst, N.C. | 98 |

**Champion of Champions**

| | |
|---|---|
| Men—Dave Starret, New Boston, Ohio | 100 |
| Women—Conni Place, Pompano Beach, Fla. | 97 |

# POLO

### U.S. POLO ASSOCIATION CHAMPIONSHIPS—1978

Open—Abercrombie and Kent, Oak Brook, Ill. (Geoffrey J. Kent, Stuart MacKenzie, Antone Herrara, Donald Wigdahl) 7, Tulsa 6
College—California-Davis defeated Xavier, 13–7, in final
Butler Handicap—Smallwood, Columbia, S.C.
Continental Cup (14 goals)—Dahlwood, Oak Brook, Ill.
Copper Cup (10 goals)—Village Farms, Gilbertsville, N.Y.
Delegates Cup (8 goals)—Boca Raton, Fla.
Gold Cup (18–22 goals)—Abercrombie and Kent
National President's Cup (8 goals)—Fairlane, Oak Brook, Ill.

# KARATE

### A.A.U. NATIONAL CHAMPIONSHIPS—1978
(Hackensack, N.J., July 22–23)

**Men's Kata**

Advanced—Domingo Llanos, Haverstraw, N.Y.
Intermediate—Domingo Olivo, Haverstraw, N.Y.
Novice—Thomas Cupo, Hawthorne, N.J.
Junior boys (16–17)—Vinny Cammarata, New York

**Men's Kumite**

Advanced—Tokey Hill, Chillicothe, Ohio
Intermediate—Humberto Fontana, Miami, Fla.
Novice—Grant Frazer, Cleveland
Junior boys (16–17)—Kevin Heard, Cleveland

**Men's Weapons Kata**

Winnter—Yao Li, Revere, Mass.

**Women's Kata**

Advanced—Ellen Beal, Barrington, N.H.
Intermediate—Barbara Merkley, Woodcliff Lake, N.J.
Novice—Irene Crevani, Mahwah, N.J.
Junior girls (16–17)—Gina Schiavone, New Rochelle, N.Y.

**Women's Kumite**

Advanced—Rosine Hatem, Methuen, Mass.
Intermediate—Debbie Mazzochetti, Rochester, N.Y.
Novice—Gwen Hoffman, Freehold, N.J.
Junior girls (16–17)—Gina Schiavone, New Rochelle, N.Y.

# JUDO

## A.A.U. NATIONAL CHAMPIONSHIPS

(Chicago, April 14–15, 1978)

**Men**

132 lb—Keith Nakasone, San Jose, Calif.
143 lb—James Martin, Sacramento, Calif.
156 lb—Steven Seck, Los Angeles
172 lb—Tefmoc Jonston-Ono, New York
189 lb—Clyde Worthen, New Milford, N.J.
Under 209 lb—Irwin Cohen, Wheeling, Ill.
Over 209 lb—John Saylor, Columbus, Ohio
Open—Michinori Ishibashi, Fort Worth, Tex.

**Women**

106 lb—Ann Marie Waddell, Hopkins, Minn.
114 lb—Lynn Lewis, Revere, Mass.
123 lb—Darlene Hill, Memphis, Tenn.
134 lb—Pamela Adams, Beverly, Mass.
145 lb—Dolores Brodie, San Jose, Calif.
Under 158 lb—Amy Kublin, Sharon, Mass.
Over 158 lb—Margaret Castro, New York
Open—Barbara Fest, Salem, Mass.

# TAE KWON DO

## A.A.U. NATIONAL CHAMPIONSHIPS

(Washington, D.C., April 8–9, 1978)

**Men**

Finweight—My Tan Nguyen, Fort Myers, Fla.
Flyweight—Mike Vasquez, Port Huron, Mich.
Bantamweight—William Kim, Honolulu
Featherweight—Oren Gautreaux, Raytown, Mo.
Lightweight—Greg Fears, Columbus, Ohio
Welterweight—Michael O'Malley, Boston
Middleweight—Larry Nell, Columbus, Ohio
Light Heavyweight—Leroy Hopkins, Baltimore
Heavyweight—John Holloway, Washington, D.C.
Forms—Dae Sung Lee, Hawaii
Outstanding Performer—Greg Fears
Team—Potomac Valley

**Women**

Finweight—Mary Hostetler, Ames, Iowa
Flyweight—Brenda Waller, Washington, D.C.
Bantamweight—Sunny Graff, Columbus, Ohio
Featherweight—Ayoka Brown, Baltimore
Lightweight—Kathy Jones, North Street, Mich.
Welterweight—Thedia Jones, Washington D.C.
Middleweight—Marcia Hall, Mountainview, Calif.
Heavyweight—Christine Coleman, Baltimore
Open—Darlene Jeffries, Sewickley, Pa.
Forms—Kathy Jones
Outstanding Performer—Ayoka Brown

# CURLING

## NATIONAL CHAMPIONS

| | |
|---|---|
| 1966 | Fargo, N.D. (Joe Zbacnik, skip; Bruce Roberts, Mike O'Leary, Gerald Toutant) |
| 1967 | Seattle (Bruce Roberts, skip; Doug Walker, Tom Fitzpatrick, John Wright) |
| 1968–69 | Superior, Wis. (Bud Somerville, skip; Bill Strum, Al Gagne, Thomas Wright) |
| 1970 | Grafton, N.D. (Art Tallackson, skip; Trueman Thompson, Raymond Holt, Glenn Gilleshammer) |
| 1971 | Edmore, N.D. (Dal Dalziel, skip; Rodney Melland, Dennis Melland, Clark Sampson) |
| 1972 | Grafton, N.D. (Robert L. LaBonte, skip; Frank L. Aasand, John O. Aasand, Ray Morgan) |
| 1973 | Winchester, Mass. (Charles Reeves, Jr., skip; Barry Blanchard, Henry Shean, Douglas Carlson) |
| 1974 | Superior, Wis. (Bud Somerville, skip; Tom Locken, Bill Strum, Bob Nichols)[1] |
| 1975 | Seattle Granite Club (Ed Risling, skip; Chuck Lundgren, Gary Schnee, Dave Tellvik) |
| 1976 | Hibbing, Minn. (Bruce Roberts, skip; Jerry Scott, Gary Kieffmall, Joe Roberts)[1] |
| 1977 | Hibbing, Minn. (Bruce Roberts, skip; Paul Pustovar, Gary Kleffman, Jerry Scott) |
| 1978 | Superior, Wis. (Bob Nichols, skip; Bob Christman, Tom Lochen, Bill Strum)[1] |

1. Won World Championship.

## WORLD CHAMPIONSHIP

(Winnipeg, Canada, March 27–April 2, 1978)

Final—United States (Bob Nichols, skip; Bob Christman, Tom Locken, Bill Strum) defeated Norway (Kristian Soerum, skip), 6–4
Semifinals—United States defeated Sweden (Tom Schaeffer, skip), 6–5; Norway defeated Canada (Mike Chernoff, skip), 6–2

## U.S. CHAMPIONSHIPS—1978

Men (Utica, N.Y., March 6–11)—Wisconsin (Superior), won all 11 matches
Women (Duluth, Feb. 22–25)—Wisconsin (Wausau: Sandy Robarge, skip; Ellen Collins, Jo Shannon, Virginia Morrison)

## OTHER MAJOR BONSPIELS—1978

Canadian Championship (Alberta)—(Mike Chernoff, skip)
Gordon Medal (Schenectady, N.Y.)—Plainfield (N.J.) C.C. (George Kornstad, skip)

# MOTORBOATING

## UNLIMITED HYDROPLANES

Champion Spark Plug Regatta (Miami, Fla., June 4, 1978)—Atlas Van Lines, Bill Muncey, La Mesa, Calif., driver; speed in final heat: 100.626 mph
Spirit of Detroit Trophy (Detroit, June 25, 1978)—Atlas Van Lines, Muncey; 106.236 mph
A.P.B.A. Gold Cup (Owensboro, Ky., July 2, 1978)—Atlas Van Lines, Muncey; 104.166 mph
Indiana Governor's Cup (Madison, Ind., July 9, 1978)—Atlas Van Lines, Muncey; 109.409 mph
Columbia Cup (Tri-Cities, Wash., July 30, 1978)—Miss Budweiser, Ron Snyder; 109.463 mph
Squire Shop Regatta (Seattle, Aug. 6, 1978)—Atlas Van Lines, Muncey; 107.463 mph
Jack-in-the-Box Regatta (San Diego, Calif., Sept. 17, 1978)—Atlas Van Lines, Muncey; 121.261 mph
1978 champion boat—Atlas Van Lines, 7,725 pts
1978 champion driver—Bill Muncey, La Mesa, Calif., 7,725 pts

## OFFSHORE RACES

Bacardi Trophy (Miami, 204 miles, May 13, 1978)—Joey Ippolito, Hallandale, Fla.; average speed: 74 mph
Grand Prix (Point Pleasant, N.J. 178 miles, July 12, 1978)—Billy Martin, Clark, N.J.; 78.43 mph

# LACROSSE

## NATIONAL INTERCOLLEGIATE CHAMPIONS

| | |
|---|---|
| 1946 | Navy |
| 1947–48 | Johns Hopkins |
| 1949 | Johns Hopkins, Navy |
| 1950 | Johns Hopkins |
| 1951 | Army, Princeton |
| 1952 | Virginia, R.P.I. |
| 1953 | Princeton |
| 1954 | Navy |
| 1955–56 | Maryland |
| 1957 | Johns Hopkins |
| 1958 | Army |
| 1959 | Army, Johns Hopkins, Maryland |
| 1960 | Navy |
| 1961 | Army, Navy |
| 1962–66 | Navy |
| 1967 | Johns Hopkins, Maryland, Navy |
| 1968 | Johns Hopkins |
| 1969 | Army, Johns Hopkins |
| 1970 | Johns Hopkins, Navy, Virginia |
| 1971[1] | Cornell |
| 1972 | Virginia |
| 1973 | Maryland |
| 1974 | Johns Hopkins |
| 1975 | Maryland |
| 1976–77 | Cornell |
| 1978 | Johns Hopkins |

1. First year of N.C.A.A. Championship Tournaments.

## NATIONAL COLLEGIATE A.A.

### DIVISION I

**Final**

(New Brunswick, N.J., May 27, 1978)
Johns Hopkins 13, Cornell 8

**Semifinals**

Johns Hopkins 19, Maryland 11
Cornell 13, Navy 7

**Quarterfinals**

Johns Hopkins 12, Hofstra 8
Cornell 12, Washington and Lee, 2
Navy defeated Army
Maryland defeated Virginia

### DIVISION II

**Final**

(Geneva, N.Y., May 20, 1978)
Roanoke 14, Hobart 13

**Semifinals**

Hobart 24, Cortland State 9
Roanoke 16, University of Maryland—Baltimore 10

**Second round**

Hobart 29, Ithaca 6
Cortland State 13, Towson 12
Maryland—Baltimore 16, Washington College 10
Roanoke 13, Adelphi 8

**First round**

Adelphi 23, Baltimore 15
Towson 24, New Haven 5
Washington College 10, Ohio Wesleyan 6
Ithaca 15, Salisbury 9
(Cortland State, Hobart, Roanoke and Maryland—Baltimore drew byes)

## U.S. WOMEN'S LACROSSE ASSOCIATION NATIONAL COLLEGIATE CHAMPIONSHIP

**Final**

(Harrisonburg, Va., May 26–28, 1978)
Penn State 9, Maryland 3

**Third place**

University of Massachusetts 5, East Stroudsburg 4, in overtime

**Fifth place**

Yale defeated Delaware

**Seventh Place**

James Madison 7, Rutgers 3

# RODEO

## RODEO COWBOYS' ASSOCIATION, ALL-AROUND COWBOY

| | |
|---|---|
| 1953 | Bill Linderman |
| 1954 | Buck Rutherford |
| 1955 | Casey Tibbs |
| 1956–59 | Jim Shoulders |
| 1960 | Harry Tompkins |
| 1961 | Benny Reynolds |
| 1962 | Tom Nesmith |
| 1963–65 | Dean Oliver |
| 1966–70 | Larry Mahan |
| 1971–72 | Phil Lyne |
| 1973 | Larry Mahan |
| 1974 | Tom Ferguson |
| 1975 | Leo Camarillo and Tom Ferguson |
| 1976–77 | Tom Ferguson |

# BILLIARDS

## THREE-CUSHION—1978

Men's world—Raymond Ceulemans, Belgium

## POCKET BILLIARDS—1978

Men's world—Ray Martin, Fair Lawn, N.J.
Women's world—Jean Balukas, Brooklyn, N.Y.

# FRISBEE

## WORLD CHAMPIONSHIPS

(Pasadena, Calif., Aug. 23–27, 1978)

Men's overall—Krae Van Sickle, New York
Women's overall—Laura Engel, Venice, Calif.
Men's distance—Joseph Youngman, L'Anse, Mich. 333 ft 1 in.
Dog "catch-and-fetch"—Dick, owned by Jim Strickler, Severna Park, Md.

# TENNIS

Lawn tennis is a comparatively modern modification of the ancient game of court tennis. Major Walter Clopton Wingfield thought that something like court tennis might be played outdoors on lawns, and in December, 1873, at Nantclwyd, Wales, he introduced his new game under the name of *Sphairistike* at a lawn party. The game was a success and spread rapidly, but the name was a total failure and almost immediately disappeared when all the players and spectators began to refer to the new game as "lawn tennis." In the early part of 1874, a young lady named Mary Ewing Outerbridge returned from Bermuda to New York, bringing with her the implements and necessary equipment of the new game, which she had obtained from a British Army supply store in Bermuda. Miss Outerbridge and friends played the first game of lawn tennis in the United States on the grounds of the Staten Island Cricket and Baseball Club in the spring of 1874.

For a few years, the new game went along in haphazard fashion until about 1880, when standard measurements for the court and standard equipment within definite limits became the rule. In 1881, the U.S. Lawn Tennis Association (whose name was changed in 1975 to U.S. Tennis Association) was formed and conducted the first national championship at Newport, R.I. The international matches for the Davis Cup began with a series between the British and United States players on the courts of the Longwood Cricket Club, Chestnut Hill, Mass., in 1900, with the home players winning.

Professional tennis, which got its start in 1926 when the French star Suzanne Lenglen was paid $50,000 for a tour, received full recognition in 1968. Staid old Wimbledon, the London home of what are considered the world championships, let the pros compete. This decision ended a long controversy over open tennis and changed the format of the competition. The United States championships at Forest Hills switched, too. Pro tours for men and women became worldwide in play that continued throughout the year.

## DAVIS CUP CHAMPIONSHIPS

No matches in 1901, 1910, 1915–18, and 1940–45.

| | |
|---|---|
| 1900 | United States 3, British Isles 0 |
| 1902 | United States 3, British Isles 2 |
| 1903 | British Isles 4, United States 1 |
| 1904 | British Isles 5, Belgium 0 |
| 1905 | British Isles 5, United States 0 |
| 1906 | British Isles 5, United States 0 |
| 1907 | Australasia 3, British Isles 2 |
| 1908 | Australasia 3, United States 2 |
| 1909 | Australasia 5, United States 0 |
| 1911 | Australasia 5, United States 0 |
| 1912 | British Isles 3, Australasia 2 |
| 1913 | United States 3, British Isles 2 |
| 1914 | Australasia 3, United States 2 |
| 1919 | Australasia 4, British Isles 1 |
| 1920 | United States 5, Australasia 0 |
| 1921 | United States 5, Japan 0 |
| 1922 | United States 4, Australasia 1 |
| 1923 | United States 4, Australasia 1 |
| 1924 | United States 5, Australasia 0 |
| 1925 | United States 5, France 0 |
| 1926 | United States 4, France 1 |
| 1927 | France 3, United States 2 |
| 1928 | France 4, United States 1 |
| 1929 | France 3, United States 2 |
| 1930 | France 4, United States 1 |
| 1931 | France 3, Great Britain 2 |
| 1932 | France 3, United States 2 |
| 1933 | Great Britain 3, France 2 |
| 1934 | Great Britain 4, United States 1 |
| 1935 | Great Britain 5, United States 0 |
| 1936 | Great Britain 3, Australia 2 |
| 1937 | United States 4, Great Britain 1 |
| 1938 | United States 3, Australia 2 |
| 1939 | Australia 3, United States 2 |
| 1946 | United States 5, Australia 0 |
| 1947 | United States 4, Australia 1 |
| 1948 | United States 5, Australia 0 |
| 1949 | United States 4, Australia 1 |
| 1950 | Australia 4, United States 1 |
| 1951 | Australia 3, United States 2 |
| 1952 | Australia 4, United States 1 |
| 1953 | Australia 3, United States 2 |
| 1954 | United States 3, Australia 2 |
| 1955 | Australia 5, United States 0 |
| 1956 | Australia 5, United States 0 |
| 1957 | Australia 3, United States 2 |
| 1958 | United States 3, Australia 2 |
| 1959 | Australia 3, United States 2 |
| 1960 | Australia 4, Italy 1 |
| 1961 | Australia 5, Italy 0 |
| 1962 | Australia 5, Mexico 0 |
| 1963 | United States 3, Australia 2 |
| 1964 | Australia 3, United States 2 |
| 1965 | Australia 4, Spain 1 |
| 1966 | Australia 4, India 1 |
| 1967 | Australia 4, Spain 1 |
| 1968 | United States 4, Australia 1 |
| 1969 | United States 5, Romania 0 |
| 1970 | United States 5, West Germany 0 |
| 1971 | United States 3, Romania 2 |
| 1972 | United States 3, Romania 2 |
| 1973 | Australia 5, United States 0 |
| 1974 | South Africa (Default by India) |
| 1975 | Sweden 3, Czechoslovakia 2 |
| 1976 | Italy 4, Chile 1 |
| 1977 | Australia 3, Italy 1 |

## FEDERATION CUP CHAMPIONSHIPS

World team competition for women conducted by International Lawn Tennis Federation

| | |
|---|---|
| 1963 | United States 2, Australia 1 |
| 1964 | Australia 2, United States 1 |
| 1965 | Australia 2, United States 1 |
| 1966 | United States 3, West Germany 0 |
| 1967 | United States 2, Britain 0 |
| 1968 | Australia 3, Netherlands 0 |
| 1969 | United States 2, Australia 1 |
| 1970 | Australia 3, West Germany 0 |
| 1971 | Australia 3, Britain 0 |
| 1972 | South Africa 2, Britain 1 |
| 1973 | Australia 3, South Africa 0 |
| 1974 | Australia 2, United States 1 |
| 1975 | Czechoslovakia 3, Australia 0 |
| 1976 | United States 2, Australia 1 |
| 1977 | United States 2, Australia 1 |

## FOUR PLAYERS WIN GRAND SLAM OF TENNIS

Only four players, two men and two women, have won the Grand Slam of Tennis by winning the Australian, French, Wimbledon, and United States singles championships. Rod Laver of Australia did it twice, in 1962 and again in 1969 when the tourneys were opens. Don Budge, an American, was the first to complete the slam in 1938. Maureen Connolly of California in 1953 was the first woman to take the four titles. Margaret Smith Court of Australia won them all in 1970.

## U.S. CHAMPIONS

### Singles—Men

**NATIONAL**

|  |  |
|---|---|
| 1881–87 | Richard D. Sears |
| 1888–89 | Henry Slocum, Jr. |
| 1890–92 | Oliver S. Campbell |
| 1893–94 | Robert D. Wrenn |
| 1895 | Fred H. Hovey |
| 1896–97 | Robert D. Wrenn |
| 1898–1900 | Malcolm Whitman |
| 1901–02 | William A. Larned |
| 1903 | Hugh L. Doherty |
| 1904 | Holcombe Ward |
| 1905 | Beals C. Wright |
| 1906 | William J. Clothier |
| 1907–11 | William A. Larned |
| 1912–13 | Maurice McLoughlin[1] |
| 1914 | R. N. Williams II |
| 1915 | William Johnston |
| 1916 | R. N. William II |
| 1917–18 | R. Lindley Murray[2] |
| 1919 | William Johnston |
| 1920–25 | Bill Tilden |
| 1926–27 | Jean Rene Lacoste |
| 1928 | Henri Cochet |
| 1929 | Bill Tilden |
| 1930 | John H. Doeg |
| 1931–32 | Ellsworth Vines |
| 1933–34 | Fred J. Perry |
| 1935 | Wilmer L. Allison |
| 1936 | Fred J. Perry |
| 1937–38 | Don Budge |
| 1939 | Robert L. Riggs |
| 1940 | Donald McNeill |
| 1941 | Robert L. Riggs |
| 1942 | Fred Schroeder |
| 1943 | Joseph Hunt |
| 1944–45 | Frank Parker |
| 1946–47 | Jack Kramer |
| 1948–49 | Richard Gonzales |
| 1950 | Arthur Larsen |
| 1951–52 | Frank Sedgman |
| 1953 | Tony Trabert |
| 1954 | Vic Seixas |
| 1955 | Tony Trabert |
| 1956 | Ken Rosewall |
| 1957 | Mal Anderson |
| 1958 | Ashley Cooper |
| 1959–60 | Neale Fraser |
| 1961 | Roy Emerson |
| 1962 | Rod Laver |
| 1963 | Rafael Osuna |
| 1964 | Roy Emerson |
| 1965 | Manuel Santana |
| 1966 | Fred Stolle |
| 1967 | John Newcombe |
| 1968 | Arthur Ashe[3] |
| 1969 | Stan Smith[3] |

**OPEN**

|  |  |
|---|---|
| 1968 | Arthur Ashe |
| 1969 | Rod Laver |
| 1970 | Ken Rosewall |
| 1971 | Stan Smith |
| 1972 | Ilie Nastase |
| 1973 | John Newcombe |
| 1974 | Jimmy Connors |
| 1975 | Manuel Orantes |
| 1976 | Jimmy Connors |
| 1977 | Guillermo Vilas |
| 1978 | Jimmy Connors |

### Singles—Women

**NATIONAL**

|  |  |
|---|---|
| 1887 | Ellen F. Hansel |
| 1888–89 | Bertha Townsend |
| 1890 | Ellen C. Roosevelt |
| 1891–92 | Mabel E. Cahill |
| 1893 | Aline M. Terry |
| 1894 | Helen R. Helwig |
| 1895 | Juliette P. Atkinson |
| 1896 | Elisabeth H. Moore |
| 1897–98 | Juliette P. Atkinson |
| 1899 | Marion Jones |
| 1900 | Myrtle McAteer |
| 1901 | Elisabeth H. Moore |
| 1902 | Marion Jones |
| 1903 | Elisabeth H. Moore |
| 1904 | May Sutton |
| 1905 | Elisabeth H. Moore |
| 1906 | Helen Homans |
| 1907 | Evelyn Sears |
| 1908 | Maud Bargar-Wallach |
| 1909–11 | Hazel V. Hotchkiss |
| 1912–14 | Mary K. Browne |
| 1915–18 | Molla Bjurstedt |
| 1919 | Hazel Hotchkiss Wightman |
| 1920–22 | Molla Bjurstedt Mallory |
| 1923–25 | Helen N. Wills |
| 1926 | Molla B. Mallory |
| 1927–29 | Helen N. Wills |
| 1930 | Betty Nuthall |
| 1931 | Helen Wills Moody |
| 1932–35 | Helen Jacobs |
| 1936 | Alice Marble |
| 1937 | Anita Lizana |
| 1938–40 | Alice Marble |
| 1941 | Sarah Palfrey Cooke |
| 1942–44 | Pauline Betz |
| 1945 | Sarah Cooke |
| 1946 | Pauline Betz |
| 1947 | Louise Brough |
| 1948–50 | Margaret Osborne duPont |
| 1951–53 | Maureen Connolly |
| 1954–55 | Doris Hart |
| 1956 | Shirley Fry |
| 1957–58 | Althea Gibson |
| 1959 | Maria Bueno |
| 1960–61 | Darlene Hard |
| 1962 | Margaret Smith |
| 1963–64 | Maria Bueno |
| 1965 | Margaret Smith |
| 1966 | Maria Bueno |
| 1967 | Billie Jean King |
| 1968–69 | Margaret Smith Court[3] |

**OPEN**

|  |  |
|---|---|
| 1968 | Virginia Wade |
| 1969–70 | Margaret Court |
| 1971–72 | Billie Jean King |
| 1973 | Margaret Court |
| 1974 | Billie Jean King |
| 1975–78 | Chris Evert |

### Doubles—Men

**NATIONAL**

| | |
|---|---|
| 1920 | Bill Johnston–C. J. Griffin |
| 1921–22 | Bill Tilden–Vincent Richards |
| 1923 | Bill Tilden–B. I. C. Norton |
| 1924 | H. O. Kinsey–R. G. Kinsey |
| 1925–26 | Vincent Richards–R. N. Williams II |
| 1927 | Bill Tilden–Frank Hunter |
| 1928 | G. M. Lott, Jr.–V. Hennessy |
| 1929–30 | G. M. Lott, Jr.–J. H. Doeg |
| 1931 | W. L. Allison–John Van Ryn |
| 1932 | E. H. Vines, Jr.–Keith Gledh |
| 1933–34 | G. M. Lott, Jr.–L. R. Stoefen |
| 1935 | W. L. Allison–John Van Ryn |
| 1936 | Don Budge–Gene Mako |
| 1937 | G. von Cramm–H. Henkel |
| 1938 | Don Budge–Gene Mako |
| 1939 | A. K. Quist–J. E. Bromwich |
| 1940–41 | Jack Kramer–F. R. Schroeder |
| 1942 | Gardnar Mulloy–Bill Talbert |
| 1943 | Jack Kramer–Frank Parker |
| 1944 | Don McNeill–Bob Falkenburg |
| 1945 | Gardnar Mulloy–Bill Talbert |
| 1946 | Gardnar Mulloy–Bill Talbert |
| 1947 | Jack Kramer–Fred Schroeder |
| 1948 | Gardnar Mulloy–Bill Talbert |
| 1949 | John Bromwich–William Sidwell |
| 1950 | John Bromwich–Frank Sedgman |
| 1951 | Frank Sedgman–Ken McGregor |
| 1952 | Vic Seixas–Mervyn Rose |
| 1953 | Mervyn Rose–Rex Hartwig |
| 1954 | Vic Seixas–Tony Trabert |
| 1955 | Kosei Kamo–Atsushi Miyagi |
| 1956 | Lewis Hoad–Ken Rosewall |
| 1957 | Ashley Cooper–Neale Fraser |
| 1958 | Ham Richardson–Alex Olmedo |
| 1959–60 | Neale Fraser–Roy Emerson |
| 1961 | Chuck McKinley–Dennis Ralston |
| 1962 | Rafael Osuna–Antonio Palafox |
| 1963–64 | Chuck McKinley–Dennis Ralston |
| 1965–66 | Fred Stolle–Roy Emerson |
| 1967 | John Newcombe–Tony Roche |
| 1968 | Stan Smith–Bob Lutz[3] |
| 1969 | Richard Crealy–Allan Stone[3] |

**OPEN**

| | |
|---|---|
| 1968 | Stan Smith–Bob Lutz |
| 1969 | Fred Stolle–Ken Rosewall |
| 1970 | Nikki Pilic–Fred Barthes |
| 1971 | John Newcombe–Roger Taylor |
| 1972 | Cliff Drysdale–Roger Taylor |
| 1973 | John Newcombe–Owen Davidson |
| 1974 | Bob Lutz–Stan Smith |
| 1975 | Jimmy Connors–Ilie Nastasc |
| 1976 | Marty Riessen–Tom Okker |
| 1977 | Frew McMillan–Bob Hewitt |
| 1978 | Bob Lutz–Stan Smith |

1. Challenge round abandoned in 1912. 2. Patriotic Tournament in 1917. 3. With the inaugural of the Open Tournament in 1968, the United States Lawn Tennis Association held a national championship at Longwood, Chestnut Hill, Mass. which barred contract professionals in 1968 and 1969.

## Doubles—Women

### NATIONAL

| | |
|---|---|
| 1924 | G. W. Wightman–Helen Wills |
| 1925 | Mary K. Browne–Helen Wills |
| 1926 | Elizabeth Ryan–Eleanor Goss |
| 1927 | L. A. Godfree–Ermyntrude Harvey |
| 1928 | Hazel Hotchkiss Wightman–Helen Wills |
| 1929 | Phoebe Watson–L. R. C. Michell |
| 1930 | Betty Nuthall–Sarah Palfrey |
| 1931 | Betty Nuthall–E. B. Wittingstall |
| 1932 | Helen Jacobs–Sarah Palfrey |
| 1933 | Betty Nuthall–Freda James |
| 1934 | Helen Jacobs–Sarah Palfrey |
| 1935 | Helen Jacobs–Sarah Palfrey Fabyan |
| 1936 | Marjorie G. Van Ryn–Carolin Babcock |
| 1937–40 | Sarah Palfrey Fabyan–Alice Marble |
| 1941 | Sarah Palfrey Cooke–Margaret Osborne |
| 1942–47 | A. Louise Brough–Margaret Osborne |
| 1948–50 | A. Louise Brough–Margaret O. duPont |
| 1951–54 | Doris Hart–Shirley Fry |
| 1955–57 | A. Louise Brough–Margaret O. duPont |
| 1958–59 | Darlene Hard–Jeanne Arth |
| 1960 | Darlene Hard–Maria Bueno |
| 1961 | Darlene Hard–Lesley Turner |
| 1962 | Darlene Hard–Maria Bueno |
| 1963 | Margaret Smith–Robyn Ebbern |
| 1964 | Karen Hantze Susman–Billie Jean Moffitt |
| 1965 | Nancy Richey–Carole Caldwell Graebner |
| 1966 | Nancy Richey–Maria Bueno |
| 1967 | Billie Jean King–Rosemary Casals |
| 1968 | Margaret Court–Maria Bueno[3] |
| 1969 | Margaret Court–Virginia Wade[3] |

### OPEN

| | |
|---|---|
| 1968 | Maria Bueno–Margaret Court |
| 1969 | Darlene Hard–Francoise Durr |
| 1970 | Margaret Court–Judy Dalton |
| 1971 | Rosemary Casals–Judy Dalton |
| 1972 | Francoise Durr–Betty Stove |
| 1973 | Margaret Court–Virginia Wade |
| 1974 | Billie Jean King–Rosemary Casals |
| 1975 | Margaret Court–Virginia Wade |
| 1976 | Linky Boshoff–Ilana Kloss |
| 1977 | Martina Navratilova–Betty Stove |
| 1978 | Billy Jean King–Martina Navratilova |

1. Challenge round abandoned in 1912. 2. Patriotic Tournament in 1917. 3. With the inaugural of the Open Tournament in 1968, the United States Lawn Tennis Association held a national championship at Longwood, Chestnut Hill, Mass. which barred contract professionals in 1968 and 1969.

## U.S. INDOOR CHAMPIONS

### Singles—Men

| | |
|---|---|
| 1964 | Charles McKinley |
| 1965 | Erik Lundquist |
| 1966 | Charles Pasarell |
| 1967 | Charles Pasarell |
| 1968 | Cliff Richey |
| 1969 | Stan Smith |
| 1970 | Ilie Nastase |
| 1971 | Clark Graebner |
| 1972 | Stan Smith |
| 1973–75 | Jimmy Connors |
| 1976 | Ilie Nastase |
| 1977 | Bjorn Borg |
| 1978 | Jimmy Connors |

### Singles—Women

| | |
|---|---|
| 1964 | Mary Ann Eisel |
| 1965 | Nancy Richey |
| 1966 | Billie Jean King |
| 1967 | Billie Jean King |
| 1968 | Billie Jean King |
| 1969 | Mary Ann Eisel |
| 1970 | Mary Ann Curtis |
| 1971 | Billie Jean King |
| 1972 | Not held |
| 1973 | Evonne Goolagong |
| 1974 | Billie Jean King |
| 1975 | Martina Navratilova |
| 1976 | Virginia Wade |
| 1977 | Not held |

### Doubles—Men

| | |
|---|---|
| 1967 | Arthur Ashe–Charles Pasarell |
| 1968 | Thomas Koch–Tom Okker |
| 1969 | Stan Smith–Bob Lutz |
| 1970 | Arthur Ashe–Stan Smith |
| 1971 | Manuel Orantes–Juan Gisbert |
| 1972 | Manuel Orantes–Andres Gimeno |
| 1973 | Juan Gisbert–Jurgen Fassbender |
| 1974 | Jimmy Connors–Frew McMillan |
| 1975 | Jimmy Connors–Ilie Nastase |
| 1976–77 | Sherwood Stewart–Fred McNair |
| 1978 | Brian Gottfried–Raul Ramirez |

### Doubles—Women

| | |
|---|---|
| 1967 | Carol Aucamp–Mary Ann Eisel |
| 1968 | Rosemary Casals–Billie Jean King |
| 1969 | Mary Ann Eisel–Valerie Ziegenfuss |
| 1970 | Peaches Bartkowicz–Nancy Richey |
| 1971 | Billie Jean King–Rosemary Casals |
| 1972 | Not held |
| 1973 | Olga Morozova–Marina Kroshina |
| 1974 | Not held |
| 1975 | Billie Jean King–Rosemary Casals |
| 1976 | Rosemary Casals–Francoise Durr |
| 1977 | Not held |
| 1978 | Not held |

## BRITISH (WIMBLEDON) CHAMPIONS

(Amateur from inception in 1877 through 1967)

### Singles—Men

| | |
|---|---|
| 1908–09 | Arthur Gore |
| 1910–13 | A. F. Wilding |
| 1914 | N. E. Brookes |
| 1919 | G. L. Patterson |
| 1920–21 | Bill Tilden |
| 1922 | G. L. Patterson |
| 1923 | William Johnston |
| 1924 | Jean Borotra |
| 1925 | Rene Lacoste |
| 1926 | Jean Borotra |
| 1927 | Henri Cochet |
| 1928 | Rene Lacoste |
| 1929 | Jean Cochet |
| 1930 | Bill Tilden |
| 1931 | S. B. Wood |
| 1932 | Ellsworth Vines |
| 1933 | J. H. Crawford |
| 1934–36 | Fred Perry |
| 1937–38 | Don Budge |
| 1939 | Robert L. Riggs |
| 1946 | Yvon Petra |
| 1947 | Jack Kramer |
| 1948 | R. Falkenburg |
| 1949 | Fred Schroeder |
| 1950 | Budge Patty |
| 1951 | Richard Savitt |
| 1952 | Frank Sedgman |
| 1953 | Vic Seixas |
| 1954 | Jaroslav Drobny |
| 1955 | Tony Trabert |
| 1956–57 | Lewis Hoad |
| 1958 | Ashley Cooper |
| 1959 | Alex Olmedo |
| 1960 | Neale Fraser |
| 1961–62 | Rod Laver |
| 1963 | Chuck McKinley |
| 1964–65 | Roy Emerson |
| 1966 | Manuel Santana |
| 1967 | John Newcombe |
| 1968–69 | Rod Laver |
| 1970–71 | John Newcombe |
| 1972 | Stan Smith |
| 1973 | Jan Kodes |
| 1974 | Jimmy Connors |
| 1975 | Arthur Ashe |
| 1976–78 | Bjorn Borg |

### Singles—Women

| | | | | | | | | | |
|---|---|---|---|---|---|---|---|---|---|
| 1919–23 | Lenglen | 1936 | Helen Jacobs | 1956 | Shirley Fry | 1969 | Ann Jones |
| 1924 | Kathleen McKane | 1937 | D. E. Round | 1957–58 | Althea Gibson | 1970 | Margaret Court |
| 1925 | Lenglen | 1938 | Helen Wills Moody | 1959–60 | Maria Bueno | 1971 | Evonne Goolagong |
| 1926 | Godfree | 1939 | Alice Marble | 1961 | Angela Mortimer | 1972–73 | Billie Jean King |
| 1927–29 | Helen Wills | 1946 | Pauline M. Betz | 1962 | Karen Susman | 1974 | Chris Evert |
| 1930 | Helen Wills Moody | 1947 | Margaret Osborne | 1963 | Margaret Smith | 1975 | Billie Jean King |
| 1931 | Frl. C. Aussen | 1948–50 | A. Louise Brough | 1964 | Maria Bueno | 1976 | Chris Evert |
| 1932–33 | Helen Wills Moody | 1951 | Doris Hart | 1965 | Margaret Smith | 1977 | Virginia Wade |
| 1934 | D. E. Round | 1952–54 | Maureen Connolly | 1966–67 | Billie Jean King | 1978 | Martina Navratilova |
| 1935 | Helen Wills Moody | 1955 | A. Louise Brough | 1968 | Billie Jean King | | |

### Doubles—Men

| | | | | | |
|---|---|---|---|---|---|
| 1953 | K. Rosewall–L. Hoad | 1962 | Fred Stolle–Bob Hewitt | 1972 | Bob Hewitt–Frew McMillan |
| 1954 | R. Hartwig–M. Rose | 1963 | Rafael Osuna–Antonio Palafox | 1973 | Jimmy Connors–Ilie Nastase |
| 1955 | R. Hartwig–L. Hoad | 1964 | Fred Stolle–Bob Hewitt | 1974 | John Newcombe–Tony Roche |
| 1956 | L. Hoad–K. Rosewall | 1965 | John Newcombe–Tony Roche | 1975 | Vitas Gerulaitis–Sandy Mayer |
| 1957 | Gardnar Mulloy–Budge Patty | 1966 | John Newcombe–Ken Fletcher | 1976 | Brian Gottfried–Raul Ramirez |
| 1958 | Sven Davidson–Ulf Schmidt | 1967 | Bob Hewitt–Frew McMillan | 1977 | Ross Case–Geoff Masters |
| 1959 | Roy Emerson–Neale Fraser | 1968–70 | John Newcombe–Tony Roche | 1978 | Frew McMillan–Bob Hewitt |
| 1960 | Dennis Ralston–Rafael Osuna | 1971 | Rod Laver–Roy Emerson | | |
| 1961 | Roy Emerson–Neale Fraser | | | | |

### Doubles—Women

| | | | | | |
|---|---|---|---|---|---|
| 1956 | Althea Gibson–Angela Buxton | 1965 | Billie Jean Moffitt–Maria Bueno | 1974 | Evonne Goolagong–Peggy Michel |
| 1957 | Althea Gibson–Darlene Hard | 1966 | Nancy Richey–Maria Bueno | 1975 | Ann Kiyomura–Kazuko Sawamatsu |
| 1958 | Althea Gibson–Maria Bueno | 1967–68 | Billie Jean King–Rosemary Casals | 1976 | Chris Evert–Martina Navratilova |
| 1959 | Darlene Hard–Jeanne Arth | 1969 | Margaret Court–Judy Tegart | 1977 | Helen Cawley–JoAnne Russell |
| 1960 | Darlene Hard–Maria Bueno | 1970–71 | Billie Jean King–Rosemary Casals | 1978 | Wendy Turnbull–Kerry Reid |
| 1961 | Karen Hantze–Billie Jean Moffitt | 1972 | Billie Jean King–Betty Stove | | |
| 1962 | Karen Hantze Susman–Billie Jean Moffitt | 1973 | Billie Jean King–Rosemary Casals | | |
| 1963 | Darlene Hard–Maria Bueno | | | | |
| 1964 | Margaret Smith–Les Turnerley | | | | |

## U.S. CHAMPIONSHIPS—1978

### Open

(Flushing, New York, Aug. 29–Sept. 10)

Men's singles—Final: Jimmy Connors, Belleville, Ill., defeated Bjorn Borg, Sweden, 6–4, 6–2, 6–2. Semifinals: Connors defeated John McEnroe, Douglaston, N.Y., 6–2, 6–2, 7–5; Borg defeated Vitas Gerulaitis, Kings Point, N.Y., 6–3, 6–2, 7–5.

Women's singles—Final: Chris Evert, Fort Lauderdale, Fla., defeated Pam Shriver, Lutherville, Md., 7–5, 6–4. Semifinals: Chris Evert defeated Wendy Turnbull, Australia, 6–3, 6–0; Pam Shriver defeated Martina Navratilova, Dallas, Tex., 7–6, 7–6.

Men's doubles—Final: Bob Lutz, San Clemente, Calif., and Stan Smith, Sea Pines, S.C., defeated Marty Riessen, Washington, D.C., and Sherwood Stewart, Goose Creek, Tex., 1–6, 7–5, 6–3.

Women's doubles—Final: Billy Jean King, New York, and Martina Navratilova, Dallas, defeated Wendy Turnbull and Kerry Reid, Australia, 7–6, 6–4.

Mixed doubles—Final: Betty Stove, Netherlands, and Frew McMillan, South Africa, defeated Billy Jean King, New York, and Ray Ruffels, Australia, 6–3, 7–6.

Women's 35—Final: Judy Alvarez defeated Nancy Reed, Winter Park, Fla., 6–3, 6–3.

Junior boys—Final: Per Hjertquist, Sweden, defeated Stefan Simonsson, Sweden, 7–6, 1–6, 7–6.

Junior girls—Final: Linda Siegel, Piedmont, Calif., defeated Ivana Madruga, Argentina, 6–3, 6–4.

### National Clay Court

(Indianapolis, Aug. 8–13)

Men's singles—Jimmy Connors, Belleville, Ill. (defeated José Higueras, Spain, 7–5, 6–1, in final)

Women's singles—Dana Gilbert, Piedmont, Calif. (defeated Viviana Gonzalez, Argentina, 6–2, 6–3, in final)

Men's doubles—Gene Mayer, Mendham, N.J., and Hank Pfister, Washington, D.C.

Women's doubles—Helena Anliot, Sweden, and Helle Sparre-Viragh, Denmark

### Other 1978 U.S. Champions

N.C.A.A. Division I—John McEnroe, Stanford; doubles: John Austin and Bruce Nichols, U.C.L.A.; team: Stanford

N.C.A.A. Division II—singles: Juan Farrow, Southern Illinois-Edwardsville; doubles: Par Svensson and Rick Goldberg, Univ. of San Diego; team: Southern Illinois-Edwardsville

N.C.A.A. Division III—singles: Chris Bussert, Kalamazoo; doubles: Chris Bussert and Jim Hosner, Kalamazoo; team: Kalamazoo

N.A.I.A.—singles: Francois Synaeghel, Belhaven (Miss.); doubles: Jeff Gibson and Bruce Gibson, East Texas State; team: East Texas State

Women's Collegiate (A.I.A.W.)—singles: Jeanne DuVall, U.C.L.A.; doubles: Kathy Jordan and Barbara Jordan, Stanford; team: Stanford

Women's Collegiate (U.S.T.A.)—singles: Stacy Margolin, So. California; doubles: Judy Acker and Sherry Acker, Florida; team: Southern California

## Tennis Earnings—1978

(U.S.T.A. listing through September 20)

### Men's

| Player | Tournaments | Total |
|---|---|---|
| Bjorn Borg | $257,641 | $569,141 |
| Vitas Gerulaitis | 348,556 | 415,316 |
| Jimmy Connors | 265,000 | 386,667 |
| Eddie Dibbs | 223,346 | 223,346 |
| Brian Gottfried | 150,397 | 202,063 |
| Wojtek Fibak | 170,179 | 189,179 |
| Raul Ramirez | 188,400 | 188,400 |
| Guillermo Vilas | 105,918 | 173,418 |
| Manuel Orantes | 100,209 | 160,209 |
| Ilie Nastase | 140,175 | 158,175 |

### Women's

| Player | Tournaments | Total |
|---|---|---|
| Martina Navratilova | $303,257 | $303,257 |
| Evonne Goolagong | 131,044 | 131,044 |
| Chris Evert | 120,411 | 120,411 |
| Virginia Wade | 116,752 | 116,752 |
| Billie Jean King | 109,267 | 109,267 |
| Wendy Turnbull | 101,633 | 101,633 |
| Betty Stove | 98,993 | 98,933 |
| Kerry Reid | 77,716 | 77,716 |
| Virginia Ruzici | 70,179 | 70,179 |
| Rosemary Casals | 59,600 | 59,600 |

## OTHER 1978 CHAMPIONSHIPS

### Wimbledon Open

(London, June 26-July 8)

Men's Singles—Final: Bjorn Borg, Sweden, defeated Jimmy Connors, Belleville, Ill., 6–2, 6–2, 6–3. Semifinals: Borg defeated Tom Okker, Netherlands, 6–4, 6–4, 6–4; Connors defeated Vitas Gerulaitis, New York, 9–7, 6–2, 6–1.

Women's singles—Final: Martina Navratilova, Dallas, defeated Chris Evert, Fort Lauderdale, Fla., 2–6, 6–4, 7–5. Semifinals: Evert defeated Virginia Wade, England, 8–6, 6–2; Navratilova defeated Evonne Goolagong, Australia, 2–6, 6–4, 6–4.

Men's doubles—Final: Frew McMillan and Bob Hewitt, South Africa, defeated John McEnroe, Douglaston, N.Y., and Peter Fleming, Chatham, N.J., 6–1, 6–4, 6–2.

Women's doubles—Final: Wendy Turnbull and Kerry Reid, Australia, defeated Virginia Ruzici, Romania, and Mima Jausovec, Yugoslavia, 4–6, 10–8, 6–3.

Mixed doubles—Final: Betty Stove, Netherlands, and Frew McMillan, defeated Billy Jean King, New York, and Ray Ruffles, Australia, 6–2, 6–2.

### French Open

(Paris, June 5-11)

Mens singles—Final: Bjorn Borg defeated Guillermo Vilas, Argentina, 6–1, 6–1, 6–3.

Women's singles—Final: Virginia Ruzici, Romania, defeated Mima Jausovec, Yugoslavia, 6–2, 6–2.

Men's doubles—Final: Hank Pfister, Bakersfield, Calif., and Gene Mayer, Mendham, N.J., defeated Jose Higueras and Manuel Orantes, Spain, 6–3, 6–2, 6–2.

Women's doubles—Final: Virginia Ruzici and Mima Jausovec defeated Lesley Bowrey, Australia, and Gail Lovera, France, 5–7, 6–4, 8–6.

### Australian Open

(Melbourne, Dec. 26, 1977-Jan. 1, 1978)

Men's singles—Final: Vitas Gerulaitis, New York, defeated John Lloyd, England, 6–3, 7–6, 5–7, 3–6, 6–2.

Women's singles—Final: Evonne Goolagong, Australia, defeated Helen Gourlay Cawley, Australia, 6–3, 6–0.

Men's doubles—Final: Ray Ruffles and Allan Stone, Australia, defeated John Alexander and Phil Dent, Australia, 7–6, 7–6.

Women's doubles—Final canceled because of rain. Honors split between Evonne Goolagong and Helen Cawley, Australia, and Chris Matison and Pam Whytcross, Australia.

### Canadian Open

(Toronto, Aug. 16-20, 1978)

Men's singles—Eddie Dibbs, Miami, Fla. (defeated José Luis Clerc, Argentina, 5–7, 6–4, 6–1, in final)

Women's singles—Regina Marsikova, Czechoslovakia (defeated Virginia Ruzici, Romania, 7–5, 6–7, 6–2, in final)

Men's doubles—Tom Okker, Netherlands, and Wojtek Fibak, Poland

## 1978 DAVIS CUP

### Zone Competition

(Eliminations started in 1977)

American Zone—South Section: Bolivia defeated Peru, 5–0; Uruguay defeated Ecuador, 3–2; Chile defeated Bolivia, 5–0; Uruguay defeated Brazil, 4–1; Chile defeated Uruguay, 4–1; Chile defeated Argentina, 3–2. North Section: South Africa defeated Colombia, 4–1; U.S. defeated South Africa, 4–1; American Zone final: U.S. defeated Chile, 3–2.

European Zone A—Israel defeated Finland, 4–0; Monaco defeated Luxembourg, 5–0; Netherlands defeated Greece, 4–1; Iran defeated Algeria, 4–1; Austria defeated Israel, 3–2; Britain defeated Monaco, 5–0; Czechoslovakia defeated Netherlands, 4–1; Poland defeated Iran, 4–1; Britain defeated Austria, 5–0; Czechoslovakia defeated Poland, 3–2; Britain defeated France, 3–2; Czechoslovakia defeated Romania, 5–0; European Zone A final: Britain defeated Czechoslovakia, 5–0.

European Zone B—Morocco defeated Norway, 4–1; Ireland defeated Portugal, 4–1; Belgium defeated Denmark, 3–2; Switzerland defeated Egypt, 5–0; Yugoslavia defeated Morocco, 5–0; Sweden defeated Ireland, 5–0; Hungary defeated Belgium, 4–1; West Germany defeated Switzerland, 5–0; Sweden defeated Yugoslavia, 3–1; Hungary defeated West Germany, 3–2; Sweden defeated Spain, 3–2; Hungary defeated Italy, 4–1; European Zone B final: Sweden defeated Hungary, 3–1.

Eastern Zone: Pakistan defeated Malaysia, 4–0; Philippines defeated Thailand, 5–0; Japan defeated Taiwan, 5–0; Korea defeated Pakistan, 3–2; Japan defeated Philippines, 4–1; India defeated Korea, 3–2; Japan defeated Indonesia, 4–1; New Zealand defeated India, 4–1; Australia defeated Japan, 5–0; Eastern Zone final: Australia defeated New Zealand, 4–0.

### Semifinals (Interzone Matches)

U.S. defeated Sweden, 3–2; Britain defeated Australia, 3–2.

## PROFESSIONAL—1978

World Championship Tennis (Dallas, May 8–12—Vitas Gerulaitis, Kings Point, N.Y. (defeated Eddie Dibbs, Miami, Fla., 6–3, 6–2, 6–1, in final); doubles (Kansas City, Mo., May 1–7): Wojtek Fibak, Poland, and Tom Okker, Netherlands (defeated Bob Lutz, San Clemente, Calif., and Stan Smith, Sea Pines, S.C., 6–7, 6–4, 6–0, 6–3, in final)

Virginia Slims Championship (Oakland, Calif., March 29–April 2)—Martina Navratilova, Dallas (defeated Evonne Goolagong, Australia, 7–6, 6–4, in final)

U.S. Pro Championship (Brookline, Mass, Aug. 22–29)—Manuel Orantes, Spain (defeated Harold Solomon, Fort Lauderdale, Fla., 6–4, 6–3, in final)

U.S. Pro Indoor Championship (Philadelphia, Jan. 24–28)—Jimmy Connors, Belleville, Ill. (defeated Roscoe Tanner, Lookout Mountain, Tenn., 6–2, 6–4, 6–3, in final)

World Team Tennis Championship—Los Angeles Strings (defeated Boston Lobsters, 3–1, in final)

# BOXING

Whether it be called pugilism, prize fighting or boxing, there is no tracing "the Sweet Science" to any definite source. Tales of rivals exchanging blows for fun, fame or money go back to earliest recorded history and classical legend. There was a mixture of boxing and wrestling called the "pancratium" in the ancient Olympic Games and in such contests the rivals belabored one another with hands fortified with heavy leather wrappings that were sometimes studded with metal. More than one Olympic competitor lost his life at this brutal exercise.

There was little law or order in pugilism until Jack Broughton, one of the early champions of England, drew up a set of rules for the game in 1743. Broughton, called "the father of English boxing," also is credited with having invented boxing gloves. However, these gloves—or "mufflers" as they were called—were used only in teaching "the manly art of self-defense" or in training bouts. All professional championship fights were contested with "bare knuckles" until 1892, when John L. Sullivan lost the heavyweight championship of the world to James J. Corbett in New Orleans in a bout in which both contestants wore regulation gloves.

The Broughton rules were superseded by the London Prize Ring Rules of 1838. The 8th Marquis of Queensberry, with the help of John G. Chambers, put forward the "Queensberry Rules" in 1866, a code that called for gloved contests. Amateurs took quickly to the Queensberry Rules, the professionals slowly.

## HISTORY OF WORLD HEAVYWEIGHT CHAMPIONSHIP FIGHTS

(Bouts in which a new champion was crowned)

*Source: Nat Fleischer's Ring Boxing Encyclopedia and Record Book*, published and copyrighted by The Ring Book Shop, Inc., 120 West 31st St., New York, N.Y. 10001.

| Date | Where held | Winner, weight, age | Loser, weight, age | Rounds | Referee |
|---|---|---|---|---|---|
| Sept. 7, 1892 | New Orleans, La. | James J. Corbett, 178 (26) | John L. Sullivan, 212 (33) | 21 | Prof. John Duffy |
| March 17, 1897 | Carson City, Nev. | Bob Fitzsimmons, 167 (34) | James J. Corbett, 183 (30) | KO 14 | George Siler |
| June 9, 1899 | Coney Island, N.Y. | James J. Jeffries, 206 (24)[1] | Bob Fitzsimmons, 167 (37) | KO 11 | George Siler |
| Feb. 23, 1906 | Los Angeles | Tommy Burns, 180 (24)[2] | Marvin Hart, 188 (29) | 20 | James J. Jeffries |
| Dec. 26, 1908 | Sydney, N.S.W. | Jack Johnson, 196 (30) | Tommy Burns, 176 (27) | KO 14 | Hugh McIntosh |
| April 5, 1915 | Havana, Cuba | Jess Willard, 230 (33) | Jack Johnson, 205½ (37) | KO 26 | Jack Welch |
| July 4, 1919 | Toledo, Ohio | Jack Dempsey, 187 (24) | Jess Willard, 245 (37) | KO 3 | Ollie Pecord |
| Sept. 23, 1926 | Philadelphia | Gene Tunney, 189 (28)[3] | Jack Dempsey, 190 (31) | 10 | Pop Reilly |
| June 12, 1930 | New York | Max Schmeling, 188 (24) | Jack Sharkey, 197 (27) | WF 4 | Jim Crowley |
| June 21, 1932 | Long Island City | Jack Sharkey, 205 (29) | Max Schmeling, 188 (26) | 15 | Gunboat Smith |
| June 29, 1933 | Long Island City | Primo Carnera, 260½ (26) | Jack Sharkey, 201 (30) | KO 6 | Arthur Donovan |
| June 14, 1934 | Long Island City | Max Baer, 209½ (25) | Primo Carnera, 263¼ (27) | KO 11 | Arthur Donovan |
| June 13, 1935 | Long Island City | Jim Braddock, 193¾ (29) | Max Baer, 209½ (26) | 15 | Jack McAvoy |
| June 22, 1937 | Chicago | Joe Louis, 197¼ (23) | Jim Braddock, 197 (31) | KO 8 | Tommy Thomas |
| June 22, 1949 | Chicago | Ezzard Charles, 181¾ (27)[4] | Joe Walcott, 195½ (35) | 15 | Davey Miller |
| Sept. 27, 1950 | New York | Ezzard Charles, 184½ (29)[5] | Joe Louis, 218 (36) | 15 | Mark Conn |
| July 18, 1951 | Pittsburgh | Joe Walcott, 194 (37) | Ezzard Charles, 182 (30) | KO 7 | Buck McTiernan |
| Sept. 23, 1952 | Philadelphia | Rocky Marciano, 184 (29)[6] | Joe Walcott, 196 (38) | KO 13 | Charley Daggert |
| Nov. 30, 1956 | Chicago | Floyd Patterson, 182¼ (21) | Archie Moore, 187¾ (42) | KO 5 | Frank Sikora |
| June 26, 1959 | New York | Ingemar Johansson, 196 (26) | Floyd Patterson, 182 (24) | KO 3 | Ruby Goldstein |
| June 20, 1960 | New York | Floyd Patterson, 190 (25) | Ingemar Johansson, 194¾ (27) | KO 5 | Arthur Mercante |
| Sept. 25, 1962 | Chicago | Sonny Liston, 214 (28) | Floyd Patterson, 189 (27) | KO 1 | Frank Sikora |
| Feb. 25, 1964 | Miami Beach, Fla. | Cassius Clay, 210 (22)[7] | Sonny Liston, 218 (30) | KO 7 | Barney Felix |
| March 4, 1968 | New York | Joe Frazier, 204½ (24)[8] | Buster Mathis, 243½ (23) | KO 11 | Arthur Mercante |
| April 27, 1968 | Oakland, Calif. | Jimmy Ellis, 197 (28)[9] | Jerry Quarry, 195 (22) | 15 | Elmer Costa |
| Feb. 16, 1970 | New York | Joe Frazier, 205 (26)[10] | Jimmy Ellis, 201 (29) | KO 5 | Tony Perez |
| Jan. 22, 1973 | Kingston, Jamaica | George Foreman, 217½ (24) | Joe Frazier, 214 (29) | KO 2 | Arthur Mercante |
| Oct. 30, 1974 | Kinshasa, Zaire | Muhammad Ali, 216½ (32) | George Foreman, 220 (26) | KO 8 | Zack Clayton |
| Feb. 15, 1978 | Las Vegas, Nev. | Leon Spinks, 197 (25) | Muhammad Ali, 224½ (36) | 15 | Howard Buck |
| June 9, 1978 | Las Vegas, Nev. | Larry Holmes, 212 (28) | Ken Norton, 220 (32) | 15 | Mills Lans |
| Sept. 15, 1978 | New Orleans | Muhammad Ali, 221 (36) | Leon Spinks, 201 (25) | 15 | Lucien Joubert |

1. Jeffries retired as champion in March 1905. He named Marvin Hart and Jack Root as leading contenders and agreed to referee their fight in Reno, Nev., on July 3, 1905, with the stipulation that he would term the winner the champion. Hart, 190 (28), knocked out Root, 171 (29), in the 12th round. 2. Burns claimed the title after defeating Hart. 3. Tunney retired as champion after defeating Tom Heeney on July 26, 1928. 4. After Louis announced his retirement as champion on March 1, 1949, Charles won recognition from the National Boxing Association as champion by defeating Walcott. 5. Charles gained undisputed recognition as champion by defeating Louis, who came out of retirement. 6. Retired as champion April 27, 1956. 7. The World Boxing Association later withdrew its recognition of Clay as champion and declared the winner of a bout between Ernie Terrell and Eddie Machen would gain its version of the title. Terrell, 199 (25), won a 15-round decision from Machen, 192 (32), in Chicago on March 5, 1965. Clay, 212¼ (25) and Terrell, 212½ (27) met in Houston on Feb. 6, 1967, Clay winning a 15-round decision. 8. Winner recognized by New York, Massachusetts, Maine, Illinois, Texas and Pennsylvania to fill vacated title when Clay was stripped of championship for failing to accept U. S. Induction. 9. Bout was final of eight-man tournament to fill Clay's place and is recognized by World Boxing Association. 10. Bout settled controversy over title. 11. Holmes won World Boxing Council title after W.B.C. had withdrawn recognition of Spinks, March 18, 1978, and awarded its title to Norton. W.B.C. said Spinks had reneged on agreement to fight Norton 12. Ali regained World Boxing Association championship.

## BARE KNUCKLE HEAVYWEIGHT CHAMPIONS

| | | | | | | | |
|---|---|---|---|---|---|---|---|
| 1719 | Jim Figg | 1740 | Jack Broughton | 1760 | Bill Stevens | 1765 | Bill Darts |
| 1734 | George Taylor | 1750 | Jack Slack | 1761 | George Meggs | 1777 | Harry Sellers |

1780 Jack Harris
1785 Tom (Jackling) Johnson
1790 Big Ben Brain
1792 Daniel Mendoza
1795 John Jackson (retired)
1802 Jem Belcher
1805 Henry Pearce (Game Chicken)
1808 John Gully (declined title)
1809 Tom Cribb received belt, not transferable, and cup
1824 Tom Spring received four cups; resigned title
1825 Jem Ward received belt, not transferable
1838 James (Deaf) Burke claimed title
1839 William Thompson (Bendigo) beat Burke; claimed championship; received belt from Jem Ward
1841 Nick Ward (Jem's brother) beat Ben Caunt, Feb. 2. In return match Caunt beat Nick Ward and received belt by subscription. It was transferable.
1845 Thompson beat Caunt and got belt
1850 Bill Perry (The Tipton Slasher), after fight with Paddock, claimed title
1851 Harry Broome won title from Perry
1853 Perry claimed title when Broome forfeited £200 to him in a match; retired from ring on Aug. 13
1857 Tom Sayers beat Perry for £200 a side and new belt
1860 Sayers retired after 42-round draw with John C. Heenan (The Benicia Boy), leaving old belt open for competition
1860 Sam Hurst (The Stalybridge Infant) beat Paddock and received belt
1861 Jem Mace beat Hurst
1862 Mace beat Tom King for £200 a side and the belt
1862 King beat Mace and claimed belt. Subsequently gave it up. Declined to meet Mace again. Mace claimed belt.
1863 King beat Heenan for £1,000 a side
1865 Joe Wormald beat Andrew Marsden for £200 a side and belt, which had been claimed by both. Belt was given to Wormald, who forfeited £120 to Mace
1866 Mace and Joe Goss fought draw with £200 a side and belt at stake
1867 Wormald received £200 forfeit from Ned O'Baldwin and claimed belt when O'Baldwin failed to appear at starting place
1867 Mace and O'Baldwin drew; £200 a side; title and belt in abeyance
1869 Mike McCoole defeated Tom Allen and claimed American championship
1870 Mace claimed world title by knocking out Allen in 10 rounds
1873 Mace retired and Allen claimed title of world champion by defeating McCoole
1876 Allen fought Joe Goss, ranked next to Mace in England. Allen was disqualified in the 27th round for fouling and Goss was recognized as world champion under London Prize Ring Rules
1880 Paddy Ryan knocked out Goss in the 87th round on May 30, near Colliers Station, W. Va., and became the first American to hold the undisputed world's bare knuckle championship
1882 John L. Sullivan knocked out Ryan in the 9th round at Mississippi City, Miss., on Feb. 7 and became the last bare knuckle champion
1889 Sullivan defeated Jake Kilrain in the last bare knuckle championship fight. The bout, on July 8 at Richburg, Miss., went 75 rounds.

## BOXING'S BIGGEST GATES

| Date | Winner, weight Loser, weight | Rounds | Site | Receipts | Attendance |
|---|---|---|---|---|---|
| Sept. 15, 1978 | Ali (221)—Spinks (201) | 15 | Superdome, New Orleans | $4,806,675 | 65,370 |
| Sept. 22, 1927 | Tunney (189½)—Dempsey (192½) (2d) | 10 | Soldier Field, Chicago | 2,658,660 | 104,943 |
| Sept. 28, 1976 | Ali (221)—Norton (217½) (2d) | 15 | Yankee Stadium, New York | 2,400,000 | 30,289 |
| June 19, 1946 | Louis (207)—Conn (187) (2d) | KO 8 | Yankee Stadium, New York | 1,925,564 | 45,266 |
| Sept. 23, 1926 | Tunney (189½)—Dempsey (190) (1st) | 10 | Sesquicentennial Stdm., Phila. | 1,895,733 | 120,757 |
| July 2, 1921 | Dempsey (188)—Carpentier (172) | KO 4 | Boyle's 30 Acres, Jersey City | 1,789,238 | 80,183 |
| Oct. 1, 1975 | Ali (224½)—Frazier (214½) (3d) | KO 14 | Manila, Philippines | 1,600,000 | 25,000 |
| March 8, 1971 | Joe Frazier (205½)—Muhammad Ali (215) | 15 | New Madison Square Garden | 1,352,951 | 20,455 |
| Oct. 30, 1974 | Ali (216½)—Foreman (220) | KO 8 | Kinshasa, Zaire | 1,200,000 | 65,000 |
| Sept. 14, 1923 | Dempsey (192½)—Firpo (216½) | KO 2 | Polo Grounds, New York | 1,188,603 | 82,000 |
| July 21, 1927 | Dempsey (194½)—Sharkey (196) | KO 7 | Yankee Stadium, New York | 1,083,530 | 75,000 |
| Jan. 28, 1974 | Ali (212) Frazier (209) (2d) | 12 | New Madison Square Garden | 1,053,688 | 20,748 |
| June 22, 1938 | Louis (198¾)—Schmeling (193) (2d) | KO 1 | Yankee Stadium, New York | 1,015,012 | 70,043 |
| Sept. 24, 1935 | Louis (199¼)—Max Baer (210½) | KO 4 | Yankee Stadium, New York | 1,000,832 | 88,150 |
| Sept. 21, 1955 | Marciano (188¼)—Moore (188) | KO 9 | Yankee Stadium, New York | 948,117 | 61,574 |
| June 25, 1948 | Louis (213½) Walcott (194¾) (2d) | KO 11 | Yankee Stadium, New York | 841,739 | 42,667 |
| June 20, 1960 | Patterson (190)—Johansson (194¾) (2d) | KO 5 | Polo Grounds, New York | 824,814 | 31,892 |
| Sept. 12, 1951 | Robinson (157½)—Turpin (159) (2d) | KO 10 | Polo Grounds, New York | 767,626 | 61,370 |
| June 12, 1930 | Schmeling (188)—Sharkey (197) (1st) | WF 4 | Yankee Stadium, New York | 749,935 | 79,222 |
| June 22, 1937 | Louis (197¼)—Braddock (197) | KO 8 | Comiskey Park, Chicago | 715,470 | 45,500 |
| July 26, 1928 | Tunney (192)—Heeney (203½) | KO 11 | Yankee Stadium, New York | 691,014 | 45,890 |
| Sept. 25, 1962 | Liston (214)—Patterson (189) (1st) | KO 1 | Comiskey Park, Chicago | 665,420 | 18,894 |
| March 4, 1968 | Frazier (206)—Mathis<br>Benvenuti (160)—Griffith (154½) | KO 11<br>15 | New Madison Square Garden | 658,503 | 18,096 |
| Feb. 16, 1970 | Joe Frazier (205)—Jimmy Ellis (201) | KO 5 | New Madison Square Garden, N.Y. | 647,997 | 18,079 |
| Feb. 25, 1964 | Clay (210½)—Liston (218) (1st) | KO 7 | Miami Beach, Fla. | 625,000 | 8,927 |
| Dec. 7, 1970 | Ali (212)—Bonavena (204) | KO 15 | New Madison Square Garden, New York | 615,401 | 19,417 |
| Sept. 29, 1941 | Louis (202¼)—Nova (202½) | KO 6 | Polo Grounds, New York | 583,711 | 56,549 |
| Sept. 23, 1957 | Basilio (153½)—Robinson (160) (1st) | 15 | Yankee Stadium, New York | 556,467 | 38,072 |
| June 19, 1936 | Schmeling (192)—Louis (198) (1st) | KO 12 | Yankee Stadium, New York | 547,541 | 42,088 |
| June 17, 1954 | Marciano (187½)—Charles (185½) (1st) | 15 | Yankee Stadium, New York | 543,092 | 47,585 |
| June 17, 1974 | Frazier (212)—Quarry (197½) (2d) | KO 5 | New Madison Square Garden, N.Y. | 517,006 | 14,611 |
| Sept. 20, 1972 | Ali (218)—Patterson (188½) (2d) | KO 7 | New Madison Square Garden, N.Y. | 512,361 | 17,378 |

NOTES: KO—won by knockout; WF—won on foul; ND—no decision; 1st—first bout; 2d—second bout; 3rd—third bout.

# OTHER WORLD BOXING TITLEHOLDERS

## Light Heavyweight

| | |
|---|---|
| 1903 | Jack Root, George Gardner |
| 1903–05 | Bob Fitzsimmons |
| 1905–12 | Philadelphia Jack O'Brien[1] |
| 1912–16 | Jack Dillon |
| 1916–20 | Battling Levinsky |
| 1920–22 | Georges Carpentier |
| 1923 | Battling Siki |
| 1923–25 | Mike McTigue |
| 1925–26 | Paul Berlenbach |
| 1926–27 | Jack Delaney[2] |
| 1927 | Mike McTigue |
| 1927–29 | Tommy Loughran |
| 1930 | Jimmy Slattery |
| 1930–34 | Maxie Rosenbloom |
| 1934–35 | Bob Olin |
| 1935–39 | John Henry Lewis |
| 1939 | Melio Bettina |
| 1939–41 | Billy Conn[2] |
| 1941 | Anton Christoforidis (NBA) |
| 1941–48 | Gus Lesnevich |
| 1948–50 | Freddie Mills |
| 1950–52 | Joey Maxim |
| 1952–61 | Archie Moore[3] |
| 1961–63 | Harold Johnson |
| 1963–65 | Willie Pastrano |
| 1965–66 | José Torres |
| 1966–67 | Dick Tiger |
| 1968 | Dick Tiger, Bob Foster |
| 1969–70 | Bob Foster |
| 1971 | Vicente Rondon (WBA), Bob Foster (WBC) |
| 1972–73 | Bob Foster (WBA, WBC) |
| 1974 | John Conteh (WBA), Bob Foster (WBC)[1 4] |
| 1975–76 | Victor Galindez (WBA), John Conteh (WBC) |
| 1977 | Victor Galindez (WBA), John Conteh (WBC)[4], Miguel Cuello (WBC) |
| 1978 | Victor Galindez (WBA), Mike Rossman (WBA), Miguel Cuello (WBC) and Mate Parlov (WBC) |

1. Retired. 2. Abandoned title. 3. NBA withdrew recognition in 1961, New York Commission in 1962; recognized thereafter only by California and Europe. 4. WBC withdrew recognition.

## Middleweight

| | |
|---|---|
| 1867–72 | Tom Chandler |
| 1872–81 | George Rooke |
| 1881–82 | Mike Donovan[1] |
| 1884–91 | Jack (Nonpareil) Dempsey |
| 1891–97 | Bob Fitzsimmons[2] |
| 1908 | Stanley Ketchel, Billy Papke |
| 1908–10 | Stanley Ketchel[3] |
| 1913 | Frank Klaus |
| 1913–14 | George Chip |
| 1914–17 | Al McCoy |
| 1917–20 | Mike O'Dowd |
| 1920–23 | Johnny Wilson |
| 1923–26 | Harry Greb |
| 1926 | Tiger Flowers |
| 1926–31 | Mickey Walker[2] |
| 1931–41 | Gorilla Jones, Ben Jeby, Marcel Thil, Lou Brouillard, Vince Dundee, Teddy Yarosz, Babe Risko, Freddy Steele, Al Hostak, Solly Kreiger, Fred Apostoli, Ceferino Garcia, Ken Overlin, Billy Soose, Tony Zale[4] |
| 1941–47 | Tony Zale |
| 1947–48 | Rocky Graziano |
| 1948 | Tony Zale |
| 1948–49 | Marcel Cerdan |
| 1949–51 | Jake LaMotta |
| 1952 | Ray Robinson, Randy Turpin |
| 1951–52 | Ray Robinson[1] |
| 1953–55 | Carl Olson |
| 1955–57 | Ray Robinson[5] |
| 1957 | Gene Fullmer, Ray Robinson |
| 1957–58 | Carmen Basilio |
| 1958–60 | Ray Robinson[6] |
| 1960–61 | Paul Pender[7] |
| 1959–62 | Gene Fullmer (NBA) |
| 1961–62 | Terry Downes[1] |
| 1962 | Paul Pender[1] |
| 1962–63 | Dick Tiger |
| 1963–65 | Joey Giardello |
| 1965–66 | Dick Tiger |
| 1966 | Emile Griffith |
| 1967 | Nino Benvenuti, Emile Griffith |
| 1968 | Emile Griffith, Nino Benvenuti |
| 1969 | Nino Benvenuti |
| 1970 | Nino Benvenuti, Carlos Monzon |
| 1971–73 | Carlos Monzon |
| 1974–75 | Carlos Monzon (WBA), Rodrigo Valdez (WBC) |
| 1976 | Carlos Monzon (WBA, WBC), Rodrigo Valdez (WBC) |
| 1977 | Carlos Monzon (WBA, WBC)[1], Rodrigo Valdez (WBA, WBC) |
| 1978 | Rodrigo Valdez, Hugo Corro |

1. Retired. 2. Abandoned title. 3. Died. 4. National Boxing Association and New York Commission disagreed on champions. Those listed were accepted by one or the other until Zale gained world-wide recognition. 5. Ended retirement in 1954. 6. NBA withdrew recognition. 7. Recognized by New York, Massachusetts, and Europe.

## Welterweight

| | |
|---|---|
| 1892–94 | Mysterious Billy Smith |
| 1894–96 | Tommy Ryan |
| 1896 | Kid McCoy[2] |
| 1896–1900 | Mysterious Billy Smith |
| 1900 | Rube Ferns |
| 1900–01 | Matty Matthews |
| 1901 | Ruby Ferns |
| 1901–04 | Joe Walcott |
| 1904 | Dixie Kid[2] |
| 1904–06 | Joe Walcott |
| 1906–07 | Honey Mellody |
| 1907 | Mike (Twin) Sullivan[2] |
| 1915–19 | Ted Lewis |
| 1919–22 | Jack Britton |
| 1922–26 | Mickey Walker |
| 1926–27 | Pete Latzo |
| 1927–29 | Joe Dundee |
| 1929–30 | Jackie Fields |
| 1930 | Young Jack Thompson |
| 1930–31 | Tommy Freeman |
| 1931 | Young Jack Thompson |
| 1931–32 | Lou Brouillard |
| 1932–33 | Jackie Fields |
| 1933 | Young Corbett 3rd |
| 1933–34 | Jimmy McLarnin, Barney Ross |
| 1934–35 | Jimmy McLarnin |
| 1935–38 | Barney Ross |
| 1938–40 | Henry Armstrong |
| 1940–41 | Fritzie Zivic |
| 1941–46 | Freddie Cochrane |
| 1946 | Marty Servo[1] |
| 1946–51 | Ray Robinson[2] |
| 1951 | Johnny Bratton (NBA) |
| 1951–54 | Kid Gavilan |
| 1954–55 | Johnny Saxton |
| 1955 | Tony DeMarco |
| 1955–56 | Carmen Basilio |
| 1956 | Johnny Saxton |
| 1956–57 | Carmen Basilio[2] |
| 1958 | Virgil Akins |
| 1959–60 | Don Jordan |
| 1960–61 | Benny (Kid) Paret |
| 1961 | Emile Griffith |
| 1961–62 | Benny (Kid) Paret |
| 1962–63 | Emile Griffith, Luis Rodriguez |
| 1963–66 | Emile Griffith[2] |
| 1966–69 | Curtis Cokes |
| 1969 | Curtis Cokes, José Napoles |
| 1970 | José Napoles, Billy Backus |
| 1971 | Billy Backus, José Napoles |
| 1972–74 | José Napoles |
| 1975 | José Napoles (WBA, WBC)[3], Angel Espada (WBA), John Stracey (WBC) |
| 1976 | Angel Espada (WBA), José Cuevas (WBA), John Stracey (WBC), Carlos Palomino (WBC) |
| 1977 | José Cuevas (WBA), Carlos Palomino (WBC) |

1. Retired. 2. Abandoned title. 3. WBA withdrew recognition.

**Lightweight**

| | |
|---|---|
| 1869–99 | Kid Lavigne |
| 1899–1902 | Frank Erne |
| 1902–08 | Joe Gans |
| 1908–10 | Battling Nelson |
| 1910–12 | Ad Wolgast |
| 1912–14 | Willie Ritchie |
| 1914–17 | Freddy Welsh |
| 1917–25 | Benny Leonard[1] |
| 1925 | Jimmy Goodrich |
| 1925–26 | Rocky Kansas |
| 1926–30 | Sammy Mandell |
| 1930 | Al Singer |
| 1930–33 | Tony Canzoneri |
| 1933–35 | Barney Ross[2] |
| 1935–36 | Tony Canzoneri |
| 1936–38 | Lou Ambers |
| 1938–39 | Henry Armstrong |
| 1939–40 | Lou Ambers |
| 1940–41 | Lew Jenkins |
| 1941–42 | Sammy Angott[1] |
| 1943–47 | Beau Jack (N.Y.), Bob Montgomery (N.Y.), Sammy Angott (NBA), Juan Zurita (NBA), Ike Williams (NBA) |
| 1947–51 | Ike Williams |
| 1951–52 | James Carter |
| 1952 | Lauro Salas |
| 1952–54 | James Carter |
| 1954 | Paddy DeMarco |
| 1954–55 | James Carter |
| 1955–56 | Wallace Smith |
| 1956–62 | Joe Brown |
| 1962–65 | Carlos Ortiz |
| 1965 | Ismael Laguna |
| 1965–68 | Carlos Ortiz |
| 1968 | Teo Cruz |
| 1969 | Teo Cruz, Mando Ramos |
| 1970 | Mando Ramos, Ismael Laguna, Ken Buchanan |
| 1971 | Ken Buchanan (WBA), Mando Ramos (WBC), Pedro Carrasco (WBC) |
| 1972 | Ken Buchanan (WBA), Roberto Duran (WBA), Pedro Carrasco (WBC), Mando Ramos (WBC), Chango Carmona (WBC), Rodolfo Gonzalez (WBC) |
| 1973 | Roberto Duran (WBA), Rodolfo Gonzalez (WBC) |
| 1974 | Roberto Duran (WBA), Rodolfo Gonzalez (WBC), Guts Ishimatsu (WBC) |
| 1975 | Roberto Duran (WBA), Guts Ishimatsu (WBC) |
| 1976 | Roberto Duran (WBA), Guts Ishimatsu (WBC), Esteban De Jesus (WBC) |
| 1977 | Robert Duran (WBA), Esteban De Jesus (WBC) |
| 1978 | Roberto Duran (WBA, WBC) |

1. Retired. 2. Abandoned title.

**Featherweight**

| | |
|---|---|
| 1889 | Dal Hawkins[1] |
| 1890 | Billy Murphy |
| 1892–1900 | George Dixon |
| 1900–01 | Terry McGovern |
| 1901 | Young Corbett[1] |
| 1901–12 | Abe Attell |
| 1912–23 | Johnny Kilbane |
| 1923 | Eugene Criqui |
| 1923–25 | Johnny Dundee[1] |
| 1925–27 | Louis (Kid) Kaplan[1] |
| 1927–28 | Benny Bass |
| 1928 | Tony Canzoneri |
| 1928–29 | Andre Routis |
| 1929–32 | Battling Battalino[1] |
| 1932 | Tommy Paul (NBA), Kid Chocolate (N.Y.) |
| 1933–36 | Freddie Miller |
| 1936–37 | Petey Sarron |
| 1937–38 | Henry Armstrong[1] |
| 1938–40 | Joey Archibald |
| 1940–41 | Harry Jefra, Joey Archibald |
| 1941–42 | Chalky Wright |
| 1942–48 | Willie Pep |
| 1948–49 | Sandy Saddler[2] |
| 1949–50 | Willie Pep |
| 1950–57 | Sandy Saddler |
| 1957–59 | Kid Bassey |
| 1959–63 | Davey Moore |
| 1963–64 | Sugar Ramos |
| 1964–67 | Vicente Saldivar[2] |
| 1968 | Howard Winstone, José Legra,[3] Paul Rojas (WBA), Sho Saijo (WBA) |
| 1969 | Sho Saijo (WBA), Johnny Famechon[3] |
| 1970 | Sho Saijo (WBA), Johnny Famechon,[3] Vicente Salvidar,[3] Kuniaki Shibata[3] |
| 1971 | Sho Saijo (WBA), Antonio Gomez (WBA), Kuniaki Shibata (WBC) |
| 1972 | Antonio Gomez (WBA), Ernesto Marcel (WBA), Kuniaki Shibata (WBC), Clemente Sanchez (WBC),[2] José Legra (WBC) |
| 1973 | Ernesto Marcel (WBA), José Legra (WBC), Eder Jofre (WBC) |
| 1974 | Ernesto Marcel (WBA)[2], Ruben Olivares (WBA), Alexis Arguello (WBA), Eder Jofre (WBC), Bobby Chacon (WBC) |
| 1975 | Alexis Arguello (WBA), Bobby Chacon (WBC), Ruben Olivares (WBC), David Kotey (WBC) |
| 1976 | Alexis Arguello (WBA),[2] David Kotey (WBC), Danny Lopez (WBC) |
| 1977 | Rafael Ortega (WBA), Danny Lopez (WBC) |
| 1978 | Rafael Ortega (WBA), Cecilio Lastra (WBA), Eusebio Pedrosa (WBA), Danny Lopez (WBC) |

1. Abandoned title. 2. Retired. 3. Recognized in Europe, Mexico, and Orient.

**Bantamweight**

| | |
|---|---|
| 1890–92 | George Dixon[1] |
| 1894–99 | Jimmy Barry[2] |
| 1899–1900 | Terry McGovern[1] |
| 1901 | Harry Harris[1] |
| 1902–03 | Harry Forbes |
| 1903–04 | Frankie Neil |
| 1904 | Joe Bowker[1] |
| 1905–07 | Jimmy Walsh[1] |
| 1910–14 | Johnny Coulon |
| 1914–17 | Kid Williams |
| 1917–20 | Pete Herman |
| 1920 | Joe Lynch |
| 1920–21 | Joe Lynch, Pete Herman, Johnny Buff |
| 1922 | Johnny Buff, Joe Lynch |
| 1923 | Joe Lynch |
| 1924 | Joe Lynch, Abe Goldstein |
| 1924 | Abe Goldstein, Eddie (Cannonball) Martin |
| 1925 | Eddie (Cannonball) Martin, Charlie (Phil) Rosenberg[3] |
| 1927–28 | Bud Taylor (NBA)[1] |
| 1929–34 | Al Brown |
| 1935 | Al Brown, Baltazar Sangchili |
| 1936 | Baltazar Sangchili, Tony Marino, Sixto Escobar |
| 1937 | Sixto Escobar, Harry Jeffra |
| 1938 | Harry Jeffra, Sixto Escobar |
| 1939–40 | Sixto Escobar[2] |
| 1940–42 | Lou Salica |
| 1942–46 | Manuel Ortiz |
| 1947 | Manuel Ortiz, Harold Dade |
| 1948–50 | Manuel Ortiz |
| 1950–52 | Vic Toweel |
| 1952–54 | Jimmy Carruthers[2] |
| 1954–55 | Robert Cohen |
| 1956 | Robert Cohen, Mario D'Agata, Raul Macias (NBA) |
| 1957 | Mario D'Agata, Alphonse Halimi |
| 1958–59 | Alphonse Halimi |
| 1959–60 | Jose Becerra[2] |
| 1960–61 | Alphonse Halimi[4] |
| 1961–62 | Johnny Caldwell[4] |
| 1961–65 | Eder Jofre |
| 1965–68 | Masahika (Fighting) Harada |
| 1968 | Masahika (Fighting) Harada, Lionel Rose |
| 1969 | Lionel Rose, Ruben Olivares |
| 1970 | Ruben Olivares, Chucho Castillo |
| 1971 | Chucho Castillo, Ruben Olivares |
| 1972 | Ruben Olivares, Rafael Herrera, Enrique Pinder |
| 1973 | Enrique Pinder (WBA), Romeo Anaya (WBA), |

| | | | | | |
|---|---|---|---|---|---|
| | Arnold Taylor (WBA) Rodolfo Martinez (WBC), Rafael Herrera (WBC) | | Martinez (WBC) | | Carlos Zarate (WBC) |
| 1974 | Arnold Taylor (WBA), Soo Hwan Hong (WBA), Rafael Herrera (WBC), Rodolfo | 1975 | Soo Hwan Hong (WBA), Alfonso Zamora (WBA), Rodolfo Martinez (WBC) | 1977 | Alfonso Zamora (WBA), Jorge Lujan (WBA), Carlos Zarate (WBC) |
| | | 1976 | Alfonso Zamora (WBA), Rodolfo Martinez (WBC), | 1978 | Jorge Lujan (WBA), Carlos Zarate (WBC) |

1. Abandoned title. 2. Retired. 3. Deprived of title for failing to make weight. 4. Recognized in Europe.

**Flyweight**

| | |
|---|---|
| 1916–23 | Jimmy Wilde |
| 1923–25 | Pancho Villa[1] |
| 1925 | Frankie Genaro |
| 1925–27 | Fidel La Barba[2] |
| 1927–31 | Corporal Izzy Schwartz, Frankie Genaro, Emile (Spider) Pladner, Midget Wolgast, Young Perez[3] |
| 1932–35 | Jackie Brown |
| 1935–38 | Bennie Lynch[4] |
| 1939 | Peter Kane[4] |
| 1943–47 | Jackie Paterson[1] |
| 1947–50 | Rinty Monaghan[2] |
| 1950 | Terry Allen |
| 1950–52 | Dado Marino |
| 1952–54 | Yoshio Shirai |
| 1954–60 | Pascual Perez |
| 1960–62 | Pone Kingpetch |
| 1962–63 | Masahika (Fighting) Harada |
| 1963–64 | Hiroyuki Ebihara |
| 1964–65 | Pone Kingpetch |
| 1965–66 | Salvatore Burrini |
| 1966 | Walter McGown, Chartchai Chionoi |
| 1966–68 | Charchai Chionoi |
| 1969 | Bernabe Villacampa, Efran Torres (WBA) |
| 1970 | Bernabe Villacampa, Chartchai Chionoi, Erbito Salavarria, Berkrerk Chartvanchai (WBA), Masao Ohba (WBA) |
| 1971 | Masao Ohba (WBA), Erbito Salavarria (WBC) |
| 1972 | Masao Ohba (WBA), Erbito Salavarria (WBC), Betulio Gonzalez (WBC), Venice Borkorsor (WBC) |
| 1973 | Masao Ohba (WBA), Chartchai Chionoi (WBA), Venice Borkorsor (WBC), Betulio Gonzalez (WBC) |
| 1974 | Chartchai Chionoi (WBA), Susumu Hanagata (WBA), Betulio Gonzalez (WBC), Shoji Oguma (WBC) |
| 1975 | Susumu Hanagata (WBA), Erbito Salavarria (WBA), Shoji Oguma (WBC), Miguel Canto (WBC) |
| 1976 | Erbito Salavarria (WBA), Alfonso Lopez (WBA), Guty Espadas (WBA), Miguel Canto (WBC) |
| 1977 | Guty Espadas (WBA), Miguel Canto (WBC) |
| 1978 | Guty Espadas (WBA), Betulio Gonzalez (WBA), Miguel Canto (WBC) |

1. Died. 2. Retired. 3. Claimants to NBA and New York Commission titles. 4. Abandoned title.

## PROFESSIONAL WEIGHT LIMITS

| | | | | | | | |
|---|---|---|---|---|---|---|---|
| Flyweight | 112 | Featherweight | 126 | Welterweight | 147 | Light heavyweight | 175 |
| Bantamweight | 118 | Lightweight | 135 | Middleweight | 160 | Heavyweight | over 175 |

## FIGHTER OF THE YEAR

Selected by *The Ring* Magazine.

| | |
|---|---|
| 1928 | Gene Tunney |
| 1929 | Tommy Loughran |
| 1930 | Max Schmeling |
| 1931 | Tommy Loughran |
| 1932 | Jack Sharkey |
| 1933 | No award |
| 1934 | Barney Ross and Tony Canzoneri |
| 1935 | Barney Ross |
| 1936 | Joe Louis |
| 1937 | Henry Armstrong |
| 1938 | Joe Louis |
| 1939 | Joe Louis |
| 1940 | Billy Conn |
| 1941 | Joe Louis |
| 1942 | Ray Robinson |
| 1943 | Fred Apostoli |
| 1944 | Beau Jack |
| 1945 | Willie Pep |
| 1946 | Tony Zale |
| 1947 | Gus Lesnevich |
| 1948 | Ike Williams |
| 1949 | Ezzard Charles |
| 1950 | Ezzard Charles |
| 1951 | Ray Robinson |
| 1952 | Rocky Marciano |
| 1953 | Bobo Olson |
| 1954 | Rocky Marciano |
| 1955 | Rocky Marciano |
| 1956 | Floyd Patterson |
| 1957 | Carmen Basilio |
| 1958 | Ingemar Johansson |
| 1959 | Ingemar Johansson |
| 1960 | Floyd Patterson |
| 1961 | Joe Brown |
| 1962 | Dick Tiger |
| 1963 | Cassius Clay |
| 1964 | Emile Griffith |
| 1965 | Dick Tiger |
| 1966 | No award |
| 1967 | Joe Frazier |
| 1968 | Nino Benvenuti |
| 1969 | Jose Napoles |
| 1970–71 | Joe Frazier |
| 1972 | Carlos Monzon and Muhammad Ali |
| 1973 | George Foreman |
| 1974–75 | Muhammad Ali |
| 1976 | George Foreman |
| 1977 | Carlos Zarate |

## MARCIANO WAS UNBEATEN AS A PRO

Rocky Marciano, heavyweight boxing champion of the world and winner of each of his 49 fights as a professional, announced his retirement from the ring on Apr. 27, 1956. He was the only heavyweight champion ever to retire without losing a professional fight.

Marciano won the title on Sept. 23, 1952, in Philadelphia, by knocking out Joe Walcott in the 13th round.

Marciano, born in Brockton, Mass., on Sept. 1, 1924, was killed in a plane crash, Aug. 31, 1969.

These were Marciano's championship fights:

| | | | |
|---|---|---|---|
| Sept. 23, 1952[1] | Joe Walcott, Philadelphia | KO | 13 |
| May 15, 1953 | Joe Walcott, Chicago | KO | 1 |
| Sept. 24, 1953 | Roland LaStarza, Polo Grounds | KO | 11 |
| June 17, 1954 | Ezzard Charles, Yankee Stad. | W | 15 |
| Sept. 17, 1954 | Ezzard Charles, Yankee Stad. | KO | 8 |
| May 16, 1955 | Don Cockell, San Francisco | KO | 9 |
| Sept. 21, 1955 | Archie Moore, Yankee Stad. | KO | 9 |

1. Won title.

# CHAMPIONSHIP BOUTS—1978

## Light Flyweight

(108–pound limit)

Yoko Gushiken, Japan, retained World Boxing Association title by stopping Aniceto Vargas, Philippines, in 14th round at Nagoyo, Japan, Jan. 29. Gushiken weighed 106¾ pounds, Vargas 106½.

Freddy Castillo, Mexico, knocked out Luis (Lumumbo) Estaba, Venezuela, in 14th round and won World Boxing Council title at Caracas, Venezuela, Feb. 19.

Netrnoi Sor Vorasigh, Thailand, outpointed Castillo at Bangkok, Thailand, May 6, and took W.B.C. title.

Gushiken, 108, knocked out Jaime Rios, Panama, in 13th round at Tokyo, May 7, and retained W.B.A. crown.

Kim Sung-jun, of Korea, knocked out Netrnoi at 2:29 of the third round and won W.B.C. championship at Seoul, Sept. 30.

## Flyweight

(112–pound limit)

Miguel Canto, Mexico, won split decision over Shoji Oguma, Japan, and retained World Boxing Council title at Koriyama City, Japan, Jan 4. Each weighed 111¾ pounds. It was Canto's 11th defense.

Canto gained unanimous decision over Oguma at Tokyo, April 18. Each weighed 112. There were no knockdowns in W.B.C. bout.

Guty Espadas, Mexico, stopped Kimio Furesawa, Japan, in 7th round at Tokyo, Jan. 2, and retained World Boxing Association championship he had won in October 1976.

Betulio Gonzalez, Venezuela, regained W.B.A. title by gaining split decision over Espadas at Maracay, Venezuela, Aug. 12. Gonzalez had held title in 1976.

## Bantamweight

(118–pound limit)

Carlos Zarate, Mexico, retained World Boxing Council title by knocking out Alberto Davila, Pomona, Calif., at 2:16 of 8th round at Inglewood, Calif., Feb. 25. It was Zarate's 6th defense of title won in 1976 and his 50th victory, 49 by knockouts. He weighed 117 pounds, Davila 117½.

Jorge Lujan, Panama, stopped Roberto Ruvaldino, Mexico, in 11th round at San Antonio, March 18, and kept World Boxing Association crown he won in 1977. Ruvaldino's seconds threw in towel at 1:59 of 11th after their fighter was knocked down. He had been floored in the 10th.

Zarate stopped Andre Hernandez, Puerto Rico, at San Juan, April 22, and kept W.B.C. title.

Zarate knocked out Emilio Hernandez, Venezuela, in 4th round at Las Vegas, Nev., June 9. It was his 8th defense of W.B.C. crown.

Lujan retained W.B.A. championship on unanimous decision over Davila in preliminary to Ali–Spinks fight at Las Vegas, Nev., Sept. 15.

## Junior Featherweight

(122–pound limit)

Wilfredo Gomez, Puerto Rico, stopped Juan Antonio Lopez, Mexico, in 7th round at San Juan, P.R., in defense of World Boxing Council title he won in May 1977. Referee halted bout because of cut above Lopez's right eye. It was 19th victory in 19 fights for Gomez.

Ricardo Cardona, Colombia, stopped Hong Soo-hwan, Korea, at 1:23 of 12th round and captured World Boxing Association crown at Seoul, South Korea, May 7. Referee stopped fight because of cuts over Hong's left eye. This was Hong's second defense after taking title from Hector Carrasquilla, Panama, in November 1977. He had outpointed Yu Kasahara in first defense.

Cardona defeated Ruben Valdez, Colombia, at Bogota, Colombia, Sept. 2, on decision in first defense of W.B.A. title.

Gomez stopped Leo Cruz, Dominican Republic, in 13th round and kept W.B.C. crown, at San Juan, P.R., Sept. 9.

## Featherweight

(128–pound limit)

Eusebio Pedrosa, Panama, took World Boxing Association title by knocking out Cecilio Lastra, Spain, at 1:46 of 13th round at Panama City, April 15. Lastra was floored 3 times in round. Each weighed 126 pounds.

Danny (Little Red) Lopez successfully defended World Boxing Council title by knocking out David Kotei, Ghana, at 1:28 of 6th round, on Ali–Spinks card at Las Vegas, Nev., Feb. 15. It was second defense by Lopez of title won in 1976.

Lopez stopped Jose DePaula, Brazil, at Los Angeles, April 23. DePaula's seconds threw in towel at 1:30 of 6th round as Lopez battered challenger for W.B.C. title.

Pedrosa stopped Ernesto Herrera, Mexico, in 12 rounds, at Mexico City, July 4, and retained W.B.A. title.

Lopez, knocked down in 1st round, kept W.B.C. title by knocking out Juan Malvarez, Argentina, in 2nd round at Las Vegas, Nev., on Ali–Spinks card, Sept. 15.

## Junior Lightweight

(130–pound limit)

Alexis Arguello, Nicaragua, won World Boxing Council title, stopping Alfredo Escalera, Puerto Rico, in 13th round at San Juan, P.R., Jan. 28. Referee halted bout at 2:36 of the round. Escalera, knocked down in 2nd round, staggered Arguello in the 8th and 12th. It was Escalera's 11th defense of title won in 1975.

Sammy Serrano, Puerto Rico, outpointed Mario Martinez and retained World Boxing Association title at San Juan, Feb. 18.

Arguello retained W.B.C. title in first defense by stopping Rey Tam, Philippines, in 5th round at Los Angeles, April 29. Tam was unbeaten in 25 fights until referee stopped bout at 1:54 of 5th. It was Arguello's 54th victory in 57 bouts.

Arguello knocked out Diego Alcala, Pasadena, Calif., at 1:50 of 1st round of W.B.C. fight at San Juan, P.R., June 3.

Serrano knocked out Young Ho, Korea, in 9th round at San Juan, July 8, and kept W.B.A. title. It was his 6th defense of crown won in 1976.

## Lightweight

(135–pound limit)

Roberto Duran, Panama, knocked out Esteban de Jesus, Puerto Rico, at 2:32 of 12th round at Las Vegas, Nev., and gained undisputed championship. Duran held World Boxing Association crown, which he won in 1972, and de Jesus had been the World Boxing Council champion since 1976. Floored by a right cross, de Jesus was up at the count of 3 in the 12th but he could not hold off Duran's attack and the referee halted the fight. It was de Jesus' 4th loss in 54 fights. In his 12th defense, Duran posted his 61st victory and 31st in a row, and his 51st knockout. Duran weighed 134¼, de Jesus 134.

## Junior Welterweight

(140–pound limit)

Antonio Cervantes, Spain, knocked out Tongta Kiatvayupakdi, Thailand, in 6th round and retained World Boxing Association title.

Cervantes, in W.B.A. title defense, stopped Norman Sekgapane, South Africa, in 9th round.

Saensak Muangsurin, Thailand, retained World Boxing Council championship by knocking out Francisco Merno, Venezuela, in 13th round.

## Welterweight

(147–pound limit)

Carlos Palomino, Huntington Beach, Calif., knocked out Mimoun Mahatar, Morocco, in 57 seconds of the 9th round and retained the World Boxing Council title at Las Vegas, Nev., March 18. Mohatar was down in 4th round. Palomino weighed 147 pounds for 6th defense of crown won in 1976. Mohatar weighed 146¼.

Jose (Pepino) Cuevas, Mexico, stopped Harold Weston, Jr., New York, in 9th round at Los Angeles. Weston suffered a broken jaw. It was the 5th defense by Cuevas since gaining title in 1976.

Palomino broke his hand midway through W.B.C. bout but outpointed Mando Muniz, Montebello, at Los Angeles, May 28.

Cuevas stopped Billy Backus, Canastota, N.Y., May 20. The W.B.A. fight was halted after the 1st round because of damage to challenger's right eye. Under California rules it is a 1st-round knockout.

Cuevas retained W.B.A. title by knocking out Pete Ranzany, Sacramento Calif., at 1:15 of 2nd round at Sacramento, Sept. 9. It was 7th defense of title by Cuevas who won title in 1976 at the age of 18, the youngest welterweight champion in history.

### Junior Middleweight

(154–pound limit)

Rocky Mattioli, Italy, knocked out Jose Duran, Spain, in 5th round and retained World Boxing Council title at Pescara, Italy, May 14. It was his 2nd defense of crown won in 1977. Duran was knocked down twice before the finish. Mattioli had knocked out Elisha Obed, the Bahamas, former champion, in the 7th round at Melbourne in his first defense.

Masashi Kudo, Japan, outpointed Eddy Gazo, Nicaragua, Aug. 9 at Tokyo and took World Boxing Association title. Gazo had won title in 1977.

### Middleweight

(160–pound limit)

Hugo Corro, Argentina, outpointed Rodrigo Valdez, Colombia, and won undisputed title (W.B.A. and W.B.C.). It was the first defense by Valdez after regaining crown in November 1977 from Bennie Briscoe, Philadelphia.

Corro outpointed Ronnie Harris, Dayton, Ohio, at Buenos Aires, Aug. 8, in first defense. It was first defeat in 28 pro bouts for Harris.

### Light Heavyweight

(175–pound limit)

Mate Parlov, Yugoslavia, knocked out Miguel Cuello, Argentina, in 9th round at Milan, Italy, Jan. 7, and won World Boxing Council championship. Cuello had gained title in May 1977.

Victor Galindez, Argentina, outpointed Alvaro (Yaqui) Lopez, Stockton, Calif., and retained World Boxing Association title, May 6 at Lido di Camaire, Italy. It was 10th defense by Galindez of title won in 1974.

Parlov kept W.B.C. crown on split decision over John Conteh, England, at Belgrade, Yugoslavia, June 17. Both judges voted for Parlov, but the referee gave nod to Conteh, former champion, who was stripped of title by W.B.C. in 1977 for failing to fight Cuello.

Mike Rossman, Turnersville, N.J., stopped Galindez in 13th round and gained W.B.A. title at Las Vegas, Nev., Sept. 15, on Spinks-Ali card. Referee halted fight when champion, who had bad cut over right eye, could not defend himself. It was first defeat for Galindez in 42 fights beginning in 1972.

### Heavyweight

Leon Spinks took the title from Mohammad Ali on a split decision at Las Vegas, Nev., Feb. 15. Ali played rope-a-dope in the early rounds, apparently believing he had no problem with the former Olympic champion from St. Louis. When the champion tried to take control later, Spinks countered successfully and apparently was awarded the advantage in a slugging final round. One judge voted for Ali, 143–142, the other for Spinks, 145–140. The referee, Howard Buck, scored the fight 144–141, for Spinks. Ali weighed 224¼ and Spinks 197.

The World Boxing Association withdrew recognition of Spinks March 18, and awarded its title to Ken Norton, San Diego, Calif. W.B.C. said Spinks had agreed to fight Norton, the winner of a bout with Jimmy Young on Nov. 5, 1977, but had chosen to meet Ali in a rematch.

In his first defense of the W.B.C. crown, Norton lost to Larry Holmes, Easton, Pa. Their bout at Las Vegas, Nev., June 9, was rated one of the best of heavyweight contests. They went into the 15th round rated even, and Holmes was given the round and the fight by two of the three judges. It was Holmes' 26th professional fight and he was unbeaten.

### Ali Gains Title for Third Time

Ali won a unanimous decision over Spinks in a rematch before the largest gate in boxing history at the Superdome in New Orleans, Sept. 15. Ali weathered a couple of early surges by Spinks and was in control of the bout from the start, outboxing the younger fighter. The referee, Lucien Joubert, and one judge scored 10 rounds for Ali, 4 for Spinks, and 1 even. The other judge voted 11–4 for Ali. Ali, 36, weighed 221 and Spinks, 25, weighed 201.

## NON-TITLE BOUTS—1978

(Heavyweights)

Larry Holmes won unanimous decision over Earnie Shavers, 33, in 12 rounds at Las Vegas, Nev., March 26. Two of three judges scored every round for Holmes; the other gave one round to Shavers.

Jimmy Young lost split decision to Osvaldo Ocasio, a 22-year-old Puerto Rican, at Las Vegas, Nev., June 9, on card with Norton-Holmes. Young weighed 220, Ocasio 205.

## JOE LOUIS' TITLE FIGHTS

| | | | |
|---|---|---|---|
| June 22, 1937[1] | Jim Braddock, Chicago | KO | 8 |
| Aug. 30, 1937 | Tommy Farr, Yankee Stadium | W | 15 |
| Feb. 23, 1938 | Nathan Mann, Mad. Sq. Garden | KO | 3 |
| April 1, 1938 | Harry Thomas, Chicago | KO | 5 |
| June 22, 1938[2] | Max Schmeling, Yankee Stadium | KO | 1 |
| Jan. 25, 1939 | John Henry Lewis, Mad. Sq. Garden | KO | 1 |
| April 17, 1939 | Jack Roper, Los Angeles | KO | 1 |
| June 28, 1939 | Tony Galento, Yankee Stadium | KO | 4 |
| Sept. 20, 1939 | Bob Pastor, Detroit | KO | 11 |
| Feb. 9, 1940 | Arturo Godoy, Mad. Sq. Garden | W | 15 |
| March 29, 1940 | Johnny Paycheck, Mad. Sq. Garden | KO | 2 |
| June 20, 1940 | Arturo Godoy, Yankee Stadium | KO | 8 |
| Dec. 16, 1940 | Al McCoy, Boston | KO | 6 |
| Jan. 31, 1941 | Red Burman, Mad. Sq. Garden | KO | 5 |
| Feb. 17, 1941 | Gus Dorazio, Philadelphia | KO | 2 |
| March, 21, 1941 | Abe Simon, Detroit | KO | 13 |
| April 8, 1941 | Tony Musto, St. Louis | KO | 9 |
| May 23, 1941 | Buddy Baer, Washington, D.C. | W disq. | 7 |
| June 18, 1941 | Billy Conn, Polo Grounds | KO | 13 |
| Sept. 29, 1941 | Lou Nova, Polo Grounds | KO | 6 |
| Jan. 9, 1942 | Buddy Baer, Madison Sq. Garden | KO | 1 |

| | | | |
|---|---|---|---|
| March 27, 1942 | Abe Simon, Madison Sq. Garden | KO | 6 |
| June 19, 1946 | Billy Conn, Yankee Stadium | KO | 8 |
| Sept. 18, 1946 | Tami Mauriello, Yankee Stadium | KO | 1 |
| Dec. 5, 1947 | Joe Walcott, Madison Sq. Garden | W | 15 |
| June 25, 1948 | Joe Walcott, Yankee Stadium | KO | 11 |
| Sept. 27, 1950[3] | Ezzard Charles, Yankee Stadium | L | 15 |

1. Won title. 2. Schmeling had stopped Louis in 12th round of non-title fight, June 19, 1936. 3. After announcing retirement as champion on March 1, 1949, Louis returned to boxing and sought to regain title in bout with Charles.

## TITLE BOUTS OF MUHAMMAD ALI (CASSIUS CLAY)

| | | | |
|---|---|---|---|
| Feb. 25, 1964[1] | Sonny Liston, Miami Beach | KO | 7 |
| (Liston failed to come out for seventh round) | | | |
| May 25, 1965 | Sonny Liston, Lewiston, Me. | KO | 1 |
| Nov. 22, 1965 | Floyd Patterson, Las Vegas | KO | 12 |
| March 29, 1966 | George Chuvalo, Toronto | W | 15 |
| May 21, 1966 | Henry Cooper, London | KO | 6 |
| Aug. 6, 1966 | Brian London, London | KO | 3 |
| Sept. 10, 1966 | Karl Mildenberger, Frankfurt, Ger. | KO | 12 |
| Nov. 14, 1966 | Cleveland Williams, Houston | KO | 3 |
| Feb. 6, 1967 | Ernie Terrell, Houston | W | 15 |
| March 22, 1967 | Zora Folley, New York | KO | 7 |
| March 8, 1971[2] | Joe Frazier, New York | L | 15 |
| Oct. 30, 1974[1] | George Foreman, Zaire | KO | 8 |
| March 24, 1975 | Chuck Wepner, Richfield, Ohio | KO | 15 |
| May 16, 1975 | Ron Lyle, Las Vegas, Nev. | KO | 11 |
| July 1, 1975 | Joe Bugner, Kuala Lumpur | W | 15 |
| Sept. 30, 1975 | Joe Frazier, Manila | KO | 14 |
| Feb. 20, 1976 | Jean-Pierre Coopman, San Juan | KO | 5 |
| April 30, 1976 | Jimmy Young, Landover, Md. | W | 15 |
| May 24, 1976 | Richard Dunn, Munich | KO | 5 |
| Sept. 28, 1976 | Ken Norton, New York | W | 15 |
| May 16, 1977 | Alfredo Evangelista, Landover, Md. | W | 15 |
| Sept. 29, 1977 | Earnie Shavers, New York | W | 15 |
| Feb. 15, 1978[3] | Leon Spinks, Las Vegas, Nev. | L | 15 |
| Sept. 15, 1978[4] | Leon Spinks, New Orleans | W | 15 |

1. Won world heavyweight championship. 2. Lost title officially. When Ali (Clay) refused induction into the United States armed services, April 18, 1967, the New York State Athletic Commission stripped him of his title and other official groups followed suit. He was convicted of draft evasion June 20, 1967, by a Federal Court and was inactive awaiting results of appeal. Ali regained license to fight in autumn of 1970, after resigning as titleholder. After losing to Frazier, United States Supreme Court reversed Federal court decision on technicalities in Justice Department's presentation of case, June 28, 1971. 3. Lost title. 4. Regained W.B.A. title.

# BOXING—AMATEUR

## A.A.U. NATIONAL CHAMPIONSHIPS

(Biloxi, Miss., April 18–22, 1978)

Light Flyweight (106 lb)—James Cullins, Bladensburg, Md.
Flyweight (112)—Mike Felde, Missoula, Mont.
Bantamweight (119)—Jackie Beard, Jackson, Tenn.
Featherweight (125)—Eiichi Jumawan, Wahiawa, Hawaii
Lightweight (132)—Melvin Paul, New Orleans
Light Welterweight (139)—Donald Curry, Fort Worth, Tex.
Welterweight (147)—Roger Leonard, U.S. Air Force
Light Middleweight (156)—J.B. Williamson, U.S. Marines
Middleweight (165)—Jeff McCracken, U.S. Marines
Light Heavyweight (178)—Elmer Martin, U.S. Navy
Heavyweight (over 178)—Greg Page, Louisville, Ky.
Outstanding Boxer—Greg Page
Sportsmanship Award—Davey Armstrong, Lightweight, Puyallup, Wash.
Team—United States Marines

## WORLD CHAMPIONSHIPS

(Belgrade, Yugoslavia, May 6–20, 1978)

Light Flyweight—Stephen Mushioki, Kenya
Flyweight—Henryk Srednicki, Poland
Bantamweight—Adolfo Horta, Cuba
Featherweight—Angel Herrera, Cuba
Lightweight—Davidson Andeh, Nigeria
Light Welterweight—Valery Lvov, U.S.S.R.
Welterweight—Valery Rachkov, U.S.S.R.
Light Middleweight—Viktor Savchenko, U.S.S.R.
Middleweight—Jose Gomez, Cuba
Light Heavyweight—Sixto Soria, Cuba
Heavyweight—Teofilo Stevenson, Cuba

# SYNCHRONIZED SWIMMING

## 1978 A.A.U. NATIONAL CHAMPIONSHIPS

**Indoor**

(City of Commerce, Calif., March 23–25)

Solo—Pam Tryon, Santa Clara (Calif.) Aquamaids
Duet—Pam Tryon and Michele Barone, Santa Clara Aquamaids
Team—Santa Clara Aquamaids

**Outdoor**

(Purchase, N.Y., July 20–23)

Solo—Linda Shelley, Santa Clara Aquamaids
Duet—Michele Barone and Pam Tryon, Santa Clara Aquamaids
Team—Santa Clara Aquamaids

## ASSOCIATION OF INTERCOLLEGIATE ATHLETICS FOR WOMEN (A.I.A.W.)—1978

Solo—Linda Shelley, San Jose State
Duet—Cary Lamb and Cindy Ott, Ohio State
Team—Ohio State

## WORLD CHAMPIONSHIPS—1978

Solo—Helen Vanderburg, Canada
Duet—Michele Calkins and Helen Vanderburg, Canada
Team—U.S. (Tami Allen, Michele Barone, Erin Barr, Michele Beaulieu, Gerry Brandly, Jane Goeppinger, Linda Shelley, Pam Tryon, Santa Clara S.C. California)

# HORSE RACING

Ancient drawings on stone and bone prove that horse racing is at least 3000 years old, but Thoroughbred Racing is a modern development. Practically every thoroughbred in training today traces its registered ancestry back to one or more of three sires that arrived in England about 1728 from the Near East and became known, from the names of their owners, as the Byerly Turk, the Darley Arabian, and the Godolphin Arabian. The Jockey Club (English) was founded at Newmarket in 1750 or 1751 and became the custodian of the Stud Book as well as the court of last resort in deciding turf affairs.

Horse racing took place in this country before the Revolution, but the great lift to the breeding industry came with the importation in 1798, by Col. John Hoomes of Virginia, of Diomed, winner of the Epsom Derby of 1780. Diomed's lineal descendants included such famous stars of the American turf as American Eclipse and Lexington. From 1800 to the time of the Civil War there were race courses and breeding establishments plentifully scattered through Virginia, North Carolina, South Carolina, Tennessee, Kentucky, and Louisiana.

The oldest stake event in North America is the Queen's Plate, a Canadian fixture that was first run in the Province of Quebec in 1836. The oldest stake event in the United States is The Travers, which was first run at Saratoga in 1864. The gambling that goes with horse racing and trickery by jockeys, trainers, owners, and track officials caused attacks on the sport by reformers and a demand among horse racing enthusiasts for an honest and effective control of some kind, but nothing of lasting value to racing came of this until the formation in 1894 of The Jockey Club.

## "TRIPLE CROWN" WINNERS IN THE UNITED STATES[1]

**(Kentucky Derby, Preakness, and Belmont Stakes)**

| Year | Horse | Owner | Year | Horse | Owner |
|---|---|---|---|---|---|
| 1919 | Sir Barton | J. K. L. Ross | 1946 | Assault | Robert J. Kleberg |
| 1930 | Gallant Fox | William Woodward | 1948 | Citation | Warren Wright |
| 1935 | Omaha | William Woodward | 1973 | Secretariat | Meadow Stable |
| 1937 | War Admiral | Samuel D. Riddle | 1977 | Seattle Slew | Karen Taylor |
| 1941 | Whirlaway | Warren Wright | 1978 | Affirmed | Louis Wolfson |
| 1943 | Count Fleet | Mrs. John Hertz | | | |

## KENTUCKY DERBY

Churchill Downs; 3-year-olds; 1 1/4 miles.

| Year | Winner | Jockey | Wt. | Win val. | Year | Winner | Jockey | Wt. | Win val. |
|---|---|---|---|---|---|---|---|---|---|
| 1875 | Aristides | O. Lewis | 100 | $2,850 | 1908 | Stone Street | A. Pickens | 117 | $4,850 |
| 1876 | Vagrant | R. Swim | 97 | 2,950 | 1909 | Wintergreen | V. Powers | 117 | 4,850 |
| 1877 | Baden Baden | W. Walker | 100 | 3,300 | 1910 | Donau | F. Herbert | 117 | 4,850 |
| 1878 | Day Star | J. Carter | 100 | 4,050 | 1911 | Meridian | G. Archibald | 117 | 4,850 |
| 1879 | Lord Murphy | C. Schauer | 100 | 3,550 | 1912 | Worth | C. H. Shilling | 117 | 4,850 |
| 1880 | Fonso | G. Lewis | 105 | 3,800 | 1913 | Donerail | R. Goose | 117 | 5,475 |
| 1881 | Hindoo | J. McLaughlin | 105 | 4,410 | 1914 | Old Rosebud | J. McCabe | 114 | 9,125 |
| 1882 | Apollo | B. Hurd | 102 | 4,560 | 1915 | Regret | J. Notter | 112 | 11,450 |
| 1883 | Leonatus | W. Donohue | 105 | 3,760 | 1916 | George Smith | J. Loftus | 117 | 9,750 |
| 1884 | Buchanan | I. Murphy | 110 | 3,990 | 1917 | Omar Khayyam | C. Borel | 117 | 16,600 |
| 1885 | Joe Cotton | E. Henderson | 110 | 4,630 | 1918 | Exterminator | W. Knapp | 114 | 14,700 |
| 1886 | Ben Ali | P. Duffy | 118 | 4,890 | 1919 | Sir Barton | J. Loftus | 112½ | 20,825 |
| 1887 | Montrose | I. Lewis | 118 | 4,200 | 1920 | Paul Jones | T. Rice | 126 | 30,375 |
| 1888 | Macbeth II | G. Covington | 115 | 4,740 | 1921 | Behave Yourself | C. Thompson | 126 | 38,450 |
| 1889 | Spokane | T. Kiley | 118 | 4,970 | 1922 | Morvich | A. Johnson | 126 | 46,775 |
| 1890 | Riley | I. Murphy | 118 | 5,460 | 1923 | Zev | E. Sande | 126 | 53,600 |
| 1891 | Kingman | I. Murphy | 122 | 4,680 | 1924 | Black Gold | J. D. Mooney | 126 | 52,775 |
| 1892 | Azra | A. Clayton | 122 | 4,230 | 1925 | Flying Ebony | E. Sande | 126 | 52,950 |
| 1893 | Lookout | E. Kunze | 122 | 4,090 | 1926 | Bubbling Over | A. Johnson | 126 | 50,075 |
| 1894 | Chant | F. Goodale | 122 | 4,020 | 1927 | Whiskery | L. McAtee | 126 | 51,000 |
| 1895 | Halma | J. Perkins | 122 | 2,970 | 1928 | Reigh Count | C. Lang | 126 | 55,375 |
| 1896 | Ben Brush | W. Simms | 117 | 4,850 | 1929 | Clyde Van Dusen | L. McAtee | 126 | 53,950 |
| 1897 | Typhoon II | F. Garner | 117 | 4,850 | 1930 | Gallant Fox | E. Sande | 126 | 50,725 |
| 1898 | Plaudit | W. Simms | 117 | 4,850 | 1931 | Twenty Grand | C. Kurtsinger | 126 | 48,725 |
| 1899 | Manuel | F. Taral | 117 | 4,850 | 1932 | Burgoo King | E. James | 126 | 52,350 |
| 1900 | Lieut. Gibson | J. Boland | 117 | 4,850 | 1933 | Brokers Tip | D. Meade | 126 | 48,925 |
| 1901 | His Eminence | J. Winkfield | 117 | 4,850 | 1934 | Cavalcade | M. Garner | 126 | 28,175 |
| 1902 | Alan-a-Dale | J. Winkfield | 117 | 4,850 | 1935 | Omaha | W. Saunders | 126 | 39,525 |
| 1903 | Judge Himes | H. Booker | 117 | 4,850 | 1936 | Bold Venture | I. Hanford | 126 | 37,725 |
| 1904 | Elwood | F. Prior | 117 | 4,850 | 1937 | War Admiral | C. Kurtsinger | 126 | 52,050 |
| 1905 | Agile | J. Martin | 122 | 4,850 | 1938 | Lawrin | E. Arcaro | 126 | 47,050 |
| 1906 | Sir Huon | R. Troxler | 117 | 4,850 | 1939 | Johnstown | J. Stout | 126 | 46,350 |
| 1907 | Pink Star | A. Minder | 117 | 4,850 | 1940 | Gallahadion | C. Bierman | 126 | 60,150 |

1. Statistics relative to thoroughbred racing in this publication are reproduced from the *American Racing Manual*, by special permission of the copyright owners, TRIANGLE PUBLICATIONS, INC. Reproduction prohibited.

| Year | Winner | Jockey | Wt. | Win val. |
|---|---|---|---|---|
| 1941 | Whirlaway | E. Arcaro | 126 | $61,275 |
| 1942 | Shut Out | W. D. Wright | 126 | 64,225 |
| 1943 | Count Fleet | J. Longden | 126 | 60,725 |
| 1944 | Pensive | C. McCreary | 126 | 64,675 |
| 1945 | Hoop Jr. | E. Arcaro | 126 | 64,850 |
| 1946 | Assault | W. Mehrtens | 126 | 96,400 |
| 1947 | Jet Pilot | E. Guerin | 126 | 92,160 |
| 1948 | Citation | E. Arcaro | 126 | 83,400 |
| 1949 | Ponder | S. Brooks | 126 | 91,600 |
| 1950 | Middleground | W. Boland | 126 | 92,650 |
| 1951 | Count Turf | C. McCreary | 126 | 98,050 |
| 1952 | Hill Gail | E. Arcaro | 126 | 96,300 |
| 1953 | Dark Star | H. Moreno | 126 | 90,050 |
| 1954 | Determine | R. York | 126 | 102,050 |
| 1955 | Swaps | W. Shoemaker | 126 | 108,400 |
| 1956 | Needles | D. Erb | 126 | 123,450 |
| 1957 | Iron Liege | W. Hartack | 126 | 107,950 |
| 1958 | Tim Tam | I. Valenzuela | 126 | 116,400 |
| 1959 | Tomy Lee | W. Shoemaker | 126 | 119,650 |
| 1960 | Venetian Way | W. Hartack | 126 | $114,850 |
| 1961 | Carry Back | J. Sellers | 126 | 120,500 |
| 1962 | Decidedly | W. Hartack | 126 | 119,650 |
| 1963 | Chateauguay | B. Baeza | 126 | 108,900 |
| 1964 | Northern Dancer | W. Hartack | 126 | 114,300 |
| 1965 | Lucky Debonair | W. Shoemaker | 126 | 112,000 |
| 1966 | Kauai King | D. Brumfield | 126 | 120,500 |
| 1967 | Proud Clarion | R. Ussery | 126 | 119,700 |
| 1968 | Forward Pass[1] | I. Valenzuela | 126 | 122,600 |
| 1969 | Majestic Prince | W. Hartack | 126 | 113,200 |
| 1970 | Dust Commander | M. Manganello | 126 | 127,800 |
| 1971 | Canonero II | G. Avila | 126 | 145,500 |
| 1972 | Riva Ridge | R. Turcotte | 126 | 140,300 |
| 1973 | Secretariat | R. Turcotte | 126 | 155,050 |
| 1974 | Cannonade | A. Cordero, Jr. | 126 | 274,000 |
| 1975 | Foolish Pleasure | J. Vasquez | 126 | 209,600 |
| 1976 | Bold Forbes | A. Cordero, Jr. | 126 | 165,200 |
| 1977 | Seattle Slew | J. Cruguet | 126 | 214,700 |
| 1978 | Affirmed | S. Cauthen | 126 | 186,900 |

1. Dancer's Image finished first but was disqualified after traces of drug were found in system.

## PREAKNESS STAKES

Pimlico; 3-year-olds; $1\frac{3}{16}$ miles; first race 1873.

| Year | Winner | Jockey | Wt. | Win val. |
|---|---|---|---|---|
| 1919 | Sir Barton | J. Loftus | 126 | $ 24,500 |
| 1930 | Gallant Fox | E. Sande | 126 | 51,925 |
| 1935 | Omaha | W. Saunders | 126 | 25,325 |
| 1936 | Bold Venture | G. Woolf | 126 | 27,325 |
| 1937 | War Admiral | C. Kurtsinger | 126 | 45,600 |
| 1941 | Whirlaway | E. Arcaro | 126 | 49,365 |
| 1943 | Count Fleet | J. Longden | 126 | 43,190 |
| 1946 | Assault | W. Mehrtens | 126 | 96,620 |
| 1948 | Citation | E. Arcaro | 126 | 91,870 |
| 1950 | Hill Prince | E. Arcaro | 126 | 56,115 |
| 1951 | Bold | E. Arcaro | 126 | 83,110 |
| 1952 | Blue Man | C. McCreary | 126 | 86,135 |
| 1953 | Native Dancer | E. Guerin | 126 | 65,200 |
| 1954 | Hasty Road | J. Adams | 126 | 91,600 |
| 1955 | Nashua | E. Arcaro | 126 | 67,550 |
| 1956 | Fabius | W. Hartack | 126 | 84,250 |
| 1957 | Bold Ruler | E. Arcaro | 126 | 65,250 |
| 1958 | Tim Tam | I. Valenzuela | 126 | 97,900 |
| 1959 | Royal Orbit | W. Harmatz | 126 | 136,200 |
| 1960 | Bally Ache | R. Ussery | 126 | $121,000 |
| 1961 | Carry Back | J. Sellers | 126 | 126,200 |
| 1962 | Greek Money | J. Rotz | 126 | 135,800 |
| 1963 | Candy Spots | W. Shoemaker | 126 | 127,500 |
| 1964 | Northern Dancer | W. Hartack | 126 | 124,200 |
| 1965 | Tom Rolfe | R. Turcotte | 126 | 128,100 |
| 1966 | Kauai King | D. Brumfield | 126 | 129,000 |
| 1967 | Damascus | W. Shoemaker | 126 | 141,500 |
| 1968 | Forward Pass | I. Valenzuela | 126 | 142,700 |
| 1969 | Majestic Prince | W. Hartack | 126 | 129,500 |
| 1970 | Personality | E. Belmonte | 126 | 151,300 |
| 1971 | Canonero II | G. Avila | 126 | 137,400 |
| 1972 | Bee Bee Bee | E. Nelson | 126 | 135,300 |
| 1973 | Secretariat | R. Turcotte | 126 | 129,900 |
| 1974 | Little Current | M. Rivera | 126 | 156,000 |
| 1975 | Master Derby | D. McHargue | 126 | 158,100 |
| 1976 | Elocutionist | J. Lively | 126 | 129,700 |
| 1977 | Seattle Slew | J. Cruguet | 126 | 138,600 |
| 1978 | Affirmed | S. Cauthen | 126 | 136,200 |

## BELMONT STAKES

Belmont Park; 3-year-olds; $1\frac{1}{2}$ miles.

Run at Jerome Park 1867 to 1890; at Morris Park 1890–94; at Belmont Park 1905–62; at Aqueduct 1963–67. Distance $1\frac{5}{8}$ miles prior to 1874; reduced to $1\frac{1}{2}$ miles, 1874; reduced to $1\frac{1}{4}$ miles, 1890; reduced to $1\frac{1}{8}$ miles, 1893; increased to $1\frac{1}{4}$ miles, 1895; increased to $1\frac{3}{8}$ miles, 1896; reduced to $1\frac{1}{4}$ miles in 1904; increased to $1\frac{1}{2}$ miles, 1926.

| Year | Winner | Jockey | Wt | Win val. |
|---|---|---|---|---|
| 1919 | Sir Barton | J. Loftus | 126 | $ 11,950 |
| 1930 | Gallant Fox | E. Sande | 126 | 66,040 |
| 1935 | Omaha | W. Saunders | 126 | 35,480 |
| 1937 | War Admiral | C. Kurtsinger | 126 | 38,020 |
| 1941 | Whirlaway | E. Arcaro | 126 | 39,770 |
| 1943 | Count Fleet | J. Longden | 126 | 35,340 |
| 1946 | Assault | W. Mehrtens | 126 | 75,400 |
| 1948 | Citation | E. Arcaro | 126 | 77,700 |
| 1950 | Middleground | W. Boland | 126 | 61,350 |
| 1951 | Counterpoint | D. Gorman | 126 | 82,000 |
| 1952 | One Count | E. Arcaro | 126 | 82,400 |
| 1953 | Native Dancer | E. Guerin | 126 | 82,500 |
| 1954 | High Gun | E. Guerin | 126 | 89,000 |
| 1955 | Nashua | E. Arcaro | 126 | 83,700 |
| 1956 | Needles | D. Erb | 126 | 83,600 |
| 1957 | Gallant Man | W. Shoemaker | 126 | 77,300 |
| 1958 | Cavan | P. Anderson | 126 | 73,440 |
| 1959 | Sword Dancer | W. Shoemaker | 126 | 93,525 |
| 1960 | Celtic Ash | W. Hartack | 126 | 96,785 |
| 1961 | Sherluck | B. Baeza | 126 | $104,900 |
| 1962 | Jaipur | W. Shoemaker | 126 | 109,550 |
| 1963 | Chateauguay | B. Baeza | 126 | 101,700 |
| 1964 | Quadrangle | M. Ycaza | 126 | 110,850 |
| 1965 | Hail to All | J. Sellers | 126 | 104,150 |
| 1966 | Amberoid | W. Boland | 126 | 117,700 |
| 1967 | Damascus | W. Shoemaker | 126 | 104,950 |
| 1968 | Stage Door Johnny | H. Gustines | 126 | 117,700 |
| 1969 | Arts and Letters | B. Baeza | 126 | 104,050 |
| 1970 | High Echelon | J. Rotz | 126 | 115,000 |
| 1971 | Pass Catcher | R. Blum | 126 | 97,710 |
| 1972 | Riva Ridge | R. Turcotte | 126 | 93,540 |
| 1973 | Secretariat | R. Turcotte | 126 | 90,120 |
| 1974 | Little Current | M. Rivera | 126 | 101,970 |
| 1975 | Avatar | W. Shoemaker | 126 | 116,160 |
| 1976 | Bold Forbes | A. Cordero, Jr. | 126 | 117,000 |
| 1977 | Seattle Slew | J. Cruguet | 126 | 109,080 |
| 1978 | Affirmed | S. Cauthen | 126 | 110,580 |

## LEADING MONEY-WINNING JOCKEYS

Steve Cauthen, a 17-year-old newcomer from Kentucky, shattered the money-winning record for jockeys in 1977. He was the first to guide his mounts to earnings of over $5 million in a year, with a total of $6,151,750. His popularity was so great that he had 2,075 mounts. He finished first on 487 of them. The list of annual leaders:

| Year | Jockey | Mts. | 1st | Amt. won |
|---|---|---|---|---|
| 1956 | Bill Hartack | 1,387 | 347 | $2,343,955 |
| 1957 | Bill Hartack | 1,238 | 341 | 3,060,501 |
| 1958 | Willie Shoemaker | 1,133 | 300 | 2,961,693 |
| 1959 | Willie Shoemaker | 1,285 | 347 | 2,843,133 |
| 1960 | Willie Shoemaker | 1,227 | 274 | 2,123,961 |
| 1961 | Willie Shoemaker | 1,256 | 304 | 2,690,819 |
| 1962 | Willie Shoemaker | 1,126 | 311 | 2,916,844 |
| 1963 | Willie Shoemaker | 1,203 | 271 | $2,526,925 |
| 1964 | Willie Shoemaker | 1,056 | 246 | 2,649,553 |
| 1965 | Braulio Baeza | 1,245 | 270 | 2,582,702 |
| 1966 | Braulio Baeza | 1,341 | 298 | 2,951,022 |
| 1967 | Braulio Baeza | 1,064 | 256 | 3,088,888 |
| 1968 | Braulio Baeza | 1,089 | 201 | 2,835,108 |
| 1969 | Jorge Velasquez | 1,442 | 258 | 2,542,305 |
| 1970 | Laffit Pincay, Jr. | 1,328 | 269 | 2,626,526 |
| 1971 | Laffit Pincay, Jr. | 1,627 | 380 | 3,784,377 |
| 1972 | Laffit Pincay, Jr. | 1,388 | 289 | 3,225,827 |
| 1973 | Laffit Pincay, Jr. | 1,444 | 350 | 4,093,492 |
| 1974 | Laffit Pincay, Jr. | 1,278 | 341 | 4,251,060 |
| 1975 | Braulio Baeza | 1,191 | 197 | 3,695,198 |
| 1976 | Angel Cordero, Jr. | 1,534 | 274 | 4,709,500 |
| 1977 | Steve Cauthen | 2,075 | 487 | 6,151,750 |

## MAN O'WAR'S RACING RECORD

| 1919 | Race | Fin. | Earnings |
|---|---|---|---|
| June 6 | Purse | 1 | $ 500 |
| June 9 | Keene Memorial Stakes | 1 | 4,200 |
| June 21 | Youthful Stakes | 1 | 3,850 |
| June 23 | Hudson Stakes | 1 | 2,825 |
| July 5 | Tremont Stakes | 1 | 4,800 |
| Aug. 2 | United States Hotel Stakes | 1 | 7,600 |
| Aug. 13 | Sanford Memorial Stakes | 2 | 700 |
| Aug. 23 | Grand Union Hotel Stakes | 1 | 7,600 |
| Aug. 30 | Hopeful Stakes | 1 | 24,600 |
| Sept. 13 | Belmont Futurity | 1 | 26,650 |

| 1920 | Race | Fin. | Earnings |
|---|---|---|---|
| May 18 | Preakness Stakes | 1 | $23,000 |
| May 29 | Withers Stakes | 1 | 4,825 |
| June 12 | Belmont Stakes | 1 | 7,950 |
| June 22 | Stuyvesant Handicap | 1 | 3,850 |
| July 10 | Dwyer Stakes | 1 | 4,850 |
| Aug. 7 | Miller Stakes | 1 | 4,700 |
| Aug. 21 | Travers Stakes | 1 | 9,275 |
| Sept. 4 | Lawrence Realization Stakes | 1 | 15,040 |
| Sept. 11 | Jockey Club Stakes | 1 | 5,850 |
| Sept. 18 | Potomac Handicap | 1 | 6,800 |
| Oct. 12 | Kenilworth Park Gold Cup | 1 | 80,000 |

**Recapitulation**

| Year | Age | Races | 1st | 2nd | Unp. | Earnings |
|---|---|---|---|---|---|---|
| 1919 | 2 | 10 | 9 | 1 | 0 | $ 83,325 |
| 1920 | 3 | 11 | 11 | 0 | 0 | 166,140 |
| **Total** | | **21** | **20** | **1** | **0** | **$249,465** |

## KELSO BIGGEST MONEY EARNER; FOREGO IS RETIRED

Forego, an 8-year old gelding, was retired July 10, 1978, just when he seemed ready to pass Kelso's record of $1,977,896 for career earnings for a race horse. Forego had raised his total earnings to $1,938,957 in 1977. However, the horse was suffering from bone chips and other ailments. When he finished fifth in his first 1978 start (on July 4), Forego's owner, Martha Gerry, decided that the gelding's racing days were over. In his 57 races, Forego finished first 34 times, second 9 times, and third 7 times. Kelso was retired in 1966 after having passed Round Table's record of $1,749,869 in 1964. The leaders as of Sept. 30, 1978:

| Horse | Starts | 1st | 2nd | 3rd | Earnings |
|---|---|---|---|---|---|
| Kelso | 63 | 39 | 12 | 2 | $1,977,896 |
| Forego | 57 | 34 | 9 | 7 | 1,938,957 |
| Round Table | 66 | 43 | 8 | 5 | 1,749,869 |
| Dahlia[1] | 48 | 15 | 3 | 7 | 1,543,139 |
| Buckpasser | 31 | 25 | 4 | 1 | 1,462,014 |
| Allez France[1] | 21 | 13 | 3 | 1 | 1,386,146 |
| Secretariat | 21 | 16 | 3 | 1 | 1,316,808 |
| Nashua | 30 | 22 | 4 | 1 | 1,288,565 |
| Exceller[2] | 26 | 13 | 3 | 4 | 1,285,922 |
| Ancient Title[2] | 56 | 24 | 11 | 9 | 1,252,791 |
| Susan's Girl[1] | 63 | 29 | 14 | 11 | 1,251,667 |
| Affirmed[2] | 18 | 15 | 3 | 0 | 1,245,018 |
| Carry Back | 61 | 21 | 11 | 11 | 1,241,165 |
| Foolish Pleasure | 26 | 16 | 4 | 3 | 1,216,705 |
| Damascus | 32 | 21 | 7 | 3 | 1,176,781 |
| Cougar II | 50 | 20 | 7 | 17 | 1,162,725 |
| Riva Ridge | 30 | 17 | 3 | 1 | 1,111,497 |
| Fort Marcy | 75 | 21 | 14 | 18 | 1,109,791 |
| Citation | 45 | 32 | 10 | 2 | 1,085,760 |
| Seattle Slew | 15 | 13 | 1 | 0 | 1,075,520 |
| Native Diver | 81 | 37 | 7 | 12 | 1,026,500 |
| Royal Glint | 52 | 21 | 9 | 4 | 1,004,815 |
| Dr. Fager | 22 | 18 | 2 | 1 | 1,002,642 |
| Swoon's Son | 51 | 30 | 10 | 3 | 970,605 |
| Roman Brother | 42 | 16 | 10 | 5 | 943,473 |
| Stymie | 131 | 35 | 33 | 28 | 918,485 |

1. Female. 2. Still active.

## THE 1978 TRIPLE CROWN

(Jockeys in parentheses)

**Kentucky Derby** (Churchill Downs, Louisville, Ky., May 6); $239,400; 3 year olds, 126 pounds, 1¼ miles—1, Affirmed (Steve Cauthen). 2, Alydar (Velasquez); 3, Believe It (E. Maple). 4, Darby Creek Road (Brumfield). 5, Esops Foibles (C. McCarron). 6, Sensitive Prince (Solomone). 7, Dr. Valeri (Rivera). 8, Hoist the Silver (Depass). 9, Chief of Dixieland (Rini). 10, Raymond Earl (Baird). 11, Special Honors (Nicolo).

Time—2:01⅕. Mutuels—1, Affirmed, owned by Harbor View Farm (Louis Wolfson), $5.60, 2.80, 2.60. 2, Alydar, owned by Calumet Farm, $2.60, 2.40. 3, Believe It, owned by Hickory Tree Stable, $2.80. Winners purse: $186,900. Margin of victory: 1½ lengths. Attendance: 131,004.

**Preakness Stakes** (Pimlico, Baltimore, Md., May 20); $188,700;

3 year olds, 126 pounds, $1\frac{3}{16}$ miles—1, Affirmed (Cauthen). 2, Alydar (Velasquez). 3, Believe It (E. Maple). 4, Noon Time Spender (Hinojosa). 5, Indigo Star (Fitzgerald). 6, Dax S. (Kurtz). 7, Track Reward (Gonzalez).

Time— 1:54⅖. Mutuels—1, Affirmed, owned by Louis Wolfson, $3.00, 2.10, 2.10. 2, Alydar, owned by Calumet Farm, $2.10, 2.10. 3, Believe It, owned by Hictory Tree Stable, $2.10. Winner's purse: $136,200. Margin of victory: neck. Attendance: 81,261.

**Belmont Stakes** (Belmont Park, Elmont, N.Y., June 10); $184,300; 3 year olds, 126 pounds, 1½ miles—1, Affirmed (Cauthen). 2, Alydar (Velasquez). 3, Darby Creek Road (Cordero). 4, Judge Advocate (Fell). 5, Noon Time Spender (R. Hernandez).

Time—2:26⅘. Mutuels—1, Affirmed, owned by Louis Wolfson, $3.20, 2.10, out. 2, Alydar, owned by Calumet Farm, $2.20, out. 3, Darby Creek Road, owned by J. W. Phillips, no show wagering. Winner's purse: $110,580. Margin of victory: head. Attendance: 65,417.

# ARCHERY

## NATIONAL FIELD ARCHERY ASSOCIATION—1978

(Aurora, Ill., July 24–29)

### Men's Freestyle

| | |
|---|---|
| Open—Paul Nazelrod, Cumberland, Md. | 2,752 |
| Open, limited—Wayne Seymour, Hattiesburg, Miss. | 2,623 |
| Amateur—Barry Velarde, Fort Knox, Ky. | 2,731 |

### Women's Freestyle

| | |
|---|---|
| Open—Beverley Stout, Clinton, Indiana | 2,643 |
| Open, limited—Sue Adamic, Canon City, Colo. | 2,410 |
| Amateur—Judy Cockerham, Winston-Salem, N.C. | 2,590 |

### Men's Barebow

| | |
|---|---|
| Open—David Hughes, Mesquite, Tex. | 2,554 |
| Amateur—Tyrus Baker, Centralia, Ill. | 2,396 |

### Women's Barebow

| | |
|---|---|
| Open—Gloria Shelley, Waterbury, Conn. | 2,399 |
| Amateur—Patti Lamb, Loves Park, Ill. | 1,982 |

## NATIONAL ARCHERY ASSOCIATION Target Competition

(Oxford, Ohio, Aug. 2–5, 1978)

### Men's Events

| | Score |
|---|---|
| Champion—Darrell Pace, Cincinnati | 2,569 |
| Intermediate boys—A. Robert Kaufhold, Lancaster, Pa. | 2,389 |

### Women's Events

| | |
|---|---|
| Champion—Luann Ryon, Riverside, Calif. | 2,487 |
| Intermediate girls—Robin Wools, Phoenix, Ariz. | 2,255 |

## Field Competition

(Mount Horeb, Wis., June 11–12, 1978)

### Men's Events

| | |
|---|---|
| Freestyle—Darrell Pace, Cincinnati | 1,010 |
| Barebow—Rick Krause, Pine Grove, Pa. | 807 |

### Women's Events

| | |
|---|---|
| Freestyle—Winnie Eicher, Duncansville, Pa. | 871 |
| Barebow—Rebecca Wallace, Palmyra, Pa. | 584 |

## WORLD CHAMPIONSHIPS

(Geneva, Switzerland, Sept. 16-17, 1978)

| | |
|---|---|
| Men's freestyle—Darrell Pace, Cincinnati | 984 |
| Women's freestyle—Anna Marie Lehmann, West Germany | 895 |
| Men's barebow—Anders Rosenberg, Sweden | 876 |
| Women's barebow—Suizuko Kobuchi, Japan | 683 |

# TABLE TENNIS

(*Source:* Ping Neuberger, Historian, U.S. Table Tennis Association.)

## 1978 U. S. Open Championship

(Oklahoma City, June 29–July 2)

Men's singles—Norio Takashima, Japan
Women's singles—Hong Ja Park, South Korea
Men's doubles—Masami Ohshima and Norio Takashima, Japan
Women's doubles—Seong Heui Kim and Hong Ja Park, South Korea
Mixed doubles—Errol Caetane and Mariann Domonkos, Canada
Senior men (over 40)—Jack Howard, Hermosa Beach, Calif.
Senior women (over 40)—Yvonne Kronlage, Ellicott City, Md.
Esquire (over 50)—Norman Schless, Niles, Ill.
Youth (under 21)—Ricky Seemiller, Pittsburgh
Youth doubles (under 21)—Eric Boggan, Merrick, N.Y., and Roger Sverdlit, Rockville Centre, N.Y.
Boys (under 17)—Eric Boggan
Girls (under 17)—Kasia Dawidowicz, Aurora, Colo.

# WRESTLING

## A.A.U. NATIONAL CHAMPIONSHIPS

### Freestyle

(Ames, Iowa, April 13–15, 1978)

105.5 lb—Bob Weaver, New York A.C.
114.5 lb—Jim Haines, Wisconsin W.C., Madison
125.5 lb—Tomiyama Hideaki, Japan
136.5 lb—Tim Cysewski, Hawkeye W.C., Iowa City
149.5 lb—Jim Humphrey, Oklahoma Underdogs
163 lb—Chuch Yagla, Hawkeye W.C.
180.5 lb—John Peterson, Athletes in Action
198 lb—Ben Peterson, Wisconsin W.C.
220 lb—Larry Bielenberg, Sunkist Kids, Arizona
Heavyweight—Greg Wojciechowski, Ohio W.C., Toledo
Team—New York Athletic Club (77 pts)
Outstanding wrestler—Tim Cysewski

## NATIONAL ASSOCIATION FOR INTERCOLLEGIATE ATHLETICS

(Whitewater, Wis., March 2–4, 1978)

118 lb—Kevin Kish, Bemidji State
126 lb—Fred Townsend, Wisconsin, Whitewater
134 lb—James Shutich, Grand Valley State
142 lb—Rich Franklin, Pacific University
150 lb—Joe Sanford, Central Washington
158 lb—Michael Abrams, Grand Valley State
167 lb—Marc Mongeon, Simon Fraser
177 lb—Darrel Landers, Southern Oregon
190 lb—Jim Blagg, Biola (Calif.)
Heavyweight—Herb Stanley, Adams State (Colo.)
Team—Southern Oregon (81.5 pts)

# TRACK AND FIELD

Running, jumping, hurdling and throwing weights—track and field sports, in other words—are as natural to young people as eating, drinking and breathing. Unorganized competition in this form of sport goes back beyond the Cave Man era. Organized competition begins with the first recorded Olympic Games in Greece, 776 B.C., when Coroebus of Elis won the only event on the program, a race of approximately 200 yards. The Olympic Games, with an ever-widening program of events, continued until "the glory that was Greece" had faded and "the grandeur that was Rome" was tarnished, and finally were abolished by decree of Emperor Theodosius I of Rome in A.D. 394. The Tailteann Games of Ireland are supposed to have antedated the first Olympic Games by some centuries, but we have no records of the specific events and winners thereof.

Professional contests of speed and strength were popular at all times and in many lands, but the widespread competition of amateur athletes in track and field sports is a comparatively modern development. The first organized amateur athletic meet of record was sponsored by the Royal Military Academy at Woolwich, England, in 1849. Oxford and Cambridge track and field rivalry began in 1864, and the English amateur championships were established in 1866. In the United States such organizations as the New York Athletic Club and the Olympic Club of San Francisco conducted track and field meets in the 1870s, and a few colleges joined to sponsor a meet in 1874. The success of the college meet led to the formation of the Intercollegiate Association of Amateur Athletes of America and the holding of an annual set of championship games beginning in 1876. The Amateur Athletic Union, organized in 1888, has been the ruling body in American amateur athletics since that time.

## WORLD RECORDS—MEN

Recognized by the International Athletic Federation in January 1977

The I.A.A.F. decided late in 1976 not to recognize records in yards except for the one-mile run. The I.A.A.F. began in 1975 to recognize two sets of records for races of 400 meters or less—hand-timed and automatically timed. General usage now goes with electrically timed records, which are used in the following tables.

### Running

| Event | Record | Holder | Home country | Where made | Date |
|---|---|---|---|---|---|
| 100 m | 0:09.95 | Jim Hines | U.S. | Mexico City | Oct. 14, 1968 |
| 200 m | 0:19.83 | Tommy Smith | U.S. | Mexico City | Oct. 16, 1968 |
| 400 m | 0:43.86 | Lee Evans | U.S. | Mexico City | Oct. 18, 1968 |
| 800 m | 1:43.5 | Alberto Juantorena | Cuba | Montreal | July 25, 1976 |
| | 1:43.4[1] | Alberto Juantorena | Cuba | Sofia, Bulgaria | Aug. 21, 1977 |
| 1,000 m | 2:13.9 | Rich Wohlhuter | U.S. | Oslo | July 30, 1974 |
| 1,500 m | 3:32.2 | Filbert Bayi | Tanzania | Christchurch, N.Z. | Feb. 2, 1974 |
| 1 mi. | 3:49.4 | John Walker | New Zealand | Göteborg, Sweden | Aug. 12, 1975 |
| 2,000 m | 4:51.4 | John Walker | New Zealand | Oslo | June 30, 1976 |
| 3,000 m | 7:35.2 | Brendan Foster | Britain | Gateshead, Eng. | Aug. 3, 1974 |
| | 7:32.1[1] | Henry Rono | Kenya | Oslo | June 27, 1978 |
| 3,000-m steeplechase | 8:08 | Anders Garderud | Sweden | Montreal | July 28, 1976 |
| | 8:05.4[1] | Henry Rono | Kenya | Seattle | May 12, 1978 |
| 5,000 m | 13:12.9 | Dick Quax | New Zealand | Stockholm | July 5, 1977 |
| | 13:08.4[1] | Henry Rono | Kenya | Berkeley, Calif. | April 8, 1978 |
| 10,000 m | 27:30 | Samson Kimombwa | Kenya | Helsinki, Finland | June 30, 1977 |
| | 27:22.5[1] | Henry Rono | Kenya | Vienna | June 11, 1978 |
| 20,000 m | 54:24.2 | Jos Hermans | Netherlands | Papendal, Neth. | May 1, 1976 |
| 25,000 m | 1:14:16.8 | Pekka Paivarinto | Finland | Oulu, Finland | May 15, 1975 |
| 30,000 m | 1:31:30 | Jim Alder | Britain | London | May 30, 1969 |
| 20,000 m | 57:24.2 | Jos Hermans | Netherlands | Papandal, Neth. | May 1, 1976 |
| 1 hour | 13 mi. 24 yd | Jos Hermans | Netherlands | Papandal, Neth. | May 1, 1976 |
| 25,000 m | 1:14:16.8 | Jos Hermans | Netherlands | Papandal, Neth. | May 1, 1976 |
| 30,000 m | 1:31:30.4 | Jim Alder | Britain | London | Sept. 5, 1970 |

### Walking

| Event | Record | Holder | Home country | Where made | Date |
|---|---|---|---|---|---|
| 20,000 m | 1:23.32 | Daniel Bautista | Mexico | Bergen, Norway | May 14, 1977 |
| 2 hours | 16 mi. 1517 yd. | Bernd Kannenberg | West Germany | Kassel, West Germany | May 11, 1974 |
| 30,000 m | 2:12.58 | Bernd Kannenberg | West Germany | Kassel, West Germany | May 11, 1974 |
| 50,000 m | 3:56.52 | Bernd Kannenberg | West Germany | Milan, Italy | Nov. 16, 1975 |
| | 3:56.39[1] | Enrique Vera | Mexico | Bergen, Norway | May 16, 1977 |

### Hurdles

| Event | Record | Holder | Home country | Where made | Date |
|---|---|---|---|---|---|
| 110 m | 0:13.24 | Rod Milburn | U.S. | Munich, W. Ger. | Sept. 7, 1972 |
| | 0:13.21[1] | Alejandro Casanas | Cuba | Sofia, Bulgaria | Sept. 21, 1977 |
| 400 m | 0:47.45 | Edwin Moses | U.S. | Westwood, Calif. | June 11, 1977 |

**Relay Races**

| Event | Record | Holder | Home country | Where made | Date |
|---|---|---|---|---|---|
| 400 m (4x100) | 0:38.03 | National Team | U.S. | Dusseldorf, W. Ger. | Sept. 3, 1977 |
| 800 m (4x200) | 1:21.5 | National Team | Italy | Barletta, It. | July 21, 1972 |
| | | (F. Ossola, P. Abeti, L. Benedetti, P. Mennea) | | | |
| | 1:20.3[1] | So. California | U.S. | Tempe, Ariz. | May 27, 1978 |
| | | (Joel Andrews, James Sanford, Billy Mullins, Clancy Edwards) | | | |
| | 1:21.4[1] | Arizona State | U.S. | Philadelphia | April 30, 1977 |
| | | (Gary Burl, Tony Darden, Gerald Burl, Herman Frazier) | | | |
| 1,600 m (4x400) | 2:56.1 | National Team | U.S. | Mexico City | Oct. 20, 1968 |
| | | (Vince Matthews, Ron Freeman, Larry James, Lee Evans) | | | |
| 3200 m. (4x800) | 7:08.6 | National Team | West Germany | Wiesbaden, W. Ger. | Aug. 13, 1966 |
| | | (Manfred Kinder, Werner Adams, Dieter Bogatski, Franz-Josef Kemper) | | | |

**Field Events**

| Event | Record | Holder | Home country | Where made | Date |
|---|---|---|---|---|---|
| High Jump | 7 ft 7¼ in. (2.32 m) | Dwight Stones | U.S. | Philadelphia | Aug. 4, 1976 |
| | 7 ft 7¾ in. (2.33 m) | Vladimir Yaschenko | U.S.S.R. | Richmond | July 3, 1977 |
| | 7 ft 8 in.[1] (2.33 m) | Vladimir Yaschenko | U.S.S.R. | Tbilisi, U.S.S.R. | June 16, 1978 |
| Long jump | 29 ft 2½ in. (8.90 m) | Bob Beamon | U.S. | Mexico City | Oct. 18, 1976 |
| Trimple jump | 58 ft 8½ in. (17.89 m) | Joao Oliveira | Brazil | Mexico City | Oct. 15, 1975 |
| Pole vault | 18 ft 8¼ in. (5.70 m) | Dave Roberts | U.S. | Eugene, Ore. | June 22, 1976 |
| | 18 ft 8¾ in.[1] (5.71 m) | Mike Tully | U.S. | Corvallis, Ore. | May 19, 1978 |
| Shot put | 72 ft 2¼ in. (22 m) | Alek. Barishnikov | U.S.S.R. | Paris | July 11, 1976 |
| | 72 ft 8 in.[1] (22.15 m) | Udo Beyer | East Germany | Goteborg, Sweden | July 6, 1978 |
| Discus throw | 232 ft 6 in. (70.86 m) | Mac Wilkins | U.S. | San Jose, Calif. | May 1, 1976 |
| | 233 ft 5 in.[1] (71.14 m) | Wolfgang Schmidt | East Germany | East Berlin | Aug. 9, 1978 |
| Javelin throw | 310 ft 4 in. (94.58 m) | Miklos Nemeth | Hungary | Montreal | July 26, 1976 |
| Hammer throw | 260 ft 2 in. (79.30 m) | Walter Schmidt | West Germany | Frankfurt, W. Ger. | Aug. 17, 1975 |
| | 263 ft 6 in.[1] | Karl-Hans Riehm | West Germany | Heidenheim, W. Ger. | Aug. 6, 1978 |
| Decathlon | 8,618 pts | Bruce Jenner | U.S. | Montreal | July 29–30, 1976 |

1. Betters listed record.

## WORLD RECORDS—WOMEN

**Running**

| Event | Record | Holder | Home country | Where made | Date |
|---|---|---|---|---|---|
| 100 m | 0.10.88 | Marlies Oelsner | East Germany | Dresden, E. Ger. | July 1, 1977 |
| 200 m | 0:22.21 | Irena Szewinska | Poland | Potsdam, E. Ger. | June 13, 1974 |
| | 0:22.06[1] | Marita Koch | East Germany | Erfurt, E. Ger. | May 28, 1978 |
| 400 m | 0:49.29 | Irena Szewinska | Poland | Montreal | July 29, 1976 |
| | 0:48.94[1] | Marita Koch | East Germany | Prague | Aug. 31, 1978 |
| 800 m | 1:54.9 | Tatyana Kazankina | U.S.S.R. | Montreal | July 26, 1976 |
| 1,500 m | 3:56 | Tatyana Kazankina | U.S.S.R. | Podolsk, U.S.S.R. | June 28, 1976 |
| 1 mi. | 4:29.5 | Paola Cacchi | Italy | Viareggio, Italy | Aug. 8, 1973 |
| | 4:23.8[1] | Natalia Maracescu | Romania | Bucharest | May 22, 1977 |
| 3,000 m | 3:27.1 | Lyudmila Bragina | U.S.S.R. | College Park, Md. | Aug. 7, 1976 |
| 5,000 m | 15:37 | Jan Merrill | U.S. | Mainz, W. Ger. | July 11, 1977 |
| | 15:08.8[1] | Lea Olafsson | Denmark | Copenhagen | May 31, 1978 |
| 10,000 m | 32:15.1 | Peg Neppel | U.S. | Westwood, Calif. | June 9, 1977 |
| | 31:45.4 | Lea Olafsson | Denmark | Copenhagen | April 6, 1978 |

**Hurdles**

| Event | Record | Holder | Home country | Where made | Date |
|---|---|---|---|---|---|
| 100 m | 0:12.59 | Annelie Ehrhardt | East Germany | Munich | Sept. 8, 1972 |
| | 0:12.48[1] | Grazyn Rabeztyn | Poland | Furth, W.G. | June 10, 1978 |
| 400 m | 0:55.63 | Karin Rossley | East Germany | Helsinki, Finland | Aug. 14, 1977 |
| | 0:54.88[1] | Tatyana Zelencova | U.S.S.R. | Prague | Sept. 2, 1978 |

**Relay Races**

| Event | Record | Holder | Home country | Where made | Date |
|---|---|---|---|---|---|
| 400 m (4x100) | 0:42.50 | National Team | East Germany | Karl Marx Stadt, E. Ger. | May 29, 1976 |
| | | (Marlies Oelsner, Renate Stecher, Carla Bodendorf, Martina Blos) | | | |
| | 0:42.27[1] | National Team | East Germany | Potsdam, E. Ger. | Aug. 19, 1978 |
| | | (Klier, Hamann, Bodendorf, Goehr) | | | |
| 800 m (4x200) | 1:32.4 | National Team | East Germany | Jena, E. Ger. | Aug. 13, 1976 |
| | | (Gudrun Berend, Marlies Oelsner, Barbel Eckert, Renate Stecher) | | | |
| | 1:31.5 | National Team | Britain | London | Aug. 20, 1977 |
| | | (Verona Elder, Donna Hartley, Sharon Colyear, Sonia Lannaman) | | | |
| 1,600 m (4x400) | 3:19.2 | National Team | East Germany | Montreal | July 31, 1976 |
| | | (Doris Maletzki, Brigitte Rohda, Ellen Streidt, Christine Bremer) | | | |
| 3,200 m (4x800) | 7:52.3 | National Team | U.S.S.R. | Podolsk, U.S.S.R. | Aug. 16, 1976 |
| | | (Tatyana Providokhina, Vera Gerasimova, Svetlana Styrkina, Tatyana Kazankina) | | | |

### Field Events

| Event | Record | Holder | Home country | Where made | Date |
|---|---|---|---|---|---|
| High jump | 6 ft 6 in. (1.98 m) | Rosemarie Ackermann | E. Germany | Dusseldorf, W. Ger. | Sept. 2, 1977 |
| | 6 ft 6¾ in. (2 m) | Rosemarie Ackermann | E. Germany | West Berlin | Aug 26, 1977 |
| | 6 ft 7¼ in.[1] (2.01 m) | Sara Simeoni | Italy | Brescia, Italy | Aug. 4, 1978 |
| Long jump | 22 ft 11¼ in. (6.99 m) | Sigrun Siegl | East Germany | Dresden, E. Ger. | May 19, 1976 |
| | 23 ft 2¼ in.[1] (7.09 m) | Vilhelmina Bardnuskena | U.S.S.R. | Prague | Aug. 29, 1978 |
| Shot put | 73 ft 2¾ in. (22.32 m) | Helena Fibingerova | Czechoslovakia | Nitra, Czech. | Aug. 20, 1977 |
| Discus throw | 231 ft 3½ in. (70.5 m) | Faina Veleva | U.S.S.R. | Sochi, U.S.S.R. | April 24, 1976 |
| | 232 ft (70.72 m) | Evelin Jahl | East Germany | East Berlin | Aug. 12, 1978 |
| Javelin throw | 226 ft 9 in. (69.12 m) | Ruth Fuchs | East Germany | East Berlin | July 12, 1976 |
| | 227 ft 5 in. (69.32 m) | Kate Schmidt | U.S. | Furth, W. Ger. | Sept. 10, 1977 |
| Pentathlon | 4,839 pts | Nadyezhda Tkachenko | U.S.S.R. | Lille, France | Sept. 9, 1977 |

1. Betters listed record.

## AMERICAN RECORDS—MEN

Officially approved by American Athletic Union as of Dec. 31, 1977, all listings are for automatic timing

### Running

| Event | Record | Holder | Where made | Date |
|---|---|---|---|---|
| 100 m | 0:09.95 | Jim Hines | Mexico City | Oct. 14, 1968 |
| 200 m | 0:19.83 | Tommie Smith | Mexico City | Oct. 16, 1968 |
| 400 m | 0:43.86 | Lee Evans | Mexico City | Oct. 16, 1968 |
| 800 m | 1:43.9 | Richard Wohlhuter | Stockholm | July 18, 1974 |
| 1,000 m | 2:13.9 | Richard Wohlhuter | Oslo | July 30, 1974 |
| 1,500 m | 3:33.1 | Jim Ryun | Los Angeles | July 18, 1967 |
| 1 mile | 3:51.1 | Jim Ryun | Bakersfield, Calif. | June 23, 1967 |
| 2,000 m | 5:01.4 | Steve Prefontaine | Coos Bay, Ore. | May 10, 1975 |
| 3,000 m | 7:44.2 | Steve Prefontaine | Oslo | Aug. 3, 1972 |
| | 7:42.6[1] | Steve Prefontaine | Milan, Italy | July 2, 1974 |
| 5,000 m | 13:15.1 | Martin Liquori | Dusseldorf, W. Ger. | Sept. 4, 1977 |
| 10,000 m | 27:43.6 | Steve Prefontaine | Eugene, Ore. | April 27, 1974 |
| 20,000 m | 59:52 | Gary Tuttle | Goleta, Calif. | July 26, 1975 |
| | 58:15[1] | Bill Rodgers | Boston | Aug. 9, 1977 |
| 25,000 m | 1:19:59.6 | Tom Fleming | Farmingdale, N.Y. | July 1, 1973 |
| 30,000 m | 1:37:33 | William Clark | Los Altos, Calif. | Feb. 13, 1971 |
| 1 hour | 12 mi. 811 yds | Gary Tuttle | Goleta, Calif. | July 26, 1975 |
| | 12 mi. 1351 yds[1] | Bill Rodgers | Boston | Aug. 9, 1977 |
| 3,000-m steeplechase | 8:23.2 | Doug Brown | Knoxville | May 11, 1974 |
| | 8:21[1] | Henry Marsh | Stockholm | July 5, 1977 |
| | 8:19.3 | Doug Brown | West Berlin | Aug. 18, 1978 |

### Hurdles

| | | | | |
|---|---|---|---|---|
| 110 m | 0:13.24 | Rod Milburn | Munich, W. Ger. | Aug. 7, 1972 |
| | 0:13.22[1] | Greg Foster | Eugene, Ore. | Jan. 2, 1978 |
| 400 m | 0:47.45 | Edwin Moses | Westwood, Calif. | June 11, 1977 |

### Relay Races

| | | | | |
|---|---|---|---|---|
| 400 m (4x100) | 0:38.03 | U.S. team (Bill Collins, Steve Riddick, Cliff Wiley, Steve Williams) | Dusseldorf, W. Ger. | Sept. 3, 1977 |
| 800 m (4x200) | 1:20.7 | So. California (Donald Quarrie, Leon Brown, Edesel Garrison, Willie Deckard) | Fresno, Calif. | May 12, 1972 |
| | 1:21.4[1] | Arizona State | Philadelphia | April 30, 1977 |
| | 1:20.3 | So. California | Tempe, Ariz. | May 27, 1978 |
| 1 mi. | 3:02.8 | Arizona State | Austin, Texas | April 2, 1977 |
| 1,600 m (4x400) | 2:56.1 | U.S. Team (Vince Matthews, Ron Freeman, Larry James, Lee Evans) | Mexico City | Oct. 20, 1968 |
| 1 mi. (4x440) | 3:02.4 | U.S. team (Ronnie Ray, Robert Taylor, Maurice Peoples, Stan Vinson) | Durham, N.C. | July 18, 1975 |
| 3,200 m (4x800) | 7:10.4 | U. of Chicago T.C. | Durham, N.C. | May 12, 1973 |

### Field Events

| | | | | |
|---|---|---|---|---|
| High jump | 7 ft 7¼ in. | Dwight Stones | Philadelphia | Aug. 4, 1976 |
| Long jump | 29 ft 2¼ in. | Robert Beamon | Mexico City | Oct. 18, 1968 |
| Triple jump | 56 ft 5¼ in. | Tommy Haynes | Mexico City | Oct. 15, 1975 |
| | 56 ft 5½ in.[1] | James Butts | Westwood, Calif. | May 7, 1978 |
| | 56 ft 6¾ in.[1] | James Butts | Helsinki, Finland | June 29, 1978 |

| Event | Record | Holder | Where made | Date |
|---|---|---|---|---|
| Pole vault | 18 ft 8¼ in. | Dave Roberts | Eugene, Ore. | June 22, 1976 |
| | 18 ft 8¾ in.[1] | Mike Tully | Corvallis, Ore. | May 20, 1978 |
| Shot put | 71 ft 8½ in. | Terry Albritton | Honolulu | Feb. 2, 1976 |
| Discus throw | 232 ft 6 in. | Mac Wilkinson | San Jose, Calif. | May 1, 1976 |
| Javelin throw | 300 ft | Mark Murro | Tempe, Ariz. | March 27, 1970 |
| Hammer throw | 235 ft 11 in. | Edward Burke | Bakersfield, Calif. | June 22, 1967 |
| | 238 ft 7 in.[1] | Scott Neilson | Seattle | April 1, 1978 |

## AMERICAN RECORDS—WOMEN

### Running

| Event | Record | Holder | Where made | Date |
|---|---|---|---|---|
| 100 m | 0:11.07 | Wyomia Tyus | Mexico City | Oct. 15, 1968 |
| 200 m | 0:22.62 | Evelyn Ashford | Westwood, Calif. | June 10, 1977 |
| | 0:22.06[1] | Brenda Morehead | Westwood, Calif. | June 10, 1978 |
| 400 m | 0:50.62 | Rosalyn Bryant | Montreal | July 28, 1976 |
| 800 m | 1:57.9 | Madeline Jackson | College Park, Md. | Aug. 7, 1976 |
| 1,500 m | 4:02.6 | Jan Merrill | Montreal | July 29, 1976 |
| 1 mi. | 4:28.2 | Francie Larrieu | Mainz, W. Ger. | June 28, 1977 |
| 3,000 m | 8:46.6 | Jan Merrill | Dusseldorf, W. Ger. | Sept. 3, 1977 |
| | 8:42.6[1] | Jan Merrill | Oslo | June 27, 1978 |
| 5,000 m | 15:37 | Jan Merrill | Mainz, W. Ger. | July 11, 1977 |
| | 15:35.5[1] | Kathy Mills | Knoxville, Tenn. | May 26, 1978 |
| 10,000 m | 33:15.1 | Peg Neppel | Westwood, Calif. | June 9, 1977 |

### Hurdles

| Event | Record | Holder | Where made | Date |
|---|---|---|---|---|
| 100 m | 0:13.24 | Jane Frederick | Sofia, Bulgaria | Aug. 19, 1977 |
| | 0:13.21 | Patty van Wolvelaere | Westwood, Calif. | May 7, 1978 |
| | 0:13.14 | Patty van Wolvelaere | Knoxville, Tenn. | May 26, 1978 |
| 400 m | 0:56.61 | Mary Ayers | Westwood, Calif. | June 11, 1977 |

### Relay Races

| Event | Record | Holder | Where made | Date |
|---|---|---|---|---|
| 400 m (4x100) | 0:42.87 | U.S. team (Barbara Ferrell, Margaret Bailes, Mildrette Netter, Wyomia Tyus) | Mexico City | Oct. 20, 1968 |
| 800 m (4x200) | 1:35.5 | U.S. team (Wyomia Tyus, Vivian Brown, Debbie Thompson, Edith McGuire) | Osaka, Japan | Oct. 25, 1964 |
| 1,600 m (4x400) | 3:22.8 | U.S. team (Debra Sapenter, Sheila Ingram, Pam Jiles, Rosalyn Bryant) | Montreal | July 31, 1976 |
| 1 mi. (4x440) | 3:30.9 | U.S. team (Robin Campbell, Cheryl Touissant, Madeline Jackson, Debra Sapenter) | Durham, N.C. | July 19, 1975 |

### Field Events

| Event | Record | Holder | Where made | Date |
|---|---|---|---|---|
| High jump | 6 ft 2¾ in. | Joni Huntley | Christchurch, N.Z. | Jan. 26, 1975 |
| | 6 ft 3 in.[1] | Louise Ritter | College Station, Tex. | April 29, 1978 |
| Long jump | 22 ft 3 in. | Kathy McMillan | Westwood, Calif. | June 12, 1976 |
| Shot put | 60 ft 6½ in. | Maren Seidler | San Jose, Calif. | March 25, 1978 |
| Discus throw | 187 ft 2 in. | Lynne Winbigler | Westwood, Calif. | June 10, 1977 |
| Javelin throw | 227 ft 5 in. | Kathy Schmidt | Furth, W. Ger. | Sept. 11, 1977 |
| Long jump | 22 ft 3 in. | Kathy McMillan | Westwood, Calif. | June 12, 1976 |
| | 22 ft 7½ in.[1] | Jodi Anderson | Westwood, Calif. | June 10, 1978 |
| Pentathlon | 4,625 pts | Jane Frederick | Sofia, Bulgaria | Aug. 19–29, 1977 |
| | 4,706 pts[1] | Jane Frederick | Czechoslovakia | June 24–25, 1978 |

1. Betters listed record.

## HISTORY OF THE RECORD FOR THE MILE RUN

| Time | Athlete | Country | Year | Location |
|---|---|---|---|---|
| 4:36.5 | Richard Webster | England | 1865 | England |
| 4:29.0 | William Chinnery | England | 1868 | England |
| 4:28.8 | Walter Gibbs | England | 1868 | England |
| 4:26.0 | Walter Slade | England | 1874 | England |
| 4:24.5 | Walter Slade | England | 1875 | London |
| 4:23.2 | Walter George | England | 1880 | London |

| Time | Athlete | Country | Year | Location |
|---|---|---|---|---|
| 4:21.4 | Walter George | England | 1882 | London |
| 4:18.4 | Walter George | England | 1884 | Birmingham, England |
| 4:18.2 | Fred Bacon | Scotland | 1894 | Edinburgh |
| 4:17.0 | Fred Bacon | Scotland | 1895 | London |
| 4:15.6 | Thomas Conneff | United States | 1895 | Travers Island, N.Y. |
| 4:15.4 | John Paul Jones | United States | 1911 | Cambridge, Mass. |
| 4:14.4 | John Paul Jones | United States | 1913 | Cambridge, Mass. |
| 4:12.6 | Norman Taber | United States | 1915 | Cambridge, Mass. |
| 4:10.4 | Paavo Nurmi | Finland | 1923 | Stockholm |
| 4:09.2 | Jules Ladoumegue | France | 1931 | Paris |
| 4:07.6 | Jack Lovelock | New Zealand | 1933 | Princeton, N.J. |
| 4:06.8 | Glenn Cunningham | United States | 1934 | Princeton, N.J. |
| 4:06.4 | Sydney Wooderson | England | 1937 | London |
| 4:06.2 | Gundar Hägg | Sweden | 1942 | Göteborg, Sweden |
| 4:06.2 | Arne Andersson | Sweden | 1942 | Stockholm |
| 4:04.6 | Gunder Hägg | Sweden | 1942 | Stockholm |
| 4:02.6 | Arne Andersson | Sweden | 1943 | Göteborg, Sweden |
| 4:01.6 | Arne Andersson | Sweden | 1944 | Malmö, Sweden |
| 4:01.4 | Gunder Hägg | Sweden | 1945 | Malmö, Sweden |
| 3:59.4 | Roger Bannister | England | 1954 | Oxford, England |
| 3:58.0 | John Landy | Australia | 1954 | Turku, Finland |
| 3:57.2 | Derek Ibbotson | England | 1957 | London |
| 3:54.5 | Herb Elliott | Australia | 1958 | Dublin |
| 3:54.4 | Peter Snell | New Zealand | 1962 | Wanganui, N.Z. |
| 3:54.1 | Peter Snell | New Zealand | 1964 | Auckland, N.Z. |
| 3:53.6 | Michel Jarzy | France | 1965 | Rennes, France |
| 3:51.3 | Jim Ryun | United States | 1966 | Berkeley, Calif. |
| 3:51.1 | Jim Ryun | United States | 1967 | Bakersfield, Calif. |
| 3:51.0 | Filbert Bayi | Tanzania | 1975 | Kingston, Jamaica |
| 3:49.4 | John Walker | New Zealand | 1975 | Göteborg, Sweden |

## WORLD'S FASTEST MILES

**Outdoors**

| Time | Athlete | Country | Date | Location |
|---|---|---|---|---|
| 3:49.4 | John Walker | New Zealand | Aug. 12, 1975 | Göteborg, Sweden |
| 3:51.0 | Filbert Bayi | Tanzania | May 17, 1975 | Kingston, Jamaica |
| 3:51.1 | Jim Ryun | United States | June 23, 1967 | Bakersfield, Calif. |
| 3:51.3 | Jim Ryun | United States | July 17, 1966 | Berkeley, Calif. |
| 3:52.0 | John Walker | New Zealand | July 11, 1977 | Dublin |
| 3:52.0 | Ben Jipcho | Kenya | July 2, 1973 | Stockholm |
| 3:52.2 | John Walker | New Zealand | 1975 | Stockholm |
| 3:52.2 | Marty Liquori[1] | United States | May 17, 1975 | Kingston, Jamaica |
| 3:52.5 | Thomas Wessinghage | West Germany | July 3, 1978 | Stockholm |
| 3:52.6 | Jozef Plachy[1] | Czechoslovakia | July 3, 1978 | Stockholm |
| 3:52.6 | Filbert Bayi[1] | Tanzania | July 2, 1973 | Stockholm |
| 3:52.8 | Jim Ryun | United States | July 29, 1972 | Toronto, Ont. |
| 3:52.8 | Steve Ovett | Britain | Sept. 20, 1978 | Oslo |
| 3:52.9 | Steve Scott[2] | United States | July 3, 1978 | Stockholm |
| 3:53.1 | Kipchoge Keino | Kenya | Sept. 10, 1967 | Kisumu |
| 3:53.1 | John Walker | New Zealand | Aug. 9, 1976 | Stockholm |
| 3:53.1 | Thomas Wessinghage[1] | W. Germany | Aug. 9, 1976 | Stockholm |
| 3:53.2 | Jim Ryun | United States | June 2, 1967 | Los Angeles, Calif. |
| 3:53.2 | Tony Waldrop | United States | April 22, 1974 | Philadelphia |
| 3:53.2 | Wilson Waigwa | Kenya | June 27, 1978 | Oslo |
| 3:53.3 | Dave Wottle | United States | June 20, 1973 | Eugene, Ore. |
| 3:53.3 | Eamonn Coghlan[2] | Ireland | May 17, 1975 | Kingston, Jamaica |
| 3:53.4 | Kipchoge Keino | Kenya | Aug. 20, 1966 | London |
| 3:53.4 | Marty Liquori[1] | United States | 1975 | Stockholm |
| 3:53.5 | Filbert Bayi[1] | Tanzania | June 27, 1978 | Oslo |
| 3:53.6 | Michel Jazy | France | June 9, 1965 | Rennes, France |
| 3:53.6 | Rod Dixon[2] | New Zealand | 1975 | Stockholm |
| 3:53.7 | Jim Ryun | United States | June 4, 1966 | Los Angeles |
| 3:53.8 | Jurgen May | East Germany | Dec. 11, 1965 | Wanganui, N.Z. |
| 3:53.8 | Bodo Tummler | W. Germany | Aug. 22, 1968 | Karlskrona, Sweden |
| 3:53.8 | Wilson Waigwa | Kenya | April 30, 1977 | Philadelphia |
| 3:53.8 | Rick Wohlhuter[3] | United States | May 17, 1975 | Kingston, Jamaica |
| 3:53.8 | Steve Scott[2] | United States | June 27, 1978 | Oslo |
| 3:53.9 | Steve Scott | United States | March 25, 1978 | Irvine, Calif. |

### Indoors

| Time | Athlete | Country | Date | Location |
|---|---|---|---|---|
| 3:54.9 | Dick Buerkle | United States | Jan. 13, 1978 | College Park, Md. |
| 3:55.0 | Tony Waldrop | United States | Feb. 17, 1974 | San Diego |
| 3:55.4 | Neil O'Shaughnessy | Ireland | Jan. 28, 1977 | Columbia, Mo. |
| 3:55.7 | Wilson Waigwa | Kenya | Feb. 8, 1977 | San Diego |
| 3:55.8 | Marty Liquori | United States | Feb. 7, 1975 | Philadelphia |
| 3:56.0 | Eamonn Coghlan | Ireland | Feb. 17, 1978 | San Diego |
| 3:56.1 | Filbert Bayi | Tanzania | Feb. 27, 1976 | New York |
| 3:56.2 | Ben Jipcho, pro | Kenya | March 22, 1975 | Los Angeles |
| 3:56.3 | Ben Jipcho, pro | Kenya | May 31, 1975 | Atlanta |
| 3:56.4 | Tony Waldrop | United States | Feb. 23, 1974 | College Park, Md. |
| 3:56.4 | Filbert Bayi | Tanzania | Feb. 15, 1975 | San Diego |
| 3:56.4 | Tom O'Hara | United States | March 6, 1964 | Chicago |
| 3:56.4 | Jim Ryun | United States | Feb. 19, 1971 | San Diego |
| 3:56.5 | Steve Scott[1] | United States | Feb. 18, 1975 | San Diego |
| 3:56.6 | Tom O'Hara | United States | Feb. 13, 1964 | New York |
| 3:56.8 | Rod Dixon | New Zealand | Feb. 21, 1976 | San Diego |
| 3:56.9 | John Walker | New Zealand | Feb. 15, 1975 | San Diego |
| 3:57.0 | Wilson Waigwa | Kenya | Feb. 15, 1975 | Oklahoma City |
| 3:57.1 | Steve Scott[1] | United States | Feb. 17, 1978 | San Diego |
| 3:57.2 | Marty Liquori | United States | Feb. 13, 1971 | Houston |
| 3:57.2 | Wilson Waigwa[1] | Kenya | Feb. 17, 1974 | San Diego |
| 3:57.5 | Jim Ryun | United States | Feb. 9, 1968 | New York |
| 3:57.5 | Filbert Bayi[1] | Tanzania | Feb. 21, 1976 | San Diego |

1. Finished second; 2. Finished third; 3. Finished fourth. NOTE: Professional marks not included.

## HISTORY OF THE POLE VAULT

(Some of early dates are the winning heights of A.A.U. champion for that year, used to show progression from one foot level to the next. Figures from A.A.U. records and *Track & Field News.*)

| | | | |
|---|---|---|---|
| 1877 | G. McNichol | 9′ | 7″ |
| 1879 | W. J. Van Houten | 10′ | 4¾″ |
| 1883 | Hugh Baxter | 11′ | 0½″ |

**Bamboo Poles**

| | | | |
|---|---|---|---|
| 1904 | Norman Dole | 12′ | 1 3/10″ |
| 1912 | Robert Gardner | 13′ | 1″ |
| 1927 | Sabin Carr | 14′ | 0″ |
| 1940 | Cornelius Warmerdam | 15′ | 1″ |
| 1942 | Cornelius Warmerdam | 15′ | 7¾″ |

**Metal Poles**

| | | | |
|---|---|---|---|
| 1957 | Bob Gutowski | 15′ | 8¼″ |
| 1960 | Don Bragg | 15′ | 9¼″ |

**Fiberglas Poles**

| | | | |
|---|---|---|---|
| 1961 | George Davis | 15′ | 10¼″ |
| 1962 | John Uelses | 16′ | 0¾″ |
| 1962 | Dave Tork | 16′ | 2″ |
| 1962 | Pentti Nikula | 16′ | 2½″ |
| 1963 | John Pennel | 16′ | 4″ |
| 1963 | Brian Sternberg | 16′ | 5″ |
| 1963 | John Pennel | 16′ | 6¾″ |
| 1963 | Brian Sternberg | 16′ | 8″ |
| 1963 | John Pennel | 16′ | 10″ |
| 1963 | John Pennel | 17′ | 0¾″ |
| 1964 | Fred Hansen | 17′ | 4″ |
| 1966 | Bob Seagren | 17′ | 5½″ |
| 1966 | John Pennel | 17′ | 6¼″ |
| 1967 | Bob Seagren | 17′ | 7″ |
| 1967 | Paul Wilson | 17′ | 7¾″ |
| 1968 | Bob Seagren | 17′ | 9″ |
| 1969 | John Pennel | 17′ | 10¼″ |
| 1970 | Wolfgang Norwig | 17′ | 10½″ |
| 1970 | Chris Papanicolaou | 18′ | 0¼″ |
| 1972 | Kjell Isaksson | 18′ | 1″ |
| 1972 | Kjell Isaksson | 18′ | 2″ |
| 1972 | Kjell Isaksson, Bob Seagren | 18′ | 4¼″ |
| 1972 | Bob Seagren | 18′ | 5¾″ |
| 1975 | Dave Roberts | 18′ | 6½″ |
| 1976 | Earl Bell | 18′ | 7¼″ |
| 1976 | Dave Roberts | 18′ | 8¼″ |
| 1978 | Mike Tully[1] | 18′ | 8¾″ |

1. Measurement in dispute.

## UNITED STATES MARATHON CHAMPIONS

(26 miles, 385 Yards)

**Boston**

| | | |
|---|---|---|
| 1970 | Ron Hill, England | 2:10:30 |
| 1971 | Alvaro Meija, Colombia | 2:18:45 |
| 1972 | Olavi Suomalainen, Finland | 2:15:39 |
| 1973 | Jon Anderson, Eugene, Ore. | 2:16:03 |
| 1974 | Neil Cusack, Ireland | 2:13:39 |
| 1975 | William H. Rodgers, Boston | 2:09:55 |
| 1976 | Jack Fultz, Arlington, Va. | 2:20:19 |
| 1977 | Jerome Drayton, Toronto | 2:14:46 |
| 1978 | William H. Rodgers, Boston | 2:10:13 |

**Amateur Athletic Union**

| | | |
|---|---|---|
| 1970 | Bob Fitts, Wisconsin | 2:24:11 |
| 1971 | Ken Moore, Portland, Ore. | 2:16:49 |
| 1972 | Edmund Norris, Brockton, Mass. | 2:24:42.8 |
| 1973 | Doug Schmenk | 2:15:48 |
| 1974 | Ron Wayne, Eugene, Ore. | 2:18:52 |
| 1975 | Gary Tuttle, Beverly Hills Strider | 2:17:27 |
| 1976 | Gary Tuttle, Los Angeles | 2:15:15 |
| 1977 | Not Held | |

## CROSS COUNTRY RACE CHAMPIONS

### Amateur Athletic Union

(10,000 Meters)

| | |
|---|---|
| 1970 | Frank Shorter, Gainesville, Fla.; Pacific Coast Club |
| 1971 | Frank Shorter, Gainesville, Fla.; Florida T.C. |
| 1972 | Frank Shorter, Gainesville, Fla.; Florida T.C. |
| 1973 | Frank Shorter, Gainesville, Fla.; Florida T.C. |
| 1974 | John Ngeno, Kenya; Colorado T.C. |
| 1975 | Greg Fredericks, Philadelphia; Colorado T.C. |
| 1976 | Rick Rojas, San Diego; Jamul Toads |
| 1977 | Nick Rose, England; Colorado T.C. |

### N.C.A.A. (University)

(6 Miles)

| | |
|---|---|
| 1972 | Neil Cusack, East Tennessee; Tennessee |
| 1973 | Steve Prefontaine, Oregon; Oregon |
| 1974 | Nick Rose, Western Kentucky; Oregon |
| 1975 | Craig Virgin, Illinois; Texas-El Paso |
| 1976 | Henry Rono, Wash. State; Texas-El Paso |
| 1977 | Henry Rono, Wash. State; Wash. State |

### N.C.A.A. (College)

(5 Miles; 4 miles prior to 1968)

| | |
|---|---|
| 1973 | Div. II: Gary Bentley, S. Dakota State; S. Dakota St. |
| | Div. III: Steve Foster, Ashland; Ashland |
| 1974 | Div. II: Garry Bentley, S. Dakota State; S.W. Missouri |
| | Div. III: David Maller, Rochester; Mount Union |
| 1975 | Div. II: Ralph Serna, Calif.-Irvine; Calif.-Irvine |
| | Div. III: Vin Fleming, Lowell; N. Central Illinois |
| 1976 | Div. II: Ralph Serna, Calif.-Irvine; Calif.-Irvine |
| | Div. III: Dale Cramer, Carleton; N. Central Illinois |

### N.A.I.A.

(5 Miles)

| | |
|---|---|
| 1972 | Mike Nixon, Pittsburgh State; Malone |
| 1973 | Tony Brien, Marymount; Eastern New Mexico |
| 1974 | Mike Boit, Eastern New Mexico; Eastern New Mexico |
| 1975 | Mike Boit, Eastern New Mexico; Edinboro State |
| 1976 | John Kebiro, Eastern New Mexico; Edinboro State |
| 1977 | Garry Henry, Pembroke State; Adams State |

## WORLD AND AMERICAN BEST PERFORMANCES IN INDOOR TRACK

The International Amateur Athletic Federation does not recognize indoor records. The following best performances, often called world records, are from lists provided by the Amateur Athletic Union of the United States and *Track & Field News*, published in Los Altos, Calif., Bert Nelson, editor and publisher.

### MEN

#### Running

| | |
|---|---|
| 50 yards—Houston McTear, Toronto, 1978 | 0:05.25 |
| 60 yards—Houston McTear, New York, 1978 | 0:06.04 |
| 70 yards—Herb McFarland, Louisville, Ky., 1975 | 0:06.7 |
| 100 yards—Don Quarrie, Pocatello, Idaho, 1971 | 0:09.3 |
| Carl Lawson, Pocatello, Idaho, 1971 | 0:09.3 |
| Cliff Branch, Pocatello, Idaho, 1972 | 0:09.3 |
| 300 yards—William Snoody, Lincoln, Neb., 1978 | 0:29.47 |
| 440 yards—Tommie Smith, Louisville, Ky., 1967 | 0:46.2 |
| Tim Dale, Princeton, N.J., 1978 | 0:47.69 |
| 500 yards—Lee Evans, College Park, Md., 1971 | 0:54.4 |
| Pro—Larry James, Salt Lake City, Utah, 1973 | 0:53.9 |
| 600 yards—Martin McGrady, New York, 1970 | 1:07.6 |
| 880 yards—Ralph Doubell, Albuquerque, N.M., 1969 | 1:47.9 |
| Mark Belger (Am.) College Park, Md., 1978 | 1:48.1 |
| Tom Von Ruden (Am.) College Park, Md., 1971 | 1:48.5 |
| 1,000 yards—Mark Winzenreid, Louisville, Ky., 1972 | 2:05.1 |
| Mile—Dick Buerkle, College Park, Md., 1978 | 3:54.9 |
| 2 miles—Emiel Puttemans, Berlin, 1973 | 8:13.2 |
| Terry O'Brien (Am.), San Diego, Calif., 1971 | 8:15.2 |
| Steve Prefontaine (Am.), San Diego, Calif., 1974 | 8:20.4 |
| 3 miles—Emiel Puttemans, Vittel, France, 1974 | 13:05.2 |
| Tracy Smith (Am.), New York, 1973 | 13:07.2 |

#### Running—Metric Distances

| | |
|---|---|
| 50 meters—Manfred Koket, East Germany, 1971 | 0:05.4 |
| Bill Gaines (Am.), Highland Park, N.J., 1968 | 0:05.4 |
| 60 meters—Houston McTear, New York, 1978 | 0:6.11 |
| 70 meters—Helmut Kornig, Germany, 1932 | 0:07.5 |
| Ira Murchison (Am.), U.S. | 0:07.5 |
| Pro—John Carlos, Pocatello, Idaho, 1974 | 0:07.3 |
| 100 meters—Eugen Ray, East Berlin, 1976 | 0:10.16 |
| Pro—Warren Edmonson, Pocatello, Idaho, 1973 | 0:10.2 |
| 200 meters—Karlh Wiesenseel, West Germany, 1978 | 0:21.11 |
| Pietro Mennea, Italy, 1978 | 0:21.11 |
| 300 meters—Pietro Mennea, Italy, 1978 | 0:32.83 |
| 400 meters—Luciano Susanj, Yugoslavia, 1973 | 0:46.38 |
| Herman Frazier, Italy, 1978 | 0:46.48 |
| 500 meters—Herman Frazier, Long Beach, Calif., 1978 | 1:01.3 |
| Pro—Lee Evans, Pocatello, Idaho, 1973 | 1:02 |
| 600 meters—Martin Bilham, England, 1969 | 1:17.7 |
| Mark Winzenreid (Am.), England, 1975 | 1:18.3 |
| 800 meters—Carlo Grippo, Italy, 1977 | 1:46.4 |
| Ted Nelson (Am.), Berlin, 1965 | 1:47.4 |
| 1,000 meters—Paul-Heinz Wellmann, West Germany, 1976 | 2:19.1 |
| Tom Von Ruden (Am.), New York, 1971 | 2:20.4 |
| Pro—Chris Fisher, Daly City, Calif., 1973 | 2:19.7 |
| 1,500 meters—Harald Norpoth, Berlin, 1971 | 3:37.8 |
| Tony Waldrop (Am.), San Diego, Calif., 1974 | 3:39.8 |
| 2,000 meters—Emiel Puttemans, Berlin, 1973 | 5:00.0 |
| 3,000 meters—Emiel Puttemans, Berlin, 1973 | 7:39.2 |
| Steve Prefontaine (Am.), San Diego, Calif., 1974 | 7:50.0 |
| 5,000 meters—Emiel Puttemans, Paris, 1976 | 13:20.8 |
| Jim Johnson (Am.), Moscow, 1974 | 13:56.4 |

#### Hurdles

| | |
|---|---|
| 50 yards—James Owens, Toronto, 1978 | 0:06.7 |
| 60 yards—Renaldo Nehemiah, New York, 1978 | 0:07.7 |
| 70 yards—Willie Davenport, 1969 | 0:07.8 |

#### Walking

| | |
|---|---|
| 1,500 meters—Todd Scully, 1978 | 5:47.9 |
| Mile—Neal Pyke, 1978 | 6:04 |
| 2 miles—Vittorio Visini, Italy, 1978 | 12:51.5 |
| Todd Scully (Am.), New York, 1977 | 13:02.5 |
| 3 miles—Antoli Soloman, Toronto, 1977 | 18:44.3 |
| Todd Scully (Am.), Toronto, 1978 | 19:40 |

#### Relays

| | |
|---|---|
| 880 yards—Stanford, Pocatello, Idaho, 1973 | 1:27.4 |
| Mile—Pacific Coast Club, Pocatello, Idaho, 1971 | 3:09.4 |
| 11-lap track—Seton Hall, College Park, Md., 1975 | 3:11.9 |
| 2 miles—Univ. of Chicago T.C., Louisville, Ky., 1974 | 7:20.8 |
| 11-lap track—Villanova, Richfield, Ohio, 1975 | 7:25.6 |
| 4 miles—Villanova, Hanover, N.H., 1976 | 16:19 |
| Sprint medley—Maccabi T.C., New York, 1976 | 2:03.2 |
| Distance medley—Villanova, Louisville, Ky., 1976 | 9:39.8 |

#### Field Events

| | |
|---|---|
| High jump—Vladimir Yashchenko, Milan, Italy, 1978 | 7 ft 8½ in. |
| Franklin Jacobs (Am.), New York, 1978 | 7 ft 7¼ in. |
| Long jump—Bob Beamon, Detroit, 1968 | 27 ft 2¾ in. |
| Triple jump—Viktor Saneyev, Moscow, 1976 | 56 ft 3½ in. |

| | |
|---|---|
| Tommy Haynes (Am.), New York, 1976 | 55 ft 5½ in. |
| Pole vault—Mike Tully, Detroit, 1978 | 18 ft 5¼ in. |
| Pro—Steve Smith, New York, 1975 | 18 ft 5 in. |
| Shotput—George Woods, Inglewood, Calif., 1974 | 72 ft 2¾ in. |
| Pro—Brian Oldfield, El Paso, 1975 | 75 ft 0 in. |
| 35-lb weight—George Frenn, Boston, 1969 | 73 ft 3½ in. |

## WOMEN

### Running

| | |
|---|---|
| 50 yards—Andrea Lynch, Toronto, 1978 | 0:05.80 |
| Deandra Carney (Am.), Toronto, 1978 | 0:05.86 |
| Kim Robinson (Am.), Toronto, 1978 | 0:05.89 |
| 60 yards—Deandra Carney, Inglewood, Calif., 1978 | 0:06.72 |
| 100 yards—Marlies Oelsner, East Germany, 1978 | 0:10.41 |
| Wilma Rudolph (Am.), Tennessee State, 1960 | 0:10.7 |
| 220 yards—Rosalyn Bryant, New York, 1977 | 0:23.4 |
| 300 yards—Rita Bottiglieri, Italy, 1978 | 0:34.2 |
| Rosalyn Bryant (Am.), New York, 1975 | 0:34.6 |
| 440 yards—Rosalyn Bryant, New York, 1977 | 0:53.5 |
| 500 yards—Rosalyn Bryant, San Diego, Calif., 1977 | 1:03.3 |
| 600 yards—Yvonne Saunders, Toronto, 1974 | 1:18.4 |
| Robin Campbell (Am.), Toronto, 1974 | 1:19.3 |
| 880 yards—Mary Decker, San Diego, Calif., 1974 | 2:02.4 |
| 1,000 yards—Mary Decker, Inglewood, Calif., 1978 | 2:23.8 |
| Mile—Francie Larrieu, Richmond, Va., 1975 | 4:28.5 |
| 2 miles—Francie Larrieu, San Diego, Calif., 1974 | 9:39.4 |

### Running—Metric Distances

| | |
|---|---|
| 50 meters—Renate Stecher, Berlin, 1974 | 0:06.19 |
| 60 meters—Marlies Oelsner, East Germany, 1978 | 0:07.12 |
| Brenda Morehead (Am.), Italy, 1978 | 0:07.32 |
| 100 meters—Marlies Oelsner, East Berlin, 1977 | 0:11.37 |
| Mamie Rallins (Am.), U.S., 1975 | 0:12.4 |
| 200 meters—Annegret Richter, West Germany, 1977 | 0:21.22 |
| 300 meters—Rita Wilden, East Germany, 1974 | 0:35.3 |
| Rosalyn Bryant (Am.), New York, 1977 | 0:38.6 |
| 400 meters—Marita Koch, Spain, 1977 | 0:51.14 |
| Sharon Dabney (Am.), Italy, 1978 | 0:53.27 |
| 500 meters—Lorna Forde, Hanover, N.H., 1978 | 1:10.5 |
| 600 meters—Verona Elder, U.K., 1974 | 1:29 |
| Robin Campbell (Am.), Moscow, 1974 | 1:30.1 |
| 800 meters—Nikolina Shtereva, Bulgaria, 1976 | 2:01.1 |
| Jane Colebrook, Spain, 1977 | 2:01.1 |
| Mary Decker (Am.), San Diego, Calif., 1974 | 2:01.8 |
| 1,000 meters—Francie Larrieu, Los Angeles, 1975 | 2:40.2 |
| 1,500 meters—Natalia Maracescu, Budapest, 1978 | 4:05 |
| Francie Larrieu (Am.), Richmond, Va., 1975 | 4:09.8 |
| 3,000 meters—Jan Merrill, Montreal, 1978 | 8:57.6 |

### Hurdles

| | |
|---|---|
| 50 yards—Johanna Klier, Toronto, 1978 | 0:06.20 |
| Deby LaPlante (Am.), Toronto, 1978 | 0:06.37 |
| 60 yards—Deby LaPlante, New York, 1978 | 0:07.53 |
| 70 yards—Mamie Rallins, Chicago, 1970 | 0:08.8 |
| Deby LaPlante, Louisville, Ky., 1976 | 0:08.8 |
| 50 meters—Annelie Ehrhardt, Berlin, 1973 | 0:06.74 |
| 60 meters—Annelie Ehrhardt, East Germany, 1974 | 0:07.9 |
| Deby LaPlante (Am.), Italy, 1978 | 0:08.25 |
| 100 meters—Annelie Ehrhardt, East Germany, 1976 | 0:13.12 |
| Patty van Wolvelaere (Am.), 1974 | 0:13.2 |

### Walking

| | |
|---|---|
| Mile—Susan Brodock, New York, 1978 | 7:01.7 |
| 1,500 meters—Susan Brodock, 1976 | 6:42.9 |

### Relays

| | |
|---|---|
| 640 yards—Atoms T.C., New York, 1976 | 1:09.7 |
| Tennessee State (Am.), Oakland, 1968 | 1:10.8 |
| 880 yards—Tennessee State, Louisville, Ky., 1978 | 1:38.5 |
| Mile—D.C. Striders, New York, 1977 | 3:45.8 |
| Atoms T.C. (Am.), Albuquerque, N.M., 1974 | 3:47.5 |
| Colorado Flyers (Am.), Albuquerque, N.M., 1978 | 3:47.3 |
| Howard University, 1978 | 3:45.1 |
| 880-yard medley—Los Angeles Mercurettes, New York, 1977 | 1:42.6 |
| 2 miles—U.S.S.R., 1972 | 8:41.6 |

### Field Events

| | |
|---|---|
| Long jump—Angela Voigt, East Berlin, 1976 | 22 ft 2¼ in. |
| Martha Watson (Am.), 1973 | 21 ft 4¾ in. |
| High jump—Rosemarie Ackerman, Berlin, 1977 | 6 ft 4¾ in. |
| Sara Simeoni, Italy, 1978 | 6 ft 4¾ in. |
| Joni Huntley (Am.), College Park, Md., | 6 ft 4 in. |
| Shotput—Helena Fibingerova, Czechoslovakia, 1977 | 73 ft 9¾ in. |
| Maren Seidler (Am.), West Germany, 1978 | 61 ft 2¼ in. |

# AMATEUR ATHLETIC UNION (A.A.U.) NATIONAL CHAMPIONSHIPS

## INDOOR

(Madison Square Garden, New York, Feb. 24, 1978)

### Men's Events

| | |
|---|---|
| 60 yd—Houston McTear, Muhammad Ali T.C., Los Angeles | 0:06.04[1] |
| 600 yd—Stan Vinson, U. of Chicago T.C. | 1:10 |
| 1,000 yd—Gideon Teror, Fairleigh Dickinson U. | 2:09.3 |
| Mile—Eamonn Coghlan, New York A.C. | 4:01.6 |
| 3 miles—Suleiman Nyambui, Tanzania | 13:09.8 |
| 2-mile walk—Todd Scully, Shore A.C., Long Branch, N.J. | 13:07.6 |
| 60-yd hurdles—Charles Foster, Phila. Pioneer Club | 0:07.11 |
| Sprint medley relay—Phila. Pioneer Club (Charles Joseph, Steve Riddick, Herman Frazier, Bill Collins) | 2:03.3 |
| Mile relay—Phila. Pioneer Club (Alfred Daley, Herman Frazier, Tom McLean, Robert Taylor) | 3:14.3 |
| 2-mile relay—Adelphi University (Bill Philips, Mark Smith, Ray Severino, Jon Williams) | 7:40.1 |
| High jump—Dwight Stones, Desert Oasis T.C. | 7 ft 4½ in.[2] |
| Pole vault—Larry Jessee, El Paso, Tex. | 17 ft 8½ in. |
| Long jump—Charlton Ehizuelen, Maccabi Union, Los Angeles | 23 ft 4½ in. |
| Triple jump—Ron Livers, San Jose State | 55 ft 3½ in. |
| Shot-put—Al Feuerbach, San Jose, Calif. | 67 ft 9 in. |
| 35-lb weight—Ed Kania, Dartmouth | 64 ft 9 in. |
| Team—Philadelphia Pioneer Club | 27 pts |

### Women's Events

| | |
|---|---|
| 60 yd—Brenda Morehead, Tennessee State | 0:06.73 |
| 220 yd—Frieda Nichols, D.C. Striders | 0:24.23 |
| 440 yd—Kim Thomas, St. John's Univ. | 0:55.53 |
| 880 yd—Debbie Vetter, Iowa State | 2:08.8 |
| Mile—Francie Larrieu, Sunnyvale, Calif. | 4:37[2] |
| 2 miles—Brenda Webb, Knoxville T.C. | 9:55.8[2] |
| Mile walk—Susan Brodock, Rialto (Calif.) Roadrunners | 7:01.7[3] |
| 60-yd hurdles—Deby LaPlante, Englewood, N.J. | 0:07.53[1] |
| 640-yd relay—Tennessee State (Brenda Morehead, Ernestine Davis, Chandra Cheeseborough, Debbie Jones) | 1:09.4[2] |
| 880-yd medley relay—Atoms T.C., Brooklyn, N.Y. (Lorna Forde, Carmen Brown, Carol Cummings, Patsy James) | 1:44.3 |
| Mile relay—Los Angeles Mercurettes (Collette Winlock, Lena Wallin, Gwen Gardner, Debbie Roberson) | 3:51.7 |
| High jump—Debbie Brill, Vancouver, B.C. | 6 ft 2 in.[2] |
| Long jump—Modupe Oshikoya, Maccabi Union T.C., Los Angeles | 20 ft 6½ in. |
| Shot-put—Maren Seidler, San Jose Stars | 61 ft[2] |

Team—Tennessee State University 20 pts
Outstanding athlete (Redbook Trophy)—Deby LaPlante

1. Betters best listed world mark. 2. Betters meet record. 3. Betters American record.

### OUTDOOR

(Los Angeles, June 8–10, 1978)

#### Men's Events

| | |
|---|---|
| 100 m—Clancy Edwards, Tobias Striders, Los Angeles | 0:10.14 |
| 200m—Clancy Edwards | 0:20.25 |
| 400 m—Maxie Parks, Athletes in Action | 0:45.15 |
| 800 m—James Robinson, Inner City A.C. | 1:45.5 |
| 1,500 m—Steve Scott, Irvine (Calif.) T.C. | 3:38.8 |
| 3,000-m steeplechase—Henry Marsh, Athletics West | 8:27.3 |
| 5,000 m—Marty Liquori, Florida Athletic Attic | 13:40.2 |
| 10,000 m—Craig Virgin, Athletics West | 28:15 |
| 5-km walk—Joseph Berendt, U.S. Army | 22:31.6 |
| 20-km walk—Todd Scully, Shore A.C., Long Branch, N.J. | 1:34:46 |
| 110-m hurdles—Renaldo Nehemiah, N.J. Flyers | 0:13.28 |
| 400-m hurdles—James Walker, Athletes in Action | 0:49.03 |
| Long jump—Arnie Robinson, San Diego SE Ghetto Striders | 27 ft 4 in. |
| Triple jump—James Butts, Athletes in Action | 55 ft 5½ in. |
| High jump—Dwight Stones, Huntington Beach, Calif. | 7 ft 6½ in. |
| Pole vault—Dan Ripley, Long Beach, Calif. | 18 ft 3 in. |
| Shot-put—Al Feuerbach, Athletics West | 67 ft 1½ in. |
| Discus—Mac Wilkins, Athletics West | 219 ft 9 in. |
| Hammer—Boris Djerassi, New York A.C. | 224 ft 3 in. |
| Javelin—Bill Schmidt, Knoxville (Tenn.) T.C. | 276 ft 9 in. |

#### Women's Events

| | |
|---|---|
| 100 m—Leleith Hodges, Texas Women's Univ. | 0:11.23 |
| 200 m—Evelyn Ashford, Maccabi T.C., Los Angeles | 0:22.66 |
| 400 m—Lorna Forde, Atoms T.C., Brooklyn, N.Y. | 0:51.04 |
| 800 m—Ruth Caldwell, Citrus College | 2:02 |
| 1,500 m—Jan Merrill, Age Group A.A., New London, Conn. | 4:09.4 |
| 3,000 m—Jan Merrill | 8:56.4 |
| 10,000 m—Ellison Goodall, Duke Univ. | 33:40.2 |
| 5,000-m walk—Susan Liers, Island T.C. | 25:46.8 |
| 10,000-m walk—Susan Brodock, So. Calif. Roadrunners | 52:18.2 |
| 100-m hurdles—Deby LaPlante, Englewood, N.J. | 0:13.19 |
| 400-m hurdles—Debbie Esser, Iowa State | 0:57.85 |
| 440-yd relay—Texas Women's Univ. (Leleith Hodges, Stephanie Brown, Karen Holmes, Ruth Simpson) | 0:44.61 |
| Mile relay—Prairie View A&M (Debra Melrose, Essie Kelley, Angela Dudley, Patricia Jackson) | 3:34.9 |
| Two-mile relay—San Jose Cindergals (Ann Regan, Diane Figliomeni, Ann Wotherspoon, Cheri Williams) | 8:41.8 |
| Sprint medley relay—Tennessee State U. T.C. | 1:37.7 |
| High jump—Louise Ritter, Texas Women's Univ. | 6 ft 1¼ in. |
| Long jump—Jodi Anderson, Naturite T.C., Los Angeles | 22 ft 7½ in. |
| Shot-put—Maren Seidler, San Jose Stars | 59 ft 8 in. |
| Discus—Lynne Winbigler, Oregon T.C. | 178 ft 6 in. |
| Javelin—Sherry Calvert, Lakewood (Calif.) Int. | 302 ft 7 in. |

#### Marathons

| | |
|---|---|
| Boston (4,212 starters, April 17, 1978)—Bill Rodgers, Boston | 2:10:13 |
| First woman to finish—Gayle Barron, Atlanta | 2:44:52 |
| U.S.T.F.F. (Drake Relays)—Charlie McMullen, Lake Ozark, Mo. | 2:15:19 |
| U.S.T.F.F. Women—Janice Arenz, St. Paul | 2:47.46 |

#### Decathlons

| | |
|---|---|
| A.A.U. (Richmond, Va., June 24–25, 1978)—Mike Hill, Boulder, Colo. | 8,004 |
| U.S.T.F.F. (Drake Relays)—John Whitson, Albuquerque, N.M. | 7,828 |
| Penn Relays—Tony Hale, Fisk University | 7,338 |
| Texas Relays—Steve Alexander, Houston | 7,750 |

#### Pentathlons

| | |
|---|---|
| A.A.U. Men's outdoor (Honolulu, July 1, 1978)—Joe Hilbe, Honolulu | 3,322 |
| A.A.U. Women's outdoor (Tempe, Ariz., June 4–5, 1978)—Modupe Oshikoya, Nigeria (U.C.L.A.) | 4,379 |
| A.A.U. Men's indoor (Bethlehem, Pa., Feb. 19, 1978)—Jim Wooding, Devon, Pa. | 3,605 |
| A.A.U. Women's indoor (Albuquerque, N.M., Feb. 2–3, 1978)—Anne Gilliland, Albuquerque, N.M. | 3,839 |

## NATIONAL COLLEGIATE ATHLETIC ASSOCIATION

#### Division I

(Eugene, Ore., June 1–3, 1978)

| | |
|---|---|
| 100 m—Clancy Edwards, So. California | 0:10.07 |
| 200 m—Clancy Edwards | 0:20.16 |
| 400 m—Billy Mullins, So. California | 0:45.33 |
| 800 m—Peter Lemashon, Texas, El Paso | 1:45.7 |
| 1,500 m—Steve Scott, California, Irvine | 3:37.6 |
| 3,000-m steeplechase—Henry Rono, Washington State | 8:12.4 |
| 5,000-m—Rudy Chapa, Oregon | 13:53.3 |
| 10,000 m—Mike Musyoki, Texas, El Paso | 28:30.9 |
| 110-m hurdles—Greg Foster, U.C.L.A. | 0:13.22 |
| 400-m hurdles—James Walker, Auburn | 0:48.92 |
| 400-m relay—Southern California (Kevin Williams, Billy Mullins, Clancy Edwards, James Sanford) | 0:39.31 |
| Mile relay—Villanova (Keith Brown, Anthony Tufariello, Glenn Bogus, Tim Dale) | 3:05.1 |
| Long jump—James Lofton, Stanford | 26 ft 11¾ in. |
| Triple jump—Ron Livers, San Jose State | 56 ft 3¼ in. |
| High jump—Franklin Jacobs, Fairleigh Dickinson | 7 ft 3 in. |
| Pole vault—Mike Tully, U.C.L.A. | 18 ft 1¾ in. |
| Shot-put—Dave Laut, U.C.L.A. | 66 ft 1¼ in. |
| Discus—Kenth Gardenkrans, Brigham Young Univ. | 210 ft |
| Hammer—Scott Neilson, Washington | 237 ft 5 in. |
| Javelin—Bob Roggy, Southern Illinois | 283 ft 9 in. |
| Team—Southern California | 59 pts |

## NATIONAL ASSOCIATION OF INTERCOLLEGIATE ATHLETICS

#### Indoor

(Kansas City, Mo., Feb. 24–25, 1978)

| | |
|---|---|
| 60 yd—Nate Johnson, Hillsdale (Mich.) | 0:06.23 |
| 440 yd—Dennis Duckworth, Jackson State | 0:49.19 |
| 600 yd—Rickey Myles, Jackson State | 1:12.01 |
| 880 yd—Evans White, Prairie View | 1:54.16 |
| 1,000 yd—Gerald Masterson, Ouachita Baptist | 2:14.44 |
| Mile—John Kebiro, Abilene Christian | 4:11.44 |
| 2 miles—John Kebiro | 9:01.49 |
| 2-mile walk—Carl Schueler, Frostburg State | 13:53.62 |
| 60-yd hurdles—Ricky Davenport, Southern U., Baton Rouge | 0:07.26[1] |
| Mile relay—Southern U., Baton Rouge (Nathaniel Epps, Kenneth August, Fred Hall, Jesse Johnson) | 3:18.92 |
| 2-mile relay—Jackson State (Daniel Watson, Michael Watson, David Melton, Joey Whitley) | 7:44.14 |
| Distance medley relay—Oklahoma Christian (Milt Gilliam, Gary Tatum, Ron Love, David Cooper) | 10:12.52 |
| Long jump—Dennis Trott, Jackson State | 25 ft 1 in. |
| High jump—Bob Bayless, Oklahoma Christian | 6 ft 10 in |
| Triple jump—Kenneth Brimmer, Jackson State | 52 ft 10¼ in. |
| Pole vault—Frank Estes, Abilene Christian | 16 ft. 6 in. |

| | |
|---|---|
| Shot-put—Franklin Gross, Adams State (Colo.) | 60 ft 7 in. |
| Team—Tie between Abilene Christian and Jackson State | 75 pts |

1. Betters N.A.I.A. record.

**Outdoor**

(Abilene, Tex., May 18–20, 1978)

| | |
|---|---|
| 100-m—Nate Johnson, Hillsdale | 0:10.37 |
| 200-m—Larry Kimbles, Texas Southern | 0:21.23 |
| 400-m—Fred Taylor, Texas Southern | 0:46.90 |
| 800-m—Evans White, Prairie View | 1:47.77 |
| 1,500-m—Steve Hills, N.W. Nazarene | 3:45.13 |
| 5,000-m—Garry Henry, Pembroke State | 14:23.25 |
| 10,000-m—Garry Henry | 30:22.18 |
| 10,000-m walk—Chris Hansen, Wisconsin-Parkside | 46:19.46 |
| 110-m hurdles—James McCraney, Southern U., Baton Rouge | 0:13.70 |
| 400-m hurdles—James McCraney | 0:51.14 |
| Mile relay—Prairie View (Clifford Terrell, Joe Johnson, Evans White, James Hunt) | 3:10.11 |
| 440-yd relay—Texas Southern (Larry Kimbles, Ricky Moxey, Fred Taylor, Kenneth Williams | 0:40.83 |
| Javelin—Jim Whitcomb, Bethany (Kan.) | 219 ft 11 in. |
| Shot-put—Frank Gross, Adams State (Colo.) | 63 ft 1 in.[1] |
| Discus—Frank Gross | 198 ft 5 in.[1] |
| Long jump—Carl Williams, Abilene Christian | 27 ft 1¼ in. |
| Triple jump—Vic White, East. Washington | 50 ft 4¼ in. |
| High jump—Vic White | 7 ft |
| Pole vault—Billy Olson, Abilene Christian | 16 ft 7 in. |
| Hammer—Harold Willers, Simon Fraser | 181 ft 11 in. |
| Team—Texas Southern | 67 pts |

1. Betters N.A.I.A. record.

**ASSOCIATION OF INTERCOLLEGIATE ATHLETICS FOR WOMEN (A.I.A.W.)**

(Knoxville, Tenn., May 25–27, 1978)

| | |
|---|---|
| 100 m—Leleith Hodges, Texas Woman's U. | 0:11.18 |
| 200 m—Evelyn Ashford, U.C.L.A. | 0:22.91 |
| 400 m—Rosalyn Bryant, Cal State, L.A. | 0:52.6 |
| 800 m—Kathy Weston, Cal State, Northridge | 2:05.6 |
| 1,500 m—Debbie Vetter, Iowa State | 4:16.1 |
| 5,000 m—Kathy Mills, Penn State | 15:35.5[1] |
| 3,000 m—Kathy Mills | 9:08.1 |
| 100-m hurdles—Patty van Wolvelaere, So. Cal. | 0:13.14[2] |
| 400-m hurdles—Debbie Esser, Iowa State | 0:57.85 |
| 400-m relay—Arizona State (Kathy Crawford, Denise Waddy, Brenda Calhoun, Val Boyer) | 0:45.40 |
| 800-m sprint medley relay—Cal State, Los Angeles (Valerie Milan, Yolanda Rich, Cynthia Mills, Rosalyn Bryant) | 1:37.29[1] |
| 1,600-m relay—Prairie View (Debra Melrose, Essie Kelley, Angie Dudly, Patricia Jackson) | 3:34.9 |
| 3,200-m relay—Cal State, Northridge (Marcia Romesser, Roma Antoniewicz, Kathy Costello, Kathy Weston) | 8:33.51[2] |
| High jump—Louise Ritter, Texas Woman's U. | 6 ft 1½ in. |
| Long jump—Modupe Oshikoya, U.C.L.A. | 21 ft 6½ in. |
| Javelin—Cathy Sulinski, Cal State, Hayward | 173 ft 1 in. |
| Discus—Ria Stalman, Texas, El Paso | 179 ft 9 in. |
| Shot-put—Jennifer Smit, Texas, El Paso | 59 ft 9½ in. |
| Pentathlon—Themis Zambryzeki, Brigham Young | 4,279 pts |
| Team—California State, Northridge | 57 pts |

1. Betters world record. 2. Betters American record.

# SQUASH RACQUETS

## 1978 U.S. Squash Racquets Assn. Champions

Singles—Mike Desaulniers, Montreal
Singles, 35's—Roger Alcaly, New York
Singles, 40's—George Morfitt, Vancouver, B.C.
Singles, 45's—Les Harding, Seattle
Singles, 50's—Henri Salaun, Boston
Singles, 55's—Dick Daly, Seattle
Class B—Peter Monaghan, Haverford, Pa.
Class C—Ed Bresnitz, New York
Doubles—Tom Page, Princeton, N.J. and Gil Mateer, Bethlehem, Pa.
Veterans doubles—Ted Simmons, St. Louis, and Mel Sokolow, New York
Senior Doubles—Gord Guyatt, Hamilton, Ont., and Barney Lawrence, Kitchener, Ont.
Collegiate singles—Mike Desaulniers, Harvard
Collegiate team—Princeton
National team—New York
Lapham Cup (singles)—United States 11, Canada 6
Grant Trophy (doubles)—Canada 4, United States 3

## 1978 U.S. Women's Squash Racquets Association Champions

Singles—Gretchen Spruance, Wilmington, Del.
Doubles—Jane Stauffer and Barbara Maltby, Philadelphia
Mixed doubles—Joyce Davenport, Philadelphia and Ralph Howe, New York
Senior singles—Goldie Edwards, Pittsburgh
Senior doubles—Jane Stauffer and Jeanne Classen, Philadelphia
Collegiate singles—Gail Ramsay, Penn State

# HORSESHOE PITCHING

## WORLD CHAMPIONSHIPS

(Des Moines, Iowa, July 28-Aug. 6, 1978)

| | | | Ringers | |
|---|---|---|---|---|
| **Men** | W | L | No. | % |
| Walter Ray William, Jr., Chino, Calif. | 34 | 1 | 2,087 | 84.1 |
| Mark Seibold, Huntington, Ind. | 29 | 6 | 2,046 | 80.9 |
| Elmer Hohl, Wellesley, Ontario | 29 | 6 | 1,932 | 78.4 |
| Albert Zadroga, Elizabeth, Pa. | 29 | 6 | 1,931 | 76.3 |
| Glen Henton, Maquokela, Iowa | 29 | 6 | 1,986 | 76.2 |
| **Women** | | | | |
| Opal Reno, Lucasville, Ohio | 11 | 0 | 555 | 82.8 |
| Lorraine Thomas | 8 | 3 | 532 | 72.8 |
| Debby Michaud | 7 | 7 | 565 | 71.7 |

**Other Champions**

Senior—Stan Manker, Ohio
Boys—Steve Hohl, Canada
Girls—Linda Pateneaude, Maine
Intermediate—Carl Steinfeldt, Rochester, N.Y.
Men's Class B—Charles Kilgore, Missouri
Men's Class C—Ken Fraser, California
Women's Class B—Helen Blutt, Montana
Women's Class C—Lil Reddon, Canada

# GAELIC SPORTS

## Irish Championships—1978

Hurling—Cork
Football—Kerry

# SWIMMING

## WORLD RECORDS—MEN

Approved September 1978 by International Swimming Federation (F.I.N.A.)
(F.I.N.A. discontinued acceptance of records in yards in 1968)

### Freestyle

| Distance | Record | Holder | Country | Where made | Date |
|---|---|---|---|---|---|
| 100 Meters | 0:49.44 | Jonty Skinner | South Africa | Philadelphia | Aug. 14, 1976 |
| 200 Meters | 1:50.29 | Bruce Furniss | U.S. | Montreal | July 19, 1976 |
| 400 Meters | 3:51:56 | Brian Goodell | U.S. | East Berlin | August 27, 1977 |
| 800 Meters | 8:01.54 | Bobby Hackett | U.S. | Long Beach, Calif. | June 21, 1976 |
| 1,500 Meters | 15:02.40 | Brian Goodell | U.S. | Montreal | July 20, 1976 |

### Backstroke

| Distance | Record | Holder | Country | Where made | Date |
|---|---|---|---|---|---|
| 100 Meters | 0:55.49 | John Naber | U.S. | Montreal | July 19, 1976 |
| 200 Meters | 1:59.19 | John Naber | U.S. | Montreal | July 24, 1976 |

### Breaststroke

| Distance | Record | Holder | Country | Where made | Date |
|---|---|---|---|---|---|
| 100 meters | 1:02.86 | Gerald Moerken | West Germany | Jonkoping, Sweden | Aug. 17, 1977 |
| 200 Meters | 2:15.11 | David Wilkie | Britain | Montreal | July 24, 1976 |

### Butterfly

| Distance | Record | Holder | Country | Where made | Date |
|---|---|---|---|---|---|
| 100 Meters | 0:54.18 | Joe Bottom | U.S. | East Berlin | Aug. 27, 1977 |
| 200 Meters | 1:59.23 | Mike Bruner | U.S. | Montreal | July 18, 1976 |

### Individual Medley

| Distance | Record | Holder | Country | Where made | Date |
|---|---|---|---|---|---|
| 200 Meters | 2:03.65 | Graham Smith | Canada | West Berlin | Aug. 24, 1978 |
| | 2:04.39 | Steve Lundquist[1] | U.S. | Woodlands, Tex. | Aug. 2, 1978 |
| | 2:05.24 | Aleksandr Sidorenko[1] | U.S.S.R. | | |
| 400 Meters | 4:20.05 | Jesse Vassallo | U.S. | West Berlin | Aug. 22, 1978 |
| | 4:23.39 | Jesse Vassalo[1] | U.S. | Woodlands, Tex. | Aug. 4, 1978 |

### Freestyle Relays

| Distance | Record | Holder | Country | Where made | Date |
|---|---|---|---|---|---|
| 400 Meters | 3:19.74 | National Team | U.S. | West Berlin | Aug. 26, 1978 |
| (Jack Babashoff, Rowdy Gaines, Jim Montgomery, David McCagg) | | | | | |
| 800 Meters | 7:20.82 | National Team | U.S. | West Berlin | Aug. 24, 1978 |
| (Bruce Furniss, Bill Forrester, Bobby Hackett, Rowdy Gains) | | | | | |

### Medley Relay

(Backstroke, breaststroke, butterfly, freestyle)

| Distance | Record | Holder | Country | Where made | Date |
|---|---|---|---|---|---|
| 400 Meters | 3:42.22 | National Team | U.S. | Montreal | July 22, 1976 |

## WORLD RECORDS—WOMEN

### Freestyle

| Distance | Record | Holder | Country | Where made | Date |
|---|---|---|---|---|---|
| 100 Meters | 0:55.41 | Barbara Krause | East Germany | East Berlin | July 5, 1978 |
| 200 Meters | 1:58.53 | Cynthia Woodhead | U.S. | West Berlin | Aug. 22, 1978 |
| | 1:59.04 | Barbara Krause[1] | East Germany | East Berlin | July 2, 1978 |
| 400 Meters | 4:06.28 | Tracey Wickham | Australia | West Berlin | Aug. 24, 1978 |
| | 4:07.06 | Kim Linehan[1] | U.S. | Woodlands, Tex. | Aug. 2, 1978 |
| 800 Meters | 8:24.62 | Tracey Wickham | Australia | Edmonton, Can. | Aug. 6, 1978 |
| | 8:30.38 | Tracey Wickham[1] | Australia | Australia | |
| 1,500 Meters | 16:14.93 | Tracey Wickham | Australia | Brisbane | Feb. 2, 1978 |

### Backstroke

| Distance | Record | Holder | Country | Where made | Date |
|---|---|---|---|---|---|
| 100 Meters | 1:01.51 | Ulrike Richter | East Germany | East Berlin | June 5, 1976 |
| 200 Meters | 2:11.93 | Linda Jezek | U.S. | West Berlin | Aug. 24, 1978 |

### Breaststroke

| Distance | Record | Holder | Country | Where made | Date |
|---|---|---|---|---|---|
| 100 Meters | 1:10.31 | Julia Bogdanova | U.S.S.R. | West Berlin | Aug. 22, 1978 |
| 200 Meters | 2:31.42 | Lina Kachushite | U.S.S.R. | West Berlin | Aug. 24, 1978 |
| | 2:33.32 | Julia Bogdanova[1] | U.S.S.R. | | |
| | 2:33.11 | Lina Kachushite[1] | U.S.S.R. | West Berlin | Aug. 24, 1978 |

### Butterfly

| Distance | Record | Holder | Country | Where made | Date |
|---|---|---|---|---|---|
| 100 Meters | 0:59.46 | Andrea Pollack | East Germany | East Berlin | July 3, 1978 |
| 200 Meters | 2:09.87 | Andrea Pollack | East Germany | East Berlin | July 4, 1978 |
| | | Tracy Caulkins | U.S. | West Berlin | Aug. 26, 1978 |

### Individual Medley

| Distance | Record | Holder | Country | Where made | Date |
|---|---|---|---|---|---|
| 200 Meters | 2:14.07 | Tracy Caulkins | U.S. | West Berlin | Aug. 20, 1978 |
| | 2:15.09 | Tracy Caulkins[1] | U.S. | Woodlands, Tex. | Aug. 2, 1978 |
| | 2:15.85 | Ulrike Tauber[1] | East Germany | | |
| 400 Meters | 4:40.83 | Tracy Caulkins | U.S. | West Berlin | Aug. 24, 1978 |

### Freestyle Relay

| | | | | | |
|---|---|---|---|---|---|
| 400 Meters | 3:43.43 | National Team | U.S. | West Berlin | Aug. 24, 1978 |
| | | (Tracy Caulkins, Stephanie Elkins, Jill Sterkel, Cynthia Woodhead) | | | |

### Medley Relay

| | | | | | |
|---|---|---|---|---|---|
| | | (Backstroke, breaststroke, butterfly, freestyle) | | | |
| 400 Meters | 4:07.95 | National Team | East Germany | Montreal | July 18, 1976 |
| | | (Ulrike Tauber, Hannelore Anke, Andrea Pollack, Korenlia Ender) | | | |

1. Time stood as record briefly in 1978.

## U.S. SHORT-COURSE SWIMMING RECORDS

(listed by Amateur Athletic Union, Jan. 1, 1978)

### MEN

#### Freestyle

| | |
|---|---|
| 100 yards—Joe Bottom, 1977 | 0:43.49 |
| 200 yards—Jim Montgomery, 1977 | 1:35.67 |
| 500 yards—Tim Shaw, 1977 | 4:17.39 |
| 500 yards—Brian Goodell, 1978 | 4:16.40 |
| 1,650 yards—Casey Converse, 1977 | 14:57.30 |
| 1,650 yards—Brian Goodell, 1978 | 14:55.53[1] |
| 1,650 yards—Brian Goodell, 1978 | 14:54.54[1] |

#### Backstroke

| | |
|---|---|
| 100 yards—John Naber, 1977 | 0:49.31 |
| 200 yards—John Naber, 1977 | 1:46.09 |

#### Breaststroke

| | |
|---|---|
| 100 yards—Scott Spann, 1977 | 0:55.19 |
| 100 yards—Graham Smith, 1977 | 0:55.10[2] |
| 200 yards—John Hencken, 1975 | 2:00.83 |
| 200 yards—Graham Smith, 1977 | 2:00.05[2] |
| 200 yards—Nick Nevid, 1978 | 2:00.53[1] |

#### Butterfly

| | |
|---|---|
| 100 yards—Joe Bottom, 1977 | 0:47.77 |
| 200 yards—Mike Bruner, 1977 | 1:45.27 |

#### Individual Medley

| | |
|---|---|
| 200 yards—Scott Spann, 1977 | 1:48.26 |
| 400 yards—Bruce Furniss, 1977 | 3:52.07 |
| 400 yards—Jesse Vassallo, 1978 | 3:51.69[1] |

#### Relays

| | |
|---|---|
| 400-yard freestyle—So. California, 1977 | 2:55.28 |
| 400-yard freestyle—Gatorade S.C., 1978 | 2:55.27[1] |
| 800-yard freestyle—So. California, 1976 | 6:33.12 |
| 800-yard freestyle—So. California, 1977 | 6:28.01[2] |
| 800-yard freestyle—Auburn, 1978 | 6:31.93[1] |
| 800-yard freestyle—Florida A.C., 1978 | 6:29.81[1] |
| 400-yard medley—Auburn, 1977 | 3:17.62 |
| 400-yard medley—Indiana, 1977 | 3:17.14 |

### WOMEN

#### Freestyle

| | |
|---|---|
| 100 yards—Jill Sterkel, 1977 | 0:49.72 |
| 100 yards—Stephanie Elkins, 1978 | 0:49.66[1] |
| 100 yards—Tracy Caulkins, 1978 | 0:49.56[1] |
| 200 yards—Jill Sterkel, 1977 | 1:47.63 |
| 200 yards—Stephanie Elkins, 1978 | 1:45.91[1] |
| 500 yards—Jennifer Hooker, 1977 | 4:42.61 |
| 500 yards—Cynthia Woodhead, 1978 | 4:39.94[1] |
| 1,650 yards—Jennifer Hooker, 1977 | 16:03.24 |
| 1,650 yards—Cynthia Woodhead, 1978 | 15:55.15[1] |

#### Relays

| | |
|---|---|
| 400-yard freestyle—U.S. Team, 1976 | 3:22.76 |
| 400-yard freestyle (club)—El Monte, 1977 | 3:23.15 |
| 400-yard freestyle (club)—Nashville Aquatics, 1978 | 3:20.69[1] |
| 400-yard medley—Nashville Aquatics, 1977 | 3:47.45 |
| 400-yard medley—U.S. Team, 1978 | 3:43.72[1] |
| 400-yard medley—Nashville Aquatics, 1978 | 3:42.54[1] |
| 800-yard freestyle—U.S. Team, 1976 | 7:15.64 |
| 800-yard freestyle (club)—Mission Viejo, 1977 | 7:19.02 |
| 800-yard freestyle (club)—Nashville Aquatics, 1978 | 7:17.62[1] |

#### Backstroke

| | |
|---|---|
| 100 yards—Tauna Vandeweghe, 1977 | 0:56.40 |
| 100 yards—Linda Jezek, 1978 | 0:54.94[1] |
| 200 yards—Linda Jezek, 1977 | 2:00.52 |
| 200 yards—Linda Jezek, 1978 | 1:59.84[1] |
| 200 yards—Linda Jezek, 1978 | 1:59.10[1] |
| 200 yards—Linda Jezek, 1978 | 1:57.97[1] |

#### Breaststroke

| | |
|---|---|
| 100 yards—Tracy Caulkins, 1977 | 1:03.08 |
| 100 yards—Tracy Caulkins, 1978 | 1:02.20[1] |
| 200 yards—Tracy Caulkins, 1977 | 2:16.97 |
| 200 yards—Tracy Caulkins, 1978 | 2:16.47[1] |
| 200 yards—Julia Bogdanova, 1978 | 2:16.21[2] |
| 200 yards—Tracy Caulkins, 1978 | 2:14.07[1] |

#### Butterfly

| | |
|---|---|
| 100 yards—Nancy Hogshead, 1977 | 0:54.57 |
| 100 yards—Diane Johannigman, 1978 | 0:54.11[1] |
| 200 yards—Alice Browne, 1977 | 1:57.83 |
| 200 yards—Nancy Hogshead, 1978 | 1:55.74[1] |

#### Individual Medley

| | |
|---|---|
| 200 yards—Tracy Caulkins, 1977 | 2:03.08 |
| 200 yards—Nancy Garapick, 1977 | 2:02.72[2] |
| 200 yards—Renee Lavorie, 1978 | 2:02.04[1] |
| 200 yards—Tracy Caulkins, 1978 | 2:00.27[1] |
| 200 yards—Tracy Caulkins, 1978 | 1:59.33[1] |
| 400 yards—Bonnie Glasgow, 1977 | 4:20.64 |
| 400 yards—Nancy Garpick, 1977 | 4:19.04[2] |
| 400 yards—Tracy Caulkins, 1978 | 4:16.76[1] |
| 400 yards—Tracy Caulkins, 1978 | 4:11.38[1] |

1. Betters listed record by American citizen, recognition pending. 2. Open American record for non-U.S. competitors.

## A.A.U. NATIONAL CHAMPIONSHIPS

### Short Course, Indoor—Men

(Austin, Tex., April 5-8, 1978)

| | |
|---|---|
| 100-yd free—Jonty Skinner, Tuscaloosa, Ala. | 0:43.64[1] |
| 200-yd free—Andy Veris, Mustang S.C., Dallas | 1:36.84 |
| 500-yd free—Brian Goodell, Mission Viejo (Calif.) S.C. | 4:16.40[2] |
| 1,650-yd free—Brian Goodell | 14:54.54[2] |
| 100-yd backstroke—Peter Rocca, Concord S.C. | 0:49.83 |
| 200-yd backstroke—Peter Rocca | 1:47.02 |
| 100-yd breaststroke—John Hencken, Santa Clara, Calif. S.C. | 0:55.27 |
| 200-yd breaststroke—Nick Nevid, Nashville (Tenn.) A.C. | 2:00.53[2] |
| 100-yd butterfly—Scott Spann, Florida Aquatic Club | 0:48.08 |
| 200-yd butterfly—Greg Jagenburg, Foxcatcher S.C. | 1:45.55[1] |
| 200-yd ind. medley—Scott Spann | 1:48.43 |
| 400-yd ind. medley—Jesse Vassallo, Mission Viejo | 3:51.69[2] |
| 400-yd medley relay—Florida Aquatic Club (Keith Dickson, Scott Spann, David McCagg, Rowdy Gaines) | 3:18.14[1] |
| 400-yd freestyle relay—Gatorade, Bloomington, Ind. (Andrew Coan, Marc Foreman, John Ebuna, John Newton) | 2:55.27[2] |
| 800-yd freestyle relay—Florida A.C. (Rowdy Gaines, David McCagg, John Hillencamp, David Larson) | 6:29.81 |
| Team—Florida Aquatic Club | 504 pts |

1. Betters meet record. 2. Betters American record.

### Short Course, Indoor—Women

| | |
|---|---|
| 100-yd free—Stephanie Elkins, Amberjax | 0:49.66[2] |
| 200-yd free—Stephanie Elkins | 1:45.91[2] |
| 500-yd. free—Cynthia Woodhead, Riverside (Calif.) A.A. | 4:39.94[2] |
| 1,650-yd free—Cynthia Woodhead | 15:55.15 |
| 100-yd backstroke—Linda Jezek, Santa Clara S.C. | 0:55.08[1] |
| 200-yd backstroke—Linda Jezek | 1:57.79[2] |
| 100-yd breaststroke—Tracy Caulkins, Nashville A.C. | 1:02.20[2] |
| 200-yd breaststroke—Tracy Caulkins | 2:14.07[2] |
| 100-yd butterfly—Diane Johannigman, Cin. Pepsi Marlins | 0:54.11[2] |
| 200-yd butterfly—Nancy Hogshead, Amberjax | 1:55.74[2] |
| 200-yd ind. medley—Tracy Caulkins | 1:59.33[2] |
| 400-yd ind. medley—Tracy Caulkins | 4:11.38[2] |
| 400-yd medley relay—Nashville (Joan Pennington, Tracy Caulkins, Karinne Miller, Amy Caulkins) | 3:42.54[2] |
| 400-yd freestyle relay—Nashville (Tracy Caulkins, Amy Caulkins, Macie Phillips, Joan Pennington) | 3:20.69[2] |
| 800-yd freestyle relay—Nashville (Joan Pennington, Macie Phillips, Amy Caulkins, Tracy Caulkins) | 7:17.62[2] |
| Team—Nashville Aquatic Club | 441 pts |

1. Betters meet record. 2. Betters American record.

### Long Course, Outdoor—Men

(The Woodlands, Tex., Aug. 2-6, 1978)

| | |
|---|---|
| 100-m free—David McCagg, Fort Myers Beach, Fla. | 0:50.79 |
| 200-m free—Bill Forrester, Auburn, Ala. | 1:51.67 |
| 400-m free—Jeff Float, Sacramento, Calif. | 3:54.32 |
| 1,500-m free—Ed Ryder, Mission Viejo, Calif. | 15:24.84 |
| 100-m backstroke—Bob Jackson, San Jose, Calif. | 0:57.22 |
| 200-m backstroke—Jesse Vassallo, Mission Viejo, Calif. | 2:03.57 |
| 100-m breaststroke—Steve Lundquist, Jonesboro, Ga. | 1:04.44 |
| 200-m breaststroke—Jeff Freeman, Los Gatos, Calif. | 2:21.78 |
| 100-m butterfly—Joe Bottom, San Ramos, Calif. | 0:54.93 |
| 200-m butterfly—Steve Gregg, Huntington Beach, Calif. | 2:00.84 |
| 200-m ind. medley—Jesse Vassallo | 2:05.90 |
| 400-m ind. medley—Jesse Vassallo | 4:23.39[1] |
| 400-m medley relay—Cummings Engine S.C., Bloomington, Ind. (Mark Kerry, Rick Hofstetter, James Halliburton, Jim Montgomery) | 3:47.84 |
| 800-m freestyle relay—Florida Aquatics (Bill Forrester, Keith Dickson, David Larson, Rowdy Gaines) | 7:30.23 |

### Long Course, Outdoor—Women

| | |
|---|---|
| 100-m free—Cynthia Woodhead, Riverside, Calif. | 0:56.73 |
| 200-m free—Cynthia Woodhead | 1:59.49[2] |
| 400-m free—Kim Linehan, Sarasota, Fla. | 4:07.66[1] |
| 800-m free—Kim Linehan | 8:31.99[2] |
| 100-m backstroke—Linda Jezek, Los Altos, Calif. | 1:03.52 |
| 200-m backstroke—Linda Jezek | 2:14.39[2] |
| 100-m breaststroke—Tracy Caulkins, Nashville, Tenn. | 1:10.97[2] |
| 200-m breaststroke—Tracy Caulkins | 2:35.23[2] |
| 100-m butterfly—Joan Pennington, Madison, Tenn. | 1:00.58[2] |
| 200-m butterfly—Tracy Caulkins | 2:10.09[2] |
| 200-m ind. medley—Tracy Caulkins | 2:15.09[1] |
| 400-m ind. medley—Tracy Caulkins | 4:47.06[2] |
| 400-m medley relay—Nashville (Tenn.) Aquatic Club (Joan Pennington, Tracy Caulkins, Karinne Miller, Jann Girard) | 4:15.15 |
| 800-m freestyle relay—Mission Viejo (Calif.) Nadadores (Diane Griebel, Kim Black, Sharyl Barnicoat, Jennifer Hooker) | 8:21.19[2] |

1. Betters listed world record. 2. Betters listed American record.

## A.A.U. NATIONAL DIVING CHAMPIONSHIPS—1978

### INDOOR

(Cleveland, Ohio, April 12-15)

**Men's Events**

| | Pts |
|---|---|
| 1-meter—Greg Louganis, El Cajon, Calif. | 811.56 |
| 3-meter—Jim Kennedy, Knoxville, Tenn. | 822.72 |
| Platform—Greg Louganis | 576.18 |
| High point leader—Phil Boggs, Ann Arbor, Mich. | 59 |

**Women's Events**

| | |
|---|---|
| 1-meter—Julie Bachman, Mobile, Ala. | 632.61 |
| 3-meter—Jenni Chandler, Birmingham, Ala. | 657.90 |
| Platform—Melissa Briley, Miami, Fla. | 350.28 |
| High point leader—Cynthia McIngvale, Dallas | 59 |

### OUTDOOR

(Mission Viejo, Calif., Aug. 2-6)

**Men's Events**

| | |
|---|---|
| 1-meter—Greg Louganis, El Cajon, Calif. | 798.87 |
| 3-meter—Jim Kennedy, Knoxville, Tenn. | 842.82 |
| Platform—Greg Louganis | 846.165 |
| High point leader—Greg Louganis | 67 |

**Women's Events**

| | |
|---|---|
| 1-meter—Cynthia Potter, Dallas | 609.87 |
| 3-meter—Jenni Chandler, Mission Viejo, Calif. | 669.24 |
| Platform—Melissa Briley, San Antonio, Tex. | 559.05 |
| High point leader—Jenni Chandler | 63 |

## NATIONAL COLLEGIATE ATHLETIC ASSOCIATION (N.C.A.A.)

### Division I

(Long Beach, Calif., March 23-25, 1978)

| | |
|---|---|
| 50-yd free—Andy Coan, Tennessee | 0:20.29 |
| 100-yd free—Andy Coan | 0:44.10 |
| 200-yd free—Bruce Furniss, So. California | 1:37.02 |

| | |
|---|---|
| 500-yd free—Brian Goodell, U.C.L.A. | 4:18.05 |
| 1,650-yd free—Brian Goodell | 14:55.53[1] |
| 100-yd backstroke—Robert Jackson, Long Beach State | 0:49.88 |
| 200-yd backstroke—Peter Rocca, Calif.-Berkeley | 1:47.48 |
| 100-yd breaststroke—Scott Spann, Auburn | 0:56.62 |
| 200-yd breaststroke—Don Smith, Calif.-Berkeley | 2:02.24 |
| 100-yd butterfly—Greg Jagenburg, Long Beach State | 0:48.77 |
| 200-yd butterfly—Greg Jagenburg | 1:46.01 |
| 200-yd ind. medley—Scott Spann | 1:49.30 |
| 400-yd ind. medley—Brian Goodell | 3:53.61 |
| 400-yd freestyle relay—Tennessee (Robert Sells, Andy Coan, John Ebuna, John Newton) | 2:55.66 |
| 400-yd medley relay—Calif.-Berkeley (Pete Rocca, Graham Smith, Par Arvidsson, Jim Fairbank) | 3:18.26 |
| 800-yd freestyle relay—Auburn (Rick Morley, David McCagg, Bill Forrester, Rowdy Gaines) | 6:31.93[1] |
| 1-m dive—Wayne Chester, Alabama | 485.10 pts |
| 3-m dive—Christopher Snode, Florida | 543.18 pts |
| Team—Tennessee | 307 pts |

1. Betters American record.

## NATIONAL ASSOCIATION OF INTERCOLLEGIATE ATHLETICS

(Portland, Ore., March 9–11, 1978)

| | |
|---|---|
| 50-yd free—James Harmon, Wisconsin, Eau Claire | 0:21.27 |
| 100-yd free—James Harmon | 0:46.27[1] |
| 200-yd free—Vic Batchelor, Simon Fraser | 1:42.94 |
| 500-yd free—Kelly Franks, Simon Fraser | 4:36.37 |
| 1,650-yd free—Kelly Franks | 16:04.51 |
| 100-yd backstroke—Ron Barnard, Pacific Lutheran | 0:54.39 |
| 200-yd backstroke—Vic Batchelor | 1:56.76 |
| 100-yd. breaststroke—Dan Jesse, Wisconsin, Stevens Point | 0:59.77 |
| 200-yd breaststroke—Craig Weishaar, Central Washington | 2:11.19 |
| 100-yd butterfly—Mark Hahto, Simon Fraser | 0:51.81 |
| 200-yd butterfly—Mark Hahto | 1:53.25 |
| 200-yd ind. medley—Vic Batchelor | 1:56.36 |
| 400-yd ind. medley—Rob Grundison, Simon Fraser | 4:09.42 |
| 400-yd freestyle relay—Drury (Tom Schaper, James Yount, Michael Scott, Michael Wagnon) | 3:08.58 |
| 800-yd freestyle relay—Simon Fraser (Rob Grundison, Gary Davis, Kelly Franks, Vic Batchelor) | 6:53.88[1] |
| 400-yd medley relay—Simon Fraser (Vic Batchelor, Derrick Hamilton, Mark Hahto, Rob Grundison) | 3:31.46 |
| 1-m dive—Tony Perriello, Clarion State | 452.94 pts |
| 3-m dive—Tony Perriello | 457.98 pts |
| Team—Simon Fraser, Burnby, British Columbia | 461 pts |

1. Betters N.A.I.A. record.

## ASSOCIATION OF INTERCOLLEGIATE ATHLETICS FOR WOMEN (A.I.A.W.)

(Durham, N.C., March 16–18, 1978)

| | |
|---|---|
| 50-yd free—Sue Hinderaker, So. California | 0:23.14[1] |
| 100-yd free—Gail Amundrud, Arizona State | 0:50.97[2] |
| 200-yd free—Gail Amundrud | 1:48.32[3] |
| 500-yd free—Bonnie Glasgow, Miami | 4:47.15[3] |
| 1,650-yd free—Valerie Lee, Stanford | 16:22.21 |
| 50-yd backstroke—Tauna Vandeweghe, U.C.L.A. | 0:27.02 |
| 100-yd backstroke—Tauna Vandeweghe | 0:57.48[3] |
| 200-yd backstroke—Cheryl Gibson, Arizona State | 2:02.41[3] |
| 50-yd breaststroke—Kim Dunson, Florida | 0:29.29 |
| 100-yd breaststroke—Kim Dunson | 1:03.59[3] |
| 200-yd breaststroke—Debbie Rudd, So. California | 2:17.11[3] |
| 50-yd butterfly—Kathy Stetler, Pittsburgh | 0:25.57 |
| 100-yd. butterfly—Diane Johannigman, Houston | 0:54.77[3] |
| 200-yd butterfly—Diane Johannigman | 1:59.88[3] |
| 100-yd ind. medley—Renee Laravie, Florida | 0:57.93[1] |
| 200-yd medley ind.—Renee Laravie | 2:02.04[1] |
| 400-yd ind. medley—Diane Johnson, Arizona | 4:21.32 |
| 200-yd freestyle relay—U.C.L.A. (Tauna Vandeweghe, Kim Worthen, Shelly Worthen, Shawn Houghton) | 1:35.62[3] |
| 400-yd freestyle relay—Arizona State (Gail Amundrud, Peggy Tosdal, Cheryl Gibson, Sue Sloan) | 3:25.66[3] |
| 800-yd freestyle relay—Florida (Louise Pfeifer, Carol Georke, Renie Mullen, Renee Laravie) | 7:27.14[3] |
| 200-yd medley relay—U.C.L.A. (Tauna Vandeweghe, Karen Melick, Shawn Houghton, LuAnn Cramer) | 1:45.80[3] |
| 400-yd medley relay—Arizona State (Melissa Belote, Pam Rogers, Peggy Tosdal, Sue Sloan) | 3:49.73[3] |
| 1-m dive—Carol Wagner, Alabama | 267.38 pts |
| 3-m dive—Julie Bachman, Michigan | 446.61 pts |
| Team—Arizona State | 533 pts |

1. Betters American record. 2. Bonnie Brown, North Carolina, set A.I.A.W. record of 0:50.80 in preliminaries. 3. Betters A.I.A.W. record.

## WORLD CHAMPIONSHIPS

(West Berlin, August 18–28, 1978)

### Men's Events

| | |
|---|---|
| 100–m freestyle—David McCagg, Fort Myers Beach, Fla. | 0:50.24 |
| 200–m freestyle—Bill Forrester, Auburn, Ala. | 1:51.02 |
| 400–m freestyle—Vladimir Salnikov, U.S.S.R. | 3:51.94 |
| 1,500–m freestyle—Vlidimir Salnikov | 15:03.99 |
| 100–m backstroke—Robert Jackson, San Jose, Calif. | 0:56.36 |
| 200–m backstroke—Jesse Vassalo, Mission Viejo, Calif. | 2:02.16 |
| 100–m breaststroke—Walter Kusch, West Germany | 1:03.56 |
| 200–m breaststroke—Nick Nevid, Elm Grove, Wis. | 2:18.37 |
| 100–m butterfly—Joe Bottom, San Ramon, Calif. | 0:54.30 |
| 200–m butterfly—Mike Bruner, Stockton, Calif. | 1:59.38 |
| 200–m ind medley—Graham Smith, Canada | 2:03.65[1] |
| 400–m ind medley—Jesse Vassallo | 4.20.05[1] |
| 400–m freestyle relay—U. S. (Jack Babashoff, Rowdy Gaines, Jim Montgomery, David McCagg) | 3:19.74[1] |
| 400–m medley relay—U. S. (Robert Jackson, Nick Nevid, Joe Bottom, David McCagg) | 3:44.63 |
| 800–m freestyle relay—U. S. (Bruce Furniss, Bill Forrester, Bobby Hackett, Rowdy Gaines) | 7:20.82[1] |

### Women's Events

| | |
|---|---|
| 100–m freestyle—Barbara Krause, East Germany | 0:55.53 |
| 200–m freestyle—Cynthia Woodhead, Riverside, Calif. | 1:58.53[1] |
| 400–m freestyle—Tracey Wickham, Australia | 4:06.28[1] |
| 800–m freestyle—Tracey Wickham | 8:24.94 |
| 100–m backstroke—Linda Jezek, Los Altos, Calif. | 1:02.55[3] |
| 200–m backstroke—Linda Jezek | 2:11.93[1] |
| 100–m breaststroke—Julia Bogdanova, U.S.S.R. | 1:10.31[1] |
| 200–m breaststroke—Lina Kachushite, U.S.S.R. | 2:31.42[1] |
| 100–m butterfly—Joan Pennington, Madison, Tenn. | 1:00.20[3] |
| 200–m butterfly—Tracy Caulkins, Nashville, Tenn. | 2:09.87[2] |
| 200–m ind. medley—Tracy Caulkins | 2:14.07[1] |
| 400–m ind. medley—Tracy Caulkins | 4:40.83[1] |
| 400–m freestyle relay—U. S. (Tracy Caulkins, Stephanie Elkins, Jill Sterkel, Cynthia Woodhead) | 3:43.43[1] |
| 500-m medley relay—U. S. (Linda Jezek, Tracy Caulkins, Joan Pennington, Cynthia Woodhead) | 4:08.21[3] |

1. World record. 2. Equals world record. 3. American record.

### Men's Diving

| | |
|---|---|
| 3 meters—Phil Boggs, U.S. | 913.95 |
| Platform—Greg Louganis, U.S. | 844.11 |

### Women's Diving

| | |
|---|---|
| 3 meters—Irina Kalinina, U.S.S.R. | 691.43 |
| Platform—Irina Kalinina | 412.71 |

# ROWING

Rowing goes back so far in history that there is no possibility of tracing it to any particular aboriginal source. The oldest rowing race still on the calendar is the "Doggett's Coat and Badge" contest among professional watermen of the Thames (England) that began in 1715. The first Oxford-Cambridge race was held at Henley in 1829. Competitive rowing in the United States began with matches between boats rowed by professional oarsmen of the New York water front. They were oarsmen who rowed the small boats that plied as ferries from Manhattan Island to Brooklyn and return, or who rowed salesmen down the harbor to meet ships arriving from Europe. Since the first salesman to meet an incoming ship had some advantage over his rivals, there was keen competition in the bidding for fast boats and the best oarsmen. This gave rise to match races.

Amateur boat clubs sprang up in the United States between 1820 and 1830 and seven students of Yale joined together to purchase a four-oared lap-streak gig in 1843. The first Harvard-Yale race was held Aug. 3, 1852, on Lake Winnepesaukee, N.H. The first time an American college crew went abroad was in 1869 when Harvard challenged Oxford and was defeated on the Thames. There were early college rowing races on Lake Quinsigamond, near Worcester, Mass., and on Saratoga Lake, N.Y., but the Intercollegiate Rowing Association in 1895 settled on the Hudson, at Poughkeepsie, as the setting for the annual "Poughkeepsie Regatta." In 1950 the I.R.A. shifted its classic to Marietta, Ohio, and in 1952 it was moved to Syracuse, N.Y. The National Association of Amateur Oarsmen, organized in 1872, has conducted annual championship regattas since that time.

## INTERCOLLEGIATE ROWING ASSOCIATION REGATTA

(Varsity Eight-Oared Shells)

Rowed at 4 miles, Poughkeepsie, N.Y., 1895–97, 1899–1916, 1925–32, 1934–41. Rowed at 3 miles, Saratoga, N.Y., 1898; Poughkeepsie, 1921–24, 1947–49; Syracuse, N.Y., 1952–1963, 1965–67. Rowed at 2,000 meters, Syracuse, N.Y., 1964 and from 1968 on. Rowed at 2 miles, Ithaca, N.Y., 1920; Marietta, Ohio, 1950–51. Suspended 1917–19, 1933, 1942–46.

| Year | Time | First | Second | Year | Time | First | Second |
|---|---|---|---|---|---|---|---|
| 1895 | 21:25 | Columbia | Cornell | 1937 | 18:33 3/5 | Washington | Navy |
| 1896 | 19:59 | Cornell | Harvard | 1938 | 18:19 | Navy | California |
| 1897 | 20:47 4/5 | Cornell | Columbia | 1939 | 18:12 3/5 | California | Washington |
| 1898 | 15:51 1/2 | Pennsylvania | Cornell | 1940 | 22:42 | Washington | Cornell |
| 1899 | 20:04 | Pennsylvania | Wisconsin | 1941 | 18:53 3/10 | Washington | California |
| 1900 | 19:44 3/5 | Pennsylvania | Wisconsin | 1947 | 13:59 1/5 | Navy | Cornell |
| 1901 | 18:53 1/5 | Cornell | Columbia | 1948 | 14:06 2/5 | Washington | California |
| 1902 | 19:03 3/5 | Cornell | Wisconsin | 1949 | 14:42 3/5 | California | Washington |
| 1903 | 18:57 | Cornell | Georgetown | 1950 | 8:07.5 | Washington | California |
| 1904 | 20:22 3/5 | Syracuse | Cornell | 1951 | 7:50.5 | Wisconsin | Washington |
| 1905 | 20:29 | Cornell | Syracuse | 1952 | 15:08.1 | Navy | Princeton |
| 1906 | 19:36 4/5 | Cornell | Pennsylvania | 1953 | 15:29.6 | Navy | Cornell |
| 1907 | 20:02 2/5 | Cornell | Columbia | 1954 | 16:04.4 | Navy[1] | Cornell |
| 1908 | 19:24 1/5 | Syracuse | Columbia | 1955 | 15:49.9 | Cornell | Pennsylvania |
| 1909 | 19:02 | Cornell | Columbia | 1956 | 16:22.4 | Cornell | Navy |
| 1910 | 20:42 1/5 | Cornell | Pennsylvania | 1957 | 15:26.6 | Cornell | Pennsylvania |
| 1911 | 20:10 4/5 | Cornell | Columbia | 1958 | 17:12.1 | Cornell | Navy |
| 1912 | 19:31 2/5 | Cornell | Wisconsin | 1959 | 18:01.7 | Wisconsin | Syracuse |
| 1913 | 19:28 3/5 | Syracuse | Cornell | 1960 | 15:57 | California | Navy |
| 1914 | 19:37 4/5 | Columbia | Pennsylvania | 1961 | 16:49.2 | California | Cornell |
| 1915 | 19:36 3/5 | Cornell | Stanford | 1962 | 17:02.9 | Cornell | Washington |
| 1916 | 20:15 2/5 | Syracuse | Cornell | 1963 | 17:24 | Cornell | Navy |
| 1920 | 11:02 3/5 | Syracuse | Cornell | 1964 | 6:31.1 | California | Washington |
| 1921 | 14:07 | Navy | California | 1965 | 16:51.3 | Navy | Cornell |
| 1922 | 13:33 3/5 | Navy | Washington | 1966 | 16:03.4 | Wisconsin | Navy |
| 1923 | 14:03 1/5 | Washington | Navy | 1967 | 16:13.9 | Pennsylvania | Wisconsin |
| 1924 | 15:02 | Washington | Wisconsin | 1968 | 6:15.6 | Pennsylvania | Washington |
| 1925 | 19:24 4/5 | Navy | Washington | 1969 | 6:30.4 | Pennsylvania | Dartmouth |
| 1926 | 19:28 3/5 | Washington | Navy | 1970 | 6:39.3 | Washington | Wisconsin |
| 1927 | 20:57 | Columbia | Washington | 1971 | 6:06 | Cornell | Washington |
| 1928 | 18:35 4/5 | California | Columbia | 1972 | 6:22.6 | Pennsylvania | Brown |
| 1929 | 22:58 | Columbia | Washington | 1973 | 6:21 | Wisconsin | Brown |
| 1930 | 21:42 | Cornell | Syracuse | 1974 | 6:33 | Wisconsin | Mass. Inst. of Technology |
| 1931 | 18:54 1/5 | Navy | Cornell | | | | |
| 1932 | 19:55 | California | Cornell | 1975 | 6:08.2 | Wisconsin | M.I.T. |
| 1934 | 19:44 | California | Washington | 1976 | 6:31 | California | Princeton |
| 1935 | 18:52 | California | Cornell | 1977 | 6:32.4 | Cornell | Pennsylvania |
| 1936 | 19:09 3/5 | Washington | California | 1978 | 6:39.5 | Syracuse | Brown |

1. Disqualified.

## NATIONAL CHAMPIONSHIPS

(Collingswood, N.J., July 21–23, 1978)

### Elite Events

| | |
|---|---|
| Singles—Jim Dietz, New York A.C. | 7:01.6 |
| Singles quarter-mile—Jim Dietz | 1:11 |
| Doubles—Tiff Wood and Greg Stone, Harvard | 6:34.6 |
| Pairs with coxswains—Tome Woodman, Philip Stekl, John Chatsky, coxswain, Univ. of Pa. | 7:14.8 |
| Pairs without coxswains—Sean Colgan and Bruce Ibbetson, Penn. | 6:48 |
| Fours with coxswains—Pennsylvania | 6:32.2 |
| Fours without coxswains—Cornell–Potomac B.C., Washington | 6:15 |
| Quadruple sculls—New York A.C. | 5:59.7 |
| Eights—Pennsylvania—Penn A.C. | 5:59.7 |
| Lightweight singles—Bill Belden, New York A.C. | 7:11.9 |
| Lightweight doubles—Larry Klecatsky and Bill Belden, New York A.C. | 6:29.5 |
| Lightweight pairs—John Sonberg and Joseph Caminiti, New York A.C. | 7:11.5 |
| Lightweight fours—New York A.C. | 6:20.4 |
| Lightweight fours with coxswains—Vesper, B.C., Philadelphia | 7:04.4 |
| Lightweight eights—New York A.C. | 6:09.4 |

### Lightweight Events

| | |
|---|---|
| ¼-mile singles—Robert Cady, Ecorse (Mich.) R.C. | 1:12.5 |
| Lightweight quads—New York A.C. | 6:06.5 |

### Intermediate Events

| | |
|---|---|
| Singles—Harborne Stuart, Harvard | 7:16.2 |
| Pairs—Tim Askin and James Stewart, London R.C. | 7:29.5 |
| Doubles—S. Williams and Bob Spousta, Potomac | 6:34.9 |
| Fours with coxswains—Worcester Polytech Inst. | 7:05.4 |
| Eights—Viking B.C. | 6:15.2 |

### Senior Events

| | |
|---|---|
| Singles—Tom Hazeltine, Undine Barge Club, Phila. | 7:16.2 |
| Doubles—Mark Hawley and Mark O'Brien, Detroit | 6:44.6 |
| Pairs—Jim Cushwa and Paul Horvat, Vesper B.C. | 7:02.2 |
| Fours with coxswains—Vesper B.C. | 6:36.8 |
| Quads—New York A.C. | 6:19 |

### Masters Events

| | |
|---|---|
| Singles A—Findley Meislahn, Cornell | 8:25.5 |
| Singles B—Mile Vega, Tampa, Fla. | 8:17.3 |
| Singles C—Gus Constant, Vesper B.C. | 8:00.6 |
| Singles D—Fred Shepherson, Malta B.C. | 8:53.4 |
| Singles E—Jerry Olrich, Cambridge (Mass.) B.C. | 9:10.7 |
| Fours with coxswains—Cambridge B.C. | 4:12.1 |

## 1978 COLLEGIATE

### Intercollegiate Rowing Association

(Lake Onondaga, Syracuse, N.Y., June 1–3)

(All races 2,000 meters)

Eights—1, Syracuse, 6:39.5; 2, Brown, 6:42.5; 3, Northeastern, 6:43.1; 4, Pennsylvania, 6:43.5; 5, Dartmouth, 6:46.0; 6, California, Berkeley, 6:50.0

| | |
|---|---|
| Second varsity eights—Pennsylvania | 6:43.3 |
| Freshmen eights—Syracuse | 7:29.3 |
| Pairs without coxswains—Rutgers (Gene Tunney, Dick Schmitt) | 7:40.2 |
| Pairs with Coxswains—Rutgers (Charles Murray, James Gilgon, Steve Gurkovich, coxswain) | 8:10.7 |
| Fours without coxswains—Oregon State | 7:04.5 |
| Fours with coxswains—Coast Guard Academy | 7:16.2 |
| Freshmen fours with coxswains—Princeton | 7:09.1 |
| Team (Jim Ten Eyck Trophy)—Pennsylvania | 239.8 pts |

# *SOFTBALL*

*Source:* Amateur Softball Association.

## Amateur Champions

| | |
|---|---|
| 1959 | Aurora (Ill.) Sealmasters |
| 1960 | Clearwater (Fla.) Bombers |
| 1961 | Aurora (Ill.) Sealmasters |
| 1962–63 | Clearwater (Fla.) Bombers |
| 1964 | Burch Gage & Tool, Detroit |
| 1965 | Aurora (Ill.) Sealmasters |
| 1966 | Clearwater (Fla.) Bombers |
| 1967 | Aurora (Ill.) Sealmasters |
| 1968 | Clearwater (Fla.) Bombers |
| 1969 | Raybestos Cardinals, Stratford, Conn. |
| 1971 | Welty Way, Cedar Rapids, Iowa |
| 1972 | Raybestos Cardinals, Stratford, Conn. |
| 1973 | Clearwater (Fla.) Bombers |
| 1974 | Santa Rosa (Calif.) |
| 1975 | Rising Sun Hotel, Reading, Pa. |
| 1976 | Raybestos Cardinals, Stratford, Conn. |
| 1977 | Billard Barbell, Reading, Pa. |
| 1978 | Redding, Pa. |

## AMATEUR SOFTBALL ASSOCIATION CHAMPIONS—1978

Men's fast pitch—Redding, Pa. (defeated Clearwater, Fla., 9–2, in final game)
Women's fast pitch—Raybestos Brakettes, Stratford, Conn. (defeated Law Equipment, Greeley, Colo., 4–0, in final)
16-inch slow pitch—Chicago Bobcats
Men's Class A fast pitch—S & K Rigging, Arcola, Ill.

## YOUTH TOURNAMENTS—1978

Boys 16–18 fast pitch—Red Wings, Rockford, Ill.
Boys 16–18 slow pitch—Bruins, Buffalo Grove, Ill.
Boys 13–15 fast pitch—Empire Bank, Springfield, Mo.
Boys 13–15 slow pitch—Valente's Deli, New York
Girls 16–18 fast pitch—Rookies, Rock Island, Ill.
Girls 16–18 slow pitch—Satellite Comets, Satellite Beach, Fla.
Girls 13–15 fast pitch—Roadrunners, St. Louis
Girls 13–15 slow pitch—Volettes, East Point, Ga.

## COLLEGIATE CHAMPIONS—1978

A.I.A.W.—U.C.L.A. (defeated Northern Colorado, 3–0, in final at Omaha)

# HARNESS RACING

Oliver Wendell Holmes, the famous Autocrat of the Breakfast Table, wrote that the running horse was a gambling toy but the trotting horse was useful and, furthermore, "horse-racing is not a republican institution; horse-trotting is." Oliver Wendell Holmes was a born-and-bred New Englander, and New England was the nursery of the harness racing sport in America. Pacers and trotters were matters of local pride and prejudice in Colonial New England, and, shortly after the Revolution, the Messenger and Justin Morgan strains produced many winners in harness racing "matches" along the turnpikes of New York, Connecticut, Rhode Island, Massachusetts, Vermont, and New Hampshire.

There was English thoroughbred blood in Messenger and Justin Morgan, and, many years later, it was blended in Rysdyk's Hambletonian, foaled in 1849. Hambletonian was not particularly fast under harness but his descendants have had almost a monopoly of prizes, titles, and records in the harness racing game. Hambletonian was purchased as a foal with its dam for a total of $124 by William Rysdyk of Goshen, N.Y., and made a modest fortune for the purchaser.

Trotters and pacers often were raced under saddle in the old days, and, in fact, the custom still survives in some places in Europe. Dexter, the great trotter that lowered the mile record from 2:19$\frac{3}{4}$ to 2:17$\frac{1}{4}$ in 1867, was said to handle just as well under saddle as when pulling a sulky. But as sulkies were lightened in weight and improved in design, trotting under saddle became less common and finally faded out in this country.

## WORLD RECORDS

Established in a Race or Against Time at One Mile

*Source:* Larry Evans, Publicity Director, United States Trotting Association.

### Trotting on Mile Track

| | Record | Holder | Driver | Where Made | Year |
|---|---|---|---|---|---|
| All Age | 1:54$\frac{4}{5}$ | Nevele Pride | Stanley Dancer | Indianapolis | 1969 |
| 2-year-old | 1:57[1] | Briscoe Hanover | James Miller | DuQuoin, Ill. | 1977 |
| 3-year-old | 1:55$\frac{3}{5}$[1] | Green Speed | Billy Haughton | DuQuoin, Ill. | 1977 |
| 4-year-old | 1:54$\frac{4}{5}$ | Nevele Pride | Stanley Dancer | Indianapolis | 1969 |

### Trotting on Half-Mile Track

| | Record | Holder | Driver | Where Made | Year |
|---|---|---|---|---|---|
| All Age | 1:56$\frac{4}{5}$[1] | Nevele Pride | Stanley Dancer | Saratoga Springs, N.Y. | 1969 |
| 2-year-old | 2:00$\frac{1}{5}$[1] | Ayres | John Simpson, Sr. | Delaware, Ohio | 1963 |
| 3-year-old | 1:58$\frac{3}{5}$[1] | Songcan | George Sholty | Delaware, Ohio | 1972 |
| 4-year-old | 1:56$\frac{4}{5}$[1] | Nevele Pride | Stanley Dancer | Saratoga Springs, N.Y. | 1969 |

### Pacing on Mile Track

| | Record | Holder | Driver | Where Made | Year |
|---|---|---|---|---|---|
| All Age | 1:52 | Steady Star | Joe O'Brien | Lexington, Ky. | 1971 |
| 2-year-old | 1:54$\frac{1}{5}$[1] | Jade Prince | Jack Kopes | Lexington, Ky. | 1976 |
| | 1:54$\frac{1}{5}$ | Fulla Strikes | Joe O'Brien | Inglewood, Calif. | 1976 |
| 3-year-old | 1:53$\frac{2}{5}$ | Windshield Wiper | Billy Haughton | Lexington, Ky | 1976 |
| 4-year-old | 1:52 | Steady Star | Joe O'Brien | Lexington, Ky. | 1971 |

### Pacing on Half-Mile Track

| | Record | Holder | Driver | Where Made | Year |
|---|---|---|---|---|---|
| All Age | 1:55$\frac{3}{5}$ | Adios Butler | Edward Cobb | Delaware, Ohio | 1963 |
| | 1:55$\frac{3}{5}$[1] | Albatross | Stanley Dancer | Delaware, Ohio | 1972 |
| 2-year-old | 1:58$\frac{4}{5}$[1] | Columbia George | Roland Beaulieu | Yonkers, N.Y. | 1969 |
| | 1:58$\frac{4}{5}$[1] | J. R. Skipper | Greg Wright | Delaware, Ohio | 1972 |
| | 1:58$\frac{4}{5}$[1] | Armbro Ranger | Joe O'Brien | Delaware, Ohio | 1975 |
| 3-year-old | 1:56$\frac{1}{5}$[1] | Governor Skipper | John Chapman | Delaware, Ohio | 1977 |
| 4-year-old | 1:55$\frac{3}{5}$[1] | Albatross | Stanley Dancer | Delaware, Ohio | 1972 |

1. Record made in race.

## HARNESS RACING RECORDS FOR THE MILE

### Trotters

| Time | Trotter, age, driver | Year |
|---|---|---|
| 2:00 | Lou Dillon, 5, Millard Sanders | 1903 |
| 1:58$\frac{1}{2}$ | Lou Dillon, 5, Millard Sanders | 1903 |
| 1:58 | Uhlan, 8, Charles Tanner | 1912 |
| 1:58 | Peter Manning, 5, T. W. Murphy | 1921 |
| 1:57$\frac{3}{4}$ | Peter Manning, 5, T. W. Murphy | 1921 |
| 1:57 | Peter Manning, 6, T. W. Murphy | 1922 |
| 1:56$\frac{3}{4}$ | Peter Manning, 6, T. W. Murphy | 1922 |
| 1:56$\frac{3}{4}$ | Greyhound, 5, Sep Palin | 1937 |
| 1:56 | Greyhound, 5, Sep Palin | 1937 |
| 1:55$\frac{1}{4}$ | Greyhound, 6, Sep Palin | 1938 |
| 1:54$\frac{4}{5}$ | Nevele Pride, 4, Stanley Dancer | 1969 |

### Pacers

| Time | Pacer, age, driver | Year |
|---|---|---|
| 2:00$\frac{1}{2}$ | John R. Gentry, 7, W.J. Andrews | 1896 |
| 1:59$\frac{1}{4}$ | Star Pointer, 8, D. McClary | 1897 |
| 1:59 | Dan Patch, 7, M. E. McHenry | 1903 |
| 1:56$\frac{1}{4}$ | Dan Patch, 7, M. E. McHenry | 1903 |
| 1:56 | Dan Patch, 8, H. C. Hersey | 1904 |
| 1:55 | Billy Direct, 4, Vic Fleming | 1938 |
| 1:55 | Adios Harry, 4, Luther Lyons | 1955 |
| 1:54$\frac{3}{5}$ | Adios Butler, 4, Paige West | 1960 |
| 1:54 | Bret Hanover, 4, Frank Ervin | 1966 |
| 1:53$\frac{3}{5}$ | Bret Hanover, 4, Frank Ervin | 1966 |
| 1:52 | Steady Star, 4, Joe O'Brien | 1971 |

# HISTORY OF TRADITIONAL HARNESS RACING STAKES

### The Hambletonian

Three-year-old trotters. One mile. Guy McKinney won first race at Syracuse in 1926; held at Goshen, N.Y., 1930–1942, 1944–1956; at Yonkers, N.Y., 1943; at Du Quoin, Ill., since 1957.

| Year | Winner | Driver | Best time | Total purse |
|---|---|---|---|---|
| 1967 | Speedy Streak | Del Cameron | 2:00 | 122,650 |
| 1968 | Nevele Pride | Stanley Dancer | 1:59⅖ | 116,190 |
| 1969 | Lindy's Pride | Howard Beissinger | 1:57⅗ | 124,910 |
| 1970 | Timothy T. | John Simpson, Jr. | 1:58⅖[1] | 143,630 |
| 1971 | Speedy Crown | Howard Beissinger | 1:57⅖ | 129,770 |
| 1972 | Super Bowl | Stanley Dancer | 1:56⅖ | 119,090 |
| 1973 | Flirth | Ralph Baldwin | 1:57⅕ | 144,710 |
| 1974 | Christopher T | Billy Haughton | 1:58⅗ | 160,150 |
| 1975 | Bonefish | Stanley Dancer | 1:59[2] | 232,192 |
| 1976 | Steve Lobell | Billy Haughton | 1:56⅖ | 263,524 |
| 1977 | Green Speed | Billy Haughton | 1:55⅗ | 284,131 |

1. By Formal Notice. 2. By Yankee Bambino.

### Little Brown Jug

Three-year-old pacers. One Mile. Raced at Delaware County Fair Grounds, Delaware, Ohio.

| Year | Winner | Driver | Best time | Total purse |
|---|---|---|---|---|
| 1967 | Best of All | Jim Hackett | 1:59[1] | 84,778 |
| 1968 | Rum Customer | William Haughton | 1:59⅗ | 104,226 |
| 1969 | Laverne Hanover | William Haughton | 2:00⅖ | 109,731 |
| 1970 | Most Happy Fella | Stanley Dancer | 1:57⅕ | 100,110 |
| 1971 | Nansemond | Herve Filion | 1:57⅖ | 102,994 |
| 1972 | Strike Out | Keith Waples | 1:56⅗ | 104,916 |
| 1973 | Melvin's Wo | Joe O'Brien | 1:57⅗ | 120,000 |
| 1974 | Ambro Omaha | Billy Haughton | 1:57 | 132,630 |
| 1975 | Seatrain | Ben Webster | 1:57 | 147,813 |
| 1976 | Keystone Ore | Stanley Dancer | 1:56⅘[2] | 153,799 |
| 1977 | Governor Skipper | John Chapman | 1:56⅕ | 150,000 |

1. By Nardin's Byrd. 2. By Armbro Ranger.

# HARNESS HORSE OF THE YEAR

Chosen in poll conducted by United States Trotting Association in conjunction with the U.S. Harness Writers Assn.

| | | | | | |
|---|---|---|---|---|---|
| 1959 | Bye Bye Byrd, Pacer | 1966 | Bret Hanover, Pacer | 1973 | Sir Dalrae, Pacer |
| 1960 | Adios Butler, Pacer | 1967 | Nevele Pride, Trotter | 1974 | Delmonica Hanover, Trotter |
| 1961 | Adios Butler, Pacer | 1968 | Nevele Pride, Trotter | 1975 | Savoir, Trotter |
| 1962 | Su Mac Lad, Trotter | 1969 | Nevele Pride, Trotter | 1976 | Keystone Ore, Pacer |
| 1963 | Speedy Scot, Trotter | 1970 | Fresh Yankee, Trotter | 1977 | Green Speed, Trotter |
| 1964 | Bret Hanover, Pacer | 1971 | Albatross, Pacer | | |
| 1965 | Bret Hanover, Pacer | 1972 | Albatross, Pacer | | |

# MAJOR STAKES

### Trotting

| | Purse |
|---|---|
| Hambletonian (DuQuoin, Ill., Sept. 2, 1978)—Speedy Somolli, driven by Howard Beissinger, won first heat in 1:55 and third in 1:57. Florida Pro won second heat in 1:55. Speedy Somolli's first-place purse: | $120,640 |
| American Trotting Championship (Roosevelt)—Kash Minibar (Jimmy Cruise); 1:59⅕ | 113,350 |
| Challenge Cup, (Roosevelt, 1½ miles)—Lola's Express (Ted Taylor) | 25,000 |
| Colonial (Liberty Bell, Sept. 16, 1978)—Florida Pro (George Sholty); 1:58⅖ | 56,675 |
| Roosevelt International (Westbury, L.I., 1¼ miles)—Cold Comfort (Peter Haughton); 2:03⅗ | 100,000 |
| Yonkers Trot (Yonkers, N.Y., Aug. 28, 1978)—Speedy Somolli (Howard Beissinger); 1:59⅗ | |

### Foreign

| | |
|---|---|
| Prix d'Amerique (Paris, 2,600 meters, Jan. 29, 1978)—Grandpre (Pierre Desire-Allaire); 3:19.9 | $118,000 |
| Canadian Pacing Derby (Greenwood, Toronto, Aug. 26, 1978)—Dream Maker (Ron Waples); 1:56⅕ | |
| Prix d'Ete (Blue Bonnet, Montreal, Aug. 28, 1978)—Abercrombie (Glen Garnsey) three heats; final: 1:54⅘ | 52,762 |

### Pacing

| | |
|---|---|
| Little Brown Jug (Delaware, Ohio, Sept. 21, 1978)—Happy Escort (Bill Popfinger) winner in four heats; final in 2:00⅘ | $49,491 |
| Adios (Meadow Lands, Pa., Aug. 12, 1978)—Abercrombie (Glen Garnsey) won first heat in 1:56⅖ and second in 1:35 | 128,663 |
| Alfred E. Driscoll (Meadowland, N.J., June 29, 1978)—Whata Baron (Lew Williams); 1:54⅘ | |
| Cane (Yonkers, July 8, 1978)—Armbro Tiger (Herve Filion) | 61,519 |
| Kentucky Pacing Derby (Louisville Downs, Sept. 16, 1978)—Scarlett Skipper (Billy Herman); 1:58⅘ | 91,887 |
| Monticello–NYC–OTB Classic (Monticello, N.Y., July 23, 1978)—Happy Lady (Jim Rankin); 1:59 | 133,082 |

# GOLF

It may be that golf originated in Holland—historians believe it did—but certainly Scotland fostered the game and is famous for it. In fact, in 1457 the Scottish Parliament, disturbed because football and golf had lured young Scots from the more soldierly exercise of archery, passed an ordinance that "futeball and golf be utterly cryit doun and nocht usit." James I and Charles I of the royal line of Stuarts were golf enthusiasts, whereby the game came to be known as "the royal and ancient game of golf."

The golf balls used in the early games were leather-covered and stuffed with feathers. Clubs of all kinds were fashioned by hand to suit individual players. The great step in spreading the game came with the change from the feather ball to the gutta-percha ball about 1850. In 1860, formal competition began with the establishment of an annual tournament for the British Open championship. There are records of "golf clubs" in the United States as far back as colonial days but no proof of actual play before John Reid and some friends laid out six holes on the Reid lawn in Yonkers, N.Y., in 1888 and played there with golf balls and clubs brought over from Scotland by Robert Lockhart. This group then formed the St. Andrews Golf Club of Yonkers, and golf was established in this country.

However, it remained a rather sedate and almost aristocratic pastime until a 20-year-old ex-caddy, Francis Ouimet of Boston, defeated two great British professionals, Harry Vardon and Ted Ray, in the United States Open championship at Brookline, Mass., in 1913. This feat put the game and Francis Ouimet on the front pages of the newspapers and stirred a wave of enthusiasm for the sport. The greatest feat so far in golf history is that of Robert Tyre Jones, Jr., of Atlanta, who won the British Open, the British Amateur, the U.S. Open, and the U.S. Amateur titles in one year, 1930.

## U.S. OPEN CHAMPIONS

| Year | Winner | Score | Where played | Year | Winner | Score | Where played |
|---|---|---|---|---|---|---|---|
| 1895 | Horace Rawlins | 173 | Newport | 1936 | Tony Manero | 282 | Baltusrol |
| 1896 | James Foulis | 152 | Shinnecock Hills | 1937 | Ralph Guldahl | 281 | Oakland Hills |
| 1897 | Joe Lloyd | 162 | Chicago | 1938 | Ralph Guldahl | 284 | Cherry Hills |
| 1898[3] | Fred Herd | 328 | Myopia | 1939 | Byron Nelson[1] | 284 | Philadelphia |
| 1899 | Willie Smith | 315 | Baltimore | 1940 | Lawson Little[1] | 287 | Canterbury |
| 1900 | Harry Vardon | 313 | Chicago | 1941 | Craig Wood | 284 | Colonial |
| 1901 | Willie Anderson[1] | 331 | Myopia | 1942–45 | No tournaments[5] | | |
| 1902 | Laurie Auchterlonie | 307 | Garden City | 1946 | Lloyd Mangrum[1] | 284 | Canterbury |
| 1903 | Willie Anderson[1] | 307 | Baltusrol | 1947 | Lew Worsham[1] | 282 | St. Louis |
| 1904 | Willie Anderson | 303 | Glen View | 1948 | Ben Hogan | 276 | Riviera |
| 1905 | Willie Anderson | 314 | Myopia | 1949 | Cary Middlecoff | 286 | Medinah |
| 1906 | Alex Smith | 295 | Onwentsia | 1950 | Ben Hogan[1] | 287 | Merion |
| 1907 | Alex Ross | 302 | Philadelphia | 1951 | Ben Hogan | 287 | Oakland Hills |
| 1908 | Fred McLeod[1] | 322 | Myopia | 1952 | Julius Boros | 281 | Northwood |
| 1909 | George Sargent | 290 | Englewood | 1953 | Ben Hogan | 283 | Oakmont |
| 1910 | Alex Smith[1] | 298 | Philadelphia | 1954 | Ed Furgol | 284 | Baltusrol |
| 1911 | John McDermott[1] | 307 | Chicago | 1955 | Jack Fleck[1] | 287 | Olympic |
| 1912 | John McDermott | 294 | Buffalo | 1956 | Cary Middlecoff | 281 | Oak Hill |
| 1913 | Francis Ouimet[1,2] | 304 | Brookline | 1957 | Dick Mayer[1] | 298 | Inverness |
| 1914 | Walter Hagen | 290 | Midlothian | 1958 | Tommy Bolt | 283 | Southern Hills |
| 1915 | Jerome D. Travers[2] | 297 | Baltusrol | 1959 | Bill Casper, Jr. | 282 | Winged Foot |
| 1916 | Charles Evans, Jr.[2] | 286 | Minikahda | 1960 | Arnold Palmer | 280 | Cherry Hills |
| 1917–18 | No tournaments[4] | | | 1961 | Gene Littler | 281 | Oakland Hills |
| 1919 | Walter Hagen[2] | 301 | Brae Burn | 1962 | Jack Nicklaus[1] | 283 | Oakmont |
| 1920 | Edward Ray | 295 | Inverness | 1963 | Julius Boros[1] | 293 | Country Club |
| 1921 | Jim Barnes | 289 | Columbia | 1964 | Ken Venturi | 278 | Congressional |
| 1922 | Gene Sarazen | 288 | Skokie | 1965 | Gary Player[1] | 282 | Bellerive |
| 1923 | R. T. Jones, Jr.[1,2] | 296 | Inwood | 1966 | Bill Casper[1] | 278 | Olympic |
| 1924 | Cyril Walker | 297 | Oakland Hills | 1967 | Jack Nicklaus | 275 | Baltusrol |
| 1925 | Willie Macfarlane[1] | 291 | Worcester | 1968 | Lee Trevino | 275 | Oak Hill |
| 1926 | R. T. Jones, Jr.[2] | 293 | Scioto | 1969 | Orville Moody | 281 | Champions G. C. |
| 1927 | Tommy Armour[1] | 301 | Oakmont | 1970 | Tony Jacklin | 281 | Hazeltine |
| 1928 | Johnny Farrell[1] | 294 | Olympia Fields | 1971 | Lee Trevino[1] | 280 | Merion |
| 1929 | R. T. Jones, Jr.[1,2] | 294 | Winged Foot | 1972 | Jack Nicklaus | 290 | Pebble Beach |
| 1930 | R. T. Jones, Jr.[2] | 287 | Interlachen | 1973 | Johnny Miller | 279 | Oakmont |
| 1931 | Billy Burke[1] | 292 | Inverness | 1974 | Hale Irwin | 287 | Winged Foot |
| 1932 | Gene Sarazen | 286 | Fresh Meadow | 1975 | Lou Graham[1] | 287 | Medinah |
| 1933 | John Goodman[2] | 287 | North Shore | 1976 | Jerry Pate | 277 | Atlanta A.C. |
| 1934 | Olin Dutra | 293 | Merion | 1977 | Hubert Green | 278 | Southern Hills |
| 1935 | Sam Parks, Jr. | 299 | Oakmont | 1978 | Andy North | 285 | Cherry Hills |

1. Winner in playoff. 2. Amateur. 3. In 1898, competition was extended to 72 holes. 4. In 1917, Jock Hutchison, with a 292, won an Open Patriotic Tournament for the benefit of the American Red Cross at Whitemarsh Valley Country Club. 5. In 1942, Ben Hogan, with a 271 won a Hale American National Open Tournament for the benefit of the Navy Relief Society and USO at Ridgemoor Country Club.

## U.S. AMATEUR CHAMPIONS

| | | | | | | | | | |
|---|---|---|---|---|---|---|---|---|---|
| 1895 | Charles B. Macdonald | 1919 | S. D. Herron | 1940 | R. D. Chapman | 1963 | Deane Beman |
| 1896–97 | H. J. Whigham | 1920 | Charles Evans, Jr. | 1941 | Marvin H. Ward | 1964 | Bill Campbell |
| 1898 | Findlay S. Douglas | 1921 | Jesse P. Guilford | 1946 | Ted Bishop | 1965[2] | Robert Murphy, Jr. |
| 1899 | H. M. Harriman | 1922 | Jess W. Sweetser | 1947 | Robert Riegel | 1966 | Gary Cowan[1] |
| 1900–01 | Walter J. Travis | 1923 | Max R. Marston | 1948 | Willie Turnesa | 1967 | Bob Dickson |
| 1902 | Louis N. James | 1924-25 | R. T. Jones Jr. | 1949 | Charles Coe | 1968 | Bruce Fleisher |
| 1903 | Walter J. Travis | 1926 | George Von Elm | 1950 | Sam Urzetta | 1969 | Steven Melnyk |
| 1904–05 | H. Chandler Egan | 1927–28 | R. T. Jones Jr. | 1951 | Billy Maxwell | 1970 | Lanny Wadkins |
| 1906 | Eben M. Byers | 1929 | H. R. Johnston | 1952 | Jack Westland | 1971 | Gary Cowan |
| 1907–08 | Jerome D. Travers | 1930 | R. T. Jones, Jr. | 1953 | Gene Littler | 1972 | Vinny Giles 3d |
| 1909 | Robert A. Gardner | 1931 | Francis Ouimet | 1954 | Arnold Palmer | 1973[3] | Craig Stadler |
| 1910 | W. C. Fownes, Jr. | 1932 | Ross Somerville | 1955–56 | Harvie Ward | 1974 | Jerry Pate |
| 1911 | Harold H. Hilton | 1933 | G. T. Dunlap, Jr. | 1957 | Hillman Robbins | 1975 | Fred Ridley |
| 1912–13 | Jerome D. Travers | 1934–35 | Lawson Little | 1958 | Charles Coe | 1976 | Bill Sander |
| 1914 | Francis Ouimet | 1936 | John W. Fischer | 1959 | Jack Nicklaus | 1977 | John Fought |
| 1915 | Robert A. Gardner | 1937 | John Goodman | 1960 | Deane Beman | 1978 | John Cook |
| 1916 | Charles Evans, Jr. | 1938 | Willie Turnesa | 1961 | Jack Nicklaus | | |
| | | 1939 | Marvin H. Ward | 1962 | Labron Harris, Jr. | | |

1. Winner in playoff. 2. Tourney switched to medal play through 1972. 3. Return to match play.

## U.S. P.G.A. CHAMPIONS

| | | | | | | | |
|---|---|---|---|---|---|---|---|
| 1916 | Jim Barnes | 1938 | Paul Runyan | 1953 | Walter Burkemo | 1967 | Don January[1] |
| 1919 | Jim Barnes | 1939 | Henry Picard | 1954 | Chick Harbert | 1968 | Julius Boros |
| 1920 | Jock Hutchison | 1940 | Byron Nelson | 1955 | Doug Ford | 1969 | Ray Floyd |
| 1921 | Walter Hagen | 1941 | Victor Ghezzi | 1956 | Jack Burke, Jr. | 1970 | Dave Stockton |
| 1922–23 | Gene Sarazen | 1942 | Sam Snead | 1957 | Lionel Hebert | 1971 | Jack Nicklaus |
| 1924–27 | Walter Hagen | 1944 | Bob Hamilton | 1958[2] | Dow Finsterwald | 1972 | Gary Player |
| 1928–29 | Leo Diegel | 1945 | Byron Nelson | 1959 | Bob Rosburg | 1973 | Jack Nicklaus |
| 1930 | Tommy Armour | 1946 | Ben Hogan | 1960 | Jay Hebert | 1974 | Lee Trevino |
| 1931 | Tom Creavy | 1947 | Jim Ferrier | 1961 | Jerry Barber[1] | 1975 | Jack Nicklaus |
| 1932 | Olin Dutra | 1948 | Ben Hogan | 1962 | Gary Player | 1976 | Dave Stockton |
| 1933 | Gene Sarazen | 1949 | Sam Snead | 1963 | Jack Nicklaus | 1977 | Lanny Wadkins[1] |
| 1934 | Paul Runyan | 1950 | Chandler Harper | 1964 | Bobby Nichols | 1978 | John Mahaffey |
| 1935 | Johnny Revolta | 1951 | Sam Snead | 1965 | Dave Marr | | |
| 1936–37 | Denny Shute | 1952 | Jim Turnesa | 1966 | Al Geiberger | | |

1. Winner in playoff. 2. Switched to medal play.

## THE MASTERS TOURNAMENT WINNERS

Augusta National Golf Club, Augusta, Ga.

| Year | Winner | Score | Year | Winner | Score | Year | Winner | Score |
|---|---|---|---|---|---|---|---|---|
| 1934 | Horton Smith | 284 | 1951 | Ben Hogan | 280 | 1965 | Jack Nicklaus | 271 |
| 1935 | Gene Sarazen[1] | 282 | 1952 | Sam Snead | 286 | 1966 | Jack Nicklaus[1] | 288 |
| 1936 | Horton Smith | 285 | 1953 | Ben Hogan | 274 | 1967 | Gay Brewer, Jr. | 280 |
| 1937 | Byron Nelson | 283 | 1954 | Sam Snead[1] | 289 | 1968 | Bob Goalby | 277 |
| 1938 | Henry Picard | 285 | 1955 | Cary Middlecoff | 279 | 1969 | George Archer | 281 |
| 1939 | Ralph Guldahl | 279 | 1956 | Jack Burke | 289 | 1970 | Billy Casper[1] | 279 |
| 1940 | Jimmy Demaret | 280 | 1957 | Doug Ford | 283 | 1971 | Charles Coody | 279 |
| 1941 | Craig Wood | 280 | 1958 | Arnold Palmer | 284 | 1972 | Jack Nicklaus | 286 |
| 1942 | Byron Nelson[1] | 280 | 1959 | Art Wall, Jr. | 284 | 1973 | Tommy Aaron | 283 |
| 1943–45 | No Tournaments | | 1960 | Arnold Palmer | 282 | 1974 | Gary Player | 278 |
| 1946 | Herman Keiser | 282 | 1961 | Gary Player | 280 | 1975 | Jack Nicklaus | 276 |
| 1947 | Jimmy Demaret | 281 | 1962 | Arnold Palmer[1] | 280 | 1976 | Ray Floyd | 271 |
| 1948 | Claude Harmon | 279 | 1963 | Jack Nicklaus | 286 | 1977 | Tom Watson | 276 |
| 1949 | Sam Snead | 282 | 1964 | Arnold Palmer | 276 | 1978 | Gary Player | 277 |
| 1950 | Jimmy Demaret | 283 | | | | | | |

1. Winner in playoff.

## U.S. WOMEN'S AMATEUR CHAMPIONS

| | | | | | | | |
|---|---|---|---|---|---|---|---|
| 1916 | Alexa Stirling | 1925 | Glenna Collett | 1936 | Pamela Barton | 1948 | Grace Lenczyk |
| 1919–20 | Alexa Stirling | 1926 | Helen Stetson | 1937 | Mrs. J. A. Page, Jr. | 1949 | Mrs. D. G. Porter |
| 1921 | Marion Hollins | 1927 | Mrs. M. B. Horn | 1938 | Patty Berg | 1950 | Beverly Hanson |
| 1922 | Glenna Collett | 1928–30 | Glenna Collett | 1939–40 | Betty Jameson | 1951 | Dorothy Kirby |
| 1923 | Edith Cummings | 1931 | Helen Hicks | 1941 | Mrs. Frank Newell | 1952 | Jacqueline Pung |
| 1924 | Dorothy Campbell Hurd | 1932–34 | Virginia Van Wie | 1946 | Mildred Zaharias | 1953 | Mary Lena Faulk |
| | | 1935 | Glenna Collett Vare | 1947 | Louise Suggs | | |

| | | | | | | | |
|---|---|---|---|---|---|---|---|
| 1954 | Barbara Romack | 1961 | Anne Quast Decker | 1967 | Lou Dill | 1974 | Cynthia Hill |
| 1955 | Patricia Lesser | | | 1968 | JoAnne G. Carner | 1975 | Beth Daniel |
| 1956 | Marlene Stewart | 1962 | JoAnne Gunderson | 1969 | Catherine Lacoste | 1976 | Donna Horton |
| 1957 | JoAnne Gunderson | 1963 | Anne Quast Welts | 1970 | Martha Wilkinson | 1977 | Beth Daniel |
| 1958 | Anne Quast | 1964 | Barbara McIntire | 1971 | Laura Baugh | 1978 | |
| 1959 | Barbara McIntire | 1965 | Jean Ashley | 1972 | Mary Ann Budke | | |
| 1960 | JoAnne Gunderson | 1966 | JoAnne Gunderson | 1973 | Carol Semple | | |

## U.S. WOMEN'S OPEN CHAMPIONS

| Year | Winner | Score | Year | Winner | Score | Year | Winner | Score |
|---|---|---|---|---|---|---|---|---|
| 1946 | Patty Berg (match play) | — | 1957 | Betsy Rawls | 299 | 1968 | Susie Berning | 289 |
| 1947 | Betty Jameson | 295 | 1958 | Mickev Wright | 290 | 1969 | Donna Caponi | 294 |
| 1948 | Mildred D. Zaharias | 300 | 1959 | Mickey Wright | 287 | 1970 | Donna Caponi | 287 |
| 1949 | Louise Suggs | 291 | 1960 | Betsy Rawls | 291 | 1971 | JoAnne Carner | 288 |
| 1950 | Mildred D. Zaharias | 291 | 1961 | Mickey Wright | 293 | 1972 | Susie Berning | 299 |
| 1951 | Betsy Rawls | 293 | 1962 | Murle Lindstrom | 301 | 1973 | Susie Berning | 290 |
| 1952 | Louise Suggs | 284 | 1963 | Mary Mills | 289 | 1974 | Sandra Haynie | 295 |
| 1953 | Betsy Rawls[1] | 302 | 1964 | Mickey Wright[1] | 290 | 1975 | Sandra Palmer | 295 |
| 1954 | Mildred D. Zaharias | 291 | 1965 | Carol Mann | 290 | 1976 | JoAnne Carner | 292 |
| 1955 | Fay Crocker | 299 | 1966 | Sandra Spuzich | 297 | 1977 | Hollis Stacy | 292 |
| 1956 | Katherine Cornelius[1] | 302 | 1967 | Catherine LaCoste | 294 | 1978 | Hollis Stacy | 289 |

1. Winner in playoff. 2. Amateur.

## BRITISH OPEN CHAMPIONS

(First tournament, held in 1860, was won by Willie Park, Sr.)

| Year | Winner | Score | Year | Winner | Score | Year | Winner | Score |
|---|---|---|---|---|---|---|---|---|
| 1920 | George Duncan | 303 | 1938 | R. A. Whitcombe | 295 | 1962 | Arnold Palmer | 276 |
| 1921 | Jock Hutchison[1] | 296 | 1939 | R. Burton | 290 | 1963 | Bob Charles[1] | 277 |
| 1922 | Walter Hagen | 300 | 1946 | Sam Snead | 290 | 1964 | Tony Lema | 279 |
| 1923 | A. G. Havers | 295 | 1947 | Fred Daly | 294 | 1965 | Peter Thomson | 285 |
| 1924 | Walter Hagen | 301 | 1948 | Henry Cotton | 283 | 1966 | Jack Nicklaus | 282 |
| 1925 | Jim Barnes | 300 | 1949 | Bobby Locke[1] | 283 | 1967 | Roberto de Vicenzo | 278 |
| 1926 | R. T. Jones, Jr. | 291 | 1950 | Bobby Locke | 279 | 1968 | Gary Player | 289 |
| 1927 | R. T. Jones, Jr. | 285 | 1951 | Max Faulkner | 285 | 1969 | Tony Jacklin | 280 |
| 1928 | Walter Hagen | 292 | 1952 | Bobby Locke | 287 | 1970 | Jack Nicklaus[1] | 283 |
| 1929 | Walter Hagen | 292 | 1953 | Ben Hogan | 282 | 1971 | Lee Trevino | 278 |
| 1930 | R. T. Jones, Jr. | 291 | 1954 | Peter Thomson | 283 | 1972 | Lee Trevino | 278 |
| 1931 | Tommy Armour | 296 | 1955 | Peter Thomson | 281 | 1973 | Tom Weiskopf | 276 |
| 1932 | Gene Sarazen | 283 | 1956 | Peter Thomson | 286 | 1974 | Gary Player | 282 |
| 1933 | Denny Shute[1] | 292 | 1957 | Bobby Locke | 279 | 1975 | Tom Watson[1] | 279 |
| 1934 | Henry Cotton | 283 | 1958 | Peter Thomson[1] | 278 | 1976 | Johnny Miller | 279 |
| 1935 | A. Perry | 283 | 1959 | Gary Player | 284 | 1977 | Tom Watson | 268 |
| 1936 | A. H. Padgham | 287 | 1960 | Kel Nagle | 278 | 1978 | Jack Nicklaus | 281 |
| 1937 | Henry Cotton | 290 | 1961 | Arnold Palmer | 284 | | | |

1. Winner in playoff.

## 1978 U.S. OPEN—MEN

(Cherry Hills, G.C., Denver, Colo., June 15–18)

| | | | | |
|---|---|---|---|---|
| Andy North, Madison, Wis. | 70 | 70 | 71 | 74—285 |
| J.C. Snead, Hot Springs, Va. | 70 | 72 | 72 | 72—286 |
| Dave Stockton, Westlake Village, Calif. | 71 | 73 | 70 | 72—286 |
| Hale Irwin, Frontenac, Mo. | 69 | 74 | 75 | 70—288 |
| Tom Weiskopf, Columbus, Ohio | 77 | 73 | 70 | 68—288 |
| Andy Bean, Lakewood, Fla. | 72 | 72 | 71 | 74—289 |
| Bill Kratzert, Fort Wayne, Ind. | 72 | 74 | 70 | 73—289 |
| Johnny Miller, Napa, Calif. | 78 | 69 | 68 | 74—289 |
| Jack Nicklaus, North Palm Beach, Fla. | 73 | 69 | 74 | 73—289 |
| Gary Player, Johannesburg, So. Africa | 71 | 71 | 70 | 77—289 |
| Tom Watson, Kansas City, Mo. | 74 | 75 | 70 | 70—289 |

Prizes—North $45,000; Snead and Stockton $19,750; Irwin and Weiskopf $13,000; Bean, Kratzert, Miller, Nicklaus, Player, and Watson $7,548

Leaders—18 holes: Irwin 69; Bob Clampett (amateur), Brigham Young University, North and Snead, 70; 36 holes: North 140, Nicklaus, Player and Snead 142; 54 holes: North 211, Player 212, Snead and Stockton 214

## P.G.A. CHAMPIONSHIP—MEN

(Oakmont, Pa. Country Club, Aug. 3–6, 1978)

| | | | | | |
|---|---|---|---|---|---|
| John Mahaffey[1] | 75 | 67 | 68 | 66—276 | $50,000 |
| Jerry Pate | 72 | 70 | 66 | 68—276 | 25,000 |
| Tom Watson | 67 | 69 | 67 | 73—276 | 25,000 |
| Gil Morgan | 76 | 71 | 66 | 67—280 | 16,000 |
| Tom Weiskopf | 73 | 67 | 69 | 71—280 | 16,000 |
| Craig Stadler | 70 | 74 | 67 | 71—282 | 10,000 |
| Andy Bean | 72 | 72 | 70 | 70—284 | 8,000 |
| Graham Marsh | 72 | 74 | 68 | 70—284 | 8,000 |
| Lee Trevino | 69 | 73 | 70 | 72—284 | 8,000 |

1. Won three-way playoff with birdie on second extra hole.

# DARTS

## U.S. OPEN—1978

John Zimnawoda, Baltimore

## 1978 MASTERS TOURNAMENT—MEN

(National Golf Club, Augusta, Ga., April 6–9)

| | | | | | |
|---|---|---|---|---|---|
| Gary Player | 72 | 72 | 69 | 64—277 | $45,000 |
| Rod Funseth | 73 | 66 | 70 | 69—278 | 21,667 |
| Hubert Green | 72 | 69 | 65 | 72—278 | 21,667 |
| Tom Watson | 73 | 68 | 68 | 69—278 | 21,667 |
| Wally Armstrong | 72 | 70 | 70 | 68—280 | 11,750 |
| Bill Kratzert | 70 | 74 | 67 | 69—280 | 11,750 |
| Jack Nicklaus | 72 | 73 | 69 | 67—281 | 10,000 |
| Hale Irwin | 73 | 67 | 71 | 71—282 | 8,500 |
| Joe Inman | 69 | 73 | 72 | 69—283 | 6,750 |
| David Graham | 75 | 69 | 67 | 72—283 | 6,750 |

## 1978 BRITISH OPEN—MEN

(St. Andrew's Royal and Ancient G.C., Scotland, July 12–15)

| | | | | | |
|---|---|---|---|---|---|
| Jack Nicklaus | 71 | 72 | 69 | 69—281 | $22,500 |
| Ben Crenshaw | 70 | 69 | 73 | 71—283 | 17,761 |
| Ray Floyd | 69 | 75 | 71 | 68—283 | 17,761 |
| Tom Kite | 72 | 69 | 72 | 70—283 | 17,761 |
| Simon Owen | 70 | 75 | 67 | 71—283 | 17,761 |
| Peter Oosterhuis | 72 | 70 | 69 | 73—284 | 9,000 |
| John Schroeder | 74 | 69 | 70 | 72—285 | 7,087 |
| Isao Aoki | 68 | 71 | 73 | 73—285 | 7,087 |
| Nick Faldo | 71 | 72 | 70 | 72—285 | 7,087 |

## OTHER LEADING 1978 TOURNAMENTS

| | |
|---|---|
| Canadian Open—Bruce Lietzke (283) | $50,000 |
| P.G.A. Seniors—Joe Jimenez, Jefferson City, Mo.[1] | 8,000 |
| Tournament of Champions—Gary Player (281) | 45,000 |
| World Series of Golf—Gil Morgan[1] (278) | 100,000 |

1. Won playoff.

## 1978 U.S. OPEN—WOMEN

(Country Club of Indianapolis, July 20–23)

| | | | | | |
|---|---|---|---|---|---|
| Hollis Stacy, Savannah, Georgia | 70 | 75 | 72 | 72—289 | $15,000 |
| JoAnne Carner, Lake Worth, Fla. | 73 | 72 | 73 | 72—290 | 7,000 |
| Sally Little, South Africa | 75 | 75 | 75 | 65—290 | 7,000 |
| Jane Blalock, Highland Beach, Fla. | 74 | 74 | 71 | 74—293 | 4,650 |
| Pam Higgins, Palm Springs, Calif. | 74 | 73 | 75 | 71—293 | 4,650 |
| Donna C. Young, Los Angeles | 68 | 78 | 73 | 75—294 | 3,260 |
| Kathy Martin, Thousand Oaks, Calif. | 76 | 74 | 71 | 73—294 | 3,260 |
| Donna White, West Palm Beach, Fla. | 72 | 72 | 79 | 71—294 | 3,260 |

Prizes—Hollis Stacy $15,000; JoAnne Carner and Sally Little $7,000; Jane Blalock and Pam Higgins $4,650; Donna Young, Kathy Martin, and Donna White $3,260

Leaders—18 holes: Young 69, Vicki Feraon, Hollis Stacy, and Alexandra Reinhardt 70; 36 holes: Nancy Lopez and Carole Semple (amateur) 144: JoAnne Carner, Donna White, and Hollis Stacy 145. 54 holes: Hollis Stacy 217, JoAnne Carner 218, Donna Young, and Jane Blalock 219

## 1978 L.P.G.A. CHAMPIONSHIP

(Nicklaus Golf Center, Mason, Ohio, June 8–11)

| | | | | | |
|---|---|---|---|---|---|
| Nancy Lopez | 71 | 65 | 69 | 70—275 | $22,500 |
| Amy Alcott | 68 | 68 | 74 | 71—281 | 14,650 |
| Judy Rankin | 67 | 73 | 71 | 72—283 | 10,510 |
| JoAnne Carner | 71 | 72 | 70 | 71—284 | 7,700 |
| JoAnn Washam | 67 | 69 | 74 | 75—285 | 6,080 |
| Sally Little | 73 | 71 | 74 | 68—286 | 4,813 |
| Donna C. Young | 73 | 72 | 71 | 70—286 | 4,813 |
| Susan Lynn | 73 | 73 | 71 | 69—286 | 4,813 |

## P.G.A. Earnings—1978

(Through Sept. 15)

| Player | Amount | Player | Amount |
|---|---|---|---|
| Tom Watson | $303,429 | Tom Kite | $149,737 |
| Andy Bean | 258,440 | John Mahaffey | 146,709 |
| Jack Nicklaus | 249,772 | Lee Elder | 146,348 |
| Lee Trevino | 215,295 | Andy North | 144,209 |
| Hubert Green | 183,906 | Mark Hayes | 134,603 |
| Hale Irwin | 178,441 | Bill Rogers | 113,071 |
| Bill Kratzert | 176,099 | Lon Hinkle | 110,666 |
| Gary Player | 170,336 | Tom Weiskopf | 110,331 |
| Jerry Pate | 167,999 | Fuzzy Zoeller | 106,055 |
| Gil Morgan | 166,599 | Bruce Lietzke | 102,450 |

## L.P.G.A. EARNINGS—1978

(Through September 15)

| Player | Amount | Player | Amount |
|---|---|---|---|
| Nancy Lopez | $156,948 | Debbie Massey | $64,851 |
| JoAnne Carner | 106,493 | Amy Alcott | 64,562 |
| Pat Bradley | 97,527 | Jan Stephenson | 61,358 |
| Jane Blalock | 90,552 | Donna C. Young | 59,093 |
| Sandra Post | 88,955 | Judy Rankin | 49,360 |
| Hollis Stacy | 85,037 | Kathy Whitworth | 47,612 |
| Sally Little | 72,986 | Debby Austin | 44,273 |
| Penny Pulz | 69,546 | JoAnn Washam | 40,882 |

## U.S.G.A. CHAMPIONSHIP—1978

(Sunnybrook G.C., Plymouth Meeting, Pa., Aug. 14–19)

Final—Cathy Sherk, Port Colborne, Ontario, defeated Judy Oliver, Pittsburgh, 4 and 3.

Semifinals—Judy Oliver defeated Mary Hafeman, West Bend, Wis., 19 holes; Cathy Sherk defeated Cindy Hill, Colorado Springs, 1 up.

Quarterfinals—Judy Oliver defeated Vicky Singleton, Oberlin, Ohio, 4 and 3; Mary Hafeman defeated Ann Swanson, Seattle, 3 and 2; Cathy Sherk defeated Pat Cornett, Salinas, Calif., 7 and 6; Cindy Hill defeated Beth Daniel, Charleston, S.C., 1 up.

## OTHER LEADING 1978 TOURNAMENTS

U.S.G.A. Public links—Kelly Fulks, Phoenix, Ariz., defeated Diana Schwab, Ketterling, Ohio, 5 and 4, in final.
U.S.G.A. Junior—Lori Castillo, Honolulu, defeated Jenny Lidback, Baton Rouge, La., 4 and 2, in final.
Collegiate (A.I.A.W.)—Deborah Petrizzi, Texas 291
British Amateur—Edwina Kennedy, Australia
Junior College—Pam Elders, Miami-Dade North, Fla.
Doherty Cup—Carolyn Hill, Placentia, Calif.
Eastern—Julie Green, Barrington, R.I. 225
Broadmoor Invitation—Tish Preuss, Colorado Springs
Southern—Ann Baker Furrow, Knoxville, Tenn.
Trans-National—Nancy Roth Syms, Colorado Springs, defeated Holly Hartley, Oceanside, Calif., 1 up, in 36-hole final.
P.G.A. Junior—Kathy Baker, Clover, S.C. 304
Western—Beth Daniel, Charleston, S.C.
Canadian Amateur—Cathy Sherk, Port Colborne, Ontario 292

## MEN'S AMATEUR—1978 RESULTS

### U.S.G.A. Championship

(Plainfield (N.J.) Country Club, Aug. 28–Sept. 3)

Final (36 holes)—John Cook, Upper Arlington, Ohio, defeated Scott Hoch, Raleigh, N.C., 5 and 4.

Semifinals—Scott Hoch defeated Bob Clampett, Carmel, Calif., 20 holes; John Cook defeated Mike Peck, Overland Park, Kan., 20 holes.

Quarterfinals—Scott Hoch defeated Bob Burke, Palm Harbor, Fla., 4 and 2; Bob Clampett defeated Steve Owen, Haines City, Fla., 4 and 2; John Cook defeated Kalua M. Akalena, Schofield Barracks, Hawaii, 5 and 3; Mike Peck defeated Griff Moody 3d, Athens, Ga., 3 and 2.

### Other Leading Tournaments

British Amateur (36 holes)—Peter McEvoy, England, defeated Paul McKellar, Scotland, 4 and 3, in final.
U.S.G.A. junior—Donald Hurter, Honolulu, defeated Keith Banes, La Miranda, Calif., 21 holes, in final.
U.S.G.A. public links—Dean Prince, Santa Rosa, Calif., defeated Tony Figueredo, Miami, 5 and 3, in final.

| | |
|---|---|
| American Senior G.A.—Dale Morey, High Point, N.C. | |
| U.S. Senior G.A.—Ed Tutwhiler, Indianapolis | 141 |
| N.C.A.A. Division I—David Edwards, Oklahoma State (54 holes) | 209 |
| N.C.A.A. Division II—Tom Brannen, Columbus College | 282 |
| N.C.A.A. Division III—Jim Quinn, Oswego | 299 |
| N.A.I.A.—Greg Brown, Point Loma (Calif.) | 290 |
| Junior College—Jim Stuart, Alexander City (Ala.) | 288 |
| American Classic—Vance Heafner, Cary, N.C. | |
| Eastern—Vance Heafner, Cary, N.C. | 281 |
| New England—Steve Robbins, Portsmouth, N.H. | 283 |
| North and South—Gary Hallberg, Barrington, Ill. | |
| Northeastern—John Cook, Upper Arlington, Ohio | |
| P.G.A. Junior—Willie Wood, Tucson, Ariz. | 289 |
| Porter Cup—Bob Clampett, Carmel, Calif. | |
| World senior—Earl Burt, Paradise Valley, Ariz. | |

### Team

| | |
|---|---|
| N.C.A.A. Division I—Oklahoma State | 1,140 |
| N.C.A.A. Division II—Columbus College | 1,174 |
| N.C.A.A. Division III—California State–Stanislaus | 1,223 |
| N.A.I.A.—Sam Houston State | 1,206 |
| World Senior—United States | 422 |

# *SALARIES AND EARNINGS OF PROFESSIONAL ATHLETES*

In the major sports the terms of contracts between the clubs and the players are not made public. The figures used in the following tables are those reported by news sources, based on general information brought about by the new era of free agents.

## Baseball Earnings

### Fielders

| Player/Team | Amount |
|---|---|
| Reggie Jackson, N.Y. Yankees | $580,000 |
| Larry Histle, Milwaukee | 525,000 |
| Oscar Gamble, California | 475,000 |
| Lyman Bostock, California | 450,000 |
| Joe Rudi, California | 440,000 |
| Bobby Bonds, Texas | 400,000 |
| Mike Schmidt, Philadelphia | 400,000 |
| Pete Rose, Cincinnati | 375,000 |
| Steve Garvey, Los Angeles | 335,000 |
| Bobby Grich, California | 330,000 |
| Gary Matthews, Atlanta | 312,000 |
| Ted Simmons, St. Louis | 300,000 |
| Richie Zisk, Texas | 295,000 |
| Sal Bando, Milwaukee | 281,000 |
| Don Baylor, California | 279,000 |
| Dave Kingman, Chicago Cubs | 275,000 |
| Gene Tenace, San Diego | 265,000 |
| Dave Cash, Montreal | 255,000 |
| Bobby Murcer, Chicago Cubs | 250,000 |

| Player/Team | Amount |
|---|---|
| Thurman Munson, N.Y. Yankees | $250,000 |
| Bill Madlock, San Francisco | 225,000 |
| Rod Carew, Minnesota | 200,000 |
| Chris Chamblis, N.Y. Yankees | 200,000 |
| Richie Hebner, Phillies | 200,000 |
| Bert Campaneris, Texas | 200,000 |
| Rick Monday, Los Angeles | 200,000 |

### Pitchers

| | |
|---|---|
| Rich Gossage, N.Y. Yankees | 458,000 |
| Mike Torrez, Boston | 358,000 |
| Rollie Fingers, San Diego | 332,000 |
| Tom Seaver, Cincinnati | 250,000 |
| George Medich, Texas | 250,000 |
| Wayne Garland, Cleveland | 230,000 |
| Ross Grimsley, Montreal | 230,000 |
| Rollie Eastwick, Philadelphia | 220,000 |
| Bill Campbell, Boston | 210,000 |
| Steve Carlton, Philadelphia | 175,000 |

## Tennis Career Earnings

### Men

| Player | Amount | Player | Amount |
|---|---|---|---|
| Jimmy Connors, 1972–77 | $1,687,974 | Stan Smith, 1969–77 | $1,148,290 |
| Ilie Nastase, 1969–77 | 1,624,956 | Manolo Orantes, 1968–77 | 1,118,114 |
| Guillermo Vilas, 1972–77 | 1,581,067 | Brian Gottfried, 1972–77 | 1,055,093 |
| Rod Laver, 1963–77 | 1,552,846 | Bjorn Borg, 1973–77 | 1,048,285 |
| Ken Rosewall, 1957–77 | 1,536,208 | | |
| Arthur Ashe, 1969–77 | 1,326,238 | | |
| Raul Ramirez, 1973–77 | 1,215,574 | | |

### Women

| Player | Amount |
|---|---|
| Chris Evert, 1973–77 | $1,479,738 |
| Billie Jean King, 1968–77 | 1,034,348 |

## Tennis Earnings—1977

These figures from United States Tennis Association include prize monies from recognized tournaments, recognized bonuses and recognized national team competitions. They do not include challenge matches, team tennis salaries or special events involving fewer than eight players.

### Men

| Player | Amount | Player | Amount |
|---|---|---|---|
| Guillermo Vilas | $800,642 | Wojtek Fibak | $238,339 |
| Jimmy Connors | 622,657 | Bob Hewitt | 234,184 |
| Brian Gottfried | 478,988 | Stan Smith | 214,134 |
| Bjorn Borg | 345,661 | Harold Solomon | 204,871 |
| Dick Stockton | 311,856 | Manolo Orantes | 200,229 |
| Ilie Nastase | 296,956 | John Alexander | 191,454 |
| Eddie Dibbs | 283,691 | Phil Dent | 170,565 |
| Vitas Gerulaitis | 274,324 | Bob Lutz | 166,641 |
| Raul Ramirez | 245,007 | Frew McMillan | 162,473 |
| Roscoe Tanner | 239,465 | Ken Rosewall | 147,798 |

### Women

| Player | Amount | Player | Amount |
|---|---|---|---|
| Chris Evert | $453,134 | Sue Barker | $180,458 |
| Martina Navratilova | 275,317 | Kerry Reid | 139,567 |
| Billie Jean King | 274,149 | Rosie Casals | 126,139 |
| Betty Stove | 229,162 | Wendy Turnbull | 98,568 |
| Virginia Wade | 193,476 | Francoise Durr | 92,703 |

## Golf Career Earnings

(Through 1977)

| Player | Amount | Player | Amount |
|---|---|---|---|
| Jack Nicklaus | $3,092,721 | Miller Barber | $1,249,864 |
| Arnold Palmer | 1,762,082 | Hale Irwin | 1,234,230 |
| Billy Casper | 1,658,468 | Johnny Miller | 1,144,065 |
| Lee Trevino | 1,620,723 | Al Geiberger | 1,077,972 |
| Tom Weiskopf | 1,563,826 | Dave Hill | 1,055,898 |
| Gene Littler | 1,383,772 | Ray Floyd | 1,039,168 |
| Bruce Crampton | 1,374,294 | Julius Boros | 1,000,642 |
| Gary Player | 1,329,307 | | |

## Golf Earnings—1977

Official money earned in Professional Golfers' Association major tournaments and such other events its Tournament Policy Board designates.

| Player | Amount | Player | Amount |
|---|---|---|---|
| Tom Watson | $310,653 | Lou Graham | $128,676 |
| Jack Nicklaus | 284,509 | Andy Boan | 127,312 |
| Lanny Wadkins | 244,882 | Rik Massengale | 126,736 |
| Hale Irwin | 221,456 | Tom Kite | 125,204 |
| Bruce Lietzke | 202,156 | Jerry McGee | 124,584 |
| Tom Weiskopf | 197,639 | Ben Crenshaw | 123,841 |
| Ray Floyd | 163,261 | Gene Littler | 119,759 |
| Miller Barber | 148,320 | Andy North | 116,794 |
| Hubert Green | 140,255 | Mark Hayes | 115,749 |
| Bill Kratzert | 134,758 | George Archer | 113,944 |

## Basketball Salaries[1]

| Player/Team | Amount |
|---|---|
| Kareem Abdul-Jabbar, Los Angeles | $625,000 |
| Pete Maravich, New Orleans | 600,000 |
| Bob McAdoo, New York | 500,000 |
| Julius Erving, Philadelphia | 500,000 |
| David Thompson, Denver | 500,000 |
| Bob Lanier, Detroit | 450,000 |
| George McGinnis, Philadelphia | 450,000 |
| Ernie DiGregorio, Los Angeles | 450,000 |
| Bill Walton, Portland | 400,000 |
| Rick Barry, Golden State | 400,000 |

1. Reported at start of 1977–78 season. The National Basketball Association said in 1976 that the average salary of league players was $109,000.

## Football Earnings

O.J. Simpson, Buffalo (1977) and San Francisco, is reported to receive top annual salary of $733,350. Several players are reported to be in brackets between $400,000 and $600,000.

The N.F.L. Management Council has released the results of a survey of players' salaries for the 1977 season. The survey covered 1,476 players who were under contract to N.F.L. clubs at the end of the regular season. It concluded that the average salary was $55,288.

**Salaries by position**[1]

| Position | Players | Average | Median[2] |
|---|---|---|---|
| Quarterbacks | 88 | $89,354 | $58,750 |
| Running backs | 182 | 60,414 | 44,895 |
| Receivers | 214 | 53,760 | 44,324 |
| Offensive linemen | 280 | 52,250 | 49,000 |
| Defensive linemen | 208 | 59,644 | 54,250 |
| Linebackers | 220 | 50,416 | 44,917 |
| Defensive backs | 225 | 47,403 | 41,250 |
| Kickers | 59 | 41,506 | 37,166 |
| | 1,476 | $55,288 | $45,563 |

1. Figures reflect preseason and regular season salary, deferred compensation earned in 1977, and pro-rated share of bonus for signing. 2. Median is mid-point: Half of players in each category received more than figure and the other half, less.

# VOLLEYBALL

## U.S. VOLLEYBALL ASSOCIATION

**National Champions—1978**

Men—Chuck's Steak House, Los Angeles
Women—Nick's Fish Market, Beverly Hills, Calif.
Senior men—Balboa Bay Club, Newport Beach, Calif.
Senior women—Nick's Fish Market, Beverly Hills, Calif.

## NATIONAL COLLEGIATE ATHLETIC ASSOCIATION

(Columbus, Ohio, May 5–6, 1978)

Final—Pepperdine defeated U.C.L.A., 15–12, 11–15, 15–8, 5–15, 15–12
Third place—Ohio State defeated Rutgers–Newark, 15–11, 15–12, 15–9

## NATIONAL ASSOCIATION FOR INTERCOLLEGIATE ATHLETICS

(Fairfax, Va., April 28–29, 1978)

Final—George Williams defeated Graceland, 15–8, 15–13, 15–5
Third place—Brigham Young defeated California Lutheran, 2–15, 15–8, 15–2

## ASSOCIATION FOR INTERCOLLEGIATE ATHLETICS FOR WOMEN

Large colleges—U.C.L.A.
Small colleges—California–Riverside

# ROLLER SKATING

## National Championships—1978

Men's singles—Paul Jones, Flint, Mich.
Women's singles—Robbie Coleman, Memphis, Tenn.
International men's singles—Lex Kane, Toledo, Ohio
International women's singles—Natalie Dunn, Bakersfield, Calif.
Men's figures—Curt Craton, Fountain Valley, Calif.
Women's figures—Patti Marshalewski, Concordville, Pa.
Pairs—Paul Price and Tina Kneisley, Brighton, Mich.
Dance—John LaBriola and Debra Coyne, Fountain Valley, Calif.
International dance—Dan Littel and Fleurette Arseneault, East Meadow, N.Y.
Speed, men—Tom Peterson, Tacoma, Wash.
Speed, women—Linda Dorso, Cincinnati

## WORLD CHAMPIONSHIPS

(Lisbon, Sept. 18–25, 1978)

Men's singles—Thomas Nieder, West Germany
Women's singles—Natalie Dunn, Bakersfield, Calif.
Dance—Fleurette Arnesault, Cambridge, Mass. and Dan Little, Farmingdale, N.Y.
Pairs—Robbie Coleman and Pat Jones, Memphis, Tenn.

# BIATHLON

## WORLD CHAMPIONSHIPS—1978

10 km—Frank Ullrich, East Germany
20 km—Odd Lirhus, Norway
Relay—East Germany

## U.S. CHAMPIONSHIPS—1978

20 km—Peter Hoag, Minneapolis
Junior 17 km—Hans Hillestad, New Paltz, N.Y.

# SOCCER

## WORLD CUP

| | | | |
|---|---|---|---|
| 1930 Uruguay | 1946 No competition | 1962 Brazil | 1978 Argentina |
| 1934 Italy | 1950 Uruguay | 1966 England | |
| 1938 Italy | 1954 West Germany | 1970 Brazil | |
| 1942 No competition | 1958 Brazil | 1974 West Germany | |

## 1978 WORLD CUP RESULTS

### FIRST ROUND

(Matches played at Buenos Aires, Cordoba, Mar del Plata, Mendoza and Rosario, Argentina, June 1–11)

**Group I**

| | W | L | T | Pts |
|---|---|---|---|---|
| Italy | 3 | 0 | 0 | 6 |
| Argentina | 2 | 1 | 0 | 4 |
| France | 1 | 2 | 0 | 2 |
| Hungary | 0 | 3 | 0 | 0 |

**Group III**

| | W | L | T | Pts |
|---|---|---|---|---|
| Austria[1] | 2 | 1 | 0 | 4 |
| Brazil | 1 | 0 | 2 | 4 |
| Spain | 1 | 1 | 1 | 3 |
| Sweden | 0 | 2 | 1 | 1 |

**Group II**

| | W | L | T | Pts |
|---|---|---|---|---|
| Poland | 2 | 0 | 1 | 5 |
| West Germany | 1 | 0 | 2 | 4 |
| Tunisia | 1 | 1 | 1 | 3 |
| Mexico | 0 | 3 | 0 | 0 |

**Group IV**

| | W | L | T | Pts |
|---|---|---|---|---|
| Peru | 2 | 0 | 1 | 5 |
| Netherlands | 1 | 1 | 1 | 3 |
| Scotland | 1 | 1 | 1 | 3 |
| Iran | 0 | 2 | 1 | 1 |

Top two teams in each group advance to second round.

1. First place decided on goals scored; Austria 3, Brazil 2.

### SECOND ROUND

**Group A**

| | W | L | T | Pts |
|---|---|---|---|---|
| Netherlands | 2 | 0 | 1 | 5 |
| Italy | 1 | 1 | 1 | 3 |
| West Germany | 0 | 1 | 2 | 2 |
| Austria | 1 | 2 | 0 | 2 |

**Group B**

| | W | L | T | Pts |
|---|---|---|---|---|
| Argentina[1] | 2 | 0 | 1 | 5 |
| Brazil | 2 | 0 | 1 | 5 |
| Poland | 1 | 2 | 0 | 2 |
| Peru | 0 | 3 | 0 | 0 |

1. Argentina gained final on higher differential between goals scored and goals allowed.

### Results of Second-round Games—Group A

June 14—Italy 0, West Germany 0; Netherlands 5, Austria 1
June 18—Italy 1, Austria 0; Netherlands 2, West Germany 2
June 21—Netherlands 2, Italy 1; Austria 3, West Germany 2

### Results of Second-round Games—Group B

June 14—Brazil 3, Peru 0; Argentina 2, Poland 0
June 18—Poland 1, Peru 0; Argentina 0, Brazil 0
June 21—Brazil 3, Poland 1; Argentina 6, Peru 0

### THIRD PLACE

(Buenos Aires, June 24)

Brazil 2, Italy 1

### CHAMPIONSHIP

(Buenos Aires, June 25)

Argentina 3, Netherlands 1 (overtime)

(Goals: Argentina: Mario Kempes (2), Daniel Bertoni; Netherlands: Dirk Nanninga)

## NORTH AMERICAN SOCCER LEAGUE
## Final Standing—1978

### NATIONAL CONFERENCE

**Eastern Division**

| | W | L | BP[1] | Pts | GF | GA |
|---|---|---|---|---|---|---|
| New York Cosmos | 24 | 4 | 68 | 212 | 88 | 39 |
| Washington Diplomats | 16 | 14 | 49 | 145 | 55 | 47 |
| Toronto Metros | 16 | 14 | 48 | 144 | 58 | 47 |
| Rochester Lancers | 14 | 16 | 47 | 131 | 47 | 52 |
| **Central Division** | | | | | | |
| Minnesota Kicks | 17 | 13 | 54 | 156 | 58 | 43 |
| Tulsa Roughnecks | 15 | 15 | 45 | 132 | 49 | 46 |
| Dallas Tornado | 14 | 16 | 47 | 131 | 51 | 53 |
| Colorado Caribous | 8 | 22 | 33 | 81 | 34 | 66 |
| **Western Division** | | | | | | |
| Vancouver Whitecaps | 24 | 6 | 55 | 199 | 68 | 29 |
| Portland Timbers | 29 | 10 | 47 | 167 | 50 | 36 |
| Seattle Sounders | 15 | 15 | 48 | 138 | 50 | 45 |
| Los Angeles Aztecs | 9 | 21 | 34 | 88 | 36 | 69 |

### AMERICAN CONFERENCE

**Eastern Division**

| | W | L | BP[1] | Pts | GF | GA |
|---|---|---|---|---|---|---|
| New England Tea Men | 19 | 11 | 51 | 165 | 62 | 39 |
| Tampa Bay Rowdies | 18 | 12 | 57 | 165 | 63 | 48 |
| Fort Lauderdale Strikers | 16 | 14 | 47 | 143 | 50 | 59 |
| Philadelphia Fury | 12 | 18 | 39 | 111 | 40 | 58 |
| **Central Division** | | | | | | |
| Detroit Express | 20 | 10 | 56 | 176 | 68 | 36 |
| Chicago Sting | 12 | 18 | 51 | 123 | 57 | 64 |
| Memphis Rogues | 10 | 20 | 41 | 101 | 43 | 58 |
| Houston Hurricane | 10 | 20 | 36 | 96 | 37 | 61 |
| **Western Division** | | | | | | |
| San Diego Sockers | 18 | 12 | 56 | 164 | 63 | 54 |
| California Surf | 13 | 17 | 37 | 115 | 43 | 49 |
| Oakland Stompers | 12 | 18 | 31 | 103 | 34 | 59 |
| San Jose Earthquakes | 8 | 22 | 35 | 83 | 36 | 81 |

1. Bonus points—awarded for each goal to a maximum of three per team per game; teams receive 6 points for each victory.

### PLAYOFFS

**Finals**

New York 1, Portland 0
New York 5, Portland 0
Fort Lauderdale 3, Tampa Bay 2
Tampa Bay 3, Fort Lauderdale 1
Tampa Bay 1, Fort Lauderdale 0 (shootout)

### CHAMPIONSHIP (SOCCER BOWL '78)

(East Rutherford, N.J., Aug. 27)

New York 3, Tampa Bay 1

Scoring: New York: Tueart, 30:42; Chinaglia, 74:30; Tueart, 76:49. Tampa Bay: Mirandihna, 76:49. Attendance: 74,901

# BARREL JUMPING—1978

World—Rowland Sylvester, Portland, Ore.
U. S.—Rowland Sylvester

### LEAGUE AWARDS

Most valuable player—Mike Flanagan, New England
Rookie of year—Gary Etherington, New York
Top offensive player—Mike Flanagan
Top defensive player—Carlos Alberto, New York
Leading scorer—Giorgio Chinaglia, New York
Goalkeeper's Cup—Phil Parkes, Vancouver
Top North American player—Bob Lenarduzzi, Vancouver

### N.C.A.A.

(December 1977)

**DIVISION I**

**Third Place**

Southern Illinois–Edwardsville 3, Brown 2

**Championship**

Hartwick 2, University of San Francisco 1

**DIVISION II**

**Third Place**

New Haven 3, Wisconsin–Green Bay 2 (2 overtimes)

**Championship**

Alabama A&M 2, Seattle Pacific 1

**DIVISION III**

**Third Place**

Babson 1, Wooster 0

**Championship**

Lock Haven State 1, Cortland State 0

### N.A.I.A.

(November 1977)

**Third Place**

Davis and Elkins 2, Erskine 0

**Championship**

Quincy 3, Keene State 0

## *FENCING*

### WORLD CHAMPIONSHIPS

*Source:* Jeffrey R. Tishman, Amateur Fencers League of America

(Hamburg, West Germany, July 12–22, 1978)

Men's foil—Didier Flament, France
Women's foil—Valentina Siderova, U.S.S.R.
Epee—Alexander Pusch, West Germany
Saber—Viktor Krovopuskov, U.S.S.R.
Men's foil team—Poland
Women's foil team—U.S.S.R.
Epee team—Hungary
Saber team—Hungary

### AMATEUR FENCERS LEAGUE OF AMERICA—U.S. CHAMPIONSHIPS

(Miami Beach, Fla., June 24-July 1, 1978)

Men's foil—Marty Lang, New York A.C.
Women's foil—Gay Dasaro, Salle Dasaro, San Jose, Calif.
Epee—Brooke Makler, Pannonia A.C., Philadelphia
Saber—Stanley Lekach, New York A.C.
Men's foil team—Pannonia A.C. (Peter Ashley, Ion Drimba, Joseph Shamash)
Women's foil team—Salle Csiszar, Philadelphia (Sharon De Biase, Nikke Franke, Jeannette Starks)
Epee team—New York A.C. (Dave Lynn, George Masin, Paul Pesthy)
Saber team—Fencers Club, New York (Stephen Blum, Stephen Kaplan, Joel Glucksman, Peter Westbrook)

**Under 19**

Men's foil—Ed McNamara, New York A.C.
Women's foil—Jana Angelakis, Tanner City Fencers Club
Epee—Michael Storm, University of Pennsylvania
Saber—Paul Friedburg, University of Pennsylvania

### INTERCOLLEGIATE CHAMPIONSHIPS
### National Collegiate Athletic Association

(Kenosha, Wis., March 16-18, 1978)

Foil—Ernest Simon, Wayne State
Epee—Bjorne Vaggo, Notre Dame
Saber—Michale Sullivan, Notre Dame
Team (3 weapon)—Notre Dame

### National Intercollegiate Women's Fencing Association

(Philadelphia, March 31–April 2, 1978)

Individual—Stacey Johnson, San Jose State
Team—San Jose State

## *EQUESTRIAN EVENTS*

### WORLD THREE-DAY

(Lexington, Ky., Sept. 14–17, 1978)

Individual Overall—Bruce Davidson, Unionville, Pa. (riding Might Tango)
Team overall—Canada (Juliet Bishop, Cathy Wedge, Elizabeth Ashton, Mark Ishoy)
Individual dressage—Michael Plumb, Chesapeake, Md. (riding Laurenson)
Team dressage—U.S. (Michael Plumb, James Wofford, Upperville, Va.; Bruce Davidson; Story Jenks, Chadd's Ford, Pa., Tad Coffin)
Individual cross-country—Bruce Davidson
Individual jumping—Bruce Davidson

### WORLD JUMPING

(Aachen, West Germany, Aug. 18–20, 1978)

Individual—Gerd Wilfang, West Germany
Team—Britain

## *PARACHUTING*

### NATIONAL CHAMPIONSHIPS—1978

(Richmond, Ind.)

Men's master overall—Bob Von Derau, U.S. Army, Fort Bragg, N.C.
Men's master accuracy—Phil Munden, U.S. Army, Fort Bragg, N.C.
Men's master style—Dennis Wise, U.S. Army, Fort Bragg, N.C.
Men's senior overall—Matt O'Gwynn, U.S. Army, Fort Bragg, N.C.
Senior men's style—Matt O'Gwynn
Women's overall—Cheryl Stearns, U.S. Army, Fort Bragg, N.C.
Women's accuracy—Cheryl Stearns
Women's style—Cheryl Stearns
10-man team—Air Freight, Elsinore, Calif.
8-man team—Golden Knights, U.S. Army, Fort Bragg, N.C.

### WORLD CHAMPIONSHIPS—1978

Men—Nicolai Usmayev, U.S.S.R.
Women—Cheryl Stearns, Fort Bragg, N.C.

# BASEBALL

The popular tradition that baseball was invented by Abner Doubleday at Cooperstown, N.Y., in 1839 has been enshrined in the Hall of Fame and National Museum of Baseball erected in that town, but research has proved that a game called "Base Ball" was played in this country and England before 1839. The first team baseball as we know it was played at the Elysian Fields, Hoboken, N.J., on June 19, 1846, between the Knickerbockers and the New York Nine. The next fifty years saw a gradual growth of baseball and an improvement of equipment and playing skill.

Historians have it that the first pitcher to throw a curve was William A. (Candy) Cummings in 1867. The Cincinnati Red Stockings were the first all-professional team, and in 1869 they played 64 games without a loss. The standard ball of the same size and weight, still the rule, was adopted in 1872. The first catcher's mask was worn in 1875. The National League was organized in 1876. The first chest protector was worn in 1885. The three-strike rule was put on the books in 1887, and the four-ball ticket to first base was instituted in 1889. The pitching distance was lengthened to 60 feet 6 inches in 1893, and the rules have been modified only slightly since that time.

The American League, under the vigorous leadership of B. B. Johnson, became a major league in 1901. Judge Kenesaw Mountain Landis, by action of the two major leagues, became Commissioner of Baseball in 1921, and upon his death (1944), Albert B. Chandler, former United States Senator from Kentucky, was elected to that office (1945). Chandler failed to obtain a new contract and was succeeded by Ford C. Frick (1951), the National League president. Frick retired after the 1965 season, and William D. Eckert, a retired Air Force lieutenant general, was named to succeed him. Eckert resigned under pressure in December, 1968. Bowie Kuhn, a New York attorney, became interim commissioner for one year in February. His appointment was made permanent with two seven-year contracts until August 1983.

## PROFESSIONAL BASEBALL GOVERNMENT

**NATIONAL LEAGUE AMERICAN LEAGUE NATIONAL ASSOCIATION**

Bowie Kuhn, *Commissioner*
Alexander Hadden, *Secretary-Treasurer*
Joseph L. Reichler, *Special Assistant to Commissioner*
John Johnson, *Administrative Officer*
Bob Wirz, *Director of Information*
75 Rockefeller Plaza, New York, N.Y. 10019

**NATIONAL LEAGUE**

Charles S. Feeney, *President*
1 Rockefeller Plaza
New York, N.Y. 10020
John J. McHale, *Vice President*
Blake Cullen, *Public Relations Director*

**AMERICAN LEAGUE**

Leland S. MacPhail, *President*
280 Park Avenue
New York, N.Y. 10017
Robert Holbrook, *Secretary*
Robert O. Fishel, *Assistant to President*
Phyllis Merhige, *Public Relations Assistant*

**NATIONAL ASSOCIATION OF PROFESSIONAL BASEBALL LEAGUES (MINOR LEAGUES)**

Robert R. Bragan, *President-Treasurer*
201 Bayshore Drive, P. O. Box A, St. Petersburg, Fla. 33731

## RECORD OF WORLD SERIES GAMES

*Source: The Book of Baseball Records,* published by Seymour Siwoff, New York City.

**Figures in parentheses for winning pitchers (WP) and losing pitchers (LP) indicate the game number in the series**

**1903**—Boston A.L. 5 (Jimmy Collins); Pittsburgh N.L. 3 (Fred Clarke). WP—Bos.: Dinneen (2, 6, 8), Young (5, 7); Pitts.: Phillippe (1, 3, 4). LP—Bos.: Young (1), Hughes (3), Dinneen (4); Pitts.: Leever (2, 6), Kennedy (5), Phillippe (7, 8).

**1904**—No series.

**1905**—New York N.L. 4 (John J. McGraw); Philadelphia A.L. 1 (Connie Mack). WP—N.Y.: Mathewson (1, 3, 5); McGinnity (4); Phila.: Bender (2). LP—N.Y.: McGinnity (2); Phila.: Plank (1, 4), Coakley (3), Bender (5).

**1906**—Chicago A.L. 4 (Fielder Jones); Chicago N.L. 2 (Frank Chance). WP—Chi.: A.L.: Altrock (1), Walsh (3, 5), White (6); Chi.: N.L.: Reulbach (2), Brown (4). LP—Chi. A.L.: White (2), Altrock (4); Chi.: N.L.: Brown (1, 6), Pfeister (3, 5).

**1907**—Chicago N.L. 4 (Frank Chance); Detroit A.L. 0 (Hugh Jennings). First game tied 3–3, 12 innings. WP—Pfeister (2), Reulbach (3), Overall (4), Brown (5). LP—Mullin (2, 5), Siever (3), Donovan (4).

**1908**—Chicago N.L. 4 (Frank Chance); Detroit A.L. 1 (Hugh Jennings). WP—Chi.: Brown (1, 4), Overall (2, 5); Det.: Mullin (3). LP—Chi.: Pfeister (3); Det.: Summers (1, 4), Donovan (2, 5).

**1909**—Pittsburgh N.L. 4 (Fred Clarke); Detroit A.L. 3 (Hugh Jennings). WP—Pitts.: Adams (1, 5, 7), Maddox (3); Det.: Donovan (2), Mullin (4, 6). LP—Pitts.: Camnitz (2), Leifield (4), Willis (6); Det.: Mullin (1), Summers (3, 5), Donovan (7).

**1910**—Philadelphia A.L. 4 (Connie Mack); Chicago N.L. 1 (Frank Chance). WP—Phila.: Bender (1), Coombs (2, 3, 5); Chi.: Brown (4). LP—Phila.: Bender (4); Chi.: Overall (1), Brown (2, 5), McIntyre (3).

**1911**—Philadelphia A.L. 4 (Connie Mack); New York N.L. 2 (John J. McGraw). WP—Phila.: Plank (2), Coombs (3), Bender (4, 6); N.Y.: Mathewson (1), Crandall (5). LP—Phila.: Bender (1), Plank (5); N.Y.: Marquard (2), Mathewson (3, 4), Ames (6).

**1912**—Boston A.L. 4 (J. Garland Stahl); New York N.L. 3 (John J. McGraw). Second game tied, 6–6, 11 innings. WP—Bos.: Wood (1, 4, 8), Bedient (5); N.Y.: Marquard (3, 6), Tesreau (7). LP—Bos.: O'Brien (3, 6), Wood (7); N.Y.: Tesreau (1, 4), Mathewson (5, 8).

**1913**—Philadelphia A.L. 4 (Connie Mack); New York N.L. 1 (John J. McGraw). WP—Phila.: Bender (1, 4), Bush (3), Plank (5); N.Y.: Mathewson (2); LP—Phila.: Plank (2); N.Y.: Marquard (1), Tesreau (3), Demaree (4), Mathewson (5).

**1914**—Boston N.L. 4 (George Stallings); Philadelphia A.L. 0 (Connie Mack). WP—Rudolph (1, 4), James (2, 3). LP—Bender (1), Plank (2), Bush (3), Shawkey (4).

**1915**—Boston A.L. 4 (Bill Carrigan); Philadelphia N.L. 1 (Pat Moran). WP—Bos.: Foster (2, 5), Leonard (3), Shore (4); Phila.: Alexander (1). LP—Bos.: Shore (1); Phila.: Mayer (2), Alexander (3), Chalmers (4), Rixey (5).

**1916**—Boston A.L. 4 (Bill Carrigan); Brooklyn N.L. 1 (Wilbert Robinson). WP—Bos.: Shore (1, 5), Ruth (2), Leonard (4); Bklyn.: Coombs (3). LP—Bos.: Mays (3); Bklyn.: Marquard (1, 4), Smith (2), Pfeffer (5).

**1917**—Chicago A.L. 4 (Clarence Rowland); New York N.L. 2 (John J. McGraw). WP—Chi.: Cicotte (1), Faber (2, 5, 6); N.Y.: Benton (3), Schupp (4). LP—Chi.: Cicotte (3), Faber (4); N.Y.: Sallee (1, 5), Anderson (2), Benton (6).

**1918**—Boston A.L. 4 (Ed Barrow); Chicago N.L. 2 (Fred Mitchell). WP—Bos.: Ruth (1, 4), Mays (3, 6); Chi.: Tyler (2), Vaughn (5). LP—Bos.: Bush (2), Jones (5); Chi.: Vaughn (1, 3), Douglas (4), Tyler (6).

**1919**—Cincinnati N.L. 5 (Pat Moran); Chicago A.L. 3 (William Gleason). WP—Cin.: Ruether (1), Sallee (2), Ring (4), Eller (5, 8); Chi.: Kerr (3, 6), Cicotte (7). LP—Cin.: Fisher (3), Ring (6), Sallee (7); Chi.: Cicotte (1, 4), Williams (2, 5, 8).

**1920**—Cleveland A.L. 5 (Tris Speaker); Brooklyn N.L. 2 (Wilbert Robinson). WP—Cleve.: Coveleski (1, 4, 7), Bagby (5), Mails (6); Bklyn.: Grimes (2), Smith (3). LP—Cleve.: Bagby (2), Caldwell (3). Bklyn.: Marquard (1), Cadore (4), Grimes (5, 7), Smith (6).

**1921**—New York N.L. 5 (John J. McGraw); New York A.L. 3 (Miller Huggins). WP—N.Y. N.L.: Barnes (3, 6), Douglas (4, 7), Nehf (8); N.Y. A.L.: Mays (1), Hoyt (2, 5). LP—N.Y. N.L.: Nehf (2, 5), Douglas (1). N.Y. A.L.: Quinn (3), Mays (4, 7), Shawkey (6), Hoyt (8).

**1922**—New York N.L. 4 (John J. McGraw); New York A.L. 0 (Miller Huggins). Second game tied 3–3, 10 innings. WP—Ryan (1), Scott (3), McQuillan (4), Nehf (5); LP—Bush (1, 5), Hoyt (3), Mays (4).

**1923**—New York A.L. 4 (Miller Huggins); New York N.L. 2 (John J. McGraw). WP—N.Y. A.L.: Pennock (2, 6), Shawkey (4), Bush (5); N.Y. N.L.:Ryan (1), Nehf (3). LP—N.Y. A.L.: Bush (1), Jones (3); N.Y. N.L.: McQuillan (2), Scott (4), Bentley (5), Nehf (6).

**1924**—Washington A.L. 4 (Bucky Harris); New York N.L. 3 (John J. McGraw). WP—Wash.: Zachary (2, 6), Mogridge (4), Johnson (9); N.Y.: Nehf (1), McQuillan (3), Bentley (5). LP—Wash.: Johnson (1, 5), Marberry (3); N.Y.: Bentley (2, 7), Barnes (4), Nehf (6).

**1925**—Pittsburgh N.L. 4 (Bill McKechnie); Washington A.L. 3 (Bucky Harris). WP—Pitts.: Aldridge (2, 5), Kremer (6, 7); Wash.: Johnson (1, 4), Ferguson (3). LP—Pitts.: Meadows (1), Kremer (3), Yde (4); Wash.: Coveleski (2, 5), Ferguson (6), Johnson (7).

**1926**—St. Louis N.L. 4 (Rogers Hornsby); New York A.L. 3 (Miller Huggins). WP—St. L.: Alexander (2, 6), Haines (3, 7); N.Y.: Pennock (1, 5), Hoyt (4). LP—St. L.: Sherdel (1, 5), Reinhart (4); N.Y.: Shocker (2), Ruether (3), Shawkey (6), Hoyt (7).

**1927**—New York A.L. 4 (Miller Huggins); Pittsburgh N.L. 0 (Donie Bush). WP—Hoyt (1), Pipgras (2), Pennock (3), Moore (4). LP—Kremer (1), Aldridge (2), Meadows (3), Miljus (4).

**1928**—New York A.L. 4 (Miller Huggins); St. Louis N.L. 0 (Bill McKechnie). WP—Hoyt (1, 4), Pipgras (2), Zachary (3). LP—Sherdel (1, 4), Alexander (2), Haines (3).

**1929**—Philadelphia A.L. 4 (Connie Mack); Chicago N.L. 1 (Joe McCarthy). WP—Phila.: Ehmke (1), Earnshaw (2), Rommel (4), Walberg (5); Chi.: Bush (3). LP—Phila.: Earnshaw (3); Chi.: Root (1), Malone (2, 5), Blake (4).

**1930**—Philadelphia A.L. 4 (Connie Mack); St. Louis N.L. 2 (Gabby Street). WP—Phila.: Grove (1, 5), Earnshaw (2, 6); St. L.: Hallahan (3), Haines (4). LP—Phila.: Walberg (3), Grove (4); St. L.: Grimes (1, 5), Rhem (2), Hallahan (6).

**1931**—St. Louis N.L. 4 (Gabby Street); Philadelphia A.L. 3 (Connie Mack). WP—St. L.: Hallahan (2, 5), Grimes (3, 7); Phila.: Grove (1, 6), Earnshaw (4). LP—St. L.: Derringer (1, 6), Johnson (4); Phila.: Earnshaw (2, 7), Grove (3), Hoyt (5).

**1932**—New York A.L. (Joe McCarthy); Chicago N.L. 0 (Charles Grimm). WP—Ruffing (1), Gomez (2), Pipgras (3), Moore (4). LP—Bush (1), Warneke (2), Root (3), May (4).

**1933**—New York N.L. 4 (Bill Terry); Washington A.L. 1 (Joe Cronin.). WP—N.Y.: Hubbell (1, 4), Schumacher (2), Luque (5); Wash.: Whitehill (3). LP—N.Y.: Fitzsimmons (3); Wash.: Stewart (1), Crowder (2), Weaver (4), Russell (5).

**1934**—St. Louis N.L. 4 (Frank Frisch); Detroit A.L. 3 (Mickey Cochrane). WP—St. L.: J. Dean (1, 7), P. Dean (3, 6); Det.: Rowe (2), Auker (4), Bridges (5). LP—St. L.: W. Walker (2, 4), J. Dean (5); Det.: Crowder (1), Bridges (3), Rowe (6), Auker (7).

**1935**—Detroit A.L. 4 (Mickey Cochrane); Chicago N.L. 2 (Charles Grimm). WP—Det.: Bridges (2, 6), Rowe (3), Crowder (4); Chi.: Warneke (1, 5); LP—Det.: Rowe (1, 5); Chi.: Root (2), French (3, 6), Carleton (4).

**1936**—New York A.L. 4 (Joe McCarthy); New York N.L. 2 (Bill Terry). WP—N.Y. A.L.: Gomez (2, 6), Hadley (3), Pearson (4); N.Y. N.L.: Hubbell (1), Schumacher (5); LP—N.Y. A.L.: Ruffing (1), Malone (5); N.Y. N.L.: Schumacher (2), Fitzsimmons (3, 6), Hubbell (4).

**1937**—New York A.L. 4 (Joe McCarthy); New York N.L. 1 (Bill Terry). WP—N.Y. A.L.: Gomez (1, 5), Ruffing (2), Pearson (3); N.Y. N.L.: Hubbell (4). LP—N.Y. A.L.: Hadley (4); N.Y. N.L.: Hubbell (1), Melton (2, 5), Schumacher (3).

**1938**—New York A.L. 4 (Joe McCarthy); Chicago N.L. 0 (Gabby Hartnett). WP—Ruffing (1, 4), Gomez (2), Pearson (3). LP—Lee (1, 4), Dean (2), Bryant (3).

**1939**—New York A.L. 4 (Joe McCarthy); Cincinnati N.L. 0 (Bill McKechnie). WP—Ruffing (1), Pearson (2), Hadley (3), Murphy (4). LP—Derringer (1), Walters (2, 4), Thompson (3).

**1940**—Cincinnati N.L. 4 (Bill McKechnie); Detroit A.L. 3 (Del Baker). WP—Cin.: Walters (2, 6), Derringer (4, 7); Det.: Newsom (1, 5), Bridges (3). LP—Cin.: Derringer (1), Turner (3), Thompson (5); Det.: Rowe (2, 6), Trout (4), Newsom (7).

**1941**—New York A.L. 4 (Joe McCarthy); Brooklyn N.L. 1 (Leo Durocher). WP—N.Y.: Ruffing (1), Russo (3), Murphy (4), Bonham (5); Bklyn: Wyatt (2). LP—N.Y.: Chandler (2); Bklyn: Davis (1), Casey (3, 4), Wyatt (5).

**1942**—St. Louis N.L. 4 (Billy Southworth); New York A.L. 1 (Joe McCarthy). WP—St. L.: Beazley (2, 5), White (3), Lanier (4); N.Y.: Ruffing (1). LP—St. L.: Cooper (1); N.Y.: Bonham (2), Chandler (3), Donald (4), Ruffing (5).

**1943**—New York A.L. 4 (Joe McCarthy); St. Louis N.L. 1 (Billy Southworth). WP—N.Y.: Chandler (1, 5), Borowy (3), Russo (4); St. L.: Cooper (2). LP—N.Y.: Bonham (2); St. L.: Lanier (1), Brazle (3), Brecheen (4), Cooper (5).

**1944**—St. Louis N.L. 4 (Billy Southworth); St. Louis A.L. 2 (Luke Sewell). WP—St. L. N.L.: Donnelly (2), Brecheen (4), Cooper (5), Lanier (6); St. L. A.L.: Galehouse (1), Kramer (3). LP—St. L. N.L.: Cooper (1), Wilks (3); St. L. A.L.: Muncrief (2), Jakucki (4), Galehouse (5), Potter (6).

**1945**—Detroit A.L. 4 (Steve O'Neill); Chicago N.L. 3 (Charles Grimm). WP—Det.: Trucks (2), Trout (4), Newhouser (5, 7); Chi.: Borowy (1, 6), Passeau (3). LP—Det.: Newhouser (1), Overmire (3), Trout (6); Chi.: Wyse (2), Prim (4), Borowy (5, 7).

**1946**—St. Louis N.L. 4 (Eddie Dyer); Boston A.L. 3 (Joe Cronin). WP—St. L.: Brecheen (2, 6, 7), Munger (4); Bos.: Johnson (1), Ferriss (3), Dobson (5). LP—St. L.: Pollet (1), Dickson (3), Brazle (5); Bos.: Harris (2, 6), Hughson (4), Klinger (7).

**1947**—New York A.L. 4 (Bucky Harris); Brooklyn N.L. 3 (Burt Shotton). WP—N.Y.: Shea (1, 5), Reynolds (2), Page (7); Bklyn.: Casey (3, 4), Branca (6). LP—N.Y.: Newsom (3), Bevens (4), Page (6); Bklyn.: Branca (1), Lombardi (2), Barney (5), Gregg (7).

**1948**—Cleveland A.L. 4 (Lou Boudreau); Boston N.L. 2 (Billy Southworth). WP—Cleve.: Lemon (2, 6), Bearden (3), Gromek (4); Bos.: Sain (1), Spahn (5). LP—Cleve.: Feller (1, 5); Bos.: Spahn (2) Bickford (3) Sain (4) Voiselle (6).

**1949**—New York A.L. 4 (Casey Stengel); Brooklyn N.L. 1 (Burt Shotton). WP—N.Y.: Reynolds (1), Page (3), Lopat (4), Raschi (5); Bklyn.: Roe (2). LP—N.Y.: Raschi (2); Bklyn.: Newcombe (1, 4), Branca (3), Barney (5).

**1950**—New York A.L. 4 (Casey Stengel); Philadelphia N.L. 0 (Eddie Sawyer). WP—Raschi (1), Reynolds (2), Ferrick (3), Ford (4). LP—Konstanty (1), Roberts (2), Meyer (3), Miller (4).

**1951**—New York A.L. 4 (Casey Stengel); New York N.L. 2 (Leo Durocher). WP—N.Y. A.L.: Lopat (2, 5), Reynolds (4), Raschi (6); N.Y. N.L.: Koslo (1), Hearn (3). LP—N.Y. A.L.: Reynolds (1), Raschi (3); N.Y. N.L.: Jansen (2, 5), Maglie (4), Koslo (6).

**1952**—New York A.L. 4 (Casey Stengel); Brooklyn N.L. 3 (Chuck Dressen). WP—N.Y.: Raschi (2, 6), Reynolds (4, 7); Bklyn.: Black (1), Roe (3), Erskine (5). LP—N.Y.: Reynolds (1), Lopat (3), Sain (5); Bklyn.: Erskine (2), Black (4, 7), Loes (6).

**1953**—New York A.L. 4 (Casey Stengel); Brooklyn N.L. 2 (Chuck Dressen). WP—N.Y.: Sain (1), Lopat (2), McDonald (5), Reynolds (6); Bklyn.: Erskine (3), Loes (4). LP—N.Y.: Raschi (3), Ford (4); Bklyn.: Labine (1, 6), Roe (2), Podres (5).

**1954**—New York N.L. 4 (Leo Durocher); Cleveland A.L. 0 (Al Lopez). WP—Grissom (1), Antonelli (2), Gomez (3), Liddle (4). LP—Lemon (1, 4), Wynn (2), Garcia (3).

**1955**—Brooklyn N.L. 4 (Walter Alston); New York A.L. 3 (Casey Stengel). WP—Bklyn.: Podres (3, 7), Labine (4), Craig (5); N.Y.: Ford (1, 6), Byrne (2). LP—Bklyn.: Newcombe (1), Loes (2), Spooner (6); N.Y.: Turley (3), Larsen (4), Grim (5), Byrne (7).

**1956**—New York A.L. 4 (Casey Stengel); Brooklyn N.L. 3 (Walter Alston). WP—N.Y.: Ford (3), Sturdivant (4), Larsen (5), Kucks (7); Bklyn.: Maglie (1), Bessent (2), Labine (6). LP—N.Y.: Ford (1), Morgan (2), Turley (6); Bklyn.: Craig (3), Erskine (4), Maglie (5), Newcombe (7).

**1957**—Milwaukee N.L. 4 (Fred Haney); New York A.L. 3 (Casey Stengel). WP—Mil.: Burdette (2, 5, 7), Spahn (4); N.Y.: Ford (1), Larsen (3), Turley (6). LP—Mil.: Spahn (1), Buhl (3), Johnson (6); N.Y.: Shantz (2), Grim (4), Ford (5), Larsen (7).

**1958**—New York A.L. 4 (Casey Stengel); Milwaukee N.L. 3 (Fred Haney). WP—N.Y.: Larsen (3), Turley (5, 7), Duren (6); Mil.: Spahn (1, 4), Burdette (2). LP—N.Y.: Duren (1), Turley (2), Ford (4); Mil.: Rush (3), Burdette (5, 7), Spahn (6).

**1959**—Los Angeles N.L. 4 (Walter Alston); Chicago A.L. 2 (Al Lopez). WP—L.A.: Podres (2), Drysdale (3), Sherry (4, 6); Chi.: Wynn (1), Shaw (5). LP—L.A.: Craig (1), Koufax (5); Chi.: Shaw (2), Donovan (3), Staley (4), Wynn (6).

**1960**—Pittsburgh N.L. 4 (Danny Murtaugh); New York A.L. 3 (Casey Stengel). WP—Pitts.: Law (1, 4), Haddix (5, 7); N.Y.: Turley (2), Ford (3, 6). LP—Pitts.: Friend (2, 6), Mizell (3); N.Y.: Ditmar (1, 5), Terry (4, 7).

**1961**—New York A.L. 4 (Ralph Houk); Cincinnati N.L. 1 (Fred Hutchinson). WP—N.Y.: Ford (1, 4), Arroyo (3), Daley (5); Cin.: Jay (2). LP—N.Y.: Terry (2); Cin.: O'Toole (1, 4), Purkey (3), Jay (5).

**1962**—New York A.L. 4 (Ralph Houk); San Francisco N.L. 3 (Al Dark). WP—N.Y.: Ford (1), Stafford (3), Terry (5, 7); S.F.: Sanford (2), Larsen (4), Pierce (6). LP—N.Y.: Terry (2), Coates (4), Ford (6); S.F.: O'Dell (1), Pierce (3), Sanford (5, 7).

**1963**—Los Angeles N.L. 4 (Walter Alston); New York A.L. 0 (Ralph Houk). WP—Koufax (1, 4), Podres (2), Drysdale (3). LP—Ford (1, 4), Downing (2), Bouton (3).

**1964**—St. Louis N.L. 4 (Johnny Keane); New York A.L. 3 (Yogi Berra). WP—St. L.: Sadecki (1), Craig (4), Gibson (5, 7); N.Y.: Stottlemyre (2), Bouton (3, 6). LP—St. L.: Gibson (2), Schultz (3), Simmons (6); N.Y.: Ford (1), Downing (4), Mikkelsen (5), Stottlemyre (7).

**1965**—Los Angeles N.L. 4 (Walter Alston); Minnesota A.L. 3 (Sam Mele). WP—L.A.: Osteen (3), Drysdale (4), Koufax (5, 7); Minn.: Grant (1, 6), Kaat (2). LP—L.A.: Drysdale (1), Koufax (2), Osteen (6); Minn.: Pascual (3), Grant (4), Kaat (5, 7).

**1966**—Baltimore A.L. 4 (Hank Bauer); Los Angeles N.L. 0 (Walter Alston). WP—Drabowsky (1), Palmer (2), Bunker (3), McNally (4). LP—Drysdale (1, 4), Koufax (2), Osteen (3).

**1967**—St. Louis N.L. 4 (Red Schoendienst); Boston A.L. 3 (Dick Williams). WP—St. L.: Gibson (1, 4, 7), Briles (3); Bos.: Lonborg (2, 5); Wyatt (6). LP—St. L.: Hughes (2), Carlton (5), Lamabe (6); Bos.: Santiago (1, 4), Bell (3), Lonborg (7).

**1968**—Detroit A.L. 4 (Mayo Smith); St. Louis N.L. 3 (Red Schoendienst). WP—Det.: Lolich (2, 5, 7), McLain (6); St. L.: Gibson (1, 4), Washburn (3), LP—Det.: McLain (1, 4), Wilson (3); St. L.: Briles (2), Hoerner (5), Washburn (6), Gibson (7).

**1969**—New York N.L. 4 (Gil Hodges); Baltimore A.L. 1 (Earl Weaver). WP—N.Y.: Koosman (2, 5), Gentry (3), Seaver (4); Balt.: Cuellar (1). LP—N.Y.: Seaver (1); Balt.: McNally (2), Palmer (3), Hall (4), Watt (5).

**1970**—Baltimore A.L. 4 (Earl Weaver); Cincinnati N.L. 1 (George Anderson) 1. WP—Balt.: Palmer (1), Phoebus (2), McNally (3), Cuellar (5); Cin.: Carroll (4). LP—Cin.: Nolan (1), Wilcox (2), Cloninger (3), Merritt (5); Balt.: Watt (4).

**1971**—Pittsburgh N.L. 4 (Danny Murtaugh); Baltimore A.L. 3 (Earl Weaver). WP—Pitts.: Blass (3, 7), Kison (4), Briles (5); Balt.: McNally (1, 6), Palmer (2). LP—Pitts.: Ellis (1), R. Johnson (2), Miller (6); Balt.: Cuellar (3, 7), Watt (4) McNally (5).

**1972**—Oakland A.L. 4 (Dick Williams); Cincinnati N.L. (George Anderson) 3. WP—Oakland: Holtzman (1), Hunter (2, 7), Fingers (4); Cincinnati: Billingham (3), Grimsley (5, 6). LP—Oakland: Odom (3), Fingers (5), Blue (6); Cincinnati: Nolan (1), Grimsley (2), Carroll (4), Bordon (7).

**1973**—Oakland A.L. 4 (Dick Williams): New York N.L. 3 (Yogi Berra). WP—Oakland: Holtzman (1, 7), Lindblad (3), Hunter (6). New York: McGraw (2), Matlack (4), Koosman (5). LP—Oakland: Fingers (2), Holtzman (4), Blue (5). New York: Matlack (1, 7) Parker (3), Seaver (6).

**1974**—Oakland A.L. 4 (Al Dark); Los Angeles N.L. 1 (Walter Alston). WP—Oakland: Fingers (1), Hunter (3), Holtzman (4), Odom (5). Los Angeles: Sutton (2). LP—Oakland: Blue (2), Los Angeles: Messersmith (1–4), Downing (3), Marshall (5).

**1975**—Cincinnati N.L. 4 (George Anderson); Boston A.L. 3 (Darrell Johnson). WP—Cincinnati: Eastwick (2-3), Gullett (5), Carroll (7); Boston: Tiant (1–4), Wise (6). LP—Cincinnati: Gullett (1), Norman (4), Darcy (6); Boston: Drago (2), Willoughby (3), Cleveland (5), Burton (7).

**1976**—Cincinnati N.L. 4 (George Anderson); New York A.L. 0 (Billy Martin). WP—Gullett (1), Billingham (2), Zachry (3), Nolan (4). LP—Alexander (1), Hunter (2), Ellis (3), Figueroa (4).

**1977**—New York A.L. 4 (Billy Martin); Los Angeles N.L. 2 (Tom Lasorda). WP—New York: Lyle (1), Torrez (3,6), Guidry (4); Los Angeles: Hooton (2), Sutton (5). LP—New York: Hunter (2), Gullett (5); Los Angeles: Rhoden (1), John (3), Rau (4), Hooton (6).

## WORLD SERIES CLUB STANDING (THROUGH 1977)

| | Series | Won | Lost | Pct. |
|---|---|---|---|---|
| Oakland (A) | 3 | 3 | 0 | 1.000 |
| New York (A) | 31 | 21 | 10 | .645 |
| St. Louis (N) | 12 | 8 | 4 | .667 |
| Pittsburgh (N) | 6 | 4 | 2 | .667 |
| Cleveland (A) | 3 | 2 | 1 | .667 |
| Boston (A) | 8 | 5 | 3 | .625 |
| Philadelphia (A) | 8 | 5 | 3 | .625 |
| Los Angeles (N) | 6 | 3 | 3 | .500 |
| Baltimore (A) | 4 | 2 | 2 | .500 |
| New York (N-Mets) | 2 | 1 | 1 | .500 |
| Milwaukee (N) | 2 | 1 | 1 | .500 |
| Boston (N) | 2 | 1 | 1 | .500 |
| Chicago (A) | 4 | 2 | 2 | .500 |
| Cincinnati (N) | 8 | 4 | 4 | .500 |
| Detroit (A) | 8 | 3 | 5 | .375 |
| New York (N-Giants) | 14 | 5 | 9 | .357 |
| Washington (A) | 3 | 1 | 2 | .333 |
| Chicago (N) | 10 | 2 | 8 | .200 |
| Brooklyn (N) | 9 | 1 | 8 | .111 |
| St. Louis (A) | 1 | 0 | 1 | .000 |
| San Francisco (N) | 1 | 0 | 1 | .000 |
| Minnesota (A) | 1 | 0 | 1 | .000 |
| Philadelphia (N) | 2 | 0 | 2 | .000 |

### Recapitulation

| | Won |
|---|---|
| American League | 44 |
| National League | 30 |

## SINGLE GAME AND SINGLE SERIES RECORDS

Most hits game—4, held by many players.
Most hits inning—2, held by many players.
Most hits series—13 (7 games) Bobby Richardson, New York A.L., 1964; Lou Brock, St. Louis N.L., 1968; 12 (6 games) Billy Martin, New York A.L., 1953; 12 (8 games) Buck Herzog, New York N.L., 1912; Joe Jackson, Chicago A.L., 1919; 10 (4 games) Babe Ruth, New York A.L., 1928; 9 (5 games) held by 8 players.
Most home runs, series—5 (6 games) Reggie Jackson, New York A.L., 1977; 4 (7 games) Babe Ruth, New York A.L., 1926; Duke Snider, Brooklyn N.L., 1952, 1955; Hank Bauer, New York A.L., 1958; Gene Tenace, Oakland A.L., 1972; 4 (4 games) Lou Gehrig, New York A.L., 1928; 3 (6 games) Babe Ruth, New York A.L., 1923; Ted Kluszewski, Chicago A.L., 1959; 3 (5 games) Donn Clendenon, New York Mets N.L., 1969; 2 (8 games) Patrick Dougherty, Boston A.L., 1903.
Most home runs, game—3, Babe Ruth, New York A.L., 1926 and 1928; Reggie Jackson, New York A.L., 1977.
Most strikeouts, series—11 (7 games) Ed Mathews, Milwaukee N.L., 1958; Wayne Garrett, New York N.L., 1973; 10 (8 games) George Kelly, New York N.L., 1921; 9 (6 games) Jim Bottomley, St. Louis N.L., 1930; 8 (5 games) Rogers Hornsby, Chicago N.L., 1929; Duke Snider, Brooklyn N.L., 1949; 7 (4 games) Bob Meusel, New York A.L., 1927.
Most stolen bases, game—3, Honus Wagner, Pittsburgh N.L., 1909; Willie Davis, Los Angeles N.L., 1965; Lou Brock, St. Louis N.L., 1967 and 1968.
Most strikeouts by pitcher, game—17, Bob Gibson, St. Louis N.L. 1968.
Most strikeouts by pitcher in succession—6, Horace Eller, Cincinnati N.L., 1919; Moe Drabowsky, Baltimore A.L., 1966.
Most strikeouts by pitcher, series—35 (7 games) Bob Gibson, St. Louis N.L., 1968, 28 (8 games) Bill Dinneen, Boston A.L., 1903; 23 (4 games) Sandy Koufax, Los Angeles, 1963; 20 (6 games) Chief Bender, Philadelphia A.L., 1911; 18 (5 games) Christy Mathewson, New York N.L., 1905.
Most bases on balls, series—11 (7 games) Babe Ruth, New York A.L., 1926; Gene Tenace, Oakland A.L., 1973; 8 (6 games) Babe Ruth, New York A.L., 1923; 7 (5 games) James Sheckard, Chicago N.L., 1910; Mickey Cochrane, Philadelphia A.L., 1929; Joe Gordon, New York A.L. 1941.

## LIFETIME WORLD SERIES RECORDS

Most hits—71, Yogi Berra, New York A.L., 1947, 1949–53, 1955–58, 1960–63.
Most runs—42, Mickey Mantle, New York A.L., 1951–53, 1955–58, 1960–64.
Most runs batted in—40, Mickey Mantle, New York A.L., 1951–53, 1955–58, 1960–64.
Most home runs—18, Mickey Mantle, New York A.L., 1951–53, 1955–58, 1960–64.
Most bases on balls—43, Mickey Mantle, New York A.L., 1951–53, 1955–58, 1960–64.
Most strikeouts—54, Mickey Mantle, New York A.L., 1951–53, 1955–58, 1960–64.
Most victories, pitcher—10, Whitey Ford, New York A.L., 1950, 1953, 1955–58, 1960–64.
Most times member of winning team—10, Yogi Berra, New York A.L., 1947, 1949–53, 1956, 1958, 1961–62.
Most victories, no defeats—6, Vernon Gomez, New York A.L., 1932, 1936(2), 1937(2), 1938.
Most shutouts—4, Christy Mathewson, New York N.L., 1905 (3), 1913.
Most innings pitched—146, Whitey Ford, New York A.L., 1950, 1953, 1955–58, 1960–1964.
Most consecutive scoreless innings—33⅔, Whitey Ford, New York A.L., 1960 (18), 1961 (14), 1962 (1⅔).
Most strikeouts by pitcher—94, Whitey Ford, New York A.L., 1950, 1953, 1955–58, 1960–64.

## LONGEST GAMES IN THE MAJORS

A 26-inning tie between the Brooklyn Dodgers and the Boston Braves on May 1, 1920, was the longest game in major league history. Played at Braves Field, Boston, the game was called because of darkness with the score 1–1. Both starting pitchers, Leon Cadore of Brooklyn and Joe Oeschger, were still in the game at the end, 3 hours and 50 minutes after it had begun. The longest game in terms of time, 7 hours and 23 minutes, was played by the New York Mets and the San Francisco Giants on May 31, 1964, in New York. The Giants won in 23 innings, 8–6. In the longest night game, the St. Louis Cards defeated the Mets at New York, 4–3, in 25 innings, Sept. 11, 1974. This game was played in 7 hours, 4 minutes.

## AMERICAN LEAGUE HOME RUN CHAMPIONS

| Year, | Player, team | No. |
|---|---|---|
| 1901 | Nap Lajoie, Phila. | 13 |
| 1902 | Ralph Seybold, Phila. | 16 |
| 1903 | Buck Freeman, Bost. | 13 |
| 1904 | Harry Davis, Phila. | 10 |
| 1905 | Harry Davis, Phila. | 8 |
| 1906 | Harry Davis, Phila. | 12 |
| 1907 | Harry Davis, Phila. | 8 |
| 1908 | Sam Crawford, Det. | 7 |
| 1909 | Ty Cobb, Det. | 9 |
| 1910 | J. Garland Stahl, Bost. | 10 |
| 1911 | Franklin Baker, Phila. | 9 |
| 1912 | Franklin Baker, Phila. | 10 |
| 1913 | Franklin Baker, Phila. | 12 |
| 1914 | Franklin Baker, Phila., and Sam Crawford, Det. | 8 |
| 1915 | Robert Roth, Chi.-Cleve. | 7 |
| 1916 | Wally Pipp, N.Y. | 12 |
| 1917 | Wally Pipp, N.Y. | 9 |
| 1918 | Babe Ruth, Bost., and Clarence Walker, Phila. | 11 |
| 1919 | Babe Ruth, Bost. | 29 |
| 1920 | Babe Ruth, N.Y. | 54 |
| 1921 | Babe Ruth, N.Y. | 59 |
| 1922 | Ken Williams, St. L. | 39 |
| 1923 | Babe Ruth, N.Y. | 41 |
| 1924 | Babe Ruth, N.Y. | 46 |
| 1925 | Bob Meusel, N.Y. | 33 |
| 1926 | Babe Ruth, N.Y. | 47 |
| 1927 | Babe Ruth, N.Y. | 60 |

| Year, | Player, team | No. |
|---|---|---|
| 1928 | Babe Ruth, N.Y. | 54 |
| 1929 | Babe Ruth, N.Y. | 46 |
| 1930 | Babe Ruth, N.Y. | 49 |
| 1931 | Lou Gehrig, N.Y., and Babe Ruth, N.Y. | 46 |
| 1932 | Jimmy Foxx, Phila. | 58 |
| 1933 | Jimmy Foxx, Phila. | 48 |
| 1934 | Lou Gehrig, N.Y. | 49 |
| 1935 | Jimmy Foxx, Phila., and Hank Greenberg, Det. | 36 |
| 1936 | Lou Gehrig, N.Y. | 49 |
| 1937 | Joe DiMaggio, N.Y. | 46 |
| 1938 | Hank Greenberg, Det. | 58 |
| 1939 | Jimmy Foxx, Bost. | 35 |
| 1940 | Hank Greenberg, Det. | 41 |
| 1941 | Ted Williams, Bost. | 37 |
| 1942 | Ted Williams, Bost. | 36 |
| 1943 | Rudy York, Det. | 34 |
| 1944 | Nick Etten, N.Y. | 22 |
| 1945 | Vern Stephens, St. L. | 24 |
| 1946 | Hank Greenberg, Det. | 44 |
| 1947 | Ted Williams, Bost. | 32 |
| 1948 | Joe DiMaggio, N.Y. | 39 |
| 1949 | Ted Williams, Bost. | 43 |
| 1950 | Al Rosen, Cleve. | 37 |
| 1951 | Gus Zernial, Chi.-Phila. | 33 |
| 1952 | Larry Doby, Cleve. | 32 |
| 1953 | Al Rosen, Cleve. | 43 |
| 1954 | Larry Doby, Cleve. | 32 |

| Year, | Player, team | No. |
|---|---|---|
| 1955 | Mickey Mantle, N.Y. | 37 |
| 1956 | Mickey Mantle, N.Y. | 52 |
| 1957 | Roy Sievers, Wash. | 42 |
| 1958 | Mickey Mantle, N.Y. | 42 |
| 1959 | Rocky Colavito, Cleve., and Harmon Killebrew, Wash. | 42 |
| 1960 | Mickey Mantle, N.Y. | 40 |
| 1961 | Roger Maris, N.Y. | 61 |
| 1962 | Harmon Killebrew, Minn. | 48 |
| 1963 | Harmon Killebrew, Minn. | 45 |
| 1964 | Harmon Killebrew, Minn. | 49 |
| 1965 | Tony Conigliaro, Bost. | 32 |
| 1966 | Frank Robinson, Balt. | 49 |
| 1967 | Carl Yastrzemski, Bost., and Harmon Killebrew, Minn. | 44 |
| 1968 | Frank Howard, Wash. | 44 |
| 1969 | Harmon Killebrew, Minn. | 49 |
| 1970 | Frank Howard, Wash. | 44 |
| 1971 | Bill Melton, Chicago | 33 |
| 1972 | Dick Allen, Chicago | 37 |
| 1973 | Reggie Jackson, Oak. | 32 |
| 1974 | Dick Allen, Chicago | 32 |
| 1975 | Reggie Jackson, Oak., and George Scott, Mil. | 36 |
| 1976 | Graig Nettles, N.Y. | 32 |
| 1977 | Jim Rice, Boston | 39 |
| 1978 | Jim Rice, Boston | 46 |

## AMERICAN LEAGUE BATTING CHAMPIONS

| Year, | Player, team | Avg. | Year, | Player, team | Avg. | Year, | Player, team | Avg. |
|---|---|---|---|---|---|---|---|---|
| 1901 | Nap Lajoie, Phila. | .422 | 1927 | Harry Heilmann, Det. | .398 | 1953 | Mickey Vernon, Wash. | .337 |
| 1902 | Ed Delahanty, Wash. | .376 | 1928 | Goose Goslin, Wash. | .379 | 1954 | Bobby Avila, Cleve. | .341 |
| 1903 | Nap Lajoie, Cleve. | .355 | 1929 | Lew Fonseca, Cleve. | .369 | 1955 | Al Kaline, Det. | .340 |
| 1904 | Nap Lajoie, Cleve. | .381 | 1930 | Al Simmons, Phila. | .381 | 1956 | Mickey Mantle, N.Y. | .353 |
| 1905 | Elmer Flick, Cleve. | .306 | 1931 | Al Simmons, Phila. | .390 | 1957 | Ted Williams, Bost. | .388 |
| 1906 | George Stone, St. L. | .358 | 1932 | Dale Alexander, Det.-Bost. | .367 | 1958 | Ted Williams, Bost. | .328 |
| 1907 | Ty Cobb, Det. | .350 | 1933 | Jimmy Foxx, Phila. | .356 | 1959 | Harvey Kuenn, Det. | .353 |
| 1908 | Ty Cobb, Det. | .324 | 1934 | Lou Gehrig, N.Y. | .363 | 1960 | Pete Runnels, Bost. | .320 |
| 1909 | Ty Cobb, Det. | .377 | 1935 | Buddy Myer, Wash. | .349 | 1961 | Norman Cash, Det. | .361 |
| 1910 | Ty Cobb, Det. | .385 | 1936 | Luke Appling, Chi. | .388 | 1962 | Pete Runnels, Bost. | .326 |
| 1911 | Ty Cobb, Det. | .420 | 1937 | Charley Gehringer, Det. | .371 | 1963 | Carl Yastrzemski, Bost. | .321 |
| 1912 | Ty Cobb, Det. | .410 | 1938 | Jimmy Foxx, Bost. | .349 | 1964 | Tony Oliva, Minn. | .323 |
| 1913 | Ty Cobb, Det. | .390 | 1939 | Joe DiMaggio, N.Y. | .381 | 1965 | Tony Oliva, Minn. | .321 |
| 1914 | Ty Cobb, Det. | .368 | 1940 | Joe DiMaggio, N.Y. | .352 | 1966 | Frank Robinson, Balt. | .316 |
| 1915 | Ty Cobb, Det. | .369 | 1941 | Ted Williams, Bost. | .406 | 1967 | Carl Yastrzemski, Bost. | .326 |
| 1916 | Tris Speaker, Cleve. | .386 | 1942 | Ted Williams, Bost. | .356 | 1968 | Carl Yastrzemski, Bost. | .301 |
| 1917 | Ty Cobb, Det. | .383 | 1943 | Luke Appling, Chi. | .328 | 1969 | Rod Carew, Minn. | .332 |
| 1918 | Ty Cobb, Det. | .382 | 1944 | Lou Boudreau, Cleve. | .327 | 1970 | Alex Johnson, Calif. | .329 |
| 1919 | Ty Cobb, Det. | .384 | 1945 | George Sternweiss, N.Y. | .309 | 1971 | Tony Oliva, Minn. | .337 |
| 1920 | George Sisler, St. L. | .407 | 1946 | Mickey Vernon, Wash. | .353 | 1972 | Rod Carew, Minn. | .318 |
| 1921 | Harry Heilmann, Det. | .394 | 1947 | Ted Williams, Bost. | .343 | 1973 | Rod Carew, Minn. | .350 |
| 1922 | George Sisler, St. L. | .420 | 1948 | Ted Williams, Bost. | .369 | 1974 | Rod Carew, Minn. | .364 |
| 1923 | Harry Heilmann, Det. | .403 | 1949 | George Kell, Det. | .343 | 1975 | Rod Carew, Minn. | .359 |
| 1924 | Babe Ruth, N.Y. | .378 | 1950 | Billy Goodman, Bost. | .354 | 1976 | George Brett, Kansas City | .333 |
| 1925 | Harry Heilmann, Det. | .393 | 1951 | Ferris Fain, Phila. | .344 | 1977 | Rod Carew, Minn. | .388 |
| 1926 | Heinie Manush, Det. | .378 | 1952 | Ferris Fain, Phila. | .327 | 1978 | Rod Carew, Minn. | .333 |

## CONSECUTIVE NO-HITTERS BY VANDER MEER

Johnny Vander Meer, a 23-year-old lefthander with the Cincinnati Reds, pitched consecutive no-hitters in June 1938, setting a mark of 18 innings of no-hit hurling. On June 11, in Cincinnati, he set down Boston without a hit as the Reds won, 3–0. Four days later, June 15, in the first night game in Brooklyn, he again held the opposition hitless as the Reds triumphed, 6–0. He was nicknamed Johnny (Double No-Hitter) Vander Meer.

## NATIONAL LEAGUE HOME RUN CHAMPIONS

| Year | Player, team | No. |
|---|---|---|
| 1876 | George Hall, Phila. Athletics | 5 |
| 1877 | George Shaffer, Louisville | 3 |
| 1878 | Paul Hines, Providence | 4 |
| 1879 | Charles Jones, Bost. | 9 |
| 1880 | James O'Rourke, Bost., and Harry Stovey, Worcester | 6 |
| 1881 | Dan Brouthers, Buffalo | 8 |
| 1882 | George Wood, Det. | 7 |
| 1883 | William Ewing, N.Y. | 10 |
| 1884 | Ed Williamson, Chi. | 27 |
| 1885 | Abner Dalrymple, Chi. | 11 |
| 1886 | Arthur Richardson, Det. | 11 |
| 1887 | Roger Connor, N.Y., and Wm. O'Brien, Wash. | 17 |
| 1888 | Roger Connor, N.Y. | 14 |
| 1889 | Sam Thompson, Phila. | 20 |
| 1890 | Tom Burns, Bklyn., and Mike Tiernan, N.Y. | 13 |
| 1891 | Harry Stovey, Bost., and Mike Tiernan, N.Y. | 16 |
| 1892 | Jim Holliday, Cin. | 13 |
| 1893 | Ed Delahanty, Phila. | 19 |
| 1894 | Hugh Duffy, Bost., and Robert Lowe, Bost. | 18 |
| 1895 | Bill Joyce, Wash. | 17 |
| 1896 | Ed Delahanty, Phila., and Sam Thompson, Phila. | 13 |
| 1897 | Nap Lajoie, Phila. | 10 |
| 1898 | James Collins, Bost. | 14 |
| 1899 | John Freeman, Wash. | 25 |
| 1900 | Herman Long, Bost. | 12 |
| 1901 | Sam Crawford, Cin. | 16 |
| 1902 | Tom Leach, Pitts. | 6 |
| 1903 | James Sheckard, Bklyn. | 9 |
| 1904 | Harry Lumley, Bklyn. | 9 |
| 1905 | Fred Odwell, Cin. | 9 |
| 1906 | Tim Jordan, Bklyn. | 12 |
| 1907 | David Brain, Bost. | 10 |
| 1908 | Tim Jordan, Bklyn. | 12 |
| 1909 | John Murray, N.Y. | 7 |
| 1910 | Fred Beck, Bost., and Frank Schulte, Chi. | 10 |
| 1911 | Frank Schulte, Chi. | 21 |
| 1912 | Henry Zimmerman, Chi. | 14 |
| 1913 | Cliff Cravath, Phila. | 19 |
| 1914 | Cliff Cravath, Phila. | 19 |
| 1915 | Cliff Cravath, Phila. | 24 |
| 1916 | Davis Robertson, N.Y., and Fred Williams, Chi. | 12 |
| 1917 | Davis Robertson, N.Y., and Cliff Cravath, Phila. | 12 |
| 1918 | Cliff Cravath, Phila. | 8 |
| 1919 | Cliff Cravath, Phila. | 12 |
| 1920 | Cy Williams, Phila. | 15 |
| 1921 | George Kelly, N.Y. | 23 |
| 1922 | Rogers Hornsby, St. L. | 42 |
| 1923 | Cy Williams, Phila. | 41 |
| 1924 | Jacques Fournier, Bklyn. | 27 |
| 1925 | Rogers Hornsby, St. L. | 39 |
| 1926 | Hack Wilson, Chi. | 21 |
| 1927 | Hack Wilson, Chi., and Cy Williams, Phila. | 30 |
| 1928 | Hack Wilson, Chi., and Jim Bottomley, St. L. | 31 |
| 1929 | Chuck Klein, Phila. | 43 |
| 1930 | Hack Wilson, Chi. | 56 |
| 1931 | Chuck Klein, Phila. | 31 |
| 1932 | Chuck Klein, Phila., and Mel Ott, N.Y. | 38 |
| 1933 | Chuck Klein, Phila. | 28 |
| 1934 | Mel Ott, N.Y., and Rip Collins, St. L. | 35 |
| 1935 | Wally Berger, Bost. | 34 |
| 1936 | Mel Ott, N.Y. | 33 |
| 1937 | Mel Ott, N.Y., and Joe Medwick, St. L. | 31 |
| 1938 | Mel Ott, N.Y. | 36 |
| 1939 | John Mize, St. L. | 28 |
| 1940 | John Mize, St. L. | 43 |
| 1941 | Dolph Camilli, Bklyn. | 34 |
| 1942 | Mel Ott, N.Y. | 30 |
| 1943 | Bill Nicholson, Chi. | 29 |
| 1944 | Bill Nicholson, Chi. | 33 |
| 1945 | Tommy Holmes, Bost. | 28 |
| 1946 | Ralph Kiner, Pitts. | 23 |
| 1947 | Ralph Kiner, Pitts., and John Mize, N.Y. | 51 |
| 1948 | Ralph Kiner, Pitts., and John Mize, N.Y. | 40 |
| 1949 | Ralph Kiner, Pitts. | 54 |
| 1950 | Ralph Kiner, Pitts. | 47 |
| 1951 | Ralph Kiner, Pitts. | 42 |
| 1952 | Ralph Kiner, Pitts., and Hank Sauer, Chi. | 37 |
| 1953 | Ed Mathews, Mil. | 47 |
| 1954 | Ted Kluszewski, Cin. | 49 |
| 1955 | Willie Mays, N.Y. | 51 |
| 1956 | Duke Snider, Bklyn. | 43 |
| 1957 | Henry Aaron, Mil. | 44 |
| 1958 | Ernie Banks, Chi. | 47 |
| 1959 | Ed Mathews, Mil. | 46 |
| 1960 | Ernie Banks, Chi. | 41 |
| 1961 | Orlando Cepeda, San Fran. | 46 |
| 1962 | Willie Mays, San Fran. | 49 |
| 1963 | Henry Aaron, Mil., and Willie McCovey, San Fran. | 44 |
| 1964 | Willie Mays, San Fran. | 47 |
| 1965 | Willie Mays, San Fran. | 52 |
| 1966 | Henry Aaron, Atlanta | 44 |
| 1967 | Henry Aaron, Atlanta | 39 |
| 1968 | Willie McCovey, San Fran. | 36 |
| 1969 | Willie McCovey, San Fran. | 45 |
| 1970 | Johnny Bench, Cin. | 45 |
| 1971 | Willie Stargell, Pitts. | 48 |
| 1972 | Johnny Bench, Cin. | 40 |
| 1973 | Willie Stargell, Pitts. | 44 |
| 1974 | Michael Schmidt, Phila. | 36 |
| 1975 | Michael Schmidt, Phila. | 38 |
| 1976 | Michael Schmidt, Phila. | 38 |
| 1977 | George Foster, Cin. | 52 |
| 1978 | George Foster, Cin. | 40 |

## NATIONAL LEAGUE BATTING CHAMPIONS

| Year | Player/Team | Avg |
|---|---|---|
| 1876 | Roscoe Barnes, Chicago | .404 |
| 1877 | Jim White, Boston | .385 |
| 1878 | Abner Dalrymple, Mil. | .356 |
| 1879 | Cap Anson, Chicago | .407 |
| 1880 | George Gore, Chicago | .365 |
| 1881 | Cap Anson, Chicago | .399 |
| 1882 | Dan Brouthers, Buffalo | .367 |
| 1883 | Dan Brouthers, Buffalo | .371 |
| 1884 | James O'Rourke, Buffalo | .350 |
| 1885 | Roger Connor, N. Y. | .371 |
| 1886 | King Kelly, Chicago | .388 |
| 1887 | Cap Anson, Chicago | .421 |
| 1888 | Cap Anson, Chicago | .343 |
| 1889 | Dan Brouthers, Boston | .373 |
| 1890 | John Glasscock, N. Y. | .336 |
| 1891 | Wm. Hamilton, Phila. | .338 |
| 1892 | Dan Brouthers, Bklyn., and Clarence Childs, Cleve. | .335 |
| 1893 | Hugh Duffy, Boston | .378 |
| 1894 | Hugh Duffy, Boston | .438 |
| 1895 | Jesse Burkett, Cleveland | .423 |
| 1896 | Jesse Burkett, Cleveland | .410 |
| 1897 | Willie Keeler, Baltimore | .432 |
| 1898 | Willie Keeler, Baltimore | .379 |
| 1899 | Ed Delahanty, Phila. | .408 |
| 1900 | Honus Wagner, Pittsburgh | .381 |
| 1901 | Jesse Burkett, St. Louis | .382 |
| 1902 | Clarence Beaumont, Pitts. | .357 |
| 1903 | Honus Wagner, Pittsburgh | .355 |
| 1904 | Honus Wagner, Pittsburgh | .349 |
| 1905 | Cy Seymour, Cincinnati | .377 |
| 1906 | Honus Wagner, Pittsburgh | .339 |
| 1907 | Honus Wagner, Pittsburgh | .350 |
| 1908 | Honus Wagner, Pittsburgh | .354 |
| 1909 | Honus Wagner, Pittsburgh | .339 |
| 1910 | Sherwood Magee, Philadelphia | .331 |
| 1911 | Honus Wagner, Pittsburgh | .334 |
| 1912 | Henry Zimmerman, Chicago | .372 |
| 1913 | Jake Daubert, Brooklyn | .350 |
| 1914 | Jake Daubert, Brooklyn | .329 |
| 1915 | Larry Doyle, N. Y. | .320 |
| 1916 | Hal Chase, Cincinnati | .339 |
| 1917 | Edd Roush, Cincinnati | .341 |
| 1918 | Zach Wheat, Brooklyn | .335 |
| 1919 | Edd Roush, Cincinnati | .321 |
| 1920 | Rogers Hornsby, St. Louis | .370 |
| 1921 | Rogers Hornsby, St. Louis | .397 |
| 1922 | Rogers Hornsby, St. Louis | .401 |
| 1923 | Rogers Hornsby, St. Louis | .384 |
| 1924 | Rogers Hornsby, St. Louis | .424 |
| 1925 | Rogers Hornsby, St. Louis | .403 |
| 1926 | Gene Hargrave, Cincinnati | .353 |
| 1927 | Paul Waner, Pittsburgh | .380 |
| 1928 | Rogers Hornsby, Boston | .387 |
| 1929 | Lefty O'Doul, Phila. | .398 |
| 1930 | Bill Terry, N. Y. | .401 |
| 1931 | Chick Hafey, St. Louis | .349 |
| 1932 | Lefty O'Doul, Brooklyn | .368 |
| 1933 | Chuck Klein, Phila. | .368 |
| 1934 | Paul Waner, Pittsburgh | .362 |
| 1935 | Arky Vaughan, Pittsburgh | .385 |
| 1936 | Paul Waner, Pittsburgh | .373 |
| 1937 | Joe Medwick, St. Louis | .374 |
| 1938 | Ernie Lombardi, Cin. | .342 |
| 1939 | John Mize, St. Louis | .349 |
| 1940 | Debs Garms, Pittsburgh | .355 |
| 1941 | Pete Reiser, Brooklyn | .343 |
| 1942 | Ernie Lombardi, Boston | .330 |
| 1943 | Stan Musial, St. Louis | .357 |
| 1944 | Dixie Walker, Brooklyn | .357 |
| 1945 | Phil Cavarretta, Chicago | .355 |

| Year | Player/Team | Avg |
|---|---|---|
| 1946 | Stan Musial, St. Louis | .365 |
| 1947 | Harry Walker, St. L.-Phila. | .363 |
| 1948 | Stan Musial, St. Louis | .376 |
| 1949 | Jackie Robinson, Brooklyn | .342 |
| 1950 | Stan Musial, St. Louis | .346 |
| 1951 | Stan Musial, St. Louis | .355 |
| 1952 | Stan Musial, St. Louis | .336 |
| 1953 | Carl Furillo, Brooklyn | .344 |
| 1954 | Willie Mays, N. Y. | .345 |
| 1955 | Richie Ashburn, Phila. | .338 |
| 1956 | Henry Aaron, Mil. | .328 |
| 1957 | Stan Musial, St. Louis | .351 |
| 1958 | Richie Ashburn, Phila. | .350 |
| 1959 | Henry Aaron, Mil. | .355 |
| 1960 | Dick Groat, Pittsburgh | .325 |
| 1961 | Roberto Clemente, Pitts. | .351 |
| 1962 | Tommy Davis, L. A. | .346 |
| 1963 | Tommy Davis, L. A. | .326 |
| 1964 | Roberto Clemente, Pitts. | .339 |
| 1965 | Roberto Clemente, Pitts. | .329 |
| 1966 | Matty Alou, Pittsburgh | .342 |
| 1967 | Roberto Clemente, Pitts. | .357 |
| 1968 | Pete Rose, Cincinnati | .335 |
| 1969 | Pete Rose, Cincinnati | .348 |
| 1970 | Rico Carty, Atlanta | .366 |
| 1971 | Joe Torre, St. Louis | .363 |
| 1972 | Billy Williams, Chicago | .333 |
| 1973 | Pete Rose, Cincinnati | .338 |
| 1974 | Ralph Garr, Atlanta | .353 |
| 1975 | Bill Madlock, Chicago | .354 |
| 1976 | Bill Madlock, Chicago | .339 |
| 1977 | Dave Parker, Pittsburgh | .338 |
| 1978 | Dave Parker, Pittsburgh | .334 |

## AMERICAN LEAGUE PENNANT WINNERS

| Year | Club | Manager | Won | Lost | Pct. |
|---|---|---|---|---|---|
| 1901 | Chicago | Clark C. Griffith | 83 | 53 | .610 |
| 1902 | Philadelphia | Connie Mack | 83 | 53 | .610 |
| 1903[1] | Boston | Jimmy Collins | 91 | 47 | .659 |
| 1904[2] | Boston | Jimmy Collins | 95 | 59 | .617 |
| 1905 | Philadelphia | Connie Mack | 92 | 56 | .622 |
| 1906[1] | Chicago | Fielder A. Jones | 93 | 58 | .616 |
| 1907 | Detroit | Hugh A. Jennings | 92 | 58 | .613 |
| 1908 | Detroit | Hugh A. Jennings | 90 | 63 | .588 |
| 1909 | Detroit | Hugh A. Jennings | 98 | 54 | .645 |
| 1910[1] | Philadelphia | Connie Mack | 102 | 48 | .680 |
| 1911[1] | Philadelphia | Connie Mack | 101 | 50 | .669 |
| 1912[1] | Boston | J. Garland Stahl | 105 | 47 | .691 |
| 1913[1] | Philadelphia | Connie Mack | 96 | 57 | .627 |
| 1914 | Philadelphia | Connie Mack | 99 | 53 | .651 |
| 1915[1] | Boston | William F. Carrigan | 101 | 50 | .669 |
| 1916[1] | Boston | William F. Carrigan | 91 | 63 | .591 |
| 1917[1] | Chicago | Clarence H. Rowland | 100 | 54 | .649 |
| 1918[1] | Boston | Ed Barrow | 75 | 51 | .595 |
| 1919 | Chicago | William Gleason | 88 | 52 | .629 |
| 1920[1] | Cleveland | Tris E. Speaker | 98 | 56 | .636 |
| 1921 | New York | Miller J. Huggins | 98 | 55 | .641 |
| 1922 | New York | Miller J. Huggins | 94 | 60 | .610 |
| 1923[1] | New York | Miller J. Huggins | 98 | 54 | .645 |
| 1924[1] | Washington | Stanley R. Harris | 92 | 62 | .597 |
| 1925 | Washington | Stanley R. Harris | 96 | 55 | .636 |
| 1926 | New York | Miller J. Huggins | 91 | 63 | .591 |
| 1927[1] | New York | Miller J. Huggins | 110 | 44 | .714 |
| 1928[1] | New York | Miller J. Huggins | 101 | 53 | .656 |
| 1929[1] | Philadelphia | Connie Mack | 104 | 46 | .693 |
| 1930[1] | Philadelphia | Connie Mack | 102 | 52 | .662 |
| 1931 | Philadelphia | Connie Mack | 107 | 45 | .704 |
| 1932[1] | New York | Joseph V. McCarthy | 107 | 47 | .695 |
| 1933 | Washington | Joseph E. Cronin | 99 | 53 | .651 |
| 1934 | Detroit | Mickey Cochrane | 101 | 53 | .656 |
| 1935[1] | Detroit | Mickey Cochrane | 93 | 58 | .616 |
| 1936[1] | New York | Joseph V. McCarthy | 102 | 51 | .667 |
| 1937[1] | New York | Joseph V. McCarthy | 102 | 52 | .662 |
| 1938[1] | New York | Joseph V. McCarthy | 99 | 53 | .651 |
| 1939[1] | New York | Joseph V. McCarthy | 106 | 45 | .702 |
| 1940 | Detroit | Delmar D. Baker | 90 | 64 | .584 |
| 1941[1] | New York | Joseph V. McCarthy | 101 | 53 | .656 |
| 1942 | New York | Joseph V. McCarthy | 103 | 51 | .669 |
| 1943[1] | New York | Joseph V. McCarthy | 98 | 56 | .636 |
| 1944 | St. Louis | Luke Sewell | 89 | 65 | .578 |
| 1945[1] | Detroit | Steve O'Neill | 88 | 65 | .575 |
| 1946 | Boston | Joseph E. Cronin | 104 | 50 | .675 |
| 1947[1] | New York | Stanley R. Harris | 97 | 57 | .630 |
| 1948[1] | Cleveland | Lou Boudreau | 97 | 58 | .626 |
| 1949[1] | New York | Casey Stengel | 97 | 57 | .630 |
| 1950[1] | New York | Casey Stengel | 98 | 56 | .636 |
| 1951[1] | New York | Casey Stengel | 98 | 56 | .636 |
| 1952[1] | New York | Casey Stengel | 95 | 59 | .617 |
| 1953[1] | New York | Casey Stengel | 99 | 52 | .656 |
| 1954 | Cleveland | Al Lopez | 111 | 43 | .721 |
| 1955 | New York | Casey Stengel | 96 | 58 | .623 |
| 1956[1] | New York | Casey Stengel | 97 | 57 | .630 |
| 1957 | New York | Casey Stengel | 98 | 56 | .636 |
| 1958[1] | New York | Casey Stengel | 92 | 62 | .597 |
| 1959 | Chicago | Al Lopez | 94 | 60 | .610 |
| 1960 | New York | Casey Stengel | 97 | 57 | .630 |
| 1961[1] | New York | Ralph Houk | 109 | 53 | .673 |
| 1962[1] | New York | Ralph Houk | 96 | 66 | .593 |
| 1963 | New York | Ralph Houk | 104 | 57 | .646 |
| 1964 | New York | Yogi Berra | 99 | 63 | .611 |
| 1965 | Minnesota | Sam Mele | 102 | 60 | .630 |
| 1966[1] | Baltimore | Hank Bauer | 97 | 63 | .606 |
| 1967 | Boston | Dick Williams | 92 | 70 | .568 |
| 1968[1] | Detroit | Mayo Smith | 103 | 59 | .636 |
| 1969 | Baltimore[3] | Earl Weaver | 109 | 53 | .673 |
| 1970[1] | Baltimore[3] | Earl Weaver | 108 | 54 | .667 |
| 1971 | Baltimore[4] | Earl Weaver | 101 | 57 | .639 |
| 1972[1] | Oakland[5] | Dick Williams | 93 | 62 | .600 |
| 1973[1] | Oakland[6] | Dick Williams | 94 | 68 | .580 |
| 1974[1] | Oakland[6] | Alvin Dark | 90 | 72 | .556 |
| 1975 | Boston[4] | Darrell Johnson | 95 | 65 | .594 |
| 1976 | New York[7] | Billy Martin | 97 | 62 | .610 |
| 1977[1] | New York[7] | Billy Martin | 100 | 62 | .617 |
| 1978 | New York[7] | Billy Martin and Bob Lemon | 100 | 63 | .613 |

1. World Series winner. 2. No World Series. 3. Defeated Minnesota, Western Division winner, in playoff. 4. Defeated Oakland, Western Division leader, in playoff. 5. Defeated Detroit, Eastern Division winner, in playoff. 6. Defeated Baltimore, Eastern Division winner, in playoff. 7. Defeated Kansas City, Western Division winner, in playoff.

## Ted Williams' Major League Batting Record

(All games with Boston Red Sox)

| | G | R | H | HR | RBI | Avg |
|---|---|---|---|---|---|---|
| 1939 | 149 | 131 | 185 | 31 | 145[1] | .327 |
| 1940 | 144 | 134[1] | 193 | 23 | 113 | .344 |
| 1941 | 143 | 135[1] | 185 | 37[1] | 120 | .406[1] |
| 1942 | 150 | 141[1] | 186 | 36[1] | 137[1] | .356[1] |
| 1946 | 150 | 142[1] | 176 | 38 | 123 | .342 |
| 1947 | 156 | 125[1] | 181 | 32[1] | 114[1] | .343[1] |
| 1948 | 137 | 124 | 188 | 25 | 127 | .369[1] |
| 1949 | 155 | 150[1] | 194 | 43[1] | 159[2] | .343 |
| 1950 | 89 | 82 | 106 | 28 | 97 | .317 |
| 1951 | 148 | 109 | 169 | 30 | 126 | .318 |
| 1952 | 6 | 2 | 4 | 1 | 3 | .400 |
| 1953 | 37 | 17 | 37 | 13 | 34 | .407 |
| 1954 | 117 | 93 | 133 | 29 | 89 | .345 |
| 1955 | 98 | 77 | 114 | 28 | 83 | .356 |
| 1956 | 136 | 71 | 138 | 24 | 82 | .345 |
| 1957 | 132 | 96 | 163 | 38 | 87 | .388[1] |
| 1958 | 129 | 81 | 135 | 26 | 85 | .328[1] |
| 1959 | 103 | 32 | 69 | 10 | 43 | .254 |
| 1960 | 113 | 56 | 98 | 29 | 72 | .316 |
| **Total** | **2292** | **1798** | **2654** | **521** | **1839** | **.344** |

1. Led league. 2. Tied for league lead.
NOTE: The years 1943–45 were spent in military service.

## NATIONAL LEAGUE PENNANT WINNERS

| Year | Club | Manager | Won | Lost | Pct |
|---|---|---|---|---|---|
| 1876 | Chicago | Albert G. Spalding | 52 | 14 | .788 |
| 1877 | Boston | Harry Wright | 31 | 17 | .646 |
| 1878 | Boston | Harry Wright | 41 | 19 | .683 |
| 1879 | Providence | George Wright | 55 | 23 | .705 |
| 1880 | Chicago | Adrian C. Anson | 67 | 17 | .798 |
| 1881 | Chicago | Adrian C. Anson | 56 | 28 | .667 |
| 1882 | Chicago | Adrian C. Anson | 55 | 29 | .655 |
| 1883 | Boston | John F. Morrill | 63 | 35 | .643 |
| 1884 | Providence | Frank C. Bancroft | 84 | 28 | .750 |
| 1885 | Chicago | Adrian C. Anson | 87 | 25 | .777 |
| 1886 | Chicago | Adrian C. Anson | 90 | 34 | .726 |
| 1887 | Detroit | W. H. Watkins | 79 | 45 | .637 |
| 1888 | New York | James J. Mutrie | 84 | 47 | .641 |
| 1889 | New York | James J. Mutrie | 83 | 43 | .659 |
| 1890 | Brooklyn | William H. McGunnigle | 86 | 43 | .667 |
| 1891 | Boston | Frank G. Selee | 87 | 51 | .630 |
| 1892 | Boston | Frank G. Selee | 102 | 48 | .680 |
| 1893 | Boston | Frank G. Selee | 86 | 44 | .662 |
| 1894 | Baltimore | Edward H. Hanlon | 89 | 39 | .695 |
| 1895 | Baltimore | Edward H. Hanlon | 87 | 43 | .669 |
| 1896 | Baltimore | Edward H. Hanlon | 90 | 39 | .698 |
| 1897 | Boston | Frank G. Selee | 93 | 39 | .705 |
| 1898 | Boston | Frank G. Selee | 102 | 47 | .685 |
| 1899 | Brooklyn | Edward H. Hanlon | 88 | 42 | .677 |
| 1900 | Brooklyn | Edward H. Hanlon | 82 | 54 | .603 |
| 1901 | Pittsburgh | Fred C. Clarke | 90 | 49 | .647 |
| 1902 | Pittsburgh | Fred C. Clarke | 103 | 36 | .741 |
| 1903 | Pittsburgh | Fred C. Clarke | 91 | 49 | .650 |
| 1904 | New York[2] | John J. McGraw | 106 | 47 | .693 |
| 1905 | New York[1] | John J. McGraw | 105 | 48 | .686 |
| 1906 | Chicago | Frank L. Chance | 116 | 36 | .763 |
| 1907 | Chicago[1] | Frank L. Chance | 107 | 45 | .704 |
| 1908 | Chicago[1] | Frank L. Chance | 99 | 55 | .643 |
| 1909 | Pittsburgh[1] | Fred C. Clarke | 110 | 42 | .724 |
| 1910 | Chicago | Frank L. Chance | 104 | 50 | .675 |
| 1911 | New York | John J. McGraw | 99 | 54 | .647 |
| 1912 | New York | John J. McGraw | 103 | 48 | .682 |
| 1913 | New York | John J. McGraw | 101 | 51 | .664 |
| 1914 | Boston[1] | George T. Stallings | 94 | 59 | .614 |
| 1915 | Philadelphia | Patrick J. Moran | 90 | 62 | .592 |
| 1916 | Brooklyn | Wilbert Robinson | 94 | 60 | .610 |
| 1917 | New York | John J. McGraw | 98 | 56 | .636 |
| 1918 | Chicago | Fred L. Mitchell | 84 | 45 | .651 |
| 1919 | Cincinnati[1] | Patrick J. Moran | 96 | 44 | .686 |
| 1920 | Brooklyn | Wilbert Robinson | 93 | 61 | .604 |
| 1921 | New York[1] | John J. McGraw | 94 | 59 | .614 |
| 1922 | New York[1] | John J. McGraw | 93 | 61 | .604 |
| 1923 | New York | John J. McGraw | 95 | 58 | .621 |
| 1924 | New York | John J. McGraw | 93 | 60 | .608 |
| 1925 | Pittsburgh[1] | William B. McKechnie | 95 | 58 | .621 |
| 1926 | St. Louis[1] | Rogers Hornsby | 89 | 65 | .578 |
| 1927 | Pittsburgh | Donie Bush | 94 | 60 | .610 |
| 1928 | St. Louis | William B. McKechnie | 95 | 59 | .617 |
| 1929 | Chicago | Joseph V. McCarthy | 98 | 54 | .645 |
| 1930 | St. Louis | Gabby Street | 92 | 62 | .597 |
| 1931 | St. Louis[1] | Gabby Street | 101 | 53 | .656 |
| 1932 | Chicago | Charles J. Grimm | 90 | 64 | .584 |
| 1933 | New York[1] | William H. Terry | 91 | 61 | .599 |
| 1934 | St. Louis[1] | Frank F. Frisch | 95 | 58 | .621 |
| 1935 | Chicago | Charles J. Grimm | 100 | 54 | .649 |
| 1936 | New York | William H. Terry | 92 | 62 | .597 |
| 1937 | New York | William H. Terry | 95 | 57 | .625 |
| 1938 | Chicago | Gabby Hartnett | 89 | 63 | .586 |
| 1939 | Cincinnati | William B. McKechnie | 97 | 57 | .630 |
| 1940 | Cincinnati[1] | William B. McKechnie | 100 | 53 | .654 |
| 1941 | Brooklyn | Leo E. Durocher | 100 | 54 | .649 |
| 1942 | St. Louis[1] | William H. Southworth | 106 | 48 | .688 |
| 1943 | St. Louis | William H. Southworth | 105 | 49 | .682 |
| 1944 | St. Louis[1] | William H. Southworth | 105 | 49 | .682 |
| 1945 | Chicago | Charles J. Grimm | 98 | 56 | .636 |
| 1946 | St. Louis[1] | Edwin H. Dyer | 98 | 58 | .628 |
| 1947 | Brooklyn | Burton E. Shotton | 94 | 60 | .610 |
| 1948 | Boston | William H. Southworth | 91 | 62 | .595 |
| 1949 | Brooklyn | Burton E. Shotton | 97 | 57 | .630 |
| 1950 | Philadelphia | Edwin M. Sawyer | 91 | 63 | .591 |
| 1951 | New York | Leo E. Durocher | 98 | 59 | .624 |
| 1952 | Brooklyn | Charles W. Dressen | 96 | 57 | .630 |
| 1953 | Brooklyn | Charles W. Dressen | 105 | 49 | .682 |
| 1954 | New York[1] | Leo E. Durocher | 97 | 57 | .630 |
| 1955 | Brooklyn[1] | Walter Alston | 98 | 55 | .641 |
| 1956 | Brooklyn | Walter Alston | 93 | 61 | .604 |
| 1957 | Milwaukee[1] | Fred Haney | 95 | 59 | .617 |
| 1958 | Milwaukee | Fred Haney | 92 | 62 | .597 |
| 1959 | Los Angeles[1] | Walter Alston | 88 | 68 | .564 |
| 1960 | Pittsburgh[1] | Danny Murtaugh | 95 | 59 | .617 |
| 1961 | Cincinnati | Fred Hutchinson | 93 | 61 | .604 |
| 1962 | San Francisco | Alvin Dark | 103 | 62 | .624 |
| 1963 | Los Angeles[1] | Walter Alston | 99 | 63 | .611 |
| 1964 | St. Louis[1] | Johnny Keane | 93 | 69 | .574 |
| 1965 | Los Angeles[1] | Walter Alston | 97 | 65 | .599 |
| 1966 | Los Angeles | Walter Alston | 95 | 67 | .586 |
| 1967 | St. Louis[1] | Red Schoendienst | 101 | 60 | .627 |
| 1968 | St. Louis | Red Schoendienst | 97 | 65 | .599 |
| 1969 | New York[1 3] | Gil Hodges | 100 | 62 | .617 |
| 1970 | Cincinnati[4] | Sparky Anderson | 102 | 60 | .630 |
| 1971 | Pittsburgh[1 5] | Danny Murtaugh | 97 | 65 | .599 |
| 1972 | Cincinnati | Sparky Anderson | 95 | 59 | .617 |
| 1973 | New York[6] | Yogi Berra | 82 | 79 | .509 |
| 1974 | Los Angeles[6] | Walter Alston | 102 | 60 | .630 |
| 1975 | Cincinnati[1 6] | Sparky Anderson | 108 | 54 | .667 |
| 1976 | Cincinnati[7] | Sparky Anderson | 102 | 60 | .630 |
| 1977 | Los Angeles[7] | Tom Lasorda | 98 | 64 | .605 |
| 1978 | Los Angeles[7] | Tom Lasorda | 95 | 67 | .586 |

1. World Series Winner. 2. No World Series. 3. Defeated Atlanta, Western Division winner, in playoff. 4. Defeated Pittsburgh, Eastern Division winner, in playoff. 5. Defeated San Francisco, Western Division winner in playoff. 6. Defeated Cincinnati, Western Division winner in playoff. 7. Defeated Philadelphia, Eastern Division winner, in playoff.

## MAJOR LEAGUE ALL-STAR GAME

| Year | Date | Winning league and manager | Runs | Losing league and manager | Runs | Winning pitcher | Losing pitcher | Site | Paid attendance |
|---|---|---|---|---|---|---|---|---|---|
| 1933 | July 6 | A.L. (Mack) | 4 | N.L. (McGraw) | 2 | Gomez | Hallahan | Chicago A.L. | 47,595 |
| 1934 | July 10 | A.L. (Cronin) | 9 | N.L. (Terry) | 7 | Harder | Mungo | New York N.L. | 48,363 |
| 1935 | July 8 | A.L. (Cochrane) | 4 | N.L. (Frisch) | 1 | Gomez | Walker | Cleveland A.L. | 69,831 |
| 1936 | July 7 | N.L. (Grimm) | 4 | A.L. (McCarthy) | 3 | J. Dean | Grove | Boston N.L. | 25,556 |
| 1937 | July 7 | A.L. (McCarthy) | 8 | N.L. (Terry) | 3 | Gomez | J. Dean | Washington A.L. | 31,391 |
| 1938 | July 6 | N.L. (Terry) | 4 | A.L. (McCarthy) | 1 | Vander Meer | Gomez | Cincinnati N.L. | 27,067 |
| 1939 | July 11 | A.L. (McCarthy) | 3 | N.L. (Hartnett) | 1 | Bridges | Lee | New York A.L. | 62,892 |
| 1940 | July 9 | N.L. (McKechnie) | 4 | A.L. (Cronin) | 0 | Derringer | Ruffing | St. Louis N.L. | 32,373 |
| 1941 | July 8 | A.L. (Baker) | 7 | N.L. (McKechnie) | 5 | E. Smith | Passeau | Detroit A.L. | 54,674 |

| Year | Date | Winning league and manager | Runs | Losing league and manager | Runs | Winning pitcher | Losing pitcher | Site | Paid attendance |
|---|---|---|---|---|---|---|---|---|---|
| 1942 | July 6 | A.L. (McCarthy) | 3 | N.L. (Durocher) | 1 | Chandler | Cooper | New York N.L. | 34,178 |
| 1943 | July 13[1] | A.L. (McCarthy) | 5 | N.L. (Southworth) | 3 | Leonard | Cooper | Philadelphia A.L. | 31,938 |
| 1944 | July 11[1] | N.L. (Southworth) | 7 | A.L. (McCarthy) | 1 | Raffensberger | Hughson | Pittsburgh N.L. | 29,589 |
| 1946 | July 9 | A.L. (O'Neill) | 12 | N.L. (Grimm) | 0 | Feller | Passeau | Boston A.L. | 34,906 |
| 1947 | July 8 | A.L. (Cronin) | 2 | N.L. (Dyer) | 1 | Shea | Sain | Chicago N.L. | 41,123 |
| 1948 | July 13 | A.L. (Harris) | 5 | N.L. (Durocher) | 2 | Raschi | Schmitz | St. Louis A.L. | 34,009 |
| 1949 | July 12 | A.L. (Boudreau) | 11 | N.L. (Southworth) | 7 | Trucks | Newcombe | Brooklyn N.L. | 32,577 |
| 1950 | July 11 | N.L. (Shotton) | 4 | A.L. (Stengel) | 3[3] | Blackwell | Gray | Chicago A.L. | 46,127 |
| 1951 | July 10 | N.L. (Sawyer) | 8 | A.L. (Stengel) | 3 | Maglie | Lopat | Detroit A.L. | 52,075 |
| 1952 | July 8 | N.L. (Durocher) | 3 | A.L. (Stengel) | 2[4] | Rush | Lemon | Philadelphia N.L. | 32,785 |
| 1953 | July 14 | N.L. (Dressen) | 5 | A.L. (Stengel) | 1 | Spahn | Reynolds | Cincinnati N.L. | 30,846 |
| 1954 | July 13 | A.L. (Stengel) | 11 | N.L. (Alston) | 9 | Stone | Conley | Cleveland A.L. | 68,751 |
| 1955 | July 12 | N.L. (Durocher) | 6 | A.L. (Lopez) | 5[5] | Conley | Sullivan | Milwaukee N.L. | 45,643 |
| 1956 | July 10 | N.L. (Alston) | 7 | A.L. (Stengel) | 3 | Friend | Pierce | Washington A.L. | 28,843 |
| 1957 | July 9 | A.L. (Stengel) | 6 | N.L. (Alston) | 5 | Bunning | Simmons | St. Louis N.L. | 30,693 |
| 1958 | July 8 | A.L. (Stengel) | 4 | N.L. (Haney) | 3 | Wynn | Friend | Baltimore A.L. | 48,829 |
| 1959[2] | July 7 | N.L. (Haney) | 5 | A.L. (Stengel) | 4 | Antonelli | Ford | Pittsburgh N.L. | 35,277 |
| | Aug. 3 | A.L. (Stengel) | 5 | N.L. (Haney) | 3 | Walker | Drysdale | Los Angeles N.L. | 55,105 |
| 1960[1] | July 11 | N.L. (Alston) | 5 | A.L. (Lopez) | 3 | Friend | Monbouquette | Kansas City A.L. | 30,619 |
| | July 13 | N.L. (Alston) | 6 | A.L. (Lopez) | 0 | Law | Ford | New York A.L. | 38,362 |
| 1961[2] | July 11 | N.L. (Murtaugh) | 5 | A.L. (Richards) | 4[6] | Miller | Wilhelm | San Francisco N.L. | 44,115 |
| | July 31 | N.L. (Murtaugh) | 1 | A.L. (Richards) | 1[7] | — | — | Boston A.L. | 31,851 |
| 1962[2] | July 10 | N.L. (Hutchinson) | 3 | A.L. (Houk) | 1 | Marichal | Pascual | Washington A.L. | 45,480 |
| | July 30 | A.L. (Houk) | 9 | N.L. (Hutchinson) | 4 | Herbert | Mahaffey | Chicago N.L. | 38,359 |
| 1963 | July 9 | N.L. (Dark) | 5 | A.L. (Houk) | 3 | Jackson | Bunning | Cleveland A.L. | 44,160 |
| 1964 | July 7 | N.L. (Alston) | 7 | A.L. (Lopez) | 4 | Marichal | Radatz | New York N.L. | 50,850 |
| 1965 | July 13 | N.L. (March) | 6 | A.L. (Lopez) | 5 | Koufax | McDowell | Minnesota A.L. | 46,706 |
| 1966 | July 12 | N.L. (Alston) | 2 | A.L. (Mele) | 1[6] | Perry | Richert | St. Louis N.L. | 49,926 |
| 1967 | July 11 | N.L. (Alston) | 2 | A.L. (Bauer) | 1[8] | Drysdale | Hunter | Anaheim A.L. | 46,309 |
| 1968 | July 9 | N.L. (Schoendienst) | 1 | A.L. (Williams) | 0 | Drysdale | Tiant | Houston N.L. | 48,321 |
| 1969 | July 23 | N.L. (Schoendienst) | 9 | A.L. (M. Smith) | 3 | Carlton | Stottlemyre | Washington A.L. | 45,259 |
| 1970 | July 14 | N.L. (Hodges) | 5 | A.L. (Weaver) | 4[5] | Osteen | Wright | Cincinnati N.L. | 51,838 |
| 1971 | July 13 | A.L. (Weaver) | 6 | N.L. (Anderson) | 4 | Blue | Ellis | Detroit A.L. | 53,559 |
| 1972 | July 25 | N.L. (Murtaugh) | 4 | A.L. (Weaver) | 3[6] | McGraw | McNally | Atlanta N.L. | 53,107 |
| 1973 | July 24[1] | N.L. (Anderson) | 7 | A.L. (Williams) | 1 | Wise | Blyleven | Kansas City A.L. | 40,849 |
| 1974 | July 23[1] | N.L. (Berra) | 7 | A.L. (Williams) | 2 | Brett | Tiant | Pittsburgh N.L. | 50,706 |
| 1975 | July 15[1] | N.L. (Dark) | 6 | A.L. (Alston) | 3 | Matlack | Hunter | Milwaukee A.L. | 51,540 |
| 1976 | July 13 | N.L. (Anderson) | 7 | A.L. (D. Johnson) | 1 | Fidrych | R. Jones | Philadelphia N.L. | 63,974 |
| 1977 | July 19[1] | N.L. (Anderson) | 7 | A.L. (Martin) | 5 | Sutton | Palmer | New York A.L. | 56,683 |
| 1978 | July 11[1] | N.L. (Lasorda) | 7 | A.L. (Martin) | 3 | Sutter | Gossage | San Diego N.L. | 51,549 |

1. Night game. 2. Two games. 3. Fourteen innings. 4. Five innings, rain. 5. Twelve innings. 6. Ten innings. 7. Called because of rain after nine innings. 8. Fifteen innings. NOTE: No game in 1945.

## MICKEY MANTLE'S MAJOR LEAGUE BATTING RECORD

(All games with New York Yankees)

| | G | R | H | HR | RBI | Avg | | G | R | H | HR | RBI | Avg | | G | R | H | HR | RBI | Avg |
|---|---|---|---|---|---|---|---|---|---|---|---|---|---|---|---|---|---|---|---|---|
| 1951 | 96 | 61 | 91 | 13 | 65 | .267 | 1958 | 150 | 127[1] | 158 | 42[1] | 97 | .304 | 1965 | 122 | 44 | 92 | 19 | 46 | .255 |
| 1952 | 142 | 94 | 171 | 23 | 87 | .311 | 1959 | 144 | 104 | 154 | 31 | 75 | .285 | 1966 | 108 | 40 | 96 | 23 | 56 | .288 |
| 1953 | 127 | 105 | 136 | 21 | 92 | .295 | 1960 | 153 | 119[1] | 145 | 40[1] | 94 | .275 | 1967 | 144 | 63 | 108 | 22 | 55 | .245 |
| 1954 | 146 | 129[1] | 163 | 27 | 102 | .300 | 1961 | 153 | 132[1] | 163 | 54 | 128 | .317 | 1968 | 144 | 57 | 103 | 18 | 54 | .237 |
| 1955 | 147 | 121 | 158 | 37[1] | 99 | .306 | 1962 | 123 | 96 | 121 | 30 | 89 | .321 | **Total** | **2401** | **1677** | **2415** | **536** | **1509** | **.298** |
| 1956 | 150 | 132[1] | 188 | 52[1] | 130[1] | .353[1] | 1963 | 65 | 40 | 54 | 15 | 35 | .314 | | | | | | | |
| 1957 | 144 | 121[1] | 173 | 34 | 94 | .365 | 1964 | 143 | 92 | 141 | 35 | 111 | .303 | | | | | | | |

1. Led league.

**World Series Record**

| | G | R | H | HR | RBI | Avg | | G | R | H | HR | RBI | Avg | | G | R | H | HR | RBI | Avg |
|---|---|---|---|---|---|---|---|---|---|---|---|---|---|---|---|---|---|---|---|---|
| 1951 | 2 | 1 | 1 | 0 | 0 | .200 | 1957 | 6 | 3 | 5 | 1 | 2 | .263 | 1963 | 4 | 1 | 2 | 1 | 1 | .133 |
| 1952 | 7 | 5 | 10 | 2 | 3 | .345 | 1958 | 7 | 4 | 6 | 2 | 3 | .250 | 1964 | 7 | 8 | 8 | 3 | 8 | .333 |
| 1953 | 6 | 3 | 5 | 2 | 7 | .208 | 1960 | 7 | 8 | 10 | 3 | 11 | .400 | **Total** | **65** | **42[1]** | **59** | **18[1]** | **40[1]** | **.257** |
| 1955 | 3 | 1 | 2 | 1 | 1 | .200 | 1961 | 2 | 0 | 1 | 0 | 0 | .167 | | | | | | | |
| 1956 | 7 | 6 | 6 | 3 | 4 | .250 | 1962 | 7 | 2 | 3 | 0 | 0 | .120 | | | | | | | |

1. Series record.

Mantle also holds World Series records for most long hits (26), most total bases (123), most strikeouts (54), most bases on balls (43), and most games played by an outfielder (63).

# NATIONAL BASEBALL HALL OF FAME

Cooperstown, N.Y.

### Fielders

| Member | Active years | Member | Active years | Member | Active years |
|---|---|---|---|---|---|
| Anson, Adrian | 1876–1897 | Dihigo, Martin[1] | 1923–1945 | Mantle, Mickey | 1951–1968 |
| Appling, Lucius | 1930–1950 | DiMaggio, Joseph | 1936–1951 | Manush, Henry | 1923–1939 |
| Averill, H. Earl | 1929–1941 | Duffy, Hugh | 1888–1906 | Maranville, Walter | 1912–1935 |
| Baker, J. Frank | 1908–1922 | Evers, John | 1902–1919 | Mathews, Edwin | 1952–1968 |
| Bancroft, David | 1915–1930 | Ewing, William | 1880–1897 | McCarthy, Thomas | 1884–1896 |
| Banks, Ernest | 1953–1971 | Flick, Elmer | 1898–1910 | McGraw, John J. | 1891–1906 |
| Beckley, Jacob | 1888–1907 | Foxx, James | 1925–1945 | Medwick, Joseph | 1932–1948 |
| Bell, James[1] | 1920–1947 | Frisch, Frank | 1919–1937 | Musial, Stanley | 1941–1963 |
| Berra, Lawrence | 1946–1965 | Gehrig, H. Louis | 1923–1939 | O'Rourke, James | 1876–1894 |
| Bottomley, James | 1922–1937 | Gehringer, Charles | 1924–1942 | Ott, Melvin | 1926–1947 |
| Boudreau, Louis | 1938–1952 | Gibson, Josh[1] | 1929–1946 | Rice, Edgar | 1915–1934 |
| Bresnahan, Roger | 1897–1915 | Goslin, Leon | 1921–1938 | Robinson, Jack | 1947–1956 |
| Brouthers, Dennis | 1879–1896 | Greenberg, Henry | 1933–1947 | Robinson, Wilbert | 1886–1902 |
| Burkett, Jesse | 1890–1905 | Hafey, Charles | 1924–1937 | Roush, Edd | 1913–1931 |
| Campanella, Roy | 1948–1957 | Hamilton, William | 1888–1901 | Ruth, George (Babe) | 1914–1935 |
| Carey, Max | 1910–1929 | Hartnett, Charles | 1922–1941 | Schalk, Raymond | 1912–1929 |
| Chance, Frank | 1898–1914 | Heilmann, Harry | 1914–1932 | Sewell, Joseph | 1920–1933 |
| Charleston, Oscar[1] | 1915–1954 | Herman, William | 1931–1947 | Simmons, Al | 1924–1944 |
| Clarke, Fred | 1894–1915 | Hooper, Harry | 1909–1925 | Sisler, George | 1915–1930 |
| Clemente, Roberto | 1955–1972 | Hornsby, Rogers | 1915–1937 | Speaker, Tristram | 1907–1928 |
| Cobb, Tyrus | 1905–1928 | Irvin, Monford M.[1] | 1939–1956 | Terry, William | 1923–1936 |
| Cochrane, Gordon | 1925–1937 | Hugh Jennings | 1891–1918 | Thompson, Samuel | 1885–1906 |
| Collins, Edward | 1906–1930 | Johnson, William[1] | 1921–1937 | Tinker, Joseph | 1902–1916 |
| Collins, James | 1895–1908 | Keeler, William | 1892–1910 | Traynor, Harold | 1920–1937 |
| Comiskey, Charles | 1882–1894 | Kelley, Joseph | 1891–1908 | Wagner, John | 1897–1917 |
| Combs, Earle | 1924–1935 | Kelly, George | 1915–1932 | Wallace, Roderick | 1894–1918 |
| Connor, Roger | 1880–1897 | Kelly, Michael | 1878–1893 | Waner, Lloyd | 1927–1945 |
| Crawford, Samuel | 1899–1917 | Kiner, Ralph | 1946–1955 | Waner, Paul | 1926–1945 |
| Cronin, Joseph | 1926–1945 | Lajoie, Napoleon | 1896–1916 | Ward, John | 1878–1894 |
| Cuyler, Hazen | 1921–1938 | Leonard, Walter[1] | 1933–1955 | Wheat, Zachariah | 1909–1927 |
| Delahanty, Edward | 1888–1903 | Lindstrom, Frederick | 1924–1936 | Williams, Theodore | 1939–1960 |
| Dickey, William | 1928–1946 | Lloyd, John Henry[1] | 1905–1931 | Youngs, Ross | 1917–1926 |

### Pitchers

| Member | Active years | Member | Active years | Member | Active years |
|---|---|---|---|---|---|
| Alexander, Grover | 1911–1930 | Haines, Jesse | 1918–1937 | Plank, Edward | 1901–1917 |
| Bender, Charles | 1903–1925 | Hoyt, Waite | 1918–1938 | Radbourne, Charles | 1880–1891 |
| Brown, Mordecai | 1903–1916 | Hubbell, Carl | 1928–1943 | Rixey, Eppa | 1912–1933 |
| Chesbro, John | 1899–1909 | Johnson, Walter | 1907–1927 | Roberts, Robin | 1948–1966 |
| Clarkson, John | 1882–1894 | Joss, Adrian | 1902–1910 | Ruffing, Charles | 1924–1947 |
| Coveleski, Stanley | 1912–1928 | Keefe, Timothy | 1880–1893 | Rusie, Amos | 1889–1901 |
| Dean, Jerome | 1930–1947 | Koufax, Sanford | 1955–1966 | Ruth, George | 1914–1933 |
| Faber, Urban | 1914–1933 | Lemon, Robert | 1946–1958 | Spahn, Warren | 1942–1965 |
| Feller, Robert | 1936–1956 | Lyons, Theodore | 1923–1946 | Vance, Arthur | 1915–1935 |
| Ford, Edward | 1950–1967 | Marquard, Richard | 1908–1925 | Waddell, George | 1897–1910 |
| Galvin, James | 1876–1892 | Mathewson, Christopher | 1900–1916 | Walsh, Edward | 1904–1917 |
| Gomez, Vernon | 1930–1943 | McGinnity, Joseph | 1899–1908 | Welch, Michael | 1880–1892 |
| Griffith, Clark | 1891–1914 | Nichols, Charles | 1890–1906 | Wynn, Early | 1939–1963 |
| Grimes, Burleigh | 1916–1934 | Paige, LeRoy (Satchel)[1] | 1926–1965 | Young, Denton | 1890–1911 |
| Grove, Robert | 1925–1941 | Pennock, Herbert | 1912–1934 | | |

### Officials and Others

| Member | Position | Member | Position |
|---|---|---|---|
| Barrow, Edward | Manager-Executive | Landis, Kenesaw M. | Commissioner |
| Bulkeley, Morgan G. | Executive | Lopez, Alfonso R. | Player-Manager |
| Cartwright, Alexander | Executive | Mack, Connie | Manager-Executive |
| Chadwick, Henry | Writer-Statistician | MacPhail, Leland S. | Executive |
| Conlan, John | Umpire | McCarthy, Joseph V. | Manager |
| Connolly, Thomas | Umpire | McKechnie, William B. | Manager |
| Cummings, William A. | Early Pitcher | Rickey, W. Branch | Manager-Executive |
| Evans, William G. | Umpire-Executive | Spalding, Albert G. | Early Player |
| Frick, Ford C. | Commissioner-Executive | Stengel, Charles D. | Player-Manager |
| Harridge, William | Executive | Weiss, George M. | Executive |
| Harris, Stanley R. | Player-Manager | Wright, George | Early Player |
| Hubbard, R. Calvin | Umpire | Wright, Harry | Manager |
| Huggins, Miller J. | Manager | | |
| Johnson, B. Bancroft | Executive | | |
| Klem, William | Umpire | | |

1. Negro League player selected by special committee.

## MOST VALUABLE PLAYERS

(Baseball Writers Association selections)

### American League

1931 Lefty Grove, Philadelphia
1932–33 Jimmy Foxx, Philadelphia
1934 Mickey Cochrane, Detroit
1935 Hank Greenberg, Detroit
1936 Lou Gehrig, New York
1937 Charley Gehringer, Detroit
1938 Jimmy Foxx, Boston
1939 Joe DiMaggio, New York
1940 Hank Greenberg, Detroit
1941 Joe DiMaggio, New York
1942 Joe Gordon, New York
1943 Spurgeon Chandler, New York
1944–45 Hal Newhouser, Detroit
1946 Ted Williams, Boston
1947 Joe DiMaggio, New York
1948 Lou Boudreau, Cleveland
1949 Ted Williams, Boston
1950 Phil Rizzuto, New York
1951 Yogi Berra, New York
1952 Bobby Shantz, Philadelphia
1953 Al Rosen, Cleveland
1954–55 Yogi Berra, New York
1956–57 Mickey Mantle, New York
1958 Jackie Jensen, Boston
1959 Nellie Fox, Chicago
1960–61 Roger Maris, New York
1962 Mickey Mantle, New York
1963 Elston Howard, New York
1964 Brooks Robinson, Baltimore
1965 Zoilo Versalles, Minnesota
1966 Frank Robinson, Baltimore
1967 Carl Yastrzemski, Boston
1968 Dennis McLain, Detroit
1969 Harmon Killebrew, Minnesota
1970 John (Boog) Powell, Baltimore
1971 Vida Blue, Oakland
1972 Dick Allen, Chicago
1973 Reggie Jackson, Oakland
1974 Jeff Burroughs, Texas
1975 Fred Lynn, Boston
1976 Thurman Munson, New York
1977 Rod Carew, Minnesota

### National League

1931 Frank Frisch, St. Louis
1932 Chuck Klein, Philadelphia
1933 Carl Hubbell, New York
1934 Dizzy Dean, St. Louis
1935 Gabby Hartnett, Chicago
1936 Carl Hubbell, New York
1937 Joe Medwick, St. Louis
1938 Ernie Lombardi, Cincinnati
1939 Bucky Walters, Cincinnati
1940 Frank McCormick, Cincinnati
1941 Dolph Camilli, Brooklyn
1942 Mort Cooper, St. Louis
1943 Stan Musial, St. Louis
1944 Marty Marion, St. Louis
1945 Phil Cavarretta, Chicago
1946 Stan Musial, St. Louis
1947 Bob Elliott, Boston
1948 Stan Musial, St. Louis
1949 Jackie Robinson, Brooklyn
1950 Jim Konstanty, Philadelphia
1951 Roy Campanella, Brooklyn
1952 Hank Sauer, Chicago
1953 Roy Campanella, Brooklyn
1954 Willie Mays, New York
1955 Roy Campanella, Brooklyn
1956 Don Newcombe, Brooklyn
1957 Henry Aaron, Milwaukee
1958–59 Ernie Banks, Chicago
1960 Dick Groat, Pittsburgh
1961 Frank Robinson, Cincinnati
1962 Maury Wills, Los Angeles
1963 Sandy Koufax, Los Angeles
1964 Ken Boyer, St. Louis
1965 Willie Mays, San Francisco
1966 Roberto Clemente, Pittsburgh
1967 Orlando Cepeda, St. Louis
1968 Bob Gibson, St. Louis
1969 Willie McCovey, San Francisco
1970 Johnny Bench, Cincinnati
1971 Joe Torre, St. Louis
1972 Johnny Bench, Cincinnati
1973 Pete Rose, Cincinnati
1974 Steve Garvey, Los Angeles
1975–76 Joe Morgan, Cincinnati
1977 George Foster, Cincinnati

## CY YOUNG AWARD

1956 Don Newcombe, Brooklyn N.L.
1957 Warren Spahn, Milwaukee N.L.
1958 Bob Turley, New York A.L.
1959 Early Wynn, Chicago A.L.
1960 Vernon Law, Pittsburgh, N.L.
1961 Whitey Ford, New York A.L.
1962 Don Drysdale, Los Angeles N.L.
1963 Sandy Koufax, Los Angeles N.L.
1964 Dean Chance, Los Angeles A.L.
1965 Sandy Koufax, Los Angeles N.L.
1966 Sandy Koufax, Los Angeles N.L.
1967 Jim Lonborg, Boston A.L.; Mike McCormick, San Francisco N.L.
1968 Dennis McLain, Detroit A.L.; Bob Gibson, St. Louis N.L.
1969 Mike Cuellar, Baltimore, and Dennis McLain, Detroit, tied in A.L.; Tom Seaver, N.Y. N.L.
1970 Jim Perry, Minnesota A.L.; Bob Gibson, St. Louis N.L.
1971 Vida Blue, Oakland A.L.; Ferguson Jenkins, Chi. N.L.
1972 Gaylord Perry, Cleveland A.L.; Steve Carlton, Phila. N.L.
1973 Jim Palmer, Baltimore A.L.; Tom Seaver, New York N.L.
1974 Catfish Hunter, Oakland A.L.; Mike Marshall, Los Angeles N.L.
1975 Jim Palmer, Baltimore A.L.; Tom Seaver, New York N.L.
1976 Jim Palmer, Baltimore A.L.; Randy Jones, San Diego N.L.
1977 Sparky Lyle, N.Y., A.L.; Steve Carlton, Phila., N.L.

## ROOKIE OF THE YEAR

(Baseball Writers Association selections)

### American League

1949 Roy Sievers, St. Louis
1950 Walt Dropo, Boston
1951 Gil McDougald, New York
1952 Harry Byrd, Philadelphia
1953 Harvey Kuenn, Detroit
1954 Bob Grim, New York
1955 Herb Score, Cleveland
1956 Luis Aparicio, Chicago
1957 Tony Kubek, New York
1958 Albie Pearson, Washington
1959 William Allison, Washington
1960 Ron Hansen, Baltimore
1961 Don Schwall, Boston
1962 Tom Tresh, New York
1963 Gary Peters, Chicago
1964 Tony Oliva, Minnesota
1965 Curt Blefary, Baltimore
1966 Tommy Agee, Chicago
1967 Rod Carew, Minnesota
1968 Stan Bahnsen, New York
1969 Lou Piniella, Kansas City
1970 Thurman Munson, New York
1971 Chris Chambliss, Cleveland
1972 Carlton Fisk, Boston
1973 Alonzo Bumbry, Baltimore
1974 Mike Hargrove, Texas
1975 Fred Lynn, Boston
1976 Mark Fidrych, Detroit
1977 Eddie Murray, Baltimore

### National League

1949 Don Newcombe, Brooklyn
1950 Sam Jethroe, Boston
1951 Willie Mays, New York
1952 Joe Black, Brooklyn
1953 Jim Gilliam, Brooklyn
1954 Wally Moon, St. Louis
1955 Bill Virdon, St. Louis
1956 Frank Robinson, Cincinnati
1957 Jack Sanford, Philadelphia
1958 Orlando Cepeda, San Francisco
1959 Willie McCovey, San Francisco
1960 Frank Howard, Los Angeles
1961 Billy Williams, Chicago
1962 Ken Hubbs, Chicago
1963 Pete Rose, Cincinnati
1964 Richie Allen, Philadelphia
1965 Jim Lefebvre, Los Angeles
1966 Tommy Helms, Cincinnati
1967 Tom Seaver, New York
1968 Johnny Bench, Cincinnati
1969 Ted Sizemore, Los Angeles
1970 Carl Morton, Montreal
1971 Earl Williams, Atlanta
1972 Jon Matlack, New York
1973 Gary Matthews, San Francisco
1974 Bake McBride, St. Louis
1975 John Montefusco, San Francisco
1976 Patrick Zachry, Cincinnati
1977 Andre Dawson, Montreal

# MAJOR LEAGUE LIFETIME RECORDS

*Source:* The Book of Baseball Records, published and copyrighted by Seymour Siwoff, New York, N.Y. 10036.

## Leading Batters

(Over 2,000 Hits)

| | Years | At bat | Hits | Avg. |
|---|---|---|---|---|
| Ty Cobb | 24 | 11,429 | 4,191 | .367 |
| Rogers Hornsby | 23 | 8,173 | 2,930 | .358 |
| Ed Delahanty | 16 | 7,493 | 2,593 | .346 |
| Dan Brouthers | 19 | 6,737 | 2,347 | .348 |
| Willie Keeler | 19 | 8,564 | 2,955 | .345 |
| Ted Williams | 19 | 7,706 | 2,654 | .344 |
| Tris Speaker | 22 | 10,208 | 3,515 | .344 |
| Billy Hamilton | 14 | 6,262 | 2,157 | .344 |
| Harry Heilmann | 17 | 7,787 | 2,660 | .342 |
| Babe Ruth | 22 | 8,399 | 2,873 | .342 |
| Jesse Burkett | 16 | 8,389 | 2,872 | .342 |
| Bill Terry | 14 | 6,428 | 2,193 | .341 |
| Lou Gehrig | 17 | 8,001 | 2,721 | .340 |
| George Sisler | 16 | 8,267 | 2,812 | .340 |
| Nap Lajoie | 21 | 9,589 | 3,251 | .339 |
| Cap Anson | 22 | 9,084 | 3,081 | .339 |
| Sam Thompson | 15 | 6,005 | 2,016 | .336 |
| Al Simmons | 20 | 8,761 | 2,927 | .334 |
| Rod Carew | 12 | 6,235 | 2,082 | .334 |
| Eddie Collins | 25 | 9,952 | 3,313 | .333 |
| Paul Waner | 20 | 9,459 | 3,152 | .333 |
| Stan Musial | 22 | 10,972 | 3,630 | .331 |
| Heinie Manush | 17 | 7,653 | 2,524 | .330 |
| Hugh Duffy | 17 | 6,999 | 2,307 | .330 |
| Honus Wagner | 21 | 10,427 | 3,430 | .329 |
| Joe DiMaggio | 13 | 6,821 | 2,214 | .325 |
| Jimmy Foxx | 20 | 8,134 | 2,646 | .325 |

## Leading Pitchers

(Over 250 Victories)

| | Years | W | L | Pct. |
|---|---|---|---|---|
| Cy Young | 22 | 511 | 315 | .619 |
| Walter Johnson | 21 | 416 | 279 | .599 |
| Grover Alexander | 20 | 373 | 208 | .642 |
| Christy Mathewson | 17 | 373 | 188 | .665 |
| James Galvin | 15 | 365 | 309 | .542 |
| Warren Spahn | 21 | 363 | 245 | .597 |
| Charles Nichols | 15 | 360 | 202 | .641 |
| Tim Keefe | 14 | 346 | 225 | .606 |
| John Clarkson | 12 | 328 | 175 | .652 |
| Eddie Plank | 17 | 325 | 190 | .631 |
| Mickey Welch | 13 | 316 | 214 | .596 |
| Hoss Radbourne | 11 | 308 | 191 | .617 |
| Lefty Grove | 20 | 300 | 141 | .680 |
| Early Wynn | 23 | 300 | 244 | .551 |
| Robin Roberts | 19 | 286 | 245 | .539 |
| Tony Mullane | 14 | 282 | 221 | .561 |
| Red Ruffing | 22 | 273 | 225 | .548 |
| Burleigh Grimes | 19 | 270 | 212 | .560 |
| Gaylord Perry | 17 | 267 | 206 | .594 |
| Bob Feller | 18 | 266 | 162 | .621 |
| Eppa Rixey | 21 | 266 | 251 | .515 |
| Gus Weyhing | 14 | 265 | 236 | .529 |
| Jim McCormick | 10 | 264 | 217 | .549 |
| Jim Kaat | 20 | 261 | 217 | .545 |
| Ted Lyons | 21 | 260 | 230 | .531 |
| Carl Hubbell | 16 | 253 | 154 | .622 |
| Red Faber | 20 | 254 | 212 | .545 |

# HOME RUN RECORDS OF HENRY AARON AND BABE RUTH

Henry Aaron broke Babe Ruth's career home run record, April 8, 1974, by hitting the ball over the left-center field fence at Atlanta for his 715th homer. He had tied Ruth's mark, April 4, at Cincinnati. Aaron, of the Atlanta Braves, hit 20 homers during the 1974 season, raising the mark to 733. Playing for Milwaukee, he added 22 in the next two seasons for a 755 total. He made 3,771 hits and scored 2,174 runs.

## HENRY AARON'S RECORD

| Year | Club | HR | Year | Club | HR |
|---|---|---|---|---|---|
| 1954 | Milwaukee (NL) | 13 | 1968 | Atlanta (NL) | 29 |
| 1955 | Milwaukee (NL) | 27 | 1969 | Atlanta (NL) | 44 |
| 1956 | Milwaukee (NL) | 26 | 1970 | Atlanta (NL) | 38 |
| 1957 | Milwaukee (NL) | 44 | 1971 | Atlanta (NL) | 47 |
| 1958 | Milwaukee (NL) | 30 | 1972 | Atlanta (NL) | 34 |
| 1959 | Milwaukee (NL) | 39 | 1973 | Atlanta (NL) | 40 |
| 1960 | Milwaukee (NL) | 40 | 1974 | Atlanta (NL) | 20 |
| 1961 | Milwaukee (NL) | 34 | 1975 | Milwaukee (AL) | 12 |
| 1962 | Milwaukee (NL) | 45 | 1976 | Milwaukee (AL) | 10 |
| 1963 | Milwaukee (NL) | 44 | | | |
| 1964 | Milwaukee (NL) | 24 | | | |
| 1965 | Milwaukee (NL) | 32 | | | |
| 1966 | Atlanta (NL) | 44 | | | |
| 1967 | Atlanta (NL) | 39 | | | |

### Totals

| | |
|---|---|
| Regular Season | 755 |
| World Series | 2 |
| Playoff Games | 3 |
| All-Star Games | 2 |
| | 762 |

Aaron also set numerous other major league records as well as National League marks. They include:

### Major League Records

| | |
|---|---|
| Most games | 3,298 |
| Most times at bat | 12,364 |
| Most runs batted in | 2,297 |
| Total bases | 6,856 |
| Most extra-base hits | 1,475 |

### National League Records

| | |
|---|---|
| Most runs | 2,107 |
| Most games | 2,503 |
| Most times at bat | 8,399 |

## BABE RUTH'S RECORD

| Year | Club | HR |
|---|---|---|
| 1914 | Boston (AL) | 0 |
| 1915 | Boston (AL) | 4 |
| 1916 | Boston (AL) | 3 |
| 1917 | Boston (AL) | 2 |
| 1918 | Boston (AL) | 11 |
| 1919 | Boston (AL) | 29 |
| 1920 | New York (AL) | 54 |
| 1921 | New York (AL) | 59 |
| 1922 | New York (AL) | 35 |
| 1923 | New York (AL) | 41 |
| 1924 | New York (AL) | 46 |
| 1925 | New York (AL) | 25 |
| 1926 | New York (AL) | 47 |
| 1927 | New York (AL) | 60 |
| 1928 | New York (AL) | 54 |
| 1929 | New York (AL) | 46 |
| 1930 | New York (AL) | 49 |
| 1931 | New York (AL) | 46 |
| 1932 | New York (AL) | 41 |
| 1933 | New York (AL) | 34 |
| 1934 | New York (AL) | 22 |
| 1935 | Boston (NL) | 6 |

### World Series

| | | |
|---|---|---|
| 1915 | Boston (AL) | 0 |
| 1916 | Boston (AL) | 0 |
| 1918 | Boston (AL) | 0 |
| 1921 | New York (AL) | 1 |
| 1922 | New York (AL) | 0 |
| 1923 | New York (AL) | 3 |
| 1926 | New York (AL) | 4 |
| 1927 | New York (AL) | 2 |
| 1928 | New York (AL) | 3 |
| 1932 | New York (AL) | 2 |

### Totals

| | |
|---|---|
| Regular season | 714 |
| World Series | 15 |
| All-Star | 1 |

(Ruth was a pitcher mainly until 1918, when he also played outfield. That was the first year he appeared at bat over 150 times. He became a regular outfielder in 1919.)

## MAJOR LEAGUE INDIVIDUAL ALL-TIME RECORDS

Highest Batting Average—.438, Hugh Duffy, Boston N.L., 1894 (Since 1900—.424, Rogers Hornsby, St. Louis N.L., 1924.)
Most Times at Bat—12,364, Henry Aaron, Milwaukee N.L., 1954–65; Atlanta N.L., 1966–74; Milwaukee A.L., 1975–76.
Most Years Batted .300 or Better—23, Ty Cobb, Detroit A.L., 1906–26, Philadelphia A.L., 1927–28.
Most hits—4,191, Ty Cobb, Detroit A.L., 1905–26, Philadelphia A.L., 1927–28.
Most Hits, Season—257, George Sisler, St. Louis A.L., 1920.
Most Hits, Game (9 innings)—7, Wilbert Robinson, Baltimore N.L., 6 singles, 1 double, 1892. Rennie Stennett, Pittsburgh N.L., 4 singles, 2 doubles, 1 triple, 1975.
Most Hits, Game (extra innings)—9, John Burnett, Cleveland A.L., 18 innings, 7 singles, 2 doubles, 1932.
Most Hits in Succession—12, Mike Higgins, Boston A.L., in four games, 1938; Walt Dropo, Detroit A.L., in three games, 1952.
Most Consecutive Games Batted Safely—56, Joe DiMaggio, New York A.L., 1941.
Most Runs—2,244, Ty Cobb, Detroit A.L., 1905–26, Philadelphia A.L., 1927–28.
Most Runs, Season—196, William Hamilton, Philadelphia N.L., 1894. (Since 1900—177, Babe Ruth, New York A.L., 1921.)
Most Runs, Game—7, Guy Hecker, Louisville A.A., 1886. (Since 1900—6, by Mel Ott, New York N.L., 1934, 1944; Johnny Pesky, Boston A.L., 1946; Frank Torre, Milwaukee N.L., 1957.)
Most Runs Batted In—2,297, Henry Aaron, Milwaukee N.L., 1954–1965; Atlanta N.L., 1966–74; Milwaukee A.L., 1975–76.
Most Runs Batted in, Season—190, Hack Wilson, Chicago N.L., 1930.
Most Runs Batted In, Game—12, Jim Bottomley, St. Louis N.L., 1924.
Most Home Runs—755, Henry Aaron, Milwaukee N.L., 1954–1965; Atlanta N.L., 1966–74; Milwaukee A.L., 1975–76.
Most Home Runs, Season—61, Roger Maris, New York A.L., 1961 (162-game season); 60, Babe Ruth, New York A.L., 1927 (154-game season)
Most Home Runs, Game—4 (see table on page 968).
Most Home Runs with Bases Filled—23, Lou Gehrig, New York A.L., 1927–39.
Most 2-Base Hits—793, Tris Speaker, Boston A.L., 1907–15, Cleveland A.L., 1916–26, Washington A.L., 1927, Philadelphia A.L., 1928.
Most 2-Base Hits, Season—67, Earl Webb, Boston A.L., 1931.
Most 2-base Hits, Game—4, by many.
Most 3-Base Hits—312, Sam Crawford, Cincinnati N.L., 1899–1902, Detroit A.L., 1903–17.
Most 3-Base Hits, Season—36, Owen Wilson, Pittsburgh N.L., 1912.
Most 3-Base Hits, Game—4, George Strief, Philadelphia A.A., 1885; William Joyce, New York N.L., 1897. (Since 1900—3, by many.)
Most Games Played—3,218. Henry Aaron, Milwaukee N.L., 1954–1965; Atlanta, N.L., 1966–74; Milwaukee A.L., 1975–76.
Most Consecutive Games Played—2,130, Lou Gehrig, New York A.L., 1925–39.
Most Bases on Balls—2,056, Babe Ruth, Boston A.L., 1914–19; New York A.L., 1920–34, Boston N.L., 1935.
Most Bases on Balls, Season—170, Babe Ruth, New York A.L., 1923.
Most Bases on Balls, Game—6, Walter Wilmot, Chicago N.L., 1891; Jimmy Foxx, Boston A.L., 1938.
Most Strikeouts—1,710, Mickey Mantle, New York A.L., 1951–68.
Most Strikeouts, Season—189, Bobby Bonds, San Francisco N.L., 1970.
Most Strikeouts, Game (9 innings)—5, by many.
Most Strikeouts, Game (extra innings)—6, Carl Weilman, St. Louis A.L., 15 innings, 1913; Don Hoak, Chicago N.L., 17 innings, 1956; Fred Reichardt, California A.L., 17, innings, 1966; Billy Cowan, California A.L., 20, 1971; Cecil Cooper, Boston A.L., 15, 1974.
Most pinch-hits, lifetime—144, Forrest Burgess, Chi.-Mil.-Cin.-Pitts. N.L., 1949, 1951–64; Chi. A.L., 1964–67.
Most Pinch-hits, season—25, Jose Morales, Montreal N.L., 1976.
Most consecutive pinch-hits—9, Dave Philley, Phil., N.L., 1958 (8), 1959 (1).
Most pinch-hit home runs, lifetime—18, Gerald Lynch, Pitt.-Cin. N.L., 1957–66.
Most pinch-hit home runs, season—6, Johnny Frederick, Brooklyn, N.L., 1932.
Most stolen bases, lifetime (since 1900)—917, Lou Brock, Chicago N.L. 1961–64; St. Louis, N.L. 1964–78.
Most stolen bases, season—156, Harry Stovey, Philadelphia, American Assn., 1888. Since 1900: 96, Ty Cobb, Detroit A.L. (156 games 1915); 118, Lou Brock, St. Louis, N.L. (162 games, 1974).
Most stolen bases, game—7, George Gore, Chicago N.L. 1881; William Hamilton, Philadelphia N.L. 1894. (Since 1900—6, Eddie Collins, Philadelphia A.L., 1912.)
Most times stealing home, lifetime—35, Ty Cobb, Detroit-Phil. A.L., 1905–28.

## MAJOR LEAGUE ALL-TIME PITCHING RECORDS

Most Games Won—511, Cy Young, Cleveland N.L., 1890–98, St. Louis N.L., 1899–1900, Boston A.L., 1901–08, Cleveland A.L., 1909–11, Boston N.L., 1911.
Most Games Won, Season—60, Hoss Radbourne, Providence N.L., 1884. (Since 1900—41, Jack Chesbro, New York A.L., 1904.)
Most Consecutive Games Won—24, Carl Hubbell, New York N.L., 1936 (16) and 1937 (8).
Most Consecutive Games Won, Season—19, Tim Keefe, New York N.L., 1888; Rube Marquard, New York N.L., 1912.
Most Years Won 20 or More Games—16, Cy Young, Cleveland N.L., 1891–98, St. Louis N.L., 1899–1900, Boston A.L., 1901–04, 1907–08.
Most Shutouts—113, Walter Johnson, Wash. A.L., 1907–27.
Most Shutouts, Season—16, Grover Alexander, Philadelphia N.L., 1916.
Most Consecutive Shutouts—6, Don Drysdale, Los Angeles, N.L., 1968.
Most Consecutive Scoreless Innings—58, Don Drysdale, Los Angeles, N.L., 1968.
Most Strikeouts—3,508, Walter Johnson, Washington A.L. 1907–27.
Most Strikeouts, Season—505, Matthew Kilroy, Baltimore A.A., 1886. (Since 1900—383, Nolan Ryan, California, A.L., 1973.)
Most Strikeouts, Game—21, Tom Cheney, Washington A.L. 1962, 16 innings. Nine innings: 19, Charles McSweeney, Providence N.L., 1884; Hugh Dailey, Chicago U.A., 1884. (Since 1900—19, Steve Carlton, St. Louis N.L. vs. New York, Sept. 15, 1969; Tom Seaver, New York N.L. vs. San Diego, April 22, 1970; Nolan Ryan, California A.L. vs. Boston, Aug. 12, 1974.)
Most Consecutive Strikeouts—10, Tom Seaver, New York N.L. vs. San Diego, April 22, 1970.
Most Games, Season—106, Mike Marshall, Los Angeles, N.L., 1974.
Most Complete Games, Season—74, William White, Cincinnati N.L., 1879. (Since 1900—48, Jack Chesbro, New York A.L., 1904.)

## OTHER LIFETIME BATTING, PITCHING, AND BASE-RUNNING RECORDS

*Source:* Baseball Record Book, published and copyrighted by *The Sporting News,* St. Louis, Mo. 63166

**Hits**

| | |
|---|---|
| Ty Cobb | 4,191 |
| Henry Aaron | 3,771 |
| Stan Musial | 3,630 |
| Tris Speaker | 3,515 |
| Honus Wagner | 3,430 |
| Eddie Collins | 3,311 |
| Willie Mays | 3,283 |
| Nap Lajoie | 3,251 |
| Pete Rose[1] | 3,164 |
| Paul Waner | 3,152 |
| Cap Anson | 3,081 |
| Al Kaline | 3,007 |
| Roberto Clemente | 3,000 |
| Edgar Rice | 2,987 |
| Sam Crawford | 2,964 |
| Willie Keeler | 2,955 |
| Frank Robinson | 2,943 |
| Jacob Beckley | 2,930 |
| Rogers Hornsby | 2,930 |
| Al Simmons | 2,927 |
| Zach Wheat | 2,884 |
| Frank Frisch | 2,880 |
| Mel Ott | 2,876 |

**Earned Run Average**

| | |
|---|---|
| Walter Johnson | 2.37 |
| Grover Alexander | 2.56 |
| Whitey Ford | 2.74 |
| Stanley Coveleski | 2.88 |
| Juan Marichal | 2.89 |
| Wilbur Cooper | 2.89 |
| Gaylord Perry[1] | 2.91 |
| Bob Gibson | 2.91 |
| Carl Mays | 2.92 |
| Don Drysdale | 2.95 |

**Runs**

| | |
|---|---|
| Ty Cobb | 2,244 |
| Henry Aaron | 2,174 |
| Babe Ruth | 2,174 |
| Willie Mays | 2,062 |
| Stan Musial | 1,949 |
| Lou Gehrig | 1,888 |
| Tris Speaker | 1,881 |
| Mel Ott | 1,859 |
| Frank Robinson | 1,829 |
| Eddie Collins | 1,818 |
| Ted Williams | 1,798 |
| Charley Gehringer | 1,773 |
| Jimmy Foxx | 1,751 |
| Honus Wagner | 1,740 |
| Willie Keeler | 1,720 |
| Cap Anson | 1,712 |
| Jesse Burkett | 1,708 |
| Billy Hamilton | 1,690 |
| Mickey Mantle | 1,677 |
| John McPhee | 1,674 |
| Pete Rose[1] | 1,657 |
| George Van Haltren | 1,650 |

**Strikeouts**

| | |
|---|---|
| Walter Johnson | 3,508 |
| Bob Gibson | 3,117 |
| Gaylord Perry[1] | 3,001 |
| Jim Bunning | 2,853 |
| Cy Young | 2,819 |
| Mickey Lolich | 2,812 |
| Tom Seaver[1] | 2,756 |
| Nolan Ryan[1] | 2,686 |
| Warren Spahn | 2,583 |
| Bob Feller | 2,581 |
| Tim Keefe | 2,538 |
| Tom Seaver[1] | 2,530 |

**Home Runs**

| | |
|---|---|
| Henry Aaron | 755 |
| Babe Ruth | 714 |
| Willie Mays | 660 |
| Frank Robinson | 586 |
| Harmon Killebrew | 573 |
| Mickey Mantle | 536 |
| Jimmy Foxx | 534 |
| Ted Williams | 521 |
| Ernie Banks | 512 |
| Ed Mathews | 512 |
| Mel Ott | 511 |
| Willie McCovey[1] | 505 |
| Lou Gehrig | 493 |
| Stan Musial | 475 |
| Willie Stargell[1] | 429 |
| Billy Williams | 426 |
| Duke Snider | 407 |
| Al Kaline | 399 |
| Carl Yastrzemski[1] | 383 |
| Frank Howard | 382 |
| Orlando Cepeda | 379 |
| Norm Cash | 377 |
| Rocky Colavito | 374 |

**Shutouts**

| | |
|---|---|
| Walter Johnson | 113 |
| Grover Alexander | 90 |
| Christy Mathewson | 83 |
| Cy Young | 77 |
| Eddie Plank | 64 |
| Warren Spahn | 63 |
| Ed Walsh | 58 |
| James Galvin | 57 |
| Bob Gibson | 56 |
| Juan Marichal | 52 |

**Strikeouts**

| | |
|---|---|
| Willie Stargell[1] | 1,746 |
| Mickey Mantle | 1,710 |
| Harmon Killebrew | 1,699 |
| Lou Brock[1] | 1,687 |
| Dick Allen | 1,556 |
| Frank Robinson | 1,532 |
| Willie Mays | 1,526 |
| Ed Mathews | 1,487 |
| Frank Howard | 1,460 |

**Bases on Balls**

| | |
|---|---|
| Babe Ruth | 2,056 |
| Ted Williams | 2,018 |
| Mickey Mantle | 1,734 |
| Mel Ott | 1,708 |
| Eddie Yost | 1,614 |
| Stan Musial | 1,599 |
| Harmon Killebrew | 1,559 |
| Lou Gehrig | 1,508 |
| Willie Mays | 1,464 |
| Jimmy Foxx | 1,452 |
| Ed Mathews | 1,444 |

**Stolen Bases**

| | |
|---|---|
| Billy Hamilton | 937 |
| Lou Brock[1] | 917 |
| Ty Cobb | 892 |
| Walter Latham | 791 |
| Harry Stovey | 744 |
| Eddie Collins | 743 |
| Max Carey | 738 |
| Honus Wagner | 720 |
| Tom Brown | 697 |
| George Davis | 632 |

1. Active player. 2. National League from 1912; American League from 1913.

## BASEBALL'S PERFECTLY PITCHED GAMES[1]

(no opposing runner reached base)

| | |
|---|---|
| John Richmond—Worcester vs. Cleveland (NL) June 12, 1880 | 1–0 |
| John M. Ward—Providence vs. Buffalo (NL) June 17, 1880 | 5–0 |
| Cy Young—Boston vs. Philadelphia (AL) May 5, 1904 | 3–0 |
| Addie Joss—Cleveland vs. Chicago (AL) Oct. 2, 1908 | 1–0 |
| Ernest Shore[2]—Boston vs. Washington (AL) June 23, 1917 | 4–0 |
| Charles Robertson—Chicago vs. Detroit (AL) April 30, 1922 | 2–0 |
| Don Larsen[3]—New York (AL) vs. Brooklyn (NL) Oct. 8, 1956 | 2–0 |
| Jim Bunning—Philadelphia vs. New York (NL) June 21, 1964 | 6–0 |
| Sandy Koufax—Los Angeles vs. Chicago (NL) Sept. 9, 1965 | 1–0 |
| Jim Hunter—Oakland vs. Minnesota (AL) May 8, 1968 | 4–0 |

1. Harvey Haddix, of Pittsburgh, pitched 12 perfect innings against Milwaukee (NL), May 26, 1959 but lost game in 13th on error and hit. 2. Shore, relief pitcher for Babe Ruth who walked first batter before being ejected by umpire, retired 26 batters who faced him and baserunner was out stealing. 3. World Series.

## BASEBALL'S TRIPLE CROWN WINNERS

(Players leading league for season in batting, runs batted in, and home runs)

**Two-Time Winners**

1922, 1925 Rogers Hornsby, St. Louis (N.L.)
1942, 1947 Ted Williams, Boston (A.L.)

**Others**

1909 Ty Cobb, Detroit (A.L.)
1912 Heinie Zimmerman, Chicago (N. L.)
1933 Jimmy Foxx, Philadelphia (A. L.)
1933 Chuck Klein, Philadelphia (N. L.)
1934 Lou Gehrig, New York (A. L.)
1937 Joe Medwick, St. Louis (N.L.)
1956 Mickey Mantle, New York (A. L.)
1966 Frank Robinson, Baltimore (A. L.)
1967 Carl Yastrzemski, Boston (A.L.)

## MAJOR LEAGUE ATTENDANCE RECORDS

Single game—78,672, San Francisco at Los Angeles (N.L.), April 18, 1958. (At Memorial Coliseum.)
Doubleheader—84,587, New York at Cleveland (A.L.), Sept. 12, 1954.
Night—78,382, Chicago at Cleveland (A.L.), Aug. 20, 1948.
Season, home—3,347,776, Los Angeles (N.L.), 1978.
Season, road—2,216,159, New York (A.L.), 1962.
Season, league—20,726,666, American League, 1978.
Season, both leagues—40,820,174, 1978.
World Series, single game—92,706, Chicago (A.L.) at Los Angeles (N.L.), Oct. 6, 1959.
World Series, all games (6)—420,784, Chicago (A.L.) and Los Angeles (N.L.), 1959.

## MOST HOME RUNS IN ONE SEASON

| HR | Player/Team | Year |
|---|---|---|
| 61 | Roger Maris, New York (AL) | 1961 |
| 60 | Babe Ruth, New York (AL) | 1927 |
| 59 | Babe Ruth, New York (AL) | 1921 |
| 58 | Jimmy Foxx, Philadelphia (AL) | 1932 |
| 58 | Hank Greenberg, Detroit (AL) | 1938 |
| 56 | Hack Wilson, Chicago (NL) | 1930 |
| 54 | Babe Ruth, New York (AL) | 1920 |
| 54 | Babe Ruth, New York (AL) | 1928 |
| 54 | Ralph Kiner, Pittsburgh (NL) | 1949 |
| 54 | Mickey Mantle, New York (AL) | 1961 |
| 52 | Mickey Mantle, New York (AL) | 1956 |
| 52 | Willie Mays, San Francisco (NL) | 1965 |
| 52 | George Foster, Cincinnati (NL) | 1977 |
| 51 | Ralph Kiner, Pittsburgh (NL) | 1947 |
| 51 | John Mize, New York (NL) | 1947 |
| 51 | Willie Mays, New York (NL) | 1955 |
| 50 | Jimmy Foxx, Boston (AL) | 1938 |
| 49 | Babe Ruth, New York (AL) | 1930 |
| 49 | Lou Gehrig, New York (AL) | 1934 |
| 49 | Lou Gehrig, New York (AL) | 1936 |
| 49 | Ted Kluszewski, Cincinnati (NL) | 1954 |
| 49 | Willie Mays, San Francisco (NL) | 1962 |
| 49 | Harmon Killebrew, Minnesota (AL) | 1964 |
| 49 | Frank Robinson, Baltimore (AL) | 1966 |
| 49 | Harmon Killebrew, Minnesota (AL) | 1969 |

## FOUR HOME RUNS IN ONE GAME

Robert L. Lowe, Boston N.L., consecutive (3d (2), 5th, 6th) May 30, 1894
Edward J. Delahanty, Phila. N.L. (1st, 5th, 7th, 9th) July 13, 1896
Lou Gehrig, New York A.L., consecutive (1st, 4th, 5th, 7th) June 3, 1932
Chuck Klein, Phila. N.L. (1st, 5th, 7th, 10th) July 10, 1936
Pat Seerey, Chicago A.L. (4th, 5th, 6th, 11th) July 18, 1948
Gil Hodges, Brooklyn N.L. (2d, 3d, 6th, 8th) Aug. 31, 1950
Joe Adcock, Milwaukee N.L. (2d, 5th, 7th, 9th) July 31, 1954
Rocky Colavito, Cleveland A.L., consecutive (3d, 5th, 6th, 9th) June 10, 1959
Willie Mays, San Francisco N.L. (1st, 3d, 6th, 8th) April 30, 1961
Michael Schmidt, Philadelphia N.L. (5th, 7th, 8th, 10th) April 17. 1976

## OTHERS HITTING 4 HOME RUNS IN SUCCESSION, 2 GAMES

| | |
|---|---|
| Jimmy Foxx, Phila A.L. | 1933 |
| Hank Greenberg, Detroit A.L. | 1938 |
| Ralph Kiner, Pittsburgh N.L. | 1949 |
| Ted Williams, Boston A.L. | 1957 |
| Charley Maxwell, Detroit A.L. | 1959 |
| John Blanchard, New York A.L. | 1961 |
| Willie Kirkland, Cleveland A.L. | 1961 |
| Mickey Mantle, New York A.L. | 1962 |
| Art Shamsky, Cincinnati, N.L. | 1966 |
| Deron Johnson, Philadelphia N.L. | 1971 |

## SANDY KOUFAX'S MAJOR LEAGUE PITCHING RECORD

(1955–57, with Brooklyn Dodgers; 1958–66, with Los Angeles Dodgers)

| | G | IP | H | BB | SO | W | L | ERA |
|---|---|---|---|---|---|---|---|---|
| 1955 | 12 | 42 | 33 | 28 | 30 | 2 | 2 | 3.00 |
| 1956 | 16 | 59 | 66 | 29 | 30 | 2 | 4 | 4.88 |
| 1957 | 34 | 104 | 83 | 51 | 122 | 5 | 4 | 3.89 |
| 1958 | 40 | 159 | 132 | 105 | 131 | 11 | 11 | 4.47 |
| 1959 | 35 | 153 | 136 | 92 | 173 | 8 | 6 | 4.06 |
| 1960 | 37 | 175 | 133 | 100 | 197 | 8 | 13 | 3.91 |
| 1961 | 42 | 256 | 212 | 96 | 269[1] | 18 | 13 | 3.52 |
| 1962 | 28 | 184 | 134 | 57 | 216 | 14 | 7 | 2.54[1] |
| 1963 | 40 | 311 | 214 | 58 | 306[1] | 25[2] | 5 | 1.88[1] |
| 1964 | 29 | 223 | 154 | 58 | 223 | 19 | 5 | 1.74[1] |
| 1965 | 43 | 336[1] | 216 | 71 | 382[1] | 26[1] | 8 | 2.04[1] |
| 1966 | 41 | 323[1] | 241 | 77 | 317 | 27[1] | 9 | 1.73[1] |
| Totals | 397 | 2,325[1] | 1,754 | 817 | 2,396 | 165 | 87 | 2.76 |

1. Led league. 2. Tied for league lead.

### World Series Record

| | G | IP | H | BB | SO | W | L | ERA |
|---|---|---|---|---|---|---|---|---|
| 1959 | 2 | 9 | 5 | 1 | 7 | 0 | 1 | 1.00 |
| 1963 | 2 | 18 | 12 | 3 | 23 | 2 | 0 | 1.50 |
| 1965 | 3 | 24 | 13 | 5 | 29 | 2 | 1 | 0.38 |
| 1966 | 1 | 6 | 6 | 2 | 2 | 0 | 1 | 1.50 |
| Totals | 8 | 57 | 36 | 11 | 61 | 4 | 3 | 0.95 |

Koufax pitched four no-hit games, more than any other man. They came in consecutive years—1962, 1963, 1964, and 1965. The 1965 no-hitter, against the Chicago Cubs, was a perfect game. Koufax won the Cy Young Award three times—more than any other pitcher.

## MAJOR LEAGUE BALL PARK STATISTICS

lf—Left-field foul line; cf—center field; rf—right-field foul line. (2)—Indicates double-header.

### American League

| Club, nickname and grounds | Distance, feet lf | cf | rf | Seating capacity | Record attendance[1] | Visiting club | Date |
|---|---|---|---|---|---|---|---|
| Baltimore Orioles—Memorial Stadium | 309 | 405 | 309 | 52,137 | 51,195 | Kansas City (night) | May 8, 1976 |
| Boston Red Sox—Fenway Park | 315 | 420 | 302 | 33,524 | 41,766 | New York (2) | Aug. 12, 1934 |
| California Angels—Anaheim Stadium | 333 | 404 | 333 | 43,204 | 44,631 | Oakland | July 4, 1971 |
| Chicago White Sox—Comiskey Park | 352 | 400 | 352 | 46,550 | 55,555 | Minnesota (2) | May 2, 1973 |
| Cleveland Indians—Municipal Stadium | 320 | 400 | 320 | 76,997 | 84,587 | New York (2) | Sept. 12, 1954 |
| Detroit Tigers—Tiger Stadium | 340 | 440 | 325 | 54,220 | 58,369 | New York (2) | July 20, 1947 |
| Kansas City Royals—Royals Stadium | 330 | 410 | 330 | 40,762 | 40,435 | New York (night) | Aug. 9, 1976 |
| Milwaukee Brewers—County Stadium | 320 | 402 | 315 | 46,000 | 55,120 | Baltimore | April 12, 1977 |
| Minnesota Twins—Metropolitan Stadium | 330 | 410 | 330 | 45,921 | 46,963 | Chicago | June 26, 1977 |
| New York Yankees—Yankee Stadium (old) | 301 | 461 | 296 | 65,010 | 81,841 | Boston (2) | May 30, 1938 |
| New York Yankees—Yankee Stadium (new) | 312 | 430 | 310 | 54,208 | 55,269 | Boston (night) | Sept. 13, 1977 |
| New York Yankees—Shea Stadium[2] | 341 | 410 | 330 | 55,300 | 53,631 | Boston (2) | July 27, 1975 |
| Oakland Athletics—Oakland Coliseum | 330 | 400 | 330 | 50,000 | 50,182 | Baltimore (night) | June 12, 1972 |
| Seattle Mariners—Kingdome | 316 | 405 | 316 | 59,059 | 57,762 | California (night) | April 6, 1977 |
| Texas Rangers—Arlington Stadium | 330 | 400 | 330 | 35,698 | 40,854 | California (night) | May 21, 1976 |
| Toronto Blue Jays—Exhibition Stadium | 330 | 400 | 330 | 40,000 | 44,649 | Chicago | April 6, 1977 |

### National League

| Club, nickname and grounds | lf | cf | rf | Seating capacity | Record attendance | Visiting club | Date |
|---|---|---|---|---|---|---|---|
| Atlanta Braves—Atlanta Stadium | 330 | 400 | 330 | 52,744 | 53,775 | Los Angeles (night) | April 8, 1974 |
| Chicago Cubs—Wrigley Field | 355 | 400 | 353 | 37,741 | 46,965 | Pittsburgh (2) | May 31, 1948 |
| Cincinnati Reds—Riverfront Stadium | 330 | 404 | 330 | 51,786 | 53,390 | Houston (day) | April 11, 1976 |
| Houston Astros—Astrodome | 330 | 400 | 330 | 45,000 | 50,908 | Los Angeles (night) | June 22, 1966 |
| Los Angeles Dodgers—Dodger Stadium | 330 | 395 | 330 | 56,000 | 55,110 | San Diego (night) | June 26, 1970 |
| Montreal Expos—Jarry Park (old) | 340 | 420 | 340 | 28,000 | 34,331 | Philadelphia | Sept. 13, 1973 |
| Montreal Expos—Olympic Stadium | 330 | 400 | 330 | 60,000 | 57,592 | Philadelphia | April 15, 1977 |
| New York Mets—Shea Stadium | 341 | 410 | 341 | 55,300 | 57,175 | Los Angeles (2) | June 13, 1965 |
| Philadelphia Phillies—Veterans Stadium | 330 | 408 | 330 | 56,581 | 63,283 | New York (night) | July 4, 1977 |
| Pittsburgh Pirates—Three Rivers Stadium | 335 | 400 | 335 | 50,230 | 51,726 | San Diego (day) | June 6, 1976 |
| St. Louis Cardinals—Busch Mem'l Stadium | 330 | 404 | 330 | 50,101 | 50,340 | Chicago (night) | July 2, 1977 |
| San Diego Padres—San Diego Stadium | 330 | 410 | 330 | 48,460 | 50,569 | St. Louis (night) | April 24, 1976 |
| San Francisco Giants—Candlestick Park | 335 | 410 | 335 | 58,000 | 56,103 | Los Angeles | May 28, 1978 |

1. Regular season in listed park. 2. Yankees played in New York National League Shea Stadium in 1974–75 while Yankee Stadium was being rebuilt.

## MAJOR LEAGUE FRANCHISE SHIFTS AND ADDITIONS

**1953**—Boston Braves (N.L.) became Milwaukee Braves. Home attendance, last season in Boston (1952), 281,278; first season in Milwaukee (1953), 1,826,397.

**1954**—St. Louis Browns (A.L.) became Baltimore Orioles. Home attendance, last season in St. Louis (1953), 297,238; first season in Baltimore (1954), 1,060,910.

**1955**—Philadelphia Athletics (A.L.) became Kansas City Athletics. Home attendance, last season in Phila. (1954), 627,100; first season in K.C. (1955), 1,393,054.

**1958**—New York Giants (N.L.) became San Francisco Giants. Home attendance, last season in New York (1957), 653,923; first season in San Francisco (1958), 1,272,625.

**1958**—Brooklyn Dodgers (N.L.) became Los Angeles Dodgers. Home attendance, last season in Brooklyn (1957), 1,028,258; first season in Los Angeles (1958), 1,845,556.

**1961**—Washington Senators (A.L.) became Minnesota Twins. Home attendance, last season in Washington (1960), 743,404; first season in Minneapolis-St. Paul (1961), 1,256,722.

**1961**—Los Angeles Angels (later renamed the California Angels) enfranchised by the American League.

**1961**—Washington Senators enfranchised by the American League (a new team, replacing the former Washington club, whose franchise was moved to Minneapolis-St. Paul).

**1962**—Houston Colt .45's (later renamed the Houston Astros) enfranchised by the National League.

**1962**—New York Mets enfranchised by the National League. Home attendance, first season (1962), 922,530.

**1966**—Milwaukee Braves (N.L.) became Atlanta Braves. Home attendance, last season in Milwaukee (1965), 555,584; first season in Atlanta (1966), 1,539,801.

**1968**—Kansas City Athletics (A.L.) became Oakland Athletics.

**1969**—Two major leagues each added two teams for totals of 12 and split into two divisions. American League additions: Kansas City Royals and Seattle Pilots; National League additions: Montreal Expos and San Diego Padres. The Division leaders met for the league championship and the two league winners met in the World Series.

**1970**—Seattle franchise was shifted to Milwaukee, with final court approval coming on March 31. Club was renamed Milwaukee Brewers.

**1971**—Washington franchise shifted at end of season to Dallas-Fort Worth Texas Rangers with field at Arlington, Tex.

**1977**—Seattle and Toronto began play in American League.

## LARSEN'S PERFECT GAME IN 1956 WORLD SERIES

Don Larsen of the New York Yankees pitched the only no-run no-hit game in World Series history in 1956 and hurled a perfect game in so doing. Facing the Brooklyn Dodgers at the Yankee Stadium in the fifth game before 64,519 on Oct. 8, Larsen retired 27 batters in a row. The Yankees won, 2 to 0.

## AMERICAN LEAGUE

### EAST DIVISION

| Team | W | L | Pct | GB |
|---|---|---|---|---|
| New York Yankees | 100 | 63 | .613 | — |
| Boston Red Sox | 99 | 64 | .607 | 1 |
| Milwaukee Brewers | 93 | 69 | .574 | 6½ |
| Baltimore Orioles | 90 | 71 | .559 | 9 |
| Detroit Tigers | 86 | 76 | .531 | 13½ |
| Cleveland Indians | 69 | 90 | .434 | 29 |
| Toronto Blue Jays | 59 | 102 | .366 | 40 |

### WEST DIVISION

| Team | W | L | Pct | GB |
|---|---|---|---|---|
| Kansas City Royals | 92 | 70 | .568 | — |
| California Angels | 87 | 75 | .537 | 5 |
| Texas Rangers | 87 | 75 | .537 | 5 |
| Minnesota Twins | 73 | 89 | .451 | 19 |
| Chicago White Sox | 71 | 90 | .441 | 20½ |
| Oakland A's | 69 | 93 | .426 | 23 |
| Seattle Mariners | 56 | 104 | .350 | 35 |

1. New York defeated Boston, 5-4, in playoff for championship of East Division.

### AMERICAN LEAGUE PLAYOFFS

**1st Game, Kansas City, Oct. 3**

| | | | | | |
|---|---|---|---|---|---|
| New York | 011 | 020 | 030—7 | 16 | 0 |
| Kansas City | 000 | 001 | 000—1 | 7 | 2 |

Beattie, Clay (6) and Munson; Leonard, Mingori (5), Hrabosky (8), Bird (9) and Porter. Winner: Beattie; Loser: Leonard. Home run: New York: Jackson. Attendance: 41,143

**2nd game, Kansas City, Oct. 4**

| | | | | | |
|---|---|---|---|---|---|
| New York | 000 | 000 | 220—4 | 12 | 1 |
| Kansas City | 140 | 000 | 32X—10 | 16 | 1 |

Figueroa, Tidrow (2), Lyle (7) and Munson; Gura, Pattin (7), Hrabosky (8) and Porter. Winner: Gura; Loser: Figueroa. Home run: Kansas City: Patek. Attendance: 41,158

**3rd game, New York, Oct. 6**

| | | | | | |
|---|---|---|---|---|---|
| Kansas City | 101 | 010 | 020—5 | 10 | 1 |
| New York | 010 | 201 | 02X—6 | 10 | 0 |

Splittorf, Bird (8), Hrabosky (8) and Porter; Hunter, Gossage (7), Winner: Gossage; Loser: Bird. Home runs: Kansas City: Brett (3), New York: Jackson, Munson. Attendance: 55,455

**4th game, New York, Oct. 7**

| | | | | | |
|---|---|---|---|---|---|
| Kansas City | 100 | 000 | 000—1 | 7 | 0 |
| New York | 010 | 001 | 00X—2 | 4 | 0 |

Leonard and Porter; Guidry, Gossage (9) and Munson. Winner: Gossage; Loser: Leonard. Home runs: New York: Nettles, White

### AMERICAN LEAGUE LEADERS

| | |
|---|---|
| Batting—Rod Carew, Minnesota | .333 |
| Runs—Ron LeFlore, Detroit | 126 |
| Hits—Jim Rice, Boston | 213 |
| Runs batted in—Jim Rice, Boston | 139 |
| Doubles—George Brett, Kansas City | 45 |
| Triples—Jim Rice, Boston | 15 |
| Home runs—Jim Rice, Boston | 46 |
| Stolen bases—Ron LeFlore, Detroit | 68 |

**Pitching**

| | |
|---|---|
| Victories—Ron Guidry, New York | 25 |
| Earned run average—Ron Guidry, New York | 1.74 |
| Strikeouts—Nolan Ryan, California | 260 |
| Shutouts—Ron Guidry, New York | 8 |

## NATIONAL LEAGUE

### EAST DIVISION

| Team | W | L | Pct | GB |
|---|---|---|---|---|
| Philadelphia Phillies | 90 | 72 | .556 | — |
| Pittsburgh Pirates | 88 | 73 | .547 | 1½ |
| Chicago Cubs | 79 | 83 | .488 | 11 |
| Montreal Expos | 76 | 86 | .469 | 14 |
| St. Louis Cardinals | 69 | 93 | .426 | 21 |
| New York Mets | 66 | 96 | .407 | 24 |

### WEST DIVISION

| Team | W | L | Pct | GB |
|---|---|---|---|---|
| Los Angeles Dodgers | 95 | 67 | .586 | — |
| Cincinnati Reds | 92 | 69 | .571 | 2½ |
| San Francisco Giants | 89 | 73 | .549 | 6 |
| San Diego Padres | 84 | 78 | .519 | 11 |
| Houston Astros | 74 | 88 | .457 | 21 |
| Atlanta Braves | 69 | 93 | .426 | 26 |

### NATIONAL LEAGUE PLAYOFFS

**1st game, Philadelphia, Oct. 4**

| | | | | | |
|---|---|---|---|---|---|
| Los Angeles | 004 | 211 | 001—9 | 13 | 1 |
| Philadelphia | 010 | 030 | 001—5 | 12 | 1 |

Hooton, Welch (5) and Yeager; Christenson, Brusstar (5), Eastwick (6), McGraw (7) and Boone; Winner: Welch; Loser: Christenson. Home runs: Los Angeles: Garvey (2), Lopes, Yeager. Philadelphia: Martin

**2nd game, Philadelphia, Oct. 5**

| | | | | | |
|---|---|---|---|---|---|
| Los Angeles | 000 | 120 | 101—4 | 8 | 0 |
| Philadelphia | 000 | 000 | 000—0 | 4 | 0 |

John and Yeager; Ruthven, Brusstar (5), Reed (7), McGraw (9) and Boone. Winner: John; Loser: Ruthven. Home run: Los Angeles: Lopes. Attendance: 60,643

**3rd game, Los Angeles, Oct. 6**

| | | | | | |
|---|---|---|---|---|---|
| Philadelphia | 040 | 003 | 101—9 | 11 | 1 |
| Los Angeles | 012 | 000 | 010—4 | 8 | 2 |

Carlton and McCarver; Sutton, Rautzhan (6), Hough (8), and Yeager; Winner: Carlton: Loser: Sutton. Home runs: Philadelphia: Carlton, Luzinski. Los Angeles: Garvey. Attendance: 55,063

**4th game, Los Angeles, Oct. 7**

| | | | | | | |
|---|---|---|---|---|---|---|
| Philadelphia | 002 | 000 | 100 | 0—3 | 8 | 2 |
| Los Angeles | 010 | 101 | 000 | 1—4 | 13 | 0 |

Lerch, Brusstar (6), Reed (7), McGraw (9) and Boone; Rau, Rhoden (6), Forster (10) and Yeager, Grote (8). Winner: Forster, Loser: McGraw. Home runs: Philadelphia: Luzinski, McBride; Los Angeles: Garvey, Cey. Attendance: 55,124

### NATIONAL LEAGUE LEADERS

| | |
|---|---|
| Batting—Dave Parker, Pittsburgh | .334 |
| Runs—Ivan DeJesus, Chicago | 104 |
| Hits—Steve Garvey, Los Angeles | 201 |
| Runs batted in—George Foster, Cincinnati | 120 |
| Doubles—Pete Rose, Cincinnati | 50 |
| Triples—Garry Templeton, St. Louis | 13 |
| Home runs—George Foster, Cincinnati | 40 |
| Stolen bases—Omar Moreno, Pittsburgh | 71 |

**Pitching**

| | |
|---|---|
| Victories—Gaylord Perry, San Diego | 25 |
| Earned run average—Craig Swan, New York | 2.43 |
| Strikeouts—Jim Richard, Houston | 303 |
| Shutouts—Bob Knepper, San Francisco | 5 |

## AMERICAN LEAGUE AVERAGES—1978

(Unofficial)

### Batting—Club

| | AB | R | H | HR | RBI | PCT |
|---|---|---|---|---|---|---|
| Milwaukee | 5536 | 804 | 1530 | 172 | 762 | .276 |
| Detroit | 5600 | 714 | 1519 | 129 | 666 | .271 |
| Kansas City | 5474 | 743 | 1469 | 97 | 694 | .268 |
| Boston | 5587 | 796 | 1493 | 170 | 739 | .267 |
| New York | 5583 | 735 | 1489 | 124 | 692 | .267 |
| Minnesota | 5524 | 666 | 1472 | 82 | 622 | .266 |
| Chicago | 5393 | 634 | 1422 | 106 | 595 | .264 |
| Cleveland | 5365 | 639 | 1400 | 105 | 597 | .261 |
| California | 5471 | 691 | 1417 | 106 | 643 | .259 |
| Baltimore | 5422 | 659 | 1397 | 154 | 613 | .258 |
| Texas | 5347 | 692 | 1352 | 132 | 649 | .253 |
| Toronto | 5430 | 590 | 1358 | 98 | 551 | .250 |
| Seattle | 5358 | 614 | 1326 | 96 | 568 | .247 |
| Oakland | 5319 | 532 | 1298 | 100 | 490 | .244 |

### Batting Leaders

| Player/team | AB | R | H | HR | RBI | PCT |
|---|---|---|---|---|---|---|
| Carew, Minn. | 564 | 86 | 188 | 5 | 71 | .333 |
| Oliver, Texas | 525 | 65 | 170 | 14 | 89 | .324 |
| Rice, Boston | 677 | 121 | 213 | 46 | 139 | .315 |
| Piniella, New York | 472 | 67 | 148 | 6 | 69 | .314 |
| Cooper, Mil. | 407 | 60 | 127 | 13 | 54 | .312 |
| Oglivie, Mil. | 469 | 71 | 142 | 18 | 72 | .303 |
| Paciorek, Seattle | 250 | 33 | 75 | 4 | 29 | .300 |
| Lemon, Chicago | 357 | 51 | 107 | 13 | 55 | .300 |
| Roberts, Seattle | 472 | 77 | 141 | 22 | 92 | .299 |
| Otis, Kan. City | 486 | 74 | 145 | 22 | 96 | .298 |
| Lynn, Boston | 541 | 75 | 161 | 22 | 82 | .298 |
| Jackson, Calif. | 387 | 49 | 115 | 6 | 57 | .297 |
| Munson, New York | 617 | 73 | 183 | 5 | 71 | .297 |
| Bostock, Calif. | 568 | 74 | 168 | 5 | 70 | .296 |
| LeFlore, Detroit | 667 | 126 | 197 | 12 | 62 | .295 |
| LaCock, Kan. City | 322 | 44 | 95 | 5 | 48 | .295 |

### Leading Pitchers

(16 or more decisions)

| Player/team | IP | H | BB | SO | W | L | ERA |
|---|---|---|---|---|---|---|---|
| Guidry, New York | 273 | 187 | 72 | 248 | 25 | 3 | 1.74 |
| Gossage, New York | 134 | 87 | 59 | 121 | 10 | 11 | 2.01 |
| Matlack, Texas | 270 | 252 | 51 | 155 | 15 | 13 | 2.30 |
| Comer, Texas | 116 | 107 | 37 | 63 | 11 | 5 | 2.32 |
| Caldwell, Mil. | 293 | 258 | 54 | 139 | 22 | 9 | 2.36 |
| Palmer, Balt. | 296 | 246 | 97 | 137 | 21 | 12 | 2.46 |
| Marshall, Minn. | 98 | 80 | 37 | 57 | 10 | 12 | 2.46 |
| Goltz, Minn. | 220 | 209 | 67 | 116 | 15 | 10 | 2.49 |
| Gura, Kan. City | 221 | 183 | 60 | 81 | 16 | 4 | 2.72 |
| LaRoche, Calif. | 95 | 73 | 48 | 69 | 10 | 9 | 2.82 |
| Eckersley, Boston | 268 | 258 | 71 | 163 | 20 | 8 | 2.99 |
| Figueroa, New York | 253 | 233 | 77 | 92 | 20 | 9 | 2.99 |
| Lacey, Oakland | 119 | 125 | 35 | 59 | 8 | 9 | 3.01 |
| Zahn, Minn. | 252 | 260 | 81 | 106 | 14 | 14 | 3.03 |
| Jenkins, Texas | 249 | 228 | 41 | 158 | 18 | 8 | 3.04 |
| Kern, Cleve. | 99 | 77 | 58 | 93 | 10 | 10 | 3.08 |
| Rozema, Detroit | 209 | 205 | 41 | 58 | 9 | 12 | 3.14 |
| Gale, Kan. City | 192 | 171 | 100 | 88 | 14 | 8 | 3.18 |
| Waits, Cleve. | 230 | 206 | 86 | 96 | 13 | 15 | 3.20 |
| Sorensen, Mil. | 280 | 277 | 50 | 77 | 18 | 12 | 3.24 |
| Keough, Oakland | 197 | 178 | 85 | 108 | 8 | 15 | 3.24 |
| Leonard, Kan. City | 294 | 281 | 78 | 180 | 21 | 17 | 3.27 |

# *JAI-ALAI*

## WORLD CHAMPIONSHIP

(San Juan de Luz, France, Aug. 31, 1978)

Doubles—Churruca, Bridgeport, Conn. and Remay, Miami, Fla.

## NATIONAL LEAGUE AVERAGES—1978

(Unofficial)

### Batting—Club

| | AB | R | H | HR | RBI | PCT |
|---|---|---|---|---|---|---|
| Chicago | 5526 | 664 | 1459 | 72 | 610 | .264 |
| Los Angeles | 5401 | 720 | 1419 | 148 | 678 | .263 |
| Houston | 5458 | 605 | 1407 | 70 | 556 | .258 |
| Philadelphia | 5449 | 708 | 1402 | 132 | 660 | .257 |
| Pittsburgh | 5405 | 684 | 1390 | 115 | 631 | .257 |
| Cincinnati | 5391 | 710 | 1378 | 136 | 671 | .256 |
| Montreal | 5530 | 633 | 1404 | 121 | 588 | .254 |
| San Diego | 5324 | 591 | 1337 | 75 | 540 | .251 |
| St. Louis | 5415 | 600 | 1351 | 78 | 569 | .250 |
| San Francisco | 5359 | 613 | 1328 | 117 | 575 | .248 |
| New York | 5434 | 607 | 1330 | 86 | 561 | .245 |
| Atlanta | 5381 | 600 | 1311 | 123 | 557 | .244 |

### Batting Leaders

| Player/team | AB | R | H | HR | RBI | PCT |
|---|---|---|---|---|---|---|
| Parker, Pitts. | 581 | 102 | 194 | 30 | 117 | .334 |
| Buckner, Chicago | 446 | 49 | 144 | 5 | 74 | .323 |
| Garvey, Los Angeles | 637 | 88 | 201 | 20 | 111 | .316 |
| Cruz, Houston | 565 | 79 | 178 | 10 | 83 | .315 |
| Richards, San Diego | 550 | 90 | 171 | 4 | 45 | .311 |
| Winfield, San Diego | 584 | 88 | 181 | 24 | 97 | .310 |
| Madlock, San Fran. | 447 | 76 | 138 | 15 | 44 | .309 |
| Ivie, San Fran. | 318 | 34 | 98 | 11 | 55 | .308 |
| Clark, San Fran. | 592 | 90 | 181 | 25 | 98 | .306 |
| Rose, Cin. | 655 | 103 | 198 | 7 | 53 | .302 |
| Burroughs, Atlanta | 488 | 72 | 147 | 23 | 77 | .301 |
| Concepcion, Cin. | 565 | 76 | 170 | 6 | 68 | .301 |
| Howe, Houston | 416 | 46 | 123 | 7 | 55 | .296 |
| Cabell, Houston | 660 | 92 | 195 | 7 | 71 | .295 |
| Smith, Los Angeles | 447 | 82 | 132 | 29 | 93 | .295 |
| Cromartie, Montreal | 607 | 76 | 179 | 10 | 56 | .295 |
| Stargell, Pitts. | 390 | 61 | 115 | 28 | 97 | .295 |

### Leading Pitchers

(16 or more decisions)

| Player/Team | IP | H | BB | SO | W | L | ERA |
|---|---|---|---|---|---|---|---|
| Rogers, Montreal | 219 | 186 | 64 | 126 | 13 | 10 | 2.47 |
| Fingers, San Diego | 107 | 83 | 29 | 72 | 6 | 12 | 2.52 |
| Vuckovich, St. Louis | 197 | 186 | 59 | 148 | 12 | 12 | 2.55 |
| Knepper, San Fran. | 260 | 216 | 85 | 147 | 17 | 11 | 2.63 |
| Hooton, Los Angeles | 237 | 196 | 61 | 104 | 19 | 10 | 2.70 |
| Forsch, Houston | 133 | 135 | 37 | 71 | 10 | 6 | 2.70 |
| Perry, San Diego | 260 | 241 | 66 | 154 | 21 | 6 | 2.73 |
| Blue, San Fran. | 258 | 233 | 70 | 171 | 18 | 10 | 2.83 |
| Carlton, Phila. | 247 | 228 | 63 | 161 | 16 | 13 | 2.84 |
| Halicki, San Fran. | 199 | 166 | 45 | 105 | 9 | 10 | 2.85 |
| Seaver, Cin. | 259 | 218 | 89 | 226 | 16 | 14 | 2.88 |
| Jones, San Diego | 253 | 262 | 64 | 71 | 13 | 14 | 2.88 |
| Niekro, Atlanta | 334 | 295 | 102 | 247 | 19 | 18 | 2.91 |
| Denny, St. Louis | 234 | 200 | 74 | 103 | 14 | 11 | 2.96 |
| Blyleven, Pitts. | 243 | 217 | 66 | 182 | 14 | 10 | 3.03 |
| Grimsley, Montreal | 262 | 231 | 69 | 84 | 20 | 11 | 3.05 |
| Richard, Houston | 275 | 192 | 141 | 303 | 18 | 11 | 3.11 |
| Sutter, Chicago | 98 | 82 | 34 | 106 | 8 | 10 | 3.19 |

# *MODERN PENTATHLON*

## NATIONAL CHAMPIONSHIPS—1978

Men's open—Greg Lesey, Napa, Calif.
Women's open—Gina Swift, Marble Falls, Tex.

## WORLD CHAMPIONSHIPS—1978

Men—Pavel Lednev, U.S.S.R.
Women—Wendy Norman, Britain
Junior men—A. Starostin, U.S.S.R.

# WORLD SERIES—1978

New York Yankees (AL) defeated Los Angeles Dodgers (NL), 4 games to 2

## 1st Game—Los Angeles, Oct. 10

| NEW YORK (A) | AB | R | H | BI |
|---|---|---|---|---|
| Rivers, cf | 4 | 0 | 0 | 0 |
| Blair, cf | 1 | 0 | 0 | 0 |
| White, lf | 4 | 0 | 1 | 0 |
| Munson, c | 4 | 1 | 0 | 0 |
| Jackson, dh | 4 | 1 | 3 | 1 |
| Piniella, rf | 4 | 2 | 1 | 1 |
| Nettles, 3b | 4 | 0 | 1 | 1 |
| Chambliss, 1b | 4 | 1 | 1 | 0 |
| Stanley, 2b | 2 | 0 | 1 | 0 |
| Johnson, ph | 1 | 0 | 0 | 0 |
| Doyle, 2b | 0 | 0 | 0 | 0 |
| Dent, ss | 4 | 0 | 1 | 2 |
| **Total** | **36** | **5** | **9** | **5** |

| LOS ANGELES (N) | AB | R | H | BI |
|---|---|---|---|---|
| Lopes, 2b | 5 | 2 | 2 | 5 |
| Russell, ss | 5 | 1 | 3 | 0 |
| Smith, rf | 5 | 0 | 1 | 1 |
| Garvey, 1b | 5 | 1 | 2 | 0 |
| Cey, 3b | 4 | 1 | 1 | 0 |
| Baker, lf | 4 | 2 | 3 | 1 |
| Monday, cf | 2 | 2 | 1 | 0 |
| North, cf | 1 | 1 | 1 | 2 |
| Lacy, dh | 3 | 0 | 1 | 1 |
| Yeager, c | 4 | 1 | 0 | 0 |
| **Total** | **38** | **11** | **15** | **10** |

| | | | | |
|---|---|---|---|---|
| **New York** | 000 | 000 | 320 | —5 |
| **Los Angeles** | 030 | 310 | 31X | —11 |

E—Dent, Lopes, Russell. DP—New York 2, Los Angeles 1. LOB—New York 6, Los Angeles 6. 2B—Monday, Stanley, North, Russell. HR—Lopes 2, Baker, Jackson.

| | IP | H | R | ER | BB | SO |
|---|---|---|---|---|---|---|
| **New York** | | | | | | |
| Figueroa (L) | 1⅔ | 5 | 3 | 3 | 1 | 0 |
| Clay | 2⅓ | 4 | 4 | 3 | 2 | 2 |
| Lindblad | 2⅓ | 4 | 3 | 3 | 0 | 1 |
| Tidrow | 1⅔ | 2 | 1 | 1 | 0 | 1 |
| **Los Angeles** | | | | | | |
| John (W) | 7⅔ | 8 | 5 | 3 | 2 | 4 |
| Forster | 1⅓ | 1 | 0 | 0 | 0 | 3 |

WP—Clay. Time of game—2:48. Attendance—55,997

UMPIRES—Ed Vargo (N), plate; Bill Haller (A), first base; John Kibler (N), second base; Marty Springstead (A), third base; Frank Pulli (N), left field; Joe Brinkman (A), right field. The umpires rotate after each game, the first base arbiter going to the plate, second base to first, etc. The plate umpire goes to right field for the following game.

## 2d Game—Los Angeles, Oct. 11

| NEW YORK (A) | AB | R | H | BI |
|---|---|---|---|---|
| White, lf | 5 | 2 | 2 | 0 |
| Thomasson, cf | 3 | 0 | 1 | 0 |
| Blair, cf | 1 | 0 | 1 | 0 |
| Munson, c | 4 | 1 | 1 | 0 |
| Jackson, dh | 4 | 0 | 1 | 3 |
| Nettles, 3b | 4 | 0 | 0 | 0 |
| Piniella, rf | 4 | 0 | 2 | 0 |
| Spencer, 1b | 4 | 0 | 1 | 0 |
| Doyle, 2b | 3 | 0 | 1 | 0 |
| Johnson, ph | 1 | 0 | 0 | 0 |
| Stanley, 2b | 0 | 0 | 0 | 0 |
| Dent, ss | 4 | 0 | 1 | 0 |
| **Total** | **37** | **3** | **11** | **3** |

| LOS ANGELES (N) | AB | R | H | BI |
|---|---|---|---|---|
| Lopes, 2b | 4 | 1 | 1 | 0 |
| Russell, ss | 4 | 0 | 1 | 0 |
| Smith, rf | 4 | 2 | 1 | 0 |
| Garvey, 1b | 3 | 0 | 1 | 0 |
| Cey, 3b | 3 | 1 | 2 | 4 |
| Baker, lf | 3 | 0 | 0 | 0 |
| Monday, cf | 3 | 0 | 0 | 0 |
| North, cf | 0 | 0 | 0 | 0 |
| Lacy, dh | 3 | 0 | 0 | 0 |
| Yeager, c | 3 | 0 | 1 | 0 |
| **Total** | **30** | **4** | **7** | **4** |

| | | | | |
|---|---|---|---|---|
| **New York** | 002 | 000 | 100 | —3 |
| **Los Angeles** | 000 | 103 | 00X | —4 |

DP—New York 1, Los Angeles 1. LOB—New York 10, Los Angeles 2. 2B—Munson, Jackson, Blair. HR—Cey. SB—White.

| | IP | H | R | ER | BB | SO |
|---|---|---|---|---|---|---|
| **New York** | | | | | | |
| Hunter (L) | 6 | 7 | 4 | 4 | 0 | 2 |
| Gossage | 2 | 0 | 0 | 0 | 0 | 0 |
| **Los Angeles** | | | | | | |
| Hooton (W) | 6 | 8 | 3 | 3 | 1 | 5 |
| Forster | 2⅓ | 3 | 0 | 0 | 1 | 3 |
| Welch | ⅔ | 0 | 0 | 0 | 0 | 1 |

Save—Welch. HBP—Jackson (by Hooton). WP—Hooton. Time of game—2:37. Attendance—55,982

## 3rd Game—New York, Oct. 13

| LOS ANGELES (N) | AB | R | H | BI |
|---|---|---|---|---|
| Lopes, 2b | 5 | 0 | 1 | 0 |
| Russell, ss | 4 | 0 | 2 | 1 |
| Smith, rf | 4 | 0 | 1 | 0 |
| Garvey, 1b | 4 | 0 | 1 | 0 |
| Cey, 3b | 3 | 0 | 0 | 0 |
| Baker, lf | 3 | 0 | 2 | 0 |
| Lacy, dh | 4 | 0 | 1 | 0 |
| North, cf | 3 | 1 | 0 | 0 |
| Yeager, c | 1 | 0 | 0 | 0 |
| Mota, ph | 0 | 0 | 0 | 0 |
| Grote, c | 0 | 0 | 0 | 0 |
| Ferguson, c | 1 | 0 | 0 | 0 |
| **Total** | **32** | **1** | **8** | **1** |

| NEW YORK (A) | AB | R | H | BI |
|---|---|---|---|---|
| Rivers, cf | 4 | 0 | 3 | 0 |
| Blair, cf | 0 | 0 | 0 | 0 |
| White, lf | 3 | 2 | 1 | 1 |
| Munson, c | 4 | 1 | 1 | 1 |
| Jackson, dh | 3 | 0 | 1 | 1 |
| Piniella, rf | 4 | 0 | 1 | 1 |
| Nettles, 3b | 4 | 1 | 1 | 0 |
| Chambliss, 1b | 3 | 0 | 1 | 0 |
| Doyle, 2b | 4 | 0 | 0 | 0 |
| Dent, ss | 4 | 1 | 1 | 1 |
| **Total** | **33** | **5** | **10** | **5** |

| | | | | |
|---|---|---|---|---|
| **Los Angeles** | 001 | 000 | 000 | —1 |
| **New York** | 110 | 000 | 30X | —5 |

E—Dent. DP—New York 2. LOB—Los Angeles 11, New York 7. 2B—Garvey. HR—White. SB—North, Piniella.

| | IP | H | R | ER | BB | SO |
|---|---|---|---|---|---|---|
| **Los Angeles** | | | | | | |
| Sutton (L) | 6⅓ | 9 | 5 | 5 | 3 | 2 |
| Rautzhan | ⅔ | 1 | 0 | 0 | 0 | 0 |
| Hough | 1 | 0 | 0 | 0 | 0 | 0 |
| **New York** | | | | | | |
| Guidry (W) | 9 | 8 | 1 | 1 | 7 | 4 |

Time of game—2:27. Attendance—56,447.

## 4th Game—New York, Oct. 14

| LOS ANGELES (N) | AB | R | H | BI |
|---|---|---|---|---|
| Lopes, 2b | 4 | 1 | 0 | 0 |
| Russell, ss | 5 | 0 | 2 | 0 |
| Smith, rf | 4 | 1 | 1 | 3 |
| Garvey, 1b | 4 | 0 | 0 | 0 |
| Cey, 3b | 4 | 0 | 1 | 0 |
| Baker, lf | 4 | 0 | 0 | 0 |
| Monday, dh | 2 | 0 | 1 | 0 |
| North, cf | 4 | 0 | 0 | 0 |
| Yeager, c | 3 | 1 | 1 | 0 |
| Davalillo, ph | 1 | 0 | 0 | 0 |
| Grote, c | 0 | 0 | 0 | 0 |
| **Total** | **35** | **3** | **6** | **3** |

| NEW YORK (A) | AB | R | H | BI |
|---|---|---|---|---|
| Blair, cf | 4 | 1 | 2 | 0 |
| Rivers, ph | 1 | 0 | 0 | 0 |
| White, lf | 3 | 2 | 1 | 0 |
| Munson, c | 3 | 1 | 2 | 1 |
| Jackson, dh | 4 | 0 | 2 | 1 |
| Piniella, rf | 5 | 0 | 1 | 1 |
| Nettles, 3b | 4 | 0 | 0 | 0 |
| Chambliss, 1b | 4 | 0 | 0 | 0 |
| Stanley, 2b | 3 | 0 | 0 | 0 |
| Spencer, ph | 1 | 0 | 0 | 0 |
| Doyle, 2b | 0 | 0 | 0 | 0 |
| Dent, ss | 4 | 0 | 1 | 0 |
| **Total** | **36** | **4** | **9** | **3** |

| | | | | | |
|---|---|---|---|---|---|
| **Los Angeles** | 000 | 030 | 000 | 0 | —3 |
| **New York** | 000 | 002 | 010 | 1 | —4 |

Two out when winning run scored

E—Russell. DP—New York 1. LOB—Los Angeles 7, New York 8. 2B—Yeager, Munson. HR—Smith. SB—Garvey, Munson. Sac.—White.

| | IP | H | R | ER | BB | SO |
|---|---|---|---|---|---|---|
| **Los Angeles** | | | | | | |
| John | 7 | 6 | 3 | 2 | 2 | 2 |
| Forster | ⅓ | 1 | 0 | 0 | 0 | 0 |
| Welch (L) | 2⅓ | 2 | 1 | 1 | 1 | 3 |
| **New York** | | | | | | |
| Figueroa | 5 | 4 | 3 | 3 | 4 | 2 |
| Tidrow | 3 | 2 | 0 | 0 | 0 | 4 |
| Gossage (W) | 2 | 0 | 0 | 0 | 1 | 2 |

HBP—Jackson (by Forster)—Time of game—3:17. Attendance—56,445.

## 5th Game—New York, Oct. 15

| LOS ANGELES (N) | AB | R | H | BI | NEW YORK (A) | AB | R | H | BI |
|---|---|---|---|---|---|---|---|---|---|
| Lopes, 2b | 4 | 2 | 2 | 0 | Rivers, cf | 5 | 2 | 3 | 1 |
| Russell, ss | 5 | 0 | 2 | 1 | Blair, cf | 1 | 1 | 0 | 0 |
| Smith, rf | 4 | 0 | 1 | 1 | White, lf | 5 | 2 | 2 | 3 |
| Garvey, 1b | 4 | 0 | 1 | 0 | Johnstone, rf | 0 | 0 | 0 | 0 |
| Cey, 3b | 3 | 0 | 1 | 0 | Munson, c | 5 | 1 | 3 | 5 |
| Baker, lf | 4 | 0 | 0 | 0 | Heath, c | 0 | 0 | 0 | 0 |
| Monday, cf | 3 | 0 | 0 | 0 | Jackson, dh | 3 | 0 | 1 | 0 |
| Lacy, dh | 4 | 0 | 0 | 0 | Piniella, rf | 4 | 0 | 1 | 1 |
| Yeager, c | 2 | 0 | 1 | 0 | Thomasson, lf | 1 | 0 | 0 | 0 |
| Oates, c | 1 | 0 | 1 | 0 | Nettles, 3b | 5 | 0 | 1 | 0 |
| **Total** | **34** | **2** | **9** | **2** | Spencer, 1b | 4 | 2 | 1 | 0 |
| | | | | | Doyle, 2b | 5 | 2 | 3 | 0 |
| | | | | | Dent, ss | 4 | 2 | 3 | 1 |
| | | | | | **Total** | **42** | **12** | **18** | **11** |

| | | | |
|---|---|---|---|
| **Los Angeles** | **1 0 1** | **0 0 0** | **0 0 0—2** |
| **New York** | **0 0 4** | **3 0 0** | **4 1 X—12** |

E—Russell, Smith, Garvey. DP—Los Angeles 2, New York 1. LOB—Los Angeles 9, New York 10. 2B—Russell, Munson, Dent. SB—Lopes, Rivers, White, Russell.

| | IP | H | R | ER | BB | SO |
|---|---|---|---|---|---|---|
| **Los Angeles** | | | | | | |
| Hooton (L) | 2⅓ | 5 | 4 | 3 | 2 | 1 |
| Rautzhan | 1⅓ | 3 | 3 | 3 | 0 | 0 |
| Hough | 4⅓ | 10 | 5 | 5 | 2 | 5 |
| **New York** | | | | | | |
| Beattie (W) | 9 | 9 | 2 | 2 | 4 | 8 |

WP—Hough. PB—Yeager. Time of game—2:56. Attendance—56,448.

## 6th Game—Los Angeles, Oct. 17

| NEW YORK (A) | AB | R | H | BI | LOS ANGELES (N) | AB | R | H | BI |
|---|---|---|---|---|---|---|---|---|---|
| Rivers, cf | 4 | 0 | 0 | 0 | Lopes, 2b | 4 | 1 | 2 | 2 |
| Blair, cf | 1 | 0 | 0 | 0 | Russell, ss | 3 | 0 | 1 | 0 |
| White, lf | 4 | 1 | 1 | 0 | Smith, rf | 4 | 0 | 0 | 0 |
| Thomasson, lf | 0 | 0 | 0 | 0 | Garvey, 1b | 4 | 0 | 0 | 0 |
| Munson, c | 5 | 0 | 1 | 0 | Cey, 3b | 4 | 0 | 1 | 0 |
| Jackson, dh | 5 | 1 | 1 | 2 | Baker, lf | 3 | 0 | 0 | 0 |
| Piniella, rf | 4 | 1 | 1 | 0 | Monday, cf | 3 | 0 | 0 | 0 |
| Johnstone, rf | 0 | 0 | 0 | 0 | Ferguson, c | 3 | 1 | 2 | 0 |
| Nettles, 3b | 4 | 1 | 1 | 0 | Davalillo, dh | 2 | 0 | 1 | 0 |
| Spencer, 1b | 3 | 1 | 0 | 0 | **Total** | **30** | **2** | **7** | **2** |
| Doyle, 2b | 4 | 2 | 3 | 2 | | | | | |
| Dent, ss | 4 | 0 | 3 | 3 | | | | | |
| **Total** | **38** | **7** | **11** | **7** | | | | | |

| | | | |
|---|---|---|---|
| **New York** | **0 3 0** | **0 0 2** | **2 0 0—7** |
| **Los Angeles** | **1 0 1** | **0 0 0** | **0 0 0—2** |

E—Ferguson. DP—New York 2. LOB—New York 6, Los Angeles 3. 2B—Doyle, Ferguson 2. HR—Lopes, Jackson. SB—Lopes. Sac—Davalillo.

| | IP | H | R | ER | BB | SO |
|---|---|---|---|---|---|---|
| **New York** | | | | | | |
| Hunter (W) | 7 | 6 | 2 | 2 | 1 | 3 |
| Gossage | 2 | 1 | 0 | 0 | 0 | 2 |
| **Los Angeles** | | | | | | |
| Sutton (L) | 5⅔ | 8 | 5 | 5 | 1 | 6 |
| Welch | 1⅓ | 2 | 2 | 2 | 1 | 2 |
| Rau | 2 | 1 | 0 | 0 | 0 | 3 |

WP—Sutton. Time of game—2:34. Attendance—55,985

**Most valuable player in series—**Bucky Dent, New York

## ROSE HITS IN 44 STRAIGHT GAMES

Pete Rose, of Cincinnati, hit safely in 44 games in a row in 1978 and equaled the National League record made by Willie Keeler in 1897. The major-league record of 56 is held by Joe DiMaggio of the New York Yankees. Rose's string began on June 14 and ended on Aug. 1 in Atlanta. The pitchers who stopped him were Larry McWilliams and Gene Garber.

During the streak, Rose made 70 hits in 182 trips to the plate, batting .385.

### LONGEST HITTING STREAKS

| Player (League) | Year | Game |
|---|---|---|
| Joe DiMaggio (A.L.) | 1941 | 56 |
| Pete Rose (N.L.) | 1978 | 44 |
| Willie Keeler (N.L.) | 1897 | 44 |
| Bill Dahlen (N.L.) | 1894 | 42 |
| George Sisler (A.L.) | 1922 | 41 |
| Ty Cobb (A.L.) | 1911 | 40 |
| Tommy Holmes (N.L.) | 1945 | 37 |
| Billy Hamilton (N.L.) | 1894 | 36 |
| Ty Cobb (A.L.) | 1917 | 35 |
| Dom DiMaggio (A.L.) | 1949 | 34 |
| George McQuinn (A.L.) | 1938 | 34 |
| George Sisler (A.L.) | 1925 | 34 |
| John Stone (A.L.) | 1930 | 34 |
| George Davis (N.L.) | 1893 | 33 |
| Rogers Hornsby (N.L.) | 1922 | 33 |
| Heinie Manush (A.L.) | 1933 | 33 |

## FORSCH, SEAVER PITCH NO-HITTERS

Bob Forsch, St. Louis Cardinals, and Tom Seaver, Cincinnati Reds, hurled no-hit games in 1978. Forsch achieved his against Philadelphia, April 16, shortly after the season began. It was the first no-hit game in a St. Louis park since 1924. Seaver had pitched six one-hit games before he finally got the no-hitter, June 18, against St. Louis.

The no-hitters:

| Date | Pitcher | Teams | BB | So | Score |
|---|---|---|---|---|---|
| April 16 | Bob Forsch | St. Louis vs. Phillies | 2 | 3 | 5–0 |
| June 18 | Tom Seaver | Cincinnati vs. St. Louis | 2 | 3 | 4–0 |

### N.L. ALL-STARS TRIUMPH AGAIN

(At San Diego Stadium, July 11)

The National League All-Stars scored 4 runs in the 8th inning and won the annual game, 7-3, from the American League. The victory was the 7th straight for the National Leaguers, who had rallied for 3 runs in the 3rd, tying the score at San Diego. The score by innings:

| | | | | | |
|---|---|---|---|---|---|
| American League | 201 | 000 | 000—3 | 8 | 1 |
| National League | 003 | 000 | 04X—7 | 10 | 0 |

Palmer, Keough (3), Sorenson (4), Kern (7), Guidry (7), Gossage (8) and Fisk, Sundberg (6); Blue, Rogers (4), Fingers (6), Sutter (7), Niekro (9) and Simmons, Boone (7). Winning pitcher: Sutter; losing pitcher: Gossage. Home runs: none. Attendance—51,549.

# CROQUET

## NATIONAL CHAMPIONSHIPS

(New York City, Sept. 13-17, 1978)

Men's singles—Richard Pearman, Bermuda

Men's doubles—E.A. (Ted) Prentis IV, New York, and Arthur Bohner, Westhampton, N.Y.

# BASEBALL—MINOR LEAGUES—1978

## CLASS AAA

### AMERICAN ASSOCIATION
**East Division**

| | W | L | Pct |
|---|---|---|---|
| Indianapolis (Reds) | 78 | 57 | .578 |
| Evansville (Tigers) | 78 | 58 | .574 |
| Springfield (Cardinals) | 70 | 66 | .515 |
| Iowa (White Sox) | 66 | 70 | .485 |

**West Division**

| | W | L | Pct |
|---|---|---|---|
| Omaha (Royals) | 66 | 69 | .489 |
| Denver (Expos) | 64 | 71 | .474 |
| Oklahoma City (Phils) | 62 | 74 | .456 |
| Wichita (Cubs) | 58 | 77 | .430 |

**PLAYOFF**

Omaha defeated Indianapolis, 4 games to 1

### INTERNATIONAL LEAGUE

| | W | L | Pct |
|---|---|---|---|
| Charleston (Astros) | 82 | 53 | .607 |
| Pawtucket (Red Sox) | 79 | 57 | .581 |
| Richmond (Braves) | 70 | 63 | .526 |
| Toledo (Twins) | 68 | 65 | .511 |
| Tidewater (Mets) | 66 | 68 | .493 |
| Rochester (Orioles) | 66 | 70 | .485 |
| Columbus (Padres) | 59 | 75 | .440 |
| Syracuse (Blue Jays) | 48 | 87 | .356 |

**PLAYOFFS**
**Semifinals**

Richmond defeated Charleston, 3 games to 1
Pawtucket defeated Toledo, 3 games to 2

**Final**

Richmond defeated Pawtucket, 4 games to 3

### PACIFIC COAST LEAGUE
**East Division**

| | W | L | Pct |
|---|---|---|---|
| Albuquerque (Dodgers) | 78 | 52 | .557 |
| Salt Lake City (Angels) | 72 | 65 | .526 |
| Phoenix (Giants) | 72 | 68 | .514 |
| Tucson (Rangers) | 69 | 71 | .493 |
| San Jose (Mariners) | 53 | 87 | .379 |

**West Division**

| | W | L | Pct |
|---|---|---|---|
| Tacoma (Yankees) | 80 | 57 | .584 |
| Portland (Indians) | 76 | 62 | .551 |
| Vancouver (A's) | 74 | 65 | .532 |
| Spokane (Brewers) | 64 | 75 | .460 |
| Hawaii (Padres) | 56 | 82 | .406 |

**PLAYOFFS**
**Semifinals**

Albuquerque defeated Salt Lake City, 3 games to 0
Tacoma and Portland tied, each winning 2 games, when series was ended because of inclement weather.

**Championship**

Albuquerque and Tacoma were declared co-champions.

### MEXICAN LEAGUE
**Division Winners**

Southeastern—Cordoba; runner-up: Mexico City Reds
Southwestern—Aguascalientes; runner-up: Durango
Northeastern—Monterrey; runner-up: Tampico
Northwestern—Saltillo; runner-up: Union Laguna

**Championship**

Aguascalientes defeated Union Laguna, 4 games to 1

## CLASS AA

Eastern League—First half: Bristol; second half: Reading. League playoff: Bristol

Southern League—Eastern Division: first half: Orlando; second half and playoff: Savannah. Western Division: both halves: Knoxville. League playoff: Knoxville, 2–1

Texas League—Eastern Division: first half: Arkansas; second half and playoff: Jacksonville. Western Division: both halves: El Paso League playoff: El Paso, 3–0

## CLASS A

California League—North Division: Lodi; South Division: Visalia. League playoff: Visalia, 3–2

Carolina League—First half: Lynchburg; second half: Peninsula. League playoff: Lynchburg, 3–0

Florida State League—North Division: first half: St. Petersburg; second half and playoff: Lakeland. South Division: first half: Fort Myers; second half and playoff: Miami. League playoff: Miami, 3–2

Midwest League—North Division: first half and playoff: Appleton; second half: Waterloo. South Division: first half: Quad Cities; second half: Burlington. League playoff: Burlington, 2–1

New York–Penn League—Yawkey Division: Oneonta; Wrigley Division: Geneva. League playoff: Geneva, 2–0

Northwest League—North Division: Grays Harbor; South Division: Eugene. League playoff: Grays Harbor, 1–0

Western Carolina League—Greenwood won both halves and championship.

## ROOKIE LEAGUES

Appalachian—Elizabethtown
Pioneer—Billings
Gulf Coast—Rangers

# BASEBALL—AMATEUR

## 1978 CHAMPIONS

N.C.A.A. Division I—Southern California
N.C.A.A. Division II—Florida Southern
N.C.A.A. Division III—Glassboro (N.J.) State
N.A.I.A.—Emporia State
American Legion—Hialeah, Fla.
Bronco League—Miami Cubans
Colt League—Waukegan, Ill.
Connie Mack League—Sachem, L.I. (N.Y.) Athletics
Little League—Final: Pintung, Taiwan, defeated Danville, Calif., 11–1; semifinals: Pintung defeated Santo Domingo, Dominican Republic, 3–0; Danville defeated Lexington, Ky., 6–5
Mickey Mantle League—Joliet (Ill.) Elks, 296
Pee Wee Reese League—Carolina Lilly, Puerto Rico
Pony League—Campbell-Moreland, Calif.
Sandy Koufax League—Baltimore Yankee-Rebels
Stan Musial League—Reading (Ohio) Tatman Taxi
Thorobred League—Arlington Heights, Ill.
Willie Mays League—Dallas Scorpions
World—Cuba

## LITTLE LEAGUE WORLD SERIES

| | | | | | |
|---|---|---|---|---|---|
| 1947 | Williamsport, Pa. | 1958 | Monterrey, Mexico | 1969 | Taiwan (Nationalist China) |
| 1948 | Lock Haven, Pa. | 1959 | Hamtramck, Mich. | 1970 | Wayne, N.J. |
| 1949 | Hammonton, N.J. | 1960 | Levittown, Pa. | 1971 | Taiwan (Nationalist China) |
| 1950 | Houston, Tex. | 1961 | El Cajon, Calif. | 1972 | Taiwan (Nationalist China) |
| 1951 | Stamford, Conn. | 1962 | San Jose, Calif. | 1973 | Taiwan (Nationalist China) |
| 1952 | Norwalk, Conn. | 1963 | Granada Hills, Calif. | 1974 | Taiwan (Nationalist China) |
| 1953 | Birmingham, Ala. | 1964 | Staten Island, N.Y. | 1975 | Lakewood Township, N.J. |
| 1954 | Schenectady, N.Y. | 1965 | Windsor Locks, Conn. | 1976 | Tokyo, Japan |
| 1955 | Morrisville, Pa. | 1966 | Houston, Tex. | 1977 | Tapei, Taiwan |
| 1956 | Roswell, N.M. | 1967 | West Tokyo, Japan | 1978 | Pintung, Taiwan |
| 1957 | Monterrey, Mexico | 1968 | Wakayama, Japan | | |

# YACHTING

## AMERICA'S CUP RECORD

First race in 1851 around Isle of Wight, Cowes, England. First defense and all others through 1920 held 30 miles off New York Bay. Races since 1930 held 30 miles off Newport, R.I. Conducted as one race only in 1851 and 1870; best four-of-seven basis, 1871; best two-of-three, 1876–1887; best three-of-five, 1893–1901; best four-of-seven, since 1930. Figures in parentheses indicate number of races won.

| Year | Winner and owner | Loser and owner |
|---|---|---|
| 1851 | AMERICA (1), John C. Stevens, U.S. | AURORA, T. Le Marchant, England[1] |
| 1870 | MAGIC (1), Franklin Osgood, U.S. | CAMBRIA, James Ashbury, England[2] |
| 1871 | COLUMBIA (2), Franklin Osgood, U.S.[3] | LIVONIA (1), James Ashbury, England |
| | SAPPHO (2), William P. Douglas, U.S. | |
| 1876 | MADELEINE (2), John S. Dickerson, U.S. | COUNTESS OF DUFFERIN, Chas. Gifford, Canada |
| 1881 | MISCHIEF (2), J. R. Busk, U.S. | ATALANTA, Alexander Cuthbert, Canada |
| 1885 | PURITAN (2), J. M. Forbes-Gen. Charles Paine, U.S. | GENESTA, Sir Richard Sutton, England |
| 1886 | MAYFLOWER (2), Gen. Charles Paine, U.S. | GALATEA, Lt. William Henn, England |
| 1887 | VOLUNTEER (2), Gen. Charles Paine, U.S. | THISTLE, James Bell et al, Scotland |
| 1893 | VIGILANT (3), C. Oliver Iselin et al., U.S. | VALKYRIE II, Lord Dunraven, England |
| 1895 | DEFENDER (3), C. O. Iselin-W. K. Vanderbilt-E. D. Morgan, U.S. | VALKYRIE III, Lord Dunraven-Lord Lonsdale-Lord Wolverton, England |
| 1899 | COLUMBIA (3), J. P. Morgan-C. O. Iselin, U.S. | SHAMROCK I, Sir Thomas Lipton, Ireland |
| 1901 | COLUMBIA (3), Edwin D. Morgan, U.S. | SHAMROCK II, Sir Thomas Lipton, Ireland |
| 1903 | RELIANCE (3), Cornelius Vanderbilt et al., U.S. | SHAMROCK III, Sir Thomas Lipton, Ireland |
| 1920 | RESOLUTE (3), Henry Walters et al., U.S. | SHAMROCK IV (2), Sir Thomas Lipton, Ireland |
| 1930 | ENTERPRISE (4), Harold S. Vanderbilt et al., U.S. | SHAMROCK V, Sir Thomas Lipton, Ireland |
| 1934 | RAINBOW (4), Harold S. Vanderbilt, U.S. | ENDEAVOUR (2), T. O. M. Sopwith, England |
| 1937 | RANGER (4), Harold S. Vanderbilt, U.S. | ENDEAVOUR II, T. O. M. Sopwith, England |
| 1958 | COLUMBIA (4), Henry Sears et al., U.S. | SCEPTRE, Hugh Goodson et al., England |
| 1962 | WEATHERLY (4), Henry D. Mercer et al., U.S. | GRETEL (1), Sir Frank Packer et al., Australia |
| 1964 | CONSTELLATION (4), New York Y.C. Syndicate, U.S. | SOVEREIGN (0), J. Anthony Bowden, England |
| 1967 | INTREPID (4), New York Y.C. Syndicate, U.S. | DAME PATTIE (0), Sydney (Aust.) Syndicate |
| 1970 | INTREPID (4), New York Y.C. Syndicate, U.S. | GRETEL II (1), Sydney (Aust.) Syndicate |
| 1974 | COURAGEOUS (4), New York N.Y. Syndicate, U.S. | SOUTHERN CROSS (0), Sydney (Aust.) Syndicate |
| 1977 | COURAGEOUS (4) New York, N.Y. Syndicate, U.S. | AUSTRALIA (0), Sun City (Aust.) Syndicate |

1. Fourteen British yachts started against America; Aurora finished second. 2. Cambria sailed against 23 U.S. yachts and finished tenth. 3. Columbia was disabled in the third race, after winning the first two; Sappho substituted and won the fourth and fifth.

## UNITED STATES YACHT RACING UNION CHAMPIONS

Adams Trophy (women)—Bonnie Shore, Ida Lewis Y.C., Newport, R.I.
Adams Memorial (women's double-handed)—Sandy Ray, Westport, Conn.–Carol Hayes, West Haven, Conn.
Sears Cup (juniors)—Mark Thompson, Jamestown, Pa.
Smythe Trophy (junior single-handed)—Richard Merriman, St. Petersburg, Fla.
Prince of Wales (club)—Galveston Bay Cruising Association
National Sea Exploring—Grant Hill–Tom Herrschaft, North Hollywood, Calif.
Mertz Trophy (women's single-handed)—Meredith O'Dowd, Riverside, R.I.
Champion of Champions—Tom Linskey, Newport Beach, Calif.

## U.S.Y.R.A. YOUTH CHAMPIONSHIPS

(Annapolis, Md., June 25–29, 1978)

Single-handed—Andrew Menkert, Washington, D.C.
Double-handed—Allen Land Peter Lindsey, Miami, Fla.

## OCEAN AND DISTANCE RACING

(Newport to Bermuda; 162 boats; 635 miles; June 16–22, 1978)

**Trophy Winners**

Bermuda Trophy (Measurement Handicap System)—Babe, Arnie Gay, Annapolis, Md.
Tamerlane Trophy—(International Offshore Rule)—Acadia, B. H. Keenan, New Orleans

# AUTO RACING

## INDIANAPOLIS 500

| Year | Winner | Car | Time | mph | Second place |
|---|---|---|---|---|---|
| 1911 | Ray Harroun | Marmon | 6:42:08 | 74.59 | Mulford |
| 1912 | Joe Dawson | National | 6:21:06 | 78.72 | Tetzloff |
| 1913 | Jules Goux | Peugeot | 6:35:05 | 75.93 | Wishart |
| 1914 | Rene Thomas | Delage | 6:03:45 | 82.47 | Duray |
| 1915 | Ralph DePalma | Mercedes | 5:33:55.51 | 89.84 | Resta |
| 1916[1] | Dario Resta | Peugeot | 3:34:17 | 84.00 | De Aleye |
| 1919 | Howard Wilcox | Peugeot | 5:40:42.87 | 88.05 | Hearne |
| 1920 | Gaston Chevrolet | Monroe | 5:38:32 | 88.62 | Thomas |
| 1921 | Tommy Milton | Frontenac | 5:34:44.65 | 89.62 | Sarles |
| 1922 | Jimmy Murphy | Murphy Special | 5:17:30.79 | 94.48 | Hartz |
| 1923 | Tommy Milton | H. C. S. Special | 5:29.50.17 | 90.95 | Hartz |
| 1924 | L. L. Corum-Joe Boyer | Dusenberg Special | 5:05:23.51 | 98.23 | Cooper |
| 1925 | Peter DePaolo | Dusenberg Special | 4:56:39.45 | 101.13 | Lewis |
| 1926[2] | Frank Lockhart | Miller Special | 4:10:14.95 | 95.904 | Hartz |
| 1927 | George Souders | Dusenberg Special | 5:07:33.08 | 97.54 | Devore |
| 1928 | Louis Meyer | Miller Special | 5:01:33.75 | 99.48 | Moore |
| 1929 | Ray Keech | Simplex Special | 5:07:25.42 | 97.58 | Louis Meyer |
| 1930 | Billy Arnold | Miller-Hartz Special | 4:58:39.72 | 100.448 | Cantlon |
| 1931 | Louis Schneider | Bowes Special | 5:10:27.93 | 96.629 | Fred Frame |
| 1932 | Fred Frame | Miller-Hartz Special | 4:48:03.79 | 104.144 | Howard Wilcox |
| 1933 | Louis Meyer | Tydol Special | 4:48:00.75 | 104.162 | Wilbur Shaw |
| 1934 | Bill Cummings | Boyle Products Special | 4:46:05.20 | 104.863 | Mauri Rose |
| 1935 | Kelly Petillo | Gilmore Special | 4:42:22.71 | 106.240 | Wilbur Shaw |
| 1936 | Louis Meyer | Ring Free Special | 4:35:03.39 | 109.069 | Horn |
| 1937 | Wilbur Shaw | Shaw-Gilmore Special | 4:24:07.80 | 113.580 | Hepburn |
| 1938 | Floyd Roberts | Burd Piston Ring Special | 4:15:58.40 | 117.200 | Wilbur Shaw |
| 1939 | Wilbur Shaw | Boyle Special | 4:20:47.39 | 115.035 | Snyder |
| 1940 | Wilbur Shaw | Boyle Special | 4:22:31.17 | 114.277 | Mays |
| 1941 | Floyd Davis-Mauri Rose | Noc Out Hose Clamp Special | 4:20:36.24 | 115.117 | Mays |
| 1946 | George Robson | Thorne Eng. Special | 4:21:26.71 | 114.820 | Jackson |
| 1947 | Mauri Rose | Blue Crown Special | 4:17:52.17 | 116.338 | Bill Holland |
| 1948 | Mauri Rose | Blue Crown Special | 4:10:23.33 | 119.814 | Bill Holland |
| 1949 | Bill Holland | Blue Crown Special | 4:07:15.97 | 121.327 | Johnny Parsons |
| 1950[3] | Johnnie Parsons | Wynn's Friction Proof Spl. | 2:46:55.97 | 124.002 | Bill Holland |
| 1951 | Lee Wallard | Belanger Special | 3:57:38.05 | 126.244 | Mike Nazaruk |
| 1952 | Troy Ruttman | Agajanian Special | 3:52:41.88 | 128.922 | Jim Rathmann |
| 1953 | Bill Vukovich | Fuel Injection Spl. | 3:53:01.69 | 128.740 | Art Cross |
| 1954 | Bill Vokovich | Fuel Injection Spl. | 3:49:17.27 | 130.840 | Jim Bryan |
| 1955 | Bob Sweikert | John Zink Special | 3:53:59.13 | 128.209 | Tony Bettenhausen |
| 1956 | Pat Flaherty | John Zink Special | 3:53:28.84 | 128.490 | Sam Hanks |
| 1957 | Sam Hanks | Belond Exhaust Special | 3:41:14.25 | 135.601 | Jim Rathmann |
| 1958 | Jimmy Bryan | Belond A-P Special | 3:44:13.80 | 133.791 | George Amick |
| 1959 | Rodger Ward | Leader Card 500 Rdstr | 3:40:49.20 | 135.857 | Jim Rathmann |
| 1960 | Jim Rathmann | Ken-Paul Special | 3:36:11.36 | 138.767 | Rodger Ward |
| 1961 | A. J. Foyt | Bowes Special | 3:35:37.49 | 139.130 | Eddie Sachs |
| 1962 | Rodger Ward | Leader Card Special | 3:33:50.33 | 140.293 | Len Sutton |
| 1963 | Parnelli Jones | Agajanian Special | 3:29:35.40 | 143.137 | Jim Clark |
| 1964 | A. J. Foyt | Offenhauser Special | 3:23:35.83 | 147.350 | Rodger Ward |
| 1965 | Jim Clark | Lotus-Ford | 3:19:05.34 | 150.686 | Parnelli Jones |
| 1966 | Graham Hill | Lola-Ford | 3:27:52.53 | 144.317 | Jim Clark |
| 1967[4] | A. J. Foyt | Coyote-Ford | 3:18:24.22 | 151.207 | Al Unser |
| 1968 | Bobby Unser | Eagle-Offenhauser | 3:16:13.76 | 152.882 | Dan Gurney |
| 1969 | Mario Andretti | STP Hawk-Ford | 3:11:14.71 | 156.867 | Dan Gurney |
| 1970 | Al Unser | P. J. Colt-Ford | 3:12:37.04 | 155.749 | Mark Donohue |
| 1971 | Al Unser | P. J. Colt-Ford | 3:10:11.56 | 157.735 | Peter Revson |
| 1972 | Mark Donohue | McLaren-Offenhauser | 3:04:05.54 | 162.962 | Al Unser |
| 1973[5] | Gordon Johncock | Eagle-Offenhauser | 2:05:26.59 | 159.036 | Billy Vukovich |
| 1974 | Johnny Rutherford | McLaren-Offenhauser | 3:09:10.06 | 158.589 | Bobby Unser |
| 1975[6] | Bobby Unser | Eagle-Offenhauser | 2:54:55.08 | 149.213 | Johnny Rutherford |
| 1976[7] | Johnny Rutherford | McLaren-Offenhauser | 1:42:52.48 | 148.725 | A. J. Foyt |
| 1977 | A. J. Foyt | Coyote-Foyt | 3:05:57.16 | 161.331 | Tom Sneva |
| 1978 | Al Unser | Lola-Cosworth | 3:05:54.99 | 161.363 | Tom Sneva |

1. 300 miles. 2. Race ended at 400 miles because of rain. 3. Race ended at 345 miles because of rain. 4. Race, postponed after 18 laps because of rain on May 30, was finished on May 31. 5. Race postponed May 28 and 29 was cut to 332.5 miles because of rain, May 30. 6. Race ended at 435 miles because of rain. 7. Race ended at 255 miles because of rain.

## U.S. AUTO CLUB NATIONAL CHAMPIONS

| | | | | | | | |
|---|---|---|---|---|---|---|---|
| 1910 | Ray Harroun | 1925 | Peter DePaolo | 1946–48 | Ted Horn | 1963–64 | A. J. Foyt |
| 1911 | Ralph Mulford | 1926 | Harry Hartz | 1949 | Johnnie Parsons | 1965–66 | Mario Andretti |
| 1912 | Ralph DePalma | 1927 | Peter DePaolo | 1950 | Henry Banks | 1967 | A. J. Foyt |
| 1913 | Earl Cooper | 1928–29 | Louis Meyer | 1951 | Tony Bettenhausen | 1968 | Bobby Unser |
| 1914 | Ralph DePalma | 1930 | Billy Arnold | | | 1969 | Mario Andretti |
| 1915 | Earl Cooper | 1931 | Louis Schneider | 1952 | Chuck Stevenson | 1970 | Al Unser |
| 1916 | Dario Resta | 1932 | Bob Carey | 1953 | Sam Hanks | 1971–72 | Joe Leonard |
| 1917 | Earl Cooper | 1933 | Louis Meyer | 1954 | Jimmy Bryan | 1973 | Roger McCluskey |
| 1918 | Ralph Mulford | 1934 | Bill Cummings | 1955 | Bob Sweikert | 1974 | Bobby Unser |
| 1919 | Howard Wilcox | 1935 | Kelly Petillo | 1956–57 | Jimmy Bryan | 1975 | A. J. Foyt |
| 1920 | Gaston Chevrolet | 1936 | Mauri Rose | 1958 | Tony Bettenhausen | 1976 | Gordon Johncock |
| 1921 | Tommy Milton | 1937 | Wilbur Shaw | | | 1977–78 | Tom Sneva |
| 1922 | James Murphy | 1938 | Floyd Roberts | 1959 | Rodger Ward | | |
| 1923 | Eddie Hearne | 1939 | Wilbur Shaw | 1960–61 | A. J. Foyt | | |
| 1924 | James Murphy | 1940–41 | Rex Mays | 1962 | Rodger Ward | | |

## NATIONAL ASSOCIATION FOR STOCK CAR AUTO RACING (NASCAR) GRAND NATIONAL CHAMPIONS

| | | | | | | | |
|---|---|---|---|---|---|---|---|
| 1949 | Red Byron | 1955 | Tim Flock | 1964 | Richard Petty | 1971–72 | Richard Petty |
| 1950 | Bill Rexford | 1956–57 | Buck Baker | 1965 | Ned Jarrett | 1973 | Benny Parsons |
| 1951 | Herb Thomas | 1958–59 | Lee Petty | 1966 | David Pearson | 1974–75 | Richard Petty |
| 1952 | Tim Flock | 1960 | Rex White | 1967 | Richard Petty | 1976–77 | Cale Yarborough |
| 1953 | Herb Thomas | 1961 | Ned Jarrett | 1968–69 | David Pearson | | |
| 1954 | Lee Petty | 1962–63 | Joe Weatherly | 1970 | Bobby Isaac | | |

## World Grand Prix Driver Champions

| | |
|---|---|
| 1950 | Giuseppe Farina, Italy, Alfa Romeo |
| 1951 | Juan Fangio, Argentina, Alfa Romeo |
| 1952 | Alberto Ascari, Italy, Ferrari |
| 1953 | Alberto Ascari, Italy, Ferrari |
| 1955 | Juan Fangio, Argentina, Maserati, Mercedes-Benz |
| 1955 | Juan Fangio, Argentina, Mercedes-Benz |
| 1956 | Juan Fangio, Argentina, Lancia-Ferrari |
| 1957 | Juan Fangio, Argentina, Masserati |
| 1958 | Mike Hawthorn, England, Ferrari |
| 1959 | Jack Brabham, Australia, Cooper |
| 1960 | Jack Brabham, Australia, Cooper |
| 1961 | Phil Hill, United States, Ferrari |
| 1962 | Graham Hill, England, BRM |
| 1963 | Jim Clark, Scotland, Lotus-Ford |
| 1964 | John Surtees, England, Ferrari |
| 1965 | Jim Clark, Scotland, Lotus-Ford |
| 1966 | Jack Brabham, Australia, Brabham-Repco |
| 1967 | Denis Hulme, New Zealand, Brabham-Repco |
| 1968 | Graham Hill, England, Lotus-Ford |
| 1969 | Jackie Stewart, Scotland, Matra-Ford |
| 1970 | Jochen Rindt, Austria, Lotus-Ford |
| 1971 | Jackie Stewart, Scotland, Tyrrell-Ford |
| 1972 | Emerson Fittipaldi, Brazil, Lotus-Ford |
| 1973 | Jackie Stewart, Scotland, Tyrrell-Ford |
| 1974 | Emerson Fittipaldi, Brazil, McLaren-Ford |
| 1975 | Niki Lauda, Austria, Ferrari |
| 1976 | James Hunt, Britain, McLaren-Ford |
| 1977 | Niki Lauda, Austria, Ferrari |
| 1978 | Mario Andretti, Nazareth, Pa., Lotus |

## THE ONE-MILE SPEED MARK

The first recorded effort for one mile was made on Jan. 12, 1904, by Henry Ford, driving a Ford "999." He established a record of 39.40 sec or 91.370 mph. All prior records were established over the flying kilometer. The first man to travel better than 100 mph was Rigolly, on July 2, 1904, at 103.56 mph. The first over 200 mph was Major H.O.D. Segrave, who drove a Sunbeam at 203.79 mph on March 29, 1927, at Daytona, Fla.

In 1947, John Cobb of London became the first person to travel more than 400 mph on land. The Englishman accomplished the feat on Sept. 16 at Bonneville, Utah, and raised the world mile record to 394.2 mph and the world kilometer mark to 393.8 mph. His car was a Railton-Mobil Special. Cobb's average speed was 9.1325 seconds per mile.

The record held by Cobb was surpassed by Britain's Donald Campbell at Lake Eyre in Australia on July 17, 1964. He drove his 30-foot, 4,250-horsepower Bluebird to two runs of 403.1 mph each. This record was beaten by Bob Summers of Ontario, Calif., who drove his 32-foot, four-engined Goldenrod to a speed of 409.227 mph at Bonneville on Nov. 12, 1965.

Craig Breedlove of Los Angeles, driving "Spirit of America," a three-wheeled, jet-powered car, at Bonneville on Aug. 5, 1963, attained a speed of 8.8355 seconds per mile, or 407.45 mph. The U.S. Auto Club created a new category for the record—jet unlimited class. The record was broken a number of times in 1964, Breedlove lifting it above 500 mph to 526.277 on Oct. 15. Again, in 1965, the mark was topped frequently—Breedlove and Art Arfons of Akron, Ohio, beating one another's records; finally, on Nov. 15, Breedlove surpassed 600 mph, achieving a standard of 600.601 at Bonneville. Gary Gabelich, driving the Blue Flame, raised the record to 622.407 mph on Oct. 23, 1970, at Bonneville. The rocket car, powered by a mixture of peroxide and natural gas, hit 617.602 on the first run and 627.287 on the second.

## U.S. AUTO CLUB

### The 1978 Triple Crown Races

**Indianapolis 500** (Indianapolis Motor Speedway, May 28)—1, Al Unser, Albuquerque, N.M.; Lola–Cosworth; 200 laps; 3 hours, 5 minutes, 54.99 seconds for average speed of 161.363 mph; first-place prize $290,364. 2, Tom Sneva, Spokane, Wash.; Penske-Cosworth; 200 laps; $112,704. 3, Gordon Johncock, Phoenix, Ariz.; Wildcat/SGD; 199 laps; $61,769. 4, Steve Krisiloff, Dana Point, Calif.; Wildcat/DGS; 198 laps; $38,704. 5, Wally Dallenbach, Basalt, Colo.; McLaren–Cosworth; 195 laps; $35,636.

**Schaefer 500** (Pocono International Raceway, Longpond, Pa., June 25)—1, Al Unser, 200 laps; 3:30:52.78; 142.261 mph; $89,296. 2, Johnny Rutherford, Fort Worth, Tex.; McLaren–Cosworth; 200 laps; $41,996. 3, Tom Sneva; 200 laps; $27,-171. 4, Wally Dallenbach; 198 laps; $16,871. 5, Larry Dickson, Marietta, Ohio; Penske-Cosworth; 196 laps; $13,021.

**California 500** (Ontario Raceway, Sept. 3)—1, Al Unser; 200 laps; 3:26:40.27; 145.158 mph; $73,400. 2, Pancho Carter, Brownsburg, Ind., Lightning; 195 laps. 3, Gordon Johncock, 194 laps. 4, Tom Bagley, Centre Hall, Pa.; Lightning; 194 laps. 5, Lee Kunzman, Guttenberg, Iowa; Fox; 180 laps.

## OTHER 1978 RACES

**Jimmy Bryan 150** (Phoenix, Ariz., March 18)—Gordon Johncock, Phoenix, Ariz.; Wildcat SDG; 1:17:04.98; 116.757 mph; $10,611.

**Datsun Twin 200** (Ontario, Calif., March 26)—Danny Ongais, Costa Mesa, Calif; Parnelli VPJ; 1:13:42.33; 162.81 mph; $18,725.

**Coors 200** (College Station, Tex., April 15)—Danny Ongais; 1:09:07.62; 173.584 mph; $16,843.

**Gabriel 200** (Trenton, N.J., April 23)—Gordon Johncock; 1:32:04.18; 129.033 mph; $11,892.

**Molson Diamond Indy** (Mosport, Ontario, 300 kilometers (186.88 miles, June 11)—Danny Ongais; 2:08:38.62; 87.164 mph; $30,635.

**Rex Mays 150** (Milwaukee, June 18)—Rick Mears, Bakersfield, Calif.; Penske-Cosworth; 1:14:34.77; 120.677 mph; $17,406.

**Norton 200** (Brooklyn, Mich., July 16)—Johnny Rutherford, Fort Worth, Tex.; McLaren-Cosworth; 1:15:01.66; 159.941 mph; $21,335.

**Gould Twin Dixie** (Atlanta, Ga., 150 miles, July 23)—Rick Mears; 1:03:43.95; 141.215 mph; $16,377.

**Texas Grand Prix** (College Station, Tex., 200 miles, Aug. 6)—A.J. Foyt, Houston, Tex.; Coyote-Ford; 159 mph.

**Tony Bettenhausen 200** (Milwaukee, Aug. 20)—Danny Ongais, 108.369 mph.

**Daily Mail Indy Trophy** (Brands Hatch, England, 120 miles, Oct. 8)—Rick Mears; 1:15:23.45; 95.79 mph; $33,451

## CHAMPIONSHIP SERIES LEADERS

(Oct. 20, 1978)

Tom Sneva 4,145 points ($270,624); Al Unser, 3,881 points ($524,696); Gordon Johncock 3,338 points ($178,854); Wally Dallenbach 2,846 points ($122,989); Steve Krisiloff 2,799 points $132,475)

## NATIONAL ASSOCIATION FOR STOCK CAR AUTO RACING (NASCAR)—1978

(Races of 400 miles or over)

**Daytona 500** (Daytona Beach, Fla., Feb. 19)—Bobby Allison, Hueytown, Ala.; Ford; 3 hours, 7 minutes, 49 seconds; average speed: 159.730 mph; winner's purse: $44,300.

**Carolina 500** (Rockingham, N.C., March 5)—David Pearson, Spartanburg, S.C.; Mercury; 4:17:17; 116.681 mph; $10,605.

**Rebel 500** (Darlington, S.C., April 9)—Benny Parsons, Detroit; Chevrolet; 3:55:50; 127.544 mph; $14,450.

**Winston 500** (Talladega, Ala., May 14)—Cale Yarborough, Timmonsville, S.C.; Oldsmobile; 3:07:53; 159.699 mph; $27,100.

**Mason-Dixon 500** (Dover, Del., May 21)—David Pearson; 4:21:38; 114.664 mph; $11,700.

**World 600** (Charlotte, N.C., May 28)—Darrell Waltrip, Owensboro, Ky.; Chevrolet; 4:20:12; 138.355 mph; $36,075.

**Gabriel 400** (Brooklyn, Mich., June 18)—Cale Yarborough; 2:40:28; 149.563 mph; $16,055.

**Firecracker 400** (Daytona Beach, Fla., July 4)—David Pearson; 2:35:30; 154.340 mph; $13,525.

**Coca-Cola 500** (Pocono, Pa., July 30)—Darrell Waltrip; 3:30:28; 142.540 mph; $14,515.

**Talladega 500** (Talladega, Ala., Aug. 6)—Lennie Pond, Chester, Va.; Oldsmobile; 2:51:43; 174.7 mph (world closed–course record for 500 miles); $19,600.

**Champion Spark Plug 400** (Cambridge Junction, Mich., Aug. 20)—David Pearson; 3:05:14; 129.586 mph; $12,000.

**Napa National 500** (Charlotte, N.C., Oct. 8)—Bobby Allison; 3:31:57; 141.826 mph); $22,725

## WINSTON CUP GRAND NATIONAL LEADERS

(Oct. 20, 1978)

Cale Yarborough, 4,334 points; Darrell Waltrip 3,953 points; Dave Marcis 3,936 points; Benny Parsons, 3,878 points; Bobby Allison 3,857 points.

## GRAND PRIX—1978

### Formula One Competition

**Argentina** (Buenos Aires, 198 miles, Jan. 15)—Mario Andretti, Nazareth, Pa.; Lotus; 1 hour, 37 minutes, 4.47 seconds; average speed: 119 miles per hour.

**Brazil** (Rio de Janeiro, 196.94 miles, Jan. 29)—Carlos Reutemann, Argentina; Ferrari; 1:49:58.86; 107.2 mph.

**South Africa** (Johannesburg, 190 miles, March 3)—Ronnie Peterson, Sweden; Lotus; 117.4 mph.

**United States West** (Long Beach, Calif., 162.7 miles, April 2)—Carlos Reutemann; 1:52:01.30; 87.10 mph.

**Monaco** (Monte Carlo, 154 miles, May 7)—Patrick Depailler, France; Tyrrell-Ford; 1:55:14.66; 80 mph.

**Belgium** (Zolder, 185.38 miles, May 21)—Mario Andretti; 1:39:54.02; 111.37 mph.

**Spain** (Madrid, 158.72 miles, June 4)—Mario Andretti; 1:41:47.06; 93.53 mph.

**Sweden** (Anderstorp, 175 miles, June 17)—Niki Lauda, Austria; Brabham; 1:41:00.60; 104.2 mph.

**France** (Le Castellet, 194 miles, July 2)—Mario Andretti; 1:38:-51.92; 118.24 mph.

**Britain** (Brands Hatch, 198.6 miles, July 16)—Carlos Reutemann; 1:42:12.39; 116.6 mph.

**Germany** (Hockenheim, 189 miles, July 30)—Mario Andretti; 1:28:00.90; 129.25 mph.

**Austria** (Zeltweg, 198.3 miles, Aug. 13)—Ronnie Peterson; 128.83 mph.

**Netherlands** (Zandevoort, 196.94 miles, Aug. 27)—Mario Andretti; 1:41:04.23; 116.923 mph.

**Italy** (Monza, 129.65 miles, Sept. 10)—Niki Lauda; 1:07:04.54; 128.95 mph. (Andretti finished first but was disqualified and placed sixth. Peterson died the following morning after injuries in crash at start, which necessitated restart and shortening of race from 52 to 40 laps.

**United States** (Watkins Glen, N.Y., 200 miles, Oct. 1)—Reutemann; 118.58 m.p.h.

**Canada** (Montreal, 197 miles Oct. 8, )—Gilles Villeneuve, Canada, Ferrari; 1:57:49.196; 99.67 mph

**Champion:** Mario Andretti, Nazareth, Pa.; Lotus, 64 points; Other point leaders: Ronnie Peterson, Sweden, Lotus, 51; Carlos Reutemann, Argentina, Ferrari, 48; Niki Lauda, Austria, Brabham, 44.

## INTERNATIONAL MOTOR SPORTS ASSOCIATION

### Camel GT Series

**24 Hours of Daytona** (Daytona Beach, Fla., Feb. 4–5, 1978)—

Toine Hezemans, Netherlands and Rolf Stommelen, West Germany; Porsche; 2,611.2 miles; average speed: 108.743 mph

**12 Hours of Sebring** (Sebring, Fla., March 20, 1978)—Brian Redman, Britain, Charles Mendoza, Tampa, Fla., and Bob Garretson, Sunnyvale, Calif.; Porsche.

### OTHER SPORTS CAR RACES

**24 Hours of Le Mans** (Le Mans, France, June 10–11, 1978)—Jean-Pierre Jaussaud and Didier Pironi, France; Renault Alpine; average speed: 130 mph

**Watkins Glen 6 Hours of Endurance** (Watkins Glen, N.Y., July 8, 1978)—John Fitzpatrick, Britain; Toine Hezemans, Netherlands; Peter Gregg, Jacksonville, Fla.; Porsche 935; average speed: 81.74 mph

**6 Hours of Talladega** (Talladega, Ala., April 2, 1978)—Peter Gregg and Brad Frisselle; Porsche 935; average speed: 116.444 mph

### INTERNATIONAL RACE OF CHAMPIONS

1977–78 Series—final race (Daytona Beach, Fla, Feb. 17, 1978)—Mario Andretti, Nazareth, Pa.

1977–78 Overall—Al Unser, 62 pts; $50,000

## GYMNASTICS

### AMATEUR ATHLETIC UNION—ELITE

(Houston, Tex., May 18–20, 1978)

**Men's Events**

| | Pts |
|---|---|
| All around—Phil Cahoy, Nebraska Gym Club | 107.20 |
| Floor exercise—Mike Silverstein, Owl G.C., Phila. | 18.95 |
| Pommel horse—Joel Ulloa, Cal State, Fullerton | 19.10 |
| Still rings—Tie between Larry Gerard, Nebraska G.C., and Mike Silverstein | 18.85 |
| Vault—Carl Antonelli, New York A.C. | 19.00 |
| Parallel bars—John Corritore, Michigan | 18.95 |
| Horizontal bar—Melvin Cooley, Univ. of Washington | 19.075 |
| Team—New York Athletic Club | 325.10 |

**Women's Events**

| | Pts |
|---|---|
| All around—Karen Lemond, Reno (Nev.) Flips | 73.80 |
| Floor exercise—Karen Lemond | 18.80 |
| Balance beam—Karen Lemond | 18.85 |
| Vault—Tie between Pam Lee, El Paso Supernovas, and Jackie Chagnovich, Utah Academy, Salt Lake City | 18.75 |
| Uneven parallel bars—Tie between Karen Lemond and Jackie Chagnovich | 18.80 |
| Team—Utah Academy, Salt Lake City | 215.05 |

### NATIONAL COLLEGIATE ATHLETIC ASSN.

**Division I**

(Eugene, Ore., April 6–8, 1978)

| | Pts |
|---|---|
| All around—Bart Conner, Oklahoma | 112.65 |
| Floor exercise—Curt Austin, Iowa State | 19.075 |
| Pommel horse—Mike Burke, N. Illinois | 19.425 |
| Still rings—Scott McEldownedy, Oregon | 19.05 |
| Vault—Ron Galimore, Louisiana State | 19.30 |
| Parallel bars—John Corritore, Michigan | 19.275 |
| Horizontal bar—Mel Cooley, Washington | 19.20 |
| Team—Oklahoma | 439.35 |

**Division II**

(North Ridge, Calif., April 1–3)

| | |
|---|---|
| All around—Casey Edwards, Wisconsin-Oshkosh | |
| Team—Illinois, Chicago Circle | 406.85 |

### ASSOCIATION OF INTERCOLLEGIATE ATHLETICS FOR WOMEN (A.I.A.W.)

(Seattle, Wash., March 30–April 1, 1978)

| | |
|---|---|
| All around—Ann Carr, Penn State | 37.85 |
| Floor exercise—Ann Carr | 19.20 |
| Balance beam—Ann Carr | 18.75 |
| Uneven parallel bars—Ann Carr | 19.0 |
| Vault—Kolleen Casey, Southwest Missouri | 19.35 |
| Team—Penn State | 147.70 |

### NATIONAL ASSOCIATION OF INTERCOLLEGIATE ATHLETICS

(Hays, Kan., March 3–4, 1978)

| | Pts |
|---|---|
| All-around—Casey Edwards, Wisconsin-Oshkosh | 52.850 |
| Floor exercise—Rob Mueller, Wisconsin-LaCrosse | 8.475 |
| High bar—Casey Edwards | 8.950 |
| Parallel bars—Casey Edwards | 8.500 |
| Pommel horse—Steve Shumski, Eastern Washington | 8.525 |
| Still rings—Casey Edwards | 9.225 |
| Vault—Casey Edwards | 9.375 |
| Team—Wisconsin-Oshkosh | 202.800 |

## CHESS

### WORLD CHAMPIONS

| | |
|---|---|
| 1894–1921 | Emanuel Lasker, Germany |
| 1921–27 | José R. Capablanca, Cuba |
| 1927–35 | Alexander A. Alekhine, U.S.S.R. |
| 1935–37 | Dr. Max Euwe, Netherlands |
| 1937–46 | Alexander A. Alekhine, U.S.S.R.[1] |
| 1948–57 | Mikhail Botvinnik, U.S.S.R. |
| 1957–58 | Vassily Smyslov, U.S.S.R. |
| 1958–60 | Mikhail Botvinnik, U.S.S.R. |
| 1960–61 | Mikhail Tal, U.S.S.R. |
| 1961–63 | Mikhail Botvinnik, U.S.S.R. |
| 1963–68 | Tigran Petrosian, U.S.S.R. |
| 1969–71 | Boris Spassky, U.S.S.R. |
| 1972–74 | Bobby Fischer, Los Angeles |
| 1975 | Bobby Fischer[2]; Anatoly Karpov, U.S.S.R. |
| 1976–78 | Anatoly Karpov, U.S.S.R.[3] |

1. Alekhine, a French citizen, died while champion. 2. Relinquished title. 3. In 1978, Karpov defeated Viktor Korchnoi 6 games to 5.

### UNITED STATES CHAMPIONS

| | |
|---|---|
| 1909–36 | Frank J. Marshall, New York |
| 1936–44 | Samuel Reshevsky, New York[1] |
| 1944–46 | Arnold S. Denker, New York |
| 1946 | Samuel Reshevsky, Boston |
| 1948 | Herman Steiner, Los Angeles |
| 1951–52 | Larry Evans, New York |
| 1954–57 | Arthur Bisguier, New York |
| 1958–61 | Bobby Fischer, Brooklyn, N.Y. |
| 1962 | Larry Evans, New York |
| 1963–67 | Bobby Fischer, New York |
| 1968 | Larry Evans, New York |
| 1969–71 | Samuel Reshevsky, Spring Valley, N.Y. |
| 1972 | Robert Byrne, Ossining, N.Y. |
| 1973 | Lubomir Kavelek, Washington; John Grefe, San Francisco |
| 1974–77 | Walter Browne, Berkeley, Calif. |
| 1978 | Lubomir Kavalek, New York |

1. In 1942, Isaac I. Kashdan of New York was co-champion for a while because of a tie with Reshevsky in that year's tournament. Reshevsky won the play-off.

# COMPREHENSIVE INDEX

## A

# B

## C

# D

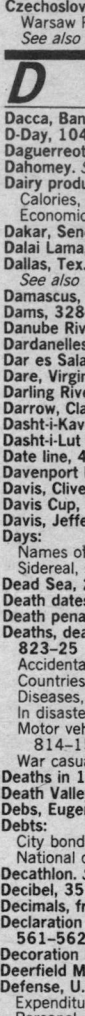

# G

## H

# I

# L



# M

# N

## O

# P

## Q



## R

# S

# T

# U

## X



## Y

# Z